Walter Van Tilburg Clark, 1909–1971
Stephen Spender, 1909–1986
Eudora Welty, b. 1909
Elizabeth Bishop, 1911–1979
J. V. Cunningham, b. 1911
Tennessee Williams, 1911–1983
John Cheever, 1912–1982
Irving Layton, b. 1912
Robert Hayden, b. 1913
Tillie Olsen, b. 1913
Muriel Rukeyser, b. 1913
Karl Shapiro, b. 1913
Jerome Weidman, b. 1913
Barbara Howes, b. 1914
Randall Jarrell, 1914–1965
Dudley Randall, b. 1914
Henry Reed, b. 1914
William Stafford, b. 1914
Dylan Thomas, 1914–1953
Tom Whitecloud, 1914–1972
Isabella Gardner, 1915–1981
Arthur Miller, b. 1915
Américo Parédes, b. 1915
Margaret Walker, b. 1915
Orson Welles, 1915–1985
Gwendolyn Brooks, b. 1917
Robert Lowell, 1917–1977
Arthur Laurents, b. 1918
Shirley Jackson, 1919–1965
Doris Lessing, b. 1919
May Swenson, 1919–1989
Edwin Morgan, b. 1920
Howard Nemerov, 1920–1991
Mary Ellen Solt, b. 1920
James Emanuel, b. 1921
Mona Van Duyn, b. 1921
Richard Wilbur, b. 1921
Philip Larkin, 1922–1985
Grace Paley, b. 1922
James Dickey, b. 1923
Mari Evans, b. 1923
Nadine Gordimer, b. 1923
Richard Hugo, 1923–1982
Edward Field, b. 1924
Vassar Miller, b. 1924
Donald Justice, b. 1925
Carolyn Kizer, b. 1925
Maxine Kumin, b. 1925
Flannery O'Connor, 1925–1964
Gerald Stern, b. 1925
A. R. Ammons, b. 1926
Robert Bly, b. 1926
Allen Ginsberg, b. 1926
James Merrill, b. 1926
Frank O'Hara, 1926–1966
W. D. Snodgrass, b. 1926
David Wagoner, b. 1926
W. S. Merwin, b. 1927
James Wright, 1927–1980
Edward Albee, b. 1928
Maya Angelou, b. 1928
Donald Hall, b. 1928
Cynthia MacDonald, b. 1928
Gabriel García Márquez, b. 1928
Cynthia Ozick, b. 1928

Anne Sexton, 1928–1974
John Hollander, b. 1929
X. J. Kennedy, b. 1929
Adrienne Rich, b. 1929
Jon Silkin, b. 1930
John Engels, b. 1931
Alice Munro, b. 1931
Linda Pastan, b. 1932
Sylvia Plath, 1932–1963
John Updike, b. 1932
Ernest Gaines, b. 1933
Etheridge Knight, b. 1933
Imamu Amiri Baraka (LeRoi Jones), b. 1934
Joanne Kyger, b. 1934
Marge Piercy, b. 1934
Sonia Sanchez, b. 1934
Mark Strand, b. 1934
Paul Zimmer, b. 1934
Ellen Gilchrist, b. 1935
Betty Keller, b. 1935
Lucille Clifton, b. 1936
Stephen Dixon, b. 1936
Andre Dubus, b. 1936
John Haines, b. 1936
H. S. (Sam) Hamod, b. 1936
Marvin Bell, b. 1937
Judith Minty, b. 1937
Luis Omar Salinas, b. 1937
Diane Wakoski, b. 1937
Dan Georgakas, b. 1938
Michael S. Harper, b. 1938
Virginia Scott, b. 1938
Margaret Atwood, b. 1939
Toni Cade Bambara, b. 1939
Seamus Heaney, b. 1939
Billy Collins, b. 1941
Simon Ortiz, b. 1941
Tino Villanueva, b. 1941
Marilyn Hacker, b. 1942
Don L. Lee, b. 1942
Sharon Olds, b. 1942
Dave Smith, b. 1942
Nikki Giovanni, b. 1943
Thomas Rabbitt, b. 1943
James Tate, b. 1943
Alice Walker, b. 1944
Joy Williams, b. 1944
Daniel Halpern, b. 1945
Carol Muske, b. 1945
Brenda Serotte, b. 1946
Maura Stanton, b. 1946
Leonard Adamé, b. 1947
Roberta Hill, b. 1947
Alan Lightman, b. 1948
Leslie Marmon Silko, b. 1948
Gary Soto, b. 1948
Olga Broumas, b. 1949
Bruce Weigl, b. 1949
Carolyn Forché, b. 1950
Chase Twichell, b. 1950
Rita Dove, b. 1952
Beth Henley, b. 1952
Naomi Shihab Nye, b. 1952
Sandra Cisneros, b. 1954
Cathy Song, b. 1955

LITERATURE

LITERATURE

An Introduction to Reading and Writing

THIRD EDITION

EDGAR V. ROBERTS
Lehman College
The City University of New York

HENRY E. JACOBS

PRENTICE HALL, ENGLEWOOD CLIFFS, NEW JERSEY 07632

Library of Congress Cataloging-in-Publication Data

Roberts, Edgar V.
    Literature : an introduction to reading and writing / Edgar
V. Roberts, Henry E. Jacobs.—3rd ed.
        p.   cm.
    Includes bibliographical references and index.
    ISBN 0-13-535683-0
    1. Literature. 2. Literature—Collections. 3. Exposition
(Rhetoric) 4. College readers. I. Jacobs, Henry E. II. Title.
PN45.R575 1991   808′.0668—dc20   91-14062 CIP

Editorial and production supervision: **John Rousselle**
Acquisitions Editor: **Kate Morgan**
Development Editor: **Leslie Taggart**
Supplements Editor: **Ann Knitel**
Copy Editor: **Anne Lesser**
Prepress Buyer: **Herb Klein**
Manufacturing Buyer: **Patrice Fraccio**
Permissions Specialist: **Mary Helen Fitzgerald**
Photo Researcher: **Kay Dellosa**
Photo Editor: **Lori Morris-Nantz**
Cover Designer: **Karen A. Stephens**

Cover photo: Kathleen Norris-Cook/The Image Bank

Credits and copyright acknowledgments appear on pp. 1631–1638,
which constitute an extension of the copyright page.

 © 1992, 1989, 1987 by Prentice-Hall, Inc.
A Simon & Schuster Company
Englewood Cliffs, New Jersey 07632

Printed in the United States of America

10 9 8 7 6 5 4 3 2 1

ISBN 0-13-535683-0

Prentice-Hall International (UK) Limited, *London*
Prentice-Hall of Australia Pty. Limited, *Sydney*
Prentice-Hall Canada Inc., *Toronto*
Prentice-Hall Hispanoamericana, S.A., *Mexico*
Prentice-Hall of India Private Limited, *New Delhi*
Prentice-Hall of Japan, Inc., *Tokyo*
Simon & Schuster Asia Pte. Ltd., *Singapore*
Editora Prentice-Hall do Brasil, Ltda., *Rio de Janeiro*

Brief Contents

Drama

Contents

Poetry

12   MEETING POETRY: AN OVERVIEW   *519*

13   CHARACTER AND SETTING: WHO, WHAT, WHERE, AND WHEN IN POETRY   *540*

14   WORDS: THE BUILDING BLOCKS OF POETRY   576

15   IMAGERY: THE POEM'S LINK TO THE SENSES   600

16   RHETORICAL FIGURES: A SOURCE OF DEPTH AND RANGE IN POETRY *622*

17   TONE: THE CREATION OF ATTITUDE IN POETRY *654*

18   PROSODY: SOUND, RHYTHM, AND RHYME IN POETRY   *677*

24   ADDITIONAL POEMS   *882*

Drama

Preface

The third edition of *Literature: An Introduction to Reading and Writing* is a unique book. Not only an excellent anthology, it is also a comprehensive guide to writing essays about literature. It therefore has a broader mission than most anthologies. Indeed, we began with the aim of incorporating literary selections within a context of writing, and we now reaffirm this aim.

The integration of reading literature and writing essays begins in Chapter 1, which has been revised extensively to highlight this goal. As in the second edition, Guy de Maupassant's famous story "The Necklace" is printed along with sample marginal comments to illustrate the process of active reading. The comments are then embodied within an expanding set of prewriting activities: journal entries, brainstorming and freewriting, general observations, selected details focusing on a major aspect to develop in an essay, an essay outline, and an early draft of an essay that has evolved out of the foregoing work. Following this section is an extensive analysis of revising through sharpening focus, stressing pertinent evidence, and clarifying language. Finally, a more advanced revision of the earlier draft is presented to demonstrate how greater breadth, emphasis, and clarity have been achieved in light of the principles developed throughout Chapter 1.

Organization

We have arranged the sections of the book in the commonly accepted order of fiction, poetry, and drama, for these genres form a natural progression from the less difficult to the more difficult, though instructors are free to make assignments from any section as they wish. We have also sought to provide a broad range of authors from a variety of cultural and ethnic groups, reflecting current critical trends of reexamining and widening the literary canon. Thus, there are works by men and women, blacks and whites, Hispanics and Native Americans, conservatives and liberals, people with strong religious convictions and others who are indifferent. We have included works by writers with secure places in the history of literature as well as by writers who are less well known.

In the sections on fiction and poetry, the chapters cover elements such as character, setting, tone, imagery, theme, and symbolism. In the drama section, the chapters deal with major categories such as tragedy and comedy. We have chosen this approach, rather than a thematic or historical one, because it permits students to analyze various aspects of literature one at a time and in depth.

The chapters each begin with general discussions of the particular elements or techniques, and include analyses—some brief, a few more extensive—of some of the works included there. References are also freely made to relevant works in other chapters. The intention of the discussions is not to preempt the student's own reading and thinking, but rather to provide specimens, or models, of how the precepts in the chapters may be realized in reading and analysis. Key terms and concepts are boldfaced, and these are gathered together and explained briefly in a comprehensive glossary at the back of the book, and also listed in the inside back cover.

The introductory material in each chapter is followed by selections to be read and studied in the context of the chapter, and also to be considered fully and independently for their content, mode, and style. When necessary for understanding, we provide brief marginal glosses and longer explanatory footnotes. Words that are defined or explained are highlighted by a small degree sign (°) in the text. Following each selection in the discussion chapters are study questions designed to help students explore and understand the selection. Some questions are factual and may be quickly answered. Others provoke extended thought and classroom discussion, and they may also serve for both in-class and out-of-class writing assignments.

The Selections and the Reading Apparatus

In the fiction section the number of stories has been expanded to a total of 53, compared with 48 and 39 in the second and first editions. All are suitable for discussion in a single classroom period, if desired, and some of the shorter stories may be read collectively in a period, with time left for discussion while the reading is still fresh in students' minds. Ten of the stories are entirely new in this edition, and one has been restored from the first edition (because of requests from users). Most stories in the section are by authors from the United States, England, and Canada, but South America, France, South Africa, ancient Greece and Rome, and Russia are also represented. In addition, we emphasize that 23 of the stories are by women, making the story selection one of the most balanced to be found in any comprehensive anthology.

Of particular note, to strengthen the connection between reading and dramatization, a number of stories are included not only because they are good, but also because they are available on videocassettes which may be used as teaching tools for support and interpretation (but not as substitutes for reading). In addition, for unique comparison we include two versions of the same subject matter—a short story and a one-act play—by the same author: Susan Glaspell's "A Jury of Her Peers" and *Trifles*. The result of these changes is a representative and challenging selection of fiction for both beginning and also more advanced students. As in the first two editions, the last chapter of the section (Chapter 11) contains a selection of stories for further study. Also, the paragraphs of all stories are numbered, by fives, for easy location and reference.

The poetry section is confined to poems in original English, written by men and women alike from all areas of English-speaking culture. There are 346 poems, many by "standard" poets such as Shakespeare, Wordsworth, Frost, Donne, Dickinson, Roethke, Bogan, Bishop, and Plath, and many by recent poets such as Song, Giovanni, Angelou, Adamé, Hacker, and Dove. The chapters are arranged according to particular characteristics or techniques (e.g., symbols, form, myth), in the expectation that the book will be used to teach important aspects of poetry. But the selections are also comprehensive enough to permit observations about the development of poetry in both England and the United States.

In the third edition our goal has been to strengthen the usefulness of these poetry chapters. Hence, almost all the introductory sections have been revised and rewritten to make them more focused and clear. If increased discussion results from these sections, the goal will have been reached. Because this book may often be used for reference as well as study and writing assignments, the length of the prosody chapter has been preserved. Any student who works with the poetry section will increasingly be able to read poetry with understanding and appreciation, and to write about it with skill, knowledge, and confidence. For further study, as in past editions, a final chapter contains many additional poems from all periods of poetry, in alphabetical order by the author's last name. For convenient reference, every fifth line of all poems is numbered.

The drama section, which includes thirteen plays and two film scenes, has also been revised to emphasize its usefulness for students. The longer and more important plays have been kept because they seem essential for any study of drama (*Oedipus the King, Hamlet, A Midsummer Night's Dream, Death of a Salesman*). Ibsen has been retained as a giant in the history of drama, but *A Doll's House* has been replaced with *An Enemy of the People* in a new translation specially prepared for this edition. Among the shorter plays, *Tea Party, Am I Blue*, and *Love Is the Doctor* (all new to the second edition) are continued. At the suggestion of a number of users of the second edition who want to introduce film into their courses, a unique feature of the third edition is the addition of a new chapter on film (Chapter 29) designed to match the introductory sections on fiction, poetry, and drama. In this new chapter we have included scenes from Welles's *Citizen Kane* and Laurents's *The Turning Point*. In effect, then, the drama sections contains fifteen separate works.

The number of short plays deserves note. Their advantage is that they may be covered within a single classroom period, and that they can also be made especially vivid by the assignment of acting parts to students for complete readings within a relatively short time. Indeed, *Tea Party* could be read and discussed in the same class. The possibilities for the shorter plays, therefore, are extensive.

As in the first two editions, every fifth line of the poetic dramas is numbered. Every fifth speech in the prose dramas is also numbered, a feature that was introduced in the second edition. This system of ready reference makes the plays consistent with the stories and poems.

To place the various works in their historical context, we include the life dates for all authors. All the authors are listed together chronologically on the inside front cover. In addition, we give the date of publication for each work in the text, along with a date of composition, when known, in parentheses.

Writing as a Major Goal of the Third Edition

Writing about literature is not a minor topic that can be addressed in a separate section at the back of the book. It is a coequal concern, and therefore we stress the study and preparation needed for good writing about the topics of all chapters. These approaches to writing, developed from tested principles of studying literature together with our own classroom experience, have been presented for more than twenty-eight years in *Writing Themes About Literature* by Edgar V. Roberts.

The skills needed for writing effective essays about literature do not represent a distinct body of knowledge. Rather, careful reading and effective writing are integrated, making this book unique. Both reading and writing ask that students be able to point to specific features to support their conclusions and make them logical.

To this end, we have supplied guides showing students the way to move from reading literature to responding and thinking, and then to planning and writing. These discussions are carefully designed to help students write confidently on the topic or technique of each chapter. In the third edition, each writing section has been revised to emphasize the actual *process* of writing: planning an essay, developing a controlling idea, selecting supporting details from the work at hand, organizing thoughts effectively, and beginning the writing process and bringing it to a conclusion. The emphasis in the revisions has been to stress the openness of the writing process and unique nature of writing for each new approach and topic, without ignoring the need to produce finished drafts ready for submission. Hence, in virtually all the chapters, we have proposed questions for discovering ideas and strategies for developing ideas. Students armed with these techniques can move forward in their writing, knowing that they may generate new ideas in the process and incorporate them in their growing and changing essays.

In these writing sections we do not simply *say* what can be done with a topic of literary study, but we also *show* ways in which it might be done. Each writing section concludes with a sample essay (sometimes more than one) to exemplify the methods and strategies discussed. Following the essay is a commentary, showing how the principles of writing presented in the discussion have been carried out. Thus, all of the writing sections may be combined with the brief exemplary discussions in the introductory sections to provide comprehensive guidance for students with papers to write.

In addition, at the end of each chapter is a set of questions designed for writing assignments. These sets were introduced into the second edition, and are changed and modified as necessary for this new edition. Many of these questions involve comparison-contrast, and for help the students may consult the discussion of this technique in Appendix B—a section that is also useful for test questions involving the comparison of two or more works. In addition, some of these end-of-chapter assignments provide students with ideas for writing their own creative works (e.g., "Write a poem" or "Compose a short scene"). The goal of these is not to demand superb poems, scenes, or stories, but rather to give students a "hands-on" experience with the literary techniques discussed in the chapters. This aspect of the assignments should therefore help students understand literature from the standpoint of their own creative writing experience.

Major Goals of This Book

The skills of reading and writing are useful far beyond the study of literature. Effective techniques acquired in the systematic use of this book will help students in every course they may ever take, and in whatever profession they follow when they leave school. Students may not have many future occasions to read the authors anthologized here, but they will always *read*—if not these authors, then other authors, and certainly always newspapers, legal documents, magazine articles, technical reports, business proposals, and much more. Although students may never be required to write again about specific literary topics like setting, structure, and metaphor, they will certainly find future situations requiring them to *write*. Indeed, the more effectively students learn to write about literature during their introduction-to-literature courses, the better they will be able to write—no matter what the topic—later on. And, we add, it is increasingly clear that the power to analyze problems and make convincing written and oral presentations is a major quality of leadership and general excellence.

While we stress the value of our book as a teaching tool, we also emphasize that literature is to be enjoyed. Sometimes we overlook the truth that study and delight are complementary processes, and that intellectual and emotional enjoyment develops not only from the immediate responses of amusement, involvement, and sympathy but also from increasing depths of understanding, assimilation, and contemplation. We therefore hope that the literature in this text will teach students about humanity, about their own perceptions, feelings, and lives, and about the timeless patterns of human existence. We hope they will take delight in such discoveries, and grow as they make them. We see the book, then, not as an end, but rather as a beginning of lifelong understanding and joy in great literature.

ACKNOWLEDGMENTS

As the book goes into the third edition, I wish to acknowledge the many people who have offered helpful advice, information, and suggestions. To name them, as Dryden says in *Absalom and Achitophel*, is to praise them. They are Professors Robert Halli, Claudia Johnson, Matthew Marino, and Matthew Winston, Eileen Allman, David Bady, Alice Griffin, Gerhard Joseph, Ruth Milberg-Kaye, Nancy Miller, Michael Paull, Scott Westrem, Mardi Valgemae, and Dan Rubey, and also Christel Bell, Linda Bridgers, Catherine Davis, Edward Hoeppner, Anna F. Jacobs, Rex Butt, Nanette Roberts, April Roberts, Eleanor Tubbs, and Eve Zarin. The skilled assistance of Jonathan Roberts has been invaluable at every stage of all the editions.

A number of other people have provided sterling guidance for the preparation of the third edition. They are: Robert Barrier, Kennesaw State College; Harryette Brown, Eastfield College; Michael Budd, Bryant College; Diane W. Gaus, Bryant College; Alice Maclin, DeKalb College; Grace McNamara, DeKalb College; James Marsden, Bryant College; Liz Meador, Wayne Community College; Joseph Urgo, Bryant College; Ralph F. Voss, University of Alabama; and Johnnie R. Williams, DeKalb College.

A word of special thanks goes to Bill Oliver, former Prentice Hall English Editor, and to Phil Miller, Editor-in-Chief, Humanities, for their imagination, foresight, support, and patience in the development and revision of this project. Of major importance has been the work of Kate Morgan, English Editor at Prentice Hall. Her inventiveness, creativeness, adaptability, understanding, firmness, and constant good humor have made working with her the greatest of pleasures. I am also deeply indebted to Leslie Taggart for her many improvements not only in the various writing sections but also in the first chapter. I also extend my thanks to Ray Mullaney, Editor-in-Chief, Development, for his pioneering work with the text, to Mary Helen Fitzgerald, for her diligent pursuit of permissions, and to Heidi Moore. Special words of thanks are reserved for John Rousselle, the production editor, and for Anne Lesser, the copy editor.

The saddest acknowledgment I make is to my associate on this project, Professor Henry E. Jacobs of the University of Alabama. His sudden death in 1986 was a stunning blow. Without him, there would have been no book, for his vision, energy, and intelligence were essential in the planning and writing of the first edition. All subsequent editions represent, as it were, a continued collaboration, even though the version that I now present is surely different in details, but not in general outline, from what we would have presented together. My memories of a superb and highly valued colleague have remained firm, and my regret and sorrow at his passing have not diminished.

EDGAR V. ROBERTS

LITERATURE

1

Introduction: Reading, Responding, and Writing About Literature

WHAT IS LITERATURE, AND WHY DO WE STUDY IT?

Broadly, we use the word **literature** to mean compositions designed to tell stories, dramatize situations, express emotions, and analyze and advocate ideas. Works composed before the invention of writing were necessarily spoken or sung, and were retained only as long as living people knew them and performed them. While many of these oral works are lost, many have also been saved and preserved as printed texts. The oral tradition of literature still exists, with many poems designed to be read aloud in their entirety, and with all plays intended to be acted and spoken by live actors. Today, however, writing and printing give life to most literature. As a result, reading and appreciating literary texts is often a totally private, silent experience.

Whatever the form in which literature is assimilated, it has much to offer, almost as many things as there are people. In fact, people often cannot explain why they enjoy reading, for goals and ideals are not easily articulated. There are, however, areas of general agreement about what the systematic and extensive reading of literature can do.

Literature helps us grow, both personally and intellectually. It provides an objective base for knowledge and understanding. It links us with the broader cultural, philosophic, and religious world of which we are a part. It enables us to recognize human dreams and struggles in different places and times that we would never otherwise know. It helps us to develop mature sensibility and compassion for the condition of *all* living things—human, animal, and vegetable. It gives us the knowledge and perception to appreciate the beauty of order and arrangement, just as a well-structured song or a beautifully painted canvas can. It provides the comparative basis from which we can see worthiness in the aims of all people, and it therefore helps us see beauty in the world around us. It exercises our emotions through interest, concern, tension, excitement, hope, fear, regret, laughter, and sympathy. Through cumulative experience in reading, literature shapes goals and values by clarifying our own identities, both positively, through acceptance of the admirable in human beings, and negatively, through rejection of the sinister. It helps us shape our judgments through the comparison of the good and the bad. Both in our everyday activities and in the decisions we make as individuals and as citizens, it enables us to develop a perspective on events occurring locally and globally, and thereby it gives us understanding and control. It encourages us to assist creative, talented people who need recognition and support. It is one of the shaping influences of life. It makes us human.

TYPES OF LITERATURE: THE GENRES

Literature may be classified into four categories or *genres:* (1) prose fiction, (2) poetry, (3) drama, and (4) nonfiction prose. While all are art forms, each with its own requirements of structure and style, usually the first three are classed as **imaginative literature.**

The genres of imaginative literature have much in common, but they also have distinguishing characteristics. **Prose fiction, or narrative fiction,** includes **novels, short stories, myths, parables, romances,** and **epics.** *Fiction* originally meant anything made up, crafted, or shaped, but as we understand the word today, it means a prose story based in the imagination of the author. Although fiction, like all imaginative literature, may introduce true historical details, it is not real history, for its purpose is primarily to interest, divert, stimulate, and instruct. The essence of fiction is **narration,** the relating or recounting of a sequence of events or actions. Works of fiction usually focus on one or a few major characters who undergo some kind of change as they interact with other characters and deal with problems. **Poetry** is more economical than prose fiction in the use of words, and it relies heavily on **imagery, figurative language,** and **sound. Drama** is literature designed to be performed by actors. Like fiction, drama may focus on a single character or a small number of characters, and it presents fictional events as if they were happening in the present, to be witnessed by an audience. Although most modern plays present dialogue in prose, on the ground that dramatic speech should be as lifelike as possible, many plays from the past, like those of ancient Greece and Renaissance England, are in poetic form.

Imaginative literature differs from **nonfiction prose,** the fourth genre, which consists of news reports, feature articles, essays, editorials, textbooks, historical and biographical works, and the like, all of which describe or interpret facts and present judgments and opinions. Major goals of nonfiction prose are truth in reporting and logic in reasoning. It bears repeating that the truth in imaginative literature, unlike that in nonfiction prose, is truth to life and human nature, not to the factual world of news, science, and history.

READING LITERATURE AND RESPONDING TO IT ACTIVELY

Do not expect a cursory reading to produce full understanding. After a quick reading of a work, it may be embarrassingly difficult to answer pointed questions or to say anything intelligent about it at all. A more careful, active reading gives us the understanding to develop well-considered answers. Obviously, we must first follow the work and understand its details, but more importantly we must respond to the words, get at the ideas, and understand the implications of what is happening. We must apply our own experiences to verify the accuracy and truth of the situation and incidents, and we must articulate our own emotional responses to the characters and their problems.

To illustrate such active responding, the following story, "The Necklace" (1884), by the French writer Guy de Maupassant, is printed with the sorts of marginal annotations that any reader might make while reading. Many of the observations, particularly at the beginning, are *assimilative*; that is, they do no more than record details and turning points in the action. But as the story progresses the comments increasingly reflect responses to the story's developing meaning. Toward the story's end, the comments are full rather than minimal, for they result not only from a first reading, but also from a second and third. Here, then, is Maupassant's "The Necklace":

GUY DE MAUPASSANT   (1850–1893)

The Necklace   *1884*

Translated by Edgar V. Roberts

She was one of those pretty and charming women, born, as if by an error of destiny, into a family of clerks and copyists. She had no dowry, no prospects, no way of getting known, courted, loved, married by a rich and distinguished man. She finally settled for a marriage with a minor clerk in the Ministry of Education.

She was a simple person, without the money to dress well, but she was as unhappy as if she had gone through bankruptcy, for women have neither rank nor race. In place of high birth or important family connections, they can rely only on their beauty, their grace, and their charm. Their inborn finesse, their elegant taste, their engaging

> "She" is pretty but poor. Apparently there is no other life for her than marriage. Without connections, she has no entry into high society, and marries an insignificant clerk.
>
> She is unhappy.
>
> A view of women that excludes the possibility of a career. In 1884, women had little else than their personalities to get ahead.

personalities, which are their only power, make working-class women the equals of the grandest ladies.

She suffered constantly, feeling herself destined for all delicacies and luxuries. She suffered because of her grim apartment with its drab walls, threadbare furniture, ugly curtains. All such things, which most other women in her situation would not even have noticed, tortured her and filled her with despair. The sight of the young country girl who did her simple housework awakened in her only a sense of desolation and lost hopes. She daydreamed of large, silent anterooms, decorated with oriental tapestries and lighted by high bronze floor lamps, with two elegant valets in short culottes dozing in large armchairs under the effects of forced-air heaters. She visualized large drawing rooms draped in the most expensive silks, with fine end tables on which were placed knickknacks of inestimable value. She dreamed of the perfume of dainty private rooms, which were designed only for intimate tête-à-têtes with the closest friends, who because of their achievements and fame would make her the envy of all other women.

She suffers because of her cheap belongings, wanting expensive things. She dreams of wealth and of how other women would envy her if she had all these fine things. But these luxuries are unrealistic and unattainable for her.

When she sat down to dinner at her round little table covered with a cloth that had not been washed for three days, in front of her husband who opened the kettle while declaring ecstatically, "Ah, good old boiled beef! I don't know anything better," she dreamed of expensive banquets with shining place settings, and wall hangings depicting ancient heroes and exotic birds in an enchanted forest. She imagined a gourmet-prepared main course carried on the most exquisite trays and served on the most beautiful dishes, with whispered gallantries which she would hear with a sphinxlike smile as she dined on the pink meat of a trout or the delicate wing of a quail.

Her husband's taste is for plain things, while she dreams of expensive gourmet food. He has adjusted to his status. She has not.

5   She had no decent dresses, no jewels, nothing. And she loved nothing but these; she believed herself born only for these. She burned with the desire to please, to be envied, to be attractive and sought after.

She lives for her unrealistic dreams, and these increase her frustration.

She had a rich friend, a comrade from convent days, whom she did not want to see anymore because she suffered so much when she returned home. She would weep for the entire day afterward with sorrow, regret, despair, and misery.

She even thinks of giving up a rich friend because she is so depressed after visiting her.

Well, one evening, her husband came home glowing and carrying a large envelope.

A new section in the story.

"Here," he said, "this is something for you."

She quickly tore open the envelope and took out a card engraved with these words:

The Chancellor of Education and Mrs. George Ramponneau request that Mr. and Mrs. Loisel do them the

An invitation to dinner at the Ministry of Education. A big plum.

honor of coming to dinner at the Ministry of Education
on the evening of January 8.

10   Instead of being delighted, as her husband had
hoped, she threw the invitation spitefully on the table,
muttering:

"What do you expect me to do with this?"

   It only upsets her.

"But honey, I thought you'd be glad. You never get
to go out, and this is a special occasion! I had a lot of
trouble getting the invitation. Everyone wants one; the
demand is high and not many clerks get invited. Everyone
important will be there."

She looked at him angrily and stated impatiently:

"What do you want me to wear to go there?"

   She declares that she hasn't anything to wear. He tries to persuade her that her theater dress might do for the occasion.

15   He had not thought of that. He stammered:

"But your theater dress. That seems nice to me . . ."

He stopped, amazed and bewildered, as his wife
began to cry. Large tears fell slowly from the corners of
her eyes to her mouth. He said falteringly:

"What's wrong? What's the matter?"

But with a strong effort she had recovered, and she
answered calmly as she wiped her damp cheeks:

20   "Nothing, except that I have nothing to wear and
therefore can't go to the party. Give your invitation to
someone else at the office whose wife will have nicer clothes
than mine."

Distressed, he responded:

"Well, all right, Mathilde. How much would a new
dress cost, something you could use at other times, but not
anything fancy?"

   Her name is Mathilde. He volunteers to pay for a new dress.

She thought for a few moments, adding things up
and thinking also of an amount that she could ask without
getting an immediate refusal and a frightened outcry from
the frugal clerk.

   She is manipulating him.

Finally she responded tentatively:

25   "I don't know exactly, but it seems to me that I could
get by on four hundred francs."

He blanched slightly at this, because he had set aside
just that amount to buy a shotgun for Sunday lark-hunts
the next summer with a few friends in the Plain of Nanterre.

   The dress will cost him his next summer's vacation. (He doesn't seem to have included her in his plans.)

However, he said:

"All right, you've got four hundred francs, but make
it a pretty dress."

As the day of the party drew near, Mrs. Loisel seemed
sad, uneasy, anxious, even though her gown was all ready.
One evening her husband said to her:

   A new section, the third in the story. The day of the party is near.

30   "What's the matter? You've been acting funny for
several days."

She answered:

"It's awful, but I don't have any jewels to wear, not a single gem, nothing to dress up my outfit. I'll look like a beggar. I'd almost rather not go to the party."

Now she complains that she doesn't have any nice jewelry. She is manipulating him again.

He responded:

"You can wear a corsage of cut flowers. This year it's all the rage. For only ten francs you can get two or three gorgeous roses."

35 She was not convinced.

"No . . . there's nothing more humiliating than looking shabby in the company of rich women."

She has a very good point, but there seems to be no way out.

But her husband exclaimed:

"God, but you're silly! Go to your friend Mrs. Forrestier, and ask her to lend you some jewelry. You know her well enough to do that."

He proposes a solution: borrow jewelry from Mrs. Forrestier, who is apparently the rich friend mentioned earlier.

She uttered a cry of joy:

40 "That's right. I hadn't thought of that."

The next day she went to her friend's house and described her problem.

Mrs. Forrestier went to her mirrored wardrobe, took out a large jewel box, opened it, and said to Mrs. Loisel: "Choose, my dear."

Mathilde will have her choice of jewels.

She saw bracelets, then a pearl necklace, then a Venetian cross of finely worked gold and gems. She tried on the jewelry in front of a mirror, and hesitated, unable to make up her mind about each one. She kept asking:

45 "Do you have anything else?"

"Certainly. Look to your heart's content. I don't know what will please you most."

Suddenly she found, in a black satin box, a superb diamond necklace, and her heart throbbed with desire for it. Her hands shook as she picked it up. She fastened it around her neck, watched it gleam at her throat, and looked at herself ecstatically.

A "superb" diamond necklace.

Then she asked, haltingly and anxiously:

"Could you lend me this, nothing but this?"

50 "Why yes, certainly."

This is what she wants, just this.

She jumped up, hugged her friend joyfully, then hurried away with her treasure.

She leaves with the "treasure."

The day of the party came. Mrs. Loisel was a success. She was prettier than anyone else, stylish, graceful, smiling, and wild with joy. All the men saw her, asked her name, sought to be introduced. All the important administrators stood in line to waltz with her. The Chancellor himself eyed her.

A new section.

The party. Mathilde is a huge success.

She danced joyfully, passionately, intoxicated with pleasure, thinking of nothing but the moment, in the triumph of her beauty, in the glory of her success, on cloud

Another judgment about women. Don't men want admiration, too?

nine with happiness made up of all the admiration, of all the aroused desire, of this victory so complete and so sweet to the heart of any woman.

She did not leave until four o'clock in the morning. Her husband, since midnight, had been sleeping in a little empty room with three other men whose wives had also been enjoying themselves.

Loisel, with other husbands, is bored, while the wives are having a ball.

55   He threw over her shoulders the shawl that he had brought for the trip home, a modest everyday wrap, the poverty of which contrasted sharply with the elegance of her evening gown. She felt it and hurried away to avoid being noticed by the other women who luxuriated in rich furs.

Ashamed of her wrap, she rushes away to avoid being seen.

Loisel tried to hold her back:

"Wait a minute. You'll catch cold outdoors. I'll call a cab."

But she paid no attention and hurried down the stairs. When they reached the street they found no carriages. They began to look for one, shouting at cabmen passing by at a distance.

They walked toward the Seine, desperate, shivering. Finally, on a quay, they found one of those old night-going buggies that are seen in Paris only after dark, as if they were ashamed of their wretched appearance in daylight.

A comedown after the nice evening. They take a wretched-looking buggy home.

60   It took them to their door, on the Street of Martyrs, and they sadly climbed the stairs to their flat. For her, it was finished. As for him, he could think only that he had to begin work at the Ministry of Education at ten o'clock.

"Street of Martyrs." Is this name significant?

Loisel is down-to-earth.

She took the shawl off her shoulders, in front of the mirror, to see herself once more in her glory. But suddenly she cried out. The necklace was no longer around her neck!

SHE HAS LOST THE NECKLACE!

Her husband, already half undressed, asked:

"What's wrong?"

She turned toward him frantically:

65   "I . . . I . . . I no longer have Mrs. Forrestier's necklace."

He stood up bewildered:

"What! . . . How! . . . It's not possible!"

And they looked in the folds of the gown, in the folds of the shawl, in the pockets, everywhere. They found nothing.

He asked:

70   "You're sure you still had it when you left the party?"

They can't find it.

"Yes. I checked it in the vestibule of the Ministry."

"But if you had lost it in the street, we would have heard it fall. It must be in the cab."

"Yes, probably. Did you notice the number?"

"No. Did you see it?"

75   "No."

Overwhelmed, they looked at each other. Finally, Loisel got dressed again:

"I'm going out to retrace all our steps," he said, "to see if I can find the necklace that way."

And he went out. She stayed in her evening dress, without the energy to get ready for bed, stretched out in a chair, drained of strength and thought.

Her husband came back at about seven o'clock. He had found nothing.

80   He went to Police Headquarters and to the newspapers to announce a reward. He went to the small cab companies, and finally he followed up even the slightest hopeful lead.

She waited the entire day, in the same enervated state, in the face of this frightful disaster.

Loisel came back in the evening, his face pale and haggard. He had found nothing.

"You'll have to write to your friend," he said, "that you broke a clasp on her necklace and that you are having it fixed. That will give us time to look around."

She wrote as he dictated.

85   At the end of a week they had lost all hope.

And Loisel, looking five years older, declared:

"We'll have to see about replacing the jewels."

The next day they took the case which had contained the necklace and went to the jeweler whose name was inside. He looked at his books:

"I wasn't the one, Madam, who sold the necklace. I only made the case."

90   Then they went from jeweler to jeweler, searching for a necklace like the other one, racking their memories, both of them sick with worry and anguish.

In a shop in the Palais-Royal, they found a necklace of diamonds that seemed to them exactly like the one they were looking for. It was priced at forty thousand francs. They could buy it for thirty-six thousand.

They got the jeweler to promise not to sell it for three days. And they made an agreement that he would buy it back for thirty-four thousand francs if the original was recovered before the end of February.

Loisel had saved eighteen thousand francs that his father had left him. He would have to borrow the rest.

He borrowed, asking a thousand francs from one, five hundred from another, five louis° here, three louis there. He wrote promissory notes, undertook ruinous obligations, did business with finance companies and the

---

He goes out to search for the necklace.

But is unsuccessful.

He really tries. He is doing his best.

Loisel's plan to explain delaying the return. He takes charge, is resourceful.

Things are hopeless.

They hunt for a replacement.

A new diamond necklace will cost 36,000 francs.

They make a deal with the jeweler. (Is Maupassant hinting that things might work out for them?)

It will take all of Loisel's inheritance plus another 18,000 francs that must be borrowed at enormous rates of interest.

° *louis:* a gold coin worth twenty francs.

whole tribe of loan sharks. He compromised himself for the remainder of his days, risked his signature without knowing whether he would be able to honor it, and, terrified by anguish over the future, by the black misery that was about to descend on him, by the prospect of all kinds of physical deprivations and moral tortures, he went to get the new necklace, and put down thirty-six thousand francs on the jeweler's counter.

95   Mrs. Loisel took the necklace back to Mrs. Forrestier, who said with an offended tone:

"You should have brought it back sooner; I might have needed it."

Mrs. Forrestier complains about the delay.

She did not open the case, as her friend feared she might. If she had noticed the substitution, what would she have thought? What would she have said? Would she not have taken her for a thief?

Is this enough justification for not telling the truth? It seems to be for the Loisels.

Mrs. Loisel soon discovered the horrible life of the needy. She did her share, however, completely, heroically. That horrifying debt had to be paid. She would pay. They dismissed the maid; they changed their address; they rented an attic flat.

A new section, the fifth.

She learned to do the heavy housework, dirty kitchen jobs. She washed the dishes, wearing away her manicured fingernails on greasy pots and encrusted baking dishes. She handwashed dirty linen, shirts, and dish towels that she hung out on the line to dry. Each morning, she took the garbage down to the street, and she carried up water, stopping at each floor to catch her breath. And, dressed in cheap house dresses, she went to the fruit dealer, the grocer, the butchers, with her basket under her arms, haggling, insulting, defending her measly cash penny by penny.

They suffer to repay their debts. Loisel works late at night. Mathilde accepts a cheap attic flat, and does all the heavy housework herself to save on domestic help.

She pinches pennies, and haggles with the local merchants.

100   They had to make installment payments every month, and, to buy more time, to refinance loans.

They struggle to meet payments.

The husband worked evenings to make fair copies of tradesmen's accounts, and late into the night he made copies at five cents a page.

Mr. Loisel moonlights to make extra money.

And this life lasted ten years.

At the end of ten years, they had paid back everything—everything—including the extra charges imposed by loan sharks and the accumulation of compound interest.

For ten years they endure.

The last section. They have finally paid back the entire debt.

Mrs. Loisel looked old now. She had become the strong, hard, and rude woman of poor households. Her hair unkempt, with uneven skirts and rough, red hands, she spoke loudly, washed floors with large buckets of water. But sometimes, when her husband was at work, she sat down near the window, and she dreamed of that evening

Mrs. Loisel (how come the narrator does not say "Mathilde"?) is roughened and aged by the work. But she has behaved "heroically" (¶ 98), and has shown her mettle.

so long ago, of that party, where she had been so beautiful and so admired.

105   What would life have been like if she had not lost that necklace? Who knows? Who knows? Life is so peculiar, so uncertain. How little a thing it takes to destroy you or to save you!

A moral? Our lives are shaped by small, uncertain things; we hang by a thread.

Well, one Sunday, when she had gone for a stroll along the Champs-Elysées to relax from the cares of the week, she suddenly noticed a woman walking with a child. It was Mrs. Forrestier, still youthful, still beautiful, still attractive.

A scene on the Champs-Elysées. She sees Jeanne Forrestier, after ten years.

Mrs. Loisel felt moved. Would she speak to her? Yes, certainly. And now that she had paid, she could tell all. Why not?

She walked closer.

"Hello, Jeanne."

110   The other gave no sign of recognition and was astonished to be addressed so familiarly by this working-class woman. She stammered:

"But . . . Madam! . . . I don't know . . . You must have made a mistake."

"No. I'm Mathilde Loisel."

Her friend cried out.

"Oh! . . . My poor Mathilde, you've changed so much."

Jeanne notes Mathilde's changed appearance.

115   "Yes. I've had some tough times since I saw you last; in fact, hardships . . . and all because of you! . . ."

"Of me . . . how so?"

"You remember the diamond necklace that you lent me to go to the party at the Ministry of Education?"

Mathilde tells Jeanne everything.

"Yes. What then?"

"Well, I lost it."

120   "How, since you gave it back to me?"

"I returned another exactly like it. And for ten years we've been paying for it. You understand that this wasn't easy for us, who have nothing. . . . Finally it's over, and I'm damned glad."

Mrs. Forrestier stopped her.

"You say that you bought a diamond necklace to replace mine?"

"Yes, you didn't notice it, eh? It was exactly like yours."

125   And she smiled with proud and childish joy.

Mrs. Forrestier, deeply moved, took both her hands.

"Oh, my poor Mathilde! But mine was only costume jewelry. At most, it was worth only five hundred francs! . . ."

*SURPRISE! The lost necklace was **not** real diamonds, and the Loisels slaved for no reason at all. But hard work and sacrifice probably brought out better qualities in Mathilde than she otherwise might have shown. Is this the moral of the story?*

READING AND RESPONDING IN A JOURNAL

The marginal comments demonstrate the active reading-responding process you should apply with everything you read. You may freely use your text margins to record your comments and questions, but you should also keep a journal for lengthier responses. The journal will be useful not only as you read, but also as you gradually shape your initial impressions into a thoughtful analysis of a work.

Your primary objective is to learn an assigned work inside and out, and then to make perceptive comments about it. To achieve this goal, you must be willing to read the work more than once. If you haven't already developed a good note-taking system, you will need to create one, so that as you read you can develop a "memory bank" of your own knowledge about a work. You can draw from this fund of ideas when you begin to write.

Whether you are preparing a particular assignment or not, you should use your journal in the ways described here. To begin, follow the *Guidelines for Reading*. Each time you read a work, new ideas will occur to you. To secure your first impressions and basic understanding, however, take the following steps as you read it for the first time.

GUIDELINES FOR READING

1. Observations for Basic Understanding
   a. Determine what is happening in the story. For a story or play, where do the actions take place? What do they show? Who is involved? Who is the major figure? Why is he or she major? What relationships do the characters have with each other? What concerns do the characters have? What do they do? Who says what to whom? What do the speeches do to advance the action and to advance your understanding of the characters? For a poem, who is talking, and to whom? What is the situation, and what does the speaker say about it? Why does the poem end how and where it does?
   b. Trace developing patterns. Make an outline or scheme for the story or main idea: What conflicts appear? Do these conflicts exist between people, groups, or ideas? How does the author resolve them? Is one force, idea, or side the winner? Why? How do you respond to the winner, or loser?
   c. Record things that you think need explaining. Write down words that are new or not immediately clear. Whenever you run across a passage that you do not quickly understand, decide whether the problem arises from unknown words. Use your dictionary and write the relevant meanings in your notebook, but be sure that these meanings clarify your understanding. Make note of special difficulties so that you may ask your instructor about them.
   d. In your journal, or on separate cards, write out in full some of the passages that you think are interesting, well written, and important. Keep these passages within easy reach, and when riding public trans-

portation, walking to class, or otherwise not occupying your time, *memorize* sentences, lines, and phrases.

    e.   Always, whenever questions occur to you, make a note of them for use in class and also in your own further study.

2.   Notes on First Impressions

    a.   Make a record of your reactions and responses, which you may derive from your marginal notations. Is there anything funny, memorable, noteworthy, or otherwise striking? Did you laugh, smile, worry, get scared, feel a thrill, learn a great deal, feel proud, find a lot to think about?

    b.   Make notes on interesting characterizations, events, techniques, and ideas. If you like a character or idea, describe what you like, and do the same for characters and ideas you don't like. Is there anything else in the work that you especially like or dislike? Are parts easy or difficult to understand? Why? Are there any surprises? What was your reaction to them? Be sure to use *your own* words in these notes.

Specimen Journal Entries

Following are some sample journal entries on "The Necklace," which follow the suggestions in the *Guidelines*. The entries are related to the responses in the margins of the story (pp. 5–12). What is important now is not the order of observation, which follows the general progress of reading, but that there are enough observations and responses to be useful later, both for additional study and for developing an essay. Notice that not only comments are recorded, but questions as well.

JOURNAL ENTRIES ON MAUPASSANT'S "THE NECKLACE"

Early in the story, Mathilde seems spoiled. She is poor, or at least lower middle class, but is unable to face her own situation.

As a dreamer, she seems harmless. Her daydreams about a fancy home, with all the expensive belongings, are not unusual. Most people dream of being well off.

She seems not to like her husband, and is embarrassed by his taste for plain food. The story contrasts her taste for trout and quail with Loisel's cheaper favorites.

Only when the Loisels get the invitation does Mathilde seem difficult. Her wish for an expensive dress (the cost of Loisel's entire vacation), and then her wanting the jewelry, are problems.

Her success at the party shows that she has the charm the speaker talks about in paragraph 2. She seems never to have had any other chances in life to exert her power.

The worst part of her personality is shown when she hurries away from the party because she is ashamed of her everyday shawl. It is Mathilde's unhappiness and unwillingness to adjust to her modest means that cause the financial downfall of the Loisels. It is her fault.

Borrowing the money to replace the necklace shows that both Loisel and

Mathilde have a strong sense of honor. Making up for the loss is good, even if it destroys them financially.

There are some nice touches, like Loisel's seeming to be five years older (paragraph 86) and his staying with the other husbands of women enjoying themselves (paragraph 54). These are done quickly but tellingly.

It's too bad that Loisel and Mathilde don't tell Jeanne that the jewels are lost. Their pride stops them—or perhaps a fear of being accused of theft.

Their ten years of slavish work (paragraphs 98–102) show how they have come down in life. Mathilde's work must all be done by hand, so she really does pitch in, and is heroic.

The attic flat (paragraph 98) shows Mathilde's strength as it also shows her becoming loud and frumpy. She does what she has to. The earlier apartment and the elegance of her imaginary rooms bring out her limitations.

The setting of the Champs-Elysées also reflects her character, for she feels free there to tell Jeanne about the disastrous loss and sacrifice (paragraph 106), producing the surprise ending.

The narrator's comment about how "little a thing it takes to destroy you or save you" (paragraph 105) is full of thought. The necklace is little, but it makes a huge problem. This creates the story's irony.

Questions: Is this story more about the surprise ending or about the character of Mathilde? Is she to be condemned or admired? Does the outcome stem from the little things that make us or break us, as the speaker suggests, or on the difficulty of rising above one's economic class, which seems true, or both? What do the speaker's remarks about women's status mean? (Remember, the story was published in 1884.) This probably isn't relevant, but wouldn't Jeanne, after hearing about the substitution, give the full value of the necklace to the Loisels, and wouldn't they then be pretty well off?

These are reasonable, if fairly full, remarks and observations about "The Necklace." You should use your journal similarly for *all* reading assignments. If your assignment is simply to learn about a work, general notes like those taken here should be enough. If you are preparing for a test, you might write pointed observations more in line with what is happening in your class, and also write and answer your own questions (see Appendix A, *Taking Examinations on Literature*). If you have a writing assignment, these entries will be the beginning of a process in which you will focus more and more closely on your topic, such as character, idea, or setting. Your journal will then be invaluable in helping you refresh your memory and develop your ideas.

WRITING ESSAYS ON LITERARY TOPICS

Writing is the sharpened, focused expression of thought and study. As you develop your writing skills, you also improve your perceptions and increase your critical faculties. Although few people ever achieve perfection in writing—a state in which words and ideas blend perfectly together—everyone can improve.

The development of your ability to think and to write about literature will also prepare you to write about other topics. Because literature itself contains the subject material, though not in a systematic way, of philosophy, religion, psychology, sociology, and politics, learning to analyze literature and to write about it will also improve your capacity to deal with these and other disciplines.

Writing begins with the search for something to say—an idea. Not all ideas are equal; some are better than others, and getting good ideas is an ability that you develop the more you think and write. Your thinking will improve the longer you engage in the analysis of literature (or of any topic). In the same way, the quality of your thought will improve as you originate ideas, see the flaws in some of your thinking processes, propose new avenues of development, secure new data to support ideas, and create new ideas. Your objective always will be to persuade your reader that your details are correct and that your conclusions are both valid and interesting.

The first stage in the writing process, *discovering ideas*, shares many of the qualities of ordinary conversation. Usually random and disorganized, conversation shifts from topic to topic, often without any apparent cause, and it is repetitive. You discover ideas for writing in the same way, jumping from idea to idea, not necessarily understanding the connections between them. As your ideas begin to take form in the first rough drafts of an essay, the process becomes more like classroom discussion, deliberately structured but also free and spontaneous. As in a classroom discussion, digressions often occur in the rough drafts of an essay. In contrast, the final result of your thinking and writing processes, the finished essay, has to stick with great determination to a specific point. In this final form, writing is the most concise and highly organized form of expression that you will ever create.

When you see a complete, polished, well-formed piece of writing, you may believe that it was always perfect, right from the beginning. Nothing could be further from the truth, for writing usually, if not always, begins in uncertainty and vagueness, and it gets into a presentable form not by magic but only by much thought and work.

If you could see the early drafts of writing you admire, you would be surprised (maybe even shocked), but you might also be encouraged to see that good writers are also human, and that their first versions are messy, uncertain, unfinished, and generally incomplete. In final drafts, many ideas are discarded and others added; new facts are introduced; early paragraphs are cut in half and assembled elsewhere with parts of other paragraphs; much paper is wadded up and thrown into wastebaskets; words are changed and misspellings corrected; sentences are revised or completely rewritten; and new writing is added to tie together the reassembled materials and make them flow smoothly together.

you read the piece several times, or you may be left with one or two overriding questions. To prepare to answer one of your questions, reread the work and jot down support for all the possible answers. Then you can see which answer has the most support, and begin developing an essay using the ideas you have gathered. If you choose the question, "Is Mathilde to be condemned or admired?" (p. 15), your possible answers might look like the following:

CONDEMNED?

She only wants to be envied and admired for being attractive (end of 1st part), not for more important qualities.

She manipulates her husband into giving her a lot of money for a party dress, but they live poorly.

She assumes that her friend would think she was a thief if she knew she was returning a different necklace.

ADMIRED?

After she cries when they get the invitation, she recovers with a "strong effort"—maybe she doesn't want her husband to feel bad.

Once she lost the necklace, "she did her share . . . completely, heroically" (paragraph 98)

From these first notes, you might decide that Mathilde is to be more condemned than admired. Thinking further, you might decide that she becomes more admirable as the story progresses. Another person might find her more admirable from the beginning. And although there seem to be only two possible answers, you might also decide that Mathilde is too complex to be wholly admired or condemned, but that both judgments are supported by some of her actions. Or, you might decide that Mathilde is more to be pitied than either condemned or admired. Trying to answer your own questions often leads you to consider new and more thoughtful ones.

Tracing Developing Patterns

You can also discover ideas by making an outline, list, or scheme for ry or main idea. What conflicts appear? Do these conflicts exist people, groups, or ideas? How does the author resolve them? Is , idea, or side the winner? Why? How do you respond to the loser?

this method, you might make a list similar to this one.

g: M. is a fish out of water. Dreams of wealth, but her life is drab usband is ordinary.

make her even more dissatisfied—almost punishes herself by lavish rooms.

All this is normal. In fact, you should think of your finished, polished essay not as something to begin with, but rather as something to achieve. How you reach your goal is up to you, because everyone has unique work habits. But you should always remember that writing is, above all, a process—a process in which you try to overcome not only the difficulties of reading and interpretation, but also the natural lethargy and resistance of the human mind.

Because writing is a process, take heart if your pathway toward a finished essay sometimes seems halting, digressive, and purposeless. Many of these ordinary difficulties in writing can be overcome if you stress to yourself that writing cannot be perfect the first time. It is important just to start—no matter how unacceptable your first efforts seem—to create a beginning, to force yourself to lock horns with the materials. You are not committed to anything you first put down on paper or on the screen of a word processor. You may throw it out and write something else, or you may write over it, or move it around, as you wish. But if you keep it buried in your mind by not beginning to write anything at all, you will have nothing to work with. In fact, the thing to do is to accept the uncertainties in the writing process and let them work for you rather than against you.

DISCOVERING IDEAS

Remember that ideas cannot be known and shaped until they take written form. Thus, the first act of the writing process is to uncover, discover, and drag out of your mind all the things you can say about a particular topic, then to write down these notions so that they may be examined later for validity and possible usefulness. You should also write down all the questions you have; later you can attempt to answer them. Use the following prewriting techniques to discover your ideas. As you attempt to get your ideas on paper, remember that writing is a process of discovery as well as creation. And, as in most fields of inquiry, the most valuable finds are often not apparent the first time you search for them.

Brainstorming

Brainstorming is a technique useful at any time during the writing process, but particularly after you have already responded to a work in writing over the course of several readings. As you read the work, you take notes in the order of events in the work. You may now begin brainstorming—letting your mind play over a particular element of the work, or over your own earlier responses to it, or over all the possibilities you sense as you consider the work in its entirety. In brainstorming, you quickly write down all the thoughts you have about the work, whether they fall into patterns, or seem disjointed, unlikely or even ridiculous. (This is also sometimes called **freewriting**.) Do not take the time to organize or criticize your thoughts. You will have the chance later to decide which of your ideas will be useful, and which should be discarded. For now, *the goal is to get all your ideas on paper.*

Suppose that after reading and responding in writing to "The Necklace," you start to wonder if Mathilde is truly honorable or if she has other motives for working so hard. Your brainstorming notes might be similar to the following:

What is honor? doing what you think you should even if you don't want to, or if it's hard—does that mean honor is different for each person?

Mathilde could have gone to her friend and told her she lost the necklace. But something didn't allow her to. Was it her honor? Or pride? Wouldn't it have been more honorable to tell her friend? Does having honor mean choosing the more difficult path, when either would probably be acceptable?

Mathilde wants others to envy her, to find her attractive. Later she tells her husband that she would feel humiliated around the rich women unless she wore jewelry. Maybe M. was more concerned about her own good name than her friend's necklace. Having a good reputation seems like it has something to do with honor. So it could be more public than I first thought. When I think of good name, though, I think more of personal qualities than appearance.

Duty. Is it the same as honor? Was it Mathilde's duty to work so hard? It seems that in the Middle Ages in Europe, it was the duty of knights to defend a lady's honor (her good name?) by fighting, or going out to slay dragons . . . or am I getting mixed up with myths?

Honor relates to these old myths, I think. They both seem bigger than any one life or person. Honor is just an idea or feeling—can an idea be larger than a life, take over someone's life?

These notes could be developed in many different ways, depending on which ideas the writer decides to pursue. The important thing here, however, is that all one's ideas should be recorded, with no initial concern about how they might seem to a reader.

After brainstorming, you decide which ideas interest you and whether there is support for them in the work. You might find that none of them prove fruitful, and might then wish to brainstorm from a different angle or perspective. Brainstorming may be used at any stage of the writing process to find a new perspective or fresh ideas.

Expanding Your Notes

In brainstorming, you do not impose any particular order on what you write. Expanding your notes, however, is a method of searching for specific characteristics that could *support or disprove* an idea you have about

the work. Brainstorming is an *all-inclusive* process, but expanding your notes is *selective*. Like brainstorming, this method can be used at any time as you write. The idea you want to test may come from your original reading notes, your brainstorming, or by thinking about the following questions:

What explanations need to be made about the characters? Which actions, scenes, and situations invite interpretation? Why so?

What assumptions do the characters and speakers reveal about life and humanity generally, about themselves, the people around them, their families, their friends, and about work, the economy, religion, politics, and the state of the world?

What manners or customs do they exhibit?

What sort of language do they use: formal or informal words, slang, or profanity?

What literary conventions and devices have you discovered, and how do these add to the work? (If an author addresses readers directly, for example, that is a **convention**; if a comparison is used, this is a **device**, which might be either a **metaphor** or a **simile**.)

For example, to try to support the idea that the attic flat shows Mathilde's strength as it also shows her becoming loud and frumpy (from the journal entry on p. 15), you might jot down the following information from "The Necklace":

M. gets strong—gives up her servant, climbs stairs carrying buckets of water, washes greasy pots, throws water around to clean floors, does all the wash by hand.

She gets loud, frumpy—argues with shopkeepers to pay cheapest pri[ce] stops caring for herself.

First she seems delicate, but after losing necklace, no way. But she [ ] lot more now. Before, she was dreamier and less practical.

What is important here is that you are writing for your[ ] details in the work support or disprove your ide[ ] supported by the text, you can move on to a ne[ ] This technique can be used any time you[ ] could serve as the basis for an essay, [ ] especially useful later, as you write t[ ] essay.

Answering Questions

Another way to form ideas a[ ] you ask yourself as you read it. It[ ] questions after each reading of a wor[ ]

Her character relates to the places in the story: the Street of the Martyrs, the dinner party scene, the attic flat. Also the places she dreams of—she fills them with the most expensive things she can think of.

They get the dinner invitation—she pouts and whines. Her husband feels discomfort, but she doesn't really harm him. She does manipulate him into buying her an expensive party dress, though.

Her dream world hurts her real life when her desire for wealth has her borrow the necklace. Losing the necklace is just plain bad luck.

The attic flat brings out her potential coarseness. But she also develops a spirit of sacrifice and cooperation. She loses, but she's actually a winner.

These observations all focus on Mathilde's character. However, you might wish to trace other patterns you find in the work you are studying. If you begin to draft an essay about one of these other patterns, be sure that you account for all the major actions and scenes that relate to your topic. Otherwise, you may miss a piece of evidence that can lead you to a new viewpoint.

Thinking by Writing

No matter what method of discovering ideas you use, it is important to realize that *unwritten thought is incomplete thought*. Make a practice of writing rough notes, sentences, or paragraphs describing your reactions whenever you read or think about a work. And always make a note of questions that occur to you. They may lead you later to the best discoveries you will make about a work.

DRAFTING THE ESSAY

As you brainstorm or use other techniques for discovering ideas, you are actually beginning to draft your essay. Although you will need to revise your ideas as connections among them become more clear, and as you reexamine the work for support for the ideas you are developing, you already have the raw materials you need to shape your topic. Before you explore your ideas more fully, however, you need to think about who will be reading your finished essay.

Considering Your Audience

In preparing to write, you have to decide how much detail to select and discuss. If your readers have not read the work you are writing about, you will need to include a brief plot summary as background. Usually, however, your audience is your instructor or the members of your class, and all of them will be familiar with the work. Such readers know the events and know who says what and when. These readers do not expect you to retell the story, but look to you rather as an *explainer* or *interpreter*.

Thus, you should introduce details from the work only if they exemplify your central idea, and you may omit details that have no bearing, even if they are important in the work itself.

Your instructor will let you know who your audience is. Whether it is your classmates or your instructor, remember that you must support all your statements with details from the work itself. Even though your audience is familiar with the work, they are not familiar with your thoughts about it. Make all of your ideas, and the connections between them, explicit to your readers.

Developing a Central Idea

By definition, an essay is *a fully developed and organized set of paragraphs that are directly connected to a central idea.* Everything in an essay should contribute to the reader's understanding of the idea. To achieve unity and completeness, each paragraph refers to the central idea and demonstrates how selected details from the work relate to and support the idea. The central idea helps the writer control and shape the essay, and it provides guidance to the reader.

A successful essay about literature is a brief but thorough (not exhaustive) examination of a literary work in light of a particular element, such as *point of view, imagery,* or *symbolism.* Typical central ideas might be (1) that a character is strong and tenacious, or (2) that the point of view makes the action seem "distant and objective," or (3) that one work is different from or better than another. All ideas included in essays on these topics must be tied to these ideas. Thus, it is a fact that Mathilde Loisel in "The Necklace" endures ten years of slavish work and sacrifice. This fact is not relevant to an essay on her character, however, unless you connect it by showing how it demonstrates one of her major traits—in this case, her strength and tenacity.

Look through all of your ideas for one or two that catch your eye for development. If you have used more than one prewriting technique, the chances are that at least a few ideas are beginning to emerge as more thought-provoking, or important, than the others.

Once you choose one that interests you, write it as a complete sentence. The complete sentence is important, for a simple phrase, such as "setting and character," does not focus thought the way a sentence does; a sentence combines a topic with some sort of outcome, such as "The setting is related to Mathilde's character." You may choose to be even more specific: "Both Mathilde's strengths and weaknesses may be connected to the real and imaginary places in the story." Because it is so vital in shaping an essay, you should always make your central idea into a sentence. A sentence will move the topic toward new exploration and discovery.

A Note on Handwriting and Word Processing

As our discussion of writing suggests, *thinking and writing are inseparable processes*. It is therefore essential to get ideas into a *visible form* so that you may ponder them and develop them further. For many people, handwriting is a psychological necessity in this process. In noting, sketching out, and drafting your responses to a work, be sure to use *only one side* of your paper or notecards. With everything on only one side, you may spread your materials out, and in this way get an overview when the time comes to begin writing.

A special word is in order about word processors, which are important for many students. Once you can handle the keyboard—the same as for a typewriter—the word processor can help you in developing ideas, for you can eliminate unworkable thoughts and put others in their places. You may move sentences and paragraphs tentatively into new contexts, test out how they look, and move them somewhere else if you do not like them. If you see spellings that are questionable, you may check them out with a dictionary and make corrections on the screen. (Because spelling, among other things, may be an element of grading, be sure that you reach an agreement with your instructor about whether to use a spell-check program.)

Studies have shown that the bottoms of pages prepared by hand or with a conventional typewriter contain many errors and awkward sentences. The reason is that writers hesitate to make improvements when they get near the end of a page because they do not want to bother starting the page over. Word processors eliminate this difficulty completely. Changes can be made anywhere in the draft, at any time, without damage to the appearance of the final draft.

In addition, with the rapid printers available today, you can print drafts, even in the initial and tentative stages. With a complete draft, you can use your pen or pencil to make additional notes, marginal corrections, arrowed lines indicating new spots for particular passages, and suggestions for further development. With the marked-up draft for guidance, you can go back to the word processor and carry out your own instructions for change and improvement. You may repeat this process as often as necessary. The result is that the machine is an additional incentive for improvement, right up to your final draft.

With a single central idea for your essay, you have a guide for accepting, rejecting, rearranging, and changing the notes you have taken. You may now choose to draft a few paragraphs quickly to see whether your idea seems valid. Or, you may decide that it would be more helpful to make an outline or list before you attempt to support your ideas in a rough draft. In either case, it is imperative that you reread your notes to see what evidence you have gathered in support of your central idea. If you find you need more ideas, you may use any of the prewriting techniques to discover them. If you need more details, jot them down as you reread the work.

Using the central idea about the story's settings as they relate to Mathilde's changing character might produce paragraphs like the following:

> The original apartment in the Street of Martyrs, and the dream world of wealthy places, both show negative sides of her character. The real-life apartment, though livable, is shabby. The furnishings all bring out her discontent. The shabbiness makes her think only of luxuriousness, and her one servant girl makes her dream of many servants. The luxury of her dream life thus heightens her unhappiness with what she has.
>
> Mathilde is coarsened during the ten years of repayment. She gives up her domestic help, and does all the heavy housework herself. She climbs stairs carrying heavy buckets of water, and throws water around to clean floors. She washes greasy and encrusted pots and pans, takes out the garbage, and does the clothes and dishes by hand. She gives up caring for her hair and hands, and wears the cheapest clothing possible. She becomes loud and argumentative, and spends much time haggling with shopkeepers to save as much money as she can. Whatever delicacy and attractiveness she had, she loses.
>
> Her Sunday walk to the Champs-Elysées is in character. This is a fashionable street, and her walk to it is similar to her earlier daydreams about wealth, for it is on this wide street that the wealthy stroll and flaunt themselves. Her meeting with Jeanne there is accidental, but it also brings out her sense of pride; that is, she confesses to the loss of the necklace, having seen things through to the complete repayment of all indebtedness. The Champs-Elysées thus brings out the surprise and irony of the story, and Mathilde's going there is totally in character, in keeping with her earlier dreams of a luxurious life.

Notice that the first and second paragraphs have come directly from earlier notes. The third paragraph was developed after the central idea was established. No attempt has been made to connect the paragraphs or make the draft read well. Even in this "discovery" draft, however, where the purpose is to write initial thoughts about the central idea, many details from the story are given in support. In the final draft, this support will be essential.

Creating a Thesis Statement

Using the central idea for guidance, we can now decide which of our earlier observations and ideas can be developed further. Our goal is to establish a number of major topics to support the central idea, and to express them in a **thesis statement**—a sentence that lists the major topics in the order they will be developed in the essay. The thesis statement functions as a plan. It connects the central idea and the list of topics in the order of presentation. Suppose we choose three ideas from the discovery draft. If we put the central idea at the left and the list of topics on the right, we have the shape of our thesis statement.

CENTRAL IDEA

The setting of "The Necklace" reflects Mathilde's character.

TOPICS

1. Real-life apartment
2. Dream surroundings
3. Attic flat

From this arrangement we can write the following sentence.

> Mathilde's character development is related to her first apartment, her dream-life mansion rooms, and her attic flat.

The thesis statement can be revised at any stage of the writing process if you find you do not have enough evidence from the work to support it.

The central idea, as we have seen, is the glue. The thesis statement lists the parts to be fastened together—that is, the topics in which the central idea is to be demonstrated and argued. To alert the audience to the essay's structure, the thesis statement is often placed at the end of the introductory paragraph.

WRITING A FIRST DRAFT

To write a first draft, you fit together the points of the thesis statement with supporting materials from your notes. You may alter, reject, and rearrange things as you wish, as long as you change the thesis statement to account for the changes (a major reason why the introduction is usually the last part of a theme to be completed). Our proposed thesis statement contains three topics (it could be two, or four, or more), which we will use in forming the body of the essay.

Just as the organization of the entire essay is based on the thesis, the form of each paragraph is based on its **topic sentence**. A topic sentence is an assertion about how a topic from the predicate of the thesis statement supports the central idea. The first topic in our example is the relationship of Mathilde's character to her first apartment, and the resulting paragraph should emphasize this relationship. Suppose we choose her trait of being constantly dissatisfied. We can then form a topic sentence by connecting the trait with the location, as follows:

> Details about the first apartment explain her dissatisfaction and depression.

Beginning with this sentence, the paragraph should show how things in the apartment, such as the furniture, the curtains, and the unwashed tablecloth, feed Mathilde's capacity for dissatisfaction.

Usually you may devote a single paragraph to each topic. However, if your topic is difficult, long, and heavily detailed, you may divide it into two or more subtopics, each devoted to single paragraphs. Should you make this division, your topic then is really a section, and each paragraph in the section should have its own topic sentence.

Once you choose your thesis statement, you can bring your observations and conclusions into sharper focus. Let us see that we can do with the second paragraph of the discovery draft.

ORIGINAL PARAGRAPH	*RESHAPED PARAGRAPH*
Mathilde is coarsened during the ten years of repayment. She gives up her domestic help, and does all the heavy housework herself. She climbs stairs carrying heavy buckets of water, and throws water around to clean floors. She washes greasy and encrusted pots and pans, takes out the garbage, and does the clothes and dishes by hand. She gives up caring for her hair and hands, and wears the cheapest clothing possible. She becomes loud and argumentative, and spends much time haggling with shopkeepers to save as much money as she can. Whatever delicacy and attractiveness she had, she loses.	The attic flat reflects the coarsening of Mathilde's character. Maupassant emphasizes the strain she endures to keep up the flat, such as throwing around heavy buckets of water to wash the floors, cleaning greasy and encrusted pots and pans, taking out the garbage, and washing clothes and dishes by hand. This makes her rough and coarse, a fact also shown by her giving up care of her hair and hands, her wearing of the cheapest dresses possible, and her becoming loud and penny-pinching in haggling with the local shopkeepers. If at the beginning she is delicate and attractive, at the end she is unpleasant and coarse.

Notice that details from the story are almost the same in each paragraph, but while the paragraph on the left is unfocused, the right-hand one connects the coarsening to Mathilde's housework in the attic flat. The paragraph on the right shows how details from a work may substantiate a unifying central idea.

Developing an Outline

All along we have been developing an *outline*—that is, a skeletal plan of organization for the essay. Some writers never use formal outlines at all, preferring to make informal lists of ideas; others rely on them constantly. Still other writers insist that they cannot make an outline until they have finished their essays. All these views can be reconciled if you realize that *a finished essay should have a tight structure*. At some point, therefore, you should create a guiding outline to develop or to shape your essay.

The outline we have been developing here is the **analytical sentence outline**. This type is easier to create than it sounds. It consists of the following:

1. An *introduction,* including the central idea and the thesis statement. Some instructors require a fusion of the two in the final draft. Therefore, make sure you ask what your instructor expects.
2. *Topic sentences* within each paragraph of the body, usually at the beginning. It is also acceptable to include a topic sentence elsewhere in a paragraph, but if you relocate it, be sure that your details make it follow naturally and logically. Usually you may devote a single paragraph to each topic. However, if your topic is difficult, long, and heavily detailed, you may divide it into two or more subtopics, each devoted to single paragraphs.
3. A *conclusion.*

When applied to the subject we have been developing, the outline looks like this:

TITLE: HOW SETTING IN "THE NECKLACE" IS RELATED
TO THE CHARACTER OF MATHILDE

1. INTRODUCTION
    a. *Central Idea:* Setting is used to show Mathilde's character.
    b. *Thesis Statement:* Her character development is related to her first apartment, her dream-life mansion rooms, and her attic flat.
2. BODY: *Topic sentences* a, b, and c (and d, e, f, if necessary)
    a. Details about her first apartment explain her dissatisfaction and depression.
    b. Her dream-life images of wealth are like the apartment because they too make her unhappy.
    c. The attic flat reflects the coarsening of her character.
3. CONCLUSION
    Topic sentence: Everything in the story, particularly the setting, is focused on the character of Mathilde.

The *conclusion* may be a summary of the body; it may evaluate the main idea; it may briefly suggest further points of discussion; or it may be a reflection on the details of the body.

You may use an outline to organize, finish, or polish your ideas at any point in the writing process. However, throughout the discussion, we have seen that much of writing is discovery. Your outline, too, can lead you to new ideas and help you to adapt materials that you had not originally planned to use.

Using the Outline

The sample essays to be developed in this book are organized according to the principles of the analytical sentence outline. To emphasize the shaping presence of these outlines, all central ideas, thesis statements, and topic sentences are underlined. In your own writing, you may wish to underline these "skeletal" sentences as a check on your organization. Unless your instructor requires the underlines, however, remove them in your final drafts.

SAMPLE ESSAY, DRAFT 1

The following essay is the first complete draft of the topic we have been developing. Although it might be considered complete, it omits a topic and some details that are included in the final draft (pp. 39–40). The first draft therefore shows how even working from an outline leaves much yet to do in the writing of a finished, polished essay. The draft, then, represents a relatively advanced but not yet completed stage of composition, which we all go through in the process of developing an acceptable piece of writing.

How Setting in "The Necklace" is Related to the Character of Mathilde Loisel°

[1] In "The Necklace" Maupassant does not give much detail about the setting. He does not even describe the necklace itself, which is the central object in his plot, but he says only that it is "superb" (paragraph 47). Rather, he uses the setting to reflect the character of the central figure, Mathilde Loisel.* All his details are presented to bring out her traits. Her character development is related to her first apartment, her dream-life mansion rooms, and her attic flat.†

[2] Details about her first apartment explain her dissatisfaction and depression. The walls are "drab," the furniture "threadbare," and the curtains "ugly" (paragraph 3). There is only a single country girl to do the housework. The tablecloth is not cleaned daily, and the best dinner dish is beef and vegetables boiled in a pot. Mathilde has no pretty dresses, but only a theater dress that she does not like. These details show her dissatisfaction about life with her low-salaried husband.

[3] Her dream-life images of wealth are like the apartment because they too make her unhappy. In her daydreams, the rooms are large, filled with expensive furniture and bric-a-brac, and draped in silk. She imagines private rooms for intimate talks, and big dinners with delicacies like trout and quail.

° See p. 5 for this story.
* Central idea.
† Thesis sentence.

With dreams of such a rich home, she feels even more despair about her modest apartment on the Street of Martyrs in Paris.

[4] The attic flat reflects the coarsening of Mathilde's character. Maupassant emphasizes the strain she endures to keep up the flat, such as throwing around heavy buckets of water to clean the floors, cleaning greasy and encrusted pots and pans, taking out the garbage, and doing dishes and washing clothes by hand. This makes her rough and coarse, a fact also shown by her giving up care of her hair and hands, her wearing of the cheapest dresses possible, and her becoming loud and penny-pinching in haggling with the local shopkeepers. If at the beginning she is delicate and attractive, at the end she is unpleasant and coarse.

[5] In summary, Maupassant focuses everything in the story, including the setting, on the character of Mathilde. Anything extra is not needed, and he does not include it. Thus he says little about the big party scene, but emphasizes the necessary detail that Mathilde was a great "success" (paragraph 52), because this detail brings out some of her early attractiveness and charm (despite her more usual unhappiness). In "The Necklace," Maupassant uses setting as a means to his end--the story of Mathilde and her needless sacrifice.

Commentary on the Essay

Upon examining this draft, the writer might notice that several parts of the essay need more thought. For example, in the second paragraph, the sentences seem more like a series of short, unconnected comments than a fully developed paragraph. Also, the last sentence of that paragraph implies that Mathilde's dissatisfaction relates mainly to her husband, not what the writer had intended. Paragraph 4 focuses too much on Mathilde's coarseness, and not enough on her sacrifice and cooperation. Finally, there is not enough support in this draft for the contention (in paragraph 5) that *everything* in the story focuses on Mathilde's character. To discover how these issues may be resolved, compare this first draft with the final draft of the essay on pp. 39–40.

REVISING THE ESSAY

After finishing your draft, you may be wondering what is left to do. You have read the work several times, discovered ideas to write about by brainstorming and asking questions, made an outline of your ideas, and written a full draft. How can you improve your writing?

The best way to begin an answer is to observe that one of the major mistakes writers make when writing about literature is to do no more than retell a story or reword an idea. Retelling a story shows only that you have read it, not that you have thought about it. You should try to produce the results of your own thinking. Writing a good essay requires you to arrange your thoughts into a pattern that can be followed by a perceptive reader.

Using Your Own Order of References

There are many ways to break the pattern of summarizing stories and to set up your own pattern of development. One is to stress *your own* order when referring to parts of a work. Do not treat things as they occur, but change them to suit your own thematic plans. Rarely, if ever, should you begin by talking about a work's opening; it is better to talk first about the conclusion or middle. If you find, as you examine your first draft, that you have followed the chronological order of the work instead of stressing your own order, you may use one of the prewriting techniques such as brainstorming to figure out new ways to connect your materials. The principle is that you should introduce references to the work only to support the points that you wish to make.

Using Literary Material as Evidence

Whenever you write, your position is like that of a detective using clues as evidence for building a case, or of a lawyer using evidence as support for an argument. Your goal should be to convince your readers of your own knowledge and the reasonableness of your conclusions.

It is vital to use evidence convincingly so that your readers can follow your ideas. Let us look briefly at two drafts of a new example to see how writing may be improved by the pointed use of details. These are from drafts of a longer essay on the character of Mathilde.

1	*2*
The major extenuating thing about Mathilde is that she seems to be isolated, locked away from other people. She and her husband do not speak to each other much, except about things. He speaks about his liking for boiled beef in a pot, and she states that she cannot accept the big invitation because she has no nice dresses. Once she gets the dress, she complains because she has no jewelry. Even when borrowing the necklace from Jeanne Forrestier, she does not say much. When she and her husband discover that the necklace is lost, they simply go over the details, and Loisel dictates a letter of explanation, which she writes in her own hand. Even when she meets Jeanne on the Champs-Elysées, she does not say a great deal about her life, but only goes	The major flaw of Mathilde's character is that she is withdrawn and uncommunicative, apparently unwilling or unable to form an intimate relationship. For example, she and her husband do not speak to each other much, except about things, such as his taste for boiled beef in a pot and her lack of a party dress and jewelry. With such a marriage, one might suppose that she would be more open with her close friend, Jeanne Forrestier, but even here Mathilde does not say much. This flaw hurts her greatly, because if she were more open she might have explained the loss and avoided the horrible sacrifice. This lack of openness, along with her self-indulgent dreaminess, is her biggest defect.

through enough details about the loss
and replacement of the necklace to
make Jeanne exclaim about the
needlessness of the ten-year sacrifice.

The answer to that difficult question of how to improve writing is to be found in a comparison of these two passages. In general, superior writers allow their minds to play on the materials. They give readers the results of their thoughts. They dare to trust their responses and are not afraid to make judgments about the work they are considering. Their principal aim in referring to actions, scenes, and characters is to develop their own thematic pattern. If you continue to revise your essay until it gives proof of these qualities, you will also be considered a superior writer.

A close comparison of the two paragraphs bears out these assertions. Although the first draft has more words than the second (159 to 120), it is more appropriate for a rough than a final draft, for the writer is doing little more than retelling the story. The paragraph is cluttered with details that do not support any conclusions. If you examine it for what you might learn about Maupassant's actual use of Mathilde's solitary traits in "The Necklace," you will find that it gives you no help at all. The writer needs to consider why these details should be shared, and should revise the paragraph according to the central idea.

On the other hand, the details in the second draft all support the declared topic. Phrases like "for example," "but even here," and "this lack" show that the writer of paragraph 2 has assumed that the audience knows the story and now wants help in interpretation. Paragraph 2 therefore guides readers *by connecting the details to the topic*. It uses these details *as evidence*, not as a retelling of actions. By contrast, paragraph 1 recounts a number of clearly relevant actions, but does not *connect* them to the topic. More details, of course, could have been added to the second draft, but they are unnecessary because the paragraph demonstrates the point with the details used. There are many things that make good writing good, but one of the more important is evident here: *In good writing, details are used only as evidence in an original pattern of thought.*

Keeping to Your Point

To show another distinction between first and second draft writing, let us consider a third example. The following paragraph is drawn from an essay on "The Idea of Economic Determinism in 'The Necklace.'" In this paragraph the writer discusses the essay as it is brought out in a number of incidents from the story. The idea is to assert that Mathilde's difficulties result not from character but rather from financial restrictions:

More important than chance in governing life is the idea that people are controlled by economic circumstances. Mathilde, as is shown right at the

Using the Present-Tense of Verbs when Referring to Actions and Ideas in a Work

Literary works spring into life in the eyes and minds of readers with each and every reading. You may therefore assume that everything happening in the works—stories, poems, and plays—takes place in the present, and in talking about literature you should generally use the *present tense of verbs*. It is thus right to say "Mathilde and her husband **work** and **economize** (not "**worked** and **economized**") for ten years to pay off the 18,000-franc debt which they **undertake** (not "**undertook**") to pay for the lost necklace."

When you consider an author's ideas, the present tense is also proper, on the principle that the words of an author are just as alive and current today (and tomorrow) as they were at the moment of writing, even though this same author may have been dead for hundreds or even thousands of years.

If you introduce historical or biographical details about a work or author, however, it is appropriate to use the *past tense* for them, because such details actually do belong to the past. Thus it is correct to state that "Shakespeare **lived** from 1564 to 1616," or that "Shakespeare **wrote** *Hamlet* in about 1599–1600."

While it is incorrect to shift tenses inappropriately when you write, it is possible to mix past and present tenses if you treat historical facts about a literary work while at the same time you are also considering it as a living text. Of prime importance is to keep things straight. Here is an example of what is acceptable:

> Because *Hamlet* **was** first **performed** in about 1600, Shakespeare most probably **wrote** it shortly before this time. In the play, a tragedy, Shakespeare **treats** an act of vengeance, but more importantly he **demonstrates** the difficulty of ever learning the exact truth. The hero, Prince Hamlet, **is** the focus of this difficulty, for the task of revenge **is assigned** to him by the Ghost of his father. Though the Ghost **claims** that his brother, Claudius, **is** his murderer, Hamlet **is** not able to verify this claim.

Here, the historical details are presented in the past tense, while all details about the play *Hamlet,* including Shakespeare as the creating author whose ideas and words are still alive, are considered in the present.

You may encounter a problem when your work introduces references to actions that have occurred prior to the time of the main action. An instance is Hemingway's "Soldier's Home," in which the main character is discontented and unsettled as a result of his combat experiences in Europe during World War I. In describing this situation, you might say something like this: "Krebs **cannot settle down** because he **is always thinking** [present tense] about the actions he **went through** [past tense] during the fighting in Europe." This use of the past influencing the present is acceptable because it corresponds to the cause-and-effect relationship brought out in the story.

As a principle, if you run into problems in managing verb tenses when discussing a work, *always consult your instructor.*

start, is born poor. Therefore she doesn't get the right doors opened for her, and her marriage is to a minor clerk. With a vivid imagination and a burning desire for luxury, seeming to be born only for the wealthy life, her poor home brings out her daydreams of expensive surroundings. She taunts her husband, Loisel, when he brings the big invitation, because she does not have a suitable (read "expensive") dress. Once she gets the dress it is jewelry that she lacks, and she borrows that and loses it. The loss of the necklace is the greatest trouble, because it forces the Loisels to borrow deeply and to lead an impoverished life for ten years.

This paragraph shows how easily writers may be diverted from their objective. The first sentence is an effective topic sentence, indicating that the writer begins with a good plan. The remaining part, however, does not follow through. The flaw is that the material of the paragraph, while an accurate account of what happens in the story, *is not tied to the topic.* Once the second sentence is under way, the paragraph gets lost in a retelling of events, and the fine opening sentence is left behind. From the example of this paragraph, we may conclude that writers cannot assume that detail alone will make an intended meaning clear. Instead they must do the connecting themselves, to make sure that all relationships are *explicitly* clear. This point cannot be overstressed.

Let us see how the problem of writing shown in the paragraph may be addressed. If the ideal paragraph can be schematized with line drawings, we might say that the paragraph's topic should be a straight line, moving toward and reaching a specific goal (explicit meaning), with an exemplifying line moving away from the straight line briefly to bring in evidence, but returning to the line after each new fact to demonstrate the relevance of the fact. Thus, the ideal scheme looks like this, with a straight line touched a number of times by an undulating line:

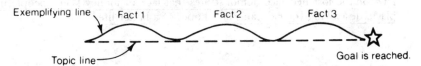

Notice that the exemplifying line, waving to illustrate how documentation or exemplification is to be used, always returns to the topic line. A scheme for the faulty paragraph on "The Necklace," however, would look like this, with the line never returning, but flying out into space:

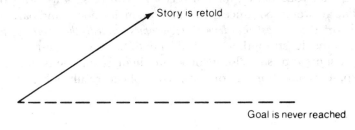

How might the faulty paragraph be improved? The best way is to remind the reader again and again of the topic, and to use examples from the text in support.

Consistently with our diagram, each time the topic is mentioned, the undulating line merges with the straight, or central-idea line. This relationship of topic to illustrative examples should prevail no matter what subject you write about. If you are analyzing *point of view*, for example, you should keep connecting your material to the speaker, or narrator, and the same applies to topics like character, point of view, or setting. According to this principle, we might revise the paragraph on economic determinism in "The Necklace" as follows, keeping as much of the original wording as we can. (Parts of sentences stressing the relationship of the examples to the topic of the paragraph are underlined.)

More important than chance in governing life is the idea that people are controlled by economic circumstances. As illustration, the speaker begins by emphasizing that Mathilde, the major character, is born poor. Therefore she doesn't get the right doors opened for her, and her marriage is to a minor clerk. In keeping with the idea, her vivid imagination and burning desire for luxury (she seems to have been born only for the wealthy life) feed on her weakness of character as she feels deep unhappiness and depression because of the contrast between her daydreams of expensive surroundings and the poor home she actually has. Their straitened economic circumstances inhibit her relationship with her husband, and she taunts him when he brings the big invitation because she does not have a suitable (read "expensive") dress. As a merging of her unrealistic dream life with actual reality, her borrowing of the necklace suggests the impossibility of overcoming economic restrictions. In the context of the idea, the ten-year sacrifice to pay for the lost necklace demonstrates that lack of money keeps people in place, destroying their dreams and hopes of a better life.

The original paragraph has been improved so that now it reaches the goal of the topic sentence. While it has also been lengthened, the length has been caused not by inessential detail but by phrases and sentences that give form and direction. You might object that if you lengthened all your paragraphs in this way, your essays would grow too bulky. The answer is to reduce the number of major points and paragraphs, on the theory that *it is better to develop a few topics pointedly than many pointlessly.* Revising done to strengthen central and topic ideas requires that you throw out some topics or else incorporate them as subpoints in the topics you keep. This assertion of your own control can result only in improvement.

CHECKING DEVELOPMENT AND ORGANIZATION

Sticking to a point is therefore one of the first requirements of a good essay. Another major step toward excellence is to make your central idea expand and grow. The word *growth* is a metaphor for *development*—the creation of new insights, the disclosure of ideas that were not at first noticeable, the expression of new, fresh, and original interpretations.

An argument here might be that you cannot be original when you are writing about someone else's work. "The author has said everything," might go the argument, "and therefore I can do little more than follow the story." This claim assumes that you have no choice in selecting material, and no opportunity to make individual thoughts and original contributions. But you have. One obvious area of originality is the development and formulation of your central idea. For example, a natural first response to "The Necklace" is that "It is about a woman who loses a borrowed necklace and endures hardship to help pay for it." Because this response refers only to the story and not to any idea, an area of thought might be introduced if the hardship is called "needless." Though better, this idea is not very original either. But an original insight can result if the topic is connected to the relationship between the dreamy, withdrawn traits of the major character and her misfortune. Thus, an idea might be that "People themselves bring about their own misfortunes." With such an idea, it is possible to do more in creating a fresh, original essay analyzing the story's development than the first response could do.

You can also develop your ability to treat your subject freshly and originally if you plan the body of the essay to build up to what you think is your most important, incisive, and well-conceived idea. As examples of such planning, the following brief topic outlines suggest how each central idea may be widened and expanded:

A. Mathilde as a Growing Character (*Character*, Chapter 4)
   1. Mathilde is at first a person with normal daydreams.
   2. Mathilde takes a risk to make her daydreams seem real.
   3. Mathilde develops by facing her mistake and working hard to right it.
B. The Idea of Economic Determinism (*Idea or Theme*, Chapter 10)
   1. Mathilde's economic class inhibits her wishes.
   2. Her economically poor married life is a damper on her character.
   3. The ten-year hardship is her punishment for trying to live beyond her means.
C. The Development of Irony in the Story (*Tone*, Chapters 8, 17)
   1. Mathilde's dissatisfaction is heightened by her dreams.
   2. The loss of the necklace ironically makes the Loisels seem poorer than they really are.
   3. Mathilde's failure to confess the loss to Jeanne makes the sacrifice needless.

D.   The Symbolic Value of the Necklace (*Symbolism and Allegory*, Chapter 9)
   1.   The necklace symbolizes economic wealth and ease.
   2.   That the necklace was false symbolizes the discrepancy between appearance and reality.
   3.   Restoring the necklace symbolizes the value of sacrifice and work.

These lists indicate how a subject may be enlarged if the exemplifying topics are treated in an increasing order of importance. Both the first and last outlines, for example, move toward ideas about moral values; the second moves toward a broad consideration of the story, and the third suggests a climax based on the story's situational irony. These suggested patterns show how two primary standards of excellence in writing—organization and growth—can be met.

   It should be clear that whenever you write, an important goal should be the development of your central idea. Constantly adhere to your topic, and constantly develop it. Nurture it and make it grow. Admittedly, in a short essay you will be able to move only a short distance with an idea, but you *should never be satisfied to leave the idea exactly where you found it.* To the degree that you can learn to develop your ideas, you will receive recognition for increasingly superior writing.

USING ACCURATE AND FORCEFUL LANGUAGE

In addition to being organized and well developed, the best writing is *accurate, insightful,* and *forceful.* The first sentences and paragraphs we write are usually weak, and they need to be rethought, recast, and reworded. Sometimes we cannot carry out this process immediately, for it may take days or even weeks for us to gain objectivity about what we say (if we ever do). As a student you usually do not have that kind of time, and thus you must acquire the habit of challenging your own statements almost as soon as you write them. Ask yourself whether they really *mean* what you intend, and if you can make them stronger.

   As an example, consider the following sentence, which was written in a student essay as a central idea about "The Necklace":

> The central idea in this story is how Mathilde and her husband respond to the loss of the necklace.

This sentence could not help the development of an essay. Because it promises no more than the retelling of the story, it needs more thought and rephrasing. Here are two revisions of the sentence that would help more:

> In the story Guy de Maupassant puts forth the idea that hard work and responsibility are basic and necessary in life.

Guy de Maupassant makes the surprise ending of the story a symbol of the need for always being truthful.

Although both new sentences deal with the same story materials, they point toward different treatments. The first would be built up out of the virtue shown by the Loisels in their sacrifice. Since the second sentence contains the word *symbol,* an essay to be developed from it would stress the mistake the Loisels make in not confessing the loss. In dealing with the symbolic meaning of their failure, such an essay would focus on the negative aspects of their characters; an essay developed from the first sentence would stress their positive aspects. Either of the two revised sentences, however, is more accurate than the original sentence, and would move a writer toward a superior composition.

Equally vital—and equally challenging and important—is to make sure to say *exactly* what you mean. If you do not focus on your subject, you may wind up saying nothing. Consider these two sentences from essays about "The Necklace":

1.   It seems as though the major character's dreams of luxury cause her to respond as she does in the story.

Using the Names of Authors

For both men and women writers, you should typically include the author's *full name* in the *first sentence* of your essay. Here are a few model first sentences:

Shirley Jackson's "The Lottery" is a story featuring both suspense and horror.

"The Lottery," by Shirley Jackson, is a story featuring both suspense and horror.

For all later references in your essay, you should use just the last names of your writers, such as *Steinbeck, Gilchrist, Crane,* or *Porter.* However, for the relatively few "giants" of literature, you should use the last names exclusively. In referring to writers like Shakespeare and Milton, for example, there is no need to include *William* or *John.*

While today's informality is such that many people use first names even for strangers, it is important never to refer to an author only by the first name, as in "**Shirley** skillfully creates suspense and horror in 'The Lottery.'" Also, never use a title before the author's name, such as "**Ms.** Jackson's 'The Lottery' is a suspenseful horror story," or "**Mr.** Shakespeare's idea is that information is uncertain." Use the last names alone.

2. This incident, although it may seem trivial or unimportant, has substantial significance in the creation of the story; by this I mean the incident that occurred is essentially what the story is all about.

Neither of these sentences goes anywhere. The first is satisfactory up to the verb "cause," but then it falls apart because the writer has lost sight of the meaning. It is best to describe *what* that response is, rather than to state nothing more than that there *is* a response. The following revision makes the sentence more specific.

> Mathilde's dreams of luxury make it impossible for her to accept her own possessions, and therefore she goes beyond her means to attend the party.

With this revision, the writer could consider the meaning of the story's early pages, and could contrast the ideas there with those in the latter part. Without the revision, it is not clear where the writer might go.

The second sentence is so vague that it confuses rather than informs. The reason, again, is that the writer has lost the topic. If we try to make things more specific, however, we may bring the dead sentence to life:

> The accidental loss of the necklace, which is trivial though costly, supports the narrator's claim that major turns in life are produced not by earthshaking events, but rather by minor ones.

When you write your own sentences, you might test them: Are you referring to an idea? State the idea directly. Are you mentioning a response or impression? Do not say simply, "The story's ending left me with a definite impression," but *state* what the impression is, like this: "The story's ending surprised me and also made me sympathetic to Mathilde's condition." Similarly, do not rest with a statement such as "I found 'The Necklace' interesting," but try to describe *what* was interesting and *why* it was interesting: "I found 'The Necklace' interesting because it shows how chance may either make or destroy people's lives." If you always name and pin down your impressions and responses, no matter how elusive they seem, your sentences will be exact and forceful.

SAMPLE ESSAY, DRAFT 2

The following essay, a revision of the draft on pp. 28–29, includes changes that create greater emphasis and unity. Some of the details in the early draft, while relevant, are not tied clearly enough to the central idea. The second draft, on the other hand, creates more introductory detail, includes another topic, and reshapes each of the paragraphs to stress the relationship of central idea to topic. Within the limits of a short assignment, the essay illustrates all the principles of organization and unity we have been discussing.

Maupassant's Use of Setting in "The Necklace" to Show the Character of Mathilde

[1] In "The Necklace" Maupassant uses setting to reflect the character and development of the major figure, Mathilde Loisel.* As a result, his setting is not particularly vivid or detailed. He does not even provide a description of the ill-fated necklace--the central object in the story--but states only that it is "superb" (paragraph 47). He includes only enough description to illuminate his central character, Mathilde. Her changing character may be related to the first apartment, the dream-life mansion rooms, the attic flat, and the public street.†

[2] Details about the modest apartment of the Loisels on the Street of Martyrs (*Rue des Martyrs*) indicate Mathilde's peevish lack of adjustment to life. Though everything is serviceable, she is unhappy with the "drab" walls, "threadbare" furniture, and "ugly" curtains (paragraph 3). She has domestic help, but wants more servants than the simple country girl who does the household chores. Her dissatisfaction is also shown by details of her irregularly cleaned tablecloth and the plain and inelegant boiled beef that her husband adores. Even her best dress, which she wears for the theater, provokes her unhappiness. All these details of the apartment establish that Mathilde's dominant character trait at the start of the story is maladjustment. She therefore seems unpleasant and unsympathetic.

[3] Like the real-life apartment, the impossibly expensive setting of her daydreams strengthens her unhappiness and her avoidance of reality. As she indulges herself, all the rooms of her fantasies are large and expensive, draped in silk and filled with nothing but the best furniture and bric-a-brac. Maupassant gives us the following description of her imaginings:

> She imagined a gourmet-prepared main course carried on the most exquisite trays and served on the most beautiful dishes, with whispered gallantries which she would hear with a sphinxlike smile as she dined on the pink meat of a trout or the delicate wing of a quail. (paragraph 4)

With dreams like this filling her mind, her despair is even greater. Ironically, this despair, together with her inability to live with reality, causes her economic and social undoing. It makes her agree to borrow the necklace (which is just as unreal as her daydreams of wealth), and losing the necklace drives her into the reality of giving up her apartment and moving into the attic flat.

Also ironically, the attic flat is related to the coarsening of her character while at the same time it brings out her best qualities of cooperativeness and honesty. Maupassant emphasizes the drudgery of the work she endures to maintain the flat, such as walking up many stairs, washing floors with large

---

* Central idea.
† Thesis sentence.

[4]
buckets of water, cleaning greasy and encrusted pots and pans, taking out the garbage, handwashing clothes, and haggling loudly with local tradespeople. All this reflects her coarsening and loss of sensibility, also shown by her giving up hair and hand care, and wearing the cheapest dresses. The things she does, however, make her heroic (paragraph 98). As she cooperates to help her husband pay back the loans, her dreams of a mansion fade, and all she has left is the memory of that one happy evening at the Minister of Education's reception. Thus the attic flat brings out her physical change for the worse at the same time that it also brings out her psychological and moral change for the better.

[5]
Her walk on the Champs Elysées illustrates another combination of traits--self-indulgence and frankness. The Champs-Elysées is the most fashionable street of Paris, and her walk to it is similar to her earlier indulgences in her dreams of wealth; she is, in effect, seeing how the upper-class people are living. But it is on this street where she meets Jeanne, and it is her frankness in confessing the loss and replacement to Jeanne that makes her, finally, completely honest. While the walk thus serves as the occasion for the story's concluding surprise and irony, Mathilde's being on the Champs-Elysées is totally in character, in keeping with her earlier reveries about luxury.

[6]
Other details in the story also have a similar bearing on Mathilde's character. For example, the story mentions little about the party scene, but emphasizes only that she was a great "success" (paragraph 52)--a judgment that shows her ability to shine if given the chance. After she and Loisel accept the fact that the necklace cannot be found, Maupassant includes details about the Parisian streets, the visits to loan sharks, and the jewelry and jewelry-case shops in order to bring out Mathilde's sense of honesty and pride as she "heroically" prepares to live the life of the poor. Thus, in "The Necklace," Maupassant uses setting to highlight Mathilde's maladjustment, her needless misfortune, her loss of youth and beauty, and finally her growth as a responsible human being.

Commentary on the Essay

Several improvements to the first draft may be seen here. The language of paragraph 2 has been revised to show more clearly that Mathilde's dissatisfaction does not seem appropriate. In paragraph 3, the irony of the story is brought out, and the writer has connected the details to the central idea in a richer pattern of ideas, showing the effects of Mathilde's despair. In paragraph 6, the fact that Mathilde "shines" at the dinner party is interpreted according to the central idea. Finally, the conclusion is now much more specific, summarizing the change in Mathilde's character rather than saying simply that the setting reveals her "needless sacrifice." In short, the second draft reflects the complexity of "The Necklace" better than the first draft. Because the writer kept thinking about and revising the first draft, the final essay is insightful, tightly structured, and forceful.

ESSAY COMMENTARIES

Throughout this book, the sample essays are followed by short commentaries that show how the essays embody the chapter's instruction and guidelines. For each essay in which a number of possible approaches are suggested, the commentary points out which one is employed, and when a sample essay uses two or more approaches, the commentary makes this fact clear. In addition, the commentary stresses key words and phrases that demonstrate the essay's thematic pattern and development. It is hoped that the commentaries will help you develop the insight necessary to use the essays as aids in your own study and writing.

To sum up, follow these guidelines whenever you do any kind of writing:

Keep returning to your points.
Use material from the work you are studying as evidence to support your argument; do not retell the story.
Include no details from the work unless you have clearly connected them to your points.
Develop your topic; make it bigger than it was when you began.
Always strive to make your statements specific, accurate, and forceful.

If you observe these guidelines, you will have a head start with all writing assignments.

RESPONDING TO LITERATURE: LIKES AND DISLIKES

The act of reading is accompanied by emotional responses that, at their simplest level, take the form of pleasure or displeasure: You either like or dislike a poem, story, or play. You have not said much, however, if all you say is no more than that. Writing about likes and dislikes should therefore require you to explain the reasons for your responses. In short, your discussion should be *informed and informative* rather than *uninformed and unexplained.*

Sometimes a first response is that a work is "boring." This reaction is usually a mask covering an incomplete and superficial first reading. It is neither informative nor informed. As you study most works, however, you will invariably get drawn into them. One word—and a common one—that describes this process is *interest;* that is, to be interested in a work is to be taken right into it emotionally. Another word is *involvement,* which suggests that one's emotions become almost enfolded in the characters, problems, and outcomes of a work. Sometimes both words are used defensively, just like the word *boring.* It is easy to say that something is "interesting," or that you get "involved" in it, and you might say just these things while hoping that no one will ask what you mean. Both "interest" and "involvement" do indeed describe genuine responses to reading, however. Once you get interested, your reading ceases to be a task or assignment, and grows into a pleasure.

Using Your Journal to Record Responses

No one can tell you what you should or should not like; liking is your own concern. While your experience of reading is still fresh, therefore, you should use your journal (discussed earlier, pp. 13–15) to record not only your observations about a work, but also your responses. Be frank in your judgment. Write down your likes and dislikes, and try to explain the reasons for your response, even if these are brief and incomplete. Here is a journal entry that explains a favorable response to Guy de Maupassant's "The Necklace":

> I like "The Necklace" because of the surprise ending. It isn't that I like Mathilde's bad luck, but I like the way Maupassant hides the most important fact in the story until the end. Mathilde does all that work and sacrifice for no reason at all, and the surprise ending makes this point strongly.

This paragraph could be expanded as a part of a developing essay. It is a clear statement of liking, followed by references to likable things in the work. This response pattern, which can be simply phrased as "I like [dislike] this work *because* . . . ," is a useful way to begin journal entries because it always requires that a response be followed with an explanation. If at first you cannot write any full sentences detailing the causes of your responses, at least make a brief list of the things you like or dislike. If you write nothing, you will probably forget your reactions; recovering them later, either for discussion or writing, will be difficult.

Responding Favorably

Usually you can equate your interest in a work with liking it. You can be more specific about favorable responses by citing one or more of the following:

> You like and admire the characters and what they do and stand for.
>
> You learn something new—something you had never known or thought before.
>
> You gain new insights into things that you already knew.
>
> You learn about characters and customs of different places, times, and ways of life.
>
> You get interested and involved in the outcome of the action or ideas, and do not want to put the work down until you have finished it.

You feel happy or thrilled because of reading the work.

You are amused and laugh often as you read.

You like the author's presentation.

You find that some of the ideas and expressions are beautiful and worth remembering.

Obviously, if you find none of these things, or find something that is distasteful, you will not like the work.

Responding Unfavorably

Although so far we have dismissed *boring* and stressed *interest, involvement,* and *liking,* it is important to know that disliking all or part of a work is normal and acceptable. You do not need to hide this response. Here, for example, are two journal responses expressing dislike for Maupassant's story "The Necklace":

1.   I do not like "The Necklace" because Mathilde seems spoiled, and I don't think she is worth reading about.

2.   "The Necklace" is not an adventure story, and I like reading only adventure stories.

These are both legitimate responses because they are based on a clear standard of judgment. The first stems from a distaste for one of the main character's unlikable traits; the second, from a preference for rapidly moving stories that evoke interest in the dangers that main characters face and overcome.

Here is a paragraph-length journal entry that might be developed from the first response. What is important is that the reasons for dislike are explained. They would need only slightly more development for use in an essay:

> I do not like "The Necklace" because Mathilde seems spoiled and I do not think she is worth reading about. She is a phony. She nags her husband because he is not rich. She never tells the truth. I dislike her for hurrying away from the party because she is afraid of being seen in her shabby coat. She is foolish and dishonest for not telling Jeanne Forrestier about losing the necklace. It is true that she works hard to pay the debt, but she also puts her husband through ten years of hardship. If Mathilde had faced facts, she might have had a better life. I do not like her and cannot like the story because of her.

As long as you include reasons for your dislike, as in this journal paragraph, you can use them again when developing your essay. In your further consideration, you will surely also expand thoughts, include new details, pick new topics for development and otherwise modify your journal entry.

You might even change your mind. However, even if you do not, it is better to record your original responses and reasons honestly than to force yourself to say you like something that you do not.

Putting Dislikes into a Larger Context

While it is important to be honest about disliking a work, it is more important to broaden your perspective and expand your taste. For example, a dislike based on the preference for only mystery or adventure stories, if generally applied, would cause a person to dislike most works of literature. This seems unnecessarily self-limiting.

By putting negative responses into a larger context, it is possible to expand the ability of liking and appreciation. Some readers might be deeply involved in personal concerns and therefore be uninterested in remote or "irrelevant" literary figures. However, if by reading about literary characters they can gain insight into general problems of life, and therefore their own concerns, they can find something to like in just about any work of literature. Other readers might like sports and therefore not read anything but sports magazines. But what probably interests them about sports is competition, so if competition or conflict can be found in a literary work, they might discover something to like in that work.

As an example, let us consider again the dislike based on a preference for adventure stories, and see if this preference can be widened. Here are some reasons for liking adventures:

1. Adventure has fast action.
2. Adventure has danger and tension, and therefore interest.
3. Adventure has daring, active, and successful characters.
4. Adventure has obstacles which the characters work hard to overcome.

No one could claim that the first three points apply to "The Necklace," but the fourth point is promising. Mathilde, the major character, works hard to overcome an obstacle: She pitches in to help her husband pay the large debt. If our student likes adventures because the characters try to gain worthy goals, then he or she can also like "The Necklace" for the same reason. The principle here is clear: if a reason for liking a favorite work or type of work can be found in another work, then there is reason to like that new work.

The following paragraph shows a possible operation of this "bridging" process of extending preferences. (The sample essay [p. 47] is also developed along these lines.)

> I usually like only adventure stories, and therefore I disliked "The Necklace" at first because it is not adventure. But one of my reasons for liking adventure is that the characters work hard to overcome difficult obstacles, like finding

buried treasure or exploring new places. Mathilde, Maupassant's main character in "The Necklace," also works hard to overcome an obstacle— helping to pay back the money and interest for the borrowed 18,000 francs used as part of the payment for the replacement necklace. I like adventure characters because they stick to things and win out. I see the same toughness in Mathilde. Her problems get more interesting as the story moves on after a slow beginning. I came to like the story.

In this way, an accepted principle of liking can be applied to another work where it also applies. A person who adapts principles in this open-minded way can redefine dislikes, no matter how slowly, and may consequently expand the ability to like and appreciate many kinds of literature.

An equally open-minded way to develop understanding and widen taste is to put dislikes in the following light: An author's creation of an *unlikable* character, situation, attitude, or expression may be deliberate. Your dislike might then result from the author's *intentions*. A first task of study is therefore to understand and explain the intention or plan. As you put the plan into your own words, you may find that you can like a work with unlikable things in it. Here is a paragraph that traces this pattern of thinking, based again on "The Necklace":

Maupassant apparently wants the reader to dislike Mathilde, and I do. At first, he shows her being unrealistic and spoiled. She lies to everyone and nags her husband. Her rushing away from the party so that no one can see her shabby coat is a form of lying. But I like the story itself because Maupassant makes another kind of point. He does not hide her bad qualities, but makes it clear that she herself is the cause of her trouble. If people like Mathilde never face the truth, they will get into bad situations. This is a good point, and I like the way Maupassant makes it. The entire story is therefore worth liking even though I still do not like Mathilde.

Neither of these two ways of broadening the contexts of response is dishonest to the original negative reactions. In the first paragraph, the writer applies one of his principles of liking to include "The Necklace." In the second, the writer considers her initial dislike in the context of the work, and discovers a basis for liking the story as a whole while still disliking the main character. The main concern in both responses is to keep an open mind despite initial dislike, and then to see if the unfavorable response can be more fully and broadly considered.

However, if you decide that your dislike overbalances any reasons you can find for liking, then you should explain your dislike. As long as you relate your response accurately to the work, and measure it by a clear standard of judgment, your dislike of even a commonly liked work is not unacceptable. What is important here is not so much that you like or dislike a particular work (you will eventually find hundreds or even thousands of works to like) *as that you develop your own abilities to analyze and express your ideas.*

WRITING ABOUT RESPONSES: LIKES AND DISLIKES

In writing about your responses, you should rely on your initial informed reactions. It is not easy to reconstruct your first responses after a lapse of time, so you will need your journal observations as your guide in the prewriting stage. Develop your essay by stressing what interests you (or does not interest you) in the work.

A major challenge is to relate the details of the work to the point you are making about your ongoing responses. You should therefore stress your involvement in the work as you bring out evidence from it. You can show your attitudes by indicating approval (or disapproval), by commenting favorably (or unfavorably) on the details, by indicating things that seem new (or shopworn) and particularly instructive (or wrong), and by giving assent to (or dissent from) ideas or expressions of feeling.

Organizing Your Essay

INTRODUCTION.   Begin by describing briefly the conditions that influence your response. Your central idea should be why you like or dislike the work. The thesis sentence should list the major causes of your response, which are to be developed in the body.

BODY.   The most common approach is to consider specific things about the work that you like or dislike. The list on pp. 42–43 may help you articulate your responses. For example, you may have admired a particular character, or maybe you became so interested in the story that you could not put it down. Also, it may be that a major idea, a fresh insight, or a particular outcome is the major point that you wish to develop. The sample paragraph on page 42 shows a surprise ending as the cause of a favorable response.

A second approach (see p. 44) is to explain any changes in your responses about the work (i.e., negative to positive and vice versa). This approach requires that you isolate the causes of the change, but it does *not* require you to follow the text from beginning to end. (1) One way to deal with such a change—the "bridge" method of transferring preference from one type of work to another—is shown in the sample essay (pp. 47–48). (2) Another way is to explain a change in terms of a new awareness or understanding that you did not have on a first reading. Thus, a first response to Poe's "The Masque of the Red Death" might have been unfavorable or neutral because, say, the story seems unnecessarily sensational and lurid. But further consideration may have led you to discover new insights that might have changed your mind, like the futility of challenging death, or the impossibility of stopping an epidemic. The essay would then demonstrate how these new insights figure into the process of your changed attitude.

CONCLUSION.   Here you might summarize the reasons for your major response. You might also face any issues brought up by a change or modification of your first reactions. For example, if you have always held certain assumptions about your taste but like the work despite these assumptions, you may wish to talk about your own change or development. This topic is personal, but in an essay about likes or dislikes, discovery about yourself is something you should aim for.

SAMPLE ESSAY

Some Reasons for Liking Maupassant's "The Necklace"°

[1]
    To me, the most likable kind of reading is adventure. Although there are many reasons for my preference, an important one is that adventure characters work hard to overcome obstacles. Because Guy de Maupassant's "The Necklace" is not adventure, I did not like it at first. But in one respect the story is like adventure: The major character Mathilde, with her husband Loisel, works hard for ten years to overcome a difficult obstacle. Thus, because Mathilde does what adventure characters also do, the story is likable.* Mathilde's appeal results from her hard work, strong character, sad fate, and also from the way our view of her changes.†

[2]
    Mathilde's hard work makes her seem good. Once she and her husband are faced with the huge debt of 18,000 francs, she works like a slave to pay it back. She gives up her servant and moves to a cheaper place. She does the household drudgery, wears cheap clothes, and bargains with shopkeepers for the lowest prices. Just like the characters in adventure stories, who do hard and unpleasant things, she does what she has to, and this makes her admirable.

[3]
    Her strong character shows her endurance, a likable trait. At first she is nagging and fussy, and she always dreams about wealth and tells lies, but she changes and gets better. She recognizes her blame in losing the necklace, and she has the toughness to help her husband redeem the debt. She sacrifices "heroically" (paragraph 98) by giving up her comfortable way of life, even though in the process she also loses her youth and beauty. Her jobs are not the exotic and glamorous ones of adventure stories, but her force of character makes her as likable as an adventure heroine.

    Her sad fate also makes her likable. In adventure stories the characters often suffer as they do their jobs. Mathilde also suffers, but in a different way,

---

° See p. 5 for this story.
* Central idea.
† Thesis sentence.

[4] because her suffering is permanent while the hardships of adventure characters are temporary. This fact makes her pitiable, and even more so because all her sacrifices are not necessary. This unfairness about her life invites the reader to take her side.

[5] The most important quality promoting admiration is the way in which Maupassant shifts our view of Mathilde. As she goes deeper into her hard life, Maupassant stresses her work and not the innermost thoughts he reveals at the beginning. In other words, the view into her character at the start, when she dreams about wealth, invites dislike; the focus at the end is on her achievements, with never a complaint--even though she still has golden memories, as the narrator tells us:

> But sometimes, when her husband was at work, she sat down near the window, and she dreamed of that evening so long ago, of that party, where she had been so beautiful and so admired. (paragraph 104)

A major quality of Maupassant's changed emphasis is that these recollections do not lead to anything unfortunate. Thus his shift in focus, from Mathilde's dissatisfaction to her willingness to accept responsibility and sacrifice, encourages the reader to like her.

[6] "The Necklace" is not an adventure story, but some of the good qualities of adventure characters are present in Mathilde. Also, the surprise revelation that the lost necklace was false is an unforgettable twist that makes her more deserving than she seems at first. Maupassant has arranged the story so that the reader finally admires Mathilde. "The Necklace" is a skillful and likable story.

Commentary on the Essay

This essay demonstrates how a reader may develop appreciation through the transferring or "bridging" of a preference for one type of work to a work that does not belong to the type (described earlier in this chapter, pp. 44–45). In the essay, the bridge is an already established taste for adventure stories, and the grounds for liking "The Necklace" is that Mathilde, the major character, shares the admirable qualities of adventure heroes and heroines.

In paragraph 1, the introduction, the grounds for transferring preference are established, and the concluding thesis sentence lists the four topics to be developed in the body.

The body first stresses how admiration is brought out by the character of Mathilde. Paragraph 2 deals with her capacity to work hard; paragraph 3 considers the equally admirable quality of endurance. The fourth paragraph describes how Mathilde's condition evokes sympathy and pity. These paragraphs hence explain the story's appeal by asserting that the major character is similar to admirable characters from works of adventure.

The fifth paragraph is constructed to demonstrate that Maupassant, as the story unfolds, alters the reader's perceptions of Mathilde, from bad to good. For this reason paragraph 5 marks a new direction from paragraphs 2, 3, and 4, because it moves away from the topic material itself—Mathilde's character—to Maupassant's *technique* in handling the topic material.

Paragraph 6, the conclusion, restates the comparison, and also introduces the surprise ending as an additional reason for liking "The Necklace." With the body and conclusion together, therefore, the essay establishes five separate reasons for approval. Three of these, which are derived directly from the major character, constitute the major grounds for liking the story; two are related to Maupassant's techniques as an author.

Throughout the essay, the central idea is brought out in words and expressions like "likable," "Mathilde's appeal," "strong character," "she does what she has to," "pitiable," and "take her side." These expressions, mixed as they are with references to many details from the story, make for shaping continuity in the essay. It is this thematic development, together with details from the story as supporting evidence, that shows how an essay on the responses of liking and disliking may be both informed and informative.

FICTION

2

Fiction: An Overview

Fiction originally meant anything made up or shaped. As we understand the word now, it refers to prose stories that authors create in their imaginations, a meaning it has retained since its first use in this sense in 1599. Because of this meaning, we distinguish fiction from works it has imitated, such as *historial accounts, reports, biographies, autobiographies, letters,* and *personal memoirs* and *meditations.* While fiction may often resemble these forms, it has a separate identity because it originates in the creative, imaginative powers. Writers of fiction may include historically accurate details, but their primary goal is to tell a story and say something significant about life.

The essence of fiction, as opposed to drama, is **narration,** the recounting or telling of a sequence of events or actions. The earliest works of fiction relied almost exclusively on narration, with speeches or dialogue being reported rather than quoted directly. Much recent fiction includes extended passages of dialogue, thereby becoming more *dramatic* even though narration is still the primary mode.

Fiction is rooted in ancient legends and myths. Local priests narrated stories about their gods and heroes, as shown in some of the narratives of ancient Egypt. Often, traveling storytellers would appear in a court or village to keep eager listeners spellbound with tales of adventurous exploits in faraway countries. Although many of these were fictionalized accounts of events and people who may not ever have existed, they were largely accepted as fact or history. An especially long tale, an **epic,** was recited over a period of days, and to aid their memories the storytellers chanted such works in poetic lines, perhaps also impressing and entertaining their listeners by playing stringed instruments.

Although the legends and epics were entertaining, they also reinforced the local religions and power structures. Myths of gods like Zeus and Athena (Greece), Jupiter and Minerva (Rome), and Baal and Ishtar

(Mesopotamia) abounded, together with stories of famous men and women like Jason, Helen of Troy, Hercules, Achilles, Odysseus, Penelope, Utu-Napishtim, Joseph, David, and Ruth. The ancient Macedonian king and general Alexander the Great (356–323 B.C.) developed many of his ideas about nobility and valor from his boyhood learning of Homer's epic about the Trojan War, *The Iliad.*

Perhaps nowhere is the moralistic-argumentative aspect of ancient storytelling better illustrated than in the **fables** of Aesop, a Greek who wrote in the sixth century B.C., and in the **parables** of Jesus as told in the Gospels of the New Testament. In these works, a short narrative is directed toward a religious, philosophic, or psychological conclusion. A Roman story of the first century A.D., "The Widow of Ephesus," by Gaius Petronius, illustrates this type of persuasive intention (pp. 70–72). Whether you agree with the narrator's ideas or not, the use of narrative events for a rhetorical and persuasive purpose is made clear right at the beginning.

Starting about 800 years ago, storytelling in Western civilization was developed to a fine art by writers such as Marie de France, a Frenchwoman who wrote in England near the end of the twelfth century, Giovanni Boccaccio (Italian, 1313–1375), and Geoffrey Chaucer (English, ca. 1340–1400). William Shakespeare (1564–1616) drew heavily on history and legend for the stories and characters in his plays.

MODERN FICTION

Fiction in the modern sense of the word did not begin to flourish until the late seventeenth and eighteenth centuries, when human beings of all social stations and ways of life became important literary topics. As one writer put it in 1709, human nature was not simple, but could be explained only with reference to many complex motives like "passion, humor, caprice, zeal, faction, and a thousand other springs."* Thus began the individual and psychological concerns that characterize fiction today. Indeed, fiction is strong because it is so real and personal. Most characters have both first and last names; the countries and cities in which they live are modeled on real places; and their actions and interactions are like those that readers themselves have experienced, could experience, or could easily imagine themselves experiencing.

Along with attention to character, fiction is also concerned with the place of individuals in their environments. In the simplest sense, environment is a backdrop or setting within which characters speak, move, and act. But more broadly, environment comprises the social, economic, and political conditions that affect the outcomes of people's lives. Fiction is

---

*Anthony Ashley Cooper, Third Earl of Shaftesbury, *Sensus Communis*, Part III, Section iii.

usually about the interactions among people, but it also involves these larger interactions—either directly or indirectly. Indeed, in a typical work of fiction there are always many forces, both small and large, that influence the ways in which characters meet and deal with their problems.

The first true works of fiction in Europe, however, were less concerned with society or politics than adventure. These were the lengthy Spanish and French **romances** of the sixteenth and seventeenth centuries. (The French word for "novel" is still *roman*.) In English the word **novel** was borrowed from French and Italian to describe these works and to distinguish them from medieval and classical romances as something that was *new* (the meaning of *novel*). In England the word **story** was used along with *novel* in reference to the new literary form.

It was natural that the increased levels of education and literacy in the eighteenth century would make possible the development of fiction. During the times of Shakespeare (1564–1616) and Dryden (1631–1700), the only way a writer could make a living from writing was to have a play accepted at a theater, and then receive either a direct payment or the proceeds of an "author's benefit." The paying audiences, however, were limited to people who lived within a short distance of the theater or who could afford the cost of travel, and who had the leisure time to attend.

Once great numbers of people could read, the paying audience for literature expanded. A writer could write a novel and receive money for it from a publisher, who could then profit from a wide sale. Readers could pick up the book at their leisure and finish it as they chose. Reading a novel could even be a social event, for people would read to each other as a means of sharing the experience. With this wider audience, authors could make a career out of writing. Fiction had arrived as a major genre of literature.

THE SHORT STORY

Because novels were long, people would spend many hours, days, or weeks reading them, with a corresponding dilution of attention. It took an American writer, Edgar Allan Poe (1809–1849) to develop a theory of the **short story,** which he described in a review of Nathaniel Hawthorne's *Twice-Told Tales.* Poe was convinced that "worldly interests" prevented people from gaining the "totality" of comprehension and response that he believed reading should provide. He added that a short, concentrated story (which he called "a brief prose tale") was ideal for producing a powerful, single impression. Thus, he concluded that the best fiction was a short story that could be read at a single sitting.

In the wake of the taste for short fiction that Poe created, many writers have worked in the form. Today, innumerable stories are printed in weekly and monthly periodicals and collections. Some of the more well-established writers, such as William Faulkner, Ernest Hemingway, Shirley Jackson, Guy de Maupassant, Flannery O'Connor, Frank O'Connor, Alice Walker, and Eudora Welty, to name only a small number, have collected their works and published them in single voumes.

ELEMENTS OF FICTION I: VERISIMILITUDE AND *DONNÉE*

Fiction, along with drama, has a basis in **realism** or **verisimilitude.** That is, the situations or characters, though they are the **invention** of writers, are similar to those that many human beings experience, know, or think. Even **fantasy,** the creation of events that are dreamlike or fantastic, is anchored in the real world, however remotely. This connection of art and life has led some critics to label fiction, and also drama, as an art of **imitation.** Shakespeare's Hamlet states that an actor attempts to portray real human beings in realistic situations (to "hold a mirror up to Nature").

The same may also be said about writers of fiction, with the provisos that reality is not easily defined, and that authors can follow many paths in imitating it. What counts in fiction is the way in which authors establish the *ground rules* for their works, whether with realistic or nonrealistic characters, places, actions, and physical and chemical laws. The assumption that authors make about the nature of their story material is called a **postulate** or a **premise**—what Henry James called a **donnée** (something given). The donnée of some stories is to resemble the everyday world as much as possible. Eudora Welty's "A Worn Path" is such a story. It tells of a woman's walking journey through a wooded area to the streets of a town, and then to the interior of a building. The events of the story are common; they could happen in life just as Welty presents them.

Once a donnée is established, it governs the directions in which the story moves. Jackson's "The Lottery," for example, contains a premise or donnée that may be phrased like this: "Suppose that a small, ordinary town held a lottery in which the 'winner' would be ritually stoned to death." Everything in Jackson's story follows from this premise. At first we seem to be reading about innocent actions in a rural American community. By the end, however, in accord with the premise, the story has moved from this everyday, realistic level into a nightmarish enactment of human indifference and cruelty.

In such ways authors may lead us into remote, fanciful, and symbolic levels of reality. In Clark's "A Portable Phonograph," for example, the futuristic donnée is that world civilization has been destroyed in a global war. In Poe's "The Masque of the Red Death," the phantasmagoric donnée is that Death may assume a human shape and claim all the revelers at a bizarre party. Literally nothing is out of bounds as long as the author makes clear the premise for the action, as in Pickthall's "The Worker in

Sandalwood," where the donnée is that miracles may overcome ordinary reality. Thus, the story makes it seem normal that Jesus, who in life had worked as a carpenter, should reappear to aid a troubled boy by miraculously completing the delicate work and carving on an unfinished cabinet.

Scenes and actions such as these, which are not realistic in our ordinary sense of the word, are normal in stories *as long as they follow the author's own stated or implied ground rules.* You may always judge a work by the standard of whether it is consistent with the premise, or the donnée, created by the writer.

While we have been speaking mainly about how the donnée refers to various levels of reality, the word may also be taken more broadly. In *futuristic* and *science fiction*, for example, there is an assumption or donnée of certain situations and technological developments (e.g., interstellar space travel) that are not presently in existence. In a *love story*, the donnée is that two people meet and overcome an obstacle of some sort (usually not a serious one) on the way to fulfilling their love. Interesting variations of this type may be seen in Lawrence's "The Horse Dealer's Daughter," Cheever's "The Season of Divorce," and Chekhov's "Lady with Lapdog." In Joyce's "Araby," only one of the major characters is in love; this is the narrator, who is telling about his boyhood crush on the sister of a friend.

There are other types, of course. An *apprenticeship* or *growth story*, for example, is about the growth of the major character, such as Jackie in "First Confession," Sarty in "Barn Burning," and Emily in "I Stand Here Ironing." In the *detective story*, a mysterious event is posited, and then the detective draws conclusions from the available evidence. A variation on the detective story may be seen in Glaspell's "A Jury of Her Peers," in which the detective work is done by two women, and not by the investigator whose business it is to find evidence.

In addition to setting levels of reality and fictional types, authors may use other controls or springboards as their données. Sometimes an initial situation may be the occasion from which the story develops (such as the social worker calling the mother to express concern about the daughter in Olsen's "I Stand Here Ironing"). Or the key may be a pattern of behavior (the boy's reactions to the people around him in O'Connor's "First Confession"), or a lie, as in Anderson's "I'm a Fool," or a lunchtime conversation, as in Atwood's "Rape Fantasies." There is always an element of control, or a donnée, that shapes the actions, and often a number of such controls operate at the same time.

ELEMENTS OF FICTION II: CHARACTER, PLOT, STRUCTURE, AND THEME

Works of fiction share a number of common elements, which we discuss in detail in the various chapters. The more significant ones are **character, plot, structure,** and **theme.**

Character

Stories, like plays, are about characters—characters who, though not real people, are drawn from life. A **character,** also discussed in detail in Chapter 4, is a reasonable facsimile of a human being, with all the good and bad traits of being human.* A story is usually concerned with a major problem that a character must face. This may involve interaction with another character, with a difficult situation, or with an idea or general circumstances which force action. The character may win, lose, or tie. He or she may learn and be the better for the experience or may miss the point and be unchanged.

Earlier we mentioned that modern fiction has accompanied the development of a psychological interest in human beings. Psychology itself has grown out of the philosophical and religious idea that people are not evil by nature, but rather that they have many inborn capacities—some for good and others for bad. People are not free of problems, and they make many mistakes in their lives, but they nevertheless are important and interesting, and are therefore worth writing about, whether male or female; young or old; white, black, tan, or yellow; rich or poor; worker or industrialist; traveler or resident; aviator, performer, mother, daughter, homemaker, prince, general, bartender, or checkout clerk.

It would therefore seem that there is nothing beyond the scope of fiction. A married couple struggling under an enormous debt, a woman meditating about her daughter's growth, a young boy learning about sin and forgiveness, a young man regretting that he cannot admit a lie, a woman surrounded by insensitive and self-seeking men, a man preserving his love for someone against overwhelming odds—all these are important because human beings are important. In fiction you may expect characters from every area of life, and, because we all share the same capacities for concern, involvement, sympathy, happiness, sorrow, exhilaration, and disappointment, you should be able to interest yourself in characters and the ways in which they deal with their circumstances.

Plot

In a well-written story, all the **actions** or **incidents, speeches, thoughts,** and **observations** are linked together to make up an entirety, sometimes called an **organic unity.** The essence of this unity is the development and resolution of a **conflict**—or conflicts—in which the

---

* Even the beings from other worlds and the lifelike robots and computers that we meet in science fiction, along with animals who populate beast fables and modern comics and films, interest us only as they exhibit human characteristics. Thus, Yogi Bear prefers honey to berries; a supremely intelligent computer with a conflicting program turns destructive; and an alien of superhuman strength riding on a spaceship tries to destroy all the human passengers. But we all know human beings with a sweet tooth; we all know that internal conflicts can produce unpredictable and destructive results; and who would say that the desire for power is not human?

protagonist, or central character, is engaged. The pattern in which the protagonist meets and resolves the conflict is called the **plot,** which has been compared to the story's *map, scheme,* or *blueprint.* The plot is based on the interactions of causes and effects as they develop **sequentially** or **chronologically.** That is, the story's actions follow one another in time as the protagonist meets and tries to overcome the forces of opposition.

Often the protagonist's struggle is directed against another character—an **antagonist,** or a group of antagonists. Just as often, however, the struggle may occur between the protagonist and opposing groups, forces, ideas, and choices—all of which make up a collective antagonist. The conflict may be carried out wherever human beings spend their lives, such as a kitchen, a bedroom, a restaurant, a town square, an estate, a workshop, or a battlefield. The conflict may also take place internally, within the mind of the protagonist.

Structure

Structure refers to the way in which a plot is assembled. Chronologically, all stories are similar because they all move from beginning to end in accord with the time it takes for causes to produce effects. But authors choose many different ways to develop their plots. While some stories, as expected, are told in chronological order, others may get pieced together through out-of-sequence and widely separated episodes, speeches, remembrances, dreams, periods of delirium, fragments of letters, overheard conversations, and the like. In dealing with structure, therefore, we deal with the *arrangement* and *development* of individual stories. Usually we study an entire story, but we may also direct our attention toward a smaller aspect of arrangement.

Theme

Fiction necessarily embodies issues and ideas. Even stories written with the goal of entertainment alone are based on an idea or position of some sort. Thus, writers of comic works are committed to the idea that human difficulties can be ironed out by discussion and humor. More serious works may force characters to make difficult moral choices, with the underlying idea that in a losing situation the only winner is the one who maintains honor and self-respect. Works designed to create mystery and suspense are based on the belief that problems have solutions, even if they may not at first seem apparent. In stories, writers may deal with the triumphs and defeats of life, the admirable and the despicable, the humorous and the pathetic, but whatever their goal, they always have things to say about human experience.

In fiction, these things take the form of an underlying **theme** or **central idea,** which helps to tie the work together. Often the author makes the theme obvious, as in the Aesop fable in which a man uses an axe to kill a fly on another person's forehead. It does not take much imagination to state the theme of this fable: The solution to a problem should not make things worse. A major theme in Maupassant's "The Necklace" is that people may be destroyed or made fortunate by the most insignificant and unpredictable of events. The accidental loss of the borrowed necklace is just such an event; this misfortune ruins the lives of both Mathilde and her husband for the following ten years.

The process of determining and describing the themes or ideas in stories is probably never complete; there is always another theme that we may discuss. Thus, in "The Necklace," one might note the additional themes that adversity brings out worth, that telling the truth is better than concealing it, that envy often produces ill fortune, or that good fortune is never recognized until it is lost. Indeed, one of the ways in which we may judge stories is to determine the degree to which they embody a number of valid and important themes.

ELEMENTS OF FICTION III: THE WRITER'S TOOLS

Narration

Writers have a number of modes of presentation, or "tools," which they may use in writing their stories. The principal tool (and the heart of fiction) is **narration,** the reporting of actions in chronological sequence. The object of narration is, as much as possible, to *render* the story, to make it clear and to bring it alive to the reader's imagination.

Style

The medium of fiction and of all literature is language, and the manipulation of language—the **style**—is a primary skill of the writer. A mark of a good style is the use of *active verbs*, and nouns that are **specific** and **concrete.** Even with the most active and graphic diction possible, writers can never render their incidents and scenes exactly, but they can indeed be judged on how vividly they tell their stories.

Point of View

One of the most important ways in which writers knit their stories together, and also an important way in which they try to interest and engage readers, is the careful control of **point of view** (see Chapter 5). Point of view is the **voice** of the story, the speaker who does the narrating. It is the way the reality of a story is made to seem authentic. It may be regarded as the story's *focus*, the *angle of vision* from which things are not only seen and reported but also judged.

A story may be told directly by a fictitious "observer" who tells us what he or she saw, heard, and concluded. This **speaker,** or **narrator—**

terms that are interchangeable—may sometimes seem to be the author speaking directly using an **authorial voice,** but just as often the speaker is an independent character—a **persona** with characteristics that separate him or her from the author. Sometimes the narrator is a participant in the story. Stories told in these ways have **first-person** points of view, for the speaker uses the "I" personal pronoun in referring to his or her position as an observer or commentator.

The other important point of view is the **third person.*** The third-person point of view may be (1) **limited,** with the focus being on one particular character and what he or she does, says, hears, thinks, and otherwise experiences, (2) **omniscient,** with the thoughts and behaviors of all the characters open and fully known by the speaker, and (3) **dramatic,** or **objective,** in which the story is confined *only* to reporting essential actions and speeches, with no commentary and no revelation of the thoughts of any of the characters.

Understanding point of view often requires subtlety—indeed, it may be one of the most difficult of all concepts in the study of fiction. We may think of it as the *total position* from which things are viewed, understood, and then communicated. The position might be simply physical: "Where was the speaker located when the events occurred," or "Does the speaker give us a close or distant view of the events?" The position might also be personal or philosophical: "Do the events illustrate a personal opinion (Maupassant's 'The Necklace')," or "embody a philosophical judgment (Hawthorne's 'Young Goodman Brown')," or "argue for a theological viewpoint ('The Prodigal Son')?"

Point of view is one of the many ways in which authors make fiction vital. By controlling point of view, an author helps us make reasonable inferences about the story's actions. Authors use point of view to raise some of the same questions in their fiction that perplex us in life. We need to evaluate what fictional narrators as well as real people tell us, for what they say is affected by their limitations, attitudes, opinions, and degree of candidness. The narrator of Petronius's "The Widow of Ephesus," for example, declares that his story illustrates the weakness and inconstancy of women. But does he really understand what he says, or does his story tell us more about his own limitations than the limitations of women? The narrator of Twain's "Luck" is convinced that his hero is a total fool, and he tells the story to convince us of this. But could we make a case that he might also be somewhat jealous of his boob hero, enough perhaps to omit some of the explanations that might give us a rounder picture? For readers, the perception of a fictional point of view can be as complex as life itself, and it may be as difficult—in fiction as in life—to evaluate our sources of information.

---

* The possibilities of a second-person point of view are discussed in Chapter 5.

Description

Together with narration, an important aspect of fiction is **description,** which brings scenes and feelings readily to the imagination of readers. Description can be both physical (places and persons) and psychological (an emotion or set of emotions). Description can interrupt action, so many writers include only as much as is necessary to highlight actions, as in Tillie Olsen's "I Stand Here Ironing," where we find a minimum of physical description, although all of us can imagine where a woman doing the week's ironing might be and what she might look like.

Other writers create extensive descriptions. Edgar Allan Poe presents detailed scenes not only to locate his actions, but also to evoke tension and excitement. Alice Munro imaginatively creates an entire nineteenth-century town in her story "Meneseteung." By the time we finish the story we have a sense of what life in her imaginary town was like over a period of several decades.

Mood and **atmosphere** are important adjuncts of descriptive writing, and to the degree that descriptions are evocative, they may reach the level of **metaphor** and **symbolism.** These characteristics of fiction are a property of all literature, and you will also encounter them in your considerations of poetry and drama.

Dialogue

Another major tool of the writer of fiction is **dialogue.** By definition, dialogue is the conversation of two people, but more than two characters may participate. The major medium of the dramatist, dialogue is just one of the means by which the fiction writer makes a story vivid and dramatic. Straight narration and description can do no more than make a secondhand assertion that a character's thoughts and responses exist, but dialogue makes everything real and firsthand.

Dialogue is hence a means of *rendering* rather than presenting. If characters feel pain or declare love, their own words may be taken as the expression of what is on their minds. Some dialogue may be terse and minimal, like that in Hemingway. Other dialogue may be expanded, depending on the situation, the personalities of the characters, and the author's intent. Dialogue may be about anything, including future plans, reactions to the past, indications of emotion, and political, social, philosophic, or religious ideas.

The language of dialogue indicates the intelligence, articulateness, educational levels, or emotional states of the speakers. Hence the author might use *grammatical mistakes, faulty pronunciation,* or *slang* to show a character of limited or disadvantaged background or a character who is trying to be seen in that light. *Dialect* shows the region from which the speaker comes, just as an *accent* indicates a place of national origin. *Jargon* and *cliché* suggest self-inflation or intellectual limitations—usually reasons for laughter. The use of *private, intimate expressions* might show people who are close to each other emotionally. Speech that is interrupted with *voiced pauses* (e.g., "er," "ah," "um," "you know"), or speech characterized by *inappropriate words* might show a character who is unsure or not in control. There are many possibilities in dialogue, but no matter what qualities you find, writers include dialogue to enable you to know their characters better.

Commentary

Writers may also include **commentary, analysis,** or **interpretation,** in the expectation that readers need at least some insight or illumination about the characters and actions. When fiction was new, authors often expressed such commentary directly. Henry Fielding (1707–1754) divided his novels into "books," and included a chapter of philosophic or artistic commentary at the beginning of each of these. In the next century, George Eliot (1819–1880) included many extensive passages of commentary in her novels.

Later writers have kept commentary at a minimum, preferring instead to concentrate on direct action and dialogue, and leaving it to readers to draw their own conclusions about meaning. One is likely, however, to encounter something like interpretive observations in first-person narrations. John Cheever's "The Season of Divorce" is such a work, as is Olsen's "I Stand Here Ironing." Observations made by dramatic speakers in works like these may be accepted at face value, but you should recognize that anything the speakers say is also a mode of character disclosure. Such commentary is therefore just as much a part of the story as the narrative incidents.

Tone and Irony

In every story one may consider **tone,** that is, the ways in which the author conveys attitudes about the story material and toward the readers. In "The Necklace," for example, Maupassant presents the bitter plight of Mathilde and her husband. *Pity* is thus an appropriate word for the author's attitude, and it is appropriate also for the reader's response. Maupassant also shows that Mathilde has brought her misfortune on herself, so the attitude is one of at least partial *satisfaction* that justice has been done. But Mathilde works hard and unselfishly; hence *admiration* tempers any inclination to condemn her. Finally, the story's conclusion shows that Mathilde's years of hard labor were unnecessary. Hence *regret* enters into the response. In a discussion of the tone of the story, it would be necessary to describe *how the author's presentation of material shapes these varying attitudes.* Usually, tone is complex in this way.

Because Mathilde's sacrifice for a period of ten years is unnecessary, her situation is *ironic*. **Irony** refers to language and situations that are inappropriate or opposite from normal expectations. **Situational irony** refers to circumstances in which punishments do not fit crimes, or in which rewards are not earned. Forces are beyond human comprehension or control. The characteristic of **dramatic irony** is that a character may perceive his or her situation in a limited way while both readers and other characters see things more broadly. In Collier's "The Chaser," the young man believes that he is about to embark upon lifelong ecstasy and romance, but Collier makes the reader aware that the character's life will be sinister. In **verbal irony,** which applies to language, what is *meant* is distinct from what is *said*. Thus, Maupassant in "The Necklace" does not *say* that Mathilde's husband is a crashing bore during the big party, but by asserting that he had been sleeping "in a little empty room with three other men whose wives had also been enjoying themselves," Maupassant makes the point with ironic force.

Symbolism and Allegory

In fiction, even an apparently ordinary thing may be understood as a **symbol;** that is, it may stand for something beyond itself. Many symbols are **universally** recognized, as with the cane in Hawthorne's "Young Goodman Brown." Because Hawthorne describes it as resembling the serpent associated with Satan, the cane symbolizes the Devil himself. Other symbols are **contextual;** that is, they become symbolic only in their individual works, as with Sammy's walking out on his job in "A & P" to protest the way the girls in swimsuits are treated. Within the context of the story, his action may be taken as a symbol of freedom of personal behavior.

When a story, in addition to maintaining its own narrative integrity, may be closely applied to another, parallel, set of situations, it is an **allegory.** "Young Goodman Brown" may be considered as an allegory of the development of hatred, distrust, and paranoia. Most stories are not allegories, however, even though they may contain sections that have allegorical parallels. Thus, the narrative of Mathilde's long servitude in Maupassant's "The Necklace" is similar to the lives and activities of many people who carry out tasks for mistaken or meaningless reasons. For this reason, "The Necklace" may be considered allegorically, even though it is not a complete allegory.

These, then, are the major tools of writers of fiction. For analytical purposes, one or another of them may be considered separately so that the artistic achievement of a particular author may be recognized. It is important to realize, however, that authors may use all the tools simultaneously. The story may be told by a character who is a witness, and thus it has a **first-person point of view.** The major **character,** the **protagonist,** goes through a series of **actions** as a result of a carefully arranged **plot.** Because of this plot, together with the author's chosen method of **narration,** the story will follow a certain kind of arrangement, or **structure,** such as a straightforward **sequence** or a disjointed series of **episodes.** One thing that the action may demonstrate is the **theme** or **central idea.** The writer's **style** may be manifested in **ironic** expressions. The description of the character's actions may reveal **irony of situation,** while at the same time this stiuation is made vivid through **dialogue** in which the character is a participant. Because the plight of the character is like the plight of many persons in the world, it is an **allegory,** and the character herself or himself may be considered as a **symbol.**

Throughout the story, no matter what characteristics we are considering, it is most important to realize that a work of fiction is an entirety, a unity. Any reading of a story should be undertaken not to break things down into parts, but to understand and assimilate the work *as a whole.* The separate analysis of various topics, to which this book is committed, is thus the means to that end, not the end itself. Finally, the study of fiction, like the study of all literature, is designed to foster our growth and our understanding of the human condition.

JOHN UPDIKE (b. 1932)

A & P°   *1961*

In walks these three girls in nothing but bathing suits. I'm in the third checkout slot, with my back to the door, so I don't see them until they're over by the bread. The one that caught my eye first was the one in the plaid green two-piece. She was a chunky kid, with a good tan and a sweet broad soft-looking can with those two crescents of white just under it, where the sun never seems to hit, at the top of the backs of her legs. I stood there with my hand on a box of HiHo crackers trying to remember if I rang it up or not. I ring it up again and the customer starts giving me hell. She's one of these cash-register-watchers, a witch about fifty with rouge on her cheekbones and no eyebrows, and I know it made her day to trip me up. She'd been watching cash registers for fifty years and probably never seen a mistake before.

By the time I got her feathers smoothed and her goodies into a bag—she gives me a little snort in passing, if she'd been born at the right time they would have burned her over in Salem—by the time I get her on her way the girls had circled around the bread and were coming back, without a pushcart, back my way along the counters, in the aisle between the checkouts and the Special bins. They didn't even have shoes on. There was this chunky one, with the two-piece—it was bright green and the seams on the bra were still sharp and her belly was still pretty pale so I guessed she just got it (the suit)—there was this one, with one of those

---

A & P: "The Great Atlantic and Pacific Tea Company," a large grocery chain still flourishing in twenty-six states.

chubby berry-faces, the lips all bunched together under her nose, this one, and a tall one, with black hair that hadn't quite frizzed right, and one of these sunburns right across under the eyes, and a chin that was too long—you know, the kind of girl other girls think is very "striking" and "attractive" but never quite makes it, as they very well know, which is why they like her so much—and then the third one, that wasn't quite so tall. She was the queen. She kind of led them, the other two peeking around and making their shoulders round. She didn't look around, not this queen, she just walked straight on slowly, on these long white prima-donna legs. She came down a little hard on her heels, as if she didn't walk in her bare feet that much, putting down her heels and then letting the weight move along to her toes as if she was testing the floor with every step, putting a little deliberate extra action into it. You never know for sure how girls' minds work (do you really think it's a mind in there or just a little buzz like a bee in a glass jar?) but you got the idea she had talked the other two into coming in here with her, and now she was showing them how to do it, walk slow and hold yourself straight.

She had on a kind of dirty-pink—beige, maybe, I don't know—bathing suit with a little nubble all over it and, what got me, the straps were down. They were off her shoulders looped loose around the cool tops of her arms, and I guess as a result the suit had slipped a little on her, so all around the top of the cloth there was this shining rim. If it hadn't been there you wouldn't have known there could have been anything whiter than those shoulders. With the straps pushed off, there was nothing between the top of the suit and the top of her head except just *her*, this clean bare plane of the top of her chest down from the shoulder bones like a dented sheet of metal tilted in the light. I mean, it was more than pretty.

She had sort of oaky hair that the sun and salt had bleached, done up in a bun that was unraveling, and a kind of prim face. Walking into the A & P with your straps down, I suppose it's the only kind of face you *can* have. She held her head so high her neck, coming up out of those white shoulders, looked kind of stretched, but I didn't mind. The longer her neck was, the more of her there was.

She must have felt in the corner of her eye me and over my shoulder Stokesie in the second slot watching, but she didn't tip. Not this queen. She kept her eyes moving across the racks, and stopped, and turned so slow it made my stomach rub the inside of my apron, and buzzed to the other two, who kind of huddled against her for relief, and then they all three of them went up the cat-and-dog-food-breakfast-cereal-macaroni-rice-raisins-seasonings-spreads-spaghetti-soft-drinks-crackers-and-cookies aisle. From the third slot I look straight up this aisle to the meat counter, and I watched them all the way. The fat one with the tan sort of fumbled with the cookies, but on second thought she put the package back. The sheep pushing their carts down the aisle—the girls were walking against the usual traffic (not that we have one-way signs or anything)—were pretty hilarious. You could see them, when Queenie's white shoulders dawned on them, kind of jerk, or hop, or hiccup, but their eyes snapped back to their own baskets and on they pushed. I bet you could set off dynamite in an A & P and the people would by and large keep reaching and checking oatmeal off their lists and muttering "Let me see, there was a third thing, began with A, asparagus, no ah, yes, applesauce!" or whatever it is they do mutter. But there was no doubt, this jiggled them. A few houseslaves in pin curlers even looked around after pushing their carts past to make sure what they had seen was correct.

You know, it's one thing to have a girl in a bathing suit down on the beach, where what with the glare nobody can look at each other much anyway, and another thing in the cool of the A & P, under the fluorescent lights, against all those stacked packages, with her feet paddling along naked over our checkerboard green-and-cream rubber-tile floor.

"Oh Daddy," Stokesie said beside me. "I feel so faint."

"Darling," I said. "Hold me tight." Stokesie's married, with two babies chalked up on his fuselage already, but as far as I can tell that's the only difference. He's twenty-two, and I was nineteen this April.

"Is it done?" he asks, the responsible married man finding his voice. I forgot to say he thinks he's going to be manager some sunny day, maybe in 1990 when it's called the Great Alexandrov and Petrooshki° Tea Company or something.

What he meant was, our town is five miles from the beach, with a big summer   10
colony out on the Point, but we're right in the middle of town, and the women generally put on a shirt or shorts or something before they get out of the car into the street. And anyway these are usually women with six children and varicose veins mapping their legs and nobody, including them, could care less. As I say, we're right in the middle of town, and if you stand at our front doors you can see two banks and the Congregational church and the newspaper store and three real-estate offices and about twenty-seven old freeloaders tearing up Central Street because the sewer broke again. It's not as if we're on the Cape,° we're north of Boston and there's people in this town haven't seen the ocean for twenty years.

The girls had reached the meat counter and were asking McMahon something. He pointed, they pointed, and they shuffled out of sight behind a pyramid of Diet Delight peaches. All that was left for us to see was old McMahon patting his mouth and looking after them sizing up their joints. Poor kids, I began to feel sorry for them, they couldn't help it.

Now here comes the sad part of the story, at least my family says it's sad, but I don't think it's so sad myself. The store's pretty empty, it being Thursday afternoon, so there was nothing much to do except lean on the register and wait for the girls to show up again. The whole store was like a pinball machine and I didn't know which tunnel they'd come out of. After a while they come around out of the far aisle, around the light bulbs, records at discount of the Caribbean Six or Tony Martin Sings or some such gunk you wonder they waste the wax on, sixpacks of candy bars, and plastic toys done up in cellophane that fall apart when a kid looks at them anyway. Around they come, Queenie still leading the way, and holding a little gray jar in her hand. Slots Three through Seven are unmanned and I could see her wondering between Stokes and me, but Stokesie with his usual luck draws an old party in baggy gray pants who stumbles up with four giant cans of pineapple juice (what do these bums *do* with all that pineapple juice? I've often asked myself) so the girls come to me. Queenie puts down the jar and I take it into my fingers icy cold. Kingfish Fancy Herring Snacks in Pure Sour Cream: 49¢. Now her hands are empty, not a ring or a bracelet, bare as God made them, and I wonder where the money's coming from. Still with that prim look she lifts a

---

Great Alexandrov and Petrooshki: Apparently a reference to the possibility that someday Russia might rule the United States.

the Cape: Cape Cod, the southeastern area of Massachusetts, a place of many resorts and beaches.

folded dollar bill out of the hollow at the center of her nubbed pink top. The jar went heavy in my hand. Really, I thought that was so cute.

Then everybody's luck begins to run out. Lengel comes in from haggling with a truck full of cabbages on the lot and is about to scuttle into that door marked MANAGER behind which he hides all day when the girls touch his eye. Lengel's pretty dreary, teaches Sunday school and the rest, but he doesn't miss that much. He comes over and says, "Girls, this isn't the beach."

Queenie blushes, though maybe it's just a brush of sunburn I was noticing for the first time, now that she was so close. "My mother asked me to pick up a jar of herring snacks." Her voice kind of startled me, the way voices do when you see the people first, coming out so flat and dumb yet kind of tony, too, the way it ticked over "pick up" and "snacks." All of a sudden I slid right down her voice into her living room. Her father and the other men were standing around in ice-cream coats and bow ties and the women were in sandals picking up herring snacks on toothpicks off a big glass plate and they were all holding drinks the color of water with olives and sprigs of mint in them. When my parents have somebody over they get lemonade and if it's a real racy affair Schlitz in tall glasses with "They'll Do It Every Time"° cartoons stenciled on.

"That's all right," Lengel said. "But this isn't the beach." His repeating this   15
struck me as funny, as if it had just occurred to him, and he had been thinking all these years the A & P was a great big dune and he was the head lifeguard. He didn't like my smiling—as I say he doesn't miss much—but he concentrates on giving the girls that sad Sunday-school-superintendent stare.

Queenie's blush is no sunburn now, and the plump one in plaid, that I liked better from the back—a really sweet can—pipes up, "We weren't doing any shopping. We just came in for the one thing."

"That makes no difference," Lengel tells her, and I could see from the way his eyes went that he hadn't noticed she was wearing a two-piece before. "We want you decently dressed when you come in here."

"We *are* decent," Queenie says suddenly, her lower lip pushing, getting sore now that she remembers her place, a place from which the crowd that runs the A & P must look pretty crummy. Fancy Herring Snacks flashed in her very blue eyes.

"Girls, I don't want to argue with you. After this come in here with your shoulders covered. It's our policy." He turns his back. That's policy for you. Policy is what the kingpins want. What the others want is juvenile delinquency.

All this while, the customers had been showing up with their carts but, you   20
know, sheep, seeing a scene, they had all bunched up on Stokesie, who shook open a paper bag as gently as peeling a peach, not wanting to miss a word. I could feel in the silence everybody getting nervous, most of all Lengel, who asks me, "Sammy, have you rung up their purchase?"

I thought and said "No" but it wasn't about that I was thinking. I go through the punches, 4, 9, GROC, TOT—it's more complicated than you think, and after you do it often enough, it begins to make a little song, that you hear words to, in my case "Hello (*bing*) there, you (*gung*) hap-py *pee*-pul (*splat*)!"—the *splat* being the drawer flying out. I uncrease the bill, tenderly as you may imagine, it just having come from between the two smoothest scoops of vanilla I had ever known were

"They'll Do It Every Time": syndicated daily and Sunday cartoon created by Jimmy Hatlo.

there, and pass a half and a penny into her narrow pink palm, and nestle the herrings in a bag and twist its neck and hand it over, all the time thinking.

The girls, and who'd blame them, are in a hurry to get out, so I say "I quit" to Lengel quick enough for them to hear, hoping they'll stop and watch me, their unsuspected hero. They keep right on going, into the electric eye; the door flies open and they flicker across the lot to their car, Queenie and Plaid and Big Tall Goony-Goony (not that as raw material she was so bad), leaving me with Lengel and a kink in his eyebrow.

"Did you say something, Sammy?"

"I said I quit."

"I thought you did." 25

"You didn't have to embarrass them."

"It was they who were embarrassing us."

I started to say something that came out "Fiddle-de-doo." It's a saying of my grandmother's, and I know she would have been pleased.

"I don't think you know what you're saying," Lengel said.

"I know you don't," I said. "But I do." I pull the bow at the back of my 30 apron and start shrugging it off my shoulders. A couple customers that had been heading for my slot begin to knock against each other, like scared pigs in a chute.

Lengel sighs and begins to look very patient and old and gray. He's been a friend of my parents for years. "Sammy, you don't want to do this to your Mom and Dad," he tells me. It's true, I don't. But it seems to me that once you begin a gesture it's fatal not to go through with it. I fold the apron, "Sammy" stitched in red on the pocket, and put it on the counter, and drop the bow tie on top of it. The bow tie is theirs, if you've ever wondered. "You'll feel this for the rest of your life," Lengel says, and I know that's true, too, but remembering how he made that pretty girl blush makes me so scrunchy inside I punch the No Sale tab and the machine whirs "pee-pul" and the drawer splats out. One advantage to this scene taking place in summer, I can follow this up with a clean exit, there's no fumbling around getting your coat and galoshes, I just saunter into the electric eye in my white shirt that my mother ironed the night before, and the door heaves itself open, and outside the sunshine is skating around on the asphalt.

I look around for my girls, but they're gone, of course. There wasn't anybody but some young married screaming with her children about some candy they didn't get by the door of a powder-blue Falcon° station wagon. Looking back in the big windows, over the bags of peat moss and aluminum lawn furniture stacked on the pavement, I could see Lengel in my place in the slot, checking the sheep through. His face was dark gray and his back stiff, as if he'd just had an injection of iron, and my stomach kind of fell as I felt how hard the world was going to be to me hereafter.

QUESTIONS

1. Consider the first eleven paragraphs as exposition, in which you learn about the location, the issues, and the participants of the conflict. Is there anything inessential? Do you learn enough to understand the story? On the basis of your conclusions, consider the nature of fictional exposition.

Falcon: small car that had recently been introduced by the Ford Motor Company.

2. From Sammy's language what do you learn about his view of himself? About his educational and class level? The first sentence, for example, is grammatically incorrect in Standard English but not uncommon in colloquial English. Point out and explain similar passages.

3. Indicate evidence in the narration that Sammy is an experienced "girl watcher." What is his estimation of the intelligence of most girls? Is this judgment consistent with what he finally does?

4. Why does Sammy say "I quit" so abruptly? What do you think he means at the end by saying that the world is going to be hard to him afterwards?

GAIUS PETRONIUS   (d. A.D. 66)

The Widow of Ephesus   (First Century A.D.)

(From The Satyricon,° Chs. 108–113)

An English version by Edgar V. Roberts

We shook hands, chatted happily, and sang loudly while the entire ship rang with our noise. Sea birds landed on the yard-arms, and Eumolpus, who was drinking too much wine, decided to amuse us with a few stories. He began by insulting women. He called them weak because he claimed they were impetuous in love and would neglect even their own children while having an illicit affair. Moreover, he said that no woman he had ever known had the moral strength to resist a handsome man. He insisted that he did not get his ideas from legend or from historical accounts about evil women. Rather, he himself had actually seen what he was talking about, and he offered to tell us a true story in illustration. We immediately urged him on, and gave him our complete attention. This is the tale he told:

"Once upon a time in the city of Ephesus, on the Coast of Asia Minor, there lived a virtuous woman whose marital fidelity was so famous that women came from far and near just to get a glimpse of her. In the course of time, her husband got sick and died, and the newly widowed lady, all by herself, arranged his funeral and burial. At the funeral she was not satisfied only to follow the cortège in the usual way, by tearing her hair and beating her breasts. No, she actually accompanied the dead body right into the tomb, and after the coffin was placed in the vault in the custom of the Greeks, she began a vigil beside it, weeping and wailing both day and night.

"She was so rigorous in her duty that she neglected to eat, and she therefore became weaker by the hour. Neither her parents nor her closest relatives could

---

° "The Widow of Ephesus" is taken from *The Satyricon*, an ancient Roman example of the novelistic form that is partially preserved in manuscript. The work consists of a series of episodes and stories held together by the adventures of Encolpius, the narrator, and a group of his friends. The story of the Widow appears after a brawl that occurs on board the ship of Lichas, a wealthy sea captain whom Encolpius had earlier robbed, and his woman friend Tryphena, a courtesan with whom Encolpius has earlier had a brief affair. Encolpius and his friends, one of whom is Eumolpus, an elderly poet and raconteur, fight against Lichas and his crew. After the fight ends and the combatants settle down, there is general joyousness on the ship. The speaker or narrator is Encolpius, who quotes Eumolpus's story.

persuade her to return home. Even the local politicians and judges could not convince her. She snubbed them, and so, with their dignity ruffled, they gave up trying.

"By this time this most amazing woman was already in the fifth day of her fast, to the sorrow of everyone in town, who believed that she would die at any moment. At her side was her faithful handmaiden, who shed as many tears as the mournful Widow did. This maiden also attended to practical matters such as refuelling and relighting the torch whenever it was about to go out. Through all the city of Ephesus, from one end to another, no one talked about anything else. All the people from richest to poorest acknowledged the Widow as the supreme example of wifely love and duty. They had never seen or heard of anyone like her.

"But regular business in Ephesus also went on, and one day the Provincial 5 Governor sentenced some local hoodlums to be crucified in the grounds next to the tomb in which the Widow stood vigil. On the night of the crucifixion a soldier was stationed there to keep away all relatives or friends who might have wanted to steal the bodies in order to bury them properly.

"As he stood guard, he saw the torchlight from the Widow's tomb, and he also heard her heartbreaking outcries. Now, curiosity is a weakness of humankind, and this soldier was typically human. He went down the stairs into the sepulchre to take a look. Imagine his shock at the sight of this pretty woman and the corpse of her husband! At first he thought he was seeing ghosts, or apparitions out of the Kingdom of Hades! But when he saw how the Widow mourned, and how she had scarred her face with her fingernails, he understood that she was near death. He therefore ran up to his station and got his supper, which he carried to her. He pleaded with the sorrowing woman to stop tearing herself apart with sobs. 'The same inescapable fate waits for all human beings,' he said, 'the final trip of all to the home of the dead.' He racked his brain for other customary words of condolence which are intended to heal the broken hearts of the bereaved.

"But the Widow, who was upset rather than consoled by this unexpected stranger, only tore at her bosom more violently, ripping out some of her hair and throwing it on the corpse. The soldier then kept repeating his soothing words, while at the same time he tempted her with the tasty food and drink of his supper. The first to yield was the Widow's handmaiden, who, beguiled by the aromatic bouquet of the wine, gratefully accepted his generous offer.

"Brought back to life by the wine and the food, the handmaiden joined the soldier in his siege against the fortress of her mistress's self-sacrifice. She cried out, 'What good can it do anyone if you starve yourself to death, if you bury yourself alive, or if you yourself speed up your own last breath before your time has truly come? Remember what the poet Virgil said:

Do you believe that ashes or buried ghosts can feel?°

My Lady, come back to life, please! Give up this crazy notion of wifely duty and, as long as you are able, enjoy the light of the sun once more. Even your dead husband, if he could speak, would advise you to get on with your life.'

"Nobody is deaf when told to eat or continue staying alive, and so the Widow,

Do . . . feel: Aeneid, IV.34

starving after her long fast, finally gave way. She refreshed herself with the food just as vigorously as her handmaiden had done.

"But everybody knows that one appetite follows another, and it should come   10 as no surprise that the soldier began wooing the Widow with the same tempting words he had used to rescue her from starvation. Although she was unparalleled for modesty, she recognized that he was an unusually handsome young man. He was also persuasive, and in addition the Widow's handmaiden quoted another line of Virgil to help him in his cause:

Would you hold out against a pleasure-giving passion?°

"Why make the story last longer? This woman stopped resisting, and she accepted the young soldier's love just as she had accepted his food. They spent the night together—and after that the next night, and the next, and the next. Naturally they kept the door of the tomb barred and bolted so that any strangers or friends passing by would conclude that the faithful wife had died upon the body of her husband.

"The soldier was enchanted both by the beauty of his new sweetheart and by their secret affair, and he bought her a few small presents out of his small pay. Every night, as soon as it was dark, he would steal away to the tomb with his gifts, and would stay there until morning.

"But one evening the parents of one of the crucified thieves took advantage of him. They watched him abandon his post to enjoy his night of love, and then they hurried to their son's cross, carried his body away, and had the final ceremony for the dead performed over it. When morning came and the soldier saw that the cross was empty, he fell into a cold sweat because he knew that the punishment for his dereliction of duty would be death. He told the Widow, and swore that he could not wait for the sentence of a court martial. He would, he said, commit suicide for his folly by falling on his sword. He then asked the Widow to put his body in the tomb after he was dead—as the final resting place not only for her husband, but also for him, her lover. The Widow, however, was resourceful as well as virtuous and dutiful.

"'No,' she cried, 'heaven forbid that I should be forced by bad luck to stand vigil at the same time beside the bodies of the only two men in the world that I ever loved. I would rather hang up a dead man on the cross than permit a living man to die.'

"After these words she told him to take her husband's corpse from the vault,   15 carry it to the empty cross, and nail it up. The soldier readily agreed to this practical scheme, and the next day everyone in town was asking how on earth the dead man had been able to climb onto the cross!"

As Eumolpus was finishing his story, Tryphena blushed until her face was red, and she tried to hide her embarrassment. The sailors were so amused that they rolled on the deck with laughter. While they laughed, Lichas sternly declared that the Provincial Governor should not have permitted such a farce. Indeed, Lichas said that the Governor's duty was to have restored the husband's corpse to the tomb, and then to have executed the Widow herself on the cross.

Would . . . passion: Aeneid, IV.38

QUESTIONS

1. Who tells the story? How is he introduced? What do you learn about him? What point does he make about his story?

2. Since there is an audience, some of whom react when the narrator is finished, what is their effect on the story?

3. What is the Widow's main virtue? How does she show this virtue upon her husband's death? What does abandoning her wish for self-sacrifice show about her?

4. Should the story be taken as a joke, as it apparently was intended, at the expense of the female protagonist? What values might make it still seem a joke? What values might make it seem more serious? In light of the misogynistic theme, to what degree are you able to like the story?

JOY WILLIAMS (b. 1944)

Taking Care   1982

Jones, the preacher, has been in love all his life. He is baffled by this because as far as he can see, it has never helped anyone, even when they have acknowledged it, which is not often. Jones's love is much too apparent and arouses neglect. He is like an animal in a traveling show who, through some aberration, wears a vital organ outside the skin, awkward and unfortunate, something that shouldn't be seen, certainly something that shouldn't be watched working. Now he sits on a bed beside his wife in the self-care unit of a hospital fifteen miles from their home. She has been committed here for tests. She is so weak, so tired. There is something wrong with her blood. Her arms are covered with bruises where they have gone into the veins. Her hip, too, is blue and swollen where they have drawn out samples of bone marrow. All of this is frightening. The doctors are severe and wise, answering Jones's questions in a way that makes him feel hopelessly deaf. They have told him that there really is no such thing as a disease of the blood, for the blood is not a living tissue but a passive vehicle for the transportation of food, oxygen and waste. They have told him that abnormalities in the blood corpuscles, which his wife seems to have, must be regarded as symptoms of disease elsewhere in the body. They have shown him, upon request, slides and charts of normal and pathological blood cells which look to Jones like canapés. They speak (for he insists) of leukocytosis,° myelocytes° and megaloblasts.° None of this takes into account the love he has for his wife! Jones sits beside her in this dim pleasant room, wearing a grey suit and his clerical collar, for when he leaves her he must visit other parishioners who are patients here. This part of the hospital is like a motel. One may wear one's regular clothes. The rooms have ice-buckets, rugs and colorful bedspreads. How he wishes that they were traveling and staying overnight, this night, in a motel. A nurse comes in with a tiny paper cup full of pills. There are three pills, or rather, capsules, and they are not for his wife but for her blood. The cup is the smallest of its type that Jones has ever seen. All perspective, all

leukocytosis: elevated number of white blood cells.
myelocytes: nuclei of nerve cells.
megaloblasts: damaged red blood cells characteristic of anemia and leukemia.

sense of time and scale seem abandoned in this hospital. For example, when Jones turns to kiss his wife's hair, he nicks the air instead.

Jones and his wife have one child, a daughter, who, in turn, has a single child, a girl, born one-half year ago. Jones's daughter has fallen in with the stars and is using the heavens, as Jones would be the first to admit, more than he ever has. It has, however, brought her only grief and confusion. She has left her husband and brought the baby to Jones. She has also given him her dog. She is going to Mexico where soon, in the mountains, she will have a nervous breakdown. Jones does not know this, but his daughter has seen it in the stars and is going out to meet it. Jones quickly agrees to care for both the baby and the dog, as this seems to be the only thing his daughter needs from him. The day of the baby's birth is secondary to the position of the planets and the terms of houses, quadrants and gradients.° Her symbol is a bareback rider. To Jones, this is a graceful thought. It signifies audacity. It also means luck. Jones slips a twenty dollar bill in the pocket of his daughter's suitcase and drives her to the airport. The plane taxis down the runway and Jones waves, holding all their luck in his arms.

One afternoon, Jones had come home and found his wife sitting in the garden, weeping. She had been transplanting flowers, putting them in pots before the first frost came. There was dirt on her forehead and around her mouth. Her light clothes felt so heavy. Their weight made her body ache. Each breath was a stone she had to swallow. She cried and cried in the weak autumn sunshine. Jones could see the veins throbbing in her neck. "I'm dying," she said. "It's taking me months to die." But after he had brought her inside, she insisted that she felt better and made them both a cup of tea while Jones potted the rest of the plants and carried them down cellar. She lay on the sofa and Jones sat beside her. They talked quietly with one another. Indeed, they were almost whispering, as though they were in a public place surrounded by strangers instead of in their own house with no one present but themselves. "It's the season," Jones said. "In fall everything slows down, retreats. I'm feeling tired myself. We need iron. I'll go to the druggist right now and buy some iron tablets." His wife agreed. She wanted to go with him, for the ride. Together they ride, through the towns, for miles and miles, even into the next state. She does not want to stop driving. They buy sandwiches and milkshakes and eat in the car. Jones drives. They have to buy more gasoline. His wife sits close to him, her eyes closed, her head tipped back against the seat. He can see the veins beating on in her neck. Somewhere there is a dreadful sound, almost audible. "First I thought it was my imagination," his wife said. "I couldn't sleep. All night I would stay awake, dreaming. But it's not in my head. It's in my ears, my eyes. They ache. Everything. My tongue. My hair. The tips of my fingers are dead." Jones pressed her cold hand to his lips. He thinks of something mad and loving better than he—running out of control, deeply in the darkness of his wife. "Just don't make me go to the hospital," she pleaded. Of course she will go there. The moment has already occurred.

Jones is writing to his daughter. He received a brief letter from her this morning, telling him where she could be reached. The foreign postmark was so large that it almost obliterated Jones's address. She did not mention either her mother or the baby, which makes Jones feel peculiar. His life seems increate as his God's life, perhaps even imaginary. His daughter tells him about the town in

---

planets . . . gradients: terms used by believers in astrology to determine the future.

which she lives. She does not plan to stay there long. She wants to travel. She will find out exactly what she wants to do and then she will come home again. The town is poor but interesting and there are many Americans there her own age. There is a zoo right on the beach. Almost all the towns, no matter how small, have little zoos. There are primarily eagles and hawks in cages. And what can Jones reply to that? He writes *Every thing is fine here. We are burning wood from the old apple tree in the fire place and it smells wonderful. Has the baby had her full series of polio shots? Take care.* Jones uses this expression constantly, usually in totally unwarranted situations, as when he purchases pipe cleaners or drives through toll booths. Distracted, Jones writes off the edge of the paper and onto the blotter. He must begin again. He will mail this on the way to the hospital. They have been taking X-rays for three days now but the pictures are cloudy. They cannot read them. His wife is now in a real sickbed with high metal sides. He sits with her while she eats her dinner. She asks him to take her good nightgown home and wash it with a bar of Ivory. They won't let her do anything now, not even wash out a few things. *You must take care.*

Jones is driving down a country road. It is the first snowfall of the season 5
and he wants to show it to the baby who rides beside him in a small cushioned car seat all her own. Her head is almost on a level with his and she looks earnestly at the landscape, sometimes smiling. They follow the road that winds tightly between fields and deep pine woods. Everything is white and clean. It has been snowing all afternoon and is doing so still, but very very lightly. Fat snowflakes fall solitary against the windshield. Sometimes the baby reaches out for them. Sometimes she gives a brief kick and cry of joy. They have done their errands. Jones has bought milk and groceries and two yellow roses which lie wrapped in tissue and newspaper in the trunk, in the cold. He must buy two on Saturday as the florist is closed on Sunday. He does not like to do this but there is no alternative. The roses do not keep well. Tonight he will give one to his wife. The other he will pack in sugar water and store in the refrigerator. He can only hope that the bud will remain tight until Sunday when he brings it into the terrible heat of the hospital. The baby rocks against the straps of her small carrier. Her lips are pursed as she watches intently the fields, the grey stalks of crops growing out of the snow, the trees. She is warmly dressed and she wears a knitted orange cap. The cap is twenty-three years old, the age of her mother. Jones found it just the other day. It has faded almost to pink on one side. At one time, it must have been stored in the sun. Jones, driving, feels almost gay. The snow is so beautiful. Everything is white. Jones is an educated man. He has read Melville, who said that white is the colorless all-color of atheism from which we shrink.° Jones does not believe this. He sees a holiness in snow, a promise. He hopes that his wife will know that it is snowing even though she is separated from the window by a curtain. Jones sees something moving across the snow, a part of the snow itself running. Although he is going slowly, he takes his foot completely off the accelerator. "Look, darling, a snowshoe rabbit." At the sound of his voice, the baby stretches open her mouth and narrows her eyes in soundless glee. The hare is splendid. So fast! It flows around invisible obstructions, something out of a kind dream. It flies across the ditch, its paws like paddles, faintly yellow, the color of raw wood. "Look, sweet,"

---

colorless . . . shrink: quotation from Chapter 42, "The Whiteness of the Whale," of *Moby Dick* (1851) by Herman Melville (1819–1891).

cries Jones, "How big he is!" But suddenly the hare is curved and falling, round as a ball, its feet and head tucked closely against its body. It strikes the road and skids upside down for several yards. The car passes around it, avoids it. Jones brakes and stops, amazed. He opens the door and trots back to the animal. The baby twists about in her seat as well as she can and peers after him. It is as though the animal had never been alive at all. Its head is broken in several places. Jones bends to touch its fur, but straightens again, not doing so. A man emerges from the woods, swinging a shotgun. He nods at Jones and picks the hare up by the ears. As he walks away, the hare's legs rub across the ground. There are small crystal stains on the snow. Jones returns to the car. He wants to apologize but he does not know to whom or for what. His life has been devoted to apologetics.° It is his profession. He is concerned with both justification and remorse. He has always acted rightly, but nothing has ever come of it. He gets in the car, starts the engine. "Oh, sweet," he says to the baby. She smiles at him, exposing her tooth. At home that night, after the baby's supper, Jones reads a story to her. She is asleep, panting in her sleep, but Jones tells her the story of al-Boraq,° the milk-white steed of Mohammed, who could stride out of the sight of mankind with a single step.

Jones sorts through a collection of records, none of which have been opened. They are still wrapped in cellophane. The jacket designs are subdued, epic. Names, instruments and orchestras are mentioned confidently. He would like to agree with their importance, for he knows that they have worth, but he is not familiar with the references. His daughter brought these records with her. They had been given to her by an older man, a professor she had been having an affair with. Naturally, this pains Jones. His daughter speaks about the men she has been involved with but no longer cares about. Where did these men come from? Where were they waiting and why have they gone? Jones remembers his daughter when she was a little girl, helping him rake leaves. What can he say? For years on April Fool's Day, she would take tobacco out of his humidor and fill it with corn flakes. Jones is full of remorse and astonishment. When he saw his daughter only a few weeks ago, she was thin and nervous. She had torn out almost all her eyebrows with her fingers from this nervousness. And her lashes. The roots of her eyes were white, like the bulbs of flowers. Her fingernails were crudely bitten, some bleeding below the quick. She was tough and remote, wanting only to go on a trip for which she had a ticket. What can he do? He seeks her in the face of the baby but she is not there. All is being both continued and resumed, but the dream is different. The dream cannot be revived. Jones breaks into one of the albums, blows the dust from the needle, plays a record. Outside it is dark. The parsonage is remote and the only buildings nearby are barns. The river cannot be seen. The music is Bruckner's *Te Deum*.° Very nice, Dedicated to God. He plays the other side. A woman, Kathleen Ferrier,° is singing in German. Jones cannot understand

---

apologetics: the explanation and defense of religion, here, specifically, of Christianity.

al-Boraq: According to the Koran, the angel Gabriel brought the prophet Mohammed to the Islamic Seventh Heaven (made up of divine light) on the mystical horse *Borak* or *al-Borak* ("lightning").

Bruckner: Anton Bruckner (1824–1896), Austrian composer and organist. His *Te Deum* for chorus, soloists, and orchestra was completed in 1884.

Kathleen Ferrier: celebrated English contralto (1912–1953), who died of cancer.

the words but the music stuns him. *Kindertotenlieder.*° It is devastating. In college he had studied only scientific German, The vocabulary of submarines, dirigibles and steam engines. Jones plays the record again and again, searching for his old grammar. At last he finds it. The wings of insects are between some of the pages. There are notes in pencil, written in his own young hand.

RENDER:
A. WAS THE TEACHER SATISFIED WITH YOU TODAY?
B. NO. HE IS NOT. MY ESSAY WAS GOOD BUT IT WAS NOT COPIED WELL.
C. I AM SORRY YOU WERE NOT INDUSTRIOUS THIS TIME FOR YOU GENERALLY ARE.

These lessons are neither of life or death. Why was he instructed in them? In the hospital, his wife waits to be translated, no longer a woman, the woman whom he loves, but a situation. Her blood moves mysteriously as constellations. She is under scrutiny and attack and she has abandoned Jones. She is a swimmer waiting to get on with the drowning. Jones is on the shore. In Mexico, his daughter walks along the beach with two men. She is acting out a play that has become her life. Jones is on the mountaintop. The baby cries and Jones takes her from the crib to change her. The dog paws the door. Jones lets him out. He settles down with the baby and listens to the record. He still cannot make out many of the words. The baby wiggles restlessly on his lap. Her eyes are a foal's eyes, navy-blue. She has grown in a few weeks to expect everything from Jones. He props her on one edge of the couch and goes to her small toy box where he keeps a bear, a few rattles and balls. On the way, he opens the door and the dog immediately enters. His heavy coat is cold, fragrant with ice. He noses the baby and she squeals.

Oft denk'ich, sie sind nur ausgegangen
Bald werden sie wieder nach Hause gelangen°

Jones selects a bright ball and pushes it gently in her direction.

It is Sunday morning and Jones is in the pulpit. The church is very old but the walls of the sanctuary have recently been painted a pale blue. In the cemetery adjoining, some of the graves are three hundred years old. It has become a historical landmark and no one has been buried there since World War I. There is a new place, not far away, which the families now use. Plots are marked not with stones but with small tablets, and immediately after any burial, workmen roll grassed sod over the new graves so that there is no blemish on the grounds, not even for a little while. Present for today's service are seventy-eight adults, eleven children and the junior choir. Jones counts them as the offertory is received. The church rolls say that there are three hundred fifty members but as far as Jones

---

Kindertotenlieder: "Songs on the Death of Children" (1901, 1904), a cycle of five songs for voice and orchestra by Gustav Mahler (1860–1911), Austrian composer and conductor. Mahler's elder daughter died three years after he completed the work.

Oft . . . gelangen: opening two lines of the fourth song in Mahler's *Kindertotenlieder*, from a poem by Friedrich Rückert (1788–1866): "Often I think they've just gone outside!/ They'll be back home again quickly!"

can see, everyone is here today. This is the day he baptizes the baby. He has made arrangements with one of the ladies to hold her and bring her up to the font at the end of the first hymn. The baby looks charming in a lacy white dress. Jones has combed her fine hair carefully, slicking it in a curl with water, but now it has dried and it sticks up awkwardly like the crest of a kingfisher. Jones bought the dress in Mammoth Mart, an enormous store which has a large metal elephant dressed in overalls dancing on the roof. He feels foolish at buying it there but he had gone to several stores and that is where he saw the prettiest dress. He blesses the baby with water from the silver bowl. He says, *We are saved not because we are worthy. We are saved because we are loved.* It is a brief ceremony. The baby, looking curiously at Jones, is taken out to the nursery. Jones begins his sermon. He can't remember when he wrote it, but here it is, typed, in front of him. *There is nothing wrong in what one does but there is something wrong in what one becomes.* He finds this questionable but goes on speaking. He has been preaching for thirty-four years. He is gaunt with belief. But his wife has a red cell count of only 2.3 millions. It is not enough! She is not getting enough oxygen! Jones is giving his sermon. Somewhere he has lost what he was looking for. He must have known once, surely. The congregation sways, like the wings of a ray in water. It is Sunday and for patients it is a holiday. The doctors don't visit. There are no tests or diagnoses. Jones would like to leave, to walk down the aisle and out into the winter, where he would read his words into the ground. Why can't he remember his life! He finishes, sits down, stands up to present communion. Tiny cubes of bread lie in a slumped pyramid. They are offered and received. Jones takes his morsel, hacked earlier from a sliced enriched loaf with his own hand. It is so dry, almost wicked. The very thought now sickens him. He chews it over and over again, but it lies unconsumed, like a muscle in his mouth.

Jones is waiting in the lobby for the results of his wife's operation. Has there ever been a time before dread? He would be grateful even to have dread back, but it has been lost, for a long time, in rapid possibility, probability and fact. The baby sits on his knees and plays with his tie. She woke very early this morning for her orange juice and then gravely, immediately, spit it all up. She seems fine now, however, her fingers exploring Jones's tie. Whenever he looks at her, she gives him a dazzling smile. He has spent most of the day fiercely cleaning the house, changing the bed-sheets and the pages of the many calendars that hang in the rooms, things he should have done a week ago. He has dusted and vacuumed and pressed all his shirts. He has laundered all the baby's clothes, soft small sacks and gowns and sleepers which froze in his hands the moment he stepped outside. And now he is waiting and watching his wristwatch. The tumor is precisely this size, they tell him, the size of his clock's face.

Jones has the baby on his lap and he is feeding her. The evening meal is lengthy and complex. First he must give her vitamins, then, because she has a cold, a dropper of liquid aspirin. This is followed by a bottle of milk, eight ounces, and a portion of strained vegetables. He gives her a rest now so that the food can settle. On his hip, she rides through the rooms of the huge house as Jones turns lights off and on. He comes back to the table and gives her a little more milk, a half jar of strained chicken and a few spoonfuls of dessert, usually cobbler, buckle or pudding. The baby enjoys all equally. She is good. She eats rapidly and neatly. Sometimes she grasps the spoon, turns it around and thrusts the wrong end into her mouth. Of course there is nothing that cannot be done incorrectly. Jones

10

adores the baby. He sniffs her warm head. Her birth is a deep error, an abstraction. Born in wedlock but out of love. He puts her in the playpen and tends to the dog. He fills one dish with water and one with horsemeat. He rinses out the empty can before putting it in the wastebasket. The dog eats with great civility. He eats a little meat and then takes some water, then meat, then water. When the dog has finished, the dishes are as clean as though they'd been washed. Jones now thinks about his own dinner. He opens the refrigerator. The ladies of the church have brought brownies, venison, cheese and apple sauce. There are turkey pies, pork chops, steak, haddock and sausage patties. A brilliant light exposes all this food. There is so much of it. It must be used. A crust has formed around the punctures in a can of Pet. There is a clear bag of chicken livers stapled shut. There are large brown eggs in a bowl. Jones stares unhappily at the beads of moisture on cartons and bottles, at the pearls of fat on the cold cooked stew. He sits down. The room is full of lamps and cords. He thinks of his wife, her breathing body deranged in tubes, and begins to shake. All objects here are perplexed by such grief.

Now it is almost Christmas and Jones is walking down by the river, around an abandoned house. The dog wades heavily through the snow, biting it. There are petals of ice on the tree limbs and when Jones lingers under them, the baby puts out her hand and her mouth starts working because she would like to have it, the ice, the branch, everything. His wife will be coming home in a few days, in time for Christmas. Jones has already put up the tree and brought the ornaments down from the attic. He will not trim it until she comes home. He wants very much to make a fine occasion out of opening the boxes of old decorations. The two of them have always enjoyed this greatly in the past. Jones will doubtlessly drop and smash a bauble, for he does every year. He tramps through the snow with his small voyager. She dangles in a shoulder sling, her legs wedged around his hip. They regard the rotting house seriously. Once it was a doctor's home and offices but long before Jones's time, the doctor, who was very respected, had been driven away because a town girl accused him of fathering her child. The story goes that all the doctor said was, "Is that so?" This incensed the town and the girl's parents, who insisted that he take the child as soon as it was born. He did and he cared for the child very well even though his practice was ruined and no one had anything to do with him. A year later the girl told the truth—that the actual father was a young college boy whom she was now going to marry. They wanted the child back, and the doctor willingly returned the infant to them. Of course it is a very old, important story. Jones has always appreciated it, but now he is annoyed at the man's passivity. He wife's sickness has changed everything for Jones. He will continue to accept but he will no longer surrender. Surely things are different for Jones now.

For insurance purposes, Jones's wife is brought out to the car in a wheelchair. She is thin and beautiful. Jones is grateful and confused. He has a mad wish to tip the orderly. Have so many years really passed? Is this not his wife, his love, fresh from giving birth? Isn't everything about to begin? In Mexico, his daughter wanders disinterestedly through a jewelry shop where she picks up a small silver egg. It opens on a hinge and inside are two figures, a bride and groom. Jones puts the baby in his wife's arms. At first the baby is alarmed because she cannot remember this person very well and she reaches for Jones, whimpering. But soon she is soothed by his wife's soft voice and she falls asleep in her arms as they drive. Jones has readied everything carefully for his wife's homecoming. The house is clean and orderly. For days he has restricted himself to only one part of the house so that his clutter will be minimal. Jones helps his wife up the steps to the door. Together they enter the shining rooms.

QUESTIONS

1. Describe the character of Jones. What is his major trait? How do you learn about it? Why does he continue to practice his profession and care for his family?

2. On the basis of this story, what can you say about the use of tenses in a narration? Why is the story told mainly in the present tense? What is the relationship here between past and present tense?

3. Explain why there are so few paragraphs in the story and why the paragraphs are rather long. Why do you think that Williams does not use more dialogue?

4. Explore the sad or depressing references and situations in the story (e.g., the ill wife, the dead rabbit, the daughter abandoning her child, the songs on the death of children). In the light of such references, how does the story make you think and feel?

ALICE WALKER   (b. 1944)

Everyday Use   *1973*

for your grandmama

I will wait for her in the yard that Maggie and I made so clean and wavy yesterday afternoon. A yard like this is more comfortable than most people know. It is not just a yard. It is like an extended living room. When the hard clay is swept clean as a floor and the fine sand around the edges lined with tiny, irregular grooves, anyone can come and sit and look up into the elm tree and wait for the breezes that never come inside the house.

Maggie will be nervous until after her sister goes: she will stand hopelessly in corners, homely and ashamed of the burn scars down her arms and legs, eying her sister with a mixture of envy and awe. She thinks her sister has held life always in the palm of one hand, that "no" is a word the world never learned to say to her.

You've no doubt seen those TV shows° where the child who has "made it" is confronted, as a surprise, by her own mother and father, tottering in weakly from backstage. (A pleasant surprise, of course: What would they do if parent and child came on the show only to curse out and insult each other?) On TV mother and child embrace and smile into each other's faces. Sometimes the mother and father weep, the child wraps them in her arms and leans across the table to tell how she would not have made it without their help. I have seen these programs.

TV shows: In the early days of television, a popular show was "This Is Your Life," which the narrator describes exactly here.

Sometimes I dream a dream in which Dee and I are suddenly brought together on a TV program of this sort. Out of a dark and soft-seated limousine I am ushered into a bright room filled with many people. There I meet a smiling, gray, sporty man like Johnny Carson who shakes my hand and tells me what a fine girl I have. Then we are on the stage and Dee is embracing me with tears in her eyes. She pins on my dress a large orchid, even though she has told me once that she thinks orchids are tacky flowers.

In real life I am a large, big-boned woman with rough, man-working hands. 5 In the winter I wear flannel nightgowns to bed and overalls during the day. I can kill and clean a hog as mercilessly as a man. My fat keeps me hot in zero weather. I can work outside all day, breaking ice to get water for washing; I can eat pork liver cooked over the open fire minutes after it comes steaming from the hog. One winter I knocked a bull calf straight in the brain between the eyes with a sledge hammer and had the meat hung up to chill before nightfall. But of course all this does not show on television. I am the way my daughter would want me to be: a hundred pounds lighter, my skin like an uncooked barley pancake. My hair glistens in the hot bright lights. Johnny Carson has much to do to keep up with my quick and witty tongue.

But that is a mistake, I know even before I wake up. Who ever knew a Johnson with a quick tongue? Who can even imagine me looking a strange white man in the eye? It seems to me I have talked to them always with one foot raised in flight, with my head turned in whichever way is farthest from them. Dee, though. She would always look anyone in the eye. Hesitation was no part of her nature.

"How do I look, Mama?" Maggie says, showing just enough of her thin body enveloped in pink skirt and red blouse for me to know she's there, almost hidden by the door.

"Come out into the yard," I say.

Have you ever seen a lame animal, perhaps a dog run over by some careless person rich enough to own a car, sidle up to someone who is ignorant enough to be kind to him? That is the way my Maggie walks. She has been like this, chin on chest, eyes on ground, feet in shuffle, ever since the fire that burned the other house to the ground.

Dee is lighter than Maggie, with nicer hair and a fuller figure. She's a woman 10 now, though sometimes I forget. How long ago was it that the other house burned? Ten, twelve years? Sometimes I can still hear the flames and feel Maggie's arms sticking to me, her hair smoking and her dress falling off her in little black papery flakes. Her eyes seemed stretched open, blazed open by the flames reflected in them. And Dee, I see her standing off under the sweet gum tree she used to dig gum out of; a look of concentration on her face as she watched the last dingy gray board of the house fall in toward the red-hot brick chimney. Why don't you do a dance around the ashes? I'd wanted to ask her. She had hated the house that much.

I used to think she hated Maggie, too. But that was before we raised the money, the church and me, to send her to Augusta° to school. She used to read to us without pity; forcing words, lies, other folks' habits, whole lives upon us two,

---

Augusta: city in eastern Georgia, the location of Paine College.

sitting trapped and ignorant underneath her voice. She washed us in a river of make-believe, burned us with a lot of knowledge we didn't necessarily need to know. Pressed us to her with the serious way she read, to shove us away at just the moment, like dimwits, we seemed about to understand.

Dee wanted nice things. A yellow organdy dress to wear to her graduation from high school; black pumps to match a green suit she'd made from an old suit somebody gave me. She was determined to stare down any disaster in her efforts. Her eyelids would not flicker for minutes at a time. Often I fought off the temptation to shake her. At sixteen she had a style of her own: and knew what style was.

I never had an education myself. After second grade the school was closed down. Don't ask me why: in 1927 colored asked fewer questions than they do now. Sometimes Maggie reads to me. She stumbles along good-naturedly, but can't see well. She knows she is not bright. Like good looks and money, quickness passed her by. She will marry John Thomas (who has mossy teeth in an earnest face) and then I'll be free to sit here and I guess just sing church songs to myself. Although I never was a good singer. Never could carry a tune. I was always better at a man's job. I used to love to milk till I was hooked in the side° in '49. Cows are soothing and slow and don't bother you, unless you try to milk them the wrong way.

I have deliberately turned my back on the house. It is three rooms, just like the one that burned, except the roof is tin; they don't make shingle roofs any more. There are no real windows, just some holes cut in the sides, like the portholes on a ship, but not round and not square, with rawhide holding the shutters up on the outside. This house is in a pasture, too, like the other one. No doubt when Dee sees it she will want to tear it down. She wrote me once that no matter where we "choose" to live, she will manage to come see us. But she will never bring her friends. Maggie and I thought about this and Maggie asked me, "Mama, when did Dee ever *have* any friends?"

She has a few. Furtive boys in pink shirts hanging about on washday after   15
school. Nervous girls who never laughed. Impressed with her they worshiped the well-turned phrase, the cute shape, the scalding humor that erupted like bubbles in lye. She read to them.

When she was courting Jimmy T she didn't have much time to pay to us, but turned all her faultfinding power on him. He *flew* to marry a cheap city girl from a family of ignorant flashy people. She hardly had time to recompose herself.

When she comes I will meet—but there they are!

Maggie attempts to make a dash for the house, in her shuffling way, but I stay her with my hand. "Come back here," I say. And she stops and tries to dig a well in the sand with her toe.

It is hard to see them clearly through the strong sun. But even the first glimpse of leg out of the car tells me it is Dee. Her feet were always neat-looking, as if God himself had shaped them with a certain style. From the other side of

---

hooked in the side: kicked by a cow.

the car comes a short, stocky man. Hair is all over his head a foot long and hanging from his chin like a kinky mule tail. I hear Maggie suck in her breath. "Uhnnnh," is what it sounds like. Like when you see the wriggling end of a snake just in front of your foot on the road. "Uhnnnh."

Dee next. A dress down to the ground, in this hot weather. A dress so loud   20
it hurts my eyes. There are yellows and oranges enough to throw back the light of the sun. I feel my whole face warming from the heat waves it throws out. Earrings gold, too, and hanging down to her shoulders. Bracelets dangling and making noises when she moves her arm up to shake the folds of the dress out of her armpits. The dress is loose and flows, and as she walks closer, I like it. I hear Maggie go "Uhnnnh" again. It is her sister's hair. It stands straight up like the wool on a sheep. It is black as night and around the edges are two long pigtails that rope about like small lizards disappearing behind her ears.

"Wa-su-zo-Tean-o!"° she says, coming on in that gliding way the dress makes her move. The short stocky yellow with the hair to his navel is all grinning and he follows up with "Asalamalakim,° my mother and my sister!" He moves to hug Maggie but she falls back, tight up against the back of my chair. I feel her trembling there and when I look up I see the perspiration falling off her chin.

"Don't get up," says Dee. Since I am stout it takes something of a push. You can see me trying to move a second or two before I make it. She turns, showing white heels through her sandals, and goes back to the car. Out she peeks next with a Polaroid. She stoops down quickly and lines up picture after picture of me sitting there in front of the house with Maggie cowering behind me. She never takes a shot without making sure the house is included. When a cow comes nibbling around the edge of the yard she snaps it and me and Maggie *and* the house. Then she puts the Polaroid in the back seat of the car, and comes up and kisses me on the forehead.

Meanwhile Asalamalakim is going through motions with Maggie's hand. Maggie's hand is as limp as a fish, and probably as cold, despite the sweat, and she keeps trying to pull it back. It looks like Asalamalakim wants to shake hands but wants to do it fancy. Or maybe he don't know how people shake hands. Anyhow, he soon gives up on Maggie.

"Well," I say, "Dee."

"No, Mama," she says. "Not 'Dee,' Wangero Leewanika Kemanjo!"   25

"What happened to 'Dee'?" I wanted to know.

"She's dead," Wangero said. "I couldn't bear it any longer, being named after the people who oppress me."

"You know as well as me you was named after your aunt Dicie," I said. Dicie is my sister. She named Dee. We called her "Big Dee" after Dee was born.

"But who was *she* named after?" asked Wangero.

"I guess after Grandma Dee," I said.   30

"And who was she named after?" asked Wangero.

"Her mother," I said, and saw Wangero was getting tired. "That's about as far back as I can trace it," I said. Though, in fact, I probably could have carried it back beyond the Civil War through the branches.

Wa-su-zo-Tean-o: greeting used by Black Muslims.
Asalamalakim: Muslim salutation meaning "Peace be with you."

"Well," said Asalamalakim, "there you are."

"Uhnnnh," I heard Maggie say.

"There I was not," I said, "before 'Dicie' cropped up in our family, so why   35
should I try to trace it that far back?"

He just stood there grinning, looking down on me like somebody inspecting
a Model A car.° Every once in a while he and Wangero sent eye signals over my
head.

"How do you pronounce this name?" I asked.

"You don't have to call me by it if you don't want to," said Wangero.

"Why shouldn't I?" I asked. "If that's what you want us to call you, we'll call
you."

"I know it might sound awkward at first," said Wangero.   40

"I'll get used to it," I said. "Ream it out again."

Well, soon we got the name out of the way. Asalamalakim had a name twice
as long and three times as hard. After I tripped over it two or three times he told
me to just call him Hakim-a-barber. I wanted to ask him was he a barber, but I
didn't really think he was, so I didn't ask.

"You must belong to those beef-cattle peoples down the road," I said. They
said "Asalamalakim" when they met you, too, but they didn't shake hands. Always
too busy: feeding the cattle, fixing the fences, putting up salt-lick shelters,° throwing
down hay. When the white folks poisoned some of the herd the men stayed up
all night with rifles in their hands. I walked a mile and a half just to see the sight.

Hakim-a-barber said, "I accept some of their doctrines, but farming and
raising cattle is not my style." (They didn't tell me, and I didn't ask, whether
Wangero (Dee) had really gone and married him.)

We sat down to eat and right away he said he didn't eat collards and pork   45
was unclean. Wangero, though, went on through the chitlins and corn bread, the
greens and everything else. She talked a blue streak over the sweet potatoes.
Everything delighted her. Even the fact that we still used the benches her daddy
made for the table when we couldn't afford to buy chairs.

"Oh, Mama!" she cried. Then turned to Hakim-a-barber. "I never knew how
lovely these benches are. You can feel the rump prints," she said, running her
hands underneath her and along the bench. Then she gave a sigh and her hand
closed over Grandma Dee's butter dish. "That's it!" she said. "I knew there was
something I wanted to ask you if I could have." She jumped up from the table
and went over in the corner where the churn stood, the milk in it clabber° by now.
She looked at the churn and looked at it.

"This churn top is what I need," she said. "Didn't Uncle Buddy whittle it
out of a tree you all used to have?"

"Yes," I said.

"Uh huh," she said happily. "And I want the dasher, too."

"Uncle Buddy whittle that, too?" asked the barber.   50

Model A car: The Ford car that replaced the Model T in the late 1920s. The Model A
was proverbial for its quality and durability.

salt-lick shelters: shelters built to prevent rain from dissolving the large blocks of rock
salt set up on poles for cattle.

clabber: curdled, turned sour.

Dee (Wangero) looked up at me.

"Aunt Dee's first husband whittled the dash," said Maggie so low you almost couldn't hear her. "His name was Henry, but they called him Stash."

"Maggie's brain is like an elephant's," Wangero said, laughing. "I can use the churn top as a centerpiece for the alcove table," she said, sliding a plate over the churn, "and I'll think of something artistic to do with the dasher."

When she finished wrapping the dasher the handle stuck out. I took it for a moment in my hands. You didn't even have to look close to see where hands pushing the dasher up and down to make butter had left a kind of sink in the wood. In fact, there were a lot of small sinks; you could see where thumbs and fingers had sunk into the wood. It was beautiful light yellow wood, from a tree that grew in the yard where Big Dee and Stash had lived.

After dinner Dee (Wangero) went to the trunk at the foot of my bed and   55
started rifling through it. Maggie hung back in the kitchen over the dishpan. Out came Wangero with two quilts. They had been pieced by Grandma Dee and then Big Dee and me had hung them on the quilt frames on the front porch and quilted them. One was in the Lone Star pattern. The other was Walk Around the Mountain. In both of them were scraps of dresses Grandma Dee had worn fifty and more years ago. Bits and pieces of Grandpa Jarrell's Paisley shirts. And one teeny faded blue piece, about the size of a penny matchbox, that was from Great Grandpa's Ezra's uniform that he wore in the Civil War.

"Mama," Wangero said sweet as a bird. "Can I have these old quilts?"

I heard something fall in the kitchen, and a minute later the kitchen door slammed.

"Why don't you take one or two of the others?" I asked. "These old things was just done by me and Big Dee from some tops your grandma pieced before she died."

"No," said Wangero. "I don't want those. They are stitched around the borders by machine."

"That'll make them last better," I said.   60

"That's not the point," said Wangero. "These are all pieces of dresses Grandma used to wear. She did all this stitching by hand. Imagine!" She held the quilts securely in her arms, stroking them.

"Some of the pieces, like those lavender ones, come from old clothes her mother handed down to her," I said, moving up to touch the quilts. Dee (Wangero) moved back just enough so that I couldn't reach the quilts. They already belonged to her.

"Imagine!" she breathed again, clutching them closely to her bosom.

"The truth is," I said, "I promised to give them quilts to Maggie, for when she marries John Thomas."

She gasped like a bee had stung her.   65

"Maggie can't appreciate these quilts!" she said. "She'd probably be backward enough to put them to everyday use."

"I reckon she would," I said. "God knows I been saving 'em for long enough with nobody using 'em. I hope she will!" I didn't want to bring up how I had offered Dee (Wangero) a quilt when she went away to college. Then she had told me they were old-fashioned, out of style.

"But they're *priceless*!" she was saying now, furiously; for she has a temper.

"Maggie would put them on the bed and in five years they'd be in rags. Less than that!"

"She can always make some more," I said. "Maggie knows how to quilt."

Dee (Wangero) looked at me with hatred. "You just will not understand.   70 The point is these quilts, *these* quilts!"

"Well," I said, stumped. "What would *you* do with them?"

"Hang them," she said. As if that was the only thing you *could* do with quilts.

Maggie by now was standing in the door. I could almost hear the sound her feet made as they scraped over each other.

"She can have them, Mama," she said, like somebody used to never winning anything, or having anything reserved for her. "I can 'member Grandma Dee without the quilts."

I looked at her hard. She had filled her bottom lip with checkerberry snuff   75 and it gave her face a kind of dopey, hangdog look. It was Grandma Dee and Big Dee who taught her how to quilt herself. She stood there with her scarred hands hidden in the folds of her skirt. She looked at her sister with something like fear but she wasn't mad at her. This was Maggie's portion. This was the way she knew God to work.

When I looked at her like that something hit me in the top of my head and ran down to the soles of my feet. Just like when I'm in church and the spirit of God touches me and I get happy and shout. I did something I never had done before: hugged Maggie to me, then dragged her on into the room, snatched the quilts out of Miss Wangero's hands and dumped them into Maggie's lap. Maggie just sat there on my bed with her mouth open.

"Take one or two of the others," I said to Dee.

But she turned without a word and went out to Hakim-a-barber.

"You just don't understand," she said, as Maggie and I came out to the car.

"What don't I understand?" I wanted to know.   80

"Your heritage," she said. And then she turned to Maggie, kissed her, and said, "You ought to try to make something of yourself, too, Maggie. It's really a new day for us. But from the way you and Mama still live you'd never know it."

She put on some sunglasses that hid everything above the tip of her nose and her chin.

Maggie smiled; maybe at the sunglasses. But a real smile, not scared. After we watched the car dust settle I asked Maggie to bring me a dip of snuff. And then the two of us sat there just enjoying, until it was time to go in the house and go to bed.

QUESTIONS

1. Describe the narrator. Who is she? What is she like? Where and how does she live? What kind of life has she had? How does the story bring out her judgments about her two daughters?

2. Describe the narrator's daughters. How are they different physically and mentally? How have their lives been different?

3. Why did Dee change her name to "Wangero"? How is this change important, and how is it reflected in her attitude toward the family artifacts?

4. Describe the importance of the phrase "everyday use" (paragraph 66). How does this phrase highlight the conflicting values in the story?

HOW TO WRITE A PRÉCIS OR ABRIDGEMENT

A *précis* is a shortening, in your own words, of the text of a written work. The closely related words *précis* and *precise* are helpful in understanding the nature of a précis—namely, a cutting down of a story into its precise, essential parts. The object is to make a short—**short**—encapsulation of the most significant details. Other words describing the précis are *abridgment, paraphrase, abstract, condensation,* and *epitome. Epitome* is particularly helpful as a description for a précis, for an epitome is a *cutting away,* so that only the important, most vital parts remain.

Uses of the Précis

Beyond enabling you to follow a story with accuracy, the précis is important in study, research, and speaking and writing. One of the best ways to study any work is to write a précis of it, for the process forces you to grasp each of the parts. Précis writing can be used in taking notes, preparing for exams, establishing and clarifying facts for any body of discourse, studying for classroom discussion, and reinforcing things learned in the past. The object of a précis should be not to tell *everything,* but only enough to give the highlights, so that any reader will know the main points of the work in question. Although you may sometimes need to condense an entire plot or epitomize an entire argument, most often you will refer to no more than parts of works, because your arguments will depend on a number of separate interpretations.

GUIDELINES FOR PRÉCIS WRITING

Following are guidelines to follow in the development of a précis.

1. **SELECTION.** Only essential details belong in a précis. For example, at the opening of the story "Everyday Use," Walker describes the narrator as a large woman who has lived a very hard life. We learn that she can kill animals for food and survival. She is fully capable of taking care of herself and her family. Writing about all these details, however, would needlessly lengthen a précis of "Everyday Use." Instead it is sufficient to say something like "Mrs. Johnson is a strong woman," because this fact is

the most vital one about her. Concentrating on only essentials enables you to achieve the shortening required of a précis. Thus, a 5,000-word story might be epitomized in 100, 200, or 400 words. Of course more details might be selected for inclusion in a longer précis. No matter how long the précis, however, you should base your selection of detail on your judgment of its importance.

2. ACCURACY.   All details in a précis should be both correct and accurate. It is important to avoid misstatement, and also to avoid using words that give a misleading impression of the original. In "The Necklace," for example, Mathilde cooperates with her husband for ten years to repay their 18,000-franc debt. In a précis it would be possible to say no more than that she "works" during this time. The word *works* is misleading, however, for it may be interpreted to mean that Mathilde gets paid for outside employment. In fact she does not. What Maupassant tells us is that Mathilde gives up her servant girl and then does all the heavy housework herself as part of her general economizing in her *own* household, not in the houses of others.

As important as the need to condense long sections of a story accurately is the need to be comprehensive. In reference to Walker's "Everyday Use," there is a concluding dispute between the mother (the narrator) and her visiting daughter about the daughter's request for two homemade quilts. Wangero wants them to adorn a wall, while the mother refuses on the grounds that she has promised them to her other daughter for "everyday use" during her approaching marriage. These details are complex, and they represent the climax of the major conflict in the story. In a précis it is important not just to explain the claims but also to present language comprehensive enough to get at the conflict. Thus, accurate and comprehensive language might be the following: "Mrs. Johnson hesitates, having already promised the quilts to Maggie for use when she gets married. Though Maggie offers to give Wangero the quilts, Mrs. Johnson insists on her original promise. Wangero then objects, claiming that the quilts will be spoiled by 'everyday use' and that her mother misunderstands the value of the family heritage." This language explains the details accurately and comprehensively—the goal of précis writing.

3. DICTION.   A précis should be an original essay and therefore it should be written *in your own words*, not those of the work you are abridging. The best way to ensure original wording is to read the work, take note of the major things that happen, and then put the work out of reach as you write. That way the temptation to borrow words can be avoided.

However, if a number of words from the text find their way into the précis even after you have tried to keep them out, then it is important to use quotation marks to set them off. As long as direct quotations are kept to a minimum, they are satisfactory. Too many quoted words, however, indicate that your précis is not original.

4. OBJECTIVITY. A précis should be scrupulously factual. Avoid explanatory or introductory material unless it is a part of the story. As much effort should be made to *avoid* conclusions in a précis as is exerted to *include* them in other kinds of writing about literature. Here is a comparative example of what to do and what to avoid:

WHAT TO DO	*WHAT TO AVOID*
Mrs. Johnson, a strong woman living on her Southern farm with her younger daughter, Maggie, is waiting for a visit by her elder daughter, Dee. Dee is returning from her home in the city, and the mother has cleaned and swept the house and yard in order to make a good impression.	Walker opens the story by building up the contrast that will soon be made apparent. Her narrator, Mrs. Johnson, is a plain, down-to-earth woman who has worked hard all her life and whose basic value is her home and possessions. The contrast is her daughter Dee, whose visit she is waiting for. Dee has left home and lived a sophisticated life in the city. Mrs. Johnson takes pride in her home, while Dee will regard the home and her mother's belongings as being of no more use than to be put on display.

The right-hand column contains a guiding topic sentence, to which the following sentences adhere. Such writing is commendable elsewhere, but not in a précis. The left-hand column is better writing *as a précis,* for it presents a selection of details only as they appear in the story, without introductory sentences. In the story there are no such introductions.

5. SENTENCES. Because a précis should be concise and factual, it is tempting to write sentences that are like short bursts of machine-gun fire. Sentences of this kind are often called "choppy." Here is an example of choppy sentences:

Dee comes in a car. She is dressed flamboyantly. She is with a strange man. He is short and bearded. She greets her mother and sister with foreign phrases. The man does, too. She immediately begins taking pictures. She snaps her mother with her sister in the background. She also takes pictures of wandering cows. She makes sure to get the house in all the shots. She kisses her mother then, on the forehead.

An entire essay consisting of sentences like these might make readers feel as though they actually have been machine-gunned. The problem is to include detail but also to remember to shape and organize your sentences. Here is a more acceptable set of sentences revised to contain the same information:

> When Dee comes, she is flamboyantly dressed, and gets out of the car with a strange, short, and bearded man. Both Dee and the man greet Mrs. Johnson and Maggie with foreign phrases. Before embracing her mother, Dee gets her Polaroid camera and takes pictures of her mother, her sister, and wandering cows, taking care to include the house in all her shots. Only then does she kiss her mother, and then only on the forehead.

This revision blends the shorter sentences together while still attempting to cover the essential details from the story. Starting the last sentence with "Only then" gets at Dee's ridiculous behavior without calling it ridiculous. Even though sentences in a précis must be almost rigidly factual, you should try to make them as graceful as possible.

WRITING A PRÉCIS

Your writing task is to condense the original work with the least possible distortion. Thus, it is necessary to keep intact the arrangement and sequence of the original. Let us suppose that a work has a surprise ending, like that in "The Necklace." In a précis, it is important to keep the same order and withhold the conclusion until the very end. It is proper, however, to introduce essential details of circumstance, such as names and places, at the beginning of the précis, even though these details are not brought out immediately in the story. For example, Maupassant does not name Mathilde right away, and he never says that she is French, but a précis of "The Necklace" would be obscure without these details.

If your assignment is a very short précis, say 100 to 150 words, you might confine everything to only one paragraph. For a longer précis, the normal principle of devoting a separate paragraph to each topic applies. If each major division, episode, scene, action, or section of the story (or play) is considered a topic, then the précis may be divided into paragraphs devoted to each of the divisions.

SAMPLE ESSAY

A Précis of Alice Walker's "Everyday Use"*

[1]   Mrs. Johnson, a strong woman living on her Southern farm with her younger daughter, Maggie, is waiting for a visit by her elder daughter, Dee. Dee is returning from her home in the city, and the mother has cleaned and swept the house and yard in order to make a good impression.

[2]   As she waits, she thinks of how independent Dee has been in the past, and of how self-confident and sophisticated she may be now. She contrasts Dee with Maggie, who is awkward, homely, and burn-scarred, and who has never left home. She also contrasts Dee with herself, thinking of Dee's many opportunities for self-improvement while she herself has never had any opportunities at all.

[3]   When Dee comes, she is flamboyantly dressed, and gets out of the car with a strange, short, and bearded man. Both Dee and the man greet Mrs. Johnson with foreign phrases. Before embracing her mother, Dee gets her Polaroid camera, and takes pictures of her mother, her sister, and wandering cows, taking care to get the house in all her shots. Only then does she kiss her mother, and then only on the forehead.

[4]   Dee soon explains that she no longer wishes to be called "Dee," but that she has taken a new name, "Wangero Leewanika Kemanjo," which she regards as her own, and not the name that previous oppressors had given her. The man she is with has an incomprehensible name, which the family understands as "Hakim-a-Barber," which he has also taken in keeping with his present philosophy.

[5]   Once greetings are past, the family sits down to eat. Wangero (Dee) is impressed with the artistic qualities of the homemade furniture, and asks for the family butter churn and dasher for display in her present home. After dinner, Wangero also asks for two homemade quilts that have been in the family for years. Mrs. Johnson hesitates, having already promised the quilts to Maggie for use when she gets married. Though Maggie offers to give Wangero the quilts, Mrs. Johnson insists on her original promise. Wangero then objects, claiming that the quilts will be spoiled by "everyday use" and that her mother misunderstands the value of the family heritage. Wangero hurriedly leaves with Hakim, while Mrs. Johnson and Maggie remain together, enjoying their snuff, until bedtime.

Commentary on the Essay

This précis, about 400 words long, illustrates the selection of major actions and the omission of interesting but inessential detail. Thus, the phrase "a strong black woman" contains four words, and it condenses

* See p. 80 for this story.

more than 150 words of detailed description in paragraph 5 of the story. By contrast, paragraph 3 of the sample essay deals with a relatively short paragraph of the story (paragraph 22). This amount of detail, however, is important because it indicates, right at Dee's entrance, her confused attitudes about her mother and the farm; the farm seems more to her like something for a scrapbook or for a wall than for real living. It is this confusion on Dee's part that underlies the major conflict of the story.

To demonstrate omissions, some materials that disclose things about Hakim's character and philosophy, to be found in paragraphs 43 through 45 of the story, are left out entirely from the précis, because they are not essential to the main characters—namely, the three women.

Each of the five paragraphs in the précis is devoted to a comparable section of "Everyday Use." Paragraphs 1 and 2 describe the story up to the appearance of Dee and her man. Paragraph 3 details Dee's activity at her entrance. Paragraph 4 treats the conversation and narrative from paragraph 24 through 44 of the story. The last paragraph condenses the dinner and post-dinner scene, featuring Dee's requests to take away family heirlooms, including the vitally important quilts.

The paragraphs of the précis require not only fidelity to the narrative development of the story, but also unity of subject matter. Thus, paragraph 1 is unified by the speaker's expectations, and paragraph 2 is unified by her contrast of her two daughters and also her contrast of herself with her returning daughter. Each of the other paragraphs is similarly unified— paragraph 3 by Dee's photography, paragraph 4 by the use of new names, and paragraph 5 by the conflicting attitudes about the disposal of family heirlooms. In any précis, similar attempts should be made to unify paragraphs.

WRITING TOPICS

1. Consider Williams's "Taking Care" as a narrative. To what extent is the author's concern less to tell a story than to reveal a character? If a major quality of a round character is the capacity to change or adapt, how does the story make Jones's adaptation apparent?

2. Consider the narrator Eumolpus's intention in telling the tale of "The Widow of Ephesus." In light of what the Widow finally does with the dead body of her husband, do you believe that the story bears out this intention? Why does the author Petronius include the responses of the other major characters who have heard the story? Why doesn't the major narrator, Encolpius, comment on the story?

3. Describe the mixture of narration and dialogue in Walker's "Everyday Use." Why do you think there is a great deal of dialogue from paragraph 24 to the end? On the basis of the mixture of dialogue and narration, what conclusions can you draw about the use that fiction makes of these elements?

4. Write a story based on a historical period you believe you know well, being as factually accurate as you can. Introduce your own fictional characters as important "movers and shakers" in your episode, dealing with their public or personal affairs, or both. While you may wish to model your characters and episodes on historical persons, you are free to exercise your imagination completely.

3

Plot and Structure: The Development and Organization of Stories

WHAT IS PLOT?

Stories are made up mostly of **actions** or **incidents** which occur in **sequence**, that is, in the order in which they happen. Once we find a sequential or **narrative** order, however, there is still more to be considered. This is **plot**, or the controls governing the development of the actions.

The English novelist E. M. Forster, in *Aspects of the Novel,* presents a memorable illustration of plot. To show a bare set of actions, he uses the following: "The king died, and then the queen died." He points out, however, that this sequence does not form a plot because it lacks *motivation* and *causation*, which he introduces in his next example: "The king died, and then the queen died of grief." With the phrase "of grief," which shows that one thing (grief) controls or overcomes another (the normal desire to live), motivation and causation enter the sequence to form a plot. In a well-plotted story, things follow or precede each other not simply because time ticks away, but more importantly because *effects* follow *causes.* Nothing is irrelevant or accidental; everything is related and deliberate.

Conflict

The controlling impulse in a connected pattern of causes and effects is **conflict,** which refers to things that a character (often the **protagonist**) must face and try to overcome (often the **antagonist**). Conflict brings out the extremes of human energy, causing characters to engage in the decisions, actions, responses, and interactions that make up most stories.

In its most elemental form, a conflict is the opposition of two people. Their conflict may take the shape of envy, hatred, anger, argument, avoidance, gossip, lies, fighting, and many other forms and actions. Conflicts may also exist between groups, although conflicts between individuals are more identifiable and therefore more suitable for stories. A more abstract kind of conflict is one in which an individual opposes larger forces such as natural objects, ideas, modes of behavior, public opinion, and the like. A difficult or even impossible *choice*—a **dilemma**—is a conflict for an individual. A conflict may also be brought out in the differences between ideas or opinions. In short, conflict shows itself in many ways.

CONFLICT, DOUBT, TENSION, AND INTEREST. Conflict is the major element of plot because opposing forces arouse *curiosity*, cause *doubt*, create *tension*, and produce *interest*. The same responses are the lifeblood of athletic competition. Consider which kind of game is more interesting: (1) One team gets so far ahead that the winner is no longer in doubt. (2) Both teams are so evenly matched that the winner is in doubt even in the final seconds. Obviously, every game should be a tense contest between teams of comparable strength. The same applies to conflict in stories. There should be uncertainty about a protagonist's success, for unless there is doubt there is no tension, and without tension there is no interest.

PLOT IN OPERATION. To see a plot in operation, let us build on Forster's description. Here is a bare plot for a story of our own: "John and Jane meet, fall in love, and get married." This is a plot because it shows cause and effect (they get married *because* they fall in love), but with no conflict, the plot is not interesting. However, let us introduce conflicting elements in this common "boy meets girl" story:

> John and Jane meet at school and fall in love. They go together for two years, and plan to marry, but a problem arises. Jane wants a career first, and after marriage she wants to be an equal contributor to the family. John understands Jane's wishes, but he wants to marry first and let her finish her studies afterward. Jane believes that this solution will not work, but is a trap from which she will never escape. This conflict interrupts their plans, and they part in regret and anger. Even though they still love each other, both marry other people and build separate lives and careers. Neither is happy even though they like and respect their spouses. The years pass, and, after children and grandchildren, Jane and John meet again. He is now a widower and she has divorced. Because their earlier conflict is no longer a barrier, they marry and try to make up for the past. Even their new happiness, however, is tinged with regret and reproach because of their earlier conflict, their unhappy solution, their lost years, and their increasing age.

Here we have a true plot because our original "boy-meets-girl" story outline contains a major conflict, from which a number of related conflicts develop. The initial difference in plans and hopes causes a parting of the characters, leading to choices that do not make them totally happy. Their later marriage produces not unqualified happiness, but regret and a sense of time irretrievably lost. These conflicting attitudes, choices, and outcomes make our short short story interesting. The situation is lifelike; the conflicts rise out of realistic aims and hopes; the outcome is true to life.

THE STRUCTURE OF FICTION

Structure describes how the writer arranges and places materials in accord with the general ideas and purpose of the work. The importance of structure may be seen graphically in the art of the painter. For example, Claude Lorrain's *Seaport, with Setting Sun* presents a scene comprising a seascape, buildings, docking area, and shore, complete with foreground figures engaged in various activities. These arrangements bring out the complexity of human existence, all in the context of urban life, commerce, and the mysteriousness of the setting sun. There is not just one set of contrasts here, but a number of them.

In prose fiction, there is usually just one major conflict. As we have seen, *plot* is concerned with the conflict; *structure* defines layout—the way a story is *shaped* to make the conflict prominent. Structure is about matters

Claude Lorrain, *Seaport with the Setting Sun.* Musée du Louvre, Paris. (Photographie Giraudon/ Art Resource)

such as placement, balance, recurring themes, true and misleading conclusions, suspense, and the imitation of models or forms like reports, letters, conversations, confessions, and the like. Thus, a story might be divided up into parts, or it might move from countryside to city, or it might develop relationships between two people from their first introduction to their falling in love. To study structure is to study these arrangements and the purposes for which they are made.

FORMAL CATEGORIES OF STRUCTURE

Many aspects of structure are common to all genres of literature. Particularly for stories and plays, however, the following aspects form a skeleton, a pattern of development.

EXPOSITION. **Exposition** is the laying out, the putting forth, of the materials in the story—the main characters, their backgrounds, their characteristics, interests, goals, limitations, potentials, and basic assumptions. It may not be limited to the story's beginning, where it is most expected, but may be found anywhere. Thus, intricacies, twists, turns, false leads, blind alleys, surprises, and other quirks may be introduced to interest, perplex, intrigue, and otherwise please readers. Whenever something new arises, to the degree that it is new it is a part of exposition. Eventually, however, the introduction of new material stops, and the story moves toward its end with only the exposition that has already been included.

COMPLICATION. The **complication** is the *onset* of the major conflict—the plot. The major participants are the protagonist and antagonist, together with whatever ideas and values they represent, such as good versus evil, freedom versus suppression, independence versus dependence, love versus hate, intelligence versus stupidity, knowledge versus ignorance, and the like.

CRISIS. The **crisis** (Greek for *turning point*) is the separation between what has gone before and what will come after, usually a decision or action undertaken to resolve the conflict. The crisis is that point in which curiosity, uncertainty, and tension are greatest. Usually the crisis is followed closely by the next stage, the *climax*. Often, in fact, the two happen so closely that they are considered to be the same.

CLIMAX. Because the **climax** (Greek for *ladder*) is a consequence of the crisis, it is the story's *high point*, which may take the shape of a decision, an action, an affirmation or denial, or an illumination or realization. It is the logical conclusion of the preceding actions; no new major developments follow it. In most stories, the climax occurs at or close to the end. For example, in Crane's "The Blue Hotel," the climax is the Swede's verbal and physical encounter with the gambler. Everything that happens prior to this confrontation leads to it: the Swede's nervousness and suspicion, his behavior at the card table, his exultation after the fistfight, his leaving the Blue Hotel, and his heavy drinking. The primitive "honor" his bullying ignites in the gambler brings his story to its sudden and disastrous end.

RESOLUTION, OR DÉNOUEMENT. The **resolution** (a releasing or untying) or **dénouement** (untying) is the finishing of things after the climax. The resolution of "The Blue Hotel" is composed of the gambler's retreat, the focus on the dead Swede, the news of the gambler's sentence, and the concluding conversation between the cowboy and the Easterner. Once the climax has occurred, there is a relaxation of tension and uncertainty, and most authors untie things as quickly as possible to avoid losing their readers' interest. Thus, Welty ends "A Worn Path" with the major character beginning her long walk home; Poe ends "The Masque of the Red Death" by asserting the "illimitable dominion" of the Red Death itself; and Twain ends "Luck" with the simple statement that the major character is a fool. Once the conflicts are finished, in other words, a brief action underscores the note of finality.

FORMAL AND ACTUAL STRUCTURE

The structure just described is a *formal* one, an ideal pattern that follows a sequential line directly from beginning to end. Most stories, however, present a *real* structure that departs from the formal pattern to greater or lesser degrees. A mystery story, for example, may hold back crucial details of exposition (because the goal is to mystify); a suspense story may keep the protagonist ignorant but provide readers with abundant details in order to maximize concern and tension about the outcome.

More realistic, less "artificial" stories might also contain structural variations. For example, Welty's "A Worn Path" produces a *double take* because the most vital detail of exposition is withheld until the story's end. During much of the story, Phoenix's conflicts seem to be against age, poverty, and environment. At the end, however, we learn that she is caring for her invalid grandson. This new detail creates an entirely new conflict—that Phoenix is fighting against hopeless illness—and our response enlarges to include heartfelt anguish. This is only one example of how an author may vary the formal structure to maximize a story's impact.

There are many other possible variants in structure. One of these is the **flashback,** in which present circumstances are explained by the selective introduction of past events. The moment at which the flashback is introduced may be a part of the resolution of the plot, and the flashback might lead you into a moment of climax, but then go from there to develop the details that are more properly part of the exposition. Let us again consider our brief plot about John and Jane, and use flashbacks to structure the story.

> Jane is now old, and a noise outside causes her to remember the argument that forced her to part with John many years before. Then she pictures in her mind the years she and John have spent happily together after they married. She then contrasts her present happiness with her memory of her earlier, less happy marriage, and from there she recalls her youthful years of courtship with John before their conflict over career plans developed. Then she looks over at John, reading in a chair, and smiles, John smiles back, and the story ends.

The structure we visualize here is that the action begins and remains in the present tense, while important parts of the past flood the protagonist's memory in flashback, though not in the order in which they happened. Flashbacks might be used structurally in other ways. Alice Munro's "Meneseteung" consists of a series of flashbacks that the narrator imagines in order to describe a probable life for the protagonist. Tillie Olsen's "I Stand Here Ironing" takes place as the narrator stands at her ironing board, but the story develops through flashbacks, memories of her daughter's growth. In short, a technique like flashback creates a unique story that departs significantly from a formal structural pattern.

You will find that the structure of each story is unique. Simple geography, for example, may govern a story's development, as in Whitecloud's "Blue Winds Dancing" (a ride from California to Wisconsin), Munro's "The Found Boat" (from a spring flood to an exploration on and beside a river), and Welty's "A Worn Path" (a walk from town to country). Parts or scenes might be carried on through conversations, as in "The Blue Hotel" and "Everyday Use," or through a ceremony witnessed by a major character, as in "Young Goodman Brown." A story may unfold in an apparently accidental way, with the characters drawing significant conclusions as they make vital discoveries about the major characters, as in Glaspell's "A Jury of Her Peers." Or there might be a dream sequence, as in Pickthall's "The Worker in Sandalwood." The possible variations are extensive.

STEPHEN CRANE   (1871–1900)

The Blue Hotel   *1898*

I

The Palace Hotel at Fort Romper was painted a light blue, a shade that is on the legs of a kind of heron, causing the bird to declare its position against any background. The Palace Hotel, then, was always screaming and howling in a way that made the dazzling winter landscape of Nebraska seem only a grey swampish hush. It stood alone on the prairie, and when the snow was falling the town two hundred yards away was not visible. But when the traveller alighted at the railway station he was obliged to pass the Palace Hotel before he could come upon the company of low clapboard houses which composed Fort Romper, and it was not to be thought that any traveller could pass the Palace Hotel without looking at it. Pat Scully, the proprietor, had proved himself a master of strategy when he chose his paints. It is true that on clear days, when the great transcontinental expresses, long lines of swaying Pullmans, swept through Fort Romper, passengers were overcome at the sight, and the cult that knows the brown-reds and the subdivisions of the dark greens of the East expressed shame, pity, horror, in a laugh. But to the citizens of this prairie town and to the people who would naturally stop there, Pat Scully had performed a feat. With this opulence and splendour, these creeds, classes, egotisms, that streamed through Romper on the rails day after day, they had no colour in common.

As if the displayed delights of such a blue hotel were not sufficiently enticing, it was Scully's habit to go every morning and evening to meet the leisurely trains that stopped at Romper and work his seductions upon any man that he might see wavering, gripsack in hand.

One morning, when a snow-crusted engine dragged its long string of freight cars and its one passenger coach to the station, Scully performed the marvel of catching three men. One was a shaky and quick-eyed Swede, with a great shining cheap valise; one was a tall bronzed cowboy, who was on his way to a ranch near the Dakota line; one was a little silent man from the East, who didn't look it, and didn't announce it. Scully practically made them prisoners. He was so nimble and merry and kindly that each probably felt it would be the height of brutality to try to escape. They trudged off over the creaking board sidewalks in the wake of the eager little Irishman. He wore a heavy fur cap squeezed tightly down on his head. It caused his two red ears to stick out stiffly, as if they were made of tin.

At last, Scully, elaborately, with boisterous hospitality, conducted them through the portals of the blue hotel. The room which they entered was small. It seemed to be merely a proper temple for an enormous stove, which, in the centre, was humming with godlike violence. At various points on its surface the iron had become luminous and glowed yellow from the heat. Beside the stove Scully's son Johnnie was playing High-Five° with an old farmer who had whiskers both grey and sandy. They were quarreling. Frequently the old farmer turned his face toward a box of sawdust—coloured brown from tobacco juice—that was behind the stove, and spat with an air of great impatience and irritation. With a loud flourish of words Scully destroyed the game of cards, and bustled his son upstairs with part of the baggage of the new guests. He himself conducted them to three basins of the coldest water in the world. The cowboy and the Easterner burnished themselves fiery red with this water, until it seemed to be some kind of metal-polish. The Swede, however, merely dipped his fingers gingerly and with trepidation. It was notable that throughout this series of small ceremonies the three travellers were made to feel that Scully was very benevolent. He was conferring

High-Five: the most commonly played card game in the United States before it was replaced in popularity by poker.

great favours upon them. He handed the towel from one to another with an air of philanthropic impulse.

Afterward they went to the first room, and, sitting about the stove, listened to Scully's officious clamour at his daughters, who were preparing the midday meal. They reflected in the silence of experienced men who tread carefully amid new people. Nevertheless, the old farmer, stationary, invincible in his chair near the warmest part of the stove, turned his face from the sawdust-box frequently and addressed a glowing commonplace to the strangers. Usually he was answered in short but adequate sentences by either the cowboy or the Easterner. The Swede said nothing. He seemed to be occupied in making furtive estimates of each man in the room. One might have thought that he had the sense of silly suspicion which comes to guilt. He resembled a badly frightened man.

Later, at dinner, he spoke a little, addressing his conversation entirely to Scully. He volunteered that he had come from New York, where for ten years he had worked as a tailor. These facts seemed to strike Scully as fascinating, and afterward he volunteered that he had lived at Romper for fourteen years. The Swede asked about the crops and the price of labour. He seemed barely to listen to Scully's extended replies. His eyes continued to rove from man to man.

Finally, with a laugh and a wink, he said that some of these Western communities were very dangerous; and after his statement he straightened his legs under the table, tilted his head, and laughed again, loudly. It was plain that the demonstration had no meaning to the others. They looked at him wondering and in silence.

II

As the men trooped heavily back into the front room, the two little windows presented views of a turmoiling sea of snow. The huge arms of the wind were making attempts—mighty, circular, futile—to embrace the flakes as they sped. A gate-post like a still man with a blanched face stood aghast amid this profligate fury. In a hearty voice Scully announced the presence of a blizzard. The guests of the blue hotel, lighting their pipes, assented with grunts of lazy masculine contentment. No island of the sea could be exempt in the degree of this little room with its humming stove. Johnnie, son of Scully, in a tone which defined his opinion of his ability as a card-player, challenged the old farmer of both grey and sandy whiskers to a game of High-Five. The farmer agreed with a contemptuous and bitter scoff. They sat close to the stove, and squared their knees under a wide board. The cowboy and the Easterner watched the game with interest. The Swede remained near the window, aloof, but with a countenance that showed signs of an inexplicable excitement.

The play of Johnnie and the grey-beard was suddenly ended by another quarrel. The old man arose while casting a look of heated scorn at his adversary. He slowly buttoned his coat, and then stalked with fabulous dignity from the room. In the discreet silence of all other men the Swede laughed. His laughter rang somehow childish. Men by this time had begun to look at him askance, as if they wished to inquire what ailed him.

A new game was formed jocosely. The cowboy volunteered to become the partner of Johnnie, and they all then turned to ask the Swede to throw in his lot with the little Easterner. He asked some questions about the game, and, learning that it wore many names, and that he had played it when it was under an alias, he accepted the invitation. He strode toward the men nervously, as if he expected to be assaulted. Finally, seated, he gazed from face to face and laughed shrilly. This laugh was so strange that the Easterner looked up quickly, the cowboy sat intent and with his mouth open, and Johnnie paused, holding the cards with still fingers.

Afterward there was a short silence. Then Johnnie said, "Well, let's get at it. Come on now!" They pulled their chairs forward until their knees were bunched under the board. They began to play, and their interest in the game caused the others to forget the manner of the Swede.

The cowboy was a board-whacker. Each time that he held superior cards he whanged them, one by one, with exceeding force, down upon the improvised table, and took the tricks with a glowing air of prowess and pride that sent thrills of indignation into the hearts of his opponents. A game with a board-whacker in it is sure to become intense. The countenances of the Easterner and the Swede were miserable whenever the cowboy thundered down his aces and kings, while Johnnie, his eyes gleaming with joy, chuckled and chuckled.

Because of the absorbing play none considered the strange ways of the Swede. They paid strict heed to the game. Finally, during a lull caused by a new deal, the Swede suddenly addressed Johnnie: "I suppose there have been a good many men killed in this room." The jaws of the others dropped and they looked at him.

"What in hell are you talking about?" said Johnnie.

The Swede laughed again his blatant laugh, full of a kind of false courage and defiance. "Oh, you know what I mean all right," he answered. 15

"I'm a liar if I do!" Johnnie protested. The card was halted, and the men stared at the Swede. Johnnie evidently felt that as the son of the proprietor he should make a direct inquiry. "Now, what might you be drivin' at, mister?" he asked. The Swede winked at him. It was a wink full of cunning. His fingers shook on the edge of the board. "Oh, maybe you think I have been to nowheres. Maybe you think I'm a tenderfoot?"

"I don't know nothin' about you," answered Johnnie, "and I don't give a damn where you've been. All I got to say is that I don't know what you're driving at. There hain't never been nobody killed in this room."

The cowboy, who had been steadily gazing at the Swede, then spoke. "What's wrong with you, mister?"

Apparently it seemed to the Swede that he was formidably menaced. He shivered and turned white near the corners of his mouth. He sent an appealing glance in the direction of the little Easterner. During these moments he did not forget to wear his air of advanced pot-valour. "They say they don't know what I mean," he remarked mockingly to the Easterner.

The latter answered after prolonged and cautious reflection. "I don't 20 understand you," he said, impassively.

The Swede made a movement then which announced that he thought he had encountered treachery from the only quarter where he had expected sympathy, if not help. "Oh, I see you are all against me. I see———"

The cowboy was in a state of deep stupefaction. "Say," he cried, as he tumbled the deck violently down upon the board, "say, what are you gittin' at, hey?"

The Swede sprang up with the celerity of a man escaping from a snake on the floor. "I don't want to fight!" he shouted, "I don't want to fight!"

The cowboy stretched his long legs indolently and deliberately. His hands were in his pockets. He spat into the sawdust-box. "Well, who the hell thought you did?" he inquired.

The Swede backed rapidly toward a corner of the room. His hands were out protectingly in front of his chest, but he was making an obvious struggle to control his fright. "Gentlemen," he quavered. "I suppose I am going to be killed before I can leave this house! I suppose I am going to be killed before I can leave this house!" In his eyes was the dying-swan° look. Through the windows could be seen the snow turning blue in the shadow of dusk. The wind tore at the house, and some loose thing beat regularly against the clapboards like a spirit tapping. 25

A door opened, and Scully himself entered. He paused in surprise as he noted the tragic attitude of the Swede. Then he said. "What's the matter here?"

The Swede answered him swiftly and eagerly: "These men are going to kill me."

"Kill you!" ejaculated Scully. "Kill you! What are you talkin'?"

The Swede made the gesture of a martyr.

Scully wheeled sternly upon his son. "What is this, Johnnie?" 30

The lad had grown sullen. "Damned if I know," he answered. "I can't make no sense of it." He began to shuffle the cards, fluttering them together with an angry snap. "He says a good many men have been killed in this room, or something like that. And he says he's goin' to be killed here too. I don't know what ails him. He's crazy, I shouldn't wonder."

Scully then looked for explanation to the cowboy, but the cowboy simply shrugged his shoulders.

"Kill you?" said Scully again to the Swede. "Kill you? Man, you're off your nut."

"Oh, I know," burst out the Swede. "I know what will happen. Yes, I'm crazy—yes. Yes, of course, I'm crazy—yes. But I know one thing—" There was a sort of sweat of misery and terror upon his face. "I know I won't get out of here alive."

The cowboy drew a deep breath, as if his mind was passing into the last stages of dissolution. "Well, I'm doggoned," he whispered to himself. 35

Scully wheeled suddenly and faced his son. "You've been troublin' this man!"

Johnnie's voice was loud with its burden of grievance. "Why, good Gawd, I ain't done nothin' to 'im."

The Swede broke in. "Gentlemen, do not disturb yourselves. I will leave this house. I will go away, because"—he accused them dramatically with his glance—"because I do not want to be killed."

Scully was furious with his son. "Will you tell me what is the matter, you young divil? What's the matter, anyhow? Speak out!"

"Blame it!" cried Johnnie in despair, "don't I tell you I don't know? He— he says we want to kill him, and that's all I know. I can't tell what ails him." 40

---

dying swan: Proverbially, a swan sings its most beautiful notes when it is about to die.

The Swede continued to repeat: "Never mind, Mr. Scully; never mind. I will leave this house. I will go away, because I do not wish to be killed. Yes, of course, I am crazy—yes. But I know one thing! I will go away. I will leave this house. Never mind, Mr. Scully; never mind, I will go away."

"You will not go 'way," said Scully. "You will not go 'way until I hear the reason of this business. If anybody has troubled you I will take care of him. This is my house. You are under my roof, and I will not allow any peaceable man to be troubled here." He cast a terrible eye upon Johnnie, the cowboy, and the Easterner.

"Never mind, Mr. Scully; never mind. I will go away. I do not wish to be killed." The Swede moved toward the door which opened upon the stairs. It was evidently his intention to go at once for his baggage.

"No, no," shouted Scully peremptorily; but the white-faced man slid by him and disappeared. "Now," said Scully severely, "what does this mane?"°

Johnnie and the cowboy cried together: "Why, we didn't do nothin' to 'im!"   45

Scully's eyes were cold. "No," he said, "you didn't?"

Johnnie swore a deep oath. "Why, this is the wildest loon I ever see. We didn't do nothin' at all. We were just sittin' here playin cards, and he————"

The father suddenly spoke to the Easterner. "Mr. Blanc," he asked, "what has these boys been doin'?"

The Easterner reflected again. "I didn't see anything wrong at all," he said at last, slowly.

Scully began to howl, "But what does it mane?" He stared ferociously at his   50
son. "I have a mind to lather you for this, me boy."

Johnnie was frantic. "Well, what have I done?" he bawled at his father.

III

"I think you are tongue-tied," said Scully finally to his son, the cowboy, and the Easterner; and at the end of this scornful sentence he left the room.

Upstairs the Swede was swiftly fastening the straps of his great valise. Once his back happened to be half turned toward the door, and, hearing a noise there, he wheeled and sprang up, uttering a loud cry. Scully's wrinkled visage showed grimly in the light of the small lamp he carried. This yellow effulgence, streaming upward, coloured only his prominent features, and left his eyes, for instance, in mysterious shadow. He resembled a murderer.

"Man! man!" he exclaimed, "have you gone daffy?"

"Oh, no! Oh, no!" rejoined the other. "There are people in this world who   55
know pretty nearly as much as you do—understand?"

For a moment they stood gazing at each other. Upon the Swede's deathly pale cheeks were two spots brightly crimson and sharply edged, as if they had been carefully painted. Scully placed the light on the table and sat himself on the edge of the bed. He spoke ruminatively. "By cracky, I never heard of such a thing in my life. It's a complete muddle. I can't, for the soul of me, think how you ever got this idea into your head." Presently he lifted his eyes and asked: "And did you sure think they were going to kill you?"

The Swede scanned the old man as if he wished to see into his mind. "I did," he said at last. He obviously suspected that this answer might precipitate an

mane: mean. Scully speaks with a slight Irish brogue (see paragraph 114).

outbreak. As he pulled on a strap his whole arm shook, the elbow wavering like a bit of paper.

Scully banged his hand impressively on the footboard of the bed. "Why, man, we're goin' to have a line of ilictric street-cars in this town next spring."

"'A line of electric street-cars,'" repeated the Swede, stupidly.

"And," said Scully, "there's a new railroad goin' to be built down from Broken Arm to here. Not to mention the four churches and the smashin' big brick schoolhouse. Then there's the big factory, too. Why, in two years Romper'll be a met-tro-*pol*-is." 60

Having finished the preparation of his baggage, the Swede straightened himself. "Mr. Scully," he said, with sudden hardihood, "how much do I owe you?"

"You don't owe me anythin'," said the old man, angrily.

"Yes, I do," retorted the Swede. He took seventy-five cents from his pocket and tendered it to Scully; but the latter snapped his fingers in disdainful refusal. However, it happened that they both stood gazing in a strange fashion at three silver pieces on the Swede's open palm.

"I'll not take your money," said Scully at last. "Not after what's been goin' on here." Then a plan seemed to strike him. "Here," he cried, picking up his lamp and moving toward the door. "Here! Come with me a minute."

"No," said the Swede, in overwhelming alarm. 65

"Yes," urged the old man. "Come on! I want you to come and see a picter— just across the hall—in my room."

The Swede must have concluded that his hour was come. His jaw dropped and his teeth showed like a dead man's. He ultimately followed Scully across the corridor, but he had the step of one hung in chains.

Scully flashed the light high on the wall of his own chamber. There was revealed a ridiculous photograph of a little girl. She was leaning against a balustrade of gorgeous decoration, and the formidable bang to her hair was prominent. The figure was as graceful as an upright sled-stake, and, withal, it was of the hue of lead. "There," said Scully, tenderly, "that's the picter of my little girl that died. Her name was Carrie. She had the purtiest hair you even saw! I was that fond of her, she———"

Turning then, he saw that the Swede was not contemplating the picture at all, but, instead, was keeping keen watch on the gloom in the rear.

"Look, man!" cried Scully, heartily. "That's the picter of my little gal that 70 died. Her name was Carrie. And then here's the picter of my oldest boy, Michael. He's a lawyer in Lincoln, an' doin' well. I gave that boy a grand eddication, and I'm glad for it now. He's a fine boy. Look at 'im now. Ain't he bold as blazes, him there in Lincoln, an honoured an' respicted gintleman! An honoured and respicted gintleman," concluded Scully with a flourish. And, so saying, he smote the Swede jovially on the back.

The Swede faintly smiled.

"Now," said the old man, "there's only one more thing." He dropped suddenly to the floor and thrust his head beneath the bed. The Swede could hear his muffled voice. "I'd keep it under me piller if it wasn't for that boy Johnnie. Then there's the old woman———Where is it now? I never put it twice in the same place. Ah, now come out with you!"

Presently he backed clumsily from under the bed, dragging with him an old coat rolled into a bundle. "I've fetched him," he muttered. Kneeling on the floor, he unrolled the coat and extracted from its heart a large yellow-brown whiskey-bottle.

His first maneuver was to hold the bottle up to the light. Reassured, apparently, that nobody had been tampering with it, he thrust it with a generous movement toward the Swede.

The weak-kneed Swede was about to eagerly clutch this element of strength,   75
but he suddenly jerked his hand away and cast a look of horror upon Scully.

"Drink," said the old man affectionately. He had risen to his feet, and now stood facing the Swede.

There was a silence. Then again Scully said: "Drink!"

The Swede laughed wildly. He grabbed the bottle, put it to his mouth; and as his lips curled absurdly around the opening and his throat worked, he kept his glance, burning with hatred, upon the old man's face.

IV

After the departure of Scully the three men, with the card-board still upon their knees, preserved for a long time an astounded silence. Then Johnnie said: "That's the dod-dangedest Swede I ever see."

"He ain't no Swede," said the cowboy, scornfully.   80

"Well, what is he then?" cried Johnnie. "What is he then?"

"It's my opinion," replied the cowboy deliberately, "he's some kind of a Dutchman." It was a venerable custom of the country to entitle as Swedes all light-haired men who spoke with a heavy tongue. In consequence the idea of the cowboy was not without its daring. "Yes, sir," he repeated. "It's my opinion this feller is some kind of Dutchman."

"Well, he says he's a Swede, anyhow," muttered Johnnie, sulkily. He turned to the Easterner: "What do you think, Mr. Blanc?"

"Oh, I don't know," replied the Easterner.

"Well, what do you think makes him act that way?" asked the cowboy.   85

"Why, he's frightened." The Easterner knocked his pipe against the rim of the stove. "He's clear frightened out of his boots."

"What at?" cried Johnnie, and the cowboy together.

The Easterner reflected over his answer.

"What at?" cried the others again.

"Oh, I don't know, but it seems to me this man has been reading dime   90
novels, and he thinks he's right out in the middle of it—the shootin' and stabbin' and all."

"But," said the cowboy, deeply scandalized, "this ain't Wyoming, ner none of them places. This is Nebrasker."

"Yes," added Johnnie, "an' why don't he wait till he gits *out West?*"

The travelled Easterner laughed. "It isn't different there even—not in these days. But he thinks he's right in the middle of hell."

Johnnie and the cowboy mused long.

"It's awful funny," remarked Johnnie at last.   95

"Yes," said the cowboy. "This is a queer game. I hope we don't git snowed in, because then we'd have to stand this here man bein' around with us all the time. That wouldn't be no good."

"I wish pop would throw him out," said Johnnie.

Presently they heard a loud stamping on the stairs, accompanied by ringing jokes in the voice of old Scully, and laughter, evidently from the Swede. The men around the stove stared vacantly at each other. "Gosh!" said the cowboy. The door flew open, and old Scully, flushed and anecdotal, came into the room. He was jabbering at the Swede, who followed him, laughing bravely. It was the entry of two roisterers from a banquet hall.

"Come now," said Scully sharply to the three seated men, "move up and give us a chance at the stove." The cowboy and the Easterner obediently sidled their chairs to make room for the new-comers. Johnnie, however, simply arranged himself in a more indolent attitude, and then remained motionless.

"Come! Git over, there," said Scully.   100

"Plenty of room on the other side of the stove," said Johnnie.

"Do you think we want to sit in the draught?" roared the father.

But the Swede here interposed with a grandeur of confidence. "No, no. Let the boy sit where he likes," he cried in a bullying voice to the father.

"All right! All right!" said Scully, deferentially. The cowboy and the Easterner exchanged glances of wonder.

The five chairs were formed in a crescent about one side of the stove. The   105
Swede began to talk; he talked arrogantly, profanely, angrily. Johnnie, the cowboy, and the Easterner maintained a morose silence, while old Scully appeared to be receptive and eager, breaking in constantly with sympathetic ejaculations.

Finally the Swede announced that he was thirsty. He moved in his chair, and said that he would go for a drink of water.

"I'll git it for you," cried Scully at once.

"No," said the Swede contemptuously. "I'll get it for myself." He arose and stalked with the air of an owner off into the executive parts of the hotel.

As soon as the Swede was out of hearing Scully sprang to his feet and whispered intensely to the others: "Upstairs he thought I was tryin' to poison 'im."

"Say," said Johnnie, "this makes me sick. Why don't you throw 'im out in   110
the snow?"

"Why, he's all right now," declared Scully. "It was only that he was from the East, and he thought this was a tough place. That's all. He's all right now."

The cowboy looked with admiration upon the Easterner. "You were straight," he said. "You were on to that there Dutchman."

"Well," said Johnnie to his father, "he may be all right now, but I don't see it. Other time he was scared, but now he's too fresh."

Scully's speech was always a combination of Irish brogue and idiom, Western twang and idiom, and scraps of curiously formal diction taken from the storybooks and newspapers. He now hurled a strange mass of language at the head of his son. "What do I keep? What do I keep? What do I keep?" he demanded, in a voice of thunder. He slapped his knee impressively, to indicate that he himself was going to make reply, and that all should heed. "I keep a hotel," he shouted. "A hotel, do you mind? A guest under my roof has sacred privileges. He is to be intimidated by none. Not one word shall he hear that would prijudice him in favor of goin' away. I'll not have it. There's no place in this here town where they can say they iver took in a guest of mine because he was afraid to stay here." He wheeled suddenly upon the cowboy and the Easterner. "Am I right?"

"Yes, Mr. Scully," said the cowboy, "I think you're right."   115

"Yes, Mr. Scully," said the Easterner, "I think you're right."

V

At six-o'clock supper, the Swede fizzed like a fire-wheel. He sometimes seemed on the point of bursting into riotous song, and in all his madness he was encouraged by old Scully. The Easterner was encased in reserve; the cowboy sat in wide-mouthed amazement, forgetting to eat, while Johnnie wrathily demolished great plates of food. The daughters of the house, when they were obliged to replenish the biscuits, approached as warily as Indians, and, having succeeded in their purpose, fled with ill-concealed trepidation. The Swede domineered the whole feast, and he gave it the appearance of a cruel bacchanal. He seemed to have grown suddenly taller; he gazed, brutally disdainful, into every face. His voice rang through the room. Once when he jabbed out harpoon-fashion with his fork to pinion a biscuit, the weapon nearly impaled the hand of the Easterner, which had been stretched quietly out for the same biscuit.

After supper, as the men filed toward the other room, the Swede smote Scully ruthlessly on the shoulder. "Well, old boy, that was a good, square meal." Johnnie looked hopefully at his father; he knew that shoulder was tender from an old fall; and, indeed, it appeared for a moment as if Scully was going to flame out over the matter, but in the end he smiled a sickly smile and remained silent. The others understood from his manner that he was admitting his responsibility for the Swede's new view-point.

Johnnie, however, addressed his parent in an aside. "Why don't you license somebody to kick you downstairs?" Scully scowled darkly by way of reply.

When they were gathered about the stove, the Swede insisted on another   120
game of High-Five. Scully gently deprecated the plan at first, but the Swede turned a wolfish glare upon him. The old man subsided, and the Swede canvassed the others. In his tone there was always a great threat. The cowboy and the Easterner both remarked indifferently that they would play. Scully said that he would presently have to go to meet the 6.58 train, and so the Swede turned menacingly upon Johnnie. For a moment their glances crossed like blades, and then Johnnie smiled and said, "Yes, I'll play."

They formed a square, with the little board on their knees. The Easterner and the Swede were again partners. As the play went on, it was noticeable that the cowboy was not board-whacking as usual. Meanwhile, Scully, near the lamp, had put on his spectacles and, with an appearance curiously like an old priest, was reading a newspaper. In time he went out to meet the 6.58 train, and, despite his precautions, a gust of polar wind whirled into the room as he opened the door. Besides scattering the cards, it chilled the players to the marrow. The Swede cursed frightfully. When Scully returned, his entrance disturbed a cosy and friendly scene. The Swede again cursed. But presently they were once more intent, their heads bent forward and their hands moving swiftly. The Swede had adopted the fashion of board-whacking.

Scully took up his paper and for a long time remained immersed in matters which were extraordinarily remote from him. The lamp burned badly, and once he stopped to adjust the wick. The newspaper, as he turned from page to page, rustled with a slow and comfortable sound. Then suddenly he heard three terrible words: "You are cheatin'!"

Such scenes often prove that there can be little of dramatic import in environment. Any room can present a tragic front: any room can be comic. This little den was now hideous as a torture-chamber. The new faces of the men themselves had changed it upon the instant. The Swede held a huge fist in front of Johnnie's face, while the latter looked steadily over it into the blazing orbs of his accuser. The Easterner had grown pallid: the cowboy's jaw had dropped in that expression of bovine amazement which was one of his important mannerisms. After the three words, the first sound in the room was made by Scully's paper as it floated forgotten to his feet. His spectacles had also fallen from his nose, but by a clutch he had saved them in air. His hand, grasping the spectacles, now remained poised awkwardly and near his shoulder. He stared at the card-players.

Probably the silence was while a second elapsed. Then, if the floor had been suddenly twitched out from under the men they could not have moved quicker. The five had projected themselves headlong toward a common point. It happened that Johnnie, in rising to hurl himself upon the Swede, had stumbled slightly because of his curiously instinctive care for the cards and the board. The loss of the moment allowed time for the arrival of Scully, and also allowed the cowboy time to give the Swede a great push which sent him staggering back. The men found tongue together, and hoarse shouts of rage, appeal, or fear burst from every throat. The cowboy pushed and jostled feverishly at the Swede, and the Easterner and Scully clung wildly to Johnnie; but through the smoky air, above the swaying bodies of the peace-compellers, the eyes of the two warriors ever sought each other in glances of challenge that were at once hot and steely.

Of course the board had been overturned, and now the whole company of   125
cards was scattered over the floor, where the boots of the men trampled the fat and painted kings and queens as they gazed with their silly eyes at the war that was waging above them.

Scully's voice was dominating the yells. "Stop now! Stop, I say! Stop, now——"

Johnnie, as he struggled to burst through the rank formed by Scully and the Easterner, was crying. "Well, he says I cheated! He says I cheated! I won't allow no man to say I cheated! If he says I cheated, he's a —— ——!"

The cowboy was telling the Swede, "Quit, now! Quit, d'ye hear——"

The screams of the Swede never ceased: "He did cheat! I saw him! I saw him——"

As for the Easterner, he was importuning in a voice that was not heeded: 130
"Wait a moment, can't you? Oh, wait a moment. What's the good of a fight over a game of cards? Wait a moment——"

In this tumult no complete sentences were clear. "Cheat"—"Quit"—"He says"—these fragments pierced the uproar and rang out sharply. It was remarkable that, whereas Scully undoubtedly made the most noise, he was the least heard of any of the riotous band.

Then suddenly there was a great cessation. It was as if each man had paused for breath; and although the room was still lighted with the anger of men, it could be seen that there was no danger of immediate conflict, and at once Johnnie, shouldering his way forward, almost succeeded in confronting the Swede. "What did you say I cheated for? What did you say I cheated for? I don't cheat, and I won't let no man say I do!"

The Swede said, "I saw you! I saw you!"

"Well," cried Johnnie, "I'll fight any man what says I cheat!"

"No, you won't," said the cowboy. "Not here."   135

"Ah, be still, can't you?" said Scully, coming between them.

The quiet was sufficient to allow the Easterner's voice to be heard. He was repeating, "Oh, wait a moment, can't you? What's the good of a fight over a game of cards? Wait a moment!"

Johnnie, his red face appearing above his father's shoulder, hailed the Swede again. "Did you say I cheated?"

The Swede showed his teeth. "Yes."

"Then," said Johnnie, "we must fight."   140

"Yes, fight," roared the Swede. He was like a demoniac. "Yes, fight! I'll show you what kind of a man I am! I'll show you who you want to fight! Maybe you think I can't fight! Maybe you think I can't! I'll show you, you skin, you card-sharp! Yes, you cheated! You cheated! You cheated!"

"Well, let's go at it, then, mister," said Johnnie coolly.

The cowboy's brow was beaded with sweat from his efforts in intercepting all sorts of raids. He turned in despair to Scully. "What are you goin' to do now?"

A change had come over the Celtic visage of the old man. He now seemed all eagerness; his eyes glowed.

"We'll let them fight," he answered stalwartly. "I can't put up with it any   145
longer. I've stood this damned Swede till I'm sick. We'll let them fight."

VI

The men prepared to go out of doors. The Easterner was so nervous that he had great difficulty in getting his arms into the sleeves of his new leather coat. As the cowboy drew his fur cap down over his ears his hands trembled. In fact, Johnnie and old Scully were the only ones who displayed no agitation. These preliminaries were conducted without words.

Scully threw open the door. "Well, come on," he said. Instantly a terrific wind caused the flame of the lamp to struggle at its wick, while a puff of black smoke sprang from the chimney-top. The stove was in mid-current of the blast, and its voice swelled to equal the roar of the storm. Some of the scarred and bedabbled cards were caught up from the floor and dashed helplessly against the farther wall. The men lowered their heads and plunged into the tempest as into a sea.

No snow was falling, but great whirls and clouds of flakes, swept up from the ground by the frantic winds, were streaming southward with the speed of bullets. The covered land was blue with the sheen of an unearthly satin, and there was no other hue save where, at the low, black railway station—which seemed incredibly distant—one light gleamed like a tiny jewel. As the men floundered into a thigh-deep drift, it was known that the Swede was bawling out something. Scully went to him, put a hand on his shoulder, and projected an ear. "What's that you say?" he shouted.

"I say," bawled the Swede again. "I won't stand much show against this gang, I know you'll all pitch on me."

Scully smote him reproachfully on the arm. "Tut, man!" he yelled. The wind   150
tore the words from Scully's lips and scattered them far alee.

"You are all a gang of———" boomed the Swede, but the storm also seized the remainder of this sentence.

Immediately turning their backs upon the wind, the men had swung around a corner to the sheltered side of the hotel. It was the function of the little house to preserve here, amid this great devastation of snow, an irregular V-shape of heavily encrusted grass, which crackled beneath the feet. One could imagine the great drifts piled against the windward side. When the party reached the comparative peace of this spot it was found that the Swede was still bellowing.

"Oh, I know what kind of a thing this is! I know you'll all pitch on me. I can't lick you all!"

Scully turned upon him panther-fashion. "You'll not have to whip all of us. You'll have to whip my son Johnnie. An' the man what troubles you durin' that time will have me to dale with."

The arrangements were swiftly made. The two men faced each other, obedient to the harsh commands of Scully, whose face, in the subtly luminous gloom, could be seen set in the austere impersonal lines that are pictured on the countenances of the Roman veterans. The Easterner's teeth were chattering, and he was hopping up and down like a mechanical toy. The cowboy stood rock-like.   155

The contestants had not stripped off any clothing. Each was in his ordinary attire. Their fists were up, and they eyed each other in a calm that had the elements of leonine cruelty in it.

During this pause, the Easterner's mind, like a film, took lasting impressions of three men—the iron-nerved master of the ceremony; the Swede, pale, motionless, terrible; and Johnnie, serene yet ferocious, brutish yet heroic. The entire prelude had in it a tragedy greater than the tragedy of action, and this aspect was accentuated by the long, mellow cry of the blizzard, as it sped the tumbling and wailing flakes into the black abyss of the south.

"Now!" said Scully.

The two combatants leaped forward and crashed together like bullocks. There was heard the cushioned sound of blows, and of a curse squeezing out from between the tight teeth of one.

As for the spectators, the Easterner's pent-up breath exploded from him with a pop of relief, absolute relief from the tension of the preliminaries. The cowboy bounded into the air with a yowl. Scully was immovable as from supreme amazement and fear at the fury of the fight which he himself had permitted and arranged.   160

For a time the encounter in the darkness was such a perplexity of flying arms that it presented no more detail than would a swiftly revolving wheel. Occasionally a face, as if illumined by a flash of light, would shine out, ghastly and marked with pink spots. A moment later, the men might have been known as shadows, if it were not for the involuntary utterance of oaths that came from them in whispers.

Suddenly a holocaust of warlike desire caught the cowboy, and he bolted forward with the speed of a broncho. "Go it, Johnnie! go it! Kill him! Kill him!"

Scully confronted him. "Kape back," he said; and by his glance the cowboy could tell that this man was Johnnie's father.

To the Easterner there was a monotony of unchangeable fighting that was an abomination. This confused mingling was eternal to his sense, which was concentrated in a longing for the end, the priceless end. Once the fighters lurched near him, and as he scrambled hastily backward he heard them breathe like men on the rack.

"Kill him, Johnnie! Kill him! Kill him! Kill him!" The cowboy's face was contorted like one of those agony masks in museums.   165

"Keep still," said Scully, icily.

Then there was a sudden loud grunt, incomplete, cut short, and Johnnie's body swung away from the Swede and fell with sickening heaviness to the grass. The cowboy was barely in time to prevent the mad Swede from flinging himself upon his prone adversary. "No, you don't," said the cowboy, interposing an arm. "Wait a second."

Scully was at his son's side. "Johnnie! Johnnie, me boy!" His voice had a quality of melancholy tenderness. "Johnnie! Can you go on with it?" He looked anxiously down into the bloody, pulpy face of his son.

There was a moment of silence, and then Johnnie answered in his ordinary voice, "Yes, I—it—yes."

Assisted by his father he struggled to his feet. "Wait a bit now till you git   170
your wind," said the old man.

A few paces away the cowboy was lecturing the Swede. "No, you don't! Wait a second!"

The Easterner was plucking at Scully's sleeve. "Oh, this is enough," he pleaded. "This is enough! Let it go as it stands. This is enough!"

"Bill," said Scully, "git out of the road." The cowboy stepped aside. "Now." The combatants were actuated by a new caution as they advanced toward collision. They glared at each other, and then the Swede aimed a lightning blow that carried with it his entire weight. Johnnie was evidently half stupid from weakness, but he miraculously dodged, and his fist sent the over-balanced Swede sprawling.

The cowboy, Scully, and the Easterner burst into a cheer that was like a chorus of triumphant soldiery, but before its conclusion the Swede has scuffed agilely to his feet and come in berserk abandon at his foe. There was another perplexity of flying arms, and Johnnie's body again swung away and fell, even as a bundle might fall from a roof. The Swede instantly staggered to a little wind-waved tree and leaned upon it, breathing like an engine, while his savage and flamelit eyes roamed from face to face as the men bent over Johnnie. There was a splendour of isolation in his situation at this time which the Easterner felt once when, lifting his eyes from the man on the ground, he beheld that mysterious and lonely figure, waiting.

"Are you any good yet, Johnnie?" asked Scully in a broken voice.   175

The son gasped and opened his eyes languidly. After a moment he answered, "No—I ain't—any good—any—more." Then, from shame, and bodily ill, he began to weep, the tears furrowing down through the blood-stains on his face. "He was too—too—too heavy for me."

Scully straightened and addressed the waiting figure.

"Stranger," he said, evenly, "it's all up with our side." Then his voice changed into that vibrant huskiness which is commonly the tone of the most simple and deadly announcements. "Johnnie is whipped."

Without replying, the victor moved off on the route to the front door of the hotel.

The cowboy was formulating new and unspellable blasphemies. The East-   180
erner was startled to find that they were out in a wind that seemed to come direct from the shadowed arctic floes. He heard again the wail of the snow as it was flung to its grave in the south. He knew now that all this time the cold had been sinking into him deeper and deeper, and he wondered that he had not perished. He felt indifferent to the condition of the vanquished man.

"Johnnie, can you walk?" asked Scully.

"Did I hurt—hurt him any?" asked the son.

"Can you walk, boy? Can you walk?"

Johnnie's voice was suddenly strong. There was a robust impatience in it. "I asked you whether I hurt him any!"

"Yes, yes, Johnnie," answered the cowboy, consolingly; "he's hurt a good deal."   185

They raised him from the ground, and as soon as he was on his feet he went tottering off, rebuffing all attempts at assistance. When the party rounded the corner they were fairly blinded by the pelting of the snow. It burned their faces like fire. The cowboy carried Johnnie through the drift to the door. As they entered, some cards again rose from the floor and beat against the wall.

The Easterner rushed to the stove. He was so profoundly chilled that he almost dared to embrace the glowing iron. The Swede was not in the room. Johnnie sank into a chair and, folding his arms on his knees, buried his face in them. Scully, warming one foot and then the other at a rim of the stove, muttered to himself with Celtic mournfulness. The cowboy had removed his fur cap, and with a dazed and rueful air he was running one hand through his tousled locks. From overhead they could hear the creaking of boards, as the Swede tramped here and there in his room.

The sad quiet was broken by the sudden flinging open of a door that led toward the kitchen. It was instantly followed by an inrush of women. They precipitated themselves upon Johnnie amid a chorus of lamentation. Before they carried their prey off to the kitchen, there to be bathed and harangued with that mixture of sympathy and abuse which is a feat of their sex, the mother straightened herself and fixed old Scully with an eye of stern reproach, "Shame be upon you, Patrick Scully!" she cried. "Your own son, too. Shame be upon you!"

"There, now! Be quiet, now!" said the old man, weakly.

"Shame be upon you, Patrick Scully!" The girls, rallying to this slogan,   190 sniffed disdainfully in the direction of those trembling accomplices, the cowboy and the Easterner. Presently they bore Johnnie away, and left the three men to dismal reflection.

VII

"I'd like to fight this here Dutchman myself," said the cowboy, breaking a long silence.

Scully wagged his head sadly. "No, that wouldn't do. It wouldn't be right. It wouldn't be right."

"Well, why wouldn't it?" argued the cowboy. "I don't see no harm in it."

"No," answered Scully, with mournful heroism. "It wouldn't be right. It was Johnnie's fight, and now we mustn't whip the man just because he whipped Johnnie."

"Yes, that's true enough," said the cowboy; "but—he better not get fresh   195 with me, because I couldn't stand no more of it."

"You'll not say a word to him," commanded Scully, and even then they heard the tread of the Swede on the stairs. His entrance was made theatric. He swept the door back with a bang and swaggered to the middle of the room. No one looked at him. "Well," he cried, insolently, at Scully, "I s'pose you'll tell me now how much I owe you?"

The old man remained stolid. "You don't owe me nothin'."

"Huh!" said the Swede, "huh! Don't owe 'im nothin'."

The cowboy addressed the Swede. "Stranger, I don't see how you come to be so gay around here."

Old Scully was instantly alert. "Stop!" he shouted, holding his hand forth, fingers upward. "Bill, you shut up!"   200

The cowboy spat carelessly into the sawdust-box. "I didn't say a word, did I?" he asked.

"Mr. Scully," called the Swede, "how much do I owe you?" It was seen that he was attired for departure, and that he had his valise in his hand.

"You don't owe me nothin'," repeated Scully in the same imperturbable way.

"Huh!" said the Swede. "I guess you're right. I guess if it was any way at all, you'd owe me somethin'. That's what I guess." He turned to the cowboy. "'Kill him! Kill him! Kill him!'" he mimicked, and then guffawed victoriously. "'Kill him!'" He was convulsed with ironical humour.

But he might have been jeering the dead. The three men were immovable and silent, staring with glassy eyes at the stove.   205

The Swede opened the door and passed into the storm, giving one derisive glance backward at the still group.

As soon as the door was closed, Scully and the cowboy leaped to their feet and began to curse. They trampled to and fro, waving their arms and smashing into the air with their fists. "Oh, but that was a hard minute!" wailed Scully. "That was a hard minute! Him there leerin' and scoffin'! One bang at his nose was worth forty dollars to me that minute! How did you stand it, Bill?"

"How did I stand it?" cried the cowboy in a quivering voice. "How did I stand it? Oh!"

The old man burst into sudden brogue. "I'd loike to take that Swade," he wailed, "and hould 'im down on a shtone flure and bate 'im to a jelly wid a shtick!"

The cowboy groaned in sympathy. "I'd like to git him by the neck and   210 hammer him"—he brought his hand down on a chair with a noise like a pistol-shot—"hammer that there Dutchman until he couldn't tell himself from a dead coyote!"

"I'd bate 'im until he———"

"I'd show *him* some things———"

And then together they raised a yearning, fanatic cry—"Oh-o-oh! if we only could———"

"Yes!"

"Yes!"   215

"And then I'd———"

"O-o-oh!"

VIII

The Swede, tightly gripping his valise, tacked across the face of the storm as if he carried sails. He was following a line of little naked, gasping trees which, he knew, must mark the way of the road. His face, fresh from the pounding of Johnnie's fists, felt more pleasure than pain in the wind and the driving snow. A number of square shapes loomed upon him finally, and he knew them as the houses of the main body of the town. He found a street and made travel along it, leaning heavily upon the wind whenever, at a corner, a terrific blast caught him.

He might have been in a deserted village. We picture the world as thick with conquering and elate humanity, but here, with the bugles of the tempest pealing, it was hard to imagine a peopled earth. One viewed the existence of man then as marvel, and conceded a glamour of wonder to these lice which were caused to cling to a whirling, fire-smitten, ice-locked, disease-stricken, space-lost bulb. The conceit of man was explained by this storm to be the very engine of life. One was a coxcomb not to die in it. However, the Swede found a saloon.

In front of it an indomitable red light was burning, and the snowflakes were   220 made blood-colour as they flew through the circumscribed territory of the lamp's shining. The Swede pushed open the door of the saloon and entered. A sanded expanse was before him, and at the end of it four men sat about a table drinking. Down one side of the room extended a radiant bar, and its guardian was leaning upon his elbows listening to the talk of the men at the table. The Swede dropped his valise upon the floor and, smiling fraternally upon the barkeeper, said, "Gimme some whisky, will you?" The man placed a bottle, a whisky-glass, and a glass of ice-thick water upon the bar. The Swede poured himself an abnormal portion of whisky and drank it in three gulps. "Pretty bad night," remarked the bartender, indifferently. He was making the pretension of blindness which is usually a distinction of his class; but it could have been seen that he was furtively studying the half-erased blood-stains on the face of the Swede. "Bad night," he said again.

"Oh, it's good enough for me," replied the Swede, hardily, as he poured himself some more whisky. The barkeeper took his coin and manoeuvred it through its reception by the highly nickelled cash-machine. A bell rang; a card labelled "20 cts." had appeared.

"No," continued the Swede, "this isn't too bad weather. It's good enough for me."

"So?" murmured the barkeeper, languidly.

The copious drams made the Swede's eyes swim, and he breathed a trifle heavier. "Yes, I like this weather. I like it. It suits me." It was apparently his design to impart a deep significance to these words.

"So?" murmured the bartender again. He turned to gaze dreamily at the   225 scroll-like birds and bird-like scrolls which had been drawn with soap upon the mirrors in back of the bar.

"Well, I guess I'll take another drink," said the Swede, presently. "Have something?"

"No, thanks; I'm not drinkin'," answered the bartender. Afterward he asked, "How did you hurt your face?"

The Swede immediately began to boast loudly. "Why, in a fight. I thumped the soul out of a man down here at Scully's hotel."

The interest of the four men at the table was at last aroused.

"Who was it?" said one.   230

"Johnnie Scully," blustered the Swede. "Son of the man what runs it. He will be pretty near dead for some weeks, I can tell you. I made a nice thing of him. I did. He couldn't get up. They carried him in the house. Have a drink?"

Instantly the men in some subtle way encased themselves in reserve. "No, thanks," said one. The group was of curious formation. Two were prominent local business men; one was the district attorney; and one was a professional gambler of the kind known as "square." But a scrutiny of the group would not have enabled an observer to pick the gambler from the men of more reputable pursuits. He was, in fact, a man so delicate in manner, when among people of fair class, and so judicious in his choice of victims, that in the strictly masculine part of the town's life he had come to be explicitly trusted and admired. People called him a thoroughbred. The fear and contempt with which his craft was regarded were undoubtedly the reason why his quiet dignity shone conspicuous above the quiet dignity of men who might be merely hatters, billiard-markers, or grocery clerks. Beyond an occasional unwary traveller who came by rail, this gambler was supposed to prey solely upon reckless and senile farmers, who, when flush with good crops, drove into town in all the pride and confidence of an absolutely invulnerable stupidity. Hearing at times in circuitous fashion of the despoilment of such a farmer, the important men of Romper invariably laughed in contempt of the victim, and if they thought of the wolf at all, it was with a kind of pride at the knowledge that he would never dare think of attacking their wisdom and courage. Besides, it was popular that this gambler had a real wife and two real children in a neat cottage in a suburb, where he led an exemplary home life; and when any one even suggested a discrepancy in his character, the crowd immediately vociferated descriptions of this virtuous family circle. Then men who led exemplary home lives, and men who did not lead exemplary home lives, all subsided in a bunch, remarking that there was nothing more to be said.

However, when a restriction was placed upon him—as, for instance, when a strong clique of members of the new Pollywog Club refused to permit him, even as a spectator, to appear in the rooms of the organization—the candour and gentleness with which he accepted the judgment disarmed many of his foes and made his friends more desperately partisan. He invariably distinguished between himself and a respectable Romper man so quickly and frankly that his manner actually appeared to be a continual broadcast compliment.

And one must not forget to declare the fundamental fact of his entire position in Romper. It is irrefutable that in all affairs outside his business, in all matters that occur eternally and commonly between man and man, this thieving cardplayer was so generous, so just, so moral, that, in a contest, he could have put to flight the consciences of nine tenths of the citizens of Romper.

And so it happened that he was seated in this saloon with the two prominent   235
local merchants and the district attorney.

The Swede continued to drink raw whisky, meanwhile babbling at the barkeeper and trying to induce him to indulge in potations. "Come on. Have a drink. Come on. What—no? Well, have a little one, then. By gawd, I've whipped a man to-night, and I want to celebrate. I whipped him good, too. Gentlemen," the Swede cried to the men at the table, "have a drink?"

"Ssh!" said the barkeeper.

The group at the table, although furtively attentive, had been pretending to be deep in talk, but now a man lifted his eyes toward the Swede and said, shortly, "Thanks. We don't want any more."

At this reply the Swede ruffled out his chest like a rooster. "Well," he exploded, "it seems I can't get anybody to drink with me in this town. Seems so, don't it? Well!"

"Ssh!" said the barkeeper.   240

"Say," snarled the Swede, "don't you try to shut me up. I won't have it. I'm a gentleman, and I want people to drink with me. And I want 'em to drink with me now. *Now*—do you understand?" He rapped the bar with his knuckles.

Years of experience had calloused the bartender. He merely grew sulky. "I hear you," he answered.

"Well," cried the Swede, "listen hard then. See those men over there? Well, they're going to drink with me, and don't you forget it. Now you watch."

"Hi!" yelled the barkeeper, "this won't do!"

"Why won't it?" demanded the Swede. He stalked over to the table, and by 245 chance laid his hand upon the shoulder of the gambler. "How about this?" he asked wrathfully. "I asked you to drink with me."

The gambler simply twisted his head and spoke over his shoulder. "My friend, I don't know you."

"Oh, hell!" answered the Swede, "come and have a drink."

"Now, my boy," advised the gambler, kindly, "take your hand off my shoulder and go 'way and mind your own business." He was a little, slim man, and it seemed strange to hear him use this tone of heroic patronage to the burly Swede. The other men at the table said nothing.

"What! You won't drink with me, you little dude? I'll make you, then! I'll make you!" The Swede had grasped the gambler frenziedly at the throat, and was dragging him from his chair. The other men sprang up. The barkeeper dashed around the corner of his bar. There was a great tumult, and then was seen a long blade in the hand of the gambler. It shot forward, and a human body, this citadel of virtue, wisdom, power, was pierced as easily as if it had been a melon. The Swede fell with a cry of supreme astonishment.

The prominent merchants and the district attorney must have at once 250 tumbled out of the place backward. The bartender found himself hanging limply to the arm of a chair and gazing into the eyes of a murderer.

"Henry," said the latter, as he wiped his knife on one of the towels that hung beneath the bar rail, "you tell 'em where to find me. I'll be home, waiting for 'em." Then he vanished. A moment afterward the barkeeper was in the street dinning through the storm for help and, moreover, companionship.

The corpse of the Swede, alone in the saloon, had its eyes fixed upon a dreadful legend that dwelt atop the cash-machine: "This registers the amount of your purchase."

IX

Months later, the cowboy was frying pork over the stove of a little ranch near the Dakota line, when there was a quick thud of hoofs outside, and presently the Easterner entered with the letters and the papers.

"Well," said the Easterner at once, "the chap that killed the Swede has got three years. Wasn't much, was it?"

"He has? Three years?" The cowboy poised his pan of pork, while he 255 ruminated upon the news. "Three years. That ain't much."

"No. It was a light sentence," replied the Easterner as he unbuckled his spurs. "Seems there was a good deal of sympathy for him in Romper."

"If the bartender had been any good," observed the cowboy, thoughtfully, "he would have gone in and cracked that there Dutchman on the head with a bottle in the beginnin' of it and stopped all this here murderin'."

"Yes, a thousand things might have happened," said the Easterner, tartly.

The cowboy returned his pan of pork to the fire, but his philosophy continued. "It's funny, ain't it? If he hadn't said Johnnie was cheatin' he'd be alive this minute. He was an awful fool. Game played for fun, too. Not for money. I believe he was crazy."

"I feel sorry for that gambler," said the Easterner.   26C

"Oh, so do I," said the cowboy. "He don't deserve none of it for killin' who he did."

"The Swede might not have been killed if everything had been square."

"Might not have been killed?" exclaimed the cowboy. "Everythin' square? Why, when he said that Johnnie was cheatin' and acted like such a jackass? And then in the saloon he fairly walked up to git hurt?" With these arguments the cowboy browbeat the Easterner and reduced him to rage.

"You're a fool!" cried the Easterner, viciously. "You're a bigger jackass than the Swede by a million majority. Now let me tell you one thing. Let me tell you something. Listen! Johnnie *was* cheating!"

"'Johnnie,'" said the cowboy, blankly. There was a minute of silence, and   26?
then he said, robustly, "Why, no. The game was only for fun."

"Fun or not," said the Easterner, "Johnnie was cheating. I saw him. I know it. I saw him. And I refused to stand up and be a man. I let the Swede fight it out alone. And you—you were simply puffing around the place wanting to fight. And then old Scully himself! We are all in it! This poor gambler isn't even a noun. He is a kind of an adverb. Every sin is the result of collaboration. We, five of us, have collaborated in the murder of this Swede. Usually there are from a dozen to forty women really involved in every murder, but in this case it seems to be only five men—you, I, Johnnie, old Scully; and that fool of an unfortunate gambler came merely as a culmination, the apex of a human movement, and gets all the punishment."

The cowboy, injured and rebellious, cried out blindly into this fog of mysterious theory: "Well, I didn't do anythin', did I?"

QUESTIONS

1. Describe the conflict in the story. Why is the Swede the major antagonist? How could he be seen as protagonist, instead of antagonist? Why do the others stress his identity as a Swede, and why is he never named?

2. Consider the Easterner's analysis (paragraph 90) as a plausible explanation of the Swede's behavior before the fight. How fully does this analysis explain these actions? How could the analysis be used in an argument that "The Blue Hotel" is a critique of conventional, dime-store views of the wild west?

3. Analyze the structure of the story. What relationship do the parts of abstract formal structure (described on pp. 97–98) have to the part divisions marked by Crane himself? Why is most of the story about events at the Blue Hotel, and why do events at the saloon, where the murder occurs, occupy only a small section? Explain, in relation to the story's structure, why we do not learn until the very end that Johnny actually *was* cheating.

4. How adequately does the Easterner's "noun-adverb" analysis in the concluding paragraphs explain the events of the story? Could such events be stopped at a certain point, or are they inevitable regardless of the Easterner's theory about collaborative control and responsibility?

EUDORA WELTY (b. 1909)

A Worn Path *1941*

It was December—a bright frozen day in the early morning. Far out in the country there was an old Negro woman with her head tied in a red rag, coming along a path through the pinewoods. Her name was Phoenix Jackson. She was very old and small and she walked slowly in the dark pine shadows, moving a little from side to side in her steps, with the balanced heaviness and lightness of a pendulum in a grandfather clock. She carried a thin, small cane made from an umbrella, and with this she kept tapping the frozen earth in front of her. This made a grave and persistent noise in the still air, that seemed meditative like the chirping of a solitary little bird.

She wore a dark striped dress reaching down to her shoe tops, and an equally long apron of bleached sugar sacks, with a full pocket: all neat and tidy, but every time she took a step she might have fallen over her shoelaces, which dragged from her unlaced shoes. She looked straight ahead. Her eyes were blue with age. Her skin had a pattern all its own of numberless branching wrinkles and as though a whole little tree stood in the middle of her forehead, but a golden color ran underneath, and the two knobs of her cheeks were illuminated by a yellow burning under the dark. Under the rag her hair came down on her neck in the frailest of ringlets, still black, and with an odor like copper.

Now and then there was a quivering in the thicket. Old Phoenix said, "Out of my way, all you foxes, owls, beetles, jack rabbits, coons and wild animals! . . . Keep out from under these feet, little bob-whites. . . . Keep the big wild hogs out of my path. Don't let none of those come running my direction. I got a long way." Under her small black-freckled hand her cane, limber as a buggy whip, would switch at the brush as if to rouse up any hiding things.

On she went. The woods were deep and still. The sun made the pine needles almost too bright to look at, up where the wind rocked. The cones dropped as light as feathers. Down in the hollow was the mourning dove—it was not too late for him.

The path ran up a hill. "Seem like there is chains about my feet, time I get   5
this far," she said, in the voice of argument old people keep to use with themselves. "Something always take a hold of me on this hill—pleads I should stay."

After she got to the top she turned and gave a full, severe look behind her where she had come. "Up through pines," she said at length. "Now down through oaks."

Her eyes opened their widest, and she started down gently. But before she got to the bottom of the hill a bush caught her dress.

Her fingers were busy and intent, but her skirts were full and long, so that before she could pull them free in one place they were caught in another. It was not possible to allow the dress to tear. "I in the thorny bush," she said. "Thorns, you doing your appointed work. Never want to let folks pass, no sir. Old eyes thought you was a pretty little *green* bush."

Finally, trembling all over, she stood free, and after a moment dared to stoop for her cane.

"Sun so high!" she cried, leaning back and looking, while the thick tears   10
went over her eyes. "The time getting all gone here."

At the foot of this hill was a place where a log was laid across the creek.

"Now comes the trial," said Phoenix.

Putting her right foot out, she mounted the log and shut her eyes. Lifting her skirt, leveling her cane fiercely before her, like a festival figure in some parade, she began to march across. Then she opened her eyes and she was safe on the other side.

"I wasn't as old as I thought," she said.

But she sat down to rest. She spread her skirts on the bank around her and folded her hands over her knees. Up above her was a tree in a pearly cloud of mistletoe. She did not dare to close her eyes, and when a little boy brought her a plate with a slice of marble-cake on it she spoke to him. "That would be acceptable," she said. But when she went to take it there was just her own hand in the air.

So she left that tree, and had to go through a barbed-wire fence. There she had to creep and crawl, spreading her knees and stretching her fingers like a baby trying to climb the steps. But she talked loudly to herself: she could not let her dress be torn now, so late in the day, and she could not pay for having her arm or leg sawed off if she got caught fast where she was.

At last she was safe through the fence and risen up out in the clearing. Big dead trees, like black men with one arm, were standing in the purple stalks of the withered cotton field. There sat a buzzard.

"Who you watching?"

In the furrow she made her way along.

"Glad this is not the season for bulls," she said, looking sideways, "and the good Lord made his snakes to curl up and sleep in the winter. A pleasure I don't see no two-headed snake coming around that tree, where it come once. It took a while to get by him, back in the summer."

She passed through the old cotton and went into a field of dead corn. It whispered and shook and was taller than her head. "Through the maze now," she said, for there was no path.

Then there was something tall, black, and skinny there, moving before her.

At first she took it for a man. It could have been a man dancing in the field. But she stood still and listened, and it did not make a sound. It was as silent as a ghost.

"Ghost," she said sharply, "who be you the ghost of? For I have heard of nary death close by."

But there was no answer—only the ragged dancing in the wind.

She shut her eyes, reached out her hand, and touched a sleeve. She found a coat and inside that an emptiness, cold as ice.

"You scarecrow," she said. Her face lighted. "I ought to be shut up for good," she said with laughter. "My senses is gone. I too old, I the oldest people I ever know. Dance, old scarecrow," she said, "while I dancing with you."

She kicked her foot over the furrow, and with mouth drawn down, shook her head once or twice in a little strutting way. Some husks blew down and whirled in steamers about her skirts.

Then she went on, parting her way from side to side with the cane, through the whispering field. At last she came to the end, to a wagon track where the silver grass blew between the red ruts. The quail were walking around like pullets, seeming all dainty and unseen.

"Walk pretty," she said. "This is the easy place. This the easy going."   30

She followed the track, swaying through the quiet bare fields, through the little strings of trees silver in their dead leaves, past cabins silver from weather, with the doors and windows boarded shut, all like old women under a spell sitting there. "I walking in their sleep," she said, nodding her head vigorously.

In a ravine she went where a spring was silently flowing through a hollow log. Old Phoenix bent and drank. "Sweet-gum makes the water sweet," she said, and drank more. "Nobody know who made this well, for it was here when I was born."

The track crossed a swampy part where the moss hung as white as lace from every limb. "Sleep on, alligators, and blow your bubbles." Then the track went into the road.

Deep, deep the road went down between the high green-colored banks. Overhead the live-oaks met, and it was as dark as a cave.

A black dog with a lolling tongue came up out of the weeds by the ditch.   35
She was meditating, and not ready, and when he came at her she only hit him a little with her cane. Over she went in the ditch, like a little puff of milkweed.

Down there, her sense drifted away. A dream visited her, and she reached her hand up, but nothing reached down and gave her a pull. So she lay there and presently went to talking. "Old woman," she said to herself, "that black dog come up out of the weeds to stall you off, and now there he sitting on his fine tail smiling at you."

A white man finally came along and found her—a hunter, a young man, with his dog on a chain.

"Well, Granny!" he laughed. "What are you doing there?"

"Lying on my back like a June-bug waiting to be turned over, mister," she said, reaching up her hand.

He lifted her up, gave her a swing in the air, and set her down. "Anything   40
broken, Granny?"

"No sir, them old dead weeds is springy enough," said Phoenix, when she had got her breath. "I thank you for your trouble."

"Where do you live, Granny?" he asked, while the two dogs were growling at each other.

"Away back yonder, sir, behind the ridge. You can't even see it from here."

"On your way home?"

"No sir, I goin to town."   45

"Why, that's too far! That's as far as I walk when I come out myself, and I get something for my trouble." He patted the stuffed bag he carried, and there hung down a little closed claw. It was one of the bob-whites, with its beak hooked bitterly to show it was dead. "Now you go on home, Granny!"

"I bound to go to town, mister," said Phoenix. "The time come around."

He gave another laugh, filling the whole landscape. "I know you old colored people! Wouldn't miss going to town to see Santa Claus!"

But something held old Phoenix very still. The deep lines in her face went into a fierce and different radiation. Without warning, she had seen with her own eyes a flashing nickel fall out of the man's pocket onto the ground.

"How old are you, Granny?" he was saying.   50

"There is no telling, mister," she said, "no telling."

Then she gave a little cry and clapped her hands and said, "Git on away from here, dog! Look! Look at that dog!" She laughed as if in admiration. "He ain't scared of nobody. He a big black dog." She whispered, "Sic him!"

"Watch me get rid of that cur," said the man. "Sic him, Pete! Sic him!"

Phoenix heard the dogs fighting, and heard the man running and throwing sticks. She even heard a gunshot. But she was slowly bending forward by that time, further and further forward, the lids stretched down over her eyes, as if she were doing this in her sleep. Her chin was lowered almost to her knees. The yellow palm of her hand came out from the fold of her apron. Her fingers slid down and along the ground under the piece of money with the grace and care they would have in lifting an egg from under a setting hen. Then she slowly straightened up, she stood erect, and the nickel was in her apron pocket. A bird flew by. Her lips moved. "God watching me the whole time. I come to stealing."

The man came back, and his own dog panted about them. "Well, I scared him off that time," he said, and then he laughed and lifted his gun and pointed it at Phoenix.   55

She stood straight and faced him.

"Doesn't the gun scare you?" he said, still pointing it.

"No, sir. I seen plenty go off closer by, in my day, and for less than what I done," she said, holding utterly still.

He smiled, and shouldered the gun. "Well, Granny," he said, "you must be a hundred years old, and scared of nothing. I'd give you a dime if I had any money with me. But you take my advice and stay home, and nothing will happen to you."

"I bound to go on my way, mister," said Phoenix. She inclined her head in the red rag. Then they went in different directions, but she could hear the gun shooting again and again over the hill.   60

She walked on. The shadows hung from the oak trees to the road like curtains. Then she smelled wood-smoke, and smelled the river, and she saw a steeple and the cabins on their steep steps. Dozens of little black children whirled around her. There ahead was Natchez shining. Bells were ringing. She walked on.

In the paved city it was Christmas time. There were red and green electric lights strung and crisscrossed everywhere, and all turned on in the daytime. Old Phoenix would have been lost if she had not distrusted her eyesight and depended on her feet to know where to take her.

She paused quietly on the sidewalk where people were passing by. A lady came along in the crowd, carrying an armful of red-, green-, and silver-wrapped presents; she gave off perfume like the red roses in hot summer, and Phoenix stopped her.

"Please, missy, will you lace up my shoe?" She held up her foot.

"What do you want, Grandma?"   65

"See my shoe," said Phoenix. "Do all right for out in the country, but wouldn't look right to go in a big building."

"Stand still then, Grandma," said the lady. She put her packages down on the sidewalk beside her and laced and tied both shoes tightly.

"Can't lace 'em with a cane," said Phoenix. "Thank you, missy. I doesn't mind asking a nice lady to tie up my shoe, when I gets out on the street."

Moving slowly and from side to side, she went into the big building, and

into a tower of steps, where she walked up and around and around until her feet
knew to stop.

She entered a door, and there she saw nailed up on the wall the document   70
that had been stamped with the gold seal and framed in the gold frame, which
matched the dream that was hung up in her head.

"Here I be," she said. There was a fixed and ceremonial stiffness over her
body.

"A charity case, I suppose," said an attendant who sat at the desk before
her.

But Phoenix only looked above her head. There was sweat on her face, the
wrinkles in her skin shone like a bright net.

"Speak up, Grandma," the woman said, "What's your name? We must have
your history, you know. Have you been here before? What seems to be the trouble
with you?"

Old Phoenix only gave a twitch to her face as if a fly were bothering her.   75

"Are you deaf?" cried the attendant.

But then the nurse came in.

"Oh, that's just old Aunt Phoenix," she said. "She doesn't come for herself—
she has a little grandson. She makes these trips just as regular as clockwork. She
lives away back off the Old Natchez Trace." She bent down. "Well, Aunt Phoenix,
why don't you just take a seat? We won't keep you standing after your long trip."
She pointed.

The old woman sat down, both upright in the chair.

"Now, how is the boy?" asked the nurse.   80

Old Phoenix did not speak.

"I said, how is the boy?"

But Phoenix only waited and stared straight ahead, her face very solemn
and withdrawn into rigidity.

"Is his throat any better?" asked the nurse. "Aunt Phoenix, don't you hear
me? Is your grandson's throat any better since the last time you came for the
medicine?"

With her hands on her knees, the old woman waited, silent, erect, and   85
motionless, just as if she were in armor.

"You mustn't take up our time this way, Aunt Phoenix," the nurse said.
"Tell us quickly about your grandson, and get it over. He isn't dead, is he?"

At last there came a flicker and then a flame of comprehension across her
face, and she spoke.

"My grandson. It was my memory had left me. There I sat and forgot why
I made my long trip."

"Forgot?" the nurse frowned. "After you came so far?"

Then Phoenix was like an old woman begging a dignified forgiveness for   90
waking up frightened in the night. "I never did go to school, I was too old at the
Surrender," she said in a soft voice. "I'm an old woman without an education. It
was my memory fail me. My little grandson, he is just the same, and I forgot it in
the coming."

"Throat never heals, does it?" said the nurse, speaking in a loud, sure voice
to old Phoenix. By now she had a card with something written on it, a little list.
"Yes. Swallowed lye. When was it—January—two, three years ago—"

Phoenix spoke unasked now. "No missy, he not dead, he just the same.

Every little while his throat begin to close up again, and he not able to swallow. He not get his breath. He not able to help himself. So the time come around, and I go on another trip for the soothing medicine."

"All right. The doctor said as long as you came to get it, you could have it," said the nurse. "But it's an obstinate case."

"My little grandson, he sit up there in the house all wrapped up, waiting by himself," Phoenix went on. "We is the only two left in the world. He suffer and it don't seem to put him back at all. He got a sweet look. He going to last. He wear a little patch quilt and peep out holding his mouth open like a little bird. I remembers so plain now. I not going to forget him again, no, the whole enduring time. I could tell him from all the others in creation."

"All right." The nurse was trying to hush her now. She brought her a bottle   95
of medicine. "Charity," she said, making a check mark in a book.

Old Phoenix held the bottle close to her eyes, and then carefully put it into her pocket.

"I thank you," she said.

"It's Christmas time, Grandma," said the attendant. "Could I give you a few pennies out of my purse?"

"Five pennies is a nickel," said Phoenix stiffly.

"Here's a nickel," said the attendant.   100

Phoenix rose carefully and held out her hand. She received the nickel and then fished the other nickel out of her pocket and laid it beside the new one. She stared at her palm closely, with her head on one side.

Then she gave a tap with her cane on the floor.

"This is what come to me to do," she said, "I going to the store and buy my child a little windmill they sells, made out of paper. He going to find it hard to believe there such a thing in the world. I'll march myself back where he waiting, holding it straight up in this hand."

She lifted her free hand, gave a little nod, turned around, and walked out of the doctor's office. Then her slow step began on the stairs, going down.

QUESTIONS

1. From the description of Phoenix, what do you conclude about her economic condition? How do you know that she has taken the path through the woods before? Is she accustomed to being alone? What do you make of her speaking to animals, and of her imagining a boy offering her a piece of cake? What does her speech show about her education and background?

2. Describe the plot of the story. With Phoenix as the protagonist, what are the obstacles ranged against her? How might Phoenix be considered to be in the grip of large and indifferent social and political forces?

3. Comment on the meaning of this dialogue between Phoenix and the hunter:

    "Doesn't the gun scare you?" he said, still pointing it.

    "No, sir, I seen plenty go off closer by, in my day, and for less than what I done," she said, holding utterly still.

4. A number of responses might be made to this story, among them admiration

for Phoenix, pity for her and her grandson and for the downtrodden generally, anger at her impoverished condition, and apprehension about her approaching senility. Do you share in any of these responses? Do you have any others?

TOM WHITECLOUD (1914–1972)

Blue Winds Dancing   *1938*

There is a moon out tonight. Moon and stars and clouds tipped with moonlight. And there is a fall wind blowing in my heart. Ever since this evening, when against a fading sky I saw geese wedge southward. They were going home. . . . Now I try to study, but against the pages I see them again, driving southward. Going home.

Across the valley there are heavy mountains holding up the night sky, and beyond the mountains there is home. Home, and peace, and the beat of drums, and blue winds dancing over snow fields. The Indian lodge will fill with my people, and our gods will come and sit among them. I should be there then. I should be at home.

But home is beyond the mountains, and I am here. Here where fall hides in the valleys, and winter never comes down from the mountains. Here where all the trees grow in rows; the palms stand stiffly by the roadsides, and in the groves the orange trees line in military rows, and endlessly bear fruit. Beautiful, yes; there is always beauty in order, in rows of growing things! But it is the beauty of captivity. A pine fighting for existence on a windy knoll is much more beautiful.

In my Wisconsin, the leaves change before the snows come. In the air there is the smell of wild rice and venison cooking; and when the winds come whispering through the forests, they carry the smell of rotting leaves. In the evenings, the loon calls, lonely; and birds sing their last songs before leaving. Bears dig roots and eat late fall berries, fattening for their long winter sleep. Later, when the first snows fall, one awakens in the morning to find the world white and beautiful and clean. Then one can look back over his trail and see the tracks following. In the woods there are tracks of deer and snowshoe rabbits, and long streaks where partridges slide to alight. Chipmunks make tiny footprints on the limbs and one can hear squirrels busy in hollow trees, sorting acorns. Soft lake waves wash the shores, and sunsets burst each evening over the lakes, and make them look as if they were afire.

That land which is my home! Beautiful, calm—where there is no hurry to get anywhere, no driving to keep up in a race that knows no ending and no goal. No classes where men talk and talk and then stop now and then to hear their own words come back to them from the students. No constant peering into the maelstrom of one's mind; no worries about grades and honors; no hysterical preparing for life until that life is half over; no anxiety about one's place in the thing they call Society.

I hear again the ring of axes in deep woods, the crunch of snow beneath my feet. I feel again the smooth velvet of ghost-birch bark. I hear the rhythm of the drums. . . . I am tired. I am weary of trying to keep up this bluff of being civilized. Being civilized means trying to do everything you don't want to, never doing anything you want to. It means dancing to the strings of custom and tradition; it means living in houses and never knowing or caring who is next door.

These civilized white men want us to be like them—always dissatisfied—getting a hill and wanting a mountain.

Then again, maybe I am not tired. Maybe I'm licked. Maybe I am just not smart enough to grasp these things that go to make up civilization. Maybe I am just too lazy to think hard enough to keep up.

Still, I know my people have many things that civilization has taken from the whites. They know how to give; how to tear one's piece of meat in two and share it with one's brother. They know how to sing—how to make each man his own songs and sing them; for their music they do not have to listen to other men singing over a radio. They know how to make things with their hands, how to shape beads into design and make a thing of beauty from a piece of birch bark.

But we are inferior. It is terrible to have to feel inferior; to have to read reports of intelligence tests, and learn that one's race is behind. It is terrible to sit in classes and hear men tell you that your people worship sticks of wood—that your gods are all false, that the Manitou forgot your people and did not write them a book.

I am tired. I want to walk again among the ghost-birches. I want to see the   10
leaves turn in autumn, the smoke rise from the lodgehouses, and to feel the blue winds. I want to hear the drums; I want to hear the drums and feel the blue whispering winds.

There is a train wailing into the night. The trains go across the mountains. It would be easy to catch a freight. They will say he has gone back to the blanket; I don't care. The dance at Christmas. . . .

A bunch of bums warming at a tiny fire talk politics and women and joke about the Relief and the WPA and smoke cigarettes. These men in caps and overcoats and dirty overalls living on the outskirts of civilization are free, but they pay the price of being free in civilization. They are outcasts. I remember a sociology professor lecturing on adjustment to society; hobos and prostitutes and criminals are individuals who never adjusted, he said. He could learn a lot if he came and listened to a bunch of bums talk. He would learn that work and a woman and a place to hang his hat are all the ordinary man wants. These are all he wants, but other men are not content to let him want only these. He must be taught to want radios and automobiles and a new suit every spring. Progress would stop if he did not want these things. I listen to hear if there is any talk of communism or socialism in the hobo jungles. There is none. At best there is a sort of disgusted philosophy about life. They seem to think there should be a better distribution of wealth, or more work, or something. But they are not rabid about it. The radicals live in the cities.

I find a fellow headed for Albuquerque, and talk road-talk with him. "It is hard to ride fruit cars. Bums break in. Better to wait for a cattle car going back to the Middle West, and ride that." We catch the next east-bound and walk the tops until we find a cattle car. Inside, we crouch near the forward wall, huddle, and try to sleep. I feel peaceful and content at last. I am going home. The cattle car rocks. I sleep.

Morning and the desert. Noon and the Salton Sea, lying more lifeless than a mirage under a somber sun in a pale sky. Skeleton mountains rearing on the skyline, thrusting out of the desert floor, all rock and shadow and edges. Desert. Good country for an Indian reservation. . . .

Yuma and the muddy Colorado. Night again, and I wait shivering for the dawn.

Phoenix. Pima country. Mountains that look like cardboard sets on a forgotten stage. Tucson, Papago country. Giant cacti that look like petrified hitchhikers along the highways. Apache country. At El Paso my road-buddy decides to go on to Houston. I leave him, and head north to the mesa country. Las Cruces and the terrible Organ Mountains, jagged peaks that instill fear and wondering. Albuquerque. Pueblos along the Rio Grande. On the boardwalk there are some Indian women in colored sashes selling bits of pottery. The stone age offering its art to the twentieth century. They hold up a piece and fix the tourist with black eyes until, embarrassed, he buys or turns away. I feel suddenly angry that my people should have to do such things for a living. . . .

Santa Fe trains are fast, and they keep them pretty clean of bums. I decide to hurry and ride passenger coaltenders. Hide in the dark, judge the speed of the train as it leaves, and then dash out, and catch it. I hug the cold steel wall of the tender and think of the roaring fire in the engine ahead, and of the passengers back in the dining car reading their papers over hot coffee. Beneath me there is a blur of rails. Death would come quick if my hands should freeze and I fall. Up over the Sangre De Cristo range, around cliffs and through canyons to Denver. Bitter cold here, and I must watch out for Denver Bob. He is a railroad bull who has thrown bums from fast freights. I miss him. It is too cold, I suppose. On north to the Sioux country.

Small towns lit for the coming Christmas. On the streets of one I see a beam-shouldered young farmer gazing into a window filled with shining silver toasters. He is tall and wears a blue shirt buttoned, with no tie. His young wife by his side looks at him hopefully. He wants decorations for his place to hang his hat to please his woman. . . .

Northward again. Minnesota, and great white fields of snow; frozen lakes, and dawn running into dusk without noon. Long forests wearing white. Bitter cold, and one night the northern lights. I am nearing home.

I reach Woodruff at midnight. Suddenly I am afraid, now that I am but twenty miles from home. Afraid of what my father will say, afraid of being looked on as a stranger by my own people. I sit by a fire and think about myself and all other young Indians. We just don't seem to fit in anywhere—certainly not among the whites, and not among the older people. I think again about the learned sociology professor and his professing. So many things seem to be clear now that I am away from school and do not have to worry about some man's opinion of my ideas. It is easy to think while looking at dancing flames.

Morning, I spend the day cleaning up, and buying some presents for my family with what is left of my money. Nothing much, but a gift is a gift, if a man buys it with his last quarter. I wait until evening, then start up the track toward home.

Christmas Eve comes in on a north wind. Snow clouds hang over the pines, and the night comes early. Walking along the railroad bed, I feel the calm peace of snowbound forests on either side of me. I take my time; I am back in a world where time does not mean so much now. I am alone; alone but not nearly so lonely as I was back on the campus at school. Those are never lonely who love the snow and the pines; never lonely when the pines are wearing white shawls and snow crunches coldly underfoot. In the woods I know there are the tracks of deer and rabbit; I know that if I leave the rails and go into the woods I shall find them. I walk along feeling glad because my legs are light and my feet seem to know that they are home. A deer comes out of the woods ahead of me, and stands silhouetted on the rails. The North, I feel, has welcomed me home. I watch him and am glad that I do not wish for a gun. He goes into the woods quietly, leaving only the design of his tracks in the snow. I walk on. Now and then I pass a field, white under the night sky, with houses at the far end. Smoke comes from the chimneys of the houses, and I try to tell what sort of wood each is burning by the smoke; some burn pine, others aspen, others tamarack. There is one from which comes black coal smoke that rises lazily and drifts out over the tops of the trees. I like to watch houses and try to imagine what might be happening in them.

Just as a light snow begins to fall I cross the reservation boundary; somehow it seems as though I have stepped into another world. Deep woods in a white-and-black winter night. A faint trail leading to the village.

The railroad on which I stand comes from a city sprawled by a lake—a city with a million people who walk around without seeing one another; a city sucking the life from all the country around; a city with stores and police and intellectuals and criminals and movies and apartment houses; a city with its politics and libraries and zoos.

Laughing, I go into the woods. As I cross a frozen lake I begin to hear the drums. Soft in the night the drums beat. It is like the pulse beat of the world. The white line of the lake ends at a black forest, and above the trees the blue winds are dancing.

I come to the outlying houses of the village. Simple box houses, etched black in the night. From one or two windows soft lamplight falls on the snow. Christmas here, too, but it does not mean much; not much in the way of parties and presents. Joe Sky will get drunk. Alex Bodidash will buy his children red mittens and a new sled. Alex is a Carlisle man, and tries to keep his home up to white standards. White standards. Funny that my people should be ever falling farther behind. The more they try to imitate whites the more tragic the result. Yet they want us to be imitation white men. About all we imitate well are their vices.

The village is not a sight to instill pride, yet I am not ashamed; one can never be ashamed of his own people when he knows they have dreams as beautiful as white snow on a tall pine.

Father and my brother and sister are seated around the table as I walk in. Father stares at me for a moment, then I am in his arms, crying on his shoulder. I give them the presents I have brought, and my throat tightens as I watch my sister save carefully bits of red string from the packages. I hide my feelings by wrestling with my brother when he strikes my shoulder in token of affection. Father looks at me, and I know he has many questions, but he seems to know why I have come. He tells me to go alone to the lodge, and he will follow.

I walk along the trail to the lodge, watching the northern lights forming in the heavens. White waving ribbons that seem to pulsate with the rhythm of the drums. Clean snow creaks beneath my feet, and a soft wind sighs through the trees, singing to me. Everything seems to say, "Be happy! You are home now— you are free. You are among friends—we are your friends; we, the trees, and the snow, and the lights." I follow the trail to the lodge. My feet are light, my heart seems to sing to the music, and I hold my head high. Across white snow fields blue winds are dancing.

25

Before the lodge door I stop, afraid, I wonder if my people will remember me. I wonder—"Am I Indian, or am I white?" I stand before the door a long time. I hear the ice groan on the lake, and remember the story of the old woman under the ice, trying to get out, so she can punish some runaway lovers. I think to myself, "If I am white I will not believe that story; If I am Indian, I will know that there is an old woman under the ice." I listen for a while, and I know that there is an old woman under the ice. I look again at the lights, and go in.

Inside the lodge there are many Indians. Some sit on benches around the walls, others dance in the center of the floor around a drum. Nobody seems to notice me. It seems as though I were among a people I have never seen before. Heavy women with long hair. Women with children on their knees—small children that watch with intent black eyes the movements of the dancers, whose small faces are solemn and serene. The faces of the old people are serene, too, and their eyes are merry and bright. I look at the old men. Straight, dressed in dark trousers and beaded velvet vests, wearing soft moccasins. Dark, lined faces intent on the music. I wonder if I am at all like them. They dance on, lifting their feet to the rhythm of the drums swaying lightly, looking upward. I look at their eyes, and am startled at the rapt attention to the rhythm of the music.

The dance stops. The men walk back to the walls, and talk in low tones or with their hands. There is little conversation, yet everyone seems to be sharing some secret. A woman looks at a small boy wandering away, and he comes back to her.

Strange, I think and then remember. These people are not sharing words— they are sharing a mood. Everyone is happy. I am so used to white people that it seems strange so many people could be together without someone talking. These Indians are happy because they are together, and because the night is beautiful outside, and the music is beautiful. I try hard to forget school and white people, and be one of these—my people. I try to forget everything but the night, and it is a part of me that I am one with my people and we are all a part of something universal. I watch eyes, and see now that the old people are speaking to me. They nod slightly, imperceptibly, and their eyes laugh into mine. I look around the room. All the eyes are friendly; they all laugh. No one questions my being here. The drums begin to beat again, and I catch the invitation in the eyes of the old men. My feet begin to lift to the rhythm, and I look out beyond the walls into the night and see the lights. I am happy. It is beautiful. I am home.

QUESTIONS

1. Describe the first section of the story in terms of the structure. Could a case be made that this first section contains its own crisis and climax and that the rest of the story is really a resolution?

2. What do you learn in the first section about the conflict in the attitudes of the narrator? What is his attitude about "civilization"? What values make him think this way? If he is the protagonist, who or what is the antagonist?

3. What does the narrator mean by saying, "I am alone; alone but not nearly so lonely as I was back on the campus at school"?

4. What is meant by the dancing of the blue winds—what kind of wisdom? What is the place for such wisdom in a computerized, industrialized society?

WRITING ABOUT THE PLOT OF A STORY

An essay about plot is an analysis of the conflict and its developments. The organization should not be modeled on sequential sections and principal events, because these invite only a retelling of the story. Instead, the organization should develop out of the important elements of conflict. Ask yourself the following questions as you look for ideas about plot for your essay.

Questions for Discovering Ideas

What is the conflict? How is it embodied in the work?

Who are the protagonist and antagonist, and how do their characteristics and interests involve them in the conflict?

If the conflict stems out of contrasting ideas or values, what are these, and how are they brought out?

Does the major character face a dilemma of any sort?

Do the characters reach their goals? Why or why not?

As a result of the outcome, are the characters successful or unsuccessful, happy or dissatisfied?

Strategies for Organizing Ideas

To keep your essay reasonably brief, you will need to be selective about what you discuss. Rather than detailing everything a character does, for example, stress the major elements in his or her conflict. Such an essay on Eudora Welty's "A Worn Path" might emphasize Phoenix as she encounters the various obstacles both in the wood and in town. When there is a conflict between two major characters, the obvious approach is to focus equally on both. For brevity, however, emphasis might be placed on just one. Thus, an essay on the plot of "The Blue Hotel" might stress the things we learn about the Swede that are important to his being a major participant in the conflict.

In addition, the plot may be analyzed more broadly in terms of impulses, goals, values, issues, and historical perspectives. Thus, you might emphasize the elements of chance working against Mathilde in Maupassant's "The Necklace," as a contrast to her dreams about wealth. A discussion of the plot of Poe's "The Masque of Red Death" might stress the haughty pride of Prospero, the major character, because the plot could not develop without his egotism. In short, when you sketch out your ideas for the essay, you have liberty of choice.

The conclusion may contain a brief summary of the points you have made. Also, a study of plot often leaves out one of the most important reasons for reading, and that is the interest and *impact* produced by a conflict. Thus, the conclusion is a fitting location for a brief consideration of effect. Additional comments might focus on whether the author has arranged things to direct your favor toward one side or the other, or whether the plot is possible or impossible, serious or comic, fair or unfair, powerful or indifferent, and so on.

SAMPLE ESSAY

The Plot of Eudora Welty's "A Worn Path"°

[1]   At first, the complexity of Eudora Welty's plot in "A Worn Path" is not clear. The main character is Phoenix Jackson, an old, poor, and frail woman; the story seems to be no more than a record of her walk to Natchez through the woods from her rural home. By the story's end, however, the plot is clear: It consists of the brave attempts of a courageous, valiant woman to carry on against overwhelming forces.* Her determination despite the great odds against her gives the story its impact. The powers ranged against her are old age, poverty, environment, and illness.†

[2]   Old age as a silent but overpowering antagonist is shown in signs of Phoenix's increasing senility. Not her mind but her feet tell her where to find the medical office in Natchez. Despite her inner strength, she is unable to explain her errand when the nursing attendant asks her. Instead she sits dumbly and unknowingly for a time, until "a flame of comprehension" comes across her face (paragraph 87). Against the power of advancing age, Phoenix is slowly losing. The implication is that soon she will lose entirely.

[3]   An equally crushing opponent is her poverty. She cannot afford to ride to town, but must walk. She has no money, and acquires her ten cents for the paper windmill by stealing and begging. The "soothing medicine" she gets for her grandson (paragraph 92) is given to her out of charity. Despite the boy's need for advanced medical care, she has no money to provide it, and the story therefore shows that her guardianship is doomed.

[4]   Closely connected to her poverty is the way through the woods, which during her walk seems to be an almost active opponent. The long hill tires her, the thornbush catches her clothes, the log endangers her balance as she crosses the creek, and the barbed-wire fence threatens to puncture her skin. Another danger on her way is the stray dog, which topples her over. Apparently not afraid, however, Phoenix carries on a cheerful monologue:

> "Out of my way, all you foxes, owls, beetles, jack rabbits, coons and wild animals! . . . Keep out from under these feet, little bobwhites. . . . Keep the big wild hogs out of my path. Don't let none of these come running my direction. I got a long way." (paragraph 3)

She prevails for the moment as she enters Natchez, but all the hazards of her walk are still there, waiting for her to return.

    The force against Phoenix which shows her plight most clearly and

---

° See p. 119 for this story.
* Central idea.
† Thesis sentence.

[5] pathetically is her grandson's incurable illness. His condition highlights her helplessness, for she is his only support. Her difficulties would be enough for one person alone, but with the grandson the odds against her are doubled. Despite her care, there is nothing anyone can do for the grandson but take the long worn path to get something to help him endure his pain.

[6] This brief description of the conflicts in "A Worn Path" only hints at the story's great power. Welty layers the details to bring out the full range of the conditions against Phoenix, who cannot win despite her determination and devotion. The most hopeless fact, the condition of the invalid grandson, is not revealed until she reaches the medical office, and this delayed final revelation makes one's heart go out to her. The plot is strong because it is so real, and Phoenix is a pathetic but memorable protagonist struggling against overwhelming odds.

Commentary on the Essay

The strategy of this essay is to explain the elements of plot in "A Worn Path" selectively, without duplicating the story's narrative order. Thus, the third aspect of conflict, the woods, might be introduced first if the story's narrative order were to be followed, but it is deferred while the more personal elements of old age and poverty are considered first. It is important to note that the essay does not consider other characters as part of Phoenix's conflict, for the other persons are helpful. Rather Phoenix's antagonist takes the shape of impersonal and unconquerable forces, like the grandson's illness.

Paragraph 1 briefly describes how one's first impressions are changed by the story's end. The thesis sentence anticipates the body by listing the four topics about to be treated. Paragraph 2 concerns Phoenix's old age; paragraph 3, her poverty; paragraph 4, the woods; and paragraph 5, her grandson's illness. The concluding paragraph (6) points out that in this set of conflicts the protagonist cannot win, except as she lives out her duty and her devotion to help her grandson. Continuing the theme of the introduction, the last paragraph also accounts for the power of the plot: By building up to Phoenix's personal affirmation against unbeatable forces, the story evokes sympathy and admiration.

WRITING ABOUT STRUCTURE IN A STORY

Your essay will be concerned with arrangement and shape. In form, the essay should not follow the part-by-part unfolding of the narrative or argument. Rather it should explain why things are where they are: "Why is this here and not there?" is the fundamental question you need to answer. Thus, it is possible to begin with a consideration of a work's crisis, and then to consider how the exposition and complication have built up to it. A vital piece of information, for example, might have been withheld in the earlier exposition (as in Jackson's "The Lottery" and Welty's "A Worn Path"), but delayed until the crisis; thus, the crisis might be heightened because there would have been less suspense if the detail had been introduced earlier. Consider the following questions as you examine the story's structure.

Questions for Discovering Ideas

Is the story structured around places, times, or events? Why?

Is the story divided into sections or parts? What are the differences among the parts? What purpose does the division serve?

Does the structure of the story depart in major ways from the formal structure of exposition, complication, crisis, climax, and resolution? What purpose do any departures serve?

Are there departures from chronological order, for example, flashbacks? What effect is achieved by the use of flashbacks?

Are any crucial details of exposition held back to achieve a certain purpose?

About a major part or important action (such as the climax): Where does it begin? End? How is it related to the other formal structural elements, such as the crisis? Is the climax an action, a realization, or a decision? To what degree does it relieve the work's tension? What is the effect of the climax on your understanding of the characters involved in it? How is this effect related to the arrangement of the climax?

Strategies for Organizing Ideas

Your essay should discuss why a story is arranged the way it is—to reveal the nature of a character's situation, or to create surprise, or to bring out maximum humor.

Your essay can also discuss the structure of no more than a part of the story, such as the climax, or the complication.

In either case, the essay is best developed in concert or agreement with what the work contains. The location of scenes is an obvious organizing element. Thus, an essay on the structure of "A Worn Path" might be based on the countryside, the town, and the medical building, where the actions of the story occur. Hawthorne's "Young Goodman Brown" and Mansfield's "Miss Brill" both take place outside (a dark forest for one and a sunny public park for the other). Maupassant's "The Necklace" begins in interiors and concludes outdoors. The locations of Updike's "A & P" are the aisles and the checkout counter of a supermarket. A structural study of any of these works might be based on these locations and their effect on the plot.

Other ways to consider structure may be derived from a work's notable aspects, such as the growing suspense and horrible conclusion of Jackson's "The Lottery," and the mystery about the father's mysterious habit in Weidman's "My Father Sits in the Dark."

In the conclusion, you may highlight the main parts of your essay. Also, you may deal briefly with the relationship of structure to the plot. If the work you have analyzed departs from chronological order, you might stress the effects of this departure. Your aim should be to focus on the success of the work as it has been brought about by the author's choices in development.

SAMPLE ESSAY

The Structure of Eudora Welty's "A Worn Path"[°]

[1] On the surface, Eudora Welty's "A Worn Path" is structured simply. The narrative is not difficult to follow, and things move sequentially. The main character is Phoenix Jackson, an old and poor woman. She walks from her rural home in Mississippi through the woods to Natchez to get a free bottle of medicine for her grandson, who is a hopeless invalid. Everything takes place in just a few hours. This action is only the frame, however, for a skillfully and powerfully structured plot.[*] The masterly control of structure is shown in the story's locations, and in the way in which the delayed revelation produces both mystery and complexity.[†]

[2] The locations in the story coincide with the increasing difficulties faced by Phoenix. The first and most obvious worn path is the rural woods with all its natural difficulties. For most people the obstacles would not be challenging, but for an old woman they are formidable. In Natchez, the location of the next part of the story, Phoenix's inability to bend over to tie her shoe demonstrates the lack of flexibility of old age. In the medical office, where the final scene takes place, two major difficulties of the plot are brought out. One is Phoenix's increasing senility, and the other is the disclosure that her grandson is an incurable invalid. This set of oppositions, the major conflicts in the plot, thus coincide with locations or scenes and show the strength of the forces opposing Phoenix.

[3] The most powerful of these conditions, the revelation about the grandson, makes the story something like a mystery. Because this detail is delayed until the end, the reader wonders for most of the story what bad thing might happen next. In fact, some parts of the story are false leads. For example, the episode with the hunter's dog is threatening, but it leads nowhere; Phoenix, with the aid of the hunter, is unharmed. That she picks up and keeps the hunter's dropped nickel might seem at first to be cause for punishment. In fact, she thinks it is, as this scene with the hunter shows:

> . . . he laughed and lifted his gun and pointed it at Phoenix.
> She stood straight and faced him.
> "Doesn't the gun scare you?" he said, still pointing it.
> "No, sir, I seen plenty go off closer by, in my day, and for less than what I done," she said, holding utterly still. (paragraphs 55–58)

[°] See p. 119 for this story.
[*] Central idea.
[†] Thesis sentence.

But the young hunter does not notice that the coin is missing, and he does not accuse her. Right up to the moment she enters the medical building, therefore, the reader is still wondering what might happen.

[4] Hence the details about the grandson, carefully concealed until the end, make the story more complex than it at first seems. Because of this concluding revelation, the reader must do a double take, and reconsider what has gone on before. Phoenix's difficult walk into town must be seen not as an ordinary errand but as a hopeless mission of mercy. Her character also bears reevaluation: She is not just a funny old woman who speaks to the woods and animals, but a brave and pathetic woman carrying on against crushing odds. These conclusions are not apparent for most of the story, and the late emergence of the carefully concealed details makes "A Worn Path" both forceful and powerful.

[5] Thus, the parts of "A Worn Path," while seemingly simple, are skillfully arranged. The key to the double take and reevaluation is Welty's withholding of the crucial detail of exposition until the very end. The result is that parts of the exposition and complication, through the speeches of the attendant and the nurse, merge with the climax near the story's end. In some respects, the detail makes it seem as though Phoenix's entire existence is a crisis, although she is not aware of this condition as she leaves the office to buy the paper windmill. It is this complex buildup and emotional peak that make the structure of "A Worn Path" the creation of a master writer.

Commentary on the Essay

To highlight the differences between essays on plot and structure, the topic of this sample essay is Welty's "A Worn Path," also analyzed in the sample essay on plot. While both essays are concerned with the conflicts of the story, the essay on plot concentrates on the opposing forces, whereas the essay on structure focuses on the placement and arrangement of the plot elements. Note that neither essay retells the story, event by event. Instead, these are analytical essays that explain the *conflict* (for plot) and the *arrangement and layout* (for structure). In both essays, the assumption is that the reader has read "A Worn Path"; hence, there is no need in the essay to tell the story again.

The introductory paragraph points out that the masterly structure accounts for the story's power. Paragraph 2 develops the topic that the geographical locations are arranged climactically to demonstrate the forces against the major character. Paragraph 3 considers how the delayed exposition about the grandson creates uncertainty about the issues and direction of the story. As supporting evidence, the paragraph cites two important details—the danger from the hunter's dog and the theft of his nickel—as structural false leads about Phoenix's troubles. Paragraph 4 deals with the complexity brought about by the delayed information: the necessary reevaluation of Phoenix's character and her mission to town. The concluding paragraph also considers this complexity, accounting for the story's power by pointing out how a number of plot elements merge near the end to bring things out swiftly and powerfully.

WRITING TOPICS

1. Compare "Everyday Use" (Chapter 2) and "Blue Winds Dancing" as stories developing plots about clashing social and racial values. In what ways are the plots similar and different?

2. What kind of story might "A Worn Path" be, structurally, if the detail about the invalid grandson were introduced at the start, before Phoenix begins her walk to town?

3. Compare the structuring of interior or exterior scenes in "The Blue Hotel," "A Worn Path," and "Blue Winds Dancing." How do these scenes bring out the various conflicts of the stories? How do characters in the interiors contribute to plot developments? What is the relationship of these characters to the major themes of the stories?

4. Select a circumstance in your life which caused you doubt, difficulty, and conflict. Making yourself anonymous (give yourself a fictitious name and fictitious location), write a brief *story* about the occasion, stressing how your conflict began, how it affected you, and how you resolved it. You might choose to describe the details in chronological order, or you might begin the story in the present tense, and introduce details in flashback.

4

Characters:
The People in Stories

Character in fiction is an extended verbal representation of a human being—the complex combination of both the inner and the outer self. Through action, speech, description, and commentary, authors portray characters who are worth caring about, rooting for, and even loving, although there are also characters at whom you may laugh or whom you may dislike or even hate.

In a story about a major character, you may expect that each action or speech, no matter how small, is part of a total portrait. Whereas in life things may "just happen," in stories all actions, interactions, speeches, and observations are deliberate. Thus, you read about important actions like a long period of work and sacrifice (Maupassant's "The Necklace"), the taking of a regular journey of mercy (Welty's "A Worn Path"), the first solo airplane flight around the world (Thurber's "The Greatest Man in the World"), or a young boy's disobedience of his father (Faulkner's "Barn Burning"). By making such actions interesting, authors help you understand and appreciate their major characters, the ones involved in the actions.

MAJOR CHARACTER TRAITS

In studying a literary character, you should determine the character's major **trait** or **traits.** A trait is a quality of mind or habitual mode of behavior, such as never repaying borrowed money, or avoiding eye contact, or always thinking oneself the center of attention. Often, traits are minor and therefore negligible. But sometimes a trait may be a person's *primary* characteristic (not only in fiction but also in life). Thus, characters may be ambitious or lazy, serene or anxious, aggressive or fearful, thoughtful or inconsiderate, open or secretive, confident or self-doubting, kind or cruel, quiet or noisy, visionary or practical, careful or careless, evenhanded or biased, straightforward or underhanded, "winners" or "losers," and so on.

With this sort of list, to which you may add at will, you can analyze and develop conclusions about character. For example, in studying Mathilde Loisel of Maupassant's "The Necklace" (pp. 5–12), you would note that at the beginning she dreams of unattainable wealth and comfort, and that she is so swept up in her visions that she scorns her comparatively good life with her reliable but dull husband. It is fair to say that this aversion to reality is her major trait. It is also a major weakness, because Maupassant shows how her dream life destroys her real life. By contrast, the narrator of Weidman's "My Father Sits in the Dark" describes how his father's mysterious musings in the darkened house form connections with a lost home and a vanished past. The trait indicates not a weakness of character, but rather strength and determination. By similarly analyzing the actions, speeches, and thoughts in the characters you encounter, you can draw conclusions about their qualities and strengths.

CIRCUMSTANCES VERSUS TRAITS

When you study a fictional person, distinguish between circumstances and character, for circumstances have value *only if they demonstrate important traits.* Thus, if Sam wins a lottery, this is very nice, but the win does not say much about his traits—not much, that is, unless we also learn that he has been spending hundreds of dollars each week for lottery tickets. In other words, making the effort to win a lottery *is* a trait, while winning *is not.*

Or, let us suppose that an author stresses the neatness of one character and the sloppiness of another. If you accept the premise that people care for their appearance according to *choice*—and that choices indicate character—you can use these details as evidence for conclusions about self-esteem or the lack of it. When reading about fictional characters, in short, look beyond circumstances, actions, and appearances and *determine what these things show about character.* Always try to get from the outside to the inside, for it is the *internal* quality that determines the *external* behavior.

TYPES OF CHARACTERS: ROUND AND FLAT

Loosely, there are two kinds of fictional characters. E. M. Forster, in *Aspects of the Novel,* calls them "round" and "flat."

Round Characters.   The basic trait of **round characters** is that they *recognize, change with,* or *adjust to* circumstances—a quality that in real life is vital to mental health. The round character—usually the major one in a story—profits from experience and undergoes a change or alteration, which may take the narrative form of (1) the performance of a particular action, (2) the realization of new strength and therefore the affirmation of previous decisions, (3) the acceptance of a new condition, or (4) the realization of previously unrecognized truths.

Round characters are relatively fully developed. For this reason, if they are also the major characters in a story, they are often given the names **hero** or **heroine.** Because many major characters are anything but heroic, however, it is preferable to use the more neutral word **protagonist**, which implies only that a character is a focus of attention, not a moral or physical giant. The protagonist is central to the action, moves against an **antagonist,** and exhibits the ability to adapt to new circumstances.

To the degree that round characters are individual and sometimes unpredictable, and because they undergo change or growth, they are **dynamic.** Minnie Wright, of Glaspell's "A Jury of Her Peers," is a case in point. We learn that as a young woman she was happy and musical, but that her marriage of twenty years deprives her and blights her. Finally, one outrageous action by her husband so enrages her that she breaks out of her subservient role and strangles him in his sleep. Her action shows her as a character undergoing radical, *dynamic* change.

Obviously, round characters are central to serious fiction, for they are the focus of conflict and interest. They may lead no more than ordinary lives, and they may face no more than the common problems of living, but they are real and human because they grow as they face their struggles. Admittedly, in brief stories we cannot learn everything there is to know, but skillful authors give us enough details to enable us to understand the dynamic processes by which round characters develop.

Flat Characters. As contrasted with round characters, **flat characters** do not grow. They remain the same because they are stupid or insensitive, or lack knowledge or insight. They end where they begin, and are **static,** not dynamic. But flat characters are not therefore worthless, for they usually highlight the development of the round characters, as with Paul's father in Cather's "Paul's Case." Usually, flat characters are minor (e.g., relatives, acquaintances, functionaries), although not all minor characters are necessarily flat.

Sometimes flat characters are prominent in certain types of literature, such as cowboy, police, and detective stories, where the focus is less on character than on performance. Such characters might be lively and engaging, even though they do not develop or change. They must be strong, tough, and clever enough to perform recurring tasks like solving crimes, overcoming villains, or finding treasures. The term **stock character** refers to characters in these repeating situations, and, to the degree that stock characters have many common traits, they are **representative** of their class, or group. Such characters, with variations in names, ages, sexes, and locations, have been constant in literature almost from the very beginnings of culture. Some regular stock characters are the insensitive father, the interfering mother, the sassy younger sister or brother, the greedy politician, the resourceful cowboy or detective, the overbearing or harassed husband, the submissive or domineering wife, the angry police captain, the lovable drunk, and the town do-gooder.

Stock characters stay flat as long as they perform only their functions and exhibit conventional and unindividual traits. When they possess no attitudes except those of their class, they are given the label **stereotype**, because they all seem to come from the same mold.

When authors bring characters into focus, however, no matter what roles they may perform, they emerge from flatness and move into roundness. For example, to most of us, checkout clerks in a grocery store are little more than flat functionaries, but Sammy, who has such a job in Updike's "A & P," is not flat, but round, because Updike shows how an incident at the checkout counter causes him to grow. Minnie Wright of "A Jury of Her Peers," as we have seen, leads an ordinary, dull life for most of her years—a flat role—but we see that dynamic processes cause her to break out of her stock role to murder her oppressor, her husband. Sarty, of "Barn Burning," is just a little boy, but he grows morally in the face of his father's revengeful custom of burning the barns of people with power over him. It is growth or development—or the absence of it—that makes characters either round or flat.

HOW IS CHARACTER DISCLOSED IN FICTION?

Authors use five distinct ways to present information about characters. Remember that you must use your own knowledge and experience to make judgments about the qualities of the characters being revealed.

1. *What the characters do.* Most commonly, authors illuminate their characters by putting them in action. What they *do*, along with the circumstances in which they do it, is our best way to understand what they *are*. For example, walking in the woods is simple recreation for most people, and it shows little about their characters. But Phoenix's walk through the woods (Welty's "A Worn Path") is a necessity that is difficult and dangerous for her. Thus, her walk, granted her age and her mission, may be taken as an expression of a loving, responsible character. Similar strength may be seen when a character faces psychological difficulties, as in Joy Williams's "Taking Care." Everything goes badly for Jones, the central character. His wife is dying, his daughter is dropping out from life, and his own religious faith is waning. Despite these incentives to

despair, however, he preserves his caring and loving role. The result is a character portrayal of enormous strength and poignancy.

As with ordinary human beings, fictional characters do not necessarily understand why they do the things they do, or articulate to themselves the ways their characters develop. Thus, Paul of "Paul's Case" goes on a week of high living with the money he has stolen from his employers. All his actions would be ordinary for a wealthy young man indulging his taste for the high things of life, but since Paul has no money of his own, they demonstrate his total departure from reality. When he faces the truth, he does not try to explain things to himself or to adjust to his real circumstances, but rather he commits suicide.

Actions may also signal qualities such as naiveté, weakness, deceit, a scheming personality, strong inner conflicts, or a realization or growth of some sort. Most of the actions of Abner Snopes in Faulkner's "Barn Burning" indicate a character of suspicion and resentment. A strong inner conflict and almost immediate growth may be seen in the two women in Glaspell's "A Jury of Her Peers." They have an obligation to the law, but they feel a stronger obligation to the accused killer, Minnie Wright. Hence they cover up their evidence even though they know beyond doubt that she is the murderer. That they form their own jury for acquittal indicates their roundness and depth.

2. *How the characters are described—both their persons and the environment they control.* Appearance and environment reveal much about a character's social and economic status, of course, but they also tell us a lot about character traits. Willa Cather describes Paul's constant attention to his personal appearance and to the conditions of his rooms, in this way stressing his fastidiousness and his aloof wish to avoid the plainness of the world around him. The same desire for elegance is a trait of Mathilde Loisel of Maupassant's "The Necklace," though the consequences of her unrealizable taste do not destroy her, but bring out her strength of character. In Walker's "Everyday Use," the mother and younger daughter devote great care to the appearance of their poor and unpretentious house, and their self-esteem is shown in this care.

3. *What the characters themselves say (and think, if the author expresses their thoughts).* The speeches of most characters are functional, being essential to keep their respective stories moving along. But even so, you can draw conclusions about what characters say. When Jackie Smurch of "The Greatest Man in the World" speaks, for example, he reveals his self-inflated and greedy nature. The three men in "A Jury of Her Peers" speak straightforwardly and directly, and these speeches suggest that their characters are similarly orderly. That they constantly ridicule the concerns of the two women, however, indicates their limitations.

Often, characters use speech to hide their motives, though we as readers should see through them immediately. The old man in Collier's

"The Chaser," for example, is a schemer, and we learn this from his language. He hopes eventually to sell his death potion to his client, Alan Austen, and hence he speaks to the youthful and romantic young man indirectly and manipulatively. To Alan he seems concerned and helpful, but to us he is a cruel merchant of death.

4. *What other characters say about them.* By studying what characters say about each other, you get not only factual information, but also enhance your understanding of character. If you make the assumption that no speeches in a story are accidental, you can make a good deal out of such conversation. Thus, the two women talking about Phoenix's condition in "A Worn Path" tell us important facts about her difficult life, but more importantly they provide a basis for conclusions about Phoenix's great strength.

Sometimes a speaker's words may ironically indicate something other than what the speaker intends, perhaps because of prejudice, stupidity, or foolishness. Nora's words about Jackie in O'Connor's "First Confession," for example, really show that Jackie is a normal little boy, while they also show Nora's own limited judgment. In "Paul's Case," Paul's teachers indicate that Paul has been hurt by the "garish fiction" he reads. Their speech indicates their lack of understanding, for the narrator corrects them by telling us that Paul hardly reads any fiction at all. In short, we learn from their incorrect analysis that Paul's serious mental troubles do not yield to easy explanations. The actresses in the local theater company, though less educated, are more accurate in their assessment, for they conclude that Paul's is indeed a "bad case."

5. *What the author says about them, speaking as storyteller or observer.* What the author, speaking with the authorial voice, says about a character is usually accurate, and the authorial voice is naturally to be accepted factually. However, when the authorial voice *interprets* actions and characteristics, as in Hawthorne's "Young Goodman Brown," the author himself or herself assumes the role of a reader or critic, and any opinions may be questioned. For this reason, authors frequently avoid interpretations and devote their skill to arranging events and speeches so that readers may draw their own conclusions.

REALITY AND PROBABILITY: VERISIMILITUDE

You are entitled to expect fictional characters to be true to life. That is, their actions, statements, and thoughts must all be what human beings are *likely* to do, say, and think under the conditions presented in the work. This expectation is often called the standard of **verisimilitude, probability,** or **plausibility.** That is, there are persons *in life* who easily do difficult or even impossible things (such as always being cheerful, or always understanding the needs of others). Such characters *in fiction* would not be true to life, however, because they do not fit within *normal* or *usual* behavior.

One should therefore distinguish between what characters may *possibly* do and what they *most frequently* or *most usually* do. Thus, in Maupassant's "The Necklace," it is possible that Mathilde could be truthful and tell her friend Jeanne Forrestier about the lost necklace. In light of her pride, honor, shame, and respectability, however, it is more in character for her and her husband to hide the fact, borrow money to buy a replacement necklace, and endure the ten-year penance to pay back the loans. Granted the possibilities of the story (either self-sacrifice or the admission of a fault), the decision she makes with her husband is the more *probable* one.

Nevertheless, probability does not rule out surprises or even exaggeration. It is not unreasonable that young Sarty would try to inform on his father in Faulkner's "Barn Burning," because he has been developing a sense of morality throughout the story. Nor do the monumental accomplishments of Granny, in Porter's "The Jilting of Granny Weatherall," seem impossible, such as having fenced 100 acres of farming land all by herself. We learn that when she was young, she developed a strong sense of determination and obligation to lead a normal life despite having been betrayed by her unfaithful lover. It is therefore not improbable that she would do everything she could to further this goal.

There are many ways of rendering probability in character. Works that attempt to mirror life—realistic, naturalistic, or "slice of life" stories like Welty's "A Worn Path"—set up the expectation that life is played out within the limits of everyday probability. Less realistic conditions establish different frameworks of probability, in which characters are *expected* to be unusual. Such an example may be seen in Hawthorne's "Young Goodman Brown." Because this story's premise or donnée is that Brown is having a nightmarish psychotic trance, his bizarre and unnatural responses are probable, just as Phoenix Jackson's speeches, influenced as they are by her approaching senility, are probable in "A Worn Path."

You might also encounter works containing *supernatural* figures, like the visiting boy in Pickthall's "The Worker in Sandalwood" and the woodland guide in "Young Goodman Brown." You may wonder whether such characters are probable or improbable. Usually, gods and goddesses like the little boy embody qualities of the best and most moral human beings, and devils like Hawthorne's guide take on attributes of the worst. However, you might remember that the devil is often given dashing and engaging qualities so that he may deceive gullible sinners and lead them into hell. The friendliness of Brown's guide is therefore a probable trait. In judging characters of this or any type, your best guide is probability, consistency, and believability.

WILLA CATHER   (1873–1947)

Paul's Case   *1905 (1904)*

A Study in Temperament

It was Paul's afternoon to appear before the faculty of the Pittsburgh High School to account for his various misdemeanors. He had been suspended a week ago, and his father had called at the Principal's office and confessed his perplexity about his son. Paul entered the faculty room suave and smiling. His clothes were a trifle outgrown, and the tan velvet on the collar of his open overcoat was frayed and worn; but for all that there was something of the dandy about him, and he wore an opal pin in his neatly knotted black four-in-hand, and a red carnation in his buttonhole. This latter adornment the faculty somehow felt was not properly significant of the contrite spirit befitting a boy under the ban of suspension.

Paul was tall for his age and very thin, with high, cramped shoulders and a narrow chest. His eyes were remarkable for a certain hysterical brilliancy, and he continually used them in a conscious, theatrical sort of way, peculiarly offensive in a boy. The pupils were abnormally large, as though he were addicted to bella-donna, but there was a glassy glitter about them which that drug does not produce.

When questioned by the Principal as to why he was there, Paul stated, politely enough, that he wanted to come back to school. This was a lie, but Paul was quite accustomed to lying; found it, indeed, indispensable for overcoming friction. His teachers were asked to state their respective charges against him, which they did with such a rancor and aggrievedness as evinced that this was not a usual case. Disorder and impertinence were among the offenses named, yet each of his instructors felt that it was scarcely possible to put into words the real cause of the trouble, which lay in a sort of hysterically defiant manner of the boy's; in the contempt which they all knew he felt for them, and which he seemingly made not the least effort to conceal. Once, when he had been making a synopsis of a paragraph at the blackboard, his English teacher had stepped to his side and attempted to guide his hand. Paul had started back with a shudder and thrust his hands violently behind him. The astonished woman could scarcely have been more hurt and embarrassed had he struck at her. The insult was so involuntary and definitely personal as to be unforgettable. In one way and another, he had made all his teachers, men and women alike, conscious of the same feeling of physical aversion. In one class he habitually sat with his hand shading his eyes; in another he always looked out of the window during the recitation; in another he made a running commentary on the lecture, with humorous intent.

His teachers felt this afternoon that his whole attitude was symbolized by his shrug and his flippantly red carnation flower, and they fell upon him without mercy, his English teacher leading the pack. He stood through it smiling, his pale lips parted over his white teeth. (His lips were continually twitching, and he had a habit of raising his eyebrows that was contemptuous and irritating to the last degree.) Older boys than Paul had broken down and shed tears under that ordeal, but his set smile did not once desert him, and his only sign of discomfort was the nervous trembling of the fingers that toyed with the buttons of his overcoat, and an occasional jerking of the other hand which held his hat. Paul was always smiling, always glancing about him, seeming to feel that people might be watching him and trying to detect something. This conscious expression, since it was as far as possible from boyish mirthfulness, was usually attributed to insolence or "smartness."

As the inquisition proceeded, one of his instructors repeated an impertinent remark of the boy's, and the Principal asked him whether he thought that a courteous speech to make to a woman. Paul shrugged his shoulders slightly and his eyebrows twitched.

"I don't know," he replied, "I didn't mean to be polite or impolite, either. I guess it's a sort of way I have, of saying things regardless."

The Principal asked him whether he didn't think that a way it would be well to get rid of. Paul grinned and said he guessed so. When he was told that he could go, he bowed gracefully and went out. His bow was like a repetition of the scandalous red carnation.

His teachers were in despair, and his drawing master voiced the feeling of them all when he declared there was something about the boy which none of them understood. He added "I don't really believe that smile of his comes altogether from insolence; there's something sort of haunted about it. The boy is not strong, for one thing. There is something wrong about the fellow."

The drawing master had come to realize that, in looking at Paul, one saw only his white teeth and the forced animation of his eyes. One warm afternoon the boy had gone to sleep at his drawing board, and his master had noted with amazement what a white, blue-veined face it was; drawn and wrinkled like an old man's about the eyes, the lips twitching even in his sleep.

His teachers left the building dissatisfied and unhappy; humiliated to have felt so vindictive toward a mere boy, to have uttered this feeling in cutting terms, and to have set each other on, as it were, in the gruesome game of intemperate reproach. One of them remembered having seen a miserable street cat set at bay by a ring of tormentors.

As for Paul, he ran down the hill whistling the Soldiers' Chorus from *Faust,*° looking wildly behind him now and then to see whether some of his teachers were not there to witness his light-heartedness. As it was now late in the afternoon and Paul was on duty that evening as usher at Carnegie Hall,° he decided that he would not go home to supper.

When he reached the concert hall the doors were not yet open. It was chilly outside, and he decided to go up into the picture gallery—always deserted at this hour—where there were some of Raffaëlli's° gay studies of Paris streets and an airy blue Venetian scene or two that always exhilarated him. He was delighted to find no one in the gallery but the old guard, who sat in the corner, a newspaper on his knee, a black patch over one eye and the other closed. Paul possessed himself of the place and walked confidently up and down, whistling under his breath. After a while he sat down before a blue Rico° and lost himself. When he bethought him to look at his watch, it was after seven o'clock, and he rose with a

---

Faust: the most popular opera of Charles Gounod (1818–1893), first produced in 1859.

Carnegie Hall: in Pittsburgh, not the more famous one in New York.

Raffaëlli: Jean-François Rafaëlli (1850–1924), impressionist painter, sculptor, and engraver, known for his scenes of Parisian life.

Rico: Martin Rico (1833–1908). Spanish painter, known for his landscapes.

start and ran downstairs, making a face at Augustus Caesar,° peering out from the cast-room, and an evil gesture at the Venus of Milo° as he passed her on the stairway.

When Paul reached the ushers' dressing-room half a dozen boys were there already, and he began excitedly to tumble into his uniform. It was one of the few that at all approached fitting, and Paul thought it very becoming—though he knew the tight, straight coat accentuated his narrow chest, about which he was exceedingly sensitive. He was always excited while he dressed, twanging all over to the tuning of the strings and preliminary flourishes of the horns in the music-room; but tonight he seemed quite beside himself, and he teased and plagued the boys until, telling him that he was crazy, they put him down on the floor and sat on him.

Somewhat calmed by his suppression, Paul dashed out to the front of the house to seat the early comers. He was a model usher. Gracious and smiling he ran up and down the aisles. Nothing was too much trouble for him; he carried messages and brought programs as though it were his greatest pleasure in life, and all the people in his section thought him a charming boy, feeling that he remembered and admired them. As the house filled, he grew more and more vivacious and animated, and the color came to his cheeks and lips. It was very much as though this were a great reception and Paul were the host. Just as the musicians came out to take their places, his English teacher arrived with checks for the seats which a prominent manufacturer had taken for the season. She betrayed some embarrassment when she handed Paul the tickets, and a *hauteur* which subsequently made her feel very foolish. Paul was startled for a moment and had the feeling of wanting to put her out; what business had she here among all these fine people and gay colors? He looked her over and decided that she was not appropriately dressed and must be a fool to sit downstairs in such togs. The tickets had probably been sent her out of kindness, he reflected, as he put down a seat for her, and she had about as much right to sit there as he had.

When the symphony began Paul sank into one of the rear seats with a long   15
sigh of relief, and lost himself as he had done before the Rico. It was not that symphonies, as such, meant anything in particular to Paul, but the first sigh of the instruments seemed to free some hilarious spirit within him; something that struggled there like the Genius in the bottle found by the Arab fisherman.° He felt a sudden zest of life; the lights danced before his eyes and the concert hall blazed into unimaginable splendor. When the soprano soloist came on, Paul forgot even the nastiness of his teacher's being there, and gave himself up to the peculiar intoxication such personages always had for him. The soloist chanced to be a German woman, by no means in her first youth, and the mother of many children; but she wore a satin gown and a tiara, and she had that indefinable air of achievement, that world-shine upon her, which always blinded Paul to any possible defects.

After a concert was over, Paul was often irritable and wretched until he got to sleep—and tonight he was even more than usually restless. He had the feeling of not being able to let down; of its being impossible to give up this delicious

Caesar . . . Milo: copies of the famous statues of Augustus in the Vatican Museum and the Venus de Milo in the Louvre.

Arab fisherman: reference to the tale of "The Fisherman and the Jinni" from *The Arabian Nights.*

excitement which was the only thing that could be called living at all. During the last number he withdrew and, after hastily changing his clothes in the dressing-room, slipped out to the side door where the singer's carriage stood. Here he began pacing rapidly up and down the walk, waiting to see her come out.

Over yonder the Schenley, in its vacant stretch, loomed big and square through the fine rain, the windows of its twelve stories glowing like those of a lighted cardboard house under a Christmas tree. All the actors and singers of any importance stayed there when they were in the city, and a number of the big manufacturers of the place lived there in the winter. Paul had often hung about the hotel, watching the people go in and out, longing to enter and leave schoolmasters and dull care° behind him forever.

At last the singer came out, accompanied by the conductor, who helped her into her carriage and closed the door with a cordial *auf Wiedersehen*,°—which set Paul to wondering whether she were not an old sweetheart of his. Paul followed the carriage over to the hotel, walking so rapidly as not to be far from the entrance when the singer alighted and disappeared behind the swinging glass doors which were opened by a Negro in a tall hat and a long coat. In the moment that the door was ajar, it seemed to Paul that he, too, entered. He seemed to feel himself go after her up the steps, into the warm, lighted building, into an exotic, a tropical world of shiny, glistening surfaces and basking ease. He reflected upon the mysterious dishes that were brought into the dining-room, the green bottles in buckets of ice, as he had seen them in the supper party pictures of the Sunday supplement. A quick gust of wind brought the rain down with sudden vehemence, and Paul was startled to find that he was still outside in the slush of the gravel driveway; that his boots were letting in the water and his scanty overcoat was clinging wet about him; that the lights in front of the concert hall were out, and that the rain was driving in sheets between him and the orange glow of the windows above him. There it was, what he wanted—tangibly before him, like the fairy world of Christmas pantomime; as the rain beat in his face, Paul wondered whether he were destined always to shiver in the black night outside looking up at it.

He turned and walked reluctantly toward the car° tracks. The end had to come some time; his father in his night-clothes at the top of the stairs, explanations that did not explain, hastily improvised fictions that were forever tripping him up, his upstairs room and its horrible yellow wallpaper, the creaking bureau with the greasy plush collar-box, and over his painted wooden bed the pictures of George Washington and John Calvin,° and the framed motto, "Feed my Lambs,"° which had been worked in red worsted by his mother, whom Paul could not remember.

Half an hour later, Paul alighted from the Negley Avenue car and went slowly down one of the side streets off the main thoroughfare. It was a highly respectable street, where all the houses were exactly alike, and where business men of moderate means begot and reared large families of children, all of whom   20

dull care: phrase from the popular seventeenth-century song "Begone, Dull Care."
auf Wiedersehen: German for "goodbye" (literally "until the seeing again").
car: streetcar.
John Calvin: John Calvin (1509–1564), a major theologian of the early Reformation in Switzerland.
"Feed my Lambs:" See John 21:15–17.

went to Sabbath-school and learned the shorter catechism, and were interested in arithmetic; all of whom were as exactly alike as their homes, and of a piece with the monotony in which they lived. Paul never went up Cordelia Street without a shudder of loathing. His home was next to the house of the Cumberland° minister. He approached it tonight with the nerveless sense of defeat, the hopeless feeling of sinking back forever into ugliness and commonness that he had always had when he came home. The moment he turned into Cordelia Street he felt the waters close above his head. After each of these orgies of living, he experienced all the physical depression which follows a debauch; the loathing of respectable beds, of common food, of a house permeated by kitchen odors; a shuddering repulsion for the flavorless, colorless mass of everyday existence; a morbid desire for cool things and soft lights and fresh flowers.

The nearer he approached the house, the more absolutely unequal Paul felt to the sight of it all: his ugly sleeping chamber, the cold bathroom with the grimy zinc tub, the cracked mirror, the dripping spiggots; his father, at the top of the stairs, his hairy legs sticking out from his nightshirt, his feet thrust into carpet slippers. He was so much later than usual that there would certainly be inquiries and reproaches. Paul stopped short before the door. He felt that he could not be accosted by his father tonight; that he could not toss again on that miserable bed. He would not go in. He would tell his father that he had no car fare, and it was raining so hard he had gone home with one of the boys and stayed all night.

Meanwhile, he was wet and cold. He went around to the back of the house and tried one of the basement windows, found it open, raised it cautiously, and scrambled down the cellar wall to the floor. There he stood, holding his breath, terrified by the noise he had made; but the floor above him was silent, and there was no creak on the stairs. He found a soap-box, and carried it over to the soft ring of light that streamed from the furnace door, and sat down. He was horribly afraid of rats, so he did not try to sleep, but sat looking distrustfully at the dark, still terrified lest he might have awakened his father. In such reactions, after one of the experiences which made days and nights out of the dreary blanks of the calendar, when his senses were deadened, Paul's head was always singularly clear. Suppose his father had heard him getting in at the window and had come down and shot him for a burglar? Then, again, suppose his father had come down, pistol in hand, and he had cried out in time to save himself, and his father had been horrified to think how nearly he had killed him? Then, again, suppose a day should come when his father would remember that night, and wish there had been no warning cry to stay his hand? With this last supposition Paul entertained himself until daybreak.

The following Sunday was fine; the sodden November chill was broken by the last flash of autumnal summer. In the morning Paul had to go to church and Sabbath-school, as always. On seasonable Sunday afternoons the burghers of Cordelia Street usually sat out on their front "stoops," and talked to their neighbors on the next stoop, or called to those across the street in neighborly fashion. The men sat placidly on gay cushions placed upon the steps that led down to the sidewalk, while the women, in their Sunday "waists,"° sat in rockers on the cramped

Cumberland: an independent, Evangelical branch of the Presbyterian Church, established in 1810.
waists: laced, close-fitting vests or jackets.

porches, pretending to be greatly at their ease. The children played in the streets; there were so many of them that the place resembled the recreation grounds of a kindergarten. The men on the steps—all in their shirt sleeves, their vests unbuttoned—sat with their legs well apart, their stomachs comfortably protruding, and talked of the prices of things, or told anecdotes of the sagacity of their various chiefs and overloads. They occasionally looked over the multitude of squabbling children, listened affectionately to their high-pitched, nasal voices, smiling to see their own proclivities reproduced in their offspring, and interspersed their legends of the iron kings with remarks about their son's progress at school, their grades in arithmetic, and the amounts they had saved in their toy banks. On this last Sunday of November, Paul sat all the afternoon on the lowest step of his "stoop," staring into the street, while his sisters, in their rockers, were talking to the minister's daughters next door about how many shirtwaists they had made in the last week, and how many waffles someone had eaten at the last church supper. When the weather was warm, and his father was in a particularly jovial frame of mind, the girls made lemonade, which was always brought out in a red-glass pitcher, ornamented with forget-me-nots in blue enamel. This the girls thought very fine, and the neighbors joked about the suspicious color of the pitcher.

Today Paul's father, on the top step, was talking to a young man who shifted a restless baby from knee to knee. He happened to be the young man who was daily held up to Paul as a model, and after whom it was his father's dearest hope that he would pattern. This young man was of a ruddy complexion, with a compressed, red mouth, and faded, near-sighted eyes, over which he wore thick spectacles, with gold bows that curved about his ears. He was clerk to one of the magnates of a great steel corporation, and was looked upon in Cordelia Street as a young man with a future. There was a story that, come five years ago—he was now barely twenty-six—he had been a trifle 'dissipated,' but in order to curb his appetites and save the loss of time and strength that a sowing of wild oats might have entailed, he had taken his chief's advice, oft reiterated to his employees, and at twenty-one had married the first woman whom he could persuade to share his fortunes. She happened to be an angular school mistress, much older than he, who also wore thick glasses, and who had now borne him four children, all nearsighted, like herself.

The young man was relating how his chief, now cruising in the Mediterranean, kept in touch with all the details of the business, arranging his office hours on his yacht just as though he were at home, and "knocking off work enough to keep two stenographers busy." His father told, in turn, the plan his corporation was considering, of putting in an electric railway plant at Cairo. Paul snapped his teeth; he had an awful apprehension that they might spoil it all before he got there. Yet he rather liked to hear these legends of the iron kings, that were told and retold on Sundays and holidays; these stories of palaces in Venice, yachts on the Mediterranean, and high play at Monte Carlo appealed to his fancy, and he was interested in the triumphs of cash boys° who had become famous, though he had no mind for the cash-boy stage. 25

After supper was over, and he had helped to dry the dishes, Paul nervously asked his father whether he could go to George's to get some help in his geometry,

cash boys: The Cash Boy, a novel by Horatio Alger (1832–1899), tells about the progress of a young boy from a $156 a year "cash boy" position to the inheritance of a million dollars.

and still more nervously asked for car fare. This latter request he had to repeat, as his father, on principle, did not like to hear requests for money, whether much or little. He asked Paul whether he could not go to some boy who lived nearer, and told him that he ought not to leave his school work until Sunday; but he gave him the dime. He was not a poor man, but he had a worthy ambition to come up in the world. His only reason for allowing Paul to usher was that he thought a boy ought to be earning a little.

Paul bounded upstairs, scrubbed the greasy odor of the dishwater from his hands with the ill-smelling soap he hated, and then shook over his fingers a few drops of violet water from the bottle he kept hidden in his drawer. He left the house with his geometry conspicuously under his arm, and the moment he got out of Cordelia Street and boarded a downtown car, he shook off the lethargy of two deadening days, and began to live again.

The leading juvenile of the permanent stock company which played at one of the downtown theaters was an acquaintance of Paul's, and the boy had been invited to drop in at the Sunday night rehearsals whenever he could. For more than a year Paul had spent every available moment loitering about Charley Edwards's dressing-room. He had won a place among Edwards's following not only because the young actor, who could not afford to employ a dresser, often found him useful, but because he recognized in Paul something akin to what churchmen term "vocation."

It was at the theater and at Carnegie Hall that Paul really lived; the rest was but a sleep and a forgetting.° This was Paul's fairy tale, and it had for him all the allurement of a secret love. The moment he inhaled the gassy, painty, dusty odor behind the scenes, he breathed like a prisoner set free, and felt within him the possibility of doing or saying splendid, brilliant things. The moment the cracked orchestra beat out the overture from *Martha*,° or jerked at the serenade from *Rigoletto*,° all stupid and ugly things slid from him, and his senses were deliciously, yet delicately fired.

Perhaps it was because, in Paul's world, the natural nearly always wore the guise of ugliness, that a certain element of artificiality seemed to him necessary in beauty. Perhaps it was because his experience of life elsewhere was so full of Sabbath-school picnics, petty economies, wholesome advice as to how to succeed in life, and the unescapable odors of cooking, that he found this existence so alluring, these smartly-clad men and women so attractive, that he was so moved by these starry apple orchards that bloomed perennially under the limelight.

It would be difficult to put it strongly enough how convincingly the stage entrance of that theater was for Paul the actual portal of Romance. Certainly none of the company ever suspected it, least of all Charley Edwards. It was very like the old stories that used to float about London of fabulously rich Jews, who had subterranean halls, with palms, and fountains, and soft lamps and richly apparelled women who never saw the disenchanting light of London day. So, in the midst of that smoke-palled city, enamored of figures and grimy toil, Paul had his secret

30

a sleep and a forgetting: from "Intimations of Immortality," an ode by William Wordsworth (1770–1850), published in 1807.

Martha: opera by Friedrich von Flotow (1812–1883), first performed in 1847, the source of "The Last Rose of Summer."

Rigoletto: one of the best known operas of Giuseppe Verdi (1813–1901), first performed in 1851.

temple, his wishing-carpet, his bit of blue-and-white Mediterranean shore bathed in perpetual sunshine.

Several of Paul's teachers had a theory that his imagination had been perverted by garish fiction; but the truth was, he scarcely ever read at all. The books at home were not such as would either tempt or corrupt a youthful mind, and as for reading the novels that some of his friends urged upon him—well, he got what he wanted much more quickly from music; any sort of music, from an orchestra to a barrel organ. He needed only the spark, the indescribable thrill that made his imagination master of his senses, and he could make plots and pictures enough of his own. It was equally true that he was not stage-struck—not, at any rate, in the usual acceptation of that expression. He had no desire to become an actor, any more than he had to become a musician. He felt no necessity to do any of these things; what he wanted was to see, to be in the atmosphere, float on the wave of it, to be carried out, blue league after blue league, away from everything.

After a night behind the scenes, Paul found the school-room more than ever repulsive; the bare floors and naked walls; the prosy men who never wore frock coats, or violets in their buttonholes; the women with their dull gowns, shrill voices, and pitiful seriousness about prepositions that govern the dative. He could not bear to have the other pupils think, for a moment, that he took these people seriously; he must convey to them that he considered it all trivial, and was there only by way of a joke, anyway. He had autographed pictures of all the members of the stock company which he showed to classmates, telling them the most incredible stories of his familiarity with these people, of his acquaintance with the soloists who came to Carnegie Hall, his suppers with them and the flowers he sent them. When these stories lost their effect, and his audience grew listless, he would bid all the boys good-by, announcing that he was going to travel for a while; going to Naples, to California, to Egypt. Then, next Monday, he would slip back, conscious and nervously smiling; his sister was ill, and he would have to defer his voyage until spring.

Matters went steadily worse with Paul at school. In the itch to let his instructors know how heartily he despised them, and how thoroughly he was appreciated elsewhere, he mentioned once or twice that he had no time to fool with theorems; adding—with a twitch of the eyebrows and a touch of that nervous bravado which so perplexed them—that he was helping the people down at the stock company; they were old friends of his.

The upshot of the matter was that the Principal went to Paul's father, and Paul was taken out of school and put to work. The manager at Carnegie Hall was told to get another usher in his stead; the door-keeper at the theater was warned not to admit him to the house; and Charley Edwards remorsefully promised the boy's father not to see him again.

The members of the stock company were vastly amused when some of Paul's stories reached them—especially the women. They were hard-working women, most of them supporting indolent husbands or brothers, and they laughed rather bitterly at having stirred the boy to such fervid and florid inventions. They agreed with the faculty and with his father, that Paul's was a bad case.

The east-bound train was plowing through a January snowstorm; the dull dawn was beginning to show gray when the engine whistled a mile out of Newark.°

Newark: New Jersey city within twenty miles of New York.

Paul started up from the seat where he had lain curled in uneasy slumber, rubbed the breath-misted window glass with his hand, and peered out. The snow was whirling in curling eddies above the white bottom lands, and the drifts lay already deep in the fields and along the fences, while here and there the long dead grass and dried weed stalks protruded black above it. Lights shone from the scattered houses, and a gang of laborers who stood beside the track waved their lanterns.

Paul had slept very little, and he felt grimy and uncomfortable. He had made the all-night journey in a day coach because he was afraid if he took a Pullman he might be seen by some Pittsburgh business man who had noticed him in Denny & Carson's office. When the whistle woke him, he clutched quickly at his breast pocket, glancing about him with an uncertain smile. But the little, clay-bespattered Italians were still sleeping, the slatternly women across the aisle were in open-mouthed oblivion, and even the crumby, crying babies were for the nonce stilled. Paul settled back to struggle with his impatience as best he could.

When he arrived at the Jersey City° station, he hurried through his breakfast, manifestly ill at ease and keeping a sharp eye about him. After he reached the Twenty-third Street station° he consulted a cabman, and had himself driven to a men's furnishing establishment which was just opening for the day. He spent upward of two hours there, buying with endless reconsidering and great care. His new street suit he put on in the fitting-room; the frock coat and dress clothes he had bundled into the cab with his new shirts. Then he drove to a hatter's and a shoe house. His next errand was at Tiffany's, where he selected silver-mounted brushes° and a scarf-pin. He would not wait to have his silver marked, he said. Lastly, he stopped at a trunk shop on Broadway, and had his purchases packed into various traveling bags.

It was a little after one o'clock when he drove up to the Waldorf, and, after settling with the cabman, went into the office. He registered from Washington; said his mother and father had been abroad, and that he had come down to await the arrival of their steamer. He told his story plausibly and had no trouble, since he offered to pay for them in advance, in engaging his rooms; a sleeping-room, sitting room and bath. 40

Not once, but a hundred times Paul had planned this entry into New York. He had gone over every detail of it with Charley Edwards, and in his scrap book at home there were pages of description about New York hotels, cut from the Sunday papers.

When he was shown to his sitting room on the eighth floor, he saw at a glance that everything was as it should be; there was but one detail in his mental picture that the place did not realize, so he rang for the bell boy and sent him down for flowers. He moved about nervously until the boy returned, putting away his new linen and fingering it delightedly as he did so. When the flowers came, he put them hastily into water, and then tumbled into a hot bath. Presently he came out of his white bathroom, resplendent in his new silk underwear, and playing with the tassels of his red robe. The snow was whirling so fiercely outside his windows that he could scarcely see across the street; but within, the air was deliciously soft and fragrant. He put the violets and jonquils on the tabouret beside

Jersey City: New Jersey city on the Hudson River, directly across from the southern tip of Manhattan.
Twenty-third Street station: Paul's final destination in Manhattan.
brushes: hairbrushes.

the couch, and threw himself down with a long sigh, covering himself with a Roman blanket. He was thoroughly tired; he had been in such haste, he had stood up to such a strain, covered so much ground in the last twenty-four hours, that he wanted to think how it had all come about. Lulled by the sound of the wind, the warm air, and the cool fragrance of the flowers, he sank into deep, drowsy retrospection.

It had been wonderfully simple; when they had shut him out of the theater and concert hall, whey they had taken away his bone, the whole thing was virtually determined. The rest was a mere matter of opportunity. The only thing that at all surprised him was his own courage—for he realized well enough that he had always been tormented by fear, a sort of apprehensive dread that, of late years, as the meshes of the lies he had told closed about him, had been pulling the muscles of his body tighter and tighter. Until now, he could not remember a time when he had not been dreading something. Even when he was a little boy, it was always there—behind him or before, or on either side. There had always been the shadowed corner, the dark place into which he dared not look, but from which something seemed always to be watching him—and Paul had done things that were not pretty to watch, he knew.

But now he had a curious sense of relief, as though he had at last thrown down the gauntlet to the thing in the corner.

Yet it was but a day since he had been sulking in the traces; but yesterday afternoon that he had been sent to the bank with Denny & Carson's deposit, as usual—but this time he was instructed to leave the book to be balanced. There was above two thousand dollars in checks, and nearly a thousand in the bank notes which he had taken from the book and quietly transferred to his pocket. At the bank he had made out a new deposit slip. His nerves had been steady enough to permit of his returning to the office, where he had finished his work and asked for a full day's holiday tomorrow, Saturday, giving a perfectly reasonable pretext. The bank book, he knew, would not be returned before Monday or Tuesday, and his father would be out of town for the next week. From the time he slipped the bank notes into his pocket until he boarded the night train for New York, he had not known a moment's hesitation. 45

How astonishingly easy it had all been; here he was, the thing done; and this time there would be no awakening, no figure at the top of the stairs. He watched the snowflakes whirling by his window until he fell asleep.

When he awoke, it was four o'clock in the afternoon. He bounded up with a start; one of his precious days gone already! He spent nearly an hour in dressing, watching every stage of his toilet carefully in the mirror. Everything was quite perfect; he was exactly the kind of boy he had always wanted to be.

When he went downstairs, Paul took a carriage and drove up Fifth Avenue toward the Park.° The snow had somewhat abated; carriages and tradesmen's wagons were hurrying soundlessly to and fro in the winter twilight; boys in woolen mufflers were shoveling off the doorsteps; the avenue stages° made fine spots of color against the white street. Here and there on the corners whole flower gardens blooming behind glass windows, against which the snow flakes stuck and melted; violets, roses, carnations, lilies of the valley—somehow vastly more lovely and

the Park: Central Park.
avenue stages: display windows.

alluring that they blossomed thus unnaturally in the snow. The Park itself was a wonderful stage winter-piece.

When he returned, the pause of the twilight had ceased, and the tune of the streets had changed. The snow was falling faster, lights streamed from the hotels that reared their many stories fearlessly up into the storm, defying the raging Atlantic winds. A long, black stream of carriages poured down the avenue, intersected here and there by other streams, tending horizontally. There were a score of cabs about the entrance of his hotel, and his driver had to wait. Boys in livery were running in and out of the awning stretched across the sidewalk, up and down the red velvet carpet laid from the door to the street. Above, about, within it all, was the rumble and roar, the hurry and toss of thousands of human beings as hot for pleasure as himself, and on every side of him towered the glaring affirmation of the omnipotence of wealth.

The boy set his teeth and drew his shoulders together in a spasm of   50
realization; the plot of all dramas, the text of all romances, the nerve-stuff of all sensations was whirling about him like the snowflakes. He burnt like a faggot in a tempest.

When Paul came down to dinner, the music of the orchestra floated up the elevator shaft to greet him. As he stepped into the thronged corridor, he sank back into one of the chairs against the wall to get his breath. The lights, the chatter, the perfumes, the bewildering medley of color—he had, for a moment, the feeling of not being able to stand it. But only for a moment; these were his own people, he told himself. He went slowly about the corridors, through the writing-rooms, smoking-rooms, reception-rooms, as though he were exploring the chambers of an enchanted palace, built and peopled for him alone.

When he reached the dining room he sat down at a table near a window. The flowers, the white linen, the many-colored wine glasses, the gay toilettes of the women, the low popping of corks, the undulating repetitions of the *Blue Danube°* from the orchestra, all flooded Paul's dream with bewildering radiance. When the roseate tinge of his champagne was added—that cold, precious, bubbling stuff that creamed and foamed in his glass—Paul wondered that there were honest men in the world at all. This was what all the world was fighting for, he reflected; this was what all the struggle was about. He doubted the reality of his past. Had he ever known a place called Cordelia Street, a place where fagged-looking business men boarded the early car? Mere rivets in a machine they seemed to Paul—sickening men, with combings of children's hair always hanging to their coats, and the smell of cooking in their clothes. Cordelia Street—Ah, that belonged to another time and country! Had he not always been thus, had he not sat here night after night, from as far back as he could remember, looking pensively over just such shimmering textures, and slowly twirling the stem of a glass like this one between his thumb and middle finger? He rather thought he had.

He was not in the least abashed or lonely. He had no special desire to meet or to know any of these people; all he demanded was the right to look on and conjecture, to watch the pageant. The mere stage properties were all he contended for. Nor was he lonely later in the evening, in his loge at the Opera. He was entirely rid of his nervous misgivings, of his forced aggressiveness, of the imperative

Blue Danube: Composed in 1866, "The Blue Danube" is perhaps the best-known waltz of Johann Strauss (1825–1899).

desire to show himself different from his surroundings. He felt now that his surroundings explained him. Nobody questioned the purple;° he had only to wear it passively. He had only to glance down at his dress coat to reassure himself that here it would be impossible for anyone to humiliate him.

He found it hard to leave his beautiful sitting room to go to bed that night, and sat long watching the raging storm from his turret window. When he went to sleep, it was with the lights turned on in his bedroom; partly because of his old timidity, and partly so that, if he should wake in the night, there would be no wretched moment of doubt, no horrible suspicion of yellow wall-paper, or of Washington and Calvin above his bed.

On Sunday morning the city was practically snow-bound. Paul breakfasted late, and in the afternoon he fell in with a wild San Francisco boy, a freshman at Yale, who said he had run down for a "little flyer" over Sunday. The young man offered to show Paul the night side of the town, and the two boys went off together after dinner, not returning to the hotel until seven o'clock the next morning. They had started out in the confiding warmth of a champagne friendship, but their parting in the elevator was singularly cool. The freshman pulled himself together to make his train, and Paul went to bed. He woke at two o'clock in the afternoon, very thirsty and dizzy, and rang for ice water, coffee, and the Pittsburgh papers.

On the part of the hotel management, Paul excited no suspicion. There was this to be said for him, that he wore his spoils with dignity and in no way made himself conspicuous. His chief greediness lay in his ears and eyes, and his excesses were not offensive ones. His dearest pleasures were the gray winter twilights in his sitting room; his quiet enjoyment of his flowers, his clothes, his wide divan, his cigarette and his sense of power. He could not remember a time when he had felt so at peace with himself. The mere release from the necessity of petty lying, lying every day and every way, restored his self-respect. He had never lied for pleasure, even at school; but to make himself noticed and admired, to assert his difference from other Cordelia Street boys; and he felt a good deal more manly, more honest, even, now that he had no need for boastful pretensions, now that he could, as his actor friends used to say, "dress the part." It was characteristic that remorse did not occur to him. His golden days went by without a shadow, and he made each as perfect as he could.

On the eighth day after his arrival in New York, he found the whole affair exploited in the Pittsburgh papers, exploited with a wealth of detail which indicated that local news of a sensational nature was at a low ebb. The firm of Denny & Carson announced that the boy's father had refunded the full amount of his theft, and that they had no intention of prosecuting. The Cumberland minister had been interviewed, and expressed his hope of yet reclaiming the motherless lad, and Paul's Sabbath-school teacher declared that she would spare no effort to that end. The rumor had reached Pittsburgh that the boy had been seen in a New York hotel, and his father had gone East to find him and bring him home.

Paul had just come in to dress for dinner; he sank into a chair, weak in the knees, and clasped his head in his hands. It was to be worse than jail, even; the tepid waters of Cordelia Street were to close over him finally and forever. The gray monotony stretched before him in hopeless, unrelieved years; Sabbath-school, Young People's Meeting, the yellow-papered room, the damp dish-towels; it all

purple: that is, clothing fit for royalty.

rushed back upon him with sickening vividness. He had the old feeling that the orchestra had suddenly stopped, the sinking sensation that the play was over. The sweat broke out on his face, and he sprang to his feet, looked about him with his white, conscious smile, and winked at himself in the mirror. With something of the childish belief in miracles with which he had so often gone to class, all his lessons unlearned, Paul dressed and dashed whistling down the corridor to the elevator.

He had no sooner entered the dining room and caught the measure of the music, than his remembrance was lightened by his old elastic power of claiming the moment, mounting with it, and finding it all sufficient. The glare and glitter about him, the mere scenic accessories had again, and for the last time, their old potency. He would show himself that he was game, he would finish the thing splendidly. He doubted, more than ever, the existence of Cordelia Street, and for the first time he drank his wine recklessly. Was he not, after all, one of these fortunate beings? Was he not still himself, and in his own place? He drummed a nervous accompaniment to the music and looked about him, telling himself over and over that it had paid.

He reflected drowsily, to the swell of the violin and the chill sweetness of   60
his wine, that he might have done it more wisely. He might have caught an outbound steamer and been well out of their clutches before now. But the other side of the world had seemed too far away and too uncertain then; he could not have waited for it; his need had been too sharp. If he had to choose over again, he would do the same thing tomorrow. He looked affectionately about the dining room, now gilded with a soft mist. Ah, it has paid indeed!

Paul was awakened the next morning by a painful throbbing in his head and feet. He had thrown himself across the bed without undressing, and had slept with his shoes on. His limbs and hands were lead heavy, and his tongue and throat were parched. There came upon him one of those fateful attacks of clear-headedness that never occurred except when he was physically exhausted and his nerves hung loose. He lay still and closed his eyes and let the tide of realities wash over him.

His father was in New York: "stopping at some joint or other," he told himself. The memory of successive summers on the front stoop fell upon him like a weight of black water. He had not a hundred dollars left, and he knew now, more than ever, that money was everything, the wall that stood between all he loathed and all he wanted. The thing was winding itself up; he had thought of that on his first glorious day in New York, and had even provided a way to snap the thread. It lay on his dressing-table now; he had got it out last night when he came blindly up from dinner,—but the shiny metal hurt his eyes, and he disliked the look of it, anyway.

He rose and moved about with a painful effort, succumbing now and again to attacks of nausea. It was the old depression exaggerated; all the world had become Cordelia Street. Yet somehow he was not afraid of anything, was absolutely calm; perhaps because he had looked into the dark corner at last, and knew. It was bad enough, what he saw there, but somehow not so bad as his long fear of it had been. He saw everything clearly now. He had a feeling that he had made the best of it, that he had lived the sort of life he was meant to live, and for half an hour he sat staring at the revolver. But he told himself that was not the way, so he went downstairs and took a cab to the ferry.

When Paul arrived at Newark, he got off the train and took another cab, directing the driver to follow the Pennsylvania tracks out of the town. The snow lay heavy on the roadways and had drifted deep in the open fields. Only here and there the dead grass or dried weed stalks projected, singularly black, above it. Once well into the country, Paul dismissed the carriage and walked, floundering along the tracks, his mind a medley of irrelevant things. He seemed to hold in his brain an actual picture of everything he had seen that morning. He remembered every feature of both his drivers, the toothless old woman from whom he had bought the red flowers in his coat, the agent from whom he had got his ticket, and all of his fellow-passengers on the ferry. His mind, unable to cope with vital matters near at hand, worked feverishly and deftly at sorting and grouping these images. They made for him a part of the ugliness of the world, of the ache in his head, and the bitter burning on his tongue. He stopped and put a handful of snow into his mouth as he walked, but that, too, seemed hot. When he reached a little hillside, where the tracks ran through a cut some twenty feet below him, he stopped and sat down.

The carnations in his coat were drooping with the cold, he noticed; all their red glory over. It occurred to him that all the flowers he had seen in the show windows that first night must have gone the same way, long before this. It was only one splendid breath they had, in spite of their brave mockery at the winter outside the glass. It was a losing game in the end, it seemed, this revolt against the homilies by which the world is run. Paul took one of the blossoms carefully from his coat and scooped a little hole in the snow, where he covered it up. Then he dozed a while, from his weak condition, seeming insensible to the cold. 65

The sound of an approaching train woke him, and he started to his feet, remembering only his resolution, and afraid lest he should be too late. He stood watching the approaching locomotive, his teeth chattering, his lips drawn away from them in a frightened smile; once or twice he glanced nervously sidewise, as though he were being watched. When the right moment came, he jumped. As he fell, the folly of his haste occurred to him with merciless clearness, the vastness of what he had left undone. There flashed through his brain, clearer than ever before, the blue of Adriatic water, the yellow of Algerian sands.

He felt something strike his chest,—his body was being thrown swiftly through the air, on and on, immeasurably far and fast, while his limbs gently relaxed. Then, because the picture-making mechanism was crushed, the disturbing visions flashed into black, and Paul dropped back into the immense design of things.

QUESTIONS

1. Why is the story called "Paul's Case"? What about it makes it a case?

2. What sort of speaker is telling the story? What concerns does the speaker have for Paul? How does the speaker describe the other characters? When does the speaker shift attention exclusively to Paul? Why?

3. Describe the character of Paul. In what ways does he seem to be physically or mentally ill? How does he grow or change? What strengths and skills or abilities does he have? What weaknesses? What do his preferences and annoyances show about him? Why does he enjoy the concerts and the theater

so? What does his meeting with the college boy in New York show about him?

4. Why does it seem to Paul that forgiveness and subsequent correction would be worse punishments for his theft than outright imprisonment?

5. What elements in the story could make it be construed as a criticism not of Paul but of early twentieth-century society at large? What future does Paul see for himself? What sorts of lives are being led by the people of Cordelia Street? To what degree is Paul's dislike of this life justified?

SUSAN GLASPELL (1882–1948)

A Jury of Her Peers°   *1917*

When Martha Hale opened the storm-door and got a cut of the north wind, she ran back for her big woolen scarf. As she hurriedly wound that round her head her eye made a scandalized sweep of her kitchen. It was no ordinary thing that called her away—it was probably further from ordinary than anything that had ever happened in Dickson County. But what her eye took in was that her kitchen was in no shape for leaving: her bread all ready for mixing, half the flour sifted and half unsifted.

She hated to see things half done; but she had been at that when the team from town stopped to get Mr. Hale, and then the sheriff came running in to say his wife wished Mrs. Hale would come too—adding, with a grin, that he guessed she was getting scary and wanted another woman along. So she had dropped everything right where it was.

"Martha!" now came her husband's impatient voice. "Don't keep folks waiting out here in the cold."

She again opened the storm-door, and this time joined the three men and the one woman waiting for her in the big two-seated buggy.

After she had the robes tucked around her she took another look at the   5
woman who sat beside her on the back seat. She had met Mrs. Peters the year before at the county fair, and the thing she remembered about her was that she didn't seem like a sheriff's wife. She was small and thin and didn't have a strong voice. Mrs. Gorman, sheriff's wife before Gorman went out and Peters came in, had a voice that somehow seemed to be backing up the law with every word. But if Mrs. Peters didn't look like a sheriff's wife, Peters made it up in looking like a sheriff. He was to a dot the kind of man who could get himself elected sheriff—a heavy man with a big voice, who was particularly genial with the law-abiding, as if to make it plain that he knew the difference between criminals and non-criminals. And right there it came into Mrs. Hale's mind, with a stab, that this man who was so pleasant and lively with all of them was going to the Wrights' now as a sheriff.

"The country's not very pleasant this time of year," Mrs. Peters at last ventured, as if she felt they ought to be talking as well as the men.

Mrs. Hale scarcely finished her reply, for they had gone up a little hill and could see the Wright place now, and seeing it did not make her feel like talking.

See also Glaspell's play *Trifles* (pp. 1018–28), with which this story may be compared.

It looked very lonesome this cold March morning. It had always been a lonesome-looking place. It was down in a hollow, and the poplar trees around it were lonesome-looking trees. The men were looking at it and talking about what had happened. The county attorney was bending to one side of the buggy, and kept looking steadily at the place as they drew up to it.

"I'm glad you came with me," Mrs. Peters said nervously, as the two women were about to follow the men in through the kitchen door.

Even after she had her foot on the door-step, her hand on the knob, Martha Hale had a moment of feeling she could not cross that threshold. And the reason it seemed she couldn't cross now was simply because she hadn't crossed it before. Time and time again it had been in her mind, "I ought to go over and see Minnie Foster"—she still thought of her as Minnie Foster, though for twenty years she had been Mrs. Wright. And then there was always something to do and Minnie Foster would go from her mind. But *now* she could come.

The men went over to the stove. The women stood close together by the door. Young Henderson, the county attorney, turned around and said, "Come up to the fire, ladies." 10

Mrs. Peters took a step forward, then stopped. "I'm not—cold," she said.

And so the two women stood by the door, at first not even so much as looking around the kitchen.

The men talked for a minute about what a good thing it was the sheriff had sent his deputy out that morning to make a fire for them, and then Sheriff Peters stepped back from the stove, unbuttoned his outer coat, and leaned his hands on the kitchen table in a way that seemed to mark the beginning of official business. "Now, Mr. Hale," he said in a sort of semi-official voice, "before we move things about, you tell Mr. Henderson just what it was you saw when you came here yesterday morning."

The county attorney was looking around the kitchen.

"By the way," he said, "has anything been moved?" He turned to the sheriff. 15 "Are things just as you left them yesterday?"

Peters looked from cupboard to sink; from that to a small worn rocker a little to one side of the kitchen table.

"It's just the same."

"Somebody should have been left here yesterday," said the county attorney.

"Oh—yesterday," returned the sheriff, with a little gesture as of yesterday having been more than he could bear to think of. "When I had to send Frank to Morris Center for that man who went crazy—let me tell you. I had my hands full *yesterday*. I knew you could get back from Omaha by today, George, and as long as I went over everything here myself—"

"Well, Mr. Hale," said the county attorney, in a way of letting what was past 20 and gone go, "tell just what happened when you came here yesterday morning."

Mrs. Hale, still leaning against the door, had that sinking feeling of the mother whose child is about to speak a piece. Lewis often wandered along and got things mixed up in a story. She hoped he would tell this straight and plain, and not say unnecessary things that would just make things harder for Minnie Foster. He didn't begin at once, and she noticed that he looked queer—as if standing in that kitchen and having to tell what he had seen there yesterday morning made him almost sick.

"Yes, Mr. Hale?" the county attorney reminded.

"Harry and I had started to town with a load of potatoes," Mrs. Hale's husband began.

Harry was Mrs. Hale's oldest boy. He wasn't with them now, for the very good reason that those potatoes never got to town yesterday and he was taking them this morning, so he hadn't been home when the sheriff stopped to say he wanted Mr. Hale to come over to the Wright place and tell the county attorney his story there, where he could point it all out. With all Mrs. Hale's other emotions came the fear now that maybe Harry wasn't dressed warm enough—they hadn't any of them realized how that north wind did bite.

"We come along this road," Hale was going on, with a motion of his hand   25
to the road over which they had just come, "and as we got in sight of the house I says to Harry, 'I'm goin' to see if I can't get John Wright to take a telephone.' You see," he explained to Henderson, "unless I can get somebody to go in with me they won't come out this branch road except for a price *I* can't pay. I'd spoke to Wright about it once before; but he put me off, saying folks talked too much anyway, and all he asked was peace and quiet—guess you know about how much he talked himself. But I thought maybe if I went to the house and talked about it before his wife, and said all the women-folks liked the telephones, and that in this lonesome stretch of road it would be a good thing—well, I said to Harry that that was what I was going to say—though I said at the same time that I didn't know as what his wife wanted made much difference to John—"

Now there he was!—saying things he didn't need to say. Mrs. Hale tried to catch her husband's eye, but fortunately the county attorney interrupted with:

"Let's talk about that a little later, Mr. Hale. I do want to talk about that, but I'm anxious now to get along to just what happened when you got here."

When he began this time, it was very deliberately and carefully:

"I didn't see or hear anything. I knocked at the door. And still it was all quiet inside. I knew they must be up—it was past eight o'clock. So I knocked again, louder, and I thought I heard somebody say, 'Come in.' I wasn't sure—I'm not sure yet. But I opened the door—this door," jerking a hand toward the door by which the two women stood, "and there, in that rocker"—pointing to it— "sat Mrs. Wright."

Everyone in the kitchen looked at the rocker. It came into Mrs. Hale's mind   30
that that rocker didn't look in the least like Minnie Foster—the Minnie Foster of twenty years before. It was a dingy red, with wooden rungs up the back, and the middle rung was gone, and the chair sagged to one side.

"How did she—look?" the county attorney was inquiring.

"Well," said Hale, "she looked—queer."

"How do you mean—queer?"

As he asked it he took out a note-book and pencil. Mrs. Hale did not like the sight of that pencil. She kept her eye fixed on her husband, as if to keep him from saying unnecessary things that would go into that note-book and make trouble.

Hale did speak guardedly, as if the pencil had affected him too.   35

"Well, as if she didn't know what she was going to do next. And kind of— done up."

"How did she seem to feel about your coming?"

"Why, I don't think she minded—one way or other. She didn't pay much

attention. I said, 'Ho' do, Mrs. Wright? It's cold, ain't it?' And she said. 'Is it?'—
and went on pleatin' at her apron.

"Well, I was surprised. She didn't ask me to come up to the stove, or to sit
down, but just set there, not even lookin' at me. And so I said: 'I want to see
John.'

"And then she—laughed. I guess you would call it a laugh.   40

"I thought of Harry and the team outside, so I said, a little sharp, 'Can I
see John?' 'No,' says she—kind of dull like. 'Ain't he home?' says I. Then she
looked at me. 'Yes,' says she, 'he's home.' 'Then why can't I see him?' I asked her,
out of patience with her now. 'Cause he's dead' says she, just as quiet and dull—
and fell to pleatin' her apron. 'Dead?' says I, like you do when you can't take in
what you've heard.

"She just nodded her head, not getting a bit excited, but rockin' back and
forth.

"'Why—where is he?' says I, not knowing *what* to say.

"She just pointed upstairs—like this"—pointing to the room above.

"I got up, with the idea of going up there myself. By this time I—didn't   45
know what to do. I walked from there to here; then I says: 'Why, what did he die
of?'

"'He died of a rope around his neck,' says she; and just went on pleatin, at
her apron."

Hale stopped speaking, and stood staring at the rocker, as if he were still
seeing the woman who had sat there the morning before. Nobody spoke; it was
as if every one were seeing the woman who had sat there the morning before.

"And what did you do then?" the county attorney at last broke the silence.

"I went out and called Harry. I thought I might—need help. I got Harry
in, and we went upstairs." His voice fell almost to a whisper. "There he was—
lying over the—"

"I think I'd rather have you go into that upstairs," the county attorney   50
interrupted, "where you can point it all out. Just go on now with the rest of the
story."

"Well, my first thought was to get that rope off. It looked—"

He stopped, his face twitching.

"But Harry, he went up to him, and he said. 'No, he's dead all right, and
we'd better not touch anything.' So we went downstairs.

"She was still sitting that same way. 'Has anybody been notified?' I asked.
'No,' says she, unconcerned.

"'Who did this, Mrs. Wright?' said Harry. He said it businesslike, and she   55
stopped pleatin' at her apron. 'I don't know,' she says. 'You don't *know*?' says
Harry. 'Weren't you sleepin' in the bed with him?' 'Yes,' says she, 'but I was on
the inside.' 'Somebody slipped a rope round his neck and strangled him, and you
didn't wake up?' says Harry. 'I didn't wake up,' she said after him.

"We may have looked as if we didn't see how that could be, for after a
minute she said, 'I sleep sound.'

"Harry was going to ask her more questions, but I said maybe that weren't
our business; maybe we ought to let her tell her story first to the coroner or the
sheriff. So Harry went fast as he could over to High Road—the Rivers' place,
where there's a telephone."

"And what did she do when she knew you had gone for the coroner?" The attorney got his pencil in his hand all ready for writing.

"She moved from that chair to this one over here"—Hale pointed to a small chair in the corner—"and just sat there with her hands held together and looking down. I got a feeling that I ought to make some conversation, so I said I had come in to see if John wanted to put in a telephone; and at that she started to laugh, and then she stopped and looked at me—scared."

At the sound of a moving pencil the man who was telling the story looked up.   60

"I dunno—maybe it wasn't scared," he hastened: "I wouldn't like to say it was. Soon Harry got back, and then Dr. Lloyd came, and you, Mr. Peters, and so I guess that's all I know that you don't."

He said that last with relief, and moved a little, as if relaxing. Everyone moved a little. The county attorney walked toward the stair door.

"I guess we'll go upstairs first—then out to the barn and around there."

He paused and looked around the kitchen.

"You're convinced there was nothing important here?" he asked the sheriff.   65
"Nothing that would—point to any motive?"

The sheriff too looked all around, as if to re-convince himself.

"Nothing here but kitchen things," he said, with a little laugh for the insignificance of kitchen things.

The county attorney was looking at the cupboard—a peculiar, ungainly structure, half closet and half cupboard, the upper part of it being built in the wall, and the lower part just the old-fashioned kitchen cupboard. As if its queerness attracted him, he got a chair and opened the upper part and looked in. After a moment he drew his hand away sticky.

"Here's a nice mess," he said resentfully.

The two women had drawn nearer, and now the sheriff's wife spoke.   70

"Oh—her fruit," she said, looking to Mrs. Hale for sympathetic understanding. She turned back to the county attorney and explained: "She worried about that when it turned so cold last night. She said the fire would go out and her jars might burst."

Mrs. Peters' husband broke into a laugh.

"Well, can you beat the women! Held for murder, and worrying about her preserves!"

The young attorney set his lips.

"I guess before we're through with her she may have something more serious   75
than preserves to worry about."

"Oh, well," said Mrs. Hale's husband, with good-natured superiority, "women are used to worrying over trifles."

The two women moved a little closer together. Neither of them spoke. The county attorney seemed suddenly to remember his manners—and think of his future.

"And yet," said he, with the gallantry of a young politician. "for all their worries, what would we do without the ladies?"

The women did not speak, did not unbend. He went to the sink and began washing his hands. He turned to wipe them on the roller towel—whirled it for a cleaner place.

"Dirty towels! Not much of a housekeeper, would you say, ladies?"   80
He kicked his foot against some dirty pans under the sink.

"There's a great deal of work to be done on a farm," said Mrs. Hale stiffly.

"To be sure. And yet"—with a little bow to her—"I know there are some Dickson County farm-houses that do not have such roller towels." He gave it a pull to expose its full length again.

"Those towels get dirty awful quick. Men's hands aren't always as clean as they might be."

"Ah, loyal to your sex, I see," he laughed. He stopped and gave her a keen   85
look. "But you and Mrs. Wright were neighbors. I suppose you were friends, too."

Martha Hale shook her head.

"I've seen little enough of her of late years. I've not been in this house—it's more than a year."

"And why was that? You didn't like her?"

"I liked her well enough," she replied with spirit. "Farmers' wives have their hands full, Mr. Henderson. And then—" She looked around the kitchen.

"Yes?" he encouraged.   90

"It never seemed a very cheerful place," said she, more to herself than to him.

"No," he agreed; "I don't think anyone would call it cheerful. I shouldn't say she had the home-making instinct."

"Well, I don't know as Wright had, either," she muttered.

"You mean they didn't get on very well?" he was quick to ask.

"No; I don't mean anything," she answered, with decision. As she turned a   95
little away from him, she added: "But I don't think a place would be any the cheerfuller for John Wright's bein' in it."

"I'd like to talk to you about that a little later, Mrs. Hale," he said. "I'm anxious to get the lay of things upstairs now."

He moved toward the stair door, followed by the two men.

"I suppose anything Mrs. Peters does'll be all right?" the sheriff inquired. "She was to take in some clothes for her, you know—and a few little things. We left in such a hurry yesterday."

The county attorney looked at the two women whom they were leaving alone there among the kitchen things.

"Yes—Mrs. Peters," he said, his glance resting on the woman who was not   100
Mrs. Peters, the big farmer woman who stood behind the sheriff's wife. "Of course Mrs. Peters is one of us," he said, in a manner of entrusting responsibility. "And keep your eye out, Mrs. Peters, for anything that might be of use. No telling; you women might come upon a clue to the motive—and that's the thing we need."

Mr. Hale rubbed his face after the fashion of a showman getting ready for a pleasantry.

"But would the women know a clue if they did come upon it?" he said; and, having delivered himself of this, he followed the others through the stair door.

The women stood motionless and silent, listening to the footsteps, first upon the stairs, then in the room above them.

Then, as if releasing herself from something strange. Mrs. Hale began to arrange the dirty pans under the sink, which the county attorney's disdainful push of the foot had deranged.

"I'd hate to have men comin' into my kitchen," she said testily—"snoopin'   105
round and criticizin'."

"Of course it's no more than their duty," said the sheriff's wife, in her manner of timid acquiescence.

"Duty's all right," replied Mrs. Hale bluffly; "but I guess that deputy sheriff that come out to make the fire might have got a little of this on." She gave the roller towel a pull. "Wish I'd thought of that sooner! Seems mean to talk about her for not having things slicked up, when she had to come away in such a hurry."

She looked around the kitchen. Certainly it was not "slicked up." Her eye was held by a bucket of sugar on a low shelf. The cover was off the wooden bucket, and beside it was a paper bag—half full.

Mrs. Hale moved toward it.

"She was putting this in there," she said to herself—slowly.   110

She thought of the flour in her kitchen at home—half sifted, half not sifted. She had been interrupted, and had left things half done. What had interrupted Minnie Foster? Why had that work been left half done? She made a move as if to finish it,—unfinished things always bothered her,—and then she glanced around and saw that Mrs. Peters was watching her—and she didn't want Mrs. Peters to get that feeling she had got of work begun and then—for some reason—not finished.

"It's a shame about her fruit," she said, and walked toward the cupboard that the county attorney had opened, and got on the chair, murmuring: "I wonder if it's all gone."

It was a sorry enough looking sight, but "Here's one that's all right," she said at last. She held it toward the light. "This is cherries, too." She looked again. "I declare I believe that's the only one."

With a sigh, she got down from the chair, went to the sink, and wiped off the bottle.

"She'll feel awful bad, after all her hard work in the hot weather. I remember   115
the afternoon I put up my cherries last summer."

She set the bottle on the table, and, with another sigh, started to sit down in the rocker. But she did not sit down. Something kept her from sitting down in that chair. She straightened—stepped back, and, half turned away, stood looking at it, seeing the woman who had sat there "pleatin' at her apron."

The thin voice of the sheriff's wife broke in upon her: "I must be getting those things from the front-room closet." She opened the door into the other room, started in, stepped back. "You coming with me, Mrs. Hale?" she asked nervously. "You—you could help me get them."

They were soon back—the stark coldness of that shut-up room was not a thing to linger in.

"My!" said Mrs. Peters, dropping the things on the table and hurrying to the stove.

Mrs. Hale stood examining the clothes the woman who was being detained   120
in town had said she wanted.

"Wright was close!"° she exclaimed, holding up a shabby black skirt that bore the marks of much making over. "I think maybe that's why she kept so much to herself. I s'pose she felt she couldn't do her part; and then, you don't enjoy things when you feel shabby. She used to wear pretty clothes and be lively—when

---

close: that is, frugal, tightfisted.

she was Minnie Foster, one of the town girls, singing in the choir. But that—oh, that was twenty years ago."

With a carefulness in which there was something tender, she folded the shabby clothes and piled them at one corner of the table. She looked up at Mrs. Peters, and there was something in the other woman's look that irritated her.

"She don't care," she said to herself. "Much difference it makes to her whether Minnie Foster had pretty clothes when she was a girl."

Then she looked again, and she wasn't so sure; in fact, she hadn't at any time been perfectly sure about Mrs. Peters. She had that shrinking manner, and yet her eyes looked as if they could see a long way into things.

"This all you was to take in?" asked Mrs. Hale.   125

"No," said the sheriff's wife; "she said she wanted an apron. Funny thing to want," she ventured in her nervous little way, "for there's not much to get you dirty in jail, goodness knows. But I suppose just to make her feel more natural. If you're used to wearing an apron—. She said they were in the bottom drawer of this cupboard. Yes—here they are. And then her little shawl that always hung on the stair door."

She took the small gray shawl from behind the door leading upstairs, and stood a minute looking at it.

Suddenly Mrs. Hale took a quick step toward the other woman.

"Mrs. Peters!"

"Yes, Mrs. Hale?"   130

"Do you think she—did it?"

A frightened look blurred the other thing in Mrs. Peters' eyes.

"Oh, I don't know," she said, in a voice that seemed to shrink away from the subject.

"Well, I don't think she did," affirmed Mrs. Hale stoutly. "Asking for an apron, and her little shawl. Worryin' about her fruit."

"Mr. Peters says—." Footsteps were heard in the room above; she stopped,   135
looked up, then went on in a lowered voice: "Mr. Peters says—it looks bad for her. Mr. Henderson is awful sarcastic in a speech, and he's going to make fun of her saying she didn't—wake up."

For a moment Mrs. Hale had no answer. Then, "Well, I guess John Wright didn't wake up—when they was slippin' that rope under his neck," she muttered.

"No, it's *strange*," breathed Mrs. Peters. "They think it was such a—funny way to kill a man."

She began to laugh; at sound of the laugh, abruptly stopped.

"That's just what Mr. Hale said," said Mrs. Hale, in a resolutely natural voice. "There was a gun in the house. He says that's what he can't understand."

"Mr. Henderson said, coming out, that what was needed for the case was a   140
motive. Something to show anger—or sudden feeling."

"Well, I don't see any signs of anger around here," said Mrs. Hale, "I don't—"

She stopped. It was as if her mind tripped on something. Her eye was caught by a dish-towel in the middle of the kitchen table. Slowly she moved toward the table. One half of it was wiped clean, the other half messy. Her eyes made a slow, almost unwilling turn to the bucket of sugar and the half empty bag beside it. Things begun—and not finished.

After a moment she stepped back, and said, in that manner of releasing herself:

"Wonder how they're finding things upstairs? I hope she had it a little more red up° up there. You know,"—she paused, and feeling gathered,—"it seems kind of *sneaking*: locking her up in town and coming out here to get her own house to turn against her!"

"But, Mrs. Hale," said the sheriff's wife, "the law is the law." 145

"I s'pose 'tis," answered Mrs. Hale shortly.

She turned to the stove, saying something about that fire not being much to brag of. She worked with it a minute, and when she straightened up she said aggressively:

"The law is the law—and a bad stove is a bad stove. How'd you like to cook on this?"—pointing with the poker to the broken lining. She opened the oven door and started to express her opinion of the oven; but she was swept into her own thoughts, thinking of what it would mean, year after year, to have that stove to wrestle with. The thought of Minnie Foster trying to bake in that oven—and the thought of her never going over to see Minnie Foster—.

She was startled by hearing Mrs. Peters say: "A person gets discouraged—and loses heart."

The sheriff's wife had looked from the stove to the sink—to the pail of 150 water which had been carried in from outside. The two women stood there silent, above them the footsteps of the men who were looking for evidence against the woman who had worked in that kitchen. That look of seeing into things, of seeing through a thing to something else, was in the eyes of the sheriff's wife now. When Mrs. Hale next spoke to her, it was gently:

"Better loosen up your things, Mrs. Peters. We'll not feel them when we go out."

Mrs. Peters went to the back of the room to hang up the fur tippet she was wearing. A moment later she exclaimed, "Why, she was piecing a quilt," and held up a large sewing basket piled high with quilt pieces.

Mrs. Hale spread some of the blocks on the table.

"It's log-cabin pattern," she said, putting several of them together, "Pretty, isn't it?"

They were so engaged with the quilt that they did not hear the footsteps on 155 the stairs. Just as the stair door opened Mrs. Hale was saying:

"Do you suppose she was going to quilt it or just knot it?"

The sheriff threw up his hands.

"They wonder whether she was going to quilt it or just knot it!"

There was a laugh for the ways of women, a warming of hands over the stove, and then the county attorney said briskly:

"Well, let's go right out to the barn and get that cleared up." 160

"I don't see as there's anything so strange," Mrs. Hale said resentfully, after the outside door had closed on the three men—"our taking up our time with little things while we're waiting for them to get the evidence. I don't see as it's anything to laugh about."

"Of course they've got awful important things on their minds," said the sheriff's wife apologetically.

They returned to an inspection of the block for the quilt. Mrs. Hale was

red up: neat.

looking at the fine, even sewing, and preoccupied with thoughts of the woman who had done that sewing, when she heard the sheriff's wife say, in a queer tone:

"Why, look at this one."

She turned to take the block held out to her.   165

"The sewing," said Mrs. Peters, in a troubled way, "All the rest of them have been so nice and even—but—this one. Why, it looks as if she didn't know what she was about!"

Their eyes met—something flashed to life, passed between them; then, as if with an effort, they seemed to pull away from each other. A moment Mrs. Hale sat there, her hands folded over that sewing which was so unlike all the rest of the sewing. Then she had pulled a knot and drawn the threads.

"Oh, what are you doing, Mrs. Hale?" asked the sheriff's wife, startled.

"Just pulling out a stitch or two that's not sewed very good," said Mrs. Hale mildly.

"I don't think we ought to touch things," Mrs. Peters said, a little helplessly.   170

"I'll just finish up this end," answered Mrs. Hale, still in that mild, matter-of-fact fashion.

She threaded a needle and started to replace bad sewing with good. For a little while she sewed in silence. Then, in that thin, timid voice, she heard:

"Mrs. Hale!"

"Yes, Mrs. Peters?"

"What do you suppose she was so—nervous about?"   175

"Oh, *I* don't know," said Mrs. Hale, as if dismissing a thing not important enough to spend much time on. "I don't know as she was—nervous. I sew awful queer sometimes when I'm just tired."

She cut a thread, and out of the corner of her eye looked up at Mrs. Peters. The small, lean face of the sheriff's wife seemed to have tightened up. Her eyes had that look of peering into something. But next moment she moved, and said in her thin, indecisive way:

"Well, I must get those clothes wrapped. They may be through sooner than we think. I wonder where I could find a piece of paper—and string."

"In that cupboard, maybe," suggested to Mrs. Hale, after a glance around.

One piece of the crazy sewing remained unripped. Mrs. Peter's back turned,   180
Martha Hale now scrutinized that piece, compared it with the dainty, accurate sewing of the other blocks. The difference was startling. Holding this block made her feel queer, as if the distracted thoughts of the woman who had perhaps turned to it to try and quiet herself were communicating themselves to her.

Mrs. Peters' voice roused her.

"Here's a bird-cage," she said. "Did she have a bird, Mrs. Hale?"

"Why, I don't know whether she did or not." She turned to look at the cage Mrs. Peters was holding up. "I've not been here in so long." She sighed. "There was a man round last year selling canaries cheap—but I don't know as she took one. Maybe she did. She used to sing real pretty herself."

Mrs. Peters looked around the kitchen.

"Seems kind of funny to think of a bird here." She half laughed—an attempt   185
to put up a barrier. "But she must have had one—or why would she have a cage? I wonder what happened to it."

"I suppose maybe the cat got it," suggested Mrs. Hale, resuming her sewing.

"No; she didn't have a cat. She's got that feeling some people have about cats—being afraid of them. When they brought her to our house yesterday, my cat got in the room, and she was real upset and asked me to take it out."

"My sister Bessie was like that," laughed Mrs. Hale.

The sheriff's wife did not reply. The silence made Mrs. Hale turn round. Mrs. Peters was examining the bird-cage.

"Look at this door," she said slowly. "It's broke. One hinge has been pulled apart."   190

Mrs. Hale came nearer.

"Looks as if someone must have been—rough with it."

Again their eyes met—startled, questioning, apprehensive. For a moment neither spoke nor stirred. Then Mrs. Hale, turning away, said brusquely:

"If they're going to find any evidence, I wish they'd be about it. I don't like this place."

"But I'm awful glad you came with me, Mrs. Hale." Mrs. Peters put the bird-   195
cage on the table and sat down. "It would be lonesome for me—sitting here alone."

"Yes, it would, wouldn't it?" agreed Mrs. Hale, a certain determined naturalness in her voice. She had picked up the sewing, but now it dropped in her lap, and she murmured in a different voice: "But I tell you what I *do* wish, Mrs.Peters. I wish I had come over sometimes when she was here. I wish—I had."

"But of course you were awful busy, Mrs. Hale. Your house—and your children."

"I could've come," retorted Mrs. Hale shortly. "I stayed away because it weren't cheerful—and that's why I ought to have come. I"—she looked around— "I've never liked this place. Maybe because it's down in a hollow and you don't see the road. I don't know what it is, but it's a lonesome place, and always was. I wish I had come over to see Minnie Foster sometimes. I can see now—" She did not put it into words.

"Well, you mustn't reproach yourself," counseled Mrs. Peters. "Somehow, we just don't see how it is with other folks till—something comes up."

"Not having children makes less work," mused Mrs. Hale, after a silence,   200
"but it makes a quiet house—and Wright out to work all day—and no company when he did come in. Did you know John Wright, Mrs. Peters?"

"Not to know him. I've seen him in town. They say he was a good man."

"Yes—good," conceded John Wright's neighbor grimly. "He didn't drink, and kept his word as well as most, I guess, and paid his debts. But he was a hard man, Mrs. Peters. Just to pass the time of day with him—." She stopped, shivered a little. "Like a raw wind that gets to the bone." Her eye fell upon the cage on the table before her, and she added, almost bitterly: "I should think she would've wanted a bird!"

Suddenly she leaned forward, looking intently at the cage. "But what do you s'pose went wrong with it?"

"I don't know," returned Mrs. Peters; "unless it got sick and died."

But after she said it she reached over and swung the broken door. Both   205
women watched it as if somehow held by it.

"You didn't know—her?" Mrs. Hale asked, a gentler note in her voice.

"Not till they brought her yesterday," said the sheriff's wife.

"She—come to think of it, she was kind of like a bird herself. Real sweet and pretty, but kind of timid and—fluttery. How—she—did—change."

That held her for a long time. Finally, as if struck with a happy thought and relieved to get back to everyday things, she exclaimed:

"Tell you what, Mrs. Peters, why don't you take the quilt in with you? It   210
might take up her mind."

"Why, I think that's a real nice idea, Mrs. Hale," agreed the sheriff's wife, as if she too were glad to come into the atmosphere of a simple kindness. "There couldn't possibly be any objection to that, could there? Now, just what will I take? I wonder if her patches are in here—and her things?"

They turned to the sewing basket.

"Here's some red," said Mrs. Hale, bringing out a roll of cloth. Underneath that was a box. "Here, maybe her scissors are in here—and her things." She held it up. "What a pretty box! I'll warrant that was something she had a long time ago—when she was a girl."

She held it in her hand a moment; then, with a little sigh, opened it.

Instantly her hand went to her nose.   215

"Why—!"

Mrs. Peters drew nearer—then turned away.

"There's something wrapped up in this piece of silk," faltered Mrs. Hale.

"This isn't her scissors," said Mrs. Peters, in a shrinking voice.

Her hand not steady, Mrs. Hale raised the piece of silk. "Oh, Mrs. Peters!"   220
she cried. "It's—"

Mrs. Peters bent closer.

"It's the bird," she whispered.

"But, Mrs. Peters!" cried Mrs. Hale. "*Look* at it! Its *neck*—look at its neck! It's all—other side *to.*"

She held the box away from her.

The sheriff's wife again bent closer.   225

"Somebody wrung its neck," said she, in a voice that was slow and deep.

And then again the eyes of the two women met—this time clung together in a look of dawning comprehension, of growing horror. Mrs. Peters looked from the dead bird to the broken door of the cage. Again their eyes met. And just then there was a sound at the outside door.

Mrs. Hale slipped the box under the quilt pieces in the basket, and sank into the chair before it. Mrs. Peters stood holding to the table. The county attorney and the sheriff came in from outside.

"Well, ladies," said the county attorney, as one turning from serious things to little pleasantries, "have you decided whether she was going to quilt it or knot it?"

"We think," began the sheriff's wife in a flurried voice, "that she was going   230
to—knot it."

He was too preoccupied to notice the change that came in her voice on that last.

"Well, that's very interesting, I'm sure," he said tolerantly. He caught sight of the bird-cage. "Has the bird flown?"

"We think the cat got it," said Mrs. Hale in a voice curiously even.

He was walking up and down, as if thinking something out.

"Is there a cat?" he asked absently.   235

Mrs. Hale shot a look up at the sheriff's wife.

"Well, not *now*," said Mrs. Peters. "They're superstitious, you know; they leave."

She sank into her chair.

The county attorney did not heed her. "No sign at all of anyone having come in from the outside," he said to Peters, in the manner of continuing an interrupted conversation. "Their own rope. Now let's go upstairs again and go over it, piece by piece. It would have to have been someone who knew just the—"

The stair door closed behind them and their voices were lost.   240

The two women sat motionless, not looking at each other, but as if peering into something and at the same time holding back. When they spoke now it was as if they were afraid of what they were saying, but as if they could not help saying it.

"She liked the bird," said Martha Hale, low and slowly. "She was going to bury it in that pretty box."

"When I was a girl," said Mrs. Peters, under her breath, "my kitten—there was a boy took a hatchet, and before my eyes—before I could get there—" She covered her face an instant. "If they hadn't held me back I would have"—she caught herself, looked upstairs where footsteps were heard, and finished weakly—"hurt him."

Then they sat without speaking or moving.

"I wonder how it would seem," Mrs. Hale at last began, as if feeling her way   245
over strange ground—"never to have had any children around?" Her eyes made a slow sweep of the kitchen, as if seeing what that kitchen had meant through all the years. "No, Wright wouldn't like the bird," she said after that—"a thing that sang. She used to sing. He killed that too." Her voice tightened.

Mrs. Peters moved uneasily.

"Of course we don't know who killed the bird."

"I knew John Wright," was Mrs. Hale's answer.

"It was an awful thing was done in this house that night, Mrs. Hale," said the sheriff's wife. "Killing a man while he slept—slipping a thing round his neck that choked the life out of him."

Mrs. Hale's hand went out to the bird cage.   250

"His neck. Choked the life out of him."

"We don't *know* who killed him," whispered Mrs. Peters wildly. "We don't *know*."

Mrs. Hale had not moved. "If there had been years and years of—nothing, then a bird to sing to you, it would be awful—still—after the bird was still."

It was as if something within her not herself had spoken, and it found in Mrs. Peters something she did not know as herself.

"I know what stillness is," she said, in a queer, monotonous voice. "When   255
we homesteaded in Dakota, and my first baby died—after he was two years old— and me with no other then—"

Mrs. Hale stirred.

"How soon do you suppose they'll be through looking for the evidence?"

"I know what stillness is," repeated Mrs. Peters, in just that same way. Then she too pulled back. "The law has got to punish crime, Mrs. Hale," she said in her tight little way.

"I wish you'd seen Minnie Foster," was the answer, "when she wore a white dress with blue ribbons, and stood up there in the choir and sang."

The picture of that girl, the fact that she had lived neighbor to that girl for 260
twenty years, and had let her die for lack of life, was suddenly more than she could bear.

"Oh, I *wish* I'd come over here once in a while!" she cried. "That was a crime! Who's going to punish that?"

"We mustn't take on," said Mrs. Peters, with a frightened look toward the stairs.

"I might 'a' *known* she needed help! I tell you, it's *queer*, Mrs. Peters. We live close together, and we live far apart. We all go through the same things—it's all just a different kind of the same thing! If it weren't—why do you and I *understand*? Why do we *know*—what we know this minute?"

She dashed her hand across her eyes. Then, seeing the jar of fruit on the table, she reached for it and choked out:

"If I was you I wouldn't *tell* her her fruit was gone! Tell her it *ain't*. Tell her 265
it's all right—all of it. Here—take this in to prove it to her! She—she may never know whether it was broke or not."

She turned away.

Mrs. Peters reached out for the bottle of fruit as if she were glad to take it—as if touching a familiar thing, having something to do, could keep her from something else. She got up, looked about for something to wrap the fruit in, took a petticoat from the pile of clothes she had brought from the front room, and nervously started winding that round the bottle.

"My!" she began, in a high, false voice, "it's a good thing the men couldn't hear us! Getting all stirred up over a little thing like a—dead canary." She hurried over that. "As if that could have anything to do with—with—My, wouldn't they *laugh*?"

Footsteps were heard on the stairs.

"Maybe they would," muttered Mrs. Hale—"maybe they wouldn't." 270

"No, Peters," said the county attorney incisively; "it's all perfectly clear, except the reason for doing it. But you know juries when it comes to women. If there was some definite thing—something to show. Something to make a story about. A thing that would connect up with this clumsy way of doing it."

In a covert way Mrs. Hale looked at Mrs. Peters. Mrs. Peters was looking at her. Quickly they looked away from each other. The outer door opened and Mr. Hale came in.

"I've got the team° round now," he said. "Pretty cold out there."

"I'm going to stay here awhile by myself," the county attorney suddenly announced. "You can send Frank out for me, can't you?" he asked the sheriff. "I want to go over everything. I'm not satisfied we can't do better."

Again, for one brief moment, the two women's eyes found one another. 275

The sheriff came up to the table.

"Did you want to see what Mrs. Peters was going to take in?"

The county attorney picked up the apron. He laughed.

"Oh, I guess they're not very dangerous things the ladies have picked out."

Mrs. Hale's hand was on the sewing basket in which the box was concealed. 280

team: team of horses pulling the buggy in which the group had come.

She felt that she ought to take her hand off the basket. She did not seem able to. He picked up one of the quilt blocks which she had piled on to cover the box. Her eyes felt like fire. She had a feeling that if he took up the basket she would snatch it from him.

But he did not take it up. With another little laugh, he turned away, saying:

"No; Mrs. Peters doesn't need supervising. For that matter, a sheriff's wife is married to the law. Ever think of it that way, Mrs. Peters?"

Mrs. Peters was standing beside the table. Mrs. Hale shot a look up at her; but she could not see her face. Mrs. Peters had turned away. When she spoke, her voice was muffled.

"Not—just that way," she said.

"Married to the law!" chuckled Mrs. Peters' husband. He moved toward the   285 door into the front room, and said to the county attorney:

"I just want you to come in here a minute, George. We ought to take a look at these windows."

"Oh—windows," said the county attorney scoffingly.

"We'll be right out, Mr. Hale," said the sheriff to the farmer, who was still waiting by the door.

Hale went to look after the horses. The sheriff followed the county attorney into the other room. Again—for one final moment—the two women were alone in that kitchen.

Martha Hale sprang up, her hands tight together, looking at that other   290 woman, with whom it rested. At first she could not see her eyes, for the sheriff's wife had not turned back since she turned away at that suggestion of being married to the law. But now Mrs. Hale made her turn back. Her eyes made her turn back. Slowly, unwillingly, Mrs. Peters turned her head until her eyes met the eyes of the other woman. There was a moment when they held each other in a steady, burning look in which there was no evasion nor flinching. Then Martha Hale's eyes pointed the way to the basket in which was hidden the thing that would make certain the conviction of the other woman—that woman who was not there and yet who had been there with them all through that hour.

For a moment Mrs. Peters did not move. And then she did it. With a rush forward, she threw back the quilt pieces, got the box, tried to put it in her handbag. It was too big. Desperately she opened it, started to take the bird out. But there she broke—she could not touch the bird. She stood there helpless, foolish.

There was the sound of a knob turning in the inner door. Martha Hale snatched the box from the sheriff's wife, and got it in the pocket of her big coat just as the sheriff and the county attorney came back into the kitchen.

"Well, Henry," said the county attorney facetiously, "at least we found out that she was not going to quilt it. She was going to—what is it you call it, ladies?"

Mrs. Hale's hand was against the pocket of her coat.

"We call it—knot it, Mr. Henderson."   295

QUESTIONS

1. Who is the major character? That is, on whom does the story focus?
2. Describe the differences between Mrs. Hale and Mrs. Peters, in terms of their status, backgrounds, and comparative strengths of character.

3. Why do the two ladies not voice their conclusions about the murderer? How does Glaspell show that they both know the murderer, the reasons, and the method? Why do they both "cover up" at the story's conclusion?

JAMES THURBER   (1894–1961)

The Greatest Man in the World   *1935*

Looking back on it now, from the vantage point of 1950, one can only marvel that it hadn't happened long before it did. The United States of America had been, even since Kitty Hawk,° blindly constructing the elaborate petard by which, sooner or later, it must be hoist.° It was inevitable that some day there would come roaring out of the skies a national hero of insufficient intelligence, background, and character successfully to endure the mounting orgies of glory prepared for aviators who stayed up a long time or flew a great distance. Both Lindbergh° and Byrd,° fortunately for national decorum and international amity, had been gentlemen; so had our other famous aviators. They wore their laurels gracefully, withstood the awful weather of publicity, married excellent women, usually of fine family, and quietly retired to private life and the enjoyment of their varying fortunes. No untoward incidents, on a worldwide scale, marred the perfection of their conduct on the perilous heights of fame. The exception to the rule was, however, bound to occur and it did, in July, 1937, when Jack ("Pal") Smurch, erstwhile mechanics' helper in a small garage in Westfield, Iowa, flew a second-hand, single-motored Bresthaven Dragon-Fly III monoplane all the way around the world, without stopping.

Never before in the history of aviation had such a flight as Smurch's ever been dreamed of. No one had even taken seriously the weird floating auxiliary gas tanks, invention of the mad New Hampshire professor of astronomy, Dr. Charles Lewis Gresham, upon which Smurch placed full reliance. When the garage worker, a slightly built, surly, unprepossessing young man of twenty-two appeared at Roosevelt Field in early July, 1937, slowly chewing a great quid of scrap tobacco, and announced "Nobody ain't seen no flyin' yet," the newspapers touched briefly and satirically upon his projected twenty-five-thousand-mile flight. Aeronautical and automotive experts dismissed the idea curtly, implying that it was a hoax, a publicity stunt. The rusty, battered, second-hand plane wouldn't go. The Gresham auxiliary tanks wouldn't work. It was simply a cheap joke.

Smurch, however, after calling on a girl in Brooklyn who worked in the flap-folding department of a large paper-box factory, a girl whom he later described as his "sweet patootie," climbed nonchalantly into his ridiculous plane at dawn of the memorable seventh of July, 1937, spat a curve of tobacco juice into the still

Kitty Hawk: in North Carolina, the location of the first heavier-than-air flight by the Wright brothers in 1903.

petard . . . hoist: that is, to be destroyed by one's own cleverness. See *Hamlet*, Act III, scene iv, lines 206–207.

Lindbergh: Charles A. Lindbergh (1902–1974), considered to be America's greatest aviation hero, made the first solo trans-Atlantic flight in May 1927.

Byrd: Richard E. Byrd, "Admiral Byrd" (1888–1957), made the first flight to the North Pole in 1926, and the first airmail flight to France in June 1927.

air, and took off, carrying with him only a gallon of bootleg gin and six pounds of salami.

When the garage boy thundered out over the ocean the papers were forced to record, in all seriousness, that a mad, unknown young man—his name was variously misspelled—had actually set out upon a preposterous attempt to span the world in a rickety, one-engined contraption, trusting to the long-distance refueling device of a crazy schoolmaster. When, nine days later, without having stopped once, the tiny place appeared above San Francisco Bay, headed for New York, spluttering and choking, to be sure, but still magnificently and miraculously aloft, the headlines, which long since had crowded everything else off the front page—even the shooting of the Governor of Illinois by the Vileti gang—swelled to unprecedented size, and the news stories began to run to twenty-five and thirty columns. It was noticeable, however, that the accounts of the epoch-making flight touched rather lightly upon the aviator himself. This was not because facts about the hero as a man were too meagre, but because they were too complete.

Reporters, who had been rushed out to Iowa when Smurch's plane was first sighted over the little French coast town of Serly-le-Mar, to dig up the story of the great man's life, had promptly discovered that the story of his life could not be printed. His mother, a sullen short-order cook in a shack restaurant on the edge of a tourists' camping ground near Westfield, met all enquiries as to her son with an angry, "Ah, the hell with him; I hope he drowns." His father appeared to be in jail somewhere for stealing spotlights and laprobes from tourists' automobiles; his younger brother, a weak-minded lad, had but recently escaped from the Preston, Iowa Reformatory and was already wanted in several Western towns for the theft of money-order blanks from post offices. These alarming discoveries were still piling up at the very time that Pal Smurch, the greatest hero of the twentieth century, blear-eyed, dead for sleep, half-starved, was piloting his crazy junk-heap high above the region in which the lamentable story of his private life was being unearthed, headed for New York under greater glory than any man of his time had ever known.

The necessity for printing some account in the papers of the young man's career and personality had led to a remarkable predicament. It was of course impossible to reveal the facts, for a tremendous popular feeling in favor of the young hero had sprung up, like a grass fire, when he was halfway across Europe on his flight around the globe. He was, therefore, described as a modest chap, taciturn, blond, popular with his friends, popular with girls. The only available snapshot of Smurch, taken at the wheel of a phony automobile in a cheap photo studio at an amusement park, was touched up so that the little vulgarian looked quite handsome. His twisted leer was smoothed into a pleasant smile. The truth was, in this way, kept from the youth's ecstatic compatriots; they did not dream that the Smurch family was despised and feared by its neighbors in the obscure Iowa town, nor that the hero himself, because of numerous unsavory exploits, had come to be regarded in Westfield as a nuisance and a menace. He had, the reporters discovered, once knifed the principal of his high school—not mortally, to be sure, but he had knifed him; and on another occasion, surprised in the act of stealing an altar-cloth from a church, he had bashed the sacristan over the head with a pot of Easter lilies; for each of these offences he had served a sentence in the reformatory.

Inwardly, the authorities, both in New York and in Washington, prayed that an understanding Providence might, however awful such a thing seemed, bring disaster to the rusty, battered plane and its illustrious pilot, whose unheard-of flight had aroused the civilized world to hosannas of hysterical praise. The authorities were convinced that the character of the renowned aviator was such that the limelight of adulation was bound to reveal him to all the world, as a congenital hooligan mentally and morally unequipped to cope with his own prodigious fame. "I trust," said the Secretary of State, at one of many secret Cabinet meetings called to consider the national dilemma, "I trust that his mother's prayer will be answered," by which he referred to Mrs. Emma Smurch's wish that her son might be drowned. It was, however, too late for that—Smurch had leaped the Atlantic and then the Pacific as if they were millponds. At three minutes after two o'clock in the afternoon of 17 July, 1937, the garage boy brought his idiotic plane into Roosevelt Field for a perfect three-point landing.

It had, of course, been out of the question to arrange a modest little reception for the greatest flier in the history of the world. He was received at Roosevelt Field with such elaborate and pretentious ceremonies as rocked the world. Fortunately, however, the worn and spent hero promptly swooned, had to be removed bodily from his plane, and was spirited from the field without having opened his mouth once. Thus he did not jeopardize the dignity of this first reception, a reception illuminated by the presence of the Secretaries of War and the Navy, Mayor Michael J. Moriarity of New York, the Premier of Canada, Governors Fanniman, Groves, McFeely, and Critchfield, and a brilliant array of European diplomats. Smurch did not, in fact, come to in time to take part in the gigantic hullabaloo arranged at City Hall for the next day. He was rushed to a secluded nursing home and confined to bed. It was nine days before he was able to get up, or to be more exact, before he was permitted to get up. Meanwhile the greatest minds in the country, in solemn assembly, had arranged a secret conference of city, state and government officials, which Smurch was to attend for the purpose of being instructed in the ethics and behavior of heroism.

On the day that the little mechanic was finally allowed to get up and dress and, for the first time in two weeks, took a great chew of tobacco, he was permitted to receive the newspapermen—this by way of testing him out. Smurch did not wait for questions. "Youse guys," he said—and the *Times* man winced—"youse guys can tell the cock-eyed world dat I put it over on Lindbergh, see? Yeh—an' made an ass o' them two frogs." The "two frogs" was a reference to a pair of gallant French fliers who, in attempting a flight only halfway round the world, had, two weeks before, unhappily been lost at sea. The *Times* man was bold enough, at this point, to sketch out for Smurch the accepted formula for interviews in cases of this kind; he explained that there should be no arrogant statements belittling the achievements of other heroes, particularly heroes of foreign nations. "Ah, the hell with that," said Smurch. "I did it, see? I did it, an' I'm talkin' about it." And he did talk about it.

None of this extraordinary interview was, of course, printed. On the contrary, the newspapers, already under the disciplined direction of a secret directorate created for the occasion and composed of statesmen and editors, gave out to a panting and restless world that "Jacky," as he had been arbitrarily nicknamed, would consent to say only that he was very happy and that anyone could have done what he did. "My achievement has been, I fear, slightly exaggerated," the *Times* man's article had him protest, with a modest smile. These newspaper stories

10

were kept from the hero, a restriction which did not serve to abate the rising malevolence of his temper. The situation was, indeed, extremely grave, for Pal Smurch was, as he kept insisting, "rarin' to go." He could not much longer be kept from a nation clamorous to lionize him. It was the most desperate crisis the United States of America had faced since the sinking of the *Lusitania.*°

On the afternoon of the twenty-seventh of July, Smurch was spirited away to a conference-room in which were gathered mayors, governors, government officials, behaviorist psychologists, and editors. He gave them each a limp, moist paw and a brief unlovely grin. "Hah ya?"° he said. When Smurch was seated, the Mayor of New York arose and, with obvious pessimism, attempted to explain what he must say and how he must act when presented to the world, ending his talk with a high tribute to the hero's courage and integrity. The Mayor was followed by Governor Fanniman of New York, who, after a touching declaration of faith, introduced Cameron Spottiswood, Second Secretary of the American Embassy in Paris, the gentlemen selected to coach Smurch in the amenities of public cere-monies. Sitting in a chair, with a soiled yellow tie in his hand and his shirt open at the throat, unshaved, smoking a rolled cigarette, Jack Smurch listened with a leer on his lips. "I get ya, I get ya," he cut in nastily. "Ya want me to ack like a softy, huh? Ya want me to ack like that—baby-faced Lindbergh, huh? Well, nuts to that, see?" Everyone took in his breath sharply; it was a sigh and a hiss. "Mr. Lindbergh," began a United States Senator, purple with rage, "and Mr. Byrd—" Smurch, who was paring his nails with a jacknife, cut in again, "Byrd!" he exclaimed. "Aw fa God's sake, dat big—" Somebody shut off his blasphemies with a sharp word. A newcomer had entered the room. Everyone stood up, except Smurch, who, still busy with his nails, did not even glance up. "Mr. Smurch," said someone sternly, "the President of the United States!" It had been thought that the presence of the Chief Executive might have a chastening effect upon the young hero, and the former had been, thanks to the remarkable co-operation of the press, secretly brought to the obscure conference room.

A great, painful silence fell. Smurch looked up, waved a hand at the President. "How ya comin?" he asked, and began rolling a fresh cigarette. The silence deepened. Someone coughed in a strained way. "Geez it's hot, ain't it?" said Smurch. He loosened two more shirt buttons, revealing a hairy chest and the tattooed word "Sadie" enclosed in a stenciled heart. The great and important men in the room, faced by the most serious crisis in recent American history, exchanged worried frowns. Nobody seemed to know how to proceed. "Come awn, come awn," said Smurch. "Let's get the hell out of here! When do I start cuttin' in on de parties, huh? And what's they goin' to be *in* it?" He rubbed a thumb and a forefinger together meaningly. "Money!" exclaimed a state senator, shocked, pale. "Yeh, money," said Pal, flipping his cigarette out of a window, "an' big money." He began rolling a fresh cigarette. "Big money," he repeated, frowning over the rice paper. He tilted back in his chair, and leered at each gentlemen, separately, the leer of an animal that knows its power, the leer of a leopard loose in a bird-and-dog shop. "Aw, fa God's sake, let's get some place where it's cooler," he said. "I been cooped up plenty for three weeks!"

Lusitania: British liner sunk by a German submarine in 1915. More than a thousand people were killed, including 128 Americans.
Hah ya: "How are you?"

Smurch stood up and walked over to an open window, where he stood staring down into the street, nine floors below. The faint shouting of newsboys floated up to him. He made out his name. "Hot dog!" he cried, grinning, ecstatic. He leaned out over the sill. "You tell 'em, babies!" he shouted down. "Hot diggity dog!" In the tense little knot of men standing behind him, a quick, mad impulse flared up. An unspoken word of appeal, of command, seemed to ring through the room. Yet it was deadly silent. Charles K. I. Brand, secretary to the Mayor of New York City, happened to be standing nearest Smurch; he looked inquiringly at the President of the United States. The President, pale, grim, nodded shortly. Brand, a tall, powerfully built man, once a tackle at Rutgers, stepped forward, seized the greatest man in the world by his left shoulder and the seat of his pants, and pushed him out of the window.

"My God, he's fallen out the window!" cried a quick-witted editor.

"Get me out of here!" cried the President. Several men sprang to his side 15 and he was hurriedly escorted out of a door toward a side-entrance of the building. The editor of the Associated Press took charge, being used to such things. Crisply he ordered certain men to leave, others to stay; quickly he outlined a story which all the papers were to agree on, sent two men to the street to handle that end of the tragedy, commanded a Senator to sob and two Congressmen to go to pieces nervously. In a word, he skillfully set the stage for the gigantic task that was to follow, the task of breaking to a grief-stricken world the sad story of the untimely, accidental death of its most illustrious and spectacular figure.

The funeral was, as you know, the most elaborate, the finest, the solemnest, and the saddest ever held in the United States of America. The monument in Arlington Cemetery, with its clean white shaft of marble and the simple device of a tiny plane on its base, is a place for pilgrims, in deep reverence, to visit. The nations of the world paid lofty tributes to little Jacky Smurch, America's greatest hero. At a given hour there were two minutes of silence throughout the nation. Even the inhabitants of the small, bewildered town of Westfield, Iowa, observed this touching ceremony; agents of the Department of Justice saw to that. One of them was especially assigned to stand grimly in the doorway of a little shack restaurant on the edge of the tourists' camping ground just outside the town. There, under his stern scrutiny, Mrs. Emma Smurch bowed her head above two hamburger steaks sizzling on her grill—bowed her head and turned away, so that the Secret Service man could not see the twisted, strangely familiar, leer on her lips.

QUESTIONS

1. Describe Jacky Smurch. What do you learn about him from his actions, the words of others, and his statements? Is he flat or round?

2. How probable is it that a person in Smurch's position would refuse to undergo the changes required of his new success? How probable that someone would push him out the window if he didn't? From your answers, what conclusions can you make about the story's level of realism?

3. Describe the humor of the story. What does Thurber ask you to laugh at? How is the laughter produced? How is the conflict linked to the humor?

4. What serious purpose underlies the story? To what degree is it true that

public relations require people to adjust their character to what is expected of them? What might happen if politicians, for example, did not scrupulously control the "image" they project before the public?

WILLIAM FAULKNER   (1897–1962)

Barn Burning   *1939*

The store in which the Justice of the Peace's court was sitting smelled of cheese. The boy, crouched on his nail keg at the back of the crowded room, knew he smelled cheese, and more; from where he sat he could see the ranked shelves close-packed with the solid, squat, dynamic shapes of tin cans whose labels his stomach read, not from the lettering which meant nothing to his mind but from the scarlet devils and the silver curve of fish—this, the cheese which he knew he smelled and the hermetic meat° which his intestines believed he smelled coming in intermittent gusts momentary and brief between the other constant one, the smell and sense just a little of fear because mostly of despair and grief, the old fierce pull of blood. He could not see the table where the Justice sat and before which his father and his father's enemy (*our enemy* he thought in that despair; *ourn! mine and his both! He's my father!*) stood, but he could hear them, the two of them that is, because his father had said no word yet:

"But what proof have you, Mr. Harris?"

"I told you. The hog got into my corn. I caught it up and sent it back to him. He had no fence that would hold it. I told him so, warned him. The next time I put the hog in my pen. When he came to get it I gave him enough wire to patch up his pen. The next time I put the hog up and kept it. I rode down to his house and saw the wire I gave him still rolled on to the spool in his yard. I told him he could have the hog when he paid me a dollar pound fee. That evening a nigger came with the dollar and got the hog. He was a strange nigger. He said, 'He say to tell you wood and hay kin burn.' I said, 'What?' 'That what he say to tell you,' the nigger said. 'Wood and hay kin burn.' That night my barn burned. I got the stock out but I lost the barn."

"Where is the nigger? Have you got him?"

"He was a strange nigger, I tell you. I don't know what became of him."   5

"But that's not proof. Don't you see that's not proof?"

"Get that boy up here. He knows." For a moment the boy thought too that the man meant his older brother until Harris said. "Not him. The little one. The boy," and, crouching, small for his age, small and wiry like his father, in patched and faded jeans even too small for him, with straight, uncombed, brown hair and eyes gray and wild as storm scud, he saw the men between himself and the table part and become a lane of grim faces, at the end of which he saw the Justice, a shabby, collarless, graying man in spectacles, beckoning him. He felt no floor under his bare feet; he seemed to walk beneath the palpable weight of the grim turning faces. His father, stiff in his black Sunday coat donned not for the trial but for the moving, did not even look at him. *He aims for me to lie,* he thought, again with that frantic grief and despair. *And I will have to do hit.*

hermetic meat: canned meat.

"What's your name, boy?" the Justice said.

"Colonel Sartoris Snopes," the boy whispered.

"Hey?" the Justice said. "Talk louder. Colonel Sartoris? I reckon anybody 10 named for Colonel Sartoris in this country can't help but tell the truth, can they?" The boy said nothing. *Enemy! Enemy!* he thought; for a moment he could not even see, could not see that the Justice's face was kindly nor discern that his voice was troubled when he spoke to the man named Harris: "Do you want me to question this boy?" But he could hear, and during those subsequent long seconds there was absolutely no sound in the crowded little room save that of quiet and intent breathing it was as if he had swung outward at the end of a grape vine, over a ravine, and at the top of the swing had been caught in a prolonged instant of mesmerized gravity, weightless in time.

"No!" Harris said violently, explosively. "Damnation! Send him out of here!" Now time, the fluid world, rushed beneath him again, the voices coming to him again through the smell of cheese and sealed meat, the fear and despair and the old grief of blood:

"This case is closed. I can't find against you, Snopes, but I can give you advice. Leave this country and don't come back to it."

His father spoke for the first time, his voice cold and harsh, level, without emphasis: "I aim to. I don't figure to stay in a country among people who . . ." he said something unprintable and vile, addressed to no one.

"That'll do," the Justice said, "Take your wagon and get out of this country before dark. Case dismissed."

His father turned, and he followed the stiff black coat, the wiry figure 15 walking a little stiffly, from where a Confederate provost's man's musket ball had taken him in the heel on a stolen horse thirty years ago, followed the two backs now, since his older brother had appeared from somewhere in the crowd, no taller than the father but thicker, chewing tobacco steadily, between the two lines of grim-faced men and out of the store and across the worn gallery and down the sagging steps and among the dogs and half-grown boys in the mild May dust, where as he passed a voice hissed:

"Barn burner!"

Again he could not see, whirling; there was a face in a red haze, moonlike, bigger than the full moon, the owner of it half again his size, he leaping in the red haze toward the face, feeling no blow, feeling no shock when his head struck the earth, scrabbling up and leaping again, feeling no blow this time either and tasting no blood, scrabbling up to see the other boy in full flight and himself already leaping into pursuit as his father's hand jerked him back, the harsh, cold voice speaking above him: "Go get in the wagon."

It stood in a grove of locusts and mulberries across the road. His two hulking sisters in their Sunday dresses and his mother and her sister in calico and sunbonnets were already in it, sitting on and among the sorry residue of the dozen and more movings which even the boy could remember—the battered stove, the broken beds and chairs, the clock inlaid with mother-of-pearl, which would not run, stopped at some fourteen minutes past two o'clock of a dead and forgotten day and time, which had been his mother's dowry. She was crying, though when she saw him she drew her sleeve across her face and began to descend from the wagon. "Get back," the father said.

"He's hurt, I got to get some water and wash his . . ."

"Get back in the wagon." his father said. He got in too, over the tail-gate.   20
His father mounted to the seat where the older brother already sat and struck the
gaunt mules two savage blows with the peeled willow, but without heat. It was not
even sadistic; it was exactly that same quality which in later years would cause his
descendants to over-run the engine before putting a motor car into motion, striking
and reining back in the same movement. The wagon went on, the store with its
quiet crowd of grimly watching men dropped behind; a curve in the road hid it.
Forever he thought. *Maybe he's done satisfied now, now that he has . . .* stopping himself,
not to say it aloud even to himself. His mother's hand touched his shoulder.

"Does hit hurt?" she said.

"Naw," he said. "Hit don't hurt. Lemme be."

"Can't you wipe some of the blood off before hit dries?"

"I'll wash tonight," he said. "Lemme be, I tell you."

The wagon went on. He did not know where they were going. None of them   25
ever did or ever asked, because it was always somewhere, always a house of sorts
waiting for them a day or two days or even three days away. Likely his father had
already arranged to make a crop on another farm before he . . . Again he had to
stop himself. He (the father) always did. There was something about his wolflike
independence and even courage when the advantage was at least neutral which
impressed strangers, as if they got from his latent ravening ferocity not so much
a sense of dependability as a feeling that his ferocious conviction in the rightness
of his own actions would be of advantage to all whose interest lay with his.

That night they camped, in a grove of oaks and beeches where a spring ran.
The nights were still cool and they had a fire against it, of a rail lifted from a
nearby fence and cut into lengths—a smalll fire, neat, niggard almost, a shrewd
fire; such fires were his father's habit and custom always, even in freezing weather.
Older, the boy might have remarked this and wondered why not a big one; why
should not a man who had not only seen the waste and extravagance of war, but
who had in his blood an inherent prodigality with material not his own, have
burned everything in sight? Then he might have gone a step farther and thought
that that was the reason; that niggard blaze was the living fruits of nights passed
during those four years in the woods hiding from all men, blue or grey, with his
strings of horses (captured horses, he called them). And older still, he might have
divined the true reason: that the element of fire spoke to some deep mainspring
of his father's being, as the element of steel or of powder spoke to other men, as
the one weapon for the preservation of integrity, else breath were not worth the
breathing, and hence to be regarded with respect and used with discretion.

But he did not think this now and he had seen those same niggard blazes
all his life. He merely ate his supper beside it and was already half asleep over his
iron plate when his father called him, and once more he followed the stiff back,
the stiff and ruthless limp, up the slope and on to the starlit road where, turning,
he could see his father against the stars but without face or depth—a shape black,
flat, and bloodless as though cut from tin in the iron folds of the frockcoat which
had not been made for him, the voice harsh like tin and without heat like tin:

"You were fixing to tell them. You would have told him." He didn't answer.
His father struck him with the flat of his hand on the side of the head, hard but
without heat, exactly as he had struck the two mules at the store, exactly as he
would strike either of them with any stick in order to kill a horse fly, his voice still
without heat or anger: "You're getting to be a man. You got to learn. You got to

learn to stick to your own blood or you ain't going to have any blood to stick to you. Do you think either of them, any man there this morning, would? Don't you know all they wanted was a chance to get at me because they knew I had them beat? Eh?" Later, twenty years later, he was to tell himself, "If I had said they wanted only truth, justice, he would have hit me again." But now he said nothing. He was not crying. He just stood there. "Answer me," his father said.

"Yes," he whispered. His father turned.

"Get on to bed. We'll be there tomorrow."

Tomorrow they were there. In the early afternoon the wagon stopped before a paintless two-room house identical almost with the dozen others it had stopped before even in the boy's ten years, and again, as on the other dozen occasions, his mother and aunt got down and began to unload the wagon, although his two sisters and his father and brother had not moved.

"Likely hit ain't fitten for hawgs," one of the sisters said.

"Nevertheless, fit it will and you'll hog it and like it," his father said. "Get out of them chairs and help your Ma unload."

The two sisters got down, big, bovine, in a flutter of cheap ribbons; one of them drew from the jumbled wagon bed a battered lantern, the other a worn broom. His father handed the reins to the older son and began to climb stiffly over the wheel. "When they get unloaded, take the team to the barn and feed them." Then he said, and at first the boy thought he was still speaking to his brother: "Come with me."

"Me?" he said.

"Yes," his father said. "You."

"Abner," his mother said. His father paused and looked back—the harsh level stare beneath the shaggy, graying, irascible brows.

"I reckon I'll have a word with the man that aims to begin tomorrow owning me body and soul for the next eight months."

They went back up the road. A week ago—or before last night, that is—he would have asked where they were going, but not now. His father had struck him before last night but never before had he paused afterward to explain why; it was as if the blow and the following calm, outrageous voice still rang, repercussed, divulging nothing to him save the terrible handicap of being young, the light weight of his few years, just heavy enough to prevent his soaring free of the world as it seemed to be ordered but not heavy enough to keep footed solid in it, to resist it and try to change the course of its events.

Presently he could see the grove of oaks and cedars and the other flowering trees and shrubs where the house would be, though not the house yet. They walked beside a fence massed with honeysuckle and Cherokee roses and came to a gate swinging open between two brick pillars, and now, beyond a sweep of drive, he saw the house for the first time and at that instant he forgot his father and the terror and despair both, and even when he remembered his father again (who had stopped) the terror and despair did not return. Because, for all the twelve movings, they had sojourned until now in a poor country, a land of small farms and fields and houses, and he had never seen a house like this before. *Hit's big as a courthouse* he thought quietly, with a surge of peace and joy whose reason he could not have thought into words, being too young for that: *They are safe from him. People whose lives are a part of this peace and dignity are beyond his touch, he no more to them than a buzzing wasp: capable of stinging for a little moment but that's all; the spell of this peace and dignity rendering even the barns and stable and cribs which belong to it impervious to the puny flames he might contrive* . . . this, the peace and joy, ebbing for an instant as he looked again at the stiff black back, the stiff and implacable limp of the figure which was not dwarfed by the house, for the reason that it had never looked big anywhere and which now, against the serene columned backdrop, had more than ever that impervious quality of something cut ruthlessly from tin, depthless, as though, sidewise to the sun, it would cast no shadow. Watching him, the boy remarked the absolutely undeviating course which his father held and saw the stiff foot come squarely down in a pile of fresh droppings where a horse had stood in the drive and which his father could have avoided by a simple change of stride. But it ebbed only for a moment, though he could not have thought this into words either, walking on in the spell of the house, which he could even want but without envy, without sorrow, certainly never with that ravening and jealous rage which unknown to him walked in the ironlike black coat before him: *Maybe he will feel it too. Maybe it will even change him now from what maybe he couldn't help but be.*

They crossed the portico. Now he could hear his father's stiff foot as it came down on the boards with clocklike finality, a sound out of all proportion to the displacement of the body it bore and which was not dwarfed either by the white door before it, as though it had attained to a sort of vicious and ravening minimum not to be dwarfed by anything—the flat, wide, black hat, the formal coat of broadcloth which had once been black but which had now that friction-glazed greenish cast of the bodies of old house flies, the lifted sleeve which was too large, the lifted hand like a curled claw. The door opened so promptly that the boy knew the Negro must have been watching them all the time, an old man with neat grizzled hair, in a linen jacket, who stood barring the door with his body, saying "Wipe yo foots, white man, fo you come in here. Major ain't home nohow."

"Get out of my way, nigger," his father said, without heat too, flinging the door back and the Negro also and entering, his hat still on his head. And now the boy saw the prints of the stiff foot on the doorsill and saw them appear on the pale rug behind the machinelike deliberation of the foot which seemed to bear (or transmit) twice the weight which the body compassed. The Negro was shouting "Miss Lula! Miss Lula!" somewhere behind them, then the boy, deluged as though by a warm wave by a suave turn of carpeted stair and a pendant glitter of chandeliers and a mute gleam of gold frames, heard the swift feet and saw her too, a lady—perhaps he had never seen her like before either—in a gray, smooth gown with lace at the throat and an apron tied at the waist and the sleeves turned back, wiping cake or biscuit dough from her hands with a towel as she came up the hall, looking not at his father at all but at the tracks on the blond rug with an expression of incredulous amazement.

"I tried," the Negro cried. "I tole him to . . ."

"Will you please go away?" she said in a shaking voice. "Major de Spain is not at home. Will you please go away?"

His father had not spoken again. He did not speak again. He did not even look at her. He just stood stiff in the center of the rug, in his hat, the shaggy iron-gray brows twitching slightly above the pebble-colored eyes as he appeared to examine the house with brief deliberation. Then with the same deliberation he turned; the boy watched him pivot on the good leg and saw the stiff foot drag

45

round the arc of the turning, leaving a final long and fading smear. His father never looked at it, he never once looked down at the rug. The Negro held the door. It closed behind them, upon the hysteric and indistinguishable woman-wail. His father stopped at the top of the steps and scraped his boot clean on the edge of it. At the gate he stopped again. He stood for a moment, planted stiffly on the stiff foot, looking back at the house. "Pretty and white, ain't it?" he said. "That's sweat. Nigger sweat. Maybe it ain't white enough yet to suit him. Maybe he wants to mix some white sweat with it."

Two hours later the boy was chopping wood behind the house within which his mother and aunt and the two sisters (the mother and aunt, not the two girls, he knew that; even at this distance and muffled by walls the flat loud voices of the two girls emanated an incorrigible idle inertia) were setting up the stove to prepare a meal, when he heard the hooves and saw the linen-clad man on a fine sorrel mare, whom he recognized even before he saw the rolled rug in front of the Negro youth following on a fat bay carriage horse—a suffused, angry face vanishing, still at full gallop, beyond the corner of the house where his father and brother were sitting in the two tilted chairs; and a moment later, almost before he could have put the axe down, he heard the hooves again and watched the sorrel mare go back out of the yard, already galloping again. Then his father began to shout one of the sisters' names, who presently emerged backward from the kitchen door dragging the rolled rug along the ground by one end while the other sister walked behind it.

"If you ain't going to tote, go on and set up the wash pot," the first said.

"You, Sarty!" the second shouted. "Set up the wash pot!" His father appeared at the door, framed against that shabbiness, as he had been against that other bland perfection, impervious to either, the mother's anxious face at his shoulder.

"Go on," the father said. "Pick it up." The two sisters stooped, broad, lethargic; stooping, they presented an incredible expanse of pale cloth and a flutter of tawdry ribbons.

"If I thought enough of a rug to have to git hit all the way from France I   50
wouldn't keep hit where folks coming in would have to tromp on hit," the first said. They raised the rug.

"Abner," the mother said. "Let me do it."

"You go back and git dinner," his father said. "I'll tend to this."

From the woodpile through the rest of the afternoon the boy watched them, the rug spread flat in the dust beside the bubbling wash pot, the two sisters stooping over it with that profound and lethargic reluctance, while the father stood over them in turn, implacable and grim, driving them though never raising his voice again. He could smell the harsh homemade lye they were using; he saw his mother come to the door once and look toward them with an expression not anxious now but very like despair; he saw his father turn, and he fell to with the axe and saw from the corner of his eye his father raise from the ground a flattish fragment of field stone and examine it and return to the pot, and this time his mother actually spoke: "Abner. Abner. Please don't. Please, Abner."

Then he was done too. It was dusk; the whippoorwills had already begun. He could smell coffee from the room where they would presently eat the cold food remaining from the mid-afternoon meal, though when he entered the house he realized they were having coffee again because there was a fire on the hearth, before which the rug now lay spread over the backs of the two chairs. The tracks of his father's foot were gone. Where they had been were now long, water-cloudy scoriations resembling the sporadic course of a Lilliputian mowing machine.

It still hung there while they ate the cold food and then went to bed, scattered without order or claim up and down the two rooms, his mother in one bed, where his father would later lie, the older brother in the other, himself, the aunt, and the two sisters on pallets on the floor. But his father was not in bed yet. The last thing the boy remembered was the depthless, harsh silhouette of the hat and coat bending over the rug and it seemed to him that he had not even closed his eyes when the silhouette was standing over him, the fire almost dead behind it, the stiff foot prodding him awake. "Catch up the mule," his father said.

When he returned with the mule his father was standing in the black door, the rolled rug over his shoulder. "Ain't you going to ride?" he said.

"No. Give me your foot."

He bent his knee into his father's hand, the wiry, surprising power flowed smoothly, rising, he rising with it, on to the mule's bare back (they had owned a saddle once; the boy could remember it though not when or where) and with the same effortlessness his father swung the rug up in front of him. Now in the starlight they retraced the afternoon's path, up the dusty road rife with honeysuckle, through the gate and up the black tunnel of the drive to the lightless house, where he sat on the mule and felt the rough warp of the rug drag across his thighs and vanish.

"Don't you want me to help?" he whispered. His father did not answer and now he heard again that stiff foot striking the hollow portico with that wooden and clocklike deliberation, that outrageous overstatement of the weight it carried. The rug, hunched, not flung (the boy could tell that even in the darkness) from his father's shoulder, struck the angle of wall and floor with a sound unbelievably loud, thunderous, then the foot again, unhurried and enormous; a light came on in the house and the boy sat, tense, breathing steadily and quietly and just a little fast, though the foot itself did not increase its beat at all, descending the steps now; now the boy could see him.

"Don't you want to ride now?" he whispered. "We kin both ride now," the light within the house altering now, flaring up and sinking. *He's coming down the stairs now,* he thought. He had already ridden the mule up beside the horse block; presently his father was up behind him and he doubled the reins over and slashed the mule across the neck, but before the animal could begin to trot the hard, thin arm came round him, the hard, knotted hand jerking the mule back to a walk.

In the first red rays of the sun they were in the lot, putting plow gear on the mules. This time the sorrel mare was in the lot before he heard it at all, the rider collarless and even bareheaded, trembling, speaking in a shaking voice as the woman in the house had done, his father merely looking up once before stooping again to the hame he was buckling, so that the man on the mare spoke to his stooping back:

"You must realize you have ruined that rug. Wasn't there anybody here, any of your women . . ." He ceased, shaking, the boy watching him, the older brother leaning now in the stable door, chewing, blinking slowly and steadily at nothing apparently. "It cost a hundred dollars. But you never had a hundred dollars. You never will. So I'm going to charge you twenty bushels of corn against your crop. I'll add it in your contract and when you come to the commissary you

55

60

can sign it. That won't keep Mrs. de Spain quiet but maybe it will teach you to wipe your feet off before you enter her house again."

Then he was gone. The boy looked at his father, who still had not spoken or even looked up again, who was now adjusting the logger-head in the hame.

"Pap," he said. His father looked at him—the inscrutable face, the shaggy brows beneath which the gray eyes glinted coldly. Suddenly the boy went toward him, fast, stopping as suddenly. "You done the best you could!" he cried. "If he wanted hit done different why didn't he wait and tell you how? He won't git no twenty bushels! He won't git none! We'll get hit and hide hit! I kin watch . . ."

"Did you put the cutter back in that straight stock like I told you?" 65

"No, sir," he said.

"Then go do it."

That was Wednesday. During the rest of that week he worked steadily, at what was within his scope and some which was beyond it, with an industry that did not need to be driven nor even commanded twice; he had this from his mother, with the difference that some at least of what he did he liked to do, such as splitting wood with the half-size axe which his mother and aunt had earned, or saved money somehow, to present him with at Christmas. In company with the two older women (and on one afternoon even one of the sisters), he built pens for the shoat and the cow which were a part of his father's contract with the landlord, and one afternoon, his father being absent, gone somewhere on one of the mules, he went to the field.

They were running a middle buster now, his brother holding the plow straight while he handled the reins, and walking beside the straining mule, the rich black soil shearing cool and damp against his bare ankles, he thought *Maybe this is the end of it. Maybe even that twenty bushels that seems hard to have to pay for just a rug will be a cheap price for him to stop forever and always from being what he used to be*; thinking, dreaming now, so that his brother had to speak sharply to him to mind the mule: *Maybe he even won't collect the twenty bushels. Maybe it will all add up and balance and vanish—corn, rug, fire; the terror and grief, the being pulled two ways like between two teams of horses—gone, done with forever and ever.*

Then it was Saturday; he looked up from beneath the mule he was harnessing 70 and saw his father in the black coat and hat. "Not that," his father said. "The wagon gear." And then, two hours later, sitting in the wagon bed behind his father and brother on the seat, the wagon accomplished a final curve, and he saw the weathered paintless store with its tattered tobacco- and patent-medicine posters and the tethered wagons and saddle animals below the gallery. He mounted the gnawed steps behind his father and brother, and there again was the lane of quiet, watching faces for the three of them to walk through. He saw the man in spectacles sitting at the plank table and he did not need to be told this was a Justice of the Peace; he sent one glare of fierce, exultant, partisan defiance at the man in collar and cravat now, whom he had seen but twice in his life, and that on a galloping horse, who now wore on his face an expression not of rage but of amazed unbelief which the boy could not have known was at the incredible circumstance of being sued by one of his own tenants, and came and stood against his father and cried at the Justice: "He ain't done it! He ain't burnt . . ."

"Go back to the wagon," his father said.

"Burnt?" the Justice said. "Do I understand this rug was burned too?"

"Does anybody here claim it was?" his father said. "Go back to the wagon."

But he did not, he merely retreated to the rear of the room, crowded as that other had been, but not to sit down this time, instead, to stand pressing among the motionless bodies, listening to the voices:

"And you claim twenty bushels of corn is too high for the damage you did to the rug?"

"He brought the rug to me and said he wanted the tracks washed out of it.   75
I washed the tracks out and took the rug back to him."

"But you didn't carry the rug back to him in the same condition it was in before you made the tracks on it."

His father did not answer, and now for perhaps half a minute there was no sound at all save that of breathing, the faint, steady suspiration of complete and intent listening.

"You decline to answer that, Mr. Snopes?" Again his father did not answer. "I'm going to find against you, Mr. Snopes. I'm going to find that you were responsible for the injury to Major de Spain's rug and hold you liable for it. But twenty bushels of corn seems a little high for a man in your circumstances to have to pay. Major de Spain claims it cost a hundred dollars. October corn will be worth about fifty cents. I figure that if Major de Spain can stand a ninety-five-dollar loss on something he paid cash for, you can stand a five-dollar loss you haven't earned yet. I hold you in damages to Major de Spain to the amount of ten bushels of corn over and above your contract with him, to be paid to him out of your crop at gathering time. Court adjourned."

It had taken no time hardly, the morning was but half begun. He thought they would return home and perhaps back to the field, since they were late, far behind all other farmers. But instead his father passed on behind the wagon, merely indicating with his hand for the older brother to follow with it, and crossed the road toward the blacksmith shop opposite, pressing on after his father, overtaking him, speaking, whispering up at the harsh, calm face beneath the weathered hat: "He won't git no ten bushels neither. He won't git one. We'll . . ." until his father glanced for an instant down on him, the face absolutely calm, the grizzled eyebrows tangled above the cold eyes, the voice almost pleasant, almost gentle:

"You think so? Well, we'll wait till October anyway."   80

The matter of the wagon—the setting of a spoke or two and the tightening of the tires—did not take long either, the business of the tires accomplished by driving the wagon into the spring branch behind the shop and letting it stand there, the mules nuzzling into the water from time to time, and the boy on the seat with the idle reins, looking up the slope and through the sooty tunnel of the shed where the slow hammer rang and where his father sat on an upended cypress bolt, easily, either talking or listening, still sitting there when the boy brought the dripping wagon up out of the branch and halted it before the door.

"Take them on to the shade and hitch," his father said. He did so and returned. His father and the smith and a third man squatting on his heels inside the door were talking, about crops and animals; the boy, squatting too in the ammoniac dust and hoof-parings and scales of rust, heard his father tell a long and unhurried story out of the time before the birth of the older brother even when he had been a professional horsetrader. And then his father came up beside him where he stood before a tattered last year's circus poster on the other side of the store, gazing rapt and quiet at the scarlet horses, the incredible poisings and convolutions of tulle and tights and the painted leers of comedians, and said, "It's time to eat."

But not at home. Squatting beside his brother against the front wall, he watched his father emerge from the store and produce from a paper sack a segment of cheese and divided it carefully and deliberately into three with his pocket knife and produce crackers from the same sack. They all three squatted on the gallery and ate slowly, without talking; then in the store again, they drank from a tin dipper tepid water smelling of the cedar bucket and of living beech trees. And still they did not go home. It was a horse lot this time, a tall rail fence upon and along which men stood and sat and out of which one by one horses were led, to be walked and trotted and then cantered back and forth along the road while the slow swapping and buying went on and the sun began to slant westward, they—the three of them—watching and listening, the older brother with his muddy eyes and his steady inevitable tobacco, the father commenting now and then on certain of the animals, to no one in particular.

It was after sundown when they reached home. They ate supper by lamplight, then, sitting on the doorstep, the boy watched the night fully accomplish, listening to the whippoorwills and the frogs, when he heard his mother's voice: "Abner! No! No! Oh, God, Oh, God, Abner!" and he rose, whirled, and saw the altered light through the door where a candle stub now burned in a bottle neck on the table and his father, still in the hat and coat, at once formal and burlesque as though dressed carefully for some shabby and ceremonial violence, emptying the reservoir of the lamp back into the five-gallon kerosene can from which it had been filled, while the mother tugged at his arm until he shifted the lamp to the other hand and flung her back, not savagely or viciously, just hard, into the wall, her hands flung out against the wall for balance, her mouth open and in her face the same quality of hopeless despair as had been in her voice. Then his father saw him standing in the door.

"Go to the barn and get that can of oil we were oiling the wagon with," he said. The boy did not move. Then he could speak. 85

"What . . ." he cried. "What are you . . ."

"Go get that oil," his father said. "Go."

Then he was moving, running, outside the house, toward the stable: this the old habit, the old blood which he had not been permitted to choose for himself, which had been bequeathed him willy nilly and which had run for so long (and who knew where, battening on what of outrage and savagery and lust) before it came to him. *I could keep on,* he thought. *I could run on and on and never look back, never need to see his face again. Only I can't. I can't,* the rusted can in his hand now, the liquid sloshing in it as he ran back to the house and into it, into the sound of his mother's weeping in the next room, and handed the can to his father.

"Ain't you going to even send a nigger?" he cried. "At least you sent a nigger before!"

This time his father didn't strike him. The hand came even faster than the 90 blow had, the same hand which had set the can on the table with almost excruciating care flashing from the can toward him too quick for him to follow it, gripping him by the back of his shirt and on to tiptoe before he had seen it quit the can, the face stooping at him in breathless and frozen ferocity, the cold, dead voice speaking over him to the older brother who leaned against the table, chewing with that steady, curious, sidewise motion of cows:

"Empty the can into the big one and go on. I'll catch up with you."

"Better tie him up to the bedpost," the brother said.

"Do like I told you," the father said. Then the boy was moving, his bunched shirt and the hard, bony hand between his shoulder-blades, his toes just touching the floor, across the room and into the other one, past the sisters sitting with spread heavy thighs in the two chairs over the cold hearth, and to where his mother and aunt sat side by side on the bed, the aunt's arms about the mother's shoulders.

"Hold him," the father said. The aunt made a startled movement. "Not you," the father said. "Lennie. Take hold of him. I want to see you do it." His mother took him by the wrist. "You'll hold him better than that. If he gets loose don't you know what he is going to do? He will go up yonder." He jerked his head toward the road. "Maybe I'd better tie him."

"I'll hold him," his mother whispered.   95

"See you do then." Then his father was gone, the stiff foot heavy and measured upon the boards, ceasing at last.

Then he began to struggle. His mother caught him in both arms, he jerking and wrenching at them. He would be stronger in the end, he knew that. But he had not time to wait for it. "Lemme go!" he cried. "I don't want to have to hit you!"

"Let him go!" the aunt said. "If he don't go, before God, I am going up there myself!"

"Don't you see I can't?" his mother cried. "Sarty! Sarty! No! No! Help me, Lizzie!"

Then he was free. His aunt grasped at him but it was too late. He whirled,   100
running, his mother stumbled forward on to her knees behind him, crying to the nearer sister: "Catch him, Net! Catch him!" But that was too late too, the sister (the sisters were twins, born at the same time, yet either of them now gave the impression of being, encompassing as much living meat and volume and weight as any other two of the family) not yet having begun to rise from the chair, her head, face, alone merely turned, presenting to him in the flying instant an astonishing expanse of young female features untroubled by any surprise even, wearing only an expression of bovine interest. Then he was out of the room, out of the house, in the mild dust of the starlit road and the heavy rifeness of honeysuckle, the pale ribbon unspooling with terrific slowness under his running feet, reaching the gate at last and turning in, running, his heart and lungs drumming, on up the drive toward the lighted house, the lighted door. He did not knock, he burst in, sobbing for breath, incapable for the moment of speech; he saw the astonished face of the Negro in the linen jacket without knowing when the Negro had appeared.

"De Spain!" he cried, panted. "Where's . . ." then he saw the white man too emerging from a white door down the hall. "Barn!" he cried. "Barn!"

"What?" the white man said. "Barn?"

"Yes!" the boy cried. "Barn!"

"Catch him!" the white man shouted.

But it was too late this time too. The Negro grasped his shirt, but the entire   105
sleeve, rotten with washing, carried away, and he was out that door too and in the drive again, and had actually never ceased to run even while he was screaming into the white man's face.

Behind him the white man was shouting. "My horse! Fetch my horse!" and he thought for an instant of cutting across the park and climbing the fence into the road, but he did not know the park nor how high the vine-massed fence might be and he dared not risk it. So he ran on down the drive, blood and breath roaring; presently he was in the road again though he could not see it. He could not hear either: the galloping mare was almost upon him before he heard her, and even then he held his course, as if the very urgency of his wild grief and need must in a moment more find him wings, waiting until the ultimate instant to hurl himself aside and into the weed-choked roadside ditch as the horse thundered past and on, for an instant in furious silhouette against the stars, the tranquil early summer night sky which, even before the shape of the horse and rider vanished, strained abruptly and violently upward: a long, swirling roar incredible and soundless, blotting the stars, and he springing up and into the road again, running again, knowing it was too late yet still running even after he heard the shot and, an instant later, two shots, pausing now without knowing he had ceased to run, crying "Pap! Pap!," running again before he knew he had begun to run, stumbling, tripping over something and scrabbling up again without ceasing to run, looking backward over his shoulder at the glare as he got up, running on among the invisible trees, panting, sobbing, "Father! Father!"

At midnight he was sitting on the crest of a hill. He did not know it was midnight and he did not know how far he had come. But there was no glare behind him now and he sat now, his back toward what he had called home for four days anyhow, his face toward the dark woods which he would enter when breath was strong again, small, shaking steadily in the chill darkness, hugging himself into the remainder of his thin, rotten shirt, the grief and despair now no longer terror and fear but just grief and despair. *Father. My father*, he thought. "He was brave!" he cried suddenly, aloud but not loud, no more than a whisper: "He was! He was in the war! He was in Colonel Sartoris' cav'ry!" not knowing that his father had gone to that war a private in the fine old European sense, wearing no uniform, admitting the authority of and giving fidelity to no man or army or flag, going to war as Malbrouck° himself did: for booty—it meant nothing and less than nothing to him if it were enemy booty or his own.

The slow constellations wheeled on. It would be dawn and then sun-up after a while and he would be hungry. But that would be tomorrow and now he was only cold, and walking would cure that. His breathing was easier now and he decided to get up and go on, and then he found that he had been asleep because he knew it was almost dawn, the night almost over. He could tell that from the whippoorwills. They were everywhere now among the dark trees below him, constant and inflectioned and ceaseless, so that, as the instant for giving over to the day birds drew nearer and nearer, there was no interval at all between them. He got up. He was a little stiff, but walking would cure that too as it would the cold, and soon there would be the sun. He went on down the hill, toward the dark woods within which the liquid silver voices of the birds called unceasing—the rapid and urgent beating of the urgent and quiring heart of the late spring night. He did not look back.

Malbrouck: hero of an old French ballad ("Malbrouck s'en va-t-en guerre"). The original Malbrouck, the English Duke of Marlborough (1650–1722) had been accused of profiteering during Queen Anne's War (1702–13).

QUESTIONS

1. Explain why Sarty's character is round rather than flat. In what ways does he change and grow? What conflicts does he face? What does he learn? How does he feel about the things his father does? Why does he leave and "not look back" at the end?

2. In the Bible, 2 Samuel, Chapters 2 and 3, Abner, the cousin of King Saul, is a powerful commander, warrior, and king maker. He is loyal to the son of King Saul and fights against the supporters of King David. Abner's death makes it possible for David to become uncontested ruler. Why do you think that Faulkner chose the name *Abner* for the father of the Snopes family? What actions of Abner Snopes make him seem heroic? Antiheroic? Why?

3. When and where is the story occurring? How does Faulkner convey this information to you?

4. Describe the characters of Sarty's mother and sisters. What do you learn about them? To what extent do any of them exhibit growth or development?

5. At the story's end, who is the rider of the horse? Who fires the three shots? Why does Faulkner not tell us the result of the shooting? (In Book I of *The Hamlet*, Faulkner explains that Abner and his other son, Flem, escape.)

WRITING ABOUT CHARACTER

Usually you will write about a major character, although you might also study a minor character or characters. After your customary overview, begin taking notes. List as many traits as you can, and also determine how the author presents details about the character, that is, actions, appearance, speeches, comments by others, authorial explanations. If there are unusual traits, determine what they show. The following questions will help you get started.

Questions for Discovering Ideas

What is the character's major trait (primary characteristic)? Minor traits?

Is the character's major trait a strength or weakness? Does it change from one to the other as the story progresses?

What circumstances, actions, or appearances demonstrate the important traits of the character?

Is the character round (dynamic)? How does the character recognize, change with, or adjust to circumstances?

Is the character the protagonist or antagonist of the story?

What is the relationship between the protagonist and antagonist?

If the character is minor (static), what function does he or she perform in the story? Is the character stereotypical? If so, does the character rise above the stereotype? How?

What do any of the other characters do, say, or think to give you insight into the character?

How does the character see himself or herself? What does the storyteller or narrator think of the character?

Is the character probable, consistent, believable? Why or why not?

Strategies for Organizing Ideas

You might select one of the following approaches to organize your ideas:

1. *Organization around central traits or major characteristics,* such as "unquestioning devotion and service" (Phoenix of "A Worn Path") or "the habit of seeing the world only on one's own terms" (Miss Brill of "Miss Brill," Snopes of "Barn Burning"). This kind of structure would show how the work embodies the trait. For example, a trait may be brought out, in one part, through speeches that characters make about the major character (as at the end of Mansfield's "Miss Brill"), and in another part through that character's own speeches and actions. Studying the trait thus enables you to focus on the different ways in which the author presents the character, and it also enables you to focus on separate parts of the work.

2. *Organization around a character's growth or change.* Such an essay would first describe a character's beginning traits, and then analyze changes or developments. *It is important to stress the actual alterations as they emerge, but at the same time to avoid merely retelling the story.* It is also important not only to describe the changing traits, but also to analyze *how* they are brought out in the work (such as the narrator's desire to reconnect himself with his Indian identity in Whitecloud's "Blue Winds Dancing," or Minnie Wright's action to overcome her long suffering).

3. *Organization around central actions, objects, or quotations that reveal primary characteristics.* Certain key incidents may stand out, along with objects closely associated with the character being analyzed. There may be key quotations spoken by the character or by someone else in the work. It is important to show how the things you choose serve as signposts or keys to understanding the character, for these guides are not to be separate topics in their own right. See the sample essay for an illustration of this type of development.

4. *Organization around qualities of a flat character or characters.* If the character is flat (such as the sisters in "Barn Burning" or the cowboy in "The Blue Hotel"), the essay might develop topics like the function and relative significance of the character, the group of which the character is representative, the relationship of the flat character to the round ones and the importance of this relationship, and any additional qualities or traits. Of major interest will be your discussion of the defects that prevent the character from developing, and the importance of these shortcomings in the author's presentation of human character.

In the conclusion, you might show how the character's traits are related to the work as a whole. If the person was good but came to a bad end, does this misfortune elevate him or her to tragic stature? If the person suffers, does this fact suggest any attitudes about the class or type of which he or she is a part? Or does it illustrate the author's general view of human life? Or both? Do the characteristics explain why the person helps or hinders other characters? How does your essay help in clearing up first-reading misunderstandings? These and similar questions may be answered in your conclusion.

SAMPLE ESSAY

The Character of Minnie Wright in Glaspell's "A Jury of Her Peers"[°]

[1]   Minnie Wright is Susan Glaspell's major character in "A Jury of Her Peers." We learn about her, however, not from seeing and hearing her, for she does not act or speak, but rather from the secondhand evidence provided by the major characters. Lewis Hale, the neighboring farmer, tells about Minnie's behavior on the morning when her husband, John, was found strangled in his bed. Martha Hale, Hale's wife, tells about Minnie's young womanhood and about how she became alienated from her nearest neighbors because of John's stingy and unfriendly ways. Both Martha and Mrs. Peters, the Sheriff's wife, make observations about her based on the condition of her kitchen. From this information we get a full portrait of Minnie, who has changed from passivity to destructive assertiveness.[*] Her change in character is indicated by her clothing, her dead canary, and her unfinished patchwork quilt.[†]

[2]   The clothes that Minnie has worn in the past and in the present indicate her character as a person of charm who has withered under neglect and contempt. Martha mentions Minnie's attractive and colorful dresses as a young woman, even recalling a white dress with blue ribbons (paragraph 258). Martha also recalls that Minnie, when young, was "sweet and pretty, but kind of timid and--fluttery" (paragraph 208). In the light of these recollections, Martha observes that Minnie had changed, and changed for the worse, during her twenty years of marriage with John Wright, who is characterized as a "raw wind that gets to the bone" (paragraph 202). As more evidence for Minnie's acceptance of her drab life, Mrs. Peters says that Minnie asks for no more than an apron and shawl when under arrest in the sheriff's home. This modest clothing, as contrasted with the colorful dresses of her youth, suggests her suppression of spirit.

Minnie's dead canary, however, while indicating her love of music, also shows the end of her suppression and the emergence of her rage. For nineteen years of marriage Minnie endures her cheerless farm home, the contempt of her husband, her life of solitude, the abandonment of her early enjoyment of

---

[°] See p. 158 for this story.
[*] Central idea.
[†] Thesis sentence.

[3] singing, a general lack of pretty things, and the recognition that she could not share the social life of the local farm women as an equal. But her buying the canary (paragraph 183) suggests the reemergence of her love of song, just as it also suggests her growth toward self-assertion. That her husband wrings the bird's neck may thus be seen as the cause not only of immediate grief (shown by the dead bird in a "pretty box" [paragraph 221]) but also of the anger that marks her change from a stock, obedient wife to a person angry enough to kill.

[4] Like her love of song, her unfinished quilt indicates her creativity. In twenty years on the farm, never having had children, she has nothing creative to do except for needlework like the quilt. Mrs. Hale comments on the beauty of Minnie's log-cabin design (paragraph 154), and observes the colorful patches of cloth in her sewing basket (paragraph 213). The inference is that even though Minnie's life has been bleak, she has been able to indulge her characteristic love of color and form--and also of warmth, granted the purpose of a quilt.

[5] Ironically, the quilt also shows Minnie's creativity in the murder of her husband. Both Mrs. Hale and Mrs. Peters interpret the breakdown of her stitching on the quilt as a sign of distress about the dead canary and also of her nervousness in planning revenge (paragraph 166). Further, even though nowhere in the story is it said that John is strangled with a quilting knot, no other conclusion is possible. Both Mrs. Hale and Mrs. Peters agree that Minnie probably intended to knot the quilt rather than sew it in a quilt stitch, and Glaspell pointedly causes the men to learn this detail also, even though they scoff at it and ignore it. In other words, we learn that Minnie's only outlet for creativity--needlework--has enabled her to perform the murder in the only way she can: She quietly puts a rope under John's neck, makes a slip-proof quilting knot, and then strangles him by drawing the knot tight. Even though her plan for the murder is deliberate (Mrs. Peters reports that the arrangement of the rope was "a funny way to kill" [paragraph 137]), Minnie is not cold or remorseless. Her passivity after the crime demonstrates that planning to evade guilt, beyond simple denial, is not in her character. She is not so diabolically creative that she plans or even understands the irony of strangling her husband just as he killed the bird by wringing its neck. Glaspell, however, has made the irony plain.

[6] It is important to emphasize again that we learn about Minnie from others. Indeed, Glaspell describes her as "that woman who was not there and yet who had been there with them all through that hour" (paragraph 290). Undeniably, then, Minnie is fully realized, round, and poignant. For the greater part of her adult life, she has been representative of women whose capacities for growth and expression are stunted by the grind of life and the cruelty and insensitivity of others. She patiently accepts her drab and colorless marriage that is so different from her youthful expectations. Amid the dreary farm surroundings, she suppresses her grudges, just as she suppresses her prettiness, colorfulness, and creativity. In short, she has been nothing more than a flat character. But the killing of the canary causes her to change and to destroy her husband in an assertive rejection of her stock role as the suffering wife. She is a patient woman whose patience finally reaches the breaking point.

Commentary on the Essay

The strategy of this essay is to use details from the story as evidence for the central idea that Minnie Wright is a round, developing character. The essay hence illustrates one of the types in the third approach described on page 191. Other organizations could also have been chosen, such as the qualities of acquiescence, fortitude, and potential for anger (no. 1), the change in Minnie from submission to vengefulness (no. 2), or the reported actions of Minnie's singing, knotting quilts, and sitting in the kitchen on the morning after the murder (another type of no. 3).

Because of the unusual fact that Minnie does not actually appear in the story, but is described only in the words of the major characters, the introductory paragraph deals with the way information is given about her. The essay thus highlights how Glaspell in "A Jury of Her Peers" uses methods 2 and 4 (see pp. 140–42) as the ways of rendering the story's main character, while not choosing methods 1 and 3.

The body is developed through inferences made from details in the story, namely Minnie's clothing (paragraph 2), her canary (3), and her quilt (4 and 5). The last paragraph, 6, summarizes a number of these details, and it also considers how Minnie transcends the stock, representative qualities of many other women in her position, and gains roundness as a result of this outbreak.

WRITING TOPICS

1. Compare the ways in which actions (or speeches, or the comments of others) are used to bring out the character traits of Sarty of "Barn Burning" and Paul of "Paul's Case."

2. Write a brief essay comparing the changes or developments of two major *round* characters in stories included in this chapter. You might deal with issues such as what the characters are like at the beginning, what conflicts they confront, deal with, or avoid, what qualities are brought out which signal the changes or developments, and so on.

3. Compare the qualities and functions of two or more *flat* characters (e.g., Paul's father, Paul's teachers, one of the men in "A Jury of Her Peers" [including John Wright], the twins in "Barn Burning"). How do they bring out qualities of the major characters? What do you discover about their own character traits?

4. Topics for brief essays:
   a. Why does Jacky Smurch not try to fit the role of "The Greatest Man in the World"? Does this absence of change make him a flat character? Consider the possibility that his absence of change indicates the roundness of his character.
   b. Why does Abner Snopes burn barns? What qualities of character do these actions reveal? In the light of your assessment of his character, how might Abner justify to himself his role as an arsonist?

    c.   To what degree does the narrator of "Paul's Case" like and understand Paul? To be baffled by him? To pity him? Why?

    d.   Consider this proposition: *To friends who haven't seen us for a time, we are round, but to ourselves and most other people, we are flat.*

5.   Write a brief story about an important decision you have made (e.g., picking a school, beginning or leaving a job, declaring a major, deciding to end a friendship, etc.). Show how your own qualities of character (to the extent that you understand them), together with your own experiences, have gone into the making of the decision. You may write more comfortably if you give yourself another name and describe your actions in the third person.

5

Point of View: The Position and Stance of the Narrator or Speaker

Point of view refers to the **voice** that authors adopt for their stories. You might also think of point of view as a work's **narrator, speaker,** or **persona**— a living personality who tells stories, presents arguments, or expresses attitudes such as love, anger, or excitement.

It is most important to recognize that authors not only try to make their works vital and interesting, but also try to bring their *presentations* to life. You may be sure that authors devote care and skill to their speaking voices—their points of view. The situation is like that of actors performing a play: The actors are always themselves, but in their roles they *impersonate* the characters they act, and temporarily *become* them.

Authors, too, impersonate characters who do the talking, with the difference that authors also *create* these impersonations, like Sammy of Updike's "A & P," the young man in Anderson's "I'm a Fool," and the unnamed speaker of Hawthorne's "Young Goodman Brown." It is almost as though the author is a ventriloquist, throwing his or her voice into the speaker or narrator who tells the story. Thus, Updike creates Sammy as a real person telling readers about an important event in his own life. We read Sammy's words, and we know that Sammy is a distinct though fictional character, but because Updike is the author we know that he is the one putting the words in Sammy's mouth. Unlike Sammy, Hawthorne's speaker tells a story about someone else, and is not easily separated from the author, even though the words we read may be different from those that Hawthorne might have chosen to use in his own person. The speaker is Hawthorne's authorial creation or impersonation for "Young Goodman Brown."

AN EXERCISE IN POINT OF VIEW:
REPORTING AN ACCIDENT

As an exercise to show that point of view is derived from lifelike situations, let us imagine that there has been an accident; two cars, driven by Alice and Bill, have collided. How might this accident be reported by a number of people?

What would Alice say?
What would Bill say?

Let us now assume that Frank, who is Bill's best friend, and Mary, who knows neither Bill nor Alice, were witnesses.

What might Frank say about who was responsible?
What might Mary say about who was responsible?

Let us finally assume that you are a reporter for a local newspaper and are sent to report on the accident. You know none of the people involved.

How will your report differ from the other reports?

A final question, which applies to all the persons in our hypothetical situation, is the degree to which all statements are designed to persuade listeners and readers of the correctness of the claims made in the respective reports.

The differences in our accident reports may be explained in terms of point of view. Obviously, because both Alice and Bill are deeply involved—each of them is a major participant, or what may be called a *major mover*—they will arrange their words to make themselves seem blameless. Frank, because he is Bill's best friend, will likely report things in Bill's favor. Mary will favor neither Alice nor Bill, but let us assume that she did not look at the colliding cars until she heard the crash; therefore her report will be restricted because she did not *actually see* everything. Most likely, *your* account as an impartial reporter will be the most reliable and objective of all, because your major interest is to learn all the details and report the truth accurately, with no concern about the personal interests of either Alice or Bill.

Above all, however, each person's report will have the "hidden agenda" of making that person seem honest, objective, intelligent, impartial, and thorough. You might also consider what the various individuals might say to a friend in ordinary conversation, or to a judge and jury when under oath. It seems clear that the ramifications of telling a story are far reaching, and the consideration of the various interests and situations can become quite subtle.

Some of these relationships may be clarified by the sketch on page 199.

CONDITIONS THAT AFFECT POINT OF VIEW

From this hypothetical situation, which is like many situations in real life, we may conclude that point of view depends on a number of things: (1) position as observer, (2) completeness and accuracy of observation, (3) degree of participation, (4) partiality or impartiality, (5) desire to draw conclusions about an action, and (6) situation of the speaker and audience at the time of the narration or monologue.

In a story, the author develops point of view in light of these same considerations. Anderson's speaker in "I'm a Fool" is a young man filled with regrets about having lied to a young woman he truly loves. Munro's speaker in "Meneseteung" declares the wish to "rescue" the memories of long-forgotten lives. For these reasons, these narrators show their own involvement and concern about the events they describe. The speaker in Jackson's "The Lottery," however, does not seem personally involved in the action. This narrator listens, sees, and reports, but is not involved personally in the cruel actions in the story's country village.

KINDS OF POINTS OF VIEW

In the various works you read you will encounter a wide variety of points of view. As a convenient way to begin your analysis, you should first determine the work's grammatical voice. Then you should study the ways in which the subject, characterization, dialogue, and form interact with the point of view.

First-Person Point of View

If the voice of the work is an "I," the author is using the **first-person point of view**—the impersonation of a fictional narrator or speaker. In our hypothetical accident, both Alice and Bill are first-person speakers. In literature, Sammy of Updike's "A & P" and the unnamed speaker of Anderson's "I'm a Fool" are also first-person speakers; in Twain's "Luck" there are two separate first-person speakers (the first "I" introduces the second "I").

Of all the points of view, the first person is potentially the most independent of the author, for such a speaker is often given a unique identity, with name, job, and economic and social positions (like Sammy).

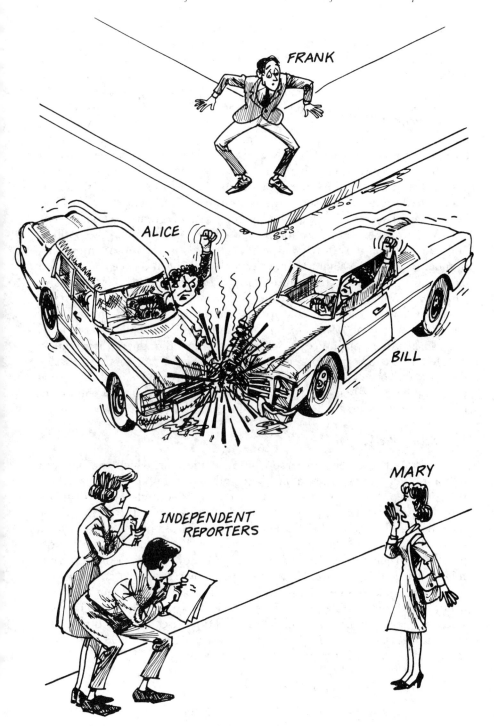

Quite often, however, the author may create a relatively neutral, uninvolved narrator who still uses the first-person voice, as with the speaker of Poe's "The Masque of the Red Death." A unique first-person narrator is the speaker of Munro's "Meneseteung." The story depends on the curiosity and sympathetic imagination of this narrator, who begins normally enough by describing her examination of various documents relating to the major character. Soon, however, the narrator shifts totally into an imaginative reconstruction—in the present tense, even though the story takes place a century earlier—of events leading up to a major event in the character's life. Though the narrator reports no firsthand material except for having visited the location of the story, she nevertheless is deeply involved, since the story results entirely from her power to articulate her imaginative vision of what the major character might have experienced.

When you encounter a first-person narrative, determine the position and ability of the narrator. First-person speakers might report things in a number of ways: (1) What they have *done, said, heard,* and *thought* (firsthand experience). (2) What they have *observed* others do and say (firsthand witness). (3) What *others have told them* (secondhand testimony and hearsay). Finally, (4) what they are able to *reconstruct* from the information they have (*hypothetical* or *imaginative* information). Their abilities, position to observe, attitudes, prejudices or self-interest, and judgment of their readers or listeners are to be considered in everything they say. When they describe their own experiences they have great authority and sometimes great power. Whatever their involvement, however, they are one of the means by which authors create an authentic, lifelike aura around their stories.

Second-Person Point of View

Although the **second-person point of view** (in which the narrator tells a listener what he or she has done and said, using the "you" personal pronoun) is possible, it is rare because in effect the second-person structure requires a first-person speaker who tells the listener—the "you" of the narration—what he or she did at a past time. Thus, a parent might tell a child what the child did during infancy, or a doctor might tell a patient with amnesia about events before the injury, or a prosecuting attorney might describe a crime to a defendant. Recently a series of "do your own" adventure books has become popular, in which readers pick out their own actions in a developing story. In practice, however, the second-person point of view is almost negligible. A. A. Milne uses it for a time at the beginning of *Winnie the Pooh*, but drops it as soon as the actions of Pooh Bear and the rest of the animals get under way.

Third-Person Point of View

If events in the work are described in the third person (*he, she, it, they*), the author is using the **third-person point of view.** It is not always easy to characterize the voice in this point of view. Sometimes the speaker may use an "I" (as in Poe's "The Masque of the Red Death") but yet still be seemingly identical with the author; at other times, however, the author may create a distinct **authorial voice,** as in Mansfield's "Miss Brill." There are three variants of the third-person point of view: dramatic or objective, omniscient, and limited omniscient.

DRAMATIC OR OBJECTIVE. The basic mode of presenting action and dialogue is the **dramatic** or **objective point of view** (also called **third-person objective**). The narrator in the dramatic point of view reports events in a way that is analogous to a hovering or tracking motion-picture camera, or to what some critics have called "a fly on the wall (or tree)." Thus, characters outdoors may be seen and heard at a distance, or up close, and when they go into an interior, such as a car or a house, the speaker continues to follow their speeches and actions. A dramatic presentation is as complete and impartial as the speaker's position as an observer allows. Let us remember that Mary, of our hypothetical accident, would give an objective description because of her impartiality, but also that her report would be incomplete because she did not see things before the accident. You, as the reporter, would also describe the accident objectively, but your report would be more detailed because you would include the results of additional observations and interviews.

In stories and poems, the dramatic point of view is like your report and Mary's: Readers, like a jury, can form their own interpretations if they are given the right evidence. Thus, Jackson's "The Lottery" (the subject of the sample essay, pp. 237–39)—a powerful example of the dramatic point of view—is an objective story about a bizarre small-town lottery. We the readers draw many conclusions about this story (such as that people are tradition-bound, insensitive, cruel, and so on), but Jackson does not *state* any of these things for us.

OMNISCIENT. The third-person point of view is **omniscient** (all-knowing) when the speaker not only presents the action and dialogue of the work, but also, like God, reports what the characters are thinking. Our hypothetical accident does not offer the possibility of an omniscient point of view, because no human being can know the unspoken thoughts of others. Authors, however, by delving into the minds of their characters, assume a stance that enables them to add dimension to the development of character and action. For example, in Munro's "Meneseteung," the speaker assumes omniscience to the extent that she explores the thoughts of her major character.

LIMITED, OR LIMITED OMNISCIENT. More common than the omniscient point of view, in which the inner workings of every character may be described, is the *limited third person,* or **limited omniscient third-person**

point of view, in which the author confines or *limits* attention to a major character. In our accident case, Frank, being Bill's friend, would be sympathetic to Bill, and thus his account would likely be third-person limited, with Bill as the center of interest. In a story, the central figure on whom things are focused is the **point-of-view character,** such as Miss Brill in "Miss Brill" by Mansfield, Paul in "Paul's Case" by Cather, and Goodman Brown in "Young Goodman Brown" by Hawthorne. Virtually everything in these stories is there because the point-of-view characters—Miss Brill, Paul, and Goodman Brown—see it, hear it, respond to it, think about it, do it or share in it, try to control it, or are controlled by it.

MINGLING POINTS OF VIEW

In some works, an author may shift the point of view in order to sustain interest, create suspense, or put the burden of response entirely upon readers. For example, Mansfield in "Miss Brill" interrupts the limited omniscient focus on Miss Brill's thoughts and reactions immediately after she is insulted. The last paragraphs are objective until the last sentence, when the limited omniscient point of view is resumed. The result is that Miss Brill is made totally alone in her grief, cut off; readers can no longer share her sorrow as they earlier shared her observations about the characters in the park. A similar shift occurs at the end of Hawthorne's "Young Goodman Brown," where the narrator objectively and almost brutally summarizes Brown's gloomy, loveless life after his nightmare about evil.

GUIDELINES FOR POINTS OF VIEW

The following list summarizes and further classifies the types of points of view. With these guidelines you should be able to distinguish differences and shades of variation in stories and poems.

1. First Person ("I" and "me"). First-person speakers are involved to at least some degree in the actions of the work. Such narrators may have (1) complete understanding, (2) partial or incorrect understanding, or (3) no understanding at all.
    a. *Major participant*
        i. telling his or her own story and thoughts as a major mover
        ii. telling a story about others and also about herself or himself as one of the major movers
        iii. telling a story mainly about others, and about himself or herself only tangentially
    b. *Minor participant, telling a story about events experienced and witnessed*

    c.   *Nonparticipating but identifiable speaker who learns about events in other ways (e.g., listening to participants, examining documents, hearing news reports). The narrator might then tell the story as a report, or as a combination report and reconstruction.*

2.   Second person ("you"). Occurs only when the speaker knows more about a character's actions than the character himself or herself, for example, parent, psychologist, lawyer. This point of view is not easily sustained, and usually is found only in brief passages.

3.   Third person ("she," "he," "it," "they"). The speaker is outside the action and is mainly a reporter of actions and speeches. Some speakers may have unique and distinguishing traits even though no separate identity is claimed for them ("the unnamed third-person narrator"). Other third-person speakers who are not separately identifiable may represent the words and views of the authors themselves ("the authorial voice").

    a.   *Dramatic or third-person objective.* Narrator reports only what can be seen and heard. Thoughts of characters are included only if they are spoken or written (dialogue, reported or overheard conversation, letters, reports, etc.).

    b.   *Omniscient.* Omniscient speaker sees all, reports all, and knows and explains, when necessary, the inner workings of the minds of any or all characters.

    c.   *Limited, or limited omniscient.* The focus is on the actions, responses, thoughts, and feelings of a single major character.

SHERWOOD ANDERSON (1876–1941)

I'm a Fool   *1924*

It was a hard jolt for me, one of the most bitterest I ever had to face. And it all came about through my own foolishness, too. Even yet sometimes, when I think of it, I want to cry or swear or kick myself. Perhaps, even now, after all this time, there will be a kind of satisfaction in making myself look cheap by telling of it.

It began at three o'clock one October afternoon as I sat in the grandstand at the fall trotting and pacing meet at Sandusky, Ohio.

To tell the truth, I felt a little foolish that I should be sitting in the grandstand at all. During the summer before I had left my home town with Harry Whitehead and, with a nigger named Burt, had taken a job as swipe° with one of the two horses Harry was campaigning through the fall race meets that year. Mother cried and my sister Mildred, who wanted to get a job as a schoolteacher in our town that fall, stormed and scolded about the house all during the week before I left. They both thought it something disgraceful that one of our family should take a

---

    swipe: groom and general handyman; the narrator describes a swipe's duties in paragraph 7.

place as a swipe with race horses. I've an idea Mildred thought my taking the place would stand in the way of her getting the job she'd been working so long for.

But after all I had to work, and there was no other work to be got. A big lumbering fellow of nineteen couldn't just hang around the house and I had got too big to mow people's lawns and sell newspapers. Little chaps who could get next to people's sympathies by their sizes were always getting jobs away from me. There was one fellow who kept saying to everyone who wanted a lawn mowed or a cistern cleaned that he was saving money to work his way through college, and I used to lay awake nights thinking up ways to injure him without being found out. I kept thinking of wagons running over him and bricks falling on his head as he walked along the street. But never mind him.

I got the place with Harry and I liked Burt fine. We got along splendid   5 together. He was a big nigger with a lazy sprawling body and soft, kind eyes, and when it came to a fight he could hit like Jack Johnson.° He had Bucephalus, a big black pacing stallion that could do 2.09 or 2.10 if he had to, and I had a little gelding named Doctor Fritz that never lost a race all fall when Harry wanted him to win.

We set out from home late in July, in a box car with the two horses and after that, until late November, we kept moving along to the race meets and the fairs. It was a peachy time for me, I'll say that. Sometimes now I think that boys who are raised regular in houses, and never have a fine nigger like Burt for best friend, and go to high schools and college, and never steal anything, or get drunk a little, or learn to swear from fellows who know how, or come walking up in front of a grand stand in their shirt sleeves and with dirty horsy pants on when the races are going on and the grand stand is full of people all dressed up— What's the use of talking about it? Such fellows don't know nothing at all. They've never had no opportunity.

But I did. Burt taught me how to rub down a horse and put the bandages on after a race and steam a horse out and a lot of valuable things for any man to know. He could wrap a bandage on a horse's leg so smooth that if it had been the same color you would think it was his skin, and I guess he'd have been a big driver, too, and got to the top like Murphy and Walter Cox and the others if he hadn't been black.

Gee whizz! it was fun. You got to a county-seat town, maybe say on a Saturday or Sunday, and the fair began the next Tuesday and lasted until Friday afternoon. Doctor Fritz would be, say, in the 2.25 trot on Tuesday afternoon and on Thursday afternoon Bucephalus would knock 'em cold in the "free-for-all" pace. It left you a lot of time to hang around and listen to horse talk, and see Burt knock some yap cold that got too gay,° and you'd find out about horses and men and pick up a lot of stuff you could use all the rest of your life, if you had some sense and salted down what you heard and felt and saw.

And then at the end of the week when the race meet was over, and Harry had run home to tend up to his livery-stable business, you and Burt hitched the two horses to carts and drove slow and steady across country, to the place for the next meeting, so as to not overheat the horses, etc., etc., you know.

Jack Johnson: (1878–1946), the first black heavyweight champion, 1910–1915.
gay: high spirited as a result of being drunk.

Gee whizz! Gosh amighty! the nice hickory-nut and beechnut and oaks and   10
other kinds of trees along the roads, all brown and red, and the good smells, and
Burt singing a song called "Deep River,"° and the country girls at the windows of
houses and everything. You can stick your colleges up your nose for all me. I
guess I know where I got my education.

Why, one of those little burgs of towns you came to on the way, say now on
a Saturday afternoon, and Burt says, "Let's lay up here." And you did.

And you took the horses to a livery stable and fed them, and you got your
good clothes out of a box and put them on.

And the town was full of farmers gaping, because they could see you were
racehorse people, and the kids maybe never see a nigger before and was afraid
and run away when the two of us walked down their main street.

And that was before prohibition and all that foolishness, and so you went
into a saloon, the two of you, and all the yaps come and stood around, and there
was always some one pretended he was horsy and knew things and spoke up and
began asking questions, and all you did was to lie and lie all you could about what
horses you had, and I said I owned them, and then some fellow said, "Will you
have a drink of whisky?" and Burt knocked his eye out the way he could say,
offhand like, "Oh, well, all right, I'm agreeable to a little nip. I'll split a quart with
you." Gee whizz!

But that isn't what I want to tell my story about. We got home late in   15
November and I promised mother I'd quit the race horses for good. There's a lot
of things you've got to promise a mother because she don't know any better.

And so, there not being any work in our town any more than when I left
there to go to the races, I went off to Sandusky and got a pretty good place taking
care of horses for a man who owned a teaming and delivery and storage and coal
and real-estate business there. It was a pretty good place with good eats, and a
day off each week, and sleeping on a cot in a big barn, and mostly just shoveling
in hay and oats to a lot of big good-enough skates of horses that couldn't have
trotted a race with a toad. I wasn't dissatisfied and I could send money home.

And then, as I started to tell you, the fall races come to Sandusky and I got
the day off and I went. I left the job at noon and had on my good clothes and
my new brown derby hat I'd bought the Saturday before, and a stand-up collar.

First of all I went downtown and walked about with the dudes. I've always
thought to myself, "Put up a good front," and so I did it. I had forty dollars in
my pockets and so I went into the West House, a big hotel, and walked up to the
cigar stand. "Give me three twenty-five cent cigars," I said. There was a lot of
horsemen and strangers and dressed-up people from other towns standing around
in the lobby and in the bar, and I mingled amongst them. In the bar there was a
fellow with a cane and a Windsor tie on, that it made me sick to look at him. I
like a man to be a man and dressed up, but not to go put on that kind of airs. So
I pushed him aside, kind of rough, and had me a drink of whisky. And then he
looked at me, as though he thought maybe he'd get gay, but he changed his mind
and didn't say anything. And then I had another drink of whisky, just to show
him something, and went out and had a hack out to the races, all to myself, and
when I got there I bought myself the best seat I could get up in the grandstand,
but didn't go in for any of these boxes. That's putting on too many airs.

"*Deep River*": well-known spiritual.

And so there I was, sitting up in the grandstand as gay as you please and looking down on the swipes coming out with their horses, and with their dirty horsy pants on and the horseblankets swung over their shoulders, same as I had been doing all the year before. I liked one thing about the same as the other, sitting up there and feeling grand and being down there and looking up at the yaps and feeling grander and more important, too.

One thing's about as good as another, if you take it just right. I've often said   20
that.

Well, right in front of me, in the grandstand that day, there was a fellow with a couple of girls and they was about my age. The young fellow was a nice guy, all right. He was the kind maybe that goes to college and then comes to be a lawyer or maybe a newspaper editor or something like that, but he wasn't stuck on himself. There are some of that kind are all right and he was one of the ones.

He had his sister with him and another girl and the sister looked around over his shoulder, accidental at first, not intending to start anything—she wasn't that kind—and her eyes and mine happened to meet.

You know how it is. Gee, she was a peach! She had on a soft dress, kind of a blue stuff and it looked carelessly made, but was well sewed and made and everything. I knew that much. I blushed when she looked right at me and so did she. She was the nicest girl I've ever seen in my life. She wasn't stuck on herself and she could talk proper grammar without being like a schoolteacher or something like that. What I mean is, she was O.K. I think maybe her father was well-to-do, but not rich to make her chesty because she was his daughter, as some are. Maybe he owned a drug store or a dry-goods store in their home town, or something like that. She never told me and I never asked.

My own people are all O.K. too, when you come to that. My grandfather was Welsh and over in the old country, in Wales he was—but never mind that.   25

The first heat of the first race come off and the young fellow setting there   25
with the two girls left them and went down to make a bet. I knew what he was up to, but he didn't talk big and noisy and let everyone around know he was a sport, as some do. He wasn't that kind. Well, he come back and I heard him tell the two girls what horse he'd bet on, and when the heat trotted they all half got to their feet and acted in the excited, sweaty way people do when they've got money down on a race, and the horse they bet on is up there pretty close at the end, and they think maybe he'll come on with a rush, but he never does because he hasn't got the old juice in him, come right down to it.

And then, pretty soon, the horses came out for the 2.18 pace and there was a horse in it I knew. He was a horse Bob French had in his string but Bob didn't own him. He was a horse owned by a Mr. Mathers down at Marietta, Ohio.

This Mr. Mathers had a lot of money and owned some coal mines or something and he had a swell place out in the country, and he was stuck on race horses, but was a Presbyterian or something, and I think more than likely his wife was one, too, maybe a stiffer one than himself. So he never raced his horses hisself, and the story round the Ohio race tracks was that when one of his horses got ready to go to the races he turned him over to Bob French and pretended to his wife he was sold.

So Bob had the horses and he did pretty much as he pleased and you can't blame Bob, at least, I never did. Sometimes he was out to win and sometimes he wasn't. I never cared much about that when I was swiping a horse. What I did want to know was that my horse had the speed and could go out in front, if you wanted him to.

And, as I'm telling you, there was Bob in this race with one of Mr. Mathers' horses, was named "About Ben Ahem"° or something like that, and was fast as a streak. He was a gelding and had a mark of 2.21, but could step in .08 or .09.

Because when Burt and I were out, as I've told you, the year before, there was a nigger Burt knew, worked for Mr. Mathers and we went out there one day when we didn't have no race on at the Marietta Fair and our boss Harry was gone home.

And so everyone was gone to the fair but just this one nigger and he took us all through Mr. Mathers' swell house and he and Burt tapped a bottle of wine Mr. Mathers had hid in his bedroom, back in a closet, without his wife knowing, and he showed us this Ahem horse. Burt was always stuck on being a driver but didn't have much chance to get to the top, being a nigger, and he and the other nigger gulped the whole bottle of wine and Burt got a little lit up.

So the nigger let Burt take this About Ben Ahem and step him a mile in a track Mr. Mathers had all to himself, right there on the farm. And Mr. Mathers had one child, a daughter, kinda sick and not very good looking, and she came home and we had to hustle to get About Ben Ahem stuck back in the barn.

I'm only telling you to get everything straight. At Sandusky, that afternoon I was at the fair, this young fellow with the two girls was fussed, being with the girls and losing his bet. You know how a fellow is that way. One of them was his girl and the other his sister. I had figured that out.

"Gee whizz," I say to myself, "I'm going to give him the dope."

He was mighty nice when I touched him on the shoulder. He and the girls were nice to me right from the start and clear to the end. I'm not blaming them.

And so he leaned back and I give him the dope on About Ben Ahem. "Don't bet a cent on this first heat because he'll go like an oxen hitched to a plow, but when the first heat is over go right down and lay on your pile." That's what I told him.

Well, I never saw a fellow treat any one sweller. There was a fat man sitting beside the little girl, that had looked at me twice by this time, and I at her, and both blushing, and what did he do but have the nerve to turn and ask the fat man to get up and change places with me so I could set with his crowd.

Gee whizz, craps amighty. There I was. What a chump I was to go and get gay up there in the West House bar, and just because that dude was standing there with a cane and that kind of a necktie on, to go and get all balled up and drink that whisky, just to show off.

Of course she would know, me setting right beside her and letting her smell of my breath. I could have kicked myself right down out of that grandstand and all around that race track and made a faster record than most of the skates of horses they had there that year.

Because that girl wasn't any mutt of a girl. What wouldn't I have give right then for a stick of chewing gum to chew, or a lozenger, or some licorice, or most

30

35

40

"About Ben Ahem": more likely "Abou Ben Adhem," from the poem "Abou Ben Adhem and the Angel" (1834) by Leigh Hunt (1784–1859).

anything. I was glad I had those twenty-five cent cigars in my pocket and right away I give that fellow one and lit one myself. Then that fat man got up and we changed places and there I was, plunked right down beside her.

They introduced themselves and the fellow's best girl, he had with him, was named Miss Elinor Woodbury, and her father was a manufacturer of barrels from a place called Tiffin, Ohio. And the fellow himself was named Wilbur Wessen and his sister was Miss Lucy Wessen.

I suppose it was their having such swell names that got me off my trolley. A fellow, just because he has been a swipe with a race horse, and works taking care of horses for a man in the teaming, delivery, and storage business isn't any better or worse than any one else. I've often thought that, and said it too.

But you know how a fellow is. There's something in that kind of nice clothes, and the kind of nice eyes she had, and the way she had looked at me, awhile before, over her brother's shoulder, and me looking back at her, and both of us blushing.

I couldn't show her up for a boob, could I?

I made a fool of myself, that's what I did. I said my name was Walter   45
Mathers from Marietta, Ohio, and then I told all three of them the smashingest lie you ever heard. What I said was that my father owned the horse About Ben Ahem and that he had let him out to this Bob French for racing purposes, because our family was proud and had never gone into racing that way, in our own name, I mean, and Miss Lucy Wessen's eyes were shining, and I went the whole hog.

I told about our place down at Marietta, and about the big stables and the grand brick house we had on a hill, up above the Ohio River, but I knew enough not to do it in no bragging way. What I did was to start things and then let them drag the rest out of me. I acted just as reluctant to tell as I could. Our family hasn't got any barrel factory, and since I've known us, we've always been pretty poor, but not asking anything of any one at that, and my grandfather, over in Wales—but never mind that.

We set there talking like we had known each other for years and years, and I went and told them that my father had been expecting maybe this Bob French wasn't on the square, and had sent me up to Sandusky on the sly to find out what I could.

And I bluffed it through I had found out all about the 2.18 pace, in which About Ben Ahem was to start.

I said he would lose the first heat by pacing like a lame cow and then he would come back and skin 'em alive after that. And to back up what I said I took thirty dollars out of my pocket and handed it to Mr. Wilbur Wessen and asked him, would he mind, after the first heat, to go down and place it on About Ben Ahem for whatever odds he could get. What I said was that I didn't want Bob French to see me and none of the swipes.

Sure enough the first heat come off and About Ben Ahem went off his   50
stride, up the back stretch, and looked like a wooden horse or a sick one, and come in to be last. Then this Wilbur Wessen went down to the betting place under the grand stand and there I was with the two girls, and when that Miss Woodbury was looking the other way once, Lucy Wessen kinda, with her shoulder you know, kinda touched me. Not just tucking down, I don't mean. You know how a woman can do. They get close, but not getting gay either. You know what they do. Gee whizz.

And then they give me a jolt. What they had done, when I didn't know, was to get together, and they had decided Wilbur Wessen would bet fifty dollars, and the two girls had gone and put in ten dollars each, of their own money, too. I was sick then, but I was sicker later.

About the gelding, About Ben Ahem, and their winning their money, I wasn't worried a lot about that. It came out O.K. Ahem stepped the next three heats like a bushel of spoiled eggs going to market before they could be found out, and Wilbur Wessen had got nine to two for the money. There was something else eating at me.

Because Wilbur come back, after he had bet the money, and after that he spent most of his time talking to that Miss Woodbury, and Lucy Wessen and I was left alone together like on a desert island. Gee, if I'd only been on the square or if there had been any way of getting myself on the square. There ain't any Walter Mathers, like I said to her and them, and there hasn't ever been one, but if there was, I bet I'd go to Marietta, Ohio, and shoot him tomorrow.

There I was, big boob that I am. Pretty soon the race was over, and Wilbur had gone down and collected our money, and we had a hack downtown, and he stood us a swell supper at the West House, and a bottle of champagne beside.

And I was with the girl and she wasn't saying much, and I wasn't saying much either. One thing I know. She wasn't stuck on me because of the lie about my father being rich and all that. There's a way you know . . . Craps amighty. There's a kind of girl you see just once in your life, and if you don't get busy and make hay, then you're gone for good and all, and might as well go jump off a bridge. They give you a look from inside of them somewhere, and it ain't no vamping, and what it means is—you want that girl to be your wife, and you want nice things around her like flowers and swell clothes, and you want her to have the kids you're going to have, and you want good music played and no ragtime. Gee whizz.

There's a place over near Sandusky, across a kind of bay, and it's called Cedar Point. And after we had supper we went over to it in a launch, all by ourselves. Wilbur and Miss Lucy and that Miss Woodbury had to catch a ten o'clock train back to Tiffin, Ohio, because, when you're out with girls like that you can't get careless and miss any trains and stay out all night, like you can with some kinds of Janes.

And Wilbur blowed himself to the launch and it cost him fifteen cold plunks, but I wouldn't never have knew if I hadn't listened. He wasn't no tin horn kind of a sport.

Over at the Cedar Point place, we didn't stay around where there was a gang of common kind of cattle at all.

There was big dance halls and dining places for yaps, and there was a beach you could walk along and get where it was dark, and we went there.

She didn't talk hardly at all and neither did I, and I was thinking how glad I was my mother was all right, and always made us kids learn to eat with a fork at the table, and not swill soup, and not be noisy and rough like a gang you see around a race track that way.

Then Wilbur and his girl went away up the beach and Lucy and I sat down in a dark place, where there was some roots of old trees the water had washed up, and after that the time, till we had to go back in the launch and they had to catch their trains, wasn't nothing at all. It went like winking your eye.

55

60

Here's how it was. The place we were setting in was dark, like I said, and there was the roots from that old stump sticking up like arms, and there was a watery smell, and the night was like—as if you could put your hand out and feel it—so warm and soft and dark and sweet like an orange.

I most cried and I most swore and I most jumped up and danced, I was so mad and happy and sad.

When Wilbur come back from being alone with his girl, and she saw him coming, Lucy she says, "We got to go to the train now," and she was most crying too, but she never knew nothing I knew, and she couldn't be so all busted up. And then, before Wilbur and Miss Woodbury got up to where we was, she put her face up and kissed me quick, and put her head up against me and she was all quivering and—Gee whizz.

Sometimes I hope I have cancer and die. I guess you know what I mean. We went in the launch across the bay to the train like that, and it was dark, too. She whispered and said it was like she and I could get out of the boat and walk on water, and it sounded foolish, but I knew what she meant.

And then quick we were right at the depot, and there was a big gang of yaps, the kind that goes to the fairs, and crowded and milling around like cattle, and how could I tell her? "It won't be long because you'll write and I'll write you." That's all she said.

I got a chance like a hay barn afire. A swell chance I got.

And maybe she would write me, down at Marietta that way, and the letter would come back, and stamped on the front of it by the U.S.A. "there ain't any such guy," or something like that, whatever they stamp on a letter that way.

And me trying to pass myself off for a big-bug and a swell—to her, as decent a little body as God ever made. Craps amighty—swell chance I got!

And then the train come in, and she got on it, and Wilbur Wessen, he come and shook hands with me, and that Miss Woodbury was nice too and bowed to me, and I at her, and the train went and I busted out and cried like a kid.

Gee, I could have run after the train and made Dan Patch° look like a freight train after a wreck but, socks amighty, what was the use? Did you ever see such a fool?

I'll bet you what—if I had an arm broke right now or a train had run over my foot—I wouldn't go to no doctor at all. I'd go set down and let her hurt and hurt—that's what I'd do.

I'll bet you what—if I hadn't a drunk that booze I'd never been such a boob as to go tell such a lie—that couldn't never be made straight to a lady like her.

I wish I had that fellow right here that had on a Windsor tie and carried a cane. I'd smash him for fair. Gosh darn his eyes. He's a big fool—that's what he is.

And if I'm not another you just go find me one and I'll quit working and be a bum and give him my job. I don't care nothing for working, and earning money, and saving it for no such boob as myself.

65

70

75

QUESTIONS

1. Describe the point of view of "I'm a Fool." How completely does the narrator describe himself? What is the level and effect of the narrator's diction? Why,

Dan Patch: one of the fastest pace horses. Dan Patch still held records at the time of the story. Proverbial for his speed, his records were not broken until well into the 1930s.

in paragraphs 8 and 11–14, does he shift to the second-person point of view?

2. What changes does the narrator undergo during the events of the story?

3. Compare the characters of Lucy and the narrator. How successful might a match have been between the two if the narrator had not made things impossible by his false stories about himself?

4. Describe the importance of location and background. How does the narrator's familiarity with racing enable him to impress the Wessens?

KATHERINE MANSFIELD (1888–1923)

Miss Brill°   *1920*

Although it was so brilliantly fine—the blue sky powdered with gold and great spots of light like white wine splashed over the Jardins Publiques°—Miss Brill was glad that she had decided on her fur. The air was motionless, but when you opened your mouth there was just a faint chill, like a chill from a glass of iced water before you sip, and now and again a leaf came drifting—from nowhere, from the sky. Miss Brill put up her hand and touched her fur. Dear little thing! It was nice to feel it again. She had taken it out of its box that afternoon, shaken out the moth-powder, given it a good brush, and rubbed the life back into the dim little eyes. "What has been happening to me?" said the sad little eyes. Oh, how sweet it was to see them snap at her again from the red eiderdown! . . . But the nose, which was of some black composition, wasn't at all firm. It must have had a knock, somehow. Never mind—a little dab of black sealing-wax when the time came—when it was absolutely necessary. . . . Little rogue! Yes, she really felt like that about it. Little rogue biting its tail just by her left ear. She could have taken it off and laid it on her lap and stroked it. She felt a tingling in her hands and arms, but that came from walking, she supposed. And when she breathed, something light and sad—no, not sad, exactly—something gentle seemed to move in her bosom.

There were a number of people out this afternoon, far more than last Sunday. And the band sounded louder and gayer. That was because the Season had begun. For although the band played all the year round on Sundays, out of season it was never the same. It was like some one playing with only the family to listen; it didn't care how it played if there weren't any strangers present. Wasn't the conductor wearing a new coat, too? She was sure it was new. He scraped with his foot and flapped his arms like a rooster about to crow, and the bandsmen sitting in the green rotunda blew out their cheeks and glared at the music. Now there came a little "flutey" bit—very pretty!—a little chain of bright drops. She was sure it would be repeated. It was; she lifted her head and smiled.

Only two people shared her "special" seat: a fine old man in a velvet coat, his hands clasped over a huge carved walking-stick, and a big old woman, sitting upright, with a roll of knitting on her embroidered apron. They did not speak.

Miss Brill: *Brill* is the name of a common deep-sea flatfish.
Jardins Publiques: public gardens or park. The setting of the story is apparently a French seaside town.

This was disappointing, for Miss Brill always looked forward to the conversation. She had become really quite expert, she thought, at listening as though she didn't listen, at sitting in other people's lives just for a minute while they talked round her.

She glanced, sideways, at the old couple. Perhaps they would go soon. Last Sunday, too, hadn't been as interesting as usual. An Englishman and his wife, he wearing a dreadful Panama hat and she button boots. And she'd gone on the whole time about how she ought to wear spectacles; she knew she needed them; but that it was no good getting any; they'd be sure to break and they'd never keep on. And he'd been so patient. He'd suggested everything—gold rims, the kind that curved round your ears, little pads inside the bridge. No, nothing would please her. "They'll always be sliding down my nose!" Miss Brill had wanted to shake her.

The old people sat on the bench, still as statues. Never mind, there was   5
always the crowd to watch. To and fro, in front of the flower-beds and the band rotunda, the couples and groups paraded, stopped to talk, to greet, to buy a handful of flowers from the old beggar who had his tray fixed to the railings. Little children ran among them, swooping and laughing; little boys with big white silk bows under their chins, little girls, little French dolls, dressed up in velvet and lace. And sometimes a tiny staggerer came suddenly rocking into the open from under the trees, stopped, stared, as suddenly sat down "flop," until its small high-stepping mother, like a young hen, rushed scolding to its rescue. Other people sat on the benches and green chairs, but they were nearly always the same, Sunday after Sunday, and—Miss Brill had often noticed—there was something funny about nearly all of them. They were odd, silent, nearly all old, and from the way they stared they looked as though they'd just come from dark little rooms or even—even cupboards!

Behind the rotunda the slender trees with yellow leaves down drooping, and through them just a line of sea, and beyond the blue sky with gold-veined clouds.

Tum-tum-tum tiddle-um! tiddle-um! tum tiddle-um tum ta! blew the band.

Two young girls in red came by and two young soldiers in blue met them, and they laughed and paired and went off arm-in-arm. Two peasant women with funny straw hats passed, gravely, leading beautiful smoke-coloured donkeys. A cold, pale nun hurried by. A beautiful woman came along and dropped her bunch of violets, and a little boy ran after to hand them to her, and she took them and threw them away as if they'd been poisoned. Dear me! Miss Brill didn't know whether to admire that or not! And now an ermine toque° and a gentleman in grey met just in front of her. He was tall, stiff, dignified, and she was wearing the ermine toque she'd bought when her hair was yellow. Now everything, her hair, her face, even her eyes, was the same colour as the shabby ermine, and her hand, in its cleaned glove, lifted to dab her lips, was a tiny yellowish paw. Oh, she was so pleased to see him—delighted! She rather thought they were going to meet that afternoon. She described where she'd been—everywhere, here, there, along by the sea. The day was so charming—didn't he agree? And wouldn't he, perhaps? . . . But he shook his head, lighted a cigarette, slowly breathed a great deep puff into her face, and, even while she was still talking and laughing, flicked the match

ermine toque: close-fitting hat made of the white fur of an ermine; here the phrase stands for the woman wearing the hat.

away and walked on. The ermine toque was alone; she smiled more brightly than ever. But even the band seemed to know what she was feeling and played more softly, played tenderly, and the drum beat, "The Brute! The Brute!" over and over. What would she do? What was going to happen now? But as Miss Brill wondered, the ermine toque turned, raised her hand as though she'd seen some one else, much nicer, just over there, and pattered away. And the band changed again and played more quickly, more gaily than ever, and the old couple on Miss Brill's seat got up and marched away, and such a funny old man with long whiskers hobbled along in time to the music and was nearly knocked over by four girls walking abreast.

Oh, how fascinating it was! How she enjoyed it! How she loved sitting here, watching it all! It was like a play. It was exactly like a play. Who could believe the sky at the back wasn't painted? But it wasn't till a little brown dog trotted on solemn and then slowly trotted off, like a little "theatre" dog, a little dog that had been drugged, that Miss Brill discovered what it was that made it so exciting. They were all on the stage. They weren't only the audience, not only looking on; they were acting. Even she had a part and came every Sunday. No doubt somebody would have noticed if she hadn't been there; she was part of the performance after all. How strange she'd never thought of it like that before! And yet it explained why she made such a point of starting from home at just the same time each week—so as not to be late for the performance—and it also explained why she had quite a queer, shy feeling at telling her English pupils how she spent her Sunday afternoons. No wonder! Miss Brill nearly laughed out loud. She was on the stage. She thought of the old invalid gentleman to whom she read the newspaper four afternoons a week while he slept in the garden. She had got quite used to the frail head on the cotton pillow, the hollowed eyes, the open mouth and the high pinched nose. If he'd been dead she mightn't have noticed for weeks; she wouldn't have minded. But suddenly he knew he was having the paper read to him by an actress! "An actress!" The old head lifted; two points of light quivered in the old eyes. "An actress—are ye?" And Miss Brill smoothed the newspaper as though it were the manuscript of her part and said gently: "Yes, I have been an actress for a long time."

The band had been having a rest. Now they started again. And what they played was warm, sunny, yet there was just a faint chill—a something, what was it?—not sadness—no, not sadness—a something that made you want to sing. The tune lifted, lifted, the light shone; and it seemed to Miss Brill that in another moment all of them, all the whole company, would begin singing. The young ones, the laughing ones who were moving together, they would begin, and the men's voices, very resolute and brave, would join them. And then she too, she too, and the others on the benches—they would come in with a kind of accompaniment—something low, that scarcely rose or fell, something so beautiful—moving. . . . And Miss Brill's eyes filled with tears and she looked smiling at all the other members of the company. Yes, we understand, we understand, she thought—though what they understood she didn't know. 10

Just at that moment a boy and girl came and sat down where the old couple had been. They were beautifully dressed; they were in love. The hero and heroine, of course, just arrived from his father's yacht. And still soundlessly singing, still with that trembling smile, Miss Brill prepared to listen.

"No, not now," said the girl, "Not here, I can't."

"But why? Because of that stupid old thing at the end there?" asked the boy. "Why does she come here at all—who wants her? Why doesn't she keep her silly old mug at home?"

"It's her fu-fur which is so funny," giggled the girl. "It's exactly like a fried whiting."

"Ah, be off with you!" said the boy in an angry whisper. Then: "Tell me, ma petite chérie—"   15

"No, not here," said the girl. "Not *yet*."

On her way home she usually bought a slice of honeycake at the baker's. It was her Sunday treat. Sometimes there was an almond in her slice, sometimes not. It made a great difference. If there was an almond it was like carrying home a tiny present—a surprise—something that might very well not have been there. She hurried on the almond Sundays and struck the match for the kettle in quite a dashing way.

But to-day she passed the baker's by, climbed the stairs, went into the little dark room—her room like a cupboard—and sat down on the red eiderdown. She sat there for a long time. The box that the fur came out of was on the bed. She unclasped the necklet quickly; quickly, without looking, laid it inside. But when she put the lid on she thought she heard something crying.

QUESTIONS

1. Describe the point of view of "Miss Brill." Who says, in paragraph 1, "Dear little thing!" about the fur? How do you justify your conclusion about the source of this and similar insights that appear throughout the story?

2. Would this story be possible if told in the first person by Miss Brill herself? What might it have been like if told by a walker in the park who observed Miss Brill and overheard the conversation about her by the boy and girl?

3. A shift in the point of view occurs when the boy and girl sit down and Miss Brill overhears them. Describe the nature of this shift. Why do you think Mansfield made the change at this point?

4. In relation to the point of view, explain the last sentence of the story: "But when she put the lid on she thought she heard something crying."

SHIRLEY JACKSON   (1919–1965)

The Lottery   *1948*

The morning of June 27th was clear and sunny, with the fresh warmth of a full summer day; the flowers were blossoming profusely and the grass was richly green. The people of the village began to gather in the square, between the post office and the bank, around ten o'clock; in some towns there were so many people that the lottery took two days and had to be started on June 26th, but in this village, where there were only about three hundred people, the whole lottery took less than two hours, so it could begin at ten o'clock in the morning and still be through in time to allow the villagers to get home for noon dinner.

The children assembled first, of course. School was recently over for the summer, and the feeling of liberty sat uneasily on most of them; they tended to gather together quietly for a while before they broke into boisterous play, and their talk was still of the classroom and the teacher, of books and reprimands. Bobby Martin had already stuffed his pockets full of stones, and the other boys soon followed his example, selecting the smoothest and roundest stones; Bobby and Harry Jones and Dickie Delacroix—the villagers pronounced this name "Dellacroy"—eventually made a great pile of stones in one corner of the square and guarded it against the raids of the other boys. The girls stood aside, talking among themselves, looking over their shoulders at the boys, and the very small children rolled in the dust or clung to the hands of their older brothers or sisters.

Soon the men began to gather, surveying their own children, speaking of planting and rain, tractors and taxes. They stood together, away from the pile of stones in the corner, and their jokes were quiet and they smiled rather than laughed. The women, wearing faded house dresses and sweaters, came shortly after their menfolk. They greeted one another and exchanged bits of gossip as they went to join their husbands. Soon the women, standing by their husbands, began to call to their children, and the children came reluctantly, having to be called four or five times. Bobby Martin ducked under his mother's grasping hand and ran, laughing, back to the pile of stones. His father spoke up sharply, and Bobby came quickly and took his place between his father and his oldest brother.

The lottery was conducted—as were the square dances, the teen-age club, the Halloween program—by Mr. Summers, who had time and energy to devote to civic activities. He was a round-faced, jovial man and he ran the coal business, and people were sorry for him, because he had no children and his wife was a scold. When he arrived in the square, carrying the black wooden box, there was a murmur of conversation among the villagers, and he waved and called, "Little late today, folks." The postmaster, Mr. Graves, followed him, carrying a three-legged stool, and the stool was put in the center of the square and Mr. Summers set the black box down on it. The villagers kept their distance, leaving a space between themselves and the stool, and when Mr. Summers said, "Some of you fellows want to give me a hand?" there was a hesitation before two men, Mr. Martin and his oldest son, Baxter, came forward to hold the box steady on the stool while Mr. Summers stirred up the papers inside it.

The original paraphernalia for the lottery had been lost long ago, and the black box now resting on the stool had been put into use even before Old Man Warner, the oldest man in town, was born. Mr. Summers spoke frequently to the villagers about making a new box, but no one liked to upset even as much tradition as was represented by the black box. There was a story that the present box had been made with some pieces of the box that had preceded it, the one that had been constructed when the first people settled down to make a village here. Every year, after the lottery, Mr. Summers began talking again about a new box, but every year the subject was allowed to fade off without anything's being done. The black box grew shabbier each year; by now it was no longer completely black but splintered badly along one side to show the original wood color, and in some places faded or stained.

Mr. Martin and his oldest son, Baxter, held the black box securely on the stool until Mr. Summers had stirred the papers thoroughly with his hand. Because so much of the ritual had been forgotten or discarded, Mr. Summers had been successful in having slips of paper substituted for the chips of wood that had been used for generations. Chips of wood, Mr. Summers had argued, had been all very well when the village was tiny, but now that the population was more than three hundred and likely to keep on growing, it was necessary to use something that would fit more easily into the black box. The night before the lottery, Mr. Summers and Mr. Graves made up the slips of paper and put them in the box, and it was then taken to the safe of Mr. Summers' coal company and locked up until Mr. Summers was ready to take it to the square next morning. The rest of the year, the box was put away, sometimes one place, sometimes another; it had spent one year in Mr. Graves's barn and another year underfoot in the post office, and sometimes it was set on a shelf in the Martin grocery and left there.

There was a great deal of fussing to be done before Mr. Summers declared the lottery open. There were the lists to make up—of heads of families, heads of households in each family, members of each household in each family. There was the proper swearing-in of Mr. Summers by the postmaster, as the official of the lottery; at one time, some people remembered, there had been a recital of some sort, performed by the official of the lottery, a perfunctory, tuneless chant that had been rattled off duly each year; some people believed that the official of the lottery used to stand just so when he said or sang it, others believed that he was supposed to walk among the people, but years and years ago this part of the ritual had been allowed to lapse. There had been, also, a ritual salute, which the official of the lottery had had to use in addressing each person who came up to draw from the box, but this also had changed with time, until now it was felt necessary only for the official to speak to each person approaching. Mr. Summers was very good at all this; in his clean white shirt and blue jeans, with one hand resting carelessly on the black box, he seemed very proper and important as he talked interminably to Mr. Graves and the Martins.

Just as Mr. Summers finally left off talking and turned to the assembled villagers, Mrs. Hutchinson came hurriedly along the path to the square, her sweater thrown over her shoulders, and slid into place in the back of the crowd. "Clean forgot what day it was," she said to Mrs. Delacroix, who stood next to her, and they both laughed softly. "Thought my old man was out back stacking wood," Mrs. Hutchinson went on, "and then I looked out the window and the kids was gone, and then I remembered it was the twenty-seventh and came a-running." She dried her hands on her apron, and Mrs. Delacroix said, "You're in time, though. They're still talking away up there."

Mrs. Hutchinson craned her neck to see through the crowd and found her husband and children standing near the front. She tapped Mrs. Delacroix on the arm as a farewell and began to make her way through the crowd. The people separated good-humoredly to let her through; two or three people said, in voices just loud enough to be heard across the crowd, "Here comes your Missus, Hutchinson," and "Bill, she made it after all." Mrs. Hutchinson reached her husband, and Mr. Summers, who had been waiting, said cheerfully, "Thought we were going to have to get on without you, Tessie." Mrs. Hutchinson said, grinning, "Wouldn't have me leave m'dishes in the sink, now, would you, Joe?," and soft laughter ran through the crowd as the people stirred back into position after Mrs. Hutchinson's arrival.

"Well, now," Mr. Summers said soberly, "guess we better get started, get this over with, so's we can go back to work. Anybody ain't here?"

"Dunbar," several people said. "Dunbar, Dunbar."

Mr. Summers consulted his list. "Clyde Dunbar," he said. "That's right. He's broke his leg, hasn't he? Who's drawing for him?"

"Me, I guess," a woman said, and Mr. Summers turned to look at her. "Wife draws for her husband," Mr. Summers said. "Don't you have a grown boy to do it for you, Janey?" Although Mr. Summers and everyone else in the village knew the answer perfectly well, it was the business of the official of the lottery to ask such questions formally. Mr. Summers waited with an expression of polite interest while Mrs. Dunbar answered.

"Horace's not but sixteen yet," Mrs. Dunbar said regretfully. "Guess I gotta fill in for the old man this year."

"Right," Mr. Summers said. He made a note on the list he was holding. Then he asked, "Watson boy drawing this year?"   15

A tall boy in the crowd raised his hand. "Here," he said. "I'm drawing for m'mother and me." He blinked his eyes nervously and ducked his head as several voices in the crowd said things like "Good fellow, Jack," and "Glad to see your mother's got a man to do it."

"Well," Mr. Summers said, "guess that's everyone. Old Man Warner make it?"

"Here," a voice said, and Mr. Summers nodded.

A sudden hush fell on the crowd as Mr. Summers cleared his throat and looked at the list. "All ready?" he called. "Now, I'll read the names—heads of families first—and the men come up and take a paper out of the box. Keep the paper folded in your hand without looking at it until everyone has had a turn. Everything clear?"

The people had done it so many times that they only half listened to the   20
directions; most of them were quiet, wetting their lips, not looking around. Then Mr. Summers raised one hand high and said, "Adams." A man disengaged himself from the crowd and came forward. "Hi, Steve," Mr. Summers said, and Mr. Adams said, "Hi, Joe." They grinned at one another humorlessly and nervously. Then Mr. Adams reached into the black box and took out a folded paper. He held it firmly by one corner as he turned and went hastily back to his place in the crowd, where he stood a little apart from his family, not looking down at his hand.

"Allen," Mr. Summers said. "Anderson. . . . Bentham."

"Seems like there's no time at all between lotteries any more," Mrs. Delacroix said to Mrs. Graves in the back row. "Seems like we got through with the last one only last week."

"Time sure goes fast," Mrs. Graves said.

"Clark. . . . Delacroix."

"There goes my old man," Mrs. Delacroix said. She held her breath while   25
her husband went forward.

"Dunbar," Mr. Summers said, and Mrs. Dunbar went steadily to the box while one of the women said, "Go on, Janey," and another said, "There she goes."

"We're next," Mrs. Graves said. She watched while Mr. Graves came around from the side of the box, greeted Mr. Summers gravely, and selected a slip of paper from the box. By now, all through the crowd there were men holding the small folded papers in their large hands, turning them over and over nervously. Mrs. Dunbar and her two sons stood together, Mrs. Dunbar holding the slip of paper.

"Harburt. . . . Hutchinson."

"Get up there, Bill," Mrs. Hutchinson said, and the people near her laughed. "Jones."   30

"They do say," Mr. Adams said to Old Man Warner, who stood next to him, "that over in the north village they're talking of giving up the lottery."

Old Man Warner snorted. "Pack of crazy fools," he said. "Listening to the young folks, nothing's good enough for *them*. Next thing you know, they'll be wanting to go back to living in caves, nobody work any more, live *that* way for a while. Used to be a saying about 'Lottery in June, corn be heavy soon.' First thing you know, we'd all be eating stewed chickweed and acorns. There's *always* been a lottery," he added petulantly. "Bad enough to see young Joe Summers up there joking with everybody."

"Some places have already quit lotteries," Mrs. Adams said.

"Nothing but trouble in *that*," Old Man Warner said stoutly. "Pack of young fools."

"Martin." And Bobby Martin watched his father go forward. "Overdyke. . . .   35
Percy."

"I wish they'd hurry," Mrs. Dunbar said to her older son. "I wish they'd hurry."

"They're almost through," her son said.

"You get ready to run tell Dad," Mrs. Dunbar said.

Mr. Summers called his own name and then stepped forward precisely and selected a slip from the box. Then he called, "Warner."

"Seventy-seventh year I been in the lottery," Old Man Warner said as he   40
went through the crowd. "Seventy-seventh time."

"Watson." The tall boy came awkwardly through the crowd. Someone said, "Don't be nervous, Jack," and Mr. Summers said, "Take your time, son."

"Zanini."

After that, there was a long pause, a breathless pause, until Mr. Summers, holding his slip of paper in the air, said, "All right, fellows." For a minute, no one moved, and then all the slips of paper were opened. Suddenly, all the women began to speak at once, saying, "Who is it?" "Who's got it?" "Is it the Dunbars?" "Is it the Watsons?" Then the voices began to say, "It's Hutchinson. It's Bill," "Bill Hutchinson's got it."

"Go tell your father," Mrs. Dunbar said to her older son.

People began to look around to see the Hutchinsons. Bill Hutchinson was   45
standing quiet, staring down at the paper in his hand. Suddenly, Tessie Hutchinson shouted to Mr. Summers, "You didn't give him time enough to take any paper he wanted. I saw you. It wasn't fair!"

"Be a good sport, Tessie," Mrs. Delacroix called, and Mrs. Graves said, "All of us took the same chance."

"Shut up, Tessie," Bill Hutchinson said.

"Well, everyone," Mr. Summers said, "that was done pretty fast, and now we've got to be hurrying a little more to get done in time." He consulted his next list. "Bill," he said, "you draw for the Hutchinson family. You got any other households in the Hutchinsons?"

"There's Don and Eva," Mrs. Hutchinson yelled. "Make *them* take their chance!"

"Daughters draw with their husbands' families, Tessie," Mr. Summers said   50
gently. "You know that as well as anyone else."

"It wasn't *fair*," Tessie said.

"I guess not, Joe," Bill Hutchinson said regretfully. "My daughter draws with her husband's family, that's only fair. And I've got no other family except the kids."

"Then, as far as drawing for families is concerned, it's you," Mr. Summers said in explanation, "and as far as drawing for households is concerned, that's you, too. Right?"

"Right," Bill Hutchinson said.

"How many kids, Bill?" Mr. Summers asked formally.   55

"Three," Bill Hutchinson said. "There's Bill, Jr., and Nancy, and little Dave. And Tessie and me."

"All right, then," Mr. Summers said. "Harry, you got their tickets back?"

Mr. Graves nodded and held up the slips of paper. "Put them in the box, then," Mr. Summers directed. "Take Bill's and put it in."

"I think we ought to start over," Mrs. Hutchinson said, as quietly as she could. "I tell you it wasn't *fair*. You didn't give him time enough to choose. *Every*-body saw that."

Mr. Graves had selected the five slips and put them in the box, and he   60
dropped all the papers but those onto the ground, where the breeze caught them and lifted them off.

"Listen, everybody," Mrs. Hutchinson was saying to the people around her.

"Ready, Bill?" Mr. Summers asked, and Bill Hutchinson, with one quick glance around at his wife and children, nodded.

"Remember," Mr. Summers said, "take the slips and keep them folded until each person has taken one. Harry, you help little Dave." Mr. Graves took the hand of the little boy, who came willingly with him up to the box. "Take a paper out of the box, Davy," Mr. Summers said. Davy put his hand into the box and laughed. "Take just *one* paper," Mr. Summers said. "Harry, you hold it for him." Mr. Graves took the child's hand and removed the folded paper from the tight fist and held it while little Dave stood next to him and looked up at him wonderingly.

"Nancy next," Mr. Summers said. Nancy was twelve, and her school friends breathed heavily as she went forward, switching her skirt, and took a slip daint-ily from the box. "Bill, Jr.," Mr. Summers said, and Billy, his face red and his feet over-large, nearly knocked the box over as he got a paper out. "Tessie," Mr. Summers said. She hesitated for a minute, looking around defiantly, and then set her lips and went up to the box. She snatched a paper out and held it be-hind her.

"Bill," Mr. Summers said, and Bill Hutchinson reached into the box and felt   65
around, bringing his hand out at last with the slip of paper in it.

The crowd was quiet. A girl whispered, "I hope it's not Nancy," and the sound of the whisper reached the edges of the crowd.

"It's not the way it used to be," Old Man Warner said clearly. "People ain't they way they used to be."

"All right," Mr. Summers said. "Open the papers. Harry, you open little Dave's."

Mr. Graves opened the slip of paper and there was a general sigh through the crowd as he held it up and everyone could see that it was blank. Nancy and Bill, Jr., opened theirs at the same time, and both beamed and laughed, turning around to the crowd and holding their slips of paper above their heads.

"Tessie," Mr. Summers said. There was a pause, and then Mr. Summers   70 looked at Bill Hutchinson, and Bill unfolded his paper and showed it. It was blank.

"It's Tessie," Mr. Summers said, and his voice was hushed. "Show us her paper, Bill."

Bill Hutchinson went over to his wife and forced the slip of paper out of her hand. It had a black spot on it, the black spot Mr. Summers had made the night before with the heavy pencil in the coal-company office. Bill Hutchinson held it up, and there was a stir in the crowd.

"All right, folks," Mr. Summers said. "Let's finish quickly."

Although the villagers had forgotten the ritual and lost the original black box, they still remembered to use stones. The pile of stones the boys had made earlier was ready; there were stones on the ground with the blowing scraps of paper that had come out of the box. Mrs. Delacroix selected a stone so large she had to pick it up with both hands and turned to Mrs. Dunbar. "Come on," she said. "Hurry up."

Mrs. Dunbar had small stones in both hands, and she said, gasping for breath, "I can't run at all. You'll have to go ahead and I'll catch up with you." 75

The children had stones already, and someone gave little Davy Hutchinson a few pebbles.

Tessie Hutchinson was in the center of a cleared space by now, and she held her hands out desperately as the villagers moved in on her. "It isn't fair," she said. A stone hit her on the side of the head.

Old Man Warner was saying, "Come on, come on, everyone." Steve Adams was in the front of the crowd of villagers with Mrs. Graves beside him.

"It isn't fair, it isn't right," Mrs. Hutchinson screamed, and then they were upon her.

QUESTIONS

1. Describe the point of view of the story. What seems to be the position from which the narrator sees and describes the events? How much extra information does the narrator provide?

2. What would the story be like if it were done with an omniscient point of view? With the first person? Could the story be as suspenseful as it is? In what other ways might the story be different with another point of view?

3. Does the conclusion of "The Lottery" seem to come as a surprise? In retrospect, what hints earlier in the story tell about what is to come?

4. A scapegoat, in the ritual of purification described in the Old Testament (Leviticus 16), was an actual goat that was released into the wilderness after having been ceremonially heaped with the "iniquities" of the people (Leviticus 16:22). What traces of such a ritual are suggested in "The Lottery"? Can you think of any other kinds of rituals that are retained today even though their purpose is now remote or even nonexistent?

5. Is the story a horror story or a surprise story, or neither or both? Explain.

ALICE MUNRO   (b. 1931)

Meneseteung   *1988*

I

> Columbine, bloodroot,
> And wild bergamot,
> Gathering armfuls,
> Giddily we go.

Offerings, the book is called. Gold lettering on a dull-blue cover. The author's full name underneath: Almeda Joynt Roth. The local paper, the *Vidette*, referred to her as "our poetess." There seems to be a mixture of respect and contempt, both for her calling and for her sex—or for their predictable conjuncture. In the front of the book is a photograph, with the photographer's name in one corner, and the date: 1865. The book was published later, in 1873.

The poetess has a long face; a rather long nose; full, somber dark eyes, which seem ready to roll down her cheeks like giant tears; a lot of dark hair gathered around her face in droopy rolls and curtains. A streak of gray hair plain to see, although she is, in this picture, only twenty-five. Not a pretty girl but the sort of woman who may age well, who probably won't get fat. She wears a tucked and braid-trimmed dark dress or jacket, with a lacy, floppy arrangement of white material—frills or a bow—filling the deep V at the neck. She also wears a hat, which might be made of velvet, in a dark color to match the dress. It's the untrimmed, shapeless hat, something like a soft beret, that makes me see artistic intentions, or at least a shy and stubborn eccentricity, in this young woman, whose long neck and forward-inclining head indicate as well that she is tall and slender and somewhat awkward. From the waist up, she looks like a young nobleman of another century. But perhaps it was the fashion.

"In 1854," she writes in the preface to her book, "my father brought us— my mother, my sister Catherine, my brother William, and me—to the wilds of Canada West (as it then was). My father was a harness-maker by trade, but a cultivated man who could quote by heart from the Bible, Shakespeare, and the writings of Edmund Burke. He prospered in this newly opened land and was able to set up a harness and leather-goods store, and after a year to build the comfortable house in which I live (alone) today. I was fourteen years old, the eldest of the children, when we came into this country from Kingston,° a town whose handsome streets I have not seen again but often remember. My sister was eleven and my brother nine. The third summer that we lived here, my brother and sister were taken ill of a prevalent fever and died within a few days of each other. My dear mother did not regain her spirits after this blow to our family. Her health declined, and after another three years she died. I then became housekeeper to my father and was happy to make his home for twelve years, until he died suddenly one morning at his shop.

Kingston: city in southeastern Ontario, on the St. Lawrence. The town of **Meneseteung** is visualized as being about 200 miles west of Kingston.

"From my earliest years I have delighted in verse and I have occupied myself—and sometimes allayed my griefs, which have been no more, I know, than any sojourner on earth must encounter—with many floundering efforts at its composition. My fingers, indeed, were always too clumsy for crochetwork, and those dazzling productions of embroidery which one sees often today—the overflowing fruit and flower baskets, the little Dutch boys, the bonneted maidens with their watering cans—have likewise proved to be beyond my skill. So I offer instead, as the product of my leisure hours, these rude posies, these ballads, couplets, reflections."

Titles of some of the poems: "Children at Their Games," "The Gypsy Fair," "A Visit to My Family," "Angels in the Snow," "Champlain at the Mouth of the Meneseteung," "The Passing of the Old Forest," and "A Garden Medley." There are some other, shorter poems, about birds and wildflowers and snowstorms. There is some comically intentioned doggerel about what people are thinking about as they listen to the sermon in church.

"Children at Their Games": The writer, a child, is playing with her brother and sister—one of those games in which children on different sides try to entice and catch each other. She plays on in the deepening twilight, until she realizes that she is alone, and much older. Still she hears the (ghostly) voices of her brother and sister calling. *Come over, come over, let Meda come over.* (Perhaps Almeda was called Meda in the family, or perhaps she shortened her name to fit the poem.)

"The Gypsy Fair": The Gypsies have an encampment near the town, a "fair," where they sell cloth and trinkets, and the writer as a child is afraid that she may be stolen by them, taken away from her family. Instead, her family has been taken away from her, stolen by Gypsies she can't locate or bargain with.

"A Visit to My Family": A visit to the cemetery, a one-sided conversation.

"Angels in the Snow": The writer once taught her brother and sister to make "angels" by lying down in the snow and moving their arms to create wing shapes. Her brother always jumped up carelessly, leaving an angel with a crippled wing. Will this be made perfect in Heaven, or will he be flying with his own makeshift, in circles?

"Champlain° at the Mouth of the Meneseteung": This poem celebrates the popular, untrue belief that the explorer sailed down the eastern shore of Lake Huron and landed at the mouth of the major river.

"The Passing of the Old Forest": A list of all the trees—their names, appearance, and uses—that were cut down in the original forest, with a general description of the bears, wolves, eagles, deer, waterfowl.

"A Garden Medley": Perhaps planned as a companion to the forest poem. Catalogue of plants brought from European countries, with bits of history and legend attached, and final Canadianness resulting from this mixture.

The poems are written in quatrains or couplets. There are a couple of attempts at sonnets, but mostly the rhyme scheme is simple—*abab* or *abcb*. The rhyme used is what was once called "masculine" ("shore"/"before"), though once in a while it is "feminine" ("quiver"/"river"). Are those terms familiar anymore?° No poem is unrhymed.

Champlain: The explorer Samuel de Champlain (1567–1635), a founder of Quebec, had traveled to the eastern regions of Lake Huron in 1615.
    anymore: See pp. 688–690.

II

> While roses cold as snow
> Bloom where those "angels" lie.
> Do they but rest below
> Or, in God's wonder, fly?

In 1879, Almeda Roth was still living in the house at the corner of Pearl and Dufferin streets, the house her father had built for his family. The house is there today; the manager of the liquor store lives in it. It's covered with aluminum siding; a closed-in porch has replaced the veranda. The woodshed, the fence, the gates, the privy, the barn—all these are gone. A photograph taken in the eighteen-eighties shows them all in place. The house and fence look a little shabby, in need of paint, but perhaps that is just because of the bleached-out look of the brownish photograph. The lace-curtained windows look like white eyes. No big shade tree is in sight, and, in fact, the tall elms that overshadowed the town until the nineteen-fifties, as well as the maples that shade it now, are skinny young trees with rough fences around them to protect them from the cows. Without the shelter of those trees, there is a great exposure—back yards, clotheslines, woodpiles, patchy sheds and barns and privies—all bare, exposed, provisional looking. Few houses would have anything like a lawn, just a patch of plantains and anthills and raked dirt. Perhaps petunias growing on top of a stump, in a round box. Only the main street is graveled; the other streets are dirt roads, muddy or dusty according to season. Yards must be fenced to keep animals out. Cows are tethered in vacant lots or pastured in back yards, but sometimes they get loose. Pigs get loose, too, and dogs roam free or nap in a lordly way on the boardwalks. The town has taken root, it's not going to vanish, yet it still has some of the look of an encampment. And, like an encampment, it's busy all the time—full of people, who, within the town, usually walk wherever they're going; full of animals, which leave horse buns, cowpats, dog turds, that ladies have to hitch up their skirts for; full of the noise of building and of drivers shouting at their horses and of the trains that come in several times a day.

I read about that life in the *Vidette*.   15

The population is younger than it is now, than it will ever be again. People past fifty usually don't come to a raw, new place. There are quite a few people in the cemetery already, but most of them died young, in accidents or childbirth or epidemics. It's youth that's in evidence in town. Children—boys—rove through the streets in gangs. School is compulsory for only four months a year, and there are lots of occasional jobs that even a child of eight or nine can do—pulling flax, holding horses, delivering groceries, sweeping the boardwalk in front of stores. A good deal of time they spend looking for adventures. One day they follow an old woman, a drunk nicknamed Queen Aggie. They get her into a wheelbarrow and trundle her all over town, then dump her into a ditch to sober her up. They also spend a lot of time around the railway station. They jump on shunting cars and dart between them and dare each other to take chances, which once in a while result in their getting maimed or killed. And they keep an eye out for any strangers coming into town. They follow them, offer to carry their bags, and direct them (for a five-cent piece) to a hotel. Strangers who don't look so prosperous are taunted and tormented. Speculation surrounds all of them—it's like a cloud of flies. Are they coming to town to start up a new business, to persuade people to invest in some scheme, to sell cures or gimmicks, to preach on the street corners? All these things are possible any day of the week. Be on your guard, the *Vidette* tells people. These are times of opportunity and danger. Tramps, confidence men, hucksters, shysters, plain thieves, are traveling the roads, and particularly the railroads. Thefts are announced: money invested and never seen again, a pair of trousers taken from the clothesline, wood from the woodpile, eggs from the henhouse. Such incidents increase in the hot weather.

Hot weather brings accidents, too. More horses run wild then, upsetting buggies. Hands caught in the wringer while doing the washing, a man lopped in two at the sawmill, a leaping boy killed in a fall of lumber at the lumberyard. Nobody sleeps well. Babies wither with summer complaint, and fat people can't catch their breath. Bodies must be buried in a hurry. One day a man goes through the streets ringing a cowbell and calling "Repent! Repent!" It's not a stranger this time, it's a young man who works at the butcher shop. Take him home, wrap him in cold wet cloths, give him some nerve medicine, keep him in bed, pray for his wits. If he doesn't recover, he must go to the asylum.

Almeda Roth's house faces on Dufferin Street, which is a street of considerable respectability. On this street merchants, a mill owner, an operator of salt wells, have their houses. But Pearl Street, which her back windows overlook and her back gate opens onto, is another story. Workmen's houses are adjacent to hers. Small but decent row houses—that is all right. Things deteriorate toward the end of the block, and the next, last one becomes dismal. Nobody but the poorest people, the unrespectable and undeserving poor, would live there at the edge of a boghole (drained since then), called the Pearl Street Swamp. Bushy and luxuriant weeds grow there, makeshift shacks have been put up, there are piles of refuse and debris and crowds of runty children, slops are flung from doorways. The town tries to compel these people to build privies, but they would just as soon go in the bushes. If a gang of boys goes down there in search of adventure, it's likely they'll get more than they bargained for. It is said that even the town constable won't go down Pearl Street on a Saturday night. Almeda Roth has never walked past the row housing. In one of those houses lives the young girl Annie, who helps her with her housecleaning. That young girl herself, being a decent girl, has never walked down to the last block or the swamp. No decent woman ever would.

But that same swamp, lying to the east of Almeda Roth's house, presents a fine sight at dawn. Almeda sleeps at the back of the house. She keeps to the same bedroom she once shared with her sister Catherine—she would not think of moving to the larger front bedroom, where her mother used to lie in bed all day, and which was later the solitary domain of her father. From her window she can see the sun rising, the swamp mist filling with light, the bulky, nearest trees floating against that mist and the trees behind turning transparent. Swamp oaks, soft maples, tamarack, bitternut.

III

Here where the river meets the inland sea,
Spreading her blue skirts from the solemn wood,
I think of birds and beasts and vanished men,
Whose pointed dwellings on these pale sands stood.

One of the strangers who arrived at the railway station a few years ago was Jarvis Poulter, who now occupies the house next to Almeda Roth's—separated from hers by a vacant lot, which he has bought, on Dufferin Street. The house is plainer than the Roth house and has no fruit trees or flowers planted around it. It is understood that this is a natural result of Jarvis Poulter's being a widower and living alone. A man may keep his house decent, but he will never—if he is a proper man—do much to decorate it. Marriage forces him to live with more ornament as well as sentiment, and it protects him, also, from the extremities of his own nature—from a frigid parsimony or a luxuriant sloth, from squalor, and from excessive sleeping, drinking, smoking, or freethinking.°

> In the interests of economy, it is believed, a certain estimable gentleman of our town persists in fetching water from the public tap and supplementing his fuel supply by picking up the loose coal along the railway track. Does he think to repay the town or the railway company with a supply of free salt?

This is the *Vidette*, full of shy jokes, innuendo, plain accusation, that no newspaper would get away with today. It's Jarvis Poulter they're talking about— though in other passages he is spoken of with great respect, as a civil magistrate, an employer, a churchman. He is close, that's all. An eccentric, to a degree. All of which may be a result of his single condition, his widower's life. Even carrying his water from the town tap and filling his coal pail along the railway track. This is a decent citizen, prosperous: a tall—slightly paunchy?—man in a dark suit with polished boots. A beard? Black hair streaked with gray. A severe and self-possessed air, and a large pale wart among the bushy hairs of one eyebrow? People talk about a young, pretty, beloved wife, dead in childbirth or some horrible accident, like a house fire or a railway disaster. There is no ground for this, but it adds interest. All he has told them is that his wife is dead.

He came to this part of the country looking for oil. The first oil well in the world was sunk in Lambton County, south of here, in the eighteen-fifties. Drilling for oil, Jarvis Poulter discovered salt. He set to work to make the most of that. When he walks home from church with Almeda Roth, he tells her about his salt wells. They are twelve hundred feet deep. Heated water is pumped down into them, and that dissolves the salt. Then the brine is pumped to the surface. It is poured into great evaporator pans over slow, steady fires, so that the water is steamed off and the pure, excellent salt remains. A commodity for which the demand will never fail.

"The salt of the earth," Almeda says.

"Yes," he says, frowning. He may think this disrespectful. She did not intend   25
it so. He speaks of competitors in other towns who are following his lead and trying to hog the market. Fortunately, their wells are not drilled so deep, or their evaporating is not done so efficiently. There is salt everywhere under this land, but it is not so easy to come by as some people think.

Does that not mean, Almeda says, that there was once a great sea?

Freethinking: an intellectual movement, begun in the eighteenth century, emphasizing reason and denying the authority of religion and the supernatural. In the nineteenth century, there were organized groups in America devoted to freethinking. See also Ibsen's *An Enemy of the People*, Act IV, speech 140 (p. 1447).

Very likely, Jarvis Poulter says. Very likely. He goes on to tell her about other enterprises of his—a brickyard, a lime kiln. And he explains to her how this operates, and where the good clay is found. He also owns two farms, whose woodlots supply the fuel for his operations.

Among the couples strolling home from church on a recent, sunny Sabbath morning we noted a certain salty gentleman and literary lady, not perhaps in their first youth but by no means blighted by the frosts of age. May we surmise?

This kind of thing pops up in the *Vidette* all the time.

May they surmise, and is this courting? Almeda Roth has a bit of money,   30 which her father left her, and she has her house. She is not too old to have a couple of children. She is a good enough housekeeper, with the tendency toward fancy iced cakes and decorated tarts which is seen fairly often in old maids. (Honorable mention at the Fall Fair.) There is nothing wrong with her looks, and naturally she is in better shape than most married women of her age, not having been loaded down with work and children. But why was she passed over in her earlier, more marriageable years, in a place that needs women to be partnered and fruitful? She was a rather gloomy girl—that may have been the trouble. The deaths of her brother and sister and then of her mother, who lost her reason, in fact, a year before she died, and lay in her bed talking nonsense—those weighed on her, so she was not lively company. And all that reading and poetry—it seemed more of a drawback, a barrier, an obsession, in the young girl than in the middle-aged woman, who needed something, after all, to fill her time. Anyway, it's five years since her book was published, so perhaps she has got over that. Perhaps it was the proud, bookish father, encouraging her?

Everyone takes it for granted that Almeda Roth is thinking of Jarvis Poulter as a husband and would say yes if he asked her. And she is thinking of him. She doesn't want to get her hopes up too much, she doesn't want to make a fool of herself. She would like a signal. If he attended church on Sunday evenings, there would be a chance, during some months of the year, to walk home after dark. He would carry a lantern. (There is as yet no street lighting in town.) He would swing the lantern to light the way in front of the lady's feet and observe their narrow and delicate shape. He might catch her arm as they step off the boardwalk. But he does not go to church at night.

Nor does he call for her, and walk with her *to* church on Sunday mornings. That would be a declaration. He walks her home, past his gate as far as hers; he lifts his hat then and leaves her. She does not invite him to come in—a woman living alone could never do such a thing. As soon as a man and woman of almost any age are alone together within four walls, it is assumed that anything may happen. Spontaneous combustion, instant fornication, an attack of passion. Brute instinct, triumph of the senses. What possibilities men and women must see in each other to infer such dangers. Or, believing in the dangers, how often they must think about the possibilities.

When they walk side by side she can smell his shaving soap, the barber's oil, his pipe tobacco, the wool and linen and leather smell of his manly clothes. The correct, orderly, heavy clothes are like those she used to brush and starch and iron for her father. She misses that job—her father's appreciation, his dark, kind authority. Jarvis Poulter's garments, his smell, his movement, all cause the skin on the side of her body next to him to tingle hopefully, and a meek shiver raises the hairs on her arms. Is this to be taken as a sign of love? She thinks of him coming into her—*their*—bedroom in his long underwear and his hat. She knows this outfit is ridiculous, but in her mind he does not look so; he has the solemn effrontery of a figure in a dream. He comes into the room and lies down on the bed beside her, preparing to take her in his arms. Surely he removes his hat? She doesn't know, for at this point a fit of welcome and submission overtakes her, a buried gasp. He would be her husband.

One thing she has noticed about married women, and that is how many of them have to go about creating their husbands. They have to start ascribing preferences, opinions, dictatorial ways. Oh, yes, they say, my husband is very particular. He won't touch turnips. He won't eat fried meat. (Or he will only eat fried meat.) He likes me to wear blue (brown) all the time. He can't stand organ music. He hates to see a woman go out bareheaded. He would kill me if I took one puff of tobacco. This way, bewildered, sidelong-looking men are made over, made into husbands, heads of households. Almeda Roth cannot imagine herself doing that. She wants a man who doesn't have to be made, who is firm already and determined and mysterious to her. She does not look for companionship. Men—except for her father—seem to her deprived in some way, incurious. No doubt that is necessary, so that they will do what they have to do. Would she herself, knowing that there was salt in the earth, discover how to get it out and sell it? Not likely. She would be thinking about the ancient sea. That kind of speculation is what Jarvis Poulter has, quite properly, no time for.

Instead of calling for her and walking her to church, Jarvis Poulter might make another, more venturesome declaration. He could hire a horse and take her for a drive out to the country. If he did this, she would be both glad and sorry. Glad to be beside him, driven by him, receiving this attention from him in front of the world. And sorry to have the countryside removed for her—filmed over, in a way, by his talk and preoccupations. The countryside that she has written about in her poems actually takes diligence and determination to see. Some things must be disregarded. Manure piles, of course, and boggy fields full of high, charred stumps, and great heaps of brush waiting for a good day for burning. The meandering creeks have been straightened, turned into ditches with high, muddy banks. Some of the crop fields and pasture fields are fenced with big, clumsy uprooted stumps, others are held in a crude stitchery of rail fences. The trees have all been cleared back to the woodlots. And the woodlots are all second growth. No trees along the roads or lanes or around the farmhouses, except a few that are newly planted, young and weedy looking. Clusters of log barns—the grand barns that are to dominate the countryside for the next hundred years are just beginning to be built—and mean-looking log houses, and every four or five miles a ragged little settlement with a church and school and store and a blacksmith shop. A raw countryside just wrenched from the forest, but swarming with people. Every hundred acres is a farm, every farm has a family, most families have ten or twelve children. (This is the country that will send out wave after wave of settlers—it's already starting to send them—to northern Ontario and the West.) It's true that you can gather wildflowers in spring in the woodlots, but you'd have to walk through herds of horned cows to get to them.

35

IV

> The Gypsies have departed.
> Their camping-ground is bare.
> Oh, boldly would I bargain now
> At the Gypsy Fair.

Almeda suffers a good deal from sleeplessness, and the doctor has given her bromides and nerve medicine. She takes the bromides, but the drops gave her dreams that were too vivid and disturbing, so she has put the bottle by for an emergency. She told the doctor her eyeballs felt dry, like hot glass, and her joints ached. Don't read so much, he said, don't study; get yourself good and tired out with housework, take exercise. He believes that her troubles would clear up if she got married. He believes this in spite of the fact that most of his nerve medicine is prescribed for married women.

So Almeda cleans house and helps clean the church, she lends a hand to friends who are wallpapering or getting ready for a wedding, she bakes one of her famous cakes for the Sunday-school picnic. On a hot Saturday in August she decides to make some grape jelly. Little jars of grape jelly will make fine Christmas presents, or offerings to the sick. But she started late in the day and the jelly is not made by nightfall. In fact, the hot pulp has just been dumped into the cheesecloth bag, to strain out the juice. Almeda drinks some tea and eats a slice of cake with butter (a childish indulgence of hers), and that's all she wants for supper. She washes her hair at the sink and sponges off her body, to be clean for Sunday. She doesn't light a lamp. She lies down on the bed with the window wide open and a sheet just up to her waist, and she does feel wonderfully tired. She can even feel a little breeze.

When she wakes up, the night seems fiery hot and full of threats. She lies sweating on her bed, and she has the impression that the noises she hears are knives and saws and axes—all angry implements chopping and jabbing and boring within her head. But it isn't true. As she comes further awake she recognizes the sounds that she has heard sometimes before—the fracas of a summer Saturday night on Pearl Street. Usually the noise centers on a fight. People are drunk, there is a lot of protest and encouragement concerning the fight, somebody will scream "Murder!" Once, there was a murder. But it didn't happen in a fight. An old man was stabbed to death in his shack, perhaps for a few dollars he kept in the mattress.

She gets out of bed and goes to the window. The night sky is clear, with no moon and with bright stars. Pegasus° hangs straight ahead, over the swamp. Her father taught her that constellation—automatically, she counts its stars. Now she can make out distinct voices, individual contributions to the row. Some people, like herself, have evidently been wakened from sleep. "Shut up!" they are yelling. "Shut up that caterwauling or I'm going to come down and tan the arse off yez!"

But nobody shuts up. It's as if there were a ball of fire rolling up Pearl   40
Street, shooting off sparks—only the fire is noise, it's yells and laughter and shrieks and curses, and the sparks are voices that shoot off alone. Two voices gradually distinguish themselves—a rising and falling howling cry and a steady throbbing,

---

Pegasus: a constellation that is at its highest point (in early evening) in autumn. Its location here, in summer, indicates the lateness of the hour.

low-pitched stream of abuse that contains all those words which Almeda associates with danger and depravity and foul smells and disgusting sights. Someone—the person crying out, "Kill me! Kill me now!"—is being beaten. A woman is being beaten. She keeps crying, "Kill me! Kill me!" and sometimes her mouth seems choked with blood. Yet there is something taunting and triumphant about her cry. There is something theatrical about it. And the people around are calling out, "Stop it! Stop that!" or "Kill her! Kill her!" in a frenzy, as if at the theater or a sporting match or a prizefight. Yes, thinks Almeda, she has noticed that before—it is always partly a charade with these people; there is a clumsy sort of parody, an exaggeration, a missed connection. As if anything they did—even a murder—might be something they didn't quite believe but were powerless to stop.

Now there is the sound of something thrown—a chair, a plank?—and of a woodpile or part of a fence giving way. A lot of newly surprised cries, the sound of running, people getting out of the way, and the commotion has come much closer. Almeda can see a figure in a light dress, bent over and running. That will be the woman. She has got hold of something like a stick of wood or a shingle, and she turns and flings it at the darker figure running after her.

"Ah, go get her!" the voices cry. "Go baste her one!"

Many fall back now; just the two figures come on and grapple, and break loose again, and finally fall down against Almeda's fence. The sound they make becomes very confused—gagging, vomiting, grunting, pounding. Then a long, vibrating, choking sound of pain and self-abasement, self-abandonment, which could come from either or both of them.

Almeda has backed away from the window and sat down on the bed. Is that the sound of murder she has heard? What is to be done, what is she to do? She must light a lantern, she must go downstairs and light a lantern—she must go out into the yard, she must go downstairs. Into the yard. The lantern. She falls over on her bed and pulls the pillow to her face. In a minute. The stairs, the lantern. She sees herself already down there, in the back hall, drawing the bolt of the back door. She falls asleep.

She wakes, startled, in the early light. She thinks there is a big crow sitting on her windowsill, talking in a disapproving but unsurprised way about the events of the night before. "Wake up and move the wheelbarrow!" it says to her, scolding, and she understands that it means something else by "wheelbarrow"—something foul and sorrowful. Then she is awake and sees that there is no such bird. She gets up at once and looks out the window. 45

Down against her fence there is a pale lump pressed—a body.

Wheelbarrow.

She puts a wrapper over her nightdress and goes downstairs. The front rooms are still shadowy, the blinds down in the kitchen. Something goes *plop, plup,* in a leisurely, censorious way, reminding her of the conversation of the crow. It's just the grape juice, straining overnight. She pulls the bolt and goes out the back door. Spiders have draped their webs over the doorway in the night, and the hollyhocks are drooping, heavy with dew. By the fence, she parts the sticky hollyhocks and looks down and she can see.

A woman's body heaped up there, turned on her side with her face squashed down into the earth. Almeda can't see her face. But there is a bare breast let loose, brown nipple pulled long like a cow's teat, and a bare haunch and leg, the haunch bearing a bruise as big as a sunflower. The unbruised skin is grayish, like a plucked, raw drumstick. Some kind of nightgown or all-purpose dress she has on. Smelling of vomit. Urine, drink, vomit.

Barefoot, in her nightgown and flimsy wrapper, Almeda runs away. She runs around the side of her house between the apple trees and the veranda; she opens the front gate and flees down Dufferin Street to Jarvis Poulter's house, which is the nearest to hers. She slaps the flat of her hand many times against the door.

"There is the body of a woman," she says when Jarvis Poulter appears at last. He is in his dark trousers, held up with braces, and his shirt is half unbuttoned, his face unshaven, his hair standing up on his head. "Mr. Poulter, excuse me. A body of a woman. At my back gate."

He looks at her fiercely. "Is she dead?"

His breath is dank, his face creased, his eyes bloodshot.

"Yes. I think murdered," says Almeda. She can see a little of his cheerless front hall. His hat on a chair. "In the night I woke up. I heard a racket down on Pearl Street," she says, struggling to keep her voice low and sensible. "I could hear this—pair. I could hear a man and a woman fighting."

He picks up his hat and puts it on his head. He closes and locks the front door, and puts the key in his pocket. They walk along the boardwalk and she sees that she is in her bare feet. She holds back what she feels a need to say next— that she is responsible, she could have run out with a lantern, she could have screamed (but who needed more screams?), she could have beat the man off. She could have run for help then, not now.

They turn down Pearl Street, instead of entering the Roth yard. Of course the body is still there. Hunched up, half bare, the same as before.

Jarvis Poulter doesn't hurry or halt. He walks straight over to the body and looks down at it, nudges the leg with the toe of his boot, just as you'd nudge a dog or a sow.

"You," he says, not too loudly but firmly, and nudges again.

Almeda tastes bile at the back of her throat.

"Alive," says Jarvis Poulter, and the woman confirms this. She stirs, she grunts weakly.

Almeda says, "I will get the doctor." If she had touched the woman, if she had forced herself to touch her, she would not have made such a mistake.

"Wait," says Jarvis Poulter. "Wait. Let's see if she can get up."

"Get up, now," he says to the woman. "Come on. Up, now. Up."

Now a startling thing happens. The body heaves itself onto all fours, the head is lifted—the hair all matted with blood and vomit—and the woman begins to bang this head, hard and rhythmically, against Almeda Roth's picket fence. As she bangs her head she finds her voice, and lets out an open-mouthed yowl, full of strength and what sounds like an anguished pleasure.

"Far from dead," says Jarvis Poulter. "And I wouldn't bother the doctor."

"There's blood," says Almeda as the woman turns her smeared face.

"From her nose," he says. "Not fresh." He bends down and catches the horrid hair close to the scalp to stop the head banging.

"You stop that now," he says. "Stop it. Gwan home now. Gwan home, where you belong." The sound coming out of the woman's mouth has stopped. He shakes her head slightly, warning her, before he lets go of her hair. "Gwan home!"

Released, the woman lunges forward, pulls herself to her feet. She can walk.

She weaves and stumbles down the street, making intermittent, cautious noises of protest. Jarvis Poulter watches her for a moment to make sure that she's on her way. Then he finds a large burdock leaf, on which he wipes his hand. He says, "There goes your dead body!"

The back gate being locked, they walk around to the front. The front gate 70 stands open. Almeda still feels sick. Her abdomen is bloated; she is hot and dizzy.

"The front door is locked," she says faintly. "I came out by the kitchen." If only he would leave her, she could go straight to the privy. But he follows. He follows her as far as the back door and into the back hall. He speaks to her in a tone of harsh joviality that she has never before heard from him. "No need for alarm," he says. "It's only the consequences of drink. A lady oughtn't to be living alone so close to a bad neighborhood." He takes hold of her arm just above the elbow. She can't open her mouth to speak to him, to say thank you. If she opened her mouth she would retch.

What Jarvis Poulter feels for Almeda Roth at this moment is just what he has not felt during all those circumspect walks and all his own solitary calculations of her probable worth, undoubted respectability, adequate comeliness. He has not been able to imagine her as a wife. Now that is possible. He is sufficiently stirred by her loosened hair—prematurely gray but thick and soft—her flushed face, her light clothing, which nobody but a husband should see. And by her indiscretion, her agitation, her foolishness, her need?

"I will call on you later," he says to her. "I will walk with you to church."

At the corner of Pearl and Dufferin streets last Sunday morning there was discovered, by a lady resident there, the body of a certain woman of Pearl Street, thought to be dead but only, as it turned out, dead drunk. She was roused from her heavenly—or otherwise—stupor by the firm persuasion of Mr. Poulter, a neighbour and a Civil magistrate, who had been summoned by the lady resident. Incidents of this sort, unseemly, troublesome, and disgraceful to our town, have of late become all too common.

V

I sit at the bottom of sleep,
As on the floor of the sea.
And fanciful Citizens of the Deep
Are graciously greeting me.

As soon as Jarvis Poulter has gone and she has heard her front gate close, Almeda 75 rushes to the privy. Her relief is not complete, however, and she realizes that the pain and fullness in her lower body come from an accumulation of menstrual blood that has not yet started to flow. She closes and locks the back door. Then, remembering Jarvis Poulter's words about church, she writes on a piece of paper, "I am not well, and wish to rest today." She sticks this firmly into the outside frame of the little window in the front door. She locks that door, too. She is trembling, as if from a great shock or danger. But she builds a fire, so that she can make tea. She boils water, measures the tea leaves, makes a large pot of tea, whose steam and smell sicken her further. She pours out a cup while the tea is still quite weak and adds to it several dark drops of nerve medicine. She sits to drink it without raising the kitchen blind. There, in the middle of the floor, is the cheesecloth bag hanging on its broom handle between the two chair backs. The grape pulp and juice has stained the swollen cloth a dark purple. *Plop, plup* into the basin beneath. She can't sit and look at such a thing. She takes her cup, the teapot, and the bottle of medicine into the dining room.

She is still sitting there when the horses start to go by on the way to church, stirring up clouds of dust. The roads will be getting hot as ashes. She is there when the gate is opened and a man's confident steps sound on her veranda. Her hearing is so sharp she seems to hear the paper taken out of the frame and unfolded—she can almost hear him reading it, hear the words in his mind. Then the footsteps go the other way, down the steps. The gate closes. An image comes to her of tombstones—it makes her laugh. Tombstones are marching down the street on their little booted feet, their long bodies inclined forward, their expressions preoccupied and severe. The church bells are ringing.

Then the clock in the hall strikes twelve and an hour has passed.

The house is getting hot. She drinks more tea and adds more medicine. She knows that the medicine is affecting her. It is responsible for her extraordinary languor, her perfect immobility, her unresisting surrender to her surroundings. That is all right. It seems necessary.

Her surroundings—some of her surroundings—in the dining room are these: walls covered with dark green garlanded wallpaper, lace curtains and mulberry velvet curtains on the windows, a table with a crocheted cloth and a bowl of wax fruit, a pinkish-gray carpet with nosegays of blue and pink roses, a sideboard spread with embroidered runners and holding various patterned plates and jugs and the silver tea things. A lot of things to watch. For every one of these patterns, decorations, seems charged with life, ready to move and flow and alter. Or possibly to explode. Almeda Roth's occupation throughout the day is to keep an eye on them. Not to prevent their alteration so much as to catch them at it—to understand it, to be a part of it. So much is going on in this room that there is no need to leave it. There is not even the thought of leaving it.

Of course, Almeda in her observations cannot escape words. She may think 80 she can, but she can't. Soon this glowing and swelling begins to suggest words—not specific words but a flow of words somewhere, just about ready to make themselves known to her. Poems, even. Yes, again, poems. Or one poem. Isn't that the idea—one very great poem that will contain everything and, oh, that will make all the other poems, the poems she has written, inconsequential, mere trial and error, mere rags? Stars and flowers and birds and trees and angels in the snow and dead children at twilight—that is not the half of it. You have to get in the obscene racket on Pearl Street and the polished toe of Jarvis Poulter's boot and the plucked-chicken haunch with its blue-black flower. Almeda is a long way now from human sympathies or fears or cozy household considerations. She doesn't think about what could be done for that woman or about keeping Jarvis Poulter's dinner warm and hanging his long underwear on the line. The basin of grape juice has overflowed and is running over her kitchen floor, staining the boards of the floor, and the stain will never come out.

She has to think of so many things at once—Champlain and the naked Indians and the salt deep in the earth but as well as the salt the money, the money-making intent brewing forever in heads like Jarvis Poulter's. Also, the brutal storms of winter and the clumsy and benighted deeds on Pearl Street. The changes of climate are often violent, and if you think about it there is no peace even in the stars. All this can be borne only if it is channeled into a poem, and the word "channeled" is appropriate, because the name of the poem will be—it *is*—"The Meneseteung." The name of the poem is the name of the river. No, in fact it is the river, the Meneseteung, that is the poem—with its deep holes and rapids and blissful pools under the summer trees and its grinding blocks of ice thrown up at the end of winter and its desolating spring floods. Almeda looks deep, deep into the river of her mind and into the tablecloth, and she sees the crocheted roses floating. They look bunchy and foolish, her mother's crocheted roses—they don't look much like real flowers. But their effort, their floating independence, their pleasure in their silly selves, does seem to her so admirable. A hopeful sign. *Meneseteung.*

She doesn't leave the room until dusk, when she goes out to the privy again and discovers that she is bleeding, her flow has started. She will have to get a towel, strap it on, bandage herself up. Never before, in health, has she passed a whole day in her nightdress. She doesn't feel any particular anxiety about this. On her way through the kitchen she walks through the pool of grape juice. She knows that she will have to mop it up, but not yet, and she walks upstairs leaving purple footprints and smelling her escaping blood and the sweat of her body that has sat all day in the closed hot room.

No need for alarm.

For she hasn't thought that crocheted roses could float away or that tombstones could hurry down the street. She doesn't mistake that for reality, and neither does she mistake anything else for reality, and that is how she knows that she is sane.

VI

I dream of you by night,
I visit you by day.
Father, Mother,
Sister, Brother,
Have you no word to say?

April 22, 1903. At her residence, on Tuesday last, between three and four o'clock in the afternoon, there passed away a lady of talent and refinement whose pen, in days gone by, enriched our local literature with a volume of sensitive, eloquent verse. It is a sad misfortune that in later years the mind of this fine person had become somewhat clouded and her behaviour, in consequence, somewhat rash and unusual. Her attention to decorum and to the care and adornment of her person had suffered, to the degree that she had become, in the eyes of those unmindful of her former pride and daintiness, a familiar eccentric, or even, sadly, a figure of fun. But now all such lapses pass from memory and what is recalled is her excellent published verse, her labours in former days in the Sunday school, her dutiful care of her parents, her noble womanly nature, charitable concerns, and unfailing religious faith. Her last illness was of mercifully short duration. She caught cold, after having become thoroughly wet from a ramble in the Pearl Street bog. (It has been said that some urchins chased her into the water, and such is the boldness and cruelty of some of our youth, and their observed persecution of this lady, that the tale cannot be entirely discounted.) The cold developed into pneumonia, and she died, attended at the last by a former neighbour, Mrs. Bert (Annie) Friels, who witnessed her calm and faithful end.

January, 1904. One of the founders of our community, an early maker and shaker of this town, was abruptly removed from our midst on Monday morning last, whilst attending to his correspondence in the office of his company. Mr. Jarvis Poulter possessed a keen and lively commercial spirit, which was instrumental in the creation of not one but several local enterprises, bringing the benefits of industry, productivity, and employment to our town.

I looked for Almeda Roth in the graveyard. I found the family stone. There was just one name on it—Roth. Then I noticed two flat stones in the ground, a distance of a few feet—six feet?—from the upright stone. One of these said "Papa," the other "Mama." Farther out from these I found two other flat stones, with the names William and Catherine on them. I had to clear away some overgrowing grass and dirt to see the full name of Catherine. No birth or death dates for anybody, nothing about being dearly beloved. It was a private sort of memorializing, not for the world. There were no roses, either—no sign of a rosebush. But perhaps it was taken out. The grounds keeper doesn't like such things, they are a nuisance to the lawnmower, and if there is nobody left to object he will pull them out.

I thought that Almeda must have been buried somewhere else. When this plot was bought—at the time of the two children's deaths—she would still have been expected to marry, and to lie finally beside her husband. They might not have left room for her here. Then I saw that the stones in the ground fanned out from the upright stone. First the two for the parents, then the two for the children, but these were placed in such a way that there was room for a third, to complete the fan. I paced out from "Catherine" the same number of steps that it took to get from "Catherine" to "William," and at this spot I began pulling grass and scrabbling in the dirt with my bare hands. Soon I felt the stone and knew that I was right. I worked away and got the whole stone clear and I read the name "Meda." There it was with the others, staring at the sky.

I made sure I had got to the edge of the stone. That was all the name there was—Meda. So it was true that she was called by that name in the family. Not just in the poem. Or perhaps she chose her name from the poem, to be written on her stone.

I thought that there wasn't anybody alive in the world but me who would know this, who would make the connection. And I would be the last person to do so. But perhaps this isn't so. People are curious. A few people are. They will be driven to find things out, even trivial things. They will put things together, knowing all along that they may be mistaken. You see them going around with notebooks, scraping the dirt off gravestones, reading microfilm, just in the hope of seeing this trickle in time, making a connection, rescuing one thing from the rubbish.

90

QUESTIONS

1. What do you learn about the speaker of this story? How does what you learn—particularly in paragraph 90—explain the narrator's concern with the story of Meda and Jarvis? How intimately does the speaker reveal the mind of Meda?

2. What "facts" form the springboard for the story? As the speaker explains it, what firsthand experiences does she have with the places of the story? What effect do her experiences have on your perceptions of the characters?

3. Particularly considering paragraphs 14, 16, 31, and 85, explain the story's shifting or developing narration. You might deal with tense, documentation, and the degree of the speaker's involvement in the developing story.

4. Describe the character development of Meda Roth. What effect does her poetry have on how you understand her? Why does the episode of the beaten woman, and its immediate aftermath, cause a change in her attitude toward Jarvis?

5. Who is the subject of paragraphs 72–73? What is the effect of these paragraphs on Meda's story? Explain how one might claim that these paragraphs (a) interrupt the story, or (b) are integral to it.

WRITING ABOUT POINT OF VIEW

Your goal is to explain how point of view contributes to making the work exactly as it is. In prewriting, therefore, consider language, authority and opportunity for observation, the involvement or detachment of the speaker, the selection of detail, interpretive commentaries, and narrative development. The following questions will help you get started.

Questions for Discovering Ideas

How is the narration made to seem real and probable? Are the actions and speeches reported authentically, as they might be seen and reported in life? How much of the story seems to result from the imaginative or creative powers of the narrator?

To what extent does the point of view make the work interesting and effective, or uninteresting and ineffective?

Is the narrator identifiable?

First-person point of view: What situation prompts the speaker to tell the story or explain the situation? What is the speaker's background?

Is the speaker talking to the reader, a listener, or herself? How does her audience affect what she is saying? Is the level of language appropriate to her and the situation? How much does she tell about herself?

To what degree is the narrator involved in the action (i.e., as a major participant, minor participant, or nonparticipating observer)? Does he make himself the center of humor or admiration? How? Does he seem aware of changes he undergoes?

Does the speaker criticize other characters? Why? Does she seem to report fairly and accurately what others have told her?

Third-person point of view: Does the author seem to be speaking in an authorial voice, or has the author adopted a special but unnamed voice for the work?

What is the speaker's level of language? Are actions, speeches, and explanations made fully or sparsely?

Does the narrator assume that the audience has any special kinds of knowledge (e.g., of art, religion, history, etc.)?

From what apparent vantage point does the speaker report action and speeches? Does this vantage point make the characters seem distant or close? How much sympathy does the speaker express for the characters?

To what degree is your interest centered on a particular character? Does the speaker give you thoughts and responses of this character (limited third person)?

If the work is third-person omniscient, how extensive is this omniscience (e.g., all the characters or just a few)? Generally, what limitations or freedoms can be attributed to this point of view?

Strategies for Organizing Ideas

Your object is to develop your analysis of how the point of view determines such aspects as situation, form, general content, and language. Answering the questions in the preceding section will enable you to decide how the point of view interacts with other elements.

An excellent way to strengthen your argument is to explore how some other point of view might affect the work you are considering (see paragraph 4 of the sample essay, p. 238). Anderson's "I'm a Fool," for example, uses a first-person narrator—a young man telling about the greatest mistake in his life. You might consider whether this story could work with a third-person narration, because the third person could state that the young man is self-critical and repentant, but with the first-person confession, we as readers learn firsthand about his emotional situation. Indeed, the story seems totally dependent on the use of the first-person narrator. Oppositely, Mansfield's "Miss Brill" employs the third-person limited point of view, with the speaker presenting an intimate portrait of the major character, but also preserving an objective and ironic distance. If Miss Brill herself were the narrator, we would get the intimacy but not the distance, and hence the story could not work. It might be another story, but not the one that Mansfield has given us.

You can see that this approach requires creative imagination, for you must speculate about a point of view that is not present. If you consider alternative points of view deeply, however, you will find that your analytical and critical abilities will be greatly enhanced.

In your conclusion you should evaluate the success of the point of view: Is it consistent, effective, truthful? What does the writer gain or lose (if anything) by the selection of point of view?

HINT: Distinguish point of view from opinion. Be careful to distinguish between *point of view* and *opinions* or *beliefs.* Point of view refers to the dramatic situation occasioning the speaking of a work, including language, audience, and perspective on events and characters, whereas an opinion is a thought about something. In examining point of view, then, you should draw conclusions about how the speaking situation of the work actually *creates* the work. Opinions and philosophical and religious judgments belong to the consideration of ideas, but have a bearing on point of view only if they influence what the narrator says.

SAMPLE ESSAY

Shirley Jackson's Dramatic Point of View in "The Lottery"°

[1]   The dramatic point of view in Shirley Jackson's "The Lottery" is essential to her success in rendering horror in the midst of the ordinary.* The story, however, is not only one of horror: it may also be called a surprise story, an allegory, or a portrayal of human insensitivity and cruelty. But the validity of all other claims for "The Lottery" hinges on the author's control over point of view to make the events develop out of a seemingly everyday, matter-of-fact situation--a control that could not be easily maintained with another point of view. The success of Jackson's point of view is achieved through her characterization, selection of details, and diction.†

[2]   Because of the dramatic point of view, Jackson succeeds in presenting the villagers as ordinary folks attending a normal, festive event--in contrast to the horror of their real purpose. The contrast depends on Jackson's speaker, who is emotionally uninvolved and who tells only enough about the 300 townsfolk and their customs to permit the conclusion that they are ordinary, common people. The principal character is a local housewife, Tessie Hutchinson, but the narrator presents little about her except that she is just as ordinary and common as everyone else--an important characteristic when she, like any other ordinary person being singled out for punishment, objects not to the lottery itself but to the "unfairness" of the drawing. So it is also with the other characters, whose brief conversations are recorded but not analyzed. This detached, reportorial method of making the villagers seem common and one-dimensional is fundamental to Jackson's dramatic point of view, and the cruel twist of the ending depends on the method.

[3]   While there could be much description, Jackson's speaker presents details only partially in order to conceal the lottery's horrible purpose. For example, the speaker presents enough information about the lottery to permit readers to understand its rules, but does not disclose that the winning prize is instant death. The short saying "Lottery in June, corn be heavy soon" is mentioned as a remnant of a long-forgotten ritual, but the speaker does not explain anything more about this connection with scapegoatism and human

---

° See p. 214 for this story.
* Central idea.
† Thesis sentence.

sacrifice (paragraph 32). None of these references seems unusual as the narrator first presents them, and it is only the conclusion that reveals, in reconsideration, their shocking ghastliness.

Without doubt, a point of view other than the dramatic would spoil Jackson's concluding horror, because it would require more explanatory detail. A first-person speaker, for example, would not be credible without explaining the situation and revealing feelings that would give away the ending. Such an "I" speaker would need to say something like "The little boys gathered rocks but seemed not to be thinking about their forthcoming use in the execution." But how would such detail affect the reader's response to the horrifying conclusion? Similarly, an omniscient narrator would need to include

[4]   details about people's reactions (how could he or she be omniscient otherwise?). A more suitable alternative might be a limited omniscient point of view confined to, say, a stranger in town, or to one of the local children. But any intelligent stranger would be asking "giveaway" questions, and any child but a tiny tot would know about the lottery's horrible purpose. Either point-of-view character would therefore require revealing the information too soon. The only possible conclusion is that the point of view that Jackson uses--the dramatic--is best for this story. Because it permits her naturally to hold back crucial details, it is essential for the suspenseful delay of horror.

Appropriate both to the suspenseful ending and also to the simple character of the villagers is the speaker's language. The words are accurate and descriptive but not elaborate. When Tessie Hutchinson appears, for example, she dries "her hands on her apron" (paragraph 8)--words that define her

[5]   everyday household status. Most of these simple, bare words may be seen as part of Jackson's similar technique of withholding detail to delay the reader's understanding. A prime example is the pile of stones, which is in truth a thoughtless and cruel preparation for the stoning, yet this conclusion cannot be drawn from the easy words describing it (paragraph 2):

> Bobby Martin had already stuffed his pockets full of stones, and the other boys soon followed his example, selecting the smoothest and roundest stones; Bobby and Harry Jones and Dickie Delacroix--the villagers pronounced this name "Dellacroy"--eventually made a great pile of stones in one corner of the square and guarded it against the raids of the other boys.

Both the nicknames and the connotation of boyhood games divert attention and obscure the horrible purpose of the stones. Even at the end, the speaker uses the word "pebbles" to describe the stones given to Tessie's son Davy (paragraph 76). The implication is that Davy is playing a game, not helping to kill his own mother!

Such masterly control over point of view is a major cause of Jackson's success in "The Lottery." Her narrative method is to establish the appearance of everyday, harmless reality, which she maintains up to the beginning of the last ominous scene. She is so successful that a reader's first response to the

[6]   stoning is that "such a killing could not take place among such common, earthy folks." Yet it is this reality that validates Jackson's vision. Horror is not to be found on moors and in haunted castles, but among everyday people

like Jackson's 300 villagers. Without her control of the dramatic point of view, there could be little of this power of suggestion, and it would not be possible to claim such success for the story.

Commentary on the Essay

The strategy of this essay is to describe how Jackson's dramatic point of view is fundamental to her success in building toward the shocking horror of the ending. Words of tribute through the essay are "success," "control," "essential," "appropriate," and "masterly." The introductory paragraph sets out three areas for exploration in the body: character, detail, and diction.

The body begins with paragraph 2, in which the aim is *not* to present a full character study (since the essay is not about character but point of view), but rather to discuss the ways in which the dramatic point of view *enables* the characters to be rendered. The topic of the paragraph is that the villagers are to be judged not as complete human beings but as "ordinary folks."

The second part of the body (paragraphs 3 and 4) emphasizes the sparseness of detail as an essential part of Jackson's purpose of delaying conclusions about the real horror of the drawing. Paragraph 4, which continues the topic of paragraph 3, shows how assertions about alternative points of view may reinforce ideas about the actual point of view chosen by the author (see p. 238). The material for the paragraph is derived from notes speculating about whether Jackson's technique of withholding detail to build toward the concluding horror (the topic of paragraph 3) could be maintained with differing points of view. A combination of analysis and imagination is therefore at work in the paragraph.

The third section of the body (paragraph 5) emphasizes that the flat, colorless diction defers awareness of what is happening; therefore the point of view is vital to the story's surprise and horror. The concluding paragraph (6) emphasizes the way in which general response to the story is conditioned by the detached, dramatic point of view.

WRITING TOPICS

1. Write a short narrative from the point of view of one of these characters:
   a. Lucy Wessen in "I'm a Fool": *How I met and lost the most wonderful man.*
   b. The baker in "Miss Brill": *My favorite customer.*
   c. Old Man Warner in "The Lottery": *People ain't the way they used to be.*
   d. Jarvis Poulter in "Meneseteung": *Why did Meda Roth really not want me to take her to church?*
2. How would the story "Meneseteung" be affected if told by narrators with the characteristics of the narrators in either "I'm a Fool" or "The Lottery"?
3. Recall a childhood occasion on which you were punished, and write an

explanation of the punishment as though you were the adult who was in the position of punishing you. Be sure to consider your childhood self objectively, in the third person. Present things from the viewpoint of the adult, and try to determine how the adult would have learned about your action, judged it, and decided on your punishment.

4. Consider the proposition that people never speak without showing their motives, and that therefore we need to judge all things that we are told.

6

Setting: Place, Objects, and Culture in Stories

Fictional characters, like all human beings, do not exist in isolation. Just as they become human by interacting with other characters, they gain identity because of their possessions, their jobs, their cultural and political allegiances, and the locations where they live, work, and love. Stories must therefore necessarily include descriptions of places, things, and backgrounds—the **setting.**

Broadly, setting is the natural, manufactured, and cultural environment in which authors make their characters live and move, including all the things and all the knowledge they use in their lives. Characters may either be helped or hurt by their immediate surroundings, and they may enter conflicts over possessions and goals. Further, as characters speak with each other, they reveal the degree to which they share the customs and ideas of their times.

SETTING AND STATEMENT

The control of setting is also one of the means by which authors create meaning, just as painters convey ideas by manipulating the forms and colors of objects and backgrounds. The totally different settings of Boucher's portrait of *Madame de Pompadour*, for example, and Hopper's *Automat* demonstrate how the same topic—a female figure—may show totally contrasting views of human life, one rarefied and pretty, the other common and dreary (pp. 242, 243). Writers manipulate literary locations in a comparable way. For example, in Welty's "A Worn Path" and Hawthorne's "Young Goodman Brown," woodland paths difficult to trace and filled with obstacles are a major topographical feature. These are of course to be expected, granted the time and circumstances of the stories, but they also convey the idea that life is difficult and uncertain. Similarly,

François Boucher, *Madame de Pompadour*. (The Wallace Collection, London)

in Glaspell's "A Jury of Her Peers," the fixtures and utensils in the kitchen of the Wright farm indicate that Midwestern homesteads early in the twentieth century were bleak and oppressive.

If the scenes and materials of setting are highlighted or emphasized, they also may be taken as symbols, through which the author expresses ideas (see also Chapter 9, pp. 326–29). For example, the shawl in Ozick's "The Shawl" has the ordinary function of providing cover, warmth, and nourishment for the baby, Magda. Because it is so prominent in the story, however, it also suggests the attempt to preserve future generations, and

Edward Hopper, *Automat*, 1927. Oil on canvas, 28⅛ × 36″. (Des Moines Art Center: Purchased with funds of the Edmundson Art Foundation Inc. 1958.2)

because its loss causes the infant to die horribly, it symbolizes the helplessness of victims in the Nazi extermination camps. Updike, in "A & P," refers to the local Congregational Church. On a symbolic level, the church indicates the decorum and restraint that people of the town are expected to exercise.

TYPES OF SETTINGS

1. NATURE AND THE OUTDOORS. The natural world often provides substance for the development of an author's meaning. It is therefore important to note natural surroundings (hills, valleys, mountains, meadows, fields, trees, lakes, streams), living creatures (birds, dogs, horses, snakes), and also the conditions in which things happen (sunlight, darkness, calm, wind, rain, snow, storm, heat)—all of which may influence character and action.

2. OBJECTS OF HUMAN MANUFACTURE AND CONSTRUCTION. To reveal or highlight qualities of character, and also to make fiction lifelike, authors include details about buildings and objects such as houses, streets, fences, park benches, toys, automobiles, phonograph records, necklaces, hair

ribbons, cash registers, and so on. The loss of a comfortable home leads a character to deep depression in Lawrence's "The Horse Dealer's Daughter." Such a loss in Maupassant's "The Necklace," however, brings out the best in characters by causing them to adjust to their economic reversal. A shabby but neat house reveals strength of character in Walker's "Everyday Use." In Cather's "Paul's Case," the dreary home of the major character, Paul, leads him into depression and flight; the impossibility of living permanently in the expensive hotel to which he flees precipitates his final downfall.

Manufactured objects also enter directly into fictional action and character. A jar of herring is a major cause of conflict in Updike's "A & P"; a broken birdcage reveals the pathetic husband–wife relationship in "A Jury of Her Peers"; a furpiece leads to heartbreak in Mansfield's "Miss Brill." O'Connor uses a few pieces of candy to demonstrate a child's liberation from guilt in "First Confession." By having her major character, Phoenix, walk to town to receive a bottle of medicine in "A Worn Path," Welty demonstrates the beauty of this character's love.

3. **CULTURAL CONDITIONS AND ASSUMPTIONS.**   Just as physical setting influences characters, so do cultural conditions and assumptions. In Márquez's "A Very Old Man with Enormous Wings," for example, the characters live in a small South American village, and the premises of their lives are therefore vastly different from our own. The broad cultural setting of Jackson's "The Lottery" is made up of two incompatible cultural assumptions—a primitive belief that the fertility of the earth requires human sacrifice, and our scientific and modern belief that such a ritual is meaningless and savage. In Clark's "The Portable Phonograph" we see that an artistic and peaceful way of life breaks down when the culture on which it depends has been destroyed.

THE USES OF SETTING

In studying setting, you should first discover all the important details, and then determine how the author uses them. Depending on the author's purpose, the amount of detail may vary. Poe provides graphic and colorful detail in "The Masque of the Red Death," so that we may follow, almost visually, the weird and bizarre action at the story's end. In some stories the setting is presented so extensively that it may be considered a virtual participant in the action. An instance of such "participation" is Welty's "A Worn Path," where woods and byways are almost active antagonists against Phoenix as she follows the path toward Natchez.

Setting and Credibility

One of the major purposes of setting is to lend **realism,** or **verisimilitude.** As the description of location and objects is more particular and detailed, the events of the work become more believable. In "The House on Mango Street," for example, Cisneros gives us representative details about a number of ramshackle residences that her speaker's family has lived in. Even futuristic, symbolic, and fantastic stories, as well as ghost stories, are more authentic if they include places and objects from everyday experience. Kafka's "A Hunger Artist," Hawthorne's "Young Goodman Brown," and Poe's "The Masque of the Red Death" are such stories. Though they make no pretenses at everyday realism, they would lose credibility if their settings were not so realistic.

Setting and Character

Setting may intersect with character as a means by which authors underscore the importance of place, circumstance, and time on human growth and change. Glaspell's setting in "A Jury of Her Peers" is the kitchen of the lonely, dreary Wright farm. Because the kitchen is a place of hard work, joylessness, and oppression, we realize that Mrs. Wright, however bright and promising she had been as a young woman, has been beaten down by the grind of her life, so much so that her outburst of anger in murdering her husband is made to seem understandable. (A similar blending of setting and character, as seen in Maupassant's "The Necklace," is explored in the sample essay in Chapter 1.)

A major aspect of setting may be found in the ways in which characters respond to social, political, and religious circumstances. How they adjust is a measure of strength or weakness. While some of the townspeople in Jackson's "The Lottery," for example, have doubted the value of the custom of the lottery, they are still acquiescent enough to engage in the ritual execution. Their acceptance indicates their lack of thought and sensitivity. In Updike's "A & P," Sammy 's strength is shown by his decision to quit his job to protest the rigorous dress code that the manager of the store imposes on the girls.

Setting and Organization

Authors often use setting as a means of organization. The actions in Jackson's "The Lottery" are all related to the place of the lottery drawing in the village square, "between the post office and the bank" (paragraph 1), and the story begins at ten o'clock in the morning and ends almost exactly at noon—in other words, according to a pattern of before, during, and immediately after the drawing. In Maupassant's "The Necklace,"

Mathilde and her husband move from an acceptable though not lavish apartment to a cheap attic flat. The story's final scene is believable because Mathilde takes a nostalgic walk on the most fashionable street in Paris, the Champs Elysées. Without this organizational shift of setting, she could not have met Jeanne Forrestier again, for their ways of life would otherwise never have crossed.

Another organizational application of place, time, and object is the **framing** or **enclosing setting.** An author opens with a particular description, and then encloses the work by returning to the same setting at the end, in this way forming a frame. An example is Welty's "A Worn Path," which begins with the major character walking toward Natchez, and ends with her walking away from it. The use of objects as a frame may be seen in Mansfield's "Miss Brill," which opens and closes with references to the heroine's shabby fur piece. Framing in this way creates a formal completeness, just as it may underscore the author's ideas about the human condition.

Setting and Atmosphere

Setting also helps to create **atmosphere** or **mood.** You will agree that an action actually *requires* no more than a functional description of setting. Thus, an action in a forest *needs* just the statement that there are trees. However, if you read descriptions of shapes, light and shadows, animals, wind, and sounds, you may be sure that the author is creating an atmosphere or mood for the action (as in Hawthorne's "Young Goodman Brown"). There are many ways of developing moods. Descriptions of bright colors (red, orange, yellow) may contribute to a mood of happiness. Darker or shaded colors, like those in Poe's "The Masque of the Red Death," may invoke gloom or augment hysteria. References to smells and sounds bring the setting even more to life by asking for additional sensory responses from the reader. The setting of a story in a small town or large city, or green or snow-covered fields, or middle-class or lower-class residences, may evoke responses to these places that contribute to the work's atmosphere.

Setting and Irony

Just as setting may reinforce character and theme, so may it ironically establish expectations that are opposite to what occurs. At the beginning of "The Lottery," for example, Jackson describes the folksiness of the assembling townspeople—details that make the conclusion ironic, for it is just these real, everyday folks who cast the stones of ritual execution. A bizarre irony is created by Poe in "The Masque of the Red Death," when Prince Prospero seals off his palace to prevent the plague, but at the same moment he seals the "Red Death" within his walls and assures the extinction of everyone within. The irony is that closed doors may as easily prevent escape as attack.

EDGAR ALLAN POE   (1809–1849)

The Masque of the Red Death   *1842*

The "Red Death" had long devastated the country. No pestilence had ever been so fatal, or so hideous. Blood was its Avatar° and its seal—the redness and the horror of blood. There were sharp pains, and sudden dizziness, and then profuse bleeding at the pores, with dissolution. The scarlet stains upon the body and especially upon the face of the victim, were the pest ban which shut him out from the aid and from the sympathy of his fellow-men. And the whole seizure, progress, and termination of the disease, were the incidents of half an hour.

But the Prince Prospero° was happy and dauntless and sagacious. When his dominions were half depopulated, he summoned to his presence a thousand hale and light-hearted friends from among the knights and dames of his court, and with these retired to the deep seclusion of one of his castellated abbeys. This was an extensive and magnificent structure, the creation of the prince's own eccentric yet august taste. A strong and lofty wall girdled it in. This wall had gates of iron. The courtiers, having entered, brought furnaces and massy hammers and welded the bolts. They resolved to leave means neither of ingress nor egress to the sudden impulses of despair or of frenzy from within. The abbey was amply provisioned. With such precautions the courtiers might bid defiance to contagion. The external world could take care of itself. In the meantime it was folly to grieve, or to think. The prince had provided all the appliances of pleasure. There were buffoons, there were improvisatori, there were ballet-dancers, there were musicians, there was Beauty, there was wine. All these and security were within. Without was the "Red Death."

It was toward the close of the fifth or sixth month of his seclusion, and while the pestilence raged most furiously abroad, that the Prince Prospero entertained his thousand friends at a masked ball of the most unusual magnificence.

It was a voluptuous scene, that masquerade. But first let me tell of the rooms in which it was held. There were seven—an imperial suite. In many palaces, however, such suites form a long and straight vista, while the folding doors slide back nearly to the walls on either hand, so that the view of the whole extent is scarcely impeded. Here the case was very different; as might have been expected from the duke's love of the *bizarre.* The apartments were so irregularly disposed that the vision embraced but little more than one at a time. There was a sharp turn at every twenty or thirty yards, and at each turn a novel effect. To the right and left, in the middle of each wall, a tall and narrow Gothic window looked out upon a closed corridor which pursued the windings of the suite. These windows were of stained glass whose color varied in accordance with the prevailing hue of

---

Avatar: model, incarnation, manifestation.
Prospero: that is, "prosperous." In Shakespeare's play *The Tempest*, the principal character is Prospero.

the decorations of the chamber into which it opened. That at the eastern extremity was hung, for example, in blue—and vividly blue were its windows. The second chamber was purple in its ornaments and tapestries, and here the panes were purple. The third was green throughout, and so were the casements. The fourth was furnished and lighted with orange—the fifth with white—the sixth with violet. The seventh apartment was closely shrouded in black velvet tapestries that hung all over the ceiling and down the walls, falling in heavy folds upon a carpet of the same material and hue. But in this chamber only, the color of the windows failed to correspond with the decorations. The panes here were scarlet—a deep blood color. Now in no one of the seven apartments was there any lamp or candelabrum, amid the profusion of golden ornaments that lay scattered to and fro or depended from the roof. There was no light of any kind emanating from lamp or candle within the suite of chambers. But in the corridors that followed the suite, there stood, opposite to each window, a heavy tripod, bearing a brazier of fire, that projected its rays through the tinted glass and so glaringly illumined the room. And thus were produced a multitude of gaudy and fantastic appearances. But in the western or black chamber the effect of the fire-light that streamed upon the dark hangings through the blood-tinted panes was ghastly in the extreme, and produced so wild a look upon the countenances of those who entered, that there were few of the company bold enough to set foot within its precincts at all.

It was in this apartment, also, that there stood against the western wall, a 5
gigantic clock of ebony. Its pendulum swung to and fro with a dull, heavy, monotonous clang; and when the minute-hand made the circuit of the face, and the hour was to be stricken, there came from the brazen lungs of the clock a sound which was clear and loud and deep and exceedingly musical, but of so peculiar a note and emphasis that, at each lapse of an hour, the musicians of the orchestra were constrained to pause, momentarily, in their performance, to hearken to the sound; and thus the waltzers perforce ceased their evolutions; and there was a brief disconcert of the whole gay company; and, while the chimes of the clock yet rang, it was observed that the giddiest grew pale, and the more aged and sedate passed their hands over their brows as if in confused revery or meditation. But when the echoes had fully ceased, a light laughter at once pervaded the assembly; the musicians looked at each other and smiled as if at their own nervousness and folly, and made whispering vows, each to the other, that the next chiming of the clock should produce in them no similar emotion; and then, after the lapse of sixty minutes (which embrace three thousand and six hundred seconds of the Time that flies), there came yet another chiming of the clock, and then were the same disconcert and tremulousness and meditation as before.

But, in spite of these things, it was a gay and magnificent revel. The tastes of the duke were peculiar. He had a fine eye for colors and effects. He disregarded the *decora*° of mere fashion. His plans were bold and fiery, and his conceptions glowed with barbaric lustre. There are some who would have thought him mad. His followers felt that he was not. It was necessary to hear and see and touch him to be *sure* that he was not.

He had directed, in great part, the movable embellishments of the seven chambers, upon occasion of this great fête,° and it was his own guiding taste which

decora: schemes, patterns.
fête: party, revel.

had given character to the masqueraders. Be sure they were grotesque. There were much glare and glitter and piquancy and phantasm—much of what has been since seen in "Hernani."° There were arabesque figures with unsuited limbs and appointments. There were delirious fancies such as the madman fashions. There were much of the beautiful, much of the wanton, much of the *bizarre*, something of the terrible, and not a little of that which might have excited disgust. To and fro in the seven chambers there stalked, in fact, a multitude of dreams. And these—the dreams—writhed in and about, taking hue from the rooms, and causing the wild music of the orchestra to seem as the echo of their steps. And, anon, there strikes the ebony clock which stands in the hall of the velvet. And then, for a moment, all is still, and all is silent save the voice of the clock. The dreams are stiff-frozen as they stand. But the echoes of the chime die away—they have endured but an instant—and a light, half-subdued laughter floats after them as they depart. And now again the music swells, and the dreams live, and writhe to and fro more merrily than ever, taking hue from the many-tinted windows through which stream the rays from the tripods. But to the chamber which lies most westwardly of the seven there are now none of the maskers who venture; for the night is waning away; and there flows a ruddier light through the blood-colored panes; and the blackness of the sable drapery appalls; and to him whose foot falls upon the sable carpet, there comes from the near clock of ebony a muffled peal more solemnly emphatic than any which reaches *their* ears who indulge in the more remote gaieties of the other apartments.

But these other apartments were densely crowded, and in them beat feverishly the heart of life. And the revel went whirlingly on, until at length there commenced the sounding of midnight upon the clock. And then the music ceased, as I have told; and the evolutions of the waltzers were quieted; and there was an uneasy cessation of all things as before. But now there were twelve strokes to be sounded by the bell of the clock; and thus it happened, perhaps that more of thought crept, with more of time, into the meditations of the thoughtful among those who revelled. And thus, too, it happened, perhaps, that before the last echoes of the last chime had utterly sunk into silence, there were many individuals in the crowd who had found leisure to become aware of the presence of a masked figure which had arrested the attention of no single individual before. And the rumor of this new presence having spread itself whisperingly around, there arose at length from the whole company a buzz, or murmur, expressive of disapprobation and surprise—then, finally, of terror, of horror, and of disgust.

In an assembly of phantasms such as I have painted, it may well be supposed that no ordinary appearance could have excited such sensation. In truth the masquerade license of the night was nearly unlimited; but the figure in question had out-Heroded Herod,° and gone beyond the bounds of even the prince's indefinite decorum. There are chords in the hearts of the most reckless which cannot be touched without emotion. Even with the utterly lost, to whom life and death are equally jests, there are matters of which no jest can be made. The whole company, indeed, seemed now deeply to feel that in the costume and bearing of the stranger neither wit nor propriety existed. The figure was tall and gaunt, and shrouded from head to foot in the habiliments of the grave. The mask which

Hernani: tragedy by Victor Hugo (1802–1885), featuring elaborate scenes and costumes.
out-Heroded Herod: quoted from Shakespeare's *Hamlet*, Act III, scene 2, line 13, in reference to extreme overacting.

concealed the visage was made so nearly to resemble the countenance of a stiffened corpse that the closest scrutiny must have had difficulty in detecting the cheat. And yet all this might have been endured, if not approved, by the mad revellers around. But the mummer had gone so far as to assume the type of the Red Death. His vesture was dabbled in *blood*—and his broad brow, with all the features of the face, was besprinkled with the scarlet horror.

When the eyes of Prince Prospero fell upon this spectral image (which, with a slow and solemn movement, as if more fully to sustain its *rôle*, stalked to and fro among the waltzers) he was seen to be convulsed, in the first moment with a strong shudder either of terror or distaste; but, in the next, his brow reddened with rage. 10

"Who dares"—he demanded hoarsely of the courtiers who stood near him—"who dares insult us with this blasphemous mockery? Seize him and unmask him—that we may know whom we have to hang, at sunrise, from the battlements!"

It was in the eastern or blue chamber in which stood the Prince Prospero as he uttered these words. They rang throughout the seven rooms loudly and clearly, for the prince was a bold and robust man, and the music had become hushed at the waving of his hand.

It was in the blue room where stood the prince, with a group of pale courtiers by his side. At first, as he spoke, there was a slight rushing movement of this group in the direction of the intruder, who, at the moment was also near at hand, and now, with deliberate and stately step, made closer approach to the speaker. But from a certain nameless awe with which the mad assumptions of the mummer had inspired the whole party, there were found none who put forth hand to seize him; so that, unimpeded, he passed within a yard of the prince's person; and, while the vast assembly, as if with one impulse, shrank from the centres of the rooms to the walls, he made his way uninterruptedly, but with the same solemn and measured step which had distinguished him from the first, through the blue chamber to the purple—through the purple to the green—through the green to the orange—through this again to the white—and even thence to the violet, ere a decided movement had been made to arrest him. It was then, however, that the Prince Prospero, maddening with rage and the shame of his own momentary cowardice, rushed hurriedly through the six chambers, while none followed him on account of a deadly terror that had seized upon all. He bore aloft a drawn dagger, and had approached, in rapid impetuosity, to within three or four feet of the retreating figure, when the latter, having attained the extremity of the velvet apartment, turned suddenly and confronted his pursuer. There was a sharp cry—and the dagger dropped gleaming upon the sable carpet, upon which, instantly afterward, fell prostrate in death the Prince Prospero. Then, summoning the wild courage of despair, a throng of the revellers at once threw themselves into the black apartment, and, seizing the mummer, whose tall figure stood erect and motionless within the shadow of the ebony clock, gasped in unutterable horror at finding the grave cerements and corpse-like mask, which they handled with so violent a rudeness, untenanted by any tangible form.

And now was acknowledged the presence of the Red Death. He had come like a thief in the night.° And one by one dropped the revellers in the blood-bedewed halls of their revel, and died each in the despairing posture of his fall. And the life of the ebony clock went out with that of the last of the gay. And the

thief in the night: 2 Peter 3:10.

flames of the tripods expired. And Darkness and Decay and the Red Death held illimitable dominion over all.

QUESTIONS

1. What is happening throughout the country in this story? What does the Prince's reaction to these events tell us about him?
2. How do the details of number, color, and lighting help create the atmosphere and mood of the story?
3. Why do the color and window of the last room disturb the revellers? To what extent does this last room reflect the plot and ideas of the story?
4. What single object is located in this last room? How is this object described? What effect does its sound have on the revellers? What do you think Poe is suggesting by this object and its effects?
5. How are the nobles dressed for the masquerade? Why is the "masked figure" remarkable? How does Prospero react to him?

WALTER VAN TILBURG CLARK   (1909–1971)

The Portable Phonograph   *1942*

The red sunset, with narrow, black cloud strips like threats across it, lay on the curved horizon of the prairie. The air was still and cold, and in it settled the mute darkness and greater cold of night. High in the air there was wind, for through the veil of the dusk the clouds could be seen gliding rapidly south and changing shapes. A sensation of torment, of two-sided, unpredictable nature, arose from the stillness of the earth air beneath the violence of the upper air. Out of the sunset, through the dead, matted grass and isolated weed stalks of the prairie, crept the narrow and deeply rutted remains of a road. In the road, in places, there were crusts of shallow, brittle ice. There were little islands of an old oiled pavement in the road too, but most of it was mud, now frozen rigid. The frozen mud still bore the toothed impress of great tanks, and a wanderer on the neighboring undulations might have stumbled, in this light, into large, partially filled-in and weed-grown cavities, their banks channeled and beginning to spread into badlands. These pits were such as might have been made by falling meteors, but they were not. They were the scars of gigantic bombs, their rawness already made a little natural by rain, seed and time. Along the road there were rakish remnants of fence. There was also, just visible, one portion of tangled and multiple barbed wire still erect, behind which was a shelving ditch with small caves, now very quiet and empty, at intervals in its back wall. Otherwise there was no structure or remnant of a structure visible over the dome of the darkling earth, but only, in sheltered hollows, the darker shadows of young trees trying again.

Under the wuthering arch of the high wind a V of wild geese fled south. The rush of their pinions sounded briefly, and the faint, plaintive notes of their expeditionary talk. Then they left a still greater vacancy. There was the smell and expectation of snow, as there is likely to be when the wild geese fly south. From the remote distance, toward the red sky, came faintly the protracted howl and quick yap-yap of a prairie wolf.

North of the road, perhaps a hundred yards, lay the parallel and deeply intrenched course of a small creek, lined with leafless alders and willows. The creek was already silent under ice. Into the bank above it was dug a sort of cell, with a single opening, like the mouth of a mine tunnel. Within the cell there was a little red of fire, which showed dully through the opening, like a reflection or a deception of the imagination. The light came from the chary burning of four blocks of poorly aged peat, which gave off a petty warmth and much acrid smoke. But the precious remnants of wood, old fence posts and timbers from the long-deserted dugouts, had to be saved for the real cold, for the time when a man's breath blew white, the moisture in his nostrils stiffened at once when he stepped out, and the expansive blizzards paraded for days over the vast open, swirling and settling and thickening, till the dawn of the cleared day when the sky was a thin blue-green and the terrible cold, in which a man could not live for three hours unwarmed, lay over the uniformly drifted swell of the plain.

Around the smoldering peat four men were seated cross-legged. Behind them, traversed by their shadows, was the earth bench, with two old and dirty army blankets, where the owner of the cell slept. In a niche in the opposite wall were a few tin utensils which caught the glint of the coals. The host was rewrapping in a piece of daubed burlap, four fine, leather-bound books. He worked slowly and very carefully, and at last tied the bundle securely with a piece of grass-woven cord. The other three looked intently upon the process, as if a great significance lay in it. As the host tied the cord, he spoke. He was an old man, his long, matted beard and hair gray to nearly white. The shadows made his brows and cheekbones appear gnarled, his eyes and cheeks deeply sunken. His big hands, rough with frost and swollen by rheumatism, were awkward but gentle at their task. He was like a prehistoric priest performing a fateful ceremonial rite. Also his voice had in it a suitable quality of deep, reverent despair, yet perhaps, at the moment, a sharpness of selfish satisfaction.

"When I perceived what was happening," he said, "I told myself, 'It is the end. I cannot take much; I will take these.'"   5

"Perhaps I was impractical," he continued. "But for myself, I do not regret, and what do we know of those who will come after us? We are the doddering remnant of a race of mechanical fools. I have saved what I love; the soul of what was good in us here; perhaps the new ones will make a strong enough beginning not to fall behind when they become clever."

He rose with slow pain and placed the wrapped volumes in the niche with his utensils. The others watched him with the same ritualistic gaze.

"Shakespeare, the Bible, *Moby Dick*,° *The Divine Comedy*,"° one of them said softly. "You might have done worse; much worse."

"You will have a little soul left until you die," said another harshly. "That is more than is true of us. My brain becomes thick, like my hands." He held the big, battered hands, with their black nails, in the glow to be seen.

Moby Dick: by Herman Melville (1819–1891), a classic American novel published in 1851.

The Divine Comedy: by Dante (1265–1321), regarded as the supreme poem of the Italian Renaissance, circulated about 1300.

"I want paper to write on," he said. "And there is none."   10

The fourth man said nothing. He sat in the shadow farthest from the fire, and sometimes his body jerked in its rags from the cold. Although he was still young, he was sick, and coughed often. Writing implied a greater future than he now felt able to consider.

The old man seated himself laboriously, and reached out, groaning at the movement, to put another block of peat on the fire. With bowed heads and averted eyes, his three guests acknowledged his magnanimity.

"We thank you, Doctor Jenkins, for the reading," said the man who had named the books.

They seemed then to be waiting for something. Doctor Jenkins understood, but was loath to comply. In an ordinary moment he would have said nothing. But the words of *The Tempest*,° which he had been reading, and the religious attention of the three, made this an unusual occasion.

"You wish to hear the phonograph,"° he said grudgingly.   15

The two middle-aged men stared into the fire, unable to formulate and expose the enormity of their desire.

The young man, however, said anxiously, between suppressed coughs, "Oh, please," like an excited child.

The old man rose again in his difficult way, and went to the back of the cell. He returned and placed tenderly upon the packed floor, where the firelight might fall upon it, an old, portable phonograph in a black case. He smoothed the top with his hand, then opened it. The lovely green-felt-covered disk became visible.

"I have been using thorns as needles," he said. "But tonight, because we have a musician among us"—he bent his head to the young man, almost invisible in the shadow—"I will use a steel needle. There are only three left."

The two middle-aged men stared at him in speechless adoration. The one   20
with the big hands, who wanted to write, moved his lips, but the whisper was not audible.

"Oh, don't," cried the young man, as if he were hurt. "The thorns will do beautifully."

"No," the old man said. "I have become accustomed to the thorns—but they are not really good. For you, my young friend, we will have good music tonight.

"After all," he added generously, and beginning to wind the phonograph, which creaked, "they can't last forever."

"No, nor we," the man who needed to write said harshly. "The needle, by all means."

"Oh, thanks," said the young man. "Thanks," he said again, in a low, excited   25
voice, and then stifled his coughing with a bowed head.

"The records, though," said the old man when he had finished winding, "are a different matter. Already they are very worn. I do not play them more than once a week. One, once a week, that is what I allow myself.

"More than a week I cannot stand it; not to hear them," he apologized.

"No, how could you?" cried the young man. "And with them here like this."

The Tempest: Shakespeare's last play, first performed about 1611.
phonograph: Early phonographs, in use before electrically driven record players, had to be wound up by hand. They played records at a speed of 78 revolutions per minute, and used steel needles that had to be changed very often. The phonograph is especially valuable to the characters in this story because they have no electricity.

"A man can stand anything," said the man who wanted to write, in his harsh, antagonistic voice.

"Please, the music," said the young man.   30

"Only the one," said the old man. "In the long run we will remember more that way."

He had a dozen records with luxuriant gold and red seals. Even in that light the others could see that the threads of the records were becoming worn. Slowly he read out the titles, and the tremendous, dead names of the composers and the artists and the orchestras. The three worked upon the names in their minds, carefully. It was difficult to select from such a wealth what they would at once most like to remember. Finally the man who wanted to write named Gershwin's "New York."°

"Oh, no," cried the sick young man, and then could say nothing more because he had to cough. The others understood him, and the harsh man withdrew his selection and waited for the musician to choose.

The musician begged Doctor Jenkins to read the titles again, very slowly, so that he could remember the sounds. While they were read, he lay back against the wall, his eyes closed, his thin, horny hand pulling at his light beard, and listened to the voices and the orchestras and the single instruments in his mind.

When the reading was done he spoke despairingly. "I have forgotten," he   35
complained. "I cannot hear them clearly."

"There are things missing," he explained.

"I know," said Doctor Jenkins. "I thought that I knew all of Shelley° by heart. I should have brought Shelley."

"That's more soul than we can use," said the harsh man. "*Moby Dick* is better."

"By God, we can understand that," he emphasized.

The doctor nodded.   40

"Still," said the man who had admired the books, "we need the absolute if we are to keep a grasp on anything.

"Anything but these sticks and peat clods and rabbit snares," he said bitterly.

"Shelley desired an ultimate absolute," said the harsh man. "It's too much," he said. "It's no good; no earthly good."

The musician selected a Debussy° nocturne. The others considered and approved. They rose to their knees to watch the doctor prepare for the playing, so that they appeared to be actually in an attitude of worship. The peat glow showed the thinness of their bearded faces, and the deep lines in them, and revealed the condition of their garments. The other two continued to kneel as the old man carefully lowered the needle onto the spinning disk, but the musician suddenly drew back against the wall again, with his knees up, and buried his face in his hands.

At the first notes of the piano the listeners were startled. They stared at   45
each other. Even the musician lifted his head in amazement, but then quickly bowed it again, strainingly, as if he were suffering from a pain he might not be able to endure. They were all listening deeply, without movement. The wet, blue-

George Gershwin (1898–1937): American composer who wrote in the jazz idiom, not in the classical manner.

Percy Bysshe Shelley (1792–1822): English poet who wrote poems about the soul, intellectual beauty, and mutability.

Claude Debussy (1862–1918): French composer. His "Nocturne" for piano was first published in 1890.

green notes tinkled forth from the old machine, and were individual, delectable presences in the cell. The individual, delectable presences swept into a sudden tide of unbearably beautiful dissonance, and then continued fully the swelling and ebbing of that tide, the dissonant inpourings, and the resolutions, and the diminishments, and the little, quiet wavelets of interlude lapping between. Every sound was piercing and singularly sweet. In all the men except the musician, there occurred rapid sequences of tragically heightened recollection. He heard nothing but what was there. At the final, whispering disappearance, but moving quietly, so that the others would not hear him and look at him, he let his head fall back in agony, as if it were drawn there by the hair, and clenched the fingers of one hand over his teeth. He sat that way while the others were silent, and until they began to breathe again normally. His drawn-up legs were trembling violently.

Quickly Doctor Jenkins lifted the needle off, to save it, and not to spoil the recollection with scraping. When he had stopped the whirling of the sacred disk, he courteously left the phonograph open and by the fire, in sight.

The others, however, understood. The musician rose last, but then abruptly, and went quickly out at the door without saying anything. The others stopped at the door and gave their thanks in low voices. The doctor nodded magnificently.

"Come again," he invited, "in a week. We will have the 'New York.'"

When the two had gone together, out toward the rimmed road, he stood in the entrance, peering and listening. At first there was only the resonant boom of the wind overhead, and then, far over the dome of the dead, dark plain, the wolf cry lamenting. In the rifts of clouds the doctor saw four stars flying. It impressed the doctor that one of them had just been obscured by the beginning of a flying cloud at the very moment he heard what he had been listening for, a sound of suppressed coughing. It was not near by, however. He believed that down against the pale alders he could see the moving shadow.

With nervous hands he lowered the piece of canvas which served as his door, and pegged it at the bottom. Then quickly and quietly, looking at the piece of canvas frequently, he slipped the records into the case, snapped the lid shut, and carried the phonograph to his couch. There, pausing often to stare at the canvas and listen, he dug earth from the wall and disclosed a piece of board. Behind this there was a deep hole in the wall, into which he put the phonograph. After a moment's consideration, he went over and reached down his bundle of books and inserted it also. Then, guardedly, he once more sealed up the hole with the board and the earth. He also changed his blankets, and the grass-stuffed sack which served as a pillow, so that he could lie facing the entrance. After carefully placing two more blocks of peat on the fire, he stood for a long time watching the stretched canvas, but it seemed to billow naturally with the first gusts of a lowering wind. At last he prayed, and got in under his blankets, and closed his smoke-smarting eyes. On the inside of the bed, next to the wall, he could feel with his hand, the comfortable piece of lead pipe.

50

QUESTIONS

1. What kind of environment is described in the first three paragraphs of this story? What has happened before the story opens? To what extent do these paragraphs establish the tone and atmosphere of the story?

2. The first three descriptive paragraphs are loaded with adjectives. In the first, for example, we find *narrow, black, still, cold, mute, dead, isolated, shallow, brittle, old, frozen, tangled, quiet,* and *empty.* What do most of these adjectives contribute to the establishment of setting and, in turn, mood?

3. How is "the host's" home described? What do the details tell us about the host, humanity, and existence in the world of the story?

4. What record do the men choose to hear? What do the phonograph and the music represent to these men?

5. What does Dr. Jenkins do with his things after the men leave? How does he readjust his bed? Why does he do these things?

CYNTHIA OZICK   (b. 1928)

The Shawl   *1980*

Stella, cold, cold the coldness of hell. How they walked on the roads together, Rosa with Magda curled up between sore breasts, Magda wound up in the shawl. Sometimes Stella carried Magda. But she was jealous of Magda. A thin girl of fourteen, too small, with thin breasts of her own, Stella wanted to be wrapped in a shawl, hidden away, asleep, rocked by the march, a baby, a round infant in arms. Magda took Rosa's nipple, and Rosa never stopped walking, a walking cradle. There was not enough milk; sometimes Magda sucked air; then she screamed. Stella was ravenous. Her knees were tumors on sticks, her elbows chicken bones.

Rosa did not feel hunger; she felt light, not like someone walking but like someone in a faint, in trance, arrested in a fit, someone who is already a floating angel, alert and seeing everything, but in the air, not there, not touching the road. As if teetering on the tips of her fingernails. She looked into Magda's face through a gap in the shawl: a squirrel in a nest, safe, no one could reach her inside the little house of the shawl's windings. The face, very round, a pocket mirror of a face: but it was not Rosa's bleak complexion, dark like cholera, it was another kind of face altogether, eyes blue as air, smooth feathers of hair nearly as yellow as the Star sewn into Rosa's coat. You could think she was one of *their* babies.

Rosa, floating, dreamed of giving Magda away in one of the villages. She could leave the line for a minute and push Magda into the hands of any woman on the side of the road. But if she moved out of line they might shoot. And even if she fled the line for half a second and pushed the shawl-bundle at a stranger, would the woman take it? She might be surprised, or afraid; she might drop the shawl, and Magda would fall out and strike her head and die. The little round head. Such a good child, she gave up screaming, and sucked now only for the taste of the drying nipple itself. The neat grip of the tiny gums. One mite of a tooth tip sticking up in the bottom gum, how shining, an elfin tombstone of white marble gleaming there. Without complaining, Magda relinquished Rosa's teats, first the left, then the right; both were cracked, not a sniff of milk. The duct crevice extinct, a dead volcano, blind eye, chill hole, so Magda took the corner of the shawl and milked it instead. She sucked and sucked, flooding the threads with wetness. The shawl's good flavor, milk of linen.

It was a magic shawl, it could nourish an infant for three days and three nights. Magda did not die, she stayed alive, although very quiet. A peculiar smell, of cinnamon and almonds, lifted out of her mouth. She held her eyes open every moment, forgetting how to blink or nap, and Rosa and sometimes Stella studied their blueness. On the road they raised one burden of a leg after another and studied Magda's face. "Aryan," Stella said, in a voice grown as thin as a string; and Rosa thought how Stella gazed at Magda like a young cannibal. And the time that Stella said "Aryan," it sounded to Rosa as if Stella had really said "Let us devour her."

But Magda lived to walk. She lived that long, but she did not walk very well, 5
partly because she was only fifteen months old, and partly because the spindles of her legs could not hold up her fat belly. It was fat with air, full and round. Rosa gave almost all her food to Magda, Stella gave nothing; Stella was ravenous, a growing child herself, but not growing much. Stella did not menstruate. Rosa did not menstruate. Rosa was ravenous, but also not; she learned from Magda how to drink the taste of a finger in one's mouth. They were in a place without pity, all pity was annihilated in Rosa, she looked at Stella's bones without pity. She was sure that Stella was waiting for Magda to die so she could put her teeth into the little thighs.

Rosa knew Magda was going to die very soon; she should have been dead already, but she had been buried away deep inside the magic shawl, mistaken there for the shivering mound of Rosa's breasts; Rosa clung to the shawl as if it covered only herself. No one took it away from her. Magda was mute. She never cried. Rosa hid her in the barracks, under the shawl, but she knew that one day someone would inform; or one day someone, not even Stella, would steal Magda to eat her. When Magda began to walk Rosa knew that Magda was going to die very soon, something would happen. She was afraid to fall asleep; she slept with the weight of her thigh on Magda's body; she was afraid she would smother Magda under her thigh. The weight of Rosa was becoming less and less; Rosa and Stella were slowly turning into air.

Magda was quiet, but her eyes were horribly alive, like blue tigers. She watched. Sometimes she laughed—it seemed a laugh, but how could it be? Magda had never seen anyone laugh. Still, Magda laughed at her shawl when the wind blew its corners, the bad wind with pieces of black in it, that made Stella's and Rosa's eyes tear. Magda's eyes were always clear and tearless. She watched like a tiger. She guarded her shawl. No one could touch it; only Rosa could touch it. Stella was not allowed. The shawl was Magda's own baby, her pet, her little sister. She tangled herself up in it and sucked on one of the corners when she wanted to be very still.

Then Stella took the shawl away and made Magda die.

Afterward Stella said: "I was cold."

And afterward she was always cold, always. The cold went into her heart: 10
Rosa saw that Stella's heart was cold. Magda flopped onward with her little pencil legs scribbling this way and that, in search of the shawl; the pencils faltered at the barracks opening, where the light began. Rosa saw and pursued. But already Magda was in the square outside the barracks, in the jolly light. It was the roll-call arena. Every morning Rosa had to conceal Magda under the shawl against a wall of the barracks and go out and stand in the arena with Stella and hundreds of others, sometimes for hours, and Magda, deserted, was quiet under the shawl, sucking on her corner. Every day Magda was silent, and so she did not die. Rosa

saw that today Magda was going to die, and at the same time a fearful joy ran
into Rosa's two palms, her fingers were on fire, she was astonished, febrile: Magda,
in the sunlight, swaying on her pencil legs, was howling. Ever since the drying up
of Rosa's nipples, ever since Magda's last scream on the road, Magda had been
devoid of any syllable; Magda was a mute. Rosa believed that something had gone
wrong with her vocal cords, with her windpipe, with the cave of her larynx; Magda
was defective, without a voice; perhaps she was deaf; there might be something
amiss with her intelligence; Magda was dumb. Even the laugh that came when the
ash-stippled wind made a clown out of Magda's shawl was only the air-blown
showing of her teeth. Even when the lice, head lice and body lice, crazed her so
that she became as wild as one of the big rats that plundered the barracks at
daybreak looking for carrion, she rubbed and scratched and kicked and bit and
rolled without a whimper. But now Magda's mouth was spilling a long viscous
rope of clamor.

"Maaaa—"

It was the first noise Magda had ever sent out from her throat since the
drying up of Rosa's nipples.

"Maaaa . . . aaa!"

Again! Magda was wavering in the perilous sunlight of the arena, scrabbling
on such pitiful little bent shins. Rosa saw. She saw that Magda was grieving for
the loss of her shawl, she saw that Magda was going to die. A tide of commands
hammered in Rosa's nipples: Fetch, get, bring! But she did not know which to go
after first, Magda or the shawl. If she jumped out into the arena to snatch Magda
up, the howling would not stop, because Magda would still not have the shawl;
but if she ran back into the barracks to find the shawl, and if she found it, and if
she came after Magda holding it and shaking it, then she would get Magda back,
Magda would put the shawl in her mouth and turn dumb again.

Rosa entered the dark. It was easy to discover the shawl. Stella was heaped   15
under it, asleep in her thin bones. Rosa tore the shawl free and flew—she could
fly, she was only air—into the arena. The sunheat murmured of another life, of
butterflies in summer. The light was placid, mellow. On the other side of the steel
fence, far away, there were green meadows speckled with dandelions and deep-
colored violets; beyond them, even farther, innocent tiger lilies, tall, lifting their
orange bonnets. In the barracks they spoke of "flowers," of "rain": excrement,
thick turd-braids, and the slow stinking maroon waterfall that slunk down from
the upper bunks, the stink mixed with a bitter fatty floating smoke that greased
Rosa's skin. She stood for an instant at the margin of the arena. Sometimes the
electricity inside the fence would seem to hum; even Stella said it was only an
imagining, but Rosa heard real sounds in the wire: grainy sad voices. The farther
she was from the fence, the more clearly the voices crowded at her. The lamenting
voices strummed so convincingly, so passionately, it was impossible to suspect them
of being phantoms. The voices told her to hold up the shawl, high; the voices told
her to shake it, to whip with it, to unfurl it like a flag. Rosa lifted, shook, whipped,
unfurled. Far off, very far, Magda leaned across her air-fed belly, reaching out
with the rods of her arms. She was high up, elevated, riding someone's shoulder.
But the shoulder that carried Magda was not coming toward Rosa and the shawl,
it was drifting away, the speck of Magda was moving more and more into the
smoky distance. Above the shoulder a helmet glinted. The light tapped the helmet

and sparkled it into a goblet. Below the helmet a black body like a domino and a pair of black boots hurled themselves in the direction of the electrified fence. The electric voices began to chatter wildly. "Maa-maa, maaamaaa," they all hummed together. How far Magda was from Rosa now, across the whole square, past a dozen barracks, all the way on the other side! She was no bigger than a moth.

All at once Magda was swimming through the air. The whole of Magda traveled through loftiness. She looked like a butterfly touching a silver vine. And the moment Magda's feathered round head and her pencil legs and balloonish belly and zigzag arms splashed against the fence, the steel voices went mad in their growling, urging Rosa to run and run to the spot where Magda had fallen from her flight against the electrified fence; but of course Rosa did not obey them. She only stood, because if she ran they would shoot, and if she tried to pick up the sticks of Magda's body they would shoot, and if she let the wolf's screech ascending now through the ladder of her skeleton break out, they would shoot; so she took Magda's shawl and filled her own mouth with it, stuffed it in and stuffed it in, until she was swallowing up the wolf's screech and tasting the cinnamon and almond depth of Magda's saliva; and Rosa drank Magda's shawl until it dried.

QUESTIONS

1. Describe how Ozick presents the setting. Why do you not receive a clear picture of how things look? Why does Ozick present the details as she does?

2. In paragraph 15, what is on the other side of the fence? Explain Ozick's description here. Why does Ozick include these details so close to the story's end?

3. What character is the center of interest in "The Shawl"? Why is she being treated as she is? What are her impressions of the conditions and circumstances around her? What are her responses to her hunger and deprivation?

4. Explain the function of the more unpleasant and brutal details. What do you need to know about the circumstances of the story to respond to these details?

SANDRA CISNEROS (b. 1954)

The House on Mango Street   *1983*

We didn't always live on Mango Street. Before that we lived on Loomis on the third floor, and before that we lived on Keeler. Before Keeler it was Paulina, and before that I can't remember. But what I remember most is moving a lot. Each time it seemed there'd be one more of us. By the time we got to Mango Street we were six—Mama, Papa, Carlos, Kiki, my sister Nenny and me.

The house on Mango Street is ours and we don't have to pay rent to anybody or share the yard with the people downstairs or be careful not to make too much noise and there isn't a landlord banging on the ceiling with a broom. But even so, it's not the house we'd thought we'd get.

We had to leave the flat on Loomis quick. The water pipes broke and the landlord wouldn't fix them because the house was too old. We had to leave fast. We were using the washroom next door and carrying water over in empty milk gallons. That's why Mama and Papa looked for a house, and that's why we moved into the house on Mango Street, far away, on the other side of town.

They always told us that one day we would move into a house, a real house that would be ours for always so we wouldn't have to move each year. And our house would have running water and pipes that worked. And inside it would have real stairs, not hallway stairs, but stairs inside like the houses on T.V. And we'd have a basement and at least three washrooms so when we took a bath we didn't have to tell everybody. Our house would be white with trees around it, a great big yard and grass growing without a fence. This was the house Papa talked about when he held a lottery ticket and this was the house Mama dreamed up in the stories she told us before we went to bed.

But the house on Mango Street is not the way they told it at all. It's small   5
and red with tight little steps in front and windows so small you'd think they were holding their breath. Bricks are crumbling in places, and the front door is so swollen you have to push hard to get in. There is no front yard, only four little elms the city planted by the curb. Out back is a small garage for the car we don't own yet and a small yard that looks smaller between the two buildings on either side. There are stairs in our house, but they're ordinary hallway stairs, and the house has only one washroom, very small. Everybody has to share a bedroom— Mama and Papa, Carlos and Kiki, me and Nenny.

Once when we were living on Loomis, a nun from my school passed by and saw me playing out front. The laundromat downstairs had been boarded up because it had been robbed two days before and the owner had painted on the wood YES WE'RE OPEN so as not to lose business.

Where do you live? she asked.

There, I said pointing up to the third floor.

You live *there*?

There. I had to look to where she pointed—the third floor, the paint peeling,   10
wooden bars Papa had nailed on the windows so we wouldn't fall out. You live *there*? The way she said it made me feel like nothing. *There.* I lived *there.* I nodded.

I knew then I had to have a house. A real house. One I could point to. But this isn't it. The house on Mango Street isn't it. For the time being, Mama says. Temporary, says Papa. But I know how those things go.

QUESTIONS

1. Why is the speaker concerned with the nature of the houses she has lived in? What feeling does she show about these houses?

2. Describe the house on Mango Street. How does the condition of this house and the other houses explain the economic circumstances of the speaker's family?

3. What is the speaker like as a character? How do you learn about her? How much do you learn?

WRITING ABOUT SETTING

In preparing to write about setting, take notes on important locations, artifacts, and customs. Determine if there is one location of action or more. Raise the following questions about how much detail is included and why.

Questions for Discovering Ideas

Are things described visually so that you can make a sketch or draw a plan (such a sketch could help you organize your essay), or are the locations left vague? Why?

What influence do the locations have upon the characters, if any? Do the locations bring characters together, push them apart, make it easy for them to be private, make intimacy and conversation difficult?

What artifacts are important in the action, and how important are they? Are they well described? Are they vital to the action?

Are things like shapes, colors, times of day, locations of the sun, conditions of light, seasons of the year, and conditions of vegetation described?

Do characters respect or mistreat the environment around them?

What cultural assumptions do the characters make about themselves? How do these assumptions affect their judgments and actions?

What conclusions do you think the author expects you to draw as a result of the world and culture that he or she has created?

Strategies for Organizing Ideas

Following are five possible approaches to essays on setting. You are free to choose the one you want, but you may find that some works invite one approach rather than others. As you develop your essay, however, you may find it necessary to introduce one or more of the other approaches. Whatever approach you use, remember to consider setting as illustration and evidence, not as an end in itself.

1. *Setting and action.* Here you explore the importance of setting in the various actions. How extensively is the setting described? Are locations essential or incidental to the actions? Does the setting serve as part of the action (e.g., places of flight or concealment; public places where people meet openly or out-of-the-way places where they meet privately; natural or environmental conditions; seasonal conditions such as searing heat or numbing cold; customs and conventions)? Do any objects cause inspiration,

difficulty, or conflict (for example, a shawl, a rundown house, a recording, a walking stick, a pretty necklace, a coin, a costume, a toy windmill, a dead bird)? How strongly do these objects influence the action?

2. *Setting and organization.* How is the setting connected to the various parts of the work? Does it undergo any changes as the action develops? Are some parts of the setting more important in the action than other parts? Is the setting apparently used as a frame or enclosure? How do objects, such as money or property, figure into the motivation of the characters? How do descriptions made at the start become important in the action later on?

3. *Setting and character.* The major issue is the degree to which setting influences and interacts with character. Are the characters happy or unhappy where they live? Do they get into discussions or arguments about their home environments? Do they want to stay or leave? Do the economic, philosophical, religious, or ethnic aspects of the setting make the characters undergo changes? What jobs do the characters perform because of their ways of life? What freedoms or restraints do these jobs cause? How does the setting influence their decisions, transportation, speech habits, eating habits, attitudes about love and honor, and general behavior?

4. *Setting and atmosphere.* To what extent does the setting contribute to moods? Does the setting go beyond the minimum needed for action or character? Are descriptive words used to paint verbal pictures, to evoke moods through references to colors, shapes, sounds, smells, or tastes? Does the setting establish a mood, say, of joy or hopelessness, lushness or sparseness? Do things happen in daylight or at night? Do the movements and locations of the characters suggest permanence or impermanence (like footsteps on a stairway, or wooden bars to keep windows from falling out)? Are things warm and pleasant, or cold and harsh? Does the atmosphere suggest that life, too, is this way?

5. *Setting and other aspects.* Earlier in this chapter, "Setting and Statement" and "Setting and Irony" are listed as important uses of setting. If the author has used setting either to reinforce or make ironic the circumstances and ideas in the work, you might consult either of these sections as guides for the body of your essay. If you perceive a contrast between setting and content, that too could be the basis of an essay such as those described in the paragraph on "Setting and Irony." If you wish to explore the symbolic implications of a setting, you might wish to consult the discussions of symbolism in Chapter 9.

When concluding, you may summarize your major points or write about related aspects of setting that you have not considered. Thus, you might have been treating the relationship of setting and action, and may wish to mention connections that the setting has with character or atmosphere. You might also point out whether your central idea about setting also applies to other major aspects of the story.

SAMPLE ESSAY

Poe's Use of Interior Setting to Augment the Eeriness of "The Masque of the Red Death"°

[1] In "The Masque of the Red Death," Edgar Allan Poe uses many details of setting to create an eerie atmosphere.* The story is about the foolishness and impossibility of trying to evade death. Poe's Prince Prospero is the example of this idea. He believes that he can lock himself away in his castle, with a thousand followers,and avoid the plague of the Red Death raging outside. At the end, however, Death invades the castle in person and destroys all the people. Poe uses interior setting to underscore this irony, and also to make Prospero's pride seem pointless and insane. The prevailing eerie mood is brought out through Poe's use of graphic description, geographical direction, evocative color, and sepulchral sound.†

[2] The height of Poe's graphic description is in the story's extensive fourth paragraph, where he describes Prince Prospero's bizarre suite of seven rooms. These rooms have different colors, each one suggesting differing moods, from subdued, to garish, to somber. The blue room is in the east, and, moving westward in an order of varying depressiveness, the next six rooms are purple, green, orange, white, violet, and finally black. The moods are determined by the narrator's explanation that each room is lighted by a "brazier of fire" throwing light through a stained glass window that provokes awe by casting a glaring, grisly light.

[3] These rooms are not only vividly described, but they are spatially arranged to complement the certainty of death. The direction of east to west suggests a movement away from life. One might observe that the blue room, in the east, is on the side of the sun rising--an optimistic idea of blue skies and new beginnings of new days. On the other hand the westernmost room, the black one, is the direction of the setting sun and the end of the day at midnight, when Death takes over. If one doubts that Poe intended this geographical direction to have meaning, it is important to note that Prospero's charge against the ghostly figure of the Red Death takes him directly from east to west--from blue to black, from life to death--on his insane rush toward doom.

[4] The most weird and garish room is the black one, on which Poe devotes the most evocative of his visual descriptions. The room is hung with black velvet tapestries, but its darkness is made flamboyant by the scarlet, "deep blood" light (Poe avoids the more neutral word "red" here). The narrator states that the room is "ghastly in the extreme" and that it produces a look of wildness (paragraph 4). Visually, this room evokes feelings of wildness, evil, and an almost ghoulish delight in blood. It is a sinister room, designed not to relax but to disturb and distress.

To these ominous locations, Poe adds the eeriness of sepulchral sounds

° See p. 247 for this story.
* Central idea.
† Thesis sentence.

by including a "gigantic clock of ebony" in the black room. He devotes an entire paragraph (the fifth) to this weird clock, and this paragraph is therefore the focal point of the story's setting. Poe's words hint that the clock is vaguely alive. It is not <u>placed</u> or <u>set</u> against the west wall, but is <u>standing</u> there (Poe's word is "stood"), as though living, and its massive pendulum is in constant, "monotonous" motion (like the beating of a ghostly heart?). Poe's implication
[5]   is that the clock represents the dismal world of death, for every hour the "clang" from its "brazen lungs" announces the chilling end of another period of life. Poe's narrator points out that the clock's musical but eerie sounds stop all revelry and create a distressed silence among the merrymakers (Poe uses the word "disconcert" twice in the paragraph to describe the clock's effect). This use of sound, having its source in this mysteriously living clock, is designed to make readers as uneasy, unsettled, and anxious as Prospero's companions.

Thus Poe's interior setting is both descriptive and evocative. The major action takes place in the rooms--the costume party attended by all Prospero's friends, except the one uninvited guest, the Red Death himself, who instantly kills all the party-goers. Prospero's last movement takes him through all the
[6]   rooms, in a ritual passage from morning to midnight, from life to death. <u>In this way, Poe employs his setting to show the folly of trying to escape death, and also to suggest that the attempt is not only foolish but also bizarre and insane.</u> The events of the story, the sustained mood, the consistent idea, are all tied together by Poe's masterly control of setting.

Commentary on the Essay

Because it treats the relationship of setting to mood or atmosphere, this essay illustrates the fourth approach we described. (For examples of the third approach, relating setting to character, see Chapter 1, pp. 28–29 and 39–40.) The essay considers those aspects of setting needed for the story, and then stresses how Poe's descriptions build the eerie mood, the irony of the major character's pretensions, and the folly of his pride. The thesis sentence announces four topics for further development.

In the body, paragraph 2 describes the physical layout of Prospero's suite of rooms, and it also points out the eerie suggestiveness of Poe's descriptions of color and light. Paragraph 3 treats Poe's geographical arrangement of the rooms, with the idea that this arrangement complements the story's movement from life to death.

Paragraphs 4 and 5 treat the last and most sinister of the rooms. Paragraph 4 stresses the mood brought out by the colors black and scarlet or "deep blood." Paragraph 5, because it deals with the clock, on which Poe presents much detail, is the high point of the essay's body. Throughout the paragraph, the topic idea is that the clock, because of its seemingly living connection with the malign world of death, is Poe's major means of achieving an atmosphere complementary to the eerie action.

The conclusion summarizes the central idea, stressing once again that Poe goes beyond simple description to heighten the eerie, macabre atmosphere of his story.

WRITING TOPICS

1. How do Dr. Jenkins and the Musician respond to the setting in "The Portable Phonograph"? How do they adjust to physical conditions? To general conditions of their destroyed world and vanished civilization?

2. Choose a story from this chapter and, first, rewrite a page or two, taking the characters out of their setting and placing them in the setting of another story, or in another setting of your choosing. Then, second, write an essay dealing with these questions: How were your characters affected by their new settings? Did you make them change slowly or rapidly? Why? As a result of your rewriting, what have you learned about the uses of setting in fiction?

3. Write a short narrative that might be included in a longer story (which you may also wish to write for the assignment). Choose *a* or *b*, or both.

   a. Relate a natural setting or type of day to a mood (for example, a nice day to happiness and satisfaction; or a cold, cloudy, rainy day to sadness). If you wish, you might create irony by relating the nice day to sadness, or the terrible day to happiness.

   b. Indicate how an object becomes the cause of conflict or reconciliation (such as the books and records in "The Portable Phonograph," the shawl in "The Shawl," or the chest in "The Worker in Sandalwood").

4. Compare and contrast how details of setting are used to establish the qualities and traits of the following characters: Mrs. Johnson of "Everyday Use," Miss Brill of "Miss Brill," Minnie Wright of "A Jury of Her Peers," Meda Roth of Menesteung," and Stella in "The Shawl." As one of your bases of comparison, introduce the ways in which Boucher and Hopper use details in their paintings (pp. 242, 243).

7

Style: The Words That Tell the Story

The word **style**, derived from the Latin word *stilus* (a writing instrument), is understood to mean the way in which writers assemble words to tell the story, develop the argument, dramatize the play, or compose the poem. Often the definition is extended to distinguish style from content. It is probably wiser, however, not to make this separation but to consider style as the placement of words in the *service* of content. The way a thing is said, in other words, cannot be separated from the thing itself.

Style is also individualistic. It is the way in which specific authors put words together under specific conditions in specific works. It is therefore possible to speak of the style of Ernest Hemingway, for example, and of Mark Twain, even though both writers are always adapting their words to the situations imagined in their works. Thus, authors may have a distinct style for narrative and descriptive passages, but their style in dialogue may be different from either of these. Indeed, it would be inferior style if a writer were to use the same manner for all of a story's varying purposes. It must therefore be emphasized that style is to be judged on its adaptability. The better the style, the more the words fit the situation. Jonathan Swift defined style as the right words in the right places. We may add that style also refers to the right words at the right time and in the right circumstances.

DICTION: CHOICE OF WORDS

Diction refers to a writer's selection of words. The selection should be accurate and explicit, so that all actions and ideas are clear. If a passage is effective, if it conveys an idea well or gets at the essence of an action vividly and powerfully, we may confidently say that the words are right. In a passage containing action, for example, there should be active verbs, whereas in a description there should be nouns and adjectives that provide locations, relationships, colors, and shapes. An explanatory or reflective passage should include words that convey thoughts, states of mind and emotion, and conditions of human relationships.

Formal, Neutral, and Informal Diction

Words fall into three basic groups, or classes, that may be called **formal** or *high*, **neutral** or *middle*, and **informal** or *low*. Formal or high diction consists of standard and elegant words (often polysyllabic), the retention of correct word order, and the absence of contractions. The sentence "It is I," for example, is formal. The following sentences from Poe's "The Masque of the Red Death" use formal language:

> They resolved to leave means neither of ingress nor egress to the sudden impulses of despair or frenzy from within. The abbey was amply provisioned. With such precautions the courtiers might bid defiance to contagion.

Note here words like *ingress, egress, provisioned, bid defiance*, and *contagion*. These words are not in ordinary, everyday vocabulary and have what we may call "elegance." Though they are accurate and apt, and though the sentences are brief and simple, the diction is *high*.

Neutral or middle diction is ordinary, everyday, but still standard vocabulary, with a shunning of longer words but with the use of contractions when necessary. The sentence "It's me," is neutral, the sort of thing many people say in preference to "It is I" when identifying themselves on the telephone. The following passage from Alice Munro's "The Found Boat" illustrates middle, neutral diction.

> What surprised them in the second place was that when the boys did actually see what boat was meant, this old flood-smashed wreck held up in the branches, they did not understand that they had been fooled, that a joke had been played on them. They did not show a moment's disappointment, but seemed as pleased at the discovery as if the boat had been whole and new. They were already barefoot, because they had been wading in the water to get lumber, and they waded in here without a stop, surrounding the boat and appraising it and paying no attention even of an insulting kind to Eva and Carol who bobbed up and down on their log. Eva and Carol had to call to them.

In this passage the words are ordinary and easy. Even the longer words, like *surprised, disappointment, surrounding, appraising*, and *insulting*, are not beyond the level of conversation, although *appraising* and *surrounding* would also be in place in a more formal passage. Essentially, however, the words do not draw attention to themselves but are centered on the topic. In a way, such words in the neutral style are like clear windows; words in the high style are more like stained glass.

Informal or low diction may range from colloquial—the language of relaxed, common activities—to the level of substandard or slang expressions. A person speaking to a close friend uses diction that would not be appropriate in public and formal situations, or even in some social situations. Low language is thus appropriate for dialogue in stories, depending on the characters speaking, and for stories told in the first-person point of view as though the speaker is talking directly to sympathetic and relaxed close friends. For example, Sammy's opening sentence in Updike's "A & P" illustrates the informal, low style:

> In walks these three girls in nothing but bathing suits.

Note the idiomatic "In walks," a singular verb, followed by a plural subject. Note also the use of "these" girls, an idiom used indefinitely to refer to specific people.

Specific-General and Concrete-Abstract Language

Specific refers to words about real things that may be readily perceived or imagined. "My dog Woofie is barking" is specific. **General** statements refer to broad classes of persons or things. Assertions like "All people like pets" and "Dogs make good pets" are generalizations. There is an ascending order from (1) very specific, to (2) less specific, to (3) general, as though the words themselves mount a stairway. Thus, *peach* is a specific fruit. *Fruit* is specific but more general because it may also include apples, oranges, and all other fruits. *Dessert* is a still more general word, which can include all sweets, including fruits and peaches, and also other things, like ice cream, that people eat at the end of their meals. *Food* is more general yet, for the word includes everything that all living creatures may eat. If you report that you are having "food" for dinner, you are being vague and overly general, but if you say that the main course is a London broil with peaches for dessert, you are being specific.

While *specific-general* refers to numbers, *concrete-abstract* refers to qualities or conditions. **Concrete** words describe qualities of immediate perception. If you say "Ice cream is cold," the word *cold* is concrete because it describes a condition that you can feel. **Abstract** words refer to broader, less palpable qualities; they may therefore apply to many separate things. Thus, ice cream may also be *sweet, creamy*, and *peachy*. If you describe it as *good*, however, you are speaking abstractly because the word *good* is far removed from ice cream itself and conveys no descriptive information about it. A wide number of things may be *good*, just as they may be *bad, fine*, "*cool*," *excellent*, and so on.

Usually, narrative and descriptive writing features specific and concrete words in preference to general and abstract ones. It stands to reason: When we confront many general and abstract words that may mean a number of things at once, we become uncertain and confused. Usually, therefore, such words are out of place in stories and novels. On the other hand, we are able to visualize and understand passages containing words about specific things and actions, for with more specificity and concreteness there is less ambiguity. Because vividness is a goal of most fiction, specific and concrete words are the writer's basic tools.

The point, however, is not that abstract and general words do not belong, but rather that *words should be appropriate in the context.* Good writers manipulate style to match their narrative and descriptive purposes. As an example, we may observe Hemingway's diction in "Soldier's Home." This story concerns the aftereffects of war on a sensitive young man who, fresh from the excitement and danger he has experienced abroad, cannot adjust to the humdrum life back home. By combining specific and abstract language to get these ideas across, Hemingway fits style to subject exactly. Thus, in paragraph 6 (p. 278), Hemingway uses abstract terms to describe the mental state of Krebs, the young veteran. We read that Krebs feels "nausea in regard to experience that is the result of untruth or exaggeration," that he goes into the "easy pose of the old soldier" when he meets another veteran, and that he "lost everything" during his time abroad. Because Hemingway does not include specific references for these words, it is not easy to understand *exactly* what he means by them, beyond conveying Krebs's general dissatisfaction.

In contrast, however, Hemingway's next paragraph describes Krebs's typical daily activities: getting out of bed, walking to the library, eating lunch, reading on the front porch, and drifting down to the local pool room. These details are specific; although Hemingway does not elaborate further on them, we know from the passage that Krebs is bogged down in aimless boredom. The two paragraphs together reflect on each other, with the specificity in paragraph 7 helping to explain the abstraction of paragraph 6. In short, Hemingway skillfully combines abstract and specific words to build up his portrait of a young man who has not developed a vision of what to do with his life.

Denotation and Connotation

Another way of understanding style is to study the author's management of denotation and connotation. **Denotation** refers to what a word means, and **connotation** to what the word suggests. It is one thing to call a person *skinny*, for example, another to use the words *thin* or *gaunt*, and still something else to say *svelte* or *shapely*. Similarly, both *cat* and *kitten* are close to each other denotatively, but *kitten* connotes more playfulness and cuteness than *cat*. If a person in a social situation behaves in ways that are *friendly, warm, polite,* or *correct,* these words all suggest slight differences in behavior, not because the words are not close in meaning, but because they have different connotations.

Through the careful choice of words, not only for denotation but also for connotation, authors create unique effects even though they might be describing similar or even identical situations. Let us look briefly at Eudora Welty's description of Phoenix Jackson in "A Worn Path" as Phoenix walks through the woods:

> Her eyes were blue with age. Her skin had a pattern all its own of numberless branching wrinkles and as though a whole little tree stood in the middle of her forehead, but a golden color ran underneath, and the two knobs of her cheeks were illumined by a yellow burning under the dark. Under the rag her hair came down on her neck in the frailest of ringlets, still black, and with an odor like copper. (paragraph 2)

Though the description skillfully portrays an aging woman, it also contains a compelling note of admiration. Specifically, the words *golden color* and *illumined* would be appropriate in the description of delicate and lovely medieval book paintings; *frailest of ringlets, still black* suggests girlishness and personal care, despite Phoenix's advancing age and weakness. With this description you might compare Sammy's words depicting the "queen" in "A & P" (paragraphs 2–4, pp. 65–66), which suggest his admiration not only of her sexual beauty but also of her grace. Shirley Jackson's briefer description of Tessie Hutchinson in "The Lottery" (paragraph 8, p. 216) is designed to reduce her to no more than an average woman of the village. The meager details are that she has a "sweater thrown over her shoulders" and that she "dried her hands on her apron." These examples demonstrate the ways in which connotation may complement an author's descriptive intentions.

RHETORIC

Broadly, **rhetoric** refers to the art of persuasive writing and, even more broadly, to the general art of writing. Any passage can be studied for its rhetorical qualities. For this reason it is necessary to develop both the methods and the descriptive vocabulary with which to carry out an analysis. Some things that may easily be done involve counting various elements in a passage and analyzing the types of sentences.

Counting

Doing a count of the number of words in a sentence—or the number of verbs, adjectives, prepositions, and adverbs; or the number of syllables in relation to the total number of words—can lead to valuable conclusions about the style, especially if the count is related to other aspects of the passage. The virtue of counting is that it is easy to do and therefore it provides a "quick opening" into at least one aspect of style. Always remember that conclusions based on a count will provide *tendencies* of a particular author rather than *absolutes*. For illustration, let us say that Author A uses words mainly of 1 or 2 syllables, whereas author B includes many words of 3, 4, and 5 syllables. Going further, let us say that A uses an average of 12 words per sentence; B uses 35. It would be fair to conclude that Author A is brief, and Author B is more expansive. This is not to say that Author A's passage would be easier or superior, however, for a long string of short sentences with short words might become choppy and tiresome and could cause your mind to wander.

Sentence Types

You can learn much about a passage by determining the sorts of sentences it contains. Though you have probably learned the basic sentence types at one time or another, let's review them here:

1. **Simple sentences** contain one subject and one verb, together with modifiers and complements. They are short, and are most appropriate for actions and declarations. Often they are idiomatic, particularly in dialogue.
2. **Compound sentences** contain two simple sentences joined by a conjunction (*and, but, for, or, nor, so,* or *yet*) and a comma, or by a semicolon without a conjunction. Frequently, compound sentences are connected as a series of three or four or more simple sentences.
3. **Complex sentences** contain a main clause and a subordinate clause. Because of the subordinate clause, the complex sentence is often suitable for describing cause-and-effect relationships in narrative, and also for analysis and reflection.
4. **Compound-complex sentences** contain two main clauses and a subordinate clause. In practice many authors produce sentences that may contain a number of subordinate clauses together with many more than two main clauses. Usually, the more clauses, the more difficult the sentence.

Loose and Periodic Sentences

A major way to describe sentences is to use the terms *loose* and *periodic*. A **loose sentence** unfolds easily, with no surprises. Most sentences in fiction and nonfiction are loose sentences. Here is an example:

> In America, the idea of equality was first applied only to white males.

Periodic sentences are arranged in an order of climax, with the concluding information or thought being withheld to make the sentence especially interesting or surprising. Usually the periodic sentence begins with a subordinate clause so that the content may be built up to the final detail, as in this sentence:

> Although in America the ideal of equality was first applied only to males of European ancestry, in this century, despite the reluctance and even the opposition of many men who have regarded equality as a mark of their own

status and not as a right for everyone, it has been extended to women and to persons of all races.

In narrative prose, sentences of this type are usually placed in spots of special importance. Often the sentence alone contains the crisis and resolution at the same moment, as in this sentence from Poe's "The Fall of the House of Usher":

> For a moment she remained trembling and reeling to and fro upon the threshold, then, with a low moaning cry, fell heavily inward upon the person of her brother, and in her violent and now final death-agonies, bore him to the floor a corpse, and a victim to the terrors he had anticipated.

Parallelism

To create interest, authors often rely on the rhetorical device called **parallelism**, which is common and easily recognized. Parallelism is the repetition of the same grammatical form (nouns, verbs, phrases, clauses) to balance expressions, conserve words, and build climaxes. Here, for example, is another sentence from Poe, from the story "The Black Cat":

> I grew, day by day, more moody, more irritable, more regardless of the feelings of others.

Arrangements like this are called *parallel* because they can be laid out graphically, according to parts of speech, in parallel lines, as in the following (with the phrase "day by day" left out):

$$I \text{ grew} \begin{cases} \text{more moody} \\ \text{more irritable} \\ \text{more regardless of the feelings of others} \end{cases}$$

Poe's sentence achieves an order of increasing severity of psychological depression developing from the personal to the social. Such an ascending order marks a deliberate attempt at climax, unlike the parallelism in the following sentence from the concluding paragraph of Clark's "The Portable Phonograph" (p. 255):

> Then quickly and quietly, looking at the piece of canvas frequently,
>
> he slipped the records into the case, snapped the lid shut,
>
> and carried the phonograph to his couch.

Here are two parallel adverbs at the beginning, both ending in *-ly*, and three past tense verbs ending in *-ed*, all of which have direct objects. The order here is time. Though the sentence is short, Clark conveys a great deal of information through the use of parallelism.

You may also see the same parallel arrangements in individual sentences within a paragraph. In the following passage from Alice Munro's "The Found Boat," for example, there are a number of sentences of identical structure that sum up the exhilaration of young people dashing naked to swim in a river. Parallel sentences begin "They felt," "They felt," "They thought," "They went running," and finally "They dipped and floated and separated":

> Nobody said a word this time, they all bent and stripped themselves. Eva, naked first, started running across the field, and then all the others ran, all five of them running bare through the knee-high hot grass, running towards the river. Not caring now about being caught but in fact leaping and yelling to call attention to themselves, if there was anybody to hear or see. They felt as if they were going to jump off a cliff and fly. They felt that something was happening to them different from anything that had happened before, and it had to do with the boat, the water, the sunlight, the dark ruined station, and each other. They thought of each other now hardly as names or people, but as echoing shrieks, reflections, all bold and white and loud and scandalous, and as fast as arrows. They went running without a break into the cold water and when it came almost to the tops of their legs they fell on it and swam. It stopped their noise. Silence, amazement, came over them in a rush. They dipped and floated and separated, sleek as mink.

Cumulatio or Accumulation.   The paragraph from "The Found Boat" also illustrates another rhetorical device used by writers, namely **cumulatio** or **accumulation**. Whereas *parallelism* refers to grammatical constructions, *cumulatio* refers to the building up of details, such as the materials in the "they" sentences in Munro's paragraph. The device is therefore a brief way of introducing much information, for once the parallel rhythm of the buildup begins, readers readily accept new material directly into the pattern. The device thus acts as a series of quick glimpses, or vignettes, and vividness is established through the parallel repetition.

Chiasmus or Antimetabole.   Also fitting into the pattern of parallelism is a device called **chiasmus** or **antimetabole**. This pattern is designed to create vividness through memorable repetition. The pattern is $A\ B\ B\ A$, which can be arranged graphically at the ends of an X (from the Greek letter *chi*):

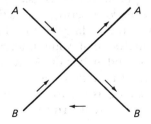

Mark Twain, in the story "Luck," creates a sentence that shows this pattern:

A   B   B   A

I drilled him and crammed him, and crammed him and drilled him.

You may not always encounter such easily detected patterns, but you should be alert to positions and arrangements that are particularly noticeable or effective. Even though you may not be able to use a technically correct name, your analysis should go well as long as you focus your attention on important aspects of effective writing in the stories that you read.

STYLE IN GENERAL

If the work is successful, you probably do not think of the style, for clear expressions and easy reading are marks of a writer's success. On consideration, however, you can begin to understand the author's achievement through a study of style. The action described in a particular passage, the relationship of the passage to the entire work, the level of the diction, the vividness of the descriptions—all these can enter into an assessment of the passage.

In the paragraph just quoted from Munro's "The Found Boat," for example, the great stylistic mastery can be perceived beyond the parallelism that we noted. The passage could be considered the climax of the story, which is, among other things, about emerging sexuality. In an almost ritualistic way, the paragraph describes young people running impetuously toward a river and diving in—an action that may be construed as sexually symbolic. Note that after the first two sentences describing action, Munro's narrator shifts the focus with four sentences of omniscient analysis describing the young people's feelings. If her intention had been to create searching psychological scrutiny, she might have selected words from the language of psychology (*libido, urge, sublimation*, and so on). Instead, she uses words that could have been in the vocabularies of the characters. Hence the young people feel "as if they were going to jump off a cliff and fly" and feel "that something was happening to them different from anything that had happened before." With these neutral words, the passage focuses on the excitement of the situation rather than on hidden psychological significance. In light of these considerations, the style of the paragraph is just right. Munro describes the actions adequately but not extensively, she objectivizes the feelings of the characters, and she avoids the sort of psychological analysis that would interrupt rather than instruct.

Observations of this kind may not occur on first reading, but on reflection you will find that the style of most passages will yield relatively full material for study. As long as the focus is on the content and also on the relationship of words to content, fruitful analysis of style will result.

MARK TWAIN (1835–1910)
[SAMUEL LANGHORNE CLEMENS]

Luck[1]   *1891*

It was at a banquet in London in honor of one of the two or three conspicuously illustrious English military names of this generation. For reasons which will presently appear, I will withhold his real name and titles and call him Lieutenant-General Lord Arthur Scoresby, Y.C., K.C.B., etc., etc. What a fascination there is in a renowned name! There sat the man, in actual flesh, whom I had heard of so many thousands of times since that day, thirty years before, when his name shot suddenly to the zenith from a Crimean battlefield,° to remain forever celebrated. It was food and drink to me to look, and look, and look at that demi-god; scanning, searching, noting: the quietness, the reserve, the noble gravity of his countenance; the simple honesty that expressed itself all over him; the sweet unconsciousness of his greatness—unconsciousness of the hundreds of admiring eyes fastened upon him, unconsciousness of the deep, loving, sincere worship welling out of the breasts of those people and flowing toward him.

The clergyman at my left was an old acquaintance of mine—clergyman now, but had spent the first half of his life in the camp and field and as an instructor in the military school at Woolwich. Just at the moment I have been talking about a veiled and singular light glimmered in his eyes and he leaned down and muttered confidentially to me—indicating the hero of the banquet with a gesture:

"Privately—he's an absolute fool."

This verdict was a great surprise to me. If its subject had been Napoleon, or Socrates, or Solomon, my astonishment could not have been greater. Two things I was well aware of: that the Reverend was a man of strict veracity and that his judgment of men was good. Therefore I knew, beyond doubt or question, that the world was mistaken about this hero: he *was* a fool. So I meant to find out, at a convenient moment, how the Reverend, all solitary and alone, had discovered the secret.

Some days later the opportunity came, and this is what the Reverend told   5
me:

About forty years ago I was an instructor in the military academy at Woolwich. I was present in one of the sections when young Scoresby underwent his preliminary examination. I was touched to the quick with pity, for the rest of the class answered up brightly and handsomely, while he—why, dear me, he didn't know *anything*, so to speak. He was evidently good, and sweet, and lovable, and guileless; and so it was exceedingly painful to see him stand there, as serene as a graven image, and deliver himself of answers which were veritably miraculous for stupidity and ignorance. All the compassion in me was aroused in his behalf. I said to myself, when he comes to be examined again he will be flung over, of course; so it will be simply a harmless act of charity to ease his fall as much as I can. I took him aside and found that he knew a little of Caesar's history; and as he didn't know anything else, I went to work and drilled him like a galley-slave on a certain line

---

[1] This is not a fancy sketch. I got it from a clergyman who was an instructor at Woolwich forty years ago, and who vouched for its truth. [Twain's note.]

Crimean battlefield: In the Crimean War (1853–1856), England was one of the allies that fought against Russia.

of stock questions concerning Caesar which I knew would be used. If you'll believe me, he went through with flying colors on examination day! He went through on that purely superficial "cram," and got compliments too, while others, who knew a thousand times more than he, got plucked. By some strangely lucky accident—an accident not likely to happen twice in a century—he was asked no question outside of the narrow limits of his drill.

It was stupefying. Well, all through his course I stood by him, with something of the sentiment which a mother feels for a crippled child; and he always saved himself—just by miracle, apparently.

Now, of course, the thing that would expose him and kill him at last was mathematics. I resolved to make his death as easy as I could; so I drilled him and crammed him, and crammed him and drilled him, just on the line of questions which the examiners would be most likely to use, and then launched him on his fate. Well, sir, try to conceive of the result: to my consternation, he took the first prize! And with it he got a perfect ovation in the way of compliments.

Sleep? There was no more sleep for me for a week. My conscience tortured me day and night. What I had done I had done purely through charity, and only to ease the poor youth's fall. I never had dreamed of any such preposterous results as the thing that had happened. I felt as guilty and miserable as Frankenstein. Here was a wooden-head whom I had put in the way of glittering promotions and prodigious responsibilities, and but one thing could happen: he and his responsibilities would all go to ruin together at the first opportunity.

The Crimean War had just broken out. Of course there had to be a war, I said to myself. We couldn't have peace and give this donkey a chance to die before he is found out. I waited for the earthquake. It came. And it made me reel when it did come. He was actually gazetted to a captaincy in a marching regiment! Better men grow old and gray in the service before they climb to a sublimity like that. And who could ever have foreseen that they would go and put such a load of responsibility on such green and inadequate shoulders? I could just barely have stood it if they had made him a cornet; but a captain—think of it! I thought my hair would turn white.

Consider what I did—I who so loved repose and inaction. I said to myself, I am responsible to the country for this, and I must go along with him and protect the country against him as far as I can. So I took my poor little capital that I had saved up through years of work and grinding economy, and went with a sigh and bought a cornetcy in his regiment, and away we went to the field.

And there—oh, dear, it was awful. Blunders?—why he never did anything *but* blunder. But, you see, nobody was in the fellow's secret. Everybody had him focused wrong, and necessarily misinterpreted his performance every time. Consequently they took his idiotic blunders for inspirations of genius. They did, honestly! His mildest blunders were enough to make a man in his right mind cry; and they did make me cry—and rage and rave, too, privately. And the thing that kept me always in a sweat of apprehension was the fact that every fresh blunder he made increased the luster of his reputation! I kept saying to myself, he'll get so high that when discovery does finally come it will be like the sun falling out of the sky.

He went right along, up from grade to grade, over the dead bodies of his superiors, until at last, in the hottest moment of the battle of———down went our colonel, and my heart jumped into my mouth, for Scoresby was next in rank! Now for it, said I: we'll all land in Sheol in ten minutes, sure.

The battle was awfully hot; the allies were steadily giving way all over the field. Our regiment occupied a position that was vital; a blunder now must be destruction. At this crucial moment, what does this immortal fool do but detach the regiment from its place and order a charge over a neighboring hill where there wasn't a suggestion of an enemy! "There you go!" I said to myself; "this *is* the end at last."

And away we did go, and were over the shoulder of the hill before the insane movement could be discovered and stopped. And what did we find? An entire and unsuspected Russian army in reserve! And what happened? We were eaten up? That is necessarily what would have happened in ninety-nine cases out of a hundred. But no; those Russians argued that no single regiment would come browsing around there at such a time. It must be the entire English army, and that the sly Russian game was detected and blocked, so they turned tail, and away they went, pell-mell, over the hill and down into the field, in wild confusion, and we after them; they themselves broke the solid Russian center in the field, and tore through, and in no time there was the most tremendous rout you ever saw, and the defeat of the allies was turned into a sweeping and splendid victory! Marshal Canrobert looked on, dizzy with astonishment, admiration, and delight; and sent right off for Scoresby, and hugged him, and decorated him on the field in presence of all the armies!

And what was Scoresby's blunder that time? Merely the mistaking his right hand for his left—that was all. An order had come to him to fall back and support our right; and, instead, he fell *forward* and went over the hill to the left. But the name he won that day as a marvelous military genius filled the world with his glory, and that glory will never fade while history books last.

He is just as good and sweet and lovable and unpretending as a man can be, but he doesn't know enough to come in when it rains. Now that is absolutely true. He is the supremest ass in the universe; and until half an hour ago nobody knew it but himself and me. He has been pursued, day by day and year by year, by a most phenomenal astonishing luckiness. He has been a shining soldier in all our wars for a generation; he has littered his whole military life with blunders, and yet has never committed one that didn't make him a knight or a baronet or a lord or something. Look at his breast; why, he is just clothed in domestic and foreign decorations. Well, sir, every one of them is the record of some shouting stupidity or other; and, taken together, they are proof that the very best thing in all this world that can befall a man is to be born lucky. I say again, as I said at the banquet, Scoresby's an absolute fool.

QUESTIONS

1. Describe Twain's style as a writer of narrative prose. What kinds of detail does he present? Does he give you enough detail about the battle during the Crimean War, for example, to justify an assertion that he describes action vividly? Or does he confine his detail to illuminate the life of Scoresby?

2. What elements in the story are amusing? How does the development of humor depend on Twain's arrangement of words?

3. Study the first paragraph. What does Twain intend after the "look, and look, and look" phrase? Why do you think he begins the story with such a description, that might even be called heroic? Contrast this paragraph with paragraph 12, where the word "blunder" is repeated.

4. Who begins the story? Who finally tells it? How does the second narrator learn about Scoresby? How does he summarize Scoresby's career?

ERNEST HEMINGWAY (1899–1961)

Soldier's Home   *1925*

Krebs went to the war from a Methodist college in Kansas. There is a picture which shows him among his fraternity brothers, all of them wearing exactly the same height and style collar. He enlisted in the Marines in 1917 and did not return to the United States until the second division returned from the Rhine in the summer of 1919.

There is a picture which shows him on the Rhine with two German girls and another corporal. Krebs and the corporal look too big for their uniforms. The German girls are not beautiful. The Rhine does not show in the picture.

By the time Krebs returned to his home town in Oklahoma the greeting of heroes was over. He came back much too late. The men from the town who had been drafted had all been welcomed elaborately on their return. There had been a great deal of hysteria. Now the reaction had set in. People seemed to think it was rather ridiculous for Krebs to be getting back so late, years after the war was over.

At first Krebs, who had been at Belleau Wood, Soissons, the Champagne, St. Mihiel and in the Argonne did not want to talk about the war at all. Later he felt the need to talk but no one wanted to hear about it. His town had heard too many atrocity stories to be thrilled by actualities. Krebs found that to be listened to at all he had to lie, and after he had done this twice he, too, had a reaction against the war and against talking about it. A distaste for everything that had happened to him in the war set in because of the lies he had told. All of the times that had been able to make him feel cool and clean inside himself when he thought of them; the times so long back when he had done the one thing, the only thing for a man to do, easily and naturally, when he might have done something else, now lost their cool, valuable quality and then were lost themselves.

His lies were quite unimportant lies and consisted in attributing to himself   5
things other men had seen, done or heard of, and stating as facts certain apocryphal incidents familiar to all soldiers. Even his lies were not sensational at the pool room. His acquaintances, who had heard detailed accounts of German women found chained to machine guns in the Argonne forest and who could not comprehend, or were barred by their patriotism from interest in, any German machine gunners who were not chained, were not thrilled by his stories.

Krebs acquired the nausea in regard to experience that is the result of untruth or exaggeration, and when he occasionally met another man who had really been a soldier and they talked a few minutes in the dressing room at a dance he fell into the easy pose of the old soldier among other soldiers: that he had been badly, sickeningly frightened all the time. In this way he lost everything.

During this time, it was late summer, he was sleeping late in bed, getting up to walk down town to the library to get a book, eating lunch at home, reading on the front porch until he became bored and then walking down through the town to spend the hottest hours of the day in the cool dark of the pool room. He loved to play pool.

In the evening he practised on his clarinet, strolled down town, read and went to bed. He was still a hero to his two young sisters. His mother would have given him breakfast in bed if he had wanted it. She often came in when he was in bed and asked him to tell her about the war, but her attention always wandered. His father was non-committal.

Before Krebs went away to the war he had never been allowed to drive the family motor car. His father was in the real estate business and always wanted the car to be at his command when he required it to take clients out into the country to show them a piece of farm property. The car always stood outside the First National Bank building where his father had an office on the second floor. Now, after the war, it was still the same car.

Nothing was changed in the town except that the young girls had grown up. 10 But they lived in such a complicated world of already defined alliances and shifting feuds that Krebs did not feel the energy or the courage to break into it. He liked to look at them, though. There were so many good-looking young girls. Most of them had their hair cut short. When he went away only little girls wore their hair like that or girls that were fast. They all wore sweaters and shirt waists with round Dutch collars. It was a pattern. He liked to look at them from the front porch as they walked on the other side of the street. He liked to watch them walking under the shade of the trees. He liked the round Dutch collars above their sweaters. He liked their silk stockings and flat shoes. He liked their bobbed hair and the way they walked.

When he was in town their appeal to him was not very strong. He did not like them when he saw them in the Greek's ice cream parlor. He did not want them themselves really. They were too complicated. There was something else. Vaguely he wanted a girl but he did not want to have to work to get her. He would have liked to have a girl but he did not want to have to spend a long time getting her. He did not want to get into the intrigue and the politics. He did not want to have to do any courting. He did not want to tell any more lies. It wasn't worth it.

He did not want any consequences. He did not want any consequences ever again. He wanted to live along without consequences. Besides he did not really need a girl. The army had taught him that. It was all right to pose as though you had to have a girl. Nearly everybody did that. But it wasn't true. You did not need a girl. That was the funny thing. First a fellow boasted how girls mean nothing to him, that he never thought of them, that they could not touch him. Then a fellow boasted that he could not get along without girls, that he had to have them all the time, that he could not go to sleep without them.

That was all a lie. It was all a lie both ways. You did not need a girl unless you thought about them. He learned that in the army. Then sooner or later you always got one. When you were really ripe for a girl you always got one. You did not have to think about it. Sooner or later it would come. He had learned that in the army.

Now he would have liked a girl if she had come to him and not wanted to talk. But here at home it was all too complicated. He knew he could never get through it all again. It was not worth the trouble. That was the thing about French girls and German girls. There was not all this talking. You couldn't talk much and you did not need to talk. It was simple and you were friends. He thought about France and then he began to think about Germany. On the whole he had liked Germany better. He did not want to leave Germany. He did not want to come home. Still, he had come home. He sat on the front porch.

He liked the girls that were walking along the other side of the street. He 15
liked the look of them much better than the French girls or the German girls. But the world they were in was not the world he was in. He would like to have one of them. But it was not worth it. They were such a nice pattern. He liked the pattern. It was exciting. But he would not go through all the talking. He did not want one badly enough. He liked to look at them all, though. It was not worth it. Not now when things were getting good again.

He sat there on the porch reading a book on the war. It was a history and he was reading about all the engagements he had been in. It was the most interesting reading he had ever done. He wished there were more maps. He looked forward with a good feeling to reading all the really good histories when they would come out with good detail maps. Now he was really learning about the war. He had been a good soldier. That made a difference.

One morning after he had been home about a month his mother came into his bedroom and sat on the bed. She smoothed her apron.

"I had a talk with your father last night, Harold," she said, "and he is willing for you to take the car out in the evenings."

"Yeah?" said Krebs, who was not fully awake. "Take the car out? Yeah?"

"Yes. Your father has felt for some time that you should be able to take the 20
car out in the evenings whenever you wished but we only talked it over last night."

"I'll bet you made him," Krebs said.

"No. It was your father's suggestion that we talk the matter over."

"Yeah. I'll bet you made him," Krebs sat up in bed.

"Will you come down to breakfast, Harold?" his mother said.

"As soon as I get my clothes on," Krebs said. 25

His mother went out of the room and he could hear her frying something downstairs while he washed, shaved and dressed to go down into the dining-room for breakfast. While he was eating breakfast his sister brought in the mail.

"Well, Hare," she said. "You old sleepy-head. What do you ever get up for?"

Krebs looked at her. He liked her. She was his best sister.

"Have you got the paper?" he asked.

She handed him *The Kansas City Star* and he shucked off its brown wrapper 30
and opened it to the sporting page. He folded *The Star* open and propped it against the water pitcher with his cereal dish to steady it, so he could read while he ate.

"Harold," his mother stood in the kitchen doorway, "Harold, please don't muss up the paper. You father can't read his *Star* if it's been mussed."

"I won't muss it," Krebs said.

His sister sat down at the table and watched him while he read.

"We're playing indoor° over at school this afternoon," she said. "I'm going to pitch."

indoor: that is, a softball game.

"Good," said Krebs. "How's the old wing?" 35

"I can pitch better than lots of the boys. I tell them all you taught me. The other girls aren't much good."

"Yeah?" said Krebs.

"I tell them all you're my beau. Aren't you my beau, Hare?"

"You bet."

"Couldn't your brother really be your beau just because he's your brother?" 40

"I don't know."

"Sure you know. Couldn't you be my beau, Hare, if I was old enough and if you wanted to?"

"Sure. You're my girl now."

"Am I really your girl?"

"Sure." 45

"Do you love me?"

"Uh, huh."

"Will you love me always?"

"Sure."

"Will you come over and watch me play indoor?" 50

"Maybe."

"Aw, Hare, you don't love me. If you loved me, you'd want to come over and watch me play indoor."

Krebs's mother came into the dining-room from the kitchen. She carried a plate with two fried eggs and some crisp bacon on it and a plate of buckwheat cakes.

"You run along, Helen," she said. "I want to talk to Harold."

She put eggs and bacon down in front of him and brought in a jug of 55
maple syrup for the buckwheat cakes. Then she sat down across the table from Krebs.

"I wish you'd put down the paper a minute, Harold," she said.

Krebs took down the paper and folded it.

"Have you decided what you are going to do yet, Harold?" his mother said, taking off her glasses.

"No," said Krebs.

"Don't you think it's about time?" His mother did not say this in a mean 60
way. She seemed worried.

"I hadn't thought about it," Krebs said.

"God has some work for every one to do," his mother said. "There can be no idle hands in His Kingdom."

"I'm not in His Kingdom," Krebs said.

"We are all of us in His Kingdom."

Krebs felt embarrassed and resentful as always. 65

"I've worried about you so much, Harold," his mother went on. "I know the temptations you must have been exposed to. I know how weak men are. I know what your own dear grandfather, my own father, told us about the Civil War and I have prayed for you. I pray for you all day long, Harold."

Krebs looked at the bacon fat hardening on his plate.

"Your father is worried, too," his mother went on. "He thinks you have lost your ambition, that you haven't got a definite aim in life. Charley Simmons, who is just your age, has a good job and is going to be married. The boys are all settling down; they're all determined to get somewhere; you can see that boys like Charley Simmons are on their way to being really a credit to the community."

Krebs said nothing.

"Don't look that way, Harold," his mother said. "You know we love you and   70
I want to tell you for your own good how matters stand. Your father does not want to hamper your freedom. He thinks you should be allowed to drive the car. If you want to take some of the nice girls out riding with you, we are only too pleased. We want you to enjoy yourself. But you are going to have to settle down to work, Harold. Your father doesn't care what you start in at. All work is honorable as he says. But you've got to make a start at something. He asked me to speak to you this morning and then you can stop in and see him at his office."

"Is that all?" Krebs said.

"Yes. Don't you love your mother, dear boy?"

"No," Krebs said.

His mother looked at him across the table. Her eyes were shiny. She started crying.

"I don't love anybody," Krebs said.   75

It wasn't any good. He couldn't tell her, he couldn't make her see it. It was silly to have said it. He had only hurt her. He went over and took hold of her arm. She was crying with her head in her hands.

"I didn't mean it," he said. "I was just angry at something. I didn't mean I didn't love you."

His mother went on crying. Krebs put his arm on her shoulder.

"Can't you believe me, mother?"

His mother shook her head.   80

"Please, please, mother. Please believe me."

"All right," his mother said chokily. She looked up at him. "I believe you, Harold."

Krebs kissed her hair. She put her face up to him.

"I'm your mother," she said. "I held you next to my heart when you were a tiny baby."

Krebs felt sick and vaguely nauseated.   85

"I know, Mummy," he said. "I'll try and be a good boy for you."

"Would you kneel and pray with me, Harold?" his mother asked.

They knelt down beside the dining-room table and Krebs's mother prayed.

"Now, you pray, Harold," she said.

"I can't," Krebs said.   90

"Try, Harold."

"I can't."

"Do you want me to pray for you?"

"Yes."

So his mother prayed for him and then they stood up and Krebs kissed his   95
mother and went out of the house. He had tried so to keep his life from being complicated. Still, none of it had touched him. He had felt sorry for his mother and she had made him lie. He would go to Kansas City and get a job and she would feel all right about it. There would be one more scene maybe before he got away. He would not go down to his father's office. He would miss that one. He wanted his life to go smoothly. It had just gotten going that way. Well, that

was all over now, anyway. He would go over to the schoolyard and watch Helen play indoor baseball.

QUESTIONS

1. Even though Hemingway is often praised for his specific writing, there are a number of vague passages in this story. Why does Hemingway include them? By what stylistic means does he control the vagueness?

2. Analyze Hemingway's sentences. What relationship is there between the things he describes and the length and complexity of his sentences?

3. Analyze Hemingway's descriptive style. What is the level of his diction? What words does he use for things and actions? How vivid are his descriptions?

4. Describe Harold Krebs. How do we learn about him? What does his relationship with his sister show about him? How does he change in the story?

JEROME WEIDMAN (b. 1913)

My Father Sits in the Dark   1934

My father has a peculiar habit. He is fond of sitting in the dark, alone. Sometimes I come home very late. The house is dark. I let myself in quietly because I do not want to disturb my mother. She is a light sleeper. I tiptoe into my room and undress in the dark. I go to the kitchen for a drink of water. My bare feet make no noise. I step into the room and almost trip over my father. He is sitting in a kitchen chair, in his pajamas, smoking his pipe.

"Hello, Pop," I say.

"Hello, son."

"Why don't you go to bed, Pa?"

"I will," he says.   5

But he remains there. Long after I am asleep I feel sure that he is still sitting there, smoking.

Many times I am reading in my room. I hear my mother get the house ready for the night. I hear my kid brother go to bed. I hear my sister come in. I hear her do things with jars and combs until she, too, is quiet. I know she has gone to sleep. In a little while I hear my mother say good night to my father. I continue to read. Soon I become thirsty. (I drink a lot of water.) I go to the kitchen for a drink. Again I almost stumble across my father. Many times it startles me. I forget about him. And there he is—smoking, sitting, thinking.

"Why don't you go to bed, Pop?"

"I will, son."

But he doesn't. He just sits there and smokes and thinks. It worries me. I   10 can't understand it. What can he be thinking about? Once I asked him.

"What are you thinking about, Pa?"

"Nothing," he said.

Once I left him there and went to bed. I awoke several hours later. I was thirsty. I went to the kitchen. There he was. His pipe was out. But he sat there, staring into a corner of the kitchen. After a moment I became accustomed to the darkness. I took my drink. He still sat and stared. His eyes did not blink. I thought he was not even aware of me. I was afraid.

"Why don't you go to bed, Pop?"

"I will, son," he said. "Don't wait up for me."   15

"But," I said, "you've been sitting here for hours. What's wrong? What are you thinking about?"

"Nothing, son," he said. "Nothing. It's just restful. That's all."

The way he said it was convincing. He did not seem worried. His voice was even and pleasant. It always is. But I could not understand it. How could it be restful to sit alone in an uncomfortable chair far into the night, in darkness?

What can it be?

I review all the possibilities. It can't be money. I know that. We haven't   20
much, but when he is worried about money he makes no secret of it. It can't be his health. He is not reticent about that either. It can't be the health of anyone in the family. We are a bit short on money, but we are long on health. (Knock wood, my mother would say.) What can it be? I am afraid I do not know. But that does not stop me from worrying.

Maybe he is thinking of his brothers in the old country. Or of his mother and two step-mothers. Or of his father. But they are all dead. And he would not brood about them like that. I say brood, but it is not really true. He does not brood. He does not even seem to be thinking. He looks too peaceful, too, well not contented, just too peaceful, to be brooding. Perhaps it is as he says. Perhaps it is restful. But it does not seem possible. It worries me.

If I only knew what he thinks about. If I only knew that he thinks at all. I might not be able to help him. He might not even need help. It may be as he says. It may be restful. But at least I would not worry about it.

Why does he just sit there, in the dark? Is his mind failing? No, it can't be. He is only fifty-three. And he is just as keen-witted as ever. In fact, he is the same in every respect. He still likes beet soup.° He still reads the second section of the *Times*° first. He still wears wing collars. He still believes that Debs° could have saved the country and that T.R.° was a tool of the moneyed interests. He is the same in every way. He does not even look older than he did five years ago. Everybody remarks about that. Well-preserved, they say. But he sits in the dark, alone, smoking, staring straight ahead of him, unblinking, into the small hours of the night.

If it is as he says, if it is restful, I will let it go at that. But suppose it is not. Suppose it is something I cannot fathom. Perhaps he needs help. Why doesn't he speak? Why doesn't he frown or laugh or cry? Why doesn't he do something? Why does he just sit there?

Finally I become angry. Maybe it is just my unsatisfied curiosity. Maybe I   25
am a bit worried. Anyway, I become angry.

Beet soup: that is, borscht, a staple food among Jewish immigrants from Eastern Europe.
Second section of the Times: that is, the financial pages of the *New York Times*.
Debs: Eugene Debs (1855–1926), labor leader and frequent presidential candidate, 1900–1920.
T.R.: Theodore Roosevelt (1858–1919), United States president, 1901–1909.

"Is something wrong, Pop?"

"Nothing, son. Nothing at all."

But this time I am determined not to be put off. I am angry.

"Then why do you sit here all alone, thinking, till late?"

"It's restful, son. I like it." 30

I am getting nowhere. Tomorrow he will be sitting there again. I will be puzzled. I will be worried. I will not stop now. I am angry.

"Well, what do you *think* about, Pa? Why do you just sit here? What's worrying you? What do you think about?"

"Nothing's worrying me, son. I'm all right. It's just restful. That's all. Go to bed, son."

My anger has left me. But the feeling of worry is still there. I must get an answer. It seems so silly. Why doesn't he tell me? I have a funny feeling that unless I get an answer I will go crazy. I am insistent.

"But what do you *think* about, Pa? What is it?" 35

"Nothing, son. Just things in general. Nothing special. Just things."

I can get no answer.

It is very late. The street is quiet and the house is dark. I climb the steps softly, skipping the ones that creak. I let myself in with my key and tiptoe into my room. I remove my clothes and remember that I am thirsty. In my bare feet I walk to the kitchen. Before I reach it I know he is there.

I can see the deeper darkness of his hunched shape. He is sitting in the same chair, his elbows on his knees, his cold pipe in his teeth, his unblinking eyes staring straight ahead. He does not seem to know I am there. He did not hear me come in. I stand quietly in the doorway and watch him.

Everything is quiet, but the night is full of little sounds. As I stand there 40 motionless I begin to notice them. The ticking of the alarm clock on the icebox. The low hum of an automobile passing many blocks away. The swish of papers moved along the street by the breeze. A whispering rise and fall of sound, like low breathing. It is strangely pleasant.

The dryness in my throat reminds me. I step briskly into the kitchen.

"Hello, Pop," I say.

"Hello, son," he says. His voice is low and dreamlike. He does not change his position or shift his gaze.

I cannot find the faucet. The dim shadow of light that comes through the window from the street lamp only makes the room seem darker. I reach for the short chain in the center of the room. I snap on the light.

He straightens up with a jerk, as though he has been struck. "What's the 45 matter, Pop?" I ask.

"Nothing," he says. "I don't like the light."

"What's the matter with the light?" I say. "What's wrong?"

"Nothing," he says. "I don't like the light."

I snap the light off. I drink my water slowly. I must take it easy, I say to myself. I must get to the bottom of this.

"Why don't you go to bed? Why do you sit here so late in the dark?" 50

"It's nice," he says. "I can't get used to lights. We didn't have lights when I was a boy in Europe."

My heart skips a beat and I catch my breath happily. I begin to think I understand. I remember the stories of his boyhood in Austria. I see the wide-beamed *kretchma*,° with my grandfather behind the bar. It is late, the customers are gone, and he is dozing. I see the bed of glowing coals, the last of the roaring fire. The room is already dark, and grows darker. I see a small boy, crouched on a pile of twigs at one side of the huge fireplace, his starry gaze fixed on the dull remains of the dead flames. The boy is my father.

I remember the pleasure of those few moments while I stood quietly in the doorway watching him.

"You mean there's nothing wrong? You just sit in the dark because you like it, Pop?" I find it hard to keep my voice from rising in a happy shout.

"Sure," he says. "I can't think with the light on."   55

I set my glass down and turn to go back to my room. "Good night, Pop," I say.

"Good night," he says.

Then I remember. I turn back. "What do you think about, Pop?" I ask.

His voice seems to come from far away. It is quiet and even again. "Nothing," he says softly. "Nothing special."

QUESTIONS

1. Why does Weidman use the present tense for most of the story? What function is served by the past tense? What might the story be like if it were entirely in the past tense?

2. What is the level of the narrator's prose? What connection does this level establish between the narrator and the reader? Why?

3. From the language that father and son use with each other, what do you learn about their relationship? What do the last several paragraphs show about the closeness or distance of father and son?

4. Explain the character of the father. How do paragraphs 20–24 and 46–52 explain his habit of sitting alone in the dark late at night?

ALICE MUNRO   (b. 1931)

The Found Boat   *1974*

At the end of Bell Street, McKay Street, Mayo Street, there was the Flood. It was the Wawanash River, which every spring overflowed its banks. Some springs, say one in every five, it covered the roads on that side of town and washed over the fields, creating a shallow choppy lake. Light reflected off the water made everything bright and cold, as it is in a lakeside town, and woke or revived in people certain vague hopes of disaster. Mostly during the late afternoon and early evening, there were people straggling out to look at it, and discuss whether it was still rising, and whether this time it might invade the town. In general, those under fifteen and over sixty-five were most certain that it would.

Eva and Carol rode out on their bicycles. They left the road—it was the end

kretchma: Kretscham, a German dialect word for a village tavern.

of Mayo Street, past any houses—and rode right into a field, over a wire fence entirely flattened by the weight of the winter's snow. They coasted a little way before the long grass stopped them, then left their bicycles lying down and went to the water.

"We have to find a log and ride on it," Eva said.

"Jesus, we'll freeze our legs off."

"Jesus, we'll freeze our legs off!" said one of the boys who were there too at the water's edge. He spoke in a sour whine, the way boys imitated girls although it was nothing like the way girls talked. These boys—there were three of them— were all in the same class as Eva and Carol at school and were known to them by name (their names being Frank, Bud and Clayton), but Eva and Carol, who had seen and recognized them from the road, had not spoken to them or looked at them or, even yet, given any sign of knowing they were there. The boys seemed to be trying to make a raft, from lumber they had salvaged from the water.

Eva and Carol took off their shoes and socks and waded in. The water was so cold it sent pain up their legs, like blue electric sparks shooting through their veins, but they went on, pulling their skirts high, tight behind and bunched so they could hold them in front.

"Look at the fat-assed ducks in wading."

"Fat-assed fucks."

Eva and Carol, of course, gave no sign of hearing this. They laid hold of a log and climbed on, taking a couple of boards floating in the water for paddles. There were always things floating around in the Flood—branches, fence-rails, logs, road signs, old lumber; sometimes boilers, washtubs, pots and pans, or even a car seat or stuffed chair, as if somewhere the Flood had got into a dump.

They paddled away from shore, heading out into the cold lake. The water was perfectly clear, they could see the brown grass swimming along the bottom. Suppose it was the sea, thought Eva. She thought of drowned cities and countries. Atlantis. Suppose they were riding in a Viking boat—Viking boats on the Atlantic were more frail and narrow than this log on the Flood—and they had miles of clear sea beneath them, then a spired city, intact as a jewel irretrievable on the ocean floor.

"This is a Viking boat," she said. "I am the carving on the front." She stuck her chest out and stretched her neck, trying to make a curve, and she made a face, putting out her tongue. Then she turned and for the first time took notice of the boys.

"Hey, you sucks!" she yelled at them. "You'd be scared to come out here, this water is ten feet deep!"

"Liar," they answered without interest, and she was.

They steered the log around a row of trees, avoiding floating barbed wire, and got into a little bay created by a natural hollow of the land. Where the bay was now, there would be a pond full of frogs later in the spring, and by the middle of summer there would be no water visible at all, just a low tangle of reeds and bushes, green, to show that mud was still wet around their roots. Larger bushes, willows, grew around the steep bank of this pond and were still partly out of the water. Eva and Carol let the log ride in. They saw a place where something was caught.

It was a boat, or part of one. An old rowboat with most of one side ripped out, the board that had been the seat just dangling. It was pushed up among the branches, lying on what would have been its side, if it had a side, the prow caught high.

Their idea came to them without consultation, at the same time:

"You guys! Hey, you guys!"

"We found you a boat!"

"Stop building your stupid raft and come and look at the boat!"

What surprised them in the first place was that the boys really did come, scrambling overland, half running, half sliding down the bank, wanting to see. 20

"Hey, where?"

"Where is it, I don't see no boat."

What surprised them in the second place was that when the boys did actually see what boat was meant, this old flood-smashed wreck held up in the branches, they did not understand that they had been fooled, that a joke had been played on them. They did not show a moment's disappointment, but seemed as pleased at the discovery as if the boat had been whole and new. They were already barefoot, because they had been wading in the water to get lumber, and they waded in here without a stop, surrounding the boat and appraising it and paying no attention even of an insulting kind to Eva and Carol who bobbed up and down on their log. Eva and Carol had to call to them.

"How do you think you're going to get it off?"

"It won't float anyway." 25

"What makes you think it will float?"

"It'll sink. Glub-blub-blub, you'll all be drownded."

The boys did not answer, because they were too busy walking around the boat, pulling at it in a testing way to see how it could be got off with the least possible damage. Frank, who was the most literate, talkative and inept of the three, began referring to the boat as *she*, an affectation which Eva and Carol acknowledged with fish-mouths of contempt.

"She's caught two places. You got to be careful not to tear a hole in her bottom. She's heavier than you'd think."

It was Clayton who climbed up and freed the boat, and Bud, a tall fat boy, 30 who got the weight of it on his back to turn it into the water so that they could half float, half carry it to shore. All this took some time. Eva and Carol abandoned their log and waded out of the water. They walked overland to get their shoes and socks and bicycles. They did not need to come back this way but they came. They stood at the top of the hill, leaning on their bicycles. They did not go on home, but they did not sit down and frankly watch, either. They stood more or less facing each other, but glancing down at the water and at the boys struggling with the boat, as if they had just halted for a moment out of curiosity, and staying longer than they intended, to see what came of this unpromising project.

About nine o'clock, or when it was nearly dark—dark to people inside the houses, but not quite dark outside—they all returned to town, going along Mayo Street in a sort of procession. Frank and Bud and Clayton came carrying the boat, upside-down, and Eva and Carol walked behind, wheeling their bicycles. The boys' heads were almost hidden in the darkness of the overturned boat, with its smell of soaked wood, cold swampy water. The girls could look ahead and see the street lights in their tin reflectors, a necklace of lights climbing Mayo Street, reaching all the way up to the standpipe. They turned onto Burns Street heading for Clayton's house, the nearest house belonging to any of them. This was not the way home for Eva or for Carol either, but they followed along. The boys were perhaps too busy carrying the boat to tell them to go away. Some younger children were still out playing, playing hopscotch on the sidewalk though they could hardly see. At this time of year the bare sidewalk was still such a novelty and delight. These children cleared out of the way and watched the boat go by with unwilling respect; they shouted questions after it, wanting to know where it came from and what was going to be done with it. No one answered them. Eva and Carol as well as the boys refused to answer or even look at them.

The five of them entered Clayton's yard. The boys shifted weight, as if they were going to put the boat down.

"You better take it round to the back where nobody can see it," Carol said. That was the first thing any of them had said since they came into town.

The boys said nothing but went on, following a mud path between Clayton's house and a leaning board fence. They let the boat down in the back yard.

"It's a stolen boat, you know," said Eva, mainly for the effect. "It must've belonged to somebody. You stole it."   35

"You was the ones who stole it then," Bud said, short of breath. "It was you seen it first."

"It was you took it."

"It was all of us then. If one of us gets in trouble then all of us does."

"Are you going to tell anybody on them?" said Carol as she and Eva rode home, along the streets which were dark between the lights now and potholed from winter.

"It's up to you, I won't if you won't."   40

"I won't if you won't."

They rode in silence, relinquishing something, but not discontented.

The board fence in Clayton's back yard had every so often a post which supported it, or tried to, and it was on these posts that Eva and Carol spent several evenings sitting, jauntily but not very comfortably. Or else they just leaned against the fence while the boys worked on the boat. During the first couple of evenings neighborhood children attracted by the sound of hammering tried to get into the yard to see what was going on, but Eva and Carol blocked their way.

"Who said you could come in here?"

"Just us can come in this yard."   45

These evenings were getting longer, the air milder. Skipping was starting on the sidewalks. Further along the street there was a row of hard maples that had been tapped. Children drank the sap as fast as it could drip into the buckets. The old man and woman who owned the trees, and who hoped to make syrup, came running out of the house making noises as if they were trying to scare away crows. Finally, every spring, the old man would come out on his porch and fire his shotgun into the air, and then the thieving would stop.

None of those working on the boat bothered about stealing sap, though all had done so last year.

The lumber to repair the boat was picked up here and there, along back lanes. At this time of year things were lying around—old boards and branches, sodden mitts, spoons flung out with the dishwater, lids of pudding pots that had been set in the snow to cool, all the debris that can sift through and survive winter. The tools came from Clayton's cellar—left over, presumably, from the time when his father was alive—and though they had nobody to advise them the boys seemed to figure out more or less the manner in which boats are built, or rebuilt. Frank was the one who showed up with diagrams from books and *Popular Mechanics* magazines. Clayton looked at these diagrams and listened to Frank read the instructions and then went ahead and decided in his own way what was to be done. Bud was best at sawing. Eva and Carol watched everything from the fence and offered criticism and thought up names. The names for the boat that they thought of were: Water Lily, Sea Horse, Flood Queen, and Caro-Eve, after them because they had found it. The boys did not say which, if any, of these names they found satisfactory.

The boat had to be tarred. Clayton heated up a pot of tar on the kitchen stove and brought it out and painted slowly, his thorough way, sitting astride the overturned boat. The other boys were sawing a board to make a new seat. As Clayton worked, the tar cooled and thickened so that finally he could not move the brush any more. He turned to Eva and held out the pot and said, "You can go in and heat this on the stove."

Eva took the pot and went up the back steps. The kitchen seemed black   50 after outside, but it must be light enough to see in, because there was Clayton's mother standing at the ironing board, ironing. She did that for a living, took in wash and ironing.

"Please may I put the tar pot on the stove?" said Eva, who had been brought up to talk politely to parents, even wash-and-iron ladies, and who for some reason especially wanted to make a good impression on Clayton's mother.

"You'll have to poke up the fire then," said Clayton's mother, as if she doubted whether Eva would know how to do that. But Eva could see now, and she picked up the lid with the stove-lifter, and took the poker and poked up a flame. She stirred the tar as it softened. She felt privileged. Then and later. Before she went to sleep a picture of Clayton came to her mind; she saw him sitting astride the boat, tar-painting, with such concentration, delicacy, absorption. She thought of him speaking to her, out of his isolation, in such an ordinary peaceful taking-for-granted voice.

On the twenty-fourth of May, a school holiday in the middle of the week, the boat was carried out of town, a long way now, off the road over fields and fences that had been repaired, to where the river flowed between its normal banks. Eva and Carol, as well as the boys, took turns carrying it. It was launched in the water from a cow-trampled spot between willow bushes that were fresh out in leaf. The boys went first. They yelled with triumph when the boat did float, when it rode amazingly down the river current. The boat was painted black, and green inside, with yellow seats, and a strip of yellow all the way around the outside. There was no name on it, after all. The boys could not imagine that it needed any name to keep it separate from the other boats in the world.

Eva and Carol ran along the bank, carrying bags full of peanut butter-and-jam sandwiches, pickles, bananas, chocolate cake, potato chips, graham crackers stuck together with corn syrup and five bottles of pop to be cooled in the river water. The bottles bumped against their legs. They yelled for a turn.   55

"If they don't let us they're bastards," Carol said, and they yelled together. "We found it! We found it!"

The boys did not answer, but after a while they brought the boat in, and Carol and Eva came crashing, panting down the bank.

"Does it leak?"

"It don't leak yet."

"We forgot a bailing can," wailed Carol, but nevertheless she got in, with Eva, and Frank pushed them off, crying. "Here's to a Watery Grave!"

And the thing about being in a boat was that it was not solidly bobbing, like a log, but was cupped in the water, so that riding in it was not like being on something in the water, but like being in the water itself. Soon they were all going out in the boat in mixed-up turns, two boys and a girl, two girls and a boy, a girl and a boy, until things were so confused it was impossible to tell whose turn came next, and nobody cared anyway. They went down the river—those who weren't riding, running along the bank to keep up. They passed under two bridges, one iron, one cement. Once they saw a big carp just resting, it seemed to smile at them, in the bridge-shaded water. They did not know how far they had gone on the river, but things had changed—the water had got shallower, and the land flatter. Across an open field they saw a building that looked like a house, abandoned. They dragged the boat up on the bank and tied it and set out across the field.

"That's the old station," Frank said. "That's Pedder Station." The others had heard this name but he was the one who knew, because his father was the station agent in town. He said that this was a station on a branch line that had been torn up, and that there had been a sawmill here, but a long time ago.

Inside the station it was dark, cool. All the windows were broken. Glass lay in shards and in fairly big pieces on the floor. They walked around finding the larger pieces of glass and tramping on them, smashing them, it was like cracking ice on puddles. Some partitions were still in place, you could see where the ticket window had been. There was a bench lying on its side. People had been here, it looked as if people came here all the time, though it was so far from anywhere. Beer bottles and pop bottles were lying around, also cigarette packages, gum and candy wrappers, the paper from a loaf of bread. The walls were covered with dim and fresh pencil and chalk writings and carved with knives.

I LOVE RONNIE COLES

I WANT TO FUCK

KILROY WAS HERE

RONNIE COLES IS AN ASS-HOLE

WHAT ARE YOU DOING HERE?

WAITING FOR A TRAIN

DAWNA MARY-LOU BARBARA JOANNE

It was exciting to be inside this large, dark, empty place, with the loud noise of breaking glass and their voices ringing back from the underside of the roof. They tipped the old beer bottles against their mouths. That reminded them that they were hungry and thirsty and they cleared a place in the middle of the floor and sat down and ate the lunch. They drank the pop just as it was, lukewarm. They ate everything there was and licked the smears of peanut butter and jam off the bread-paper in which the sandwiches had been wrapped.

They played Truth or Dare.

"I dare you to write on the wall, I am a Stupid Ass, and sign your name."

"Tell the truth—what is the worst lie you ever told?"

"Did you ever wet the bed?"

"Did you ever dream you were walking down the street without any clothes on?"

"I dare you to go outside and pee on the railway sign."

It was Frank who had to do that. They could not see him, even his back,   70
but they knew he did it, they heard the hissing sound of his pee. They all sat still,
amazed, unable to think of what the next dare would be.

"I dare everybody," said Frank from the doorway. "I dare—Everybody."

"What?"

"Take off all our clothes."

Eva and Carol screamed.

"Anybody who won't do it has to walk—has to *crawl*—around this floor on   75
their hands and knees."

They were all quiet, till Eva said, almost complacently, "What first?"

"Shoes and socks."

"Then we have to go outside, there's too much glass here."

They pulled off their shoes and socks in the doorway, in the sudden blinding
sun. The field before them was bright as water. They ran across where the tracks
used to go.

"That's enough, that's enough," said Carol. "Watch out for thistles!"   80

"Tops! Everybody take off their tops!"

"I won't! We won't, will we, Eva?"

But Eva was whirling round and round in the sun where the track used to
be. "I don't care, I don't care! Truth or Dare! Truth or Dare!"

She unbuttoned her blouse as she whirled, as if she didn't know what her
hand was doing, she flung it off.

Carol took off hers. "I wouldn't have done it, if you hadn't!"   85

"Bottoms!"

Nobody said a word this time, they all bent and stripped themselves. Eva,
naked first, started running across the field, and then all the others ran, all five
of them running bare through the knee-high hot grass, running towards the river.
Not caring now about being caught but in fact leaping and yelling to call attention
to themselves, if there was anybody to hear or see. They felt as if they were going
to jump off a cliff and fly. They felt that something was happening to them
different from anything that had happened before, and it had to do with the boat,
the water, the sunlight, the dark ruined station, and each other. They thought of
each other now hardly as names or people, but as echoing shrieks, reflections, all
bold and white and loud and scandalous, and as fast as arrows. They went running
without a break into the cold water and when it came almost to the tops of their
legs they fell on it and swam. It stopped their noise. Silence, amazement, came
over them in a rush. They dipped and floated and separated, sleek as mink.

Eva stood up in the water her hair dripping, water running down her face.
She was waist deep. She stood on smooth stones, her feet fairly wide apart, water
flowing between her legs. About a yard away from her Clayton also stood up, and
they were blinking the water out of their eyes, looking at each other. Eva did not
turn or try to hide; she was quivering from the cold of the water, but also with
pride, shame, boldness, and exhilaration.

Clayton shook his head violently, as if he wanted to bang something out of
it, then bent over and took a mouthful of river water. He stood up with his cheeks
full and made a tight hole of his mouth and shot the water at her as if it was
coming out of a hose, hitting her exactly, first one breast and then the other.
Water from his mouth ran down her body. He hooted to see it, a loud self-

conscious sound that nobody would have expected, from him. The others looked
up from wherever they were in the water and closed in to see.

Eva crouched down and slid into the water, letting her head go right under. 90
She swam, and when she let her head out, downstream, Carol was coming after
her and the boys were already on the bank, already running into the grass, showing
their skinny backs, their white, flat buttocks. They were laughing and saying things
to each other but she couldn't hear, for the water in her ears.

"What did he do?" said Carol.

"Nothing."

They crept in to shore. "Let's stay in the bushes till they go," said Eva. "I
hate them anyway. I really do. Don't you hate them?"

"Sure," said Carol, and they waited, not very long, until they heard the boys
still noisy and excited coming down to the place a bit upriver where they had left
the boat. They heard them jump in and start rowing.

"They've got all the hard part, going back," said Eva, hugging herself and 95
shivering violently. "Who cares? Anyway. It never was our boat."

"What if they tell?" said Carol.

"We'll say it's all a lie."

Eva hadn't thought of this solution until she said it, but as soon as she did
she felt almost light-hearted again. The ease and scornfulness of it did make them
both giggle, and slapping themselves and splashing out of the water they set about
developing one of those fits of laughter in which, as soon as one showed signs of
exhaustion, the other would snort and start up again, and they would make
helpless—soon genuinely helpless—faces at each other and bend over and grab
themselves as if they had the worst pain.

QUESTIONS

1. Consider the details used in passages of description in the story. What kinds
    of details are included?

2. What is the level of diction in the dialogue of the story? From the dialogue,
    what do you learn about the various speakers?

3. Study paragraph 10. What does the paragraph tell you about Eva as a
    limited-point-of-view center of interest? How?

4. Consider the last paragraph in the story as a paragraph of action. What
    verbs are used and how well do they help you visualize and imagine the
    sounds of the scene? What is the effect of the verb "snort"?

5. From the lifestyle and artifacts mentioned, what do you learn about the time
    of the events and the economic level of the town? What is the effect of the
    facts that it is early springtime, that the water is still cold, but that in May
    the water is swimmable? What are the implications for summer?

WRITING ABOUT STYLE

In prewriting, you should consider the selected passage in the context of
the entire story. If you can answer questions such as the following, you

will readily assemble materials for your essay on the style of a passage from a story.

Questions for Discovering Ideas

What sort of passage is it? Narrative? Descriptive? Does it contain dialogue?

Is there a speaker with clearly established characteristics? How does the passage reflect his or her personality?

Do you need a dictionary to discover the meaning of any words? Are there any unusual words? Any especially difficult or uncommon words? Do any of the words distract you?

Is there any slang? Are any words used only in particular occupations or ways of life (such as technical words about horses, words from other languages, and so on)? Are there any contractions? Do they indicate a conversational, intimate level of speech?

Are the words the most common ones that might be used? Can you think of more difficult ones? Easier ones? More accurate ones? Are there many short words? Long words?

Can you easily imagine the situations described by the words? If you have difficulty, to what degree does it stem out of the level of diction?

Are the sentences long or short? Is there any variation in length? Can you observe any relationship between length and topic material?

Are the sentences simple, compound, or complex? Does one type predominate? Why?

Are there any noteworthy rhetorical devices? Are there any sentences that are *periodic* as opposed to *loose*? What effect is gained by this sentence or sentences? What other rhetorical devices are used? How are they used? What is their effect?

Strategies for Organizing Ideas

In your essay you should describe and evaluate the style of the passage. Always remember to consider the style in relationship to the other circumstances of the work. For example, suppose the speaker has just returned home after a long and painful journey, or has just finished a race with a close competitor, or is recalling an event of the long-distant past, or is anticipating future happiness or frustration. Throughout your analysis, you should keep such conditions constantly in mind.

To focus your essay, you might wish to single out one aspect of style, or to discuss everything, depending on the length of the assignment. Be sure to treat things like *levels of diction*, categories like *specific-general* or *concrete-abstract*, the degree of *simplicity* or *complexity*, *length*, *numbers* of words (an approach that is relatively easy for a beginning), and *denotation-connotation*. In discussing rhetorical aspects, go as far as you can with the nomenclature at your command. Consider things like sentence types and rhetorical devices you can describe. If you can draw attention to the elements in a parallel structure by using grammatical terms, do so. If you are able to detect the ways in which the sentences are kept simple or made complex, describe these ways. Be sure to use examples from the passage to illustrate your point; indent them and leave spaces between them and your own material.

The sort of essay envisaged here is designed to sharpen your levels of awareness at your own stage of development as a reader. Later, to the degree that you will have gained sharper perceptions and a wider descriptive vocabulary, you will be able to enhance the sophistication of your analyses.

In your conclusion, make evaluations of the author's style. To what extent has your analysis increased or reinforced your appreciation of the author's technique? Does the passage take on any added importance as a result of your study? Is there anything elsewhere in the work comparable to the content, words, or ideas that you have discussed in the passage?

Numbers for Easy Reference

Include a copy of your passage at the beginning of your essay, as in the example. For your reader's convenience, number the sentences in the passage, and use these numbers as they become relevant in your essay.

SAMPLE ESSAY

Mark Twain's Blending of Style and Purpose in "Luck"°

[1] The battle was awfully hot; the allies were steadily giving way all over the field. [2] Our regiment occupied a position that was vital; a blunder now must be destruction. [3] At this crucial moment, what [14] does this immortal fool do but detach the regiment from its place and order a charge over a neighboring hill where there wasn't a suggestion of an enemy! [4] "There you go!" I said to myself; "this *is* the end at last."

[5] And away we did go, and were over the shoulder of the hill before the insane movement could be discovered and stopped. [6] And what did we find? [7] An entire and unsuspected Russian army in reserve! [8] And what happened? [9] We were eaten up? [10] That is necessarily what would have happened in ninety-nine cases out of a hundred. [11] But no; those Russians argued that no single regiment would come browsing around there at such a time. [12] It must be the entire English army, and that the sly Russian game was detected and [15] blocked; so they turned tail, and away they went, pell-mell, over the hill and down into the field, in wild confusion, and we after them; they themselves broke the solid Russian center in the field, and tore through, and in no time there was the most tremendous rout you ever saw, and the

° See p. 275 for this story.

defeat of the allies was turned into a sweeping and splendid victory! [13] Marshall Canrobert looked on, dizzy with astonishment, admiration, and delight; and sent right off for Scoresby, and hugged him, and decorated him on the field in presence of all the armies!

[1].   Appearing close to the end of "Luck," these two paragraphs are important in Twain's satiric design to puncture the bubble of Scoresby, a widely recognized and decorated British hero who is nothing more than a lucky boob. In the story, the paragraphs come as a climax. By presenting a brief account of a decisive battle in the Crimean War, in which Scoresby's regiment figures prominently, they bring out his stupidity and luck to the highest degree. Though the passages are narrative, the mark of Twain's style is to underscore how the hero's blundering foolishness is always saved by luck.* In every respect--description, word level, use of general and abstract diction, grammatical patterns, and the narrator's involvement--the passage embodies Twain's satiric and comic goal.†

[2]   The descriptions in the paragraphs are directed toward the idiocy of the main character. In fact, the descriptions are not about the battle at all. The military matter presented in the thirteen sentences is that the allies are giving way, that Scoresby orders a charge, and that the Russians turn tail and dash away. There is no report of clashing soldiers and dying men and horses beyond the claim that the Russians themselves "tore through" their own ranks, and there are no vivid words, beyond these, describing the circumstances of victory. Indeed, the descriptions are minimal, containing just enough to exemplify Scoresby's lucky blunder, but no more. The paragraphs would be unsuccessful as an account of a battle, but as part of this story they serve Twain's purpose superbly.

[3]   In keeping with the exposé, Twain uses a middle, or neutral, level of diction. The words are not unusual or difficult. What could be more ordinary, for example, than words like *battle, awfully, steadily, occupied, discovered, stopped, argued,* and *victory*? One may grant that *splendid, astonishment, pell-mell, immortal,* and *crucial* are not common in everyday speech, but in this context they are appropriate, for they fall within the vocabulary of responses to battle. Because of their aptness, they enable the reader to focus on the subject and on the narrator's expressions of humor, and in this respect they fit the middle level of diction.

[4]   Not only is the level neutral, but many words are general and abstract, in accord with the intention of the story to debunk Scoresby. The "allies were steadily giving way," for example, and the "movement" of many individuals is described as "insane." These broad words are fitting for groups and mass actions, but not for specific individuals. When the Russians conclude from Scoresby's senseless charge that their "game" is "detected," they turn "tail" and run "pell-mell," dashing in such "wild confusion" that there is "the most tremendous rout you ever saw," resulting in "sweeping and splendid victory"-- all general and abstract words. Even the "hero," Scoresby, is not detailed anywhere as a specific leader and fighter; it is as though he is less significant than the gigantic forces of blind stupidity he unleashes. The last sentence of

* Central idea.
† Thesis sentence.

the paragraphs, the thirteenth, continues in this mode with the abstract but worshipful responses of the commander, Marshall Canrobert; he is "dizzy with astonishment, admiration, and delight." These abstract words reflect the public renown of Scoresby, which we, as the narrator's listeners, know to be misplaced. Both general and abstract words thus jell perfectly with Twain's debunking humor.

[5] Grammatically, as well, there is great emphasis on the contrast between Scoresby's stupidity and his success. Twain's first two sentences are neatly balanced with contrasting ideas: Sentence 1 tells us that the battle is "hot" (part 1) and that the allies are losing (part 2). Sentence 2 tells us that the regiment is important (part 1) and that a mistake would be disastrous (part 2). But as the battle descends into the sweeping chaos caused by the charge of Scoresby's regiment, the grammar takes on the same chaotic pattern. Sentence 12, containing all the battle details, is eighty-one words long. It is broken up by semicolons and commas into a variety of separate statements and structures describing the pell-mell retreat and victory. In other words, the sentence has the same wildness, sweep, and madness of the events being described--a blending of grammar and subject.

[6] The major quality of Twain's style in the passage, however, is the amused, debunking language contributed directly by the narrator. The narrator's ideas keep the passage short, and his words frame the suspense and anticlimax of the battle, as is shown in the first paragraph (sentences 1–4). He tells us (sentence 3) that the "immortal fool" orders a mistaken charge. His lamenting prediction, "this is the end at last" (sentence 4), is designed for full dramatic and suspenseful effect. The narrator's involvement is also shown by his simply phrased questions just before he tells about the results of the charge: "And what did we find?" "And what happened?" "We were eaten up?" His continual effect on the language is apparent in his reconstruction of the military logic of the Russians, and his attitude is most amusingly shown by the word "browsing" (sentence 11) which suggests grazing animals, not charging armies. This word emphasizes the dimwittedness of Scoresby's command to attack. Throughout the paragraphs, the speaker thus lends his own wry insights to the language. The skill, naturally, belongs to Twain.

[7] In all respects, the passage is a model of the right use of words in the right places. If the writing were about an actual military combat, it would be poor. But because it is part of a comic exposé of a fortunate fool, it is hard to imagine a better way to put things. Twain's speaker gives us what we need to know: namely that Scoresby has a Midas touch in everything he does, no matter how potentially disastrous. The sentences are clear and direct, and convey the facts about Scoresby that show his imbecility. Even the longest and most confused sentence, the twelfth, is appropriate to the confusion that Scoresby converts to triumph. For these reasons, the paragraphs are examples of accurate, purposeful narrative prose.

Commentary on the Essay

This essay shows how separate stylistic topics may be unified. Important in this objective are the transitions from paragraph to paragraph, such as "not only . . . but," "in keeping with the exposé," "as well," and "in all respects." These transition phrases enable reader concentration to move smoothly from one topic to the next.

The beginning of the essay demonstrates the importance of relating the passage being studied to the work as a whole. Because the central idea is connected to Twain's debunking objective, the point is made that style and satiric intention are merged and integrated.

In the body, paragraph 2 treats the absence of specifically descriptive words, explaining this lack by reference to the satiric subject. Paragraph 3 treats the neutral diction, making the point that this language is appropriate because it permits a direct focus on the asinine blunders of the major character. Twain's use of general and abstract language is treated in paragraph 4, the point being that this language is appropriate because the story exposes the emptyheadedness of Scoresby. In paragraph 5, the subject is the grammar of the passage, indicating that the movement from balance to chaos complements the chaos of the battle. Paragraph 6, the last of the body, is designed as the high point of the discussion of style, asserting that the most important aspect of the writing is the narrative speaker. It is this speaker whose ideas and words permit Twain to keep the narrative brief while emphasizing his hero's blundering stupidity. Paragraph 7, the last, is a tribute to Twain's style, emphasizing again how his satiric objective governs word choices.

WRITING TOPICS

1. Write an essay on the differences in style between the two narrators in "Luck." What purpose do the two narrators serve?

2. Write an essay that answers the following questions: To what degree are the narrative and descriptive styles of "Soldier's Home" appropriate to the nature of the story? What would be the effect on the story if the style of Faulkner in "Barn Burning" (Chapter 4), or Updike in "A & P" (Chapter 2), or Whitecloud in "Blue Winds Dancing" (Chapter 3) were used?

3. "The Found Boat" is characterized by full descriptions, so that the reader needs to imagine few details. Would this style be appropriate in "My Father Sits in the Dark"? Why or why not?

4. Write two brief character sketches, or a description of an action, to be included in a longer story. Make the first favorable, and the second negative. Analyze your word choices in the contrasting accounts: What kinds of words do you select, and on what principles do you select them? On the basis of your answers, what can you conclude about the development of a fiction writer's style?

8

Tone: Attitude and Control in Fiction

Tone refers to the methods by which writers and speakers reveal attitudes or feelings. It is an aspect of everything spoken and written, such as earnest declarations of love, requests to pass a dish at dinner, or letters from government offices threatening penalties if fines are not paid. Because tone is often equated with *attitude*, it is important to realize that tone refers *not* to attitudes themselves but rather to those techniques and modes of presentation that *reveal* or *create* attitudes.

The concept of *tone* is borrowed from the phrase *tone of voice* in speech. Tone of voice reflects attitudes toward a particular object or situation, and also toward listeners. Let us suppose that Mary has a difficult assignment, on which she expects to work all day. Things go well, and she finishes quickly. She happily tells her friend Anne, "I'm so pleased. I needed only two hours for that." Then she decides to buy tickets for a popular play, and must wait through a long and slow line. After getting her tickets, she tells the people at the end of the line, "I'm so pleased. I needed only two hours for that." The sentences are the same, but by changing her emphasis, Mary indicates her impatience with her long wait, and also shows her sympathy with the people still in line. By controlling the *tone* of her statements, in other words, Mary conveys totally different attitudes.

TONE WITHIN STORIES

As this story about Mary indicates, an attitude itself may be summarized with a word or phrase (satisfaction, indignation; love, contempt; deference, command; and so on), but the study of tone examines those aspects of situation, language, action, and background that *bring out* the attitude. In Poe's "The Masque of the Red Death," for example, Prince Prospero declares outrage at the intruder costumed as the Red Death. His words indicate anger and intimidation:

> "Who dares"—he demanded hoarsely of the courtiers who stood near him—"who dares insult us with this blasphemous mockery? Seize him and unmask him—that we may know whom we have to hang, at sunrise, from the battlements!" (paragraph 11)

Prospero's commands show that he is judge, jury, and executioner, and gives no chance for appeal. In contrast, at the end of "A Worn Path," the attendant offers Phoenix "a few pennies," but Phoenix wants more. A recipient of charity, but also an independent sort, Phoenix makes her request indirectly (paragraph 99):

> "Five pennies is a nickel," said Phoenix stiffly.

This request is less imperious than Prince Prospero's, but it is nevertheless demanding. Though Phoenix is not a literary master, she is a master of tone in this conversational situation.

TONE AND AUTHORIAL ATTITUDES

THE APPARENT AUTHORIAL ATTITUDE TOWARD THE MATERIAL.   By reading a story carefully, we may discover the author's attitude or attitudes toward the subject matter. In "The Story of an Hour," for example, Kate Chopin sympathetically portrays a young wife's secret wishes for freedom, just as she also humorously reveals the unwitting smugness that often pervades men's relationships with women. In "The Hammon and the Beans," Parédes shows revulsion against the effects of poverty, and pity for the dead young girl who might have been saved with proper health care. In a broader perspective, authors may create situations and characters that indicate amused affection (Atwood's "Rape Fantasies") or deep admiration (Williams's "Taking Care"). A vitally important authorial tone is that of irony (see pp. 303–05).

THE APPARENT AUTHORIAL ATTITUDE TOWARD READERS.   Authors recognize that readers are participants in the creative act, and that all elements of a story—word choice, characterization, allusiveness, levels of reality—must take reader response into account. When Hawthorne's woodland guide in "Young Goodman Brown" refers to King Philip's War, for example (p. 334), Hawthorne assumes that his readers know that this war was savagely greedy and cruel. By not explaining this part of history, he indicates respect for the knowledge of his readers, and he also assumes identity with readers by relying on their agreement with his interpretation.

Authors always make similar considerations about readers, by implicitly complimenting them on their knowledge and also by satisfying their desire to be interested, stimulated, and pleased. Updike in "A & P" (p. 65) assumes that readers understand his use of Sammy's diction to reveal Sammy as a perceptive and independent but insecure young man. In "Soldier's Home," Hemingway assumes that readers connect Krebs's discontent with the viciousness and frustration of trench warfare in World War I. Such authorial consideration for readers is a vital aspect of tone.

THE FICTIONAL EXPRESSION OF ATTITUDES

Beyond general authorial tone, there are many dramatically rendered expressions of attitude. For example, Alan's farewell in Collier's "The Chaser" (see the sample essay, p. 322), is "Thank you again. . . . Goodbye." This is courteous and ordinary speech, and it suggests that Alan is still uncomplicated and unsophisticated. In contrast, however, the old man responds with the words "Au revoir," a French phrase meaning "until we meet again." Although this salutation is not uncommon, it indicates the old man's cynicism, for he has been telling Alan about an untraceable and deadly poison. His implication is that Alan will one day get tired of his sweetheart, and then will return to buy the poison to kill her. Thus, these two statements of farewell, as ordinary as they are, are ominous.

In addition, characters interact, and their tone dramatically shows their judgments about other characters and situations. The brusque young woman in Mansfield's "Miss Brill" (p. 211) compares Miss Brill's fur muff to a "fried whiting," an insult that she makes sure Miss Brill herself hears (paragraph 14). Her speech indicates contempt, indifference, and cruelty. A complicated control of tone occurs in Glaspell's "A Jury of Her Peers," where the two major characters, Mrs. Hale and Mrs. Peters, decide to cover up the conclusive evidence that Minnie Wright has murdered her husband. When Mrs. Peters agrees to this obstruction of justice, however, she speaks innocently and offhandedly about the possible embarrassment of the situation:

> "My!" she began, in a high, false voice, "it's a good thing the men couldn't hear us! Getting all stirred up over a little thing like a—dead canary." She hurried over that. "As if that could have anything to do with— with— My, wouldn't they *laugh*?" (paragraph 267)

Notice that she does not make any statement violating legal principles. Instead, she takes advantage of her knowledge that men scoff at feminine things, like Minnie's quilting knots, and therefore she anticipates the men's amusement. But we know that by these words she has joined Mrs. Hale in sympathizing with Minnie and in hiding the evidence.

LAUGHTER, COMEDY, AND FARCE

A major aspect of tone is laughter and the methods of comedy and farce. Everyone likes to laugh, but not everyone can explain laughter. It is clear that smiles, shared laughter, and good human relationships go together, so that laughter is essential to mental health. Laughter is unplanned, often unpredictable, personal, and idiosyncratic. It resists close analysis. Despite the difficulty of explaining laughter, however, we may note a number of common elements:

1. *An object to laugh at.* There must be something to laugh at, whether a person, thing, situation, custom, a habit of speech or dialect, or an arrangement of words.

2. *Incongruity.* Human beings normally know what to expect under given conditions, and anything contrary to these expectations is *incongruous* and may therefore generate laughter. When the temperature is 100°F, for example, you expect people to dress lightly. If you see a person dressed in a heavy overcoat, a warm hat, a muffler, and large gloves, who is waving his arms and stamping his feet to keep warm, this person violates your expectations. Because his garments and behavior are *inappropriate* or *incongruous*, you would probably laugh at him. A student in a language class once wrote about the "congregation of verbs." This inadvertent verbal mistake is called a **malapropism,** after Mrs. Malaprop, a character in Sheridan's eighteenth-century play *The Rivals.* He meant the "conjugation" of verbs, of course, but used a word more appropriate to people in church than to a grammatical list. Incongruity is common to these laughter-producing examples. In the literary creation of such verbal slips, the tone is directed against the speaker, for the amusement of both readers and author alike.

3. *Safety and/or goodwill.* Seeing a person slipping on a banana peel and hurtling through the air may cause laughter as long as we ourselves are not that person, for laughter depends on insulation from danger and pain. In farce, where much physical abuse takes place (such as falling through trapdoors or being hit in the face by cream pies), the abuse never harms the participants. The incongruity of such situations causes laughter, and immunity from pain and injury prevents grave or even horrified responses. Goodwill enters into laughter in romantic comedy or in any other work where you are drawn into general sympathy with the major figures, such as Rosie and Vlashkin in Paley's "Goodbye and Good Luck" (p. 498). As the author leads the characters toward recognizing their love, your involvement produces happiness, smiles, and even sympathetic laughter.

4. *Unfamiliarity, newness, uniqueness, spontaneity.* Laughter depends on seeing something new or unique, or on experiencing a known thing freshly. Because laughter is prompted by flashes of insight, or sudden revelations, it is always spontaneous, but it is not lost just because a thing

is well known. Indeed, the task of the comic writer is to develop ordinary materials to a point when spontaneity frees readers to laugh. Thus, it is possible to read and reread O'Connor's "First Confession" (p. 487) and laugh each time because, even though you know what happens, the story shapes your acceptance of how reconciliation penetrates a wall of anger and guilt. Young Jackie's experience is and always will be comic because it is so spontaneous and incongruous.

IRONY

One of the most human traits is the capacity to have two or more attitudes toward someone or something. We know that people are not perfect, but we love a number of them anyway. Therefore we speak to them not only with love and praise, but also with banter and criticism. On occasion, you may have given mildly insulting greeting cards to your loved ones, in the expectation of amusing rather than affronting them. As you share smiles and laughs, you also remind them of your affection.

The word **irony** describes such contradictory statements or situations. Irony is natural to human beings who are aware of life's ambiguities and complexities. It develops from the realization that life does not always measure up to promise, that friends and loved ones are sometimes angry and bitter toward each other, that the universe contains incomprehensible mysteries, that doubt exists even in the certainty of knowledge and faith, and that human character is built through chagrin, regret, and pain as much as through emulation and praise. In expressing an idea ironically, writers pay the greatest compliment to their readers, for they assume that readers have sufficient skill and understanding to discover the real meaning of quizzical or ambiguous statements and situations.

The major types of irony are *verbal, situational,* and *dramatic.* In **verbal irony** one thing is said and another is meant. For example, one of the American astronauts was asked how he would feel if his safety equipment broke down during reentry. He answered, "A thing like that could ruin your whole day." His words would have been appropriate for day-to-day minor mishaps, but since failed safety equipment would cause his death, his answer was ironic (doubly so since the loss in 1986 of the space shuttle *Challenger*). This form of verbal irony is **understatement.** By contrast, **overstatement,** or **hyperbole,** is deliberate exaggeration for effect, as in the priest's responses to the boy Jackie in "First Confession" (p. 491, paragraphs 38–50). While the priest makes his hyperbolic responses to Jackie's confessions of planned slaughter, readers smile, chuckle, and laugh.

Often verbal irony is ambiguous, having double meaning or **double entendre.** Midway through "Young Goodman Brown," for example, the woodland guide leaves Brown alone while stating, "when you feel like moving again, there is my staff to help you along" (paragraph 40). The word "staff" is ambiguous, for it refers to the staff that resembles a serpent (paragraph 13). The word therefore suggests that the devilish guide is leaving Brown not only with a real staff, but also with the spirit of evil (unlike the divine "staff" of Psalm 23 that gives comfort). Ambiguity of course may be used in relation to any topic. Quite often double entendre is used in statements about sexuality and love, usually for the amusement of listeners or readers.

The term **situational irony,** or **irony of situation,** refers to conditions emphasizing that human beings have little or no control over their lives or anything else. The forces of opposition may be psychological, social, cultural, political, or environmental. In Atwood's "Rape Fantasies," for example, the narrator Estelle states her inability to understand why men cannot be satisfied by human relationships with women rather than rapacious ones. Though "Rape Fantasies" is not a sociological document, Estelle's uneasiness underscores the irony of the political and social conditions that produce rape. The situational irony of traditional marriage is brought out in Chopin's "The Story of an Hour." Because Louise Mallard, the main character, believes that her husband's death has released her from her servile role as wife, her heart fails when she sees her husband alive. The irony is that the doctors conclude that her death results from the shock of joy, not of disappointment.

A special kind of situational irony that emphasizes the pessimistic and fatalistic side of life is **cosmic irony,** or **irony of fate.** By the standard of cosmic irony, the universe is indifferent to individuals, who are subject to blind chance, accident, uncontrollable emotions, perpetual misfortune, and misery. Even if things temporarily go well, people's lives end badly, and their best efforts do not rescue them or make them happy. A story illustrating cosmic irony is "The Hammon and the Beans" by Parédes. Among the impoverished Mexican-American families living near the border in Texas, the little girl Chonita dies without a chance to fulfill her potential for a productive, happy life. Her death is no more than a minor statistic—an insignificant part of a gigantic pattern of social and political neglect. Her situation is cosmically ironic, for the implication of "The Hammon and the Beans" is that human beings are caught in a web of adverse circumstances from which there is no escape.

Like cosmic irony, **dramatic irony** is a special kind of situational irony. It happens when a character perceives a situation in a limited way while the audience, including other characters, sees it in greater perspective. The character therefore is able to understand things in only one way, whereas the audience can perceive two ways. Alan Austen in "The Chaser" is locked into such irony. He believes that the only potion he will ever need is the one to win him love; the old man and the readers know that one day he will return for the poison. The classic example of dramatic irony is the play *Oedipus Rex* by the ancient Greek dramatist Sophocles.

All his life Oedipus has been driven by Fate, which he can never escape. As the play drags to its climax and Oedipus believes that he is about to discover the murderer of his father, the audience knows—as he does not—that he is approaching his own self-destruction: As he condemns the murderer, he also condemns himself.

KATE CHOPIN (1851–1904)

The Story of an Hour   *1894*

Knowing that Mrs. Mallard was afflicted with a heart trouble, great care was taken to break to her as gently as possible the news of her husband's death.

It was her sister Josephine who told her, in broken sentences: veiled hints that revealed in half concealing. Her husband's friend Richards was there, too, near her. It was he who had been in the newspaper office when intelligence of the railroad disaster was received, with Brently Mallard's name leading the list of "killed." He had only taken the time to assure himself of its truth by a second telegram, and had hastened to forestall any less careful, less tender friend in bearing the sad message.

She did not hear the story as many women have heard the same, with a paralyzed inability to accept its significance. She wept at once, with sudden, wild abandonment, in her sister's arms. When the storm of grief had spent itself she went away to her room alone. She would have no one follow her.

There stood, facing the open window, a comfortable, roomy armchair. Into this she sank, pressed down by a physical exhaustion that haunted her body and seemed to reach into her soul.

She could see in the open square before her house the tops of trees that   5
wee all aquiver with the new spring life. The delicious breath of rain was in the air. In the street below a peddler was crying his wares. The notes of a distant song which some one was singing reached her faintly, and countless sparrows were twittering in the eaves.

There were patches of blue sky showing here and there through the clouds that had met and piled one above the other in the west facing her window.

She sat with her head thrown back upon the cushion of the chair, quite motionless, except when a sob came up into her throat and shook her, as a child who has cried itself to sleep continues to sob in its dreams.

She was young, with a fair, calm face, whose lines bespoke repression and even a certain strength. But now there was a dull stare in her eyes, whose gaze was fixed away off yonder on one of those patches of blue sky. It was not a glance of reflection, but rather indicated a suspension of intelligent thought.

There was something coming to her and she was waiting for it, fearfully. What was it? She did not know; it was too subtle and elusive to name. But she felt it, creeping out of the sky, reaching toward her through the sounds, the scents, the color that filled the air.

Now her bosom rose and fell tumultuously. She was beginning to recognize   10
this thing that was approaching to possess her, and she was striving to beat it back with her will—as powerless as her two white slender hands would have been.

When she abandoned herself a little whispered word escaped her slightly parted lips. She said it over and over under her breath: "free, free, free!" The vacant stare and the look of terror that had followed it went from her eyes. They stayed keen and bright. Her pulses beat fast, and the coursing blood warmed and relaxed every inch of her body.

She did not stop to ask if it were or were not a monstrous joy that held her. A clear and exalted perception enabled her to dismiss the suggestion as trivial.

She knew that she would weep again when she saw the kind, tender hands folded in death; the face that had never looked save with love upon her, fixed and gray and dead. But she saw beyond that bitter moment a long procession of years to come that would belong to her absolutely. And she opened and spread her arms out to them in welcome.

There would be no one to live for during those coming years; she would live for herself. There would be no powerful will bending hers in that blind persistence with which men and women believe they have a right to impose a private will upon a fellow-creature. A kind intention or a cruel intention made the act seem no less a crime as she looked upon it in that brief moment of illumination.

And yet she had loved him—sometimes. Often she had not. What did it   15
matter! What could love, the unsolved mystery, count for in face of this possession of self-assertion which she suddenly recognized as the strongest impulse of her being!

"Free! Body and soul free!" she kept whispering.

Josephine was kneeling before the closed door with her lips to the keyhole, imploring for admission. "Louise, open the door! I beg; open the door—you will make yourself ill. What are you doing, Louise? For heaven's sake open the door."

"Go away. I am not making myself ill." No; she was drinking in a very elixir of life through that open window.

Her fancy was running riot along those days ahead of her. Spring days, and summer days, and all sorts of days that would be her own. She breathed a quick prayer that life might be long. It was only yesterday she had thought with a shudder that life might be long.

She arose at length and opened the door to her sister's importunities. There   20
was a feverish triumph in her eyes, and she carried herself unwittingly like a goddess of Victory. She clasped her sister's waist, and together they descended the stairs. Richards stood waiting for them at the bottom.

Some one was opening the front door with a latchkey. It was Brently Mallard who entered, a little travel-stained, composedly carrying his grip-sack and umbrella. He had been far from the scene of accident, and did not even know there had been one. He stood amazed at Josephine's piercing cry: at Richards' quick motion to screen him from the view of his wife.

But Richards was too late.

When the doctors came they said she had died of heart disease—of joy that kills.

QUESTION

1. What do we learn about Louise's husband? How has he justified her responses? How are your judgments about him controlled by the context of the story?

2 Analyze the tone of paragraph 5. How is the imagery here (and in the following paragraphs) appropriate for her developing mood?

3. What is the apparent attitude of the narrator toward the institution of marriage, and what elements of tone make this apparent?

4. What do Louise's sister and Richards have in common? How do their attitudes contribute to the irony of the story?

5. Consider the tone of the last paragraph. What judgment is being made about how men view their importance to women?

AMÉRICO PARÉDES (b. 1915)

The Hammon and the Beans   *1963*

Once we lived in one of my grandfather's houses near Fort Jones.° It was just a block from the parade grounds, a big frame house painted a dirty yellow. My mother hated it, especially because of the pigeons that cooed all day about the eaves. They had fleas, she said. But it was a quiet neighborhood at least, too far from the center of town for automobiles and too near for musical, night-roaming drunks.

At this time Jonesville-on-the-Grande was not the thriving little city that it is today. We told off our days by the routine on the post. At six sharp the flag was raised on the parade grounds to the cackling of the bugles, and a field piece thundered out a salute. The sound of the shot bounced away through the morning mist until its echoes worked their way into every corner of town. Jonesville-on-the-Grande woke to the cannon's roar, as if to battle, and the day began.

At eight the whistle from the post laundry sent us children off to school. The whole town stopped for lunch with the noon whistle, and after lunch everybody went back to work when the post laundry said that it was one o'clock, except for those who could afford to be old-fashioned and took the siesta. The post was the town's clock, you might have said, or like some insistent elder person who was always there to tell you it was time.

At six the flag came down, and we went to watch through the high wire fence that divided the post from the town. Sometimes we joined in the ceremony, standing at salute until the sound of the cannon made us jump. That must have been when we had just studied about George Washington in school, or recited "The Song of Marion's Men"° about Marion the Fox and the British cavalry that chased him up and down the broad Santee. But at other times we stuck out our tongues and jeered at the soldiers. Perhaps the night before we had hung at the edges of a group of old men and listened to tales about Aniceto Pizaña and the

Fort Jones: The setting of Fort Jones and Jonesville-on-the-Grande in Texas is fictional. The story takes place in the mid-1920s, one of the most turbulent periods of Mexican history and only a few years after the deaths of two of the greatest heroes of the Mexican revolution— Pancho Villa (1877–1923) and Emiliano Zapata (ca. 1879–1919).

"Song of Marion's Men": A poem by William Cullen Bryant (1794–1878) about Colonel Francis Marion (ca. 1732–1795), who was a leader of irregular guerilla forces in South Carolina during the Revolutionary War. Because of his hit-and-run tactics, involving his hiding in the swamps near the "broad Santee" river in South Carolina, Marion was nicknamed the "Swamp Fox."

"border troubles,"° as the local paper still called them when it referred to them gingerly in passing.

It was because of the border troubles, ten years or so before, that the soldiers 5 had come back to old Fort Jones. But we did not hate them for that; we admired them even, at least sometimes. But when we were thinking about the border troubles instead of Marion the Fox we hooted them and the flag they were lowering, which for the moment was theirs alone, just as we would have jeered an opposing ball team, in a friendly sort of way. On these occasions even Chonita would join in the mockery, though she usually ran home at the stroke of six. But whether we taunted or saluted, the distant men in khaki uniforms went about their motions without noticing us at all.

The last word from the post came in the night when a distant bugle blew. At nine it was all right because all the lights were on. But sometimes I heard it at eleven when everything was dark and still, and it made me feel that I was all alone in the world. I would even doubt that I was me, and that put me in such a fright that I felt like yelling out just to make sure I was really there. But next morning the sun shone and life began all over again. With its whistles and cannon shots and bugles blowing. And so we lived, we and the post, side by side with the wire fence in between.

The wandering soldiers whom the bugle called home at night did not wander in our neighborhood, and none of us ever went into Fort Jones. None except Chonita. Every evening when the flag came down she would leave off playing and go down towards what was known as the "lower" gate of the post, the one that opened not on Main Street but against the poorest part of town. She went into the grounds and to the mess halls and pressed her nose against the screens and watched the soldiers eat. They sat at long tables calling to each other through food-stuffed mouths.

"Hey bud, pass the coffee!"

"Give me the ham!"

"Yeah, give me the beans!" 10

After the soldiers were through the cooks came out and scolded Chonita, and then they gave her packages with things to eat.

Chonita's mother did our washing, in gratefulness—as my mother put it— for the use of a vacant lot of my grandfather's which was a couple of blocks down the street. On the lot was an old one-room shack which had been a shed long ago, and this Chonita's father had patched up with flattened-out pieces of tin. He was a laborer. Ever since the end of the border troubles there had been a development boom in the Valley, and Chonita's father was getting his share of the good times. Clearing brush and building irrigation ditches he sometimes pulled down as much as six dollars a week. He drank a good deal of it up, it was true. But corn was just a few cents a bushel in those days. He was the breadwinner, you might say, while Chonita furnished the luxuries.

Chonita was a poet too. I had just moved into the neighborhood when a boy came up to me and said, "Come on! Let's go hear Chonita make a speech."

She was already on top of the alley fence when we got there, a scrawny little girl of about nine, her bare dirty feet clinging to the fence almost like hands. A

border troubles: The most serious border incidents occured in 1916, when Pancho Villa was responsible for deaths of Americans on both sides of the border. He made repeated raids into New Mexico and Texas.

dozen other kids were there below her, waiting. Some were boys I knew at school; five or six were her younger brothers and sisters.

"Speech! Speech!" they all cried. "Let Chonita make a speech! Talk in English, Chonita!"

They were grinning and nudging each other except for her brothers and sisters, who looked up at her with proud serious faces. She gazed out beyond us all with a grand, distant air and then she spoke.

"Give me the hammon and the beans!" she yelled. "Give me the hammon and the beans!"

She leaped off the fence and everybody cheered and told her how good it was and how she could talk English better than the teachers at the grammar school.

I thought it was a pretty poor joke. Every evening almost, they would make her get up on the fence and yell, "Give me the hammon and the beans!" And everybody would cheer and make her think she was talking English. As for me, I would wait there until she got it over with so we could play at something else. I wondered how long it would be before they got tired of it all. I never did find out because just about that time I got the chills and fever, and when I got up and around Chonita wasn't there anymore.

In later years I thought of her a lot, especially during the thirties when I was growing up. Those years would have been just made for her. Many's the time I have seen her in my mind's eyes, in the picket lines demanding not bread, not cake, but the hammon and the beans. But it didn't work out that way.

One night Doctor Zapata came into our kitchen through the back door. He set his bag on the table and said to my father, who had opened the door for him, "Well, she is dead."

My father flinched. "What was it?" he asked.

The doctor had gone to the window and he stood with his back to us, looking out toward the light of Fort Jones. "Pneumonia, flu, malnutrition, worms, the evil eye," he said without turning around. "What the hell difference does it make?"

"I wish I had known how sick she was," my father said in a very mild tone. "Not that it's really my affair, but I wish I had."

The doctor snorted and shook his head.

My mother came in and I asked her who was dead. She told me. It made me feel strange but I did not cry. My mother put her arm around my shoulders. "She is in Heaven now," she said. "She is happy."

I shrugged her arm away and sat down in one of the kitchen chairs.

"They're like animals," the doctor was saying. He turned round suddenly and his eyes glistened in the light. "Do you know what that brute of a father was doing when I left? He was laughing! Drinking and laughing with his friends."

"There's no telling what the poor man feels," my mother said.

My father made a deprecatory gesture. "It wasn't his daughter anyway."

"No?" the doctor said. He sounded interested.

"This is the woman's second husband," my father explained. "First one died before the girl was born, shot and hanged from a mesquite limb. He was working too close to the tracks the day the Olmito train was derailed."

"You know what?" the doctor said. "In classical times they did things better. Take Troy, for instance. After they stormed the city they grabbed the babies by the heels and dashed them against the wall. That was more humane."

My father smiled. "You sound very radical. You sound just like your relative down there in Morelos."°

"No relative of mine," the doctor said. "I'm a conservative, the son of a   35
conservative, and you know that I wouldn't be here except for that little detail."

"Habit," my father said. "Pure habit, pure tradition. You're a radical at heart."

"It depends on how you define radicalism," the doctor answered. "People tend to use words too loosely. A dentist could be called a radical, I suppose. He pulls up things by the roots."

My father chuckled.

"Any bandit in Mexico nowadays can give himself a political label," the doctor went on, "and that makes him respectable. He's a leader of the people."

"Take Villa, now—" my father began.   40

"Villa was a different type of man," the doctor broke in.

"I don't see any difference."

The doctor came over to the table and sat down. "Now look at it this way," he began, his finger in front of my father's face. My father threw back his head and laughed.

"You'd better go to bed and rest," my mother told me. "You're not completely well, you know."

So I went to bed, but I didn't go to sleep, not right away. I lay there for a   45
long time while behind my darkened eyelids Emiliano Zapata's cavalry charged down to the broad Santee, where there were grave men with hoary hairs.° I was still awake at eleven when the cold voice of the bugle went gliding in and out of the dark like something that couldn't find its way back to wherever it had been. I thought of Chonita in Heaven, and I saw her in her torn and dirty dress, with a pair of bright wings attached, flying round and round like a butterfly shouting, "Give me the hammon and the beans!"

Then I cried. And whether it was the bugle, or whether it was Chonita or what, to this day I do not know. But cry I did, and I felt much better after that.

QUESTIONS

1. How does Parédes establish the setting of the story? What is the significance of the fort? Of the "dirty yellow" paint? Of the vacant lot and the shack?

2. Is Chonita round or flat? To what extent does the author make her symbolic and representative?

3. What is the tone of the story (some possibilities: ironic, cynical, resigned, bitter, resentful)? What techniques does Parédes use to control the tone?

4. How does Doctor Zapata's attitude toward Chonita's death, and the words he uses to announce it, help to control the tone?

5. How does the tale of Chonita's brief life and her death fit into the political, social, and broadly human framework of the story?

Morelos: the home state of Zapata.
Grave men with hoary hairs: Cf. lines 49–52 of Bryant's "Song of Marion's Men:"
> Grave Men there are by broad Santee,
>   Grave men with hoary hairs;
> Their hearts are all with Marion,
>   For Marion are their prayers.

6. Describe the irony of the situation in which the Mexican-American children are taught United States history, but learn nothing about the political movements represented by Villa and Zapata.

7. Near the end of Bryant's "Song of Marion's Men," the following four lines appear:

> And lovely ladies greet our band [i.e., of soldiers]
> With kindliest welcoming,
> And smiles like those of summer,
> And tears like those of spring.

—lines 53–56

Contrast these lines with the narrator's vision of Chonita in heaven.

JOHN COLLIER (1901–1980)

The Chaser   *1940*

Alan Austen, as nervous as a kitten, went up certain dark and creaky stairs in the neighborhood of Pell Street, and peered about for a long time on the dim landing before he found the name he wanted written obscurely on one of the doors.

He pushed open this door, as he had been told to do, and found himself in a tiny room, which contained no furniture but a plain kitchen table, a rocking-chair, and an ordinary chair. On one of the dirty buff-coloured walls were a couple of shelves, containing in all perhaps a dozen bottles and jars.

An old man sat in the rocking-chair, reading a newspaper. Alan, without a word, handed him the card he had been given. "Sit down, Mr. Austen," said the old man very politely. "I am glad to make your acquaintance."

"Is it true," asked Alan, "that you have a certain mixture that has—er—quite extraordinary effects?"

"My dear sir," replied the old man, "my stock in trade is not very large—I don't deal in laxatives and teething mixtures—but such as it is, it is varied. I think nothing I sell has effects which could be precisely described as ordinary." 5

"Well, the fact is . . ." began Alan.

"Here, for example," interrupted the old man, reaching for a bottle from the shelf. "Here is a liquid as colourless as water, almost tasteless, quite imperceptible in coffee, wine, or any other beverage. It is also imperceptible to any known method of autopsy."

"Do you mean it is a poison?" cried Alan, very much horrified.

"Call it a glove-cleaner if you like," said the old man indifferently. "Maybe it will clean gloves. I have never tried. One might call it a life-cleaner. Lives need cleaning sometimes."

"I want nothing of that sort," said Alan. 10

"Probably it is just as well," said the old man. "Do you know the price of this? For one teaspoonful, which is sufficient, I ask five thousand dollars. Never less. Not a penny less."

"I hope all your mixtures are not as expensive," said Alan apprehensively.

"Oh dear, no," said the old man. "It would be no good charging that sort of price for a love potion, for example. Young people who need a love potion very seldom have five thousand dollars. Otherwise they would not need a love potion."

"I am glad to hear that," said Alan.

"I look at it like this," said the old man. "Please a customer with one article, and he will come back when he needs another. Even if it *is* more costly. He will save up for it, if necessary."

"So," said Alan, "you really do sell love potions?"

"If I did not sell love potions," said the old man, reaching for another bottle, "I should not have mentioned the other matter to you. It is only when one is in a position to oblige that one can afford to be so confidential."

"And these potions," said Alan. "They are not just—just—er—"

"Oh, no," said the old man. "Their effects are permanent, and extended far beyond the mere casual impulse. But they include it. Oh, yes, they include it. Bountifully, insistently. Everlastingly."

"Dear me!" said Alan, attempting a look of scientific detachment. "How very interesting!"

"But consider the spiritual side," said the old man.

"I do, indeed," said Alan.

"For indifference,' said the old man, "they substitute devotion. For scorn, adoration. Give one tiny measure of this to the young lady—its flavour is imperceptible in orange juice, soup, or cocktails—and however gay and giddy she is, she will change altogether. She will want nothing but solitude and you."

"I can hardly believe it," said Alan. "She is so fond of parties."

"She will not like them any more," said the old man. "She will be afraid of the pretty girls you may meet."

"She will actually be jealous?" cried Alan in a rapture. "Of me?"

"Yes, she will want to be everything to you."

"She is, already. Only she doesn't care about it."

"She will, when she has taken this. She will care intensely. You will be her sole interest in life."

"Wonderful!" cried Alan.

"She will want to know all you do," said the old man. "All that has happened to you during the day. Every word of it. She will want to know what you are thinking about, why you smile suddenly, why you are looking sad."

"That is love!" cried Alan.

"Yes," said the old man. "How carefully she will look after you! She will never allow you to be tired, to sit in a draught, to neglect your food. If you are an hour late, she will be terrified. She will think you are killed, or that some siren has caught you."

"I can hardly imagine Diana like that!" cried Alan, overwhelmed with joy.

"You will not have to use your imagination," said the old man. "And, by the way, since there are always sirens, if by any chance you *should*, later on, slip a little, you need not worry. She will forgive you, in the end. She will be terribly hurt, of course, but she will forgive you—in the end."

"That will not happen," said Alan fervently.

"Of course not," said the old man. "But, it it did, you need not worry. She would never divorce you. Oh, no! And, of course, she will never give you the least, the very least, grounds for—uneasiness."

"And how much," said Alan, "is this wonderful mixture?"

"It is not as dear," said the old man, "as the glove-cleaner, or life-cleaner, as I sometimes call it. No. That is five thousand dollars, never a penny less. One has to be older than you are, to indulge in that sort of thing. One has to save up for it."

"But the love potion?" said Alan.   40

"Oh, that," said the old man, opening the drawer in the kitchen table, and taking out a tiny, rather dirty-looking phial. "That is just a dollar."

"I can't tell you how grateful I am," said Alan, watching him fill it.

"I like to oblige," said the old man. "Then customers come back, later in life, when they are better off, and want more expensive things. Here you are. You will find it very effective."

"Thank you again," said Alan. "Good-bye."

"Au revoir," said the old man.   45

QUESTIONS

1. Summarize the plot of this story. What are the qualities of the poison that the old man tells Austen about? What are the powers of the love potion? What is the connection between the love potion and the so-called glove cleaner?

2. Are the two characters static or dynamic? Round or flat? To what extent does their characterization focus the story and control the tone?

3. How is the setting of the story described? How does this description contribute to the mood of the story and the characterization of the old man?

4. How do the words of the story control the tone and attitude? What words help us form an attitude toward Alan Austen? Toward the old man?

5. To what extent is the story ironic? What do we and the old man know that Alan Austen doesn't?

6. What point does this story make about love? Youth? Desire? How can the story be taken as a commentary about the need for love relationships that preserve individuality as well as romantic commitment?

MARGARET ATWOOD (b. 1939)

Rape Fantasies   *1977*

The way they're going on about it in the magazines you'd think it was just invented, and not only that but it's something terrific, like a vaccine for cancer. They put it in capital letters on the front cover, and inside they have these questionnaires like the ones they used to have about whether you were a good enough wife or an endomorph or an ectomorph, remember that? with the scoring upside down on page 73, and then these numbered do-it-yourself dealies, you know? RAPE, TEN THINGS TO DO ABOUT IT, like it was ten new hairdos or something. I mean, what's so new about it?

So at work they all have to talk about it because no matter what magazine you open, there it is, staring you right between the eyes, and they're beginning to have it on the television, too. Personally I'd prefer a June Allyson° movie anytime but they don't make them any more and they don't even have them that much on the Late Show. For instance, day before yesterday, that would be Wednesday, thank god it's Friday as they say, we were sitting around in the women's lunch room—the *lunch* room, I mean you'd think you could get some peace and quiet in there—and Chrissy closes up the magazine she's been reading and says, "How about it, girls, do you have rape fantasies?"

The four of us were having our game of bridge the way we always do, and I had a bare twelve points counting the singleton with not that much of a bid in anything. So I said one club, hoping Sondra would remember about the one club convention, because the time before when I used that she thought I really meant clubs and she bid us up to three, and all I had was four little ones with nothing higher than a six, and we went down two and on top of that we were vulnerable. She is not the world's best bridge player. I mean, neither am I but there's a limit.

Darlene passed but the damage was done, Sondra's head went round like it was on ball bearings and she said, "*What* fantasies?"

"Rape fantasies," Chrissy said. She's a receptionist and she looks like one;   5
she's pretty but cool as a cucumber, like she's been painted all over with nail polish, if you know what I mean. Varnished. "It says here all women have rape fantasies."

"For Chrissake, I'm eating an egg sandwich," I said, "and I bid one club and Darlene passed."

"You mean, like some guy jumping you in an alley or something," Sondra said. She was eating her lunch, we all eat our lunches during the game, and she bit into a piece of that celery she always brings and started to chew away on it with this thoughtful expression in her eyes and I knew we might as well pack it in as far as the game was concerned.

"Yeah, sort of like that," Chrissy said. She was blushing a little, you could see it even under her makeup.

"I don't think you should go out alone at night," Darlene said, "you put yourself in a position," and I may have been mistaken but she was looking at me. She's the oldest, she's forty-one though you wouldn't know it and neither does she, but I looked it up in the employees' file. I like to guess a person's age and then look it up to see if I'm right. I let myself have an extra pack of cigarettes if I am, though I'm trying to cut down. I figure it's harmless as long as you don't tell. I mean, not everyone has access to that file, it's more or less confidential. But it's all right if I tell you, I don't expect you'll ever meet her, though you never know, it's a small world. Anyway.

"For *heaven's* sake, it's only *Toronto*," Greta said. She worked in Detroit for   10
three years and she never lets you forget it, it's like she thinks she's a war hero or something, we should all admire her just for the fact that she's still walking this earth, though she was really living in Windsor° the whole time, she just worked in Detroit. Which for me doesn't really count. It's where you sleep, right?

June Allyson: actress (b. 1917) known for her bright smile and scratchy voice. She specialized in "sweet" movie and musical roles, 1943–1959, and still appears regularly in TV commercials.

Windsor: city south of Detroit, noted as the only place where any portion of Canada is south of the United States.

"Well, do you?" Chrissy said. She was obviously trying to tell us about hers but she wasn't about to go first, she's cautious, that one.

"I certainly don't," Darlene said, and she wrinkled up her nose, like this, and I had to laugh. "I think it's disgusting." She's divorced, I read that in the file too, she never talks about it. It must've been years ago anyway. She got up and went over to the coffee machine and turned her back on us as though she wasn't going to have anything more to do with it.

"Well," Greta said. I could see it was going to be between her and Chrissy. They're both blondes, I don't mean that in a bitchy way but they do try to outdress each other. Greta would like to get out of Filing, she'd like to be a receptionist too so she could meet more people. You don't meet much of anyone in Filing except other people in Filing. Me, I don't mind it so much, I have outside interests.

"Well," Greta said, "I sometimes think about, you know my apartment? It's got this little balcony, I like to sit out there in the summer and I have a few plants out there. I never bother that much about locking the door to the balcony, it's one of those sliding glass ones, I'm on the eighteenth floor for heaven's sake, I've got a good view of the lake and the CN Tower and all. But I'm sitting around one night in my housecoat, watching TV with my shoes off, you know how you do, and I see this guy's feet, coming down past the window, and the next thing you know he's standing on the balcony, he's let himself down by a rope with a hook on the end of it from the floor above, that's the nineteenth, and before I can even get up off the chesterfield he's inside the apartment. He's all dressed in black with black gloves on"—I knew right away what show she got the black gloves off because I saw the same one—"and then he, well, you know."

"You know what?" Chrissy said, but Greta said, "And afterwards he tells me   15 that he goes all over the outside of the apartment building like that, from one floor to another, with his rope and his hook . . . and then he goes out to the balcony and tosses his rope, and he climbs up it and disappears."

"Just like Tarzan," I said, but nobody laughed.

"Is that all?" Chrissy said. "Don't you ever think about, well, I think about being in the bathtub, with no clothes on . . ."

"So who takes a bath in their clothes?" I said, you have to admit it's stupid when you come to think of it, but she just went on, ". . . with lots of bubbles, what I use is Vitabath, it's more expensive but it's so relaxing, and my hair pinned up, and the door opens and this fellow's standing there. . . ."

"How'd he get in?" Greta said.

"Oh, I don't know, through a window or something. Well, I can't very well   20 get out of the bathtub, the bathroom's too small and besides he's blocking the doorway, so I just *lie* there, and he starts to very slowly take his own clothes off, and then he gets into the bathtub with me."

"Don't you scream or anything?" said Darlene. She'd come back with her cup of coffee, she was getting really interested. "I'd scream like bloody murder."

"Who'd hear me?" Chrissy said. "Besides, all the articles say it's better not to resist, that way you don't get hurt."

"Anyway you might get bubbles up your nose," I said, "from the deep breathing," and I swear all four of them looked at me like I was in bad taste, like I'd insulted the Virgin Mary or something. I mean, I don't see what's wrong with a little joke now and then. Life's too short, right?

"Listen," I said, "those aren't *rape* fantasies. I mean, you aren't getting *raped*, it's just some guy you haven't met formally who happens to be more attractive than Derek Cummins"—he's the Assistant Manager, he wears elevator shoes or at any rate they have these thick soles and he has this funny way of talking, we call him Derek Duck—"and you have a good time. Rape is when they've got a knife or something and you don't want to."

"So what about you, Estelle," Chrissy said, she was miffed because I laughed   25
at her fantasy, she thought I was putting her down. Sondra was miffed too, by this time she'd finished her celery and she wanted to tell about hers, but she hadn't got in fast enough.

"All right, let me tell you one," I said. "I'm walking down this dark street at night and this fellow comes up and grabs my arm. Now it so happens that I have a plastic lemon in my purse, you know how it always says you should carry a plastic lemon in your purse? I don't really do it, I tried it once but the darn thing leaked all over my chequebook, but in this fantasy I have one, and I say to him, "You're intending to rape me, right?" and he nods, so I open my purse to get the plastic lemon, and I can't find it! My purse is full of all this junk, Kleenex and cigarettes and my change purse and my lipstick and my driver's licence, you know the kind of stuff: so I ask him to hold out his hands, like this, and I pile all this junk into them and down at the bottom there's the plastic lemon, and I can't get the top off. So I hand it to him and he's very obliging, he twists the top off and hands it back to me, and I squirt him in the eye."

I hope you don't think that's too vicious. Come to think of it, it is a bit mean, especially when he was so polite and all.

"*That's* your rape fantasy?" Chrissy says, "I don't believe it."

"She's a card," Darlene says, she and I are the ones that've been here the longest and she never will forget the time I got drunk at the office party and insisted I was going to dance under the table instead of on top of it, I did a sort of Cossack number° but then I hit my head on the bottom of the table—actually it was a desk—when I went to get up, and I knocked myself out cold. She's decided that's the mark of an original mind and she tells everyone new about it and I'm not sure that's fair. Though I did do it.

"I'm being totally honest," I say. I always am and they know it. There's no   30
point in being anything else, is the way I look at it, and sooner or later the truth will out so you might as well not waste the time, right? "You should hear the one about the Easy-Off Cleaner."

But that was the end of the lunch hour, with one bridge game shot to hell, and the next day we spent most of the time arguing over whether to start a new game or play out the hands we had left over from the day before, so Sondra never did get a chance to tell about her rape fantasy.

It started me thinking though, about my own rape fantasies. Maybe I'm abnormal or something, I mean I have fantasies about handsome strangers coming in through the window too, like Mr. Clean, I wish one would, please god somebody without flat feet and big sweat marks on his shirt, and over five feet five, believe me being tall is a handicap though it's getting better, tall guys are starting to like someone whose nose reaches higher than their belly button. But if you're being totally honest you can't count those as rape fantasies. In a real rape fantasy, what

---

Cossack number: a Ukrainian folk dance movement performed in a squatting position, with much hand clapping.

you should feel is this anxiety, like when you think about your apartment building catching on fire and whether you should use the elevator or the stairs or maybe just stick your head under a wet towel, and you try to remember everything you've read about what to do but you can't decide.

For instance, I'm walking along this dark street at night and this short, ugly fellow comes up and grabs my arm, and not only is he ugly, you know, with a sort of puffy nothing face, like those fellows you have to talk to in the bank when your account's overdrawn—of course I don't mean they're all like that—but he's absolutely covered in pimples. So he gets me pinned against the wall, he's short but he's heavy, and he starts to undo himself and the zipper gets stuck. I mean, one of the most significant moments in a girl's life, it's almost like getting married or having a baby or something, and he sticks the zipper.

So I say, kind of disgusted, "Oh for Chrissake," and he starts to cry. He tells me he's never been able to get anything right in his entire life, and this is the last straw, he's going to go jump off a bridge.

"Look," I say, I feel so sorry for him, in my rape fantasies I always end up 35 feeling sorry for the guy, I mean there has to be something *wrong* with them, if it was Clint Eastwood° it'd be different but worse luck it never is. I was the kind of little girl who buried dead robins, know what I mean? It used to drive my mother nuts, she didn't like me touching them, because of the germs I guess. So I say, "Listen, I know how you feel. You really should do something about those pimples, if you got rid of them you'd be quite good looking, honest; then you wouldn't have to go around doing stuff like this. I had them myself once," I say, to comfort him, but in fact I did, and it ends up I give him the name of my old dermatologist, the one I had in high school, that was back in Leamington,° except I used to go to St. Catharine's for the dermatologist. I'm telling you, I was really lonely when I first came here; I thought it was going to be such a big adventure and all, but it's a lot harder to meet people in a city. But I guess it's different for a guy.

Or I'm lying in bed with this terrible cold, my face is all swollen up, my eyes are red and my nose is dripping like a leaky tap, and this fellow comes in through the window and *he* has a terrible cold too, it's a new kind of flu that's been going around. So he says, "I'b goig do rabe you"—I hope you don't mind me holding my nose like this but that's the way I imagine it—and he lets out this terrific sneeze, which slows him down a bit, also I'm no object of beauty myself, you'd have to be some kind of pervert to want to rape someone with a cold like mine, it'd be like raping a bottle of LePages mucilage the way my nose is running. He's looking wildly around the room, and I realize it's because he doesn't have a piece of Kleenex! "Id's ride here," I say, and I pass him the Kleenex, god knows why he even bothered to get out of bed, you'd think if you were going to go around climbing in windows you'd wait till you were healthier, right? I mean, that takes a certain amount of energy. So I ask him why doesn't he let me fix him a NeoCitran and scotch, that's what I always take, you still have the cold but you don't feel it, so I do and we end up watching the Late Show together. I mean, they aren't all sex maniacs, the rest of the time they must lead a normal life. I figure they enjoy watching the Late Show just like anybody else.

Clint Eastwood: born 1930, star of many tough-guy detective and western movies; most famous as "Dirty Harry" (1971).
Leamington: in Ontario on the north shore of Lake Erie, southeast of Windsor.

I do have a scarier one though . . . where the fellow says he's hearing angel voices that're telling him he's got to kill me, you know, you read about things like that all the time in the papers. In this one I'm not in the apartment where I live now, I'm back in my mother's house in Leamington and the fellow's been hiding in the cellar, he grabs my arm when I go downstairs to get a jar of jam and he's got hold of the axe too, out of the garage, that one is really scary. I mean, what do you say to a nut like that?

So I start to shake but after a minute I get control of myself and I say, is he sure the angel voices have got the right person, because I hear the same angel voices and they've been telling me for some time that I'm going to give birth to the reincarnation of St. Anne who in turn has the Virgin Mary and right after that comes Jesus Christ and the end of the world, and he wouldn't want to interfere with that, would he? So he gets confused and listens some more, and then he asks for a sign and I show him my vaccination mark, you can see it's sort of an odd-shaped one, it got infected because I scratched the top off, and that does it, he apologizes and climbs out the coal chute° again, which is how he got in in the first place, and I say to myself there's some advantage in having been brought up a Catholic even though I haven't been to church since they changed the service into English,° it just isn't the same, you might as well be a Protestant. I must write to Mother and tell her to nail up that coal chute, it always has bothered me. Funny, I couldn't tell you at all what this man looks like but I know exactly what kind of shoes he's wearing, because that's the last I see of him, his shoes going up the coal chute, and they're the old-fashioned kind that lace up the ankles, even though he's a young fellow. That's strange, isn't it?

Let me tell you though I really sweat until I see him safely out of there and I go upstairs right away and make myself a cup of tea. I don't think about that one much. My mother always said you shouldn't dwell on unpleasant things and I generally agree with that, I mean, dwelling on them doesn't make them go away. Though not dwelling on them doesn't make them go away either, when you come to think of it.

Sometimes I have these short ones where the fellow grabs my arm but I'm   40
really a Kung-Fu° expert, can you believe it, in real life I'm sure it would just be a conk on the head and that's that, like getting your tonsils out, you'd wake up and it would be all over except for the sore places, and you'd be lucky if your neck wasn't broken or something, I could never even hit the volleyball in gym and a volleyball is fairly large, you know?—and I just go *zap* with my fingers into his eyes and that's it, he falls over, or I flip him against a wall or something. But I could never really stick my fingers in anyone's eyes, could you? It would feel like hot jello and I don't even like cold jello, just thinking about it gives me the creeps. I feel a bit guilty about that one, I mean how would you like walking around knowing someone's been blinded for life because of you?

But maybe it's different for a guy.

coal chute: trough for delivering coal from a truck into a basement coal bin. Estelle's remark indicates that the chute was not fastened over the opening to the bin, thus permitting an illegal entry.

into English: In accord with the Second Vatican Council (1962–1965), the Latin Mass was replaced by vernacular languages in the late 1960s.

Kung-Fu: elaborate self-defense system developed in China, similar to Karate.

The most touching one I have is when the fellow grabs my arm and I say, sad and kind of dignified, "You'd be raping a corpse." That pulls him up short and I explain that I've just found out I have leukaemia and the doctors have only given me a few months to live. That's why I'm out pacing the streets alone at night, I need to think, you know, come to terms with myself. I don't really have leukaemia but in the fantasy I do, I guess I chose that particular disease because a girl in my grade four class died of it, the whole class sent her flowers when she was in the hospital. I didn't understand then that she was going to die and I wanted to have leukaemia too so I could get flowers. Kids are funny, aren't they? Well, it turns out that he has leukaemia himself, and *he* only has a few months to live, that's why he's going around raping people, he's very bitter because he's so young and his life is being taken from him before he's really lived it. So we walk along gently under the street lights, it's spring and sort of misty, and we end up going for coffee, we're happy we've found the only other person in the world who can understand what we're going through, it's almost like fate, and after a while we just sort of look at each other and our hands touch, and he comes back with me and moves into my apartment and we spend our last months together before we die, we just sort of don't wake up in the morning, though I've never decided which one of us gets to die first. If it's him I have to go on and fantasize about the funeral, if it's me I don't have to worry about that, so it just about depends on how tired I am at the time. You may not believe this but sometimes I even start crying. I cry at the end of movies, even the ones that aren't all that sad, so I guess it's the same thing. My mother's like that too.

The funny thing about these fantasies is that the man is always someone I don't know, and the statistics in the magazines, well, most of them anyway, they say it's often someone you do know, at least a little bit, like your boss or something— I mean, it wouldn't be *my* boss, he's over sixty and I'm sure he couldn't rape his way out of a paper bag, poor old thing, but it might be someone like Derek Duck, in his elevator shoes, perish the thought—or someone you just met, who invites you up for a drink, it's getting so you can hardly be sociable any more, and how are you supposed to meet people if you can't trust them even that basic amount? You can't spend your whole life in the Filing Department or cooped up in your own apartment with all the doors and windows locked and the shades down. I'm not what you would call a drinker but I like to go out now and then for a drink or two in a nice place, even if I am by myself, I'm with Women's Lib on that even though I can't agree with a lot of the other things they say. Like here for instance, the waiters all know me and if anyone, you know, bothers me . . . I don't know why I'm telling you all this, except I think it helps you get to know a person, especially at first, hearing some of the things they think about. At work they call me the office worry wart, but it isn't so much like worrying, it's more like figuring out what you should do in an emergency, like I said before.

Anyway, another thing about it is that there's a lot of conversation, in fact I spend most of my time, in the fantasy that is, wondering what I'm going to say and what he's going to say, I think it would be better if you could get a conversation going. Like, how could a fellow do that to a person he's just had a long conversation with, once you let them know you're human, you have a life too, I don't see how they could go ahead with it, right? I mean, I know it happens but I just don't understand it, that's the part I really don't understand.

QUESTIONS

1. What elements of the various rape fantasies are comic? How is the comedy brought out (e.g., through subject matter, circumstances of description, attitudes and understanding of the characters, comments by the narrator)?
2. What do the various fantasies of Estelle have in common, and what do they show about her? How does Atwood control the tone so as to keep Estelle from considering rape as a problem in psychology or criminology?
3. Describe the story's tone. How does tone affect your perception of Estelle?
4. Consider the tone of the very last paragraph. What is Atwood's apparent attitude toward the subject? How is it tempered by her attitude toward Estelle?
5. Studies point out that rape is an act of violence. What do the women in the story do to deflect the seriousness of the potential violence involved?

WRITING ABOUT TONE

In preparing to write about tone, you will, as always, need to begin with a careful reading, noting those elements of the story that touch particularly on attitudes or authorial consideration. For example, you may be studying Collier's "The Chaser," where it is necessary to consider whether the story asks too much of the reader: Is the old man's prediction really the horror at the end of the road for *all* romantic love? In this respect the story may cause a certain mental squirming. But is this right? Does Collier want the squirming to occur? Perhaps if the question is phrased another way, the tone might be more adequately understood. If Alan Austen confuses "overly possessive love" for "romantic love," the story may seem less disturbing. Depending on the story, your devising and answering such questions can help you understand the degree of an author's control over tone. Similar questions apply when you study internal qualities such as style and characterization.

Questions for Discovering Ideas

Do all the speeches seem right for speaker and situation?

Are all descriptions appropriate, all actions believable?

If the story is comic, is the writer laughing too? In serious situations, is there evidence of understanding and sympathy? Does the writer ask you to lament the human condition?

What kind of character is the speaker? Is he or she intelligent? Friendly? Idealistic? Realistic?

Do any words seem unusual or especially noteworthy, such as dialect, polysyllabic words, foreign words or phrases that the author assumes you know, or especially connotative or emotive words?

Strategies for Organizing Ideas

You will want to discuss the dominant moods or impressions of the story (for example, the cynicism of "The Chaser" or the comedy of "Rape Fantasies"). You might show how the author creates the overall mood of the story by using the language of ordinary people, pointing out the pretentiousness of various speakers, or calling on the reader's ability to visualize experience. Some of the things you could address are these:

1. *Audience, situation, and characters.* Is any person or group directly addressed by the narrator? What attitude is expressed (love, respect, condescension, confidentiality, confidence, etc.)? What is the basic situation in the story? Do you find irony? If so, what kind is it? What does the irony show (optimism or pessimism, for example)? How is the situation controlled to shape your responses? That is, can actions, situations, or characters be seen as expressions of attitude, or as embodiments of certain favorable or unfavorable ideas or positions? What is the nature of the speaker or persona? Why does the speaker speak exactly as he or she does? How is the speaker's character manipulated to show apparent authorial attitude and to elicit reader response? Does the story promote respect, admiration, dislike, or other feelings about character or situation? How?

2. *Descriptions, diction.* Analysis of descriptions and diction is stylistic, but your concern here is to relate style to attitude. Are there any systematic references, such as to colors, sounds, noises, natural scenes, and so on, that collectively reflect an attitude? Do connotative meanings of words control response in any way? What knowledge is the narrator expected to have about history, nature, psychology? To what degree does the diction require readers to have a large or technical vocabulary? Do speech or dialect patterns indicate attitudes about speakers or their condition of life? Are speech patterns normal and standard, or slang or substandard? What is the effect of these patterns? Are there unusual or particularly noteworthy expressions? If so, what attitudes do these show? Does the author use verbal irony? To what effect?

3. *Humor.* Is the story funny? How funny, how intense? How is the humor achieved? Does the humor develop out of incongruous situations or language, or both? Is there an underlying basis of attack in the humor, or are the objects of laughter still respected or even loved despite having humor directed against them?

4. *Ideas.* Ideas may be advocated, defended mildly, or attacked. Which do you have in the story you've been studying? How does the author make his or her attitude clear—directly, by statement, or indirectly, through understatement, overstatement, or the language of a character? In what ways does the story assume a common ground of assent between author and reader? That is, what common assumptions do you find about

religious views, political ideas, moral and behavioral standards, and so on? Is it easy to give assent (temporary or permanent) to these ideas, or is any concession needed by the reader to approach the story? (For example, a major subject of "First Confession" [p. 487] is the proper preparation for a child taking first confession in the Catholic faith. Not everyone can grant the importance of this action, but even a skeptical reader might find common ground in the psychological situation of the story, or in the desire to learn as much as possible about human beings.)

5. *Unique characteristics of the story.* Each story has unique properties that contribute to the tone. Thus, Collier's "The Chaser" is developed almost entirely through the dialogue between the old man and Austen. The tone of the story is therefore illustrated by the attitudes and interests of each character, almost as though the story is a drama. A reversal of roles is found in Glaspell's "A Jury of Her Peers" in which the focus is on how the two women prove to be better detectives than their husbands, who are searching the farmhouse. Without these women, we would have no story; the author invites us to perceive the irony of this fact. In other stories there might be some recurring word or essay that seems special. For example, Mark Twain in "Luck" (p. 275) develops a passage centering on the word *blunder*, and thereby makes his attitude clear about the boob hero, Scoresby (paragraph 12). When you study any story, be alert to bring out such special and unique things.

The conclusion may summarize your main points, and from there go on to redefinitions, explanations, or afterthoughts, together with ideas reinforcing earlier points. You might also mention some other major aspect of the story's tone that you did not develop in the body.

SAMPLE ESSAY

The Situational and Verbal Irony of Collier's "The Chaser"°

[1] John Collier's "The Chaser" is based on the situational irony of the unreal hope of youth as opposed to the extreme disillusion of age and experience. Collier builds the brief story almost entirely in dialogue between a young man, Alan Austen, who is deeply in love and wants to possess his sweetheart entirely, and an unnamed old man who believes in a life free of romantic encumbrances. The situation reflects disillusionment so completely that the story may in fact be called cynical.* This attitude is made plain by the circumstances of the two main characters, the sales method of the old man, and his use of double meaning.†

The circumstances of the two men establish the story's dominant tone of cynicism. Austen, the young man full of illusions and unreal expectations,

° See p. 311 for this story.
* Central idea.
† Thesis sentence.

[2] has come to the old man to buy a love potion so that his sweetheart, Diana, will love him with slavelike adoration. Collier makes clear that the old man, a seller of magic brews, has seen many young men in the grips of romantic desire before, just like Austen, and he therefore knows that their possessive love will eventually bore and anger them. He knows, because he has already seen these disillusioned customers return to buy the "chaser," which is a deadly, untraceable poison, so that they could kill the women for whom they previously bought the love potion. Thus, Collier creates the ironic situation of the story--the beginning of an inevitable process in which Austen, like other young men before him, is made to appear so unrealistic and self-defeating that his enthusiastic passion will someday change into hate and murderousness. The tone of the story could hardly be more cynical and pessimistic.

[3] The sales method used by the old man reveals his cynical understanding of men like Austen. Collier makes clear that the old man knows why Austen has come. Thus, before showing his love potion, the old man describes the untraceable poison. His ultimate aim is to sell the expensive poison, and he is using the love potion as inexpensive "bait," or what retailers call a "loss leader." By this means Collier shows the old man's art of manipulation, for even though Austen is horrified by the poison, the seed has been planted in his mind. He will always know, when his love for Diana is lost, that he has the choice of "cleaning" his life, as the old man reminds him. This unscrupulous sales method effectively corrupts Austen in advance. Such a calculation on the old man's part is grimly cynical.

[4] Supporting the tone of cynicism in the old man's sales technique is his use of double meaning. His concluding words, "Au revoir" (i.e., "until I see you again"), for example, mean that he expects a future meeting when Austen will return to buy the poison to kill Diana. His speech acknowledging Austen's gratitude shows the same double edge. He says,

> I like to oblige. . . . Then customers come back, later in life, when they are better off, and want more expensive things. (paragraph 43)

Clearly the "expensive" thing he is talking about is the poison, the "chaser." Through such speeches of double meaning, the old man is calmly and politely, but cynically, telling Austen that his love will not last and that it will eventually irritate him to the point where he will want to murder Diana rather than to continue living with her potion-induced possessiveness.

[5] Before "The Chaser" is dismissed as hopelessly cynical, however, it must be said that the only possible result of Austen's idea of love would be just such cynicism. The old man's descriptions of the total enslavement of Diana that Austen has dreamed about would leave no breathing room for either Austen or Diana. This sort of love would exclude everything else in life, and would soon be suffocating rather than pleasing. It would be normal to want freedom from such psychological imprisonment, even if the prison is of one's own making. Under these conditions, the cynical tone of "The Chaser" suggests that the desire to be totally possessing and possessed--to "want nothing but solitude" and the loved one--can lead only to disaster for both man and woman. The old man's cynicism and the young man's desire thus point toward an ideal of love that permits interchange, individuality, and un-

derstanding. Even though this better ideal is not described anywhere in the story, it is compatible with Collier's situational irony. Thus, cynical as the story unquestionably is, it does not exclude an idealism of tolerant and more human love.

Commentary on the Essay

This essay presents a possible way to describe a story's presentation of pessimism and cynicism while not assenting to that story's negative situational irony. Therefore the essay illustrates how a consideration of tone can aid the development of objective literary judgment.

The introductory paragraph indicates that the aspect of tone to be discussed will be an ironic situation—youthful but unrealistic hope in the context of aged cynicism. The thesis sentence indicates that the body of the essay will deal with (1) this situation and how it is related to (2) the sales method of a major character—the old man—and (3) his speeches containing double meaning.

The second paragraph establishes the situational irony by describing the desires of Austen and the cynical attitude of the old man. In the third paragraph the topic is the sinister manipulation of Austen as a result of the old man's skillful and subtle salesmanship. By stressing that the old man plants the seeds of corruption in Austen, this paragraph continues the topic of the tone of cynicism which is the thematic basis of the essay. The subject of the fourth paragraph, the last in the body, is Collier's use of double meaning in the speeches of the old man to emphasize that Austen will someday want to kill his wife.

The concluding paragraph is a reflective one. In view of the cynical tone of the story, this paragraph suggests that a more realistic and optimistic attitude about love is possible—a view that while not perceivable in the story is also not incompatible with it.

WRITING TOPICS

1. Write an essay comparing and contrasting the modes of presentation of Mrs. Mallard in "The Story of an Hour" and Mrs. Wright in "A Jury of Her Peers." How does the presentation control your understanding of their conditions and your attitudes toward them?

2. Consider a short story in which the narrator is the central character (for example, "Rape Fantasies," "A & P," "First Confession," "Everyday Use," "Blue Winds Dancing," "I Stand Here Ironing"). Write an essay showing how the language of the characters establishes your attitudes toward them. Be sure to emphasize the relationship between their language and your responses.

3. Assume that you are writing a story involving, say, a student, a supervisor, or a politician. Write a fragment treating your character with dramatic irony; that is, your character thinks he or she knows all the details about a situation,

but really does not (e.g., a woman declares her interest in a man without realizing that he is engaged to another woman, or the supervisor expresses distrust in a person who is one of the best workers in the firm). What action, words, and situations do you choose to make your irony clear?

9

Symbolism and Allegory: Keys to Extended Meaning

Symbolism and **allegory** are modes of expression designed to extend and expand meaning. **Symbolism,** to be considered first, is derived from a Greek word meaning "to throw together" (*syn*, together, and *ballein*, to throw). A symbol pulls or draws together (1) a specific thing and (2) ideas, values, persons, or ways of life, into a direct relationship that normally would not be apparent. A symbol might also be regarded as a *substitute* for the elements being signified, as a flag stands for the ideals of a nation.

In stories—and also in poems and plays—a symbol is usually a person, object, place, action, group, artwork, or situation. It has its own identity, and may function at an ordinary level of reality. Often there is a close relationship between the symbol and the things it stands for, but the symbol may also have no apparent connection. What is important is that symbols extend beyond their immediate identity and point toward additional levels of meaning.

To test whether something is a symbol, you need to judge whether it consistently refers beyond itself to a significant idea, emotion, or quality. For example, the ancient mythological character Sisyphus is widely recognized as a symbol. In the ancient Greek mythological underworld, Sisyphus is forever doomed to roll a large boulder up a high hill. Just as he gets it to the top, it rolls down, and then he is fated to roll it up again—and again—and again—because the rock always rolls back. The plight of Sisyphus is a symbol of the human condition: A person rarely if ever completes anything. Work must always be done over and over from day to day and from generation to generation, and the same problems confront humanity throughout all time. Because of such fruitless effort, life seems to have little or no meaning. Nevertheless, there is hope. People who meet frustration, as Sisyphus does, stay involved and active, and even if they are only temporarily successful, their work makes their lives meaningful. A writer referring to Sisyphus would expect us to understand how this ancient mythological figure symbolizes these conditions.

Universal Symbols

Many symbols like the myth of Sisyphus are *generally* or *universally* recognized, and are therefore **cultural** or **universal.** They embody ideas and emotions that writers and readers share as heirs of the same historical and cultural tradition. When using these symbols, a writer assumes that readers already know what the symbol represents. Thus, ordinary water, the substance in the sacrament of baptism, is a recognized symbol of life. When clear water spouts up in a fountain, it symbolizes optimism (as upwelling, bubbling life). A stagnant pool symbolizes the pollution and diminution of life. Water is also understood as a symbol of sexuality. Thus, lovers may meet by a quiet lake, a cascading waterfall, a murmuring stream, a wide river, or a stormy sea. The condition of the water in each instance may symbolize their romantic relationship.

Contextual Symbols

Objects and descriptions that are not universal symbols can be called symbols only if they are made so *within individual stories*. These are **private, authorial,** or **contextual** symbols. Unlike universal symbols, these gain their symbolic meaning within the *context* of a specific story. For example, the standing clock in the black room in Poe's "The Masque of the Red Death" (p. 247) is used there to symbolize not only the passage of time but also the sinister forces of death. Similarly, the chrysanthemums tended by Elisa in Steinbeck's "The Chrysanthemums" seem at first nothing more than prized flowers. As the story progresses, however, the flowers gain symbolic significance. The traveling tinsmith's apparent interest in them is the wedge he uses to get a small mending job from Elisa. Her description of the care needed in planting and tending them suggests that they signify her qualities of kindness, love, orderliness, femininity, and motherliness. At the story's end, after the tinsmith has dumped the flowers at the side of the road, we conclude that her values have also been dumped and that she has been used and deceived. Like Poe's clock, Steinbeck's chrysanthemums are a major contextual symbol. But there is no carryover, for if you find these objects in other stories, they are not symbolic unless the authors of the other stories invest them with symbolic meaning.

DETERMINING WHAT IS SYMBOLIC

To determine whether a particular object, action, or character is a symbol, you need to judge the importance the author gives to it. If the thing is prominent, and also maintains a constancy of meaning, you may justify interpreting it as a symbol. For example, Miss Brill's fur piece in Mansfield's "Miss Brill" (p. 211) is shabby and moth-eaten. It has no value. But because Mansfield makes it especially important at both the beginning and ending of the story, it contextually symbolizes Miss Brill's poverty and isolation. At the end of Welty's "A Worn Path" (p. 124), Phoenix, the major character, plans to spend all her money for a toy windmill for her sick grandson. Readers will note that the windmill is small and fragile, like her life and that of her grandson, but that Phoenix wants to give the boy a little pleasure despite their poverty and hopelessness. For these reasons the windmill is a *contextual* or authorial symbol of her strong character, generous nature, and pathetic existence.

ALLEGORY

An **allegory** is like a symbol because both use one thing to refer to something else. The term is derived from the Greek word *allegorein*, which means "to speak so as to imply other than what is said." Allegory, however, is more sustained than symbolism. An allegory is to a symbol as a motion picture is to a still picture. In form, an allegory is a complete and self-sufficient narrative, but it also signifies another series of events or conditions. While some stories are allegories from beginning to end, many stories that are not allegories may nevertheless contain brief sections or episodes that are *allegorical*.

Allegories and the allegorical method do not exist simply to enable authors to engage in literary exercises. Rather, thinkers and writers have concluded almost from the beginning of time that readers learn and memorize *stories* more easily than *moral lessons*. In addition, thought and expression have not always been free. The threat of censorship and the danger of reprisal have sometimes caused authors to express their views indirectly in the form of allegory rather than to write directly and risk political attack or accusations of libel. The double meaning of many allegories is hence based in both need and reality.

THE NATURE AND APPLICATION OF ALLEGORY

As you study a story for allegory, you should determine how either an entire narrative or a brief episode may be construed as having an extended, allegorical meaning. The continued popularity of George Lucas's film *Star Wars* and its sequels, for example, is attributable at least partly to its being an allegory about the conflict between good and evil. Obi Wan Kenobi (intelligence) enlists the aid of Luke Skywalker (heroism, boldness), and instructs him in "the force" (moral or religious faith). Thus armed and guided, Skywalker opposes the powers of Darth Vader (evil) to rescue the Princess Leia (purity and goodness) with the aid of the latest spaceships and weaponry (technology). The story is accompanied by ingenious visual effects and almost tactile sound effects and music, and hence as an adventure film it stands by itself. With the obvious allegorical overtones, however, it stands for any person's quest for self-fulfillment.

To apply a part of the allegory more specifically, let us consider that the evil Vader has the power to imprison Skywalker for a time, and that Skywalker must exert all his skill and strength to get free and to overcome Vader. In the allegorical application of the episode, this temporary imprisonment signifies those moments of doubt, discouragement, and depression that people experience while trying to better themselves through education, work, self-improvement, friendship, marriage, and so on.

Almost from the beginning of recorded literature, heroic deeds have been represented in allegorical forms. From ancient Greece, the allegorical hero Jason sails the Argo to distant lands to gain the golden fleece (those who take risks are rewarded). From Anglo-Saxon England, the hero Beowulf saves the kingdom by killing Grendel and his monstrous mother (victory comes to those who rely on the forces of good). From seventeenth-century England, Bunyan's *The Pilgrim's Progress* tells how the hero Christian overcomes difficulties and temptations while traveling from this world to the next (belief, perseverance, and resistance to temptation will save the faithful). As long as the parallel interconnections are close and consistent, like those mentioned here, an extended allegorical interpretation is valid.

FABLE, PARABLE, AND MYTH

Three additional forms that are close to allegory, but which are special types, are fable, parable, and myth.

FABLE. The **fable** is an old and popular form. It is usually short, and often features animals with human traits (which are called **beast fables**), to which writers and editors attach "morals" or explanations. Aesop (sixth century B.C.) was reputedly a slave who composed fables in ancient Greece. His fable of "The Fox and the Grapes," for example, signifies the trait of belittling things we cannot have. More recent contributions to the fable tradition are Walt Disney's "Mickey Mouse" and Walt Kelly's "Pogo."

PARABLE. The **parable** is a short, simple allegory with a moral or religious bent. Parables are most often associated with Jesus, who used them to embody his own unique religious insights and truths. His parables of the Good Samaritan and the Prodigal Son, for example, are interpreted to show God's love, concern, understanding, and forgiveness.

MYTH. A **myth** is a story, like the myth of Sisyphus, that is associated with the religion, philosophy, and collective psychology of various societies or cultures. Myths embody truths for prescientific societies, and codify the social and cultural values of the civilization in which they are composed. Sometimes, unfortunately, the words *myth* and *mythical* are used to mean "fanciful" or "untrue." Such disparagement reflects a limited understanding of the psychological, philosophical, and scientific truths embedded in myths. In fact, the truths of mythology are not to be found literally in the stories themselves, but rather in their symbolic or allegorical interpretations.

ALLUSION IN SYMBOLISM AND ALLEGORY

Universal or cultural symbols and allegories often allude to other works from our cultural heritage, such as the Bible, ancient history and literature, and works of the British and American traditions. Sometimes understanding a story may require knowledge of politics and current events.

If a reference is not immediately clear to you, you will need a dictionary or other reference work. The scope of your college dictionary will surprise you. If you cannot find an entry there, however, try one of the major encyclopedias, or ask your reference librarian, who can direct you to shelves loaded with helpful books. A few standard guides are *The Oxford Companion to English Literature*, *The Oxford Companion to Classical Literature*, and William Rose Benet's *The Reader's Encyclopedia*. A useful aid in finding biblical references is *Cruden's Complete Concordance*, which in various editions has been used by readers since 1737, though *Strong's Exhaustive Concordance*, another classic, is fuller and more up to date. These concordances list all the major words used in the King James Bible, so that you may easily locate the chapter and verse of any biblical quotation. If you still have trouble after using sources like these, see your instructor.

AESOP

The Fox and the Grapes (ca. 6th C. B.C.)

A hungry Fox came into a vineyard where there hung delicious clusters of ripe Grapes, his mouth watered to be at them; but they were nailed up to a trellis so high, that with all his springing and leaping he could not reach a single bunch. At last, growing tired and disappointed, "Let who will take them!" says he "they are but green and sour; so I'll e'en let them alone."

QUESTIONS

1. How much do you learn about the characteristics of the fox? How are these characteristics related to the moral or message of the fable?
2. What is the conflict in the fable? What is the resolution?

3. In your own words, explain the meaning of the fable. Is the "sour grape" explanation a satisfactory excuse, or is it a rationalization for failure?

4. From your reading of "The Fox and the Grapes," explain the characteristics of the fable as a type of literature.

THE GOSPEL OF ST. LUKE 15:11–32

The Parable of the Prodigal Son   (*ca.* A.D. *90*)

11 And he [Jesus] said, A certain man had two sons:

12 And the younger of them said to *his* father, Father, give me the portion of goods that falleth *to me*. And he divided unto them *his* living.°

13 And not many days after the younger son gathered all together, and took his journey into a far country,° and there wasted his substance with riotous living.

14 And when he had spent all, there arose a mighty famine in that land; and he began to be in want.

15 And he went and joined himself to a citizen of that country; and he sent him into his fields to feed swine.°

16 And he would fain have filled his belly with the husks° that the swine did eat: and no man gave unto him.

17 And when he came to himself, he said, How many hired servants of my father's have bread enough and to spare, and I perish with hunger!

18 I will arise and go to my father, and will say unto him, Father, I have sinned against heaven, and before thee.

19 And am no more worthy to be called thy son: make me as one of thy hired servants.

20 And he arose, and came to his father. But when he was yet a great way off, his father saw him, and had compassion, and ran, and fell on his neck, and kissed him.

21 And the son said unto him, Father, I have sinned against heaven, and in thy sight, and am no more worthy to be called thy son.

22 But the father said to his servants, Bring forth the best robe, and put *it* on him; and put a ring on his hand, and shoes on *his* feet:

23 And bring hither the fatted calf,° and kill *it*; and let us eat, and be merry:

24 For this my son was dead, and is alive again; he was lost, and is found. And they began to be merry.

25 Now his elder son was in the field: and as he came and drew nigh to the house, he heard music and dancing.

26 And he called one of the servants, and asked what these things meant.

divided . . . his living: one-third of the father's estate; the son had to renounce all further claim.

far country: countries of the Jewish dispersal, or *diaspora*, in the areas bordering the Mediterranean Sea.

feed swine: In Jewish custom, pigs were unclean.

husks: pods of the carob tree, the eating of which was thought to be penitential.

fatted calf: grain-fed calf.

27 And he said unto him, Thy brother is come; and thy father hath killed the fatted calf, because he hath received him safe and sound.

28 And he was angry, and would not go in: therefore came his father out, and intreated him.

29 And he answering said to *his* father, Lo, these many years do I serve thee, neither transgressed I at any time thy commandment: and yet thou never gavest me a kid, that I might make merry with my friends:

30 But as soon as this thy son was come, which hath devoured thy living with harlots, thou hast killed for him the fatted calf.

31 And he said unto him, Son, thou art ever with me, and all that I have is thine.

32 It was meet° that we should make merry, and be glad: for this thy brother was dead, and is alive again: and was lost, and is found.

QUESTIONS

1. Describe the character of the Prodigal Son. Is he flat or round, representative or individual? Why is it necessary that the character be considered representatively, even though he has individual characteristics?

2. What is the plot? What is the antagonism against which the Prodigal Son contends? Why is it necessary that the brother resent the brother's return?

3. What is the resolution of the parable? Why is there no "they lived happily ever after" ending?

4. Using verse numbers, analyze the structure of the parable. What determines your division of the parts? Do these parts coincide with the development of the plot? Describe the relationship of plot to structure in the parable.

5. What is the point of view here? How does the emphasis shift with verse 22?

6. On the basis of the fact that there are many characteristics here of many stories you have read write a description of the parable as a type of literature.

NATHANIEL HAWTHORNE   (1804–1864)

Young Goodman Brown   *1835*

Young Goodman Brown came forth at sunset, into the street of Salem village,° but put his head back, after crossing the threshold, to exchange a parting kiss with his young wife. And Faith, as the wife was aptly named, thrust her own pretty head into the street, letting the wind play with the pink ribbons of her cap, while she called to Goodman Brown.

"Dearest heart," whispered she, softly and rather sadly, when her lips were close to his ear, "prithee, put off your journey until sunrise, and sleep in your own bed to-night. A lone woman is troubled with such dreams and such thoughts, that she's afeared of herself, sometimes. Pray, tarry with me this night, dear husband, of all nights in the year!"

meet: appropriate.
Salem village: in Massachusetts, about fifteen miles north of Boston. The time of the story is the late seventeenth or early eighteenth century.

"My love and my Faith," replied young Goodman Brown, "of all nights in the year, this one night must I tarry away from thee. My journey, as thou callest it, forth and back again, must needs be done 'twixt now and sunrise. What, my sweet, pretty wife, dost thou doubt me already, and we but three months married!"

"Then God bless you!" said Faith with the pink ribbons, "and may you find all well, when you come back."

"Amen!" cried Goodman Brown. "Say thy prayers, dear Faith, and go to bed at dusk, and no harm will come to thee." 5

So they parted; and the young man pursued his way, until, being about to turn the corner by the meeting-house, he looked back and saw the head of Faith still peeping after him, with a melancholy air, in spite of her pink ribbons.

"Poor little Faith!" thought he, for his heart smote him. "What a wretch am I, to leave her on such an errand! She talks of dreams, too. Methought, as she spoke, there was trouble in her face, as if a dream had warned her what work is to be done to-night. But no, no! 't would kill her to think it. Well; she's a blessed angel on earth; and after this one night, I'll cling to her skirts and follow her to Heaven."

With this excellent resolve for the future, Goodman Brown felt himself justified in making more haste on his present evil purpose. He had taken a dreary road, darkened by all the gloomiest trees of the forest, which barely stood aside to let the narrow path creep through, and closed immediately behind. It was all as lonely as could be; and there is this peculiarity in such a solitude, that the traveller knows not who may be concealed by the innumerable trunks and the thick boughs overhead; so that, with lonely footsteps, he may yet be passing through an unseen multitude.

"There may be a devilish Indian behind every tree," said Goodman Brown to himself; and he glanced fearfully behind him, as he added, "What if the devil himself should be at my very elbow!"

His head being turned back, he passed a crook of the road, and looking forward again, beheld the figure of a man, in grave and decent attire, seated at the foot of an old tree. He arose at Goodman Brown's approach, and walked onward, side by side with him. 10

"You are late, Goodman Brown," said he. "The clock of the Old South° was striking, as I came through Boston; and that is full fifteen minutes agone."

"Faith kept me back awhile," replied the young man, with a tremor in his voice, caused by the sudden appearance of his companion, though not wholly unexpected.

It was now deep dusk in the forest, and deepest in that part of it where these two were journeying. As nearly as could be discerned, the second traveller was about fifty years old, apparently in the same rank of life as Goodman Brown, and bearing a considerable resemblance to him, though perhaps more in expression than features. Still, they might have been taken for father and son. And yet, though the elder person was as simply clad as the younger, and as simple in manner too, he had an indescribable air of one who knew the world, and would not have felt abashed at the governor's dinner-table, or in King William's° court, were it possible that his affairs should call him thither. But the only thing about

---

Old South: The Old South Church, in Boston, is still there.

King William: William III was king from 1688 to 1701. William IV was King of England from 1830 to 1837.

him that could be fixed upon as remarkable, was his staff, which bore the likeness of a great black snake, so curiously wrought, that it might almost be seen to twist and wriggle itself like a living serpent. This, of course, must have been an ocular deception, assisted by the uncertain light.

"Come, Goodman Brown!" cried his fellow-traveller, "this is a dull pace for the beginning of a journey. Take my staff, if you are so soon weary."

"Friend," said the other, exchanging his slow pace for a full stop, "having   15
kept covenant by meeting thee here, it is my purpose now to return whence I came. I have scruples, touching the matter thou wot'st of."°

"Sayest thou so?" replied he of the serpent, smiling apart. "Let us walk on, nevertheless, reasoning as we go, and if I convince thee not, thou shalt turn back. We are but a little way in the forest, yet."

"Too far, too far!" exclaimed the goodman, unconsciously resuming his walk. "My father never went into the woods on such an errand, nor his father before him. We have been a race of honest men and good Christians, since the days of the martyrs.° And shall I be the first of the name of Brown that ever took this path and kept—"

"Such company, thou wouldst say," observed the elder person, interrupting his pause. "Well said, Goodman Brown! I have been as well acquainted with your family as ever a one among the Puritans; and that's no trifle to say. I helped your grandfather, the constable, when he lashed the Quaker woman so smartly through the streets of Salem. And it was I that brought your father a pitch-pine knot, kindled at my own hearth, to set fire to an Indian village, in King Philip's war.° They were my good friends, both; and many a pleasant walk have we had along this path, and returned merrily after midnight. I would fain be friends with you, for their sake."

"If it be as thou sayest," replied Goodman Brown, "I marvel they never spoke of these matters. Or, verily, I marvel not, seeing that the least rumor of the sort would have driven them from New England. We are a people of prayer, and good works to boot, and abide no such wickedness."

"Wickedness or not," said the traveller with twisted staff, "I have a very   20
general acquaintance here in New England. The deacons of many a church have drunk the communion wine with me; the selectmen, of divers towns, make me their chairman; and a majority of the Great and General Court are firm supporters of my interest. The governor and I, too—but these are state secrets."

"Can this be so!" cried Goodman Brown, with a stare of amazement at his undisturbed companion. "Howbeit, I have nothing to do with the governor and council; they have their own ways, and are no rule for a simple husbandman like me. But, were I to go on with thee, how should I meet the eye of that good old man, our minister, at Salem village? Oh, his voice would make me tremble, both Sabbath-day and lecture-day!"

Thus far, the elder traveller had listened with due gravity, but now burst

Thou wot'st: You know.

days of the martyrs: the martyrdoms of Protestants in England during the reign of Queen Mary (1553–1558).

King Philip's war: This war (1675–1676), infamous for the atrocities committed by the New England settlers, resulted in the suppression of Indian tribal life, and prepared the way for unlimited settlement of New England by European immigrants. "Philip" was the English name of Chief Metacomet of the Wampanoag tribe.

into a fit of irrepressible mirth, shaking himself so violently, that his snakelike staff actually seemed to wriggle in sympathy.

"Ha! ha! ha!" shouted he, again and again; then composing himself, "Well, go on, Goodman Brown, go on; but, prithee, don't kill me with laughing!"

"Well, then, to end the matter at once," said Goodman Brown, considerably nettled, "there is my wife, Faith. It would break her dear little heart; and I'd rather break my own!"

"Nay, if that be the case," answered the other, "e'en go thy ways, Goodman Brown. I would not, for twenty old women like the one hobbling before us, that Faith should come to any harm."

25

As he spoke, he pointed his staff at a female figure on the path, in whom Goodman Brown recognized a very pious and exemplary dame, who had taught him his catechism in youth, and was still his moral and spiritual adviser, jointly with the minister and Deacon Gookin.

"A marvel, truly, that Goody° Cloyse should be so far in the wilderness, at nightfall!" said he. "But, with your leave, friend, I shall take a cut through the woods, until we have left this Christian woman behind. Being a stranger to you, she might ask whom I was consorting with, and whither I was going."

"Be it so," said his fellow-traveller. "Betake you to the woods, and let me keep the path."

Accordingly, the young man turned aside, but took care to watch his companion, who advanced softly along the road, until he had come within a staff's length of the old dame. She, meanwhile, was making the best of her way, with singular speed for so aged a woman, and mumbling some indistinct words, a prayer, doubtless, as she went. The traveller put forth his staff, and touched her withered neck with what seemed the serpent's tail.

"The devil!" screamed the pious old lady.

30

"Then Goody Cloyse knows her old friend?" observed the traveller, confronting her, and leaning on his writhing stick.

"Ah, forsooth, and is it your worship, indeed?" cried the good dame. "Yea, truly is it, and in the very image of my old gossip,° Goodman Brown, the grandfather of the silly fellow that now is. But, would your worship believe it? My broomstick hath strangely disappeared, stolen, as I suspect, by that unhanged witch, Goody Cory,° and that, too, when I was all anointed with the juice of smallage and cinquefoil and wolf's-bane—"°

"Mingled with fine wheat and the fat of a new-born babe," said the shape of old Goodman Brown.

"Ah, your worship knows the recipe," cried the old lady, cackling aloud. "So, as I was saying, being all ready for the meeting, and no horse to ride on, I made up my mind to foot it; for they tell me there is a nice young man to be taken into communion to-night. But now your good worship will lend me your arm, and we shall be there in a twinkling."

Goody: shortened form of "goodwife," a respectful name for a married woman of low rank. A "Goody Cloyse" was one of the women sentenced to execution by Hawthorne's great grandfather, Judge John Hathorne.

gossip: from "good sib" or "good relative."

Goody Cory: name of a woman who was also sent to execution by Judge Hathorne.

smallage and cinquefoil and wolf's-bane: plants commonly used by witches in making ointments.

"That can hardly be," answered her friend. "I will not spare you my arm,   35
Goody Cloyse, but here is my staff, if you will."

So saying, he threw it down at her feet, where, perhaps, it assumed life,
being one of the rods which its owner had formerly lent to the Egyptian Magi.°
Of this fact, however, Goodman Brown could not take cognizance. He had cast
up his eyes in astonishment, and looking down again, beheld neither Goody Cloyse
nor the serpentine staff, but his fellow-traveller alone, who waited for him as
calmly as if nothing had happened.

"That old woman taught me my catechism!" said the young man; and there
was a world of meaning in this simple comment.

They continued to walk onward, while the elder traveller exhorted his
companion to make good speed and persevere in the path, discoursing so aptly,
that his arguments seemed rather to spring up in the bosom of his auditor, than
to be suggested by himself. As they went he plucked a branch of maple, to serve
for a walking-stick, and began to strip it of the twigs and little boughs, which were
wet with evening dew. The moment his fingers touched them, they became
strangely withered and dried up, as with a week's sunshine. Thus the pair
proceeded, at a good free pace, until suddenly, in a gloomy hollow of the road,
Goodman Brown sat himself down on the stump of a tree, and refused to go any
farther.

"Friend," said he, stubbornly, "my mind is made up. Not another step will
I budge on this errand. What if a wretched old woman do choose to go to the
devil, when I thought she was going to Heaven! Is that any reason why I should
quit my dear Faith, and go after her?"

"You will think better of this by and by," said his acquaintance, composedly.   40
"Sit here and rest yourself a while; and when you feel like moving again, there is
my staff to help you along."

Without more words, he threw his companion the maple stick, and was as
speedily out of sight as if he had vanished into the deepening gloom. The young
man sat a few moments by the roadside, applauding himself greatly, and thinking
with how clear a conscience he should meet the minister, in his morning walk, nor
shrink from the eye of good old Deacon Gookin. And what calm sleep would be
his, that very night, which was to have been spent so wickedly, but purely and
sweetly now, in the arms of Faith! Amidst these pleasant and praiseworthy
meditations, Goodman Brown heard the tramp of horses along the road, and
deemed it advisable to conceal himself within the verge of the forest, conscious of
the guilty purpose that had brought him thither, though now so happily turned
from it.

On came the hoof-tramps and the voices of the riders, two grave old voices,
conversing soberly as they drew near. These mingled sounds appeared to pass
along the road, within a few yards of the young man's hiding-place; but owing,
doubtless, to the depth of the gloom, at that particular spot, neither the travellers
nor their steeds were visible. Though their figures brushed the small boughs by
the wayside, it could not be seen that they intercepted, even for a moment, the
faint gleam from the strip of bright sky, athwart which they must have passed.
Goodman Brown alternately crouched and stood on tiptoe, pulling aside the
branches, and thrusting forth his head as far as he durst, without discerning so

---

lent to the Egyptian Magi: See Exodus 7:10–12.

much as a shadow. It vexed him the more, because he could have sworn, were such a thing possible, that he recognized the voices of the minister and Deacon Gookin, jogging° along quietly, as they were wont to do, when bound to some ordination or ecclesiastical council. While yet within hearing, one of the riders stopped to pluck a switch.

"Of the two, reverend Sir," said the voice like the deacon's, "I had rather miss an ordination dinner than to-night's meeting. They tell me that some of our community are to be here from Falmouth and beyond, and others from Connecticut and Rhode Island; besides several of the Indian powwows,° who, after their fashion, know almost as much deviltry as the best of us. Moreover, there is a goodly young woman to be taken into communion."

"Mighty well, Deacon Gookin!" replied the solemn old tones of the minister. "Spur up, or we shall be late. Nothing can be done, you know, until I get on the ground."

The hoofs clattered again, and the voices, talking so strangely in the empty air, passed on through the forest, where no church had ever been gathered, nor solitary Christian prayed. Whither, then, could these holy men be journeying, so deep into the heathen wilderness? Young Goodman Brown caught hold of a tree, for support, being ready to sink down on the ground, faint and over-burthened with the heavy sickness of his heart. He looked up to the sky, doubting whether there really was a Heaven above him. Yet, there was the blue arch, and the stars brightening in it. 45

"With Heaven above, and Faith below, I will yet stand firm against the devil!" cried Goodman Brown.

While he still gazed upward, into the deep arch of the firmament, and had lifted his hands to pray, a cloud, though no wind was stirring, hurried across the zenith, and hid the brightening stars. The blue sky was still visible, except directly overhead, where this black mass of cloud was sweeping swiftly northward. Aloft in the air, as if from the depths of the cloud, came a confused and doubtful sound of voices. Once, the listener fancied that he could distinguish the accents of town's people of his own, men and women, both pious and ungodly, many of whom he had met at the communion-table, and had seen others rioting at the tavern. The next moment, so indistinct were the sounds, he doubted whether he had heard aught but the murmur of the old forest, whispering without a wind. Then came a stronger swell of those familiar tones, heard daily in the sunshine, at Salem village, but never, until now, from a cloud at night. There was one voice, of a young woman, uttering lamentations, yet with an uncertain sorrow, and entreating for some favor, which, perhaps, it would grieve her to obtain. And all the unseen multitude, both saints and sinners, seemed to encourage her onward.

"Faith!" shouted Goodman Brown, in a voice of agony and desperation; and the echoes of the forest mocked him, crying—"Faith! Faith!" as if bewildered wretches were seeking her, all through the wilderness.

The cry of grief, rage, and terror was yet piercing the night, when the unhappy husband held his breath for a response. There was a scream, drowned immediately in a louder murmur of voices fading into far-off laughter, as the dark

jogging: riding a horse at a slow trot.
powwow: a Narragansett Indian word describing a ritual ceremony of dancing, incantation, and magic.

cloud swept away, leaving the clear and silent sky above Goodman Brown. But something fluttered lightly down through the air, and caught on the branch of a tree. The young man seized it and beheld a pink ribbon.

"My Faith is gone!" cried he, after one stupefied moment. "There is no good on earth, and sin is but a name. Come, devil! for to thee is this world given." 50

And maddened with despair, so that he laughed loud and long, did Goodman Brown grasp his staff and set forth again, at such a rate, that he seemed to fly along the forest path, rather than to walk or run. The road grew wilder and drearier, and more faintly traced, and vanished at length, leaving him in the heart of the dark wilderness, still rushing onward, with the instinct that guides mortal man to evil. The whole forest was peopled with frightful sounds; the creaking of the trees, the howling of wild beasts, and the yell of Indians; while, sometimes, the wind tolled like a distant church bell, and sometimes gave a broad roar around the traveller, as if all Nature were laughing him to scorn. But he was himself the chief horror of the scene, and shrank not from its other horrors.

"Ha! ha! ha!" roared Goodman Brown, when the wind laughed at him. "Let us hear which will laugh loudest! Think not to frighten me with your deviltry! Come witch, come wizard, come Indian powwow, come devil himself! and here comes Goodman Brown. You may as well fear him as he fear you!"

In truth, all through the haunted forest, there could be nothing more frightful than the figure of Goodman Brown. On he flew, among the black pines, brandishing his staff with frenzied gestures, now giving vent to an inspiration of horrid blasphemy, and now shouting forth such laughter, as set all the echoes of the forest laughing like demons around him. The fiend in his own shape is less hideous than when he rages in the breast of man. Thus sped the demoniac on his course, until, quivering among the trees, he saw a red light before him, as when the felled trunks and branches of a clearing have been set on fire, and throw up their lurid blaze against the sky, at the hour of midnight. He paused, in a lull of the tempest that had driven him onward, and heard the swell of what seemed a hymn, rolling solemnly from a distance, with the weight of many voices. He knew the tune. It was a familiar one in the choir of the village meeting-house. The verse died heavily away, and was lengthened by a chorus, not of human voices, but of all the sounds of the benighted wilderness, pealing in awful harmony together. Goodman Brown cried out; and his cry was lost to his own ear, by its unison with the cry of the desert.

In the interval of silence, he stole forward, until the light glared full upon his eyes. At one extremity of an open space, hemmed in by the dark wall of the forest, arose a rock, bearing some rude, natural resemblance either to an altar or a pulpit, and surrounded by four blazing pines, their tops aflame, their stems untouched, like candles at an evening meeting. The mass of foliage, that had overgrown the summit of the rock, was all on fire, blazing high into the night, and fitfully illuminating the whole field. Each pendent twig and leafy festoon was in a blaze. As the red light arose and fell, a numerous congregation alternately shone forth, then disappeared in shadow, and again grew, as it were, out of the darkness, peopling the heart of the solitary woods at once.

"A grave and dark-clad company!" quoth Goodman Brown. 55

In truth, they were such. Among them, quivering to-and-fro, between gloom and splendor, appeared faces that would be seen, next day, at the council-board of the province, and others which, Sabbath after Sabbath, looked devoutly heavenward, and benignantly over the crowded pews, from the holiest pulpits in the land. Some affirm that the lady of the governor was there. At least, there were high dames well known to her, and wives of honored husbands, and widows a great multitude, and ancient maidens, all of excellent repute, and fair young girls, who trembled lest their mothers should espy them. Either the sudden gleams of light, flashing over the obscure field, bedazzled Goodman Brown, or he recognized a score of the church members of Salem village, famous for their especial sanctity. Good old Deacon Gookin had arrived, and waited at the skirts of that venerable saint, his reverend pastor. But, irreverently consorting with these grave, reputable, and pious people, these elders of the church, these chaste dames and dewy virgins, there were men of dissolute lives and women of spotted fame, wretches given over to all mean and filthy vice, and suspected even of horrid crimes. It was strange to see, that the good shrank not from the wicked, nor were the sinners abashed by the saints. Scattered, also, among their pale-faced enemies, were the Indian priests, or powwows, who had often scared their native forest with more hideous incantations than any known to English witchcraft.

"But, where is Faith?" thought Goodman Brown; and, as hope came into his heart, he trembled.

Another verse of the hymn arose, a slow and mournful strain, such as the pious love, but joined to words which expressed all that our nature can conceive of sin, and darkly hinted at far more. Unfathomable to mere mortals is the lore of fiends. Verse after verse was sung, and still the chorus of the desert swelled between, like the deepest tone of a mighty organ. And, with the final peal of that dreadful anthem, there came a sound, as if the roaring wind, the rushing streams, the howling beasts, and every other voice of the unconverted wilderness were mingling and according with the voice of guilty man, in homage to the prince of all. The four blazing pines threw up a loftier flame, and obscurely discovered shapes and visages of horror on the smoke-wreaths, above the impious assembly. At the same moment, the fire on the rock shot redly forth, and formed a glowing arch above its base, where now appeared a figure. With reverence be it spoken, the apparition bore no slight similitude, both in garb and manner, to some grave divine of the New England churches.

"Bring forth the converts!" cried a voice, that echoed through the field and rolled into the forest.

At the word, Goodman Brown stepped forth from the shadow of the trees, and approached the congregation, with whom he felt a loathful brotherhood, by the sympathy of all that was wicked in his heart. He could have well-nigh sworn, that the shape of his own dead father beckoned him to advance, looking downward from a smoke-wreath, while a woman, with dim features of despair, threw out her hand to warn him back. Was it his mother? But he had no power to retreat one step, nor to resist, even in thought, when the minister and good old Deacon Gookin seized his arms, and led him to the blazing rock. Thither came also the slender form of a veiled female, led between Goody Cloyse, that pious teacher of the catechism, and Martha Carrier, who had received the devil's promise to be queen of hell. A rampant hag was she! And there stood the proselytes, beneath the canopy of fire.

"Welcome, my children," said the dark figure, "to the communion of your race! Ye have found, thus young, your nature and your destiny. My children, look behind you!"

They turned; and flashing forth, as it were, in a sheet of flame, the fiend-worshippers were seen; the smile of welcome gleamed darkly on every visage.

"There," resumed the sable form, "are all whom ye have reverenced from youth. Ye deemed them holier than yourselves, and shrank from your own sin, contrasting it with their lives of righteousness and prayerful aspirations heavenward. Yet, here are they all, in my worshipping assembly! This night it shall be granted you to know their secret deeds; how hoary-bearded elders of the church have whispered wanton words to the young maids of their households; how many a woman, eager for widow's weeds, has given her husband a drink at bedtime, and let him sleep his last sleep in her bosom; how beardless youths have made haste to inherit their father's wealth; and how fair damsels—blush not, sweet ones!—have dug little graves in the garden, and bidden me, the sole guest, to an infant's funeral. By the sympathy of your human hearts for sin, ye shall scent out all the places—whether in church, bed-chamber, street, field, or forest—where crime has been committed, and shall exult to behold the whole earth one stain of guilt, one mighty blood-spot. Far more than this! It shall be yours to penetrate, in every bosom, the deep mystery of sin, the fountain of all wicked arts, and which inexhaustibly supplies more evil impulses than human power—than my power, at its utmost!—can make manifest in deeds. And now, my children, look upon each other."

They did so; and, by the blaze of the hell-kindled torches, the wretched man beheld his Faith, and the wife her husband, trembling before that unhallowed altar.

"Lo! there ye stand, my children," said the figure, in a deep and solemn   65
tone, almost sad, with its despairing awfulness, as if his once angelic nature° could yet mourn for our miserable race. "Depending upon one another's hearts, ye had still hoped that virtue were not all a dream! Now are ye undeceived!—Evil is the nature of mankind. Evil must be your only happiness. Welcome, again, my children, to the communion of your race!"

"Welcome!" repeated the fiend-worshippers, in one cry of despair and triumph.

And there they stood, the only pair, as it seemed, who were yet hesitating on the verge of wickedness, in this dark world. A basin was hollowed, naturally, in the rock. Did it contain water, reddened by the lurid light? or was it blood? or, perchance, a liquid flame? Herein did the Shape of Evil dip his hand, and prepare to lay the mark of baptism upon their foreheads, that they might be partakers of the mystery of sin, more conscious of the secret guilt of others, both in deed and thought, than they could now be of their own. The husband cast one look at his pale wife, and Faith at him. What polluted wretches would the next glance show them to each other, shuddering alike at what they disclosed and what they saw!

"Faith! Faith!" cried the husband. "Look up to Heaven, and resist the Wicked One!"

Whether Faith obeyed, he knew not. Hardly had he spoken, when he found himself amid calm night and solitude, listening to a roar of the wind, which died heavily away through the forest. He staggered against the rock, and felt it chill

---

once angelic nature: Lucifer ("light bearer"), another name for the Devil, led the traditional revolt of the angels, and was thrown into hell as his punishment. See Isaiah 14:12–15.

and damp, while a hanging twig, that had been all on fire, besprinkled his cheek
with the coldest dew.

The next morning, young Goodman Brown came slowly into the street of   70
Salem village staring around him like a bewildered man. The good old minister
was taking a walk along the grave-yard, to get an appetite for breakfast and
meditate his sermon, and bestowed a blessing, as he passed, on Goodman Brown.
He shrank from the venerable saint, as if to avoid an anathema. Old Deacon
Gookin was at domestic worship, and the holy words of his prayer were heard
through the open window. "What God doth the wizard pray to?" quoth Goodman
Brown. Goody Cloyse, that excellent old Christian, stood in the early sunshine, at
her own lattice, catechising a little girl, who had brought her a pint of morning's
milk. Goodman Brown snatched away the child, as from the grasp of the fiend
himself. Turning the corner by the meetinghouse, he spied the head of Faith,
with the pink ribbons, gazing anxiously forth, and bursting into such joy at the
sight of him that she skipt along the street, and almost kissed her husband before
the whole village. But Goodman Brown looked sternly and sadly into her face,
and passed on without a greeting.

Had Goodman Brown fallen asleep in the forest, and only dreamed a wild
dream of a witch-meeting?

Be it so, if you will. But, alas! it was a dream of evil omen for young
Goodman Brown. A stern, a sad, a darkly meditative, a distrustful, if not a
desperate man did he become, from the night of that fearful dream. On the
Sabbath day, when the congregation were singing a holy psalm, he could not
listen, because an anthem of sin rushed loudly upon his ear, and drowned all the
blessed strain. When the minister spoke from the pulpit, with power and fervid
eloquence, and with his hand on the open Bible, of the sacred truths of our
religion, and of saint-like lives and triumphant deaths, and of future bliss or
misery unutterable, then did Goodman Brown turn pale, dreading lest the roof
should thunder down upon the gray blasphemer and his hearers. Often, awaking
suddenly at midnight, he shrank from the bosom of Faith, and at morning or
eventide, when the family knelt down in prayer, he scowled, and muttered to
himself, and gazed sternly at his wife, and turned away. And when he had lived
long, and was borne to his grave, a hoary corpse, followed by Faith, an aged
woman, and children and grandchildren, a goodly procession, besides neighbors
not a few, they carved no hopeful verse upon his tombstone; for his dying hour
was gloom.

QUESTIONS

1. Near the end of the story the narrator asks the following: "Had Goodman
   Brown fallen asleep in the forest, and only dreamed a wild dream of a witch-
   meeting?" What is the answer? If Goodman Brown's visions come out of his
   own dreams (mind, subconscious), what do they tell us about him?

2. Is Goodman Brown round or flat? To what extent is he a symbolic "everyman"
   or representative of humankind?

3. Consider Hawthorne's use of symbolism, such as sunset and night, the
   walking stick, the witches' sabbath, the marriage to Faith, and the vague
   shadows amid the darkness, together with other symbols that you may find.

4. What details establish the two settings? What characterizes Salem? The woods? Why might we be justified in seeing the forest as a symbolic setting?

5. To what extent are the people, objects, and events in Goodman Brown's adventure invested with enough *consistent* symbolic resonance to justify calling his episode in the woods an allegory? Consider Brown's wife, Faith, as an allegorical figure. What do you make of Brown's statements that "I'll cling to her skirts and follow her to Heaven" (paragraph 7) and "Faith kept me back awhile" (paragraph 12). In this same light, consider the other characters Brown meets in the forest, the sunset, the walk into the forest, and the staff "which bore the likeness of a great black snake."

MARJORIE PICKTHALL   (1883–1922)

The Worker in Sandalwood   1923

I like to think of this as a true story, but you who read may please yourselves, siding either with the curé,° who says Hyacinthe dreamed it all, and did the carving himself in his sleep, or with Madame. I am sure that Hyacinthe thinks it true, and so does Madame, but then she has the cabinet, with the little birds and the lilies carved at the corners. Monsieur le curé shrugs his patient shoulders; but then he is tainted with the infidelities of cities, good man, having been three times to Montreal, and once, in an electric car, to Saint Anne. He and Madame still talk it over whenever they meet, though it happened so many years ago, and each leaves the other forever unconvinced. Meanwhile the dust gathers in the infinite fine lines of the little birds' feathers, and softens the lily stamens where Madame's duster may not go; and the wood, ageing, takes on a golden gleam as of immemorial sunsets: that pale red wood, heavy with the scent of the ancient East; the wood that Hyacinthe loved.

It was the only wood of that kind which had ever been seen in Terminaison.° Pierre L'Oreillard brought it into the workshop one morning; a small heavy bundle wrapped in sacking, and then in burlap, and then in fine soft cloths. He laid it on a pile of shavings, and unwrapped it carefully and a dim sweetness filled the dark shed and hung heavily in the thin winter sunbeams.

Pierre L'Oreillard rubbed the wood respectfully with his knobby fingers. "It is sandalwood," he explained to Hyacinthe, pride of knowledge making him expansive; "a most precious wood° that grows in warm countries, thou great goblin. Smell it, *imbécile*. It is sweeter than cedar. It is to make a cabinet for the old Madame at the big house. Thy great hands shall smooth the wood, *nigaud*,° and I—I, Pierre the cabinet-maker, shall render it beautiful." Then he went out, locking the door behind him.

When he was gone, Hyacinthe laid down his plane, blew on his stiff fingers, and shambled slowly over to the wood. He was a great clumsy boy of fourteen, dark-faced, very slow of speech, dull-eyed and uncared for. He was clumsy because

curé: parish priest.
Terminaison: (literally, the "ending"), a town imagined as a part of French Canada.
a most precious wood: Sandalwood is still rare and precious: it is grown mainly in India and yields to exquisite detail in carving and decoration.
nigaud: simpleton.

it is impossible to move gracefully when you are growing very big and fast on quite insufficient food. He was dull-eyed because all eyes met his unlovingly; uncared for, because none knew the beauty of his soul. But his heavy young hands could carve simple things, like flowers and birds and beasts, to perfection, as the curé pointed out. Simon has a tobacco-jar, carved with pine-cones and squirrels, and the curé has a pipe whose bowl is the bloom of a moccasin-flower, that I have seen. But it is all very long ago. And facts, in these lonely villages, easily become transfigured, touched upon their gray with a golden gleam.

"Thy hands shall smooth the wood, *nigaud*, and I shall render it beautiful," said Pierre L'Oreillard, and went off to drink brandy at the Cinq Chateaux.   5

Hyacinthe knew that the making of the cabinet would fall to him, as most of the other work did. He also touched the strange sweet wood, and at last laid his cheek against it, while the fragrance caught his breath. "How it is beautiful," said Hyacinthe, and for a moment his eyes glowed and he was happy. Then the light passed, and with bent head he shuffled back to his bench through a foam of white shavings curling almost to his knees.

"Madame perhaps will want the cabinet next week, for that is Christmas," said Hyacinthe, and fell to work harder than ever, though it was so cold in the shed that his breath hung like a little silver cloud and the steel stung his hands. There was a tiny window to his right, through which, when it was clear of frost, one looked on Terminaison, and that was cheerful and made one whistle. But to the left, through the chink of the ill-fitting door, there was nothing but the forest and the road dying away in it, and the trees moving heavily under the snow. Yet, from there came all Hyacinthe's dumb dreams and slow reluctant fancies, which he sometimes found himself able to tell—in wood, not in words.

Brandy was good at the Cinq Chateaux, and Pierre L'Oreillard gave Hyacinthe plenty of directions, but no further help with the cabinet.

"That is to be finished for Madame on the festival, *gros escargot!*"° said he, cuffing Hyacinthe's ears furiously, "finished, and with a prettiness about the corners, hearest thou, *ourson?*° I suffer from a delicacy of the constitution and a little feebleness in the legs on these days, so that I cannot handle the tools. I must leave this work to thee, *gâcheur.*° See it is done properly, and stand up and touch a hand to thy cap when I address thee, *orvet,*° great slow-worm."

"Yes, monsieur," said Hyacinthe, wearily.   10

It is hard, when you do all the work, to be cuffed into the bargain, and fourteen is not very old. He went to work on the cabinet with slow, exquisite skill, but on the eve of Noel, he was still at work, and the cabinet unfinished. It meant a thrashing from Pierre if the morrow came and found it still unfinished, and Pierre's thrashings were cruel. But it was growing into a thing of perfection under his slow hands, and Hyacinthe would not hurry over it.

"Then work on it all night, and show it to me all completed in the morning, or thy bones shall mourn thy idleness," said Pierre with a flicker of his little eyes. And he shut Hyacinthe into the workshop with a smoky lamp, his tools, and the sandalwood cabinet.

It was nothing unusual. The boy had often been left before to finish a piece

gros escargot: big snail.
ourson: bear cub.
gâcheur: bungler, spoiler.
orvet: blind worm, slow worm.

of work overnight while Pierre went off to his brandies. But this was Christmas Eve, and he was very tired. The cold crept into the shed until the scent of the sandalwood could not make him dream himself warm, and the roof cracked sullenly in the forest. There came upon Hyacinthe one of those awful, hopeless despairs that children know. It seemed to be a living presence that caught up his soul and crushed it in black hands. "In all the world, nothing!" said he, staring at the dull flame; "no place, no heart, no love! O kind God, is there a place, a love for me in another world?"

I cannot endure to think of Hyacinthe, poor lad, shut up despairing in the workshop with his loneliness, his cold, and his hunger, on the eve of Christmas. He was but an overgrown, unhappy child, and for unhappy children no aid, at this season, seems too divine for faith. So Madame says, and she is very old and very wise. Hyacinthe even looked at the chisel in his hand, and thought that by a touch of that he might lose it all, all, and be at peace, somewhere not far from God; only it was forbidden. Then came the tears, and great sobs that sickened and deafened him, so that he scarcely heard the gentle rattling of the latch.

At least, I suppose it came then, but it may have been later. The story is all   15
so vague here, so confused with fancies that have spoiled the first simplicity. I think that Hyacinthe must have gone to the door, opening it upon the still woods and the frosty stars, and the lad who stood outside must have said: "I see you are working late, comrade. May I come in?" or something like it.

Hyacinthe brushed his ragged sleeve across his eyes, and opened the door wider with a little nod to the other to enter. Those little lonely villages strung along the great river see strange wayfarers adrift inland from the sea. Hyacinthe said to himself that surely here was such a one.

Afterwards he told the curé that for a moment he had been bewildered. Dully blinking into the stranger's eyes, he lost for a flash the first impression of youth and received one of some incredible age or sadness. But this also passed and he knew that the wanderer's eyes were only quiet, very quiet, like the little pools in the wood where the wild does went to drink. As he turned within the door, smiling at Hyacinthe and shaking some snow from his fur cap, he did not seem more than sixteen or so.

"It is very cold outside," he said. "There is a big oak tree on the edge of the fields that has split in the frost and frightened all the little squirrels asleep there. Next year it will make an even better home for them. And see what I found close by!" He opened his fingers, and showed Hyacinthe a little sparrow lying unruffled in his palm.

"*Pauvrette!*"° said the dull Hyacinthe. "*Pauvrette!* Is it then dead?" He touched it with a gentle forefinger.

"No," answered the strange boy, "it is not dead. We'll put it here among the   20
shavings, not far from the lamp, and it will be well by morning."°

He smiled at Hyacinthe again, and the shambling lad felt dimly as if the scent of sandalwood had deepened, and the lamp-flame burned clearer. But the stranger's eyes were only quiet, quiet.

"Have you come far?" asked Hyacinthe. "It is a bad season for travelling, and the wolves are out in the woods."

Pauvrette: poor little thing.
. . . by morning: See Psalms 84:4.

"A long way," said the other; "a long, long way. I heard a child cry. . . ."

"There is no child here," answered Hyacinthe, shaking his head. "Monsieur L'Oreillard is not fond of children, he says they cost too much money. But if you have come far, you must be cold and hungry, and I have no food or fire. At the Cinq Chateaux you will find both!"

The stranger looked at him again with those quiet eyes, and Hyacinthe 25
fancied his face was familiar. "I will stay here," he said, "you are very late at work and you are unhappy."

"Why, as to that," answered Hyacinthe, rubbing again at his cheeks and ashamed of his tears, "most of us are sad at one time or another, the good God knows. Stay here and welcome if it pleases you, and you may take a share of my bed, though it is no more than a pile of balsam boughs and an old blanket, in the loft. But I must work at this cabinet, for the drawer must be finished and the handles put on and these corners carved, all by the holy morning; or my wages will be paid with a stick."

"You have a hard master," put in the other boy, "if he would pay you with blows upon the feast of Noel."

"He is hard enough," said Hyacinthe; "but once he gave me a dinner of sausages and white wine, and once, in the summer, melons. If my eyes will stay open, I will finish this by morning, but indeed I am sleepy. Stay with me an hour or so, comrade, and talk to me of your wanderings, so that the time may pass more quickly."

"I will tell you of the country where I was a child," answered the stranger.

And while Hyacinthe worked, he told—of sunshine and dust; of the shadows 30
of vine-leaves on the flat white walls of a house; of rosy doves on the flat roof; of the flowers that come in the spring, crimson and blue, and the white cyclamen in the shadow of the rocks; of the olive, the myrtle and almond; until Hyacinthe's slow fingers ceased working, and his sleepy eyes blinked wonderingly.

"See what you have done, comrade," he said at last; "you have told of such pretty things that I have done no work for an hour. And now the cabinet will never be finished, and I shall be beaten."

"Let me help you," smiled the other; "I also was bred a carpenter."°

At first Hyacinthe would not, fearing to trust the sweet wood out of his own hands, but at length he allowed the stranger to fit in one of the little drawers, and so deftly was the work done, that Hyacinthe pounded his fists on the bench in admiration. "You have a pretty knack," he cried; "it seemed as if you did but hold the drawer in your hands a moment, and hey! ho! it jumped into its place!"

"Let me fit in the other little drawers, while you go and rest a while," said the wanderer. So Hyacinthe curled up among the shavings, and the stranger fell to work upon the little cabinet of sandalwood.

Here begins what the curé will have it is a dream within a dream. Sweetest 35
of dreams was ever dreamed, if that is so. Sometimes I am forced to think with him, but again I see as clearly as with old Madame's eyes, that have not seen the earthly light for twenty years, and with her and Hyacinthe, I say "Credo."°

Hyacinthe said that he lay upon the shavings in the sweetness of the

. . . bred a carpenter: See Matthew 13:55.
Credo: "I believe," the opening words of the *Credo* section of the traditional Mass ("Credo in unum Deum . . ." ["I believe in one God . . ."]).

sandalwood, and was very tired. He thought of the country where the stranger had been a boy; of the flowers on the hills; of the laughing leaves of aspen, and poplar; of the golden flowering anise and the golden sun upon the dusty roads, until he was warm. All the time through these pictures, as through a painted veil, he was aware of that other boy with the quiet eyes, at work upon the cabinet, smoothing, fitting, polishing. "He does better work than I," thought Hyacinthe, but he was not jealous. And again he thought, "It is growing towards morning. In a little while I will get up and help him." But he did not, for the dream of warmth and the smell of the sandalwood held him in a sweet drowse. Also he said that he thought the stranger was singing as he worked, for there seemed to be a sense of some music in the shed, though he could not tell whether it came from the other boy's lips, or from the shabby old tools as he used them, or from the stars. "The stars are much paler," thought Hyacinthe, "and soon it will be morning, and the corners are not carved yet. I must get up and help this kind one in a little moment. Only I am so tired, and the music and the sweetness seem to wrap me and fold me close, so that I may not move."

He lay without moving, and behind the forest there shone a pale glow of some indescribable colour that was neither green nor blue, while in Terminaison the church bells began to ring. "Day will soon be here!" thought Hyacinthe, immovable in that deep dream of his, "and with day will come Monsieur L'Oreillard and his stick. I must get up and help, for even yet the corners are not carved."

But he did not get up. Instead, he saw the stranger look at him again, smiling as if he loved him, and lay his brown finger lightly upon the four empty corners of the cabinet. And Hyacinthe saw the little squares of reddish wood ripple and heave and break, as little clouds when the wind goes through the sky. And out of them thrust forth little birds, and after them the lilies, for a moment living, but even while Hyacinthe looked, growing hard and reddish-brown and settling back into the sweet wood. Then the stranger smiled again, and laid all the tools neatly in order, and, opening the door quietly, went away into the woods.

Hyacinthe lay still among the shavings for a long time, and then he crept slowly to the door. The sun, not yet risen, set its first beams upon the delicate mist of frost afloat beneath the trees, and so all the world was aflame with spendid gold. Far away down the road a dim figure seemed to move amid the glory, but the flow and the splendour were such that Hyacinthe was blinded. His breath came sharply as the glow beat in great waves on the wretched shed; on the foam of shavings; on the cabinet with the little birds and the lilies carved at the corners.

He was too pure of heart° to feel afraid. But, "Blessed be the Lord," 40 whispered Hyacinthe, clasping his slow hands, "for He hath visited and redeemed His people.° But who will believe?"

Then the sun of Christ's day rose gloriously, and the little sparrow came from his nest among the shavings and shook his wings to the light.°

QUESTIONS

1. What point of view is employed in the story? Who is the narrator? To what extent does the narrator know more than we might expect? Why does the narrator repeat that the events happened "very long ago"?

pure of heart: See Matthew 5:8.
His people: See Luke 1:68.
wings to the light: See Malachi 4:2.

2. Describe Hyacinthe. How does he deal with his life? How does he react to L'Oreillard's treatment? Why does the "strange child" appear to him?

3. Why does the narrator stress the quality of Hyacinthe's work? Why does the narrator stress that Hyacinthe dreamed the events? To what extent do these points of emphasis keep the story from becoming too fantastic or sentimentalized?

4. To what extent does the setting work symbolically to establish mood and tone? Consider the time of year, the specific night, the description of the shed in which Hyacinthe works, the forest, and the animals noted throughout.

5. Consider the symbolism associated with the "quiet" stranger: his homeland, his training as a carpenter, the sparrow he revives, the heightening of the lamp-flame, and the warming of the workshop.

6. Would you consider this story an allegory, a myth, a fable, a parable, or simply symbolic? Explain your answer.

JOHN STEINBECK (1902–1968)

The Chrysanthemums   *1937*

The high grey-flannel fog of winter closed off the Salinas Valley° from the sky and from all the rest of the world. On every side it sat like a lid on the mountains and made of the great valley a closed pot. On the broad, level land floor the gang plows bit deep and left the black earth shining like metal where the shares had cut. On the foothill ranches across the Salinas River, the yellow stubble fields seemed to be bathed in pale cold sunshine, but there was no sunshine in the valley now in December. The thick willow scrub along the river flamed with sharp and positive yellow leaves.

It was a time of quiet and of waiting. The air was cold and tender. A light wind blew up from the southwest so that the farmers were mildly hopeful of a good rain before long; but fog and rain do not go together.

Across the river, on Henry Allen's foothill ranch there was little work to be done, for the hay was cut and stored and the orchards were plowed up to receive the rain deeply when it should come. The cattle on the higher slopes were becoming shaggy and rough-coated.

Elisa Allen, working in her flower garden, looked down across the yard and saw Henry, her husband, talking to two men in business suits. The three of them stood by the tractor shed, each man with one foot on the side of the little Fordson.° They smoked cigarettes and studied the machines as they talked.

Elisa watched them for a moment and then went back to her work. She was   5
thirty-five. Her face was lean and strong and her eyes were as clear as water. Her figure looked blocked and heavy in her gardening costume, a man's black hat pulled low down over her eyes, clodhopper shoes, a figured print dress almost completely covered by a big corduroy apron with four big pockets to hold the

Salinas Valley: in Monterey County, California, about 50 miles south of San José. Steinbeck was born in Salinas, and his home there is open to the public.
Fordson: a tractor manufactured by the Ford Motor Company, with large rear steel-lugged wheels.

snips, the trowel and scratcher, the seeds and the knife she worked with. She wore heavy leather gloves to protect her hands while she worked.

She was cutting down the old year's chrysanthemum stalks with a pair of short and powerful scissors. She looked down toward the men by the tractor shed now and then. Her face was eager and mature and handsome; even her work with the scissors was over-eager, over-powerful. The chrysanthemum stems seemed too small and easy for her energy.

She brushed a cloud of hair out of her eyes with the back of her glove, and left a smudge of earth on the cheek in doing it. Behind her stood the neat white farm house with red geraniums close-banked around it as high as the windows. It was a hard-swept looking little house, with hard-polished windows, and a clean mud-mat on the front steps.

Elisa cast another glance toward the tractor shed. The strangers were getting into their Ford coupe. She took off a glove and put her strong fingers down into the forest of new green chrysanthemum sprouts that were growing around the old roots. She spread the leaves and looked down among the close-growing stems. No aphids were there, no sowbugs or snails or cutworms. Her terrier fingers destroyed such pests before they could get started.

Elisa started at the sound of her husband's voice. He had come near quietly, and he leaned over the wire fence that protected her flower garden from cattle and dogs and chickens.

"At it again," he said. "You've got a strong new crop coming."   10

Elisa straightened her back and pulled on the gardening glove again. "Yes. They'll be strong this coming year." In her tone and on her face there was a little smugness.

"You've got a gift with things," Henry observed. "Some of those yellow chrysanthemums you had this year were ten inches across. I wish you'd work out in the orchard and raise some apples that big."

Her eyes sharpened. "Maybe I could do it, too. I've a gift with things, all right. My mother had it. She could stick anything in the ground and make it grow. She said it was having planters' hands that knew how to do it."

"Well, it sure works with flowers," he said.

"Henry, who were those men you were talking to?"   15

"Why, sure, that's what I came to tell you. They were from the Western Meat Company. I sold those thirty head of three-year-old steers. Got nearly my own price, too."

"Good," she said. "Good for you."

"And I thought," he continued, "I thought how it's Saturday afternoon, and we might go to Salinas for dinner at a restaurant, and then to a picture show—to celebrate, you see."

"Good," she repeated. "Oh, yes. That will be good."

Henry put on his joking tone. "There's fights tonight. How'd you like to go   20 to the fights?"

"Oh, no," she said breathlessly. "No, I wouldn't like fights."

"Just fooling, Elisa. We'll go to a movie. Let's see. It's two now. I'm going to take Scotty and bring down those steers from the hill. It'll take us maybe two hours. We'll go in town about five and have dinner at the Cominos Hotel. Like that?"

"Of course I'll like it. It's good to eat away from home."

"All right, then. I'll go get up a couple of horses."

She said, "I'll have plenty of time to transplant some of these sets, I guess." 25

She heard her husband calling Scotty down by the barn. And a little later she saw the two men ride up the pale yellow hillside in search of the steers.

There was a little square sandy bed kept for rooting the chrysanthemums. With her trowel she turned the soil over and over, and smoothed it and patted it firm. Then she dug ten parallel trenches to receive the sets. Back at the chrysanthemum bed she pulled out the little crisp shoots, trimmed off the leaves of each one with her scissors and laid it on a small orderly pile.

A squeak of wheels and plod of hoofs came from the road. Elisa looked up. The country road ran along the dense bank of willows and cottonwoods that bordered the river, and up this road came a curious vehicle, curiously drawn. It was an old spring-wagon, with a round canvas top on it like the cover of a prairie schooner. It was drawn by an old bay horse and a little grey-and-white burro. A big stubble-bearded man sat between the cover flaps and drove the crawling team. Underneath the wagon, between the hind wheels, a lean and rangy mongrel dog walked sedately. Words were painted on the canvas in clumsy, crooked letters. "Pots, pans, knives, sisors, lawn mores. Fixed." Two rows of articles and the triumphantly definitive "Fixed" below. The black paint had run down in little sharp points beneath each letter.

Elisa, squatting on the ground, watched to see the crazy, loose-jointed wagon pass by. But it didn't pass. It turned into the farm road in front of her house, crooked old wheels skirling and squeaking. The rangy dog darted from between the wheels and ran ahead. Instantly the two ranch shepherds flew out at him. Then all three stopped, and with stiff and quivering tails, with taut straight legs, with ambassadorial dignity, they slowly circled, sniffing daintily. The caravan pulled up to Elisa's wire fence and stopped. Now the newcomer dog, feeling outnumbered, lowered his tail and retired under the wagon with raised hackles and bared teeth.

The man on the wagon seat called out. "That's a bad dog in a fight when 30 he gets started."

Elisa laughed. "I see he is. How soon does he generally get started?"

The man caught up her laughter and echoed it heartily. "Sometimes not for weeks and weeks," he said. He climbed stiffly down, over the wheel. The horse and the donkey dropped like unwatered flowers.

Elisa saw that he was a very big man. Although his hair and beard were greying, he did not look old. His worn black suit was wrinkled and spotted with grease. The laughter had disappeared from his face and eyes the moment his laughing voice ceased. His eyes were dark and they were full of the brooding that gets in the eyes of teamsters and of sailors. The calloused hands he rested on the wire fence were cracked, and every crack was a black line. He took off his battered hat.

"I'm off my general road, ma'am," he said. "Does this dirt road cut over across the river to the Los Angeles highway?"

Elisa stood up and shoved the thick scissors in her apron pocket. "Well, yes, 35 it does, but it winds around and then fords the river. I don't think your team could pull through the sand."

He replied with some asperity, "It might surprise you what them beasts can pull through."

"When they get started?" she asked.

He smiled for a second. "Yes. When they get started."

"Well," said Elisa, "I think you'll save time if you go back to the Salinas road and pick up the highway there."

He drew a big finger down the chicken wire and made it sing. "I ain't in any hurry, ma'am. I go from Seattle to San Diego and back every year. Takes all my time. About six months each way. I aim to follow nice weather." 40

Elisa took off her gloves and stuffed them in the apron pocket with the scissors. She touched the under edge of her man's hat, searching for fugitive hairs. "That sounds like a nice kind of a way to live," she said.

He leaned confidentially over the fence. "Maybe you noticed the writing on my wagon. I mend pots and sharpen knives and scissors. You got any of them things to do?"

"Oh, no," she said quickly. "Nothing like that." Her eyes hardened with resistance.

"Scissors is the worst thing," he explained. "Most people just ruin scissors trying to sharpen 'em, but I know how. I got a special tool. It's a little bobbit kind of thing, and patented. But it sure does the trick."

"No. My scissors are all sharp." 45

"All right, then. Take a pot," he continued earnestly, "a bent pot, or a pot with a hole. I can make it like new so you don't have to buy no new ones. That's a saving for you."

"No," she said shortly. "I tell you I have nothing like that for you to do."

His face fell to an exaggerated sadness. His voice took on a whining undertone. "I ain't had a thing to do today. Maybe I won't have no supper tonight. You see I'm off my regular road. I know folks on the highway clear from Seattle to San Diego. They save their things for me to sharpen up because they know I do it so good and save them money."

"I'm sorry," Elisa said irritably. "I haven't anything for you to do."

His eyes left her face and fell to searching the ground. They roamed about until they came to the chrysanthemum bed where she had been working. "What's them plants, ma'am?" 50

The irritation and resistance melted from Elisa's face. "Oh, those are chrysanthemums, giant whites and yellows. I raise them every year, bigger than anybody around here."

"Kind of a long-stemmed flower? Looks like a quick puff of colored smoke?" he asked.

"That's it. What a nice way to describe them."

"They smell kind of nasty till you get used to them," he said.

"It's a good bitter smell," she retorted, "not nasty at all." 55

He changed his tone quickly. "I like the smell myself."

"I had ten-inch blooms this year," she said.

The man leaned farther over the fence. "Look. I know a lady down the road a piece, has got the nicest garden you ever seen. Got nearly every kind of flower but no chrysanthemums. Last time I was mending a copper-bottom washtub for her (that's a hard job but I do it good), she said to me, 'If you ever run acrost some nice chrysanthemums I wish you'd try to get me a few seeds.' That's what she told me."

Elisa's eyes grew alert and eager. "She couldn't have known much about chrysanthemums. You can raise them from seed, but it's much easier to root the little sprouts you see there."

"Oh," he said. "I s'pose I can't take none to her, then." 60

"Why yes you can," Elisa cried. "I can put some in damp sand, and you can carry them right along with you. They'll take root in the pot if you keep them damp. And then she can transplant them."

"She'd sure like to have some, ma'am. You say they're nice ones?"

"Beautiful," she said. "Oh, beautiful." Her eyes shone. She tore off the battered hat and shook out her dark pretty hair. "I'll put them in a flower pot, and you can take them right with you. Come into the yard."

While the man came through the picket gate Elisa ran excitedly along the geranium-bordered path to the back of the house. And she returned carrying a big red flower pot. The gloves were forgotten now. She kneeled on the ground by the starting bed and dug up the sandy soil with her fingers and scooped it into the bright new flower pot. Then she picked up the little pile of shoots she had prepared. With her strong fingers she pressed them into the sand and tamped around them with her knuckles. The man stood over her. "I'll tell you what to do," she said. "You remember so you can tell the lady."

"Yes, I'll try to remember." 65

"Well, look. These will take root in about a month. Then she must set them out, about a foot apart in good rich earth like this, see?" She lifted a handful of dark soil for him to look at. "They'll grow fast and tall. Now remember this. In July tell her to cut them down, about eight inches from the ground."

"Before they bloom?" he asked.

"Yes, before they bloom." Her face was tight with eagerness. "They'll grow right up again. About the last of September the buds will start."

She stopped and seemed perplexed. "It's the budding that takes the most care," she said hesitantly. "I don't know how to tell you." She looked deep into his eyes, searchingly. Her mouth opened a little, and she seemed to be listening. "I'll try to tell you," she said. "Did you ever hear of planting hands?"

"Can't say I have, ma'am." 70

"Well, I can only tell you what it feels like. It's when you're picking off the buds you don't want. Everything goes right down into your fingertips. You watch your fingers work. They do it themselves. You can feel how it is. They pick and pick the buds. They never make a mistake. They're with the plant. Do you see? Your fingers and the plant. You can feel that, right up your arm. They know. They never make a mistake. You can feel it. When you're like that you can't do anything wrong. Do you see that? Can you understand that?"

She was kneeling on the ground looking up at him. Her breast swelled passionately.

The man's eyes narrowed. He looked away self-consciously. "Maybe I know," he said. "Sometimes in the night in the wagon there—"

Elisa's voice grew husky. She broke in on him. "I've never lived as you do, but I know what you mean. When the night is dark—why, the stars are sharp-pointed, and there's quiet. Why, you rise up and up! Every pointed star gets driven into your body. It's like that. Hot and sharp and—lovely."

Kneeling there, her hand went out toward his legs in the greasy black 75 trousers. Her hesitant fingers almost touched the cloth. Then her hand dropped to the ground. She crouched low like a fawning dog.

He said, "It's nice, just like you say. Only when you don't have no dinner, it ain't."

She stood up then, very straight, and her face was ashamed. She held the flower pot out to him and placed it gently in his arms. "Here. Put it in your wagon, on the seat, where you can watch it. Maybe I can find something for you to do."

At the back of the house she dug in the can pile and found two old and battered aluminum saucepans. She carried them back and gave them to him. "Here, maybe you can fix these."

His manner changed. He became professional. "Good as new I can fix them." At the back of his wagon he set a little anvil, and out of an oily tool box dug a small machine hammer. Elisa came through the gate to watch him while he pounded out the dents in the kettles. His mouth grew sure and knowing. At a difficult part of the work he sucked his under-lip.

"You sleep right in the wagon?" Elisa asked.   80

"Right in the wagon, ma'am. Rain or shine. I'm dry as a cow in there."

"It must be nice," she said. "It must be very nice. I wish women could do such things."

"It ain't the right kind of a life for a woman."

Her upper lip raised a little, showing her teeth. "How do you know? How can you tell?" she said.

"I don't know ma'am," he protested. "Of course I don't know. Now here's   85
your kettles, done. You don't have to buy no new ones."

"How much?"

"Oh, fifty cents'll do. I keep my prices down and my work good. That's why I have all them satisfied customers up and down the highway."

Elisa brought him a fifty-cent piece from the house and dropped it in his hand. "You might be surprised to have a rival some time. I can sharpen scissors, too. And I can beat the dents out of little pots. I could show you what a woman might do."

He put his hammer back in the oily box and shoved the little anvil out of sight. "It would be a lonely life for a woman, ma'am, and a scarey life, too, with animals creeping under the wagon all night." He climbed over the single-tree, steadying himself with a hand on the burro's white rump. He settled himself in the seat, picked up the lines. "Thank you kindly, ma'am," he said. "I'll do like you told me; I'll go back and catch the Salinas road."

"Mind," she called, "if you're long in getting there, keep the sand damp."   90

"Sand, ma'am? . . . Sand? Oh, sure. You mean round the chrysanthemums. Sure I will." He clucked his tongue. The beasts leaned luxuriously into their collars. The mongrel dog took his place between the back wheels. The wagon turned and crawled out the entrance road and back the way it had come, along the river.

Elisa stood in front of her wire fence watching the slow progress of the caravan. Her shoulders were straight, her head thrown back, her eyes half-closed, so that the scene came vaguely into them. Her lips moved silently, forming the words "Good-bye—good-bye." Then she whispered, "That's a bright direction. There's a glowing there." The sound of her whisper startled her. She shook herself free and looked about to see whether anyone had been listening. Only the dogs had heard. They lifted their heads toward her from their sleeping in the dust, and then stretched out their chins and settled asleep again. Elisa turned and ran hurriedly into the house.

In the kitchen she reached behind the stove and felt the water tank. It was full of hot water from the noonday cooking. In the bathroom she tore off her soiled clothes and flung them into the corner. And then she scrubbed herself with a little block of pumice, legs and thighs, loins and chest and arms, until her skin was scratched and red. When she had dried herself she stood in front of a mirror in her bedroom and looked at her body. She tightened her stomach and threw out her chest. She turned and looked over her shoulder at her back.

After a while she began to dress, slowly. She put on her newest underclothing and her nicest stockings and the dress which was the symbol of her prettiness. She worked carefully on her hair, pencilled her eyebrows and rouged her lips.

Before she was finished she heard the little thunder of hoofs and the shouts of Henry and his helper as they drove the red steers into the corral. She heard the gate bang shut and set herself for Henry's arrival. 95

His step sounded on the porch. He entered the house calling "Elisa, where are you?"

"In my room, dressing. I'm not ready. There's hot water for your bath. Hurry up. It's getting late."

When she heard him splashing in the tub, Elisa laid his dark suit on the bed, and shirt and socks and tie beside it. She stood his polished shoes on the floor beside the bed. Then she went to the porch and sat primly and stiffly down. She looked toward the river road where the willow-line was still yellow with frosted leaves so that under the high grey fog they seemed a thin band of sunshine. This was the only color in the grey afternoon. She sat unmoving for a long time. Her eyes blinked rarely.

Henry came banging out of the door, shoving his tie inside his vest as he came. Elisa stiffened and her face grew tight. Henry stopped short and looked at her. "Why—why, Elisa. You look so nice!"

"Nice? You think I look nice? What do you mean by 'nice'?" 100

Henry blundered on. "I don't know. I mean you look different, strong and happy."

"I am strong? Yes, strong. What do you mean 'strong'?"

He looked bewildered. "You're playing some kind of a game," he said helplessly. "It's a kind of a play. You look strong enough to break a calf over your knee, happy enough to eat it like watermelon."

For a second she lost her rigidity. "Henry! Don't talk like that. You didn't know what you said." She grew complete again. "I'm strong," she boasted. "I never knew before how strong."

Henry looked down toward the tractor shed, and when he brought his eyes back to her, they were his own again. "I'll get out the car. You can put on your coat while I'm starting." 105

Elisa went into the house. She heard him drive to the gate and idle down his motor, and then she took a long time to put on her hat. She pulled it here and pressed it there. When Henry turned the motor off she slipped into her coat and went out.

The little roadster bounced along on the dirt road by the river, raising the birds and driving the rabbits into the brush. Two cranes flapped heavily over the willow-line and dropped into the river-bed.

Far ahead on the road Elisa saw a dark speck. She knew.

She tried not to look as they passed it, but her eyes would not obey. She whispered to herself sadly. "He might have thrown them off the road. That wouldn't have been much trouble, not very much. But he kept the pot," she explained. "He had to keep the pot. That's why he couldn't get them off the road."

The roadster turned a bend and she saw the caravan ahead. She swung full   110 around toward her husband so she could not see the little covered wagon and the mismatched team as the car passed them.

In a moment it was over. The thing was done. She did not look back. She said loudly, to be heard above the motor, "It will be good, tonight, a good dinner."

"Now you're changed again," Henry complained. He took one hand from the wheel and patted her knee. "I ought to take you in to dinner oftener. It would be good for both of us. We get so heavy out on the ranch."

"Henry," she asked, "could we have wine at dinner?"

"Sure we could. Say! That will be fine."

She was silent for a little while; then she said, "Henry, at those prize fights,   115 do the men hurt each other very much?"

"Sometimes a little, not often. Why?"

"Well, I've read how they break noses, and blood runs down their chests. I've read how the fighting gloves get heavy and soggy with blood."

He looked around at her. "What's the matter, Elisa? I didn't know you read things like that." He brought the car to a stop, then turned to the right over the Salinas River bridge.

"Do any women ever go to the fights?" she asked.

"Oh, sure, some. What's the matter, Elisa? Do you want to go? I don't think   120 you'd like it, but I'll take you if you really want to go."

She relaxed limply in the seat. "Oh, no. No. I don't want to go. I'm sure I don't." Her face was turned away from him. "It will be enough if we can have wine. It will be plenty." She turned up her coat collar so he could not see that she was crying weakly—like an old woman.

QUESTIONS

1. What point of view is used in the story? What are the advantages of this point of view?

2. Consider the symbolism of the setting in this story with respect to the Salinas Valley, the time of year, and the description of the Allen house. What do these things tell us about Elisa Allen and her world?

3. To what extent is Steinbeck's description of Elisa in paragraphs 5 and 6 symbolic? What is she wearing? What do her clothes hide or suppress?

4. What do the chrysanthemums symbolize for Elisa? What do they symbolize *about* her? What role do these flowers play in her life?

5. How does Elisa's character or sense of self change during the episode in which she washes and dresses for dinner? To what extent is this washing-dressing episode symbolic? How would you explain the symbolism?

6. Consider the symbolic impact of Elisa's seeing the chrysanthemum sprouts at the roadside. What does her reaction tell us about her values?

WRITING ABOUT SYMBOLISM OR ALLEGORY

Test the story to determine parallels that may genuinely establish the presence of symbolism or allegory by applying the following questions.

Questions for Discovering Ideas

Symbols: Does a person, object, place, or situation in the story seem to have more than one layer of meaning? If so, does it refer consistently to a significant idea, emotion, or quality?

Does the person, object, place, or situation seem to be important in the story, judging by the way the author treats it? Why do you think so?

Do you recognize any universal symbols in the story? What do they represent?

Is it possible to make parallel lists to show how qualities of the symbol line up with the qualities of a character or action? Here is such a list for the symbol of the toy windmill in Welty's "A Worn Path":

QUALITIES OF THE WINDMILL	COMPARABLE QUALITIES IN PHOENIX AND HER LIFE
1. Cheap	1. Poor, but she gives all she has for the windmill
2. Breakable	2. Old, and not far from death
3. A gift	3. Generous
4. Not practical	4. Needs some relief from reality and practicality
5. Colorful	5. Needs something new and cheerful

Allegory: Does the story seem to have an extended symbolic meaning that underlies all of the action? Or does part of the story seem to have an allegorical meaning? Why do you think so?

Does the author make any allusions that lead you to believe he or she is implying a symbolic or allegorical meaning in the story?

Can you use a diagram such as the one for *Star Wars* on page 356 to show correspondences between characters, actions, objects, or ideas to an allegorical meaning?

Strategies for Organizing Ideas

One way to begin is to decide on a central idea and then see if the supporting details can be construed as symbols. A general idea about "Young Goodman Brown," for example, is that fanaticism darkens and limits the human soul. An early incident in the story may be used as a symbol of this idea. Specifically, when Goodman Brown enters the woods,

STAR WARS	Luke Skywalker	Obi Wan Kenobi	Darth Vader	Princess Leia	Capture	Escape, and defeat of Vader
ALLEGORICAL APPLICATION TO MORALITY AND FAITH	Forces of good	Education and faith	Forces of evil	Object to be saved, ideals to be rescued and restored	Doubt, spiritual negligence	Restoration of faith
ALLEGORICAL APPLICATION TO PERSONAL AND GENERAL CONCERNS	Individual in pursuit of goals	The means by which goals may be reached	Obstacles to be overcome	Occupation, happiness, goals	Temporary failure, depression, discouragement, disappointment	Success

he resolves "to stand firm against the devil," and he then looks up "to heaven above." As he looks, a "black mass of cloud" appears to hide the "brightening stars." Within the limits of our central idea, the cloud may be seen as a symbol, just like the widening path or the night walk itself. As long as you make solid connections in this way, your symbolic ascriptions will be acceptable.

Also, for your essay development, you will need to prepare justifications for your symbols or allegorical parallels. In "The Masque of the Red Death," for example, Prince Prospero's seemingly impregnable "castellated abbey" is a line of defense against the plague raging the countryside. But the Red Death in a human shape easily invades the castle and conquers Prospero and his misguided guests. If you were to treat the abbey as a symbol, it would be important to apply it to measures that people take (medicine, escapist activity, etc.) to keep death distant and remote. In the same way, in an allegorical treatment of "Young Goodman Brown," you would need to establish a connecting link, perhaps something like the following: People lose ideals and forsake principles not because they are evil, but because they misunderstand the people around them.

There are a number of other strategies for discussing symbolism and allegory. You might use one exclusively, or a combination. If you want to write about symbolism, you might consider the following:

1. *The meaning of a major symbol.* Here you interpret the symbol and what it stands for. Answer questions like these: Is the symbol contextual or universal? How do you decide? How do you derive your interpretation of the symbolic meaning? What is the extent of the meaning? Does the symbol undergo modification or new applications if it reappears? How does the symbol affect your understanding of the total story? Does the symbol bring out any ironies? How does the symbol add strength and depth to the story?

2. *The development and relationship of symbols.* For two or more symbols: How do the symbols connect with each other (like night and the cloud in "Young Goodman Brown" as symbols of a darkening mind)? What additional meanings do the symbols develop? Are they complementary, contradictory, or ironic (the windmill and the medicine in "A Worn Path," for example, are ironic because the windmill suggests cheer while the medicine suggests hopelessness)? Do the symbols control the form of the story? How? (For example, in "The Worker in Sandalwood" the concluding episode begins in doubt during the night of Christmas Eve and ends in success on the morning of Christmas Day. By contrast, the conclusion of Joyce's "Araby" [p. 368] begins in anticipation during the day and ends in disillusionment at night.) May these contrasting times be viewed symbolically in relationship to the development of the two stories? Other questions are whether the symbols fit naturally or artificially into the context of the story, or whether and how the writer's symbols make for unique qualities or excellences.

If you write about allegory, you might use one of the following approaches:

1. *The application and meaning of the allegory.* Does the allegory (fable, parable, myth) refer to anyone or anything specific? How may it be more generally applied to ideas or to qualities of human character, not only of its own time but of our own? Does it illustrate, either closely or loosely, particular philosophies or religious views? If so, what are these? How do you know? If the allegory seems outdated, how much can be salvaged for people today?

2. *The consistency of the allegory.* Is the allegory used consistently throughout the story, or is it intermittent? Explain and illustrate this use. Would it be correct to call your story *allegorical* rather than an *allegory*? Can you determine how parts of the story are introduced for their allegorical importance? Examples are the natural obstacles in the woods in Welty's "A Worn Path," which are allegorical equivalents of life's difficulties, and the entertainment scene in "The Masque of the Red Death," which corresponds to the ways people try to avoid the realities of disease and death.

In the conclusion, you might summarize main points, describe general impressions, explain the impact of the symbolic or allegorical methods, indicate personal responses, or suggest further lines of thought and application. You might also assess the quality and appropriateness of the symbolism or allegory (such as the opening of "Young Goodman Brown" being in darkness, with the closing in gloom).

SAMPLE ESSAY

Allegory and Symbolism in Hawthorne's "Young Goodman Brown"[°]

[1]   It is hard to read beyond the third paragraph of Nathaniel Hawthorne's "Young Goodman Brown" without finding allegory and symbolism. The opening at first seems realistic. Goodman Brown, a young Puritan, leaves his home in colonial Salem to take an overnight trip. His wife's name, "Faith," however, suggests a symbolic reading, and as soon as Brown goes into the forest, his journey becomes an allegorical trip into evil. The idea that Hawthorne shows by this trip is that rigid belief destroys even the best human qualities.[*] He develops this thought in the allegory and in many symbols, particularly the sunset, the walking stick, and the path.[†]

    The allegory is about how people develop destructive ideas. Most of the story is dreamlike and unreal, and the ideas that Brown gains are also unreal. At the weird "witch meeting" in the dream forest, he concludes that

[°] See p. 332 for this story.
[*] Central idea.
[†] Thesis sentence.

everyone he knows is sinful, and he then permits mistrust and loathing to distort his previous love for his wife and neighbors. As a result, the rest of his life is harsh and gloomy. The location of the story in colonial Salem indicates that Hawthorne's allegorical target is the overly zealous pursuit of religious principles which dwell on sinfulness rather than on love. However, modern readers may also apply the allegory to the ways in which people uncritically accept *any* ideal (most often political loyalties or racial or national prejudices), and thereby reject the rights and integrity of others. If people like Brown apply a rigid standard, they can condemn anyone, particularly if they never try to understand those they condemn. In this way, Hawthorne's allegory applies to any narrow-minded acceptance of ideals or systems that exclude the importance of love, understanding, and tolerance.

[2]

Hawthorne's attack on such dehumanizing belief is found not just in the allegory, but also in his many symbols. For example, the seventh word in the story, "sunset," may be taken as a symbol. In reality, sunset merely indicates the end of day. Coming at the beginning of the story, however, it suggests that Goodman Brown is beginning his long night of hatred, his spiritual death. For him the night will never end because his final days are shrouded in "gloom" (paragraph 72).

[3]

The next symbol, the guide's walking stick or staff, suggests the arbitrariness of the standard by which Brown judges his neighbors. Hawthorne's description indicates the symbolic nature of this staff:

[4]

> . . . the only thing about him [the guide] that could be fixed upon as remarkable, was his staff, which bore the likeness of a great black snake, so curiously wrought, that it might almost be seen to twist and wriggle itself like a living serpent. This, of course, must have been an ocular deception, assisted by the uncertain light. (paragraph 13)

The serpent symbolically suggests Satan, who in Genesis (3:1–7) is the originator of all evil, but the phrase "ocular deception" creates an interesting and realistic ambiguity about the symbol. Since the perception of the snake may depend on nothing more than the "uncertain" light, the staff may be less symbolic of evil than of the tendency to find evil where it does not exist (and could the light itself symbolize the tentative, temporary condition of all human knowledge?).

In the same vein, the path through the forest is a major symbol of the destructive mental confusion that overcomes Brown. As he walks, the path grows "wilder and drearier, and more faintly traced," and "at length" it vanishes (paragraph 51). This is like the biblical description of the "broad" way that leads "to Destruction" (Matthew 7:13). As a symbol, the path shows that most human acts are bad, while a small number, like the "narrow" way to life (Matthew 7:14), are good. Goodman Brown's path is at first clear, as though sin is at first unique and unusual. Soon, however, it is so indistinct that he can see only sin wherever he turns. The symbol suggests that, as people follow evil, their moral vision becomes blurred and they cannot choose the right way even if it is in front of them, and they soon fall prey to "the instinct that guides mortal man to evil" (paragraph 51).

[5]

Through Hawthorne's allegory and symbols, then, "Young Goodman

Brown" presents the paradox of how outwardly noble beliefs can backfire destructively. Goodman Brown dies in gloom because he believes that his wrong vision is real. This form of evil is the hardest to stop, because wrongdoers who are convinced of their own goodness are beyond reach. In view [6] of such self-righteous evil, whether cloaked in the apparent virtues of Puritanism or of some other blindly rigorous doctrine (political as well as religious), Hawthorne writes that "the fiend in his own shape is less hideous than when he rages in the breast of man" (paragraph 53). Young Goodman Brown thus is the central symbol of the story. He is one of those who think they walk in light but who really create their own darkness.

Commentary on the Essay

The introduction justifies the treatment of allegory and symbolism on the grounds that Hawthorne early in the story invites such a reading. The central idea relates Hawthorne's method to the idea that rigid belief destroys the best human qualities. The thesis sentence outlines two major areas of discussion: (1) allegory and (2) symbolism.

Paragraph 2 considers the allegory as a criticism of rigid Puritan morality. The major thread running through each of the major parts of the paragraph is the hurtful effect of monomaniacal views like those of Brown. Paragraphs 3, 4, and 5 deal with three major symbols: sunset, the staff, and the path. The aim of this discussion is to show the meaning and applicability of these symbols to Hawthorne's attack on unquestioning belief. Throughout these three paragraphs the central idea—the relationship of rigidity to destructiveness—is stressed. Hawthorne's allusions to both the Old and New Testaments are pointed out in paragraphs 4 and 5. The last paragraph raises questions leading to the conclusion that Brown himself symbolizes Hawthorne's idea that the primary cause of evil is the inability to separate reality from unreality.

Should you be discussing any story as allegory, the structure of paragraph 2 would be useful as a guide either for a single paragraph or, as expanded, for an entire essay. If "Young Goodman Brown" were to be considered further as an allegory, for example, additional topics might be Brown's gullibility, the meaning of Faith and the requirements for maintaining it, and the causes for preferring to think evil rather than good of other people. The point is that the more extensive the analysis of any allegory, the more separate points may be explored.

WRITING TOPICS

1. Write an essay on the allegorical method of *The Prodigal Son* and of other allegories included in the Gospel According to Luke, such as *The Bridegroom* (5:34–35), *The Garments and the Wineskins* (5:36–39), *The Sower* (8:4–15), *The Good Samaritan* (10:25–37), *The Ox in the Well* (14:5–6), *The Watering of Animals on the Sabbath* (13:15–17), *The Rich Fool* (12:16–21), *Lazarus* (16:19–31), *The Widow and the Judge* (18:1–8), and *The Pharisee and the Publican* (18:9–14).

2. Compare and contrast the symbolism in Steinbeck's "The Chrysanthemums" (p. 347) and Munro's "The Found Boat" (p. 286). To what degree do the stories rely on contextual symbols? On universal symbols? On the basis of your comparison, what is the case for asserting that realism and fantasy are directly related to the nature of the symbolism employed by the writer?

3. On the basis of "The Parable of the Prodigal Son" and "The Worker in Sandalwood," why do you think that religious stories and parables rely heavily on symbolism and allegory?

4. Write a brief story using a *universal symbol* such as the flag (patriotism, love of country, a certain type of politics), water (regeneration, life), or the hydrogen bomb (the end of life on earth). By arranging actions and dialogue, make clear the issues conveyed by your symbol, and also try to resolve the conflicts that the symbol might raise among your characters.

5. Write a brief story in which you develop your own *contextual symbol.* You might, for example, demonstrate how holding a job brings out character strengths that are not at first apparent, or how neglecting to care for the inside or outside of a house indicates a character's decline. The principle is to take something that may at first seem normal and ordinary, and then to make that thing symbolic as your story progresses.

10

Idea or Theme: The Meaning and the Message in Fiction

The word **idea** refers to the result or results of general and abstract thinking. Synonymous words are *concept, thought, opinion,* and *principle.* In literary study the consideration of ideas gets us involved in *meaning, interpretation, explanation,* and *significance.* Though ideas are usually extensive and complex, separate ideas may be named by a single word, such as *justice, right, good, love, piety, causation,* and, not unsurprisingly, *idea* itself.

IDEAS NEED THE FORM OF ASSERTIONS

Although a single word may provide a title, an idea is not operative until we phrase it as a sentence or **assertion.** In other words, an idea needs a subject and a predicate to get it moving so that we can use it as a basis of understanding. An assertion of an idea is not the same as an ordinary sentence, such as "It's a nice day." This observation may be true (depending on the weather), but it cannot be called an *idea.* Rather, an idea should indicate *thought* about the day's quality, such as "A nice day requires blue sky, a warm sun, and light breezes." Because this sentence deals with an assertion about "nice," it lends itself to the consideration of the idea of a nice day.

In studying literature, you should always phrase ideas as assertions. For example, you might claim that an idea in Lawrence's "The Horse Dealer's Daughter" is "love," but it would be difficult to go far with this unless you make an assertion like "This story demonstrates the idea that love is both irresistible and irrational." With this assertion you could explain the unlikely and sudden development of love between Mabel and Dr. Jack Fergusson. Similarly, for Eudora Welty's "A Worn Path" you might make the following assertion based on the character Phoenix Jackson: "Phoenix embodies the idea that caring for others gives no reward but the continuation of the duty itself."

362

Although we have noted only one idea in these stories, there are usually many separate ideas. When one of the ideas seems to be the major one, it is called the **theme.** Loosely, the words *theme* and *major idea* or *central idea* are the same.

IDEAS IN LITERATURE:
VALUES AND THE HUMAN CONDITION

In fiction, ideas are of interest because they concern people in their lives—the ways in which they *actually* lead them, *should* lead them, or *ought to be allowed* to lead them. This means that ideas are not ends in themselves. Rather they apply to the human side of things, and usually they are presented along with the expression or implication that certain things should be highly valued.

As a general rule, **values** are embodied in stories coincidentally with ideas. For example, the idea of justice may be considered abstractly and broadly, as Plato does in his *Republic* when developing his concept of the most just government. In comparison, justice is also a subject of Ernest J. Gaines in "The Sky Is Gray," but Gaines is not abstract and speculative, like Plato. Rather he is personal. Gaines's idea is that human beings are equal regardless of race, and he asserts the need for equal treatment by showing that the boy narrator has needs, difficulties, discomforts, and pains that are the same as those of all human beings, regardless of race. In short, to talk about Gaines's idea is also to talk about his values.

THE PLACE OF IDEAS IN LITERATURE

Because writers of fiction are usually not systematic philosophers, it would be a mistake to go "message hunting" as though their stories contained nothing but ideas. Indeed, there is much benefit and pleasure to be derived from savoring a story, from being taken up in the developing pattern of conflict and interest, from following its implications and suggestions, and from listening to the sounds of its words—to name only a few of the things for which literature is treasured.

All these reservations aside, ideas are vital to understanding and appreciation, for it is indisputable that writers have ideas and want to communicate them. For example, in "The Horse Dealer's Daughter" Lawrence directs sympathy at the sudden development of overpowering love between two unlikely characters. This love is unusual, and the story is therefore effective, but the story is also provocative because it raises the idea that love pushes aside other decisions that people make. Gaines in "The Sky Is Gray" describes the extraordinary difficulty and pain experienced by a young child and his mother on what should be no more than a simple visit to a dentist, but the story embodies *ideas* about the need for equality, the strength of human character, and the beauty of human kindness.

DISTINGUISHING BETWEEN IDEAS AND ACTIONS

As you analyze stories for ideas, it is important to avoid the trap of confusing ideas and actions. Such a trap is contained in the following sentence about Updike's "A & P" (p. 65): "The major character, Sammy, quits his job to protest the way his boss mistreats the girls." This sentence successfully describes the story's major action, but it does not express an *idea*. Indeed, it *obstructs* understanding because it focuses only on what happens and does not introduce an idea to connect characters and events. The necessary connection might be achieved with sentences like "'A & P' illustrates the idea that making a protest imposes difficulty," or "'A & P' demonstrates that individual rights are more important than arbitrary regulations." A study based on these connecting formulations could be focused on ideas, and would not be sidetracked into simply retelling Updike's story.

In a similar way, you should distinguish between ideas and situations. For example, in Joyce's "Araby," the narrator concludes by describing his frustration and embarrassment at the "Araby" Bazaar in Dublin. This is a *situation*, but it is not the *idea* brought out by the situation. Joyce's idea is rather that immature love causes unreal dreams and hopes that result only in disappointment and self-reproach. In this way, it is most important to separate the various circumstances in a story from the guiding idea or ideas that the writer is illustrating.

HOW DO YOU FIND IDEAS?

Ideas do not just leap out from the page and announce their presence. To determine an idea, you need to consider the meaning of what you read, and then develop explanatory and comprehensive assertions. There is no rule requiring that your assertions must be the same as those that others might make. People notice different things, and individual formulations vary. In Joyce's "Araby," for example, an initial expression of the story's idea might take any of the following forms: (1) The force of sexual attraction is strong and begins early in life. (2) The attraction leads some individuals to the idealization of the loved one. (3) Sexual feelings are private and may cause embarrassment and shame. Although any one of these choices could be an idea around which to study "Araby," they all have in common the idealization by the narrator of his friend's sister. In studying for ideas, you should follow a similar process—making a number of formulations for an idea, and then selecting one for further development.

As you read, you should be alert to the various ways in which authors convey ideas. Thus, one author might prefer an indirect way through a character's speeches; another may prefer direct statement. In practice, authors may employ all the following methods.

Direct Statements by the Authorial Voice

Although writers of fiction are mainly interested in rendering action, dialogue, and situation, they sometimes, through their authorial voices, state ideas to guide us and deepen our understanding. Such authorial ideas are usually brief but are nevertheless crucial. In the second paragraph of "The Necklace," for example (p. 5), Maupassant's authorial voice presents the idea that women have only charm and beauty to get on in the world. Ironically, however, Maupassant uses the story to show that for the major character Mathilde, nothing is effective, for her charm cannot prevent disaster. Poe, in "The Masque of the Red Death," asserts a key idea that "there are matters of which no jest can be made" (p. 249, paragraph 9). This idea is expressed as authorial commentary just as the Red Death has invaded the party, and it demonstrates the futility of Prospero's attempts to overcome death.

Direct Statements by the First-Person Speaker

First-person narrators or speakers frequently express ideas along with their depiction of actions and situations. (See also Chapter 5, pp. 198–200.) Because they are part of a dramatic presentation, the ideas may be right or wrong, well considered or thoughtless, or brilliant of half-baked, depending on the speaker. The narrator of Atwood's "Rape Fantasies," for example (p. 313), is not noteworthy for her intelligence, yet she voices penetrating ideas about the relationships of men and women. In Whitecloud's "Blue Winds Dancing" (p. 125), the unnamed narrator expresses ideas and values that have become alien during our times, when increasing urbanization is separating human beings' from the natural world. A somewhat half-baked speaker, but yet an interesting one, is Sammy, the narrator of Updike's "A & P" (p. 65), who seems engulfed in intellectual commonplaces, particularly in his insinuation about the intelligence of women (paragraph 2). In his defense, however, Sammy *acts* upon a worthy idea about rights of expression and dress.

Dramatic Statements Made by Characters

In many stories, characters express their own views, which may be admirable or contemptible. Through such dramatic speeches, you may encounter thirteen ways of looking at a blackbird, and must do considerable interpreting and evaluating yourself. For example, Old Man Warner in "The Lottery" (p. 214) states that the lottery is valuable even though we learn from the narrator that the beliefs underlying it have long been forgotten. Because Warner is a zealous and noisy person, however, his words show that outdated ideas continue to do harm even when there is strong reason to abandon them and develop new ones. The unnamed young man in the dentist's office in "The Sky Is Gray" speaks in contradictions, but when he amplifies them in his bitterness we learn a number of his ideas about the failure of America to live up to its professed principles of equality.

Figurative Language

Usually figurative language is considered an exclusive property of poetry, but it also abounds in fiction. In Joyce's "Araby," for example, the narrator uses a beautiful figure of speech to describe his youthful admiration for his friend's sister. He says that his body "was like a harp and her words and gestures were like fingers running upon the wires." Another notable figure occurs at the opening of Mansfield's "Miss Brill," when the narrator likens a sunny day to gold and white wine—a lovely comparison conveying the idea that the world is a place of beauty and happiness—an idea that contrasts ironically with the indifference and cruelty that Miss Brill experiences.

Characters Who Stand for Ideas

Characters often engage in actions that are so typical that they stand out as representatives of ideas and values. Thus, Mathilde's story in Maupassant's "The Necklace" is so powerful that she comes to stand for the idea that unrealizable dreams may invade and damage the real world. Two diverse or opposed characters may represent contrasting ideas, as with Sammy and Lengel of Updike's "A & P," who stand for opposing views about rights of expression.

In effect, characters who stand for ideas may assume symbolic status, as in Hawthorne's "Young Goodman Brown," where the protagonist symbolizes the alienation accompanying overzealousness, or in "The Shawl," where the small child Magda embodies the vulnerability and helplessness of human beings in the face of dehumanizing state brutality. In this way, such characters may be equated directly with particular ideas, and to talk about them is a shorthand way of talking about the ideas.

The Story Itself as It Represents Ideas

One of the most important ways in which authors express ideas is to make them an inseparable part of a story's total impression. The art of painting is instructive here, for a painting may usually be taken in by a

Pablo Picasso, *Guernica*, 1937. Oil on canvas, 11'5½" × 25'5¾". (Museo del Prado, Madrid)

single view (though individual sections may be studied separately). Thus, the broken and distorted figures in Picasso's *Guernica*, which can be comprehended together, all emphasize the idea that war creates horror and suffering for both human beings and beasts (p. 367).

Comparably, when a story is considered in its totality, various actions and characters may be seen to embody a major idea. In "The Sky Is Gray," for example, Gaines makes objective the idea that the urgency of ending racial barriers overrides the historical reasons for their existence. Although he does not use these exact words, the story powerfully embodies this idea. The conclusion of "Blue Winds Dancing" drives the point home that human beings will not accept anything new when they truly believe that their own way of life is of equal or superior value. Most stories represent ideas in a similar way. Even "escape literature," which is designed to help readers forget about their own problems, contains plots that stem out of conflicts between good and evil, love and hate, good spies and bad, earthlings and aliens, and so on. Such stories in fact *do* embody ideas and themes, even though they admittedly are not intended to strike readers with the boldness and originality of their ideas.

JAMES JOYCE   (1882–1941)

Araby   *1914*

North Richmond Street,° being blind,° was a quiet street except at the hour when the Christian Brothers' School set the boys free. An uninhabited house of two storeys stood at the blind end, detached from its neighbours in a square ground. The other houses of the street, conscious of decent lives within them, gazed at one another with brown imperturbable faces.

The former tenant of our house, a priest, had died in the back drawing room. Air, musty from having long been enclosed, hung in all the rooms, and the waste room behind the kitchen was littered with old useless papers. Among these I found a few paper-covered books, the pages of which were curled and damp: *The Abbott*, by Walter Scott, *The Devout Communicant*° and *The Memoirs of Vidocq*.° I liked the last best because its leaves were yellow. The wild garden behind the house contained a central apple-tree and a few straggling bushes under one of which I found the late tenant's rusty bicycle-pump. He had been a very charitable priest; in his will he had left all his money to institutions and the furniture of his house to his sister.

When the short days of winter came dusk fell before we had well eaten our dinners. When we met in the street the houses had grown sombre. The space of sky above us was the colour of ever-changing violet and towards it the lamps of

---

North Richmond Street: Name of a real street in Dublin on which Joyce lived as a boy.
blind: dead-end street.
The Devout Communicant: a book of meditations by Pacificus Baker, published 1873.
The Memoirs of Vidocq: published 1829, the story of François Vidocq, a Parisian chief of detectives.

the street lifted their feeble lanterns. The cold air stung us and we played till our bodies glowed. Our shouts echoed in the silent street. The career of our play brought us through the dark muddy lanes behind the houses where we ran the gauntlet of the rough tribes from the cottages, to the back doors of the dark dripping gardens where odours arose from the ashpits, to the dark odorous stables where a coachman smoothed and combed the horse or shook music from the buckled harness. When we returned to the street light from the kitchen windows had filled the areas. If my uncle was seen turning the corner we hid in the shadow until we had seen him safely housed. Or if Mangan's sister came out on the doorstep to call her brother in to his tea we watched her from our shadow peer up and down the street. We waited to see whether she would remain or go in and, if she remained, we left our shadow and walked up to Mangan's steps resignedly. She was waiting for us, her figure defined by the light from the half-opened door. Her brother always teased her before he obeyed and I stood by the railings looking at her. Her dress swung as she moved her body and the soft rope of her hair tossed from side to side.

Every morning I lay on the floor in the front parlor watching her door. The blind was pulled down within an inch of the sash so that I could not be seen. When she came out on the doorstep my heart leaped. I ran to the hall, seized my books and followed her. I kept her brown figure always in my eye and, when we came near the point at which our ways diverged, I quickened my pace and passed her. This happened morning after morning. I had never spoken to her, except for a few casual words, and yet her name was like a summons to all my foolish blood.

Her image accompanied me even in places the most hostile to romance. On Saturday evenings when my aunt went marketing I had to go to carry some of the parcels. We walked through the flaring street, jostled by drunken men and bargaining women, amid the curses of labourers, the shrill litanies of shop-boys who stood on guard by the barrels of pigs' cheeks, the nasal chanting of street singers, who sang a *come-all-you* about O'Donovan Rossa,° or a ballad about the troubles in our native land. These noises converged in a single sensation of life for me: I imagined that I bore my chalice safely through the throng of foes. Her name sprang to my lips at moments in strange prayers and praises which I myself did not understand. My eyes were often full of tears (I could not tell why) and at times a flood from my heart seemed to pour itself out into my bosom. I thought little of the future. I did not know whether I would ever speak to her or not or, if I spoke to her, how I could tell her of my confused adoration. But my body was like a harp and her words and gestures were like fingers running upon the wires.

One evening I went into the back drawing-room in which the priest had died. It was a dark rainy evening and there was no sound in the house. Through one of the broken panes I heard the rain impinge upon the earth, the fine incessant needles of water playing in the sodden beds. Some distant lamp or lighted window gleamed below me. I was thankful that I could see so little. All my senses seemed to desire to veil themselves and, feeling that I was about to slip from them, I pressed the palms of my hands together until they trembled, murmuring: *O love! O love!* many times.

O'Donovan Rossa: popular ballad about Jeremiah O'Donovan (1831–1915), a leader in the movement to free Ireland from English control.

At last she spoke to me. When she addressed the first words to me I was so confused that I did not know what to answer. She asked me was I going to *Araby*.° I forget whether I answered yes or no. It would be a splendid bazaar, she said; she would love to go.

—And why can't you? I asked.

While she spoke she turned a silver bracelet round and round her wrist. She could not go, she said, because there would be a retreat° that week in her convent. Her brother and two other boys were fighting for their caps and I was alone at the railings. She held one of the spikes, bowing her head towards me. The light from the lamp opposite our door caught the white curve of her neck, lit up her hair that rested there and, falling, lit up the hand upon the railing. It fell over one side of her dress and caught the white border of a petticoat, just visible as she stood at ease.

—It's well for you, she said.   10

—If I go, I said, I will bring you something.

What innumerable follies laid waste my waking and sleeping thoughts after that evening! I wished to annihilate the tedious intervening days. I chafed against the work of school. At night in my bedroom and by day in the classroom her image came between me and the page I strove to read. The syllables of the word *Araby* were called to me through the silence in which my soul luxuriated and cast an Eastern enchantment over me. I asked for leave to go to the bazaar on Saturday night. My aunt was surprised and hoped it was not some Freemason° affair. I answered few questions in class. I watched my master's face pass from amiability to sternness; he hoped I was not beginning to idle. I could not call my wandering thoughts together. I had hardly any patience with the serious work of life which, now that it stood between me and my desire, seemed to me child's play, ugly monotonous child's play.

On Saturday morning I reminded my uncle that I wished to go to the bazaar in the evening. He was fussing at the hall-stand, looking for the hatbrush, and answered me curtly:

—Yes, boy, I know.

As he was in the hall I could not go into the front parlour and lie at the   15
window. I left the house in bad humour and walked slowly towards the school. The air was pitilessly raw and already my heart misgave me.

When I came home to dinner my uncle had not yet been home. Still, it was early. I sat staring at the clock for some time and, when its ticking began to irritate me, I left the room. I mounted the staircase and gained the upper part of the house. The high cold empty gloomy rooms liberated me and I went from room to room singing. From the front window I saw my companions playing below in the street. Their cries reached me weakened and indistinct and, leaning my forehead against the cool glass, I looked over at the dark house where she lived. I may have stood there for an hour, seeing nothing but the brown-clad figure cast by my imagination, touched discreetly by the lamplight at the curved neck, at the hand upon the railing and at the border below the dress.

Araby: A bazaar advertised as "Araby in Dublin," a "Grand Oriental Fete," was held in Dublin from May 14–19, 1894.

   retreat: a special time set aside for concentrated religious instruction, discussion, and prayer.

   Freemason: and therefore Protestant.

When I came downstairs again I found Mrs. Mercer sitting at the fire. She was an old garrulous woman, a pawnbroker's widow, who collected used stamps for some pious purpose. I had to endure the gossip of the tea-table. The meal was prolonged beyond an hour and still my uncle did not come. Mrs. Mercer stood up to go: she was sorry she couldn't wait any longer, but it was after eight o'clock and she did not like to be out late, as the night air was bad for her. When she had gone I began to walk up and down the room, clenching my fists. My aunt said:

—I'm afraid you may put off your bazaar for this night of Our Lord.

At nine o'clock I heard my uncle's latchkey in the halldoor. I heard him talking to himself and heard the hall-stand rocking when it had received the weight of his overcoat. I could interpret these signs. When he was midway through his dinner I asked him to give me the money to go to the bazaar. He had forgotten.

—The people are in bed and after their first sleep now, he said.   20

I did not smile. My aunt said to him energetically:

—Can't you give him the money and let him go? You've kept him late enough as it is.

My uncle said he was very sorry he had forgotten. He said he believed in the old saying: *All work and no play makes Jack a dull boy*. He asked me where I was going and, when I had told him a second time he asked me did I know *The Arab's Farewell to his Steed*.° When I left the kitchen he was about to recite the opening lines of the piece to my aunt.

I held a florin° tightly in my hand as I strode down Buckingham Street towards the station. The sight of the streets thronged with buyers and glaring with gas recalled to me the purpose of my journey. I took my seat in a third-class carriage of a deserted train. After an intolerable delay the train moved out of the station slowly. It crept onward among ruinous houses and over the twinkling river. At Westland Row Station a crowd of people pressed to the carriage doors; but the porters moved them back, saying that it was a special train for the bazaar. I remained alone in the bare carriage. In a few minutes the train drew up beside an improvised wooden platform. I passed out on to the road and saw by the lighted dial of a clock that it was ten minutes to ten. In front of me was a large building which displayed the magical name.

I could not find any sixpenny entrance and, fearing that the bazaar would   25
be closed, I passed in quickly through a turnstile, handing a shilling to a weary-looking man. I found myself in a big hall girdled at half its height by a gallery. Nearly all the stalls were closed and the greater part of the hall was in darkness. I recognized a silence like that which pervades a church after a service. I walked into the centre of the bazaar timidly. A few people were gathered about the stalls which were still open. Before a curtain, over which the words *Café Chantant* were written in coloured lamps, two men were counting money on a salver. I listened to the fall of the coins.

Remembering with difficulty why I had come I went over to one of the stalls and examined porcelain vases and flowered tea-sets. At the door of the stall a young lady was talking and laughing with two young gentlemen. I remarked their English accents and listened vaguely to their conversation.

The Arab's Farewell to his Steed: poem by Caroline Norton (1808–1877).
   florin: a two-shilling coin in the 1890s (when the story takes place), worth perhaps ten dollars in today's money.

—O, I never said such a thing!

—O, but you did!

—O, but I didn't!

—Didn't she say that? 30

—Yes I heard her.

—O, there's a . . . fib!

Observing me the young lady came over and asked me did I wish to buy anything. The tone in her voice was not encouraging; she seemed to have spoken to me out of a sense of duty. I looked humbly at the great jars that stood like eastern guards at either side of the dark entrance to the stall and murmured:

—No, thank you.

The young lady changed the position of one of the vases and went back to 35 the two young men. They began to talk of the same subject. Once or twice the young lady glanced at me over her shoulder.

I lingered before her stall, though I knew my stay was useless, to make my interest in her wares seem the more real. Then I turned away slowly and walked down the middle of the bazaar. I allowed the two pennies to fall against the sixpence in my pocket. I heard a voice call from one end of the gallery that the light was out. The upper part of the hall was now completely dark.

Gazing up into the darkness I saw myself as a creature driven and derided by vanity; and my eyes burned with anguish and anger.

QUESTIONS

1. Describe what you consider to be the story's major idea.

2. How might the bazaar, "Araby," be considered symbolically in the story? To what extent does this symbol embody the story's central idea?

3. Consider the attitude of the speaker toward his home as indicated in the first paragraph. Why do you think the speaker uses the word *blind* to describe the dead-end street? What relationship exists between the speaker's pain at the end of the story to the ideas in the first paragraph?

4. Who is the narrator? About how old is he at the time of the story? About how old when he tells the story? What effect is produced by this difference in age between narrator-as-character and narrator-as-storyteller?

D. H. LAWRENCE (1885–1930)

The Horse Dealer's Daughter   1922

"Well, Mabel, and what are you going to do with yourself?" asked Joe, with foolish flippancy. He felt quite safe himself. Without listening for an answer, he turned aside, worked a grain of tobacco to the tip of his tongue, and spat it out. He did not care about anything, since he felt safe himself.

The three brothers and the sister sat round the desolate breakfast table, attempting some sort of desultory consultation. The morning's post had given the final tap to the family fortunes, and all was over. The dreary dining-room itself, with its heavy mahogany furniture, looked as it were waiting to be done away with.

But the consultation amounted to nothing. There was a strange air of ineffectuality about the three men, as they sprawled at table, smoking and reflecting vaguely on their own condition. The girl was alone, a rather short, sullen-looking young woman of twenty-seven. She did not share the same life as her brothers. She would have been good-looking, save for the impassive fixity of her face, "bulldog," as her brothers called it.

There was a confused tramping of horses' feet outside. The three men all sprawled round in their chairs to watch. Beyond the dark holly-bushes that separated the strip of lawn from the high-road, they could see a cavalcade of shire horses swinging out of their own yard, being taken for exercise. This was the last time. These were the last horses that would go through their hands. The young men watched with critical, callous look. They were all frightened at the collapse of their lives, and the sense of disaster in which they were involved left them no inner freedom.

Yet they were three fine, well-set fellows enough. Joe, the eldest, was a man of thirty-three, broad and handsome in a hot, flushed way. His face was red, he twisted his black moustache over a thick finger, his eyes were shallow and restless. He had a sensual way of uncovering his teeth when he laughed, and his bearing was stupid. Now he watched the horses with a glazed look of helplessness in his eyes, a certain stupor of downfall.

The great draught-horses swung past. They were tied head to tail, four of them, and they heaved along to where a lane branched off from the highroad, planting their great hoofs floutingly in the fine black mud, swinging their great rounded haunches sumptuously, and trotting a few sudden steps as they were led into the lane, round the corner. Every movement showed a massive, slumbrous strength, and a stupidity which held them in subjection. The groom at the head looked back, jerking the leading rope. And the cavalcade moved out of sight up the lane, the tail of the last horse, bobbed up tight and stiff, held out taut from the swinging great haunches as they rocked behind the hedges in a motionlike sleep.

Joe watched with glazed hopeless eyes. The horses were almost like his own body to him. He felt he was done for now. Luckily, he was engaged to a woman as old as himself, and therefore her father, who was steward of a neighbouring estate, would provide him with a job. He would marry and go into harness. His life was over, he would be a subject animal now.

He turned uneasily aside, the retreating steps of the horses echoing in his ears. Then, with foolish restlessness, he reached for the scraps of bacon-rind from the plates, and making a faint whistling sound, flung them to the terrier that lay against the fender. He watched the dog swallow them, and waited till the creature looked into his eyes. Then a faint grin came on his face, and in a high, foolish voice he said:

"You won't get much more bacon, shall you, you little b———?"

The dog faintly and dismally wagged its tail, then lowered its haunches, circled round, and lay down again.

There was another helpless silence at the table. Joe sprawled uneasily in his seat, not willing to go till the family conclave was dissolved. Fred Henry, the second brother, was erect, clean-limbed, alert. He had watched the passing of the horses with more *sang-froid*.° If he was an animal, like Joe, he was an animal which controls, not one which is controlled. He was master of any horse, and he carried himself with a well-tempered air of mastery. But he was not master of the situations of life. He pushed his coarse brown moustache upwards, off his lip, and glanced irritably at his sister, who sat impassive and inscrutable.

"You'll go and stop with Lucy for a bit, shan't you?" he asked. The girl did not answer.

"I don't see what else you can do," persisted Fred Henry.

"Go as a skivvy,"° Joe interpolated laconically.

The girl did not move a muscle.   15

"If I was her, I should go in for training for a nurse," said Malcolm, the youngest of them all. He was the baby of the family, a young man of twenty-two, with a fresh, jaunty *museau*.°

But Mabel did not take any notice of him. They had talked at her and round her for so many years, that she hardly heard them at all.

The marble clock on the mantel-piece softly chimed the half-hour, the dog rose uneasily from the hearthrug and looked at the party at the breakfast table. But still they sat on in ineffectual conclave.

"Oh, all right," said Joe suddenly, *à propos* of nothing. "I'll get a move on."

He pushed back his chair, straddled his knees with a downward jerk, to get   20
them free, in horsey fashion, and went to the fire. Still he did not go out of the room; he was curious to know what the others would do or say. He began to charge his pipe, looking down at the dog and saying, in a high, affected voice:

"Going wi' me? Going wi' me are ter? Tha'rt goin' further than tha counts on just now, dost hear?"

The dog faintly wagged its tail, the man stuck out his jaw and covered his pipe with his hands, and puffed intently, losing himself in the tobacco, looking down all the while at the dog, with an absent brown eye. The dog looked up at him in mournful distrust. Joe stood with his knees stuck out, in real horsey fashion.

"Have you had a letter from Lucy?" Fred Henry asked of his sister.

"Last week," came the neutral reply.

"And what does she say?"   25

There was no answer.

"Does she *ask* you to go and stop there?" persisted Fred Henry.

"She says I can if I like."

"Well, then, you'd better. Tell her you'll come on Monday."

This was received in silence.   30

"That's what you'll do then, is it?" said Fred Henry, in some exasperation.

But she made no answer. There was a silence of futility and irritation in the room. Malcolm grinned fatuously.

"You'll have to make up your mind between now and next Wednesday," said Joe loudly, "or else find yourself lodgings on the kerbstone."

The face of the young woman darkened, but she sat on immutable.

"Here's Jack Fergusson!" exclaimed Malcolm, who was looking aimlessly out   35
of the window.

---

sang-froid: unconcern (literally, cold blood).
skivvy: British slang for housemaid.
museau: French for nose, snout.

"Where?" exclaimed Joe, loudly.

"Just gone past."

"Coming in?"

Malcolm craned his neck to see the gate.

"Yes," he said.   40

There was a silence. Mabel sat on like one condemned, at the head of the table. Then a whistle was heard from the kitchen. The dog got up and barked sharply. Joe opened the door and shouted:

"Come on."

After a moment, a young man entered. He was muffled up in overcoat and a purple woolen scarf, and his tweed cap, which he did not remove, was pulled down on his head. He was of medium height, his face was rather long and pale, his eyes looked tired.

"Hello, Jack! Well, Jack!" exclaimed Malcolm and Joe. Fred Henry merely said "Jack!"

"What's doing?" asked the newcomer, evidently addressing Fred Henry.   45

"Same. We've got to be out by Wednesday—Got a cold?"

"I have—got it bad, too."

"Why don't you stop in?"

"*Me* stop in? When I can't stand on my legs, perhaps I shall have a chance." The young man spoke huskily. He had a slight Scotch accent.

"It's a knock-out, isn't it," said Joe boisterously, "if a doctor goes round   50
croaking with a cold. Looks bad for the patients, doesn't it?"

The young doctor looked at him slowly.

"Anything the matter with *you*, then?" he asked, sarcastically.

"Not as I know of. Damn your eyes, I hope not. Why?"

"I thought you were very concerned about the patients, wondered if you might be one yourself."

"Damn it, no, I've never been patient to no flaming doctor, and hope I   55
never shall be," returned Joe.

At this point Mabel rose from the table, and they all seemed to become aware of her existence. She began putting the dishes together. The young doctor looked at her, but did not address her. He had not greeted her. She went out of the room with the tray, her face impassive and unchanged.

"When are you off then, all of you?" asked the doctor.

"I'm catching the eleven-forty," replied Malcolm. "Are you goin' down wi' th' trap,° Joe?"

"Yes, I've told you I'm going down wi' th' trap, haven't I?"

"We'd better be getting her in then.—So long, Jack, if I don't see you before   60
I go," said Malcolm, shaking hands.

He went out, followed by Joe, who seemed to have his tail between his legs.

"Well, this is the devil's own," exclaimed the doctor, when he was left alone with Fred Henry. "Going before Wednesday, are you?"

"That's the orders," replied the other.

"Where, to Northampton?"

"That's it."   65

"The devil!" exclaimed Fergusson, with quiet chagrin.

trap: small wagon.

And there was silence between the two.

"All settled up, are you?" asked Fergusson.

"About."

There was another pause.

"Well, I shall miss yer, Freddy boy," said the young doctor.

"And I shall miss thee, Jack," returned the other.

"Miss you like hell," mused the doctor.

Fred Henry turned aside. There was nothing to say. Mabel came in again, to finish clearing the table.

"What are *you* going to do then, Miss Pervin?" asked Fergusson. "Going to your sister's, are you?"

Mabel looked at him with her steady, dangerous eyes, that always made him uncomfortable, unsettling his superficial ease.

"No," she said.

"Well, what in the name of fortune *are* you going to do? Say what you *mean* to do," cried Fred Henry, with futile intensity.

But she only averted her head, and continued her work. She folded the white table-cloth, and put on the chenille cloth.

"The sulkiest bitch that ever trod!" muttered her brother.

But she finished her task with perfectly impassive face, the young doctor watching her interestedly all the while. Then she went out.

Fred Henry stared after her, clenching his lips, his blue eyes fixing in sharp antagonism, as he made a grimace of sour exasperation.

"You could bray her into bits, and that's all you'd get out of her," he said, in a small, narrowed tone.

The doctor smiled faintly.

"What's she *going* to do then?" he asked.

"Strike me if *I* know!" returned the other.

There was a pause. Then the doctor stirred.

"I'll be seeing you to-night, shall I?" he said to his friend.

"Ay—where's it to be? Are we going over to Jessdale?"

"I don't know. I've got such a cold on me. I'll come round to the Moon and Stars, anyway."

"Let Lizzie and May miss their night for once, eh?"

"That's it—if I feel as I do now."

"All's one—"

The two young men went through the passage and down to the back door together. The house was large, but it was servantless now, and desolate. At the back was a small bricked house-yard, and beyond that a big square, gravelled fine and red, and having stables on two sides. Sloping, dank, winter-dark fields stretched away on the open sides.

But the stables were empty. Joseph Pervin, the father of the family, had been a man of no education, who had become a fairly large horse dealer. The stables had been full of horses, there was a great turmoil and come-and-go of horses and of dealers and grooms. Then the kitchen was full of servants. But of late things had declined. The old man had married a second time, to retrieve his fortunes. Now he was dead and everything was gone to the dogs, there was nothing but debt and threatening.

For months, Mabel had been servantless in the big house, keeping the home together in penury for her ineffectual brothers. She had kept house for ten years. But previously, it was with unstinted means. Then, however brutal and coarse everything was, the sense of money had kept her proud, confident. The men might be foul-mouthed, the women in the kitchen might have bad reputations, her brothers might have illegitimate children. But so long as there was money, the girl felt herself established, and brutally proud, reserved.

No company came to the house, save dealers and coarse men. Mabel had no associates of her own sex, after her sister went away. But she did not mind. She went regularly to church, she attended to her father. And she lived in the memory of her mother, who had died when she was fourteen, and whom she had loved. She had loved her father, too, in a different way, depending upon him, and feeling secure in him, until at the age of fifty-four he married again. And then she had set hard against him. Now he had died and left them all hopelessly in debt.

She had suffered badly during the period of poverty. Nothing, however, could shake the curious sullen, animal pride that dominated each member of the family. Now, for Mabel, the end had come. Still she would not cast about her. She would follow her own way just the same. She would always hold the keys of her own situation. Mindless and persistent, she endured from day to day. Why should she think? Why should she answer anybody? It was enough that this was the end, and there was no way out. She need not pass any more darkly along the main street of the small town, avoiding every eye. She need not demean herself any more, going into the shops and buying the cheapest food. This was at an end. She thought of nobody, not even of herself. Mindless and persistent, she seemed in a sort of ecstasy to be coming nearer to her fulfilment, her own glorification, approaching her dead mother, who was glorified.°

In the afternoon she took a little bag, with shears and sponge and a small scrubbing brush, and went out. It was a grey, wintry day, with saddened, dark-green fields and an atmosphere blackened by the smoke of foundries not far off. She went quickly, darkly along the causeway, heeding nobody, through the town to the churchyard.

There she always felt secure, as if no one could see her, although as a matter   100
of fact she was exposed to the stare of everyone who passed along under the churchyard wall. Nevertheless, once under the shadow of the great looming church, among the graves, she felt immune from the world, reserved within the thick churchyard wall as in another country.

Carefully she clipped the grass from the grave, and arranged the pinky-white, small chrysanthemums in the tin cross. When this was done, she took an empty jar from a neighbouring grave, brought water, and carefully, most scrupulously sponged the marble headstone and the coping-stone.

It gave her sincere satisfaction to do this. She felt in immediate contact with the world of her mother. She took minute pains, went through the park in a state bordering on pure happiness, as if in performing this task she came into a subtle, intimate connection with her mother. For the life she followed here in the world was far less real than the world of death she inherited from her mother.

The doctor's house was just by the church. Fergusson, being a mere hired assistant, was slave to the countryside. As he hurried now to attend to the outpatients

who was glorified: See Romans 8:17,30.

in the surgery, glancing across the graveyard with his quick eye, he saw the girl at her task at the grave. She seemed so intent and remote, it was like looking into another world. Some mystical element was touched in him. He slowed down as he walked, watching her as if spell-bound.

She lifted her eyes, feeling him looking. Their eyes met. And each looked again at once, each feeling, in some way, found out by the other. He lifted his cap and passed on down the road. There remained distinct in his consciousness, like a vision, the memory of her face, lifted from the tombstone in the churchyard, and looking at him with slow, large, portentous eyes. It *was* portentous, her face. It seemed to mesmerise him. There was a heavy power in her eyes which laid hold of his whole being, as if he had drunk some powerful drug. He had been feeling weak and done before. Now the life came back into him, he felt delivered from his own fretted, daily self.

He finished his duties at the surgery as quickly as might be, hastily filling   105
up the bottles of the waiting people with cheap drugs. Then, in perpetual haste, he set off again to visit several cases in another part of his round, before teatime. At all times he preferred to walk, if he could, but particularly when he was not well. He fancied the motion restored him.

The afternoon was falling. It was grey, deadened, and wintry, with a slow, moist, heavy coldness sinking in and deadening all the faculties. But why should he think or notice? He hastily climbed the hill and turned across the dark-green fields, following the black cinder-track. In the distance, across a shallow dip in the country, the small town was clustered like smouldering ash, a tower, a spire, a heap of low, raw, extinct houses. And on the nearest fringe of the town, sloping into the dip, was Oldmeadow, the Pervins' house. He could see the stables and the outbuildings distinctly, as they lay towards him on the slope. Well, he would not go there many more times! Another resource would be lost to him, another place gone: the only company he cared for in the alien, ugly little town he was losing. Nothing but work, drudgery, constant hastening from dwelling to dwelling among the colliers and the iron-workers. It wore him out, but at the same time he had a craving for it. It was a stimulant to him to be in the homes of the working people, moving as it were through the innermost body of their life. His nerves were excited and gratified. He could come so near, into the very lives of the rough, inarticulate, powerfully emotional men and women. He grumbled, he said he hated the hellish hole. But as a matter of fact it excited him, the contact with the rough, strongly-feeling people was a stimulant applied direct to his nerves.

Below Oldmeadow, in the green, shallow, soddened hollow of fields, lay a square, deep pond. Roving across the landscape, the doctor's quick eye detected a figure in black passing through the gate of the field, down towards the pond. He looked again. It would be Mabel Pervin. His mind suddenly became alive and attentive.

Why was she going down there? He pulled up on the path on the slope above, and stood staring. He could just make sure of the small black figure moving in the hollow of the failing day. He seemed to see her in the midst of such obscurity, that he was like a clairvoyant, seeing rather with the mind's eye than with ordinary sight. Yet he could see her positively enough, whilst he kept his eye attentive. He felt, if he looked away from her, in the thick, ugly falling dusk, he would lose her altogether.

He followed her minutely as she moved, direct and intent, like something transmitted rather than stirring in voluntary activity, straight down the field towards the pond. There she stood on the bank for a moment. She never raised her head. Then she waded slowly into the water.

He stood motionless as the small black figure walked slowly and deliberately towards the centre of the pond, very slowly, gradually moving deeper into the motionless water, and still moving forward as the water got up to her breast. Then he could see her no more in the dusk of the dead afternoon.   110

"There!" he exclaimed. "Would you believe it?"

And he hastened straight down, running over the wet, soddened fields, pushing through the hedges, down into the depression of callous wintry obscurity. It took him several minutes to come to the pond. He stood on the bank, breathing heavily. He could see nothing. His eyes seemed to penetrate the dead water. Yes, perhaps that was the dark shadow of her black clothing beneath the surface of the water.

He slowly ventured into the pond. The bottom was deep, soft clay, he sank in, and the water clasped dead cold round his legs. As he stirred he could smell the cold, rotten clay that fouled up into the water. It was objectionable in his lungs. Still, repelled and yet not heeding, he moved deeper into the pond. The cold water rose over his thighs, over his loins, upon his abdomen. The lower part of his body was all sunk in the hideous cold element. And the bottom was so deeply soft and uncertain, he was afraid of pitching with his mouth underneath. He could not swim, and was afraid.

He crouched a little, spreading his hands under the water and moving them round, trying to feel for her. The dead cold pond swayed upon his chest. He moved again, a little deeper, and again, with his hands underneath, he felt all around under the water. And he touched her clothing. But it evaded his fingers. He made a desperate effort to grasp it.

And so doing he lost his balance and went under, horribly, suffocating in   115
the foul earthy water, struggling madly for a few moments. At last, after what seemed an eternity, he got his footing, rose again into the air and looked around. He gasped, and knew he was in the world. Then he looked at the water. She had risen near him. He grasped her clothing, and drawing her nearer, turned to take his way to land again.

He went very slowly, carefully, absorbed in the slow progress. He rose higher, climbing out of the pond. The water was not only about his legs; he was thankful, full of relief to be out of the clutches of the pond. He lifted her and staggered on to the bank, out of the horror of wet, grey clay.

He laid her down on the bank. She was quite unconscious and running with water. He made the water come from her mouth, he worked to restore her. He did not have to work very long before he could feel the breathing begin again in her; she was breathing naturally. He worked a little longer. He could feel her live beneath his hands; she was coming back. He wiped her face, wrapped her in his overcoat, looked round into the dim, dark-grey world, then lifted her and staggered down the bank and across the fields.

It seemed an unthinkably long way, and his burden so heavy he felt he would never get to the house. But at last he was in the stable-yard, and then in the house-yard. He opened the door and went into the house. In the kitchen he laid her down on the hearthrug, and called. The house was empty. But the fire was burning in the grate.

Then again he kneeled to attend to her. She was breathing regularly, her eyes were wide open as if conscious, but there seemed something missing in her look. She was conscious in herself, but unconscious of her surroundings.

He ran upstairs, took blankets from a bed, and put them before the fire to   120
warm. Then he removed her saturated, earthy-smelling clothing, rubbed her dry with a towel, and wrapped her naked in the blankets. Then he went into the dining-room, to look for spirits. There was a little whiskey. He drank a gulp himself, and put some into her mouth.

The effect was instantaneous. She looked full into his face, as if she had been seeing him for some time, and yet had only just become conscious of him.

"Dr. Fergusson?" she said.

"What?" he answered.

He was divesting himself of his coat, intending to find some dry clothing upstairs. He could not bear the smell of the dead, clayey water, and he was mortally afraid for his own health.

"What did I do?" she asked.   125

"Walked into the pond," he replied. He had begun to shudder like one sick, and could hardly attend to her. Her eyes remained full on him, he seemed to be going dark in his mind, looking back at her helplessly. The shuddering became quieter in him, his life came back in him, dark and unknowing, but strong again.

"Was I out of my mind?" she asked, while her eyes were fixed on him all the time.

"Maybe, for the moment," he replied. He felt quiet, because his strength had come back. The strange fretful strain had left him.

"Am I out of my mind now?" she asked.

"Are you?" he reflected a moment. "No," he answered truthfully, "I don't   130
see that you are." He turned his face aside. He was afraid, now, because he felt dazed, and felt dimly that her power was stronger than his, in this issue. And she continued to look at him fixedly all the time. "Can you tell me where I shall find some dry things to put on?" he asked.

"Did you dive into the pond for me?" she asked.

"No," he answered. "I walked in. But I went in overhead as well."

There was silence for a moment. He hesitated. He very much wanted to go upstairs to get into dry clothing. But there was another desire in him. And she seemed to hold him. His will seemed to have gone to sleep, and left him, standing there slack before her. But he felt warm inside himself. He did not shudder at all, though his clothes were sodden on him.

"Why did you?" she asked.

"Because I didn't want you to do such a foolish thing," he said.   135

"It wasn't foolish," she said, still gazing at him as she lay on the floor, with a sofa cushion under her head. "It was the right thing to do. *I* knew best, then."

"I'll go and shift these wet things," he said. But still he had not the power to move out of her presence, until she sent him. It was as if she had the life of his body in her hands, and he could not extricate himself. Or perhaps he did not want to.

Suddenly she sat up. Then she became aware of her own immediate condition. She felt the blankets about her, she knew her own limbs. For a moment it seemed as if her reason were going. She looked round, with wild eye, as if seeking something. He stood still with fear. She saw her clothing lying scattered.

"Who undressed me?" she asked, her eyes resting full and inevitable on his face.

"I did," he replied, "to bring you round." 140

For some moments she sat and gazed at him awfully, her lips parted.

"Do you love me then?" she asked.

He only stood and stared at her, fascinated. His soul seemed to melt.

She shuffled forward on her knees, and put her arms round him, round his legs, as he stood there, pressing her breasts against his knees and thighs, clutching him with strange, convulsive certainty, pressing his thighs against her, drawing him to her face, her throat, as she looked up at him with flaring, humble eyes of transfiguration, triumphant in first possession.

"You love me," she murmured, in strange transport, yearning and triumphant 145 and confident. "You love me. I know you love me, I know."

And she was passionately kissing his knees, through the wet clothing, passionately and indiscriminately kissing his knees, his legs, as if unaware of everything.

He looked down at the tangled wet hair, the wild, bare, animal shoulders. He was amazed, bewildered, and afraid. He had never thought of loving her. He had never wanted to love her. When he rescued her and restored her, he was a doctor, and she was a patient. He had had no single personal thought of her. Nay, this introduction of the personal element was very distasteful to him, a violation of his professional honour. It was horrible to have her there embracing his knees. It was horrible. He revolted from it, violently. And yet—and yet—he had not the power to break away.

She looked at him again, with the same supplication of powerful love, and that same transcendent, frightening light of triumph. In view of the delicate flame which seemed to come from her face like a light, he was powerless. And yet he had never intended to love her. He had never intended. And something stubborn in him could not give way.

"You love me," she repeated, in a murmur of deep, rhapsodic assurance. "You love me."

Her hands were drawing him, drawing him down to her. He was afraid, 150 even a little horrified. For he had, really, no intention of loving her. Yet her hands were drawing him towards her. He put out his hand quickly to steady himself, and grasped her bare shoulder. A flame seemed to burn the hand that grasped her soft shoulder. He had no intention of loving her: his whole will was against his yielding. It was horrible— And yet wonderful was the touch of her shoulder, beautiful the shining of her face. Was she perhaps mad? He had a horror of yielding to her. Yet something in him ached also.

He had been staring away at the door, away from her. But his hand remained on her shoulder. She had gone suddenly very still. He looked down at her. Her eyes were now wide with fear, with doubt, the light was dying from her face, a shadow of terrible greyness was returning. He could not bear the touch of her eyes' question upon him, and the look of death behind the question.

With an inward groan he gave way, and let his heart yield towards her. A sudden gentle smile came on his face. And her eyes, which never left his face, slowly, slowly filled with tears. He watched the strange water rise in her eyes, like some slow fountain coming up. And his heart seemed to burn and melt away in his breast.

He could not bear to look at her any more. He dropped on his knees and caught her head with his arms and pressed her face against his throat. She was very still. His heart, which seemed to have broken, was burning with a kind of agony in his breast. And he felt her slow, hot tears wetting his throat. But he could not move.

He felt the hot tears wet his neck and the hollows of his neck, and he remained motionless, suspended through one of man's eternities. Only now it had become indispensable to him to have her face pressed close to him; he could never let her go again. He could never let her head go away from the close clutch of his arm. He wanted to remain like that for ever, with his heart hurting him in a pain that was also life to him. Without knowing, he was looking down on her damp, soft brown hair.

Then, as it were suddenly, he smelt the horrid stagnant smell of the water. 155
And at the same moment she drew away from him and looked at him. Her eyes were wistful and unfathomable. He was afraid of them, and he fell to kissing her, not knowing what he was doing. He wanted her eyes not to have that terrible, wistful, unfathomable look.

When she turned her face to him again, a faint delicate flush was glowing, and there was again dawning that terrible shining of joy in her eyes, which really terrified him, and yet which he now wanted to see, because he feared the look of doubt still more.

"You love me?" she said, rather faltering.

"Yes." The word cost him a painful effort. Not because it wasn't true. But because it was too newly true, the *saying* seemed to tear open again his newly-torn heart. And he hardly wanted it to be true, even now.

She lifted her face to him, and he bent forward and kissed her on the mouth gently, with the one kiss that is an eternal pledge. And as he kissed her his heart strained again in his breast. He never intended to love her. But now it was over. He had crossed over the gulf to her, and all that he had left behind had shrivelled and become void.

After the kiss, her eyes again slowly filled with tears. She sat still, away from 160
him, with her face drooped aside, and her hands folded in her lap. The tears fell very slowly. There was complete silence. He too sat there motionless and silent on the hearthrug. The strange pain of his heart that was broken seemed to consume him. That he should love her? That this was love! That he should be ripped open in this way!—Him, a doctor!—How they would all jeer if they knew!—It was agony to him to think they might know.

In the curious naked pain of the thought he looked again to her. She was sitting there drooped into a muse. He saw a tear fall, and his heart flared hot. He saw for the first time that one of her shoulders was quite uncovered, one arm bare, he could see one of her small breasts; dimly, because it had become almost dark in the room.

"Why are you crying?" he asked, in an altered voice.

She looked up at him, and behind her tears the consciousness of her situation for the first time brought a dark look of shame to her eyes.

"I'm not crying, really," she said, watching him half frightened.

He reached his hand, and softly closed it on her bare arm. 165

"I love you! I love you!" he said in a soft, low vibrating voice, unlike himself.

She shrank, and dropped her head. The soft, penetrating grip of his hand on her arm distressed her. She looked up at him.

"I want to go," she said. "I want to go and get you some dry things."

"Why?" he said. "I'm all right."

"But I want to go," she said. "And I want you to change your things."   170

He released her arm, and she wrapped herself in the blanket, looking at him rather frightened. And still she did not rise.

"Kiss me," she said wistfully.

He kissed her, but briefly, half in anger.

Then, after a second, she rose nervously, all mixed up in the blanket. He watched her in her confusion, as she tried to extricate herself and wrap herself up so that she could walk. He watched her relentlessly, as she knew.

And as she went, the blanket trailing, and as he saw a glimpse of her feet   175
and her white leg, he tried to remember her as she was when he had wrapped her in the blanket. But then he didn't want to remember, because she had been nothing to him then, and his nature revolted from remembering her as she was when she was nothing to him.

A tumbling muffled noise from within the dark house startled him. Then he heard her voice:—"There are clothes." He rose and went to the foot of the stairs, and gathered up the garments she had thrown down. Then he came back to the fire, to rub himself down and dress. He grinned at his own appearance, when he had finished.

The fire was sinking, so he put on coal. The house was now quite dark, save for the light of a street-lamp that shone in faintly from beyond the holly trees. He lit the gas with matches he found on the mantel-piece. Then he emptied the pockets of his own clothes, and threw all his wet things in a heap into the scullery. After which he gathered up her sodden clothes, gently, and put them in a separate heap on the copper-top in the scullery.

It was six o'clock on the clock. His own watch had stopped. He ought to be back to the surgery. He waited, and still she did not come down. So he went to the foot of the stairs and called:

"I shall have to go."

Almost immediately he heard her coming down. She had on her best dress   180
of black voile, and her hair was tidy, but still damp. She looked at him—and in spite of herself, smiled.

"I don't like you in those clothes," she said.

"Do I look a sight?" he answered.

They were shy of one another.

"I'll make you some tea," she said.

"No, I must go."   185

"Must you?" And she looked at him again with the wide, strained, doubtful eyes. And again, from the pain of his breast, he knew how he loved her. He went and bent to kiss her, gently, passionately, with his heart's painful kiss.

"And my hair smells so horrible," she murmured in distraction. "And I'm so awful, I'm so awful! Oh, no, I'm too awful." And she broke into bitter, heartbroken sobbing. "You can't want to love me, I'm horrible."

"Don't be silly, don't be silly," he said, trying to comfort her, kissing her, holding her in his arms. "I want you, I want to marry you, we're going to be married, quickly, quickly—to-morrow if I can."

But she only sobbed terribly, and cried.

"I feel awful. I feel awful. I feel I'm horrible to you."   190

"No, I want you, I want you," was all he answered blindly, with that terrible intonation which frightened her almost more than her horror lest he should *not* want her.

QUESTIONS

1. What idea is Lawrence illustrating by the breakup of the Pervin household?

2. What does the comparison of Joe Pervin and the draft horses mean with regard specifically to Joe, and generally to people without love?

3. What kind of person is Mabel? How do her brothers treat her? How does she feel about her brothers? What dilemma does she face as the story begins?

4. What effect does Mabel have on Fergusson as he watches her in her home, in the churchyard, and at the pond? What does this effect contribute to Lawrence's ideas about love?

5. What do Mabel and Fergusson realize as he revives and warms her? How do their responses signify their growth as characters?

6. Why does the narrator tell us at the story's end that Fergusson "had no intention of loving" Mabel? What idea does this repeated assertion convey?

7. In this story, there is an extensive exploration of the ambiguous feelings of both Fergusson and Mabel after they realize their love. Why does Lawrence explore these feelings so extensively?

ERNEST J. GAINES   (b. 1933)

The Sky Is Gray   1968

1

Go'n be coming in a few minutes. Coming round that bend down there full speed. And I'm go'n get out my handkerchief and wave it down, and we go'n get on it and go.

I keep on looking for it, but Mama don't look that way no more. She's looking down the road where we just come from. It's a long old road, and far 's you can see you don't see nothing but gravel. You got dry weeds on both sides, and you got trees on both sides, and fences on both sides, too. And you got cows in the pastures and they standing close together. And when we was coming out here to catch the bus I seen the smoke coming out of the cows's noses.

I look at my mama and I know what she's thinking. I been with Mama so much, just me and her, I know what she's thinking all the time. Right now it's home—Auntie and them. She's thinking if they got enough wood—if she left enough there to keep them warm till we get back. She's thinking if it go'n rain and if any of them go'n have to go out in the rain. She's thinking 'bout the hog— if he go'n get out, and if Ty and Val be able to get him back in. She always worry like that when she leaves the house. She don't worry too much if she leave me there with the smaller ones, 'cause she know I'm go'n look after them and look after Auntie and everything else. I'm the oldest and she say I'm the man.

I look at my mama and I love my mama. She's wearing that black coat and that black hat and she's looking sad. I love my mama and I want put my arm round her and tell her. But I'm not supposed to do that. She say that's weakness and that's crybaby stuff, and she don't want no crybaby round her. She don't want you to be scared, either. 'Cause Ty's scared of ghosts and she's always whipping him. I'm scared of the dark, too, but I make 'tend I ain't. I make 'tend I ain't 'cause I'm the oldest, and I got to set a good sample for the rest. I can't ever be scared and I can't ever cry. And that's why I never said nothing 'bout my teeth. It's been hurting me and hurting me close to a month now, but I never said it. I didn't say it 'cause I didn't want act like a crybaby, and 'cause I know we didn't have enough money to go have it pulled. But, Lord, it been hurting me. And look like it wouldn't start till at night when you was trying to get yourself little sleep. Then soon 's you shut your eyes—ummm-ummm, Lord, look like it go right down to your heartstring.

"Hurting, hanh?" Ty'd say. 5

I'd shake my head, but I wouldn't open my mouth for nothing. You open your mouth and let that wind in, and it almost kill you.

I'd just lay there and listen to them snore. Ty there, right 'side me, and Auntie and Val over by the fireplace. Val younger than me and Ty, and he sleeps with Auntie. Mama sleeps round the other side with Louis and Walker.

I'd just lay there and listen to them, and listen to that wind out there, and listen to that fire in the fireplace. Sometimes it'd stop long enough to let me get little rest. Sometimes it just hurt, hurt, hurt. Lord, have mercy.

2

Auntie knowed it was hurting me. I didn't tell nobody but Ty, 'cause we buddies and he ain't go'n tell nobody. But some kind of way Auntie found out. When she asked me, I told her no, nothing was wrong. But she knowed it all the time. She told me to mash up a piece of aspirin and wrap it in some cotton and jugg it down in that hole. I did it, but it didn't do no good. It stopped for a little while, and started right back again. Auntie wanted to tell Mama, but I told her, "Uh-uh." 'Cause I knowed we didn't have any money, and it just was go'n make her mad again. So Auntie told Monsieur Bayonne, and Monsieur Bayonne came over to the house and told me to kneel down 'side him on the fireplace. He put his finger in his mouth and made the Sign of the Cross on my jaw. The tip of Monsieur Bayonne's finger is some hard, 'cause he's always playing on that guitar. If we sit outside at night we can always hear Monsieur Bayonne playing on his guitar. Sometimes we leave him out there playing on the guitar.

Monsieur Bayonne made the Sign of the Cross over and over on my jaw, 10 but that didn't do no good. Even when he prayed and told me to pray some, too, that tooth still hurt me.

"How you feeling?" he say.

"Same," I say.

He kept on praying and making the Sign of the Cross and I kept on praying, too.

"Still hurting?" he say.

"Yes, sir." 15

Monsieur Bayonne mashed harder and harder on my jaw. He mashed so hard he almost pushed me over on Ty. But then he stopped.

"What kind of prayers you praying, boy?" he say.

"Baptist," I say.

"Well, I'll be—no wonder that tooth still killing him. I'm going one way and he pulling the other. Boy, don't you know any Catholic prayers?"

"I know 'Hail Mary,'" I say.   20

"Then you better start saying it."

"Yes, sir."

He started mashing on my jaw again, and I could hear him praying at the same time. And, sure enough, after while it stopped hurting me.

Me and Ty went outside where Monsieur Bayonne's two hounds was and we started playing with them. "Let's go hunting," Ty say. "All right," I say; and we went on back in the pasture. Soon the hounds got on a trail, and me and Ty followed them all 'cross the pasture and then back in the woods, too. And then they cornered this little old rabbit and killed him, and me and Ty made them get back, and we picked up the rabbit and started on back home. But my tooth had started hurting me again. It was hurting me plenty now, but I wouldn't tell Monsieur Bayonne. That night I didn't sleep a bit, and first thing in the morning Auntie told me to go back and let Monsieur Bayonne pray over me some more. Monsieur Bayonne was in his kitchen making coffee when I got there. Soon 's he seen me he knowed what was wrong.

"All right, kneel down there 'side that stove," he say. "And this time make   25
sure you pray Catholic. I don't know nothing 'bout that Baptist, and I don't want know nothing 'bout him."

3

Last night Mama say, "Tomorrow we going to town."

"It ain't hurting me no more," I say. "I can eat anything on it."

"Tomorrow we going to town," she say.

And after she finished eating, she got up and went to bed. She always go to bed early now. 'Fore Daddy went in the Army,° she used to stay up late. All of us sitting out on the gallery or round the fire. But now, look like soon 's she finish eating she go to bed.

This morning when I woke up, her and Auntie was standing 'fore the   30
fireplace. She say: "Enough to get there and back. Dollar and a half to have it pulled. Twenty-five for me to go, twenty-five for him. Twenty-five for me to come back, twenty-five for him. Fifty cents left. Guess I get little piece of salt meat with that."

"Sure can use it," Auntie say. "White beans and no salt meat ain't white beans."

"I do the best I can," Mama say.

They was quiet after that, and I made 'tend I was still asleep.

"James, hit the floor," Auntie say.

I still made 'tend I was asleep. I didn't want them to know I was listening.   35

"All right," Auntie say, shaking me by the shoulder. "Come on. Today's the day."

I pushed the cover down to get out, and Ty grabbed it and pulled it back.

Daddy went in the Army: The time of the story is about 1942, early in World War II, when millions of men were being drafted into the armed services.

"You, too, Ty," Auntie say.

"I ain't getting no teef pulled," Ty say.

"Don't mean it ain't time to get up," Auntie say. "Hit it, Ty." 40

Ty got up grumbling.

"James, you hurry up and get in your clothes and eat your food," Auntie say. "What time y'all coming back?" she say to Mama.

"That 'leven o'clock bus," Mama say. "Got to get back in that field this evening."

"Get a move on you, James," Auntie say.

I went in the kitchen and washed my face, then I ate my breakfast. I was 45 having bread and syrup. The bread was warm and hard and tasted good. And I tried to make it last a long time.

Ty came back there grumbling and mad at me.

"Got to get up," he say. "I ain't having no teefes pulled. What I got to be getting up for?"

Ty poured some syrup in his pan and got a piece of bread. He didn't wash his hands, neither his face, and I could see that white stuff in his eyes.

"You the one getting your teef pulled," he say. "What I got to get up for. I bet if I was getting a teef pulled, you wouldn't be getting up. Shucks; syrup again. I'm getting tired of this old syrup. Syrup, syrup, syrup. I'm go'n take with the sugar diabetes. I want me some bacon sometime."

"Go out in the field and work and you can have your bacon," Auntie say. 50 She stood in the middle door looking at Ty. "You better be glad you got syrup. Some people ain't got that—hard's time is."

"Shucks," Ty say. "How can I be strong."

"I don't know too much 'bout your strength," Auntie say; "but I know where you go'n be hot at, you keep that grumbling up. James, get a move on you; your mama waiting."

I ate my last piece of bread and went in the front room. Mama was standing 'fore the fireplace warming her hands. I put on my coat and my cap, and we left the house.

4

I look down there again, but it still ain't coming. I almost say, "It ain't coming yet," but I keep my mouth shut. 'Cause that's something else she don't like. She don't like for you to say something just for nothing. She can see it ain't coming. I can see it ain't coming, so why say it ain't coming. I don't say it, I turn and look at the river that's back of us. It's so cold the smoke's just raising up from the water. I see a bunch of pool-doos not too far out—just on the other side of the lilies. I'm wondering if you can eat pool-doos.° I ain't too sure, 'cause I ain't never ate none. But I done ate owls and blackbirds, and I done ate redbirds,° too. I didn't want kill the redbirds, but she made me kill them. They had two of them back there. One in my trap, one in Ty's trap. Me and Ty was go'n play with them and let them go, but she made me kill them 'cause we needed the food.

pool-doos: Pool-doo is a local Louisiana pronunciation of the French *poule d'eau*, or "bird of water." It refers to a marsh hen, or bird of the rail family—most likely the American Coot.

redbirds: cardinals.

"I can't," I say. "I can't."   55

"Here," she say. "Take it."

"I can't," I say. "I can't. I can't kill him, Mama, please."

"Here," she say. "Take this fork, James."

"Please, Mama, I can't kill him," I say.

I could tell she was go'n hit me. I jerked back, but I didn't jerk back soon   60
enough.

"Take it," she say.

I took it and reached in for him, but he kept on hopping to the back.

"I can't, Mama," I say. The water just kept on running down my face. "I
can't," I say.

"Get him out of there," she say.

I reached in for him and he kept on hopping to the back. Then I reached   65
in farther, and he pecked me on the hand.

"I can't, Mama," I say.

She slapped me again.

I reached in again, but he kept on hopping out my way. Then he hopped
to one side and I reached there. The fork got him on the leg and I heard his leg
pop. I pulled my hand out 'cause I had hurt him.

"Give it here," she say, and jerked the fork out my hand.

/ She reached in and got the little bird right in the neck. I heard the fork go   70
in his neck, and I heard it go in the ground. She brought him out and helt him
right in front of me.

"That's one," she say. She shook him off and gived me the fork. "Get the
other one."

"I can't, Mama," I say, "I'll do anything, but don't make me do that."

She went to the corner of the fence and broke the biggest switch over there
she could find. I knelt 'side the trap, crying. /

"Get him out of there," she say.

"I can't, Mama."   75

She started hitting me 'cross the back. I went down on the ground, crying.

"Get him," she say.

"Octavia?" Auntie say.

'Cause she had come out of the house and she was standing by the tree
looking at us.

"Get him out of there," Mama say.   80

"Octavia," Auntie say, "explain to him. Explain to him. Just don't beat him.
Explain to him."

But she hit me and hit me and hit me.

I'm still young—I ain't no more than eight; but I know now; I know why I
had to do it. (They was so little, though. They was so little. I 'member how I
picked the feathers off them and cleaned them and helt them over the fire. Then
we all ate them. Ain't had but a little bitty piece each, but we all had a little bitty
piece, and everybody just looked at me 'cause they was so proud.) Suppose she
had to go away? That's why I had to do it. Suppose she had to go away like Daddy
went away? Then who was go'n look after us? They had to be somebody left to
carry on. I didn't know it then, but I know it now. Auntie and Monsieur Bayonne
talked to me and made me see.

5

Time I see it I get out my handkerchief and start waving. It's still 'way down there, but I keep waving anyhow. Then it come up and stop and me and Mama get on. Mama tell me go sit in the back while she pay. I do like she say, and the people look at me. When I pass the little sign that say "White" and "Colored," I start looking for a seat. I just see one of them back there, but I don't take it, 'cause I want my mama to sit down herself. She comes in the back and sit down, and I lean on the seat. They got seats in the front, but I know I can't sit there, 'cause I have to sit back of the sign. Anyhow, I don't want sit there if my mama go'n sit back here.

They got a lady sitting 'side my mama and she looks at me and smiles little bit. I smile back, but I don't open my mouth, 'cause the wind'll get in and make that tooth ache. The lady take out a pack of gum and reach me a slice, but I shake my head. The lady just can't understand why a little boy'll turn down gum, and she reach me a slice again. This time I point to my jaw. The lady understands and smiles little bit, and I smile little bit, but I don't open my mouth, though.

They got a girl sitting 'cross from me. She got on a red overcoat and her hair's plaited in one big plait. First, I make 'tend I don't see her over there, but then I start looking at her little bit. She make 'tend she don't see me, either, but I catch her looking that way. She got a cold, and every now and then she h'ist that little handkerchief to her nose. She ought to blow it, but she don't. Must think she's too much a lady or something.

Every time she h'ist that little handkerchief, the lady 'side her say something in her ear. She shakes her head and lays her hands in her lap again. Then I catch her kind of looking where I'm at. I smile at her little bit. But think she'll smile back? Uh-uh. She just turn up her little old nose and turn her head. Well, I show her both of us can turn us head. I turn mine too and look out at the river.

The river is gray. The sky is gray. They have pool-doos on the water. The water is wavy, and the pool-doos go up and down. The bus go round a turn, and you got plenty trees hiding the river. Then the bus go round another turn, and I can see the river again.

I look toward the front where all the white people sitting. Then I look at that little old gal again. I don't look right at her, 'cause I don't want all them people to know I love her. I just look at her little bit, like I'm looking out that window over there. But she knows I'm looking that way, and she kind of look at me, too. The lady sitting 'side her catch her this time, and she leans over and says something in her ear.

"I don't love him nothing," that little old gal says out loud.

Everybody back there hear her mouth, and all of them look at us and laugh.

"I don't love you, either," I say. "So you don't have to turn up your nose, Miss."

"You the one looking," she say.

"I wasn't looking at you," I say. "I was looking out that window, there."

"Out that window, my foot," she say. "I seen you. Everytime I turned round you was looking at me."

"You must of been looking yourself if you seen me all them times," I say.

"Shucks," she say, "I got me all kind of boyfriends."

"I got girlfriends, too," I say.

"Well, I just don't want you getting your hopes up," she say.

I don't say no more to that little old gal 'cause I don't want have to bust her   100
in the mouth. I lean on the seat where Mama sitting, and I don't even look that
way no more. When we get to Bayonne, she jugg her little old tongue out at me.
I make 'tend I'm go'n hit her, and she duck down 'side her mama. And all the
people laugh at us again.

6

Me and Mama get off and start walking in town. Bayonne is a little bitty
town. Baton Rouge is a hundred times bigger than Bayonne. I went to Baton
Rouge once—me, Ty, Mama, and Daddy. But that was 'way back yonder, 'fore
Daddy went in the Army. I wonder when we go'n see him again. I wonder when.
Look like he ain't ever coming back home. . . . Even the pavement all cracked in
Bayonne. Got grass shooting right out the sidewalk. Got weeds in the ditch, too;
just like they got at home.

It's some cold in Bayonne. Look like it's colder than it is home. The wind
blows in my face, and I feel that stuff running down my nose. I sniff. Mama says
use that handkerchief. I blow my nose and put it back.

We pass a school and I see them white children playing in the yard. Big old
red school, and them children just running and playing. Then we pass a café, and
I see a bunch of people in there eating. I wish I was in there 'cause I'm cold.
Mama tells me keep my eyes in front where they belong.

We pass stores that's got dummies, and we pass another café, and then we
pass a shoe shop, and that bald-head man in there fixing on a shoe. I look at him
and I butt into that white lady, and Mama jerks me in front and tells me stay
there.

We come up to the courthouse, and I see the flag waving there. This flag   105
ain't like the one we got at school. This one here ain't got but a handful of stars.°
One at school got a big pile of stars—one for every state. We pass it and we turn
and there it is—the dentist office. Me and Mama go in, and they got people sitting
everywhere you look. They even got a little boy in there younger than me.

Me and Mama sit on that bench, and a white lady come in there and ask me
what my name is. Mama tells her and the white lady goes on back. Then I hear
somebody hollering in there. Soon 's that little boy hear him hollering, he starts
hollering, too. His mama pats him and pats him, trying to make him hush up, but
he ain't thinking 'bout his mama.

The man that was hollering in there comes out holding his jaw. He is a big
old man and he's wearing overalls and a jumper.

"Got it, hanh?" another man asks him.

The man shakes his head—don't want open his mouth.

"Man, I thought they was killing you in there," the other man says. "Hollering   110
like a pig under a gate."

The man don't say nothing. He just heads for the door, and the other man
follows him.

"John Lee," the white lady says. "John Lee Williams."

handful of stars: The Confederate flag contains thirteen stars. At the time of the story,
the American flag had forty-eight.

The little boy juggs his head down in his mama's lap and holler more now. His mama tells him go with the nurse, but he ain't thinking 'bout his mama. His mama tells him again, but he don't even hear her. His mama picks him up and takes him in there, and even when the white lady shuts the door I can still hear little old John Lee.

"I often wonder why the Lord let a child like that suffer," a lady says to my mama. The lady's sitting right in front of us on another bench. She's got on a white dress and a black sweater. She must be a nurse or something herself, I reckon.

"Not us to question," a man says. 115

"Sometimes I don't know if we shouldn't," the lady says.

"I know definitely we shouldn't," the man says. The man looks like a preacher. He's big and fat and he's got on a black suit. He's got a gold chain, too.

"Why?" the lady says.

"Why anything?" the preacher says.

"Yes," the lady says. "Why anything?" 120

"Not us to question," the preacher says.

The lady looks at the preacher a little while and looks at Mama again.

"And look like it's the poor who suffers the most," she says. "I don't understand it."

"Best not to even try," the preacher says. "He works in mysterious ways— wonders to perform."°

Right then little John Lee bust out hollering, and everybody turn they head 125 to listen.

"He's not a good dentist," the lady says. "Dr. Robillard is much better. But more expensive. That's why most of the colored people come here. The white people go to Dr. Robillard. Y'all from Bayonne?"

"Down the river," my mama says. And that's all she go'n say, 'cause she don't talk much. But the lady keeps on looking at her, and so she says, "Near Morgan."

"I see," the lady says.

7

"That's the trouble with the black people in this country today," somebody else says. This one here's sitting on the same side me and Mama's sitting, and he is kind of sitting in front of that preacher. He looks like a teacher or somebody that goes to college. He's got on a suit, and he's got a book that he's been reading. "We don't question is exactly our problem," he says. "We should question and question and question—question everything."

The preacher just looks at him a long time. He done put a toothpick or 130 something in his mouth, and he just keeps on turning it and turning it. You can see he don't like that boy with that book.

"Maybe you can explain what you mean," he says.

"I said what I meant," the boy says. "Question everything. Every stripe, every star, every word spoken. Everything."

"It 'pears to me that this young lady and I was talking 'bout God, young man," the preacher says.

°*He works . . . perform*: an allusion to the well-known hymn "God moves in a mysterious way / His wonders to perform," by William Cowper (1731–1800).

"Question Him, too," the boys says.

"Wait," the preacher says. "Wait now." 135

"You heard me right," the boy says. "His existence as well as everything else. Everything."

The preacher just looks across the room at the boy. You can see he's getting madder and madder. But mad or no mad, the boy ain't thinking 'bout him. He looks at that preacher just 's hard 's the preacher looks at him.

"Is this what they coming to?" the preacher says. "Is this what we educating them for?"

"You're not educating me," the boy says. "I wash dishes at night so that I can go to school in the day. So even the words you spoke need questioning."

The preacher just looks at him and shakes his head. 140

"When I come in this room and seen you there with your book, I said to myself, 'There's an intelligent man.' How wrong a person can be."

"Show me one reason to believe in the existence of a God," the boy says.

"My heart tells me," the preacher says.

"'My heart tells me,'" the boys says. "'My heart tells me.' Sure, 'My heart tells me.' And as long as you listen to what your heart tells you, you will have only what the white man gives you and nothing more. Me, I don't listen to my heart. The purpose of the heart is to pump blood throughout the body, and nothing else."

"Who's your paw, boy?" the preacher says. 145

"Why?"

"Who is he?"

"He's dead."

"And you mom?"

"She's in Charity Hospital with pneumonia. Half killed herself, working for 150 nothing."

"And 'cause he's dead and she's sick, you mad at the world?"

"I'm not mad at the world. I'm questioning the world. I'm questioning it with cold logic, sir. What do words like Freedom, Liberty, God, White, Colored mean? I want to know. That's why *you* are sending us to school, to read and to ask questions. And because we ask these questions, you call us mad. No sir, it is not us who are mad."

"You keep saying 'us'?"

"'Us.' Yes—us. I'm not alone."

The preacher just shakes his head. Then he looks at everybody in the 155 room—everybody. Some of the people look down at the floor, keep from looking at him. I kind of look 'way myself, but soon 's I know he done turn his head, I look that way again.

"I'm sorry for you," he says to the boy.

"Why?" the boy says. "Why not be sorry for yourself? Why are you so much better off than I am? Why aren't you sorry for these other people in here? Why not be sorry for the lady who had to drag her child into the dentist office? Why not be sorry for the lady sitting on that bench over there? Be sorry for them. Not for me. Some way or the other I'm going to make it."

"No, I'm sorry for you," the preacher says.

"Of course, of course," the boy says, nodding his head. "You're sorry for me because I rock that pillar you're leaning on."

"You can't ever rock the pillar I'm leaning on, young man. It's stronger than anything man can ever do." 160

"You believe in God because a man told you to believe in God," the boy says. "A white man told you to believe in God. And why? To keep you ignorant so he can keep his feet on your neck."

"So now we the ignorant?" the preacher says.

"Yes," the boy says. "Yes." And he opens his book again.

The preacher just looks at him sitting there. The boy done forgot all about him. Everybody else make 'tend they done forgot the squabble, too.

Then I see that preacher getting up real slow. Preacher's a great big 165 old man and he got to brace himself to get up. He comes over where the boy is sitting.

He just stands there a little while looking down at him, but the boy don't raise his head.

"Get up, boy," preacher says.

The boy looks up at him, then he shuts his book real slow and stands up. Preacher just hauls back and hit him in the face. The boy falls back 'gainst the wall, but he straightens himself up and looks right back at that preacher.

"You forgot the other cheek," he says.°

The preacher hauls back and hit him again on the other side. But this time the boy braces himself and don't fall.

"That hasn't changed a thing," he says. 170

The preacher just looks at the boy. The preacher's breathing real hard like he just run up a big hill. The boy sits down and opens his book again.

"I feel sorry for you," the preacher says. "I never felt so sorry for a man before."

The boy makes 'tend he don't even hear that preacher. He keeps on reading his book. The preacher goes back and gets his hat off the chair.

"Excuse me," he says to us. "I'll come back some other time. Y'all, please excuse me."

And he looks at the boy and goes out the room. The boy h'ist his hand up 175 to his mouth one time to wipe 'way some blood. All the rest of the time he keeps on reading. And nobody else in there say a word.

8

Little John Lee and his mama come out the dentist office, and the nurse calls somebody else in. Then little bit later they come out, and the nurse calls another name. But fast 's she calls somebody in there, somebody else comes in the place where we sitting, and the room stays full.

The people coming in now, all of them wearing big coats. One of them says something 'bout sleeting, another one says he hope not. Another one says he think it ain't nothing but rain. 'Cause, he says, rain can get awful cold this time of year.

All round the room they talking. Some of them talking to people right by them, some of them talking to people clear 'cross the room, some of them talking to anybody'll listen. It's a little bitty room, no bigger than us kitchen, and I can see everybody in there. The little old room's full of smoke, 'cause you got two old men smoking pipes over by that side door. I think I feel my tooth thumping me

other cheek: Matthew 5:39.

some, and I hold my breath and wait. I wait and wait, but it don't thump me no more. Thank God for that.

I feel like going to sleep, and I lean back 'gainst the wall. But I'm scared to go to sleep. Scared 'cause the nurse might call my name and I won't hear her. And Mama might go to sleep, too, and she'll be mad if neither one of us heard the nurse.

I look up at Mama. I love my mama. I love my mama. And when cotton   180
come I'm go'n get her a new coat. And I ain't go'n get a black one, either. I think I'm go'n get her a red one.

"They got some books over there," I say. "Want read one of them?"

Mama looks at the books, but she don't answer me.

"You got yourself a little man there," the lady says.

Mama don't say nothing to the lady, but she must've smiled, 'cause I seen the lady smiling back. The lady looks at me a little while, like she's feeling sorry for me.

"You sure got that preacher out here in a hurry," she says to that boy.   185

The boy looks up at her and looks in his book again. When I grow up I want be just like him. I want clothes like that and I want keep a book with me, too.

"You really don't believe in God?" the lady says.

"No," he says.

"But why?" the lady says.

"Because the wind is pink," he says.   190

"What?" the lady says.

The boy don't answer her no more. He just reads in his book.

"Talking 'bout the wind is pink," that old lady says. She's sitting on the same bench with the boy and she's trying to look in his face. The boy makes 'tend the old lady ain't even there. He just keeps on reading. "Wind is pink," she says again. "Eh, Lord, what children go'n be saying next?"

The lady 'cross from us bust out laughing.

"That's a good one," she says. "The wind is pink. Yes sir, that's a good   195
one."

"Don't you believe the wind is pink?" the boys says. He keeps his head down in the book.

"Course I believe it, honey," the lady says. "Course I do." She looks at us and winks her eye. "And what color is grass, honey?"

"Grass? Grass is black."

She bust out laughing again. The boy looks at her.

"Don't you believe grass is black?" he says.   200

The lady quits her laughing and looks at him. Everybody else looking at him, too. The place quiet, quiet.

"Grass is green, honey," the lady says. "It was green yesterday, it's green today, and it's go'n be green tomorrow."

"How do you know it's green?"

"I know because I know."

"You don't know it's green," the boy says. "You believe it's green because   205
someone told you it was green. If someone had told you it was black you'd believe it was black."

"It's green," the lady says. "I know green when I see green."

"Prove it's green," the boy says.

"Sure, now," the lady says. "Don't tell me it's coming to that."

"It's coming to just that," the boy says. "Words mean nothing. One means no more than the other."

"That's what it all coming to?" that old lady says. That old lady got on a turban and she got on two sweaters. She got a green sweater under a black sweater. I can see the green sweater 'cause some of the buttons on the other sweater's missing. 210

"Yes, ma'am," the boy says. "Words mean nothing. Action is the only thing. Doing. That's the only thing."

"Other words, you want the Lord to come down here and show Hisself to you?" she says.

"Exactly, ma'am," he says.

"You don't mean that, I'm sure?" she says.

"I do, ma'am," he says. 215

"Done, Jesus," the old lady says, shaking her head.

"I didn't go 'long with that preacher at first," the other lady says; "but now— I don't know. When a person say the grass is black, he's either a lunatic or something's wrong."

"Prove to me that it's green," the boy says.

"It's green because the people say it's green."

"Those same people say we're citizens of these United States," the boy says. 220

"I think I'm a citizen," the lady says.

"Citizens have certain rights," the boy says. "Name me one right that you have. One right, granted by the Constitution, that you can exercise in Bayonne."

The lady don't answer him. She just looks at him like she don't know what he's talking 'bout. I know I don't.

"Things changing," she says.

"Things are changing because some black men have begun to think with their brains and not their hearts," the boy says. 225

"You trying to say these people don't believe in God?"

"I'm sure some of them do. Maybe most of them do. But they don't believe that God is going to touch these white people's hearts and change things tomorrow. Things change through action. By no other way."

Everybody sit quiet and look at the boy. Nobody says a thing. Then the lady 'cross the room from me and Mama just shakes her head.

"Let's hope that not all your generation feel the same way you do," she says.

"Think what you please, it doesn't matter," the boy says. "But it will be men who listen to their heads and not their hearts who will see that your children have a better chance than you had." 230

"Let's hope they ain't all like you, though," the old lady says. "Done forgot the heart absolutely."

"Yes ma'am, I hope they aren't all like me," the boy says. "Unfortunately, I was born too late to believe in your God. Let's hope that the ones who come after will have your faith—if not in your God, then in something else, something definitely that they can lean on. I haven't anything. For me, the wind is pink, the grass is black."

9

The nurse comes in the room where we all sitting and waiting and says the doctor won't take no more patients till one o'clock this evening.° My mama jumps up off the bench and goes up to the white lady.

"Nurse, I have to go back in the field this evening," she says.

"The doctor is treating his last patient now," the nurse says. "One o'clock   235
this evening."

"Can I at least speak to the doctor?" my mama asks.

"I'm his nurse," the lady says.

"My little boy's sick," my mama says. "Right now his tooth almost killing him."

The nurse looks at me. She's trying to make up her mind if to let me come in. I look at her real pitiful. The tooth ain't hurting me at all, but Mama say it is, so I make 'tend for her sake.

"This evening," the nurse says, and goes on back in the office.   240

"Don't feel 'jected, honey," the lady says to Mama. "I been round them a long time—they take you when they want to. If you was white, that's something else; but we the wrong color."

Mama don't say nothing to the lady, and me and her go outside and stand 'gainst the wall. It's cold out there. I can feel that wind going through my coat. Some of the other people come out of the room and go up the street. Me and Mama stand there a little while and we start walking. I don't know where we going. When we come to the other street we just stand there.

"You don't have to make water, do you?" Mama says.

"No, ma'am," I say.

We go on up the street. Walking real slow. I can tell Mama don't know   245
where she's going. When we come to a store we stand there and look at the dummies. I look at a little boy wearing a brown overcoat. He's got on brown shoes, too. I look at my old shoes and look at his'n again. You wait till summer, I say.

Me and Mama walk away. We come up to another store and we stop and look at them dummies, too. Then we go on again. We pass a café where the white people in there eating. Mama tells me keep my eyes in front where they belong, but I can't help from seeing them people eat. My stomach starts to growling 'cause I'm hungry. When I see people eating, I get hungry; when I see a coat, I get cold.

A man whistles at my mama when we go by a filling station. She makes 'tend she don't even see him. I look back and I feel like hitting him in the mouth. If I was bigger, I say; if I was bigger, you'd see.

We keep on going. I'm getting colder and colder, but I don't say nothing. I feel that stuff running down my nose and I sniff.

"That rag," Mama says.

I get it out and wipe my nose. I'm getting cold all over now—my face, my   250
hands, my feet, everything. We pass another little café, but this'n for white people, too, and we can't go in there, either. So we just walk. I'm so cold now I'm 'bout ready to say it. If I knowed where we was going I wouldn't be so cold, but I don't know where we going. We go, we go, we go. We walk clean out of Bayonne. Then we cross the street and we come back. Same thing I seen when I got off the bus

evening: local dialect for *afternoon.*

this morning. Same old trees, same old walk, same old weeds, same old cracked pave—same old everything.

I sniff again.

"That rag," Mama says.

I wipe my nose real fast and jugg that handkerchief back in my pocket 'fore my hand gets too cold. I raise my head and I can see David's hardware store. When we come up to it, we go in. I don't know why, but I'm glad.

It's warm in there. It's so warm in there you don't ever want to leave. I look for the heater, and I see it over by them barrels. Three white men standing round the heater talking in Creole.° One of them comes over to see what my mama want.

"Got any axe handles?" she says.   255

Me, Mama and the white man start to the back, but Mama stops me when we come up to the heater. She and the white man go on. I hold my hands over the heater and look at them. They go all the way to the back, and I see the white man pointing to the axe handles 'gainst the wall. Mama takes one of them and shakes it like she's trying to figure how much it weighs. Then she rubs her hand over it from one end to the other end. She turns it over and looks at the other side, then she shakes it again, and shakes her head and puts it back. She gets another one and she does it just like she did the first one, then she shakes her head. Then she gets a brown one and do it that, too. But she don't like this one, either. Then she gets another one, but 'fore she shakes it or anything, she looks at me. Look like she's trying to say something to me, but I don't know what it is. All I know is I done got warm now and I'm feeling right smart better. Mama shakes this axe handle just like she did the others, and shakes her head and says something to the white man. The white man just looks at his pile of axe handles, and when Mama pass him to come to the front, the white man just scratch his head and follows her. She tells me come on and we go on out and start walking again.

We walk and walk, and no time at all I'm cold again. Look like I'm colder now 'cause I can still remember how good it was back there. My stomach growls and I suck it in to keep Mama from hearing it. She's walking right 'side me, and it growls so loud you can hear it a mile. But Mama don't say a word.

10

When we come up to the courthouse, I look at the clock. It's got quarter to twelve. Mean we got another hour and a quarter to be out here in the cold. We go and stand 'side a building. Something hits my cap and I look up at the sky. Sleet's falling.

I look at Mama standing there. I want stand close 'side her, but she don't like that. She say that's crybaby stuff. She say you got to stand for yourself, by yourself.

"Let's go back to that office," she says.   260

We cross the street. When we get to the dentist office I try to open the door, but I can't. I twist and twist, but I can't. Mama pushes me to the side and she twist the knob, but she can't open the door, either. She turns 'way from the door. I look at her, but I don't move and I don't say nothing. I done seen her like this before and I'm scared of her.

Creole: the French Cajun dialect in Louisiana.

"You hungry?" she says. She says it like she's mad at me, like I'm the cause of everything.

"No, ma'am," I say.

"You want eat and walk back, or you rather don't eat and ride?"

"I ain't hungry," I say. 265

I ain't just hungry, but I'm cold, too. I'm so hungry and cold I want to cry. And look like I'm getting colder and colder. My feet done got numb. I try to work my toes, but I don't even feel them. Look like I'm go'n die. Look like I'm go'n stand right here and freeze to death. I think 'bout home. I think 'bout Val and Auntie and Ty and Louis and Walker. It's 'bout twelve o'clock and I know they eating dinner now. I can hear Ty making jokes. He done forgot 'bout getting up early this morning and right now he's probably making jokes. Always trying to make somebody laugh. I wish I was right there listening to him. Give anything in the world if I was home round the fire.

"Come on," Mama says.

We start walking again. My feet so numb I can't hardly feel them. We turn the corner and go on back up the street. The clock on the courthouse starts hitting for twelve.

The sleet's coming down plenty now. They hit the pave and bounce like rice. Oh, Lord; oh, Lord, I pray. Don't let me die, don't let me die, don't let me die, Lord.

11

Now I know where we going. We going back of town where the colored 270 people eat. I don't care if I don't eat. I been hungry before. I can stand it. But I can't stand the cold.

I can see we go'n have a long walk. It's 'bout a mile down there. But I don't mind. I know when I get there I'm go'n warm myself. I think I can hold out. My hands numb in my pockets and my feet numb, too, but if I keep moving I can hold out. Just don't stop no more, that's all.

The sky's gray. The sleet keeps on falling. Falling like rain now—plenty, plenty. You can hear it hitting the pave. You can see it bouncing. Sometimes it bounces two times 'fore it settles.

We keep on going. We don't say nothing. We just keep on going, keep on going.

I wonder what Mama's thinking. I hope she ain't mad at me. When summer come I'm go'n pick plenty cotton and get her a coat. I'm go'n get her a red one.

I hope they'd make it summer all the time. I'd be glad if it was summer all 275 the time—but it ain't. We got to have winter, too. Lord, I hate the winter. I guess everybody hate the winter.

I don't sniff this time. I get out my handkerchief and wipe my nose. My hand's so cold I can hardly hold the handkerchief.

I think we getting close, but we ain't there yet. I wonder where everybody is. Can't see a soul but us. Look like we the only two people moving round today. Must be too cold for the rest of the people to move round in.

I can hear my teeth. I hope they don't knock together too hard and make that bad one hurt. Lord, that's all I need, for that bad one to start off.

I hear a church bell somewhere. But today ain't Sunday. They must be ringing for a funeral or something.

I wonder what they doing at home. They must be eating. Monsieur Bayonne   280
might be there with his guitar. One day Ty played with Monsieur Bayonne's guitar
and broke one of the strings. Monsieur Bayonne was some mad with Ty. He say
Ty wasn't go'n ever 'mount to nothing. Ty can go just like Monsieur Bayonne
when he ain't there. Ty can make everybody laugh when he starts to mocking
Monsieur Bayonne.

I used to like to be with Mama and Daddy. We used to be happy. But they
took him in the Army. Now, nobody happy no more. . . . I be glad when Daddy
comes home.

Monsieur Bayonne say it wasn't fair for them to take Daddy and give Mama
nothing and give us nothing. Auntie say, "Shhh, Etienne. Don't let them hear you
talk like that." Monsieur Bayonne say, "It's God truth. What they giving his
children? They have to walk three and a half miles to school hot or cold. That's
anything to give for a paw? She's got to work in the field rain or shine just to
make ends meet. That's anything to give for a husband?" Auntie say, "Shhh,
Etienne, shhh." "Yes, you right," Monsieur Bayonne say. "Best don't say it in front
of them now. But one day they go'n find out. One day." "Yes, I suppose so,"
Auntie say. "Then what, Rose Mary?" Monsieur Bayonne say. "I don't know,
Etienne," Auntie say. "All we can do is us job, and leave everything else in His
hand . . ."

We getting closer, now. We getting closer. I can even see the railroad tracks.

We cross the tracks, and now I see the café. Just to get in there, I say. Just
to get in there. Already I'm starting to feel little better.

12

We go in. Ahh, it's good. I look for the heater; there 'gainst the wall. One   285
of them little brown ones. I just stand there and hold my hands over it. I can't
open my hands too wide 'cause they almost froze.

Mama's standing right 'side me. She done unbuttoned her coat. Smoke rises
out of the coat, and the coat smells like a wet dog.

I move to the side so Mama can have more room. She opens out her hands
and rubs them together. I rub mine together, too, 'cause this keeps them from
hurting. If you let them warm too fast, they hurt you sure. But if you let them
warm just little bit at a time, and you keep rubbing them, they be all right every
time.

They got just two more people in the café. A lady back of the counter, and
a man on this side the counter. They been watching us even since we come in.

Mama gets out the handkerchief and count up the money. Both of us know
how much money she's got there. Three dollars. No, she ain't got three dollars,
'cause she had to pay us way up here. She ain't got but two dollars and a half left.
Dollar and a half to get my tooth pulled, and fifty cents for us to go back on, and
fifty cents worth of salt meat.

She stirs the money round with her finger. Most of the money is change   290
'cause I can hear it rubbing together. She stirs it and stirs it. Then she looks at
the door. It's still sleeting. I can hear it hitting 'gainst the wall like rice.

"I ain't hungry, Mama," I say.

"Got to pay them something for they heat," she says.

She takes a quarter out the handkerchief and ties the handkerchief up again.
She looks over her shoulder at the people, but she still don't move. I hope she

don't spend the money. I don't want her spending it on me. I'm hungry, I'm almost starving I'm so hungry, but I don't want her spending the money on me.

She flips the quarter over like she's thinking. She's must be thinking 'bout us walking back home. Lord, I sure don't want walk home. If I thought it'd do any good to say something, I'd say it. But Mama makes up her own mind 'bout things.

She turns 'way from the heater right fast, like she better hurry up and spend   295
the quarter 'fore she change her mind. I watch her go toward the counter. The man and the lady look at her, too. She tells the lady something and the lady walks away. The man keeps on looking at her. Her back's turned to the man, and she don't even know he's standing there.

The lady puts some cakes and a glass of milk on the counter. Then she pours a cup of coffee and sets it 'side the other stuff. Mama pays her for the things and comes on back where I'm standing. She tells me sit down at the table 'gainst the wall.

The milk and the cake's for me; the coffee's for Mama. I eat slow and I look at her. She's looking outside at the sleet. She's looking real sad. I say to myself, I'm go'n make all this up one day. You see, one day, I'm go'n make all this up. I want say it now; I want tell her how I feel right now; but Mama don't like for us to talk like that.

"I can't eat all this," I say.

They ain't got but just three little old cakes there. I'm so hungry right now, the Lord knows I can eat a hundred times three, but I want my mama to have one.

Mama don't even look my way. She knows I'm hungry, she knows I want it.   300
I let it stay there a little while, then I get it and eat it. I eat just on my front teeth, though, 'cause if cake touch that back tooth I know what'll happen. Thank God it ain't hurt me at all today.

After I finish eating I see the man go to the juke box. He drops a nickel in it, then he just stand there a little while looking at the record. Mama tells me keep my eyes in front where they belong. I turn my head like she say, but then I hear the man coming toward us.

"Dance, pretty?" he says.

Mama gets up to dance with him. But 'fore you know it, she done grabbed the little man in the collar and done heaved him 'side the wall. He hit the wall so hard he stop the juke box from playing.

"Some pimp," the lady back of the counter says. "Some pimp."

The little man jumps up off the floor and starts toward my mama. 'Fore   305
you know it, Mama done sprung open her knife and she's waiting for him.

"Come on," she says. "Come on. I'll gut you from your neighbo° to your throat. Come on."

I go up to the little man to hit him, but Mama makes me come and stand 'side her. The little man looks at me and Mama and goes on back to the counter.

"Some pimp," the lady back of the counter says. "Some pimp." She starts laughing and pointing at the little man. "Yes sir, you a pimp, all right. Yes sir-ree."

neighbo: navel.

13

/"Fasten that coat, let's go," Mama says.

"You don't have to leave," the lady says. 310

Mama don't answer the lady, and we right out in the cold again. I'm warm right now—my hands, my ears, my feet—but I know this ain't go'n last too long. It done sleet so much now you got ice everywhere you look. /

We cross the railroad tracks, and soon's we do, I get cold. That wind goes through this little old coat like it ain't even there. I got on a shirt and a sweater under the coat, but that wind don't pay them no mind. I look up and I can see we got a long way to go. I wonder if we go'n make it 'fore I get too cold.

We cross over to walk on the sidewalk. They got just one sidewalk back here, and it's over there.

After we go just a little piece, I smell bread cooking. I look, then I see a baker shop. When we get closer, I can smell it more better. I shut my eyes and make 'tend I'm eating. But I keep them shut too long and I butt up 'gainst a telephone post. Mama grabs me and see if I'm hurt. I ain't bleeding or nothing and she turns me loose.

I can feel I'm getting colder and colder, and I look up to see how far we 315 still got to go. Uptown is 'way up yonder. A half mile more, I reckon. I try to think of something. They say think and you won't get cold. I think of that poem, "Annabel Lee."° I ain't been to school in so long—this bad weather—I reckon they done passed "Annabel Lee" by now. But passed it or not, I'm sure Miss Walker go'n make me recite it when I get there. That woman don't never forget nothing. I ain't never seen nobody like that in my life.

I'm still getting cold. "Annabel Lee" or no "Annabel Lee," I'm still getting cold. But I can see we getting closer. We getting there gradually.

Soon 's we turn the corner, I see a little old white lady up in front of us. She's the only lady on the street. She's all in black and she's got a long black rag over her head.

"Stop," she says.

Me and Mama stop and look at her. She must be crazy to be out in all this bad weather. Ain't got but a few other people out there, and all of them's men.

"Y'all done ate?" she says. 320

"Just finish," Mama says.

"Y'all must be cold then?" she says.

"We headed for the dentist," Mama says. "We'll warm up when we get there."

"What dentist?" the old lady says. "Mr. Bassett?"

"Yes, ma'am," Mama says. 325

"Come on in," the old lady says. "I'll telephone him and tell him y'all coming."

Me and Mama follow the old lady in the store. It's a little bitty store, and it don't have much in there. The old lady takes off her head rag and folds it up.

"Helena?" somebody calls from the back.

"Yes, Alnest?" the old lady says.

"Annabel Lee": poem (1849) by Edgar Allan Poe (1809–1849).

"Did you see them?"   330
"They're here. Standing beside me."
"Good. Now you can stay inside."
The old lady looks at Mama. Mama's waiting to hear what she brought us in here for. I'm waiting for that, too.
"I saw y'all each time you went by," she says. "I came out to catch you, but you were gone."
"We went back of town," Mama says.   335
"Did you eat?"
"Yes, ma'am."
The old lady looks at Mama a long time, like she's thinking Mama might be just saying that. Mama looks right back at her. The old lady looks at me to see what I have to say. I don't say nothing. I sure ain't going 'gainst my mama.
"There's food in the kitchen," she says to Mama. "I've been keeping it warm."
Mama turns right around and starts for the door.   340
"Just a minute," the old lady says. Mama stops. "The boy'll have to work for it. It isn't free."
"We don't take no handout," Mama says.
"I'm not handing out anything," the old lady says. "I need my garbage moved to the front. Ernest has a bad cold and can't go out there."
"James'll move it for you," Mama says.
"Not unless you eat," the old lady says. "I'm old, but I have my pride, too,   345
you know."
Mama can see that she ain't go'n beat this old lady down, so she just shakes her head.
"All right," the old lady says. "Come into the kitchen."
She leads the way with that rag in her hand. The kitchen is a little bitty little old thing, too. The table and the stove just 'bout fill it up. They got a little room to the side. Somebody in there laying 'cross the bed—'cause I can see one of his feet. Must be the person she was talking to: Ernest or Alnest—something like that.
"Sit down," the old lady says to Mama. "Not you," she says to me. "You have to move the cans."
"Helena?" the man says in the other room.   350
"Yes, Alnest?" the old lady says.
"Are you going out there again?"
"I must show the boy where the garbage is, Alnest," the old lady says.
"Keep that shawl over your head," the old man says.
"You don't have to remind me, Alnest. Come, boy," the old lady says.   355
We go out in the yard. Little old back yard ain't no bigger than the store or the kitchen. But it can sleet here just like it can sleet in any big back yard. And 'fore you know it, I'm trembling.
"There," the old lady says, pointing to the cans. I pick up one of the cans and set it right back down. The can's so light, I'm go'n see what's inside of it.
"Here," the old lady says. "Leave that can alone."
I look back at her standing there in the door. She's got that black rag wrapped round her shoulders, and she's pointing one of her little old fingers at me.
"Pick it up and carry it to the front," she says. I go by her with the can, and   360
she's looking at me all the time. I'm sure the can's empty. I'm sure she could've

carried it herself—maybe both of them at the same time. "Set it on the sidewalk by the door and come back for the other one," she says.

I go and come back, and Mama looks at me when I pass her. I get the other can and take it to the front. It don't feel a bit heavier than that first one. I tell myself I ain't go'n be nobody's fool, and I'm go'n look inside this can to see just what I been hauling. First, I look up the street, then down the street. Nobody coming. Then I look over my shoulder toward the door. That little old lady done slipped up there quiet 's mouse, watching me again. Look like she knowed what I was go'n do.

"Ehh, Lord," she says. "Children, children. Come in here, boy, and go wash your hands."

I follow her in the kitchen. She points toward the bathroom, and I go in there and wash up. Little bitty old bathroom, but it's clean, clean. I don't use any of her towels; I wipe my hands on my pants legs.

When I come back in the kitchen, the old lady done dished up the food. Rice, gravy, meat—and she even got some lettuce and tomato in a saucer. She even got a glass of milk and a piece of cake there, too. It looks so good, I almost start eating 'fore I say my blessing.

"Helena?" the old man says.   365

"Yes, Alnest?"

"Are they eating?"

"Yes," she says.

"Good," he says. "Now you'll stay inside."

The old lady goes in there where he is and I can hear them talking. I look   370
at Mama. She's eating slow like she's thinking. I wonder what's the matter now. I reckon she's thinking 'bout home.

The old lady comes back in the kitchen.

"I talked to Dr. Bassett's nurse," she says. "Dr. Bassett will take you as soon as you get there."

"Thank you, ma'am," Mama says.

"Perfectly all right," the old lady says. "Which one is it?"

Mama nods toward me. The old lady looks at me real sad. I look sad, too.   375

"You're not afraid, are you?" she says.

"No, ma'am," I say.

"That's a good boy," the old lady says. "Nothing to be afraid of. Dr. Bassett will not hurt you."

When me and Mama get through eating, we thank the old lady again.

"Helena, are they leaving?" the old man says.   380

"Yes, Alnest."

"Tell them I say good-bye."

"They can hear you, Alnest."

"Good-bye both mother and son," the old man says. "And may God be with you."

Me and Mama tell the old man good-bye, and we follow the old lady in the   385
front room. Mama opens the door to go out, but she stops and comes back in the store.

"You sell salt meat?" she says.

"Yes."

"Give me two bits worth."

"That isn't very much salt meat," the old lady says.

"That's all I have," Mama says.   390

The old lady goes back of the counter and cuts a big piece off the chunk. Then she wraps it up and puts it in a paper bag.

"Two bits," she says.

"That looks like awful lot of meat for a quarter," Mama says.

"Two bits," the old lady says. "I've been selling salt meat behind this counter twenty-five years. I think I know what I'm doing."

"You got a scale there," Mama says.   395

"What?" the old lady says.

"Weigh it," Mama says.

"What?" the old lady says. "Are you telling me how to run my business?"

"Thanks very much for the food," Mama says.

"Just a minute," the old lady says.   400

"James," Mama says to me. I move toward the door.

"Just one minute, I said," the old lady says.

Me and Mama stop again and look at her. The old lady takes the meat out of the bag and unwraps it and cuts 'bout half of it off. Then she wraps it up again and juggs it back in the bag and gives the bag to Mama. Mama lays the quarter on the counter.

"Your kindness will never be forgotten," she says. "James," she says to me.

We go out, and the old lady comes to the door to look at us. After we go a   405 little piece I look back, and she's still there watching us.

The sleet's coming down heavy, heavy now, and I turn up my coat collar to keep my neck warm. My mama tells me turn it right back down.

"You not a bum," she says. "You a man."

QUESTIONS

1. What does Gaines establish by using the eight-year-old boy, James, as the narrator who tells the story in the present tense and in his own dialect?

2. Why does James describe the family's need to kill and eat the small birds?

3. What is the major action in the story? What is the result of James and his mother Octavia taking the trip to the dentist? What is gained by the delays, which require the boy and his mother to wait in the office and then to walk out into the cold and sleet?

4. What is the significance of the discussions of suffering occasioned by the protesting child in the dentist's office? What ideas does the young man present (section 7)? When the minister hits him and reproaches him, what is demonstrated about the old and new ideas professed by African-Americans?

5. What values are represented by the elderly couple in the store? Why doesn't the woman phone Dr. Robillard, the "better" but "more expensive" dentist? Why doesn't Octavia accept the portion of salt meat the woman first offers her? What causes the woman to cut the salt meat in half?

WRITING ABOUT MEANING IN FICTION

Most likely you will wish to write about a major idea or theme, but you may also get interested in one of the many other ideas you find. Asking

questions like the following ones as you brainstorm and develop preliminary drafts will help you find ideas to write about.

Questions for Discovering Ideas

Is the idea personal, social, political, economic, scientific, ethical, esthetic, or
religious?

How pervasive in the story is the idea (throughout for a major idea,
intermittently, or just once for a secondary idea)?

How can character, action, dialogue, statement, description, scene, structure,
and development be related to the idea?

Are there contradictory statements? Implications? Images? Symbols?

Is the idea asserted directly, indirectly, dramatically, ironically?

What value or values are embodied in the idea?

Strategies for Organizing Ideas

Remember that in well-written stories (also poems or plays), things
are introduced only as they have a bearing on the idea. In this sense, the
idea is like a key in music, or like a continuous thread tying together
actions, characters, statements, symbols, and dialogue. As readers, we can
trace such a thread, with all the variations that writers work upon them.

As you write about ideas, you may find yourself relying most heavily
on the direct statements of the authorial voice, or on a combination of
these and your interpretation of characters and action. Or you might
focus exclusively on a first-person speaker and use his or her ideas to
develop your analysis. You should plan to make clear the sources of your
details and to distinguish the sources from your own commentary. Establish
patterns like these:

1. In "The Horse Dealer's Daughter," the anonymous narrator describes the
    reservations that Mabel and Dr. Fergusson have about their newfound love.
    This description shows Lawrence's idea that love not only creates the
    excitement of commitment to another person, but also brings out reservations
    about the possible loss of control over one's life. [Here the first sentence
    refers to a statement by the story's narrator. The second sentence interprets
    this statement.]

2. Near the end of "A Jury of Her Peers," the county attorney draws attention
    to the "strange way" in which John Wright was strangled. Because both
    women would know, upon seeing the rope used in the murder, that the
    knot was a type used in quilting (a familiar occupation of rural women), this
    language vividly shows Glaspell's idea that the interests and knowledge of
    men and women are widely separated. [Here the source of the detail in the
    first sentence is a character's dramatic statement. The second sentence is
    interpretive.]

3. The speaker in "Araby" states that the boys from the Christian Brothers
    School, when school lets out, are like inmates just released from prison. This
    comparison, coming at the beginning, sounds a note of irony that comple-
    ments the somewhat embarrassing revelations that the speaker makes in the

story. [Here the first sentence locates the source as the first-person narrator; the second is interpretive.]

4. In O'Connor's "First Confession," the priest's tolerant, good-humored treatment of Jackie, as contrasted with the harsh, intimidating treatment by the others, shows the idea that religious incentive is best implanted by kindness and understanding, not by fear [Here the idea, expressed as a single sentence, is derived from a consideration of the work as a whole.]

Locating sources in this way keeps the lines of your conclusions clear, helping your reader verify and follow your arguments.

Your general goal is to define an idea and show its importance in the story. Each separate story, poem, or play will invite its own approach, but here are a number of strategies you might use to organize your essay.

1. *Analyzing the idea as it applies to character.* Example: "Minnie Wright is an embodiment of the idea that a life lived amid cruelty and insensitivity will lead to alienation, unhappiness, despair, and even to violence."

2. *Showing how actions bring out the idea.* Example: "That Mabel and Dr. Fergusson fall in love rather than go their separate ways indicates Lawrence's idea that love is so strong it literally rescues human lives."

3. *Showing how dialogue and separate speeches bring out the idea.* Example: "The priest's responses to Jackie's confession show in operation the idea that kindness and understanding are the best means to encourage religious commitment."

4. *Showing how the story's structure is determined by the idea.* Example: "The idea that horror may exist in ordinary things leads to a structure in which Jackson introduces seemingly commonplace people, builds suspense about an impending misfortune, and develops a conclusion of mob destructiveness."

5. *Treating variations or differing manifestations of the idea.* Example: "The idea that overzealousness leads to destruction is shown in Brown's nightmarish distortion of reality, his rejection of others, and his dying gloom."

6. *Dealing with a combination of these (together with any other significant aspect).* Example: "The idea in 'Araby' that devotion is complex and contradictory is shown in the narrator's romantic mission as a carrier of parcels, his outcries to love in the back room of his house, and his self-reproach and shame at the story's end." [Here the idea is traced through speech and action.]

In your conclusion you might begin with a summary, together with your evaluation of the validity or force of the idea. If you have been convinced by the author's ideas, you might say that the author has expressed the idea forcefully and convincingly, or else you might show the relevance of the idea to current conditions. If you do not like the idea, it is never enough just to state your disagreement; you should include reasons, and should demonstrate the shortcomings or limitations of the idea. If you wish to mention a related idea, whether in the story you have studied or in some other story, you might introduce that here, but be sure to stress the connections.

SAMPLE ESSAY

The Idea in D. H. Lawrence's "The Horse Dealer's Daughter" That Human Destiny Is to Love°

[1]
There are many ideas in "The Horse Dealer's Daughter" about the love between men and women. The story suggests that love is a part of the uncontrollable and emotional side of human life, and that love cannot exist without a physical basis. It also suggests that love transforms life into something new, that love gives security, that only love gives meaning to life, and that love is not only something to live for but something to be feared. The one idea that takes in all these is that loving is an essential part of human nature and that it is human destiny to love.* This idea is embodied negatively in characters who are without love, and positively in characters who find love.†

[2]
In the first part of the story, loveless characters are negative and incomplete. Their lack of love causes them to be sullen, argumentative, and even cruel. Their lives are similar to those of the draft horses on the Pervin farm, who move with a "massive, slumbrous strength, and a stupidity which [holds] them in subjection" (paragraph 6). The idea is brought across with force, for the story implies that time is running out on people in this condition, and unless they find love they are doomed to misery. And the love they find must be real, for the underlying theme is that anything short of that is an evasion and will hasten their doom. Joe, the eldest of the Pervin brothers, is the major example of what can happen without love, for even though he is planning to marry, he is doing so without love. His motives are thus destroying him. As the narrator says, in emphasizing the story's major idea, Joe's "life was over, he would be a subject animal" like the horses (paragraph 7).

[3]
The idea that life is impossible without love is exemplified most fully in Mabel Pervin, the "horse dealer's daughter." She is alone among the males in the Pervin family, and the character for whom the story is named. Just as the father's death is breaking up the family, so is it forcing her toward drastic action. She assumes that the loss of, first, her mother and, now, her father has deprived her of all love. Therefore her attempt to drown herself in the brackish waters, which she undertakes soon after attending to her mother's grave, symbolically demonstrates the idea that a life without love has no constructive purpose and is in effect a kind of death.

Rather than ending life, however, the murky pond illustrates the idea that love begins life. Dr. Fergusson, who rescues Mabel, is her destiny, despite the fact that the two have never considered each other before as lovers.

° See p. 372 for this story.
* Central idea.
† Thesis sentence.

[4]
Jack has been introduced as a person leading a life of "quiet desperation." His common cold, which is mentioned when he first appears, suggests the idea that the soul without love is sick. When Jack leaves the Pervin house, his route is aimless and without any eagerly sought goal, and his seeing Mabel go into the water is not deliberate but accidental. When he acts heroically, therefore, he saves not only Mabel but also himself. The rescue thus underscores the idea that once love is found, it restores life.

[5]
But love is also complex, and when it comes it creates new problems- certainly an idea that is compatible with human destiny. As Lawrence shows his characters finding each other, he shows that love brings out new and strange emotions, and it upsets the habits and attitudes of a lifetime. Indeed, there is a strong element of fear in love; it changes life so completely that no one can ever be the same after experiencing it. We see this kind of fearful change in Dr. Jack Fergusson. The narrator tells us that the doctor "had no intention of loving" Mabel, but that destiny drives him into this state. The final paragraph of the story indicates the mixture of desire and terror that love and change can produce:

> "No, I want you, I want you," was all he answered, blindly, with that terrible intonation which frightened her almost more than the horror lest he should *not* want her. (paragraph 191)

Thus, the story forcefully makes the point that the human destiny driving people toward love is both exhilarating and fearsome at the same time.

[6]
This realistic presentation of human emotions raises Lawrence's treatment of his idea above the popular and romantic conception of love. Love creates problems as great as those it solves, but it also builds a platform of emotional strength from which these new problems can be attacked. This strength can be achieved only when men and women know love, because only then, in keeping with Lawrence's idea, are they living life as it was destined to be lived. The problems facing them then are the real ones that men and women should face, since such problems are a natural result of destiny. By contrast, men and women without love, like those at the beginning of the story, have never reached fulfillment. Consequently, they face problems that are irrelevant to life as it should be lived. The entire story of Mabel and Jack is an illustration of the idea that it is the destiny of men and women to love.

Commentary on the Essay

This essay follows the sixth strategy (p. 406) by showing how separate components from the story exhibit the idea's pervasiveness. Throughout, citations of actions, speeches, circumstances, and narrator's observations are used as evidence for the various conclusions. Transitions between paragraphs are effected by phrases like "The idea that . . ." (3), "however" (4), "But" (5), and "This" (6), all of which emphasize the continuity of the topic.

The introductory paragraph first illustrates a number of ideas about love that the story suggests, and then produces a comprehensive statement of the theme which is made the central idea. This assertion is developed as it applies (1) to characters without love and (2) to those who find it. In the body of the essay, paragraphs 2 and 3 emphasize the emptiness of the lives of characters without love. The relationship of these two paragraphs to the main idea is that if the characters are not living in accord with human destiny, they are cut off from life. Thus, Joe is dismissed in the story as a "subject animal," and Mabel, his sister, attempts suicide. These details are brought out in support of the essay's central idea. Paragraphs 4 and 5 treat the positive aspects of the main idea, focusing on the renewing effect of love on both Mabel and Jack, but also on the complexity of their emotional responses to their newly realized love. The last paragraph evaluates the idea or theme of the story, and concludes that it is realistic and well balanced.

WRITING TOPICS

1. What changes does the narrator in "The Sky Is Gray" undergo which suggest growth or change? How do the behaviors of the older folks around him (the men in the hardware store, the "pimp," the minister, the kind old folks in the store) register with him? What alterations might these behaviors eventually cause in him?

2. On the basis of ideas, write an essay criticizing a story in this anthology which you dislike or to which you are indifferent. You might consult the section in Chapter 1 on "Likes and Dislikes" (pp. 41–49) to get ideas about how to proceed. Explain how your responses are conditioned by your own beliefs and values, and be sure that your criticism is based accurately in the story.

3. Compare two stories with similar or contrasting themes (examples: "Lady with Lapdog" and "The Season of Divorce"; "Goodbye and Good Luck" and "Araby"; "Miss Brill" and "Meneseteung"; "The Shawl" and "The Portable Phonograph"; "I Stand Here Ironing" and "Barn Burning"; etc.). For help in developing your essay, consult Appendix B on the technique of comparison-contrast.

4. Select an idea that particularly interests you, and write a story showing how characters may or may not live up to the idea. If you have difficulty getting started, you might use one of these possible ideas:

   a. Interest and enthusiasm are hard to maintain for long.

   b. People always want more than they have or need.

   c. The concerns of adults are different from those of children.

   d. It is awkward to confront another person about a grievance.

   e. Making a decision is difficult because it often requires a complete change in life's directions.

11

Additional Stories

TONI CADE BAMBARA   (b. 1939)

Raymond's Run   *1970*

I don't have much work to do around the house like some girls. My mother does that. And I don't have to earn my pocket money by hustling; George runs errands for the big boys and sells Christmas cards. And anything else that's got to get done, my father does. All I have to do in life is mind my brother Raymond, which is enough.

Sometimes I slip and say my little brother Raymond. But as any fool can see he's much bigger and he's older too. But a lot of people call him my little brother cause he needs looking after cause he's not quite right. And a lot of smart mouths got lots to say about that too, especially when George was minding him. But now, if anybody has anything to say to Raymond, anything to say about his big head, they have to come by me. And I don't play the dozens° or believe in standing around with somebody in my face doing a lot of talking. I much rather just knock you down and take my chances even if I am a little girl with skinny arms and a squeaky voice, which is how I got the name Squeaky. And if things get too rough, I run. And as anybody can tell you, I'm the fastest thing on two feet.

There is no track meet that I don't win the first-place medal. I used to win the twenty-yard dash when I was a little kid in kindergarten. Nowadays, it's the fifty-yard dash. And tomorrow I'm subject to run the quarter-meter relay all by myself and come in first, second, and third. The big kids call me Mercury° cause I'm the swiftest thing in the neighborhood. Everybody knows that—except two people who know better, my father and me. He can beat me to Amsterdam Avenue° with me having a two-fire-hydrant head start and him running with his

---

the dozens: children's game in which the participants chant insults at each other.

Mercury: ancient Roman god of travel, portrayed with winged sandals to show his speed.

Amsterdam Avenue: All the street references, except for 34th Street (paragraph 5), are to places in Harlem.

hands in his pockets and whistling. But that's private information. Cause can you imagine some thirty-five-year-old man stuffing himself into PAL shorts to race little kids?° So as far as everyone's concerned, I'm the fastest and that goes for Gretchen, too, who has put out the tale that she is going to win the first-place medal this year. Ridiculous. In the second place, she's got short legs. In the third place, she's got freckles. In the first place, no one can beat me and that's all there is to it.

I'm standing on the corner admiring the weather and about to take a stroll down Broadway so I can practice my breathing exercises, and I've got Raymond walking on the inside close to the buildings, cause he's subject to fits of fantasy and starts thinking he's a circus performer and that the curb is a tightrope strung high in the air. And sometimes after a rain he likes to step down off his tightrope right into the gutter and slosh around getting his shoes and cuffs wet. Then I get hit when I get home. Or sometimes if you don't watch him he'll dash across traffic to the island in the middle of Broadway and give the pigeons a fit. Then I have to go behind him apologizing to all the old people sitting around trying to get some sun and getting all upset with the pigeons fluttering around them, scattering their newspapers and upsetting the wax paper lunches in their laps. So I keep Raymond on the inside of me, and he plays like he's driving a stagecoach which is O.K. by me so long as he doesn't run me over or interrupt my breathing exercises, which I have to do on account of I'm serious about my running, and I don't care who knows it.

Now some people like to act like things come easy to them, won't let on that they practice. Not me. I'll high-prance down 34th Street like a rodeo pony to keep my knees strong even if it does get my mother uptight so that she walks ahead like she's not with me, don't know me, is all by herself on a shopping trip, and I am somebody else's crazy child. Now you take Cynthia Procter for instance. She's just the opposite. If there's a test tomorrow, she'll say something like, "Oh, I guess I'll play handball this afternoon and watch television tonight," just to let you know she ain't thinking about the test. Or like last week when she won the spelling bee for the millionth time, "A good thing you got 'receive,' Squeaky, cause I would have got it wrong. I completely forgot about the spelling bee." And she'll clutch the lace on her blouse like it was a narrow escape. Oh, brother. But of course when I pass her house on my early morning trots around the block, she is practicing the scales on the piano over and over and over and over. Then in music class she always lets herself get bumped around so she falls accidently on purpose onto the piano stool and is so surprised to find herself sitting there that she decides just for fun to try out the ole keys. And what do you know—Chopin's waltzes just spring out of her fingertips and she's the most surprised thing in the world. A regular prodigy. I could kill people like that. I stay up all night studying the words for the spelling bee. And you can see me any time of day practicing running. I never walk if I can trot, and shame on Raymond if he can't keep up. But of course he does, cause if he hangs back someone's liable to walk up to him and get smart, or take his allowance from him, or ask him where he got that great big pumpkin head. People are so stupid sometimes.

So I'm strolling down Broadway breathing out and breathing in on counts

5

°*PAL . . . little kids*: reference to children's racing events sponsored by the Police Athletic League.

of seven, which is my lucky number, and here comes Gretchen and her sidekicks: Mary Louise, who used to be a friend of mine when she first moved to Harlem from Baltimore and got beat up by everybody till I took up for her on account of her mother and my mother used to sing in the same choir when they were young girls, but people ain't grateful, so now she hangs out with the new girl Gretchen and talks about me like a dog; and Rosie, who is as fat as I am skinny and has a big mouth where Raymond is concerned and is too stupid to know that there is not a big deal of difference between herself and Raymond and that she can't afford to throw stones. So they are steady coming up Broadway and I see right away that it's going to be one of those Dodge City scenes° cause the street ain't that big and they're close to the buildings just as we are. First I think I'll step into the candy store and look over the new comics and let them pass. But that's chicken and I've got a reputation to consider. So then I think I'll just walk straight on through them or even over them if necessary. But as they get to me, they slow down. I'm ready to fight, cause like I said I don't feature a whole lot of chitchat, I much prefer to just knock you down right from the jump and save everybody a lotta precious time.

"You signing up for the May Day races?" smiles Mary Louise, only it's not a smile at all. A dumb question like that doesn't deserve an answer. Besides, there's just me and Gretchen standing there really, so no use wasting my breath talking to shadows.

"I don't think you're going to win this time," says Rosie, trying to signify with her hands on her hips all salty, completely forgetting that I have whupped her behind many times for less salt than that.

"I always win cause I'm the best," I say straight at Gretchen who is, as far as I'm concerned, the only one talking in this ventriloquist-dummy routine. Gretchen smiles, but it's not a smile, and I'm thinking that girls never really smile at each other because they don't know how and don't want to know how and there's probably no one to teach us how, cause grownup girls don't know either. Then they all look at Raymond who has just brought his mule team to a standstill. And they're about to see what trouble they can get into through him.

"What grade you in now, Raymond?"   10

"You got anything to say to my brother, you say it to me, Mary Louise Williams of Raggedy Town, Baltimore."

"What are you, his mother?" sasses Rosie.

"That's right, Fatso. And the next word out of anybody and I'll be *their* mother too." So they just stand there and Gretchen shifts from one leg to the other and so do they. Then Gretchen puts her hands on her hips and is about to say something with her freckle-face self but doesn't. Then she walks around me looking me up and down but keeps walking up Broadway, and her sidekicks follow her. So me and Raymond smile at each other and he says, "Giddyap" to his team and I continue with my breathing exercises, strolling down Broadway toward the ice man on 145th with not a care in the world cause I am Miss Quicksilver herself.

I take my time getting to the park on May Day because the track meet is the last thing on the program. The biggest thing on the program is the Maypole dancing, which I can do without, thank you, even if my mother thinks it's a shame

Dodge City scenes: The location of "Gunsmoke," a popular TV Western serial, was Dodge City. The opening of the show focused on the protagonist and another man in a showdown gunfight.

I don't take part and act like a girl for a change. You'd think my mother'd be grateful not to have to make me a white organdy dress with a big satin sash and buy me new white baby-doll shoes that can't be taken out of the box till the big day. You'd think she'd be glad her daughter ain't out there prancing around a Maypole getting the new clothes all dirty and sweaty and trying to act like a fairy or a flower or whatever you're supposed to be when you should be trying to be yourself, whatever that is, which is, as far as I am concerned, a poor black girl who really can't afford to buy shoes and a new dress you only wear once a lifetime cause it won't fit next year.

I was once a strawberry in a Hansel and Gretel pageant when I was in 15 nursery school and didn't have no better sense than to dance on tiptoe with my arms in a circle over my head doing umbrella steps and being a perfect fool just so my mother and father could come dressed up and clap. You'd think they'd know better than to encourage that kind of nonsense. I am not a strawberry. I do not dance on my toes. I run. That is what I am all about. So I always come late to the May Day program, just in time to get my number pinned on and lay in the grass till they announce the fifty-yard dash.

I put Raymond in the little swings, which is a tight squeeze this year and will be impossible next year. Then I look around for Mr. Pearson, who pins the numbers on. I'm really looking for Gretchen if you want to know the truth, but she's not around. The park is jam-packed. Parents in hats and corsages and breastpocket handkerchiefs peeking up. Kids in white dresses and light blue suits. The parkees unfolding chairs and chasing the rowdy kids from Lenox as if they had no right to be there. The big guys with their caps on backwards, leaning against the fence swirling the basketballs on the tips of their fingers, waiting for all these crazy people to clear out the park so they can play. Most of the kids in my class are carrying bass drums and glockenspiels and flutes. You'd think they'd put in a few bongos or something for real like that.

Then here comes Mr. Pearson with his clipboard and his cards and pencils and whistles and safety pins and fifty million other things he's always dropping all over the place with his clumsy self. He sticks out in a crowd because he's on stilts. We used to call him Jack and the Beanstalk to get him mad. But I'm the only one that can outrun him and get away, and I'm too grown for that silliness now.

"Well, Squeaky," he says, checking my name off the list and handing me number seven and two pins. And I'm thinking he's got no right to call me Squeaky, if I can't call him Beanstalk.

"Hazel Elizabeth Deborah Parker," I correct him and tell him to write it down on his board.

"Well, Hazel Elizabeth Deborah Parker, going to give someone else a break 20 this year?" I squint at him real hard to see if he is seriously thinking I should lose the race on purpose just to give someone else a break. "Only six girls running this time," he continues, shaking his head sadly like it's my fault all of New York didn't turn out in sneakers. "That new girl should give you a run for your money." He looks around the park for Gretchen like a periscope in a submarine movie. "Wouldn't it be a nice gesture if you were . . . to ahhh . . ."

I give him such a look he couldn't finish putting that idea into words. Grownups got a lot of nerve sometimes. I pin number seven to myself and stomp away, I'm so burnt. And I go straight for the track and stretch out on the grass while the band winds up with "Oh, the Monkey Wrapped His Tail Around the Flagpole,"° which my teacher calls by some other name. The man on the loudspeaker is calling everyone over to the track and I'm on my back looking at the sky, trying to pretend I'm in the country, but I can't, because even grass in the city feels hard as sidewalk, and there's just no pretending you are anywhere but in a "concrete jungle" as my grandfather says.

The twenty-yard dash takes all of two minutes cause most of the little kids don't know no better than to run off the track or run the wrong way or run smack into the fence and fall down and cry. One little kid, though, has got the good sense to run straight for the white ribbon up ahead so he wins. Then the second-graders line up for the thirty-yard dash and I don't even bother to turn my head to watch cause Raphael Perez always wins. He wins before he even begins by psyching the runners, telling them they're going to trip on their shoelaces and fall on their faces or lose their shorts or something, which he doesn't really have to do since he is very fast, almost as fast as I am. After that is the forty-yard dash which I use to run when I was in first grade. Raymond is hollering from the swings cause he knows I'm about to do my thing cause the man on the loudspeaker has just announced the fifty-yard dash, although he might just as well be giving a recipe for angel food cake cause you can hardly make out what he's saying for the static. I get up and slip off my sweat pants and then I see Gretchen standing at the starting line, kicking her legs out like a pro. Then as I get into place I see that ole Raymond is on line on the other side of the fence, bending down with his fingers on the ground just like he knew what he was doing. I was going to yell at him but then I didn't. It burns up your energy to holler.

Every time, just before I take off in a race, I always feel like I'm in a dream, the kind of dream you have when you're sick with fever and feel all hot and weightless. I dream I'm flying over a sandy beach in the early morning sun, kissing the leaves of the trees as I fly by. And there's always the smell of apples, just like in the country when I was little and used to think I was a choo-choo train, running through the fields of corn and chugging up the hill to the orchard. And all the time I'm dreaming this, I get lighter and lighter until I'm flying over the beach again, getting blown through the sky like a feather that weighs nothing at all. But once I spread my fingers in the dirt and crouch over the Get on Your Mark, the dream goes and I am solid again and am telling myself, Squeaky you must win, you must win, you are the fastest thing in the world, you can even beat your father up Amsterdam if you really try. And then I feel my weight coming back just behind my knees then down to my feet then into the earth and the pistol shot explodes in my blood and I am off and weightless again, flying past the other runners, my arms pumping up and down and the whole world is quiet except for the crunch as I zoom over the gravel in the track. I glance to my left and there is no one. To the right, a blurred Gretchen, who's got her chin jutting out as if it would win the race all by itself. And on the other side of the fence is Raymond with his arms down to his side and the palms tucked up behind him, running in his very own style, and it's the first time I ever saw that and I almost stop to watch my brother Raymond on his first run. But the white ribbon is bouncing toward

Oh . . . Flagpole: the first line of obscene lyrics to Sousa's "Washington Post" march.

me and I tear past it, racing into the distance till my feet with a mind of their own start digging up footfuls of dirt and brake me short. Then all the kids standing on the side pile on me, banging me on the back and slapping my head with their May Day programs, for I have won again and everybody on 151st Street can walk tall for another year.

"In first place . . ." the man on the loudspeaker is clear as a bell now, but then he pauses and the loudspeaker starts to whine. Then static. And I lean down to catch my breath and here comes Gretchen walking back, for she's overshot the finish line too, huffing and puffing with her hands on her hips taking it slow, breathing in steady time like a real pro and I sort of like her a little for the first time. "In first place . . ." and then three or four voices get all mixed up on the loudspeaker and I dig my sneaker into the grass and stare at Gretchen who's staring back, we both wondering just who did win. I can hear old Beanstalk arguing with the man on the loudspeaker and then a few others running their mouths about what the stopwatches say. Then I hear Raymond yanking at the fence to call me and I wave to shush him, but he keeps rattling the fence like a gorilla in a cage like in them gorilla movies, but then like a dancer or something he starts climbing up nice and easy but very fast. And it occurs to me, watching how smoothly he climbs hand over hand and remembering how he looked running with his arms down to his side and with the wind pulling his mouth back and his teeth showing and all, it occurred to me that Raymond would make a very fine runner. Doesn't he always keep up with me on my trots? And he surely knows how to breathe in counts of seven cause he's always doing it at the dinner table, which drives my brother George up the wall. And I'm smiling to beat the band cause if I've lost this race, or if me and Gretchen tied, or even if I've won, I can always retire as a runner and begin a whole new career as a coach with Raymond as my champion. After all, with a little more study I can beat Cynthia and her phony self at the spelling bee. And if I bugged my mother, I could get piano lessons and become a star. And I have a big rep as the baddest thing around. And I've got a roomful of ribbons and medals and awards. But what has Raymond got to call his own?

So I stand there with my new plans, laughing out loud by this time as 25 Raymond jumps down from the fence and runs over with his teeth showing and his arms down to the side, which no one before him has quite mastered as a running style. and by the time he comes over I'm jumping up and down so glad to see him—my brother Raymond, a great runner in the family tradition. But of course everyone thinks I'm jumping up and down because the men on the loudspeaker have finally gotten themselves together and compared notes and are announcing "In first place—Miss Hazel Elizabeth Deborah Parker." (Dig that.) "In second place—Miss Gretchen P. Lewis." And I look at Gretchen wondering what the "P" stands for. And I smile. Cause she's good, no doubt about it. Maybe she'd like to help me coach Raymond; she obviously is serious about running, as any fool can see. And she nods to congratulate me and then she smiles. And I smile. We stand there with this big smile of respect between us. It's about as real a smile as girls can do for each other, considering we don't practice real smiling every day, you know, cause maybe we too busy being flowers or fairies or strawberries instead of something honest and worthy of respect . . . you know . . . like being people.

JOHN CHEEVER   (1912–1982)

The Season of Divorce   *1973*

My wife has brown hair, dark eyes, and a gentle disposition. Because of her gentle disposition, I sometimes think that she spoils the children. She can't refuse them anything. They always get around her. Ethel and I have been married for ten years. We both come from Morristown, New Jersey, and I can't even remember when I first met her. Our marriage has always seemed happy and resourceful to me. We live in a walk-up in the East Fifties. Our son, Carl, who is six, goes to a good private school, and our daughter, who is four, won't go to school until next year. We often find fault with the way we were educated, but we seem to be struggling to raise our children along the same lines, and when the time comes, I suppose they'll go to the same school and colleges that we went to.

Ethel graduated from a women's college in the East, and then went for a year to the University of Grenoble. She worked for a year in New York after returning from France, and then we were married. She once hung her diploma above the kitchen sink, but it was a short-lived joke and I don't know where the diploma is now. Ethel is cheerful and adaptable, as well as gentle, and we both come from that enormous stratum of the middle class that is distinguished by its ability to recall better times. Lost money is so much a part of our lives that I am sometimes reminded of expatriates, of a group who have adapted themselves energetically to some alien soil but who are reminded, now and then, of the escarpments of their native coast. Because our lives are confined by my modest salary, the surface of Ethel's life is easy to describe.

She gets up at seven and turns the radio on. After she is dressed, she rouses the children and cooks the breakfast. Our son has to be walked to the school bus at eight o'clock. When Ethel returns from this trip, Carol's hair has to be braided. I leave the house at eight-thirty, but I know that every move that Ethel makes for the rest of the day will be determined by the housework, the cooking, the shopping, and the demands of the children. I know that on Tuesdays and Thursdays she will be at the A & P between eleven and noon, that on every clear afternoon she will be on a certain bench in a playground from three until five, that she cleans the house on Mondays, Wednesdays, and Fridays, and polishes the silver when it rains. When I return at six, she is usually cleaning the vegetables or making some other preparation for dinner. Then when the children have been fed and bathed, when the dinner is ready, when the table in the living room is set with food and china, she stands in the middle of the room as if she has lost or forgotten something, and this moment of reflection is so deep that she will not hear me if I speak to her, or the children if they call. Then it is over. She lights the four white candles in their silver sticks, and we sit down to a supper of corned-beef hash or some other modest fare.

We go out once or twice a week and entertain about once a month. Because of practical considerations, most of the people we see live in our neighborhood. We often go around the corner to the parties given by a generous couple named Newsome. The Newsomes' parties are large and confusing, and the arbitrary impulses of friendship are given a free play.

We became attached at the Newsomes' one evening, for reasons that I've   5
never understood, to a couple named Dr. and Mrs. Trencher. I think that Mrs.

Trencher was the aggressor in this friendship, and after our first meeting she telephoned Ethel three or four times. We went to their house for dinner, and they came to our house, and sometimes in the evening when Dr. Trencher was walking their old dachshund, he would come up for a short visit. He seemed like a pleasant man to have around. I've heard other doctors say that he's a good physician. The Trenchers are about thirty; at least he is. She is older.

I'd say that Mrs. Trencher is a plain woman, but her plainness is difficult to specify. She is small, she has a good figure and regular features, and I suppose that the impression of plainness arises from some inner modesty, some needlessly narrow view of her chances. Dr. Trencher doesn't smoke or drink, and I don't know whether there's any connection or not, but the coloring in his slender face is fresh—his cheeks are pink, and his blue eyes are clear and strong. He has the singular optimism of a well-adjusted physician—the feeling that death is a chance misfortune and that the physical world is merely a field for conquest. In the same way that his wife seems plain, he seems young.

The Trenchers live in a comfortable and unpretentious private house in our neighborhood. The house is old-fashioned; its living rooms are large, its halls are gloomy, and the Trenchers don't seem to generate enough human warmth to animate the place, so that you sometimes take away from them, at the end of an evening, an impression of many empty rooms. Mrs. Trencher is noticeably attached to her possessions—her clothes, her jewels, and the ornaments she's bought for the house—and to Fräulein, the old dachshund. She feeds Fräulein scraps from the table, furtively, as if she has been forbidden to do this, and after dinner Fräulein lies beside her on the sofa. With the play of green light from a television set on her drawn features and her thin hands stroking Fräulein, Mrs. Trencher looked to me one evening like a good-hearted and miserable soul.

Mrs. Trencher began to call Ethel in the mornings for a talk or to ask her for lunch or a matinee. Ethel can't go out in the day and she claims to dislike long telephone conversations. She complained that Mrs. Trencher was a tireless and aggressive gossip. Then late one afternoon Dr. Trencher appeared at the playground where Ethel takes our two children. He was walking by, and he saw her and sat with her until it was time to take the children home. He came again a few days later, and then his visits with Ethel in the playground, she told me, became a regular thing. Ethel thought that perhaps he didn't have many patients and that with nothing to do he was happy to talk with anyone. Then, when we were washing dishes one night, Ethel said thoughtfully that Trencher's attitude toward her seemed strange. "He stares at me," she said. "He sighs and stares at me." I know what my wife looks like in the playground. She wears an old tweed coat, overshoes, and Army gloves, and a scarf is tied under her chin. The playground is a fenced and paved lot between a slum and the river. The picture of the well-dressed, pink-cheeked doctor losing his heart to Ethel in this environment was hard to take seriously. She didn't mention him then for several days, and I guessed that he had stopped his visits. Ethel's birthday came at the end of the month, and I forgot about it, but when I came home that evening, there were a lot of roses in the living room. They were a birthday present from Trencher, she told me. I was cross at myself for having forgotten her birthday, and Trencher's roses made me angry. I asked her if she'd seen him recently.

"Oh, yes," she said, "he still comes to the playground nearly every afternoon. I haven't told you, have I? He's made his declaration. He loves me. He can't live without me. He'd walk through fire to hear the notes of my voice." She laughed. "That's what he said."

"When did he say this?"

"At the playground. And walking home. Yesterday."

"How long has he known?"

"That's the funny part about it," she said. "He knew before he met me at the Newsomes' that night. He saw me waiting for a crosstown bus about three weeks before that. He just saw me and he said that he knew then, the minute he saw me. Of course, he's crazy."

I was tired that night and worried about taxes and bills, and I could think of Trencher's declaration only as a comical mistake. I felt that he was a captive of financial and sentimental commitments, like every other man I know, and that he was no more free to fall in love with a strange woman he saw on a street corner than he was to take a walking trip through French Guiana or to recommence his life in Chicago under an assumed name. His declaration, the scene in the playground, seemed to me to be like those chance meetings that are a part of the life of any large city. A blind man asks you to help him across the street, and as you are about to leave him, he seizes your arm and regales you with a passionate account of his cruel and ungrateful children; or the elevator man who is taking you up to a party turns to you suddenly and says that his grandson has infantile paralysis. The city is full of accidental revelation, half-heard cries for help, and strangers who will tell you everything at the first suspicion of sympathy, and Trencher seemed to me like the blind man or the elevator operator. His declaration had no more bearing on the business of our lives than these interruptions.

Mrs. Trencher's telephone conversations had stopped, and we had stopped visiting the Trenchers, but sometimes I would see him in the morning on the crosstown bus when I was late going to work. He seemed understandably embarrassed whenever he saw me, but the bus was always crowded at that time of day, and it was no effort to avoid one another. Also, at about that time I made a mistake in business and lost several thousand dollars for the firm I work for. There was not much chance of my losing my job, but the possibility was always at the back of my mind, and under this and under the continuous urgency of making more money the memory of the eccentric doctor was buried. Three weeks passed without Ethel's mentioning him, and then one evening, when I was reading, I noticed Ethel standing at the window looking down into the street.

"He's really there," she said.

"Who?"

"Trencher. Come here and see."

I went to the window. There were only three people on the sidewalk across the street. It was dark and it would have been difficult to recognize anyone, but because one of them, walking toward the corner, had a dachshund on a leash, it could have been Trencher.

"Well, what about it?" I said. "He's just walking the dog."

"But he wasn't walking the dog when I first looked out of the window. He was just standing there, staring up at this building. That's what he says he does. He says that he comes over here and stares up at our lighted windows."

"When did he say this?"

"At the playground."

"I thought you went to another playground."

10

15

20

"Oh, I do, I do, but he followed me. He's crazy, darling. I know he's crazy, but I feel so sorry for him. He says that he spends night after night looking up at our windows. He says that he sees me everywhere—the back of my head, my eyebrows—that he hears my voice. He says that he's never compromised in his life and that he isn't going to compromise about this. I feel so sorry for him, darling. I can't help but feel sorry for him."

For the first time then, the situation seemed serious to me, for in his helplessness I knew that he might have touched an inestimable and wayward passion that Ethel shares with some other women—an inability to refuse any cry for help, to refuse any voice that sounds pitiable. It is not a reasonable passion, and I would almost rather have had her desire him than pity him. When we were getting ready for bed that night, the telephone rang, and when I picked up and said hello, no one answered. Fifteen minutes later, the telephone rang again, and when there was no answer this time, I began to shout and swear at Trencher, but he didn't reply—there wasn't even the click of a closed circuit—and I felt like a fool. Because I felt like a fool, I accused Ethel of having led him on, of having encouraged him, but these accusations didn't affect her, and when I finished them, I felt worse, because I knew that she was innocent, and that she had to go out on the street to buy groceries and air the children, and that there was no force of law that could keep Trencher from waiting for her there, or from staring up at our lights.

We went to the Newsomes' one night the next week, and while we were taking off our coats, I heard Trencher's voice. He left a few minutes after we arrived, but his manner—the sad glance he gave Ethel, the way he sidestepped me, the sorrowful way that he refused the Newsomes when they asked him to stay longer, and the gallant attentions he showed his miserable wife—made me angry. Then I happened to notice Ethel and saw that her color was high, that her eyes were bright, and that while she was praising Mrs. Newsome's new shoes, her mind was not on what she was saying. When we came home that night, the baby-sitter told us crossly that neither of the children had slept. Ethel took their temperatures. Carol was all right, but the boy had a fever of a hundred and four. Neither of us got much sleep that night, and in the morning Ethel called me at the office to say that Carl had bronchitis. Three days later, his sister came down with it.

For the next two weeks, the sick children took up most of our time. They had to be given medicine at eleven in the evening and again at three in the morning, and we lost a lot of sleep. It was impossible to ventilate or clean the house, and when I came in, after walking through the cold from the bus stop, it stank of cough syrups and tobacco, fruit cores and sickbeds. There were blankets and pillows, ashtrays, and medicine glasses everywhere. We divided the work of sickness reasonably and took turns at getting up in the night, but I often fell asleep at my desk during the day, and after dinner Ethel would fall asleep in a chair in the living room. Fatigue seems to differ for adults and children only in that adults recognize it and so are not overwhelmed, and when we were tired, we were unreasonable, cross, and the victims of transcendent depressions. One evening after the worst of the sickness was over, I came home and found some roses in the living room. Ethel said that Trencher had brought them. She hadn't let him in. She had closed the door in his face. I took the roses and threw them out. We didn't quarrel. The children went to sleep at nine, and a few minutes after nine I went to bed. Sometime later, something woke me.

A light was burning in the hall. I got up. The children's room and the living room were dark. I found Ethel in the kitchen sitting at the table, drinking coffee.

"I've made some fresh coffee," she said. "Carol felt croupy again, so I steamed her. They're both asleep now."

"How long have you been up?"

"Since half past twelve," she said. "What time is it?"

"Two."

I poured myself a cup of coffee and sat down. She got up from the table and rinsed her cup and looked at herself in a mirror that hangs over the sink. It was a windy night. A dog was wailing somewhere in an apartment below ours, and a loose radio antenna was brushing against the kitchen window.

"It sounds like a branch," she said.

In the bare kitchen light, meant for peeling potatoes and washing dishes, she looked very tired.

"Will the children be able to go out tomorrow?"

"Oh, I hope so," she said. "Do you realize that I haven't been out of this apartment in over two weeks?" She spoke bitterly and this startled me.

"It hasn't been quite two weeks."

"It's been over two weeks," she said.

"Well, let's figure it out," I said. "The children were taken sick on a Saturday night. That was the fourth. Today is the—"

"Stop it, stop it," she said. "I know how long it's been. I haven't had my shoes on in two weeks."

"You make it sound pretty bad."

"It is. I haven't had on a decent dress or fixed my hair."

"It could be worse."

"My mother's cooks had a better life."

"I doubt that."

"My mother's cooks had a better life," she said loudly.

"You'll wake the children."

"My mother's cooks had a better life. They had pleasant rooms. No one could come into the kitchen without their permission." She knocked the coffee grounds into the garbage and began to wash the pot.

"How long was Trencher here this afternoon?"

"A minute. I've told you."

"I don't believe it. He was in here."

"He was not. I didn't let him in. I didn't let him in because I looked so badly. I didn't want to discourage him."

"Why not?"

"I don't know. He may be a fool. He may be insane but the things he's told me have made me feel marvelously, he's made me feel marvelously."

"Do you want to go?"

"Go? Where would I go?" She reached for the purse that is kept in the kitchen to pay for groceries and counted out of it two dollars and thirty-five cents. "Ossining? Montclair?"

"I mean with Trencher."

"I don't know, I don't know," she said, "but who can say that I shouldn't? What harm would it do? What good would it do? Who knows. I love the children but that isn't enough, that isn't nearly enough. I wouldn't hurt them, but would I hurt them so much if I left you? Is divorce so dreadful and of all the things that hold a marriage together how many of them are good?" She sat down at the table.

"In Grenoble," she said, "I wrote a long paper on Charles Stuart in French. A professor at the University of Chicago wrote me a letter. I couldn't read a French newspaper without a dictionary today, I don't have the time to follow any newspaper, and I am ashamed of my incompetence, ashamed of the way I look. Oh, I guess I love you, I do love the children, but I love myself, I love my life, it has some value and some promise for me and Trencher's roses make me feel that I'm losing this, that I'm losing my self-respect. Do you know what I mean, do you understand what I mean?"

"He's crazy," I said.

"Do you know what I mean? Do you understand what I mean?"

"No," I said. "No."

Carl woke up then and called for his mother. I told Ethel to go to bed. I turned out the kitchen light and went into the children's room. 65

The children felt better the next day, and since it was Sunday, I took them for a walk. The afternoon sun was clement and pure, and only the colored shadows made me remember that it was midwinter, that the cruise ships were returning, and that in another week jonquils would be twenty-five cents a bunch. Walking down Lexington Avenue, we heard the drone bass of a church organ sound from the sky, and we and the others on the sidewalk looked up in piety and bewilderment, like a devout and stupid congregation, and saw a formation of heavy bombers heading for the sea. As it got late, it got cold and clear and still, and on the stillness the waste from the smokestacks along the East River seemed to articulate, as legibly as the Pepsi-Cola plant, whole words and sentences. Halcyon. Disaster. They were hard to make out. It seemed the ebb of the year—an evil day for gastritis, sinus, and respiratory disease—and remembering other winters, the markings of the light convinced me that it was the season of divorce. It was a long afternoon, and I brought the children in before dark.

I think that the seriousness of the day affected the children, and when they returned to the house, they were quiet. The seriousness of it kept coming to me with the feeling that this change, like a phenomenon of speed, was affecting our watches as well as our hearts. I tried to remember the willingness with which Ethel had followed my regiment during the war, from West Virginia to the Carolinas and Oklahoma, and the day coaches and rooms she had lived in, and the street in San Francisco where I said goodbye to her before I left the country, but I could not put any of this into words, and neither of us found anything to say. Sometime after dark, the children were bathed and put to bed, and we sat down to our supper. At about nine o'clock, the doorbell rang, and when I answered it and recognized Trencher's voice on the speaking tube, I asked him to come up.

He seemed distraught and exhilarated when he appeared. He stumbled on the edge of the carpet. "I know that I'm not welcome here," he said in a hard voice, as if I were deaf. "I know that you don't like me here. I respect your feelings. This is your home. I respect a man's feelings about his home. I don't usually go to a man's home unless he asks me. I respect your home. I respect your marriage. I respect your children. I think everything ought to be aboveboard. I've come here to tell you that I love your wife."

"Get out," I said.

"You've got to listen to me," he said. "I love your wife. I can't live without 70 her. I've tried and I can't. I've even thought of going away—of moving to the West Coast—but I know that it wouldn't make any difference. I want to marry her. I'm not romantic. I'm matter-of-fact. I'm very matter-of-fact. I know that you have two children and that you don't have much money. I know that there are problems of custody and property and things like that to be settled. I'm not romantic. I'm hardheaded. I've talked this all over with Mrs. Trencher, and she's agreed to give me a divorce. I'm not underhanded. Your wife can tell you that. I realize all the practical aspects that have to be considered—custody, property, and so forth. I have plenty of money. I can give Ethel everything she needs, but there are the children. You'll have to decide about them between yourselves. I have a check here. It's made out to Ethel. I want her to take it and go to Nevada. I'm a practical man and I realize that nothing can be decided until she gets her divorce."

"Get out of here!" I said. "Get the hell out of here!"

He started for the door. There was a potted geranium on the mantelpiece, and I threw this across the room at him. It got him in the small of the back and nearly knocked him down. The pot broke on the floor. Ethel screamed. Trencher was still on his way out. Following him, I picked up a candlestick and aimed it at his head, but it missed and bounced off the wall. "Get the hell out of here!" I yelled, and he slammed the door. I went back into the living room. Ethel was pale but she wasn't crying. There was a loud rapping on the radiator, a signal from the people upstairs for decorum and silence—urgent and expressive, like the communications that prisoners send to one another through the plumbing in a penitentiary. Then everything was still.

We went to bed, and I woke sometime during the night. I couldn't see the clock on the dresser, so I don't know what time it was. There was no sound from the children's room. The neighborhood was perfectly still. There were no lighted windows anywhere. Then I knew that Ethel had wakened me. She was lying on her side of the bed. She was crying.

"Why are you crying?" I asked.

"Why am I crying?" she said. "Why am I crying?" And to hear my voice and to speak set her off again, and she began to sob cruelly. She sat up and slipped her arms into the sleeves of a wrapper and felt along the table for a package of cigarettes. I saw her wet face when she lighted a cigarette. I heard her moving around in the dark.

"Why do you cry?"

"Why do I cry? Why do I cry?" she asked impatiently. "I cry because I saw an old woman cuffing a little boy on Third Avenue. She was drunk. I can't get it out of my mind." She pulled the quilt off the foot of our bed and wandered with it toward the door. "I cry because my father died when I was twelve and because my mother married a man I detested or thought that I detested. I cry because I had to wear an ugly dress—a hand-me-down dress—to a party twenty years ago, and I didn't have a good time. I cry because of some unkindness that I can't remember. I cry because I'm tired—because I'm tired and I can't sleep." I heard her arrange herself on the sofa and then everything was quiet.

I like to think that the Trenchers have gone away, but I still see Trencher now and then on a crosstown bus when I'm late going to work. I've also seen his wife, going into the neighborhood lending library with Fräulein. She looks old. I'm not good at judging ages, but I wouldn't be surprised to find that Mrs. Trencher is fifteen years older than her husband. Now when I come home in the evenings, Ethel is still sitting on the stool by the sink cleaning vegetables. I go with her into the children's room. The light there is bright. The children have built something out of an orange crate, something preposterous and ascendant, and their sweetness, their compulsion to build, the brightness of the light are reflected perfectly and increased in Ethel's face. Then she feeds them, bathes them, and sets the table, and stands for a moment in the middle of the room, trying to make some connection between the evening and the day. Then it is over. She lights the four candles, and we sit down to our supper.

ANTON CHEKHOV (1860–1904)

Lady with Lapdog   *1899*

Translated by David Magarshack

I

The appearance on the front of a new arrival—a lady with a lapdog—became the topic of general conversation. Dmitry Dmitrich Gurov, who had been a fortnight in Yalta and got used to its ways, was also interested in new arrivals. One day, sitting on the terrace of Vernet's restaurant, he saw a young woman walking along the promenade; she was fair, not very tall, and wore a toque; behind her trotted a white pomeranian.

Later he came across her in the park and in the square several times a day. She was always alone, always wearing the same toque, followed by the white pomeranian. No one knew who she was, and she became known simply as the lady with the lapdog.

"If she's here without her husband and without any friends," thought Gurov, "it wouldn't be a bad idea to strike up an acquaintance with her."

He was not yet forty, but he had a twelve-year-old daughter and two schoolboy sons. He had been married off when he was still in his second year at the university, and his wife seemed to him now to be almost twice his age. She was a tall, black-browed woman, erect, dignified, austere, and, as she liked to describe herself, a "thinking person." She was a great reader, preferred the new "advanced" spelling, called her husband by the more formal "Dimitry" and not the familiar "Dmitry"; and though he secretly considered her not particularly intelligent, narrow-minded, and inelegant, he was afraid of her and disliked being at home. He had been unfaithful to her for a long time, he was often unfaithful to her, and that was why, perhaps, he almost always spoke ill of women, and when men discussed women in his presence, he described them as *the lower breed*.

He could not help feeling that he had had enough bitter experience to have   5
the right to call them as he pleased, but all the same without *the lower breed* he could not have existed a couple of days. He was bored and ill at ease among men, with whom he was reticent and cold, but when he was among women he felt at ease, he knew what to talk about with them and how to behave, even when he was silent in their company he experienced no feeling of constraint. There was something attractive, something elusive in his appearance, in his character and his

whole person that women found interesting and irresistible; he was aware of it, and was himself drawn to them by some irresistible force.

Long and indeed bitter experience had taught him that every new affair, which at first relieved the monotony of life so pleasantly and appeared to be such a charming and light adventure, among decent people and especially among Muscovites, who are so irresolute and so hard to rouse, inevitably developed into an extremely complicated problem and finally the whole situation became rather cumbersome. But at every new meeting with an attractive woman he forgot all about this experience, he wanted to enjoy life so badly and it all seemed so simple and amusing.

And so one afternoon, while he was having dinner at a restaurant in the park, the woman in the toque walked in unhurriedly and took a seat at the table next to him. The way she looked, walked and dressed, wore her hair, told him that she was of good social standing, that she was married, that she was in Yalta for the first time, that she was alone and bored. . . . There was a great deal of exaggeration in the stories about the laxity of morals among the Yalta visitors, and he dismissed them with contempt, for he knew that such stories were mostly made up by people who would gladly have sinned themselves if they had had any idea how to go about it; but when the woman sat down at the table three yards away from him he remembered these stories of easy conquests and excursions to the mountains and the tempting thought of a quiet and fleeting affair, an affair with a strange woman whose very name he did not know, suddenly took possession of him.

He tried to attract the attention of the dog by calling softly to it, and when the pomeranian came up to him he shook a finger at it. The pomeranian growled. Gurov again shook a finger at it.

The woman looked up at him and immediately lowered her eyes.

"He doesn't bite," she said and blushed.   10

"May I give him a bone?" he asked, and when she nodded, he said amiably: "Have you been long in Yalta?"

"About five days."

"And I am just finishing my second week here."

They said nothing for the next few minutes.

"Time flies," she said without looking at him, "and yet it's so boring here."   15

"That's what one usually hears people saying here. A man may be living in Belev and Zhizdra or some other God-forsaken hole and he isn't bored, but the moment he comes here all you hear from him is 'Oh, it's so boring! Oh, the dust!' You'd think he'd come from Granada!"

She laughed. Then both went on eating in silence, like complete strangers; but after dinner they strolled off together, and they embarked on the light playful conversation of free and contented people who do not care where they go or what they talk about. They walked, and talked about the strange light that fell on the sea; the water was of such a soft and warm lilac, and the moon threw a shaft of gold across it. They talked about how close it was after a hot day. Gurov told her that he lived in Moscow, that he was a graduate in philology but worked in a bank, that he had at one time thought of singing in a private opera company but had given up the idea, that he owned two houses in Moscow. . . . From her he learnt that she had grown up in Petersburg, but had got married in the town of S——, where she had been living for the past two years, that she would stay another month in Yalta, and that her husband, who also needed a rest, might join her. She was quite unable to tell him what her husband's job was, whether he served in the offices of the provincial governor or the rural council, and she found this rather amusing herself. Gurov also found out that her name and patronymic were Anna Sergeyevna.

Later, in his hotel room, he thought about her and felt sure that he would meet her again the next day. It had to be. As he went to bed he remembered that she had only recently left her boarding school, that she had been a schoolgirl like his own daughter; he recalled how much diffidence and angularity there was in her laughter and her conversation with a stranger—it was probably the first time in her life she had found herself alone, in a situation when men followed her, looked at her, and spoke to her with only one secret intention, an intention she could hardly fail to guess. He remembered her slender, weak neck, her beautiful grey eyes.

"There's something pathetic about her, all the same," he thought as he fell asleep.

II

A week had passed since their first meeting. It was a holiday. It was close indoors, while in the streets a strong wind raised clouds of dust and tore off people's hats. All day long one felt thirsty, and Gurov kept going to the terrace of the restaurant, offering Anna Sergeyevna fruit drinks and ices. There was nowhere to go. 20

In the evening, when the wind had dropped a little, they went to the pier to watch the arrival of the steamer. There were a great many people taking a walk on the landing pier; some were meeting friends, they had bunches of flowers in their hands. It was there that two peculiarities of the Yalta smart set at once arrested attention: the middle-aged women dressed as if they were still young girls and there was a great number of generals.

Because of the rough sea the steamer arrived late, after the sun had set, and she had to swing backwards and forwards several times before getting alongside the pier. Anna Sergeyevna looked at the steamer and the passengers through her lorgnette, as though trying to make out some friends, and when she turned to Gurov her eyes were sparkling. She talked a lot, asked many abrupt questions, and immediately forgot what it was she had wanted to know; then she lost her lorgnette in the crowd of people.

The smartly dressed crowd dispersed; soon they were all gone, the wind had dropped completely, but Gurov and Anna were still standing there as though waiting to see if someone else would come off the boat. Anna Sergeyevna was no longer talking. She was smelling her flowers without looking at Gurov.

"It's a nice evening," he said. "Where shall we go now? Shall we go for a drive?"

She made no answer. 25

Then he looked keenly at her and suddenly put his arms round her and kissed her on the mouth. He felt the fragrance and dampness of the flowers and immediately looked around him fearfully: had anyone seen them?

"Let's go to your room," he said softly.

And both walked off quickly.

It was very close in her hotel room, which was full of the smell of the scents she had bought in a Japanese shop. Looking at her now, Gurov thought: "Life is full of strange encounters!" From his past he preserved the memory of carefree, good-natured women, whom love had made gay and who were grateful to him for the happiness he gave them, however short-lived; and of women like his wife, who made love without sincerity, with unnecessary talk, affectedly, hysterically, with such an expression, as though it were not love or passion, but something much more significant; and of two or three very beautiful, frigid women, whose faces suddenly lit up with a predatory expression, an obstinate desire to take, to snatch from life more than it could give; these were women no longer in their first youth, capricious, unreasoning, despotic, unintelligent women, and when Gurov lost interest in them, their beauty merely aroused hatred in him and the lace trimmings on their négligés looked to him then like the scales of a snake.

But here there was still the same diffidence and angularity of inexperienced youth—an awkward feeling; and there was also the impression of embarrassment, as if someone had just knocked at the door. Anna Sergeyevna, this lady with the lapdog, apparently regarded what had happened in a peculiar sort of way, very seriously, as though she had become a fallen women—so it seemed to him, and he found it odd and disconcerting. Her features lengthened and drooped, and her long hair hung mournfully on either side of her face; she sank into thought in a despondent pose, like a woman taken in adultery in an old painting.

"It's wrong," she said. "You'll be the first not to respect me now."

There was a water-melon on the table. Gurov cut himself a slice and began to eat it slowly. At least half an hour passed in silence.

Anna Sergeyevna was very touching; there was an air of pure, decent, naïve woman about her, a woman who had very little experience of life; the solitary candle burning on the table scarcely lighted up her face, but it was obvious that she was unhappy.

"But, darling, why should I stop respecting you?" Gurov asked. "You don't know yourself what you're saying."

"May God forgive me," she said, and her eyes filled with tears. "It's terrible."

"You seem to wish to justify yourself."

"How can I justify myself? I am a bad, despicable creature. I despise myself and have no thought of justifying myself. I haven't deceived my husband, I've deceived myself. And not only now. I've been deceiving myself for a long time. My husband is, I'm sure, a good and honest man, but, you see, he is a flunkey. I don't know what he does at his office, all I know is that he is a flunkey. I was only twenty when I married him, I was eaten up by curiosity, I wanted something better. There surely must be a different kind of life, I said to myself. I wanted to live. To live, to live! I was burning with curiosity. I don't think you know what I am talking about, but I swear I could no longer control myself, something was happening to me, I could not be held back, I told my husband I was ill, and I came here. . . . Here too I was going about as though in a daze, as though I was mad, and now I've become a vulgar worthless woman whom everyone has a right to despise."

Gurov could not help feeling bored as he listened to her; he was irritated by her naïve tone of voice and her repentance, which was so unexpected and so out of place; but for the tears in her eyes, he might have thought that she was joking or play-acting.

30

35

"I don't understand," he said gently, "what it is you want."

She buried her face on his chest and clung close to him.   40

"Please, please believe me," she said. "I love a pure, honest life. I hate immorality. I don't know myself what I am doing. The common people say 'the devil led her astray,' I too can now say about myself that the devil has led me astray."

"There, there . . ." he murmured.

He gazed into her staring, frightened eyes, kissed her, spoke gently and affectionately to her, and gradually she calmed down and her cheerfulness returned; both of them were soon laughing.

Later, when they went out, there was not a soul on the promenade, the town with its cypresses looked quite dead, but the sea was still roaring and dashing itself against the shore; a single launch tossed on the waves, its lamp flickering sleepily.

They hailed a cab and drove to Oreanda.   45

"I've just found out your surname, downstairs in the lobby," said Gurov. "Von Diederitz. Is your husband a German?"

"No. I believe his grandfather was German. He is of the Orthodox faith himself."

In Oreanda they sat on a bench not far from the church, looked down on the sea, and were silent. Yalta could scarcely be seen through the morning mist. White clouds lay motionless on the mountain tops. Not a leaf stirred on the trees, the cicadas chirped, and the monotonous, hollow roar of the sea, coming up from below, spoke of rest, of eternal sleep awaiting us all. The sea had roared like that down below when there was no Yalta or Oreanda, it was roaring now, and it would go on roaring as indifferently and hollowly when we were here no more. And in this constancy, in this complete indifference to the life and death of each one of us, there is perhaps hidden the guarantee of our eternal salvation, the never-ceasing movement of life on earth, the never-ceasing movement towards perfection. Sitting beside a young woman who looked so beautiful at the break of day, soothed and enchanted by the sight of all that fairy-land scenery—the sea, the mountains, the clouds, the wide sky—Gurov reflected that, when you came to think of it, everything in the world was really really beautiful, everything but our own thoughts and actions when we lose sight of the higher aims of existence and our dignity as human beings.

Someone walked up to them, a watchman probably, looked at them, and went away. And there seemed to be something mysterious and also beautiful in this fact, too. They could see the Theodosia boat coming towards the pier, lit up by the sunrise, and with no lights.

"There's dew on the grass," said Anna Sergeyevna, breaking the silence.   50

"Yes. Time to go home."

They went back to town.

After that they met on the front every day at twelve o'clock, had lunch and dinner together, went for walks, admired the sea. She complained of sleeping badly and of her heart beating uneasily, asked the same questions, alternately worried by feelings of jealousy and by fear that he did not respect her sufficiently. And again and again in the park or in the square, when there was no one in sight, he would draw her to him and kiss her passionately. The complete idleness, these kisses in broad daylight, always having to look round for fear of someone watching them, the heat, the smell of the sea, and the constant looming into sight of idle, well-dressed, and well-fed people seemed to have made a new man of him; he told Anna Sergeyevna that she was beautiful, that she was desirable, made passionate love to her, never left her side, while she was often lost in thought and kept asking him to admit that he did not really respect her, that he was not in the least in love with her and only saw in her a vulgar woman. Almost every night they drove out of town, to Oreanda or to the waterfall; the excursion was always a success, and every time their impressions were invariably grand and beautiful.

They kept expecting her husband to arrive. But a letter came from him in which he wrote that he was having trouble with his eyes and implored his wife to return home as soon as possible. Anna Sergeyevna lost no time in getting ready for her journey home.

"It's a good thing I'm going," she said to Gurov. "It's fate."   55

She took a carriage to the railway station, and he saw her off. The drive took a whole day. When she got into the express train, after the second bell, she said:

"Let me have another look at you. . . . One last look. So."

She did not cry, but looked sad, just as if she were ill, and her face quivered.

"I'll be thinking of you, remembering you," she said. "Good-bye. You're staying, aren't you? Don't think badly of me. We are parting for ever. Yes, it must be so, for we should never have met. Well, good-bye. . . ."

The train moved rapidly out of the station; its lights soon disappeared, and   60 a minute later it could not even be heard, just as though everything had conspired to put a quick end to this sweet trance, this madness. And standing alone on the platform gazing into the dark distance, Gurov listened to the chirping of the grasshoppers and the humming of the telegraph wires with a feeling as though he had just woken up. He told himself that this had been just one more affair in his life, just one more adventure, and that it too was over, leaving nothing but a memory. He was moved and sad, and felt a little penitent that the young woman, whom he would never see again, had not been happy with him; he had been amiable and affectionate with her, but all the same in his behavior to her, in the tone of his voice and in his caresses, there was a suspicion of light irony, the somewhat coarse arrogance of the successful male, who was, moreover, almost twice her age. All the time she called him good, wonderful, high-minded; evidently she must have taken him to be quite different from what he really was, which meant that he had involuntarily deceived her.

At the railway station there was already a whiff of autumn in the air; the evening was chilly.

"Time I went north, too," thought Gurov, as he walked off the platform. "High time!"

III

At home in Moscow everything was already like winter: the stoves were heated, and it was still dark in the morning when the children were getting ready to go to school and having breakfast, so that the nurse had to light the lamp for a short time. The frosts had set in. When the first snow falls and the first day one goes out for a ride in a sleigh, one is glad to see the white ground, the white roofs, the air is so soft and wonderful to breathe, and one remembers the days of one's youth. The old lime trees and birches, white with rime, have such a benignant look, they are nearer to one's heart than cypresses and palms, and beside them one no longer wants to think of mountains and the sea.

Gurov had been born and bred in Moscow, and he returned to Moscow on a fine frosty day; and when he put on his fur coat and warm gloves and took a walk down Petrovka Street, and when on Saturday evening he heard the church bells ringing, his recent holiday trip and the places he had visited lost their charm for him. Gradually he became immersed in Moscow life, eagerly reading three newspapers a day and declaring that he never read Moscow papers on principle. Once more, he could not resist the attraction of restaurants, clubs, banquets, and anniversary celebrations, and once more he felt flattered that well-known lawyers and actors came to see him and that in the Medical Club he played cards with a professor as his partner. Once again he was capable of eating a whole portion of the Moscow speciality of sour cabbage and meat served in a frying-pan. . . .

Another month and, he thought, nothing but a memory would remain of Anna Sergeyevna; he would remember her as through a haze and only occasionally dream of her with a wistful smile, as he did of the others before her. But over a month passed, winter was at its height, and he remembered her as clearly as though he had only parted from her the day before. His memories haunted him more and more persistently. Every time the voices of his children doing their homework reached him in his study in the stillness of the evening, every time he heard a popular song or some music in a restaurant, every time the wind howled in the chimney—it all came back to him: their walks on the pier, early morning with the mist on the mountains, the Theodosia boat, and the kisses. He kept pacing the room for hours remembering it all and smiling, and then his memories turned into daydreams and the past mingled in his imagination with what was going to happen. He did not dream of Anna Sergeyevna, she accompanied him everywhere like his shadow and followed him wherever he went. Closing his eyes, he saw her as clearly as if she were before him, and she seemed to him lovelier, younger, and tenderer than she had been; and he thought that he too was much better than he had been in Yalta. In the evenings she gazed at him from the bookcase, from the fireplace, from the corner—he heard her breathing, the sweet rustle of her dress. In the street he followed women with his eyes, looking for anyone who resembled her. . . .

He was beginning to be overcome by an overwhelming desire to share his memories with someone. But at home it was impossible to talk of his love, and outside his home there was no one he could talk to. Not the tenants who lived in his house, and certainly not his colleagues in the bank. And what was he to tell them? Had he been in love then? Had there been anything beautiful, poetic, edifying, or even anything interesting about his relations with Anna Sergeyevna? So he had to talk in general terms about love and women, and no one guessed what he was driving at, and his wife merely raised her black eyebrows and said:

"Really, Dimitry, the role of a coxcomb doesn't suit you at all!"

One evening, as he left the Medical Club with his partner, a civil servant, he could not restrain himself, and said:

"If you knew what a fascinating woman I met in Yalta!"

The civil servant got into his sleigh and was about to be driven off, but suddenly he turned round and called out:

"I say!"

"Yes?"

"You were quite right: the sturgeon *was* a bit off."

These words, so ordinary in themselves, for some reason hurt Gurov's feelings: they seemed to him humiliating and indecent. What savage manners! What faces! What stupid nights! What uninteresting, wasted days! Crazy gambling at cards, gluttony, drunkenness, endless talk about one and the same thing. Business that was of no use to anyone and talk about one and the same thing absorbed the greater part of one's time and energy, and what was left in the end was a sort of dock-tailed, barren life, a sort of nonsensical existence, and it was impossible to escape from it, just as though you were in a lunatic asylum or a convict chaingang!

Gurov lay awake all night, fretting and fuming, and had a splitting headache the whole of the next day. The following nights too he slept badly, sitting up in bed thinking, or walking up and down his room. He was tired of his children, tired of the bank, he did not feel like going out anywhere or talking about anything. 75

In December, during the Christmas holidays, he packed his things, told his wife that he was going to Petersburg to get a job for a young man he knew, and set off for the town of S——. Why? He had no very clear idea himself. He wanted to see Anna Sergeyevna, to talk to her, to arrange a meeting, if possible.

He arrived in S—— in the morning and took the best room in a hotel, with a fitted carpet of military grey cloth and an inkstand grey with dust on the table, surmounted by a horseman with raised hand and no head. The hall porter supplied him with all the necessary information: Von Diederitz lived in a house of his own in Old Potter's Street, not far from the hotel. He lived well, was rich, kept his own carriage horses, the whole town knew him. The hall-porter pronounced the name: Dridiritz.

Gurov took a leisurely walk down Old Potter's Street and found the house. In front of it was a long grey fence studded with upturned nails.

"A fence like that would make anyone wish to run away," thought Gurov, scanning the windows and the fence.

As it was a holiday, he thought, her husband was probably at home. It did not matter either way, though, for he could not very well embarrass her by calling at the house. If he were to send in a note it might fall into the hands of the husband and ruin everything. The best thing was to rely on chance. And he kept walking up and down the street and along the fence, waiting for his chance. He watched a beggar enter the gate and the dogs attack him; then, an hour later, he heard the faint indistinct sounds of a piano. That must have been Anna Sergeyevna playing. Suddenly the front door opened and an old woman came out, followed by the familiar white pomeranian. Gurov was about to call to the dog, but his heart began to beat violently and in his excitement he could not remember its name. 80

He went on walking up and down the street, hating the grey fence more and more, and he was already saying to himself that Anna Sergeyevna had forgotten him and had perhaps been having a good time with someone else, which was indeed quite natural for a young woman who had to look at that damned fence from morning till night. He went back to his hotel room and sat on the sofa for a long time, not knowing what to do, then he had dinner and after dinner a long sleep.

"How stupid and disturbing it all is," he thought, waking up and staring at the dark windows: it was already evening. "Well, I've had a good sleep, so what now? What am I going to do tonight?"

He sat on a bed covered by a cheap grey blanket looking exactly like a hospital blanket, and taunted himself in vexation:

"A *lady* with a lapdog! Some adventure, I must say! Serves you right!"

At the railway station that morning he had noticed a poster announcing in huge letters the first performance of *The Geisha Girl* at the local theatre. He recalled it now, and decided to go to the theatre.

"Quite possibly she goes to first nights," he thought.

The theatre was full. As in all provincial theatres, there was a mist over the chandeliers and the people in the gallery kept up a noisy and excited conversation; in the first row of the stalls stood the local dandies with their hands crossed behind their backs; here, too, in the front seat of the Governor's box, sat the Governor's daughter, wearing a feather boa, while the Governor himself hid modestly behind the portière so that only his hands were visible; the curtain stirred, the orchestra took a long time tuning up. Gurov scanned the audience eagerly as they filed in and occupied their seats.

Anna Sergeyevna came in too. She took her seat in the third row, and when Gurov glanced at her his heart missed a beat and he realized clearly that there was no one in the world nearer and dearer or more important to him than that little woman with the stupid lorgnette in her hand, who was in no way remarkable. That woman lost in a provincial crowd now filled his whole life, was his misfortune, his joy, and the only happiness that he wished for himself. Listening to the bad orchestra and the wretched violins played by second-rate musicians, he thought how beautiful she was. He thought and dreamed.

A very tall, round-shouldered young man with small whiskers had come in with Anna Sergeyevna and sat down beside her; he nodded at every step he took and seemed to be continually bowing to someone. This was probably her husband, whom in a fit of bitterness at Yalta she had called a flunkey. And indeed there was something of a lackey's obsequiousness in his lank figure, his whiskers, and the little bald spot on the top of his head. He smiled sweetly, and the gleaming insignia of some scientific society which he wore in his buttonhole looked like the number on a waiter's coat.

In the first interval the husband went out to smoke and she was left in her seat. Gurov, who also had a seat in the stalls, went up to her and said in a trembling voice and with a forced smile:

"Good evening!"

She looked up at him and turned pale, then looked at him again in panic, unable to believe her eyes, clenching her fan and lorgnette in her hand and apparently trying hard not to fall into a dead faint. Both were silent. She sat and he stood, frightened by her embarrassment and not daring to sit down beside her. The violinists and the flautist began tuning their instruments, and they suddenly felt terrified, as though they were being watched from all the boxes. But a moment later she got up and walked rapidly towards one of the exits; he followed her, and both of them walked aimlessly along corridors and up and down stairs. Figures in all sorts of uniforms—lawyers, teachers, civil servants, all wearing badges— flashed by them; ladies, fur coats hanging on pegs, the cold draught bringing with it the odour of cigarette-ends. Gurov, whose heart was beating violently, thought:

"Oh, Lord, what are all these people, that orchestra, doing here?"

At that moment, he suddenly remembered how after seeing Anna Sergeyevna off he had told himself that evening at the station that all was over and that they would never meet again. But how far they still were from the end!

She stopped on a dark, narrow staircase with a notice over it: "To the Upper Circle." 95

"How you frightened me!" she said, breathing heavily, still looking pale and stunned. "Oh, dear, how you frightened me! I'm scarcely alive. Why did you come? Why?"

"But, please, try to understand, Anna," he murmured hurriedly. "I beg you, please, try to understand. . . ."

She looked at him with fear, entreaty, love, looked at him intently, so as to fix his features firmly in her mind.

"I've suffered so much," she went on, without listening to him. "I've been thinking of you all the time. The thought of you kept me alive. And yet I tried so hard to forget you—why, oh, why did you come?"

On the landing above two schoolboys were smoking and looking down, but 100 Gurov did not care. He drew Anna Sergeyevna towards him and began kissing her face, her lips, her hands.

"What are you doing? What are you doing?" she said in horror, pushing him away. "We've both gone mad. You must go back tonight, this minute. I implore you, by all that's sacred . . . Somebody's coming!"

Somebody was coming up the stairs.

"You must go back," continued Anna Sergeyevna in a whisper. "Do you hear? I'll come to you in Moscow. I've never been happy, I'm unhappy now, and I shall never be happy, never! So please don't make me suffer still more. I swear I'll come to you in Moscow. But now we must part. Oh, my sweet, my darling, we must part!"

She pressed his hand and went quickly down the stairs, looking back at him all the time, and he could see from the expression in her eyes that she really was unhappy. Gurov stood listening for a short time, and when all was quiet he went to look for his coat and left the theatre.

IV

Anna Sergeyevna began going to Moscow to see him. Every two or three months 105 she left the town of S——, telling her husband that she was going to consult a Moscow gynaecologist, and her husband believed and did not believe her. In Moscow she stayed at the Slav Bazaar and immediately sent a porter in a red cap to inform Gurov of her arrival. Gurov went to her hotel, and no one in Moscow knew about it.

One winter morning he went to her hotel as usual (the porter had called with his message at his house the evening before, but he had not been in). He had his daughter with him, and he was glad of the opportunity of taking her to school, which was on the way to the hotel. Snow was falling in thick wet flakes.

"It's three degrees above zero," Gurov was saying to his daughter, "and yet it's snowing. But then, you see, it's only warm on the earth's surface, in the upper layers of the atmosphere the temperature's quite different."

"Why isn't there any thunder in winter, Daddy?"

He explained that, too. As he was speaking, he kept thinking that he was going to meet his mistress and not a living soul knew about it. He led a double life: one for all who were interested to see, full of conventional truth and conventional deception, exactly like the lives of his friends and acquaintances; and another which went on in secret. And by a kind of strange concatenation of circumstances, possibly quite by accident, everything that was important, interesting, essential, everything about which he was sincere and did not deceive himself, everything that made up the quintessence of his life, went on in secret, while everything that was a lie, everything that was merely the husk in which he hid himself to conceal the truth, like his work at the bank, for instance, his discussions at the club, his ideas of the lower breed, his going to anniversary functions with his wife—all that happened in the sight of all. He judged others by himself, did not believe what he saw, and was always of the opinion that every man's real and most interesting life went on in secret, under cover of night. The personal, private life of an individual was kept a secret, and perhaps that was partly the reason why civilized man was so anxious that his personal secrets should be respected.

Having seen his daughter off to her school, Gurov went to the Slav Bazaar. He took off his fur coat in the cloakroom, went upstairs, and knocked softly on the door. Anna Sergeyevna, wearing the grey dress he liked most, tired out by her journey and by the suspense of waiting for him, had been expecting him since the evening before; she was pale, looked at him without smiling, but was in his arms the moment he went into the room. Their kiss was long and lingering, as if they had not seen each other for two years.

"Well," he asked, "how are you getting on there? Anything new?"

"Wait, I'll tell you in a moment. . . . I can't . . . ."

She could not speak because she was crying. She turned away from him and pressed her handkerchief to her eyes.

"Well, let her have her cry," he thought, sitting down in an armchair. "I'll wait."

Then he rang the bell and ordered tea; while he was having his tea, she was still standing there with her face to the window. She wept because she could not control her emotions, because she was bitterly conscious of the fact that their life was so sad: they could only meet in secret, they had to hide from people, like thieves! Was not their life ruined?

"Please stop crying!" he said.

It was quite clear to him that their love would not come to an end for a long time, if ever. Anna Sergeyevna was getting attached to him more and more strongly, she worshipped him, and it would have been absurd to tell her that all this would have to come to an end one day. She would not have believed it, anyway.

He went up to her and took her by the shoulders, wishing to be nice to her, to make her smile; and at that moment he caught sight of himself in the looking glass.

His hair was already beginning to turn grey. It struck him as strange that he should have aged so much, that he should have lost his good looks in the last few years. The shoulders on which his hands lay were warm and quivering. He felt so sorry for this life, still so warm and beautiful, but probably soon to fade and wilt like his own. Why did she love him so? To women he always seemed different from what he was, and they loved in him not himself, but the man their imagination conjured up and whom they had eagerly been looking for all their lives; and when they discovered their mistake they still loved him. And not one of them had ever been happy with him. Time had passed, he had met women, made love to them, parted from them, but not once had he been in love; there had been everything between them, but no love.

It was only now, when his hair was beginning to turn grey, that he had   120 fallen in love properly, in good earnest for the first time in his life.

He and Anna Sergeyevna loved each other as people do who are very dear and near, as man and wife or close friends love each other; they could not help feeling that fate itself had intended them for one another, and they were unable to understand why he should have a wife and she a husband; they were like two migrating birds, male and female, who had been caught and forced to live in separate cages. They had forgiven each other what they had been ashamed of in the past, and forgave each other everything in their present, and felt that this love of theirs had changed them both.

Before, when he felt depressed, he had comforted himself by all sorts of arguments that happened to occur to him on the spur of the moment, but now he had more serious things to think of, he felt profound compassion, he longed to be sincere, tender. . . .

"Don't cry, my sweet," he said. "That'll do, you've had your cry. . . . Let's talk now, let's think of something."

Then they had a long talk. They tried to think how they could get rid of the necessity of hiding, telling lies, living in different towns, not seeing one another for so long. How were they to free themselves from their intolerable chains?

"How? How?" he asked himself, clutching at his head. "How?"

And it seemed to them that in only a few more minutes a solution would be   125 found and a new, beautiful life would begin; but both of them knew very well that the end was still a long, long way away and that the most complicated and difficult part was only just beginning.

STEPHEN DIXON   (b. 1936)

All Gone   *1990*

He says goodbye, we kiss at the door, he rings for the elevator, I say "I'll call you when I find out about the tickets," he says "Anytime, as I'll be in all day working on that book jacket I'm behind on," waves to me as the elevator door opens and I shut the door.

I find out about the tickets and call him and he doesn't answer. Maybe he hasn't gotten home yet, though he usually does in half an hour. But it's Saturday and the subway's always much slower on weekends, and I call him half an hour later and he doesn't answer.

He could have got home and I missed him because he right away might have gone out to buy some necessary art supply or something, and I call him an hour later and he doesn't answer. I do warm-ups, go out and run my three miles along the river, come back and shower and call him and he doesn't answer. I dial him every half hour after that for the next three hours and then call Operator and she checks and says his phone's in working order.

I call his landlord and say "This is Maria Pierce, Eliot Schulter's good friend for about the last half-year—you know me. Anyway, could you do me a real big favor and knock on his door? I know it's an inconvenience but he's only one flight up and you see, he should be home and doesn't answer and I've been phoning and phoning him and am getting worried. I'll call you back in fifteen minutes. If he's in and for his own reasons didn't want to answer the phone or it actually is out of order, could you have him call me at home?"

I call the landlord back in fifteen minutes and he says "I did what you said and he didn't answer. That would've been enough for me. But you got me worried also, so I went downstairs for his duplicate keys and opened his door just a ways and yelled in for him and then walked in and he wasn't there, though his place looked okay." 5

"Excuse me, I just thought of something. Was his night light on?"

"You mean the little small-watt-bulb lamp on his fireplace mantel?"

"That's the one. He always keeps it on at night to keep away burglars who like to jump in from his terrace."

"What burglars jumping in from where? He was never robbed that I know."

"The tenant before him said she was. Was it on?" 10

"That's different. Yes. I thought he'd forgotten about the light, so I shut if off. I was thinking about his electricity cost, but you think I did wrong?"

"No. It only means he never got home. Thanks."

I call every half hour after that till around six, when he usually comes to my apartment. But he never comes here without our first talking on the phone during the afternoon about all sorts of things: how our work's going, what the mail brought, what we might have for dinner that evening and do later and if there's anything he can pick up on the way here and so on. The concert's at eight and I still have to pick up the tickets from my friend who's giving them to me and can't go herself because her baby's sick and her husband won't go without her. I call her and say "I don't see how we can make the concert. Eliot's not here, hasn't called, doesn't answer his phone and from what his landlord said, I doubt he ever got home after he left me this morning."

"Does he have any relatives or close friends in the city for you to call?"

"No, he would have gone to his apartment directly—I know him. He had important work to finish, and the only close person other than myself to him is his mother in Seattle." 15

"Maybe he did get home but got a very sudden call to drop everything and fly out to her, so he didn't have the time to phone you, or when he did, your line was busy."

"No, we're close enough that he'd know it would worry me. He'd have called from the airport, someplace."

"Your line still could have been busy all the times you were trying to get him. But I'm sure everything's okay, and don't worry about the tickets. Expensive as they are, I'll put them down as a total loss. Though if you are still so worried about him, phone the police in his neighborhood or even his mother in Seattle."

"Not his mother. There's no reason and I'd just worry her and Eliot would get angry at me. But the police is a good idea."

I call the police station in his precinct. The officer who answers says "We've nothing on a Mr. Schulter. But being that you say he left your apartment this morning, phone your precinct station," and she gives me the number. I call it and 20 the officer on duty says "Something did come in today about someone of his name—let me think."

"Oh no."

"Hey, take it easy. It could be nothing. I'm only remembering that I saw an earlier bulletin, but what it was went right past me. What's your relationship to him before I start searching for it?"

"His closest friend. We're really very very close and his nearest relative is three thousand miles from here."

"Well, I don't see it in front of me. I'll locate it, though don't get excited when I'm away. It could be nothing. I might even be wrong. It was probably more like a Mr. Fullter or Schulton I read about, but not him. Want me to phone you back?"

"I'll wait, thanks."

"Let me take your number anyway, just in case I get lost."

He goes, comes back in a minute. "Now take it easy. It's very serious. He had no I.D. on him other than this artist society card with only his signature on it, which we were checking into, so we're grateful you called."

"Please, what is it?"

"According to this elderly witness, he was supposedly thrown on the subway tracks this morning and killed."

I scream, break down, hang up, pound the telephone table with my fists, the officer calls back and says "If you could please revive yourself, Miss, we'd like you to come to the police station here and then, if you could by the end of the night sometime, to the morgue to identify your friend."

I say no, I could never go to the morgue, but then go with my best friend. She stays outside the body room when I go in, look and say "That's him." Later I call Eliot's mother and the next day her brother comes to the city and takes care of the arrangements to have Eliot flown to Seattle and his apartment closed down and most of his belongings sold or given away or put on the street. The uncle asks if I'd like to attend the funeral, but doesn't mention anything about providing air fare or where I would stay. Since I don't have much money saved and also think I'll be out of place there and maybe even looked down upon by his family I've never seen, I stay here and arrange on that same funeral day a small ceremony in the basement of a local church, where I and several of our friends and his employers speak about Eliot and read aloud excerpts of his letters to a couple of us and listen to parts of my opera records he most liked to play and for a minute bow our heads, hold hands and pray.

According to that elderly witness, Eliot was waiting for a train on the downtown platform of my stop when he saw a young man speaking abusively to a girl of about fifteen. When the girl continued to ignore him, he made several obscene gestures and said he was going to throw her to the platform and force her to do all sorts of sordid things to him and if he couldn't get her to do them there because people were watching, then in the men's room upstairs. The girl was frightened and started to walk away. The young man grabbed her wrist, started to twist it, stopped and said he would rip her arm off if she gave him a hard time, but didn't let go. There were a few people on the platform. Nobody said anything or tried to help her and in fact all of them except Eliot and this elderly man eventually moved to the other end of the platform or at least away from what was going on. Then Eliot went over to the young man, who was still

25

30

holding the girl by her wrist, and very politely asked him to let her alone. Something like "Excuse me, I don't like to interfere in anyone's problems. But if this young lady doesn't want to be bothered by you, then I would really think you'd let her go."

"Listen, I know her, so mind your business," the young man said and she said to Eliot "No he don't." Then out of nowhere a friend of the young man ran down the subway stairs and said to him "What's this chump doing, horning in on your act?" The elderly man got up from a bench and started for the upstairs to get help. "You stay right here, grandpa," the first young man said, "or you'll get thrown on your back too." The elderly man stopped. Eliot said to the young men "Please, nobody should be getting thrown on their backs. And I hate to get myself any more involved in this but for your own good you fellows ought to go now or just leave everybody here alone."

"And for your own good," one of the young men said, "you'd be wiser moving your ass out of here."

"I can only move it once I know this girl's out of danger with you two."   35

"She'll be plenty out of danger when you move your ass out of here, now move."

"Believe me, I'd like to, but how can I? Either you leave her completely alone now or I'll have to get the police."

That's when they jumped him, beat him to the ground and, when he continued to fight back with his feet, fists and butting his head, picked him up and threw him on the tracks. He landed on his head and cracked his skull and something like a blood clot suddenly shot through to the brain, a doctor later said. The girl had already run away. The young men ran the opposite way. The elderly man shouted at Eliot to get up, then at people to jump down to the tracks to help Eliot up, then ran in the direction the young men went to the token booth upstairs and told the attendant inside that an unconscious man was lying on the tracks and for her to do something quick to prevent a train from running over him. She phoned from the booth. He ran back to the platform and all the way to the other end of it yelling to the people around him "Stop the train. Man on the tracks, stop the local train." When the downtown local entered the station a minute later, he and most of the people along the platform screamed and waved the motorman to stop the train because someone was on the tracks. The train came to a complete stop ten feet from Eliot. A lot of the passengers were thrown to the floor and the next few days a number of them sued the city for the dizzy spells and sprained fingers and ripped clothes they said they got from the sudden train stop and also for the days and weeks they'd have to miss from their jobs because of their injuries. Anyway, according to that same doctor who examined Eliot at the hospital, he was dead a second or two after his head hit the train rail.

For a week after the funeral I go into my own special kind of mourning: seeing nobody, never leaving the apartment or answering phone calls, eating little and drinking too much, but mostly just sleeping or watching television while crying and lying in bed. Then I turn the television off, answer every phone call, run along the river for twice as many miles than I usually do, go out for a big restaurant dinner with a friend and return to my job.

The Saturday morning after the next Saturday after that I sit on the bench   40
near the place on the subway platform where Eliot was thrown off. I stay there from eight to around one, on the lookout for the two young men. I figure they

live in the neighborhood and maybe every Saturday have a job or something to go to downtown and after a few weeks they'll think everything's forgotten about them and their crime and they can go safely back to their old routines, like riding the subway to work at the station nearest their homes. The descriptions I have of them are the ones the elderly witness gave. He said he was a portrait painter or used to be and so he was absolutely exact about their height, age, looks, mannerisms and hair color and style and clothes. He also made detailed drawings of the men for the police, which I have copies of from the newspaper, and which so far haven't done the police any good in finding them.

What I'm really looking out for besides those descriptions are two young men who will try and pick up or seriously annoy or molest a teen-age girl on the platform or do that to any reasonably young woman, including me. If I see them and I'm sure it's them I'll summon a transit policeman to arrest them and if there's none around then I'll follow the young men, though discreetly, till I see a policeman. And if they try and molest or terrorize me on the bench and no policeman's around, I'll scream at the top of my lungs till someone comes and steps in, and hopefully a policeman. But I just want those two young men caught, that's all, and am willing to risk myself a little for it, and though there's probably not much chance of it happening, I still want to give it a good try.

I do this every Saturday morning for months. I see occasional violence on the platform, like a man slapping his woman friend in the face or a mother hitting her infant real hard, but nothing like two or even one man of any description close to those young men terrorizing or molesting a woman or girl or even trying to pick one up. I do see men, both old and young, and a few who look no more than nine years old or ten, leer at women plenty as if they'd like to pick them up or molest them. Some men, after staring at a woman from a distance, then walk near to her when the train comes just to follow her through the same door into the car. But that's as far as it goes on the platform. Maybe when they both get in the car and especially when it's crowded, something worse happens. I know that a few times a year when I ride the subway, a pull or poke from a man has happened to me.

A few times a man has come over to the bench and once even a woman who looked manly and tried to talk to me, but I brushed them off with silence or a remark. Then one morning a man walks over when I'm alone on the bench and nobody else is around. I'm not worried, since he has a nice face and is decently dressed and I've seen him before here waiting for the train and all it seems he wants now is to sit down. He's a big man, so I move over a few inches to the far end of the bench to give him more room.

"No," he says, "I don't want to sit—I'm just curious. I've seen you in this exact place almost every Saturday for the last couple of months and never once saw you get on the train. Would it be too rude—"

"Yes."

"All right. I won't ask it. I'm sorry."

"No, go on, ask it. What is it you want to know? Why I sit here? Well I've been here every Saturday for more than three months straight, if you're so curious to know, and why you don't see me get on the car is none of your business, okay?"

"Sure," he says, not really offended or embarrassed. "I asked for and got it and should be satisfied. Excuse me," and he walks away and stands near the edge

45

of the platform, never turning around to me. When the local comes, he gets on it.

Maybe I shouldn't have been that sharp with him, but I don't like to be spoken to by men I don't know, especially in subways.

Next Saturday around the same time he comes downstairs again and stops by my bench. 50

"Hello," he says.

I don't say anything and look the other way.

"Still none of my business why you sit here every Saturday like this?"

I continue to look the other way.

"I should take a hint, right?" 55

"Do you think that's funny?"

"No."

"Then what do you want me to do, call a policeman?"

"Of course not. I'm sorry and I am being stupid."

"Look, I wouldn't call a policeman. You seem okay. You want to be friendly 60 or so it seems. You're curious besides, which is good. But to me it is solely my business and not yours why I am here and don't want to talk to you and so forth and I don't know why you'd want to persist in it."

"I understand," and he walks away, stays with his back to me and gets on the train when it comes.

Next Saturday he walks down the stairs and stays near the platform edge about ten feet away reading a book. Then he turns to me and seems just about to say something and I don't know what I'm going to say in return, if anything, because he does seem polite and nice and intelligent and I actually looked forward a little to seeing and speaking civilly to him, when the train comes. He waves to me and gets on it. I lift my hand to wave back but quickly put it down. Why start?

Next Saturday he runs down the stairs to catch the train that's pulling in. He doesn't even look at me this time, so in a rush is he to get on the car. He gets past the doors just before they close and has his back to me when the train leaves. He must be late for someplace.

The next Saturday he comes down the stairs and walks over to me with two containers of coffee or tea while the train's pulling in. He keeps walking to me while the train doors open, close, and the train goes. I look at the advertisement clock. He's about fifteen minutes earlier than usual.

"How do you like your coffee if I can ask, black or regular? Or maybe you 65 don't want any from me, if you do drink coffee, which would of course be all right too."

"Regular, but I don't want any, thanks."

"Come on, take it, it's not toxic and I can drink my coffee any old way. And it'll perk you up, not that you need perking up and certainly not from me," and he gives me a container. "Sugar?" and I say "Really, this is—" and he says "Come on: sugar?" and I nod and he pulls out of his jacket pocket a couple of sugar packets and a stirring stick. "I just took these on the way out of the shop without waiting for a bag, don't ask me why. The stick's probably a bit dirty, do you mind?" and I shake my head and wipe the stick though there's nothing on it. "Mind if I sit and have my coffee also?" and I say "Go ahead. It's not my bench and all that and I'd be afraid to think what you'd pull out of your pocket if I said no—probably your own bench and cocktail table," and he says "Don't be silly," and sits.

He starts talking about the bench, how the same oak one has been here for at least thirty years because that's how long he's lived in the neighborhood, then about the coffee, that it's good though always from the shop upstairs a little bitter, then why he happens to see me every Saturday: that he's recently divorced and has a child by that marriage who he goes to in Brooklyn once a week to spend the whole day with. He seems even nicer and more intelligent than I thought and comfortable to be with and for the first time I think he's maybe even goodlooking when before I thought his ears stuck out too far and he had too thin a mouth and small a nose. He dresses well anyway and has a nice profile and his hair's stylish and neat and his face shaven clean which I like and no excessive jewelry or neck chain which I don't and in his other jacket pocket are a paperback and small ribbon-wrapped package, the last I guess a present for his little girl.

His train comes and when the doors open I say "Shouldn't you get on it?" and he says "I'll take the next one if you don't mind," and I say "I don't think it's up to me to decide," and he hunches his shoulders and gives me that expression "Well I don't know what to say," and the train goes and when it's quiet again he continues the conversation, now about what I think of something that happened in Africa yesterday which he read in the paper today. I tell him I didn't read it and that maybe when I do read my paper it won't be the same as his and so might not have that news story and he says "What paper you read?" and I tell him and he says "Same one—front page, left-hand column," and I say "Anyway, on Saturdays I don't, and for my own reasons, have time for the newspaper till I get home later and really also don't have the time to just sit here and talk," and he says "Of course, of course," but seriously, as if he believes me, and we're silent for a while, drinking our coffees and looking at the tracks.

We hear another train coming and I say "I think you better get on this one," 70 and he says "Okay. It's been great and I hope I haven't been too much of a nuisance," and I say "You really haven't at all," and he says "Mind if I ask your name?" and I say "Your train," and he yells to the people going into the subway car "Hold the door," and gets up and says to me "Mine's Vaughn," and shakes my hand and says "Next week," and runs to the train with his container and he's not past the door a second when the man who kept it open for him lets it close.

I picture him on his way to Brooklyn, reading his book, later in Prospect Park with his daughter as he said they would do if the good weather holds up and in an indoor ice-skating rink if it doesn't, and then go back to my lookout. People spit and throw trash on the tracks, a drunk or crazy man urinates on the platform, a boy defaces the tile wall with a marker pen and tells me to go shoot myself when I very politely suggest he stop, there's almost a fight between a man trying to get off the train and the one blocking his way who's trying to get on, which I doubt would have happened if both sides of the double door had opened, but again no sign of my two young men.

Vaughn's not there the next Saturday and the Saturday after that and the third Saturday he's not there I begin thinking that I'm thinking more about him than I do of anybody or thing and spending more time looking at the staircase and around the platform for him than I do for those young men. I've gradually lost interest in finding them and over the last four months my chances have gotten worse and worse that I'll even recognize them if they ever do come down here and as far as their repeating that harassing-the-girl incident at this particular station, well forget it, and I leave the station at noon instead of around my usual two and decide that was my last Saturday there.

A month later I meet Vaughn coming out of a supermarket when I'm going in. He's pulling a shopping cart filled with clean laundry at the bottom and two big grocery bags on top. It's Saturday, we're both dressed in T- shirts and shorts for the warm weather now, and I stop him by saying "Vaughn, how are you?" He looks at me as if he doesn't remember me. "Maybe because you can't place me anywhere else but on a subway bench. Maria Pierce. From the subway station over there."

"That's right. Suddenly your face was familiar, but you never gave me your name. What's been happening?" and I say "Nothing much I guess," and he says "You don't wait in subway stations anymore for whatever you were waiting for those days?" and I say "How would you know? You stopped coming yourself there and to tell you the truth I was sort of looking forward to a continuation of that nice chat we last had."

"Oh, let me tell you what went wrong. My ex-wife, giving me a day's notice, changed jobs and locations and took my daughter to Boston with her. I could have fought it, but don't like arguments. I only get to see her when I get up there, which hasn't happened yet, and maybe for August if I want."

"That's too bad. I remember how devoted you were."

"I don't know it's so bad. I'm beginning to enjoy my freedom every Saturday, as much as I miss my kid. But I got to go. Ice cream in the bag will soon be melting," and he says goodbye and goes.

If I knew his last name I might look him up in the phone book and call him and say something like "Since we live in the same neighborhood, would you care to have a cup of coffee one of these days? I owe you one and I'll even, if you're still curious, let you in on my big secret why I every Saturday for months waited at our favorite subway station." Then I think no, even if I did have his phone number. I gave him on the street a couple of openings to make overtures about seeing me again and he didn't take them because he didn't want to or whatever his reasons but certainly not because of his melting ice cream.

Several weeks later I read in the newspaper that those two young men got caught. They were in the Eighth Street subway station and tried to molest a policewoman dressed like an artist with even a sketchbook and drawing pen, and two plain-clothesmen were waiting nearby. The police connected them up with Eliot's death. The two men later admitted to being on my subway platform that day but said they only started a fight with him because he tried to stop one of them from making a date with a girl the young man once knew. They said they told Eliot to mind his business, he refused, so they wrestled him to the ground and then said he could get up if he didn't make any more trouble. Eliot said okay, got up and immediately swung at them, missed, lost his footing and before either of them could grab him away, fell to the tracks. They got scared and ran to the street. They don't know the girl's last name or where she lives except that it's somewhere in the Bronx.

I buy all the newspapers that day and the next. One of them has a photo of the young men sticking their middle fingers up to the news photographers. They don't look anything like the young men I was on the lookout for, so either the witness's description of them or the printing of the photograph was bad, because I don't see how they could have physically changed so much in just a few months.

I continue to read the papers for weeks after that, hoping to find something about the young men going to trial, but don't. Then a month later a co-worker of mine who knew about Eliot and me says she saw on the television last night that the young men were allowed to plead guilty to a lesser charge of negligent manslaughter or something and got off with a jail term of from one to three years. "It seems the elderly man, that main witness to Eliot's murder, died of a fatal disease a while ago and the young woman witness could never be found. As for molesting the policewoman, that charge was dropped, though the news reporter never said why."

ANDRE DUBUS (b. 1936)

The Curse   *1988*

Mitchell Hayes was forty-nine years old, but when the cops left him in the bar with Bob, the manager, he felt much older. He did not know what it was like to be very old, a shrunken and wrinkled man, but he assumed it was like this: fatigue beyond relieving by rest, by sleep. He also was not a small man: his weight moved up and down in the hundred and seventies and he was five feet, ten inches tall. But now his body seemed short and thin. Both stood at one end of the bar; he was a large blackhaired man, and there was nothing in front of him but an ash tray he was using. He looked at Mitchell at the cash register and said: "Forget it. You heard what Smitty said."

Mitchell looked away, at the front door. He had put the chairs upside down on the table. He looked from the door past Bob to the empty space of floor at the rear; sometimes people danced there, to the jukebox. Opposite Bob, on the wall behind the bar, was a telephone; Mitchell looked at it. He had told Smitty there were five guys and when he moved to the phone one of them stepped around the corner of the bar and shoved him: one hand against Mitchell's chest, and it pushed him backward; he nearly fell. That was when they were getting rough with her at the bar. When they took her to the floor Mitchell looked once at her sounds, then looked down at the duckboard he stood on, or at the belly or chest of a young man in front of him.

He knew they were not drunk. They had been drinking before they came to his place, a loud popping of motorcycles outside, then walking into the empty bar, young and sunburned and carrying helmets and wearing thick leather jackets in August. They stood in front of Mitchell and drank drafts. When he took their first order he thought they were on drugs and later, watching them, he was certain. They were not relaxed, in the way of most drinkers near closing time. Their eyes were quick, alert as wary animals, and they spoke loudly, with passion, but their passion was strange and disturbing, because they were only chatting, bantering. Mitchell knew nothing of the effects of drugs, so could not guess what was in their blood. He feared and hated drugs because of his work and because he was the stepfather of teenagers: a boy and a girl. He gave last call and served them and leaned against the counter behind him.

Then the door opened and the girl walked in from the night, a girl he had never seen, and she crossed the floor toward Mitchell. He stepped forward to tell her she had missed last call, but before he spoke she asked for change for the cigarette machine. She was young, he guessed nineteen to twenty-one, and deeply tanned and had dark hair. She was sober and wore jeans and a dark blue tee shirt. He gave her the quarters but she was standing between two of the men and she did not get to the machine.

When it was over and she lay crying on the cleared circle of floor, he left   5
the bar and picked up the jeans and tee shirt beside her and crouched and handed them to her. She did not look at him. She lay the clothes across her breasts and what Mitchell thought of now as her wound. He left her and dialed 911, then Bob's number. He woke up Bob. Then he picked up her sneakers from the floor and placed them beside her and squatted near her face, her crying. He wanted to speak to her and touch her, hold a hand or press her brow, but he could not.

The cruiser was there quickly, the siren coming east from town, then slowing and deepening as the car stopped outside. He was glad Smitty was one of them; he had gone to high school with Smitty. The other was Dave, and Mitchell knew him because it was a small town. When they saw the girl Dave went out to the cruiser to call for an ambulance, and when he came back he said two other cruisers had those scumbags and were taking them in. The girl was still crying and could not talk to Smitty and Dave. She was crying when a man and woman lifted her onto a stretcher and rolled her out the door and she vanished forever in a siren.

Bob came in while Smitty and Dave were sitting at the bar drinking coffee and Smitty was writing his report; Mitchell stood behind the bar. Bob sat next to Dave as Mitchell said: "I could have stopped them, Smitty."

"That's our job," Smitty said. "You want to be in the hospital now?"

Mitchell did not answer. When Smitty and Dave left, he got a glass of Coke from the cobra and had a cigarette with Bob. They did not talk. Then Mitchell washed his glass and Bob's cup and they left, turning off the lights. Outside Mitchell locked the front door, feeling the sudden night air after almost ten hours of air conditioning. When he had come to work the day had been very hot, and now he thought it would not have happened in winter. They had stopped for a beer on their way somewhere from the beach; he had heard them say that. But the beach was not the reason. He did not know the reason, but he knew it would not have happened in winter. The night was cool and now he could smell trees. He turned and looked at the road in front of the bar. Bob stood beside him on the small porch.

"If the regulars had been here," Bob said.   10

He turned and with his hand resting on the wooden rail he walked down the ramp to the ground. At his car he stopped and looked over its roof at Mitchell.

"You take it easy," he said.

Mitchell nodded. When Bob got in his car and left, he went down the ramp and drove home to his house on a street that he thought was neither good nor bad. The houses were small and there were old large houses used now as apartments for families. Most of the people had work, most of the mothers cared for their children, and most of the children were clean and looked like they lived in homes, not caves like some he saw in town. He worried about the older kids, one group of them anyway. They were idle. When he was a boy in a town farther up the Merrimack River, he and his friends committed every mischievous act he could recall on afternoons and nights when they were idle. His stepchildren were not part of that group. They had friends from the high school. The front porch light was on for him and one in the kitchen at the rear of the house. He went in the front door and switched off the porch light and walked through the living and dining rooms to the kitchen. He got a can of beer from the refrigerator, turned out the light, and sat at the table. When he could see, he took a cigarette from Susan's pack in front of him.

Down the hall he heard Susan move on the bed then get up and he hoped it wasn't for the bathroom but for him. He had met her eight years ago when he had given up on ever marrying and having kids, then one night she came into the bar with two of her girl friends from work. She made six dollars an hour going to homes of invalids, mostly what she called her little old ladies, and bathing them. She got the house from her marriage, and child support the guy paid for a few months till he left town and went south. She came barefoot down the hall and stood in the kitchen doorway and said: "Are you all right?"

"No."   15

She sat across from him, and he told her. Very soon she held his hand. She was good. He knew if he had fought all five of them and was lying in pieces in a hospital bed she would tell him he had done the right thing, as she was telling him now. He liked her strong hand on his. It was a professional hand and he wanted from her something he had never wanted before: to lie in bed while she bathed him. When they went to bed he did not think he would be able to sleep, but she kneeled beside him and massaged his shoulders and rubbed his temples and pressed her hands on his forehead. He woke to the voices of Marty and Joyce in the kitchen. They had summer jobs, and always when they woke him he went back to sleep till noon, but now he got up and dressed and went to the kitchen door. Susan was at the stove, her back to him, and Marty and Joyce were talking and smoking. He said good morning, and stepped into the room.

"What are you doing up?" Joyce said.

She was a pretty girl with her mother's wide cheekbones and Marty was a tall good-looking boy, and Mitchell felt as old as he had before he slept. Susan was watching him. Then she poured him a cup of coffee and put it at his place and he sat. Marty said: "You getting up for the day?"

"Something happened last night. At the bar." They tried to conceal their excitement, but he saw it in their eyes. "I should have stopped it. I think I *could* have stopped it. That's the point. There were these five guys. They were on motorcycles but they weren't bikers. Just punks. They came in late, when everybody else had gone home. It was a slow night anyway. Everybody was at the beach."

"They rob you?" Marty said.   20

"No. A girl came in. Young. Nice looking. You know: just a girl, minding her business."

They nodded, and their eyes were apprehensive.

"She wanted cigarette change, that's all. Those guys were on dope. Coke or something. You know: they were flying in place."

"Did they rape her?" Joyce said.

"Yes, honey."   25

"The *fuckers*."

Susan opened her mouth then closed it and Joyce reached quickly for Susan's pack of cigarettes. Mitchell held his lighter for her and said: "When they started getting rough with her at the bar I went for the phone. One of them stopped me. He shoved me, that's all. I should have hit him with a bottle."

Marty reached over the table with his big hand and held Mitchell's shoulder.

"No, Mitch. Five guys that mean. And coked up or whatever. No way. You wouldn't be here this morning."

"I don't know. There was always a guy with me. But just one guy, taking turns."   30

"Great," Joyce said. Marty's hand was on Mitchell's left shoulder; she put hers on his right hand.

"They took her to the hospital," he said. "The guys are in jail."

"They are?" Joyce said.

"I called the cops. When they left."

"You'll be a good witness," Joyce said.   35

He looked at her proud face.

"At the trial," she said.

The day was hot but that night most of the regulars came to the bar. Some of the younger ones came on motorcycles. They were a good crowd: they all worked, except the retired ones and no one ever bothered the women, not even the young ones with their summer tans. Everyone talked about it: some had read the newspaper story, some had heard the story in town, and they wanted to hear it from Mitchell. He told it as often as they asked but he did not finish it because he was working hard and could not stay with any group of customers long enough.

He watched their faces. Not one of them, even the women, looked at him as if he had not cared enough for the girl, or was a coward. Many of them even appeared sympathetic, making him feel for moments that he was a survivor of something horrible, and when that feeling left him he was ashamed. He felt tired and old, making drinks and change, moving and talking up and down the bar. At the stool at the far end Bob drank coffee and whenever Mitchell looked at him he smiled or nodded and once raised his right fist, with the thumb up.

Reggie was drinking too much. He did that two or three times a month and   40
Mitchell had to shut him off and Reggie always took it humbly. He was a big gentle man with a long brown beard. But tonight shutting off Reggie demanded from Mitchell an act of will, and when the eleven o'clock news came on the television and Reggie ordered another shot and a draft, Mitchell pretended not to hear him. He served the customers at the other end of the bar, where Bob was. He could hear Reggie calling: Hey Mitch; shot and a draft, Mitch. Mitchell was close to Bob now. Bob said softly: "He's had enough."

Mitchell nodded and went to Reggie, leaned closer to him so he could speak quietly, and said: "Sorry, Reggie. Time for coffee. I don't want you dead out there."

Reggie blinked at him.

"Okay, Mitch." He pulled some bills from his pocket and put them on the bar. Mitchell glanced at them and saw at least a ten dollar tip. When he rang up Reggie's tab the change was sixteen dollars and fifty cents, and he dropped the coins and shoved the bills into the beer mug beside the cash register. The mug was full of bills, as it was on most nights, and he kept his hand in there, pressing Reggie's into the others, and saw the sunburned young men holding her down on the floor and one kneeling between her legs, spread and held, and he heard their cheering voices and her screaming and groaning and finally weeping and weeping and weeping, until she was the siren crying then fading into the night. From the floor behind him, far across the room, he felt her pain and terror and grief, then her curse upon him. The curse moved into his back and spread down and up his spine, into his stomach and legs and arms and shoulders until he quivered with it. He wished he were alone so he could kneel to receive it.

GABRIEL GARCÍA MÁRQUEZ   (b. 1928)

A Very Old Man with Enormous Wings   *1971*

Translated by Gregory Rabassa

A TALE FOR CHILDREN

On the third day of rain they had killed so many crabs inside the house that Pelayo had to cross his drenched courtyard and throw them into the sea, because the newborn child had a temperature all night and they thought it was due to the stench. The world had been sad since Tuesday. Sea and sky were a single ash-gray thing and the sands of the beach, which on March nights glimmered like powdered light, had become a stew of mud and rotten shellfish. The light was so weak at noon that when Pelayo was coming back to the house after throwing away the crabs, it was hard for him to see what it was that was moving and groaning in the rear of the courtyard. He had to go very close to see that it was an old man, a very old man, lying face down in the mud, who, in spite of his tremendous efforts, couldn't get up, impeded by his enormous wings.

Frightened by that nightmare, Pelayo ran to get Elisenda, his wife, who was putting compresses on the sick child, and he took her to the rear of the courtyard. They both looked at the fallen body with mute stupor. He was dressed like a ragpicker. There were only a few faded hairs left on his bald skull and very few teeth in his mouth, and his pitiful condition of a drenched great-grandfather had taken away any sense of grandeur he might have had. His huge buzzard wings, dirty and half-plucked, were forever entangled in the mud. They looked at him so long and so closely that Pelayo and Elisenda very soon overcame their surprise and in the end found him familiar. Then they dared speak to him, and he answered in an incomprehensible dialect with a strong sailor's voice. That was how they skipped over the inconvenience of the wings and quite intelligently concluded that he was a lonely castaway from some foreign ship wrecked by the storm. And yet, they called in a neighbor woman who knew everything about life and death to see him, and all she needed was one look to show them their mistake.

"He's an angel," she told them. "He must have been coming for the child, but the poor fellow is so old that the rain knocked him down."

On the following day everyone knew that a flesh-and-blood angel was held captive in Pelayo's house. Against the judgment of the wise neighbor woman, for whom angels in those times were the fugitive survivors of a celestial conspiracy, they did not have the heart to club him to death. Pelayo watched over him all afternoon from the kitchen, armed with his bailiff's club, and before going to bed he dragged him out of the mud and locked him up with the hens in the wire chicken coop. In the middle of the night, when the rain stopped, Pelayo and

Elisenda were still killing crabs. A short time afterward the child woke up without a fever and with a desire to eat. Then they felt magnanimous and decided to put the angel on a raft with fresh water and provisions for three days and leave him to his fate on the high seas. But when they went out into the courtyard with the first light of dawn, they found the whole neighborhood in front of the chicken coop having fun with the angel, without the slightest reverence, tossing him things to eat through the openings in the wire as if he weren't a supernatural creature but a circus animal.

Father Gonzaga arrived before seven o'clock, alarmed at the strange news. By that time onlookers less frivolous than those at dawn had already arrived and they were making all kinds of conjectures concerning the captive's future. The simplest among them thought that he should be named mayor of the world. Others of sterner mind felt that he should be promoted to the rank of five-star general in order to win all wars. Some visionaries hoped that he could be put to stud in order to implant on earth a race of winged wise men who could take charge of the universe. But Father Gonzaga, before becoming a priest, had been a robust woodcutter. Standing by the wire, he reviewed his catechism in an instant and asked them to open the door so that he could take a close look at that pitiful man who looked more like a huge decrepit hen among the fascinated chickens. He was lying in a corner drying his open wings in the sunlight among the fruit peels and breakfast leftovers that the early risers had thrown him. Alien to the impertinences of the world, he only lifted his antiquarian eyes and murmured something in his dialect when Father Gonzaga went into the chicken coop and said good morning to him in Latin. The parish priest had his first suspicion of an imposter when he saw that he did not understand the language of God or know how to greet His ministers. Then he noticed that seen close up he was much too human: he had an unbearable smell of the outdoors, the back side of his wings was strewn with parasites and his main feathers had been mistreated by terrestrial winds, and nothing about him measured up to the proud dignity of angels. Then he came out of the chicken coop and in a brief sermon warned the curious against the risks of being ingenuous. He reminded them that the devil had the bad habit of making use of carnival tricks in order to confuse the unwary.° He argued that if wings were not the essential element in determining the difference between a hawk and an airplane, they were even less so in the recognition of angels. Nevertheless, he promised to write a letter to his bishop so that the latter would write to his primate so that the latter would write to the Supreme Pontiff° in order to get the final verdict from the highest courts.

His prudence fell on sterile hearts. The news of the captive angel spread with such rapidity that after a few hours the courtyard had the bustle of a marketplace and they had to call in troops with fixed bayonets to disperse the mob that was about to knock the house down. Elisenda, her spine all twisted from sweeping up so much marketplace trash, then got the idea of fencing in the yard and charging five cents admission to see the angel.

The curious came from far away. A traveling carnival arrived with a flying acrobat who buzzed over the crowd several times, but no one paid any attention to him because his wings were not those of an angel but, rather, those of a sidereal

He . . . the unwary: See *Hamlet*, Act II, scene 2, lines 573–578, for a further explanation of this power of the devil.
Supreme Pontiff: the Pope in Rome.

bat. The most unfortunate invalids on earth came in search of health: a poor woman who since childhood had been counting her heartbeats and had run out of numbers; a Portuguese man who couldn't sleep because the noise of the stars disturbed him; a sleepwalker who got up at night to undo the things he had done while awake; and many others with less serious ailments. In the midst of that shipwreck disorder that made the earth tremble, Pelayo and Elisenda were happy with fatigue, for in less than a week they had crammed their rooms with money and the line of pilgrims waiting their turn to enter still reached beyond the horizon.

The angel was the only one who took no part in his own act. He spent his time trying to get comfortable in his borrowed nest, befuddled by the hellish heat of the oil lamps and sacramental candles that had been placed along the wire. At first they tried to make him eat some mothballs, which, according to the wisdom of the wise neighbor woman, were the food prescribed for angels. But he turned them down, just as he turned down the papal lunches that the penitents brought him, and they never found out whether it was because he was an angel or because he was an old man that in the end he ate nothing but eggplant mush. His only supernatural virtue seemed to be patience. Especially during the first days, when the hens pecked at him, searching for the stellar parasites that proliferated in his wings, and the cripples pulled out feathers to touch their defective parts with, and even the most merciful threw stones at him, trying to get him to rise so they could see him standing. The only time they succeeded in arousing him was when they burned his side with an iron for branding steers, for he had been motionless for so many hours that they thought he was dead. He awoke with a start, ranting in his hermetic language and with tears in his eyes, and he flapped his wings a couple of times, which brought on a whirlwind of chicken dung and lunar dust and a gale of panic that did not seem to be of this world. Although many thought that his reaction had been one not of rage but of pain, from then on they were careful not to annoy him, because the majority understood that his passivity was not that of a hero taking his ease but that of a cataclysm in repose.

Father Gonzaga held back the crowd's frivolity with formulas of maidservant inspiration while awaiting the arrival of a final judgment on the nature of the captive. But the mail from Rome showed no sense of urgency. They spent their time finding out if the prisoner had a navel, if his dialect had any connection with Aramaic, how many times he could fit on the head of a pin, or whether he wasn't just a Norwegian with wings. Those meager letters might have come and gone until the end of time if a providential event had not put an end to the priest's tribulations.

It so happened that during those days, among so many other carnival attractions, there arrived in town the traveling show of the woman who had been changed into a spider for having disobeyed her parents. The admission to see her was not only less than the admission to see the angel, but people were permitted to ask her all manner of questions about her absurd state and to examine her up and down so that no one would ever doubt the truth of her horror. She was a frightful tarantula the size of a ram and with the head of a sad maiden. What was most heart-rending, however, was not her outlandish shape but the sincere affliction with which she recounted the details of her misfortune. While still practically a child she had sneaked out of her parents' house to go to a dance, and while she was coming back through the woods after having danced all night without

10

permission, a fearful thunderclap rent the sky in two and through the crack came the lightning bolt of brimstone that changed her into a spider. Her only nourishment came from the meatballs that charitable souls chose to toss into her mouth. A spectacle like that, full of so much human truth and with such a fearful lesson, was bound to defeat without even trying that of a haughty angel who scarcely deigned to look at mortals. Besides, the few miracles attributed to the angel showed a certain mental disorder, like the blind man who didn't recover his sight but grew three new teeth, or the paralytic who didn't get to walk but almost won the lottery, and the leper whose sores sprouted sunflowers. Those consolation miracles, which were more like mocking fun, had already ruined the angel's reputation when the woman who had been changed into a spider finally crushed him completely. That was how Father Gonzaga was cured forever of his insomnia and Pelayo's courtyard went back to being as empty as during the time it had rained for three days and crabs walked through the bedrooms.

The owners of the house had no reason to lament. With the money they saved they built a two-story mansion with balconies and gardens and high netting so that crabs wouldn't get in during the winter, and with iron bars on the windows so that angels wouldn't get in. Pelayo also set up a rabbit warren close to town and gave up his job as bailiff for good, and Elisenda bought some satin pumps with high heels and many dresses of iridescent silk, the kind worn on Sunday by the most desirable women in those times. The chicken coop was the only thing that didn't receive any attention. If they washed it down with creolin° and burned tears of myrrh° inside it every so often, it was not in homage to the angel but to drive away the dungheap stench that still hung everywhere like a ghost and was turning the new house into an old one. At first, when the child learned to walk, they were careful that he not get too close to the chicken coop. But then they began to lose their fears and got used to the smell, and before the child got his second teeth he'd gone inside the chicken coop to play, where the wires were falling apart. The angel was no less standoffish with him than with other mortals, but he tolerated the most ingenious infamies with the patience of a dog who had no illusions. They both came down with chicken pox at the same time. The doctor who took care of the child couldn't resist the temptation to listen to the angel's heart, and he found so much whistling in the heart and so many sounds in his kidneys that it seemed impossible for him to be alive. What surprised him most, however, was the logic of his wings. They seemed so natural on that completely human organism that he couldn't understand why other men didn't have them too.

When the child began school it had been some time since the sun and rain had caused the collapse of the chicken coop. The angel went dragging himself about here and there like a stray dying man. They would drive him out of the bedroom with a broom and a moment later find him in the kitchen. He seemed to be in so many places at the same time that they grew to think that he'd been duplicated, that he was reproducing himself all through the house, and the exasperated and unhinged Elisenda shouted that it was awful living in that hell full of angels. He could scarcely eat and his antiquarian eyes had also become so foggy that he went about bumping into posts. All he had left were the bare

creolin: creosote-based disinfectant.
myrrh: fragrant plant resin used in making incense and perfume.

cannulae° of his last feathers. Pelayo threw a blanket over him and extended him the charity of letting him sleep in the shed, and only then did they notice that he had a temperature at night, and was delirious with the tongue twisters of an old Norwegian. That was one of the few times they became alarmed, for they thought he was going to die and not even the wise neighbor woman had been able to tell them what to do with dead angels.

And yet he not only survived his worst winter, but seemed improved with the first sunny days. He remained motionless for several days in the farthest corner of the courtyard, where no one would see him, and at the beginning of December some large, stiff feathers began to grow on his wings, the feathers of a scarecrow, which looked more like another misfortune of decrepitude. But he must have known the reason for those changes, for he was quite careful that no one should notice them, that no one should hear the sea chanteys that he sometimes sang under the stars. One morning Elisenda was cutting some bunches of onions for lunch when a wind that seemed to come from the high seas blew into the kitchen. Then she went to the window and caught the angel in his first attempts at flight. They were so clumsy that his fingernails opened a furrow in the vegetable patch and he was on the point of knocking the shed down with the ungainly flapping that slipped on the light and couldn't get a grip on the air. But he did manage to gain altitude. Elisenda let out a sigh of relief, for herself and for him, when she saw him pass over the last houses, holding himself up in some way with the risky flapping of a senile vulture. She kept watching him even when she was through cutting the onions and she kept on watching until it was no longer possible for her to see him, because then he was no longer an annoyance in her life but an imaginary dot on the horizon of the sea.

ELLEN GILCHRIST (b. 1935)

The Song of Songs   *1989*

It was Christmas morning. A bright clear day. Almost cool. The city of New Orleans lay in peace. Sleeeeep in heavenly peeeeace. Sleep in heavenly peace.° Strains of hymns from midnight mass echoed in the ears of the faithful. For unto us a child is born. Unto us a son is given.° The smell of lilies and candles. Morning. Children were waking. Cats prowled the marble floors of the mansions of the Garden District and the lesser mansions of the Lower Garden District and the Victorian houses of the university section.

Barrett Clare had slept like a baby on two Valiums and a Seconal, safe in the high bedroom of the biggest whitest house on State Street. She had fought for that house. If it had been up to him, Charlie Clare would have settled for the old Phipps place, that tacky brick box.

She opened her eyes. The sun was slanting in the wooden shutters, casting bright demarcations over everything on the floor, her red wool dress, her De Liso Debs, her satin, hand-embroidered slip, her underpants, her bra. She had slept alone in the walnut bed. I have always been alone, she thought, and rose from

cannulae: hollow central stems of feathers.
Sleeeeep . . . peace: from the Christmas hymn "Silent Night."
For . . . given: chorus from *Messiah* (1741) by George Frideric Handel (1685–1759).

the bed, shaking off the fuzzy feeling of the drugs, worrying that Charles was already awake, looking for her. Her baby, her one and only love, her boy. Damn, she thought, and shook her head again. The Seconal was too much. That was going too far. Still, it was better than not sleeping. It was better than dreams.

She picked up the slacks she had been wearing the day before and squeezed them in her hand. She had been wearing them when the tall blond boy came with his terrible message. That nightmare. Only it was true. He had come out of nowhere at eleven o'clock in the morning on Christmas Eve to tell her where her mother was. Her real mother, the one that had borne her into the world and given her away. She never touched me, Barrett had told Gustave over and over. No, I know she didn't. I would remember if she had. No one can remember that far back, he would say, and move around ever so gradually in his old brown chair. An enormous response from Gustave. She never touched me, Barrett would insist. I know. I would know. They got me from the home when I was five days old. I weighed eight pounds. I was a huge baby. I was alone when I was born and I have been alone ever since. She had me and then she never even looked at me. Gustave would move again in his chair. When she talked of *it* at least he listened. Well, he always listened. He was a wonderful doctor. A member of the Academy. He was the best. The very best. The best that money could buy.

Where was he now that she needed him? Where had he gone to? How dare 5
he leave town at Christmas. Why couldn't they find him? They could find him if they really wanted to. She sat down on the bed and rang his answering service.

"You know you can find him. You must tell him it's an emergency. Tell him it's Barrett, Barrett Clare. You must reach him for me. All right, I'll be waiting. Yes, please try." She hung up. Who do they think they are? Those answering-service people.

Amanda McCamey is my mother. I'll call her on the phone. The thought was like an arrow. It flew across the room and disappeared. No, it's her place to call me. If she knows where I am. Your mother is named Amanda McCamey and she is up in Arkansas and she is going to have a baby any day now. That is what the blond boy said. I am going there now. I will tell her that I told you.

I'll go too, she had answered. I will go and talk to her. You can't go, he said. She is going to have a baby. She doesn't know you know. She doesn't know I'm here.

I want to tell someone, Barrett thought. I need to tell someone who my mother is. She is so beautiful. Didn't I touch her? That day at Loyola? When Brummette introduced us. I think I touched her. I think I shook her hand. She called me Shelley. She thought my name was Shelley. Why hasn't she called me if she knows who I am? Here is your mother, the blond boy said. And now I am taking her away.

A rush of fuzziness passed across her brain. She shook her head. She picked 10
up Charlie's coat from the chair and started going through the pockets looking for a cigarette. He had come in from Vail at three or four. He had tried to get in bed with her. "It was a snowstorm, baby. They closed the airport. I couldn't help it."

"Get out of here, you bastard. Don't get near me."

"It's Christmas," he said.

"Go away, Charlie."

She went into the dressing room and washed her face and hands. She combed her hair. She looked deep into the mirror, searching her face for the face of her mother. It was there. Yes, anyone could see it. I could go on living, she thought. If it never would be Christmas. If I never had to hang that dead tree in the window. Well, Charles will be waking up. I must act normal. I must act like everything's okay. It's Christmas morning. She laughed at that. Suddenly her sadness and self-absorption seemed the silliest thing in all New Orleans.

She went downstairs and found Charles and Charlie in the breakfast room. 15
Charlie still looked drunk. He was reading the paper. Charles had already started opening his presents. "Daddy slept with me," he said. "In my bed." He tore open a package containing a white shirt with his initials on the cuffs. He pulled it out of the package and took the pins out and tried it on. He was five years old, a sturdy wild little boy, excitable, hard to control.

The shirt was too big. The cuffs came down and hid his new Rolex watch. "It hides my watch," he said. "It doesn't fit. You have to take it back."

"You aren't supposed to be opening things yet," Charlie said. "I told you to wait for her. Is Lorraine coming, Barrett? Are we going to have breakfast?"

"She'll be here later. She has to cook for her family. I'll make breakfast. How was Vail?" He didn't answer. She rolled up the sleeves of her robe and set the table with red placemats and a set of Christmas china Charlie's sister had given them the year before. In a while she put a breakfast of bacon and eggs on the plates.

"Let's sit together now," she said. "Let's hold hands and say grace. Charles, do you want to say the prayer?" They were holding hands around the table. She could feel the thick wiry hair on Charlie's hand, tough reddish blond hair. Wire, she thought. Like his mind. A piece of wire. I'll put that in a poem.

At least there's Patsy, he was thinking. God love her soft little buns. God 20
love her laughter.

"Lord make us thankful for these and all our many other blessings, for Christ's sake, amen. Ahh, men. That's what old maids say, isn't it, Daddy?"

"You all go on and eat," Barrett said. "I'm going upstairs for a while." She reached over and hugged the little boy. "I love you, Sweetie Pie," she said. "Don't you ever forget that." Charlie sighed and put butter on a biscuit. He took a bite and put the other half on Charles's plate. They were beautiful plates, white porcelain decorated with holly. "I love you too, Charlie," she said. "No matter what you do." She gave him a very small kiss on the cheek.

"Don't you want to see your presents?"

"Not yet," she said. She unrolled the sleeves of her robe and walked out of the kitchen past the painted porch swing. she was the only woman in town with a porch swing in her kitchen. She walked into the hall and up the stairs past the stained-glass window depicting Saint George slaying the dragon. She walked into Charlie's room and took a pistol with handmade wooden handles out of a gun case and walked over to the window looking out on the avenue. Now I will pull the trigger and blow my old blue and brown coiled-up brains all over the Pande Camaroon and some will spill on the Andrew Wyeth and, why not, some of them can move out onto the balcony and festoon the iron railings. You know, they will say, those old railings New Orleans is so famous for? Yes, it will make a good story around town. It will make everybody's day. They'll forget themselves in the story of my willfulness.

She put the gun in her mouth and sucked the barrel. It was a game she 25 liked to play. It was the only power she knew she had. The phone was ringing, a lovely ring, soft, like bells. Barrett took it down from its hanger on the wall. "Is this Barrett Clare?" the voice said. The voice was tearing into her ears. "This is Amanda McCamey. I am your mother. If this is Mrs. Charles Clare. If you are an adopted child. I am your mother. Oh, forgive me, oh, my God, forgive me. I need you so terribly dreadfully much. Will you talk to me? Will you let me talk to you?"

"This is me," she said. "I knew you would call me up. I've been waiting all day."

"I've been waiting all my life," the voice said. "Forgive me for calling you instead of coming there. I should have come. But I can't come for several days, perhaps a week. Will you come to me? Will you come to where I am? Will you bring your little boy? Your father will be here. I will have him here. He's the one that found you. I'll send him for you. Oh, yes, that's what I'll do."

"No," Barrett said. "Don't do that. I'll come today. Tell me where to go. Tell me how to get there." There was a sound on the other end, like sobbing, or something else, something she had never heard. "Don't cry," she said to her mother. "I am going to come to where you are as fast as I can get there. And I'm bringing Charles, my little boy. I will stay a long long time . . . I might come and stay forever. I might not ever leave. Can you hear me? I know you. Do you know that? I know who you are."

"How is that? How do you know?"

"I mean we met. At Loyola. Don Brummette introduced us. I used to read   30
everything you wrote. I guess I had a crush on you that year."

"What do you look like? How could I not have known? I can't remember. So many things have happened today. A friend of mine was in a terrible wreck, someone I love. And everything else. Are you really coming here? You will come to me? You will come here?"

"I'm coming as soon as I can pack a bag and leave. I look like you. Yes, I think I look like you. We will look in a mirror. The two of us. We will look at one another. Tell me where you are. How to get there. How to go."

"Here's Katie," Amanda said. "She's my friend. She'll tell you what to do." Then a woman named Katie got on the phone and told Barrett how to get to Fayetteville, Arkansas, from New Orleans, Louisiana. It was not that simple. "I'll be there this afternoon," Barrett said. "Tell my mother that I love her. Tell her I'll be there very soon." She put the phone back on the wall and picked the gun up off the dresser and walked across the room and put it back into the case and turned the key. Then she took the key and walked out on the balcony and threw it far out into the branches of a Japanese magnolia tree. Then she ran down the stairs to her husband and her child.

Charlie was sitting on the floor in a sea of wrapping paper drinking a brandy and playing with Charles. The great hanging tree for which the Clares were famous on State Street swayed softly above him. "Well," he said. "You're going to join us. How charming of you, Barrett."

"My mother just called me on the phone," she said. "My real mother. The   35
one who had me. I'm going there today and taking Charles with me. Now get up please and help me. I want you to call and charter us a plane. She lives up in Arkansas. It's a long way and inaccessible. Do it right now, Charlie. This is not a joke. Something's happened to her. She needs me."

"Your mother?"

"Yes, my mother. Please get me a plane right now, Charlie. While I pack. Charles, you are going with me somewhere. We're going to see your grandmother. Your real grandmother. Someone you've never seen." The child did not move, but her husband, Charlie, got up. He came toward her, reaching out to her. "All right," he said. "That's wonderful. What else? What else can I do?"

"What will we wear?" Charles said. "What will we take to wear?"

"It doesn't matter what we wear," she said. "We're going to see my mother. My mother. I'm going to see my mother." She picked him up off the floor and hugged him fiercely and danced him around the room. I exist, she was singing inside her head. I am here. I am really here. Everything that happens from this day forward will be better. Whatever happens next will be better and better and better. My mother is waiting for me.

A woman named Katie met them at the airport and drove them to a house   40
on top of a small mountain overlooking the university. "It was brave of you to come like this," Katie said. "What a brave thing to do."

"Where are we?" Charles said. "I don't know where we are."

Then they turned into a driveway and Barrett's mother was standing in the doorway of a small wooden house. A tall woman with hair that fell like a cascade almost to her waist. She walked out across the yard and took her daughter into her arms.

NADINE GORDIMER   (b. 1923)

The Moment Before the Gun Went Off   *1988*

Marais Van der Vyver shot one of his farm laborers, dead. An accident, there are accidents with guns every day of the week—children playing a fatal game with a father's revolver in the cities where guns are domestic objects, nowadays, hunting mishaps like this one, in the country—but these won't be reported all over the world. Van der Vyver knows his will be. He knows that the story of the Afrikaner farmer—regional leader of the National Party and commandant of the local security commando—shooting a black man who worked for him will fit exactly *their* version of South Africa, it's made for them. They'll be able to use it in their boycott and divestment campaigns, it'll be another piece of evidence in their truth about the country. The papers at home will quote the story as it has appeared in the overseas press, and in the back and forth he and the black man will become those crudely drawn figures on anti-apartheid banners, units in statistics of white brutality against blacks quoted at the United Nations—he, whom they will gleefully be able to call "a leading member" of the ruling Party.

People in the farming community understand how he must feel. Bad enough to have killed a man, without helping the Party's, the government's, the country's enemies as well. They see the truth of that. They know, reading the Sunday papers, that when Van der Vyver is quoted saying he is "terribly shocked," he will "look after the wife and children," none of those Americans and English, and none of those people at home who want to destroy the white man's power will believe him. And how they will sneer when he even says of the farm boy (according to one paper, if you can trust any of those reporters), "He was my friend, I always took him hunting with me." Those city and overseas people don't know it's true:

farmers usually have one particular black boy they like to take along with them in the lands; you could call it a kind of friend, yes, friends are not only your own white people, like yourself, whom you take into your house, pray with in church, and work with on the Party committee. But how can those others know that? They don't want to know it. They think all blacks are like the bigmouth agitators in town. And Van der Vyver's face in the photographs, strangely opened by distress— everyone in the district remembers Marais Van der Vyver as a little boy who would go away and hide himself if he caught you smiling at him, and everyone knows him now as a man who hides any change of expression round his mouth behind a thick, soft mustache, and in his eyes by always looking at some object in hand, a leaf or a crop fingered, pen or stone picked up, while concentrating on what he is saying, or while listening to you. It just goes to show what shock can do; when you look at the newspaper photographs you feel like apologizing, as if you had stared in on some room where you should not be.

There will be an inquiry; there had better be, to stop the assumption of yet another case of brutality against farm workers, although there's nothing in doubt— an accident, and all the facts fully admitted by Van der Vyver. He made a statement when he arrived at the police station with the dead man in his *bakkie*. Captain Beetge knows him well, of course; he gave him brandy. He was shaking, this big, calm, clever son of Willem Van der Vyver, who inherited the old man's best farm. The black was stone dead, nothing to be done for him. Beetge will not tell anyone that after the brandy Van der Vyver wept. He sobbed, snot running onto his hands, like a dirty kid. The captain was ashamed for him, and walked out to give him a chance to recover himself.

Marais Van der Vyver left his house at three in the afternoon to cull a buck from the family of kudu he protects in the bush areas of his farm. He is interested in wildlife and sees it as the farmers' sacred duty to raise game as well as cattle. As usual, he called at his shed to pick up Lucas, a twenty-year-old farmhand who had shown mechanical aptitude and whom Van der Vyver himself had taught to maintain tractors and other farm machinery. He hooted, and Lucas followed the familiar routine, jumping onto the back of the truck. He liked to travel standing up there, spotting game before his employer did. He would lean forward, bracing against the cab below him.

Van der Vyver had a rifle and .30 caliber ammunition beside him in the cab. The rifle was one of his father's, because his own was at the gunsmith's in town. Since his father died (Beetge's sergeant wrote "passed on") no one had used the rifle, and so when he took it from a cupboard he was sure it was not loaded. His father had never allowed a loaded gun in the house, he himself had been taught since childhood never to ride with a loaded weapon in a vehicle. But this gun was loaded. On a dirt track, Lucas thumped his fist on the cab roof three times to signal: look left. Having seen the white-ripple-marked flank of a kudu, and its fine horns raking through disguising bush, Van der Vyver drove rather fast over a pothole. The jolt fired the rifle. Upright, it was pointing straight through the cab roof at the head of Lucas. The bullet pierced the roof and entered Lucas's brain by way of his throat.

That is the statement of what happened. Although a man of such standing in the district, Van der Vyver had to go through the ritual of swearing that it was the truth. It has gone on record, and will be there in the archive of the local police

5

station as long as Van der Vyver lives, and beyond that, through the lives of his children, Magnus, Helena, and Karel—unless things in the country get worse, the example of black mobs in the town spreads to the rural areas and the place is burned down as many urban police stations have been. Because nothing the government can do will appease the agitators and the whites who encourage them. Nothing satisfies them, in the cities: blacks can sit and drink in white hotels now, the Immorality Act has gone, blacks can sleep with whites . . . It's not even a crime anymore.

Van der Vyver has a high, barbed security fence round his farmhouse and garden which his wife, Alida, thinks spoils completely the effect of her artificial stream with its tree ferns beneath the jacarandas. There is an aerial soaring like a flagpole in the backyard. All his vehicles, including the truck in which the black man died, have aerials that swing their whips when the driver hits a pothole: they are part of the security system the farmers in the district maintain, each farm in touch with every other by radio, twenty-four hours out of twenty-four. It has already happened that infiltrators from over the border have mined remote farm roads, killing white farmers and their families out on their own property for a Sunday picnic. The pothole could have set off a land mine, and Van der Vyver might have died with his farm boy. When neighbors use the communications system to call up and say they are sorry about "that business" with one of Van der Vyver's boys, there goes unsaid: it could have been worse.

It is obvious from the quality and fittings of the coffin that the farmer has provided money for the funeral. And an elaborate funeral means a great deal to blacks; look how they will deprive themselves of the little they have, in their lifetime, keeping up payments to a burial society so they won't go in boxwood to an unmarked grave. The young wife is pregnant (of course) and another little one, a boy wearing red shoes several sizes too large, leans under her jutting belly. He is too young to understand what has happened, what he is witnessing that day, but neither whines nor plays about; he is solemn without knowing why. Blacks expose small children to everything, they don't protect them from the sight of fear and pain the way whites do theirs. It is the young wife who rolls her head and cries like a child, sobbing on the breast of this relative and that. All present work for Van der Vyver or are the families of those who work; in the weeding and harvest seasons, the women and children work for him too, carried at sunrise to the fields, wrapped in their blankets, on a truck, singing. The dead man's mother is a woman who can't be more than in her late thirties (they start bearing children at puberty), but she is heavily mature in a black dress, standing between her own parents, who were already working for old Van der Vyver when Marais, like their daughter, was a child. The parents hold her as if she were a prisoner or a crazy woman to be restrained. But she says nothing, does nothing. She does not look up; she does not look at Van der Vyver, whose gun went off in the truck, she stares at the grave. Nothing will make her look up; there need be no fear that she will look up, at him. His wife, Alida, is beside him. To show the proper respect, as for any white funeral, she is wearing the navy blue and cream hat she wears to church this summer. She is always supportive, although he doesn't seem to notice it; this coldness and reserve—his mother says he didn't mix well as a child—she accepts for herself but regrets that it has prevented him from being nominated, as he should be, to stand as the Party's parliamentary candidate for the district.

He does not let her clothing, or that of anyone else gathered closely, make contact with him. He, too, stares at the grave. The dead man's mother and he stare at the grave in communication like that between the black man outside and the white man inside the cab the moment before the gun went off.

The moment before the gun went off was a moment of high excitement 10 shared through the roof of the cab, as the bullet was to pass, between the young black man outside and the white farmer inside the vehicle. There were such moments, without explanation, between them, although often around the farm the farmer would pass the young man without returning a greeting, as if he did not recognize him. When the bullet went off what Van der Vyver saw was the kudu stumble in fright at the report and gallop away. Then he heard the thud behind him, and past the window saw the young man fall out of the vehicle. He was sure he had leapt up and toppled—in fright, like the buck. The farmer was almost laughing with relief, ready to tease, as he opened his door, it did not seem possible that a bullet passing through the roof could have done harm.

The young man did not laugh with him at his own fright. The farmer carried him in his arms, to the truck. He was sure, sure he could not be dead. But the young black man's blood was all over the farmer's clothes, soaking against his flesh as he drove.

How will they ever know, when they file newspaper clippings, evidence, proof, when they look at the photographs and see his face—guilty! guilty! they are right!—how will they know, when the police stations burn with all the evidence of what has happened now, and what the law made a crime in the past? How could they know that *they do not know*. Anything. The young black callously shot through the negligence of the white man was not the farmer's boy; he was his son.

LANGSTON HUGHES (1902–1967)

Slave on the Block   1938

They were people who went in for Negroes—Michael and Anne—the Carraways. But not in the social-service, philanthropic sort of way, no. They saw no use in helping a race that was already too charming and naive and lovely for words. Leave them unspoiled and just enjoy them, Michael and Anne felt. So they went in for the Art of Negroes—the dancing that had such jungle life about it, the songs that were so simple and fervent, the poetry that was so direct, so real. They never tried to influence that art, they only bought it and raved over it, and copied it. For they were artists, too.

In their collection they owned some Covarrubias originals. Of course Covarrubias wasn't a Negro, but how he caught the darky spirit! They owned all the Robeson records and all the Bessie Smith. And they had a manuscript of Countee Cullen's. They saw all the plays with or about Negroes, read all the books, and adored the Hall Johnson Singers. They had met Doctor DuBois, and longed to meet Carl Van Vechten. Of course they knew Harlem like their own backyard, that is, all the speakeasies and night clubs and dance halls, from the Cotton Club and the ritzy joints where Negroes couldn't go themselves, down to places like the Hot Dime, where white folks couldn't get in—unless they knew the man. (And tipped heavily.)

They were acquainted with lots of Negroes, too—but somehow the Negroes didn't seem to like them very much. Maybe the Carraways gushed over them too soon. Or maybe they looked a little like poor white folks, although they were really quite well off. Or maybe they tried too hard to make friends, dark friends, and the dark friends suspected something. Or perhaps their house in the Village was too far from Harlem, or too hard to find, being back in one of those queer and expensive little side streets that had once been alleys before the art invasion came. Anyway, occasionally, a furtive Negro might accept their invitation for tea, or cocktails; and sometimes a lesser Harlem celebrity or two would decorate their rather slow parties; but one seldom came back for more. As much as they loved Negroes, Negroes didn't seem to love Michael and Anne.

But they were blessed with a wonderful colored cook and maid—until she took sick and died in her room in their basement. And then the most marvellous ebony boy walked into their life, a boy as black as all the Negroes they'd ever known put together.

"He *is* the jungle," said Anne when she saw him.   5

"He's 'I Couldn't Hear Nobody Pray,'" said Michael.

For Anne thought in terms of pictures: she was a painter. And Michael thought in terms of music: he was a composer for the piano. And they had a most wonderful idea of painting pictures and composing music that went together, and then having a joint "concert-exhibition" as they would call it. Her pictures and his music. The Carraways, a sonata and a picture, a fugue and a picture. It would be lovely, and such a novelty, people would have to like it. And many of their things would be Negro. Anne had painted their maid six times. And Michael had composed several themes based on the spirituals, and on Louis Armstrong's jazz. Now here was this ebony boy. The essence in the flesh.

They had nearly missed the boy. He had come, when they were out, to gather up the things the cook had left, and take them to her sister in Jersey. It seems that he was the late cook's nephew. The new colored maid had let him in and given him the two suitcases of poor dear Emma's belongings, and he was on his way to the Subway. That is, he was in the hall, going out just as the Carraways, Michael and Anne, stepped in. They could hardly see the boy, it being dark in the hall, and he being dark, too.

"Hello," they said. "Is this Emma's nephew?"

"Yes'm," said the maid. "Yes'm."   10

"Well, come in," said Anne, "and let us see you. We loved your aunt so much. She was the best cook we ever had."

"You don't know where I could get a job, do you?" said the boy. This took Michael and Anne back a bit, but they rallied at once. So charming and naive to ask right away for what he wanted.

Anne burst out, "You know, I think I'd like to paint you."

Michael said, "Oh, I say now, that would be lovely! He's so utterly Negro."

The boy grinned.   15

Anne said, "Could you come back tomorrow?"

And the boy said, "Yes, indeed. I sure could."

The upshot of it was that they hired him. They hired him to look after the garden, which was just about as big as Michael's grand piano—only a little square behind the house. You know those Village gardens. Anne sometimes painted it. And occasionally they set the table there for four on a spring evening. Nothing grew in the garden really, practically nothing. But the boy said he could plant things. And they had to have some excuse to hire him.

The boy's name was Luther. He had come from the South to his relatives in Jersey, and had had only one job since he got there, shining shoes for a Greek in Elizabeth. But the Greek fired him because the boy wouldn't give half his tips over to the proprietor.

"I never heard of a job where I had to pay the boss, instead of the boss paying me," said Luther. "Not till I got here."

"And then what did you do?" said Anne.

"Nothing. Been looking for a job for the last four months."

"Poor boy," said Michael; "poor, dear boy."

"Yes," said Anne. "You must be hungry." And they called the cook to give him something to eat.

Luther dug around in the garden a little bit that first day, went out and bought some seeds, came back and ate some more. They made a place for him to sleep in the basement by the furnace. And the next day Anne started to paint him, after she'd bought the right colors.

"He'll be good company for Mattie," they said. "She claims she's afraid to stay alone at night when we're out, so she leaves." They suspected, though, that Mattie just liked to get up to Harlem. And they thought right. Mattie was not as settled as she looked. Once out, with the Savoy open until three in the morning, why come home? That was the way Mattie felt.

In fact, what happened was that Mattie showed Luther where the best and cheapest hot spots in Harlem were located. Luther hadn't even set foot in Harlem before, living twenty-eight miles away, as he did, in Jersey, and being a kind of quiet boy. But the second night he was there Mattie said, "Come on, let's go. Working for white folks all day, I'm tired. They needn't think I was made to answer telephones all night." So out they went.

Anne noticed that most mornings Luther would doze almost as soon as she sat him down to pose, so she eventually decided to paint Luther asleep. "The Sleeping Negro," she would call it. Dear, natural childlike people, they would sleep anywhere they wanted to. Anyway, asleep, he kept still and held the pose.

And he *was* an adorable Negro. Not tall, but with a splendid body. And a slow and lively smile that lighted up his black, black face, for his teeth were very white, and his eyes, too. Most effective in oil and canvas. Better even than Emma had been. Anne could stare at him at leisure when he was asleep. One day she decided to paint him nude, or at least half nude. A slave picture, that's what she would do. The market at New Orleans for a background. And call it "The Boy on the Block."

So one morning when Luther settled down in his sleeping pose, Anne said, "No," she had finished that picture. She wanted to paint him now representing to the full the soul and sorrow of his people. She wanted to paint him as a slave about to be sold. And since slaves in warm climates had no clothes, would he please take off his shirt.

Luther smiled a sort of embarrassed smile and took off his shirt.

"Your undershirt, too," said Anne. But it turned out that he had on a union suit, so he had to go out and change altogether. He came back and mounted the box that Anne said would serve just then for a slave block, and she began to sketch. Before luncheon Michael came in, and went into rhapsodies over Luther on the box without a shirt, about to be sold into slavery. He said he must put him into music right now. And he went to the piano and began to play something that sounded like Deep River in the jaws of a dog, but Michael said it was a modern slave plaint, 1850 in terms of 1933. Vieux Carré° remembered on 135th Street, Slavery in the Cotton Club.

Anne said, "It's too marvellous!" And they painted and played till dark, with rest periods in between for Luther. Then they all knocked off for dinner. Anne and Michael went out later to one of Lew Leslie's new shows. And Luther and Mattie said, "Thank God!" and got dressed up for Harlem.

Funny, they didn't like the Carraways. They treated them nice and paid them well. "But they're too strange," said Mattie, "they makes me nervous."

"They is mighty funny," Luther agreed. 35

They didn't understand the vagaries of white folks, neither Luther nor Mattie, and they didn't want to be bothered trying.

"I does my work," said Mattie. "After that I don't want to be painted, or asked to sing songs, nor nothing like that."

The Carraways often asked Luther to sing, and he sang. He knew a lot of southern worksongs and reels, and spirituals and ballads.

> *"Dear Ma, I'm in hard luck:*
> *Three days since I et,*
> *And the stamp on this letter's*
> *Gwine to put me in debt."*

The Carraways allowed him to neglect the garden altogether. About all Luther did was pose and sing. And he got tired of that.

Indeed, both Luther and Mattie became a bit difficult to handle as time 40 went on. The Carraways blamed it on Mattie. She had got hold of Luther. She was just simply spoiling a nice simple young boy. She was old enough to know better. Mattie was in love with Luther.

At least, he slept with her. The Carraways discovered this one night about one o'clock when they went to wake Luther up (the first time they'd ever done such a thing) and ask him if he wouldn't sing his own marvellous version of John Henry for a man who had just come from Saint Louis and was sailing for Paris tomorrow. But Luther wasn't in his own bed by the furnace. There was a light in Mattie's room, so Michael knocked softly. Mattie said, "Who's that?" And Michael poked his head in, and here were Luther and Mattie in bed together!

Of course, Anne condoned them. "It's so simple and natural for Negroes to make love." But Mattie, after all, was forty if she was a day. And Luther was only a kid. Besides Anne thought that Luther had been ever so much nicer when he first came than he was now. But from so many nights at the Savoy, he had become a marvellous dancer, and he was teaching Anne the Lindy Hop to Cab Calloway's records. Besides, her picture of "The Boy on the Block" wasn't anywhere near done. And he did take pretty good care of the furnace. So they kept him. At least, Anne kept him, although Michael said he was getting a little bored with the same Negro always in the way.

For Luther had grown a bit familiar lately. He smoked up all their cigarettes,

Vieux Carré: the old quarter of New Orleans.

drank their wine, told jokes on them to their friends, and sometimes even came upstairs singing and walking about the house when the Carraways had guests in who didn't share their enthusiasm for Negroes, natural or otherwise.

Luther and Mattie together were a pair. They quite frankly lived with one another now. Well, let that go. Anne and Michael prided themselves on being different; artists, you know, and liberal-minded people—maybe a little scatter-brained, but then (secretly, they felt) that came from genius. They were not ordinary people, bothering about the liberties of others. Certainly, the last thing they would do would be to interfere with the delightful simplicity of Negroes.

But Mattie must be giving Luther money and buying him clothes. He was   45
really dressing awfully well. And on her Thursday afternoons off she would come back loaded down with packages. As far as the Carraways could tell, they were all for Luther.

And sometimes there were quarrels drifting up from the basement. And often, all too often, Mattie had moods. Then Luther would have moods. And it was pretty awful having two dark and glowering people around the house. Anne couldn't paint and Michael couldn't play.

One day, when she hadn't seen Luther for three days, Anne called downstairs and asked him if he wouldn't please come up and take off his shirt and get on the box. The picture was almost done. Luther came dragging his feet upstairs and humming:

> *"Before I'd be a slave*
> *I'd be buried in ma grave*
> *And go home to my Jesus*
> *And be free."*

And that afternoon he let the furnace go almost out.

That was the state of things when Michael's mother (whom Anne had never liked) arrived from Kansas City to pay them a visit. At once neither Mattie nor Luther liked her either. She was a mannish old lady, big and tall, and inclined to be bossy. Mattie, however, did spruce up her service, cooked delicious things, and treated Mrs. Carraway with a great deal more respect than she did Anne.

"I never play with servants," Mrs. Carraway had said to Michael, and Mattie must have heard her.

But Luther, he was worse than ever. Not that he did anything wrong, Anne   50
thought, but the way he did things! For instance, he didn't need to sing now all the time, especially since Mrs. Carraway had said she didn't like singing. And certainly not songs like "You Rascal, You."

But all things end! With the Carraways and Luther it happened like this: One forenoon, quite without a shirt (for he expected to pose) Luther came sauntering through the library to change the flowers in the vase. He carried red roses. Mrs. Carraway was reading her morning scripture from the Health and Life.

"Oh, good morning," said Luther. "How long are you gonna stay in this house?"

"I never liked familiar Negroes," said Mrs. Carraway, over her nose glasses.

"Huh!" said Luther. "That's too bad! I never liked poor white folks."

Mrs. Carraway screamed, a short, loud, dignified scream. Michael came   55 running in bathrobe and pyjamas. Mrs. Carraway grew tall. There was a scene. Luther talked. Michael talked. Anne appeared.

"Never, never, never," said Mrs. Carraway, "have I suffered such impudence from servants—and a nigger servant—in my own son's house."

"Mother, Mother, Mother," said Michael. "Be calm. I'll discharge him." He turned on the nonchalant Luther. "Go!" he said, pointing toward the door. "Go, go!"

"Michael," Anne cried, "I haven't finished 'The Slave on the Block.'" Her husband looked nonplussed. For a moment he breathed deeply.

"Either he goes or I go," said Mrs. Carraway, firm as a rock.

"He goes," said Michael with strength from his mother.   60

"Oh!" cried Anne. She looked at Luther. His black arms were full of roses he had brought to put in the vases. He had on no shirt. "Oh!" His body was ebony.

"Don't worry 'bout me!" said Luther. "I'll go."

"Yes, we'll go," boomed Mattie from the doorway, who had come up from below, fat and belligerent. "We've stood enough foolery from you white folks! Yes, we'll go. Come on, Luther."

What could she mean, "stood enough"? What had they done to them, Anne and Michael wondered. They had tried to be kind. "Oh!"

"Sneaking around knocking on our door at night," Mattie went on. "Yes,   65 we'll go. Pay us! Pay us! Pay us!" So she remembered the time they had come for Luther at night. That was it.

"I'll pay you," said Michael. He followed Mattie out.

Anne looked at her black boy.

"Goody-bye," Luther said. "You fix the vases."

He handed her his armful of roses, glanced impudently at old Mrs. Carraway and grinned—grinned that wide, beautiful, white-toothed grin that made Anne say when she first saw him, "He looks like the jungle." Grinned, and disappeared in the dark hall, with no shirt on his back.

"Oh," Anne moaned distressfully, "my 'Boy on the Block'!"   70

"Huh!" snorted Mrs. Carraway.

FRANZ KAFKA   (1883–1924)

A Hunger Artist   *1924*

Translated by Willa and Edwin Muir

During these last decades the interest in professional fasting has markedly diminished. It used to pay very well to stage such great performances under one's own management, but today that is quite impossible. We live in a different world now. At one time the whole town took a lively interest in the hunger artist; from day to day of his fast the excitement mounted; everybody wanted to see him at least once a day; there were people who bought season tickets for the last few days and sat from morning till night in front of his small barred cage; even in the nighttime there were visiting hours, when the whole effect was heightened by torch flares; on fine days the cage was set out in the open air, and then it was the children's special treat to see the hunger artist; for their elders he was often just a joke that happened to be in fashion, but the children stood openmouthed, holding each other's hands for greater security, marveling at him as he sat there pallid in black tights, with his ribs sticking out so prominently, not even on a seat but down among straw on the ground, sometimes giving a courteous nod, answering questions with a constrained smile, or perhaps stretching an arm through the bars so that one might feel how thin it was, and then again withdrawing deep into himself, paying no attention to anyone or anything, not even to the all-important striking of the clock that was the only piece of furniture in his cage, but merely staring into vacancy with half-shut eyes, now and then taking a sip from a tiny glass of water to moisten his lips.

Besides casual onlookers there were also relays of permanent watchers selected by the public, usually butchers, strangely enough, and it was their task to watch the hunger artist day and night, three of them at a time, in case he should have some secret recourse to nourishment. This was nothing but a formality, instituted to reassure the masses, for the initiates knew well enough that during his fast the artist would never in any circumstances, not even under forcible compulsion, swallow the smallest morsel of food; the honor of his profession forbade it. Not every watcher, of course, was capable of understanding this, there were often groups of night watchers who were very lax in carrying out their duties and deliberately huddled together in a retired corner to play cards with great absorption, obviously intending to give the hunger artist the chance of a little refreshment, which they supposed he could draw from some private hoard. Nothing annoyed the artist more than such watchers; they made him miserable; they made his fast seem unendurable; sometimes he mastered his feebleness sufficiently to sing during their watch for as long as he could keep going, to show them how unjust their suspicions were. But that was of little use; they only wondered at his cleverness in being able to fill his mouth even while singing. Much more to his taste were the watchers who sat close up to the bars, who were not content with the dim night lighting of the hall but focused him in the full glare of the electric pocket torch given them by the impresario. The harsh light did not trouble him at all, in any case he could never sleep properly, and he could always drowse a little, whatever the light, at any hour, even when the hall was thronged with noisy onlookers. He was quite happy at the prospect of spending a sleepless night with such watchers; he was ready to exchange jokes with them, to tell them stories out of his nomadic life, anything at all to keep them awake and demonstrate to them again that he had no eatables in his cage and that he was fasting as not one of them could fast. But his happiest moment was when the morning came and an enormous breakfast was brought them, at his expense, on which they flung themselves with the keen appetite of healthy men after a weary night of wakefulness. Of course there were people who argued that this breakfast was an unfair attempt to bribe the watchers, but that was going rather too far, and when they were invited to take on a night's vigil without a breakfast, merely for the sake of the cause, they made themselves scarce, although they stuck stubbornly to their suspicions.

Such suspicions, anyhow, were a necessary accompaniment to the profession of fasting. No one could possibly watch the hunger artist continuously, day and night, and so no one could produce first-hand evidence that the fast had really been rigorous and continuous; only the artist himself could know that, he was therefore bound to be the sole completely satisfied spectator of his own fast. Yet for other reasons he was never satisfied; it was not perhaps mere fasting that had brought him to such skeleton thinness that many people had regretfully to keep away from his exhibitions, because the sight of him was too much for them, perhaps it was dissatisfaction with himself that had worn him down. For he alone knew, what no other initiate knew, how easy it was to fast. It was the easiest thing in the world. He made no secret of this, yet people did not believe him, at the best they set him down as modest; most of them, however, thought he was out for publicity or else was some kind of cheat who found it easy to fast because he had discovered a way of making it easy, and then had the impudence to admit the fact, more or less. He had to put up with all that, and in the course of time had got used to it, but his inner dissatisfaction always rankled, and never yet, after any term of fasting—this must be granted to his credit—had he left the cage of his own free will. The longest period of fasting was fixed by his impresario at forty days, beyond that term he was not allowed to go, not even in great cities, and there was good reason for it, too. Experience had proved that for about forty days the interest of the public could be stimulated by a steadily increasing pressure of advertisement, but after that the town began to lose interest, sympathetic support began notably to fall off; there were of course local variations as between one town and another or one country and another, but as a general rule forty days marked the limit. So on the fortieth day the flower-bedecked cage was opened, enthusiastic spectators filled the hall, a military band played, two doctors entered the cage to measure the results of the fast, which were announced through a megaphone, and finally two young ladies appeared, blissful at having been selected for the honor, to help the hunger artist down the few steps leading to a small table on which was spread a carefully chosen invalid repast. And at this very moment the artist always turned stubborn. True, he would entrust his bony arms to the outstretched helping hands of the ladies bending over him, but stand up he would not. Why stop fasting at this particular moment, after forty days of it? He had held out for a long time, an illimitably long time; why stop now, when he was in his best fasting form, or rather, not yet quite in his best fasting form? Why should he be cheated of the fame he would get for fasting longer, for being not only the record hunger artist of all time, which presumably he was already, but for beating his own record by a performance beyond human imagination, since he felt that there were no limits to his capacity for fasting? His public pretended to admire him so much, why should it have so little patience with him; if he could endure fasting longer, why shouldn't the public endure it? Besides, he was tired, he was comfortable sitting in the straw, and now he was supposed to lift himself to his full height and go down to a meal the very thought of which gave him a nausea that only the presence of the ladies kept him from betraying, and even that with an effort. And he looked up into the eyes of the ladies who were apparently so friendly and in reality so cruel, and shook his head, which felt too heavy on its strengthless neck. But then there happened yet again what always happened. The impresario came forward, without a word—for the band made speech impossible—lifted his arms in the air above the artist, as if inviting Heaven to look down upon its creature here in the straw, this suffering martyr, which indeed he was, although in quite another sense; grasped him around the emaciated waist, with exaggerated caution, so that the frail condition he was in might be appreciated; and committed him to the care of the blenching ladies, not without secretly giving him a shaking so that his legs and body tottered and swayed. The artist now submitted completely; his head lolled on his breast as if it had landed there by chance; his body was hollowed out; his legs in a spasm of self-preservation clung close to each other at the knees, yet scraped on the ground as if it were not really solid ground, as if they were only trying to find solid ground; and the whole weight of his body, a featherweight after all, relapsed onto one of the ladies, who, looking around for help and panting a little—this post of honor was not at all what she had expected it to be—first stretched her neck as far as she could to keep her face at least free from contact with the artist, then finding this impossible, and her more fortunate companion not coming to her aid but merely holding extended in her own trembling hand the little bunch of knucklebones that was the artist's, to the great delight of the spectators burst into tears and had to be replaced by an attendant who had long been stationed in readiness. Then came the food, a little of which the impresario managed to get between the artist's lips, while he sat in a kind of half-fainting trance, to the accompaniment of cheerful patter designed to distract the public's attention from the artist's condition; after that, a toast was drunk to the public, supposedly prompted by a whisper from the artist in the impresario's ear; the band confirmed it with a mighty flourish, the spectators melted away, and no one had any cause to be dissatisfied with the proceedings, no one except the hunger artist himself, he only, as always.

So he lived for many years, with small regular intervals of recuperation, in visible glory, honored by the world, yet in spite of that troubled in spirit, and all the more troubled because no one would take his trouble seriously. What comfort could he possibly need? What more could he possibly wish for? And if some good-natured person, feeling sorry for him, tried to console him by pointing out that his melancholy was probably caused by fasting, it could happen, especially when he had been fasting for some time, that he reacted with an outburst of fury and to the general alarm began to shake the bars of his cage like a wild animal. Yet the impresario had a way of punishing these outbreaks which he rather enjoyed putting into operation. He would apologize publicly for the artist's behavior, which was only to be excused, he admitted, because of the irritability caused by fasting; a condition hardly to be understood by well-fed people; then by natural transition he went on to mention the artist's equally incomprehensible boast that he could fast for much longer than he was doing; he praised the high ambition, the good will, the great self-denial undoubtedly implicit in such a statement; and then quite simply countered it by bringing out photographs, which were also on sale to the public, showing the artist on the fortieth day of a fast lying in bed almost dead from exhaustion. This perversion of the truth, familiar to the artist though it was, always unnerved him afresh and proved too much for him. What was a consequence of the premature ending of his fast was here presented as the cause of it! To fight against this lack of understanding, against a whole world of nonunderstanding, was impossible. Time and again in good faith he stood by the bars listening to the impresario, but as soon as the photographs appeared he always let go and sank with a groan back onto his straw, and the reassured public could once more come close and gaze at him.

A few years later when the witnesses of such scenes called them to mind, they often failed to understand themselves at all. For meanwhile the aforementioned change in public interest had set in; it seemed to happen almost overnight; there may have been profound causes for it, but who was going to bother about

5

that; at any rate the pampered hunger artist suddenly found himself deserted one fine day by the amusement-seekers, who went streaming past him to other more-favored attractions. For the last time the impresario hurried him over half Europe to discover whether the old interest might still survive here and there; all in vain; everywhere, as if by secret agreement, a positive revulsion from professional fasting was in evidence. Of course it could not really have sprung up so suddenly as all that, and many premonitory symptoms which had not been sufficiently remarked or suppressed during the rush and glitter of success now came retrospectively to mind, but it was now too late to take any countermeasures. Fasting would surely come into fashion again at some future date, yet that was no comfort for those living in the present. What, then, was the hunger artist to do? He had been applauded by thousands in his time and could hardly come down to showing himself in a street booth at village fairs, and as for adopting another profession, he was not only too old for that but too fanatically devoted to fasting. So he took leave of the impresario, his partner in an unparalleled career, and hired himself to a large circus; in order to spare his own feelings he avoided reading the conditions of his contract.

A large circus with its enormous traffic in replacing and recruiting men, animals, and apparatus can always find a use for people at any time, even for a hunger artist, provided of course that he does not ask too much, and in this particular case anyhow it was not only the artist who was taken on but his famous and long-known name as well; indeed considering the peculiar nature of his performance, which was not impaired by advancing age, it could not be objected that here was an artist past his prime, no longer at the height of his professional skill, seeking a refuge in some quiet corner of a circus; on the contrary, the hunger artist averred that he could fast as well as ever, which was entirely credible, he even alleged that if he were allowed to fast as he liked, and this was at once promised him without more ado, he could astound the world by establishing a record never yet achieved, a statement that certainly provoked a smile among the other professionals, since it left out of account the change in public opinion, which the hunger artist in his zeal conveniently forgot.

He had not, however, actually lost his sense of the real situation and took it as a matter of course that he and his cage should be stationed, not in the middle of the ring as a main attraction, but outside, near the animal cages, on a site that was after all easily accessible. Large and gaily painted placards made a frame for the cage and announced what was to be seen inside it. When the public came thronging out in the intervals to see the animals, they could hardly avoid passing the hunger artist's cage and stopping there for a moment, perhaps they might even have stayed longer had not those pressing behind them in the narrow gangway, who did not understand why they should be held up on their way toward the excitements of the menagerie, made it impossible for anyone to stand gazing quietly for any length of time. And that was the reason why the hunger artist, who had of course been looking forward to these visiting hours as the main achievement of his life, began instead to shrink from them. At first he could hardly wait for the intervals; it was exhilarating to watch the crowds come streaming his way, until only too soon—not even the most obstinate self-deception, clung to almost consciously, could hold out against the fact—the conviction was borne in upon him that these people, most of them, to judge from their actions, again and again, without exception, were all on their way to the menagerie. And the first sight of them from the distance remained the best. For when they reached his cage he was at once deafened by the storm of shouting and abuse that arose from the two contending factions, which renewed themselves continuously, of those who wanted to stop and stare at him—he soon began to dislike them more than the others—not out of real interest but only out of obstinate self-assertiveness, and those who wanted to go straight on to the animals. When the first great rush was past, the stragglers came along, and these, whom nothing could have prevented from stopping to look at him as long as they had breath, raced past with long strides, hardly even glancing at him, in their haste to get to the menagerie in time. And all too rarely did it happen that he had a stroke of luck, when some father of a family fetched up before him with his children, pointed a finger at the hunger artist, and explained at length what the phenomenon meant, telling stories of earlier years when he himself had watched similar but much more thrilling performances, and the children, still rather uncomprehending, since neither inside nor outside school had they been sufficiently prepared for this lesson—what did they care about fasting?—yet showed by the brightness of their intent eyes that new and better times might be coming. Perhaps, said the hunger artist to himself many a time, things would be a little better if his cage were set not quite so near the menagerie. that made it too easy for people to make their choice, to say nothing of what he suffered from the stench of the menagerie, the animals' restlessness by night, the carrying past of raw lumps of flesh for the beasts of prey, the roaring at feeding times, which depressed him continually. But he did not dare to lodge a complaint with the management; after all, he had the animals to thank for the troops of people who passed his cage, among whom there might always be one here and there to take an interest in him, and who could tell where they might schedule him if he called attention to his existence and thereby to the fact that, strictly speaking, he was only an impediment on the way to the menagerie.

A small impediment, to be sure, one that grew steadily less. People grew familiar with the strange idea that they could be expected, in times like these, to take an interest in a hunger artist, and with this familiarity the verdict went out against him. He might fast as much as he could, and he did so; but nothing could save him now, people passed him by. Just try to explain to anyone the art of fasting! Anyone who has no feeling for it cannot be made to understand it. The fine placards grew dirty and illegible, they were torn down; the little notice board telling the number of fast days achieved, which at first was changed carefully every day, had long stayed at the same figure, for after the first few weeks even this small task seemed pointless to the staff; and so the artist simply fasted on and on, as he had once dreamed of doing, and it was no trouble to him, just as he had always foretold, but no one counted the days, no one, not even the artist himself, knew what records he was already breaking, and his heart grew heavy. And when once in a while some leisurely passer-by stopped, made merry over the old figure on the board, and spoke of swindling, that was in its way the stupidest lie ever invented by indifference and inborn malice, since it was not the hunger artist who was cheating, he was working honestly, but the world was cheating him of his reward.

Many more days went by, however, and that too came to an end. An overseer's eye fell on the cage one day and he asked the attendants why this perfectly good cage should be left standing there unused with dirty straw inside it; nobody knew, until one man, helped out by the notice board, remembered about the hunger artist. They poked into the straw with sticks and found him in it. "Are you still fasting?" asked the overseer, "when on earth do you mean to stop?" "Forgive me, everybody," whispered the hunger artist; only the overseer, who had his ear to the bars, understood him. "Of course," said the overseer, and tapped his forehead with a finger to let the attendants know what state the man was in, "we forgive you." "I always wanted you to admire my fasting," said the hunger artist. "We do admire it," said the overseer, affably. "But you shouldn't admire it," said the hunger artist. "Well then we don't admire it," said the overseer, "but why shouldn't we admire it?" "Because I have to fast, I can't help it," said the hunger artist. "What a fellow you are," said the overseer, "and why can't you help it?" "Because," said the hunger artist, lifting his head a little and speaking, with his lips pursed, as if for a kiss, right into the overseer's ear, so that no syllable might be lost, "because I couldn't find the food I liked. If I had found it, believe me, I should have made no fuss and stuffed myself like you or anyone else." These were his last words but in his dimming eyes remained the firm though no longer proud persuasion that he was still continuing to fast.

"Well, clear this out now!" said the overseer, and they buried the hunger 10 artist, straw and all. Into the cage they put a young panther. Even the most insensitive felt it refreshing to see this wild creature leaping around the cage that had so long been dreary. The panther was all right. The food he liked was brought him without hesitation by the attendants; he seemed not even to miss his freedom; his noble body, furnished almost to the bursting point with all that it needed, seemed to carry freedom around with it too; somewhere in his jaws it seemed to lurk; and the joy of life streamed with such ardent passion from his throat that for the onlookers it was not easy to stand the shock of it. But they braced themselves, crowded around the cage, and did not want ever to move away.

DORIS LESSING (b. 1919)

The Old Chief Mshlanga   *1951*

They were good, the years of ranging the bush over her father's farm which, like every white farm, was largely unused, broken only occasionally by small patches of cultivation. In between, nothing but trees, the long sparse grass, thorn and cactus and gully, grass and outcrop and thorn. And a jutting piece of rock which had been thrust up from the warm soil of Africa unimaginable eras of time ago, washed into hollows and whorls by sun and wind that had travelled so many thousands of miles of space and bush, would hold the weight of a small girl whose eyes were sightless for anything but a pale willowed river, a pale gleaming castle— a small girl singing: "Out flew the web and floated wide, the mirror cracked from side to side . . ."

Pushing her way through the green aisles of the mealie° stalks, the leaves arching like cathedrals veined with sunlight far overhead, with the packed red earth underfoot, a fine lace of red starred witchweed would summon up a black bent figure croaking premonitions: the Northern witch, bred of cold Northern forests, would stand before her among the mealie fields, and it was the mealie

---

mealie: a word for corn in Southern Africa.

fields that faded and fled, leaving her among the gnarled roots of an oak, snow falling thick and soft and white, the woodcutter's fire glowing red welcome through crowding tree trunks.

A white child, opening its eyes curiously on a sun-suffused landscape, a gaunt and violent landscape, might be supposed to accept it as her own, to take the msasa trees and the thorn trees as familiars, to feel her blood running free and responsive to the swing of the seasons.

This child could not see a msasa tree, or the thorn, for what they were. Her books held tales of alien fairies, her rivers ran slow and peaceful, and she knew the shape of the leaves of an ash or an oak, the names of the little creatures that lived in English streams, when the words "the veld"° meant strangeness, though she could remember nothing else.

Because of this, for many years, it was the veld that seemed unreal; the sun was a foreign sun, and the wind spoke a strange language.

The black people on the farm were as remote as the trees and the rocks. They were an amorphous black mass, mingling and thinning and massing like tadpoles, faceless, who existed merely to serve, to say "Yes, Baas,"° take their money and go. They changed season by season, moving from one farm to the next, according to their outlandish needs, which one did not have to understand, coming from perhaps hundreds of miles North or East, passing on after a few months—where? Perhaps even as far away as the fabled gold mines of Johannesburg, where the pay was so much better than the few shillings a month and the double handful of mealie meal twice a day which they earned in that part of Africa.

The child was taught to take them for granted: the servants in the house would come running a hundred yards to pick up a book if she dropped it. She was called "Nkosikaas"—Chieftainess, even by the black children her own age.

Later, when the farm grew too small to hold her curiosity, she carried a gun in the crook of her arm and wandered miles a day, from vlei° to vlei, from *kopje* to *kopje*,° accompanied by two dogs: the dogs and the gun were an armour against fear. Because of them she never felt fear.

If a native came into sight along the kaffir° paths half a mile away, the dogs would flush him up a tree as if he were a bird. If he expostulated (in his uncouth language which was by itself ridiculous) that was cheek. If one was in a good mood, it could be a matter for laughter. Otherwise one passed on, hardly glancing at the angry man in the tree.

On the rare occasions when white children met together they could amuse themselves by hailing a passing native in order to make a buffoon of him; they could set the dogs on him and watch him run; they could tease a small black child as if he were a puppy—save that they would not throw stones and sticks at a dog without a sense of guilt.

Later still, certain questions presented themselves in the child's mind: and because the answers were not easy to accept, they were silenced by an even greater arrogance of manner.

5

10

veld: also *veldt*, a vast, open grass-covered area used for grazing.
Baas: boss.
vlei: a slough or pond (valley).
kopje: a small hill covered with vegetation and rocks. Usually pronounced "copy."
kaffir: pejorative word for the various Bantu peoples and their languages.

It was even impossible to think of the black people who worked about the house as friends, for if she talked to one of them, her mother would come running anxiously: "Come away; you mustn't talk to natives."

It was this instilled consciousness of danger, of something unpleasant, that made it easy to laugh out loud, crudely, if a servant made a mistake in his English of if he failed to understand an order—there is a certain kind of laughter that is fear, afraid of itself.

One evening, when I was about fourteen, I was walking down the side of a mealie field that had been newly ploughed, so that the great red clods showed fresh and tumbling to the vlei beyond, like a choppy red sea; it was that hushed and listening hour, when the birds send long sad calls from tree to tree, and all the colours of earth and sky and leaf are deep and golden. I had my rifle in the curve of my arm, and the dogs were at my heels.

In front of me, perhaps a couple of hundred yards away, a group of three 15 Africans came into sight around the side of a big antheap. I whistled the dogs close in to my skirts and let the gun swing in my hand, and advanced, waiting for them to move aside, off the path, in respect for my passing. But they came on steadily, and the dogs looked up at me for the command to chase. I was angry. It was "cheek" for a native not to stand off a path, the moment he caught sight of you.

In front walked an old man, stooping his weight on to a stick, his hair grizzled white, a dark red blanket slung over his shoulders like a cloak. Behind him came two young men, carrying bundles of pots, assegais, hatchets.

The group was not a usual one. They were not natives seeking work. These had an air of dignity, of quietly following their own purpose. It was the dignity that checked my tongue. I walked quietly on, talking softly to the growling dogs, till I was ten paces away. Then the old man stopped, drawing his blanket close.

"Morning, Nkosikaas," he said, using the customary greeting for any time of the day.

"Good morning," I said. "Where are you going?" My voice was a little truculent.

The old man spoke in his own language, then one of the young men stepped 20 forward politely and said in careful English: "My Chief travels to see his brothers beyond the river."

A Chief! I thought, understanding the pride that made the old man stand before me like an equal—more than an equal, for he showed courtesy, and I showed none.

The old man spoke again, wearing dignity like an inherited garment, still standing ten paces off, flanked by his entourage, not looking at me (that would have been rude) but directing his eyes somewhere over my head at the trees.

"You are the little Nkosikaas from the farm of Baas Jordan?"

"That's right," I said.

"Perhaps your father does not remember," said the interpreter for the old 25 man, "but there was an affair with some goats. I remember seeing you when you were . . ." The young man held his hand at knee level and smiled.

We all smiled.

"What is your name?" I asked.

"This is Chief Mshlanga," said the young man.

"I will tell my father that I met you," I said.

The old man said: "My greetings to your father, little Nkosikaas."   30

"Good morning," I said politely, finding the politeness difficult, from lack of use.

"Morning, little Nkosikaas," said the old man, and stood aside to let me pass.

I went by, my gun hanging awkwardly, the dogs sniffing and growling, cheated of their favorite game of chasing natives like animals.

Not long afterwards I read in an old explorer's book the phrase: "Chief Mshlanga's country." It went like this: "Our destination was Chief Mshlanga's country, to the north of the river; and it was our desire to ask his permission to prospect for gold in his territory."

The phrase "ask his permission" was so extraordinary to a white child,   35 brought up to consider all natives as things to use, that it revived those questions, which could not be suppressed: they fermented slowly in my mind.

On another occasion one of those old prospectors who still move over Africa looking for neglected reefs, with their hammers and tents, and pans for sifting gold from crushed rock, came to the farm and, in talking of the old days, used that phrase again: "This was the Old Chief's country," he said. "It stretched from those mountains over there way back to the river, hundreds of miles of country." That was his name for our district: "The Old Chief's Country"; he did not use our name for it—a new phrase which held no implication of usurped ownership.

As I read more books about the time when this part of Africa was opened up, not much more than fifty years before, I found Old Chief Mshlanga had been a famous man, known to all the explorers and prospectors. But then he had been young: or maybe it was his father or uncle they spoke of—I never found out.

During that year I met him several times in the part of the farm that was traversed by natives moving over the country. I learned that the path up the side of the big red field where the birds sang was the recognized highway for migrants. Perhaps I even haunted it in the hope of meeting him: being greeted by him, the exchange of courtesies, seemed to answer the questions that troubled me.

Soon I carried a gun in a different spirit; I used it for shooting food and not to give me confidence. And now the dogs learned better manners. When I saw a native approaching, we offered and took greetings; and slowly that other landscape in my mind faded, and my feet struck directly on the African soil, and I saw the shapes of tree and hill clearly, and the black people moved back, as it were, out of my life: it was as if I stood aside to watch a low intimate dance of landscape and men, a very old dance, whose steps I could not learn.

But I thought: this is my heritage, too; I was bred here; it is my country as   40 well as the black man's country; and there is plenty of room for all of us, without elbowing each other off the pavements and roads.

It seemed it was only necessary to let free that respect I felt when I was talking with old Chief Mshlanga, to let both black and white people meet gently, with tolerance for each other's differences: it seemed quite easy.

Then, one day, something new happened. Working in our house as servants were always three natives: cook, houseboy, garden boy. They used to change as the farm natives changed: staying for a few months then moving on to a new job, or back home to their kraals.° They were thought of as "good" or "bad" natives; which meant: how did they behave as servants? Were they lazy, efficient, obedient,

kraals: fenced-in native villages.

or disrespectful? If the family felt good-humoured, the phrase was: "What can you expect from raw black savages?" If we were angry, we said: "These damned niggers, we would be much better off without them."

One day, a white policeman was on his rounds of the district, and he said laughingly: "Did you know you have an important man in your kitchen?"

"What!" exclaimed my mother sharply. "What do you mean?"

"A Chief's son." The policeman seemed amused. "He'll boss the tribe when the old man dies." 45

"He'd better not put on a Chief's son act with me," said my mother.

When the policeman left, we looked with different eyes at our cook: he was a good worker, but he drank too much at week-ends—that was how we knew him.

He was a tall youth, with very black skin, like black polished metal, his tightly-growing black hair parted white man's fashion at one side, with a metal comb from the store stuck into it; very polite, very distant, very quick to obey an order. Now that it had been pointed out, we said: "Of course, you can see. Blood always tells."

My mother became strict with him now she knew about his birth and prospects. Sometimes, when she lost her temper, she would say: "You aren't the Chief yet, you know." And he would answer her very quietly, his eyes on the ground: "Yes, Nkosikaas."

One afternoon he asked for a whole day off, instead of the customary half-day, to go home next Sunday. 50

"How can you go home in one day?"

"It will take me half an hour on my bicycle," he explained.

I watched the direction he took; and the next day I went off to look for this kraal; I understood he must be Chief Mshlanga's successor: there was no other kraal near enough our farm.

Beyond our boundaries on that side the country was new to me. I followed unfamiliar paths past *kopjes* that till now had been part of the jagged horizon, hazed with distance. This was Government land, which had never been cultivated by white men; at first I could not understand why it was that it appeared, in merely crossing the boundary, I had entered a completely fresh type of landscape. It was a wide green valley, where a small river sparkled, and vivid water-birds darted over the rushes. The grass was thick and soft to my calves, the trees stood tall and shapely.

I was used to our farm, whose hundreds of acres of harsh eroded soil bore trees that had been cut for the mine furnaces and had grown thin and twisted, where the cattle had dragged the grass flat, leaving innumerable criss-crossing trails that deepened each season into gullies, under the force of the rains. 55

This country had been left untouched, save for prospectors whose picks had struck a few sparks from the surface of the rocks as they wandered by; and for migrant natives whose passing had left, perhaps, a charred patch on the trunk of a tree where their evening fire had nestled.

It was very silent: a hot morning with pigeons cooing throatily, the midday shadows lying dense and thick with clear yellow spaces of sunlight between and in all that wide green park-like valley, not a human soul but myself.

I was listening to the quick regular tapping of a woodpecker when slowly a chill feeling seemed to grow up from the small of my back to my shoulders, in a constricting spasm like a shudder, and at the roots of my hair a tingling sensation began and ran down over the surface of my flesh, leaving me goosefleshed and cold, though I was damp with sweat. Fever? I thought; then uneasily, turned to look over my shoulder; and realized suddenly that this was fear. It was extraordinary, even humiliating. It was a new fear. For all the years I had walked by myself over this country I had never known a moment's uneasiness; in the beginning because I had been supported by a gun and the dogs, then because I had learnt an easy friendliness for the Africans I might encounter.

I had read of this feeling, how the bigness and silence of Africa, under the ancient sun, grows dense and takes shape in the mind, till even the birds seem to call menacingly, and a deadly spirit comes out of the trees and the rocks. You move warily, as if your very passing disturbs something old and evil, something dark and big and angry that might suddenly rear and strike from behind. You look at groves of entwined trees, and picture the animals that might be lurking there; you look at the river running slowly, dropping from level to level through the vlei, spreading into pools where at night the bucks come to drink, and the crocodiles rise and drag them by their soft noses into underwater caves. Fear possessed me. I found I was turning round and round, because of that shapeless menace behind me that might reach out and take me; I kept glancing at the files of *kopjes* which, seen from a different angle, seemed to change with every step so that even known landmarks, like a big mountain that had sentinelled my world since I first became conscious of it, showed an unfamiliar sunlit valley among its foothills. I did not know where I was. I was lost. Panic seized me. I found I was spinning round and round, staring anxiously at this tree and that, peering up at the sun which appeared to have moved into an eastern slant, shedding the sad yellow light of sunset. Hours must have passed! I looked at my watch and found that this state of meaningless terror had lasted perhaps ten minutes.

The point was that it was meaningless. I was not ten miles from home: I had only to take my way back along the valley to find myself at the fence; away among the foothills of the *kopjes* gleamed the roof of a neighbor's house, and a couple of hours' walking would reach it. This was the sort of fear that contracts the flesh of a dog at night and sets him howling at the full moon. It had nothing to do with what I thought or felt; and I was more disturbed by the fact that I could become its victim than of the physical sensation itself: I walked steadily on, quietened, in a divided mind, watching my own pricking nerves and apprehensive glances from side to side with a disgusted amusement. Deliberately I set myself to think of this village I was seeking, and what I should do when I entered it—if I could find it, which was doubtful, since I was walking aimlessly and it might be anywhere in the hundreds of thousands of acres of bush that stretched about me. With my mind on that village, I realized that a new sensation was added to the fear: loneliness. Now such a terror of isolation invaded me that I could hardly walk; and if it were not that I came over the crest of a small rise and saw a village below me, I should have turned and gone home. It was a cluster of thatched huts in a clearing among trees. There were neat patches of mealies and pumpkins and millet, and cattle grazed under some trees at a distance. Fowls scratched among the huts, dogs lay sleeping on the grass, and goats friezed a *kopje* that jutted up beyond a tributary of the river lying like an enclosing arm round the village.

As I came close I saw the huts were lovingly decorated with patterns of yellow and red and ochre mud on the walls; and the thatch was tied in place with plaits of straw.

60

This was not at all like our farm compound, a dirty and neglected place, a temporary home for migrants who had no roots in it.

And now I did not know what to do next. I called a small black boy, who was sitting on a lot playing a stringed gourd, quite naked except for the strings of blue beads round his neck, and said: "Tell the Chief I am here." The child stuck his thumb in his mouth and stared shyly back at me.

For minutes I shifted my feet on the edge of what seemed a deserted village, till at last the child scuttled off, and then some women came. They were draped in bright cloths, with brass glinting in their ears and on their arms. They also stared, silently; then turned to chatter among themselves.

I said again: "Can I see Chief Mshlanga?" I saw they caught the name: they   65
did not understand what I wanted. I did not understand myself.

At last I walked through them and came past the huts and saw a clearing under a big shady tree, where a dozen old men sat cross-legged on the ground, talking. Chief Mshlanga was leaning back against the tree, holding a gourd in his hand, from which he had been drinking. When he saw me, not a muscle of his face moved, and I could see he was not pleased: perhaps he was afflicted with my own shyness, due to being unable to find the right forms of courtesy for the occasion. To meet me, on our own farm, was one thing; but I should not have come here. What had I expected? I could not join them socially: the thing was unheard of. Bad enough that I, a white girl, should be walking the veld alone as a white man might: and in this part of the bush where only Government officials had the right to move.

Again I stood, smiling foolishly, while behind me stood the groups of brightly clad, chattering women, their faces alert with curiosity and interest, and in front of me sat the old men, with old lined faces, their eyes guarded, aloof. It was a village of ancients and children and women. Even the two young men who kneeled beside the Chief were not those I had seen with him previously: the young men were all away working on the white men's farms and mines, and the Chief must depend on relatives who were temporarily on holiday for his attendants.

"The small white Nkosikaas is far from home," remarked the old man at last.

"Yes," I agreed, "it is far." I wanted to say: "I have come to pay you a friendly visit, Chief Mshlanga." I could not say it. I might now be feeling an urgent helpless desire to get to know these men and women as people, to be accepted by them as a friend, but the truth was I had set out in a spirit of curiosity: I had wanted to see the village that one day our cook, the reserved and obedient young man who got drunk on Sundays, would one day rule over.

"The child of Nkosi Jordan is welcome," said Chief Mshlanga.   70

"Thank you," I said, and could think of nothing more to say. There was a silence, while the flies rose and began to buzz around my head: and the wind shook a little in the thick green tree that spread its branches over the old men.

"Good morning," I said at last. "I have to return now to my home."

"Morning, little Nkosikaas," said Chief Mshlanga.

I walked away from the indifferent village, over the rise past the staring amber-eyed goats, down through the tall stately trees into the great rich green valley where the river meandered and the pigeons cooed tales of plenty and the woodpecker tapped softly.

The fear was gone; the loneliness had set into stiff-necked stoicism; there was now a queer hostility in the landscape, a cold, hard, sullen indomitability that walked with me, as strong as a wall, as intangible as smoke; it seemed to say to me: you walk here as a destroyer. I went slowly homewards, with an empty heart: I had learned that if one cannot call a country to heel like a dog, neither can one dismiss the past with a smile in an easy gush of feeling, saying: I could not help it, I am also a victim.

75

I only saw Chief Mshlanga once again.

One night my father's big red land was trampled down by small sharp hooves, and it was discovered that the culprits were goats from Chief Mshlanga's kraal. This had happened once before, years ago.

My father confiscated all the goats. Then he sent a message to the old Chief that if he wanted them he would have to pay for the damage.

He arrived at our house at the time of sunset one evening, looking very old and bent now, walking stiffly under his regally draped blanket, leaning on a big stick. My father sat himself down in his big chair below the steps of the house; the old man squatted carefully on the ground before him, flanked by his two young men.

The palaver was long and painful, because of the bad English of the young man who interpreted, and because my father could not speak dialect, but only kitchen kaffir.

80

From my father's point of view, at least two hundred pounds' worth of damage had been done to the crop. He knew he could not get the money from the old man. He felt he was entitled to keep the goats. As for the old Chief, he kept repeating angrily: "Twenty goats! My people cannot lose twenty goats! We are not rich; like the Nkosi Jordan, to lose twenty goats at once."

My father did not think of himself as rich, but rather as very poor. He spoke quickly and angrily in return, saying that the damage done meant a great deal to him, and that he was entitled to the goats.

At last it grew so heated that the cook, the Chief's son, was called from the kitchen to be interpreter, and now my father spoke fluently in English, and our cook translated rapidly so that the old man could understand how very angry my father was. The young man spoke without emotion, in a mechanical way, his eyes lowered, but showing how he felt his position by a hostile uncomfortable set of the shoulders.

It was now in the late sunset, the sky a welter of colours, the birds singing their last songs, and the cattle, lowing peacefully, moving past us towards their sheds for the night. It was the hour when Africa is most beautiful; and here was this pathetic, ugly scene, doing no one any good.

At last my father stated finally: "I'm not going to argue about it. I am keeping the goats."

85

The old Chief flashed back in his own language: "That means that my people will go hungry when the dry season comes."

"Go to the police, then," said my father, and looked triumphant.

There was, of course, no more to be said.

The old man sat silent, his head bent, his hands dangling helplessly over his withered knees. Then he rose, the young men helping him, and he stood facing my father. He spoke once again, very stiffly; and turned away and went home to his village.

"What did he say?" asked my father of the young man, who laughed   90
uncomfortably and would not meet his eyes.

"What did he say?" insisted my father.

Our cook stood straight and silent, his brows knotted together. Then he
spoke. "My father says: All this land, this land you call yours, is his land, and
belongs to our people."

Having made this statement, he walked off into the bush after his father,
and we did not see him again.

Our next cook was a migrant from Nyasaland, with no expectations of
greatness.

Next time the policeman came on his rounds he was told this story. He   95
remarked: "That kraal has no right to be there; it should have been moved long
ago. I don't know why no one has done anything about it. I'll have a chat with
the Native Commissioner next week. I'm going over for tennis on Sunday, anyway."

Some time later we heard that Chief Mshlanga and his people had been
moved two hundred miles east, to a proper Native Reserve; the Government land
was going to be opened up for white settlement soon.

I went to see the village again, about a year afterwards. There was nothing
there. Mounds of red mud, where the huts had been, had long swathes of rotting
thatch over them, veined with the red galleries of the white ants. The pumpkin
vines rioted everywhere, over the bushes, up the lower branches of trees so that
the great golden balls rolled underfoot and dangled overhead: it was a festival of
pumpkins. The bushes were crowding up, the new grass sprang vivid green.

The settler lucky enough to be allotted the lush warm valley (if he chose to
cultivate this particular section) would find, suddenly, in the middle of a mealie
field, the plants were growing fifteen feet tall, the weight of the cobs dragging at
the stalks, and wonder what unsuspected vein of richness he had struck.

FLANNERY O'CONNOR   (1925–1964)

A Good Man Is Hard to Find   *1953*

The grandmother didn't want to go to Florida. She wanted to visit some of her
connections in east Tennessee and she was seizing at every chance to change
Bailey's mind. Bailey was the son she lived with, her only son. He was sitting on
the edge of his chair at the table, bent over the orange sports section of the *Journal.*
"Now look here, Bailey," she said, "see here, read this," and she stood with one
hand on her thin hip and the other rattling the newspaper at his bald head. "Here
this fellow that calls himself The Misfit is aloose from the Federal Pen and headed
toward Florida and you read here what it says he did to these people. Just you
read it. I wouldn't take my children in any direction with a criminal like that
aloose in it. I couldn't answer to my conscience if I did."

Bailey didn't look up from his reading so she wheeled around then and
faced the children's mother, a young woman in slacks, whose face was as broad
and innocent as a cabbage and was tied round with a green head-kerchief that
had two points on the top like rabbit's ears. She was sitting on the sofa, feeding
the baby his apricots out of a jar. "The children have been to Florida before," the

old lady said. "You all ought to take them somewhere else for a change so they would see different parts of the world and be broad. They never have been to east Tennessee."

The children's mother didn't seem to hear her but the eight-year-old boy, John Wesley, a stocky child with glasses, said, "If you don't want to go to Florida, why dontcha stay at home?" He and the little girl, June Star, were reading the funny papers on the floor.

"She wouldn't stay at home to be queen for a day," June Star said without raising her yellow head.

"Yes and what would you do if this fellow, The Misfit, caught you?" the   5
grandmother asked.

"I'd smack his face," John Wesley said.

"She wouldn't stay at home for a million bucks," June Star said. "Afraid she'd miss something. She has to go everywhere we go."

"All right, Miss," the grandmother said. "Just remember that the next time you want me to curl your hair."

June Star said her hair was naturally curly.

The next morning the grandmother was the first one in the car, ready to   10
go. She had her big black valise that looked like the head of a hippopotamus in one corner, and underneath it she was hiding a basket with Pitty Sing, the cat, in it. She didn't intend for the cat to be left alone in the house for three days because he would miss her too much and she was afraid he might brush against one of the gas burners and accidentally asphyxiate himself. Her son, Bailey, didn't like to arrive at a motel with a cat.

She sat in the middle of the back seat with John Wesley and June Star on either side of her. Bailey and the children's mother and the baby sat in the front and they left Atlanta at eight forty-five with the mileage on the car at 55890. The grandmother wrote this down because she thought it would be interesting to say how many miles they had been when they got back. It took them twenty minutes to reach the outskirts of the city.

The old lady settled herself comfortably, removing her white cotton gloves and putting them up with her purse on the shelf in front of the back window. The children's mother still had on slacks and still had her head tied up in a green kerchief, but the grandmother had on a navy blue straw sailor hat with a bunch of white violets on the brim and a navy blue dress with a small white dot in the print. Her collar and cuffs were white organdy trimmed with lace and at her neckline she had pinned a purple spray of cloth violets containing a sachet. In case of an accident, anyone seeing her dead on the highway would know at once that she was a lady.

She said she thought it was going to be a good day for driving, neither too hot nor too cold, and she cautioned Bailey that the speed limit was fifty-five miles an hour and that the patrolmen hid themselves behind billboards and small clumps of trees and sped out after you before you had a chance to slow down. She pointed out interesting details of the scenery: Stone Mountain; the blue granite that in some places came up to both sides of the highway; the brilliant red clay banks slightly streaked with purple; and the various crops that made rows of green lacework on the ground. The trees were full of silver-white sunlight and the meanest of them sparkled. The children were reading comic magazines and their mother had gone back to sleep.

"Let's go through Georgia fast so we won't have to look at it much," John Wesley said.

"If I were a little boy," said the grandmother, "I wouldn't talk about my native state that way. Tennessee has the mountains and Georgia has the hills." 15

"Tennessee is just a hillbilly dumping ground," John Wesley said, "and Georgia is a lousy state too."

"You said it," June Star said.

"In my time," said the grandmother, folding her thin veined fingers, "children were more respectful of their native states and their parents and everything else. People did right then. Oh look at the cute little pickaninny!" she said and pointed to a Negro child standing in the door of a shack. "Wouldn't that make a picture, now?" she asked and they all turned and looked at the little Negro out of the back window. He waved.

"He didn't have any britches on," June said.

"He probably didn't have any," the grandmother explained. "Little niggers 20 in the country don't have things like we do. If I could paint, I'd paint that picture," she said.

The children exchanged comic books.

The grandmother offered to hold the baby and the children's mother passed him over the front seat to her. She set him on her knee and bounced him and told him about the things they were passing. She rolled her eyes and screwed up her mouth and stuck her leathery thin face into his smooth bland one. Occasionally he gave her a faraway smile. They passed a large cotton field with five or six graves fenced in the middle of it, like a small island. "Look at the graveyard!" the grandmother said, pointing it out. "That was the old family burying ground. That belonged to the plantation."

"Where's the plantation?" John Wesley asked.

"Gone With the Wind," said the grandmother. "Ha. Ha."

When the children finished all the comic books they had brought, they 25 opened the lunch and ate it. The grandmother ate a peanut butter sandwich and an olive and would not let the children throw the box and the paper napkins out the window. When there was nothing else to do they played a game by choosing a cloud and making the other two guess what shape it suggested. John Wesley took one the shape of a cow and June Star guessed a cow and John Wesley said, no, an automobile, and June Star said he didn't play fair, and they began to slap each other over the grandmother.

The grandmother said she would tell them a story if they would keep quiet. When she told a story, she rolled her eyes and waved her head and was very dramatic. She said once when she was a maiden lady she had been courted by a Mr. Edgar Atkins Teagarden from Jasper, Georgia. She said he was a very good-looking man and a gentleman and that he brought her a watermelon every Saturday afternoon with his initials cut in it, E. A. T. Well, one Saturday, she said, Mr. Teagarden brought the watermelon and there was nobody at home and he left it on the front porch and returned in his buggy to Jasper, but she never got the watermelon, she said, because a nigger boy ate it when he saw the initials, E. A. T.! This story tickled John Wesley's funny bone and he giggled and giggled but June Star didn't think it was any good. She said she wouldn't marry a man that just brought her a watermelon on Saturday. The grandmother said she would have done well to marry Mr. Teagarden because he was a gentleman and had bought Coca-Cola stock when it first came out and that he had died only a few years ago, a very wealthy man.

They stopped at The Tower for barbecued sandwiches. The Tower was a part stucco and part wood filling station and dance hall set in a clearing outside of Timothy. A fat man named Red Sammy Butts ran it and there were signs stuck here and there on the building and for miles up and down the highway saying, TRY RED SAMMY'S FAMOUS BARBECUE. NONE LIKE FAMOUS RED SAMMY'S! RED SAM! THE FAT BOY WITH THE HAPPY LAUGH. A VETERAN! SAMMY'S YOUR MAN!

Red Sammy was lying on the bare ground outside The Tower with his head under a truck while a gray monkey about a foot high, chained to a small chinaberry tree, chattered nearby. The monkey sprang back into the tree and got on the highest limb as soon as he saw the children jump out of the car and run toward him.

Inside, The Tower was a long dark room with a counter at one end and tables at the other and dancing space in the middle. They all sat down at a broad table next to the nickelodeon and Red Sam's wife, a tall burnt-brown woman with hair and eyes lighter than her skin, came and took their order. The children's mother put a dime in the machine and played "The Tennessee Waltz," and the grandmother said the tune always made her want to dance. She asked Bailey if he would like to dance but he only glared at her. He didn't have a naturally sunny disposition like she did and trips made him nervous. The grandmother's brown eyes were very bright. She swayed her head from side to side and pretended she was dancing in her chair. June Star said play something she could tap to so the children's mother put in another dime and played a fast number and June Star stepped out onto the dance floor and did her tap routine.

"Ain't she cute?" Red Sam's wife said, leaning over the counter. "Would you like to come be my little girl?"

"No I certainly wouldn't," June Star said. "I wouldn't live in a broken-down place like this for a million bucks!" and she ran back to the table.

"Ain't she cute?" the woman repeated, stretching her mouth politely.

"Aren't you ashamed?" hissed her grandmother.

Red Sam came in and told his wife to quit lounging on the counter and hurry with these people's order. His khaki trousers reached just to his hip bones and his stomach hung over them like a sack of meal swaying under his shirt. He came over and sat down at a table nearby and let out a combination sigh and yodel. "You can't win," he said. "You can't win," and he wiped his sweating red face with a gray handkerchief. "These days you don't know who to trust," he said. "Ain't that the truth?"

"People are certainly not nice like they used to be," said the grandmother.

"Two fellers come in here last week," Red Sammy said, "driving a Chrysler. It was a old beat-up car but it was a good one and these boys looked all right to me. Said they worked at the mill and you know I let them fellers charge the gas they bought? Now why did I do that?"

"Because you're a good man!" the grandmother said at once.

"Yes'm, I suppose so," Red Sam said as if he were struck with the answer.

His wife brought the orders, carrying the five plates all at once without a tray, two in each hand and one balanced on her arm. "It isn't a soul in this green world of God's that you can trust," she said. "And I don't count anybody out of that, not nobody," she repeated, looking at Red Sammy.

"Did you read about that criminal, The Misfit, that's escaped?" asked the   40
grandmother.

"I wouldn't be a bit surprised if he didn't attack this place right here," said
the woman. "If he hears about it being here, I wouldn't be none surprised to see
him. If he hears it's two cent in the cash register, I wouldn't be a tall surprised if
he . . ."

"That'll do," Red Sam said. "Go bring these people their Co'Colas," and the
woman went off to get the rest of the order.

"A good man is hard to find," Red Sammy said. "Everything is getting
terrible. I remember the day you could go off and leave your screen door
unlatched. Not no more."

He and the grandmother discussed better times. The old lady said that in
her opinion Europe was entirely to blame for the way things were now. She said
the way Europe acted you would think we were made of money and Red Sam
said it was no use talking about it, she was exactly right. The children ran outside
into the white sunlight and looked at the monkey in the lacy chinaberry tree. He
was busy catching fleas on himself and biting each one carefully between his teeth
as if it were a delicacy.

They drove off again into the hot afternoon. The grandmother took cat   45
naps and woke up every few minutes with her own snoring. Outside of Toombsboro
she woke up and recalled an old plantation that she had visited in this neighborhood
once when she was a young lady. She said the house had six white columns across
the front and that there was an avenue of oaks leading up to it and two little
wooden trellis arbors on either side in front where you sat down with your suitor
after a stroll in the garden. She recalled exactly which road to turn off to get to
it. She knew that Bailey would not be willing to lose any time looking at an old
house, but the more she talked about it, the more she wanted to see it once again
and find out if the little twin arbors were still standing. "There was a secret panel
in this house," she said craftily, not telling the truth but wishing that she were,
"and the story went that all the family silver was hidden in it when Sherman° came
through but it was never found . . ."

"Hey!" John Wesley said, "Let's go see it! We'll find it! We'll poke all the
woodwork and find it! Who lives there? Where do you turn off at? Hey Pop, can't
we turn off there?"

"We never have seen a house with a secret panel!" June Star shrieked. "Let's
go to the house with the secret panel! Hey, Pop, can't we go see the house with
the secret panel!"

"It's not far from here, I know," the grandmother said. "It wouldn't take
over twenty minutes."

Bailey was looking straight ahead. His jaw was as rigid as a horseshoe. "No,"
he said.

The children began to yell and scream that they wanted to see the house   50
with the secret panel. John Wesley kicked the back of the front seat and June Star
hung over her mother's shoulder and whined desperately into her ear that they
never had any fun even on their vacation, and that they could never do what THEY

Sherman: William Tecumseh Sherman (1820–1891), Union general during the Civil
War.

wanted to do. The baby began to scream and John Wesley kicked the back of the seat so hard that his father could feel the blows in his kidney.

"All right!" he shouted, and drew the car to a stop at the side of the road. "Will you all shut up? Will you all just shut up for one second? If you don't shut up, we won't go anywhere."

"It would be very educational for them," the grandmother murmured.

"All right," Bailey said, "but get this: this is the only time we're going to stop for anything like this. This is the one and only time."

"The dirt road that you have to turn down is about a mile back," the grandmother directed. "I marked it when we passed."

"A dirt road," Bailey groaned.   55

After they had turned around and were headed toward the dirt road, the grandmother recalled other points about the house, the beautiful glass over the front doorway and the candle-lamp in the hall. John Wesley said that the secret panel was probably in the fireplace.

"You can't go inside this house," Bailey said. "You don't know who lives there."

"While you all talk to the people in front, I'll run around behind and get in a window," John Wesley suggested.

"We'll all stay in the car," his mother said.

They turned onto the dirt road and the car raced roughly along in swirl of   60
pink dust. The grandmother recalled the times when there were no paved roads and thirty miles was a day's journey. The dirt road was hilly and there were sudden washes in it and sharp curves on dangerous embankments. All at once they would be on a hill, looking down over the blue tops of trees for miles around, then the next minute, they would be in a red depression with the dust-coated trees looking down on them.

"This place had better turn up in a minute," Bailey said, "or I'm going to turn around."

The road looked as if no one had traveled on it in months.

"It's not much farther," the grandmother said and just as she said it, a horrible thought came to her. The thought was so embarrassing that she turned red in the face and her eyes dilated and her feet jumped up, upsetting her valise in the corner. The instant the valise moved, the newspaper top she had over the basket under it rose with a snarl and Pitty Sing, the cat, sprang onto Bailey's shoulder.

The children were thrown to the floor and their mother, clutching the baby, was thrown out the door onto the ground; the old lady was thrown into the front seat. The car turned over once and landed right-side-up in a gulch on the side of the road. Bailey remained in the driver's seat with the cat—gray-striped with a broad white face and an orange nose—clinging to his neck like a caterpillar.

As soon as the children saw they could move their arms and legs, they   65
scrambled out of the car, shouting, "We've had an ACCIDENT!" The grandmother was curled up under the dashboard, hoping she was injured so that Bailey's wrath would not come down on her all at once. The horrible thought she had had before the accident was that the house she had remembered so vividly was not in Georgia but in Tennessee.

Bailey removed the cat from his neck with both hands and flung it out the window against the side of a pine tree. Then he got out of the car and started looking for the children's mother. She was sitting against the side of the red gutted ditch, holding the screaming baby, but she only had a cut down her face and a broken shoulder. "We've had an ACCIDENT!" the children screamed in a frenzy of delight.

"But nobody's killed," June Star said with disappointment as the grandmother limped out of the car, her hat still pinned to her head but the broken front brim standing up at a jaunty angle and the violet spray hanging off the side. They all sat down in the ditch, except the children, to recover from the shock. They were all shaking.

"Maybe a car will come along," said the children's mother hoarsely.

"I believe I have injured an organ," said the grandmother, pressing her side, but no one answered her. Bailey's teeth were clattering. He had on a yellow sport shirt with bright blue parrots designed in it and his face was as yellow as the shirt. The grandmother decided that she would not mention that the house was in Tennessee.

The road was about ten feet above and they could see only the tops of the   70
trees on the other side of it. Behind the ditch they were sitting in there were more woods, tall and dark and deep. In a few minutes they saw a car some distance away on top of a hill, coming slowly as if the occupants were watching them. The grandmother stood up and waved both arms dramatically to attract their attention. The car continued to come on slowly, disappeared around a bend and appeared again, moving even slower, on top of the hill they had gone over. It was a big black battered hearse-like automobile. There were three men in it.

It came to a stop just over them and for some minutes, the driver looked down with a steady expressionless gaze to where they were sitting, and didn't speak. Then he turned his head and muttered something to the other two and they got out. One was a fat boy in black trousers and a red sweat shirt with a silver stallion embossed on the front of it. He moved around on the right side of them and stood staring, his mouth partly open in a kind of loose grin. The other had on khaki pants and a blue striped coat and a gray hat pulled down very low, hiding most of his face. He came around slowly on the left side. Neither spoke.

The driver got out of the car and stood by the side of it, looking down at them. He was an older man than the other two. His hair was just beginning to gray and he wore silver-rimmed spectacles that gave him a scholarly look. He had a long creased face and didn't have on any shirt or undershirt. He had on blue jeans that were too tight for him and was holding a black hat and a gun. The two boys also had guns.

"We've had an ACCIDENT!" the children screamed.

The grandmother had the peculiar feeling that the bespectacled man was someone she knew. His face was as familiar to her as if she had known him all her life but she could not recall who he was. He moved away from the car and began to come down the embankment, placing his feet carefully so that he wouldn't slip. He had on tan and white shoes and no socks, and his ankles were red and thin. "Good afternoon," he said. "I see you all had a little spill."

"We turned over twice!" said the grandmother.   75

"Oncet," he corrected. "We seen it happen. Try their car and see will it run, Hiram," he said quietly to the boy with the gray hat.

"What you got that gun for?" John Wesley asked, "Whatcha gonna do with that gun?"

"Lady," the man said to the children's mother, "would you mind calling them children to sit down by you? Children make me nervous. I want all you all to set down right together there where you're at."

"What are you telling us what to do for?" June Star asked.

Behind them the line of woods gaped like a dark open mouth. "Come here," said their mother. 80

"Look here now," Bailey began suddenly, "we're in a predicament! We're in . . ."

The grandmother shrieked. She scrambled to her feet and stood staring. "You're The Misfit!" she said. "I recognized you at once."

"Yes'm" the man said, smiling slightly as if he were pleased in spite of himself to be known, "but it would have been better for all of you, lady, if you hadn't reckernized me."

Bailey turned his head sharply and said something to his mother that shocked even the children. The old lady began to cry and The Misfit reddened.

"Lady," he said, "don't you get upset: Sometimes a man says things he don't mean. I don't reckon he meant to talk to you thataway." 85

"You wouldn't shoot a lady, would you?" the grandmother said and removed a clean handkerchief from her cuff and began to slap at her eyes with it.

The Misfit pointed the toe of his shoe into the ground and made a little hole and then covered it up again. "I would hate to have to," he said.

"Listen," the grandmother almost screamed, "I know you're a good man. You don't look a bit like you have common blood. I know you must come from nice people!"

"Yes mam," he said, "finest people in the world." When he smiled he showed a row of strong white teeth. "God never made a finer woman than my mother and my daddy's heart was pure gold," he said. The boy with the red sweat shirt had come around behind them and was standing with his gun at his hip. The Misfit squatted down on the ground. "Watch them children, Bobby Lee," he said. "You know they make me nervous." He looked at the six of them huddled together in front of him and he seemed to be embarrassed as if he couldn't think if anything to say. "Ain't a cloud in the sky," he remarked, looking up at it. "Don't see no sun but don't see no cloud neither."

"Yes, it's a beautiful day," said the grandmother. "Listen," she said, "you shouldn't call yourself The Misfit because I know you're a good man at heart. I can just look at you and tell." 90

"Hush!" Bailey yelled. "Hush! Everybody shut up and let me handle this!" He was squatting in the position of a runner about to sprint forward but he didn't move.

"I pre-chate that, lady," The Misfit said and drew a little circle in the ground with the butt of his gun.

"It'll take a half a hour to fix this here car," Hiram called, looking over the raised hood of it.

"Well, first you and Bobby Lee get him and that little boy to step over yonder with you," The Misfit said, pointing to Bailey and John Wesley. "The boys want to ask you something," he said to Bailey. "Would you mind stepping back in them woods there with them?"

"Listen," Bailey began, "we're in a terrible predicament. Nobody realizes   95
what this is," and his voice cracked. His eyes were as blue and intense as the
parrots in his shirt and he remained perfectly still.

The grandmother reached up to adjust her hat brim as if she were going to
the woods with him but it came off in her hand. She stood staring at it and after
a second she let it fall to the ground. Hiram pulled Bailey up by the arm as if he
were assisting an old man. John Wesley caught hold of his father's hand and
Bobby Lee followed. They went off toward the woods and just as they reached
the dark edge, Bailey turned and supporting himself against a gray naked pine
trunk, he shouted, "I'll be back in a minute, Mamma, wait on me!"

"Come back this instant!" his mother shrilled but they all disappeared into
the woods.

"Bailey Boy!" the grandmother called in a tragic voice but she found she
was looking at The Misfit squatting on the ground in front of her. "I just know
you're a good man," she said desperately. "You're not a bit common!"

"Nome, I ain't a good man," The Misfit said after a second as if he had
considered her statement carefully, "but I ain't the worst in the world neither. My
daddy said I was different breed of dog from my brothers and sisters. 'You know,'
Daddy said, 'it's some that can live their whole life out without asking about it and
it's others has to know why it is, and this boy is one of the latters. He's going to
be into everything!'" He put on his black hat and looked up suddenly and then
away deep into the woods as if he were embarrassed again. "I'm sorry I don't have
on a shirt before you ladies," he said, hunching his shoulders slightly. "We buried
our clothes that we had on when we escaped and we're just making do until we
can get better. We borrowed these from some folks we met," he explained.

"That's perfectly all right," the grandmother said. "Maybe Bailey has an   100
extra shirt in his suitcase."

"I'll look and see terrectly," the Misfit said.

"Where are they taking him?" the children's mother screamed.

"Daddy was a card himself," the Misfit said. "You couldn't put anything over
on him. He never got in trouble with the Authorities though. Just had the knack
of handling them."

"You could be honest too if you'd only try," said the grandmother. "Think
how wonderful it would be to settle down and live a comfortable life and not have
to think about somebody chasing you all the time."

The Misfit kept scratching in the ground with the butt of his gun as if he   105
were thinking about it. "Yes'm, somebody is always after you," he murmured.

The grandmother noticed how thin his shoulder blades were just behind his
hat because she was standing up looking down on him. "Do you ever pray?" she
asked.

He shook his head. All she saw was the black hat wiggle between his shoulder
blades. "Nome," he said.

There was a pistol shot from the woods, followed closely by another. Then
silence. The old lady's head jerked around. She could hear the wind move through
the tree tops like a long satisfied insuck of breath. "Bailey Boy!" she called.

"I was a gospel singer for a while," The Misfit said. "I been most everything.
Been in the arm service, both land and sea, at home and abroad, been twict
married, been an undertaker, been with the railroads, plowed Mother Earth, been
in a tornado, seen a man burnt alive oncet," and he looked up at the children's

mother and the little girl who were sitting close together, their faces white and their eyes glassy; "I even seen a woman flogged," he said.

"Pray, pray," the grandmother began, "pray, pray . . ." 110

"I never was a bad boy that I remember of," The Misfit said in an almost dreamy voice, "but somewheres along the line I done something wrong and got sent to the penitentiary. I was buried alive," and he looked up and held her attention to him by a steady stare.

"That's when you should have started to pray," she said. "What did you do to get sent to the penitentiary that first time?"

"Turn to the right, it was a wall," The Misfit said, looking up again at the cloudless sky. "Turn to the left, it was a wall. Look up it was a ceiling, look down it was a floor. I forgot what I done, lady. I set there and set there, trying to remember what it was I done and I ain't recalled it to this day. Oncet in a while, I would think it was coming to me, but it never come."

"Maybe they put you in by mistake," the old lady said vaguely.

"Nome," he said. "It wasn't no mistake. They had the papers on me." 115

"You must have stolen something," she said.

The Misfit sneered slightly. "Nobody had nothing I wanted," he said. "It was a head-doctor at the penitentiary said what I had done was kill my daddy but I know that for a lie. My daddy died in nineteen ought nineteen of the epidemic flu and I never had a thing to do with it. He was buried in the Mount Hopewell Baptist churchyard and you can go there and see for yourself."

"If you would pray," the old lady said, "Jesus would help you."

"That's right," The Misfit said.

"Well then, why don't you pray?" she asked trembling with delight suddenly. 120

"I don't want no hep," he said. "I'm doing all right by myself."

Bobby Lee and Hiram came ambling back from the woods. Bobby Lee was dragging a yellow shirt with bright blue parrots in it.

"Throw me that shirt, Bobby Lee," The Misfit said. The shirt came flying at him and landed on his shoulder and he put it on. The grandmother couldn't name what the shirt reminded her of. "No, lady," The Misfit said while he was buttoning it up. "I found out the crime don't matter. You can do one thing or you can do another, kill a man or take a tire off his car, because sooner or later you're going to forget what it was you done and just be punished for it."

The children's mother had begun to make heaving noises as if she couldn't get her breath. "Lady," he asked, "would you and that little girl like to step off yonder with Bobby Lee and Hiram and join your husband?"

"Yes, thank you," the mother said faintly. Her left arm dangled helplessly 125 and she was holding the baby, who had gone to sleep, in the other. "Hep that lady up, Hiram," The Misfit said as she struggled to climb out of the ditch, "and Bobby Lee, you hold onto that little girl's hand."

"I don't want to hold hands with him," June Star said. "He reminds me of a pig."

The fat boy blushed and laughed and caught her by the arm and pulled her off into the woods after Hiram and her mother.

Alone with The Misfit, the grandmother found that she had lost her voice. There was not a cloud in the sky nor any sun. There was nothing around her but woods. She wanted to tell him that he must pray. She opened and closed her mouth several times before anything came out. Finally she found herself saying,

"Jesus, Jesus," meaning Jesus will help you, but the way she was saying it, it sounded as if she might be cursing.

"Yes'm," The Misfit said as if he agreed. "Jesus thown everything off balance. It was the same case with Him as with me except He hadn't committed any crime and they could prove I had committed one because they had the papers on me. Of course," he said, "they never shown me any papers. That's why I sign myself now. I said long ago, you get you a signature and sign everything you do and keep a copy of it. Then you'll know what you done and you can hold up the crime to the punishment and see do they match and in the end you'll have something to prove you ain't been treated right. I call myself The Misfit," he said, "because I can't make what all I done wrong fit what all I gone through in punishment."

There was a piercing scream from the woods, followed closely by a pistol   130
report. "Does it seem right to you, lady, that one is punished a heap and another ain't punished at all?"

"Jesus!" the old lady cried. "You've got good blood! I know you wouldn't shoot a lady! I know you come from nice people! Pray! Jesus, you ought not to shoot a lady: I'll give you all the money I've got!"

"Lady," The Misfit said, looking beyond her far into the woods, "there never was a body that give the undertaker a tip."

There were two more pistol reports and the grandmother raised her head like a parched old turkey hen crying for water and called, "Bailey Boy, Bailey Boy!" as if her heart would break.

"Jesus was the only One that ever raised the dead," The Misfit continued, "and He shouldn't have done it. He thown everything off balance. If He did what He said then it's nothing for you to do but thow away everything and follow Him, and if He didn't, then it's nothing for you to do but enjoy the few minutes you got left the best way you can—by killing somebody or burning down his house or doing some other meanness to him. No pleasure but meanness," he said and his voice had become almost a snarl.

"Maybe He didn't raise the dead," the old lady mumbled, not knowing what   135
she was saying and feeling so dizzy that she sank down in the ditch with her legs twisted under her.

"I wasn't there so I can't say He didn't." The Misfit said, "I wisht I had of been there," he said, hitting the ground with his fist. "It ain't right I wasn't there because if I had of been there I would of known. Listen lady," he said in a high voice, "if I had of been there I would of known and I wouldn't be like I am now." His voice seemed about to crack and the grandmother's head cleared for an instant. She saw the man's face twisted close to her own as if he were going to cry and she murmured, "Why you're one of my babies. You're one of my own children!" She reached out and touched him on the shoulder. The Misfit sprang back as if a snake had bitten him and shot her three times through the chest. Then he put his gun down on the ground and took off his glasses and began to clean them.

Hiram and Bobby Lee returned from the woods and stood over the ditch, looking down at the grandmother who half sat and half lay in a puddle of blood with her legs crossed under her like a child's and her face smiling up at the cloudless sky.

Without his glasses, The Misfit's eyes were red-rimmed and pale and defenseless-looking. "Take her off and thow her where you thown the others," he said, picking up the cat that was rubbing itself against his leg.

"She was a talker, wasn't she?" Bobby Lee said, sliding down the ditch with a yodel.

"She would of been a good woman," The Misfit said, "if it had been somebody   140
there to shoot her every minute of her life."

"Some fun!" Bobby Lee said.

"Shut up, Bobby Lee," The Misfit said. "It's no real pleasure in life."

FRANK O'CONNOR (1903–1966)

First Confession   1951

All the trouble began when my grandfather died and my grandmother—my father's mother—came to live with us. Relations in the one house are a strain at the best of times, but, to make matters worse, my grandmother was a real old countrywoman and quite unsuited to the life in town. She had a fat, wrinkled old face, and, to Mother's great indignation, went round the house in bare feet—the boots had her crippled, she said. For dinner she had a jug of porter° and a pot of potatoes with—sometimes—a bit of salt fish, and she poured out the potatoes on the table and ate them slowly, with great relish, using her fingers by way of a fork.

Now, girls are supposed to be fastidious, but I was the one who suffered most from this. Nora, my sister, just sucked up to the old woman for the penny she got every Friday out of the old-age pension, a thing I could not do. I was too honest, that was my trouble; and when I was playing with Bill Connell, the sergeant-major's son, and saw my grandmother steering up the path with the jug of porter sticking out from beneath her shawl I was mortified. I made excuses not to let him come into the house, because I could never be sure what she would be up to when we went in.

When Mother was at work and my grandmother made the dinner I wouldn't touch it. Nora once tried to make me, but I hid under the table from her and took the bread-knife with me for protection. Nora let on to be very indignant (she wasn't, of course, but she knew Mother saw through her, so she sided with Gran) and came after me. I lashed out at her with the bread-knife, and after that she left me alone. I stayed there till Mother came in from work and made my dinner, but when Father came in later Nora said in a shocked voice: "Oh, Dadda, do you know what Jackie did at dinnertime?" Then, of course, it all came out; Father gave me a flaking; Mother interfered, and for days after that he didn't speak to me and Mother barely spoke to Nora. And all because of that old woman! God knows, I was heart-scalded.

Then, to crown my misfortune, I had to make my first confession and communion. It was an old woman called Ryan who prepared us for these. She was about the one age with Gran; she was well-to-do, lived in a big house on Montenotte, wore a black cloak and bonnet, and came every day to school at three o'clock when we should have been going home, and talked to us of hell. She may

porter: a dark-brown beer.

have mentioned the other place as well, but that could only have been by accident, for hell had the first place in her heart.

She lit a candle, took out a new half-crown, and offered it to the first boy   5
who would hold one finger—only one finger!—in the flame for five minutes by the school clock. Being always very ambitious I was tempted to volunteer, but I thought it might look greedy. Then she asked were we afraid of holding one finger—only one finger!—in a little candle flame for five minutes and not afraid of burning all over in roasting hot furnaces for all eternity. "All eternity! Just think of that! A whole lifetime goes by and it's nothing, not even a drop in the ocean of your sufferings." The woman was really interesting about hell, but my attention was all fixed on the half-crown. At the end of the lesson she put it back in her purse. It was a great disappointment; a religious woman like that, you wouldn't think she'd bother about a thing like a half-crown.

Another day she said she knew a priest who woke one night to find a fellow he didn't recognize leaning over the end of his bed. The priest was a bit frightened—naturally enough—but he asked the fellow what he wanted, and the fellow said in a deep, husky voice that he wanted to go to confession. The priest said it was an awkward time and wouldn't it do in the morning, but the fellow said that last time he went to confession, there was one sin he kept back, being ashamed to mention it, and now it was always on his mind. Then the priest knew it was a bad case, because the fellow was after making a bad confession and committing a mortal sin. He got up to dress, and just then the cock crew in the yard outside, and—lo and behold!—when the priest looked round there was no sign of the fellow, only a smell of burning timber, and when the priest looked at his bed didn't he see the print of two hands burned in it? That was because the fellow had made a bad confession. This story made a shocking impression on me.

But the worst of all was when she showed us how to examine our conscience. Did we take the name of the Lord, our God, in vain? Did we honour our father and our mother? (I asked her did this include grandmothers and she said it did.) Did we love our neighbours as ourselves? Did we covet our neighbour's goods? (I thought of the way I felt about the penny that Nora got every Friday.) I decided that, between one thing and another, I must have broken the whole ten commandments, all on account of that old woman, and so far as I could see, so long as she remained in the house I had no hope of ever doing anything else.

I was scared to death of confession. The day the whole class went I let on to have a toothache, hoping my absence wouldn't be noticed; but at three o'clock, just as I was feeling safe, along comes a chap with a message from Mrs. Ryan that I was to go to confession myself on Saturday and be at the chapel for communion with the rest. To make it worse, Mother couldn't come with me and sent Nora instead.

Now, that girl had ways of tormenting me that Mother never knew of. She held my hand as we went down the hill, smiling sadly and saying how sorry she was for me, as if she were bringing me to the hospital for an operation.

"Oh, God help us!" she moaned. "Isn't it a terrible pity you weren't a good   10
boy? Oh, Jackie, my heart bleeds for you! How will you ever think of all your sins? Don't forget you have to tell him about the time you kicked Gran on the shin."

"Lemme go!" I said, trying to drag myself free of her. "I don't want to go to confession at all."

"But sure, you'll have to go to confession, Jackie," she replied in the same regretful tone. "Sure, if you didn't the parish priest would be up to the house, looking for you. 'Tisn't, God knows, that I'm not sorry for you. Do you remember the time you tried to kill me with the bread-knife under the table? And the language you used to me? I don't know what he'll do with you at all, Jackie. He might have to send you up to the bishop."

I remember thinking bitterly that she didn't know the half of what I had to tell—if I told it. I knew I couldn't tell it, and understood perfectly why the fellow in Mrs. Ryan's story made a bad confession; it seemed to me a great shame that people wouldn't stop criticizing him. I remember that steep hill down to the church, and the sunlit hillsides beyond the valley of the river, which I saw in the gaps between the houses like Adam's last glimpse of Paradise.°

Then, when she had manœuvered me down the long flight of steps to the chapel yard, Nora suddenly changed her tone. She became the raging malicious devil she really was.

"There you are!" she said with a yelp of triumph, hurling me through the church door. "And I hope he'll give you the penitential psalms, you dirty little caffler."

I knew then I was lost, given up to eternal justice. The door with the coloured-glass panels swung shut behind me, the sunlight went out and gave place to deep shadow, and the wind whistled outside so that the silence within seemed to crackle like ice under my feet. Nora sat in front of me by the confession box. There were a couple of old women ahead of her, and then a miserable-looking poor devil came and wedged me in at the other side, so that I couldn't escape even if I had the courage. He joined his hands and rolled his eyes in the direction of the roof, muttering aspirations in an anguished tone, and I wondered had he a grandmother too. Only a grandmother could account for a fellow behaving in that heartbroken way, but he was better off than I, for he at least could go and confess his sins; while I would make a bad confession and then die in the night and be continually coming back and burning people's furniture.

Nora's turn came, and I heard the sound of something slamming, and then her voice as if butter wouldn't melt in her mouth, and then another slam, and out she came. God, the hypocrisy of women! Her eyes were lowered, her head was bowed, and her hands were joined very low down on her stomach, and she walked up the aisle to the side altar looking like a saint. You never saw such an exhibition of devotion, and I remembered the devilish malice with which she had tormented me all the way from our door, and wondered were all religious people like that, really. It was my turn now. With the fear of damnation in my soul I went in, and the confessional door closed of itself behind me.

It was pitch-dark and I couldn't see priest or anything else. Then I really began to be frightened. In the darkness it was a matter between God and me, and He had all the odds. He knew what my intentions were before I even started; I had no chance. All I had ever been told about confession got mixed up in my mind, and I knelt to one wall and said: "Bless me, father, for I have sinned; this is my first confession." I waited for a few minutes, but nothing happened, so I tried it on the other wall. Nothing happened there either. He had me spotted all right.

Adam's last glimpse of Paradise: Genesis 3:23–24.

It must have been then that I noticed the shelf at about one height with my head. It was really a place for grown-up people to rest their elbows, but in my distracted state I thought it was probably the place you were supposed to kneel. Of course, it was on the high side and not very deep, but I was always good at climbing and managed to get up all right. Staying up was the trouble. There was room only for my knees, and nothing you could get a grip on but a sort of wooden moulding a bit above it. I held on to the moulding and repeated the words a little louder, and this time something happened all right. A slide was slammed back; a little light entered the box, and a man's voice said: "Who's there?"

"'Tis me, father," I said for fear he mightn't see me and go away again. I   20
couldn't see him at all. The place the voice came from was under the moulding, about level with my knees, so I took a good grip of the moulding and swung myself down till I saw the astonished face of a young priest looking up at me. He had to put his head on one side to see me, and I had to put mine on one side to see him, so we were more or less talking to one another upside-down. It struck me as a queer way of hearing confessions, but I didn't feel it my place to criticize.

"Bless me, father, for I have sinned; this is my first confession," I rattled off all in one breath, and swung myself down the least shade more to make it easier for him.

"What are you doing up there?" he shouted in an angry voice, and the strain the politeness was putting on my hold of the moulding, and the shock of being addressed in such an uncivil tone, were too much for me. I lost my grip, tumbled, and hit the door an unmerciful wallop before I found myself flat on my back in the middle of the aisle. The people who had been waiting stood up with their mouths open. The priest opened the door of the middle box and came out, pushing his biretta back from his forehead; he looked something terrible. Then Nora came scampering down the aisle.

"Oh, you dirty little caffler!" she said. "I might have known you'd do it. I might have known you'd disgrace me. I can't leave you out of my sight for one minute."

Before I could even get to my feet to defend myself she bent down and gave me a clip across the ear. This reminded me that I was so stunned I had even forgotten to cry, so that people might think I wasn't hurt at all, when in fact I was probably maimed for life. I gave a roar out of me.

"What's all this about?" the priest hissed, getting angrier than ever and   25
pushing Nora off me. "How dare you hit the child like that, you little vixen?"

"But I can't do my penance with him, father," Nora cried, cocking an outraged eye up to him.

"Well, go and do it, or I'll give you some more to do," he said, giving me a hand up. "Was it coming to confession you were, my poor man?" he asked me.

"'Twas, father," said I with a sob.

"Oh," he said respectfully, "a big hefty fellow like you must have terrible sins. Is this your first?"

"'Tis, father," said I.

"Worse and worse," he said gloomily. "The crimes of a lifetime. I don't know will I get rid of you at all today. You'd better wait now till I'm finished with these old ones. You can see by the looks of them they haven't much to tell."

"I will, father," I said with something approaching joy.

The relief of it was really enormous. Nora stuck out her tongue at me from behind his back, but I couldn't even be bothered retorting. I knew from the very moment that man opened his mouth that he was intelligent above the ordinary. When I had time to think, I saw how right I was. It only stood to reason that a fellow confessing after seven years would have more to tell than people that went every week. The crimes of a lifetime, exactly as he said. It was only what he expected, and the rest was the cackle of old women and girls with their talk of hell, the bishop, and the penitential psalms. That was all they knew. I started to make my examination of conscience, and barring the one bad business of my grandmother it didn't seem so bad.

The next time, the priest steered me into the confession box himself and left the shutter back the way I could see him get in and sit down at the further side of the grille from me.

"Well, now," he said, "what do they call you?" 35

"Jackie, father," said I.

"And what's a-trouble to you, Jackie?"

"Father," I said, feeling I might as well get it over while I had him in good humour, "I had it all arranged to kill my grandmother."

He seemed a bit shaken by that, all right, because he said nothing for quite a while.

"My goodness," he said at last, "that'd be a shocking thing to do. What put 40 that into your head?"

"Father," I said, feeling very sorry for myself, "she's an awful woman."

"Is she?" he asked. "What way is she awful?"

"She takes porter, father," I said, knowing well from the way Mother talked of it that this was a mortal sin, and hoping it would make the priest take a more favourable view of my case.

"Oh, my!" he said, and I could see he was impressed.

"And snuff, father," said I. 45

"That's a bad case, sure enough, Jackie," he said.

"And she goes round in her bare feet, father," I went on in a rush of self-pity, "and she knows I don't like her, and she gives pennies to Nora and none to me, and my da sides with her and flakes me, and one night I was so heartscalded I made up my mind I'd have to kill her."

"And what would you do with the body?" he asked with great interest.

"I was thinking I could chop that up and carry it away in a barrow I have," I said.

"Begor, Jackie," he said, "do you know you're a terrible child?" 50

"I know, father," I said, for I was just thinking the same thing myself. "I tried to kill Nora too with a bread-knife under the table, only I missed her."

"Is that the little girl that was beating you just now?" he asked.

"'Tis, father."

"Someone will go for her with a bread-knife one day, and he won't miss her," he said rather cryptically. "You must have great courage. Between ourselves, there's a lot of people I'd like to do the same to but I'd never have the nerve. Hanging is an awful death."

"Is it, father?" I asked with the deepest interest—I was always very keen on 55 hanging. "Did you ever see a fellow hanged?"

"Dozens of them," he said solemnly. "And they all died roaring."

"Jay!" I said.

"Oh, a horrible death!" he said with great satisfaction. "Lots of fellows I saw killed their grandmothers too, but they all said 'twas never worth it."

He had me there for a full ten minutes talking, and then walked out the chapel yard with me. I was genuinely sorry to part with him, because he was the most entertaining character I'd ever met in the religious line. Outside, after the shadow of the church, the sunlight was like the roaring of waves on a beach; it dazzled me; and when the frozen silence melted and I heard the screech of trams on the road my heart soared. I knew now I wouldn't die in the night and come back, leaving marks on my mother's furniture. It would be a great worry to her, and the poor soul had enough.

Nora was sitting on the railing, waiting for me, and she put on a very sour puss when she saw the priest with me. She was made jealous because a priest had never come out of the church with her.

"Well," she asked coldly, after he left me, "what did he give you?"

"Three Hail Marys," I said.

"Three Hail Marys," she repeated incredulously. "You mustn't have told him anything."

"I told him everything," I said confidently.

"About Gran and all?"   65

"About Gran and all."

(All she wanted was to be able to go home and say I'd made a bad confession.)

"Did you tell him you went for me with the bread-knife?" she asked with a frown.

"I did to be sure."

"And he only gave you three Hail Marys?"   70

"That's all."

She slowly got down from the railing with a baffled air. Clearly, this was beyond her. As we mounted the steps back to the main road she looked at me suspiciously.

"What are you sucking?" she asked.

"Bullseyes."

"Was it the priest gave them to you?"   75

"'Twas."

"Lord God," she wailed bitterly, "some people have all the luck! 'Tis no advantage to anybody trying to be good. I might just as well be a sinner like you."

TILLIE OLSEN (b. 1913)

I Stand Here Ironing   *1953–1954*

I stand here ironing, and what you asked me moves tormented back and forth with the iron.

"I wish you would manage the time to come in and talk with me about your daughter. I'm sure you can help me understand her. She's a youngster who needs help and whom I'm deeply interested in helping."

"Who needs help." . . . Even if I came, what good would it do? You think because I am her mother I have a key, or that in some way you could use me as a key? She has lived for nineteen years. There is all that life that has happened outside of me, beyond me.

And when is there time to remember, to sift, to weigh, to estimate, to total? I will start and there will be an interruption and I will have to gather it all together again. Or I will become engulfed with all I did or did not do, with what should have been and what cannot be helped.

She was a beautiful baby. The first and only one of our five that was beautiful at birth. You do not guess how new and uneasy her tenancy in her now-loveliness. You did not know her all those years she was thought homely, or see her poring over her baby pictures, making me tell her over and over how beautiful she had been—and would be, I would tell her—and was now, to the seeing eye. But the seeing eyes were few or nonexistent. Including mine. 5

I nursed her. They feel that's important nowadays. I nursed all the children, but with her, with all the fierce rigidity of first motherhood, I did like the books then said. Though her cries battered me to trembling and my breasts ached with swollenness, I waited till the clock decreed.

Why do I put that first? I do not even know if it matters, or if it explains anything.

She was a beautiful baby. She blew shining bubbles of sound. She loved motion, loved light, loved color and music and textures. She would lie on the floor in her blue overalls patting the surface so hard in ecstasy her hands and feet would blur. She was a miracle to me, but when she was eight months old I had to leave her daytimes with the woman downstairs to whom she was no miracle at all, for I worked or looked for work and for Emily's father, who "could no longer endure" (he wrote in his good-bye note) "sharing want with us."

I was nineteen. It was the pre-relief, pre-WPA world of the depression. I would start running as soon as I got off the streetcar, running up the stairs, the place smelling sour, and awake or asleep to startle awake, when she saw me she would break into a clogged weeping that could not be comforted, a weeping I can hear yet.

After a while I found a job hashing at night so I could be with her days, and it was better. But it came to where I had to bring her to his family and leave her. 10

It took a long time to raise the money for her fare back. Then she got chicken pox and I had to wait longer. When she finally came, I hardly knew her, walking quick and nervous like her father, looking like her father, thin, and dressed in a shoddy red that yellowed her skin and glared at the pockmarks. All the baby loveliness gone.

She was two. Old enough for nursery school they said, and I did not know then what I know now—the fatigue of the long day, and the lacerations of group life in the kinds of nurseries that are only parking places for children.

Except that it would have made no difference if I had known. It was the only place there was. It was the only way we could be together, the only way I could hold a job.

And even without knowing, I knew. I knew the teacher that was evil because all these years it has curdled into my memory, the little boy hunched in the corner, her rasp, "why aren't you outside, because Alvin hits you? that's no reason, go out, scaredy." I knew Emily hated it even if she did not clutch and implore "don't go Mommy" like the other children, mornings.

She always had a reason why we should stay home. Momma, you look sick.   15
Momma, I feel sick. Momma, the teachers aren't there today, they're sick. Momma,
we can't go, there was a fire there last night. Momma, it's a holiday today, no
school, they told me.

But never a direct protest, never rebellion. I think of our others in their
three-, four-year-oldness—the explosions, the tempers, the denunciations, the
demands—and I feel suddenly ill. I put the iron down. What in me demanded
that goodness in her? And what was the cost, the cost to her of such goodness?

The old man living in the back once said in his gentle way: "You should
smile at Emily more when you look at her." What *was* in my face when I looked
at her? I loved her. There were all the acts of love.

It was only with the others I remembered what he said, and it was the face
of joy, and not of care or tightness or worry I turned to them—too late for Emily.
She does not smile easily, let alone almost always as her brothers and sisters do.
Her face is closed and sombre, but when she wants, how fluid. You must have
seen it in her pantomimes, you spoke of her rare gift for comedy on the stage
that rouses a laughter out of the audience so dear they applaud and applaud and
do not want to let her go.

Where does it come from, that comedy? There was none of it in her when
she came back to me that second time, after I had had to send her away again.
She had a new daddy now to learn to love, and I think perhaps it was a better
time.

Except when we left her alone nights, telling ourselves she was old enough.   20
"Can't you go some other time, Mommy, like tomorrow?" she would ask.
"Will it be just a little while you'll be gone? Do you promise?"

The time we came back, the front door open, the clock on the floor in the
hall. She rigid awake. "It wasn't just a little while. I didn't cry. Three times I called
you, just three times, and then I ran downstairs to open the door so you could
come faster. The clock talked loud. I threw it away, it scared me what it talked."

She said the clock talked loud again that night I went to the hospital to have
Susan. She was delirious with the fever that comes before red measles, but she
was fully conscious all the week I was gone and the week after we were home
when she could not come near the new baby or me.

She did not get well. She stayed skeleton thin, not wanting to eat, and night
after night she had nightmares. She would call for me, and I would rouse from
exhaustion to sleepily call back: "You're all right, darling, go to sleep, it's just a
dream," and if she still called, in a sterner voice, "now go to sleep, Emily, there's
nothing to hurt you." Twice, only twice, when I had to get up for Susan anyhow,
I went in to sit with her.

Now when it is too late (as if she would let me hold and comfort her like I   25
do the others) I get up and go to her at once at her moan or restless stirring.
"Are you awake, Emily? Can I get you something?" And the answer is always the
same: "No, I'm all right, go back to sleep, Mother."

They persuaded me at the clinic to send her away to a convalescent home
in the country where "she can have the kind of food and care you can't manage
for her, and you'll be free to concentrate on the new baby." They still send children
to that place. I see pictures on the society page of sleek young women planning
affairs to raise money for it, or dancing at the affairs, or decorating Easter eggs
or filling Christmas stockings for the children.

They never have a picture of the children so I do not know if the girls still wear those gigantic red bows and the ravaged looks on the every other Sunday when parents can come to visit "unless otherwise notified"—as we were notified the first six weeks.

Oh it is a handsome place, green lawns and tall trees and fluted flower beds. High up on the balconies of each cottage the children stand, the girls in their red bows and white dresses, the boys in white suits and giant red ties. The parents stand below shrieking up to be heard and the children shriek down to be heard, and between them the invisible wall "Not To Be Contaminated by Parental Germs or Physical Affection."

There was a tiny girl who always stood hand in hand with Emily. Her parents never came. One visit she was gone. "They moved her to Rose Cottage" Emily shouted in explanation. "They don't like you to love anybody here."

She wrote once a week, the labored writing of a seven-year-old. "I am fine. 30
How is the baby. If I write my leter nicly I will have a star. Love." There never was a star. We wrote every other day, letters she could never hold or keep but only hear read—once. "We simply do not have room for children to keep any personal possessions," they patiently explained when we pieced one Sunday's shrieking together to plead how much it would mean to Emily, who loved so to keep things, to be allowed to keep her letters and cards.

Each visit she looked frailer. "She isn't eating," they told us.

(They had runny eggs for breakfast or mush with lumps, Emily said later, I'd hold it in my mouth and not swallow. Nothing ever tasted good, just when they had chicken.)

It took us eight months to get her released home, and only the fact that she gained back so little of her seven lost pounds convinced the social worker.

I used to try to hold and love her after she came back, but her body would stay stiff, and after a while she'd push away. She ate little. Food sickened her, and I think much of life too. Oh she had physical lightness and brightness, twinkling by on skates, bouncing like a ball up and down up and down over the jump rope, skimming over the hill; but these were momentary.

She fretted about her appearance, thin and dark and foreign-looking at a 35
time when every little girl was supposed to look or thought she should look a chubby blonde replica of Shirley Temple. The doorbell sometimes rang for her, but no one seemed to come and play in the house or be a best friend. Maybe because we moved so much.

There was a boy she loved painfully through two school semesters. Months later she told me how she had taken pennies from my purse to buy him candy. "Licorice was his favorite and I brought him some every day, but he still liked Jennifer better'n me. Why, Mommy?" The kind of question for which there is no answer.

School was a worry to her. She was not glib or quick in a world where glibness and quickness were easily confused with ability to learn. To her overworked and exasperated teachers she was an overconscientious "slow learner" who kept trying to catch up and was absent entirely too often.

I let her be absent, though sometimes the illness was imaginary. How different from my now-strictness about attendance with the others. I wasn't working. We had a new baby, I was home anyhow. Sometimes, after Susan grew old enough, I would keep her home from school, too, to have them all together.

Mostly Emily had asthma, and her breathing, harsh and labored, would fill the house with a curiously tranquil sound. I would bring the two old dresser mirrors and her boxes of collections to her bed. She would select beads and single earrings, bottle tops and shells, dried flowers and pebbles, old postcards and scraps, all sorts of oddments; then she and Susan would play Kingdom, setting up landscapes and furniture, peopling them with action.

Those were the only times of peaceful companionship between her and   40
Susan. I have edged away from it, that poisonous feeling between them, that terrible balancing of hurts and needs I had to do between the two, and did so badly, those earlier years.

Oh there are conflicts between the others too, each one human, needing, demanding, hurting, taking—but only between Emily and Susan, no, Emily toward Susan that corroding resentment. It seems so obvious on the surface, yet it is not obvious. Susan, the second child, Susan, golden- and curly-haired and chubby, quick and articulate and assured, everything in appearance and manner Emily was not; Susan, not able to resist Emily's precious things, losing or sometimes clumsily breaking them; Susan telling jokes and riddles to company for applause while Emily sat silent (to say to me later; that was *my* riddle, Mother, I told it to Susan); Susan, who for all the five years' difference in age was just a year behind Emily in developing physically.

I am glad for that slow physical development that widened the difference between her and her contemporaries, though she suffered over it. She was too vulnerable for that terrible world of youthful competition, of preening and parading, of constant measuring of yourself against every other, of envy, "If I had that copper hair," "If I had that skin. . . ." She tormented herself enough about not looking like the others, there was enough of the unsureness, the having to be conscious of words before you speak, the constant caring—what are they thinking of me? without having it all magnified by the merciless physical drives.

Ronnie is calling. He is wet and I change him. It is rare there is such a cry now. That time of motherhood is almost behind me when the ear is not one's own but must always be racked and listening for the child cry, the child call. We sit for a while and I hold him, looking out over the city spread in charcoal with its soft aisles of light, "Shoogily," he breathes and curls closer. I carry him back to bed, asleep. *Shoogily.* A funny word, a family word, inherited from Emily, invented by her to say: *comfort.*

In this and other ways she leaves her seal, I say aloud. And startle at my saying it. What do I mean? What did I start to gather together, to try and make coherent? I was at the terrible, growing years. War years. I do not remember them well. I was working, there were four smaller ones now, there was not time for her. She had to help be a mother, a housekeeper, and shopper. She had to set her seal. Mornings of crisis and near hysteria trying to get lunches packed, hair combed, coats and shoes found, everyone to school or Child Care on time, the baby ready for transportation. And always the paper scribbled on by a smaller one, the book looked at by Susan then mislaid, the homework not done. Running out to that huge school where she was one, she was lost, she was a drop; suffering over the unpreparedness, stammering and unsure in her classes.

There was so little time left at night after the kids were bedded down. She   45
would struggle over books, always eating (it was in those years she developed her enormous appetite that is legendary in our family) and I would be ironing, or

preparing food for the next day, or writing V-mail to Bill, or tending the baby. Sometimes, to make me laugh, or out of her despair, she would imitate happenings or types at school.

I think I said once: "Why don't you do something like this in the school amateur show?" One morning she phoned me at work, hardly understandable through the weeping: "Mother, I did it. I won, I won; they gave me first prize; they clapped and clapped and wouldn't let me go."

Now suddenly she was Somebody, and as imprisoned in her difference as she had been in anonymity.

She began to be asked to perform at other high schools, even in colleges, then at city and statewide affairs. The first one we went to, I only recognized her that first moment when thin, shy, she almost drowned herself into the curtains. Then: Was this Emily? The control, the command, the convulsing and deadly clowning, the spell, then the roaring, stamping audience, unwilling to let this rare and precious laughter out of their lives.

Afterwards: You ought to do something about her with a gift like that—but without money or knowing how, what does one do? We have left it all to her, and the gift has as often eddied inside, clogged and clotted, as been used and growing.

She is coming. She runs up the stairs two at a time with her light graceful 50
step, and I know she is happy tonight. Whatever it was that occasioned your call did not happen today.

"Aren't you ever going to finish the ironing, Mother? Whistler painted his mother in a rocker. I'd have to paint mine standing over an ironing board." This is one of her communicative nights and she tells me everything and nothing as she fixes herself a plate of food out of the icebox.

She is so lovely. Why did you want me to come in at all? Why were you concerned? She will find her way.

She starts up the stairs to bed. "Don't get me up with the rest in the morning." "But I thought you were having midterms." "Oh, those," she comes back in, kisses me, and says quite lightly, "in a couple of years when we'll all be atom-dead they won't matter a bit.

She has said it before. She *believes* it. But because I have been dredging the past, and all that compounds a human being is so heavy and meaningful in me, I cannot endure it tonight.

I will never total it all. I will never come in to say: She was a child seldom 55
smiled at. Her father left me before she was a year old. I had to work her first six years when there was work, or I sent her home and to his relatives. There were years she had care she hated. She was dark and thin and foreign-looking in a world where the prestige went to blondeness and curly hair and dimples, she was slow where glibness was prized. She was a child of anxious, not proud, love. We were poor and could not afford for her the soil of easy growth. I was a young mother, I was a distracted mother. There were the other children pushing up, demanding. Her younger sister seemed all that she was not. There were years she did not want me to touch her. She kept too much in herself, her life was such she had to keep too much in herself. My wisdom came too late. She has much to her and probably little will come of it. She is a child of her age, of depression, of war, of fear.

Let her be. So all that is in her will not bloom—but in how many does it? There is still enough left to live by. Only help her to know—help make it so there is cause for her to know—that she is more than this dress on the ironing board, helpless before the iron.

GRACE PALEY (b. 1922)

Goodbye and Good Luck   *1959*

I was popular in certain circles, says Aunt Rose. I wasn't no thinner then, only more stationary in the flesh. In time to come, Lillie, don't be surprised—change is a fact of God. From this no one is excused. Only a person like your mama stands on one foot, she don't notice how big her behind is getting and sings in the canary's ear for thirty years. Who's listening? Papa's in the shop. You and Seymour, thinking about yourself. So she waits in a spotless kitchen for a kind word and thinks—poor Rosie. . . .

Poor Rosie! If there was more life in my little sister, she would know my heart is a regular college of feelings and there is such information between my corset and me that her whole married life is a kindergarten.

Nowadays you could find me any time in a hotel, uptown or downtown. Who needs an apartment to live like a maid with a dustrag in the hand, sneezing? I'm in very good with the bus boys, it's more interesting than home, all kinds of people, everybody with a reason.

And my reason, Lillie, is a long time ago I said to the forelady, "Missus, if I can't sit by the window, I can't sit." "If you can't sit, girlie," she says politely, "go stand on the street corner." And that's how I got unemployed in novelty wear.

For my next job I answered an ad which said: "Refined young lady, medium salary, cultural organization." I went by trolley to the address, the Russian Art Theater of Second Avenue where they played only the best Yiddish plays. They needed a ticket seller, someone like me, who likes the public but is very sharp on crooks. The man who interviewed me was the manager, a certain type.

Immediately he said: "Rosie Lieber, you surely got a build on you!"

"It takes all kinds, Mr. Krimberg."

"Don't misunderstand me, little girl," he said. "I appreciate, I appreciate. A young lady lacking fore and aft, her blood is so busy warming the toes and the finger tips, it don't have time to circulate where it's most required."

Everybody likes kindness. I said to him: "Only don't be fresh, Mr. Krimberg, and we'll make a good bargain."

We did: Nine dollars a week, a glass of tea every night, a free ticket once a week for Mama, and I could go watch rehearsals any time I wanted.

My first nine dollars was in the grocer's hands ready to move on already, when Krimberg said to me, "Rosie, here's a great gentleman, a member of this remarkable theater, wants to meet you, impressed no doubt by your big brown eyes."

And who was it, Lillie? Listen to me before my very eyes was Volodya Vlashkin, called by the people of those days the Valentino of Second Avenue. I took one look, and I said to myself: Where did a Jewish boy grow up so big? "Just outside Kiev," he told me.

How? "My mama nursed me till I was six. I was the only boy in the village to have such health."

"My goodness, Vlashkin, six years old! She must have had shredded wheat there, not breasts, poor woman."

"My mother was beautiful," he said. "She had eyes like stars."   15

He had such a way of expressing himself, it brought tears.

To Krimberg, Vlashkin said after this introduction: "Who is responsible for hiding this wonderful young person in a cage?"

"That is where the ticket seller sells."

"So, David, go in there and sell tickets for a half hour. I have something in mind in regards to the future of this girl and this company. Go, David, be a good boy. And you, Miss Lieber, please, I suggest Feinberg's for a glass of tea. The rehearsals are long. I enjoy a quiet interlude with a friendly person."

So he took me there, Feinberg's, then around the corner, a place so full of   20
Hungarians, it was deafening. In the back room was a table of honor for him. On the tablecloth embroidered by the lady of the house was "Here Vlashkin Eats." We finished one glass of tea in quietness, out of thirst, when I finally made up my mind what to say.

"Mr. Vlashkin, I saw you a couple weeks ago, even before I started working here, in *The Sea Gull*. Believe me, if I was that girl, I wouldn't look even for a minute on the young bourgeois fellow. He could fall out of the play altogether. How Chekhov could put him in the same play as you, I can't understand."

"You liked me?" he asked, taking my hand and kindly patting it. "Well, well, young people still like me . . . so, and you like the theater too? Good. And you, Rose, you know you have such a nice hand, so warm to the touch, such a fine skin, tell me, why do you wear a scarf around your neck? You only hide your young, young throat. These are not olden times, my child, to live in shame."

"Who's ashamed?" I said, taking off the kerchief, but my hand right away went to the kerchief's place, because the truth is, it really was olden times, and I was still of a nature to melt with shame.

"Have some more tea, my dear."

"No, thank you, I am a samovar already."   25

"Dorfmann!" he hollered like a king. "Bring this child a seltzer with fresh ice!"

In weeks to follow I had the privilege to know him better and better as a person—also the opportunity to see him in his profession. The time was autumn; the theater full of coming and going. Rehearsing without end. After *The Sea Gull* flopped *The Salesman from Istanbul* played, a great success.

Here the ladies went crazy. On the opening night, in the middle of the first scene, one missus—a widow or her husband worked too long hours—began to clap and sing out, "Oi, oi, Vlashkin." Soon there was such a tumult, the actors had to stop acting. Vlashkin stepped forward. Only not Vlashkin to the eyes . . . a younger man with pitch-black hair, lively on restless feet, his mouth clever. A half a century later at the end of the play he came out again, a gray philosopher, a student of life from only reading books, his hands as smooth as silk. . . I cried to think who I was—nothing—and such a man could look at me with interest.

Then I got a small raise, due to he kindly put in a good word for me, and also for fifty cents a night I was given the pleasure together with cousins, in-laws, and plain stage-struck kids to be part of a crowd scene and to see like he saw every single night the hundreds of pale faces waiting for his feelings to make them laugh or bend down their heads in sorrow.

The sad day came, I kissed my mama goodbye. Vlashkin helped me to get   30
a reasonable room near the theater to be more free. Also my outstanding friend
would have a place to recline away from the noise of the dressing rooms. She
cried and she cried. "This is a different way of living, Mama," I said. "Besides I
am driven by love."

"You! You, a nothing, a rotten hole in a piece of cheese, are you telling me
what is life?" she screamed.

Very insulted, I went away from her. But I am good-natured—you know
fat people are like that—kind, and I thought to myself, poor Mama . . . it is true
she got more of an idea of life than me. She married who she didn't like, a sick
man, his spirit already swallowed up by God. He never washed. He had an
unhappy smell. His teeth fell out, his hair disappeared, he got smaller, shriveled
up little by little, till goodbye and good luck he was gone and only came to Mama's
mind when she went to the mailbox under the stairs to get the electric bill. In
memory of him and out of respect for mankind, I decided to live for love.

Don't laugh, you ignorant girl.

Do you think it was easy for me? I had to give Mama a little something.
Ruthie was saving up together with your papa for linens, a couple knives and
forks. In the morning I had to do piecework if I wanted to keep by myself. So I
made flowers. Before lunch time every day a whole garden grew on my table.

This was my independence, Lillie dear, blooming, but it didn't have no roots   35
and its face was paper.

Meanwhile Krimberg went after me too. No doubt observing the success of
Vlashkin, he thought, "Aha, open sesame . . ." Others in the company similar.
After me in those years were the following: Krimberg I mentioned. Carl Zimmer,
played innocent young fellows with a wig. Charlie Peel, a Christian who fell in the
soup by accident, a creator of beautiful sets. "Color is his middle name," says
Vlashkin, always to the point.

I put this in to show you your fat old aunt was not crazy out of loneliness.
In those noisy years I had friends among interesting people who admired me for
reasons of youth and that I was a first-class listener.

The actresses—Raisele, Marya, Esther Leopold—were only interested in
tomorrow. After them was the rich men, producers, the whole garment center;
their past is a pincushion, future the eye of a needle.

Finally the day came, I no longer could keep my tact in my mouth. I said:
"Vlashkin, I hear by carrier pigeon you have a wife, children, the whole combination."

"True, I don't tell stories. I make no pretense."   40

"That isn't the question. What is this lady like? It hurts me to ask, but tell
me, Vlashkin . . . a man's life is something I don't clearly see."

"Little girl, I have told you a hundred times, this small room is the convent
of my troubled spirit. Her I come to your innocent shelter to refresh myself in
the midst of an agonized life."

"Ach, Vlashkin, serious, serious, who is this lady?"

"Rosie, she is a fine woman of the middle classes, a good mother to my
children, three in number, girls all, a good cook, in her youth handsome, now no
longer young. You see, could I be more frank? I entrust you, dear, with my soul."

It was some few months later at the New Year's ball of the Russian Artists   45
Club, I met Mrs. Vlashkin, a woman with black hair in a low bun, straight and

too proud. She sat at a small table speaking in a deep voice to whoever stopped a moment to converse. Her Yiddish was perfect, each word cut like a special jewel. I looked at her. She noticed me like she notices everybody, cold like Christmas morning. Then she got tired. Vlashkin called a taxi and I never saw her again. Poor woman, she did not know I was on the same stage with her. The poison I was to her role, she did not know.

Later on that night in front of my door I said to Vlashkin, "No more. This isn't for me. I am sick from it all. I am no home breaker."

"Girlie," he said, "don't be foolish."

"No, no, goodbye, good luck," I said. "I am sincere."

So I went and stayed with Mama for a week's vacation and cleaned up all the closets and scrubbed the walls till the paint came off. She was very grateful, all the same her hard life made her say. "Now we see the end. If you live like a bum, you are finally a lunatic."

After this few days I came back to my life. When we met, me and Vlashkin, we said only hello and goodbye, and then for a few sad years, with the head we nodded as if to say, "Yes, yes, I know who you are."

Meanwhile in the field was a whole new strategy. Your mama and your grandmama brought around—boys. Your own father had a brother, you never even seen him. Ruben. A serious fellow, his idealism was his hat and his coat, "Rosie, I offer you a big new free happy unusual life." How? "With me, we will raise up the sands of Palestine to make a nation. That is the land of tomorrow for us Jews." "Ha-ha, Ruben, I'll go tomorrow then." "Rosie!" says Ruben. "We need strong women like you, mothers and farmers." "You don't fool me, Ruben, what you need is dray horses. But for that you need more money." "I don't like your attitude, Rose." "In that case, go and multiply. Goodbye."

Another fellow: Yonkel Gurstein, a regular sport, dressed to kill, with such an excitable nature. In those days—it looks to me like yesterday—the youngest girls wore undergarments like Battle Creek, Michigan. To him it was a matter of seconds. Where did he practice, a Jewish boy? Nowadays I suppose it is easier, Lillie? My goodness, I ain't asking you nothing—touchy, touchy. . . .

Well, by now you must know yourself, honey whatever you do, life don't stop. It only sits a minute and dreams a dream.

While I was saying to all these silly youngsters "no, no, no," Vlashkin went to Europe and toured a few seasons . . . Moscow, Prague, London, even Berlin—already a pessimistic place. When he came back he wrote a book, you could get from the library even today, *The Jewish Actor Abroad*. If someday you're interested enough in my lonesome years, you could read it. You could absorb a flavor of the man from the book. No, no, I am not mentioned. After all, who am I?

When the book came out I stopped him in the street to say congratulations. But I am not a liar, so I pointed out, too, the egotism of many parts—even the critics said something along such lines.

"Talk is cheap," Vlashkin answered me. "But who are the critics? Tell me, do they create? Not to mention," he continues, "there is a line in Shakespeare in one of the plays from the great history of England. It says, 'Self-loving is not so vile a sin, my liege, as self-neglecting.'° This idea also appears in modern times in

self-loving . . . self-neglecting: Henry V, 2.4. 74–75.

the moralistic followers of Freud. . . . Rosie, are you listening? You asked a question. By the way, you look very well. How come no wedding ring?"

I walked away from this conversation in tears. But this talking in the street opened the happy road up for more discussions. In regard to many things. . . . For instance, the management—very narrow-minded—wouldn't give him any more certain young men's parts. Fools. What youngest man knew enough about life to be as young as him?

"Rosie, Rosie," he said to me one day, "I see by the clock on your rosy, rosy face you must be thirty."

"The hands are slow, Vlashkin. On a week before Thursday I was thirty-four."

"Is that so? Rosie, I worry about you. It has been on my mind to talk to you. You are losing your time. Do you understand it? A woman should not lose her time." 60

"Oi, Vlashkin, if you are my friend, what is time?"

For this he had no answer, only looked at me surprised. We went instead, full of interest but not with our former speed, up to my new place on Ninety-fourth Street. The same pictures on the wall, all of Vlashkin, only now everything painted red and black, which was stylish, and new upholstery.

A few years ago there was a book by another member of that fine company, an actress, the one that learned English very good and went uptown—Marya Kavkaz, in which she says certain things regarding Vlashkin. Such as, he was her lover for eleven years, she's not ashamed to write this down. Without respect for him, his wife and children, or even others who also may have feelings in the matter.

Now, Lillie, don't be surprised. This is called a fact of life. An actor's soul must be like a diamond. The more faces it got the more shining is his name. Honey, you will no doubt love and marry one man and have a couple kids and be happy forever till you die tired. More than that, a person like us don't have to know. But a great artist like Volodya Vlashkin . . . in order to make a job on the stage, he's got to practice. I understand it now, to him life is like a rehearsal.

Myself, when I saw him in *The Father-in-law*—an older man in love with a darling young girl, his son's wife, played by Raisele Maisel—I cried. What he said to this girl, how he whispered such sweetness, how all his hot feelings were on his face . . . Lillie, all this experience he had with me. The very words were the same. You can image how proud I was. 65

So the story creeps to an end.

I noticed it first on my mother's face, the rotten handwriting of time, scribbled up and down her cheeks, across her forehead back and forth—a child could read—it said, old, old, old. But it troubled my heart most to see these realities scratched on Vlashkin's wonderful expression.

First the company fell apart. The theater ended. Esther Leopold died from being very aged. Krimberg had a heart attack. Marya went to Broadway. Also Raisele changed her name to Roslyn and was a big comical hit in the movies. Vlashkin himself, no place to go, retired. It said in the paper, "an actor without peer, he will write his memoirs and spend his last years in the bosom of his family among his thriving grandchildren, the apple of his wife's doting eye."

This is journalism.

We made for him a great dinner of honor. At this dinner I said to him, for the last time, I thought, "Goodbye, dear friend, topic of my life, now we part." 70

And to myself I said further: Finished. This is your lonesome bed. A lady what they call fat and fifty. You made it personally. From this lonesome bed you will finally fall to a bed not so lonesome, only crowded with a million bones.

And now comes? Lillie, guess.

Last week, washing my underwear in the basin, I get a buzz on the phone. "Excuse me, is this the Rose Lieber formerly connected with the Russian Art Theater?"

"It is."

"Well, well, how do you do, Rose? This is Vlashkin."

"Vlashkin! Volodya Vlashkin?"   75

"In fact. How are you, Rose?"

"Living, Vlashkin, thank you."

"You are all right? Really, Rose? Your health is good? You are working?"

"My health, considering the weight it must carry, is first-class. I am back for some years now where I started, in novelty wear."

"Very interesting."   80

"Listen, Vlashkin, tell me the truth, what's on your mind?"

"My mind? Rosie, I am looking up an old friend, an old warmhearted companion of more joyful days. My circumstances, by the way, are changed. I am retired, as you know. Also I am a free man."

"What? What do you mean?"

"Mrs. Vlashkin is divorcing me."

"What come over her? Did you start drinking or something from melan-   85
choly?"

"She is divorcing me for adultery."

"But, Vlashkin, you should excuse me, don't be insulted, but you got maybe seventeen, eighteen years on me, and even me, all this nonsense—this daydreams and nightmares—is mostly for the pleasure of conversation alone."

"I pointed all this out to her. My dear, I said, my time is past, my blood is as dry as my bones. The truth is, Rose, she isn't accustomed to have a man around all day, reading out loud from the papers the interesting events of our time, waiting for breakfast, waiting for lunch. So all day she gets madder and madder. By nighttime a furious old lady gives me my supper. She has information from the last fifty years to pepper my soup. Surely there was a Judas in that theater, saying every day, 'Vlashkin, Vlashkin, Vlashkin . . .' and while my heart was circulating with his smiles he was on the wire passing the dope to my wife."

"Such a foolish end, Volodya, to such a lively story. What is your plans?"

"First, could I ask you for dinner and the theater—uptown, of course? After   90
this . . . we are old friends. I have money to burn. What your heart desires. Others are like grass, the north wind of time has cut out their heart. Of you, Rosie, I recreate only kindness. What a woman should be to a man, you were to me. Do you think, Rosie, a couple of old pals like us could have a few good times among the material things of this world?"

My answer, Lillie, in a minute was altogether. "Yes, yes, come up," I said. "Ask the room by the switchboard, let us talk."

So he came that night and every night in the week, we talked of his long life. Even at the end of time, a fascinating man. And like men are, too, till time's end, trying to get away in one piece.

"Listen, Rosie," he explains the other day. "I was married to my wife, do you realize, nearly half a century. What good was it? Look at the bitterness. The more I think of it, the more I think we would be fools to marry."

"Volodya Vlashkin," I told him straight, "when I was young I warmed your cold back many a night, no questions asked. You admit it, I didn't make no demands. I was softhearted. I didn't want to be called Rosie Lieber, a breaker up of homes. But now, Vlashkin, you are a free man. How could you ask me to go with you on trains to stay in strange hotels, among Americans, not your wife? Be ashamed."

So now, darling Lillie, tell this story to your mama from your young mouth. She don't listen to a word from me. She only screams, "I'll faint, I'll faint," Tell her after all I'll have a husband, which, as everybody knows, a woman should have at least one before the end of the story. 95

My goodness, I am already late. Give me a kiss. After all, I watched you grow from a plain seed. So give me a couple wishes on my wedding day. A long and happy life. Many years of love. Hug Mama, tell her from Aunt Rose, goodbye and good luck.

KATHERINE ANNE PORTER (1890–1980)

The Jilting of Granny Weatherall   *1930*

She flicked her wrist neatly out of Doctor Harry's pudgy careful fingers and pulled the sheet up to her chin. The brat ought to be in knee breeches. Doctoring around the country with spectacles on his nose! "Get along now, take your schoolbooks and go. There's nothing wrong with me."

Doctor Harry spread a warm paw like a cushion on her forehead where the forked green vein danced and made her eyelids twitch. "Now, now, be a good girl, and we'll have you up in no time."

"That's no way to speak to a woman nearly eighty years old just because she's down. I'd have you respect your elders, young man."

"Well, Missy, excuse me." Doctor Harry patted her cheek. "But I've got to warn you, haven't I? You're a marvel, but you must be careful or you're going to be good and sorry."

"Don't tell me what I'm going to be. I'm on my feet now, morally speaking. It's Cornelia. I had to go to bed to get rid of her." 5

Her bones felt loose, and floated around in her skin, and Doctor Harry floated like a balloon around the foot of the bed. He floated and pulled down his waistcoat and swung his glasses on a cord. "Well, stay where you are, it certainly can't hurt you."

"Get along and doctor your sick." said Granny Weatherall. "Leave a well woman alone. I'll call for you when I want you. . . . Where were you forty years ago when I pulled through milk-leg and double pneumonia? You weren't even born. Don't let Cornelia lead you on." she shouted, because Doctor Harry appeared to float up to the ceiling and out. "I pay my own bills, and I don't throw my money away on nonsense!"

She meant to wave good-by, but it was too much trouble. Her eyes closed of themselves, it was like a dark curtain drawn around the bed. The pillow rose and floated under her, pleasant as a hammock in a light wind. She listened to the leaves rustling outside the window. No, somebody was swishing newspapers: no, Cornelia and Doctor Harry were whispering together. She leaped broad awake, thinking they whispered in her ear.

"She was never like this, *never* like this!" "Well, what can we expect?" "Yes, eighty years old. . . ."

Well, and what if she was? She still had ears. It was like Cornelia to whisper   10
around doors. She always kept things secret in such a public way. She was always being tactful and kind. Cornelia was dutiful; that was the trouble with her. Dutiful and good: "So good and dutiful," said Granny, "that I'd like to spank her." She saw herself spanking Cornelia and making a fine job of it.

"What'd you say, Mother?"

Granny felt her face tying up in hard knots.

"Can't a body think, I'd like to know?"

"I thought you might want something."

"I do. I want a lot of things. First off, go away and don't whisper."   15

She lay and drowsed, hoping in her sleep that the children would keep out and let her rest a minute. It had been a long day. Not that she was tired. It was always pleasant to snatch a minute now and then. There was always so much to be done, let me see: tomorrow.

Tomorrow was far away and there was nothing to trouble about. Things were finished somehow when the time came; thank God there was always a little margin over for peace: then a person could spread out the plan of life and tuck in the edges orderly. It was good to have everything clean and folded away, with the hair brushes and tonic bottles sitting straight on the white embroidered linen: the day started without fuss and the pantry shelves laid out with rows of jelly glasses and brown jugs and white stone-china jars with blue whirligigs and words painted on them: coffee, tea, sugar, ginger, cinnamon, allspice: and the bronze clock with the lion on top nicely dusted off. The dust that lion could collect in twenty-four hours! The box in the attic with all those letters tied up, well she'd have to go through that tomorrow. All those letters—George's letters and John's letters and her letters to them both—lying around for the children to find afterwards made her uneasy. Yes, that would be tomorrow's business. No use to let them know how silly she had been once.

While she was rummaging around she found death in her mind and it felt clammy and unfamiliar. She had spent so much time preparing for death there was no need for bringing it up again. Let it take care of itself now. When she was sixty she had felt very old, finished, and went around making farewell trips to see her children and grandchildren, with a secret in her mind: This is the very last of your mother, children! Then she made her will and came down with a long fever. That was all just a notion like a lot of other things, but it was lucky too, for she had once for all got over the idea of dying for a long time. Now she couldn't be worried. She hoped she had better sense now. Her father had lived to be one hundred and two years old and had drunk a noggin of strong hot toddy on his last birthday. He told the reporters it was his daily habit, and he owed his long life to that. He had made quite a scandal and was very pleased about it. She believed she'd just plague Cornelia a little.

"Cornelia! Cornelia!" No footsteps, but a sudden hand on her cheek. "Bless you, where have you been?"

"Here, mother."   20

"Well, Cornelia, I want a noggin of hot toddy."

"Are you cold, darling?"

"I'm chilly, Cornelia. Lying in bed stops the circulation. I must have told you that a thousand times."

Well, she could just hear Cornelia telling her husband that Mother was getting childish and they'd have to humor her. The thing that most annoyed her was that Cornelia thought she was deaf, dumb, and blind. Little hasty glances and tiny gestures tossed around her and over her head saying, "Don't cross her, let her have her way, she's eighty years old," and she sitting there as if she lived in a thin glass cage. Sometimes Granny almost made up her mind to pack up and move back to her own house where nobody could remind her every minute that she was old. Wait, wait, Cornelia, till your own children whisper behind your back!

In her day she had kept a better house and had got more work done. She wasn't too old yet for Lydia to be driving eighty miles for advice when one of the children jumped the track, and Jimmy still dropped in and talked things over: "Now, Mammy, you've a good business head, I want to know what you think of this? . . ." Old Cornelia couldn't change the furniture around without asking. Little things, little things! They had been so sweet when they were little. Granny wished the old days were back again with the children young and everything to be done over. It had been a hard pull, but not too much for her. When she thought of all the food she had cooked, and all the clothes she had cut and sewed, and all the gardens she had made—well, the children showed it. There they were, made out of her, and they couldn't get away from that. Sometimes she wanted to see John again and point to them and say, Well, I didn't do so badly, did I? But that would have to wait. That was for tomorrow. She used to think of him as a man, but now all the children were older than their father, and he would be a child beside her if she saw him now. It seemed strange and there was something wrong in the idea. Why, he couldn't possibly recognize her. She had fenced in a hundred acres once, digging the post holes herself and clamping the wires with just a negro boy to help. That changed a woman. John would be looking for a young woman with the peaked Spanish comb in her hair and the painted fan. Digging post holes changed a woman. Riding country roads in the winter when women had their babies was another thing: sitting up nights with sick horses and sick negroes and sick children and hardly ever losing one. John, I hardly ever lost one of them! John would see that in a minute, that would be something he could understand, she wouldn't have to explain anything!

It made her feel like rolling up her sleeves and putting the whole place to rights again. No matter if Cornelia was determined to be everywhere at once, there were a great many things left undone on this place. She would start tomorrow and do them. It was good to be strong enough for everything, even if all you made melted and changed and slipped under your hands, so that by the time you finished you almost forgot what you were working for. What was it I set out to do? she asked herself intently, but she could not remember. A fog rose over the valley, she saw it marching across the creek swallowing the trees and moving up the hill like an army of ghosts. Soon it would be at the near edge of the orchard, and then it was time to go in and light the lamps. Come in children, don't stay out in the night air.

Lighting the lamps had been beautiful. The children huddled up to her and breathed like little calves waiting at the bars in the twilight. Their eyes followed the match and watched the flame rise and settle in a blue curve, then they moved away from her. The lamp was lit, they didn't have to be scared and hang on to mother any more. Never, never, never more. God, for all my life I thank Thee. Without Thee, my God, I could never have done it. Hail, Mary, full of grace.

I want you to pick all the fruit this year and see that nothing is wasted. There's always someone who can use it. Don't let good things rot for want of using. You waste life when you waste good food. Don't let things get lost. It's bitter to lose things. Now, don't let me get to thinking, not when I am tired and taking a little nap before supper. . . .

The pillow rose about her shoulders and pressed against her heart and the memory was being squeezed out of it: oh, push down the pillow, somebody: it would smother her if she tried to hold it. Such a fresh breeze blowing and such a green day with no threats in it. But he had not come, just the same. What does a woman do when she has put on the white veil and set out the white cake for a man and he doesn't come? She tried to remember. No, I swear he never harmed me but in that. He never harmed me but in that . . . and what if he did? There was the day, the day, but a whirl of dark smoke rose and covered it, crept up and over into the bright field where everything was planted so carefully in orderly rows. That was hell, she knew hell when she saw it. For sixty years she had prayed against remembering him and against losing her soul in the deep pit of hell, and now the two things were mingled in one and the thought of him was a smoky cloud from hell that moved and crept in her head when she had just got rid of Doctor Harry and was trying to rest a minute. Wounded vanity, Ellen, said a sharp voice in the top of her mind. Don't let your wounded vanity get the upper hand of you. Plenty of girls get jilted. You were jilted, weren't you. Then stand up to it. Her eyelids wavered and let in streamers of blue-gray light like tissue paper over her eyes. She must get up and pull the shades down or she'd never sleep. She was in bed again and the shades were not down. How could that happen? Better turn over, hide from the light, sleeping in the light gave you nightmares. "Mother, how do you feel now?" and a stinging wetness on her forehead. But I don't like having my face washed in cold water!

Hapsy? George? Lydia? Jimmy? No, Cornelia, and her features were swollen [30] and full of little puddles. "They're coming, darling, they'll all be here soon." Go wash your face, child, you look funny.

Instead of obeying, Cornelia knelt down and put her head on the pillow. She seemed to be talking but there was no sound. "Well, are you tongue-tied? Whose birthday is it? Are you going to give a party?"

Cornelia's mouth moved urgently in strange shapes. "Don't do that, you bother me, daughter."

"Oh, no, Mother, Oh, no. . . ."

Nonsense. It was strange about children. They disputed your every word. "No what, Cornelia?"

"Here's Doctor Harry." [35]

"I won't see that boy again. He just left five minutes ago."

"That was this morning, Mother. It's night now. Here's the nurse."

"This is Doctor Harry, Mrs. Weatherall. I never saw you look so young and happy!"

"Ah, I'll never be young again—but I'd be happy if they'd let me lie in peace and get rested."

She thought she spoke up loudly, but no one answered. A warm weight on 40
her forehead, a warm bracelet on her wrist, and a breeze went on whispering,
trying to tell her something. A shuffle of leaves in the everlasting hand of God.
He blew on them and they danced and rattled. "Mother, don't mind, we're going
to give you a little hypodermic." "Look here, daughter, how do ants get in this
bed? I saw sugar ants yesterday." Did you send for Hapsy too?

It was Hapsy she really wanted. She had to go a long way back through a
great many rooms to find Hapsy standing with a baby on her arm. She seemed to
herself to be Hapsy also, and the baby on Hapsy's arm was Hapsy and himself
and herself, all at once, and there was no surprise in the meeting. Then Hapsy
melted from within and turned flimsy as gray gauze and the baby was a gauzy
shadow, and Hapsy came up close and said, "I thought you'd never come," and
looked at her very searchingly and said, "You haven't changed a bit!" They leaned
forward to kiss, when Cornelia began whispering from a long way off, "Oh, is
there anything you want to tell me? Is there anything I can do for you?"

Yes, she had changed her mind after sixty years and she would like to see
George. I want you to find George. Find him and be sure to tell him I forgot him.
I want him to know I had my husband just the same and my children and my
house like any other woman. A good house too and a good husband that I loved
and fine children out of him. Better than I hoped for even. Tell him I was given
back everything he took away and more. Oh, no, oh, God, no, there was something
else besides the house and the man and the children. Oh, surely they were not
all? What was it? Something not given back. . . . Her breath crowded down under
her ribs and grew into a monstrous frightening shape with cutting edges; it bored
up into her head, and the agony was unbelievable: Yes, John, get the doctor now,
no more talk, my time has come.

When this one was born it should be the last. The last. It should have been
born first, for it was the one she had truly wanted. Everything came in good time.
Nothing left out, left over. She was strong, in three days she would be as well as
ever. Better. A woman needed milk in her to have her full health.

"Mother, do you hear me?"

"I've been telling you—" 45

"Mother, Father Connolly's here."

"I went to Holy Communion only last week. Tell him I'm not so sinful as
all that."

"Father just wants to speak to you."

He could speak as much as he pleased. It was like him to drop in and inquire
about her soul as if it were a teething baby, and then stay on for a cup of tea and
a round of cards and gossip. He always had a funny story of some sort, usually
about an Irishman who made his little mistakes and confessed them, and the point
lay in some absurd thing he would blurt out in the confessional showing his
struggles between native piety and original sin. Granny felt easy about her soul.
Cornelia, where are your manners? Give Father Connolly a chair. She had her
secret comfortable understanding with a few favorite saints who cleared a straight
road to God for her. All as surely signed and sealed as the papers for the new
Forty Acres. Forever . . . heirs and assigns forever. Since the day the wedding
cake was not cut, but thrown out and wasted. The whole bottom dropped out of
the world, and there she was blind and sweating with nothing under her feet and
the walls falling away. His hand had caught her under the breast, she had not

fallen, there was the freshly polished floor with the green rug on it, just as before. He had cursed like a sailor's parrot and said. "I'll kill him for you." Don't lay a hand on him, for my sake leave something to God. "Now, Ellen, you must believe what I tell you. . . ."

So there was nothing, nothing to worry about any more, except sometimes 50 in the night one of the children screamed in a nightmare, and they both hustled out shaking and hunting for the matches and calling, "There, wait a minute, here we are!" John, get the doctor now. Hapsy's time has come. But there was Hapsy standing by the bed in a white cap. "Cornelia, tell Hapsy to take off her cap. I can't see her plain."

Her eyes opened very wide and the room stood out like a picture she had seen somewhere. Dark colors with the shadow rising towards the ceiling in long angles. The tall black dresser gleamed with nothing on it but John's picture, enlarged from a little one, with John's eyes very black when they should have been blue. You never saw him, so how do you know how he looked? But the man insisted the copy was perfect, it was very rich and handsome. For a picture, yes, but it's not my husband. The table by the bed had a linen cover and a candle and a crucifix. The light was blue from Cornelia's silk lampshades. No sort of light at all, just frippery. You had to live forty years with kerosene lamps to appreciate honest electricity. She felt very strong and she saw Doctor Harry with a rosy nimbus around him.

"You look like a saint, Doctor Harry, and I vow that's as near as you'll ever come to it."

"She's saying something."

"I heard you, Cornelia. What's all this carrying-on?"

"Father Connolly's saying—" 55

Cornelia's voice staggered and bumped like a cart in a bad road. It rounded corners and turned back again and arrived nowhere. Granny stepped up in the cart very lightly and reached for the reins, but a man sat beside her and she knew him by his hands, driving the cart. She did not look in his face, for she knew without seeing, but looked instead down the road where the trees leaned over and bowed to each other and a thousand birds were singing a Mass. She felt like singing too, but she put her hand in the bosom of her dress and pulled out a rosary, and Father Connolly murmured Latin in a very solemn voice and tickled her feet. My God, will you stop that nonsense? I'm a married woman. What if he did run away and leave me to face the priest by myself? I found another a whole world better. I wouldn't have exchanged my husband for anybody except St. Michael himself, and you may tell him that for me with a thank you in the bargain.

Light flashed on her closed eyelids, and a deep roaring shook her. Cornelia, is that lightning? I hear thunder. There's going to be a storm. Close all the windows. Call the children in. . . "Mother, here we are, all of us." "Is that you, Hapsy?" "Oh, no, I'm Lydia. We drove as fast as we could." Their faces drifted above her, drifted away. The rosary fell out of her hands and Lydia put it back. Jimmy tried to help, their hands fumbled together, and Granny closed two fingers around Jimmy's thumb. Beads wouldn't do, it must be something alive. She was so amazed her thoughts ran round and round. So, my dear Lord, this is my death and I wasn't even thinking about it. My children have come to see me die. But I can't, it's not time. Oh, I always hated surprises. I wanted to give Cornelia the amethyst set—Cornelia, you're to have the amethyst set, but Hapsy's to wear it when she wants, and, Doctor Harry, do shut up. Nobody sent for you. Oh, my dear Lord, do wait a minute. I meant to do something about the Forty Acres, Jimmy doesn't need it and Lydia will later on with that worthless husband of hers. I meant to finish the altar cloth and send six bottles of wine to Sister Borgia for her dyspepsia. I want to send six bottles of wine to Sister Borgia, Father Connolly, now don't let me forget.

Cornelia's voice made short turns and tilted over and crashed. "Oh, Mother, oh, Mother, oh, Mother. . . ."

"I'm not going, Cornelia. I'm taken by surprise. I can't go."

You'll see Hapsy again. What about her? "I thought you'd never come."   60
Granny made a long journey outward, looking for Hapsy. What if I don't find her? What then? Her heart sank down and down, there was no bottom to death, she couldn't come to the end of it. The blue light from Cornelia's lampshade drew into a tiny point in the center of her brain, it flickered and winked like an eye, quietly it fluttered and dwindled. Granny lay curled down within herself, amazed and watchful, staring at the point of light that was herself; her body was now only a deeper mass of shadow in an endless darkness and this darkness would curl around the light and swallow it up. God, give a sign!

For the second time there was no sign. Again no bridegroom and the priest in the house. She could not remember any other sorrow because this grief wiped them all away. Oh, no, there's nothing more cruel than this—I'll never forgive it. She stretched herself with a deep breath and blew out the light.

LESLIE MARMON SILKO   (b. 1948)

Lullaby   *1981*

The sun had gone down but the snow in the wind gave off its own light. It came in thick tufts like new wool—washed before the weaver spins it. Ayah reached out for it like her own babies had, and she smiled when she remembered how she had laughed at them. She was an old woman now, and her life had become memories. She sat down with her back against the wide cottonwood tree, feeling the rough bark on her back bones; she faced east and listened to the wind and snow sing a high-pitched Yeibechei song. Out of the wind she felt warmer, and she could watch the wide fluffy snow fill in her tracks, steadily, until the direction she had come from was gone. By the light of the snow she could see the dark outline of the big arroyo° a few feet away. She was sitting on the edge of Cebolleta Creek, where in the springtime the thin cows would graze on grass already chewed flat to the ground. In the wide deep creek bed where only a trickle of water flowed in the summer, the skinny cows would wander, looking for new grass along winding paths splashed with manure.

Ayah pulled the old Army blanket over her head like a shawl. Jimmie's blanket—the one he had sent to her. That was a long time ago and the green wool was faded, and it was unraveling on the edges. She did not want to think about Jimmie. So she thought about the weaving and the way her mother had done it. On the tall wooden loom set into the sand under a tamarack tree for

arroyo: narrow ravine or streambed.

shade. She could see it clearly. She had been only a little girl when her grandma gave her the wooden combs to pull the twigs and burrs from the raw, freshly washed wool. And while she combed the wool, her grandma sat beside her, spinning a silvery strand of yarn around the smooth cedar spindle. Her mother worked at the loom with yarns dyed bright yellow and red and gold. She watched them dye the yarn in boiling black pots full of beeweed petals, juniper berries, and sage. The blankets her mother made were soft and woven so tight that rain rolled off them like birds' feathers. Ayah remembered sleeping warm on cold windy nights, wrapped in her mother's blankets on the hogan's° sandy floor.

The snow drifted now, with the northwest wind hurling it in gusts. It drifted up around her black overshoes—old ones with little metal buckles. She smiled at the snow which was trying to cover her little by little. She could remember when they had no black rubber overshoes; only the high buckskin leggings that they wrapped over their elkhide moccasins. If the snow was dry or frozen, a person could walk all day and not get wet; and in the evenings the beams of the ceiling would hang with lengths of pale buckskin leggings, drying out slowly.

She felt peaceful remembering. She didn't feel cold any more. Jimmie's blanket seemed warmer than it had ever been. And she could remember the morning he was born. She could remember whispering to her mother, who was sleeping on the other side of the hogan, to tell her it was time now. She did not want to wake the others. The second time she called to her, her mother stood up and pulled on her shoes; she knew. They walked to the old stone hogan together, Ayah walking a step behind her mother. She waited alone, learning the rhythms of the pains while her mother went to call the old woman to help them. The morning was already warm even before dawn and Ayah smelled the bee flowers blooming and the young willow growing at the springs. She could remember that so clearly, but his birth merged into the births of the other children and to her it became all the same birth. They named him for the summer morning and in English they called him Jimmie.

It wasn't like Jimmie died. He just never came back, and one day a dark 5 blue sedan with white writing on its doors pulled up in front of the boxcar shack where the rancher let the Indians live. A man in a khaki uniform trimmed in gold gave them a yellow piece of paper and told them that Jimmie was dead. He said the Army would try to get the body back and then it would be shipped to them; but it wasn't likely because the helicopter had burned after it crashed. All of this was told to Chato because he could understand English. She stood inside the doorway holding the baby while Chato listened. Chato spoke English like a white man and he spoke Spanish too. He was taller than the white man and he stood straighter too. Chato didn't explain why; he just told the military man they could keep the body if they found it. The white man looked bewildered; he nodded his head and he left. Then Chato looked at her and shook his head, and then he told her, "Jimmie isn't coming home anymore," and when he spoke, he used the words to speak of the dead. She didn't cry then, but she hurt inside with anger. And she mourned him as the years passed, when a horse fell with Chato and broke his leg, and the white rancher told them he wouldn't pay Chato until he could work again. She mourned Jimmie because he would have worked for his father then; he would have saddled the big bay horse and ridden the fence lines each day, with wire

hogan: Navajo Indian dwelling made of earth and timbers.

cutters and heavy gloves, fixing the breaks in the barbed wire and putting the stray cattle back inside again.

She mourned him after the white doctors came to take Danny and Ella away. She was at the shack alone that day they came. It was back in the days before they hired Navajo women to go with them as interpreters. She recognized one of the doctors. She had seen him at the children's clinic at Cañoncito about a month ago. They were wearing khaki uniforms and they waved papers at her and a black ball-point pen, trying to make her understand their English words. She was frightened by the way they looked at the children, like the lizard watches the fly. Danny was swinging on the tire swing on the elm tree behind the rancher's house, and Ella was toddling around the front door, dragging the broomstick horse Chato made for her. Ayah could see they wanted her to sign the papers, and Chato had taught her to sign her name. It was something she was proud of. She only wanted them to go, and to take their eyes away from her children.

She took the pen from the man without looking at his face and she signed the papers in three different places he pointed to. She stared at the ground by their feet and waited for them to leave. But they stood there and began to point and gesture at the children. Danny stopped swinging. Ayah could see his fear. She moved suddenly and grabbed Ella into her arms; the child squirmed, trying to get back to her toys. Ayah ran with the baby toward Danny; she screamed for him to run and then she grabbed him around his chest and carried him too. She ran south into the foothills of juniper trees and black lava rock. Behind her she heard the doctors running, but they had been taken by surprise, and as the hills became steeper and the cholla cactus were thicker, they stopped. When she reached the top of the hill, she stopped to listen in case they were circling around her. But in a few minutes she heard a car engine start and they drove away. The children had been too surprised to cry while she ran with them. Danny was shaking and Ella's little fingers were gripping Ayah's blouse.

She stayed up in the hills for the rest of the day, sitting on a black lava boulder in the sunshine where she could see for miles all around her. The sky was light blue and cloudless, and it was warm for late April. The sun warmth relaxed her and took the fear and anger away. She lay back on the rock and watched the sky. It seemed to her that she could walk into the sky, stepping through clouds endlessly. Danny played with little pebbles and stones, pretending they were birds' eggs and then little rabbits. Ella sat at her feet and dropped fistfuls of dirt into the breeze, watching the dust and particles of sand intently. Ayah watched a hawk soar high above them, dark wings gliding; hunting or only watching, she did not know. The hawk was patient and he circled all afternoon before he disappeared around the high volcanic peak the Mexicans called Guadalupe.

Late in the afternoon, Ayah looked down at the gray boxcar shack with the paint all peeled from the wood; the stove pipe on the roof was rusted and crooked. The fire she had built that morning in the oil drum stove had burned out. Ella was asleep in her lap now and Danny sat close to her complaining that he was hungry; he asked when they could go to the house. "We will stay up here until your father comes," she told him, "because those white men were chasing us." The boy remembered then and he nodded at her silently.

If Jimmie had been there he could have read those papers and explained   10
to her what they said. Ayah would have known then, never to sign them. The

doctors came back the next day and they brought a BIA° policeman with them. They told Chato they had her signature and that was all they needed. Except for the kids. She listened to Chato sullenly; she hated him when he told her it was the old woman who died in the winter, spitting blood; it was her old grandma who had given the children this disease. "They don't spit blood," she said coldly. "The whites lie." She held Ella and Danny close to her, ready to run to the hills again. "I want a medicine man first," she said to Chato, not looking at him. He shook his head. "It's too late now. The policeman is with them. You signed the paper." His voice was gentle.

It was worse than if they had died: to lose the children and to know that somewhere, in a place called Colorado, in a place full of sick and dying strangers, her children were without her. There had been babies that died soon after they were born, and one that died before he could walk. She had carried them herself, up to the boulders and great pieces of the cliff that long ago crashed down from Long Mesa; she laid them in the crevices of sandstone and buried them in fine brown sand with round quartz pebbles that washed down the hills in the rain. She had endured it because they had been with her. But she could not bear this pain. She did not sleep for a long time after they took her children. She stayed on the hill where they had fled the first time, and she slept rolled up in the blanket Jimmie had sent her. She carried the pain in her belly and it was fed by everything she saw: the blue sky of their last day together and the dust and pebbles they played with; the swing in the elm tree and broomstick horse choked life from her. The pain filled her stomach and there was no room for food or for her lungs to fill with air. The air and the food would have been theirs.

She hated Chato, not because he let the policeman and doctors put the screaming children in the government car, but because he had taught her to sign her name. Because it was like the old ones always told her about learning their language or any of their ways: it endangered you. She slept alone on the hill until the middle of November when the first snows came. Then she made a bed for herself where the children had slept. She did not lie down beside Chato again until many years later, when he was sick and shivering and only her body could keep him warm. The illness came after the white rancher told Chato he was too old to work for him anymore, and Chato and his old woman should be out of the shack by the next afternoon because the rancher had hired new people to work there. That had satisfied her. To see how the white man repaid Chato's years of loyalty and work. All of Chato's fine-sounding English talk didn't change things.

It snowed steadily and the luminous light from the snow gradually diminished into the darkness. Somewhere in Cebolleta a dog barked and other village dogs joined with it. Ayah looked in the direction she had come, from the bar where Chato was buying the wine. Sometimes he told her to go on ahead and wait; and then he never came. And when she finally went back looking for him, she would find him passed out at the bottom of the wooden steps to Azzie's Bar. All the wine would be gone and most of the money too, from the pale blue check that came to them once a month in a government envelope. It was then that she would look at his face and his hands, scarred by ropes and the barbed wire for all those years, and she would think, this man is a stranger; for forty years she had smiled at him

BIA: Bureau of Indian Affairs.

and cooked his food, but he remained a stranger. She stood up again, with the snow almost to her knees, and she walked back to find Chato.

It was hard to walk in the deep snow and she felt the air burn in her lungs. She stopped a short distance from the bar to rest and readjust the blanket. But this time he wasn't waiting for her on the bottom step with his old Stetson hat° pulled down and his shoulders hunched up in his long wool overcoat.

She was careful not to slip on the wooden steps. When she pushed the door open, warm air and cigarette smoke hit her face. She looked around slowly and deliberately, in every corner, in every dark place that the old man might find to sleep. The bar owner didn't like Indians in there, especially Navajos, but he let Chato come in because he could talk Spanish like he was one of them. The men at the bar stared at her, and the bartender saw that she left the door open wide. Snowflakes were flying inside like moths and melting into a puddle on the oiled wood floor. He motioned to her to close the door, but she did not see him. She held herself straight and walked across the room slowly, searching the room with every step. The snow in her hair melted and she could feel it on her forehead. At the far corner of the room, she saw red flames at the mica window of the old stove door; she looked behind the stove just to make sure. The bar got quiet except for the Spanish polka music playing on the jukebox. She stood by the stove and shook the snow from her blanket and held it near the stove to dry. The wet wool smell reminded her of new-born goats in early March, brought inside to warm near the fire, she felt calm.

In past years they would have told her to get out. But her hair was white now and her face was wrinkled. They looked at her like she was a spider crawling slowly across the room. They were afraid; she could feel the fear. She looked at their faces steadily. They reminded her of the first time the white people brought her children back to her that winter. Danny had been shy and hid behind the thin white woman who brought them. And the baby had not known her until Ayah took her into her arms, and then Ella had nuzzled close to her as she had when she was nursing. The blonde woman was nervous and kept looking at a dainty gold watch on her wrist. She sat on the bench near the small window and watched the dark snow clouds gather around the mountains; she was worrying about the unpaved road. She was frightened by what she saw inside too: the strips of venison drying on a rope across the ceiling and the children jabbering excitedly in a language she did not know. So they stayed for only a few hours. Ayah watched the government car disappear down the road and she knew they were already being weaned from these lava hills and from this sky. The last time they came was in early June, and Ella stared at her the way the men in the bar were now staring. Ayah did not try to pick her up; she smiled at her instead and spoke cheerfully to Danny. When he tried to answer her, he could not seem to remember and he spoke English words with the Navajo. But he gave her a scrap of paper that he had found somewhere and carried in his pocket; it was folded in half, and he shyly looked up at her and said it was a bird. She asked Chato if they were home for good this time. He spoke to the white woman and she shook her head. "How much longer?" he asked, and she didn't know; but Chato saw how she stared at the boxcar shack. Ayah turned away then. She did not say good-bye.

She felt satisfied that the men in the bar feared her. Maybe it was her face

Stetson hat: high, broad-brimmed hat worn by Western cowboys.

and the way she held her mouth with teeth clenched tight, like there was nothing anyone could do to her now. She walked north down the road, searching for the old man. She did this because she had the blanket, and there would be no place for him except with her and the blanket in the old adobe barn near the arroyo. They always slept there when they came to Cebolleta. If the money and the wine were gone, she would be relieved because then they could go home again; back to the old hogan with a dirt roof and rock walls where she herself had been born. And the next day the old man could go back to the few sheep they still had, to follow along behind them, guiding them, into dry sandy arroyos where sparse grass grew. She knew he did not like walking behind old ewes when for so many years he rode big quarter horses and worked with cattle. But she wasn't sorry for him; he should have known all along what would happen.

There had not been enough rain for their garden in five years; and that was when Chato finally hitched a ride into the town and brought back brown boxes of rice and sugar and big tin cans of welfare peaches. After that, at the first of the month they went to Cebolleta to ask the postmaster for the check; and then Chato would go to the bar and cash it. They did this as they planted the garden every May, not because anything would survive the summer dust, but because it was time to do this. The journey passed the days that smelled silent and dry like the caves above the canyon with yellow painted buffaloes on their walls.

He was walking along the pavement when she found him. He did not stop or turn around when he heard her behind him. She walked beside him and she noticed how slowly he moved now. He smelled strong of woodsmoke and urine. Lately he had been forgetting. Sometimes he called her by his sister's name and she had been gone for a long time. Once she had found him wandering on the road to the white man's ranch, and she asked him why he was going that way; he laughed at her and said, "You know they can't run that ranch without me," and he walked on determined, limping on the leg that had been crushed many years before. Now he looked at her curiously, as if for the first time, but he kept shuffling along, moving slowly along the side of the highway. His gray hair had grown long and spread out on the shoulders of the long overcoat. He wore the old felt hat pulled down over his ears. His boots were worn out at the toes and he had stuffed pieces of an old red shirt in the holes. The rags made his feet look like little animals up to their ears in snow. She laughed at his feet, the snow muffled the sound of her laugh. He stopped and looked at her again. The wind had quit blowing and the snow was falling straight down; the southeast sky was beginning to clear and Ayah could see a star.

"Let's rest awhile," she said to him. They walked away from the road and up the slope to the giant boulders that had tumbled down from the red sandrock mesa throughout the centuries of rainstorms and earth tremors. In a place where the boulders shut out the wind, they sat down with their backs against the rock. She offered half of the blanket to him and they sat wrapped together. 20

The storm passed swiftly. The clouds moved east. They were massive and full, crowding together across the sky. She watched them with the feeling of horses—steely blue-gray horses startled across the sky. The powerful haunches pushed into the distances and the tail hairs streamed white mist behind them. The sky cleared. Ayah saw that there was nothing between her and the stars. The light was crystalline. There was no shimmer, no distortion through earth haze. She breathed the clarity of the night sky; she smelled the purity of the half moon and the stars. He was lying on his side with his knees pulled up near his belly for warmth. His eyes were closed now, and in the light from the stars and the moon, he looked young again.

She could see it descend out of the night sky: an icy stillness from the edge of the thin moon. She recognized the freezing. It came gradually, sinking snowflake by snowflake until the crust was heavy and deep. It had the strength of the stars in Orion, and its journey was endless. Ayah knew that with the wine he would sleep. He would not feel it. She tucked the blanket around him, remembering how it was when Ella had been with her; and she felt the rush so big inside her heart for the babies. And she sang the only song she knew to sing for babies. She could not remember if she had ever sung it to her children, but she knew that her grandmother had sung it and her mother had sung it:

> *The earth is your mother,*
> *she holds you.*
> *The sky is your father,*
> *he protects you.*
> *Sleep,*
> *sleep.*
> *Rainbow is your sister,*
> *she loves you.*
> *The winds are your brothers,*
> *they sing to you.*
> *Sleep,*
> *sleep.*
> *We are together always*
> *We are together always*
> *There never was a time*
> *when this*
> *was not so.*

POETRY

12

Meeting Poetry: An Overview

Poetry and **poem** describe a wide variety of spoken and written forms, styles, and patterns, and also a wide variety of subjects. Because of this variety, it is not possible to make a single, comprehensive definition. The origin of the word is the Greek word *poiema*, that is, "something made or fashioned [in words]"—a meaning which we may apply to both poetry and poems. Naturally, a **poet** was, and is, a person who does the making or fashioning. Rather than to seek brief definitions that limit more than explain, however, we believe that the best way to understand poetry is to read it, learn it, experience it, and enjoy it. As your understanding deepens you will develop your own ideas and definitions.

Let us begin right away with a poem based on the life of students and teachers alike.

BILLY COLLINS   (b. 1941)

Schoolsville   *1985*

Glancing over my shoulder at the past,
I realize the number of students I have taught
is enough to populate a small town.

I can see it nestled in a paper landscape,
chalk dust flurrying down in winter,   5
nights dark as a blackboard.

The population ages but never graduates.
On hot afternoons they sweat the final in the park
and when it's cold they shiver around stoves
reading disorganized essays out loud.   10
A bell rings on the hour and everybody zigzags
in the streets with their books.

I forgot all their last names first and their
first names last in alphabetical order.
But the boy who always had his hand up   15
is an alderman and owns the haberdashery.
The girl who signed her papers in lipstick
leans against the drugstore, smoking,
brushing her hair like a machine.

Their grades are sewn into their clothes   20
like references to Hawthorne.°   *i.e.,* The Scarlet Letter
The A's stroll along with other A's.
The D's honk whenever they pass another D.

All the creative writing students recline
on the courthouse lawn and play the lute.   25
Wherever they go, they form a big circle.

Needless to say, I am the mayor.
I live in the white colonial at Maple and Main.
I rarely leave the house. The car deflates
in the driveway. Vines twirl around the porchswing.   30

Once in a while a student knocks on the door
with a term paper fifteen years late
or a question about Yeats or double-spacing.
And sometimes one will appear in a window pane
to watch me lecturing the wall paper,   35
quizzing the chandelier, reprimanding the air.

QUESTIONS

1. What school experiences are here? Why is the poem entitled "Schoolsville"?
2. Describe the profession, current situation, and characteristics of the speaker. What attitudes do you find about the speaker, and about the speaker's past students?
3. Are the details of school experiences appropriate, exaggerated, funny? What things indicate a sense of affection in the poem?
4. Compare the details of this poem with those in Roethke's "Dolor" (p. 590). What similarities do you find? What differences?

This poem shows us much about poetry. The topic material is drawn from the life we have all experienced in various schools or colleges. The references are introduced not to tell a story, but to make assertions. The connecting element is therefore the fanciful and comic but also affectionate views the speaker expresses about the sameness and also the changes that characterize school life. The details in the poem are sharply observed and recorded, such as the chalk dust flurrying down like snow, the girl who signs her name in lipstick, and the students forming a circle. The poem is arranged in lines, but does not follow measured rhythmical patterns, nor does it rhyme. Once we have read and followed the poem, we will not forget it, and it will echo in our minds as time passes. Like all good poetry, in short, this poem is alive, and if we read it sensitively it will become a part of us.

THE NATURE OF POETRY

"Schoolsville" is unique; it is at once serious and original, and it is also amusing. There is no other poem like it. Indeed, all good poems are unique, and because this is so we cannot formulate a single definition of poetry to account for all poems. Nevertheless, we can offer a number of descriptive statements about poetry that may be helpful. To begin with, poems are imaginative works expressed in words that are used with the utmost *compression, force,* and *economy.* Unlike prose, which is expansive and exhaustive, most poems are *brief* but also *comprehensive,* offering us *high points* of *thought, feeling, reflection,* and *resolution.* Poems may take just about *any coherent and developed shape,* from a line of a single word to lines of twenty, thirty, or more words, and these lines may be organized into *any number of repeating or nonrepeating patterns.* Some poems make us *think,* give us *new and unexpected insights,* and generally *instruct* us; other poems *arouse our emotions, surprise us, amuse us,* and *inspire us.* Ideally, reading and understanding poetry should prompt us to *reexamine, reinforce,* and *reshape our ideas, our attitudes, our feelings,* and *our lives.*

POETRY OF THE ENGLISH LANGUAGE

Today, most nations with their own languages, such as France, Germany, and Japan, have their own literatures, including poetry, with unique characteristics and histories. In this anthology, however, we are concerned with poetry in our own language by American, British, and Canadian poets.

The earliest poems in English date back to late in the period of *Old English* (A.D. 450–1100). Many of these early English poems reflect the influence of Christianity. Indeed, the most famous poem, the epic *Beowulf,* was probably interpreted as a Christian allegory even though it concerns the secular themes of adventure, courage, and war. Ever since the *Middle English* period (A.D. 1100–1500), poets have written about many other subjects, even though religious themes have also maintained their importance. Today, we may find poetry on virtually all topics, ranging from sexuality, love, society, individuality, warfare, strong drink, government and politics, worship, and music, to special and unusual topics like fishing, computers, exotic birds, and automobile smashups.

In short, poetry is alive and flourishing. Some people read it aloud in front of audiences, friends, and families, and others silently read it alone in the privacy of their rooms. Set to music and sung aloud, it is exceedingly powerful. Francis Scott Key's "The Star-Spangled Banner," for example, in which he wrote about events in a battle in the War of 1812, has become our national anthem. More recently, musical groups like the Beatles and U2, along with the solo singer Bruce Springsteen, have gained great popularity by expressing ideas that huge masses of people have taken to heart. Ever since the 1960s, people devoted to civil rights have been unified and empowered by the simple lyrics of "We Shall Overcome," not only in the United States but throughout the world. The strength and vitality of poetry could be similarly documented time and time again.

HOW POETRY WORKS

With poetry, as with any other form of literature, the more effort we put into understanding, the greater will be our reward. Poems are often about subjects that we have never experienced directly ourselves. We have never met the poet, never had his or her exact experiences, and never thought about things in exactly the same way. To recapture the experience of the poem, we need to understand the language, ideas, attitudes, and frames of reference that will make the poem come alive. Consider the following poem by an American poet.

RANDALL JARRELL   (1914–1965)

The Death of the Ball Turret Gunner   *1945*

From my mother's sleep I fell into the State
And I hunched in its belly till my wet fur froze.
Six miles from earth, loosed from its dream of life,
I woke to black flak and the nightmare fighters.
When I died they washed me out of the turret with a hose.   5

To understand and appreciate this poem, we need to know a number of things. The topic is the violent death of a gunner on a World War II bomber, imagined as being told by the dead gunner himself. The poet, Jarrell, tells us in a note that "a ball turret was a Plexiglas sphere set into the belly of a B-17 or B-24 [both large, four-engine, high-altitude, precision-bombing aircraft] and inhabited by two .50-calibre machine guns and one man, a short small man. When this gunner tracked with his machine guns a fighter attacking his bomber from below, he revolved with the turret; hunched upside-down in his little sphere, he looked like a fetus in the womb. The fighters which attacked him were armed with cannon firing exploding shells. The hose was a steam hose." We add that *Flak* (an acronym from the German word for anti-aircraft gun, **FL**ieger**A**bwehr**K**anone) describes the high-altitude explosions of anti-aircraft shells fired from the ground.

This explanation helps us understand and experience Jarrell's poem. It does not make us smile, like Collins's "Schoolsville," but instead it dramatizes the grisly reality of aerial warfare. The opening comparison draws a parallel between an infant in the womb and the gunner in his little sphere. Thus, the "wet fur" of line 2 refers to the fur collar of a flight jacket, and it also suggests the hair of an unborn or newly born infant or animal. Expanding on this comparison, the poem suggests that the gunner is typical of young men who fight in war and die before they become adults. The gunner's death is particularly horrible. His identity is reduced to insignificance by the image of his mangled and shapeless remains being washed "out of the turret with a hose." Although there is no explicitly stated message or moral, we may easily conclude that Jarrell is saying that war is mindless, brutal, indifferent, and wasteful.

HOW TO READ A POEM

Carefully, *thoughtfully*, and *sympathetically*—these words sum up the best approach to reading poetry. The economy and compression of poetry mean that every part of the poem must carry some of the impact and meaning, and thus every part repays careful attention. There should be an interaction between the poem and you, the reader. You cannot sit back and expect the poem (or the poet) to do all the work. The poem contributes its language, imagery, rhythms, ideas, and all the other aspects that make it poetry, but you, the reader, will need to open your mind to the poem's impact.

No single technique for reading poetry can guarantee a valuable and enjoyable experience, but we can suggest general approaches that will help you read, absorb, and appreciate poems. Earlier, in Chapter 1, we suggested a number of steps that you might take with any work of literature (pp. 13–15). These are also applicable for studying poetry. In addition, read each poem more than once, keeping a number of objectives in mind:

1. *Read straight through to get a general sense of what the poem is about.* In this first reading, do not stop to puzzle out difficult passages or obscure words; just read through from beginning to ending.

2. *Develop an understanding of the basic meaning and organization of the poem.* As you read and reread the poem, study the following:

a.   THE TITLE. The title usually supplies important information. The title "The Death of the Ball Turret Gunner" tells about the subject and the stances of the poem; the title of Robert Frost's "Stopping by Woods on a Snowy Evening" tells us about the poem's setting and situation.

b. THE SPEAKER. The poem is usually dramatic, with a speaker who may be "inside," as a person directly involved in the action (like the gunner in "The Death of the Ball Turret Gunner"), or "outside," as in "Sir Patrick Spens," in which the speaker is an observer uninvolved in the action, much like a third-person speaker in prose fiction (see also Chapter 5, pp. 200–202).

c. THE MEANING OF BOTH FAMILIAR AND UNFAMILIAR WORDS. Some poems are written in a style that is immediately clear to you, but with other poems you will need to look up unfamiliar words (and sometimes even familiar words) and references. You therefore will need help from dictionaries, encyclopedias, reference works on mythology, and so on. Take as much time as you need for looking things up, for when you are finished you should have developed a fairly clear grasp of the poem's content. If you are unable to locate a reference, or if you continue having difficulty even after using your sources, be sure to ask your instructor.

d. THE SETTING AND SITUATION OF THE POEM. Some poems establish their settings and circumstances vividly. "Stopping by Woods on a Snowy Evening," for example, describes a scene in which the speaker stops his horse-drawn sleigh by a woods in the evening, during a snowfall, so that he may watch the snow pile up amid the trees. Although many poems do not establish setting and situation so clearly or so quickly, you should always try to figure out as much as you can about the *where* and *when* of a given poem.

e. THE SUBJECT AND THEME OF THE POEM. The **subject** indicates the general or specific topic; the **theme** refers to the idea or ideas that the poem explores. Jarrell's poem announces its subject in the title. The theme, however, usually must be inferred. In this poem it is about the senseless brutality of war, the poignancy of the loss of young lives, the callousness and indifference of the living toward the dead, and the suddenness with which war forces young people to face cruelty and horror.

f. THE BASIC FORM AND DEVELOPMENT OF THE POEM. Some poems, like "Sir Patrick Spens," are narratives; others, like "Death of the Ball Turret Gunner," are personal statements; still others may be speeches to another person. The poems may be laid out in a sonnet form, or may develop in two-line sequences (couplets). They may contain stanzas, each of which is unified by a particular action or thought. Try to determine the form and to trace the way in which the poem unfolds, part by part.

3. *Read the poem aloud, sounding each word clearly in your mind.* This reading will give you the chance to hear the music of the poem, and to assess the contributions that rhythm, rhyme, and sound make to the total effect. If you read "Death of the Ball Turret Gunner" aloud, for example, you will notice the impact of rhyming *froze* with *hose* and the suggestion of the percussive sounds of cannon fire in the repeated and rhyming *l, a,* and *k* sounds of *black flak* (for further discussion of sounds in poetry, see pp. 677–90).

4. *Prepare a* PARAPHRASE *of the poem, and make an* EXPLICATION *of the ideas and themes that you have discovered there.* A paraphrase is a restatement of the poem in your own words (for more on paraphrasing, see Chapter 2, pp. 87–93, and also pp. 533–35 in this chapter). Paraphrasing helps you crystallize your understanding. An explication, either of brief passages or of the entire poem, goes beyond paraphrase to consider the significance of anything and everything in the poem.

STUDYING POETRY

Let us now look at a poem in some detail. We have already noted that poems may be narratives; that is, they tell stories. As an example, the following poem was composed orally as a song sometime during the late Middle Ages or early Renaissance, when ordinary people got much of their information about the outside world from roving balladeers who sang the news to them. It tells a story that is probably true, or that is at least based on a real event.

ANONYMOUS

Sir Patrick Spens   *Fifteenth century*

The king sits in Dumferline town,
   Drinking the blood-red wine:
"O where will I get a good sailor
   To sail this ship of mine?"

Up and spoke and eldern° knight   *old, elderly*   5
   Sat at the king's right knee:
"Sir Patrick Spens is the best sailor
   That sails upon the sea."

The king has written a braid° letter   *large*
   And signed it wi° his hand,   *with*   10
And sent it to Sir Patrick Spens,
   Was walking on the sand.

The first line that Sir Patrick read,
   A loud laugh laughèd he;
The next line that Sir Patrick read,   15
   A tear blinded his eye.

"O who is this has done this deed,
   This ill deed done to me,
To send me out this time o' the year,
   To sail upon the sea?   20

"Make haste, make haste, my merry men all,
  Our good ship sails the morn."
"O say not so, my master dear,
  For I fear a deadly storm.

Late late yestere'en° I saw the new moon   *last evening* 25
  Wi' the old moon in her arm,
And I fear, I fear, my dear master,
  That we will come to harm."

O our Scots nobles were right loath
  To wet their cork-heeled shoon,°   *shoes* 30
But long ere a'° the play were played   *all*
  Their hats they swam aboon.°   *above*

O long, long may their ladies sit,
  Wi' their fans into their hand,
Or e'er they see Sir Patrick Spens   35
  Come sailing to the land.

O long, long may the ladies stand,
  Wi' their gold combs in their hair,
Waiting for their own dear lords,
  For they'll see them no more.   40

Half o'er, half o'er to Aberdour
  It's fifty fathom deep,
And there lies good Sir Patrick Spens,
  Wi' the Scots lords at his feet.

    "Sir Patrick Spens" is a type of poem called a **narrative ballad.** A narrative tells a story, and the term *ballad* defines the poem's shape or form. The first two stanzas set up the situation: The king needs a sailor to undertake a vital mission, and an old knight—one of the king's close advisers—suggests the appointment of Sir Patrick Spens. We know that this knight is a powerful adviser since he sits "at the king's right knee."

    The rest of the poem focuses on the feelings and eventual deaths of Sir Patrick and his men. The third stanza provides a transition from the king to Sir Patrick. The king writes a letter ordering Sir Patrick to sea, and Sir Patrick reads it. On reading the first line, Sir Patrick laughs— maybe because the king begins by flattering him, or maybe because Sir Patrick at first believes that an order to go to sea at an obvious time of danger is nothing more than a grim joke. But when he reads the next line and realizes that the order is real, he foresees disaster. He weeps at the prospect of danger, and wonders who (among the king's advisers) is responsible for sending him seaward "this time o' the year." Our sense of impending calamity is increased when we learn that Sir Patrick's crew is also frightened (lines 23–28).

The shipwreck, which is described in stanza 8, is presented with ironic understatement. There is no description of the storm or of the crew's panic, nor does the speaker describe the masts splitting or the ship sinking under the waves. Although these horrors are omitted, the floating hats are grim evidence of destruction and death. The remainder of the poem continues in this vein of understatement. In stanzas 9 and 10 the focus shifts back to the land, and to the ladies who will wait a "long, long" time (forever) for Sir Patrick and his men to return. The poem ends with a vision of Sir Patrick and the "Scots lords" lying "fifty fathom deep."

On first reflection, "Sir Patrick Spens" tells a sad tale without complications. The subject seems to be no more than the unfortunate drowning of Sir Patrick and his crew of sailors and Scots noblemen, and one might therefore claim that the poem does not have a clear theme. Even the understated irony of the floating hats and the waiting ladies is reasonably straightforward and unambiguous. However, you might consider what the poem suggests about the conflict between individual judgment and obedience to authority. Sir Patrick knows the risks when he sets sail, yet he still obeys the king's command. There are contradictory and conflicting forces at work here. In addition, there is a suggestion in lines 5 and 32 of political infighting. The "eldern knight" is in effect responsible for dooming the ship. Moreover, the "play" being "played" suggests that a political game is taking place over and beyond the grim game of the men caught in the deadly storm (if Sir Patrick knows the danger, would not the knight also know it, and would this knight not also know the consequences of choosing Sir Patrick?). These political motives are not spelled out, but are implied. Thus, the poem is not only a sad tale, but is also a poignant dramatization of how power operates, of how a loyal person responds to a tragic dilemma, and of the pitiful consequences of that response.

In reading poetry, then, let the individual poem be your guide. Get all the words, try to understand dramatic situations, follow the emotional cues provided for you by the poet, and try to develop explanations for everything that is happening. If you find implications in the poem that you believe are important (as with the discussion in the previous paragraph about the political overtones of "Sir Patrick Spens") be sure to support your observations carefully. Resist the temptation to "uncover" unusual or farfetched elements in the poem (as a student once did by claiming that Frost's "Stopping by Woods on a Snowy Evening" is a celebration of Santa Claus, stopping on Christmas Eve for a brief rest before carrying out his mission to deliver presents throughout the world). Draw only those conclusions that the poem itself will support.

POEMS FOR STUDY

WILLIAM SHAKESPEARE   (1564–1616)

Sonnet 55:
Not Marble, Nor the Gilded Monuments   *1609*

Not marble, nor the gilded monuments
Of princes, shall outlive this powerful rhyme;
But you shall shine more bright in these contents
Than unswept stone, besmeared with sluttish time.
When wasteful war shall statues overturn,   5
And broils root out the work of masonry,
Nor° Mars his° sword nor war's quick fire shall burn   *Neither; Mars's*
The living record of your memory.
'Gainst death and all-oblivious enmity
Shall you pace forth; your praise shall still find room   10
Even in the eyes of all posterity
That wear this world out to the ending doom.°   *Judgment day*
So, till the judgment that yourself arise,
You live in this, and dwell in lovers' eyes.

QUESTIONS

1. Who is the speaker of the poem, and who is being addressed?
2. What powers of destruction does the speaker mention? What, according to
    the speaker, will survive these powers?
3. What does "the living record of your memory" (line 8) mean?
4. What is the poem's subject? Theme?

EMILY DICKINSON   (1830–1886)

Because I Could Not Stop for Death   *1890 (ca. 1863)*

Because I could not stop for Death—
He kindly stopped for me—
The Carriage held but just Ourselves—
And Immortality.

We slowly drove—He knew no haste   5
And I had put away
My labor and my leisure too,
For His Civility—

We passed the School, where Children strove
At Recess—in the Ring—   10

We passed the Fields of Gazing Grain—
We passed the Setting Sun—

Or rather—He passed Us—
The Dews drew quivering and chill—
For only Gossamer,° my Gown—   *thin fabric*   15
My Tippet°—only Tulle°—   *cape, scarf; thin silk*

We passed before a House that seemed
A Swelling of the Ground—
The Roof was scarcely visible—
The Cornice—in the Ground—   20

Since then—'tis Centuries—and yet
Feels shorter than the Day
I first surmised the Horses' Heads
Were toward Eternity—

QUESTIONS

1. Who is the speaker and what is she like? Why couldn't she stop for death?
   What perspective does her present position give the poem?

2. In what unusual ways does the poem characterize death?

3. What does the carriage represent? Where is it headed? Who are the riders?
   What is meant by the things the carriage passes?

4. What is represented by the house in line 17? Why does the poet use the
   word *house* in preference to some other word?

A. E. HOUSMAN   (1859–1936)

Loveliest of Trees, the Cherry Now   1896

Loveliest of trees, the cherry now
Is hung with bloom along the bough,
And stands about the woodland ride°   *path*
Wearing white for Eastertide.

Now, of my threescore years and ten,   5
Twenty will not come again,
And take from seventy springs a score,
It only leaves me fifty more.

And since to look at things in bloom
Fifty springs are little room,   10
About the woodland I will go
To see the cherry hung with snow.

QUESTIONS

1.   How old is the speaker? How can you tell? Why does he assume he will live seventy years ("threescore years and ten")?

2.   How would you describe the speaker's perception or sense of time? What is the effect of the words *only* (line 8) and *little* (line 10)?

3.   What ideas about time, beauty, and life does this poem explore? What does it suggest about the way we should live?

THOMAS HARDY   (1840–1928)

The Man He Killed   *1902*

"Had he and I but met
   By some old ancient inn,
We should have sat us down to wet
   Right many a nipperkin!°   *half-pint cup*

"But ranged as infantry,   5
   And staring face to face,
I shot at him as he at me,
   And killed him in his place.

"I shot him dead because—
   Because he was my foe.   10
Just so: my foe of course he was;
   That's clear enough; although

"He thought he'd 'list,° perhaps,   *enlist*
   Off-hand like—just as I—
Was out of work—had sold his traps°—   *possessions*   15
   No other reason why.

"Yes; quaint and curious war is!
   You shoot a fellow down
You'd treat if met where any bar is,
   Or help to half-a-crown."°   20

THE MAN HE KILLED.   20 *half a crown*: today about 40 cents, but at the time, the equivalent of $10 or $20.

QUESTIONS

1.   Who and what is the speaker? What do you learn about him from his language?

2.   What situation and event is the speaker recalling and relating?

3.   What is the effect produced by repeating the word *because* in lines 9 and 10 and using the word *although* in line 12?

4.   What is the speaker's attitude toward his "foe" and toward what he has done?

5. What point, if any, does this poem make about war? How are this poem and
    Jarrell's "The Death of the Ball Turret Gunner" similar and different?

ROBERT FROST   (1874–1963)

Stopping by Woods on a Snowy Evening   *1923*

Whose woods these are I think I know.
His house is in the village though;
He will not see me stopping here
To watch his woods fill up with snow.

My little horse must think it queer   5
To stop without a farmhouse near
Between the woods and frozen lake
The darkest evening of the year.

He gives his harness bells a shake
To ask if there is some mistake.   10
The only other sound's the sweep
Of easy wind and downy flake.

The woods are lovely, dark and deep,
But I have promises to keep,
And miles to go before I sleep,   15
And miles to go before I sleep.

QUESTIONS

1. What do we learn about the speaker? Where is he? What is he doing?
2. What is the setting (place, weather, time) of this poem?
3. Why does the speaker want to watch the "woods fill up with snow"?
4. What evidence suggests that the speaker is embarrassed or self-conscious
    about stopping? Consider the words *though* in line 2 and *must* in line 5.
5. The last stanza offers two alternative attitudes and courses of action. What
    are they? Which does the speaker choose?
6. To what extent do the sound and rhyme of this poem contribute to its
    impact? Note especially the *s* sounds in line 11 and the *w* sounds in line 12.

LOUIS MACNEICE   (1907–1963)

Snow   *1935*

The room was suddenly rich and the great bay-window was
Spawning snow and pink roses against it
Soundlessly collateral and incompatible:
World is suddener than we fancy it.

World is crazier and more of it than we think,   5
Incorrigibly plural. I peel and portion
A tangerine and spit the pips and feel
The drunkenness of things being various.

And the fire flames with a bubbling sound for world
Is more spiteful and gay than one supposes—   10
On the tongue on the eyes on the ears in the palms of one's hands—
There is more than glass between the snow and the huge roses.

QUESTIONS

1. Where is the speaker at the time of the poem? What is the contrast between the roses and the snow? Why is this contrast important?

2. What words describe snow in lines 1–3? What words in lines 4, 5, 6, 8, and 10 describe the world generally? Why does the speaker choose these words rather than more descriptive or pictorial ones?

3. Granted the nature of the poem, what is the meaning of the last line?

4. What similarities and differences do you find between "Snow" and "Stopping by Woods on a Snowy Evening"?

JAMES WRIGHT   (1927–1980)

Two Hangovers   *1963*

NUMBER ONE
I slouch in bed.
Beyond the streaked trees of my window,
All groves are bare.
Locusts and poplars change to unmarried women   5
Sorting slate from anthracite
Between railroad ties:
The yellow-bearded winter of the depression
Is still alive somewhere, an old man
Counting his collection of bottle caps   10
In a tarpaper shack under the cold trees
Of my grave.

I still feel half drunk,
And all those old women beyond my window
Are hunching toward the graveyard.   15

Drunk, mumbling Hungarian,
The sun staggers in,
And his big stupid face pitches
Into the stove.
For two hours I have been dreaming   20
Of green butterflies searching for diamonds

In coal seams;
And children chasing each other for a game
Through the hills of fresh graves.
But the sun has come home drunk from the sea,   25
And a sparrow outside
Sings of the Hanna Coal Co. and the dead moon.
The filaments of cold light bulbs tremble
In music like delicate birds.
Ah, turn it off.   30

NUMBER TWO: I TRY TO WAKEN AND GREET THE WORLD ONCE AGAIN
In a pine tree,
A few yards away from my window sill,
A brilliant blue jay is springing up and down, up and down,
On a branch.   35
I laugh, as I see him abandon himself
To entire delight, for he knows as well as I do
That the branch will not break.

QUESTIONS

1. What do we learn about the speaker in hangover "Number One"? What is
   his physical condition? Where is he? What is he trying to do?

2. How does the speaker's condition affect the way he views the trees outside
   his window? The world? His own life?

3. Do you think the sun really "staggers in" and falls "into the stove"? What
   does the sun stand for in "Number One"?

4. Find all the images of death and desolation that you can in "Number One."
   Why do you suppose these images are so dominant?

5. Why is hangover "Number Two" so much shorter than "Number One"?

6. How does the speaker's mood and perspective change from "Number One"
   to "Number Two"? How do you account for this shift?

PARAPHRASING POETRY

The **paraphrase** is especially useful in the study of poetry. It fixes both
the general shape and the details of a poem in your mind, and also reveals
the poetic devices at work. A comparison of the original poem with the
paraphrase highlights the techniques and the language that make the
poem effective.

To make a paraphrase, you rewrite the poem in prose, in your own
words. You need to make careful decisions about what details to include—
an amount that you determine partly by the length of the poem and partly
by the total length of your paraphrase. When you deal with lyrics, sonnets,
and other short poems, you may include all the details, and thus your

paraphrase may be as long as the work, or even longer. Paraphrases of long poems, however, will be shorter than the originals because some details must be summarized briefly while others may be cut out entirely.

It is vital to make your paraphrase accurate, and also to use *only your own words*. To make sure that your words are all your own, read through the poem several times. Then, put the poem out of sight and write your paraphrase. Once you've finished, check yourself both for accuracy and vocabulary. If you find that you've borrowed too many of the poem's words, select alternative ones that provide the same content, or else use quotation marks to set off the original words (but do not overuse quotations).

Above all, remain faithful to the poem, but *avoid drawing conclusions and making unnecessary explanations*. It would be wrong in a paraphrase of Jarrell's "Death of the Ball Turret Gunner," for example, to state that "this poem makes a forceful argument against the brutal and wasteful deaths caused by war." This assertion describes the poem's theme, but it does not reflect the poem's *actual content*.

Organizing Your Paraphrase

In paraphrasing a poem, your task is to rewrite the work in your own words with as little distortion as possible. Your organization should reflect the form or development of the poem. Paraphrase material in the order in which it occurs. When dealing with short poems, organize your paraphrase to reflect the poem's development line by line or stanza by stanza. In paraphrasing Shakespeare's "Not Marble, Nor the Gilded Monuments," for example, you would want to follow the natural subdivisions of the sonnet and deal in sequence with each quatrain and then with the couplet. With longer poems, look for natural divisions like groups of related stanzas, verse paragraphs, or other units suggested by the work. In every situation, the shape of the poem should determine the structure of your paraphrase.

SAMPLE ESSAY

A Paraphrase of Thomas Hardy's "The Man He Killed"

[1] If the man I killed had met me in an inn, we would have sat down together and had many drinks. Because we belonged to armies of warring foot soldiers lined up on a battlefield, however, we shot at each other, and my shot killed him.

[2] The reason I killed him, I think, was that he and I were enemies--just that. But as I think of it, I realize that he had enlisted in just the way I did. Perhaps he did it on a whim, or perhaps he had lost his job and sold everything he owned. There was no other reason to enlist.

[3] Being at war is certainly unusual and strange. You are forced to kill a man for whom you would buy a drink, or whom you would help out with half a crown in a time of need.

Commentary on the Essay

Because Hardy's poem is short, the paraphrase attempts to include all its details. The organization closely follows the poem's development. Paragraph 1, for example, restates the contents of the first two stanzas. Paragraph 2 restates stanzas 3 and 4. Finally, the last paragraph paraphrases the last stanza. This stanza is given its own paragraph because it contains the reflections made by the poem's "I" speaker. It concludes the paraphrase just as the last stanza concludes the poem.

Notice that the sample essay does not (1) abstract details from the poem, such as "The dead man might have become a dependable and important friend in peacetime" for stanza 5, or (2) extend details, such as "We would have gotten acquainted, had drinks together, told many stories, and done quite a bit of laughing" for stanza 1 (even though both stanzas suggest these details). Although the poem is a dramatization of strong antiwar sentiments, a sentence such as "By his very directness, the narrator brings out the senselessness and brutality of warfare," which discusses these feelings, would be out of place. What is needed is a short restatement of the poem to demonstrate the essay writer's understanding of the poem's content, and no more.

WRITING AN EXPLICATION OF POETRY

Explication, which means to explain and interpret, gives you an opportunity to show your understanding of a poem, for an explication goes beyond the assimilation required for a paraphrase. A complete explication requires that a poem be examined and explained word by word and line by line—a technique that is also, obviously, exhaustive (and exhausting). Thus, a full explication of a poem like "The Man He Killed" might take twenty or thirty pages (yes, pages). Many sentences would be needed, for example, to consider questions like the following.

Questions for Discovering Ideas ("The Man He Killed")

Why does the speaker hesitate in stanza 3, when he tries to explain why he killed his "foe"?

What sort of ideas of war's justification that he may have heard from others is he unable to reproduce in his own words?

After he explains that the other man was his foe, why does he go on to repeat the phrase?

How do his hesitation and his subsequent insistence show his true feelings?
Does he himself really understand his true feelings?

Because of the obvious need to keep essays within limits, such detailed explication should be limited to a few lines of poetry or to a stanza. The goal is to demonstrate your ability to understand the poem, not your capacity to write about it forever.

The more manageable technique to use is the **general explication,** which devotes attention to the meaning of individual parts in relationship to the entire work, as in the discussion of "Sir Patrick Spens" (pp. 526–27). Literally everything in the poem could be the subject of your essay. Because your reading is general, however, and because you are not expected to go into exhaustive detail, you will need to be selective. Therefore you should study things like the general content, the main idea, difficult or unusual words or expressions, and noteworthy elements of style, character, humor, and the like.

Strategies for Organizing Ideas

In a general explication essay, you demonstrate your ability (1) to follow the essential details of the poem (the same as in paraphrase), (2) to understand the issues and the meaning the poem reveals, (3) to explain some of the relationships of content to technique, and (4) to note and discuss especially important or unique aspects of the poem.

The first thing to include in the essay is a brief explanation of what the poem contains—not by exact paraphrase, but by using your own organizing elements. Hence, if the speaker is "inside" the poem as a first-person involved "I," you do not need to reproduce this voice yourself, as with the sample essay paraphrasing "The Man He Killed." Instead, *describe* the poem in your own words, as in the second paragraph of the following sample essay.

Next, go on to explicate the poem in relationship to your central idea. No matter what order of discussion you choose, keep stressing your central idea with each new topic. Thus, you may wish to follow your description by discussing what you consider to be the poem's meaning, or even by presenting two or more possible interpretations. You might also wish to bring in significant techniques. For example, in "Sir Patrick Spens" a noteworthy technique is the unintroduced quotations (i.e., quotations appearing without any "he said" or "quoth he" phrases) as the ballad writer's means of dramatizing the commands and responses of Sir Patrick and his doomed crew.

You might also introduce special topics, like the crewman who explains that bad luck is about to follow the phenomenon of the new moon having "the old moon in her arm" (line 26). Such a reference to superstition in the poem might include the explanation of the crewman's assumptions, the relationship of his uneasiness to the remainder of the poem, and also how the ballad writer attains narrative brevity. In short, discuss those aspects of meaning and technique that bear upon the interpretation you wish to assert.

To reinforce the thematic structure of your essay in the conclusion, you may stress your major idea again. Especially in a general explication, there will be parts of the poem that you will not have discussed. You might therefore mention what might be gained from an exhaustive discussion of various parts of the poem (do not, however, begin to exhaust any subject in the conclusion of an essay). The last stanza of Hardy's "The Man He Killed," for example, contains the words "quaint and curious" in reference to war. These words are unusual, particularly because the speaker might have chosen "hateful," "destructive," or other similar words. Why did Hardy have his speaker make such a choice? With brief attention to such a problem, you may conclude.

SAMPLE ESSAY

An Explication of Hardy's "The Man He Killed"°

[1] Thomas Hardy's "The Man He Killed" exposes the senselessness of war.* It does this through a silent contrast between the needs of ordinary people, as represented by a young man--the speaker--who has killed an enemy soldier in battle, and the antihuman and unnatural deaths of war. Of major note in this contrast are the circumstances described by the speaker, his language, his similarity with the dead man, and his typical concerns and wishes.†

[2] The speaker begins by contrasting the circumstances of warfare with those of peace. He does not identify himself, but his speech reveals that he is an ordinary sort--one of "the people"--who enjoys drinking in a bar and who prefers friendship and helpfulness to violence. If he and the man he killed had met in an inn, he says, they would have shared many drinks, but because they met on a battlefield they shot at each other, and he killed the other man. The speaker tries to justify the killing, but can produce no stronger reason than that the dead man was his "foe." Once he states this reason, he again thinks of the similarities between himself and the dead man, and then concludes that warfare is "quaint and curious" (line 17) because one is forced to kill a person he would have befriended if they had met during a time of peace.

To make the irony of warfare clear, the poem uses easy, colloquial language to bring out the speaker's ordinary qualities. His manner of speech is conversational, as in "We should have sat us down" (line 3), and "'list"

° For this poem, see p. 530.
* Central idea.
† Thesis sentence.

[3] (for "enlist," line 13), and his use of "you" in the last stanza. Also, his word choices, shown in words like "nipperkin," "traps," and "fellow" (lines 4, 15, and 18), are common and informal. This language is important, because it establishes that the speaker is an ordinary man who has been thrown into an unnatural role because of war.

[4] As another means of stressing the grim stupidity of war, the poem makes clear that the two men--the live soldier who killed and the dead soldier who was killed--were so alike that they could have been brothers or even twins. They had similar ways of life, similar economic troubles, similar wishes to help other people, and similar motives in doing things like enlisting in the army. Symbolically, at least, the "man he killed" is the speaker himself, and hence warfare forces not only homicide, but suicide. The poem thus raises the question of why two people who are almost identical should be shoved into opposing battle lines to try to kill each other. This question is rhetorical, for the obvious answer is that there is no good reason at all.

[5] Because the speaker (and also, very likely, the dead man) is shown as a person embodying the virtues of friendliness and helpfulness, Hardy's poem is a strong disapproval of war. Clearly, political reasons for violence as policy are irrelevant to the characters and concerns of the men who fight. They, like the speaker, would prefer to follow their own needs rather than distant and nameless political leaders. The failure of complex but irrelevant political explanations is brought out most clearly in the third stanza, in which the speaker tries to give a reason for shooting the other man. Hardy's use of punctuation --the dashes--stresses the fact that the speaker has no ideological commitment to the cause he served when killing. Thus the speaker stops at the word "because--" and gropes for a good reason (line 9). Not being subtle or articulate, he can say only "Because he was my foe. / Just so: my foe of course he was; / That's clear enough" (lines 10–12). These short bursts of language indicate that he cannot explain things to himself or to anyone else except in the most obvious and trite terms, and in apparent embarrassment he inserts "of course" as an expected way of emphasizing hostility even though he felt none toward the man he killed.

[6] A reading thus shows the power of Hardy's dramatic argument in the poem. Hardy does not establish closely detailed reasons against war as a policy, but rather dramatizes the idea that all political arguments are unimportant in view of the central and glaring brutality of war--the killing of human beings by human beings. Hardy's speaker is not able to express deep feelings; rather he is confused and perplexed because he is an average sort whose idea of life is to live and let live and to enjoy a drink in a bar with friends. But it is this very commonness that stresses the point that everyone is victimized by war--both those who die and those who are forced to kill. Once the poem is finished, the thoughtful reader reflects that it is a powerful argument for peace and reconciliation.

Commentary on the Essay

This explication begins by stating a central idea about "The Man He Killed," and then indicates the topics to follow that will develop the idea.

Although nowhere does the speaker state that war is senseless, the essay takes the position that the poem embodies this idea. A more detailed examination of the themes of the poem might develop the idea by contrasting the ways in which individuals are caught up in social and political forces that send them to war, or the contrast between individuality and the state. In this essay, however, the simple statement of the idea is sufficient.

Paragraph 2 describes the major details of the poem, with guiding words like "the speaker begins," "he says," and "he again thinks." Thus, the paragraph goes over the poem, like a paraphrase, but explains how things occur, as is appropriate for an explication. Paragraph 3 is devoted to the speaker's words and idioms, with the idea that his conversational manner is part of the poem's contrasting method of argument.

Paragraph 4 is an extension of paragraph 3 inasmuch as it points out the similarities of the speaker and the man he killed. If the situation were reversed, in other words, the dead man might say exactly the same things about the present speaker. It is this affinity that underlies the idea that war is not only senseless, but also suicidal. Paragraph 5 treats the style of the poem's fourth stanza. The last paragraph goes over the main idea of the essay and concludes with a brief tribute to the poem as an argument.

The entire essay, therefore, represents a reading and explanation of the high points of the poem. It stresses a particular interpretation, and briefly shows how various aspects of the poem bear it out.

WRITING TOPICS

1. Skim the titles of poems listed in the table of contents. Judging by the subjects of these poems, describe and discuss the possible range of subject matter for poetry. What topics seem most suitable? Why? Do any topics seem to be ruled out? Why? What additional subject matter would you suggest as possible topics for poems?

2. How accurate is the proposition that poetry is a particularly compressed form of expression? To support your position, you might refer to poems such as "The Man He Killed," "Snow," and "Stopping by Woods on a Snowy Evening."

3. Write two poems about the future and your own future plans. In one, begin with the assumption that the world is stable and will go on forever. In the other, assume that you have received the news that a large asteroid is out of orbit and is hurtling toward the earth at great speed, and that a collision, expected in six months, will bring untold destruction and perhaps even the end of life on earth. After composing your poems, write a brief explanation of how and why they differ in terms of language, references, attitudes towards friends, family, country, religion, and so on.

13

Character and Setting: Who, What, Where, and When in Poetry

Poets, like other writers, bring their works alive through the interactions of fictional characters who experience love and hatred, pleasure and pain, and all the conditions and situations that life offers. As in narrative fiction, poetic characters are created and defined by what they say, what they do, how they react to other characters, and what other characters say about them. Because poetry may be developed in many ways other than narrative, however, our concern with character development in poems is to see it in relation to someone or something else—such as the interactions of speakers with listeners or with the reader, the inner conflicts of a speaker discussing the state of his or her spirit, and the issues of love, hate, admiration, emulation, idea, action, and so on, that are brought out in the experiences people have with each other and with society.

In addition, we may also find the *setting* of a poem to be one of the major means of measuring character (see Chapter 6, pp. 241–65). Poetic protagonists, like those in stories, are necessarily influenced by the things around them, the places they inhabit, and the times in which they live. Poems therefore abound with references to events and situations, and also to objects such as beaches, forests, battlefields, graveyards, teaspoons, museums, paintings, and so on. However, whereas in fiction we consider setting in a number of different ways, in poetry we focus on the interactions of character with object, place, and time. The period that people have spent in a relationship, their relative wealth or poverty, their social and economic circumstances—all have a bearing on what they are like.

CHARACTERS IN POETRY

The Speaker or Persona

The most significant of the three character types in poetry is the *speaker*, also called the *persona* (plural *personae*, a term that comes from the Latin word meaning "mask"). In prose fiction, we use "speaker" and "persona" for this character too, but we often prefer the word *narrator* because of the obvious role of storyteller. This distinction emphasizes the personal and psychological importance of the speakers of poems. Sometimes the role is so clear that the speaker may be taken as a distinct character, with individual characteristics and a well-imagined and detailed life and background. In Emily Dickinson's "Because I Could Not Stop for Death," for example (p. 528), the speaker states that she has been dead for hundreds of years and is now looking back from eternity to the moment of her death. Her calm acceptance of death as a friendly ally invites us to interpret death as being different from the more common view involving anguish, pain, and bereavement.

Alternatively, certain poetic speakers act as the embodiment of a position or stance that the poet selects to present a case or advance an argument. The poet is thus the undeniable speaker, but the voice we hear may be considered a brief dramatization of the poet's personality or need. Donne in his *Holy Sonnets* adopts such a stance—a suppliant or penitent praying for divine favor (pp. 852–54). In these sonnets Donne is not creating a separate dramatic character in deep religious anguish, but is expressing many of his own hopes and fears.

One of the first things to decide in reading a poem is whether the speaker is *inside* or *outside* the poem. Determine the **point of view** used by the poet (see Chapter 6, pp. 196–240). The speaker is *inside* the poem if the point of view is first person. Here is such a poem, written by an unknown poet.

Western Wind, When Will Thou Blow?   *Fifteenth century?*

Western wind, when will thou blow?
The small rain down can rain.
Christ, if my love were in my arms,
And I in my bed again.

In this poem the "my" and "I" pronouns indicate that the speaker is *inside* the poem speaking in the first person, wishing for warm spring rains and the renewal of life and love that is signaled by spring.

The speaker is *outside* the poem, however, if the third person is used. In such poems, the speaker is not involved with the action, but simply describes what is happening to others, as with this anonymous Scots ballad.

Bonny George Campbell   *Late sixteenth century*

High upon Highlands
  And low upon Tay.°
Bonny George Campbell
  Rode out on a day.

But toom° came his saddle,   *empty*   5
  All bloody to see,
Oh, home came his good horse,
  But never came he.

Down came his old mother,
  Greeting full sair°   *weeping full sore*   10
And down came his bonny wife,
  Wringing her hair.

Saddled, and bridled,
  And booted rode he;
And home came his good horse,   15
  But never came he.

"My meadow lies green,
  And my corn is unshorn,°   *grain is not harvested*
My barn is to build°   *yet to be built*
  And my babe is unborn."   20

Saddled, and bridled,
  And booted rode he;
Toom home came the saddle,
  But never came he.

BONNY GEORGE CAMPBELL.   2 *Tay:* Loch Tay, a lake in Perth County, in central Scotland, about 60 miles north of Glasgow.

QUESTIONS

1. What can you deduce about the character, social status, way of life, and feelings of the three persons mentioned in the poem?

2. What happened to George Campbell? Why must you infer the exact details?

3. Why do quotation marks enclose the fifth stanza? Who is the speaker here? What effect has George Campbell's absence had on this speaker?

In this ballad the speaker is not involved, and limits his or her perspective to the people left behind, who loved Campbell. They do not learn his fate beyond what they learn from the bloody saddle—nor do we—because the speaker does not assume an omniscient stance to tell us. However, the speaker does describe the effects upon Campbell's mother and wife, even quoting the wife's lamentation because Campbell's death has deprived her of husband, breadwinner, and father of her unborn child. By avoiding entering the poem as an "I," the speaker maintains objectivity and lets the details speak for themselves.

Poets have used many sorts of speakers to voice their poems. This anthology contains poems spoken by kings and dukes, husbands and wives, lovers and killers, shepherds, secretaries, civil servants, children, beggars, and almost every other kind of person you can imagine. In addition, you will meet speakers who are gods, historical figures, mythological heroes and heroines, corpses, and ghosts. The speaker does not even have to be human, for animals can be the speakers, or clouds, buildings, whirlwinds, computers, or whatever the poet's imagination may create.

It's not enough only to identify the speaker, for we must also find out what the speaker does, together with any other facts we can discover. An obvious place to begin is the title. Take, for example, Marlowe's "The Passionate Shepherd to His Love" (p. 547). This title tells us that the speaker herds sheep for a living, that he has a lady love, and that he is full of desire and hope. In addition to the title, we should also look at the speaker's diction, for speakers either intentionally or unintentionally provide us with autobiographical information. In "Loveliest of Trees" by A. E. Housman (p. 529), the speaker reveals that he is twenty years old, that he doesn't think his remaining fifty years (assuming a lifetime of seventy years, the biblical life expectancy) will give him enough time to experience and observe life fully, that he enjoys the flowering of spring, that he knows enough of church rituals to claim that the whiteness of cherry blossoms coincides with the liturgical color of white for Easter, and that he is meditative and somber rather than extroverted and hilarious. All this is quite a bit of information from so short a poem.

If we look at all poems with the same care, we will be able to discover many other details. Grammatical forms, together with word levels, may define the speaker's social class or educational level. Similarly, the selection of topics may indicate the speaker's emotional state, self-esteem, knowledge, attitudes, habits, hobbies, and much more.

The Listener

The second type of character we encounter in poetry is the **listener**— a person, not the reader, whom a speaker addresses directly and who is therefore "inside" the poem. Occasionally we find poems in the form of a **dialogue** between two persons, so that the characters are *both* speakers and listeners, as in Hardy's "The Workbox" (p. 660). Whatever the form, the speaker-listener relationship underlines the dramatic nature of much poetry. In effect, we as readers become an audience, hearing either conversational exchanges or one-way conversations. The speakers of course identify themselves with the "I" pronoun, and address their listeners with the pronouns "thou-thy-thee" and "you-your-yours."

In poems in which the only words are the speaker's, the listener hears the speaker's words without response, as in the "The Passionate Shepherd to His Love" by Marlowe and "The Nymph's Reply to the Shepherd" by Raleigh (included in this chapter's Poems for Study). A variation is that the listener may not be present, but may instead be the speaker's intended recipient. In this case the speaker is like a letter writer and the listener is the "addressee." Such a listener is the "thou-thee-thine" of Ben Jonson's well-known "Drink to Me, Only, with Thine Eyes," in which the speaker is addressing compliments to a woman.

BEN JONSON   (1573–1637)

Drink to Me, Only, with Thine Eyes   *1616*

Drink to me, only, with thine eyes,
   And I will pledge° with mine;   *drink a toast*
Or leave a kiss but in the cup,
   And I'll not look for wine.
The thirst that from the soul doth rise   5
   Doth ask a drink divine:
But might I of Jove's nectar° sup
   I would not change° for thine.   *exchange it [i.e., nectar]*

I sent thee, late, a rosy wreath,
   Not so much honoring thee,   10
As giving it a hope, that there
   It could not withered be.
But thou thereon did'st only breathe,
   And sent'st it back to me:
Since when° it grows, and smells, I swear,   *that time, then*   15
   Not of itself, but thee.

DRINK TO ME, ONLY, WITH THINE EYES.   7 *Jove's nectar:* Jove, or Jupiter, was the principal Roman god. Nectar (a word meaning "overcoming death") was the drink of the gods; a human being who drank it would become immortal.

QUESTIONS

1. Who is the speaker? What do you learn about him, his knowledge, his wit, and his concern for the listener?

2. What has the speaker sent to the listener before he begins the poem? What did she do, and why is he still writing to her?

3. How may the poem be seen as an attempt to "top" the listener's disdain? Explain why the speaker seems just as interested in showing his wittiness as in pleasing the listener with his compliments.

This poem demonstrates that the silent listener, while not making direct responses, may nevertheless have done something to prompt the speaker to create the poem. It is clear that Jonson's listener has returned the speaker's gift of a "rosy wreath," and thus has spurned him. The poem may therefore be seen at least partly as the speaker's attempt, by demonstrating his wit, to ingratiate himself once again in his woman friend's good graces. With similar poems involving a speaker and a silent listener, we should be prepared to consider both the dramatic situation and the listener's possible responses.

A related but distinct type of situation involving a listener is the **dramatic monologue,** in which the speaker talks directly to a present listener who reacts to what the speaker says, and who therefore directly affects the course of the poem. Browning's "My Last Duchess" is such a poem (p. 557), in which the speaker, the Duke, addresses the "you" listener who has been given the task of arranging financial terms with the Duke about the dowry to be awarded him by the "Count" upon his forthcoming marriage to the Count's daughter.

Ultimately, of course, we as readers are the listeners of all poems. In this capacity we are usually the poet's uninvolved, outside audience. Sometimes, however, the poet may address us directly in our role as readers, as in this brief dedicatory poem that Ben Jonson uses to begin his book of epigrams published in 1616.

To the Reader   *1616*

Pray thee, take care, that tak'st my book in hand,
To read it well: that is, to understand.

In this couplet Jonson establishes intimacy with us by using the second-person singular pronoun "thee." Though we are clearly *outside* the poem, Jonson invites us *inside* by asking us to read well and understand all his forthcoming poems. As much as a poet can, he therefore closes the distance that sometimes exists between poem and reader.

Only rarely do poets address us directly, as Jonson does. For this reason it is important to determine what is meant when a poet uses the "you" pronoun. Often the "you" may refer to the speaker himself or herself, and not to listeners or to us as readers. The speaker of Hardy's "The Man He Killed," for example, uses such a conversational *you* as a reference to himself and to people generally (p. 530). Similarly, Richard Hugo's "Degrees of Gray in Philipsburg" (p. 564) begins "You might come here Sunday on a whim." The *you* in this poem is neither the reader nor an inside listener. Rather it is an oblique or indirect way for the speaker to talk about himself. Most of the time, in other words, we are not so much listeners as spectators. In poems like Hardy's "The Workbox" and Browning's "My Last Duchess," we are almost literally an audience, whereas in a poem like Housman's "Loveliest of Trees," we are outside listeners, eavesdropping as the speaker meditates on time, death, and beauty. Most poems will put us, as readers, into situations like the one in Housman's poem.

The Participants, Major and Minor

Because poetry is dramatic, it often concerns not only speakers and listeners, but also major and minor participants. Thus, we are concerned in poetry with actions, responses, appearances, and speeches—and how we learn about them. As in narrative fiction, the speaker is usually a reliable observer whose accuracy about action and character is not to be questioned. The speaker of "Sir Patrick Spens" (p. 525), is such a reliable guide, for he or she is straightforward and objective in describing the action of the king, the adviser, Sir Patrick, the crew member, the Scots lords, and the ladies who wait in vain for the ship to return. We may take as true what the poem tells us about these characters. In some poems, however, we should be alert for subjectivity and distortion in the speaker's views of others—also as in prose fiction. In "My Last Duchess," a notable example (p. 557), the speaker talks extensively about his dead wife, the Duchess, who is one of the three central participants in the poem's action even though she is not alive at the time of the monologue. The poem soon makes clear that we cannot accept the accuracy of the Duke's account. We must therefore use our judgments to discover her true character and the nature of her actions despite his distortions and deliberate lies.

SETTING AND CHARACTER IN POETRY

The people in poetry, like all people, do not exist in a vacuum. When they speak, act, and react, they reflect the time, place, thought, social conventions, and general circumstances of their lives. Love poetry, for example, is not about desire alone, but rather about love within the possible ranges provided by the culture and the environment. Religion, economic circumstances, leisure, and the condition of the natural world may all enter into a speaking lover's pronouncements. Thus, the speaker of "The Passionate Shepherd to His Love" (p. 547) speaks of time to be spent in open nature with his lady love, listening to bird songs and sharing the sights of "valleys, groves, hills, and fields." Here his use of setting as an Arcadian dream world—without work, without illness, without want— reinforces his desire for his woman friend. In contrast, the speaker of Hardy's "The Walk" (p. 561) speaks about Nature when his beloved is infirm, and can no longer share the view of the "hilltop tree / By the gated ways" that the two enjoyed when the world was young and beautiful for them both. Although both poems are about love, one ignores the real world of age and ill health, while the other confronts it.

Poetic settings are of course not confined to romantic relationships, but may bring out political, philosophical, and religious thoughts, as in Gray's "Elegy Written in a Country Churchyard" (p. 549). Here, the early evening hour, bringing the end of day "in darkness," causes the speaker to think of the "rude forefathers of the hamlet" in their churchyard graves. This fact prompts him to compare human pretentions with the ultimate fact of death, and he draws conclusions about lost human potential. The interaction here is a complex one, involving the constant interweaving of character and history with natural and cultural situations and images. A poem similarly connecting character and setting is Words- worth's "Lines Composed . . . Above Tintern Abbey" (p. 553). This poem, based on the relationship of the past, present, and future of the speaker to the natural scenes he describes, is a model of the fusion in poetry of setting and character.

It is no exaggeration to say that setting interacts in a virtually infinite number of ways with character. As motivation, the Duke's displays of valuable art in Browning's "My Last Duchess" forms a setting which exposes for us this individual's greed, lust for power, and cruelty. Blake's "London" (p. 553) introduces the vision of streets and walls, together with the sounds of cries, sighs, and curses, to evoke a response of repulsion and rejection. As the representation of a philosophical judgment, the setting of Arnold's "Dover Beach" (p. 559) demonstrates life's changeability and impermanence. The speaker's solution is to establish fidelity as something permanent amid the surroundings of change, dissolution, and brutality. To a greater or lesser degree, each poem will offer similar connections of setting and character.

POEMS FOR STUDY

CHRISTOPHER MARLOWE (1564–1593)

The Passionate Shepherd to His Love   *1599*

Come live with me and be my love,
And we will all the pleasures prove°   *test*
That valleys, groves, hills, and fields,
Woods, or steepy mountain yields.

And we will sit upon the rocks,   5
Seeing the shepherds feed their flocks,
By shallow rivers to whose falls
Melodious birds sing madrigals.

And I will make thee beds of roses
And a thousand fragrant posies,   10
A cap of flowers, and a kirtle°   *long dress*
Embroidered all with leaves of myrtle;

A gown made of the finest wool
Which from our pretty lambs we pull;
Fair lined slippers for the cold,   15
With buckles of the purest gold;

A belt of straw and ivy buds,
With coral clasps and amber studs;
And if these pleasures may thee move,
Come live with me, and be my love.   20

The shepherds' swains° shall dance and sing   *lovers*
For thy delight each May morning:
If these delights thy mind may move,
Then live with me and be my love.

QUESTIONS

1. Describe the speaker. What does he do? What is he like? What does he want?
2. Who is the listener? What is the relationship between speaker and listener?
3. What specific gifts, and what sort of world, does the speaker offer the listener?
4. What is realistic/unrealistic about the speaker's description of life? What do you think is the speaker's understanding of reality?

SIR WALTER RALEIGH (1552–1618)

The Nymph's Reply to the Shepherd   *1600*

If all the world and love were young,
And truth in every shepherd's tongue,
These pretty pleasures might me move
To live with thee and be thy love.

Time drives the flocks from field to fold°   *fenced field*   5
When rivers rage and rocks grow cold,
And Philomel° becometh dumb;   *the nightingale*
The rest complains of cares to come.

The flowers do fade, and wanton fields
To wayward winter reckoning yields;   10

A honey tongue, a heart of gall,
Is fancy's spring, but sorrow's fall.

Thy gowns, thy shoes, thy beds of roses,
Thy cap, thy kirtle,° and thy posies°   *long dress; flowers and poems*
Soon break, soon wither, soon forgotten—   15
In folly ripe, in reason rotten.

Thy belt of straw and ivy buds,
Thy coral clasps and amber studs,
All these in me no means can move
To come to thee and be thy love.   20

But could youth last and love still° breed,   *always*
Had joys no date nor age no need,
Then these delights my mind might move
To live with thee and be thy love.

QUESTIONS

1. Who is the speaker? What do we learn about the speaker? Who is the listener?
2. How are the ideas of love and the world in this poem different from those in Marlowe's poem?
3. To what extent is this poem a parody (an imitation that makes fun) of Marlowe's poem? To what extent is it a refutation of Marlowe's poem?
4. Determine the steps of the speaker's logical argument in this poem.

THOMAS GRAY   (1716–1771)

Elegy Written in a Country Churchyard   *1751*

The curfew tolls the knell of parting day,
  The lowing herd wind slowly o'er the lea,
The ploughman homeward plods his weary way,
  And leaves the world to darkness and to me.

Now fades the glimm'ring landscape on the sight,   5
  And all the air a solemn stillness holds,
Save where the beetle wheels his droning flight,
  And drowsy tinklings lull the distant folds;

Save that from yonder ivy-mantled tower
  The moping owl does to the moon complain   10
Of such as wand'ring near her secret bower
  Molest her ancient solitary reign.

Beneath those rugged elms, that yew-tree's shade,
  Where heaves the turf in many a mold'ring heap,

Each in his narrow cell forever laid,   15
   The rude forefathers of the hamlet sleep.

The breezy call of incense-breathing morn,
   The swallow twitt'ring from the straw-built shed,
The cock's shrill clarion, or the echoing horn,°   *hunting horn*
   No more shall rouse them from their lowly bed.   20

For them no more the blazing hearth shall burn,
   Or busy housewife ply her evening care;
No children run to lisp their sire's return,
   Or climb his knees the envied kiss to share.

Oft did the harvest to their sickle yield,   25
   Their furrow oft the stubborn glebe° has broke;   *church land*
How jocund did they drive their team afield!
   How bowed the woods beneath their sturdy stroke!

Let not Ambition mock their useful toil
   Their homely joys, and destiny obscure;   30
Nor Grandeur hear with a disdainful smile
   The short and simple annals of the poor.

The boast of heraldry, the pomp of power,
   And all that beauty, all that wealth e'er gave,
Awaits alike th'inevitable hour.   35
   The paths of glory lead but to the grave.

Nor you, ye proud, impute to these the fault,
   If mem'ry o'er their tomb no trophies raise,
Where through the long-drawn aisle and fretted vault
   The pealing anthem swells the note of praise.   40

Can storied urn or animated bust
   Back to its mansion call the fleeting breath?
Can Honor's voice provoke the silent dust,
   Or Flatt'ry soothe the dull cold ear of death?

Perhaps in this neglected spot is laid   45
   Some heart once pregnant with celestial fire;
Hands that the rod of empire might have swayed,
   Or waked to ecstasy the living lyre.

But Knowledge to their eyes her ample page
   Rich with the spoils of time did ne'er unroll;   50
Chill Penury repressed their noble rage,
   And froze the genial current of the soul.

Full many a gem of purest ray serene,
   The dark unfathomed caves of ocean bear;
Full many a flower is born to blush unseen,   55
   And waste its sweetness on the desert air.

Some village Hampden,° that with dauntless breast
    The little tyrant of his fields withstood;
Some mute inglorious Milton here may rest,
    Some Cromwell guiltless of his country's blood.   60

Th'applause of list'ning senates to command,
    The threats of pain and ruin to despise,
To scatter plenty o'er a smiling land,
    And read their hist'ry in a nation's eyes

Their lot forbade: nor circumscribed alone   65
    Their growing virtues, but their crimes confined;
Forbade to wade through slaughter to a throne,
    And shut the gates of mercy on mankind,

The struggling pangs of conscious truth to hide,
    To quench the blushes of ingenuous shame,   70
Or heap the shrine of luxury and pride
    With incense kindled at the Muse's flame.

Far from the madding° crowd's ignoble strife,   *raving*
    Their sober wishes never learned to stray;
Along the cool sequestered vale of life   75
    They kept the noiseless tenor of their way.

Yet ev'n these bones from insult to protect
    Some frail memorial still erected nigh,
With uncouth° rhymes and shapeless sculpture decked,   *uneducated, unsophisticated*
    Implores the passing tribute of a sigh.   80

Their names, their years, spelt by th'unlettered Muse,
    The place of fame and elegy supply;
And many a holy text around she strews,
    That teach the rustic moralist to die.

For who to dumb forgetfulness a prey,   85
    This pleasing anxious being e'er resigned,
Left the warm precincts of the cheerful day,
    Nor cast one longing ling'ring look behind?

On some fond breast the parting soul relies,
    Some pious drops the closing eye requires;   90
Ev'n from the tomb the voice of Nature cries,
    Ev'n in our ashes live their wonted fires.

For thee, who mindful of th'unhonored dead
    Dost in these lines their artless tale relate;
If chance, by lonely contemplation led,   95
    Some kindred spirit shall inquire thy fate.

ELEGY WRITTEN IN A COUNTRY CHURCHYARD.   57 *Hampden:* John Hampden
(1594–1643), English statesman who defended the rights of the people against King Charles
I and who died in the English Civil War of 1642–1646.

Haply some hoary-headed swain may say,
   "Oft have we seen him at the peep of dawn
Brushing with hasty steps the dews away
   To meet the sun upon the upland lawn.   100

"There, at the foot of yonder nodding beech
   That wreathes its old fantastic° roots so high,   *natural, following nature*
His listless length at noontide would he stretch
   And pore upon the brook that babbles by.

"Hard by yon wood, now smiling as in scorn,   105
   Mutt'ring his wayward fancies he would rove,
Now drooping, woeful wan, like one forlorn,
   Or crazed with care, or crossed in hopeless love.

"One morn I missed him on the 'customed hill,
   Along the heath and near his fav'rite tree;   110
Another came; nor yet beside the rill,
   Nor up the lawn, nor at the wood was he;

"The next with dirges due in sad array
   Slow through the church-way path we saw him borne.
Approach and read (for thou canst read) the lay,   115
   Graved on the stone beneath yon aged thorn."

THE EPITAPH

Here rests his head upon the lap of earth
   A youth to fortune and to fame unknown;
Fair Science frowned not on his humble birth,
   And Melancholy marked him for her own.   120

Large was his bounty, and his soul sincere,
   Heav'n did a recompense as largely send:
He gave to mis'ry all he had, a tear:
   He gain'd from Heav'n ('twas all he wished) a friend.

No farther seek his merits to disclose,   125
   Or draw his frailties from their dread abode,
(There they alike in trembling hope repose)
   The bosom of his Father and his God.

QUESTIONS

1. What is the time of day of the speaker's meditation? What is happening in nature as the poem opens? Whom is the speaker addressing?

2. Who are the people buried in the church graveyard? What point does Gray make about the contributions they might have made if they had not died?

3. How does Gray's use of sights and sounds complement the poem's mood?

4. Who is "thee" (line 93)? What happens to him? Why is he included in the poem?

WILLIAM BLAKE (1757–1827)

London 1794

I wander thro' each charter'd° street,
Near where the charter'd Thames does flow,
And mark in every face I meet
Marks of weakness, marks of woe.

In every cry of every Man, 5
In every Infant's cry of fear,
In every voice, in every ban,° *public pronouncement*
The mind-forg'd manacles I hear.

How the Chimney-sweeper's cry
Every blackning Church appalls;° 10
And the hapless Soldier's sigh
Runs in blood down Palace walls.

But most thro' midnight streets I hear
How the youthful Harlot's curse
Blasts the new-born Infant's tear, 15
And blights with plagues the Marriage hearse.

LONDON.   1 *charter'd:* privileged, licensed, authorized.   10 *appalls:* weakens, makes
pale, shocks.

QUESTIONS

1. What does London represent to the speaker? How do the persons who live
   there contribute to the poem's ideas about the state of humanity?

2. What sounds does the speaker mention as a part of the London scene?
   Characterize these sounds in relation to the poem's main idea.

3. Because of the tension in the poem between civilized activity (as represented
   in the chartering of the street and the river) and free human impulses,
   explain how the poem might be considered revolutionary.

4. The poem appeared in *Songs of Experience*, published in 1794. Explain the
   appropriateness of his including the poem in a collection so named.

WILLIAM WORDSWORTH (1770–1850)

*Lines Composed a Few Miles Above Tintern Abbey on Revisiting
the Banks of the Wye During a Tour, June 13, 1798°* 1798

Five years have past; five summers, with the length
Of five long winters! and again I hear
These waters, rolling from their mountain-springs

LINES COMPOSED ABOVE TINTERN ABBEY.   Wordsworth first visited the valley
of the Wye in southwest England in August 1793 at age twenty-three. On this second visit
he was accompanied by his sister Dorothy (the "friend" in line 115).

With a soft inland murmur.—Once again
Do I behold these steep and lofty cliffs,   5
That on a wild secluded scene impress
Thoughts of more deep seclusion, and connect
The landscape with the quiet of the sky.
The day is come when I again repose
Here, under this dark sycamore, and view   10
These plots of cottage-ground, these orchard-tufts,
Which at this season, with their unripe fruits,
Are clad in one green hue, and lose themselves
'Mid groves and copses. Once again I see
These hedge-rows, hardly hedge-rows, little lines   15
Of sportive wood run wild; these pastoral farms,
Green to the very door; and wreaths of smoke
Sent up, in silence, from among the trees!
With some uncertain notice, as might seem
Of vagrant dwellers in the houseless woods,   20
Or of some Hermit's cave, where by his fire
The Hermit sits alone.
                              These beauteous forms,
Through a long absence, have not been to me
As is a landscape to a blind man's eye:
But oft, in lonely rooms, and 'mid the din   25
Of towns and cities, I have owed to them
In hours of weariness, sensations sweet,
Felt in the blood, and felt along the heart;
And passing even into my purer mind,
With tranquil restoration:—feelings too   30
Of unremembered pleasure: such, perhaps,
As have no slight or trivial influence
On that best portion of a good man's life,
His little, nameless, unremembered acts
Of kindness and of love. Nor less, I trust,   35
To them I may have owed another gift,
Of aspect more sublime; that blessed mood,
In which the burden of the mystery,
In which the heavy and the weary weight
Of all this unintelligible world,   40
Is lightened:—that serene and blessed mood,
In which the affections gently lead us on,—
Until, the breath of this corporeal frame
And even the motion of our human blood
Almost suspended, we are laid asleep   45
In body, and become a living soul:
While with an eye made quiet by the power
Of harmony, and the deep power of joy,
We see into the life of things.
                              If this
Be but a vain belief, yet, oh!—how oft—   50

In darkness and amid the many shapes
Of joyless daylight; when the fretful stir
Unprofitable, and the fever of the world,
Have hung upon the beatings of my heart—
How oft, in spirit, have I turned to thee,   55
O sylvan Wye! thou wanderer thro' the woods,
How often has my spirit turned to thee!
    And now, with gleams of half extinguished thought,
With many recognitions dim and faint,
And somewhat of a sad perplexity,   60
The picture of the mind revives again:
While here I stand, not only with the sense
Of present pleasure, but with pleasing thoughts
That in this moment there is life and food
For future years. And so I dare to hope,   65
Though changed, no doubt, from what I was when first
I came among these hills; when like a roe
I bounded o'er the mountains, by the sides
Of the deep rivers, and the lonely streams,
Wherever nature led: more like a man   70
Flying from something that he dreads, than one
Who sought the thing he loved. For nature then
(The coarser pleasures of my boyish days,
And their glad animal movements all gone by)
To me was all in all.—I cannot paint   75
What then I was. The sounding cataract
Haunted me like a passion: the tall rock,
The mountain, and the deep and gloomy wood,
Their colours, and their forms, were then to me
An appetite; a feeling and a love,   80
That had no need of a remoter charm,
By thought supplied, nor any interest
Unborrowed from the eye.—That time is past,
And all its aching joys are now no more,
And all its dizzy raptures. Not for this   85
Faint I, nor mourn nor murmur; other gifts
Have followed; for such loss, I would believe,
Abundant recompense. For I have learned
To look on nature, not as in the hour
Of thoughtless youth; but hearing oftentimes   90
The still, sad music of humanity,
Nor harsh nor grating, though of ample power
To chasten and subdue. And I have felt
A presence that disturbs me with the joy
Of elevated thoughts; a sense sublime   95
Of something far more deeply interfused,
Whose dwelling is the light of setting suns,
And the round ocean, and the living air,
And the blue sky, and in the mind of man;

A motion and a spirit, that impels   100
All thinking things, all objects of all thought,
And rolls through all things. Therefore am I still
A lover of the meadows and the woods,
And mountains; and of all that we behold
From this green earth; of all the mighty world   105
Of eye, and ear,—both what they half create,
And what perceive; well pleased to recognize
In nature and the language of the sense,
The anchor of my purest thoughts, the nurse,
The guide, the guardian of my heart, and soul   110
Of all my mortal being.
                            Nor perchance,
If I were not thus taught, should I the more
Suffer my genial spirits to decay:
For thou art with me here upon the banks
Of this fair river; thou my dearest Friend,   115
My dear, dear Friend; and in thy voice I catch
The language of my former heart, and read
My former pleasures in the shooting lights
Of thy wild eyes. Oh! yet a little while
May I behold in thee what I was once,   120
My dear, dear Sister! and this prayer I make,
Knowing that Nature never did betray
The heart that loved her; 'tis her privilege,
Through all the years of this our life, to lead
From joy to joy: for she can so inform   125
The mind that is within us, so impress
With quietness and beauty, and so feed
With lofty thoughts, that neither evil tongues,
Rash judgments, nor the sneers of selfish men,
Nor greetings where no kindness is, nor all   130
The dreary intercourse of daily life,
Shall e'er prevail against us, or disturb
Our cheerful faith that all which we behold
Is full of blessings. Therefore let the moon
Shine on thee in thy solitary walk;   135
And let the misty mountain-winds be free
To blow against thee: and, in after years,
When these wild ecstasies shall be matured
Into a sober pleasure; when thy mind
Shall be a mansion for all lovely forms,   140
Thy memory be as a dwelling-place
For all sweet sounds and harmonies; oh! then,
If solitude, or fear, or pain, or grief,
Should be thy portion, with what healing thoughts
Of tender joy wilt thou remember me,   145
And these my exhortations! Nor, perchance—
If I should be where I no more can hear

Thy voice, nor catch from thy wild eyes these gleams
Of past existence—wilt thou then forget
That on the banks of this delightful stream   150
We stood together; and that I, so long
A worshipper of Nature, hither came
Unwearied in that service: rather say
With warmer love—oh! with far deeper zeal
Of holier love. Nor wilt thou then forget,   155
That after many wanderings, many years
Of absence, these steep woods and lofty cliffs,
And this green pastoral landscape, were to me
More dear, both for themselves and for thy sake!

QUESTIONS

1. What is the opening scene? How much time has elapsed since the speaker viewed the scene? What has it meant to him in the past?

2. To the speaker, what is the relationship between remembered scenes and the development of moral behavior?

3. What effect does the speaker consider that this present experience will have on him in future years?

4. In lines 93–111, how successful is the speaker in making concrete his ideas about the moral forces he perceives along with his vision of the natural scenes?

5. What is the power that the speaker attributes to Nature? Characterize the "cheerful faith" described in lines 133–134.

ROBERT BROWNING (1812–1889)

My Last Duchess°   *1842*

FERRARA

That's my last Duchess painted on the wall,
Looking as if she were alive. I call
That piece a wonder, now: Frà Pandolf's° hands
Worked busily a day, and there she stands.
Will't please you sit and look at her? I said   5
"Frà Pandolf" by design, for never read
Strangers like you that pictured countenance,
The depth and passion of its earnest glance,
But to myself they turned (since none puts by

MY LAST DUCHESS.   The poem is based on incidents in the life of Alfonso II, Duke of Ferrara, whose first wife died in 1561. Some claimed she was poisoned. The Duke negotiated his second marriage to the daughter of the Count of Tyrol through an agent. 3 *Frà Pandolf:* an imaginary painter who is also a monk.

The curtain I have drawn for you, but I)   10
And seemed as they would ask me, if they durst,°   *dared*
How such a glance came there; so, not the first
Are you to turn and ask thus. Sir, 'twas not
Her husband's presence only, called that spot
Of joy into the Duchess' cheek: perhaps   15
Frà Pandolf chanced to say "Her mantle laps
Over my lady's wrist too much," or "Paint
Must never hope to reproduce the faint
Half-flush that dies along her throat": such stuff
Was courtesy, she thought, and cause enough   20
For calling up that spot of joy. She had
A heart—how shall I say?—too soon made glad,
Too easily impressed; she liked whate'er
She looked on, and her looks went everywhere.
Sir, 'twas all one! My favor at her breast,   25
The dropping of the daylight in the West,
The bough of cherries some officious fool
Broke in the orchard for her, the white mule
She rode with round the terrace—all and each
Would draw from her alike the approving speech,   30
Or blush, at least. She thanked men—good! but thanked
Somehow—I know not how—as if she ranked
My gift of a nine-hundred-years-old name
With anybody's gift. Who'd stoop to blame
This sort of trifling? Even had you skill   35
In speech—(which I have not)—to make your will
Quite clear to such an one, and say, "Just this
Or that in you disgusts me; here you miss,
Or there exceed the mark"—and if she let
Herself be lessoned so, nor plainly set   40
Her wits to yours, forsooth, and made excuse
—E'en then would be some stooping; and I choose
Never to stoop. Oh sir, she smiled, no doubt,
Whene'er I passed her; but who passed without
Much the same smile? This grew; I gave commands;   45
Then all smiles stopped together. There she stands
As if alive. Will't please you rise? We'll meet
The company below, then. I repeat,
The Count your master's known munificence
Is ample warrant that no just pretense   50
Of mine for dowry will be disallowed;
Though his fair daughter's self, as I avowed
At starting, is my object. Nay, we'll go
Together down, sir. Notice Neptune,° though,
Taming a sea horse, thought a rarity,   55
Which Claus of Innsbruck° cast in bronze for me!

54 *Neptune:* Roman god of the sea.   56 *Claus of Innsbruck*: an imaginary sculptor.

QUESTIONS

1. Who is the speaker? The listener? What is the setting and situation?
2. What third character is described? How is your judgment about this character different from the speaker's? How do you account for the difference?
3. Characterize the speaker. How does Browning's use of detail and speech cause you to make your judgments?

MATTHEW ARNOLD (1822–1888)

Dover Beach   *1867 (1849)*

The sea is calm tonight.
The tide is full, the moon lies fair
Upon the straits—on the French coast the light
Gleams and is gone; the cliffs of England stand,
Glimmering and vast, out in the tranquil bay.   5
Come to the window, sweet is the night air!
Only, from the long line of spray
Where the sea meets the moon-blanched land,
Listen! you hear the grating roar
Of pebbles which the waves draw back, and fling,   10
At their return, up the high strand,
Begin, and cease, and then again begin,
With tremulous cadence slow, and bring
The eternal note of sadness in.

Sophocles long ago   15
Heard it on the Aegean, and it brought
Into his mind the turbid ebb and flow
Of human misery; we
Find also in the sound a thought,
Hearing it by this distant northern sea.   20

The Sea of Faith
Was once, too, at the full, and round earth's shore
Lay like the folds of a bright girdle furled.
But now I only hear
Its melancholy, long, withdrawing roar,   25
Retreating, to the breath
Of the night wind, down the vast edges drear
And naked shingles° of the world.   *beaches*

Ah, love, let us be true
To one another! for the world, which seems   30
To lie before us like a land of dreams,
So various, so beautiful, so new,
Hath really neither joy, nor love, nor light,
Nor certitude, nor peace, nor help for pain;

And we are here as on a darkling plain   35
Swept with confused alarms of struggle and flight,
Where ignorant armies clash by night.

QUESTIONS

1. What words and details establish the setting?
2. Where are the speaker and listener? What can they see? Hear?
3. What sort of movement may be topographically traced in the first six lines
   of the poem, so that the scene finally focuses on the speaker and the listener?
4. What is meant by comparing the English Channel to the Aegean Sea, and
   relating the Aegean surf to the thought of Sophocles?
5. What faith remains after the loss of religious faith? Defend the claim that
   the faith is the speaker's commitment to personal fidelity rather than love.

CHRISTINA ROSSETTI (1830–1894)

A Christmas Carol   *1872*

In the bleak mid-winter
    Frosty wind made moan,
Earth stood hard as iron,
    Water like a stone;
Snow had fallen, snow on snow,   5
    Snow on snow,
In the bleak mid-winter
    Long ago.

Our God, Heaven cannot hold Him
    Nor earth sustain;   10
Heaven and earth shall flee away
    When He comes to reign:
In the bleak mid-winter
    A stable-place sufficed°   *see Luke 2:7*
The Lord God Almighty   15
    Jesus Christ.

Enough for Him whom cherubim
    Worship night and day,
A breastful of milk
    And a mangerful of hay;   20
Enough for Him whom angels
    Fall down before,
The ox and ass and camel
    Which adore.

Angels and archangels   25
    May have gathered there,

Cherubim and seraphim
  Throng'd the air,
But only His mother
  In her maiden bliss   30
Worshipped the Beloved
  With a kiss.

What can I give Him,
  Poor as I am?
If I were a shepherd°   *see Luke 2:8–20*   35
  I would bring a lamb,
If I were a wise man°   *see Matthew 2:1–12*
  I would do my part,—
Yet what I can I give Him,
  Give my heart.   40

QUESTIONS

1. Why does Rossetti stress the bitterness and bleakness of the winter setting?
2. Why does the speaker emphasize the simplicity of the birthplace of "The Lord God Almighty"? What is the origin and tradition of this setting?
3. How does the fourth stanza prepare you for the speaker's description of her own condition in stanza 5?
4. How does the speaker's gift reveal her character and condition?

THOMAS HARDY   (1840–1928)

The Walk   *1913*

You did not walk with me
Of late to the hilltop tree
  By the gated ways,
  As in earlier days;
  You were weak and lame,   5
  So you never came,
And I went alone, and I did not mind,
Not thinking of you as left behind.

  I walked up there today
  Just in the former way;   10
    Surveyed around
    The familiar ground
    By myself again:
    What difference, then?
Only that underlying sense   15
Of the look of a room on returning thence.

QUESTIONS

1. What relationship does the speaker have to the person being addressed?
2. Why did the speaker's companion not walk to the hilltop tree? Does the speaker admit to being in solitude even though the most recent walk was done alone? How does his conclusion reveal his character?
3. Consider the final two lines. What impression do they convey about the location where the couple used to walk?

THOMAS HARDY   (1840–1928)

Channel Firing   *1914*

That night your great guns, unawares,
Shook all our coffins° as we lay,
And broke the chancel window-squares,
We thought it was the Judgment Day

And sat upright. While drearisome   5
Arose the howl of wakened hounds:
The mouse let fall the altar-crumb,
The worms drew back into the mounds,

The glebe° cow drooled. Till God called, "No;
It's gunnery practice out at sea   10
Just as before you went below;
The world is as it used to be:

"All nations striving strong to make
Red war yet redder. Mad as hatters
They do no more for Christés sake   15
Than you who are helpless in such matters.

"That this is not the judgment hour
For some of them's a blessed thing,
For if it were they'd have to scour
Hell's floor for so much threatening. . . .   20

"Ha, ha. It will be warmer when
I blow the trumpet (if indeed
I ever do; for you are men,
And rest eternal sorely need)."

So down we lay again. "I wonder,   25
Will the world ever saner be,"
Said one, "than when He sent us under
In our indifferent century!"

CHANNEL FIRING.   2 *coffins:* It has been common practice in England for hundreds of years to bury people in the floors or basements of churches.   9 *glebe:* a parcel of land adjoining and belonging to a church. Cows were grazed there to keep the grass short.

And many a skeleton shook his head.
"Instead of preaching forty year,"   30
My neighbor Parson Thirdly said,
"I wish I had stuck to pipes and beer."

Again the guns disturbed the hour,
Roaring their readiness to avenge,
As far inland as Stourton Tower.°   35
And Camelot,° and starlit Stonehenge.°

35 *Stourton Tower:* tower commemorating King Alfred the Great's defeat of the Danes in
A.D. 879.   36 *Camelot:* legendary seat of King Arthur's court.   *Stonehenge:* group of
standing stones on Salisbury Plain, probably built as a place of worship before 1000 B.C.

QUESTIONS

1. Who is the speaker in this poem? What is the setting? The situation?
2. To whom does the *your* in line 1 refer? The *our* in line 2?
3. What has awakened the speaker and his companions? What mistake have
    they made?
4. What three other voices are heard in the poem? How are their traits revealed?
5. What ideas about war and the nature of humanity does this poem explore?

C. DAY LEWIS   (1904–1972)

Song   *1935*

Come, live with me and be my love,
And we will all the pleasures prove
Of peace and plenty, bed and board,
That chance employment may afford.

I'll handle dainties on the docks   5
And thou shalt read of summer frocks:
At evening by the sour canals
We'll hope to hear some madrigals.

Care on thy maiden brow shall put
A wreath of wrinkles, and thy foot   10
Be shod with pain: not silken dress
But toil shall tire thy loveliness.

Hunger shall make thy modest zone
And cheat fond death of all but bone—
If these delights thy mind may move,   15
Then live with me and be my love.

QUESTIONS

1. What is the connection and contrast between this poem and Marlowe's "Passionate Shepherd to His Love"?
2. To what other poems in this chapter is this poem related? How?
3. Who is the speaker in this poem? The listener?
4. What is the effect of words like *chance employment* (line 4), *read* (line 6), and *hope* (line 8)?

RICHARD HUGO   (1923–1982)

Degrees of Gray in Philipsburg   1973

You might come here Sunday on a whim.
Say your life broke down. The last good kiss
you had was years ago. You walk these streets
laid out by the insane, past hotels
that didn't last, bars that did, the tortured try   5
of local drivers to accelerate their lives.
Only churches are kept up. The jail
turned 70 this year. The only prisoner
is always in, not knowing what he's done.

The principal supporting business now   10
is rage. Hatred of the various grays
the mountain sends, hatred of the mill,
The Silver Bill repeal, the best liked girls
who leave each year for Butte. One good
restaurant and bars can't wipe the boredom out.   15
The 1907 boom, eight going silver mines,
a dance floor built on springs—
all memory resolves itself in gaze,
in panoramic green you know the cattle eat
on two stacks high above the town,   20
two dead kilns, the huge mill in collapse
for fifty years that won't fall finally down.

Isn't this your life? That ancient kiss
still burning out your eyes? Isn't this defeat
so accurate, the church bell simply seems   25
a pure announcement: ring and no one comes?
Don't empty houses ring? Are magnesium
and scorn sufficient to support a town,
not just Philipsburg, but towns
of towering blondes, good jazz and booze   30
the world will never let you have
until the town you came from dies inside?

Say no to yourself. The old man, twenty
when the jail was built, still laughs
although his lips collapse. Someday soon,   35
he says, I'll go to sleep and not wake up.
You tell him no. You're talking to yourself.
The car that brought you here still runs.
The money you buy lunch with,
no matter where it's mined, is silver   40
and the girl who serves your food
is slender and her red hair lights the wall.

QUESTIONS

1. How does the speaker characterize Philipsburg? What was the past like there? Why has so much changed? Who is the "you" addressed in line 1?

2. What is life like in the town now? What is the principal supporting business?

3. What does the speaker think should characterize a living, as opposed to a dead, town? What does his thought tell you about his character?

4. How can this poem be seen as a philosophic reflection on the ability of human beings to endure and adjust even though new circumstances change previous ways of life?

JAMES MERRILL (b. 1926)

Laboratory Poem   *1958*

Charles used to watch Naomi, taking heart
And a steel saw, open up turtles, live.
While she swore they felt nothing, he would gag
At blood, at the blind twitching, even after
The murky dawn of entrails cleared, revealing   5
Contours he knew, egg-yellows like lamps paling.

Well then. She carried off the beating heart
To the kymograph° and rigged it there, a rag
In fitful wind, now made to strain, now stopped
By her solutions tonic or malign°   10
Alternately in which it would be steeped.
What the heart bore, she noted on a chart.

For work did not stop only with the heart.
He thought of certain human hearts, their climb

LABORATORY POEM.   8 *kymograph:* an instrument that measures pulsations or variations of pressure and records them on a revolving scroll of paper.   10 *tonic or malign:* healthful or poisonous, virtuous or evil.

Through violence into exquisite disciplines   15
Of which, as it now appeared, they all expired.
Soon she would fetch another and start over,
Easy in the presence of her lover.

QUESTIONS

1. What can you determine about the speaker here? Is he or she *inside* or *outside* the poem? Engaged in the action or detached?

2. Who are the two characters in the poem? What are they like? What is their relationship? What are they doing?

3. Which character's thoughts does the speaker relate? What are they? What does this character conclude about science? Human endeavor?

4. What is the setting of the poem? The situation? The event described? What aspects of human existence does the poem explore?

JAMES WRIGHT   (1927–1980)

A Blessing   *1963*

Just off the highway to Rochester, Minnesota,
Twilight bounds softly forth on the grass.
And the eyes of those two Indian ponies
Darken with kindness.
They have come gladly out of the willows   5
To welcome my friend and me.
We step over the barbed wire into the pasture
Where they have been grazing all day, alone.
They ripple tensely, they can hardly contain their happiness
That we have come.   10
They bow shyly as wet swans. They love each other.
There is no loneliness like theirs.
At home once more,
They begin munching the young tufts of spring in the darkness.
I would like to hold the slenderer one in my arms.   15
For she has walked over to me
And nuzzled my left hand.
She is black and white,
Her mane falls wild on her forehead,
And the light breeze moves me to caress her long ear   20
That is delicate as the skin over a girl's wrist.
Suddenly I realize
That if I stepped out of my body I would break
Into blossom.

QUESTIONS

1. What has happened just before the poem opens? Account for the poet's use of the present tense in his descriptions.

2. Is the setting specific or general? What happens as the poem progresses?

3. What realization overtakes the speaker? How does this realization constitute a "blessing," and what does it show about his character?

4. To what degree is it necessary for the poet to include all the detail of the first twenty-one lines before the realization of the last three?

MARGE PIERCY   (b. 1934)

Wellfleet° Sabbath   *1988*

The hawk eye of the sun slowly shuts.
The breast of the bay is softly feathered
dove grey. The sky is barred like the sand
when the tide trickles out.

The great doors of the sabbath are swinging   5
open over the ocean, loosing the moon
floating up slow distorted vast, a copper
balloon just sailing free.

The wind slides over the waves, patting
them with its giant hand, and the sea   10
stretches its muscles in the deep,
purrs and rolls over.

The sweet beeswax candles flicker
and sigh, standing between the phlox
and the roast chicken. The wine shines   15
its red lantern of joy.

Here on this piney sandspit, the Shekinah°
comes on the short strong wings of the seaside
sparrow raising her song and bringing
down the fresh clean night.   20

WELLFLEET SABBATH. *Wellfleet:* a town close to the northern tip of Cape Cod, Massachusetts.   17 *Shekinah:* in the Jewish faith, a visible sign or manifestation of divinity.

QUESTIONS

1. What is the speaker's dominant mood? Explain how the poet's descriptive words for both outside and inside contribute to this mood.

2. What is the time of day and week? How does what is happening outside influence what is happening inside?

3. Where is the speaker? Who, if anyone, is being addressed? What is the reader's relationship to the poem?

MAURA STANTON   (b. 1946)

The Conjurer   1975

In a mayonnaise jar I keep the tiny
people I shrank with my magic; I didn't
know they'd hold each other's hands & cry
so sharply when I said, no, the spell's
irreversible, do you eat grass or breadcrumbs?   5
Two are lovers who claim the air's bad
down there, & bite my fingers when I offer
a ride. They don't understand me.
I keep the jar by a window, washing
soot off the glass walls periodically . . .   10
When I gave them a flower, some ants
in the stamen attacked viciously,
gnawing the man-in-the-fur-cap's leg
completely off, while the others squealed
at the punched lid for his rescue: 15
I thumbed the ant dead, but were they grateful?
Lately they've begun to irritate me,
refusing raw meat, demanding more privacy
as if they were parrots who need cage covers
for daytime sleep. The awkward lovers   20
break apart at my shadow, nonchalant . . .
They're weaving something out of grass,
a blanket maybe, growing thin to save
their stalks, eating only breadcrumbs.
Don't they see? I could dump them   25
out into a real garden, let them tunnel
through the weeds to an anthill.
One night I dreamed those lovers crawled
inside my left ear with candles,
trying to find my brain in a fog.   30
They moved deep among the stalactites
searching for the magic spell they thought
I'd lost in sleep. I knew better.
Still, I woke with something resurrected
in my memory, maybe only a trick,   35
yes, a trick, I'll tell them to close
their eyes I've something for them.

QUESTIONS

1. Who is the speaker? What is the speaker's occupation? How does the speaker treat the other characters in the poem? Why? What "trick" is in store for the other characters?
2. What attitude does the speaker exhibit toward the other characters in the poem? What is the attitude of these characters toward the speaker?
3. Characterize the speaker. On what elements of the poem do you base your conclusions?
4. What is the level of reality in the poem?

WRITING ABOUT CHARACTER AND SETTING IN POETRY

Writing about character and setting involves many of the same considerations whether you deal with prose fiction or poetry. You might therefore review the material on character presented in Chapter 4 (pp. 137–95). However, there are some important differences between the two writing tasks. One of these is the way you find out about characters. In prose fiction, you can usually judge a character by the details the narrator gives you about his or her actions, words, thoughts, appearance, opinions, and the like. In poetry, however, the speaker is less likely to present fully detailed information. Consequently, many conclusions about characters in poems must be inferred from the suggestions and hints the speaker gives us along with the details.

Another difference between writing about character in fiction and poetry concerns the types of character. In fiction you have a broad range of options for writing: You may choose to write about the protagonist, the antagonist, the narrator, or any of the incidental characters. By contrast, in poetry you are usually limited to the speaker or to one of the characters described by the speaker (although you may sometimes be able to discuss the listener, too). In writing about Browning's "My Last Duchess," for example, you could focus on either the Duke or the Duchess, for you learn enough from the poem to write about either.

In planning and prewriting, you should find out as much as you can about the characters and their relationship to their situations, that is, to the action, emotion, ideas, setting, and other characters in the poem. Answering the following questions will help you find a focus.

Questions for Discovering Ideas

About the speaker

Who is the speaker? What is he or she doing? What has already occurred? What does he or she say about himself or herself? About others?

What judgments and opinions does the speaker express? How knowledgeable is the speaker?

What do the speaker's choice of words reveal about his or her education and social standing? Does the language give us an idea about his or her deeply held assumptions? What tone of voice is suggested in the speaker's presentation?

How deeply involved is the speaker with the action or thought of the poem and with the other characters?

About other characters

How does the character respond to the surroundings?

What is he or she trying to gain?

How is the character affected by others and how do others respond to him or her?

What degree of control does the character seem to exert, and what does this effort reveal?

How does the character speak and behave, and what do you learn from these words and actions?

Usually you may rely on the views expressed by the speaker, although you might also find distorted or slanted presentations, as with the Duke-speaker in Browning's "My Last Duchess." When you perceive an obvious bias, be sure to take it into consideration when interpreting the speaker's views.

Strategies for Organizing Ideas

When you write about a single character, the central idea will usually provide a focused conclusion about his or her personality or status. If you are writing about the Duke in "My Last Duchess," for example, your idea might be that he is arrogant, cruel, greedy, and power-mad. In writing about Sir Patrick Spens, your idea would most probably be concerned with the qualities of Sir Patrick that are brought out by his fidelity to the king's command, even to the point of self-sacrifice. If the topic is a set of characters, the central idea should express some relationship or common-ality among them. Thus, the characters in "Bonny George Campbell" respond with grief to Campbell's sudden and unexpected death, and the characters in "London" to illustrate the withering effects that discrimina-tory law and religion produce in human beings.

You might wish to organize your essay according to one of the following approaches:

1. *Character as revealed by action.* Often the speaker describes himself or herself as a major character or major mover in the action of the poem. What does the action reveal about him or her? In Stanton's "The Conjurer," the speaker reveals that he or she has miniaturized a number of people,

and is keeping them in a bottle. What does this action show? In Gray's "Elegy Written in a Country Churchyard," there is not much action, but we may conclude that the speaker is entering the churchyard at the close of day, and that his meditation among the tombstones is brought about by the quiet and solemnity of his surroundings. This beginning action causes him to think of a number of other actions involving his judgments about life, glory, fame, fortune, and religious dedication. What do his speculations and conclusions reveal about his character?

In a parallel way, the speaker of Wordsworth's "Tintern Abbey" lines has returned to a scene visited five years before. His thoughts on the occasion deal with his actions as a child and an adult, prompting him to connect Nature with the development of his own identity as a human being. In the light of this spectrum of action, what conclusions might we make about his character?

2. *Character as revealed by interaction.* Poems that are based in a clearly defined dramatic situation will yield best to this sort of treatment. "My Last Duchess" is a fine example, as are Hardy's "Channel Firing" and Jonson's "Drink to Me, Only, with Thine Eyes." The dramatic situation in Hardy's "The Walk" is that the speaker is talking directly to a presumably infirm listener who has not been able to go on the walk that the two had shared in times of mutual good health. What do the speaker's descriptions and attitudes toward the listener tell us about his character? What do you learn about relationships from this and other poems? How have these relationships affected the characters involved?

3. *Character as revealed by circumstance or setting.* The essay based on the interrelationship of character and setting presupposes that conditions of time, place, artifact, money, family, culture, and history influence character and motivation, and also that individual and collective traits are developed as people try to control and alter the world around them. For instance, the speaker of Wright's "A Blessing" describes a moment of looking at the world around him, and at the end of the poem he feels as though he is about to "break / Into blossom." What leads to the interaction enabling him to reach this happy conclusion? How do the things and animals that he sees produce this effect? Why does he feel safe rather than frightened in the pasture? Why does he believe in the benevolence of the two ponies, and, in turn, why do the ponies treat him with affection? What aspects of character enable him to step over the barbed wire without fear, and to believe that the experience is really a "blessing"? Would such an experience have been possible at a more suspicious, less civilized time, when people stepping uninvited onto property might have been considered intruders? In short, how has setting in the very broadest sense entered into the character of the speaker?

In dealing with the interrelationship of character and external situation, you might be able to organize the body of your essay by relying on certain aspects of the setting. Thus, you might select the details about time in past, present, and future as presented in Wordsworth's "Tintern Abbey" lines. Similarly, the details about the roaring surf and the dim lights in Arnold's "Dover Beach" would provide the thematic links for a discussion of the speaker's sense of alienation, loss, and dedication. In such ways, you may use aspects of setting not only as topics to shed light on character but also as shaping and guiding influences for your essay.

Whatever strategy you choose, remember that your organization will finally be determined by the poem you are writing about. Each poem will suggest its own avenues of exploration, helping you in this way to shape your essay. Your goal, as always, is to support your central idea logically and coherently.

In the conclusion you might summarize your major points about the character or characters, and you might also tie your conclusions into an assessment of the poem as a whole. Thus, you might briefly discuss the connection between character and character, character and environment, character and death, character and greed, character and love, and so on, and deal with these topics generally as you bring your essay to a close.

SAMPLE ESSAY

The Character of the Duke in Browning's "My Last Duchess"°

[1] In this dramatic monologue, Browning skillfully develops the character of his speaker, who holds the high position of Duke of Ferrara (in Italy) during the sixteenth century, a period of aristocratic absolutism. Because the Duke is at the top of the aristocracy, he also has the power to exert absolute control, whether for good or for bad. Browning's Duke is bad; not only is he bad, but he is totally evil.* Browning does not make a direct accusation, but he does not need to. The Duke reveals his evil nature as he carries on his one-way conversation with the listener, who is apparently an envoy of a less powerful aristocrat, the Count, whose daughter the Duke is going to marry. The Duke's evil character is brought out by his indulgence in power, his intimidation of others, his manipulation of his dead wife the Duchess, and his general contempt for other people.†

[2] The Duke's indulgence in power, the basis of his evil, is apparent in his use of indirect speech. On the surface, Browning makes him seem intelligent, civilized, gracious, and friendly. The Duke begins his dramatic monologue by pointing out to his listener the beauty of a painting of his "last Duchess," but his entire speech--comprising the entire poem--reveals the horror of his self-indulgence. Although his description of how he treated the Duchess is indirect, it is threatening enough to show us that he delights in his own evil. When he says that "I gave commands; / Then all smiles stopped

° For this poem, see p. 557.
* Central idea.
† Thesis sentence.

together" (lines 45-46), he is actually bragging about his power. He is coldly horrible, the more so because Browning makes clear that he covers over his absolute evil with quiet words and a love of good art.

[3]

Another of the Duke's horrible qualities is the way he intimidates people. Although at first it seems that he is doing no more than discussing his dead wife and the life he had with her, it is clear at the poem's end that all the time he has been intimidating both his listener and also the listener's master, the Count. The last nine lines (lines 48-56), indicate that his *monologue* should have been a *dialogue*, in which he should have negotiated the terms for money and property that he is to receive as dowry from the Count. The fact that he has talked only about how he got rid of his "last Duchess" shows his arrogance and disregard for the Count's goodwill. Thus, there is no mention of dowry until lines 48-53, when the Duke states that he will make a "just pretense" for a dowry which of course the Count will honor (for "just pretense," read a demand for most of the Count's money and land). In addition, the Duke's commands, "Will't please you rise? We'll meet / The company below then" (lines 47–48), indicates that the negotiation that never began is now over, and that the envoy is totally in his power. This is intimidation, and the character who intimidates by describing one of his own death sentences is totally ruthless and inhuman.

[4]

In addition to the Duke's ruthless intimidation, the evil characteristic of manipulation and control is brought out in his description of his treatment of the Duchess. If we look through his words at what the Duchess was really like, we may conclude that she was even-tempered and pleasant to all--the soul of graciousness and courtesy. In fact, it would be hard to say that she was anything but perfect. But the Duke, rather than indicating pleasure with her, states that she was ungrateful to him because she was not submissive. So he complains that the smile she gave to others was the same as the smile she gave to him (it probably was not; we may conclude that her smile to him probably covered fear):

> O sir, she smiled, no doubt,
> Whene'er I passed her; but who passed without
> Much the same smile? (lines 43-45)

These lines show that the Duke is a manipulator of the worst sort and that the poor Duchess was in an impossible situation under his power. It would not be difficult to imagine that he would have complained also if she had smiled only at him and not at others--thereby leaving herself open to the Duke's perverted judgment that she did not show the graciousness toward others that he expected from his wife. No matter how good she was, there is no way she could have pleased such a monster. He would have manipulated her into an unfavorable position, in his eyes, that would have justified his giving the "commands" to remove her.

Perhaps the worst of this monster's traits is the contempt he shows for people by thinking of them not as human beings but rather as things. Most notable is the way he thinks of the Duchess; he calls her painting a "piece" (line 3) to hang on a wall, looking "as if she were alive" (line 2). He does not even name her, or recognize her humanity by calling her "the *late* Duchess,"

[5] and he speaks about the bronze statue of Neptune "taming a sea horse" (line 55) as being equal to her (it is worth noting that the subject of this statue is domination). This same contempt for people is shown in his claim that his interest in the Count's daughter is the "fair daughter's self" (line 52), while the rest of the poem makes clear that he looks on the new bride as no more than the means to additional wealth and power. Oddly, also, he seems to think of himself less as a person than as a "nine-hundred-years-old name" (line 33), and it is this intangible thing that he prizes above everything else. In other words, he views even his own humanity with contempt.

Browning's Duke, then, is a monster, a person with absolute power but without the kindness and understanding to use it for anyone but himself. His complaints about the dead Duchess are meaningless, for they are no more than pretexts for his cruel self-indulgence. He is at the top of the aristocratic power structure, and therefore he is able to do what he wants without reprisal.

[6] People must defer to him and obey him, but only because he makes everyone afraid. His intimidation, his manipulation, his lust for power--all govern him, and leave him unable to look at human beings as anything more than pawns in his self-indulgent game for control over everything he sees. He is an example of the old saying that absolute power corrupts absolutely, and his character is therefore a frightening portrait of evil.

Commentary on the Essay

Because the subject of the discussion, the Duke, is the speaker, the essay is based partially on details presented by him, but is also partially based on interpretations of detail. The principal topic is the interaction the Duke has with the subject of the poem—the "last Duchess"—in addition to his interaction with the listener, who is a representative of an inferior aristocrat, and whom he therefore treats with contempt. Elements of setting are also introduced to illuminate the Duke's character: his works of art, his absolute power, the prestige of his name, title, wealth. The essay thus demonstrates how character may be analyzed with reference (1) to interactions between persons, and also (2) to connections of persons with their environment.

The central idea is that the Duke is evil. This point is made in the first paragraph, with sufficient accompanying detail to explain that the Duke's position enables him to exercise absolute power. Paragraph 2 brings out that indulgence in power is one of the Duke's primary evil traits; paragraphs 3, 4, and 5 bring out traits of intimidation, manipulation, and contempt. The final paragraph, 6, contains the summary, but it also asserts that the Duke's justifications for killing his wife are meaningless in the light of his greed and desire for power.

As the essay develops, transitions are effected by phrases such as "another," "in addition," "perhaps the worst," "this same," and "then." The assertions in the essay are supported by references to specific details from the poem, quotations from the poem (with line numbers noted), and interpretations of details.

WRITING TOPICS

1. Write an essay comparing the speakers of the various "passionate shepherd" poems (by Marlowe, Raleigh, and Lewis). How are the speakers alike, and how are they different? How do their words and references indicate their characters? How do the speakers influence your judgments of the poems in which they appear?

2. Write an essay discussing the relationships among location, thought, and character as asserted in the poems by Gray, Blake, Arnold, and Wordsworth contained in this chapter (or others). What importance do place and time have on life and character? How do responses to time, historical period, and place influence ideas about how to live?

3. Write a short poem, biographical or autobiographical, showing how a certain time, place, or experience has shaped a present quality of your character and/or a certain decision about your life, friendships, and goals.

14

Words: The Building Blocks of Poetry

Poems are constructed of words. Words create the rhythm, rhyme, meter, and stanza form of poems. They define the speaker, the other characters, the setting, and the situation. They also carry the ideas and the emotions. For this reason, each poet seeks the perfect and indispensable word, the word that looks right, sounds right, and conveys all the compressed meanings, overtones, and emotions that the poem requires.

WORDS AND MEANING

All systems of communication are based on signs that have acquired conventional and accepted meanings. In any language, words are the signifiers for thoughts, things, or actions. Life, and poetry, would be simpler (and less interesting) if there were an exact one-to-one correspondence between words and the ideas they signify. We find an approximation of this close correspondence in artificial language systems such as chemical equations and computer languages. Such correspondence, however, is not characteristic of English or any other language. Instead, words have the independent (and wonderful) habit of acquiring a vast array of different meanings.

Most of us recognize the slippery nature of words at some level, even if we have not devoted much time to thinking about language. Much of our humor is built on the ambiguities of words and phrases. When Shakespeare's Mercutio (in *Romeo and Juliet*) says, "Seek for me tomorrow and you shall find me a grave man," the joke works because *grave* has two entirely different meanings, both of which come into play. In reading poetry, we recognize this ambiguity and understand that poets rejoice in the shifty nature of language.

DENOTATION AND CONNOTATION

Because of the vitality of individual words in poetry, we will consider denotation and connotation in more detail here than we do in our previous discussion (see Chapter 7, pp. 266–98). **Denotation** refers to the standard dictionary meaning of a word; it indicates conventional correspondences between a sign (the word) and an idea. We might expect that denotation would be fairly straightforward. However, most English words have multiple denotations. The word *house*, for example, can refer to a home, a chamber of congress, a theater, an audience, a fraternity, an astrological reference, and a brothel. Although context often makes the denotation of *house* more specific, the different meanings give this simple word some built-in ambiguity. The situation becomes far more complicated with a word like *fall*, which has over fifty different definitions or denotations. As a verb, *fall* means descend, hang down, succumb to temptation, be overthrown, killed, and chopped down. As a noun, the word denotes a descent, a season of the year, a slope, the state of sin, a capture, and even a hairpiece, among other things. In prose, a writer usually tries to limit the denotative value of *fall* to one of these meanings. Poets, however, frequently hold on to as many useful and appropriate denotations as possible.

Denotation presents us with problems because of the way words gain new meanings and lose old ones over long periods of time. Language changes slowly, but the shift can be dramatic over several centuries. In reading poems written before the nineteenth century, we often encounter words that have changed meaning so completely that a modern dictionary is not much help. Consider the word *vegetable* in Andrew Marvell's "To His Coy Mistress." The speaker asserts that "My vegetable love should grow / Vaster than empires and more slow." Our first impulse may be to imagine a giant and passionate cabbage. When we turn to a modern dictionary, we discover that "vegetable" is an adjective that means "plant-like," but "plantlike love" does not get us much beyond "vegetable love." A reference to the *Oxford English Dictionary* (*OED*), however, tells us that "vegetable" was used as an adjective in the seventeenth century to mean "living or growing like a plant." Thus, we find out that "vegetable love" can be an emotion that grows slowly and steadily larger.

Connotation refers to the emotional, psychological, or social overtones that words carry in addition to their denotations. We can see connotation at work in the synonyms *childish* and *childlike*. According to the dictionary, these two adjectives both denote the state of being like a child. Nevertheless, the two words connote or imply very different sets of characteristics. *Childish* suggests a person who is bratty, stubborn, immature, silly, and petulant. *Childlike*, on the other hand, describes a person who is innocent, charming, and unaffected. These very different descriptions are based entirely on the connotations of the two words; the denotations make little distinction.

We encounter the manipulation of connotation all the time, even though we may be unaware of it. Advertising depends to a large extent on the skillful management of connotation. This manipulation may be as simple as calling a "used" car "previously owned" to avoid the negative connotations of the word *used*. On the other hand, it may be as sophisticated as the current use of the words *lite* or *light* to describe specific foods and drinks. In all these products, the word *lite* means dietetic, low-calorie, or even weak. The distinction—and the selling point—is found in connotation. Imagine how difficult it would be to sell a drink called "dietetic beer" or "weak beer." *Light* and *lite*, however, carry none of the negative connotations of *weak* or *dietetic*. Instead, *lite* suggests a product that is pleasant, sparkling, bright, and healthy. "Weak beer" would grow dusty on the shelves; "lite beer" sells very well indeed.

Denotation and connotation are especially significant in poetry. Poets often make a single word carry as many appropriate and effective denotations and connotations as possible. To put it another way, poets often use *packed* or *loaded* words that carry a broad range of meaning and association. In reading poems, we "unpack" these loaded words and enjoy the play of language. With this in mind, take a look at the following poem by Robert Graves.

ROBERT GRAVES   (1895–1985)

The Naked and the Nude   *1957*

For me, the naked and the nude
(By lexicographers° construed
As synonyms that should express
The same deficiency of dress
Or shelter) stand as wide apart   5
As love from lies, or truth from art.

Lovers without reproach will gaze
On bodies naked and ablaze;
The Hippocratic° eye will see
In nakedness, anatomy;   10
And naked shines the Goddess when
She mounts her lion among men.

The nude are bold, the nude are sly
To hold each treasonable eye.

THE NAKED AND THE NUDE.   2 *lexicographers*: people who write dictionaries.   9
Hippocratic: medical; the adjective derives from Hippocrates, an ancient Greek considered the father of medicine.

While draping by a showman's trick   15
Their dishabille° in rhetoric,
They grin a mock-religious grin
Of scorn at those of naked skin.

The naked, therefore, who compete
Against the nude may know defeat;   20
Yet when they both together tread
The briary pastures of the dead,
By Gorgons° with long whips pursued,
How naked go the sometime nude!

16 *dishabille*: being carelessly or partly dressed.   23 *Gorgons*: mythological female monsters
with snakes for hair.

QUESTIONS

1. How does the speaker explain the denotations and connotations of *naked*
    and *nude* in the first stanza? What is indicated by the fact that the word
    naked is derived from the Old English *nacod* whereas *nude* comes from the
    Latin *nudus*?

2. What examples of "the naked" and "the nude" do the second and third
    stanzas provide? What do the examples have in common?

3. How do the connotations of words like *sly, draping, dishabille, rhetoric,* and
    grin contribute to the poem's ideas about "the nude"?

4. What is the meaning of "briary pastures of the dead" in the last stanza?

"The Naked and the Nude" explores the connotative distinctions
between two words that share a common denotation. The title also suggests
that the poem will be about people. If the speaker were simply considering
the words, she or he would say *naked* and *nude* instead of "*the* naked and
the nude." The speaker's use of *the* signifies a double focus on human
conditions and values as well as language.

The denotations of the two words are identical. A dictionary defines
naked as nude or without clothing, and *nude* as without clothing or naked.
Lines 1–5 of the poem express this commonality. The speaker observes
that "lexicographers" consider naked and nude to be "synonyms that
should express / The same deficiency of dress" (lines 2–4). Although these
lines establish the common meaning of the words, they also question this
commonality through the use of elevated and complex words. By using
the terms *lexicographers, construed, express,* and *deficiency,* the poet implies
that the connection between "the naked" and "the nude" is artificial and
sophisticated.

In the rest of the poem, Graves develops this distinction, linking the
word *naked* to the virtues of love, truth, innocence, and honesty, while
connecting *nude* to lies, artifice, hypocrisy, and deceit. At the end, he
visualizes a classical underworld in which the moment of truth will arrive.

All pretentiousness will disappear, and the nude will finally lose their sophistication and become merged with the naked. The implication is that trickery and artifice will disappear in the face of ultimate reality. A thorough study of the words in the poem bears out the consistency of Graves's idea, not only about the two title words, but also about the layers of history, usage, and philosophy that constantly weigh upon human life and thought.

DICTION

English is one of the world's richest languages. Usually we can find half a dozen words that mean pretty much the same thing *denotatively*, but that *connotatively* provide the opportunity for many degrees or shades of meaning, as with *naked* and *nude*. Writers in English are therefore blessed with a wealth of word choices. **Diction** refers to the specific words selected by a writer to produce a desired effect. We discuss diction at some length in Chapter 7 (pp. 266–70); you might review this material. Again, however, word choice is so important in poetry that the subject deserves special attention here.

Types of Words: Specific/General and Concrete/Abstract

The distinctions among these types of words are centrally important to poetry because the choices determine immediacy and impact. **Specific** words refer to objects or conditions that may be seen or imagined; **general** words signify broad classes of persons or things. Similarly, **concrete** words describe conditions or qualities that are exact and vivid; **abstract** words refer to circumstances that are difficult to envision. These distinctions become clear when we consider some of the differences between Housman's "Loveliest of Trees" (p. 529) and Richard Eberhart's "The Fury of Aerial Bombardment" (p. 591). Many of the terms and images that Housman uses, such as "three score years and ten" and "Cherry . . . hung with bloom," are specific and concrete; they evoke an exact sense of time and a precise visualization. By contrast, Eberhart's terms, such as "infinite spaces" and "eternal truth," are general and abstract. It is hard to envision them with clarity and exactness. This is not to claim superiority for Housman over Eberhart, but simply to note differences in word choice in light of differing objectives.

In fact, poets may use any of the four types, depending on the effect they wish to achieve. As a general principle, poems using mainly general and abstract words are detached and cerebral, often dealing in an impersonal manner with universal questions or emotions. Poems using mainly specific and concrete words, on the other hand, are usually more immediate, familiar, and compelling. For the most part, poets employ a mixture of words, as in Theodore Roethke's "Dolor," for example (p. 590), which uses specific and concrete words to define a series of more abstract emotional states.

Levels of Diction

Like other writers, poets may choose from three levels of diction: *high* or *formal, middle* or *neutral,* and *low* or *informal.* **Formal diction** is elevated and elaborate; it follows the rules of syntax exactly and avoids idioms, colloquialisms, contractions, and slang. Beyond such correctness, formal language is characterized by complex words and a lofty tone. Graves uses formal diction in "The Naked and the Nude" when the speaker asserts that the terms are "By lexicographers construed / As synonyms that should express / The same deficiency of dress." These Latinate words stiffen and generalize the subject of the passage. We find *lexicographers* instead of *dictionary writers, construed* (from Latin) instead of *thought* (native English), *express* (from Latin) instead of *say* or *show* (native English), and *deficiency* (Latin) instead of *lack* (English).

Middle, or **neutral diction,** maintains the correct language and word order of formal diction but avoids the elaborate words and elevated tone. For example, Emily Dickinson's "Because I Could Not Stop for Death" (p. 528) is almost entirely in neutral diction.

Informal, or **low diction,** is the plain language of everyday use; it is relaxed, conversational, and colloquial. Poems using informal diction often include common and simple words, idiomatic expressions, some slang, and contractions. Informal diction is characteristic of Thomas Hardy's "The Man He Killed" (p. 530), where the poet uses words and phrases like "many a nipperkin," "He thought he'd 'list," and "off-hand like." In general, formal diction uses the longer words of Latin, Greek, and French derivation; informal diction uses words from historical English together with the shorter words from the Latinate languages. A good college-level dictionary (note that in English we use the French word for *dictionary*; our word would have been *wordbook*) will provide you with etymologies, so that as an exercise you might derive the origins of a number of words in a poem.

In the eighteenth century, many writers tried to give the English language something of the dignity of ancient Latin, which was at the time the international language of intellectual discourse. They therefore believed that only formal diction was appropriate for poetry. These writers developed rules about the subjects and styles that were suitable. Common life and colloquial language were usually excluded. These rules of **poetic decorum** (appropriateness, suitability) made it necessary to use elevated language rather than common words and phrases. The development of scientific terminology also influenced the choice of language. In the scientific mode, poets of the time used genus-species phrases like "lowing herd" for cattle (Gray) and "finny prey" for fish (Pope). In this formal vein, Thomas Gray, in the "Sonnet on the Death of Richard West," described the sun rising as "reddening Phoebus lifts his golden fire." Alexander Pope, one of the greatest English poets, maintained these rules of decorum, and made fun of them at the same time, in his mock-epic poem *The Rape of the Lock,* and more fully in a mock-critical work entitled *The Art of Sinking in Poetry.* In *The Rape of the Lock,* for example, he refers to a pair of scissors as a "glittering forfex." Similarly, he elevates the simple act of pouring coffee with the following couplet:

> From silver spouts the grateful liquors glide,
> While China's earth receives the smoking tide.

The comic mode here is that the elaborate phrases "China's earth" for "cups" and "smoking tide" for "coffee" create a verbal anticlimax that causes amusement.

Special Types of Diction

In addition to the three levels of diction already described, poets and writers may use four special types of words and phrases: *idiom, dialect, slang,* and *jargon.*

Idiom and **idioms** refer to words and phrases that are peculiar but correct for a given language. Standard idioms are constant, and we therefore hardly notice them. Thus, for example, we speak about being "*in* love," and walking "*along* a road," and so on. The proper use of such prepositions, along with the phrases which they govern, is one element characterizing the idiom of standard English. Sometimes idioms, along with words, have passed out of use. Thus, Shakespeare writes that "In me thou seest the glowing of such fire / That on the ashes of *his* youth doth lie." Here the *his* was the correct word for the *its* that we use today. Poets may select idiomatic expressions to create special qualities in their poems. For example, Paul Zimmer, in "The Day Zimmer Lost Religion" (p. 985), wryly uses the phrase "ready for him now," an idiom from the boxing world describing a fighter in top condition. Linda Pastan uses "gives me an A" and "I'm dropping out," both phrases from school life, to create comic effects in "Marks" (p. 944). E. E. Cummings was fond of using idioms for satiric effect, as in "she being Brand/ - new" (p. 666) and "next to of course god america i" (p. 901). Popular idioms enable poets to achieve levels of colloquial and substandard diction, depending on their purposes, but we must note again that standard language is also dependent on the proper and correct use of standard idioms.

Dialect refers to the words and pronunciation of a particular region or group. We can recognize certain common dialects such as Brooklynese, American black English, Yiddish English, Texan, southern, and Scottish

English. Dialect is concerned with whether we refer to a *pail* (general American) or a *bucket* (southern), or sit down on a *sofa* (eastern) or a *couch* (general American) or *davenport* (midwestern), and drink *soda* (eastern), *pop* (midwestern), *soda pop* (a confused midwesterner living in the east, or a confused easterner living in the midwest), or *tonic* (Bostonian), or use all the standard verb forms. The anonymous "Bonny George Campbell" (p. 542), Sanchez's "right on: white america" (p. 954), and Brooks's "We Real Cool" (p. 701) illustrate the use of dialect in poems.

Slang refers to informal and substandard vocabulary and idiom. It is made up of spontaneous words and phrases which may exist for a time and then vanish. For a brief period recently, for example, the word "bad" was used as a slang form for "good." Slang has a way of persisting, however, as may be seen in the many phrases that Americans have developed to describe dying, such as "kick the bucket," "croak," "be wasted," "be disappeared," and "be offed." A non-native speaker of English would have difficulty understanding that a person who "kicked the bucket" or was "offed" had actually died.

Even when slang becomes widely accepted, it usually goes no further than colloquial or conversational levels. If it is introduced into a standard context it will mar and jar, as in Larkin's "Next, Please" (p. 834), where the speaker describes the female statue at the bow of a ship as "a figurehead with golden tits." Because the poem is designed to expose the fatuousness of unreal hopes, the slang word creates a jarring, clashing, deflating effect that is complementary to this intention.

Jargon refers to words and idioms developed by a particular group to fit their own special needs. Without some kind of initiation, people not in the group cannot understand the jargon. Usually such groups are specific professions or trades. For example, lawyers, plumbers, astronauts, doctors, and football players all have terms and phrases that are particular to their trades. Jargon becomes interesting when it moves into the mainstream of English or is used in literature. Two poems in this chapter that illustrate the poetic use of jargon are Henry Reed's "Naming of Parts" and Richard Eberhart's "The Fury of Aerial Bombardment." Both poems use technical terms for firearms to establish the authenticity of their references and therefore to reinforce their judgments about the subject of warfare.

SYNTAX

Syntax refers to *word order* and *sentence structure*. Normal English word order is firmly fixed in a subject–verb–object sequence. At the simplest level, we say "John (*subject*) throws (*verb*) the ball (*object*)." This order is so vital that any change has a significant impact on meaning: "Dog bites man" is not the same as "Man bites dog."

Most of the time, poets follow normal word order. In "The Lamb," for example, Blake creates a simple, easy order in keeping with the poem's purpose of presenting a childlike praise of God. Many modern poets like James Wright go out of their way to create ordinary, everyday syntax, on the theory that a poem's sentence structures should not get in the way of the reader's perceptions.

Yet, just as good poets always explore the limits of ideas, so also do they sometimes explore the many possibilities of English syntax. In Donne's "Holy Sonnet 14," for example (p. 586), line 7 is "Reason, Your viceroy in me, me should defend." If one were to write this sentence as prose, it would read "Reason, which is Your viceroy in me, should defend me." But note that Donne drops out the "which is," thus making an appositive instead of a relative clause. In the predicate, he places the direct object *me* before and not after the verb. The resulting emphasis on the pronoun *me* is appropriate to the personal–divine relationship that is the topic of the sonnet. (The alteration also meets the demand of the poem's rhyme scheme.)

A noteworthy syntactic variation occurs in Roethke's "Dolor" (p. 590), in which the opening verb ("have known") is followed not by the usual one or two direct objects, but rather by six. In addition, there is syntactic ambiguity in the poem, because a number of these noun–objects also are modified by prepositional phrases, all containing nouns (e.g., "of multigraph, paper-clip, comma"), together with an appositive phrase (containing nouns) in line 2. By the time we reach line 5 we have become uncertain about where the various nouns belong, syntactically. This syntactic bewilderment is in keeping with the poem's idea that school and office routines produce disjunction, purposelessness, and depression.

These examples illustrate a general technique. There are many other ways in which poets shape and vary word order to create emphasis. As a general rule, you should be alert to determine the effects of all the combinations you encounter.

An area of syntax especially important in poetry is the way in which rhetoric influences sentence structures. A fundamental and easily recognized device is **parallelism,** the duplication of forms and word order (see also pp. 272–73). The simplest kind of parallelism is the **repetition** of the same words and phrases, to be seen in Blake's "The Lamb." Through the use of the same *forms* of *different* words, parallelism produces lines or portions of lines that impress our minds strongly, as in this passage from Robinson's "Richard Cory," in which there are four parallel past-tense verbs:

> So on we *worked*, and *waited* for the light,
> And *went* without the meat, and *cursed* the bread;

The final two lines of this poem demonstrate how parallelism may embody a contrasting situation or idea (**antithesis**), and therefore may facilitate surprise, climax, and great power:

> And Richard Cory, one calm summer night,
> *Went* home and *put* a bullet through his head.

A major characteristic of parallelism is the packing of words (the *compression* of poetry), for by using a parallel structure the poet makes a single word or phrase function a number of times, with no need for repetition. We have observed the opening verb phrase in Roethke's "Dolor," which, though used once, controls six parallel direct objects (nouns) in the first eight lines. At the end of Donne's "Holy Sonnet 14," parallelism permits Donne to omit the italicized words added and bracketed in the last line:

> for I,
> Except You enthrall me, never shall be free,
> Nor [*shall I*] ever [*be*] chaste, except You ravish me.

Note also that parallelism and antithesis make possible the unique A–B–B–A ordering of these two lines, with the pattern *enthrall* (verb)–*free* (adjective)–*chaste* (adjective)–*ravish* (verb). This pattern, called **chiasmus** or **antimetabole,** is a common means by which poets create unity and emphasis (see also p. 273).

POEMS FOR STUDY

BEN JONSON (1572–1632)

On My First Son°   1616 (1603?)

Farewell, thou child of my right hand,° and joy;
My sin was too much hope of thee, loved boy;
Seven years thou wert lent to me, and I thee pay,
Exacted by thy fate, on the just day.
Oh, could I lose all father, now! For why   5
Will man lament the state he should envy?
To have so soon scaped° world's, and flesh's rage,   *escaped*

ON MY FIRST SON. Jonson's eldest son, also named Benjamin, died on his seventh birthday in 1603. 1 *child of my right hand*: a literal translation of the Hebrew name Benjamin (*ben* means "son of" and *jamin* means "right hand").

And, if no other misery, yet age?
Rest in soft peace, and, asked, say here doth lie
Ben Jonson his° best piece of poetry,   *Jonson's*   10
For whose sake, henceforth, all his vows be such,
As what he loves may never like too much.

QUESTIONS

1. What special language is evoked by the phrase "child of my right hand"?

2. What does the speaker mean by "all father" (line 5)? What point does he make about his sadness and his son's present state in lines 5–8?

3. What kind of special diction is reflected in "Rest in soft peace" and "here doth lie" (line 9)? Where are such phrases normally found?

4. The speaker calls his son "his best piece of poetry" (line 10). Look up the derivation of the word *poet* and explain this assertion.

JOHN DONNE   (1572–1631)

Holy Sonnet 14: Batter My Heart, Three-Personed God   *1633*

Batter my heart, three-personed God; for You
As yet but knock, breathe, shine, and seek to mend;
That I may rise and stand, o'erthrow me, and bend
Your force to break, blow, burn and make me new.
I, like an usurped° town, to another due,   *stolen*   5
Labor to admit You, but Oh, to no end;
Reason, Your viceroy in me, me should defend,
But is captived, and proves weak or untrue.
Yet dearly I love You, and would be loved fain,°   *gladly*
But am betrothed unto Your enemy.   10
Divorce me, untie or break that knot again;
Take me to You, imprison me, for I,
Except You enthrall me, never shall be free,
Nor ever chaste, except you ravish me.

QUESTIONS

1. What kind of God is suggested by the words *batter, knock, overthrow,* and *break*? What does "three-personed God" mean?

2. With which person of God might the verbs *knock* and *break* be associated? The verbs *breathe* and *blow*? The verbs *shine* and *burn*?

3. What is the effect of the altered word order at the ends of lines 7 and 9?

4. Explain the words *enthrall* (line 13) and *ravish* (line 14) to resolve the apparent paradox or contradiction in the last two lines.

WILLIAM BLAKE (1757–1827)

The Lamb 1789

Little Lamb, who made thee?
Dost thou know who made thee?
Gave thee life & bid thee feed,
By the stream & o'er the mead;
Gave thee clothing of delight, 5
Softest clothing wooly bright;
Gave thee such a tender voice,
Making all the vales rejoice!
    Little Lamb who made thee?
    Dost thou know who made thee? 10

Little Lamb I'll tell thee,
Little Lamb I'll tell thee!
He is called by thy name,
For he calls himself a Lamb:
He is meek & he is mild, 15
He became a little child:
I a child & thou a lamb,
We are calléd by his name.
    Little Lamb God bless thee.
    Little Lamb God bless thee. 20

QUESTIONS

1. Who or what is the speaker in this poem? The listener? How are they related?

2. What is the effect of repetition in the poem?

3. How would you characterize the diction in this poem? High, middle, or low? Abstract or concrete? How is it consistent with the speaker?

4. What are the connotations of *softest, bright, tender, meek,* and *mild*? What do these words imply about the Creator?

5. Describe the characteristics of God imagined in this poem. Contrast the image here with the image of God in Donne's "Batter My Heart."

LEWIS CARROLL (1832–1898)

Jabberwocky° 1871

'Twas brillig, and the slithy toves
    Did gyre and gimble in the wabe;
All mimsy were the borogoves,
    And the mome raths outgrabe.

JABBERWOCKY.   The poem, which appears in the first chapter of *Through the Looking Glass*, is full of nonsense words that Carroll made up with the sound (rather than the sense) in mind. Alice admits that the poem makes some sense even though she does not know the words: "It seems very pretty . . . but it's rather hard to understand! . . . Somehow it seems to fill my head with ideas—only I don't exactly know what they are!"

"Beware the Jabberwock, my son!   5
   The jaws that bite, the claws that catch!
Beware the Jubjub bird, and shun
   The frumious Bandersnatch!"

He took his vorpal sword in hand;
   Long time the manxome foe he sought—   10
So rested he by the Tumtum tree,
   And stood awhile in thought.

And, as in uffish thought he stood,
   The Jabberwock, with eyes of flame,
Came whiffling through the tulgey wood,   15
   And burbled as it came!

One, two! One, two! And through and through
   The vorpal blade went snicker-snack!
He left it dead, and with its head
   He went galumphing back.   20

"And hast thou slain the Jabberwock?
   Come to my arms, my beamish boy!
O frabjous day! Callooh! Callay!"
   He chortled in his joy.

'Twas brillig, and the slithy toves   25
   Did gyre and gimble in the wabe;
All mimsy were the borogoves,
   And the mome raths outgrabe.

QUESTIONS

1. Summarize in your own words the story that this poem tells.
2. Humpty Dumpty begins to explain or explicate this poem for Alice in Chapter 6 of *Through the Looking Glass*. He explains that " 'brillig' means four o'clock in the afternoon—the time when you begin *broiling* things for dinner." He also explains that " 'slithy' means 'lithe' and 'slimy.' 'Lithe' is the same as 'active.' You see it's like a portmanteau—there are two meanings packed into one word." Go through the poem and determine what combinations of words are packed into these portmanteau words. *Brillig*, for example, might be seen as a combination of *broiling*, *brilliant*, and *light*.

EDWIN ARLINGTON ROBINSON (1869–1935)

Richard Cory   *1897*

Whenever Richard Cory went down town,
We people on the pavement looked at him:
He was a gentleman from sole to crown,
Clean favored, and imperially slim.

And he was always quietly arrayed,   5
And he was always human when he talked;
But still he fluttered pulses when he said,
'Good-morning,' and he glittered when he walked.

And he was rich—yes, richer than a king—
And admirably schooled in every grace: 10
In fine, we thought that he was everything
To make us wish that we were in his place.

So on we worked, and waited for the light,
And went without the meat, and cursed the bread;
And Richard Cory, one calm summer night,   15
Went home and put a bullet through his head.

QUESTIONS

1. What is the effect of using *down town, pavement, meat,* and *bread* in connection with the people who admire Richard Cory?

2. What are the connotations and implications of the name *Richard Cory?* Of the word *gentleman?*

3. Why does the poet use "sole to crown" instead of "head to toe" and "imperially slim" instead of "very thin" to describe Cory?

4. What effect does repetition produce in this poem? Consider especially the six lines that begin with "And."

5. What positive characteristic does Richard Cory possess (at least from the perspective of the speaker) besides wealth?

WALLACE STEVENS (1879–1955)

Disillusionment of Ten O'Clock   *1923*

The houses are haunted
By white night-gowns.
None are green,
Or purple with green rings,
Or green with yellow rings,   5
Or yellow with blue rings.
None of them are strange,
With socks of lace
And beaded ceintures.°   *belts*
People are not going   10
To dream of baboons and periwinkles.
Only, here and there, an old sailor,
Drunk and asleep in his boots,
Catches tigers
In red weather.   15

QUESTIONS

1. Is the "Ten O'Clock" here morning or night? How can you tell?
2. What do "haunted" and "white night-gowns" suggest about the people who live in the houses? What do the negative images in lines 3–9 suggest?
3. To whom are these people contrasted in lines 12–15?
4. What are the connotations of "socks with lace" and "beaded ceintures"? With which character in the poem would you associate these things?
5. What is the effect of using words and images like *baboons, periwinkles, tigers,* and *red weather* in lines 11–15? Who will dream of these things?
6. Explain the term *disillusionment* and explore its relation to the point that this poem makes about dreams, images, and imagination.

THEODORE ROETHKE   (1907–1963)

Dolor   *1943*

I have known the inexorable sadness of pencils,
Neat in their boxes, dolor of pad and paper-weight,
All the misery of manila folders and mucilage,
Desolation in immaculate public places,
Lonely reception room, lavatory, switchboard,   5
The unalterable pathos of basin and pitcher,
Ritual of multigraph, paper-clip, comma,
Endless duplication of lives and objects.
And I have seen dust from the walls of institutions,
Finer than flour, alive, more dangerous than silica,   10
Sift, almost invisible, through long afternoons of tedium,
Dropping a fine film on nails and delicate eyebrows,
Glazing the pale hair, the duplicate grey standard faces.

QUESTIONS

1. What does *dolor* mean? What words objectify the concept?
2. Why does "Dolor" not contain the fourteen lines usual in a sonnet?
3. What institutions, conditions, and places does the speaker associate with "dolor"? What do these have in common?
4. Describe the relationships of sentence structures and lines in "Dolor."

HENRY REED   (b. 1914)

Naming of Parts   *1946*

To-day we have naming of parts. Yesterday,
We had daily cleaning. And to-morrow morning,
We shall have what to do after firing. But to-day,

To-day we have naming of parts. Japonica
Glistens like coral in all of the neighboring gardens,   5
   And to-day we have naming of parts.

This is the lower sling swivel. And this
Is the upper sling swivel, whose use you will see,
When you are given your slings. And this is the piling swivel,
Which in your case you have not got. The branches   10
Hold in the gardens their silent, eloquent gestures,
   Which in our case we have not got.

This is the safety-catch, which is always released
With an easy flick of the thumb. And please do not let me
See anyone using his finger. You can do it quite easy   15
If you have any strength in your thumb. The blossoms
Are fragile and motionless, never letting anyone see
   Any of them using their finger.

And this you can see is the bolt. The purpose of this
Is to open the breech, as you see. We can slide it   20
Rapidly backwards and forwards: we call this
Easing the spring. And rapidly backwards and forwards
The early bees are assaulting and fumbling the flowers:
   They call it easing the Spring.

They call it easing the Spring: it is perfectly easy   25
If you have any strength in your thumb: like the bolt,
And the breech, and the cocking-piece, and the point of balance,
Which in our case we have not got; and the almond-blossom
Silent in all of the gardens and the bees going backwards and forwards,
   For to-day we have naming of parts.   30

QUESTIONS

1. There may be two speakers in this poem, or one speaker repeating the words of another and adding his own thoughts. What two voices do you hear?

2. What is the setting? The situation? How do these affect the speaker?

3. How and why is jargon used in the poem? With what set of "parts" is the jargon initially associated? How does this change?

4. How are phrases like "easing the spring" (lines 22, 24, 25) and "point of balance" (27) used ambiguously? What is the effect of repetition?

RICHARD EBERHART   (b. 1904)

The Fury of Aerial Bombardment   *1947*

You would think the fury of aerial bombardment
Would rouse God to relent; the infinite spaces
Are still silent. He looks on shock-pried faces.
History, even, does not know what is meant.

You would feel that after so many centuries   5
God would give man to repent; yet he can kill
As Cain could, but with multitudinous will,
No farther advanced than in his ancient furies.

Was man made stupid to see his own stupidity?
Is God by definition indifferent, beyond us all?   10
Is the eternal truth man's fighting soul
Wherein the Beast ravens in its own avidity?

Of Van Wettering I speak, and Averill,
Names on a list, whose faces I do not recall
But they are gone to early death, who late in school   15
Distinguished the belt feed lever from the belt holding pawl.

QUESTIONS

1. Who or what is the speaker in this poem? What does the last stanza tell you
   about him? (Eberhart was a gunnery instructor during World War II.)

2. What type and level of diction predominate in lines 1–12? What observations
   about God are made in these lines? Compare the image of God presented
   here with the one found in Donne's "Batter My Heart, Three-Personed
   God" and Blake's "The Lamb." What similarities or differences do you find?

3. How does the level and type of diction change in the last stanza? What is
   the effect of these changes? How is jargon used here?

4. Compare this poem with Thomas Hardy's "Channel Firing" (p. 562). How
   are the ideas in the poems similar?

MAXINE KUMIN   (b. 1925)

Hello, Hello Henry   *1982*

My neighbor in the country, Henry Manley,
with a washpot warming on his woodstove,
with a heifer and two goats and yearly chickens,
has outlasted Stalin, Roosevelt and Churchill
but something's stirring in him in his dotage.   5

Last fall he dug a hole and moved his privy
and a year ago in April reamed his well out.
When the county sent a truck and poles and cable,
his daddy ran the linemen off with birdshot
and swore he'd die by oil lamp, and did.   10

Now you tell me that all yesterday in Boston
you set your city phone at mine, and had it ringing
inside a dead apartment for three hours
room after empty room, to keep yours busy.
I hear it in my head, that ranting summons.   15

That must have been about the time that Henry
walked up two miles, shy as a girl come calling,
to tell me he has a phone now, 264, ring two.
It rang one time last week—wrong number.
He'd be pleased if one day I would think to call him. 20

Hello, hello Henry? Is that you?

QUESTIONS

1. What does the poem's level of diction contribute to your response?
2. What words in this poem are appropriate for a country location? What do the words show about Henry Manley? About the conditions on Henry's farm?
3. Who is the speaker? What does the selection of words indicate about the speaker's character and state of mind?
4. Whom is the speaker addressing? How does the listener enter into the action of the poem in the third stanza? What is the meaning of the listener's action?

WRITING ABOUT DICTION AND SYNTAX IN POETRY

In setting out to write an essay on a poem's diction or syntax, you will usually be looking for a connection between one of these elements and another element of poetry, such as character, setting, or ideas. Consequently, you cannot begin to develop your own ideas about the impact of language until you have a clear general understanding of the poem you have chosen to consider.

First note down as much as you can about the speaker, the listener, the other characters, the setting and situation, the subject, and the ideas of the poem. You may use little of this material in your essay, but it will help shape your response to questions of diction and syntax. Moreover, you will find that the diction and syntax contribute to the development and impact of these other elements. Thus, you are likely to end up writing about word choice or language in connection with some other crucial element of poetry.

Once you understand the general meaning and impact, move back through the poem and examine it word by word and sentence by sentence. Look for any consistent patterns of diction or syntax that relate to the elements you have already considered. If you were planning to write about diction in Frost's "Stopping by Woods on a Snowy Evening" (p. 531), for example, you might isolate the following words and phrases connected with setting and situation: "woods," "fill up with snow," "without a farmhouse," "between the woods and frozen lake," "sound's the sweep," "easy wind," "downy flake," "lovely," "dark," and "deep." Some of these are quite straightforward, but others lend themselves to further investigation and explanation. You might consider the implications of "fill up," "without a farmhouse near," and "between the woods and frozen lake"; these phrases all suggest more than they say. In addition, you might deal with the connotative values of words like *woods, darkest, sweep, easy, downy,* and *deep.* A careful analysis of the diction employed here will lead you to a series of connected discoveries about Frost's language. These discoveries, in turn, can produce the raw materials for an essay about the link between diction and setting in "Stopping by Woods."

As you develop your ideas, look for any effective and consistent patterns of word choice, connotation, repetition, or the like that help create and reinforce the conclusions you have already reached about the poem. You might ask yourself the following questions:

Questions for Discovering Ideas

Does the poem contain many loaded or connotative words in connection with any single element like setting, speaker, or theme?

Does the poem contain a large number of general and abstract or specific and concrete words? What is the effect of these choices?

Is the level of diction in the poem elevated, neutral, or informal, and how does this level affect your perception of the speaker, subject, and the like?

Does the poem contain examples of special diction such as jargon? If so, how do these help shape your response to the poem as a whole?

Can you find instances of abnormal English word order in the poem, and if so, what is the effect of these alterations?

Has the poet used any striking patterns of sentence structure such as parallelism or repetition? If so, what is the effect?

These questions isolate places to begin an exploration of diction or syntax with an eye to writing an effective essay. Eventually, you should focus your efforts on a single aspect of word choice or language. Once you deal with these six questions, however, the most fruitful area of investigation should be clear.

Strategies for Organizing Ideas

When you have narrowed your examination down to one or two specific areas of diction or syntax, list relevant words, phrases, and sentences, and investigate the full range of meaning and effect produced by the examples. At this point, begin to look for examples that work in similar ways or produce similar effects. Doing this will allow you to group related examples together as you organize your notes. Eventually, you will want to reorganize your initial list of instances and explanations so that related examples are grouped together in units that will become paragraphs when you write the essay.

Finally, you will be ready to formulate a tentative central idea and arrange your examples in the most effective way to support this thesis. The central idea will naturally emerge from your investigation of the specific group or groups of examples of diction or syntax that prove to be most fruitful and interesting. Since diction and syntax contribute to the general impact and meaning of the poem, your thesis and examples will almost always relate to conclusions you have reached about the poem through other avenues of exploration. If you are writing an essay about "The Naked and the Nude," for example, your central idea might assert that Graves employs words with multiple denotations and connotations to emphasize the moral and lexical distinctions between "the naked" and "the nude." Such a formulation makes a clear connection between diction and meaning.

There are many different ways that your material can be organized. If you choose to deal with only one aspect of diction, such as connotative words or jargon, you might treat these in the order in which they appear in the poem. When you deal with two or three different aspects of diction and syntax, however, you can group related examples together regardless of where they occur. Thus, you might treat examples of multiple denotation, then connotation, and finally jargon in a series of paragraphs. In this instance, the organization of the essay is controlled by the types of material under consideration rather than by the order in which the words occur in the poem.

Alternatively, you might deal with the impact of diction or syntax on a series of other elements, such as character, setting, or situation. In such a paper you would focus on a single type of lexical or syntactic device as it relates to these different elements in sequence. Thus, you might discuss the link between connotation and character, then setting, and finally situation in sequential paragraphs. Whatever organization you select initially, keep in mind that each poem will finally suggest its own avenues of exploration and strategies of organization.

The conclusion should bring the essay to a strong and assertive close. Here, you can summarize the conclusions you have reached about the impact of diction or syntax in the poem. You can also consider the larger implications of your ideas in connection with the thoughts and emotions conveyed by the poem and evoked in your reading.

SAMPLE ESSAY

Diction and Character in Edwin Arlington Robinson's "Richard Cory"°

In "Richard Cory," Edwin Arlington Robinson makes a general observation about the human condition; namely, that nothing can ensure happiness. Robinson explores this idea by focusing on a central character--Richard

° See p. 588 for this poem.

Cory--who seems to have everything: wealth, status, dignity, taste, respect, and humanity. Cory's suicide at the end of the poem, however, reveals that these things cannot be equated with happiness. Robinson sets us up for the

[1]   surprising reversal in the last two lines--the suicide--by creating a gulf between Cory and the people of the town who admire and envy him. This distinction is produced, at least in part, through Robinson's use of loaded words that demean the general populace and elevate the central character.* The speaker and his or her fellow workers have words associated with them that connote their common lot, while Richard Cory is described in terms that imply nobility and privilege.†

For the most part, the poem focuses on Richard Cory. This character is seen, however, from the perspective of the townspeople, who wished "that we were in his place" (line 12). Robinson skillfully employs words in connection with these common folk to suggest their low status and impoverished way of life. In the first line of the poem, for example, the speaker places himself or herself and these other people "down town." The phrase denotes the central business district of a city. Nevertheless, it also carries all the denotations

[2]   and connotations of the word *down*. The term thus implies that Cory's journey to town is a descent or a lowering "down" and that the people exist continually in this "down" condition. We find a similar instance of loaded diction in the term *pavement* (line 2). Robinson employs *pavement* instead of *sidewalk* to create a stronger sense of inferiority for the speaker and the common people. Pavement can mean sidewalk, but it can also mean street or roadbed. The net effect of the term *pavement* here is to place "we people" even lower than Richard Cory--literally on the street.

In contrast to these few examples of diction that suggest the negative status of the people, the poem overflows with terms that connote Richard Cory's elevated status. Many of these words and phrases also carry the suggestion of nobility or royalty. These implications begin with the title of the poem and the name "Richard Cory." *Richard* contains the word *rich*, thus implying wealth and privileged status through sound. It is also the name of

[3]   a number of English kings, including Richard the Lion Hearted ("Richard Coeur de Lion"). The name *Cory* is equally connotative. On first reading, it reminds us of the word *core*, the central or innermost part of anything. The name thus points toward Cory's singular position and significance in the town and in the poem. Through sound, *Cory* also suggests both the French word *cour* (court) and the English word *court*. The name "Richard Cory" thus begins a process of association through sound and implication that links the central character of this poem with images of kingship and elegance.

We find similarly loaded words throughout the first stanza of the poem. The speaker describes Richard Cory as "a gentleman from sole to crown" (line 3). *Gentleman* denotes a civilized and well-mannered individual, but it also means "highborn" or "noble" in older usage. The phrase "from sole to crown" means "from head to toe," but it connotes a great deal more than that.

[4]   *Sole* means both "the bottom of a shoe or foot" and "alone" or "singular"; thus, the word suggests Cory's isolation and separation from the common

---

* Central idea.
† Thesis sentence.

folk. The word is also a pun and a homonym on *soul*, implying that Cory's gentility is inward as well as external. The final touch is the word *crown*. In context, the term denotes the top of the head, but its aristocratic and royal connotations are self-evident.

[5]

The speaker also describes Cory as "clean favored" and "imperially slim" (line 4). "Clean favored," instead of the more common *good-looking*, connotes crisp and untouched features; it again suggests that Cory is set apart and isolated. More to the point, the term *favored* also means "preferred," "elevated," "honored," and "privileged." "Imperially slim," instead of *thin*, is equally connotative of wealth and status. While both terms denote the same physical condition, *slim* connotes elegance, wealth, and choice, whereas *thin* suggests poverty, disease, and necessity. The adverb *imperially*, like *crown*, makes an explicit connection between Cory and emperors.

[6]

Although instances of this type of diction taper off after the first stanza, Robinson employs enough similar terms in the rest of the poem to sustain the connotative link between Richard Cory and royalty. In the second stanza, for example, we find "quietly arrayed" and "glittered." Both carry elevated and imperial connotations. *Arrayed* means "dressed," but it is not a verb we associate with commonplace clothing. Rather, it implies elegant finery. "Quietly arrayed" means dressed with taste and modesty, but *quietly* also suggests solitude and introversion. *Glittered* works against *quietly*; it connotes richness of dress and manner, suggesting that the man himself is golden. In the third stanza, the deliberate cliché "richer than a king" again clearly links Richard Cory to royalty. The speaker also notes that Cory was "schooled in every grace" (line 10). The phrase means that Cory was trained in manners and social niceties, but *grace* also connotes privilege and nobility, because it is the formal title used when addressing a monarch or member of the nobility (as in "Your Grace").

[7]

In conclusion, we can see that Robinson uses loaded words and connotation to lower the common folk and elevate the central character in "Richard Cory." The words linked with the speaker and the other townspeople have demeaning and negative implications. At the same time, the poet uses a series of words and phrases that connote royalty and privilege in connection with Cory. This careful manipulation of diction widens the gulf between Richard Cory and the speaker. It also heightens our sense that Cory is possessed of aristocratic looks, manners, taste, and breeding. The network of associations between Cory and royalty built through this skillful diction shapes our image of the central figure and thus makes the ending of the poem that much more shocking. The diction reinforces the poem's message that wealth, looks, breeding, and status cannot ensure happiness.

Commentary on the Essay

This essay deals with the ways in which Robinson uses loaded and connotative words to define and differentiate the townspeople and the central character in "Richard Cory." The opening paragraph makes a general assertion about the theme of the poem, connects character to this assertion, and argues that Robinson manipulates diction to achieve specific effects in connection with character. The central idea and the thesis sentence both assert that the poet employs diction to demean the common people (and the speaker of the poem) and to elevate Richard Cory.

The body of the essay in five paragraphs deals with several instances of word choice and diction. The organization illustrates a modified version of the first strategy discussed above. The examples of connotative words are arranged to reflect partly the characters they define and partly the order in which they appear in the poem. Thus, paragraph 2 discusses the common people and the speaker in connection with two loaded terms: *down town* and *pavement.*

The next four paragraphs (3–6) focus on Richard Cory and words or phrases that suggest royalty and privilege. The examples of diction examined here are taken up in the order in which they appear in the poem. Thus, paragraph 3 considers Cory's name, and the fourth explores the connotative effects of *gentleman* and "sole to crown." Paragraphs 5 and 6 continue this process, examining instances of diction that sustain the association between Richard Cory and nobility. Taken together, the four paragraphs devoted to this central character illustrate Robinson's consistent manipulation of diction to enoble and isolate Cory.

The conclusion of the essay summarizes the observations about word choice and connotation made in the body. It also ties these observations back into a general consideration of character and theme. The conclusion asserts that Robinson's management of diction contributes to the isolation of Richard Cory from the other characters in the poem and that it adds to the impact of Cory's suicide in the last two lines. In this way, the words and phrases examined in the essay are linked to the poem's exploration of ideas about the human condition.

WRITING TOPICS

1. Using the poems of Reed and Eberhart in this chapter, Jarrell (p. 522), and Owen (pp. 604, 657), study the words that these poets use to indicate the weapons and actions of warfare. Write an essay which considers these questions. How are the poets similar? How are they different? What details do they select commonly, and separately? How do their word choices assist them in making their various points about war as action, tragedy, and horror?

2. Write an essay in which you consider the sound qualities of the invented words in "Jabberwocky." Some obvious choices are "brillig," "frumious," "vorpal," and "manxome," but you are free to choose any or all of them. What is the relationship between the sound and apparent meaning of these words? What effect do the surrounding normal words and normal word order have upon the special words? How does Carroll succeed in creating a narrative "structure" even though the key words are, on the surface, nonsense?

3. Write a short poem describing a violent crime and commenting on it. Then, assume that you are the "perpetrator" of the crime, and write another poem

on the same topic. Even though you describe the same situation, how do your words differ, and why have you made these different choices? Explain the other different word choices you have made, with perhaps a discussion of words that you considered using but rejected.

15

Imagery: The Poem's Link to the Senses

In literature, **imagery** refers to words that trigger your **imagination** to recall and recombine **images**—memories or mental pictures of sights, sounds, tastes, smells, sensations of touch, and motions. The process is active, and even vigorous, for when particular words or descriptions produce images, you are applying your own experiences with life and language to your understanding of the poems you are reading. In effect, *you are recreating the work in your own way through the controlled stimulation produced by the poet's words*. Imagery, in short, is a channel to your active imagination, and along this channel, poets, like all writers, bring their works directly into your consciousness.

For example, reading the word *lake* in a poem may cause you to imagine or visualize a particular lake that you remember vividly. Your mental picture—or image—may be a distant view of calm waters reflecting blue sky, a nearby view of gentle waves rippled by the wind, a view of the lake bottom from a boat, or an overhead view of a sandy and sunlit shoreline. Similarly, the words *rose, apple, hot dog, malted milk,* and *pizza* all cause you to to visualize these things, and, in addition, may cause you to recall their smells and tastes. Active and graphic words like *row, swim,* and *dive* stimulate you to picture moving images of someone performing these actions.

RESPONSES AND THE WRITER'S USE OF DETAIL

In studying imagery we describe and interpret our imaginative reconstruction of the pictures and impressions evoked by the work's images. We let the poet's words simmer and percolate in our minds. To get our imaginations stirring, we might follow Coleridge in this description from "Kubla Khan" (lines 37–41):

A damsel with a dulcimer
In a vision once I saw:
It was an Abyssinian maid,
And on her dulcimer she played,
Singing of Mount Abora.

We do not read about the color of the young woman's clothing, or anything else about her appearance except that she is playing a stringed instrument, a dulcimer, and that she is singing a song about a mountain in a foreign, remote land. But Coleridge's image is enough. From it we can imagine a vivid, exotic picture of a young woman from a distant land singing, together with the loveliness of her song (even though we never hear it or understand it). The image lives.

IMAGERY, IDEAS, AND ATTITUDES

Poets use images to do more with your active imagination than prompt you to recreate sensory impressions. They also transfer their own ideas by the *authenticating* effects of the vision and perceptions underlying them, in this way helping you to widen your understanding, to give you new ways of seeing the world, or to strengthen your old ways of seeing it. Langston Hughes, in "Theme for English B," for example (p. 668), develops the idea that human beings are equal. Rather than stating the idea directly, he uses images of everyday, ordinary activities that his speaker shares in common with most human beings (line 21):

. . . I like to eat, sleep, drink, and be in love.

These images of action form an equalizing link that is not only true, but unarguable. Such use of imagery is one of the strongest means by which literature reinforces ideas.

In addition, as you form mental pictures from a poet's images, you also respond with appropriate attitudes and feelings. Thus the phrase "beside a lake, beneath the trees," in Wordsworth's "Daffodils," prompts both the visualization of a wooded lakeshore and also the related pleasantness of outdoor relaxation and happiness (p. 829). A contrasting artistic visualization is to be found in Herkomer's painting *Hard Times*, where all the images—the tired faces, the heavy load, the tools, the bleak road, the leafless trees—point toward the harsh life of the worker and his family, causing a response of sadness and sympathy (p. 602). Similar negative imagery is used by Jonathan Swift in the poem "Description of the Morning," which triggers unpleasant responses by offering images of street hawkers, thieves, bill collectors, and hesitant schoolboys (p. 692). By such a use of imagery, artists and poets not only create sensory vividness, but also direct and control the attitudes of their audience.

Sir Hubert von Herkomer (1849–1914), *Hard Times.* (© Manchester City Art Galleries)

CLASSIFICATION OF IMAGERY

SIGHT.   Sight is the most significant of our senses, for it is the key to our remembrance of other impressions. Therefore, the most frequently occurring literary imagery is to things we can visualize either exactly or approximately—**visual images.** Masefield in "Cargoes" (the subject of the sample essay, p. 618) asks us to recreate mental pictures or images of oceangoing merchant vessels from three periods of human history.

JOHN MASEFIELD   (1878–1967)

Cargoes   *1902*

Quinquereme° of Nineveh° from distant Ophir,°
Rowing home to haven in sunny Palestine,
With a cargo of ivory,

CARGOES.   1 *quinquereme*: the largest of the ancient ships. It was powered by three tiers of oars, and was named "quinquereme" because five men operated each vertical oar station. Two oars were taken by two men each, while the third was taken by one man alone. *Nineveh*: capital of ancient Assyria, an "exceeding great city" (Jonah 3:3). *Ophir.* Ophir probably was in Africa, and was known for its gold (I Kings 10:22; I Chron. 29:4). Masefield echoes some of the biblical verses in his first stanza.

And apes and peacocks,°
Sandalwood, cedarwood,° and sweet white wine.   5

Stately Spanish galleon coming from the Isthmus,°
Dipping through the Tropics by the palm-green shores,
With a cargo of diamonds,
Emeralds, amethysts,
Topazes, and cinnamon, and gold moidores.°   10

Dirty British coaster with a salt-caked smoke-stack,
Butting through the Channel in the mad March days,
With a cargo of Tyne coal,°
Road-rails, pig-lead,
Firewood, iron-ware, and cheap tin trays.   15

4 *apes and peacocks*: I Kings 10:22, and II Chron. 9:21.   5 *cedarwood*: I Kings 9:11.
6 *Isthmus*: the Isthmus of Panama.   10 *moidores*: coins in use in Portugal and Brazil
during the early times of new world exploration.   13 *Tyne coal*: Newcastle-upon-Tyne, a
coal-producing center in northern England.

QUESTIONS

1. Consider the images that you find in each of the stanzas as they picture life
    during three periods of history: Ancient Israel at the time of Solomon (ca.
    950 B.C.), sixteenth-century Spain, and modern England. What do these
    images tell you about Masefield's interpretation of modern commercial life?

2. To what senses do most of the images refer (e.g., sight, taste, etc.)?

3. There are no complete sentences in this poem. Why do you think that
    Masefield included only the verbals ("rowing," "dipping," "butting") to begin
    the second line of each of the stanzas, rather than finite verbs?

4. As historical reality, the quinquereme was likely rowed by slaves, and the
    Spanish galleon likely carried cargoes seized from Central American natives.
    How might these unpleasant details affect the impressions intended for
    stanzas 1 and 2?

Masefield's images in "Cargoes" are vivid as they stand, and need no
more detailed amplification. In order to reconstruct them imaginatively,
we do not need ever to have seen the ancient biblical lands or waters, or
ever to have seen or handled the cheap commodities on a modern
merchantship. We have seen enough in our lives both in reality and in
pictures to *imagine* places and objects like these, and hence Masefield is
successful in implanting his visual images into our minds.

SOUND. **Auditory images** are images appealing to our experiences
with sound. For such images, let us consider Wilfred Owen's "Anthem for
Doomed Youth."

WILFRED OWEN   (1893–1918)

Anthem for Doomed Youth   *1920*

What passing-bells for these who die as cattle?
Only the monstrous anger of the guns.
Only the stuttering rifles' rapid rattle
Can patter out their hasty orisons.°   *prayers*
No mockeries for them from prayers or bells,   5
Nor any voice of mourning save the choirs—
The shrill, demented choirs of wailing shells;
And bugles calling for them from sad shires.

What candles may be held to speed them all?
Not in the hands of boys, but in their eyes   10
Shall shine the holy glimmers of good-byes.
The pallor of girls' brows shall be their pall;
Their flowers the tenderness of patient minds,
And each slow dusk a drawing-down of blinds.

QUESTIONS

1. What is the predominant type of imagery in the first eight lines? How does
    the imagery change in the last six lines?

2. Describe the contrast between images usually associated with death as
    observed in religious funerals and death on the battlefield. How does this
    contrast affect your ability to experience and understand this poem?

3. Consider these images: "holy glimmers of good-byes"; "pallor of girls' brows";
    "patient minds"; "drawing-down of blinds." Who is being considered in these
    images? What is their relationship to the doomed youth?

In asking what "passing bells" may be tolled for "those who die as cattle,"
Owen's speaker is referring to the traditional tolling of a parish church
bell to announce the death of a parishioner. Such ceremony suggests
peace and order, when there is time to pay respect to the dead. But the
poem then points out that the only sound for those fallen in battle is the
"rapid rattle" of "stuttering" rifles—in other words, not the dignified
sounds of peace, but the horrifying noises of war. Owen's auditory images
evoke corresponding sounds in our imaginations, and help us experience
the poem and hate the uncivilized depravity of war.

SMELL, TASTE, AND TOUCH.   In addition to sight and sound, you will
also find images from the other senses. An **olfactory image** refers to smell,
a **gustatory image** to taste, and a **tactile image** to touch. A great deal of
love poetry, for example, includes observations about the fragrances of
flowers. As a twist on this common olfactory imagery, Shakespeare's
speaker in Sonnet 130, "My Mistress' Eyes," candidly admits that the

breath of his woman friend is not the same as the scent of roses (lines 7–8).

Images derived from and referring to taste—gustatory images—are also common, though less frequent than those to sight and sound. In lines 5 and 10 of Masefield's "Cargoes," for example, there are references to "sweet white wine" and "cinnamon." Although the poem includes these things as cargoes, the words themselves also register in our minds as gustatory images because they appeal to our sense of taste.

Tactile images of touch and texture are not as common because touch is difficult to render except in terms of effects. The speaker of Lowell's "Patterns," for example (p. 932), uses tactile imagery when imagining a never-to-happen embrace with her fiancé, who we learn has been killed in war. Her imagery records the effect of the embrace ("bruised"), while her feelings are expressed in metaphors ("aching, melting"):

> And the buttons of his waistcoat bruised my body as he clasped me
> Aching, melting, unafraid. (lines 51–52)

Tactile images are not uncommon in love poetry, where references to touch and feeling are natural. Because references to erotic love might easily verge on pornography, however, love poetry usually deals with yearning and hope (as in Keats's "Bright Star," p. 629) rather than sexual fulfillment.

IMAGES OF MOTION AND ACTIVITY. References to movement are also images. Images of general motion are *kinetic* (remember that *motion pictures* are also called "cinema"); the term **kinesthetic** is applied to human or animal movement. Imagery of motion is closely related to visual images, for motion is most often seen. Masefield's British coaster, for example, is a visual image, but when it goes "Butting through the channel," the motion makes it also kinetic. When Hardy's corpses sit upright at the beginning of "Channel Firing" (p. 562), the image is kinesthetic, as is the action of Amy Lowell's speaker walking in the garden after hearing about her fiancé's death. Both types may be seen at the conclusion of the following poem, Elizabeth Bishop's "The Fish."

ELIZABETH BISHOP (1911–1979)

The Fish   *1946*

I caught a tremendous fish
and held him beside the boat
half out of water, with my hook
fast in a corner of his mouth.

He didn't fight   5
He hadn't fought at all.
He hung a grunting weight,
battered and venerable
and homely. Here and there
his brown skin hung in strips   10
like ancient wallpaper,
and its pattern of darker brown
was like wallpaper:
shapes like full-blown roses
stained and lost through age.   15
He was speckled with barnacles,
fine rosettes of lime,
and infested
with tiny white sea-lice,
and underneath two or three   20
rags of green weed hung down.
While his gills were breathing in
the terrible oxygen
—the frightening gills,
fresh and crisp with blood,   25
that can cut so badly—
I thought of the coarse white flesh
packed in like feathers,
the big bones and the little bones,
the dramatic reds and blacks   30
of his shiny entrails,
and the pink swim-bladder
like a big peony.
I looked into his eyes
which were far larger than mine   35
but shallower, and yellowed,
the irises backed and packed
with tarnished tinfoil
seen through the lenses
of old scratched isinglass.   40
They shifted a little, but not
to return my stare.
—It was more like the tipping
of an object toward the light.
I admired his sullen face,   45
the mechanism of his jaw,
and then I saw
that from his lower lip
—if you could call it a lip—
grim, wet, and weaponlike,   50
hung five old pieces of fish-line,
or four and a wire leader
with the swivel still attached,

with all their five big hooks
grown firmly in his mouth.   55
A green line, frayed at the end
where he broke it, two heavier lines,
and a fine black thread
still crimped from the strain and snap
when it broke and he got away.   60
Like medals with their ribbons
frayed and wavering,
a five-haired beard of wisdom
trailing from his aching jaw.
I stared and stared   65
and victory filled up
the little rented boat,
from the pool of bilge
where oil had spread a rainbow
around the rusted engine   70
to the bailer rusted orange,
the sun-cracked thwarts,
the oarlocks on their strings,
the gunnels—until everything
was rainbow, rainbow, rainbow!   75
And I let the fish go.

QUESTIONS

1. Describe the images of actions in the poem. What is unusual about them?
2. What impression does the fish make upon the speaker? Is the fish beautiful? Ugly? Why is the fish described in such detail?
3. What do the "five old pieces of fish-line" indicate about the fish?
4. How is the rainbow being formed around the engine of the boat? What does this rainbow suggest to the speaker?
5. To what degree does it seem right for the fish to be free? Does the speaker have a right to keep the fish? Why does the speaker let the fish go?

The kinetic images at the end of "The Fish" are those of victory filling the boat (difficult to visualize) and the oil spreading to make a rainbow (easier to visualize). The kinesthetic images are readily imagined— the speaker's staring, observing, and letting the fish go—and they are vivid and real. The final gesture is the necessary outcome of the observed contrast between the deteriorating artifacts of human beings and the natural world of the fish, and it is a vivid expression of the right of the natural world to exist without the intervention of human civilization. Bishop's kinetic and kinesthetic imagery, in short, are designed to objectivize the need for freedom not only for human beings but for all creatures.

The range of objects or activities that poets employ as imagery is both vast and unpredictable. Indeed, an important quality about imagery is its very unpredictability. At a first reading of "The Pulley," by George Herbert, for example, you might be hard put to explain the connection between the title and the poem itself. Here is the poem.

GEORGE HERBERT (1593–1633)

The Pulley   *1633*

When God at first made man,
Having a glass of blessings standing by,
  "Let us," said he, "pour on him all we can.
Let the world's riches, which dispersed lie,
  Contract into a span."°   5

So strength first made a way;
Then beauty flowed, then wisdom, honor, pleasure.
  When almost all was out, God made a stay,
Perceiving that, alone of all his treasure,
  Rest° in the bottom lay.   10

"For if I should," said he,
"Bestow this jewel also on my creature,
  He would adore my gifts instead of me.
And rest in Nature, not the God of Nature;
  So both should losers be.   15

"Yet let him keep the rest,
But keep them with repining restlessness.
  Let him be rich and weary, that at least,
If goodness lead him not, yet weariness
  May toss him to my breast."   20

THE PULLEY.   5 *span*: that is, within the control of human beings.   10 *rest*: (1) repose, security; (2) all that remains.

QUESTIONS

1. Describe the dramatic scene of the poem. Who is doing what?
2. What are the particular "blessings" that God confers on humanity, according to the speaker? Why should these be considered as blessings?
3. To what extent is it true or possible, as Herbert suggests, that "repining restlessness" might be the means that leads human beings to become religious?
4. Consider the image of the pulley as the means, or device, by which God has arranged that people will become worshipful.

The connection between title and poem becomes clear if we recall that pulleys, because they increase mechanical advantage, may enable large and heavily resistant objects to be moved easily by only a small force.

Herbert's image of the pulley makes the human race such a resistant object. People, according to Herbert's speaker, have been blessed with so much that they can easily neglect God. But God nevertheless has mechanical advantage because human beings are never satisfied with all their blessings. God's hold is human restlessness and dissatisfaction, and God uses these conditions to pull human beings away from their worldly preoccupations toward faith and adoration. Using this mechanical image, Herbert makes the unpredictable relevant. Indeed, once we have finished "The Pulley," the image somehow seems no longer unusual or unpredictable at all, because it so aptly illustrates the connection between human behavior and divine power. Herbert, in other words, has chosen and developed his image in a masterly way.

The areas from which kinetic and kinesthetic imagery may be derived are almost too varied to describe. Occupations, trades, professions, businesses, recreational activities—all these might furnish images. One poet introduces references from gardening, another from money and banking, another from modern real estate developments, another from life within jungles. The freshness, newness, and surprise of literature result from the many and varied areas from which poets draw their images.

POEMS FOR STUDY

WILLIAM SHAKESPEARE   (1564–1616)

Sonnet 130: My Mistress' Eyes Are Nothing Like the Sun   *1609*

My mistress'° eyes are nothing like the sun;	*woman friend*	
Coral is far more red than her lips' red;		
If snow be white, why then her breasts are dun;		
If hairs be wires, black wires grow on her head.		
I have seen roses damasked,° red and white,	*set in an elaborate bouquet*	5
But no such roses see I in her cheeks;		
And in some perfumes is there more delight		
Than in the breath that from my mistress reeks.		
I love to hear her speak, yet well I know		
That music hath a far more pleasing sound;		10
I grant I never saw a goddess go;		
My mistress, when she walks, treads on the ground.		
And yet, by heaven, I think my love as rare		
As any she belied with false compare.		

QUESTIONS

1. To what does the speaker negatively compare his mistress's eyes? Lips? Breasts? Hair? Cheeks? Breath? Voice? Walk? What kinds of images are created in these negative comparisons?

2. What conventional images does this poem ridicule? What sort of poem is Shakespeare mocking by using the negative images in lines 1–12?

3. In the light of the last two lines, do you think the speaker intends the images as insults? If not as insults, how should they be taken?

4. Are most of the images auditory, olfactory, visual, or kinesthetic? Explain.

5. What point does this poem make about love poetry? About human relationships? How does the imagery contribute to the development of both points?

RICHARD CRASHAW (1613–1649)

On Our Crucified Lord, Naked and Bloody   *1646*

Th' have° left Thee naked,° Lord, O that they had;   *they have*
This garment too I would they had denied.
Thee with Thyself they have too richly clad,
Opening the purple° wardrobe of Thy side.°
   O never could be found garments too good   5
   For Thee to wear, but these, of Thine own blood.

ON OUR CRUCIFIED LORD, NAKED AND BLOODY.   1 *naked*: See Mark 15:24.
3–4 *Thee . . . side*: John 20:34.   4 *purple*: Mark 15:17.

QUESTIONS

1. Explain the contradiction and irony in the poem. Why does clothing made by human beings seem unworthy of being draped upon the crucified Lord?

2. What is meant by "this garment" in line 2? What is the relationship between this phrase and "Thee with Thyself" in line 3?

3. Does the emphasis on the blood of Christ in this poem seem appropriate or inappropriate for a devotional poem?

WILLIAM BLAKE (1757–1827)

The Tyger°   *1794*

Tyger! Tyger! burning bright
In the forests of the night,
What immortal hand or eye
Could frame thy fearful symmetry?

In what distant deeps or skies   5
Burnt the fire of thine eyes?
On what wings dare he aspire?
What the hand, dare seize the fire?

THE TYGER   The title refers not only to a tiger, but to any large, wild, ferocious cat.

And what shoulder, & what art,
Could twist the sinews of thy heart?　　　　　　　　　　　10
And when thy heart began to beat,
What dread hand? & what dread feet?

What the hammer? what the chain?
In what furnace was thy brain?
What the anvil? what dread grasp　　　　　　　　　　　15
Dare its deadly terrors clasp?

When the stars threw down their spears,
And water'd heaven with their tears,
Did he smile his work to see?
Did he who made the Lamb make thee?　　　　　　　　　20

Tyger! Tyger! burning bright
In the forests of the night,
What immortal hand or eye
Dare frame thy fearful symmetry?

QUESTIONS

1. What do the associations of the image of "burning" suggest? Why is the burning done at night rather than day? What does night suggest?

2. Describe the kinesthetic images of lines 4–20. What ideas is Blake's speaker representing by these images? What attributes does the speaker suggest may belong to the blacksmith-type initiator of these actions?

3. Line 20 presents the kinesthetic image of a creator. What is implied about the mixture of good and evil in the world? What answer does the poem offer? Why does Blake phrase this line as a question rather than an assertion?

4. Stanza 6 repeats stanza 1 with only one change of imagery of action. Contrast these stanzas, stressing the difference between *could* in line 4 and *dare* in 24.

SAMUEL TAYLOR COLERIDGE (1772–1834)

Kubla Khan　　　　　　　　　　　　　　　　　　*1816*

In Xanadu did Kubla Khan
A stately pleasure dome decree:
Where Alph,° the sacred river, ran
Through caverns measureless to man
　Down to a sunless sea.　　　　　　　　　　　　　　　5
So twice five miles of fertile ground
With walls and towers were girdled round:
And there were gardens bright with sinuous rills,

KUBLA KHAN.　　　3 *Alph*: possibly a reference to the river Alpheus in Greece, as described by the ancient writers Virgil and Pausanias.

Where blossomed many an incense-bearing tree;
And here were forest ancient as the hills,   10
Enfolding sunny spots of greenery.

But oh! that deep romantic chasm which slanted
Down the green hill athwart a cedarn cover!
A savage place! as holy and enchanted
As e'er beneath a waning moon was haunted   15
By woman wailing for her demon lover!
And from this chasm, with ceaseless turmoil seething,
As if this earth in fast thick pants were breathing,
A mighty fountain momently was forced:
Amid whose swift half-intermitted burst   20
Huge fragments vaulted like rebounding hail,
Or chaffy grain beneath the thresher's flail:
And 'mid these dancing rocks at once and ever
It flung up momently the sacred river.
Five miles meandering with a mazy motion   25
Through wood and dale the sacred river ran,
Then reached the caverns measureless to man,
And sank in tumult to a lifeless ocean:
And 'mid this tumult Kubla heard from far
Ancestral voices prophesying war!   30
   The shadow of the dome of pleasure
   Floated midway on the waves;
   Where was heard the mingled measure
   From the fountain and the caves.
It was a miracle of rare device,   35
A sunny pleasure dome with caves of ice!

   A damsel with a dulcimer
   In a vision once I saw:
   It was an Abyssinian maid,
   And on her dulcimer she played   40
   Singing of Mount Abora.°
Could I revive within me
Her symphony and song,
To such a deep delight 'twould win me,
That with music loud and long,   45
I would build that dome in air,
That sunny dome! those caves of ice!
And all who heard should see them there,
And all should cry, Beware! Beware!
His flashing eyes, his floating hair!   50
Weave a circle round him thrice,
And close your eyes with holy dread,
For he on honeydew hath fed,
And drunk the milk of Paradise.

41 *Mount Abora*: a mountain of Coleridge's imagination. But see John Milton's *Paradise Lost*,
IV, lines 268–284.

QUESTIONS

1. How many of the poem's images might be sketched or visualized? Which ones would be panoramic landscapes? Which might be close-ups?
2. What is the effect of auditory images such as "wailing," "fast thick pants," "tumult," "ancestral voices prophesying war," and "mingled measure"?
3. When Coleridge was writing this poem, he was recalling it from a dream. At line 54 he was interrupted, and when he resumed he could write no more. How might an argument be made that the poem is finished?
4. How do lines 35–36 establish the pleasure dome as a place of mysterious oddity? What is the effect of the words *miracle* and *rare*? The effect of combining the images "sunny" with "caves of ice"?
5. Why does the speaker yearn for the power of the singing Abyssinian maid? What kinesthetic images end the poem? How are these images important in the speaker's desire to reconstruct the vision of the pleasure dome?

GERARD MANLEY HOPKINS (1844–1889)

Spring   *1877*

Nothing is so beautiful as Spring—
   When weeds, in wheels, shoot long and lovely and lush;
   Thrush's eggs look little low heavens, and thrush
Through the echoing timber does so rinse and wring
The ear, it strikes like lightnings to hear him sing;   5
   The glassy peartree leaves and blooms, they brush
   The descending blue; that blue is all in a rush
With richness; the racing lambs too have fair their fling.

What is all this juice and all this joy?
   A strain of the earth's sweet being in the beginning   10
In Eden garden.—Have, get, before it cloy,
   Before it cloud, Christ, lord, and sour with sinning,
Innocent mind and Mayday in girl and boy,
   Most, O maid's child, thy choice and worthy the winning.

QUESTIONS

1. What images does the speaker mention as support for his first line, "Nothing is so beautiful as Spring"? Are these images those that you would normally expect? To what degree do they seem to be new or unusual?
2. What images of motion and activity do you find in the poem? Are these mainly static or dynamic? What do these suggest about the speaker's view of spring?
3. What is the relationship between "Eden garden" in line 11 and the scene described in lines 1–8? To what extent are spring and "innocent mind and Mayday" a glimpse of the Garden of Eden?

4. Christ is mentioned in lines 12 and 14 (as "maid's child"). Do these references seal the poem off from readers who are not Christian? Why or why not?

EZRA POUND   (1885–1972)

In a Station of the Metro°   *1916*

The apparition of these faces in the crowd;
Petals on a wet, black bough.

IN A STATION OF THE METRO.   *Metro*: the Paris subway.

QUESTIONS

1. Is the image of the wet, black bough happy or sad? If the petals were on a tree in the sunlight, what would be the effect?
2. What is the meaning of the image suggested by *apparition*? Does it suggest a positive or negative view of human life?
3. This poem contains only two lines. Is it proper to consider it as a poem nevertheless? If it is not a poem, what is it?

H. D. (HILDA DOOLITTLE)   (1886–1961)

Heat   *1916*

O wind, rend open the heat,
cut apart the heat,
rend it to tatters.

Fruit cannot drop
through this thick air—   5
fruit cannot fall into heat
that presses up and blunts
the points of pears
and rounds of grapes.

Cut the heat—   10
plough through it,
turning it on either side
of your path.

QUESTIONS

1. What is the meaning of the images of rending and cutting?
2. In 4–9, is it true that fruit cannot fall? If not, what is the meaning of the image that heat may blunt the points of pears and rounds of grapes?

3. Discuss the image of a plough as a cutter and separator of heat.
4. In light of the images, what impression of heat does the poet express?

T. S. ELIOT (1888–1965)

Preludes   *1910*

I

The winter evening settles down
With smell of steaks in passageways.
Six o'clock.
The burnt-out ends of smoky days.
And now a gusty shower wraps   5
The grimy scraps
Of withered leaves about your feet
And newspapers from vacant lots;
The showers beat
On broken blinds and chimney-pots,   10
And at the corner of the street
A lonely cab-horse steams and stamps.
And then the lighting of the lamps.

II

The morning comes to consciousness
Of faint stale smells of beer   15
From the sawdust-trampled street
With all its muddy feet that press
To early coffee-stands.
With the other masquerades
That time resumes,   20
One thinks of all the hands
That are raising dingy shades
In a thousand furnished rooms.

III

You tossed a blanket from the bed,
You lay upon your back, and waited;   25
You dozed, and watched the night revealing
The thousand sordid images
Of which your soul was constituted;
They flickered against the ceiling.
And when all the world came back   30
And the light crept up between the shutters
And you heard the sparrows in the gutters,
You had such a vision of the street,
As the street hardly understands;
Sitting along the bed's edge, where   35

You curled the papers from your hair,
Or clasped the yellow soles of feet
In the palms of both soiled hands.

IV

His soul stretched tight across the skies
That fade behind a city block,   40
Or trampled by insistent feet
At four and five and six o'clock;
And short square fingers stuffing pipes,
And evening newspapers, and eyes
Assured of certain certainties,   45
The conscience of a blackened street
Impatient to assume the world.

I am moved by fancies that are curled
Around these images, and cling:
The notion of some infinitely gentle   50
Infinitely suffering thing.

Wipe your hand across your mouth, and laugh;
The worlds revolve like ancient women
Gathering fuel in vacant lots.

QUESTIONS

1. From what locations are the images in stanza 1 derived? How do the images shift in the second stanza? What is the connection between the images in stanza 2 and stanza 3?

2. Who is the "you" in stanza 3? What images are associated with this listener?

3. Who is the "His" of stanza 4? How do the images develop in this stanza? What is meant particularly in the images of lines 46–47?

4. What is the nature of the bodily imagery in the poem? The urban imagery? What impressions do these images cause?

5. In lines 48–51, what does the speaker conclude? How do the last two unnumbered stanzas constitute a contrast of attitude?

WRITING ABOUT IMAGERY

Questions for Discovering Ideas

In preparing to write you should work with a thoughtfully developed set of notes, dealing with issues such as the following.

Is the imagery primarily visual (shapes, colors), auditory (sounds), olfactory (smells), tactile (touch and texture), gustatory (taste), kinetic or kinesthetic (motion), or a combination of these?

Do the images stand out in detail? Are they vivid? How is this vividness achieved?

Within a group of images, say visual or auditory, do the images pertain to one location or area rather than another (natural scenes rather than interiors, snowy scenes rather than grassy ones; loud and harsh sounds rather than quiet and civilized ones, etc.)?

Are the images derived from reality or imagination? What characteristics of either world are observable?

What responses and ideas are produced by the images? How are they integrated within the respective works?

With answers to questions like these, you will have virtually ready-made material to be turned directly into the body of your essay.

Strategies for Organizing Ideas

You should connect a brief overview of the poem to your plan for the body of your essay, such as that the writer uses images to strengthen ideas about war, character, love, and so on, or that the writer relies predominantly on images of sight, sound, and action. You might choose to deal exclusively with one of the following aspects, or, equally likely, you may combine your approaches, as you wish.

1. *Images suggesting ideas and/or moods.* The emphasis in such an essay is on the results of the imagery. What ideas or moods are evoked by the images? (The auditory images beginning "Anthem for Doomed Youth," for example, all point toward a condemnation of war's brutal cruelty. The visual images of "Preludes" all point toward a loss of principle and vitality in modern urban life.) Do the images promote approval or disapproval? Cheerfulness? Melancholy? Are the images drab, exciting, vivid? How? Why? Are they conducive to humor, or surprise? How does the writer achieve these effects? Are the images consistent, or are they ambiguous? (For example, the images in Masefield's "Cargoes" indicate first approval and then disapproval, with no ambiguity. By contrast, Shakespeare's images in "My Mistress' Eyes" might be construed as insults, but in context, they may be seen as compliments.)

2. *The types of images.* Here the emphasis is on the categories of images themselves. Is there a predominance of a particular type of image, such as references to sight, or is there a blending? Is there a bunching of types at particular points in the poem or story? If so, why? Is there any shifting as the work develops (as, for example, in Owen's "Anthem for Doomed Youth," where the auditory images first evoke loudness and harshness, but later bring out quietness and sorrow)? Are the images appropriate, granting the nature and apparent intent of the work? Do they assist in making the ideas seem convincing? If there seems to be any inappropriateness, what is its effect?

3. *Systems of images.* Here the emphasis should be on the areas from which the images are drawn. This is another way of considering the appropriateness of the imagery. Is there a pattern of similar or consistent images, such as darkness and dinginess (Eliot's "Preludes") or color and activity (Hopkins's "Spring")? Do all the images adhere consistently to a particular frame of reference, such as a sunlit garden (Lowell's "Patterns"), an extensive recreational forest and garden (Coleridge's "Kubla Khan" [p. 611]), dreary urban scenes (Eliot's "Preludes"), a graveyard (Hardy's "Channel Firing" [p. 562]), or a darkened forest (Blake's "The Tyger")? What is unusual or unique about the set of images? What unexpected or new responses do they produce?

Beyond a recapitulation of your major points, the conclusion is the place for additional insights. It would not be proper to go too far in new directions here, but you might briefly take up one or more of the conclusions you do not develop in the body. In short, what have you learned from your study of imagery in the poem about which you have written?

SAMPLE ESSAY

The Images of John Masefield's Poem "Cargoes"°

[1]
In the three-stanza poem "Cargoes," John Masefield develops imagery to create a negative impression of modern commercial life.* There is a contrast between the first two stanzas and the third, with the first two idealizing the romantic, distant past and the third demeaning the modern, gritty, grimy present. Masefield's images are thus both positive and lush, on the one hand, and negative and stark, on the other.†

[2]
The most evocative and pleasant images in the poem are in the first stanza. The speaker asks that we imagine a "Quinquereme of Nineveh from distant Ophir" (line 1), an ocean-going, many-oared vessel loaded with treasure for the biblical King Solomon. As Masefield identifies the cargo, the visual images are rich and romantic (lines 3–5):

With a cargo of ivory,
And apes and peacocks,
Sandalwood, cedarwood, and sweet white wine.

Ivory suggests richness, which is augmented by the exotic "apes and peacocks" in all their exciting strangeness. The "sandalwood, cedarwood, and sweet white wine" evoke pungent smells and tastes. The "sunny" light of ancient Palestine (line 2) not only illuminates the imaginative scene (visual),

° For this poem, see p. 602.
* Central idea.
† Thesis sentence

but invites readers to imagine the sun's warming touch (tactile). The references to animals and birds also suggest the sounds that these creatures would make (auditory). Thus, in this lush first stanza, images derived from all the senses are introduced to create impressions of a glorious past.

[3]

Almost equally lush are the images of the second stanza, which completes the poem's first part. Here the visual imagery evokes the royal splendor of a tall-masted, full-sailed galleon (line 6) at the height of Spain's commercial power in the sixteenth century. The galleon's cargo suggests great wealth, with sparkling diamonds and amethysts, and Portuguese "gold moidores" gleaming in open chests (line 10). With cinnamon in the second stanza's bill of lading (line 10), Masefield includes the image of a pleasant-tasting spice.

[4]

The negative imagery of the third stanza is in stark contrast to the first two stanzas. Here the poem draws the visual image of a modern "Dirty British coaster" (line 11) to focus on the griminess and suffocation of modern civilization. This spray-swept ship is loaded with materials that pollute the earth with noise and smoke. The smoke-stack of the coaster (line 11) and the firewood it is carrying suggest the creation of choking smog. The Tyne coal (line 13) and road-rails (line 14) suggest the noise and smoke of puffing railroad engines. As if this were not enough, the "pig-lead" (line 14) to be used in various industrial processes indicates not just more unpleasantness, but also something more poisonous and deadly. In contrast to the lush and stately imagery of the first two stanzas, the images in the third stanza invite the conclusion that people now, when the "Dirty British coaster" butts through the English Channel, are surrounded and threatened by visual, olfactory, and auditory pollution.

[5]

The poem thus establishes a romantic past and ugly present through images of sight, smell, and sound. The images of motion also emphasize this view: In stanzas 1 and 2 the quinquereme is "rowing" and the galleon is "dipping." These kinetic images suggest dignity and lightness. The British coaster, however, is "butting," an image indicating bull-like hostility and stupid force. These, together with all the other images, focus the poem's negative views of today's consumer-oriented society. The facts that life for both the ancient Palestinians and the Renaissance Spaniards included slavery (of those men rowing the quinquereme) and piracy (by those Spanish "explorers" who robbed and killed the natives of the isthmus) should probably not be emphasized as a protest against Masefield's otherwise valid contrasts in images. His final commentary may hence be thought of as the banging of his "cheap tin trays" (line 15), which makes a percussive climax of the oppressive images filling too large a portion of modern lives.

Commentary on the Essay

The method illustrated in this sample essay is the first (p. 617), the use of images to develop ideas and moods. All the examples—derived directly from the poem—emphasize the qualities of Masefield's images. This method permits the introduction of imagery drawn from all the senses in order to demonstrate Masefield's ideas about the past and the present. Other approaches might have concentrated exclusively on Masefield's visual images, or upon his images drawn from trade and commerce. Because Masefield uses auditory and gustatory images, but does not develop them extensively, these images might be appropriately devoted to short paragraph-length essays.

The introductory paragraph of the essay presents the central idea that Masefield uses his images climactically to lead to his negative view of modern commercialism. The thesis sentence indicates that the topics to be developed are those of [1] lushness, and [2] starkness.

Paragraphs 2 and 3 form a unit stressing the lushness and exoticism of stanza 1 and the wealth and colorfulness of stanza 2. In particular, paragraph 2 uses words like *lush, evocative, rich, exotic, pungent,* and *romantic* to characterize the pleasing mental pictures the images invoke. Although the paragraph indicates enthusiastic responses to the images, however, it does not go beyond the limits of the images themselves.

Paragraph 4 stresses the contrast of Masefield's images in stanza 3 with those of stanzas 1 and 2. To this end the paragraph illustrates the imaginative reconstruction needed to develop an understanding of this contrast. The unpleasantness, annoyance, and even the danger of the cargoes mentioned in stanza 3 are therefore emphasized as the qualities evoked by the images.

The last paragraph demonstrates that the imagery of motion—not much stressed in the poem—is in agreement with the rest of Masefield's imagery. As a demonstration of the need for fair, impartial judgment, the conclusion introduces the possible objection that Masefield's imagistic portraits may be slanted because they include not a full but rather a partial view of their respective historical periods. Thus, the concluding paragraph adds balance to the analysis illustrated in paragraphs 2, 3, and 4.

WRITING TOPICS

1. In the last six lines of "Anthem for Doomed Youth," the images referring to the homes of the dead soldiers are particularly effective in the poem's condemnation of war. Write an essay explaining why they are effective. If Owen had chosen more violent images, how might the poem have been different?

2. Based on the poems in this chapter by Crashaw, Blake, Coleridge, H. D., and Hopkins, write an essay discussing the poetic use of images drawn from the natural world. What sorts of references do the poets make? What attitudes do they express about the details they select? What is the relationship between the images and religious views? What judgments about God and nature do the poets show by their images?

3. Considering the imagery of Eliot's "Preludes," write an essay explaining how imagery may be considered as a powerful kind of statement. As you develop your thoughts, be sure to consider the dramatic nature of Eliot's images, and to account for the impressions and ideas that they create. You may also

wish to introduce references to images from other poems that are relevant to your points.

4. Write a poem describing one of these:

   a. Athletes who have just completed an exhausting run.

   b. Children getting out of school for the day.

   c. Your recollection of having been lost as a child.

   d. The antics of your dog, cat, horse, or other pet.

   e. A particularly good meal you had recently.

   f. A good concert, rock or otherwise.

   g. Driving to work/school on a rainy/snowy day.

   Then, write an analysis of the images you selected for your poem, and explain your choices. Are the details the things that stand out in your mind? What do you recall best—sight, smell, sound, action? What is the relationship between your images and the ideas you express in your poem?

5. Study the reproduction of Herkomer's painting *Hard Times* (p. 602). Then write an essay comparing and contrasting the artistic techniques with Hopkins's poem "Spring" (p. 613) and Pound's "In a Station of the Metro" (p. 614), along with other poems that you may wish to include. What similarities and differences do you find in subject matter, treatment, arrangement, and general idea? On the basis of your comparison, what relationships do you perceive between poetic and painterly techniques?

16

Rhetorical Figures:
A Source of Depth
and Range in Poetry

Figurative language refers to expressions that conform to particular patterns and arrangements of thought. These patterns, or **rhetorical figures**, are the tools that help make literary works effective, persuasive, and forceful. Although rhetorical figures, also called **devices,** may be used in any kind of work, they are more common in poetry than in prose.

The two most important figures are **metaphor** and **simile**. Others are **paradox, apostrophe, personification, synecdoche** and **metonymy, synthesia,** the **pun** (or **paronomasia**), and **overstatement** and **understatement.** All these figures are modes of comparison, and they may be expressed in single words, phrases, clauses, and also entire structures. The use of figures enables poets to extend and deepen their range of subject matter in ways similar to the operation of symbolism (see pp. 326–61, 999). Indeed, the word **metaphorical** is often broadly applied to most rhetorical figures, including symbols.

METAPHOR AND SIMILE

A **metaphor** (a "carrying out of a change") is the direct verbal equation of something unknown with something known, so that the unknown may be explained and made clear. A metaphor by Shakespeare that has become a favorite is "All the world's a stage, / And all the men and women merely players," whereby Shakespeare's character Jacques (from *As You Like It,* II.7) explains aspects of human life (the unknown) by equating them with the life of the theater (the known). Shakespeare's metaphor does not state that the world is *like* a stage, but that it literally *is* a stage.

While a metaphor thus merges identities, a **simile** (the "showing of similarity or oneness") explains the unknown by showing its *similarity* to the known. A simile is distinguishable from a metaphor because it is introduced by "like" with nouns and "as" (also "as if" and "as though") with clauses. Campion's sentence "Her brows like bended bows do stand," from the poem "Cherry Ripe" (p. 899), points out that the young woman being described is able to put down potential offenders with frowns that are as effective as arrows shot from a bow. Because the simile is introduced by "like," the emphasis of the figure is on the *similarity* of her eyebrows to bows and arrows, not on the *identification* of the two.

IMAGERY, METAPHOR, AND SIMILE

To see the relationship of metaphor and simile to imagery (see also Chapter 15, pp. 600–621), you should remember that imagery requires readers to use their imaginations to recall experiences suggested by language. The images in the work arise as a function of the topic material. By duplicating the images intellectually and emotionally, through the use of imagination, readers may understand and verify the poet's ideas.

Metaphors and similes go beyond imagery by introducing comparisons that may be unusual, unpredictable, and even surprising. They connect the thing or things unknown and to be communicated—such as qualities of love or the excitement of unexpected discovery—with a new insight that is made objective through the comparison of a simile or the equation of a metaphor. For example, in "A Valediction: Forbidding Mourning," Donne's speaker points out that a trip away from a loved one is not really a separation, but is instead just a thinning out, like the hammering of the malleable element gold. How many people have ever thought that love is like a metal? But is it not true that the comparison emphasizes the permanence of the bond between two lovers, and also that *gold* itself suggests how valuable the bond is? Such a figure extends knowledge and awareness by introducing new perspectives that otherwise would not come to light. First and foremost, then, metaphors and similes are a mode of expression, but more importantly they are one of the ways in which great literature leads us to see the world originally and freshly.

For example, to communicate a character's joy and excitement, the sentence "She was happy" is accurate but not interesting or effective. A more vivid way of saying the same thing is to use an image of an action, such as, "She jumped for joy." This image gives us a concrete picture of an action which a person might perform as a demonstration of happiness. But an even better way of communicating a happy state is the following simile: "She felt as if she had just inherited five million tax-free dollars." Because readers easily understand the combination of excitement, disbelief, exhilaration, and joy that such an event would bring, they also understand—and feel—the character's happiness. It is the simile that evokes this perception, for no simple description can help a reader comprehend the same degree of emotion.

As a poetic example, let us refer to John Keats's poem "On First Looking into Chapman's Homer." Keats wrote the poem after he first read the Elizabethan writer John Chapman's translation of the *Iliad* and the *Odyssey,* epic poems attributed to the ancient Greek epic poet Homer. His main idea is that Chapman not only translated Homer's words but also transmitted his greatness. A brief paraphrase of the poem is this:

> I have enjoyed much art and read much European literature, and have been told that Homer is the best writer of all, but not knowing Greek, I could not genuinely appreciate his works until I discovered them in Chapman's translation. To me, this experience was exciting and awe-inspiring.

This paraphrase destroys the poem's sense of exhilaration and discovery. Contrast the second sentence of the paraphrase with the last six lines of the sonnet as Keats writes them.

JOHN KEATS (1795–1821)

On First Looking into Chapman's Homer   *1816*

Much have I travell'd in the realms of gold,
  And many goodly states and kingdoms seen;
  Round many western islands have I been
Which bards in fealty to Apollo° hold.
Oft of one wide expanse had I been told   5
  That deep-brow'd Homer ruled as his demesne;°
  Yet did I never breathe its pure serene°
Till I heard Chapman speak out loud and bold:
Then felt I like some watcher of the skies
  When a new planet swims into his ken;°   10
Or like stout Cortez° when with eagle eyes
  He star'd at the Pacific—and all his men
Look'd at each other with a wild surmise—
  Silent, upon a peak in Darien.

ON FIRST LOOKING INTO CHAPMAN'S HOMER.   George Chapman (ca. 1560–1634) published his translations of Homer's *Iliad* in 1612 and *Odyssey* in 1614–1615. 4 *bards . . . Apollo:* writers who are sworn subjects of Apollo, the Greek god of light, music, poetry, prophecy, and the sun.   6 *demesne:* realm, estate.   7 *serene:* a clear expanse of air; also grandeur, clarity; rulers were also sometimes called "serene majesty."   10 *ken:* field of sight.   11 *Cortez:* Hernando Cortez (1485–1547), a Spanish general and the conqueror of Mexico. Keats has confused him with Vasco de Balboa (ca. 1475–1519), the first European to see the Pacific Ocean (in 1510) from Darien, an old name for the Isthmus of Panama.

QUESTIONS

1. What is being discovered in this poem? To what extent is this process of discovery a universal experience?

2. Explain the metaphor of land and travel that Keats develops in lines 1–6. Be careful to consider the words *realms, states, kingdoms, islands, expanse,* and *demesne.*

3. How successfully does Keats convey a sense of excitement through the similes in lines 9–10 and 11–14? Create a simile of your own to express a feeling about discovery; how does yours compare with Keats's?

4. Describe the metaphor of *swims* in line 10. What might have been the impact if Keats had used words such as *drifts, floats, flows,* or *wanders?*

If all we had of the poem were our paraphrase, we would probably pay little attention to it, for it carries no sense of stimulation or discovery. But let us notice the strength of the poem, particularly the two powerful similes in the last six lines ("like some watcher" and "like stout Cortez"). We should not just read these similes and pass them by, but should use our imaginations to experience them. In mulling them over, we might suppose that we actually *are* an astronomer just discovering a new planet, and that we actually *are* the first Europeans to see the Pacific Ocean. As we imagine ourselves in these roles, we should think of our accompanying amazement, wonder, excitement, anticipation, joy, and sense of accomplishment. If we imagine these feelings, then Keats has unlocked experiences that the relatively unpromising title does not suggest. He has given us something new. He has enlarged us.

VEHICLE AND TENOR

To describe the relationship between a writer's ideas and the metaphors and similes chosen to objectify them, two useful terms have been coined by I. A. Richards (in *The Philosophy of Rhetoric*). First is the *tenor,* which is the totality of ideas and attitudes not only of the literary speaker but also of the author. Second is the *vehicle,* or the details that carry the tenor. The vehicle of the five-million-dollar simile is the description of the inheritance, while the tenor is joy. Similarly, the tenor of the similes in the last six lines of Keats's sonnet is awe and wonder; the vehicle is the reference to astronomical and geographical discovery.

CHARACTERISTICS OF METAPHORICAL LANGUAGE

It would be difficult to find any good piece of writing that does not employ metaphorical language to at least some extent. Such language is most vital, however, in imaginative writing, particularly poetry, where it compresses thought, promotes understanding, and shapes response.

As we have seen in the chapter on imagery (pp. 600–621), images are embodied in words or descriptions denoting sense experience that lead to many associations. A single word naming a flower, say *rose*, evokes a positive response. But *rose* is not a metaphor or simile until its associations are used in a comparative or analogical way, as in "A Red, Red Rose" by Robert Burns.

ROBERT BURNS   (1759–1796)

A Red, Red Rose   *1796*

O my Luve's like a red, red rose,
  That's newly sprung in June:
O my Luve's like the melodie
  That's sweetly play'd in tune.

As fair art thou, my bonnie lass,   5
  So deep in luve am I;
And I will luve thee still, my Dear,
  Till a'° the seas gang° dry.   *all; go*

Till a' the seas gang dry, my Dear,
  And the rocks melt wi'° the sun: *with*   10
And I will luve thee still, my Dear,
  While the sands o' life shall run.

And fare thee weel, my only Luve!
  And fare thee weel, awhile!
And I will come again, my Luve,   15
  Tho' it were ten thousand mile!

QUESTIONS

1. In light of the character and background of the speaker, do the two similes that open the poem seem common or unusual? If they are no more than ordinary comparisons, does that fact diminish their value? How and why?
2. Describe the shift of listener envisioned after the first stanza. How are the last three stanzas related to the first?
3. Consider the metaphors concerning time and travel. How do the metaphors assist in the comprehension of the speaker's character?

    In the first stanza the speaker is telling us about his sweetheart. We know that a devoted lover could probably say things forever, but the poet knows that we would quickly get bored with a lengthy disquisition. For this reason the similes make for power and also for brevity. To dwell on the rose, the speaker asks us to bring to our minds all the possible associations that we might have with roses, in addition to those already mentioned. After winter's drabness and leaflessness, springtime's lush growth marks a new beginning, an entirely new and colorful earth as contrasted with the monochrome dullness of winter. Thus, the rose suggests loveliness, colorfulness, the end of dreariness, love, and the seasonal fertility of the earth. Once we have expanded upon the simile in this way, we have come close to comprehending the speaker's enthusiasm.

To see how metaphorical language may compress the thought of writers, let us briefly consider Shakespeare's Sonnet 30. Shakespeare's opening metaphor equates the business of a law court with personal reverie and self-evaluation.

WILLIAM SHAKESPEARE (1564–1616)

Sonnet 30: When to the Sessions of Sweet Silent Thought   *1609*

When to the sessions° of sweet silent thought	*holding of court*
I summon° up remembrance of things past,	*call to a legal hearing*
I sigh the lack of many a thing I sought,	
And with old woes new wail° my dear time's waste:	*lament again*
Then can I drown an eye (un-used to flow)	5
For precious friends hid in death's dateless° night,	*endless*
And weep afresh love's long since cancelled° woe,	*paid in full*
And moan th'expense° of many a vanished sight.	*cost, loss*
Then can I grieve at grievances foregone,	
And heavily° from woe to woe tell° o'er	*sadly; count* 10
The sad account of fore-bemoanèd moan,	
Which I new pay, as if not paid before.	
But if the while I think on thee (dear friend)	
All losses are restored, and sorrows end.	

QUESTIONS

1. Explain the metaphor of "sessions" and "summon" in lines 1–2. Where are the *sessions* being held? What is a *summons* for remembrance?

2. What is the metaphor brought out by the word *cancelled* in line 7? In what sense might a "woe" of love be cancelled? Explain the metaphor of *expense* in line 8.

3. What type of transaction does Shakespeare refer to in the metaphor of lines 9–12? What understanding does the metaphor provide about the sadness and regret that a person feels about past mistakes and sorrows?

4. What role does the speaker assign to the "dear friend" of line 13 in relation to the metaphors of the poem?

The word *sessions* is the legal name for that period of time (a *sitting*) in which judges, juries, lawyers, and witnesses carry out the court's business (i.e., "The court is now in *session*"; think also of "school is now in *session*"). The word *summon* is the legal command for a person to appear before a court, usually to stand as a defendant for an alleged wrongdoing. Through these metaphors, the speaker says that in moments of reflection he (assuming a male speaker) thinks about past sorrows and regrets, and wonders whether he always did the right things. In a way, the speaker asks us to visualize his "sweet silent thought" as though he is sitting as a combination lawyer-judge over his memories, which he has commanded to reappear. The implication of this metaphor is that the total experience of a person is constantly alive and present; that the memory is like an entire society with wrongs, shortcomings, and transgressions; that judgment and reassessment are constant living processes; and that the consciousness of individuals is not an unchanging, solid state, but is instead a series of conflicting or contrasting impulses.

This development of Shakespeare's metaphor may seem like more than Shakespeare intended; indeed, we have used more words in prose than he uses in verse. Once we have understood his language, however, our minds are unlocked, and we may then allow ourselves this kind of expansion as we consider the full ramifications of the comparison or equation.

OTHER RHETORICAL FIGURES

Paradox.   A **paradox** is a device in which contradiction reveals unexpected truth. The wit of the figure is hence that the contradiction is not a contradiction at all. The second line of Sir Thomas Wyatt's sonnet "I Find No Peace," for example (p. 632), shows two paradoxes. One contrasts fear and hope, the other fire and ice: "I fear and hope; I burn and freeze like ice." These paradoxes reflect the contradictory states of people in love. On the one hand they want to love, but on the other they are apprehensive about the changes their feelings bring about. There is also the idea that a lover may be unsure that love is being returned. The paradox thus brings to life both the satisfaction and uncertainty of people who wage the "war" of love and personal commitment.

Apostrophe.   The **apostrophe** (originally a "turning away," or redirection of attention to something new) is a dramatic device whereby the speaker addresses a real or imagined listener who is not present. When used, it creates the situation of a public speech, with the readers as an audience. The speaker may thus develop ideas and attitudes that might arise naturally on a public occasion, as in Wordsworth's sonnet "London, 1802," which is addressed to the long dead English poet Milton. In Keats's sonnet "Bright Star," the speaker addresses a distant and inanimate object, yet through apostrophe the speaker proceeds as though it has human understanding and divine power.

JOHN KEATS   (1795–1822)

Bright Star   *1838 (1819)*

Bright star! would I were steadfast as thou art—
  Not in lone splendor hung aloft the night,
And watching, with eternal lids apart,
  Like Nature's patient, sleepless eremite,°   *hermit*
The moving waters at their priestlike task   5
  Of pure ablution round earth's human shores,
Or gazing on the new soft-fallen mask
  Of snow upon the mountains and the moors;
No—yet still steadfast, still unchangeable,
  Pillowed upon my fair love's ripening breast,   10
To feel forever its soft fall and swell,
  Awake forever in a sweet unrest,
    Still, still to hear her tender-taken breath,
    And so live ever—or else swoon to death.

QUESTIONS

1. With what topic is the speaker concerned in this sonnet? How does he compare himself with the distant star?

2. What qualities does the speaker attribute specifically to the star? What sort of role does he seem to assign to it? In light of this role, and the qualities needed to serve in it, how might the star be compared to a divine and benign presence?

3. In light of the stress put on the words "forever" and "ever" in lines 11–14, how appropriate is the choice of the star as the subject of the apostrophe in the poem?

In this sonnet the poet addresses the star as though it is a person or god, an object of adoration, and the poem is therefore like a petitional prayer. The star is idealized with qualities that the speaker wishes to establish in himself. One quality is steadfastness of position; a second is eternal watchfulness and fidelity. The point of the apostrophe is thus to dramatize the speaker's yearning and to stress the permanence of space and eternity as contrasted with the impermanence of life on earth. We as readers are witnesses, for we may well imagine the speaker looking at the night sky and connecting its vastness and mystery to our own lives.

    PERSONIFICATION.   Going hand in hand with apostrophe is the device of **personification**, which is the attribution of human characteristics to nonhuman things or abstractions. To personify things is a normal human habit. At various times, people have believed in pantheism—namely, that spirits inhabit things such as trees, mountains, lakes, and even roadways, which can be addressed as deities. In poetry, poets build on this trait to explore the relationships between people and their environments, their ideals, or their inner lives. In "Bright Star," as we have just seen, Keats personifies the star addressed by the speaker. Shakespeare, in Sonnet 146, "Poor Soul, the Center of My Sinful Earth" (p. 959), personifies his own soul so that he can deal with earthly versus heavenly concerns. Other major examples of personification are Keats's poems "To Autumn" and "Ode on a Grecian Urn," and Shelley's "Ode to the West Wind" (pp. 637, 830, 746).

SYNECDOCHE AND METONYMY.   These figures are close in purpose and effect. **Synecdoche** (taking one thing out of another) is a device in which a part stands for the whole, or a whole for a part, like the expression "All hands aboard" to signify that a ship's crew should return to ship. **Metonymy** (a transfer of name) refers to the substitution of one thing for another closely identified thing, like "the White House" signifying the policies and activities of the president. The objective of both devices is to express new ideas and insights in a new perspective. Because synecdoche and metonymy extend meaning in this way, they are similar to metaphor and simile.

Synecdoche may be seen in Keats's "To Autumn," where the gourd and hazel shells in lines 7–8, which are single instances of ripe produce, stand for the entire autumnal harvest. In Wordsworth's "London, 1802" (p. 636), the phrase "thy heart" (line 13) is a synecdoche referring to the entire person and mind of Milton. Metonymy may be seen in Keats's "To Autumn" (again), when the "granary floor," the place where grain is stored, is used with the transferred meaning of the harvest stored there. In "Exit, Pursued by a Bear" (p. 638), Ogden Nash metonymically uses brand names, the names of artists, and the names of cities to mean objects, artworks, and places. Thus, "Chippendale" is a metonym for a valuable piece of ornate antique furniture, and "Picasso" is a metonym substituting the name of the artist for the work of art. Nash's entire poem is built up with such metonyms, which cumulatively symbolize the cultured civilization that may so easily be destroyed by global war.

SYNESTHESIA.   A figure that also transfers one thing to another, and which therefore resembles synecdoche and metonymy, is **synesthesia** (*together feeling*), which is the union of separate sensations or feelings. With this device, a poet describes one type of perception or thought with words appropriate to another. In "The Garden," for example, Andrew Marvell speaks of a "green thought" in reference to thinking that is conducive to life and the nurture of living things. A thought obviously cannot be green—who has ever *seen* any thought, let alone a *green* one? Nevertheless, "green thought" makes vivid sense. Of all poets, Keats is the one who makes most use of synesthesia, as, for example, in the "Ode to a Nightingale" (p. 744), where a plot of ground is "melodious," a draught of wine tastes of "Dance, and Provençal song, and sunburnt mirth," and beaded bubbles of wine "wink" at the brim of a glass.

THE PUN, OR PARONOMASIA.   Another transferring figure is the **pun** (which probably originally meant a *point* or a *puncture*), or **paronomasia.** A pun is a wordplay in which the writer surprisingly reveals that words with totally different meanings have similar or even identical sounds. Because puns can be outrageous, and often require a little bit of thinking, people often groan when they hear them (even while they probably are enjoying them). Also, because puns seem to play only with sound, they have not always enjoyed critical acclaim, but good puns may always be relished because they work with sounds to *reveal* ideas. John Gay, for example, utilizes clever and complex puns in the following song, sung by the gang of thieves in *The Beggar's Opera* (1728).

JOHN GAY (1685–1732)

Let Us Take the Road   1728

Let us take the road.
  Hark! I hear the sound of coaches!
  The hour of attack approaches,
To your arms, brave boys, and load.
    See the ball I hold! *[holding up a bullet]*   5
  Let the chymists° toil like asses,   *alchemists*
  Our fire their fire surpasses,
    And turns all our lead to gold.

QUESTIONS

1. What traits are shown by the singers of this poem? Why do they not seem frightening, despite their "profession" of theft?
2. Describe the puns in the poem. What kind of knowledge is needed to explain them fully? How many puns are there? How are they connected? Why do the puns seem particularly witty and also outrageous?

Here *fire, lead,* and *gold* are puns. *Lead* was the "base" or "low" metal that the medieval alchemists ("chymists") tried to transform into *gold,* using the heat from their *fires.* The puns develop because the gang of cutthroats singing the song is about to go out to rob people riding in horse-drawn coaches. Hence their "lead" is in the form of bullets, which will be transformed into the "gold" coins they steal. Their "fire" is not the alchemists' fire, but rather the fire of pistols. Through these puns, Gay's villains thus charm us by their wit, even though the threatening situation they describe would be terrifying in real life.

OVERSTATEMENT AND UNDERSTATEMENT.   Two devices conferring emphasis are **overstatement**, or **hyperbole**, and **understatement.** Overstatement,
also called the *overreacher*, is exaggeration for effect. In "London, 1802,"
for example (p. 636), Wordsworth declares that England is a "fen of
stagnant waters." That is, the country and its people make up collectively
a stinking, smelly, polluted marsh, a muddy dump. What Wordsworth
establishes by this overstatement is his judgment that England in 1802
needed a writer to unite the people around noble moral and political
ideas, just as Milton had once done.

On the other side of the scale, understatement is the deliberate
underplaying or undervaluing of a thing for purposes of emphasis. One
of the most famous poetic understatements is in Andrew Marvell's "To
His Coy Mistress" (p. 825):

> The grave's a fine and private place,
> But none, I think, do there embrace.

Here the understatement grimly emphasizes the eternity of death by
contrasting the permanent privacy of the grave with the temporary privacy
of a trysting place sought by lovers. Another ironic use of understatement
is in lines 17–20 of Ogden Nash's "Exit, Pursued by a Bear," where the
speaker indicates that the "lion and the lizard" cannot hear "heavenly
harmonies." In this figure Nash emphasizes that the people have been
killed who once inhabited the rooms where such melodies were played,
and therefore he emphasizes the ignorance and horror of war.

POEMS FOR STUDY

SIR THOMAS WYATT   (1503–1542)

I Find No Peace   *1557*

I find no peace, and all my war is done,
  I fear and hope, I burn and freeze like ice;
  I fly above the wind yet can I not arise;
  And naught I have and all the world I season.
That looseth nor locketh holdeth me in prison,°   5
  And holdeth me not, yet I can scape° nowise;   *escape*
  Nor letteth me live nor die at my devise,°   *choice*
  And yet of death it giveth none occasion.

I FIND NO PEACE.   5 *that . . . prison*: that is, "that which neither lets me go nor
contains me holds me in prison." At the time of Wyatt, *-eth* was used for the third person
singular present tense.

Without eyen° I see, and without tongue I plain;°   *eyes*
  I desire to perish, and yet I ask health;   10
  I love another, and thus I hate myself;
I feed me in sorrow, and laugh in all my pain.
  Likewise displeaseth me both death and life°
  And my delight is causer of this strife.

9 *plain*: express desires about love.   13 *likewise . . . life*: literally, "it is displeasing to me, in the same way, both death and life." That is "both death and life are equally distasteful to me."

QUESTIONS

1. What situation is the speaker reflecting upon? What metaphors and similes express his feelings? How successful are these figures?

2. How many paradoxes are in the poem? What is their cumulative effect? What is the topic of the paradoxes in lines 1–4? In lines 5–8? Why does the speaker declare that hating himself is a consequence of loving another? Why is it ironic that his "delight" is the "causer of this strife"?

3. To what extent do you think the paradoxes express the feelings of a person in love, particularly because in the sixteenth century, the free and unchaperoned meetings of lovers were not easily arranged?

WILLIAM SHAKESPEARE   (1564–1616)

Sonnet 18: Shall I Compare Thee to a Summer's Day?   *1609*

Shall I compare thee to a summer's day?
Thou art more lovely and more temperate:
Rough winds do shake the darling buds of May,
And summer's lease hath all too short a date:
Sometime too hot the eye of heaven° shines,   *the sun*   5
And often is his gold complexion dimmed;
And every fair from fair some-time declines,
By chance, or nature's changing course untrimmed;
But thy eternal summer shall not fade,
Nor lose possession of that fair thou owest°;   *ownest*   10
Nor shall Death brag thou wander'st in his shade,
When in eternal lines to time thou growest,
  So long as men can breathe or eyes can see,
  So long lives this, and this gives life to thee.

QUESTIONS

1. What is a possible dramatic situation out of which this poem springs?

2. Is the comparison offered in the first line a common or uncommon one?

3. What are the metaphors in lines 1–8 designed to assert? Why is the speaker emphasizing the brevity of life?

4. What is meant by *temperate* (line 2)? What sense of fragility is brought out by the metaphor of "darling buds of May"?

5. What is the metaphorical meaning of *lease* and *date* in line 4?

6. In lines 5 and 6, what happens to the sun, and why is the comparison appropriate to the person being addressed?

7. How does the topic shift in line 9? What is the new metaphor in line 11?

JOHN DONNE (1572–1631)

A Valediction: Forbidding Mourning   *1633*

As virtuous men pass mildly away,
    And whisper to their souls to go,
Whilst some of their sad friends do say
    The breath goes now, and some say, No;

So let us melt, and make no noise,   5
    No tear-floods, nor sigh-tempests move,
'Twere profanation° of our joys
    To tell the laity° our love.

Moving of th'earth° brings harm and fears,   *earthquakes*
    Men reckon what it did and meant: 10
But trepidation° of the spheres,
    Though greater far, is innocent.

Dull sublunary lovers' love
    (Whose soul is sense°) cannot admit
Absence, because it doth remove   15
    Those things which elemented it.

But we by a love so much refined
    That our selves know not what it is,
Inter-assured of the mind,
    Care less, eyes, lips, and hands to miss.   20

Our two souls therefore, which are one,
    Though I must go, endure not yet
A breach, but an expansion
    Like gold to airy thinness beat.°

A VALEDICTION: FORBIDDING MOURNING.   7, 8 *profanation . . . laity*: as though the lovers are priests of love, whose love is a mystery.   11 *trepidation*: Before Sir Isaac Newton explained the precession of the equinoxes, it was assumed that the positions of heavenly bodies should be constant and perfectly circular. The clearly observable irregularities (caused by the slow wobbling of the earth's axis) were explained by the concept of *trepidation*, or a trembling or oscillation that occurred in the outermost of the spheres surrounding the earth.   14 *soul is sense*: lovers whose attraction is totally physical.   24 *gold to airy thinness beat*: a reference to the malleability of gold.

If they be two, they are two so   25
   As stiff twin compasses° are two;
Thy soul, the fixt foot, makes no show
   To move, but doth, if th'other do.

And though it in the center sit,
   Yet when the other far doth roam,   30
It leans and harkens after it,
   And grows erect, as that comes home.

Such wilt thou be to me, who must
   Like th'other foot, obliquely run;
Thy firmness draws my circle just,°   35
   And makes me end where I begun.

26 *compasses*: a compass used for drawing circles.   35 *just*: perfectly round.

QUESTIONS

1. What is the situation envisioned as the occasion for the poem? Who is talking to whom? What is their relationship?
2. What is the intention of the first two stanzas? What is the effect of the phrases "tear-floods" and "sigh-tempests"?
3. Describe the effect of the opening simile about men on their deathbeds.
4. What is the metaphor of stanza 3 (lines 9–12)? In what sense might the "trepidation of the spheres" be less harmful than the parting of the lovers?
5. In lines 13–20 there is a comparison making the love of the speaker and his sweetheart superior to the love of average lovers. What is the basis for the speaker's claim?
6. What is the comparison begun by the word *refined* in line 17 and continued by the simile in line 24?

HENRY KING (1592–1669)

Sic Vita°   *1657*

Like to the falling of a star,
Or as the flights of eagles are,
Or like the fresh spring's gaudy hue,
Or silver drops of morning dew,
Or like a wind that chafes the flood,   5
Or bubbles which on water stood:
Even such is man, whose borrowed light
Is straight called in, and paid to night.
   The wind blows out, the bubble dies;
   The spring entombed in autumn lies: 10
   The dew dries up, the star is shot;
   The flight is past, and man forgot.

SIC VITA. (Latin): Such is life.

QUESTIONS

1. How many similes do you find in lines 1–6? Describe the range of references; that is, from what sources are the similes derived? What do all these similes (and references) have in common?

2. Explain the two metaphors in lines 7–8. (One is brought out by the words *borrowed, called in,* and *paid*; the other by *light* and *night.*)

3. Explain the continuation in lines 9–12 of the similes in 1–6. Do you think that these last four lines are essential, or might the poem have been successfully concluded with line 8? Explain.

4. What point does this poem make about humanity? In what ways do the similes in the poem help explore these ideas and bring them to life?

WILLIAM WORDSWORTH   (1770–1850)

London, 1802   *1807 (1802)*

Milton! thou should'st be living at this hour:
England hath need of thee: she is a fen°   bog, marsh
Of stagnant waters: altar, sword, and pen,
Fireside, the heroic wealth of hall and bower,
Have forfeited their ancient English dower°   widow's inheritance   5
Of inward happiness. We are selfish men;
Oh! raise us up, return to us again;
And give us manners,° virtue, freedom, power.
Thy soul was like a star, and dwelt apart:
Thou hadst a voice whose sound was like the sea: 10
Pure as the naked heavens, majestic, free,
So didst thou travel on life's common way,
In cheerful godliness; and yet thy heart
The lowliest duties on herself did lay.

LONDON, 1802.   8 *manners:* customs, moral modes of social and political conduct.

QUESTIONS

1. What is the effect of Wordworth's apostrophe to Milton? What elements of Milton's career as a writer does Wordsworth emphasize?

2. In lines 3 and 4, the device of metonymy is used. How does Wordsworth judge the respective institutions represented by the details?

3. Consider the use of overstatement, or hyperbole, from lines 2–6. What effect does Wordsworth achieve by using the device as extensively as he does here?

4. What effect does Wordsworth make through his use of overstatement in his praise of Milton in lines 9–14? What does he mean by the metonymic references to *soul* (line 9) and *heart* (line 13)?

JOHN KEATS (1795–1821)

To Autumn   *1820 (1819)*

Season of mists and mellow fruitfulness!
  Close bosom-friend of the maturing sun;
Conspiring with him how to load and bless
  With fruit the vines that round the thatch-eaves run;
To bend with apples the mossed cottage-trees,   5
  And fill all fruit with ripeness to the core;
    To swell the gourd, and plump the hazel shells
With a sweet kernel; to set budding more,
  And still more, later flowers for the bees,
  Until they think warm days will never cease,   10
    For Summer has o'erbrimmed their clammy cells.

Who hath not seen thee oft amid thy store?
  Sometimes whoever seeks abroad may find
Thee sitting careless on a granary floor,
  Thy hair soft-lifted by the winnowing wind,   15
Or on a half-reaped furrow sound asleep,
Drowsed with the fume of poppies, while thy hook
  Spares the next swath and all its twinèd flowers;
And sometimes like a gleaner thou dost keep
  Steady thy laden head across a brook;   20
  Or by a cider-press, with patient look,
  Thou watchest the last oozings hours by hours.

Where are the songs of Spring? Ay, where are they?
  Think not of them, thou hast thy music too,—
While barred clouds bloom the soft-dying day,   25
  And touch the stubble-plains with rosy hue;
Then in a wailful choir the small gnats mourn
  Among the river sallows, borne aloft
  Or sinking as the light wind lives or dies;
And full-grown lambs loud bleat from hilly bourn;   30
  Hedge-crickets sing; and now with treble soft
  The redbreast whistles from a garden-croft;
  And gathering swallows twitter in the skies.

QUESTIONS

1. How is personification used in the first stanza? How does it change in the second? What is the effect of such personification?

2. How does Keats structure the poem to accord with his apostrophe to autumn? That is, in what ways may the stanzas be distinguished by the type of discourse addressed to the season?

3. Analyze Keats's metonymy in stanza 1 and synecdoche in stanza 2. What effects does he achieve with these devices?

4.   How, through the use of images, does Keats develop his idea that autumn is a season of "mellow fruitfulness"?

T. S. ELIOT   (1888–1965)

Eyes That Last I Saw in Tears   *1924*

Eyes that last I saw in tears
Through division
Here in death's dream kingdom
The golden vision reappears
I see the eyes but not the tears   5
This is my affliction

This is my affliction
Eyes I shall not see again
Eyes of decision
Eyes I shall not see unless   10
At the door of death's other kingdom
Where, as in this,
The eyes outlast a little while
A little while outlast the tears
And hold us in derision.   15

QUESTIONS

1.   What do *eyes* and *tears* signify as a synecdoche and as a metonymy?
2.   What is the cause of the tears (line 2)? What is meant by the eyes outlasting the tears (lines 13, 14)? Why should the eyes "hold us in derision"? In line 9 the eyes are "of decision." What does this synecdoche mean?
3.   Explain the paradox of the speaker's declaration in line 5 that he sees the eyes but not the tears. Why does he say that this is his "affliction"?
4.   Why might the entire poem be considered a paradox? What happened in life? What does the speaker look forward to in death?
5.   What is the distinction in the poem between "death's dream kingdom" and "death's other kingdom"?

OGDEN NASH   (1902–1970)

Exit, Pursued by a Bear   *1954*

Chipmunk chewing the Chippendale,°
Mice on the Meissen° shelf,

EXIT, PURSUED BY A BEAR.   The title is a stage direction in Shakespeare's *The Winter's Tale* (Act III, scene 3, 58). The character is torn apart by the bear. When this poem was first published, the atomic bomb had existed for nine years, and the hydrogen bomb for two. In late 1953, Russia, which is sometimes symbolized by a bear, announced that it possessed the hydrogen bomb.   1 *Chippendale:* ornate furniture made by Thomas

Pigeon stains on the Aubusson,°
Spider lace on the delf.°

Squirrel climbing the Sheraton,°   5
Skunk on the Duncan Phyfe,°
Silverfish in the Gobelins°
And the calfbound volumes of *Life.*

Pocks on the pink Picasso,
Dust on the four Cézannes,   10
Kit on the keys of the Steinway,
Cat on the Louis Quinze.°

Rings on the Adam° mantel
From a thousand bygone thirsts,
Mold on the Henry Millers°   15
And the Ronald Firbank° firsts.

The lion and the lizard°
No heavenly harmonies hear
From the high-fidelity speaker
Concealed behind the Vermeer.   20

Jamshid° squats in a cavern
Screened by a waterfall,
Catered by Heinz and Campbell,
And awaits the fireball.

Chippendale (1718–1779).   2 *Meissen:* expensive chinaware made in Meissen, Germany.
Also called "Dresden China."   3 *Aubusson:* carpet imported from France.   4 *delf:*
expensive pottery made in Delft, The Netherlands.   5 *Sheraton:* furniture made by
Thomas Sheraton (1751–1806).   6 *Duncan Phyfe:* furniture made by Duncan Phyfe
(1768–1854), a Scotsman who came to America in 1783.   7 *Gobelins:* rare and exquisitely
crafted tapestries made by Gobelin of Paris.   12 *Louis Quinze:* furniture made in France
during the reign of Louis XV (1710–1774).   13 *Adam:* Robert Adam (1728–1792) was
one of the most famous English architects.   15 *Henry Miller:* American author (1891–
1980).   16 *Ronald Firbank:* Arthur Ainsley Ronald Firbank (1886–1926), British author.
17 *The lion and the lizard:* See Edward Fitzgerald's (1809–1883) version of *The Rubáiyát of
Omar Khayyám,* stanza 18, particularly in reference to Nash's last stanza.   21 *Jamshid:* a
reference to the legendary Persian hero Jamshid, who found a cup containing the elixir of
life and lived for 700 years. At one point in the story Jamshid remained hidden for a
hundred years. Note also the reference to Fitzgerald's *Rubáiyát,* stanza 18.

QUESTIONS

1. In relationship to the serious subject matter of the poem, what is the effect
    of the title? What is the possible pun on the word *bear?*

2. What location is the speaker describing? How is metonymy used to suggest
    the wealth of the collections of household items and art? What sort of
    lifestyle is suggested by the metonymy?

3. Why is it that animals rather than people are living with the expensive
    artifacts? Judging from line 14, how long has this situation existed?

4. How might the situation presented in the poem be considered as a paradox?

LANGSTON HUGHES   (1902–1967)

Harlem   *1951*

What happens to a dream deferred?

Does it dry up
like a raisin in the sun?
Or fester like a sore—
And then run?   5
Does it stink like rotten meat?
Or crust and sugar over—
like a syrupy sweet?

Maybe it just sags
like a heavy load.   10

Or does it explode?

QUESTIONS

1. In the light of the black experience with the "American Dream," what do you think is meant by the phrase "dream deferred"?
2. Explain the structure of the poem in terms of the speaker's questions and answers. How is the structure here similar to the one in Shakespeare's sonnet, "Shall I Compare Thee to a Summer's Day?" (p. 633)?
3. Explain the similes in lines 3, 4, 6, 8, and 10. Why are these apt comparisons? What sorts of human actions are implied in these figures?
4. What is the meaning of the metaphor in line 11? Why do you think Hughes shifted from similes to a metaphor in this line?

ELIZABETH BISHOP   (1911–1979)

Rain Towards Morning   *1947*

The great light cage has broken up in the air,
freeing, I think, about a million birds
whose wild ascending shadows will not be back,
and all the wires come falling down.
No cage, no frightening birds; the rain   5
is brightening now. The face is pale
that tried the puzzle of their prison
and solved it with an unexpected kiss,
whose freckled unsuspected hands alit.

QUESTIONS

1. What sort of personal situation is being described in the poem? How much does the poet allow you to learn about the situation? Do you discover enough to determine the general pattern of what is happening?

2. Describe the effect of the overstatement in lines 1–4. In light of the "kiss," which is more powerful: understatement or overstatement?

3. What is the meaning of the "great light cage" in lines 1–4? What is the "puzzle" of the birds' prison in line 7?

4. How can the "face" of line 6 and the "kiss" in line 8 be explained, through the figure of synecdoche, to have "hands" in line 9? What do these figures suggest about the nature of the experience being described?

5. Explain the paradox of how rain can be brightening (line 6).

SYLVIA PLATH   (1932–1963)

Metaphors   *1960*

I'm a riddle in nine syllables,
An elephant, a ponderous house,
A melon strolling on two tendrils.
O red fruit, ivory, fine timbers!
This loaf's big with its yeasty rising.   5
Money's new-minted in this fat purse.
I'm a means, a stage, a cow in calf.
I've eaten a bag of green apples,
Boarded the train there's no getting off.

QUESTIONS

1. What evidence can you find in the poem that the speaker here is a woman?

2. The speaker calls herself a "riddle in nine syllables." What is the answer to the riddle? Why nine syllables (as opposed to eight or ten)? In what sense is the poem also a riddle? How are the answers to both riddles related?

3. Which of the metaphors do you find amusing, shocking, or demeaning? What do these suggest about the speaker's attitude toward herself?

4. What aspect of the speaker's condition is captured in the "bag of green apples" metaphor (line 8)? What two meanings are suggested by the *stage* metaphor (line 7)? Why is the *train* metaphor (line 9) appropriate to the speaker's condition and the results of that condition?

MARGE PIERCY   (b. 1934)

A Work of Artifice   *1973*

The bonsai tree
in the attractive pot
could have grown eighty feet tall
on the side of a mountain
till split by lightning.   5

But a gardener
carefully pruned it.
It is nine inches high.
Every day as he
whittles back the branches   10
the gardener croons,
It is your nature
to be small and cozy
domestic and weak;
how lucky, little tree,   15
to have a pot to grow in.
With living creatures
one must begin very early
to dwarf their growth:
the bound feet,   20
the crippled brain,
the hair in curlers,
the hands you
love to touch.

QUESTIONS

1. What is a bonsai tree? In what ways is it an apt metaphor for women? The
   tree "could have grown eighty feet tall." What would be the comparable
   growth and development of a woman?

2. What do you make of the gardener's song (lines 12–16)? If the bonsai tree
   were able to respond, would it accept the gardener's consolation? What
   conclusions about women's lives are implied by the metaphor of the tree?

3. How does the poem shift at line 17? To what extent do the next images
   (lines 20–24) embody women's lives? How are the images metaphorical?

JUDITH MINTY   (b. 1937)

Conjoined   *1981*

a marriage poem

The onion in my cupboard, a monster, actually
two joined under one transparent skin:
each half-round, then flat and deformed
where it pressed and grew against the other.

An accident, like the two-headed calf rooted   5
in one body, fighting to suck at its mother's teats;
or like those other freaks, Chang and Eng,° twins

CONJOINED.   7 *Chang and Eng*: born in 1811, the original and most famous Siamese
twins. Although they were never separated, they nevertheless fathered twenty-two children.
They died in 1874.

joined at the chest by skin and muscle, doomed
to live, even make love, together for sixty years.

Do you feel the skin that binds us   10
together as we move, heavy in this house?
To sever the muscle could free one,
but might kill the other. Ah, but men
don't slice onions in the kitchen, seldom see
what is invisible. We cannot escape each other.   15

QUESTIONS

1. What are the two things—the "us" and "we" of lines 10 and 11—that are conjoined? Since this is "a marriage poem," might they be the man and the woman? Why might they also be considered as the body and soul of the speaker; or the desire to be married and subordinated, on the one hand, and to be free and in control of destiny, on the other?

2. Explore the metaphor of the onion and the similes of the two-headed calf and the Siamese twins. Why do you think the poet introduces the words *monster, accident,* and *freaks* into these figures in lines 1, 5, and 7? In what sense do you believe that these words are applicable to the nature and plight of women?

3. Is it true that *all* "men / don't slice onions in the kitchen, seldom see / what is invisible"? Explain.

DIANE WAKOSKI (b. 1937)

Inside Out   *1965*

I walk the purple carpet into your eye,
carrying the silver butter server,
but a truck rumbles by,
        leaving its black tire prints on my foot,
and old images—   5
        the sound of banging screen doors on hot afternoons
        and a fly buzzing over Kool-Aid spilled on the sink—
flicker, as reflections on the metal surface.

Come in, you said,
inside your paintings, inside the blood factory, inside the   10
old songs that line your hands, inside
eyes that change like a snowflake every second,

inside spinach leaves holding that one piece of gravel,

inside the whiskers of a cat,

inside your old hat, and most of all inside your mouth where you   15
grind the pigments with your teeth, painting

with a broken bottle on the floor, and painting
with an ostrich feather on the moon that rolls out of my mouth.

You cannot let me walk inside you too long
inside the veins where my small feet touch   20
bottom.
You must reach inside and pull me
like a silver bullet°
from your arm.

INSIDE OUT.   23 *silver bullet*: According to legend, silver bullets were used to kill
vampires. The Lone Ranger, of the radio and television series popular in the 1940s and
1950s, always used silver bullets as a trademark of his pursuit of justice.

QUESTIONS

1. What "inside out" details of the listener's anatomy does the speaker mention?
    What do you think is meant by the poem's title?
2. Consider details of the eye and the veins as synecdoche, and the paintings
    and the old hat as metonymy. In the determination of the poem's charac-
    terization of the "you" inside the poem, what do these details stand for?
3. Consider the truck's black tire prints on the speaker's foot (lines 3–4) as an
    instance of synesthesia, that is, the application of one set of sensuous
    references to another sense. What might this figure mean? Do the same for
    the mouth with the ground pigments (lines 15–16), the ostrich feather and
    the rolling moon (line 18), and the walk inside the veins (lines 19–20).
4. What is meant by lines 19–24? Why, after the establishment of so personal
    and intimate a relationship, might the speaker express the reservations that
    are contained here? How might these lines be interpreted as a reflection
    upon the paradoxical nature of the love relationship generally?
5. Describe the paradox of the purple carpet and the silver butter server.

WRITING ABOUT RHETORICAL FIGURES

When you begin planning to write about metaphors, similes, and other
rhetorical figures, you will not know what direction your essay will take.
Thus, you will need to record your discoveries as you study the work.
Determine the use, line by line, of metaphors or similes, if these are the
objects of your study, or of other rhetorical figures. Obviously, similes are
the easiest figure to recognize because of the "like" or "as" with which
they begin. Metaphors may be recognizable because of the transference
of the subject or vehicle to the actual meaning or tenor. If the subject is
memory, for example, but the poem speaks of law courts, you are looking
at a metaphor. Similarly, if the poet is addressing an absent person, or a
natural object, or if you find clear double meanings in words, you may
have apostrophe, personification, or puns.

Questions for Discovering Ideas

What figures does the work contain?

Where do they occur? Under what circumstances?

How extensive are they?

How do you recognize them? Are they signaled by a single word, like "bows" in Campion's "Cherry Ripe," or are they more extensively detailed, as in Shakespeare's "When to the Sessions of Sweet Silent Thought"?

What effect do the figures have on the experiences and attitudes of the poem?

Structurally, how are the figures developed? How do they rise out of the situation? Are the figures the major means of development, or are they no more than an embellishment of a more discursive or conversational mode? How do they relate to other aspects of the poem?

How vivid are the figures? How obvious? How unusual? What kind of effort is needed to understand them in context?

Is one type of figure used in a particular section while another predominates in another? Why?

If you have discovered a number of figures, what relationships can you find among them (such as the judicial and financial connections in Shakespeare's Sonnet 30)?

What ideas do the figures bring out? How important are they as an aspect of the poem's ideas?

How do they broaden, deepen, or otherwise assist in making the ideas in the poem forceful?

In short, how appropriate and meaningful are the figures in the poem, and how well do they assist you in your understanding and appreciation?

Strategies for Organizing Ideas

For this essay, two types of compositions are possible. One is a full-scale essay. The other, because some rhetorical figures may occupy only a small part of the poem, is a single paragraph. Let us consider the single paragraph first.

1. *A paragraph.* For a single paragraph you need only one topic, such as the opening paradox and metonym that begin Eliot's "Eyes That Last I Saw in Tears" (p. 638). The goal should be to deal with the single figure and its relationship to the poem's main idea. Thus, the figure should be described, and its meaning and implications should be discussed. It is important to begin with a comprehensive topic sentence, such as one that explains the cleverness of the puns in Gay's "Let Us Take the Road" (p. 631), or the use of synesthesia in Keats's "Ode to a Nightingale" (p. 744).

2. *A full-length essay.* One type of essay might examine just one figure, supposing that the figure is pervasive enough in the poem to justify a full treatment. The second type of essay might explore the meaning and effect of two or more figures, with the various parts of the body of the essay

being taken up with each of the figures. The unity of this second kind of essay is achieved by the linking of a series of two or three different rhetorical devices to a single idea or emotion conveyed in the poem.

In the introduction, you should relate the quality of the figures to the general nature of the work you are studying. Thus, metaphors and similes of suffering might be appropriate to a religious, redemptive work; those of sunshine and cheer might be right for a romantic one. If there is any discrepancy between the metaphorical language and the topic, you would find it necessary to consider that contrast as a possible central idea, for your writer would clearly be developing an ironic perspective. Suppose that the topic of the poem is love, but the figures put you in mind of darkness and cold: What would the writer be saying about the quality of love? You should also try to justify any claims that you make about the figures. For example, one of the similes in Coleridge's "Kubla Khan" compares the sounds of a "mighty fountain" to the breathing of the earth in "fast thick pants." How is this simile to be taken? As a reference to the animality of the earth? As a suggestion that the fountain, and the earth, are dangerous? Or simply as a comparison suggesting immense, forceful noise? How do you explain the answer or answers you select? Your introduction is the place to establish ideas and justifications of this sort.

The following approaches for discussing rhetorical figures are not mutually exclusive, and you may combine them as you wish. Most likely, the essay you write will bring in most of the following classifications.

1. *Interpret the meaning and effect of the figures.* Here you explain how the figures enable you to make an interpretation. In stanza 2 of "A Valediction: Forbidding Mourning," for example, Donne introduces a metaphor equating the condition of love with the structure of the church:

'Twere profanation of our joys
To tell the laity our love.

Here Donne emphasizes the private, mystical relationship of two lovers, drawing the metaphor from the religious tradition any explanation of religious mysteries is considered a desecration. The idea Donne is promoting is that love is rare, heaven-sent, private, privileged, and so fragile that it would be hurt if it were made public. This interpretive approach is a direct one, requiring that metaphors, similes, or other figures be explained and expanded, with the introduction of necessary references and allusions to make your expansion fully meaningful.

2. *Analyze the frames of reference and their appropriateness to the subject matter.* Here you classify and locate the sources and types of the references, and determine the appropriateness of these to the subject matter of the poem. Questions are similar to those you might ask in a study of imagery: Does the writer refer extensively to nature, science, warfare, politics, business, reading? For example, Shakespeare in Sonnet 30, as we have

seen, expands a metaphor equating personal reverie with courtroom proceedings. Because such proceedings are public and methodical, whereas personal self-evaluation is private and relatively unplanned, how appropriate is the metaphor? Does Shakespeare make it seem right as he develops it in the poem? How? In considering any metaphors and similes in the work you analyze, you would need similarly to classify according to sources and to try to determine the appropriateness of this body of figures to the poet's ideas.

3. *Focus on the interests and sensibilities of the poet.* In a way this approach is like the second one, but the emphasis here is on what the selectivity of the writer might show about his or her vision and interests. You might begin by listing the figures in the poem and then determining the sources, just as you would do in discussing the sources of images generally. But then you should raise questions like the following: Does the writer use figures derived from one sense rather than another (i.e., sight, hearing, taste, smell, touch)? Does he or she record color, brightness, shadow, shape, depth, height, number, size, slowness, speed, emptiness, fullness, richness, drabness? Has the writer relied on the associations of figures of sense? Do metaphors and similes referring to green plants and trees, to red roses, or to rich fabrics, for example, suggest that life is full and beautiful, or do references to touch suggest amorous warmth? This approach is designed to help you to draw whatever conclusions you can about the author's—or the speaker's—taste or sensibility as a result of your study.

4. *Examine the effect of one figure on the other figures and ideas of the poem.* The assumption of this approach is that each literary work is unified and organically whole, so that each part is closely related and inseparable from everything else. Usually it is best to pick a figure that occurs at the beginning of the poem and then to determine how this figure influences your perception of the rest of the poem. In an analysis of this sort, your aim is to consider the relationship of part to parts, and part to whole. The beginning of Donne's "A Valediction: Forbidding Mourning," for example, contains a simile comparing the parting of the speaker and his woman friend to the quiet dying of "virtuous men." What is the effect of this comparison upon the rest of the poem? To help you in approaching such a question, you might substitute a totally different detail, such as, here, the violent death of a condemned criminal, or the slaughter of a domestic animal, rather than the deaths of "virtuous men." Such suppositions, which would clearly be out of place and inappropriate, may help you to understand and then explain the poet's rhetorical figures.

In your conclusion you might summarize your main points, describe your general impressions, try to describe the impact of the figures, indicate your personal responses, or show what might further be done along the lines you have been developing in the body. If you know other works by the same writer, or other works by other writers with comparable or contrasting figures, you might briefly consider this other work and the light it might shed on your present analysis.

SAMPLE PARAGRAPH

Wordsworth's Use of Overstatement in "London, 1802"°

Through overstatement, Wordsworth emphasizes his tribute to Milton as a master of idealistic thought. The speaker's claim that England is "a fen / Of stagnant waters" (lines 2–3) is overstated, just as the implication that people ("we") in England have no "manners, virtue, freedom, [or] power" (line 8). With the overstatement, however, Wordsworth makes the case that the nation's well-being depends on the constant flow of creative thoughts by persons of great ideas. Because Milton was clearly the greatest of these, in the view of Wordsworth's speaker, the overstatement stresses the importance of voices of leadership. Milton is the model, and the overstated need lays the foundation in the real political and moral world for a revival of Milton's ideas. Thus, through overstatement, Wordsworth emphasizes the importance of Milton, and in this way pays tribute to him.

Commentary on the Paragraph

This sample illustrates how a single rhetorical figure may become the basis of a short paragraph. The rhetorical figure you choose to write about does not have to be prominent in the poem. The topic is Wordsworth's use of overstatement in "London, 1802." The detail of overstatement selected from the poem is Wordsworth's assertion about the immoral state of his country in 1802. The goal of the paragraph is not to describe the details of the figure, however, but to show how the figure affects Wordsworth's poetic tribute to Milton. Even in a short writing assignment make sure you support your major point in a direct, clear way.

SAMPLE ESSAY

A Study of Shakespeare's Metaphors in Sonnet 30°

[1]   In this sonnet Shakespeare's speaker stresses the sadness and regret of remembered experience, but he states that a person with these feelings may be cheered by the thought of a friend. His metaphors, cleverly used, create new and fresh ways of seeing personal life in this perspective.* He

° See p. 636 for this poem.
° See p. 627 for this poem.
* Central idea.

presents metaphors drawn from the public and business world of law courts, money, and banking or money-handling.†

[2] The courtroom metaphor of the first four lines shows that memories of past experience are constantly present and influential. Like a judge commanding defendants to appear in court, the speaker "summon[s]" his memory of "things past" to appear on trial before him. This metaphor suggests that people are their own judges and that their ideals and morals are like laws by which they measure themselves. The speaker finds himself guilty of wasting his time in the past. Removing himself, however, from the strict punishment that a real judge might require, he does not condemn himself for his "dear time's waste," but instead laments it (line 4). The metaphor is thus used to indicate that a person's consciousness is made up just as much of self-doubt and reproach as by more positive influences.

[3] With the closely related reference to money in the next group of four lines, Shakespeare shows that living is a lifelong investment and is valuable for this reason. According to the money metaphor, living requires the spending of emotions and commitment to others. When friends move away and loved ones die, it is as though this expenditure has been lost. Thus, the speaker's dead friends are "precious" because he invested time and love in them, and the "sights" that have "vanished" from his eyes make him "moan" because he went to great "expense" for them (line 8).

[4] Like the money metaphor, the metaphor of banking or money-handling in the next four lines emphasizes the fact that life's experiences are on deposit in the mind. They are recorded there, and may be withdrawn in moments of "sweet silent thought" just as a depositor may withdraw money. Thus, the speaker states that he counts out his woes just as a merchant or banker counts money: "And heavily from woe to woe *tell* o'er" (line 10). Because strong emotions still accompany his memories of mistakes made long ago, he pays again with "new" woe the accounts that he has already paid with old woe in the past. The metaphor suggests that the past is so much a part of the present that a person never finishes paying both the principal and interest of past emotional investments. Because of this combination of banking and legal figures, the speaker indicates that his memory puts him in double jeopardy, for the thoughts of his losses overwhelm him in the present just as much as they did in the past.

[5] The legal, financial, and money-handling metaphors combine in the last two lines to show how a healthy present life may overcome past regrets. The "dear friend" being addressed in these lines has the resources (financial) to settle all the emotional judgments that the speaker as a self-judge has made against himself (legal). It is as though the friend is a rich patron who rescues him from emotional bankruptcy (legal and financial) and the possible doom resulting from the potential sentence of emotional misery and depression (legal).

In these metaphors, therefore, Shakespeare's references are drawn from everyday public and business actions, but his use of them is creative and unusual. In particular, the idea of line 8 ("And moan th'expense of many a

---

† Thesis sentence.

[6]

vanished sight") stresses that people spend much emotional energy on others. Without such personal commitment, one cannot have precious friends and loved ones. In keeping with this metaphor of money and investment, one could measure life not in months or years, but in the spending of emotion and involvement in personal relationships. Shakespeare, by inviting readers to explore the values brought out by his metaphors, gives new insights into the nature and value of life.

Commentary on the Essay

This essay treats the three classes of metaphors that Shakespeare introduces in Sonnet 30. It thus illustrates the second approach (p. 646). But the aim of the discussion is not to explore the extent and nature of the comparison between the metaphors and the personal situations spoken about in the sonnet. Instead the goal is to explain how the metaphors develop Shakespeare's meaning. This method therefore also illustrates the first approach (p. 646).

In addition to providing a brief description of the sonnet, the introduction brings out to the central idea and the thesis sentence. Paragraph 2 deals with the meaning of Shakespeare's courtroom metaphor. His money metaphor is explained in paragraph 3. Paragraph 4 considers the banking, or money-handling, figure. The fifth paragraph shows how Shakespeare's last two lines bring together the three separate strands, or classes, of metaphor. The conclusion comments generally on the creativity of Shakespeare's metaphors, and it also amplifies the way in which the money metaphor leads toward an increased understanding and valuation of life.

Throughout the essay, transitions from one topic to the next are brought about by linking words in the topic sentences. In paragraph 3, for example, the words "closely related" and "next group" move the reader from paragraph 2 to the new content. In paragraph 4, the words effecting the transition are "like the money metaphor" and "the next four lines." The opening sentence of paragraph 5 refers collectively to the subjects of paragraphs 2, 3, and 4, thereby focusing them on the new topic of paragraph 5.

SAMPLE ESSAY

Paradox in Sir Thomas Wyatt's "I Find No Peace"°

Wyatt's sonnet "I Find No Peace" is built on paradox. The first-person speaker is describing the effects his lover has upon him, and he indicates forcefully that he is caught between commitment, on the one hand, and the

° See p. 632 for this poem.

Writing About Rhetorical Figures **651**

desire to be free, on the other. Because of his conflict, he describes his own conditions of amazement, dismay, and amusement, but he states also that he is reconciled to his contrary states. His situation blends naturally with the rhetorical pattern of paradox.* In the poem, the paradox is extended to the speaker's personal reactions, his attitude toward his beloved, and his general public situation.†

[2]
The speaker's personal reactions are most vividly described within the contrary states defined by paradox. Thus the speaker at the beginning declares his satisfaction at having won his "war" because he has apparently convinced his sweetheart to love him. But at the same time he can never really be sure of her. Hence he also states the paradox that he can "find no peace." Throughout the sonnet the speaker develops these contradictory emotional states. He is at the height of desire, but he cannot find consummation. He therefore speaks ambiguously of his sexual frustration (line 7, where he cannot "live nor die at ... [his] devise," with *die* being a sexual pun), and the frustration in turn continues his uncertainty. Throughout, in almost every line, the speaker stresses other paradoxes that point out his inner anguish.

[3]
In the speaker's descriptions of his attitude toward his beloved, the same paradoxes are apparent. He calls her his "delight," for example (line 14), and yet he confesses that he is blind to whatever human faults she might possess ("Without eyen I see," line 9). He would like to pursue his quest further but does not want to offend, and thus he states, "without tongue I plain" (line 9). In short, his sweetheart is also a human being to whom he must grant individuality and freedom. Because of the gap between this recognition and his desire, he paradoxically experiences the joy of love and the pain of uncertainty.

[4]
Finally, the speaker claims that his attempts to carry on normally in life are also afflicted with his paradoxical personal condition. In line 12 the speaker explains that he continues to eat and also to laugh; that is, his life has not stopped, and he goes about his affairs. But all the time he is at meals, which should be a joyful time, he is in sorrow, and even when he is laughing, he is also in pain. In this way, the poet develops the paradox in which a person functioning well publicly is personally torn and uncertain.

[5]
The poem thus stresses the paradoxical effects of intense love in all major phases of the speaker's life. The human basis of the paradoxes is the difficulty that people have in truly knowing each other, even the ones they love most dearly. In the poem, this inability to know the true mind of the beloved, even though she is "all the world" to the speaker (line 4), creates the uncertainty out of which the paradoxes arise. This state is convincingly real, particularly because of the speaker's intensity of feeling. Wyatt's complete incorporation of paradox into the sonnet therefore dramatizes the conflicting feelings of a person in love. Paradox here is precisely fitted to the subject of the poem.

* Central idea.
† Thesis sentence.

Commentary on the Essay

This sample illustrates how a pervasive rhetorical figure may be divided for consideration in a full-length essay. The figure chosen is paradox because it is so prominent in "I Find No Peace." For any other poem in which any particular figure is important, the same method might be followed. If the essay were to be based on two or more figures, each one of these might form a separate part or paragraph in the body.

In the introduction to this particular essay, attention is focused on the figure of paradox and its importance in the situation described in the poem. The central idea proposes the argument that idea and figure are blended. The thesis sentence lists three areas of the poem to be explored in the body. Paragraph 2 describes the paradox as developed in the speaker's perception of his own condition as a lover. Because the sonnet is primarily about the speaker rather than about his love, this paragraph is the longest in the body of the essay. Paragraph 3 is concerned with the paradox as it affects the speaker's descriptions of his beloved. His difficulty results from the fact that she is an individual, and hence he cannot control her as much as his love would dictate. Paragraph 4, the shortest of the body, is concerned with the sparse information that the speaker discloses about his public life as it is affected by the paradox of his private turmoil. The conclusion briefly summarizes the main topics of the body, and then it attempts to explain the paradoxes in terms of this difficulty people have in knowing each other. The last sentence is a restatement of the central idea.

WRITING TOPICS

1. Study the simile of the "stiff twin compasses" in Donne's "A Valediction: Forbidding Mourning." Using such a compass, or a drawing of one, write an essay which demonstrates the accuracy of Donne's descriptions. What light does the simile shed on the relationship of two lovers? How does it emphasize any or all of these aspects of love: closeness, immediacy, extent, importance, duration, intensity?

2. Consider some of the metaphors and similes in the poems included in this chapter. Write an essay that answers the following questions. How effective are the figures you select? (Examples: the bonsai tree [Piercy], the Siamese twins [Minty], the explosive [Hughes], the summer's day [Shakespeare].) What insights do the figures provide within the contexts of their respective poems? How appropriate are they? Might they be expanded more fully, and if they were, what would be the effect?

3. Consider some of the other rhetorical figures to be found in the poems of this chapter. On the basis of the figures you select, write an essay describing the importance of figures in creating emphasis and in extending and deepening the ideas of poetry.

4. Write a poem in which you create a governing metaphor or simile. An example might be: My girl- or boyfriend is like (a) an opening flower, (b) a difficult book, (c) an insoluble mathematical problem, (d) a bill that cannot be paid, (e) a slow-moving chess game. Another example: Teaching a person how to do a particular job is like (a) shoveling heavy snow, (b) climbing a mountain during a landslide, (c) having someone force you underwater when you're gasping for breath. When you finish, describe the relationship between your comparison and the development and structure of your poem.

17

Tone: The Creation of Attitude in Poetry

Tone (also discussed in Chapter 8 in relationship to fiction) is the means by which poets control attitudes and feelings. You may remember that the term is borrowed from the *tone of voice* of speech. In the study of tone in poetry, the object is to consider *the ways in which poets express and control attitudes*. Literally everything in a poem helps convey attitudes. The poet's stance toward the material and toward readers is one of the most important aspects. In establishing a speaker or an authorial voice, the poet must develop a character to do the speaking in relation to the purpose of the poem: How much self-awareness will this speaker have? How many traits? What kind of background? What kind of relationship will be established between the speaker and the readers? How much knowledge will speaker and readers share? What interests and assumptions will be attributed to the readers? All these enter into the writing of the poem and therefore into the poem's tone.

In addition, things like *irony, understatement, overstatement*, the creation of either *seriousness* or *humor*, the use of *diction* and the control of *connotation*, and the *images, similes*, and *metaphors*, are a part of tone. For a comparison with art, refer briefly to Leger's painting "The City" (facing page). The figures, signs, stairs, and pole in the painting are all features of contemporary city life. Because Leger does not complete them, but rather cuts them up or leaves them partially hidden, he conveys the idea that modern urban life is truncated, incomplete, and sinister. In short, the tone of the painting depends on the form and arrangement of detail.

The same control of texture is necessary in poetry. The sentences must be just long enough, no shorter and no longer, to achieve the poet's intended effect. If a conversational style is established, overly formal words must be avoided. Similarly, in a formal style slang must not intrude, nor should there be any rollicking rhythms or frivolous rhymes. Whatever the style, ambiguities should be deliberate, not unintentional. In all such

Fernand Leger (1881–1955), *The City*, 1919. Oil on canvas, 90¾ × 117¼". (Philadelphia Museum of Art: A. E. Gallatin Collection)

features that collectively make up the tone of a poem, the poet's consistency is of primary importance. If anything falls short, the poem sinks, and the poet will have failed.

TONE, CHOICE, AND READER RESPONSE

Remember that a major rhetorical objective of poets is to shape, enrich, stimulate, inform, and generally affect readers. Thus, poets may begin their poems with perhaps not much more than a brief idea, a vague feeling, or a fleeting impression. Then, in the light of their developing design, their own attitudes, and their judgment of possible reader responses, they *choose* what to say—the form of the material, and the words and phrases to express it. The poem "Theme for English B," by Langston Hughes (the topic of the sample essay), illustrates almost in outline form the process by which a poet determines reader response in order to gain acceptance. Hughes's speaker lays out those common interests shared by him and his intended reader, his English teacher. In this way Hughes establishes grounds for acceptance of his ideas of human equality.

In order to balance poetic intention with the full range of reader responses, the poet must exert the greatest skill. Control over tone is essential, so that readers may respond with appropriate recognition, understanding, and emotion. In the long run, readers might not accept all the ideas in the poem, but the successful poem will have gained the reader's acceptance—at least for a time—because the poet's control over tone will have been right.

Each poem, in short, attempts to evoke *total* responses, which any interfering lapse of tone might destroy. Such lapses may take the form of an objectionable assumption about the qualities of a person or idea in the poem, a misinterpretation of how readers may take an idea, an uncertain expression, or some ambiguity that creates a misimpression. Let us look at a poem that misses in controlling tone, and misses badly.

CORNELIUS WHUR   (1782–1853)

The First-Rate Wife   *1837*

This brief effusion I indite,
  And my vast wishes send,
That thou mayst be directed right,
And have ere long within thy sight
  A most *enchanting* friend!   5

The *maiden* should have *lovely face*,
  And be of *genteel mien*;
If not, within thy dwelling place,
There may be vestige of disgrace,
  Not much admired—when seen.   10

Nor will thy dearest be complete
  Without *domestic* care;
If otherwise, howe'er discreet,
Thine eyes will very often meet
  What none desire to share!   15

And further still—thy future *dear*,
  Should have some *mental* ray;
If not, thou mayest drop a tear,
Because no *real sense* is there
  To charm life's dreary day!   20

QUESTIONS

1. What is the situation of the poem? Who is the speaker? The listener? How does the poem's tone reveal the speaker's character?

2. What requirements does the speaker create for the "first-rate wife"? In light of the tone, to what degree does the poem constitute an insult toward women?

3. How might lines 14 and 15 be interpreted as a possible threat if the woman as a wife does not take care of the house?

The form of "The First-Rate Wife" is that of advice given by a male speaker to a male listener about those traits which make a young lady a first-rate wife. In stanza 1 the speaker sets himself up as an advice-giver. In stanzas 2, 3, and 4, he asserts that the three requirements are beauty, neatness, and intelligence. From the tone of the speaker's remarks, it is clear that he regards the decision to marry as being comparable to the hiring of a housekeeper or the buying of a diverting book. Note the tone of the phrase "some *mental* ray," for example. The word *some* does not mean "a great deal," but in this instance is more like "*at least* some," as though it would be unreasonable to expect anything more of a woman. From the tone of the last three lines it is clear that the speaker's requirement for intelligence does not mean that the woman should be the man's intellectual equal, but rather that she should be charming enough to rescue him from dreariness and boredom. Even allowing for the fact that the poem was written in the nineteenth century and represents a traditional masculine view of marriage, "The First-Rate Wife" will probably offend readers. Do you wonder why you probably never heard of Cornelius Whur before?

TONE AND THE NEED FOR CONTROL

"The First-Rate Wife" emphasizes the need for the poet to be in control over the entire situation of the poem. The speaker must be aware of his or her situation, and should not, like Cornelius Whur's speaker, demonstrate any smugness or insensitivity, unless the poet is deliberately revealing the shortcomings of the speaker by dramatizing them for the reader's amusement, as E. E. Cummings does in the poem "Next to of course God" (p. 901). In a poem with well-controlled tone, details and situations should be factually correct; observations should be both logical and fair, within the poem's structure, and should also be comprehensive and generally applicable. The following poem illustrates a firm control over tone.

WILFRED OWEN (1893–1918)

Dulce et Decorum Est°   *1920 (1918)*

Bent double, like old beggars under sacks,
Knock-kneed, coughing like hags, we cursed through sludge,
Till on the haunting flares we turned our backs
And towards our distant rest began to trudge.
Men marched asleep. Many had lost their boots   5

DULCE ET DECORUM EST. The Latin title comes from Horace's *Odes*, Book 3, line 13: *Dulce et decorum est pro patria mori* ("It is sweet and honorable to die [while fighting] for [one's] country"). See the poem's last line.

But limped on, blood-shod. All went lame; all blind;
Drunk with fatigue; deaf even to the hoots
Of tired, outstripped Five-Nines° that dropped behind.

Gas! GAS!° Quick, boys!—An ecstasy of fumbling,
Fitting the clumsy helmets° just in time;   10
But someone still was yelling out and stumbling
And flound'ring like a man in fire or lime . . .
Dim, through the misty panes and thick green° light,
As under a green sea, I saw him drowning.
In all my dreams, before my helpless sight,   15
He plunges at me, guttering, choking, drowning.

If in some smothering dreams you too could pace
Behind the wagon that we flung him in,
And watch the white eyes writhing in his face,
His hanging face, like a devil's sick of sin;   20
If you could hear, at every jolt, the blood
Come gargling from the froth-corrupted lungs,
Obscene as cancer, bitter as the cud
Of vile, incurable sores on innocent tongues,—
My friend, you would not tell with such high zest   25
To children ardent for some desperate glory,
The old Lie: Dulce et decorum est
Pro patria mori.

8 *Five-Nines:* 5.9 caliber artillery shells that made a hooting sound just before landing.
Gas: In January 1917, Owen was subjected to a German gas attack while leading a scouting
mission in France.   10 *helmets:* Soldiers carried gas masks as a part of normal battle
equipment.   13 *thick green:* The chlorine gas used in gas attacks has a greenish yellow
color.

QUESTIONS

1. What is the scene described in lines 1–8? What expressions does the speaker
    use to indicate his attitude toward the conditions?

2. What does the title of the poem mean? What attitude or conviction does it
    embody?

3. Does the speaker really mean "my friend" in line 25? In what tone of voice
    might this phrase be spoken?

4. What is the tonal relationship between the patriotic fervor of the Latin
    phrase and the images of the poem? How does the tonal contrast create the
    dominant tone of the poem?

The tone of "Dulce et Decorum Est" never once lapses. The poet
intends the description to evoke a response of horror, for he contrasts the
strategic goals of warfare with the speaker's experience with the up-close
terror of death in battle. The speaker's language skillfully emphasizes first
the dreariness and fatigue of warfare (with words like *sludge, trudge, lame,*

and *blind*) and second the agony of violent death from chlorine (embodied in the participles *guttering, choking, drowning, smothering,* and *writhing*). With these details established, the concluding attack against the "glory" of war is difficult to refute, even if warfare is undertaken in preservation of one's country. Although the details about the agonized death may distress or discomfort a sensitive reader, they are not designed to do that alone, but instead are integral to the poem's argument. Ultimately, it is the contrast between the high ideals of the Latin phrase and the realities of death during a gas attack that creates the dominant tone of the poem. The Latin phrase treats war and death in the abstract; the poem brings images of battle and death vividly alive. The resultant tone is that of controlled bitterness and irony.

COMMON GROUNDS OF ASSENT

This is not to say that all those reading the poem will deny that war is ever necessary. The issues of politics and warfare are far too complex for that. But the poem does show another important aspect of tone—namely, the degree to which the poet judges and tries to control the readers' responses through the establishment of a *common ground of assent*. An appeal to a bond of commonly held interests, concerns, and assumptions is essential if a poet is to maintain an effective tone. Owen, for example, does not create arguments against the necessity of a just war. Instead, he bases the poem upon realistic details about the writhing, spastic death suffered by the speaker's comrade, and he appeals to emotions that everyone, pacifist and militarist alike, would feel—horror at the contemplation of violent death. Even assuming a widely divergent audience, in other words, the *tone* of the poem is successful because it is based on commonly acknowledged facts and commonly felt emotions. Knowing a poem like this one, even advocates of a strong military would need to defend their ideas on the grounds of *prevention* of just such needless, ugly deaths. Owen has wisely and carefully considered the responses of his readers, and has controlled speaker, situation, detail, and argument in order to make the poem acceptable for the broadest possible spectrum of opinion.

TONE AND IRONY

Irony is a mode of indirection, a means of establishing an assertion by the emphasis on a discrepancy or opposite (see also pp. 303–5). Thus, Owen uses the title "Dulce et Decorum Est" to emphasize that death in warfare is not fitting and noble, but rather demeaning and horrible. The title ironically reminds us of eloquent holiday speeches at the tombs of unknown soldiers, but as we have seen, it also reminds us of the reality of the agonized death of Owen's soldier. As an aspect of tone, therefore, irony is a powerful way of conveying attitudes, for it draws your attention to at least two ways of seeing the situation being presented, and through such a perspective it enables you not only to understand, but also to feel.

SITUATIONAL IRONY.   Poetry shares with fiction and drama the various kinds of ironies that poets believe may afflict human life. "The Workbox," by Thomas Hardy, illustrates a skillful manipulation of irony.

THOMAS HARDY   (1840–1928)

The Workbox   *1914*

"See, here's the workbox, little wife,
　That I made of polished oak."
He was a joiner,° of village life;   *cabinetmaker*
　She came of borough° folk.

He holds the present up to her   5
　As with a smile she nears
And answers to the profferer,
　"'Twill last all my sewing years!"

"I warrant it will. And longer too.
　'Tis a scantling° that I got   10
Off poor John Wayward's coffin, who
　Died of they knew not what.

"The shingled pattern that seems to cease
　Against your box's rim
Continues right on in the piece   15
　That's underground with him.

"And while I worked it made me think
　Of timber's varied doom:
One inch where people eat and drink,
　The next inch in a tomb.   20

"But why do you look so white, my dear,
　And turn aside your face?
You knew not that good lad, I fear,
　Though he came from your native place?"

"How could I know that good young man,   25
　Though he came from my native town,
When he must have left far earlier than
　I was a woman grown?"

THE WORKBOX.   4,5 *village, borough:* a village was small and rustic; a borough was larger and more sophisticated.   10 *scantling:* a small leftover piece of wood.

"Ah, no. I should have understood!
  It shocked you that I gave
To you one end of a piece of wood
  Whose other is in a grave?"

30

"Don't, dear, despise my intellect,
  Mere accidental things
Of that sort never have effect
  On my imaginings."

35

Yet still her lips were limp and wan,
  Her face still held aside,
As if she had known not only John,
  But known of what he died.

40

QUESTIONS

1. Who does most of the speaking in this poem? What does the tone of the speeches show about the characters of the man and the wife? What does the tone indicate about the poet's attitude toward them?

2. In lines 21–40, what does the dialogue indicate about the wife's knowledge of John and about her possible earlier relationship with him? Why does the wife deny such knowledge? What does the last stanza suggest about her? Why is a mystery preserved about the cause of John's death?

3. In lines 17–20, the man describes the "varied doom" of timber. What sort of irony is suggested by the symbolism of the wood made into the workbox?

4. In what way is the irony described by the man more complex than he realizes?

5. The narrator, or speaker, of the poem speaks only in lines 3–7 and 37–40. How much of the explanation he gives is essential? How much indicates his attitude? How might the poem have been more effectively concluded?

"The Workbox" is a little domestic drama of deception and sadness. The extremely complex details are evidence of **situational irony,** that is, an awareness that human beings do not control themselves but are rather controlled by powerful, overwhelming forces—in this case, both death and earlier feelings and commitments. Beyond this irony evolving out of the domestic scene, Hardy also emphasizes symbolically the direct connection that death has with the living. As a result of the husband's gift made of the same wood with which he has also made a coffin for the dead man, the wife will live all the rest of her days with the constant reminder of this man. Her future will be characterized by regret and also by the apparently endless need to deny her true emotions.

DRAMATIC IRONY.   In addition to situational irony, the deception practiced by the wife reveals that the husband is in a situation of **dramatic irony.** The character understands one set of circumstances while the readers understand, in greater perspective, something completely different. In this poem, the husband does not know that the wife is not being truthful or open about her earlier relationship with the dead man. The tone of "The Workbox" suggests that the husband may be suspicious, however. By his emphasis on the piece of wood, he may be trying to draw her out. But he does not actually *know* the true circumstances, and hence he is unsure of his wife's attitude toward him. Because of this mixture of dramatic and situational irony, Hardy has created a poem of great complexity.

VERBAL IRONY.   Poetry may also contain **verbal irony,** that is, ambiguous language. "she being Brand / -new" by E. E. Cummings (p. 666) is filled with double meaning. Using terms of breaking in a new car, the speaker of the poem is actually describing a sexual encounter, and the entire poem is a virtuoso piece of double entendre. Another example of verbal irony may be seen in Theodore Roethke's "My Papa's Waltz" (p. 669), in which the speaker uses the name of this orderly, stately dance to describe his childhood memory of his father's whirling him around the kitchen in wild, boisterous drunkenness.

SATIRE

Satire, of major importance as an aspect of tone, is designed to expose human follies and vices. In method, a satiric poem may be bitter and vituperative in its attack, but quite often it employs humor and irony, on the grounds that anger turns readers away while a comic tone more easily gains agreement. The speaker of a satiric poem either may attack folly and vice *directly*, or may dramatically *embody* the folly or vice, and thus serve as an illustration of the subject of satire. An example of the first type is the following short poem by Alexander Pope, in which the speaker directly attacks a listener who has claimed identity as a poet, but whom the speaker considers as nothing more than a fool. The speaker cleverly uses insult as the tone of attack.

ALEXANDER POPE   (1688–1744)

Epigram from the French   *1732*

Sir, I admit your general rule
That every poet is a fool:
But you yourself may serve to show it,
That every fool is not a poet.

An example of the second type of satiric poem is the following short epigram by the same poet, in which the speaker is an actual embodiment of the subject of attack.

ALEXANDER POPE (1688–1744)

Epigram. Engraved on the Collar of a Dog which I gave to his Royal Highness 1738 (1737)

I am his Highness' dog at Kew:°   one of the royal palaces, near London
Pray tell me sir, whose dog are you?

Here the speaker is the king's dog at the palace at Kew, and the listener an unknown dog. Pope's satire is directed not against canine habits, however, but against human class pretentiousness. The tone of the first line ridicules derived, not earned, status; the tone of the second line implies an unwillingness to recognize the listener until the question of rank is resolved. Pope, by using the dog as a speaker, reduces such snobbishness to an absurdity. Another satiric poem attacking pretentiousness is "next to of course God" by E. E. Cummings (p. 901), where the speaker voices a set of patriotic platitudes, and in doing so illustrates Cummings's satiric point that such claims are often void of understanding and thought. Satiric tone may thus range widely, sometimes being objective, comic, and distant; sometimes deeply concerned and scornful; and sometimes dramatic, ingenuous, and revelatory. Always, however, the satiric mode confronts and exposes.

POEMS FOR STUDY

ANNE BRADSTREET (1612–1672)

The Author to Her Book 1678

Thou ill-formed offspring of my feeble brain,
Who after birth did'st by my side remain,
Till snatched from thence by friends, less wise than true,
Who thee abroad exposed to public view;
Made thee in rags, halting, to the press to trudge,   5
Where errors were not lessened, all may judge.
At thy return my blushing was not small,
My rambling brat° (in print) should mother call;

THE AUTHOR TO HER BOOK.   8 *brat:* The word here emphasizes the insignificance rather than the unpleasant aspects of a child.

I cast thee by as one unfit for light,
Thy visage was so irksome in my sight;   10
Yet being mine own, at length affection would
Thy blemishes amend, if so I could:
I washed thy face, but more defects I saw,
And rubbing off a spot, still made a flaw.
I stretched thy joints to make thee even feet,°   *regular poetic meter*   15
Yet still thou run'st more hobbling than is meet;
In better dress to trim thee was my mind,
But nought save homespun cloth, in the house I find.
In this array, 'mongst vulgars may'st thou roam;
In critics hands beware thou dost not come;   20
And take thy way where yet thou art not known.
If for thy Father asked, say thou had'st none;
And for thy Mother, she alas is poor,
Which caused her thus to send thee out of door.

QUESTIONS

1. What is the tone of the speaker's references to those friends who "exposed"
    her book to "public view" (that is, circulated it without her consent)? How
    does this tone indicate her ambiguous feelings about them?

2. How does the speaker excuse the fact that she is issuing her book of poetry
    on her own initiative? How does the tone produce humor? How does the
    tone of the concluding metaphor encourage you to smile, or even to laugh?

3. What attitude toward herself does the speaker express? How do you react
    to this attitude? How do you think you are expected by the poet to react?

4. What is the tone of the extended metaphor of the child in lines 11–18?

ANNE FINCH, COUNTESS OF WINCHILSEA   (1661–1720)

To the Nightingale   *1713*

Exert thy voice, sweet harbinger° of spring!   *forerunner, herald*
    This moment is thy time to sing,
    This moment I attend to praise,
And set my numbers to thy lays.°   *ballads*
    Free as thine shall be my song   5
    As thy music, short or long.
Poets, wild as thee, were born,
    Pleasing best when unconfined,
    When to please is least designed,
Soothing but their cares to rest;   10
    Cares do still their thoughts molest,
    And still the unhappy poet's breast,
Like thine, when best he sings, is placed against a thorn.°

TO THE NIGHTINGALE.   13 *thorn:* a reference to the (untrue) legend that nightingales
sing most sweetly only when they are in pain because of thorns.

She begins. Let all be still!
  Muse, thy promise now fulfil!   15
Sweet, oh sweet! still sweeter yet!
Can thy words such accents fit,
Canst thou syllables refine,
Melt a sense that shall retain
Still some spirit of the brain,   20
Till with sounds like these it join?
  'Twill not be! then change thy note,
  Let division° shake thy throat.
Hark! division now she tries,
Yet as far the Muse outflies.   25
  Cease then, prithee, cease thy tune!
  Trifler, wilt thou sing till June?
Till thy business all lies waste,
And the time of building's past?
  Thus we poets that have speech,   30
Unlike what thy forests teach,
  If a fluent vein be shown
  That's transcendent to our own,
Criticize, reform, or preach,
Or censure what we cannot reach.   35

23 *division:* in music, the rapid singing of many notes.

QUESTIONS

1. What is the tone of the speaker's description of the nightingale? Is the tone consistent or mixed? How do you know?

2. For what reasons does the speaker admire the song of the bird? Describe the tone of the speaker's description of the bird's song as noted from lines 14–25. Why does the speaker censure the bird in lines 26–29? What attitude toward the speaker does the poet intend by the tone of these lines?

3. What is the tone of the connection the speaker makes between the song of the nightingale and the works of poets? What ideas does the speaker derive from this connection about the future of poetic creativity?

4. In lines 11–13 what is the tone of the speaker's metaphor of the thorn? How does the tone reveal the speaker's attitude toward herself?

5. What is the purpose of lines 30–35? What does the tone of these lines show about the speaker's attitude toward herself?

ARTHUR O'SHAUGHNESSY   (1844–1881)

A Love Symphony   *1881*

Along the garden° ways just now   *a green area*
  I heard the flowers speak;
The white rose told me of your brow,
  The red rose of your cheek;

The lily of your bended head,   5
   The bindweed of your hair;
Each looked its loveliest and said
   You were more fair.

I went into the wood anon,°   *later, soon after*
   And heard the wild birds sing   10
How sweet you were; they warbled on,
   Piped, trilled the self-same thing,
Thrush, blackbird, linnet, without pause
   The burden did repeat,
And still began again because   15
   You were more sweet.

And then I went down to the sea,
   And heard it murmuring too,
Part of an ancient mystery,
   All made of me and you.   20
How many a thousand years ago
   I loved, and you were sweet—
Longer I could not stay, and so
   I fled back to your feet.

QUESTIONS

1. What is the "symphony" of love? What is the tone of the speaker's descriptions of the symphony as coming from flowers, birds, and the sea?

2. What is the tone of the phrase "ancient mystery / All made of me and you" (lines 19–20)? Compare this use of the idea of religious mysteriousness and love with the use in John Donne's "The Canonization" (p. 849) and Anne Finch's "To Mr. Finch, Now Earl of Winchelsea" (p. 775). What common attitudes about love do these three poems contain? What differences?

3. What tone is expressed about the loved one in lines 23–24? In the light of his tone in describing her qualities, what sort of relationship is he celebrating?

e. e. cummings   (1894–1962)

she being Brand / -new   1926

she being Brand

-new;and you
know consequently a
little stiff i was
careful of her and(having   5

thoroughly oiled the universal
joint tested my gas felt of

her radiator made sure her springs were O.
K.)i went right to it flooded-the-carburetor cranked her

up,slipped the   10
clutch(and then somehow got into reverse she
kicked what
the hell)next
minute i was back in neutral tried and

again slo-wly;bare,ly nudg. ing(my   15

lev-er Right-
oh and her gears being in

A 1 shape passed
from low through
second-in-to-high like   20
greasedlightning) just as we turned the corner of Divinity

avenue i touched the accelerator and give

her the juice,good

        (it
was the first ride and believe i we was   25
happy to see how nice she acted right up to
the last minute coming back down by the Public
Gardens i slammed on
the

internalexpanding   30
&
externalcontracting
brakes Bothatonce and

brought allofher tremB
-ling   35
to a:dead.

stand-
;Still)

QUESTIONS

1. How extensive is the verbal irony, the double entendre, in this poem? This
   poem is considered comic. Do you agree? Why or why not?

2. How do the spacing and alignment affect your reading of the poem? How
   does the unexpected and sometimes absent punctuation—such as in line 15,
   "again slo-wly;bare,ly nudg. ing(my"—contribute to the humor?

3. Can this poem in any respect be called off-color or bawdy? How might you
   refute such charges in light of the tone the speaker uses to equate a first
   sexual experience with the breaking in of a new car?

LANGSTON HUGHES   (1902–1967)

Theme for English B   *1959*

The instructor said,

    Go home and write
    a page tonight.
    And let that page come out of you—
    Then, it will be true.   5

I wonder if it's that simple?

I am twenty-two, colored, born in Winston-Salem.
I went to school there, then Durham, then here
to this college on the hill above Harlem.°
I am the only colored student in my class.   10
The steps from the hill lead down to Harlem,
through a park, then I cross St. Nicholas,
Eighth Avenue, Seventh, and I come to the Y,
the Harlem Branch Y, where I take the elevator
up to my room, sit down, and write this page: 15

It's not easy to know what is true for you or me
at twenty-two, my age. But I guess I'm what
I feel and see and hear. Harlem, I hear you:
hear you, hear me—we two—you, me talk on this page.
(I hear New York, too.) Me—who?   20

Well, I like to eat, sleep, drink, and be in love.
I like to work, read, learn, and understand life.
I like a pipe for a Christmas present,
or records—Bessie,° bop,° or Bach.°

I guess being colored doesn't make me not like   25
the same things other folks like who are other races.
So will my page be colored that I write?
Being me, it will not be white.
But it will be
a part of you, instructor.   30
You are white—
yet a part of me, as I am a part of you.
That's American.

Sometimes perhaps you don't want to be a part of me.
Nor do I often want to be a part of you.   35

THEME FOR ENGLISH B.   9 *college . . . Harlem:* a reference to Columbia University in
the Columbia Heights section of New York City. The other streets and buildings mentioned
in lines 11–14 refer to specific places in the same vicinity.   24 *Bessie:* Bessie Smith (ca.
1898–1937), American jazz singer, famed as the "Empress of the Blues."   *bop:* a type of
popular music which was in vogue in the 1940s through the 1960s.   *Bach:* Johann Sebastian
Bach (1685–1750), German composer, considered the master of the baroque style of music.

But we are, that's true!
As I learn from you,
I guess you learn from me—
although you're older—and white—
and somewhat more free.   40

This is my page for English B.

QUESTIONS

1. What is the tone of the speaker's self-assessment? What does the tone indicate about his feelings toward the situation in the class and at the Y?

2. What tone is implicit in the fact that the speaker, in response to a theme assignment, has composed a poem rather than a prose essay?

3. What is the tone of lines 21–24, where the speaker indicates his likes? In what way may the characteristics brought out in these lines serve as an argument for social and political equality?

4. How does the tone in lines 27–40, particularly lines 34–36, prevent the statements of the speaker from becoming overly assertive or strident?

THEODORE ROETHKE (1907–1963)

My Papa's Waltz   *1942*

The whiskey on your breath
Could make a small boy dizzy;
But I hung on like death:
Such waltzing was not easy.

We romped until the pans   5
Slid from the kitchen shelf;
My mother's countenance
Could not unfrown itself.

The hand that held my wrist
Was battered on one knuckle;   10
At every step you missed
My right ear scraped a buckle.

You beat time on my head
With a palm caked hard by dirt,
Then waltzed me off to bed   15
Still clinging to your shirt.

QUESTIONS

1. What is the tone of the speaker's opening description of his father? What is the tone of the phrases "like death" and "such waltzing"?

2. What is the "waltz" the speaker describes? What is the tone of his words describing it in lines 5–15?

3. What does the reference to his "mother's countenance" contribute to the tone? What situation is suggested by the selection of the word "unfrown"?

4. What does the tone of the physical descriptions of the father contribute to your understanding of the speaker's attitude toward his childhood experiences as his father's dancing partner?

LUCILLE CLIFTON   (b. 1936)

homage to my hips   *1987*

these hips are big hips
they need space to
move around in.
they don't fit into little
petty places. these hips   5
are free hips.
they don't like to be held back.
these hips have never been enslaved.
they go where they want to go.
they do what they want to do.   10
these hips are mighty hips.
these hips are magic hips.
i have known them
to put a spell on a man and
spin him like a top!   15

QUESTIONS

1. What is unusual about the subject matter? Because people sometimes feel embarrassment about their hips, what attitudes does the speaker express here?

2. How do the words "enslaved," "want to go," "want to do," "mighty," and "spell" define the poem's ideas about the relationship between mentality and physicality?

3. What about the subject and the diction of this poem makes it funny?

X. J. KENNEDY   (b. 1929)

John while swimming in the ocean   *1986*

John while swimming in the ocean
Rubbed sharks' backs with suntan lotion.
Now those sharks have skin of bronze
In their bellies—namely, John's.

QUESTIONS

1. What is the "action" of the poem? Why is it ludicrous?
2. What do the rhymes contribute to the poem's comic tone?
3. In light of the tone, what attitude is expressed about beach and ocean culture?

APHRA BEHN   (1640–1689)

Love Armed   *1665*

Love in Fantastic Triumph sat,
Whilst Bleeding Hearts around him flowed,
For whom Fresh pains he did Create,
And strange Tyrannic power he showed;
From thy Bright Eyes he took his fire,   5
Which round about, in sport he hurled;
But 'twas from mine he took desire,
Enough to undo the Amorous World

From me he took his sighs and tears,
From thee his Pride and Cruelty;   10
From me his Languishments and Fears,
And every Killing Dart from thee;
Thus thou and I, the God° have armed.   *Cupid, god of love*
And set him up a Deity;
But my poor Heart alone is harmed,   15
Whilst thine the Victor is, and free.

QUESTIONS

1. What do the speaker and the beloved each supply to their love? Who suffers more?
2. What attitude does the poem express about love?

WRITING ABOUT TONE IN POETRY

In preparing to write about tone, you will, as always, need to begin with a careful reading. As you study, it is important to note those elements of the work that touch particularly on attitudes or authorial consideration. Thus, for example, you may be studying Hughes's "Theme For English B," where it is necessary to consider the force of the poet's claim for equality. How serious is the claim? Does the speaker's apparent matter-of-factness make him seem less than enthusiastic? Or does this tone indicate that equality is so fundamental a right that its realization should be an everyday part of life? Depending on the work, your devising and answering such questions can help you understand the degree to which authors show control of tone.

Similar questions apply when you study internal qualities such as style and characterization.

Questions for Discovering Ideas

Do all the speeches seem right for the speaker and situation? Are all descriptions appropriate, all actions believable?

If the work is comic, does the writer seem to be laughing too?

In serious situations, is there evidence of understanding and sympathy? Does the writer ask you to lament the human condition?

What kind of character is the speaker? Is he or she intelligent? Friendly? Idealistic? Realistic?

Do any words seem unusual or especially noteworthy, such as dialect, polysyllabic words, foreign words or phrases that the author assumes you know, or especially connotative or emotive words?

Strategies for Organizing Ideas

In the essay, you should examine all aspects bearing on the tone. Some of the things to cover might be these:

1. *The audience, situation, and characters.* Is any person or group directly addressed by the speaker? What attitude is expressed (love, respect, condescension, confidentiality, confidence, etc.)? What is the basic situation in the work? Do you find irony? If so, what kind is it? What does the irony show (optimism or pessimism, for example)? How is the situation controlled to shape your responses? That is, can actions, situations, or characters be seen as expressions of attitude or as embodiments of certain favorable or unfavorable ideas or positions? What is the nature of the speaker or persona? Why does the speaker seem to speak exactly as he or she does? How is the speaker's character manipulated to show apparent authorial attitude and to elicit reader response? Does the work promote respect, admiration, dislike, or other feelings about character or situation? How?

2. *Descriptions, diction.* Your concern here is to relate style to attitude. Are there any systematic references, such as to colors, sounds, noises, natural scenes, and so on, that collectively reflect an attitude? Do connotative meanings of words control response in any way? Is any special knowledge of references or unusual words expected of readers? What is the extent of this knowledge? Do speech or dialect patterns indicate attitudes about speakers or their condition of life? Are speech patterns normal and standard, or slang or substandard? What is the effect of these patterns? Are there unusual or particularly noteworthy expressions? If so, what attitudes do these show? Does the author use verbal irony? To what effect?

3. *Humor.* Is the work funny? How funny, how intense? How is the

humor achieved? Does the humor develop out of incongruous situations or language, or both? Is there an underlying basis of attack in the humor, or are the objects of laughter still respected or even loved despite having humor directed against them?

4. *Ideas.* Ideas may be advocated, defended mildly, or attacked. Which do you have in the work you have been studying? How does the author make his or her attitude clear—directly, by statement, or indirectly, through understatement, overstatement, or the language of a character? In what ways does the work assume a common ground of assent between author and reader? That is, are there apparently common assumptions about religious views, political ideas, moral and behavioral standards, and so on? Are these commonly assumed ideas readily acceptable, or is any concession needed by the reader to approach the work? (For example, a major subject of "Dover Beach" is that absolute belief in the truth of Christianity has been lost. This subject may not be important to everyone, but even an irreligious reader, or a follower of another faith, may find common ground in the poem's psychological situation, or in the desire to learn as much as possible about so important a phenomenon of modern Western society.)

5. *Unique characteristics.* Each work has unique properties that contribute to the tone. Anne Bradstreet, for example, in "The Author to Her Book," introduces the metaphor of her work as an unwanted child that she is sending out into the world. Her apology hence introduces a tone of amused but sincere self-effacement that the reader must consider. Theodore Roethke's "My Papa's Waltz" is a brief narrative in which the speaker's feelings about memories of his childhood participation in his father's boisterously drunken behavior must be inferred from understatement like "waltz." Hardy's "Channel Firing" develops from the comic idea that the firing of guns at sea is so loud it could awaken the dead. Be alert for such special circumstances in the poem you are studying, and as you plan and develop your essay, take these things into account.

The conclusion may summarize your main points, and go on to any needed redefinitions, explanations, or afterthoughts, together with ideas reinforcing earlier points. If you have changed your mind, or have discovered new ideas, a brief account of these would also be appropriate. Finally, you might mention some other major aspect of the work's tone that you did not develop in the body.

SAMPLE ESSAY

The Tone of Confidence in "Theme for English B" by Langston Hughes°

"Theme for English B" grows from the situational irony of racial differences. The situation is unequal opportunity, seen from the perspective of a college student from the oppressed race. This situation might easily produce

° For this poem, see p. 668.

[1] bitterness, anger, outrage, or vengefulness. However, the poem contains none of these. It is not angry or indignant; it is not an appeal for revenge or revolution. It is rather a declaration of personal independence and individuality. The tone is one of objectivity, daring, occasional playfulness, but above all, confidence.* These attitudes are made plain in the speaker's situation, the ideas, the poetic form, the diction, and the expressions.†

[2] Hughes's treatment of the situation is objective, factual, and personal, not emotional or political. The poem contains a number of factual details presented clearly, like these: The speaker is black in an otherwise all-white College English class. He has come from North Carolina, and is now living alone at the Harlem YMCA, away from family and roots. He is also, at 22, an older student. The class is for freshman (English B), yet he is the age of many seniors. All this is evidence of disadvantage, yet the speaker does no more than present the facts objectively, without comment. He is in control, presenting the details straightforwardly, in a tone of total objectivity.

[3] Hughes's thoughts about equality--the idea underlying the poem--are presented in the same objective, cool manner. The speaker writes to his instructor as an equal, not as an inferior. In describing himself he does not deal in abstractions, but rather in reality. Thus he defines himself in language descriptive of everyday abilities, needs, activities, and likes. He is cool and direct here, for his presentation takes the form of a set of inclusive principles emphasizing the sameness and identity of everyone regardless of race or background. The idea is that everyone should put away prejudices and begin to treat people as people, not as representatives of any race. By causing the speaker to avoid emotionalism and controversy, Hughes makes counterarguments difficult if not impossible. He is so much in control that the facts themselves carry his argument for equality.

[4] The selection of a poetic form demonstrates bravery and confidence. The title here is the key, for it does not promise the most exciting of topics. Normally, in fact, one would expect nothing much more than a short prose theme in response to an English assignment, so a poem is unexpected and therefore daring and original, particularly one like this that touches on the topic of equality and identity. The wit, ability, and skill of the speaker's use of the form demonstrate the self-confidence and self-sufficiency that embody the theoretical basis for equality.

[5] Hughes's diction is in keeping with the tone of confidence and daring. The words are simple, showing the speaker's confidence in the truth and power of his ideas. Almost all the words are short, of no more than one or two syllables. This high proportion of short words reflects a conscious attempt to keep the diction clear and direct. A result is that Hughes avoids ambiguity, as the following section of the poem shows:

> Well, I like to eat, sleep, drink, and be in love.
> I like to work, read, learn, and understand life.
> I like a pipe for a Christmas present,
> or records--Bessie, bop, or Bach. (lines 21-24)

* Central idea.
† Thesis sentence.

With the exception of what it means to "understand life," these words are descriptive, and are free of emotional overtones. They reflect the speaker's confidence in his belief that equality should replace inequality and prejudice.

[6]
A number of the speaker's phrases and expressions also show this same confidence. Although most of the material is expressed straightforwardly, one can perceive playfulness and irony. In lines 18-20 there seems to be a deliberate use of confusing language to bring about a verbal merging of the identities of the speaker, the instructor, Harlem, and the greater New York area:

> Harlem, I hear you:
> hear you, hear me--we two--you, me talk on this page.
> (I hear New York, too.) Me--who? (lines 18-20)

The speaker's confidence is so strong that he writes an expression that seems almost childish. This expression is in the second line of the following excerpt:

> I guess being colored doesn't make me not like
> the same things other folks like who are other races. (lines 25-26)

There is also whimsicality in the way in which the speaker treats the irony of the black-white situation: "So will my page be colored that I write?" (line 27).

Underlying this last expression is an awareness that, despite the claim that people are equal and are tied to each other by common humanity, there are also strong differences among individuals. The speaker is confidently asserting grounds for independence as well as equality.

[7]
Thus, an examination of "Theme for English B" reveals vitality and confidence. The poem is a statement of trust and an almost open challenge on the personal level to the unachieved ideal of equality. Hughes is saying that since it is American to have such ideals, there is nothing to do but to live up to them. He makes this point through the deliberate simplicity of the speaker's words and descriptions. Yet the poem is not without irony, particularly at the end, where the speaker mentions that the instructor is "somewhat more free" than he is. "Theme for English B" is complex and engaging. It shows the speaker's confidence through objectivity, daring, and playfulness.

Commentary on the Essay

Because this essay embodies a number of approaches by which tone may be studied in any work (situation, common ground, diction, special characteristics), it is typical of many essays that use a combined, eclectic approach. The central idea is that the dominant attitude in "Theme for English B" is the speaker's confidence, and that this confidence is shown in the similar but separable attitudes of objectivity, daring, and playfulness. The purpose of the essay is to discuss how Hughes makes plain these and other related attitudes in five separate aspects of the poem.

Paragraph 2 deals with situational irony in relation to the social and political circumstance of racial discrimination (see approach 1). Paragraph 3 considers the objectivity with which Hughes considers the idea of equality (approach 4).

The fourth paragraph is particularly instructive, for it shows how a topic that might ordinarily be taken for granted, such as the basic form of expression, can be seen as a unique feature of tone (approach 5). The paragraph contrasts the expected student response (no more than a brief prose essay) with the actual response (the poem itself, with its interesting twists and turns).

Paragraphs 5 and 6 consider how Hughes's word choices exhibit his attempts at clarity, objectivity, playfulness, and confidence (approach 2). The attention given in these paragraphs to Hughes's monosyllabic words is justified by their importance in the poem's tone.

The concluding paragraph stresses again the attitude of confidence in the poem, and also notes additional attitudes of trust, challenge, ingenuousness, irony, daring, and playfulness.

WRITING TOPICS

1. Consider "A Love Symphony," "she being Brand / -new," "The Workbox," and "The First-Rate Wife" as poems about love. What similarities do you find among the poems? That is, do the poets state that love creates joy, satisfaction, distress, embarrassment, trouble? How does the tone of each of the poems enable you to draw your conclusions? What differences do you find in the ways the poets either control or do not control tone?

2. Consider the tone of "My Papa's Waltz." Some readers have concluded that the speaker is expressing fond memories of his childhood experiences with his father. Others believe that the speaker is ambiguous about the father, and that he therefore blocks out remembered pain as he also describes boisterousness in the kitchen. On the basis of the poem's tone, what are your conclusions about the way in which the poem should be interpreted?

3. Write a poem about something that has made you either glad or angry. Try to create the same feelings in your reader, but create them through your rendering of situation and your choices of the right words. (Possible topics: a social injustice, an unfair grade, a compliment you have received on a task well done, the landing of a good job, the winning of a game, a good book or movie, and so on.)

4. What judgments about modern city life do you think that Leger conveys in his painting *The City* (p. 655)? If the tone of paintings may be considered as being similar to the tone of poetry, in what ways is *The City* then comparable to the presentation of detail in Blake's "London" (p. 553), Eliot's "Preludes" (p. 615), Swift's "A Description of the Morning" (p. 692) and Sandburg's "Chicago" (p. 955)—together with any other poems you wish to include in the comparison?

18

Prosody: Sound, Rhythm, and Rhyme in Poetry

Prosody refers to the study of sounds and rhythms in poetry. Poets, being especially attuned to language, select words not just for content but also for sound, and they arrange words so that important ideas and climaxes of sound coincide. Sensitive readers, when reading poetry aloud, interpret the lines and develop an appropriate speed and expressiveness of delivery—a proper rhythm. Indeed, some people think of rhythm and sound as the *music* of poetry, since it refers to measured sounds much like rhythms and tempos in music. Like music, poetry requires some regularity of beat, but the tempo and loudness may be freer and less regular, and also a reader may linger over certain sounds and words, depending on their position in a line. Prosody is the word most often used in reference to sound and rhythm, but other descriptive words are **metrics, versification,** and **mechanics of verse.**

It is important to realize that *prosody can never be separated from the content of a poem.* It is significant only as it supports and underscores content. Alexander Pope wrote that "the sound must seem an echo to the sense." In short, words count—not only for their meanings, but also for their sounds and their contributions to a poem's rhythmical flow. Thus, the study of prosody is an attempt to determine how poets arrange the sounds of their poems to make sound complement content.

WHAT TO CONSIDER IN STUDYING PROSODY

To consider prosody you need a few basic linguistic facts. Words are made up of individually meaningful sounds (*segmental phonemes*), which we call simply **segments.** Thus, in the word *top* there are three segments: *t, o,* and *p.* When you hear these three sounds in order, you recognize the sounds as the word *top.* It takes three alphabetical letters—*t, o,* and *p*—to spell (**graph**) *top*, because each letter is identical with a segment. Sometimes it takes more than one letter to spell a segment. In the word *enough*, for example, there are four segments (*e, n, ŭ, f*) *but six letters: e, n, ou*, and *gh*. The last two segments (*ŭ* and *f*) require two letters each (two letters forming one segment are called a **digraph**). In the word *through* there are three segments but *seven* letters. To be correctly spelled in this word, the $\overline{oo}$ segment must have four letters (*ough*). Note, however, that in the word *flute* the $\overline{oo}$ segment requires only one letter, *u*.

Individual sounds in combination make up words, and separate words in combination make up lines of poetry. When we study the combined flow of words, we are concerned with **rhythm,** and when we study the effects of various segments in relationship to the rhythms and the content, we are concerned with **sound,** more specifically **alliteration, assonance,** and **rhyme.**

DISTINGUISHING SOUNDS FROM SPELLING

It is important—vital—to distinguish between spelling, or **graphics,** and pronunciation, or **phonetics.** Not all English sounds are spelled and pronounced in the same way, as with *top*. Thus, the letter *s* has three very different sounds in the words, *sweet, sugar,* and *flows: s, sh* (as in *sharp*) and *z*. On the other hand, the words *shape, ocean, nation, sure,* and *machine* use different letters or combinations of letters (as digraphs) to spell the same *sh* sound.

Vowel sounds may also be spelled in different ways. The *e* sound, for example, can be spelled *i* in *machine, ee* in *speed, ea* in *eat, e* in *even,* and *y* in *funny,* yet the vowel sounds in *eat, break,* and *bear* are not the same even though they are spelled the same. Remember this: With both consonants and vowel sounds, *do not confuse spellings with sounds.*

POETRY AND PROSE: RHYTHM

Rhythm in speech is a combination of vocal speeds, rises and falls, starts and stops, vigor and slackness, and relaxation and tension. Every spoken utterance is rhythmical, but in ordinary speech and in the reading of prose, rhythm is usually less important than the flow of ideas. Rhythm is more significant in poetry, because poetry is so emotionally charged, compact, and intense. This is not to say that writers of prose ignore sound and rhythm, but rather that poets habitually devote great attention and skill to these qualities of language. Poets invite readers to stop at words, to linger over sounds, to slow down at times and to speed up at others. As language becomes more dramatic and intense, it also becomes more rhythmical. When you read poetry, therefore, you give great attention to individual words; your units of expression are shorter than in prose; your voice goes through a wider range of pitch; and you rely on greater ranges of dramatic intensity.

The unit of rhythm in poetry and prose is the **syllable,** which consists of a single strand of sound such as *a* in "a table," *fine* in "fine linen," *sleds* in "new sleds," and *flounce* in "the little girls flounce into the room." (While "a" is a syllable of only one segment, "flounce" consists of six segments: *f*, *l*, *ow*, *n*, *t*, and *s*). The rhythm of English poetry in the **closed form** (see also pp. 723–34) is determined by the measured relationship of heavily stressed to less heavily stressed syllables. In pronouncing words, you give some syllables more force and intensity than others (note the comparative intensities of the syllables as you say "the bucket," for example, or "the old oaken bucket"). For our purposes, the more intense syllables are given **heavy stress;** the relatively less intense syllables are given **light stress.** In closed-form verse, poets regularize the syllables into patterns called **feet,** which normally consist of one heavily stressed syllable and one or more lightly stressed syllables.

There are various types of feet, each with a definite pattern. Poets of traditional or closed forms usually fill their lines with a specific number of the same feet, and that number determines the **meter,** or measure of that line. Thus, five feet in a line are **pentameter,** four are **tetrameter,** three are **trimeter,** and two are **dimeter.** (To these may be added the less common line lengths **hexameter,** a six-foot line, **heptameter** or **the septenary,** seven feet, and **octameter,** eight feet.) In terms of **accent** or **beat,** a trimeter line has three beats (or heavy stresses), a pentameter line five beats, and so on.

Frequently, rhetorical needs cause poets to **substitute** other feet for the regular foot established in the poem. Whether there is **substitution** or not, however, the number and kind of feet in each line constitute the metrical description of that line. To discover the prevailing metrical system in any poem, you **scan** the poem. The act of scanning is called **scansion.**

A Notational System to Indicate Rhythms

In scansion, it is important to use an agreed-upon notational system to record stress or accent. A heavy or primary accent is commonly indicated by a prime mark or **acute accent** (´). A light accent may be indicated by a bowl-like half circle called a **breve** (˘), or by a raised circle or degree sign (°). To separate one foot from another, a **virgule** (/) or slash is used. Thus, the following line, from Coleridge's "The Rime of the Ancient Mariner," may be schematized formally in this way:

Wá - tĕr, / wá - tĕr, / év - ĕry whére,

Here the virgules show that the line may be divided into two two-syllable feet and one three-syllable foot.

METRICAL FEET

Equipped with this knowledge, you are ready to scan poems and determine the rhythmical patterns of feet. The most important ones, the specific names of which are derived from Greek poetry, may be generally classed as the two-syllable foot, the three-syllable foot, and the imperfect (or one-syllable) foot.

The Two-Syllable Foot

1. IAMB.   This is a light stress followed by a heavy stress:

the winds

The iamb is the most common foot in English poetry because it most nearly reflects natural speech while also elevating speech to poetry. It is the most versatile of poetic feet, capable of great variation. Even within the same line, iambic feet may vary in intensity, so that they may support or undergrid the shades of meaning designed by the poet. For example, in this line from Wordsworth, each foot is unique:

The winds / that will / be howl- / ing at / all hours.

Even though *will* and *at* are stressed syllables, they are not as heavily stressed as *winds, howl-,* and *hours* (indeed, they are also less strong than *all,* which is in an unstressed position in the concluding iamb). Such variability, approximating the stresses and rhythms of actual speech, makes the iamb suitable for both serious or light verse, and it therefore helps poets focus attention on ideas and emotions. If used with skill, it never becomes monotonous, for it does not distract readers by drawing attention to its own rhythm.

2. TROCHEE.   This is a heavy accent followed by a light:

flow - er

Rhythmically, most English words are trochaic

(examples: *water, snowfall, author, willow, morning,*

early, follow, singing, presence, something)

unless they have prefixes

(e.g., *sublime, because, impel)*

or are borrowed from another language and are still pronounced as in that language

(e.g., *machine, technique, garage, chemise).*

Because trochaic rhythm has often been called *falling, dyning, light,* or *anticlimactic,* whereas iambic rhythm is *rising, elevating, serious,* and *climactic,* poets have preferred the iambic foot. They therefore have arranged various placements of two-syllable words, using single syllable words and a variety of other means, so that the stressed syllable is at the end of the foot, as in Shakespeare's

hĭs bénd - / ĭng sĭ́ck - /lĕ's cŏm - / pắss cŏ́mel,

in which three successive trochaic words are arranged to match the iambic meter.

3. Spondee.   The **spondee**—also called a **hovering accent**—consists of two successive, equally heavy accents, as in *men's eyes* in Shakespeare's line:

Whĕn, ĭn / dĭs -gráce / wĭth fŏr - / tŭne ănd / mén's éyes.

The spondee is mainly a substitute foot in English verse because successive spondees invariably develop as iambs or trochees. For this reason it is virtually impossible within traditional metrical patterns for an entire poem to be written in spondees (but see Gwendolyn Brooks's poem "We Real Cool," p. 701). As a substitute, however, the spondee creates emphasis. The usual way to indicate the spondaic foot is to link the two syllables together with chevronlike marks ($\wedge$).

4. Pyrrhic.   The **pyrrhic** consists of two unstressed syllables (even though one of them may be in a normally stressed position), as in *on their* in Pope's line:

Nŏw sléep - /ĭng flŏcks / ŏn thĕir / sŏft fléec - / ĕs líe.

The pyrrhic is made up of weakly accented words such as prepositions (e.g., *on, to*) and articles (*the, a*). Like the spondee, it is usually substituted for an iamb or trochee, and therefore a complete poem cannot be in pyrrhics. As a substitute foot, however, the pyrrhic acts as a kind of rhythmic catapult to move the reader swiftly to the next strongly accented syllable, and therefore it undergirds the ideas conveyed by more important words.

The Three-Syllable Foot

1. Anapaest.   This consists of two light stresses followed by a heavy:

bў thĕ dáwn's / eăr - lў líght. (Key)

2. Dactyl.   This is a heavy stress followed by two lights:

gréen as our / hópe in it, / whíte as our / faíth in it. (Swinburne)

The Imperfect Foot

The imperfect foot consists of a single syllable, (´). by itself, or (˘) by itself. This foot is a variant or substitute occurring in a poem in which one of the major feet forms the metrical pattern. The second line of "The Star-Spangled Banner," for example, is anapaestic, but it contains an imperfect foot at the end:

What so proud -/ly we hailed/at the twi-/light's last gleam-/ing.

Uncommon Meters

In many poems you might encounter variants other than those just described. Poets like Browning, Tennyson, Poe, and Swinburne experimented with uncommon meters. Other poets manipulated pauses or **caesurae** (discussed later) to create the effects of uncommon meters. For these reasons, you might need to refer to metrical feet such as the following:

1. Amphibrach.   A light, heavy, and light:

Ah feed me / and fill me / with pleas - sure (Swinburne).

2. Amphimacer or Cretic.   A heavy, light, and heavy:

Love is best (Browning).

3. Bacchius or Bacchic.   A light stress followed by two heavy stresses:

Some late lark / [sing - ing] (Henley).

4. Dipodic or Syzygy.   Dipodic measure (literally, "two feet" combining to make one) develops in longer lines when a poet submerges two regular feet under a stronger beat, so that a "galloping" or "rollicking" rhythm results. The following line from Masefield's "Cargoes," for example, may be scanned as trochaic hexameter, with the concluding foot being an iamb:

Quin-que / reme of / Nin-e- /veh from / dis-tant / O-phir.

In reading, however, a stronger beat is superimposed, which makes one foot out of two—dipodic measure or syzygy:

Quinquereme of / Nineveh from / distant Ophir

OTHER RHYTHMIC DEVICES

Accentual, Strong-Stress, and "Sprung" Rhythms

Accentual or strong-stress lines are historically derived from the poetry of Old English (see pp. 521–22). At that time, each line was divided in two, with two major stresses occurring in each half. In the nineteenth century, Gerard Manley Hopkins (1844–1889) developed what he called "sprung" rhythm, a rhythm in which the major stresses would be released or "sprung" from the line. The method is complex, but one characteristic is the juxtaposing of one-syllable stressed words, as in this line from "Pied Beauty":

With swi̊ft, slo̊w; swe̊et, so̊ur; ådåzzle, di̊m;

Here a number of elements combine to create six major stresses in the line, which contains only nine syllables. Many of Hopkins's lines combine alliteration and strong stresses in this way to create the same effect of heavy emphasis.

A parallel instance of strongly stressed lines may be seen in "We Real Cool" by Gwendolyn Brooks (p. 701). In this poem the effect is achieved by the exclusive use of monosyllabic stressed words combined with internal rhyme, repetition, and alliteration.

The Caesura, or Pause

Whenever we speak, we utter a number of syllables without pause of any sort, and stop only after a definite group of meaningful words is finished. These groups of words, rhythmically, are **cadence groups.** In poetry, the short or heavy pause separating cadence groups is called a **caesura** (plural **caesurae**). For scansion, the caesura may be noted by two diagonal lines or virgules (//) to distinguish it from the single virgule separating feet. Sometimes the caesura coincides with the end of a foot, as in this line by William Blake ("To Mrs. Anna Flaxman"):

Wi̊th hands / di̊ - vi̊ne // he̊ mov'd / the̊ ge̊n - / tle̊ So̊d./

The caesura, however, may fall within a foot, and there may be more than one in a line, as in this line by Ben Jonson:

Thoů art / no̊t, //Pe̊ns - / hurst, // bui̊lt / to̊ e̊n - / vi̊ous show./

When a caesura ends a line, usually marked by a comma, semicolon, or period, that line is **end-stopped,** as in this line which opens Keats's "Endymion" (1818):

Å thi̊ng / of beau - / tẙ // is̊ / å jo̊y / for - ev̊ -er. //

If a line has no punctuation at the end and runs over to the next line, it is called **run-on.** A term also used to indicate run-on lines is **enjambement.** The following passage, a continuation of the line from Keats, contains three run-on lines:

> Its loveliness increases; // it will never
> Pass into nothingness; // but still will keep
> A bower quiet for us, // and a sleep
> Full of sweet dreams, // . . .

Emphasis by Formal Substitution

Most closed-form poems follow a regular pattern that may be formally analyzed according to the regular feet we have been describing here. For interest and emphasis, however (and also perhaps because of the natural rhythms of English speech), poets may **substitute** other feet for the regular feet of the poem. For example, the following line is from the "January" Eclogue of Edmund Spenser's *Shepherd's Calendar.* Although the pattern of the poem is iambic pentameter (i.e., five iambs per line), Spenser includes two substitute feet in the line:

$$\text{Áll ĭn / ă sún - / shine day, / ăs díd / bĕ - fáll./}$$

In the first foot, *Áll ĭn* is a trochee, and *shine day* is a spondee. These are *formal substitutions*; that is, Spenser uses separate, formally structured feet in place of the normal iambic feet. The effect is to move from "All" to "sunshine day" in a rapid, climactic sweep, in keeping with the idea that a springlike day in winter is an indescribable pleasure.

Emphasis by Rhetorical Substitution

The effects provided by formal substitution may also be achieved by the manipulation of the caesura. If the pauses are arranged within feet, they may create the actual *hearing* of trochees, amphibrachs, and other variant feet even though the line may scan regularly in the dominant meter. This variation is **rhetorical substitution.** A noteworthy example in an iambic pentameter line is this one from Pope's *Essay on Man:*

$$\text{Hĭs ác-/tĭons',//pás-/sĭons,//bĕ-/ing's,//úse/ănd énd.}$$

Ordinarily there is one caesura in a line of this type (after the fourth syllable), but in this one Pope has made three, each producing a strong pause. The line is regularly iambic, but in reading, the effect is different. Because of the caesurae after the third, fifth, and seventh syllables, the rhythm produces an amphibrach, a trochee, another trochee, and an amphimacer, thus:

His ac-tions',//pas-sions',//be-ing's,//use and end.
AMPHIBRACH   TROCHEE   TROCHEE   AMPHIMACER

Thus, the spoken substitutions produced by the caesurae in this regular line produce the effect of substitution and therefore tension and interest.

When studying rhythm, your main concern in noting substitutions is to determine the formal metrical pattern, and then to analyze the formal and rhetorical variations on this pattern and their principal techniques and effects. Always try to show how these variations have enabled the poet to get points across and to achieve emphasis.

SEGMENTAL POETIC DEVICES

Once you have completed your analysis of rhythms, you may go on to consider the segmental poetic devices in the poem. Usually these devices are used to create emphasis, but sometimes in context they may echo or imitate some of the things being described. The segmental devices most common in poetry are *assonance, alliteration, onomatopoeia,* and *euphony and cacophony.*

Assonance

The repetition of identical **vowel** sounds in different words—for example, the short *i* in "swift Camilla skims"—is called **assonance.** It is a strong means of emphasis, as in the following line, where the *ŭ* sound connects the two words *lull* and *slumber,* and the short *i* connects *him, in,* and *his:*

And more, to lull him in his slumber soft.

In some cases, poets may use assonance elaborately, as in the first line of Pope's *An Essay on Criticism:*

'Tis hard to say, if greater want of skill.

Here the line is formed and balanced with the short *i* in *'Tis, if,* and *skill.* The *ä* in *hard* and *want* forms another, internal frame, and *ā* in *say* and *greater* creates still another frame. Such a balanced use of vowels is unusual, however, for in most lines assonance occurs primarily as a means of highlighting important words, without such elaborate patterning.

Alliteration

Like assonance, **alliteration** is a means of highlighting ideas by the selection of words containing the same **consonant** sound—for example, the repeated *m* in Spenser's "*M*ixed with a *m*ur*m*uring wind," or the *s* sound in Waller's "Your never-failing *s*word made war to *c*ease," which emphasizes the connection between the words "sword" and "cease."

There are two kinds of alliteration. Most commonly, alliteration is regarded as the repetition of identical consonant sounds that begin syllables in close proximity—for example, in Pope's lines "La*b*orious, heavy, *b*usy, *b*old, and *b*lind," and "While *p*ensive *p*oets *p*ainful vigils keep." Used judiciously, alliteration gives strength to ideas by emphasizing key words, but too much can *c*ause *c*omic and *c*atastrophic *c*onsequences. The second form of alliteration occurs when a poet repeats identical or similar consonant sounds that do not begin syllables but nevertheless create a pattern—for example, the *z* segment in the line "In the*s*e place*s* free*z*ing bree*z*es ea*s*ily cau*s*e snee*z*es," or the *b*, *m*, and *p* segments (all of which are made *b*ila*b*ially, that is, with both lips) in "The *m*u*mb*ling and *m*ur*m*uring *b*eggar throws *p*egs and *p*e*bb*les in the *b*u*bb*ling *p*ool." Such patterns, apparently deliberately organized, are hard to overlook.

Onomatopoeia

Onomatopoeia is a blending of consonant and vowel sounds designed to *imitate* or *suggest* a situation or action. It is made possible in poetry because many words in English are **echoic** in origin; that is, they are verbal echoes of the actions they describe, such as *buzz*, *bump*, *slap*, and so on. Poe used such words to create onomatopoeia in "The Bells," where through the combined use of assonance and alliteration he imitates the kinds of bells he celebrates. Thus, wedding bells sound softly with "molten golden notes" ($\bar{o}$); alarm bells "clang and clash and roar" (*kl*). David Wagoner includes imitative words like *tweedledy*, *thump*, and *wheeze* to suggest the sounds of the music produced by the protagonist of his "March for a One-Man Band."

Euphony and Cacophony

Words describing smooth or jarring sounds, particularly those resulting from consonants, are **euphony** and **cacophony.** Euphony ("good sound") refers to words containing consonants that permit an easy and smooth flow of spoken sound. Although there is no rule that some consonants are inherently more pleasant than others, students of poetry often cite sounds like *m, n, ng, l, v,* and *z*, together with *w* and *y*, as being especially easy on the ears. The opposite of euphony is cacophony ("bad sound"), in which percussive and choppy sounds make for particularly vigorous and noisy pronunciation. It is the combination of words and sounds that creates harshness, as in tongue twisters like "black bug's blood" and "selfish shellfish in a sushi dish." Obviously, unintentional cacophony is a mark of imperfect control. When a poet deliberately creates it for effect, however, as in Tennyson's line "The bare black cliff clang'd round him," Pope's "The hoarse, rough verse should like the torrent roar," and Coleridge's "Huge fragments vaulted like rebounding hail, / Or chaffy grain beneath the thresher's flail," cacophony is a mark of poetic skill. Although poets generally aim at easily flowing, euphonious lines, cacophony does have a place, always depending on the poet's intention and subject matter.

RHYME AND ITS FUNCTIONS

Rhyme is the repetition of identical or similar concluding syllables in different words, most often at the ends of lines. Words with the same concluding vowel sounds rhyme; such rhymes are a special kind of assonance. Thus, *day* rhymes with *weigh, grey, bouquet,* and *matinee.* Rhyme may also combine assonance and identical consonant sounds, as in *ache, bake, break,* and *opaque,* or *turn, yearn, fern,* and *adjourn.* As these examples illustrate, rhyme is predominantly a function of *sound* rather than spelling; *the words do not have to be spelled the same way or look alike to rhyme.*

Rhyme is not a universal feature of poetry; thousands of excellent poems have been written without any rhymes whatsoever. Indeed, many contemporary poets have abandoned rhyme in favor of other ways of joining sound and sense, because they find rhyme too restrictive or artificial. Nevertheless, rhyme has been an important aspect of poetry for hundreds of years, and it remains a valid and useful poetic technique today.

When rhyme is employed to good effect, it is much more than a simple ornament. It adds to a poem's sensory impact by providing a pleasing network of related sounds that echo in the mind. Through rhyme, sound may join with sense in a coherent whole. Rhyme can also contribute significantly to the impression that a poem makes on our memories. In its simplest form, it jingles in the mind, with rhymes like *bells* and *tells,* but rhyme can also provide emphasis and reinforce ideas. It is a powerful way of clinching a thought by the physical link of related sounds.

Rhyme is closely connected with the degree to which a given poem moves us or leaves us flat. Whenever rhyme is employed with skill and originality, it leads the mind into fresh, unusual, and even surprising turns of thought. Poets may thus be judged on their rhymes. Some rhymers are satisfied with easy rhymes, or **cliché rhymes,** like *trees* and *breeze* (a rhyme criticized by Pope). But good rhymes and good poets go together, in creative cooperation. For example, the seventeenth-century poet John Dryden, who wrote volumes of rhyming couplets, acknowledged that the need to find rhymes inspired ideas that he had not anticipated. In this sense, rhyme has been—and still is—a vital element of poetic creativity.

TYPES OF RHYMES

The effects of rhyme are closely connected with those of rhythm and meter. Rhymes that are produced with one-syllable words—like *moon, June, tune,* and *soon*—or with multisyllabic words in which the accent falls on the last syllable—like *combine, decline, refine, consign,* and *repine*—are called **heavy-stress rhyme, accented rhyme,** or **rising rhyme.** In general, rising rhyme lends itself to serious effects. The accenting of heavy stress rhyme appears in the opening lines of Robert Frost's "Stopping by Woods on a Snowy Evening" (p. 531):

Whose woods / these are / I think / I *know*

His house / is in / the vil - / lage *though.*

Here, the rhyming sounds are produced by one-syllable words—*know* and *though*—that occur in the final accented positions of the lines (which are iambic tetrameter with initial spondees).

Rhymes using words of two or more syllables in which the accent falls on any syllable other than the last are called **trochaic,** or **double rhyme** for rhymes of two syllables and **dactylic,** or **triple rhyme** for rhymes of three syllables. Less technically, these types of rhymes are also called **falling,** or **dying rhymes;** this is probably because the energy of pronunciation drops away on the light accent or accents following the heavy accent.

In general, double and triple rhymes lend themselves more readily to amusing or light poetry than they do to serious verse. The accents of falling rhyme may be seen in lines 2 and 4 of the first stanza of "Miniver Cheevy" by Edwin Arlington Robinson:

> Miniver Cheevy, child of scorn
>   Grew lean while he assailed the *seasons*;
> He wept that he was ever born,
>   And he had *reasons.*

In this poem the effect of the double rhyme is humorous, thus helping to make Miniver Cheevy seem ridiculous and pathetic. Occasionally, however, double rhyme can be used successfully in a serious poem, as in Robert Herrick's "To the Virgins, to Make Much of Time":

> Gather ye rosebuds while ye may,
>   Old time is still *a-flying*;
> And this same flower that smiles today
>   Tomorrow will be *dying.*

A-flying and *dying* (our italics) are both double rhymes; indeed, Herrick uses falling rhymes in the second and fourth lines of every stanza of this poem. Though the falling rhymes lighten the tone, they do not modify the seriousness of the poem's idea.

Dactylic, or **triple rhyme** is extremely rare and almost always humorous in effect. It may be seen in these lines from Robert Browning's "The Pied Piper of Hamlin."

> Small feet were *pattering*, wooden shoes *clattering*,
> Little hands clapping and little tongues *chattering*.
> And, like fowls in a farm-yard where barley is *scattering*,

Here, the words that end the lines, *clattering, chattering,* and *scattering,* are all instances of triple rhyme. The first line also offers an example of **internal rhyme,** the presence of a rhyming word within a line of verse. In this case, *pattering* rhymes with *clattering* and also maintains the triple rhyme pattern.

VARIATIONS IN RHYME

Traditionally, a wide latitude of rhyming forms has been accepted in English. Perfect rhyming words, where both the vowel and the consonant sounds rhyme, are called **exact rhymes.** Not all rhymes, however, are exact. In poetry we often find words that *almost* rhyme. In most of these instances, the vowel segments are different while the consonants are the same. This type of rhyme is variously called **slant rhyme, near rhyme, half rhyme,** or **off rhyme.** In employing slant rhyme, a poet can pair *bleak* with *broke* or *could* with *solitude.* Emily Dickinson uses slant rhyme extensively in "To Hear an Oriole Sing"; in the second stanza of the poem she rhymes *Bird, unheard,* and *Crowd. Bird* and *unheard* make up an exact rhyme, but the vowel and consonant shift in *Crowd* produces a slant rhyme.

Another variant that shows up in poetry written in English is **eye rhyme,** or **sight rhyme.** In these instances, we find the pairing of words that look alike but do not sound alike. Thus, according to eye rhyme, "I *wind* [a clock]" may be joined to "The North *Wind*," or *bough* may be rhymed with *cough, dough, enough,* and *tough.* Ben Jonson's "To Celia" begins with a typical eye rhyme:

> Come, my Celia, let us *prove*,
> While we can, the sports of *love*.

Prove and *love* look as though they ought to rhyme, but when the lines are read aloud, we realize that they do not. As in all instances of eye rhyme, the spelling is more important than the sound.

RHYME SCHEMES

A **rhyme scheme** refers to a poem's pattern of rhyming sounds, which is indicated by alphabetical letters. Each repeated letter indicates a rhyme, so that lines ending with *love* and *dove*, for example, are marked *a a*. A poem's first rhyme receives an *a*, and each new rhyming sound is assigned a new letter. Thus, lines ending with the words *love, moon, thicket, dove, June, picket, above, croon* and *wicket* are schematized as *a b c, a b c, a b c*.

To formulate a rhyme scheme or pattern, include the meter and the number of feet in each line as well as the letters indicating rhymes. Here is such a formulation:

Iambic pentameter: *a b a b. c d c d. e f e f.*

This scheme shows that all the lines in the poem are iambic, with five feet in each. Pauses separating the units indicates a stanzaic pattern of three 4-line units, or **quatrains,** with the rhymes falling on the first and third, and the second and fourth, lines of each quatrain.

Should the number of feet in the lines of a poem or **stanza** vary, show this fact by using a number in front of each letter:

Iambic: *4a 3b 4a 3b 5a 5a 4b*

This formulation shows an intricate pattern of rhymes and line lengths in a stanza of seven lines. The first, third, fifth, and sixth lines rhyme, and vary from four to five feet. The second, fourth, and seventh lines also rhyme, and vary from three to four feet.

The absence of a rhyme sound is indicated by an *x*. Thus, you formulate the rhyme scheme of **ballad measure** like this:

Iambic: *4x 3a 4x 3a*

The formulation shows that the quatrain alternates iambic tetrameter with trimeter. In this ballad quatrain, only lines 2 and 4 rhyme; there is no end rhyme in lines 1 and 3.

POEMS FOR STUDY

WILLIAM SHAKESPEARE   (1564–1616)

Sonnet 73: That Time of Year Thou Mayst in Me Behold   1609

That time of year thou mayst in me behold
When yellow leaves, or none, or few, do hang
Upon those boughs which shake against the cold,

Bare ruined choirs,° where late the sweet birds sang.
In me thou see'st the twilight of such day   5
As after sunset fadeth in the west;
Which by and by black night doth take away,
Death's second self,° that seals up all in rest.
In me thou see'st the glowing of such fire,
That on the ashes of his° youth doth lie,   *its*   10
As the death-bed whereon it must expire,
Consumed with that which it was nourished by,°
  This thou perceivest, which makes thy love more strong,
  To love that well which thou must leave ere long.

SONNET 73.   4 *choirs*: the part of a church just in front of the altar.   8 *Death's* . . .
self; That is, night is a mirror image of death inasmuch as it brings the sleep of rest just as
death brings the sleep of actual death.   12 *Consumed* . . . *by*: That is, the ashes of the fuel
burned at the fire's height now prevent the fire from continuing, and in fact extinguish it.

QUESTIONS

1. Describe the content of lines 1–4, 5–8, and 9–12. What connects these three
   sections? How does the concluding couplet relate to the first twelve lines?

2. Analyze the iambic pentameter of the poem. Consider the spondees in lines
   2 (*do hang*), 4 (*bare ru-* and *birds sang*), 5 (*such day*), 7 (*black night*), 8 (*death's
   sec-*), 9 (*such fire*), 10 (*doth lie*), 11 (*death-bed*), 13 (*more strong*), and 14 (*ere
   long*). What is the effect of these substitutions on the poem's ideas?

3. How does the enjambement of lines 1–3 and 5–6 permit these lines to seem
   to conclude *as lines* even though grammatically they carry over to form
   sentences?

4. In lines 2, 5, 6, and 9, where does Shakespeare place the caesurae? What
   relationship is there between the rhythms produced by these caesurae and
   the content of lines 1–12? In lines 13 and 14, how do the rising stressed
   caesurae relate to the content?

ROBERT HERRICK   (1591–1674)

Upon Julia's Voice   *1648*

So smooth, so sweet, so silv'ry is thy voice,
As, could they hear, the damned would make no noise,
But listen to thee (walking in thy chamber)
Melting melodious words, to lutes of amber.

QUESTIONS

1. How do the words *silv'ry* and *amber* contribute to the praise of Julia's voice?
   How powerful does the speaker claim her voice is?

2. What is the "joke" of the poem? How can the praise of Julia's voice be interpreted as general praise for Julia herself?

3. How and where is alliteration used in the poem? Which of the alliterative sounds best complement the words praising the sweetness of Julia's voice?

JONATHAN SWIFT (1667–1745)

A Description of the Morning   *1709*

Now hardly here and there a hackney-coach
Appearing, showed the ruddy morn's approach.
Now Betty from her master's bed had flown.
And softly stole to discompose her own.
The slip-shod 'prentice from his master's door   5
Had pared the dirt, and sprinkled round the floor.
Now Moll had whirled her mop with dextrous airs,
Prepared to scrub the entry and the stairs.
The youth with broomy stumps began to trace
The kennel's edge,° where wheels had worn the place.   10
The small-coal man° was heard with cadence deep,   *charcoal seller*
Till drowned in shriller notes of chimney-sweep.
Duns° at his lordship's gate began to meet;   *bill collectors*
And brickdust Moll had screamed through half the street.
The turnkey° now his flock returning sees,   15
Duly let out a-nights to steal for fees.
The watchful bailiffs take their silent stands,
And schoolboys lag° with satchels in their hands.

A DESCRIPTION OF THE MORNING.   10 *kennel's edge*: that is, the edge of the gutter. Swift annotated this line "To find old Nails."   15 *turnkey*: an entrepreneur, operating a jail for profit, who allowed prisoners to go free at night so that they might bring him a night's booty to pay for the necessities provided them in jail.   18 *schoolboys lag*: cf. Shakespeare's *As You Like It*, Act II, scene 7, lines 145–147.

QUESTIONS

1. What antiheroic images of life in London are presented in this poem? What attitude is shown toward "his lordship"?

2. Analyze the poem for alliterative patterns. What is their effect?

3. Make the same kind of analysis for assonance. How many different assonantal patterns are there? What is their effect?

4. Iambic rhyming couplets are often called "heroic." How does Swift's choice of this form affect the subject matter of the poem?

ALFRED, LORD TENNYSON   (1809–1892)

From *Idylls of the King: The Passing of Arthur*   1869 (1842)

But, as he walked, King Arthur panted hard,
Like one that feels a nightmare on his bed   345
When all the house is mute. So sighed the King,
Muttering and murmuring at his ear, "Quick, quick!
I fear it is too late, and I shall die."
But the other swiftly strode from ridge to ridge,
Clothed with his breath, and looking, as he walked,   350
Larger than human on the frozen hills.
He heard the deep behind him, and a cry
Before. His own thought drove him like a goad.
Dry clashed his harness in the icy caves
And barren chasms, and all to left and right   355
The bare black cliff clanged round him, as he based
His feet on juts of slippery crag that rang
Sharp-smitten with the dint of armèd heels—
And on a sudden, lo! the level lake,
And the long glories of the winter moon.   360

Then saw they how there hove a dusky barge,
Dark as a funeral scarf from stem to stern,
Beneath them; and descending they were ware°   *aware*
That all the decks were dense with stately forms,
Black-stoled, black-hooded, like a dream—by these   365
Three Queens with crowns of gold: and from them rose
A cry that shivered to the tingling stars,
And, as it were one voice, an agony
Of lamentation, like a wind that shrills
All night in a waste land, where no one comes,   370
Or hath come, since the making of the world.

Then murmured Arthur, "Place me in the barge."
So to the barge they came. There those three Queens
Put forth their hands, and took the King, and wept.
But she, that rose the tallest of them all   375
And fairest, laid his head upon her lap,
And loosed the shattered casque,° and chafed his hands,   *helmet*
And called him by his name, complaining loud,
And dropping bitter tears against a brow
Striped with dark blood: for all his face was white   380
And colorless, and like the withered moon
Smote by the fresh beam of the springing east;
And all his greaves and cuisses° dashed with drops   *pieces of armor*
Of onset;° and the light and lustrous curls—   *blood*
That made his forehead like a rising sun   385

High from the dais-throne—were parched with dust:
Or, clotted into points and hanging loose,
Mixed with the knightly growth that fringed his lips.
So like a shattered column lay the King:
Not like that Arthur who, with lance in rest,   390
From spur to plume a star of tournament,
Shot through the lists at Camelot, and charged
Before the eyes of ladies and of kings.

QUESTIONS

1. How does Tennyson develop the mood of depression and loss associated
    with the dying of Arthur? What is the effect of the concluding simile?
2. Analyze the patterns of assonance and alliteration in the passage. What
    patterns are developed most extensively? What effects are thus achieved?
3. Describe Tennyson's use of onomatopoeia in lines 349–360, 369–371, and
    380–383. What segments contribute to this effect?

EDGAR ALLAN POE   (1809–1849)

The Bells   *1849*

                          I
Hear the sledges with the bells—
          Silver bells!
What a world of merriment their melody foretells!
How they tinkle, tinkle, tinkle,
    In the icy air of night!   5
While the stars that oversprinkle
All the heavens, seem to twinkle
  With a crystalline delight;
      Keeping time, time, time,
      In a sort of Runic rhyme,   10
To the tintinnabulation that so musically wells
      From the bells, bells, bells, bells,
        Bells, bells, bells—
From the jingling and the tinkling of the bells.

                          II
Hear the mellow wedding bells—   15
          Golden bells!
What a world of happiness their harmony foretells!
    Through the balmy air of night
    How they ring out their delight!—
      From the molten-golden notes,   20

And all in tune,
What a liquid ditty floats
To the turtle-dove that listens, while she gloats
On the moon!
Oh, from out the sounding cells, 25
What a gush of euphony voluminously wells!
How is swells!
How it dwells
On the Future!—how it tells
Of the rapture that impels 30
To the swinging and the ringing
Of the bells, bells, bells—
Of the bells, bells, bells, bells,
Bells, bells, bells—
To the rhyming and the chiming of the bells! 35

III

Hear the loud alarum bells—
Brazen bells!
What a tale of terror, now, their turbulency tells!
In the startled ear of night
How they scream out their affright! 40
Too much horrified to speak,
They can only shriek, shriek,
Out of tune,
In a clamorous appealing to the mercy of the fire,
In a mad expostulation with the deaf and frantic fire, 45
Leaping higher, higher, higher,
With a desperate desire,
And a resolute endeavor
Now—now to sit, or never,
By the side of the pale-faced moon, 50
Oh, the bells, bells, bells!
What a tale their terror tells
Of Despair!
How they clang, and clash, and roar!
What a horror they outpour 55
On the bosom of the palpitating air!
Yet the ear, it fully knows,
By the twanging
And the clanging,
How the danger ebbs and flows; 60
Yet the ear distinctly tells,
In the jangling
And the wrangling,
How the danger sinks and swells,
By the sinking or the swelling in the anger of the bells— 65
Of the bells,—

Of the bells, bells, bells, bells,
    Bells, bells, bells—
In the clamor and the clangor of the bells!

       IV
  Hear the tolling of the bells—   70
     Iron bells!
What a world of solemn thought their monody compels!
  In the silence of the night,
  How we shiver with affright
At the melancholy menace of their tone!   75
  For every sound that floats
  From the rust within their throats
    Is a groan.
    And the people—ah, the people—
    They that dwell up in the steeple,   80
     All alone,
  And who tolling, tolling, tolling,
   In that muffled monotone,
  Feel a glory in so rolling
    On the human heart a stone—   85
They are neither man nor woman—
They are neither brute nor human—
    They are Ghouls:—
  And their king it is who tolls:—
  And he rolls, rolls, rolls,   90
    Rolls
    A paean from the bells!
And his merry bosom swells
   With the paean of the bells!
And he dances, and he yells;   95
Keeping time, time, time,
In a sort of Runic rhyme,
   To the paean of the bells—
  Of the bells:
Keeping time, time, time,   100
In a sort of Runic rhyme,
   To the throbbing of the bells—
  Of the bells, bells, bells—
   To the sobbing of the bells;
Keeping time, time, time,   105
  As he knells, knells, knells,
In a happy Runic rhyme,
   To the rolling of the bells—
  Of the bells, bells, bells:—
   To the tolling of the bells—   110
Of the bells, bells, bells, bells,
   Bells, bells, bells—
To the moaning and the groaning of the bells.

QUESTIONS

1. What kinds of bells does Poe extol in each of the stanzas? What metals and images does he associate with each type of bell? How appropriate are these? Why do you think the stanzas become progressively longer?

2. What segmental sounds does Poe utilize as imitative of the various bells? What differences in vowels are observable between the silver sledge bells, for example, and the brass ("brazen") alarum bells? Between the vowels describing the iron bells and the golden bells?

3. What is the effect of the repetition of the word *bells* throughout? What onomatopoeic effect is created by these repetitions?

4. Describe the pattern of rhymes in this poem.

EMILY DICKINSON   (1830–1886)

To Hear an Oriole Sing   *1891 (ca. 1862)*

To hear an Oriole sing
May be a common thing—
Or only a divine.

It is not of the Bird
Who sings the same, unheard,   5
As unto Crowd—

The Fashion of the Ear
Attireth that it hear
In Dun, or fair—

So whether it be Rune,   10
Or whether it be none
Is of within.

The "Tune is in the Tree—"
The Skeptic—showeth me—
"No Sir! In Thee!"   15

QUESTIONS

1. What can you deduce about the speaker? The listener? Who speaks in line 13? To whom is line 15 addressed?

2. Formulate the rhyme scheme of this poem. How does it help subdivide the poem into cohesive units of thought? To what extent does it unify the poem?

3. Locate all the slant rhymes in this poem. What effect do these have on your reading and perception? How is the rhyme here like the oriole's song?

4. To what degree does rhyme reinforce meaning? Note especially the rhyme words in the final stanza.

CHRISTINA ROSSETTI   (1830–1894)

Echo   *1862*

Come to me in the silence of the night;
  Come in the speaking silence of a dream;
Come with soft rounded cheeks and eyes as bright
    As sunlight on a stream;
      Come back in tears,   5
O memory, hope, love of finished years.

O dream how sweet, too sweet, too bitter sweet,
  Whose wakening should have been in Paradise,
Where souls brimful of love abide and meet;
    Where thirsty longing eyes   10
      Watch the slow door
That opening, letting in, lets out no more.

Yet come to me in dreams, that I may live
  My very life again though cold in death;
Come back to me in dreams, that I may give   15
    Pulse for pulse, breath for breath:
      Speak low, lean low,
As long ago, my love, how long ago.

QUESTIONS

1. In what ways is present reality contrasted with memory in this poem? In what ways is the real world contrasted with dreams?

2. To what extent does repetition contribute to the fusion of sound and sense in this poem? How are alliteration and assonance used?

3. What type of rhyme predominates? How does rhyme advance the meaning and impact? In this regard, consider especially *night—bright, sweet—meet*, and *death—breath*. Also consider that rhyme itself is a kind of echo.

GERARD MANLEY HOPKINS   (1844–1889)

God's Grandeur   *1877*

The world is charged with the grandeur of God.
  It will flame out, like shining from shook foil;
  It gathers to a greatness, like the ooze of oil
Crushed. Why do men then now not reck his rod?°
Generations have trod, have trod, have trod;   5
  And all is seared with trade; bleared, smeared with toil;
  And wears man's smudge and shares man's smell: the soil

GOD'S GRANDEUR.   4 *reck his rod*: God as king holds a scepter, making official laws through scriptures which people ("men") disobey.

Is bare now, nor can foot feel, being shod.
And for all this, nature is never spent;
   There lives the dearest freshness deep down things;   10
And though the last lights off the black West went
   Oh, morning, at the brown brink eastward, springs—
Because the Holy Ghost over the bent
   World broods with warm breast and with ah! bright wings.

QUESTIONS

1. What is the contrast between the assertions in lines 1–4 and 5–8? How do lines 9–14 develop out of this contrast?

2. Analyze Hopkins's use of alliteration. What alliterative patterns occur? How do these affect meter and emphasis? On the basis of your analysis, describe "sprung rhythm" as used by Hopkins.

3. What instances of assonance, repetitions, and internal rhyme do you find?

FRANCIS THOMPSON _ (1859–1907)

To a Snowflake   *1897*

What heart could have thought you?
Past our devisal
(O filigree petal!)
Fashioned so purely,
Fragilely, surely,   5
From what Paradisal
Imagineless metal,
Too costly for cost?
Who hammered you, wrought you
From argentine° vapour?—   *silver*   10
"God was my shaper.
Passing surmisal,
He hammered, He wrought me.
From curled silver vapour,
To lust of His mind:—   15
Thou could'st not have thought me!
So purely, so palely,
Tinily, surely,
Mightily, frailly,
Insculped and embossed,   20
With His hammer of wind,
And His graver of frost."

QUESTIONS

1. The poem is in dimeter (lines consisting of two feet). Why is this short line appropriate to the subject?

2. What is the prevailing metrical pattern? How is this meter appropriate for the subject of a snowflake? Would iambs have been more or less appropriate? What variations on the predominant foot can you find? Why do you think the poet made the last three lines conclude with stressed syllables?

3. Why are some of the rhymes placed on heavy stressed syllables even though most of the rhymes are linked with falling or trochaic rhythms?

4. Compare this poem with Blake's "The Lamb" (p. 587) and "The Tyger" (p. 610). To which of the two Blake poems is "To a Snowflake" more similar? Why? In what ways is Thompson's poem different from those of Blake?

T. S. ELIOT (1888–1965)

Macavity: The Mystery Cat   1939

Macavity's a Mystery Cat: he's called the Hidden Paw—
For he's the master criminal who can defy the Law.
He's the bafflement of Scotland Yard, the Flying Squad's despair:
For when they reach the scene of the crime—*Macavity's not there!*

Macavity, Macavity, there's no one like Macavity,   5
He's broken every human law, he breaks the law of gravity.
His powers of levitation would make a fakir stare,
And when you reach the scene of crime—*Macavity's not there!*
You may seek him in the basement, you may look up in the air—
But I tell you once and once again, *Macavity's not there!*   10

Macavity's a ginger cat, he's very tall and thin;
You would know him if you saw him, for his eyes are sunken in.
His brow is deeply lined with thought, his head is highly domed;
His coat is dusty from neglect, his whiskers are uncombed.
He sways his head from side to side, with movements like a snake;   15
And when you think he's half asleep, he's always wide awake.

Macavity, Macavity, there's no one like Macavity,
For he's a fiend in feline shape, a monster of depravity.
You may meet him in a by-street, you may see him in the square—
But when a crime's discovered, then *Macavity's not there!*   20

He's outwardly respectable. (They say he cheats at cards.)
And his footprints are not found in any file of Scotland Yard's.
And when the larder's looted, or the jewel-case is rifled,
Or when the milk is missing, or another Peke's been stifled,°
Or the greenhouse glass is broken, and the trellis past repair—   25
Ay, there's the wonder of the thing! *Macavity's not there!*

MACAVITY: THE MYSTERY CAT.   24 *Peke's been stifled*: A Pekinese dog (a small animal, with silky hair) has been found dead.

And when the Foreign Office find a Treaty's gone astray,
Or the Admiralty lose some plans and drawings by the way,
There may be a scrap of paper in the hall or on the stair—
But it's useless to investigate—*Macavity's not there!*   30
And when the loss has been disclosed, the Secret Service say:
"It *must* have been Macavity!"—but he's a mile away.
You'll be sure to find him resting, or a-licking of his thumbs,
Or engaging in doing complicated long division sums.

Macavity, Macavity, there's no one like Macavity,   35
There never was a Cat of such deceitfulness and suavity.
He always has an alibi, and one or two to spare:
At whatever time the deed took place—MACAVITY WASN'T THERE!
And they say that all the Cats whose wicked deeds are widely known
(I might mention Mungojerrie, I might mention Griddlebone)   40
Are nothing more than agents for the Cat who all the time
Just controls their operations: the Napoleon of Crime!

QUESTIONS

1. What are some of Macavity's major "crimes" as a master criminal and "mystery cat"? How, if the "crimes" had been attributed to a human being, would they be grievous wrongs? Since they are attributed to a cat, how do they add to the comic qualities of the poem?

2. What is the basic metrical foot of the poem? How many feet are contained in each of the lines? What is the norm?

3. Once you begin reading and getting into the lines, what new kind of pattern emerges? How many major stresses appear in each line? In light of the nature of the poem, how is the dipodic rhythm appropriate?

GWENDOLYN BROOKS (b. 1917)

We Real Cool   1959

The Pool Players.
Seven at the Golden Shovel.

We real cool. We
Left school. We

Lurk late. We
Strike straight. We

Sing sin. We   5
Thin gin. We

Jazz June. We
Die soon.

QUESTIONS

1. What is the major idea of the poem? Who is the speaker? How is the last sentence a climax? How is this sentence consistent with the declarations in lines 1–7? How is the poet's attitude made clear?
2. Describe the patterning of stresses in the poem. Explain the absence of light stresses. What method is employed to achieve the constant strong stresses?

JAMES EMANUEL   (b. 1921)

The Negro   *1968*

Never saw him.
Never can.
Hypothetical,
Haunting man:

Eyes a-saucer,   5
Yessir bossir,
Dice a-clicking.
Razor flicking.

The-ness froze him
In a dance.   10
A-ness never
Had a chance.

QUESTIONS

1. What are the attributes of the black man in lines 1–4, 5 and 6, and 7 and 8? What attitude does the poem convey about the plight of the man?
2. What is the meaning of *The-ness* and *A-ness* in the third stanza?
3. What metrical foot is dominant? Why do you think the poet chose this foot in preference to a foot having a rising rhythm, such as the iamb?

EDWIN ARLINGTON ROBINSON   (1869–1935)

Miniver Cheevy   *1910*

Miniver Cheevy, child of scorn,
   Grew lean while he assailed the seasons;
He wept that he was ever born,
   And he had reasons.

Miniver loved the days of old   5
   When swords were bright and steeds were prancing;

The vision of a warrior bold
  Would set him dancing.

Miniver sighed for what was not,
  And dreamed, and rested from his labors;   10
He dreamed of Thebes° and Camelot,°
  And Priam's° neighbors.

Miniver mourned the ripe renown
  That made so many a name so fragrant;
He mourned Romance, now on the town,   15
  And Art, a vagrant.

Miniver loved the Medici,°
  Albeit he had never seen one;
He would have sinned incessantly
  Could he have been one.   20

Miniver cursed the commonplace
  And eyed a khaki suit with loathing;
He missed the medieval grace
  Of iron clothing.

Miniver scorned the gold he sought,   25
  But sore annoyed was he without it;
Miniver thought, and thought, and thought,
  And thought about it.

Miniver Cheevy, born too late,
  Scratched his head and kept on thinking;   30
Miniver coughed, and called it fate,
  And kept on drinking.

MINIVER CHEEVY.   11 *Thebes*: a city in Greece prominent in Greek legend and
mythology in connection with Cadmus and Oedipus.   *Camelot*: legendary seat of the
Round Table and capital of Britain during the reign of King Arthur.   12 *Priam's*: Priam
was the king of Troy during the Trojan War.   17 *Medici*: wealthy Italian family that
ruled Florence from the fifteenth to the eighteenth century. During the Renaissance,
Lorenzo de'Medici was an important patron of the arts.

QUESTIONS

1. What is the speaker's attitude toward the central character? How does rhyme
    help define this attitude?

2. How does repetition reinforce the image of the central character and the
    speaker's attitude? Consider the beginning of each stanza and lines 27–28.

3. What rhyme predominates in lines 2 and 4 of each stanza? How does this
    rhyme help make sound echo sense?

LANGSTON HUGHES   (1902–1967)

Let America Be America Again   *1936*

Let America be America again.
Let it be the dream it used to be.
Let it be the pioneer on the plain
Seeking a home where he himself is free.

(America never was America to me.)   5

Let America be the dream the dreamers dreamed—
Let it be that great strong land of love
Where never kings connive nor tyrants scheme
That any man be crushed by one above.

(It never was America to me.)   10

O, let my land be a land where Liberty
Is crowned with no false patriotic wreath,
But opportunity is real, and life is free,
Equality is in the air we breathe.

(There's never been equality for me,   15
Nor freedom in this "homeland of the free.")

Say who are you that mumbles in the dark?
And who are you that draws your veil across the stars?
I am the poor white, fooled and pushed apart,
I am the Negro bearing slavery's scars.   20
I am the red man driven from the land,
I am the immigrant clutching the hope I seek—
And finding only the same old stupid plan
Of dog eat dog, of mighty crush the weak.

I am the young man, full of strength and hope,   25
Tangled in that ancient endless chain
Of profit, power, gain, of grab the land!
Of grab the gold! Of grab the ways of satisfying need!
Of work the men! Of take the pay!
Of owning everything for one's own greed!   30

I am the farmer, bondsman to the soil.
I am the worker sold to the machine.
I am the Negro, servant to you all.
I am the people, worried, hungry, mean—
Hungry yet today despite the dream.   35
Beaten yet today—O, Pioneers!
I am the man who never got ahead,
The poorest worker bartered through the years.

Yet I'm the one who dreamt our basic dream
In the Old World while still a serf of kings,   40
Who dreamt a dream so strong, so brave, so true,
That even yet its mighty daring sings
In every brick and stone, in every furrow turned
That's made America the land it has become.
O, I'm the man who sailed those early seas   45
In search of what I meant to be my home—
For I'm the one who left dark Ireland's shore,
And Poland's plain, and England's grassy lea,
And torn from Black Africa's strand I came
To build a "homeland of the free."   50
The free?

A dream—
Still beckoning to me!

O, let America be America again—
The land that never has been yet—   55
And yet must be—
The land where *every* man is free.
The land that's mine—
The poor man's, Indian's, Negro's, ME—
Who made America,   60
Whose sweat and blood, whose faith and pain,
Whose hand at the foundry, whose plow in the rain,
Must bring back our mighty dream again.

Sure, call me any ugly name you choose—
The steel of freedom does not stain.   65
From those who live like leeches on the people's lives,
We must take back our land again,
America!

O, yes,
I say it plain,   70
America never was America to me,
And yet I swear this oath—
America will be!
An ever-living seed,
Its dream   75
Lies deep in the heart of me.

We, the people, must redeem
Our land, the mines, the plants, the rivers,
The mountains and the endless plain—
All, all the stretch of these great green states—   80
And make America again!

QUESTIONS

1. In light of the poet's ideas, what is the effect of the changing stanzaic patterns? After the opening, fairly regular quatrains, why do the groupings become irregular?

2. What is the effect of the refrains in lines 5, 10, and 15–16? Why does the poet stop using the refrain after the third quatrain and not bring it out again until line 71?

3. Describe the use of alliteration. In phrases like "pushed apart" and "slavery's scars," together with other phrases, how does the alliteration emphasize the poet's ideas?

4. Describe the use of assonance, rhyme, and slant rhyme. What is gained by the slant rhymes?

BARBARA HOWES   (b. 1914)

Death of a Vermont Farm Woman   *1954*

Is it time now to go away?
July is nearly over; hay
Fattens the barn, the herds are strong,
Our old fields prosper; these long
Green evenings will keep death at bay.   5

Last winter lingered; it was May
Before a flowering lilac spray
Barred cold for ever. I was wrong.
        Is it time now?

Six decades vanished in a day!   10
I bore four sons: one lives; they
Were all good men; three dying young
Was hard on us. I have looked long
For these hills to show me where peace lay.
        Is it time now?   15

QUESTIONS

1. What does this poem suggest about the life of "A Vermont Farm Woman"? About the lives of many women?

2. How many different rhyme sounds are used in this poem? What is the effect of using so few?

3. To what extent does rhyme divide the poem into coherent units of thought and tie the whole poem together?

4. Normally, repetition of the same rhyming word is judged to be a flaw in poetry. To what extent is that the case in this poem?

ISABELLA GARDNER (1915–1981)

At a Summer Hotel   *1979*

I am here with my bountiful womanful child
to be soothed by the sea not roused by these roses roving wild.
My girl is gold in the sun and bold in the dazzling water,
She drowses on the blond sand and in the daisy fields my daughter
dreams. Uneasy in the drafty shade I rock on the veranda   5
reminded of Europa Persephone Miranda.°

AT A SUMMER HOTEL.   6 *Europa Persephone Miranda*: Europa is a princess in Greek
mythology who attracted the attention of Zeus, the king of the gods. He took the form of a
bull and carried her over the sea to Crete. She bore him three sons. Persephone, in Greek
mythology, is the daughter of Zeus and Demeter, the goddess of fertility. She attracted the
attention of Hades, the god of the underworld, who forcibly carried her off and married
her. Miranda is an innocent young woman in Shakespeare's *The Tempest* who was exiled on
an island for twelve years with her father, Prospero. One of his servants—the beastly
Caliban—attempted to rape her.

QUESTIONS

1. Why is the speaker "uneasy" (line 5)? How do the references to Europa,
   Persephone, and Miranda help define this uneasiness?
2. To what extent do alliteration and repetition unify the lines and make the
   sound echo sense? Note especially the *b* and *ful* sounds in line 1, the *s* and *r*
   sounds in line 2, and the *d* and *dr* sounds in lines 4–5.
3. What is the effect of internal rhyme in this poem?
4. What kind of rhyme (rising or falling, exact or slant) is in lines 1–2? To
   what extent does this rhyme highlight the poem's central idea? What rhyme
   is in lines 3–6? How does this rhyme affect the poem's tone and impact?

DAVID WAGONER (b. 1926)

March for a One-Man Band   *1983*

He's *a boom a blat* in the uniform
Of an army *tweedledy* band *a toot*
Complete with medals *a honk* cornet
Against *a thump* one side of his lips
And the other stuck with *a sloop a tweet*   5
A whistle *a crash* on top of *a crash*
A helmet *a crash* a cymbal a drum
At his *bumbledy* knee and a *rimshot* flag
A click he stands at attention *a wheeze*
And plays the Irrational Anthem *bang.*   10

QUESTIONS

1. What attitude does the speaker convey about the one-man band? Why is the Anthem "Irrational" rather than "National"?

2. Describe the onomatopoeic effect of the italicized percussive words. What is the purpose of the rhythms that these words cause?

3. What ambiguity is suggested by the "bang" of line 10? How does this ambiguity make the poem seem more than simply an entertaining display of sounds?

WRITING ABOUT PROSODY

Because studying prosody requires a good deal of specific detail and description, it is best to limit your study to a short poem or to a short passage from a long poem. A sonnet, a stanza of a lyric poem, or fragment from a long poem will usually be sufficient. If you choose a fragment, it should be self-contained, such as an entire speech or short episode or scene (as in the example from Tennyson chosen for the sample essay on pp. 711–17).

The analysis of even a short poem, however, can grow long because of the need to describe word positions and stresses, and also to determine the various effects. For this reason you do not have to exhaust your topic. Try to make your discussion representative of the prosody of your poem or passage.

Your first reading in preparation for your essay should be for comprehension. On second and third readings, make notes of sounds, accents, and rhymes by reading the poem aloud. To perceive sounds, one student helped herself by reading aloud in an exaggerated way in front of a mirror. If you have privacy, or are not self-conscious, you might do the same. Let yourself go a bit. As you dramatize your reading (maybe even in front of fellow students), you will find that heightened levels of reading also accompany the poet's expression of important ideas. Mark these spots for later analysis, so that you will be able to make good points about the relationship of the poem's prosody to its content.

In planning your essay, it is vitally important to prepare study sheets, so that your observations will be correct, for if your factual analysis is wrong, your writing will go astray. Experience has shown that it is best to make four triple-spaced copies of the poem or passage (with carbon paper or photocopy). These will be for the separate analysis of rhythm, assonance, alliteration, and rhyme. If you have been assigned just one of these, of course, only one copy will be necessary. Leave spaces between syllables and words for marking out the various feet of the poem. Ultimately, this duplication of the passage, with your markings, should be included as a first page, as in the sample essays.

Carry out your study of the passage in the following way.

Discovering Ideas

Number each line of the passage, regardless of length, beginning with *1*, so that you may use these numbers as location references in your essay.

Determine the formal pattern of feet, using the short acute accent for heavily stressed syllables (´). and the breve for lightly stressed syllables (˘). Use chevrons to mark spondees (⋀).

Indicate the separate feet by a diagonal line or virgule (/). Indicate caesurae and end-of-line pauses by double virgules (//).

Use colored pencils to underline, circle, make boxes, or otherwise mark the formal and rhetorical substitutions that you discover. Because such substitutions may occur throughout the poem, develop a numbering system for each type (e.g., 1 = spondee, 7 = trochee, etc., as in the sample worksheet, p. 712). Provide a key to your numbers at the bottom of the page.

Do the same for alliteration, assonance, onomatopoeia, and rhyme. It has proved particularly effective to draw lines to connect the repeating sounds, for these effects will be close together in the poem, and your connections will dramatize this closeness. The use of a separate color for each separate effect is particularly useful, for the distinctions of differing colors simplify exact observations.

Use your worksheets as a reference for your reader. In writing your essay, however, you will need to make your examples specific by making brief quotations, as in the examples (i.e., words, phrases, and entire lines, with proper marks and accents). Do not rely on line numbers alone.

Once you have analyzed the various effects in your poem, and you have recorded these on your worksheets and in your notes, you will be ready to formulate a central idea and organization. The focus of the essay should reflect what you have found to be the most significant features of prosody in relationship to some other element of the poem, such as speaker, tone, or ideas. Thus, in planning an essay about T. S. Eliot's "Macavity," you might decide to argue that the dipodic rhythm contributes to the humor of the poem, and makes the "Napoleon of Crime" seem comic.

Strategies for Organizing Ideas

Depending on your assignment, you might wish to show the operation of all the component elements of prosody, or you may wish to focus on just one aspect. It would be possible, for example, to devote an entire essay to the discussion of (1) regular meter, (2) one particular variation in meter, such as the anapaest or spondee, (3) the caesura, (4) assonance, (5) alliteration, (6) onomatopoeia, or (7) rhyme. For brevity of illustration, we here treat rhythm and segments together in one essay, and rhyme in a separate essay.

After a brief description of the poem (such as that it is a sonnet, a two-stanza lyric, an iambic pentameter description of a character or action, a dipodic burlesque poem, and so on) establish the scope of your essay. You might wish to discuss all aspects of rhythm or sound, or perhaps just one, such as the poet's use of regular meter, a particular substitution, alliteration, or assonance. Your central idea will outline the thought you wish to carry out through your prosodic analysis, such as that regularity of meter is consistent with a happy, firm vision of love or life, or that frequent spondees emphasize the solidity of the speaker's wish to love, or that particular sounds echo some of the poem's actions.

1. *Rhythm.* You might first establish the formal metrical pattern. What is the dominant metrical foot and line length? Are some lines shorter than the pattern? What relationship do the variable lengths have with the subject matter? If the poem is a lyric, or a sonnet, is the poet successful in placing important words and syllables in stressed positions in order to achieve emphasis? Try to relate line lengths to whatever exposition and development of ideas and whatever rising and falling emotions you find. It is also important to look for either repeating or varying metrical patterns as the subject matter reaches peaks or climaxes. Generally, deal with the relationship between the formal rhythmical pattern and the poet's ideas and attitudes.

When noting substitutions, you might analyze the formal variations and the principal effects of these, as nearly as you can determine what the effects are. If you concentrate on only one substitution, describe any apparent pattern in its use, that is, its locations, recurrences, and effects on meaning.

For caesurae, treat the effectiveness of the poet's control. Can you see any pattern of use? Are the pauses regular, or do they seem randomly placed? Describe noticeable principles of placement, such as (1) the creation of rhythmical similarities in various parts of the poem, (2) the development of particular rhetorical effects, or (3) the creation of interest through rhythmical variety. Do the caesurae lead to important ideas and attitudes? Are the lines all end-stopped, or do you discover enjambement? How do these rhythmical characteristics aid in the poet's expression of subject matter?

2. *Segmental effects.* Here you might discuss, collectively or separately, the use and effects of assonance, alliteration, onomatopoeia, and cacophony and euphony. Be sure to establish that the instances you choose have really occurred systematically enough within the poem to be grouped as a pattern. You should illustrate sounds by including relevant words within parentheses. You might wish to make separate paragraphs on alliteration, assonance, and any other seemingly important pattern. Also, because space in an essay is always at a premium, you might wish to concentrate on only one noteworthy effect, like a certain pattern of assonance, rather than on everything in the poem. Throughout your discussion, always keep foremost the relationship between content and sound.

Note: To make illustrations clear, underline all sounds to which you are calling attention. If you use an entire word to illustrate a sound, underline only the sound and not the entire word, but put the word within quotation marks (for example, The poet uses a t ["tip," "top," and "terrific"]). When you refer to entire words containing particular segments, however, underline these words (for example, "The poet uses a t in tip, top, and terrific").

3. *Rhyme.* This discussion should include a description of the major features of rhyme, including the scheme and variants, the lengths and rhythms of the rhyming words, and noteworthy segmental characteristics. In discussing the grammatical features of the rhymes, you might note the kinds of words (i.e., verbs, nouns, etc.) used for rhymes: Are they all the same? Does one form predominate? Is there variety? Can you determine the grammatical positions of the rhyming words? How may these characteristics be related to the idea or theme of the poem?

You might also discuss the qualities of the rhyming words. Are the words specific? Concrete? Abstract? Are there any striking rhymes? Any surprises? Any rhymes that are particularly clever and witty? Do any rhymes give unique comparisons or contrasts? How?

Generally, you might also note striking or unique rhyming effects. Without becoming overly subtle or farfetched, you can make valid and interesting conclusions. Do any sounds in the rhyming words appear in patterns of assonance or alliteration elsewhere in the poem to an appreciable degree? Do the rhymes enter into any onomatopoeic effects? Broadly, can you detect any aspects of rhyme that are uniquely effective because they are at one with the thought and mood of the poem?

In your conclusion, you might try to develop a short evaluation of the poet's prosodic performance. If we accept the premise that poetry is designed not only to inform, but also to transfer attitudes and to stimulate, to what degree did the prosodic techniques of the poem contribute to these goals? Without going into excessive detail (and in effect writing another essay), what more can you say here? What has been the value of your study to your understanding and appreciating the poem? If you think your analysis has helped you to develop new awareness of the poet's craft, it would be appropriate to state what you have learned.

SAMPLE ESSAY

A Study of Tennyson's Rhythm and Segments in "The Passing of Arthur," 349–360°

Note: *For illustration, this essay analyzes a passage from Tennyson's "The Passing of Arthur," which is part of* **Idylls of the King.** *Containing 469 lines, "The Passing of Arthur" describes the last battle and death of Arthur, legendary king of early Britain.*

° See p. 693 for this poem.

After the fight, in which Arthur has been mortally wounded by the traitor Mordred, only Arthur and his follower Sir Bedivere remain alive. Arthur commands Bedivere to throw the royal sword Excalibur into the lake from which Arthur had originally received it. After great hesitation and some false claims, Bedivere does throw the sword into the lake, and a hand rises out of the water to catch it. Bedivere then carries Arthur to the lakeshore, where the dying king is taken aboard a magical funeral barge. In the passage selected for discussion (lines 349–360), Tennyson describes Bedivere carrying Arthur down the hills and cliffs from the battlefield to the lake below.

1. RHYTHMICAL ANALYSIS

But thĕ o- / thĕr swift- / lў stróde / / from ridge / to ridge, / /   1

Clothed with / his breath, / / and look- / ing, / / as / he walk'd, / /   2

Lár-gĕr / than hŭ- / man / / on / the fro- / zen hills. / /   3

Hĕ heárd / the deép / bĕ-hínd / him, / / and / a crý   4

Bĕ-fóre. / / His own / thought drove / him / / like / a goád. / /   5

Dry clash'd / his hár- / nĕss / / in / the í / cy caves   6

And bár- rĕn / chásms, / / and all / to left / and right   7

The báre / black cliff / clang'd round / him, / / as / he based   8

His feét / on júts / of slíp- / pĕ-rў crág / / that ráng   9

Sharp- smit- / tĕn / / with / the / dínt / of ár- / mĕd heéls— / /   10

And ón / a súd- / dĕn, / / lo! / / the lév- / eĺ lake, / /   11

And the / long glór- / iĕs / / of / the wín- / ter moón. / /   12

---

1 = Anapaest, or effect of anapaest.   4 = Effect of imperfect foot.
2 = Amphibrach, or the effect   5 = Pyrrhic.
    of amphibrach.   6 = Trochee, or the effect
3 = Spondee.   of trochee.

2. ALLITERATION

But the other (s) wiftly (s) trode from ridge to ridge,   1

Clothed with his breath, and looking, as (h) e walked,   2

Larger than (h) uman on the frozen (h) ills.   3

(H) e (h) eard the deep be (h) ind (h) im, and a cry   4

Before. (H) is own thought drove him like a goad.   5

Dry (c) lashed (h) is (h) arness in the icy (c) aves   6

And (b) arren (ch) asms, and all to left and right   7

The (b) are (b) (l) ack (c) (l) iff (c) (l) anged round him, as he (b) ased   8

His feet on juts of s (l) ippery (c) rag that rang   9

Sharp-smitten with the dint of armed heels—   10

And on a sudden, (l) o! the (l) evel, (l) ake,   11

And the (l) ong g (l) ories of the winter moon.   12

〰〰〰〰 = s   ———— = b

- - - - - - = h   〜〜〜〜 = l as second consonant
                                              sound in words

············ = k   —·—·—· = l

3. ASSONANCE

But the other sw ⓘ ftly str ⓞ de from r ⓘ dge to r ⓘ dge,   1

Cl ⓞ thed w ⓘ th h ⓘ s breath, and looking, as he walked,   2

Larger than human on the fr ⓞ zen hills.   3

He heard the deep beh ⓘ nd him, and a cr ⓨ   4

Before. His ⓞw n thought dr ⓞ ve him l ⓘ ke a g oa d.   5

Dr ⓨ clashed his harness in the ⓘ cy caves   6

And barren ch ⓐ sms, and all to left and r ⓘ ght   7

The bare bl ⓐ ck cliff cl ⓐ nged round him, as he based   8

H ⓘ s feet on juts of sl ⓘ ppery cr ⓐ g that r ⓐ ng   9

Sh ⓐr p-sm ⓘ tten w ⓘ th the d ⓘ nt of ⓐr med heels—   10

And on a sudden, lo, the level lake,   11

And the long glories of the winter moon!   12

―――――― = ō *   •—·—·—·—· = ä

------------ = ī   ⌇⌇⌇⌇⌇⌇ = ĭ

•••••••••• = a

* Pronunciation symbols as in *Webster's New World Dictionary*, 3d ed.

[1]
This passage describes the ordeal of Sir Bedivere as he carries the dying Arthur from the mountainous heights, where he was wounded, down to the lake, where the king will be sent to his final rest. Tennyson devotes great attention to the ghostly, deserted landscape, emphasizing the bleakness and hostility of the scenes. The passage is unrhymed iambic pentameter—blank verse. But Tennyson's verse is alive; it constantly augments his descriptions and conveys an impression of Bedivere's mood, whether of anguish or relaxation.* The control over prosody enables a true blending of sound and sense, as may be seen in Tennyson's use of rhythm and in his manipulation of segmental devices, including onomatopoeia.†

[2]
Tennyson controls his meter to emphasize Bedivere's exertions and moods. In line 1 the meter is regular, except for an anapaest in the first foot. This regularity may be interpreted as emphasizing the swiftness and sure-footedness of Bedivere. But he is about to undergo a severe test, and the rhythm quickly becomes irregular, as though to strain the pentameter verse in illustration of Bedivere's exertions. Tennyson therefore uses variations to highlight key words. For example, he uses the effect of anapaests in a number of lines. In line 2 he emphasizes the chill air and Bedivere's vitality in the following way:

Clothed with / his breath,//

The image is one of being surrounded by one's own breath that vaporizes on hitting the cold air, and the rhythmical variation—a trochaic substitution in the first foot—enables the voice to build up to the word *breath*, a most effective internal climax.

[3]
Tennyson uses something like the same rhythmical effect in line 3. He emphasizes the *frozen hills* by creating a caesura in the middle of the third foot, and then by making the heavy stress of the third foot fall on the preposition *on*, which with *the* creates in effect the two unstressed syllables of an anapaest including the first, stressed, syllable of *frozen*. The effect is that the voice builds up to the word and thus emphasizes the extreme conditions in which Bedivere is walking:

// on / the fro - / zen hills.//

Tennyson uses this rhythmical effect twelve times in the passage. It is one of his major means of rhetorical emphasis.

[4]
Perhaps the most effective metrical variation is the spondee, which appears in lines 5, 6, 8, (twice), 10, and 12. These substitutions, occurring mainly in the section in which Sir Bedivere is forcing his way down the frozen hills, permit the lines to ring out, as in:

The bare / black cliff / clang'd round /

and

Dry clash'd / his har - / ness.

* Central idea.
† Thesis sentence.

The best use of the spondee is in line 5, where the stresses reach a climax on the word *drove*, which suggests the torment Bedivere is feeling:

His own / thought drove / him //

There is other substitution, too, both formal and rhetorical, and the tension these variations create keeps the responsive reader aware of Bedivere's tasks. One type of variation is the appearance of amphibrachic rhythm, which [5] is produced in lines 2, 3, 4, 6, 7, and 11. The effect is achieved by a pattern which complements the rhetorical anapaests. A caesura in the middle of a foot leaves the three preceding syllables as a light, heavy, and light, the rhythmical form of the amphibrach. In line 2, for example, it appears thus:

// and look - / ing //

In line 6 it takes this form:

/ his har - / ness //

Still another related variation is that of the apparently imperfect feet in [6] lines 5, 8, 11, and 12. These imperfect feet are produced by a caesura, which isolates the syllable, as *him* is in line 8:

The bare / black cliff / clang'd round / him,//

[6] In line 11 the syllable (on the word *lo!*) is surrounded by two caesurae, and is therefore thrust into a position of great stress:

And on / a sud - / den // lo! // the lev - / el lake

Other, less significant substitutions are the trochees in lines 3 and 7, and the pyrrhic in line 12. All the described variations support the heroic action described in the passage.

Many of the variations described are produced by Tennyson's handling of his sentence structure, which results in a free placement of the caesurae and in a free use of end-stopping and enjambement. It is interesting that four of the first five lines are end-stopped (two by commas, two by periods). Bedivere is exerting himself during these lines and apparently he is making short tests to gather strength for his ordeal. The ordeal comes during the next four lines, when he makes his precarious descent; none of the lines containing [7] this description is end-stopped. Bedivere is disturbed (being goaded by "his own thought"), but he must keep going, and we may presume that the free sentence structure and the free metrical variation enforce his difficulty and mental disturbance. But in the last two lines, when he has reached the lake, the lines "relax" with falling caesurae exactly at the fifth syllable. In other words, the sentence structure of the last two lines is regular, an effect designed to indicate the return to order and beauty after the previous, rugged chaos.

This rhythmical virtuosity is accompanied by a similarly brilliant control over segmental devices. Alliteration is the most obvious, permitting Tennyson

[8] to tie key words and their signifying actions together, as in the *s*'s in "*s*wiftly *s*trode" in line 1, or the *b*'s in "*b*arren," "*b*are," "*b*lack," and "*b*ased" in lines 7 and 8. Other notable examples are the aspirated *h*'s in lines 2–6 (*h*e, *h*uman, *h*ills, *h*eard, be*h*ind, *h*im, *h*is, *h*arness); the *k*'s in lines 6–9 (*c*lash'd, *c*aves, *c*hasms, *c*liff, *c*lang'd, *c*rag); and the *l*'s in lines 11 and 12 (*l*o, *l*evel, *l*ake, *l*ong, g*l*ories). One might compare these *l*'s with the *l*'s in the more anguished context of lines 8 and 9, where the sounds appear as the second segment in the heavy, ringing words there (b*l*ack, c*l*iff, c*l*ang'd, s*l*ippery). The sounds are the same, and the emphasis is similar, but the effects are different.

[9] Assonance is also present throughout the passage. In the first five lines, for example, the *ō* appears in six words. The first three *ō*s are in descriptive or metaphoric words (str*o*de, cl*o*thed, fr*o*zen), while the last three are in words describing the pain and anguish that Bedivere experiences as a result of his efforts in the barren landscape (*o*wn, dr*o*ve, g*o*ad). The *o* therefore ties the physical to the psychological. Other patterns of assonance are the *ă* in lines 7, 8, and 9 (ch*a*sms, cl*a*ng'd, bl*a*ck, cr*a*g, r*a*ng), the *ä* of line 10 (sh*a*rp, *a*rmed), the *ī* of lines 4–7 (beh*i*nd, cr*y*, l*i*ke, dr*y*, *i*cy, r*i*ght), and the short *i* of lines 1 and 2, and 9 and 10 (sw*i*ftly, r*i*dge, w*i*th, h*i*s, sl*i*ppery, sm*i*tten, w*i*th, d*i*nt). One might remark also that in the last two lines, which describe the level lake and the moon, Tennyson introduces a number of relaxed *ō* and *ōo* and similar vowel sounds (*ô, u, ō, ô, u, ōo*).

[10] The last two lines are, in fact, onomatopoeic, since the liquid *l* sounds suggest the gentle lapping of waves on a lake shore. There are other examples of onomatopoeia, too. In line 2 Tennyson brings out the detail of Sir Bedivere's walking in the presumably cold air "Clothed with his breath," and in the following five lines Tennyson employs many words with the aspirate *h* (e.g., *h*is *h*arness); in this context, these sounds suggest Sir Bedivere's labored breath as he carries his royal burden. Similarly, the explosive stops *b* and *k*, *d*, and *t* in lines 6–10 seem to be imitative of the sounds of Sir Bedivere's feet on the "juts of slippery crag."

[11] This short passage is filled with many examples of poetic excellence. The sounds and the rhythms of the words and lines, put into this context by Tennyson, actually speak along with the meaning; they emphasize the grandeur of Arthur and his faithful follower, and for one brief moment bring out the magic that Tennyson associated with the fading past.

Commentary on the Essay

This essay presents a full discussion of the prosody of the passage from Tennyson. Paragraphs 2 through 7 discuss the relationship of the rhythm to the content. Note that prosody is not discussed in isolation, but as it serves Tennyson's purpose in describing the action and scenes of the passage. Thus, paragraph 4 refers to the use of the spondee as a means of reinforcing the ideas.

Paragraphs 8 and 9 present a discussion of the alliteration and assonance of the passage, and paragraph 10 considers onomatopoeia.

SAMPLE ESSAY

The Rhymes in Christina Rossetti's "Echo"°

	n	
1	*Come* to me in the silence of the *night*;	5a
	n	
2	*Come* in the speaking silence of a *dream*;	5b
	adj	
3	*Come* with soft rounded cheeks and eyes as *bright*	5a
	n	
4	As sunlight on a *stream*;	3b
	n	
5	*Come* back in *tears*,	2c
	n	
6	O memory, hope, love of finished *years*.	5c
	adj	
7	O *dream* how *sweet*, too *sweet*, too bitter *sweet*,	5d
	n	
8	Whose wakening should have been in *Paradise*,	5e
	v	
9	Where souls brimful of love abide and *meet*;	5d
	n	
10	Where thirsty longing *eyes*	3e
	n	
11	Watch the slow *door*	2f
	adv	
12	That opening, letting in, lets out no *more*.	5f
	v	
13	Yet *come* to me in *dreams*, that I may *live*	5g
	n	
14	My very life again though cold in *death*;	5h
	v	
15	*Come* back to me in *dreams*, that I may *give*	5g
	n	
16	Pulse for pulse, *breath* for *breath*:	3h

° See p. 698 for this poem.

adv
17   Speak *low*, lean *low*,   2i

adj
18 As *long ago*, my love, how *long ago*.   5i

[1] In the three-stanza lyric poem "Echo," Christina Rossetti uses rhyme as a way of saying that one might regain in dreams a love that is lost in reality.* As the dream of love is to the real love, so is an echo to an original sound. From this comparison comes the title of the poem and also Rossetti's unique use of rhyme. Aspects of her rhyme are the lyric pattern, the forms and qualities of the rhyming words, and the special use of repetition.†

[2] The rhyme pattern is simple, and, like rhyme generally, it may be thought of as a pattern of echoes. Each stanza contains four lines of alternating rhymes concluded by a couplet, as follows: 5a, 5b, 5a, 3b, 2c, 5c (iambic). There are nine separate rhymes throughout the poem, three in each stanza. Only two words are used for each rhyme; no rhyme is used twice. Of the eighteen rhyming words, sixteen—almost all—are of one syllable. The remaining two words consist of two and three syllables. With such a great number of single-syllable words, the rhymes are all rising ones, on the accented halves of iambic feet, and the end-of-line emphasis is on simple words.

[3] The grammatical forms and positions of the rhyming words lend support to the inward, introspective subject matter. Although there is variety, more than half the rhyming words are nouns. There are ten in all, and eight are placed as the objects of prepositions. Such enclosure helps the speaker emphasize her yearning to relive her love within dreams. Also, the repeated verb "come" in stanzas one and three is in the form of commands to the absent lover. A careful study shows that most of the verbal energy in the stanzas is in the first parts of the lines, leaving the rhymes to occur in elements modifying the verbs, as in these lines:

Come to me in the silence of the *night*; (1)

Yet come to me in dreams, that I may *live* (13)

My very life again though cold in *death*; (14)

Most of the other rhymes are also in such internalized positions. The free rhyming verbs occur in subordinate clauses, and the nouns that are not the objects of prepositions are the subject (10) and object (11) of the same subordinate clause.

The qualities of the rhyming words are also consistent with the poem's emphasis on the speaker's internal life. Most of the words are impressionistic. Even the concrete words—*stream, tears, eyes, door,* and *breath*—reflect the speaker's mental condition rather than describe reality. In this regard, the

* Central idea.
† Thesis sentence.

[4] rhyming words of 1 and 3 are effective. These are *night* and *bright*, which contrast the bleakness of the speaker's condition, on the one hand, with the vitality of her inner life, on the other. Another effective contrast is in 14 and 16, where *death* and *breath* are rhymed. This rhyme may be taken to illustrate the sad fact that even though the speaker's love is past, it can yet live in present memory just as an echo continues to sound.

It is in emphasizing how memory echoes experience that Rossetti creates the special use of rhyming words. There is an ingenious but not obtrusive repetition of a number of words—echoes. The major echoing word is of course the verb *come*, which appears six times at the beginnings of lines in stanzas 1 and 3. But rhyming words, stressing as they do the ends of lines, are also repeated systematically. The most notable is *dream*, the rhyming word in 2.

[5] Rossetti repeats the word in 7 and uses the plural in 13 and 15. In 7 the rhyming word *sweet* is the third use of the word, a climax of "how *sweet*, too *sweet*, too bitter *sweet*." Concluding the poem, Rossetti repeats *breath* (16), *low* (17), and the phrase *long ago* (18). This special use of repetition justifies the title "Echo," and it also stresses the major idea that it is only in one's memory that past experience has reality, even if dreams are no more than echoes.

Thus rhyme is not just ornamental in "Echo," but integral. The skill of Rossetti here is the same as in her half-serious, half-mocking poem "Eve," even though the two poems are totally different. In "Eve," she uses very plain rhyming words together with comically intended double rhymes. In "Echo," her subject might be called fanciful and maybe even morbid, but the easiness

[6] of the rhyming words, like the diction of the poem generally, keeps the focus on regret and yearning rather than self-indulgence. As in all rhyming poems, Rossetti's rhymes emphasize the conclusions of her lines. The rhymes go beyond this effect, however, because of the internal repetition—echoes—of the rhyming words. "Echo" is a poem in which rhyme is inseparable from meaning.

Commentary on the Essay

Throughout the essay, illustrative words are italicized, and numbers are used to indicate the lines from which the illustrations are drawn. The introductory paragraph asserts that rhyme is important in Rossetti's poem. It also attempts to explain the title, "Echo." The thesis sentence indicates the four topics to be developed in the body.

Paragraph 2 deals with the mechanical, mathematical aspects of the poem's rhyme. The high number of monosyllabic rhyming words is used to explain the rising, heavy-stress rhyme.

The third paragraph treats the grammar of the rhymes. For example, an analysis and count reveal that there are ten rhyming nouns and three rhyming verbs. The verb of command "come" is mentioned to show that most of the rhyming words exist within groups modifying this word, and three lines from the poem illustrate this fact. The grammatical analysis is related to the internalized nature of the subject of the poem.

Paragraph 4 emphasizes the impressionistic nature of the rhyming words and also points out two instances in which rhymes stress the contrast between real life and the speaker's introspective life.

Paragraph 5 deals with repetitions within the poem of five rhyming words. This repetition is seen as a pattern of echoes, in keeping with the title of the poem.

In the concluding paragraph, the rhymes in "Echo" are compared briefly with those in "Eve," another poem by Christina Rossetti. The conclusion is that Rossetti is a skilled rhymer because she uses rhyme appropriately in both poems. At the end of the essay the central idea is reiterated.

WRITING TOPICS

1. For Shakespeare's Sonnet 73, analyze the ways in which Shakespeare creates his iambics. That is, what is the relationship of lightly accented syllables to the heavily accented ones? Where does Shakespeare use articles (*the*), pronouns (*this*, *his*), prepositions (*upon*, *against*, *of*), relative clause markers (*which*, *that*) and adverb clause markers (*as*, *when*) in relation to syllables of heavy stress? Determine the number and placement of one-syllable words and two-syllable words in the sonnet. On the basis of this study, how would you characterize Shakespeare's control of the iambic foot?

2. Compare the sounds used in Poe's "The Bells" with those of Wagoner's "March for a One-Man Band." What effects are achieved by each poet? What is the relationship in each poem between sound and content? Which poem do you prefer on the basis of sound? Why?

3. The poems "Barbara Allan," "Miniver Cheevy," and "At a Summer Hotel" all utilize falling, or trochaic, rhyme. What is the effect of this rhyming pattern in the three poems? How do the poems achieve seriousness, despite the fact that trochaic rhyme is often used generally to complement humorous and light verse?

4. Try writing a limerick. If you are at a loss for a topic, use one of the following lines to begin:

   There once was a man in a rowboat.
   Two happy friends tried to study.
   A fellow walked into a bar.

   Once you have finished, use the same topic and detail for a poem in iambics. Describe the differences and challenges you encounter because of the differences between the rollicking form of the limerick and the more steady pace of the iambics. How do you handle the differnt demands of the form? What can you say about the iambic foot as a result of this experience?

5. Try writing a few short poems using comic rhymes. An example of what might be done is the following set of lines in which an anonymous poet was finding rhymes for the Irish town of Tipperary:

The stubborn muse he could not vary,
For still the lines would run contrary
Whene'er he thought on Tipperary.

Some words for rhyming: *bookcase, Schenectady, computer, seven, Chanhassen, grammar*, and so on. If you find trouble with exact rhymes, see what you can do with slant rhymes and eye rhymes. The idea is to use your ingenuity. Have fun.

19

Form: The Shape of the Poem

Poetry is tightly compressed and highly rhythmical language, and it always exists under self-imposed restrictions, or conventions (see also Chapter 18, pp. 677–722). The goal of poets has been not only to *say* something important and moving, but also to say it with intelligence, wit, insight, and skill. Poets have therefore traditionally exercised their verbal powers within a variety of clearly recognizable shapes or forms—**closed-form poetry.** Since the middle of the last century, many poets have rejected the more obvious conventions, thereby producing poems which follow patterns of thought and emotion that appear to be spontaneous and free—**open-form poetry.**

CLOSED AND OPEN FORMS

The terms *closed* and *open* refer to structure and technique rather than to content or ideas. **Closed-form poetry** is written in specific and traditional patterns of *rhyme, meter, line length,* and *line groupings.* In the closed form, the **stanza** is the poetic analogue of the paragraph. It consists of a number of lines connected by subject or theme, and often grouped or separated both topically and visually. Examples of closed form that have been used for hundreds of years are *ballads, sonnets, couplets, blank verse, limericks, hymns, odes,* and *lyrics.*

    Open-form poetry, on the other hand, refers to poems that avoid traditional patterns of organization and do not rely on meter, rhyme, line length, or stanzas to produce order. An open-form poem often presents an apparently indiscriminate blending of long and short lines, no rhyme scheme, and no distinct stanzas at all. Open-form poetry, however, is not disorganized or chaotic. The poet has instead sought new ways to arrange words and lines, new ways to express thoughts and feelings, and new ways to order poetic experience.

CLOSED-FORM POETRY: THE BUILDING BLOCKS

In closed-form poetry the basic building block is the *line of verse*. Various numbers of lines may be grouped together through rhyme to form stanzas or sections of poems which in turn are assembled to create traditional forms.

BLANK VERSE.   The most common single line in English poetry is **blank verse,** or *unrhymed iambic pentameter* (see pp. 679–80). Shakespeare's plays use blank verse extensively, and Milton's long epic, *Paradise Lost,* uses it exclusively. An example of Shakespeare's blank verse is this speech from the first act of *Hamlet,* where the prince tells his mother that his sorrow over his father's death is real and not superficial:

Seems, madam? nay it is. I know not "seems."
'Tis not alone my inky cloak good mother,
Nor customary suits of solemn black,
Nor windy suspiration of forced breath,
No, nor the fruitful river of the eye,°   *tears*
Nor the dejected havior° of the visage,°   *appearance; face*
Together with all forms, moods, shapes of grief,
That can denote me truly: these indeed seem,
For they are actions, that a man might play,
But I have that within which passes show,
These but the trappings and the suits of woe.   *(Act I, scene 2, lines 76–86)*

While these lines are linked together to make up the entire speech, each one creates an identifiable unit of thought and grammatical coherence. (The rhyming lines mark the conclusion, not a new form.) In the footsteps of Shakespeare, poets of English have used blank verse again and again, for without forsaking its poetic identity as a closed form, it most closely resembles normal speech.

THE COUPLET.   The basic two-line building block of poetic form is the **couplet.** The two lines usually rhyme, and usually are of the same length, although English translations of biblical poetry contain couplets unified by parallel ideas and assertions, not by meter and rhyme. Some couplets may be extremely short; even single-word lines like "Flee/Me" or "Night/Flight" can comprise a couplet. However, couplets are most often in iambic pentameter or iambic tetrameter. They are used in larger units or forms of poetry, such as stanzas, sonnet conclusions, and entire poems, and for this reason are one of the most versatile of closed forms. For example, the following couplet by John Dryden (1631–1700) is justly considered one of the best in the language:

Great Wits are sure to Madness near ally'd;
And thin Partitions do their Bounds divide.

Ever since the fourteenth century, when Chaucer used them, couplets have been a regular feature of English poetry. In the seventeenth and eighteenth centuries, the five-stress couplet was considered particularly appropriate for epic, or heroic, poetry. For this reason it is often called the **heroic couplet.** Also because the period is considered the neoclassic age of literature, the form is also called the **neoclassic couplet.** It was used with consummate skill by Dryden, and also by Alexander Pope (1685–1744).

Usually, the heroic couplet expresses a complete idea and is grammatically self-sufficient. It thrives on the rhetorical strategies of **parallelism** and **antithesis.** Look, for example, at these lines from Pope's "The Rape of the Lock," his great mock-epic poem:

> Here *Britain's* Statesmen oft the Fall foredoom
> Of Foreign Tyrants, and of Nymphs at home;
> Here Thou, Great *Anna*! whom three Realms obey,
> Dost sometimes Counsel take—and sometimes *Tea*.   [italics added]

These lines describe activities at Hampton Court, the royal palace and residence of Queen Anne (reigned 1701–1714). Notice that the first couplet allows Pope to link *"Britain's* Statesmen" with two related but antithetical events: the fall of nations and the fall of young women. Similarly, the second heroic couplet allows for the parallel and comic linking of royal meetings of state (*Counsel*) and tea time (in the early eighteenth century, *tea* was pronounced "tay"). The example thus demonstrates how the heroic couplet may place contrasting actions and situations in amusing and ironic parallels.

THE TERCET, OR TRIPLET. A three-line stanza is called a **tercet,** or **triplet.** Tercets may be written in any uniform line length or meter, usually with a single rhyming sound (*a a a, b b b,* and so on), which in effect creates short stanzaic units. The following poem is written in iambic tetrameter triplets.

ALFRED, LORD TENNYSON (1809–1892)

The Eagle   *1851*

He clasps the crag with crooked hands;
Close to the sun in lonely lands,
Ring'd with the azure world, he stands.

The wrinkled sea beneath him crawls;
He watches from his mountain walls.
And like a thunderbolt he falls.

5

The lines are of even length, with the rhyming sounds being repeated three times in each stanza. In the first tercet we view the eagle, as though at a distance. In the second, the perspective shifts, and we see through the eagle's eyes and follow his actions. In this tercet the verbs are active: The sea "crawls" and the eagle "falls." While the two tercets and the shift in perspective divide the poem, alliteration pulls things back together. This is especially true of the *k* sound in *clasps, crag, crooked, close,* and *crawls,* and the *w* sound in *with, world, watches,* and *walls.*

Terza Rima. An exception to the triple rhyme of the tercet is **terza rima,** in which stanzas are interlocked through a pattern that requires the center termination in one tercet to be rhymed twice in the next, as follows: *a b a, b c b, c d c, d e d,* and so on. You can see an example of terza rima in Shelley's "Ode to the West Wind" (p. 746).

The Villanelle. Still another exception to the *a a a* pattern of the tercet is the **villanelle,** in which every triplet in the poem is rhymed *a b a* (for an example, see Dylan Thomas's "Do Not Go Gentle Into That Good Night," p. 749). As these two forms illustrate, the tercet, like the couplet, is adaptable. No single definition or illustration can adequately encompass the variability of these traditional stanza patterns.

The Quatrain. The most adaptable and popular building block in English and American poetry is the four-line **quatrain.** This stanza has been popular for hundreds of years and has lent itself to a great many variations. Like couplets and triplets, quatrains may be written in any line length and meter; even the line lengths *within* a quatrain may vary. The determining factor is always the rhyme scheme, and even that can vary significantly, given the demands of the form and the desires of the poet. Quatrains may be rhymed *a a a a,* but they can also be rhymed *a b a b, a b b a, a a b a,* or even *a b c b.* All these variations are determined, at least in part, by the larger patterns or forms that quatrains are used to build. Quatrains are basic components of many traditional closed forms, including ballads and sonnets.

COMMON TYPES OF CLOSED-FORM POETRY

Over the centuries, English and American poetry has evolved or appropriated many traditional closed forms, all of them determined by some combination of meter, rhyme scheme, line length, and stanza form. Most of them involve a combination of the basic building blocks of poetic form, such as the couplet, tercet, and quatrain. The following are the more common traditional forms.

The Italian, or Petrarchan Sonnet

The **sonnet** is one of the most durable and popular traditional forms. All sonnets are fourteen lines long. Initially, they were an Italian poetic form (*sonnetto* means "little song") popularized by Petrarch (1304–1374), who wrote long collections or *cycles* of sonnets. The form and style of Petrarch's sonnets were adapted to English poetry in the early sixteenth century, and with variations have been used ever since. The **Italian,** or **Petrarchan sonnet** is in iambic pentameter and is composed of two quatrains and two tercets. The first eight lines are the **octave** (an eight-line unit of thought) and the last six form the **sestet.**

The rhyme scheme of the octave is usually fixed in an *a b b a, a b b a* pattern. The sestet offers a number of rhyming possibilities, including *c d c, c d c* and *c d e, c d e*. In terms of structure and meaning, the octave usually presents a problem or dilemma, and the sestet offers a resolution. As a result, there is often a clear shift or turn in thought from the octave to the sestet, as in Milton's "When I Consider How My Light Is Spent" (p. 739).

The English, or Shakespearean Sonnet

The **English,** or **Shakespearean sonnet,** named after its most famous practitioner, is written in iambic pentameter and has the following rhyme scheme: *a b a b, c d c d, e f e f, g g*. Shakespeare recognized that there are fewer rhyming words in English than in Italian, and hence he based his form on seven rhymes rather than the five of the Italian sonnet. As indicated by the rhyme scheme, the Shakespearean sonnet contains three quatrains and a concluding couplet. The pattern of thought therefore shifts from the octave-sestet organization of the Italian sonnet to a four-part argument on a single thought or emotion. Each quatrain usually contains a separate development of the sonnet's central idea, with the couplet providing a conclusion, climax, and resolution. Shakespeare's Sonnet 116, "Let Me Not to the Marriage of True Minds" (p. 732), is an example of the English sonnet.

The Ballad

The **ballad,** which originated in folk literature, is the oldest continuously used closed form in English poetry. A ballad consists of a long series of quatrains in which lines of iambic tetrameter alternate with iambic trimeter. Normally, only the second and fourth lines of each stanza contain rhyming words, and so the rhyme scheme is *x a x a, x b x b, x c x c*, and so on. The ballad of tradition was a lengthy narrative, designed for singing, like the anonymous ballads "Sir Patrick Spens" (p. 525) and "Barbara Allan" (p. 884). Often a single tune was used over and over again by subsequent balladeers, and many of the tunes have survived to the present day.

Common Measure or Hymnal Stanza

Common measure is probably derived from the ballad stanza. It shares with the ballad the alternation of four-beat and three-beat iambic lines, but adds a second rhyme to each quatrain: *a b a b, c d c d,* and so on. As with the ballad, the building block of common measure is the quatrain. The measure is often used in hymns, so it is sometimes called the **hymnal stanza.** Many of Emily Dickinson's poems, including "Because I Could Not Stop for Death" (p. 528), are written in common measure.

The Song, or Lyric

The **lyric** is a free stanzaic form that was originally designed to be sung to a repeating melody. The structure and rhyme scheme of the first stanza are therefore duplicated in all subsequent stanzas. After the ballad, it is one of the oldest traditional closed poetic forms. The individual stanzas of a lyric may be built from any combination of single lines, couplets, triplets, and quatrains. The line lengths may shift, and a great deal of metrical variation is common.

There is theoretically no limit to the number of stanzas in a lyric, although there are usually no more than five or six. We can find a great deal of variation in the structure. A. E. Housman's "Loveliest of Trees, the Cherry Now" (p. 529), for example, is a lyric made up of three quatrains containing two couplets each. It is in iambic tetrameter and rhymes *a a b b.* The second and third stanza repeat the same pattern. Christina Rossetti's "Echo" (p. 698) is also a lyric, but its structure is different from that of Housman's poem. Here, the structural formulation of each stanza is iambic: *5a 5b 5a 3b 2c 5c.* Lyrics can have very complex and ingenious stanzaic structures. John Donne's "The Canonization" (p. 849), for instance, contains five stanzas that reflect the following pattern: *Iambic: 5a 4b 5b 5a 4c 4c 4c 4a 3a.* The nine-line stanza contains three different rhymes and three different line lengths. Nevertheless, the same intricate pattern is repeated in each of the five stanzas.

The Ode

The **ode** is a more complex stanzaic form than the lyric, with varying line lengths and intricate rhyme schemes. Some odes have repeating patterns; others offer no duplication and introduce a new structure in each stanza. Although some odes were designed to be set to music, most do not fit repeating melodies. There is no set form for the ode. Poets have developed their own structure according to their needs. John Keats's great odes were particularly congenial to his ideas, as in the "Ode to a Nightingale" (p. 744), which consists of ten stanzas in iambic pentameter with the repeating form *a b a b c d e 3c d e.*

Haiku

The **haiku** originated in Japan, where it has been a favored poetic form for hundreds of years. In its original form, the haiku imposed strict rules on the writer: The poem must be only three lines long and have a total of seventeen syllables in a pattern of *five, seven,* and *five* syllables per line. The traditional subject matter was nature and the seasons. Today English-language poets have treated many different subjects in haiku, and have also taken liberties with the syllabic count. Because of the rigid pattern, haiku poetry must aim for objectivity, simplicity, and clarity, and should be judged by these standards. The following anonymous haiku illustrates some of these qualities.

Spun in high, dark clouds

Spun in high, dark clouds,
Snow forms vast webs of white flakes
And drifts lightly down.

In the tradition of haiku, the subject of this poem is derived from nature. The major metaphor equates gathering snow with the webs of spiders or silkworms. To supply a degree of tension, the lines contrast "high" with "down," and "dark" with "white." Because of the enforced brevity of the haiku form, the diction is simple and, except for the word *forms,* is of English derivation (*form* is a word derived from French). In addition, the words are mainly monosyllabic, and the form therefore crowds sixteen words into the seventeen-syllable form. Most English haiku contain a similar preponderance of one-syllable words.

Some Other Closed-Form Types

Many other closed forms have enjoyed long popularity. One of these, the **epigram,** is a short and witty poem that usually makes a humorous or satiric point. Epigrams are two to four lines long and are often written in couplets. The form was developed by the Roman poet Martial (A.D. 40–102) and has remained popular to the present. Humorous **epitaphs,** lines composed to mark the death of someone, can also be epigrams. The following epitaph-epigram was written to commemorate John Hewet and Sara Drew, who were killed by lightning on July 31, 1718, while helping bring in the harvest; it is followed by a selection of epigrams.

ALEXANDER POPE   (1688–1744)

Epitaph on the Stanton-Harcourt Lovers   *1718*

Here lie two poor Lovers, who had the mishap,
Though very chaste people, to die of a Clap.

SAMUEL TAYLOR COLERIDGE   (1772–1834)

What Is an Epigram?   *1802*

What is an epigram? a dwarfish whole,
Its body brevity, and wit its soul.

e. e. cummings   (1894–1962)

A Politician   *1944*

a politician is an arse upon
which everyone has sat except a man.

J. V. CUNNINGHAM   (b. 1911)

Epitaph for Someone or Other   *1950*

Naked I came, naked I leave the scene,
And naked was my pastime in between.

QUESTIONS

1. What do these four epigrams have in common? To what extent do they
   share a common tone and form?
2. Consider the relationship between epigrams and the couplets that close
   English sonnets or the heroic couplets of the eighteenth century. Look at
   the concluding couplets of Shakespeare's sonnets in this text (use the index)
   and look at Alexander Pope's couplets in the extract from "The Rape of the
   Lock" (p. 725). To what extent do these couplets have effects similar to those
   produced by epigrams?

Another popular closed-form type is the **limerick.** Like the epigram,
the limerick is usually comic, the humor often being reinforced by double
or falling rhymes (see pp. 688–89). In addition, most limericks today are
bawdy and sexual. We do not know who invented the limerick as a form,
but it was popularized by Edward Lear (1812–1888), an English artist and
humorist. Limericks are always five lines long and the dominant foot is

the *anapaest* (˘˘´). The structure of most limericks may thus be described as *anapaestic, with variations: 3a 3a 2b 2b 3a.* Here are a few limericks for your enyoyment.

A diner while dining at Crewe,
Found a rather large mouse in his stew.
  Said the waiter, "Don't shout
  And wave it about,
Or the rest will be wanting one too."

There once was a man from Tarentum
Who gnashed his false teeth till he bent 'em.
  When asked the cost
  Of what he had lost,
He said "I can't say, for I rent 'em."

Humorous closed forms continue to be devised by enterprising writers. Although none has become as popular as the limerick, they illustrate both the pleasures and the agonies of working within closed forms. The **clerihew,** invented in the late nineteenth century by Edmund Clerihew Bentley (1875–1956), is related to the epigram. Clerihews are usually composed of two couplets and focus on a well-known person, who is named in the first line. Here are two clerihews, both written by Bentley and published in 1937.

George the Third
Ought never to have occurred.
One can only wonder
At so grotesque a blunder.

Alfred, Lord Tennyson
Lived upon venison:
Not cheap, I fear,
Because venison's deer.

QUESTIONS

1. What do these clerihews have in common? To what extent do they share a common tone and structure?
2. Write several clerihews about contemporary figures and share them with your class. Try to maintain the tone and style of Bentley's work.

As a final illustration of humorous closed form, we offer the **double dactyl,** devised in the 1960s by Anthony Hecht and John Hollander. The form is related to that of the epigram, limerick, and clerihew, and the rules that govern this form are fairly complex; they dictate the meter, line length, and specific content of lines 1, 2, and 6 or 7. Here is an example:

ANTHONY HECHT   (b. 1923)

Nominalism   *1967*

Higgledy-piggledy
Juliet Capulet
Cherished the tenderest
Thoughts of a rose:

"What's in a name?" said she,   5
Etymologically,
"Save that all Montagues
Stink in God's nose."

CLOSED FORM AND MEANING

Although traditional closed forms seem restrictive to many contemporary
poets, they provide a framework within which a poet can express ideas,
attitudes, and feelings. The poet's challenge is to take an existing framework and breathe new life into it by arranging images, emotions, and
ideas. A skillful poet uses the demands of a closed form to his or her own
ends. With this in mind, let us look at the way a specific closed form may
be employed to shape thoughts and emotions.

WILLIAM SHAKESPEARE   (1564–1616)

Sonnet 116: Let Me Not to the Marriage of True Minds   *1609*

Let me not to the marriage of true minds	
Admit impediments.° Love is not love	
Which alters when it alteration finds,	
Or bends with the remover to remove:	
Oh, no! it is an ever-fixèd mark,	5
That looks on tempests and is never shaken;	
It is the star to every wandering bark,°	*small ship*
Whose worth's unknown, although his height° be taken	*altitude*
Love's not Time's fool,° though rosy lips and cheeks	*slave*
Within his° bending sickle's compass come;	*Time's* 10
Love alters not with his brief hours and weeks,	
But bears it out even to the edge of doom.°	*The Last Judgment*
If this be error and upon me proved,	
I never writ, nor no man ever loved.	

SONNET 116.   2 *impediments*: a reference to "The Order of Solemnization of
Matrimony" in the Anglican *Book of Common Prayer*: "I require that if either of you know of
any impediment why ye may not be lawfully joined together in Matrimony, ye do now
confess it."

QUESTIONS

1. Describe the restrictions imposed by this closed form. To what extent is the poem's argument imposed by the form?
2. What is the poem's meter? Rhyme scheme? Structure?
3. Describe the varying ideas about love explored in the three quatrains.
4. What does the concluding couplet contribute to the poem's argument about love?

We immediately recognize that this poem is a Shakespearean sonnet. It is in iambic pentameter and contains three quatrains and a concluding couplet, rhyming *a b a b, c d c d, e f e f, g g*. The topic is that real love is a "marriage of true minds." The sonnet puts forward the idea that such love exists independently of earthly time and change.

Shakespeare's sonnet form provides the organization for the poem's argument, with each quatrain advancing a new perspective on the central thought. The first quatrain presents the sonnet's *thesis*: True and permanent love is based on the "marriage of true minds." The rhetorical strategy is negation, for the speaker tells us what true love is *not*. The allusion to the Anglican marriage ceremony (in the term *impediments*) makes the tone public and ceremonial, as though the lines were being spoken during a wedding or a formal social occasion.

In lines 5–8 the speaker illustrates the permanence of true love by introducing a nautical and navigational metaphor. Love is comparable to an unchanging landmark and a constant star—the Pole Star—both of which unfailingly guide sailors to port. The quatrain thus reverses the rhetorical strategy of the first, for it tells what true love *is* rather than what it is *not*.

The third quatrain returns to the negative strategy of the first. Here Time is personified as a reaper whose sickle inevitably cuts down all living things. Though the hand of death destroys lovers, however, it cannot disjoin them, for their love will endure beyond them, "even to the edge" of historical time when "doom," or the day of judgment, will take place.

The final couplet sums up the argument by offering an irrefutable logical proposition: If the speaker can be proved wrong, then he never wrote and no man ever loved. Because these last conditions contradict experience, the reader is left to conclude that the speaker's arguments are both valid and true.

As this brief exposition demonstrates, Shakespeare brings out his ideas brilliantly within the space of the closed form. This is not to say either that he exhausts his topic, or that he wants to. The ideas of the third quatrain, for example, about how love transcends time, could be greatly expanded. A philosophical analysis of the topic would need to deal extensively with Platonic ideas about reality—whether it exists in *particulars* or *universals*. Such a discussion would require many pages and chapters.

But that is not Shakespeare's interest here. He rather chooses the restricted form of a quatrain, and within this framework he strongly asserts that human love has the power to exceed mortal restrictions. Similarly, the poem's very last line, if it became the topic of a prose disquisition, might require the introduction of evidence about the poet's own writing, and also about many examples of human love. But the two lines are enough here, within the restrictions of the poem. One might add the most readers find Shakespeare's poem interesting and vital, while extensive philosophical disquisitions often drop into laps as readers fall asleep.

The closed poetic form therefore may be viewed as a natural function of characteristic poetic compression. No matter what form a poet chooses— couplet, sonnet, song, ballad, ode—that form imposes restrictions, and it therefore challenges and shapes the poet's thought. The poet of the closed form shares with all writers the need to make ideas seem logical and well supported, but the challenge of the form is to make all this happen *within the form itself*. The thought must be developed clearly and also fully, and there should be no lingering doubts once the poem is completed. The words must seem absolutely right, as though they were the easiest and most natural ones on earth that could be selected. All this means that when we look at good poems in the closed form, we may be sure that they represent the ultimate degree of poetic thought, discipline, and skill.

OPEN-FORM POETRY

As we noted earlier, poets writing in open rather than closed forms avoid the ready-made patterns of traditional structures such as the ballad or sonnet. Similarly, they do not use traditional rhyme schemes or regular meters to organize their poems. Instead, they employ other ways of organizing words, lines, and sentences into cohesive and effective poetic statements. In many respects, open forms have come to dominate modern poetry.

Open-form poetry was once termed **free verse** (from the French *vers libre*) to signify its freedom from regular metrical rules and its dependence on the rhythms of spoken language. That term is misleading, however. While open-form poetry is indeed liberated from rigid demands of meter, rhyme, and stanza, there is nothing accidental or haphazard about the poems; they have patterns, but these patterns are nontraditional.

OPEN FORM AND MEANING

By giving up the shaping power of traditional devices, poets writing in open forms accept the need to create new kinds of fusion between form and content. They hence base their poems on devices such as rhythm and cadence, line lengths and breaks, pauses, and the groupings of words and phrases. They also isolate individual words and/or phrases into single lines, and freely emphasize their ideas through the manipulation of spaces separating words and sentences. They may even write poems that look exactly like prose, and are printed in paragraphs instead of stanzas or lines. These **prose poems** rely on the cadences of language and the progression of images to convey the poetic experience. As a general rule, we should remember that open-form poetry is neither disorganized nor formless. On the contrary, each poem embodies its own principles of structure.

We can see an early instance of open-form poetry in Walt Whitman's "Reconciliation." It was written as part of *Drum Taps*, a collection of fifty-three poems about the poet's reactions to Civil War battles in Virginia.

WALT WHITMAN (1819–1892)

Reconciliation   *1865, 1881*

Word over all, beautiful as the sky,
Beautiful that war and all its deeds of carnage must in time be utterly lost,
That the hands of the sisters Death and Night incessantly softly wash again, and
   ever again, this soil'd world;
For my enemy is dead, a man divine as myself is dead,
I look where he lies white-faced and still in the coffin—I draw near,   5
Bend down and touch lightly with my lips the white face in the coffin.

QUESTIONS

1. How do individual lines, varying line lengths, punctuation, pauses, and cadences create rhythm and organize the images and ideas in this poem?
2. To what extent do alliteration, assonance, and the repetition of words unify the poem and reinforce its content?
3. What is the "word" referred to in line 1? What does the speaker find "beautiful" about this "word" and the passage of time?
4. What instances of personification can you find? What do these personified figures do? What does the speaker do in lines 5–6? Why does he do this?

Whitman's "Reconciliation" shows the power of open-form poetry. There is no dominant meter, rhyme scheme, or stanza pattern. Instead, the poet uses individual lines and varying line lengths to organize and emphasize the images, ideas, and emotions. He also uses repetition, alliteration, and assonance to make internal line connections.

Without going into every aspect of the poem we may note the unifying elements in the first few lines. The *word over all* (i.e., reconciliation, peace) is linked to the second line by the repetition of the words *beautiful* and *all*; *beautiful* is grammatically complemented by the clauses *that . . . lost* (line 2) and *That . . . world* (line 3). The reconciling word is thus connected to the image of the two personified figures, Death and Night, who "wash" war and carnage (bloodshed) out of "this soil'd world."

In the third line, unity and emphasis are created through the repetition of *again* and the alliteration on the *ly* sound of *incessantly* and *softly*, the *s* sound in *hands, sisters, incessantly, softly,* and *soil'd,* and the *d* sound in *hands, Death, soil'd,* and *World.* One may also note the unifying assonance patterns of $\breve{\imath}$ in *its, in, sisters, incessantly,* and *this,* and $\bar{\imath}$ in *sky, time,* and *Night.* The pauses of the line, or "junctures," create remarkable internal rhythms that coincide with the thought: *That the hands // of the sisters // Death and Night // incessantly // softly // wash again // and ever again // this soil'd world.*

This selective analysis demonstrates that open-form poetry creates its own unity. While some of the unifying elements, such as alliteration and assonance, are also a property of closed-form poetry, many are unique to poetry of the open form, such as the repetitions, the reliance on grammatical structures, and the careful control of rhythms. The concept of the open form is that the topic itself shapes the appearance of the final poem. Unity is there—development is there—but the open form demands that there be as many shapes and forms as there are topics.

VISUAL POETRY AND CONCRETE POETRY

In **visual poetry,** much of the impact comes from the appearance of the poem as a shape on the page. Some visual poetry seeks to strike a balance between the pleasures of seeing and those of hearing the poem. Other visual poetry, however, abandons sound completely and invests all its impact in our perception of the visual image or picture. To some degree, visual poetry sacrifices the pleasure of hearing the poem, since the impact of the form depends on *sight.*

Visual poetry is not a recent development. The Chinese have been producing it for thousands of years, and there are surviving examples from ancient Greece. Even in the English tradition, visual poetry dates back to the seventeenth century when ingenious writers created poems in the shapes of squares, circles, triangles, stars, and the like. This type of poetry, called **shaped verse,** was usually more ingenious than significant. There was rarely an organic connection between the shape and the sense of the poem. Exceptional poets, however, produced shaped verse in which the visual image and the meaning strikingly echo each other.

Picture poems experienced a revival after World War II, when visual poetry reentered the literary landscape with the birth of a new movement called **concrete poetry.** Poets in this tradition focus their attention almost completely on the medium from which the poem is created. In the case of printed work, this means that the writers pay far more attention to the visual arrangement of letters, words, lines, and white spaces than they do to content. Concrete poetry represents a fusion of writing with painting or graphic design, and the emphasis is on the visual. Form is both the means and the end of creation.

FORM AND MEANING IN VISUAL POETRY

In reading visual and concrete poetry, you should seek correspondences between the image and the words. In your consideration, include the shape of the poem, the connotations of this shape, the varying line lengths, the placement of individual words and phrases, and the use of space. A superb example of seventeenth-century visual poetry is George Herbert's "Easter Wings," a religious poem that offers two different pictures that are both relevant to the content (p. 738).

This poem is an admission of sin and a prayer for redemption. It compares humanity's loss of Eden ("wealth and store") to the speaker's spiritual state as a petitioner seeking salvation through the Good Friday sacrifice. When viewed sideways, the poem resembles a pair of angel's wings. The image is thus linked with the title of the poem, and it connotes atonement, grace, and salvation.

The correspondence between shape and meaning goes even further. Herbert reinforces the ideas in various lines by the careful manipulation of line lengths. Thus, in discussing the spiritual history of humanity, the original "wealth and store" of Eden are described in the poem's longest (widest) line. As the fall from grace is described, the lines get progressively shorter (thinner), until humanity's fallen state is reached in the narrowest, "most poor" line (line 5). This same pattern is repeated in lines 11–15 to portray the sinful state that has left the speaker spiritually "most thin." In the second half of each stanza, this pattern is reversed, and the lines gradually expand, echoing the speaker's prayers for grace and salvation. Thus, the full lengths of lines 10 and 20 reflect the original states of grace, described in lines 1 and 11, and the glorious wealth of redemption.

POEMS FOR STUDY

GEORGE HERBERT   (1593–1633)

Easter Wings   *1633*

Lord, who createdst man in wealth and store,°   *abundance*
  Though foolishly he lost the same,
    Decaying more and more
      Till he became
        Most poor: 5
        With thee
        O let me rise
      As larks, harmoniously,
    And sing this day thy victories:
Then shall the fall further the flight in me.   10

My tender age in sorrow did I begin:
  And still with sicknesses and shame
    Thou didst so punish sin,
      That I became
        Most thin.   15
        With thee
        Let me combine,
      And feel this day thy victory;
    For, if I imp° my wing on thine,
Affliction shall advance the flight in me.   20

EASTER WINGS.   19 *imp*: to repair a falcon's wing or tail by grafting on a feather.

QUESTIONS

1. What does the poem look like when viewed sideways? When viewed straight on? How do these two images echo and emphasize the poem's content?

2. How does the typographical arrangement of the lines of this poem echo the sense? As a starting point, consider lines 5 and 15. How are typography, shape, and meaning fused in these lines?

3. What do lines 1–5 tell you about humanity's spiritual history? What do lines 11–15 tell you about the speaker's spiritual state? How are these parallel?

JOHN MILTON (1608–1674)

When I Consider How My Light Is Spent°

1655

When I consider how my light is spent
  Ere half my days, in this dark world and wide,
  And that one talent° which is death to hide,
  Lodged with me useless, though my soul more bent
To serve therewith my Maker, and present   5
  My true account, lest he returning chide;
  "Doth God exact day-labor, light denied?"
  I fondly° ask; but Patience to prevent°   *foolishly; forestall*
That murmur, soon replies, "God doth not need
  Either man's work or his own gifts; who best   10
  Bear his mild yoke, they serve him best. His state
Is kingly. Thousands at his bidding speed
  And post o'er land and ocean without rest;
  They also serve who only stand and wait."

WHEN I CONSIDER HOW MY LIGHT IS SPENT. Milton began to go blind in the late 1640s and was completely blind by 1651.   3 *talent*: both a skill and a reference to the talents discussed in the parable in Matthew 25:14–30.

QUESTIONS

1. What is the meter of this poem? The rhyme scheme? The closed form?
2. To what extent do the two major divisions of this form organize the poem's ideas?
3. What problem is raised in the octave? What are the speaker's complaints? Who is the speaker in the sestet? How are the earlier conflicts resolved?
4. Explore the word *talent* and relate its various meanings to the poem as a whole. To understand the term fully, see Matthew 25:14–30.

PERCY BYSSHE SHELLEY (1792–1822)

Ozymandias

1818

I met a traveller from an antique land,
Who said—"Two vast and trunkless legs of stone
Stand in the desert. . . . Near them, on the sand,
Half sunk, a shattered visage lies, whose frown,
And wrinkled lip, and sneer of cold command,   5
Tell that its sculptor well those passions read
Which yet survive, stamped on these lifeless things,
The hand that mocked them, and the heart that fed;
And on the pedestal, these words appear;

'My name is Ozymandias, King of Kings, 10
Look on my Works, ye Mighty, and despair!'
Nothing beside remains. Round the decay
Of that colossal Wreck, boundless and bare
The lone and level sands stretch far away."

QUESTIONS

1. What is the meter of this poem? The rhyme scheme? What traditional closed form is modified here? How do the modifications affect the poem?

2. To what extent are content and meaning shaped by the closed form? What is described in the octave? In the sestet?

3. Characterize Ozymandias (thought to be Ramses II, Pharoah of Egypt, who died in 1225 B.C.) from the way he is portrayed in this poem.

CLAUDE MCKAY (1890–1948)

In Bondage 1922

I would be wandering in distant fields
Where man, and bird, and beast, lives leisurely,
And the old earth is kind, and ever yields
Her goodly gifts to all her children free;
Where life is fairer, lighter, less demanding, 5
And boys and girls have time and space for play
Before they come to years of understanding—
Somewhere I would be singing, far away.
For life is greater than the thousand wars
Men wage for it in their insatiate lust, 10
And will remain like the eternal stars,
When all that shines to-day is drift and dust.

But I am bound with you in your mean graves,
O black men, simple slaves of ruthless slaves.

QUESTIONS

1. What is the meter of this poem? The rhyme scheme? The form? To what extent does the form organize the speaker's thoughts?

2. Lines 1–8 present a conditional (rather than actual) situation that the speaker desires. What word signals this nature? What is the speaker's wish?

3. What point does the speaker make about life in lines 9–12?

4. How does the couplet undermine the rest of the poem? What single word conveys this reversal? How effectively do the rhymes clinch the poem's meaning? What is the speaker telling us about the lives of black people?

JOHN DRYDEN (1631–1700)

To the Memory of Mr. Oldham   *1684*

Farewell, too little and too lately known,
Whom I began to think and call my own:
For sure our souls were near allied, and thine
Cast in the same poetic mold with mine.
One common note on either lyre did strike,   5
And knaves and fools we both abhorred alike.
To the same goal did both our studies drive;
The last set out the soonest did arrive.
Thus Nisus° fell upon the slipp'ry place,
While his young friend performed and won the race.   10
O early ripe! to thy abundant store
What could advancing age have added more?
It might (what nature never gives the young)
Have taught the numbers of thy native tongue.
But satire needs not those, and wit will shine   15
Through the harsh cadence of a rugged line;
A noble error, and but seldom made,
When poets are by too much force betrayed.
Thy gen'rous fruits, though gathered ere their prime,
Still showed a quickness; and maturing time   20
But mellows what we write to the dull sweets of rhyme.
Once more, hail and farewell;° farewell, thou young.
But ah too short, Marcellus° of our tongue;
Thy brows with ivy and with laurels° bound;
But fate and gloomy night encompass thee around.   25

TO THE MEMORY OF MR. OLDHAM.   John Oldham (1653–1683) was a young poet
whom Dryden admired.   9 *Nisus:* a character in Vergil's *Aeneid* who slipped in a pool of
blood while running a race, thus allowing his best friend to win.   22 *hail and farewell:* an
echo of the Latin phrase "ave atque vale" spoken by gladiators about to fight.
23 *Marcellus:* a Roman general who was adopted by the Emperor Augustus as his successor
but died at the age of twenty.   24 *laurels:* a plant sacred to Apollo, the Greek god of
poetry; the traditional prize given to poets is a wreath of laurel.

QUESTIONS

1. What is the meter of this poem? Rhyme scheme? Closed form? How does
    the form control the tempo? Why is this tempo appropriate?

2. What does the speaker reveal about himself in lines 1–10? About Oldham?
    About his relationship with Oldham? What did the two have in common?

3. What is the effect of Dryden's frequent classical allusions? What pairs of
    rhyming words most effectively clinch ideas?

JEAN TOOMER   (1894–1967)

Reapers   *1923*

Black reapers with the sound of steel on stones
Are sharpening scythes. I see them place the hones
In their hip-pockets as a thing that's done,
And start their silent swinging, one by one.
Black horses drive a mower through the weeds,   5
And there, a field rat, startled, squealing bleeds,
His belly close to ground. I see the blade,
Blood-stained, continue cutting weeds and shade.

QUESTIONS

1. What is the poem's meter? The rhyme scheme? The form? What is the
    difference between Toomer's use of the form and Dryden's?

2. How do the images of this poem relate to each other? How does the image
    of the bleeding field rat and the "blood-stained" blade heighten the impact?

3. How does alliteration unify this poem and make sound echo sense? Note
    especially the *s* and *b* sounds, and the phrase *silent swinging*.

GEORGE HERBERT   (1593–1633)

Virtue°   *1633*

Sweet day, so cool, so calm, so bright,
The bridal of the earth and sky:
The dew shall weep thy fall tonight;
    For thou must die.

Sweet rose, whose hue, angry° and brave,°   *red; splendid*   5
Bids the rash° gazer wipe his eye:
Thy root is ever in its grave,
    And thou must die.

Sweet spring, full of sweet days and roses,
A box where sweets° compacted lie: *perfumes*   10
My music shows ye have your closes,°
    And all must die.

Only a sweet and virtuous soul,
Like seasoned timber, never gives;°

VIRTUE.   *Virtue*: (1) divine Power operating both outside and inside an individual; a
characteristic quality or property; (2) conformity to divine and moral laws.   6 *rash*: eager
or sympathetic.   11 *closes*: A *close* is the conclusion of a musical composition.   14 *never
gives*: that is, never gives in, never deteriorates and collapses (like rotted timber).

But though the whole world turn to coal,°   15
    Then chiefly lives.

15 *turn to coal*: universal fire at the Day of Judgment.

QUESTIONS

1. What is the rhyme scheme of this poem? The meter? The form?
2. What points does the speaker make about the day, the rose, spring, and the "sweet and virtuous soul"?
3. To what extent do the rhyme scheme and stanzaic structure of this poem shape and reinforce the poem's theme?

ROBERT FROST (1874–1963)

Desert Places   *1936*

Snow falling and night falling fast, oh, fast
In a field I looked into going past,
And the ground almost covered smooth in snow,
But a few weeds and stubble showing last.

The woods around it have it—it is theirs.   5
All animals are smothered in their lairs.
I am too absent-spirited to count;
The loneliness includes me unawares.

And lonely as it is that loneliness
Will be more lonely ere it will be less—   10
A blanker whiteness of benighted snow
With no expression, nothing to express.

They cannot scare me with their empty spaces
Between stars—on stars where no human race is.
I have it in me so much nearer home   15
To scare myself with my own desert places.

QUESTIONS

1. What is the meter? The rhyme scheme? The form?
2. What setting and situation are established in lines 1–4? What does the snow affect here? What does it affect in lines 5–8? In lines 9–12?
3. What different kinds of "desert places" is this poem about? Which kind is the most important? Most frightening?
4. How does the type of rhyme (rising or falling) change in the last stanza? How does this change affect the tone and impact of the poem?

5. How does the stanzaic pattern of this poem organize the progression of the speaker's thoughts, feelings, and conclusions?

JOHN KEATS (1795–1821)

Ode to a Nightingale   *1819*

1

My heart aches, and a drowsy numbness pains
　My sense, as though of hemlock° I had drunk,   *a poisonous herb*
Or emptied some dull opiate to the drains
　One minute past, and Lethe-wards° had sunk:
'Tis not through envy of thy happy lot,   5
　But being too happy in thine happiness,—
　　That thou, light-winged Dryad° of the trees,
　　　In some melodious plot
Of beechen green, and shadows numberless,
　　Singest of summer in full-throated ease.   10

2

O, for a draught of vintage! that hath been
　Cool'd a long age in the deep-delved earth,
Tasting of Flora° and the country green,
　Dance, and Provençal song, and sunburnt mirth!
O for a beaker full of the warm South,   15
　Full of the true, the blushful Hippocrene,°
　　With beaded bubbles winking at the brim,
　　　And purple-stainèd mouth;
That I might drink, and leave the world unseen,
　　And with thee fade away into the forest dim: 20

3

Fade far away, dissolve, and quite forget
　What thou among the leaves hast never known,
The weariness, the fever, and the fret
　Here, where men sit and hear each other groan;
Where palsy shakes a few, sad, last gray hairs,   25
　Where youth grows pale, and spectre-thin, and dies;
　　Where but to think is to be full of sorrow
　　　And leaden-eyed despairs,
Where Beauty cannot keep her lustrous eyes,
　　Or new Love pine at them beyond to-morrow.   30

ODE TO A NIGHTINGALE.   4 *Lethe-wards*: toward the river of forgetfulness in Hades, the underworld of Greek mythology.   7 *Dryad*: in Greek mythology, a semidivine tree spirit.   13 *Flora*: the Roman goddess of flowers.   16 *Hippocrene*: the fountain of the Muses on Mt. Helicon in Greek mythology; the phrase thus refers to both the waters of poetic inspiration and a cup of wine.

4

Away! away! for I will fly to thee,
  Not charioted by Bacchus° and his pards,°   *leopards*
But on the viewless wings of Poesy,°   *poetry*
  Though the dull brain perplexes and retards:
Already with thee! tender is the night,   35
  And haply the Queen-Moon is on her throne,
    Cluster'd around by all her starry Fays;°   *fairies*
      But here there is no light,
  Save what from heaven is with the breezes blown
  Through verdurous glooms and winding mossy ways.   40

5

I cannot see what flowers are at my feet,
  Nor what soft incense hangs upon the boughs,
But, in embalmed° darkness, guess each sweet   *fragrant*
  Wherewith the seasonable month endows
The grass, the thicket, and the fruit-tree wild;   45
  White hawthorn, and the pastoral eglantine;°   *honeysuckle*
    Fast fading violets cover'd up in leaves;
      And mid-May's eldest child,
  The coming musk-rose, full of dewy wine,
    The murmurous haunt of flies on summer eves.   50

6

Darkling° I listen; and, for many a time   *in the dark*
  I have been half in love with easeful Death,
Call'd him soft names in many a musèd rhyme,
  To take into the air my quiet breath;
Now more than ever seems it rich to die,   55
  To cease upon the midnight with no pain,
    While thou art pouring forth thy soul abroad
      In such an ecstasy!
  Still wouldst thou sing, and I have ears in vain—
  To thy high requiem become a sod.   60

7

Thou wast not born for death, immortal Bird!
  No hungry generations tread thee down;
The voice I hear this passing night was heard
  In ancient days by emperor and clown:
Perhaps the self-same song that found a path   65
  Through the sad heart of Ruth,° when, sick for home,
    She stood in tears amid the alien corn;°   *wheat, grain*
      The same that oft-times hath

32 *Bacchus*: the Greek god of wine.   66 *Ruth*: the widow of Boaz in the biblical Book of
Ruth.

Charm'd magic casements, opening on the foam
   Of perilous seas, in faery lands forlorn.   70

                    8

Forlorn! the very word is like a bell
   To toll me back from thee to my sole self!
Adieu! the fancy° cannot cheat so well   *imagination*
   As she is fam'd to do, deceiving elf.
Adieu! adieu! thy plaintive anthem fades   75
   Past the near meadows, over the still stream,
      Up the hill-side; and now 'tis buried deep
         In the next valley-glades:
Was it a vision, or a waking dream?
   Fled is that music:—Do I wake or sleep?   80

QUESTIONS

1. Formulate the structure (meter of each line and rhyme scheme) of the stanzas. What traditional form is employed here?

2. What is the speaker's mental and emotional state in stanza 1? What similes are employed to describe this condition?

3. What does the speaker want in stanza 2? Whom does he want to join? Why? From what aspects of the world (stanza 3) does he want to escape?

4. How do the speaker's mood and perspective change in stanza 4? How does he achieve this transition? What characterizes the world that the speaker enters in stanza 5? What senses are employed to describe this world?

5. What does the speaker establish about the nightingale's song in the seventh stanza? What does the song come to symbolize?

PERCY BYSSHE SHELLEY   (1792–1822)

Ode to the West Wind   *1820*

                    I

O wild West Wind, thou breath of Autumn's being,
Thou, from whose unseen presence the leaves dead
Are driven, like ghosts from an enchanter fleeing,

Yellow, and black, and pale, and hectic° red,
Pestilence-stricken multitudes: O Thou,   5
Who chariotest to their dark wintry bed

The winged seeds, where they lie cold and low,
Each like a corpse within its grave, until
Thine azure sister of the Spring° shall blow

ODE TO THE WEST WIND.   4 *hectic*: a tubercular fever that produces flushed cheeks.
9 *Spring*: the wind that will blow in the spring.

Her clarion o'er the dreaming earth, and fill   10
(Driving sweet buds like flocks to feed in air)
With living hues and odours plain and hill:

Wild Spirit, which art moving everywhere;
Destroyer and Preserver; hear, O hear!

II

Thou on whose stream, 'mid the steep sky's commotion,   15
Loose clouds like Earth's decaying leaves are shed,
Shook from the tangled boughs of Heaven and Ocean,

Angels of rain and lightning: there are spread
On the blue surface of thine aery surge,
Like the bright hair uplifted from the head   20

Of some fierce Maenad,° even from the dim verge
Of the horizon to the zenith's height,
The locks of the approaching storm. Thou Dirge

Of the dying year, to which this closing night
Will be the dome of a vast sepulchre,   25
Vaulted with all thy congregated might

Of vapours,° from whose solid atmosphere   *clouds*
Black rain and fire and hail will burst: O hear!

III

Thou who didst waken from his summer dreams
The blue Mediterranean, where he lay,   30
Lulled by the coil of his crystalline streams,

Beside a pumice isle in Baiae's bay,°
And saw in sleep old palaces and towers
Quivering within the wave's intenser day,

All overgrown with azure moss and flowers   35
So sweet, the sense faints picturing them! Thou
For whose path the Atlantic's level powers

Cleave themselves into chasms, while far below
The sea-blooms and the oozy woods which wear
The sapless foliage of the ocean, know   40

Thy voice, and suddenly grow grey with fear,
And tremble and despoil themselves: O hear!

---

21 *Maenad*: a frenzied female worshipper of Dionysus, the god of wine and fertility in
Greek mythology.   32 *Baiae's bay*: a bay of the Mediterranean Sea west of Naples,
famous for the elaborate villas built on the shore by Roman emperors.

IV

If I were a dead leaf thou mightest bear;
If I were a swift cloud to fly with thee;
A wave to pant beneath thy power, and share   45

The impulse of thy strength, only less free
Than thou, O Uncontrollable! If even
I were as in my boyhood, and could be

The comrade of thy wanderings over Heaven,
As then, when to outstrip thy skiey speed   50
Scarce seemed a vision; I would ne'er have striven

As thus with thee in prayer in my sore need,
Oh! lift me as a wave, a leaf, a cloud!
I fall upon thorns of life! I bleed!

A heavy weight of hours has chained and bowed   55
One too like thee: tameless, and swift, and proud.

V

Make me thy lyre,° even as the forest is:
What if my leaves are falling like its own!
The tumult of thy mighty harmonies

Will take from both a deep, autumnal tone,   60
Sweet though in sadness. Be thou, Spirit fierce,
My spirit! Be thou me, impetuous one!

Drive my dead thoughts over the universe
Like withered leaves to quicken a new birth!
And, by the incantation of this verse,   65

Scatter, as from an unextinguished hearth
Ashes and sparks, my words among mankind!
Be through my lips to unawakened Earth

The trumpet of a prophecy! O Wind,
If Winter comes, can Spring be far behind?   70

57 *Lyre*: an Aeolian harp, a musical device which is sounded by the wind blowing across
strings.

QUESTIONS

1. Formulate the structure (meter of each line and rhyme scheme) of the
   stanzas. What two traditional closed forms are combined in this poem?

2. How many times (and where) is the *e* rhyme of the first stanza repeated as
   a rhyme sound throughout the poem? What is the effect of this repetition?

3. What aspect of the natural world does the wind affect in the first section of
   the poem? The second section? The third?

4. What does the speaker assert (in section 4) that time has done to him? What does he want from the West Wind? What does he want to become?

5. To what extent are the speaker's thoughts and feelings organized by the poem's five sections? What is the logical progression from section to section?

6. What does the West Wind symbolize? Compare this poem to Keats's "Ode to a Nightingale." How are the nightingale's song and the West Wind related to each other as symbols?

DYLAN THOMAS   (1914–1953)

Do Not Go Gentle Into That Good Night   *1951*

Do not go gentle into that good night,
Old age should burn and rave at close of day;
Rage, rage against the dying of the light.

Though wise men at their end know dark is right,
Because their words had forked no lightning they   5
Do not go gentle into that good night.

Good men, the last wave by, crying how bright
Their frail deeds might have danced in a green bay,
Rage, rage against the dying of the light.

Wild men who caught and sang the sun in flight,   10
And learn, too late, they grieved it on its way,
Do not go gentle into that good night.

Grave men, near death, who see with blinding sight
Blind eyes could blaze like meteors and be gay,
Rage, rage against the dying of the light.   15

And you, my father, there on the sad height,
Curse, bless, me now with your fierce tears, I pray.
Do not go gentle into that good night.
Rage, rage against the dying of the light.

QUESTIONS

1. This poem is written in a traditional closed form called the **villanelle,** which was developed in France during the Middle Ages. A villanelle may be nineteen lines long. There are additional rules governing the length and structure of stanzas, the rhyme scheme, and the repetition of complete lines. Try to formulate these rules. To look at another example, see Roethke's "The Waking" (p. 953).

2. What do you conclude about the speaker, listener, and situation here?

3. What four different kinds of men does the speaker discuss in lines 4–15? What do they have in common?

4. What puns and connotative words can you find in this poem? Consider the *good* of "good night" and the word *grave* (line 13).

DUDLEY RANDALL   (b. 1914)

Ballad of Birmingham°   *1966*

(On the bombing of a church in Birmingham, Alabama, 1963)

"Mother dear, may I go downtown
Instead of out to play,
And march the streets of Birmingham
In a Freedom March today?"

"No, baby, no, you may not go,   5
For the dogs are fierce and wild,
And clubs and hoses, guns and jails
Aren't good for a little child."

"But, mother, I won't be alone.
Other children will go with me,   10
And march the streets of Birmingham
To make our country free."

"No, baby, no, you may not go,
For I fear those guns will fire.
But you may go to church instead   15
And sing in the children's choir."

She has combed and brushed her night-dark hair,
And bathed rose petal sweet,
And drawn white gloves on her small brown hands,
And white shoes on her feet.   20

The mother smiled to know her child
Was in the sacred place,
But that smile was the last smile
To come upon her face.

For when she heard the explosion,   25
Her eyes grew wet and wild.
She raced through the streets of Birmingham
Calling for her child.

She clawed through bits of glass and brick,
Then lifted out a shoe   30

BALLAD OF BIRMINGHAM.   Four black children were killed when the 16th Street
Baptist Church in Birmingham, Alabama, was bombed in 1963. A man was finally indicted
for the murders in 1977 and convicted in 1982.

"Oh, here's the shoe my baby wore,
But, baby, where are you?"

QUESTIONS

1. Formulate the structure (meter, rhyme scheme, stanza form) of this poem. What traditional closed form is employed here?

2. Who is the speaker in stanzas 1 and 3? In stanzas 2 and 4? How are quotation and repetition employed to create tension?

3. What ironies do you find in the mother's assumptions? In the poem as a whole? In the society pictured in the poem?

4. Compare the poem to "Sir Patrick Spens" (p. 525) and to "Barbara Allan" (p. 884). How are the structures of all three alike? To what extent do all three deal with the same type of subject matter?

e. e. cummings (1894–1962)

Buffalo Bill's Defunct°   1923

Buffalo Bill's
defunct
       who used to
       ride a watersmooth-silver
               stallion   5
and break onetwothreefourfive pigeonsjustlikethat
                     Jesus
he was a handsome man
            and what i want to know is
how do you like your blueeyed boy   10
Mister Death

BUFFALO BILL'S DEFUNCT.   The poem has no title; it is usually referred to as
"Portrait" or by its first two lines. Buffalo Bill (William F. Cody, 1846–1917) was an
American plainsman, hunter, army scout, sharpshooter, and showman whose Wild West
show began touring the world in 1883; he became a symbol of the Wild West.

QUESTIONS

1. What is the effect of devoting a whole line to *Buffalo Bill's* (line 1), *defunct* (line 2), *stallion* (line 5), *Jesus* (line 7), and *Mister Death* (line 11)? How does this technique reflect and emphasize the content of the poem?

2. How does the typographical arrangement of line 6 contribute to the fusion of sound and sense? What other examples of this technique do you find?

3. Explain the denotations and connotations of *defunct*. What would be lost (or gained) by using the term *dead* or *deceased* instead?

4. To what extent is this poem a "portrait" of Buffalo Bill? What do we learn about him? Is the portrait respectful, mocking, or something in between?

WILLIAM CARLOS WILLIAMS   (1883–1963)

The Dance   *1944*

In Breughel's° great picture, The Kermess,
the dancers go round, they go round and
around, the squeal and the blare and the
tweedle of bagpipes, a bugle and fiddles
tipping their bellies (round as the thick-   5
sided glasses whose wash they impound)
their hips and their bellies off balance
to turn them. Kicking and rolling about
the Fair Grounds, swinging their butts, those
shanks must be sound to bear up under such   10
rollicking measures, prance as the dance
in Breughel's great picture, The Kermess.

THE DANCE.   1 *Breughel's:* Pieter Breughel (ca. 1525–1569), a Flemish painter. *The
Kermess* shows peasants dancing in celebration of the anniversary of the founding of a
church (*church mass*).

QUESTIONS

1.   What effect is produced by repeating the first line as the last line?
2.   How do repetition, alliteration, assonance, onomatopoeia, and internal rhyme

Pieter Brueghel the Elder, *La Kermesse.* Kunsthistorisches Museum, Vienna. (Art Resource)

affect the tempo, feeling, and meaning of the poem? How do the numerous participles (like *tipping, kicking, rolling*) make sound echo sense?

3. What words are capitalized? What effect is produced by omitting the capital letters at the beginning of each line? How does this typographical choice reinforce the sound and the sense of the poem?

4. Most of the lines of this poem are run-on rather than end-stopped, and many of them end with fairly weak words such as *and, the, about,* and *such.* What effect is produced through these techniques?

5. How successful is Williams in making the words and sentence rhythms echo the visual rhythms in Breughel's painting? Why is this open form more appropriate to the images of the poem than any closed form could be?

ALLEN GINSBERG (b. 1926)

A Supermarket in California   *1955*

What thoughts I have of you tonight, Walt Whitman,° for
I walked down the sidestreets under the trees with a headache
self-conscious looking at the full moon.
  In my hungry fatigue, and shopping for images, I went
into the neon fruit supermarket, dreaming of your enumera-   5
tions!°
What peaches and what penumbras! Whole families
shopping at night! Aisles full of husbands! Wives in the
avocados, babies in the tomatoes!—and you, Garcia Lorca,° what
were you doing down by the watermelons?   10

I saw you, Walt Whitman, childless, lonely old grubber,
poking among the meats in the refrigerator and eyeing the
grocery boys.
  I heard you asking questions of each: Who killed the pork
chops? What price bananas? Are you my Angel?   15
  I wandered in and out of the brilliant stacks of cans
following you, and followed in my imagination by the store
detective.
  We strode down the open corridors together in our solitary
fancy tasting artichokes, possessing every frozen delicacy, and   20
never passing the cashier.

Where are we going, Walt Whitman? The doors close in
an hour. Which way does your beard point tonight?
  (I touch your book and dream of our odyssey in the supermarket
and feel absurd.)   25
  Will we walk all night through solitary streets? The trees

A SUPERMARKET IN CALIFORNIA.   1 *Walt Whitman*: American poet (1819–1892)
who experimented with open forms and significantly influenced the development of
twentieth-century poetry.   5 *enumerations*: Many of Whitman's poems contain long lists.
9 *García Lorca*: Spanish surrealist poet and playwright (1896–1936) whose later poetry
became progressively more like prose.

add shade to shade, lights out in the houses, we'll both be
lonely.

Will we stroll dreaming of the lost America of love past blue
automobiles in driveways, home to our silent cottage?   30
   Ah, dear father, graybeard, lonely old courage-teacher,
what America did you have when Charon° quit poling his ferry
and you got out on a smoking bank and stood watching the
boat disappear on the black waters of Lethe?°

32 *Charon*: boatman in Greek mythology who ferried the souls of the dead across the river
Styx into Hades, the underworld.   34 *Lethe*: the river of forgetfulness in Hades. The
dead drank from this river and forgot their former lives.

QUESTIONS

1. Where is the speaker? What is he doing? What is his condition?

2. What effect is produced by placing Whitman and Lorca in the market?

3. To what extent do we find Whitman-like enumerations in this work? What
    is the effect of such enumerations?

4. Why is this a poem? What poetic devices are employed here? To what extent
    might it make more sense to consider this prose rather than poetry?

NIKKI GIOVANNI   (b. 1943)

Nikki-Rosa   1968

childhood remembrances are always a drag
if you're Black
you always remember things like living in Woodlawn°
with no inside toilet
and if you become famous or something   5
they never talk about how happy you were to have your mother
all to yourself and
how good the water felt when you got your bath from one of those
big tubs that folk in chicago barbecue in
and somehow when you talk about home   10
it never gets across how much you
understood their feelings
as the whole family attended meetings about Hollydale
and even though you remember
your biographers never understand   15
your father's pain as he sells his stock
and another dream goes
and though you're poor it isn't poverty that
concerns you
and though they fought a lot   20

NIKKI-ROSA.   3 *Woodlawn*: a predominantly black suburb of Cincinnati, Ohio.

it isn't your father's drinking that makes any difference
but only that everybody is together and you
and your sister have happy birthdays and very good christmasses
and I really hope no white person ever has cause to write about me
because they never understand Black love is Black wealth and they'll   25
probably talk about my hard childhood and never understand that
all the while I was quite happy

QUESTIONS

1. To what extent do individual lines, caesurae, and cadences create a rhythm
   and reinforce the sense of this poem?

2. What points does the speaker make about childhood in general, the child-
   hoods of blacks, and his or her own childhood?

3. What ideas about the ways in which whites understand or misunderstand
   blacks does this poem explore?

MAY SWENSON (1919–1989)

Women   *1968*

```
Women                    Or they
   should be                should be
      pedestals                little horses
         moving                   those wooden
            pedestals                sweet                                    5
               moving                  oldfashioned
                  to the                 painted
                     motions              rocking
                        of men            horses

              the gladdest things in the toyroom                             10

                  The                    feelingly
                 pegs                   and then
                of their               unfeelingly
               ears                   To be
              so familiar           joyfully                                 15
             and dear             ridden
            to the trusting      rockingly
           fists                ridden until
          To be chafed        the restored

egos dismount and the legs stride away                                       20

Immobile                 willing
   sweetlipped              to be set
      sturdy                  into motion
         and smiling            Women
            women                  should be                                 25
               should always          pedestals
                  be waiting            to men
```

QUESTIONS

1. Is this poem an instance of closed form, open form, or visual poetry? In what different ways or sequences can it be read? How do the different sequences change the meaning?

2. How well does the image of the poem reinforce its meaning? Would the effect be different if the columns of words were straight instead of undulating?

3. To what extent do repetition and alliteration help to organize the poem and underscore its sense? Note especially *w, m, f, r,* and *s* sounds.

4. What does this poem *say* that women should be? Does it mean what it says? How are men characterized? In what way is this poem ironic?

MARY ELLEN SOLT   (b. 1920)

Forsythia   *1966*

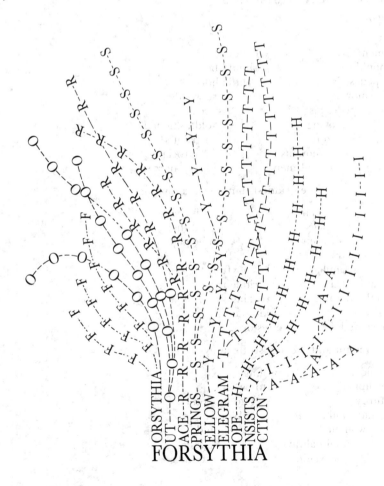

FORSYTHIA

QUESTIONS

1. Is this a poem or is it rather what is called in art a "wordwork"? What does this work tell you about forsythia?

2. When this work was originally published, it was printed over a square of yellow. What additional visual effect might have been produced by this color?

3. What is the meaning of the dots and dashes between each letter of "FORSYTHIA"? What is the link between this device and the word "TEL-EGRAM"?

EDWIN MORGAN   (b. 1920)

The Computer's First Christmas Card   *1968*

```
jollymerry
hollyberry
jollyberry
merryholly
happyjolly
jollyjelly
jellybelly
bellymerry
hollyheppy
jollyMolly
marryJerry
merryHarry
hoppyBarry
heppyJarry
boppyheppy
berryjorry
jorryjolly
moppyjelly
Mollymerry
Jerryjolly
bellyboppy
jorryhoppy
hollymoppy
Barrymerry
Jarryhappy
happyboppy
boppyjolly
jollymerry
merrymerry
merrymerry
merryChris
ammerryasa
Chrismerry
asMERRYCHR
YSANTHEMUM
```

QUESTIONS

1. To what extent is the effect of this work visual? What aspects or devices link it to a computer?

2. The writer (or computer) has generated some interesting word variations and images. What is the logic of the movement from line to line?

3. How successful is this work in conveying ideas or images of Christmas? How far away from Christmas does "the computer" wander? What do you make of the fact that the work ends "asMERRYCHR / YSANTHEMUM"?

4. Why might you consider this a poem?

JOHN HOLLANDER   (b. 1929)

Swan and Shadow   1969

```
                    Dusk
                 Above the
             water hang the
                        loud
                        flies                                        5
                    Here
                  O so
                   gray
                   then
                What            A pale signal will appear            10
                When            Soon before its shadow fades
              Where            Here in this pool of opened eye
              In us        No Upon us As at the very edges
                of where we take shape in the dark air
                  this object bares its image awakening
                ripples of recognition that will
                brush darkness up into light
   even after this bird this hour both drift by atop the perfect sad instant now
                    already passing out of sight
                toward yet-untroubled reflection                    20
                this image bears its object darkening
                into memorial shades Scattered bits of
              light            No of water Or something across
              water            Breaking up No Being regathered
              soon            Yet by then a swan will have         25
                gone            Yes out of mind into what
                  vast
                   pale
                   hush
                   of a                                             30
                   place
                    past
        sudden dark as
             if a swan
                sang                                                35
```

QUESTIONS

1. How effectively and consistenly does the shape image reinforce the meaning?
2. What specific words, phrases, and lines are emphasized by the typographical arrangement? To what extent does this effect give added impact to the poem?
3. How well does the structure echo the verbal images of the poem?
4. Do you find John Hollander's experiment with shaped verse as successful as George Herbert's in "Easter Wings" (p. 738)? If so, demonstrate how it succeeds. If not, explain why.

WRITING ABOUT FORM IN POETRY

In an essay about form in poetry you should aim to demonstrate a relationship between the structure and content of the poem you have selected. Do not discuss form or shape in isolation, for then your essay will be no more than a detailed description. As with essays about meter, sound, and rhyme, composition follows a double process of discovery, in which you investigate both the sense and the form of your poem.

The first thing to do in prewriting is to examine the poem's main ideas. Consider the various elements that contribute to the poem's impact and effectiveness: the speaker, listener, setting, situation, diction, imagery, rhetorical devices, and the like. Once you understand these, it will be easier to establish a connection between form and content.

You may find it helpful to prepare a worksheet much like the ones for writing about prosody (pp. 711–14, 718–19). In this case the worksheet will highlight structural elements. For closed forms, these will include the rhyme scheme, meter, line lengths, and stanzaic pattern. They may also include significant words and phrases linking stanzas together. The worksheet for an open-form poem should indicate variables such as rhythm and phrases, pauses and enjambements, significant words that are isolated or emphasized through typography, and patterns of repeated sounds, phrases, and images.

As you consider the relationship between the form and content of a poem, you might also consider the following questions.

Questions for Discovering Ideas

CLOSED FORM

What is the predominant meter? Line length? Rhyme scheme? To what extent do these establish and/or reinforce the form?

What is the form of each stanza or unit? What building blocks make up the stanza or the poem? How many stanzas or divisions does the poem contain? Is the pattern established in the first stanza or unit repeated?

What is the form of the poem, such as a ballad or sonnet? To what degree does the poem follow the traditional form, and what variations does it introduce? What is the effect of the variations?

How effectively does the structure create or reinforce the poem's internal logic? Can you find and explain a logical progression from unit to unit?

To what extent does the form organize the images of the poem? Are key images developed *within* single units or stanzas? Do images recur in several units?

To what extent does the form organize and bring out the ideas or emotions of the poem?

OPEN FORM

What does the poem look like on the page? How does its shape reflect its meaning?

How does the poet use variable line lengths, spaces, punctuation, capitalization, and the like to shape the poem? How do these variables contribute to the poem's sense and impact?

What rhythms are built into the poem through language or typography? How are these cadences relevant to the poem's content?

What is the poem's progression of ideas, images, and/or emotions? How is the logic created and what does it contribute?

How does form or typography isolate or group, and thus emphasize, various words and phrases? What is the effect of such emphasis? To what extent is this technique one of the organizing principles of the poem?

What words and sounds form patterns? To what degree do the patterns create order and structure? How do they underscore the sense of the poem?

Strategies for Organizing Ideas

In developing your central idea, it is not enough simply to assert that form organizes and underscores meaning. You should explain *how* this occurs. If you are planning an essay on Shakespeare's Sonnet 116, "Let Me Not to the Marriage of True Minds," for example, you might argue that form controls meaning. Such an assertion, while true, is not an adequate central idea. A better formulation might be this: "The sonnet form organizes the speaker's thoughts into a three-part argument in which each quatrain examines a different aspect of love's permanence, and the couplet provides a conclusion."

Sometimes the formulation of a central idea involves a two-step connection between form and content. In planning an essay on Williams's "The Dance," for instance, you might decide that meaning is most effectively reinforced and echoed through rhythm. Hence, you would focus on the ways in which form creates rhythm, and your central idea would link form to rhythm and meaning. Above all, make sure that the evidence you are developing is clearly relevant to your main idea. If you find that your examples are leading you into digressions, you should rethink the essay and make revisions to bring your digressions into your main line of thought.

Early in one of the paragraphs, it is important to describe the formal characteristics of your poem, using schemes and numbers. With closed forms, this paragraph will detail such standard features as the traditional form, meter, rhyme scheme, stanzaic structure, and number of stanzas. With open-form poetry, the paragraph should focus on the most striking and significant features of the verse. The problem of this sort of paragraph is to present the essential information while preserving the central idea of your essay. Most likely, you can succeed if you relate the form to the poem's development of ideas.

The order in which you deal with your topics is entirely up to you. It may be that you have uncovered a good deal of information about a technical feature such as alliteration, or rhyme, or you may wish to stress the ways in which words or types of phrases and clauses form a developing pattern of ideas. Always be sure that your references to form are integrated with a discussion of the poem's content. Remember that you are not making a paraphrase or a general explication of the poem, but rather that you are demonstrating how the poet has used the form—either an open or a closed one—in the service of meaning.

The conclusion of your essay might contain any additional observations about shape or structure that seem relevant. It should also include a summation of your argument. Here, as in all essays about literature, you should make sure that you reach an actual conclusion rather than simply a stopping point.

SAMPLE ESSAY

Form and Meaning in George Herbert's "Virtue"°

[1] George Herbert's devotional four-stanza poem, or song, "Virtue" (1633), contrasts the mortality of worldly things with the immortality of the "virtuous soul." In light of much religious poetry, there is nothing particularly unusual about this contrast. What is unusual, however, is the simplicity and directness of Herbert's expressions, and the way in which he integrates his ideas within the confinement of his stanzaic song pattern. Each part of the poem organizes the images logically and underscores the supremacy of life and ultimate reality over death.* Through the skillful use of line and stanza groupings, rhyme scheme, and repeated sounds and words, Herbert's stanzas create a structural and visual distinction between the "sweet" soul and the rest of creation.†

Herbert's control over lines within the stanzas is particularly strong. Each stanza follows the same basic *a b a b* rhyme scheme. Since some rhyme

° See p. 742 for this poem.
* Central idea.
† Thesis sentence.

[2]

sounds and words are repeated throughout the first three stanzas, however, the structure of the poem may be formulated as *4a 4b 4a 2b, 4c 4b 4c 2b, 4d 4b 4d 2b, 4e 4f 4e 2f.* Each stanza thus contains three lines of iambic tetrameter with a final line of iambic dimeter--an unusual pattern that creates a unique emphasis. In the first three stanzas, the two-beat lines stress the phrase "must die"; in the last stanza the contrast is made on the words "then lives." These rhythms require a sensitive reading, and they powerfully underscore Herbert's view of how life conquers death.

[3]

Like individual lines, Herbert's stanzaic structure provides the poem's pattern of organization and logic. The first stanza focuses on the image of the "Sweet day," comparing the day to "The bridal of the earth and sky" (line 2) and asserting that the day inevitably "must die." Similarly, the second stanza focuses on the image of a "Sweet rose," and asserts that it too "must die." The third stanza shifts to the image of "Sweet spring." Here the poet blends the images of the first two stanzas into the third by noting that the "Sweet spring" is "full of sweet days and roses" (line 9). The stanza concludes with the summarizing claim that "all must die." In this way, the third stanza is the climax of Herbert's imagery of beauty and mortality. The last stanza introduces a new image--"a sweet and virtuous soul"-- and an assertion which is the opposite of the ideas expressed in the previous three. Although the day, the rose, and the spring "must die," the soul "never" deteriorates, but "chiefly lives" even though "the whole world turn to coal" (line 15). With its key image of the "virtuous soul," this last stanza marks the logical conclusion of Herbert's argument. The pattern of organization of the lyric form allows this key image of the one thing that lives to be separated structurally from the images of things that die.

[4]

This structural organization of images and ideas is repeated and reinforced by other techniques that Herbert employs within the poem's form. The rhyme scheme, for example, links the first three stanzas while isolating the fourth. That the *b* rhyme is repeated at the ends of the second and fourth lines of each of the first three stanzas makes these stanzas into a complete unit. The fourth stanza, however, is different, both in content and in rhyme. The stanza introduces the concept of immortality, and it also introduces entirely new rhymes, replacing the *b* rhyme with an *f* rhyme. Thus, the rhyme scheme, by sound alone, parallels the poem's imagery and logic.

[5]

As a complement to the rhyming sounds, the poem also demonstrates organizing patterns of assonance. Most notable is the $\overline{oo}$ sound, which is repeated throughout the first three stanzas in the words *cool, dew, whose, hue, root,* and *music.* In Herbert's time, the sound was also prominent in the word *thou,* so that in the first three stanzas the $\overline{oo}$, which is not unlike a moan (certainly appropriate to things that die), is repeated eight times. In the last stanza there is a stress on the $\overline{o}$ sound, in *only, soul, though, whole,* and *coal.* While *oh* may also be a moan, in this context it is more like an exclamation, in keeping with the triumph contained in the final line.

In addition, the repetition of key words and phrases also distinguishes the first three stanzas from the last stanza. Each of the first three stanzas begins with *sweet* and ends with *must die.* These repetitions stress both the beauty and the mortality of worldly things. In the last stanza, however, this

[6] pattern of repetition is abandoned, just as the stress on immortality transcends mortality. The *sweet* that begins each of the first three stanzas is replaced by *Only* (line 13). Similarly, *must die* is replaced with *chiefly lives*. Both substitutions create a striking separation between this final stanza and the three previous stanzas. More important, the shift in the verbal pattern emphasizes the conceptual transition from death to the virtuous soul's immortality.

[7] It is therefore clear that the lyric form of Herbert's "Virtue" provides an organizational pattern for the poem's images and ideas. At the same time, the pattern of stanzas and the rhyme scheme allow the poet to draw a valid structural distinction between the corruptible world and the immortal soul. The closed form of this poem is not arbitrary or incidental; it is an integral way of asserting the singularity of the key image, the "sweet and virtuous soul."

Commentary on the Essay

The introductory paragraph establishes the groundwork of the essay—the treatment of form in relationship to content. The main idea is that each part of the poem represents a complete blending of image, logic, and meaning.

Paragraph 2, the first in the body, demonstrates how the poem's schematic formulation is integrated into Herbert's contrast of death and life. In this respect the paragraph demonstrates how a formal enumeration may be integrated within an essay's thematic development.

The focus of paragraph 3 is the organization of both images and ideas from stanza to stanza. Here, the essay demonstrates that the image of the "virtuous soul" and the idea of immortality are isolated and emphasized through the stanzaic pattern. Paragraph 4 begins with a transitional sentence that repeats part of the essay's central idea and, at the same time, connects it to paragraph 3. In the same way, paragraph 4 is closely tied to both paragraphs 1 and 3. The main topic here, the rhyme scheme of "Virtue," is introduced in the second sentence, which asserts that it also reinforces the division between mortality and immortality. On much the same topic, paragraph 5, which introduces Herbert's use of the technical element of assonance, may be seen as integral in the poem's blending of form and content.

Paragraph 6 takes up the last structural element mentioned in the introduction—the repetition of key words and phrases. Transition between the previous paragraph and this one is established with the first phrase of the opening sentence: "In addition." The paragraph also asserts that repeated words and phrases underscore the poem's division between mortality and immortality.

Paragraph 7, the conclusion, provides a brief overview and summation of the essay's argument. In addition, it concludes that form in "Virtue" is neither arbitrary nor incidental, but rather an integral part of the poem's meaning.

WRITING TOPICS

1.   Describe the use of the ode form as exemplified by Shelley's "Ode to the West Wind" and Keats's "Ode to a Nightingale." What patterns of regularity do you find? What differences do you find in the form and content of the poems? How do you account for these differences?

2.   How do Cummings, Thomas, Randall, and Dryden use different forms to consider the subject of death (in "Buffalo Bill's defunct," "Do Not Go Gentle Into That Good Night," "Ballad of Birmingham," and "To the Memory of Mr. Oldham")? What differences in form and treatment do you find? What similarities do you find, despite these differences?

3.   Write a "visual" poem, and explain the principles on which you develop your lines. Some possible topics (just to get you started):

     A "boom box," a duck, a beer bottle, a sweater, a snow shovel, a skunk.

     After creating your poem, write a short essay that considers these questions: How serious does the visual form enable your poem to become? What are the strengths and limitations of the visual form, according to the experience you have acquired in writing such a poem?

4.   Write a haiku. Be sure to fit your poem to the 5-7-5 pattern of syllables. What challenges and problems do you encounter in this form? Once you have completed your haiku (which, to be traditional, should be concerned with nature), try to cut the number of syllables to 4-5-4. Explain how you establish the first haiku pattern, and also explain how you go about cutting the total number of syllables. Be sure to explain the kinds and lengths of your words.

5.   Consider the structural arrangement and shaping of the following works: Brueghel's *La Kermesse* (*The Kermess*, p. 752), Hollander's "Swan and Shadow" (p. 758), Wagoner's "March for a One-Man Band" (p. 707), Ginsberg's "A Supermarket in California" (p. 753), and Williams's "The Dance" (p. 752). How do both painter and poets utilize topic, arrangement, shape, and space to draw your attention to their primary ideas? How does Hollander's "Swan and Shadow" blend poetic and artistic techniques? (You may consider other poems, and/or stories, in your discussion.)

20

Symbolism and Allusion: Windows to a Wide Expanse of Meaning

Symbolism refers to the use of symbols in literary works. As we noted earlier (Chapter 9, pp. 326–61), a **symbol** has meaning in and of itself, but it also stands for something else, like the flag for the country or the school song for the school. Symbols occur in stories as well as in poems, but poetry relies more heavily on symbolism than fiction because it is more concise and because it comprises more forms than fiction, which is always reliant on a narrative structure.

In a broad sense, almost all words are symbols, for they stand for various objects without actually being those objects. When we say *horse*, for example, or *tree*, these words are not horses or trees, but are only symbols for those things. They direct our minds to things in the real world that we have seen and can therefore imagine easily. In literature, however, symbolism implies a special relationship that extends beyond our ordinary understanding of words, descriptions, and arguments.

SYMBOLISM AS A WINDOW TO GREATER MEANING

Symbolism goes beyond the close referral of word to thing; it is more like a window through which one can get a glimpse at the extensive world outside. Because poetry is a compact form of expression, it relies heavily on brief references and on hitting the high points of experience. Symbolism is therefore one of its primary characteristics. It is a shorthand way of referring to extensive ideas or attitudes that otherwise would be impossible to state in the relatively brief format of poetry. Thus, William Butler Yeats, who believed that the city of Constantinople, or Byzantium, represented a pinnacle of human civilization, used the city as a symbol of human achievement in peace, politics, and particularly art and literature. His poem "Sailing to Byzantium" (p. 984) does not expand upon the full meaning and interpretation of this idea, for it would take a long history and a detailed analysis of Byzantine art and literature to do that. But the poem does use Byzantium as a symbol of excellence—a standard by which Yeats measures what he thought was the declining state of twentieth-century civilization. The use of symbols, in other words, is a means of encapsulating or crystallizing information—a means of saying a great deal within a short space.

HOW DOES SYMBOLISM OPERATE?

Symbolism thus expands meaning beyond the normal connotation of words. For example, at the time of William Blake (1757–1827), the word *tiger* meant not only the specific animal we know today as a tiger, but also, generally, any large, predatory cat, with a connotation of wildness, predation, and fierceness. By using the tiger as a symbol in "The Tyger," Blake builds upon the connotation to make the animal a stand-in for negativism and evil in the world—the savage, wild forces that lurk in the uncivilized human heart. Thus, the tiger as a symbol is more meaningful than either the denotation or the connotation of the word would indicate. A visual comparison may be made with Goya's "The Colossus," in which the giant pugilistic figure dominating the scattering figures symbolizes the sinister combinations of anger and ruthlessness unleashed in warfare (p. 767).

GENERAL, CULTURAL, OR UNIVERSAL SYMBOLS.   In poetry, some symbols possess a ready-made, clearly agreed-upon meaning. These kinds of symbols are those described in Chapter 9 as **general, cultural,** or **universal symbols.** Many such symbols, like the tiger, are drawn directly from the world of nature. Springtime and morning are universal symbols signifying beginnings, growth, hope, optimism, and love. A reference to spring is normal and appropriate in a love poem. If the topic were death, however, the symbol of spring would still be appropriate as the basis of ironic observations about the untimeliness with which death claims its victims.

Cultural symbols are drawn from history and custom. Because the Judeo-Christian religion has been so important for the last three thousand years, many religious symbols have been taken up by poets. References to the lamb, Eden, Egyptian bondage, shepherds, exile, the Temple, blood, water, bread, the cross, and wine—all Jewish and/or Christian symbols— appear over and over again in poetry of the English language. Sometimes these symbols occur in purely devotional poems. At other times they may be contrasted with symbols of warfare and corruption to show how extensively people neglect their moral and religious obligations.

Francisco Goya, *The Colossus.* (Museo del Prado, Madrid)

PRIVATE, AUTHORIAL, AND CONTEXTUAL SYMBOLS.   Symbols that are not widely or universally recognized are termed **private, authorial,** or **contextual symbols** (also discussed in Chapter 9). Some of these have a natural relationship with things being symbolized. Snow, for example, is cold and white, and when it falls it covers everything. A poet can thus exploit this quality and make snow a symbol. At the beginning of the extensive poem "The Waste Land," for example, T. S. Eliot uses the symbol of snow ironically to symbolize a retreat from life, an intellectual and moral hibernation. Another poem using snow as a symbol linking the living and the dead both literally and figuratively is the following one:

VIRGINIA SCOTT   (b. 1938)

Snow   1977

A doe stands at the roadside,
spirit of those who have lived here
and passed known through our memory.
The doe stands at the edge of the icy road,
then darts back into the woods.   5

Snow falling,
mother-spirit hovering,
white on the drops in the road and fields,
light from the windows
of the old house   10
brightening the snow.

Presences: mother,
grandmother,
here in their place
at the foot of *Ben Lomond,*   15
green trees black in the hemlock night.

The doe stands at the edge of the icy road,
then darts back into the woods.

Golden Grove, New Brunswick, Canada
January 5, 1977

QUESTIONS

1. How is snow described? How and where is it seen? As a symbol, what does
   it signify in relationship to the doe, the memory of persons, the mother-
   spirit, the old house, the light, the presences, the mountains, and the trees?

2. Explain the structural purpose for which the doe is mentioned three times
   in the poem, with lines 17 and 18 repeating 4 and 5. As a symbol, what
   might the doe signify?

3. What are the relationships between memory of the past and existence in the
   present? What does the symbolism contribute to your understanding of these
   relationships?

   This poem describes a real circumstance at a real place at a real time;
the poet has even provided an actual location and date, just as we do
when writing a letter. We may therefore presume that the snow was real
snow, falling at a time in the evening when lights had been put on in the
nearby house. This detail by itself would be sufficient as a realistic image.
But as Scott develops the poem, the snow symbolizes the link between the
speaker's memory of the past and perception of the present. The reality

of the moment is suffused with the memory of the people—"mother, / grandmother"—who "lived here." The poet is meditating on the idea that individuals, though they may often be alone like the speaker, are never alone as long as they have a vivid memory of the past. Just as the snow covers the scene, the past and present are always connected.

At the poem's conclusion, the doe darting into the woods suggests a linking of the present with the future (i.e., as long as there are woods, there will be does darting into them). Both the snow and the deer are private and contextual symbols, for they are established and developed within the poem, and do not possess symbolic value elsewhere. Through the symbolism, therefore, the poet has converted a private moment into an idea of general significance.

Similarly, references to other ordinary materials may be symbolic if the poet emphasizes them sufficiently. Keats, in "La Belle Dame Sans Merci," for example (p. 778), opens and closes the poem with the image of withered sedge, or grass. What might seem like an appropriate detail therefore becomes symbolic of the sense of loss and bewilderment felt by people when the persons they love seem to be unreal, faithless, and destructive to them rather than genuine, loyal, and supportive.

THE INTRODUCTION OF SYMBOLS

SINGLE WORDS. Poets may introduce symbols into their poems in many ways. With general and universal symbols, a single word is often sufficient, as with references to the lamb, shepherd, cross, blood, bread, and wine, or to summer and winter, or to drought and flood, morning and night, heat and shade, storm and calm, or feast and famine. Reference to a nightingale may be taken as an example of how a single word may become instantly symbolic. Because the bird has such a beautiful song, it frequently symbolizes natural, unspoiled beauty as contrasted with the contrived attempts by human beings to create beauty. Keats refers to the bird in this way in his "Ode to a Nightingale," and compares the eternal beauty of this singer with his own mortality.

Anne Finch, in her poem addressed "To the Nightingale" (p. 664), makes a similar comparison of the human poet and the bird, drawing attention to the fact that the "unhappy poet's breast, / Like thine, when best he sings, is plac'd against a thorn." Here the symbol emphasizes the claim that poetic expression originates in the deep pain and feeling of poets. By contrast, T. S. Eliot uses the less idealistic aspects of the bird in "Sweeney Among the Nightingales." Here Eliot refers to the song not as a symbol of beauty, but rather as a backdrop for the horror of the murder of the ancient king Agamemnon. The only contribution the nightingales make as a symbol is their droppings—a staining, dirtying commentary on human affairs. Despite Eliot's usage, however, poets usually emphasize the lovelier aspects of the bird in their symbols.

ACTIONS.   Not only words but also actions may be presented as symbols. In Virginia Scott's "Snow," as we have just observed, the doe darting into the darkening woods symbolizes both the renewal and the mystery of life. In Thomas Hardy's "In Time of 'The Breaking of Nations'" (p. 780), the action of the man plowing a field symbolizes the continued life and vitality of the folk, the people, despite political and military changes that are constantly raging in the world.

SETTING.   Sometimes, a setting or natural scene may be symbolic. For example, Randall Jarrell's brief poem "The Death of the Ball Turret Gunner" (p. 522) unites the ball turret of a World War II high-altitude bomber with a mother's womb, symbolically indicating that war and brutal death are the human lot from the very beginning of life. Similarly, the "elfin grot" (grotto) of the "lady in the meads" in Keats's "La Belle Dame Sans Merci" is an unreal and magical, womblike location symbolizing both the allure and the disappointment that sometimes characterize sexual attraction.

CHARACTERS.   The many characters or people in poetry may also reach symbolic status if the poet designs them to represent ideas or values. In E. E. Cummings's "In Just-," for example, the balloonman is such a figure (p. 786). Although the balloonman is not extensively visualized, Cummings includes enough detail about him to indicate that he symbolizes the basic and primitive vitality, joy, and sexuality with which children are literally called out of childhood. The fairy child of "La Belle Dame Sans Merci" is a symbol of the mystery of love. The figures in Hardy's "In Time of 'The Breaking of Nations'" are symbolic of the poet's faith in the power of unimportant people to endure even though "Dynasties pass."

SITUATIONS.   In addition, situations, circumstances, or conditions may be symbolic. The condition of Jarrell's ball turret gunner, exposed and helpless 6 miles in the air, may be understood as a symbol of the condition of all people in the age of fear and anxiety produced by the threat of global wars and technologically diabolical destructiveness. The speaker of Anne Finch's "To Mr. F., Now Earl of W." symbolizes human confrontation with the emotion of a love so strong that it transcends human capacity for expression, and hence must remain unexpressed and private.

QUALITIES OF SYMBOLS

Just as symbols may be expressed in these various ways, the meanings of the symbols may be placed on a continuum of qualities from good to bad, high to low, favorable to unfavorable. For example, Cummings's old balloonman of "In Just-" is on the positive end, symbolizing the irresistible and joyful call of growth and sexuality. Outright horror is suggested by the symbol of the rough beast slouching towards Bethlehem in Yeats's "The Second Coming" (p. 781). While the beast shares a common birthplace with Jesus, it is in ironic contrast because it represents the extremes of anger, hatred, and brutality that in Yeats's judgment are dominant in twentieth-century politics, even long before the development of nuclear warfare.

ALLUSION IN POETRY

Just as symbolism enriches meaning, so also does **allusion.** Also discussed in Chapter 9, *allusion* is the adaptation and assimilation of (1) unacknowledged brief quotations from other works and (2) references to historical events and any aspect of human culture—art, music, literature, and so on. It is a means of recognizing both the literary tradition and the broader cultural environment of which the poem is a part. In addition it assumes a common bond of knowledge between the poet and the reader. On the one hand, allusion compliments the past, and on the other it salutes the reader who is able to recognize it and find new meaning in it in its new context.

Allusions may be seen in no more than a single word, provided that the word is unusual enough or associative enough to bear the weight of the reference. Virginia Scott's "Snow," for example, speaks of "green trees black in the hemlock night." *Hemlock*, of course, refers to a type of evergreen tree observed by the speaker, but hemlock was also the poison drunk by Socrates when he was executed by the ancient Athenians. Just about any reference to hemlock calls to mind the death of Socrates and also the idea that death is oblivion and the common end of all life. At the beginning of "Ode to a Nightingale" (pp. 744–46), Keats's speaker describes a numbness that might come "As though of hemlock . . . [he] had drunk." Here the allusion is placed in the context of a wish to be connected and united to the universal spirit not of oblivion but of creative power.

Allusions may also be longer, consisting of extensive phrases or also of descriptions or situations. When these are made, they add their own interest and power before the poet moves on to other ideas. Line 6 of Scott's "Snow," for example, is simply "Snow falling." This phrase is descriptive and accurate, but it also is a direct quotation from the first line of Robert Frost's poem "Desert Places" (p. 743). The contexts are of course different. Frost's line introduces the topic of the speaker's fear of bleakness, unconcern, coldness—his "desert places"—while in "Snow," as we stated earlier, Scott is referring to the continuity of the past and the present. There is bleakness and isolation in Scott's scene, but her old house also throws light on the snow, and the dead are fondly remembered because their spirit and memory are as alive as the doe who darts back into the woods. By making the allusion, Scott actually emphasizes the difference between her idea and Frost's.

THE SOURCES OF ALLUSIONS.   Allusions may be drawn from just about any area of life, history, and art. Sometimes symbols are allusions as well as symbols. In "The Second Coming," Yeats's "lion body and the head of a man" is a descriptive allusion to the sphinx, which was an ancient mythical monster that destroyed those who could not solve its riddle. As Yeats uses the description he is referring to the monstrous aspects of the figure as a means of focusing on both the horror and mystery, the brutality and coldness, that often infest human political institutions.

As works become well known and popular, they become a source of allusions for subsequent writers. One of Robert Frost's most famous lines, for example, is the conclusion of "Stopping by Woods on a Snowy Evening": "And miles to go before I sleep." This line is so often quoted that it has become a metaphor for having a task to complete before one may rest or relax in recreational activities. Isabella Gardner alludes to the line in her "Collage of Echoes," a poem which is deliberately built out of allusions. Interestingly enough, Frost's line itself alludes to a line in Keats's sonnet "Keen Fitful Gusts," where Keats says, "The stars are very cold about the sky, / And I have many miles on foot to fare." Any allusion to Frost is therefore also an indirect allusion to Keats's lines.

ALLUSIONS AND THE ORIGINAL CONTEXT.   If an allusion is made to a literary work, it carries with it the entire context of the work from which it is drawn. Perhaps the richest storehouses of such ready-made stories and quotations are the King James version of the Bible and the plays of Shakespeare. In "Ode to a Nightingale," Keats alludes to the biblical story of Ruth who, he says, was "sick with tears amid the alien corn." This allusion is particularly rich, because Ruth became the mother of Jesse. According to the Gospel of Matthew it was from the line of Jesse that King David was born, and it was from the house of David that Jesus was born. Thus, Keats's nightingale is not only a symbol of natural beauty, but through this biblical allusion it becomes symbolic of regeneration and redemption, much in keeping with Keats's assertion that the bird was not born for death. In Yeats's "The Second Coming," the reference to the "blood-dimmed tide" suggests the soliloquy in the second act of Shakespeare's *Macbeth*, when Macbeth, after murdering Duncan, asks if there is enough water in Neptune's ocean to wash the blood from his hands. His immediate, guilt-ridden response is that Duncan's blood on his hands will instead stain the ocean, turning the green of the water to red. This image of crime being so bloody that it can stain the water of the ocean is thus the allusion of Yeats's "blood-dimmed tide," for Yeats's authorial speaker is just as concerned about the global implications of evil as is Shakespeare's Macbeth.

Allusions are therefore an important means by which poets broaden the context and deepen the meaning of their poems. The issues raised by a poet in a specific poem, in other words, are not important only there, but are linked through allusion to issues raised earlier by other thinkers, or brought out by previous events, places, or persons. With connections made through allusions, poets clarify the significance and applicability of their own ideas. The situations in their works are not confined only to their time and place, but are general problems for many times and places. Allusion is hence not literary "theft," but is rather a means of literary enrichment.

STUDYING FOR SYMBOL AND ALLUSION

As you study poetry for its symbols and allusions, it is important to realize that these devices do not come ready-marked with special notice and fanfare. A decision to call a feature of the poem *symbolic* is based on qualities within the poem: Perhaps an item of major importance is introduced at a climactic part of the poem, or a description has something noteworthy or unusual about it, such as the connection between "stony silence" and the "rough beast" in Yeats's "The Second Coming." When such a connection occurs, the element may no longer be taken just literally, but should be read as a symbol.

Even after you have found a hint such as this, however, you will have to think in order to learn its symbolic value. Thus, the "rough beast" raises questions about what Yeats means. In the poem's context the phrase might refer to the person or persons hinted at in traditional interpretations of the New Testament as the "anti-Christ." In a secular frame of reference, the associations of blankness and pitilessness suggest that some aspect of brutality and suppression is being suggested. Still further, however, if the twentieth century were not a period in which millions of people have been persecuted and exterminated in military and secret police operations, even these associations might make the "rough beast" quizzical but not necessarily symbolic. But because of the rightness of the application, together with the traditional biblical associations, the figure clearly should be construed as a symbol.

As you can see, the interpretation of a symbol requires that you identify and objectivize the person, thing, situation, or action in question. To the degree that the element can be seen as general and representative— characteristic of the condition of a large number of human beings—it assumes the nature of a symbol, for it then stands definitely for something universal. As a rule, the more ideas that you can associate with the element, the more likely it is to be a symbol.

In one respect, then, identification of an allusion is simple. Either a word, situation, or phrase is an allusion or it is not, and hence the matter is easily settled once a source is located. The problem comes in determining how the allusion affects the context of the poem you are reading. Thus, we have determined that Virginia Scott alludes to Robert Frost's "Desert Places" by using the phrase "Snow falling" in the poem "Snow." Once this allusion is established, its purpose must still be determined. Thus, the allusion might mean that the situation in "Snow" is the same as in Frost's poem, namely that the authorial speaker is making observations about interior blankness—the "desert places" of the mind, or soul. On the other hand, the poet may be using the allusion in a new sense—for example, Frost uses the fall snow to symbolize a coldness of spirit, whereas Scott uses it, more warmly, to connect the natural scene to the memory of family. In other words, once the presence of an allusion is established, the business of reading and understanding still continues.

POEMS FOR STUDY

GEORGE HERBERT   (1593–1633)

The Collar°   *1633*

I struck the board, and cry'd, "No more;
    I will abroad!
What? shall I ever sigh and pine?
My lines and life are free; free as the road,
  Loose as the wind, as large as store,   5
    Shall I be still in suit?°
  Have I no harvest but a thorn°
 To let me blood, and not restore
What I have lost with cordial fruit?
    Sure there was wine   10
  Before my sighs did dry it: there was corn
  Before my tears did drown it.
  Is the year only lost to me?
  Have I no bays° to crown it?
No flowers, no garlands gay? all blasted?   15
    All wasted?
  Not so, my heart: but there is fruit,
    And thou hast hands.

THE COLLAR.   *collar:* (1) the collar worn by a member of the clergy; (2) the collar of the harness of a draft animal such as a horse; (3) a restraint placed on prisoners; (4) a pun on *choler* (yellow bile), a bodily substance that was thought to cause quick rages.   6 *in suit:* waiting upon a person of power to gain favor or position.   7 *thorn:* See Mark 15:17. 14 *bays:* laurel crowns to signify victory and honor.

Recover all thy sigh-blown age
On double pleasures: leave thy cold dispute   20
Of what is fit, and not; forsake thy cage;
    Thy rope of sands,
Which petty thoughts have made, and made to thee
  Good cable, to enforce and draw,
    And be thy law,   25
  While thou didst wink and wouldst not see.
    Away; take heed:
    I will abroad.
Call in thy death's head there: tie up thy fears.
    He that forbears   30
  To suit° and serve his need,   *follow*
  Deserves his load."
But as I rav'd and grew more fierce and wild
    At every word,
  Me thought I heard one calling, "Child:"   35
  And I replied, "*My Lord.*"

QUESTIONS

1. What is the opening situation? Why is the speaker angry? Against what role in life is he complaining?

2. In light of the many possible meanings of *collar* (see note), explain the title as a symbol in the poem.

3. Explain the symbolism of the thorn (line 7), blood (line 8), wine (line 10), bays (line 14), flowers and garlands (line 15), cage (line 21), rope of sands (line 22), death's head (line 29), and the dialogue in lines 35 and 36.

ANNE FINCH, COUNTESS OF WINCHILSEA   (1661–1720)

To Mr. F[inch], Now Earl of W[inchilsea]   *1689*

Who going abroad, had desired Ardelia° to write some verses upon whatever subject she thought fit, against his return in the evening.

No sooner, Flavio,° were you gone,
But your injunction thought upon,
  Ardelia took the pen;

TO MR. F., NOW EARL OF W.   *Ardelia:* the name Anne Finch used in her personal poems in reference to herself, so that she could use the third person to refer to her feelings and attitudes. The name suggests warmth and devotion (ardency).   1 *Flavio:* the name that she assigned to Mr. Finch, her husband. The name *Flavio* was common in ancient Rome. Cnaeus Flavianus, a Roman of the fourth century B.C., was particularly known for his justice and leadership.

Designing to perform the task
Her Flavio did so kindly ask,   5
   Ere he returned again.

Unto Parnassus° straight she sent,
And bid the messenger, that went
   Unto the Muses' court,°
Assure them she their aid did need,   10
And begg'd they'd use their utmost speed,
   Because the time was short.

The hasty summons was allow'd:
And being well-bred they rose and bow'd,
   And said they'd post away: 15
That well they did Ardelia know,
And that no female's voice below
   They sooner would obey.

That many of that rhyming train°   *poets*
On like occasions sought in vain   20
   Their industry t' excite:
But for Ardelia all they'd leave.
Thus flatt'ring can the Muse deceive
   And wheedle us to write.

Yet since there was such haste requir'd,   25
To know the subject 'twas desired
   On which they must infuse,°   *give judgment*
That they might temper words and rules,
And with their counsel carry tools
   As country doctors use.   30

Wherefore to cut off all delays,
'Twas soon replied, a husband's praise
   (Tho' in these looser times)
Ardelia gladly would rehearse
A husband's who indulged her verse,   35
   And now requir'd her rhymes.

"A husband!" echo'd all around:
And to Parnassus sure that sound
   Had never yet been sent.
Amazement in each face was read,   40
In haste th' affrighted sisters fled,
   And into council went.

Erato° cried, "since Grizel's° days,

---

7 *Parnassus:* Mount Parnassus was the home of the nine muses and was also sacred to
Apollo, the god of poetry, music, and dance.   9 *Muses' court:* the court of the muses,
who governed art, music, literature, and the sciences.   43 *Erato:* the muse of lyrical love
poetry.   *Grizel:* Griselda, in Chaucer's "Clerk's Tale," was known for her patient and
forgiving love of her husband, Walter.

Since Troy-town pleas'd, and Chevy Chase,°
  No such design was known;"   45
And 'twas their business to take care
It reach'd not to the public ear,
  Or got about the town.

Nor came where evening beaux° were met,   *dandies*
O'er billet-doux° and chocolate,   *love letters* 50
  Lest it destroyed the house:
For in that place who could dispense
(That wore his clothes with common sense)
  With mention of a spouse?

'Twas put unto the vote at last,   55
And in the negative it passed,
  None to her aid should move;
Yet since Ardelia was a friend,
Excuses 'twas agreed to send
  Which plausible might prove: 60

That Pegasus° of late had been
So often rid thro' thick and thin
  With neither fear nor wit,
In panegyric° been so spurr'd,   *poems of praise*
He could not from the stall be stirr'd,   65
  Nor would endure a bit.

Melpomene° had given a bond
By the new house° alone to stand
  And write alone of war and strife;
Thalia,° she had taken fees   70
And stipends from the patentees,
  And durst not for her life.

Urania° only liked the choice;
Yet not to thwart the public voice,
  She whispering did impart: 75
"They need no foreign aid invoke,
No help to draw a moving stroke,
  Who dictate from the heart."

---

44 *Troy-town, Chevy Chase:* Ancient Troy ("Troy-town") was besieged by the Greeks. Hector, the most famous Trojan hero, was deeply loved by his wife, Andromache. In the late medieval ballad of Chevy Chase, the Douglases and Percies made war against each other and were mourned by their wives (Child Ballads A57; B55–56).   61 *Pegasus:* the famous winged horse of Greek mythology.   67 *Melpomene:* the muse of tragedy.   68 *new house:* There were two authorized or "patent" theaters in London in 1689. The "new house" was the Drury Lane Theater, built in 1673. "Patentees" (line 71) were the managers; a dramatist who contracted to write plays for them could not do the same for someone else without breaking the contract. The allusion may be to the well-publicized breach of contract by the poet laureate John Dryden in 1682.   70 *Thalia:* the muse of pastoral poetry and also of comedy.   73 *Urania:* The muse of astronomers; hence the muse closest to heaven.

"Enough!" the pleas'd Ardelia cried:
And slighting ev'ry Muse beside,   80
  Consulting now her breast.
Perceived that ev'ry tender thought
Which from abroad she vainly sought
  Did there in silence rest:

And should unmov'd that post maintain,   85
Till in his quick return again,
  Met in some neighb'ring grove,
(Where vice nor vanity appear)
Her Flavio them alone might hear
  In all the sounds of love.   90

For since the world does so despise
Hymen's° endearments and its ties,
  They should mysterious be:
Till we that pleasure too possess
(Which makes their fancied happiness)   95
  Of stolen secrecy.

92 *Hymen:* the Greek god of marriage.

QUESTIONS

1. What situation prompts the speaker to write the poem? What imaginary journey does Ardelia make, and for what reason?

2. Describe the development of Ardelia's mission to the muses. At what point does the narrative change to describe Ardelia's analysis of her love for Flavio?

3. Why is the response of the muses comic? Upon what usual assessment of married love is the muses' response based (see lines 91, 92)?

4. Describe the poet's symbolic use of allusions in lines 43 and 44. What do these symbols represent? What do the beaux symbolize (line 49)? How may the situation between Ardelia and Flavio be seen as symbolic?

JOHN KEATS   (1795–1821)

La Belle Dame Sans Merci: A Ballad°   *1820 (1819)*

1

O what can ail thee, knight at arms,
  Alone and palely loitering?
The sedge has wither'd from the lake,
  And no birds sing.

LA BELLE DAME SANS MERCI: French for "The beautiful lady without pity" (that is, "The heartless woman"). "La Belle Dame Sans Merci" is the title of a medieval poem by Alain Chartier; Keats's poem bears no other relationship to the medieval poem, which was thought at the time to have been by Chaucer.

2

O what can ail thee, knight at arms,   5
 So haggard and so woe-begone?
The squirrel's granary is full,
 And the harvest's done.

3

I see a lily on thy brow
 With anguish moist and fever dew,   10
And on thy cheeks a fading rose
 Fast withereth too.

4

I met a lady in the meads,°   *meadows*
 Full beautiful, a fairy's child;
Her hair was long, her foot was light,   15
 And her eyes were wild.

5

I made a garland for her head,
 And bracelets too, and fragrant zone;°   *belt*
She look'd at me as she did love,
 And made sweet moan.   20

6

I set her on my pacing steed,
 And nothing else saw all day long,
For sidelong would she bend, and sing
 A fairy's song.

7

She found me roots of relish° sweet,   *magical potion* 25
 And honey wild, and manna° dew, *see Exodus 16:14–36*
And sure in language strange she said—
 I love thee true.

8

She took me to her elfin grot,°   *grotto*
 And there she wept, and sigh'd full sore,   30
And there I shut her wild wild eyes
 With kisses four.

9

And there she lullèd me asleep,
 And there I dream'd—Ah! woe betide!
The latest° dream I ever dream'd   *last* 35
 On the cold hill's side.

10

I saw pale kings, and princes too,
 Pale warriors, death pale were they all;
They cried—"La belle dame sans merci
 Hath thee in thrall!"°   *slavery* 40

11

I saw their starv'd lips in the gloam
  With horrid warning gapèd wide,
And I awoke and found me here
  On the cold hill's side.

12

And this is why I sojourn here,   45
  Alone and palely loitering,
Though the sedge is wither'd from the lake,
  And no birds sing.

QUESTIONS

1. Who is the speaker of stanzas 1–3? Who speaks after that?
2. In light of the dreamlike content of the poem, how can the knight's experience be viewed as symbolic? What is being symbolized?
3. Consider *relish* (line 25), *honey* (line 26), and *manna* (line 26) as symbols. Are they realistic or mythical? What does the allusion to manna signify? What is symbolized by the "pale kings, and princes too" and "Pale warriors"?
4. Consider the poem's setting as symbols of the knight's state of mind.

THOMAS HARDY   (1840–1928)

In Time of "The Breaking of Nations"°   *1916 (1915)*

Only a man harrowing clods
  In a slow silent walk,
With an old horse that stumbles and nods
  Half asleep as they stalk.

Only thin smoke without flame   5
  From the heaps of couch grass:°   *quack grass*
Yet this will go onward the same
  Though Dynasties pass.

Yonder a maid and her wight°   *fellow*
  Come whispering by;   10
War's annals will fade into night
  Ere their story die.

IN TIME OF "THE BREAKING OF NATIONS." See Jeremiah 51:20, "with you I break nations in pieces."

QUESTIONS

1. What does Hardy symbolize by the man, horse, smoke, and couple? How realistic and vivid are these symbols? Are they universal or contextual?

2. How does Hardy show that the phrase "breaking of nations" is to be taken symbolically? What meaning is gained by the biblical allusion of this phrase?

3. Contrast the structure of stanza 1 with that of stanzas 2 and 3. How does the form of stanzas 2 and 3 enable Hardy to emphasize the main idea?

4. How does the speaker show his evaluation of the life of the common people? You might consider that at the time (1915), World War I was raging in Europe.

WILLIAM BUTLER YEATS   (1865–1939)

The Second Coming°   *1920 (1919)*

Turning and turning in the widening gyre°
The falcon cannot hear the falconer;
Things fall apart; the center cannot hold;
Mere anarchy is loosed upon the world,
The blood-dimmed tide° is loosed, and everywhere   5
The ceremony of innocence is drowned;
The best lack all conviction, while the worst
Are full of passionate intensity.

Surely some revelation is at hand;
Surely the Second Coming is at hand.   10
The Second Coming! Hardly are those words out

THE SECOND COMING. The phrase "second coming" has been traditionally used to refer to expectations of the return of Jesus for the salvation of believers, as described in the New Testament. The prophecies foretold that Christ's return would be preceded by famine, epidemics, wars between nations, and general civil disturbance. Yeats believed that human history could be measured in cycles of approximately 2,000 years (see line 19, "twenty centuries"). According to this system, the birth of Jesus ended the Greco-Roman cycle and in 1919, when Yeats wrote "The Second Coming," it appeared to him that the Christian period was ending and a new era was about to take its place. The New Testament expectation was that Jesus would reappear. Yeats, by contrast, holds that the disruptions of the twentieth century were preceding a takeover by the forces of evil. 1 *gyre:* a radiating spiral, cone, or vortex. Yeats used the intersecting of two of these shapes as a visual symbol of his cyclic theory. As one gyre spiraled and widened out, to become dissipated, one period of history would end; at the same time a new gyre, closer to the center, would begin and spiral in a reverse direction to the starting point of the old gyre. A drawing of this plan looks like this:

The falcon of line 2 is at the broadest, centrifugal point of one gyre, symbolically illustrating the end of a cycle. The "indignant desert birds" of line 17 "reel" in a tighter circle, symbolizing the beginning of the new age in the new gyre.   5 *blood-dimmed tide:* quotation from Shakespeare's *Macbeth*, Act II, scene 2, lines 60–63.

When a vast image out of *Spiritus Mundi*°
Troubles my sight; somewhere in sands of the desert
A shape with lion body and the head of a man,°
A gaze blank and pitiless as the sun,   15
Is moving its slow thighs, while all about it
Reel shadows of the indignant desert birds.
The darkness drops again; but now I know
That twenty centuries of stony sleep
Were vexed to nightmare by a rocking cradle,   20
And what rough beast, its hour come round at last,
Slouches towards Bethlehem to be born?

12 *Spiritus Mundi:* literally, the spirit of the world, a collective human consciousness that
furnished writers and thinkers with a common fund of images and symbols. Yeats referred
to this collective repository as "a great memory passing on from generation to generation."
14 *lion body and the head of a man:* that is, the Sphinx, which in ancient Egypt symbolized
the pharaoh as a spirit of the sun. Because of this pre-Christian origin, the reincarnation
of a sphinx could therefore represent qualities associated in New Testament books like
Revelation (11, 13, 17), Mark (13:14–20), and 2 Thessalonians (2:1–12) with a monstrous,
superhuman, satanic figure. For a picture of the Sphinx, see p. 808.

QUESTIONS

1. Consider the following as symbols: the gyre, the falcon, the "blood-dimmed tide," the ceremony of innocence, the "worst" who are "full of passionate intensity." What ideas and values do these symbolize in the poem?

2. Why does Yeats capitalize the phrase "Second Coming"? To what does this phrase refer? Explain the irony of Yeats's use of the phrase in this poem.

3. Contrast the symbols of the falcon of line 2 and the desert birds of line 17. Considering that these are realistically presented, how does the realism contribute to their identity as symbols?

4. What is symbolized by the sphinx being revealed as a "rough beast"? What is the significance of the beast's going "to Bethlehem to be born"?

ROBINSON JEFFERS   (1887–1962)

The Purse-Seine   *1937*

1

Our sardine fishermen work at night in the dark of the moon; daylight or
   moonlight
They could not tell where to spread the net, unable to see the phosphorescence
   of the shoals of fish.
They work northward from Monterey, coasting Santa Cruz; off New Year's Point
   or off Pigeon Point
The look-out man will see some lakes of milk-color light on the seas's night-purple;
   he points, and the helmsman

Turns the dark prow, the motorboat circles the gleaming shoal and drifts out   5
    her seine-net. They close the circle
And purse the bottom of the net, then with great labor haul it in.

2

                                      I cannot tell you
How beautiful the scene is, and a little terrible, then, when the crowded fish
Know they are caught, and wildly beat from one wall to the other of their closing
    destiny the phosphorescent
Water to a pool of flame, each beautiful slender body sheeted with flame, like a   10
    live rocket
A comet's tail wake of clear yellow flame; while outside the narrowing
Floats and cordage of the net great sea-lions come up to watch, sighing in the
    dark; the vast walls of night
Stand erect to the stars.

3

                        Lately I was looking from a night mountain-top
On a wide city, the colored splendor, galaxies of light: how could I help but recall   15
    the seine-net
Gathering the luminous fish? I cannot tell you how beautiful the city appeared,
    and a little terrible.
I thought, We have geared the machines and locked all together into
    interdependence; we have built the great cities; now
There is no escape. We have gathered vast populations incapable of free survival,
    insulated
From the strong earth, each person in himself helpless, on all dependent. The
    circle is closed, and the net
Is being hauled in. They hardly feel the cords drawing, yet they shine already.   20
    The inevitable mass-disasters
Will not come in our time nor in our children's, but we and our children
Must watch the net draw narrower, government take all powers—or revolution,
    and the new government
Take more than all, add to kept bodies kept souls—or anarchy, the mass-disasters.

4

                These things are Progress;
Do you marvel our verse is troubled or frowning, while it keeps its reason? Or it   25
    lets go, lets the mood flow
In the manner of the recent young men into mere hysteria, splintered gleams,
    crackled laughter. But they are quite wrong.
There is no reason for amazement: surely one always knew that cultures decay,
    and life's end is death.

QUESTIONS

1. Describe how the purse-seine is used to haul in the sardines. What is the speaker's reaction to the scene as described in stanza 2?

2. How does the speaker explain that the purse-seine is a symbol? What does it symbolize? What do the sardines symbolize?

3. Compare the ideas of Jeffers with those of Yeats in "The Second Coming." Are the ideas of Jeffers more or less methodical?

4. Is the statement at the end to be taken as a fact or as a resigned acceptance of that fact? Does the poem offer any solution to the problem?

5. How may the sea lions of line 12, and their sighs, be construed as a symbol?

T. S. ELIOT   (1888–1965)

Sweeney Among the Nightingales°   *1918*

ὤμοι, πέπληγμαι καιρίαν πληγὴν ἔσω.

Apeneck Sweeney spreads his knees
Letting his arms hang down to laugh,
The zebra strips along his jaw
Swelling to maculate° giraffe.   *dirty, stained*

The circles of the stormy moon   5
Slide westward toward the River Plate,°
Death and the Raven° drift above
And Sweeney guards the hornèd gate.°

Gloomy Orion° and the Dog°
Are veiled; and hushed the shrunken seas;   10
The person in the Spanish cape
Tries to sit on Sweeney's knees

Slips and pulls the tablecloth
Overturns a coffee-cup,
Reorganized upon the floor   15
She yawns and draws a stocking up;

The silent man in mocha brown°   *Sweeney*
Sprawls at the window sill and gapes;

SWEENEY AMONG THE NIGHTINGALES.   Eliot wrote two other works featuring Sweeney. These are "Sweeney Erect" (a poem) and *Sweeney Agonistes* (a drama). The character represents the grosser aspects of modern human beings. In the play, Sweeney says "Birth, and copulation, and death. / That's all, that's all, that's all." Sweeney is also the name of a hero of Irish legend and folklore.   The Greek epigraph below the title is from Aeschylus, *Agamemnon*, line 1348, and may be translated "Alas I am struck with a mortal blow within." This is the off-stage cry of Agamemnon when he is being murdered. 6 *River Plate:* The River Plate, or Rio de la Plata, is the large estuary extending from the Atlantic Ocean to Buenos Aires. It separates Argentina and Uruguay.   7 *Raven:* a bird of ill omen; also the constellation Corvus.   8 *hornèd gate:* one of the two gates of the underworld, according to Virgil, *Aeneid*, book 6:1192–1193. The usual guardian of the gates was the three-headed dog, Cerberus.   9 *Orion:* a mythological Greek giant and hunter. Because of a misunderstanding, he was killed by Artemis, the Goddess of the Moon and of the Hunt. Orion is also one of the most prominent winter constellations. *Dog:* Orion's dog. The "dog star," Sirius, is in the constellation Canis Major, east of Orion, and it is the brightest star in the sky.

The waiter brings in oranges
Bananas figs and hothouse grapes;   20

The silent vertebrate in brown°   *Sweeney*
Contracts and concentrates, withdraws;
Rachel *née* Rabinovitch
Tears at the grapes with murderous paws;

She and the lady in the cape   25
Are suspect, thought to be in league;
Therefore the man with heavy eyes
Declines the gambit, shows fatigue,

Leaves the room and reappears
Outside the window, leaning in,   30
Branches of wistaria
Circumscribe a golden grin;

The host with someone indistinct°
Converses at the door apart,
The nightingales are singing near   35
The Convent of the Sacred Heart,

And sang within the bloody° wood
When Agamemnon cried aloud,
And let their liquid siftings fall
To stain the stiff dishonored shroud.   40

33 *someone indistinct:* a murderer, corresponding to Aegisthus, the murderer of Agamemnon.
37 *bloody:* A pun: (1) covered with blood; (2) a vulgar word in British slang.

QUESTIONS

1. What does Sweeney represent as a symbol? Why does the poet use as the epigraph the passage from Aeschylus in which Agamemnon cries out in the pain of death? Why do you think the speaker describes Sweeney as "apeneck" (line 1) and as a "vertebrate in brown" (line 21)?

2. Why does Eliot include references to constellations? Consider also the geography (i.e., South America, Greece, the underworld). What is the effect of this broad set of references upon the symbolic meaning of the central incidents involving Agamemnon and Sweeney?

3. In stanza 2, how might the references to the moon, westward, the raven, and hornèd gate be considered as symbols? What do these symbols represent?

4. How does the speaker describe "Rachel *née* Rabinovitch"? Knowing that Sweeney is the name of a hero of Irish folklore, what do you make of Eliot's selection of that name for his antihero?

5. What are the host and the "indistinct" man conferring about? What is going to happen to Sweeney?

6. What do nightingales usually symbolize? What do they represent here? How may this use of the nightingales be considered as ironic?

e. e. cummings   (1894–1962)

In Just-   *1923*

in Just-
spring   when the world is mud-
luscious the little
lame balloonman

whistles   far   and wee   5

and eddieandbill come
running from marbles and
piracies and it's
spring

when the world is puddle-wonderful   10

the queer
old balloonman whistles
far   and   wee
and bettyandisbel come dancing

from hop-scotch and jump-rope and   15

it's
spring
and
    the
        goat-footed°   20

balloonMan   whistles
far
and
wee

IN JUST-.   20 *goat-footed:* The mythological Greek god Pan, a free-spirited and lascivious god who presides over fields, forests, and herds, was portrayed with the body of a man and the legs of a goat.

QUESTIONS

1. Explain the following as symbols: spring, mud-luscious, marbles, puddle-wonderful, hop-scotch. What does the whistle of the balloonman symbolize?
2. In what way is the balloonman symbolic?
3. Besides the balloonman, there are four other characters in the poem. Who are they? Why does Cummings run their names together? What impulses do these characters represent symbolically?
4. Read the poem aloud. Taking into account the spacing and alignment, how does the physical arrangement on the page influence your perception?

ISABELLA GARDNER   (1915–1981)

Collage of Echoes   *1979*

I have no promises to keep
Nor miles to go before I sleep,°
For miles of years I have made promises
and (mostly) kept them.
    It's time I slept.   5
Now I lay me down to sleep°
With no promises to keep.
    My sleaves are ravelled°
    I have travelled.°

COLLAGE OF ECHOES.   *2 miles to go before I sleep:* see Robert Frost, "Stopping by
Woods on a Snowy Evening" (p. 531), lines 13–16.   6 *Now I lay me down to sleep:* from
the child's prayer: Now I lay me down to sleep; / I pray the Lord my soul to keep. / If I
should die before I wake, / I pray the Lord my soul to take.   8 *My sleaves are ravelled:*
See *Macbeth*, Act II, scene 2, line 37: "Sleep that knits up the ravelled sleave of care."
9 *I have travelled:* See Keats, "On First Looking into Chapman's Homer" (p. 624).

QUESTIONS

1. Given the allusions in the poem, what do you conclude about the speaker's
   judgment of the reader's knowledge of literature?

2. How reliant is "Collage of Echoes" upon the contexts being echoed? How
   do the echoes assist in enabling enjoyment and appreciation of the poem?

3. In relation to the speaker's character as demonstrated in the poem, consider
   the phrases "(mostly) kept them," "With no promises to keep," and "My
   sleaves are ravelled." What do they show about the speaker's self-assessment?
   In what way might these phrases be considered comic?

X. J. KENNEDY   (b. 1929)

Old Men Pitching Horseshoes   *1985*

Back in a yard where ringers groove a ditch,
These four in shirtsleeves congregate to pitch
Dirt-burnished iron. With appraising eye,
One sizes up a peg, hoists and lets fly—
A clang resounds as though a smith had struck   5
Fire from a forge. His first blow, out of luck,
Rattles in circles. Hitching up his face,
He swings, and weight once more inhabits space,
Tumbles as gently as a new-laid egg.
Extended iron arms surround their peg   10
Like one come home to greet a long-lost brother.
Shouts from one outpost. Mutters from the other.

Now changing sides, each withered pitcher moves
As his considered dignity behooves
Down the worn path of earth where August flies   15
And sheaves of air in warm distortions rise.
To stand ground, fling, kick dust with all the force
Of shoes still hammered to a living horse.

QUESTIONS

1. How does the poet show that pitching horseshoes is a symbol? As symbols,
   why are old men chosen rather than young men?

2. Discuss the effects of the words *congregate, outpost, withered, sheaves, kick dust,*
   and *force.* What do these words contribute to the poem's symbolism?

3. Compare the topic of this poem with the concluding lines of Eliot's "Preludes"
   (p. 615). How is the symbolism of these poems similar? Different?

CAROL MUSKE   (b. 1945)

Real Estate   *1981*

You think you earned this space on earth,
but look at the gold face of the teen-age
pharaoh,° smug as a Shriner, in his box

with no diploma, a plot flashy enough
for Manhattan.° Early death, then what.   5
a task dragging a sofa into the grave,
a couple of floor lamps, the alarm set

for another century. Someday we'll heed
the testament of that paid escort watching
himself in all the ballroom mirrors: slide   10

with each slide of the old trombone,
be good to the bald, press up against
the ugly duck-like.° Time is never old,

never lies. What a past you'd have
if you'd only admit to it: the real estate   15

REAL ESTATE.   3 *teen-age pharaoh:* Tutankhamen, the Egyptian "boy king" of the
fourteenth century B.C. The discovery of his tomb in 1922, when hundreds of precious
household objects were found with the sarcophagus, showed the lavishness of Egyptian
royal burials. The mummy of King Tut was covered with a mask of gold and colored
metals.   5 *Manhattan:* In 1981 a large number of treasures from Tutankhamen's tomb
were displayed at the Metropolitan Museum of Art in Manhattan.   13 *ugly duck-like:*
"The Ugly Duckling" is a children's story by Hans Christian Andersen.

your family dabbled in for generations,
the vacant lots° developed like the clan

overbite—through years of sudden
foreclosure. Who knows what it costs?
First you stand for the national anthem,   20

then you start waltzing around without
strings, reminding yourself of yourself,
expecting to live in that big city
against daddy's admonition: buy land°

get some roots down under those spike   25
heels, let the river bow and scrape as
it enters the big front door of your property.

17 *vacant lots:* See T. S. Eliot, "Preludes," concluding lines.   24 *buy land:* See Robert
Frost's poem "Build Soil" (1932).

QUESTIONS

1. Who is speaking? Who is being addressed? What sort of person is the speaker? What does she think of old age? Of sex? What advice does she offer?

2. What does "the teen-age pharaoh" symbolize? Why does the poet mention modern objects that might be found in a comparable tomb of a person of the twentieth century? What might these things symbolize?

3. What does the "paid escort" (line 9) symbolize? What does the "old trombone" symbolize? What does the choice of these symbolize about the traditional role of women with regard to men? What attitude is conveyed by this choice?

4. Consider the ambiguity of lines 25–27. What might "roots" and "property" signify as the means of causing the "river" to "bow and scrape"? Why is it difficult to understand these lines without symbolic explanations?

5. Consider the allusion in line 24 to Robert Frost's "Build Soil" (1932). Frost delivered his poem at Columbia University just before the party conventions of 1932. The United States was in its worst economic depression. Frost spoke about agriculture, world politics, and the need for developing the nation's resources. In comparison, what does Muske achieve by the allusion?

WRITING ABOUT SYMBOLISM AND ALLUSION IN POETRY

As you read your poem, take notes and make all the observations you can about the presence of symbols or allusions or both. Explanatory notes will help you in establishing basic information, but you also need to explain meanings and create interpretations in your own words. Use a dictionary to build up your understanding of words or phrases that require further study. For allusions, you might check out original sources to determine original contexts. Try to determine the ways in which your poem is similar to, or different from, the original work or source, and then determine the purpose served by the allusion.

Questions for Discovering Ideas

To perceive symbols: What events or occasions in your life have developed symbolic meanings through repeated experience? What is it that makes an object, event, or individual symbolic to you?

In the poem:

What elements may be taken as symbols? Look for noteworthy or highlighted things; are they general or universal in nature, or particular and contextual?

Can you support your claim through brief freewriting?

How many symbols might there be in the poem? What is their nature?

Would the poem work in the same way if the element were not symbolic?

Strategies for Organizing Ideas

You might begin with a brief description of the poem and of the symbolism or allusions in it. A symbol might be central to the poem, or an allusion might be introduced at a particularly important point. Your central idea might take you in a number of directions, such as that the symbolism is based on objects like flowers and natural scenes, or that it stems out of an action or set of actions, or that it is developed from an initial situation the poem establishes. Or, the symbols may be universal, or they may be contextual. Or, they may be applicable particularly to personal life, or political or social life. Allusions may emphasize the differences between your poem and the work or event being alluded to, or they may highlight the situation presented in your poem. Also, you might make a point that the symbols and/or allusions make your poem seem optimistic, or pessimistic, and so on.

Some possible approaches for the essay, which may be combined as the need arises, are these:

1. *The meaning of symbols or allusions.* This approach is the most natural one to take for an essay on symbolism or allusion. If you have discovered a symbol or symbols, or allusions, you explain the meaning as best you can. In effect, you are writing about the poem's ideas as they are developed through the various symbols and allusions. Thus, you will need to answer questions like these: What is the poem's major idea? How do you know that your interpretation is valid? How do the poem's symbols and allusions contribute to your interpretation? How pervasive, how applicable, are these devices? If you have discovered many symbols and allusions, which

ones predominate? What do they mean? Why are some more important than others? What connects them with each other and with the poem's main idea? How are you able to make conclusions about all this?

2. *The importance of symbols or allusions to the form of the poem.* Here the goal is to determine how symbolism or allusion is related to the poetic structure. Where does the symbol occur in the poem? If it is early, how do the following parts relate to the ideas of the symbol? What sort of logical or chronological function does the symbol serve in the development of the poem? Is the symbol repeated, and if so, to what effect? If the symbol is introduced later in the poem, has it been anticipated earlier? How do you know? Can the symbol be considered as being climactic? What might the structure of the poem have been like if the symbolism had not been used? (Answering this question can help you judge how the symbol influences the poem's structure.) Many of these same questions might also be applied to an allusion or allusions. In addition, for an allusion, it would be important to compare the contexts of your work and the original to determine how the poet has used the allusion as a part of the poem's form or structure.

3. *The relationship between the literal and the symbolic.* The object here is to describe the literal nature of the symbols, and then to determine their appropriateness to the poem's context. If the symbol emerges as a part of a narrative, what is its literal function? If the symbol is a person, object, or setting, what physical aspects are described? Are colors included? Shapes? Sizes? Sounds? In the light of this actual description, how applicable is the symbol to the ideas it embodies? How appropriate is the literal condition to the symbolic? The answers to questions like these should lead not so much to a detailed account of the meaning of the symbols, but rather to an account of their appropriateness to the topics and ideas of the poem.

4. *Implications and resonances of symbols and allusions.* We have used the term *resonance* elsewhere to refer to the complex of suggestions and associations and implications that are brought out by a particular aspect of literature. The term is rather vague, but in a major respect it is at the very heart of literary experience. Here, particularly, it could be a fruitful direction to take for an essay. Ideas to explore would be about the chain of thinking that is brought out through the symbolism or allusiveness. In following the chain, you also follow a process of thought similar to the poet's, except that you are free to move in your own direction as long as you base your discussion in the symbols and allusions. If the poet is speaking in general terms about the end of an era, for example, as in "The Second Coming" and "The Purse-Seine," then you could include your own thoughts about the observations. It is not easy to summon the knowledge and authority to contradict the work of a poet, but if you can point out shortcomings in the thought of the symbols or allusions, you should go right ahead.

Your conclusion might contain a summary of the main points. If your poem is particularly rich in symbols or allusions, you might also briefly consider some of the elements that you did not consider fully in the body, and try to tie these together with those you have already discussed. It would also be appropriate to introduce any responses you developed as a result of your study.

SAMPLE ESSAY

Symbol and Allusion in Yeats's "The Second Coming"°

[1]
William Butler Yeats's "The Second Coming" is a prophetic poem that lays out reasons for being scared about the future. The poem's symbolism and allusiveness combine traditional materials from ancient history and literature together with Yeats's own visual scheme designed to explain the rise and fall of civilizations. These devices are arranged to explain both the disruption of our present but old culture, and also the installation of a fearsome new one.* To make his prophecies clear, Yeats describes major symbols and allusions separately, and combines them as a reflection of horror.†

[2]
Yeats's first symbol, the gyre, or rather two gyres interconnecting, is pervasive in the poem, for it indicates the cyclical nature of political changes. Flying outward at the widest point of the gyre--symbolizing our present era --a falcon is used by Yeats to introduce the idea that "the center cannot hold." The "desert birds," hovering around the "lion body and the head of a man" (the sphinx-like figure) show a tighter circle in a second gyre, symbolizing a new stage of human existence. Thus the widening symbolic gyre in line 1 is interpenetrating with the narrowing gyre pointing at the "rough beast." This blending and intersecting show that new things blend into old things, while separating from them at the same time. The spatial and geometrical symbolism thus illustrates that the order of the past is breaking up, while the future order is about to take the shape of the past--but at its worst, not at its best.

[3]
Embodying this horror-to-be, the second major symbol is the sphinx-like creature moving its slow thighs in the sands of the desert. The attributes of the creature--a monster, really--are blankness and pitilessness. Yeats describes it as a "rough beast," with the "indignant desert birds," perhaps vultures, flying in circles above it. This description of the symbol emphasizes the brutal nature of the new age. Yeats wrote the poem in 1919, right after the conclusion of World War I, which had seen particularly mindless and vicious trench warfare. The disruption of life caused by this war was a disturbing indicator that the new period would be one of political repression and continued brutality.

It is this forthcoming brutality that makes ironic the poem's major al-

° For this poem, see p. 781.
* Central idea.
† Thesis sentence.

[4]   lusion--the "second coming." Yeats alludes to the second coming in the poem's title, and also in lines 9 and 10:

> Surely some revelation is at hand;
> Surely the Second Coming is at hand.

The allusion is to the usual understanding of New Testament prophecies about the return of Christ at the end of historical time, when the Kingdom will come on earth. In the Bible, war and rumors of war are claimed as being the signs indicating that the return, or "second coming," is near. Thus far, both the biblical signs and the observations of Yeats coincide. The twist, however, is that Yeats is suggesting in the allusion that after breakup of the present age, the new age will be marked not by God's Kingdom but by the "rough beast." Because Yeats describes the beast as a sphinx, his model is the kind of despotism known in ancient Egypt, when power was held absolutely by the pharaoh, and when few people were granted any freedom or civil rights.

[5]   A unique aspect of Yeats's symbolism and allusiveness is that he fuses the two together. The "ceremony of innocence," for example (line 6), refers to the ritual of communion and also to its symbolic value of regeneration. By indicating that it is being drowned, he thus doubles the impact of his assertion that tradition is being lost and brutalized. The *Spiritus Mundi* is an abstract allusion to a common human bond of images and characteristics, but because of the image of brutality it produces, as a symbol it demonstrates that horror is a normal condition of human life. In addition, the "blood-dimmed tide" is an allusion to Shakespeare's Macbeth, who symbolically has stained the ocean red with King Duncan's blood. The "blood-dimmed tide" therefore both allusively and symbolically indicates the global importance of the forthcoming age of evil.

[6]   "The Second Coming" is therefore rich in symbols that are both traditional and also personal to Yeats, but there are additional symbols and allusions. The most easily visualized of these is the falcon out of control, flying higher and higher and farther away from the falconer, to symbolize the anarchy that Yeats mentions in line 4 as being "loosed" in the world. An example of a symbol being used ironically is the reference to Bethlehem where, according to Matthew and Luke, Jesus, the "Prince of Peace," was born. In "The Second Coming," Yeats asserts that the new birth will not lead to peace, but instead will bring about a future age of repression and brutality. The poem thus offers a complex and disturbing fabric of symbol and allusion.

Commentary on the Essay

This essay combines the topics of symbolism and allusion, and illustrates how each may be treated. The introduction briefly characterizes the poem and asserts that the arguments are made through the use of symbols and allusions. The central idea is about the replacement of the old by the new, and the thesis sentence lists two major symbols and allusions to be discussed in the body. Paragraph 2 describes the shape of the symbol, thus illustrating method 2 as just described, and also explains it, illustrating method 1. Paragraph 3 considers the "rough beast" as a symbol of emerging brutality. Paragraph 4 treats the title's allusion to New Testament prophetic tradition, showing how Yeats makes his point by reversing the outcome that tradition had predicted. Paragraph 5 demonstrates the complexity of Yeats's poem by stressing how he fuses symbolism and allusion as a common topic. The sixth and last paragraph summarizes and characterizes the body briefly, and proceeds to illustrate the richness of "The Second Coming" with brief reference to additional symbols and allusions.

WRITING TOPICS

1. Analyze the ways in which Keats, Herbert, and Jeffers use symbols to convey the fact and idea of capture and thralldom ("La Belle Dame Sans Merci," "The Collar," and "The Purse-Seine"). What major symbols do the three poets use? How appropriate is each symbol in its respective poem? How do the poets use the symbols to focus on the problems they present in their poems?

2. Describe the differences in the ways in which Anne Finch, E. E. Cummings, T. S. Eliot, and W. B. Yeats use allusions in "To Mr. Finch," "In Just-," "Sweeney Among the Nightingales," and "The Second Coming." How possible is it to understand these poems without an explanation of the allusions? How extensive should explanations be? To what extent does the allusiveness make the poems difficult? Challenging? Interesting? Enriching?

3. Write a poem in which you develop a major symbol, as Jeffers does in "The Purse-Seine" and Kennedy does in "Old Men Pitching Horseshoes." Some symbols you might consider are these:

> Atomic waste, or nuclear weapons
> Foreign-made cars
> A superstar athlete
> A computer
> A dog staring out a window as the children leave for school

Now, write an essay describing the process of your creation. How do you begin? How much detail is necessary? How many conclusions do you need to bring out about your symbol? When do you think you have said enough? Too much? How do you know?

4. Write a poem in which you make your own allusions to things in your own experience, such as school, an activity, a team, a book, a movie character, or a recent artistic or political event. What assumptions do you make about your reader when you bring out your allusions? How do you make the allusion (i.e., by a quotation, a name, a title, an indirect reference)? How does your allusion deepen your meaning? How does your allusion increase your own power of expression?

21

Myth: Systems of Symbolic Allusion in Poetry

The word **myth** comes to us from the Greek word *muthos*, meaning a story or narrative. Throughout the ages, people have developed myths because they want to know who they are, where they have been, where they are going, how the world got the way it is, and whether anyone "up there" cares. Mythical stories and characters do exactly that. They comprise narrative systems that account for the history, culture, religion, and collective psychology of individual societies and civilizations. They satisfy our need to explain, organize, and humanize conditions that are otherwise mysterious and even frightening.

Although many myths originated in primitive times, they still provide a wealth of material and allusion in literature and art. The world around us seems more rich, awesome, and divine when we know that many events, places, creatures, trees, and flowers are important in the beautiful stories and legends that we have inherited from the past.

A single story is a **myth** (like the *Myth of Sisyphus*). **Mythology** refers collectively to all the stories together, either of a group or of all groups (*Greek mythology*, or the *mythology of the Ancient Near East*). A system of beliefs and religious or historical doctrines is a **mythos** (the *Islamic Mythos*, or the *Buddhist Mythos*).

MYTH, SCIENCE, AND BELIEF

As you might expect, myth and science overlap, since both attempt to provide explanations for the universe as we see it. At the beginnings of civilizations, almost all the vital questions were answered by myths, such as those about the existence of gods, the creation of the world, the formation of humankind, the origins of lightning and thunder, the causes of earthquakes and volcanoes, and birth, death, and sexuality.

As Western civilization became progressively more educated and sophisticated, however, particularly since the time of Copernicus (1473–1543), scientific discoveries largely replaced myths as the means of explaining the "how's" of life and existence. Thus we understand today that lightning and thunder are produced by the friction of electrically charged clouds being buffeted in high winds, not by great and powerful gods like Zeus or Thor hurling lightning bolts from the sky. Wherever there are volcanic eruptions, we know the cause to be molten lava deep within the earth's crust being vented violently through fissures in the volcanoes. (Nevertheless, on the "Big Island" of Hawaii, many people will say that the originator is a mythical goddess named *Pele*.)

But even though myths are not scientific, they should not be dismissed as superstition and falsehood. While we know an immense amount scientifically about *how* things happen as they do, we do not really know *why* they happen. For instance, although cosmologists tell us a great deal about the early stages of the universe and the development of galaxies, stars, the solar system, and our earth, they do not even approach answering the imponderable religious and philosophical questions about causes that myths seek to explain.

THE POWER OF MYTH, AND SYMBOLIC MYTHICAL TRUTH

Even when science does provide illumination, there is still a place for myth, for myths are ingrained into our human consciousness—into our very thought patterns. Thus we know that the earth is always half in sunlight and half in shadow because it makes a complete rotation on its axis every twenty-four hours. Despite this absolute scientific knowledge, we continue to use the words "the sun rises" and "the sun sets" to explain the phenomena of day and night, as though we still believed the mythical stories about a flat earth with the sun turning about it. Such mythically originated language is inseparable from our minds. Even the belief that science and technology can solve all earthly problems may be seen as a myth. Human beings, in short, are **mythopoeic**—that is, not only do we live with myths, but we *habitually* create them.

Almost every culture embraces a mythology, either by developing its own or else by absorbing the mythology of another people and adapting it to its own ends. The ancient Romans, for example, assimilated the whole body of Greek mythology. Most Roman myths and mythic figures, such as Jupiter, Minerva, and Ulysses, parallel those in Greek mythology (such as Zeus, Athena, and Odysseus).

It is therefore important to realize that myths express truth *symbolically* even if mythical heroes and stories themselves are scientifically or historically inadmissible. The truths are not to be found in the actual lore itself but rather in what the lore shows about our existence here on earth. Thus, when we read about the problems of the ancient Theban king Oedipus, we may safely assume that the specific details of his life (if he ever actually did live) did not happen just as Sophocles dramatizes them in *Oedipus the King*. But we find in the play a powerful rendering of how human beings make mistakes and how they must pay for them. In short, the truth of the Oedipus myth is psychological, not literal and historical.

MYTH AS CONCEPT AND PERSPECTIVE

We may broaden our consideration somewhat by adding that myths also imply a special perspective about how people see their place and purpose in the world. This kind of myth may be constructive and generative. Thus, at one time most North Americans accepted the myth that Nature was limitless and wild, and in need of being conquered. With this concept foremost in mind, settlers moved into every available corner of the land— to build, farm, create industries, and establish a new way of life. Without such an inspiring myth, people would have stayed put, and the nation would never have achieved its current prominence.

This is not to say that all myths are permanently positive and generative; indeed, some myths may become destructive. Thus, the once-positive myth of limitless and inexhaustible Nature has led us into the massive problems we face today with environmental exploitation and degradation. A new attitude is in the process of coming into existence— that the earth is no longer inimical, in need of taming, but is beautiful, tender, and fragile, in need of conservation. The Ansel Adams photograph "Forest Floor, Yosemite Valley" is a visual embodiment of this attitude (p. 798). While the reasons for the changing attitude are largely scientific, the attitude itself marks a new *mythos*—that of a caring relationship for Nature, with all the consequent approaches to preserving wild animals, the land, and natural resources.

MYTHOLOGICAL THEMES OR MOTIFS

Since myths address our human need to know, it is not surprising to find that many civilizations, separated by time and space, have parallel myths, such as the many stories accounting for the creation of the universe. The details of these myths are different, but the *patterns* are similar inasmuch as they all posit both an original time and action of creation, and a creator god or gods who also take part in human history. The principal god is perceived as a shaper, a model, a divine artisan, who is the ultimate cause of the orderly systems we find in the world, such as life, daylight, tides, warmth, fertility, harvests, morality, and social stability.

Ansel Adams, *Forest Floor, Yosemite Valley*. (Photograph by Ansel Adams. Copyright © 1992 by the trustees of the Ansel Adams Publishing Rights Trust. All rights reserved.)

One of the most crucial of all myths involves sin, disobedience, and evil, which are usually blamed for natural calamities, the death of the year, and the death of living creatures. A corollary of the myth is that a god-hero or goddess-heroine must undergo a sacrifice to atone for sin and to ensure the coming of spring and renewed vitality. In *The Golden Bough*, a massive collection and analysis of mythic stories, Sir James Frazer (1854–1941) compares a series of mythical death–renewal motifs. Among such sacrificed and reborn gods are Thammuz (Babylonia), Attis (Phrygia), Osiris (Egypt), and Adonis, Dionysus, and Persephone (Greece). Again, the specific myths take different forms, but they reflect the same mysteries, fears, and hopes.

Scholars and anthropologists like Frazer were among the first to observe the interrelationships among myths produced by diverse cultures. The Swiss psychoanalyst Carl Gustav Jung (1875–1961) offered an explanation for this duplication. He noticed that images, characters, and events similar to those in literature, mythology, and religion also occurred in the dreams of his patients. He termed these recurring images **archetypes** (from the Greek word meaning "model" or "first mold") and developed a theory that all human beings share in a universal or collective unconscious mind. Even if Jung's theory is ignored, the fact remains that specific types of mythic creatures such as dragons and centaurs, archetypal mother–daughter and father–son stories, and narratives involving sacrifices, heroic quests, and trips to the underworld recur throughout various mythologies and pervade our literature.

MYTHOLOGY AND LITERATURE

When writing was invented, the first written works recorded already existing mythologies. The early Greek poet Homer, for example (perhaps a mythical figure himself), told about the mythical gods and heroes of the Trojan war. Homer did not actually write (tradition says he was blind), but other writers recorded and transmitted his epics. The Latin writer Ovid (43 B.C.–A.D. 17) received a large body of mythology, and wrote poetic stories based on it. The results of this assimilation of myth into poetry was a combination of literature and religion that served the double purpose of teaching and entertaining. In this way, poets throughout antiquity used mythology as a mine for ideas, images, and symbols.

Though almost two thousand years have passed since the time of Ovid, writers and artists have not abandoned the use of mythology. In every generation since the earliest Anglo-Saxon poems and legends, poets of English have retold and updated mythological stories. Indeed, many of the poems in this chapter are from the twentieth century. Modern poetry utilizing mythology, however, is no longer primarily designed to reinforce the religious mythos of society. Instead, it uses mythology to link past and present, to dramatize important concerns, and to symbolize universal patterns of thought.

Most Western poets who use mythological material in their verse turn to long-standing bodies of myth, particularly those of Greco-Roman, Norse-Teutonic, and Judeo-Christian origin. These systems of mythology are **public** or **universal,** since they are part of a vast common heritage. Like universal symbols, they make up a reservoir of material that all writers are free to employ.

LEARNING ABOUT MYTHOLOGICAL REFERENCES IN POETRY

When poets make references to a myth, as in poems like Tennyson's "Ulysses" and Parker's "Penelope," both of which refer to the myth of Odysseus (Ulysses), they assume that readers already understand some-thing about the stories and characters. With these poems, readers are expected to know enough of Homer's *Odyssey* to recall that this hero fought in the Trojan War for ten years, and then spent ten years returning home.

In other words, during most of his reign as king of Ithaca he was a warrior and adventurer—an absentee ruler—but at the same time his queen, Penelope, stayed at home.

While you may often have enough background in mythology to understand all the poet's references, you may sometimes need to fill in or reinforce your knowledge. A good place to start is a dictionary or general encyclopedia, where you will find brief identifications of mythic figures and a key to further reading. Eventually you will want access to more detailed information. Two well-known books that retell the stories of Greco-Roman mythology are Thomas Bullfinch's *The Age of Fable* and Edith Hamilton's *Mythology*. There are also many classical dictionaries, such as the *Oxford Classical Dictionary*. John Keats learned much mythology from Lemprière's *Classical Dictionary*, an eighteenth-century guide which comprehensively locates all the ancient literature on which the mythological stories are based. Many libraries have this book on their reference shelves, and you cannot do better than to follow Keats, and use it. Similarly, if you find allusions to the myths of *Paul Bunyan* and *Johnny Appleseed*, you would want a collection of American folk tales. References to *Odin, Thor, the Valkyries*, or *Asgard* should lead you to a collection of Norse-Teutonic mythology.

STUDYING MYTHOLOGY IN POETRY

We are now ready to look at a poem that is built upon a myth. The poem is by William Butler Yeats, and it draws on Greco-Roman mythology.

WILLIAM BUTLER YEATS   (1865–1939)

Leda and the Swan   *1924 (1923)*

A sudden blow: the great wings beating still
Above the staggering girl, her thighs caressed
By the dark webs, her nape caught in his bill,
He holds her helpless breast upon his breast.

How can those terrified vague fingers push   5
The feathered glory from her loosening thighs?
And how can body, laid in that white rush,
But feel the strange heart beating where it lies?

A shudder in the loins engenders there
The broken wall, the burning roof and tower   10
And Agamemnon dead.
                        Being so caught up,
So mastered by the brute blood of the air,
Did she put on his knowledge with his power
Before the indifferent beak could let her drop?   15

QUESTIONS

1. What mythic event does the poem retell? Who was Leda? The swan? Who were Leda's children? What events are alluded to in lines 10 and 11?

2. How is Leda described? What words suggest her helplessness? What phrases suggest the swan's mystery and divinity?

3. What question is raised in the last two lines? To what extent does the poem provide an answer to this question?

Yeats's poem, a sonnet, focuses on a specific event of ancient Greek mythology—the King of the gods, Zeus, having taken the form of a swan, rapes Leda, a Spartan queen (although the two central characters are identified only in the title). According to the myth, this violent event was a starting point not only of Greek civilization, but also of humanity's angers and troubles. One of the children born of the rape was Helen of Troy, whose abduction by Paris was the cause of the Trojan War. Thus, Yeats's phrase "the broken wall, the burning roof and tower" refers to Troy's destruction. Another child was Clytemnestra, the wife and queen of Agamemnon, the leader of the Greek forces fighting against Troy. Because Agamemnon sacrificed their daughter Iphigenia as a part of the war effort, Clytemnestra vowed revenge, and had him murdered when he returned home from the Trojan War. (See also Eliot's "Sweeney Among the Nightingales," p. 784.)

After a graphic recounting of the swan's attack on Leda, and a brief reference to the sack of Troy and the death of Agamemnon, Yeats's concluding lines raise a central issue stemming from the myth. While Leda took on some of Zeus's divine power with the rape (through the process of childbearing), the poem asks whether she also "put on" some of his divine knowledge—whether she acquired Zeus's foreknowledge of the fall of Troy, the murder of Agamemnon, and, by extension, the subsequent events in history. Of course, the question is rhetorical and the answer is negative.

If all the poem did were to question the ancient myth in this way, it would be of limited interest for modern readers. But it does more than that; it directs our attention to concerns of today's world. Thus, we may conclude from Yeats's use of the myth that human beings, like Leda, do not have preknowledge, but have only their own culture, experience, and intelligence as their guides. If divine beings exist, they have no interest in human affairs, but are rather uninvolved and "indifferent" (line 15). By extension the myth suggests that the burden of civilization is on human beings themselves, and that if knowledge and power are ever to be combined for constructive goals, that blending must be a human achievement.

Yeats thus employs mythic material in this sonnet to raise a searching question about the nature of existence, knowledge, and power. The historical process is embodied in the rape, the children born out of it, and their troubles. As the central figure of the myth, Leda is the focal point of circumstances and concerns that have extended from the distant past to the present, and that will likely extend into the future.

Because most myths similarly embody recurring issues, they have great value for modern readers. Rukeyser's "Myth," for example, uses the ancient myth about Oedipus to shed light amusingly on misperceptions about male–female relationships. Edward Field's "Icarus" (one of a number of Icarus poems we include here) uses the ancient Icarus myth to decry the impact of modern society upon individuals. In these and in other poems based in mythological topics, you may look for such original ways in which poets receive something old and make it new. Myths do not belong only to the past, but are alive and well in the present.

POEMS FOR STUDY

ALFRED, LORD TENNYSON   (1809–1892)

Ulysses   *1842 (1833)*

It little profits that an idle king,
By this still hearth, among these barren crags,
Matched with an aged wife, I mete and dole
Unequal laws° unto a savage race,   *rewards and punishments*
That hoard, and sleep, and feed, and know not me.   5

   I cannot rest from travel; I will drink
Life to the lees.° All times I have enjoyed   *dregs*
Greatly, have suffered greatly, both with those
That loved me, and alone; on shore, and when
Through scudding drifts the rainy Hyades°   10
Vexed the dim sea. I am become a name;
For always roaming with a hungry heart
Much have I seen and known—cities of men
And manners, climates, councils, governments,
Myself not least, but honored of them all—   15
And drunk delight of battle with my peers,
Far on the ringing plains of windy Troy.
I am a part of all that I have met;
Yet all experience is an arch wherethrough
Gleams that untraveled world whose margin fades   20
Forever and forever when I move.
How dull it is to pause, to make an end,
To rust unburnished, not to shine in use!
As though to breathe were life! Life piled on life

ULYSSES.   10 *Hyades:* nymphs who were placed among the stars by Zeus, the king of the gods. The name means "rain," and the rising of the stars was thought to precede a storm.

Were all too little, and of one to me   25
Little remains; but every hour is saved
From that eternal silence, something more,
A bringer of new things; and vile it were
For some three suns to store and hoard myself,
And this gray spirit yearning in desire   30
To follow knowledge like a sinking star,
Beyond the utmost bound of human thought.

    This is my son, mine own Telemachus,
To whom I leave the scepter and the isle—°
Well-loved of me, discerning to fulfill   35
This labor, by slow prudence to make mild
A rugged people, and through soft degrees
Subdue them to the useful and the good.
Most blameless is he, centered in the sphere
Of common duties, decent not to fail   40
In offices of tenderness, and pay
Meet adoration to my household gods,
When I am gone. He works his work, I mine.

    There lies the port; the vessel puffs her sail;
There gloom the dark, broad seas. My mariners,   45
Souls that have toiled, and wrought, and thought with me—
That ever with a frolic welcome took
The thunder and the sunshine, and opposed
Free hearts, free foreheads—you and I are old;
Old age hath yet his honor and his toil.   50
Death closes all; but something ere the end,
Some work of noble note, may yet be done,
Not unbecoming men that strove with Gods.
The lights begin to twinkle from the rocks;
The long day wanes; the slow moon climbs; the deep   55
Moans round with many voices. Come, my friends,
'Tis not too late to seek a newer world.
Push off, and sitting well in order smite
The sounding furrows; for my purpose holds
To sail beyond the sunset, and the baths   60
Of all the western stars, until I die.
It may be that the gulfs will wash us down;
It may be we shall touch the Happy Isles,°
And see the great Achilles,° whom we knew.

Though much is taken, much abides; and though   65
We are not now that strength which in old days
Moved earth and heaven, that which we are, we are—
One equal temper of heroic hearts,

34 *isle:* Ithaca, the island realm ruled by Odysseus.   63 *Happy Isles:* the Elysian Fields,
dwelling place of mortals who have been made immortal by the gods.   64 *Achilles:* Greek
hero of the Trojan War who killed Hector and was, in turn, killed by Paris.

Made weak by time and fate, but strong in will
To strive, to seek, to find, and not to yield.   70

QUESTIONS

1. Who is the speaker of the poem? What is his attitude toward his life in
    Ithaca? What key phrases and adjectives in lines 1–5 establish this attitude?
2. Who is Telemachus? What is the speaker's attitude toward him? How are
    the speaker and Telemachus different?
3. What aspects of Ulysses are emphasized in this poem? To what extent does
    he become symbolic? What does he symbolize?

DOROTHY PARKER   (1893–1967)

Penelope   *1936*

In the pathway of the sun,
  In the footsteps of the breeze,
Where the world and sky are one,
  He shall ride the silver seas,
    He shall cut the glittering wave.   5
I shall sit at home, and rock;
Rise, to heed a neighbor's knock;
Brew my tea, and snip my thread;
Bleach the linen for my bed.
    They will call him brave.   10

QUESTIONS

1. How does the speaker describe her life? How is her life different from that
    of the male figure described in lines 1–5?
2. To what extent is Penelope a symbol? What does she symbolize? How does
    our knowledge of the myth deepen our response to this symbolism?

W. S. MERWIN   (b. 1927)

Odysseus   *1960*

Always the setting forth was the same,
Same sea, same dangers waiting for him
As though he had got nowhere but older.
Behind him on the receding shore
The identical reproaches, and somewhere   5
Out before him, the unravelling patience
He was wedded to. There were the islands
Each with its woman and twining welcome

To be navigated, and one to call "home."
The knowledge of all that he betrayed   10
Grew till it was the same whether he stayed
Or went. Therefore he went. And what wonder
If sometimes he could not remember
Which was the one who wished on his departure
Perils that he could never sail through,   15
And which, improbable, remote, and true,
Was the one he kept sailing home to?

QUESTIONS

1. What aspects of the Odysseus myth are evoked in this poem? What point does the poem make about Odysseus's experiences?

2. To what extent is Odysseus symbolic of a specific kind of life and attitude toward life? How does our knowledge of Odysseus contribute to the impact and meaning of the poem?

3. Compare this poem with Parker's "Penelope." How is the same mythic material used toward different ends in these poems?

4. Compare this poem with Tennyson's "Ulysses." Explain how and why the same mythic figure can be used to convey such different ideas.

MARGARET ATWOOD   (b. 1939)

Siren Song   *1974*

This is the one song everyone
would like to learn: the song
that is irresistible:

the song that forces men
to leap overboard in squadrons   5
even though they see the beached skulls

the song nobody knows
because anyone who has heard it
is dead, and the others can't remember.

Shall I tell you the secret   10
and if I do, will you get me
out of this bird suit?

I don't enjoy it here
squatting on this island
looking picturesque and mythical   15

with these two feathery maniacs,
I don't enjoy singing
this trio, fatal and valuable.

I will tell the secret to you,
to you, only to you.   20
Come closer. This song

is a cry for help: Help me!
Only you, only you can,
you are unique

at last, Alas   25
it is a boring song
but it works every time.

QUESTIONS

1. Who were the sirens in Greek mythology? What effect did their song have?
2. Who is the speaker in this poem? What is the effect of her colloquial diction?
    What does she tell you about her song?
3. Who is the "you" referred to in lines 10–24? What does the speaker say
    about her life? What "works every time"? To what extent is the conclusion
    amusing?

OLGA BROUMAS   (b. 1949)

Circe   *1977*

The Charm

The fire bites, the fire bites.   Bites
to the little death.   Bites

till she comes to nothing.   Bites
on her own sweet tongue. She goes on.   Biting.   5

The Anticipation

They tell me a woman waits, motionless
till she's wooed.   I wait

spiderlike, effortless as they weave
even my web for me, tying the cord in knots   10

with their courting hands. Such power
over them.   And the spell

their own.   Who could release them?   Who
would untie the cord

with a cloven hoof?   15

The Bite

What I wear in the morning pleases
me: green shirt, skirt of wine.   I am wrapped

in myself as the smell of night
wraps round my sleep when I sleep   20

outside.   By the time
I get to the corner

bar, corner store, corner construction
site, I become divine.   I turn

men into swine.   Leave   25
them behind me whistling, grunting, wild.

QUESTIONS

1. Who was Circe? What powers did she have?
2. Who or what is the speaker in this poem? What is the connection between the speaker and Circe? Why is the poem entitled "Circe"?
3. What do Circe and the speaker symbolize in the poem? What is the source of Circe's power in the myth and the poem? What does this power symbolize?
4. What is the "fire" (lines 1–5)? Who are "they" (lines 6–15)? What is the effect of "spiderlike" (line 9) and "courting hands" (line 11)? What is "the spell" (line 12)? What is the significance of "a cloven hoof" (line 15)?
5. What is the speaker's attitude toward herself in lines 16–26? What happens to her in these lines? What happens to the men she encounters?

MURIEL RUKEYSER   (b. 1913)

Myth   *1978*

Long afterward, Oedipus, old and blinded, walked the
roads.   He smelled a familiar smell.   It was
the Sphinx.°   Oedipus said, "I want to ask one question.
Why didn't I recognize my mother?"   "You gave the
wrong answer," said the Sphinx.   "But that was what   5
made everything possible," said Oedipus.   "No," she said.
"When I asked, What walks on four legs in the morning,
two at noon, and three in the evening, you answered,
Man.   You didn't say anything about woman."
"When you say Man," said Oedipus, "you include women   10
too. Everyone knows that."   She said, "That's what
you think."

Sphinx: For a representation of the Sphinx at Gîza in Egypt, see p. 808.

QUESTIONS

1. Who was Oedipus? The Sphinx? According to this poem, what was wrong with Oedipus's answer to the Riddle of the Sphinx?

The great sphinx at Gîza, Egypt. (Archivi Alinari/Art Resource)

2. What elements and techniques in this work allow you to consider it a poem?
3. What two myths and meanings of *myth* are embodied in the title?
4. To what extent does the poem's colloquial language revitalize the mythic material?

POEMS ABOUT ICARUS

The next five poems, written between 1933 and 1963, all draw on the same mythic material—the story of the death of Icarus—to create symbolic resonance, meaning, and impact. According to Greek myth, Icarus was the son of Daedalus, an inventor and craftsman who was employed by Minos, the king of Crete, to design and build a labyrinth in which the king wanted to imprison the Minotaur, a monster that was half man and half bull. With Daedalus's help, Theseus killed the Minotaur and freed Athens from its annual tribute of sacrificial youths. As punishment for helping Theseus, Minos imprisoned Daedalus and Icarus in a tower. He also posted guards permanently on all roads and at the seaport to prevent escape. Daedalus realized that he and Icarus could escape only by air, so he fashioned two pairs of wings made of feathers and wax. As father and son were about to fly away from Crete and imprisonment, Daedalus warned Icarus not to fly too near the sun, because the heat would melt the wax and destroy the wings. In the glory of flight, however, Icarus forgot his father's warnings and began to soar higher and higher toward the sun. Icarus continued to mount upward, despite his father's passionate cries, until the wax melted and the wings fell apart; he plunged into the sea and drowned.

Although all the following poems feature Icarus as the central mythic figure, the focus and the symbolic resonance is different in each. Each poet went to the common storehouse of Greek mythology, selected the story and the figure of Icarus, and shaped these materials according to his or her own poetic goals. These goals are different in each poem. Thus, Icarus is used in various ways to illustrate and symbolize ideas about pride, daring, suffering, creativity, idealism, society, and the tedium of daily life. Each of the "Icarus" poems offers its own meaning, impact, and poetic experience. Taken together, however, the group of poems illustrates the way myth can be used for very different effects in various poetic contexts. As you study these poems, try to answer the following questions.

1. What is Icarus's symbolic meaning or value in the myth? What qualities or characteristics does Icarus represent in mythology?
2. On what aspects of the Icarus myth does each poet focus? Some possibilities include character, action, motivation, emotion, death, suffering, or the implications of the action.
3. To what extent does the allusion to Icarus contribute symbolic resonance and meaning to each poem? In what ways is the poetic effect of the mythic allusion different in each?
4. How do such poetic elements as diction, meter, rhyme, tone, and form help to reshape the myth and the figure of Icarus in each poem?
5. What themes or ideas are explored in each poem? Explain the connection between the Icarus myth and the meaning in each poem.

STEPHEN SPENDER (1909–1986)

Icarus   1933

He will watch the hawk with an indifferent eye
  Or pitifully;
Nor on those eagles that so feared him, now
  Will strain his brow;
Weapons men use, stone, sling and strong-thewed bow   5
  He will not know.

This aristocrat, superb of all instinct,
  With death close linked
Had paced the enormous cloud, almost had won
  War on the sun;   10
Till now, like Icarus mid-ocean-drowned,
  Hands, wings, are found.

W. H. AUDEN   (1907–1973)

Musée des Beaux Arts°   *1940*

About suffering they were never wrong,
The Old Masters: how well they understood
Its human position; how it takes place
While someone else is eating or opening a window or just walking dully along;
How, when the aged are reverently, passionately waiting   5
For the miraculous birth, there always must be
Children who did not specially want it to happen, skating
On a pond at the edge of the wood:
They never forgot
That even the dreadful martyrdom must run its course   10
Anyhow in a corner, some untidy spot
Where the dogs go on with their doggy life and the torturer's horse
Scratches its innocent behind on a tree.
In Brueghel's° *Icarus*, for instance: how everything turns away
Quite leisurely from the disaster; the ploughman may   15
Have heard the splash, the forsaken cry,
But for him it was not an important failure; the sun shone
As it had to on the white legs disappearing into the green
Water; and the expensive delicate ship that must have seen

MUSÉE DES BEAUX ARTS: "Museum of Fine Arts."   14 *Brueghel:* Pieter Brueghel or
Breughel (ca. 1525–1569) was a Flemish painter whose subjects included the Nativity ("the
miraculous birth"), the Crucifixion ("the dreadful martyrdom"), and the fall of Icarus. See
pp. 752 and 811 for two other poems based on the work of Brueghel.

Pieter Brueghel the Elder, *Landscape with the Fall of Icarus.* Museo di Belle Arti,
Brussels. (Scala/Art Resource)

Something amazing, a boy falling out of the sky,   20
Had somewhere to get to and sailed calmly on.

ANNE SEXTON (1928–1974)

To a Friend Whose Work Has Come to Triumph°   *1962*

Consider Icarus, pasting those sticky wings on,
testing that strange little tug at his shoulder blade,
and think of that first flawless moment over the lawn
of the labyrinth. Think of the difference it made!
There below are the trees, as awkward as camels;   5
and here are the shocked starlings pumping past
and think of innocent Icarus who is doing quite well:
larger than a sail, over the fog and the blast
of the plushy ocean, he goes. Admire his wings!
Feel the fire at his neck and see how casually   10
he glances up and is caught, wondrously tunneling
into that hot eye. Who cares that he fell back to the sea?
See him acclaiming the sun and come plunging down
while his sensible daddy goes straight into town.

TO A FRIEND WHOSE WORK HAS COME TO TRIUMPH. The title alludes to and
reverses the title of a poem by William Butler Yeats, "To a Friend Whose Work Has Come
to Nothing" (1914).

WILLIAM CARLOS WILLIAMS (1883–1963)

Landscape with the Fall of Icarus   *1962*

According to Brueghel°
when Icarus fell
it was spring

a farmer was ploughing
his field   5
the whole pageantry

of the year was
awake tingling
near

the edge of the sea   10
concerned
with itself

LANDSCAPE WITH THE FALL OF ICARUS.   1 *Brueghel:* See the note for line 14 in
Auden's "Musée des Beaux Arts," p. 810.

sweating in the sun
that melted
the wings' wax   15

unsignificantly
off the coast
there was

a splash quite unnoticed
this was   20
Icarus drowning

EDWARD FIELD   (b. 1924)

Icarus   *1963*

Only the feathers floating around the hat
Showed that anything more spectacular had occurred
Than the usual drowning. The police preferred to ignore
The confusing aspects of the case,
And the witnesses ran off to a gang war.   5
So the report filed and forgotten in the archives read simply
"Drowned," but it was wrong: Icarus
Had swum away, coming at last to the city
Where he rented a house and tended the garden.

"That nice Mr. Hicks" the neighbors called him,   10
Never dreaming that the gray, respectable suit
Concealed arms that had controlled huge wings
Nor that those sad, defeated eyes had once
Compelled the sun. And had he told them
They would have answered with a shocked, uncomprehending stare.   15
No, he could not disturb their neat front yards;
Yet all his books insisted that this was a horrible mistake:
What was he doing aging in a suburb?
Can the genius of the hero fall
To the middling stature of the merely talented?   20

And nightly Icarus probes his wound
And daily in his workshop, curtains carefully drawn,
Constructs small wings and tries to fly
To the lighting fixture on the ceiling:
Fails every time and hates himself for trying.   25

He had thought himself a hero, had acted heroically,
And dreamt of his fall, the tragic fall of the hero;
But now rides commuter trains,
Serves on various committees,
And wishes he had drowned.   30

WRITING ABOUT MYTH IN POETRY

An essay on myth in poetry will normally connect the mythic material in a poem to some other consideration, such as speaker, tone, or meaning. This suggests a two-part exploration of the poem, one concerned with its general sense, and the other concerned with the ways in which myth shapes and controls that sense. Be sure to consider the mythological content and its relationship to other elements, including speaker, character, action, setting, situation, imagery, form, and meaning.

As you reexamine the poem, you are looking for the ways in which myth enriches the poem and focuses its meaning. The following questions should help:

Questions for Discovering Ideas

To what extent does the title identify the mythic content of the poem and thus provide a key for understanding?

Does the poem retell a myth? In other words, how much of the poem's action, setting, and situation are borrowed from mythology? What is the significance of the action in the myth? To what extent is this material symbolic? How does the poet reshape the action and its significance to his or her own ends?

Are the speaker or any of the characters drawn from mythology? If so, what qualities and characteristics of the mythic figures are evoked in the poem? To what extent does our understanding of the myth explain the speaker, characters, situations, and ideas in the poem?

If the characters are drawn from mythology, how are they symbolic in the myth, apart from the poem? What aspects of this symbolism are carried into the poem? How does the poem maintain, undercut, increase, or change the symbolism?

Beyond character and action, what mythic images occur in the poem? How do these affect the poem's meaning and impact?

How do the various formal elements of poetry such as diction, rhyme, meter, and form reshape the mythic material and affect the meaning and impact of the myth? Do specific words and phrases, for instance, undercut or reinforce the ideas and implications that we find in the myth itself? Does the rhyme (if any) lead us to deal with the mythic content seriously or humorously? Does the tone of the poem support or undercut the implications of the myth?

Generally, how does the mythic content help create and clarify the poem?

Your answers to these and other questions will usually point toward the specific area in which the myth and the poem interact most profoundly.

The introduction should state the essay's idea and the way the idea will be supported in the body. If, for example, you find that the poem retells a myth in order to make a point about history or society, your central idea may reflect that connection. Similarly, if the poem employs a mythical speaker or character to convey ideas about war or heroism, your essay will focus on the linkage among myth, character, and those ideas.

The central idea should identify the important mythic aspects of the poem, link them with other relevant poetic elements, and make an assertion about the effect of this connection. It is not enough merely to assert that a given poem contains a great deal of mythic material. If you are writing an essay about Yeats's "Leda and the Swan," for example, you might be tempted to form a central idea that argues that "William Butler Yeats's 'Leda and the Swan' retells the myth of Leda's rape by Zeus and the consequences of that event." That sentence does not tell the reader anything about the *way* myth works in the poem. Nor does it provide a basis for moving beyond simple summary and paraphrase. A more effective formulation of a central idea might read as follows: "In Yeats's 'Leda and the Swan,' the myth of Leda's rape by Zeus and the consequences of that rape are employed to illustrate the historical process and to question the connection between knowledge and power." This sentence points to a specific connection between mythological content and the poem's effect, and it gives a clear direction to the essay.

Strategies for Organizing Ideas

Early in the essay, you might want to summarize briefly the relevant parts of your poem's mythical elements. For the most part, however, the essay should focus on the poem (and the mythic material within the poem) rather than on the myth itself.

Various strategies can be employed to organize the body of the essay. You might decide to echo the organization of the poem, and shape the central paragraphs to reflect the line-by-line or stanza-by-stanza logic of the poem (as in the discussion of "Leda and the Swan" on p. 800). Alternatively, you might choose an organization based on a series of different mythic elements or figures. If a poem alludes to Odysseus, his wife Penelope, and his son Telemachus, for instance, you might devote a paragraph or two to the way each figure shapes the poem's impact and meaning. As a third option, you might use the relevant elements of poetry as the focal points of organization. Thus, if you argue that diction, rhyme, and tone shape the mythological material to produce significant effects, you would deal with each element in turn.

To bring your essay to a convincing and assertive close, you might summarize your major points. At the same time, you might draw your reader's attention to the significance of your observations and to any further implications that might arise from the unique fusion of myth and the poem you have considered.

SAMPLE ESSAY

Myth and Meaning in Dorothy Parker's "Penelope"°

[1] Dorothy Parker's short lyric poem "Penelope" uses mythic allusion and symbolism to criticize conventional social perspectives about the roles of women and men. Her speaker is the mythic figure Penelope, the wife of King Odysseus of the ancient realm of Ithaca. Not only is Penelope the speaker, but she is also the poem's major figure. Parker uses her to assert that society has consistently misjudged and undervalued women's lives.* Her assertions are brought out through the poem's title, its mythic resonance, its diction, and its view of the representative lives of Odysseus and Penelope themselves.†

[2] The key to the poem's mythic resonance is the title, "Penelope." As the only place where the mythological speaker of the poem is named, the title alludes to the Homeric account in *The Odyssey* that Penelope waits at home in Ithaca for twenty years while her husband adventures in the Trojan War and struggles against the Sea God, Poseidon, to return home. The life Penelope leads is filled with trouble. Her palace is occupied by boorish suitors who assume that Odysseus is dead and that his kingship is vacant. They therefore demand that Penelope choose a new husband. Only Penelope and Telemachus, her son, cling to the hope that Odysseus is still alive. Penelope keeps the arrogant suitors at bay by promising to marry one of them after she finishes weaving a shroud for Odysseus's father. In order to delay this eventuality, she works at the loom each day and unravels the work each night. Thus, she lives a domestic but stressful life for ten years while she bravely resists both despair and the demands of the suitors.

[3] Although the title refers directly to Penelope, the poem itself draws on mythic material that relates to both Penelope and Odysseus. Lines 1–5 evoke the memory of Odysseus; his wanderings and adventures are alluded to in phrases like "He shall ride the silver seas" (line 4) and "He shall cut the glittering wave" (line 5). Because Odysseus is not identified by name, but only by the pronoun "he," readers may see this male figure as a symbol for all men who leave home and pursue an active life of adventure. The adjectives and verbs in these lines make this active life seem attractive and exciting. Such phrases as "the pathway of the sun" (line 1) and "the footsteps of the breeze" (line 2) add romance and mystery to the male's distant wanderings. The adjectives *silver* and *glittering* connote splendor and glory; the verbs *ride* and *cut* reinforce the active and violent nature of the male's adventure. In the same lines, however, one may perceive a subtle undercutting of the heroic figure. Many of the phrases, like "ride the silver seas," suggest that some of the Homeric lines are clichés. The implication is that an overglorified image of active heroes like Odysseus is both trite and inaccurate.

Just as the language about Odysseus also refers to men generally, the language about Penelope has general meaning for women. In lines 6–9 Pe-

° See p. 804 for this poem.
* Central idea.
† Thesis sentence.

[4] nelope, the speaker, contrasts her own life to the active life of males. Here we find no adjectives at all; the woman's existence is thus rendered drab and tedious. In addition, the verbs represent passive and domestic activities: *sit, rock, rise, brew, snip*, and *bleach*. These last two verbs are especially effective. The phrase "snip my thread" (line 8) is the only allusion to Penelope's unhappy existence in Ithaca. It refers to her daring deception of the suitors through weaving and unraveling the shroud. At the same time, *snip* is contrasted with the verb *cut* used earlier in the poem. While the words are synonyms, they carry very different connotations, for *cut* implies a degree of violence while *snip* suggests careful and delicate activity. *Bleach* is equally connotative; although it refers directly to "the linen for my bed," it is consistent with the view that Penelope's life is faded and colorless.

[5] The final line of the poem ironically crystallizes its message and clarifies the speaker's attitude toward the different roles that men and women play. Here, the speaker asserts that "They will call him brave." *They* refers to society, to the world at large, and to generations of readers who have admired Odysseus in Homer's *Iliad* and *Odyssey*. The speaker assures us that he--both Odysseus in particular and the active male in general--will be admired by society. The meter of the line places a great deal of stress on the word *him*, thus emphasizing the speaker's irony at her realization that society ignores or dismisses the quiet bravery of women. In myth and in life, the woman's role often demands more courage and conviction than the man's. Certainly Penelope's desperate existence for ten years in Ithaca, besieged in her own home by arrogant suitors who ignore her wishes, testifies to the strength and bravery of women.

[6] This poem thus employs mythic figures and events to criticize the distorted perception of the roles historically played by men and women. Odysseus, as a symbol for all men, is presented as a heroic figure, but he too is human, and not all his adventures may be described without triteness. Parker's point is not so much to demean him and his life, however, as to emphasize that women, too, have their own kinds of heroism. Biology and destiny may have traditionally confined women to sit at home and weave tapestries while men go to fight and wander in distant lands, but waiting takes courage, and meeting domestic challenges takes courage. Penelope and Odysseus lived at a time of the old ways, but if Parker's poem is understood properly, it is time for the old ways to be reviewed and altered. Penelope is right to express annoyance and irony when considering how history will tell her story. Our knowledge of her courageous survival in Ithaca during the absence of Odysseus adds significantly to the truth and depth of her feelings.

Commentary on the Essay

The major rhetorical purpose of this essay is not to explain the emotions of the distant past, but rather to show how the poet uses the myth to shed new light on conventional attitudes toward male–female relationships. As a guide for your own writing aims, therefore, the essay illustrates how the mythological material may lead to vital ideas for development.

The body of the essay is organized along the lines of the first strategy mentioned on page 814; it follows the organization of the poem itself. Thus, paragraph 2 focuses on the title, paragraph 3 on lines 1–5, paragraph 4 on lines 6–9, and paragraph 5 on the last line. Each of the paragraphs also advances a specific aspect of the essay's central idea. In paragraph 2 Penelope is identified, and the relevant mythic material is reviewed. Logically, the information in this paragraph is essential for the remainder of the essay.

In paragraph 3, the title and its mythic resonance are used to introduce Odysseus and the symbol of the heroic male. Here, the point is that Parker's diction undercuts the active male while seeming to glorify him. The first sentence of paragraph 4 provides a transition from Odysseus and heroic males to Penelope and the perceived passiveness of women. Again, the essay explores the way diction and mythic allusion in the poem demonstrate that there is more to the lives of women than usually is claimed. Paragraph 5 looks at the poem's final line in relation to the contrasted lives of heroic men and passive women. Here, the essay takes up tone and meter to reveal the speaker's attitude toward these contrasting lives and society's misperception of them.

The conclusion goes quickly over the essay's basic points, but it emphasizes how the poem, with its ancient myth, brings new light to a traditional problem. The conclusion is, therefore, a brief personal essay, a consideration of the poem's ideas and their current importance.

WRITING TOPICS

1. In the poems "Ulysses," "Penelope," "Odysseus," "Siren Song," and "Circe," the poets evoke the same myth but for different purposes. What are these purposes? What views do you find about adventure, domesticity, and sexuality? What attitudes toward figures in the myth (Odysseus, Penelope, the Siren, Circe) do the poets bring out? How does word choice, selection of detail, and point of view influence each poet's conclusions?

2. The myth of Icarus is used by Spender, Auden, Sexton, Williams, and Field. Basing your conclusions on two or more of their poems, what similarities and differences can you describe? How do the poets present the myth? How do they use the myth to create unusual or surprising endings, and to comment on contemporary but also permanent attitudes about life and the sufferings of others?

3. What point does Muriel Rukeyser's "Myth" make about both men and women and their attitudes toward each other? How does our knowledge of the Oedipus myth (see Sophocles's play *Oedipus the King* in the drama section) help clarify these aspects of the poem? In what respects is the poem particularly contemporary?

4. Select a story from among the many myths, traditions, and historical events that are a part of our heritage (e.g., Oedipus, Jason, Romulus and Remus,

Antigone, Sisyphus, the fight between God and Satan, the Captivity in Egypt and the Exodus, the Babylonian Captivity, Robin Hood, Beaver stealing fire from the Pines (Nez Percé legend), Paul Bunyan, Davy Crockett, the Amistad affair, the Forty-Niners, the Lone Ranger, the log cabin, the American West, the homesteaders, the Rough Riders, etc.). Write a poem based on the story, and attempt to present your own view about its importance, timeliness, intelligence, and truth. What kinds of detail do you select? How do you give the figures mythic status? How do you make your own attitudes apparent by your arrangement of detail and your word choice (see, for example, how Broumas and Rukeyser present their figures).

Theme: Idea, Motif, and Meaning in Poetry

Theme, idea, motif, and *meaning* (see also Chapter 10, pp. 362–409, are all concerned with the significance of poetry. These words are elusive, and the shades of meaning among them are not easily distinguished. First, by **idea** we mean a *concept, principle, scheme, method, idealization,* or *archetype.* An idea may yield to extensive description and definition, such as the *idea of goodness,* the *idea of time,* and so on.

When we use the word **theme** (*something placed*), we refer to an idea, image, principle, or **motif** (*something that moves*) that, like a melody in music, is *embodied and developed within a literary work.* The theme of Wordsworth's "Daffodils" is that intense experiences with Nature provide energy for the human mind and spirit. Wordsworth introduces the theme by describing his impressions at having seen masses of springtime daffodils. At the end of the poem he brings out the motif by emphasizing how the remembered vision is a constant source of psychological and spiritual joy:

> For oft, when on my couch I lie
> In vacant or in pensive mood,
> They flash upon that inward eye
> Which is the bliss of solitude;
> And then my heart with pleasure fills,
> And dances with the daffodils.

> (lines 19–24)

In this way, Wordsworth develops his theme, or motif, by drawing general conclusions about his specific experience.

Going up the scale from idea, theme, and motif, we arrive at **meaning,** the word referring comprehensively to the body of significances and ideas within the poem. Meaning is the poem's *sense* or *message.* It implies that we may condense or encapsulate the poem's entire sense, and phrase it concisely. But even when we try to grasp a poem's meaning, it is important to recognize the limitations of our effort. Our sentence is no more than our sentence. It demonstrates our perception and comprehension, but only the poem itself contains its *entire* meaning. We know that individual poems are made up of separate parts, that each part has its own meaning, and that the various parts together make up the whole. Because poetry, like literature generally, is a *time art*, it always takes time for the poem to unfold, and we cannot hold the entire poem in our minds simultaneously. When we go on to new lines, the content of early lines is in our minds, but it recedes as we follow the patterning of words, rhythms, and sounds. It is therefore possible to say that meaning in a poem develops, but difficult to claim that a reader can achieve a comprehensive, instantaneous understanding of the meaning.

Then, too, individual parts shift in meaning, depending on individual response. Sometimes we read poetry as though it always has an absolute meaning that will invariably be true for all readers. But while we continue to ask and try to answer questions about what we read—as the best way to understand individual poems—we realize that readers may *approach* understanding while never completely *reaching* it.

There is also a question of time and delayed comprehension and impact. Some lines that we read today may not impress us fully, whereas at a later time these same lines may burst upon us with great meaning and power. One of the American presidents (Eisenhower) once introduced a new legislative proposal by quoting the following couplet from "An Essay on Criticism" by Alexander Pope:

> Be not the *first* by whom the *New* are try'd,
> Nor yet the *last* to lay the *Old* aside.

Everyone who studies Pope's poem reads this passage, in which he discusses the need to develop discrimination about new literary fashions. But someone on the president's staff thought it was a meaningful justification for new proposals to address the nation's needs. This is a clear example of a way in which the understanding of a meaning can emerge when the time and circumstances make the idea shine out for all to see.

But even after we complete all our analyses of a poem, we have not touched it. It remains exactly as it was, and it always maintains its own identity. Our understanding of it may grow, however, and this is why we keep trying to reach it. A dancer was once asked why she danced. Her response was that if she could explain her reasons in words, she would not need to dance. The meaning of poetry is something like that. No matter how well we follow a poem's intricate threads of theme or motif, or how comprehensively we determine the meaning of the poem's individual parts, the poem is still out there—dancing. We see it and try to understand it, but it evidences techniques and meaning that evade our total grasp and comprehension. This is what leads Archibald MacLeish, in his poem "Ars Poetica," to claim that "A poem should not mean / But be" (p. 833). Nevertheless, before poems reach such an ideal and almost mystical state in our eyes, we need to confront them and assimilate them as best we can.

SUBJECT AND MEANING

To determine the total effect of poems, we begin with the basic things we have been working with throughout this book. The first of these is **subject.** Subjects are often general, and may include such broad categories as love, death, war, art, youth, age, work, and nature. Thomas Hardy's "Channel Firing" (p. 562) and Wilfred Owen's "Dulce et Decorum Est" (p. 657), for example, share the same subject—war.

But the subject of a poem is only the beginning of our comprehension, for subjects alone are static. To move us, poems must take us somewhere. In prose, ideas are established directly and openly. For example, a major point in our Declaration of Independence is that human beings have the inalienable rights of life, liberty, and the pursuit of happiness. In poetry, however, points are made dramatically and indirectly. Even if we grant that many poems may have no *overt* intention to express ideas (poems are not newspaper articles, or sermons), it is nevertheless true that most poems are based in views about their subjects that we may consider as a major aspect of their meaning.

Thus, Hardy's "Channel Firing" and Owen's "Dulce et Decorum Est" are both powerful and dramatic poems. They share a common thread of hostility toward war as a human institution. But in addition, both poems are strong statements of ideas. Hardy's poem asserts that war is a perpetual condition, and that despite the perversity of war it will likely continue to threaten all the positive and noble achievements that humanity has created. Owen's poem, briefly dramatizing the death of a soldier in a wartime gas attack, asserts that war is obscene, and that ideas about war's nobility are unreal and untrue. Both poems, in short, contain clear ideas.

Moreover, no matter what the subject, poems achieve much of their impact through the strength of their ideas. For example, Andrew Marvell's "To His Coy Mistress" and Robert Herrick's "To the Virgins, to Make Much of Time" both concern the subject of love within the context of passing time. But while Herrick's poem argues that the pressure of eventual death should lead people toward delight in marriage, Marvell's poem asserts that this same pressure should lead toward the full but desperate pursuit of pleasures through the "iron gates of life." These ideas, like those of Hardy and Owen, are not frivolous expressions of idle poetic moments, but are deeply felt ideas that people should know, think about, and apply or not apply, as they wish, to their own lives.

STRATEGIES FOR DEALING WITH MEANING

So that we may approach comprehension of poetic meaning, we need to consider a poem's ideas together with its intellectual and emotional impact. In effect, meaning involves us in a transfer of experience from the poet's mind to our own. It is no exaggeration to claim that the structure and development of a poem also produces a corresponding development of thoughts, reactions, considerations, and emotions in readers. To get at meaning, then, is to get at all the ways in which poetry brings these effects about.

An initial understanding of meaning can therefore be gained by a close sentence-by-sentence reading. But for most poems the meaning emerges as a result of comprehending not only the direct statements but also the results of the poet's technique. In the various chapters of this book we have studied many of these elements of technique separately: speaker, character, setting and situation, action, diction, sound, imagery, metaphor and simile, tone, meter, rhyme, form, symbol, allusion, and others.

SPEAKER.   The identity and circumstances of the speaker significantly affects a poem's meaning. It is essential for us to understand, for example, that the speaker of Hardy's "Channel Firing" is a corpse who has been awakened in his grave by the noise of "great guns" at sea, and that the speaker in Sharon Olds's "35/10" is a mother brushing her daughter's hair. The attitudes and ironies so essential to the meanings of these poems would not be clear if we did not know who these speakers are and what they are doing at the "time" of the poems. Similarly, it is important to determine whether a speaker is trustworthy. Thus, in Browning's "My Last Duchess" the speaker presents himself as a friendly and intelligent man of integrity, but his words betray him as intimidating, cold, cruel, and heartless. In short, each poem produces its own unique speaker, whose circumstances have a vital bearing on content and meaning.

CHARACTER, SETTING, ACTION.   The characters, settings, and actions in a poem do much to shape the meaning. A poem that is set in a graveyard and that refers to gunnery practice at sea ("Channel Firing") conveys a different meaning from one that tells about a walk through the woodland in spring (Housman's "Loveliest of Trees") or that tells about a mother brushing her daughter's hair at bedtime (Olds's "35/10"). Even if all three poems dealt with the common subject of death, their radically different contexts and actions would produce a new perspective, a different emotional response, a new experience, and a different meaning.

DICTION.   The words of a poem—denotation, connotation, diction, and syntax—all shape a poem's total meaning and emotional impact. In

Robert Herrick's "To the Virgins, to Make Much of Time," for example, the speaker advises virgins to gather "rosebuds," which could easily be interpreted as an invitation to promiscuous sexuality. However, the poem concludes on the advice to "go marry," and thereby it places the urgency of sex in a context of socially and religiously approved behavior. By contrast, in Ben Jonson's "To Celia," the speaker urges "sports of love" and "love's fruit," but provides no additional context. Thus, "To Celia" primarily advises seduction, whereas "To the Virgins" provides happy but mature advice about life, even though both poems similarly belong to the "seize the day" or **carpe diem** tradition of love poetry.

IMAGERY AND RHETORICAL FIGURES. Imagery, metaphor, simile, and other devices of language make abstract ideas and situations concrete and immediate. We have stressed how Keats creates a sense of excitement through his simile of the "watcher of the skies" in "On First Looking into Chapman's Homer" (p. 624). Beyond such uses, a poet may use imagery and metaphorical language to reinforce or to negate what appears to be the speaker's major thrust. In Owen's "Dulce et Decorum Est," for example, soldiers are described as "Bent double, like old beggars under sacks." The simile is consistent with the rest of the poem; it defines the speaker's dislike of the drudgery and difficulty of war, and it shapes the poem's point that war is humiliating, dehumanizing, and horrible. In contrast, the first part of Dorothy Parker's "Penelope" (p. 804) contains clichéd images that undercut the heroic ideal. The poem thereby emphasizes the negative truth that heroes, while pursuing their goals, may also be self-centered and neglectful.

TONE. The tone of a poem has a significant effect on the expression of ideas. In Arthur O'Shaughnessy's "A Love Symphony," for example (p. 665), the speaker's admiration for the listener is clear, unambiguous, and unreserved, as indicated by phrases like "You were more sweet." There is no question about the content of his poem. Tone may sometimes create ambiguity, however, or it may even work against the stated purpose of the speaker, as in the Duke's mentioning the marriage settlement in "My Last Duchess." The Duke speaks of the Count's "known munificence" as justification for his "just" claims, while we conclude that the Duke's demands will be onerous. Through irony, therefore, Browning makes it clear that the Duke is an inhuman monster. Irony is also present in Marvell's "To His Coy Mistress," in which the carpe diem mode is colored by the speaker's many details about death and eternity. In short, although the ostensible purpose of Marvell's speaker is persuasion and seduction, the tone makes the poem not happy and loving but rather somber and desperate.

RHYTHM, METER, AND SOUND. Devices like rhythm, alliteration, assonance, and onomatopoeia shape meaning significantly in tandem with other elements. Rhythm and meter may throw particularly important words into strong positions of emphasis, and therefore they may shape our perception of the importance of particular ideas. The last line of Parker's "Penelope," for example, is "They will call him brave." The meter literally demands that "him" be accented, thus underscoring the powerful irony of this line, and of the poem. Similarly, meaning can be refined through the skillful use of alliteration, assonance, and the repetition of identical or similar sounds. In Pope's line "The sound must seem an echo to the sense," for example, the alliteration of the *s* sound connected the key words "sound," "seem," and "sense." The words are important in themselves, but they are made more emphatic, in the context, by Pope's linking them by sound.

RHYME, STRUCTURE, AND FORM.   Rhyme may be employed to clinch ideas, regulate the tone, and thus shape meaning. The falling or double rhymes in Herrick's "To the Virgins" lighten the tone and thus modify the poem's message. Form, too, can provide a method for ordering and shaping a poem's theme and meaning. The coherent units or stanzas of a closed form often reflect specific steps in the poem's expression of meaning. Such is the case in Spenser's *Amoretti 75*, "One Day I Wrote Her Name upon the Strand." In this poem the formal divisions of the sonnet reflect a logical pattern that moves from an action to a reaction and finally to an explanation.

SYMBOL AND ALLUSION.   Poets employ symbol and allusion as a short-hand way of conveying complex ideas and a great deal of information as quickly and economically as possible. In "To the Virgins," for example, two symbols—rosebuds and flowers—point beyond themselves to human sexuality, marriage and families, and full engagement with life. The symbols thus carry much of the poem's impact and message. Allusion can be equally important. In "To His Coy Mistress" we find geographic and biblical allusions that are crucial in shaping the meaning of the first part of the poem's argument.

Admittedly, these eight areas form a large number of variables to consider as you work toward an understanding of a poem's central idea and meaning. Keep in mind, however, that this is an outside number of approaches, and that as you study you will probably focus not on all but rather on just a few. In addition, you will eventually be able to evaluate the impact of many of these elements on meaning rather quickly. The point to remember about analyzing poetic meaning, however, is that all elements of poetry—statements and techniques—are available, and you can introduce any element that is relevant to assist you in developing your comprehension.

POEMS FOR STUDY

BEN JONSON (1572–1632)

To Celia°   *1606*

Come my Celia, let us prove,°   *try*
While we may, the sports of love;
Time will not be ours forever;
He at length our good will sever.
Spend not then his gifts in vain.   5
Suns that set may rise again;
But if once we lose this light,
'Tis with us perpetual night.
Why should we defer our joys?
Fame° and rumor are but toys.   *reputation*   10
Cannot we delude the eyes
Of a few poor household spies,
Or his° easier ears beguile,   *Celia's husband*
So removed by our wile?
'Tis no sin love's fruit to steal;   15
But the sweet theft to reveal,
To be taken, to be seen,
These have crimes accounted been.

TO CELIA. The poem is from Jonson's play *Volpone;* it is spoken by Volpone (the name
means "the fox") to Celia, a married woman whom he is trying to seduce.

QUESTIONS

1. What is the speaker like? What is his attitude toward time? Love? Celia?
2. What is personified in lines 3–5? What power does this force have?
3. This type of poem is called *carpe diem* (Latin for "seize the day"). How is the
   idea of "seizing the day" relevant to the first eight lines of this poem?
4. How does the speaker's argument change in the last ten lines? What assertions
   does the poem make about time, love, reputation, and crime?
5. What is the tone of the poem? How does it affect the meaning?

ANDREW MARVELL (1621–1678)

To His Coy Mistress   *1681*

Had we but world enough, and time,
This coyness, lady, were no crime.
We would sit down, and think which way
To walk, and pass our long love's day.

Thou by the Indian Ganges° side   5
Shouldst rubies find; I by the tide
Of Humber° would complain. I would
Love you ten years before the flood,°   *Noah's flood*
And you should, if you please, refuse
Till the conversion of the Jews.°   10
My vegetable love should grow
Vaster than empires and more slow;
An hundred years should go to praise
Thine eyes, and on thy forehead gaze;
Two hundred to adore each breast,   15
But thirty thousand to the rest;
An age at least to every part,
And the last age should show your heart.
For, lady, you deserve this state,
Nor would I love at lower rate.   20
   But at my back I always hear
Time's wingéd chariot hurrying near;
And yonder all before us lie
Deserts of vast eternity.
Thy beauty shall no more be found,   25
Nor, in thy marble vault, shall sound
My echoing song; then worms shall try
That long-preserved virginity,
And your quaint honor turn to dust,
And into ashes all my lust: 30
The grave's a fine and private place,
But none, I think, do there embrace.
   Now therefore, while the youthful hue
Sits on thy skin like morning dew,
And while thy willing soul transpires   35
At every pore with instant fires,
Now let us sport us while we may,
And now, like amorous birds of prey,
Rather at once our time devour
Than languish in his slow-chapped° power.   *slow-jawed*   40
Let us roll all our strength and all
Our sweetness up into one ball,
And tear our pleasures with rough strife
Thorough° the iron gates of life: *through*
Thus, though we cannot make our sun   45
Stand still, yet we will make him run.

TO HIS COY MISTRESS.   5 *Ganges:* a large river that runs across most of India.
7 *Humber:* a small river that runs through the north of England to the North Sea.
10 *Jews:* Traditionally, this conversion is supposed to occur just before the Last Judgment.

QUESTIONS

1. In lines 1 through 20 the speaker sets up a hypothetical situation and the
   first part of a pseudo-logical proof: If *A* then *B*. What specific words indicate
   the logic of this section? What hypothetical situation is established?

2. How do geographic and biblical allusions affect our sense of time and place?

3. In lines 21 through 32 the speaker refutes the hypothetical condition set up in the first twenty lines. What word indicates that this is a refutation? How does imagery help create and reinforce meaning here?

4. The last part of the poem (lines 33–46) presents the speaker's "logical" conclusion. What words indicate that this is a conclusion? What is the conclusion?

ROBERT HERRICK   (1591–1674)

To the Virgins, to Make Much of Time   *1648*

Gather ye rosebuds while ye may,
  Old time is still a-flying;
And this same flower that smiles today
  Tomorrow will be dying.

The glorious lamp of heaven, the sun,   5
  The higher he's a-getting,
The sooner will his race be run,
  And nearer he's to setting.

That age is best which is the first,
  When youth and blood are warmer;   10
But being spent, the worse, and worst
  Times still succeed the former.

Then be not coy, but use your time,
  And, while ye may, go marry;
For, having lost but once your prime,   15
  You may forever tarry.

QUESTIONS

1. What does the title of this poem tell us? What can we deduce about the speaker? To whom is the poem addressed?

2. What point does this poem make about time? Life? Love?

3. How does symbolism help shape the message and meaning of the poem? Consider especially "rosebuds," "flower," and "the sun."

4. How do rhyme and tone help create and focus the meaning of this poem?

5. Compare this poem to Jonson's "To Celia" and Marvell's "To His Coy Mistress" as *carpe diem* poems. How are the tone and message of this poem similar to and different from those in the poems by Jonson and Marvell?

EDMUND SPENSER   (1552–1599)

Amoretti 75: One Day I Wrote Her Name upon the Strand   *1595*

One day I wrote her name upon the strand,°   *beach*
But came the waves and washèd it away:
Again I wrote it with a second hand,
But came the tide and made my pains his prey.
"Vain man," said she, "that doest in vain assay,   5
A mortal thing so to immortalize,
For I myself shall like to this decay,
And eek° my name be wiped out likewise."   *also, indeed*
"Not so," quod° I, "let baser things devise,   *said*
To die in dust, but you shall live by fame: 10
My verse your virtues rare shall eternize,
And in the heavens write your glorious name.
Where whenas death shall all the world subdue,
Our love shall live, and later life renew."

QUESTIONS

1. What action is described in the first quatrain? What point does the speaker's mistress make about this action in the second quatrain?

2. What is the subject of this poem? What is its theme?

3. How do rhyme, meter, and form contribute to the poem's meaning?

MARIANNE MOORE   (1887–1982)

Poetry°   *1921*

I, too, dislike it: there are things that are important beyond all this fiddle.
    Reading it, however, with a perfect contempt for it, one discovers in
    it after all, a place for the genuine.
        Hands that can grasp, eyes
        that can dilate, hair that can rise   5
            if it must, these things are important not because a

high-sounding interpretation can be put upon them but because they are
    useful. When they become so derivative as to become unintelligible,
    the same thing may be said for all of us, that we
        do not admire what   10
        we cannot understand: the bat
            holding on upside down or in quest of something to

POETRY. In the most recent edition of her *Collected Poems*, Moore deleted everything in
this poem following "genuine" in line 3.

eat, elephants pushing, a wild horse taking a roll, a tireless wolf under
  a tree, the immovable critic twitching his skin like a horse that feels a
      flea, the base-
    ball fan, the statistician—   15
      nor is it valid
        to discriminate against 'business documents and

school-books';° all these phenomena are important. One must make a distinction
  however: when dragged into prominence by half poets, the result is not poetry, 20
  nor till the poets among us can be
    'literalists of
    the imagination'°—above
      insolence and triviality and can present

for inspection, 'imaginary gardens with real toads in them', shall we have 25
  it. In the meantime, if you demand on the one hand,
  the raw material of poetry in
    all its rawness and
    that which is on the other hand
      genuine, you are interested in poetry.   30

QUESTIONS

1. What is the tone of this poem? How do words like *fiddle* (line 1) and *perfect contempt* (line 2) affect the tone and meaning?
2. What is the subject of this poem? The theme?
3. How does the speaker modify his or her initial assertion about poetry? What can poetry provide? What is its value? How should we experience it?
4. What is meant by poems "we cannot understand" (line 11)? How does imagery clarify the assertion about incomprehensible things?

18–19 *'business . . . school-books'*: The phrase is quoted from the Russian novelist, Leo Tolstoy (1828–1910). Moore's original note cites a passage in Tolstoy's *Diaries* (1917) in which he discusses the difference between prose and poetry: "Where the boundary between prose and poetry lies, I shall never be able to understand. . . . Poetry is verse: prose is not verse. Or else poetry is everything with the exception of business documents and school books" (p. 96).   22–23 *literalists of the imagination:* Moore's original note refers to W. B. Yeats's discussion of William Blake in *Ideas of Good and Evil* (1903), where Yeats observes that Blake was "a too literal realist of imagination" (p. 182).

WILLIAM WORDSWORTH   (1770–1850)

Daffodils (I Wandered Lonely as a Cloud)°   *1807 (1804)*

I wandered lonely as a cloud
That floats on high o'er vales and hills,
When all at once I saw a crowd,
A host, of golden daffodils;

Beside the lake, beneath the trees,   5
Fluttering and dancing in the breeze.

Continuous as the stars that shine
And twinkle on the milky way,
They stretched in never-ending line
Along the margin of a bay: 10
Ten thousand saw I at a glance,
Tossing their heads in sprightly dance.

The waves beside them danced; but they
Out-did the sparkling waves in glee;
A poet could not but be gay,   15
In such a jocund° company;   *cheerful, merry*
I gazed—and gazed—but little thought
What wealth the show to me had brought:

For oft, when on my couch I lie
In vacant or in pensive mood,   20
They flash upon that inward eye
Which is the bliss of solitude;
And then my heart with pleasure fills,
And dances with the daffodils.

*Written at Town-end, Grasmere. The Daffodils grew and still grow on the margin of
Ullswater, and probably may be seen to this day as beautiful in the month of March, nodding
their golden heads beside the dancing and foaming waves. [Wordsworth's note. Wordsworth
also pointed out that lines 21 and 22, the "best lines," were by his wife, Mary.]*

QUESTIONS

1. Describe the poem's specific occasion. Why does the speaker specify that he
   was alone?

2. What is the significance of the verbs and verbals describing the flowers?
   What idea about Nature is suggested by these words?

3. How has the scene affected the speaker? In what way? For how long? What
   general conclusion about human beings and Nature does the poem invite us
   to draw?

JOHN KEATS (1795–1821)

Ode on a Grecian Urn   *1820 (1819)*

1

Thou still unravish'd bride of quietness,
   Thou foster-child of silence and slow time,
Sylvan historian, who canst thus express
A flowery tale more sweetly than our rhyme:
What leaf-fring'd legend° haunts about thy shape   *border and tale*   5

The Krater of Thanagra. Fourth century B.C., showing a wedding procession and musicians. National Museum, Athens. (Archivi Alinari/Art Resource)

Of deities or mortals, or of both,
  In Tempe° or the dales of Arcady?°
What men or gods are these? What maidens loth?
What mad pursuit? What struggle to escape?
  What pipes and timbrels? What wild ecstasy?

10

2

Heard melodies are sweet, but those unheard
  Are sweeter; therefore, ye soft pipes, play on;
Not to the sensual ear, but, more endear'd,
  Pipe to the spirit ditties of no tone:

ODE ON A GRECIAN URN. The imaginary Grecian urn to which the poem is addressed combines design motifs from many different existing urns. This imaginary one is decorated with a border of leaves and trees, men (or gods) chasing women, a young musician sitting under a tree, lovers, and a priest and congregation leading a heifer to sacrifice.   7 *Tempe:* a beautiful rustic valley in Greece.   *Arcady:* refers to the valleys of Arcadia, a state in ancient Greece known for its beauty and peacefulness.

Fair youth, beneath the trees, thou canst not leave   15
  Thy song, nor ever can those trees be bare;
    Bold lover, never, never canst thou kiss,
Though winning near the goal—yet, do not grieve;
    She cannot fade, though thou hast not thy bliss,
  For ever wilt thou love, and she be fair!   20

3

Ah, happy, happy boughs! that cannot shed
  Your leaves, nor ever bid the spring adieu;
And, happy melodist, unwearied,
  For ever piping songs for ever new;
More happy love! more happy, happy love!   25
  For ever warm and still to be enjoy'd,
    For ever panting, and for ever young;
All breathing human passion far above,
  That leaves a heart high-sorrowful and cloy'd,
    A burning forehead, and a parching tongue.   30

4

Who are these coming to the sacrifice?
  To what green altar, O mysterious priest,
Lead'st thou that heifer lowing at the skies,
  And all her silken flanks with garlands drest?
What little town by river or sea shore,   35
  Or mountain-built° with peaceful citadel,   *built on a mountain*
    Is emptied of this folk, this pious morn?
And, little town, thy streets for evermore
  Will silent be; and not a soul to tell
    Why thou art desolate, can e'er return.   40

5

O Attic shape! Fair attitude! with brede°   *braid, pattern*
  Of marble men and maidens overwrought,°   *ornamented*
With forest branches and the trodden weed;
  Thou, silent form, dost tease us out of thought
As doth eternity: Cold Pastoral!   45
  When old age shall this generation waste,
    Thou shalt remain, in midst of other woe
Than ours, a friend to man, to whom thou say'st,
  "Beauty is truth, truth beauty,"—that is all
    Ye know on earth, and all ye need to know.   50

QUESTIONS

1. What is the dramatic situation? What does the speaker see and do?

2. What does the speaker call the urn in the first stanza? What is suggested in these lines about the urn's relationship to time and change? To poetry?

3. What are "unheard melodies" (line 11) and "ditties of no tone" (line 14)? Why are these "sweeter" than songs heard by "the sensual ear" (line 13)? What central contrast is created through this comparison?

4. What do the trees, the musician, and the lovers have in common? How are they all related to the real world of time and change?

ARCHIBALD MACLEISH (1892–1982)

Ars Poetica   *1926*

A poem should be palpable and mute
As a globed fruit,

Dumb
As old medallions to the thumb,

Silent as the sleeve-worn stone   5
Of casement ledges where the moss has grown—

A poem should be wordless
As the flight of birds.
        ***

A poem should be motionless in time
As the moon climbs.   10

Leaving, as the moon releases
Twig by twig the night-entangled trees,

Leaving, as the moon behind the winter leaves,
Memory by memory the mind—

A poem should be motionless in time   15
As the moon climbs.
        ***

A poem should be equal to:
Not true.

For all the history of grief
An empty doorway and a maple leaf   20

For love
The leaning grasses and two lights above the sea—

A poem should not mean
But be.

QUESTIONS

1. What does the first section (lines 1–8) assert that a poem should be? How are similes employed to make this assertion clearer and more concrete?

2. How can a poem be "mute" (line 1), "dumb" (line 3), "silent" (line 5), and "wordless" (line 7)? Since a poem (and this poem) must be made of words, how can this paradox be resolved?

3. What does the second section (lines 9–16) assert about a poem? How are symbolism and simile used to clarify this assertion? How can something be

"motionless" and "climb" at the same time? What is the effect of repetition in this section?

4. What does the third section (lines 17–24) assert about a poem? What symbolizes "all the history of grief" here? What symbolizes "love"? Why are these two examples of symbolism included?

5. Generally, what does this poem assert about poetry? To what extent does "Ars Poetica" embody and illustrate its own ideas and total meaning?

PHILIP LARKIN   (1922–1985)

Next, Please   1955

Always too eager for the future, we
Pick up bad habits of expectancy.
Something is always approaching; every day
Till then we say,

Watching from a bluff the tiny, clear,   5
Sparkling armada of promises draw near.
How slow they are! And how much time they waste,
Refusing to make haste!

Yet still they leave us holding wretched stalks
Of disappointment, for, though nothing balks   10
Each big approach, leaning with brasswork prinked,°   *adorned*
Each rope distinct,

Flagged, and the figurehead with golden tits
Arching our way, it never anchors; it's
No sooner present than it turns to past.   15
Right to the last

We think each one will heave to and unload
All good into our lives, all we are owed
For waiting so devoutly and so long.
But we are wrong: 20

Only one ship is seeking us, a black-
Sailed unfamiliar, towing at her back
A huge and birdless silence. In her wake
No waters breed or break.

QUESTIONS

1. What is the subject of the poem? The theme? What point does it make about time, expectation, human nature, and the way we live our lives?

2. What cliché does the extended metaphor that begins in the second stanza ironically revitalize and reverse? How does this metaphor make the total meaning of the poem clearer and more palpable?

3. How do meter, rhyme, and diction help create meaning? Consider, for example, the metrical variation in the fourth line of each stanza, rhyming pairs such as *waste-haste* and *wake-break*, or words such as *bluff* and *armada*.

4. Compare this poem to the three carpe diem poems in this chapter. To what extent is "Next, Please" a carpe diem poem?

DONALD JUSTICE (b. 1925)

On the Death of Friends in Childhood 1960

We shall not ever meet them bearded in heaven,
Nor sunning themselves among the bald of hell;
If anywhere, in the deserted schoolyard at twilight,
Forming a ring, perhaps, or joining hands
In games whose very names we have forgotten,   5
Come, memory, let us seek them there in the shadows.

QUESTIONS

1. What is the subject of this poem: the living, or the dead? How accurate is the title as a guide to subject and theme?
2. What point (if any) does this poem make about death? Time? Memory? The living?
3. How do imagery, diction, rhetoric and tone contribute to the total meaning of this poem? Consider phrases like "bearded in heaven" and "sunning themselves among the bald of hell." What is personified in the last line?

LINDA PASTAN (b. 1932)

Ethics 1980

In ethics class so many years ago
our teacher asked this question every fall:
if there were a fire in a museum
which would you save, a Rembrandt painting
or an old woman who hadn't many   5
years left anyhow? Restless on hard chairs
caring little for pictures or old age
we'd opt one year for life, the next for art
and always half-heartedly. Sometimes
the woman borrowed my grandmother's face   10
leaving her usual kitchen to wander
some drafty, half-imagined museum.
One year, feeling clever, I replied
why not let the woman decide herself?
Linda, the teacher would report, eschews   15
the burdens of responsibility.
This fall in a real museum I stand
before a real Rembrandt, old woman,

or nearly so, myself. The colors
within this frame are darker than autumn,   20
darker even than winter—the browns of earth,
though earth's most radiant elements burn
through the canvas. I know now that woman
and painting and season are almost one
and all beyond saving by children.   25

QUESTIONS

1. What can we surmise about the speaker in this poem? How does this knowledge contribute to our understanding of theme?

2. What are the two settings, situations, and actions presented here? How are they related? How much time has passed between them? How does the contrast between them help create meaning?

3. How has the passage of time changed the speaker's attitudes? What does she now realize about "woman / and painting and season" (lines 23–24)? About children?

4. What is the subject of this poem? The theme? What point does it make about art, life, time, and values?

DONALD HALL   (b. 1928)

Whip-poor-will   *1981*

As the last light
of June withdraws
the whip-poor-will sings
his clear brief notes
by the darkening house, then   5
rises abruptly from sandy
ground, a brown bird
in the near-night, soaring
over shed and woodshed
to far dark fields. When   10
he returns at dawn,
in my sleep I hear
his three syllables make
a man's name, who slept
fifty years in this bed   15
and ploughed these fields:
Wes-ley-Wells . . . Wes-
ley-Wells . . .
                It is good
to wake early in high   20
summer with work to do,
and look out the window

at a ghost bird lifting away
to drowse all morning
in his grassy hut.   25

QUESTIONS

1. What is a whip-poor-will? How does its song figure into the poem? Why does the speaker stress that he hears the name *Wesley Wells* not when waking but when asleep?

2. Who was Wesley Wells? What connection is established between him and the speaker's home and life? To what degree is the information presented about Wesley Wells sufficient to establish this connection?

3. Why is so much attention given to the flying and singing habits of the bird?

4. How comparable is this poem to Keats's "Ode to a Nightingale" (p. 744)? How do birds and their songs serve to bring out major ideas in both poems?

SHARON OLDS (b. 1942)

35/10   *1984*

Brushing out my daughter's dark
silken hair before the mirror
I see the grey gleaming on my head,
the silver-haired servant behind her. Why is it
just as we begin to go   5
they begin to arrive, the fold in my neck
clarifying as the fine bones of her
hips sharpen? As my skin shows
its dry pitting, she opens like a small
pale flower on the tip of a cactus;   10
as my last chances to bear a child
are falling through my body, the duds among them,
her full purse of eggs, round and
firm as hard-boiled yolks, is about
to snap its clasp. I brush her tangled   15
fragrant hair at bedtime. It's an old
story—the oldest we have on our planet—
the story of replacement.

QUESTIONS

1. Who is the speaker in this poem? What is she doing? What is the setting?

2. How does the speaker contrast her own state of being to her daughter's stage of life? How are images, metaphors, and similes used to clarify this contrast? How does this contrast help convey the poem's meaning?

3. What point does this poem make about life and nature? To what extent does the last sentence clarify (or overclarify) the poem's theme?

WRITING ABOUT THEME AND MEANING IN POETRY

When you plan an essay about meaning, you will be dealing with the topic, statement, and experience of the poem.

Always keep foremost in mind that your essay should connect the poem's theme and meaning to other poetic elements, such as speaker, imagery, metaphor, symbol, or tone. The following questions should be helpful in planning the focus and finding the information necessary for such an essay.

Questions for Discovering Ideas

What does the title of the poem tell you about subject and meaning?

What do you learn about the speaker? How does the speaker shape and communicate theme?

How do the other characters in the poem (if any) affect theme and meaning?

What impact do setting, situation, and action have on theme?

How does diction affect theme? How are multiple denotations and connotations employed? To what extent are special types of diction or word order used?

How do imagery, metaphor, simile, and other rhetorical devices help determine the impact and theme of the poem?

What is the poem's tone? What effect does tone have on theme?

What role do rhythm, meter, sound, and rhyme play (if any) in shaping and emphasizing important words and ideas?

How does the form of the poem shape its theme and your response?

How do symbol, allusion, or myth contribute to the poem's theme and impact?

You will find poems for which all these questions are relevant, for some poets employ every element and device in the poetic repertoire to create meaning and impact. Other poems will offer useful information in only a few of these areas. It is unlikely that you will be able to deal with all the various elements, for such a treatment would grow long, and would tend to become unwieldy and fragmented. Instead, look for major elements that have the most profound impact on the poem's theme and on your ability to consider the poem as an emotional as well as an intellectual experience.

Strategies for Organizing Ideas

In your essay, be careful to distinguish between subject and theme. In planning to write about Larkin's "Next, Please," for example, you might write the following: "'Next, Please' makes a clear assertion about human habits of expectation." This sentence describes the poem's *subject*, and might even be a good beginning sentence for your essay. It is not, however, a good central idea because it tells the reader nothing about the poem's theme or meaning. A better central idea might be, "'Next, Please' exposes the futility of those who hope for a better future while ignoring the things they have in the present." This sentence summarizes the theme of the poem and makes a strong statement on which to build an effective paper.

Next, you can focus on the relationship between your idea and the ways in which the poem creates meaning. Use the information you gain from answering the ten questions we listed. Look for the links between the meaning and the methods of the poem, and plan your organization. Thus, if you find that a poem's theme is established through symbol and allusion, your plan should express this connection by relating meaning to these elements. Such a plan might be (1) theme, (2) theme and symbol, and (3) theme and allusion. Or it might be that the poet's meaning is made plain through a dominant image or metaphor. You might then plan to develop the idea part by part, and show how the metaphor develops it, or you might want to stress the metaphor itself as it grows and develops as support for the poem's idea, as in the sample essay.

In general, your organization will depend on your observations about the poem. As you organize and develop your paragraphs, keep in mind the following structural patterns. They will be useful for almost all the poems you encounter:

1. The poem may convey meaning through *direct statement*. In such a case you might organize your essay to reflect the line-by-line or sentence-by-sentence structure of the poem itself.
2. You might find that the *logic* of the speaker's argument most effectively creates meaning. To follow such a pattern of logic, for example, would be useful in an essay about the meaning of Andrew Marvell's "To His Coy Mistress."
3. The poet's use of a *single element*, such as a metaphor or simile, or a set of consistent references (such as explorers, bankers, darkness, rain), might bring out the poem's meaning. Your organization might reflect the ways the element works and develops in the poem.
4. Finally, it might be that a number of *different poetic elements* (such as rhythm, rhyme, metaphor, level of language, imagery, and so on) work together to shape theme and impact. The structure of an essay dealing with such elements can be based on a sequential discussion of each element as it contributes to meaning.

In short, each poem offers unique methods and modes of rendering experience that can be used in the controlling and shaping of your essay. The four structural patterns just noted can be modified and combined. To accommodate the specific poem you are considering, you should always be prepared to adjust whatever plan you choose.

In your conclusion, you have the opportunity to pull all the strands of the essay together and to reaffirm the connection between the poem's method and meaning. This is most conveniently done through a summary of your major points. The conclusion is also the place where you can consider additional aspects of the poem's theme and impact. The ideas and experiences you develop when you read a poem often suggest additional ideas. Similarly, you might want to consider the extent to which your own circumstances (such as age, sex, race, or religion) help determine the meaning and impact that the poem has for you.

SAMPLE ESSAY

Metaphor and Meaning in Philip Larkin's "Next, Please"°

[1] Philip Larkin's "Next, Please" exposes the futility of those who hope for a better future while ignoring the things they have in the present. The idea is borne out in the poem's assertions that the fulfillment of our expectations is slow and rare but that disappointment and death are certain.* This theme is conveyed through the single extended metaphor of an "armada of promises" that begins in the second stanza and runs throughout the rest of the poem; within the metaphor, diction and meter reinforce the meaning of the poem and the moment of human experience that it creates.†

[2] The poem announces its subject and begins to develop its theme through the title and the direct statements of the first stanza. The title refers to the human desire to move on and to look ahead. It suggests that we are never satisfied with what we have, but always expect happiness just around the corner. These implications are brought into focus in the first stanza, where the speaker notes that we are "Always too eager for the future" and that "we / Pick up bad habits of expectancy" (lines 1-2). Our habitual focus on the promise of the future is captured in the speaker's observation that "every day / *Till then* we say" (lines 3-4). By using the pronouns *we* (and *us*) here and throughout, the speaker states that human beings habitually indulge in wishful thinking.

[3] To this point, the speaker has isolated a specific human characteristic --our belief that better things will happen. Beginning in the second stanza, however, the poem asserts that these "bad habits of expectancy" leave us disappointed. The poem makes this point through an extended metaphor that is based on a hidden cliché: "someday my ship will come in." The cliché expresses the belief that we will get everything we want or deserve "someday" in the future. Larkin's metaphor, however, shows us that the cliché is wrong; the metaphor draws out the cliché into a dramatic experience to suggest that our hopes for the future inevitably lead to failure and death.

The extended metaphor creates meaning by placing us in a dramatic situation that we can experience. We are "Watching from a bluff" as the "tiny, clear, / Sparkling armada of promises draws near" (lines 5-6). Our ship has

° See p. 834 for this poem.
* Central idea.
† Thesis sentence.

[4]
become an entire fleet. Even at this early point, however, the diction begins to undercut the cliché and our habit of expectation. We are watching from a *bluff* rather than a cliff; a *bluff* is a hill, but it is also an attempt to mislead or deceive through false confidence. The word thus suggests that our hopes for the future stand on self-deception and false confidence. *Armada* is similarly loaded. For British and American readers, the term evokes the memory of the Spanish Armada that sailed against England in 1588 and was destroyed by sea battles and storms. Overtones of failure and destruction are thus built into the metaphor.

[5]
The metaphor makes the poem's meaning vivid and immediate through a wealth of detail. We notice that the "armada of promises" moves very slowly: "How slow they are! And how much time they waste, / Refusing to make haste" (lines 7-8). As the metaphor is extended, more and more details are brought to our attention; we read progressively more of each ship as the speaker mentions the shining "brasswork," "Each rope distinct," the flag, and "the figurehead with golden tits / Arching our way" (lines 11-14). Through such details, the metaphor suggests that the fleet draws ever closer. Even as it approaches, however, the failure of such promise is also established: "Yet still they leave us holding wretched stalks / Of disappointment" (lines 9-10). This image--within the metaphor--leaves us standing on the "bluff" holding wilted flowers and hopes.

[6]
This disappointment is brought into explicit focus as the "armada" metaphor continues in the fourth stanza. We see that the fleet "never anchors"; "it's / No sooner present than it turns to past" (lines 14-15). Most of these words carry double meanings. *It*, for example, refers to both the ships and time. *Turns to* indicates both a change of course and the inevitable transformation of the present into the past. Similarly, *present* and *past* signify both the physical status of the ships and the movement of time. The metaphor thus conveys the experience of disappointment both in terms of the "armada of promises" and the time we waste waiting for future reward.

[7]
The last two stanzas of "Next, Please" conclude the armada metaphor and expand on the theme of inevitable disappointment. The fifth stanza summarizes the development of the metaphor, and thus the entire poem; the speaker observes that we always expect one of these ships to "heave to" and to deliver "All good into our lives" (line 18). The last line of the stanza, however, completely undercuts all hope. Here, we sense the impact of a metrical technique that Larkin has employed throughout. The poem is mostly in iambic pentameter, but the fourth line of each stanza is cut short to two or three feet. This metrical falling-off parallels the feeling of disappointment. Like the "armada" and the future, each stanza fails to deliver what we expect. The force of this device strikes us at the close of the fifth stanza, where the final two-beat line bleakly tells us, "But we are wrong" (line 20). The metaphor and the falling meter make it clear that our ship will never "heave to" and deliver. There is, however, "one ship" that "is seeking us" (line 21). It is not a ship full of good things; instead, it is a "black- / Sailed unfamiliar" ship "towing at her back / A huge and birdless silence" (lines 22-23). This is the only ship that will come in for us if we passively await the future--the ship of death.

"Next, Please" thus tells us that a life spent in passive expectation and

[8]
hope for the future will offer only disappointment and death. The poem lets us experience this meaning through an extended metaphor, in which an "armada of promises" approaches and then leaves without yielding anything but disappointment. The meaning of the poem becomes our movement through the metaphor, and our experience of the metaphor is disappointment and a vision of death. At the same time, the poem implies that we should live in and for the present, making the most of what we have. To this extent, "Next, Please" may be considered a carpe diem poem; it suggests that we should "seize" today, which is real, rather than hope for tomorrow, which is unreal.

Commentary on the Essay

The essay illustrates the need to combine and adjust abstract strategies of organization in dealing with a specific poem. It combines a focus on a specific poetic element (metaphor) with secondary interest in two other elements (diction and meter). The essay thus represents a modification and combination of the third and fourth organizational plans noted earlier (p. 839). Basically, however, it traces the development of theme and meaning through the progressive stages of a dominant and central metaphor.

The introduction briefly explains how the poem establishes its subject. It also indicates that in the body the essay will deal with the way metaphor, diction, and meter combine to create meaning.

Paragraph 2 deals primarily with the subject of the poem; it grows directly out of the first two sentences of the introduction. This discussion is essential because it provides the foundation for the essay's subsequent treatment of theme and meaning.

Paragraphs 3 through 7 grow out of the last two sentences of the introduction; they treat the connection between metaphor and meaning, and they take up the secondary subjects of diction and meter. Paragraph 3 provides transition from subject to theme, introduces the dominant metaphor, and explains the hidden cliché on which the metaphor is based. Paragraph 4 examines the way that the "armada" metaphor begins to create a palpable experience and how diction immediately begins to undercut the promise of the future. The first sentence of this paragraph links it both to the introduction and to the previous paragraph through its reference to metaphor and meaning.

Paragraph 5 sustains the focus on the link between metaphor and meaning through attention to the details that the speaker mentions in the second, third, and fourth stanzas of the poem. Again, the first sentence connects this paragraph to both the introduction and the previous paragraph. Similarly, the concluding sentence leads into paragraph 6, which takes up the next stage of the extended metaphor and the articulation of disappointment. This focus on the end of the metaphor and on the experience of disappointment is continued in paragraph 7, which explores the impact of the poem's meter on the poet's assertion that waiting produces only death.

The concluding paragraph briefly considers the implications of the poem's meaning, offers a second and implied theme for the poem, and connects "Next, Please" to the long-standing carpe diem poetic tradition. The value of this paragraph as an example is that it is more than a summary, leaving the reader with new thoughts to ponder after completing the essay.

WRITING TOPICS

1. Compare two or all of the following poems: Jonson's "To Celia," Herrick's "To the Virgins, to Make Much of Time" (and also "Corinna's Going A-Maying," in Chapter 24), and Marvell's "To His Coy Mistress" as carpe diem poems. How well does each poem express the central idea of the carpe diem tradition? How are the tone and ideas of the poems similar, and how are they different? To what degree is it accurate to say that these poems are not about seduction but rather about life and values?

2. On the basis of ideas about age, change, and the loss of time and life, compare Pastan's "Ethics," Olds's "35/10," Wordsworth's "Daffodils," and Justice's "On the Death of Friends in Childhood." How do the ideas of the poems merge, even though they are about different subjects? Which of the poems do you prefer? Why?

3. Keats's line "Beauty is truth, truth beauty" from his "Ode on a Grecian Urn" has generated considerable discussion. What do you think it means? How does the material in the poem support Keats's idea? Would the idea be tenable if it had come early in the poem rather than late? Why?

4. Write your own poem in which you stress a particular idea. You might write about a friend or acquaintance who has endured an illness, performed an important service, admitted a mistake or failure, or succeeded in a task. Other possible topics are a social, religious, or political issue or some aspect of education, work, or community life. When you finish, explain how you go about making the situation clear to your reader, and how you use the situation to bring out your ideas. Do not neglect the title as one of the means of expressing ideas.

23

Poetic Careers: The Work of Three Poets

We have looked at poetry in terms of its elements and effects. Let us now consider a collection of poems by three individual poets: John Donne (1572–1631), Emily Dickinson (1830–1886), and Robert Frost (1874–1963). Donne, one of the most important English poets of the seventeenth century, developed what we call the *metaphysical* or philosophical style. Emily Dickinson and Robert Frost are both American poets and New Englanders; Dickinson is one of the prominent poetic voices of nineteenth-century American poetry, and Frost is recognized as one of the poetic giants of twentieth-century America. While the poems included here cannot present full pictures of poetic careers, they do provide an opportunity to read and consider a body of works by individual poets. We have chosen poems that illustrate the central concerns and major characteristics of each poet's work. Thus, the material provides an opportunity to look for common themes and techniques or for sudden shifts of concern within a poet's career.

JOHN DONNE (1572–1631)

Traditionally, scholars have argued that John Donne had two poetic careers, one as a love poet and satirist in his youth and another as a religious poet after he became an Anglican priest in 1615. Such a clear division cannot be maintained, however, since Donne wrote a great deal of religious verse before 1615 and very little poetry at all after that year. Donne's poetry does fall into two broad categories—love poetry and religious verse—but his style remains constant.

Donne was born to a Roman Catholic family in a newly Protestant land; religion thus had a significant impact on his life even before he took holy orders. Although he attended both Oxford and Cambridge universities between 1584 and 1590, his Catholicism barred him from receiving degrees. In 1591 Donne moved to London and enrolled at the law school at Lincoln's Inn, where he studied science, philosophy, law, languages, and literature. All these subjects (and more) were worked into his poetry. During these years Donne had a reputation as a wit and a ladies' man; he wrote many love poems and satires, and circulated them among his friends (very little of his poetry was published until 1633).

In 1593 Donne converted to Anglicanism (the official state religion in England) and began to rise in aristocratic circles. He became private secretary to Sir Thomas Egerton (an important court official) in 1598, and was on the verge of a brilliant career when he eloped (in 1601) with Egerton's sixteen-year-old niece, Anne More. This destroyed his chances for advancement; the girl's father had Donne dismissed from court, had him jailed, and barred his further employment. Donne spent the next fourteen years writing poetry, eking out a meager living at various jobs, and desperately seeking royal employment. King James I (reigned 1603–1625) was sympathetic, but he refused to help Donne, believing that Donne's proper place was as a priest in the Anglican Church.

Donne finally gave in to this inevitability; in 1615 he took holy orders and began a meteoric rise in the church. In 1621 he was appointed dean of St. Paul's Cathedral in London, the most fashionable church in seventeenth-century England. He became a famous preacher—over 130 of his sermons were published—and the noble and wealthy flocked to his services. Donne remained a powerful speaker and poet up to his death in May 1631; he previewed his own funeral sermon before the king on February 25, 1631, and supposedly wrote his last poem eight days before his death.

Donne's poetry is commonly termed *metaphysical*, a word used to describe poetry that is highly intellectual and characterized by complexity, subtlety and elaborate imagery. The label was made by the poet-critic John Dryden (1631–1700), who asserted in *A Discourse Concerning the Origin and Progress of Satire* (1693) that Donne's love poetry "affects the metaphysics" and "perplexes the minds of the fair sex with nice [i.e., careful] speculations of philosophy." Although Dryden originally used the word to disparage Donne's work, it has come to signify both the style of his verse and a "school" of poetry.

Poetic Characteristics. In *poetic style*, Donne's poetry represents a radical departure from earlier Elizabethan verse. He rebelled against the smooth rhythms, flowery language, and conventional imagery of the sixteenth century. His poems are characterized by abrupt beginnings, dramatic shifts in tone, irregular rhythms, puns, paradoxes, and rigorous logic. Their major characteristic, however, is the *metaphysical conceit*. A **conceit** is an elaborate metaphor, and a **metaphysical conceit** is an extended comparison that links two unrelated fields or subjects in a surprising and revealing conjunction of ideas. Above all else, Donne's poems illustrate *wit*, the ability to advance a complex or even outrageous argument through subtle logic, unusual analogy, and diverse allusion.

In terms of *diction and language*, Donne's verse is equally unconventional. The poems include a great deal of harsh language and numerous terms borrowed from various fields of learning, including alchemy, law, theology, philosophy, and geography. The characteristic *poetic forms* for both the love poetry and the religious verse include the lyric and the sonnet. The stanzaic structure of Donne's lyrics is quite inventive, with varying line lengths and complex rhyme schemes.

POETIC SUBJECTS.   Donne's love poetry, written mostly between 1590 and 1615, established the metaphysical style. These poems are ingenious, and overflow with images and allusions. Taken as a group, they suggest that passion is both wonderful and dangerous and that love is a mystery much like religion. They also imply that lovers can and should be self-sufficient and separate from the public world.

The religious verse maintains the characteristics of the love poetry but shifts the ground from human passion to divine love. In the Holy Sonnets, for instance, Donne uses a traditional poetic form normally associated with love poetry to consider human sin and divine grace. In these poems Donne often employs the techniques of religious meditation, focusing at first on a specific time or event and then considering the meaning of that event in connection with his own spiritual state. In "At the Round Earth's Imagined Corners," for example, Donne begins with a vivid meditation on the moment of the Last Judgment. The Hymns, like the Holy Sonnets, maintain the metaphysical style and deal with spiritual matters. The "Hymn to God the Father," for instance, plays repeatedly with a pun on Donne's name. Similarly, the "Hymn to God My God, In My Sickness," (not included here) supposedly written eight days before Donne died in May 1631, is full of puns, paradoxes, convoluted logic, and metaphysical conceits.

BIBLIOGRAPHIC SOURCES.   Donne's poetry received little attention during his lifetime. Although an awareness of Donne's work was growing in the late 1800s, two events in the twentieth century dramatically rekindled interest in his poetry. One was the publication of Sir Herbert Grierson's complete edition of *The Poems of John Donne* (1912) and the other was T. S. Eliot's spirited defense of Donne and metaphysical poetry (see, for example, Eliot's essay, "The Metaphysical Poets," published in 1921 and reprinted in 1960 in his *Selected Essays*). Although Donne's verse may have seemed unpoetic and overly complex to earlier generations, it appeals with great strength to the sensibilities of the contemporary world. More recent editions of Donne's work include Helen Gardner's edition of *The

Divine Poems (1952) and of *The Elegies and the Songs and Sonnets* (1965). Significant critical discussions of Donne's work may be found in Cleanth Brooks, *The Well-Wrought Urn* (1932), Helen White, *The Metaphysical Poets* (1936), J. B. Leishman, *The Monarch of Wit* (1951), Louis L. Martz, *The Poetry of Meditation* (1954), Richard E. Hughes, *The Progress of the Soul* (1968), John Carey, *John Donne: Life, Mind, and Art* (1981), and George Parfitt, *John Donne: A Literary Life* (1989). Refer to the index for additional poems by Donne.

The Good Morrow   *1633*

I wonder, by my troth, what thou and I
Did, till we loved! Were we not weaned till then,
But sucked on country pleasures, childishly?
Or snorted we in the seven sleepers' den?°
T'was so; But this, all pleasures fancies be.   5
If ever any beauty I did see,
Which I desired, and got, t'was but a dream of thee.

And now good morrow to our waking souls,
Which watch not one another out of fear;
For love all love of other sights controls,   10
And makes one little room an everywhere.
Let sea-discoverers to new worlds have gone,
Let maps to other,° worlds on worlds have shown,
Let us possess one world; each hath one, and is one.

My face in thine eye, thine in mine appears,°   15
And true plain hearts do in the faces rest;
Where can we find two better hemispheres
Without sharp North, without declining West?
Whatever dies was not mixed equally;°
If our two loves be one, or thou and I   20
Love so alike that none do slacken, none can die.

THE GOOD MORROW.   4 *seven sleepers' den:* a reference to the miracle of the seven Christian youths who took shelter in a cave to avoid religious persecution by the Emperor Decius (ca. A.D. 250) and were sealed inside. The young men supposedly slept for about 185 years and emerged in perfect health during the reign of Theodosius II (ca. A.D. 435). 13 *other:* others, that is, other discoverers.   15 *My face . . . appears:* Each face is reflected in the pupils of the other lover's eyes.   19 *Whatever . . . equally:* Scholastic philosophy argues that elements which are either perfectly balanced or united will never change or decay; hence, such a mixture cannot die.

Song   *1633*

Go and catch a falling star,
  Get with child a mandrake root,°
Tell me where all past years are,
  Or who cleft the Devil's foot,
Teach me to hear mermaids singing,   5
  Or to keep off envy's stinging,
      And find
      What wind
Serves to advance an honest mind.

If thou beest born to strange sights,   10
  Things invisible to see,
Ride ten thousand days and nights,
  Till age snow white hairs on thee,
Thou, when thou return'st, wilt tell me
All strange wonders that befell thee,   15
      And swear
      Nowhere
Lives a woman true, and fair.

If thou findst one, let me know,
  Such a pilgrimage were sweet;   20
Yet do not, I would not go,
  Though at next door we might meet;
Though she were true when you met her,
And last till you write your letter,
      Yet she   25
      Will be
False, ere I come, to two, or three.

SONG.   2 *mandrake root:* The mandrake, or mandragora, is a European narcotic herb
once considered an aphrodisiac. The fleshy, forked root was thought to resemble the
human form.

The Sun Rising   *1633*

    Busy old fool, unruly sun,
    Why dost thou thus,
Through windows and through curtains call on us?
Must to thy motions lovers' seasons run?
    Saucy pedantic wretch, go chide   5
    Late school boys and sour prentices,°   *apprentices*
To tell court huntsmen that the King will ride,
Call country ants to harvest offices;°   *duties*
Love, all alike, no season knows nor clime,
Nor hours, days, months, which are the rags of time.   10

    Thy beams, so reverend and strong
    Why shouldst thou think?
I could eclipse and cloud them with a wink,
But that I would not lose her sight so long;

If her eyes have not blinded thine,   15
   Look, and tomorrow late, tell me,
  Whether both the Indias of spice and mine°
  Be where thou leftst them, or lie here with me.
Ask for those kings whom thou saw'st yesterday,
And thou shalt hear, All here in one bed lay.   20

   She is all states, and all princes, I,
    Nothing else is.
Princes do but play us; compared to this,
All honor's mimic, all wealth alchemy.°   *counterfeit*
   Thou, sun, art half as happy as we,   25
    In that the world's contracted thus;
  Thine age asks ease, and since thy duties be
  To warm the world, that's done in warming us.
Shine here to us, and thou art everywhere;
This bed thy center° is, these walls, thy sphere.   30

THE SUN RISING.   17 *Indias of spice and mine:* the India of "spice" is East India or the
East Indies; the India of "mine" or gold is the West Indies.   30 *center:* the central point
of the sun's orbit.

The Canonization   *1633*

For God's sake hold your tongue,° and let me love,
   Or chide my palsy, or my gout,
My five gray hairs, or ruined fortune, flout,
  With wealth your state, your mind with arts improve,
   Take you a course,° get you a place,°   5
   Observe His Honor, or His Grace,
Or the King's real, or his stamped face°
   Contemplate,—what you will, approve,°   *test, try*
   So you will let me love.

Alas, alas, who's injured by my love?   10
   What merchant's ships have my sighs drowned?
Who says my tears have overflowed his ground?
   When did my colds a forward spring remove?
    When did the heats which my veins fill
    Add one more to the plaguy bill?°   15
Soldiers find wars, and lawyers find out still
   Litigious men, which quarrels move,
   Though she and I do love.

Call us what you will, we are made such by love;
   Call her one, me another fly,   20

THE CANONIZATION.   1 *your tongue:* "Your" refers to either the public world in
general or a specific but unheard critic who attacks the speaker's love.   5 *course:* a course
of action.   *place:* office or position, probably at court.   7 *stamped face:* the king's
portrait on coins.   15 *plaguy bill:* a weekly list of people who have died from the plague.

We're tapers too, and at our own cost die,°
   And we in us find the eagle and the dove.°
      The phoenix riddle° hath more wit
      By us,—we two being one, are it.
So, to one neutral thing both sexes fit.   25
   We die and rise the same, and prove
   Mysterious by this love.

We can die by it, if not live by love,
   And if unfit for tombs and hearse
Our legend be, it will be fit for verse;   30
   And if no piece of chronicle we prove,
      We'll build in sonnets pretty rooms;
      As well a well-wrought urn becomes°   *befits, suits*
The greatest ashes, as half-acre tombs,
   And by these hymns, all shall approve°   35
   Us canonized for love:

And thus invoke us: "You whom reverend love
   Made one another's hermitage;
You, to whom love was peace, that now is rage;
   Who did the whole world's soul contract, and drove   40
      Into the glasses of your eyes
      (So made such mirrors, and such spies,
That they did all to you epitomize)
   Countries, towns, courts: Beg from above
   A pattern of your love!"°   45

20–21 *fly . . . die:* Both flies and candles are symbols of the brevity of life. Since the word *die* was a common euphemism in the seventeenth century for sexual orgasm, the line suggests that each sex act shortens the lovers' lives.   22 *eagle and the dove:* proverbial symbols of male strength and female mildness.   23 *phoenix riddle:* the riddle of the phoenix's perpetuation; the phoenix is a mythological Arabian bird—only one exists at a time—that lives for a thousand years and then burns itself to ashes on a funeral pyre. A new phoenix then miraculously rises from the ashes of the old. The phoenix thus symbolizes immortality, death, and resurrection, and the rekindling of sexual desire. 35 *hymns . . . approve:* The hymns refer to the speaker's poetry and this poem in particular. The idea is that succeeding generations will confirm ("approve") the sainthood of the lovers in a new religion of love because of this poem.   37–45 *"You . . . love":* These lines are spoken by lovers in succeeding generations who are praying to the lover-saints that the speaker and his beloved have become. Hence, *You* (line 37) refers to the speaker and his mistress.

A Fever   *1633*

Oh do not die, for I shall hate
   All women so, when thou art gone,
That thee I shall not celebrate,°   *mourn*
   When I remember, thou wast one.

But yet thou canst not die, I know;   5
    To leave this world behind, is death;
But when thou from this world wilt go,
    The whole world vapours° with thy breath.   *evaporates*

Or if, when thou, the world's soul, goest,
    It stay, 'tis but thy carcase then;   10
The fairest woman, but thy ghost,
    But corrupt worms, the worthiest men.

O wrangling schools,° that search what fire
    Shall burn this world, had none the wit
Unto this knowledge to aspire,   15
    That this her fever might be it?

And yet she cannot waste by this,
    Nor long bear this torturing wrong,
For much corruption needful is,
    To fuel such a fever long.°   *for long*   20

These burning fits but meteors be,
    Whose matter in thee is soon spent:
Thy beauty, and all parts which are thee,
    Are unchangeable firmament.°

Yet 'twas of my mind, seizing thee,   25
    Though it in thee cannot persever:°   *persist*
For I had rather owner be
    Of thee one hour, than all else ever.

A FEVER.   13 *wrangling schools:* competing sects of pagan and Christian philosophy that debated what sort of fire would ultimately destroy the world.   24 *firmament:* the vault of heaven and the stars.

The Flea   *1633*

Mark° but this flea, and mark in this,   *note, look at*
How little that which thou deniest me is;
It sucked me first, and now sucks thee,
And in this flea our two bloods mingled be;
Thou know'st that this cannot be said°   *called*   5
A sin, nor shame, nor loss of maidenhead,
    Yet this enjoys before it woo,°   *marry*
    And pampered swells with one blood made of two,°
    And this, alas, is more than we would do.

Oh stay, three lives in one flea spare,   10
Where we almost, yea more than married, are.

THE FLEA.   8 *two:* The flea has bitten both the speaker and the lady and thus mingles their blood; the image also suggests pregnancy.

This flea is you and I, and this
Our marriage bed and marriage temple is;
Though parents grudge, and you,° w'are met,
And cloister'd in these living walls of jet,   15
   Though use° make you apt to kill me   *custom*
   Let not to that, self-murder added be,
   And sacrilege, three sins in killing three.

Cruel and sudden, hast thou since
Purpled thy nail, in blood of innocence?°   20
Wherein could this flea guilty be,
Except in that drop which it sucked from thee?
Yet thou triumph'st, and say'st that thou
Find'st not thy self nor me the weaker now;
   'Tis true, then learn how false fears be;   25
   Just so much honor, when thou yield'st to me,
   Will waste, as this flea's death took life from thee.

14 *you:* You [the lady] also "grudge" or resent the idea of premarital sex.   20 *innocence:*
a possible allusion to Herod's slaughter of the innocents (Matthew 2:16).

Holy Sonnet 6: This Is My Play's Last Scene   *1633*

This is my play's last scene; here heavens appoint
My pilgrimage's last mile; and my race
Idly, yet quickly run, hath this last pace,
My span's last inch, my minute's last point,
And gluttonous Death will instantly unjoint   5
My body, and soul, and I shall sleep a space,
But my ever-waking part° shall see that face,   *the soul*
Whose fear already shakes my every joint.
Then, as my soul, t'heaven her first seat, takes flight,
And earth-borne body, in the earth shall dwell,   10
So, fall my sins, that all may have their right,
To where they are bred, and would press me, to hell.
Impute me righteous, thus purged of evil,
For thus I leave the world, the flesh, and devil.

Holy Sonnet 7: At the Round Earth's Imagined Corners   *1633*

At the round earth's imagined corners, blow
Your trumpets, angels,° and arise, arise

AT THE ROUND EARTH'S IMAGINED CORNERS.   1–2 *At . . . angels:* The lines
combine the image of the angels or winds drawn at the four corners of old maps with an
allusion to the four angels mentioned in Revelations 7:1.

From death, you numberless infinities
Of souls, and to your scattered bodies go,
All whom the flood did, and fire shall o'erthrow,   5
All whom war, dearth, age, agues, tyrannies,
Despair, law, chance, hath slain, and you whose eyes
Shall behold God, and never taste death's woe.°
But let them sleep, Lord, and me mourn a space,
For, if above all these, my sins abound,   10
'Tis late to ask abundance of Thy grace,
When we are there. Here on this lowly ground,
Teach me how to repent; for that's as good
As if Thou hadst sealed my pardon with Thy blood.

7–8 *you whose eyes . . . woe:* a reference to those people who are still living on the day of the Last Judgment and thus move directly from life to judgment without experiencing death.

Holy Sonnet 10: Death Be Not Proud   *1633*

Death, be not proud, though some have callèd thee
Mighty and dreadful, for thou art not so;
For those whom thou think'st thou dost overthrow
Die not, poor Death, nor yet canst thou kill me.
From rest and sleep, which but thy pictures° be,   *imitations*   5
Much pleasure; then from thee much more must flow,
And soonest our best men with thee do go,
Rest of their bones, and soul's delivery.
Thou art slave to fate, chance, kings, and desperate men,
And dost with poison, war, and sickness dwell,   10
And poppy° or charms can make us sleep as well   *opium*
And better than thy stroke; why swell'st° thou then?   *puff up with pride*
One short sleep past, we wake eternally°   *on Judgment Day*
And death shall be no more; Death, thou shalt die.

A Hymn to God the Father   *1633 (1623?)*

Wilt Thou forgive that sin where I begun,
    Which is my sin, though it were done before?
Wilt Thou forgive those sins through which I run,
    And do them still, though still I do deplore?
        When Thou hast done, Thou hast not done,   5
            For I have more.

Wilt Thou forgive that sin by which I won
    Others to sin and made my sin their door?

Wilt Thou forgive that sin which I did shun
  A year or two, but wallowed in a score?   10
    When Thou hast done, Thou hast not done,
      For I have more.

I have a sin of fear, that when I have spun
  My last thread, I shall perish on the shore;
Swear by Thy Self, that at my death Thy sun   15
  Shall shine as it shines now and heretofore;
    And, having done that, Thou hast done,
      I have no more.

EMILY DICKINSON (1830–1886)

Emily Dickinson lived in the small, religious, and tradition-bound community of Amherst, Massachusetts. Her life was shaped by a combination of public submission and poetic rebellion against authority. Although she spent three years at school—two at Amherst Academy and one at South Hadley Seminary for Women (now Mount Holyoke College)—she was largely self-taught and her life was restricted to Amherst and her family home. After 1862 she became progressively more reclusive.

Although Dickinson never married or had a love affair that we know about, much of her poetry is concerned with love and the psychology of human relationships. This choice of subject may have resulted from her relationships with three men around whom she built an emotional life in her poetry. The first was Benjamin Newton, a young law student whom she met in 1848 and who began to direct her reading. This guidance was cut short when Newton married and moved away; he died of tuberculosis in 1856. Scholars have assumed that Newton is one of the two persons referred to in Dickinson's "I Never Lost as Much But Twice," written about 1858.

The second man in Dickinson's life was the Reverend Charles Wadsworth, a minister whom she met in 1855. Because Wadsworth was married, a romantic involvement never occurred. But her poetry was most prolific during this period, and focuses directly on love, marriage, and relationships. "I Cannot Live with You" (ca. 1862), for example, seems to deal with Dickinson's internalized relationship with Wadsworth. The relationship ended in 1862, when Wadsworth accepted a ministry in San Francisco.

After Wadsworth left, Dickinson became even more reclusive. In 1862 she began to correspond with Thomas Wentworth Higginson, a literary critic who had written an article encouraging young writers. Dickinson wrote to him, enclosing some of her poetry and asking if her verses were "alive" and ready for publication. She may have viewed

Higginson initially as another mentor, but she soon discovered that his literary judgments were conventional and traditional. Ironically, Higginson became one of the first editors of her work after her death in 1886.

We can never know the exact connection between the events in Dickinson's life and the poems she wrote. She began writing poetry in her early twenties; her earliest efforts were occasional poems and valentines. She did not begin writing in earnest until around 1858, and between 1858 and 1861 she wrote about 300 poems. At this point she seems to have experienced a burst of creative energy; she wrote 366 poems in 1862, 141 in 1863, 174 in 1864, and about 80 in 1865. After 1865 she wrote about 20 poems a year until her death. In all there are 1,775 poems from her pen. Since she produced about one-third of her total poetic work in the three years between 1862 and 1864, we can only surmise that this prodigious output was connected in some way with the loss of Reverend Wadsworth. It was, no doubt, also connected with her growth as a poet and her increasing skepticism about the values of her family and community.

POETIC CHARACTERISTICS. Dickinson's *poetic style* might best be described as metaphysical. Her poetry is simple and passionate and at the same time economical and concentrated. We see in her verse, as in Donne's, an elliptical style that produces both concentration of language and the rapid movement of thoughts and images. In terms of *language and diction*, Dickinson's verse is full of grammatical irregularities and eccentricities of punctuation. The most obvious is her frequent abandonment of conventional punctuation in favor of the dash. She even developed a special length of dash that helps to control the rhythm and pauses in her poetry.

The *poetic forms* that Dickinson frequently used are common measure and ballad stanza (see p. 727). She may have gained her interest in these forms from the Protestant hymnal, the major poetic text of her youth. Within these quatrain forms, Dickinson achieves remarkable flexibility and variation through the skillful use of metrical substitution and slant rhyme. Although these irregularities annoyed Dickinson's first editors, they have since been recognized as important and effective elements of her poetry.

POETIC SUBJECTS. For *poetic subjects*, Dickinson turned to her immediate world of village and garden, and to her inner life of emotion and skepticism. The characteristic subjects of her poetry include love, nature, faith, death, and immortality. Beyond these, however, her poems also chart her inner growth, the world that she created for herself in her own mind, and a broad range of psychological insights. Her ideas are witty, unconventional, and rebellious.

Of Dickinson's 1,775 poems, only seven were published during her lifetime, anonymously and in obscure periodicals. She may have rejected further publication because of editors' tendencies to "adjust" her verse or because of Higginson's discouraging advice. In any event, she stopped publishing early on and wrote for herself. After her death, her sister Lavinia was amazed to find boxes of small, handwritten and bound pamphlets of verse that contained about twenty poems each. Lavinia recognized the significance of her sister's work and eventually turned some of the poems over to Mabel L. Todd and Higginson for editing and publication. They produced three volumes of Dickinson's work (published in 1890, 1891, and 1896), each containing about 100 poems. In these editions, the editors eliminated slant rhymes, smoothed out the meter, revised those metaphors that struck them as outrageous, and regularized the punctuation.

BIBLIOGRAPHIC SOURCES.   The well-intended but destructive adjustments to Dickinson's poetry remained intact until 1955, when the Harvard University Press published Thomas H. Johnson's three-volume edition of her poems. Johnson went back to the manuscripts to establish the original text of each poem (with variants), and his edition is definitive. Important critical and biographical studies include Charles R. Anderson, *Emily Dickinson's Poetry* (1960), Ruth Miller, *The Poetry of Emily Dickinson* (1968), Richard B. Sewall, *The Life of Emily Dickinson* (1974), Joanne F. Diehl, *Dickinson and the Romantic Imagination* (1981), Antonina C. Mossberg, *Emily Dickinson: When a Writer Is a Daughter* (1982), Susan Juhasz, *The Undiscovered Continent: Emily Dickinson and the Space of the Mind* (1983), E. Miller Budick, *Emily Dickinson and the Life of Language: A Study in Symbolic Poetics* (1985), Sharon Leder and Andrea Abbott, *The Language of Exclusion* (1987), Joanne Dobson, *Dickinson and the Strategies of Reticence* (1989), and Gary L. Stonum, *The Dickinson Sublime* (1990). One of the hour-long programs in the PBS "Voices and Visions" series (1987) features her work. Refer to the index for additional poems by Dickinson.

I Never Lost as Much But Twice   *1890 (ca. 1858)*

I never lost as much but twice,
And that was in the sod.
Twice have I stood a beggar
Before the door of God!

Angels—twice descending   5
Reimbursed my store—
Burglar! Banker—Father!
I am poor once more!

Success Is Counted Sweetest

1878, 1890 (ca. 1859)

Success is counted sweetest
By those who ne'er succeed.
To comprehend a nectar
Requires sorest need.

Not one of all the purple Host   5
Who took the Flag today
Can tell the definition
So clear of Victory

As he defeated–dying–
On whose forbidden ear   10
The distant strains of triumph
Burst agonized and clear!

"Faith" Is a Fine Invention

1891 (ca. 1860)

"Faith" is a fine invention
When Gentlemen can *see*–
But *Microscopes* are prudent
In an Emergency.

I Taste a Liquor Never Brewed

1861, 1891 (ca. 1860)

I taste a liquor never brewed–
From Tankards scooped in Pearl–
Not all the Frankfort Berries°   *grapes*
Yield such an Alcohol!

Inebriate of Air–am I–   5
And Debauchee of Dew–
Reeling–thro endless summer days–
From inns of Molten Blue–

When "Landlords" turn the drunken Bee
Out of the Foxglove's door–   10
When Butterflies–renounce their "drams"–
I shall but drink the more!

Till Seraphs swing their snowy Hats–
And Saints–to windows run–
To see the little Tippler   15
From Manzanilla° come!

I TASTE A LIQUOR NEVER BREWED   16 *Manzanilla:* a pale sherry from Spain.
Dickinson may also have been thinking of Manzanillo, a Cuban city often associated with
rum.

Safe in Their Alabaster Chambers   *1862, 1890 (1861)*

Safe in their Alabaster Chambers–
Untouched by Morning–
And untouched by Noon–
Lie the meek members of the Resurrection–
Rafter of Satin–and Roof of Stone!   5

Grand go the Years–in the Crescent–above them–
Worlds scoop their Arcs–
And Firmaments–row–
Diadems–drop–and Doges°–surrender–
Soundless as dots–on a Disc of Snow–   10

SAFE IN THEIR ALABASTER CHAMBERS.   9 *Doges:* Renaissance rulers of the
Italian city-states of Venice and Genoa.

Wild Nights–Wild Nights!   *1890 (ca. 1861)*

Wild Nights–Wild Nights!
Were I with thee
Wild Nights should be
Our luxury!

Futile–the Winds–   5
To a Heart in port–
Done with the Compass–
Done with the Chart!

Rowing in Eden–
Ah, the Sea!   10
Might I but moor–Tonight–
In Thee!

There's a Certain Slant of Light   *1890 (ca. 1861)*

There's a certain Slant of light,
Winter Afternoons–
That oppresses, like the Heft
Of Cathedral Tunes–

Heavenly Hurt, it gives us–   5
We can find no scar,
But internal difference,
Where the Meanings, are–

None may teach it–Any–
'Tis the Seal Despair–
An imperial affliction
Sent us of the Air–

10

When it comes, the Landscape listens–
Shadows–hold their breath–
When it goes, 'tis like the Distance
On the look of Death–

15

The Soul Selects Her Own Society

1890 (ca. 1862)

The Soul selects her own Society–
Then–shuts the Door–
To her divine Majority–
Present no more–

Unmoved–she notes the Chariots–pausing–
At her low Gate–
Unmoved–an Emperor be kneeling
Upon her Mat–

5

I've known her–from an ample nation–
Choose One–
Then–close the Valves of her attention–
Like Stone–

10

Some Keep the Sabbath Going to Church

1864 (ca. 1862)

Some keep the Sabbath going to Church–
I keep it, staying at Home–
With a Bobolink for a Chorister–
And an Orchard, for a Dome–

Some keep the Sabbath in Surplice–
I just wear my Wings–
And instead of tolling the Bell, for Church,
Our little Sexton–sings.

5

God preaches, a noted Clergyman–
And the sermon is never long,
So instead of getting to Heaven, at last–
I'm going, all along.

10

After Great Pain, a Formal Feeling Comes   1929 (ca. 1862)

After great pain, a formal feeling comes—
The Nerves sit ceremonious, like Tombs—
The stiff Heart questions was it He, that bore,
And Yesterday, or Centuries before?

The Feet, mechanical, go round—   5
Of Ground, or Air, or Ought°—   *anything, nothing*
A Wooden way
Regardless grown,
A Quartz contentment, like a stone—

This is the Hour of Lead—   10
Remembered, if outlived,
As Freezing persons, recollect the Snow—
First—Chill—then Stupor—then the letting go—

Much Madness Is Divinest Sense   1890 (ca. 1862)

Much Madness is divinest Sense—
To a discerning Eye—
Much Sense—the starkest Madness—
'Tis the Majority
In this, as All, prevail—   5
Assent—and you are sane—
Demur—you're straightway dangerous—
And handled with a Chain—

I Heard a Fly Buzz—When I Died   1896 (ca. 1862)

I heard a Fly buzz—when I died—
The Stillness in the Room
Was like the Stillness in the Air—
Between the Heaves of Storm—

The Eyes around—had wrung them dry—   5
And Breaths were gathering firm
For that last Onset—when the King
Be witnessed—in the Room—

I willed my Keepsakes—Signed away
What portion of me be   10
Assignable—and then it was
There interposed a Fly—

With Blue—uncertain stumbling Buzz—
Between the light—and me—
And then the Windows failed—and then   15
I could not see to see—

I Like to See It Lap the Miles   *1891 (ca. 1862)*

I like to see it lap the Miles—
And lick the Valleys up—
And stop to feed itself at Tanks—
And then—prodigious step

Around a Pile of Mountains—   5
And supercilious peer
In Shanties—by the sides of Roads—
And then a Quarry pare

To fit its sides
And crawl between   10
Complaining all the while
In horrid—hooting stanza—
Then chase itself down Hill—

And neigh like Boanerges°—
Then—prompter than a Star   15
Stop—docile and omnipotent
At its own stable door—

I LIKE TO SEE IT LAP THE MILES.   14 *Boanerges:* a surname meaning "the sons of
thunder" that appears in Mark 3:17.

I Cannot Live with You   *1890 (ca. 1862)*

I cannot live with You—
It would be Life—
And Life is over there—
Behind the Shelf

The Sexton keeps the Key to—   5
Putting up
Our Life—His Porcelain—
Like a Cup—

Discarded of the Housewife—
Quaint—or Broke—   10
A newer Sevres° pleases—   *a fine French porcelain*
Old Ones crack—

I could not die—with You—
For One must wait
To shut the Other's Gaze down—   15
You—could not—

And I—Could I stand by
And see You—freeze—
Without my Right of Frost—
Death's privilege?   20

Nor could I rise—with You—
Because Your Face
Would put out Jesus'—
That New Grace

Glow plain—and foreign   25
On my homesick Eye—
Except that You than He
Shone closer by—

They'd judge Us—How—
For You—served Heaven—You know,   30
Or sought to—
I could not—

Because You saturated Sight—
And I had no more Eyes
For sordid excellence   35
As Paradise

And were You lost, I would be—
Though My Name
Rang loudest
On the Heavenly fame—   40

And were You—saved—
And I—condemned to be
Where You were not—
That self—were Hell to Me—

So We must meet apart—   45
You there—I—here—
With just the Door ajar
That Oceans are—and Prayer—
And that White Sustenance—
Despair—   50

One Need Not Be a Chamber—To Be Haunted   1891 (ca. 1863)

One need not be a Chamber—to be Haunted—
One need not be a House—

The Brain has Corridors—surpassing
Material Place—

Far safer, of a Midnight Meeting   5
External Ghost
Than its interior Confronting—
That Cooler Host.

Far safer, through an Abbey gallop,
The Stones a'chase—   10
Than Unarmed, one's a'self encounter—
In lonesome Place—

Ourself behind ourself, concealed—
Should startle most—
Assassin hid in our Apartment   15
Be Horror's least.

The Body—borrows a Revolver—
He bolts the Door—
O'erlooking a superior spectre—
Or More—   20

The Bustle in a House   *1890 (ca. 1866)*

The Bustle in a House
The Morning after Death
Is solemnest of industries
Enacted upon Earth—

The Sweeping up the Heart   5
And putting Love away
We shall not want to use again
Until Eternity.

My Triumph Lasted Till the Drums   *1935 (ca. 1872)*

My Triumph lasted till the Drums
Had left the Dead alone
And then I dropped my Victory
And chastened stole along
To where the finished Faces   5
Conclusion turned on me
And then I hated Glory
And wished myself were They.

What is to be is best descried
When it has also been–   10
Could Prospect taste of Retrospect
The tyrannies of Men
Were Tenderer–diviner
The Transitive toward.
A Bayonet's contrition   15
Is nothing to the Dead.

The Heart Is the Capital of the Mind   *1929 (ca. 1876)*

The Heart is the Capital of the Mind–
The Mind is a single State–
The Heart and the Mind together make
A single Continent–

One–is the Population–   5
Numerous enough–
This ecstatic Nation
Seek–it is Yourself.

My Life Closed Twice Before Its Close   *1896*

My life closed twice before its close;
It yet remains to see
If Immortality unveil
A third event to me,

So huge, so hopeless to conceive   5
As these that twice befel.
Parting is all we know of heaven,
And all we need of hell.

ROBERT FROST (1874–1963)

When Robert Frost's first book of poems, *A Boy's Will*, was published in
England in 1913, he was virtually unknown in the United States. At the
time Ezra Pound wrote, "it is a sinister thing that so American . . . a talent
. . . should have to be exported before it can find due encouragement
and recognition." Time, of course, brought Frost all the encouragement
and recognition he could want. He eventually received over twenty

honorary degrees and four Pulitzer Prizes. Indeed, he came as close as possible to becoming America's official poet when he read "The Gift Outright" at the inauguration of President John F. Kennedy in 1961. In his own lifetime Frost became one of the most visible and admired American poets. His poetry continues to earn him that recognition.

Frost, who presented himself as the quintessential New Englander in person and in his poetry, was born in San Francisco on March 26, 1874. His father had moved the family west so that he could write for the *San Francisco Bulletin;* when his father died in 1885, Frost's mother brought the family back to Lawrence, Massachusetts. Frost attended Lawrence High School, studied classics, began writing poetry, and graduated in 1892 as co-valedictorian with Eleanor White, whom he married in 1895. After high school, he attended Dartmouth College for seven weeks and then turned to newspaper work and schoolteaching; he continued to write poetry, little of which was published. He returned to college after his marriage, attending classes at Harvard from 1897 to 1899, but he left without a degree.

In 1900 Frost's grandfather gave him a farm in Derry, New Hampshire, and for the next twelve years he farmed, wrote poetry, and taught English at Pinkerton Academy. The life was hard and the poetry mostly ignored. In 1912 he sold the farm to devote himself to writing. He moved to England, where he met a number of emerging and established poets, including Ezra Pound and W. B. Yeats. His first two books of poetry were published in England and received favorable reviews. These books, *A Boy's Will* (1913) and *North of Boston* (1914), were published in the United States in 1915, and Frost finally began to receive recognition at home.

That same year Frost and his family returned to the United States and took up residence on a farm near Franconia, New Hampshire. More books of poetry and greater acclaim followed quickly. In 1916 he published *Mountain Interval,* a book containing "The Road Not Taken," "Birches," and "'Out, Out—.'" He also became poet-in-residence at Amherst College, a relationship that would continue sporadically for much of his life. He began to develop his public persona as the wry and philosophical country poet. Later, it became more difficult to separate this public mask from what Randall Jarrell calls "The Other Frost," the often agonized and troubled man whose voice is heard in many poems.

More books of poetry and more recognition followed throughout Frost's life. In 1923 he published *Selected Poems* and *New Hampshire.* The latter book, for which Frost won a Pulitzer Prize, contains some of his best-known work: "Stopping by Woods on a Snowy Evening." "Fire and Ice," and "Nothing Gold Can Stay." These were followed by *West-Running Brook* (1928), *Collected Poems* (1930), *A Further Range* (1936), *A Witness Tree* (1942), *Steeple Bush* (1947), *Complete Poems* (1949), *Aforesaid* (1954), and *In the Clearing* (1962).

POETIC CHARACTERISTICS.   Frost's *poetic style* remained fairly consistent throughout his career; we do not see significant development or change in his work. We can find a clear sense of the land, of history, and of human nature. The poetry seems, at first, to be simple, lucid, straightforward, and descriptive. Further reading, however, reveals subtleties of wit and irony that often underlie his meditations on common events or objects.

Frost's *language and diction* are conversational; his words are plain and his phrases simple and direct. More often than not, he uses and refines the natural speech patterns and rhythms of New England, polishing the language that people actually speak to a compact and terse poetic texture.

In *poetic structure*, Frost's poems often move from an event or an object, through a metaphor, to an idea, in a smooth, uninterrupted flow. Within this pattern, Frost usually describes a complete event rather than a single vision. The heart of the process is the image or metaphor. Frost's metaphors are sparse and careful; they are brought sharply into focus and skillfully interwoven with the whole poem. Frost himself saw the metaphor as the beginning of the process. In *Education by Poetry* (1931) he wrote that "poetry begins in trivial metaphors, pretty metaphors, 'grace' metaphors, and goes on to the profoundest thinking that we have. Poetry provides the one permissible way of saying one thing and meaning another."

Frost's poems also reflect traditional *poetic forms* and meters. The poet once asserted that writing "free verse" was like playing tennis without a net. Consequently, we find conventional rhyme schemes and clear iambic meters in much of his work. Similarly, we find such closed forms as couplets, terza rima, quatrains, and blank verse.

POETIC SUBJECTS.   Frost's *poetic subjects* are generally common and rural events, objects, and characters: digging gardens, mending walls, cutting wood; snow, trees, insects, spring, and fall; children, parents, husbands and wives. Often, the poems move from these objects, events, or characters to philosophical generalizations about life and death, survival and responsibility, nature and humanity, that are so simple and right as to verge on the obvious.

BIBLIOGRAPHIC SOURCES.   The standard edition of Frost's work is *The Poetry of Robert Frost* (1969), edited by Edward Connery Lathem. The standard biography was written in three volumes by Lawrence Thompson: *Robert Frost: The Early Years* (1966), *The Years of Triumph* (1970), and *The Later Years* (1977). The last volume was completed after Thompson's death by R. H. Winnick. Useful criticism of the poetry includes Reuben Brower, *The Poetry of Robert Frost* (1963), J. F. Lynan, *The Pastoral Art of Robert Frost* (1964), Philip L. Gerber, *Robert Frost* (1966), Reginald Cook, *Robert Frost: A Living Voice* (1975), John C. Kemp, *Robert Frost and New England* (1979),

Richard Wakefield, *Robert Frost and the Opposing Light* (1985), and George Monteiro, *Robert Frost and the New England Renaissance* (1988). One of the PBS "Voices and Visions" series (1987) features his work. Refer to the index for additional poems by Frost.

The Tuft of Flowers   *1906*

I went to turn the grass once after one
Who mowed it in the dew before the sun.

The dew was gone that made his blade so keen
Before I came to view the leveled scene.

I looked for him behind an isle of trees;   5
I listened for his whetstone on the breeze.

But he had gone his way, the grass all mown,
And I must be, as he had been,—alone,

'As all must be,' I said within my heart,
'Whether they work together or apart.'   10

But as I said it, swift there passed me by
On noiseless wing a bewildered butterfly,

Seeking with memories grown dim o'er night
Some resting flower of yesterday's delight.

And once I marked his flight go round and round,   15
As where some flower lay withering on the ground.

And then he flew as far as eye could see,
And then on tremulous wing came back to me.

I thought of questions that have no reply,
And would have turned to toss the grass to dry;   20

But he turned first, and led my eye to look
At a tall tuft of flowers beside a brook,

A leaping tongue of bloom the scythe had spared
Beside a reedy brook the scythe had bared.

The mower in the dew had loved them thus,   25
By leaving them to flourish, not for us,

Nor yet to draw one thought of ours to him,
But from sheer morning gladness at the brim.

The butterfly and I had lit upon,
Nevertheless, a message from the dawn,   30

That made me hear the wakening birds around,
And hear his long scythe whispering to the ground,

And feel a spirit kindred to my own;
So that henceforth I worked no more alone;

But glad with him, I worked as with his aid,   35
And weary, sought at noon with him the shade;

And dreaming, as it were, held brotherly speech
With one whose thought I had not hoped to reach.

'Men work together,' I told him from the heart,
'Whether they work together or apart.'   40

Mending Wall   *1914*

Something there is that doesn't love a wall,
That sends the frozen-ground-swell under it,
And spills the upper boulders in the sun;
And makes gaps even two can pass abreast.
The work of hunters is another thing: 5
I have come after them and made repair
Where they have left not one stone on a stone,
But they would have the rabbit out of hiding,
To please the yelping dogs. The gaps I mean,
No one has seen them made or heard them made,   10
But at spring mending-time we find them there.
I let my neighbor know beyond the hill;
And on a day we meet to walk the line
And set the wall between us once again.
We keep the wall between us as we go.   15
To each the boulders that have fallen to each.
And some are loaves and some so nearly balls
We have to use a spell to make them balance:
'Stay where you are until our backs are turned!'
We wear our fingers rough with handling them.   20
Oh, just another kind of outdoor game,
One on a side. It comes to little more:
There where it is we do not need the wall:
He is all pine and I am apple orchard.
My apple trees will never get across   25
And eat the cones under his pines, I tell him.
He only says, 'Good fences make good neighbors.'
Spring is the mischief in me, and I wonder
If I could put a notion in his head:
'*Why* do they make good neighbors? Isn't it   30
Where there are cows? But here there are no cows.

Before I built a wall I'd ask to know
What I was walling in or walling out,
And to whom I was like to give offense.
Something there is that doesn't love a wall,   35
That wants it down.' I could say 'Elves' to him,
But it's not elves exactly, and I'd rather
He said it for himself. I see him there
Bringing a stone grasped firmly by the top
In each hand, like an old-stone savage armed.   40
He moves in darkness as it seems to me,
Not of woods only and the shade of trees.
He will not go behind his father's saying,
And he likes having thought of it so well
He says again, 'Good fences make good neighbors.'   45

Birches   *1915*

When I see birches bend to left and right
Across the lines of straighter darker trees,
I like to think some boy's been swinging them.
But swinging doesn't bend them down to stay
As ice-storms do. Often you must have seen them   5
Loaded with ice a sunny winter morning
After a rain. They click upon themselves
As the breeze rises, and turn many-colored
As the stir cracks and crazes their enamel.
Soon the sun's warmth makes them shed crystal shells   10
Shattering and avalanching on the snow-crust—
Such heaps of broken glass to sweep away
You'd think the inner dome of heaven had fallen.
They are dragged to the withered bracken by the load,
And they seem not to break; though once they are bowed   15
So low for long, they never right themselves:
You may see their trunks arching in the woods
Years afterwards, trailing their leaves on the ground
Like girls on hands and knees that throw their hair
Before them over their heads to dry in the sun.   20
But I was going to say when Truth broke in
With all her matter-of-fact about the ice-storm
I should prefer to have some boy bend them
As he went out and in to fetch the cows—
Some boy too far from town to learn baseball,   25
Whose only play was what he found himself,
Summer or winter, and could play alone.
One by one he subdued his father's trees
By riding them down over and over again

Until he took the stiffness out of them,   30
And not one but hung limp, not one was left
For him to conquer. He learned all there was
To learn about not launching out too soon
And so not carrying the tree away
Clear to the ground. He always kept his poise   35
To the top branches, climbing carefully
With the same pains you use to fill a cup
Up to the brim, and even above the brim.
Then he flung outward, feet first, with a swish,
Kicking his way down through the air to the ground.   40
So was I once myself a swinger of birches.
And so I dream of going back to be.
It's when I'm weary of considerations,
And life is too much like a pathless wood
Where your face burns and tickles with the cobwebs   45
Broken across it, and one eye is weeping
From a twig's having lashed across it open.
I'd like to get away from earth awhile
And then come back to it and begin over.
May no fate willfully misunderstand me   50
And half grant what I wish and snatch me away
Not to return. Earth's the right place for love:
I don't know where it's likely to go better.
I'd like to go by climbing a birch tree,
And climb black branches up a snow-white trunk   55
Toward Heaven, till the tree could bear no more,
But dipped its top and set me down again.
That would be good both going and coming back.
One could do worse than be a swinger of birches.

The Road Not Taken   1915

Two roads diverged in a yellow wood,
And sorry I could not travel both
And be one traveler, long I stood
And looked down one as far as I could
To where it bent in the undergrowth;   5

Then took the other, as just as fair,
And having perhaps the better claim,
Because it was grassy and wanted wear;
Though as for that the passing there
Had worn them really about the same,   10
And both that morning equally lay
In leaves no step had trodden black.
Oh, I kept the first for another day!

Yet knowing how way leads on to way,
I doubted if I should ever come back.   15

I shall be telling this with a sigh
Somewhere ages and ages hence:
Two roads diverged in a wood, and I—
I took the one less traveled by,
And that has made all the difference.   20

'Out, Out—'   *1916*

The buzz saw snarled and rattled in the yard
And made dust and dropped stove-length sticks of wood,
Sweet-scented stuff when the breeze drew across it.
And from there those that lifted eyes could count
Five mountain ranges one behind the other   5
Under the sunset far into Vermont.
And the saw snarled and rattled, snarled and rattled,
As it ran light, or had to bear a load.
And nothing happened: day was all but done.
Call it a day, I wish they might have said   10
To please the boy by giving him the half hour
That a boy counts so much when saved from work.
His sister stood beside them in her apron
To tell them 'Supper.' At the word, the saw,
As if to prove saws knew what supper meant,   15
Leaped out at the boy's hand, or seemed to leap—
He must have given the hand. However it was,
Neither refused the meeting. But the hand!
The boy's first outcry was rueful laugh,
As he swung toward them holding up the hand   20
Half in appeal, but half as if to keep
The life from spilling. Then the boy saw all—
Since he was old enough to know, big boy
Doing a man's work, though a child at heart—
He saw all spoiled. 'Don't let him cut my hand off—   25
The doctor, when he comes. Don't let him, sister!'
So. But the hand was gone already.
The doctor put him in the dark of ether.
He lay and puffed his lips out with his breath.
And then—the watcher at his pulse took fright.   30
No one believed. They listened at his heart.
Little—less—nothing!—and that ended it.
No more to build on there. And they, since they
Were not the one dead, turned to their affairs.

Fire and Ice   *1920*

Some say the world will end in fire,
Some say in ice.
From what I've tasted of desire
I hold with those who favor fire.
But if it had to perish twice,   5
I think I know enough of hate
To say that for destruction ice
Is also great
And would suffice.

Nothing Gold Can Stay   *1923*

Nature's first green is gold,
Her hardest hue to hold.
Her early leaf's a flower;
But only so an hour.
Then leaf subsides to leaf.   5
So Eden sank to grief,
So dawn goes down to day.
Nothing gold can stay.

Misgiving   *1923*

All crying, 'We will go with you, O Wind!'
The foliage follow him, leaf and stem;
But a sleep oppresses them as they go,
And they end by bidding him stay with them.

Since ever they flung abroad in spring   5
The leaves had promised themselves this flight,
Who now would fain seek sheltering wall,
Or thicket, or hollow place for the night.

And now they answer his summoning blast
With an ever vaguer and vaguer stir,   10
Or at utmost a little reluctant whirl
That drops them no further than where they were.

I only hope that when I am free
As they are free to go in quest
Of the knowledge beyond the bounds of life   15
It may not seem better to me to rest.

Acquainted with the Night   *1928*

I have been one acquainted with the night.
I have walked out in rain—and back in rain.
I have outwalked the furthest city light.

I have looked down the saddest city lane.
I have passed by the watchman on his beat   5
And dropped my eyes, unwilling to explain.

I have stood still and stopped the sound of feet
When far away an interrupted cry
Came over houses from another street,

But not to call me back or say good-by;   10
And further still at an unearthly height,
One luminary clock against the sky

Proclaimed the time was neither wrong nor right.
I have been one acquainted with the night.

Design   *1936*

I found a dimpled spider, fat and white,
On a white heal-all,° holding up a moth
Like a white piece of rigid satin cloth—
Assorted characters of death and blight
Mixed ready to begin the morning right,   5
Like the ingredients of a witches' broth—
A snow-drop spider, a flower like a froth,
And dead wings carried like a paper kite.

What had that flower to do with being white,
The wayside blue and innocent heal-all?   10
What brought the kindred spider to that height,
Then steered the white moth thither in the night?
What but design of darkness to appall?—
If design govern in a thing so small.

DESIGN.   2 *heal-all:* a flower, usually blue, thought to have healing powers.

A Considerable Speck   *1942*

(Microscopic)

A speck that would have been beneath my sight
On any but a paper sheet so white
Set off across what I had written there.

And I had idly poised my pen in air
To stop it with a period of ink   5
When something strange about it made me think.
This was no dust speck by my breathing blown,
But unmistakably a living mite
With inclinations it could call its own.
It paused as with suspicion of my pen,   10
And then came racing wildly on again
To where my manuscript was not yet dry;
Then paused again and either drank or smelt—
With loathing, for again it turned to fly.
Plainly with an intelligence I dealt.   15
It seemed too tiny to have room for feet,
Yet must have had a set of them complete
To express how much it didn't want to die.
It ran with terror and with cunning crept.
It faltered: I could see it hesitate;   20
Then in the middle of the open sheet
Cower down in desperation to accept
Whatever I accorded it of fate.
I have none of the tenderer-than-thou
Collectivistic regimenting love   25
With which the modern world is being swept
But this poor microscopic item now!
Since it was nothing I knew evil of
I let it lie there till I hope it slept.
I have a mind myself and recognize   30
Mind when I meet with it in any guise.
No one can know how glad I am to find
On any sheet the least display of mind.

WRITING ABOUT A POET'S WORK

It is difficult to write an effective essay on a poet's entire career based on a small selection of the poet's verse. It is both possible and reasonable, however, to write about a limited number of poems by a single author. There are three potential approaches to this type of essay: biographical, developmental, and comparative.

The *biographical essay* is perhaps the least productive; it seeks to relate poems to specific events or stages in a poet's life. Thus, you might attempt an essay that connects specific events in Emily Dickinson's life with specific poems; this type of essay requires extensive biographical research.

The *developmental essay* traces the growth of a single image, concept, or technique throughout a poet's career. Such an essay presupposes both development and the ability to look at a poet's work in the order in which it was written. An essay of this type might focus, for example, on Frost's use of snow imagery or Dickinson's employment of slant rhyme. In either case, the object would be to discover, assert, and prove through examples that development occurred over the poet's creative life.

The *comparative essay* is perhaps the easiest to formulate and the most common, since it neither assumes development nor requires biographical research (see Appendix B for an additional discussion of comparison as a strategy). Like the developmental essay, the comparative essay focuses on a specific element, image, idea, or technique in a poet's work; however, the object is to assert *continuity* or *commonality* rather than development and to use each work to clarify the others. Thus, such an essay will usually argue that a poet uses the same devices or addresses the same concerns in a similar way in a number of his or her poems to establish related ideas or emotions. Such an essay might deal with snow imagery in three of Robert Frost's poems, biblical allusions in four of Donne's poems, or the subject of death in four of Dickinson's poems.

Almost any essay dealing with a number of poems by the same author will inevitably focus on a specific element of the poems rather than attempt a wholesale treatment. The potential subjects for this type of essay include virtually every aspect of poetry. Thus, you might choose to work with speaker, setting and situation, diction, imagery, tone, rhythm, rhyme and form, symbol, allusion, or theme. The choice, of course, is never completely arbitrary; you should look for an element or technique that strikes you as especially significant and effective.

Prewriting strategies for either a developmental or comparative essay include selecting a poet, an approach, and a focus. These choices are not always easy, but some investigation of the works at hand will usually help you narrow the options considerably. As you plan the essay, you should remember that your aim is to discover development or commonality. With this in mind, you might consider the following questions in connection with a given poet.

Questions for Discovering Ideas

Are the speakers in the poems similar or related to each other? Does the speaker remain constant throughout the poems, develop gradually, or change radically from poem to poem? To what extent do the speakers share a common tone or attitude? Do tone and attitude remain constant, or do they change?

Do the poems have common or similar settings or situations? Are these established vividly and quickly, or left undeveloped? To what extent do setting and situation produce similar effects in a number of poems by the same author?

Can you find common threads of diction, imagery, metaphor, simile, symbol, or allusion in a number of poems by the same author? Are these common devices always used the same way and to the same effect, or do the method and impact change?

Does the poet's use of the elements of form—rhythm, rhyme, meter, stanza—remain constant or develop? Does form consistently reinforce meaning?

Does the connection between form and content remain constant or become less or more effective?

Does the poet deal with the same subject or convey similar ideas in a significant number of poems? To what extent do the poet's attitudes toward this subject and treatment of the idea remain constant or change? To what extent can you see logical connection or development among the poems in question?

These questions obviously cover a broad range of topics. In actual practice, however, the poems at hand will usually direct you to specific areas of consideration rather quickly. As you answer the questions that seem relevant to the poems, the focus of the essay should begin to emerge.

Once you have chosen a poet, isolated an area of interest, and selected a series of poems for examination, you can begin to shape a tentative central idea for the essay. As usual, this is probably the most difficult step in the prewriting process. Discovering an area of commonality or development is only half the battle; you must go on to assert a central fact about this common thread. It is not enough, for example, to argue in an essay that "we find the idea of death in three of Emily Dickinson's poems" or that "snow imagery recurs in a number of Robert Frost's poems." Rather, you must link the common thread to an assertion about its effect, impact, or significance. Thus, you might formulate a tentative thesis that argues that "death is presented in a number of Emily Dickinson's poems as the natural and welcome end to a life of toil" or that "the common image of snow in many of Robert Frost's poems grows progressively more grim and ironic throughout his career." Notice that both these formulations identify an area of commonality *and* make an assertion about that area. The first thesis would produce a comparative essay, the second a developmental one.

Having formulated a tentative central idea, go back through the poet's work and reexamine those poems that offer support and illustration. Look for aspects of specific poems that will eventually form the body of the essay. During this stage you may find it necessary to revise or refocus the thesis several times to solidify the connection between the essay's central idea and the supporting details.

Strategies for Organizing Ideas

The introductory paragraph should indicate, at least indirectly, the type of approach that will be taken in the essay. After reading the first paragraph, a reader should be able to tell if the essay is biographical, developmental, or comparative. The introduction should also specify which poems will be examined to support the central idea of the essay.

The organization of the body of the essay is determined almost completely by the strategy outlined in the introduction. A biographical essay would probably be organized around crucial events in the poet's life and key poems that reflect those events. A developmental essay would naturally consider a number of the author's poems in chronological order, based on approximate or exact dates of composition. A comparative essay, on the other hand, might take up one poem at a time in almost any order.

As with other essays, the main thrust of the body is to support and prove the assertion made in the introduction. To do this with conviction, you should normally plan to work with no more than three to five poems. Thus, one effective strategy for organizing the body of the essay is to deal with one poem at a time, stanza by stanza or unit by unit, focusing on the aspect under consideration. Be especially careful to provide clear transitions between your treatments of each poem and to tie each separate discussion back into the central idea and the introductory paragraph so that your essay does not break down into three or four disjointed discussions. In addition, discussions of poems later in the essay should be connected to earlier ones through comparison or contrast.

The conclusion should pull together all the strands of your argument and provide an overview. This can be done by summarizing the main points and observations. At the same time, you might use the conclusion to relate your argument to a broader consideration of the poet's work. Thus, an essay on the speaker in three of Frost's poems might conclude with a sentence or two that connects this narrative voice with the dominant tones or moods of Frost's poetry.

SAMPLE ESSAY

Images of Expanding and Contracting Space in John Donne's Love Poetry°

[1]   John Donne's love poetry has extended images and metaphors that emphasize the mystery and the power of love. Images that expand or contract space recur in much of this poetry; they help to create a private and separate world for the lovers and to demonstrate the power of love.* We can see this skillful and effective use of spatial imagery in "The Good Morrow," "The Sun Rising," and "The Flea."†

[2]   "The Good Morrow," a three-stanza lyric spoken by a lover to his mistress, contains spatial images that illustrate both the expansion and the contraction of space to create a private world of love. The central image in this poem is the world or the globe; this image is skillfully manipulated to demonstrate the power of love. The speaker introduces the image in the second stanza when he asserts "For love all love of other sights controls, / And makes one little room an everywhere" (lines 10–11). This image suggests that love is powerful enough to expand "one little room" into an entire world that con-

° See "The Good Morrow" (p. 847), "The Sun Rising" (p. 848), and "The Flea" (p. 851).
* Central idea.
† Thesis sentence.

tains everything the lovers might desire. In the rest of the stanza, the image of the world becomes even more explicit:

> Let sea-discoverers to new worlds have gone,
> Let maps to other, worlds on worlds have shown,
> Let us possess one world; each hath one, and is one. (lines 12–14)

The movement of the spatial imagery here is complex but consistent. These lines make a clear distinction between the public world of "sea-discoverers" or "maps" and the private world of the lovers. The speaker asserts that the lovers should "possess" their own world; each lover is a world and "hath" the other lover-world. More to the point, the movement here is inward and progressively contracting, from the actual globe to maps and finally to the lovers as little worlds.

[3]   This contraction of the world and space--the movement inward--is continued in the third stanza with the image of reflected faces: "My face in thine eye, thine in mine appears, / And true plain hearts do in the faces rest" (lines 15–16). At first, this image of reflected faces and hearts seems to depart from the spatial imagery of the second stanza. The connection, however, is established when we realize that eyes are spheres or globes, and that the reflection occurs on the outward half or "hemisphere" of the eyes. This witty contraction of worlds to eyes is brought home in the next two lines: "Where can we find two better hemispheres / Without sharp North, without declining West?" (lines 17–18). Here, the image finally contracts to a single world or globe, and the lovers become that world. Thus, the poem simultaneously contracts global space to the physical presence of the lovers and expands their "little room" into a total cosmos.

[4]   We find a similar manipulation of spatial imagery in "The Sun Rising," another three-stanza lyric spoken by a lover. This time, however, the poem is addressed to the sun, which has awakened the lover and his mistress. In stanza 1 the speaker establishes the distinction between the lovers and the outside world--the "school boys," "sour prentices," "huntsmen," and "country ants." The second stanza returns to images of expanding and contracting space that define love as self-sufficient and all-encompassing. Here the speaker tells the sun:

> Look, and tomorrow late, tell me,
> Whether both the Indias of spice and mine
> Be where thou leftst them, or lie here with me.
> Ask for those kings whom thou saw'st yesterday,
> And thou shalt hear, All here in one bed lay. (lines 16–20)

In this instance, the image contracts space, pulling most of the world into the bed and into the lovers themselves. The lady becomes both the East Indies of spices and the West Indies of gold. Similarly, the speaker becomes all the kings of the earth.

This imagery of spatial contraction becomes far more vivid in the last stanza of "The Sun Rising," when the speaker asserts that "She is all states, and all princes, I, / Nothing else is" (lines 21–22). The woman thus becomes

[5] the world and the speaker the ruler of "all states." The spatial contraction, pulling "all states" into bed with the speaker, underscores the irrelevance of the world at large and the importance of the lovers as a self-contained world. The speaker goes on, in lines 25 and 26, to argue that the sun should be happy "that the world's contracted thus" since warming it will be that much easier. And in the concluding two lines, the lovers and their bed become not only the world but also the center of the solar system: "Shine here to us, and thou art everywhere; / This bed thy center is, these walls, thy sphere" (lines 29–30). The movement of the image in this poem, as in "The Good Morrow," is thus both contracting and expanding. The outer world--the Indies, all kings, all states, all princes--is pulled into the room, the bed, and the physical being of the lovers. At the same time, the bed and the lovers expand to become a world unto themselves and the center of the solar system; the walls of their room become the outer limits of the sun's orbit. In this way, the spatial imagery creates a tone of comic outrageousness that helps define the power of love.

[6] Although "The Flea" is a very different type of poem than either "The Good Morrow" or "The Sun Rising," similar images of spatial manipulation emphasize the singularity and power of love. Unlike the other two lyrics, "The Flea" is a song of seduction spoken by an eager lover to an unwilling lady. Again, however, space expands and contracts to create a private (and in this case amusing) world for the lovers. Reduced to its basic logic, the poem asserts that the loss of virginity is no more significant than a flea bite. The master image of the poem is the flea and the blood of the eager lover and resistant lady that has been "mingled" in the flea. Indeed, the first stanza is given over to the image of the flea biting each lover and swelling "with one blood made of two" (line 8).

[7] The speaker does not begin to manipulate spatial imagery until the second stanza of "The Flea," where images of expanding and contracting space become both amusing and bizarre. Working from the premise established in the first stanza, that the flea contains both the speaker's and the lady's blood, the flea suddenly becomes all three beings: "Oh stay, three lives in one flea spare, / Where we almost, yea more than married, are" (lines 10–11). In terms of the dramatic situation, the lady is about to kill the flea; the speaker argues that they are married within the flea since their bloods are "mingled." This sets up one of Donne's most outrageous spatial images:

This flea is you and I, and this
Our marriage bed and marriage temple is;
Though parents grudge, and you, w'are met,
And cloister'd in these living walls of jet. (lines 12–15)

This manipulation of space and place is obviously witty and bizarre, but it is also consistent with the images of expanding and contracting space that occur in "The Good Morrow" and "The Sun Rising." Here the lovers contract or the flea expands until it has become both a "marriage bed and marriage temple." At the end of the passage we see that the image and the outrageous logic create the lovers' private world; they are "met / And cloister'd" within the black sides of the flea.

In each of these poems, images of space are thus manipulated to dem-

onstrate the power of love and the private world of the lovers. In all three instances, extended metaphors establish the power of love (or desire) to contract the whole world into one bed or to expand a little room (or even a little·
[8]   flea) into an everywhere. Such imagery is consistent with the attitude toward love expressed throughout Donne's songs and sonnets; love and passion are private, powerful, and mysterious. Images of expanding and contracting space are simply one of the many techniques that Donne employs to emphasize and describe the miracle of love.

Commentary on the Essay

The sample is a comparative essay that deals with a common thread of imagery that runs through a number of Donne's poems. The introduction establishes the blueprint for the entire essay. The first sentence announces the focus—images and metaphors—and makes a generalization about Donne's love poetry. The second sentence establishes the central idea of the essay: images of expanding and contracting space demonstrate both the private world of lovers and the power of love. At the same time, the formulation of this sentence makes it clear that the essay is comparative rather than developmental or biographical; the statement makes no claims for development and avoids any reference to the poet's life. Finally, the last sentence of the introduction specifies the poems that will be discussed to support the central idea in the body of the essay.

The body—paragraphs 2 through 7—takes up the three poems mentioned at the close of the introduction in the order in which they are noted. Thus, paragraphs 2 and 3 deal with "The Good Morrow," 4 and 5 with "The Sun Rising," and 6 and 7 with "The Flea." Each of these two-paragraph units is organized the same way. In each, the topic sentence (the first sentence in paragraphs 2, 4, and 6) names the poem, makes a general observation about the poem, and restates part of the central idea of the essay. Thus, each separate discussion is tied back into the introduction. In addition, the topic sentences in paragraphs 4 and 6 establish transition from poem to poem (and discussion to discussion) by using transitional words like *similar, another,* and *although.* In this way, each discussion is linked to the previous one. One additional linking device is employed in each discussion; at some point in each, the poem under discussion is directly compared with the poem or poems previously discussed. All these strategies help to unify the essay.

Within the body of this essay two paragraphs are devoted to each poem. This need not always be the case; in many instances you can make the necessary point using one paragraph for each poem. Here, however, there is too much material to cover each poem in a single paragraph. Thus, each two-paragraph unit is organized to follow the structure of the poem itself; the first paragraph deals with material in earlier stanzas, and the second with examples in later stanzas. The second paragraph in each unit also begins with a topic sentence that connects the material to the central idea and provides transition from the previous paragraph. In this way, each paragraph in the essay returns to the "straight line" of the central idea.

The conclusion (paragraph 8) restates the central idea of the essay and summarizes the major point illustrated with each poem. In addition, it relates these observations about spatial imagery to the broader context of Donne's love poetry. Thus, the essay ends as it began, with a general assertion about Donne's songs and sonnets.

WRITING TOPICS

On John Donne
1. Themes and ideas in Donne's religious poems.
2. Donne's use of metaphor and simile.
3. Donne's use of specific and general words in two or three poems.

On Emily Dickinson
4. Dickinson's characteristic brevity in her poems.
5. Dickinson's use of personal but not totally disclosed subject matter.
6. Dickinson's ideas about (a) death, or (b) religion, or (c) personal pain.
7. Dickinson's humor and irony.

On Robert Frost
8. Frost's use of topics based on recollections and reflections of personal experience.
9. Frost's characteristic pattern of structure, moving from specific to general, in a number of poems.
10. Frost's use of images drawn from everyday rural life.

24

Additional Poems

LEONARD ADAMÉ (b. 1947)

My Grandmother Would Rock Quietly and Hum   *1973*

in her house
she would rock quietly and hum
until her swelled hands
calmed

in summer   5
she wore thick stockings
sweaters
and grey braids

(when "el cheque" came
we went to Payless°   *a grocery store*   10
and I laughed greedily
when given a quarter)

mornings,
sunlight barely lit
the kitchen   15
and where
there were shadows
it was not cold

she quietly rolled
flour tortillas—   20
the "papas"°   *potatoes*
cracking in hot lard
would wake me

she had lost her teeth
and when we ate   25

she had bread
soaked in "café"°   *coffee*

always her eyes
were clear
and she could see   30
as I cannot yet see—
through her eyes
she gave me herself

she would sit
and talk   35
of her girlhood—
of things strange to me:
   México
   epidemics
   relatives shot   40
    her father's hopes
    of this country—
how they sank
with cement dust
to his insides   45

now
when I go
to the old house
the worn spots
by the stove   50
echo of her shuffling
and
México
still hangs in her
fading   55
calendar pictures

A. R. AMMONS (b. 1926)

80-Proof   *1975*

A fifth of me's me:
the rest's chaser:
35 lbs.'s
my true self: but
chuck 10 lbs. or so for bones,   5
what's left's
steaks & chops &
chicken fat,
two-over-easy & cream-on-the-side:
strip off a sheath of hide,   10

strip out nerves & veins
& permeable membranes,
what's left's a greasy spot:
the question's
whether   15
to retain
the shallow stain
or go 100% spiritual
and fifth by fifth
achieve a whole,   20
highly transcendental.

MAYA ANGELOU   (b. 1928)

My Arkansas   *1978*

There is a deep brooding
in Arkansas.
Old crimes like moss pend
from poplar trees.
The sullen earth   5
is much too
red for comfort.

Sunrise seems to hesitate
and in that second
lose its   10
incandescent aim, and
dusk no more shadows
than the noon.
The past is brighter yet.

Old hates and   15
ante-bellum° lace, are rent
but not discarded.
Today is yet to come
in Arkansas.
It writhes. It writhes in awful   20
waves of brooding.

MY ARKANSAS.   16 *ante-bellum:* before the U.S. Civil War (1861–1865).

ANONYMOUS

Barbara Allan   *Sixteenth century*

It was in and about the Martinmas° time,   *November 11*
    When the green leaves were a-fallin',
That Sir John Graeme in the West Country
    Fell in love with Barbara Allan.

He sent his man down through the town   5
   To the place where she was dwellin':
"O haste and come to my master dear,
   Gin° ye be Barbara Allan."   *if*

O slowly, slowly rose she up,
   To the place where he was lyin',   10
And when she drew the curtain by:
   "Young man, I think you're dyin'."

"O it's I'm sick, and very, very sick,
   And 'tis all for Barbara Allan."
"O the better for me ye shall never be,   15
   Though your heart's blood were a-spillin'."

"O dinna ye mind,° young man," said she,   *don't you recall*
   "When ye the cups were fillin',
That ye made the healths° go round and round,   *toasts*
   And slighted Barbara Allan?"   20

He turned his face unto the wall,
   And death with him was dealin':
"Adieu, adieu,° my dear friends all,   *farewell*
   And be kind to Barbara Allan."

And slowly, slowly, rose she up,   25
   And slowly, slowly left him;
And sighing said she could not stay,
   Since death of life had reft° him.   *bereft, taken from*

She had not gone a mile but twa,°   *two*
   When she heard the dead-bell knellin',   30
And every jow° that the dead-bell ga'ed°   *stroke; made*
   It cried, "Woe to Barbara Allan!"

"O mother, mother, make my bed,
   O make it soft and narrow:
Since my love died for me today,   35
   I'll die for him tomorrow."

ANONYMOUS

Lord Randal   *Sixteenth century*

"Oh, where have you been, Lord Randal, my son?
Oh, where have you been, my handsome young man?"
"Oh, I've been to the wildwood; mother, make my bed soon,
I'm weary of hunting and I fain° would lie down."   *gladly*

"And whom did you meet there, Lord Randal, my son?   5
And whom did you meet there, my handsome young man?"
"Oh, I met with my true love; mother, make my bed soon,
I'm weary of hunting and I fain would lie down."

"What got you for supper, Lord Randal, my son?
What got you for supper, my handsome young man?" 10
"I got eels boiled in broth; mother, make my bed soon,
I'm weary of hunting and I fain would lie down."

"And who got your leavings, Lord Randal, my son?
And who got your leavings, my handsome young man?"
"I gave them to my dogs; mother, make my bed soon, 15
I'm weary of hunting and I fain would lie down."

"And what did your dogs do, Lord Randal, my son?
And what did your dogs do, my handsome young man?"
"Oh, they stretched out and died; mother, make my bed soon,
I'm weary of hunting and I fain would lie down." 20

"Oh, I fear you are poisoned, Lord Randal, my son,
Oh, I fear you are poisoned, my handsome young man."
"Oh, yes, I am poisoned; mother, make my bed soon,
For I'm sick at my heart and I fain would lie down."

"What will you leave your mother, Lord Randal, my son? 25
What will you leave your mother, my handsome young man?"
"My house and my lands; mother, make my bed soon,
For I'm sick at my heart and I fain would lie down."

"What will you leave your sister, Lord Randal, my son?
What will you leave your sister, my handsome young man?" 30
"My gold and my silver; mother, make my bed soon,
For I'm sick at my heart and I fain would lie down."

"What will you leave your brother, Lord Randal, my son?
What will you leave your brother, my handsome young man?"
"My horse and my saddle; mother, make my bed soon, 35
For I'm sick at my heart and I fain would lie down."

"What will you leave your true-love, Lord Randal, my son?
What will you leave your true-love, my handsome young man?"
"A halter to hang her; mother, make my bed soon,
For I'm sick at my heart and I want to lie down." 40

ANONYMOUS

The Three Ravens   *Sixteenth century*

There were three ravens sat on a tree,
   Down a down, hay down, hay down,
There were three ravens sat on a tree,
   With a down,
There were three ravens sat on a tree, 5

They were as black as they might be,
　With a down, derry, derry, derry, down, down.°

The one of them said to his mate,
"Where shall we our breakfast take?

"Down in yonder green field   10
There lies a knight slain under his shield.

"His hounds they lie down at his feet,
So well they can their master keep.

"His hawks they fly so eagerly,°   *fiercely*
There's no fowl° dare him come nigh."   *bird*   15

Down there comes a fallow° doe,   *light brown*
As great with young as she might go,°   *walk*

She lifted up his bloody head,
And kissed his wounds that were so red.

She got him up upon her back,   20
And carried him to earthen lake.°   *pit*

She buried him before the prime,°   *morning prayer service*
She was dead herself ere evensong time.°
God send every gentleman
Such hawks, such hounds, and such a lemman.°   *mistress*   25

THE THREE RAVENS.   7 *down:* In singing this ballad, the first line of each stanza is
repeated three times and the refrain is repeated as in stanza 1.
23 *evensong time:* the time for the evening prayer service.

W. H. AUDEN   (1907–1973)

The Unknown Citizen   *1940*

(To JS/07/M/378
This Marble Monument
Is Erected by the State)

He was found by the Bureau of Statistics to be
One against whom there was no official complaint,
And all the reports on his conduct agree
That, in the modern sense of an old-fashioned word, he was a saint,
For in everything he did he served the Greater Community.   5

Except for the War till the day he retired
He worked in a factory and never got fired,
But satisfied his employers, Fudge Motors Inc.
Yet he wasn't a scab° or odd in his views.   *strikebreaker*
For his Union reports that he paid his dues,   10

(Our report on his Union shows it was sound)
And our Social Psychology workers found
That he was popular with his mates° and liked a drink.   *co-workers*
The Press are convinced that he bought a paper every day
And that his reactions to advertisements were normal in every way.   15
Policies taken out in his name prove that he was fully insured,
And his Health-card shows he was once in hospital but left it cured.
Both Producers Research and High-Grade Living declare
He was fully sensible to the advantages of the Instalment Plan
And had everything necessary to the Modern Man,   20
A phonograph, a radio, a car and a frigidaire.
Our reseachers into Public Opinion are content
That he held the proper opinions for the time of year;
When there was peace, he was for peace; when there was war, he went.
He was married and added five children to the population,   25
Which our Eugenist says was the right number for a parent of his generation,
And our teachers report that he never interfered with their education.
Was he free? Was he happy? The question is absurd:
Had anything been wrong, we should certainly have heard.

IMAMU AMIRI BARAKA (LEROI JONES)   (b. 1934)

Ka 'Ba   1969

A closed window looks down
on a dirty courtyard, and black people
call across or scream across or walk across
defying physics in the stream of their will

Our world is full of sound   5
Our world is more lovely than anyone's
tho we suffer, and kill each other
and sometimes fail to walk the air

We are beautiful people
with african imaginations   10
full of masks and dances and swelling chants
with african eyes, and noses, and arms,
though we sprawl in grey chains in a place
full of winters, when what we want is sun.

We have been captured,   15
brothers. And we labor
to make our getaway, into
the ancient image, into a new

correspondence with ourselves
and our black family. We need magic   20
now we need the spells, to raise up
return, destroy, and create. What will be

the sacred words?

MARVIN BELL   (b. 1937)

Things We Dreamt We Died For   *1969*

Flags of all sorts.
The literary life.
Each time we dreamt we'd done
the gentlemanly thing,
covering our causes   5
in closets full of bones
to remove ourselves forever
from dearest possibilities,
the old weapons re-injured us,
the old armies conscripted us,   10
and we gave in to getting even,
a little less like us
if a lot less like others.
Many, thus, gained fame
in the way of great plunderers,   15
retiring to the university
to cultivate grand plunder-gardens
in the service of literature,
the young and no more wars.
Their continuing tributes   20
make them our greatest saviours,
whose many fortunes are followed
by the many who have not one.

EARLE BIRNEY   (b. 1904)

Can. Lit.°   *1962*

(or *them able leave her ever*)

since we'd always sky about
when we had eagles they flew out
leaving no shadow bigger than wren's
to trouble even our broodiest hens
too busy bridging loneliness   5
to be alone
we hacked in railway ties
what Emily° etched in bone
                                                                               10
we French & English never lost
our civil war

CAN LIT. The title is an abbreviation for "Canadian Literature."   8 *Emily:* Emily
Dickinson (1830–1886), American poet (see pp. 854–64).

endure it still
a bloody civil bore

the wounded sirened off
no Whitman° wanted
it's only by our lack of ghosts   15
we're haunted

14 *Whitman:* Walt Whitman (1819–1892), American poet.

WILLIAM BLAKE   (1757–1827)

The Sick Rose   *1794*

O Rose thou art sick.
The invisible worm
That flies in the night,
In the howling storm:

Has found out thy bed   5
Of crimson joy:
And his dark secret love
Does thy life destroy.

WILLIAM BLAKE   (1757–1827)

Ah Sun-flower   *1794*

Ah Sun-flower! weary of time,
Who countest the steps of the Sun,
Seeking after that sweet golden clime
Where the traveller's journey is done;

Where the Youth pined away with desire,   5
And the pale Virgin shrouded in snow,
Arise from their graves and aspire,
Where my Sun-flower wishes to go.

ROBERT BLY   (b. 1926)

Snowfall in the Afternoon   *1962*

1.
The grass is half-covered with snow.
It was the sort of snowfall that starts in late afternoon.
And now the little houses of the grass are growing dark.

2.
If I reached my hands down, near the earth
I could take handfuls of darkness!   5
A darkness was always there, which we never noticed.

3.
As the snow grows heavier, the cornstalks fade further away,
And the barn moves nearer to the house.
The barn moves all alone in the growing storm.

4.
The barn is full of corn, and moving toward us now,   10
Like a hulk blown toward us in a storm at sea;
All the sailors on deck have been blind for many years.

LOUISE BOGAN   (1879–1970)

Women   *1923*

Women have no wilderness in them,
They are provident instead,
Content in the tight hot cell of their hearts
To eat dusty bread.

They do not see cattle cropping red winter grass,   5
They do not hear
Snow water going down under culverts
Shallow and clear.

They wait, when they should turn to journeys,
They stiffen, when they should bend.   10
They use against themselves that benevolence
To which no man is friend.

They cannot think of so many crops to a field
Or of clean wood cleft by an axe.
Their love is an eager meaninglessness   15
Too tense, or too lax.

They hear in every whisper that speaks to them
A shout and a cry.
As like as not, when they take life over their door-sills
They should let it go by.   20

ARNA BONTEMPS   (1902–1973)

A Black Man Talks of Reaping   *1940*

I have sown beside all waters in my day.
I planted deep, within my heart the fear
that wind or fowl would take the grain away.
I planted safe against this stark, lean year.

I scattered seed enough to plant the land   5
in rows from Canada to Mexico

but for my reaping only what the hand
can hold at once is all that I can show.

Yet what I sowed and what the orchard yields
my brother's sons are gathering stalk and root;   10
small wonder then my children glean in fields
they have not sown, and feed on bitter fruit.

ANNE BRADSTREET   (1612–1672)

To My Dear and Loving Husband   *1678*

If ever two were one, then surely we.
If ever man were loved by wife, then thee;
If ever wife was happy in a man,
Compare with me ye women if you can.
I prize thy love more than whole mines of gold,   5
Or all the riches that the East doth hold.
My love is such that rivers cannot quench,
Nor ought but love from thee give recompense.
Thy love is such I can no way repay;
The heavens reward thee manifold, I pray.   10
Then while we live, in love let's so persever,
That when we live no more we may live ever.

ROBERT BRIDGES   (1844–1930)

Nightingales   *1893*

　Beautiful must be the mountains whence ye come,
And bright in the fruitful valleys the streams, wherefrom
　　Ye learn your song:
Where are those starry woods? O might I wander there,
　Among the flowers, which in that heavenly air   5
　　Bloom the year long!

　Nay, barren are those mountains and spent the streams:
Our song is the voice of desire, that haunts our dreams,
　　A throe of the heart,
Whose pining visions dim, forbidden hopes profound,   10
　No dying cadence nor long sigh can sound,
　　For all our art.

　Alone, aloud in the raptured ear of men
We pour our dark nocturnal secret; and then,
　　As night is withdrawn   15
From these sweet-springing meads° and bursting boughs of May.   *meadows*
　Dream, while the innumerable choir of day
　　Welcome the dawn.

GWENDOLYN BROOKS   (b. 1917)

Primer for Blacks   *1980*

Blackness
is a title,
is a preoccupation,
is a commitment Blacks
are to comprehend—   5
and in which you are
to perceive your Glory.

The conscious shout
of all that is white is
"It's Great to be white."   10
The conscious shout
of the slack in Black is
"It's Great to be white."
Thus all that is white
has white strength and yours.   15

The word Black
has geographic power,
pulls everybody in:
Blacks here—
Blacks there—   20
Blacks wherever they may be.
And remember, you Blacks, what they told you—
remember your Education:
"one Drop—one Drop
maketh a brand new Black."   25
      Oh mighty Drop.
——And because they have given us kindly
so many more of our people

Blackness
stretches over the land.   30
Blackness—
the Black of it,
the rust-red of it,
the milk and cream of it,
the tan and yellow-tan of it,   35
the deep-brown middle-brown high-brown of it,
the "olive" and ochre of it—
Blackness
marches on.

The huge, the pungent object of our prime out-ride   40
is to Comprehend,
to salute and to Love the fact that we are Black,
which *is* our "ultimate Reality,"

which is the lone ground
from which our meaningful metamorphosis,   45
from which our prosperous staccato,
group of individual, can rise.

Self-shriveled Blacks.
Begin with gaunt and marvelous concession:
YOU are our costume and our fundamental bone.   50

    All of you—
    You COLORED ones,
    you NEGRO ones,
those of you who proudly cry
    "I'm half INDian"—   55
    those of you who proudly screech
    "I'VE got the blood of George WASHington in
      MY veins"—

ALL of you—
    you proper Blacks,   60
you half-Blacks,
you wish-I-weren't Blacks,
Niggeroes and Niggerenes.

You.

ELIZABETH BARRETT BROWNING   (1806–1861)

Sonnets from the Portuguese: Number 43   *1850*

How do I love thee? Let me count the ways.
I love thee to the depth and breadth and height
My soul can reach, when feeling out of sight
For the ends of Being and ideal Grace.
I love thee to the level of every day's   5
Most quiet need, by sun and candelight.
I love thee freely, as men strive for Right;
I love thee purely, as they turn from Praise.
I love thee with the passion put to use
In my old griefs, and with my childhood's faith.   10
I love thee with a love I seemed to lose
With my lost saints,—I love thee with the breath,
Smiles, tears, of all my life!—and, if God choose,
I shall but love thee better after death.

ROBERT BROWNING (1812–1889)

Soliloquy of the Spanish Cloister   *1842*

1

Gr-r-r—there go, my heart's abhorrence!
    Water your damned flowerpots, do!
If hate killed men, Brother Lawrence,
    God's blood, would not mine kill you!
What? your myrtle bush wants trimming?   5
    Oh, that rose has prior claims—
Needs its leaden vase filled brimming?
    Hell dry you up with its flames!

2

At the meal we sit together:
    Salve tibi!° I must hear   *Hail to thee!* 10
Wise talk of the kind of weather,
    Sort of season, time of year:
Not a plenteous cork crop: scarcely
    Dare we hope oak-galls, I doubt:
What's the Latin name for "parsley"?   15
    What's the Greek name for Swine's Snout?

3

Whew! We'll have our platter burnished,
    Laid with care on our own shelf!
With a fire-new spoon we're furnished,
    And a goblet for ourself,   20
Rinsed like something sacrificial
    Ere 'tis fit to touch our chaps°   *jaws*
Marked with L. for our initial!
    (He-he! There his lily snaps!)

4

Saint, forsooth! While brown Dolores   25
    Squats outside the Convent bank
With Sanchicha, telling stories,
    Steeping tresses in the tank,
Blue-black, lustrous, thick like horsehairs,
    —Can't I see his dead eye glow,   30
Bright as 'twere a Barbary corsair's?°   *pirate's*
    (That is, if he'd let it show!)

5

When he finishes refection,°   *dinner*
    Knife and fork he never lays
Cross-wise, to my recollection,   35
    As do I, in Jesu's praise.

I the Trinity illustrate,
    Drinking watered orange-pulp—
In three sips the Arian° frustrate;   *Anti-Trinitarian (a heretic)*
    While he drains his at one gulp.   40

6

Oh, those melons? If he's able
    We're to have a feast! so nice!
One goes to the Abbot's table,
    All of us get each a slice.
How go on your flowers? None double?   45
    Not one fruit-sort can you spy?
Strange!—And I, too, at such trouble,
    Keep them close-nipped on the sly!

7

There's a great text in Galatians,°   *perhaps 3:10 or 5:19–21*
    Once you trip on it, entails   50
Twenty-nine distinct damnations,
    One sure, if another fails:
If I trip him just a-dying,
    Sure of heaven as sure can be,
Spin him round and send him flying   55
    Off to hell, a Manichee?°   *heretic*

8

Or, my scrofulous° French novel   *pornographic*
    On gray paper with blunt type!
Simply glance at it, you grovel
    Hand and foot in Belial's° gripe: *the Devil*   60
If I double down its pages
    At the woeful sixteenth print,
When he gathers his greengages,
    Ope a sieve and slip it in't?

9

Or, there's Satan!—one might venture   65
    Pledge one's soul to him, yet leave
Such a flaw in the indenture°   *contract*
    As he'd miss till, past retrieve,
Blasted lay that rose-acacia
    We're so proud of! *Hy, Zy, Hine . . .*   70
'St, there's Vespers! *Plena gratiâ*°   *full of grace*
    Ave, Virgo!° Gr-r-r—you swine!   *Hail Virgin*

ROBERT BURNS   (1759–1796)

To a Mouse   *1786*

ON TURNING HER UP IN HER NEST WITH
THE PLOW, NOVEMBER, 1785

Wee, sleekit,° cow'rin', tim'rous beastie,   *sleek*
O, what a panic's in thy breastie!
Thou need na start awa sae hasty,
    Wi' bickering brattle!°   *scamper*
I wad be laith° to rin an' chase thee   *loath*   5
    Wi' murd-ring pattle!°   *plowstaff*

I'm truly sorry man's dominion
Has broken Nature's social union,
An' justifies that ill opinion
    Which makes thee startle   10
At me, thy poor, earth-born companion,
    An' fellow mortal!

I doubt na, whiles,° but thou may thieve;   *sometimes*
What then? poor beastie, thou maun° live!   *must*
A daimen-icker° in a thrave°   15
    'S a sma' request:
I'll get a blessin' wi' the lave,°   *remainder*
    And never miss 't!

Thy wee-bit housie, too, in ruin!
Its silly° wa's the win's are strewin'!   *feeble*   20
An' naething, now, to big° a new ane,   *build*
    O' foggage° green!   *moss*
An' bleak December's winds ensuin',
    Baith snell° an' keen!   *bitter*

Thou saw the fields laid bare and waste,   25
An' weary winter comin' fast,
An' cozie here, beneath the blast,
    Thou thought to dwell,
Till crash! The cruel coulter° passed   *cutter-blade*
    Out-through thy cell.   30

That wee-bit heap o'leaves an' stibble°   *stubble*
Has cost thee money a weary nibble!
Now thou's turned out, for a' thy trouble,
    But° house or hald,°   *Without; hold*
To thole° the winter's sleety dribble,   *endure*   35
    An' cranreuch° cauld!   *hoarfrost*

But Mousie, thou art no thy lane,°   *not alone*
In proving foresight may be vain:

TO A MOUSE.   15 *daimen-icker:* an occasional ear of corn.   *thrave:* a unit of measure
for unthreshed grain, equal to twenty-four sheaves.

The best-laid schemes o' mice an' men
    Gang aft a-gley,°   *go often awry*   40
An' lea'e us nought but grief an' pain,
    For promised joy.

Still thou art blest compared wi' me!
The present only toucheth thee:
But och! I backward cast my e'e   45
    On prospects drear!
An forward though I canna see,
    I guess an' fear!

GEORGE GORDON, LORD BYRON   (1788–1824)

The Destruction of Sennacherib°   *1815*

The Assyrian came down like the wolf on the fold,
And his cohorts were gleaming in purple and gold;
And the sheen of their spears was like stars on the sea,
When the blue wave rolls nightly on deep Galilee.

Like the leaves of the forest when summer is green,   5
That host with their banners at sunset were seen:
Like the leaves of the forest when autumn hath blown,
That host on the morrow lay withered and strown.

For the Angel of Death spread his wings on the blast,
And breathed in the face of the foe as he passed;   10
And the eyes of the sleepers waxed deadly and chill,
And their hearts but once heaved—and for ever grew still!

And there lay the steed with his nostril all wide,
But through it there rolled not the breath of his pride;
And the foam of his gasping lay white on the turf,   15
And cold as the spray of the rock-beating surf.

And there lay the rider distorted and pale,
With the dew on his brow, and the rust on his mail;
And the tents were all silent, the banners alone,
The lances unlifted, the trumpet unblown.   20

And the widows of Ashur° are loud in their wail,
And the idols are broke in the temple of Baal;°
And the might of the Gentile, unsmote by the sword,
Hath melted like snow in the glance of the Lord!

THE DESTRUCTION OF SENNACHERIB. Sennacherib was king of the ancient Near Eastern empire of Assyria from 705 to 681 B.C. He laid seige to Jerusalem in about 702 B.C., even though King Hezekiah had already rendered tribute to Assyria. According to 2 Kings 19:35–36, a miracle occurred to save the besieged Hebrews: "the angel of the Lord went out and smote . . . [185,000 Assyrian soldiers]; and when they [the Hebrews] arose early in the morning, behold, they [the Assyrians] were all dead corpses."   21 *Ashur:* the land of the Assyrians.   22 *Baal:* a god who supposedly controlled weather and storms.

THOMAS CAMPION   (1567–1620)

Cherry Ripe   *1617*

There is a garden in her face,
Where roses and white lilies grow;
A heavenly paradise is that place,
Wherein all pleasant fruits do flow.
There cherries grow, which none may buy   5
Till "Cherry ripe" themselves do cry.

Those cherries fairly do enclose
Of orient pearl a double row;
Which when her lovely laughter shows,
They look like rosebuds filled with snow.   10
Yet them nor peer nor prince can buy
Till "Cherry ripe" themselves do cry.

Her eyes like angels watch them still;
Her brows like bended bows do stand,
Threatening with piercing frowns to kill   15
All that attempt, with eye or hand,
Those sacred cherries to come nigh
Till "Cherry ripe" themselves do cry.

LUCILLE CLIFTON   (b. 1936)

this morning
(for the girls of eastern high school)   *1987*

this morning
this morning
            i met myself
coming in

a bright   5
jungle girl
shining
quick as a snake
a tall
tree girl a   10
me girl
            i met myself
this morning
coming in

and all day   15
i have been

a black bell
ringing
i survive
        survive   20
survive

LUCILLE CLIFTON   (b. 1936)

the poet   *1987*

i beg my bones to be good but
they keep clicking music and
i spin in the center of myself
a foolish frightful woman
moving my skin against the wind and   5
tap dancing for my life.

STEPHEN CRANE   (1871–1900)

Do Not Weep, Maiden, for War Is Kind   *1896, 1899 (1895)*

Do not weep, maiden, for war is kind.
Because your lover threw wild hands toward the sky
And the affrighted steed ran on alone,
Do not weep.
War is kind.   5

    Hoarse, booming drums of the regiment
    Little souls who thirst for fight,
    These men were born to drill and die
    The unexplained glory flies above them
    Great is the battle-god, great, and his kingdom—   10
    A field where a thousand corpses lie.

Do not weep, babe, for war is kind.
Because your father tumbled in the yellow trenches,
Raged at his breast, gulped and died,
Do not weep.   15
War is kind.

    Swift, blazing flag of the regiment
    Eagle with crest of red and gold,
    These men were born to drill and die
    Point for them the virtue of slaughter   20
    Make plain to them the excellence of killing
    And a field where a thousand corpses lie.

Mother whose head hung humble as a button
On the bright splendid shroud of your son,

Do not weep.   25
War is kind.

COUNTEE CULLEN   (1903–1946)

Yet Do I Marvel   *1925*

I doubt not God is good, well-meaning, kind,
And did He stoop to quibble could tell why
The little buried mole continues blind,
Why flesh that mirrors Him must some day die.
Make plain the reason tortured Tantalus°   5
Is baited by the fickle fruit, declare
If merely brute caprice dooms Sisyphus°
To struggle up a never-ending stair.
Inscrutable His ways are, and immune
To catechism by a mind too strewn   10
With petty cares to slightly understand
What awful brain compels His awful hand.
Yet do I marvel at this curious thing:
To make a poet black, and bid him sing!

YET I DO MARVEL.   5 *Tantalus:* a figure in Greek mythology condemned to eternal
hunger and thirst. He stood in Hades chin deep in water with a fruit-laden branch just
above his head, but could never eat or drink.   7 *Sisyphus:* a figure in Greek mythology
condemned to eternally useless labor. He was fated to roll a huge boulder up a hill in the
underworld, but each time he neared the top, the stone slipped and he had to begin anew.
See also pp. 326–27.

e. e. cummings   (1894–1962)

next to of course god america i   *1926*

"next to of course god america i
love you land of the pilgrims' and so forth oh
say can you see by the dawn's early my
country 'tis of centuries come and go
and are no more what of it we should worry   5
in every language even deafanddumb
thy sons acclaim your glorious name by gorry
by jingo by gee by gosh by gum
why talk of beauty what could be more beaut-
iful than these heroic happy dead   10
who rushed like lions to the roaring slaughter
they did not stop to think they died instead
then shall the voice of liberty be mute?"

He spoke. And drank rapidly a glass of water

e. e. cummings   (1894–1962)

if there are any heavens   *1931*

if there are any heavens my mother will(all by herself)have
one.   It will not be a pansy heaven nor
a fragile heaven of lilies-of-the-valley but
it will be a heaven of blackred roses

my father will be(deep like a rose   5
tall like a rose)

standing near my

swaying over her
(silent)
with eyes which are really petals and see   10

nothing with the face of a poet really which
is a flower and not a face with
hands
which whisper
This is my beloved my   15

              (suddenly in sunlight

he will bow,

& the whole garden will bow)

JAMES DICKEY   (b. 1923)

The Performance   *1967*

The last time I saw Donald Armstrong
He was staggering oddly off into the sun,
Going down, off the Philippine Islands.
I let my shovel fall, and put that hand
Above my eyes, and moved some way to one side   5
That his body might pass through the sun,

And I saw how well he was not
Standing there on his hands,
On his spindle-shanked forearms balanced,
Unbalanced, with his big feet looming and waving   10
In the great, untrustworthy air
He flew in each night, when it darkened.

Dust fanned in scraped puffs from the earth
Between his arms, and blood turned his face inside out,
To demonstrate its suppleness   15
Of veins, as he perfected his role.

Next day, he toppled his head off
On an island beach to the south,

And the enemy's two-handed sword
Did not fall from anyone's hands   20
At that miraculous sight,
As the head rolled over upon
Its wide-eyed face, and fell
Into the inadequate grave

He had dug for himself, under pressure.   25
Yet I put my flat hand to my eyebrows
Months later, to see him again
In the sun, when I learned how he died,
And imagined him, there,
Come, judged, before his small captors,   30

Doing all his lean tricks to amaze them—
The back somersault, the kip-up—
And at last, the stand on his hands,
Perfect, with his feet together,
His head down, evenly breathing,   35
As the sun poured up from the sea

And the headsmen broke down
In a blaze of tears, in that light
Of the thin, long human frame
Upside down in its own strange joy,   40
And, if some other one had not told him,
Would have cut off the feet

Instead of the head,
And if Armstrong had not presently risen
In kingly, round-shouldered attendance,   45
And then knelt down in himself
Beside his hacked, glittering grave, having done
All things in this life that he could.

JAMES DICKEY (b. 1923)

Kudzu   *1964*

Japan invades. Far Eastern vines
Run from the clay banks they are

Supposed to keep from eroding,
Up telephone poles,
Which rear, half out of leafage,   5
As though they would shriek,
Like things smothered by their own
Green, mindless, unkillable ghosts.

In Georgia, the legend says
That you must close your windows   10

At night to keep it out of the house.
The glass is tinged with green, even so,

As the tendrils crawl over the fields.
The night the kudzu has
Your pasture, you sleep like the dead.   15
Silence has grown Oriental
And you cannot step upon ground:
Your leg plunges somewhere
It should not, it never should be,
Disappears, and waits to be struck   20

Anywhere between sole and kneecap:
For when the kudzu comes,

The snakes do, and weave themselves
Among its lengthening vines,
Their spade heads resting on leaves,   25
Growing also, in earthly power
And the huge circumstance of concealment.
One by one the cows stumble in,
Drooling a hot green froth,
And die, seeing the wood of their stalls   30

Strain to break into leaf.
In your closed house, with the vine

Tapping your window like lightning,
You remember what tactics to use.
In the wrong yellow fog-light of dawn   35
You herd them in, the hogs,
Head down in their hairy fat,
The meaty troops, to the pasture.
The leaves of the kudzu quake
With the serpents' fear, inside   40

The meadow ringed with men
Holding sticks, on the country roads.

The hogs disappear in the leaves.
The sound is intense, subhuman,
Nearly human with purposive rage.   45
There is no terror
Sound from the snakes.
No one can see the desperate, futile
Striking under the leaf heads.
Now and then, the flash of a long   50

Living vine, a cold belly,
Leaps up, torn apart, then falls

Under the tussling surface.
You have won, and wait for frost,
When, at the merest touch
Of cold, the kudzu turns   55
Black, withers inward and dies,
Leaving a mass of brown strings
Like the wires of a gigantic switchboard.
You open your windows,   60

With the lightning restored to the sky
And no leaves rising to bury

You alive inside your frail house,
And you think, in the opened cold,
Of the surface of things and its terrors,   65
And of the mistaken, mortal
Arrogance of the snakes

JAMES DICKEY (b. 1923)

The Lifeguard   *1962*

In a stable of boats I lie still,
From all sleeping children hidden.
The leap of a fish from its shadow
Makes the whole lake instantly tremble.
With my foot on the water, I feel   5
The moon outside

Take on the utmost of its power.
I rise and go out through the boats.
I set my broad sole upon silver,
On the skin of the sky, on the moonlight,   10
Stepping outward from earth onto water
In quest of the miracle

This village of children believed
That I could perform as I dived
For one who had sunk from my sight.   15
I saw his cropped haircut go under.
I leapt, and my steep body flashed
Once, in the sun.

Dark drew all the light from my eyes.
Like a man who explores his death   20
By the pull of his slow-moving shoulders,
I hung head down in the cold,
Wide-eyed, contained, and alone
Among the weeds,

And my fingertips turned into stone   25
From clutching immovable blackness.

Time after time I leapt upward
Exploding in breath, and fell back
From the change in the children's faces
At my defeat.   30

Beneath them I swam to the boathouse
With only my life in my arms
To wait for the lake to shine back
At the risen moon with such power
That my steps on the light of the ripples   35
Might be sustained.

Beneath me is nothing but brightness
Like the ghost of a snowfield in summer.
As I moved toward the center of the lake,
Which is also the center of the moon,   40
I am thinking of how I may be
The saviour of one

Who has already died in my care.
The dark trees fade from around me.
The moon's dust hovers together.   45
I call softly out, and the child's
Voice answers through blinding water.
Patiently, slowly,

He rises, dilating to break
The surface of stone with his forehead.   50
He is one I do not remember
Having ever seen in his life.
The ground I stand on is trembling
Upon his smile.

I wash the black mud from my hands.   55
On a light given off by the grave
I kneel in the quick of the moon
At the heart of a distant forest
And hold in my arms a child
Of water, water, water.   60

H. D. (HILDA DOOLITTLE) (1886–1961)

Pear Tree   *1916*

Silver dust
lifted from the earth,
higher than my arms reach,
you have mounted,
O silver,   5
higher than my arms reach
you front us with great mass;

no flower ever opened
so staunch a white leaf,
no flower ever parted silver   10
from such rare silver;

O white pear,
your flower-tufts
thick on the branch
bring summer and ripe fruits   15
in their purple hearts.

RITA DOVE   (b. 1952)

Ö°   *1980*

Shape the lips to an *o*, say *a*.
That's *island*.

One word of Swedish has changed the whole neighborhood.
When I look up, the yellow house on the corner
is a galleon stranded in flowers. Around it   5
the wind. Even the high roar of a leaf-mulcher
could be the horn-blast from a ship
as it skirts the misted shoals.

We don't need much more to keep things going.
Families complete themselves   10
and refuse to budge from the present,
the present extends its glass forehead to sea
(backyard breezes, scattered cardinals)

and if, one evening, the house on the corner
took off over the marshland,   15
neither I nor my neighbor
would be amazed. Sometimes

a word is found so right it trembles
at the slightest explanation.
You start out with one thing, end   20
up with another, and nothing's
like it used to be, not even the future.

Ö: the Swedish word for "island," pronounced as explained in lines 1 and 2.

MICHAEL DRAYTON   (1563–1631)

Since There's No Help   *1619*

Since there's no help, come let us kiss and part;
Nay, I have done, you get no more of me,
And I am glad, yea glad with all my heart

That thus so cleanly I myself can free;
Shake hands forever, cancel all our vows,   5
And when we meet at any time again,
Be it not seen in either of our brows
That we one jot of former love retain.
Now at the last gasp of love's latest breath,
When, his pulse failing, passion speechless lies,   10
When faith is kneeling by his bed of death,
And innocence is closing up his eyes;
Now if thou wouldst, when all have given him over,
From death to life thou mightst him yet recover.

PAUL LAURENCE DUNBAR   (1872–1906)

Sympathy   *1895*

I know what the caged bird feels, alas!
When the sun is bright on the upland slopes;
When the wind stirs soft through the springing grass
And the river flows like a stream of glass;
When the first bird sings and the first bud opes,   5
And the faint perfume from its chalice steals—
I know what the caged bird feels!

I know why the caged bird beats his wing
Till its blood is red on the cruel bars;
For he must fly back to his perch and cling   10
When he fain would be on the bough a-swing;
And a pain still throbs in the old, old scars
And they pulse again with a keener sting—
I know why he beats his wing!

I know why the caged bird sings, ah me,   15
When his wing is bruised and his bosom sore,
When he beats his bars and would be free;
It is not a carol of joy or glee,
But a prayer that he sends from his heart's deep core,
But a plea, that upward to Heaven he flings—   20
I know why the caged bird sings!

RICHARD EBERHART   (b. 1904)

The Groundhog   *1936*

In June, amid the golden fields,
I saw a groundhog lying dead.
Dead lay he; my senses shook,
And mind outshot our naked frailty.

There lowly in the vigorous summer   5
His form began its senseless change,
And made my senses waver dim
Seeing nature ferocious in him.
Inspecting close his maggots' might
And seething cauldron of his being,   10
Half with loathing, half with a strange love,
I poked him with an angry stick.
The fever arose, became a flame
And Vigour circumscribed the skies,
Immense energy in the sun,   15
And through my frame a sunless trembling.
My stick had done nor good nor harm.
Then stood I silent in the day
Watching the object, as before;
And kept my reverence for knowledge   20
Trying for control, to be still,
To quell the passion of the blood;
Until I had bent down on my knees
Praying for joy in the sight of decay.
And so I left; and I returned   25
In Autumn strict of eye, to see
The sap gone out of the groundhog,
But the bony sodden hulk remained.
But the year had lost its meaning,
And in intellectual chains   30
I lost both love and loathing,
Mured up in the wall of wisdom.
Another summer took the fields again
Massive and burning, full of life,
But when I chanced upon the spot   35
There was only a little hair left,
And bones bleaching in the sunlight
Beautiful as architecture;
I watched them like a geometer,
And cut a walking stick from a birch.   40
It has been three years, now.
There is no sign of the groundhog.
I stood there in the whirling summer,
My hand capped a withered heart,
And thought of China and of Greece,   45
Of Alexander° in his tent;
Of Montaigne° in his tower,
Of Saint Theresa° in her wild lament.

THE GROUNDHOG.   46 *Alexander:* Alexander the Great (356–323 B.C.), king of
Macedonia and conquerer of virtually the entire civilized world.   47 *Montaigne:* Michel
de Montaigne (1553–1592), French essayist and commentator on human nature and
society.   48 *Saint Theresa:* Theresa de Avila (1515–1582), Spanish religious mystic,
writer, and founder of a religious order.

T. S. ELIOT   (1888–1965)

The Love Song of J. Alfred Prufrock°   *1915 (1910–1911)*

S'io credesse che mia risposta fosse
A persona che mai tornasse al mondo,
Questa fiamma staria senza più scosse.
Ma perciocche giammai di questo fondo
Non torno vivo alcun, s'i'odo il vero,
Senza tema d'infamia ti rispondo.°

Let us go then, you and I
When the evening is spread out against the sky
Like a patient etherized upon a table;
Let us go, through certain half-deserted streets,
The muttering retreats   5
Of restless nights in one-night cheap hotels
And sawdust restaurants with oyster shells;
Streets that follow like a tedious argument
Of insidious intent
To lead you to an overwhelming question . . .   10
Oh, do not ask, "What is it?"
Let us go and make our visit.

In the room the women come and go
Talking of Michelangelo.°

The yellow fog that rubs its back upon the windowpanes,   15
The yellow smoke that rubs its muzzle on the windowpanes
Licked its tongue into the corners of the evening,
Lingered upon the pools that stand in drains,
Let fall upon its back the soot that falls from chimneys,
Slipped by the terrace, made a sudden leap,   20
And seeing that it was a soft October night,
Curled once about the house, and fell asleep.

And indeed there will be time
For the yellow smoke that slides along the street,
Rubbing its back upon the windowpanes;   25
There will be time, there will be time°
To prepare a face to meet the faces that you meet;
There will be time to murder and create,

THE LOVE SONG OF J. ALFRED PRUFROCK. The poem is a monologue spoken by
Prufrock; the name is invented but suggests a businessman.   EPIGRAPH: The Italian
epigraph is quoted from Dante's *Inferno* (Canto 27, lines 61–66) and is spoken by a man
who relates his evil deeds to Dante because he assumes that Dante will never return to the
world: "If I believed that my response were made to a person who would ever revisit the
world, this flame would stand motionless. But since none has ever returned from this
depth alive, if I hear the truth, I answer you without fear of infamy."
14 *Michelangelo:* one of the greatest Italian Renaissance painters and sculptors (1475–1564).
The name suggests that the women are cultured, or at least pretending to be so.
26 *time:* a possible allusion to Andrew Marvell's "To His Coy Mistress" (p. 825).

And time for all the works and days° of hands
That lift and drop a question on your plate;   30
Time for you and time for me,
And time yet for a hundred indecisions,
And for a hundred visions and revisions,
Before the taking of a toast and tea.

In the room the women come and go   35
Talking of Michelangelo.

And indeed there will be time
To wonder, "Do I dare?" and, "Do I dare?"
Time to turn back and descend the stair,
With a bald spot in the middle of my hair—   40
(They will say: "How his hair is growing thin!")
My morning coat, my collar mounting firmly to the chin,
My necktie rich and modest, but asserted by a simple pin—
(They will say: "But how his arms and legs are thin!")
Do I dare   45
Disturb the universe?
In a minute there is time
For decisions and revisions which a minute will reverse.

For I have known them all already, known them all—
Have known the evenings, mornings, afternoons,   50
I have measured out my life with coffee spoons;
I know the voices dying with a dying fall°
Beneath the music from a farther room.
    So how should I presume?

And I have known the eyes already, known them all—   55
The eyes that fix you in a formulated phrase,
And when I am formulated, sprawling on a pin,
When I am pinned and wriggling on the wall,
Then how should I begin
To spit out all the butt-ends of my days and ways?   60
And how should I presume?

And I have known the arms already, known them all—
Arms that are braceleted and white and bare
(But in the lamplight, downed with light brown hair!)
Is it perfume from a dress   65
That makes me so digress?
Arms that lie along a table, or wrap about a shawl.
    And should I then presume?
    And how should I begin?

Shall I say, I have gone at dusk through narrow streets   70
And watched the smoke that rises from the pipes

---

29 *works and days:* the title of a poem about farming by the Greek poet Hesiod. Here the
phrase ironically refers to social gestures.   52 *dying fall:* an allusion to a speech by
Orsino in Shakespeare's *Twelfth Night* (Act I, scene 1, line 4).

Of lonely men in shirt-sleeves, leaning out of windows? . . .

I should have been a pair of ragged claws
Scuttling across the floors of silent seas.

And the afternoon, the evening, sleeps so peacefully!   75
Smoothed by long fingers,
Asleep . . . tired . . . or it malingers,°
Stretched on the floor, here beside you and me.
Should I, after tea and cakes and ices,
Have the strength to force the moment to its crisis?   80
But though I have wept and fasted, wept and prayed,
Though I have seen my head (grown slightly bald) brought in upon a platter,°
I am no prophet—and here's no great matter;
I have seen the moment of my greatness flicker,
And I have seen the eternal Footman hold my coat, and snicker,   85
And in short, I was afraid.

And would it have been worth it, after all,
After the cups, the marmalade, the tea,
Among the porcelain, among some talk of you and me,
Would it have been worth while,   90
To have bitten off the matter with a smile,
To have squeezed the universe into a ball°
To roll it toward some overwhelming question,
To say: "I am Lazarus,° come from the dead,
Come back to tell you all, I shall tell you all"—   95
If one, setting a pillow by her head,
    Should say: "That is not what I meant at all.
    That is not it, at all."

And would it have been worth it, after all,
Would it have been worth while,   100
After the sunsets and the dooryards and the sprinkled streets,
After the novels, after the teacups, after the skirts that trail along the floor—
And this, and so much more?—
It is impossible to say just what I mean!
But as if a magic lantern threw the nerves in patterns on a screen: 105
Would it have been worth while
If one, setting a pillow or throwing off a shawl,
And turning toward the window, should say:
    "That is not it at all,
    That is not what I meant, at all."   110

No! I am not Prince Hamlet,° nor was meant to be;
Am an attendant lord, one that will do
To swell a progress,° start a scene or two,

---

77 *malingers:* pretends to be ill.   82 *platter:* as was the head of John the Baptist; see Mark
6:17–28 and Matthew 14:3–11.   92 *ball:* another allusion to Marvell's "Coy Mistress."
94 *Lazarus:* See John 11:1–44.   111 *Prince Hamlet:* the hero of Shakespeare's play
Hamlet.   113 *swell a progress:* enlarge a royal procession.

Advise the prince; no doubt, an easy tool,
Deferential, glad to be of use,   115
Politic, cautious, and meticulous;
Full of high sentence,° but a bit obtuse;
At times, indeed, almost ridiculous—
Almost, at times, the Fool.

I grow old . . . I grow old . . .   120
I shall wear the bottoms of my trousers rolled.°

Shall I part my hair behind? Do I dare to eat a peach?
I shall wear white flannel trousers, and walk upon the beach.
I have heard the mermaids singing, each to each.

I do not think that they will sing to me.   125

I have seen them riding seaward on the waves
Combing the white hair of the waves blown back
When the wind blows the water white and black.

We have lingered in the chambers of the sea
By sea-girls wreathed with seaweed red and brown   130
Till human voices wake us, and we drown.

117 *sentence:* ideals, opinions, sentiment.   121 *rolled:* a possible reference to cuffs, which
were becoming fashionable in 1910.

JOHN ENGELS (b. 1931)

Naming the Animals   *1981*

Since spring I've seen two deer,
one lashed to a fender. The other fed
in a clearing on the back slope
of Bean Hill, his big rack° still   *antlers*
in velvet. The shot buck bled,   5

its tongue frozen
to the rusty hood.
But the other, in its simpler stance,
felt merely the delicate itch
of antler skin.   10

And three does, mildly alert,
cocked ears toward where I watched from
in the hemlocks. I saw, of course,
five deer; but I
count only what by plain necessity of death   15

or feeding is oblivious to me,
does not watch back.

MARI EVANS (b. 1923)

I Am a Black Woman   *1970*

I am a black woman
the music of my song
some sweet arpeggio of tears
is written in a minor key
and I   5
can be heard humming in the night
Can be heard
   humming
in the night

I saw my mate leap screaming to the sea   10
and I/with these hands/cupped the lifebreath
from my issue in the canebrake
I lost Nat's swinging body° in a rain of tears

and heard my son scream all the way from Anzio°
for Peace he never knew.... I   15
learned Da Nang° and Pork Chop Hill°
in anguish
Now my nostrils know the gas
and these trigger tire/d fingers
seek the softness in my warrior's beard   20

I
am a black woman
tall as a cypress
strong
beyond all definition still   25
defying place
and time
and circumstance
   assailed
      impervious   30
         indestructible

Look
   on me and be
renewed

I AM A BLACK WOMAN.   13 *Nat's swinging body:* Nat Turner was hanged in 1831 for
leading a slave revolt in Southampton, Virginia.   14 *Anzio:* seacoast town in Italy, the
scene of fierce fighting between the Allies and the Germans in 1944 during World War II.
16 *Da Nang:* major American military base in South Vietnam, frequently attacked during
the Vietnam War.   *Pork Chop Hill:* site of a bloody battle between U.N. and Communist
forces during the Korean War (1950–1953).

CAROLYN FORCHÉ (b. 1950)

Because One Is Always Forgotten   *1981*

IN MEMORIAM, JOSÉ RUDOLFO VIERA
1939–1981: EL SALVADOR

When Viera was buried we knew it had come to an end,
his coffin rocking into the ground like a boat or a cradle.

I could take my heart, he said, and give it to a *campesino*°   peasant
and he would cut it up and give it back:

you can't eat heart in those four dark   5
chambers where a man can be kept years.

A boy soldier in the bone-hot sun works his knife
to peel the face from a dead man

and hang it from the branch of a tree
flowering with such faces.   10

The heart is the toughest part of the body.
Tenderness is in the hands.

DAN GEORGAKAS (b. 1938)

Hiroshima Crewman   *1969*

Somewhere in California
his body humbled by a hair shirt,
a vow of silence on his lips,
a Hiroshima crewman tries to find a life.
If he should ever choose to break his peace,   5
he might speak of death by fire
no Nazi ordered; he might tell how
war produces many brands of
Auschwitz soap and Dachau lampshade.

NIKKI GIOVANNI (b. 1943)

Woman   *1978*

she wanted to be a blade
of grass amid the fields
but he wouldn't agree
to be the dandelion

she wanted to be a robin singing   5
through the leaves

but he refused to be
her tree

she spun herself into a web
  and looking for a place to rest
turned to him
but he stood straight
declining to be her corner

                                    10

she tried to be a book
but he wouldn't read
she turned herself into a bulb
but he wouldn't let her grow

                                    15

she decided to become
a woman
and though he still refused
to be a man
she decided it was all
right

                                    20

MARILYN HACKER   (b. 1942)

Sonnet Ending with a Film Subtitle   *1979*

For Judith Landry

Life has its nauseating ironies:
The good die young, as often has been shown;
Chaste spouses catch Venereal Disease;
And feminists sit by the telephone.
Last night was rather bleak, tonight is starker.   5
I may stare at the wall till half-past-one.
My friends are all convinced Dorothy Parker
Lives, but is not well, in Marylebone.°   *a district in London*
I wish that I could imitate my betters
And fortify my rhetoric with guns.   10
Some day we women all will break our fetters
And raise our daughters to be Lesbians.
(I wonder if the bastard kept my letters?)
Here follow untranslatable French puns.

JOHN HAINES   (b. 1936)

Little Cosmic Dust Poem   *1985*

Out of the debris of dying stars,
this rain of particles
that waters the waste with brightness;

the sea-wave of atoms hurrying home,
collapse of the giant,
unstable guest who cannot stay;   5

the sun's heart reddens and expands,
his mighty aspiration is lasting,
as the shell of his substance
one day will be white with frost.   10

In the radiant field of Orion°
great hordes of stars are forming,
just as we see every night,
fiery and faithful to the end.

Out of the cold and fleeing dust   15
that is never and always,
the silence and waste to come—

this arm, this hand,
my voice, your face, this love.

LITTLE COSMIC DUST POEM. 11 *Orion:* a prominent winter constellation. Recent
observations have led scientists to conclude that stars are being formed in the nebulous
area in the "sword" of the constellation.

DONALD HALL (b. 1928)

Scenic View   *1981*

Every year the mountains
get paler and more distant—
trees less green, rock piles
disappearing—as emulsion
from a billion Kodaks   5
sucks color out.
In fifteen years
Monadnock and Kearsarge,
the Green Mountains
and the White, will turn   10
invisible, all
tint removed
atom by atom to albums
in Medford and Greenwich,
while over the valleys   15
the still intractable granite
rears with unseeable peaks
fatal to airplanes.

DANIEL HALPERN   (b. 1945)

Snapshot of Hue   *1982*

For Robert Stone

They are riding bicycles on the other side
of the Perfume River.

A few months ago the bridges were down
and there was no one on the streets.

There were the telling piles on corners,   5
debris that contained a little of everything.

There was nothing not under cover—
even the sky remained impenetrable

day after day. And if you were seen
on the riverbank you were knocked down.   10

It is clear today. The litter in the streets
has been swept away. It couldn't have been

that bad, one of us said, the river barely moving,
the bicycles barely moving, the sun posted above.

H. S. (SAM) HAMOD   (b. 1936)

Leaves   *1973*
(for Sally)

Tonight, Sally and I are making stuffed
grapeleaves, we get out a package, it's
drying out, I've been saving it in the freezer, it's
one of the last things my father ever picked in this
life—they're over five years old   5
and up to now
we just kept finding packages of them in the
freezer, as if he were still picking them
somewhere packing them
carefully to send to us   10
making sure they didn't break into pieces.
                            ***

"To my Dar Garnchildn
Davd and Lura
from Thr Jido"
twisted on tablet paper   15
between the lines
in this English lettering
hard for him even to print,

I keep this small torn record,
this piece of paper stays in the upstairs storage,
one of the few pieces of American
my father ever wrote. We find his Arabic letters
all over the place, even in the files we find
letters to him in English, one I found from Charles Atlas
telling him, in 1932,
"Of course, Mr. Hamod, you too can build
your muscles like mine . . ."

       ***

Last week my mother told me, when I was
asking why I became a poet, "But don't you remember,
your father made up poems, don't you remember him
singing in the car as we drove—those were poems."
Even now, at night, I sometimes
get out the Arabic grammar book
though it seems so late.

FRANCES E. W. HARPER (1825–1911)

She's Free!

1854

How say that by law we may torture and chase
A woman whose crime is the hue of her face?—
With her step on the ice, and her arm on her child,
The danger was fearful, the pathway was wild. . . .
But she's free! yes, free from the land where the slave,
From the hand of oppression, must rest in the grave;
Where bondage and blood, where scourges and chains,
Have placed on our banner indelible stains. . . .

The bloodhounds have miss'd the scent of her way,
The hunter is rifled and foiled of his prey,
The cursing of men and clanking of chains
Make sounds of strange discord on Liberty's plains. . . .
Oh! poverty, danger and death she can brave,
For the child of her love is no longer a slave.

MICHAEL S. HARPER (b. 1938)

Called

1975

Digging the grave
through black dirt,
gravel and rocks
that will hold her down,
we speak of her heat

which has driven her out
over the highway
in her first year.

A fly glides from her mouth
as we take her four legs,   10
and the great white neck
muddled at the lakeside
bends gracefully into the arc
of her tongue, colorless, now,
and we set her in the bed   15
of earth and rock
which will hold her as the sun
sets over her shoulders.

You had spoken of her brother,
100 lbs or more,   20
and her slight frame
from the diet of chain
she had broken;
on her back
as the spade cools her brow   25
with black dirt, rocks,
sand, white tongue,
what pups does she hold
that are seeds unspayed
in her broken body;   30
what does her brother say
to the seed gone out over
the prairie, on the hunt
of the unreturned:
and what do we say   35
to the master of the dog dead,
heat, highway, this bed
on the shoulder
of the road west
where her brother called, calls   40

ROBERT HAYDEN   (b. 1913)

Those Winter Sundays   *1962*

Sundays too my father got up early
and put his clothes on in the blueblack cold,
then with cracked hands that ached
from labor in the weekday weather made
banked fires blaze. No one ever thanked him.   5

I'd wake and hear the cold splintering, breaking,
When the rooms were warm, he'd call,
and slowly I would rise and dress,
fearing the chronic angers of that house,

Speaking indifferently to him,   10
who had driven out the cold
and polished my good shoes as well.
What did I know, what did I know
of love's austere and lonely offices?

roles, duties

SEAMUS HEANEY (b. 1939)

Valediction   *1966*

Lady with the frilled blouse
And simple tartan skirt,
Since you have left the house
Its emptiness has hurt
All thought. In your presence   5
Time rode easy, anchored
On a smile; but absence
Rocked love's balance, unmoored
The days. They buck and bound
Across the calendar   10
Pitched from the quiet sound
Of your flower-tender
Voice. Need breaks on my strand;
You've gone, I am at sea.
Until you resume command   15
Self is in mutiny.

GEORGE HERBERT (1593–1633)

Love (III)°   *1633*

Love bade me welcome: yet my soul drew back,
    Guilty of dust and sin.
But quick-eyed Love, observing me grow slack
    From my first entrance in,
Drew nearer to me, sweetly questioning   5
    If I lacked° anything.

LOVE (III). cf. I John 4:8: "He that loveth not knoweth not God; for God is love."
6 *lacked:* wanted; the phrase is a standard question asked by innkeepers.

"A guest," I answered, "worthy to be here":
 Love said, "You shall be he."
"I, the unkind, ungrateful? Ah, my dear,
 I cannot look on thee."   10
Love took my hand, and smiling did reply,
 "Who made the eyes but I?"

"Truth, Lord; but I have marred them; let my shame
 Go where it doth deserve."
"And know you not," says Love, "who bore the blame?"   15
 "My dear, then I will serve."
"You must sit down," says Love, "and taste my meat."°
 So I did sit and eat.

17 *and taste my meat:* Job 12:11: "Doth not the ear try words? and the mouth taste his
meat?" Here, meat refers to food in general.   17–18 *You must sit down . . . eat:* Luke 13:37:
"Blessed are those servants, whom the Lord when he cometh shall find watching: verily I
say unto you, that he shall gird himself, and make them to sit down to meat, and will come
forth and serve them."

ROBERT HERRICK (1591–1674)

Corinna's Going A-Maying   *1648*

Get up! get up for shame! the blooming morn
Upon her wings presents the god unshorn°   *Apollo, god of the sun*
 See how Aurora° throws her fair   *Roman goddess of dawn*
 Fresh-quilted colors through the air:
 Get up, sweet slug-a-bed, and see   5
 The dew bespangling herb and tree.
Each flower has wept and bowed toward the east
Above an hour since, yet you not dressed;
 Nay, not so much as out of bed?
 When all the birds have matins° said,   *morning prayers* 10
 And sung their thankful hymns, 'tis sin,
 Nay, profanation to keep in,
Whenas a thousand virgins on this day
Spring, sooner than the lark, to fetch in May.°   *May Day*

Rise, and put on your foliage, and be seen   15
To come forth, like the springtime, fresh and green,
 And sweet as Flora.° Take no care   *Roman goddess of flowers*
 For jewels for your gown or hair;
 Fear not; the leaves will strew
 Gems in abundance upon you;   20
Besides, the childhood of the days has kept,
Against you come, some orient° pearls unwept;   *eastern*
 Come and receive them while the light
 Hangs on the dew-locks of the night,

And Titan° on the eastern hill   *the sun*   25
   Retires himself, or else stands still
Till you come forth. Wash, dress, be brief in praying:
Few beads° are best when once we go a-Maying.   *prayers, rosaries*

Come, my Corinna, come; and, coming, mark°   *note*
How each field turns° a street, each street a park   *turns into*   30
   Made green and trimmed with trees: see how
   Devotion gives each house a bough
   Or branch: each porch, each door ere this,
   An ark, a tabernacle is,
Made up of whitethorn neatly interwove,   35
As if here were those cooler shades of love.
   Can such delights be in the street
   And open fields, and we not see 't?
   Come, we'll abroad; and let's obey
   The proclamation made for May,   40
And sin no more, as we have done, by staying;
But, my Corinna, come, let's go a-Maying.

There's not a budding boy or girl this day
But is got up and gone to bring in May;
   A deal° of youth, ere this, is come   *great many*   45
   Back, and with whitethorn laden home.
   Some have dispatched their cakes and cream
   Before that we have left to dream;
And some have wept, and wooed, and plighted troth,
And chose their priest, ere we can cast off sloth.   50
   Many a green-gown° has been given,   *green with grass stains*
   Many a kiss, both odd and even;
   Many a glance, too, has been sent
   From out the eye, love's firmament;
Many a jest told of the keys betraying   55
This night, and locks picked; yet we're not a-Maying.

Come, let us go while we are in our prime,
And take the harmless folly of the time.
   We shall grow old apace, and die
   Before we know our liberty.
   Our life is short, and our days run   60
   As fast away as does the sun;
And, as a vapor or a drop of rain
Once lost, can ne'er be found again;
   So when or you or I are made
   A fable, song, or fluting shade,   65
   All love; all liking, all delight
   Lies drowned with us in endless night.
Then while time serves, and we are but decaying,
Come, my Corinna, come, let's go a-Maying.   70

ROBERTA HILL (b. 1947)

Dream of Rebirth   *1970*

We stand on the edge of wounds, hugging canned meat,
waiting for owls to come grind
nightsmell in our ears. Over fields,
darkness has been rumbling. Crows gather.
Our luxuries are hatred. Grief. Worn-out hands   5
carry the pale remains of forgotten murders.
If I could only lull or change this slow hunger,
this midnight swollen four hundred years.

Groping within us are cries yet unheard.
We are born with cobwebs in our mouths   10
bleeding with prophecies.
Yet within this interior, a spirit kindles
moonlight glittering deep into the sea.
These seeds take root in the hush
of dusk. Songs, a thin echo, heal the salted marsh,   15
and yield visions untrembling in our grip.

GERARD MANLEY HOPKINS (1844–1889)

The Windhover°   *1918 (1877)*

To Christ Our Lord

I caught this morning morning's minion,° king-   *darling*
    dom of daylight's dauphin,° dapple-dawn-drawn Falcon, in his riding
   Of the rolling level underneath him steady air, and striding
High there, how he rung upon the rein of a wimpling wing
In his ecstasy! then off, off forth on swing,   5
   As a skate's heel sweeps smooth on a bow-bend: the hurl and gliding
   Rebuffed the big wind. My heart in hiding
Stirred for a bird,—the achieve of, the mastery of the thing!

Brute beauty and valour and act, oh, air, pride, plume, here
   Buckle!° AND the fire that breaks from thee then, a billion   *join*   10
Times told lovelier, more dangerous. O my chevalier!°   *knight*

   No wonder of it: shéer plód makes plough down sillion°
Shine, and blue-beak embers, ah my dear,
   Fall, gall themselves, and gash gold-vermilion.

THE WINDHOVER: The title refers to a kestrel or falcon that glides or hovers in the wind.   2 *dauphin:* prince, heir to the throne of France.   12 *sillion:* the ridge of earth between two plowed furrows in a field.

GERARD MANLEY HOPKINS (1844–1889)

Pied Beauty

(1918) 1877

Glory be to God for dappled things—
　For skies of couple-colour as a brinded cow;
　　For rose-moles all in stipple upon trout that swim;
Fresh-firecoal chestnut-falls;° finches' wings;
　Landscape plotted and pieced°—fold,° fallow,° and plough;
　　And áll trádes, their gear and tackle and trim.

All things counter,° original, spare,° strange;
　Whatever is fickle, freckled (who knows how?)
　　With swift, slow; sweet, sour; adazzle, dim;
He fathers-forth whose beauty is past change:
　　　　　　Praise him.

PIED BEAUTY.　　4 *Chestnut-falls:* the meat of a roasted chestnut.　　5 *pieced:* divided
into fields of different colors, depending on the crops or use.　　*fold:* an enclosed field for
animals. *fallow:* a plowed but unplanted field.　　7 *counter:* opposed, as in contrasting
patterns. *spare:* rare.

JULIA WARD HOWE (1819–1910)

Battle Hymn of the Republic

1862

Mine eyes have seen the glory of the coming of the Lord;
He is trampling out the vintage where the grapes of wrath are stored:
He hath loosed the fateful lightning of His terrible swift sword;
　His truth is marching on!
　　Glory! glory! hallelujah!
　　Glory! glory! hallelujah!
　　Glory! glory! hallelujah!
　　　Our God is marching on!

I have seen Him in the watch-fire of a hundred circling camps,
They have builded Him an altar in the evening dews and damps;
I can read His righteous sentence by the dim and flaring lamps;
　His day is marching on!
　　Glory! etc.

I have read a fiery gospel writ in burnished rows of steel:
"As ye deal with my contemners so with you my grace shall deal!"
Let the Hero born of woman crush the serpent with his heel,
　Since God is marching on!
　　Glory! etc.

He has sounded forth the trumpet that shall never call retreat;
He is sifting out the hearts of men before His judgment seat;

Oh! be swift, my soul, to answer Him, be jubilant, my feet!
  Our God is marching on!
    Glory! etc.

In the beauty of the lilies Christ was born across the sea,
With a glory in his bosom that transfigures you and me;   25
As he died to make men holy, let us die to make men free.
  While God is marching on!
    Glory! etc.

LANGSTON HUGHES (1902–1967)

Negro   *1958*

I am a Negro:
  Black as the night is black,
  Black like the depths of my Africa.

I've been a slave:
  Caesar told me to keep his door-steps clean.   5
  I brushed the boots of Washington.

I've been a worker:
  Under my hand the pyramids arose.
  I made mortar for the Woolworth Building.

I've been a singer: 10
  All the way from Africa to Georgia
  I carried my sorrow songs.
  I made ragtime.

I've been a victim:
  The Belgians cut off my hands in the Congo.   15
  They lynch me still in Mississippi.

I am a Negro:
  Black as the night is black,
  Black like the depths of my Africa.

ROBINSON JEFFERS (1887–1962)

The Answer   *1937*

Then what is the answer?—Not to be deluded by dreams.
To know that great civilizations have broken down into violence, and their tyrants
  come, many times before.

When open violence appears, to avoid it with honor or choose the least ugly
    faction; these evils are essential.
To keep one's own integrity, be merciful and uncorrupted and not wish for evil;
    and not be duped
By dreams of universal justice or happiness. These dreams will not be fulfilled.   5
To know this, and know that however ugly the parts appear the whole remains
    beautiful. A severed hand
Is an ugly thing, and man dissevered from the earth and stars and his history
    . . . for contemplation or in fact . . .

Often appears atrociously ugly. Integrity is wholeness, the greatest beauty is
Organic wholeness, the wholeness of life and things, the divine beauty of the
    universe. Love that, not man
Apart from that, or else you will share man's pitiful confusions, or drown in
    despair   10
    when his days darken.

CAROLYN KIZER (b. 1925)

Night Sounds   *1984*

imitated from the Chinese

The moonlight on my bed keeps me awake;
Living alone now, aware of the voices of evening,
A child weeping at nightmares, the faint love-cries of a woman,
Everything tinged by terror or nostalgia.

No heavy, impassive back to nudge with one foot   5
While coaxing, "Wake up and hold me,"
When the moon's creamy beauty is transformed
Into a map of impersonal desolation.

But, restless in this mock dawn of moonlight
That so chills the spirit, I alter our history: 10
You were never able to lie quite peacefully at my side,
Not the night through. Always withholding something.

Awake before morning, restless and uneasy,
Trying not to disturb me, you would leave my bed
While I lay there rigidly, feigning sleep.   15
Still—the night was nearly over, the light not as cold
As a full cup of moonlight.

And there were the lovely times when, to the skies' cold *No*
You cried to me, *Yes!* Impaled me with affirmation.
Now when I call out in fear, not in love, there is no answer.   20
Nothing speaks in the dark but the distant voices,
A child with the moon on his face, a dog's hollow cadence.

ETHERIDGE KNIGHT   (b. 1933)

Haiku°   *1968*

1

Eastern guard tower
glints in sunset; convicts rest
like lizards on rocks.

2

The piano man
is sting at 3 am   5
his songs drop like plum.

3

Morning sun slants cell.
Drunks stagger like cripple flies
On Jailhouse floor.

4

To write a blues song   10
is to regiment riots
and pluck gems from graves.

5

A bare pecan tree
slips a pencil shadow down
a moonlit snow slope.   15

6

The falling snow flakes
Can not blunt the hard aches nor
Match the steel stillness.

7

Under moon shadows
A tall boy flashes knife and   20
Slices star bright ice.

8

In the August grass
Struck by the last rays of sun
The cracked teacup screams.

9

Making jazz swing in   25
Seventeen syllables AIN'T
No square poet's job.

HAIKU. The haiku is a Japanese lyric verse form consisting of three lines that total
seventeen syllables, divided 5-7-5. See the discussion on p. 729.

MAXINE KUMIN   (b. 1925)

Woodchucks   *1972*

Gassing the woodchucks didn't turn out right.
The knockout bomb from the Feed and Grain Exchange
was featured as merciful, quick at the bone
and the case we had against them was airtight,
both exits shoehorned shut with puddingstone,   5
but they had a sub-sub-basement out of range.

Next morning they turned up again, no worse
for the cyanide than we for our cigarettes
and state-store Scotch, all of us up to scratch.
They brought down the marigolds as a matter of course   10
and then took over the vegetable patch
nipping the broccoli shoots, beheading the carrots.

The food from our mouths, I said, righteously thrilling
to the feel of the .22, the bullet's neat noses.
I, a lapsed pacifist fallen from grace   15
puffed with Darwinian pieties° for killing,
now drew a bead on the littlest woodchuck's face.
He died down in the everbearing roses.

Ten minutes later I dropped the mother. She
flipflopped in the air and fell, her needle teeth   20
still hooked in a leaf of early Swiss chard.
Another baby next. O one-two-three
the murderer inside me rose up hard,
the hawkeye killer came on stage forthwith.

There's one chuck left. Old wily fellow, he keeps   25
me cocked and ready day after day after day.
All night I hunt his humped-up form. I dream
I sight along the barrel in my sleep.
If only they'd all consented to die unseen
gassed underground the quiet Nazi way.°   30

WOODCHUCKS.   16 *Darwinian pieties:* Charles Darwin (1809–1892) was a British
naturalist who formulated the theory of evolution; the piety is "survival of the fittest."
30 *gassed . . . way:* a reference to the extermination of millions of people in gas chambers
by the Nazis during World War II.

JOANNE KYGER   (b. 1934)

Destruction   *1980*

First of all do you remember the way a bear goes through
a cabin when nobody is home? He goes through
the front door. I mean he really goes *through* it. Then

he takes the cupboard off the wall and eats a can of lard.

He eats all the apples, limes, dates, bottled decaffeinated   5
coffee, and 35 pounds of granola. The asparagus soup cans
fall to the floor. Yum! He chomps up Norwegian crackers
stashed for the winter. And the bouillon, salt, pepper,
paprika, garlic, onions, potatoes.

                              He rips the Green Tara   10
poster from the wall. Tries the Coleman Mustard, spills
the ink, tracks in the flour. Goes up stairs and takes
a shit. Rips open the water bed, eats the incense and
drinks the perfume. Knocks over the Japanese tansu
and the Persian miniature of a man on horseback watching   15
a woman bathing.

                    Knocks *Shelter, Whole Earth Catalogue,*
Planet Drum, Northern Mists, Truck Tracks, and
Women's Sports into the oozing water bed mess.

                               He goes   20
down stairs and out the back wall. He keeps on going
for a long way and finds a good cave to sleep it all off.
Luckily he ate the whole medicine cabinet, including stash
of LSD, Peyote, Psilocybin, Amanita, Benzedrine, Valium
and aspirin.   25

IRVING LAYTON   (b. 1912)

Rhine Boat Trip°   1977

The castles on the Rhine
are all haunted
by the ghosts of Jewish mothers
looking for their ghostly children

And the clusters of grapes   5
in the sloping vineyards
are myriads of blinded eyes
staring at the blind sun

The tireless Lorelei°
can never comb from their hair   10
the crimson beards
of murdered rabbis

RHINE BOAT TRIP: The title refers to the Rhine River, which flows through Germany.
9 *Lorelei:* legendary seductive nymphs who lived in the cliffs overlooking the Rhine, and
whose singing lured sailors to shipwreck.

However sweetly they sing
one hears only
the low wailing of cattle-cars°   15
moving invisibly across the land

15 *cattle-cars:* railroad cars designed to transport cattle but used by the Nazis to transport
Jews from the cities of Europe to extermination camps.

DON L. LEE (b. 1942)

Change Is Not Always Progress (for Africa & Africans)   1970

Africa.

don't let them
steal
your face   or
take your circles   5
and make them squares.

don't let them
steel
your body   as to put
100 stories of concrete on you   10

so that you
            arrogantly
scrape
the

sky.   15

ALAN P. LIGHTMAN (b. 1948)

In Computers   1982 (1981)

In the magnets of computers will
   be stored

   Blend of sunset over wheat
      fields.
   Low thunder of gazelle.   5
   Light, sweet wind on high
      ground.
   Vacuum stillness spreading from
      a thick snowfall.

Men will sit in rooms   10
upon the smooth, scrubbed earth

or stand in tunnels on the moon
and instruct themselves in how it
    was.
Nothing will be lost.   15
Nothing will be lost.

RICHARD LOVELACE   (1618–1657)

To Lucasta, Going to the Wars   *1649*

Tell me not, Sweet, I am unkind
That from the nunnery
Of thy chaste breast and quiet mind,
To war and arms I fly.

True, a new mistress now I chase,   5
The first foe in the field;
And with a stronger faith embrace
A sword, a horse, a shield.

Yet this inconstancy is such
As you too shall adore;   10
I could not love thee, Dear, so much,
Loved I not honor more.

AMY LOWELL   (1874–1925)

Patterns   *1916*

I walk down the garden paths,
And all the daffodils
Are blowing, and the bright blue squills.
I walk down the patterned garden-paths
In my stiff, brocaded gown.   5
With my powdered hair and jewelled fan,
I too am a rare
Pattern. As I wander down
The garden paths.
My dress is richly figured,   10
And the train
Makes a pink and silver stain
On the gravel, and the thrift
Of the borders.
Just a plate of current fashion   15
Tripping by in high-heeled, ribboned shoes.
Not a softness anywhere about me,

Only whalebone° and brocade.
And I sink on a seat in the shade
Of a lime tree. For my passion   20
Wars against the stiff brocade.
The daffodils and squills
Flutter in the breeze
As they please.
And I weep;   25
For the lime-tree is in blossom
And one small flower has dropped upon my bosom.

And the plashing of waterdrops
In the marble fountain
Comes down the garden-paths.   30
The dripping never stops.
Underneath my stiffened gown
Is the softness of a woman bathing in a marble basin,
A basin in the midst of hedges grown
So thick, she cannot see her lover hiding,   35
But she guesses he is near,
And the sliding of the water
Seems the stroking of a dear
Hand upon her.
What is Summer in a fine brocaded gown!   40
I should like to see it lying in a heap upon the ground.
All the pink and silver crumpled up on the ground.

I would be the pink and silver as I ran along the paths,
And he would stumble after,
Bewildered by my laughter.   45
I should see the sun flashing from his sword-hilt and buckles on his shoes.
I would choose
To lead him in a maze along the patterned paths,
A bright and laughing maze for my heavy-booted lover.
Till he caught me in the shade,   50
And the buttons of his waistcoat bruised my body as he clasped me,
Aching, melting, unafraid.
With the shadows of the leaves and the sundrops,
And the plopping of the waterdrops,
All about us in the open afternoon—   55
I am very like to swoon
With the weight of this brocade,
For the sun sifts through the shade.

Underneath the fallen blossom
In my bosom,   60
Is a letter I have hid.

PATTERNS.   18 *whalebone:* Bones from whales were used to make extremely rigid
corsets for women.

It was brought to me this morning by a rider from the Duke.
Madam, we regret to inform you that Lord Hartwell
Died in action Thursday se'nnight.°
As I read it in the white, morning sunlight,   65
The letters squirmed like snakes.
"Any answer, Madam," said my footman.
"No," I told him.
"See that the messenger takes some refreshment.

No, no answer."   70
And I walked into the garden,
Up and down the patterned paths,
In my stiff, correct brocade.
The blue and yellow flowers stood up proudly in the sun,
Each one.   75
I stood upright too,
Held rigid to the pattern
By the stiffness of my gown.
Up and down I walked.
Up and down.   80

In a month he would have been my husband.
In a month, here, underneath this lime,
We would have broken the pattern;
He for me, and I for him,
He as Colonel, I as Lady,   85
On this shady seat.
He had a whim
That sunlight carried blessing.
And I answered, "It shall be as you have said."
Now he is dead.   90

In Summer and In Winter I shall walk
Up and down
The patterned garden-paths
In my stiff, brocaded gown.
The squills and daffodils   95
Will give peace to pillared roses, and to asters, and to snow.
I shall go
Up and down,
In my gown.
Gorgeously arrayed,   100
Boned and stayed.
And the softness of my body will be guarded from embrace
By each button, hook, and lace.
For the man who should loose me is dead,

64 *se'nnight:* seven nights, hence a week ago.

Fighting with the Duke in Flanders,° 105
In a pattern called a war.
Christ! What are patterns for?

105 *Flanders:* a place of frequent warfare in Belgium. The speaker's clothing (lines 5, 6) suggests the time of the Duke of Marlborough's Flanders campaigns of 1702–1710. The Battle of Waterloo (1815) was also fought nearby under the Duke of Wellington. During World War I, fierce fighting against the Germans occurred in Flanders in 1914 and 1915, with great loss of life.

ROBERT LOWELL (1917–1977)

For the Union Dead° *1960*

"Relinquunt omnia servare rem publicam."°

The old South Boston Aquarium stands
in a Sahara of snow now. Its broken windows are boarded.
The bronze weathervane cod has lost half its scales.
The airy tanks are dry.

Once my nose crawled like a snail on the glass; 5
my hand tingled
to burst the bubbles
drifting from noses of the cowed, compliant fish.

My hand draws back. I often sigh still
for the dark downward and vegetating kingdom 10
of the fish and reptile. One morning last March,
I pressed against the new barbed and galvanized

fence on the Boston Common. Behind their cage,
yellow dinosaur steamshovels were grunting
as they cropped up tons of mush and grass 15
to gouge their underworld garage.

Parking spaces luxuriate like civic
sandpiles in the heart of Boston.
A girdle of orange, Puritan-pumpkin colored girders
braces the tingling Statehouse, 20

FOR THE UNION DEAD: The poem was first published in 1959 with the title, "Colonel Shaw and the Massachusetts 54th." Robert Gould Shaw (1837–1863) was the commander of the first regiment of blacks formed in the Union to fight in the Civil War. He was killed leading an attack at Fort Wagner in South Carolina. The "Civil War relief" in bronze described in the poem was sculpted by Augustus Saint-Gaudens (1848–1907), dedicated in 1897, and stands on the Boston Common (a central park or green) across from the Massachusetts State House. EPIGRAPH: The Latin epigraph inscribed on the sculpture means, "They give up everything to serve the republic."

shaking over the excavations, as it faces Colonel Shaw
and his bell-cheeked Negro infantry
on St. Gaudens' shaking Civil War relief,
propped by a plank splint against the garage's earthquake.

Two months after marching through Boston,   25
half the regiment was dead;
at the dedication,
William James° could almost hear the bronze Negroes breathe.

Their monument sticks like a fishbone
in the city's throat.   30
Its Colonel is as lean
as a compass-needle.

He has an angry wrenlike vigilance,
a greyhound's gentle tautness;
he seems to wince at pleasure,   35
and suffocate for privacy.

He is out of bounds now. He rejoices in man's lovely,
peculiar power to choose life and die—
when he leads his black soldiers to death,
he cannot bend his back.   40

On a thousand small town New England greens,
the old white churches hold their air
of sparse, sincere rebellion; frayed flags
quilt the graveyards of the Grand Army of the Republic.°

The stone statues of the abstract Union Soldier   45
grow slimmer and younger each year—
wasp-waisted, they doze over muskets
and muse through their sideburns . . .

Shaw's father wanted no monument
except the ditch,   50
where his son's body was thrown
and lost with his "niggers."

The ditch is nearer.
There are no statues for the last war° here;
on Boylston Street,° a commercial photograph   55
shows Hiroshima° boiling

over a Mosler Safe, the "Rock of Ages"
that survived the blast. Space is nearer.

28 *William James:* American philosopher and psychologist (1842–1910) who taught at
Harvard.   44 *Grand Army of the Republic:* an organization, founded in 1866, of men who
served in the Union Army and Navy.   54 *last war:* World War II.
55 *Boylston Street:* a street in Boston.   56 *Hiroshima:* Japanese city on which the United
States dropped the first atomic bomb during World War II on August 6, 1945.

Where I crouch to my television set,
the drained faces of Negro school-children rise like balloons.   60

Colonel Shaw
is riding on his bubble,
he waits
for the blesséd break.

The Aquarium is gone. Everywhere,   65
giant finned cars nose forward like fish;
a savage servility
slides by on grease.

CYNTHIA MACDONALD   (b. 1928)

The Lobster   *1980*

This lobster flown in from Maine to Houston
Lies in a wooden box on cracked ice.
Its green not the green of deep water,
But of decay. Its stalk eyes, which should be
Grains of black caviar, are beads of phlegm.   5
Through the cracks in its shell, the meat
Shines like oil on water or mother-of-pearl.

I see exactly what it is, yet must wrap it up
In my finest linen handkerchief—the one with
The border and initials pulled by Filipino nuns—   10
And take it home to keep in my bureau drawer;
So that its smell invades my private places,
And lobster mold begins to form on the edges of fabrics.

I throw open the doors and jalousies, hoping to
Dilute the crustacean air, and you walk in. I had not   15
Expected to see you again: we had decided.
We inventory everything and redecide: you will stay.
The lobster, smooth and green as deep water, is
Crawling over the blue silk scarf when we
Open the drawer. We cook it for dinner,   20
In water laved with peppercorns and fennel, and spread
A sheet on the table, anticipating the complete repast.

CLAUDE MCKAY   (1890–1948)

The White City   *1922*

I will not toy with it nor bend an inch.
Deep in the secret chambers of my heart
I muse my life-long hate, and without flinch

I bear it nobly as I live my part.
My being would be a skeleton, a shell,   5
If this dark Passion that fills my every mood,
And makes my heaven in the white world's hell,
Did not forever feed me vital blood.
I see the mighty city through a mist—
The strident trains that speed the goaded mass,   10
The poles and spires and towers vapor-kissed,
The fortressed port through which the great ships pass,
The tides, the wharves, the dens I contemplate,
Are sweet like wanton loves because I hate.

EDNA ST. VINCENT MILLAY   (1892–1950)

What Lips My Lips Have Kissed, and Where, and Why   *1923*

What lips my lips have kissed, and where, and why,
I have forgotten, and what arms have lain
Under my head till morning; but the rain
Is full of ghosts tonight, that tap and sigh
Upon the glass and listen for reply,   5
And in my heart there stirs a quiet pain
For unremembered lads that not again
Will turn to me at midnight with a cry.
Thus in the winter stands the lonely tree,
Nor knows what birds have vanished one by one,   10
Yet knows it boughs more silent than before:
I cannot say what loves have come and gone,
I only know that summer sang in me
A little while, that in me sings no more.

VASSAR MILLER   (b. 1924)

Loneliness   *1963*

So deep is this silence
that the insects, the birds,
the talk of the neighbors in the distance,
the whir of the traffic, the music
are only its voices   5
and do not contradict it.

So deep is this crying
that the silence, the hush,
the quiet, the stillness, the not speaking,
the never hearing a word   10
are only the surge
of its innumerable waters.

This silence, this crying,
O my God, is my country
with Yours the sole footstep besides my own.   15
Save me amid its landscapes
so terrible, strange
I am almost in love with them!

JOHN MILTON   (1608–1674)

O Nightingale!   *1630*

O Nightingale, that on yon bloomy Spray
  Warbl'st at eve, when all the Woods are still,
  Thou with fresh hope the Lover's heart dost fill,
  While the jolly hours lead on propitious *May*
Thy liquid notes that close the eye of Day,   5
  First heard before the shallow Cuckoo's bill,
  Portend success in love; O, if *Jove's* will
  Have linkt that amorous power to thy soft lay,
Now timely sing, ere the rude Bird of Hate
  Foretell my hopeless doom in some Grove nigh: 10
  As thou from year to year hast sung too late
For my relief; yet hadst no reason why.
  Whether the Muse, or Love call thee his mate,
  Both them I serve, and of their train am I.

THOMAS MOORE   (1779–1852)

Believe Me, If All Those Endearing Young Charms   *1834*

Believe me, if all those endearing young charms,
  Which I gaze on so fondly to-day,
Were to change by tomorrow, and fleet° in my arms,   *vanish*
  Like fairy gifts fading away!
Thou wouldst still be adored, as this moment thou art,   5
  Let thy loveliness fade as it will,
And around the dear ruin each wish of my heart
  Would entwine itself verdantly still.

It is not while beauty and youth are thine own,
  And thy cheeks unprofaned by a tear,   10
That the fervor and faith of a soul may be known,
  To which time will but make thee more dear!
Oh the heart that has truly loved never forgets,
  But as truly loves on to the close,
As the sunflower turns to her god when he sets   15
  The same look which she turned when he rose!

OGDEN NASH   (1902–1971)

Very Like a Whale°   1934

One thing that literature would be greatly the better for
Would be a more restricted employment by authors of simile and metaphor.
Authors of all races, be they Greeks, Romans, Teutons or Celts,
Can't seem just to say that anything is the thing it is but have to go out of their
    way to say that it is like something else.
What does it mean when we are told   5
That the Assyrian came down like a wolf on the fold?
In the first place, George Gordon Byron° had had enough experience
To know that it probably wasn't just one Assyrian, it was a lot of Assyrians.
However, as too many arguments are apt to induce apoplexy and thus hinder
    longevity,
We'll let it pass as one Assyrian for the sake of brevity.   10
Now then, this particular Assyrian; the one whose cohorts were gleaming in purple
    and gold,
Just what does the poet mean when he says he came down like a wolf on the
    fold?
In heaven and earth more than is dreamed of in our philosophy there are a great
    many things,
But I don't imagine that among them there is a wolf with purple and gold cohorts
    or purple and gold anythings.
No, no, Lord Byron, before I'll believe that this Assyrian was actually like a wolf   15
    I must have some kind of proof;
Did he run on all fours and did he have a hairy tail and a big red mouth and big
    white teeth and did he say Woof woof woof?
Frankly I think it very unlikely, and all you were entitled to say, at the very most,
Was that the Assyrian cohorts came down like a lot of Assyrian cohorts about to
    destroy the Hebrew host.
But that wasn't fancy enough for Lord Byron, oh dear me no, he had to invent a
    lot of figures of speech and then interpolate them.
With the result that whenever you mention Old Testament soldiers to people they   20
    say Oh yes, they're the ones that a lot of wolves dressed up in gold and purple
    ate them.
That's the kind of thing that's being done all the time by poets, from Homer to
    Tennyson;
They're always comparing ladies to lilies° and veal to venison.
How about the man who wrote,
Her little feet stole in and out like mice beneath her petticoat?°
Wouldn't anybody but a poet think twice   25
Before stating that his girl's feet were mice?

VERY LIKE A WHALE: See *Hamlet*, Act III, scene 2, line 358. 7 *George Gordon Byron:* See
Byron, "The Destruction of Sennacherib," (p. 898), which Nash is satirizing in this poem.
22 *ladies:* See Campion, "Cherry Ripe," stanza 1, and also Burns, "A Red, Red Rose."
24 *little feet . . . petticoat:* In Sir John Suckling's, "A Ballad upon a Wedding" (1641), the
following lines appear: "Her feet beneath her petticoat/Like little mice stole in and out."
Also in a poem by Robert Herrick complimenting the feet of Susanna Southwell (1648), he
wrote: "Her pretty feet/Like snails did creep."

Then they always say things like that after a winter storm
The snow is a white blanket. Oh it is, is it, all right then, you sleep under a six-
    inch blanket of snow and I'll sleep under a half-inch blanket of unpoetical
    blanket material and we'll see which one keeps warm.
And after that maybe you'll begin to comprehend dimly
What I meant by too much metaphor and simile.   30

HOWARD NEMEROV   (1920–1991)

Life Cycle of Common Man   *1960*

Roughly figured, this man of moderate habits,
This average consumer of the middle class,
Consumed in the course of his average life span
Just under half a million cigarettes,
Four thousand fifths of gin and about   5
A quarter as much vermouth; he drank
Maybe a hundred thousand cups of coffee,
And counting his parents' share it cost
Something like half a million dollars
To put him through life. How many beasts   10
Died to provide him with meat, belt and shoes
Cannot be certainly said.
                         But anyhow,
It is in this way that a man travels through time,
Leaving behind him a lengthening trail   15
Of empty bottles and bones, of broken shoes,
Frayed collars and worn out or outgrown
Diapers and dinnerjackets, silk ties and slickers.

Given the energy and security thus achieved,
He did . . . ? What? The usual things, of course,   20
The eating, dreaming, drinking and begetting,
And he worked for the money which was to pay
For the eating, et cetera, which were necessary
If he were to go on working for the money, et cetera,
But chiefly he talked. As the bottles and bones   25
Accumulated behind him, the words proceeded
Steadily from the front of his face as he
Advanced into the silence and made it verbal.
Who can tally the tale of his words? A lifetime
Would barely suffice for their repetition;   30
If you merely printed all his commas the result
Would be a very large volume, and the number of times
He said "thank you" or "very little sugar, please,"
Would stagger the imagination. There were also
Witticisms, platitudes, and statements beginning   35
"It seems to me" or "As I always say."

Consider the courage in all that, and behold the man
Walking into deep silence, with the ectoplastic
Cartoon's balloon of speech proceeding
Steadily out of the front of his face, the words   40
Borne along on the breath which is his spirit
Telling the numberless tale of his untold Word
Which makes the world his apple, and forces him to eat.

NAOMI SHIHAB NYE   (b. 1952)

Where Children Live   *1982*

Homes where children live exude a pleasant rumpledness,
like a bed made by a child, or a yard littered with balloons.

To be a child again one would need to shed details
till the heart found itself dressed in the coat with a hood.
Now the heart has taken on gloves and mufflers,   5
the heart never goes outside to find something to "do."
And the house takes on a new face, dignified.
No lost shoes blooming under bushes.
No chipped trucks in the drive.
Grown-ups like swings, leafy plants, slow-motion back and forth.   10
While the yard of a child is strewn with the corpses
of bottle-rockets and whistles,
anything whizzing and spectacular, brilliantly short-lived.

Trees in children's yards speak in clearer tongues.
Ants have more hope. Squirrels dance as well as hide.   15
The fence has a reason to be there, so children can go in and out.
Even when the children are at school, the yards glow
with the leftovers of their affection,
the roots of the tiniest grasses curl toward one another
like secret smiles.   20

FRANK O'HARA   (1926–1966)

Poem   *1952*

The eager note on my door said "Call me,
call when you get in!" so I quickly threw
a few tangerines into my overnight bag,
straightened my eyelids and shoulders, and

headed straight for the door. It was autumn   5
by the time I got around the corner, oh all

unwilling to be either pertinent or bemused, but
the leaves were brighter than grass on the sidewalk!

Funny, I thought, that the lights are on this late
and the hall door open; still up at this hour, a   10
champion jai-alai player like himself? Oh fie!
for shame! What a host, so zealous! And he was

there in the hall, flat on a sheet of blood that
ran down the stairs. I did appreciate it. There are few
hosts who so thoroughly prepare to greet a guest   15
only casually invited, and that several months ago.

SIMON ORTIZ   (b. 1941)

A Story of How a Wall Stands   1976

At Acu there is a wall almost 400 years old which
supports hundreds of tons of dirt and bones—it's a
graveyard built on a steep incline—and it looks like
it's about to fall down the incline but will not for a long time.

My father, who works with stone,
says, "That's just the part you see,
the stones which seem to be
just packed in on the outside,"
and with his hands put the stone and mud   5
in place. "Underneath
what looks like loose stone,
there is stone woven together."
He ties one hand over the other,
fitting like the bones of his hands   10
and fingers. "That's what is
holding it together."

"It is built that carefully,"
he says, "the mud mixed
to a certain texture," patiently   15
"with the fingers," worked
in the palm of his hand. "So that
placed between the stones, they hold
together for a long, long time."

He tells me those things,   20
the story of them worked
with his fingers, in the palm
of his hands, working the stone
and the mud until they become
the wall that stands a long, long time.   25

AMÉRICO PARÉDES (b. 1915)

Guitarreros 1964

Black against twisted black
The old mesquite
Rears up against the stars
Branch bridle hanging,
While the bull comes down from the mountain 5
Driven along by your fingers,
Twenty nimble stallions prancing up and down the *redil°* of   *the "web" of music*
     the guitars.
One leaning on the trunk, one facing—
Now the song:
Not cleanly flanked, not pacing, 10
But in a stubborn yielding that unshapes
And shapes itself again;
Hard-mouthed, zigzagged, thrusting,
Thrown, not sung,
One to the other. 15
The old man listens in his cloud
Of white tobacco smoke.
"It was so," he says,
"In the old days it was so."

DOROTHY PARKER (1893–1967)

Résumé 1936

Razors pain you;
Rivers are damp;
Acids stain you;
And drugs cause cramp.
Guns aren't lawful; 5
Nooses give;
Gas smells awful;
You might as well live.

LINDA PASTAN (b. 1932)

Marks 1978

My husband gives me an A
for last night's supper,
an incomplete for my ironing,
a B plus in bed.
My son says I am average, 5

an average mother, but if
I put my mind to it
I could improve.
My daughter believes
in Pass/Fail and tells me   10
I pass. Wait 'til they learn
I'm dropping out.

MARGE PIERCY   (b. 1934)

The Secretary Chant   *1973*

My hips are a desk.
From my ears hang
chains of paper clips.
Rubber bands form my hair.
My breasts are wells of mimeograph ink.   5
My feet bear casters.
Buzz. Click.
My head is a badly organized file.
My head is a switchboard
where crossed lines crackle.   10
Press my fingers
and in my eyes appear
credit and debit.
Zing. Tinkle.
My navel is a reject button.   15
From my mouth issue canceled reams.
Swollen, heavy, rectangular
I am about to be delivered
of a baby
Xerox machine.   20
File me under W
because I wonce
was
a woman.

MARGE PIERCY   (b. 1934)

Will We Work Together?   *1980*

You wake in the early grey
morning in bed alone and curse
me, that I am only
sometimes there. But when
I am with you, I light   5
up the corners, I am bright

as a fireplace roaring
with love, every bone in my back
and my fingers is singing
like a tea kettle on the boil.   10
My heart wags me, a big dog
with a bigger tail. I am
a new coin printed with
your face. My body wears
sore before I can express   15
on yours the smallest part
of what moves me. Words
shred and splinter.
I want to make with you
some bold new thing   20
to stand in the marketplace,
the statue of a goddess
laughing, armed and wearing
flowers and feathers. Like sheep
of whose hair is made   25
blankets and coats, I want
to force from this fierce sturdy
rampant love some useful thing.

SYLVIA PLATH   (1932–1962)

Last Words   *1971 (1961)*

I do not want a plain box, I want a sarcophagus
With tigery stripes, and a face on it
Round as the moon, to stare up.
I want to be looking at them when they° come
Picking among the dumb minerals, the roots,   5
I see them already—the pale, star-distance faces.
Now they are nothing, they are not even babies.
I imagine them without fathers or mothers, like the first gods.
They will wonder if I was important.
I should sugar and preserve my days like fruit!   10
My mirror is clouding over—
A few more breaths, and it will reflect nothing at all.
The flowers and the faces whiten to a sheet.

I do not trust the spirit. It escapes like steam
In dreams, through mouth-hole or eye-hole. I can't stop it.   15
One day it won't come back. Things aren't like that.
They stay, their little particular lusters
Warmed by much handling. They almost purr.

LAST WORDS.   4 *they:* possibly archeologists exploring the speaker's tomb or stone
coffin ("sarcophagus").

When the soles of my feet grow cold,
The blue eye of my turquoise will comfort me.   20
Let me have my copper cooking pots, let my rouge pots
Bloom about me like night flowers, with a good smell.
They will roll me up in bandages, they will store my heart
Under my feet in a neat parcel.°
I shall hardly know myself. It will be dark,   25
And the shine of these small things sweeter than the face of Ishtar.°

19–24 *When . . . parcel:* The objects and procedures here refer to the household goods
normally entombed with a body in ancient Egypt and to the preparation of a mummy.
27 *Ishtar:* Ancient Babylonian goddess of fertility, love, and war.

SYLVIA PLATH   (1932–1962)

Mirror   *1965 (1961)*

I am silver and exact. I have no preconceptions.
Whatever I see I swallow immediately
Just as it is, unmisted by love or dislike.
I am not cruel, only truthful—
The eye of a little god, four-cornered.   5
Most of the time I meditate on the opposite wall.
It is pink, with speckles. I have looked at it so long
I think it is a part of my heart. But it flickers.
Faces and darkness separate us over and over.

Now I am a lake. A woman bends over me,   10
Searching my reaches for what she really is.
Then she turns to those liars, the candles or the moon.
I see her back, and reflect it faithfully.
She rewards me with tears and an agitation of hands.
I am important to her. She comes and goes.   15
Each morning it is her face that replaces the darkness.
In me she has drowned a young girl, and in me an old woman
Rises toward her day after day, like a terrible fish.

EZRA POUND   (1885–1972)

The River-Merchant's Wife: A Letter°   *1926 (1915)*

While my hair was still cut straight across my forehead
I played about the front gate, pulling flowers.
You came by on bamboo stilts, playing horse,
You walked about my seat, playing with blue plums.

THE RIVER-MERCHANTS WIFE: A LETTER. Freely translated from the Chinese of Li
Po (701–762).

And we went on living in the village of Chokan:°   5
Two small people, without dislike or suspicion.

At fourteen I married My Lord you.
I never laughed, being bashful.
Lowering my head, I looked at the wall.
Called to, a thousand times, I never looked back.   10

At fifteen I stopped scowling,
I desired my dust to be mingled with yours
Forever and forever and forever.
Why should I climb the look out?

At sixteen you departed,   15
You went into far Ku-tō-en,° by the river of swirling eddies,
And you have been gone five months.
The monkeys make sorrowful noise overhead.

You dragged your feet when you went out.
By the gate now, the moss is grown, the different mosses,   20
Too deep to clear them away!
The leaves fall early this autumn, in wind.
The paired butterflies are already yellow with August

Over the grass in the West garden;
They hurt me, I grow older.   25
If you are coming down through the narrows of the river Kiang,
Please let me know beforehand,
And I will come out to meet you
        As far as Chō-fū-Sa.°

5 *Chokan:* a suburb of Nanking, China.   16 *Ku-tō-en:* an island several hundred miles up the Kiang River from Nanking.   29 *Chō-fū-Sa:* a beach near Ku-tō-en.

E. J. PRATT (1882–1964)

The Shark   *1923*

He seemed to know the harbour,
So leisurely he swam;
His fin,
Like a piece of sheet-iron,
Three-cornered,   5
And with knife-edge,
Stirred not a bubble
As it moved
With its base-line on the water.

His body was tubular   10
And tapered
And smoke-blue,

And as he passed the wharf
He turned,
And snapped at a flat-fish   15
That was dead and floating.
And I saw the flash of a white throat,
And a double row of white teeth,
And eyes of metallic grey,
Hard and narrow and slit.   20

Then out of the harbour,
With that three-cornered fin
Shearing without a bubble the water
Lithely,
Leisurely,   25
He swam—
That strange fish,
Tubular, tapered, smoke-blue,
Part vulture, part wolf,
Part neither—for his blood was cold.   30

THOMAS RABBITT (b. 1943)

Gargoyle   *1981*

He looks down to watch the river twist
Like a dead vein into the suburbs.
From his height it is all flat, stone-grey
And ugly. He knows he himself is hideous,
Sterile, the artist's pleasantry set up   5
To scare off devils. He knows nothing.
He is stunning in his pure impossibility.
Enough cherry trees blossom along the river.
Enough paired lovers gaze through the pink air.
Drab birds, disguised as money, sing prettily   10
And the sun blinds itself in the water.
He hears laughter. He knows nothing.
When the lovers glance up, they take him in.
Their looks are incidental, monumental, sweeping.

JOHN CROWE RANSOM (1888–1974)

Bells for John Whiteside's Daughter   *1924*

There was such speed in her little body,
And such lightness in her footfall,
It is no wonder her brown study
Astonishes us all.

Her wars were bruited in our high window.   5
We looked among orchard trees and beyond
Where she took arms against her shadow,
Or harried unto the pond.

The lazy geese, like a snow cloud
Dripping their snow on the green grass,   10
Tricking and stopping, sleepy and proud,
Who cried in goose, Alas,

For the tireless heart within the little
Lady with rod that made them rise
From their noon apple-dreams and scuttle   15
Goose-fashion under the skies!

But now go the bells, and we are ready,
In one house we are sternly stopped
To say we are vexed at her brown study,
Lying so primly propped.   20

ADRIENNE RICH   (b. 1929)

Diving into the Wreck   *1972*

First having read the book of myths,
and loaded the camera,
and checked the edge of the knife-blade,
I put on
the body-armor of black rubber   5
the absurd flippers
the grave and awkward mask.
I am having to do this
not like Cousteau with his
assiduous team   10
aboard the sun-flooded schooner
but here alone.

There is a ladder.
The ladder is always there
hanging innocently   15
close to the side of the schooner.
We know what it is for,
we who have used it.
otherwise
it is a piece of maritime floss   20
some sundry equipment.

I go down.
Rung after rung and still
the oxygen immerses me

the blue light   25
the clear atoms
of our human air.
I go down.
My flippers cripple me,
I crawl like an insect down the ladder   30
and there is no one
to tell me when the ocean
will begin.

First the air is blue and then
it is bluer and then green and then   35
black I am blacking out and yet
my mask is powerful
it pumps my blood with power
the sea is another story
the sea is not a question of power   40
I have to learn alone
to turn my body without force
in the deep element.

And now: it is easy to forget
what I came for   45
among so many who have always
lived here
swaying their crenellated fans
between the reefs
and besides   50
you breathe differently down here.

I came to explore the wreck.
The words are purposes.
The words are maps.
I came to see the damage that was done   55
and the treasures that prevail.
I stroke the beam of my lamp
slowly along the flank
of something more permanent
than fish or weed   60

the thing I came for:
the wreck and not the story of the wreck
the thing itself and not the myth
the drowned face always staring
toward the sun   65
the evidence of damage
worn by salt and sway into this threadbare beauty
the ribs of the disaster
curving their assertion
among the tentative haunters.   70

This is the place.
And I am here, the mermaid whose dark hair
streams black, the merman in his armored body.
We circle silently
about the wreck   75
we dive into the hold.
I am she; I am he

whose drowned face sleeps with open eyes
whose breasts still bear the stress
whose silver, copper, vermeil cargo lies   80
obscurely inside barrels
half-wedged and left to rot
we are the half-destroyed instruments
that once held to a course
the water-eaten log   85
the fouled compass

We are, I am, you are
by cowardice or courage
the one who find our way
back to this scene   90
carrying a knife, a camera
a book of myths
in which
our names do not appear.

THEODORE ROETHKE   (1908–1963)

I Knew a Woman   *1958*

I knew a woman, lovely in her bones,
When small birds sighed, she would sigh back at them;
Ah, when she moved, she moved more ways than one:
The shapes a bright container can contain!
Of her choice virtues only gods should speak,   5
Or English poets who grew up on Greek
(I'd have them sing in chorus, cheek to cheek).

How well her wishes went! She stroked my chin,
She taught me Turn, and Counter-turn, and Stand;
She taught me Touch, that undulant white skin;   10
I nibbled meekly from her proffered hand;
She was the sickle; I, poor I, the rake,
Coming behind her for her pretty sake
(But what prodigious mowing we did make).

Love likes a gander, and adores a goose: 15
Her full lips pursed, the errant note to seize;
She played it quick, she played it light and loose;

My eyes, they dazzled at her flowing knees;
Her several parts could keep a pure repose,
Or one hip quiver with a mobile nose   20
(She moved in circles, and those circles moved).

Let seed be grass, and grass turn into hay:
I'm martyr to a motion not my own;
What's freedom for? To know eternity.
I swear she cast a shadow white as stone.   25
But who would count eternity in days?
These old bones live to learn her wanton ways:
(I measure time by how a body sways).

THEODORE ROETHKE   (1908–1963)

The Waking   *1953*

I wake to sleep, and take my waking slow.
I feel my fate in what I cannot fear.
I learn by going where I have to go.

We think by feeling. What is there to know?
I hear my being dance from ear to ear.   5
I wake to sleep, and take my waking slow.

Of those so close beside me, which are you?
God bless the Ground! I shall walk softly there,
And learn by going where I have to go.

Light takes the Tree; but who can tell us how?   10
The lowly worm climbs up a winding stair;
I wake to sleep, and take my waking slow.

Great Nature has another thing to do
To you and me; so take the lively air,
And, lovely, learn by going where to go.   15

This shaking keeps me steady. I should know.
What falls away is always. And is near.
I wake to sleep, and take my waking slow.
I learn by going where I have to go.

LUIS OMAR SALINAS   (b. 1937)

In a Farmhouse   *1973*

Fifteen miles
out of Robstown
with the Texas sun
fading in the distance

I sit in the bedroom   5
profoundly,
animated by the day's work
in the cottonfields.

I made two dollars and
thirty cents today   10
I am eight years old
and I wonder
how the rest of the Mestizos°
do not go hungry
and if one were to die   15
of hunger
what an odd way
to leave for heaven.

IN A FARMHOUSE.   13 *Mestizos:* persons of mixed Spanish and Amerindian ancestry.

SONIA SANCHEZ   (b. 1934)

right on: white america   *1970*

this country might have
been a pio
  neer land
once.
  but.   there ain't   5
no mo
    indians   blowing
custer's° mind
    with a different
image of america.   10
        this country
might have
      needed shoot/
outs/ daily/
    once.   15
     but. there ain't
no mo real/ white/   allamerican
        bad/guys.
just
   u & me.   20
     blk/ and un/armed.
this country might have

RIGHT ON: WHITE AMERICA.   8 *custer's:* General George Armstrong Custer (1839–1876) was killed in his "last stand" at the Little Bighorn in Montana during a battle with Sioux Indians.

been a pion
        eer land.   once.
                and it still is.   25
check out
     the falling
gun/shells   on our blk/tomorrows.

CARL SANDBURG (1878–1967)

Chicago   *1916*

    Hog Butcher for the World,
    Tool Maker, Stacker of Wheat,
    Player with Railroads and the Nation's Freight Handler;
    Stormy, husky, brawling,
    City of the Big Shoulders: 5

They tell me you are wicked and I believe them, for I have seen your painted
    women under the gas lamps luring the farm boys.
And they tell me you are crooked and I answer: Yes, it is true I have seen the
    gunman kill and go free to kill again.
And they tell me you are brutal and my reply is: On the faces of women and
    children I have seen the marks of wanton hunger.
And having answered so I turn once more to those who sneer at this my city,
    and I give them back the sneer and say to them:
Come and show me another city with lifted head singing so proud to be alive   10
    and coarse and strong and cunning.
Flinging magnetic curses amid the toil of piling job on job, here is a tall bold
    slugger set vivid against the little soft cities;
Fierce as a dog with tongue lapping for action, cunning as a savage pitted against
    the wilderness,
        Bareheaded,
        Shoveling,
        Wrecking,   15
        Planning,
        Building, breaking, rebuilding,
Under the smoke, dust all over his mouth, laughing with white teeth,
Under the terrible burden of destiny laughing as a young man laughs,
Laughing even as an ignorant fighter laughs who has never lost a battle,   20
Bragging and laughing that under his wrist is the pulse, and under his ribs the
    heart of the people,
        Laughing!
Laughing the stormy, husky, brawling laughter of Youth, half-naked, sweating,
    proud to be Hog Butcher, Tool Maker, Stacker of Wheat, Player with Railroads
    and Freight Handler to the Nation.

SIEGFRIED SASSOON (1886–1967)

Dreamers *1918*

Soldiers are citizens of death's grey land,
   Drawing no dividend from time's to-morrows.
In the great hour of destiny they stand,
   Each with his feuds, and jealousies, and sorrows.

  Soldiers are sworn to action; they must win 5
  Some flaming, fatal climax with their lives.
Soldiers are dreamers; when the guns begin
   They think of firelit homes, clean beds, and wives.

I see them in foul dug-outs, gnawed by rats,
   And in the ruined trenches, lashed with rain, 10
Dreaming of things they did with balls and bats,
   And mocked by hopeless longing to regain
Bank-holidays,° and picture shows, and spats,
   And going to the office in the train.

DREAMERS.   13 *Bank-holidays:* legal holidays in Great Britain.

ALAN SEEGER (1888–1916)

I Have a Rendezvous with Death *1916*

I have a rendezvous with Death
At some disputed barricade,
When Spring comes back with rustling shade
And apple blossoms fill the air—
I have a rendezvous with Death 5
When Spring brings back blue days and fair.

It may be he shall take my hand
And lead me into his dark land
And close my eyes and quench my breath—
It may be I shall pass him still. 10
I have a rendezvous with Death
On some scarred slope of battered hill,
When Spring comes round again this year
And the first meadow flowers appear.

God knows 'twere better to be deep 15
Pillowed in silk and scented down,
Where Love throbs out in blissful sleep,
Pulse nigh to pulse and breath to breath,
Where hushed awakenings are dear. . . .
But I've a rendezvous with Death 20
At midnight in some flaming town,

When Spring trips north again this year,
And I to my pledged word am true,
I shall not fail that rendezvous.

BRENDA SEROTTE   (b. 1946)

My Mother's Face   *1991*

Dressing for work
I glanced in the mirror
startled to see my mother's face
white, with the mouth turned down
her red frizzled hair   5
wild in all directions.
She turned sideways
to study my dress
standing tiptoe like I do
craning her long neck   10
in a futile attempt to see my feet.
Then without warning, the tears
rolling from the outer corners down
past slightly pitted cheeks
past that inverted smile   15
into the cave of her bosom
which heaved a sigh so forlorn
so weighted with loss
that had I not been standing silent
I would have surely thought it was me.   20

ANNE SEXTON   (1928–1974)

Three Green Windows   *1966 (1962)*

Half awake in my Sunday nap
I see three green windows
in three different lights—
one west, one south, one east.
I have forgotten that old friends are dying.   5
I have forgotten that I grow middle-aged.
At each window such rustlings!
The trees persist, yeasty and sensuous,
as thick as saints.
I see three wet gargoyles covered with birds.   10
Their skins shine in the sun like leather.

I'm on my bed as light as a sponge.
Soon it will be summer.

She is my mother.
She will tell me a story and keep me asleep   15
against her plump and fruity skin.
I see leaves—
leaves that are washed and innocent,
leaves that never knew a cellar,
born in their own green blood   20
like the hands of mermaids.

I do not think of the rusty wagon on the walk.
I pay no attention to the red squirrels
that leap like machines beside the house.
I do not remember the real trunks of the trees   25
that stand beneath the windows
as bulky as artichokes.
I turn like a giant,
secretly watching, secretly knowing,
secretly naming each elegant sea.   30

I have misplaced the Van Allen belt,°
the sewers and the drainage,
the urban renewal and the suburban centers.
I have forgotten the names of the literary critics.
I know what I know.   35
I am the child I was,
living the life that was mine.
I am young and half asleep.
It is a time of water, a time of trees.

THREE GREEN WINDOWS.   31 *Van Allen belt:* radiation belt around the earth, named
after its discoverer, American astrophysicist James A. Van Allen (b. 1914).

WILLIAM SHAKESPEARE   (1564–1616)

Fear No More the Heat o' the Sun°   *1623 (ca. 1609)*

Fear no more the heat o' the sun,
  Nor the furious winter's rages;
Thou thy worldly task hast done,
  Home art gone, and ta'en° thy wages: *taken*
Golden lads and girls all must,   5
As° chimney-sweepers, come to dust.   *like*

Fear no more the frown o' the great;
  Thou art past the tyrant's stroke;
Care no more to clothe and eat;
  To thee the reed is as the oak;   10

FEAR NO MORE THE HEAT O' THE SUN. A dirge or lament sung over the supposedly
dead body of Imogen in Act IV of Shakespeare's *Cymbeline*.

The scepter, learning, physic, must
All follow this, and come to dust.

Fear no more the lightning flash,
   Nor the all-dreaded thunder stone;°
Fear not slander, censure rash;   15
   Thou hast finished joy and moan:°   *sadness*
All lovers young, all lovers must
Consign to thee, and come to dust.

No exorciser harm thee!
Nor no witchcraft charm thee!   20
Ghost unlaid forbear thee!
Nothing ill come near thee!
Quiet consummation have;
And renownéd be thy grave!

14 *thunder stone:* The sound of thunder was believed to be caused by stones falling from the sky.

WILLIAM SHAKESPEARE   (1564–1616)

Sonnet 29: When in Disgrace with Fortune and Men's Eyes   *1609*

When, in disgrace with Fortune and men's eyes,
I all alone beweep my outcast state,
And trouble deaf heaven with my bootless° cries,   *futile, useless*
And look upon myself and curse my fate,
Wishing me like to one more rich in hope,   5
Featured like him, like him with friends possessed,
Desiring this man's art and that man's scope,
With what I most enjoy contented least,
Yet in these thoughts myself almost despising;
Haply I think on thee, and then my state,   10
(Like to the lark at break of day arising)
From sullen earth sings hymns at heaven's gate,
For thy sweet love remembered such wealth brings
That then I scorn to change my state with kings.

WILLIAM SHAKESPEARE   (1564–1616)

Sonnet 146: Poor Soul, The Center of My Sinful Earth   *1609*

Poor soul, the center of my sinful earth,
Thrall° to these rebel powers that thee array,°   *captive*
Why dost thou pine within and suffer dearth
Painting thy outward walls so costly gay?

POOR SOUL.   2 *array:* surround or dress out, as in a military formation.

Why so large cost having so short a lease,   5
Dost thou upon thy fading mansion spend?
Shall worms, inheritors of this excess,
Eat up thy charge? Is this thy body's end?
Then, soul, live thou upon thy servant's loss,°
And let that pine to aggravate thy store;°   10
Buy terms° divine in selling hours of dross°   *periods; refuse*
Within be fed, without be rich no more:
So shalt thou feed on Death, that feeds on men,
And Death once dead, there's no more dying then.

9 *thy servant's loss:* the loss of the body.   10 *let . . . store:* let the body ("that") dwindle
("pine") to increase ("aggravate") the riches ("store") of the soul.

KARL SHAPIRO   (b. 1913)

Auto Wreck   *1941*

Its quick soft silver bell beating, beating,
And down the dark one ruby flare
Pulsing out red light like an artery,
The ambulance at top speed floating down
Past beacons and illuminated clocks   5
Wings in a heavy curve, dips down,
And brakes speed, entering the crowd.
The doors leap open, emptying light;
Stretchers are laid out, the mangled lifted
And stowed into the little hospital.   10
Then the bell, breaking the hush, tolls once,
And the ambulance with its terrible cargo
Rocking, slightly rocking, moves away,
As the doors, an afterthought, are closed.

We are deranged, walking among the cops   15
Who sweep glass and are large and composed.
One is still making notes under the light.
One with a bucket douches ponds of blood
Into the street and gutter.
One hangs lanterns on the wrecks that cling,   20
Empty husks of locusts, to iron poles.
Our throats were tight as tourniquets,
Our feet were bound with splints, but now,
Like convalescents intimate and gauche,
We speak through sickly smiles and warn   25
With the stubborn saw of common sense,
The grim joke and the banal resolution.
The traffic moves around with care,
But we remain, touching a wound
That opens to our richest horror.   30

Already old, the question Who shall die?
Becomes unspoken Who is innocent?
For death in war is done by hands;
Suicide has cause and stillbirth, logic;
And cancer, simple as a flower, blooms.   35
But this invites the occult mind,
Cancels our physics with a sneer,
And spatters all we knew of dénouement
Across the expedient and wicked stones.

SIR PHILIP SIDNEY (1554–1586)

Astrophil and Stella, Number 71   *1591*

Who will in fairest book of Nature know,
How Virtue may best lodged in beauty be,
Let him but learn of Love to read in thee,
Stella, those fair lines, which true goodness show.
There shall he find all vices' overthrow,   5
Not by rude force, but sweetest sovereignty
Of reason, from whose light those night birds fly;
That inward sun in thine eyes shineth so.
And not content to be Perfection's heir
Thyself, dost strive all minds that way to move,   10
Who mark in thee what is in thee most fair.
So while thy beauty draws the heart to love,
As fast thy Virtue bends that love to good:
"But ah," desire still cries, "give me some food."

JON SILKIN (b. 1930)

Worm   *1971*

Look out, they say, for yourself.
The worm doesn't. It is blind
As a sloe; its death by cutting,
Bitter. Its oozed length is ringed,
With parts swollen. Cold and blind   5
It is graspable, and writhes
In your hot hand; a small snake, unvenomous.
Its seeds furred and moist
It sexes by lying beside another,
In its eking conjunction of seed   10
Wriggling and worm-like.
Its ganglia are in its head,
And if this is severed
It must grow backwards.

It is lowly, useful, pink. It breaks   15
Tons of soil, gorging the humus
Its whole length; its shit a fine cast
Coiled in heaps, a burial mound, or like a shell
Made by a dead snail.
It has a life, which is virtuous   20
As a farmer's, making his own food.
Passionless as a hoe, sometimes, persistent.
Does not want to kill a thing.

LESLIE MARMON SILKO   (b. 1948)

Where Mountain Lion Lay Down with Deer   *1974*

I climb the black rock mountain
   stepping from day to day
           silently.
I smell the wind for my ancestors
   pale blue leaves   5
   crushed wild mountain smell.
Returning
  up the gray stone cliff
  where I descended
        a thousand years ago.   10

Returning to faded black stone
  where mountain lion lay down with deer.
It is better to stay up here
          watching wind's reflection
          in tall yellow flowers.   15
The old ones who remember me are gone
      the old songs are all forgotten
and the story of my birth.
How I danced in snow-frost moonlight
     distant stars to the end of the Earth,   20
How I swam away
      in freezing mountain water
      narrow mossy canyon tumbling down
         out of the mountain
          out of the deep canyon stone   25
       down
         the memory
           spilling out
           into the world.

DAVE SMITH (b. 1942)

Bluejays

1981

She tries to call them down,
quicknesses of air.
They bitch and scorn,
they roost away from her.

It isn't that she's brutal.
She's just a girl. Worse,   5
her touch is total.
Her play is dangerous.

Darkly they spit each at each,
from tops of pine and spruce.   10
Her words are shy and sweet,
but it's no use.

Ragged, blue, shrill,
they dart around like boys.
They fear the beautiful   15
but do not fly away.

STEVIE SMITH (1902–1971)

Not Waving But Drowning

1957

Nobody heard him, the dead man,
But still he lay moaning:
I was much further out than you thought
And not waving but drowning.

Poor chap, he always loved larking   5
And now he's dead
It must have been too cold for him his heart gave way,
They said.

Oh, no no no, it was too cold always
(Still the dead one lay moaning)   10
I was much too far out all my life
And not waving but drowning.

W. D. SNODGRASS (b. 1926)

Lobsters in the Window

1963

First, you think they are dead.
Then you are almost sure
One is beginning to stir.

Out of the crushed ice, slow
As the hands of a schoolroom clock,   5
He lifts his one great claw
And holds it over his head;
Now, he is trying to walk.

But like a run-down toy;
Like the backward crabs we boys   10
Splashed after in the creek,
Trapped in jars or a net,
And then took home to keep.
Overgrown, retarded, weak,
He is fumbling yet   15
From the deep chill of his sleep

As if, in a glacial thaw,
Some ancient thing might wake
Sore and cold and stiff
Struggling to raise one claw   20
Like a defiant fist;
Yet wavering, as if
Starting to swell and ache
With that thick peg in the wrist.

I should wave back, I guess.   25
But still in his permanent clench
He's fallen back with the mass
Heaped in their common trench
Who stir, but do not look out
Through the rainstreaming glass.   30
Hear what the newsboys shout,
Or see the raincoats pass.

CATHY SONG   (b. 1955)

Lost Sister   *1983*

1

In China,
even the peasants
named their first daughters
Jade—°
the stone that in the far fields   5
could moisten the dry season,
could make men move mountains
for the healing green of the inner hills
glistening like slices of winter melon.

LOST SISTER.   4 *Jade:* Both the mineral and the name are considered signs of good
fortune and health in China.

And the daughters were grateful: 10
they never left home.
To move freely was a luxury
stolen from them at birth.
Instead, they gathered patience,
learning to walk in shoes   15
the size of teacups,°
without breaking—
the arc of their movements
as dormant as the rooted willow,
as redundant as the farmyard hens.   20
But they traveled far
in surviving,
learning to stretch the family rice,
to quiet the demons,
the noisy stomachs.   25

2

There is a sister
across the ocean,
who relinquished her name,
diluting jade green
with the blue of the Pacific.   30
Rising with a tide of locusts,
she swarmed with others
to inundate another shore.
In America,
there are many roads   35
and women can stride along with men.

But in another wilderness,
the possibilities,
the loneliness,
can strangulate like jungle vines.   40
The meager provisions and sentiments
of once belonging—
fermented roots, Mah-Jongg° tiles and firecrackers—
set but a flimsy household
in a forest of nightless cities.   45
A giant snake rattles above,
spewing black clouds into your kitchen.
Dough-faced landlords
slip in and out of your keyholes,
making claims you don't understand,   50

16 *teacups:* Traditionally, girls' feet were bound at the age of seven in China because
minuscule feet were considered beautiful and aristocratic. The binding inhibited the
natural growth of the feet and made it painful and difficult to walk.
43 *Mah-Jongg:* a Chinese game played with 144 domino-like tiles marked in suits, counters,
and dice.

tapping into your communication systems
of laundry lines and restaurant chains.

You find you need China:
your one fragile identification,
a jade link   55
handcuffed to your wrist.
You remember your mother
who walked for centuries,
footless—
and like her,   60
you have left no footprints,
but only because
there is an ocean in between,
the unremitting space of your rebellion.

GARY SOTO (b. 1948)

Oranges   *1984*

The first time I walked
With a girl, I was twelve,
Cold, and weighted down
With two oranges in my jacket.
December. Frost cracking   5
Beneath my steps, my breath
Before me, then gone,
As I walked toward
Her house, the one whose
Porch light burned yellow   10
Night and day, in any weather.
A dog barked at me, until
She came out pulling
At her gloves, face bright
With rouge. I smiled,   15
Touched her shoulder, and led
Her down the street, across
A used car lot and a line
Of newly planted trees,
Until we were breathing   20
Before a drugstore. We
Entered, the tiny bell
Bringing a saleslady
Down a narrow aisle of goods.
I turned to the candies   25
Tiered like bleachers,
And asked what she wanted—
Light in her eyes, a smile

Starting at the corners
Of her mouth. I fingered   30
A nickel in my pocket,
And when she lifted a chocolate
That cost a dime,
I didn't say anything.
I took the nickel from   35
My pocket, then an orange,
And set them quietly on
The counter. When I looked up,
The lady's eyes met mine,
And held them, knowing   40
Very well what it was all
About.

       Outside,
A few cars hissing past,
Fog hanging like old   45
Coats between the trees.
I took my girl's hand
In mine for two blocks,
Then released it to let
Her unwrap the chocolate.   50
I peeled my orange
That was so bright against
The gray of December
That, from some distance,
Someone might have thought   55
I was making a fire in my hands.

GARY SOTO (b. 1948)

Kearney Park   *1985*

True Mexicans or not, let's open our shirts
And dance, a spark of heels
Chipping at the dusty cement. The people
Are shiny like the sea, turning
To the clockwork of rancheras,   5
The accordion wheezing, the drum-tap
Of work rising and falling.
Let's dance with our hats in hand.
The sun is behind the trees,
Behind my stutter of awkward steps   10
With a woman who is a brilliant arc of smiles,
An armful of falling water. Her skirt
Opens and closes. My arms
Know no better but to flop

On their own, and we spin, dip 15
And laugh into each other's faces—
Faces that could be famous
On the coffee table of my abuelita.° *little grandmother*
But grandma is here, at the park, with a beer
At her feet, clapping 20
And shouting, "Dance, hijo,° dance!" *son, child*
Laughing, I bend, slide, and throw up
A great cloud of dust,
Until the girl and I are no more.

EDMUND SPENSER   (1552–1599)

Amoretti° 54: Of This World's Theater in Which We Stay 1595

Of this world's theater in which we stay,
My love like the spectator idly sits,
Beholding me that all the pageants° play, *roles*
Disguising diversly my troubled wits.
Sometimes I joy when glad occasion fits, 5
And mask in mirth like to a comedy:
Soon after when my joy to sorrow flits,
I wail and make my woes a tragedy.
Yet she, beholding me with constant eye,
Delights not in my mirth nor rues° my smart: *regrets* 10
But when I laugh, she mocks, and when I cry
She laughs and hardens evermore her heart.
What then can move her? if not mirth nor moan,
She is no woman, but a senseless stone.

AMORETTI 54. *Amoretti* means "little loves" or "little love songs."

WILLIAM STAFFORD   (b. 1914)

Traveling Through the Dark 1960

Traveling through the dark I found a deer
dead on the edge of the Wilson River road.
It is usually best to roll them into the canyon:
that road is narrow; to swerve might make more dead.

By glow of the tail-light I stumbled back of the car 5
and stood by the heap, a doe, a recent killing;
she had stiffened already, almost cold.
I dragged her off; she was large in the belly.

My fingers touching her side brought me the reason—
her side was warm; her fawn lay there waiting, 10

alive, still, never to be born.
Beside that mountain road I hesitated.

The car aimed ahead its lowered parking lights;
under the hood purred the steady engine.
I stood in the glare of the warm exhaust turning red;   15
around our group I could hear the wilderness listen.
I thought hard for us all—my only swerving—,
then pushed her over the edge into the river.

GERALD STERN   (b. 1925)

Burying an Animal on the Way to New York   *1977*

Don't flinch when you come across a dead animal lying on the road;
you are being shown the secret of life.
Drive slowly over the brown flesh;
you are helping to bury it.
If you are the last mourner there will be no caress   5
at all from the crushed limbs
and you will have to slide over the dark spot imagining
the first suffering all by yourself
Shreds of spirit and little ghost fragments will be spread out
for two miles above the white highway.   10
Slow down with your radio off and your window open
to hear the twittering as you go by.

WALLACE STEVENS   (1879–1955)

The Emperor of Ice-Cream   *1923*

Call the roller of big cigars,
The muscular one, and bid him whip
In kitchen cups concupiscent curds.
Let the wenches dawdle in such dress
As they are used to wear, and let the boys   5
Bring flowers in last month's newspapers.
Let be be finale° of seem.
The only emperor is the emperor of ice-cream.
Take from the dresser of deal,°
Lacking the three glass knobs, that sheet   10
On which she embroidered fantails° once
And spread it so as to cover her face.
If her horny feet protrude, they come
To show how cold she is, and dumb.

THE EMPEROR OF ICE-CREAM.   7 *finale:* the grand conclusion.   9 *deal:*
unfinished pine or fir used to make cheap furniture.   11 *fantails:* fantail pigeons.

Let the lamp affix its beam.   15
The only emperor is the emperor of ice-cream.

MARK STRAND   (b. 1934)

The Remains   *1969*

I empty myself of the names of others.
I empty my pockets, I empty my shoes and leave them beside
the road. At night I turn back the clocks; I open the family
album and look at myself as a boy.

What good does it do? The hours have done their job.   5
I say my own name. I say goodbye.
The words follow each other downwind.
I love my wife but send her away.

My parents rise out of their thrones
into the milky rooms of clouds. How can I sing?   10
Time tells me what I am. I change and I am the same.
I empty myself of my life and my life remains.

JONATHAN SWIFT   (1667–1745)

A Riddle (The Vowels)   *1746*

We are little airy Creatures,
All of different Voice and Features;
One of us in Glass is set,
One of us you'll find in Jet.
T'other you may see in Tin,   5
And the fourth a Box within.
If the fifth you shou'd pursue,
It can never fly from you.

JAMES TATE   (b. 1943)

The Blue Booby   *1969*

The blue booby lives
on the bare rocks
of Galápagos°
and fears nothing.
It is a simple life: 5

THE BLUE BOOBY.   3 *Galápagos:* islands in the Pacific Ocean on the equator about
600 miles west of Ecuador where many unique species of animals live.

they live on fish,
and there are few predators.
Also, the males do not
make fools of themselves
chasing after the young
ladies. Rather,   10
they gather the blue
objects of the world
and construct from them

a nest—an occasional   15
Gaulois° package,
a string of beads,
a piece of cloth from
a sailor's suit. This
replaces the need for   20
dazzling plumage;
in fact, in the past
fifty million years
the male has grown
considerably duller,   25
nor can he sing well.
The female, though,

asks little of him—
the blue satisfies her
completely, has   30
a magical effect
on her. When she returns
from her day of
gossip and shopping,
she sees he has found her   35
a new shred of blue foil:
for this she rewards him
with her dark body,
the stars turn slowly
in the blue foil beside them   40
like the eyes of a mild savior.

16 *Gaulois:* a brand of French cigarettes with a blue package.

ALFRED, LORD TENNYSON (1809–1892)

Tithonus   *1860*

  The woods decay, the woods decay and fall,
The vapors weep their burthen to the ground,
Man comes and tills the field and lies beneath,
And after many a summer dies the swan.

Me only cruel immortality   5
Consumes; I wither slowly in thine arms,
Here at the quiet limit of the world,
A white-haired shadow roaming like a dream
The ever-silent spaces of the East,
Far-folded mists, and gleaming halls of morn.   10
   Alas! for this gray shadow, once a man—
So glorious in his beauty and thy choice,
Who madest him thy chosen, that he seemed
To his great heart none other than a God!
I asked thee, "Give me immortality."   15
Then didst thou grant mine asking with a smile,
Like wealthy men who care not how they give.
But thy strong Hours indignant worked their wills,
And beat me down and marred and wasted me,
And though they could not end me, left me maimed   20
To dwell in presence of immortal youth,
Immortal age beside immortal youth,
And all I was in ashes. Can thy love,
Thy beauty, make amends, though even now,
Close over us, the silver star, thy guide,   25
Shines in those tremulous eyes that fill with tears
To hear me? Let me go; take back thy gift.
Why should a man desire in any way
To vary from the kindly race of men,
Or pass beyond the goal of ordinance   30
Where all should pause, as is most meet for all?
   A soft air fans the cloud apart; there comes
A glimpse of that dark world where I was born.
Once more the old mysterious glimmer steals
From thy pure brows, and from thy shoulders pure,   35
And bosom beating with a heart renewed.
Thy cheek begins to redden through the gloom,
Thy sweet eyes brighten slowly close to mine,
Ere yet they blind the stars, and the wild team
Which love thee, yearning for thy yoke, arise,   40
And shake the darkness from their loosened manes,
And beat the twilight into flakes of fire.
   Lo! ever thus thou growest beautiful
In silence, then before thine answer given
Departest, and thy tears are on my cheek.   45
   Why wilt thou ever scare me with thy tears,
And make me tremble lest a saying learnt,
In days far-off, on that dark earth, be true?
"The Gods themselves cannot recall their gifts."
   Ay me! ay me! with what another heart   50
In days far-off, and with what other eyes
I used to watch—if I be he that watched—
The lucid outline forming round thee; saw

The dim curls kindle into sunny rings;
Changed with thy mystic change, and felt my blood   55
Glow with the glow that slowly crimsoned all
Thy presence and thy portals, while I lay,
Mouth, forehead, eyelids, growing dewy-warm
With kisses balmier than half-opening buds
Of April, and could hear the lips that kissed   60
Whispering I knew not what of wild and sweet,
Like that strange song I heard Apollo sing,
While Ilion like a mist rose into towers.
　　Yet hold me not forever in thine East;
How can my nature longer mix with thine?   65
Coldly thy rose shadows bathe me, cold
Are all thy lights, and cold my wrinkled feet
Upon thy glimmering thresholds, when the steam
Floats up from those dim fields about the homes
Of happy men that have the power to die,   70
And grassy barrows of the happier dead.
Release me, and restore me to the ground.
Thou seest all things, thou wilt see my grave;
Thou wilt renew thy beauty morn by morn,
I earth in earth forget these empty courts,   75
And thee returning on thy silver wheels.

DYLAN THOMAS (1914–1953)

A Refusal to Mourn the Death, by Fire, of a Child in London   *1946*

Never until the mankind making
Bird beast and flower
Fathering and all humbling darkness
Tells with silence the last light breaking
And the still hour   5
Is come of the sea tumbling in harness

And I must enter again the round
Zion of the water bead
And the synagogue of the ear of corn
Shall I let pray the shadow of a sound   10
Or sow my salt seed
In the least valley of sackcloth to mourn

The majesty and burning of the child's death.
I shall not murder
The mankind of her going with a grave truth   15
Nor blaspheme down the stations of the breath
With any further
Elegy of innocence and youth.

Deep with the first dead lies London's daughter,
Robed in the long friends,   20
The grains beyond age, the dark veins of her mother,
Secret by the unmourning water
Of the riding Thames.°
After the first death, there is no other.

A REFUSAL TO MOURN.   23 *Thames:* the River Thames, which flows through
London.

CHASE TWICHELL   (b. 1950)

Blurry Cow   *1983*

Two cows stand transfixed
by a trough of floating leaves,
facing as if into the camera,
black and white. One stamps
at the hot sting of a deerfly.   5

Seen from the window of a train,
the hoof lifts forever
over hay crosshatched by speed,
and the scales of the haunches
balance. The rest is lost: 10
the head a sudden slur of light,
the dog loping along the tracks
toward a farm yard
where a woman wavers
in her mirage of laundry.   15
A blurry cow, of all things,
strays into the mind's eye,
the afterimage
of this day on earth.

MONA VAN DUYN   (b. 1921)

Advice to a God   *1971*

Before you leave her, the woman who thought you lavish,
whose body you led to parade without a blush
the touching vulgarity of the *nouveau-riche,*

whose every register your sexual coin
crammed full, whose ignorant bush mistook for sunshine   5
the cold, brazen battering of your rain,

rising, so little spent, strange millionaire
who feels in his loins' pocket clouds of power
gathering again for shower upon golden shower,

say to her, since she loves you, "Those as unworldly   10
as you are fated, and I can afford, to be
may find in Love's bed the perfect economy,

but, in all of his other places, a populace
living in fear of his management, his excess
of stingy might and extravagant helplessness.   15

Turn from him, Danae. I am greater by far,
whose flower reseeds without love for another flower,
whose seas part without loneliness, whose air

brightens or darkens heartlessly. By chance
I have come to you, and a progeny of events,   20
all that the mind of man calls consequence,

will follow my coming, slaughter and marriage, intrigue,
enchantment, definition of beauty, hag
and hero, a teeming, throwaway catalogue

of the tiniest, riskiest portion of my investment.   25
Yet pity your great landlord, for if I lent
so much as an ear to you, one loving tenant,

your bankrupt scream as I leave might tempt me to see
all creation in the ungainly, ungodly
throes of your individuality."   30

TINO VILLANUEVA (b. 1941)

Day-Long Day   *1972*

Again the drag of pisca,° pisca . . . pisca . . .
Daydreams border on sun-fed hallucinations,
eyes and hands automatically discriminate
whiteness of cotton from field of vision.
Pisca, pisca.
                        "Un Hijo del Sol,"°
                        Genaro Gonzales°

Third-generation timetable.
Sweat day-long dripping into open space;

DAY-LONG DAY.   EPIGRAPH: *pisca:* picking cotton.   *Un Hijo del Sol:* A Son of the
Sun. *Genaro Gonzales:* Hispanic author, born 1949.

sun blocks out the sky, suffocates the only breeze.
From el amo desgraciado,° a sentence:

"I wanna a bale a day, and the boy here   5
don't hafta go to school."
*   *   *
In time-binding motion—
a family of sinews and backs,
row-trapped,
zigzagging through summer-long rows   10
of cotton: Lubbock by way of Wharton.°
"Está como si escupieran fuego,"° a mother moans
in sweat-patched jeans,
stooping
with unbending dreams.   15
"Estudia para que no seas burro como nosotros,"°
our elders warn, their gloves and cuffs
leaf-stained by seasons.
*   *   *
Bronzed and blurry-eyed by
the blast of degrees,   20
we blend into earth's rotation.
And sweltering toward Saturday, the
day-long day is sunstruck by 6:00 P.M.
One last chug-a-lug from a water jug
old as granddad.   25
Day-long sweat dripping into open space:
Wharton by way of Lubbock.

4 *el amo desgraciado:* the despicable boss.   11 *Lubbock . . . Wharton:* cities on opposite sides
of Texas.   12 *Está . . . fuego:* "It's as if they are spewing fire."   16 *Estudia . . . nosotros:*
"Study so that you will not be a burro like us."

DIANE WAKOSKI   (b. 1937)

The Ring   *1977*

I carry it on my keychain, which itself
is a big brass ring
large enough for my wrist,
holding keys for safe-deposit box,
friends' apartments,   5
my house, office and faithless car.

I would like to wear it,
the only ornament on my plain body,
but it is a relic,
the husband gone to other wives,   10
and it could never be a symbol of sharing,

but like the gold it's made of, stands for possession, power,
the security of a throne.

So, on my keyring,
dull from resting in my dark purse,   15
it hangs, reminding me of failure, of beauty I once had,
of more ancient searches for an enchanted ring.

I understand, now, what that enchantment is, though.
It is being loved.
Or, conversely, loving so much that you feel loved.   20
And the ring hangs there
with my keys,
reminding of failure.

This vain head full of roses,
crystal,   25
bleeding lips,
a voice doomed to listen, forever,
to itself.

ALICE WALKER (b. 1944)

Revolutionary Petunias   1972

Sammy Lou of Rue
sent to his reward
the exact creature who
murdered her husband,
using a cultivator's hoe   5
with verve and skill;
and laughed fit to kill
in disbelief
at the angry, militant
pictures of herself   10
the Sonneteers quickly drew:
not any of them people that
she knew.
A backwoods woman
her house was papered with   15
funeral home calendars and
faces appropriate for a Mississippi
Sunday School. She raised a George,
a Martha, a Jackie and a Kennedy. Also
a John Wesley Junior.°   20

REVOLUTIONARY PETUNIAS.   18–20 *George . . . Junior:* The children are named
after George and Martha Washington, Jackie and John Fitzgerald Kennedy (1917–1963,
thirty-fifth U.S. president), and John Wesley (1703–1791), English evangelical preacher
who founded Methodism.

"Always respect the word of God,"
she said on her way to she didn't
know where, except it would be by
electric chair, and she continued
"Don't yall forgit to *water*   25
my purple petunias."

MARGARET WALKER   (b. 1915)

Iowa Farmer   1942

I talked to a farmer one day in Iowa.
We looked out far over acres of wheat.
He spoke with pride and yet not boastfully;
he had no need to fumble for his words.
He knew his land and there was love for home   5
within the soft serene eyes of his son.
His ugly house was clean against the storm;
there was no hunger deep within the heart
nor burning riveted within the bone,
but here they ate a satisfying bread.   10
Yet in the Middle West where wheat was plentiful;
where grain grew golden under sunny skies
and cattle fattened through the summer heat
I could remember more familiar sights.

EDMUND WALLER   (1606–1687)

Go, Lovely Rose   1645

Go, lovely rose!
Tell her that wastes her time and me
  That now she knows,
When I resemble° her to thee,   *compare*
How sweet and fair she seems to be.   5

  Tell her that's young,
And shuns to have her graces spied,
  That hadst thou sprung
In deserts, where no men abide,
Thou must have uncommended died.   10

  Small is the worth
Of beauty from the light retired;
  Bid her come forth,
Suffer herself to be desired,
And not blush so to be admired.   15

  Then die! that she
The common fate of all things rare
  May read in thee;

How small a part of time they share
That are so wondrous sweet and fair.   20

ROBERT PENN WARREN   (1905–1989)

Heart of Autumn   *1978*

Wind finds the northwest gap, fall comes.
Today, under gray cloud-scud and over gray
Wind-flicker of forest, in perfect formation, wild geese
Head for a land of warm water, the *boom*, the lead pellet.

Some crumple in air, fall. Some stagger, recover control,   5
Then take the last glide for a far glint of water. None
Knows what has happened. Now, today, watching
How tirelessly *V* upon *V* arrows the season's logic,

Do I know my own story? At least, they know
When the hour comes for the great wing-beat. Sky-strider,   10
Star-strider—they rise, and the imperial utterance,
Which cries out for distance, quivers in the wheeling sky.

That much they know, and in their nature know
The path of pathlessness, with all the joy
Of destiny fulfilling its own name.   15
I have known time and distance, but not why I am here.

Path of logic, path of folly, all
The same—and I stand, my face lifted now skyward,
Hearing the high beat, my arms outstretched in the tingling
Process of transformation, and soon tough legs,   20

With folded feet, trail in the sounding vacuum of passage,
And my heart is impacted with a fierce impulse
To unwordable utterance—
Toward sunset, at a great height.

BRUCE WEIGL   (b. 1949)

Song of Napalm   *1985*

For My Wife

After the storm, after the rain stopped pounding,
We stood in the doorway watching horses
Walk off lazily across the pasture's hill.
We stared through the black screen,
Our vision altered by the distance   5
So I thought I saw a mist

Kicked up around their hooves when they faded
Like cut-out horses
Away from us.
The grass was never more blue in that light, more   10
Scarlet; beyond the pasture
Trees scraped their voices in the wind, branches
Criss-crossed the sky like barbed-wire
But you said they were only branches.

Okay. The storm stopped pounding.   15
I am trying to say this straight: for once
I was sane enough to pause and breathe
Outside my wild plans and after the hard rain
I turned my back on the old curses, I believed
They swung finally away from me . . .   20

But still the branches are wire
And thunder is the pounding mortar,
Still I close my eyes and see the girl
Running from her village, napalm
Stuck to her dress like jelly,   25
Her hands reaching for the no one
Who waits in waves of heat before her.

So I can keep on living,
So I can stay here beside you,
I try to imagine she runs down the road and wings   30
Beat inside her until she rises
Above the stinking jungle and her pain
Eases, and your pain, and mine.
But the lie swings back again.
The lie works only as long as it takes to speak   35
And the girl runs only so far
As the napalm allows
Until her burning tendons and crackling
Muscles draw her up
Into that final position   40
Burning bodies so perfectly assume. Nothing
Can change that; she is burned behind my eyes
And not your good love and not the rain-swept air
And not the jungle green
Pasture unfolding before us can deny it.   45

PHYLLIS WHEATLEY   (1754–1784)

On Being Brought from Africa to America   1773

'Twas mercy brought me from my *Pagan* land,
Taught my benighted soul to understand
That there's a God, that there's a *Saviour* too:

Once I redemption neither sought nor knew.
Some view our sable race with scornful eye,   5
"Their colour is a diabolic die."
Remember, *Christians*, *Negroes*, black as *Cain*,
May be refin'd, and join th' angelic train.

RICHARD WILBUR   (b. 1921)

Ballade for the Duke of Orleans   *1961*

who offered a prize at Blois, circa 1457, for
the best ballade employing the line "Je
meurs de soif auprès de la fontaine."°

Flailed from the heart of water in a bow,
He took the falling fly; my line went taut;
Foam was in uproar where he drove below;
In spangling air I fought him and was fought.
Then, wearied to the shallows, he was caught,   5
Gasped in the net, lay still and stony-eyed.
It was no feeling iris I had sought.
I die of thirst, here at the fountain-side.

Down in the harbor's flow and counter-flow
I left my ships with hopes and heroes fraught.   10
Ten times more golden than the sun could show,
Calypso° gave the darkness I besought.
Oh, but her fleecy touch was dearly bought:
All spent, I wakened by my only bride,
Beside whom every vision is but nought,   15
And die of thirst, here at the fountain-side.

Where does that Plenty dwell, I'd like to know,
Which fathered poor Desire, as Plato taught?
Out on the real and endless waters go
Conquistador and stubborn Argonaut.   20
Where Buddha bathed, the golden bowl he brought
Gilded the stream, but stalled its living tide.
The sunlight withers as the verse is wrought.
I die of thirst, here at the fountain-side.

ENVOI

Duke, keep your coin. All men are born distraught,   25
And will not for the world be satisfied.
Whether we live in fact, or but in thought,
We die of thirst, here at the fountain-side.

BALLADE. The refrain line in French means "I am dying of thirst beside the fountain."
12 *Calypso:* Sea nymph in Homer's *Odyssey* with whom Odysseus lives for seven years.

RICHARD WILBUR (b. 1921)

The Sirens   *1950*

I never knew the road
From which the whole earth didn't call away,
With wild birds rounding the hill crowns,
Haling out of the heart an old dismay,
Or the shore somewhere pounding its slow code,   5
Or low-lighted towns
Seeming to tell me, stay.

Lands I have never seen
And shall not see, loves I will not forget,
All I have missed, or slighted, or foregone   10
Call to me now. And weaken me. And yet
I would not walk a road without a scene.
I listen going on,
The richer for regret.

WILLIAM CARLOS WILLIAMS (1883–1963)

The Red Wheelbarrow   *1923*

so much depends
upon

a red wheel
barrow

glazed with rain   5
water

beside the white
chickens.

WILLIAM WORDSWORTH (1770–1850)

Lines Written in Early Spring   *1798*

I heard a thousand blended notes,
While in a grove I sate° reclined,   *sat*
In that sweet mood when pleasant thoughts
Bring sad thoughts to the mind.

To her fair works did Nature link   5
The human soul that through me ran;
And much it grieved my heart to think
What man has made of man.

Through primrose tufts, in that green bower,
The periwinkle° trailed its wreaths;   10
And 'tis my faith that every flower
Enjoys the air it breathes.

The birds around me hopped and played,
Their thoughts I cannot measure—
But the least motion which they made,   15
It seemed a thrill of pleasure.

The budding twigs spread out their fan,
To catch the breezy air;
And I must think, do all I can,
That there was pleasure there.   20

If this belief from heaven be sent,
If such be Nature's holy plan,
Have I not reason to lament
What man has made of man?

LINES WRITTEN IN EARLY SPRING.   10 *periwinkle:* a trailing evergreen plant with
blue or white flowers.

WILLIAM WORDSWORTH (1770–1850)

The Solitary Reaper   *1807*

Behold her, single in the field,
Yon solitary Highland Lass!
Reaping and singing by herself;
Stop here, or gently pass!

Alone she cuts and binds the grain,   5
And sings a melancholy strain;
O listen! for the Vale profound
Is overflowing with the sound.

No Nightingale did ever chaunt
More welcome notes to weary bands   10
Of travelers in some shady haunt,
Among Arabian sands;
A voice so thrilling ne'er was heard
In springtime from the Cuckoo bird,
Breaking the silence of the seas   15
Among the farthest Hebrides.°

Will no one tell me what she sings?°
Perhaps the plaintive numbers flow

THE SOLITARY REAPER.   16 *Hebrides:* a group of islands belonging to and off the
west coast of Scotland.   17 *Will . . . sings:* The speaker does not understand Scots Gaelic,
the language in which the woman sings.

For old, unhappy, far-off things,
And battles long ago;   20
Or is it some more humble lay,
Familiar matter of today?
Some natural sorrow, loss, or pain,
That has been, and may be again?

Whate'er the theme, the Maiden sang   25
As if her song could have no ending;
I saw her singing at her work,
And o'er the sickle bending—
I listened, motionless and still;
And, as I mounted up the hill,   30
The music in my heart I bore,
Long after it was heard no more.

WILLIAM BUTLER YEATS   (1865–1939)

Sailing to Byzantium°   *1927*

1

That is no country for old men. The young
In one another's arms, birds in the trees
—Those dying generations—at their song,
The salmon-falls, the mackerel-crowded seas,
Fish, flesh, or fowl, commend all summer long   5
Whatever is begotten, born, and dies.
Caught in that sensual music all neglect
Monuments of unaging intellect.

2

An aged man is but a paltry thing.
A tattered coat upon a stick, unless   10
Soul clap its hands and sing, and louder sing
For every tatter in its mortal dress,
Nor is there singing school but studying
Monuments of its own magnificence;
And therefore I have sailed the seas and come   15
To the holy city of Byzantium.

3

O sages standing in God's holy fire
As in the gold mosaic of a wall,
Come from the holy fire, perne in a gyre,°
And be the singing-masters of my soul.   20

SAILING TO BYZANTIUM. In Yeats's private mythology, Byzantium (called
Constantinople in Roman times and Istanbul today) symbolizes art, artifice, sophistication,
and eternity as opposed to the natural world and physicality.   19 *perne in a gyre:* turning
about in a spiral motion. See the diagram on p. 781.

Consume my heart away; sick with desire
And fastened to a dying animal
It knows not what it is; and gather me
Into the artifice of eternity.

4

Once out of nature I shall never take   25
My bodily form from any natural thing,
But such a form as Grecian goldsmiths make
Of hammered gold and gold enameling
To keep a drowsy Emperor awake;
Or set upon a golden bough to sing   30
To lords and ladies of Byzantium
Of what is past, or passing, or to come.

PAUL ZIMMER   (b. 1934)

The Day Zimmer Lost Religion   *1973*

The first Sunday I missed Mass on purpose
I waited all day for Christ to climb down
Like a wiry flyweight° from the cross and
Club me on my irreverent teeth, to wade into
My blasphemous gut and drop me like a   5
Red hot thurible,° the devil roaring in
Reserved seats until he got the hiccups.

It was a long cold way from the old days
When cassocked and surpliced° I mumbled Latin
At the old priest and rang his obscure bell.   10
A long way from the dirty wind that blew
The soot like venial sins° across the schoolyard
Where God reigned as a threatening,
One-eyed triangle high in the fleecy sky.

The first Sunday I missed Mass on purpose   15
I waited all day for Christ to climb down
Like the playground bully, the cuts and mice
Upon his face agleam, and pound me
Till my irreligious tongue hung out.
But of course He never came, knowing that   20
I was grown up and ready for Him now.

THE DAY ZIMMER LOST RELIGION.   3 *flyweight:* a boxer weighing less than 112
pounds.   *thurible:* a censer, container in which incense is burned.   9 *cassocked and*
surpliced: wearing the traditional garb of an altar boy during Mass.   12 *venial sins:* minor
inadvertent sins.

DRAMA

25

Drama: An Overview

"Doing" or "acting" is now—and always has been—the major characteristic of **drama.** The word itself is derived from the Greek word *dran*, which means "to do" or "to act." The actors in a play act or *perform* the various actions—and also *mimic* the emotions of the major characters—in order to create a maximum impact on the living people who make up the audience. Drama is therefore an imitative, or **mimetic,** art. Although the word *drama* sometimes means a single **play,** it may also refer to a group of plays ("Elizabethan drama") or to all plays collectively ("world drama"). While drama shares many characteristics with fiction and poetry, the most important difference is that plays are written to be presented by actors on a stage before an audience.

AN ABBREVIATED HISTORY OF DRAMA

Drama evolved from the rites of early cultures. Prehistoric people would perform religious rituals in which they acted out their deepest fears, strongest desires, and greatest achievements. A successful hunt, for instance, might have been followed by a rite of thanksgiving in which the hunt was symbolically reenacted. During the winter, people might have acted out the coming of spring and the regeneration of the earth, to reassure themselves that such a rebirth would occur.

Our earliest extant plays were written by a number of dramatists who lived during the sixth, fifth, and fourth centuries B.C. in the Greek city-state of Athens. These writers retained much of the earlier ritualistic quality, for they retold many of the ancient myths (e.g., Agamemnon, Oedipus, Antigone) and offered their plays for performance during the Athenian religious festivals. But the Greek playwrights also shaped drama into its modern form by increasing the number of characters and dividing the action into separate scenes.

Drama retained connections with religion and ritual throughout much of its subsequent history. After the breakup of the Roman Empire in the West (fifth century A.D.), drama languished for centuries, only to emerge again in the medieval churches of England and other Western European countries as part of the Mass. As medieval and early Renaissance drama evolved outside the churches, it was still linked to Christianity, especially the **mystery plays,** which dramatized many biblical stories (e.g., Adam and Eve, Cain and Abel, Noah, Abraham and Isaac, Herod, and the Shepherds Abiding in the Field), and the **morality plays,** which show the way to live a Christian life. With the increasing secularization of society during and after the Renaissance, drama departed from these religious foundations, and rendered the twists and turns of human conflicts. To the degree that modern drama deals with behavioral and ethical problems, however, it is still connected with the ritualistic and religious concerns on which it was originally based.

PERFORMANCE: THE LIFE OF A PLAY

A person who writes plays is a **dramatist** or a **playwright** (a term combining *play* with the word *wright*—a worker or builder). The text of a play consists of dialogue, monologue, and stage directions. **Dialogue** is the conversation of two or more characters. A **monologue** is spoken by a single character who is usually alone on stage. **Stage directions** are the playwright's instructions about vocal expression, "body language," stage appearance, lighting, and similar matters.

What distinguishes drama from all other written forms is the acting or staging—the **performance.** It is performance that brings about movement, immediacy, and excitement. Actors bring the characters and the dialogue to life—loving or hating, strutting or cringing, shouting or whispering, laughing or crying, and inspiring or deceiving. Actors give their bodies to the characters, providing vocal quality and inflection, gestures, and facial expressions. Actors move about the stage according to a pattern called **blocking.** Actors also engage in **stage business**—gestures or movements that keep the production active, dynamic, and often funny.

It is also the actors who bring the play to life through the wearing of **costumes** and the use of **makeup,** which help the audience understand the social status, time period, occupation, and mentality of the characters. Costumes may be used realistically (a king in rich robes, a salesman in a rumpled business suit), or symbolically (the use of black clothing for a character suffering depression). Makeup is used to enhance an actor's facial features, but it may also help to fix the illusion of youth or age, or may emphasize a character's joy or sorrow.

In the theater, all aspects of performance are controlled by the

director, the person who plans the production in association with the **producer,** and who directs the actors to move, speak, and act in ways that are consistent with his or her vision of the play. When a play calls for special effects, such as Molière's *Love Is the Doctor*, the director works with specialists such as musicians, choreographers, and sound technicians to enhance and enliven the performance.

Most modern plays are performed on a **proscenium stage** (like a room with one wall missing so that the audience may look in on the action), a **thrust stage** (an acting area that projects into the audience), or a **theater-in-the-round** (an area that is surrounded by the audience). On whatever kind of stage, the modern theater is likely to provide **scenery** and **properties** (or **props**), which locate the action in place and time and underscore the ideas of the director. The **sets** (the appurtenances for a particular scene) may be changed a number of times during a performance, as in *An Enemy of the People*, or a single set may be used throughout, as in *Oedipus the King*.

The modern theater also relies heavily on **lighting.** Lights were not used in the theater until the seventeenth century. Before then, plays were performed during the day and under the sky, in inn-yards and courtyard-like theaters like the Globe Theatre in London, in which many of Shakespeare's plays were first performed. Because open-air performances were dependent on favorable weather, plays were eventually taken indoors, and theaters then relied on candles, and later on gaslight, for lighting effects (yes, some theaters burned down). The development of electric lights in the late nineteenth century revolutionized dramatic productions. For today's performances, producers may use spotlights, filters, dimmers, and other lighting technology to emphasize various parts of the stage, to shape the mood of a scene, and to highlight individual characters. In productions of plays like *The Glass Menagerie* and *Death of a Salesman*, lighting is even used to indicate changes in time or place.

The **audience** too plays a significant role in a theatrical performance. The reactions of spectators to the onstage action provide feedback to the actors, and thus continually alter the delivery and pace of the performance. Similarly, the audience, sitting together in a darkened auditorium, offers a communal response to the events taking place on stage. Thus, drama *in the theater* is the most immediate and accessible of the literary arts. There is no narrator, as in prose fiction, and no speaker, as in poetry, between us and the stage action.

TYPES OF DRAMA

The ancient Athenian Greek philosopher and critic Aristotle (384–322 B.C.), in his *Poetics*, divides drama into **tragedy** and **comedy.** Tragedy recounts an individual's downfall; it begins high and ends low. Comedy describes the regeneration of an individual or group; it begins in doubt and ends in success. (Although tragedy is normally considered sad and comedy happy, the brief definitions here have more to do with patterns of action than with our emotional responses. For more complete discussions of tragedy and comedy, see pp. 1046 and 1291).

Pure forms of tragedy and comedy have rarely been written since the ancient classical period, and most British and American plays offer a mixture of the two forms. For example, Shakespeare's tragedies include witty and humorous scenes, and his comedies often deal with serious and threatening problems. In many plays written before the twentieth century, however, one type or the other predominates. When the patterns and emotions are truly mixed, the play is called a **tragicomedy,** a term first used by the Roman playwright Plautus around 186 B.C. Today the term encompasses a broad range of plays that mix tragic and comic effects. In many ways, tragicomedy is the dominant form of twentieth-century drama.

Other forms of drama that have evolved from tragedy and comedy include **farce, melodrama,** and **social drama.** Farce is a form of comedy crammed full of slapstick stage business and extravagant dialogue, with rapid shifts in action and emotion. Chekhov's *The Bear* is a good example of farce. Melodrama is a debased form of tragedy with a happy ending. The adversities in melodrama all grow out of plot rather than character— the mortgage is due, the family business is failing, the daughter has been kidnapped by the villain. The hero always arrives just in time to pay the mortgage, save the business, and rescue the heroine, while the villain leaves the stage saying something like "Curses, foiled again!"

Social drama, sometimes called *problem drama*, evolved in the nineteenth century. This type of play explores social problems and the individual's place in society. The plays can be tragic, comic, or mixed. Examples of social drama are Ibsen's *An Enemy of the People*, Glaspell's *Trifles*, and Miller's *Death of a Salesman*.

One further distinction will be helpful in your exploration of drama. **Full-length plays** are dramas that usually contain three or five separate acts (as in *An Enemy of the People*) or a long series of separate scenes (as in *Oedipus the King* and *The Glass Menagerie*). Such plays, designed for a full performance of about three or more hours in the theater, make possible a complete and in-depth development of character, conflict, and idea. Full-length plays containing separate acts, like *Hamlet* and *Death of a Salesman*, are also subdivided. Sometimes these subdivisions, or **scenes,** are not noted in the text, but often they are given formal scene numbers. Characteristic of scenes are a coherent action, a unified setting, and a fixed group of characters.

Shorter dramas, usually **one-act plays,** do not permit extensive development and subdivision because they are by definition more limited and confined than full-length plays. If you consider parallels with fiction, the full-length play is analogous to the novel; the one-act play is like the short story. The short play is appropriate for brief performances. Sometimes an evening at the theater is made up of two or three one-acters. In addition, the one-act play may be used for studio and classroom performance, or, for that matter, for adaptation as hour or half-hour performances for film or television. Usually, one-act plays like *Before Breakfast* and *The Bear* flow smoothly from beginning to end without a break. On the other hand, somewhat longer short plays, like *Love Is the Doctor* and *Am I Blue*, may contain formal scene and act divisions. *Love Is the Doctor* is unique because it features **French scenes,** in which a new scene begins each time a character enters or leaves the stage.

Given all these terms and types, you should keep in mind that classification is not the goal of reading or seeing plays. It is less important to identify *Am I Blue* as a comedy or *Before Breakfast* as a melodramatic tragedy than it is to feel and understand the experiences and ideas that each play offers us.

THE BASIC ELEMENTS OF DRAMATIC LITERATURE

In the following sections we consider the basic elements of dramatic literature: *plot, character, point of view, setting, language, tone, symbolism,* and *theme* or *meaning.* Poetic drama, such as Sophocles's *Oedipus the King* and Shakespeare's *Hamlet* and *A Midsummer Night's Dream*, add elements that characterize poetry, such as *meter* and *rhyme.* All these elements have remained relatively constant throughout the history of drama. Aristotle identifies six components of drama: plot, character, language, spectacle, thought, and song. Modern drama cannot be judged exclusively on the basis of Aristotle's six aspects, but his list illustrates the continuity of dramatic elements and techniques.

Plot, Action, and Conflict

Plot, in drama as in fiction, is an ordered chain of physical, emotional, or intellectual events that ties the action together (see also Chapter 3, pp. 94–135). It is a planned sequence of interrelated actions that begins in a state of imbalance, grows out of conflict, reaches a peak of complication, and resolves into some new situation. It is, of course, easy to oversimplify the idea of plot in a play. Dramatic plots are often more complicated than a single movement toward a single solution or resolution. Some plays have **double plots**—two different but related lines of action going on at the same time. Other plays offer a **main plot,** together with a **subplot** that comments, either directly or indirectly, on the main plot. In *A Midsummer Night's Dream* four separate plots are woven together to form a single story.

The mainspring of plot in a play is **conflict,** which can be physical, psychological, social, or all three. It can involve a character's struggle against another person, against the environment, or against himself or herself. Most commonly, the conflict in a play is a combination of these general types. In Albee's *The Sandbox*, for example, Grandma is in conflict with her family, society, and death. Similarly, the hero in *Hamlet* is in conflict with himself, his enemies, and his society—all at the same time. Conflict in drama can be more explicit than in prose fiction because we actually see the clash of wills and characters on stage or on the page.

In a classic full-length play, sometimes also called a **regular play** (a play conforming to *rule*), we may trace a five-stage *plot structure*—exposition, complication, crisis or climax, catastrophe, and resolution. The German critic Gustav Freytag (1816–1895) compares this pattern to a pyramid, in which the rising action (exposition and complication) leads up to the point of crisis or climax and is followed by the falling action (the catastrophe and resolution).

The Freytag Pyramid of Plot Structure

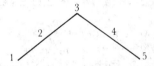

1. Exposition or Introduction
2. Complication and Development
3. Climax or Crisis
4. Falling Action, Catastrophe
5. Resolution or Dénouement

In the first of these stages, the **exposition,** the audience receives essential background information; we are introduced to the characters, the situations, and the conflicts. In *Oedipus the King* this material is conveyed in the prologue. Other playwrights might have several characters discuss the people in the play and the crucial events that have occurred before the beginning of the play's action. In *Hamlet*, for example, the conversations of Barnardo, Marcellus, and Horatio provide critical information. Other plays distribute the information throughout the entire action, as in *Trifles*.

In the second stage, the **complication,** the conflicts grow heated and the plot becomes more involved. As the complication develops, the situation becomes more and more tightly knotted, leading to the most excruciating part of the play—the **crisis** or **climax**—which is the *turning point* or *high point*. In this third stage the hero or heroine faces an agonizing decision, and almost simultaneously chooses a course of action (for better or worse) that determines the outcome.

The pyramid begins its downward slope in stage 4, the **catastrophe.** The catastrophe (not to be confused with our modern use of the term to mean "disaster") is the moment of revelation when all the pieces fall into place. It is often caused by the discovery of certain information or events that have been unknown to most of the characters up to that instant. During the final stage, the **resolution,** conflicts are resolved, lives are straightened out or ended, and loose ends are tied up.

Since the days of Shakespeare, English dramatists have generally been more concerned with *dramatic effect* than with *dramatic form.* As a result, many plays in English do not perfectly follow the regular structure outlined here. The pattern is rather an ideal model, which individual dramatists may vary according to their needs. You should therefore be prepared for plays that offer little exposition, have no dénouement, compress the crisis-climax-catastrophe-resolution into a short space, or modify the formal pattern in some other significant way.

Character

A **character** is a person created by the playwright to carry the action, language, ideas, and emotions of the play. Many of the types of characters that populate prose fiction are also found in drama (see Chapter 4, pp. 137–95). In drama as in fiction, for instance, we find both *round* and *flat* characters. A **round character,** like Shakespeare's Hamlet and Ibsen's Dr. Thomas Stockmann, undergoes a change or development as the play progresses. On the other hand, a **flat character,** like Molière's Lisette, is undeveloped, even though he or she may be interesting, vital, and amusing. As in fiction, dramatic characters can also be considered **static**—that is, fixed and unchanging—or **dynamic**—that is, growing and developing.

Because drama depends on conflict as fully as fiction does, we also find protagonists and antagonists in plays. The **protagonist** is usually the central character in the action. The **antagonist** opposes the protagonist and is often the villain. A classic opposition of this type may be seen in *Hamlet,* in which Prince Hamlet is the protagonist while his uncle, King Claudius, is the antagonist. The play develops as Hamlet the protagonist tries first to confirm, and then to punish, the villainy of his uncle, the antagonist.

There are also characters who set off or highlight the protagonist, and others who are in the main peripheral to the action. The first of these types, called a **foil,** is a character whose behavior and attitudes contrast to the protagonist's. In *Hamlet,* for instance, both Laertes and Fortinbras are foils to the prince. The second type, called a **choric figure,** is rooted in the choruses of Greek tragedy, and is usually played by a single character, often a friend or confidant of the protagonist, such as Horatio in *Hamlet.* This type of character is sometimes called a **raisonneur** (the French word meaning *reasoner*) if he or she also provides commentary about the major actions of the play.

Dramatic characters may be **realistic, nonrealistic, symbolic,** and **stereotyped,** or **stock.** Realistic characters are normally accurate imitations of individualized men and women; they are given backgrounds, person-alities, desires, motivations, and thoughts. Nonrealistic characters are usually stripped of such individualizing touches; they are often undevel-oped and symbolic. All the characters in *The Sandbox* are nonrealistic. Symbolic characters represent an idea, a way of life, moral values, or some other abstraction. The two women in *Tea Party* thus symbolize the agonized loneliness of old age; Dr. Fillpocket in *Love Is the Doctor* symbolizes cynicism, greed, charlatanism, and the misuse of responsibility.

Stereotyped or stock characters have been used in drama (and other types of literature) throughout the ages. In effect they serve as a shortcut in characterization for both dramatist and audience. The general types developed in classical and Renaissance drama are the *bumpkin*, the *braggart*, the *trickster*, the *victim*, the *stubborn father*, the *shrewish wife*, the *lusty youth*, and the *prodigal son*. Modern drama continues these stereotypes, and it has also invented many of its own, such as the *hardboiled detective*, the *loner cowboy*, the *honest policeman*, and the *whore with a heart of gold*.

The major difference between characters in fiction or poetry and characters in drama is the way they are unfolded. Playwrights do not have the fiction writer's freedom to tell us directly about a character. We learn about characters in plays by paying attention to their words and actions, by listening to what other characters say about them, and by watching what other characters do to them.

Point of View and Perspective

Point of view in drama is strikingly different from the comparable element in fiction and poetry (see also Chapter 6, pp. 196–240). With the exceptions of works like Tennessee Williams's *The Glass Menagerie*, plays rarely have narrators, and it is difficult for a playwright to sustain a perspective that is exclusively first-person-protagonist or third-person-omniscient. Instead, playwrights employ the **dramatic point of view** in which we receive only the information contained in the speeches and actions. The key to the dramatic point of view is that the playwright gives us the objective raw materials—the action and the words—but arranges them in such a way that we ourselves must draw all the conclusions.

Within these limits playwrights do have techniques to lead an audience to see things from a specific character's perspective. In O'Neill's *Before Breakfast*, the entire play is a monologue spoken by the major character, Mrs. Rowland. Another commonly used device is the **soliloquy,** in which the hero or villain reveals his or her thoughts directly to the audience. The soliloquies of sixteenth- and seventeenth-century plays are common techniques for revealing the thoughts and emotions of characters. In the twentieth century, soliloquies have again become an important element in experimental and nonrealistic drama. Another device, called the **aside,** allows a character to address brief remarks to the audience—or to another character—which the other characters do not hear.

Setting, Sets, and Scenery

In the text of a play, the **setting** (or **set**) is usually described in the opening stage directions. (Compare Chapter 5, pp. 241–65.) Its function is to establish the play in a specific time and place, and it may also determine the play's level of reality. In a production, the scenery is the first thing we see on the stage, and it brings the written directions to life through backdrops, furnishings, props, and lighting.

Like characters, the setting may be realistic or nonrealistic. A **realistic setting** requires extensive scenery and stage furniture, for the object is to create as real an environment as possible. In *Trifles*, for example, the setting is a realistic rendering of an early twentieth-century Nebraska farm kitchen. A **nonrealistic setting** is nonrepresentational and often symbolic, as in *The Sandbox*, where the scenery consists of a sandbox and a number of chairs. Often such scenery is produced in a **unit set**—a series of platforms, rooms, stairs, and exits that form the locations for all the play's actions, as in *The Glass Menagerie*.

Most one-act plays make do with a single setting and with action that is relatively short. Many of the plays in this anthology, for example, limit their action to a single time and place. That time may be as short as the fifteen or so minutes required for a performance of *Tea Party*, for example, or it may be visualized as happening in an hour (*Am I Blue*), an afternoon (*Love Is the Doctor*), or an entire day (*The Sandbox*). The underlying theory of time and place here is that the illusion of reality is enhanced if the time of the play is arranged to coincide with the length of the show.

Many full-length plays also confine the action to a single setting and a limited time, as with Sophocles's *Oedipus the King*, which takes place, in presumably less than a day, before the royal palace in the ancient Greek city of Thebes. Other longer plays may extend time while being set in the same location, as in *The Glass Menagerie*, in which the extended time of action all occurs in the apartment home of the Wingfields. Some full-length plays change settings frequently just as they also stretch out time. *Hamlet* takes place in a number of different locations, including battlements, a throne room, a bed chamber, and a graveyard (all these scene changes put great strain on a production committed to realistic scene design).

Diction, Imagery, Style, and Language

Most of what we learn about characters, relationships, and conflict is conveyed through dramatic language (see also Chapter 7, pp. 266–98). Characters tell us what they think, hope, fear, and desire. Their dialogue may reflect the details of their daily lives or their deepest thoughts about life and death. Their words must fit the circumstances, the time, and the place of the play. Thus, it would be as wrong for Miller's Willy Loman to speak in Elizabethan blank verse as it would be for Shakespeare's Hamlet to speak in modern American English. This fitting of language to dramatic circumstances is called **decorum.**

The words and rhetorical devices of a play delineate character, emotion, and theme, much as they do in fiction and poetry. Dramatists may employ words that have wide-ranging connotations (or associations) or that acquire many layers of meaning. Such is the case with the words *trifle* and *knot* in Glaspell's play *Trifles.* Similarly, playwrights may have their characters speak in similes or metaphors that contribute significantly to the impact and meaning of the play. Again in *Trifles*, one of the characters compares another to a bird, and this simile grows to become one of the play's central symbols.

Dramatists may also employ accents, dialects, idiom, jargon, and clichés to indicate character traits. The characters in *The Sandbox*, for example, speak in clichés that mark their limitations and shortcomings. The Gravedigger in *Hamlet* speaks in an Elizabethan dialect which distinguishes his life and interests from those of the upper-class persons in the play. Most of the characters in *The Glass Menagerie* speak in dialect, complete with slang expressions, that locates them in the southern United States at the time of the action. In short, playwrights may use any and all stylistic and rhetorical devices of language as they bring character, emotion, conflict, and ideas to their plays.

Tone and Atmosphere

Tone in drama, as in other literature, signifies the way moods and attitudes are created and presented (see also Chapter 8, pp. 299–325). In plays, tone may be conveyed directly to the spectator through voice and through the stage gestures that accompany dialogue, such as rolling one's eyes, throwing up one's hands, shaking one's head, jumping for joy, and staggering backward in grief. Even silence can be an effective device for creating tone and mood.

Whereas voice and movement establish tone on the stage, we have no such exacting guides while reading a play. Sometimes a playwright indicates the tone of specific lines through stage directions. In *The Sandbox*, for instance, Albee prefaces many speeches with directions such as *whining*, *vaguely*, *impatiently*, and *mocking*. These are cues to tone designed for the actors, but which also help readers. When such directions are lacking, the diction, tempo, imagery, and context all become clues to the tone of specific speeches and whole plays.

Tone may create an atmosphere or mood that dominates a play. Let us take the opening scene of *Hamlet*, in which Shakespeare uses tempo and diction to create an atmosphere of fear and apprehension. It is dark and close to midnight, and Francisco, one of the guards, carries a torch:

BARNARDO. Who's there?
FRANCISCO. Nay, answer me. Stand and unfold yourself.

BARNARDO. Long live the king!
FRANCISCO. Barnardo?
BARNARDO. He.

Notice the short lines, the questions, and the choppy and rapid exchange. The tone of the dialogue is anxious and questioning. The exchange thus suggests nervousness, tension, and insecurity. When Hamlet later says that things are bad in Denmark, these opening phrases have established a groundwork which confirms his conclusion.

In the determination of tone, it is important to distinguish between the tone of an individual character and the playwright's tone that shapes our total response to the play. Specific characters may be sincere, sarcastic, joyful, or resigned, but the entire drama may reflect only one or even none of these tones. In *Trifles*, for instance, the tones of some speeches are noted as *resentful, apologetic,* or *mild*. The play as a whole, however, is predominantly bitter and ironic.

One of the most common methods employed by playwrights to control the tone of the play is **dramatic irony.** This type of **situational** (as opposed to **verbal**) irony may be created in any circumstance where the audience knows more than the characters in a play or when one or two characters know more than the others. In *Trifles*, one of the male characters mockingly dismisses the women's concerns by noting that "women are used to worrying about such trifles." The line acquires vast dramatic irony as we watch Mrs. Hale and Mrs. Peters achieve understanding through careful attention to the "trifles" that the men ignore. Such dramatic irony, when used consistently, creates an ironic tone for the entire work. This is the situation in *Oedipus the King*, where the audience always knows more than the protagonist, and almost every line is ironic.

Symbolism and Allegory

As in fiction and poetry, dramatic **symbols** represent meaning or significance beyond the intrinsic identity of the symbol itself (see also Chapter 9, pp. 326–61). Symbols in drama can be persons, settings, objects, actions, situations, or statements. Playwrights have access to both universal and private symbols. **Universal symbols**—such as crosses, flags, snakes, flowers—are generally understood by the audience or reader regardless of the context in which they appear. In Act V of *Hamlet*, for example, we recognize Yorick's skull as a symbol of death. **Private symbols** develop their impact only within the context of a specific play or even a particular scene. We often don't realize that such objects or actions are symbolic when they first occur; they acquire symbolic meaning through context and continued action. *The Sandbox*, for instance, opens with a "large child's sandbox with a toy pail and shovel" on stage. Initially, this object has no symbolic meaning for us. As the play goes on, however, we realize that the sandbox represents the beach, a refuse pile, the childishness we habitually associate with old age, and the grave.

When a play may be found to offer consistent and sustained symbols that refer to general human experiences, that play may be considered an **allegory,** and may be read allegorically. Keller's *Tea Party* dramatizes the preparations that two elderly women make for a young newspaperboy who avoids their party. As an allegory, the play deals with the pathos of the old, who live out their lives with lost memories and hopeless expectations. A more cheerful reading may be applied to Chekhov's *The Bear*, which allegorizes the triumph of love, desire, and life over disappointment, renunciation, and death.

Subject and Theme

Although most playwrights are not primarily concerned to persuade or propagandize their audience, they do write their plays with a design to dramatize ideas about the human condition (see also Chapter 10, pp. 362–409). The aspects of humanity a playwright explores constitute the play's **subject.** Plays may thus be *about* love, religion, hatred, war, ambition, death, envy, or anything else that is part of the human condition.

The ideas that the play dramatizes about its subject make up the play's **theme** or meaning. Thus, a play might explore the idea that love will always find a way or that marriage can be destructive, that pride always leads to disaster, or that grief can be conquered through strength and a commitment to life. The theme is the end result of all the other elements of drama; it is one of the things we are left to think about after we have read a play or seen a production.

As a result, we must pay careful attention to the words, actions, and attitudes of the characters. Frequently, the protagonist and his or her conflicts embody much of the meaning. Hamlet's attempts to prove that his uncle is guilty of murder, and his extended soliloquies of self-accusation, bring forward one of the central ideas in the play: that revenge in a Christian society is questionable and irreligious, and definitely extralegal or illegal.

Since theme is created and conveyed through all the other elements of drama, it is often difficult to isolate and identify. Even short plays may have complex themes, as in Molière's *Love Is the Doctor*, which farcically explores the themes that freedom seeks ways out of suppression, that love is one of the most powerful and inventive of human emotions, and that deceit is thoroughly infused within the human spirit and may be as strong as life itself.

Full-length plays may contain even more thematic strands. Ibsen creates such complexity in *An Enemy of the People*, where he deals with themes of idealism, egotism, betrayal, self-interest, hypocrisy, and deceit. Some plays may even explore contradictory themes, thus complicating analysis still further. For instance, Sophocles's *Oedipus the King* is built on the idea that human beings cannot escape the destiny preordained for them by the gods, or by the fates, or by fortune. At the same time, however, it also explores the idea that fate is the result of an individual's personality and choices. These are contradictory themes, but no more contradictory, perhaps, than life itself.

HOW TO READ A PLAY

The clear difference between the text of a play and its production might lead you to ask why we bother to *read* plays. There are, of course, many answers. The most obvious is that you may never get a chance actually to *see* the performance of a play you want to learn. Then, reading a play can be as exciting and rewarding as reading a novel, a short story, or a poem. In reading, we have the chance to imagine settings, costumes, and action with a degree of scope and vividness that the stage rarely duplicates. We also read plays to familiarize ourselves with important literature. Plays are not simply maps to production; they are a significant and valuable part of our literary heritage. Dramas like *Oedipus the King, Hamlet, Death of a Salesman*, and *The Glass Menagerie* have become cultural touchstones of other works of literature, art, film, and television. Finally, we read plays in order to have the time to study and understand them. Only through reading do we have the opportunity to look at the parts that make up the whole, and to determine how they fit together to create a moving and meaningful experience.

Reading a play, as opposed to watching a performance, carries both advantages and disadvantages. The major *disadvantage* is that you lack the immediacy of live theater. You do not hear the whispers of the murderer and the ranting of the madman, or see the strutting of the soldier and the furtive glances of the conspirators. You do not have the splendor of the palace or the shock of an emptied stage, the spotlight that rivets the audience's attention on a single defiant gesture, the blare of trumpets, or the pathos of the beggar's rags.

The major *advantage* of reading is that you may consider each element in the play at length, and may "stage" the play in your own imagination. In the theater, the action rushes by at the director's pace. There is no opportunity to turn back to an interesting scene or to reconsider an important speech. In addition, a performance always represents someone else's interpretation. The director and the actors have already made choices that emphasize certain avenues of exploration and cut off others. Reading a play lets you avoid these problems. You read at whatever tempo you choose; you turn back and reread a particular speech or scene until you are comfortable with your own reactions. Also you have the freedom to explore those implications or ideas that strike you as interesting. No one else has limited the scope of your considerations.

Try to use the advantages of reading and study to compensate for the disadvantages. You have time and freedom to read carefully, reflect deeply, and follow your thoughts. Rely on your experiences in watching theatrical productions, movies, and television to enhance your reading. Stage the play as fully as you can in the theater of your mind. Become the director, the set designer, the lighting technician, the costume designer, and all the actors. Build whatever mental sets you like, dress your actors as you see fit, and move the characters across the stage of your mind.

Finally, remember that all drama is based, at least in part, on the stage conventions of its own age and theatrical environment. A **stage convention** is a traditional or customary method of presentation (often unrealistic) that is accepted by audiences or readers and allows a playwright to limit and simplify material. Most stage conventions reflect either the physical conditions of the theater or the prejudices of society in a given age. Many of these conventions are explained in the introductions to specific plays, which provide information about drama in a given period. The *chorus* in Greek tragedy, for instance, was made up of fifteen men who changed their speeches in unison. While to us this is not realistic, it is a conventional device of Greek tragedy that allows the playwright to express the reactions of the common people. The *soliloquy* is a similarly unrealistic convention of the Elizabethan stage; it permits the characters to reveal thoughts and feelings directly to the audience. Such a convention may strike you as a disruption of the action, but it reflects both the intimacy of the Elizabethan theaters (when some of the audience sat right on the stage) and the audience's acceptance of such a break in the flow of the play. As increasingly skilled readers of plays, we must accept stage conventions on their own terms, just as we do the conventions of film and television.

BETTY KELLER, *TEA PARTY*

Betty Keller has brought a wide variety of experiences to her work for the theater, including such unlikely jobs as adjusting insurance claims, farming, assisting a photographer, and serving as a prison matron. She worked as a director in many theatrical workshops in Vancouver, British Columbia, and for four years was a principal director with Playhouse Holiday in Vancouver. She taught drama and theater at the Windsor Secondary School in North Vancouver until 1974, the year she published the collection of short plays and sketches from which *Tea Party* is selected. More recently she has published a biography of the Canadian naturalist and writer Ernest Thompson Seton.

Brief as *Tea Party* is, it illustrates the power of drama to depict character and situation and to convey emotion. The main characters are two lonely elderly sisters who have outlived their friends and relatives and have no one except the people who occasionally come to their house to perform various services, such as delivering the paper and reading the meters. The sketch presents their plight deftly and succinctly, touching with great tenderness on the pathos of their loneliness.

Tea Party is too short to present difficult choices for the characters, and hence they hardly get the opportunity to go through the responses and changes that are found in full-length plays. Both Alma and Hester are individualized, however, as they carry on a minor controversy about names and dates from their long-vanished past. Beyond this, in Alma's last speech, which ends the sketch, one might find a hint of the awareness and recognition that we expect of round, developed dramatic characters. Even though the paperboy is not a speaking part, his unkindness to the sisters is clearly shown, and in this way Keller dramatizes the poignant situation of persons whom life has passed by. It is difficult to find a play that conveys so much of life and feeling in so short a span of time and action.

BETTY KELLER (b. 1930)

Tea Party   *1974*

CHARACTERS

Alma Evans: *seventy-five years old, small and spare framed. Her clothing is simple but not outdated, her grey hair cut short and neat. She walks with the aid of a cane, although she would not be classed as a cripple.*

Hester Evans: *seventy-nine years old. There is little to distinguish her physically from her sister, except perhaps a face a little more pinched and pain-worn. She sits in a wheelchair; but although her legs may be crippled, her mind certainly is not.*

The Boy: *in his early teens, seen only fleetingly.*

SCENE. *The sitting room of the Evans sisters' home. The door to the street is on the rear wall Upstage Left,° a large window faces the street Upstage Center. On the right wall is the door to the kitchen; on the left, a door to the remainder of the house. Downstage Left is an easy chair, Upstage Right a sofa, Downstage Right a tea trolley. The room is crowded with the knickknacks gathered by its inhabitants in three-quarters of a century of living.*

[*At rise,* ALMA *is positioning* HESTER'S *wheelchair Upstage Left.* ALMA'S *cane is on* HESTER'S *lap.*]

Upstage Left: To visualize stage locations, assume that the stage directions are described from the viewpoint of an actor facing the audience. Thus "Right" is actually to the left of the audience, and "Left" is right. "Downstage" refers to the front of the stage, while "Upstage" is the back. The terms *down* and *up* were established at a time when stages were tilted toward the audience, so that spectators at floor level could have as complete a view as possible of the entire stage.

HESTER.   That's it.

[ALMA *takes her cane from* HESTER. *They both survey the room.*]

ALMA.   I think I'll sit on the sofa . . . at the far end.
HESTER.   Yes. That will be cosy. Then he can sit on this end between us.

[ALMA *sits on the Downstage Right end of the sofa. They both study the effect.*]

ALMA.   But then he's too close to the door, Hester!

[HESTER *nods, absorbed in the problem.*]

ALMA.   [*moving to the Upstage Left end of sofa.*] Then I'd better sit here.   5
HESTER.   But now he's too far away from me, Alma.

[ALMA *stands; both of them study the room again.*]

ALMA.   But if I push the tea trolley in front of you, he'll have to come to
you, won't he?
HESTER.   Oh, all right, Alma. You're sure it's today?
ALMA.   [*pushing the tea trolley laden with cups and napkins, etc. to* HESTER.] The
first Thursday of the month.
HESTER.   You haven't forgotten the chocolate biscuits?°   10
ALMA.   No dear, they're on the plate. I'll bring them in with the tea. [*Goes
to the window, peering up the street to the Right.*]
HESTER.   And cocoa?
ALMA.   I remembered.
HESTER.   You didn't remember for Charlie's visit.
ALMA.   Charlie drinks tea, Hester. I didn't make cocoa for him because he   15
drinks tea.
HESTER.   Oh. He didn't stay last time anyway.
ALMA.   It was a busy day. . . .
HESTER.   Rushing in and out like that. I was going to tell him about father
and the *Bainbridge* . . . and he didn't stay.
ALMA.   What about the *Bainbridge*?
HESTER.   Her maiden voyage out of Liverpool . . . when father was gone   20
three months and we thought he'd gone down with her.
ALMA.   That wasn't the *Bainbridge*.
HESTER.   Yes, it was. It was the *Bainbridge*. I remember standing on the
dock in the snow when she finally came in. That was the year I'd begun first form,
and I could spell out the letters on her side.
ALMA.   It was her sister ship, the *Heddingham*.
HESTER.   The *Bainbridge*. You were too young to remember. Let's see, the
year was . . .
ALMA.   Mother often told the story. It was the *Heddingham* and her engine   25
broke down off Cape Wrath beyond the Hebrides.
HESTER.   It was 1902 and you were just four years old.
ALMA.   The *Heddingham,* and she limped into port on January the fifth.
HESTER.   January the fourth just after nine in the morning, and we stood

10 *chocolate biscuits:* chocolate cookies.

in the snow and watched the *Bainbridge* nudge the pier, and I cried and the tears froze on my cheeks.

ALMA. The *Heddingham*.

HESTER. Alma, mother didn't cry, you know. I don't think she ever cried. My memory of names and places is sharp so that I don't confuse them as some others I could mention, but sometimes I can't remember things like how people reacted. But I remember that day. There were tears frozen on my cheeks but mother didn't cry.

ALMA. [*nodding.*] She said he didn't offer a word of explanation. Just marched home beside her.

HESTER. [*smiling.*] He never did say much. . . . Is he coming yet?

ALMA. No, can't be much longer though. Almost half past four.

HESTER. Perhaps you'd better bring in the tea. Then it will seem natural.

ALMA. Yes dear, I know. [*Exits out door Upstage Right.*] Everything's ready.

HESTER. What will you talk about?

ALMA. [*re-entering with the teapot*] I thought perhaps . . . [*carefully putting down the teapot.*] . . . perhaps brother George!

HESTER. And the torpedo? No, Alma, he's not old enough for that story!

ALMA. He's old enough to know about courage. I thought I'd show him the medal, too. [*She goes to the window, peers both ways worriedly, then carries on towards the kitchen.*]

HESTER. Not yet? He's late to-night. You're sure it's today?

ALMA. He'll come. It's the first Thursday. [*Exit.*]

HESTER. You have his money?

ALMA. [*returning with the plate of biscuits.*] I've got a twenty dollar bill, Hester.

HESTER. Alma!

ALMA. Well, we haven't used that one on him. It was Dennis, the last one, who always had change. We could get two visits this way, Hester.

HESTER. Maybe Dennis warned him to carry change for a twenty.

ALMA. It seemed worth a try. [*Goes to the window again.*] Are you going to tell him about the *Heddingham*?

HESTER. The *Bainbridge*. Maybe . . . or maybe I'll tell him about the day the Great War ended. Remember, Alma, all the noise, the paper streamers . . .

ALMA. And father sitting silent in his chair.

HESTER. It wasn't the same for him with George gone. Is he coming yet?

ALMA. No dear, maybe he's stopped to talk somewhere. [*looking to the right.*] . . . No . . . no, there he is, on the Davis' porch now!

HESTER. I'll pour then. You get the cocoa, Alma.

ALMA. [*going out.*] It's all ready, I just have to add hot water.

HESTER. Don't forget the marshmallows!

ALMA. [*reappearing*] Oh, Hester, what if he comes in and just sits down closest to the door? He'll never stay!

HESTER. You'll have to prod him along. For goodness sakes, Alma, get his cocoa!

[*ALMA disappears.*]

HESTER. He must be nearly here. He doesn't go to the Leschynskis, and the Blackburns don't get home till after six.

ALMA. [*returning with the cocoa.*] Here we are! Just in . . .

[*The BOY passes the window. There is a slapping sound as the newspaper lands on the porch.*]

[*ALMA and HESTER look at the door and wait, hoping to hear a knock, but they both know the truth. Finally, ALMA goes to the door, opens it and looks down at the newspaper.*]

ALMA.   He's gone on by.
HESTER.   You must have had the day wrong.   60
ALMA.   No, he collected at the Davis'.
HESTER.   [*after a long pause.*] He couldn't have forgotten us.
ALMA.   [*still holding the cocoa, she turns from the door.*] He's collecting at the Kerighan's now. [*She closes the door and stands forlornly.*]
HESTER.   Well, don't stand there with that cocoa! You look silly. [*ALMA brings the cocoa to the tea trolley.*] Here's your tea. [*ALMA takes the cup, sits on the Upstage Left end of the sofa. There is a long silence.*]
HESTER.   I think I'll save that story for the meter man.   65
ALMA.   The *Heddingham?*
HESTER.   The *Bainbridge.*
ALMA.   [*after a pause.*] They don't read the meters for two more weeks.

SLOW BLACKOUT

QUESTIONS

1.   What is the major conflict in this play? The minor conflict?

2.   Why do the two sisters discuss their seating arrangements in preparation for the visit of the paperboy to collect money for the papers? How do we learn that they have made these arrangements a number of times before?

3.   What does Alma's planned use of the twenty-dollar bill show about her character? What does the discussion about the bill and the previous paperboy, together with the discussion about the present paperboy, indicate about the women's self-awareness of what they are doing to have company for tea?

4.   For your understanding of the characters of the two sisters, what is achieved by their controversy about the names *Bainbridge* and *Heddingham?*

GENERAL QUESTIONS

1.   Consider the setting of *Tea Party.* How does this description aid your visualization of the action, of the tasks each of the women performs in their household? Based on the setting, what conclusions can you draw about the relationship of objects and spatial arrangements to the action and development of a play?

2.   Consider the women particularly with regard to their age. In the light of their health and their isolation, how does *Tea Party* present the circumstances of the aged? How can the play be construed as a sociological/political argument, with the elderly as the focus?

ANTON CHEKHOV, *THE BEAR*

Anton Chekhov was born in Taganrog in southern Russia in 1860, the son of a merchant and grandson of a serf. He entered medical school in Moscow in 1879, graduating in 1884. While studying he was also helping to support the family, and he made money by writing scores of stories, jokes, and other potboilers under a variety of pen names, one of which was "The Doctor Without Patients." *The Bear* belongs to the end of this early period, ten years before Chekhov's association with the Moscow Arts Theatre at the end of the century (see also p. 1400).

Chekhov minimized this play, referring to it as a "joke" and also as a "vaudeville"—both words suggesting a farcical work with little form or substance. However, he was also pleased with it, because it was widely appreciated and made him good money. Three months after its first performance in 1888 he was so happy with its earnings that he likened *The Bear* to a "milk cow" because it supplied him with money day in and day out.

The Bear is a farce, a dramatic form designed preeminently to make people laugh, and it therefore contains extravagant language and boisterous and sudden action. But there is also an underlying seriousness that sustains the humor. In their way, both Smirnov and Mrs. Popov have been failures; they could possibly sink into lives of depression and futility, and both are on a very fine wire as the play begins. Chekhov makes clear that Mrs. Popov is filled with resentment at her unfaithful and now dead husband, and also that she is chafing under her self-imposed resolution to lead a live of mourning and self-denial in his memory. Smirnov is having difficulty with creditors, and admits that his relationships with the many women he has known have ended unhappily. He is therefore both cynical and angry.

The climax of the play is the improbable and preposterous challenge that Smirnov offers to Mrs. Popov, resolved by the equally sudden and preposterous outcome. Despite the improbabilities of the play, however, the actions are not impossible because they are a manifestation of the true internal needs of the major participants. Even Chekhov's friend Leo Tolstoy, who criticized some of Chekhov's late plays, found *The Bear* irresistible. He laughed heartily at the farcical and romantic outcome, thereby joining the laughter of the generations since his time.

ANTON CHEKHOV   (1860–1904)

The Bear: A Joke in One Act   *1900*

CAST OF CHARACTERS

> Mrs. Popov. *A widow of seven months, Mrs. Popov is small and pretty, with dimples. She is a landowner. At the start of the play, she is pining away in memory of her dead husband.*
> Grigory Stepanovich Smirnov. *Easily angered and loud, Smirnov is older. He is a landowner, too, and a gentleman farmer of some substance.*
> Luka. *Luka is Mrs. Popov's footman (a servant whose main tasks were to wait table*

and attend the carriages, in addition to general duties). *He is old enough to feel secure in telling Mrs. Popov what he thinks.*
    Gardener, Coachman, Workmen, *who enter at the end.*

SCENE. *The drawing room of* MRS. POPOV's *country home.*

[MRS. POPOV, *in deep mourning, does not remove her eyes from a photograph.*]

    LUKA.   It isn't right, madam ... you're only destroying yourself.... The chambermaid and the cook have gone off berry picking; every living being is rejoicing; even the cat knows how to be content, walking around the yard catching birds, and you sit in your room all day as if it were a convent, and you don't take pleasure in anything. Yes, really! Almost a year has passed since you've gone out of the house!
    MRS. POPOV.   And I shall never go out.... What for? My life is already ended. *He* lies in his grave; I have buried myself in these four walls ... we are both dead.
    LUKA.   There you go again! Your husband is dead, that's as it was meant to be, it's the will of God, may he rest in peace.... You've done your mourning and that will do. You can't go on weeping and mourning forever. My wife died when her time came, too.... Well? I grieved, I wept for a month, and that was enough for her; the old lady wasn't worth a second more. [*Sighs.*] You've forgotten all your neighbors. You don't go anywhere or accept any calls. We live, so to speak, like spiders. We never see the light. The mice have eaten my uniform. It isn't as if there weren't any nice neighbors—the district is full of them ... there's a regiment stationed at Riblov, such officers—they're like candy—you'll never get your fill of them! And in the barracks, never a Friday goes by without a dance; and, if you please, the military band plays music every day.... Yes, madam, my dear lady: you're young, beautiful, in the full bloom of youth—if only you took a little pleasure in life ... beauty doesn't last forever, you know! In ten years' time, you'll be wanting to wave your fanny in front of the officers—and it will be too late.
    MRS. POPOV.   [*determined.*] I must ask you never to talk to me like that! You know that when Mr. Popov died, life lost all its salt for me. It may seem to you that I am alive, but that's only conjecture! I vowed to wear mourning to my grave and not to see the light of day.... Do you hear me? May his departed spirit see how much I love him.... Yes, I know, it's no mystery to you that he was often mean to me, cruel ... and even unfaithful, but I shall remain true to the grave and show him I know how to love. There, beyond the grave, he will see me as I was before his death....
    LUKA.   Instead of talking like that, you should be taking a walk in the   5
garden or have Toby or Giant harnessed and go visit some of the neighbors ...
    MRS. POPOV.   Ai! [*She weeps.*]
    LUKA.   Madam! Dear lady! What's the matter with you! Christ be with you!
    MRS. POPOV.   Oh, how he loved Toby! He always used to ride on him to visit the Korchagins or the Vlasovs. How wonderfully he rode! How graceful he was when he pulled at the reins with all his strength! Do you remember? Toby, Toby! Tell them to give him an extra bag of oats today.
    LUKA.   Yes, madam.

[*Sound of loud ringing.*]

MRS. POPOV. [*shudders.*] Who's that? Tell them I'm not at home!   10
LUKA.   Of course, madam. [*He exits.*]
MRS. POPOV. [*alone. Looks at the photograph.*] You will see, Nicholas, how much I can love and forgive . . . my love will die only when I do, when my poor heart stops beating. [*Laughing through her tears.*] Have you no shame? I'm a good girl, a virtuous little wife. I've locked myself in and I'll be true to you to the grave, and you . . . aren't you ashamed, you chubby cheeks? You deceived me, you made scenes, for weeks on end you left me alone . . .
LUKA. [*enters, alarmed.*] Madam, somebody is asking for you. He wants to see you. . . .
MRS. POPOV.   But didn't you tell them that since the death of my husband, I don't see anybody?
LUKA.   I did, but he didn't want to listen; he spoke about some very   15
important business.
MRS. POPOV.   I am *not at home*!
LUKA.   That's what I told him . . . but . . . the devil . . . he cursed and pushed past me right into the room . . . he's in the dining room right now.
MRS. POPOV. [*losing her temper.*] Very well, let him come in . . . such manners! [*LUKA goes out.*] How difficult these people are! What does he want from me? Why should he disturb my peace? [*Sighs.*] But it's obvious I'll have to go live in a convent. . . . [*Thoughtfully.*] Yes, a convent. . . .
SMIRNOV. [*enters while speaking to LUKA.*] You idiot, you talk too much. . . . Ass! [*Sees MRS. POPOV and changes to dignified speech.*] Madam, may I introduce myself: retired lieutenant of the artillery and landowner, Grigory Stepanovich Smirnov! I feel the necessity of troubling you about a highly important matter. . . .
MRS. POPOV. [*refusing her hand.*] What do you want?   20
SMIRNOV.   Your late husband, whom I had the pleasure of knowing, has remained in my debt for two twelve-hundred-ruble notes. Since I must pay the interest at the agricultural bank tomorrow, I have come to ask you, madam, to pay me the money today.
MRS. POPOV.   One thousand two hundred. . . . And why was my husband in debt to you?
SMIRNOV.   He used to buy oats from me.
MRS. POPOV. [*sighing, to LUKA.*] So, Luka, don't you forget to tell them to give Toby an extra bag of oats.

[*LUKA goes out.*]

[*To SMIRNOV.*] If Nikolai, my husband, was in debt to you, then it goes without saying that I'll pay; but please excuse me today. I haven't any spare cash. The day after tomorrow, my steward will be back from town and I will give him instructions to pay you what is owed; until then I cannot comply with your wishes. . . . Besides, today is the anniversary—exactly seven months ago my husband died, and I'm in such a mood that I'm not quite disposed to occupy myself with money matters.
SMIRNOV.   And I'm in such a mood that if I don't pay the interest tomorrow,   25
I'll be owing so much that my troubles will drown me. They'll take away my estate!
MRS. POPOV.   You'll receive your money the day after tomorrow.

SMIRNOV.   I don't want the money the day after tomorrow. I want it today.

MRS. POPOV.   You must excuse me. I can't pay you today.

SMIRNOV.   And I can't wait until after tomorrow.

MRS. POPOV.   What can I do, if I don't have it now?   30

SMIRNOV.   You mean to say you can't pay?

MRS. POPOV.   I can't pay. . . .

SMIRNOV.   Hm! Is that your last word?

MRS. POPOV.   That is my last word.

SMIRNOV.   Positively the last?   35

MRS. POPOV.   Positively.

SMIRNOV.   Thank you very much. We'll make a note of that. [*Shrugs his shoulders.*] And people want me to be calm and collected! Just now, on the way here, I met a tax officer and he asked me: why are you always so angry, Grigory Stepanovich? Goodness' sake, how can I be anything but angry? I need money desperately . . . I rode out yesterday early in the morning, at daybreak, and went to see all my debtors; and if only one of them had paid his debt . . . I was dog-tired, spent the night God knows where—a Jewish tavern beside a barrel of vodka. . . . Finally I got here, fifty miles from home, hoping to be paid, and you treat me to a "mood." How can I help being angry?

MRS. POPOV.   It seems to me that I clearly said: My steward will return from the country and then you will be paid.

SMIRNOV.   I didn't come to your steward, but to you! What the hell, if you'll pardon the expression, would I do with your steward?

MRS. POPOV.   Excuse me, my dear sir, I am not accustomed to such profane   40
expressions nor to such a tone. I'm not listening to you any more. [*Goes out quickly.*]

SMIRNOV.   [*alone.*] Well, how do you like that? "A mood." . . . "Husband died seven months ago"! Must I pay the interest or mustn't I? I ask you: Must I pay, or must I not? So, your husband's dead, and you're in a mood and all that finicky stuff . . . and your steward's away somewhere; may he drop dead. What do you want me to do? Do you think I can fly away from my creditors in a balloon or something? Or should I run and bash my head against the wall? I go to Gruzdev—and he's not at home; Yaroshevich is hiding, with Kuritsin it's a quarrel to the death and I almost throw him out the window; Mazutov has diarrhea, and this one is in a "mood." Not one of these swine wants to pay me! And all because I'm too nice to them. I'm a sniveling idiot, I'm spineless, I'm an old lady! I'm too delicate with them! So, just you wait! You'll find out what I'm like! I won't let you play around with me, you devils! I'll stay and stick it out until she pays. Rrr! . . . How furious I am today, how furious! I'm shaking inside from rage and I can hardly catch my breath. . . . Damn it! My God, I even feel sick! [*He shouts.*] Hey, you!

LUKA.   [*enters.*] What do you want?

SMIRNOV.   Give me some beer or some water! [*LUKA exits.*] What logic is there in this! A man needs money desperately, it's like a noose around his neck—and she won't pay because, you see, she's not disposed to occupy herself with money matters! . . . That's the logic of a woman! That's why I never did like and do not like to talk to women. I'd rather sit on a keg of gunpowder than talk to a woman. Brr! . . . I even have goose pimples, this broad has put me in such a rage! All I have to do is see one of those spoiled bitches from a distance, and I get so angry it gives me a cramp in the leg. I just want to shout for help.

LUKA. [*entering with water.*] Madam is sick and won't see anyone.

SMIRNOV. Get out! [*LUKA goes.*] Sick and won't see anyone! No need to see   45
me . . . I'll stay and sit here until you give me the money. You can stay sick for a
week, and I'll stay for a week . . . if you're sick for a year, I'll stay a year. . . . I'll
get my own back, dear lady! You can't impress me with your widow's weeds and
your dimpled cheeks . . . we know all about those dimples! [*Shouts through the
window.*] Semyon, unharness the horses! We're not going away quite yet! I'm
staying here! Tell them in the stable to give the horses some oats! You brute, you
let the horse on the left side get all tangled up in the reins again! [*Teasing.*] "Never
mind" . . . I'll give you a never mind! [*Goes away from the window.*] Shit! The heat
is unbearable and nobody pays up. I slept badly last night and on top of everything
else this broad in mourning is "in a mood" . . . my head aches . . . [*Drinks, and
grimaces.*] Shit! This is water! What I need is a drink! [*Shouts.*] Hey, you!

LUKA. [*Enters.*] What is it?

SMIRNOV. Give me a glass of vodka. [*LUKA goes out.*] Oaf! [*Sits down and
examines himself.*] Nobody would say I was looking well! Dusty all over, boots dirty,
unwashed, unkept, straw on my waistcoat. . . . The dear lady probably took me
for a robber. [*Yawns.*] It's not very polite to present myself in a drawing room
looking like this; oh well, who cares? . . . I'm not here as a visitor but as a creditor,
and there's no official costume for creditors. . . .

LUKA. [*enters with vodka.*] You're taking liberties, my good man. . . .

SMIRNOV. [*angrily.*] What?

LUKA. I . . . nothing . . . I only . . .   50

SMIRNOV. Who are you talking to? Shut up!

LUKA. [*aside.*] The devil sent this leech. An ill wind brought him. . . . [*LUKA
goes out.*]

SMIRNOV. Oh how furious I am! I'm so mad I could crush the whole world
into a powder! I even feel faint! [*Shouts.*] Hey, you!

MRS. POPOV [*enters, eyes downcast*]. My dear sir, in my solitude, I have long
ago grown unaccustomed to the masculine voice and I cannot bear shouting. I
must request you not to disturb my peace and quiet!

SMIRNOV. Pay me my money and I'll go.   55

MRS. POPOV. I told you in plain language: I haven't any spare cash now;
wait until the day after tomorrow.

SMIRNOV. And I also told you respectfully, in plain language: I don't need
the money the day after tomorrow, but today. If you don't pay me today, then
tomorrow I'll have to hang myself.

MRS. POPOV. But what can I do if I don't have the money? You're so
strange!

SMIRNOV. Then you won't pay me now? No?

MRS. POPOV. I can't. . . .   60

SMIRNOV. In that case, I can stay here and wait until you pay. . . . [*Sits down.*]
You'll pay the day after tomorrow? Excellent! In that case I'll stay here until the
day after tomorrow. I'll sit here all that time . . . [*Jumps up.*] I ask you: Have I got
to pay the interest tomorrow, or not? Or do you think I'm joking?

MRS. POPOV. My dear sir, I ask you not to shout! This isn't a stable!

SMIRNOV. I wasn't asking you about a stable but about this: Do I have to
pay the interest tomorrow or not?

MRS. POPOV. You don't know how to behave in the company of a lady!

SMIRNOV. No, I don't know how to behave in the company of a lady! 65

MRS. POPOV. No, you don't! You are an ill-bred, rude man! Respectable people don't talk to a woman like that!

SMIRNOV. Ach, it's astonishing! How would you like me to talk to you? In French, perhaps? [*Lisps in anger.*] *Madame, je vous prie*° . . . how happy I am that you're not paying me the money. . . . Ah, pardon, I've made you uneasy! Such lovely weather we're having today! And you look so becoming in your mourning dress. [*Bows and scrapes.*]

MRS. POPOV. That's rude and not very clever!

SMIRNOV. [*teasing.*] Rude and not very clever! I don't know how to behave in the company of ladies. Madam, in my time I've seen far more women than you've seen sparrows. Three times I've fought duels over women; I've jilted twelve women, nine have jilted me! Yes! There was a time when I played the fool; I became sentimental over women, used honeyed words, fawned on them, bowed and scraped. . . . I loved, suffered, sighed at the moon; I became limp, melted, shivered . . . I loved passionately, madly, every which way, devil take me, I chattered away like a magpie about the emancipation of women, ran through half my fortune as a result of my tender feelings; but now, if you will excuse me, I'm on to your ways! I've had enough! Dark eyes, passionate eyes, ruby lips, dimpled cheeks; the moon, whispers, bated breath—for all that I wouldn't give a good goddamn. Present company excepted, of course, but all women, young and old alike, are affected clowns, gossips, hateful, consummate liars to the marrow of their bones, vain, trivial, ruthless, outrageously illogical, and as far as this is concerned [*taps on his forehead.*], well, excuse my frankness, any sparrow could give pointers to a philosopher in petticoats! Look at one of those romantic creatures: muslin, ethereal demigoddess, a thousand raptures, and you look into her soul— a common crocodile! [*Grips the back of a chair; the chair cracks and breaks.*] But the most revolting part of it all is that this crocodile imagines that she has, above everything, her own privilege, a monopoly on tender feelings. The hell with it— you can hang me upside down by that nail if a woman is capable of loving anything besides a lapdog. All she can do when she's in love is slobber! While the man suffers and sacrifices, all her love is expressed in playing with her skirt and trying to lead him around firmly by the nose. You have the misfortune of being a woman, you know yourself what the nature of a woman is like. Tell me honestly: Have you ever in your life seen a woman who is sincere, faithful, and constant? You never have! Only old and ugly ladies are faithful and constant! You're more liable to meet a horned cat or a white woodcock than a faithful woman!

MRS. POPOV. Pardon me, but in your opinion, who is faithful and constant 70 in love? The man?

SMIRNOV. Yes, the man!

MRS. POPOV. The man! [*Malicious laugh.*] Men are faithful and constant in love! That's news! [*Heatedly.*] What right have you to say that? Men are faithful and constant! For that matter, as far as I know, of all the men I have known and now know, my late husband was the best. . . . I loved him passionately, with all my being, as only a young intellectual woman can love; I gave him my youth, my happiness, my life, my fortune; he was my life's breath; I worshipped him as if I

Madame, je vous prie: I beg you, Madam.

were a heathen, and ... and, what good did it do—this best of men himself deceived me shamelessly at every step of the way. After his death, I found his desk full of love letters; and when he was alive—it's terrible to remember—he used to leave me alone for weeks at a time, and before my eyes he flirted with other women and deceived me. He squandered my money, made a mockery of my feelings ... and, in spite of all that, I loved him and was true to him ... and besides, now that he is dead, I am still faithful and constant. I have shut myself up in these four walls forever and I won't remove these widow's weeds until my dying day. ...

SMIRNOV. [*laughs contemptuously.*] Widow's weeds! ... I don't know what you take me for! As if I didn't know why you wear that black outfit and bury yourself in these four walls! Well, well! It's no secret, so romantic! When some fool of a poet passes by this country house, he'll look up at your window and think: "Here lives the mysterious Tamara, who, for the love of her husband, buried herself in these four walls." We know these tricks!

MRS. POPOV. [*flaring.*] What? How dare you say that to me?

SMIRNOV. You may have buried yourself alive, but you haven't forgotten to   75
powder yourself!

MRS. POPOV. How dare you use such expressions with me?

SMIRNOV. Please don't shout. I'm not your steward! You must allow me to call a spade a spade. I'm not a woman and I'm used to saying what's on my mind! Don't you shout at me!

MRS. POPOV. I'm not shouting, you are! Please leave me in peace!

SMIRNOV. Pay me my money and I'll go.

MRS. POPOV. I won't give you any money!   80

SMIRNOV. Yes, you will.

MRS. POPOV. To spite you, I won't pay you anything. You can leave me in peace!

SMIRNOV. I don't have the pleasure of being either your husband or your fiancé, so please don't make scenes! [*Sits down.*] I don't like it.

MRS. POPOV. [*choking with rage.*] You're sitting down?

SMIRNOV. Yes, I am.   85

MRS. POPOV. I ask you to get out!

SMIRNOV. Give me my money ... [*Aside.*] Oh, I'm so furious! Furious!

MRS. POPOV. I don't want to talk to impudent people! Get out of here! [*Pause.*] You're not going? No?

SMIRNOV. No.

MRS. POPOV. No?   90

SMIRNOV. No!

MRS. POPOV. We'll see about that. [*Rings.*]

[*LUKA enters.*]

Luka, show the gentleman out!

LUKA. [*goes up to SMIRNOV.*] Sir, will you please leave, as you have been asked. You mustn't ...

SMIRNOV. [*jumping up.*] Shut up! Who do you think you're talking to? I'll make mincemeat out of you!

LUKA. [*his hand to his heart.*] Oh my God! Saints above! [*Falls into chair.*] Oh,   95
I feel ill! I can't catch my breath!

MRS. POPOV. Where's Dasha? Dasha! [*She shouts.*] Dasha! Pelagea! Dasha!
[*She rings.*]

LUKA. Oh! They've all gone berry picking . . . there's nobody at home . . .
I'm ill! Water!

MRS. POPOV. Will you please get out!

SMIRNOV. Will you please be more polite?

MRS. POPOV. [*clenches her fist and stamps her feet.*] You're nothing but a crude   100
bear! A brute! A monster!

SMIRNOV. What? What did you say?

MRS. POPOV. I said that you were a bear, a monster!

SMIRNOV. [*advancing toward her.*] Excuse me, but what right do you have to
insult me?

MRS. POPOV. Yes, I am insulting you . . . so what? Do you think I'm afraid
of you?

SMIRNOV. And do you think just because you're one of those romantic   105
creations, that you have the right to insult me with impunity? Yes? I challenge
you!

LUKA. Lord in Heaven! Saints above! . . . Water!

SMIRNOV. Pistols!

MRS. POPOV. Do you think just because you have big fists and you can
bellow like a bull, that I'm afraid of you? You're such a bully!

SMIRNOV. I challenge you! I'm not going to let anybody insult me, and I
don't care if you are a woman, a delicate creature!

MRS. POPOV. [*trying to get a word in edgewise.*] Bear! Bear! Bear!   110

SMIRNOV. It's about time we got rid of the prejudice that only men must
pay for their insults! Devil take it, if women want to be equal, they should behave
as equals! Let's fight!

MRS. POPOV. You want to fight! By all means!

SMIRNOV. This minute!

MRS. POPOV. This minute! My husband had some pistols . . . I'll go and
get them right away. [*Goes out hurriedly and then returns.*] What pleasure I'll have
putting a bullet through that thick head of yours! The hell with you! [*She goes out.*]

SMIRNOV. I'll shoot her down like a chicken! I'm not a little boy or a   115
sentimental puppy. I don't care if she is delicate and fragile.

LUKA. Kind sir! Holy father! [*kneels.*] Have pity on a poor old man and go
away from here! You've frightened her to death and now you're going to shoot
her?

SMIRNOV. [*not listening to him.*] If she fights, then it means she believes in
equality of rights and emancipation of women. Here the sexes are equal! I'll shoot
her like a chicken! But what a woman! [*Imitates her.*] "The hell with you! . . . I'll
put a bullet through that thick head of yours! . . ." What a woman! How she
blushed, her eyes shone . . . she accepted my challenge! To tell the truth, it was
the first time in my life I've seen a woman like that. . . .

LUKA. Dear sir, please go away! I'll pray to God on your behalf as long as
I live!

SMIRNOV. That's a woman for you! A woman like that I can understand! A real woman! Not a sour-faced nincompoop but fiery, gunpowder! Fireworks! I'm even sorry to have to kill her!

LUKA. [*weeps.*] Dear sir . . . go away! 120

SMIRNOV. I positively like her! Positively! Even though she has dimpled cheeks, I like her! I'm almost ready to forget about the debt. . . . My fury has diminished. Wonderful woman!

MRS. POPOV. [*enters with pistols.*] Here they are, the pistols. Before we fight, you must show me how to fire. . . . I've never had a pistol in my hands before . . .

LUKA. Oh dear Lord, for pity's sake. . . . I'll go and find the gardener and the coachman. . . . What did we do to deserve such trouble? [*Exit.*]

SMIRNOV. [*examining the pistols.*] You see, there are several sorts of pistols . . . there are special dueling pistols, the Mortimer with primers. Then there are Smith and Wesson revolvers, triple action with extractors . . . excellent pistols! . . . they cost a minimum of ninety rubles a pair. . . . You must hold the revolver like this . . . [*Aside.*] What eyes, what eyes! A woman to set you on fire!

MRS. POPOV. Like this? 125

SMIRNOV. Yes, like this . . . then you cock the pistol . . . take aim . . . put your head back a little . . . stretch your arm out all the way . . . that's right . . . then with this finger press on this little piece of goods . . . and that's all there is to do . . . but the most important thing is not to get excited and aim without hurrying . . . try to keep your arm from shaking.

MRS. POPOV. Good . . . it's not comfortable to shoot indoors. Let's go into the garden.

SMIRNOV. Let's go. But I'm giving you advance notice that I'm going to fire into the air.

MRS. POPOV. That's the last straw! Why?

SMIRNOV. Why? . . . Why . . . because it's my business, that's why. 130

MRS. POPOV. Are you afraid? Yes? Aahhh! No, sir. You're not going to get out of it that easily! Be so good as to follow me! I will not rest until I've put a hole through your forehead . . . that forehead I hate so much! Are you afraid?

SMIRNOV. Yes, I'm afraid.

MRS. POPOV. You're lying! Why don't you want to fight?

SMIRNOV. Because . . . because you . . . because I like you.

MRS. POPOV. [*laughs angrily.*] He likes me! He dares say that he likes me! 135
[*Points to the door.*] Out!

SMIRNOV. [*loads the revolver in silence, takes cap and goes; at the door, stops for half a minute while they look at each other in silence; then he approaches* MRS. POPOV *hesitantly.*] Listen. . . . Are you still angry? I'm extremely irritated, but, do you understand me, how can I express it . . . the fact is, that, you see, strictly speaking . . . [*He shouts.*] Is it my fault, really, for liking you? [*Grabs the back of a chair, which cracks and breaks.*] Why the hell do you have such fragile furniture! I like you! Do you understand? I . . . I'm almost in love with you!

MRS. POPOV. Get away from me—I hate you!

SMIRNOV. God, what a woman! I've never in my life seen anything like her! I'm lost! I'm done for! I'm caught like a mouse in a trap!

MRS. POPOV. Stand back or I'll shoot!

SMIRNOV. Shoot! You could never understand what happiness it would be 140
to die under the gaze of those wonderful eyes, to be shot by a revolver which was

held by those little velvet hands. . . . I've gone out of my mind! Think about it and decide right away, because if I leave here, then we'll never see each other again! Decide . . . I'm a nobleman, a respectable gentleman, of good family. I have an income of ten thousand a year. . . . I can put a bullet through a coin tossed in the air . . . I have some fine horses. . . . Will you be my wife?

MRS. POPOV.   [*indignantly brandishes her revolver.*] Let's fight! I challenge you!

SMIRNOV.   I'm out of my mind . . . I don't understand anything . . . [*Shouts.*] Hey, you, water!

MRS. POPOV.   [*shouts.*] Let's fight!

SMIRNOV.   I've gone out of my mind. I'm in love like a boy, like an idiot! [*He grabs her hand, she screams with pain.*] I love you! [*Kneels.*] I love you as I've never loved before! I've jilted twelve women, nine women have jilted me, but I've never loved one of them as I love you. . . . I'm weak, I'm a limp rag. . . . I'm on my knees like a fool, offering you my hand. . . . Shame, shame! I haven't been in love for five years, I vowed I wouldn't; and suddenly I'm in love, like a fish out of water. I'm offering my hand in marriage. Yes or no? You don't want to? You don't need to! [*Gets up and quickly goes to the door.*]

MRS. POPOV.   Wait!   145

SMIRNOV.   [*stops.*] Well?

MRS. POPOV.   Nothing . . . you can go . . . go away . . . wait. . . . No, get out, get out! I hate you! But—don't go! Oh, if you only knew how furious I am, how angry! [*Throws revolver on table.*] My fingers are swollen from that nasty thing. . . . [*Tears her handkerchief furiously.*] What are you waiting for? Get out!

SMIRNOV.   Farewell!

MRS. POPOV.   Yes, yes, go away! [*Shouts.*] Where are you going? Stop. . . . Oh, go away! Oh, how furious I am! Don't come near me! Don't come near me!

SMIRNOV.   [*approaching her.*] How angry I am with myself! I'm in love like a   150 student. I've been on my knees. . . . It gives me the shivers. [*Rudely.*] I love you! A lot of good it will do me to fall in love with you! Tomorrow I've got to pay the interest, begin the mowing of the hay. [*Puts his arm around her waist.*] I'll never forgive myself for this. . . .

MRS. POPOV.   Get away from me! Get your hands away! I . . . hate you! I . . . challenge you!

[*Prolonged kiss, LUKA enters with an ax, the GARDENER with a rake, the COACHMAN with a pitchfork, and WORKMEN with cudgels.*]

LUKA.   [*catches sight of the pair kissing.*] Lord in heaven! [*Pause.*]

MRS. POPOV.   [*lowering her eyes.*] Luka, tell them in the stable not to give Toby any oats today.

CURTAIN

QUESTIONS

1. What kind of life did Mrs. Popov have with her late husband? What did she learn about him after his death? How has this knowledge affected her?

2. Why does Smirnov come to the house? What is he like, and how do you draw conclusions about him? What does he say about women, and why does he present these conclusions?

3. Of what importance is Luka? What is he like as a character? How do his responses highlight both the action and also the emotions developing between Smirnov and Mrs. Popov?

4. What leads Mrs. Popov to call Smirnov a bear, a brute, a monster? What is his immediate response?

5. What is the significance of Toby? To what extent does he symbolize the shifting of Mrs. Popov's emotions in the course of the play?

GENERAL QUESTIONS

1. Where in the play were you moved to laughter? Analyze those moments and try to determine the circumstances and causes of laughter.

2. From this play, what conclusions can you draw about the nature of farce as a dramatic form? Consider such things as the breaking chairs, the shouting, the improbable challenge, the unlikely attitude of Smirnov toward being shot, the sudden shift of feelings, and so on.

3. Even though Smirnov and Mrs. Popov have declared their intentions to remain single, they fall in love. How does Chekhov's presentation of their characters make their reversal of feelings seem normal and logical, although sudden, unexpected, and surprising?

4. What are the major ideas or themes in *The Bear*? You might consider topics such as the strength of allegiances that the living make to the dead, the difficulty of keeping resolutions, the nature and power of strong emotions, the need to observe expected and conventional behaviors, and so on.

SUSAN GLASPELL, *TRIFLES*

Susan Glaspell, playwright and writer of fiction, grew up in Iowa and moved to the Northeast in her thirties. She helped found the Provincetown Players (Cape Cod, Massachusetts) in 1914, and wrote most of her plays for that company. Much of her work—both plays and short stories—is strongly feminist. It deals with the roles that women play (or are forced to play) in society and with the relationships between men and women. She wrote or co-authored over ten plays for the Provincetown Players, including *Women's Honor* (1918), *Bernice* (1919), *The Inheritors* (1921), and *The Verge* (1921). After 1922, however, she gave up the theater and turned almost exclusively to fiction. The one exception was *Alison's House* (1930), a play loosely based on the life and family of Emily Dickinson, for which Glaspell won a Pulitzer Prize.

   Trifles (1916) is Glaspell's best-known play; she wrote it in ten days for the Provincetown Players, and it was produced by them in 1916. For her topic, she was inspired by a murder trial she covered while working as a reporter for a Des Moines newspaper. A year after the play she rewrote it as a short story entitled "A Jury of Her Peers," which appears in Chapter 4 (pp. 158–72).

Although *Trifles* concerns a murder investigation, the play is not a murder mystery; the audience and the characters identify the killer almost as soon as the play begins. The action of the play is concerned with discovering a motive. In terms of theme, the play explores the reasons that such a murder might occur and the differing abilities of men and women to understand those reasons. The men—the County Attorney and the Sheriff—look for signs of violent rage. The women—Mrs. Hale and Mrs. Peters—draw their conclusions from the "trifles" they find in the kitchen. Finally, the women must decide what to do with their evidence and how to judge the killer. Their decisions embody the play's major themes with regard to the role of women in marriage and society. *Trifles* eloquently and forcefully dramatizes the disastrous consequences not only of marriage, but of any human institution founded on shortsightedness and inequality.

SUSAN GLASPELL   (1882–1948)

Trifles   *1916*

CAST OF CHARACTERS

George Henderson, *county attorney*
Henry Peters, *sheriff*
Lewis Hale, *a neighboring farmer*
Mrs. Peters
Mrs. Hale

SCENE. *The kitchen in the now abandoned farmhouse of JOHN WRIGHT, a gloomy kitchen, and left without having been put in order—unwashed pans under the sink, a loaf of bread outside the bread-box, a dish-towel on the table—other signs of incompleted work. At the rear the outer door opens and the SHERIFF comes in followed by the COUNTY ATTORNEY and HALE. The SHERIFF and HALE are men in middle life, the COUNTY ATTORNEY is a young man; all are much bundled up and go at once to the stove. They are followed by the two women—the SHERIFF's wife first; she is a slight wiry woman, a thin nervous face. MRS. HALE is larger and would ordinarily be called more comfortable looking, but she is disturbed now and looks fearfully about as she enters. The women have come in slowly, and stand close together near the door.*

COUNTY ATTORNEY.   [*Rubbing his hands.*] This feels good. Come up to the fire, ladies.
MRS. PETERS.   [*After taking a step forward.*] I'm not—cold.
SHERIFF.   [*Unbuttoning his overcoat and stepping away from the stove as if to mark the beginning of official business.*] Now, Mr. Hale, before we move things about, you explain to Mr. Henderson just what you saw when you came here yesterday morning.
COUNTY ATTORNEY.   By the way, has anything been moved? Are things just as you left them yesterday?
SHERIFF.   [*Looking about.*] It's just the same. When it dropped below zero last

5

night I thought I'd better send Frank out this morning to make a fire for us—no use getting pneumonia with a big case on, but I told him not to touch anything except the stove—and you know Frank.

COUNTY ATTORNEY.   Somebody should have been left here yesterday.

SHERIFF.   Oh—yesterday. When I had to send Frank to Morris Center for that man who went crazy—I want you to know I had my hands full yesterday. I knew you could get back from Omaha by today and as long as I went over everything here myself—

COUNTY ATTORNEY.   Well, Mr. Hale, tell just what happened when you came here yesterday morning.

HALE.   Harry and I had started to town with a load of potatoes. We came along the road from my place and as I got here I said, "I'm going to see if I can't get John Wright to go in with me on a party telephone." I spoke to Wright about it once before and he put me off, saying folks talked too much anyway, and all he asked was peace and quiet—I guess you know about how much he talked himself; but I thought maybe if I went to the house and talked about it before his wife, though I said to Harry that I didn't know as what his wife wanted made much difference to John—

COUNTY ATTORNEY.   Let's talk about that later, Mr. Hale. I do want to talk   10
about that, but tell now just what happened when you got to the house.

HALE.   I didn't hear or see anything; I knocked at the door, and still it was all quiet inside. I knew they must be up, it was past eight o'clock. So I knocked again, and I thought I heard somebody say, "Come in." I wasn't sure, I'm not sure yet, but I opened the door—this door [*Indicating the door by which the two women are still standing.*] and there in that rocker—[*Pointing to it.*] sat Mrs. Wright.

[*They all look at the rocker.*]

COUNTY ATTORNEY.   What—was she doing?

HALE.   She was rockin' back and forth. She had her apron in her hand and was kind of—pleating it.

COUNTY ATTORNEY.   And how did she—look?

HALE.   Well, she looked queer.   15

COUNTY ATTORNEY.   How do you mean—queer?

HALE.   Well, as if she didn't know what she was going to do next. And kind of done up.

COUNTY ATTORNEY.   How did she seem to feel about your coming?

HALE.   Why, I don't think she minded—one way or other. She didn't pay much attention. I said, "How do, Mrs. Wright, it's cold, ain't it?" And she said, "Is it?"—and went on kind of pleating at her apron. Well, I was surprised; she didn't ask me to come up to the stove, or to set down, but just sat there, not even looking at me, so I said, "I want to see John." And then she—laughed. I guess you would call it a laugh. I thought of Harry and the team outside, so I said a little sharp: "Can't I see John?" "No," she says, kind o' dull like. "Ain't he home?" says I. "Yes," says she, "he's home." "Then why can't I see him?" I asked her, out of patience. "'Cause he's dead," says she. "*Dead?*" says I. She just nodded her head, not getting a bit excited, but rockin' back and forth. "Why—where is he?" says I, not knowing what to say. She just pointed upstairs—like that. [*himself pointing to the room above.*] I got up, with the idea of going up there. I walked from there to here—then I says, "Why, what did he die of?" "He died of a rope round his neck," says she, and just went on pleatin' at her apron. Well, I went out and called Harry. I thought I might—need help. We went upstairs and there he was lyin'—

COUNTY ATTORNEY. I think I'd rather have you go into that upstairs, where   20
you can point it all out. Just go on now with the rest of the story.

HALE. Well, my first thought was to get that rope off. It looked . . . [*Stops, his face twitches.*] . . . but Harry, he went up to him, and he said, "No, he's dead all right, and we'd better not touch anything." So we went back downstairs. She was still sitting that same way. "Has anybody been notified?" I asked. "No," says she, unconcerned. "Who did this, Mrs. Wright?" said Harry. He said it businesslike—and she stopped pleatin' of her apron. "I don't know," she says. "You don't *know*?" says Harry. "No," says she. "Weren't you sleepin' in the bed with him?" says Harry. "Yes," says she, "but I was on the inside." "Somebody slipped a rope round his neck and strangled him and you didn't wake up?" says Harry. "I didn't wake up," she said after him. We must 'a looked as if we didn't see how that could be, for after a minute she said, "I sleep sound." Harry was going to ask her more questions but I said maybe we ought to let her tell her story first to the coroner, or the sheriff, so Harry went fast as he could to Rivers' place, where there's a telephone.

COUNTY ATTORNEY. And what did Mrs. Wright do when she knew that you had gone for the coroner?

HALE. She moved from that chair to this one over here [*Pointing to a small chair in the corner.*] and just sat there with her hands held together and looking down. I got a feeling that I ought to make some conversation, so I said I had come in to see if John wanted to put in a telephone, and at that she started to laugh, and then she stopped and looked at me—scared. [*The COUNTY ATTORNEY, who has had his notebook out, makes a note.*] I dunno, maybe it wasn't scared. I wouldn't like to say it was. Soon Harry got back, and then Dr. Lloyd came, and you, Mr. Peters, and so I guess that's all I know that you don't.

COUNTY ATTORNEY. [*Looking around.*] I guess we'll go upstairs first—and then out to the barn and around there. [*To the SHERIFF.*] You're convinced that there was nothing important here—nothing that would point to any motive.

SHERIFF. Nothing here but kitchen things.   25

[*The COUNTY ATTORNEY, after again looking around the kitchen, opens the door of a cupboard closet. He gets up on a chair and looks on a shelf. Pulls his hand away, sticky.*]

COUNTY ATTORNEY. Here's a nice mess.

[*The women draw nearer.*]

MRS. PETERS. [*To the other woman.*] Oh, her fruit; it did freeze. [*To the LAWYER.*] She worried about that when it turned so cold. She said the fire'd go out and her jars would break.

SHERIFF. Well, can you beat the women! Held for murder and worryin' about her preserves.

COUNTY ATTORNEY. I guess before we're through she may have something more serious than preserves to worry about.

HALE. Well, women are used to worrying over trifles.   30

[*The two women move a little closer together.*]

COUNTY ATTORNEY. [*With the gallantry of a young politician.*] And yet, for all their worries, what would we do without the ladies? [*The women do not unbend. He goes to the sink, takes a dipperful of water from the pail and pouring it into a basin, washes his hands. Starts to wipe them on the roller-towel, turns it for a cleaner place.*] Dirty towels! [*Kicks his foot against the pans under the sink.*] Not much of a housekeeper, would you say, ladies?

MRS. HALE.   [*Stiffly.*] There's a great deal of work to be done on a farm.

COUNTY ATTORNEY.   To be sure. And yet [*with a little bow to her.*] I know there are some Dickson county farmhouses which do not have such roller towels.

[*He gives it a pull to expose its full length again.*]

MRS. HALE.   Those towels get dirty awful quick. Men's hands aren't always as clean as they might be.

COUNTY ATTORNEY.   Ah, loyal to your sex, I see. But you and Mrs. Wright   35
were neighbors. I suppose you were friends, too.

MRS. HALE.   [*Shaking her head.*] I've not seen much of her of late years. I've not been in this house—it's more than a year.

COUNTY ATTORNEY.   And why was that? You didn't like her?

MRS. HALE.   I liked her all well enough. Farmers' wives have their hands full, Mr. Henderson. And then—

COUNTY ATTORNEY.   Yes—?

MRS. HALE.   [*Looking about.*] It never seemed a very cheerful place.   40

COUNTY ATTORNEY.   No—it's not cheerful. I shouldn't say she had the homemaking instinct.

MRS. HALE.   Well, I don't know as Wright had, either.

COUNTY ATTORNEY.   You mean that they didn't get on very well?

MRS. HALE.   No, I don't mean anything. But I don't think a place'd be any cheerfuller for John Wright's being in it.   45

COUNTY ATTORNEY.   I'd like to talk more of that a little later. I want to get the lay of things upstairs now.

[*He goes to the left, where three steps lead to a stair door.*]

SHERIFF.   I suppose anything Mrs. Peters does'll be all right. She was to take in some clothes for her, you know, and a few little things. We left in such a hurry yesterday.

COUNTY ATTORNEY.   Yes, but I would like to see what you take, Mrs. Peters, and keep an eye out for anything that might be of use to us.

MRS. PETERS.   Yes, Mr. Henderson.

[*The women listen to the men's steps on the stairs, then look about the kitchen.*]

MRS. HALE.   I'd hate to have men coming into my kitchen, snooping around and criticising.

[*She arranges the pans under sink which the LAWYER had shoved out of place.*]

MRS. PETERS.   Of course it's no more than their duty.   50

MRS. HALE.   Duty's all right, but I guess that deputy sheriff that came out to make the fire might have got a little of this on. [*Gives the roller towel a pull.*] Wish I'd thought of that sooner. Seems mean to talk about her for not having things slicked up when she had to come away in such a hurry.

MRS. PETERS. [*Who had gone to a small table in the left rear corner of the room, and lifted one end of a towel that covers a pan.*] She had bread set.

[*Stands still.*]

MRS. HALE. [*Eyes fixed on a loaf of bread beside the breadbox, which is on a low shelf at the other side of the room. Moves slowly toward it.*] She was going to put this in there. [*Picks up loaf, then abruptly drops it. In a manner of returning to familiar things.*] It's a shame about her fruit. I wonder if it's all gone. [*Gets up on the chair and looks.*] I think there's some here that's all right, Mrs. Peters. Yes—here; [*Holding it toward the window.*] this is cherries, too. [*Looking again.*] I declare I believe that's the only one. [*Gets down, bottle in her hand. Goes to the sink and wipes it off on the outside.*] She'll feel awful bad after all her hard work in the hot weather. I remember the afternoon I put up my cherries last summer.

[*She puts the bottle on the big kitchen table, center of the room. With a sigh, is about to sit down in the rocking-chair. Before she is seated realizes what chair it is; with a slow look at it, steps back. The chair which she has touched rocks back and forth.*]

MRS. PETERS. Well, I must get those things from the front room closet. [*She goes to the door at the right, but after looking into the other room, steps back.*] You coming with me, Mrs. Hale? You could help me carry them.

[*They go in the other room; reappear, MRS. PETERS carrying a dress and skirt, MRS. HALE following with a pair of shoes.*]

MRS. PETERS. My, it's cold in there.   55

[*She puts the clothes on the big table and hurries to the stove.*]

MRS. HALE. [*Examining the skirt.*] Wright was close. I think maybe that's why she kept so much to herself. She didn't even belong to the Ladies Aid. I suppose she felt she couldn't do her part, and then you don't enjoy things when you feel shabby. She used to wear pretty clothes and be lively, when she was Minnie Foster, one of the town girls singing in the choir. But that—oh, that was thirty years ago. This all you was to take in?

MRS. PETERS. She said she wanted an apron. Funny thing to want, for there isn't much to get you dirty in jail, goodness knows. But I suppose just to make her feel more natural. She said they was in the top drawer in this cupboard. Yes, here. And then her little shawl that always hung behind the door. [*Opens stair door and looks.*] Yes, here it is.

[*Quickly shuts door leading upstairs.*]

MRS. HALE. [*Abruptly moving toward her.*] Mrs. Peters?
MRS. PETERS. Yes, Mrs. Hale?
MRS. HALE. Do you think she did it?   60
MRS. PETERS. [*In a frightened voice.*] Oh, I don't know.
MRS. HALE. Well, I don't think she did. Asking for an apron and her little shawl. Worrying about her fruit.
MRS. PETERS. [*Starts to speak, glances up, where footsteps are heard in the room above. In a low voice.*] Mr. Peters says it looks bad for her. Mr. Henderson is awful sarcastic in a speech and he'll make fun of her sayin' she didn't wake up.

Mrs. Hale.   Well, I guess John Wright didn't wake when they was slipping that rope under his neck.

Mrs. Peters.   No, it's strange. It must have been done awful crafty and still. They say it was such a—funny way to kill a man, rigging it all up like that.

Mrs. Hale.   That's just what Mr. Hale said. There was a gun in the house. He says that's what he can't understand.

Mrs. Peters.   Mr. Henderson said coming out that what was needed for the case was a motive; something to show anger, or—sudden feeling.

Mrs. Hale.   [*Who is standing by the table.*] Well, I don't see any signs of anger around here. [*She puts her hand on the dish towel which lies on the table, stands looking down at table, one half of which is clean, the other half messy.*] It's wiped to here. [*Makes a move as if to finish work, then turns and looks at loaf of bread outside the breadbox. Drops towel. In that voice of coming back to familiar things.*] Wonder how they are finding things upstairs. I hope she had it a little more red-up° up there. You know, it seems kind of *sneaking*. Locking her up in town and then coming out here and trying to get her own house to turn against her!

Mrs. Peters.   But Mrs. Hale, the law is the law.

Mrs. Hale.   I s'pose 'tis. [*Unbuttoning her coat.*] Better loosen up your things, Mrs. Peters. You won't feel them when you go out.

[*Mrs. Peters takes off her fur tippet,° goes to hang it on hook at back of room, stands looking at the under part of the small corner table.*]

Mrs. Peters.   She was piecing a quilt.

[*She brings the large sewing basket and they look at the bright pieces.*]

Mrs. Hale.   It's log cabin pattern. Pretty, isn't it? I wonder if she was goin' to quilt it or just knot it?

[*Footsteps have been heard coming down the stairs. The Sheriff enters followed by Hale and the County Attorney.*]

Sheriff.   They wonder if she was going to quilt it or just knot it!

[*The men laugh; the women look abashed.*]

County Attorney.   [*Rubbing his hands over the stove.*] Frank's fire didn't do much up there, did it? Well, let's go out to the barn and get that cleared up.

[*The men go outside.*]

Mrs. Hale.   [*Resentfully.*] I don't know as there's anything so strange, our takin' up our time with little things while we're waiting for them to get the evidence. [*She sits down at the big table smoothing out a block with decision.*] I don't see as it's anything to laugh about.

Mrs. Peters.   [*Apologetically.*] Of course they've got awful important things on their minds.

[*Pulls up a chair and joins Mrs. Hale at the table.*]

---

red-up: neat, arranged in order.   *tippet:* scarf-like garment of fur or wool for the neck and shoulders.

MRS. HALE. [*Examining another block.*] Mrs. Peters, look at this one. Here, this is the one she was working on, and look at the sewing! All the rest of it has been so nice and even. And look at this! It's all over the place! Why, it looks as if she didn't know what she was about!

[*After she has said this they look at each other, then start to glance back at the door. After an instant MRS. HALE has pulled at a knot and ripped the sewing.*]

MRS. PETERS. Oh, what are you doing, Mrs. Hale?

MRS. HALE. [*Mildly.*] Just pulling out a stitch or two that's not sewed very good. [*Threading a needle.*] Bad sewing always made me fidgety.

MRS. PETERS. [*Nervously.*] I don't think we ought to touch things.   80

MRS. HALE. I'll just finish up this end. [*Suddenly stopping and leaning forward.*] Mrs. Peters?

MRS. PETERS. Yes, Mrs. Hale?

MRS. HALE. What do you suppose she was so nervous about?

MRS. PETERS. Oh—I don't know. I don't know as she was nervous. I sometimes sew awful queer when I'm just tired. [*MRS. HALE starts to say something, looks at MRS. PETERS, then goes on sewing.*] Well I must get these things wrapped up. They may be through sooner than we think. [*Putting apron and other things together.*] I wonder where I can find a piece of paper, and string.

MRS. HALE. In that cupboard, maybe.   85

MRS. PETERS. [*Looking in cupboard.*] Why, here's a bird-cage. [*Holds it up.*] Did she have a bird, Mrs. Hale?

MRS. HALE. Why, I don't know whether she did or not—I've not been here for so long. There was a man around last year selling canaries cheap, but I don't know as she took one; maybe she did. She used to sing real pretty herself.

MRS. PETERS. [*Glancing around.*] Seems funny to think of a bird here. But she must have had one, or why would she have a cage? I wonder what happened to it?

MRS. HALE. I s'pose maybe the cat got it.

MRS. PETERS. No, she didn't have a cat. She's got that feeling some people   90
have about cats—being afraid of them. My cat got in her room and she was real upset and asked me to take it out.

MRS. HALE. My sister Bessie was like that. Queer, ain't it?

MRS. PETERS. [*Examining the cage.*] Why, look at this door. It's broke. One hinge is pulled apart.

MRS. HALE. [*Looking too.*] Looks as if someone must have been rough with it.

MRS. PETERS. Why, yes.

[*She brings the cage forward and puts it on the table.*]

MRS. HALE. I wish if they're going to find any evidence they'd be about it.   95
I don't like this place.

MRS. PETERS. But I'm awful glad you came with me, Mrs. Hale. It would be lonesome for me sitting here alone.

MRS. HALE. It would, wouldn't it? [*Dropping her sewing.*] But I tell you what I do wish, Mrs. Peters. I wish I had come over sometimes when *she* was here. I—*Looking around the room.*]—wish I had.

MRS. PETERS. But of course you were awful busy, Mrs. Hale—your house and your children.

MRS. HALE. I could've come. I stayed away because it weren't cheerful—and that's why I ought to have come. I—I've never liked this place. Maybe because it's down in a hollow and you don't see the road. I dunno what it is, but it's a lonesome place and always was. I wish I had come over to see Minnie Foster sometimes. I can see now—

[*Shakes her head.*]

MRS. PETERS. Well, you mustn't reproach yourself, Mrs. Hale. Somehow we just don't see how it is with other folks until—something comes up. 100

MRS. HALE. Not having children makes less work—but it makes a quiet house, and Wright out to work all day, and no company when he did come in. Did you know John Wright, Mrs. Peters?

MRS. PETERS. Not to know him; I've seen him in town. They say he was a good man.

MRS. HALE. Yes—good; he didn't drink, and kept his word as well as most, I guess, and paid his debts. But he was a hard man, Mrs. Peters. Just to pass the time of day with him—[*Shivers.*] Like a raw wind that gets to the bone. [*Pauses, her eye falling on the cage.*] I should think she would 'a wanted a bird. But what do you suppose went with it?

MRS. PETERS. I don't know, unless it got sick and died.

[*She reaches over and swings the broken door, swings it again, both women watch it.*]

MRS. HALE. You weren't raised round here, were you? [*MRS. PETERS shakes her head.*] You didn't know—her? 105

MRS. PETERS. Not till they brought her yesterday.

MRS. HALE. She—come to think of it, she was kind of like a bird herself—real sweet and pretty, but kind of timid and—fluttery. How—she—did—change. [*Silence; then as if struck by a happy thought and relieved to get back to everyday things.*] Tell you what, Mrs. Peters, why don't you take the quilt in with you? It might take up her mind.

MRS. PETERS. Why, I think that's a real nice idea, Mrs. Hale. There couldn't possibly be any objection to it, could there? Now, just what would I take? I wonder if her patches are in here—and her things.

[*They look in the sewing basket.*]

MRS. HALE. Here's some red. I expect this has got sewing things in it. [*Brings out a fancy box.*] What a pretty box. Looks like something somebody would give you. Maybe her scissors are in here. [*Opens box. Suddenly puts her hand to her nose.*] Why—[*MRS. PETERS bends nearer, then turns her face away.*] There's something wrapped up in this piece of silk.

MRS. PETERS. Why, this isn't her scissors. 110

MRS. HALE. [*Lifting the silk.*] Oh, Mrs. Peters—it's—

[*MRS. PETERS bends closer.*]

MRS. PETERS. It's the bird.

MRS. HALE. [*Jumping up.*] But, Mrs. Peters—look at it! Its neck! Look at its neck! It's all—other side *to*.

MRS. PETERS.   Somebody—wrung—its—neck.

[*Their eyes meet. A look of growing comprehension, of horror. Steps are heard outside. MRS. HALE slips box under quilt pieces, and sinks into her chair. Enter SHERIFF and COUNTY ATTORNEY. MRS. PETERS rises.*]

COUNTY ATTORNEY.   [*As one turning from serious things to little pleasantries.*] Well,   115
ladies, have you decided whether she was going to quilt it or knot it?

MRS. PETERS.   We think she was going to—knot it.

COUNTY ATTORNEY.   Well, that's interesting, I'm sure. [*Seeing the bird-cage.*]
Has the bird flown?

MRS. HALE.   [*Putting more quilt pieces over the box.*] We think the—cat got it.

COUNTY ATTORNEY.   [*Preoccupied.*] Is there a cat?

[*MRS. HALE glances in a quick covert way at MRS. PETERS.*]

MRS. PETERS.   Well, not *now*. They're superstitious, you know. They leave.   120

COUNTY ATTORNEY.   [*To SHERIFF PETERS, continuing an interrupted conversation.*]
No sign at all of anyone having come from the outside. Their own rope. Now let's
go up again and go over it piece by piece. [*They start upstairs.*] It would have to
have been someone who knew just the—

[*MRS. PETERS sits down. The two women sit there not looking at one another, but as if peering into something and at the same time holding back. When they talk now it is in the manner of feeling their way over strange ground, as if afraid of what they are saying, but as if they cannot help saying it.*]

MRS. HALE.   She liked the bird. She was going to bury it in that pretty box.

MRS. PETERS.   [*In a whisper.*] When I was a girl—my kitten—there was a boy
took a hatchet, and before my eyes—and before I could get there—[*Covers her
face an instant.*] If they hadn't held me back I would have—[*Catches herself, looks
upstairs where steps are heard, falters weakly.*]—hurt him.

MRS. HALE.   [*With a slow look around her.*] I wonder how it would seem never
to have had any children around. [*Pause.*] No, Wright wouldn't like the bird—a
thing that sang. She used to sing. He killed that, too.

MRS. PETERS.   [*Moving uneasily.*] We don't know who killed the bird.   125

MRS. HALE.   I knew John Wright.

MRS. PETERS.   It was an awful thing was done in this house that night, Mrs.
Hale. Killing a man while he slept, slipping a rope around his neck that choked
the life out of him.

MRS. HALE.   His neck. Choked the life out of him.

[*Her hand goes out and rests on the bird-cage.*]

MRS. PETERS.   [*With rising voice.*] We don't know who killed him. We don't
know.

MRS. HALE.   [*Her own feeling not interrupted.*] If there'd been years and years   130
of nothing, then a bird to sing to you, it would be awful—still, after the bird was
still.

MRS. PETERS.   [*Something within her speaking.*] I know what stillness is. When
we homesteaded in Dakota, and my first baby died—after he was two years old,
and me with no other then—

MRS. HALE.   [*Moving.*] How soon do you suppose they'll be through, looking for the evidence?·

MRS. PETERS.   I know what stillness is. [*Pulling herself back.*] The law has got to punish crime, Mrs. Hale.

MRS. HALE.   [*Not as if answering that.*] I wish you'd seen Minnie Foster when she wore a white dress with blue ribbons and stood up there in the choir and sang. [*A look around the room.*] Oh, I *wish* I'd come over here once in a while! That was a crime! That was a crime! Who's going to punish that?

MRS. PETERS.   [*Looking upstairs.*] We mustn't—take on.   135

MRS. HALE.   I might have known she needed help! I know how things can be—for women. I tell you, it's queer, Mrs. Peters. We live close together and we live far apart. We all go through the same things—it's all just a different kind of the same thing. [*Brushes her eyes, noticing the bottle of fruit, reaches out for it.*] If I was you I wouldn't tell her her fruit was gone. Tell her it *ain't.* Tell her it's all right. Take this in to prove it to her. She—she may never know whether it was broke or not.

MRS. PETERS.   [*Takes the bottle, looks about for something to wrap it in; takes petticoat from the clothes brought from the other room, very nervously begins winding this around the bottle. In a false voice.*] My, it's a good thing the men couldn't hear us. Wouldn't they just laugh! Getting all stirred up over a little thing like a—dead canary. As if that could have anything to do with—with—wouldn't they *laugh!*

[*The men are heard coming down stairs.*]

MRS. HALE.   [*Under her breath.*] Maybe they would—maybe they wouldn't.

COUNTY ATTORNEY.   No, Peters, it's all perfectly clear except a reason for doing it. But you know juries when it comes to women. If there was some definite thing. Something to show—something to make a story about—a thing that would connect up with this strange way of doing it—

[*The women's eyes meet for an instant. Enter HALE from outer door.*]

HALE.   Well, I've got the team° around. Pretty cold out there.   140

COUNTY ATTORNEY.   I'm going to stay here a while by myself. [*To the SHERIFF.*] You can send Frank out for me, can't you? I want to go over everything. I'm not satisfied that we can't do better.

SHERIFF.   Do you want to see what Mrs. Peters is going to take in?

[*The COUNTY ATTORNEY goes to the table, picks up the apron, laughs.*]

COUNTY ATTORNEY.   Oh, I guess they're not very dangerous things the ladies have picked out. [*Moves a few things about, disturbing the quilt pieces which cover the box. Steps back.*] No, Mrs. Peters doesn't need supervising. For that matter, a sheriff's wife is married to the law. Ever think of it that way, Mrs. Peters?

MRS. PETERS.   Not—just that way.

SHERIFF.   [*Chuckling.*] Married to the law. [*Moves toward the other room.*] I just   145
want you to come in here a minute, George. We ought to take a look at these windows.

COUNTY ATTORNEY.   [*Scoffingly.*] Oh, windows!

SHERIFF.   We'll be right out, Mr. Hale.

[*HALE goes outside. The SHERIFF follows the COUNTY ATTORNEY into the other room. Then*

team: team of horses drawing a wagon.

MRS. HALE *rises, hands tight together, looking intensely at* MRS. PETERS, *whose eyes make a slow turn, finally meeting* MRS. HALE'S. *A moment* MRS. HALE *holds her, then her own eyes point the way to where the box is concealed. Suddenly* MRS. PETERS *throws back quilt pieces and tries to put the box in the bag she is wearing. It is too big. She opens box, starts to take bird out, cannot touch it, goes to pieces, stands there helpless. Sound of a knob turning in the other room.* MRS. HALE *snatches the box and puts it in the pocket of her big coat. Enter* COUNTY ATTORNEY *and* SHERIFF.]

> COUNTY ATTORNEY. [*Facetiously.*] Well, Henry, at least we found out that she was not going to quilt it. She was going to—what is it you call it, ladies?
>
> MRS. HALE. [*Her hand against her pocket.*] We call it—knot it, Mr. Henderson.

CURTAIN

QUESTIONS

1. How does the first entrance of the characters establish a distinction between the men and women in the play? What is suggested by the different reactions of the men and women to the freezing of the preserves?

2. What does Mr. Hale report to the County Attorney in his extended narrative? How observant is he? How accurate?

3. What is needed to make a strong legal case against Mrs. Wright? What does the Sheriff determine about the kitchen? What do his conclusions show you about the men?

4. What conclusions do the women draw about the bad sewing in the quilt? What does Mrs. Hale do about it? At this point, what conclusions might she be drawing about the murder?

5. Of what importance are Mrs. Hale's descriptions (a) of Minnie Foster (Mrs. Wright) as a young woman and (b) of the Wrights's marriage?

6. What do the women deduce from the broken birdcage and the dead bird? How are these symbolic, and what do they symbolize?

7. Assuming that Minnie Wright is the murderer of her husband, how did she do it? What things in the play enable you to solve the crime? What information do the women have, not possessed by the men, that permits them to make the right inferences about the crime?

8. What does Mrs. Hale do with the "trifles" of evidence? Why? How is her reaction to the evidence different from that of Mrs. Peters? What conflict develops between these women? How is it resolved?

9. Why does Mrs. Hale feel guilt about her relationship with Minnie Wright? To what degree does her guilt shape her decisions and actions?

GENERAL QUESTIONS

1. To what does the title of this play refer? How does this irony of the word *trifles* help shape the play's meaning?

2. What are the men like? Are they round or flat? How observant are they? What is their attitude toward their jobs? Toward their own importance? Toward the women and "kitchen things"?

3. What is Mrs. Hale like? How observant is she? What is her attitude toward the men and their work, and toward herself?

4. Some critics argue that Minnie Wright is the most important character in the play, even though she never appears on stage. Do you agree with this assertion? Why do you think Glaspell did not want her to appear as a speaking character?

5. How is symbolism employed to establish and underscore the play's meaning? Consider especially the birdcage, the dead bird, and the repeated assertion that Mrs. Wright was going to "knot" (tie) rather than "quilt" (sew) the quilt.

EUGENE O'NEILL, *BEFORE BREAKFAST*

Eugene O'Neill is one of America's greatest playwrights. He wrote more than forty plays, won three Pulitzer Prizes, and received the Nobel Prize for literature in 1936. The son of a well-known actor, in his youth he traveled about the world as a seaman, studied briefly at Princeton and Harvard, and began writing plays in 1912. The first of his plays to be produced, *Bound East for Cardiff*, was acted by the Provincetown Players at the Wharf Theater in Provincetown, Massachusetts, in 1916. O'Neill maintained a close connection with this company for several years, providing them with ten one-act plays between 1916 and 1920. His later (and longer) works include *The Emperor Jones* (1920), *Anna Christie* (1921), *Desire Under the Elms* (1924), *Strange Interlude* (1928), *Mourning Becomes Electra* (1931), and *The Iceman Cometh* (1946). O'Neill also wrote an auto-biographical play, *A Long Day's Journey Into Night* (1936), which was suppressed at his request until after his death. When it was staged on Broadway in 1956, it won him a third Pulitzer Prize in drama, and it was later made into a film starring Katherine Hepburn.

Before Breakfast, though one of O'Neill's earliest plays, shows his characteristic control of conflict, character, setting, and point of view. The play was first staged in December 1916, by the Provincetown Players at the Playwright's Theater in New York City's Greenwich Village (where Christopher Street, the address of the Rowlands's apartment, is located). There is little action in the play, and yet it is charged with conflict. The plot is simple and straightforward—a wife onstage harangues her offstage husband for twenty minutes before breakfast. The conflict between them is longstanding and bitter, and it is resolved in the play's horrifying conclusion.

Above all, *Before Breakfast* illustrates O'Neill's skillful employment of the dramatic point of view. By giving Mrs. Rowland every word spoken onstage, O'Neill causes the audience to understand everything as it is filtered through her characteristic pettiness and selfishness. Indeed, the play is a *bravura* piece for a gifted actress. Finally, however, the audience (and the reader) must determine both the validity and the limitations of her perspective.

Setting is equally important in *Before Breakfast*. O'Neill uses the single stage setting, described at length in the opening stage directions, to show the audience (or tell the reader) a great deal about the characters and their lives. The Rowlands's flat is in Greenwich Village, the location of New York University and a traditional haunt of artists, artisans, poets, novelists, dramatists, actors, singers, and dancers, and it therefore suggests the type of life that Alfred Rowland is seeking to attain. The implications of the setting are confirmed throughout the rest of the play.

EUGENE O'NEILL   (1888–1953)

Before Breakfast   *1916*

CHARACTERS

>   Mrs. Rowland, *The Wife*
>   Mr. Alfred Rowland, *The Husband*

SCENE. *A small room serving both as kitchen and dining room in a flat on Christopher Street, New York City. In the rear, to the right, a door leading to the outer hallway. On the left of the doorway, a sink, and a two-burner gas stove. Over the stove, and extending to the left wall, a wooden closet for dishes, etc. On the left, two windows looking out on a fire escape where several potted plants are dying of neglect. Before the windows, a table covered with oilcloth. Two cane-bottomed chairs are placed by the table. Another stands against the wall to the right of door in rear. In the right wall, rear, a doorway leading into a bedroom. Farther forward, different articles of a man's and a woman's clothing are hung on pegs. A clothes line is strung from the left corner, rear, to the right wall, forward.*

It is about eight-thirty in the morning of a fine, sunshiny day in the early fall.

Mrs. Rowland enters from the bedroom, yawning, her hands still busy putting the finishing touches on a slovenly toilet by sticking hairpins into her hair which is bunched up in a drab-colored mass on top of her round head. She is of medium height and inclined to a shapeless stoutness, accentuated by her formless blue dress, shabby and worn. Her face is characterless, with small regular features and eyes of a nondescript blue. There is a pinched expression about her eyes and nose and her weak, spiteful mouth. She is in her early twenties but looks much older.

She comes to the middle of the room and yawns, stretching her arms to their full length. Her drowsy eyes stare about the room with the irritated look of one to whom a long sleep has not been a long rest. She goes wearily to the clothes hanging on the right and takes an apron from a hook. She ties it about her waist, giving vent to an exasperated "damn" when the knot fails to obey her clumsy fingers. Finally gets it tied and goes slowly to the gas stove and lights one burner. She fills the coffee pot at the sink and sets it over the flame. Then slumps down into a chair by the table and puts a hand over her forehead as if she were suffering from headache. Suddenly her face brightens as though she had remembered something, and she casts a quick glance at the dish closet; then looks sharply at the bedroom door and listens intently for a moment or so.

MRS. ROWLAND. [*In a low voice.*] Alfred! Alfred! [*There is no answer from the next room and she continues suspiciously in a louder tone.*] You needn't pretend you're asleep. [*There is no reply to this from the bedroom, and, reassured, she gets up from her chair and tiptoes cautiously to the dish closet. She slowly opens one door, taking great care to make no noise, and slides out, from their hiding place behind the dishes, a bottle of Gordon gin and a glass. In doing so she disturbs the top dish, which rattles a little. At this sound she starts guiltily and looks with sulky defiance at the doorway to the next room.*]

[*Her voice trembling.*] Alfred!

[*After a pause, during which she listens for any sound, she takes the glass and pours out a large drink and gulps it down; then hastily returns the bottle and glass to their hiding place. She closes the closet door with the same care as she had opened it, and, heaving a great sigh of relief, sinks down into her chair again. The large dose of alcohol she has taken has an almost immediate effect. Her features become more animated, she seems to gather energy, and she looks at the bedroom door with a hard, vindictive smile on her lips. Her eyes glance quickly about the room and are fixed on a man's coat and vest which hang from a hook at right. She moves stealthily over to the open doorway and stands there, out of sight of anyone inside, listening for any movement.*]

[*Calling in a half-whisper.*] Alfred!

[*Again there is no reply. With a swift movement she takes the coat and vest from the hook and returns with them to her chair. She sits down and takes the various articles out of each pocket but quickly puts them back again. At last, in the inside pocket of the vest, she finds a letter.*]

[*Looking at the handwriting—slowly to herself.*] Hmm! I knew it.

[*She opens the letter and reads it. At first her expression is one of hatred and rage, but as she goes on to the end it changes to one of triumphant malignity. She remains in deep thought for a moment, staring before her, the letter in her hands, a cruel smile on her lips. Then she puts the letter back in the pocket of the vest, and still careful not to awaken the sleeper, hangs the clothes up again on the same hook, and goes to the bedroom door and looks in.*]

[*In a loud, shrill voice.*] Alfred! [*Still louder.*] Alfred! [*There is a muffled, yawning groan from the next room.*] Don't you think it's about time you got up? Do you want to stay in bed all day? [*Turning around and coming back to her chair.*] Not that I've got any doubts about your being lazy enough to stay in bed forever. [*She sits down and looks out of the window, irritably.*] Goodness knows what time it is. We haven't even got any way of telling the time since you pawned your watch like a fool. The last valuable thing we had, and you knew it. It's been nothing but pawn, pawn, pawn, with you—anything to put off getting a job, anything to get out of going to work like a man. [*She taps the floor with her foot nervously, biting her lips.*]

[*After a short pause.*] Alfred! Get up, do you hear me? I want to make that bed before I go out. I'm sick of having this place in a continual muss on your account. [*With a certain vindictive satisfaction.*] Not that we'll be here long unless you manage to get some money some place. Heaven knows I do my part—and more— going out to sew every day while you play the gentleman and loaf around bar rooms with that good-for-nothing lot of artists from the Square.°

5

Square: Washington Square, at the center of Greenwich Village.

[*A short pause during which she plays nervously with a cup and saucer on the table.*]

And where are you going to get money, I'd like to know? The rent's due this week and you know what the landlord is. He won't let us stay a minute over our time. You say you *can't* get a job. That's a lie and you know it. You never even look for one. All you do is moon around all day writing silly poetry and stories that no one will buy—and no wonder they won't. I notice I can always get a position, such as it is; and it's only that which keeps us from starving to death.

[*Gets up and goes over to the stove—looks into the coffee pot to see if the water is boiling; then comes back and sits down again.*]

You'll have to get money to-day some place. I can't do it all, and I won't do it all. You've got to come to your senses. You've got to beg, borrow, or steal it somewheres. [*With a contemptuous laugh.*] But where, I'd like to know? You're too proud to beg, and you've borrowed the limit, and you haven't the nerve to steal.

[*After a pause—getting up angrily.*] Aren't you up yet, for heaven's sake? It's just like you to go to sleep again, or pretend to. [*She goes to the bedroom door and looks in.*] Oh, you are up. Well, it's about time. You needn't look at me like that. Your airs don't fool me a bit any more. I know you too well—better than you think I do—you and your goings-on. [*Turning away from the door—meaningly.*] I know a lot of things, my dear. Never mind what I know, now. I'll tell you before I go, you needn't worry. [*She comes to the middle of the room and stands there, frowning.*]

[*Irritably.*] Hmm! I suppose I might as well get breakfast ready—not that   10 there's anything much to get. [*Questioningly.*] Unless you have some money? [*She pauses for an answer from the next room which does not come.*] Foolish question! [*She gives a short, hard laugh.*] I ought to know you better than that by this time. When you left here in such a huff last night I knew what would happen. You can't be trusted for a second. A nice condition you came home in! The fight we had was only an excuse for you to make a beast of yourself. What was the use pawning your watch if all you wanted with the money was to waste it in buying drink?

[*Goes over to the dish closet and takes out plates, cups, etc., while she is talking.*]

Hurry up! It don't take long to get breakfast these days, thanks to you. All we got this morning is bread and butter and coffee; and you wouldn't even have that if it wasn't for me sewing my fingers off. [*She slams the loaf of bread on the table with a bang.*]

The bread's stale. I hope you'll like it. *You* don't deserve any better, but I don't see why *I* should suffer.

[*Going over to the stove.*] The coffee'll be ready in a minute, and you needn't expect me to wait for you.

[*Suddenly with great anger.*] What on earth are you doing all this time? [*She goes over to the door and looks in.*] Well, you're *almost* dressed at any rate. I expected to find you back in bed. That'd be just like you. How awful you look this morning! For heaven's sake, shave! You're disgusting! You look like a tramp. No wonder no one will give you a job. I don't blame them—when you don't even look halfway decent. [*She goes to the stove.*] There's plenty of hot water right here. You've got no excuse. [*Gets a bowl and pours some of the water from the coffee pot into it.*] Here.

[*He reaches his hand into the room for it. It is a sensitive hand with slender fingers. It trembles and some of the water spills on the floor.*]

[*Tauntingly.*] Look at your hand tremble! You'd better give up drinking. You   15
can't stand it. It's just your kind that get the D.T.'s. *That would be* the last straw!
[*Looking down at the floor.*] Look at the mess you've made of this floor—cigarette
butts and ashes all over the place. Why can't you put them on a plate? No, you
wouldn't be considerate enough to do that. You never think of me. You don't
have to sweep the room and that's all you care about.

[*Takes the broom and commences to sweep viciously, raising a cloud of dust. From the inner
room comes the sound of a razor being stropped.*]°

[*Sweeping.*] Hurry up! It must be nearly time for me to go. If I'm late I'm
liable to lose my position, and then I couldn't support you any longer. [*As an
afterthought she adds sarcastically.*] And then you'd have to go to work or something
dreadful like that. [*Sweeping under the table.*] What I want to know is whether you're
going to look for a job to-day or not. You know your family won't help us any
more. They've had enough of you, too. [*After a moment's silent sweeping.*] I'm about
sick of all this life. I've a good notion to go home, if I wasn't too proud to let
them know what a failure you've been—you, the millionaire Rowland's only son,
the Harvard graduate, the poet, the catch of the town—Huh! [*With bitterness.*]
There wouldn't be many of them now envy my catch if they knew the truth. What
has our marriage been, I'd like to know? Even before your *millionaire* father died
owing every one in the world money, you certainly never wasted any of your time
on your wife. I suppose you thought I'd ought to be glad you were *honorable*
enough to marry me—after getting me into trouble. You were ashamed of me
with your fine friends because my father's only a grocer, that's what you were. At
least he's honest, which is more than any one could say about yours. [*She is sweeping
steadily toward the door. Leans on her broom for a moment.*]

You hoped every one'd think you'd been forced to marry me, and pity you,
didn't you? You didn't hesitate much about telling me you loved me, and making
me believe your lies, before it happened, did you? You made me think you didn't
want your father to buy me off as he tried to do. I know better now. I haven't
lived with you all this time for nothing. [*Somberly.*] It's lucky the poor thing was
born dead, after all. What a father you'd have been!

[*Is silent, brooding moodily for a moment—then she continues with a sort of savage joy.*]

But I'm not the only one who's got you to thank for being unhappy. There's
one other, at least, and *she* can't hope to marry you now. [*She puts her head into the
next room.*] How about Helen? [*She starts back from the doorway, half frightened.*]
Don't look at me that way! Yes, I read her letter. What about it? I got a
right to. I'm your wife. And I know all there is to know, so don't lie. You needn't
stare at me so. You can't bully me with your superior airs any longer. Only for
me you'd be going without breakfast this very morning. [*She sets the broom back in
the corner—whiningly.*] You never did have any gratitude for what I've done. [*She
comes to the stove and puts the coffee into the pot.*] The coffee's ready. I'm not going to
wait for you. [*She sits down in her chair again.*]

[*After a pause—puts her hand to her head—fretfully.*] My head aches so this   20
morning. It's a shame I've got to go to work in a stuffy room all day in my

---

stropped: Alfred is using a leather strap to sharpen a straight razor, the kind barbers still
use, with a very sharp steel blade that is hinged to a handle.

condition. And I wouldn't if you were half a man. By rights I ought to be lying on my back instead of you. You know how sick I've been this last year; and yet you object when I take a little something to keep up my spirits. You even didn't want me to take that tonic I got at the drug store. [*With a hard laugh.*] I know you'd be glad to have me dead and out of your way; then you'd be free to run after all these silly girls that think you're such a wonderful, misunderstood person— this Helen and the others. [*There is a sharp exclamation of pain from the next room.*]

[*With satisfaction.*] There! I knew you'd cut yourself. It'll be a lesson to you. You know you oughtn't to be running around nights drinking with your nerves in such an awful shape. [*She goes to the door and looks in.*]

What makes you so pale? What are you staring at yourself in the mirror that way for? For goodness sake, wipe that blood off your face! [*With a shudder.*] It's horrible. [*In relieved tones.*] There, that's better. I never could stand the sight of blood. [*She shrinks back from the door a little.*] You better give up trying and go to a barber shop. Your hand shakes dreadfully. Why do you stare at me like that? [*She turns away from the door.*] Are you still mad at me about that letter? [*Defiantly.*] Well, I had a right to read it. I'm your wife. [*She comes to the chair and sits down again. After a pause.*]

I knew all the time you were running around with someone. Your lame excuses about spending the time at the library didn't fool me. Who is this Helen, anyway? One of those artists? Or does she write poetry, too? Her letter sounds that way. I'll bet she told you your things were the best ever, and you believed her, like a fool. Is she young and pretty? I was young and pretty, too, when you fooled me with your fine, poetic talk; but life with you would soon wear anyone down. What I've been through!

[*Goes over and takes the coffee off the stove.*] Breakfast is ready. [*With a contemptuous glance.*] Breakfast! [*Pours out a cup of coffee for herself and puts the pot on the table.*] Your coffee'll be cold. What are you doing—still shaving, for heaven's sake? You'd better give it up. One of these mornings you'll give yourself a serious cut. [*She cuts off bread and butters it. During the following speeches she eats and sips her coffee.*]

I'll have to run as soon as I've finished eating. One of us has got to work. [*Angrily.*] Are you going to look for a job to-day or aren't you? I should think some of your fine friends would help you, if they really think you're so much. But I guess they just like to hear you talk. [*Sits in silence for a moment.*]   25

I'm sorry for this Helen, whoever she is. Haven't you got any feelings for other people? What will her family say? I see she mentions them in her letter. What is she going to do—have the child—or go to one of those doctors? That's a nice thing, I must say. Where can she get the money? Is she rich? [*She waits for some answer to this volley of questions.*]

Hmm! You won't tell me anything about her, will you? Much I care. Come to think of it, I'm not so sorry for her after all. She knew what she was doing. She isn't any schoolgirl, like I was, from the looks of her letter. Does she know you're married? Of course, she must. All your friends know about your unhappy marriage. I know they pity you, but they don't know my side of it. They'd talk different if they did.

[*Too busy eating to go on for a second or so.*]

This Helen must be a fine one, if she knew you were married. What does she expect, then? That I'll divorce you and let her marry you? Does she think I'm crazy enough for that—after all you've made me go through? I guess not! And you can't get a divorce from me and you know it. No one can say *I've* ever done anything wrong. [*Drinks the last of her cup of coffee.*]

She deserves to suffer, that's all I can say. I'll tell you what I think; I think your Helen is no better than a common street-walker, that's what I think. [*There is a stifled groan of pain from the next room.*]

Did you cut yourself again? Serves you right. [*Gets up and takes off her apron.*] 30
Well, I've got to run along. [*Peevishly.*] This is a fine life for me to be leading! I won't stand for your loafing any longer. [*Something catches her ear and she pauses and listens intently.*] There! You've overturned the water all over everything. Don't say you haven't. I can hear it dripping on the floor. [*A vague expression of fear comes over her face.*] Alfred! Why don't you answer me?

[*She moves slowly toward the room. There is the noise of a chair being overturned and something crashes heavily to the floor. She stands, trembling with fright.*]

Alfred! Alfred! Answer me! What is it you knocked over? Are you still drunk? [*Unable to stand the tension a second longer she rushes to the door of the bedroom.*] Alfred!

[*She stands in the doorway looking down at the floor of the inner room, transfixed with horror. Then she shrieks wildly and runs to the other door, unlocks it and frenziedly pulls it open, and runs shrieking madly into the outer hallway.*]

[*The curtain falls.*]

QUESTIONS

1. What does the setting tell you about the Rowlands?
2. What image of Mrs. Rowland is presented in the opening stage directions? How are adjectives employed to shape your initial response to her? To what extent does the rest of the play sustain or alter this initial image?
3. How does Mrs. Rowland treat Alfred? What tone does she use in speaking to him? What does she complain about? What does she accuse Alfred of being and doing?
4. What happened during Mrs. Rowland's premarital affair with Alfred? Why do you suppose that she didn't let Alfred's father "buy her off"?
5. Where is the crisis of the play? Which character comes to a crisis? What actions and descriptions indicate that the character and play have reached a crisis?
6. Mrs. Rowland precipitates the climax of this play with her discussion of Alfred's affair with Helen. What do we learn about Helen? What pushes Alfred over the edge?

GENERAL QUESTIONS

1. How does the setting define the characters, their relationship, and their life? What details of setting are most significant?
2. Is Mrs. Rowland flat or round? Static or dynamic? Individualized or ster-

eotyped? Why does she have no first name? What is the effect of these choices?

3.   Why is Alfred Rowland kept off stage (except for his hand) and given no dialogue? How does this affect the play?

4.   Alfred Rowland is presented from his wife's point of view. How accurate is this portrait? To what degree does Alfred seem to justify his wife's accusations?

5.   Why does O'Neill present the history of Alfred's family and his relationship with Mrs. Rowland out of chronological order? What is the effect of this method of presentation?

WRITING ABOUT THE ELEMENTS OF DRAMA

Although some aspects of drama, such as lighting and stage movement, are singularly theatrical, drama shares a number of elements with prose fiction and poetry. The planning and the writing processes you use in drama are very similar to those you employ for essays on fiction or poetry. Thus, in the following discussion we refer to pages earlier in the text that discuss strategies for writing about specific elements.

As you plan an essay on drama, select a play and an appropriate element or series of elements. It would be inappropriate, for example, to attempt an essay about character development in *The Sandbox* (pp. 1465–71), because this play does not get deeply into the various characters. Be certain to choose elements that are clearly defined and have a decided effect on your reading of the play.

Once you select the play, choose a focus for your essay. This focus, which is your central idea, asserts something about a single element or about the relationship among elements in the play. For example, you might argue that a given character is flat, static, nonrealistic, and symbolic of good or evil. Or, to prove relationship among elements, you might want to claim that the meaning of a play is shaped and emphasized through setting and symbolism. In either event, the following questions will help you determine a focus, gather the raw materials, and form a thesis for your essay.

Questions for Discovering Ideas

PLOT, ACTION, CONFLICT.   (See also pp. 94–135.) How do actions and conflicts unfold? What are the conflicts? Which one is central? How is it resolved? What kind of conflict is it? Does it suggest any universal patterns of behavior? For plot, to what extent can you determine separate stages of development? What is the climax? The catastrophe? How are they anticipated or foreshadowed? Does the plot have a second plot or subplot? If so, how does it relate to the main plot? Is a significant pattern of action repeated? If so, what is the effect? To what extent do these parallel or repetitive patterns relate to theme and meaning? How do they control your emotional responses to the play?

CHARACTER. (See also pp. 137–95.) What central idea can you formulate to express a character's personality, function, or the connection between the character and the play's meaning? Is the character round or flat? Static or dynamic? Individualized or stereotyped? Realistic or nonrealistic? Is the protagonist (or antagonist) a choric, or incidental, character? Symbolic in any way? How is the character described in the stage directions? By other characters? By himself or herself? What does the character say? Do? Think? What is the character's attitude toward the environment? The action? Other characters? Himself or herself? To what extent does he or she articulate and/or embody key ideas in the play?

Referring to Plays and Parts of Plays

When you write about a play, always underline (or *italicize*) the title, just as you would for any printed book. In referring to particular speeches, you should assume that your reader may be using a text different from yours. You should therefore provide the specific numerical information necessary to enable your reader to find the exact location, regardless of text.

For a play with act, scene, and line or speech numbers, refer to *act* (Roman numeral), *scene* (Arabic numeral), and *line* or *speech* number (Arabic numeral).

Spell out the words *Act*, *scene*, and *line* (for poetry) or *speech* (for prose) in the *body* of your essay. Examples are Act I. scene 3. speech 4, or Act I. scene 1. line 33. Examples are *Act I, scene 3, speech 4*, or *Act I, scene 1, line 33*. In the body of your essay, when referring to materials in the play, spell out these references, such as "This action occurs in scene 4 of Act III (line 17, or speech 34)."

When making quotations, however, including **block quotations** (which you set apart from your own writing), include the numbers in parentheses following the quotation. Examples are I.1.33 (when no word precedes the last number, it is ordinarily understood to refer to a line), or I.3, speech 4 (for the sake of clarity, it is best to spell out that you are referring to a speech number).

When a play is divided into acts but not scenes, or if the play contains only one act, the best principle is to spell things out completely. Thus, a play like *Death of a Salesman*, which contains two acts and an epilogue, may be referred to as Act I, speech 348, or Epilogue, speech 5, both in your text and in block quotations. If the play is like *The Glass Menagerie*, which contains only numbered scenes, spell things out similarly, such as Scene I, speech 29. In referring to a one-act play like *The Bear*, refer simply to the speech or line number, such as Speech 265.

STAGE DIRECTIONS. If you refer to a stage direction, use the line or speech number immediately preceding the direction, and abbreviate "stage direction" as *s.d.*, as in Scene I, speech 16, s.d. Your reader will then know that you are referring to the stage direction following speech 16 in Scene 1. If there are stage directions at the very opening of the play, before the speeches begin (as in *The Glass Menagerie* and *Before Breakfast*), use a *0* and then a decimal point followed by an Arabic numeral to refer to the paragraph of directions. Thus 0.3, s.d. refers to the third paragraph of directions at the play's beginning.

PREFACES, SCENE DIRECTIONS, AND CASTS OF CHARACTERS. Some plays contain prefatory material, such as the "Production Notes" at the beginning of *The Glass Menagerie*. In referring to such introductions, use the title and then the paragraph number to which you refer (example, "In the 'Production Notes,' Williams describes *The Glass Menagerie* as a 'memory play' (paragraph 1)."

For scene directions at the beginning of acts or scenes, the most certain way is to spell out the circumstances, such as "The scene directions for Act III of *An Enemy of the People* describe the shabby editorial offices of *The People's Messenger*."

For the cast of characters, the same principle applies: Spell out what you mean, such as "the cast of characters," "the *Characters* list," or "the *Dramatis Personae*."

The important thing about referring to parts of plays is that you be clear and exact. The guidance offered here will cover most of the situations you encounter, but complications and exceptions will inevitably occur. When they do, always seek the advice of your instructor.

POINT OF VIEW AND PERSPECTIVE. (See also pp. 196–240.) Does the playwright present things from the perspective of an individual character? How does such a perspective affect the play's structure and meaning? Why is this point of view useful or striking? What does it suggest about characters? Theme? To what extent does your reaction to the play correspond with or diverge from this perspective? If characters speak in a soliloquy or monologue, do you sympathize with the character? What information does the character convey? What is he or she trying to prove? What is the tone of the speech? What do these devices contribute to your response to the play? Generally, what does the perspective contribute to your understanding of the play's meaning?

SETTING, SETS, AND PROPS. (See also pp. 241–65.) How do setting and objects help to establish the time, place, characters, lifestyle, values, or ideas of the play? Is the setting realistic or nonrealistic? To what extent may it be symbolic? What details and objects are specified, and what do they tell you about the time, place, characters, way of life, and values? To what extent do they contribute to the tone, atmosphere, impact, and meaning of the play?

DICTION, IMAGERY, STYLE. (See also pp. 266–70, 576–99, and 600–621) What level of diction and types of dialect, jargon, slang, or clichés are used by the characters? To what extent do these techniques define the characters and support or undercut their ideas? What connotative words or phrases do you find repeated in the play or spoken at a significant moment? What striking or consistent threads of imagery, metaphor, tone, or meaning? How do all these aspects of language shape your reaction to the play?

TONE AND ATMOSPHERE. (See also pp. 299–325.) How is the tone established and what impact does it have on the play's meaning? By what clues in stage directions, diction, imagery, rhetorical devices, tempo and context does the playwright convey his or her tone throughout the play? Individual characters' tones? How does tone articulate its meaning—directly, or indirectly through irony? To what degree do you as a reader or spectator know more than many of the onstage characters?

SYMBOLISM AND ALLEGORY. (See also pp. 326–61 and 765–94.) What are the symbols and how do they contribute to the play's ideas and impact? Which characters, objects, settings, situations, actions, words or phrases, and/or costumes seem to be symbolic? What do they symbolize? Are they universal or contextual symbols? Are they instantly symbolic or do they accumulate symbolic meaning? Is the symbolism extensive and consistent enough to form an allegorical system? If so, what are the two levels of meaning addressed by the allegory? To what extent does the symbolism or allegory shape the play's meaning and your response?

THEME. (See also pp. 362–409 and 819–43.) What does the play mean, and how is the meaning most strikingly communicated? What key ideas does the play explore, and what aspects of the play convey these ideas most emphatically? All of the preceding questions will be helpful in discovering which elements have the most profound impact on meaning.

Strategies for Organizing Ideas

Your essay should be focused on a central idea and developed through the use of examples and details that you discuss point by point. You can make use of carefully chosen quotations to help illustrate your assertions. When you use quotations, always explain in your own words exactly how they advance your argument.

A broad array of strategies for organizing your essay is available. If you are writing about the theme of loneliness and frustration in Keller's *Tea Party*, for example, you might select a number of objects or occurrences as the launching point for your discussion. Some of these might be the tea trolley and the sofa, or the bringing in of the cocoa and the paperboy's rapid movement past the window. Should you be discussing the specific crimes and guilt of Claudius in *Hamlet*, you might choose (1) the testimony of the Ghost to Hamlet, (2) Claudius's reaction to the players' scene, (3) his speech as he is praying, and (4) his poisoning of the cup, to show how these actions convincingly establish his villainy. For such essays, you might devote separate paragraphs to each element, or you might use two or more paragraphs for each element as you expand on your ideas.

Similar strategies might be listed for every possible type of essay on drama. In dealing with character in Glaspell's *Trifles*, for example, you might claim that a number of symbolic props help establish and reinforce the character of Minnie Wright or the ideas about marriage conveyed in the play. You might then use separate paragraphs to discuss these related symbols, such as Minnie's clothes, her dead canary, and her unfinished quilt. Similarly, in writing about language in plays like Chekhov's *The Bear* or Albee's *The Sandbox*, you would need to establish how the particular play connects qualities of speech to revelations about topics such as character and idea. Thus, in *The Sandbox*, much use is made of clichés, repetition, and connotative words, all of which have a relationship to the traits of the characters. In *The Bear*, Smirnov's constant use of exclamations, shouts, and profanity establish his irascibility, at least until close to the play's end. There are many possibilities and choices. Each play and topic will offer a variety of effective methods; any organization that is logical, clear, and convincing will help you produce a strong essay.

The conclusion should reinforce what you have advanced as your central idea. At the same time, the conclusion should relate the topics to the meaning or impact of the play as a whole. Thus, your conclusion should relate the points you make about aspects such as tone, character, plot, or language to overall meaning.

FIRST SAMPLE ESSAY

O'Neill's Use of Negative Descriptions and Stage Directions in *Before Breakfast*° to Reveal the Character of Mrs. Rowland

[1]   In the one-act play *Before Breakfast*, Eugene O'Neill dramatizes the suicidal crisis of a worsening husband-wife relationship. The story is clear. Mrs. Rowland, when still a young girl, was naive and opportunistic. She used her sexuality to seduce and then marry Alfred Rowland, who was the heir of his father's millions. Her resulting pregnancy ended in stillbirth. As if this were not enough, Alfred's father died not a millionaire, but a pauper deeply in debt. During the years of these disappointments, it is clear that Mrs. Rowland has lost whatever pleasantness she once possessed, and has de-

° See p. 1030 for this play.

scended into a state of personal neglect, alcoholism, and bitter selfishness.*
To bring out these traits early in the play, O'Neill relies heavily on negative
descriptions and stage directions.†

[2]
O'Neill's descriptions of Mrs. Rowland's personal neglect emphasize
her loss of self-esteem. The directions indicate that she has allowed her figure
to become a "shapeless stoutness," and that she has left her hair a "drab-
colored mass." This neglect of her physical person is capped off, according
to O'Neill's description, by her blue dress, which is "shabby and worn" and
"formless" (0.1, s.d.). Clearly, the shabbiness and excessive wear may result
from poverty, and thus show little about her character, but the formlessness
of the dress indicates a characteristic lack of concern about appearance,
also shown by her present physical condition and the miserable attention she
gives her hair. This slovenly image shows how she wants to appear in public,
because she is dressed and ready to go to work for the day. O'Neill's uncomplimentary descriptions thus define her absence of self-respect.

Similarly uncomplimentary, O'Neill's directions about her sneaking, furtive behavior reveal her dependence on alcohol. A serious sign of distress,
even though it might also be funny on stage, is the direction indicating that
she takes out a bottle of gin, which she keeps hidden behind dishes in a
"dish closet" (speech 1, s.d.). With this stage direction O'Neill symbolizes
the weakest trait of the secret drinker, which he also shows in the direction
that Mrs. Rowland brightens up once she has taken a stiff jolt of gin:

[3]
The large dose of alcohol she has taken has an almost immediate effect.
Her features become more animated, she seems to gather energy, and
she looks at the bedroom with a hard, vindictive smile on her lips.
(speech 2, s.d.)

It is safe to assume that these stage directions, on the morning of the play's
action, would also have applied to her behavior on many previous mornings.
In short, O'Neill is telling us through the stage directions that Mrs. Rowland
is a secret alcoholic.

[4]
The furtiveness of her drinking also shows up in her search of Alfred's
clothing, which also shows her selfishness and bitterness. When she me-
thodically empties his pockets, and uncovers the letter that we soon learn is
from his mistress, the stage directions show that she unhesitatingly and un-
derhandedly reads the letter through. Then O'Neill directs the actress to form
"a cruel smile on her lips" as she thinks about what to do with this new
information (speech 4, s.d.). As with the drinking, we see Mrs. Rowland rifling
through his things only this once, but the action suggests that this secretive
prying is a regular feature of her life. However, it is her discovery on this
morning--before breakfast--which is the key to the action, because her extensive monologue against her husband, which constitutes most of the play,
allows her to vent all her hatred by reproaching him about his lack of work,
his neglect of her, the time he spends with friends, his love affair, and so on.

While O'Neill uses these early stage directions and descriptions to convey a character portrait of Mrs. Rowland's unpleasantness, he provides a
certain balance in her speeches and additional actions. He makes her a

---

* Central idea.
† Thesis sentence.

[5] master of harangue, but there is nothing either in the directions or in her speeches to indicate that she wants to drive Alfred to suicide. Indeed, her horror at his suicide is genuine--just as it concludes the play with an incredible shock. In addition, on the positive side, her speeches show that despite her alcoholism and anger she is actually functioning in the outside world--as a seamstress--and that it is she who provides the meager money on which the couple is living (speech 6). In addition, she is working despite the fact that she has been feeling ill for a period of time before the play's action (speech 20). She also has enough concern for Alfred to bring him hot water for shaving (speech 14, s.d.).

[6] It is clear that O'Neill wants us to conclude that if Mrs. Rowland were a supportive person, Alfred might not be the nervous alcoholic who cuts his throat in the bathroom. However, the play does not make clear that he ever could have been better, even with the maximum support of a perfect wife. Certainly, Mrs. Rowland is not supportive. The stage directions and speeches show that she is limited by her weakness and bitterness. With such character traits, she has unquestionably never given Alfred any support at all, and probably never could. Everything that O'Neill tells us about her indicates that she is petty and selfish, and that she originally married Alfred expecting to receive and not to give.

[7] As things stand at the beginning of the play, then, Alfred is at the brink of despair, and Mrs. Rowland's bitter and reproachful speeches drive him into the pit of suicide. Despite all the spitefulness that O'Neill attributes to her character through the stage descriptions and directions, however, it is not possible to say that she is the cause of Alfred's suicide. O'Neill shows that Mrs. Rowland is an unpleasant, spiteful, and messy whiner, but it is not possible to reach any conclusions beyond this characterization.

Commentary on the Essay

This essay is designed to show how specifically dramatic conventions may be considered in reference to the analysis of character. Although the essay refers briefly to the speeches of the main character, Mrs. Rowland, it stresses those descriptions and directions that O'Neill designs specifically for the actress performing the role. The essay thus indicates one way to carry on a discussion of a play, as distinguished from a story or poem.

The introductory paragraph contains enough of the story about Mrs. Rowland and her husband to make sense of the following material about the stage directions and descriptions. The thesis statement lists the topics to be pursued in the body of the essay. Throughout the body, paragraph transitions are effected by words such as *similarly, also, while,* and *then.*

Paragraph 2, the first of the body, deals with O'Neill's directions concerning Mrs. Rowland's slovenly appearance and personal care. As distinguished from her personal appearance, paragraphs 3 and 4 are concerned with directions about her behavior—first her drinking and then her search of Alfred's clothing. The conclusion is that her actions show both weakness and underhanded selfishness. Paragraph 5 briefly attempts to consider how O'Neill uses Mrs. Rowland's speeches and other actions to balance the totally negative portrait he builds up through the negative stage directions.

Paragraphs 6 and 7 jointly form a conclusion to the essay. Paragraph 6 considers how the stage directions lead no further than that the marriage of the Rowlands is a terrible one. Paragraph 7, the last of the essay, continues the thread of the argument of paragraph 6, with the additional thought that O'Neill's directions do not warrant the conclusion that Mrs. Rowland's spiteful character is the cause of her husband's suicide.

SECOND SAMPLE ESSAY

The Idea of Love's Power in Chekhov's *The Bear*°

[1]   In the one-act farce *The Bear*, Anton Chekhov shows a man and woman who have never met before falling suddenly in love. With such an unlikely main action, ideas may seem unimportant, or even nonexistent. Though the play is admittedly farcical and unrealistic, it nevertheless embodies a number of significant ideas. Some of these are that responsibility to life is stronger than to death, that people may justify even the most stupid and contradictory actions, that love makes people do foolish things, and that lifelong commitments may be made with hardly any thought at all. One of the play's major ideas is that love and desire are powerful enough to overcome even the strongest obstacles.* This idea is shown as the force of love conquers commitment to the dead, renunciation of womankind, unfamiliarity, and anger.†

[2]   Commitment to her dead husband is the obstacle to love shown in Mrs. Popov. She states that she has made a vow never to see daylight because of her mourning (speech 4), and she spends her time staring at her husband's picture and sacrificing her life to her faithfulness. Her devotion to the dead is so intense that she claims to be dead herself out of sympathy: "My life is already ended. *He* lies in his grave; I have buried myself in these four walls . . . we are both dead" (speech 2). In her, Chekhov has created a strong obstacle so that he might illustrate the power of all-conquering love. By the play's end, Mrs. Popov's embracing Smirnov is a visual example of the idea (speech 151, s.d.).

[3]   Renunciation of women is the obstacle for Smirnov. He tells Mrs. Popov that women have made him bitter and that he no longer gives "a good goddamn" about them (speech 69). His disillusioned words apparently make him an impossible candidate for love. But, in keeping with Chekhov's idea, Smirnov soon confesses his sudden and uncontrollable love at the peak of his anger against Mrs. Popov. Within him, the force of love operates so strongly that he would even claim happiness at being shot by the "little velvet hands" of Mrs. Popov (speech 140).

As if these personal causes were not enough to stop love, a genuinely real obstacle is that the two people are strangers. Not only have they never

° See p. 1007 for this play.
* Central idea.
† Thesis sentence.

[4] met, but they have never even heard of each other. According to the main idea, however, this unfamiliarity is no major problem. Chekhov is dramatizing the power of love, and shows that it is strong enough to overcome even a lack of familiarity or friendship. Indeed, that Smirnov and Mrs. Popov are total strangers may be irrelevant to the idea about love's strength.

[5] Anger and the threat of violence, however, make the greatest obstacle. The two characters become so irritated with each other over Smirnov's demand for payment that, as an improbable climax of their heated words, Smirnov challenges Mrs. Popov, a woman, to a duel! He shouts, "And do you think just because you're one of those romantic creations, that you have the right to insult me with impunity? Yes? I challenge you!" (speech 105). Along with their own personal barriers against loving, it would seem that the threat of shooting each other, even if poor Luka could stop them, would cause lifelong hatred. And yet love knocks down all these obstacles, in line with Chekhov's idea that love's power is, like a flood, irresistible.

[6] The idea is not new or surprising. It is the subject of popular songs, stories, other plays, movies, and TV shows. What is surprising about Chekhov's use of the idea is that love in *The Bear* overcomes such unlikely conditions, and wins so suddenly. These conditions bring up an interesting and closely related idea: Chekhov is showing that intensely negative feeling may lead not to hatred but rather to love. In the speeches of Smirnov and Mrs. Popov, one can see hurt, disappointment, regret, frustration, annoyance, anger, rage, and self-destructiveness. Yet at the high point of these negative feelings, love takes over. It is as though hostility finally collapses because it is the nature of people to prefer loving to hating. *The Bear* is an uproariously farcical dramatization of the power of love, and it is made better because it is founded on a truthful judgment of the way people really are.

Commentary on the Essay

This essay shows how separate components of *The Bear* exhibit the pervasiveness of the idea selected for discussion. An initial difficulty that the essay deals with is that the play is unrealistic because it is a farce, and therefore that it might not contain any genuine ideas. The essay asserts that even a farce may be seriously based in ideas, and therefore that the discussion can go forward. The particularly dramatic elements used as support in the essay are dialogue, farcical situations and actions, and soliloquies.

The introduction states the major idea that love has the power to surmount great obstacles. The thesis sentence lists the four obstacles to be explored in the body.

As the operative aspects of Chekhov's idea, paragraphs 2 through 5 detail the nature of each of the obstacles. The obstacle of paragraph 2, Mrs. Popov's commitment to her husband's memory, is "strong." The one in paragraph 3, Smirnov's dislike of women, is seemingly "impossible." The one in paragraph 4, their being total strangers, is a "genuinely real" difficulty. In paragraph 5, the obstacle of anger is more likely to produce "hatred" than love.

There are two objectives in the concluding paragraph. One is to reassert the central idea—a brief summary. The second is to build on the idea by suggesting another related and important idea. The conclusion therefore demonstrates a major quality not only of drama but of literature generally—that a consequence of one idea is the exploration of other ideas.

Throughout the essay, transitions between paragraphs are effected by phrases like "these personal causes" (4), "greatest obstacle" (5), and "The idea" (6), all of which emphasize the continuity of the topic.

WRITING TOPICS

1. *Tea Party* might be considered a sentimental work, on the grounds that the two elderly characters are presented to evoke sympathy and anguish, not to resemble the life of real persons. Write an essay defending the play against this judgment. As you write your defense, make references to Keller's characterizations and her development of character.

2. *The Bear* is one of Chekhov's most popular plays. Read another Chekhov play (for example, *The Cherry Orchard, The Seagull, Three Sisters, Uncle Vanya*) and compare it to *The Bear* (characters with characters, dialogue with dialogue, situations with situations, and so on). In light of your comparison, write an essay in which you explain and justify the continued popularity of *The Bear*.

3. *Before Breakfast* is set in an apartment in Greenwich Village in lower Manhattan around 1916. It was performed in Greenwich Village in December 1916. Write an essay that deals with the following questions:
   a. What do you make of this convergence of settings—artistic and realistic?
   b. What could O'Neill assume about his original audience's reaction to the setting?

4. Write an essay that considers the following questions. Is Glaspell's *Trifles* about crime? Rural life? Marriage? The roles of rural and frontier women? The way men regard women (even today)? The way in which anger that is bottled up must eventually explode? Write an essay detailing your response, using specific details from the play as evidence in your argument. To what degree is the situation in the play realistic? If it were to be presented as a play about a similar rural murder in the 1990s, what freedom would the women have to explore the kitchen?

5. Read the story "A Jury of Her Peers" (Chapter 4, pp. 158–72), which Susan Glaspell wrote a year after her play *Trifles*. Write an essay describing the differences you find between the story and the play (for example, the openings of the two works, the various descriptions of how the women react to their discoveries in the kitchen, the amounts of detail used in the play and in the story). Based on your findings, describe some of the characteristics of drama as opposed to fiction.

6. On the basis of the plays included in this chapter, plan and write an essay dealing with the characteristics of the dramatic form. You might wish to consider topics like the use of dialogue, monologue, soliloquy, action, vocal ranges, staging, comparative lengths of plays, pauses in speech, stage directions, laughter, seriousness, and the means by which the dramatists get you interested in characters and situations.

26

Tragedy: Affirmation Through Loss

THE ORIGIN AND NATURE OF TRAGEDY

"A tragedy is a sad story." "A tragedy is a story that ends in death." "A tragedy is the story of the downfall of an individual." Everyone has notions about what constitutes tragedy. Common to most definitions is the element that something bad—usually fatal—happens to the main character.

The idea that the protagonist in tragedy has to suffer and die originated in the belief that sacrifice leads to redemption and renewal. Tragedy, like drama in general, evolved from prehistoric rites celebrating the end of winter and the return of spring. In these rites, the ritual sacrifice of a god or hero would be reenacted to ensure the land's fruitfulness after winter's barrenness. Thus, while the god/hero suffered death, the community was restored and revitalized.

At some point in prehistory the ritual began including narrative choral songs in which the myth of the god/hero was retold. According to Aristotle (384–322 B.C.), the shift from the narrative to the dramatic mode occurred when the ancient Athenian writer Thespis (ca. 534 B.C.) singled out a member of the chorus—the first actor—to speak separately in the person of the god/hero. As the actor took the central role, the chorus also assumed a role, such as a group of soldiers, worshippers, or citizens.

This conceptual shift in the ritual, whereby the actor became impersonator, made drama possible, for the god/hero could now interact with the chorus. Aristotle tells us that a second actor was added by Aeschylus (525–456 B.C.) and a third by Sophocles (ca. 496–406 B.C.). These actors could play as many different parts as the playwright wished, but the number of players was limited (in the plays of Sophocles) to a chorus and three actors.

By the time of Sophocles, tragedy had developed its own form and style. Aristotle, who attended many tragedies in the Great Theater of Dionysus in Athens, analyzed and described the characteristics of tragedy in his great critical work *The Poetics*. In Chapter 6 he states that tragedy is "an imitation of an action that is serious, complete, and of a certain magnitude; in language embellished with each kind of artistic ornament; . . . in the form of a drama, not of narrative; through pity and fear effecting the proper purgation of these emotions."[1] Bear in mind that Aristotle is not establishing "rules" for writing tragedies, but is rather offering a comprehensive description based on the tragedies he has seen. It is interesting to note that most of the examples he cites throughout *The Poetics* are from Sophocles's *Oedipus the King*, the first play in this chapter.

An analysis of the separate parts of Aristotle's definition will help you to be a successful reader and critic of tragedies. Let us begin with Aristotle's assertion that a tragedy is "serious, complete, and of a certain magnitude." "Serious" indicates that the subject matter must be elevated and that the characters must be royal and aristocratic rather than common—in other words, that the characters must be important and worth considering. By "complete" Aristotle means that the story must have a beginning, a middle, and an end that make a logical, causal, and artistic whole. The playwright need not dramatize *everything* about the story, but rather is free to present no more than *one* of the most significant aspects, for the "magnitude" of the plot suggests that the play must be of "a length which can be easily embraced by memory" (Chapter 7). Thus, the actual *story* of Oedipus covers the protagonist's whole life, but the *play* itself dramatizes only part of the last day of his reign as king of Thebes (Sophocles's other plays about Oedipus concern later episodes of this mythical life).

The tragedy must be acted out rather than told. By "action," Aristotle means the complete working out of a single motivation from its beginning in activity to its conclusion in the perception (or recognition) of a truth. Thus, in *Oedipus*, the action develops from the hero's wish, as King of Thebes, to save this royal city from the plague, and to do it by expelling the former king's murderer. (Oedipus, we all know, is that murderer, but he learns this fact only in the course of the play.) Similarly, in *Hamlet* the action grows out of Hamlet's resolution to purify Denmark by avenging the murder of his father. In dramatizing the complete working out of an original motive, the tragic action moves from purpose (or activity), through emotion (or *pathos*), and finally to perception. Aristotle uses the term "plot" to describe this whole process.

Perhaps the most interesting part of Aristotle's description of tragedy is his assertion that tragic drama arouses fear and pity in the spectators and leads to a **purgation (catharsis)** of these emotions. Here, Aristotle addresses himself to the reasons we appreciate tragedy. The pity and fear that the play evokes in us allow us to experience these emotions vicariously in an extreme form. At the end of the tragedy, these emotions have been washed out of (purged from) our psyche, and we are renewed.

---

[1] S. H. Butcher, *Aristotle's Theory of Poetry and Fine Art*, 4th ed. (London: Macmillan, 1932). All quotations are from this edition.

The purgation of fear and pity may also be explained with reference to the Freytag pyramid (see p. 994). Looking at the pyramid, we see that fear and anxiety are most heavy during the tension and uncertainty (stages one and two) leading up to the climax, and pity and regret are the major emotions after the climax during the "falling action" (stage four). In other words, just as the tragedy has a clearly perceivable form, it produces a similar patterning of emotions in the spectators or readers.

Aristotle narrows his description of tragedy still further in other chapters of *The Poetics*. He asserts, for example, that the hero's misfortunes are brought about not by "vice" or "depravity," but rather by an "error" or "frailty" (Chapter 13). The Greek term for error or frailty is **hamartia,** which is sometimes translated as "tragic flaw." The idea of hamartia is that any human being might make mistakes, regardless of social station. We, as an audience of normally imperfect human beings, can thus identify with the hero or heroine, and sympathize with his or her predicament. If the disaster were brought about by evil or viciousness, instead of feeling pity we would be happy to see a villain destroyed. On the other hand, if the protagonist were a pure soul, without fault, then we would be indignant at the fall of an innocent person, but would also be unable to involve ourselves completely with the character. Thus, the tragic hero is a character the audience easily identifies with: neither evil nor saintly but somewhere in between, possessing virtues and faults, a character who makes crucial mistakes that begin the process of the tragic fall.

This is not to say that concepts and philosophies about fate, fortune, the gods, and circumstances do not play a role in the misfortunes of the hero. The Greeks believed that the gods intervened in the affairs of human beings for their own purposes, which ordinary mortals do not understand. Similarly, Shakespeare causes Hamlet to speak about the "divinity that shapes our ends," as though external rather than internal forces control life. In *Death of a Salesman*, Arthur Miller introduces the power of economics in the life of the hero, and suggests that misfortune results from social class and economic forces, over which few of us have any control.

The issue of whether external or internal forces bring about the ups and downs of life is closely related to the problem of free will as opposed to destiny, a question that has perennially occupied philosophers. In tragedy, the question leads to what is often called the "tragic dilemma"; that is, a situation in which the protagonist faces two equally difficult or unacceptable choices, either one of which leads to disaster. Thus, Oedipus must ignore the problems of Thebes and thereby be a bad king, or take the lead in discovering and eliminating the cause of these problems (himself). Hamlet must either become a murderous avenger, contrary to his own good nature, or avoid the entire situation and retreat into ineffectiveness or suicide. Once the protagonist chooses, the destructive result is inevitable. It may seem, therefore, that divinity, fate, or destiny is operating even though the protagonist has apparently exercised free will.

To complete the tragic sequence of events, Aristotle introduces two additional elements—the reversal of action and the growth of understanding or self-knowledge. He calls the **reversal** of action or intention the **peripeteia:** that instant when there is "a change by which the action veers around to its opposite" (Chapter 11). In the best tragedies, according to Aristotle, the reversal occurs simultaneously with understanding, a moment that he calls the **"recognition" (anagnorisis).** Indeed, this element is most important, because it is an affirmative signal in the midst of negative events. The protagonist realizes his or her own place in the universal scheme of things, acknowledging the errors that have led to tragedy, and accepting the degree to which he or she is responsible. In effect, the tragic hero, even though not responsible for the disintegrating state of affairs, shoulders the responsibility and accepts the consequences, no matter how catastrophic they are. Without this affirmation, we would have works that might be described as sad, pathetic, or despairing. With the affirmation, however, we have tragedy—the dramatic form which illustrates the heights that human beings can reach even in the lowest depths of adversity.

To this point, we have described tragedy largely with reference to Aristotle and *The Poetics*. This description is not limited to Greek tragedy. You will also learn that not all tragedy is "Aristotelian" in structure, nor is Aristotle's analysis totally descriptive of all later tragedies. Every age has redefined and refashioned tragedy to its own ends and images. In England during the Renaissance, for example, Shakespeare and his contemporaries wrote tragedies with reference to history rather than myth, and to medieval rather than Aristotelian traditions. Similarly, the eighteenth century saw the growth of middle-class tragic protagonists and **domestic tragedy.** In the twentieth century, tragedy has been reformulated to include both working-class protagonists and antiheroes. Thus Arthur Miller names his hero "Loman" (that is, "low man"), as if to emphasize the gulf between modern human beings and kings and princes. Modern tragedians have loosened the structure of tragic plots, lowered the level of language, and also have stressed the mechanistic nature of the universe and the hopelessness and inevitability of misfortune. Nevertheless, in the end, modern and ancient tragedies meet on common ground, with both asserting that this dramatic form must lead to learning, to recognition and understanding, and to affirmation.

LANGUAGE AND TONE IN TRAGEDY

Just as character and action are important, so also are language and tone. Greek tragedy was always written in verse. As a result, Aristotle asserts in *The Poetics* that lofty diction and poetic ornaments are necessary to tragedies. This description is true, for the most part, until the late eighteenth century, on the assumption that just as tragic protagonists are important and elevated, so also is the language that they speak. Roman tragedy is poetic. English Renaissance and Restoration tragedy is written mostly in blank verse and heroic couplets. This does not mean that all tragedy before the nineteenth century is written completely in verse, for Shakespeare and most of his contemporaries mixed verse and prose. *Hamlet*, for example, shifts between blank verse and prose, depending on the characters and the circumstances. The Elizabethan playwrights also included characters from all social classes in their tragedies, thus making colloquial diction appropriate in many instances—the graveyard scene in *Hamlet* (Act V, scene 1) is a good example. In the twentieth century, tragedy has become a great deal less elevated. The shift to the common man or woman as the tragic protagonist has led to a concurrent shift from poetry to colloquial and conversational dialogue. The characters in Miller's *Death of a Salesman*, for example, speak the idiomatic American English of the 1940s.

The tone of tragedy is frequently ironic. One of the most important reasons is dramatic irony (Chapter 25, p. 999). As readers or spectators, we almost always know more than the tragic protagonist. We know, for instance, that Oedipus killed his father and that Claudius murdered his brother—long before the tragic heroes in either play learn these things. Thus, we see the ironic futility of many actions and statements. For example, a tragic protagonist's greatest strength may also be one of his or her greatest weaknesses. We can see this in Oedipus's determination to unmask a murderer and save his country at all costs. It is similarly ironic that the best characters in tragedy—the most sensitive, intelligent, or honest—are the ones who suffer the most and often die. Perhaps the most effective twist of irony in tragedy is the irony of *anagnorisis*, or recognition. Increased self-knowledge and understanding must occur, but they never come until the protagonist has passed the point of no return; recognition is thus both necessary and ironically useless in averting disaster.

THE THEATER OF SOPHOCLES

In Athens, during Sophocles's lifetime (ca. 496–406 B.C.), plays were performed in the Great Theater of Dionysus during the festival of Dionysus (the god of fertility and wine) in late March or early April. A typical Dionysian festival (a **Dionysia**) lasted five or six days and was an occasion for dramatic productions and an annual theatrical competition. Three tragedians (writers of tragedy) and three to five comedic playwrights were chosen to compete. Each of the comedic writers supplied one play; each of the tragedians wrote three related tragedies (a **trilogy**) and one **satyr play,** a short comic interlude.

The congregation (and audience) for the festival was enormous; all citizens of Athens and all visitors normally attended. The first two or three days were devoted to religious processions and poetry contests. The last three days were given over to the playwrights' competition. On each of these days (the festival began at dawn), the spectators watched three tragedies, a satyr play, and a comedy or two. At the end of the festival, prizes were awarded to the playwrights judged best in tragedy and in comedy.

The Great Theater of Dionysus, in which Sophocles's plays were first performed, was a vast semicircular open-air amphitheater built into the side of a hill and seating twenty thousand spectators (see illustration). The central circle, called the **orchestra,** was the area where the chorus sang its lyrical interludes (odes) and performed dances. Originally, the spectators simply sat on the hills surrounding and overlooking the orchestra. Later, wooden seats and then stone seats were installed. Behind the orchestra a small building called the **skene** (in Latin, the *scaena,* from which we get the word "scene") was used as a dressing room and a place for actors to await their cues. The skene was merely a tent at first and later, a wooden building. Eventually it became a permanent stone building, its front facing the audience and decorated with paintings. A crane installed on top enabled the actors playing gods to be lowered from the "heavens" or

Ancient theater at Epidauros, Greece. (Gian Berto Vanni/Art Resource)

raised up from the "earth." This piece of machinery, often used by inept playwrights to end their plays quickly with the appearance of a god, led to the Latin term *deus ex machina* ("god from the machine"), which is now used to describe an illogical event that solves all the problems in a work. The skene had three doors for entrances and exits: one in the center and one each on the left and the right. Eventually, a **colonnade** (a row of columns) was built behind the skene at the Great Theater to provide a permanent backdrop that suggested a palace or a temple. Some theater historians argue that a raised wooden stage (called the **proskenion** or, in Latin, the **proscenium**) was constructed in front of the skene to separate the actors from the chorus and make them more visible to the audience.

Plays were performed in this theater in broad daylight without any scenery and with a minimum of props. To establish a time or place for the action, the playwright had a character mention the location or time of day. The plays of Sophocles were usually performed by a chorus of fifteen men (including the **choragos,** or choral leader) and three male actors. All parts, including women's roles, were played by men. The three actors could play as many different characters as the playwright required simply by withdrawing into the skene, changing masks, and reentering as a new character. Thus, in a play like *Oedipus the King* a single actor would most likely play both a prophet and a messenger. Mute (silent) characters, like Oedipus's daughters, were not considered roles and thus did not count in the total number of actors.

The chorus entered and exited the orchestra along an aisle, called the **parados,** on each side of the skene. The actors could enter the playing area either from the skene or by way of the parados, and could perform in the orchestra, on the wooden stage, or even on the roof of the skene. The chorus was restricted to the orchestra, and always stood between the audience and the actors. This placing of the chorus helped to emphasize its double role as both participants and reactors to the action. The chorus thus played an important role in the play and at the same time guided audience reaction to the drama.

The actors in classical Greek theater performed in stylized masks (called **personae** in Latin, from which we derive the word "person"). These masks had built-in megaphones to amplify the actors' voices. According to tradition, the actors also wore thick-soled shoes, called **cothurni** or **buskins,** that elevated their height and stylized their appearance. The Athenian audience accepted the stylization (or **conventions**) of their drama as we accept the conventions of grand opera, Westerns, or situation comedies.

Plays written during the age of Sophocles are usually divided into five distinct sections: *prologue, parados, episodia, stasimon,* and *exodos.* The **prologue** occurs before the first choral ode; it contains much exposition. The **parados** is also the name of the first lyrical ode the chorus chants after entering the orchestra for the first time; it presents the initial problems and attitudes of the chorus. The middle part of the play is made up of numerous **episodia** (episodes) and **stasima** (choric odes; the singular is **stasimon**). Each episode begins after a choral ode and ends with another. The episodes are often debates between the tragic protagonist and another character; the stasima are choral reactions to these debates. The **exodos** (exit) is the scene that follows the last choral ode of the play; it contains both the resolution of the drama and the departure (*exodos*) of the actors.

SOPHOCLES, *OEDIPUS THE KING*

When Sophocles dramatized the story of Oedipus, the myth was already hundreds of years old. Most of the Athenians who thronged to the Great Theater of Dionysus around 430 B.C. to watch Sophocles' new play would have known many details of Oedipus's history: the prophecy delivered before his birth; his exposure as an infant on Mount Cithaeron; his upbringing in Corinth as the adopted son of Merope and Polybus; the murder of Laius at the place where three roads meet; his defeat of the Sphinx; his marriage to Jocasta; and his twenty-year reign as king of Thebes. In dramatizing this very well-known story, Sophocles was consistent with the playwriting practices of his age; these, in fact, continued throughout the entire classical period. The dramatists in England during the age of Shakespeare, like the classical Greek tragedians, put no special value on originality or timeliness. Rather, they sought new ways to dramatize old and valued tales.

This practice of dramatizing well-known stories had a profound effect on the shape and impact of plays like *Oedipus the King*. Let us consider what Sophocles lost and what he gained. For one thing, he could not change the basic shape of the story or alter any significant details of Oedipus's life. Thus, Sophocles gave up any possibility of creating suspense about the resolution or of adding a surprise ending. At the same time, however, much could be gained. Sophocles could assume, for example, that his audience would be familiar with the characters in the Oedipus story, so he could focus on nuances of phrasing and characterization and on conflict and meaning. Most important, Sophocles could use his audience's knowledge to create dramatic irony. Early in *Oedipus the King*, for example, when Oedipus curses the murderer of Laius: "may he wear out his life unblest and evil" (line 253), the audience knows that the curse will fall on him, but Oedipus does not know this. The play is full of this kind of dramatic irony. Indeed, *Oedipus* is like a murder mystery in which the reader knows who did it right from the beginning. The pleasure and the agony are produced as we watch Oedipus the detective move step by step through a process of discovery that will ultimately lead to the guilty person—himself.

The mythic material that Sophocles worked with in shaping *Oedipus the King* is the story of Oedipus—from the oracle delivered before the tragic hero's birth, to his ultimate expulsion from Thebes, and to his old age. In forming a play from this material, Sophocles had to create a unified plot that limited the action to a single motivation and a single process of fall from prosperity to adversity. Sophocles did this by dramatizing only the final hours of Oedipus's reign as king. These last hours take us from Apollo's prophecy that Thebes will be saved from the plague only through the expulsion of the murderer of Laius to Oedipus's discovery that he is that murderer. The remainder of Oedipus's story is told through conversations and debates; characters discuss events that happened years before the "present time" of the dramatized day. By choosing to dramatize only part of the last day of Oedipus's reign, Sophocles was able to produce a highly cohesive play that maintains the traditional **unities** of **place, time,** and **action.** The entire play occurs in the courtyard in front of the royal palace of Thebes, and the elapsed time within the play covers only part of a single day. Unity of action is achieved by the focus on a single story and a single motivation: the need to save Thebes from the plague by expelling the murderer of Laius.

Oedipus the King conforms in most respects to Aristotle's description of tragedy. Two aspects of this description are especially noteworthy: the reversal (or *peripeteia*) and the recognition (or *anagnorisis*). The play is full of reversals of action or intention. The messenger from Corinth, for example, thinks that he is releasing Oedipus from fear when he discloses that Merope and Polybus are not his real parents; in fact, the result is exactly the opposite of what the messenger intends. In some ways, the entire play is built on the idea of *peripeteia*. Oedipus vows to save the city by rooting out the murderer of Laius, and ultimately discovers that he is that murderer. Obviously, the intention and the action have been reversed. The recognition of truth in *Oedipus* is tightly bound up with this central reversal. The *peripeteia* of Oedipus's action and intention occurs simultaneously with his own recognition of his errors, sins, guilt, and destiny.

At the end of *Oedipus the King* we are left with a puzzle. We must decide if Oedipus's tragic fall is produced by forces beyond his control, or by aspects of his character that led to errors in judgment and action. The play offers support for both interpretations. On the one hand, Oedipus's destiny was prophesied before his birth by the oracle of Apollo. Does this mean that he was destined to murder his father and marry his mother, or does it mean that the gods simply knew the future? On the other hand, Oedipus's rage, his overweening pride (*hubris*), and his compulsive need to know the truth drive him inexorably toward destruction. Sophocles has left us this central problem to ponder on our own.

SOPHOCLES (ca. 496–406 B.C.)

Oedipus the King

ca. 430 B.C.

Translated by Thomas Gould

CHARACTERS

> Oedipus,° *The King of Thebes*
> Priest of Zeus, *Leader of the Suppliants*
> Creon, *Oedipus's Brother-in-law*
> Chorus, *a Group of Theban Elders*
> Choragos, *Spokesman of the Chorus*
> Tiresias, *a blind Seer or Prophet*
> Jocasta, *The Queen of Thebes*
> Messenger, *from Corinth, once a Shepherd*
> Herdsman, *once a Servant of Laius*
> Second Messenger, *a Servant of Oedipus*

MUTES

> Suppliants, *Thebans seeking Oedipus's help*
> Attendants, *for the Royal Family*
> Servants, *to lead Tiresias and Oedipus*
> Antigone, *Daughter of Oedipus and Jocasta*
> Ismene, *Daughter of Oedipus and Jocasta*

[*The action takes place during the day in front of the royal palace in Thebes. There are two altars (left and right) on the Proscenium and several steps leading down to the Orchestra. As the play opens, Thebans of various ages who have come to beg Oedipus for help are sitting on these steps and in part of the Orchestra. These suppliants are holding branches of laurel or olive which have strips of wool° wrapped around them. Oedipus enters from the palace (the central door of the Skene).*]

PROLOGUE

OEDIPUS.   My children, ancient Cadmus'° newest care,
   why have you hurried to those seats, your boughs
   wound with the emblems of the suppliant?
   The city is weighed down with fragrant smoke,
   with hymns to the Healer° and the cries of mourners.
   I thought it wrong, my sons, to hear your words   5

Oedipus: The name means "swollen foot." It refers to the mutilation of Oedipus's feet done by his father, Laius, before the infant was sent to Mount Cithaeron to be put to death by exposure.   Stage direction: *wool:* Branches wrapped with wool are traditional symbols of prayer or supplication.   *Cadmus:* Oedipus's great great grandfather (although he does not know this) and the founder of Thebes.   5 *Healer:* Apollo, god of prophecy, light, healing, justice, purification, and destruction.

through emissaries, and have come out myself,
I, Oedipus, a name that all men know.

[OEDIPUS *addresses the* PRIEST.]

Old man—for it is fitting that you speak
for all—what is your mood as you entreat me,   10
fear or trust? You may be confident
that I'll do anything. How hard of heart
if an appeal like this did not rouse my pity!

PRIEST. You, Oedipus, who hold the power here,
you see our several ages, we who sit   15
before your altars—some not strong enough
to take long flight, some heavy in old age,
the priests, as I of Zeus,° and from our youths
a chosen band. The rest sit with their windings
in the markets, at the twin shrines of Pallas,°   20
and the prophetic embers of Ismēnos.°
Our city, as you see yourself, is tossed
too much, and can no longer lift its head
above the troughs of billows red with death.
It dies in the fruitful flowers of the soil,   25
it dies in its pastured herds, and in its women's
barren pangs. And the fire-bearing god°
has swooped upon the city, hateful plague,
and he has left the house of Cadmus empty.
Black Hades° is made rich with moans and weeping.   30
Not judging you an equal of the gods,
do I and the children sit here at your hearth,
but as the first of men, in troubled times
and in encounters with divinities.
You came to Cadmus' city and unbound   35
the tax we had to pay to the harsh singer,°
did it without a helpful word from us,
with no instruction; with a god's assistance
you raised up our life, so we believe.
Again now Oedipus, our greatest power,   40

18 *Zeus:* father and king of the gods.   20 *Pallas:* Athena, goddess of wisdom, arts, crafts,
and war.   21 *Ismēnos:* a reference to the temple of Apollo near the river Ismēnos in
Thebes. Prophecies were made here by "reading" the ashes of the altar fires.   27 *fire-
bearing god:* contagious fever viewed as a god.   30 *Black Hades:* refers to both the
underworld, where the spirits of the dead go, and the god of the underworld.   36 *harsh
singer:* the Sphinx, a monster with a woman's head, a lion's body, and wings. The "tax" that
Oedipus freed Thebes from was the destruction of all the young men who failed to solve
the Sphinx's riddle and were subsequently devoured. The Sphinx always asked the same
riddle: "What goes on four legs in the morning, two legs at noon, and three legs in the
evening, and yet is weakest when supported by the largest number of feet?" Oedipus
discovered the correct answer—man, who crawls in infancy, walks in his prime, and uses a
stick in old age—and thus ended the Sphinx's reign of terror. The Sphinx destroyed
herself when Oedipus answered the riddle. Oedipus's reward for freeing Thebes of the
Sphinx was the throne and the hand of the recently widowed Jocasta. (A photograph of a
Sphinx built in ancient Egypt appears on p. 808.)

we plead with you, as suppliants, all of us,
to find us strength, whether from a god's response,
or learned in some way from another man.
I know that the experienced among men
give counsels that will prosper best of all.   45
Noblest of men, lift up our land again!
Think also of yourself; since now the land
calls you its Savior for your zeal of old,
oh let us never look back at your rule
as men helped up only to fall again!   50
Do not stumble! Put our land on firm feet!
The bird of omen was auspicious then,
when you brought that luck; be that same man again!
The power is yours; if you will rule our country,
rule over men, not in an empty land.   55
A towered city or a ship is nothing
if desolate and no man lives within.
OEDIPUS. Pitiable children, oh I know, I know
the yearnings that have brought you. Yes, I know
that you are sick. And yet, though you are sick,   60
there is not one of you so sick as I.
For your affliction comes to each alone,
for him and no one else, but my soul mourns
for me and for you, too, and for the city.
You do not waken me as from a sleep,   65
for I have wept, bitterly and long,
tried many paths in the wanderings of thought,
and the single cure I found by careful search
I've acted on: I sent Menoeceus' son,
Creon, brother of my wife, to the Pythian   70
halls of Phoebus,° so that I might learn
what I must do or say to save this city.
Already, when I think what day this is,
I wonder anxiously what he is doing.
Too long, more than is right, he's been away.   75
But when he comes, then I shall be a traitor
if I do not do all that the god reveals.
PRIEST. Welcome words! But look, those men have signaled
that it is Creon who is now approaching!
OEDIPUS. Lord Apollo! May he bring Savior Luck,   80
a Luck as brilliant as his eyes are now!
PRIEST. His news is happy, it appears. He comes,
forehead crowned with thickly berried laurel.°
OEDIPUS. We'll know, for he is near enough to hear us.

[*Enter* CREON *along one of the Parados.*]

70–71 *Pythian . . . Phoebus:* the temple of Phoebus Apollo's oracle or prophet at Delphi.
83 *laurel:* Creon is wearing a garland of laurel leaves, sacred to Apollo.

Lord, brother in marriage, son of Menoeceus! 85
What is the god's pronouncement that you bring?
CREON.   It's good. For even troubles, if they chance
    to turn out well, I always count as lucky.
OEDIPUS.   But what was the response? You seem to say
    I'm not to fear—but not to take heart either. 90
CREON.   If you will hear me with these men present,
    I'm ready to report—or go inside.

[CREON *moves up the steps toward the palace.*]

OEDIPUS.   Speak out to all! The grief that burdens me
    concerns these men more than it does my life.
CREON.   Then I shall tell you what I heard from the god. 95
    The task Lord Phoebus sets for us is clear:
    drive out pollution sheltered in our land,
    and do not shelter what is incurable.
OEDIPUS.   What is our trouble? How shall we cleanse ourselves?
CREON.   We must banish or murder to free ourselves 100
    from a murder that blows storms through the city.
OEDIPUS.   What man's bad luck does he accuse in this?
CREON.   My Lord, a king named Laius ruled our land
    before you came to steer the city straight.
OEDIPUS.   I know. So I was told—I never saw him. 105
CREON.   Since he was murdered, you must raise your hand
    against the men who killed him with their hands.
OEDIPUS.   Where are they now? And how can we ever find
    the track of ancient guilt now hard to read?
CREON.   In our own land, he said. What we pursue, 110
    that can be caught; but not what we neglect.
OEDIPUS.   Was Laius home, or in the countryside—
    or was he murdered in some foreign land?
CREON.   He left to see a sacred rite, he said;
    He left, but never came home from his journey. 115
OEDIPUS.   Did none of his party see it and report—
    someone we might profitably question?
CREON.   They were all killed but one, who fled in fear,
    and he could tell us only one clear fact.
OEDIPUS.   What fact? One thing could lead us on to more 120
    if we could get a small start on our hope.
CREON.   He said that bandits chanced on them and killed him—
    with the force of many hands, not one alone.
OEDIPUS.   How could a bandit dare so great an act—
    unless this was a plot paid off from here! 125
CREON.   We thought of that, but when Laius was killed,
    we had no one to help us in our troubles.
OEDIPUS.   It was your very kingship that was killed!
    What kind of trouble blocked you from a search?
CREON.   The subtle-singing Sphinx asked us to turn 130
    from the obscure to what lay at our feet.

OEDIPUS.   Then I shall begin again and make it plain.
It was quite worthy of Phoebus, and worthy of you,
to turn our thoughts back to the murdered man,
and right that you should see me join the battle   135
for justice to our land and to the god.
Not on behalf of any distant kinships,
it's for myself I will dispel this stain.
Whoever murdered him may also wish
to punish me—and with the selfsame hand.   140
In helping him I also serve myself.
Now quickly, children: up from the altar steps,
and raise the branches of the suppliant!
Let someone go and summon Cadmus' people:
say I'll do anything.

　　　　　　　　　　　[Exit an ATTENDANT *along one of the Parados.]*

　　　　　　　　　　　Our luck will prosper   145
if the god is with us, or we have already fallen.
PRIEST.   Rise, my children; that for which we came,
he has himself proclaimed he will accomplish.
May Phoebus, who announced this, also come
as Savior and reliever from the plague.   150

[Exit OEDIPUS *and* CREON *into the Palace. The* PRIEST *and the* SUPPLIANTS *exit left and right along the Parados. After a brief pause, the* CHORUS *(including the* CHORAGOS*) enters the Orchestra from the Parados.]*

PARADOS

Strophe 1°

CHORUS.   Voice from Zeus,° sweetly spoken, what are you
that have arrived from golden
Pytho° to our shining
Thebes? I am on the rack, terror
　　shakes my soul.   155
Delian Healer,° summoned by "iē!"
I await in holy dread what obligation, something new
or something back once more with the revolving years,
　　you'll bring about for me.
Oh tell me, child of golden Hope,   160
　　deathless Response!

151,162 *Strophe, Antistrophe:* These stanzaic units refer to movements, counter-movements, and gestures that the Chorus performed while singing or chanting in the orchestra.
151 *Voice from Zeus:* a reference to Apollo's prophecy. Zeus taught Apollo how to prophesy.
153 *Pytho:* Delphi.　　156 *Delian Healer:* Apollo.

Antistrophe 1°

I appeal to you first, daughter of Zeus,
    deathless Athena,
    and to your sister who protects this land,
    Artemis,° whose famous throne is the whole circle   165
    of the marketplace,
and Phoebus, who shoots from afar: iō!
Three-fold defenders against death, appear!
If ever in the past, to stop blind ruin
    sent against the city,   170
you banished utterly the fires of suffering,
    come now again!

Strophe 2

Ah! Ah! Unnumbered are the miseries
I bear. The plague claims all
our comrades. Nor has thought found yet a spear   175
by which a man shall be protected. What our glorious
earth gives birth to does not grow. Without a birth
from cries of labor
    do the women rise.
One person after another   180
    you may see, like flying birds,
faster than indomitable fire, sped
to the shore of the god that is the sunset.°

Antistrophe 2

And with their deaths unnumbered dies the city.
Her children lie unpitied on the ground,   185
spreading death, unmourned.
Meanwhile young wives, and gray-haired mothers with them,
on the shores of the altars, from this side and that,
suppliants from mournful trouble,
    cry out their grief.   190
A hymn to the Healer shines,
    the flute a mourner's voice.
Against which, golden goddess, daughter of Zeus,
    send lovely Strength.

Strophe 3

Cause raging Ares°—who,   195
    armed now with no shield of bronze,
burns me, coming on amid loud cries—

---

165 *Artemis:* goddess of virginity, childbirth, and hunting.   183 *god . . . sunset:* Hades,
god of the underworld.   195 *Ares:* god of war and destruction.

to turn his back and run from my land,
with a fair wind behind, to the great
    hall of Amphitritē,°   200
or to the anchorage that welcomes no one,
Thrace's troubled sea!
If night lets something get away at last,
    it comes by day.
Fire-bearing god   205
    you who dispense the might of lightning,
Zeus! Father! Destroy him with your thunderbolt!

[*Enter* OEDIPUS *from the palace.*]

Antistrophe 3

Lycēan Lord!° From your looped
    bowstring, twisted gold,
I wish indomitable missiles might be scattered   210
and stand forward, our protectors; also fire-bearing
radiance of Artemis, with which
    she darts across the Lycian mountains.
I call the god whose head is bound in gold,
with whom this country shares its name,   215
Bacchus,° wine-flushed, summoned by "euoi!,"
    Maenads' comrade,
to approach ablaze
    with gleaming . . . . . .
pine, opposed to that god-hated god.   220

Episode 1

OEDIPUS.   I hear your prayer. Submit to what I say
    and to the labors that the plague demands
    and you'll get help and a relief from evils.
    I'll make the proclamation, though a stranger
    to the report and to the deed. Alone,   225
    had I no key, I would soon lose the track.
    Since it was only later that I joined you,
    to all the sons of Cadmus I say this:
    whoever has clear knowledge of the man
    who murdered Laius, son of Labdacus,   230
    I command him to reveal it all to me—
    nor fear if, to remove the charge, he must
    accuse himself: his fate will not be cruel—
    he will depart unstumbling into exile.
    But if you know another, or a stranger,   235
    to be the one whose hand is guilty, speak:
    I shall reward you and remember you.

200 *Amphitritē:* the Atlantic Ocean.   208 *Lycēan Lord:* Apollo.   216 *Bacchus:* Dionysus,
god of fertility and wine.

But if you keep your peace because of fear,
and shield yourself or kin from my command,
hear you what I shall do in that event: 240
I charge all in this land where I have throne
and power, shut out that man—no matter who—
both from your shelter and all spoken words,
nor in your prayers or sacrifices make
him partner, nor allot him lustral° water.   245
All men shall drive him from their homes: for he
is the pollution that the god-sent Pythian
response has only now revealed to me.
In this way I ally myself in war
with the divinity and the deceased.°   250
And this curse, too, against the one who did it,
whether alone in secrecy, or with others:
may he wear out his life unblest and evil!
I pray this, too: if he is at my hearth
and in my home, and I have knowledge of him,   255
may the curse pronounced on others come to me.
All this I lay to you to execute,
for my sake, for the god's, and for this land
now ruined, barren, abandoned by the gods.
Even if no god had driven you to it,   260
you ought not to have left this stain uncleansed,
the murdered man a nobleman, a king!
You should have looked! But now, since, as it happens,
It's I who have the power that he had once,
and have his bed, and a wife who shares our seed,   265
and common bond had we had common children
(had not his hope of offspring had back luck—
but as it happened, luck lunged at his head);
because of this, as if for my own father,
I'll fight for him, I'll leave no means untried,   270
to catch the one who did it with his hand,
for the son of Labdacus, of Polydōrus,
of Cadmus before him, and of Agēnor.°
This prayer against all those who disobey:
the gods send out no harvest from their soil,   275
nor children from their wives. Oh, let them die
victims of this plague, or of something worse.
Yet for the rest of us, people of Cadmus,
we the obedient, may Justice, our ally,
and all the gods, be always on our side!   280
CHORAGOS.   I speak because I feel the grip of your curse:
    the killer is not I. Nor can I point
    to him. The one who set us to this search,

---

245 *lustral:* purifying.   250 *the deceased:* Laius.   272–73 *son . . . Agēnor:* refers to Laius
by citing his genealogy.

Phoebus, should also name the guilty man.
OEDIPUS.   Quite right, but to compel unwilling gods—   285
   no man has ever had that kind of power.
CHORAGOS.   May I suggest to you a second way?
OEDIPUS.   A second or a third—pass over nothing!
CHORAGOS.   I know of no one who sees more of what
   Lord Phoebus sees than Lord Tiresias.   290
   My Lord, one might learn brilliantly from him.
OEDIPUS.   Nor is this something I have been slow to do.
   At Creon's word I sent an escort—twice now!
   I am astonished that he has not come.
CHORAGOS.   The old account is useless. It told us nothing.   295
OEDIPUS.   But tell it to me. I'll scrutinize all stories.
CHORAGOS.   He is said to have been killed by travelers.
OEDIPUS.   I have heard, but the one who did it no one sees.
CHORAGOS.   If there is any fear in him at all,
   he won't stay here once he has heard that curse.   300
OEDIPUS.   He won't fear words: he had no fear when he did it.

[*Enter* TIRESIAS *from the right, led by a* SERVANT *and two of Oedipus's* ATTENDANTS.]

CHORAGOS.   Look there! There is the man who will convict him!
   It's the god's prophet they are leading here,
   one gifted with the truth as no one else.
OEDIPUS.   Tiresias, master of all omens—   305
   public and secret, in the sky and on the earth—
   your mind, if not your eyes, sees how the city
   lives with a plague, against which Thebes can find
   no Saviour or protector, Lord, but you.
   For Phoebus, as the attendants surely told you,   310
   returned this answer to us: liberation
   from the disease would never come unless
   we learned without a doubt who murdered Laius—
   put them to death, or sent them into exile.
   Do not begrudge us what you may learn from birds   315
   or any other prophet's path you know!
   Care for yourself, the city, care for me,
   care for the whole pollution of the dead!
   We're in your hands. To do all that he can
   to help another is man's noblest labor.   320
TIRESIAS.   How terrible to understand and get
   no profit from the knowledge! I knew this,
   but I forgot, or I had never come.
OEDIPUS.   What's this? You've come with very little zeal.
TIRESIAS.   Let me go home! If you will listen to me,   325
   You will endure your troubles better—and I mine.
OEDIPUS.   A strange request, not very kind to the land
   that cared for you—to hold back this oracle!
TIRESIAS.   I see your understanding comes to you
   inopportunely. So that won't happen to me . . .   330

OEDIPUS.   Oh, by the gods, if you understand about this,
    don't turn away! We're on our knees to you.
TIRESIAS.   None of you understands! I'll never bring
    my grief to light—I will not speak of yours.
OEDIPUS.   You know and won't declare it! Is your purpose   335
    to betray us and to destroy this land!
TIRESIAS.   I will grieve neither of us. Stop this futile
    cross-examination. I'll tell you nothing!
OEDIPUS.   Nothing? You vile traitor! You could provoke
    a stone to anger! You still refuse to tell?   340
    Can nothing soften you, nothing convince you?
TIRESIAS.   You blamed anger in me—you haven't seen.
    Can nothing soften you, nothing convince you?
OEDIPUS.   Who wouldn't fill with anger, listening
    to words like yours which now disgrace this city?   345
TIRESIAS.   It will come, even if my silence hides it.
OEDIPUS.   If it will come, then why won't you declare it?
TIRESIAS.   I'd rather say no more. Now if you wish,
    respond to that with all your fiercest anger!
OEDIPUS.   Now I am angry enough to come right out   350
    with this conjecture: you, I think, helped plot
    the deed; you did it—even if your hand
    cannot have struck the blow. If you could see,
    I should have said the deed was yours alone.
TIRESIAS.   Is that right! Then I charge you to abide   355
    by the decree you have announced: from this day
    say no word to either these or me,
    for you are the vile polluter of this land!
OEDIPUS.   Aren't you appalled to let a charge like that
    come bounding forth? How will you get away?   360
TIRESIAS.   You cannot catch me. I have the strength of truth.
OEDIPUS.   Who taught you this? Not your prophetic craft!
TIRESIAS.   You did. You made me say it. I didn't want to.
OEDIPUS.   Say what? Repeat it so I'll understand.
TIRESIAS.   I made no sense? Or are you trying me?   365
OEDIPUS.   No sense I understood. Say it again!
TIRESIAS.   I say you are the murderer you seek.
OEDIPUS.   Again that horror! You'll wish you hadn't said that.
TIRESIAS.   Shall I say more, and raise your anger higher?
OEDIPUS.   Anything you like! Your words are powerless.   370
TIRESIAS.   You live, unknowing, with those nearest to you
    in the greatest shame. You do not see the evil.
OEDIPUS.   You won't go on like that and never pay!
TIRESIAS.   I can if there is any strength in truth.
OEDIPUS.   In truth, but not in you! You have no strength,   375
    blind in your ears, your reason, and your eyes.
TIRESIAS.   Unhappy man! Those jeers you hurl at me
    before long all these men will hurl at you.

OEDIPUS. You are the child of endless night; it's not
    for me or anyone who sees to hurt you.   380
TIRESIAS. It's not my fate to be struck down by you.
    Apollo is enough. That's his concern.
OEDIPUS. Are these inventions Creon's or your own?
TIRESIAS. No, your affliction is yourself, not Creon.
OEDIPUS. Oh success!—in wealth, kingship, artistry,   385
    in any life that wins much admiration—
    the envious ill will stored up for you!
    to get at my command, a gift I did not
    seek, which the city put into my hands,
    my loyal Creon, colleague from the start,   390
    longs to sneak up in secret and dethrone me.
    So he's suborned this fortuneteller—schemer!
    deceitful beggar-priest!—who has good eyes
    for gains alone, though in his craft he's blind.
    Where were your prophet's powers ever proved?   395
    Why, when the dog who chanted verse° was here,
    did you not speak and liberate this city?
    Her riddle wasn't for a man chancing by
    to interpret; prophetic art was needed,
    but you had none, it seems—learned from birds   400
    or from a god. I came along, yes I,
    Oedipus the ignorant, and stopped her—
    by using thought, not augury from birds.
    And it is I whom you now wish to banish,
    so you'll be close to the Creontian throne.   405
    You—and the plot's concocter—will drive out
    pollution to your grief: you look quite old
    or you would be the victim of that plot!
CHORAGOS. It seems to us that this man's words were said
    in anger, Oedipus, and yours as well.   410
    Insight, not angry words, is what we need,
    the best solution to the god's response.
TIRESIAS. You are the king, and yet I am your equal
    in my right to speak. In that I too am Lord,
    for I belong to Loxias,° not you.   415
    I am not Creon's man. He's nothing to me.
    Hear this, since you have thrown my blindness at me:
    Your eyes can't see the evil to which you've come,
    nor where you live, nor who is in your house.
    Do you know your parents? Now knowing, you are   420
    their enemy, in the underworld and here.
    A mother's and a father's double-lashing
    terrible-footed curse will soon drive you out.
    Now you can see, then you will stare into darkness.

396 *dog . . . verse:* the Sphinx.   415 *Loxias:* Apollo.

What place will not be harbor to your cry,   425
or what Cithaeron° not reverberate
when you have heard the bride-song in your palace
to which you sailed? Fair wind to evil harbor!
Nor do you see how many other woes
will level you to yourself and to your children.   430
So, at my message, and at Creon, too,
splatter muck! There will never be a man
ground into wretchedness as you will be.

OEDIPUS.   Am I to listen to such things from him!
May you be damned! Get out of here at once!   435
Go! Leave my palace! Turn around and go!

[*TIRESIAS begins to move away from OEDIPUS.*]

TIRESIAS.   I wouldn't have come had you not sent for me.

OEDIPUS.   I did not know you'd talk stupidity,
or I wouldn't have rushed to bring you to my house.

TIRESIAS.   Stupid I seem to you, yet to your parents   440
who gave you natural birth I seemed quite shrewd.

OEDIPUS.   Who? Wait! Who is the one who gave me birth?

TIRESIAS.   This day will give you birth,° and ruin too.

OEDIPUS.   What murky, riddling things you always say!

TIRESIAS.   Don't you surpass us all at finding out?   445

OEDIPUS.   You sneer at what you'll find has brought me greatness.

TIRESIAS.   And that's the very luck that ruined you.

OEDIPUS.   I wouldn't care, just so I saved the city.

TIRESIAS.   In that case I shall go. Boy, lead the way!

OEDIPUS.   Yes, let him lead you off. Here, underfoot,   450
you irk me. Gone, you'll cause no further pain.

TIRESIAS.   I'll go when I have said what I was sent for.
Your face won't scare me. You can't ruin me.
I say to you, the man whom you have looked for
as you pronounced your curses, your decrees   455
on the bloody death of Laius—he is here!
A seeming stranger, he shall be shown to be
a Theban born, though he'll take no delight
in that solution. Blind, who once could see,
a beggar who was rich, through foreign lands   460
he'll go and point before him with a stick.
To his beloved children, he'll be shown
a father who is also brother; to the one
who bore him, son and husband; to his father,
his seed-fellow and killer. Go in   465
and think this out; and if you find I've lied,
say then I have no prophet's understanding!

[*Exit TIRESIAS, led by a SERVANT. OEDIPUS exits into the palace with his ATTENDANTS.*]

426 *Cithaeron:* reference to the mountain on which Oedipus was to be exposed as an infant.
443 *give you birth:* that is, identify your parents.

STASIMON 1

Strophe 1

CHORUS.   Who is the man of whom the inspired
     rock of Delphi° said
  he has committed the unspeakable   470
    with blood-stained hands?
Time for him to ply a foot
mightier than those of the horses
    of the storm in his escape;
upon him mounts and plunges the weaponed   475
son of Zeus,° with fire and thunderbolts,
and in his train the dreaded goddesses
of Death, who never miss.

Antistrophe 1

The message has just blazed,
    gleaming from the snows   480
of Mount Parnassus: we must track
    everywhere the unseen man.
He wanders, hidden by wild
forests, up through caves
    and rocks, like a bull,   485
anxious, with an anxious foot, forlorn.
He puts away from him the mantic° words come from earth's
navel,° at its center, yet these live
forever and still hover round him.

Strophe 2

Terribly he troubles me,   490
    the skilled interpreter of birds!°
I can't assent, nor speak against him.
    Both paths are closed to me.
I hover on the wings of doubt,
    not seeing what is here nor what's to come.   495
What quarrel started in the house of Labdacus°
or in the house of Polybus,°
    either ever in the past
    or now, I never
heard, so that . . . with this fact for my touchstone   500

---

469 *rock of Delphi:* Apollo's oracle at Delphi.   476 *son of Zeus:* Apollo.   487 *mantic:*
prophetic.   487–88 *earth's navel:* Delphi.   491 *interpreter of birds:* Tiresias. The Chorus
is troubled by his accusations.   496 *house of Labdacus:* the line of Laius.   497 *Polybus:*
Oedipus's foster father.

I could attack the public
    fame of Oedipus, by the side of the Labdaceans
an ally, against the dark assassination.

Antistrophe 2

No, Zeus and Apollo
    understand and know things   505
mortal; but that another man
    can do more as a prophet than I can—
for that there is no certain test,
    though, skill to skill,
one man might overtake another.   510
No, never, not until
    I see the charges proved,
when someone blames him shall I nod assent.
For once, as we all saw, the winged maiden° came
against him: he was seen then to be skilled,   515
    proved, by that touchstone, dear to the people. So,
never will my mind convict him of the evil.

EPISODE 2

[*Enter* CREON *from the right door of the skene and speaks to the* CHORUS.]

CREON. Citizens, I hear that a fearful charge
    is made against me by King Oedipus!
    I had to come. If, in this crisis,   520
    he thinks that he has suffered injury
    from anything that I have said or done,
    I have no appetite for a long life—
    bearing a blame like that! It's no slight blow
    the punishment I'd take from what he said: 525
    it's the ultimate hurt to be called traitor
    by the city, by you, by my own people!
CHORAGOS. The thing that forced that accusation out
    could have been anger, not the power of thought.
CREON. But who persuaded him that thoughts of mine   530
    had led the prophet into telling lies?
CHORAGOS. I do not know the thought behind his words.
CREON. But did he look straight at you? Was his mind right
    when he said that I was guilty of this charge?
CHORAGOS. I have no eyes to see what rulers do.   535
    But here he comes himself out of the house.

[*Enter* OEDIPUS *from the palace.*]

OEDIPUS. What? You here? And can you really have

514 *winged maiden:* the Sphinx.

the face and daring to approach my house
when you're exposed as its master's murderer
and caught, too, as the robber of my kingship?   540
Did you see cowardice in me, by the gods,
or foolishness, when you began this plot?
Did you suppose that I would not detect
your stealthy moves, or that I'd not fight back?
It's your attempt that's folly, isn't it—   545
tracking without followers or connections,
kingship which is caught with wealth and numbers?
CREON.   Now wait! Give me as long to answer back!
   Judge me for yourself when you have heard me!
OEDIPUS.   You're eloquent, but I'd be slow to learn   550
   from you, now that I've seen your malice toward me.
CREON.   That I deny. Hear what I have to say.
OEDIPUS.   Don't you deny it! You are the traitor here!
CREON.   If you consider mindless willfulness
   a prized possession, you are not thinking sense.   555
OEDIPUS.   If you think you can wrong a relative
   and get off free, you are not thinking sense.
CREON.   Perfectly just, I won't say no. And yet
   what is this injury you say I did you?
OEDIPUS.   Did you persuade me, yes or no, to send   560
   someone to bring that solemn prophet here?
CREON.   And I still hold to the advice I gave.
OEDIPUS.   How many years ago did your King Laius . . .
CREON.   Laius! Do what? Now I don't understand.
OEDIPUS.   Vanish—victim of a murderous violence?   565
CREON.   That is a long count back into the past.
OEDIPUS.   Well, was this seer then practicing his art?
CREON.   Yes, skilled and honored just as he is today.
OEDIPUS.   Did he, back then, ever refer to me?
CREON.   He did not do so in my presence ever.   570
OEDIPUS.   You did inquire into the murder then.
CREON.   We had to, surely, though we discovered nothing.
OEDIPUS.   But the "skilled" one did not say this then? Why not?
CREON.   I never talk when I am ignorant.
OEDIPUS.   But you're not ignorant of your own part.   575
CREON.   What do you mean? I'll tell you if I know.
OEDIPUS.   Just this: if he had not conferred with you
   he'd not have told about my murdering Laius.
CREON.   If he said that, you are the one who knows.
   But now it's fair that you should answer me.   580
OEDIPUS.   Ask on! You won't convict me as the killer.
CREON.   Well then, answer. My sister is your wife?
OEDIPUS.   Now there's a statement that I can't deny.
CREON.   You two have equal power in this country?
OEDIPUS.   She gets from me whatever she desires.   585
CREON.   And I'm a third? The three of us are equals?

OEDIPUS.   That's where you're treacherous to your kinship!
CREON.   But think about this rationally, as I do.
 First look at this: do you think anyone
 prefers the anxieties of being king   590
 to untroubled sleep—if he has equal power?
 I'm not the kind of man who falls in love
 with kingship. I am content with a king's power.
 And so would any man who's wise and prudent.
 I get all things from you, with no distress;   595
 as king I would have onerous duties, too.
 How could the kingship bring me more delight
 than this untroubled power and influence?
 I'm not misguided yet to such a point
 that profitable honors aren't enough.   600
 As it is, all wish me well and all salute;
 those begging you for something have me summoned,
 for their success depends on that alone.
 Why should I lose all this to become king?
 A prudent mind is never traitorous.   605
 Treason's a thought I'm not enamored of;
 nor could I join a man who acted so.
 In proof of this, first go yourself to Pytho°
 and ask if I brought back the true response.
 Then, if you find I plotted with that portent   610
 reader,° don't have me put to death by your vote
 only—I'll vote myself for my conviction.
 Don't let an unsupported thought convict me!
 It's not right mindlessly to take the bad
 for good or to suppose the good are traitors.   615
 Rejecting a relation who is loyal
 is like rejecting life, our greatest love.
 In time you'll know securely without stumbling,
 for time alone can prove a just man just,
 though you can know a bad man in a day.   620
CHORAGOS.   Well said, to one who's anxious not to fall.
 Swift thinkers, Lord, are never safe from stumbling.
OEDIPUS.   But when a swift and secret plotter moves
 against me, I must make swift counterplot.
 If I lie quiet and await his move,   625
 he'll have achieved his aims and I'll have missed.
CREON.   You surely cannot mean you want me exiled!
OEDIPUS.   Not exiled, no. Your death is what I want!
CREON.   If you would first define what envy is . . .
OEDIPUS.   Are you still stubborn! Still disobedient? 630
CREON.   I see you cannot think!
OEDIPUS.   For me I can.
CREON.   You should for me as well!

608 *Pytho:* Delphi. 610–11 *portent reader:* Apollo's oracle or prophet.

OEDIPUS.   But you're a traitor!
CREON.   What if you're wrong?
OEDIPUS.   Authority must be maintained.
CREON.   Not if the ruler's evil.
OEDIPUS.   Hear that, Thebes!
CREON.   It is my city too, not yours alone!   635
CHORAGOS.   Please don't, my Lords! Ah, just in time, I see
    Jocasta there, coming from the palace.
    With her help you must settle your quarrel.

[*Enter JOCASTA from the Palace.*]

JOCASTA.   Wretched men! What has provoked this ill-
    advised dispute? Have you no sense of shame,   640
    with Thebes so sick, to stir up private troubles?
    Now go inside! And Creon, you go home!
    Don't make a general anguish out of nothing!
CREON.   My sister, Oedipus your husband here
    sees fit to do one of two hideous things: 645
    to have me banished from the land—or killed!
OEDIPUS.   That's right: I caught him, Lady, plotting harm
    against my person—with a malignant science.
CREON.   May my life fail, may I die cursed, if I
    did any of the things you said I did!   650
JOCASTA.   Believe his words, for the god's sake, Oedipus,
    in deference above all to his oath
    to the gods. Also for me, and for these men!

KOMMOS°

Strophe 1

CHORUS.   Consent, with will and mind,
    my king, I beg of you!   655
OEDIPUS.   What do you wish me to surrender?
CHORUS.   Show deference to him who was not feeble in time past
    and is now great in the power of his oath!
OEDIPUS.   Do you know what you're asking?
CHORUS.   Yes.
OEDIPUS.   Tell me then.
CHORUS.   Never to cast into dishonored guilt, with an unproved   660
    assumption, a kinsman who has bound himself by curse.
OEDIPUS.   Now you must understand, when you ask this,
    you ask my death or banishment from the land.

Kommos: a dirge or lament sung by the Chorus and one or more of the chief characters.

Strophe 2

CHORUS. No, by the god who is the foremost of all gods,
 the Sun! No! Godless,   665
   friendless, whatever death is worst of all,
 let that be my destruction, if this
   thought ever moved me!
 But my ill-fated soul
   this dying land   670
 wears out—the more if to these older troubles
 she adds new troubles from the two of you!
OEDIPUS. Then let him go, though it must mean my death,
 or else disgrace and exile from the land.
 My pity is moved by your words, not by his—   675
 he'll only have my hate, wherever he goes.
CREON. You're sullen as you yield; you'll be depressed
 when you've passed through this anger. Natures like yours
 are hardest on themselves. That's as it should be.
OEDIPUS. Then won't you go and let me be?
CREON.   I'll go.   680
 Though you're unreasonable, they know I'm righteous.

                 [Exit CREON.*]*

Antistrophe 1

CHORUS. Why are you waiting, Lady?
 Conduct him back into the palace!
JOCASTA. I will, when I have heard what chanced.   685
CHORUS. Conjectures—words alone, and nothing based on thought.
 But even an injustice can devour a man.
JOCASTA. Did the words come from both sides?
CHORUS.   Yes.
JOCASTA.   What was said?
CHORUS. To me it seems enough! enough! the land already troubled, 690
 that this should rest where it has stopped.
OEDIPUS. See what you've come to in your honest thought,
 in seeking to relax and blunt my heart?

Antistrophe 2

CHORUS. I have not said this only once, my Lord.
 That I had lost my sanity,   695
   without a path in thinking—
 be sure this would be clear
   if I put you away
 who, when my cherished land
   wandered crazed   700
 with suffering, brought her back on course.
 Now, too, be a lucky helmsman!

JOCASTA.   Please, for the god's sake, Lord, explain to me
    the reason why you have conceived this wrath?
OEDIPUS.   I honor you, not them,° and I'll explain   705
    to you how Creon has conspired against me.
JOCASTA.   All right, if that will explain how the quarrel started.
OEDIPUS.   He says I am the murderer of Laius!
JOCASTA.   Did he claim knowledge or that someone told him?
OEDIPUS.   Here's what he did: he sent that vicious seer   710
    so he could keep his own mouth innocent.
JOCASTA.   Ah then, absolve yourself of what he charges!
    Listen to this and you'll agree, no mortal
    is ever given skill in prophecy.
    I'll prove this quickly with one incident.   715
    It was foretold to Laius—I shall not say
    by Phoebus himself, but by his ministers—
    that when his fate arrived he would be killed
    by a son who would be born to him and me.
    And yet, so it is told, foreign robbers   720
    murdered him, at a place where three roads meet.
    As for the child I bore him, not three days passed
    before he yoked the ball-joints of its feet,°
    then cast it, by others' hands, on a trackless mountain.
    That time Apollo did not make our child   725
    a patricide, or bring about what Laius
    feared, that he be killed by his own son.
    That's how prophetic words determined things!
    Forget them. The things a god must track
    he will himself painlessly reveal.   730
OEDIPUS.   Just now, as I was listening to you, Lady,
    what a profound distraction seized my mind!
JOCASTA.   What made you turn around so anxiously?
OEDIPUS.   I thought you said that Laius was attacked
    and butchered at a place where three roads meet.   735
JOCASTA.   That is the story, and it is told so still.
OEDIPUS.   Where is the place where this was done to him?
JOCASTA.   The land's called Phocis, where a two-forked road
    comes in from Delphi and from Daulia.
OEDIPUS.   And how much time has passed since these events?   740
JOCASTA.   Just prior to your presentation here
    as king this news was published to the city.
OEDIPUS.   Oh, Zeus, what have you willed to do to me?
JOCASTA.   Oedipus, what makes your heart so heavy?
OEDIPUS.   No, tell me first of Laius' appearance,   745
    what peak of youthful vigor he had reached.
JOCASTA.   A tall man, showing his first growth of white.
    He had a figure not unlike your own.

---

705 *them:* the Chorus.   723 *ball-joints of its feet:* the ankles.

OEDIPUS. Alas! It seems that in my ignorance
    I laid those fearful curses on myself.   750
JOCASTA. What is it, Lord? I flinch to see your face.
OEDIPUS. I'm dreadfully afraid the prophet sees.
    But I'll know better with one more detail.
JOCASTA. I'm frightened too. But ask: I'll answer you.
OEDIPUS. Was his retinue small, or did he travel   755
    with a great troop, as would befit a prince?
JOCASTA. There were just five in all, one a herald.
    There was a carriage, too, bearing Laius.
OEDIPUS. Alas! Now I see it! But who was it,
    Lady, who told you what you know about this?   760
JOCASTA. A servant who alone was saved unharmed.
OEDIPUS. By chance, could he be now in the palace?
JOCASTA. No, he is not. When he returned and saw
    you had the power of the murdered Laius,
    he touched my hand and begged me formally   765
    to send him to the fields and to the pastures,
    so he'd be out of sight, far from the city.
    I did. Although a slave, he well deserved
    to win this favor, and indeed far more.
OEDIPUS. Let's have him called back in immediately.   770
JOCASTA. That can be done, but why do you desire it?
OEDIPUS. I fear, Lady, I have already said
    too much. That's why I wish to see him now.
JOCASTA. Then he shall come; but it is right somehow
    that I, too, Lord, should know what troubles you.   775
OEDIPUS. I've gone so deep into the things I feared
    I'll tell you everything. Who has a right
    greater than yours, while I cross through this chance?
    Polybus of Corinth was my father,
    my mother was the Dorian Meropē.   780
    I was first citizen, until this chance
    attacked me—striking enough, to be sure,
    but not worth all the gravity I gave it.
    This: at a feast a man who'd drunk too much
    denied, at the wine, I was my father's son.   785
    I was depressed and all that day I barely
    held it in. Next day I put the question
    to my mother and father. They were enraged
    at the man who'd let this fiction fly at me.
    I was much cheered by them. And yet it kept   790
    grinding into me. His words kept coming back.
    Without my mother's or my father's knowledge
    I went to Pytho. But Phoebus sent me away
    dishonoring my demand. Instead, other
    wretched horrors he flashed forth in speech.   795
    He said that I would be my mother's lover,
    show offspring to mankind they could not look at,

and be his murderer whose seed I am.°
When I heard this, and ever since, I gauged
the way to Corinth by the stars alone,   800
running to a place where I would never see
the disgrace in the oracle's words come true.
But I soon came to the exact location
where, as you tell of it, the king was killed.
Lady, here is the truth. As I went on,   805
when I was just approaching those three roads,
a herald and a man like him you spoke of
came on, riding a carriage drawn by colts.
Both the man out front and the old man himself°
tried violently to force me off the road.   810
The driver, when he tried to push me off,
I struck in anger. The old man saw this, watched
me approach, then leaned out and lunged down
with twin prongs° at the middle of my head!
He got more than he gave. Abruptly—struck   815
once by the staff in this my hand—he tumbled
out, head first, from the middle of the carriage.
And then I killed them all. But if there is
a kinship between Laius and this stranger,
who is more wretched than the man you see?   820
Who was there born more hated by the gods?
For neither citizen nor foreigner
may take me in his home or speak to me.
No, they must drive me off. And it is I
who have pronounced these curses on myself!   825
I stain the dead man's bed with these my hands,
by which he died. Is not my nature vile?
Unclean?—if I am banished and even
in exile I may not see my own parents,
or set foot in my homeland, or else be yoked   830
in marriage to my mother, and kill my father,
Polybus, who raised me and gave me birth?
If someone judged a cruel divinity
did this to me, would he not speak the truth?
You pure and awful gods, may I not ever   835
see that day, may I be swept away
from men before I see so great and so
calamitous a stain fixed on my person!
CHORAGOS.   These things seem fearful to us, Lord, and yet,
until you hear it from the witness, keep hope!   840
OEDIPUS.   That is the single hope that's left to me,
to wait for him, that herdsman—until he comes.
JOCASTA.   When he appears, what are you eager for?

---

798 *be . . . am:* that is, murder my father.   809 *old man himself:* Laius.   813–14 *lunged
. . . prongs:* Laius strikes Oedipus with a two-pronged horse goad or whip.

OEDIPUS.   Just this: if his account agrees with yours
    then I shall have escaped this misery.   845
JOCASTA.   But what was it that struck you in my story?
OEDIPUS.   You said he spoke of robbers as the ones
    who killed him. Now: if he continues still
    to speak of many, then I could not have killed him.
    One man and many men just do not jibe.   850
    But if he says one belted man, the doubt
    is gone. The balance tips toward me. I did it.
JOCASTA.   No! He told it as I told you. Be certain.
    He can't reject that and reverse himself.
    The city heard these things, not I alone.   855
    But even if he swerves from what he said,
    he'll never show that Laius' murder, Lord,
    occurred just as predicted. For Loxias
    expressly said my son was doomed to kill him.
    The boy—poor boy—he never had a chance   860
    to cut him down, for he was cut down first.
    Never again, just for some oracle
    will I shoot frightened glances right and left.
OEDIPUS.   That's full of sense. Nonetheless, send a man
    to bring that farm hand here. Will you do it?   865
JOCASTA.   I'll send one right away. But let's go in.
    Would I do anything against your wishes?

        [*Exit* OEDIPUS *and* JOCASTA *through the central door into the palace.*]

STASIMON 2

Strophe 1

CHORUS.   May there accompany me
    the fate to keep a reverential purity in what I say,
    in all I do, for which the laws have been set forth   870
    and walk on high, born to traverse the brightest,
    highest upper air; Olympus° only
    is their father, nor was it
    mortal nature
    that fathered them, and never will   875
    oblivion lull them into sleep;
    the god in them is great and never ages.

Antistrophe 1

The will to violate, seed of the tyrant,
if it has drunk mindlessly of wealth and power,

872 *Olympus:* Mount Olympus, home of the gods, treated as a god.

without a sense of time or true advantage,   880
mounts to a peak, then
plunges to an abrupt . . . destiny,
where the useful foot
is of no use. But the kind
of struggling that is good for the city   885
I ask the god never to abolish.
The god is my protector: never will I give that up.

Strophe 2

But if a man proceeds disdainfully
    in deeds of hand or word
and has no fear of Justice   890
    or reverence for shrines of the divinities
(may a bad fate catch him
    for his luckless wantonness!),
if he'll not gain what he gains with justice
and deny himself what is unholy,   895
or if he clings, in foolishness, to the untouchable
(what man, finally, in such an action, will have strength
enough to fend off passion's arrows from his soul?),
if, I say, this kind of
    deed is held in honor—   900
why should I join the sacred dance?

Antistrophe 2

No longer shall I visit and revere
    Earth's navel,° the untouchable,
nor visit Abae's° temple,
    or Olympia,°   905
if the prophecies are not matched by events
    for all the world to point to.
No, you who hold the power, if you are rightly called
Zeus the king of all, let this matter not escape you
and your ever-deathless rule,   910
for the prophecies to Laius fade . . .
and men already disregard them;
nor is Apollo anywhere
    glorified with honors.
Religion slips away.   915

---

903 *Earth's navel:* Delphi.   904 *Abae:* a town in Phocis where there was another oracle of
Apollo.   905 *Olympia:* site of the oracle of Zeus.

EPISODE 3

[*Enter* JOCASTA *from the palace carrying a branch wound with wool and a jar of incense. She is attended by two women.*]

JOCASTA. Lords of the realm, the thought has come to me
    to visit shrines of the divinities
    with suppliant's branch in hand and fragrant smoke.
    For Oedipus excites his soul too much
    with alarms of all kinds. He will not judge   920
    the present by the past, like a man of sense.
    He's at the mercy of all terror-mongers.

[*JOCASTA approaches the altar on the right and kneels.*]

    Since I can do no good by counseling,
    Apollo the Lycēan!—you are the closest—
    I come a suppliant, with these my vows,   925
    for a cleansing that will not pollute him.
    For when we see him shaken we are all
    afraid, like people looking at their helmsman.

[*Enter a* MESSENGER *along one of the Parados. He sees* JOCASTA *at the altar and then addresses the* CHORUS.]

MESSENGER. I would be pleased if you would help me, stranger.
    Where is the palace of King Oedipus?   930
    Or tell me where he is himself, if you know.
CHORUS. This is his house, stranger. He is within.
    This is his wife and mother of his children.
MESSENGER. May she and her family find prosperity,
    if, as you say, her marriage is fulfilled.   935
JOCASTA. You also, stranger, for you deserve as much
    for your gracious words. But tell me why you've come.
    What do you wish? Or what have you to tell us?
MESSENGER. Good news, my Lady, both for your house and
        husband.
JOCASTA. What is your news? And who has sent you to us?   940
MESSENGER. I come from Corinth. When you have heard my
        news
    you will rejoice, I'm sure—and grieve perhaps.
JOCASTA. What is it? How can it have this double power?
MESSENGER. They will establish him their king, so say
    the people of the land of Isthmia.°   945
JOCASTA. But is old Polybus not still in power?
MESSENGER. He's not, for death has clasped him in the tomb.
JOCASTA. What's this? Has Oedipus' father died?
MESSENGER. If I have lied then I deserve to die.

945 *land of Isthmia:* Corinth, which was on an isthmus.

JOCASTA.   Attendant! Go quickly to your master,   950
and tell him this.

[*Exit an* ATTENDANT *into the palace.*]

Oracles of the gods!
Where are you now? The man whom Oedipus
fled long ago, for fear that he should kill him—
he's been destroyed by chance and not by him!

[*Enter* OEDIPUS *from the palace.*]

OEDIPUS.   Darling Jocasta, my beloved wife,   955
Why have you called me from the palace?
JOCASTA.   First hear what this man has to say. Then see
what the god's grave oracle has come to now!
OEDIPUS.   Where is he from? What is this news he brings me?
JOCASTA.   From Corinth. He brings news about your father: 960
that Polybus is no more! that he is dead!
OEDIPUS.   What's this, old man? I want to hear you say it.
MESSENGER.   If this is what must first be clarified,
please be assured that he is dead and gone.
OEDIPUS.   By treachery or by the touch of sickness?   965
MESSENGER.   Light pressures tip agéd frames into their sleep.
OEDIPUS.   You mean the poor man died of some disease.
MESSENGER.   And of the length of years that he had tallied.
OEDIPUS.   Aha! Then why should we look to Pytho's vapors,°
or to the birds that scream above our heads?°   970
If we could really take those things for guides,
I would have killed my father. But he's dead!
He is beneath the earth, and here am I,
who never touched a spear. Unless he died
of longing for me and I "killed" him that way!   975
No, in this case, Polybus, by dying, took
the worthless oracle to Hades with him.
JOCASTA.   And wasn't I telling you that just now?
OEDIPUS.   You were indeed. I was misled by fear.
JOCASTA.   You should not care about this anymore.   980
OEDIPUS.   I must care. I must stay clear of my mother's bed.
JOCASTA.   What's there for man to fear? The realm of chance
prevails. True foresight isn't possible.
His life is best who lives without a plan.
This marriage with your mother—don't fear it.   985
How many times have men in dreams, too, slept
with their own mothers! Those who believe such things
mean nothing endure their lives most easily.

969 *Pytho's vapors:* the prophecies of the oracle at Delphi.   970 *birds . . . heads:* the
prophecies derived from interpreting the flights of birds.

OEDIPUS.   A fine, bold speech, and you are right, perhaps,
    except that my mother is still living,   990
    so I must fear her, however well you argue.
JOCASTA.   And yet your father's tomb is a great eye.
OEDIPUS.   Illuminating, yes. But I still fear the living.
MESSENGER.   Who is the woman who inspires this fear?
OEDIPUS.   Meropē, Polybus' wife, old man.   995
MESSENGER.   And what is there about her that alarms you?
OEDIPUS.   An oracle, god-sent and fearful, stranger.
MESSENGER.   Is it permitted that another know?
OEDIPUS.   It is. Loxias once said to me
    I must have intercourse with my own mother   1000
    and take my father's blood with these my hands.
    So I have long lived far away from Corinth.
    This has indeed brought much good luck, and yet,
    to see one's parents' eyes is happiest.
MESSENGER.   Was it for this that you have lived in exile?   1005
OEDIPUS.   So I'd not be my father's killer, sir.
MESSENGER.   Had I not better free you from this fear,
    my Lord? That's why I came—to do you service.
OEDIPUS.   Indeed, what a reward you'd get for that!
MESSENGER.   Indeed, this is the main point of my trip,   1010
    to be rewarded when you get back home.
OEDIPUS.   I'll never rejoin the givers of my seed!°
MESSENGER.   My son, clearly you don't know what you're doing.
OEDIPUS.   But how is that, old man? For the gods' sake, tell me!
MESSENGER.   If it's because of them you won't go home.   1015
OEDIPUS.   I fear that Phoebus will have told the truth.
MESSENGER.   Pollution from the ones who gave you seed?
OEDIPUS.   That is the thing, old man, I always fear.
MESSENGER.   Your fear is groundless. Understand that.
OEDIPUS.   Groundless? Not if I was born their son.   1020
MESSENGER.   But Polybus is not related to you.
OEDIPUS.   Do you mean Polybus was not my father?
MESSENGER.   No more than I. We're both the same to you.
OEDIPUS.   Same? One who begot me and one who didn't?
MESSENGER.   He didn't beget you any more than I did.   1025
OEDIPUS.   But then, why did he say I was his son?
MESSENGER.   He got you as a gift from my own hands.
OEDIPUS.   He loved me so, though from another's hands?
MESSENGER.   His former childlessness persuaded him.
OEDIPUS.   But had you bought me, or begotten me?   1030
MESSENGER.   Found you. In the forest hallows of Cithaeron.
OEDIPUS.   What were you doing traveling in that region?
MESSENGER.   I was in charge of flocks which grazed those mountains.
OEDIPUS.   A wanderer who worked the flocks for hire?

1012 *givers of my seed:* that is, my parents. Oedipus still thinks Meropē and Polybus are his parents.

MESSENGER. Ah, but that day I was your savior, son.   1035
OEDIPUS. From what? What was my trouble when you took me?
MESSENGER. The ball-joints of your feet might testify.
OEDIPUS. What's that? What makes you name that ancient trouble?
MESSENGER. Your feet were pierced and I am your rescuer.
OEDIPUS. A fearful rebuke those tokens left for me!   1040
MESSENGER. That was the chance that names you who you are.
OEDIPUS. By the gods, did my mother or my father do this?
MESSENGER. That I don't know. He might who gave you to me.
OEDIPUS. From someone else? You didn't chance on me?
MESSENGER. Another shepherd handed you to me.   1045
OEDIPUS. Who was he? Do you know? Will you explain!
MESSENGER. They called him one of the men of—was it Laius?
OEDIPUS. The one who once was king here long ago?
MESSENGER. That is the one! The man was shepherd to him.
OEDIPUS. And is he still alive so I can see him?   1050
MESSENGER. But you who live here ought to know that best.
OEDIPUS. Does any one of you now present know
     about the shepherd whom this man has named?
     Have you seen him in town or in the fields? Speak out!
     The time has come for the discovery!   1055
CHORAGOS. The man he speaks of, I believe, is the same
     as the field hand you have already asked to see.
     But it's Jocasta who would know this best.
OEDIPUS. Lady, do you remember the man we just
     now sent for—is that the man he speaks of?   1060
JOCASTA. What? The man he spoke of? Pay no attention!
     His words are not worth thinking about. It's nothing.
OEDIPUS. With clues like this within my grasp, give up?
     Fail to solve the mystery of my birth?
JOCASTA. For the love of the gods, and if you love your life,   1065
     give up this search! My sickness is enough.
OEDIPUS. Come! Though my mothers for three generations
     were in slavery, you'd not be lowborn!
JOCASTA. No, listen to me! Please! Don't do this thing!
OEDIPUS. I will not listen; I will search out the truth.   1070
JOCASTA. My thinking is for you—it would be best.
OEDIPUS. This "best" of yours is starting to annoy me.
JOCASTA. Doomed man! Never find out who you are!
OEDIPUS. Will someone go and bring that shepherd here?
     Leave her to glory in her wealthy birth!   1075
JOCASTA. Man of misery! No other name
     shall I address you by, ever again.

     [*Exit* JOCASTA *into the palace after a long pause.*]

CHORAGOS. Why has your lady left, Oedipus.
     hurled by a savage grief? I am afraid
     disaster will come bursting from this silence.   1080
OEDIPUS. Let it burst forth! However low this seed

of mine may be, yet I desire to see it.
She, perhaps—she has a woman's pride—
is mortified by my base origins.
But I who count myself the child of Chance,   1085
the giver of good, shall never know dishonor.
She is my mother,° and the months my brothers
who first marked out my lowness, then my greatness.
I shall not prove untrue to such a nature
by giving up the search for my own birth.   1090

STASIMON 3

Strophe

CHORUS.   If I have mantic power
and excellence in thought,
by Olympus,
        you shall not, Cithaeron, at tomorrow's
full moon,   1095
fail to hear us celebrate you as the countryman
of Oedipus, his nurse and mother,
or fail to be the subject of our dance,
        since you have given pleasure
to our king.   1100
Phoebus, whom we summon by "iē!,"
may this be pleasing to you!

Antistrophe

Who was your mother, son?
which of the long-lived nymphs
after lying with Pan,°   1105
        the mountain roaming . . . Or was it a bride
of Loxias?°
For dear to him are all the upland pastures.
Or was it Mount Cyllēnē's lord,°
or the Bacchic god,°   1110
        dweller of the mountain peaks,
who received you as a joyous find
from one of the nymphs of Helicon,
the favorite sharers of his sport?

EPISODE 4

OEDIPUS.   If someone like myself, who never met him,   1115
        may calculate—elders, I think I see
the very herdsman we've been waiting for.

1087 *She . . . mother:* Chance is my mother.   1105 *Pan:* god of shepherds and woodlands,
half man and half goat.   1107 *Loxias:* Apollo.   1109 *Mount Cyllēnē's lord:* Hermes,
messenger of the gods.   1110 *Bacchic god:* Dionysus.

His many years would fit that man's age,
and those who bring him on, if I am right,
are my own men. And yet, in real knowledge,   1120
you can outstrip me, surely: you've seen him.

[*Enter the old* HERDSMAN *escorted by two of Oedipus's* ATTENDANTS. *At first, the* HERDSMAN
will not look at OEDIPUS.]

CHORAGOS.   I know him, yes, a man of the house of Laius,
    a trusty herdsman if he ever had one.
OEDIPUS.   I ask you first, the stranger come from Corinth:
    is this the man you spoke of?
MESSENGER.   That's he you see.   1125
OEDIPUS.   Then you, old man. First look at me! Now answer:
    did you belong to Laius' household once?
HERDSMAN.   I did. Not a purchased slave but raised in the palace.
OEDIPUS.   How have you spent your life? What is your work?
HERDSMAN.   Most of my life now I have tended sheep.   1130
OEDIPUS.   Where is the usual place you stay with them?
HERDSMAN.   On Mount Cithaeron. Or in that district.
OEDIPUS.   Do you recall observing this man there?
HERDSMAN.   Doing what? Which is the man you mean?
OEDIPUS.   This man right here. Have you had dealings with him?   1135
HERDSMAN.   I can't say right away. I don't remember.
MESSENGER.   No wonder, master. I'll bring clear memory
    to his ignorance. I'm absolutely sure
    he can recall it, the district was Cithaeron,
    he with a double flock, and I, with one,   1140
    lived close to him, for three entire seasons,
    six months long, from spring right to Arcturus.°
    Then for the winter I'd drive mine to my fold,
    and he'd drive his to Laius' pen again.
    Did any of the things I say take place?   1145
HERDSMAN.   You speak the truth, though it's from long ago.
MESSENGER.   Do you remember giving me, back then,
    a boy I was to care for as my own?
HERDSMAN.   What are you saying? Why do you ask me that?
MESSENGER.   There, sir, is the man who was that boy!   1150
HERDSMAN.   Damn you! Shut your mouth! Keep your silence!
OEDIPUS.   Stop! Don't you rebuke his words.
    Your words ask for rebuke far more than his.
HERDSMAN.   But what have I done wrong, most royal master?
OEDIPUS.   Not telling of the boy of whom he asked.   1155
HERDSMAN.   He's ignorant and blundering toward ruin.
OEDIPUS.   Tell it willingly—or under torture.

1142 *from spring right to Arcturus:* That is, from spring to early fall, when the summer star
Arcturus (in the constellation Boötes) is no longer visible in the early evening sky. It does
not rise at night again until the following spring.

HERDSMAN.   Oh god! Don't—I am old—don't torture me!
OEDIPUS.   Here! Someone put his hands behind his back!
HERDSMAN.   But why? What else would you find out, poor man?   1160
OEDIPUS.   Did you give him the child he asks about?
HERDSMAN.   I did. I wish that I had died that day!
OEDIPUS.   You'll come to that if you don't speak the truth.
HERDSMAN.   It's if I speak that I shall be destroyed.
OEDIPUS.   I think this fellow struggles for delay.   1165
HERDSMAN.   No, no! I said already that I gave him.
OEDIPUS.   From your own home, or got from someone else?
HERDSMAN.   Not from my own. I got him from another.
OEDIPUS.   Which of these citizens? What sort of house?
HERDSMAN.   Don't—by the gods!—don't, master, ask me more!   1170
OEDIPUS.   It means your death if I must ask again.
HERDSMAN.   One of the children of the house of Laius.
OEDIPUS.   A slave—or born into the family?
HERDSMAN.   I have come to the dreaded thing, and I shall say it.
OEDIPUS.   And I to hearing it, but hear I must.   1175
HERDSMAN.   He was reported to have been—his son.
     Your lady in the house could tell you best.
OEDIPUS.   Because she gave him to you?
HERDSMAN.   Yes, my lord.
OEDIPUS.   What was her purpose?
HERDSMAN.   I was to kill the boy.
OEDIPUS.   The child she bore?
HERDSMAN.   She dreaded prophecies.   1180
OEDIPUS.   What were they?
HERDSMAN.   The word was that he'd kill his parents.
OEDIPUS.   Then why did you give him up to this old man?
HERDSMAN.   In pity, master—so he would take him home,
     to another land. But what he did was save him
     for this supreme disaster. If you are the one   1185
     he speaks of—know your evil birth and fate!
OEDIPUS.   Ah! All of it was destined to be true!
     Oh light, now may I look my last upon you,
     shown monstrous in my birth, in marriage monstrous,
     a murderer monstrous in those I killed.   1190
                                        [*Exit* OEDIPUS, *running into the palace.*]

STASIMON 4

Strophe 1

CHORUS.   Oh generations of mortal men,
     while you are living, I will
          appraise your lives at zero!
     What man
     comes closer to seizing lasting blessedness   1195

than merely to seize its semblance,
and after living in this semblance, to plunge?
With your example before us,
with your destiny, yours,
    suffering Oedipus, no mortal   1200
can I judge fortunate.

Antistrophe 1

For he,° outranging everybody,
shot his arrow° and became the lord
    of wide prosperity and blessedness,
oh Zeus, after destroying   1205
the virgin with the crooked talons,°
singer of oracles; and against death,
in my land, he arose a tower of defense.
From which time you were called my king
and granted privileges supreme—in mighty   1210
Thebes the ruling lord.

Strophe 2

But now—whose story is more sorrowful than yours?
Who is more intimate with fierce calamities,
with labors, now that your life is altered?
Alas, my Oedipus, whom all men know: 1215
one great harbor°—
one alone sufficed for you,
as son and father,
when you tumbled,° plowman° of the woman's chamber.
How, how could your paternal   1220
    furrows, wretched man,
endure you silently so long.

Antistrophe 2

Time, all-seeing, surprised you living an unwilled life
and sits from of old in judgment on the marriage, not a marriage,
where the begetter is the begot as well.   1225
Ah, son of Laius . . . ,
would that—oh, would that
I had never seen you!
I wail, my scream climbing beyond itself

1202 *he:* Oedipus.   1203 *shot his arrow:* took his chances; made a guess at the Sphinx's
riddle.   1206 *virgin . . . talons:* the Sphinx.   1216 *one great harbor:* metaphorical
allusion to Jocasta's body.   1219 *tumbled:* were born and had sex.   *plowman:* Plowing is
used here as a sexual metaphor.

from my whole power of voice. To say it straight: 1230
    from you I got new breath—
but I also lulled my eye to sleep.°

EXODOS

[*Enter the* SECOND MESSENGER *from the palace.*]

SECOND MESSENGER.   You who are first among the citizens,
    what deeds you are about to hear and see!
    What grief you'll carry, if, true to your birth,   1235
    you still respect the house of Labdacus!
    Neither the Ister nor the Phasis river
    could purify this house, such suffering
    does it conceal, or soon must bring to light—
    willed this time, not unwilled. Griefs hurt worst   1240
    which we perceive to be self-chosen ones.
CHORAGOS.   They were sufficient, the things we knew before,
    to make us grieve. What can you add to those?
SECOND MESSENGER.   The thing that's quickest said and quickest heard:
    our own, our royal one, Jocasta's dead.   1245
CHORAGOS.   Unhappy queen! What was responsible?
SECOND MESSENGER.   Herself. The bitterest of these events
    is not for you, you were not there to see,
    but yet, exactly as I can recall it,
    you'll hear what happened to that wretched lady.   1250
    She came in anger through the outer hall,
    and then she ran straight to her marriage bed,
    tearing her hair with the fingers of both hands.
    Then, slamming shut the doors when she was in,
    she called to Laius, dead so many years,   1255
    remembering the ancient seed which caused
    his death, leaving the mother to the son
    to breed again an ill-born progeny.
    She mourned the bed where she, alas, bred double—
    husband by husband, children by her child.   1260
    From this point on I don't know how she died,
    for Oedipus then burst in with a cry,
    and did not let us watch her final evil.
    Our eyes were fixed on him. Wildly he ran
    to each of us, asking for his spear   1265
    and for his wife—no wife: where he might find
    the double mother-field, his and his children's.
    He raved, and some divinity then showed him—
    for none of us did so who stood close by.
    With a dreadful shout—as if some guide were leading—   1270

1232 *I . . . sleep:* I failed to see the corruption you brought.

he lunged through the double doors; he bent the hollow
bolts from the sockets, burst into the room,
and there we saw her, hanging from above,
entangled in some twisted hanging strands.
He saw, was stricken, and with a wild roar   1275
ripped down the dangling noose. When she, poor woman,
lay on the ground, there came a fearful sight:
he snatched the pins of worked gold from her dress,
with which her clothes were fastened: these he raised
and struck into the ball-joints of his eyes.°   1280
He shouted that they would no longer see
the evils he had suffered or had done,
see in the dark those he should not have seen,
and know no more those he once sought to know.
While chanting this, not once but many times   1285
he raised his hand and struck into his eyes.
Blood from his wounded eyes poured down his chin,
not freed in moistening drops, but all at once
a stormy rain of black blood burst like hail.
These evils, coupling them, making them one,   1290
have broken loose upon both man and wife.
The old prosperity that they had once
was true prosperity, and yet today,
mourning, ruin, death, disgrace, and every
evil you could name—not one is absent.   1295
CHORAGOS.   Has he allowed himself some peace from all this grief?
SECOND MESSENGER.   He shouts that someone slide the bolts and show
    to all the Cadmeians the patricide,
    his mother's—I can't say it, it's unholy—
    so he can cast himself out of the land,   1300
    not stay and curse his house by his own curse.
    He lacks the strength, though, and he needs a guide,
    for his is a sickness that's too great to bear.
    Now you yourself will see: the bolts of the doors
    are opening. You are about to see   1305
    a vision even one who hates must pity.

[*Enter the blinded* OEDIPUS *from the palace, led in by a household* SERVANT.]

CHORAGOS.   This suffering sends terror through men's eyes,
    terrible beyond any suffering
    my eyes have touched. Oh man of pain,
    what madness reached you? Which god from far off,   1310
    surpassing in range his longest spring,
        struck hard against your god-abandoned fate?
    Oh man of pain,
    I cannot look upon you—though there's so much
    I would ask you, so much to hear,   1315

1280 *ball-joints of his eyes:* his eyeballs. Oedipus blinds himself in both eyes at the same time.

so much that holds my eyes—
    so awesome the convulsions you send through me.
OEDIPUS. Ah! Ah! I am a man of misery.
    Where am I carried? Pity me! Where
    is my voice scattered abroad on wings?   1320
        Divinity, where has your lunge transported me?
CHORAGOS. To something horrible, not to be heard or seen.

KOMMOS

Strophe 1

OEDIPUS. Oh, my cloud
    of darkness, abominable, unspeakable as it attacks me,
    not to be turned away, brought by an evil wind!   1325
    Alas!
    Again alas! Both enter me at once:
    the sting of the prongs,° the memory of evils!
CHORUS. I do not marvel that in these afflictions
    you carry double griefs and double evils.   1330

Antistrophe 1

OEDIPUS. Ah, friend,
    so you at least are there, resolute servant!
    Still with a heart to care for me, the blind man.
    Oh! Oh!
    I know that you are there. I recognize   1335
    even inside my darkness, that voice of yours.
CHORUS. Doer of horror, how did you bear to quench
    your vision? What divinity raised your hand?

Strophe 2

OEDIPUS. It was Apollo there, Apollo, friends,
    who brought my sorrows, vile sorrows to their perfection,   1340
        these evils that were done to me.
    But the one who struck them with his hand,
        that one was none but I, in wretchedness.
    For why was I to see
    when nothing I could see would bring me joy?   1345
CHORUS. Yes, that is how it was.
OEDIPUS. What could I see, indeed,
    or what enjoy—what greeting
    is there I could hear with pleasure, friends?
    Conduct me out of the land   1350
        as quickly as you can!

1328 *prongs:* refers to both the whip that Laius used and the two gold pins Oedipus used
to blind himself.

Conduct me out, my friends,
    the man utterly ruined,
supremely cursed,
    the man who is by gods   1355
the most detested of all men!
CHORUS. Wretched in disaster and in knowledge:
    oh, I could wish you'd never come to know!

Antistrophe 2

OEDIPUS. May he be destroyed, whoever freed the savage shackles
    from my feet when I'd been sent to the wild pasture,   1360
        whoever rescued me from murder
    and became my savior—
        a bitter gift:
    if I had died then,
    I'd not have been such grief to self and kin.   1365
CHORUS. I also would have had it so.
OEDIPUS. I'd not have returned to be my father's
    murderer; I'd not be called by men
    my mother's bridegroom.
    Now I'm without a god,   1370
        child of a polluted parent,
    fellow progenitor with him
        who gave me birth in misery.
    If there's an evil that
        surpasses evils, that   1375
    has fallen to the lot of Oedipus.

CHORAGOS. How can I say that you have counseled well?
    Better not to be than live a blind man.
OEDIPUS. That this was not the best thing I could do—
    don't tell me that, or advise me any more!   1380
    Should I descend to Hades and endure
    to see my father with these eyes? Or see
    my poor unhappy mother? For I have done,
    to both of these, things too great for hanging.
    Or is the sight of children to be yearned for,   1385
    to see new shoots that sprouted as these did?
    Never, never with these eyes of mine!
    Nor city, nor tower, nor holy images
    of the divinities! For I, all-wretched,
    most nobly raised—as no one else in Thebes—   1390
    deprived myself of these when I ordained
    that all expel the impious one—god-shown
    to be polluted, and the dead king's son!°
    Once I exposed this great stain upon me,
    could I have looked on these with steady eyes?   1395

1391–1393 *I . . . son:* Oedipus refers to his own curse against the murderer as well as his
sins of patricide and incest.

No! No! And if there were a way to block
the source of hearing in my ears, I'd gladly
have locked up my pitiable body,
so I'd be blind and deaf. Evils shut out—
that way my mind could live in sweetness.   1400
Alas, Cithaeron,° why did you receive me?
Or when you had me, not killed me instantly?
I'd not have had to show my birth to mankind.
Polybus, Corinth, halls—ancestral,
they told me—how beautiful was your ward,   1405
a scar that held back festering disease!
Evil my nature, evil my origin.
You, three roads, and you, secret ravine,
you oak grove, narrow place of those three paths
that drank my blood° from these my hands, from him   1410
who fathered me, do you remember still
the things I did to you? When I'd come here,
what I then did once more? Oh marriages! Marriages!
You gave us life and when you'd planted us
you sent the same seed up, and then revealed   1415
fathers, brothers, sons, and kinsman's blood,
and brides, and wives, and mothers, all the most
atrocious things that happen to mankind!
One should not name what never should have been.
Somewhere out there, then, quickly, by the gods,   1420
cover me up, or murder me, or throw me
to the ocean where you will never see me more!

[*Oedipus moves toward the Chorus and they back away from him.*]

Come! Don't shrink to touch this wretched man!
Believe me, do not be frightened! I alone
of all mankind can carry these afflictions.   1425

[*Enter Creon from the palace with Attendants.*]

Choragos.   Tell Creon what you wish for. Just when we need him
   he's here. He can act, he can advise you.
   He's now the land's sole guardian in your place.
Oedipus.   Ah! Are there words that I can speak to him?
   What ground for trust can I present? It's proved   1430
   that I was false to him in everything.
Creon.   I have not come to mock you, Oedipus,
   nor to reproach you for your former falseness.
   You men, if you have no respect for sons
   of mortals, let your awe for the all-feeding   1435
   flames of lordly Hēlius° prevent

1401 *Cithaeron:* the mountain on which the infant Oedipus was supposed to be exposed.
1410 *my blood:* that is, the blood of my father, Laius.   1436 *Hēlius:* the sun.

your showing unconcealed so great a stain,
abhorred by earth and sacred rain and light.
Escort him quickly back into the house!
If blood kin only see and hear their own   1440
afflictions, we'll have no impious defilement.
OEDIPUS.   By the gods, you've freed me from one terrible fear,
so nobly meeting my unworthiness:
grant me something—not for me; for you!
CREON.   What do you want that you should beg me so?   1445
OEDIPUS.   To drive me from the land at once, to a place
where there will be no man to speak to me!
CREON.   I would have done just that—had I not wished
to ask first of the god what I should do.
OEDIPUS.   His answer was revealed in full—that I,   1450
the patricide, unholy, be destroyed.
CREON.   He said that, but our need is so extreme,
it's best to have sure knowledge what must be done.
OEDIPUS.   You'll ask about a wretched man like me?
CREON.   Is it not time you put your trust in the god?   1455
OEDIPUS.   But I bid you as well, and shall entreat you.
Give her who is within what burial
you will—you'll give your own her proper rites;
but me—do not condemn my fathers' land
to have me dwelling here while I'm alive,   1460
but let me live on mountains—on Cithaeron
famed as mine, for my mother and my father,
while they yet lived, made it my destined tomb,
and I'll be killed by those who wished my ruin!
And yet I know: no sickness will destroy me,   1465
nothing will: I'd never have been saved
when left to die unless for some dread evil.
Then let my fate continue where it will!
As for my children, Creon, take no pains
for my sons—they're men and they will never lack   1470
the means to live, wherever they may be—
but my two wretched, pitiable girls,
who never ate but at my table, never
were without me—everything that I
would touch, they'd always have a share of it—   1475
please care for them! Above all, let me touch
them with my hands and weep aloud my woes!
Please, my Lord!
Please, noble heart! Touching with my hands,
I'd think I held them as when I could see.   1480

[*Enter* ANTIGONE *and* ISMENE *from the palace with* ATTENDANTS.]

What's this?
Oh gods! Do I hear, somewhere, my two dear ones

sobbing? Has Creon really pitied me
and sent to me my dearest ones, my children?
Is that it? 1485
CREON. Yes, I prepared this for you, for I knew
you'd feel this joy, as you have always done.
OEDIPUS. Good fortune, then, and, for your care, be guarded
far better by divinity than I was!
Where are you, children? Come to me! Come here 1490
to these my hands, hands of your brother, hands
of him who gave you seed, hands that made
these once bright eyes to see now in this fashion.

[OEDIPUS *embraces his daughters.*]

He, children, seeing nothing, knowing nothing,
he fathered you where his own seed was plowed. 1495
I weep for you as well, though I can't see you,
imagining your bitter life to come,
the life you will be forced by men to live.
What gatherings of townsmen will you join,
what festivals, without returning home 1500
in tears instead of watching holy rites?
And when you've reached the time for marrying,
where, children, is the man who'll run the risk
of taking on himself the infamy
that will wound you as it did my parents? 1505
What evil is not here? Your father killed
his father, plowed the one who gave him birth,
and from the place where he was sown, from there
he got you, from the place he too was born.
These are the wounds: then who will marry you? 1510
No man, my children. No, it's clear that you
must wither in dry barrenness, unmarried.

[OEDIPUS *addresses* CREON.]

Son of Menoeceus! You are the only father
left to them—we two who gave them seed
are both destroyed: watch that they don't become 1515
poor, wanderers, unmarried—they are your kin.
Let not my ruin be their ruin, too!
No, pity them! You see how young they are,
bereft of everyone, except for you.
Consent, kind heart, and touch me with your hand! 1520

[CREON *grasps* OEDIPUS's *right hand.*]

You, children, if you had reached an age of sense,
I would have counseled much. Now, pray you may live
always where it's allowed, finding a life
better than his was, who gave you seed.

CREON. Stop this now. Quiet your weeping. Move away, into the house.   1525
OEDIPUS. Bitter words, but I obey them.
CREON.   There's an end to all things.
OEDIPUS. I have first this request.
CREON.   I will hear it.
OEDIPUS. Banish me from my homeland.
CREON.   You must ask that of the god.
OEDIPUS. But I am the gods' most hated man!
CREON.   Then you will soon get what you
  want.
OEDIPUS. Do you consent?
CREON.   I never promise when, as now, I'm ignorant.   1530
OEDIPUS. Then lead me in.
CREON.   Come. But let your hold fall from your children.
OEDIPUS. Do not take them from me, ever!
CREON.   Do not wish to keep all of the
  power. You had power, but that power did not follow you through life.

[*OEDIPUS's daughters are taken from him and led into the palace by* ATTENDANTS. *OEDIPUS
is led into the palace by a* SERVANT. CREON *and the other* ATTENDANTS *follow. Only the* CHORUS
remains.]

CHORUS. People of Thebes, my country, see: here is that Oedipus—
  he who "knew" the famous riddle, and attained the highest power,   1535
  whom all citizens admired, even envying his luck!
  See the billows of wild troubles which he has entered now!
  Here is the truth of each man's life: we must wait, and see his end,
  scrutinize his dying day, and refuse to call him happy
  till he has crossed the border of his life without pain.   1540

[*Exit the* CHORUS *along each of the Parados.*]

QUESTIONS

Prologue and Parados

1. What is the situation in Thebes as the play begins? Why does Oedipus want
    to find Laius's murderer?

Episode 1 and Stasimon 1

2. How does Oedipus react to Tiresias's refusal to speak? How is this reaction
    characteristic of Oedipus? What other instances of this sort of behavior can
    you find in Oedipus's story?
3. When Tiresias does speak, he answers the central question of the play and
    tells the truth. Why doesn't Oedipus recognize this as the truth?

Episode 2 and Stasimon 2

4. What does Oedipus accuse Creon of doing? How does Creon defend himself?
    Do you find Creon's defense convincing? Why?

5. What is Jocasta's attitude toward oracles and prophecy? Why does she have this attitude? How does it contrast with the attitude of the chorus?

6. At what point in the play does Oedipus begin to suspect that he killed Laius? What details make him begin to suspect himself?

Episode 3 and Stasimon 3

7. What news does the messenger from Corinth bring? Why does this news seem to be good at first? How is this situation reversed?

Episode 4 and Stasimon 4

8. What do you make of the coincidence that the same herdsman (1) saved the infant Oedipus from death, (2) was with Laius at the place where three roads meet and was the lone survivor of the attack, and (3) will now be the agent to destroy Oedipus?

9. What moral does the chorus see in Oedipus's life?

Exodos

10. Why does Oedipus blind himself? What is the significance of the instruments that he uses to blind himself?

11. Who or what does Oedipus blame for his tragic life and destruction?

GENERAL QUESTIONS

1. In *Oedipus*, the peripeteia, anagnorisis, and catastrophe all occur at the same moment. When is this moment? Who is most severely affected by it?

2. Sophocles tells the events of Oedipus's life out of chronological order. Put all the events of his life in chronological order and consider how you might dramatize them. Why does Sophocles's ordering of these events produce an effective play?

3. Each episode of the play introduces new conflicts: Oedipus against the plague, against Tiresias, against Creon. What is the central conflict of the play? Why is it central?

4. All the violent acts of this play—the suicide of Jocasta and the blinding of Oedipus—occur offstage and are reported rather than shown. What are the advantages and disadvantages of dealing with violence this way?

5. Discuss the use of coincidences in the play. How do you react to them? Do they seem convincing or forced, given the plot of the play?

6. Explore the ways in which Sophocles employs dramatic irony, with reference to three specific examples.

7. Consider that *Oedipus* is a tragedy of both the individual and the state. What do you think will happen to Thebes after Oedipus is exiled?

8. Discuss the functions of the chorus and the Choragos. What do the choral odes contribute to the play?

9. Early in the play Oedipus begins a search for a murderer. How does the object of his search change as the play progresses? Why does it change?

THE THEATER OF SHAKESPEARE

In the early part of the English Renaissance, religious drama fused with rediscovered Roman drama and neoclassical European drama to produce **Tudor interludes** (monarchs of the Tudor family ruled England from 1485 to 1603). These interludes were short tragedies, comedies, or history plays that were performed by students or professional actors. The religious drama and the interludes, in turn, gave birth to the first generation of Elizabethan playwrights: Christopher Marlowe, Thomas Kyd, Robert Greene, George Peele, Thomas Lodge, and John Lyly. These were the men whose plays William Shakespeare watched and acted in when he first arrived in London from Stratford-upon-Avon in the early 1590s.

The latter part of the English Renaissance (1580–1642) was the golden age of British drama. During the reigns of Queen Elizabeth I (1558–1603) and King James I (1603–1625) the theater in England reached a pinnacle of development. Greek and Roman drama were, for the most part, lost to the world for almost a thousand years from the fall of Rome in A.D. 476 until the Renaissance. As a consequence, drama was "reinvented" in England and Europe during the Middle Ages. Not surprisingly, it once again developed in a religious context. The first dramas were short dialogues (called **tropes**) which were inserted into the Catholic mass to dramatize passages of the Gospel. As these tropes grew longer and more complicated, they evolved into mystery plays, miracle plays, and finally morality plays. **Mystery plays** are dramatizations of Bible stories; **miracle plays** provide enactments of saints' lives. **Morality plays** teach the principles of Christian life and salvation. Although originally performed by the clergy, after the thirteenth century the plays were taken over by the craft guilds (medieval unions) and, still later, by professional actors.

The Elizabethan public theater also represents the high point of a long process of development and refinement. Before 1576 plays were performed by traveling companies of professional players on temporary stages set up in inn yards or in bear-baiting or bull-baiting arenas. Plays were also performed at court, in the great halls of aristocratic houses, in the law courts, and at universities. All these locations contributed to the ultimate shape and design of the Elizabethan public theaters.

The Globe Theater (see illustration on p. 1096), most famous of the Elizabethan public theaters, was built on the south bank of the Thames River in 1599 by members of the Lord Chamberlain's Men, the acting company to which Shakespeare belonged. It was an octagonal building with a central courtyard open to the sky. The stage thrust about 30 feet out into the yard from one of the eight sides of the building. On the remaining seven sides were three floors of galleries. Spectators sat in these galleries or, for much less money, stood in the yard around the stage. These people were called *groundlings* because they stood on the ground. Compared with the massive Greek theaters, the Globe was relatively small,

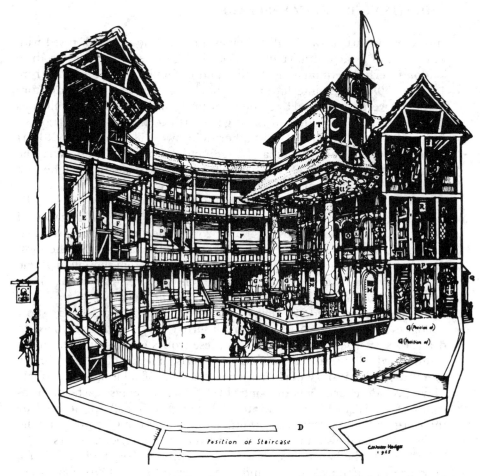

The Globe Playhouse,
1599-1613

A CONJECTURAL

RECONSTRUCTION

KEY

AA Main entrance
B   The Yard
CC Entrances to lowest gallery
D   Entrances to staircase and upper galleries
E   Corridor serving the different sections of the middle gallery
F   Middle gallery ('Twopenny Rooms')
G   'Gentlemen's Rooms' or 'Lords' Rooms'
H   The stage

J   The hanging being put up round the stage
K   The 'Hell' under the stage
L   The stage trap, leading down to the Hell
MM Stage doors
N   Curtained 'place behind the stage'
O   Gallery above the stage, used as required sometimes by musicians, sometimes by spectators, and often as part of the play
P   Back-stage area (the tiring-house)
Q   Tiring-house door
R   Dressing-rooms
S   Wardrobe and storage
T   The hut housing the machine for lowering enthroned gods, etc., to the stage
U   The 'Heavens'
W   Hoisting the playhouse flag

From C. Walter Hodges, *The Globe Restored*.

with no spectators being more than seventy feet from the stage action. Theater historians, however, estimate that the Globe could hold more than two thousand spectators and perhaps as many as three thousand (assuming that the groundlings were packed tightly together). Recent excavations in London at the sites of both the Globe and the nearby Rose theaters promise fascinating new information about theaters and theater-going in Shakespeare's day. For example, recovered nutshells are direct evidence of the confections enjoyed by Elizabethan audiences as they watched the performances.

The stage in the Globe was a *thrust stage* that extended far into the yard and was raised about five feet from the ground. The area below the stage was called the "Hell." In the center of the stage, leading to this Hell, was a trapdoor that was used for the entrances and exits of devils, monsters, or ghosts. On the left and right of the stage were two pillars holding up the "Heavens," both a decorated roof and also a hut that concealed machinery to lower and raise gods and goddesses. These pillars were probably used in productions to support small props and to provide hiding places for characters observing other characters. Behind the stage was a **tiring house** and storage area where actors changed their costumes and awaited their cues. Two or three doors led from the tiring house onto the stage. In addition, there was an area at the rear of stage center where a curtained enclosure could be set up when it was necessary to indicate interior scenes. On the second floor, at the rear of the stage, was a **gallery** that was used by musicians, actors (as in the "balcony" scene in Shakespeare's *Romeo and Juliet*), or spectators.

Plays were performed in the afternoon. As in the Athenian theater, there was neither artificial lighting nor scenery. However, extensive props and elaborate costumes were used. As in Greek drama, women were excluded from the Elizabethan stage; all women's roles were played by boys. Because of these performance conditions and the physical shape of the Elizabethan theater, a number of dramatic conventions developed over time. On the Elizabethan stage, for example, costumes were stylized to permit instant recognition of various characters. Kings always wore a robe and a crown and carried a sceptre; fools wore *motley* (multicolored) clothing; and ghosts wore leather. Since plays were performed without lights or scenery, time and place were also established through convention or dialogue. Shakespeare would indicate a night scene by having the actors carry candles or torches. Often, a character would simply state the time and place. For example, in Act II, scene 4, line 13 of *As You Like It*, the heroine says, "Well, this is the forest of Arden." In the first scene of *Hamlet*, Horatio informs the audience that it is dawn by saying, "But look, the morn in russet mantle clad / Walks o'er the dew of yon high eastward hill" (lines 166–167).

The actors in the Elizabethan theaters used no masks. Instead, they developed conventional expressions and gestures. These conventions sometimes led to overacting. Shakespeare alludes to this in *Hamlet*, Act III, scene 2, when Hamlet advises the traveling actors not to "mouth" their lines "as many of your players do" and not to "saw the air too much with your hands" (lines 1–4). Hamlet also condemns actors who "tear a passion to tatters, to very rags, to split the ears of the groundlings . . ." (lines 9–10).

The closeness of the spectators to the thrust stage may have led to two additional conventions that are important to Elizabethan and Shakespearean drama. One of these, called an **aside,** allows a character to make a brief remark directly to the audience or to another character without the rest of the characters hearing the lines. In the other, called a **soliloquy,** a single character alone on stage speaks his or her thoughts or plans at length directly to the spectators. For example, in Hamlet's second soliloquy (Act II, scene 2, lines 524–580), the prince criticizes his emotional detachment from his father's murder and tells us how he plans to test Claudius's guilt. These two conventions, by giving the audience information that is withheld from the other characters, bring about dramatic irony.

The small size of the Globe theater and the thrust of its stage made for intimate performances. The actors had a great deal of playing space: the rear of the stage, the upper gallery, and also the very front of the stage. There was no barrier or separation between the audience and the actors (no orchestra and chorus) as there were in the Greek theater, and no proscenium and curtain as there are in most twentieth-century theaters. Consequently, in the Elizabethan theater there was much interaction between actors and spectators. The plays were performed rapidly, without intermissions or indications of changes in scene or act other than an occasional rhymed couplet. With no curtain to raise or lower and no scenery to change, shifts in scene were indicated by having one group of characters walk off one side of the stage and another group walk on from the opposite side at the same time. This type of scene change produced rapid shifts in time and place and made for great fluidity and fast pacing.

WILLIAM SHAKESPEARE, *HAMLET*

William Shakespeare, the greatest English playwright and poet, was born in 1564 in Stratford-upon-Avon. He attended the Stratford grammar school, married in 1582, had three children, and moved to London without his family sometime between 1585 and 1592. During this period he began to act professionally and to write poetry and plays; by 1595 he was recognized as a major writer of comedies and tragedies. He eventually became associated with the leading theatrical company of Elizabethan England, the Lord Chamberlain's Men, and wrote thirty-seven plays:

sixteen comedies or tragicomedies, eleven tragedies, and ten historical dramas.

When Shakespeare's acting company first staged *Hamlet* in 1600 or 1601 at the Globe Theater, it is more than likely that the Elizabethan audience already knew the story of the Danish prince who avenges his father's murder and is killed in the process. There is evidence that a play based on the Hamlet story, now lost, had been written and performed before 1589. If this is the case, then most of the spectators would have known that King Claudius had murdered the old King Hamlet and married the dead king's wife. Since only Claudius and Hamlet (and later Horatio) possess information about the murder, the audience knew a great deal more than most of the characters. Thus, the play was open to the same kinds of dramatic irony that we find in *Oedipus the King*.

Even if the spectators did not know the Hamlet story, they would have been familiar with the traditions and conventions of **revenge tragedy.** The Elizabethans had been introduced to this type of drama in the 1570s and early 1580s, when the plays of Seneca, a Roman playwright (4 B.C.– A.D. 65), were performed in translation. The audience was also familiar with Thomas Kyd's *Spanish Tragedy* (ca. 1587), the first English revenge tragedy and the most popular play of the English Renaissance. Thus, the spectators expected to see key features and conventions of revenge tragedy in *Hamlet*. They expected, for example, a ghost who calls for vengeance and a revenger who pretends to be insane at least part of the time. They also expected that the revenge itself would be postponed until the end or close to the end. Above all else, the audience understood that the revenger—in this case Hamlet—would die. Since personal blood vengeance was forbidden by both Church and state, a successful revenger was automatically condemned as an outlaw. The conventions of revenge tragedy thus dictate that a revenger—no matter how good the man or how just the cause—has to die. In the light of this convention, it is possible to see Hamlet's fall partly as the result of circumstances beyond his control and partly as the result of his commitment to personal blood revenge.

Although prepared for *Hamlet* by the traditional formulas of revenge tragedy, the Elizabethan audience could not have anticipated a protagonist of Hamlet's depth and complexity. Traditionally, revengers are presented as flat characters who have a single fixation on justice through personal vengeance. Hamlet, however, is much deeper. He is acutely aware of the political and moral corruption of the Danish court, and he reflects on the fallen state of humanity and also contemplates suicide. In addition, Hamlet learns and changes. Although he does not have the focused *anagnorisis* that Oedipus experiences, he does learn that he must look beyond reason and philosophy for ways of coping with the world. He also learns to be patient and to trust in Providence. In the last scene he calmly awaits events with a new understanding that "there's a divinity that shapes our ends" (line 10) and that "the readiness is all" (line 205).

In modern times, attempts have been made to see Hamlet as an Aristotelian tragic protagonist, brought to his death by some aspect of his character that leads him into error. To some scholars Hamlet's *hamartia*, or "fatal flaw," is his tendency to overrationalize or his mother fixation (an Oedipal complex). Most critics, however, claim that the prince's downfall may be found in the deferring of revenge brought about by his "inability to act." The facts in the play do not bear out this interpretation. Although Hamlet chastises himself for delay, he wastes almost no time at all. Once he has been urged to revenge by the ghost, he uses both his pretended madness and "The Murder of Gonzago"—the play-within-a-play—in an attempt to confirm the ghost's accusations against Claudius. And once this confirmation has been gained, Hamlet acts almost immediately. Although he cannot bring himself to kill an unarmed man at prayers, minutes later he kills a person, Polonius, who he assumes is Claudius, behind the curtain in the Queen's chamber. This accidental murder complicates Hamlet's revenge, because it turns Laertes into a revenger and also lets Claudius know that Hamlet is trying to kill him. Hamlet's revenge is further complicated and delayed by Claudius's counterplots; the king sends Hamlet off to England immediately after the death of Polonius.

Just as Hamlet does not perfectly fit Aristotle's conception of a tragic protagonist, so the play itself does not conform to Aristotle's description of a tragedy (see pp. 1047–49). We may find a single motive or action in Hamlet's desire to avenge his father's murder and cleanse the state. This motivation, however, does not account for all the events in the play. The story of Polonius and his family, for example, is at least partly irrelevant to this motive. Also, Shakespeare does not follow the unities of time and place; the play covers several months (some have suggested years), and scenes change from place to place. Perhaps the most radical departure from Aristotelian standards is Shakespeare's use of comic elements. Whereas Aristotle called for absolutely pure forms of comedy and tragedy, English drama offered a mixture of elements and modes. Thus, *Hamlet* presents a great deal of humor in characters like Polonius, Osric, and the gravediggers. In addition, Hamlet's remarks are often quite funny.

Finally, *Hamlet*, like *Oedipus the King*, touches our lives and raises ever-present questions about living and dying, truth and honor, art and nature, and responsibility to ourselves, our families, and the state. In the years since Shakespeare wrote *Hamlet*, it has remained among the most popular, most moving, and most effective plays in the world. It has been translated into scores of languages, and it has successfully held the stage from Shakespeare's day to our own. Beyond its stage popularity, *Hamlet* has become one of the central documents of western civilization. Somehow, we all know about *Hamlet*, even if we have never read the play or seen a performance. This fact testifies to Shakespeare's consummate skill as a poet and playwright.

WILLIAM SHAKESPEARE (1564–1616)

The Tragedy of Hamlet, Prince of Denmark   *ca. 1600*

Edited by Alice Griffin°

CHARACTERS

>Claudius, *King of Denmark*
>Hamlet, *Son to the former, and nephew to the present King*
>Polonius, *Lord Chamberlain*
>Horatio, *Friend to Hamlet*
>Laertes, *Son to Polonius*
>Valtemand ⎫
>Cornelius ⎪
>Rosencrantz ⎬ *Courtiers*
>Guildenstern ⎪
>Osric ⎭
>
>A Gentleman
>A Priest
>Marcellus ⎫ *Officers*
>Barnardo ⎭
>Francisco, *a Soldier*
>Reynaldo, *Servant to Polonius*
>Players
>Two Clowns, *gravediggers*
>Fortinbras, *Prince of Norway*
>A Norwegian Captain
>English Ambassadors
>Gertrude, *Queen of Denmark, mother to Hamlet*
>Ophelia, *Daughter to Polonius*
>Ghost of Hamlet's Father
>Lords, Ladies, Officers, Soldiers, Sailors, Messengers, Attendants
>
>[*SCENE: Elsinore*]

ACT 1

Scene 1. *[A platform on the battlements of the castle]*

Enter BARNARDO and FRANCISCO, two Sentinels

BARNARDO.   Who's there?
FRANCISCO.   Nay, answer me. Stand and unfold° yourself.
BARNARDO.   Long live the king.
FRANCISCO.   Barnardo?

Professor Griffin's text for *Hamlet* was the Second Quarto (edition) published in 1604, with modifications based on the First Folio, published in 1623. Stage directions in those editions are printed here without brackets; added stage directions are printed within brackets. We have edited Griffin's notes for this text.   2 *unfold:* reveal.

BARNARDO. He.   5
FRANCISCO. You come most carefully upon your hour.
BARNARDO. 'Tis now struck twelve, get thee to bed Francisco.
FRANCISCO. For this relief much thanks, 'tis bitter cold,
     And I am sick at heart.
BARNARDO. Have you had quiet guard?
FRANCISCO.   Not a mouse stirring.   10
BARNARDO. Well, good night:
     If you do meet Horatio and Marcellus,
     The rivals° of my watch, bid them make haste.

Enter HORATIO and MARCELLUS.

FRANCISCO. I think I hear them. Stand ho, who is there?
HORATIO. Friends to this ground.
MARCELLUS.   And liegemen° to the Dane.°   15
FRANCISCO. Give you good night.
MARCELLUS.   O, farewell honest soldier,
     Who hath relieved you?
FRANCISCO.   Barnardo hath my place;
     Give you good night.   *Exit FRANCISCO*
MARCELLUS. Holla, Barnardo!
BARNARDO.   Say,
     What, is Horatio there?
HORATIO.   A piece of him.
BARNARDO. Welcome Horatio, welcome good Marcellus.   20
HORATIO. What, has this thing appeared again tonight?
BARNARDO. I have seen nothing.
MARCELLUS. Horatio says 'tis but our fantasy,°
     And will not let belief take hold of him,
     Touching this dreaded sight twice seen of us,   25
     Therefore I have entreated him along
     With us to watch the minutes of this night,
     That if again this apparition come,
     He may approve° our eyes and speak to it.
HORATIO. Tush, tush, 'twill not appear.
BARNARDO.   Sit down awhile,   30
     And let us once again assail your ears,
     That are so fortified against our story,
     What we have two nights seen.
HORATIO.   Well, sit we down,
     And let us hear Barnardo speak of this.
BARNARDO. Last night of all,   35
     When yon same star that's westward from the pole°
     Had made his course t'illume that part of heaven
     Where now it burns, Marcellus and myself,
     The bell then beating one—

---

13 *rivals:* partners.   15 *liegemen:* subjects.   *Dane:* King of Denmark.   23 *fantasy:*
imagination.   29 *approve:* prove reliable.   36 *pole:* North Star.

Enter GHOST.

MARCELLUS. Peace, break thee off, look where it comes again.	40

BARNARDO.   In the same figure like the king that's dead.

MARCELLUS.   Thou art a scholar, speak to it Horatio.

BARNARDO.   Looks a' not like the king? mark it Horatio.

HORATIO.   Most like, it harrows me with fear and wonder.

BARNARDO.   It would be spoke to.

MARCELLUS.   Question it Horatio.   45

HORATIO.   What art thou that usurp'st° this time of night,
    Together with that fair and warlike form,
    In which the majesty of buried Denmark°
    Did sometimes° march? by heaven I charge thee speak.

MARCELLUS.   It is offended.

BARNARDO.   See, it stalks away.   50

HORATIO.   Stay, speak, speak, I charge thee speak.   *Exit GHOST.*

MARCELLUS.   'Tis gone and will not answer.

BARNARDO.   How now Horatio, you tremble and look pale,
    Is not this something more than fantasy?
    What think you on't?   55

HORATIO.   Before my God I might not this believe,
    Without the sensible and true avouch°
    Of mine own eyes.

MARCELLUS.   Is it not like the king?

HORATIO.   As thou art to thyself.
    Such was the very armour he had on,   60
    When he the ambitious Norway° combated:
    So frowned he once, when in an angry parle°
    He smote the sledded Polacks° on the ice.
    'Tis strange.

MARCELLUS.   Thus twice before, and jump° at this dead hour,   65
    With martial stalk hath he gone by our watch.

HORATIO.   In what particular thought to work, I know not,
    But in the gross and scope° of mine opinion,
    This bodes some strange eruption to our state.

MARCELLUS.   Good now sit down, and tell me he that knows,   70
    Why this same strict and most observant watch
    So nightly toils the subject° of the land,
    And why such daily cast of brazen cannon
    And foreign mart,° for implements of war,
    Why such impress° of shipwrights, whose sore° task   75
    Does not divide the Sunday from the week,
    What might be toward° that this sweaty haste

---

46 *usurp'st:* wrongfully occupy (both the time and the shape of the dead king).   48 *buried
Denmark:* the buried King of Denmark.   49 *sometimes:* formerly.   57 *Sensible . . . avouch:*
assurance of the truth of the senses.   61 *Norway:* King of Norway.   62 *parle:* parley,
verbal battle.   63 *sledded Polacks:* Poles on sleds.   65 *jump:* just.   68 *gross and scope:*
general view.   72 *toils the subject:* makes the subjects toil.   74 *mart:* trade.   75 *impress:*
conscription.   *sore:* difficult.   77 *toward:* forthcoming.

Doth make the night joint-labourer with the day,
Who is't that can inform me?

HORATIO.   That can I.

At least the whisper goes so; our last king,   80
Whose image even but now appeared to us,
Was as you know by Fortinbras of Norway,
Thereto pricked on by a most emulate° pride,
Dared to the combat; in which our valiant Hamlet
(For so this side of our known world esteemed him)   85
Did slay this Fortinbras, who by a sealed compact,°
Well ratified by law and heraldy,°
Did forfeit (with his life) all those his lands
Which he stood seized° of, to the conqueror:
Against the which a moiety competent°   90
Was gagèd° by our King, which had returned
To the inheritance of Fortinbras,
Had he been vanquisher; as by the same co-mart,°
And carriage of the article designed,°
His fell to Hamlet; now sir, young Fortinbras,   95
Of unimprovèd mettle° hot and full,
Hath in the skirts° of Norway here and there
Sharked up° a list of lawless resolutes°
For food and diet to some enterprise
That hath a stomach° in't, which is no other,   100
As it doth well appear unto our state,
But to recover of us by strong hand
And terms compulsatory, those foresaid lands
So by his father lost; and this I take it,
Is the main motive of our preparations,   105
The source of this our watch, and the chief head°
Of this post-haste and romage° in the land.

BARNARDO.   I think it be no other, but e'en so;
Well may it sort° that this portentous figure
Comes armèd through our watch so like the king   110
That was and is the question of these wars.

HORATIO.   A mote it is to trouble the mind's eye:
In the most high and palmy° state of Rome,
A little ere the mightest Julius fell,
The graves stood tenantless, and the sheeted dead   115
Did squeak and gibber in the Roman streets,
As stars with trains of fire,° and dews of blood,

83 *emulate:* rivaling.   86 *compact:* treaty.   87 *law and heraldy:* heraldic law regulating
combats.   89 *seized:* possessed.   90 *moiety competent:* equal amount.   91 *gagèd:*
pledged.   93 *co-mart:* joint bargain.   94 *carriage . . . designed:* intent of the treaty
drawn up.   96 *unimprovèd mettle:* untested (1) metal (2) spirit.   97 *skirts:* outskirts.
98 *Sharked up:* gathered up indiscriminately (as a shark preys).   *lawless resolutes:*
determined outlaws.   100 *stomach:* show of courage.   106 *head:* fountainhead.
107 *romage:* bustle (rummage).   109 *sort:* turn out.   113 *palmy:* triumphant.
117 *stars . . . fire:* meteors.

Disasters° in the sun; and the moist star,°
Upon whose influence Neptune's empire stands,
Was sick almost to doomsday with eclipse.   120
And even the like precurse° of feared events,
As harbingers preceding still° the fates
And prologue to the omen° coming on,
Have heaven and earth together demonstrated
Unto our climatures° and countrymen.   125

Enter GHOST.

But soft, behold, lo where it comes again.
I'll cross° it though it blast me: *Spreads his arms.*
                        stay illusion,
If thou hast any sound or use of voice,
Speak to me.
If there be any good thing to be done   130
That may to thee do ease, and grace° to me,
Speak to me.
If thou art privy° to thy country's fate
Which happily° foreknowing may avoid,
O speak: 135
Or if thou hast uphoarded in thy life
Extorted treasure in the womb of earth,
For which they say you spirits oft walk in death,

                                                            The cock crows.

    Speak of it, stay and speak. Stop it Marcellus.
MARCELLUS.   Shall I strike at it with my partisan?°   140
HORATIO.   Do, if it will not stand
BARNARDO.   'Tis here.
HORATIO.   'Tis here.
MARCELLUS. 'Tis gone.   *Exit GHOST.*
We do it wrong being so majestical,
To offer it the show of violence,
For it is as the air, invulnerable,   145
And our vain blows malicious mockery.°
BARNARDO.   It was about to speak when the cock crew.°
HORATIO.   And then it started like a guilty thing,
Upon a fearful summons; I have heard,
The cock that is the trumpet to the morn,   150
Doth with his lofty and shrill-sounding throat
Awake the god of day, and at his warning

---

118 *Disasters:* unfavorable portents.   *moist star:* moon.   121 *precurse:* portent.
122 *still:* always.   123 *omen:* disaster.   125 *climatures:* regions.   127 *cross:* (1) cross its
path (2) spread my arms to make a cross of my body (to ward against evil).   131 *grace:*
(1) honor (2) blessedness.   133 *art privy:* know secretly of.   134 *happily:* perhaps.
140 *partisan:* spear.   146 *malicious mockery:* mockery because they only imitate harm.
147 *cock crew:* (traditional signal for ghosts to return to their confines).

Whether in sea or fire, in earth or air,°
Th'extravagant and erring° spirit hies°
To his confine, and of the truth herein   155
This present object made probation.°
MARCELLUS.   It faded on the crowing of the cock.
Some say that ever 'gainst° that season comes
Wherein our Saviour's birth is celebrated
This bird of dawning singeth all night long,   160
And then they say no spirit dare stir abroad,
The nights are wholesome,° then no planets strike,°
No fairy takes,° nor witch hath power to charm,
So hallowed, and so gracious is that time.
HORATIO.   So have I heard and do in part believe it.   165
But look, the morn in russet° mantle clad
Walks o'er the dew of yon high eastward hill:
Break we our watch up and by my advice
Let us impart what we have seen tonight
Unto young Hamlet, for upon my life   170
This spirit dumb to us, will speak to him:
Do you consent we shall acquaint him with it,
As needful in our loves,° fitting our duty?
MARCELLUS.   Let's do't I pray, and I this morning know
Where we shall find him most convenient.   *Exeunt.°* 175

Scene 2. [A room of state in the castle]

Flourish.° Enter CLAUDIUS *King of Denmark,* GERTRUDE *the Queen, [members of the] Council:
as* POLONIUS; *and his son* LAERTES, HAMLET, [VALTEMAND *and* CORNELIUS] *cum aliis.°*

KING.   Though yet of Hamlet our dear brother's death
The memory be green, and that it us befitted
To bear our hearts in grief, and our whole kingdom
To be contracted in one brow of woe,
Yet so far hath discretion fought with nature,°   5
That we° with wisest sorrow think on him
Together with remembrance of ourselves:°
Therefore our sometime° sister,° now our queen,
Th'imperial jointress° to this warlike state,
Have we as 'twere with a defeated joy,   10
With an auspicious, and a dropping eye,°

153 *sea . . . air:* the four elements (inhabited by spirits, each indigenous to a particular
element).   154 *extravagant and erring:* going beyond its bounds (vagrant) and wandering.
hies: hastens.   156 *made probation:* gave proof.   158 *'gainst:* just before.
162 *wholesome:* healthy (night air was considered unhealthy).   *strike:* exert evil influence
163 *takes:* bewitches.   166 *russet:* reddish.   173 *needful . . . loves:* urged by our
friendship.   175 stage direction: *Exeunt:* all exit.   stage direction: *Flourish:* fanfare of
trumpets.   *cum aliis:* with others.   5 *nature:* natural impulse (of grief).   6 *we:* royal
plural. The King speaks not only for himself, but for his entire government.
7 *remembrance of ourselves:* reminder of our duties.   8 *sometime:* former.   *sister:* sister-in-
law.   9 *jointress:* widow who inherits the estate.   11 *auspicious . . . eye:* one eye happy,
the other tearful.

With mirth in funeral, and with dirge in marriage,
In equal scale weighing delight and dole,
Taken to wife: nor have we herein barred
Your better wisdoms,° which have freely gone   15
With this affair along—for all, our thanks.
Now follows that you know, young Fortinbras,
Holding a weak supposal of our worth,°
Or thinking by our late dear brother's death
Our state to be disjoint and out of frame,°   20
Colleaguèd° with this dream of his advantage,°
He hath not failed to pester us with message
Importing the surrender of those lands
Lost by his father, with all bands° of law,
To our most valiant brother—so much for him: 25
Now for ourself, and for this time of meeting,
Thus much the business is. We have here writ
To Norway, uncle of young Fortinbras—
Who impotent and bed-rid scarcely hears
Of this his nephew's purpose—to suppress   30
His further gait° herein, in that the levies,
The lists, and full proportions are all made
Out of his subject:° and we here dispatch
You good Cornelius, and you Valtemand,
For bearers of this greeting to old Norway,   35
Giving to you no further personal power
To business with the king, more than the scope
Of these delated° articles allow:
Farewell, and let your haste commend your duty.°
CORNELIUS, VALTEMAND.   In that, and all things, will we show our duty.   40
KING.   We doubt it nothing, heartily farewell.

Exeunt VALTEMAND *and* CORNELIUS.

And now Laertes what's the news with you?
You told us of some suit, what is't Laertes?
You cannot speak of reason to the Dane
And lose your voice;° what wouldst thou beg Laertes,   45
That shall not be my offer, not thy asking?°
The head is not more native° to the heart,
The hand more instrumental to the mouth,
Than is the throne of Denmark to thy father.
What wouldst thou have Laertes?

14–15 *barred . . . wisdoms:* failed to seek and abide by your good advice.   18 *weak . . .
worth:* low opinion of my ability in office.   20 *out of frame:* tottering.   21 *Colleaguèd:*
supported.   *advantage:* superiority.   24 *bands:* bonds.   31 *gait:* progress.
31–33 *levies . . . subject:* Taxes, conscriptions, and supplies are all obtained from his
subjects.   38 *delated:* accusing.   39 *haste . . . duty:* prompt departure signify your
respect.   45 *lose your voice:* speak in vain.   46 *offer . . . asking:* grant even before
requested.   47 *native:* related.

LAERTES.   My dread lord,   50
   Your leave and favour° to return to France,
   From whence, though willingly I came to Denmark,
   To show my duty in your coronation,
   Yet now I must confess, that duty done,
   My thoughts and wishes bend again toward France,   55
   And bow them to your gracious leave and pardon.°
KING.   Have you your father's leave? What says Polonius?
POLONIUS.   He hath my lord wrung from me my slow leave
   By laboursome petition, and at last
   Upon his will I sealed my hard consent.°   60
   I do beseech you give him leave to go.
KING.   Take thy fair hour Laertes, time be thine,
   And thy best graces spend it at thy will.
   But now my cousin° Hamlet, and my son—
HAMLET.   [*Aside.*] A little more than kin,° and less than kind.°   65
KING.   How is it that the clouds still hang on you?
HAMLET.   Not so my lord, I am too much in the sun.°
QUEEN.   Good Hamlet cast they nighted colour° off
   And let thine eye look like a friend on Denmark,°
   Do not for ever with they vailèd° lids   70
   Seek for thy noble father in the dust,
   Thou know'st 'tis common, all that lives must die,
   Passing through nature to eternity.
HAMLET.   Ay madam, it is common.°
QUEEN.   If it be,
   Why seems it so particular with thee?   75
HAMLET.   Seems, madam? nay it is, I know not "seems."
   'Tis not alone my inky cloak good mother,
   Nor customary suits of solemn black,
   Nor windy suspiration of forced breath,
   No, nor the fruitful river in the eye,°   80
   Nor the dejected haviour° of the visage,
   Together with all forms, moods, shapes of grief,
   That can denote me truly: these indeed seem,
   For they are actions that a man might play,°
   But I have that within which passes show,   85
   These but the trappings and the suits of woe.°

51 *leave and favour:* kind permission.   56 *pardon:* allowance.   60 *Upon . . . consent:* (1)
At his request, I gave my grudging consent. (2) On the soft sealing wax of his (legal) will, I
stamped my approval.   64 *cousin:* kinsman (used for relatives outside the immediate
family).   65 *more than kin:* too much of a kinsman, being both uncle and stepfather.
less than kind: (1) unkind because of being a kin (proverbial) and taking the throne from
the former king's son (2) unnatural (as it was considered incest to marry the wife of one's
dead brother).   67 *in the sun:* (1) in presence of the king (often associated metaphorically
with the sun) (2) proverbial: "out of heaven's blessing into the warm sun" (3) of a "son."
68 *nighted colour:* black.   69 *Denmark:* the King of Denmark.   70 *vailèd:* downcast.
74 *common:* (1) general (2) vulgar.   79–80 *windy . . . eye:* (hyperbole used to describe
exaggerated sighs and tears).   81 *haviour:* behavior.   84 *play:* act.   86 *trappings . . .*
woe: outward, superficial costumes of mourning.

KING. 'Tis sweet and commendable in your nature Hamlet,
    To give these mourning duties to your father:
    But you must know your father lost a father,
    That father lost, lost his, and the survivor bound   90
    In filial obligation for some term
    To do obsequious sorrow:° but to persever
    In obstinate condolement,° is a course
    Of impious stubbornness, 'tis unmanly grief,
    It shows a will most incorrect to heaven,   95
    A heart unfortified, a mind impatient,
    An understanding simple and unschooled:
    For what we know must be, and is as common
    As any the most vulgar thing to sense,°
    Why should we in our peevish opposition   100
    Take it to heart? Fie, 'tis a fault to heaven,
    A fault against the dead, a fault to nature,
    To reason most absurd, whose common theme
    Is death of fathers, and who still° hath cried
    From the first corse,° till he that died today,   105
    "This must be so." We pray you throw to earth
    This unprevailing° woe, and think of us
    As of a father, for let the world take note
    You are the most immediate° to our throne,
    And with no less nobility of love   110
    Than that which dearest father bears his son,
    Do I impart toward you. For your intent
    In going back to school in Wittenberg,
    It is most retrograde° to our desire,
    And we beseech you, bend you° to remain   115
    Here in the cheer and comfort of our eye,
    Our chiefest courtier, cousin, and our son.
QUEEN. Let not thy mother lose her prayers Hamlet,
    I pray thee stay with us, go not to Wittenberg.
HAMLET. I shall in all my best obey you madam.   120
KING. Why 'tis a loving and a fair reply,
    Be as ourself in Denmark. Madam come,
    This gentle and unforced accord of Hamlet
    Sits smiling to my heart, in grace whereof,
    No jocund health that Denmark drinks today,   125
    But the great cannon to the clouds shall tell,

---

92 *do obsequious sorrow:* express sorrow befitting obsequies or funerals.   93 *condolement:*
grief.   99 *As any . . . sense:* as the most ordinary thing the senses can perceive.
104 *still:* always.   105 *corse:* corpse (of Abel, also, ironically, the first fratricide).
107 *unprevailing:* useless.   109 *most immediate:* next in succession (though Danish kings
were elected by the council, an Elizabethan audience might feel that Hamlet, not Claudius,
should be king).   114 *retrograde:* movement (of planets) in a reverse direction.
115 *beseech . . . you:* hope you will be inclined.

And the king's rouse° the heaven shall bruit° again,
Re-speaking earthly thunder; come away.

Flourish, Exeunt all but HAMLET.

HAMLET. O that this too too sullied° flesh would melt,   130
    Thaw and resolve itself into a dew,
    Or that the Everlasting had not fixed
    His canon° 'gainst self-slaughter. O God, God,
    How weary, stale, flat, and unprofitable
    Seems to me all the uses of this world!   135
    Fie on't, ah fie, 'tis an unweeded garden
    That grows to seed, things rank° and gross in nature
    Possess it merely.° That it should come to this,
    But two months dead, nay not so much, not two,
    [So excellent a king, that was to this
    Hyperion° to a satyr,° so loving to my mother]   140
    That he might not beteem° the winds of heaven
    Visit her face too roughly—heaven and earth,
    Must I remember? why, she would hang on him
    As if increase of appetite had grown
    By what it fed on,° and yet within a month—   145
    Let me not think on't: Frailty, thy name is woman—
    A little month or ere those shoes were old
    With which she followed my poor father's body
    Like Niobe° all tears, why she, even she—
    O God, a beast that wants° discourse of reason   150
    Would have mourned longer—married with my uncle,
    My father's brother, but no more like my father
    Than I to Hercules: within a month,
    Ere yet the salt of most unrighteous° tears
    Had left the flushing° in her gallèd° eyes,   155
    She married. O most wicked speed, to post°
    With such dexterity to incestuous° sheets:
    It is not, nor it cannot come to good,
    But break my heart, for I must hold my tongue.

Enter HORATIO, MARCELLUS *and* BARNARDO.

HORATIO.   Hail to your lordship.
HAMLET.   I am glad to see you well;   160
    Horatio, or I do forget my self.

---

127 *rouse:* toast that empties the wine cup.   *bruit:* sound.   129 *sullied:* tainted.
132 *canon:* divine edict.   136 *rank:* (1) luxuriant, excessive (2) bad-smelling.
137 *merely:* entirely.   140 *Hyperion:* god of the sun.   *satyr:* part-goat, part-man
woodland deity (noted for lust).   141 *beteem:* allow.   144–145 *As if . . . on:* as if the
more she fed, the more her appetite increased.   149 *Niobe:* (who boasted of her children
before Leto and was punished by their destruction; Zeus changed the weeping mother to a
stone dropping continual tears).   150 *wants:* lacks.   154 *unrighteous:* (because untrue).
155 *flushing:* redness.   *gallèd:* rubbed sore.   156 *post:* rush.   157 *incestuous:* (the
church forbade marriage to one's brother's widow).

HORATIO. The same my lord, and your poor servant ever.

HAMLET. Sir my good friend, I'll change° that name with you:
　And what make you from Wittenberg, Horatio?
　Marcellus. 165

MARCELLUS. My good lord.

HAMLET. I am very glad to see you: good even, sir.
　But what in faith make you from Wittenberg?

HORATIO. A truant disposition, good my lord.

HAMLET. I would not hear your enemy say so, 170
　Nor shall you do mine ear that violence
　To make it truster of your own report
　Against yourself. I know you are no truant,
　But what is your affair in Elsinore?
　We'll teach you to drink deep ere you depart. 175

HORATIO. My Lord, I came to see your father's funeral.

HAMLET. I prithee do not mock me, fellow student,
　I think it was to see my mother's wedding.

HORATIO. Indeed my lord it followed hard upon.

HAMLET. Thrift, thrift, Horatio, the funeral baked meats° 180
　Did coldly° furnish forth the marriage tables.
　Would I had met my dearest° foe in heaven
　Or ever I had seen that day Horatio.
　My father, methinks I see my father.

HORATIO. Where my lord?

HAMLET.　　　　　　　　In my mind's eye Horatio. 185

HORATIO. I saw him once, a' was a goodly° king.

HAMLET. A' was a man, take him for all in all,
　I shall not look upon his like again.

HORATIO. My lord, I think I saw him yesternight.

HAMLET. Saw? Who? 190

HORATIO. My lord, the king your father.

HAMLET.　　　　　　　　The king my father?

HORATIO. Season your admiration° for a while
　With an attent ear till I may deliver
　Upon the witness of these gentlemen
　This marvel to you.

HAMLET.　　　　　　　　For God's love let me hear! 195

HORATIO. Two nights together had these gentlemen,
　Marcellus and Barnardo, on their watch
　In the dead waste and middle of the night,
　Been thus encountered. A figure like your father
　Armed at point exactly, cap-a-pe,° 200
　Appears before them, and with solemn march,
　Goes slow and stately by them; thrice he walked
　By their oppressed° and fear-surprisèd eyes

163 *change:* exchange (and be called your friend).　180 *funeral baked meats:* food
prepared for the funeral.　181 *coldly:* when cold.　182 *dearest:* direst.　186 *goodly:*
handsome.　192 *Season your admiration:* control your wonder.　200 *at point . . . cap-a-pe:*
in every detail, head to foot.　203 *oppressed:* overcome by horror.

Within his truncheon's° length, whilst they distilled°
Almost to jelly with the act of fear,   205
Stand dumb and speak not to him; this to me
In dreadful secrecy° impart they did,
And I with them the third night kept the watch,
Where as they had delivered, both in time,
Form of the thing, each word made true and good,   210
The apparition comes: I knew your father,
These hands are not more like.

HAMLET.   But where was this?
MARCELLUS.   My lord upon the platform where we watch.
HAMLET.   Did you not speak to it?
HORATIO.   My lord I did,
But answer made it none, yet once methought   215
It lifted up it° head, and did address
Itself to motion° like as it would speak:
But even then the morning cock crew loud,
And at the sound it shrunk in haste away
And vanished from our sight.
HAMLET.   'Tis very strange.   220
HORATIO.   As I do live my honoured lord 'tis true,
And we did think it writ down in our duty
To let you know of it.
HAMLET.   Indeed indeed sirs, but this troubles me.
Hold you the watch tonight?
ALL.   We do my lord.   225
HAMLET.   Armed say you?
ALL.   Armed my lord.
HAMLET.   From top to toe?
ALL.   My lord from head to foot.
HAMLET.   Then saw you not his face.
HORATIO.   O yes my lord, he wore his beaver° up.   230
HAMLET.   What, looked he frowningly?
HORATIO.   A countenance more in sorrow than in anger.
HAMLET.   Pale, or red?
HORATIO.   Nay, very pale.
HAMLET.   And fixed his eyes upon you?
HORATIO.   Most constantly.
HAMLET.   I would I had been there.   235
HORATIO.   It would have much amazed you.
HAMLET.   Very like, very like, stayed it long?
HORATIO.   While one with moderate haste might tell° a hundred.
MARCELLUS, BARNARDO.   Longer, longer.
HORATIO.   Not when I saw't.
HAMLET.   His beard was grizzled,° no?   240

204 *truncheon:* staff (of office).   *distilled:* dissolved.   207 *in dreadful secrecy:* as a dread
secret.   216 *it:* its.   216–217 *address . . . motion:* start to move.   230 *beaver:* visor.
238 *tell:* count.   240 *grizzled:* grey.

HORATIO.   It was as I have seen it in his life,
    A sable silvered.°
HAMLET.   I will watch tonight;
    Perchance 'twill walk again.
HORATIO.   I warr'nt it will.
HAMLET.   If it assume my noble father's person,
    I'll speak to it though hell itself should gape   245
    And bid me hold my peace;° I pray you all
    If you have hitherto concealed this sight
    Let it be tenable° in your silence still,
    And whatsoever else shall hap tonight,
    Give it an understanding but no tongue.   250
    I will requite your loves, so fare you well:
    Upon the platform 'twixt eleven and twelve
    I'll visit you.
ALL.   Our duty to your honour.
HAMLET.   Your loves, as mine to you:° farewell.   *Exeunt.*
    My father's spirit (in arms) all is not well,   255
    I doubt° some foul play, would the night were come;
    Till then sit still my soul, foul deeds will rise,
    Though all the earth o'erwhelm them, to men's eyes.   *Exit.*

/ Scene 3. *[Polonius's chambers]*

Enter LAERTES and OPHELIA his sister.

LAERTES.   My necessaries are embarked, farewell,
    And sister, as the winds give benefit
    And convoy° is assistant, do not sleep
    But let me hear from you.
OPHELIA.   Do you doubt that?
LAERTES.   For Hamlet, and the trifling of his favour,   5
    Hold it a fashion, and a toy in blood,°
    A violet in the youth of primy nature,°
    Forward,° not permanent, sweet, not lasting,
    The perfume and suppliance of° a minute,
    No more.
OPHELIA.   No more but so?
LAERTES.   Think it no more.   10
    For nature crescent° does not grow alone
    In thews and bulk,° but as this temple waxes°
    The inward service of the mind and soul

---

242 *A sable silvered:* black flecked with grey.   245–246 *though hell . . . peace:* despite the risk of hell (for speaking to a demon) warning me to be silent.   248 *tenable:* held, kept. 254 *Your loves . . . you:* offer your friendship (rather than duty) in exchange for mine. 256 *doubt:* fear.   3 *convoy:* conveyance.   6 *toy in blood:* whim of the passions.   7 *youth of primy nature:* early spring.   8 *Forward:* premature.   9 *suppliance of:* supplying diversion for.   11 *nature crescent:* man as he grows.   12 *thews and bulk:* sinews and body.   *temple waxes:* body grows (1 Cor. 6:19).

Grows wide withal.° Perhaps he loves you now,
And now no soil nor cautel° doth besmirch   15
The virtue of his will:° but you must fear,
His greatness weighed,° his will is not his own,
For he himself is subject to his birth:
He may not as unvalued persons° do,
Carve° for himself, for on his choice depends   20
The sanctity and health of this whole state,
And therefore must his choice be circumscribed
Unto the voice and yielding° of that body
Whereof he is the head. Then if he says he loves you,
It fits your wisdom so far to believe it   25
As he in his particular act and place
May give his saying deed,° which is no further
Than the main voice of Denmark goes withal.
Then weigh what loss your honour may sustain
If with too credent° ear you list° his songs,   30
Or lose your heart, or your chaste treasure open
To his unmast'red importunity.°
Fear it Ophelia, fear it my dear sister,
And keep you in the rear of your affection,
Out of the shot and danger of desire.   35
The chariest° maid is prodigal enough
If she unmask her beauty to the moon.
Virtue itself 'scapes not calumnious strokes.
The canker galls the infants° of the spring
Too oft before their buttons° be disclosed,   40
And in the morn and liquid dew of youth
Contagious blastments° are most imminent.
Be wary then, best safety lies in fear,
Youth to itself rebels,° though none else near.
OPHELIA.   I shall the effect° of this good lesson keep   45
As watchman to my heart: but good my brother,
Do not as some ungracious° pastors do,
Show me the steep and thorny way to heaven,
Whiles like a puffed and reckless libertine
Himself the primrose path of dalliance treads,   50
And recks not his own rede.°

Enter POLONIUS.

14 *withal:* at the same time.   15 *cautel:* deceit.   16 *will:* desire.   17 *weighed:*
considered.   19 *unvalued persons:* common people.   20 *Carve:* choose (as does the one
who carves the food).   23 *voice and yielding:* approving vote.   26–27 *in his . . . deed:*
limited by personal responsibilities and rank, may perform what he promises.
30 *credent:* credulous.   *list:* listen to.   31–32 *your chaste . . . importunity:* lose your
virginity to his uncontrolled persistence.   36 *chariest:* most cautious.   39 *canker . . .*
infants: cankerworm or caterpillar harms the young plants.   40 *buttons:* buds.
42 *blastments:* blights.   44 *to itself rebels:* lusts by nature.   45 *effect:* moral.
47 *ungracious:* lacking God's grace.   51 *recks . . . rede:* does not follow his own advice.

LAERTES.   O fear me not,°
  I stay too long, but here my father comes:
  A double blessing is a double grace,
  Occasion smiles upon a second leave.°
POLONIUS.   Yet here Laertes? aboard, aboard for shame,   55
  The wind sits in the shoulder of your sail,
  And you are stayed for: there, my blessing with thee,
  And these few precepts in thy memory
  Look thou character.° Give thy thoughts no tongue,
  Nor any unproportioned thought his act: 60
  Be thou familiar, but by no means vulgar:°
  Those friends thou hast, and their adoption tried,°
  Grapple them unto thy soul with hoops of steel,
  But do not dull° thy palm with entertainment
  Of each new-hatched unfledged° comrade. Beware   65
  Of entrance to a quarrel, but being in,
  Bear't that th'opposèd may beware of thee.
  Give every man thy ear, but few thy voice:
  Take each man's censure,° but reserve thy judgment.
  Costly thy habit° as thy purse can buy,   70
  But not expressed in fancy;° rich, not gaudy,
  For the apparel oft proclaims the man,
  And they in France of the best rank and station,
  Are of a most select and generous chief° in that:
  Neither a borrower nor a lender be,   75
  For loan oft loses both itself and friend,
  And borrowing dulls the edge of husbandry;°
  This above all, to thine own self be true
  And it must follow as the night the day,
  Thou canst not then be false to any man.   80
  Farewell, my blessing season° this in thee.
LAERTES.   Most humbly do I take my leave my lord.
POLONIUS.   The time invites you, go, your servants tend.°
LAERTES.   Farewell Ophelia, and remember well
  What I have said to you.
OPHELIA.   'Tis in my memory locked,   85
  And you yourself shall keep the key of it.
LAERTES.   Farewell.   *Exit* LAERTES.
POLONIUS.   What is't Ophelia he hath said to you?
OPHELIA.   So please you, something touching the Lord Hamlet.
POLONIUS.   Marry,° well bethought: 90
  'Tis told me he hath very oft of late

---

fear me not: Don't worry about me.   54 *Occasion . . . leave:* opportunity favors a second
leave-taking.   59 *character:* write, impress, imprint.   61 *vulgar:* indiscriminately
friendly.   62 *adoption tried:* loyalty proved.   64 *dull:* get callouses on.   65 *new-
hatched, unfledged:* new and untested.   69 *censure:* opinion.   70 *habit:* clothing.
71 *expressed in fancy:* so fantastic as to be ridiculous.   74 *select . . . chief:* judicious and
noble eminence.   77 *husbandry:* thrift.   81 *season:* bring to maturity.   83 *tend:*
attend, wait.   90 *Marry:* (a mild oath, from "By the Virgin Mary").

Given private time to you, and you yourself
Have of your audience been most free and bounteous.
If it be so, as so 'tis put on me,
And that in way of caution, I must tell you,   95
You do not understand yourself so clearly
As it behooves my daughter, and your honour.
What is between you? give me up the truth.

OPHELIA.   He hath my lord of late made many tenders°
Of his affection to me.   100

POLONIUS.   Affection, puh, you speak like a green girl
Unsifted° in such perilous circumstance.
Do you believe his tenders as you call them?

OPHELIA.   I do not know my lord what I should think.

POLONIUS.   Marry, I will teach you; think yourself a baby   105
That you have ta'en these tenders° for true pay
Which are not sterling.° Tender yourself more dearly,°
Or (not to crack the wind of the poor phrase,
Running it thus°) you'll tender me a fool.°

OPHELIA.   My lord he hath importuned me with love   110
In honourable fashion.

POLONIUS.   Ay, fashion you may call it, go to, go to.

OPHELIA.   And hath given countenance° to his speech, my lord,
With almost all the holy vows of heaven.

POLONIUS.   Ay, springes° to catch woodcocks.° I do know   115
When the blood burns, how prodigal the soul
Lends the tongue vows: these blazes daughter,
Giving more light than heat, extinct in both,
Even in their promise, as it is a-making,°
You must not take for fire. From this time   120
Be something scanter of your maiden presence,
Set your entreatments at a higher rate
Than a command to parle;° for Lord Hamlet,
Believe so much in him that he is young,
And with a larger tether may he walk   125
Than may be given you: in few° Ophelia,
Do not believe his vows, for they are brokers°
Not of that dye which their investments° show,
But mere implorators° of unholy suits,
Breathing° like sanctified and pious bonds,°   130

---

99 *tenders:* offers (see lines 106–109).   102 *Unsifted:* untested.   106 *tenders:* offers (of
money).   107 *sterling:* genuine (currency).   *Tender . . . dearly:* hold yourself at a higher
value.   108–109 *crack . . . thus:* make the phrase lose its breath.   109 *tender . . . fool:* (1)
make me look foolish (2) present me with a baby.   113 *countenance:* confirmation.
115 *springes:* snares.   *woodcocks:* snipelike birds (believed to be stupid and therefore easily
trapped).   118–119 *extinct . . . a-making:* losing both appearance, because of brevity, and
substance, because of broken promises.   122–123 *Set . . . parle:* Don't rush to negotiate a
surrender as soon as the besieger asks for a discussion of terms.   126 *few:* short.
127 *brokers:* (1) business agents (2) procurers.   128 *investments:* (1) business ventures (2)
clothing.   129 *implorators:* solicitors.   130 *Breathing:* speaking softly.   *bonds:* pledges.

The better to beguile. This is for all,
I would not in plain terms from this time forth
Have you so slander any moment leisure
As to give words or talk with the Lord Hamlet.
Look to't I charge you, come your ways.°   135
OPHELIA.   I shall obey, my lord.   [*Exeunt.*]

Scene 4. [*The platform on the battlements*]

Enter HAMLET, HORATIO and MARCELLUS.

HAMLET.   The air bites shrewdly,° it is very cold.
HORATIO.   It is a nipping and an eager° air.
HAMLET.   What hour now?
HORATIO.   I think it lacks of twelve.
MARCELLUS.   No, it is struck.
HORATIO.   Indeed? I heard it not: it then draws near the season,°   5
Wherein the spirit held his wont to walk.

A flourish of trumpets, and two pieces [of ordnance] go off.

What does this mean my lord?
HAMLET.   The king doth wake° tonight and takes his rouse,°
Keeps wassail° and the swagg'ring up-spring° reels:
And as he drains his draughts of Rhenish° down,   10
The kettle-drum and trumpet thus bray out
The triumph of his pledge.°
HORATIO.   Is it a custom?
HAMLET.   Ay marry is't,
But to my mind, though I am native here
And to the manner born,° it is a custom   15
More honoured in the breach than the observance.°
This heavy-headed revel east and west
Makes us traduced and taxed of° other nations:
They clepe° us drunkards, and with swinish phrase
Soil our addition,° and indeed it takes   20
From our achievements, though performed at height,°
The pith and marrow of our attribute.°
So oft it chances in particular men,
That for some vicious mole of nature° in them,
As in their birth, wherein they are not guilty   25
(Since nature cannot choose his origin),

135 *come your ways:* come along.   1 *shrewdly:* piercingly.   2 *eager:* sharp.   5 *season:*
time, period.   8 *wake:* stay awake.   *rouse:* drinks that empty the cup.   9 *Keeps*
wassail: holds drinking bouts.   *up-spring:* a vigorous German dance.   10 *Rhenish:*
Rhine wine.   12 *triumph . . . pledge:* victory of emptying the cup with one draught.
15 *to . . . born:* accustomed to the practice since birth.   16 *More . . . observance:* better to
break than to observe.   18 *traduced and taxed of:* defamed and taken to task by.
19 *clepe:* call.   19–20 *with swinish . . . addition:* blemish our reputation by comparing us to
swine.   21 *at height:* to the maximum.   22 *attribute:* reputation.   24 *mole of nature:*
natural blemish.

By the o'ergrowth of some complexion,°
Oft breaking down the pales° and forts of reason,
Or by some habit, that too much o'er-leavens°
The form of plausive° manners—that these men,   30
Carrying I say the stamp of one defect,
Being nature's livery,° or fortune's star,°
His virtues else be they as pure as grace,
As infinite as man may undergo,
Shall in the general censure° take corruption   35
From that particular fault: the dram of evil
Doth all the noble substance of a doubt,
To his own scandal.°

Enter GHOST.

HORATIO.   Look my lord, it comes.
HAMLET.   Angels and ministers of grace defend us:
     Be thou a spirit of health, or goblin damned,°   40
     Bring with thee airs from heaven, or blasts from hell,
     Be thy intents wicked, or charitable,
     Thou com'st in such a questionable° shape,
     That I will speak to thee. I'll call thee Hamlet,
     King, father, royal Dane. O answer me,   45
     Let me not burst in ignorance, but tell
     Why thy canonized° bones hearsèd° in death
     Have burst their cerements°? why the sepulchre,
     Wherein we saw thee quietly interred
     Hath oped his ponderous and marble jaws,   50
     To cast thee up again? What may this mean
     That thou, dead corse, again in complete steel
     Revisits thus the glimpses of the moon,
     Making night hideous, and we fools of nature°
     So horridly to shake our disposition   55
     With thoughts beyond the reaches of our souls,
     Say why is this? wherefore? what should we do?   *GHOST beckons HAMLET.*
HORATIO.   It beckons you to go away with it,
     As if it some impartment did desire°
     To you alone.
MARCELLUS.   Look with what courteous action   60
     It waves you to a more removèd ground,

---

27 *o'er growth . . . complexion:* overbalance of one of the body's four humors or fluids
believed to determine temperament.   18 *pales:* defensive enclosures.   29 *too much o'er-*
leavens: excessively modifies (like too much leaven in bread).   30 *plausive:* pleasing.
32 *nature's livery:* marked by nature.   *fortune's star:* destined by chance.   35 *general*
censure: public opinion.   36–38 *the dram . . . scandal:* the minute quantity of evil casts
doubt upon his noble nature, to his shame.   40 *spirit . . . damned:* true ghost or demon
from hell.   43 *questionable:* question-raising.   47 *canonized:* buried in accordance with
church edict.   *hearsèd:* entombed.   48 *cerements:* waxed cloth wrappings.   54 *fools of*
nature: mocked by our natural limitations when faced with the supernatural.   59 *some . . .*
desire: desired to impart something.

But do not go with it.

HORATIO.   No, by no means.

HAMLET.   It will not speak, then I will follow it.

HORATIO.   Do not my lord.

HAMLET.   Why what should be the fear?
I do not set my life at a pin's fee,°   65
And for my soul, what can it do to that
Being a thing immortal as itself;
It waves me forth again, I'll follow it.

HORATIO.   What if it tempt you toward the flood my lord,
Or to the dreadful summit of the cliff   70
That beetles o'er° his base into the sea,
And there assume some other horrible form
Which might deprive your sovereignty of reason,°
And draw you into madness? think of it,
The very place puts toys of desperation,°   75
Without more motive, into every brain
That looks so many fathoms to the sea
And hears it roar beneath.

HAMLET.   It waves me still:
Go on, I'll follow thee.

MARCELLUS.   You shall not go my lord.

HAMLET.   Hold off your hands.   80

HORATIO.   Be ruled, you shall not go.

HAMLET.   My fate cries out,
And makes each petty artire° in this body
As hardy as the Nemean lion's° nerve;°
Still am I called, unhand me gentlemen,
By heaven I'll make a ghost of him that lets° me: 85
I say away; go on, I'll follow thee.   *Exeunt* GHOST *and* HAMLET.

HORATIO.   He waxes desperate° with imagination.

MARCELLUS.   Let's follow, 'tis not fit thus to obey him.

HORATIO.   Have after—to what issue will this come?

MARCELLUS.   Something is rotten in the state of Denmark.   90

HORATIO.   Heaven will direct it.

MARCELLUS.   Nay, let's follow him.   *Exeunt.*

Scene 5. [Another part of the platform]

Enter GHOST *and* HAMLET.

HAMLET.   Whither wilt thou lead me? Speak, I'll go no further.

GHOST.   Mark me.

HAMLET.   I will.

GHOST.   My hour is almost come

---

65 *fee:* value.   71 *beetles o'er:* overhangs.   73 *deprive . . . reason:* dethrone your reason
from its sovereignty.   75 *toys of desperation:* desperate whims.   82 *artire:* ligament.
83 *Nemean lion:* (killed by Hercules as one of his twelve labors).   *nerve:* sinew.   85 *lets:*
prevents.   87 *waxes desperate:* grows frantic.

When I to sulphurous and tormenting flames
   Must render up myself.
HAMLET.   Alas poor ghost.
GHOST.   Pity me not, but lend thy serious hearing   5
   To what I shall unfold.
HAMLET.   Speak, I am bound° to hear.
GHOST.   So art thou to revenge, when thou shalt hear.
HAMLET.   What?
GHOST.   I am thy father's spirit,
   Doomed for a certain term to walk the night,   10
   And for the day confined to fast in fires,
   Till the foul crimes done in my days of nature°
   Are burnt and purged away: but that I am forbid
   To tell the secrets of my prison-house,
   I could a tale unfold whose lightest word   15
   Would harrow up thy soul, freeze thy young blood,
   Make thy two eyes like stars start from their spheres,°
   Thy knotted and combinèd locks to part,
   And each particular hair to stand an end,
   Like quills upon the fretful porpentine:°   20
   But this eternal blazon° must not be
   To ears of flesh and blood; list, list, O list:
   If though didst ever thy dear father love—
HAMLET.   O God!
GHOST.   Revenge his foul and most unnatural murder.   25
HAMLET.   Murder?
GHOST.   Murder most foul, as in the best it is,
   But this most foul, strange and unnatural.
HAMLET.   Haste me to know't, that I with wings as swift
   As meditation or the thoughts of love,   30
   May sweep to my revenge.
GHOST.   I find thee apt,°
   And duller shouldst thou be than the fat° weed
   That rots itself in ease on Lethe wharf,°
   Wouldst thou not stir in this; now Hamlet hear,
   'Tis given out, that sleeping in my orchard,°   35
   A serpent stung me, so the whole ear of Denmark
   Is by a forgèd process° of my death
   Rankly abused:° but know thou noble youth,
   The serpent that did sting thy father's life
   Now wears his crown.
HAMLET.   O my prophetic soul!   40
   My uncle?

---

6 *bound:* obliged by duty.   12 *crimes . . . nature:* sins committed during my life on earth.
17 *spheres:* (1) orbits (according to Ptolemy, each planet was confined to a sphere revolving
around the earth) (2) sockets.   19 *an:* on.   20 *fretful porpentine:* angry porcupine.
21 *eternal blazon:* revelation about eternity.   31 *apt:* ready.   32 *fat:* slimy.   33 *Lethe
wharf:* the banks of Lethe (river in Hades from which spirits drank to forget their past
lives).   35 *orchard:* garden.   37 *process:* account.   38 *abused:* deceived.

GHOST. Ay, that incestuous, that adulterate° beast,
With witchcraft of his wit, with traitorous gifts,
O wicked wit and gifts, that have the power
So to seduce; won to his shameful lust   45
The will of my most seeming-virtuous queen;
O Hamlet, what a falling-off was there,
From me whose love was of that dignity
That it went hand in hand, even with the vow
I made to her in marriage, and to decline   50
Upon° a wretch whose natural gifts were poor
To° those of mine;
But virtue, as it never will be moved,
Though lewdness court it in a shape of heaven,°
So lust, though to a radiant angle linked,   55
Will sate itself in a celestial bed
And prey on garbage.
But soft, methinks I scent the morning air,
Brief let me be; sleeping within my orchard,
My custom always of the afternoon,   60
Upon my secure° hour thy uncle stole
With juice of cursèd hebona° in a vial,
And in the porches of my ears did pour
The leperous° distilment, whose effect
Holds such an enmity with blood of man,   65
That swift as quicksilver it courses through
The natural gates and alleys of the body,
And with a sudden vigour it doth posset°
And curd, like eager° droppings into milk,
The thin and wholesome° blood; so did it mine,   70
And a most instant tetter° barked about°
Most lazar°-like with vile and loathsome crust
All my smooth body.
Thus was I sleeping by a brother's hand,
Of life, of crown, of queen at once dispatched,   75
Cut off even in the blossoms of my sin,
Unhouseled, disappointed, unaneled,°
No reck'ning° made, but sent to my account°
With all my imperfections on my head;
O horrible, O horrible, most horrible!   80
If thou hast nature in thee bear it not,
Let not the royal bed of Denmark be

---

42 *adulterate:* adulterous.   50–51 *decline Upon:* descend to.   52 *To:* compared to.
54 *shape of heaven:* angelic appearance.   61 *secure:* unsuspecting.   62 *hebona:* poisonous
sap of the ebony or henbane.   64 *leperous:* leprosy-causing.   68 *posset:* curdle.
69 *eager:* sour.   70 *wholesome:* healthy.   71 *tetter:* skin eruption.   *barked about:*
covered (like bark on a tree).   72 *lazar:* leper.   77 *Unhouseled ... unaneled:* without
final sacrament, unprepared (without confession) and lacking extreme unction (anointing).
78 *reck'ning:* (1) accounting (2) payment of my bill (3) confession and absolution.
account: judgment.

A couch for luxury° and damnèd incest.
But howsoever thou pursues this act,
Taint not thy mind, nor let thy soul contrive   85
Against thy mother aught;° leave her to heaven,
And to those thorns that in her bosom lodge
To prick and sting her. Fare thee well at once,
The glow-worm shows the matin° to be near
And 'gins to pale this uneffectual fire:°   90
Adieu, adieu, adieu, remember me.   *Exit.*

HAMLET.   O all you host of heaven! O earth! what else?
And shall I couple° hell? O fie! Hold, hold my heart,
And you my sinews, grow not instant old,
But bear me stiffly up; remember thee?   95
Ay thou poor ghost, whiles memory holds a seat
In this distracted globe.° Remember thee?
Yea, from the table° of my memory
I'll wipe away all trivial fond° records,
All saws of books,° all forms, all pressures° past   100
That youth and observation copied there,
And thy commandment all alone shall live
Within the book and volume of my brain,
Unmixed with baser matter, yes by heaven:
O most pernicious woman!   105
O villain, villain, smiling damnèd villain!
My tables,° meet° it is I set it down
That one may smile, and smile, and be a villain,
At least I am sure it may be so in Denmark.
So uncle, there you are: now to my word,°   110
It is 'Adieu, adieu, remember me.'
I have sworn't.

Enter HORATIO and MARCELLUS.

HORATIO.   My lord, my lord!
MARCELLUS.   Lord Hamlet!
HORATIO.   Heaven secure° him.
HAMLET.   So be it.
MARCELLUS.   Illo, ho, ho, my lord!   115
HAMLET.   Hillo, ho, ho, boy, come° bird, come.
MARCELLUS.   How is't my noble lord?
HORATIO.   What news my lord?
HAMLET.   O, wonderful!
HORATIO.   Good my lord, tell it.

---

83 *luxury:* lust.   86 *aught:* anything.   89 *matin:* dawn.   90 *'gins . . . fire:* his light
becomes ineffective, made pale by day.   93 *couple:* engage in a contest against.
97 *distracted globe:* (his head).   98 *table:* tablet, "table-book."   99 *fond:* foolish.
100 *saws of books:* maxims (sayings) copied from books.   *forms, pressures:* ideas,
impressions.   107 *tables:* See note for line 98.   *meet:* fitting.   110 *word:* motto (to
guide my actions).   113 *secure:* protect.   116 *Hillo . . . come:* falconer's cry with which
Hamlet replies to their calls.

HAMLET.   No, you will reveal it.

HORATIO.   Not I my lord, by heaven.

MARCELLUS.   Nor I my lord.   120

HAMLET.   How say you then, would heart of man once think it?
    But you'll be secret?

BOTH.   Ay, by heaven, my lord.

HAMLET.   There's ne'er a villain dwelling in all Denmark
    But he's an arrant° knave.

HORATIO.   There needs no ghost my lord, come from the grave   125
    To tell us this.

HAMLET.   Why right, you are in the right,
    And so without more circumstance° at all
    I hold it fit that we shake hands and part,
    You, as your business and desire shall point you,
    For every man hath business and desire   130
    Such as it is, and for my own poor part,
    Look you, I will go pray.

HORATIO.   These are but wild and whirling words my lord.

HAMLET.   I am sorry they offend you, heartily,
    Yes faith, heartily.

HORATIO.   There's no offence my lord.   135

HAMLET.   Yes by Saint Patrick, but there is Horatio,
    And much offence too: touching this vision here,
    It is an honest° ghost, that let me tell you:
    For your desire to know what is between us,
    O'ermaster't as you may. And now good friends,   140
    As you are friends, scholars, and soldiers,
    Give me one poor request.

HORATIO.   What is't, my lord? we will.

HAMLET.   Never make known what you have seen tonight.

BOTH.   My lord we will not.

HAMLET.   Nay, but swear't.

HORATIO.   In faith   145
    My lord, not I.

MARCELLUS.   Nor I my lord, in faith.

HAMLET.   Upon my sword.

MARCELLUS.   We have sworn my lord already.

HAMLET.   Indeed, upon my sword,° indeed.

GHOST.   Swear.   *Ghost cries under the stage.*

HAMLET.   Ha, ha, boy, say'st thou so, art thou there, truepenny°?   150
    Come on, you hear this fellow in the cellarage,
    Consent to swear.

HORATIO.   Propose the oath my lord.

HAMLET.   Never to speak of this that you have seen.
    Swear by my sword.

---

124 *arrant:* thoroughgoing.   127 *circumstance:* ceremony.   138 *honest:* true (not a devil
in disguise).   148 *sword:* (the cross-shaped hilt).   150 *truepenny:* old pal.

GHOST. [*Beneath.*] Swear.   155
HAMLET.   Hic et ubique?° then we'll shift our ground:
   Come hither gentlemen,
   And lay your hands again upon my sword,
   Swear by my sword
   Never to speak of this that you have heard.   160
GHOST. [*Beneath.*] Swear by his sword.
HAMLET.   Well said old mole, canst work i'th' earth so fast?
   A worthy pioner°—once more remove,° good friends.
HORATIO.   O day and night, but this is wondrous strange.
HAMLET.   And therefore as a stranger give it welcome.   165
   There are more things in heaven and earth Horatio,
   Than are dreamt of in your philosophy.
   But come,
   Here as before, never so help you mercy,
   How strange or odd some'er I bear myself,   170
   (As I perchance hereafter shall think meet
   To put an antic disposition on°)
   That you at such times seeing me, never shall
   With arms encumbered° thus, or this head-shake,
   Or by pronouncing of some doubtful phrase,   175
   As "Well, well, we know," or "We could and if we would,"
   Or "If we list° to speak," or "There be and if they might,"
   Or such ambiguous giving out, to note
   That you know aught of me; this do swear,
   So grace and mercy at your need help you.   180
GHOST. [*Beneath.*] Swear.   [*They swear.*]
HAMLET.   Rest, rest, perturbed spirit: so gentlemen,
   With all my love I do commend me to you,°
   And what so poor a man as Hamlet is,
   May do t'express his love and friending to you   185
   God willing shall not lack: let us go in together,
   And still° your fingers on your lips I pray.
   The time is out of joint: O cursèd spite,
   That ever I was born to set it right.
   Nay come, let's go together.   *Exeunt.*   190

ACT 2

Scene 1. [*Polonius's chambers*]

Enter old POLONIUS *with his man* REYNALDO.

POLONIUS.   Give him this money, and these notes Reynaldo.
REYNALDO.   I will my lord.

---

156 *Hic et ubique:* here and everywhere.   163 *pioner:* digger (army trencher).   *remove:*
move elsewhere.   172 *put . . . on:* assume a mad or grotesque behavior.
174 *encumbered:* folded.   177 *list:* please.   183 *commend . . . you:* put myself in your
hands.   187 *still:* always.

POLONIUS. You shall do marvellous° wisely, good Reynaldo,
  Before you visit him, to make inquire
  Of his behaviour.
REYNALDO.   My lord, I did intend it.   5
POLONIUS. Marry, well said, very well said; look you sir,
  Inquire me first what Danskers° are in Paris,
  And how, and who, what means, and where they keep,°
  What company, at what expense, and finding
  By this encompassment° and drift of question   10
  That they do know my son, come you more nearer
  Than your particular demands° will touch it,
  Take you as 'twere some distant knowledge of him,
  As thus, "I know his father, and his friends,
  And in part him"—do you mark this, Reynaldo?   15
REYNALDO. Ay, very well my lord.
POLONIUS. 'And in part him, but,' you may say, 'not well,
  But if't be he I mean, he's very wild,
  Addicted so and so;' and there put on him
  What forgeries° you please, marry none so rank°   20
  As may dishonour him, take heed of that,
  But sir, such wanton, wild, and usual slips,
  As are companions noted and most known
  To youth and liberty.
REYNALDO.   As gaming my lord.
POLONIUS. Ay, or drinking, fencing, swearing,   25
  Quarrelling, drabbing°—you may go so far.
REYNALDO. My lord, that would dishonour him.
POLONIUS. Faith no, as you may season it in the charge.°
  You must not put another scandal on him,
  That he is open to incontinency,°   30
  That's not my meaning, but breathe his faults so quaintly°
  That they may seem the taints of° liberty,
  The flash and outbreak of a fiery mind,
  A savageness in unreclaimèd blood,°
  Of general assault.°
REYNALDO.   But my good lord—   35
POLONIUS. Wherefore° should you do this?
REYNALDO.   Ay my lord,
  I would know that.
POLONIUS.   Marry sir, here's my drift,
  And I believe it is a fetch of warrant:°
  You laying these slight sullies on my son,

---

3 *marvellous:* wonderfully.   7 *danskers:* Danes.   8 *keep:* lodge.   10 *encompassment:*
roundabout way.   12 *particular demands:* specific questions.   20 *forgeries:* inventions.
rank: excessive.   26 *drabbing:* whoring.   28 *season . . . charge:* temper the charge as you
make it.   30 *incontinency:* uncontrolled lechery.   31 *quaintly:* delicately.   32 *taints of:*
blemishes due to.   34 *unreclaimèd blood:* unbridled passion.   35 *general assault:*
attacking all (young men).   36 *Wherefore:* why.   38 *fetch of warrant:* trick guaranteed to
succeed.

As 'twere a thing a little soiled i'th' working,°   40
Mark you, your party in converse, him you would sound,
Having ever seen° in the prenominate crimes°
The youth you breathe of guilty, be assured
He closes with you in this consequence,°
"Good sir," or so, or "friend," or "gentleman,"   45
According to the phrase, or the addition°
Of man and country.

REYNALDO.   Very good my lord.

POLONIUS.   And then sir, does a'° this, a' does, what was I
       about to say?
By the mass I was about to say something,
Where did I leave?   50

REYNALDO.   At "closes in the consequence,"
       At "friend, or so, and gentleman."

POLONIUS.   At "closes in the consequence," ay marry,
He closes thus, "I know the gentleman,
I saw him yesterday, or th'other day,
Or then, or then, with such or such, and as you say,   55
There was a' gaming, there o'ertook in's rouse,°
There falling out at tennis," or perchance
"I saw him enter such a house of sale,"
Videlicet,° a brothel, or so forth. See you now,
Your bait of falsehood takes this carp of truth,   60
And thus do we of wisdom, and of reach,°
With windlasses,° and with assays of bias,°
By indirections find directions out:
So by my former lecture and advice
Shall you my son; you have me, have you not?   65

REYNALDO.   My lord I have.

POLONIUS.   God bye ye, fare ye well.

REYNALDO.   Good my lord.

POLONIUS.   Observe his inclination in yourself.°

REYNALDO.   I shall my lord.

POLONIUS.   And let him ply° his music.

REYNALDO.   Well my lord.   70

POLONIUS.   Farewell.

                                         Exit REYNALDO.

Enter OPHELIA.

                How now Ophelia, what's the matter?

OPHELIA.   O my lord, my lord, I have been so affrighted.

POLONIUS.   With what, i'th'name of God?

---

40 *working:* handling.   42 *Having ever seen:* if he has ever seen.   *prenominate crimes:*
aforenamed sins.   44 *closes . . . consequence:* comes to terms with you as follows.
46 *addition:* title, form of address.   48 *'a:* he.   56 *o'ertook in's rouse:* overcome by
drunkenness.   59 *Videlicet:* namely.   61 *reach:* far-reaching knowledge.
62 *windlasses:* roundabout approaches.   *assays of bias:* indirect attempts.   68 *in yourself:*
personally.   70 *ply:* practice.

OPHELIA.   My lord, as I was sewing in my closet,°
    Lord Hamlet with his doublet all unbraced,°   75
    No hat upon his head, his stockings fouled,
    Ungart'red, and down-gyvèd° to his ankle,
    Pale as his shirt, his knees knocking each other,
    And with a look so piteous in purport°
    As if he had been loosèd out of hell   80
    To speak of horrors, he comes before me.
POLONIUS.   Mad for thy love?
OPHELIA.   My lord I do not know,
    But truly I do fear it.
POLONIUS.   What said he?
OPHELIA.   He took me by the wrist, and held me hard,
    Then goes he to the length of all his arm,°   85
    And with his other hand thus o'er his brow,
    He falls to such perusal of my face
    As° a' would draw it; long stayed he so,
    At last, a little shaking of mine arm,
    And thrice his head thus waving up and down,   90
    He raised a sigh so piteous and profound
    As it did seem to shatter all his bulk,°
    And end his being; that done, he lets me go,
    And with his head over his shoulder turned
    He seemed to find his way without his eyes,   95
    For out adoors he went without their helps,
    And to the last bended their light on me.
POLONIUS.   Come, go with me, I will go seek the king,
    This is the very ecstasy° of love,
    Whose violent property fordoes itself,°   100
    And leads the will to desperate undertakings
    As oft as any passion under heaven
    That does afflict our natures: I am sorry.
    What, have you given him any hard words of late?
OPHELIA.   No my good lord, but as you did command   105
    I did repel his letters, and denied
    His access to me.
POLONIUS.   That hath made him mad.
    I am sorry that with better heed and judgment
    I had not quoted° him. I feared he did but trifle
    And meant to wrack° thee, but beshrew my jealousy:°   110
    By heaven it is as proper to our age
    To cast beyond ourselves in our opinions,°

---

74 *closet:* private room.   75 *doublet all unbraced:* jacket all unfastened.   77 *down-gyvèd:*
down around his ankles (like prisoners' fetters or gyves).   79 *purport:* expression.
85 *goes . . . arm:* holds me at arm's length.   88 *As:* as if.   92 *bulk:* body.   99 *ecstasy:*
madness.   100 *Whose . . . itself:* that, by its violent nature, destroys the lover.
109 *quoted:* observed.   110 *wrack:* ruin.   *beshrew my jealousy:* curse my suspicion.
111–112 *proper . . . opinions:* natural for old people to read more into something than is
actually there.

As it is common for the younger sort
To lack discretion; come, go we to the king,
This must be known, which being kept close, might move   115
More grief to hide, than hate to utter love.°   [*Exeunt.*]

Scene 2. [*A room in the Castle*]

Flourish. Enter KING *and* QUEEN, ROSENCRANTZ *and* GUILDENSTERN, *cum aliis.*

KING.   Welcome dear Rosencrantz and Guildenstern.
Moreover° that we much did long to see you,
The need we have to use you did provoke
Our hasty sending. Something have you heard
Of Hamlet's transformation—so call it.   5
Sith° nor th'exterior nor the inward man
Resembles that it was. What it should be,
More than his father's death, that thus hath put him
So much from th'understanding of himself,
I cannot dream of: I entreat you both,   10
That being of so young days° brought up with him,
And sith so neighboured to his youth and haviour,
That you vouchsafe your rest° here in our court
Some little time, so by your companies
To draw him on to pleasures, and to gather   15
So much as from occasion you may glean,
Whether aught to us unknown afflicts him thus,
That opened° lies within our remedy.
QUEEN.   Good gentlemen, he hath much talked of you,
And sure I am, two men there are not living   20
To whom he more adheres. If it will please you
To show us so much gentry° and good will,
As to expend your time with us awhile,
For the supply and profit of our hope,
Your visitation shall receive such thanks   25
As fits a king's remembrance.
ROSENCRANTZ.   Both your majesties
Might by the sovereign power you have of us,
Put your dread pleasures more into command
Than to entreaty.
GUILDENSTERN.   But we both obey,
And here give up ourselves in the full bent,°   30
To lay our service freely at your feet
To be commanded.
KING.   Thanks Rosencrantz, and gentle Guildenstern.

115–116 *being kept . . . love:* if kept secret, might cause more grief than if we risked the
king's displeasure.   2 *Moreover:* in addition to the fact.   6 *Sith:* since.   11 *of . . .
days:* from your early days.   13 *vouchsafe your rest:* agree to stay.   18 *Opened:*
discovered.   22 *gentry:* courtesy.   30 *in the full bent:* to the utmost (in archery, bending
the bow).

QUEEN.   Thanks Guildenstern, and gentle Rosencrantz.
　And I beseech you instantly to visit　　　　　　　　　　　　　　35
　My too much changèd son. Go some of you
　And bring these gentlemen where Hamlet is.
GUILDENSTERN.   Heavens make our presence and our practices°
　Pleasant and helpful to him.
QUEEN.　　　　　　　　　Ay, amen.

　　　　　　　　　　Exeunt ROSENCRANTZ *and* GUILDENSTERN.

Enter POLONIUS.

POLONIUS.   Th'ambassadors from Norway my good lord,　　　　40
　Are joyfully returned.
KING.   Thou still° hast been the father of good news.
POLONIUS.   Have I, my lord? Assure you, my good liege,
　I hold my duty as I hold my soul,
　Both to my God and to my gracious king;　　　　　　　　45
　And I do think, or else this brain of mine
　Hunts not the trail of policy° so sure
　As it hath used to do, that I have found
　The very cause of Hamlet's lunacy.
KING.   O speak of that, that do I long to hear.　　　　　　　50
POLONIUS.   Give first admittance to th' ambassadors,
　My news shall be the fruit° to that great feast.
KING.   Thyself do grace to them, and bring them in.　　　*[Exit* POLONIUS.*]*
　He tells me my dear Gertrude, he hath found
　The head and source of all your son's distemper.　　　　　55
QUEEN.   I doubt° it is no other but the main,
　His father's death and our o'erhasty marriage.
KING.   Well, we shall sift him.

Enter POLONIUS, VALTEMAND, *and* CORNELIUS.

　　　　　　　　　　Welcome, my good friends.
　Say Valtemand, what from our brother Norway?
VALTEMAND.   Most fair return of greetings and desires;　　　60
　Upon our first,° he sent out to suppress
　His nephew's levies, which to him appeared
　To be a preparation 'gainst the Polack,
　But better looked into, he truly found
　It was against your highness, whereat grieved
　That so his sickness, age, and impotence　　　　　　　　65
　Was falsely borne in hand,° sends out arrests
　On Fortinbras, which he in brief obeys,
　Receives rebuke from Norway, and in fine,°
　Makes vow before his uncle never more　　　　　　　　70
　To give th'assay° of arms against your majesty:

---

38 *practices:* (1) actions (2) plots.　　42 *still:* always.　　47 *policy:* (1) politics (2) plots.
52 *fruit:* dessert.　　56 *doubt:* suspect.　　61 *first:* first presentation.　　67 *borne in hand:*
deceived.　　69 *fine:* finishing.　　71 *assay:* test.

Whereon old Norway, overcome with joy,
Gives him threescore thousand crowns in annual fee,
And his commission to employ those soldiers
So levied (as before) against the Polack,   75
With an entreaty herein further shown,
That it might please you to give quiet pass°
Through your dominions for this enterprise,
On such regards of safety and allowance
As therein are set down.   [*Giving a paper.*]

KING.   It likes° us well,   80
And at our more considered time,° we'll read,
Answer, and think upon this business:
Meantime, we thank you for your well-took labour,
Go to your rest, at night we'll feast together.
Most welcome home.   *Exeunt* AMBASSADORS.

POLONIUS.   This business is well ended.   85
My liege and madam, to expostulate°
What majesty should be, what duty is,
Why day is day, night night, and time is time,
Were nothing but to waste night, day, and time.
Therefore since brevity is the soul of wit,°   90
And tediousness the limbs and outward flourishes,°
I will be brief. Your noble son is mad:
Mad call I it, for to define true madness,
What is't but to be nothing else but mad?
But let that go.

QUEEN.   More matter, with less art.   95

POLONIUS.   Madam, I swear I use no art at all:
That he is mad 'tis true: 'tis true, 'tis pity,
And pity 'tis 'tis true: a foolish figure,°
But farewell it, for I will use no art.
Mad let us grant him then, and now remains   100
That we find out the cause of this effect,
Or rather say, the cause of this defect,
For this effect defective comes by cause:
Thus it remains, and the remainder thus.
Perpend.°   105
I have a daughter, have while she is mine,
Who in her duty and obedience, mark,
Hath given me this, now gather and surmise.
[*Reads.*] "To the celestial, and my soul's idol, the most
beautified° Ophelia,"—   110
That's an ill phrase, a vile phrase, "beautified" is a vile
phrase, but you shall hear. Thus: [*Reads.*]
    "In her excellent white bosom, these," &c.—

77 *pass:* passage.   80 *likes:* pleases.   81 *at . . . time:* when time is available for
consideration.   86 *expostulate:* discuss.   90 *wit:* understanding.   91 *tediousness . . .*
flourishes: embellishments and flourishes cause tedium.   98 *figure:* rhetorical figure.
105 *Perpend:* consider.   110 *beautified:* beautiful.

QUEEN.   Came this from Hamlet to her?

POLONIUS.   Good madam stay awhile, I will be faithful.   [*Reads.*]   115

       "Doubt thou the stars are fire,
         Doubt that the sun doth move,°
       Doubt° truth to be a liar,
         But never doubt I love.

    O dear Ophelia, I am ill at these numbers, I have not   120
art to reckon° my groans, but that I love thee best, O
most best, believe it. Adieu.

       Thine evermore, most dear lady, whilst
         this machine° is to° him, Hamlet."

This in obedience hath my daughter shown me,   125
And more above hath his solicitings,
As they fell out by time, by means, and place,
All given to mine ear.

KING.   But how hath she
Received his love?

POLONIUS.   What do you think of me?

KING.   As of a man faithful and honourable.   130

POLONIUS.   I would fain prove so. But what might you think
When I had seen this hot love on the wing,
As I perceived it (I must tell you that)
Before my daughter told me, what might you,
Or my dear majesty your queen here think,   135
If I had played the desk or table-book,°
Or given my heart a winking° mute and dumb,
Or looked upon this love with idle° sight,
What might you think? No, I went round to work,
And my young mistress this I did bespeak,   140
"Lord Hamlet is a prince out of thy star,°
This must not be:" and then I prescripts° gave her
That she should lock herself from his resort,°
Admit no messengers, receive no tokens:
Which done, she took the fruits of my advice,   145
And he repellèd, a short tale to make,
Fell into a sadness, then into a fast,
Thence to a watch,° thence into a weakness,
Thence to a lightness,° and by this declension,
Into the madness wherein now he raves,   150
And all we mourn for.

KING.   Do you think 'tis this?

QUEEN.   It may be very like.

POLONIUS.   Hath there been such a time, I would fain know that,

---

117 *move:* (as it was believed to do, around the earth).   118 *Doubt:* suspect.
121 *reckon:* express in meter.   124 *machine:* body.   *to:* attached to.   136 *played . . .*
book: kept it concealed as in a desk or personal notebook.   137 *given . . . winking:* had my
heart shut its eyes to the matter.   138 *idle:* unseeing.   141 *out . . . star:* out of your
sphere (above you in station).   142 *prescripts:* orders.   143 *resort:* company.
148 *watch:* sleeplessness.   149 *lightness:* lightheadedness.

That I have positively said "Tis so,"
When it proved otherwise?

KING.   Not that I know.   155

POLONIUS. Take this, from this, if this be otherwise;

[*Points to his head and shoulder.*]

If circumstances lead me, I will find
Where truth is hid, though it were hid indeed
Within the center.

KING.   How may we try° it further?

POLONIUS. You know sometimes he walks four hours together   160
Here in the lobby.

QUEEN.   So he does indeed.

POLONIUS. At such a time, I'll loose° my daughter to him.
Be you and I behind an arras° then,
Mark the encounter: if he love her not,
And be not from his reason fall'n thereon,   165
Let me be no assistant for a state,°
But keep a farm and carters.

KING.   We will try it.

Enter HAMLET reading on a book.

QUEEN. But look where sadly the poor wretch comes reading.

POLONIUS. Away, I do beseech you both away,
I'll board him presently,° O give me leave.   *Exeunt KING and QUEEN.*   170
How does my good Lord Hamlet?

HAMLET. Well, God-a-mercy.

POLONIUS. Do you know me, my lord?

HAMLET. Excellent well, you are a fishmonger.°

POLONIUS. Not I my lord.   175

HAMLET. Then I would you were so honest a man.

POLONIUS. Honest, my lord?

HAMLET. Ay sir, to be honest as this world goes, is to be one
man picked out of ten thousand.

POLONIUS. That's very true, my lord.   180

HAMLET. For if the sun breed maggots° in a dead dog, being a good
kissing carrion°—have you a daughter?

POLONIUS. I have my lord.

HAMLET. Let her not walk i'th'sun:° conception° is a blessing, but as
your daughter may conceive, friend look to'it.   185

POLONIUS. [*Aside.*] How say you by that? Still harping on my daughter,
yet he knew me not at first, a' said I was a fishmonger.

---

159 *try:* test.   162 *loose:* (1) release (2) turn loose.   163 *arras:* hanging tapestry.
166 *assistant . . . state:* state official.   170 *board him presently:* approach him immediately.
174 *fishmonger:* (1) fish dealer (2) pimp.   181 *breed maggots* (in the belief that the rays of
the sun caused maggots to breed in dead flesh).   182 *kissing carrion:* piece of flesh for
kissing.   184 *Let . . . sun:* (1) (proverbial: "out of God's blessing, into the warm sun") (2)
because the sun is a breeder (3) don't let her go near me (with a pun on "sun" and "son").
conception: (1) understanding (2) pregnancy.

A' is far gone, far gone, and truly in my youth, I suffered
much extremity for love, very near this. I'll speak to him
again. What do you read my lord?   190
HAMLET.   Words, words, words.
POLONIUS.   What is the matter my lord?
HAMLET.   Between who?
POLONIUS.   I mean the matter° that you read, my lord.
HAMLET.   Slanders sir; for the satirical rogue says here, that old men   195
have grey beards, that their faces are wrinkled, their eyes
purging thick amber and plum-tree gum,° and that they
have a plentiful lack of wit, together with most weak
hams. All which sir, though I most powerfully and
potently believe, yet I hold it not honesty° to have it thus set   200
down, for yourself sir shall grow old as I am: if like a crab
you could go backward.
POLONIUS.   [*Aside.*] Though this be madness, yet there is method
in't.
Will you walk out of the air° my lord?   205
HAMLET.   Into my grave.
POLONIUS.   [*Aside.*] Indeed that's out of the air; how pregnant°
sometimes his replies are, a happiness° that often
madness hits on, which reason and sanity could not so
prosperously° be delivered of. I will leave him, and   210
suddenly contrive the means of meeting between him
and my daughter. My honourable lord, I will most
humbly take leave of you.
HAMLET.   You cannot sir take from me anything that I will more
willingly part withal: except my life, except my life,   215
except my life.
POLONIUS.   Fare you well my lord.
HAMLET.   These tedious old fools.

Enter ROSENCRANTZ and GUILDENSTERN.

POLONIUS.   You go to seek the Lord Hamlet, there he is.
ROSENCRANTZ.   [*To Polonius.*] God save you sir.   [*Exit POLONIUS.*]   220
GUILDENSTERN.   My honoured lord.
ROSENCRANTZ.   My most dear lord.
HAMLET.   My excellent good friends, how dost thou Guildenstern?
Ah Rosencrantz, good lads, how do you both?
ROSENCRANTZ.   As the indifferent° children of the earth.   225
GUILDENSTERN.   Happy, in that we are not over-happy:
On Fortune's cap we are not the very button.°
HAMLET.   Nor the soles of her shoe?

---

194 *matter:* (1) content (Polonius's meaning) (2) cause of a quarrel (Hamlet's interpretation).
197–198 *purging . . . gum:* exuding a viscous yellowish discharge.   200 *honesty:* decency.
205 *out . . . air:* (in the belief that fresh air was bad for the sick).   207 *pregnant:* full of
meaning.   208 *happiness:* aptness.   210 *prosperously:* successfully.   225 *indifferent:*
ordinary.   227 *on Fortune's . . . button:* we are not at the height of our fortunes.

ROSENCRANTZ.   Neither my lord.

HAMLET.   Then you live about her waist, or in the middle of her   230
5   favours?

GUILDENSTERN.   Faith, her privates° we.

HAMLET.   In the secret parts of Fortune? O most true, she is a
       strumpet.° What news?

ROSENCRANTZ.   None my lord, but that the world's grown honest.   235

HAMLET.   Then is doomsday near: but your news is not true. Let me
       question more in particular: what have you my good
       friends, deserved at the hands of Fortune, that she sends
       you to prison hither?

GUILDENSTERN.   Prison, my lord?   240

HAMLET.   Denmark's a prison.

ROSENCRANTZ.   Then is the world one.

HAMLET.   A goodly one, in which there are many confines, wards,°
       and dungeons; Denmark being one o'th'worst.

ROSENCRANTZ.   We think not so my lord.   245

HAMLET.   Why then 'tis none to you; for there is nothing either good
       or bad, but thinking makes it so: to me it is a prison.

ROSENCRANTZ.   Why then your ambition makes it one: 'tis too narrow for
       your mind.

HAMLET.   O God, I could be bounded in a nutshell, and count   250
       myself a king of infinite space; were it not that I have bad
       dreams.

GUILDENSTERN.   Which dreams indeed are ambition: for the very substance
       of the ambitious, is merely the shadow of a dream.

HAMLET.   A dream itself is but a shadow.   255

ROSENCRANTZ.   Truly, and I hold ambition of so airy and light a quality,
       that it is but a shadow's shadow.

HAMLET.   Then are our beggars bodies, and our monarchs and
       outstretched heroes the beggars' shadows:° shall we to th'
       court? for by my fay,° I cannot reason.   260

BOTH.   We'll wait upon° you.

HAMLET.   No such matter. I will not sort° you with the rest of my
       servants: for to speak to you like an honest man, I am most
       dreadfully attended. But in the beaten way of friendship,
       what make you at Elsinore?   265

ROSENCRANTZ.   To visit you my lord, no other occasion.

HAMLET.   Beggar that I am, I am even poor in thanks, but I thank
       you, and sure dear friends, my thanks are too dear a
       halfpenny:° were you not sent for? is it your own inclining?
       is it a free° visitation? come, come, deal justly with me,   270
       come, come, nay speak.

---

232 *privates:* (1) intimate friends (2) private parts.   234 *strumpet:* inconstant woman,
giving favor to many.   243 *wards:* cells.   258–259 *Then are . . . shadows:* then beggars
are the true substance and ambitious kings and heroes the elongated shadows of beggars'
bodies (for only a real substance can cast a shadow).   260 *fay:* faith.   261 *wait upon:*
attend.   262 *sort:* class.   268–269 *too dear a halfpenny:* worth not even a halfpenny (as I
have no influence).   270 *free:* voluntary.

GUILDENSTERN. What should we say my lord?

HAMLET. Anything but to th'purpose: you were sent for, and there
is a kind of confession in your looks, which your modesties
have not craft enough to colour: I know the good king and   275
queen have sent for you.

ROSENCRANTZ. To what end my lord?

HAMLET. That you must teach me: but let me conjure° you, by the
rights of our fellowship, by the consonancy of our youth,°
by the obligation of our ever-preserved love, and by what   280
more dear a better proposer can charge you withal,° be
even and direct with me whether you were sent for or no.

ROSENCRANTZ. [*Aside to Guildenstern.*] What say you?

HAMLET. Nay then, I have an eye of° you: If you love me,
hold not off.   285

GUILDENSTERN. My lord, we were sent for.

famous HAMLET. I will tell you why, so shall my anticipation prevent° your
discovery,° and your secrecy to the king and queen moult
no feather.° I have of late, but wherefore I know not, lost all
my mirth, forgone all custom of exercises: and indeed it   290
goes so heavily with my disposition, that this goodly
frame the earth, seems to me a sterile promontory, this
most excellent canopy the air, look you, this brave°   *—dim world view, negative*
o'erhanging firmament, this majestical roof fretted° with
golden fire,° why it appeareth nothing to me but a foul and   295
pestilent congregation of vapours.° What a piece of work is
a man! How noble in reason, how infinite in faculties,° in
form and moving, how express° and admirable in action,
how like an angel in apprehension, how like a god: the
beauty of the world; the paragon of animals; and yet to   300
me, what is this quintessence of dust? Man delights not
me, no, nor woman neither, though by your smiling, you
seem to say so.

ROSENCRANTZ. My lord, there was no such stuff in my thoughts.

HAMLET. Why did ye laugh then, when I said 'man delights not me'?   305

ROSENCRANTZ. To think, my lord, if you delight not in man, what lenten
entertainment° the players shall receive from you: we coted°
them on the way, and hither are they coming to offer you
service.

HAMLET. He that plays the king shall be welcome, his majesty shall   310
have tribute of me, the adventurous knight° shall use his
foil and target,° the lover shall not sigh gratis,° the humorous

---

278 *conjure:* appeal to.   279 *consonancy . . . youth:* agreement in our ages.   281 *withal:*
with.   284 *of:* on.   287 *prevent:* forestall.   288 *discovery:* disclosure.
288–289 *moult no feather:* change in no way.   293 *brave:* splendid.   294 *fretted:*
ornamented with fretwork.   295 *golden fire:* stars.   296 *pestilent . . . vapours:* (clouds
were believed to carry contagion).   297 *faculties:* physical powers.   298 *express:* well
framed.   306–307 *lenten entertainment:* meager treatment.   307 *coted:* passed.
311 *adventurous knight:* knight errant (a popular stage character).   312 *foil and target:*
sword blunted for stage fighting, and small shield.   312 *gratis:* (without applause).

hall end his part in peace,° the clown shall make
   ugh whose lungs are tickle o'th'sere,° and the lady
      y her mind freely: or the blank verse shall halt° for't.   315
   What players are they?
ROSENCRANTZ.   Even those you were wont to take such delight in, the
   tragedians of the city.
HAMLET.   How chances it they travel? Their residence° both in
   reputation and profit was better both ways.   320
ROSENCRANTZ.   I think their inhibition comes by the means of the late
   innovation.°
HAMLET.   Do they hold the same estimation they did when I was in
   the city; are they so followed?
ROSENCRANTZ.   No indeed are they not.   325
HAMLET.   How comes it? Do they grow rusty?
ROSENCRANTZ.   Nay, their endeavour keeps in the wonted pace; but there
   is sir an aery° of children, like eyases,° that cry out on the
   top of question,° and are most tyrannically° clapped for't:
   these are now the fashion, and so berattle° the common   330
   stages° (so they call them) that many wearing rapiers° are
   afraid of goose-quills,° and dare scarce come thither.
HAMLET.   What, are they children? Who maintains 'em? How are
   they escoted°? Will they pursue the quality no longer than
   they can sing°? Will they not say afterwards if they should   335
   grow themselves to common players (as it is most like, if
   their means are not better) their writers do them wrong, to
   make them exclaim against their own succession°?
ROSENCRANTZ.   Faith, there has been much to-do on both sides: and the
   nation holds it no sin to tarre° them to controversy. There   340
   was for a while, no money bid for argument,° unless the
   poet and the player went to cuffs in the question.°
HAMLET.   Is't possible?
GUILDENSTERN.   O there has been much throwing about of brains.
HAMLET.   Do the boys carry it away°?   345
ROSENCRANTZ.   Ay, that they do my lord, Hercules and his load too.°

312–313 *humorous man:* eccentric character with a dominant trait, caused by an excess of
one of the four humors, or bodily fluids.   313 *in peace:* without interruption.
314 *tickle o'th'sere:* attuned to respond to laughter, as the finely adjusted gunlock responds
to the touch of the trigger (fr. hunting).   315 *halt:* limp (if she adds her own opinions
and spoils the meter).   319 *residence:* i.e., in a city theatre.   321–322 *inhibition . . .
innovation:* i.e., they were forced out of town by a more popular theatrical fashion. The
following speeches allude to the "War of the Theatres" (1601–1602) between the child and
adult acting companies.   328 *aery:* nest.   *eyases:* young hawks.   328–329 *that cry . . .
question:* whose shrill voices can be heard above all others.   329 *tyrannically:* strongly.
330 *berattle:* berate.   330–331 *common stages:* public playhouses (the children's companies
performed in private theatres).   331 *wearing rapiers:* (worn by gentlemen).   332 *goose-
quills:* pens (of satirical dramatists who wrote for the children).   334 *escoted:* supported.
334–335 *pursue . . . sing:* continue acting only until their voices change.   338 *succession:*
inheritance.   340 *tarre:* provoke.   341 *bid for argument:* paid for the plot of a proposed
play.   342 *went . . . question:* came to blows on the subject.   345 *carry it away:* carry off
the prize.   346 *Hercules . . . too:* (Shakespeare's own company at the Globe Theatre,
whose sign was Hercules carrying the globe of the world).

HAMLET.   It is not very strange, for my uncle is king of Denmark,
   and those that would make mows° at him while my father
   lived, give twenty, forty, fifty, a hundred ducats apiece
   for his picture in little.° 'Sblood,° there is something in this   350
   more than natural, if philosophy° could find it out.

A flourish for the Players.

GUILDENSTERN.   There are the players.
HAMLET.   Gentlemen, you are welcome to Elsinore: your hands,
   come then, th'appurtenance° of welcome is fashion and
   ceremony; let me comply with you in this garb,° lest my   355
   extent° to the players, which I tell you must show fairly
   outwards, should more appear like entertainment than
   yours.° You are welcome: but my uncle-father, and aunt-
   mother, are deceived.
GUILDENSTERN.   In what my dear lord?   360
HAMLET.   I am but mad north-north-west; when the wind is southerly,
   I know a hawk from a handsaw.°

Enter POLONIUS.

POLONIUS.   Well be with you, gentlemen.
HAMLET.   Hark you Guildenstern, and you too, at each ear a hearer:
   that great baby you see there is not yet out of his swaddling   365
   clouts.°
ROSENCRANTZ.   Happily° he is the second time come to them, for they say
   an old man is twice a child.
HAMLET.   I will prophesy, he comes to tell me of the players, mark
   it.—You say right sir, a Monday morning, 'twas then   370
   indeed.
POLONIUS.   My lord, I have news to tell you.
HAMLET.   My lord, I have news to tell you. When Roscius° was an
   actor in Rome—
POLONIUS.   The actors are come hither, my lord.   375
HAMLET.   Buz, buz.°
POLONIUS.   Upon my honour.
HAMLET.   Then came each actor on his ass—
POLONIUS.   The best actors in the world, either for tragedy, comedy,
   history, pastoral, pastoral-comical, historical-pastoral,   380
   tragical-historical, tragical-comical-historical-pastoral,
   scene individable,° or poem unlimited.° Seneca cannot be

---

348 *mows:* mouths, grimaces.   350 *little:* a miniature.   *'Sblood:* by God's blood.
351 *philosophy:* science.   354 *appurtenance:* accessory.   355 *comply . . . garb:* observe the
formalities with you in this style.   356 *extent:* i.e., of welcome.   357–358 *should . . .
yours:* should appear more hospitable than yours.   362 *I know . . . handsaw:* I can tell the
difference between two things that are unlike ("hawk" = (1) bird of prey (2) mattock,
pickaxe; "handsaw" = (1) hernshaw or heron bird (2) small saw).   356–366 *swaddling
clouts:* strips of cloth binding a newborn baby.   367 *Happily:* perhaps.   373 *Roscius:*
famous Roman actor.   376 *Buz, buz:* (contemptuous).   382 *scene individable:* play
observing the unities (time, place, action).   *poem unlimited:* play ignoring the unities.

too heavy, nor Plautus° too light for the law of writ, and the
liberty:° these are the only men.

HAMLET. O Jephthah,° judge of Israel, what a treasure hadst thou.   385

POLONIUS. What a treasure had he, my lord?

HAMLET. Why
    'One fair daughter and no more,
      The which he lovèd passing° well.'

POLONIUS. [*Aside.*] Still on my daughter.   390

HAMLET. Am I not i'th' right, old Jephthah?

POLONIUS. If you call me Jephthah my lord, I have a daughter that I
love passing well.

HAMLET. Nay, that follows not.

POLONIUS. What follows then, my lord?   395

HAMLET. Why
    "As by lot, God wot,"
and then you know
    "It came to pass, as most like° it was:"
the first row° of the pious chanson will show you more, for   400
look where my abridgement° comes.

Enter four or five PLAYERS.

You are welcome masters, welcome all. I am glad to see
thee well: welcome, good friends. O my old friend, why
thy face is valanced° since I saw thee last, com'st thou to
beard me in Denmark? What, my young lady° and   405
mistress? by'r lady, your ladyship is nearer to heaven than
when I saw you last, by the altitude of a chopine.° Pray
God your voice, like a piece of uncurrent° gold, be not
cracked within the ring.° Masters, you are all welcome:
we'll e'en to't like French falconers, fly at any thing we see:°   410
we'll have a speech straight. Come give us a taste of your
quality: come, a passionate speech.

I. PLAYER. What speech, my good lord?

HAMLET. I heard thee speak me a speech once, but it was never
acted, or if it was, not above once, for the play I remember   415
pleased not the million, 'twas caviary to the general,° but it
was (as I received it, and others, whose judgments in such
matters cried in the top of mine°) an excellent play, well
digested in the scenes, set down with as much modesty as

382–383 *Seneca, Plautus:* Roman writers of tragedy and comedy, respectively.
383–384 *law . . . liberty:* "rules" regarding the unities and those exercising freedom from
the unities.   385 *Jephthah:* (who was forced to sacrifice his only daughter because of a
rash promise: Judges 11:29–39).   389 *passing:* surpassingly.   399 *like:* likely.
400 *row:* stanza.   401 *abridgement:* (the players who will cut short my song).
404 *valanced:* fringed with a beard.   405 *lady:* boy playing women's role.   407 *chopine:*
thick-soled shoe.   408 *uncurrent:* not legal tender.   409 *ring:* (1) ring enclosing the
design on a gold coin (to crack it within the ring [to steal the gold] made it "uncurrent")
(2) sound.   410 *fly . . . see:* undertake any difficulty.   416 *caviary . . . general:* like
caviar, too rich for the general public.   418 *cried . . . mine:* spoke with more authority
than mine.

cunning.° I remember one said there were no sallets° in the 420
lines, to make the matter savoury, nor no matter in the
phrase that might indict the author of° affection, but called
it an honest method, as wholesome as sweet, and by very
much more handsome than fine:° one speech in't I chiefly
loved, 'twas Aeneas' tale to Dido, and thereabout of it 425
especially where he speaks of Priam's slaughter.° If it live in
your memory begin at this line, let me see, let me see:
  "The rugged Pyrrhus,° like th'Hyrcanian beast"°—
'tis not so: it begins with Pyrrhus—
  "The rugged Pyrrhus, he whose sable° arms, 430
Black as his purpose, did the night resemble
When he lay couched in th'ominous horse,°
Hath now this dread and black complexion smeared
With heraldy more dismal: head to foot
Now is he total gules,° horridly tricked° 435
With blood of fathers, mothers, daughters, sons,
Baked and impasted° with the parching° streets,
That lend a tyrannous and damnèd light
To their lord's murder. Roasted in wrath and fire,
And thus o'er-sizèd° with coagulate gore, 440
With eyes like carbuncles,° the hellish Pyrrhus
Old grandsire Priam seeks;"
So proceed you.
POLONIUS. 'Fore God, my lord, well spoken, with good accent and
  good discretion.° 445
I. PLAYER. "Anon he finds him,
Striking too short at Greeks, his antique° sword,
Rebellious to his arm, lies where it falls,
Repugnant to command;° unequal matched,
Pyrrhus at Priam drives, in rage strikes wide, 450
But with the whiff and wind of his fell° sword,
Th'unnerved father falls: then senseless Ilium,°
Seeming to feel this blow, with flaming top
Stoops to his base; and with a hideous crash
Takes prisoner Pyrrhus' ear. For lo, his sword 455
Which was declining on the milky head
Of reverend Priam, seemed i'th'air to stick;
So as a painted° tyrant Pyrrhus stood,

419–420 *modesty as cunning:* moderation as skill.   420 *sallets:* spicy bits.   422 *indict . . .*
of: charge . . . with.   424 *handsome than fine:* dignified than finely wrought.
426 *Priam's slaughter:* the murder of the King of Troy (as told in the Aeneid).
428 *Pyrrhus:* son of Achilles.   *Hyrcanian beast:* tiger noted for fierceness.   430 *sable:*
black.   432 *horse:* the hollow wooden horse used by the Greeks to enter Troy.
435 *gules:* red.   *horridly tricked:* horribly decorated.   437 *impasted:* coagulated.
parching: (because the city was on fire).   440 *o'er-sizèd:* covered over.   441 *carbuncles:*
red gems.   445 *discretion:* interpretation.   447 *antique:* ancient.   449 *Repugnant to*
command: refusing to obey its commander.   451 *fell:* savage.   452 *senseless Ilium:*
unfeeling Troy.   458 *painted:* pictured.

And like a neutral to his will and matter,°
Did nothing: 460
But as we often see, against° some storm,
A silence in the heavens, the rack° stand still,
The bold winds speechless, and the orb° below
As hush as death, anon the dreadful thunder
Doth rend the region, so after Pyrrhus' pause,   465
A rousèd vengeance sets him new awork,
And never did the Cyclops'° hammers fall
On Mars's armour, forged for proof eterne,°
With less remorse than Pyrrhus' bleeding sword
Now falls on Priam.   470
Out, out, thou strumpet Fortune: all you gods,
In general synod° take away her power,
Break all the spokes and fellies from her wheel,°
And bowl the round nave° down the hill of heaven
As low as to the fiends."°   475

POLONIUS.   This is too long.

HAMLET.   It shall to the barber's with your beard; prithee say on: he's
    for a jig, or a tale of bawdry, or he sleeps. Say on, come to
    Hecuba.

I. PLAYER.   "But who, ah woe, had seen the mobled° queen—"   480

HAMLET.   "The mobled queen"?

POLONIUS.   That's good, "mobled queen" is good.

I. PLAYER.   "Run barefoot up and down, threat'ning the flames
    With bissom rheum,° a clout° upon that head
    Where late the diadem stood, and for a robe,   485
    About her lank and all o'er-teemèd° loins,
    A blanket in the alarm of fear caught up—
    Who this had seen, with tongue in venom steeped,
    'Gainst Fortune's state° would treason have pronounced;
    But if the gods themselves did see her then,   490
    When she saw Pyrrhus make malicious sport
    In mincing with his sword her husband's limbs,
    The instant burst of clamour that she made,
    Unless things mortal move them not at all,
    Would have made milch° the burning eyes of heaven,   495
    And passion in the gods."

POLONIUS.   Look whe'r° he has not turned° his colour, and has tears in's
    eyes, prithee no more.

HAMLET.   'Tis well, I'll have thee speak out the rest of this soon.

---

459 *like . . . matter:* unmoved by either his purpose or its achievement.   461 *against:*
before.   462 *rack:* clouds.   463 *orb:* earth.   467 *Cyclops:* workmen of Vulcan,
armorer of the gods.   468 *for proof eterne:* to be eternally invincible.   472 *synod:*
assembly.   473 *fellies . . . wheel:* curved pieces of the rim of the wheel that fortune turns,
representing a man's fortunes.   474 *nave:* hub.   475 *fiends:* i.e., of hell.   480 *mobled:*
muffled in a scarf.   484 *bissom rheum:* binding tears.   *clout:* cloth.   486 *o'erteemed:*
worn out by excessive childbearing.   489 *state:* reign.   495 *milch:* milky, moist.
497 *whe'r:* whether.   *turned:* changed.

Good my lord, will you see the players well bestowed;° do   500
you hear, let them be well used, for they are the abstract°
and brief chronicles° of the time; after your death you were
better have a bad epitaph than their ill report while you
live.

POLONIUS. My lord, I will use them according to their desert.°   505

HAMLET. God's bodkin° man, much better. Use every man after° his
desert, and who shall 'scape whipping? Use them after
you own honour and dignity: the less they deserve, the
more merit is in your bounty. Take them in.

POLONIUS. Come sirs.   *Exeunt* POLONIUS *and* PLAYERS.   510

HAMLET. Follow him friends, we'll hear a play tomorrow; [*Stops the
First Player.*] dost thou hear me, old friend, can you play
The Murder of Gonzago?

I. PLAYER Ay my lord.

HAMLET. We'll ha't tomorrow night. You could for a need° study a   515
speech of some dozen or sixteen lines, which I would set
down and insert in't, could you not?

I. PLAYER. Ay my lord.

HAMLET. Very well, follow that lord, and look you mock him not.

                                        [*Exit* FIRST PLAYER.]

[*To Rosencrantz and Guildenstern.*] My good friends, I'll   520
leave you till night, you are welcome to Elsinore.

ROSENCRANTZ. Good my lord.   [*Exeunt* ROSENCRANTZ *and* GUILDENSTERN.]

HAMLET. Ay so, God bye to you, now I am alone.
O what a rogue and peasant slave am I.
Is it not monstrous that this player here,
But in a fiction, in a dream of passion,°   525
Could force his soul so to his own conceit°
That from her working all his visage wanned,°
Tears in his eyes, distraction in his aspect,
A broken voice, and his whole function° suiting
With forms° to his conceit; and all for nothing,   530
For Hecuba!
What's Hecuba to him, or he to Hecuba,
That he should weep for her? what would he do,
Had he the motive and the cue for passion
That I have? he would drown the stage with tears,   535
And cleave the general ear° with horrid speech,
Make mad the guilty and appal the free,°
Confound° the ignorant, and amaze indeed
The very faculties of eyes and ears; yet I,   540

---

500 *bestowed:* lodged.   501 *abstract:* summary (noun).   502 *brief chronicles:* history in
brief.   505 *desert:* merit.   506 *God's bodkin:* God's little body, the communion wafer (an
oath).   *after:* according to.   515 *for a need:* if necessary.   526 *dream of passion:*
portrayal of emotion.   527 *conceit:* imagination.   528 *wanned:* grew pale.
530 *function:* bearing.   531 *With forms:* in appearance.   537 *general ear:* ears of all in
the audience.   538 *free:* innocent.   539 *Confound:* confuse.

A dull and muddy-mettled° rascal, peak°
Like John-a-dreams,° unpregnant of° my cause,
And can say nothing; no, not for a king,
Upon whose property and most dear life,
A damned defeat was made: am I a coward?   545
Who calls me villain, breaks my pate° across,
Plucks off my beard° and blows it in my face,
Tweaks me by the nose, gives me the lie i'th'throat
As deep as to the lungs,° who does me this?
Ha, 'swounds,° I should take it; for it cannot be   550
But I am pigeon-livered,° and lack gall
To make oppression bitter, or ere this
I should ha' fatted all the region kites°
With this slave's offal: bloody, bawdy villain,
Remorseless, treacherous, lecherous, kindless° villain!   555
O vengeance!
Why what an ass am I, this is most brave,°
That I, the son of a dear father murdered,
Prompted to my revenge by heaven and hell,
Must like a whore unpack my heart with words,   560
And fall a-cursing like a very drab,°
A scullion,° fie upon't, foh.
About, my brains; hum, I have heard,
That guilty creatures sitting at a play,
Have by the very cunning of the scene   565
Been struck so to the soul, that presently°
They have proclaimed their malefactions:
For murder, though it have no tongue, will speak
With most miraculous organ:/I'll have these players
Play something like the murder of my father   570
Before mine uncle, I'll observe his looks,
I'll tent° him to the quick, if a' do blench°
I know my course./The spirit that I have seen
May be a devil, and the devil hath power
T'assume a pleasing shape, yea, and perhaps   575
Out of my weakness, and my melancholy,
As he is very potent with such spirits,
Abuses me to damn me; I'll have grounds
More relative than this: the play's the thing
Wherein I'll catch the conscience of the king.   *Exit.*

---

541 *muddy-mettled:* dull-spirited.   *peak:* pine, mope.   542 *John-a-dreams:* a daydreaming
fellow.   *unpregnant of:* unstirred by.   546 *pate:* head.   547 *Plucks . . . beard:* (a way
of giving insult).   548–549 *gives . . . lungs:* insults me by calling me a liar of the worst
kind (the lungs being deeper than the throat).   550 *'swounds:* God's wounds.
551 *pigeon-livered:* meek and uncouraged.   553 *region kites:* vultures of the upper air.
555 *kindless:* unnatural.   557 *brave:* fine.   561 *drab:* whore.   562 *scullion:* kitchen
wench.   566 *presently:* immediately.   572 *tent:* probe.   *blench:* flinch.

[ACT 3]

Scene 1. [A room in the castle]

Enter KING, QUEEN, POLONIUS, OPHELIA, ROSENCRANTZ, GUILDENSTERN, and LORDS.

KING.   And can you by no drift of conference°
    Get from him why he puts on this confusion,°
    Grating so harshly all his days of quiet
    With turbulent and dangerous lunacy?
ROSENCRANTZ.   He does confess he feels himself distracted,   5
    But from what cause, a' will by no means speak.
GUILDENSTERN.   Nor do we find him forward to be sounded,°
    But with a crafty madness keeps aloof
    When we would bring him on to some confession
    Of his true state.
QUEEN.   Did he receive you well?   10
ROSENCRANTZ.   Most like a gentleman.
GUILDENSTERN.   But with much forcing of his disposition.°
ROSENCRANTZ.   Niggard of question,° but of our demands
    Most free in his reply.
QUEEN.   Did you assay° him
    To any pastime?   15
ROSENCRANTZ.   Madam, it so fell out that certain players
    We o'er-raught° on the way: of these we told him,
    And there did seem in him a kind of joy
    To hear of it: they are here about the court,
    And as I think, they have already order   20
    This night to play before him.
POLONIUS.   'Tis most true,
    And he beseeched me to entreat your majesties
    To hear and see the matter.°
KING.   With all my heart, and it doth much content me
    To hear him so inclined.   25
    Good gentlemen, give him a further edge,°
    And drive his purpose into these delights.
ROSENCRANTZ.   We shall my lord.   *Exeunt ROSENCRANTZ and GUILDENSTERN.*
KING.   Sweet Gertrude, leave us too,
    For we have closely° sent for Hamlet hither,
    That he, as 'twere by accident, may here   30
    Affront° Ophelia;
    Her father and myself, lawful espials,°

---

1 *drift of conference:* turn of conversation.   2 *puts . . . confusion:* seems so distracted ("puts on" indicates the king's private suspicion that Hamlet is playing mad).   7 *forward . . . sounded:* disposed to be sounded out.   12 *forcing . . . disposition:* forcing himself to be so. 13 *Niggard of question:* unwilling to talk.   14 *assay:* tempt.   17 *o'er-raught:* overtook. 23 *matter:* i.e., of the play.   26 *give . . . edge:* encourage his keen interest.   29 *closely:* secretly.   31 *Affront:* meet face to face with.   32 *espials:* spies.

Will so bestow° ourselves, that seeing unseen,
We may of their encounter frankly° judge,
And gather by him as he is behaved,   35
If't be th'affliction of his love or no
That thus he suffers for.

QUEEN.   I shall obey you.
And for your part Ophelia, I do wish
That your good beauties be the happy cause
Of Hamlet's wildness, so shall I hope your virtues   40
Will bring him to his wonted° way again,
To both your honours.

OPHELIA.   Madam, I wish it may.   [*Exit* QUEEN.]

POLONIUS.   Ophelia, walk you here—Gracious,° so please you,
We will bestow ourselves—read on this book,°
That show of such an exercise° may colour°   45
Your loneliness; we are oft to blame in this,
'Tis too much proved,° that with devotion's visage
And pious action, we do sugar o'er
The devil himself.

KING.   [*Aside.*] O 'tis too true,°
How smart a lash that speech doth give my conscience.   50
The harlot's cheek, beautied with plast'ring art,
Is not more ugly to° the thing that helps it,
Than is my deed to my most painted word:°
O heavy burden!

POLONIUS.   I hear him coming, let's withdraw my lord.   *Exeunt.*   55

Enter HAMLET.

HAMLET.   To be, or not to be, that is the question,
Whether 'tis nobler in the mind° to suffer
The slings and arrows of outrageous fortune,
Or to take arms against a sea of troubles,
And by opposing, end them: to die, to sleep,   60
No more; and by a sleep, to say we end
The heart-ache, and the thousand natural shocks
That flesh is heir to; 'tis a consummation
Devoutly to be wished. To die, to sleep,
To sleep, perchance to dream, ay there's the rub,°   65
For in that sleep of death what dreams may come
When we have shuffled off this mortal coil°
Must give us pause—there's the respect°

33, 44 *bestow:* place.   34 *frankly:* freely.   41 *wonted:* customary.   43 *Gracious:* i.e.,
Your Grace.   44 *book:* (of prayer).   45 *exercise:* religious exercise.   *colour:* make
plausible.   47 *'Tis . . . proved:* it is all too apparent.   49 *'tis too true:* (the king's first
indication that he is guilty).   52 *to:* compared to.   51–53 *harlot's cheek . . . word:* just as
the harlot's cheek is even uglier by contrast to the makeup that tries to beautify it, so my
deed is uglier by contrast to the hypocritical words under which I hide it.   57 *nobler in
the mind:* best, according to "sovereign" reason.   65 *rub:* obstacle.   67 *mortal coil:*
(1) turmoil of mortal life (2) coil of flesh encircling the body.   68 *respect:* consideration.

That makes calamity of so long life:°
For who would bear the whips and scorns of time,   70
Th'oppressor's wrong, the proud man's contumely,°
The pangs of disprized love, the law's delay,°
The insolence of office,° and the spurns
That patient merit of th'unworthy takes,
When he himself might his quietus° make   75
With a bare bodkin;° who would fardels° bear,
To grunt and sweat under a weary life,
But that the dread of something after death,
The undiscovered° country, from whose bourn°
No traveller returns, puzzles the will,   80
And makes us rather bear those ills we have,
Than fly to others that we know not of.
Thus conscience does make cowards of us all,
And thus the native hue° of resolution
Is sicklied o'er with the pale cast of thought,   85
And enterprises of great pitch° and moment,°
With this regard° their currents turn awry,°
And lose the name of action. Soft you now,
The fair Ophelia—Nymph, in thy orisons°
Be all my sins remembered.

OPHELIA.   Good my lord,   90
　How does your honour for this many a day°?
HAMLET.   I humbly thank you: well, well, well.
OPHELIA.   My lord, I have remembrances of yours
　That I have longèd long to re-deliver,
　I pray you now receive them.
HAMLET.   No, not I,   95
　I never gave you aught.
OPHELIA.   My honoured lord, you know right well you did,
　And with them words of so sweet breath° composed
　As made the things more rich: their perfume lost,
　Take these again, for to the noble mind   100
　Rich gifts wax° poor when givers prove unkind.
　There my lord.
HAMLET.   Ha, ha, are you honest°?
OPHELIA.   My lord.
HAMLET.   Are you fair°?   105
OPHELIA.   What means your lordship?

---

69 *makes calamity of so long life:* makes living long a calamity.　71 *contumely:* contempt.
72 *law's delay:* longevity of lawsuits.　73 *office:* officials.　75 *quietus:* settlement of his
debt.　76 *bare bodkin:* mere dagger.　*fardels:* burdens.　79 *undiscovered:* unknown,
unexplored.　*bourn:* boundary.　84 *native hue:* natural complexion.　86 *pitch:*
height, excellence.　*moment:* importance.　87 *regard:* consideration.　*their currents
turn awry:* change their course.　89 *orisons:* prayers (referring to her prayer book).
91 *this . . . day:* all these days.　98 *breath:* speech.　101 *wax:* grow.　103 *honest:*
(1) chaste (2) truthful.　105 *fair:* (1) beautiful (2) honorable.

HAMLET.   That if you be honest and fair, your honesty should admit
   no discourse to your beauty.°

OPHELIA.   Could beauty my lord, have better commerce than with
   honesty?   110

HAMLET.   Ay truly, for the power of beauty will sooner transform
   honesty° from what it is to a bawd,° than the force of
   honesty can translate beauty into his likeness. This was
   sometime° a paradox, but now the time gives it proof. I did
   love you once.   115

OPHELIA.   Indeed my lord, you made me believe so.

HAMLET.   You should not have believed me, for virtue cannot so
   inoculate our old stock, but we shall relish of it.° I loved
   you not.

OPHELIA.   I was the more deceived.   120

HAMLET.   Get thee to a nunnery,° why wouldst thou be a breeder of
   sinners? I am myself indifferent honest,° but yet I could
   accuse me of such things, that it were better my mother
   had not borne me: I am very proud, revengeful, ambitious,
   with more offences at my beck,° than I have thoughts   125
   to put them in, imagination to give them shape, or time to
   act them in: what should such fellows as I do, crawling
   between earth and heaven? we are arrant° knaves all,
   believe none of us, go thy ways to a nunnery. Where's
   your father?   130

OPHELIA.   At home my lord.

HAMLET.   Let the doors be shut upon him, that he may play the fool
   no where but in's own house. Farewell.

OPHELIA.   O help him, you sweet heavens.

HAMLET.   If thou dost marry, I'll give thee this plague° for thy dowry: 135
   be thou as chaste as ice, as pure as snow, thou shalt not
   escape calumny; get thee to a nunnery, go, farewell. Or if
   thou wilt needs marry, marry a fool, for wise men know
   well enough what monsters° you make of them: to a nunnery
   go, and quickly too, farewell.   140

OPHELIA.   O heavenly powers, restore him.

HAMLET.   I have heard of your paintings too, well enough. God hath
   given you one face, and you make yourselves another: you
   jig,° you amble, and you lisp,° you nick-name God's
   creatures, and make your wantonness your ignorance;° go to,   145

107–108 *admit . . . beauty:* (1) not allow communication with your beauty (2) not allow your
beauty to be used as a trap (Hamlet may have overheard the Polonius–Claudius plot or
spotted their movement behind the arras).   112 *honesty:* chastity.   *bawd:* procurer,
pimp.   114 *sometime:* once.   118 *inoculate . . . it:* change our sinful nature (as a tree is
grafted to improve it) but we will keep our old taste (as will the fruit of the grafted tree).
121 *nunnery:* (1) cloister (2) slang for "brothel" (cf. "bawd" above).   122 *indifferent honest:*
reasonably virtuous.   125 *beck:* beckoning.   128 *arrant:* absolute.   135 *plague:* curse.
139 *monsters:* horned cuckolds (men whose wives were unfaithful).   144 *jig:* walk in a
mincing way.   *lisp:* put on affected speech.   145 *make your . . . ignorance:* excuse your
caprices as being due to ignorance.

I'll no more on't, it hath made me mad. I say we will have
no moe° marriage. Those that are married already, all but
one shall live, the rest shall keep as they are: to a nunnery,
go.   *Exit* HAMLET.

OPHELIA.   O what a noble mind is here o'erthrown!   150
    The courtier's, soldier's, scholar's, eye, tongue, sword,
    Th'expectancy and rose° of the fair state,
    The glass° of fashion, and the mould of form,°
    Th'observed of all observers, quite quite down,
    And I of ladies most deject and wretched,   155
    That sucked the honey of his music vows,
    Now see that noble and most sovereign° reason
    Like sweet bells jangled, out of tune and harsh,
    That unmatched form and feature° of blown° youth
    Blasted with ecstasy.° O woe is me,   160
    T'have seen what I have seen, see what I see.

Enter KING *and* POLONIUS.

KING.   Love? his affections° do not that way tend,
    Nor what he spake, though it lacked form a little,
    Was not like madness. There's something in his soul
    O'er which his melancholy sits on brood,   165
    And I do doubt,° the hatch and the disclose°
    Will be some danger; which for to prevent,
    I have in quick determination
    Thus set it down: he shall with speed to England,
    For the demand of our neglected° tribute: 170
    Haply° the seas, and countries different,
    With variable° objects, shall expel
    This something°-settled matter in his heart,
    Whereon his brains still beating puts him thus
    From fashion of himself.° What think you on't?   175
POLONIUS.   It shall do well. But yet do I believe
    The origin and commencement of his grief
    Sprung from neglected° love. How now Ophelia?
    You need not tell us what Lord Hamlet said,
    We heard it all. My lord, do as you please,   180
    But if you hold it fit, after the play,
    Let his queen-mother all alone entreat him
    To show his grief, let her be round° with him,
    And I'll be placed (so please you) in the ear

---

147 *moe:* more.   152 *expectancy and rose:* fair hope.   153 *glass:* mirror.   *mould of
form:* model of manners.   157 *sovereign:* (because it should rule).   159 *feature:* external
appearance.   159 *blown:* flowering.   160 *Blasted with ecstasy:* blighted by madness.
162 *affections:* emotions, afflictions.   166 *doubt:* fear.   165–166 *on brood . . . hatch . . .
disclose:* (metaphor of a hen sitting on eggs).   170 *neglected:* (being unpaid).
171 *Haply:* perhaps.   172 *variable:* varied.   173 *something-:* somewhat-.   175 *fashion
of himself:* his usual self.   178 *neglected:* unrequited.   183 *round:* direct.

Of° all their conference. If she find° him not,   185
To England send him: or confine him where
Your wisdom best shall think.

KING.   It shall be so,
Madness in great ones must not unwatched go.   *Exeunt.*

Scene 2. *[A hall in the castle]*

Enter HAMLET and three of the PLAYERS.

HAMLET.   Speak the speech° I pray you as I pronounced it to you,
  trippingly on the tongue, but if you mouth it° as many of
  your players do, I had as lief the town-crier spoke my
  lines. Nor do not saw the air too much with your hand
  thus, but use all gently, for in the very torrent, tempest,   5
  and as I may say, whirlwind of your passion, you must
  acquire and beget° a temperance that may give it smoothness.
  O it offends me to the soul, to hear a robustious°
  periwig-pated° fellow tear a passion to tatters, to very rags,
  to split the ears of the groundlings,° who for the most part   10
  are capable of° nothing but inexplicable dumb shows° and
  noise: I would have such a fellow whipped for o'erdoing
  Termagant:° it out-herods Herod,° pray you avoid it.

I. PLAYER.   I warrant you honour.

HAMLET.   Be not too tame neither, but let your own discretion be   15
  your tutor, suit the action to the word, the word to the
  action, with this special observance, that you o'erstep not
  the modesty° of nature: for any thing so o'erdone, is from°
  the purpose of playing, whose end both at the first, and
  now, was and is, to hold as 'twere the mirror up to nature,   20
  to show virtue her own feature, scorn° her own image, and
  the very age and body of the time his form and pressure.°
  Now this overdone, or come tardy off,° though it make the
  unskilful° laugh, cannot but make the judicious grieve, the
  censure of the which one,° must in your allowance°   25
  o'erweigh a whole theatre of others. O there be players
  that I have seen play, and heard others praise, and that
  highly (not to speak it profanely) that neither having
  th'accent of Christians, nor the gait of Christian, pagan,

184–185 *in the ear Of:* so as to overhear.   185 *find:* find out.   1 *the speech:* i.e., that
Hamlet has inserted.   2 *mouth it:* deliver it slowly and overdramatically.   7 *acquire and
beget:* achieve for yourself and instill in other actors.   8 *robustious:* boisterous.
9 *periwig-pated:* wig-wearing.   10 *groundlings:* audience who paid least and stood on the
ground floor.   11 *capable of:* able to understand.   *dumb shows:* pantomimed synopses
of the action to follow (as below).   13 *Termagant:* violent, ranting character in the guild
or mystery plays.   *out-herods Herod:* outdoes even Herod, King of Judea (who
commanded the slaughter of the innocents and who was a ranting tyrant in the mystery
plays).   18 *modesty:* moderation.   *from:* away from.   21 *scorn:* that which should be
scorned.   22 *age . . . pressure:* shape of the times in its accurate impression.   23 *come
tardy off:* understated, underdone.   24 *unskilful:* unsophisticated.   25 *one:* the
judicious.   *allowance:* estimation.

nor man, have so strutted and bellowed, that I have   30
thought some of nature's journeymen° had made men, and
not made them well, they imitated humanity so
abominably.

I. PLAYER. I hope we have reformed that indifferently° with us, sir.

HAMLET. O reform it altogether, and let those that play your clowns   35
speak no more than is set down for them,° for there be of
them that will themselves laugh, to set on some quantity
of barren° spectators to laugh too, though in the meantime,
some necessary question° of the play be then to be considered:
that's villainous, and shows a most pitiful ambition   40
in the fool that uses it. Go make you ready.   *Exeunt PLAYERS.*

Enter POLONIUS, ROSENCRANTZ, and GUILDENSTERN.

How now my lord, will the king hear this piece of work?

POLONIUS. And the queen too, and that presently.

HAMLET. Bid the players make haste.   *Exit POLONIUS.*
Will you two help to hasten them?   45

ROSENCRANTZ. Ay my lord.   *Exeunt they two.*

HAMLET. What ho, Horatio!

Enter HORATIO.

HORATIO. Here sweet lord, at your service.

HAMLET. Horatio, thou art e'en as just° a man
As e'er my conversation coped withal.°   50

HORATIO. O my dear lord.

HAMLET.   Nay, do not think I flatter,
For what advancement may I hope from thee,
That no revenue hast but thy good spirits
To feed and clothe thee? Why should the poor be flattered?
No, let the candied° tongue lick° absurd pomp,   55
And crook the pregnant° hinges of the knee
Where thrift may follow fawning.° Dost thou hear,
Since my dear soul was mistress of her choice,
And could of men distinguish her election,°
Sh'hath sealed° thee for herself, for thou hast been   60
As one in suff'ring all that suffers nothing,
A man that Fortune's buffets° and rewards
Hast ta'en with equal thanks; and blest are those
Whose blood° and judgment are so well co-mingled,
That they are not a pipe for Fortune's finger   65

---

31 *journeymen:* artisans working for others and not yet masters of their trades.
34 *indifferently:* reasonably well.   36 *speak no more . . . them:* stick to their lines.
38 *barren:* witless.   39 *question:* dialogue.   49 *just:* well balanced.   50 *coped withal:*
had to do with.   55–57 *candied . . . fawning:* (metaphor of a dog licking and fawning for
candy).   55 *candied:* flattering.   *lick:* pay court to.   56–57 *crook . . . fawning:*
obsequiously kneel when personal profit may ensue.   56 *pregnant:* quick in motion.
59 *election:* choice.   60 *sealed:* confirmed.   62 *buffets:* blows.   64 *blood:* passions.

To sound what stop° she please:° give me that man
That is not passion's slave, and I will wear him
In my heart's core, ay in my heart of heart,
As I do thee. Something too much of this.
There is a play tonight before the king,   70
One scene of it comes near the circumstance
Which I have told thee of my father's death.
I prithee when thou seest that act afoot,
Even with the very comment° of thy soul
Observe my uncle: if his occulted° guilt   75
Do not itself unkennel° in one speech,
It is a damnèd ghost° that we have seen,
And my imaginations are as foul
As Vulcan's stithy;° give him heedful note,
For I mine eyes will rivet to his face,   80
And after we will both our judgments join
In censure of his seeming.°
HORATIO.   Well my lord,
If a' steal aught the whilst this play is playing,
And 'scape detecting, I will pay° the theft.   *Sound a flourish.*
HAMLET.   They are coming to the play. I must be idle,°   85
Get you a place.

Enter Trumpets and Kettledrums, KING, QUEEN, POLONIUS, OPHELIA, ROSENCRANTZ, GUILDENSTERN, and other LORDS attendant, with his GUARD carrying torches. Danish March.

KING.   How fares° our cousin Hamlet?
HAMLET.   Excellent i'faith, of the chameleon's dish: I eat the air,°
     promise-crammed, you cannot feed capons so.°
KING.   I have nothing with° this answer Hamlet, these words are   90
     not mine.°
HAMLET.   No, nor mine now. [*To Polonius.*] My lord, you played
     once i'th'university you say?
POLONIUS.   That did I my lord, and was accounted a good actor.
HAMLET.   What did you enact?   95
POLONIUS.   I did enact Julius Caesar, I was killed i'th'Capitol, Brutus
     killed me.
HAMLET.   It was a brute part of him to kill so capital a calf there. Be
     the players ready?
ROSENCRANTZ.   Ay my lord, they stay upon your patience.°   100

66 *sound . . . please:* play whatever tune she likes.   *stop:* finger hole in wind instrument for varying the sound.   74 *very comment:* acutest observation.   75 *occulted:* hidden. 76 *unkennel:* force from hiding.   77 *damnèd ghost:* devil (not the ghost of my father). 79 *Vulcan's stithy:* the forge of the blacksmith of the gods.   82 *censure . . . seeming:* (1) judgment of his appearance (2) disapproval of his pretending.   84 *pay:* i.e., for.   85 *be idle:* act mad.   87 *fares:* does, but Hamlet takes it to mean "eats" or "dines."   88 *eat the air:* the chameleon supposedly ate air, but Hamlet also puns on "heir."   89 *you cannot . . . so:* (1) even a capon cannot feed on air and your promises (2) like a capon stuffed with food before being killed, I am stuffed (fed up) with your promises.   90 *nothing with:* nothing to do with.   91 *not mine:* not in answer to my question.   100 *stay . . . patience:* await your permission.

QUEEN. Come hither my dear Hamlet, sit by me.

HAMLET. No, good mother, here's metal more attractive.°

POLONIUS. [*To the King.*] O ho, do you mark that?

HAMLET. Lady, shall I lie in your lap?

OPHELIA. No my lord.   105

HAMLET. I mean, my head upon your lap?

OPHELIA. Ay my lord.

HAMLET. Do you think I meant country° matters?

OPHELIA. I think nothing my lord.

HAMLET. That's a fair thought to lie between maids' legs.   110

OPHELIA. What is, my lord?

HAMLET. Nothing.

OPHELIA. You are merry my lord.

HAMLET. Who, I?

OPHELIA. Ay my lord.   115

HAMLET. O God, your only jig-maker: what should a man do but be
merry, for look you how cheerfully my mother looks, and
my father died within's two hours.

OPHELIA. Nay, 'tis twice two months my lord.

HAMLET. So long? Nay then let the devil wear black, for I'll have a   120
suit of sables;° O heavens, die two months ago, and not
forgotten yet? Then there's hope a great man's memory
may outlive his life half a year, but by'r lady° a' must build
churches then, or else shall a' suffer not thinking on,° with
the hobby-horse,° whose epitaph is "For O, for O, the   125
hobby-horse is forgot."

*The trumpets sound. The Dumb Show° follows. Enter a King and a Queen, very lovingly,
the Queen embracing him, and he her. She kneels and makes show of protestation unto him.
He takes her up, and declines his head upon her neck. He lies him down upon a bank of
flowers; she seeing him asleep leaves him: anon comes in another man, takes off his crown,
kisses it, pours poison in the sleeper's ears, and leaves him: the Queen returns, finds the King
dead, and makes passionate action. The poisoner with some three or four mutes° comes in
again, seeming to condole with her. The dead body is carried away. The poisoner wooes the
Queen with gifts: she seems harsh and unwilling awhile, but in the end accepts his love.
Exeunt.*

OPHELIA. What means this, my lord?

HAMLET. Marry, this is miching mallecho,° it means mischief.

OPHELIA. Belike this show imports the argument° of the play.

Enter PROLOGUE.

---

102 *metal more attractive:* (1) iron more magnetic (2) stuff ("mettle") more beautiful.
108 *country:* rustic, sexual (with a pun on a slang word for the female sexual organ).
121 *sables:* (1) rich fur (2) black mourning garb.   123 *by'r lady:* by Our Lady (the Virgin
Mary).   124 *not thinking on:* being forgotten.   125 *hobby-horse:* (1) character in the May
games (2) slang for "prostitute."   126 stage direction: *Dumb Show:* pantomimed synopsis
of the action to follow.   126 stage direction: *mutes:* actors without speaking parts.
128 *miching mallecho:* skulking mischief.   129 *imports the argument:* signifies the plot.

HAMLET. We shall know by this fellow: the players cannot keep   130
counsel,° they'll tell all.
OPHELIA. Will a' tell us what this show meant?
HAMLET. Ay, or any show that you will show him. Be not you
ashamed to show, he'll not shame to tell you what it
means.   135
OPHELIA. You are naught,° you are naught, I'll mark the play.
PROLOGUE. For us and for our tragedy,
        Here stooping to your clemency,
        We beg your hearing patiently.   [*Exit.*]
HAMLET. Is this a prologue, or the posy° of a ring?   140
OPHELIA. 'Tis brief, my lord.
HAMLET. As woman's love.

Enter Player KING and QUEEN.

PLAYER KING. Full thirty times hath Phoebus' cart° gone round
        Neptune's salt wash,° and Tellus' orbèd ground,°
        And thirty dozen moons with borrowed sheen   145
        About the world have times twelve thirties been,
        Since love our hearts, and Hymen° did our hands
        Unite commutual,° in most sacred bands.
PLAYER QUEEN. So many journeys may the sun and moon
        Make us again count o'er ere love be done,   150
        But woe is me, you are so sick of late,
        So far from cheer, and from your former state,
        That I distrust you:° yet though I distrust,
        Discomfort you, my lord, it nothing must.
        For women fear too much, even as they love,   155
        And women's fear and love hold quantity,°
        In neither aught, or in extremity:°
        Now what my love is, proof° hath made you know,
        And as my love is sized, my fear is so.
        Where love is great, the littlest doubts are fear,   160
        Where little fears grow great, great love grows there.
PLAYER KING. Faith, I must leave thee love, and shortly too,
        My operant° powers their functions leave° to do,
        And thou shalt live in this fair world behind,
        Honoured, beloved, and haply° one as kind   165
        For husband shalt thou—
PLAYER QUEEN.   O confound the rest:
        Such love must needs be treason in my breast.
        In second husband let me be accurst,

---

131 *counsel:* a secret.   136 *naught:* naughty, lewd.   140 *posy:* motto (engraved in a
ring).   143 *Phoebus' cart:* chariot of the sun.   144 *wash:* sea.   *Tellus'* . . . *ground:* the
earth (Tellus was a Roman earth goddess).   147 *Hymen:* Roman god of marriage.
148 *commutual:* mutually.   153 *distrust you:* am worried about you.   156 *quantity:*
proportion.   157 *In neither . . . extremity:* their love and fear are either absent or
excessive.   158 *proof:* experience.   163 *operant:* vital.   *leave:* cease.   165 *haply:*
perhaps.

None wed the second, but who killed the first.
HAMLET. [*Aside.*] That's wormwood,° wormwood. 170
PLAYER QUEEN. The instances° that second marriage move°
    Are base respects of thrift,° but none of love.
    A second time I kill my husband dead,
    When second husband kisses me in bed.
PLAYER KING. I do believe you think what now you speak, 175
    But what we do determine, oft we break:
    Purpose is but the slave to memory,
    Of violent birth but poor validity:°
    Which now like fruit unripe sticks on the tree,
    But fall unshaken when they mellow be. 180
    Most necessary 'tis that we forget
    To pay ourselves what to ourselves is debt:°
    What to ourselves in passion we propose,
    The passion ending, doth the purpose lose.
    The violence of either grief or joy 185
    Their own enactures° with themselves destroy:
    Where joy most revels, grief doth most lament;
    Grief joys, joy grieves, on slender accident.
    This world is not for aye,° nor 'tis not strange
    That even our loves should with our fortunes change: 190
    For 'tis a question left us yet to prove,
    Whether love lead fortune, or else fortune love.°
    The great man down, you mark his favourite flies,
    The poor advanced, makes friends of enemies:
    And hitherto doth love on fortune tend, 195
    For who not needs, shall never lack a friend,
    And who in want a hollow friend doth try,
    Directly seasons him° his enemy.
    But orderly to end where I begun,
    Our wills and fates do so contrary run, 200
    That our devices still° are overthrown,
    Our thoughts are ours, their ends none of our own.
    So think thou wilt no second husband wed,
    But die thy thoughts when thy first lord is dead.
PLAYER QUEEN. Nor earth to me give food, nor heaven light, 205
    Sport and repose lock from me day and night,
    To desperation turn my trust and hope,
    An anchor's° cheer in prison be my scope,
    Each opposite that blanks° the face of joy,
    Meet what I would have well, and it destroy, 210

---

170 *wormwood:* bitter (like the herb). 171 *instances:* causes. *move:* motivate.
172 *respects of thrift:* consideration of profit. 178 *validity:* strength. 181–182 *Most . . .*
debt: we are easy creditors to ourselves and forget our fo mer promises (debts).
186 *enactures:* fulfillments. 189 *aye:* ever. 192 *fortun° love:* fortune lead love.
198 *seasons him:* causes him to become. 201 *devices still:* plans always. 208 *anchor's:*
hermit's. 209 *opposite that blanks:* contrary event that pales.

Both here and hence° pursue me lasting strife,
    If once a widow, ever I be wife.
HAMLET.   If she should break it now.
PLAYER KING.   'Tis deeply sworn: sweet, leave me here awhile,
    My spirits grow dull, and fain° I would beguile   215
    The tedious day with sleep.   *Sleeps.*
PLAYER QUEEN.   Sleep rock thy brain.
    And never come mischance between us twain.   *Exit.*
HAMLET.   Madam, how like you this play?
QUEEN.   The lady doth protest too much methinks.
HAMLET.   O but she'll keep her word.   220
KING.   Have you heard the argument°? Is there no offence in't?
HAMLET.   No, no, they do but jest, poison in jest, no offence
    i'th'world.
KING.   What do you call the play?
HAMLET.   The Mouse-trap. Marry, how? Tropically:° this play is the   225
    image of a murder done in Vienna: Gonzago is the duke's
    name, his wife Baptista, you shall see anon, 'tis a knavish
    piece of work, but what of that? Your majesty, and we
    that have free° souls, it touches us not: let the galled jade
    winch,° our withers are unwrung.°   230

Enter LUCIANUS.

    This is one Lucianus, nephew to the king.
OPHELIA.   You are as good as a chorus,° my lord.
HAMLET.   I could interpret between you and your love, if I could see
    the puppets dallying.
OPHELIA.   You are keen my lord, you are keen.°   235
HAMLET.   It would cost you a groaning to take off mine edge.
OPHELIA.   Still better and worse.°
HAMLET.   So you mistake° your husbands. Begin, murderer. Pox,°
    leave thy damnable faces° and begin. Come, the croaking
    raven doth bellow for revenge.   240
LUCIANUS.   Thoughts black, hands apt, drugs fit, and time agreeing,
    Confederate season, else no creature seeing,°
    Thou mixture rank, of midnight weeds collected,
    With Hecate's° ban° thrice blasted, thrice infected,
    Thy natural magic, and dire property,   245
    On wholesome° life usurps immediately.   *Pours the poison in his ears.*
HAMLET.   A' poisons him i'th'garden for's estate, his name's Gonzago,
    the story is extant, and written in very choice

211 *here and hence:* in this world and the next.   215 *fain:* gladly.   221 *argument:* plot.
225 *Tropically:* figuratively.   229 *free:* innocent.   229–230 *galled jade winch:* chafed old
horse wince (from its sores).   230 *withers are unwrung:* (1) shoulders are unchafed (2)
consciences are clear.   232 *chorus:* actor who introduced the action.   235 *keen:* (1)
sharp (Ophelia's meaning) (2) sexually excited (Hamlet's interpretation).   237 *better and
worse:* better wit but a worse meaning, with a pun on "better" and "bitter."   238 *mistake:*
mis-take.   *Pox:* a plague on it.   239 *faces:* exaggerated facial expressions.
242 *Confederate . . . seeing:* no one seeing me except time, my confederate.   244 *Hecate:*
goddess of witchcraft.   *ban:* evil spell.   246 *wholesome:* healthy.

Italian, you shall see anon how the murderer gets the love
of Gonzago's wife.   250
OPHELIA.   The king rises.
HAMLET.   What, frighted with false fire°?
QUEEN.   How fares my lord?
POLONIUS.   Give o'er the play.
KING.   Give me some light. Away!   255
ALL.   Lights, lights, lights!   *Exeunt all but* HAMLET *and* HORATIO.
HAMLET.   Why, let the stricken deer go weep,
          The hart ungallèd° play,°
     For some must watch while some must sleep,
          Thus runs the world away.   260
     Would not this° sir, and a forest of feathers,° if the rest of my
     fortunes turn Turk with° me, with two Provincial roses° on
     my razed° shoes, get me a fellowship° in a cry° of players?
HORATIO.   Half a share.°
HAMLET.   A whole one, I.   265
     For thou dost know, O Damon° dear,
          This realm dismantled was
     Of Jove° himself, and now reigns here
          A very very—pajock.°
HORATIO.   You might have rhymed.°   270
HAMLET.   O good Horatio, I'll take the ghost's word for a thousand
     pound. Didst perceive?
HORATIO.   Very well my lord.
HAMLET.   Upon the talk of the poisoning?
HORATIO.   I did very well note him.   275

Enter ROSENCRANTZ *and* GUILDENSTERN.

HAMLET.   Ah ha, come, some music. Come, the recorders.°
     For if the king like not the comedy,
     Why then belike he likes it not, perdy.°
     Come, some music.
GUILDENSTERN.   Good my lord, vouchsafe me a word with you.   280
HAMLET.   Sir, a whole history.
GUILDENSTERN.   The king, sir—
HAMLET.   Ay sir, what of him?
GUILDENSTERN.   Is in his retirement, marvellous distempered.
HAMLET.   With drink sir?   285

---

252 *false fire:* discharge of blanks (not gunpowder).   257–258 *deer . . . play:* (the belief
that a wounded deer wept, abandoned by the others).   258 *ungallèd:* unhurt.
261 *this:* i.e., sample (of my theatrical talent).   *feathers:* plumes (worn by actors).
262 *turn Turk with:* cruelly turn against.   *Provincial roses:* rosettes named for Provins,
France.   263 *razed:* slashed, decorated with cutouts.   *fellowship:* partnership.   *cry:*
pack, troupe.   264 *share:* divisions of profits among members of a theatrical production
company.   266 *Damon:* legendary ideal friend to Pythias.   268 *Jove:* (Hamlet's father).
269 *pajock:* peacock (associated with lechery).   270 *rhymed:* (used "ass" instead of
"pajock").   276 *recorders:* soft-toned woodwind instruments, similar to flutes.
278 *perdy:* by God (*par dieu*).

GUILDENSTERN.   No my lord, with choler.°

HAMLET.   Your wisdom should show itself more richer to signify
     this to the doctor: for, for me to put him to his purgation,°
     would perhaps plunge him into more choler.

GUILDENSTERN.   Good my lord, put your discourse into some frame,° and   290
     start not so wildly from my affair.

HAMLET.   I am tame sir, pronounce.

GUILDENSTERN.   The queen your mother, in most great affliction of spirit,
     hath sent me to you.

HAMLET.   You are welcome.   295

GUILDENSTERN.   Nay good my lord, this courtesy is not of the right breed.°
     If it shall please you to make me a wholesome° answer, I
     will do your mother's commandment: if not, your pardon°
     and my return shall be the end of my business.

HAMLET.   Sir I cannot.   300

ROSENCRANTZ.   What, my lord?

HAMLET.   Make you a wholesome answer: my wit's diseased. But
     sir, such answer as I can make, you shall command, or
     rather as you say, my mother: therefore no more, but to
     the matter. My mother you say.   305

ROSENCRANTZ.   Then thus she says, your behaviour hath struck her into
     amazement and admiration.°

HAMLET.   O wonderful son that can so 'stonish a mother. But is there
     no sequel at the heels of this mother's admiration? Impart.

ROSENCRANTZ.   She desires to speak with you in her closet°   310
     ere you go to bed.

HAMLET.   We shall obey, were she ten times our mother. Have you
     any further trade with us?

ROSENCRANTZ.   My lord, you once did love me.

HAMLET.   And do still, by these pickers and stealers.°   315

ROSENCRANTZ.   Good my lord, what is your cause of distemper? You do
     surely bar the door upon your own liberty, if you deny
     your griefs to your friend.°

HAMLET.   Sir, I lack advancement.

ROSENCRANTZ.   How can that be, when you have the voice° of the king   320
     himself for your succession in Denmark?

HAMLET.   Ay sir, but 'while the grass grows'°—the proverb is
     something musty.°

Enter the PLAYERS with recorders.

     O the recorders, let me see one. To withdraw° with you,

---

286 *choler:* anger.   288 *purgation:* (1) purging of excessive bile (2) judicial investigations
(3) purgatory.   290 *frame:* order.   296 *breed:* (1) species (2) manners.
297 *wholesome:* reasonable.   298 *pardon:* permission to depart.   307 *admiration:*
wonder.   310 *closet:* private room, bedroom.   315 *pickers and stealers:* hands (from the
prayer, "Keep my hands from picking and stealing").   317–318 *deny . . . friend:* refuse to
let your friend know the cause of your suffering.   320 *voice:* vote.   322 *while . . .
grows:* (the proverb ends: "the horse starves").   323 *something musty:* somewhat too old
and trite (to finish).   324 *withdraw:* speak privately.

why do you go about to recover the wind of me,° as if you   325
would drive me into a toil°?

GUILDENSTERN.   O my lord, if my duty be too bold, my love is too
unmannerly.°

HAMLET.   I do not well understand that. Will you play
upon this pipe°?   330

GUILDENSTERN.   My lord I cannot.

HAMLET.   I pray you.

GUILDENSTERN.   Believe me. I cannot.

HAMLET.   I do beseech you.

GUILDENSTERN.   I know no touch of it° my lord.   335

HAMLET.   It is as easy as lying; govern these ventages° with your
fingers and thumb, give it breath with your mouth, and it
will discourse most eloquent music. Look you, these are
the stops.

GUILDENSTERN.   But these cannot I command to any utt'rance of harmony,   340
I have not the skill.

HAMLET.   Why look you now how unworthy a thing you make of
me: you would play upon me, you would seem to know
my stops, you would pluck out the heart of my mystery,
you would sound me from my lowest note to the top of my   345
compass:° and there is much music, excellent voice in this
little organ,° yet cannot you make it speak. 'Sblood, do you
think I am easier to be played on than a pipe? Call me what
instrument you will, though you can fret° me, you cannot
play upon me.   350

Enter POLONIUS.

God bless you sir.

POLONIUS.   My lord, the queen would speak with you, and presently.

HAMLET.   Do you see yonder cloud that's almost in shape of a camel?

POLONIUS.   By th'mass and 'tis, like a camel indeed.

HAMLET.   Methinks it is like a weasel.   355

POLONIUS.   It is backed like a weasel.

HAMLET.   Or like a whale?

POLONIUS.   Very like a whale.

HAMLET.   Then I will come to my mother by and by.°
[*Aside.*] They fool me to the top of my bent.°   360
I will come by and by.

POLONIUS.   I will say so.   *Exit.*

HAMLET.   "By and by" is easily said.
Leave me, friends.   [*Exeunt all but HAMLET.*]

---

325 *recover . . . me:* drive me toward the wind, as with a prey, to avoid its scenting the
hunter.   326 *toil:* snare.   327–328 *is too unmannerly:* makes me forget my good
manners.   330 *pipe:* recorder.   335 *know . . . it:* have no skill at fingering it.
336 *ventages:* holes, stops.   346 *compass:* range.   347 *organ:* musical instrument.
349 *fret:* (1) irritate (2) play an instrument that has "frets" or bars to guide the fingering.
359 *by and by:* very soon.   360 *fool me . . . bent:* force me to play the fool to my utmost.

'Tis now the very witching time of night.   365
When churchyards yawn,° and hell itself breathes out
Contagion° to this world: now could I drink hot blood,
And do such bitter business as the day
Would quake to look on: soft, now to my mother—
O heart, lose not thy nature,° let not ever   370
The soul of Nero° enter this firm bosom,
Let me be cruel, not unnatural.
I will speak daggers to her, but use none:
My tongue and soul in this be hypocrites,°
How in my words somever she be shent,°   375
To give them seals,° never my soul consent.   *Exit.*

Scene 3. [A room in the castle]

Enter KING, ROSENCRANTZ, *and* GUILDENSTERN.

KING. I like him not, nor stands it safe with us
      To let his madness range. Therefore prepare you,
      I your commission will forthwith dispatch,°
      And he to England shall along with you:
      The terms of our estate° may not endure   5
      Hazard so near's° as doth hourly grow
      Out of his brows.°
GUILDENSTERN.   We will ourselves provide:°
      Most holy and religious fear it is
      To keep those many many bodies safe
      That live and feed upon your majesty.   10
ROSENCRANTZ. The single and peculiar° life is bound
      With all the strength and armour of the mind
      To keep itself from noyance,° but much more
      That spirit, upon whose weal° depends and rests
      The lives of many; the cess° of majesty   15
      Dies not alone, but like a gulf° doth draw
      What's near it, with it. O 'tis a massy wheel
      Fixed on the summit of the highest mount,
      To whose huge spokes, ten thousand lesser things
      Are mortised° and adjoined, which when it falls,   20
      Each small annexment, petty consequence,
      Attends° the boist'rous ruin. Never alone
      Did the king sigh, but with a general groan.

366 *churchyards yawn:* graves open.   367 *Contagion:* (1) evil (2) diseases.   370 *nature:*
natural affection.   371 *Nero:* (who killed his mother).   374 *My tongue . . . hypocrites:* I
will speak cruelly but intend no harm.   375 *shent:* chastised.   376 *give them seals:*
confirm them with action (as a legal "deed" is confirmed with a "seal").   3 *forthwith
dispatch:* immediately have prepared.   5 *terms . . . estate:* circumstances of my royal office.
6 *near's:* near us.   7 *brows:* effronteries.   *provide:* prepare.   11 *peculiar:* individual.
13 *noyance:* harm.   14 *weal:* well-being.   15 *cess:* cessation, death.   16 *gulf:*
whirlpool.   20 *mortised:* securely fitted.   22 *Attends:* accompanies.

KING. Arm° you I pray you, to this speedy voyage,
    For we will fetters put about this fear,   25
    Which now goes too free-footed.
ROSENCRANTZ.   We will haste us.

                        Exeunt [ROSENCRANTZ *and* GUILDENSTERN.]

Enter POLONIUS.

POLONIUS. My lord, he's going to his mother's closet:
    Behind the arras I'll convey myself
    To hear the process.° I'll warrant she'll tax him home,
    And as you said, and wisely was it said,   30
    'Tis meet° that some more audience than a mother,
    Since nature makes them partial, should o'erhear
    The speech of vantage;° fare you well my liege,°
    I'll call upon you ere you go to bed,
    And tell you what I know.
KING.   Thanks, dear my lord.   *Exit* [POLONIUS.] 35
    O my offence is rank, it smells to heaven,
    It hath the primal eldest curse° upon't,
    A brother's murder. Pray can I not,
    Though inclination be as sharp as will:°
    My stronger guilt defeats my strong intent,   40
    And like a man to double business bound,
    I stand in pause where I shall first begin,
    And both neglect; what if this cursèd hand
    Were thicker than itself with brother's blood,
    Is there not rain enough in the sweet heavens   45
    To wash it white as snow? Whereto serves mercy
    But to confront the visage of offence°?
    And what's in prayer but this two-fold force,
    To be forestallèd° ere we come to fall,
    Or pardoned being down? Then I'll look up,   50
    My fault is past. But O what form of prayer
    Can serve my turn? "Forgive me my foul murder":
    That cannot be, since I am still possessed
    Of those effects° for which I did the murder:
    My crown, mine own ambition, and my queen.   55
    May one be pardoned and retain th'offence?
    In the corrupted currents of this world,
    Offence's gilded hand may shove by justice,
    And oft 'tis seen the wicked prize itself
    Buys out the law;° but 'tis not so above,   60
    There is no shuffling,° there the action lies

---

24 *Arm:* prepare.   29 *the process:* what proceeds.   31 *meet:* fitting.   33 *of vantage:*
from an advantageous position.   *liege:* lord.   37 *primal . . . curse:* curse of Cain.
39 *inclination . . . will:* my desire to pray is as strong as my determination to do so.
47 *confront . . . offence:* plead in man's behalf against sin (at the Last Judgment).
49 *forestallèd:* prevented.   54 *effects:* results.   59–60 *wicked . . . law:* fruits of the crime
bribe the judge.   61 *shuffling:* evasion.

In his true nature,° and we ourselves compelled
Even to the teeth and forehead of our faults°
To give in evidence. What then? What rests°?
Try what repentance can. What can it not?   65
Yet what can it, when one can not repent?
O wretched state? O bosom black as death!
O limèd soul, that struggling to be free,
Art more engaged;° help, angels, make assay:°
Bow stubborn knees, and heart with strings of steel,   70
Be soft as sinews of the new-born babe,
All may be well.   *[He kneels.]*

Enter HAMLET.

HAMLET. Now might I do it pat,° now a' is a-praying,
And now I'll do't, [*Draws his sword.*] and so a' goes to heaven,
And so am I revenged: that would be scanned:°   75
A villain kills my father, and for that,
I his sole son, do this same villain send
To heaven.
Why, this is hire and salary, not revenge.
A' took my father grossly,° full of bread,°   80
With all his crimes° broad blown,° as flush° as May,
And how his audit° stands who knows save heaven,
But in our circumstance and course of thought,
'Tis heavy° with him: and am I then revenged
To take him in the purging of his soul,   85
when he is fit and seasoned° for his passage?
No.   *[Sheathes his sword.]*
Up sword, and know thou a more horrid hent,°
When he is drunk asleep, or in his rage,
Or in th'incestuous pleasure of his bed,   90
At game, a-swearing, or about some act
That has no relish° of salvation in't,
Then trip him that his heels may kick at heaven,
And that his soul may be as damned and black
As hell whereto it goes; my mother stays,   95
This physic° but prolongs thy sickly days.   *Exit.*
KING. [*Rises.*] My words fly up, my thoughts remain below,
Words without thoughts never to heaven go.   *Exit.*

61–62 *action . . . nature:* (1) deed is seen in its true nature (2) legal action is sustained
according to the truth.   63 *to the teeth . . . faults:* meeting our sins face to face.
64 *rests:* remains.   68–69 *limèd . . . engaged:* like a bird caught in lime (a sticky substance
spread on twigs as a snare), the soul in its struggle to clear itself only becomes more
entangled.   69 *make assay:* I'll make an attempt.   73 *pat:* opportunely.   75 *would be
scanned:* needs closer examination.   80 *grossly:* unpurified (by final rites).   *bread:* self-
indulgence.   81 *crimes:* sins.   *broad blown:* in full flower.   *flush:* lusty.   82 *audit:*
account.   84 *heavy:* grievous.   86 *seasoned:* ready (prepared).   88 *horrid hent:*
horrible opportunity ("hint") for seizure ("hent") by me.   92 *relish:* taste.   96 *physic:*
(1) medicine (2) purgation of your soul by prayer.

Scene 4. [The queen's closet]

Enter QUEEN and POLONIUS.

POLONIUS. A' will come straight, look you lay home° to him,
    Tell him his pranks have been too broad° to bear with,
    And that your grace hath screened and stood between
    Much heat° and him. I'll silence me° even here:
    Pray you be round with him.   5
HAMLET. [*Within.*] Mother, mother, mother.
QUEEN.   I'll war'nt you,
    Fear me not. Withdraw, I hear him coming. [*POLONIUS hides behind the arras.*]

Enter HAMLET.

HAMLET. Now mother, what's the matter?
QUEEN. Hamlet, thou hast thy father much offended.
HAMLET. Mother, you have my father much offended.   10
QUEEN. Come, come, you answer with an idle° tongue.
HAMLET. Go, go, you question with a wicked tongue.
QUEEN. Why, how now Hamlet?
HAMLET.   What's the matter now?
QUEEN. Have you forgot me?
HAMLET.   No by the rood,° not so,
    You are the queen, your husband's brother's wife,   15
    And would it were not so, you are my mother.
QUEEN. Nay, then I'll set those to you that can speak.°
HAMLET. Come, come, and sit you down, you shall not budge,
    You go not till I set you up a glass°
    Where you may see the inmost part of you.   20
QUEEN. What wilt thou do? Thou wilt not murder me?
    Help, help, ho!
POLONIUS. [*Behind the arras.*] What ho! help, help, help!
HAMLET. How now, a rat? dead for a ducat,° dead.

Kills POLONIUS [through the arras.]

POLONIUS. O I am slain!
QUEEN. O me, what hast thou done?
HAMLET.   Nay I know not,   25
    Is it the king?
QUEEN. O what a rash and bloody deed is this!
HAMLET. A bloody deed, almost as bad, good mother,
    As kill a king, and marry with his brother.
QUEEN. As kill a king?
HAMLET.   Ay lady, it was my word.   30
    [*To Polonius.*] Thou wretched, rash, intruding fool, farewell,

1 *lay home:* thrust home; speak sharply.   2 *broad:* unrestrained.   4 *heat:* anger.
silence me: hide in silence.   11 *idle:* foolish.   14 *rood:* cross.   17 *speak:* i.e., to you as
you should be spoken to.   19 *glass:* looking glass.   23 *for a ducat:* I wager a ducat (an
Italian gold coin).

I took thee for thy better,° take thy fortune,
Thou find'st to be too busy is some danger.
[*To the Queen.*] Leave wringing of your hands, peace, sit you down,
And let me wring your heart, for so I shall   35
If it be made of penetrable stuff,
If damnèd custom° have not brazed° it so,
That it be proof° and bulwark against sense.°
QUEEN.   What have I done, that thou dar'st wag thy tongue
    In noise so rude against me?
HAMLEY.   Such an act   40
    That blurs the grace and blush of modesty,
Calls virtue hypocrite, takes off the rose°
From the fair forehead of an innocent love
And sets a blister there,° makes marriage vows
As false as dicers' oaths, O such a deed,   45
As from the body of contraction° plucks
The very soul, and sweet religion makes
A rhapsody° of words; heaven's face does glow,°
Yea this solidity and compound mass°
With heated visage, as against the doom,°   50
Is thought-sick at the act.
QUEEN.   Ay me, what act,
    That roars so loud, and thunders in the index°?
HAMLET.   Look here upon this picture, and on this,
    The counterfeit presentment° of two brothers:
See what a grace was seated on this brow,   55
Hyperion's° curls, the front° of Jove himself,
An eye like Mars, to threaten and command,
A station° like the herald Mercury,
New-lighted on a heaven-kissing hill,
A combination and a form indeed,   60
Where every god did seem to set his seal
To give the world assurance of a man.
This was your husband. Look you now what follows.
Here is your husband, like a mildewed ear,°
Blasting° his wholesome brother. Have you eyes?   65
Could you on this fair mountain leave to feed,°
And batten° on this moor? Ha! Have you eyes?
You cannot call it love, for at your age
The hey-day in the blood° is tame, it's humble,

---

32 *thy better:* the king.   37 *custom:* habit.   *brazed:* brass-plated (brazened).   38 *proof:* armor.   *sense:* sensibility.   42 *rose:* (symbol of perfection and innocence).   44 *blister there:* (whores were punished by being branded on the forehead).   46 *body of contraction:* marriage contract.   48 *rhapsody:* (meaningless) mixture.   *glow:* blush.   49 *solidity . . . mass:* solid earth, compounded of the four elements.   50 *against the doom:* expecting Judgment Day.   52 *index:* (1) table of contents (2) prologue.   54 *counterfeit presentment:* painted likeness.   56 *Hyperion:* Greek sun god.   *front:* forehead.   58 *station:* bearing.   64 *ear:* i.e., of grain.   65 *Blasting:* blighting.   66 *leave to feed:* leave off feeding.   67 *batten:* gorge yourself.   69 *hey-day in the blood:* youthful passion.

And waits upon the judgment, and what judgment 70
Would step from this to this? Sense° sure you have
Else could you not have motion,° but sure that sense
Is apoplexed,° for madness would not err,
Nor sense to ecstasy was ne'er so thralled°
But it reserved some quantity of choice 75
To serve in such a difference.° What devil was't
That thus hath cozened you at hoodman-blind°?
Eyes without feeling, feeling without sight,
Ears without hands or eyes, smelling sans all,°
Or but a sickly part of one true sense 80
Could not so mope:° O shame, where is thy blush?
Rebellious hell,
If thou canst mutine in a matron's bones,
To flaming youth let virtue be as wax
And melt in her own fire. Proclaim no shame 85
When the compulsive° ardour gives the charge,°
Since frost itself as actively doth burn,
And reason panders will.°
QUEEN.   O Hamlet, speak no more,
Thou turn'st my eyes into my very soul,
And there I see such black and grainèd° spots 90
As will not leave their tinct.°
HAMLET.   Nay, but to live
In the rank sweat of an enseamèd° bed,
Stewed in corruption, honeying, and making love
Over the nasty sty.
QUEEN.   O speak to me no more,
These words like daggers enter in mine ears, 95
No more, sweet Hamlet.
HAMLET.   A murderer and a villain,
A slave that is not twentieth part the tithe°
Of your precedent lord, a vice° of kings,
A cutpurse° of the empire and the rule,
That from a shelf the precious diadem stole 100
And put it in his pocket.
QUEEN.   No more.
HAMLET. A king of shreds and patches—

Enter the GHOST in his night-gown.°

71 *Sense:* perception by the senses.   72 *motion:* impulse.   73 *apoplexed:* paralyzed.
74 *sense . . . thralled:* sensibility was never so enslaved by madness.   76 *in . . . difference:*
where the difference was so great.   77 *cozened . . . blind:* cheated you at blindman's bluff.
79 *sans all:* without the other senses.   81 *so mope:* be so dull.   86 *compulsive:*
compelling.   *gives the charge:* attacks.   88 *panders will:* pimps for lust.   90 *grainèd:*
dyed in grain, unfading.   91 *leave their tinct:* lose their color.   92 *enseamèd:* greasy.
97 *tithe:* one-tenth part.   98 *vice:* buffoon (like the character of Vice in the morality
plays).   99 *cutpurse:* pickpocket.   102.1 stage direction: *night-gown:* dressing gown.

Save me and hover o'er me with your wings,
You heavenly guards. What would your gracious figure?
QUEEN. Alas, he's mad.   105
HAMLET. Do you not come your tardy son to chide,
That lapsed in time and passion° lets go by
Th'important acting of your dread command?
O say!
GHOST. Do not forget: this visitation   110
Is but to whet thy almost blunted purpose.
But look, amazement on thy mother sits,
O step between her and her fighting soul,
Conceit° in weakest bodies strongest works,
Speak to her Hamlet.
HAMLET.   How is it with you lady?   115
QUEEN. Alas, how is't with you,
That you do bend your eye on vacancy,°
And with th'incorporal° air do hold discourse?
Forth at your eyes your spirits° wildly peep,
And as the sleeping soldiers in th'alarm,   120
Your bedded° hairs, like life in excrements,°
Start up and stand an° end. O gentle son,
Upon the heat and flame of thy distemper
sprinkle cool patience. Whereon do you look?
HAMLET. On him, on him, look you how pale he glares,   125
His form and cause conjoined, preaching to stones,
Would make them capable.° Do not look upon me,
Lest with this piteous action you convert
My stern effects,° then what I have to do
Will want° true colour,° tears perchance for blood.   130
QUEEN. To whom do you speak this?
HAMLET.   Do you see nothing there?
QUEEN. Nothing at all, yet all that is I see.
HAMLET. Nor did you nothing hear?
QUEEN.   No, nothing but ourselves.
HAMLET. Why look you there, look how it steals away,
My father in his habit as he lived,°   135
Look where he goes, even now out at the portal.   *Exit* [GHOST.]
QUEEN. This is the very coinage of your brain,
This bodiless creation ecstasy
Is very cunning in.°
HAMLET.   Ecstasy?

---

107 *lapsed . . . passion:* having let time elapse and passion cool.   114 *Conceit:* imagination.
117 *vacancy:* (she cannot see the ghost).   118 *incorporal:* bodiless.   119 *spirits:* vital
forces.   121 *bedded:* lying flat.   *excrements:* outgrowths (of the body).   122 *an:* on.
127 *capable:* i.e., of feeling pity.   128–129 *convert . . . effects:* transform my outward signs
of sternness.   130 *want:* lack.   *colour:* (1) complexion (2) motivation.   135 *habit . . .
lived:* clothing he wore when alive.   138–139 *bodiless . . . cunning in:* madness (ecstasy) is
very skillful in causing an affected person to hallucinate.

My pulse as yours doth temperately keep time,   140
And makes as healthful music. It is not madness
That I have uttered; bring me to the test
And I the matter will re-word, which madness
Would gambol° from. Mother, for love of grace,
Lay not that flattering unction° to your soul,   145
That not your trespass but my madness speaks,
It will but skin and film the ulcerous place,
Whiles rank corruption mining° all within,
Infects unseen. Confess yourself to heaven,
Repent what's past, avoid what is to come,   150
And do not spread the compost° on the weeds
To make them ranker. Forgive me this my virtue,°
For in the fatness° of these pursy° times
Virtue itself of vice must pardon beg,
Yea curb and woo° for leave to do him° good.   155

QUEEN.   O Hamlet, thou hast cleft my heart in twain.
HAMLET.   O throw away the worser part of it,
And live the purer with the other half.
Good night, but go not to my uncle's bed,
Assume° a virtue if you have it not.   160
That monster custom, who all sense doth eat
Of habits evil,° is angel yet in this,
That to the use° of actions fair and good,
He likewise gives a frock or livery
That aptly° is put on. Refrain tonight,   165
And that shall lend a kind of easiness
To the next abstinence, the next more easy:
For use° almost can change the stamp° of nature,
And either . . . the° devil, or throw him out
With wondrous potency: once more good night,   170
And when you are desirous to be blessed,
I'll blessing beg of you. For this same lord,°
I do repent; but heaven hath pleased it so
To punish me with this, and this with me,
That I must be their scourge and minister.°   175
I will bestow° him and will answer well°
The death I gave him; so again good night.
I must be cruel only to be kind;
This bad begins, and worse remains behind.°

[handwritten annotations: "★ key speech", "seems more important than to have her repent for her sins", "to Hamlet"]

144 *gambol:* leap.   145 *unction:* salve.   148 *mining:* undermining.   151 *compost:*
manure.   152 *virtue:* sermon on virtue.   153 *fatness:* grossness.   *pursy:* flabby.
155 *curb and woo:* bow and plead.   *him:* vice.   160 *Assume:* put on the guise of.
161–162 *all sense . . . evil:* confuses the sense of right and wrong in a habitué.   163 *use:*
habit.   165 *aptly:* readily.   168 *use:* habit.   *stamp:* form.   169 *either . . . the:* (word
omitted, for which "tame," "curls," and "quell" have been suggested).   172 *lord:*
Polonius.   175 *their . . . minister:* heaven's punishment and agent of retribution.
176 *bestow:* stow away.   *answer well:* assume full responsibility for.   179 *bad . . . behind:*
is a bad beginning to a worse end to come.

One word more, good lady.

QUEEN.   What shall I do?   180

HAMLET.   Not this by no means that I bid you do:
Let the bloat° king tempt you again to bed,
Pinch wanton on your cheek, call you his mouse,
And let him for a pair of reechy° kisses,
Or paddling in your neck with his damned fingers,   185
Make you to ravel° all this matter out
That I essentially am not in madness,
But mad in craft. 'Twere good you let him know,
For who that's but a queen, fair, sober, wise,
Would from a paddock, from a bat, a gib,°   190
Such dear concernings hide? who would do so?
No, in despite of sense and secrecy,
Unpeg the basket on the house's top,
Let the birds fly, and like the famous ape,
To try conclusions° in the basket creep,   195
And break your own neck down.°

QUEEN.   Be thou assured, if words be made of breath,
And breath of life, I have no life to breathe
What thou hast said to me.

HAMLET.   I must to England, you know that.

QUEEN.   Alack,   200
I had forgot: 'tis so concluded on.

HAMLET.   There's letters sealed, and my two school-fellows,
Whom I will trust as I will adders fanged,
They bear the mandate, they must sweep my way
And marshal me to knavery:° let it work,   205
For 'tis the sport to have the enginer°
Hoist with his own petar,° and't shall go hard
But I will delve one yard below their mines,
And blow them at the moon: O 'tis most sweet
When in one line two crafts directly meet.°   210
This man shall set me packing,°
I'll lug the guts into the neighbour room;
Mother good night indeed. This counsellor
Is now most still, most secret, and most grave,
Who was in life a foolish prating knave.   215

---

182 *bloat:* bloated with dissipation.   184 *reechy:* filthy.   186 *ravel:* unravel.
190 *paddock, bat, gib:* toad, bat, tomcat ("familiars" or demons in animal shape that attend on witches).   193–196 *Unpeg . . . down:* (the story refers to an ape that climbs to the top of a house and opens a basket of birds; when the birds fly away, the ape crawls into the basket, tries to fly, and breaks his neck. The point is that if she gives away Hamlet's secret, she harms herself).   195 *try conclusions:* experiment.   204–205 *sweep . . . knavery:* (like the marshal who went before a royal procession, clearing the way, so Rosencrantz and Guildenstern clear Hamlet's path to some unknown evil).   206 *enginer:* maker of war engines.   207 *Hoist . . . petar:* blown up by his own bomb.   210 *in one . . . meet:* the digger of the mine and the digger of the countermine meet halfway in their tunnels.
211 *packing:* (1) i.e., my bags (2) rushing away (3) plotting.

Come sir, to draw toward an end with you.
Good night mother. *Exit HAMLET tugging in POLONIUS.*

[ACT 4]

Scene 1. *[A room in the castle]*

Enter KING and QUEEN with ROSENCRANTZ and GUILDENSTERN.

KING. There's matter in these sighs, these profound heaves,
    You must translate, 'tis fit we understand them.
    Where is your son?
QUEEN. Bestow this place on us° a little while.

Exeunt ROSENCRANTZ and GUILDENSTERN.

    Ah mine own lord, what have I seen tonight! 5
KING. What, Gertrude? How does Hamlet?
QUEEN. Mad as the sea and wind when both contend
    Which is the mightier, in his lawless fit,
    Behind the arras hearing something stir,
    Whips out his rapier, cries "A rat, a rat," 10
    And in this brainish apprehension° kills
    The unseen good old man.
KING.   O heavy deed!
    It had been so with us° had we been there:
    His liberty is full of threats to all,
    To you yourself, to us, to every one. 15
    Alas, how shall this bloody deed be answered?
    It will be laid to us,° whose providence°
    Should have kept short,° restrained, and out of haunt°
    This mad young man; but so much was our love,
    We would not understand what was most fit, 20
    But like the owner of a foul disease,
    To keep it from divulging,° let it feed
    Even on the pith of life: where is he gone?
QUEEN. To draw apart the body he hath killed,
    O'er whom his very madness, like some ore 25
    Among a mineral of metals base,°
    Shows itself pure: a' weeps for what is done.
KING. O Gertrude, come away:
    The sun no sooner shall the mountains touch,
    But we will ship him hence and this vile deed 30
    We must with all our majesty and skill
    Both countenance° and excuse. Ho Guildenstern!

4 *Bestow . . . us:* leave us. 11 *brainish apprehension:* insane delusion. 13 *us:* me (royal plural). 17 *laid to us:* blamed on me. *providence:* foresight. 18 *short:* tethered by a short leash. *out of haunt:* away from others. 22 *divulging:* being divulged. 25–26 *ore . . . base:* pure ore (such as gold) in a mine of base metal. 32 *countenance:* defend.

Enter Rosencrantz *and* Guildenstern.

> Friends both, go join you with some further aid;
> Hamlet in madness hath Polonius slain,
> And from his mother's closet hath he dragged him.   35
> Go seek him out, speak fair, and bring the body
> Into the chapel; I pray you haste in this.   *Exeunt Gent[lemen.]*
> Come Gertrude, we'll call up our wisest friends,
> And let them know both what we mean to do
> And what's untimely done: [so haply slander,]   40
> Whose whisper o'er the world's diameter,
> As level° as the cannon to his blank°
> Transports his° poisoned shot, may miss our name,
> And hit the woundless° air. O come away,
> My soul is full of discord and dismay.   *Exeunt.*   45

Scene 2. *[Another room in the castle]*

Enter Hamlet.

Hamlet. Safely stowed.
> *Gentlemen within*: Hamlet, Lord Hamlet!
> But soft, what noise, who calls on Hamlet?
> O here they come.

Enter Rosencrantz *and* Guildenstern.

Rosencrantz. What have you done my lord with the dead body?
Hamlet. Compounded it with dust whereto 'tis kin.   5
Rosencrantz. Tell us where 'tis that we may take it thence,
> And bear it to the chapel.
Hamlet. Do not believe it.
Rosencrantz. Believe what?
Hamlet. That I can keep your counsel° and not mine own.° Besides,   10
> to be demanded of° a sponge, what replication° should be
> made by the son of a king?
Rosencrantz. Take you me for a sponge, my lord?
Hamlet. Ay sir, that soaks up the king's countenance,° his rewards,
> his authorities. But such officers do the king best service in   15
> the end; he keeps them like an apple in the corner of his
> jaw, first mouthed to be last swallowed: when he needs
> what you have gleaned, it is but squeezing you, and
> sponge, you shall be dry again.
Rosencrantz. I understand you not my lord.   20
Hamlet. I am glad of it: a knavish speech sleeps in° a foolish ear.
Rosencrantz. My lord, you must tell us where the body is, and go with
> us to the king.

---

42 *As level:* with a straight aim.   *blank:* while bull's-eye at the target's center.   43 *his:*
slander's.   44 *woundless:* invulnerable.   10 *counsel:* (1) advice (2) secret.   *keep . . .*
own: follow your advice and not keep my own secret.   11 *demanded of:* questioned by.
replication: reply to a charge.   14 *countenance:* favor.   21 *sleeps in:* means nothing to.

HAMLET. The body is with the king, but the king° is not with the
    body. The king is a thing—   25
GUILDENSTERN. A thing my lord?
HAMLET. Of nothing, bring me to him. Hide fox, and all after.°   *Exeunt.*

Scene 3. *[Another room in the castle.]*

Enter KING and two or three.

KING. I have sent to seek him, and to find the body:
    How dangerous is it that this man goes loose,
    Yet must not we put the strong law on him,
    He's loved of the distracted multitude,°
    Who like not in° their judgment, but their eyes,   5
    And where 'tis so, th'offender's scourge° is weighed
    But never the offence: to bear all° smooth and even,
    This sudden sending him away must seem
    Deliberate pause:° diseases desperate grown,
    By desperate appliance° are relieved,   10
    Or not at all.

Enter ROSENCRANTZ and all the rest.

           How now, what hath befallen?
ROSENCRANTZ. Where the dead body is bestowed my lord,
    We cannot get from him.
KING.   But where is he?
ROSENCRANTZ. Without, my lord, guarded,° to know your pleasure.
KING. Bring him before us.
ROSENCRANTZ.   Ho, bring in the lord.   15

Enter HAMLET (guarded) and GUILDENSTERN.

KING. Now Hamlet, where's Polonius?
HAMLET. At supper.
KING. At supper? where?
HAMLET. Not where he eats, but where a' is eaten: a certain
    convocation of politic° worms are e'en° at him. Your worm is your   20
    only emperor for diet, we fat all creatures else to fat us,
    and we fat ourselves for maggots. Your fat king and your
    lean beggar is but variable service,° two dishes but to one
    table, that's the end.
KING. Alas, alas.   25
HAMLET. A man may fish with the worm that hath eat of a king, and
    eat of the fish that hath fed of that worm.
KING. What dost thou mean by this?

---

24 *king . . . king:* Hamlet's father . . . Claudius.   27 *Hide fox . . . after:* (cry in a children's
game, like hide-and-seek).   4 *distracted multitude:* confused mob.   5 *in:* according to.
6 *scourge:* punishment.   7 *bear all:* carry out everything.   9 *Deliberate pause:* considered
delay.   10 *appliance:* remedy.   14 *guarded:* (Hamlet is under guard until he boards the
ship).   20 *politic:* (1) statesmanlike (2) crafty.   *e'en:* even now.   23 *variable service:*
different types of food.

HAMLET. Nothing but to show you how a king may go a progress°
through the guts of a beggar.   30

KING. Where is Polonius?

HAMLET. In heaven, send thither to see. If your messenger find him
not there, seek him i'th'other place yourself: but if indeed
you find him not within this month, you shall nose him as
you go up the stairs into the lobby.   35

KING. [*To Attendants.*] Go seek him there.

HAMLET. A' will stay till you come.   [*Exeunt.*]

KING. Hamlet, this deed, for thine especial safety—
Which we do tender,° as we dearly grieve
For that which thou hast done—must send thee hence   40
With fiery quickness. Therefore prepare thyself,
The bark is ready, and the wind at help,°
Th'associates tend,° and every thing is bent
For England.

HAMLET.   For England.

KING.   Ay Hamlet.

HAMLET.   Good.

KING. So is it if thou knew'st our purposes.   45

HAMLET. I see a cherub° that sees them: but come, for England.
Farewell dear mother.

KING. Thy loving father, Hamlet.

HAMLET. My mother: father and mother is man and wife, man and
wife is one flesh, and so my mother: come, for England.   *Exit.* 50

KING. [*To ROSENCRANTZ and GUILDENSTERN.*]
Follow him at foot,° tempt him with speed aboard,
Delay it not, I'll have him hence tonight.
Away, for every thing is sealed and done
That else leans on° th'affair, pray you make haste.   [*Exeunt.*]
And England,° if my love thou hold'st at aught°—   55
As my great power thereof may give thee sense,
Since yet thy cicatrice° looks raw and red
After the Danish sword, and thy free awe
Pays homage° to us—thou mayst not coldly set°
Our sovereign process,° which imports at full   60
By letters congruing° to that effect,
The present° death of Hamlet. Do it England,
For like the hectic° in my blood he rages,
And thou must cure me; till I know 'tis done,
Howe'er my haps,° my joys were ne'er begun.   *Exit.* 65

29 *go a progress:* make a splendid royal journey from one part of the country to another.
39 *tender:* cherish.   42 *at help:* helpful.   43 *tend:* wait.   46 *cherub:* (considered the
watchmen of heaven).   51 *at foot:* at his heels.   54 *leans on:* relates to.   55 *England:*
King of England.   *my love . . . aught:* you place any value on my favor.   57 *cicatrice:*
scar.   58–59 *free . . . homage:* awe which you, though free, still show by paying homage.
59 *coldly set:* lightly estimate.   60 *process:* command.   61 *congruing:* agreeing.
62 *present:* immediate.   63 *hectic:* fever.   65 *haps:* fortunes.

Scene 4. [A plain in Denmark]

Enter FORTINBRAS with his army over the stage.

FORTINBRAS. Go captain, from me greet the Danish king,
    Tell him that by his license, Fortinbras
    Craves the conveyance° of a promised march
    Over his kingdom. You know the rendezvous:
    If that his majesty would aught with us,   5
    We shall express our duty in his eye,°
    And let him know so.
CAPTAIN.   I will do't, my lord.
FORTINBRAS. Go softly° on.   *Exit.*

Enter HAMLET, ROSENCRANTZ, [GUILDENSTERN,] etc.

HAMLET. Good sir whose powers° are these?
CAPTAIN. They are of Norway sir.
HAMLET. How purposed sir I pray you?   10
CAPTAIN. Against some part of Poland.
HAMLET. Who commands them sir?
CAPTAIN. The nephew to old Norway, Fortinbras.
HAMLET. Goes it against the main° of Poland sir,   15
    Or for some frontier?
CAPTAIN. Truly to speak, and with no addition,
    We go to gain a little patch of ground
    That hath in it no profit but the name.°
    To pay five ducats, five, I would not farm it;   20
    Nor will it yield to Norway or the Pole
    A ranker° rate, should it be sold in fee.°
HAMLET. Why then the Polack never will defend it.
CAPTAIN. Yes, it is already garrisoned.
HAMLET. Two thousand souls, and twenty thousand ducats   25
    Will not debate the question of° this straw:°
    This is th'imposthume of much wealth and peace,°
    That inward breaks, and shows no cause without
    Why the man dies. I humbly thank you sir.
CAPTAIN. God bye you sir.   *[Exit.]*
ROSENCRANTZ.   Will't please you go my lord?   30
HAMLET. I'll be with you straight, go a little before.

                      [Exeunt all but HAMLET.]

    How all occasions do inform against me,
    And spur my dull revenge. What is a man
    If his chief good and market° of his time
    Be but to sleep and feed? a beast, no more: 35

3 *conveyance of:* escort for.   6 *in his eye:* face to face.   8 *softly:* slowly.   9 *powers:* troops.   15 *main:* body.   19 *name:* glory.   22 *ranker:* higher (as annual interest on the total).   *in fee:* outright.   26 *debate . . . of:* settle the dispute over.   *straw:* triviality.
27 *imposthume . . . peace:* swelling discontent (inner abscess) resulting from too much wealth and peace.   34 *market:* profit.

Sure he that made us with such large discourse,°
Looking before and after,° gave us not
That capability and god-like reason
To fust° in us unused. Now whether it be
Bestial oblivion,° or some craven° scruple   40
Of thinking too precisely on th'event°—
A thought which quartered hath but one part wisdom,
And ever three parts coward—I do not know
Why yet I live to say "This thing's to do,"
Sith I have cause, and will, and strength, and means   45
To do't; examples gross° as earth exhort me:
Witness this army of such mass and charge,°
Led by a delicate and tender° prince,
Whose spirit with divine ambition puffed,
Makes mouths° at the invisible event,°   50
Exposing what is mortal, and unsure,
To all that fortune, death, and danger dare,
Even for an egg-shell. Rightly to be great,
Is not to stir without great argument,
But greatly to find quarrel in a straw   55
When honour's at the stake.° How stand I then
That have a father killed, a mother stained,
Excitements° of my reason, and my blood,
And let all sleep, while to my shame I see
The imminent death of twenty thousand men,   60
That for a fantasy and trick° of fame
Go to their graves like beds, fight for a plot
Whereon the numbers cannot try the cause,°
Which is not tomb enough and continent°
To hide the slain. O from this time forth,   65
My thoughts be bloody, or be nothing worth.   *Exit.*

Scene 5. *[A room in the castle]*

Enter QUEEN, HORATIO *and a* GENTLEMAN.

QUEEN.   I will not speak with her.
GENTLEMAN.   She is importunate, indeed distract,°
   Her mood will needs be° pitied.
QUEEN.   What would she have?
GENTLEMAN.   She speaks much of her father, says she hears
   There's tricks i'th'world, and hems,° and beats her heart,   5

36 *discourse:* power of reasoning.   37 *Looking . . . after:* seeing causes and effects.
39 *fust:* grow moldy.   40 *Bestial oblivion:* forgetfulness, as a beast forgets its parents.
craven: cowardly.   41 *event:* outcome.   46 *gross:* obvious.   47 *charge:* expense.
48 *delicate and tender:* gentle and young.   50 *mouths:* faces.   *event:* outcome.
53–56 *Rightly . . . stake:* the truly great do not fight without just cause ("argument"), but it
is nobly ("greatly") done to fight even for a trifle if honor is at stake.   58 *Excitements:*
incentives.   61 *fantasy and trick:* illusion and trifle.   63 *Whereon . . . cause:* too small to
accommodate all the troops fighting for it.   64 *continent:* container.   2 *distract:* insane.
3 *will needs be:* needs to be.   5 *hems:* coughs.

Spurns enviously at straws,° speaks things in doubt°
That carry but half sense: her speech is nothing,
Yet the unshapèd use of it doth move
The hearers to collection;° they aim° at it,
And botch° the words up fit to their own thoughts,   10
Which as her winks, and nods, and gestures yield them,
Indeed would make one think there might be thought,
Though nothing sure, yet much unhappily.
HORATIO. 'Twere good she were spoken with, for she may strew
Dangerous conjectures in ill-breeding minds.   15
QUEEN. Let her come in.   *Exit* GENTLEMAN.
[*Aside.*] To my sick soul, as sin's true nature is,°
Each toy° seems prologue to some great amiss,°
So full of artless jealousy° is guilt,
It spills itself, in fearing to be spilt.   20

Enter OPHELIA, *distracted.*°

OPHELIA. Where is the beauteous majesty of Denmark?
QUEEN. How now Ophelia?
OPHELIA. [*Sings.*] How should I your true love know
                From another one?
                By his cockle hat and staff,°   25
                And his sandal shoon.°
QUEEN. Alas sweet lady, what imports this song?
OPHELIA. Say you? nay, pray you mark.
        [*Sings.*] He is dead and gone, lady,
                He is dead and gone,   30
                At his head a grass-green turf,
                At his heels a stone.
    O ho.
QUEEN. Nay but Ophelia—
OPHELIA.   Pray you mark.
        [*Sings.*] White his shroud as the mountain snow—

Enter KING.

QUEEN. Alas, look here my lord.   35
OPHELIA. [*Sings.*] Larded° all with sweet flowers,
                Which bewept to the ground did not go,
                With true-love showers.
KING. How do you, pretty lady?
OPHELIA. Well, God 'ild° you. They say the owl was a baker's   40

---

6 *Spurns . . . straws:* reacts maliciously to trifles.   *in doubt:* ambiguous.   9 *collection:*
inference.   *aim:* guess.   10 *botch:* patch.   17 *as sin's . . . is:* as is natural for the
guilty.   18 *toy:* trifle.   *amiss:* disaster.   19 *artless jealousy:* uncontrollable suspicion.
20 stage direction: *distracted:* insane.   25 *cockle hat and staff:* (marks of the pilgrim, the
cockle shell symbolizing his journey to the shrine of St. James; the pilgrim was a common
metaphor for the lover).   26 *shoon:* shoes.   36 *Larded:* trimmed.   40 *God 'ild:* God
yield (reward).

daughter.° Lord, we know what we are, but know not what
we may be. God be at your table.°

KING   Conceit° upon her father.

OPHELIA.   Pray you let's have no words of this, but when they ask
you what it means, say you this: 45
[*Sings.*] Tomorrow is Saint Valentine's day,
    All in the morning betime,°
    And I a maid at your window
      To be your Valentine.
Then up he rose, and donned his clo'es,   50
    And dupped° the chamber door,
Let in the maid, that out a maid,
      Never departed more.

KING.   Pretty Ophelia.

OPHELIA.   Indeed, la, without an oath I'll make an end on't.   55
[*Sings.*] By Gis° and by Saint Charity,
    Alack and fie for shame,
Young men will do't, if they come to't,
    By Cock° they are to blame.
Quoth she, Before you tumbled me,   60
    You promised me to wed.

(He answers)
    So would I ha' done, by yonder sun,
    An° thou hadst not come to my bed.

KING.   How long hath she been thus?   65

OPHELIA.   I hope all will be well. We must be patient, but I cannot
choose but weep to think they would lay him i'th'cold
ground. My brother shall know of it, and so I thank you
for your good counsel. Come, my coach: good night
ladies, good night. Sweet ladies, good night, good night.   [*Exit* OPHELIA.]   70
                                                                  [*Exit* HORATIO.]

KING.   Follow her close, give her good watch I pray you.
O this is the poison of deep grief, it springs
All from her father's death, and now behold:
O Gertrude, Gertrude,
When sorrows come, they come not single spies,   75
But in battalions: first her father slain,
Next, your son gone, and he most violent author
Of his own just remove, the people muddied,°
Thick and unwholesome in their thoughts and whispers
For good Polonius' death: and we have done but greenly°   80
In hugger-mugger° to inter him: poor Ophelia
Divided from herself and her fair judgment,
Without the which we are pictures or mere beasts,

40–41 *owl . . . daughter:* (in a medieval legend, a baker's daughter was turned into an owl
because she gave Jesus short weight on a loaf of bread).   42 *God . . . table:* (a blessing at
dinner).   43 *Conceit:* thinking.   47 *betime:* early (because the first woman a man saw
on Valentine's Day would be his true love).   51 *dupped:* opened.   56 *Gis:* contraction
of "Jesus."   59 *Cock:* (vulgarization of "God" in oaths).   64 *An:* if.   78 *muddied:*
stirred up.   80 *done but greenly:* acted like amateurs.   81 *hugger-mugger:* secret haste.

Last, and as much containing° as all these,
Her brother is in secret come from France,   85
Feeds on his wonder,° keeps himself in clouds,°
And wants not buzzers° to infect his ear
With pestilent speeches of his father's death,
Wherein necessity, of matter beggared,
Will nothing stick our person to arraign°   90
In ear and ear:° O my dear Gertrude, this
Like to a murdering-piece° in many places
Gives me superfluous death.   *A noise within.*

QUEEN.   Alack, what noise is this?
KING.   Attend!   *Enter a MESSENGER.*
Where are my Switzers°? Let them guard the door.   95
What is the matter?
MESSENGER.   Save yourself, my lord.
The ocean, overpeering of his list,°
Eats not the flats° with more impiteous haste
Than young Laertes in a riotous head°
O'erbears your officers: the rabble call him lord,   100
And as the world were now but to begin,
Antiquity forgot, custom not known,
The ratifiers and props of every word,
They cry "Choose we, Laertes shall be king!"
Caps, hands, and tongues applaud it to the clouds,   105
"Laertes shall be king, Laertes king!"   *A noise within.*
QUEEN.   How cheerfully on the false trail they cry.
O this is counter,° you false Danish dogs.
KING.   The doors are broke.

Enter LAERTES with others.

LAERTES.   Where is this king? Sirs, stand you all without.°   110
DANES.   No, let's come in.
LAERTES.   I pray you give me leave.°
DANES.   We will, we will.   *[They retire.]*
LAERTES.   I thank you, keep the door. O thou vile king,
Give me my father.
QUEEN.   Calmly, good Laertes.
LAERTES.   That drop of blood that's calm proclaims me bastard,   115
Cries cuckold° to my father, brands° the harlot
Even here between the chaste unsmirchèd brows
Of my true mother.

84 *containing:* i.e., cause for sorrow.   86 *Feeds . . . wonder:* sustains himself by wondering
about his father's death.   *clouds:* gloom, obscurity.   87 *wants not buzzers:* lacks not
whispering gossips.   89–90 *Wherein . . . arraign:* in which the tellers, lacking facts, will
not hesitate to accuse me.   91 *In ear and ear:* whispering from one ear to another.
92 *murdering-piece:* small cannon shooting shrapnel, to inflict numerous wounds.
95 *Switzers:* Swiss guards.   97 *overpeering . . . list:* rising above its usual limits.   98 *flats:*
lowlands.   99 *head:* armed force.   108 *counter:* following the scent backward.
110 *without:* outside.   111 *leave:* i.e., to enter alone.   116 *cuckold:* betrayed husband.
brands: (so harlots were punished).

KING.   What is the cause Laertes,
   That thy rebellion looks so giant-like?
   Let him go Gertrude, do not fear° our person,   120
   There's such divinity° doth hedge a king,
   That treason can but peep to° what it would,
   Acts little of his° will. Tell me Laertes,
   Why thou art this incensed. Let him go Gertrude.
   Speak man.   125
LAERTES.   Where is my father?
KING.   Dead.
QUEEN.   But not by him.
KING.   Let him demand his fill.
LAERTES.   How came he dead? I'll not be juggled with.
   To hell allegiance, vows to the blackest devil,
   Conscience and grace, to the profoundest pit.   130
   I dare damnation: to this point I stand,
   That both the worlds I give to negligence,°
   Let come what comes, only I'll be revenged
   Most throughly for my father.
KING.   Who shall stay you?
LAERTES.   My will, not all the world's:°   135
   And for my means, I'll husband° them so well,
   They shall go far with little.
KING.   Good Laertes,
   If you desire to know the certainty
   Of your dear father, is't writ in your revenge
   That swoopstake,° you will draw both friend and foe,   140
   Winner and loser?
LAERTES.   None but his enemies.
KING.   Will you know them then?
LAERTES.   To his good friends thus wide I'll ope my arms,
   And like the kind life-rend'ring pelican,°
   Repast them with my blood.
KING.   Why now you speak   145
   Like a good child, and a true gentleman.
   That I am guiltless of your father's death,
   And am most sensibly° in grief for it,
   It shall as level° to your judgment 'pear
   As day does to your eye.   150

   [*A noise within.*]

   [*Crowd shouts.*] Let her come in.
LAERTES.   How now, what noise is that?

---

120 *fear:* i.e., for.   121 *divinity:* divine protection.   122 *peep to:* strain to see.
123 *his:* treason's.   132 *both . . . negligence:* I care nothing for this world or the next.
135 *world's:* i.e., will.   136 *husband:* economize.   140 *swoopstake:* sweeping in all the
stakes in a game, both of winner and loser.   144 *pelican:* (the mother pelican was
believed to nourish her young with blood pecked from her own breast).   148 *sensibly:*
feelingly.   149 *level:* plain.

O heat, dry up my brains, tears seven time salt,
Burn out the sense and virtue° of mine eye!
By heaven, thy madness shall be paid with weight,°
Till our scale turn the beam,° O rose of May,   155
Dear maid, kind sister, sweet Ophelia:
O heavens, is't possible a young maid's wits
Should be as mortal as an old man's life?
Nature is fine in love, and where 'tis fine,
It sends some previous instance of itself   160
after the thing it loves.°
OPHELIA. [*Sings.*] They bore him barefaced on the bier,
        Hey non nonny, nonny, hey nonny:
        And in his grave rained many a tear—
Fare you well my dove.   165
LAERTES. Hadst thou thy wits, and didst persuade revenge,
It could not move thus.
OPHELIA. You must sing "adown adown," and you call him adown-a.
O how the wheel becomes it.° It is the false steward that
stole his master's daughter.   170
LAERTES. This nothing's more than matter.°
OPHELIA. There's rosemary,° that's for remembrance, pray you love
remember: and there is pansies, that's for thoughts.
LAERTES. A document° in madness, thoughts and remembrance
fitted.°   175
OPHELIA. There's fennel for you, and columbines.° There's rue° for
you, and here's some for me, we may call it herb of grace°
o'Sundays: O, you must wear your rue with a difference.°
There's a daisy,° I would give you some violets,° but they
withered all when my father died: they say a' made a good   180
end;
      [*Sings.*] For bonny sweet Robin is all my joy.
LAERTES. Thought and affliction, passion, hell itself,
She turns to favour and to prettiness.
OPHELIA. [*Sings.*] And will a' not come again,   185
        And will a' not come again?
          No, no, he is dead,
          Go to thy death-bed,
        He never will come again.

---

153 *sense and virtue:* feeling and power.　　154 *with weight:* with equal weight.　　155 *turn the beam:* outweigh the other side.　　159–161 *Nature . . . loves:* filial love that is so refined and pure sends some precious token (her wits) after the beloved dead.　　169 *wheel becomes it:* refrain ("adown") suits the subject (Polonius's fall).　　171 *more than matter:* more eloquent than sane speech.　　172 *There's rosemary:* (given to Laertes; she may be distributing imaginary or real flowers).　　174 *document:* lesson.　　*thoughts . . . fitted:* thoughts of revenge matched with remembrance of Polonius.　　176 *fennel, columbines:* (given to the king, symbolizing flattery and ingratitude).　　*rue:* (given to the queen, symbolizing sorrow or repentance).　　177 *herb of grace:* (because it symbolizes repentance). 178 *with a difference:* for a different reason (Ophelia's is for sorrow and the queen's for repentance).　　179 *daisy:* (symbolizing dissembling).　　*violets:* (symbolizing faithfulness).

His beard was as white as snow,   190
All flaxen was his poll,°
    He is gone, he is gone,
    And we cast away moan,
God ha' mercy on his soul.
And of all Christian souls, I pray God. God bye you.   195

Exit OPHELIA.

LAERTES.   Do you see this, O God?
KING.   Laertes, I must commune with your grief,
    Or you deny me right: go but apart,
    Make choice of whom your wisest friends you will,
    And they shall hear and judge 'twixt you and me;   200
    If by direct or by collateral° hand
    They find us touched,° we will our kingdom give,
    Our crown, our life, and all that we call ours
    To you in satisfaction; but if not,
    Be you content to lend your patience to us,   205
    And we shall jointly labour with your soul
    To give it due content.
LAERTES.   Let this be so.
    His means of death, his obscure funeral,
    No trophy,° sword, nor hatchment° o'er his bones,
    No noble rite, nor formal ostentation,°   210
    Cry° to be heard as 'twere from heaven to earth,
    That I must call't in question.
KING.   So you shall,
    And where th'offence is, let the great axe fall.
    I pray you go with me.   [*Exeunt.*]

Scene 6. [Another room in the castle]

Enter HORATIO *and others.*

HORATIO.   What are they that would speak with me?
GENTLEMAN.   Seafaring men sir, they say they have letters for you.
HORATIO.   Let them come in.   [*Exit* ATTENDANT.]
    I do not know from what part of the world
    I should be greeted, if not from Lord Hamlet.   5

Enter SAILORS.

SAILOR.   God bless you sir.
HORATIO.   Let him bless thee too.
SAILOR.   A' shall sir, an't please him. There's a letter for you sir, it
    came from th'ambassador that was bound for England, if
    your name be Horatio, as I am let to know it is.   10

191 *flaxen . . . poll:* white was his head.   201 *collateral:* indirect.   202 *touched:* tainted
with guilt.   209 *trophy:* memorial.   *hatchment:* tablet displaying coat of arms.
210 *ostentation:* ceremony.   211 *Cry:* cry out.

HORATIO. [*Reads the letter.*] "Horatio, when thou shalt have
overlooked° this, give these fellows some means to the king,
they have letters for him. Ere we were two days old at sea,
a pirate of very warlike appointment° gave us chase.
Finding ourselves too slow of sail, we put on a compelled   15
valour, and in the grapple° I boarded them. On the instant
they got clear of our ship, so I alone became their prisoner.
They have dealt with me like thieves of mercy,° but they
knew what they did. I am to do a good turn for them. Let
the king have the letters I have sent, and repair° thou to me   20
with as much speed as thou wouldst fly death. I have
words to speak in thine ear will make thee dumb, yet are
they much too light for the bore° of the matter. These good
fellows will bring thee where I am. Rosencrantz and
Guildenstern hold their course for England. Of them I   25
have much to tell thee. Farewell.
           He that thou knowest thine, Hamlet."
Come, I will give you way° for these your letters,
And do't the speedier that you may direct me
To him from whom you brought them.   *Exeunt.*   30

Scene 7. [Another room in the castle]

Enter KING *and* LAERTES.

KING. Now must your conscience my acquittance seal,°
And you must put me in your heart for friend,
Sith you have heard and with a knowing ear,
That he which hath your noble father slain
Pursued my life.
LAERTES.   It well appears: but tell me   5
Why you proceeded not against these feats
So crimeful and so capital in nature,
As by your safety, greatness, wisdom, all things else,
You mainly were stirred up.°
KING.   O for two special reasons,
Which may to you perhaps seem much unsinewed,°   10
But yet to me they're strong. The queen his mother
Lives almost by his looks, and for myself,
My virtue or my plague, be it either which,
She's so conjunctive° to my life and soul,
That as the star moves not but in his sphere,°   15
I could not but by her. The other motive,
Why to a public count° I might not go,

12 *overlooked:* read over.   14 *appointment:* equipment.   16 *in the grapple:* when the
pirate ship hooked onto ours.   18 *of mercy:* merciful.   20 *repair:* come.   23 *bore:*
size, caliber.   28 *way:* access (to the king).   1 *my acquittance seal:* confirm my acquittal.
9 *mainly . . . up:* were strongly urged.   10 *much unsinewed:* very weak.   14 *conjunctive:*
closely allied.   15 *in his sphere:* (referring to the Ptolemaic belief that each planet, fixed
in its own sphere, revolved around the earth).   17 *count:* accounting.

Is the great love the general gender° bear him,
Who dipping all his faults in their affection,
Would like the spring that turneth wood to stone,°   20
Convert his gyves to graces,° so that my arrows,
Too slightly timbered° for so loud a wind,
Would have reverted to my bow again,
And not where I had aimed them.

LAERTES.   And so have I a noble father lost,   25
A sister driven into desperate terms,°
Whose worth, if praises may go back° again,
Stood challenger on mount of all the age
For her perfections.° But my revenge will come.

KING.   Break not your sleeps for that, you must not think   30
That we are made of stuff so flat and dull,
That we can let our beard be shook with danger,
And think it pastime. You shortly shall hear more,
I loved your father, and we love ourself,
And that I hope will teach you to imagine—   35

Enter a MESSENGER with letters.

How now. What news?
MESSENGER.   Letters my lord, from Hamlet.
These to your majesty, this to the queen.
KING.   From Hamlet? Who brought them?
MESSENGER.   Sailors my lord they say, I saw them not:
They were given me by Claudio, he received them   40
Of him that brought them.
KING.   Laertes you shall hear them:
Leave us.   *Exit [MESSENGER]*
[*Reads*] "High and mighty, you shall know I am set naked° on
your kingdom. Tomorrow shall I beg leave to see your kingly
eyes, when I shall, first asking your pardon° thereunto,   45
recount the occasion of my sudden and more strange return
                                    Hamlet."
What should this mean? Are all the rest come back?
Or is it some abuse,° and no such thing?
LAERTES.   Know you the hand?
KING.   'Tis Hamlet's character.° "Naked,"   50
And in a postscript here he says "alone."
Can you devise° me?

---

18 *general gender:* common people.   20 *the spring . . . stone:* (the baths of King's Newnham
in Warwickshire were described as being able to turn wood into stone because of their high
concentrations of lime).   21 *Convert . . . graces:* regard his fetters (had he been
imprisoned) as honors.   22 *slightly timbered:* light-shafted.   26 *desperate terms:* madness.
27 *go back:* i.e., before her madness.   28–29 *challenger . . . perfections:* like a challenger on
horseback, ready to defend against the world her claim to perfection.   43 *naked:* without
resources.   45 *pardon:* permission.   49 *abuse:* deception.   50 *character:* handwriting.
52 *devise me:* explain it.

LAERTES. I am lost in it my lord, but let him come,
  It warms the very sickness in my heart
  That I shall live and tell him to his teeth,   55
  "Thus didest thou."
KING.   If it be so Laertes—
  As how should it be so? how otherwise?—
  Will you be ruled by me?
LAERTES.   Ay my lord,
  So you will not o'errule me to a peace.
KING. To thine own peace: if he be now returned,   60
  As checking at° his voyage, and that he means
  No more to undertake it, I will work him
  To an exploit, now ripe in my device,°
  Under the which he shall not choose but fall:
  And for his death no wind of blame shall breathe,   65
  But even his mother shall uncharge the practice,°
  And call it accident.
LAERTES.   My lord, I will be ruled,
  The rather if you could devise it so
  That I might be the organ.°
KING.   It falls right.
  You have been talked of since your travel much,   70
  And that in Hamlet's hearing, for a quality
  Wherein they say you shine: your sum of parts°
  Did not together pluck such envy from him
  As did that one, and that in my regard
  Of the unworthiest siege.°
LAERTES.   What part is that my lord?   75
KING. A very riband° in the cap of youth,
  Yet needful too, for youth no less becomes°
  The light and careless livery° that it wears,
  Than settled age his sables° and his weeds°
  Importing health and graveness; two months since,°   80
  Here was a gentleman of Normandy—
  I have seen myself, and served against the French,
  And they can° well on horseback—but this gallant
  Had witchcraft in't, he grew unto his seat,
  And to such wondrous doing brought his horse,   85
  As had he been incorpsed and demi-natured°
  With the brave beast. So far he topped my thought,
  That I in forgery of° shapes and tricks
  Come short of what he did.

61 *checking at:* altering the course of (when the falcon forsakes one quarry for another).
63 *ripe in my device:* already planned by me.   66 *uncharge the practice:* acquit the plot (of
treachery).   69 *organ:* instrument.   72 *your sum of parts:* all your accomplishments.
75 *siege:* rank.   76 *riband:* decoration.   77 *becomes:* befits.   78 *livery:* clothing
(denoting rank or occupation).   79 *sables:* fur-trimmed gowns.   *weeds:* garments.
80 *since:* ago.   83 *can:* can do.   86 *incorpsed . . . natured:* made into one body, sharing
half its nature.   88 *in forgery of:* imagining.

LAERTES.   A Norman was't?

KING.   A Norman.   ,   90

LAERTES.   Upon my life, Lamord.

KING.   The very same.

LAERTES.   I know him well, he is the brooch° indeed
    And gem of all the nation.

KING.   He made confession° of you,
    And gave you such a masterly report   95
    For art and exercise in your defence,
    And for your rapier most especial,
    That he cried out 'twould be a sight indeed
    If one could match you; the scrimers° of their nation
    He swore had neither motion, guard, nor eye,   100
    If you opposed them; sir this report of his
    Did Hamlet so envenom° with his envy,
    That he could nothing do but wish and beg
    Your sudden coming o'er to play with him.
    Now out of this—

LAERTES.   What out of this, my lord?   105

KING.   Laertes, was your father dear to you?
    Or are you like the painting of a sorrow,
    A face without a heart?

LAERTES.   Why ask you this?

KING.   Not that I think you did not love your father,
    But that I know love is begun by time,   110
    And that I see in passages of proof,°
    Time qualifies° the spark and fire of it:
    There lives within the very flame of love
    A kind of wick or snuff that will abate it,°
    And nothing is at a like goodness still,°   115
    For goodness growing to a plurisy,°
    Dies in his own too-much. That we would do
    We should do when we would: for this "would"° changes,
    And hath abatements and delays as many
    As there are tongues, are hands, are accidents,   120
    And then this "should"° is like a spendthrift sigh,
    That hurts by easing;° but to the quick° of th'ulcer:
    Hamlet comes back, what would you undertake
    To show yourself in deed your father's son
    More than in words?

LAERTES.   To cut his throat i'th'church.   125

KING.   No place indeed should murder sanctuarize,°

92 *brooch:* ornament.   94 *confession:* report.   99 *scrimers:* fencers.   102 *envenom:*
poison.   111 *passages of proof:* examples drawn from experience.   112 *qualifies:*
weakens.   114 *snuff . . . it:* charred end of the wick that will diminish the flame.
115 *still:* always.   116 *plurisy:* excess.   118 *"would":* will to act.   121 *"should":*
reminder of one's duty.   121–122 *spendthrift . . . easing:* A sigh which, though giving
temporary relief, wastes life, as each sigh draws a drop of blood away from the heart (a
common Elizabethan belief).   122 *quick:* most sensitive spot.   126 *murder sanctuarize:*
give sanctuary to murder.

Revenge should have no bounds: but good Laertes,
Will you do this, keep close within your chamber:
Hamlet returned shall know you are come home,
We'll put on° those shall praise your excellence,   130
And set a double varnish on the fame
The Frenchman gave you, bring you in fine° together,
And wager on your heads; he being remiss,°
Most generous, and free from all contriving,
Will not peruse the foils, so that with ease,   135
Or with a little shuffling, you may choose
A sword unbated,° and in a pass of practice°
Requite him for your father.

LAERTES.   I will do't,
And for the purpose, I'll anoint my sword.
I bought an unction° of a mountebank°   140
So mortal,° that but dip a knife in it,
Where it draws blood, no cataplasm° so rare,
Collected from all simples° that have virtue°
Under the moon,° can save the thing from death
That is but scratched withal: I'll touch my point   145
With this contagion, that if I gall° him slightly,
It may be death.

KING.   Let's further think of this,
Weigh what convenience both of time and means
May fit us to our shape;° if this should fail,
And that our drift° look through° our bad performance,   150
'Twere better not assayed; therefore this project
Should have a back or second that might hold
If this did blast in proof;° soft, let me see,
We'll make a solemn wager on your cunnings°—
I ha't: 155
When in your motion you are hot and dry,
As make your bouts more violent to that end,
And that he calls for drink, I'll have prepared him
A chalice for the nonce,° whereon but sipping,
If he by chance escape your venomed stuck,°   160
Our purpose may hold there; but stay, what noise?

Enter QUEEN.

How, sweet queen?
QUEEN.   One woe doth tread upon another's heel,

---

130 *put on:* incite.   132 *in fine:* finally.   133 *remiss:* easy-going.   137 *unbated:* not
blunted (the edges and points were blunted for fencing).   *pass of practice:* (1) match for
exercise (2) treacherous thrust.   140 *unction:* ointment.   *mountebank:* quack doctor,
medicine man.   141 *mortal:* deadly.   142 *cataplasm:* poultice.   143 *simples:* herbs.
virtue: power (of healing).   144 *Under the moon:* (when herbs were supposed to be
collected to be most effective).   146 *gall:* scratch.   149 *shape:* plan.   150 *drift:* aim.
look through: be exposed by.   153 *blast in proof:* fail when tested (as a bursting cannon).
154 *cunnings:* skills.   159 *nonce:* occasion.   160 *stuck:* thrust.

So fast they follow; your sister's drowned, Laertes.

LAERTES.   Drowned! O where?   165

QUEEN.   There is a willow grows aslant a brook,
That shows his hoar° leaves in the glassy stream,
There with fantastic garlands did she make
Of crow-flowers,° nettles, daisies, and long purples,°
That liberal° shepherds give a grosser name,   170
But our cold° maids do dead men's fingers call them.
There on the pendent boughs her coronet weeds°
Clamb'ring to hang, an envious sliver° broke,
When down her weedy trophies and herself
Fell in the weeping brook: her clothes spread wide,   175
And mermaid-like awhile they bore her up,
Which time she chanted snatches of old tunes,
As one incapable of° her own distress,
Or like a creature native and indued
Unto° that element: but long it could not be   180
Till that her garments, heavy with their drink,
Pulled the poor wretch from her melodious lay
To muddy death.

LAERTES.   Alas, then she is drowned?

QUEEN.   Drowned, drowned.

LAERTES.   Too much of water hast thou, poor Ophelia,   185
And therefore I forbid my tears; but yet
It is our trick, nature her custom holds,
Let shame say what it will; when these° are gone,
The woman will be out.° Adieu my lord,
I have a speech o' fire that fain would blaze,   190
But that this folly douts it.°   *Exit.*

KING.   Let's follow, Gertrude,
How much I had to do to calm his rage;
Now fear I this will give it start again,
Therefore let's follow.   *Exeunt.*

[ACT 5]

Scene 1. *[A churchyard]*

Enter two CLOWNS.°

1. CLOWN.   Is she to be buried in Christian burial,° when she wilfully
seeks her own salvation?°

167 *hoar:* grey (on the underside).   169 *crow-flowers:* buttercups.   *long purples:*
spikelike early orchid.   170 *liberal:* libertine.   171 *cold:* chaste.   172 *coronet weeds:*
garland of weeds.   173 *envious sliver:* malicious branch.   178 *incapable of:* unable to
understand.   179–180 *indued Unto:* endowed by nature to exist in.   188 *these:* i.e.,
tears.   189 *woman . . . out:* womanly habits will be out of me.   191 *folly douts it:* tears
put it out.   0.2 Stage direction: *clowns:* rustics.   1 *Christian burial:* consecrated ground
within a churchyard (where suicides were not allowed burial).   2 *salvation:* i.e.,
"damnation." The gravediggers make a number of such "mistakes," later termed
"malapropisms."

2. CLOWN. I tell thee she is, therefore make her grave straight.° The
crowner hath sat on her,° and finds it Christian burial.

1. CLOWN. How can that be, unless she drowned herself in her own   5
defence?°

2. CLOWN. Why, 'tis found so.

1. CLOWN. It must be "se offendendo,"° it cannot be else: for here lies
the point: if I drown myself wittingly, it argues an act,
and an act hath three branches, it is to act, to do, and to   10
perform; argal,° she drowned herself wittingly.

2. CLOWN. Nay, but hear you, goodman delver.

1. CLOWN. Give me leave: here lies the water, good. Here stands the
man, good. If the man go to this water and drown himself,
it is, will he nill he,° he goes, mark you that. But if the   15
water come to him, and drown him, he drowns not
himself. Argal, he that is not guilty of his own death, shortens not his own
life.

2. CLOWN. But is this law?

1. CLOWN. Ay marry is't, crowner's quest° law.   20

2. CLOWN. Will you ha' the truth on't? If this had not been a
gentlewoman, she would have been buried out o'Christian
burial.

1. CLOWN. Why there thou say'st, and the more pity that great folk
should have countenance° in this world to drown or hang   25
themselves more than their even-Christen.° Come, my
spade; there is no ancient gentlemen but gardeners,
ditchers and grave-makers; they hold up Adam's profession.

2. CLOWN. Was he a gentleman?

1. CLOWN. A' was the first that ever bore arms.°   30

2. CLOWN. Why, he had none.

1. CLOWN. What, art a heathen? How dost thou understand the
Scripture? The Scripture says Adam digged; could he dig
without arms? I'll put another question to thee; if thou
answerest me not to the purpose, confess thyself—   35

2. CLOWN. Go to.

1. CLOWN. What is he that builds stronger than either the mason, the
shipwright, or the carpenter?

2. CLOWN. The gallows-maker, for that frame outlives a thousand
tenants.   40

1. CLOWN. I like thy wit well in good faith, the gallows does well, but
how does it well? It does well to those that do ill. Now
thou dost ill to say the gallows is built stronger than the
church. Argal, the gallows may do well to thee.° To't
again, come.   45

---

3 *straight:* straightaway, at once.   4 *crowner . . . her:* coroner has ruled on her case.
5–6 *her own defence:* (as self-defense justifies homicide, so may it justify suicide).   8 *"se offendendo":* (he means *"se defendendo,"* in self-defense).   11 *argal:* (corruption of "ergo"
= therefore).   15 *will he nill he:* will he or will he not (willy nilly).   20 *quest:* inquest.
25 *countenance:* privilege.   26 *even-Christen:* fellow Christian.   30 *arms:* (with a pun on
"coat of arms").   44 *to thee:* i.e., by hanging you.

2. CLOWN. 'Who builds stronger than a mason, a shipwright, or a
    carpenter?'
1. CLOWN. Ay, tell me that, and unyoke.°
2. CLOWN. Marry, now I can tell.
1. CLOWN. To't.   50
2. CLOWN. Mass,° I cannot tell.
1. CLOWN. Cudgel thy brains no more about it, for your dull ass will
    not mend his pace with beating, and when you are asked
    this question next, say "a grave-maker:" the houses he
    makes last till doomsday. Go get thee to Yaughan,° and   55
    fetch me a stoup° of liquor.   [*Exit 2. CLOWN.*]

Enter HAMLET and HORATIO afar off.

1. CLOWN. (*Sings.*) In youth when I did love, did love,
             Methought it was very sweet,
             To contract oh the time for a° my behove,°
             O methought there a was nothing a meet.°   60
HAMLET. Has this fellow no feeling of his business, that a'sings in
    grave-making?
HORATIO. Custom hath made it in him a property of easiness.°
HAMLET. 'Tis e'en so, the hand of little employment hath the
    daintier sense.°   65
1. CLOWN. (*Sings.*) But age with his stealing steps
             Hath clawed me in his clutch,
             And hath shipped me intil° the land,
             As if I had never been such.   [*Throws up a skull.*]
HAMLET. That skull had a tongue in it, and could sing once: how the   70
    knave jowls° it to the ground, as if'twere Cain's jaw-bone,°
    that did the first murder. This might be the pate of a
    politician, which this ass now o'erreaches;° one that
    would circumvent° God, might it not?
HORATIO. It might my lord.   75
HAMLET. Or of a courtier, which could say "Good morrow sweet
    lord, how dost thou good lord?" This might be my lord
    such-a-one, that praised my lord such-a-one's horse, when
    a'meant to beg it, might it not?
HORATIO. It might my lord.   80
HAMLET. Why e'en so, and now my Lady Worm's, chopless,° and
    knocked about the mazzard° with a sexton's spade; here's
    fine revolution an° we had the trick° to see't. Did these

---

48 *unyoke:* unharness (your wits, after this exertion).   51 *Mass:* by the mass.
55 *Yaughan:* probably a local innkeeper.   56 *stoup:* stein, drinking mug.   59 *oh, a:* (he
grunts as he works).   *behove:* benefit.   60 *meet:* suitable.   63 *Custom . . . easiness:*
being accustomed to it has made him indifferent.   65 *daintier sense:* finer sensibility
(being uncalloused).   68 *intil:* into.   71 *jowls:* casts (with obvious pun).   *Cain's jawbone:* the jawbone of an ass with which Cain murdered Abel.   73 *o'erreaches:* (1) reaches
over (2) gets the better of.   74 *would circumvent:* tried to outwit.   81 *chopless:* lacking
the lower jaw.   82 *mazzard:* head.   83 *an:* if.   *trick:* knack.

bones cost no more the breeding, but to play at loggets°
with them? Mine ache to think on't.   85
1. CLOWN.   (*Sings.*) A pick-axe and a spade, a spade,
             For and a shrouding sheet,
             O a pit of clay for to be made
             For such a guest is meet.°   [*Throws up another skull.*]
HAMLET.   There's another: why may not that be the skull of a   90
lawyer? Where be his quiddities° now, his quillets,° his
cases, his tenures,° and his tricks? Why does he suffer this
rude knave now to knock him about the sconce° with a
dirty shovel, and will not tell him of his action of battery?
Hum, this fellow might be in's time a great buyer of land,   95
with his statutes,° his recognizances,° his fines,° his double
vouchers,° his recoveries:° is this the fine° of his fines, and
the recovery° of his recoveries, to have his fine pate full of
fine dirt? Will his vouchers vouch him no more of his
purchases, and double ones too, than the length and   100
breadth of a pair of indentures?° The very conveyances° of
his lands will scarcely lie in this box,° and must th'inheritor°
himself have no more, ha?
HORATIO.   Not a jot more my lord.
HAMLET.   Is not parchment made of sheep-skins?   105
HORATIO.   Ay my lord, and of calves'-skins too.
HAMLET.   They are sheep and calves which seek out assurance° in
that. I will speak to this fellow. Whose grave's this, sirrah?
1. CLOWN.   Mine sir:
    [*Sings.*] O a pit of clay for to be made   110
          For such a guest is meet.
HAMLET.   I think it be thine indeed, for thou liest in't.
1. CLOWN.   You lie out on't° sir, and therefore 'tis not yours; for my
part I do not lie in't, and yet it is mine.
HAMLET.   Thous dost lie in't, to be in't and say it is thine: 'tis for the   115
dead, not for the quick,° therefore thou liest.
1. CLOWN.   'Tis a quick lie sir, 'twill away again from me to you.
HAMLET.   What man dost thou dig it for?
1. CLOWN.   For no man sir.
HAMLET.   What woman then?   120
1. CLOWN.   For none neither.
HAMLET.   Who is to be buried in't?
1. CLOWN.   One that was a woman sir, but rest her soul she's dead.
HAMLET.   How absolute° the knave is, we must speak by the card,° or

---

84 *loggets:* game in which small pieces of wood were thrown at fixed stakes.   89 *meet:*
fitting.   91 *quiddities:* subtle definition.   *quillets:* minute distinctions.   92 *tenures:*
property holdings.   93 *sconce:* head.   96 *statutes:* mortgages.   *recognizances:*
promissory bonds.   96–97 *fines, recoveries:* legal processes for transferring real estate.
97 *vouchers:* persons who vouched for a title to real estate.   97 *fine:* end.   98 *recovery:*
attainment.   100–101 *length . . . indentures:* contracts in duplicate, which spread out,
would just cover his grave.   101 *conveyances:* deeds.   102 *box:* the grave.   *inheritor:*
owner.   107 *assurance:* (1) security (2) transfer of land.   113 *on:* of.   116 *quick:*
living.   124 *absolute:* precise.   *by the card:* exactly to the point (card on which compass
points are marked).

equivocation° will undo us. By the lord, Horatio, this   125
three years I have took note of it, the age is grown so
picked,° that the toe of the peasant comes so near the heel of
the courtier, he galls his kibe.° How long hast thou been
grave-maker?

1. CLOWN.   Of all the days i'th'year I came to't that day that our last   130
king Hamlet overcame Fortinbras.

HAMLET.   How long is that since?

1. CLOWN.   Cannot you tell that? Every fool can tell that. It was the very day
that young Hamlet was born: he that is mad and
sent into England.   135

HAMLET.   Ay marry, why was he sent into England?

1. CLOWN.   Why because a' was mad: a' shall recover his wits there, or
if a' do not, 'tis no great matter there.

HAMLET.   Why?

1. CLOWN.   'Twill not be seen in him there, there the men are as mad   140
as he.

HAMLET.   How came he mad?

1. CLOWN.   Very strangely they say.

HAMLET.   How strangely?

1. CLOWN.   Faith, e'en with losing his wits.   145

HAMLET.   Upon what ground?

1. CLOWN.   Why here in Denmark: I have been sexton here man and
boy thirty years.

HAMLET.   How long will a man lie i'ith'earth ere he rot?

1. CLOWN.   Faith, if a' be not rotten before a' die, as we have many   150
pocky° corses nowadays that will scarce hold the laying in,
a' will last you some eight year, or nine year. A tanner will
last you nine year.

HAMLET.   Why he more than another?

1. CLOWN.   Why sir, his hide is so tanned with his trade, that a' will   155
keep out water a great while; and your water is a sore°
decayer of your whoreson dead body. Here's a skull now:
this skull hath lain you i'th'earth three-and-twenty years.

HAMLET.   Whose was it?

1. CLOWN.   A whoreson mad fellow's it was, whose do you think it   160
was?

HAMLET.   Nay, I know not.

1. CLOWN.   A pestilence on him for a mad rogue, a' poured a flagon of
Rhenish° on my head once; this same skull sir, was sir,
Yorick's skull, the king's jester.   165

HAMLET.   This?

1. CLOWN.   E'en that.

HAMLET.   Let me see. [*Takes the skull.*] Alas poor Yorick, I knew him
Horatio, a fellow of infinite jest, of most excellent fancy,°

---

125 *equivocation:* ambiguity.   127 *picked:* fastidious ("picky").   128 *galls his kibe:* chafes
the sore on the courtier's heel.   151 *pocky:* rotten (with venereal disease).   156 *sore:*
grievous.   164 *Rhenish:* Rhine wine.   169 *fancy:* imagination.

he hath borne me on his back a thousand times: and now 170
how abhorred in my imagination it is: my gorge rises at it.
Here hung those lips that I have kissed I know not how
oft. Where be your gibes now? your gambols, your songs,
your flashes of merriment, that were wont to set the table
on a roar?° not one now to mock your own grinning? quite 175
chop-fallen?° Now get you to my lady's chamber, and tell
her, let her paint an inch thick, to this favour° she must
come. Make her laugh at that. Prithee Horatio, tell me one
thing.

HORATIO.   What's that, my lord? 180

HAMLET.   Dost thou think Alexander looked o' this fashion
i'th'earth?

HORATIO.   E'en so.

HAMLET.   And smelt so? pah.   [*Puts down the skull.*]

HORATIO.   E'en so my lord. 185

HAMLET.   To what base uses we may return, Horatio. Why may not
imagination trace the noble dust of Alexander, til a'find it
stopping a bung-hole?°

HORATIO.   'Twere to consider too curiously,° to consider so.

HAMLET.   No faith, not a jot, but to follow him thither with modesty° 190
enough, and likelihood to lead it; as thus: Alexander died,
Alexander was buried, Alexander returneth to dust, the
dust is earth, of earth we make loam,° and why of that loam
whereto he was converted, might they not stop a
beer-barrel? 195

Imperious Caesar, dead and turned to clay,
Might stop a hole to keep the wind away.
O that that earth which kept the world in awe,
Should patch a wall t'expel the winter's flaw.°

But soft, but soft awhile, here comes the king, 200
The queen, the courtiers.

Enter KING, QUEEN, LAERTES, *[Doctor of Divinity], and a coffin, with Lords attendant.*

Who is this they follow?
And with such maimèd° rites? This doth betoken
The corse they follow did with desp'rate hand
Fordo it° own life; 'twas of some estate.°
Couch° we awhile, and mark.   [*They retire.*] 205

HAMLET.   That is Laertes,
A very noble youth: mark.

LAERTES.   What ceremony else?

DOCTOR.   Her obsequies have been as far enlarged

---

175 *on a roar:* roaring with laughter.   176 *chop-fallen:* (a) lacking a lower jaw (2) dejected,
"down in the mouth."   177 *favour:* appearance.   188 *bung-hole:* hole in a cask.
189 *curiously:* minutely.   190 *modesty:* moderation.   193 *loam:* a clay mixture used as
plaster.   199 *flaw:* windy gusts.   202 *maimèd:* abbreviated.   204 *Fordo it:* destroy its.
estate: social rank.   205 *Couch:* hide.

As we have warranty: her death was doubtful,°   210
And but that great command o'ersways the order,
She should in ground unsanctified have lodged
Til the last trumpet: for charitable prayers,
Shards,° flints and pebbles should be thrown on her:
Yet here she is allowed her virgin crants,°   215
Her maiden strewments,° and the bringing home
Of° bell and burial.

LAERTES.   Must there no more be done?

DOCTOR.   No more be done:
We should profane the service of the dead,
To sing sage requiem° and such rest to her   220
As to peace-parted souls.

LAERTES.   Lay her i'th'earth,
And from her fair and unpolluted flesh
May violets spring: I tell thee churlish priest,
A minist'ring angel shall my sister be,
When thou liest howling.

HAMLET.   What, the fair Ophelia?   225

QUEEN.   [*Scattering flowers.*] Sweets to the sweet, farewell.
I hoped thou shouldst have been my Hamlet's wife:
I thought thy bride-bed to have decked, sweet maid,
And not have strewed thy grave.

LAERTES.   O treble woe
Fall ten times treble on that cursèd head   230
Whose wicked deed thy most ingenious sense°
Deprived thee of. Hold off the earth awhile,
Till I have caught her once more in mine arms;   *Leaps in the grave.*
Now pile your dust upon the quick° and dead,
Till of this flat a mountain you have made   235
T'o'ertop old Pelion,° or the skyish head
Of blue Olympus.

HAMLET.   [*Comes forward.*] What is he whose grief
Bears such an emphasis? whose phrase of sorrow
Conjures the wand'ring stars,° and makes them stand
Like wonder-wounded hearers? This is I,   240
Hamlet the Dane.   *HAMLET leaps in after LAERTES.*

LAERTES.   [*Grapples with him.*] The devil take thy soul.

HAMLET.   Thou pray'st not well,
I prithee take thy fingers from my throat,
For though I am not splenitive° and rash,
Yet have I in me something dangerous,   245
Which let thy wiseness fear; hold off thy hand.

---

210 *doubtful:* suspicious.   214 *Shards:* bits of broken pottery.   215 *crants:* garland.
216 *strewments:* flowers strewn on the grave.   216–217 *bringing home Of:* laying to rest
with.   220 *sage requiem:* solemn dirge.   231 *sense:* mind.   234 *quick:* live.
236 *Pelion:* mountain (on which the Titans placed Mt. Ossa, to scale Mt. Olympus and
reach the gods).   239 *Conjures . . . stars:* casts a spell over the planets.   244 *splenitive:*
quick-tempered (anger was thought to originate in the spleen).

KING. Pluck them asunder.
QUEEN.   Hamlet, Hamlet!
ALL. Gentlemen!
HORATIO.   Good my lord, be quiet.

[*Attendants part them, and they come out of the grave.*]

HAMLET. Why, I will fight with him upon this theme
    Until my eyelids will no longer wag.   250
QUEEN. O my son, what theme?
HAMLET. I loved Ophelia, forty thousand brothers
    Could not with all their quantity of love
    Make up my sum. What wilt thou do for her?
KING. O he is mad, Laertes.   255
QUEEN. For love of God, forbear° him.
HAMLET. 'Swounds,° show me what thou't do:
    Woo't° weep? woo't fight? woo't fast? woo't tear thyself?
    Woo't drink up eisel?° eat a crocodile?°
    I'll do't. Dost thou come here to whine?   260
    To outface me with leaping in her grave?
    Be buried quick with her, and so will I.
    And if thou prate of mountains, let them throw
    Millions of acres on us, till our ground,
    Singeing his pate against the burning zone,°   265
    Make Ossa° like a wart. Nay, an thou'lt mouth,
    I'll rant as well as thou.
QUEEN.   This is mere° madness,
    And thus awhile the fit will work on him:
    Anon as patient as the female dove
    When that her golden couplets° are disclosed,   270
    His silence will sit drooping.
HAMLET.   Hear you sir,
    What is the reason that you use me thus?
    I loved you ever; but it is no matter.
    Let Hercules himself do what he may,
    The cat will mew, and dog will have his day.   *Exit* HAMLET.   275
KING. I pray thee good Horatio, wait upon him.   [*HORATIO follows.*]
    [*Aside to Laertes.*] Strengthen your patience in our last night's speech,
    We'll put the matter to the present push°—
    Good Gertrude, set some watch over your son—
    This grave shall have a living monument:°   280
    An hour of quiet shortly shall we see,
    Till then, in patience our proceeding be.   *Exeunt.*

---

256 *forbear:* be patient with.   257 *'Swounds:* corruption of "God's wounds."   258 *Woo't:*
wilt thou.   259 *eisel:* vinegar (thought to reduce anger and encourage melancholy).
crocodile: (associated with hypocritical tears).   265 *burning zone:* sun's sphere.
266 *Ossa:* (see above, line 236 n.).   267 *mere:* absolute.   270 *golden couplets:* fuzzy
yellow twin fledglings.   278 *present push:* immediate test.   280 *living monument:* (1)
lasting tombstone (2) living sacrifice (Hamlet) to memorialize it.

Scene 2. [A hall in the castle]

Enter HAMLET and HORATIO.

HAMLET.   So much for this sir, now shall you see the other;
    You do remember all the circumstance.
HORATIO.   Remember it my lord!
HAMLET.   Sir, in my heart there was a kind of fighting
    That would not let me sleep; methought I lay   5
    Worse than the mutines in the bilboes.° Rashly—
    And praised be rashness for it: let us know,
    Our indiscretion sometimes serves us well
    When our deep plots do pall,° and that should learn us
    There's a divinity that shapes our ends,   10
    Rough-hew them how we will—
HORATIO.   That is most certain.
HAMLET.   Up from my cabin,
    My sea-gown° scarfed about me, in the dark
    Groped I to find out them, had my desire,
    Fingered° their packet, and in fine° withdrew   15
    To mine own room again, making so bold,
    My fears forgetting manners, to unseal
    Their grand commission; where I found, Horatio—
    Ah royal knavery—an exact command,
    Larded° with many several sorts of reasons,   20
    Importing Denmark's health, and England's too,
    With ho, such bugs and goblins in my life,°
    That on the supervise,° no leisure bated,°
    No, not to stay° the grinding of the axe,
    My head should be struck off.
HORATIO.   Is't possible?   25
HAMLET.   Here's the commission, read it at more leisure.
    But wilt thou hear now how I did proceed?
HORATIO.   I beseech you.
HAMLET.   Being thus be-netted round with villainies,
    Ere I could make a prologue to my brains,   30
    They had begun the play.° I sat me down,
    Devised a new commission, wrote it fair°—
    I once did hold it, as our statists° do,
    A baseness° to write fair, and laboured much
    How to forget that learning, but sir now   35
    It did me yeoman's° service: wilt thou know

6 *mutines . . . bilboes:* mutineers in shackles.   9 *pall:* fail.   13 *sea-gown:* short-sleeved
knee-length gown worn by seamen.   15 *Fingered:* got my fingers on.   *in fine:* to finish.
20 *Larded:* embellished.   22 *bugs . . . life:* imaginary evils attributed to me, like imaginary
goblins ("bugs") meant to frighten children.   23 *supervise:* looking over (the commission).
leisure bated: delay excepted.   24 *stay:* await.   30–31 *Ere . . . play:* Before I could
outline the action in my mind, my brains started to play their part.   32 *wrote it fair:*
wrote a finished (neat) copy, a "fair copy."   33 *statists:* statesmen.   34 *baseness:* mark of
humble status.   36 *yeoman's:* (in the sense of "faithful").

Th'effect of what I wrote?

HORATIO.   Ay, good my lord.

HAMLET. An earnest conjuration° from the king,
As England was his faithful tributary,
As love between them like the palm might flourish,   40
As peace should still her wheaten garland wear
And stand a comma° 'tween their amities,
And many such like "as'es"° of great charge,°
That on the view and know of these contents,
Without debatement further, more or less,   45
He should those bearers put to sudden death,
Not shriving° time allowed.

HORATIO.   How was this sealed?

HAMLET. Why even in that was heaven ordinant,°
I had my father's signet° in my purse,
Which was the model° of that Danish seal: 50
Folded the writ up in the form of th'other,
Subscribed° it, gave't th'impression,° placed it safely,
The changeling° never known: now the next day
Was our sea-fight, and what to this was sequent
Thou knowest already.   55

HORATIO. So Guildenstern and Rosencrantz go to't.

HAMLET. Why man, they did make love to this employment,°
They are not near my conscience, their defeat
Does by their own insinuation° grow:
'Tis dangerous when the baser nature comes   60
Between the pass° and fell° incensed points
Of mighty opposites.

HORATIO.   Why, what a king is this!

HAMLET. Does it not, think thee, stand me now upon°—
He that hath killed my king, and whored my mother,
Popped in between th'election° and my hopes,   65
Thrown out his angle° for my proper° life,
And with such cozenage°—is't not perfect conscience
To quit° him with this arm? And is't not to be damned,
To let this canker of our nature° come
In further evil?   70

HORATIO. It must be shortly known to him from England
What is the issue of the business there.

HAMLET. It will be short, the interim is mine,

38 *conjuration:* entreaty (he parodies the rhetoric of such documents).   42 *comma:*
connection.   43 *as'es:* (1) the "as" clauses in the commission (2) asses.   *charge:* (1)
weight (in the clauses) (2) burdens (on the asses).   47 *shriving:* confession and absolution.
48 *was heaven ordinant:* it was divinely ordained.   49 *signet:* seal.   50 *model:* replica.
52 *Subscribed:* signed.   *impression:* i.e., of the seal.   53 *changeling:* substitute (baby imp
left when an infant was spirited away).   57 *did . . . employment:* asked for it.
59 *insinuation:* intrusion.   61 *pass:* thrust.   *fell:* fierce.   63 *stand . . . upon:* become
incumbent upon me now.   65 *election:* (the Danish king was so chosen).   66 *angle:*
fishing hook.   *proper:* very own.   67 *cozenage:* deception.   68 *quit:* repay, requite.
69 *canker of our nature:* cancer of humanity.

And a man's life's no more than to say "One."°
But I am very sorry good Horatio,   75
That to Laertes I forgot myself;
For by the image of my cause, I see
The portraiture of his;° I'll court his favours:
But sure the bravery° of his grief did put me
Into a towering passion.

HORATIO.   Peace, who comes here?   80

Enter young OSRIC.

OSRIC.   Your lordship is right welcome back to Denmark.
HAMLET.   I humbly thank you sir. [*Aside to Horatio.*] Dost know this
   water-fly?
HORATIO.   No my good lord.
HAMLET.   Thy state is the more gracious,° for 'tis a vice to know him: 85
   he hath much land, and fertile: let a beast be lord of beasts,
   and his crib shall stand at the king's mess;° 'tis a chough,°
   but as I say, spacious in the possession of dirt.
OSRIC.   Sweet lord, if your lordship were at leisure, I should
   impart a thing to you from his majesty.   90
HAMLET.   I will receive it sir, with all diligence of spirit; put your
   bonnet° to his right use, 'tis for the head.
OSRIC.   I thank your lordship, it is very hot.
HAMLET.   No, believe me, 'tis very cold, the wind is northerly.
OSRIC.   It is indifferent° cold my lord indeed.   95
HAMLET.   But yet methinks it is very sultry and hot for my
   complexion.°
OSRIC.   Exceedingly, my lord, it is very sultry, as 'twere, I cannot
   tell how: but my lord, his majesty bade me signify to you
   that a' has laid a great wager on your head. Sir, this is the   100
   matter—
HAMLET.   [*Moves him to put on his hat.*] I beseech you remember—
OSRIC.   Nay good my lord, for mine ease,° in good faith. Sir, here
   is newly come to court Laertes, believe me, an absolute
   gentleman, full of most excellent differences,° of very soft   105
   society, and great showing: indeed to speak feelingly of
   him, he is the card° or calendar of gentry: for you shall find
   in him the continent of what part a gentleman would see.°
HAMLET.   Sir, his definement° suffers no perdition° in you, though I
   know to divide him inventorially would dozy°   110

74 *to say "One":* to score one hit in fencing.   77–78 *by the image . . . his:* in the depiction
of my situation, I see the reflection of his.   79 *bravery:* ostentation.   85 *gracious:*
favorable.   86–87 *let a beast . . . mess:* An ass who owns enough property can eat with the
king.   87 *chough:* chattering bird, jackdaw.   92 *bonnet:* hat.   95 *indifferent:*
reasonably.   97 *complexion:* temperament.   103 *for mine ease:* for my own comfort.
105 *differences:* accomplishments.   107 *card:* shipman's compass card.   108 *continent
. . . see:* (continuing the marine metaphor) (1) geographical continent (2) all the qualities a
gentleman would look for.   109–116 *Sir . . . more:* (Hamlet outdoes Osric in affected
speech).   109 *definement:* description.   *perdition:* loss.   110 *dozy:* dizzy.

th'arithmetic of memory, and yet but yaw neither,° in
respect of his quick sail,° but in the verity of extolment,° I
take him to be a soul of great article,° and his infusion° of
such dearth and rareness, as to make true diction of him,
his semblable° is his mirror, and who else would trace° him,   115
his umbrage,° nothing more.°

OSRIC. Your lordship speaks most infallibly of him.

HAMLET. The concernancy° sir? why do we wrap the gentleman in
our more rawer breath?°

OSRIC. Sir?   120

HORATIO. Is't not possible to understand in another tongue?° You
will do't sir, really.

HAMLET. What imports the nomination° of this gentleman?

OSRIC. Of Laertes?

HORATIO. His purse is empty already, all's golden words are spent.   125

HAMLET. Of him, sir.

OSRIC. I know you are not ignorant—

HAMLET. I would you did sir, yet in faith if you did, it would not
much approve me.° Well, sir.

OSRIC. You are not ignorant of what excellence Laertes is—   130

HAMLET. I dare not confess that, lest I should compare with him in
excellence, but to know a man well were to know himself.°

OSRIC. I mean sir for his weapon, but in the imputation° laid on
him by them in his meed,° he's unfellowed.°

HAMLET. What's his weapon?   135

OSRIC. Rapier and dagger.

HAMLET. That's two of his weapons—but well.

OSRIC. The king sir, hath wagered with him six Barbary horses,
against which he has impawned,° as I take it, six French
rapiers and poniards,° with their assigns,° as girdle, hangers,°   140
and so. Three of the carriages° in faith are very dear to
fancy,° very responsive to the hilts, most delicate carriages,
and of very liberal conceit.°

HAMLET. What call you the carriages?

HORATIO. I knew you must be edified by the margent° ere you had   145
done.

111–112 *yaw . . . sail:* (1) moving in an unsteady course (as another boat would do, trying
to catch up with Laertes' "quick sail") (2) staggering to one trying to list his
accomplishments.   112 *in . . . extolment:* to praise him truthfully.   113 *article:* scope.
infusion: essence.   114–116 *as to make . . . more:* to describe him truly I would have to
employ his mirror to depict his only equal—himself, and who would follow him is only a
shadow.   115 *semblable:* equal.   *trace:* (1) describe (2) follow.   116 *umbrage:* shadow.
118 *concernancy:* relevance.   119 *rawer breath:* crude speech.   121 *Is't not . . . tongue:*
Cannot Osric understand his own way of speaking when used by another?
123 *nomination:* naming.   128–129 *if you did . . . me:* If you found me to be "not
ignorant," it would prove little (as you are no judge of ignorance).   132 *to know . . .
himself:* to know a man well, one must first know oneself.   133 *imputation:* repute.
134 *meed:* worth.   *unfellowed:* unequaled.   139 *impawned:* staked.   140 *poniards:*
daggers.   *assigns:* accessories.   140 *girdle, hangers:* belt, straps attached thereto, from
which swords were hung.   141 *carriages:* hangers.   141–142 *dear to fancy:* rare in
design.   143 *liberal conceit:* elaborate conception.   145 *margent:* marginal note.

OSRIC.   The carriages sir, are the hangers.

HAMLET.   The phrase would be more germane to the matter, if we
could carry a cannon by our sides: I would it might be
hangers till then, but on: six Barbary horses against six   150
French swords, their assigns, and three liberal-conceited
carriages—that's the French bet against the Danish. Why
is this all "impawned" as you call it?

OSRIC.   The king sir, hath laid sir, that in a dozen passes between
yourself and him, he shall not exceed you three hits°; he   155
hath laid on twelve for nine, and it would come to
immediate trial, if your lordship would vouchsafe the
answer.°

HAMLET.   How if I answer no?

OSRIC.   I mean my lord, the opposition of your person in trial.   160

HAMLET.   Sir, I will walk here in the hall; if it please his majesty, it is
the breathing time° of day with me; let the foils be brought,
the gentleman willing, and the king hold his purpose, I
will win for him an I can, if not, I will gain nothing but my
shame and the odd hits.   165

OSRIC.   Shall I re-deliver you° e'en so?

HAMLET.   To this effect sir, after what flourish your nature will.°

OSRIC.   I commend° my duty to your lordship.

HAMLET.   Yours, yours.   [*Exit* OSRIC.]

He does well to commend it himself, there are no tongues   170
else for's turn.°

HORATIO.   This lapwing° runs away with the shell on his head.

HAMLET.   A' did comply° sir, with his dug° before a' sucked it: thus
has he—and many more of the same bevy that I know the
drossy° age dotes on—only got the tune of the time, and   175
out of an habit of encounter,° a kind of yeasty collection,°
which carries them through and through the most fond
and winnowed° opinions; and do but blow them to their
trial, and bubbles are out.°

Enter a LORD.

LORD.   My lord, his majesty commended him to you by young   180
Osric, who brings back to him that you attend him in
the hall. He sends to know if your pleasure hold to play
with Laertes, or that you will take longer time.

HAMLET.   I am constant to my purposes, they follow the king's

---

154–155 *laid . . . three hits:* wagered that in twelve bouts Laertes must win three more than
Hamlet.   158 *answer:* acceptance of the challenge (Hamlet interprets as "reply").
165 *breathing time:* exercise period.   166 *re-deliver you:* take back your answer.
167 *after . . . will:* embellished as you wish.   168 *commend:* offer (Hamlet interprets as
"praise").   170–171 *no tongues . . . turn:* no others who would.   172 *lapwing:* (reported
to be so precocious that it ran as soon as hatched).   173 *comply:* observe the formalities
of courtesy.   *dug:* mother's breast.   175 *drossy:* frivolous.   176 *habit of encounter:*
habitual association (with others as frivolous).   176 *yeasty collection:* frothy assortment of
phrases.   177–178 *fond and winnowed:* trivial and considered.   178–179 *blow . . . out:*
blow on them to test them and they are gone.

pleasure, if his fitness speaks,° mine is ready: now or   185
whensoever, provided I be so able as now.
LORD. The king, and queen, and all are coming down.
HAMLET. In happy time.
LORD. The queen desires you to use some gentle entertainment°
to Laertes, before you fall to play.   190
HAMLET. She well instructs me.   [*Exit* LORD.]
HORATIO. You will lose this wager, my lord.
HAMLET. I do not think so, since we went into France, I have been in
continual practice, I shall win at the odds; but thou
wouldst not think how ill all's here about my heart: but it   195
is no matter.
HORATIO. Nay good my lord—
HAMLET. It is but a foolery, but it is such a kind of gaingiving° as
would perhaps trouble a woman.
HORATIO. If your mind dislike any thing, obey it. I will forestall their   200
repair° hither, and say you are not fit.
HAMLET. Not a whit, we defy augury;° there is a special providence
in the fall of a sparrow.° If it be now, 'tis not to come:
if it be not to come, it will be now; if it be not now,
yet it will come—the readiness is all. Since no man has   205
aught of what he leaves, what is't to leave betimes?° let
be.

A table prepared. Trumpets, Drums, and officers with cushions. Enter KING, QUEEN, *and
all the state,* [OSRIC], *foils daggers, and* LAERTES.

KING. Come Hamlet, come and take this hand from me.
[*Puts Laertes' hand into Hamlet's.*]
HAMLET. Give me your pardon sir, I have done you wrong,
But pardon't as you are a gentleman.   210
This presence knows, and you must needs have heard,
How I am punished with a sore distraction.°
What I have done
That might your nature, honour, and exception°
Roughly awake, I here proclaim was madness: 215
Was't Hamlet wronged Laertes? never Hamlet.
If Hamlet from himself be ta'en away,
And when he's not himself, does wrong Laertes,
Then Hamlet does it not, Hamlet denies it:
Who does it then? his madness. If't be so,   220
Hamlet is of the faction that is wronged,
His madness is poor Hamlet's enemy.
Sir, in this audience,

---

185 *his fitness speaks:* it agrees with his convenience.   189 *gentle entertainment:* friendly
treatment.   198 *gaingiving:* misgiving.   201 *repair:* coming.   202 *augury:* omens.
202–203 *special . . . sparrow:* ("Are not two sparrows sold for a farthing? and one of them
shall not fall on the ground without your Father": Matthew 10:29).   206 *betimes:* early
(before one's time).   212 *sore distraction:* grievous madness.   214 *exception:* disapproval.

Let my disclaiming from a purposed evil,
Free me so far in your most generous thoughts,   225
That I have shot my arrow o'er the house
And hurt my brother.°

LAERTES.   I am satisfied in nature,
Whose motive in this case should stir me most
To my revenge, but in my terms of honour
I stand aloof, and will no reconcilement,   230
Till by some elder masters of known honour
I have a voice and precedent° of peace
To keep my name ungored:° but till that time,
I do receive your offered love, like love,
And will not wrong it.

HAMLET.   I embrace it freely,   235
And will this brother's wager frankly° play.
Give us the foils: come on.

LAERTES.   Come, one for me.

HAMLET.   I'll be your foil° Laertes, in mine ignorance
Your skill shall like a star i'th' darkest night
Stick fiery off° indeed.   240

LAERTES.   You mock me sir.

HAMLET. No, by this hand.

KING.   Give them the foils young Osric. Cousin° Hamlet,
You know the wager.

HAMLET.   Very well my lord.
Your grace has laid the odds o'th'weaker side.

KING.   I do not fear it, I have seen you both,   245
But since he is bettered,° we have therefore odds.

LAERTES.   This is too heavy: let me see another.°

HAMLET.   This likes° me well, these foils have all a° length?

OSRIC.   Ay my good lord.   *Prepare to play.*

KING.   Set me the stoups° of wine upon that table: 250
If Hamlet give the first or second hit,
Or quit in answer of° the third exchange,
Let all the battlements their ordnance fire.
The king shall drink to Hamlet's better breath,
And in the cup an union° shall he throw,   255
Richer than that which four successive kings
In Denmark's crown have worn: give me the cups,
And let the kettle° to the trumpet speak,

226–227 *That I have . . . brother:* (that it was accidental).   232 *voice and precedent:* opinion
based on precedent.   233 *name ungored:* reputation uninjured. Laertes says that he
cannot accept Hamlet's apology formally until he is assured that his acceptance will not
harm his honor or damage his reputation.   236 *frankly:* freely.   238 *foil:* (1) the
blunted sword with which they fence (2) leaf of metal set under a jewel to make it shine
more brilliantly.   240 *Stick fiery off:* show in shining contrast.   242 *Cousin:* kinsman.
246 *bettered:* either (a) judged to be better, or (b) better trained.   247 *another:* (the
unbated and poisoned sword).   248 *likes:* pleases.   *all a:* all the same.   250 *stoups:*
goblets.   252 *quit in answer of:* score a draw in.   255 *union:* large pearl.   258 *kettle:*
kettledrum.

The trumpet to the cannoneer without,
The cannons to the heavens, the heaven to earth, 260
"Now the king drinks to Hamlet." Come begin.
And you the judges bear a wary eye. *Trumpets the while.*
HAMLET. Come on sir.
LAERTES. Come my lord. *They play.*
HAMLET. One.
LAERTES. No.
HAMLET. Judgment.
OSRIC. A hit, a very palpable hit.

Flourish. Drum, trumpets and shot. A piece° goes off.

LAERTES. Well, again.
KING. Stay, give me drink. Hamlet, this pearl is thine. 265
Here's to thy health: give him the cup.
HAMLET. I'll play this bout first, set it by a while.
Come. *[They play.]*
Another hit. What say you?
LAERTES. A touch, a touch, I do confess't.
KING. Our son shall win.
QUEEN. He's fat° and scant of breath. 270
Here Hamlet, take my napkin,° rub thy brows. *[She takes HAMLET's cup.]*
The queen carouses° to thy fortune, Hamlet.
HAMLET. Good madam.
KING. Gertrude, do not drink.
QUEEN. I will my lord, I pray you pardon me.
KING. *[Aside.]* It is the poisoned cup, it is too late. 275
HAMLET. I dare not drink yet madam: by and by.
QUEEN. Come, let me wipe thy face.
LAERTES. *[To the King.]* My lord, I'll hit him now.
KING. I do not think't.
LAERTES. *[Aside.]* And yet 'tis almost 'gainst my conscience.
HAMLET. Come for the third Laertes, you do but dally, 280
I pray you pass° with your best violence,
I am afeard you make a wanton of me.°
LAERTES. Say you so? Come on. *Play.*
OSRIC. Nothing neither way. *[They break off.]*
LAERTES. Have at you now.° *[Wounds HAMLET.]*

In scuffling they change rapiers.

KING. Part them, they are incensed. 285
HAMLET. Nay, come again. *[The QUEEN falls.]*
OSRIC. Look to the queen there, ho!

[HAMLET wounds LAERTES.]

264.1 stage direction: *piece:* i.e., a cannon.   270 *fat:* sweating (sweat was thought to be
melted body fat).   271 *napkin:* handkerchief.   272 *carouses:* drinks.   281 *pass:*
thrust.   282 *make a wanton of me:* are indulging me like a spoiled child.   285 *Have . . .
now:* (the bout is over when Laertes attacks Hamlet and catches him off guard).

HORATIO.   They bleed on both side. How is it, my lord?

OSRIC.   How is't, Laertes?

LAERTES.   Why as a woodcock° to my own springe,° Osric,
   I am justly killed with mine own treachery.   290

HAMLET.   How does the queen?

KING.   She sounds° to see them bleed.

QUEEN.   No. no, the drink, the drink, O my dear Hamlet,
   The drink, the drink, I am poisoned.   *[Dies.]*

HAMLET.   O villainy! ho! let the door be locked,
   Treachery, seek it out!   295

LAERTES.   It is here Hamlet. Hamlet, thou art slain,
   No medicine in the world can do thee good,
   In thee there is not half an hour of life,
   The treacherous instrument is in thy hand,
   Unbated° and envenomed. The foul practice°   300
   Hath turned itself on me, lo, here I lie
   Never to rise again: thy mother's poisoned:
   I can no more: the king, the king's to blame.

HAMLET.   The point envenomed too:
   Then venom, to thy work.   *Hurts the KING.*   305

ALL.   Treason! treason!

KING.   O yet defend me friends, I am but hurt.°

HAMLET.   Here, thou incestuous, murderous, damnèd Dane,
   Drink off this potion: is thy union here?
   Follow my mother.   *KING dies.*   310

LAERTES.   He is justly served,
   It is a poison tempered° by himself:
   Exchange forgiveness with me, noble Hamlet,
   Mine and my father's death come not upon thee,°
   Nor thine on me.   *Dies.*

HAMLET.   Heaven make thee free° of it, I follow thee.   315
   I am dead, Horatio; wretched queen, adieu.
   You that look pale, and tremble at this chance,
   That are but mutes,° or audience to this act,
   Had I but time, as this fell sergeant° Death
   Is strict in his arrest, O I could tell you—   320
   But let it be; Horatio, I am dead,
   Thou livest, report me and my cause aright
   To the unsatisfied.°

HORATIO.   Never believe it;
   I am more an antique Roman° than a Dane:
   Here's yet some liquor left.

---

289 *woodcock:* snipe-like bird (believed to be foolish and therefore easily trapped).
springe: trap.   291 *sounds:* swoons.   300 *Unbated:* not blunted.   *practice:* plot.
307 *but hurt:* only wounded.   311 *tempered:* mixed.   313 *come . . . thee:* are not to be
blamed on you.   315 *free:* guiltless.   318 *mutes:* actors without speaking parts.
319 *fell sergeant:* cruel sheriff's officer.   323 *unsatisfied:* uninformed.   324 *antique
Roman:* ancient Roman (who considered suicide honorable).

HAMLET.   As thou'rt a man,   325
    Give me the cup, let go, by heaven I'll ha't.
    O God, Horatio, what a wounded name,
    Things standing thus unknown, shall live behind me.
    If thou didst ever hold me in thy heart,
    Absènt thee from felicity awhile,   330
    And in this harsh world draw thy breath in pain
    To tell my story.   *A march afar off, and shot within.*
                    What warlike noise is this?
OSRIC. Young Fortinbras with conquest come from Poland,
    To th'ambassadors of England gives
    This warlike volley.
HAMLET.   O I die Horatio,   335
    The potent poison quite o'er-crows° my spirit,
    I cannot live to hear the news from England,
    But I do prophesy th'election° lights
    On Fortinbras, he has my dying voice,°
    So tell him, with th'occurrents more and less°   340
    Which have solicited°—the rest is silence.   *Dies.*
HORATIO. Now cracks a noble heart: good night sweet prince,
    And flights of angels sing thee to thy rest.
    Why does the drum come hither?

Enter FORTINBRAS and English Ambassadors, with drum, colours, and attendants.

FORTINBRAS. Where is this sight?
HORATIO.   What is it you would see?   345
    If aught of woe, or wonder, cease your search.
FORTINBRAS. This quarry cries on havoc.° O proud death,
    What feast is toward° in thine eternal cell,
    That thou so many princes at a shot
    So bloodily hast struck?   350
AMBASSADOR.   The sight is dismal,
    And our affairs from England come too late;
    The ears° are senseless that should give us hearing,
    To tell him his commandment is fulfilled,
    That Rosencrantz and Guildenstern are dead:
    Where should we have our thanks?
HORATIO.   Not from his mouth,   355
    Had it th'ability of life to thank you;
    He never gave commandment for their death;
    But since so jump° upon this bloody question,
    You from the Polack wars, and you from England
    Are here arrived, give order that these bodies   360
    High on a stage be placèd to the view,

---

336 *o'er-crows:* overpowers, conquers.   338 *election:* (for king of Denmark).   339 *voice:*
vote.   340 *occurrents more and less:* events great and small.   341 *solicited:* incited me.
347 *quarry . . . havoc:* heap of dead bodies proclaims slaughter done here.   348 *toward:* in
preparation.   352 *ears:* (of Claudius).   358 *jump:* opportunely.

And let me speak to th'yet unknowing world
How these things came about; so shall you hear
Of carnal, bloody and unnatural acts,
Of accidental judgments, casual° slaughters,   365
Of deaths put on° by cunning and forced cause,°
And in this upshot, purposes mistook,
Fall'n on th'inventors' heads:° all this can I
Truly deliver.

FORTINBRAS.   Let us haste to hear it,
And call the noblest to the audience.   370
For me, with sorrow I embrace my fortune;
I have some rights of memory° in this kingdom,
Which now to claim my vantage° doth invite me.

HORATIO.   Of that I shall have also cause to speak,
And from his mouth whose voice will draw on more:°   375
But let this same° be presently performed,
Even while men's minds are wild,° lest more mischance
On° plots and errors happen.

FORTINBRAS.   Let four captains
Bear Hamlet like a soldier to the stage,
For he was likely, had he been put on,°   380
To have proved most royal; and for his passage,°
The soldiers' music and the rite of war
Speak loudly for him:
Take up the bodies, such a sight as this,
Becomes the field, but here shows much amiss.   385
Go bid the soldiers shoot.

Exeunt marching: after the which a peal of ordnance are shot off.

365 *casual:* unpremeditated.   366 *put on:* prompted by.   *forced cause:* being forced to
act in self-defense.   367–368 *purposes . . . heads:* plots gone wrong and destroying their
inventors.   372 *of memory:* remembered.   373 *vantage:* advantageous position.
375 *draw on more:* influence more (votes).   376 *this same:* this telling of the story.
377 *wild:* upset.   378 *On:* on top of.   380 *put on:* i.e., put on the throne.
381 *passage:* i.e., to the next world.

QUESTIONS

Act I

1. Discuss the various ways in which the first scene of *Hamlet* shows you that
    something is wrong in Denmark.

2. What impression does Claudius make in scene 2? Is he a rational man? A
    good administrator? A competent ruler? A loving husband and uncle?

3. What does Hamlet reveal about his own mental state in his first soliloquy?

4. What attitude toward Ophelia's relationship with Hamlet do Laertes and
    Polonius share? What do they want Ophelia to do? Why?

5. What does the ghost tell Hamlet? What does the ghost want Hamlet to do

and not to do? Why does Hamlet need proof that the ghost's words are true?

Act II

6. What does Polonius think is the cause of Hamlet's madness? What do Polonious's diagnosis and his handling of the situation show us about him?

7. What does Hamlet accuse himself of in the soliloquy that begins "O what a rogue and peasant slave am I" (Act II, scene 2, lines 524–580)? To what extent is his self-accusation justified?

Act III

8. How do you react to Hamlet's treatment of Ophelia in the first scene of Act III? What evidence might indicate that Hamlet knows that Claudius and Polonius are watching and listening to everything that occurs?

9. Hamlet sets up the performance of "The Murder of Gonzago"—the play-within-a-play—to test Claudius's guilt. What is the relationship between the events of this play-within-a-play and the events of *Hamlet?*

10. How does Claudius react to "The Murder of Gonzago"? What does this reaction tell Hamlet? Why do you suppose Claudius did not react to the dumb show presented at the beginning of the play-within-a-play?

11. What is Hamlet's reason for not killing Claudius at prayer?

12. How does Hamlet treat his mother during their confrontation in her closet? Is Hamlet's behavior overly nasty or justified? Why does the ghost reappear during this confrontation?

13. What crimes or sins does Hamlet accuse Gertrude of committing?

Act IV

14. Do you think Laertes's desire to avenge his father's murder is any more or less justified than Hamlet's desire?

15. How does Claudius plan to use Laertes's desire for revenge to manipulate him? To what extent does Laertes unwittingly allow himself to be used by Claudius?

Act V

16. The conversation between the two clowns (grave-diggers) and between Hamlet and the first clown is seen as comic relief—a humorous episode designed to ease tension. Why is comic relief appropriate at this point?

17. How does this scene of comic relief reflect and broaden the play's themes?

18. Why does Hamlet describe Osric as a "water-fly"? How does Shakespeare use Osric's language and behavior to characterize him?

19. Discuss the lessons that Hamlet tells Horatio he has learned about life. How does this understanding change Hamlet? Why is it ironic?

20. How is Gertrude killed? Hamlet? Laertes? Claudius? Why does Hamlet insist that Horatio not commit suicide?

GENERAL QUESTIONS

1. Describe the character of Claudius. Do you consider him purely evil or merely a flawed human? Why? To what degree can you justify calling this play "The Tragedy of Claudius, King of Denmark"?

2. Characterize Horatio. Why does Hamlet admire and trust him? How is he different from Polonius or Rosencrantz and Guildenstern?

3. Describe Rosencrantz and Guildenstern. Are they round or flat? How does Claudius use them? Why do they cooperate with Claudius? How does Hamlet arrange their deaths? To what extent can this action be justified?

4. Evaluate Polonius's character. Is he a wise counselor? A fool? Sincere? Self-serving? Hypocritical? What are his motives? How is he like Rosencrantz and Guildenstern? How is his death like their deaths?

5. *Hamlet* is full of conflicts that oppose people to other people, to society, and to themselves. List all the conflicts you can find in the play. Decide which of these is the central conflict, and explain your choice.

6. What is the crisis of *Hamlet*? When does it occur? Whom does it affect? What is the catastrophe? The resolution?

7. In Act IV, Claudius notes that "sorrows come . . . in battalions." By the end of the play these sorrows include the deaths of Polonius, Rosencrantz, Guildenstern, Ophelia, Laertes, Gertrude, Claudius, and Hamlet. To what degree can Claudius be held responsible for all the sorrows of the play? Which sorrows are primarily Hamlet's responsibility?

8. Is *Hamlet* a tragedy of the state as well as a tragedy of the individual? In what condition is Denmark at the beginning of the play? Is the condition of Denmark better or worse at the end?

THE THEATER OF ARTHUR MILLER

When we shift to the twentieth-century theater of Arthur Miller, we abandon the masks of the Greek theater and the soliloquies of the Elizabethan stage for drama that mixes realism and nonrealism (this genre is examined in Chaper 28). By **realistic drama,** we mean plays that present an image of the world as we know it. This world is populated by salesmen, workers, bankers, housewives, lawyers, and thieves instead of kings, revengers, and soothsayers. In addition, these plays are spoken in the colloquial language of our own lives instead of in choric odes or blank verse.

With the nineteenth-century movement into realism, the drama required both a theater and a stage that could accommodate plays reflecting middle-class lives and values. Thus, the theater became the darkened auditorium in which we sit in rows and face a proscenium arch and a vast curtain that separate us from the acting areas. When the curtain rises, we often see a room resembling one we might live in or visit. This **box set**

Stage set for *Death of a Salesman*. (Billy Rose Theatre Collection; The New York Public Library at Lincoln Center; Astor, Lenox and Tilden Foundation)

signals an attempt to make settings look as much like the real world as possible.

Today, stage settings have been embellished with the full range of sound and lighting effects made possible by modern technology. This technological revolution has been especially significant in the area of lighting, which is managed by a switchboard (now computerized) that can be programmed to control hundreds or even thousands of lights in any combination and intensity. Lighting can establish times, places, moods, atmospheres, and effects. It can also divide the stage or a unit set into different acting areas simply through the illumination of one section and the darkening of the rest. As a result, lighting has become an element of set design, especially when the dramatist uses a *scrim*, which permits great variety in the portrayal of scenes and great rapidity in scene changes.

Since the 1940s, playwrights and theatrical designers have often eliminated the proscenium arch and the curtain, and have experimented with stages and sets inspired by earlier ages of the theater. Thus, we find classical Greek and Roman staging reflected in the contemporary **arena stage**, and medieval staging imitated in **theater in the round.** Similarly, many newer theaters offer a thrust stage loosely based on the model of the Elizabethan theaters. Miller's *Death of a Salesman*, for example, utilizes elements of the traditional box set combined with a thrust stage in the form of an extended **apron** that projects from the forestage.

ARTHUR MILLER, *DEATH OF A SALESMAN*

Arthur Miller, one of the dominant American playwrights from the 1940's to the present time, was born in New York City in 1915 and educated at the University of Michigan, where he wrote and staged his first plays. His early dramas include *The Man Who Had All the Luck* (1944), *All My Sons* (1947), *Death of a Salesman* (1949), *An Enemy of the People* (1951, an adaptation of the play by Henrik Ibsen), *The Crucible* (1953), and *A View from the Bridge* (1955). Many of these combine Miller's interests in family relationships and social issues. *All My Sons,* for instance, explores the relationship between Joe Keller, a war profiteer who allowed damaged engines to be put into U.S. military aircraft, and his son Chris, an army pilot returning home from World War II. The play also investigates Joe Keller's guilt and his emerging realization that the pilots who died because of his faulty engines were "all my sons." These sorts of thematic concerns reveal the extent to which Miller was influenced by Henrik Ibsen (see p. 1404). Miller's later work includes *The Misfits* (1961, a screenplay), *After the Fall* (1964), *Incident at Vichy* (1964), *The Price* (1968), and *The Archbishop's Ceiling* (1976).

Death of a Salesman, which opened on February 10, 1949, in New York City, is similar to both *Oedipus* and the traditional *well-made play* (see p. 1405) in several respects. For one thing, it dramatizes the end of a much longer story. The stage action in the present (in Acts I and II) covers about twenty-four hours, from Monday evening to Tuesday evening. The story, however, goes back as far as Willy Loman's childhood, and Willy's memories of past events constantly impose themselves on the present. Additionally, at least one of the central conflicts stems from a secret known only to Willy and his son, Biff, but withheld from the rest of the characters and from us for most of the play. This secret, however, is not the linchpin of the play, as it would be in a well-made play.

In writing a tragedy about the struggles and failures of Willy Loman, Miller effectively redefines the nature of the tragic protagonist. In a *New York Times* essay published several weeks after the Broadway opening of the play, Miller argued that "the common man is as apt a subject for tragedy in its highest sense as kings were."[2] He asserted that tragedy springs from the individual's quest for a proper place in the world and from his readiness "to lay down his life, if need be, to secure one thing— his sense of personal dignity." Willy is certainly flawed: he is weak, dishonest, and self-deluded. But Miller links his protagonist's *hamartia* with this quest for dignity: "the flaw or crack in the character is really nothing . . . but his inherent unwillingness to remain passive in the face of what he conceives to be a challenge to his dignity, his image of his rightful status."

---

[2] "Tragedy and the Common Man," *The New York Times*, February 27, 1949, sec. 2, p. 1.

Death of a Salesman is constructed primarily from Willy Loman's point of view. At first, Miller wanted to call the play "The Inside of His Head," and his initial vision was of "an enormous face the height of the proscenium arch that would appear and open up, and we would see the inside of a man's head."[3] The play contains two types of time and action: real and remembered. Present events are enacted and described realistically. Such action, however, often triggers Willy's memory of the past. Sometimes, past events occur simultaneously with present action; thus, in Act I Willy speaks with his dead brother (whom he is remembering) while at the same time he plays cards with Charley. At other times, past events take over the play completely, although Willy still continues to exist in the present. Willy's past is always with him—as he remembers it or reconstructs it—shaping the way he reacts to the present.

Like the acting of past events, the setting of *Death of a Salesman* is symbolic and nonrealistic (see p. 997). It is designed to allow fluid transitions between present and past, between current action and memory. The Loman house is a framework with three rooms (or acting areas) on three levels: the kitchen, the sons' bedroom, and Willy's bedroom. The forestage and apron are used for all scenes away from the house and for "memory" scenes. In the present, the house is hemmed in by apartment houses and lit with an "angry glow of orange," thus suggesting that Willy's present existence is urbanized and claustrophobic. When memory takes over, however, the apartment houses disappear (a technique of lighting), and the orange glow gives way to pastoral colors and the shadows of leaves—the setting of dreams.

Death of a Salesman is very much about dreams, illusions, and self-deception. Dreams pervade Willy's thoughts, conversation, family, and house. The central dream (and illusion) is the American dream of success and wealth through selling the self. This dream is recapitulated in a series of smaller dreams (illusions, lies) that Willy and his sons build out of thin air. Throughout the play, these dreams are destroyed when confronted with reality. Willy's dream of a "New York City job" and a salary, for example, collides with reality in his disastrous encounter with his younger and unsympathetic boss. Only Linda escapes the tyranny of dreams. While she serves and supports Willy completely, she remains firmly planted in the reality of house payments, insurance premiums, and her husband's need for dignity and "attention" as his world falls apart.

At the end of the play, we are left with a number of questions about the degree to which Willy recognizes and understands the corruption and the illusory nature of the American dream, his own dreams, and his self-image. He does understand that he has run out of lies and has nothing left to sell. He also understands—according to Miller—his alienation from true values:

[3] Arthur Miller, "Introduction to the Collected Plays," *Arthur Miller's Collected Plays* (New York: Viking, 1957), 23.

> Had Willy been unaware of his separation from values that endure he would
> have died contentedly while polishing his car. . . . But he was agonized by
> his awareness of being in a false position, so constantly haunted by the
> hollowness of all he had placed his faith in, so aware, in short, that he must
> somehow be filled with his spirit or fly apart, that he staked his life on the
> ultimate assertion.[4]

Yet at the end of the play, Willy is still in the grip of delusions of glory
for Biff and for himself. He imagines that his insurance money will make
Biff "magnificent." Similarly, he dreams that his funeral will be massive.
Both visions are delusions, for Biff has already abandoned the business
world, and the funeral is attended by only five people. In the *Requiem*
scene, Biff states that Willy's dreams were illusory: "He had all the wrong
dreams. All, all wrong" (speech 16). Only Happy remains trapped in
selfishness and his own petty version of Willy's dream: "He had a good
dream. It's the only dream you can have—to come out number-one man"
(speech 25).

ARTHUR MILLER   (b. 1915)

Death of a Salesman   *1949*

CHARACTERS

Willy Loman
Linda, *his wife*
Biff ⎫
Happy ⎭ *his sons*
Uncle Ben
Charley
Bernard
The Woman
Howard Wagner
Jenny
Stanley
Miss Forsythe
Letta

The action takes place in WILLY LOMAN'*s house and yard and in various places he visits in
the New York and Boston of today.*

ACT 1

*A melody is heard, played upon a flute. It is small and fine, telling of grass and trees and
the horizon. The curtain rises.*

[4] Ibid., pp. 34–35.

Before us is the Salesman's house. We are aware of towering, angular shapes behind it, surrounding it on all sides. Only the blue light of the sky falls upon the house and forestage; the surrounding area shows an angry glow of orange. As more light appears, we see a solid vault of apartment houses around the small, fragile-seeming home. An air of the dream clings to the place, a dream rising out of reality. The kitchen at center seems actual enough, for there is a kitchen table with three chairs, and a refrigerator. But no other fixtures are seen. At the back of the kitchen there is a draped entrance, which leads to the living-room. To the right of the kitchen, on a level raised two feet, is a bedroom furnished only with a brass bedstead and a straight chair. On a shelf over the bed a silver athletic trophy stands. A window opens onto the apartment house at the side.

Behind the kitchen, on a level raised six and a half feet, is the boys' bedroom, at present barely visible. Two beds are dimly seen, and at the back of the room a dormer window. (This bedroom is above the unseen living-room.) At the left a stairway curves up to it from the kitchen.

The entire setting is wholly or, in some places, partially transparent. The roof-line of the house is one-dimensional; under and over it we see the apartment buildings. Before the house lies an apron, curving beyond the forestage into the orchestra. This forward area serves as the back yard as well as the locale of all Willy's imaginings and of his city scenes. Whenever the action is in the present the actors observe the imaginary wall-lines, entering the house only through its door at the left. But in the scenes of the past these boundaries are broken, and characters enter or leave a room by stepping "through" a wall onto the forestage.

[From the right, WILLY LOMAN, The Salesman, enters, carrying two large sample cases. The flute plays on. He hears but is not aware of it. He is past sixty years of age, dressed quietly. Even as he crosses the stage to the doorway of the house, his exhaustion is apparent. He unlocks the door, comes into the kitchen, and thankfully lets his burden down, feeling the soreness of his palms. A word-sigh escapes his lips—it might be "Oh, boy, oh, boy." He closes the door, then carries his cases out into the living-room, through the draped kitchen doorway.]

[LINDA, his wife, has stirred in her bed at the right. She gets out and puts on a robe, listening. Most often jovial, she has developed an iron repression of her exceptions to WILLY's behavior—she more than loves him, she admires him, as though his mercurial nature, his temper, his massive dreams and little cruelties, served her only as sharp reminders of the turbulent longings within him, longings which she shares but lacks the temperament to utter and follow to their end.]

LINDA. [*hearing WILLY outside the bedroom, calls with some trepidation*] Willy!

WILLY. It's all right. I came back.

LINDA. Why? What happened? [*slight pause*] Did something happen, Willy?

WILLY. No, nothing happened.

LINDA. You didn't smash the car, did you?   5

WILLY. [*with casual irritation*] I said nothing happened. Didn't you hear me?

LINDA. Don't you feel well?

WILLY. I'm tired to the death. [*The flute has faded away. He sits on the bed beside her, a little numb.*] I couldn't make it. I just couldn't make it, Linda.

LINDA. [*very carefully, delicately*] Where were you all day? You look terrible.

WILLY. I got as far as a little above Yonkers.° I stopped for a cup of coffee.   10
Maybe it was the coffee.

LINDA. What?

Yonkers: Yonkers is immediately north of New York City, touching the city limits of the Bronx. Because Willy lives in Brooklyn, to the south, he got no more than thirty or thirty-five miles from home.

WILLY. [*after a pause*] I suddenly couldn't drive any more. The car kept going off onto the shoulder, y'know?

LINDA. [*helpfully*] Oh. Maybe it was the steering again. I don't think Angelo knows the Studebaker.

WILLY. No, it's me, it's me. Suddenly I realize I'm goin' sixty miles an hour and I don't remember the last five minutes. I'm—I can't seem to—keep my mind to it.

LINDA. Maybe it's your glasses. You never went for your new glasses.   15

WILLY. No, I see everything. I came back ten miles an hour. It took me nearly four hours from Yonkers.

LINDA. [*resigned*] Well, you'll just have to take a rest, Willy, you can't continue this way.

WILLY. I just got back from Florida.

LINDA. But you didn't rest your mind. Your mind is overactive, and the mind is what counts, dear.

WILLY. I'll start out in the morning. Maybe I'll feel better in the morning.   20 [*She is taking off his shoes.*] These goddam arch supports are killing me.

LINDA. Take an aspirin. Should I get you an aspirin? It'll soothe you.

WILLY. [*with wonder*] I was driving along, you understand? And I was fine. I was even observing the scenery. You can imagine, me looking at scenery, on the road every week of my life. But it's so beautiful up there, Linda, the trees are so thick, and the sun is warm. I opened the windshield and just let the warm air bathe over me. And then all of a sudden I'm goin' off the road! I'm tellin' ya, I absolutely forgot I was driving. If I'd've gone the other way over the white line I might've killed somebody. So I went on again—and five minutes later I'm dreamin' again, and I nearly—[*He presses two fingers against his eyes.*] I have such thoughts, I have such strange thoughts.

LINDA. Willy, dear. Talk to them again. There's no reason why you can't work in New York.

WILLY. They don't need me in New York. I'm the New England man. I'm vital in New England.

LINDA. But you're sixty years old. They can't expect you to keep traveling   25 every week.

WILLY. I'll have to send a wire to Portland. I'm supposed to see Brown and Morrison tomorrow morning at ten o'clock to show the line. Goddammit, I could sell them! [*He starts putting on his jacket.*]

LINDA. [*taking the jacket from him*] Why don't you go down to the place tomorrow and tell Howard you've simply got to work in New York? You're too accommodating, dear.

WILLY. If old man Wagner was alive I'd a been in charge of New York now! That man was a prince, he was a masterful man. But that boy of his, that Howard, he don't appreciate. When I went north the first time, the Wagner Company didn't know where New England was!

LINDA. Why don't you tell those things to Howard, dear?

WILLY. [*encouraged*] I will, I definitely will. Is there any cheese?   30

LINDA. I'll make you a sandwich.

WILLY. No, go to sleep. I'll take some milk. I'll be up right away. The boys in?

LINDA. They're sleeping. Happy took Biff on a date tonight.

WILLY. [*interested*] That so?

LINDA. It was so nice to see them shaving together, one behind the other, in the bathroom. And going out together. You notice? The whole house smells of shaving lotion.

WILLY. Figure it out. Work a lifetime to pay off a house. You finally own it, and there's nobody to live in it.

LINDA. Well, dear, life is a casting off. It's always that way.

WILLY. No, no, some people—some people accomplish something. Did Biff say anything after I went this morning?

LINDA. You shouldn't have criticized him, Willy, especially after he just got off the train. You mustn't lose your temper with him.

WILLY. When the hell did I lose my temper? I simply asked him if he was making any money. Is that a criticism?

LINDA. But, dear, how could he make any money?

WILLY. [*worried and angered*] There's such an undercurrent in him. He became a moody man. Did he apologize when I left this morning?

LINDA. He was crestfallen, Willy. You know how he admires you. I think if he finds himself, then you'll both be happier and not fight any more.

WILLY. How can he find himself on a farm? Is that a life? A farmhand? In the beginning, when he was young, I thought, well, a young man, it's good for him to tramp around, take a lot of different jobs. But it's more than ten years now and he has yet to make thirty-five dollars a week!

LINDA. He's finding himself, Willy.

WILLY. Not finding yourself at the age of thirty-four is a disgrace!

LINDA. Shh!

WILLY. The trouble is he's lazy, goddammit!

LINDA. Willy, please!

WILLY. Biff is a lazy bum!

LINDA. They're sleeping. Get something to eat. Go on down.

WILLY. Why did he come home? I would like to know what brought him home.

LINDA. I don't know. I think he's still lost, Willy. I think he's very lost.

WILLY. Biff Loman is lost. In the greatest country in the world a young man with such—personal attractiveness, gets lost. And such a hard worker. There's one thing about Biff—he's not lazy.

LINDA. Never.

WILLY. [*with pity and resolve*] I'll see him in the morning; I'll have a nice talk with him. I'll get him a job selling. He could be big in no time. My God! Remember how they used to follow him around in high school? When he smiled at one of them their faces lit up. When he walked down the street . . . [*He loses himself in reminiscences.*]

LINDA. [*trying to bring him out of it*] Willy, dear, I got a new kind of American-type cheese today. It's whipped.

WILLY. Why do you get American when I like Swiss?

LINDA. I just thought you'd like a change—

WILLY. I don't want a change! I want Swiss cheese. Why am I always being contradicted?

LINDA. [*with a covering laugh*] I thought it would be a surprise.

WILLY. Why don't you open a window in here, for God's sake?

LINDA.   [*with infinite patience*] They're all open dear.

WILLY.   The way they boxed us in here. Bricks and windows, windows and bricks.

LINDA.   We should've bought the land next door.   65

WILLY.   The street is lined with cars. There's not a breath of fresh air in the neighborhood. The grass don't grow any more, you can't raise a carrot in the back yard. They should've had a law against apartment houses. Remember those two beautiful elm trees out there? When I and Biff hung the swing between them?

LINDA.   Yeah, like being a million miles from the city.

WILLY.   They should've arrested the builder for cutting those down. They massacred the neighborhood. [*lost*] More and more I think of those days, Linda. This time of year it was lilac and wisteria. And then the peonies would come out, and the daffodils. What fragrance in this room!

LINDA.   Well, after all, people had to move somewhere.

WILLY.   No, there's more people now.   70

LINDA.   I don't think there's more people. I think—

WILLY.   There's more people! That's what's ruining this country! Population is getting out of control. The competition is maddening! Smell the stink from that apartment house! And another one on the other side . . . How can they whip cheese?

[*On WILLY's last line, BIFF and HAPPY raise themselves up in their beds, listening.*]

LINDA.   Go down, try it. And be quiet.

WILLY.   [*turning to LINDA, guiltily*] You're not worried about me, are you, sweetheart?

BIFF.   What's the matter?   75

HAPPY.   Listen!

LINDA.   You've got too much on the ball to worry about.

WILLY.   You're my foundation and my support, Linda.

LINDA.   Just try to relax, dear. You make mountains out of molehills.

WILLY.   I won't fight with him any more. If he wants to go back to Texas,   80
let him go.

LINDA.   He'll find his way.

WILLY.   Sure. Certain men just don't get started till later in life. Like Thomas Edison, I think. Or B. F. Goodrich.° One of them was deaf. [*He starts for the bedroom doorway.*] I'll put my money on Biff.

LINDA.   And Willy—if it's warm Sunday we'll drive in the country. And we'll open the windshield, and take lunch.

WILLY.   No, the windshields don't open on the new cars.

LINDA.   But you opened it today.   85

WILLY.   Me? I didn't. [*He stops.*] Now isn't that peculiar! Isn't that a re-markable— [*He breaks off in amazement and fright as the flute is heard distantly.*]

LINDA.   What, darling?

WILLY.   That is the most remarkable thing.

LINDA.   What, dear?

Thomas Edison, B. F. Goodrich: Thomas A. Edison (1847–1931) was an American inventor who developed the electric light and the phonograph. Benjamin Franklin Goodrich (1841–1888) founded the B. F. Goodrich Rubber and Tire Company. It was Edison who suffered from deafness.

WILLY. I was thinking of the Chevvy. [*slight pause*] Nineteen twenty-eight   90
... when I had that red Chevvy— [*Breaks off.*] That funny? I coulda sworn I was
driving that Chevvy today.

LINDA. Well, that's nothing. Something must've reminded you.

WILLY. Remarkable. Ts. Remember those days? The way Biff used to
simonize that car? The dealer refused to believe there was eighty thousand miles
on it. [*He shakes his head.*] Heh! [*to Linda*] Close your eyes, I'll be right up. [*He
walks out of the bedroom.*]

HAPPY. [*to BIFF*] Jesus, maybe he smashed up the car again!

LINDA. [*calling after WILLY*] Be careful on the stairs, dear! The cheese is on
the middle shelf! [*She turns, goes over to the bed, takes his jacket, and goes out of the
bedroom.*]

[*Light has risen on the boys' room. Unseen, WILLY is heard talking to himself, "Eighty thousand
miles," and a little laugh. BIFF gets out of bed, comes downstage a bit, and stands attentively.
BIFF is two years older than his brother HAPPY, well built, but in these days bears a worn air
and seems less self-assured. He has succeeded less, and his dreams are stronger and less
acceptable than HAPPY's. HAPPY is tall, powerfully made. Sexuality is like a visible color on
him, or a scent that many women have discovered. He, like his brother, is lost, but in a different
way, for he has never allowed himself to turn his face toward defeat and is thus more confused
and hard-skinned, although seemingly more content.*]

HAPPY. [*getting out of bed*] He's going to get his license taken away if he   95
keeps that up. I'm getting nervous about him, y'know, Biff?

BIFF. His eyes are going.

HAPPY. No, I've driven with him. He sees all right. He just doesn't keep
his mind on it. I drove into the city with him last week. He stops at a green light
and then it turns red and he goes. [*He laughs.*]

BIFF. Maybe he's color-blind.

HAPPY. Pop? Why he's got the finest eye for color in the business. You
know that.

BIFF. [*sitting down on his bed*] I'm going to sleep.   100

HAPPY. You're not still sour on Dad, are you, Biff?

BIFF. He's all right, I guess.

WILLY. [*underneath them, in the living-room*] Yes, sir, eighty thousand miles—
eighty-two thousand!

BIFF. You smoking?

HAPPY. [*holding out a pack of cigarettes*] Want one?   105

BIFF. [*taking a cigarette*] I can never sleep when I smell it.

WILLY. What a simonizing job, heh!

HAPPY. [*with deep sentiment*] Funny, Biff y'know? Us sleeping in here again?
The old beds. [*He pats his bed affectionately.*] All the talk that went across those two
beds, huh? Our whole lives.

BIFF. Yeah. Lotta dreams and plans.

HAPPY. [*with a deep and masculine laugh*] About five hundred women would   110
like to know what was said in this room.

[*They share a soft laugh.*]

BIFF. Remember that big Betsy something—what the hell was her name—
over on Bushwick Avenue?

HAPPY. [*combing his hair*] With the collie dog!

BIFF. That's the one. I got you in there, remember?

HAPPY. Yeah, that was my first time—I think. Boy, there was a pig! [*They laugh, almost crudely.*] You taught me everything I know about women. Don't forget that.

BIFF. I bet you forgot how bashful you used to be. Especially with girls. 115

HAPPY. Oh, I still am, Biff.

BIFF. Oh, go on.

HAPPY. I just control it, that's all. I think I got less bashful and you got more so. What happened, Biff? Where's the old humor, the old confidence? [*He shakes* BIFF's *knee.* BIFF *gets up and moves restlessly about the room.*] What's the matter?

BIFF. Why does Dad mock me all the time?

HAPPY. He's not mocking you, he— 120

BIFF. Everything I say there's a twist of mockery on his face. I can't get near him.

HAPPY. He just wants you to make good, that's all. I wanted to talk to you about Dad for a long time, Biff. Something's—happening to him. He—talks to himself.

BIFF. I noticed that this morning. But he always mumbled.

HAPPY. But not so noticeable. It got so embarrassing I sent him to Florida. And you know something? Most of the time he's talking to you.

BIFF. What's he say about me? 125

HAPPY. I can't make it out.

BIFF. What's he say about me?

HAPPY. I think the fact that you're not settled, that you're still kind of up in the air . . .

BIFF. There's one or two other things depressing him, Happy.

HAPPY. What do you mean? 130

BIFF. Never mind. Just don't lay it all to me.

HAPPY. But I think if you just got started—I mean—is there any future for you out there?

BIFF. I tell ya, Hap, I don't know what the future is. I don't know—what I'm supposed to want.

HAPPY. What do you mean?

BIFF. Well, I spent six or seven years after high school trying to work 135 myself up. Shipping clerk, salesman, business of one kind or another. And it's a measly manner of existence. To get on that subway on the hot mornings in summer. To devote your whole life to keeping stock, or making phone calls, or selling or buying. To suffer fifty weeks of the year for the sake of a two-week vacation, when all you really desire is to be outdoors, with your shirt off. And always to have to get ahead of the next fella. And still—that's how you build a future.

HAPPY. Well, you really enjoy it on a farm? Are you content out there?

BIFF. [*with rising agitation*] Hap, I've had twenty or thirty different kinds of jobs since I left home before the war, and it always turns out the same. I just realized it lately. In Nebraska when I herded cattle, and the Dakotas, and Arizona, and now in Texas. It's why I came home now, I guess, because I realized it. This farm I work on, it's spring there now, see? And they've got about fifteen new colts. There's nothing more inspiring or—beautiful than the sight of a mare and a new colt. And it's cool there now, see? Texas is cool now, and it's spring. And whenever spring comes to where I am, I suddenly get the feeling, my God, I'm not gettin' anywhere! What the hell am I doing, playing around with horses, twenty-eight dollars a week! I'm thirty-four years old, I oughta be makin' my future. That's when I come running home. And now, I get here, and I don't know what to do with myself. [*after a pause*] I've always made a point of not wasting my life, and everytime I come back here I know that all I've done is to waste my life.

HAPPY. You're a poet, you know that, Biff? You're a—you're an idealist!

BIFF. No, I'm mixed up very bad. Maybe I oughta get married. Maybe I oughta get stuck into something. Maybe that's my trouble. I'm like a boy. I'm not married, I'm not in business, I just—I'm like a boy. Are you content, Hap? You're a success, aren't you? Are you content?

HAPPY. Hell, no! 140

BIFF. Why? You're making money, aren't you?

HAPPY. [*moving about with energy, expressiveness*] All I can do now is wait for the merchandise manager to die. And suppose I get to be merchandise manager? He's a good friend of mine, and he just built a terrific estate on Long Island. And he lived there about two months and sold it, and now he's building another one. He can't enjoy it once it's finished. And I know that's just what I would do. I don't know what the hell I'm workin' for. Sometimes I sit in my apartment—all alone. And I think of the rent I'm paying. And it's crazy. But then, it's what I always wanted. My own apartment, a car, and plenty of women. And still, goddammit, I'm lonely.

BIFF. [*with enthusiasm*] Listen, why don't you come out West with me?

HAPPY. You and I, heh?

BIFF. Sure, maybe we could buy a ranch. Raise cattle, use our muscles. Men 145
built like we are should be working out in the open.

HAPPY. [*avidly*] The Loman Brothers, heh?

BIFF. [*with vast affection*] Sure, we'd be known all over the counties!

HAPPY. [*enthralled*] That's what I dream about, Biff. Sometimes I want to just rip my clothes off in the middle of the store and outbox thát goddam merchandise manager. I mean I can outbox, outrun, and outlift anybody in that store, and I have to take orders from those common, petty sons-of-bitches till I can't stand it any more.

BIFF. I'm tellin' you, kid, if you were with me I'd be happy out there.

HAPPY. [*enthused*] See, Biff, everybody around me is so false that I'm 150
constantly lowering my ideals . . .

BIFF. Baby, together we'd stand up for one another, we'd have someone to trust.

HAPPY. If I were around you—

BIFF. Hap, the trouble is we weren't brought up to grub for money. I don't know how to do it.

HAPPY. Neither can I!

BIFF. Then let's go! 155

HAPPY. The only thing is—what can you make out there?

BIFF. But look at your friend. Builds an estate and then hasn't the peace of mind to live in it.

HAPPY.   Yeah, but when he walks into the store the waves part in front of him. That's fifty-two thousand dollars a year coming through the revolving door, and I got more in my pinky finger than he's got in his head.

BIFF.   Yeah, but you just said—

HAPPY.   I gotta show some of those pompous, self-important executives over   160
there that Hap Loman can make the grade. I want to walk into the store the way he walks in. Then I'll go with you, Biff. We'll be together yet, I swear. But take those two we had tonight. Now weren't they gorgeous creatures?

BIFF.   Yeah, yeah, most gorgeous I've had in years.

HAPPY.   I get that any time I want, Biff. Whenever I feel disgusted. The only trouble is, it gets like bowling or something. I just keep knockin' them over and it doesn't mean anything. You still run around a lot?

BIFF.   Naa. I'd like to find a girl—steady, somebody with substance.

HAPPY.   That's what I long for.

BIFF.   Go on! You'd never come home.   165

HAPPY.   I would! Somebody with character, with resistance! Like Mom, y'know? You're gonna call me a bastard when I tell you this. That girl Charlotte I was with tonight is engaged to be married in five weeks. [*He tries on his new hat.*]

BIFF.   No kiddin'!

HAPPY.   Sure, the guy's in line for the vice-presidency of the store. I don't know what gets into me, maybe I just have an overdeveloped sense of competition or something, but I went and ruined her, and furthermore I can't get rid of her. And he's the third executive I've done that to. Isn't that a crummy characteristic? And to top it all, I go to their weddings! [*Indignantly, but laughing*] Like I'm not supposed to take bribes. Manufacturers offer me a hundred-dollar bill now and then to throw an order their way. You know how honest I am, but it's like this girl, see. I hate myself for it. Because I don't want the girl, and, still, I take it and—I love it!

BIFF.   Let's go to sleep.

HAPPY.   I guess we didn't settle anything, heh?   170

BIFF.   I just got one idea that I think I'm going to try.

HAPPY.   What's that?

BIFF.   Remember Bill Oliver?

HAPPY.   Sure, Oliver is very big now. You want to work for him again?

BIFF.   No, but when I quit he said something to me. He put his arm on my   175
shoulder and he said, "Biff, if you ever need anything, come to me."

HAPPY.   I remember that. That sounds good.

BIFF.   I think I'll go to see him. If I could get ten thousand or even seven or eight thousand dollars I could buy a beautiful ranch.

HAPPY.   I bet he'd back you. 'Cause he thought highly of you, Biff. I mean, they all do. You're well liked, Biff. That's why I say to come back here, and we both have the apartment. And I'm tellin' you, Biff, any babe you want . . .

BIFF.   No, with a ranch I could do the work I like and still be something. I just wonder though. I wonder if Oliver still thinks I stole that carton of basketballs.

HAPPY.   Oh, he probably forgot that long ago. It's almost ten years. You're   180
too sensitive. Anyway, he didn't really fire you.

BIFF.   Well, I think he was going to. I think that's why I quit. I was never sure whether he knew or not. I know he thought the world of me, though. I was the only one he'd let lock up the place.

WILLY. [*below*] You gonna wash the engine, Biff?
HAPPY. Shh!

[*BIFF looks at HAPPY, who is gazing down, listening. WILLY is mumbling in the parlor.*]

HAPPY. You hear that?

[*They listen. WILLY laughs warmly.*]

BIFF. [*growing angry*] Doesn't he know Mom can hear that?   185
WILLY. Don't get your sweater dirty, Biff!

[*A look of pain crosses BIFF's face.*]

HAPPY. Isn't that terrible! Don't leave again, will you? You'll find a job
here. You gotta stick around. I don't know what to do about him, it's getting
embarrassing.
WILLY. What a simonizing job!
BIFF. Mom's hearing that!
WILLY. No kiddin', Biff, you got a date? Wonderful!   190
HAPPY. Go on to sleep. But talk to him in the morning, will you?
BIFF. [*reluctantly getting into bed*] With her in the house. Brother!
HAPPY. [*getting into bed*] I wish you'd have a good talk with him.

[*The light on their room begins to fade.*]

BIFF. [*to himself in bed*] That selfish, stupid . . .
HAPPY. Sh . . . Sleep, Biff.   195

[*Their light is out. Well before they have finished speaking, WILLY's form is dimly seen below
in the darkened kitchen. He opens the refrigerator, searches in there, and takes out a bottle
of milk. The apartment houses are fading out, and the entire house and surroundings become
covered with leaves. Music insinuates itself as the leaves appear.*]

WILLY. Just wanna be careful with those girls, Biff, that's all. Don't make
any promises. No promises of any kind. Because a girl, y'know, they always believe
what you tell 'em, and you're very young, Biff, you're too young to be talking
seriously to girls.

[*Light rises on the kitchen. WILLY, talking, shuts the refrigerator door and comes downstage
to the kitchen table. He pours milk into a glass. He is totally immersed in himself, smiling
faintly.*]

WILLY. Too young entirely, Biff. You want to watch your schooling first.
Then when you're all set, there'll be plenty of girls for a boy like you. [*He smiles
broadly at a kitchen chair.*] That so? The girls pay for you? [*He laughs.*] Boy, you
must really be makin' a hit.

[*WILLY is gradually addressing—physically—a point offstage, speaking through the wall of
the kitchen, and his voice has been rising in volume to that of a normal conversation.*]

WILLY. I been wondering why you polish the car so careful. Ha! Don't
leave the hubcaps, boys. Get the chamois to the hubcaps. Happy, use newspaper
on the windows, it's the easiest thing. Show him how to do it, Biff! You see,
Happy? Pad it up, use it like a pad. That's it, that's it, good work. You're doin' all

right, Hap. [*He pauses, then nods in approbation for a few seconds, then looks upward.*] Biff, first thing we gotta do when we get time is clip that big branch over the house. Afraid it's gonna fall in a storm and hit the roof. Tell you what. We get a rope and sling her around, and then we climb up there with a couple of saws and take her down. Soon as you finish the car, boys, I wanna see ya. I got a surprise for you, boys.

BIFF.   [*offstage*] Whatta ya got, Dad?

WILLY.   No, you finish first. Never leave a job till you're finished—remember   200 that. [*looking toward the "big trees"*] Biff, up in Albany I saw a beautiful hammock. I think I'll buy it next trip, and we'll hang it right between those two elms. Wouldn't that be something? Just swingin' there under those branches. Boy, that would be . . .

[*YOUNG BIFF and YOUNG HAPPY appear from the direction WILLY was addressing. HAPPY carries rags and a pail of water. BIFF, wearing a sweater with a block "S," carries a football.*]

BIFF.   [*pointing in the direction of the car offstage*] How's that, Pop, professional?

WILLY.   Terrific. Terrific job, boys. Good work, Biff.

HAPPY.   Where's the surprise, Pop?

WILLY.   In the back seat of the car.

HAPPY.   Boy! [*He runs off.*]   205

BIFF.   What is it, Dad? Tell me, what'd you buy?

WILLY.   [*laughing, cuffs him*] Never mind, something I want you to have.

BIFF.   [*turns and starts off*] What is it, Hap?

HAPPY.   [*offstage*] It's a punching bag!

BIFF.   Oh, Pop!   210

WILLY.   It's got Gene Tunney's° signature on it!

[*HAPPY runs onstage with a punching bag.*]

BIFF.   Gee, how'd you know we wanted a punching bag?

WILLY.   Well, it's the finest thing for the timing.

HAPPY.   [*lies down on his back and pedals with his feet*] I'm losing weight, you notice, Pop?

WILLY.   [*to HAPPY*] Jumping rope is good too.   215

BIFF.   Did you see the new football I got?

WILLY.   [*examining the ball*] Where'd you get a new ball?

BIFF.   The coach told me to practice my passing.

WILLY.   That so? And he gave you the ball, heh?

BIFF.   Well, I borrowed it from the locker room. [*He laughs confidentially.*]   220

WILLY.   [*laughing with him at the theft*] I want you to return that.

HAPPY.   I told you he wouldn't like it!

BIFF.   [*angrily*] Well, I'm bringing it back!

WILLY.   [*stopping the incipient argument, to HAPPY*] Sure, he's gotta practice with a regulation ball, doesn't he? [*to BIFF*] Coach'll probably congratulate you on your initiative!

BIFF.   Oh, he keeps congratulating my initiative all the time, Pop.   225

Gene Tunney: James Joseph Tunney, a boxer who won the heavyweight championship from Jack Dempsey in 1926 and retired undefeated in 1928.

WILLY. That's because he likes you. If somebody else took that ball there'd be an uproar. So what's the report, boys, what's the report?

BIFF. Where'd you go this time, Dad? Gee we were lonesome for you.

WILLY. [*pleased, puts an arm around each boy and they come down to the apron*] Lonesome, heh?

BIFF. Missed you every minute.

WILLY. Don't say? Tell you a secret, boys. Don't breathe it to a soul. 230 Someday I'll have my own business, and I'll never have to leave home any more.

HAPPY. Like Uncle Charley, heh?

WILLY. Bigger than Uncle Charley! Because Charley is not—liked. He's liked, but he's not—well liked.

BIFF. Where'd you go this time, Dad?

WILLY. Well, I got on the road, and I went north to Providence. Met the Mayor.

BIFF. The Mayor of Providence! 235

WILLY. He was sitting in the hotel lobby.

BIFF. What'd he say?

WILLY. He said, "Morning!" And I said, "You got a fine city here, Mayor." And then he had coffee with me. And then I went to Waterbury. Waterbury is a fine city. Big clock city, the famous Waterbury clock. Sold a nice bill there. And then Boston—Boston is the cradle of the Revolution. A fine city. And a couple of other towns in Mass., and on to Portland and Bangor and straight home!

BIFF. Gee, I'd love to go with you sometime, Dad.

WILLY. Soon as summer comes. 240

HAPPY. Promise?

WILLY. You and Hap and I, and I'll show you all the towns. America is full of beautiful towns and fine, upstanding people. And they know me, boys, they know me up and down New England. The finest people. And when I bring you fellas up, there'll be open sesame for all of us, 'cause one thing, boys: I have friends. I can park my car in any street in New England, and the cops protect it like their own. This summer, heh?

BIFF and HAPPY. [*together*] Yeah! You bet!

WILLY. We'll take our bathing suits.

HAPPY. We'll carry your bags, Pop! 245

WILLY. Oh, won't that be something! Me comin' into the Boston stores with you boys carryin' my bags. What a sensation!

[*BIFF is prancing around, practicing passing the ball.*]

WILLY. You nervous, Biff, about the game?

BIFF. Not if you're gonna be there.

WILLY. What do they say about you in school, now that they made you captain?

HAPPY. There's a crowd of girls behind him everytime the classes change. 250

BIFF. [*taking WILLY's hand*] This Saturday, Pop, this Saturday—just for you, I'm going to break through for a touchdown.

HAPPY. You're supposed to pass.

BIFF. I'm takin' one play for Pop. You watch me, Pop, and when I take off my helmet, that means I'm breakin' out. Then you watch me crash through that line!

WILLY. [*kisses* BIFF] Oh, wait'll I tell this in Boston!

[BERNARD *enters in knickers. He is younger than* BIFF, *earnest and loyal, a worried boy.*]

BERNARD.   Biff, where are you? You're supposed to study with me today.   255
WILLY.   Hey, looka Bernard. What're you lookin' so anemic about, Bernard?
BERNARD.   He's gotta study, Uncle Willy. He's got Regents° next week.
HAPPY.   [*tauntingly, spinning* BERNARD *around*] Let's box, Bernard!
BERNARD.   Biff! [*He gets away from* HAPPY.] Listen, Biff, I heard Mr. Birnbaum
say that if you don't start studyin' math he's gonna flunk you, and you won't
graduate. I heard him!
WILLY.   You better study with him, Biff. Go ahead now.   260
BERNARD.   I heard him!
BIFF.   Oh, Pop, you didn't see my sneakers! [*He holds up a foot for* WILLY *to
look at.*]
WILLY.   Hey, that's a beautiful job of printing!
BERNARD.   [*wiping his glasses*] Just because he printed University of Virginia
on his sneakers doesn't mean they've got to graduate him, Uncle Willy!
WILLY.   [*angrily*] What're you talking about? With scholarships to three uni-   265
versities they're gonna flunk him?
BERNARD.   But I heard Mr. Birnbaum say—
WILLY.   Don't be a pest, Bernard! [*to his boys*] What an anemic!
BERNARD.   Okay, I'm waiting for you in my house, Biff.

[BERNARD *goes off. The* LOMANS *laugh.*]

WILLY.   Bernard is not well liked, is he?
BIFF.   He's liked, but he's not well liked.   270
HAPPY.   That's right, Pop.
WILLY.   That's just what I mean. Bernard can get the best marks in school,
y'understand, but when he gets out in the business world, y'understand, you are
going to be five times ahead of him. That's why I thank Almighty God you're
both built like Adonises. Because the man who makes an appearance in the
business world, the man who creates personal interest, is the man who gets ahead.
Be liked and you will never want. You take me, for instance. I never have to wait
in line to see a buyer. "Willy Loman is here!" That's all they have to know, and I
go right through.
BIFF.   Did you knock them dead, Pop?
WILLY.   Knocked 'em cold in Providence, slaughtered 'em in Boston.
HAPPY.   [*on his back, pedaling again*] I'm losing weight, you notice, Pop?   275

[LINDA *enters, as of old, a ribbon in her hair, carrying a basket of washing.*]

LINDA.   [*with youthful energy*] Hello, dear!
WILLY.   Sweetheart!
LINDA.   How'd the Chevvy run?
WILLY.   Chevrolet, Linda, is the greatest car ever built. [*to the boys*] Since
when do you let your mother carry wash up the stairs?
BIFF.   Grab hold there, boy!   280
HAPPY.   Where to, Mom?

Regents: A statewide high school proficiency examination administered in New York State.

LINDA. Hang them up on the line. And you better go down to your friends, Biff. The cellar is full of boys. They don't know what to do with themselves.

BIFF. Ah, when Pop comes home they can wait!

WILLY. [*laughs appreciatively*] You better go down and tell them what to do, Biff.

BIFF. I think I'll have them sweep out the furnace room. 285

WILLY. Good work, Biff.

BIFF. [*goes through wall-line of kitchen to doorway at back and calls down*] Fellas! Everybody sweep out the furnace room! I'll be right down!

VOICES. All right! Okay, Biff.

BIFF. George and Sam and Frank, come out back! We're hangin' up the wash! Come on, Hap, on the double! [*He and HAPPY carry out the basket.*]

LINDA. The way they obey him! 290

WILLY. Well, that's training, the training. I'm tellin' you, I was sellin' thousands and thousands, but I had to come home.

LINDA. Oh, the whole block'll be at that game. Did you sell anything?

WILLY. I did five hundred gross in Providence and seven hundred gross in Boston.

LINDA. No! Wait a minute, I've got a pencil. [*She pulls pencil and paper out of her apron pocket.*] That makes your commission . . . Two hundred—my God! Two hundred and twelve dollars!

WILLY. Well, I didn't figure it yet, but . . . 295

LINDA. How much did you do?

WILLY. Well, I—I did—about a hundred and eighty gross in Providence. Well, no—it came to—roughly two hundred gross on the whole trip.

LINDA. [*without hesitation*] Two hundred gross. That's . . . [*She figures.*]

WILLY. The trouble was that three of the stores were half closed for inventory in Boston. Otherwise I woulda broke records.

LINDA. Well, it makes seventy dollars and some pennies. That's very good. 300

WILLY. What do we owe?

LINDA. Well, on the first there's sixteen dollars on the refrigerator—

WILLY. Why sixteen?

LINDA. Well, the fan belt broke, so it was a dollar eighty.

WILLY. But it's brand new. 305

LINDA. Well, the man said that's the way it is. Till they work themselves in, y'know.

[*They move through the wall-line into the kitchen.*]

WILLY. I hope we didn't get stuck on that machine.

LINDA. They got the biggest ads of any of them!

WILLY. I know, it's a fine machine. What else?

LINDA. Well, there's nine-sixty for the washing machine. And for the vacuum cleaner there's three and a half due on the fifteenth. Then the roof, you got twenty-one dollars remaining. 310

WILLY. It don't leak, does it?

LINDA. No, they did a wonderful job. Then you owe Frank for the carburetor.

WILLY. I'm not going to pay that man! That goddam Chevrolet, they ought to prohibit the manufacture of that car!

LINDA.   Well, you owe him three and a half. And odds and ends, comes to around a hundred and twenty dollars by the fifteenth.

WILLY.   A hundred and twenty dollars! My God, if business don't pick up   315
I don't know what I'm gonna do!

LINDA.   Well, next week you'll do better.

WILLY.   Oh, I'll knock 'em dead next week. I'll go to Hartford. I'm very well liked in Hartford. You know, the trouble is, Linda, people don't seem to take to me.

[*They move onto the forestage.*]

LINDA.   Oh, don't be foolish.

WILLY.   I know it when I walk in. They seem to laugh at me.

LINDA.   Why? Why would they laugh at you? Don't talk that way, Willy.   320

[*WILLY moves to the edge of the stage. LINDA goes into the kitchen and starts to darn stockings.*]

WILLY.   I don't know the reason for it, but they just pass me by. I'm not noticed.

LINDA.   But you're doing wonderful, dear. You're making seventy to a hundred dollars a week.

WILLY.   But I gotta be at it ten, twelve hours a day. Other men—I don't know—they do it easier. I don't know why—I can't stop myself—I talk too much. A man oughta come in with a few words. One thing about Charley. He's a man of few words, and they respect him.

LINDA.   You don't talk too much, you're just lively.

WILLY.   [*smiling*] Well, I figure, what the hell, life is short, a couple of jokes.   325
[*to himself*] I joke too much! [*The smile goes.*]

LINDA.   Why? You're—

WILLY.   I'm fat. I'm very—foolish to look at, Linda. I didn't tell you, but Christmas time I happened to be calling on F. H. Stewarts, and a salesman I know, as I was going in to see the buyer I heard him say something about—walrus. And I—I cracked him right across the face. I won't take that. I simply will not take that. But they do laugh at me. I know that.

LINDA.   Darling . . .

WILLY.   I gotta overcome it. I know I gotta overcome it. I'm not dressing to advantage, maybe.

LINDA.   Willy, darling, you're the handsomest man in the world—   330

WILLY.   Oh, no, Linda.

LINDA.   To me you are. [*slight pause*] The handsomest.

[*From the darkness is heard the laughter of a woman. WILLY doesn't turn to it, but it continues through LINDA's lines.*]

LINDA.   And the boys, Willy. Few men are idolized by their children the way you are.

[*Music is heard as behind a scrim, to the left of the house, THE WOMAN, dimly seen, is dressing.*]

WILLY.   [*with great feeling*] You're the best there is, Linda, you're a pal, you know that? On the road—on the road I want to grab you sometimes and just kiss the life outa you.

[*The laughter is loud now, and he moves into a brightening area at the left, where* THE WOMAN *has come from behind the scrim and is standing, putting on her hat, looking into a "mirror" and laughing.*]

WILLY. Cause I get so lonely—especially when business is bad and there's   335
nobody to talk to. I get the feeling that I'll never sell anything again, that I won't
make a living for you, or a business, a business for the boys. [*He talks through* THE
WOMAN'*s subsiding laughter;* THE WOMAN *primps at the "mirror."*] There's so much I
want to make for—
THE WOMAN. Me? You didn't make me, Willy. I picked you.
WILLY. [*pleased*] You picked me?
THE WOMAN. [*who is quite proper-looking,* WILLY'*s age*] I did. I've been sitting
at that desk watching all the salesmen go by, day in, day out. But you've got such
a sense of humor, and we do have such a good time together, don't we?
WILLY. Sure, sure. [*He takes her in his arms.*] Why do you have to go now?
THE WOMAN. It's two o'clock . . .   340
WILLY. No, come on in! [*He pulls her.*]
THE WOMAN. . . . my sisters'll be scandalized. When'll you be back?
WILLY. Oh, two weeks about. Will you come up again?
THE WOMAN. Sure thing. You do make me laugh. It's good for me. [*She
squeezes his arm, kisses him.*] And I think you're a wonderful man.
WILLY. You picked me, heh?   345
THE WOMAN. Sure. Because you're so sweet. And such a kidder.
WILLY. Well, I'll see you next time I'm in Boston.
THE WOMAN. I'll put you right through to the buyers.
WILLY. [*slapping her bottom*] Right. Well, bottoms up!
THE WOMAN. [*slaps him gently and laughs*] You just kill me, Willy. [*He suddenly*   350
grabs her and kisses her roughly.] You kill me. And thanks for the stockings. I love a
lot of stockings. Well, good night.
WILLY. Good night. And keep your pores open!
THE WOMAN. Oh, Willy!

[THE WOMAN *bursts out laughing, and* LINDA'*s laughter blends in.* THE WOMAN *disappears
into the dark. Now the area at the kitchen table brightens.* LINDA *is sitting where she was at
the kitchen table, but now is mending a pair of her silk stockings.*]

LINDA. You are, Willy. The handsomest man. You've got no reason to feel
that—
WILLY. [*coming out of* THE WOMAN'*s dimming area and going over to* LINDA] I'll
make it all up to you, Linda, I'll—
LINDA. There's nothing to make up, dear. You're doing fine, better than—   355
WILLY. [*noticing her mending*] What's that?
LINDA. Just mending my stockings. They're so expensive—
WILLY. [*angrily, taking them from her*] I won't have you mending stockings in
this house! Now throw them out!

[LINDA *puts the stockings in her pocket.*]

BERNARD. [*entering on the run*] Where is he? If he doesn't study!
WILLY. [*moving to the forestage, with great agitation*] You'll give him the an-   360
swers!

BERNARD   I do, but I can't on a Regents! That's a state exam! They're liable
to arrest me!

WILLY.   Where is he? I'll whip him, I'll whip him!

LINDA.   And he'd better give back that football, Willy, it's not nice.

WILLY.   Biff! Where is he? Why is he taking everything?

LINDA.   He's too rough with the girls, Willy. All the mothers are afraid of   365
him!

WILLY.   I'll whip him!

BERNARD.   He's driving the car without a license!

[*THE WOMAN's laugh is heard.*]

WILLY.   Shut up!

LINDA.   All the mothers—

WILLY.   Shut up!   370

BERNARD.   [*backing quietly away and out*] Mr. Birnbaum says he's stuck up.

WILLY.   Get outa here!

BERNARD.   If he doesn't buckle down he'll flunk math! [*He goes off.*]

LINDA.   He's right, Willy, you've gotta—

WILLY.   [*exploding at her*] There's nothing the matter with him! You want   375
him to be a worm like Bernard? He's got spirit, personality . . .

[*As he speaks, LINDA, almost in tears, exits into the living-room. WILLY is alone in the kitchen, wilting and staring. The leaves are gone. It is night again, and the apartment houses look down from behind.*]

WILLY.   Loaded with it. Loaded! What is he stealing? He's giving it back, isn't he? Why is he stealing? What did I tell him? I never in my life told him anything but decent things.

[*HAPPY in pajamas has come down the stairs; WILLY suddenly becomes aware of HAPPY's presence.*]

HAPPY.   Let's go now, come on.

WILLY.   [*sitting down at the kitchen table*] Huh! Why did she have to wax the floors herself? Everytime she waxes the floors she keels over. She knows that!

HAPPY.   Shh! Take it easy. What brought you back tonight?

WILLY.   I got an awful scare. Nearly hit a kid in Yonkers. God! Why didn't   380
I go to Alaska with my brother Ben that time! Ben! That man was a genius, that man was success incarnate! What a mistake! He begged me to go.

HAPPY.   Well, there's no use in—

WILLY.   You guys! There was a man started with the clothes on his back and ended up with diamond mines!

HAPPY.   Boy, someday I'd like to know how he did it.

WILLY.   What's the mystery? The man knew what he wanted and went out and got it! Walked into a jungle, and comes out, the age of twenty-one, and he's rich! The world is an oyster, but you don't crack it open on a mattress!

HAPPY.   Pop, I told you I'm gonna retire you for life.   385

WILLY.   You'll retire me for life on seventy goddam dollars a week? And your women and your car and your apartment, and you'll retire me for life! Christ's sake, I couldn't get past Yonkers today! Where are you guys, where are you? The woods are burning! I can't drive a car!

[CHARLEY *has appeared in the doorway. He is a large man, slow of speech, laconic, immovable. In all he says, despite what he says, there is pity, and now, trepidation. He has a robe over pajamas, slippers on his feet. He enters the kitchen.*]

CHARLEY. Everything all right?

HAPPY. Yeah, Charley, everything's . . .

WILLY. What's the matter?

CHARLEY. I heard some noise. I thought something happened. Can't we do   390
something about the walls? You sneeze in here, and in my house hats blow off.

HAPPY. Let's go to bed, Dad. Come on.

[CHARLEY *signals to* HAPPY *to go.*]

WILLY. You go ahead, I'm not tired at the moment.

HAPPY. [*to* WILLY] Take it easy, huh? [*He exits.*]

WILLY. What're you doin' up?

CHARLEY. [*sitting down at the kitchen table opposite* WILLY] Couldn't sleep good.   395
I had a heartburn.

WILLY. Well, you don't know how to eat.

CHARLEY. I eat with my mouth.

WILLY. No, you're ignorant. You gotta know about vitamins and things like
that.

CHARLEY. Come on, let's shoot. Tire you out a little.

WILLY. [*hesitantly*] All right. You got cards?   400

CHARLEY. [*taking a deck from his pocket*] Yeah, I got them. Someplace. What
is it with those vitamins?

WILLY. [*dealing*] They build up your bones. Chemistry.

CHARLEY. Yeah, but there's no bones in a heartburn.

WILLY. What are you talkin' about? Do you know the first thing about it?

CHARLEY. Don't get insulted.   405

WILLY. Don't talk about something you don't know anything about.

[*They are playing. Pause.*]

CHARLEY. What're you doin' home?

WILLY. A little trouble with the car.

CHARLEY. Oh. [*Pause*] I'd like to take a trip to California.

WILLY. Don't say.   410

CHARLEY. You want a job?

WILLY. I got a job, I told you that. [*after a slight pause*] What the hell are
you offering me a job for?

CHARLEY. Don't get insulted.

WILLY. Don't insult me.

CHARLEY. I don't see no sense in it. You don't have to go on this way.   415

WILLY. I got a good job. [*slight pause*] What do you keep comin' in for?

CHARLEY. You want me to go?

WILLY. [*after a pause, withering*] I can't understand it. He's going back to
Texas again. What the hell is that?

CHARLEY. Let him go.

WILLY. I got nothin' to give him, Charley, I'm clean, I'm clean.   420

CHARLEY. He won't starve. None a them starve. Forget about him.

WILLY.   Then what have I got to remember?

CHARLEY.   You take it too hard. To hell with it. When a deposit bottle is broken you don't get your nickel back.

WILLY.   That's easy enough for you to say.

CHARLEY.   That ain't easy for me to say.   425

WILLY.   Did you see the ceiling I put up in the living-room?

CHARLEY.   Yeah, that's a piece of work. To put up a ceiling is a mystery to me. How do you do it?

WILLY.   What's the difference?

CHARLEY.   Well, talk about it.   430

WILLY.   You gonna put up a ceiling?

CHARLEY.   How could I put up a ceiling?

WILLY.   Then what the hell are you bothering me for?

CHARLEY.   You're insulted again.

WILLY.   A man who can't handle tools is not a man. You're disgusting.

CHARLEY.   Don't call me disgusting, Willy.   435

[UNCLE BEN, *carrying a valise and an umbrella, enters the forestage from around the right corner of the house. He is a stolid man, in his sixties, with a mustache and an authoritative air. He is utterly certain of his destiny, and there is an aura of far places about him. He enters exactly as* WILLY *speaks.*]

WILLY.   I'm getting awfully tired, Ben.

[BEN's *music is heard.* BEN *looks around at everything.*]

CHARLEY.   Good, keep playing; you'll sleep better. Did you call me Ben?

[BEN *looks at his watch.*]

WILLY.   That's funny. For a second there you reminded me of my brother Ben.

BEN.   I only have a few minutes. [*He strolls, inspecting the place.* WILLY *and* CHARLEY *continue playing.*]

CHARLEY.   You never heard from him again, heh? Since that time?   440

WILLY.   Didn't Linda tell you? Couple of weeks ago we got a letter from his wife in Africa. He died.

CHARLEY.   That so.

BEN.   [*chuckling*] So this is Brooklyn, eh?

CHARLEY.   Maybe you're in for some of his money.

WILLY.   Naa, he had seven sons. There's just one opportunity I had with   445
that man . . .

BEN.   I must make a train, William. There are several properties I'm looking at in Alaska.

WILLY.   Sure, sure! If I'd gone with him to Alaska that time, everything would've been totally different.

CHARLEY.   Go on, you'd froze to death up there.

WILLY.   What're you talking about?

BEN.   Opportunity is tremendous in Alaska, William. Surprised you're not   450
up there

WILLY.   Sure, tremendous.

CHARLEY. Heh?

WILLY. There was the only man I ever met who knew the answers.

CHARLEY. Who?

BEN. How are you all? 455

WILLY. [*taking a pot, smiling*] Fine, fine.

CHARLEY. Pretty sharp tonight.

BEN. Is Mother living with you?

WILLY. No, she died a long time ago.

CHARLEY. Who? 460

BEN. That's too bad. Fine specimen of a lady, Mother.

WILLY. [*to CHARLEY*] Heh?

BEN. I'd hoped to see the old girl.

CHARLEY. Who died?

BEN. Heard anything from Father, have you? 465

WILLY. [*unnerved*] What do you mean, who died?

CHARLEY. [*taking a pot*] What're you talkin' about?

BEN. [*looking at his watch*] William, it's half-past eight!

WILLY. [*As though to dispel his confusion he angrily stops CHARLEY's hand.*] That's my build!

CHARLEY. I put the ace— 470

WILLY. If you don't know how to play the game I'm not gonna throw my money away on you!

CHARLEY. [*rising*] It was my ace, for God's sake!

WILLY. I'm through, I'm through!

BEN. When did Mother die?

WILLY. Long ago. Since the beginning you never knew how to play cards. 475

CHARLEY. [*picks up the cards and goes to the door*] All right! Next time I'll bring a deck with five aces.

WILLY. I don't play that kind of game!

CHARLEY. [*turning to him*] You ought to be ashamed of yourself!

WILLY. Yeah?

CHARLEY. Yeah! [*He goes out.*] 480

WILLY. [*slamming the door after him*] Ignoramus!

BEN. [*as WILLY comes toward him through the wall-line of the kitchen*] So you're William.

WILLY. [*shaking BEN's hand*] Ben! I've been waiting for you so long! What's the answer? How did you do it?

BEN. Oh, there's a story in that.

[*LINDA enters the forestage, as of old, carrying the wash basket.*]

LINDA. Is this Ben? 485

BEN. [*gallantly*] How do you do, my dear.

LINDA. Where've you been all these years? Willy's always wondered why you—

WILLY. [*pulling BEN away from her impatiently*] Where is Dad? Didn't you follow him? How did you get started?

BEN. Well, I don't know how much you remember.

WILLY. Well, I was just a baby, of course, only three or four years old— 490

BEN. Three years and eleven months.

WILLY.   What a memory, Ben!

BEN.   I have many enterprises, William, and I have never kept books.

WILLY.   I remember I was sitting under the wagon in—was it Nebraska?

BEN.   It was South Dakota, and I gave you a bunch of wild flowers.   495

WILLY.   I remember you walking away down some open road.

BEN.   [*laughing*] I was going to find Father in Alaska.

WILLY.   Where is he?

BEN.   At that age I had a very faulty view of geography, William. I discovered after a few days that I was heading due south, so instead of Alaska, I ended up in Africa.

LINDA.   Africa!   500

WILLY.   The Gold Coast!

BEN.   Principally diamond mines.

LINDA.   Diamond mines!

BEN.   Yes, my dear. But I've only a few minutes—

WILLY.   No! Boys! Boys! [*YOUNG BIFF and HAPPY appear.*] Listen to this. This   505
is your Uncle Ben, a great man! Tell my boys, Ben!

BEN.   Why, boys, when I was seventeen I walked into the jungle, and when I was twenty-one I walked out. [*He laughs.*] And by God I was rich.

WILLY.   [*to the boys*] You see what I been talking about? The greatest things can happen!

BEN.   [*glancing at his watch*] I have an appointment in Ketchikan Tuesday week.

WILLY.   No, Ben. Please tell about Dad. I want my boys to hear. I want them to know the kind of stock they spring from. All I remember is a man with a big beard, and I was in Mamma's lap, sitting around a fire, and some kind of high music.

BEN.   His flute. He played the flute.   510

WILLY.   Sure, the flute, that's right!

[*New music is heard, a high, rollicking tune.*]

BEN.   Father was a very great and a very wild-hearted man. We would start in Boston, and he'd toss the whole family into the wagon, and then he'd drive the team right across the country; through Ohio, and Indiana, Michigan, Illinois, and all the Western states. And we'd stop in the towns and sell the flutes that he'd made on the way. Great inventor, Father. With one gadget he made more in a week than a man like you could make in a lifetime.

WILLY.   That's just the way I'm bringing them up, Ben—rugged, well liked, all-around.

BEN.   Yeah? [*to BIFF*] Hit that, boy—hard as you can. [*He pounds his stomach.*]

BIFF.   Oh, no, sir!   515

BEN.   [*taking boxing stance*] Come on, get to me! [*He laughs.*]

BIFF.   Okay! [*He cocks his fists and starts in.*]

WILLY.   Go to it, Biff! Go ahead, show him!

LINDA.   [*to WILLY*] Why must he fight, dear?

BEN.   [*sparring with BIFF*] Good boy! Good boy!   520

WILLY.   How's that, Ben, heh?

HAPPY.   Give him the left, Biff!

LINDA.   Why are you fighting?

BEN. Good boy! [*suddenly comes in, trips BIFF, and stands over him, the point of his umbrella poised over BIFF's eye.*]

LINDA. Look out, Biff! 525

BIFF. Gee!

BEN. [*patting BIFF's knee*] Never fight fair with a stranger, boy. You'll never get out of the jungle that way. [*taking LINDA's hand and bowing*] It was an honor and a pleasure to meet you, Linda.

LINDA. [*withdrawing her hand coldly, frightened*] Have a nice—trip.

BEN. [*to WILLY*] And good luck with your—what do you do?

WILLY. Selling. 530

BEN. Yes. Well . . . [*He raises his hand in farewell to all.*]

WILLY. No, Ben, I don't want you to think . . . [*He takes BEN's arm to show him.*] It's Brooklyn, I know, but we hunt too.

BEN. Really, now.

WILLY. Oh, sure, there's snakes and rabbits and—that's why I moved out here. Why, Biff can fell any one of these trees in no time! Boys! Go right over to where they're building the apartment house and get some sand. We're gonna rebuild the entire front stoop right now! Watch this, Ben!

BIFF. Yes, sir! On the double, Hap! 535

HAPPY. [*as he and BIFF run off*] I lost weight, Pop, you notice?

[*CHARLEY enters in knickers, even before the boys are gone.*]

CHARLEY. Listen, if they steal any more from that building the watchman'll put the cops on them!

LINDA. [*to WILLY*] Don't let Biff . . .

[*BEN laughs lustily.*]

WILLY. You shoulda seen the lumber they brought home last week. At least a dozen six-by-tens worth all kinds a money.

CHARLEY. Listen, if that watchman— 540

WILLY. I gave them hell, understand. But I got a couple of fearless characters there.

CHARLEY. Willy, the jails are full of fearless characters.

BEN. [*clapping WILLY on the back, with a laugh at CHARLEY*] And the stock exchange, friend!

WILLY. [*joining in BEN's laughter*] Where are the rest of your pants?

CHARLEY. My wife bought them. 545

WILLY. Now all you need is a golf club and you can go upstairs and go to sleep. [*to BEN*] Great athlete! Between him and his son Bernard they can't hammer a nail!

BERNARD. [*rushing in*] The watchman's chasing Biff!

WILLY. [*angrily*] Shut up! He's not stealing anything!

LINDA. [*alarmed, hurrying off left*] Where is he? Biff, dear! [*She exits.*]

WILLY. [*moving toward the left, away from BEN*] There's nothing wrong. What's the matter with you? 550

BEN. Nervy boy. Good!

WILLY. [*laughing*] Oh, nerves of iron, that Biff!

CHARLEY. Don't know what it is. My New England man comes back and he's bleedin', they murdered him up there.

WILLY. It's contacts, Charley, I got important contacts!

CHARLEY. [*sarcastically*] Glad to hear it, Willy. Come in later, we'll shoot a   555
little casino. I'll take some of your Portland money. [*He laughs at* WILLY *and exits.*]

WILLY. [*turning to* BEN] Business is bad, it's murderous. But not for me, of
course.

BEN. I'll stop by on my way back to Africa.

WILLY. [*longingly.*] Can't you stay a few days? You're just what I need, Ben,
because I—I have a fine position here, but I—well, Dad left when I was such a
baby and I never had a chance to talk to him and I still feel—kind of temporary
about myself.

BEN. I'll be late for my train.

[*They are at opposite ends of the stage.*]

WILLY. Ben, my boys—can't we talk? They'd go into the jaws of hell for   560
me, see, but I—

BEN. William, you're being first-rate with your boys. Outstanding, manly
chaps!

WILLY. [*hanging on to his words*] Oh, Ben, that's good to hear! Because
sometimes I'm afraid that I'm not teaching them the right kind of—Ben, how
should I teach them?

BEN. [*giving great weight to each word, and with a certain vicious audacity*] William, when I walked into the jungle, I was seventeen. When I walked out I was
twenty-one. And, by God, I was rich! [*He goes off into darkness around the right corner
of the house.*]

WILLY. . . . was rich! That's just the spirit I want to imbue them with! To
walk into a jungle! I was right! I was right! I was right!

[BEN *is gone, but* WILLY *is still speaking to him as* LINDA, *in her nightgown and robe, enters
the kitchen, glances around for* WILLY, *then goes to the door of the house, looks out and sees
him. Comes down to his left. He looks at her.*]

LINDA. Willy, dear? Willy?   565

WILLY. I was right!

LINDA. Did you have some cheese? [*He can't answer.*] It's very late, darling.
Come to bed, heh?

WILLY. [*looking straight up*] Gotta break your neck to see a star in this yard.

LINDA. You coming in?

WILLY. Whatever happened to that diamond watch fob? Remember? When   570
Ben came from Africa that time? Didn't he give me a watch fob with a diamond
in it?

LINDA. You pawned it, dear. Twelve, thirteen years ago. For Biff's radio
correspondence course.

WILLY. Gee, that was a beautiful thing. I'll take a walk.

LINDA. But you're in your slippers.

WILLY. [*starting to go around the house at the left*] I was right! I was! [*Half to
LINDA, as he goes, shaking his head*] What a man! There was a man worth talking to.
I was right!

LINDA. [*calling after* WILLY] But in your slippers, Willy!   575

[WILLY *is almost gone when* BIFF, *in his pajamas, comes down the stairs and enters the kitchen.*]

BIFF.   What is he doing out there?

LINDA.   Sh!

BIFF.   God Almighty, Mom, how long has he been doing this?

LINDA.   Don't, he'll hear you.

BIFF.   What the hell is the matter with him?   580

LINDA.   It'll pass by morning.

BIFF.   Shouldn't we do anything?

LINDA.   Oh, my dear, you should do a lot of things, but there's nothing to do, so go to sleep.

[*HAPPY comes down the stairs and sits on the steps.*]

HAPPY.   I never heard him so loud, Mom.

LINDA.   Well, come around more often; you'll hear him. [*She sits down at the*   585
table and mends the lining of WILLY's jacket.]

BIFF.   Why didn't you ever write me about this, Mom?

LINDA.   How would I write to you? For over three months you had no address.

BIFF.   I was on the move. But you know I thought of you all the time. You know that, don't you, pal?

LINDA.   I know, dear, I know. But he likes to have a letter. Just to know that there's still a possibility for better things.

BIFF.   He's not like this all the time, is he?   590

LINDA.   It's when you come home he's always the worst.

BIFF.   When I come home?

LINDA.   When you write you're coming, he's all smiles, and talks about the future, and—he's just wonderful. And then the closer you seem to come, the more shaky he gets, and then, by the time you get here, he's arguing, and he seems angry at you. I think it's just that maybe he can't bring himself to—to open up to you. Why are you so hateful to each other? Why is that?

BIFF.   [*evasively*] I'm not hateful, Mom.

LINDA.   But you no sooner come in the door than you're fighting!   595

BIFF.   I don't know why. I mean to change. I'm tryin', Mom, you understand?

LINDA.   Are you home to stay now?

BIFF.   I don't know. I want to look around, see what's doin'.

LINDA.   Biff, you can't look around all your life, can you?

BIFF.   I just can't take hold, Mom. I can't take hold of some kind of a life.   600

LINDA.   Biff, a man is not a bird, to come and go with the springtime.

BIFF.   Your hair . . . [*He touches her hair.*] Your hair got so gray.

LINDA.   Oh, it's been gray since you were in high school. I just stopped dyeing it, that's all.

BIFF.   Dye it again, will ya? I don't want my pal looking old. [*He smiles.*]

LINDA.   You're such a boy! You think you can go away for a year and . . .   605
You've got to get it into your head now that one day you'll knock on this door and there'll be strange people here—

BIFF.   What are you talking about? You're not even sixty, Mom.

LINDA.   But what about your father?

BIFF.   [*lamely*] Well, I meant him, too.

HAPPY.   He admires Pop.

LINDA. Biff, dear, if you don't have any feeling for him, then you can't   610
have any feeling for me.

BIFF. Sure I can, Mom.

LINDA. No. You can't just come to see me, because I love him. [*with a threat,
but only a threat, of tears*] He's the dearest man in the world to me, and I won't have
anyone making him feel unwanted and low and blue. You've got to make up your
mind now, darling, there's no leeway any more. Either he's your father and you
pay him that respect, or else you're not to come here. I know he's not easy to get
along with—nobody knows that better than me—but . . .

WILLY. [*from the left, with a laugh*] Hey, hey, Biffo!

BIFF. [*starting to go out after WILLY*] What the hell is the matter with him?
[*HAPPY stops him.*]

LINDA. Don't—don't go near him!   615

BIFF. Stop making excuses for him! He always, always wiped the floor with
you. Never had an ounce of respect for you.

HAPPY. He's always had respect for—

BIFF. What the hell do you know about it?

HAPPY. [*surlily*] Just don't call him crazy!

BIFF. He's got no character—Charley wouldn't do this. Not in his own   620
house—spewing out that vomit from his mind.

HAPPY. Charley never had to cope with what he's got to.

BIFF. People are worse off than Willy Loman. Believe me, I've seen them!

LINDA. Then make Charley your father, Biff. You can't do that, can you?
I don't say he's a great man. Willy Loman never made a lot of money. His name
was never in the paper. He's not the finest character that ever lived. But he's a
human being, and a terrible thing is happening to him. So attention must be paid.
He's not to be allowed to fall into his grave like an old dog. Attention, attention
must be finally paid to such a person. You called him crazy—

BIFF. I didn't mean—

LINDA. No, a lot of people think he's lost his—balance. But you don't have   625
to be very smart to know what his trouble is. The man is exhausted.

HAPPY. Sure!

LINDA. A small man can be just as exhausted as a great man. He works for
a company thirty-six years this March, opens up unheard-of-territories to their
trademark, and now in his old age they take his salary away.

HAPPY. [*indignantly*] I didn't know that, Mom.

LINDA. You never asked, my dear! Now that you get your spending money
someplace else you don't trouble your mind with him.

HAPPY. But I gave you money last—   630

LINDA. Christmas time, fifty dollars! To fix the hot water it cost ninety-
seven fifty! For five weeks he's been on straight commission,° like a beginner, an
unknown!

BIFF. Those ungrateful bastards!

LINDA. Are they any worse than his sons? When he brought them business,
when he was young, they were glad to see him. But now his old friends, the old
buyers that loved him so and always found some order to hand him in a pinch—

---

straight commission: refers to the fact that Willy is receiving no salary, only a commission
(percentage) on the sales he makes.

they're all dead, retired. He used to be able to make six, seven calls a day in Boston. Now he takes his valises out of the car and puts them back and takes them out again and he's exhausted. Instead of walking he talks now. He drives seven hundred miles, and when he gets there no one knows him any more, no one welcomes him. And what goes through a man's mind, driving seven hundred miles home without having earned a cent? Why shouldn't he talk to himself? Why? When he has to go to Charley and borrow fifty dollars a week and pretend to me that it's his pay? How long can that go on? How long? You see what I'm sitting here and waiting for? And you tell me he has no character? The man who never worked a day but for your benefit? When does he get the medal for that? Is this his reward—to turn around at the age of sixty-three and find his sons, who he loved better than his life, one a philandering bum—

HAPPY. Mom!

LINDA. That's all you are, my baby! [*To Biff*] And you! What happened to   635
the love you had for him? You were such pals! How you used to talk to him on the phone every night! How lonely he was till he could come home to you!

BIFF. All right, Mom. I'll live here in my room, and I'll get a job. I'll keep away from him, that's all.

LINDA. No, Biff. You can't stay here and fight all the time.

BIFF. He threw me out of this house, remember that.

LINDA. Why did he do that? I never knew why.

BIFF. Because I know he's a fake and he doesn't like anybody around who   640
knows!

LINDA. Why a fake? In what way? What do you mean?

BIFF. Just don't lay it all at my feet. It's between me and him—that's all I have to say. I'll chip in from now on. He'll settle for half my pay check. He'll be all right. I'm going to bed. [*He starts for the stairs.*]

LINDA. He won't be all right.

BIFF. [*turning on the stairs, furiously*] I hate this city and I'll stay here. Now what do you want?

LINDA. He's dying, Biff.   645

[*HAPPY turns quickly to her, shocked.*]

BIFF. [*after a pause*] Why is he dying?

LINDA. He's been trying to kill himself.

BIFF. [*with great horror*] How?

LINDA. I live from day to day.

BIFF. What're you talking about?   650

LINDA. Remember I wrote you that he smashed up the car again? In February?

BIFF. Well?

LINDA. The insurance inspector came. He said that they have evidence. That all these accidents in the last year—weren't—weren't—accidents.

HAPPY. How can they tell that? That's a lie.

LINDA. It seems there's a woman . . . [*She takes a breath as*]   655
⎧ BIFF. [*sharply but contained*] What woman?
⎨ LINDA. [*simultaneously*] . . . and this woman . . .
⎩ LINDA. What?

BIFF. Nothing. Go ahead.

LINDA.   What did you say?   660
BIFF.   Nothing. I just said what woman?
HAPPY.   What about her?
LINDA.   Well, it seems she was walking down the road and saw his car. She says that he wasn't driving fast at all, and that he didn't skid. She says he came to that little bridge, and then deliberately smashed into the railing, and it was only the shallowness of the water that saved him.
BIFF.   Oh, no, he probably just fell asleep again.
LINDA.   I don't think he fell asleep.   665
BIFF.   Why not?
LINDA.   Last month . . . [*with great difficulty*] Oh, boys, it's so hard to say a thing like this! He's just a big stupid man to you, but I tell you there's more good in him than in many other people. [*She chokes, wipes her eyes.*] I was looking for a fuse. The lights blew out, and I went down the cellar. And behind the fuse box— it happened to fall out—was a length of rubber pipe—just short.
HAPPY.   No kidding?
LINDA.   There's a little attachment on the end of it. I knew right away. And sure enough, on the bottom of the water heater there's a new little nipple on the gas pipe.
HAPPY.   [*angrily*] That—jerk.   670
BIFF.   Did you have it taken off?
LINDA.   I'm—I'm ashamed to. How can I mention it to him? Every day I go down and take away that little rubber pipe. But, when he comes home, I put it back where it was. How can I insult him that way? I don't know what to do. I live from day to day, boys. I tell you, I know every thought in his mind. It sounds so old-fashioned and silly, but I tell you he put his whole life into you and you've turned your backs on him. [*She is bent over in the chair, weeping, her face in her hands.*] Biff, I swear to God! Biff, his life is in your hands!
HAPPY.   [*to* BIFF] How do you like that damned fool!
BIFF.   [*kissing her*] All right, pal, all right. It's all settled now. I've been remiss. I know that, Mom. But now I'll stay, and I swear to you, I'll apply myself. [*kneeling in front of her, in a fever of self-reproach*] It's just—you see, Mom, I don't fit in business. Not that I won't try. I'll try, and I'll make good.
HAPPY.   Sure you will. The trouble with you in business was you never tried   675
to please people.
BIFF.   I know, I—
HAPPY.   Like when you worked for Harrison's. Bob Harrison said you were tops, and then you go and do some damn fool thing like whistling whole songs in the elevator like a comedian.
BIFF.   [*against* HAPPY] So what? I like to whistle sometimes.
HAPPY.   You don't raise a guy to a responsible job who whistles in the elevator!
LINDA.   Well, don't argue about it now.   680
HAPPY.   Like when you'd go off and swim in the middle of the day instead of taking the line around.
BIFF.   [*his resentment rising*] Well, don't you run off? You take off sometimes, don't you? On a nice summer day?
HAPPY.   Yeah, but I cover myself!
LINDA.   Boys!

HAPPY. If I'm going to take a fade the boss can call any number where   685
I'm supposed to be and they'll swear to him that I just left. I'll tell you something
that I hate to say, Biff, but in the business world some of them think you're crazy.

BIFF. [*angered*] Screw the business world!

HAPPY. All right, screw it! Great, but cover yourself!

LINDA. Hap, Hap!

BIFF. I don't care what they think! They've laughed at Dad for years, and
you know why? Because we don't belong in this nuthouse of a city! We should be
mixing cement on some open plain, or—or carpenters. A carpenter is allowed to
whistle!

[*WILLY walks in from the entrance of the house, at left.*]

WILLY. Even your grandfather was better than a carpenter. [*pause. They*   690
watch him.] You never grew up. Bernard does not whistle in the elevator, I assure
you.

BIFF. [*as though to laugh WILLY out of it*] Yeah, but you do, Pop.

WILLY. I never in my life whistled in an elevator! And who in the business
world thinks I'm crazy?

BIFF. I didn't mean it like that, Pop. Now don't make a whole thing out of
it, will ya?

WILLY. Go back to the West! Be a carpenter, a cowboy, enjoy yourself!

LINDA. Willy, he was just saying—   695

WILLY. I heard what he said!

HAPPY. [*trying to quiet WILLY*] Hey, Pop, come on now . . .

WILLY. [*continuing over HAPPY's line*] They laugh at me, heh? Go to Filene's,
go to the Hub, go to Slattery's,° Boston. Call out the name Willy Loman and see
what happens! Big shot!

BIFF. All right, Pop.

WILLY. Big!   700

BIFF. All right!

WILLY. Why do you always insult me?

BIFF. I didn't say a word. [*to LINDA*] Did I say a word?

LINDA. He didn't say anything, Willy.

WILLY. [*going to the doorway of the living room*] All right, good night, good   705
night.

LINDA. Willy, dear, he just decided . . .

WILLY. [*to BIFF*] If you get tired hanging around tomorrow, paint the ceiling
I put up in the living-room.

BIFF. I'm leaving early tomorrow.

HAPPY. He's going to see Bill Oliver, Pop.

WILLY. [*interestedly*] Oliver? For what?   710

BIFF. [*with reserve, but trying, trying*] He always said he'd stake me. I'd like
to go into business, so maybe I can take him up on it.

LINDA. Isn't that wonderful?

WILLY. Don't interrupt. What's wonderful about it? There's fifty men in
the City of New York who'd stake him. [*to BIFF*] Sporting goods?

BIFF. I guess so. I know something about it and—

Filene's, the Hub, Slattery's: department stores in New England.

WILLY.   He knows something about it! You know sporting goods better than   715
Spalding, for God's sake! How much is he giving you?

BIFF.   I don't know. I didn't even see him yet, but—

WILLY.   Then what're you talkin' about?

BIFF.   [*getting angry*] Well, all I said was I'm gonna see him, that's all!

WILLY.   [*turning away*] Ah, you're counting your chickens again.

BIFF.   [*starting left for the stairs*] Oh, Jesus, I'm going to sleep!   720

WILLY.   [*calling after him*] Don't curse in this house!

BIFF.   [*turning*] Since when did you get so clean?

HAPPY.   [*trying to stop them*] Wait a . . .

WILLY.   Don't use that language to me! I won't have it!

HAPPY.   [*grabbing BIFF, shouts*] Wait a minute! I got an idea. I got a feasible   725
idea. Come here, Biff, let's talk this over now, let's talk some sense here. When I
was down in Florida last time, I thought of a great idea to sell sporting goods. It
just came back to me. You and I, Biff—we have a line, the Loman Line. We train
a couple of weeks, and put on a couple of exhibitions, see?

WILLY.   That's an idea!

HAPPY.   Wait! We form two basketball teams, see? Two waterpolo teams.
We play each other. It's a million dollars' worth of publicity. Two brothers, see?
The Loman Brothers. Displays in the Royal Palms—all the hotels. And banners
over the ring and the basketball court: "Loman Brothers." Baby, we could sell
sporting goods!

WILLY.   That is a one-million-dollar idea!

LINDA.   Marvelous!

BIFF.   I'm in great shape as far as that's concerned.   730

HAPPY.   And the beauty of it is, Biff, it wouldn't be like a business. We'd be
out playin' ball again . . .

BIFF.   [*enthused*] Yeah, that's . . .

WILLY.   Million-dollar . . .

HAPPY.   And you wouldn't get fed up with it, Biff. It'd be the family again.
There'd be the old honor, and comradeship, and if you wanted to go off for a
swim or somethin'—well, you'd do it! Without some smart cooky gettin' up ahead
of you!

WILLY.   Lick the world! You guys together could absolutely lick the civilized   735
world.

BIFF.   I'll see Oliver tomorrow. Hap, if we could work that out . . .

LINDA.   Maybe things are beginning to—

WILLY.   [*wildly enthused, to LINDA*] Stop interrupting! [*to BIFF*] But don't wear
sport jacket and slacks when you see Oliver.

BIFF.   No, I'll—

WILLY.   A business suit, and talk as little as possible, and don't crack any   740
jokes.

BIFF.   He did like me. Always liked me.

LINDA.   He loved you!

WILLY.   [*to LINDA*] Will you stop! [*to BIFF*] Walk in very serious. You are not
applying for a boy's job. Money is to pass. Be quiet, fine, and serious. Everybody
likes a kidder, but nobody lends him money.

HAPPY.   I'll try to get some myself, Biff. I'm sure I can.

WILLY.   I see great things for you kids. I think your troubles are over. But   745 remember, start big and you'll end big. Ask for fifteen. How much you gonna ask for?

BIFF. Gee, I don't know—

WILLY. And don't say "Gee." "Gee" is a boy's word. A man walking in for fifteen thousand dollars does not say "Gee!"

BIFF. Ten, I think, would be top though.

WILLY. Don't be so modest. You always started too low. Walk in with a big laugh. Don't look worried. Start off with a couple of your good stories to lighten things up. It's not what you say, it's how you say it—because personality always wins the day.

LINDA. Oliver always thought the highest of him—   750

WILLY. Will you let me talk?

BIFF. Don't yell at her, Pop, will ya?

WILLY. [*angrily*] I was talking, wasn't I?

BIFF. I don't like you yelling at her all the time, and I'm tellin' you, that's all.

WILLY. What're you, takin' over this house?   755

LINDA. Willy—

WILLY. [*turning on her*] Don't take his side all the time, godammit!

BIFF. [*furiously*] Stop yelling at her!

WILLY. [*suddenly pulling on his cheek, beaten down, guilt ridden*] Give my best to Bill Oliver—he may remember me.

[*He exits through the living-room doorway.*]

LINDA. [*her voice subdued*] What'd you have to start that for? [*BIFF turns*   760
away.] You see how sweet he was as soon as you talked hopefully? [*She goes over to*
BIFF.] Come up and say good night to him. Don't let him go to bed that way.

HAPPY. Come on, Biff, let's buck him up.

LINDA. Please, dear. Just say good night. It takes so little to make him happy. Come. [*She goes through the living-room doorway, calling upstairs from within the living-room.*] Your pajamas are hanging in the bathroom, Willy!

HAPPY. [*looking toward where LINDA went out*] What a woman! They broke the mold when they made her. You know that, Biff?

BIFF. He's off salary. My God, working on commission!

HAPPY. Well, let's face it: he's no hot-shot selling man. Except that some-   765
times, you have to admit, he's a sweet personality.

BIFF. [*deciding*] Lend me ten bucks, will ya? I want to buy some new ties.

HAPPY. I'll take you to a place I know. Beautiful stuff. Wear one of my striped shirts tomorrow.

BIFF. She got gray. Mom got awful old. Gee, I'm gonna go in to Oliver tomorrow and knock him for a—

HAPPY. Come on up. Tell that to Dad. Let's give him a whirl. Come on.

BIFF. [*steamed up*] You know, with ten thousand bucks, boy!   770

HAPPY. [*as they go into the living-room*] That's the talk, Biff, that's the first time I've heard the old confidence out of you! [*from within the living-room, fading off*] You're gonna live with me, kid, and any babe you want just say the word . . .
[*The last lines are hardly heard. They are mounting the stairs to their parents' bedroom.*]

LINDA. [*entering her bedroom and addressing WILLY, who is in the bathroom. She is straightening the bed for him.*] Can you do anything about the shower? It drips.

WILLY. [*from the bathroom*] All of a sudden everything falls to pieces! Goddam plumbing, oughta be sued, those people. I hardly finished putting it in and the thing . . . [*His words rumble off.*]

LINDA. I'm just wondering if Oliver will remember him. You think he might?

WILLY. [*coming out of the bathroom in his pajamas*] Remember him? What's   775 the matter with you, you crazy? If he'd've stayed with Oliver he'd be on top by now! Wait'll Oliver gets a look at him. You don't know the average caliber any more. The average young man today—[*He is getting into bed*]—is got a caliber of zero. Greatest thing in the world for him was to bum around.

[*BIFF and HAPPY enter the bedroom. Slight pause.*]

WILLY. [*stops short, looking at BIFF*] Glad to hear it, boy.
HAPPY. He wanted to say good night to you, sport.
WILLY. [*to BIFF*] Yeah. Knock him dead, boy. What'd you want to tell me?
BIFF. Just take it easy, Pop. Good night. [*He turns to go.*]
WILLY. [*unable to resist*] And if anything falls off the desk while you're   780 talking to him—like a package or something—don't you pick it up. They have office boys for that.
LINDA. I'll make a big breakfast—
WILLY. Will you let me finish? [*to BIFF*] Tell him you were in the business in the West. Not farm work.
BIFF. All right, Dad.
LINDA. I think everything—
WILLY. [*going right through her speech*] And don't undersell yourself. No less   785 than fifteen thousand dollars.
BIFF. [*unable to bear him*] Okay. Good night, Mom. [*He starts moving.*]
WILLY. Because you got a greatness in you, Biff, remember that. You got all kinds a greatness . . . [*He lies back, exhausted.*]

[*BIFF walks out.*]

LINDA. [*calling after BIFF*] Sleep well, darling!
HAPPY. I'm gonna get married, Mom. I wanted to tell you.
LINDA. Go to sleep, dear.   790
HAPPY. [*going*] I just wanted to tell you.
WILLY. Keep up the good work. [*HAPPY exits.*] God . . . remember that Ebbets Field° game? The championship of the city?
LINDA. Just rest. Should I sing to you?
WILLY. Yeah. Sing to me. [*LINDA hums a soft lullaby.*] When that team came out—he was the tallest, remember?
LINDA. Oh, yes. And in gold.   795

[*BIFF enters the darkened kitchen, takes a cigarette, and leaves the house. He comes downstage into a golden pool of light. He smokes, staring at the night.*]

WILLY. Like a young god. Hercules—something like that. And the sun, the sun all around him. Remember how he waved to me? Right up from the field,

Ebbets Field: the baseball stadium of the Brooklyn Dodgers before they moved to Los Angeles in 1958. Biff had played there in a city championship football game. See II.210 (p. 1248).

with the representatives of three colleges standing by? And the buyers I brought, and the cheers when he came out—Loman, Loman, Loman! God Almighty, he'll be great yet. A star like that, magnificent, can never really fade away!

[*The light on* WILLY *is fading. The gas heater begins to glow through the kitchen wall, near the stairs, a blue flame beneath red coils.*]

LINDA. [*timidly*] Willy dear, what has he got against you?
WILLY. I'm so tired. Don't talk any more.

[BIFF *slowly returns to the kitchen. He stops, stares toward the heater.*]

LINDA. Will you ask Howard to let you work in New York?
WILLY. First thing in the morning. Everything'll be all right.   800

[BIFF *reaches behind the heater and draws out a length of rubber tubing. He is horrified and turns his head toward* WILLY'S *room, still dimly lit, from which the strains of* LINDA's *desperate but monotonous humming rise.*]

WILLY. [*staring through the window into the moonlight*] Gee, look at the moon moving between the buildings!

[BIFF *wraps the tubing around his hand and quickly goes up the stairs.*]

ACT 2

[*Music is heard, gay and bright. The curtain rises as the music fades away.* WILLY, *in shirt sleeves, is sitting at the kitchen table, sipping coffee, his hat in his lap.* LINDA *is filling his cup when she can.*]

WILLY. Wonderful coffee. Meal in itself.
LINDA. Can I make you some eggs?
WILLY. No. Take a breath.
LINDA. You look so rested, dear.
WILLY. I slept like a dead one. First time in months. Imagine, sleeping till   5
ten on a Tuesday morning. Boys left nice and early, heh?
LINDA. They were out of here by eight o'clock.
WILLY. Good work!
LINDA. It was so thrilling to see them leaving together. I can't get over the shaving lotion in this house!
WILLY. [*smiling*] Mmm—
LINDA. Biff was very changed this morning. His whole attitude seemed to   10
be hopeful. He couldn't wait to get downtown to see Oliver.
WILLY. He's heading for a change. There's no question, there simply are certain men that take longer to get—solidified. How did he dress?
LINDA. His blue suit. He's so handsome in that suit. He could be a—anything in that suit!

[WILLY *gets up from the table.* LINDA *holds his jacket for him.*]

WILLY. There's no question, no question at all. Gee, on the way home tonight I'd like to buy some seeds.

LINDA.   [*laughing*] That'd be wonderful. But not enough sun gets back there. Nothing'll grow any more.

WILLY.   You wait, kid, before it's all over we're gonna get a little place out   15
in the country, and I'll raise some vegetables, a couple of chickens . . .

LINDA.   You'll do it yet, dear.

[*WILLY walks out of his jacket, LINDA follows him.*]

WILLY.   And they'll get married, and come for a weekend. I'd build a little guest house. 'Cause I got so many fine tools, all I'd need would be a little lumber and some peace of mind.

LINDA.   [*joyfully*] I sewed the lining . . .

WILLY.   I could build two guest houses, so they'd both come. Did he decide how much he's going to ask Oliver for?

LINDA.   [*getting him into the jacket*] He didn't mention it, but I imagine ten   20
or fifteen thousand. You going to talk to Howard today?

WILLY.   Yeah. I'll put it to him straight and simple. He'll just have to take me off the road.

LINDA.   And Willy, don't forget to ask for a little advance, because we've got the insurance premium. It's the grace period now.

WILLY.   That's a hundred . . . ?

LINDA.   A hundred and eight, sixty-eight. Because we're a little short again.

WILLY.   Why are we short?   25

LINDA.   Well, you had the motor job on the car . . .

WILLY.   That goddam Studebaker!

LINDA.   And you got one more payment on the refrigerator . . .

WILLY.   But it just broke again!

LINDA.   Well, it's old, dear.   30

WILLY.   I told you we should've bought a well-advertised machine. Charley bought a General Electric and it's twenty years old and it's still good, that son-of-a-bitch.

LINDA.   But, Willy—

WILLY.   Whoever heard of a Hastings refrigerator? Once in my life I would like to own something outright before it's broken! I'm always in a race with the junkyard! I just finished paying for the car and it's on its last legs. The refrigerator consumes belts like a goddam maniac. They time those things. They time them so when you finally paid for them, they're used up.

LINDA.   [*buttoning up his jacket as he unbuttons it*] All told, about two hundred dollars would carry us, dear. But that includes the last payment on the mortgage. After this payment, Willy, the house belongs to us.

WILLY.   It's twenty-five years!   35

LINDA.   Biff was nine years old when we bought it.

WILLY.   Well, that's a great thing. To weather a twenty-five year mortgage is—

LINDA.   It's an accomplishment.

WILLY.   All the cement, the lumber, the reconstruction I put in this house! There ain't a crack to be found in it any more.

LINDA.   Well, it served its purpose.   40

WILLY.   What purpose? Some stranger'll come along, move in, and that's that. If only Biff would take this house, and raise a family . . . [*He starts to go.*] Good-by, I'm late.

LINDA. [*suddenly remembering*] Oh, I forgot! You're supposed to meet them for dinner.

WILLY. Me?

LINDA. At Frank's Chop House on Forty-eighth near Sixth Avenue.

WILLY. Is that so! How about you? 45

LINDA. No, just the three of you. They're gonna blow you to a big meal!

WILLY. Don't say! Who thought of that?

LINDA. Biff came to me this morning, Willy, and he said, "Tell Dad, we want to blow him to a big meal." Be there six o'clock. You and your two boys are going to have dinner.

WILLY. Gee whiz! That's really somethin'. I'm gonna knock Howard for a loop, kid. I'll get an advance, and I'll come home with a New York job. Goddammit, now I'm gonna do it!

LINDA. Oh, that's the spirit, Willy! 50

WILLY. I will never get behind a wheel the rest of my life!

LINDA. It's changing, Willy, I can feel it changing!

WILLY. Beyond a question. G'by, I'm late. [*He starts to go again.*]

LINDA. [*calling after him as she runs to the kitchen table for a handkerchief*] You got your glasses?

WILLY. [*feels for them, then comes back in*] Yeah, yeah, got my glasses. 55

LINDA. [*giving him the handkerchief*] And a handkerchief.

WILLY. Yeah, handkerchief.

LINDA. And your saccharine?

WILLY. Yeah, my saccharine.

LINDA. Be careful on the subway stairs. 60

[*She kisses him, and a silk stocking is seen hanging from her hand. WILLY notices it.*]

WILLY. Will you stop mending stockings? At least while I'm in the house. It gets me nervous. I can't tell you. Please.

[*LINDA hides the stocking in her hand as she follows WILLY across the forestage in front of the house.*]

LINDA. Remember, Frank's Chop House.

WILLY. [*passing the apron*] Maybe beets would grow out there.

LINDA. [*laughing*] But you tried so many times.

WILLY. Yeah. Well, don't work hard today. [*He disappears around the right 65 corner of the house.*]

LINDA. Be careful!

[*As WILLY vanishes, LINDA waves to him. Suddenly the phone rings. She runs across the stage and into the kitchen and lifts it.*]

LINDA. Hello? Oh, Biff! I'm so glad you called, I just . . . Yes, sure, I just told him. Yes, he'll be there for dinner at six o'clock, I didn't forget. Listen, I was just dying to tell you. You know that little rubber pipe I told you about? That he connected to the gas heater? I finally decided to go down the cellar this morning and take it away and destroy it. But it's gone! Imagine? He took it away himself, it isn't there! [*She listens.*] When? Oh, then you took it. Oh—nothing, it's just that I'd hoped he'd taken it away himself. Oh, I'm not worried, darling, because this morning he left in such high spirits, it was like the old days! I'm not afraid any more. Did Mr. Oliver see you? . . . Well, you wait there then. And make a nice impression on him, darling. Just don't perspire too much before you see him. And have a nice time with Dad. He may have big news too! . . . That's right, a New York job. And be sweet to him tonight, dear. Be loving to him. Because he's only a little boat looking for a harbor. [*She is trembling with sorrow and joy.*] Oh, that's wonderful, Biff, you'll save his life. Thanks, darling. Just put your arm around him when he comes into the restaurant. Give him a smile. That's the boy . . . Good-by, dear . . . You got your comb? . . . That's fine. Good-by, Biff dear.

[*In the middle of her speech,* HOWARD WAGNER, *thirty-six, wheels in a small typewriter table on which is a wire-recording machine and proceeds to plug it in. This is on the left forestage. Light slowly fades on* LINDA *as it rises on* HOWARD. HOWARD *is intent on threading the machine and only glances over his shoulder as* WILLY *appears.*]

WILLY.   Pst! Pst!
HOWARD.   Hello, Willy, come in.
WILLY.   Like to have a little talk with you, Howard.   70
HOWARD.   Sorry to keep you waiting. I'll be with you in a minute.
WILLY.   What's that, Howard?
HOWARD.   Didn't you ever see one of these? Wire recorder.
WILLY.   Oh. Can we talk a minute?
HOWARD.   Records things. Just got delivery yesterday. Been driving me   75
crazy, the most terrific machine I ever saw in my life. I was up all night with it.
WILLY.   What do you do with it?
HOWARD.   I bought it for dictation, but you can do anything with it. Listen to this. I had it home last night. Listen to what I picked up. The first one is my daughter. Get this. [*He flicks the switch and "Roll out the Barrel" is heard being whistled.*] Listen to that kid whistle.
WILLY.   That is lifelike, isn't it?
HOWARD.   Seven years old. Get that tone.
WILLY.   Ts, ts. Like to ask a little favor if you . . .   80

[*The whistling breaks off, and the voice of* HOWARD'S DAUGHTER *is heard.*]

HIS DAUGHTER.   "Now you, Daddy."
HOWARD.   She's crazy for me! [*Again the same song is whistled.*] That's me! Ha!
[*He winks.*]
WILLY.   You're very good!

[*The whistling breaks off again. The machine runs silent for a moment.*]

HOWARD.   Sh! Get this now, this is my son.
HIS SON.   "The capital of Alabama is Montgomery; the capital of Arizona   85
is Phoenix; the capital of Arkansas is Little Rock; the capital of California is Sacramento . . ." [*and on, and on*]
HOWARD.   [*holding up five fingers*] Five years old, Willy!
WILLY.   He'll make an announcer some day!
HIS SON.   [*continuing*] "The capital . . ."

HOWARD.   Get that—alphabetical order! [*The machine breaks off suddenly.*] Wait
a minute. The maid kicked the plug out.

WILLY.   It certainly is a—   90

HOWARD.   Sh, for God's sake!

HIS SON.   "It's nine o'clock, Bulova watch time. So I have to go to sleep."

WILLY.   That really is—

HOWARD.   Wait a minute! The next is my wife.

[*They wait.*]

HOWARD'S VOICE.   "Go on, say something." [*pause*] "Well, you gonna talk?"   95

HIS WIFE.   "I can't think of anything."

HOWARD'S VOICE.   "Well, talk—it's turning."

HIS WIFE.   [*shyly, beaten*] "Hello." [*Silence*] "Oh, Howard, I can't talk into
this . . ."

HOWARD.   [*snapping the machine off*] That was my wife.

WILLY.   That is a wonderful machine. Can we—   100

HOWARD.   I tell you, Willy, I'm gonna take my camera, and my bandsaw,
and all my hobbies, and out they go. This is the most fascinating relaxation I ever
found.

WILLY.   I think I'll get one myself.

HOWARD.   Sure, they're only a hundred and a half. You can't do without it.
Supposing you wanna hear Jack Benny,° see? But you can't be at home at that
hour. So you tell the maid to turn the radio on when Jack Benny comes on, and
this automatically goes on with the radio . . .

WILLY.   And when you come home you . . .

HOWARD.   You can come home twelve o'clock, one o'clock, any time you   105
like, and you get yourself a Coke and sit yourself down, throw the switch, and
there's Jack Benny's program in the middle of the night!

WILLY.   I'm definitely going to get one. Because lots of time I'm on the
road, and I think to myself, what I must be missing on the radio!

HOWARD.   Don't you have a radio in the car?

WILLY.   Well, yeah, but who ever thinks of turning it on?

HOWARD.   Say, aren't you supposed to be in Boston?

WILLY.   That's what I want to talk to you about, Howard. You got a minute?   110

[*He draws a chair in from the wing.*]

HOWARD.   What happened? What're you doing here?

WILLY.   Well . . .

HOWARD.   You didn't crack up again, did you?

WILLY.   Oh, no. No . . .

HOWARD.   Geez, you had me worried there for a minute. What's the trouble?   115

WILLY.   Well, tell you the truth, Howard, I've come to the decision that I'd
rather not travel any more.

HOWARD.   Not travel! Well, what'll you do?

WILLY.   Remember, Christmas time, when you had the party here? You
said you'd try to think of some spot for me here in town.

HOWARD.   With us?

Jack Benny: (1894–1974), vaudeville, radio, television and movie comedian.

WILLY. Well, sure.   120

HOWARD. Oh, yeah, yeah. I remember. Well, I couldn't think of anything for you, Willy.

WILLY. I tell ya, Howard. The kids are all grown up, y'know. I don't need much any more. If I could take home—well, sixty-five dollars a week, I could swing it.

HOWARD. Yeah, but Willy, see I—

WILLY. I tell ya why, Howard. Speaking frankly and between the two of us, y'know—I'm just a little tired.

HOWARD. Oh, I could understand that, Willy. But you're a road man, Willy,   125
and we do a road business. We've only got a half-dozen salesmen on the floor here.

WILLY. God knows, Howard, I never asked a favor of any man. But I was with the firm when your father used to carry you up here in his arms.

HOWARD. I know that, Willy, but—

WILLY. Your father came to me the day you were born and asked me what I thought of the name of Howard, may he rest in peace.

HOWARD. I appreciate that, Willy, but there just is no spot here for you. If I had a spot I'd slam you right in, but I just don't have a single solitary spot.

[*He looks for his lighter. WILLY has picked it up and gives it to him. Pause.*]

WILLY. [*with increasing anger*] Howard, all I need to set my table is fifty   130
dollars a week.

HOWARD. But where am I going to put you, kid?

WILLY. Look, it isn't a question of whether I can sell merchandise, is it?

HOWARD. No, but it's a business, kid, and everybody's gotta pull his own weight.

WILLY. [*desperately*] Just let me tell you a story, Howard—

HOWARD. 'Cause you gotta admit, business is business.   135

WILLY. [*angrily*] Business in definitely business, but just listen for a minute. You don't understand this. When I was a boy—eighteen, nineteen—I was already on the road. And there was a question in my mind as to whether selling had a future for me. Because in those days I had a yearning to go to Alaska. See, there were three gold strikes in one month in Alaska, and I felt like going out. Just for the ride, you might say.

HOWARD. [*barely interested*] Don't say.

WILLY. Oh, yeah, my father lived many years in Alaska. He was an adventurous man. We've got quite a little streak of self-reliance in our family. I thought I'd go out with my older brother and try to locate him, and maybe settle in the North with the old man. And I was almost decided to go, when I met a salesman in the Parker House.° His name was Dave Singleman. And he was eighty-four years old, and he'd drummed merchandise in thirty-one states. And old Dave, he'd go up to his room, y'understand, put on his green velvet slippers—I'll never forget—and pick up his phone and call the buyers, and without ever leaving his room, at the age of eighty-four, he made his living. And when I saw that, I realized that selling was the greatest career a man could want. 'Cause what could be more satisfying than to be able to go, at the age of eighty-four, into twenty or thirty

---

Parker House: a hotel in Boston.

different cities, and pick up a phone, and be remembered and loved and helped by so many different people? Do you know? when he died—and by the way he died the death of a salesman, in his green velvet slippers in the smoker of the New York, New Haven and Hartford, going into Boston—when he died, hundreds of salesmen and buyers were at his funeral. Things were sad on a lotta trains for months after that. [*He stands up. HOWARD has not looked at him.*] In those days there was personality in it, Howard. There was respect, and comradeship, and gratitude in it. Today, it's all cut and dried, and there's no chance for bringing friendship to bear—or personality. You see what I mean? They don't know me any more.

HOWARD. [*moving away, to the right*] That's just the thing, Willy.

WILLY. If I had forty dollars a week—that's all I'd need. Forty dollars, Howard. 140

HOWARD. Kid, I can't take blood from a stone, I—

WILLY. [*desperation is on him now*] Howard, the year Al Smith° was nominated, your father came to me and—

HOWARD. [*starting to go off*] I've got to see some people, kid.

WILLY. [*stopping him*] I'm talking about your father! There were promises made across this desk! You mustn't tell me you've got people to see—I put thirty-four years into this firm, Howard, and now I can't pay my insurance! You can't eat the orange and throw the peel away—a man is not a piece of fruit! [*after a pause*] Now pay attention. Your father—in 1928 I had a big year. I averaged a hundred and seventy dollars a week in commissions.

HOWARD. [*impatiently*] Now, Willy, you never averaged— 145

WILLY. [*banging his hand on the desk*] I averaged a hundred and seventy dollars a week in the year of 1928! And your father came to me—or rather, I was in the office here—it was right over this desk—and he put his hand on my shoulder—

HOWARD. [*getting up*] You'll have to excuse me, Willy, I gotta see some people. Pull yourself together. [*going out*] I'll be back in a little while.

[*On HOWARD's exit, the light on his chair grows very bright and strange.*]

WILLY. Pull myself together! What the hell did I say to him? My God, I was yelling at him! How could I! [*WILLY breaks off, staring at the light, which occupies the chair, animating it. He approaches this chair, standing across the desk from it.*] Frank, Frank, don't you remember what you told me that time? How you put your hand on my shoulder, and Frank . . . [*He leans on the desk and as he speaks the dead man's name he accidentally switches on the recorder, and instantly*]

HOWARD'S SON. ". . . of New York is Albany. The capital of Ohio is Cincinnati, the capital of Rhode Island is . . ." [*The recitation continues.*]

WILLY. [*leaping away with fright, shouting*] Ha! Howard! Howard! Howard! 150

HOWARD. [*rushing in*] What happened?

WILLY. [*pointing at the machine, which continues nasally, childishly, with the capital cities*] Shut it off! Shut it off!

HOWARD. [*pulling the plug out*] Look, Willy . . .

WILLY. [*pressing his hands to his eyes*] I gotta get myself some coffee. I'll get some coffee . . .

Al Smith: Alfred E. Smith was governor of New York State (1919–1921, 1923–1929) and the Democratic presidential candidate defeated by Herbert Hoover in 1928.

[*WILLY starts to walk out. HOWARD stops him.*]

HOWARD.   [*rolling up the cord*] Willy, look . . .   155
WILLY.   I'll go to Boston.
HOWARD.   Willy, you can't go to Boston for us.
WILLY.   Why can't I go?
HOWARD.   I don't want you to represent us. I've been meaning to tell you
for a long time now.
WILLY.   Howard, are you firing me?   160
HOWARD.   I think you need a good long rest, Willy.
WILLY.   Howard—
HOWARD.   And when you feel better, come back, and we'll see if we can
work something out.
WILLY.   But I gotta earn money, Howard. I'm in no position to—
HOWARD.   Where are your sons? Why don't your sons give you a hand?   165
WILLY.   They're working on a very big deal.
HOWARD.   This is no time for false pride, Willy. You go to your sons and
you tell them that you're tired. You've got two great boys, haven't you?
WILLY.   Oh, no question, no question, but in the meantime . . .
HOWARD.   Then that's that, heh?
WILLY.   All right, I'll go to Boston tomorrow.   170
HOWARD.   No, no.
WILLY.   I can't throw myself on my sons. I'm not a cripple!
HOWARD.   Look, kid, I'm busy this morning.
WILLY.   [*grasping HOWARD's arm*] Howard, you've got to let me go to Boston!
HOWARD.   [*hard, keeping himself under control*] I've got a line of people to see   175
this morning. Sit down, take five minutes, and pull yourself together, and then
go home, will ya? I need the office, Willy. [*He starts to go, turns, remembering the
recorder, starts to push off the table holding the recorder.*] Oh, yeah. Whenever you can
this week, stop by and drop off the samples. You'll feel better, Willy, and then
come back and we'll talk. Pull yourself together, kid, there's people outside.

[*HOWARD exits, pushing the table off left. WILLY stares into space, exhausted. Now the music
is heard—BEN's music—first distantly, then closer. As WILLY speaks, BEN enters from the
right. He carries valise and umbrella.*]

WILLY.   Oh, Ben, how did you do it? What is the answer? Did you wind up
the Alaska deal already?
BEN.   Doesn't take much time if you know what you're doing. Just a short
business trip. Boarding ship in an hour. Wanted to say good-by.
WILLY.   Ben, I've got to talk to you.
BEN.   [*glancing at his watch*] Haven't much time, William.
WILLY.   [*crossing the apron to BEN*] Ben, nothing's working out. I don't know   180
what to do.
BEN.   Now, look here, William. I've bought timberland in Alaska and I need
a man to look after things for me.
WILLY.   God, timberland! Me and my boys in those grand outdoors!
BEN.   You've a new continent at your doorstep, William. Get out of these
cities, they're full of talk and time payments and courts of law. Screw on your fists
and you can fight for a fortune up there.

WILLY.   Yes, yes! Linda, Linda!

[*LINDA enters as of old, with the wash.*]

LINDA.   Oh, you're back?   185
BEN.   I haven't much time.
WILLY.   No, wait! Linda, he's got a proposition for me in Alaska.
LINDA.   But you've got—[*to BEN*] He's got a beautiful job here.
WILLY.   But in Alaska, kid, I could—
LINDA.   You're doing well enough, Willy!   190
BEN.   [*to LINDA*] Enough for what, my dear?
LINDA.   [*frightened of BEN and angry at him*] Don't say those things to him!
Enough to be happy right here, right now. [*to WILLY, while BEN laughs*] Why must
everybody conquer the world? You're well liked, and the boys love you, and
someday—[*to BEN*]—why old man Wagner told him just the other day that if he
keeps it up he'll be a member of the firm, didn't he, Willy?
WILLY.   Sure, sure. I am building something with this firm, Ben, and if a
man is building something he must be on the right track, mustn't he?
BEN.   What are you building? Lay your hand on it. Where is it?
WILLY.   [*hesitantly*] That's true, Linda, there's nothing.   195
LINDA.   Why? [*to BEN*] There's a man eighty-four years old—
WILLY.   That's right, Ben, that's right. When I look at that man I say, what
is there to worry about?
BEN.   Bah!
WILLY.   It's true, Ben. All he has to do is go into any city, pick up the
phone, and he's making his living and you know why?
BEN.   [*picking up his valise*] I've got to go.   200
WILLY.   [*holding BEN back*] Look at this boy!

[*BIFF, in his high school sweater, enters carrying suitcase. HAPPY carries BIFF's shoulder
guards, gold helmet, and football pants.*]

WILLY.   Without a penny to his name, three great universities are begging
for him, and from there the sky's the limit, because it's not what you do, Ben. It's
who you know and the smile on your face! It's contacts, Ben, contacts! The whole
wealth of Alaska passes over the lunch table at the Commodore Hotel,° and that's
the wonder, the wonder of this country, that a man can end with diamonds here
on the basis of being liked! [*He turns to BIFF*] And that's why when you get out on
that field today it's important. Because thousands of people will be rooting for
you and loving you. [*to BEN, who has again begun to leave*] And Ben! when he walks
into a business office his name will sound out like a bell and all the doors will
open to him! I've seen it, Ben, I've seen it a thousand times! You can't feel it with
your hand like timber, but it's there!
BEN.   Good-by, William.
WILLY.   Ben, am I right? Don't you think I'm right? I value your advice.
BEN.   There's a new continent at your doorstep, William. You could walk   205
out rich. Rich! [*He is gone.*]
WILLY.   We'll do it here, Ben! You hear me? We're gonna do it here!

[*YOUNG BERNARD rushes in. The gay music of the Boys is heard.*]

Commodore Hotel: a large hotel in New York City.

BERNARD. Oh, gee, I was afraid you left already!

WILLY. Why? What time is it?

BERNARD. It's half-past one!

WILLY. Well, come on, everybody! Ebbets Field next stop! Where's the   210
pennants? [*He rushes through the wall-line of the kitchen and out into the dining-room.*]

LINDA. [*to BIFF*] Did you pack fresh underwear?

BIFF. [*who has been limbering up*] I want to go!

BERNARD. Biff, I'm carrying your helmet, ain't I?

HAPPY. No, I'm carrying the helmet.

BERNARD. Oh, Biff, you promised me.   215

HAPPY. I'm carrying the helmet.

BERNARD. How am I going to get in the locker room?

LINDA. Let him carry the shoulder guards. [*She puts her coat and hat on in the kitchen.*]

BERNARD. Can I, Biff? 'Cause I told everybody I'm going to be in the locker room.

HAPPY. In Ebbets Field it's the clubhouse.   220

BERNARD. I meant the clubhouse. Biff!

HAPPY. Biff!

BIFF. [*grandly, after a slight pause.*] Let him carry the shoulder guards.

HAPPY. [*as he gives BERNARD the shoulder guards*] Stay close to us now.

[*WILLY rushes in with the pennants.*]

WILLY. [*handing them out*] Everybody wave when Biff comes out on the field.   225
[*HAPPY and BERNARD run off.*] You set now, boy?

[*The music has died away.*]

BIFF. Ready to go, Pop. Every muscle is ready.

WILLY. [*at the edge of the apron*] You realize what this means?

BIFF. That's right, Pop.

WILLY. [*feeling BIFF's muscles*] You're comin' home this afternoon captain of the All-Scholastic Championship Team of the City of New York.

BIFF. I got it, Pop. And remember, pal, when I take off my helmet, that   230
touchdown is for you.

WILLY. Let's go! [*He is starting out, with his arm around BIFF, when CHARLEY enters, as of old, in knickers.*] I got no room for you, Charley.

CHARLEY. Room? For what?

WILLY. In the car.

CHARLEY. You goin' for a ride? I wanted to shoot some casino.

WILLY. [*furiously*] Casino! [*incredulously*] Don't you realize what today is?   235

LINDA. Oh, he knows, Willy. He's just kidding you.

WILLY. That's nothing to kid about!

CHARLEY. No, Linda, what's goin' on?

LINDA. He's playing in Ebbets Field.

CHARLEY. Baseball in this weather?   240

WILLY. Don't talk to him. Come on, come on! [*He is pushing them out.*]

CHARLEY. Wait a minute, didn't you hear the news?

WILLY. What?

CHARLEY. Don't you listen to the radio? Ebbets Field just blew up.

WILLY. You go to hell! [*CHARLEY laughs. Pushing them out.*] Come on, come 245
on! We're late.

CHARLEY. [*as they go*] Knock a homer, Biff, knock a homer!

WILLY. [*the last to leave, turning to CHARLEY*] I don't think that was funny,
Charley. This is the greatest day of his life.

CHARLEY. Willy, when are you going to grow up?

WILLY. Yeah, heh? When this game is over, Charley, you'll be laughing out
the other side of your face. They'll be calling him another Red Grange.° Twenty-
five thousand a year.

CHARLEY. [*kidding*] Is that so? 250

WILLY. Yeah, that's so.

CHARLEY. Well, then, I'm sorry, Willy. But tell me something.

WILLY. What?

CHARLEY. Who is Red Grange?

WILLY. Put up your hands. Goddam you, put up your hands! 255

[*CHARLEY, chuckling, shakes his head and walks away, around the left corner of the stage.
WILLY follows him. The music rises to a mocking frenzy.*]

WILLY. Who the hell do you think you are, better than everybody else?
You don't know everything, you big, ignorant, stupid. . . . Put up your hands!

[*Light rises, on the right side of the forestage, on a small table in the reception room of
CHARLEY's office. Traffic sounds are heard. BERNARD, now mature, sits whistling to himself.
A pair of tennis rackets and an overnight bag are on the floor beside him.*]

WILLY. [*offstage*] What are you walking away for? Don't walk away! If you're
going to say something say it to my face! I know you laugh at me behind my back.
You'll laugh out of the other side of your goddam face after this game. Touchdown!
Touchdown! Eighty thousand people! Touchdown. Right between the goal posts.

[*BERNARD is a quiet, earnest, but self-assured young man. WILLY's voice is coming from right
upstage now. BERNARD lowers his feet off the table and listens. JENNY, his father's secretary,
enters.*]

JENNY. [*distressed*] Say, Bernard, will you go out in the hall?

BERNARD. What is that noise? Who is it?

JENNY. Mr. Loman. He just got off the elevator. 260

BERNARD. [*getting up*] Who's he arguing with?

JENNY. Nobody. There's nobody with him. I can't deal with him any more,
and your father gets all upset everytime he comes. I've got a lot of typing to do,
and your father's waiting to sign it. Will you see him?

WILLY. [*entering*] Touchdown! Touch—[*He sees JENNY.*] Jenny, Jenny, good
to see you. How're ya? Workin'? Or still honest?

JENNY. Fine. How've you been feeling?

WILLY. Not much any more, Jenny. Ha, ha! [*He is surprised to see the rackets.*] 265

BERNARD. Hello, Uncle Willy.

WILLY. [*almost shocked*] Bernard! Well, look who's here! [*He comes quickly,
guiltily, to BERNARD and warmly shakes his hand.*]

Red Grange: Harold Edward Grange (1903–1991), all-America halfback (1923–1925) at the
University of Illinois.

BERNARD.   How are you? Good to see you.

WILLY.   What are you doing here?

BERNARD.   Oh, just stopped off to see Pop. Get off my feet till my train   270
leaves. I'm going to Washington in a few minutes.

WILLY.   Is he in?

BERNARD.   Yes, he's in his office with the accountants. Sit down.

WILLY.   [*sitting down*] What're you going to do in Washington?

BERNARD.   Oh, just a case I've got there, Willy.

WILLY.   That so? [*Indicating the rackets*] You going to play tennis there?   275

BERNARD.   I'm staying with a friend who's got a court.

WILLY.   Don't say. His own tennis court. Must be fine people, I bet.

BERNARD.   They are, very nice. Dad tells me Biff's in town.

WILLY.   [*with a big smile*] Yeah, Biff's in. Working on a very big deal, Bernard.

BERNARD.   What's Biff doing?   280

WILLY.   Well, he's been doing very big things in the West. But he decided
to establish himself here. Very big. We're having dinner. Did I hear your wife had
a boy?

BERNARD.   That's right. Our second.

WILLY.   Two boys! What do you know!

BERNARD.   What kind of a deal has Biff got?

WILLY.   Well, Bill Oliver—very big sporting-goods man—he wants Biff very   285
badly. Called him in from the West. Long distance, carte blanche, special deliveries.
Your friends have their own private tennis court?

BERNARD.   You still with the old firm, Willy?

WILLY.   [*after a pause*] I'm—I'm overjoyed to see how you made the grade,
Bernard, overjoyed. It's an encouraging thing to see a young man really—really—
Looks very good for Biff—very—[*He breaks off, then*] Bernard— [*He is so full of
emotion, he breaks off again.*]

BERNARD.   What is it, Willy?

WILLY.   [*small and alone*] What—what's the secret?

BERNARD.   What secret?   290

WILLY.   How—how did you? Why didn't he ever catch on?

BERNARD.   I wouldn't know that, Willy.

WILLY.   [*confidentially, desperately*] You were his friend, his boyhood friend.
There's something I don't understand about it. His life ended after that Ebbets
Field game. From the age of seventeen nothing good ever happened to him.

BERNARD.   He never trained himself for anything.

WILLY.   But he did, he did. After high school he took so many correspon-   295
dence courses. Radio mechanics; television; God knows what, and never made the
slightest mark.

BERNARD.   [*taking off his glasses*] Willy, do you want to talk candidly?

WILLY.   [*rising, faces* BERNARD] I regard you as a very brilliant man, Bernard.
I value your advice.

BERNARD.   Oh, the hell with the advice, Willy. I couldn't advise you. There's
just one thing I've always wanted to ask you. When he was supposed to graduate,
and the math teacher flunked him—

WILLY.   Oh, that son-of-a-bitch ruined his life.

BERNARD.   Yeah, but, Willy, all he had to do was go to summer school and   300
make up that subject.

WILLY. That's right, that's right.

BERNARD. Did you tell him not to go to summer school?

WILLY. Me? I begged him to go. I ordered him to go!

BERNARD. Then why wouldn't he go?

WILLY. Why? Why! Bernard, that question has been trailing me like a ghost   305
for the last fifteen years. He flunked the subject, and laid down and died like a
hammer hit him!

BERNARD. Take it easy, kid.

WILLY. Let me talk to you—I got nobody to talk to. Bernard, Bernard, was
it my fault? Y'see? It keeps going around in my mind, maybe I did something to
him. I got nothing to give him.

BERNARD. Don't take it so hard.

WILLY. Why did he lay down? What is the story there? You were his friend!

BERNARD. Willy, I remember, it was June, and our grades came out. And   310
he'd flunked math.

WILLY. That son-of-a-bitch!

BERNARD. No, it wasn't right then. Biff just got very angry, I remember,
and he was ready to enroll in summer school.

WILLY. [*surprised*] He was?

BERNARD. He wasn't beaten by it at all. But then, Willy, he disappeared
from the block for almost a month. And I got the idea that he'd gone up to New
England to see you. Did he have a talk with you then?

[*WILLY stares in silence.*]

BERNARD. Willy?   315

WILLY. [*with a strong edge of resentment in his voice*] Yeah, he came to Boston.
What about it?

BERNARD. Well, just that when he came back—I'll never forget this, it
always mystifies me. Because I'd thought so well of Biff, even though he'd always
taken advantage of me. I loved him, Willy, y'know? And he came back after that
month and took his sneakers—remember the sneakers with "University of Virginia"
printed on them? He was so proud of those, wore them every day. And he took
them down in the cellar, and burned them up in the furnace. We had a fist fight.
It lasted at least half an hour. Just the two of us, punching each other down the
cellar, and crying right through it. I've often thought of how strange it was that I
knew he'd given up his life. What happened in Boston, Willy?

[*WILLY looks at him as at an intruder.*]

BERNARD. I just bring it up because you asked me.

WILLY. [*angrily*] Nothing. What do you mean, "What happened?" What's
that got to do with anything?

BERNARD. Well, don't get sore.   320

WILLY. What are you trying to do, blame it on me? If a boy lays down is
that my fault?

BERNARD. Now, Willy, don't get—

WILLY. Well, don't—don't talk to me that way! What does that mean, "What
happened?"

[*CHARLEY enters. He is in his vest, and he carries a bottle of bourbon.*]

CHARLEY. Hey, you're going to miss that train. [*He waves the bottle.*]

BERNARD. Yeah, I'm going. [*He takes the bottle.*] Thanks, Pop. [*He picks up*   325
his rackets and bag.] Good-by, Willy, and don't worry about it. You know, "If at first
you don't succeed . . ."

WILLY. Yes, I believe in that.

BERNARD. But sometimes, Willy, it's better for a man just to walk away.

WILLY. Walk away?

BERNARD. That's right.

WILLY. But if you can't walk away?   330

BERNARD. [*after a slight pause*] I guess that's when it's tough. [*extending his
hand*] Good-by, Willy.

WILLY. [*shaking BERNARD's hand*] Good-by, boy.

CHARLEY. [*an arm on BERNARD's shoulder*] How do you like this kid? Gonna
argue a case in front of the Supreme Court.

BERNARD. [*protesting*] Pop!

WILLY. [*genuinely shocked, pained, and happy*] No! The Supreme Court!   335

BERNARD. I gotta run. 'By, Dad!

CHARLEY. Knock 'em dead, Bernard!

[*BERNARD goes off.*]

WILLY. [*as CHARLEY takes out his wallet*] The Supreme Court! And he didn't
even mention it!

CHARLEY. [*counting out money on the desk*] He don't have to—he's gonna do
it.

WILLY. And you never told him what to do, did you? You never took any   340
interest in him.

CHARLEY. My salvation is that I never took any interest in anything. There's
some money—fifty dollars. I got an accountant inside.

WILLY. Charley, look . . . [*with difficulty*] I got my insurance to pay. If you
can manage it—I need a hundred and ten dollars.

[*CHARLEY doesn't reply for a moment; merely stops moving.*]

WILLY. I'd draw it from my bank but Linda would know, and I . . .

CHARLEY. Sit down, Willy.

WILLY. [*moving toward the chair*] I'm keeping an account of everything,   345
remember. I'll pay every penny back. [*He sits.*]

CHARLEY. Now listen to me, Willy . . .

WILLY. I want you to know I appreciate . . .

CHARLEY. [*sitting down on the table*] Willy, what're you doin'? What the hell
is goin' on in your head?

WILLY. Why? I'm simply . . .

CHARLEY. I offered you a job. You can make fifty dollars a week. And I   350
won't send you on the road.

WILLY. I've got a job.

CHARLEY. Without pay? What kind of job is a job without pay? [*He rises.*]
Now, look, kid, enough is enough. I'm no genius but I know when I'm being
insulted.

WILLY. Insulted!

CHARLEY. Why don't you want to work for me?

WILLY. What's the matter with you? I've got a job.   355

CHARLEY. Then what're you walkin' in here every week for?

WILLY. [*getting up*] Well, if you don't want me to walk in here—

CHARLEY. I am offering you a job.

WILLY. I don't want your goddam job!

CHARLEY. When the hell are you going to grow up?   360

WILLY. [*furiously*] You big ignoramus, if you say that to me again I'll rap
you one! I don't care how big you are! [*He's ready to fight.*]

[*Pause.*]

CHARLEY. [*kindly, going to him*] How much do you need, Willy?

WILLY. Charley, I'm strapped. I'm strapped. I don't know what to do. I
was just fired.

CHARLEY. Howard fired you?

WILLY. That snotnose. Imagine that? I named him. I named him Howard.   365

CHARLEY. Willy, when're you gonna realize that them things don't mean
anything? You named him Howard, but you can't·sell that. The only thing you
got in this world is what you can sell. And the funny thing is that you're a salesman,
and you don't know that.

WILLY. I've tried to think otherwise, I guess. I always felt that if a man was
impressive, and well liked, that nothing—

CHARLEY. Why must everybody like you? Who liked J. P. Morgan?° Was he
impressive? In a Turkish bath he'd look like a butcher. But with his pockets on
he was very well liked. Now listen, Willy, I know you don't like me, and nobody
can say I'm in love with you, but I'll give you a job because—just for the hell of
it, put it that way. Now what do you say?

WILLY. I—I just can't work for you, Charley.

CHARLEY. What're you, jealous of me?   370

WILLY. I can't work for you, that's all, don't ask me why.

CHARLEY. [*angered, takes out more bills*] You been jealous of me all your life,
you damned fool! Here, pay your insurance. [*He puts the money in* WILLY'S *hand.*]

WILLY. I'm keeping strict accounts.

CHARLEY. I've got some work to do. Take care of yourself. And pay your
insurance.

WILLY. [*moving to the right*] Funny, y'know? After all the highways, and the   375
trains, and the appointments, and the years, you end up worth more dead than
alive.

CHARLEY. Willy, nobody's worth nothin' dead. [*after a slight pause*] Did you
hear what I said?

[WILLY *stands still, dreaming.*]

CHARLEY. Willy!

WILLY. Apologize to Bernard for me when you see him. I didn't mean to
argue with him. He's a fine boy. They're all fine boys, and they'll end up big—all
of them. Someday they'll all play tennis together. Wish me luck, Charley. He saw
Bill Oliver today.

J. P. Morgan: John Pierpont Morgan (1837–1913) was the founder of U.S. Steel and the
head of a gigantic family fortune that was enlarged by his son, John Pierpont Morgan
(1867–1943). Charley is probably referring to the son.

CHARLEY.   Good luck.

WILLY.   [*on the verge of tears*] Charley, you're the only friend I got. Isn't   380
that a remarkable thing? [*He goes out.*]

CHARLEY.   Jesus!

[*CHARLEY stares after him a moment and follows. All light blacks out. Suddenly raucous music is heard, and a red glow rises behind the screen at right. STANLEY, a young waiter, appears, carrying a table, followed by HAPPY, who is carrying two chairs.*]

STANLEY.   [*putting the table down*] That's all right, Mr. Loman. I can handle it myself. [*He turns and takes the chairs from HAPPY and places them at the table.*]

HAPPY.   [*glancing around.*] Oh, this is better.

STANLEY.   Sure, in the front there you're in the middle of all kinds a noise. Whenever you got a party, Mr. Loman, you just tell me and I'll put you back here. Y'know, there's a lotta people they don't like it private, because when they go out they like to see a lotta action around them because they're sick and tired to stay in the house by theirself. But I know you, you ain't from Hackensack.° You know what I mean?

HAPPY.   [*sitting down*] So how's it coming, Stanley?   385

STANLEY.   Ah, it's a dog's life. I only wish during the war they'd a took me in the Army. I coulda been dead by now.

HAPPY.   My brother's back, Stanley.

STANLEY.   Oh, he come back, heh? From the Far West.

HAPPY.   Yeah, big cattle man, my brother, so treat him right. And my father's coming too.

STANLEY.   Oh, your father too!   390

HAPPY.   You got a couple of nice lobsters?

STANLEY.   Hundred per cent, big.

HAPPY.   I want them with claws.

STANLEY.   Don't worry. I don't give you no mice. [*HAPPY laughs.*] How about some wine? It'll put a head on the meal.

HAPPY.   No. You remember, Stanley, that recipe I brought you from   395
overseas? With the champagne in it?

STANLEY.   Oh, yeah, sure. I still got it tacked up yet in the kitchen. But that'll have to cost a buck apiece anyways.

HAPPY.   That's all right.

STANLEY.   What'd you, hit a number or somethin'?

HAPPY.   No, it's a little celebration. My brother is—I think he pulled off a big deal today. I think we're going into business together.

STANLEY.   Great! That's the best for you. Because a family business, you   400
know what I mean?—that's the best.

HAPPY.   That's what I think.

STANLEY.   'Cause what's the difference? Somebody steals? It's in the family. Know what I mean? [*sotto voce*°] Like this bartender here. The boss is goin' crazy what kinda leak he's got in the cash register. You put it in but it don't come out.

HAPPY.   [*raising his head*] Sh!

STANLEY.   What?

Hackensack: a city in northeastern New Jersey; Stanley uses the name as a reference to unsophisticated visitors to New York City.   *sotto voce:* spoken in an undertone or "stage" whisper.

HAPPY.   You notice I wasn't lookin' right or left, was I?   405
STANLEY.   No.
HAPPY.   And my eyes are closed.
STANLEY.   So what's the—?
HAPPY.   Strudel's comin'.
STANLEY.   [*catching on, looks around*] Ah, no, there's no—   410

[*He breaks off as a furred, lavishly dressed GIRL enters and sits at the next table. Both follow her with their eyes.*]

STANLEY.   Geez, how'd ya know?
HAPPY.   I got radar or something. [*staring directly at her profile*] Oooooooo
. . . Stanley.
STANLEY.   I think that's for you, Mr. Loman.
HAPPY.   Look at that mouth. Oh God. And the binoculars.
STANLEY.   Geez, you got a life, Mr. Loman.   415
HAPPY.   Wait on her.
STANLEY.   [*going to the GIRL's table*] Would you like a menu, ma'am?
GIRL.   I'm expecting someone, but I'd like a—
HAPPY.   Why don't you bring her—excuse me, miss, do you mind? I sell
champagne, and I'd like you to try my brand. Bring her a champagne, Stanley.
GIRL.   That's awfully nice of you.   420
HAPPY.   Don't mention it. It's all company money. [*He laughs.*]
GIRL.   That's a charming product to be selling, isn't it?
HAPPY.   Oh, gets to be like everything else. Selling is selling, y'know.
GIRL.   I suppose.
HAPPY.   You don't happen to sell, do you?   425
GIRL.   No, I don't sell.
HAPPY.   Would you object to a compliment from a stranger? You ought to
be on a magazine cover.
GIRL.   [*looking at him a little archly*] I have been.

[*STANLEY comes in with a glass of champagne.*]

HAPPY.   What'd I say before, Stanley? You see? She's a cover girl.
STANLEY.   Oh, I could see, I could see.   430
HAPPY.   [*to the GIRL*] What magazine?
GIRL.   Oh, a lot of them. [*She takes the drink.*] Thank you.
HAPPY.   You know what they say in France, don't you? "Champagne is the
drink of the complexion"—Hya, Biff!

[*BIFF has entered and sits with HAPPY.*]

BIFF.   Hello, kid. Sorry I'm late.
HAPPY.   I just got here. Uh, Miss—?   435
GIRL.   Forsythe.
HAPPY.   Miss Forsythe, this is my brother.
BIFF.   Is Dad here?
HAPPY.   His name if Biff. You might've heard of him. Great football player.
GIRL.   Really? What team?   440
HAPPY.   Are you familiar with football?
GIRL.   No. I'm afraid I'm not.

HAPPY.   Biff is quarterback with the New York Giants.

GIRL.   Well, that is nice, isn't it? [*She drinks.*]

HAPPY.   Good health.   445

GIRL.   I'm happy to meet you.

HAPPY.   That's my name. Hap. It's really Harold, but at West Point they called me Happy.

GIRL.   [*now really impressed*] Oh, I see. How do you do? [*She turns her profile.*]

BIFF.   Isn't Dad coming?

HAPPY.   You want her?   450

BIFF.   Oh, I could never make that.

HAPPY.   I remember the time that idea would never come into your head. Where's the old confidence, Biff?

BIFF.   I just saw Oliver—

HAPPY.   Wait a minute. I've got to see that old confidence again. Do you want her? She's on call.

BIFF.   Oh, no. [*He turns to look at the GIRL.*]   455

HAPPY.   I'm telling you. Watch this. [*turning to the GIRL*] Honey? [*She turns to him.*] Are you busy?

GIRL.   Well, I am . . . but I could make a phone call.

HAPPY.   Do that, will you, honey? And see if you can get a friend. We'll be here for a while. Biff is one of the greatest football players in the country.

GIRL.   [*standing up*] Well, I'm certainly happy to meet you.

HAPPY.   Come back soon.   460

GIRL.   I'll try.

HAPPY.   Don't try, honey, try hard.

[*The GIRL exits. STANLEY follows, shaking his head in bewildered admiration.*]

HAPPY.   Isn't that a shame now? A beautiful girl like that? That's why I can't get married. There's not a good woman in a thousand. New York is loaded with them, kid!

BIFF.   Hap, look—

HAPPY.   I told you she was on call!   465

BIFF.   [*strangely unnerved*] Cut it out, will ya? I want to say something to you.

HAPPY.   Did you see Oliver?

BIFF.   I saw him all right. Now look, I want to tell Dad a couple of things and I want you to help me.

HAPPY.   What? Is he going to back you?

BIFF.   Are you crazy? You're out of your goddam head, you know that?   470

HAPPY.   Why? What happened?

BIFF.   [*breathlessly*] I did a terrible thing today, Hap. It's been the strangest day I ever went through. I'm all numb, I swear.

HAPPY.   You mean he wouldn't see you?

BIFF.   Well, I waited six hours for him, see? All day. Kept sending my name in. Even tried to date his secretary so she'd get me to him, but no soap.

HAPPY.   Because you're not showin' the old confidence, Biff. He remembered   475 you, didn't he?

BIFF.   [*stopping HAPPY with a gesture*] Finally, about five o'clock, he comes out. Didn't remember who I was or anything. I felt like such an idiot, Hap.

HAPPY.   Did you tell him my Florida idea?

BIFF. He walked away. I saw him for one minute. I got so mad I could've torn the walls down! How the hell did I ever get the idea I was a salesman there? I even believed myself that I'd been a salesman for him! And then he gave me one look and—I realized what a ridiculous lie my whole life has been! We've been talking in a dream for fifteen years. I was a shipping clerk.

HAPPY. What'd you do?

BIFF. [*with great tension and wonder*] Well, he left, see. And the secretary   480
went out. I was all alone in the waiting-room. I don't know what came over me, Hap. The next thing I know I'm in his office—paneled walls, everything. I can't explain it. I—Hap, I took his fountain pen.

HAPPY. Geez, did he catch you?

BIFF. I ran out. I ran down all eleven flights. I ran and ran and ran.

HAPPY. That was an awful dumb—what'd you do that for?

BIFF. [*agonized*] I don't know, I just—wanted to take something. I don't know. You gotta help me, Hap, I'm gonna tell Pop.

HAPPY. You crazy? What for?   485

BIFF. Hap, he's got to understand that I'm not the man somebody lends that kind of money to. He thinks I've been spiting him all these years and it's eating him up.

HAPPY. That's just it. You tell him something nice.

BIFF. I can't.

HAPPY. Say you got a lunch date with Oliver tomorrow.

BIFF. So what do I do tomorrow?   490

HAPPY. You leave the house tomorrow and come back at night and say Oliver is thinking it over. And he thinks it over for a couple of weeks, and gradually it fades away and nobody's the worse.

BIFF. But it'll go on forever!

HAPPY. Dad is never so happy as when he's looking forward to something!

[*WILLY enters.*]

HAPPY. Hello, scout!

WILLY. Gee, I haven't been here in years!   495

[*STANLEY has followed WILLY in and sets a chair for him. STANLEY starts off but HAPPY stops him.*]

HAPPY. Stanley!

[*STANLEY stands by, waiting for an order.*]

BIFF. [*going to WILLY with guilt, as to an invalid*] Sit down, Pop. You want a drink?

WILLY. Sure, I don't mind.

BIFF. Let's get a load on.

WILLY. You look worried.   500

BIFF. N-no. [*to STANLEY*] Scotch all around. Make it doubles.

STANLEY. Doubles, right. [*He goes.*]

WILLY. You had a couple already, didn't you?

BIFF. Just a couple, yeah.

WILLY. Well, what happened, boy? [*nodding affirmatively, with a smile*] Every-   505
thing go all right?

BIFF. [*takes a breath, then reaches out and grasps* WILLY's *hand*] Pal . . . [*He is smiling bravely, and* WILLY *is smiling too.*] I had an experience today.

HAPPY. Terrific, Pop.

WILLY. That so? What happened?

BIFF. [*high, slightly alcoholic, above the earth*] I'm going to tell you everything from first to last. It's been a strange day. [*Silence. He looks around, composes himself as best he can, but his breath keeps breaking the rhythm of his voice.*] I had to wait quite a while for him, and—

WILLY. Oliver?   510

BIFF. Yeah, Oliver. All day, as a matter of cold fact. And a lot of— instances—facts, Pop, facts about my life came back to me. Who was it, Pop? Who ever said I was a salesman with Oliver?

WILLY. Well, you were.

BIFF. No, Dad, I was a shipping clerk.

WILLY. But you were practically—

BIFF. [*with determination*] Dad, I don't know who said it first, but I was never   515
a salesman for Bill Oliver.

WILLY. What're you talking about?

BIFF. Let's hold on to the facts tonight, Pop. We're not going to get anywhere bullin' around. I was a shipping clerk.

WILLY. [*angrily*] All right, now listen to me—

BIFF. Why don't you let me finish?

WILLY. I'm not interested in stories about the past or any crap of that kind   520
because the woods are burning, boys, you understand? There's a big blaze going on all around. I was fired today.

BIFF. [*shocked*] How could you be?

WILLY. I was fired, and I'm looking for a little good news to tell your mother, because the woman has waited and the woman has suffered. The gist of it is that I haven't got a story left in my head, Biff. So don't give me a lecture about facts and aspects. I am not interested. Now what've you got to say to me?

[STANLEY *enters with three drinks. They wait until he leaves.*]

WILLY. Did you see Oliver?

BIFF. Jesus, Dad!

WILLY. You mean you didn't go up there?   525

HAPPY. Sure he went up there.

BIFF. I did. I—saw him. How could they fire you?

WILLY. [*on the edge of his chair*] What kind of a welcome did he give you?

BIFF. He won't even let you work on commission?

WILLY. I'm out! [*driving*] So tell me, he gave you a warm welcome?   530

HAPPY. Sure, Pop, sure!

BIFF. [*driven*] Well, it was kind of—

WILLY. I was wondering if he'd remember you. [*to* HAPPY] Imagine, man doesn't see him for ten, twelve years and gives him that kind of a welcome!

HAPPY. Damn right!

BIFF. [*trying to return to the offensive*] Pop, look—   535

WILLY. You know why he remembered you, don't you? Because you impressed him in those days.

BIFF. Let's talk quietly and get this down to the facts, huh?

WILLY. [*as though BIFF had been interrupting*] Well, what happened? It's great news, Biff. Did he take you into his office or'd you talk in the waiting-room?

BIFF. Well, he came in, see, and—

WILLY. [*with a big smile*] What'd he say? Betcha he threw his arm around 540 you.

BIFF. Well, he kinda—

WILLY. He's a fine man. [*to HAPPY*] Very hard man to see, y'know.

HAPPY. [*agreeing*] Oh, I know.

WILLY. [*to BIFF*] Is that where you had the drinks?

BIFF. Yeah, he gave me a couple of—no, no! 545

HAPPY. [*cutting in*] He told him my Florida idea.

WILLY. Don't interrupt. [*to BIFF*] How'd he react to the Florida idea?

BIFF. Dad, will you give me a minute to explain?

WILLY. I've been waiting for you to explain since I sat down here! What happened? He took you into his office and what?

BIFF. Well—I talked. And—and he listened, see. 550

WILLY. Famous for the way he listens, y'know. What was his answer?

BIFF. His answer was—[*He breaks off, suddenly angry.*] Dad, you're not letting me tell you what I want to tell you!

WILLY. [*accusing, angered*] You didn't see him, did you?

BIFF. I did see him!

WILLY. What'd you insult him or something? You insulted him, didn't you? 555

BIFF. Listen, will you let me out of it, will you just let me out of it!

HAPPY. What the hell!

WILLY. Tell me what happened!

BIFF. [*to HAPPY*] I can't talk to him!

[*A single trumpet note jars the ear. The light of green leaves stains the house, which holds the air of night and a dream. YOUNG BERNARD enters and knocks on the door of the house.*]

YOUNG BERNARD. [*frantically*] Mrs. Loman, Mrs. Loman! 560

HAPPY. Tell him what happened!

BIFF. [*to HAPPY*] Shut up and leave me alone!

WILLY. No, no! You had to go and flunk math!

BIFF. What math? What're you talking about?

YOUNG BERNARD. Mrs. Loman, Mrs. Loman! 565

[*LINDA appears in the house, as of old.*]

WILLY. [*wildly*] Math, math, math!

BIFF. Take it easy, Pop!

YOUNG BERNARD. Mrs. Loman!

WILLY. [*furiously*] If you hadn't flunked you'd've been set by now!

BIFF. Now, look, I'm gonna tell you what happened, and you're going to 570 listen to me.

YOUNG BERNARD. Mrs. Loman!

BIFF. I waited six hours—

HAPPY. What the hell are you saying?

BIFF. I kept sending in my name but he wouldn't see me. So finally he . . .

[*He continues unheard as light fades low on the restaurant.*]

YOUNG BERNARD.   Biff flunked math!   575

LINDA.   No!

YOUNG BERNARD.   Birnbaum flunked him! They won't graduate him!

LINDA.   But they have to. He's gotta go to the university. Where is he? Biff!
Biff!

YOUNG BERNARD.   No, he left. He went to Grand Central.

LINDA.   Grand—You mean he went to Boston!   580

YOUNG BERNARD.   Is Uncle Willy in Boston?

LINDA.   Oh, maybe Willy can talk to the teacher. Oh, the poor, poor boy!

[*Light on house area snaps out.*]

BIFF.   [*at the table, now audible, holding up a gold fountain pen*] . . . so I'm washed
up with Oliver, you understand? Are you listening to me?

WILLY.   [*at a loss*] Yeah, sure. If you hadn't flunked—

BIFF.   Flunked what? What're you talking about?   585

WILLY.   Don't blame everything on me! I didn't flunk math—you did! What
pen?

HAPPY.   That was awful dumb, Biff, a pen like that is worth—

WILLY.   [*seeing the pen for the first time*] You took Oliver's pen?

BIFF.   [*weakening*] Dad, I just explained it to you.

WILLY.   You stole Bill Oliver's fountain pen!   590

BIFF.   I didn't exactly steal it! That's just what I've been explaining to you!

HAPPY.   He had it in his hand and just then Oliver walked in, so he got
nervous and stuck it in his pocket!

WILLY.   My God, Biff!

BIFF.   I never intended to do it, Dad!

OPERATOR'S VOICE.   Standish Arms, good evening!   595

WILLY.   [*shouting*] I'm not in my room!

BIFF.   [*frightened*] Dad, what's the matter? [*He and HAPPY stand up.*]

OPERATOR.   Ringing Mr. Loman for you!

WILLY.   I'm not there, stop it!

BIFF.   [*horrified, gets down on one knee before WILLY*] Dad, I'll make good, I'll   600
make good. [*WILLY tries to get to his feet. BIFF holds him down.*] Sit down now.

WILLY.   No, you're no good, you're no good for anything.

BIFF.   I am, Dad, I'll find something else, you understand? Now don't worry
about anything. [*He holds up WILLY's face.*] Talk to me, Dad.

OPERATOR.   Mr. Loman does not answer. Shall I page him?

WILLY.   [*attempting to stand, as though to rush and silence the OPERATOR*] No, no,
no!

HAPPY.   He'll strike something, Pop.   605

WILLY.   No, no . . .

BIFF.   [*desperately, standing over WILLY*] Pop, listen! Listen to me! I'm telling
you something good. Oliver talked to his partner about the Florida idea. you
listening? He—he talked to his partner, and he came to me . . . I'm going to be
all right, you hear? Dad, listen to me, he said it was just a question of the amount!

WILLY.   Then you . . . got it?

HAPPY.   He's gonna be terrific, Pop!

WILLY.   [*trying to stand*] Then you got it, haven't you? You got it! You got   610
it!

BIFF. [*agonized, holds WILLY down*] No, no. Look, Pop. I'm supposed to have lunch with them tomorrow. I'm just telling you this so you'll know that I can still make an impression, Pop. And I'll make good somewhere, but I can't go tomorrow, see?

WILLY. Why not? You simply—

BIFF. But the pen, Pop!

WILLY. You give it to him and tell him it was an oversight!

HAPPY. Sure, have lunch tomorrow! 615

BIFF. I can't say that—

WILLY. You were doing a crossword puzzle and accidentally used his pen!

BIFF. Listen, kid, I took those balls years ago, now I walk in with his fountain pen? That clinches it, don't you see? I can't face him like that! I'll try elsewhere.

PAGE'S VOICE. Paging Mr. Loman!

WILLY. Don't you want to be anything? 620

BIFF. Pop, how can I go back?

WILLY. You don't want to be anything, is that what's behind it?

BIFF. [*now angry at WILLY for not crediting his sympathy*] Don't take it that way! You think it was easy walking into that office after what I'd done to him? A team of horses couldn't have dragged me back to Bill Oliver!

WILLY. Then why'd you go?

BIFF. Why did I go? Why did I go? Look at you! Look at what's become 625
of you!

[*Off left, THE WOMAN laughs.*]

WILLY. Biff, you're going to go to that lunch tomorrow, or—

BIFF. I can't go. I've got no appointment!

HAPPY. Biff, for . . . !

WILLY. Are you spiting me?

BIFF. Don't take it that way! Goddammit! 630

WILLY. [*strikes BIFF and falters away from the table*] You rotten little louse! Are you spiting me?

THE WOMAN. Someone's at the door, Willy!

BIFF. I'm no good, can't you see what I am?

HAPPY. [*separating them*] Hey, you're in a restaurant! Now cut it out, both of you! [*The girls enter.*] Hello, girls, sit down.

[*THE WOMAN laughs, off left.*]

MISS FORSYTHE. I guess we might as well. This is Letta. 635

THE WOMAN. Willy, are you going to wake up?

BIFF. [*ignoring WILLY*] How're ya, miss, sit down. What do you drink?

MISS FORSYTHE. Letta might not be able to stay long.

LETTA. I gotta get up very early tomorrow. I got jury duty. I'm so excited! Were you fellows ever on a jury?

BIFF. No, but I been in front of them! [*The girls laugh.*] This is my father. 640

LETTA. Isn't he cute? Sit down with us, Pop.

HAPPY. Sit him down, Biff!

BIFF. [*going to him*] Come on, slugger, drink us under the table. To hell with it! Come on, sit down, pal.

[*On BIFF's last insistence, WILLY is about to sit.*]

THE WOMAN.   [*now urgently*] Willy, are you going to answer the door!

[*THE WOMAN's call pulls WILLY back. He starts right, befuddled.*]

BIFF.   Hey, where are you going?   645
WILLY.   Open the door.
BIFF.   The door?
WILLY.   The washroom . . . the door . . . where's the door?
BIFF.   [*leading WILLY to the left*] Just go straight down.

[*WILLY moves left.*]

THE WOMAN.   Willy, Willy, are you going to get up, get up, get up, get   650
up?

[*WILLY exits left.*]

LETTA.   I think it's sweet you bring your daddy along.
MISS FORSYTHE.   Oh, he isn't really your father!
BIFF.   [*at left, turning to her resentfully*] Miss Forsythe, you've just seen a prince
walk by. A fine, troubled prince. A hard-working, unappreciated prince. A pal,
you understand? A good companion. Always for his boys.
LETTA.   That's so sweet.
HAPPY.   Well, girls, what's the program? We're wasting time. Come on, Biff.   655
Gather round. Where would you like to go?
BIFF.   Why don't you do something for him?
HAPPY.   Me!
BIFF.   Don't you give a damn for him, Hap?
HAPPY.   What're you talking about? I'm the one who—
BIFF.   I sense it, you don't give a good goddam about him. [*He takes the*   660
rolled-up hose from his pocket and puts it on the table in front of HAPPY.] Look what I
found in the cellar, for Christ's sake. How can you bear to let it go on?
HAPPY.   Me? Who goes away? Who runs off and—
BIFF.   Yeah, but he doesn't mean anything to you. You could help him—I
can't! Don't you understand what I'm talking about? He's going to kill himself,
don't you know that?
HAPPY.   Don't I know it! Me!
BIFF.   Hap, help him! Jesus . . . help him . . . Help me, help me, I can't bear
to look at his face! [*Ready to weep, he hurries out, up right.*]
HAPPY.   [*staring after him*] Where are you going?   665
MISS FORSYTHE.   What's he so mad about?
HAPPY.   Come on, girls, we'll catch up with him.
MISS FORSYTHE.   [*as HAPPY pushes her out*] Say, I don't like that temper of his!
HAPPY.   He's just a little overstrung, he'll be all right!
WILLY.   [*off left, as THE WOMAN laughs*] Don't answer! Don't answer!   670
LETTA.   Don't you want to tell your father—
HAPPY.   No, that's not my father. He's just a guy. Come on, we'll catch Biff,
and, honey, we're going to paint this town! Stanley, where's the check! Hey,
Stanley!

[*They exit. STANLEY looks toward left.*]

STANLEY.   [*calling to* HAPPY *indignantly*] Mr. Loman! Mr. Loman!

[STANLEY *picks up a chair and follows them off. Knocking is heard off left.* THE WOMAN *enters, laughing.* WILLY *follows her. She is in a black slip; he is buttoning his shirt. Raw, sensuous music accompanies their speech.*]

WILLY.   Will you stop laughing? Will you stop?

THE WOMAN.   Aren't you going to answer the door? He'll wake the whole   675
hotel.

WILLY.   I'm not expecting anybody.

THE WOMAN.   Whyn't you have another drink, honey, and stop being so damn self-centered?

WILLY.   I'm so lonely.

THE WOMAN.   You know you ruined me, Willy? From now on, whenever you come to the office, I'll see that you go right through to the buyers. No waiting at my desk any more, Willy. You ruined me.

WILLY.   That's nice of you to say that.   680

THE WOMAN.   Gee, you are self-centered! Why so sad? You are the saddest, self-centeredest soul I ever did see-saw. [*She laughs. He kisses her.*] Come on inside, drummer boy. It's silly to be dressing in the middle of the night. [*As knocking is heard*] Aren't you going to answer the door?

WILLY.   They're knocking on the wrong door.

THE WOMAN.   But I felt the knocking! And he heard us talking in here. Maybe the hotel's on fire!

WILLY.   [*his terror rising*] It's a mistake.

THE WOMAN.   Then tell him to go away!   685

WILLY.   There's nobody there.

THE WOMAN.   It's getting on my nerves, Willy. There's somebody standing out there and it's getting on my nerves!

WILLY.   [*pushing her away from him*] All right, stay in the bathroom here, and don't come out. I think there's a law in Massachusetts about it, so don't come out. It may be that new room clerk. He looked very mean. So don't come out. It's a mistake, there's no fire.

[*The knocking is heard again. He takes a few steps away from her, and she vanishes into the wing. The light follows him, and now he is facing* YOUNG BIFF, *who carries a suitcase.* BIFF *steps toward him. The music is gone.*]

BIFF.   Why didn't you answer?

WILLY.   Biff! What are you doing in Boston?   690

BIFF.   Why didn't you answer? I've been knocking for five minutes, I called you on the phone—

WILLY.   I just heard you. I was in the bathroom and had the door shut. Did anything happen home?

BIFF.   Dad—I let you down.

WILLY.   What do you mean?

BIFF.   Dad . . .   695

WILLY.   Biffo, what's this about? [*putting his arm around* BIFF] Come on, let's go downstairs and get you a malted.

BIFF.   Dad, I flunked math.

WILLY.   Not for the term?

BIFF.   The term. I haven't got enough credits to graduate.

WILLY.   You mean to say Bernard wouldn't give you the answers?   700

BIFF.   He did, he tried, but I only got a sixty-one.

WILLY.   And they wouldn't give you four points?

BIFF.   Birnbaum refused absolutely. I begged him, Pop, but he won't give me those points. You gotta talk to him before they close the school. Because if he saw the kind of man you are, and you just talked to him in your way, I'm sure he'd come through for me. The class came right before practice, see, and I didn't go enough. Would you talk to him? He'd like you, Pop. You know the way you could talk.

WILLY.   You're on. We'll drive right back.

BIFF.   Oh, Dad, good work! I'm sure he'll change it for you!   705

WILLY.   Go downstairs and tell the clerk I'm checkin' out. Go right down.

BIFF.   Yes, sir! See, the reason he hates me, Pop—one day he was late for class so I got up at the blackboard and imitated him. I crossed my eyes and talked with a lithp.

WILLY.   [*laughing*] You did? The kids like it?

BIFF.   They nearly died laughing!

WILLY.   Yeah? What'd you do?   710

BIFF.   The thquare root of thixthy twee is . . . [*WILLY bursts out laughing; BIFF joins him.*] And in the middle of it he walked in!

[*WILLY laughs and THE WOMAN joins in offstage.*]

WILLY.   [*without hesitation*] Hurry downstairs and—

BIFF.   Somebody in there?

WILLY.   No, that was next door.

[*THE WOMAN laughs offstage.*]

BIFF.   Somebody got in your bathroom!   715

WILLY.   No, it's the next room, there's a party—

THE WOMAN.   [*enters, laughing. She lisps this.*] Can I come in? There's something in the bathtub, Willy, and it's moving!

[*WILLY looks at BIFF, who is staring open-mouthed and horrified at THE WOMAN.*]

WILLY.   Ah—you better go back to your room. They must be finished painting by now. They're painting her room so I let her take a shower here. Go back, go back . . . [*He pushes her.*]

THE WOMAN.   [*resisting*] But I've got to get dressed, Willy, I can't—

WILLY.   Get out of here! Go back, go back . . . [*suddenly striving for the ordinary*] This is Miss Francis, Biff, she's a buyer. They're painting her room. Go back, Miss Francis, go back . . .   720

THE WOMAN.   But my clothes, I can't go out naked in the hall!

WILLY.   [*pushing her offstage*] Get outa here! Go back, go back!

[*BIFF slowly sits down on his suitcase as the argument continues offstage.*]

THE WOMAN.   Where's my stockings? You promised me stockings, Willy!

WILLY.   I have no stockings here!

THE WOMAN. You had two boxes of size nine sheers for me, and I want them! 725

WILLY. Here, for God's sake, will you get outa here!

THE WOMAN. [*enters holding a box of stockings*] I just hope there's nobody in the hall. That's all I hope. [*To BIFF*] Are you football or baseball?

BIFF. Football.

THE WOMAN. [*angry, humiliated*] That's me too. G'night. [*she snatches her clothes from WILLY, and walks out.*]

WILLY. [*after a pause*] Well, better get going. I want to get to the school first thing in the morning. Get my suits out of the closet. I'll get my valise. [*BIFF doesn't move.*] What's the matter? [*BIFF remains motionless, tears falling*] She's a buyer. Buys for J. H. Simmons. She lives down the hall—they're painting. You don't imagine—[*He breaks off. After a pause*] Now listen, pal, she's just a buyer. She sees merchandise in her room and they have to keep it looking just so . . . [*Pause. Assuming command*] All right, get my suits. [*BIFF doesn't move.*] Now stop crying and do as I say. I gave you an order. Biff, I gave you an order! Is that what you do when I give you an order? How dare you cry! [*putting his arm around BIFF*] Now look, Biff, when you grow up you'll understand about these things. You mustn't— you mustn't overemphasize a thing like this. I'll see Birnbaum first thing in the morning. 730

BIFF. Never mind.

WILLY. [*getting down beside BIFF*] Never mind! He's going to give you those points. I'll see to it.

BIFF. He wouldn't listen to you.

WILLY. He certainly will listen to me. You need those points for the U. of Virginia.

BIFF. I'm not going there. 735

WILLY. Heh? If I can't get him to change that mark you'll make it up in summer school. You've got all summer to—

BIFF. [*his weeping breaking from him*] Dad . . .

WILLY. [*infected by it*] Oh, my boy . . .

BIFF. Dad . . .

WILLY. She's nothing to me, Biff. I was lonely, I was terribly lonely. 740

BIFF. You—you gave her Mama's stockings! [*His tears break through and he rises to go.*]

WILLY. [*grabbing for BIFF*] I gave you an order!

BIFF. Don't touch me, you—liar!

WILLY. Apologize for that!

BIFF. You fake! You phony little fake! [*Overcome, he turns quickly and weeping fully goes out with his suitcase. WILLY is left on the floor on his knees.*] 745

WILLY. I gave you an order! Biff, come back here or I'll beat you! Come back here! I'll whip you!

[*STANLEY comes quickly in from the right and stands in front of WILLY.*]

WILLY. [*shouts at STANLEY*] I gave you an order . . .

STANLEY. Hey, let's pick it up, pick it up, Mr. Loman. [*He helps WILLY to his feet.*] Your boys left with the chippies. They said they'll see you home.

[*A SECOND WAITER watches some distance away.*]

WILLY. But we were supposed to have dinner together.

[*Music is heard, WILLY's theme.*]

STANLEY. Can you make it?   750

WILLY. I'll—sure, I can make it. [*suddenly concerned about his clothes*] Do I—I look all right?

STANLEY. Sure, you look all right. [*He flicks a speck off WILLY's lapel.*]

WILLY. Here—here's a dollar.

STANLEY. Oh, your son paid me. It's all right.

WILLY. [*putting it in STANLEY's hand*] No, take it. You're a good boy.   755

STANLEY. Oh, no, you don't have to . . .

WILLY. Here—here's some more, I don't need it any more. [*after a slight pause*] Tell me—is there a seed store in the neighborhood?

STANLEY. Seeds? You mean like to plant?

[*As WILLY turns, STANLEY slips the money back into his jacket pocket.*]

WILLY. Yes. Carrots, peas . . .

STANLEY. Well, there's hardware stores on Sixth Avenue, but it may be   760
too late now.

WILLY. [*anxiously*] Oh, I'd better hurry. I've got to get some seeds. [*He starts off to the right.*] I've got to get some seeds, right away. Nothing's planted. I don't have a thing in the ground.

[*WILLY hurries out as the light goes down. STANLEY moves over to the right after him, watches him off. The other waiter has been staring at WILLY.*]

STANLEY. [*to the WAITER*] Well, whatta you looking at?

[*The WAITER picks up the chairs and moves off right. STANLEY takes the table and follows him. The light fades on this area. There is a long pause, the sound of the flute coming over. The light gradually rises on the kitchen, which is empty. HAPPY appears at the door of the house, followed by BIFF. HAPPY is carrying a large bunch of long-stemmed roses. He enters the kitchen, looks around for LINDA. Not seeing her, he turns to BIFF, who is just outside the house door, and makes a gesture with his hands, indicating "Not here, I guess." He looks into the living-room and freezes. Inside, LINDA, unseen, is seated, WILLY's coat on her lap. She rises ominously and quietly and moves toward HAPPY, who backs up into the kitchen, afraid.*]

HAPPY. Hey, what're you doing up? [*LINDA says nothing but moves toward him implacably.*] Where's Pop? [*He keeps backing to the right, and now LINDA is in full view in the doorway to the living-room.*] Is he sleeping?

LINDA. Where were you?

HAPPY. [*trying to laugh it off*] We met two girls, Mom, very fine types. Here,   765
we brought you some flowers. [*offering them to her*] Put them in your room, Ma.

[*She knocks them to the floor at BIFF's feet. He has now come inside and closed the door behind him. She stares at BIFF, silent.*]

HAPPY. Now what'd you do that for? Mom, I want you to have some flowers—

LINDA. [*cutting HAPPY off, violently to BIFF*] Don't you care whether he lives or dies?

HAPPY. [*going to the stairs*] Come upstairs, Biff.

BIFF. [*with a flare of disgust, to* HAPPY] Go away from me! [*to* LINDA] What do you mean, lives or dies? Nobody's dying around here, pal.

LINDA. Get out of my sight! Get out of here! 770

BIFF. I wanna see the boss.

LINDA. You're not going near him!

BIFF. Where is he? [*He moves into the living-room and* LINDA *follows.*]

LINDA. [*shouting after* BIFF] You invite him for dinner. He looks forward to it all day—[BIFF *appears in his parents' bedroom, looks around, and exits.*]—and then you desert him there. There's no stranger you'd do that to!

HAPPY. Why? He had a swell time with us. Listen, when I—[LINDA *comes* 775 *back into the kitchen.*]—desert him I hope I don't outlive the day!

LINDA. Get out of here!

HAPPY. Now look, Mom . . .

LINDA. Did you have to go to women tonight? You and your lousy rotten whores!

[BIFF *re-enters the kitchen.*]

HAPPY. Mom, all we did was follow Biff around trying to cheer him up! [*to* BIFF] Boy, what a night you gave me!

LINDA. Get out of here, both of you, and don't come back! I don't want 780 you tormenting him any more. Go on now, get your things together! [*to* BIFF] You can sleep in his apartment. [*She starts to pick up the flowers and stops herself.*] Pick up this stuff, I'm not your maid any more. Pick it up, you bum, you!

[HAPPY *turns his back to her in refusal.* BIFF *slowly moves over and gets down on his knees, picking up the flowers.*]

LINDA. You're a pair of animals! Not one, not another living soul would have had the cruelty to walk out on that man in a restaurant!

BIFF. [*not looking at her*] Is that what he said?

LINDA. He didn't have to say anything. He was so humiliated he nearly limped when he came in.

HAPPY. But, Mom, he had a great time with us—

BIFF. [*cutting him off violently*] Shut up! 785

[*Without another word,* HAPPY *goes upstairs.*]

LINDA. You! You didn't even go in to see if he was all right!

BIFF. [*still on the floor in front of* LINDA, *the flowers in his hand; with self-loathing*] No. Didn't. Didn't do a damned thing. How do you like that, heh? Left him babbling in a toilet.

LINDA. You louse. You . . .

BIFF. Now you hit it on the nose! [*He gets up, throws the flowers in the wastebasket.*] The scum of the earth, and you're looking at him!

LINDA. Get out of here! 790

BIFF. I gotta talk to the boss, Mom. Where is he?

LINDA. You're not going near him. Get out of this house!

BIFF. [*with absolute assurance, determination*] No. We're gonna have an abrupt conversation, him and me.

LINDA. You're not talking to him!

[*Hammering is heard from outside the house, off right. BIFF turns toward the noise.*]

LINDA. [*suddenly pleading*] Will you please leave him alone? 795
BIFF. What's he doing out there?
LINDA. He's planting the garden!
BIFF. [*quietly*] Now? Oh, my God!

[*BIFF moves outside, LINDA following. The light dies down on them and comes up on the center of the apron as WILLY walks into it. He is carrying a flashlight, a hoe, and a handful of seed packets. He raps the top of the hoe sharply to fix it firmly, and then moves to the left, measuring off the distance with his foot. He holds the flashlight to look at the seed packets, reading off the instructions. He is in the blue of night.*]

WILLY. Carrots . . . quarter-inch apart. Rows . . . one-foot rows. [*He measures it off.*] One foot. [*He puts down a package and measures off.*] Beets. [*He puts down another package and measures again.*] Lettuce. [*He reads the package, puts it down.*] One foot—[*He breaks off as BEN appears at the right and moves slowly down to him.*] What a proposition, ts, ts. Terrific, terrific. 'Cause she's suffered, Ben, the woman has suffered. You understand me? A man can't go out the way he came in, Ben, a man has got to add up to something. You can't, you can't—[*BEN moves toward him as though to interrupt.*] You gotta consider, now. Don't answer so quick. Remember, it's a guaranteed twenty-thousand-dollar proposition. Now look, Ben, I want you to go through the ins and outs of this thing with me. I've got nobody to talk to, Ben, and the woman has suffered, you hear me?
BEN. [*standing still, considering*] What's the proposition? 800
WILLY. It's twenty thousand dollars on the barrelhead. Guaranteed, gilt-edged, you understand?
BEN. You don't want to make a fool of yourself. They might not honor the policy.
WILLY. How can they dare refuse? Didn't I work like a coolie to meet every premium on the nose? And now they don't pay off? Impossible!
BEN. It's called a cowardly thing, William.
WILLY. Why? Does it take more guts to stand here the rest of my life 805
ringing up a zero?
BEN. [*yielding*] That's a point, William. [*He moves, thinking, turns.*] And twenty thousand—that *is* something one can feel with the hand, it is there.
WILLY. [*now assured, with rising power*] Oh, Ben, that's the whole beauty of it! I see it like a diamond, shining in the dark, hard and rough, that I can pick up and touch in my hand. Not like—like an appointment! This would not be another damned-fool appointment, Ben, and it changes all the aspects. Because he thinks I'm nothing, see, and so he spites me. But the funeral—[*straightening up*] Ben, that funeral will be massive! They'll come from Maine, Massachusetts, Vermont, New Hampshire! All the old-timers with the strange license plates—that boy will be thunder-struck, Ben, because he never realized—I am known! Rhode Island, New York, New Jersey—I am known, Ben, and he'll see it with his eyes once and for all. He'll see what I am, Ben! He's in for a shock, that boy!
BEN. [*coming down to the edge of the garden*] He'll call you a coward.
WILLY. [*suddenly fearful*] No, that would be terrible.
BEN. Yes. And a damned fool. 810
WILLY. No, no, he mustn't, I won't have that! [*He is broken and desperate.*]

BEN.   He'll hate you, William.

[*The gay music of the Boys is heard.*]

WILLY.   Oh, Ben, how do we get back to all the great times? Used to be so full of light, and comradeship, the sleigh-riding in winter, and the ruddiness on his cheeks. And always some kind of good news coming up, always something nice coming up ahead. And never even let me carry the valises in the house, and simonizing, simonizing that little red car! Why, why can't I give him something and not have him hate me?

BEN.   Let me think about it. [*He glances at his watch.*] I still have a little time. Remarkable proposition, but you've got to be sure you're not making a fool of yourself.

[BEN *drifts upstage and goes out of sight.* BIFF *comes down from the left.*]

WILLY.   [*suddenly conscious of* BIFF, *turns and looks up at him, then begins picking up the packages of seeds in confusion*] Where the hell is that seed? [*Indignantly*] You can't see nothing out here! They boxed in the whole goddam neighborhood!   815

BIFF.   There are people all around here. Don't you realize that?

WILLY.   I'm busy. Don't bother me.

BIFF.   [*taking the hoe from* WILLY] I'm saying good-by to you, Pop. [WILLY *looks at him, silent, unable to move.*] I'm not coming back any more.

WILLY.   You're not going to see Oliver tomorrow?

BIFF.   I've got no appointment, Dad.   820

WILLY.   He put his arm around you, and you've got no appointment?

BIFF.   Pop, get this now, will you? Everytime I've left it's been a fight that sent me out of here. Today I realized something about myself and I tried to explain it to you and I—I think I'm just not smart enough to make any sense out of it for you. To hell with whose fault it is or anything like that. [*He takes* WILLY's *arm.*] Let's just wrap it up, heh? Come on in, we'll tell Mom. [*He gently tries to pull* WILLY *to left.*]

WILLY.   [*frozen, immobile, with guilt in his voice*] No, I don't want to see her.

BIFF.   Come on! [*He pulls again, and* WILLY *tries to pull away.*]

WILLY.   [*highly nervous*] No, no, I don't want to see her.   825

BIFF.   [*tries to look into* WILLY's *face, as if to find the answer there*] Why don't you want to see her?

WILLY.   [*more harshly now*] Don't bother me, will you?

BIFF.   What do you mean, you don't want to see her? You don't want them calling you yellow, do you? This isn't your fault; it's me, I'm a bum. Now come inside! [WILLY *strains to get away.*] Did you hear what I said to you?

[WILLY *pulls away and quickly goes by himself into the house.* BIFF *follows.*]

LINDA.   [*to* WILLY] Did you plant, dear?

BIFF.   [*at the door, to* LINDA] All right, we had it out. I'm going and I'm not   830 writing any more.

LINDA.   [*going to* WILLY *in the kitchen*] I think that's the best way, dear. 'Cause there's no use drawing it out, you'll just never get along.

[WILLY *doesn't respond.*]

BIFF.   People ask where I am and what I'm doing, you don't know, and you don't care. That way it'll be off your mind and you can start brightening up again. All right? That clears it, doesn't it? [WILLY *is silent, and* BIFF *goes to him.*] You gonna wish me luck, scout? [*He extends his hand.*] What do you say?

LINDA.   Shake his hand, Willy.

WILLY.   [*turning to her, seething with hurt*] There's no necessity to mention the pen at all, y'know.

BIFF.   [*gently*] I've got no appointment, Dad.   835

WILLY.   [*erupting fiercely*] He put his arm around . . . ?

BIFF.   Dad, you're never going to see what I am, so what's the use of arguing? If I strike oil I'll send you a check. Meantime forget I'm alive.

WILLY.   [*to* LINDA] Spite, see?

BIFF.   Shake hands, Dad.   840

WILLY.   Not my hand.

BIFF.   I was hoping not to go this way.

WILLY.   Well, this is the way you're going. Good-by.

[BIFF *looks at him a moment, then turns sharply and goes to the stairs.*]

WILLY.   [*stops him with*] May you rot in hell if you leave this house!

BIFF.   [*turning*] Exactly what is it that you want from me?

WILLY.   I want you to know, on the train, in the mountains, in the valleys,   845
wherever you go, that you cut down your life for spite!

BIFF.   No, no.

WILLY.   Spite, spite, is the word of your undoing! And when you're down and out, remember what did it. When you're rotting somewhere beside the railroad tracks, remember, and don't you dare blame it on me!

BIFF.   I'm not blaming it on you!

WILLY.   I won't take the rap for this, you hear?

[HAPPY *comes down the stairs and stands on the bottom step, watching.*]

BIFF.   That's just what I'm telling you!   850

WILLY.   [*sinking into a chair at the table, with full accusation*] You're trying to put a knife in me—don't think I don't know what you're doing!

BIFF.   All right, phony! Then let's lay it on the line. [*He whips the rubber tube out of his pocket and puts it on the table.*]

HAPPY.   You crazy—

LINDA.   Biff! [*She moves to grab the hose, but* BIFF *holds it down with his hand.*]

BIFF.   Leave it here! Don't move it!   855

WILLY.   [*not looking at it*] What is that?

BIFF.   You know goddam well what that is.

WILLY.   [*caged, wanting to escape*] I never saw that.

BIFF.   You saw it. The mice didn't bring it into the cellar! What is this supposed to do, make a hero out of you? This supposed to make me sorry for you?

WILLY.   Never heard of it.   860

BIFF.   There'll be no pity for you, you hear it? No pity!

WILLY.   [*to* LINDA] You hear the spite!

BIFF.   No, you're going to hear the truth—what you are and what I am!

LINDA.   Stop it!

WILLY. Spite!   865

HAPPY. [*coming down toward BIFF*] You cut it now!

BIFF. [*to HAPPY*] The man don't know who we are! The man is gonna know! [*to WILLY*] We never told the truth for ten minutes in this house!

HAPPY. We always told the truth!

BIFF. [*turning on him*] You big blow, are you the assistant buyer? You're one of the two assistants to the assistant, aren't you?

HAPPY. Well, I'm practically—   870

BIFF. You're practically full of it! We all are! And I'm through with it. [*to WILLY*] Now hear this, Willy, this is me.

WILLY. I know you!

BIFF. You know why I had no address for three months? I stole a suit in Kansas City and I was in jail. [*to LINDA, who is sobbing*] Stop crying. I'm through with it.

[*LINDA turns from them, her hands covering her face.*]

WILLY. I suppose that's my fault!

BIFF. I stole myself out of every good job since high school!   875

WILLY. And whose fault is that?

BIFF. And I never got anywhere because you blew me so full of hot air I could never stand taking orders from anybody! That's whose fault it is!

WILLY. I hear that!

LINDA. Don't, Biff!

BIFF. It's goddam time you heard that! I had to be boss big shot in two   880 weeks, and I'm through with it!

WILLY. Then hang yourself! For spite, hang yourself!

BIFF. No! Nobody's hanging himself, Willy! I ran down eleven flights with a pen in my hand today. And suddenly I stopped, you hear me? And in the middle of that office building, do you hear this? I stopped in the middle of that building and I saw—the sky. I saw the things that I love in this world. The work and the food and time to sit and smoke. And I looked at the pen and said to myself, what the hell am I grabbing this for? Why am I trying to become what I don't want to be? What am I doing in an office, making a contemptuous, begging fool of myself, when all I want is out there, waiting for me the minute I say I know who I am! Why can't I say that, Willy?

[*He tries to make WILLY face him, but WILLY pulls away and moves to the left.*]

WILLY. [*with hatred, threateningly.*] The door of your life is wide open!

BIFF. Pop! I'm a dime a dozen, and so are you!

WILLY. [*turning on him now in an uncontrolled outburst*] I am not a dime a   885 dozen! I am Willy Loman, and you are Biff Loman!

[*BIFF starts for WILLY, but is blocked by HAPPY. In his fury, BIFF seems on the verge of attacking his father.*]

BIFF. I am not a leader of men, Willy, and neither are you. You were never anything but a hard-working drummer who landed in the ash can like all the rest of them! I'm one dollar an hour, Willy! I tried seven states and couldn't raise it. A buck an hour! Do you gather my meaning? I'm not bringing home any prizes any more, and you're going to stop waiting for me to bring them home!

WILLY. [*directly to* BIFF] You vengeful, spiteful mut!

[BIFF *breaks from* HAPPY. WILLY, *in fright, starts up the stairs.* BIFF *grabs him.*]

BIFF. [*at the peak of his fury*] Pop I'm nothing! I'm nothing, Pop. Can't you understand that? There's no spite in it any more. I'm just what I am, that's all.

[BIFF'*s fury has spent itself, and he breaks down, sobbing, holding on to* WILLY, *who dumbly fumbles for* BIFF'*s face.*]

WILLY. [*astonished*] What're you doing? What're you doing? [*to* LINDA] Why is he crying?

BIFF. [*crying, broken*] Will you let me go, for Christ's sake? Will you take   890
that phony dream and burn it before something happens? [*Struggling to contain himself, he pulls away and moves to the stairs.*] I'll go in the morning. Put him—put him to bed. [*Exhausted,* BIFF *moves up the stairs to his room.*]

WILLY. [*after a long pause, astonished, elevated*] Isn't that—isn't that remarkable? Biff—he likes me!

LINDA. He loves you, Willy!

HAPPY. [*deeply moved*] Always did, Pop.

WILLY. Oh, Biff! [*staring wildly*] He cried! Cried to me. [*He is choking with his love, and now cries out his promise.*] That boy—that boy is going to be magnificent!

[BEN *appears in the light just outside the kitchen.*]

BEN. Yes, outstanding, with twenty thousand behind him.   895

LINDA. [*sensing the racing of his mind, fearfully, carefully*] Now come to bed, Willy. It's all settled now.

WILLY. [*finding it difficult not to rush out of the house*] Yes, we'll sleep. Come on. Go to sleep, Hap.

BEN. And it does take a great kind of a man to crack the jungle.

[*In accents of dread,* BEN'*s idyllic music starts up.*]

HAPPY. [*his arm around* LINDA] I'm getting married, Pop, don't forget it. I'm changing everything. I'm gonna run that department before the year is up. You'll see, Mom. [*He kisses her.*]

BEN. The jungle is dark but full of diamonds, Willy.   900

[WILLY *turns, moves, listening to* BEN.]

LINDA. Be good. You're both good boys, just act that way, that's all.

HAPPY. 'Night, Pop. [*He goes upstairs.*]

LINDA. [*to* WILLY] Come, dear.

BEN. [*with greater force*] One must go in to fetch a diamond out.

WILLY. [*to* LINDA, *as he moves slowly along the edge of the kitchen, toward the*   905
door] I just want to get settled down, Linda. Let me sit alone for a little.

LINDA. [*almost uttering her fear*] I want you upstairs.

WILLY. [*taking her in his arms*] In a few minutes, Linda. I couldn't sleep right now. Go on, you look awful tired. [*He kisses her.*]

BEN. Not like an appointment at all. A diamond is rough and hard to the touch.

WILLY. Go on now. I'll be right up.

LINDA. I think this is the only way, Willy.   910

WILLY.   Sure, it's the best thing.

BEN.   Best thing!

WILLY.   The only way. Everything is gonna be—go on, kid, get to bed. You look so tired.

LINDA.   Come right up.

WILLY.   Two minutes.   915

[*LINDA goes into the living-room, then reappears in her bedroom. WILLY moves just outside the kitchen door.*]

WILLY.   Loves me. [*wonderingly*] Always loved me. Isn't that a remarkable thing? Ben, he'll worship me for it!

BEN.   [*with promise*] It's dark there, but full of diamonds.

WILLY.   Can you imagine that magnificence with twenty thousand dollars in his pocket?

LINDA.   [*calling from her room*] Willy! Come up!

WILLY.   [*calling into the kitchen*] Yes! Yes. Coming! It's very smart, you   920
realize that, don't you, sweetheart? Even Ben sees it. I gotta go, baby. 'By! 'By! [*going over to BEN, almost dancing*] Imagine? When the mail comes he'll be ahead of Bernard again!

BEN.   A perfect proposition all around.

WILLY.   Did you see how he cried to me? Oh, if I could kiss him, Ben!

BEN.   Time, William, time!

WILLY.   Oh, Ben, I always knew one way or another we were gonna make it, Biff and I!

BEN.   [*looking at his watch*] The boat. We'll be late. [*He moves slowly off into*   925
the darkness.]

WILLY.   [*elegiacally, turning to the house*] Now when you kick off, boy, I want a seventy-yard boot, and get right down the field under the ball, and when you hit, hit low and hit hard, because it's important, boy. [*He swings around and faces the audience.*] There's all kinds of important people in the stands, and the first thing you know . . . [*suddenly realizing he is alone*] Ben! Ben, where do I . . . ? [*He makes a sudden movement of search.*] Ben, how do I . . . ?

LINDA.   [*calling*] Willy, you coming up?

WILLY.   [*uttering a gasp of fear, whirling about as if to quiet her*] Sh! [*He turns around as if to find his way; sounds, faces, voices, seem to be swarming in upon him and he flicks at them, crying*] Sh! Sh! [*Suddenly music, faint and high, stops him. It rises in intensity, almost to an unbearable scream. He goes up and down on his toes, and rushes off around the house.*] Shhh!

LINDA.   Willy?

[*There is no answer. LINDA waits. BIFF gets up off his bed. He is still in his clothes. HAPPY sits up. BIFF stands listening.*]

LINDA.   [*with real fear*] Willy, answer me! Willy!   930

[*There is the sound of a car starting and moving away at full speed.*]

LINDA.   No!

BIFF.   [*rushing down the stairs*] Pop!

[*As the car speeds off, the music crashes down in a frenzy of sound, which becomes the soft pulsation of a single cello string. BIFF slowly returns to his bedroom. He and HAPPY gravely don their jackets. LINDA slowly walks out of her room. The music has developed into a dead march. The leaves of day are appearing over everything. CHARLEY and BERNARD somberly dressed, appear and knock on the kitchen door. BIFF and HAPPY slowly descend the stairs to the kitchen as CHARLEY and BERNARD enter. All stop a moment when LINDA, in clothes of mourning, bearing a little bunch of roses, comes through the draped doorway into the kitchen. She goes to CHARLEY and takes his arm. Now all move toward the audience, through the wall-line of the kitchen. At the limit of the apron, LINDA lays down the flowers, kneels, and sits back on her heels. All stare down at the grave.]*

REQUIEM

CHARLEY. It's getting dark, Linda.

[*LINDA doesn't react. She stares at the grave.*]

BIFF. How about it, Mom? Better get some rest, heh? They'll be closing the gate soon.

[*LINDA makes no move. Pause.*]

HAPPY. [*deeply angered*] He had no right to do that. There was no necessity for it. We would've helped him.

CHARLEY. [*grunting*] Hmmm.

BIFF. Come along, Mom.   5

LINDA. Why didn't anybody come?

CHARLEY. It was a very nice funeral.

LINDA. But where are all the people he knew? Maybe they blame him.

CHARLEY. Naa. It's a rough world, Linda. They wouldn't blame him.

LINDA. I can't understand it. At this time especially. First time in thirty-   10
five years we were just about free and clear. He only needed a little salary. He was even finished with the dentist.

CHARLEY. No man only needs a little salary.

LINDA. I can't understand it.

BIFF. There were a lot of nice days. When he'd come home from a trip; or on Sundays, making the stoop; finishing the cellar; putting on the new porch; when he built the extra bathroom; and put up the garage. You know something, Charley, there's more of him in that front stoop than in all the sales he ever made.

CHARLEY. Yeah. He was a happy man with a batch of cement.

LINDA. He was so wonderful with his hands.   15

BIFF. He had all the wrong dreams. All, all, wrong.

HAPPY. [*almost ready to fight BIFF*] Don't say that!

BIFF. He never knew who he was.

CHARLEY. [*stopping HAPPY's movement and reply. To BIFF*] Nobody dast blame this man. You don't understand. Willy was a salesman. And for a salesman, there is no rock bottom to the life. He don't put a bolt to a nut, he don't tell you the law or give you medicine. He's a man way out there in the blue, riding on a smile and a shoeshine. And when they start not smiling back—that's an earthquake. And then you get yourself a couple of spots on your hat, and you're finished.

Nobody dast blame this man. A salesman is got to dream, boy. It comes with the territory.

BIFF. Charley, the man didn't know who he was. 20

HAPPY. [*infuriated*] Don't say that!

BIFF. Why don't you come with me, Happy?

HAPPY. I'm not licked that easily. I'm staying right in this city, and I'm gonna beat this racket! [*He looks at* BIFF, *his chin set.*] The Loman Brothers!

BIFF. I know who I am, kid.

HAPPY. All right, boy. I'm gonna show you and everybody else that Willy 25 Loman did not die in vain. He had a good dream. It's the only dream you can have—to come out number-one man. He fought it out here, and this is where I'm gonna win it for him.

BIFF. [*with a hopeless glance at* HAPPY, *bends toward his mother*] Let's go, Mom.

LINDA. I'll be with you in a minute. Go on, Charley. [*He hesitates.*] I want to, just for a minute. I never had a chance to say good-by.

[CHARLEY *moves away, followed by* HAPPY. BIFF *remains a slight distance up and left of* LINDA. *She sits there, summoning herself. The flute begins, not far away, playing behind her speech.*]

LINDA. Forgive me, dear. I can't cry. I don't know what it is, but I can't cry. I don't understand it. Why did you ever do that? Help me, Willy, I can't cry. It seems to me that you're just on another trip. I keep expecting you. Willy, dear, I can't cry. Why did you do it? I search and search and I search, and I can't understand it, Willy. I made the last payment on the house today. Today, dear. And there'll be nobody home. [*A sob rises in her throat.*] We're free and clear. [*sobbing more fully, released*] We're free. [BIFF *comes slowly toward her.*] We're free . . . We're free . . .

[BIFF *lifts her to her feet and moves out up right with her in his arms.* LINDA *sobs quietly.* BERNARD *and* CHARLEY *come together and follow them, followed by* HAPPY. *Only the music of the flute is left on the darkening stage as over the house the hard towers of the apartment buildings rise into sharp focus, and*

The curtain falls.]

QUESTIONS

Act I

1. What do you learn about Willy from the first stage direction?

2. What instances of stealing are in the play? Why do Biff and Happy steal? Where did they learn about stealing? How is stealing related to salesmanship?

3. In Act I Willy claims that "I never in my life told him [Biff] anything but decent things." Is this assertion true? What does it show you about Willy?

Act II and Requiem

4. What does Willy's difficulty with machines—especially his car, the refrigerator, and Howard's wire recorder—suggest about him? To what extent are these machines symbolic?

5. When Willy sees Bernard in Charley's office, he asks, "What—what's the secret?" What secret is he asking about? Does such a secret exist?

6. In Act II Willy buys seeds and tries to plant a garden at night. Why is Willy so disturbed that "nothing's planted" and "I don't have a thing in the ground"? What do this garden and having "things in the ground" mean to Willy?

7. In Act II, speech 267, Biff claims that "we never told the truth for ten minutes in this house!" What does he mean? To what extent is he right?

8. Linda's last line in the play—"We're free . . . we're free"—seems to refer to the house mortgage. In what other ways, however, might you take it?

GENERAL QUESTIONS

1. How does Miller use lighting, the set, blocking, and music to differentiate between action in the present and "memory" action?

2. The stage directions are full of information that cannot be played. In describing Happy, for example, Miller notes that "sexuality is like a color on him." What is the function of such stage directions?

3. How is Willy's suicide foreshadowed throughout the play? To what extent does this foreshadowing create tension?

4. Which characters are "real" and which are "hallucinations" that spring from Willy's memory? What are the major differences between these two groups?

5. Which characters are symbolic and what do they symbolize?

6. Describe the character of Willy Loman. What are his good qualities? In what ways does he have heroic stature? What are his bad qualities? To what extent is his "fall" the result of his flaws, and to what extent is it caused by circumstances beyond his control?

7. How is the relationship between Charley and Bernard different from the one between Willy and his sons? Why is this difference important?

8. Discuss Linda's character and role. In what ways is she supportive of Willy? In what ways does she encourage his deceptions and self-delusions?

9. What sort of person is Happy? What has he inherited from Willy? How is he a debasement of Willy? To what degree is he successful or happy?

10. Willy claims that success in business is based not on "what you do" but on "who you know and the smile on your face! It's contacts. . . . a man can end up with diamonds on the basis of being well liked." How does the play support or reject this assertion?

11. Most of Willy's memories—Ben's visit, Boston, the football game—are from 1928. Why does Willy's memory return to 1928? Why is the contrast between 1928 and the present significant for Willy and for the play as a whole?

WRITING ABOUT TRAGEDY

As you plan and write an essay about tragedy, keep in mind all the elements of drama. A full discussion of traditional approaches to these elements—plot, character, point of view, setting, language, tone, symbol, and theme—can be found in Chapter 25 (pp. 993–1001). Review this material before you begin your essay.

While the basic elements remain consistent in tragedy, the form also requires a few special considerations. In planning and writing about tragedy, think about the following questions to help you focus your ideas.

Questions for Discovering Ideas

Plot and conflict: At what point does the downfall become inevitable (the crisis/climax)? Explore this point in detail. To what degree do the conflicts shape or accelerate the tragic action?

Character: What is the connection between the protagonist's strengths and weaknesses? To what extent does the protagonist bring on or cooperate with his or her own destruction? What key characteristics and behavior patterns ensure both the protagonist's heroic stature and fall? Pay special attention to the protagonist in relation to the major antagonists.

Tone: To what degree is the play ironic? Do you know more about what is going on than the protagonist? Than most of the characters? If so, how does this knowledge affect the play's impact and meaning?

All the traditional elements of drama, along with the special considerations just noted, can provide fruitful areas of investigation for planning and writing an essay about tragic drama. In the remainder of this discussion, however, we are going to introduce two new ways of writing about literature: an examination of a problem and a close reading of a passage. Both of these approaches have universal application. They can be employed to write about prose fiction, poetry, or any type of dramatic literature. Our discussion will naturally focus on tragedy—specifically *Hamlet*—and the plays in which problem solving and close reading can generate effective essays about tragic drama. Keep in mind, however, that both approaches work well in writing about any kind of literature.

AN ESSAY ABOUT A PROBLEM

A **problem** is any question you cannot answer easily and correctly about a body of material that you know. The question, "Who is the major character in *Hamlet*?" is not a problem, because the obvious answer is Hamlet.

Let us, however, ask another question: "Why is it *correct* to say that Hamlet is the major character?" This question is not as easy as the first, and for this reason it is a problem. It requires that we think about our answer, even though we do not need to search very far. Hamlet is the title character. He is involved in most of the actions of the play. He is so much the center of our liking and concern that his death causes sadness and regret. To "solve" this problem has required a set of responses, all of which provide answers to the question "why?" With variation, most readers of Shakespeare's play would likely be satisfied with these answers.

More complex, however, and more typical of most problems, are questions like these: "Why does Hamlet talk of suicide in his first soliloquy?" "Why does he treat Ophelia so coarsely in the 'nunnery' scene?" "Why does he delay in avenging his father's death?" It is with questions like these that essays on a problem are normally concerned. Simple factual responses do not answer such questions. A good deal of thought, together with a number of interpretations knitted together into a whole essay, is required.

The Usefulness of Problem Solving

The process of framing and then solving problems is one of the most valuable tools that you can bring to any text. You will encounter many problems and questions in classroom discussions, but you should also make it your regular task to ask and answer your own questions. Developing your answers will take you creatively into understanding that you do not anticipate at first. If you carry out this question-answer process, you will find that you are constantly isolating key issues, testing possible solutions, and organizing your thinking.

The first step in planning an essay on a problem is choosing an appropriate problem and framing a tentative solution. These processes need not be difficult. Most works of literature offer a multitude of problems that can be solved or explained in a number of ways. The problem, of course, should be of some significance. This can be a difficult distinction; your best guide is your own sense of what needs explaining in the play. The problem (or question) of why Claudius murders his brother would not generate an effective essay because the solution is too obvious. A more fruitful question might be why Rosencrantz and Guildenstern cooperate with Claudius and become spies. While the solution to this problem may seem obvious, you should consider not only motivation, but also circumstances and the degree to which these men understand what is going on in Denmark.

Strategies for Organizing Ideas

The first purpose in an essay about a problem is to convince your reader that your solution is a good one. This you do by making sound conclusions from supporting evidence. In nonscientific subjects like literature you rarely find absolute proofs, so your conclusions will not be *proved* in the way you prove triangles congruent. But your organization, your use of facts from the text, your interpretations, and your application of general or specific knowledge should all make your conclusions convincing. Your basic strategy is thus *persuasion*.

Because problems and solutions change with works, each essay on a problem is different from any other. Despite these differences, however, you may adapt a number of common strategies. You might use one or more of these, keeping in mind that your goal is to solve your problem in the most direct, convenient way.

STRATEGY 1: DEMONSTRATE THAT CONDITIONS FOR A SOLUTION ARE FULFILLED. In effect, this development is the most basic in writing—namely, illustration. You first explain that certain conditions need to exist for your solution to be plausible. Your central idea—really a brief answer to the question—is that the conditions do indeed exist. Your development is to show how the conditions may be found in the work.

Suppose that you are writing on the problem of why Hamlet delays revenge against his uncle, Claudius. Suppose that, in your introduction, you make the point that Hamlet delays because he is never sure that Claudius is guilty. This is your "solution" to the problem. In your essay you support your answer by showing the flimsiness of the information Hamlet receives about the crime (i.e., the two visits from the Ghost and Claudius's distress at the play within the play). Once you have "attacked" these sources of data on the grounds that they are unreliable, you have succeeded because your solution is consistent with the details of the play.

STRATEGY 2: ANALYZE WORDS IN THE PHRASING OF THE PROBLEM. Another good approach is to explore the meaning and limits of important words or phrases in the question. Your object is to clarify the words and show how applicable they are. You may wish to define the words and to show whether they have any special meaning.

Such attention to words might give you enough material for all or part of your essay. Thus, an essay on the problem of Hamlet's delay might focus on a treatment of the word *delay*: What, really, does *delay* mean? For Hamlet, is there a difference between reasonable and unreasonable delay? Does Hamlet delay unreasonably? Is his delay the result of a psychological fault? Would speedy revenge be more or less reasonable than the delay? By the time you answer such pointed questions, you will also have written a goodly portion of your full essay.

STRATEGY 3: REFER TO LITERARY CONVENTIONS OR EXPECTATIONS. What appears to be a problem can often be treated as a normal characteristic, given the particular work you are studying. In this light, the best argument is to establish that the problem can be solved by reference to the literary mode or conventions of a work, or to the work's own self-limitations. A problem about the artificiality of the choruses in *Oedipus the King*, for example, might be resolved by reference to the fact that choruses were a normal feature of Greek drama. In a similar manner, the knowledge that delay is a convention of all revenge tragedy might provide a key to the problem of Hamlet's apparent procrastination. Similarly, a question about the differing functions of Tom in *The Glass Menagerie* (pp. 1474–1524) can be explained by the free use that Tennessee Williams makes of nonrealistic stage conventions.

Strategy 4: Argue Against Possible Objections. With this strategy, you raise your own objections and then argue against them. This strategy, called **procatalepsis** or **anticipation,** helps you sharpen your arguments, for *anticipating* and dealing with objections forces you to make analyses and use facts that you might otherwise overlook. Although procatalepsis may be used point by point throughout your essay, you may find it most useful at the end.

The situation to imagine is that someone is raising objections to your solution to the problem. It is then your task to show that the objections (1) are not accurate or valid, (2) are not strong or convincing, or (3) are based on unusual rather than usual conditions (on an exception and not the rule). Here are some examples of these approaches. The objections raised are underlined, so that you can easily distinguish them from the answers.

1. *The objection is not accurate or valid.* Here you reject the objection by showing that either the interpretation or the conclusions are wrong and also by emphasizing that the evidence supports your solution.

> Although Hamlet's delay is reasonable, the claim might be made that his duty is to kill Claudius in revenge immediately after the Ghost's accusations. This claim is not persuasive because it assumes that Hamlet knows everything the audience knows. The audience accepts the Ghost's word that Claudius is guilty, but from Hamlet's position there is every reason to doubt the Ghost and not to act. Would it not seem foolish and insane for Hamlet to kill Claudius, who is king legally, and then to claim that he did it because the Ghost told him to do so? The argument for speedy revenge is not good, because it is based on an incorrect view of Hamlet's situation.

2. *The objection is not strong or convincing.* Here you *concede* that the objection has some truth or validity, but you then try to show that it is weak and that your own solution is stronger.

> One might claim that Claudius's distress at the play within the play is evidence for his guilt and that therefore Hamlet should carry out his revenge right away. This argument has merit, and Hamlet's speech after Claudius has fled the scene ("I'll take the Ghost's word for a thousand pound") shows that the "conscience of the king" has been caught. But the king's guilty behavior is not a strong cause for killing him. Hamlet could justifiably ask for an investigation of his father's death on these grounds, but he could not justify a revenge killing. Claudius could not be convicted in any court on the testimony that he was disturbed at seeing the Murder of Gonzago. Even after the play within the play, the reasons for delay are stronger than for action.

3. *The objection is based on unusual rather than usual conditions.* Here you reject the objection on the grounds that it could be valid only if normal conditions were suspended. The objection depends on an exception, not a rule.

> The case for quick action is simple: Hamlet should kill Claudius right after seeing the Ghost (I.3), or else after seeing the King's reaction to the stage murder of Gonzago (III.2) or else after seeing the Ghost again (III.4). This argument wrongly assumes that due process does not exist in the Denmark of Hamlet and Claudius. Redress under these circumstances, goes the argument, must be both personal and extralegal. However, the fact is that Hamlet's Denmark is a civilized place where legality and the rules of evidence are precious. Thus, Hamlet cannot rush out to kill Claudius, because he knows that the King has not had anything close to due process. The argument for quick action is poor because it rests on an exception being made from civilized law.

You might wish to combine several of these strategies in your essay. Thus, if we assume that your argument is that Hamlet's delay is reasonable, you might first consider the word *delay* (strategy 2). Then you might use strategy 1 to explain the reasons Hamlet does delay. Finally, to answer objections to your argument, you might show that he acts when he feels justified in acting (strategy 4).

Remember that writing an essay on a problem requires you to argue a position: Either there is a solution or there is not. To develop your position requires that you show the steps to your conclusion. Your general thematic form is thus (1) a description of the conditions that need to be met for the solution you propose, and then (2) a demonstration that these conditions exist. If you assert that there is no solution, then your form would be the same for the first part, but your second part—the development—would show that these conditions have *not* been met.

In the essay's conclusion, affirm the validity of your solution in view of the supporting evidence. You might do this by reemphasizing your strongest points, or you might simply present a brief summary. Or you might think of your argument as still continuing and thus use the strategy of procatalepsis to raise and answer possible objections to your solution, as in the last paragraph of the sample essay.

SAMPLE ESSAY

The Problem of Hamlet's Apparent Delay in Shakespeare's *Hamlet*°

For hundreds of years, readers and spectators of Shakespeare's *Hamlet* have been puzzled by the Prince's failure to take quick action against Claudius. Early in the play, the ghost calls on his son to "Revenge his foul and

° See p. 1101 for this play.

[1] most unnatural murder" (I.5.25). Hamlet, however, waits until the end of the play to gain his vengeance. This is the problem: how can we account for Hamlet's delay? The solution is found in a demonstration that there is no unjustified delay and that Hamlet acts as quickly as possible at almost every point.* This becomes evident when we examine the conventions of revenge tragedy, the actual "call to revenge," and the steps that Hamlet takes to achieve vengeance.†

[2] Revenge tragedy conventionally requires that vengeance be delayed until the closing moments of the play. Given this limitation, Shakespeare had to justify the wide gap of time between the call to revenge in Act I and the killing of Claudius in Act V. We find such justification in the unreliability of the ghost's initial accusation, Hamlet's need for additional evidence, and the events that occur after this evidence is obtained.

[3] The ghost's accusations and demands are straightforward: He accuses his brother of murdering him and he calls on his son for vengeance. Shakespeare is careful, however, to establish that this testimony is not necessarily to be trusted. Horatio voices doubts about the ghost's veracity and motives; he warns Hamlet that the spirit might "assume some other horrid form / Which might deprive your sovereignty of reason, / And draw you into madness" (I.4.72–74). Hamlet himself questions the ghost's reliability:

> The spirit that I have seen
> may be a devil, and the devil hath power
> T'assume a pleasing shape, yea, and perhaps
> Out of my weakness, and my melancholy
> As he is very potent with such spirits,
> Abuses me to damn me; I'll have grounds
> More relative than this.   (II.2.573–79)

The prince thus cannot act simply on the unsupported word of the ghost; he needs more evidence.

[4] There is no delay at this point in the play; Hamlet quickly begins to develop ways to gain corroboration. Immediately after speaking with the ghost, he decides to use pretended madness as a "cover" for his investigation. He swears his companions to silence and warns them not to react knowingly if he subsequently appears to be mad:

> . . . never so help you mercy,
> How strange or odd some'er I bear myself,
> (As I perchance hereafter shall think meet
> To put an antic disposition on)
> That you at such times seeing me, never shall
> . . . note
> That you know aught of me   (I.5.169–79)

---

* Central idea.
† Thesis sentence.

By the close of Act I Hamlet has already mapped out a campaign to gain further information by taking on an "antic disposition." He assumes that such a pose will make him less suspect and make others less careful.

[5] When we next encounter Hamlet, he has already established his "antic disposition" with most of the court. Polonius, for example, is convinced that the prince is "mad" for love and tells Claudius that "I have found / The very cause of Hamlet's lunacy" (II.2.48–49). In the soliloquy that ends Act II, the prince tells us exactly how he plans to test Claudius:

> I'll have these players
> Play something like the murder of my father
> Before mine uncle, I'll observe his looks,
> I'll tent him to the quick, if a' do blench
> I know my course. (II.2.569–73)

Again, we find no delay in Hamlet's behavior. Once a method of testing the ghost's charges is developed, it is put to use immediately. Hamlet tells the First Player that "We'll ha't [the play] tomorrow night" (II.2.515).

[6] "The Mousetrap" provides the information Hamlet needs to proceed with his vengeance. The king interrupts the performance immediately after the villain pours poison into the ears of the player-king: a reenactment of Claudius's original crime. Now Hamlet has corroborating evidence; he says, "I'll take the ghost's word for a thousand pound" (III.2.271–72). Moreover, he is psychologically ready to act against the king, for he asserts that he could "drink hot blood, / And do such bitter business as the day / Would quake to look on" (III.2.367–69). Hamlet even has a chance to gain revenge. In the very next scene Claudius is unguarded and appears to be praying. When Hamlet enters and sees this unexpected opportunity, he determines to act: "Now might I do it pat, now a' is a-praying, / And now I'll do't" (III.3.73–74).

[7] Hamlet has motive, means, evidence, and opportunity, but does not act. Here--and only here--one might accuse him of delay. Again, however, Shakespeare is careful to justify Hamlet's hesitancy. The prince does not want to send the soul of Claudius to heaven by killing him while he is in such a state of grace. Rather, he wants the revenge to match the cruel way in which Claudius killed old king Hamlet without giving him a chance to repent his sins:

> Up sword, and know thou a more horrid hent,
> When he is drunk asleep, or in his rage,
> Or in th'incestuous pleasure of his bed,
> At game, a-swearing, or about some act
> That has no relish of salvation in't,
> Then trip him that his heels may kick at heaven,
> And that his soul may be as damned and black
> As hell whereto it goes. (III.3.88–95)

Hamlet's decision to defer revenge here is in keeping with the peculiar "justice" of personal blood vengeance. The retribution must match or exceed the original crime.

[8] From this point on, there is no question of delay. Rather, Hamlet acts or reacts to every situation as the opportunity presents itself. During his confrontation with Gertrude, for example, he hears a noise behind the arras and instantly stabs the eavesdropper. He hopes that Claudius is his victim. When the spy turns out to be Polonius, Hamlet's quest for vengeance becomes more difficult. The murder of Polonius lets the king know that Hamlet is perfectly sane and trying to kill him. As a result, Claudius begins a counterplot that makes it impossible for Hamlet to act. He had already decided to send Hamlet off to England and execution; he now determines to send the prince away at dawn that very day. Thus, Hamlet has no further opportunity to act before he is sent to England "under guard."

[9] Hamlet leaves the court in Act IV and does not return until Act V. In the interval, he works with speed and cunning to escape the intended execution and to return to Denmark. When he encounters Claudius at Ophelia's funeral, the king is guarded and surrounded by attendants. Again, Hamlet is forced by circumstances to wait. He makes it clear to Horatio, however, that he will seize the next opportunity; he asserts that "the readiness is all" (V.2.205). This is followed immediately by the rigged fencing match and the bloodbath that ends the play. Hamlet finally gains revenge by stabbing and poisoning the king.

[10] Thus, we see the problem of Hamlet's delay is really no problem at all. The prince acts in accordance with the internal "justice" of revenge as quickly as circumstances permit once he is satisfied that the ghost's accusations are true. Although the text of the play supports this solution, critics might still argue that procrastination is an issue because Hamlet twice accuses himself of delay. Such an objection does not take into consideration that Hamlet's perception of time and action is distorted by his eagerness for vengeance. From Hamlet's subjective point of view, any break in activity is delay. From our objective viewpoint, however, delay is finally not an issue.

Commentary on the Essay

The introductory paragraph raises the problem of Hamlet's apparent delay and offers a brief statement of the solution (the central idea). The thesis sentence outlines the steps of the argument that will validate the solution and it provides an overall plan for the essay.

This plan is developed in paragraphs 2 through 9 in exactly the same order in which the issues are raised in the introduction. Paragraph 2 deals with the conventions of revenge tragedy, and paragraph 3 takes up the reliability of the ghost. Paragraphs 4 through 6 deal with Hamlet's attempts to corroborate the ghost's accusations, and paragraphs 7, 8, and 9 consider the subsequent action. Note that each paragraph in the argument grows naturally out of the one that precedes it just as all the paragraphs are linked back to the introductory paragraph.

The concluding paragraph asserts that the original problem is solved; the paragraph then summarizes the steps of the solution. It also continues the argument by raising and then dealing with a possible objection to the proposed solution.

The general structure of the essay illustrates strategy 1 described on pages 1279–81. The second paragraph, however, makes brief use of strategy 3 in its reference to the conventions of revenge tragedy. Finally, the concluding paragraph offers an example of *procatalepsis*, or strategy 4.

AN ESSAY ON A CLOSE READING OF A PASSAGE

An essay on a close reading is a detailed study of a passage of prose or verse that may be part of a longer work—in this chapter, a play—or it may be an entire short poem. The close-reading essay is specific because it focuses on the selected passage. It is also general because you do not focus on a single topic (such as *character, setting,* or *theme*), but rather deal with *all* the elements to be found in the passage. If the passage describes a person, for example, you must discuss character, but your emphasis should be on what the passage itself brings out about the character. *The passage dictates the content of your essay.*

In planning an essay on a close reading of a passage from a play, your first step is to isolate several important passages and explore their significance to the play as a whole. You may find that specific passages relate most clearly to the character, tone, theme, or some other element. In these instances, you can direct your exploration along these lines. At an early point in prewriting, you can choose a specific passage and begin to consider both its meaning and its significance in the larger context of the play.

During this stage of prewriting, focus on the general meaning and impact of the passage. Who speaks it? What is it about? What does it tell you about the speaker or the world of the play? Once these issues are clear, develop a set of notes on your observations that can be organized later into paragraphs. Try to reach some specific and focused conclusions about the passage: Does it (1) describe a scene, (2) develop a character, (3) present an action, (4) reveal a character's thoughts, (5) advance an argument, or (6) introduce an idea? What is the thematic content of the passage? In this respect, how does it relate to earlier and later parts of the whole text? (To deal with this question, you may assume that your reader is familiar with the entire work.) Following are some obvious points to consider while you develop your materials.

Strategies for Organizing Ideas

For an Early Passage. For an early passage, you may expect that the author is setting things in motion (exposition, complication). Thus, you should try to determine how themes, characterizations, and arguments in the passage are related to later developments. Always assume that everything is there for a purpose, and then find that purpose.

FOR A LATER, MIDPOINT PASSAGE.   For a passage close to the midpoint of the play, a character's fortunes may be taking either an expected or an unexpected turn. If the change is unexpected, you should explain how the passage focuses the various themes or ideas and then propels them toward the forthcoming crisis/climax (the turning point or high point). It may be that the work features surprises, and the passage thus acquires a different meaning on second reading. Or it may be that the speaker has one set of assumptions while the readers have others, and that the passage marks a point of increasing self-awareness on the part of the speaker. Any part of any work is part of a whole, and it is therefore your task to determine the extent to which the passage (1) builds on what has happened previously, and (2) prepares the way for the outcome of the work.

FOR A CONCLUDING PASSAGE.   You may assume that a passage at or near the end of the work is designed to solve problems or to be a focal point or climax for all the situations and ideas that have been building up. You will need to show how the passage brings together all details, ideas, and themes. What is happening? Is any action described in the passage a major action, or a step leading to the major action? Has everything in the passage been prepared for earlier, or are there any surprises?

In an essay of this type, begin by quoting the entire passage just as it appears in the text. It is also helpful to number the lines for easy reference. Because the close-reading essay is concerned with details, you might have a problem developing a thematic structure. You can overcome this difficulty if you begin to work with either a generalization about the passage or a thesis based on the relationship of the passage to the work. Suppose, for example, that the passage is factually descriptive or that it introduces a major character or raises a major idea. Any one of these observations may serve as a thesis.

Develop the body of the essay according to what you find in the passage. If, for example, you have a passage of character description you might analyze what is said about the character, together with a comparison of how this information is modified later. In addition, you might consider how the characteristics described affect other characters or later events in the work. If the passage introduces a theme, you might demonstrate how the idea is established in the passage and then developed throughout the work. The aim here is to focus on details in the passage and also on the relationship of these details to the entire work.

The conclusion of your essay may summarize your argument and bring it to an effective close. In addition, you may use the conclusion to deal with secondary issues that arise in the passage but do not merit full consideration. There may be specific phrases or underlying assumptions, for example, that are found in the passage. The conclusion is the place for you to mention these concerns.

SAMPLE ESSAY

Appearance and Reality in Shakespeare's *Hamlet*:°
A Close Reading of *Hamlet*, I.2.76–86.

Seems, madam? nay it is. I know not "seems."	76
'Tis not alone my inky cloak good mother,	77
Nor customary suits of solemn black,	78
Nor windy suspiration of forced breath,	79
No, nor the fruitful river of the eye,	80
Nor the dejected havior of the visage,	81
Together with all forms, moods, shapes of grief,	82
That can denote me truly: these indeed seem,	83
For they are actions, that a man might play,	84
But I have that within which passes show,	85
These but the trappings and the suits of woe.	86

[1] This passage from Shakespeare's *Hamlet* is spoken by the prince during his first appearance on stage in Act I. Gertrude--his mother--has just tried to convince Hamlet that death is "common" to all humanity and that he "seems" to be taking his father's death too much to heart. Hamlet's entire speech grows out of Gertrude's use of the word "seems." In this passage, Shakespeare introduces one of the play's central ideas--that there is a difference between appearance and reality.* This concept is stated directly in the first line, is amplified in the rest of the passage, and shows up repeatedly throughout the play in the ways characters present themselves and in the actions they perform.†

[2] The discrepancy between appearance and reality is introduced explicitly in Hamlet's first line: "Seems, madam? nay, it is." In this statement, Hamlet opposes "seems" to "is." Thus, he introduces a direct contrast between those things that seem to be and those that actually exist. This explicit opposition of illusion or appearance ("seems") and reality ("is") becomes the cornerstone for the rest of the passage.

Hamlet expands on the idea of a difference between appearance and reality in lines 77–86 with reference to the outward trappings of mourning. He begins by listing five of the traditional signs of grief: an "inky cloak" (77); "suits of solemn black" (78); sighs, or the "windy suspiration of forced breath" (79); tears, or "the fruitful river of the eye" (80); and sad looks, or "the dejected

° See p. 1101 for this play.
* Central idea.
† Thesis sentence.

[3] [be]havior of the visage" (81). Having listed these items, Hamlet goes on to identify them in three separate lines as the outward displays of mourning. First, he calls them the "forms, moods, shapes of grief" (82). In line 84 he also notes that "they are actions that a man might play." And in line 86 he labels this list as "the trappings [costumes] and the suits of woe." These three lines thus show that the five signs of grief are all outward shows. Appearance (as opposed to reality) is especially emphasized in the words forms, shapes, play, and trappings. Finally, Hamlet brings his speech to its logical climax and conclusion by contrasting all these appearances of grief with his own real and internal feelings: "I have that within which [sur]passes show" (line 85). Again, we have the direct contrast between appearance ("show") and reality ("that within").

[4] The idea raised in this passage is central to our understanding of *Hamlet;* the difference between appearance and reality shows up repeatedly in characters and situations throughout the play. Claudius, for example, appears to be a loving uncle, a good king, and a reasonable man. He is actually a murderer and a usurper who fears Hamlet and plots continually against him. Rosencrantz and Guildenstern put on the appearance of innocent school friends, but they are actually tools of Claudius, and they willingly spy on Hamlet. We find a similar discrepancy between the appearance and the reality of actions and events. In Act III, for example, Claudius appears to be praying for forgiveness and repenting his crimes. In actuality, however, he can neither pray nor repent because he is "still possessed / Of those effects for which I did the murder" (III.3.53–54). Similarly, the duel between Hamlet and Laertes seems to be a straightforward fencing match but is actually a complicated trap by which Claudius plans to have Hamlet killed by sword or poison.

[5] On its primary level, therefore, Hamlet's speech clearly contains his assertions about the depth of his own grief. But on further analysis, we see that it raises one of the central issues in the entire play: the difference between appearance and reality, and the confusion this discrepancy produces in the personal, social, and political world. Because characters and events in *Hamlet* are rarely what they appear to be, the passage provides a key to our understanding of Shakespeare's tragedy.

Commentary on the Essay

Although the essay deals extensively with the actual words in the passage being analyzed, it focuses on content rather than style. Since the passage is Hamlet's first extended speech, we might have chosen an essay that examined the ways in which Hamlet's character is established. Instead, the essay deals with one of the play's major themes: the difference between appearance and reality. The introduction places the passage in its immediate context, states the central idea of the essay, and notes the steps in which this thesis will be discussed.

The body takes up the specific ways in which the concept of a discrepancy between appearance and reality is expressed in the passage and developed throughout the play. Paragraph 2 deals with Hamlet's explicit statement of the idea, and paragraph 3 discusses his illustration of the concept with reference to the trappings of grief. Paragraph 4 demonstrates the relationship of this idea to character and situation elsewhere in the text. The conclusion brings the arguments of the essay together, concluding on the note of the importance of the major contrast between appearance and reality.

WRITING TOPICS

1. Much has been made of the contrast in *Oedipus the King* between seeing and blindness. Write an essay which considers this contrast as it is related to the character of Oedipus. How are blindness and seeing reversed, with regard to his understanding about the curse on the city, his attempts to ferret out the guilty ones, his awakening perceptions of his own responsibility and guilt, and his self-blinding? To what degree is Tiresias to be compared and contrasted with Oedipus?

2. Develop an argument for one of these assertions:
   a. Oedipus's fall is the result of fate, predestination, and the gods, and would happen despite his character.
   b. Oedipus's fall is the result only of his character, and has nothing to do with fate or the gods.

3. Write an essay considering the degree to which Gertrude and Ophelia in *Hamlet* justify Hamlet's assertion, "Frailty, thy name is woman" (I.2.146). Questions you might take into account concern the status of these women, their power to exert their own individuality and to make their own decisions, Gertrude as a royal queen and Ophelia as an aristocratic daughter, their ability to undergo the pain of being bereaved, Hamlet's own feelings about the death of his father, and so on.

4. Hamlet, Laertes, and Fortinbras are all young men whose fathers have been killed and who set out to avenge these deaths. Their courses of action, however, are different. In an essay, compare and contrast how each man deals with his father's death. Which approach seems most reasonable to you? Most emotional? Most effective?

5. *Death of a Salesman* was successfully produced in the People's Republic of China in 1983, and was revived on Broadway in 1984, not to mention the successful Lee J. Cobb and Dustin Hoffman television productions of the 1950s and 1980s. How do you account for the continuing interest in the play from the time it was first produced until the present moment, in contemporary America and in other cultures?

6. Write an essay discussing the ways in which *Death of a Salesman* comments on American life and values. What specific shortcomings of American life does Miller expose and attack? To what degree does Willy Loman represent these shortcomings, and how may he be seen also as an innocent victim? To what degree might Willy's death be seen as a redemption, and therefore as a defense of American life?

7. Considering *Oedipus the King*, *Hamlet*, and *Death of a Salesman*, write an essay describing the nature of tragedy. Try to include references to the nature of

the tragic protagonists, the situations they face, their solutions to their problems, their reactions to the consequences of their actions, and their worthiness of character. Whenever possible, compare and contrast the actions and speeches of Oedipus, Hamlet, and Willy Loman as evidence in your discussion.

27

Comedy: Restoring the Balance

The term **comedy** comes from the Greek word *komos*, which means "celebration," "revel," or "merrymaking." As the word suggests, comedy began as a ritual celebration, a time of merrymaking in which social restrictions were released, appetites were indulged, bizarre behavior was encouraged, and the world was turned upside down. The original *komos* may have been a religious revel celebrating the cyclical rebirth of Dionysus, the god of fertility and wine. His death and rebirth trace the movement from winter to spring, sterility to fertility, and adversity to prosperity. Comedy thus has an ancient and ongoing association with celebrations of rebirth.

Comedy is often considered to be the opposite of tragedy, and in many ways this perception is accurate. The mask of comedy smiles, while that of tragedy frowns. Comedy opens with problems and adversity and moves toward a successful outcome. Tragedy, on the other hand, begins in prosperity and focuses on the fall of the major protagonist. The language of tragedy can be elevated and heroic, whereas the language of comedy can be witty or bawdy, artificially elegant or stridently colloquial. Tragedy often ends in death, and comedy frequently closes with marriages. But the gulf between tragedy and comedy is not as great as we might think. Many tragedies contain potentially comic plots, and many comedies are filled with tragic potential. Indeed, tragedy may be seen as an abortive or incomplete comedy in which affairs go wrong, and comedy can be considered a tragedy in which the truth is discovered, the hero saves the day, or the villain confesses in time to avert disaster.

OLD AND NEW COMEDY

Classical Greek and Roman comedy is traditionally divided into two general types: old and new comedy. **Old comedy,** exemplified by the plays of Aristophanes (ca. 448–388 B.C.), was satirical and involved extensive attacks on individuals and on the society at large. The plays were very topical and at least partly improvised; the language was witty and biting.

Many elements of old comedy survive to this day, especially the use of satire and witty language. For the most part, however, old comedy was replaced by **new comedy** in the third century B.C. New comedy, developed by the Greek dramatist Menander (ca. 342–291 B.C.), was romantic rather than satirical. It employed stock characters such as young lovers, stubborn fathers, jealous husbands, and clever slaves, and the action depended more on plot than on language or character.

Roman new comic plays tended to be short, violent, and bawdy. They often involved young lovers whose relationship was prevented or blocked. The **blocking agent,** or obstruction to true love, could be almost anything—a rival lover, an angry father, a family feud, an old law, a previously arranged marriage, or a difference in social class.

There are many funny elements in these plays, such as the overblown sighs of the divided lovers, the ranting of the offended father, the confusion of mistaken identities. The comedy, however, derives from the pattern of the action: the initial problem, the outrageous plots hatched by the characters to circumvent the blocking agents, and the ultimate victory of young love. In these plays the resolution frequently represents the victory of youth over age and the passing of control from one generation to the next.

COMIC AND FUNNY: THE PATTERN OF COMEDY

Although dictionaries often give *funny* as a synonym for *comic*, there is an essential difference between the two terms. Words like "funny," "amusing," or "humorous" define our emotional reactions to things rather than the things themselves, and the reaction always depends on context. While we usually react with laughter to an actor repeatedly knocked on the head with a wooden paddle during a slapstick routine, the sight of a man being beaten with a baseball bat on the street is horrifying rather than amusing. "Comic," the adjective derived from "comedy," does not signify an emotional response. Rather, it means that a literary work conforms to the patterns and characteristics of comedy. Many comedies are, in fact, very funny; we react with amusement to the witty remarks, bawdy jokes, foolish characters, silly mistakes, and other devices of plot, action, and language that occur in comic drama. At heart, however, comedy and the term "comic" suggests a *pattern of action*, growing out of character or situation, that leads to a specific kind of catastrophe and resolution.

Comedies begin in adversity; during their exposition, we usually learn that something is amiss. These initial problems can be the result of character or circumstance; they can be individual or social. They can involve thwarted love, eccentric behavior, corruption in society, or a combination of ingredients. As the play moves from exposition to complication, these problems usually get much worse. In comedy, complication is often fueled by confusion, misunderstanding, mistakes in identity, coincidences that stretch our credulity, errors in judgment, and excessive or unreasonable behavior.

The climax of a comedy occurs when these confusions reach a peak, misunderstanding is dominant, pressure is at a high point, choices must be made, and solutions must be found. The catastrophe unties the knots and resolves the complications. In comedy, the catastrophe is frequently a sudden revelation of truth in which some key fact, identity, or event is explained to the characters and the audience at the same time.

In most comedies, the events of the catastrophe resolve the initial problems and allow for the comic resolution of the play. This comic resolution frequently involves setting things right at every level of action: individual lives are straightened out, new families are formed through marriages, and a healthy social order is established.

Two key features of the comic pattern are *education* and *change*. In many comedies at least some of the characters learn something about themselves, their society, or the way to live and love. This education makes it possible for the characters (and thus, the society) to change for the better. In other comedies, however, the *audience* is educated, and the playwright hopes that change will occur in the world rather than on the stage.

CHARACTERS IN COMEDY

Characters in comedy are far more limited than in tragedy, because comedies deal with groups or representative types rather than with individuals of heroic stature. In comedy, we usually do not find characters with the depth or individuality of Hamlet or Oedipus. Instead, there are stock characters who represent classes, types, and generations. In Shakespeare's *A Midsummer Night's Dream*, for instance, most of the characters are representative stock figures. Egeus is a conventional indignant father; similarly, Hermia and Lysander (along with Helena and Demetrius) are typical young lovers.

LANGUAGE IN COMEDY

As in other types of literature, comic dramatists use language to delineate character, to establish tone and mood, and to express ideas and feelings. In comedy, however, language is also one of the most important vehicles for creating humor. Some comedies are characterized by elegant and witty language, others by bawdy jokes and puns.

Characters in comedy tend either to be masters of language or to be mastered by it. Those who are skillful with language, such as Lisette in *Love Is the Doctor*, can use a witty phrase like a knife to satirize their friends and foes. Those who are unskilled with language, such as Bottom in *A Midsummer Night's Dream*, bungle through a speech with their misuse of words and inadvertent puns. Both types of characters are amusing; we smile a knowing smile with the wits and laugh out loud at the bunglers.

TYPES OF COMEDY

Differences in comic style, content, and intent that have evolved over the centuries make it possible to divide comedy into various types. The broadest of these divisions, based on both style and content, separates all comic literature into high comedy and low comedy. **High comedy** (a term coined by George Meredith in 1877 in *The Idea of Comedy*) is witty, graceful, and sophisticated. The complications and problems grow out of character rather than situation, and the appeal is to the intellect.

In **low comedy** emphasis is on funny remarks and outrageous circumstances. Plays of this type are often full of physical humor—seven men hide in different places in the same room, or a poor soul gets whacked each time a carpenter turns around with a plank. Complications develop from plot and situation rather than from character.

A special type of low comedy is **farce** (a word derived from the Latin word *farsus*, meaning "stuffed"). A farce is a boisterous physical comedy overflowing with silly characters, improbable happenings, wild clowning, and bawdy jokes. In farce, the focus is on action and extravagant language.

Commedia dell'arte and slapstick comedy are specific kinds of farce. **Commedia dell'arte,** which developed in Italy in the sixteenth century, is broadly humorous farce. The stock characters—the fool, the young lovers, the old man with a young wife or daughter, the quack physician and lawyer, the soldier, the clever servant—are derived from the new comedy. They have, in turn, become constant features of much subsequent comedy. **Slapstick comedy** is a low form of farce that depends almost entirely on exaggerated facial expressions and on stage business involving props such as pies, water pails, dough, or toilet paper, and also involving wild and improbable actions like falling, hiding, tumbling, or tripping. The name is derived from the double paddle ("slap stick") that reverberated loudly when Roman comic actors used to strike each other.

Another distinction, based on content and the playwright's intent, divides comedy into satires and romances. **Satiric comedy** is designed to ridicule vices and follies. The playwright of satiric comedy assumes the perspective of a rational and moderate observer measuring human life against a moderate norm. The audience is invited to share this viewpoint as they, along with the dramatist, heap scorn upon the vicious and laugh loudly at the eccentric and the foolish.

Romantic comedy is more gentle and sympathetic. Deriving from Roman new comedy, it presents young lovers trying to overcome opposition and achieve a successful union. Its aim is amusement and entertainment rather than ridicule and reform. Although vice and folly may be exposed in romantic comedy, especially in the characters blocking the young lovers, the dominant impulse is toleration and amused indulgence.

Related to romantic comedy is the **comedy of manners,** a type that developed in the sixteenth century and flourished in the seventeenth. The comedy of manners examines and satirizes attitudes and customs in the light of high intellectual and moral standards. The dialogue is witty and sophisticated, with characters often being measured according to their linguistic and intellectual powers. The love plots, while usually cast in the pattern of the youthful lovers versus blocking forces, bear a note of seriousness and reality. Seriousness is so evident in some of the comedies written in Restoration England (1660–1700), in fact, that one might consider them not only as plays of manners but also of problems.

Many of the types of comedy just discussed still flourish. Romantic comedies, comedies of manners, farces, and slapstick comedy may be found on innumerable stages and movie screens. Often in a trivialized form (Will Mr. Smith get the contract signed in order to save his job? Will Jimmy get Dad's car fixed before the dented fender is discovered?), the types find their ways into the many "sitcoms" (*situation comedies*) that regularly occupy prime-time television programs.

Other types of modern and contemporary comedy include **ironic comedy, realistic comedy,** and **comedy of the absurd.** All of these usually shun the happy endings of traditional comedy. In many of them, the blocking agents are successful and the protagonists are defeated. Often, the initial problem—either a realistic or an absurdist dilemma—remains unresolved. Such comedies, which began to appear in the late nineteenth century, illustrate the complexities and absurdities of modern life and the funny but futile efforts that people make when coming to grips with existence.

In view of the various kinds of comedies you will encounter, it is most important to realize that comedies are rarely pure forms of one type. High comedies might include crude physical humor, especially with characters marked out for audience disapproval. Low comedies may sometimes contain wit and elegance. Satiric comedies might deal with successful young lovers. Romantic comedies may mock the vices and follies of weird and eccentric characters. Farce and slapstick comedy may also satirize social values and conventions.

WILLIAM SHAKESPEARE, *A MIDSUMMER NIGHT'S DREAM*

In Chapter 26 we discuss Shakespeare's age and theater and his career as a dramatist. *A Midsummer Night's Dream* was written fairly early in his career, in 1594 or 1595. It is a romantic comedy that explores the tribulations of thwarted love and the chaos of mad infatuation and irrational love. The central plot concerns the misadventures and eventual harmony of four conventional and representative young lovers: indeed, it is difficult to tell the young men apart. This central line of action, which owes a great deal to Roman new comedy, involves blocked love, a journey of circumvention and education that takes the lovers from the world of laws and problems into an imaginary world of chaos and transformations, and an ultimate victory for young love back in the world of daylight and order.

The play demonstrates Shakespeare's skillful interweaving of four separate plots, four groups of characters, and four styles of language into one coherent comedy. The **overplot**—the action that establishes the time frame for the entire play—concerns Duke Theseus, the ruler of Athens, and Hippolyta, his fiancée and the queen of the Amazons. These characters are the rulers and they speak predominantly in blank verse (unrhymed iambic pentameter; see p. 724).

The two connected **middle plots** concern the adventures of the four lovers and the actions of the fairies, specifically Oberon and Titania. The four lovers are middle-class figures, and their plot line embodies both social and individual problems; they speak predominantly in rhymed iambic pentameter couplets (see pp. 724–25). Oberon and Titania, the king and queen of the fairies, embody the supernatural forces of nature. Although they and the other fairies speak in both blank verse and rhymed couplets, the fairies are the only characters who also sing songs and speak in iambic tetrameter.

The **low plot** presents the adventures of the Athenian workingmen who try to put on a play in honor of the marriage of Hippolyta and Theseus. These laborers are often called "the mechanicals" because of their trades. Their plot contains much of the low comedy in the play, and they are the only group of characters who speak in prose.

The subject of *A Midsummer Night's Dream* is love; each plot explores the nature of love, the madness of irrational or unthinking love, and the harmony necessary for regenerative love. In the overplot, the relationship between Theseus and Hippolyta illustrates love that has moved from madness of war to rational harmony. As such, they represent the dynastic continuity of the state, the order of the daylight world of Athens, and the rigor of the law, a rigor that is softened in the course of the play.

The four lovers of the middle plot present young love at its most passionate, insistent, and unthinking. For them, love is a blind and all-powerful force. During their long night in the woods of illusion outside Athens, their passions are redirected three times by Oberon and his servant, Puck. Each change demonstrates anew the power of blind passion. Ultimately, these adventures drive the lovers into a semblance of rationality in which each recognizes and accepts his or her appropriate mate.

The second middle plot, the action involving Oberon and Titania, offers three related explorations of love's madness and the restoration of reason and order to love. The central relationship, between the king and queen of the fairies, is in a shambles because Titania has become infatuated with the "changeling" child that she claims was given to her, but that she may actually have stolen. In either event, Oberon also wants the boy, but Titania's passionate fixation leads her to defy her husband, and their discord produces chaos and disaster throughout nature. In order to cure this infatuation and teach her a lesson, Oberon causes Titania to fall madly in love with a monster, and then he cures her of all love madness. Titania's restored rationality brings her back into subservience to Oberon, the proper state for a wife according to Elizabethan males.

The examination of love in the low plot occurs partly in Titania's relationship with Bottom—the most hilarious instance of love madness in the play—and partly in "The most lamentable comedy and most cruel death of Pyramus and Thisby," the play that the mechanicals perform at court in celebration of the marriages. This wildly funny tragedy echoes the central plot of *A Midsummer Night's Dream* and demonstrates, again, the dangers of love. It also emphasizes the happy and harmonious marriages and rapprochements that occur at the other levels of action.

While *A Midsummer Night's Dream* is chiefly about love, it also explores other ideas and topics. Chief among these is the complicated relationship of perception, imagination, dreaming, passion, and art (or drama, or illusion). In the last act Theseus asserts that "The lunatic, the lover, and the poet" are all related through the powers of passion, imagination, and dreaming. By the same token, the movement from the "real" world of Athens to the dreamlike and illusory world of Oberon and Titania raises questions about the relationship between illusion (or dreaming or art or drama) and reality.

Many of these concerns come together in the low plot, specifically in the mechanicals' understanding (or ignorance) of dramatic representation and their abysmal production of *Pyramus and Thisby*. These "actors" and their aristocratic audience give Shakespeare an opportunity to investigate the nature of dramatic illusion, the degree to which audiences understand the imitative quality of theater, and the connection between art and life.

WILLIAM SHAKESPEARE   (1564–1616)

A Midsummer Night's Dream   *1600 (ca. 1594)*

Edited by Alice Griffin°

[*THE NAMES OF THE ACTORS*]

> Theseus, *Duke of Athens*
> Egeus, *father of Hermia*
> Lysander, *beloved of Hermia*
> Demetrius, *in love with Hermia, favoured by Egeus*
> Philostrate, *Master of the Revels to Theseus*
>
> Peter Quince, *a carpenter* (*Prologue*)*
> Nick Bottom, *a weaver* (*Pyramus*)*
> Francis Flute, *a bellows-mender* (*Thisby*)*
> Tom Snout, *a tinker* (*Wall*)*
> Snug, *a joiner* (*Lion*)*
> Robin Starveling, *a tailor* (*Moonshine*)*
>
> Hippolyta, *Queen of the Amazons, betrothed to Theseus*
> Hermia, *daughter of Egeus, in love with Lysander*
> Helena, *in love with Demetrius*
>
> Oberon, *King of the Fairies*
> Titania, *Queen of the Fairies*
> Puck, *or* Robin Goodfellow
> Peaseblossom ⎫
> Cobweb   ⎬ *Fairies*
> Moth   ⎪
> Mustardseed ⎭

Other Fairies attending Oberon and Titania. Attendants on Theseus and Hippolyta.

Scene: *Athens, and a wood nearby*

ACT 1

[Scene 1. Athens. The palace of Theseus]

Enter THESEUS, HIPPOLYTA,° [PHILOSTRATE,] WITH OTHERS.

THESEUS.   Now fair Hippolyta, our nuptial hour
   Draws on apace: four happy days bring in

Professor Griffin's text for *A Midsummer Night's Dream* is the First Quarto (edition) published in 1600, with modifications based on the Quarto edition of 1619 and the First Folio, published in 1623. Stage directions in those editions are printed here without brackets; added stage directions are printed within brackets. We have edited Griffin's notes for this text.   * Characters played in the interlude.   0.3 Stage direction: *Theseus, Hippolyta:* In Greek legend, Theseus captured the Amazon Queen Hippolyta and brought her to Athens where they were married.

Another moon: but O, methinks how slow
This old moon wanes! she lingers° my desires,
Like to a stepdame or a dowager,°   5
Long withering out° a young man's revenue.

HIPPOLYTA. Four days will quickly steep themselves in night:
Four nights will quickly dream away the time:
And then the moon, like to a silver bow
New-bent in heaven, shall behold the night   10
Of our solemnities.

THESEUS.   Go Philostrate,
Stir up the Athenian youth to merriments,
Awake the pert° and nimble spirit of mirth,
Turn melancholy forth to funerals:
The pale companion° is not for our pomp.   [*Exit* PHILOSTRATE.]   15
Hippolyta, I wooed thee with my sword,
And won thy love doing thee injuries;
But I will wed thee in another key,
With pomp, with triumph,° and with revelling.

Enter EGEUS *and his daughter* HERMIA, LYSANDER *and* DEMETRIUS.

EGEUS. Happy be Theseus, our renownèd duke.   20
THESEUS. Thanks good Egeus:° what's the news with thee?
EGEUS. Full of vexation come I, with complaint
Against my child, my daughter Hermia.
Stand forth Demetrius. My noble lord,
This man hath my consent to marry her.   25
Stand forth Lysander. And my gracious duke,
This man hath bewitched the bosom of my child.
Thou, thou Lysander, thou hast given her rhymes,
And interchanged love tokens with my child:
Thou hast by moonlight at her window sung,   30
With feigning voice, verses of feigning° love,
And stol'n the impression of her fantasy°
With bracelets of thy hair, rings, gauds,° conceits,°
Knacks,° trifles, nosegays, sweetmeats—messengers
Of strong prevailment in unhardened youth.   35
With cunning hast thou filched my daughter's heart,
Turned her obedience, which is due to me,
To stubborn harshness. And my gracious duke,
Be it so° she will not here before your grace
Consent to marry with Demetrius,   40
I beg the ancient privilege of Athens:
As she is mine, I may dispose of her:

---

4 *lingers:* delays the fulfillment of.   5 *dowager:* a widow supported by her dead husband's
heirs.   6 *withering out:* (1) depleting (2) growing withered.   13 *pert:* lively.
15 *companion:* fellow (contemptuous).   19 *triumph:* public festival.   21 *Egeus:*
(trisyllabic).   31 *feigning:* (1) deceptive (2) desirous ("faining").   32 *stol'n . . . fantasy:*
stealthily imprinted your image upon her fancy.   33 *gauds:* trinkets.   *conceits:* either
(a) love poetry, or (b) love tokens.   34 *Knacks:* knick-knacks.   39 *Be it so:* if it be that.

Which shall be, either to this gentleman,
Or to her death, according to our law
Immediately° provided in that case.   45
THESEUS.   What say you, Hermia? Be advised, fair maid.
To you your father should be as a god:
One that composed your beauties: yea and one
To whom you are but as a form in wax
By him imprinted, and within his power   50
To leave the figure, or disfigure it:
Demetrius is a worthy gentleman.
HERMIA.   So is Lysander.
THESEUS.   In himself he is:
But in this kind, wanting your father's voice,°
The other must be held the worthier.   55
HERMIA.   I would my father looked but with my eyes.
THESEUS.   Rather your eyes must with his judgment look.
HERMIA.   I do entreat your grace to pardon me.
I know not by what power I am made bold,
Nor how it may concern my modesty,   60
In such a presence, here to plead my thoughts:
But I beseech your grace that I may know
The worst that may befall me in this case,
If I refuse to wed Demetrius.
THESEUS.   Either to die the death, or to abjure   65
For ever the society of men.
Therefore fair Hermia, question your desires,
Know of your youth,° examine well your blood,°
Whether, if you yield not to your father's choice,
You can endure the livery° of a nun,   70
For aye° to be in shady cloister mewed,°
To live a barren sister all your life,
Chanting faint hymns to the cold fruitless moon.°
Thrice blessèd they that master so their blood,
To undergo such maiden pilgrimage: 75
But earthlier happy° is the rose distilled,°
Than that which, withering on the virgin thorn,
Grows, lives, and dies, in single blessedness.
HERMIA.   So will I grow, so live, so die my lord,
Ere I will yield my virgin patent° up   80
Unto his lordship, whose unwishèd yoke
My soul consents not to give sovereignty.
THESEUS.   Take time to pause, and by the next moon,
The sealing day betwixt my love and me,

45 *Immediately:* precisely.   54 *in . . . voice:* in this respect, lacking your father's approval.
68 *Know . . . youth:* ask yourself as a young person.   68 *blood:* passions.   70 *livery:*
habit.   71 *aye:* ever.   *mewed:* shut up.   73 *moon:* (the moon goddess Diana
represented unmarried chastity).   76 *earthlier happy:* more happy on earth.   *distilled:*
i.e., into perfume (thus its essence is passed on, as to a child).   80 *patent:* privilege.

For everlasting bond of fellowship, 85
Upon that day either prepare to die
For disobedience to your father's will,
Or else to wed Demetrius, as he would,
Or on Diana's altar to protest°
For aye, austerity and single life. 90
DEMETRIUS.   Relent, sweet Hermia, and Lysander, yield
Thy crazèd° title to my certain right.
LYSANDER.   You have her father's love, Demetrius:
Let me have Hermia's: do you marry him.
EGEUS.   Scornful Lysander, true, he hath my love: 95
And what is mine, my love shall render him.
And she is mine, and all my right of her
I do estate° unto Demetrius.
LYSANDER.   I am, my lord, as well derived° as he,
As well possessed:° my love is more than his: 100
My fortunes every way as fairly ranked
(If not with vantage) as° Demetrius':
And, which is more than all these boasts can be,
I am beloved of beauteous Hermia.
Why should not I then prosecute my right? 105
Demetrius, I'll avouch it to his head,°
Made love to Nedar's daughter, Helena,
And won her soul: and she, sweet lady, dotes,
Devoutly dotes, dotes in idolatry,
Upon this spotted° and inconstant man. 110
THESEUS.   I must confess that I have heard so much,
And with Demetrius thought to have spoke thereof:
But being over-full of self-affairs,
My mind did lose it. But Demetrius come,
And come Egeus, you shall go with me: 115
I have some private schooling for you both.
For you fair Hermia, look you arm yourself,
To fit your fancies to your father's will;
Or else the law of Athens yields you up
(Which by no means we may extenuate) 120
To death or to a vow of single life.
Come my Hippolyta, what cheer my love?
Demetrius and Egeus, go along:
I must employ you in some business
Against° our nuptial, and confer with you 125
Of something nearly° that concerns yourselves.
EGEUS.   With duty and desire we follow you.
                    Exeunt.° Manent° LYSANDER *and* HERMIA.

89 *protest:* vow.   92 *crazèd:* flawed.   98 *estate:* transfer.   99 *well derived:* well born.
100 *well possessed:* wealthy.   102 *with vantage, as:* better, than.   106 *avouch . . . head:*
prove it to his face.   110 *spotted:* stained (by betrayal of Helena).   125 *Against:* in
preparation for.   126 *nearly:* closely.   127 stage direction: *Exeunt:* they exit.
Manent: they remain.

LYSANDER.   How now my love? Why is your cheek so pale?
　　How chance the roses there do fade so fast?
HERMIA.   Belike° for want of rain, which I could well   130
　　Beteem° them from the tempest of my eyes,
LYSANDER.   Ay me, for aught that I could ever read,
　　Could ever hear by tale or history,
　　The course of true love never did run smooth;
　　But either it was different in blood—   135
HERMIA.   O cross! too high° to be enthralled to low.°
LYSANDER.   Or else misgraffèd° in respect of years—
HERMIA.   O spite! too old to be engaged to young.
LYSANDER.   Or else it stood upon the choice of friends—
HERMIA.   O hell! to choose love by another's eyes.   140
LYSANDER.   Or if there were a sympathy in choice,
　　War, death, or sickness did lay siege to it;
　　Making it momentany° as a sound,
　　Swift as a shadow, short as any dream,
　　Brief as the lightning in the collied° night,   145
　　That, in a spleen,° unfolds both heaven and earth;
　　And ere a man hath power to say "Behold,"
　　The jaws of darkness do devour it up:
　　So quick bright things come to confusion.
HERMIA.   If then true lovers have been ever crossed,°   150
　　It stands as an edict in destiny:
　　Then let us teach our trial patience,°
　　Because it is a customary cross,
　　As due to love as thoughts and dreams and sighs,
　　Wishes and tears; poor Fancy's° followers.   155
LYSANDER.   A good persuasion: therefore hear me, Hermia:
　　I have a widow aunt, a dowager,
　　Of great revenue, and she hath no child:
　　From Athens is her house remote seven leagues,
　　And she respects° me as her only son: 160
　　There gentle Hermia, may I marry thee,
　　And to that place the sharp Athenian law
　　Cannot pursue us. If thou lov'st me then,
　　Steal forth thy father's house tomorrow night:
　　And in the wood, a league without the town,   165
　　Where I did meet thee once with Helena
　　To do observance to a morn of May,°
　　There will I stay° for thee.
HERMIA.　　　　　　　　　My good Lysander,
　　I swear to thee, by Cupid's strongest bow,

130 *Belike:* likely.   131 *Beteem:* (1) pour out on (2) allow.   136 *high:* highborn.
enthralled to low: made a slave to one of low birth.   137 *misgraffèd:* badly joined.
143 *momentany:* momentary.   145 *collied:* black as coal.   146 *in a spleen:* impulsively, in
a sudden outburst.   150 *ever crossed:* evermore thwarted.   152 *teach . . . patience:* teach
ourselves to be patient.   155 *Fancy:* love (sometimes infatuation).   160 *respects:*
regards.   167 *do . . . May:* celebrate May Day.   168 *stay:* wait.

By his best arrow, with the golden head,° 170
By the simplicity of Venus' doves,
By that which knitteth souls and prospers loves,
And by that fire which burned the Carthage queen,
When the false Troyan° under sail was seen,
By all the vows that ever men have broke, 175
(In number more than ever women spoke)
In that same place thou has appointed me,
Tomorrow truly will I meet with thee.
LYSANDER. Keep promise love: look, here comes Helena.

Enter HELENA.
HERMIA. God speed fair Helena: whither away? 180
HELENA. Call you me fair? That fair again unsay.
Demetrius loves your fair:° O happy fair!
Your eyes are lodestars,° and your tongue's sweet air°
More tuneable than lark to shepherd's ear,
When wheat is green, when hawthorn buds appear. 185
Sickness is catching: O were favour° so,
Yours would I catch, fair Hermia, ere I go,
My ear should catch your voice,° my eye your eye,°
My tongue should catch your tongue's sweet melody.
Were the world mine, Demetrius being bated,° 190
The rest I'ld give to be to you translated.°
O teach me how you look, and with what art
You sway the motion of Demetrius' heart.
HERMIA. I frown upon him; yet he loves me still.
HELENA. O that your frowns would teach my smiles such skill. 195
HERMIA. I give him curses; yet he gives me love.
HELENA. O that my prayers could such affection move.
HERMIA. The more I hate, the more he follows me.
HELENA. The more I love, the more he hateth me.
HERMIA. His folly, Helena, is no fault of mine. 200
HELENA. None but your beauty; would that fault were mine.
HERMIA. Take comfort: he no more shall see my face:
Lysander and myself will fly this place.
Before the time I did Lysander see,
Seemed Athens as a paradise to me: 205
O then, what graces in my love do dwell,
That he hath turned a heaven unto a hell!
LYSANDER. Helen, to you our minds we will unfold:
Tomorrow night, when Phoebe° doth behold
Her silver visage in the wat'ry glass,° 210

170 *golden head:* (The arrow with the gold head causes love).   173–174 *Carthage Queen
. . . false Troyan:* Dido, who burned herself to death on a funeral pyre when Trojan Aeneas
deserted her.   182 *your fair:* i.e., beauty.   183 *lodestars:* guiding stars.   *air:* music.
186 *favour:* appearance.   188 *My ear . . . voice:* my ear should catch the tone of your
voice.   *my eye your eye:* my eye should catch the way you glance.   190 *bated:* subtracted,
excepted.   191 *translated:* transformed.   209 *Phoebe:* Diana, the moon.   210 *wat'ry
glass:* mirror of the water.

Decking with liquid pearl the bladed grass
(A time that lovers' flights doth still° conceal)
Through Athens gates have we devised to steal.

HERMIA.   And in the wood, where often you and I
   Upon faint primrose beds were wont to lie,   215
   Emptying our bosoms of their counsel° sweet,
   There my Lysander and myself shall meet,
   And thence from Athens turn away our eyes,
   To see new friends and stranger companies.°
   Farewell, sweet playfellow: pray thou for us: 220
   And good luck grant thee thy Demetrius.
   Keep word Lysander: we must starve our sight
   From lovers' food,° till morrow deep midnight.

LYSANDER.   I will my Hermia.   *Exit* HERMIA.
                Helena adieu:
   As you on him, Demetrius dote on you.°   *Exit* LYSANDER.   225

HELENA.   How happy some, o'er other some, can be!
   Through Athens I am thought as fair as she.
   But what of that? Demetrius thinks not so:
   He will not know what all but he do know.
   And as he errs, doting on Hermia's eyes,   230
   So I, admiring of his qualities.
   Things base and vile, holding no quantity.°
   Love can transpose to form and dignity.
   Love looks not with the eyes, but with the mind:
   And therefore is winged Cupid painted blind.   235
   Nor hath Love's mind of any judgment taste:
   Wings, and no eyes, figure° unheedy haste.
   And therefore is Love said to be a child:
   Because in choice he is so oft beguiled.
   As waggish boys in game themselves forswear: 240
   So the boy Love is perjured everywhere.
   For ere Demetrius looked on Hermia's eyne,°
   He hailed down oaths that he was only mine.
   And when this hail some heat from Hermia felt,
   So he dissolved, and show'rs of oaths did melt.   245
   I will go tell him of fair Hermia's flight:
   Then to the wood will he tomorrow night
   Pursue her: and for this intelligence,°
   If I have thanks, it is a dear expense:°
   But herein mean I to enrich my pain,   250
   To have his sight° thither and back again.   *Exit.*

---

212 *still:* always.   216 *counsel:* secrets.   219 *stranger companies:* the companionship of
strangers.   223 *lovers' food:* the sight of the loved one.   225 *As . . . you:* As you dote on
Demetrius, so may Demetrius also dote on you.   232 *holding no quantity:* out of
proportion.   237 *figure:* symbolize.   242 *eyne:* eyes.   248 *intelligence:* information.
249 *dear expense:* costly outlay (on Demetrius' part).   250–251 *But . . . sight:* but I will be
rewarded just by the sight of him.

[Scene 2. Quince's house]

Enter QUINCE the Carpenter; and SNUG the Joiner; and BOTTOM the Weaver; and FLUTE the Bellows-mender; and SNOUT the Tinker; and STARVELING the Tailor.°

QUINCE. Is all our company here?

BOTTOM. You were the best to call them generally,° man by man, according to the scrip.

QUINCE. Here is the scroll of every man's name which is thought
fit, through all Athens, to play in our interlude° before   5
the duke and the duchess, on his wedding-day at night.

BOTTOM. First good Peter Quince, say what the play treats on,
then read the names of the actors: and so grow to a point.

QUINCE. Marry,° our play is "The most lamentable comedy, and
most cruel death of Pyramus and Thisby."   10

BOTTOM. A very good piece of work I assure you, and a merry. Now
good Peter Quince, call forth your actors by the scroll.
Masters, spread yourselves.

QUINCE. Answer as I call you. Nick Bottom the weaver?

BOTTOM. Ready: name what part I am for, and proceed.   15

QUINCE. You, Nick Bottom, are set down for Pyramus.

BOTTOM. What is Pyramus? A lover, or a tyrant?

QUINCE. A lover that kills himself, most gallant, for love.

BOTTOM. That will ask some tears in the true performing of it. If I
do it, let the audience look to their eyes: I will move   20
storms: I will condole° in some measure. To the rest—
yet my chief humour° is for a tyrant. I could play Ercles°
rarely, or a part to tear a cat in, to make all split.°

    The raging rocks
    And shivering shocks,   25
    Shall break the locks
      Of prison gates,
    And Phibbus' car°
    Shall shine from far,
    And make and mar   30
      The foolish Fates.

This was lofty. Now name the rest of the players. This is
Ercles' vein, a tyrant's vein: a lover is more condoling.

QUINCE. Francis Flute, the bellows-mender?

FLUTE. Here Peter Quince.   35

QUINCE. Flute, you must take Thisby on you.

0.2 Stage direction: the low characters' names describe their work: *Quince:* quoins, wooden wedges used in building.   *Snug:* fitting snugly, suiting a joiner of furniture.   *Bottom:* bobbin or core on which yarn is wound.   *Flute:* mender of fluted church organs and bellows.   *Snout:* spout (of the kettles he mends).   *Starveling:* (tailors being traditionally thin).   2 *generally:* Bottom often uses the wrong word; here he means the opposite: "severally, one-by-one."   5 *interlude:* short play.   9 *Marry:* indeed (mild oath, corruption of "by the Virgin Mary").   21 *condole:* lament.   22 *humour:* inclination. *Ercles:* Hercules (typified by ranting).   23 *tear . . . split:* (terms for ranting and raging on the stage).   28 *Phibbus' car:* Phoebus Apollo's chariot.

FLUTE.   What is Thisby? A wand'ring knight?

QUINCE.   It is the lady that Pyramus must love.

FLUTE.   Nay faith, let not me play a woman: I have a beard
    coming.   40

QUINCE.   That's all one:° you shall play it in a mask, and you may
    speak as small° as you will.

BOTTOM.   And° I may hide my face, let me play Thisby too: I'll speak
    in a monstrous little voice; "Thisne, Thisne," "Ah
    Pyramus, my lover dear, thy Thisby dear, and lady   45
    dear."

QUINCE.   No, no, you must play Pyramus: and Flute, you Thisby.

BOTTOM.   Well, proceed.

QUINCE.   Robin Starveling, the tailor?

STARVELING.   Here Peter Quince.   50

QUINCE.   Robin Starveling, you must play Thisby's mother. Tom
    Snout, the tinker?

SNOUT.   Here Peter Quince.

QUINCE.   You, Pyramus' father; myself, Thisby's father; Snug the
    joiner, you the lion's part: and I hope here is a play   55
    fitted.°

SNUG.   Have you the lion's part written? Pray you, if it be, give
    it me: for I am slow of study.

QUINCE.   You may do it extempore: for it is nothing but roaring.

BOTTOM.   Let me play the lion too. I will roar, that° I will do any   60
    man's heart good to hear me. I will roar, that I will make
    the duke say "Let him roar again: let him roar again."

QUINCE.   And you should do it too terribly, you would fright the
    duchess and the ladies, that they would shriek: and
    that were enough to hang us all.   65

ALL.   That would hang us, every mother's son.

BOTTOM.   I grant you, friends, if you should fright the ladies out of
    their wits, they would have no more discretion but to
    hang us: but I will aggravate° my voice so, that I will roar
    you as gently as any sucking dove: I will roar you and   70
    'twere° any nightingale.

QUINCE.   You can play no part but Pyramus: for Pyramus is a
    sweet-faced man; a proper° man as one shall see in a
    summer's day; a most lovely gentleman-like man: therefore
    you must needs play Pyramus.   75

BOTTOM.   Well: I will undertake it. What beard were I best to play
    it in?

QUINCE.   Why, what you will.

BOTTOM.   I will discharge it in either your straw-colour beard, your
    orange-tawny beard, your purple-in-grain° beard, or your   80

---

41 *That's all one:* never mind.   42 *small:* softly.   43 *And:* if.   56 *fitted:* cast.
60 *that:* so that.   69 *aggravate:* (he means "moderate").   70–71 *and 'twere:* as if it were.
73 *proper:* handsome.   80 *purple-in-grain:* dyed permanently purple.

French-crown-colour° beard, your perfit yellow.

QUINCE. Some of your French crowns° have no hair at all; and
then you will play barefaced. But masters here are your
parts, and I am to entreat you, request you, and desire
you, to con° them by tomorrow night: and meet me in the   85
palace wood, a mile without the town, by moonlight;
there will we rehearse: for if we meet in the city, we
shall be dogged with company, and our devices° known.
In the meantime, I will draw a bill of properties,° such
as our play wants. I pray you fail me not.   90

BOTTOM. We will meet, and there we may rehearse most obscenely°
and courageously. Take pain, be perfit: adieu.

QUINCE. At the duke's oak we meet.

BOTTOM. Enough: hold, or cut bow-strings.°   *Exeunt.*

ACT 2

[Scene 1. A wood near Athens]

Enter a FAIRY at one door, and ROBIN GOODFELLOW [Puck] at another.

PUCK. How now spirit, whither wander you?

FAIRY. Over hill, over dale,
    Thorough bush, thorough brier,
Over park, over pale,°
    Thorough flood, thorough fire: 5
I do wander everywhere,
Swifter than the moon's sphere:
And I serve the Fairy Queen,
To dew ° her orbs° upon the green.
The cowslips° tall her pensioners° be,   10
In their gold coats, spots you see:
Those be rubies, fairy favours:°
In those freckles live their savours.°
I must go seek some dewdrops here,
And hang a pearl in every cowslip's ear.   15
Farewell thou lob° of spirits: I'll be gone,
Our queen and all her elves come here anon.

PUCK. The king doth keep his revels here tonight.
Take heed the queen come not within his sight.
For Oberon is passing fell° and wrath,   20

---

81 *French-crown-colour:* golden, like French crowns (gold coins). 82 *French crowns:* bald
heads believed to be caused by syphilis, the "French" disease. 85 *con:* learn by heart.
88 *devices:* plans. 89 *bill of properties:* list of stage props. 91 *obscenely:* (he may mean
"fittingly," or "obscurely"). 94 *hold, or cut bow-strings* (meaning uncertain, but equivalent
to "fish, or cut bait"). 4 *pale:* enclosure. 9 *dew:* bedew. *orbs:* fairy rings (circles of
high grass). 10 *cowslips:* primroses. *pensioners:* royal bodyguards. 12 *favours:* gifts.
13 *savours:* perfumes. 16 *lob:* lout, lubber. 20 *passing fell:* surpassingly fierce.

Because that she, as her attendant, hath
A lovely boy, stol'n from an Indian king:
She never had so sweet a changeling.°
And jealous Oberon would have the child
Knight of his train, to trace° the forests wild.   25
But she, perforce,° withholds the lovèd boy,
Crowns him with flowers, and makes him all her joy.
And now, they never meet in grove or green,
By fountain clear, or spangled starlight sheen,
But they do square,° that all their elves for fear   30
Creep into acorn cups, and hide them there.

FAIRY.   Either I mistake your shape and making quite,
     Or else you are that shrewd and knavish sprite
     Called Robin Goodfellow. Are not you he
     That frights the maidens of the villagery,   35
     Skim milk,° and sometimes labour in the quern,°
     And bootless° make the breathless housewife churn,
     And sometime make the drink to bear no barm,°
     Mislead night-wanderers, laughing at their harm?
     Those that Hobgoblin call you, and sweet Puck,   40
     You do their work, and they shall have good luck.
     Are not you he?

PUCK.   Thou speakest aright;
     I am that merry wanderer of the night.
     I jest to Oberon, and make him smile,
     When I a fat and bean-fed horse beguile,   45
     Neighing in likeness of a filly foal;
     And sometime lurk I in a gossip's° bowl,
     In very likeness of a roasted crab,°
     And when she drinks, against her lips I bob,
     And on her withered dewlap° pour the ale.   50
     The wisest aunt, telling the saddest tale,
     Sometime for three-foot stool mistaketh me:
     Then slip I from her bum, down topples she,
     And "tailor"° cries, and falls into a cough;
     And then the whole quire° hold their hips and laugh,   55
     And waxen° in their mirth, and neeze,° and swear
     A merrier hour was never wasted° there.
     But room° fairy: here comes Oberon.

FAIRY.   And here, my mistress. Would that he were gone.

---

23 *changeling:* creature exchanged by fairies for a stolen baby (among the fairies, the stolen child).   25 *trace:* traverse.   26 *perforce:* by force.   30 *square:* quarrel.   36 *Skim milk:* steals the cream off the milk.   *quern:* handmill for grinding grain.   37 *bootless:* without result.   38 *barm:* foamy head (therefore the drink was flat).   47 *gossip's:* old woman's.   48 *crab:* crabapple (often put into ale).   50 *dewlap:* loose skin hanging about the throat.   54 *"tailor":* (variously explained: perhaps the squatting position of the tailor, or "tailard"—one with a tail).   55 *quire:* choir, group.   56 *waxen:* increase. *neeze:* sneeze.   57 *wasted:* spent.   58 *room:* make room.

Enter [OBERON] the KING OF FAIRIES, at one door with his TRAIN, and the QUEEN
[TITANIA], *at another, with hers.*

OBERON. Ill met by moonlight, proud Titania. 60
QUEEN. What, jealous Oberon? Fairy, skip hence.
  I have forsworn his bed and company.
OBERON. Tarry, rash wanton.° Am not I thy lord?
QUEEN. Then I must be thy lady: but I know
  When thou hast stol'n away from fairyland, 65
  And in the shape of Corin° sat all day,
  Playing on pipes of corn,° and versing love
  To amorous Phillida.° Why art thou here
  Come from the farthest steep of India?
  But that, forsooth, the bouncing Amazon,° 70
  Your buskined° mistress and your warrior love,
  To Theseus must be wedded; and you come,
  To give their bed joy and prosperity.
OBERON. How canst thou thus, for shame, Titania,
  Glance at my credit with° Hippolyta, 75
  Knowing I know thy love to Theseus?
  Didst thou not lead him through the glimmering night,
  From Perigenia, whom he ravishèd?
  And make him with fair Aegles break his faith,
  With Ariadne, and Antiopa°? 80
QUEEN. These are the forgeries of jealousy:
  And never, since the middle summer's spring,°
  Met we on hill, in dale, forest, or mead,
  By pavèd° fountain, or by rushy brook,
  Or in the beachèd margent° of the sea, 85
  To dance our ringlets to the whistling wind,
  But with thy brawls thou hast disturbed our sport.
  Therefore the winds, piping to us in vain,
  As in revenge, have sucked up from the sea
  Contagious° fogs: which falling in the land, 90
  Hath every pelting° river made so proud,
  That they have overborne their continents.°
  The ox hath therefore stretched his yoke in vain,
  The ploughman lost his sweat, and the green corn°
  Hath rotted, ere his youth attained a beard:° 95
  The fold° stands empty in the drownèd field,

63 *Tarry, rash wanton:* wait, headstrong one. 66–68 *Corin, Phillida:* (traditional names in
pastoral literature for a shepherd and his loved one, respectively). 67 *corn:* wheat
straws. 70 *Amazon:* Hippolyta. 71 *buskined:* wearing boots. 75 *Glance . . . credit
with:* hint at my favors from. 78–80 *Perigenia . . . Antiopa:* women that Theseus
supposedly loved and deserted. 82 *middle . . . spring:* beginning of midsummer.
84 *pavèd:* with a pebbly bottom. 85 *margent:* margin, shore. 88–117 *Therefore . . .
original:* (the disturbance in nature reflects the discord between Oberon and Titania).
90 *Contagious:* spreading pestilence. 91 *pelting:* paltry. 92 *overborne their continents:*
overflown the banks which contain them. 94 *corn:* grain. 95 *beard:* the tassels on
ripened grain. 96 *fold:* enclosure for livestock.

And crows are fatted with the murrion° flock.
The nine men's morris° is filled up with mud:
And the quaint mazes° in the wanton green,°
For lack of tread, are undistinguishable.   100
The human mortals want° their winter here,
No night is now with hymn or carol blest;
Therefore the moon, the governess of floods,
Pale in her anger, washes all the air,
That rheumatic diseases do abound.   105
And thorough this distemperature,° we see
The seasons alter: hoary-headed frosts
Fall in the fresh lap of the crimson rose,
And on old Hiems'° thin and icy crown,
An odorous chaplet° of sweet summer buds   110
Is, as in mockery, set. The spring, the summer,
The childing° autumn, angry winter change
Their wonted liveries:° and the mazèd° world,
By their increase, now knows not which is which:
And this same progeny of evils comes   115
From our debate, from our dissension:
We are their parents and original.
OBERON.   Do you amend it then: it lies in you.
Why should Titania cross her Oberon?
I do but beg a little changeling boy,   120
To be my henchman.°
QUEEN.   Set your heart at rest.
The fairy land buys not the child of me.
His mother was a vot'ress° of my order:
And in the spicèd Indian air, by night,
Full often hath she gossiped by my side.   125
And sat with me on Neptune's yellow sands,
Marking th' embarkèd traders° on the flood:
When we have laughed to see the sails conceive,
And grow big-bellied with the wanton° wind:
Which she, with pretty and with swimming gait,   130
Following (her womb then rich with my young squire)
Would imitate, and sail upon the land,
To fetch me trifles, and return again,
As from a voyage, rich with merchandise.
But she, being mortal, of that boy did die,   135
And for her sake, do I rear up her boy:
And for her sake, I will not part with him.

---

97 *murrion:* dead from murrain, a cattle disease.   98 *nine men's morris:* game played on
squares cut in the grass on which stones or disks are moved.   99 *quaint mazes:* intricate
paths.   *wanton green:* luxuriant grass.   101 *want:* lack.   106 *distemperature:* upset in
nature.   109 *Hiems:* god of winter.   110 *odorous chaplet:* sweet-smelling wreath.
112 *childing:* fruitful.   113 *wonted liveries:* accustomed dress.   *mazèd:* amazed.
121 *henchman:* attendant.   123 *vot'ress:* vowed and devoted follower.   127 *traders:*
merchant ships.   129 *wanton:* sportive.

OBERON.   How long within this wood intend you stay?

QUEEN.   Perchance till after Theseus' wedding day.
    If you will patiently dance in our round,°   140
    And see our moonlight revels, go with us:
    If not, shun me, and I will spare° your haunts.

OBERON.   Give me that boy, and I will go with thee.

QUEEN.   Not for thy fairy kingdom. Fairies away
    We shall chide downright, if I longer stay.   145

Exeunt [TITANIA *and her* TRAIN.]

OBERON.   Well, go thy way. Thou shalt not from this grove,
    Till I torment thee for this injury.
    My gentle Puck come hither: thou rememb'rest,
    Since° once I sat upon a promontory,
    And heard a mermaid, on a dolphin's back,   150
    Uttering such dulcet and harmonious breath,
    That the rude° sea grew civil° at her song,
    And certain stars shot madly from their spheres,
    To hear the sea-maid's music.

PUCK.   I remember.

OBERON.   That very time, I saw (but thou couldst not)   155
    Flying between the cold moon and the earth,
    Cupid, all armed: a certain aim he took
    At a fair Vestal,° thronèd by the west,
    And loosed his love-shaft smartly from his bow,
    As it should pierce a hundred thousand hearts: 160
    But I might see young Cupid's fiery shaft
    Quenched in the chaste beams of the wat'ry moon:
    And the imperial vot'ress° passèd on,
    In maiden meditation, fancy-free.°
    Yet marked I where the bolt° of Cupid fell.   165
    It fell upon a little western flower;
    Before, milk-white; now purple with love's wound,
    And maidens call it love-in-idleness.°
    Fetch me that flow'r: the herb I showed thee once.
    The juice of it, on sleeping eyelids laid,   170
    Will make or man or woman madly dote
    Upon the next live creature that it sees.
    Fetch me this herb, and be thou here again
    Ere the leviathan° can swim a league.

PUCK.   I'll put a girdle round about the earth,   175
    In forty minutes.   [*Exit.*]

OBERON.   Having once this juice,
    I'll watch Titania when she is asleep,

---

140 *round:* round dance.   142 *spare:* shun.   149 *Since:* when.   152 *rude:* rough.
civil: calm.   158 *Vestal:* virgin, probable reference to Queen Elizabeth.   162 *imperial vot'ress:* royal devotee (Queen Elizabeth) of Diana.   164 *fancy-free:* free from love.
165 *bolt:* arrow.   168 *love-in-idleness:* pansy.   174 *leviathan:* whale.

And drop the liquor of it in her eyes:
The next thing then she waking looks upon,
(Be it on lion, bear, or wolf, or bull,   180
On meddling monkey, or on busy° ape)
She shall pursue it, with the soul of love.
And ere I take this charm from off her sight
(As I can take it with another herb)
I'll make her render up her page to me.   185
But who comes here? I am invisible,
And I will overhear their conference.

Enter DEMETRIUS, HELENA *following him.*

DEMETRIUS.   I love thee not: therefore pursue me not.
    Where is Lysander and fair Hermia?
    The one I'll slay: the other slayeth me.   190
    Thou told'st me they were stol'n unto this wood:
    And here am I, and wood° within this wood:
    Because I cannot meet my Hermia.
    Hence, get thee gone, and follow me no more.
HELENA.   You draw me, you hard-hearted adamant:°   195
    But yet you draw not iron, for my heart
    Is true as steel. Leave you your power to draw,
    And I shall have no power to follow you.
DEMETRIUS.   Do I entice you? Do I speak you fair°?
    Or rather do I not in plainest truth   200
    Tell you I do not, nor I cannot love you?
HELENA.   And even for that, do I love you the more:
    I am your spaniel: and Demetrius,
    The more you beat me, I will fawn on you.
    Use me but as your spaniel: spurn me, strike me,   205
    Neglect me, lose me: only give me leave,
    Unworthy as I am, to follow you.
    What worser place can I beg in your love
    (And yet a place of high respect with me)
    Than to be usèd as you use your dog.   210
DEMETRIUS.   Tempt not too much the hatred of my spirit,
    For I am sick, when I do look on thee.
HELENA.   And I am sick, when I look not on you.
DEMETRIUS.   You do impeach° your modesty too much,
    To leave the city and commit yourself   215
    Into the hands of one that loves you not,
    To trust the opportunity of night,
    And the ill counsel of a desert° place,
    With the rich worth of your virginity.
HELENA.   Your virtue is my privilege:° for that°   220

181 *busy:* mischievous.   192 *wood:* crazy.   195 *adamant:* (1) magnet (2) impenetrably
hard lodestone.   199 *you fair:* to you in a kindly way.   214 *impeach:* discredit.
218 *desert:* deserted.   220 *Your . . . privilege:* your attraction is my excuse (for coming).
for that: because.

It is not night, when I do see your face,
Therefore I think I am not in the night.
Nor doth this wood lack worlds of company,
For you, in my respect,° are all the world.
Then how can it be said I am alone,   225
When all the world is here to look on me?
DEMETRIUS. I'll run from thee and hide me in the brakes,°
    And leave thee to the mercy of wild beasts.
HELENA. The wildest hath not such a heart as you.
    Run when you will: the story shall be changed;   230
    Apollo flies, and Daphne° holds the chase:
    The dove pursues the griffin:° the mild hind°
    Makes speed to catch the tiger. Bootless° speed,
    When cowardice pursues, and valour flies.
DEMETRIUS. I will not stay° thy questions. Let me go: 235
    Or if thou follow me, do not believe
    But I shall do thee mischief in the wood.   [*Exit* DEMETRIUS.]
HELENA. Ay, in the temple, in the town, the field,
    You do me mischief. Fie Demetrius,
    Your wrongs do set a scandal on my sex: 240
    We cannot fight for love, as men may do:
    We should be wooed, and were not made to woo.
    I'll follow thee and make a heaven of hell,
    To die upon the hand I love so well.   *Exit.*
OBERON. Fare thee well nymph. Ere he do leave this grove,   245
    Thou shalt fly him, and he shall seek thy love.

Enter PUCK.

    Hast thou the flower there? Welcome wanderer.
PUCK. Ay, there it is.
OBERON.   I pray thee give it me.
    I know a bank where the wild thyme blows,
    Where oxlips and the nodding violet grows,   250
    Quite over-canopied with luscious woodbine,
    With sweet musk-roses, and with eglantine:
    There sleeps Titania, sometime of the night,
    Lulled in these flowers, with dances and delight:
    And there the snake throws° her enamelled skin,   255
    Weed° wide enough to wrap a fairy in.
    And with the juice of this, I'll streak her eyes,
    And make her full of hateful fantasies.
    Take thou some of it, and seek through this grove:
    A sweet Athenian lady is in love   260
    With a disdainful youth: anoint his eyes.
    But do it when the next thing he espies

224 *respect:* regard.   227 *brakes:* thickets.   231 *Apollo . . . Daphne:* (in Ovid, Apollo
pursues Daphne, who turns into a laurel tree).   232 *griffin:* legendary beast with the
head of an eagle and the body of a lion.   *hind:* doe.   233 *Bootless:* useless.   235 *stay:*
wait for.   255 *throws:* casts off.   256 *weed:* garment.

May be the lady. Thou shalt know the man
By the Athenian garments he hath on.
Effect it with some care, that he may prove   265
More fond° on her, than she upon her love:
And look thou meet me ere the first cock crow.
PUCK.   Fear not my lord: your servant shall do so.   *Exeunt.*

[Scene 2. Another part of the wood]

Enter TITANIA Queen of Fairies with her train.

QUEEN.   Come, now a roundel° and a fairy song:
Then, for the third part of a minute, hence—
Some to kill cankers in the musk-rose buds,
Some war with reremice° for their leathren wings,
To make my small elves coats, and some keep back   5
The clamorous owl, that nightly hoots and wonders
At our quaint° spirits. Sing me now asleep:
Then to your offices,° and let me rest.

Fairies sing.

You spotted snakes with double° tongue,
    Thorny hedgehogs be not seen,   10
Newts and blind-worms° do no wrong,
    Come not near our Fairy Queen.

    Philomele,° with melody,
    Sing in our sweet lullaby,
Lulla, lulla, lullaby, lulla, lulla, lullaby.   15
    Never harm,
    Nor spell, nor charm,
Come our lovely lady nigh.
So good night, with lullaby.
1. FAIRY.   Weaving spiders come not here: 20
    Hence you long-legged spinners, hence:
    Beetles black approach not near:
    Worm nor snail do no offence.
    Philomele, with melody, &c.   *She sleeps.*
2. FAIRY.   Hence away: now all is well: 25
    One aloof stand sentinel.   *[Exeunt fairies.]*

Enter OBERON [and applies the flower juice to TITANIA's eyelids.]

OBERON.   What thou seest, when thou dost wake,
    Do it for thy true love take:
    Love and languish for his sake.

---

266 *fond:* doting, madly in love.   1 *roundel:* dance in a ring.   4 *reremice:* bats.
7 *quaint:* dainty.   8 *offices:* duties.   9 *double:* forked.   11 *blind-worms:* legless lizards.
13 *Philomele:* the nightingale.

Be it ounce,° or cat, or bear,   30
Pard,° or boar with bristled hair,
In thy eye that shall appear,
When thou wak'st, it is thy dear:
Wake when some vile thing is near.   [*Exit.*]

Enter LYSANDER *and* HERMIA.

LYSANDER. Fair love, you faint with wand'ring in the wood: 35
  And to speak troth° I have forgot our way.
  We'll rest us Hermia, if you think it good,
  And tarry for the comfort of the day.
HERMIA. Be't so Lysander: find you out a bed:
  For I upon this bank will rest my head.   40
LYSANDER. One turf shall serve as pillow for us both,
  One heart, one bed, two bosoms, and one troth.°
HERMIA. Nay good Lysander: for my sake, my dear,
  Lie further off yet; do not lie so near.
LYSANDER. O take the sense, sweet, of my innocence:°   45
  Love takes the meaning in love's conference.°
  I mean that my heart unto yours is knit,
  So that but one heart we can make of it:
  Two bosoms interchainèd with an oath,
  So then two bosoms and a single troth.   50
  Then by your side no bed-room me deny:
  For lying so, Hermia, I do not lie.
HERMIA. Lysander riddles very prettily.
  Now much beshrew° my manners and my pride,
  If Hermia meant to say Lysander lied.   55
  But gentle friend, for love and courtesy,
  Lie further off, in human modesty:
  Such separation as may well be said
  Becomes a virtuous bachelor and a maid,
  So far be distant, and good night sweet friend: 60
  Thy love ne'er alter till thy sweet life end.
LYSANDER. Amen, amen, to that fair prayer say I,
  And then end life, when I end loyalty.
  Here is my bed: sleep give thee all his rest.
HERMIA. With half that wish, the wisher's eyes be pressed.°   65

                                                              They sleep.

Enter PUCK.

PUCK. Through the forest have I gone,
  But Athenian found I none,
  On whose eyes I might approve°

---

30 *ounce:* lynx.   31 *Pard:* leopard.   36 *troth:* truth.   42 *troth:* true love.   45 *take*
. . . *innocence:* understand the innocence of my remark.   46 *Love . . . conference:* love
enables lovers to understand each other when they converse.   54 *beshrew:* curse.
65 *pressed:* i.e., by sleep.   68 *approve:* test.

This flower's force in stirring love.
Night and silence. Who is here?   70
Weeds° of Athens he doth wear:
This is he (my master said)
Despisèd the Athenian maid:
And here the maiden, sleeping sound,
On the dank and dirty ground.   75
Pretty soul, she durst not lie
Near this lack-love, this kill-courtesy.
Churl, upon thy eyes I throw
All the power this charm doth owe:°
When thou wak'st, let love forbid   80
Sleep his seat on thy eyelid.°
So awake when I am gone:
For I must now to Oberon.   *Exit.*

Enter DEMETRIUS and HELENA running.

HELENA.   Stay, thou kill me, sweet Demetrius.
DEMETRIUS.   I charge thee hence, and do not haunt me thus.   85
HELENA.   O, wilt thou darkling° leave me? Do not so.
DEMETRIUS.   Stay on thy peril: I alone will go.   *Exit DEMETRIUS.*
HELENA.   O, I am out of breath in this fond° chase:
     The more my prayer, the lesser is my grace.°
     Happy is Hermia, wheresoe'er she lies: 90
     For she hath blessèd and attractive eyes.
     How came her eyes so bright? Not with salt tears:
     If so, my eyes are oft'ner washed than hers.
     No, no: I am as ugly as a bear:
     For beasts that meet me run away for fear.   95
     Therefore no marvel, though Demetrius
     Do as a monster, fly my presence thus.
     What wicked and dissembling glass° of mine,
     Made me compare with Hermia's sphery eyne°!
     But who is here? Lysander, on the ground?   100
     Dead, or asleep? I see no blood, no wound.
     Lysander, if you live, good sir awake.
LYSANDER.   [*Wakes.*] And run through fire, I will for thy sweet sake.
     Transparent° Helena, nature shows art,
     That through thy bosom, makes me see thy heart.   105
     Where is Demetrius? O how fit a word
     Is that vile name to perish on my sword!
HELENA.   Do not say so, Lysander, say not so.
     What though he love your Hermia? Lord, what though?
     Yet Hermia still loves you: then be content.   110
LYSANDER.   Content with Hermia? No: I do repent

71 *Weeds:* garments.   79 *owe:* own.   80–81 *forbid . . . eyelid:* make you sleepless (with love).   86 *darkling:* in the dark.   88 *fond:* foolishly doting.   89 *my grace:* favor shown to me.   98 *glass:* looking glass.   99 *sphery eyne:* starry eyes.   104 *Transparent:* radiant.

The tedious minutes I with her have spent.
Not Hermia, but Helena I love.
Who will not change a raven for a dove?
The will of man is by his reason swayed:°   115
And reason says you are the worthier maid.
Things growing are not ripe until their season:
So I, being young, till now ripe° not to reason.
And touching now the point° of human skill,°
Reason becomes the marshal to my will,   120
And leads me to your eyes; where I o'erlook
Love's stories, written in love's richest book.

HELENA.   Wherefore° was I to this keen mockery born?
When at your hands did I deserve this scorn?
Is't not enough, is't not enough, young man,   125
That I did never, no, nor never can,
Deserve a sweet look from Demetrius' eye,
But you must flout° my insufficiency?
Good troth you do me wrong, good sooth you do,
In such disdainful manner me to woo.   130
But fare you well: perforce I must confess,
I thought you lord of more true gentleness.°
O, that a lady, of one man refused,
Should of another, therefore be abused!   *Exit.*

LYSANDER.   She sees not Hermia. Hermia, sleep thou there,   135
And never mayst thou come Lysander near.
For, as a surfeit of the sweetest things
The deepest loathing to the stomach brings:
Or as the heresies that men do leave,
Are hated most of those they did deceive: 140
So thou, my surfeit and my heresy,
Of all be hated; but the most, of me:
And all my powers, address your love and might,
To honour Helen, and to be her knight.   *Exit.*

HERMIA.   [*Wakes.*] Help me Lysander, help me: do thy best   145
To pluck this crawling serpent from my breast.
Ay me, for pity. What a dream was here?
Lysander, look how I do quake with fear.
Methought a serpent eat my heart away,
And you sat smiling at his cruel prey.°   150
Lysander: what, removed? Lysander, lord!
What, out of hearing, gone? No sound, no word?
Alack, where are you? Speak, and if you hear:
Speak, of° all loves. I swoon almost with fear.
No? Then I well perceive you are not nigh: 155
Either death, or you, I'll find immediately.   *Exit.*

---

115 *swayed:* ruled.   118 *ripe:* mature.   119 *point:* peak.   *skill:* knowledge.
123 *Wherefore:* why.   128 *flout:* mock.   132 *lord ... gentleness:* more of a gentleman.
150 *prey:* preying.   154 *of:* for the sake of.

ACT 3

[Scene 1. The wood]

Enter the CLOWNS *[*QUINCE, SNUG, BOTTOM, FLUTE, SNOUT, *and* STARVELING.*]*

BOTTOM.   Are we all met?

QUINCE.   Pat, pat: and here's a marvellous convenient place for
   our rehearsal. This green plot shall be our stage, this
   hawthorn brake° our tiring-house,° and we will do it in
   action, as we will do it before the duke.   5

BOTTOM.   Peter Quince?

QUINCE.   What sayest thou, bully° Bottom?

BOTTOM.   There are things in this Comedy of Pyramus and Thisby
   that will never please. First, Pyramus must draw a sword
   to kill himself; which the ladies cannot abide. How   10
   answer you that?

SNOUT.   By'r lakin,° a parlous° fear.

STARVELING.   I believe we must leave the killing out, when all is done.

BOTTOM.   Not a whit: I have a device to make all well. Write me
   a prologue, and let the prologue seem to say, we will   15
   do no harm with our swords, and that Pyramus is not
   killed indeed: and for the more better assurance, tell
   them that I Pyramus am not Pyramus, but Bottom the
   weaver: this will put them out of fear.

QUINCE.   Well, we will have such a prologue, and it shall be   20
   written in eight and six.°

BOTTOM.   No, make it two more: let it be written in eight and
   eight.

SNOUT.   Will not the ladies be afeared of the lion?

STARVELING.   I fear it, I promise you.   25

BOTTOM.   Masters, you ought to consider with yourselves, to bring
   in (God shield us) a lion among ladies, is a most dreadful
   thing. For there is not a more fearful wild-fowl than
   your lion living: and we ought to look to't.

SNOUT.   Therefore another prologue must tell he is not a lion.   30

BOTTOM.   Nay, you must name his name, and half his face must be
   seen through the lion's neck, and he himself must speak
   through, saying thus, or to the same defect:° "Ladies,"
   or "Fair ladies—I would wish you," or "I would request
   you," or "I would entreat you, not to fear,   35
   not to tremble: my life for yours. If you think I come
   hither as a lion, it were pity of my life. No, I am no
   such thing: I am a man as other men are." And there
   indeed let him name his name, and tell them plainly he
   is Snug the joiner.   40

---

4 *brake:* thicket.   *tiring-house:* dressing room.   7 *bully:* "old pal."   12 *By'r lakin:* mild
oath, "by Our Lady."   *parlous:* awful, perilous.   21 *eight and six:* alternate lines of eight
and six syllables (the ballad meter).   33 *defect:* (he means "effect").

QUINCE.   Well, it shall be so, but there is two hard things: that is,
    to bring the moonlight into a chamber: for you know,
    Pyramus and Thisby meet by moonlight.

SNOUT.   Doth the moon shine that night we play our play?

BOTTOM.   A calendar, a calendar: look in the almanac: find out   45
    moonshine, find out moonshine.

QUINCE.   Yes, it doth shine that night.

BOTTOM.   Why then may you leave a casement of the great
    chamber window, where we play, open; and the moon may
    shine in at the casement.   50

QUINCE.   Ay, or else one must come in with a bush of thorns° and
    a lantern, and say he comes to disfigure,° or to present,
    the person of Moonshine. Then, there is another thing;
    we must have a wall in the great chamber: for Pyramus
    and Thisby, says the story, did talk through the chink   55
    of a wall.

SNOUT.   You can never bring in a wall. What say you, Bottom?

BOTTOM.   Some man or other must present wall: and let him have
    some plaster, or some loam, or some rough-cast° about
    him, to signify wall; and let him hold his fingers thus: 60
    and through that cranny, shall Pyramus and Thisby whisper.

QUINCE.   If that may be, then all is well. Come, sit down every
    mother's son, and rehearse your parts. Pyramus, you
    begin: when you have spoken your speech, enter into that
    brake, and so every one according to his cue.   65

Enter PUCK.

PUCK.   What hempen homespuns° have we swagg'ring here,
    So near the cradle of the Fairy Queen?
    What, a play toward°? I'll be an auditor,
    An actor too perhaps, if I see cause.

QUINCE.   Speak Pyramus. Thisby stand forth.   70

PYRAMUS.   Thisby, the flowers of odious savours sweet—

QUINCE.   "Odorous, odorous."

PYRAMUS.   —odours savours sweet,
    So hath thy breath, my dearest Thisby dear.
    But hark, a voice: stay thou but here awhile,   75
    And by and by I will to thee appear.   *Exit PYRAMUS.*
                                                              [*Exit.*]
PUCK.   A stranger Pyramus than e'er played here.

THISBY.   Must I speak now?

QUINCE.   Ay marry must you. For you must understand he goes
    but to see a noise that he heard, and is to come again.   80

THISBY.   Most radiant Pyramus, most lily-white of hue,
    Of colour like the red rose, on triumphant brier,

---

51 *bush of thorns:* bundle of firewood (the man in the moon was supposed to have been
placed there as a punishment for gathering wood on Sundays).   52 *disfigure:* (he means
"figure," symbolize).   59 *rough-cast:* coarse plaster of lime and gravel.   66 *hempen
homespuns:* wearers of clothing spun at home from hemp.   68 *toward:* in preparation.

Most brisky juvenal,° and eke most lovely Jew,°
    As true as truest horse, that yet would never tire,
    I'll meet thee Pyramus, at Ninny's tomb.   85
QUINCE. "Ninus' tomb,"° man: why, you must not speak that yet.
    That you answer to Pyramus. You speak all your part
    at once, cues and all. Pyramus, enter; your cue is past:
    it is "never tire."
THISBY. O—As true as truest horse, that yet would never tire.   90

Enter PYRAMUS with the ass-head [followed by PUCK].

PYRAMUS. If I were fair, Thisby, I were only thine.
QUINCE. O monstrous! O strange! We are haunted. Pray masters,
    fly masters. Help!   *The clowns all exeunt.*
PUCK. I'll follow you: I'll lead you about a round,°
    Through bog, through bush, through brake, through brier.   95
    Sometime a horse I'll be, sometime a hound,
        A hog, a headless bear, sometime a fire,
    And neigh, and bark, and grunt, and roar, and burn,
    Like horse, hound, hog, bear, fire, at every turn.   *Exit.*
BOTTOM. Why do they run away? This is a knavery of them to   100
    make me afeared.

Enter SNOUT.

SNOUT. O Bottom, thou art changed. What do I see on thee?
BOTTOM. What do you see? You see an ass-head of your own, do
    you?   *[Exit SNOUT.]*

Enter QUINCE.

QUINCE. Bless thee Bottom, bless thee. Thou art translated.°   *Exit.*   105
BOTTOM. I see their knavery. This is to make an ass of me, to
    fright me if they could: but I will not stir from this
    place, do what they can. I will walk up and down here,
    and will sing that they shall hear I am not afraid.
        [*Sings.*] The woosel° cock, so black of hue,   110
                With orange tawny bill,
            The throstle,° with his note so true,
                The wren, with little quill.°
TITANIA. What angel wakes me from my flow'ry bed?
BOTTOM. [*Sings.*] The finch, the sparrow, and the lark,   115
                The plain-song° cuckoo gray:
            Whose note full many a man doth mark,
                And dares not answer, nay.
    For indeed, who would set his wit to° so foolish a bird?

83 *brisky juvenal:* lively youth.   *Jew:* diminutive of either "juvenal" or "jewel."
86 *Ninus' tomb:* (tomb of the founder of Nineveh, and meeting place of the lovers in Ovid's
version of the Pyramus story).   94 *about a round:* in circles, like a round dance (round
about).   105 *translated:* transformed.   110 *woosel:* ousel, blackbird.   112 *throstle:*
thrush.   113 *quill:* piping note.   116 *plain-song:* sounding a simple unvaried note.
119 *set . . . to:* match his wit against.

Who would give a bird the lie,° though he cry "cuckoo"° 120
    never so°?
TITANIA. I pray thee, gentle mortal, sing again.
    Mine ear is much enamoured of thy note:
    So is mine eye enthrallèd to thy shape,
    And thy fair virtue's force (perforce°) doth move me, 125
    On the first view to say, to swear, I love thee.
BOTTOM. Methinks mistress, you should have little reason for
    that. And yet, to say the truth, reason and love keep
    little company together now-a-days. The more the pity,
    That some honest neighbours will not make them friends. 130
    Nay, I can gleek° upon occasion.
TITANIA. Thou art as wise as thou art beautiful.
BOTTOM. Not so neither: but if I had wit enough to get out of
    this wood, I have enough to serve mine own turn.
TITANIA. Out of this wood do not desire to go: 135
    Thou shalt remain here, whether thou wilt or no.
    I am a spirit of no common rate:°
    The summer still doth tend upon my state,°
    And I do love thee: therefore go with me.
    I'll give thee fairies to attend on thee: 140
    And they shall fetch thee jewels from the deep,
    And sing, while thou on pressèd flowers dost sleep:
    And I will purge thy mortal grossness so,
    That thou shalt like an airy spirit go.
    Peaseblossom, Cobweb, Moth,° and Mustardseed! 145

Enter four FAIRIES.

PEASEBLOSSOM. Ready.
COBWEB. And I.
MOTH.   And I.
MUSTARDSEED.   And I.
ALL.   Where shall we go?
TITANIA. Be kind and courteous to this gentleman,
    Hop in his walks and gambol° in his eyes,
    Feed him with apricocks° and dewberries,° 150
    With purple grapes, green figs, and mulberries.
    The honey-bags steal from the humblebees,°
    And for night-tapers, crop° their waxen thighs,
    And light them at the fiery glow-worm's eyes,
    To have my love to bed and to arise: 155
    And pluck the wings from painted butterflies,
    To fan the moonbeams from his sleeping eyes.

---

120 *Who . . . lie:* who could call a bird a liar. *"cuckoo":* (which sounded like "cuckold" = a
deceived husband).   121 *never so:* i.e., often.   125 *perforce:* by force.   131 *gleek:* joke
satirically.   137 *rate:* rank, value   138 *still . . . state:* always serves as an attendant in my
royal train.   145 *Moth:* mote (so pronounced), tiny speck.   149 *gambol in:* caper
before.   150 *apricocks:* apricots.   *dewberries:* blackberries.   152 *humblebees:*
bumblebees.   153 *crop:* clip.

Nod to him elves, and do him courtesies.

PEASEBLOSSOM. Hail, mortal.

COBWEB. Hail. 160

MOTH. Hail.

MUSTARDSEED. Hail.

BOTTOM. I cry your worships mercy,° heartily: I beseech your
worship's name.

COBWEB. Cobweb. 165

BOTTOM. I shall desire you of more acquaintance, good Master
Cobweb: if I cut my finger,° I shall make bold with you.
Your name, honest gentleman?

PEASEBLOSSOM. Peaseblossom.

BOTTOM. I pray you commend me° to Mistress Squash,° your mother, 170
and to Master Peascod,° your father. Good Master Peaseblossom,
I shall desire you of more acquaintance, too.
Your name I beseech you sir?

MUSTARDSEED. Mustardseed.

BOTTOM. Good Master Mustardseed, I know your patience well. 175
That same cowardly giant-like ox beef hath devoured
many a gentleman of your house. I promise you, your
kindred hath made my eyes water ere now. I desire you
of more acquaintance, good Master Mustardseed.

TITANIA. Come wait upon him: lead him to my bower. 180
The moon methinks looks with a wat'ry eye:
And when she weeps, weeps every little flower,
Lamenting some enforcèd° chastity.
Tie up my lover's tongue, bring him silently. *Exeunt.*

[Scene 2. Another part of the wood]

Enter [OBERON,] King of Fairies, solus.°

OBERON. I wonder if Titania be awaked;
Then what it was that next came in her eye,
Which she must dote on in extremity.

Enter PUCK.

Here comes my messenger. How now, mad spirit?
What night-rule° now about this haunted grove? 5

PUCK. My mistress with a monster is in love.
Near to her close and consecrated bower,
While she was in her dull° and sleeping hour,
A crew of patches,° rude mechanicals,°
That work for bread upon Athenian stalls,° 10

---

163 *I . . . mercy:* I respectfully beg your pardons.   167 *cut my finger:* (cobwebs were used
to stop bleeding).   170 *commend me:* offer my respects.   *Squash:* unripe peapod.
171 *Peascod:* ripe peapod.   183 *enforcèd:* violated.   Stage direction: *solus:* alone.
5 *night-rule:* diversion ("misrule") in the night.   8 *dull:* drowsy.   9 *patches:* fools.
mechanicals: workers.   10 *stalls:* shops.

Were met together to rehearse a play,
Intended for great Theseus' nuptial day:
The shallowest thickskin of that barren sort,°
Who Pyramus presented in their sport,
Forsook his scene and entered in a brake: 15
When I did him at this advantage take,
An ass's nole° I fixèd on his head.
Anon° his Thisby must be answerèd,
And forth my mimic° comes. When they him spy,
As wild geese, that the creeping fowler° eye,   20
Or russet-pated choughs,° many in sort,°
Rising and cawing at the gun's report,
Sever themselves and madly sweep the sky,
So at his sight away his fellows fly:
And at our stamp, here o'er and o'er one falls: 25
He murder cries, and help from Athens calls.
Their sense thus weak, lost with their fears thus strong,
Made senseless things begin to do them wrong.
For briers and thorns at their apparel snatch:
Some° sleeves, some hats; from yielders, all things catch.°   30
I led them on in this distracted° fear,
And left sweet Pyramus translated there:
When in that moment (so it came to pass)
Titania waked, and straightway loved an ass.
OBERON.   This falls out better than I could devise.   35
    But has thou yet latched° the Athenian's eyes
    With the love-juice, as I did bid thee do?
PUCK.   I took him sleeping (that is finished too)
    And the Athenian woman by his side;
    That when he waked, of force° she must be eyed.   40

Enter DEMETRIUS and HERMIA.

OBERON.   Stand close:° this is the same Athenian.
PUCK.   This is the woman: but not this the man.
DEMETRIUS.   O why rebuke you him that loves you so?
    Lay breath so bitter on your bitter foe.
HERMIA.   Now I but chide: but I should use thee worse,   45
    For thou, I fear, hast given me cause to curse.
    If thou hast slain Lysander in his sleep,
    Being o'er shoes in blood, plunge in the deep,
    And kill me too.
    The sun was not so true unto the day,   50
    As he to me. Would he have stolen away

---

13 *barren sort:* stupid crew.   17 *nole:* head, noodle.   18 *Anon:* presently.   19 *mimic:*
actor.   20 *fowler:* hunter of fowl.   21 *russet-pated choughs:* grey-headed jackdaws.
sort: a flock.   30 *Some:* ie., snatch.   *from yielders . . . catch:* (everything joins in to harm
the weak).   31 *distracted:* maddened.   36 *latched:* moistened.   40 *of force:* by
necessity.   41 *close:* hidden.

From sleeping Hermia? I'll believe as soon
This whole° earth may be bored,° and that the moon
May through the center creep, and so displease
Her brother's noontide with th' Antipodes.°   55
It cannot be but thou hast murdered him.
So should a murderer look; so dead,° so grim.

DEMETRIUS.   So should the murdered look, and so should I,
Pierced through the heart with your stern cruelty.
Yet you, the murderer, look as bright, as clear,   60
As yonder Venus in her glimmering sphere.°

HERMIA.   What's this to my Lysander? Where is he?
Ah good Demetrius, wilt thou give him me?

DEMETRIUS.   I had rather give his carcass to my hounds.

HERMIA.   Out dog, out cur! Thou driv'st me past the bounds   65
Of maiden's patience. Hast thou slain him then?
Henceforth be never numbered among men.
O, once tell true: tell true, even for my sake:
Durst thou have looked upon him, being awake?
And hast thou killed him sleeping? O brave touch°!   70
Could not a worm,° an adder, do so much?
An adder did it: for with doubler tongue°
Than thine, thou serpent, never adder stung.

DEMETRIUS.   You spend your passion on a misprised mood:°
I am not guilty of Lysander's blood: 75
Nor is he dead, for aught that I can tell.

HERMIA.   I pray thee, tell me then that he is well.

DEMETRIUS.   And if I could, what should I get therefore?

HERMIA.   A privilege never to see me more:
And from thy hated presence part I so: 80
See me no more, whether he be dead or no.   *Exit.*

DEMETRIUS.   There is no following her in this fierce vein.
Here therefore for a while I will remain.
So sorrow's heaviness doth heavier grow
For debt that bankrout sleep doth sorrow owe°   85
Which now in some slight measure it will pay,
If for his tender° here I make some stay.°   *Lie down.*

OBERON.   What hast thou done? Thou hast mistaken quite,
And laid the love-juice on some true-love's sight.
Of thy misprision° must perforce° ensue   90
Some true love turned, and not a false turned true.

PUCK.   Then fate o'errules, that one man holding troth,

---

53 *whole:* solid.   *be bored:* have a hole bored through it.   55 *Her brother's . . . Antipodes:*
the noon of her brother sun, by appearing among the Antipodes (the people on the other
side of the earth).   57 *dead:* deadly.   61 *sphere:* (in the Ptolemaic system, each planet
moved in its own sphere around the earth).   70 *brave touch:* splendid stroke (ironic).
71 *worm:* snake.   72 *doubler tongue:* (1) tongue more forked (2) more deceitful speech.
74 *on . . . mood:* in mistaken anger.   85 *For debt . . . owe:* because sleep cannot pay the
debt of repose he owes the man who is kept awake by sorrow.   87 *tender:* offer.   *stay:*
pause.   90 *misprision:* mistake.   *perforce:* of necessity.

A million fail, confounding° oath on oath.°
OBERON.   About the wood, go swifter than the wind,
    And Helena of Athens look thou find.   95
    All fancy-sick° she is, and pale of cheer,°
    With sighs of love, that costs the fresh blood dear.
    By some illusion see thou bring her here:
    I'll charm his eyes against she do appear.°
PUCK.   I go, I go, look how I go.   100
    Swifter than arrow from the Tartar's bow.°   *Exit.*
OBERON.   Flower of this purple dye,
    Hit with Cupid's archery,
    Sink in apple of his eye:
    When his love he doth espy,   105
    Let her shine as gloriously
    As the Venus of the sky.
    When thou wak'st, if she be by,
    Beg of her for remedy.

Enter PUCK.

PUCK.   Captain of our fairy band,   110
    Helena is here at hand,
    And the youth, mistook by me,
    Pleading for a lover's fee.°
    Shall we their fond pageant° see?
    Lord, what fools these mortals be!   115
OBERON.   Stand aside. The noise they make
    Will cause Demetrius to awake.
PUCK.   Then will two at once woo one:
    That must needs be sport alone.°
    And those things do best please me   120
    That befall prepost'rously.

Enter LYSANDER and HELENA.

LYSANDER.   Why should you think that I should woo in scorn?
        Scorn and derision never come in tears.
    Look when I vow, I weep: and vows so born,
        In their nativity all truth appears.°   125
        How can these things in me seem scorn to you,
        Bearing the badge° of faith to prove them true?
HELENA.   You do advance your cunning more and more.
        When truth kills truth,° O devilish-holy fray!
    These vows are Hermia's. Will you give her o'er?   130

---

93 *confounding:* destroying.   *oath on oath:* one oath after another.   96 *fancy-sick:*
lovesick.   *cheer:* face.   99 *against . . . appear:* in preparation for her appearance.
101 *Tartar's bow:* (the Tartars, who used powerful Oriental bows, were famed as archers).
113 *fee:* reward.   114 *fond pageant:* foolish spectacle.   119 *alone:* unique.
124–125 *vows . . . appears:* vows born in weeping must be true ones.   127 *badge:* (1)
outward signs (2) family crest.   129 *truth kills truth:* former true love is killed by vows of
present true love.

Weigh oath with oath, and you will nothing weigh.
Your vows to her and me, put in two scales,
Will even weigh: and both as light as tales.
LYSANDER.   I had no judgment, when to her I swore.
HELENA.   Nor none, in my mind, now you give her o'er.   135
LYSANDER.   Demetrius loves her: and he loves not you.
DEMETRIUS.   (*Awakes.*) O Helen, goddess, nymph, perfect, divine,
To what, my love, shall I compare thine eyne!
Crystal is muddy. O, how ripe in show,
Thy lips, those kissing cherries, tempting grow!   140
That pure congealèd white, high Taurus'° snow,
Fanned with the eastern wind, turns to a crow,
When thou hold'st up thy hand. O let me kiss
This princess of pure white,° this seal of bliss.
HELENA.   O spite! O hell! I see you all are bent   145
To set against me, for your merriment.
If you were civil,° and knew courtesy,
You would not do me thus much injury.
Can you not hate me, as I know you do,
But you must join in souls° to mock me too?   150
If you were men, as men you are in show,
You would not use a gentle lady so;
To vow, and swear, and superpraise my parts,°
When I am sure you hate me with your hearts.
You both are rivals, and love Hermia: 155
And now both rivals, to mock Helena.
A trim° exploit, a manly enterprise,
To conjure tears up in a poor maid's eyes
With your derision. None of noble sort
Would so offend a virgin, and extort°   160
A poor soul's patience, all to make you sport.
LYSANDER.   You are unkind, Demetrius: be not so.
For you love Hermia: this you know I know.
And here, with all good will, with all my heart,
In Hermia's love I yield you up my part: 165
And yours of Helena to be bequeath,
Whom I do love, and will do to my death.
HELENA.   Never did mockers waste more idle breath.
DEMETRIUS.   Lysander, keep thy Hermia: I will none.°
If e'er I loved her, all that love is gone.   170
My heart to her but as guest-wise sojourned:°
And now to Helen is it home returned,
There to remain.
LYSANDER.   Helen, it is not so.

---

141 *Taurus:* mountain range in Asia Minor.   144 *princess . . . white:* sovereign example of
whiteness (her hand).   147 *civil:* well behaved.   150 *join in souls:* agree in spirit.
153 *parts:* qualities.   157 *trim:* fine (ironic).   160 *extort:* wring.   169 *none:* have none
of her.   171 *to her . . . sojourned:* visited her only as a guest.

DEMETRIUS. Disparage not the faith thou dost not know,
    Lest to thy peril thou aby it dear.° 175
    Look where thy love comes: yonder is thy dear.

Enter HERMIA.

HERMIA. Dark night, that from the eye his function takes,
    The ear more quick of apprehension makes.
    Wherein it doth impair the seeing sense,
    It pays the hearing double recompense. 180
    Thou art not by mine eye, Lysander, found:
    Mine ear, I thank it, brought me to thy sound.
    But why unkindly didst thou leave me so?
LYSANDER. Why should he stay, whom love doth press to go?
HERMIA. What love could press Lysander from my side? 185
LYSANDER. Lysander's love, that would not let him bide—
    Fair Helena: who more engilds the night
    Than all your fiery oes and eyes of light.°
    Why seek'st thou me? Could not this make thee know,
    The hate I bare thee made me leave thee so? 190
HERMIA. You speak not as you think: it cannot be.
HELENA. Lo: She is one of this confederacy.
    Now I perceive they have conjoined all three,
    To fashion this false sport in spite of° me.
    Injurious° Hermia, most ungrateful maid, 195
    Have you conspired, have you with these contrived
    To bait° me with this foul derision?
    Is all the counsel° that we two have shared,
    The sisters' vows, the hours that we have spent,
    When we have chid the hasty-footed time 200
    For parting us; O, is all forgot?
    All schooldays' friendship, childhood innocence?
    We Hermia, like two artificial° gods,
    Have with our needles created both one flower,
    Both on one sampler,° sitting on one cushion, 205
    Both warbling of one song, both in one key;
    As if our hands, our sides, voices, and minds
    Had been incorporate.° So we grew together,
    Like to a double cherry, seeming parted,
    But yet an union in partition, 210
    Two lovely berries moulded on one stem:
    So with two seeming bodies, but one heart,
    Two of the first, like coats in heraldry,
    Due but to one, and crownèd with one crest.°

---

175 *aby it dear:* buy it at a high price. 188 *oes . . . light:* stars. 194 *in spite of:* to spite.
195 *Injurious:* insulting. 197 *bait:* attack. 198 *counsel:* secrets. 203 *artificial:* skilled
in art. 205 *sampler:* work of embroidery. 208 *incorporate:* in one body.
213–214 *Two . . . crest:* (the two bodies being) like double coats of arms joined under one
crest (with one heart).

And will you rent° our ancient love asunder,   215
To join with men in scorning your poor friend?
It is not friendly, 'tis not maidenly.
Our sex, as well as I, may chide you for it;
Though I alone do feel the injury.

HERMIA.   I am amazèd at your passionate words: 220
I scorn you not. It seems that you scorn me.

HELENA.   Have you not set Lysander, as in scorn,
To follow me, and praise my eyes and face?
And made your other love, Demetrius
(Who even but now did spurn° me with his foot)   225
To call me goddess, nymph, divine, and rare,
Precious, celestial? Wherefore speaks he this
To her he hates? And wherefore doth Lysander
Deny your love, so rich within his soul,
And tender° me (forsooth) affection,   230
But by your setting on, by your consent?
What though I be not so in grace° as you,
So hung upon with love, so fortunate,
But miserable most, to love unloved?
This you should pity, rather than despise.   235

HERMIA.   I understand not what you mean by this.

HELENA.   Ay, do. Persèver, counterfeit sad° looks:
Make mouths upon° me when I turn my back:
Wink each at other, hold the sweet jest up.
This sport well carried, shall be chronicled.°   240
If you have any pity, grace, or manners,
You would not make me such an argument.°
But fare ye well: 'tis partly my own fault:
Which death or absence soon shall remedy.

LYSANDER.   Stay, gentle Helena: hear my excuse,   245
My love, my life, my soul, fair Helena.

HELENA.   O excellent!

HERMIA.   Sweet, do not scorn her so.

DEMETRIUS.   If she cannot entreat,° I can compel.

LYSANDER.   Thou canst compel no more than she entreat.
Thy threats have no more strength than her weak prayers.   250
Helen, I love thee, by my life I do:
I swear by that which I will lose for thee,
To prove° him false that says I love thee not.

DEMETRIUS.   I say I love thee more than he can do.

LYSANDER.   If thou say so, withdraw, and prove° it too.   255

DEMETRIUS.   Quick, come.

HERMIA.   Lysander, whereto tends all this?

---

215 *rent:* rend, tear.   225 *spurn:* kick.   230 *tender:* offer.   232 *in grace:* favored.
237 *sad:* serious.   238 *mouths upon:* faces at.   240 *chronicled:* written down in the
history books.   242 *argument:* subject (of your mockery).   248 *entreat:* sway you by
entreaty.   253, 255 *prove:* i.e., by a duel.

LYSANDER. Away, you Ethiope.°
DEMETRIUS.   No, no, sir,
  Seem to break loose: take on° as you would follow;
  But yet come not.° You are a tame man, go.
LYSANDER. Hang off,° thou cat, thou burr: vile thing, let loose;   260
  Or I will shake thee from me like a serpent.
HERMIA. Why are you grown so rude? What change is this,
  Sweet love?
LYSANDER.   Thy love? Out, tawny Tartar, out:
  Out, loathèd med'cine: O hated potion, hence!
HERMIA. Do you not jest?
HELENA.   Yes sooth: and so do you.   265
LYSANDER. Demetrius, I will keep my word° with thee.
DEMETRIUS. I would I had your bond.° For I perceive
  A weak bond holds you. I'll not trust your word.
LYSANDER. What? Should I hurt her, strike her, kill her dead?
  Although I hate her, I'll not harm her so.   270
HERMIA. What? Can you do me greater harm than hate?
  Hate me, wherefore°? O me, what news,° my love?
  Am not I Hermia? Are not you Lysander?
  I am as fair now, as I was erewhile.°
  Since night, you loved me; yet since night, you left me.   275
  Why then, you left me—O, the gods forbid—
  In earnest, shall I say?
LYSANDER.   Ay, by my life:
  And never did desire to see thee more.
  Therefore be out of hope, of question, of doubt:
  Be certain: nothing truer: 'tis no jest   280
  That I do hate thee, and love Helena.
HERMIA. O me, you juggler,° you canker blossom,°
  You thief of love: what, have you come by night,
  And stol'n my love's heart from him?
HELENA.   Fine, i' faith.   285
  Have you no modesty, no maiden shame,
  No touch of bashfulness? What, will you tear
  Impatient answers from my gentle tongue?
  Fie, fie, you counterfeit, you puppet,° you.
HERMIA. Puppet? Why so—ay, that way goes the game.
  Now I perceive that she hath made compare   290
  Between our statures, she hath urged her height,
  And with her personage, her tall personage,
  Her height (forsooth) she hath prevailed with him.

---

257 *Ethiope:* (because she is a brunette).   258–259 *Seem . . . not:* You only seem to break
loose from Hermia and pretend to follow me to a duel, but you actually hold back.
260 *Hang off:* let go.   266 *keep my word:* i.e., to duel.   267 *bond:* written agreement.
272 *wherefore:* why.   *what news:* what's the matter.   274 *erewhile:* a short while ago.
282 *juggler:* deceiver.   *canker blossom:* worm that causes canker in blossoms.
288 *puppet:* (Hermia is short and Helena tall).

And are you grown so high in his esteem,
Because I am so dwarfish and so low?   295
How low am I, thou painted maypole? Speak:
How low am I? I am not yet so low,
But that my nails can reach unto thine eyes.
HELENA.   I pray you, though you mock me, gentlemen,
Let her not hurt me. I was never curst:°   300
I have no gift at all in shrewishness:
I am a right maid for my cowardice:°
Let her not strike me. You perhaps may think,
Because she is something lower than myself,
That I can match her.
HERMIA.   Lower? Hark again.   305
HELENA.   Good Hermia, do not be so bitter with me,
I evermore did love you Hermia.
Did ever keep your counsels, never wronged you;
Save that in love unto Demetrius,
I told him of your stealth unto this wood.   310
He followed you: for love I followed him.
But he hath chid me hence, and threatened me
To strike me, spurn me, nay to kill me too;
And now, so° you will let me quiet go,
To Athens will I bear my folly back,   315
And follow you no further. Let me go.
You see how simple and how fond° I am.
HERMIA.   Why, get you gone. Who is't that hinders you?
HELENA.   A foolish heart, that I leave here behind.
HERMIA.   What, with Lysander?
HELENA.   With Demetrius.   320
LYSANDER.   Be not afraid: she shall not harm thee Helena.
DEMETRIUS.   No sir: she shall not, though you take her part.
HELENA.   O when she's angry, she is keen and shrewd.°
She was a vixen when she went to school:
And though she be but little, she is fierce.   325
HERMIA.   "Little" again? Nothing but "low" and "little"?
Why will you suffer her to flout° me thus?
Let me come to her.
LYSANDER.   Get you gone, you dwarf;
You minimus,° of hind'ring knot-grass° made;
You bead, you acorn.
DEMETRIUS.   You are too officious   330
In her behalf that scorns your services.
Let her alone: speak not of Helena,
Take not her part. For if thou dost intend°

---

300 *curst:* bad-tempered.   302 *right . . . cowardice:* true woman in being cowardly.
314 *so:* if.   317 *fond:* foolish.   323 *keen and shrewd:* sharp and malicious.   327 *flout:*
mock.   329 *minimus:* smallest of creatures.   *knot-grass:* weed believed to stunt the
growth if eaten.   333 *intend:* extend.

Never so little show of love to her,
Thou shalt aby it.°
LYSANDER.   Now she holds me not: 335
Now follow, if thou dar'st, to try whose right,
Of thine or mine, is most in Helena.°
DEMETRIUS.   Follow? Nay, I'll go with thee, cheek by jowl.

Exeunt LYSANDER *and* DEMETRIUS.

HERMIA.   You, mistress, all this coil is long of° you.
Nay, go not back.
HELENA.   I will not trust you, I,   340
Nor longer stay in your curst company
Your hands than mine are quicker for a fray:
My legs are longer though, to run away.   [*Exit.*]
HERMIA.   I am amazed,° and know not what to say.   *Exit.*
OBERON.   This is thy negligence: still thou mistak'st,   345
Or else commit'st thy knaveries wilfully.
PUCK.   Believe me, king of shadows, I mistook.
Did not you tell me I should know the man
By the Athenian garments he had on?
And so far blameless proves my enterprise,   350
That I have 'nointed an Athenian's eyes:
And so far am I glad it so did sort,°
As this their jangling I esteem a sport.
OBERON.   Thou seest these lovers seek a place to fight;
Hie therefore Robin, overcast the night,   355
The starry welkin° cover thou anon
With drooping fog as black as Acheron,°
And lead these testy° rivals so astray,
As° one come not within another's way.
Like to Lysander sometime frame thy tongue: 360
Then stir Demetrius up with bitter wrong:°
And sometime rail thou like Demetrius:
And from each other look thou lead them thus;
Till o'er their brows death-counterfeiting sleep
With leaden legs and batty wings doth creep: 365
Then crush this herb into Lysander's eye;
Whose liquor hath this virtuous° property,
To take from thence all error with his might,
And make his eyeballs roll with wonted° sight.
When they next wake, all this derision°   370
Shall seem a dream, and fruitless vision,
And back to Athens shall the lovers wend,

---

335 *aby it:* buy it dearly.   336–337 *try . . . Helena:* prove by fighting which of us has most
right to Helena.   339 *coil is long of:* turmoil is because of.   344 *amazed:* confused.
352 *sort:* turn out.   356 *welkin:* sky.   357 *Acheron:* one of the four rivers in the
underworld.   358 *testy:* irritable.   359 *As:* so that.   361 *wrong:* insult.
367 *virtuous:* potent.   369 *wonted:* (previously) accustomed.   370 *derision:* laughable
interlude.

With league whose date° till death shall never end.
Whiles I in this affair do thee employ,
I'll to my queen and beg her Indian boy: 375
And then I will her charmèd eye release
From monster's view, and all things shall be peace.

PUCK.   My fairy lord, this must be done with haste,
For night's swift dragons cut the clouds full fast:
And yonder shines Aurora's harbinger,°   380
At whose approach, ghosts wand'ring here and there,
Troop home to churchyards: damnèd spirits all,
That in crossways° and floods° have burial,
Already to their wormy beds are gone:
For fear lest day should look their shames upon,   385
They wilfully themselves exile from light,
And must for aye consort° with black-browed night.

OBERON.   But we are spirits of another sort.
I with the morning's love have oft made sport,°
And like a forester, the groves may tread   390
Even till the eastern gate all fiery red,
Opening on Neptune, with fair blessèd beams,
Turns into yellow gold his salt green streams.
But notwithstanding, haste, make no delay:
We may effect this business yet ere day.   [*Exit.*]   395

PUCK.   Up and down, up and down,
I will lead them up and down.
I am feared in field and town.
Goblin, lead them up and down.
Here comes one.   400

Enter LYSANDER.

LYSANDER.   Where art thou, proud Demetrius? Speak thou now.
PUCK.   Here villain, drawn° and ready. Where art thou?
LYSANDER.   I will be with thee straight.
PUCK.   Follow me then
To plainer° ground.   [*Exit LYSANDER.*]

Enter DEMETRIUS.

DEMETRIUS.   Lysander, speak again.
Thou runaway, thou coward, art thou fled?   405
Speak: in some bush? Where dost thou hide thy head?
PUCK.   Thou coward, art thou bragging to the stars,
Telling the bushes that thou look'st for wars,
And wilt not come? Come recreant,° come thou child,

---

373 *date:* term.   380 *Aurora's harbinger:* the morning star heralding Aurora, the dawn.
383 *crossways:* crossroads, where suicides were buried.   *floods:* those who drowned.
387 *aye consort:* ever associate.   389 *morning's . . . sport:* hunted with Cephalus (beloved of
Aurora and himself devoted to his wife Procris, whom he killed by accident; "sport" also =
"amorous dalliance," and "love" = Aurora's love for Oberon).   402 *drawn:* with sword
drawn.   404 *plainer:* more level.   409 *recreant:* oath-breaker, coward.

I'll whip thee with a rod. He is defiled   410
That draws a sword on thee.
DEMETRIUS.   Yea, art thou there?
PUCK.   Follow my voice: we'll try no manhood° here.   *Exeunt.*

[*Enter* LYSANDER.]

LYSANDER.   He goes before me and still dares me on:
When I come where he calls, then he is gone
The villain is much lighter-heeled than I;   415
I followed fast: but faster he did fly,
That fallen am I in dark uneven way,
And here will rest me. (*Lie down.*) Come thou gentle day,
For if but once thou show me thy grey light.
I'll find Demetrius and revenge this spite.   [*Sleeps.*]   420

Enter PUCK *and* DEMETRIUS.

PUCK.   Ho, ho, ho! Coward, why com'st thou not?
DEMETRIUS.   Abide° me, if thou dar'st, for well I wot°
Thou run'st before me, shifting every place,
And dar'st not stand, nor look me in the face.
Where art thou now?
PUCK.   Come hither: I am here.   425
DEMETRIUS.   Nay then thou mock'st me. Thou shalt buy this dear,°
If ever I thy face by daylight see.
Now go thy way. Faintness constraineth me
To measure out my length on this cold bed.
By day's approach look to be visited.   [*Lies down and sleeps.*]   430

Enter HELENA.

HELENA.   O weary night, O long and tedious night,
Abate° thy hours; shine comforts° from the east,
That I may back to Athens by daylight,
From these that my poor company detest:
And sleep, that sometimes shuts up sorrow's eye.   435
Steal me awhile from mine own company.   *Sleeps.*
PUCK.   Yet but three? Come one more,
Two of both kinds makes up four.
Here she comes, curst° and sad.
Cupid is a knavish lad,   440
Thus to make poor females mad.

Enter HERMIA.

HERMIA.   Never so weary, never so in woe,
Bedabbled with the dew, and torn with briers:
I can no further crawl, no further go:

---

412 *try no manhood:* test no valor.   422 *Abide:* wait for.   *wot:* know.   426 *buy this dear:* pay dearly for this.   432 *Abate:* shorten.   *shine comforts:* may comforts shine. 439 *curst:* cross.

My legs can keep no pace with my desires.   445
Here will I rest me till the break of day.
Heavens shield Lysander, if they mean a fray.   [*Lies down and sleeps.*]

PUCK.   On the ground,
 Sleep sound:
 I'll apply   450
 To your eye,
Gentle lover, remedy.   [*Squeezes the love-juice on* LYSANDER'S *eyelids.*]
 When thou wak'st,
 Thou tak'st
 True delight   455
 In the sight
Of thy former lady's eye:
And the country proverb known,
That every man should take his own,
In your waking shall be shown.   460
 Jack shall have Jill:
 Naught shall go ill:
The man shall have his mare again, and all shall be well.

[*Exit* PUCK. *The lovers remain asleep on stage.*]

ACT 4

[Scene 1. The wood]

Enter [TITANIA] QUEEN OF FAIRIES, *and* [BOTTOM THE] CLOWN, *and* FAIRIES, *and the* KING [OBERON] *behind them* [*unseen*].

TITANIA.   Come sit thee down upon this flow'ry bed,
 While I thy amiable° cheeks do coy,°
 And stick musk-roses in thy sleek smooth head,
 And kiss thy fair large ears, my gentle joy.
BOTTOM.   Where's Peaseblossom?   5
PEASEBLOSSOM.   Ready.
BOTTOM.   Scratch my head, Peaseblossom. Where's Mounsieur
 Cobweb?
COBWEB.   Ready.
BOTTOM.   Mounsieur Cobweb, good mounsieur, get you your weapons   10
 in your hand, and kill me a red-hipped humblebee on
 the top of a thistle: and good mounsieur, bring me the
 honey-bag. Do not fret yourself too much in the action,
 mounsieur: and good mounsieur have a care the honey-
 bag break not, I would be loath to have you overflowen   15
 with a honey bag, signior. Where's Mounsieur
 Mustardseed?
MUSTARDSEED.   Ready.

2 *amiable:* lovely.   *coy:* caress.

BOTTOM.   Give me your neaf,° Mounsieur Mustardseed. Pray you
leave your curtsy,° good mounsieur.   20
MUSTARDSEED.   What's your will?
BOTTOM.   Nothing, good mounsieur, but to help Cavalery° Cobweb
to scratch. I must to the barber's mounsieur, for
methinks I am marvellous hairy about the face. And I am
such a tender ass, if my hair do but tickle me, I must   25
scratch.
TITANIA.   What, will thou hear some music, my sweet love?
BOTTOM.   I have a reasonable good ear in music. Let's have the tongs°
and the bones.°
TITANIA.   Or say, sweet love, what thou desirest to eat.   30
BOTTOM.   Truly, a peck of provender. I could munch your good
dry oats. Methinks I have a great desire to a bottle° of hay.
Good hay, sweet hay, hath no fellow.
TITANIA.   I have a venturous fairy that shall seek
The squirrel's hoard, and fetch thee new nuts.   35
BOTTOM.   I had rather have a handful or two of dried pease. But
I pray you, let none of your people stir me: I have an
exposition of° sleep come upon me.
TITANIA.   Sleep thou, and I will wind thee in my arms.
Fairies, be gone, and be all ways° away.   *[Exeunt FAIRIES.]*   40
So doth the woodbine the sweet honeysuckle
Gently entwist: the female ivy so
Enrings the barky fingers of the elm.
O how I love thee! how I dote on thee!   *[They sleep.]*

Enter ROBIN GOODFELLOW [PUCK.]

OBERON.   *[Advances.]* Welcome good Robin. Seest thou this sweet sight?   45
Her dotage now I do begin to pity.
For meeting her of late behind the wood,
Seeking sweet favours° for this hateful fool,
I did upbraid her and fall out with her.
For she his hairy temples then had rounded   50
With coronet of fresh and fragrant flowers
And that same dew which sometime° on the buds
Was wont to° swell like round and orient° pearls,
Stood now within the pretty flowerets' eyes,
Like tears that did their own disgrace bewail.   55
When I had at my pleasure taunted her,
And she in mild terms begged my patience,
I then did ask of her her changeling child:
Which straight she gave me, and her fairy sent

19 *neaf:* fist.   20 *leave your curtsy:* either (a) stop bowing, or (b) replace your hat.
22 *Cavalery:* (he means "cavalier").   29 *tongs:* crude music made by striking tongs with a
piece of metal.   *bones:* pieces of bone held between the fingers and clapped together
rhythmically.   32 *bottle:* bundle.   38 *exposition of:* (he means "disposition to").   40 *all
ways:* in every direction.   48 *favours:* bouquets as love tokens.   52 *sometime:* formerly.
53 *Was wont to:* used to.   *orient:* (where the most beautiful pearls came from).

To bear him to my bower in fairy land. 60
And now I have the boy, I will undo
This hateful imperfection of her eyes.
And gentle Puck, take this transformèd scalp
From off the head of this Athenian swain;
That he awaking when the other do, 65
May all to Athens back again repair,°
And think no more of this night's accidents,°
But as the fierce vexation of a dream.
But first I will release the Fairy Queen.
  Be as thou wast wont to be: 70
  See, as thou wast wont to see.
  Dian's bud o'er Cupid's flower°
  Hath such force and blessèd power.
Now my Titania, wake you, my sweet queen.
TITANIA. My Oberon, what visions have I seen! 75
Methought I was enamoured of an ass.
OBERON. There lies your love.
TITANIA.   How came these things to pass?
O, how mine eyes do loathe his visage now!
OBERON. Silence awhile Robin, take off this head:
Titania, music call, and strike more dead 80
Than common sleep of all these five the sense.°
TITANIA. Music, ho music! such as charmeth sleep.
PUCK. Now, when thou wak'st, with thine own fools' eyes peep.
OBERON. Sound music: *Music still.*°
         come my queen, take hands with me,
And rock the ground whereon these sleepers be.   [*Dance.*] 85
Now thou and I are new in amity,
And will tomorrow midnight solemnly
Dance in Duke Theseus' house triumphantly,°
And bless it to all fair prosperity.
There shall the pairs of faithful lovers be 90
Wedded, with Theseus, all in jollity.
PUCK.   Fairy King, attend and mark:
  I do hear the morning lark.
OBERON. Then my queen, in silence sad,°
  Trip we after the night's shade: 95
  We the globe can compass soon,
  Swifter than the wand'ring moon.
TITANIA. Come my lord, and in our flight,
  Tell me how it came this night,
  That I sleeping here was found, 100
  With these mortals on the ground.   *Exeunt.*

---

66 *repair:* return.   67 *accidents:* incidents.   72 *Dian's bud . . . flower:* (Diana's bud counteracts the effects of love-in-idleness, the pansy).   80–81 *strike . . . sense:* Make these five (the lovers and Bottom) sleep more soundly.   84.1 stage direction: *still:* continuously.   88 *triumphantly:* in celebration.   94 *sad:* serious.

Wind° horns. Enter THESEUS, HIPPOLYTA, EGEUS *and all his train.*

THESEUS.   Go one of you, find out the forester:
    For now our observation° is performed.
    And since we have the vaward° of the day,
    My love shall hear the music of my hounds.   105
    Uncouple° in the western valley, let them go:
    Dispatch I say, and find the forester.   *[Exit an* ATTENDANT.*]*
    We will, fair queen, up to the mountain's top,
    And mark the musical confusion
    Of hounds and echo in conjunction.   110
HIPPOLYTA.   I was with Hercules and Cadmus° once,
    When in a wood of Crete they bayed the bear,°
    With hounds of Sparta:° never did I hear
    Such gallant chiding. For besides the groves,
    The skies, the fountains, every region near   115
    Seemed all one mutual cry. I never heard
    So musical a discord, such sweet thunder.
THESEUS.   My hounds are bred out of the Spartan kind:
    So flewed, so sanded:° and their heads are hung
    With ears that sweep away the morning dew,   120
    Crook-kneed, and dewlapped° like Thessalian bulls:
    Slow in pursuit; but matched in mouth like bells,
    Each under each.° A cry° more tuneable
    Was never holloa'd to, nor cheered with horn,
    In Crete, in Sparta, nor in Thessaly.   125
    Judge when you hear. But soft.° What nymphs are these?
EGEUS.   My lord, this is my daughter here asleep,
    And this Lysander, this Demetrius is,
    This Helena, old Nedar's Helena.
    I wonder of their being here together.   130
THESEUS.   No doubt they rose up early to observe
    The rite of May: and hearing our intent,
    Came here in grace° of our solemnity.
    But speak Egeus, is not this the day
    That Hermia should give answer of her choice?   135
EGEUS.   It is, my lord.
THESEUS.   Go bid the huntsmen wake them with their horns.

Shout within: wind horns. They all start up.

    Good morrow, friends. Saint Valentine is past.

101.1 stage direction: *wind:* blow, sound.   103 *observation:* observance of the May Day
rites.   104 *vaward:* vanguard, earliest part.   106 *Uncouple:* unleash (the dogs).
111 *Cadmus:* mythical builder of Thebes.   112 *bayed the bear:* brought the bear to bay, to
its last stand.   113 *hounds of Sparta:* (a breed famous for their swiftness and quick scent).
119 *flewed, so sanded:* with hanging cheeks, so sand-colored.   121 *dewlapped:* with skin
hanging from the chin.   122–23 *matched . . . each:* with each voice matched for harmony
with the next in pitch, like bells in a chime.   123 *cry:* pack of dogs.   126 *soft:* wait.
133 *grace:* honor.

Begin these wood-birds but to couple now?°
LYSANDER.   Pardon, my lord.   [*They kneel.*]
THESEUS.   I pray you all, stand up.   140
 I know you two are rival enemies.
 How comes this gentle concord in the world,
 That hatred is so far from jealousy,°
 To sleep by hate° and fear no enmity?
LYSANDER.   My lord, I shall reply amazedly,   145
 Half sleep, half waking. But as yet, I swear,
 I cannot truly say how I came here.
 But as I think—for truly would I speak,
 And now I do bethink me, so it is—
 I came with Hermia hither. Our intent   150
 Was to be gone from Athens, where we might,
 Without° the peril of the Athenian law—
EGEUS.   Enough, enough, my lord: you have enough.
 I beg the law, the law upon his head:
 They would have stol'n away, they would, Demetrius,   155
 Thereby to have defeated you and me:
 You of your wife, and me of my consent:
 Of my consent that she should be your wife.
DEMETRIUS.   My lord, fair Helen told me of their stealth,
 Of this their purpose hither, to this wood,   160
 And I in fury hither followed them;
 Fair Helena in fancy° following me.
 But my good lord, I wot not by what power
 (But by some power it is) my love to Hermia,
 Melted as the snow, seems to me now   165
 As the remembrance of an idle gaud,°
 Which in my childhood I did dote upon:
 And all the faith, the virtue of my heart,
 The object and the pleasure of mine eye,
 Is only Helena. To her, my lord,   170
 Was I betrothed ere I saw Hermia:
 But like a sickness,° did I loathe this food.
 But as in health, come° to my natural taste,
 Now I do wish it, love it, long for it.
 And will for evermore be true to it.   175
THESEUS.   Fair lovers, you are fortunately met.
 Of this discourse we more will hear anon.
 Egeus, I will overbear your will:
 For in the temple, by and by,° with us,
 These couples shall eternally be knit.   180
 And for the morning now is something worn,°

138–139 *Saint . . . now:* (birds traditionally chose their mates on St. Valentine's Day).
143 *jealousy:* suspicion. 144 *hate:* one it hates. 152 *Without:* beyond. 162 *in fancy:*
out of doting love. 166 *idle gaud:* trifling toy. 172 *sickness:* sick person. 173 *come:*
i.e., back. 179 *by and by:* immediately. 181 *something worn:* somewhat worn on.

Our purposed hunting shall be set aside.
Away with us to Athens. Three and three,
We'll hold a feast in great solemnity.
Come Hippolyta.   185

Exeunt Duke [Hippolyta, Egeus] *and* Lords.

DEMETRIUS. These things seem small and undistinguishable,
      Like far-off mountains turnèd into clouds.
HERMIA. Methinks I see these things with parted° eye,
      When everything seems double.
HELENA.   So methinks:
      And I have found Demetrius, like a jewel,   190
      Mine own, and not mine own.°
DEMETRIUS.   Are you sure
      That we are awake? It seems to me,
      That yet we sleep, we dream. Do not you think
      The duke was here, and bid us follow him?
HERMIA. Yea, and my father.
HELENA.   And Hippolyta.   195
LYSANDER. And he did bid us follow to the temple.
DEMETRIUS. Why then, we are awake: let's follow him,
      And by the way let us recount our dreams.   *Exeunt Lovers.*
BOTTOM. (*Wakes.*) When my cue comes, call me, and I will answer.
      My next is "Most fair Pyramus." Hey ho. Peter Quince?   200
      Flute the bellows-mender? Snout the tinker? Starveling?
      God's my life! Stol'n hence, and left me asleep? I have
      had a most rare vision. I have had a dream, past the wit
      of man to say what dream it was. Man is but an ass, if he
      go about° to expound this dream. Methought I was—   205
      there is no man can tell what. Methought I was, and
      methought I had—but man is but a patched fool,° if he
      will offer to say what methought I had. The eye of man
      hath not heard, the ear of man hath not seen, man's hand is
      not able to taste, his tongue to conceive, nor his   210
      heart to report, what my dream was. I will get Peter
      Quince to write a ballad of this dream: it shall be called
      Bottom's Dream; because it hath no bottom: and I
      will sing it in the latter end of our play, before the duke.
      Peradventure, to make it the more gracious, I shall sing   215
      it at her° death.

Exit.

[Scene 2. Athens, Quince's house]

Enter Quince, Flute, Snout, *and* Starveling.

QUINCE. Have you sent to Bottom's house? Is he come home yet?

---

188 *parted:* divided (each eye seeing a separate image).   190–191 *like . . . own:* like a
person who finds a jewel: the finder is the owner, but insecurely so.   205 *go about:*
attempt.   207 *patched fool:* fool dressed in motley.   216 *her:* Thisby's.

STARVELING.   He cannot be heard of. Out of doubt he is transported.°
FLUTE.   If he come not, then the play is marred. It goes not forward,
    doth it?
QUINCE.   It is not possible. You have not a man in all Athens able   5
    to discharge° Pyramus but he.
FLUTE.   No, he hath simply the best wit of any handicraft man in Athens.
QUINCE.   Yea, and the best person too, and he is a very paramour
    for a sweet voice.
FLUTE.   You must say "paragon." A paramour is (God bless us)   10
    a thing of naught.°

Enter SNUG THE JOINER.

SNUG.   Masters, the duke is coming from the temple, and there
    is two or three lords and ladies more married. If our
    sport had gone forward, we had all been made men.°
FLUTE.   O sweet bully Bottom. Thus hath he lost sixpence a day°   15
    during his life: he could not have 'scaped sixpence a day.
    And the duke had not given him sixpence a day for playing
    Pyramus, I'll be hanged. He would have deserved it.
    Sixpence a day in Pyramus, or nothing.

Enter BOTTOM.

BOTTOM.   Where are these lads? Where are these hearts?   20
QUINCE.   Bottom! O most courageous° day! O most happy hour!
BOTTOM.   Masters, I am to discourse wonders: but ask me not what.
    For if I tell you, I am not true Athenian. I will tell you
    everything, right as it fell out.
QUINCE.   Let us hear, sweet Bottom.   25
BOTTOM.   Not a word of me. All that I will tell you is, that the
    duke hath dined. Get your apparel together, good
    strings to your beards, new ribbands to your pumps, meet
    presently° at the palace, every man look o'er his part: for
    the short and the long is, our play is preferred.° In any   30
    case, let Thisby have clean linen: and let not him that
    plays the lion pare his nails, for they shall hang out for
    the lion's claws. And most dear actors, eat no onions nor
    garlic, for we are to utter sweet breath: and I do not
    doubt but to hear them say it is a sweet comedy. No more   35
    words: away, go away.   *Exeunt.*

---

2 *transported:* carried away (by spirits).   6 *discharge:* portray.   11 *of naught:* wicked,
naughty.   14 *made men:* men made rich.   15 *sixpence a day:* i.e., as a pension.
21 *courageous:* (he may mean "auspicious").   29 *presently:* immediately.
30 *preferred:* recommended (for presentation).

ACT 5

[Scene 1. The palace of Theseus]

Enter THESEUS, HIPPOLYTA, *and* PHILOSTRATE, *and his* LORDS.

HIPPOLYTA. 'Tis strange, my Theseus, that these lovers speak of.
THESEUS. More strange than true. I never may believe
    These antick° fables, nor these fairy toys.°
    Lovers and madmen have such seething brains,
    Such shaping fantasies,° that apprehend   5
    More than cool reason ever comprehends.
    The lunatic, the lover, and the poet,
    Are of imagination all compact.°
    One sees more devils than vast hell can hold:
    That is the madman. The lover, all as frantic,   10
    Sees Helen's beauty in a brow of Egypt.°
    The poet's eye, in a fine frenzy rolling,
    Doth glance from heaven to earth, from earth to heaven.
    And as imagination bodies forth
    The forms of things unknown, the poet's pen   15
    Turns them to shapes, and gives to airy nothing,
    A local habitation and a name.
    Such tricks hath strong imagination,
    That if it would but apprehend some joy,
    It comprehends° some bringer of that joy.   20
    Or in the night, imagining some fear,
    How easy is a bush supposed a bear.
HIPPOLYTA. But all the story of the night told over,
    And all their minds transfigured so together,
    More witnesseth than fancy's images,°   25
    And grows to something of great constancy:°
    But howsoever, strange and admirable.°

Enter LOVERS: LYSANDER, DEMETRIUS, HERMIA, *and* HELENA.

THESEUS. Here come the lovers, full of joy and mirth.
    Joy, gentle friends, joy and fresh days of love
    Accompany your hearts.
LYSANDER.   More° than to us   30
    Wait in your royal walks, your board, your bed.
THESEUS. Come now, what masques,° what dances shall we have,
    To wear away this long age of three hours
    Between our after-supper° and bed-time?

---

3 *antick:* fantastic.   *fairy toys:* trivial fairy stories.   5 *fantasies:* imaginations.   8 *of . . . compact:* totally composed of imagination.   11 *a brow of Egypt:* the swarthy face of a gypsy (believed to come from Egypt).   20 *comprehends:* includes.   25 *More . . . images:* testifies that it is more than just imagination.   26 *constancy:* certainty.   27 *admirable:* to be wondered at.   30 *More:* even more (joy and love).   32, 40 *masques:* lavish courtly entertainments combining song and dance.   34 *after-supper:* late supper.

Where is our usual manager of mirth?   35
What revels are in hand? Is there no play,
To ease the anguish of a torturing hour?
Call Philostrate.
PHILOSTRATE.   Here, mighty Theseus.
THESEUS. Say, what abridgment° have you for this evening?
What masque,° what music? How shall we beguile   40
The lazy time, if not with some delight?
PHILOSTRATE.   There is a brief° how many sports are ripe:°
Make choice of which your highness will see first.

[*Gives a paper.*]

THESEUS.   "The battle with the Centaurs, to be sung
By an Athenian eunuch to the harp."   45
We'll none of that. That have I told my love
In glory of my kinsman Hercules.
"The riot of the tipsy Bacchanals,
Tearing the Thracian singer in their rage."°
That is an old device: and it was played   50
When I from Thebes came last a conqueror.
"The thrice three Muses mourning for the death
Of Learning, late deceased in beggary."
That is some satire keen and critical,
Not sorting with° a nuptial ceremony.   55
"A tedious brief scene of young Pyramus
And his love Thisby; very tragical mirth."
Merry and tragical? Tedious and brief?
That is hot ice and wondrous strange snow.
How shall we find the concord of this discord?   60
PHILOSTRATE.   A play there is, my lord, some ten words long,
Which is as brief as I have known a play:
But by ten words, my lord, it is too long,
Which makes it tedious: for in all the play
There is not one word apt, one player fitted.°   65
And tragical, my noble lord, it is:
For Pyramus therein doth kill himself.
Which when I saw rehearsed, I must confess,
Made mine eyes water; but more merry tears
The passion of loud laughter never shed.   70
THESEUS.   What are they that do play it?
PHILOSTRATE.   Hard-handed men, that work in Athens here,
Which never laboured in their minds till now:
And now have toiled their unbreathed° memories
With this same play, against° your nuptial.   75

39 *abridgment:* either (a) diversion to make the hours seem shorter or (b) short
entertainment.   42 *brief:* list.   *ripe:* ready.   48–49 *riot . . . rage:* (The singer Orpheus
of Thrace was torn limb from limb by the Maenads, frenzied female priests of Bacchus).
55 *sorting with:* befitting.   65 *fitted:* (well) cast.   74 *unbreathed:* unpracticed,
unexercised.   75 *against:* in preparation for.

THESEUS.   And we will hear it.
PHILOSTRATE.   No, my noble lord,
 It is not for you. I have heard it over,
 And it is nothing, nothing in the world;
 Unless you can find sport in their intents,
 Extremely stretched and conned° with cruel pain.   80
 To do your service.
THESEUS.   I will hear that play.
 For never anything can be amiss,
 When simpleness and duty tender° it.
 Go bring them in, and take your places, ladies.   [*Exit* PHILOSTRATE.]
HIPPOLYTA.   I love not to see wretchedness o'ercharged,°   85
 And duty in his service perishing.
THESEUS.   Why, gentle sweet, you shall see no such thing.
HIPPOLYTA.   He says they can do nothing in this kind.°
THESEUS.   The kinder we, to give them thanks for nothing.
 Our sport shall be to take what they mistake.   90
 And what poor duty cannot do, noble respect
 Takes it in might, not merit.°
 Where I have come, great clerks° have purposèd
 To greet me with premeditated welcomes;
 Where I have seen them shiver and look pale,   95
 Make periods in the midst of sentences,
 Throttle° their practised accent in their fears,
 And in conclusion dumbly have broke off,
 Not paying me a welcome. Trust me, sweet,
 Out of this silence yet I picked a welcome: 100
 And in the modesty of fearful duty°
 I read as much as from the rattling tongue
 Of saucy and audacious eloquence.
 Love, therefore, and tongue-tied simplicity,
 In° least, speak most, to my capacity.°   105

[*Enter* PHILOSTRATE.]

PHILOSTRATE.   So please your grace, the Prologue is addressed.°
THESEUS.   Let him approach.

Flourish trumpets. Enter the PROLOGUE *[*QUINCE*].*

PROLOGUE.   If we offend, it is with our good will.
  That you should think, we come not to offend,
  But with good will. To show our simple skill,   110
  That is the true beginning of our end.

80 *stretched and conned:* strained and memorized. 83 *tender:* offer. 85 *wretchedness o'ercharged:* poor fellows taxing themselves too much. 88 *in this kind:* of this sort.
91–92 *noble . . . merit:* a noble nature considers the sincerity of effort rather than the skill of execution. 93 *clerks:* scholars. 97 *Throttle:* choke on. 101 *fearful duty:* subjects whose devotions gave them stage fright. 105 *In:* i.e., saying. *capacity:* way of thinking. 106 *addressed:* ready. 108–117 *If . . . know:* (Quince's blunders in punctuation exactly reverse the meaning).

Consider then, we come but in despite.°
We do not come, as minding to content you,
Our true intent is. All for your delight,
We are not here. That you should here repent you,   115
The actors are at hand: and by their show,
You shall know all, that you are like to know.°

THESEUS.   This fellow doth not stand upon points.°

LYSANDER.   He hath rid his prologue like a rough colt: he knows
not the stop.° A good moral my lord: it is not enough   120
to speak; but to speak true.

HIPPOLYTA.   Indeed he hath played on his prologue like a child on a
recorder:° a sound, but not in government.°

THESUS.   His speech was like a tangled chain: nothing impaired, but
all disordered. Who is next?   125

Enter PYRAMUS and THISBY, WALL, MOONSHINE, and LION.

PROLOGUE.   Gentles, perchance you wonder at this show,
But wonder on, till truth make all things plain.
This man is Pyramus, if you would know:
This beauteous lady, Thisby is certain.
This man, with lime and rough-cast,° doth present   130
Wall, that vile wall which did these lovers sunder:
And through Wall's chink, poor souls, they are content
To whisper. At the which, let no man wonder.
This man, with lantern, dog, and bush of thorn,
Presenteth Moonshine. For if you will know,   135
By moonshine did these lovers think no scorn
To meet at Ninus' tomb, there, there to woo:
This grisly beast (which Lion hight° by name)
The trusty Thisby, coming first by night,
Did scare away, or rather did affright: 140
And as she fled, her mantle she did fall:°
Which Lion vile with bloody mouth did stain.
Anon comes Pyramus, sweet youth and tall,°
And finds his trusty Thisby's mantle slain:
Whereat, with blade, with bloody blameful blade,   145
He bravely broached° his boiling bloody breast.
And Thisby, tarrying in mulberry shade,
His dagger drew, and died. For all the rest,
Let Lion, Moonshine, Wall, and lovers twain.
At large° discourse, while here they do remain.   150

THESEUS.   I wonder if the lion be to speak.

---

112 *despite:* malice.   181 *stand upon points:* (1) pay attention to punctuation (2) bother
about the niceties (of expression).   120 *stop:* (1) halt (2) period.   123 *recorder:* flutelike
wind instrument.   *in government:* well managed.   130 *rough-cast:* rough plaster made
of lime and gravel.   138 *hight:* is called.   141 *fall:* let fall.   143 *tall:* brave.
146 *broached:* opened (Shakespeare parodies the overuse of alliteration in the earlier
bombastic Elizabethan plays).   150 *At large:* in full.

DEMETRIUS.   No wonder, my lord: one lion may, when many asses do.

Exeunt [PROLOGUE, PYRAMUS,] LION, THISBY, MOONSHINE.

WALL.   In this same interlude° it doth befall
    That I, one Snout by name, present a wall:
    And such a wall, as I would have you think,   155
    That had in it a crannied hole or chink:
    Through which the lovers, Pyramus and Thisby,
    Did whisper often, very secretly.
    This loam, this rough-cast, and this stone doth show
    That I am that same wall: the truth is so.   160
    And this the cranny is, right and sinister,°
    Through which the fearful lovers are to whisper.
THESEUS.   Would you desire lime and hair to speak better?
DEMETRIUS.   It is the wittiest° partition° that ever I heard discourse,
    my lord.   165

Enter PYRAMUS.

THESEUS.   Pyramus draws near the wall: silence.
PYRAMUS.   O grim-looked night, O night with hue so black,
      O night, which ever art when day is not:
      O night, O night, alack, alack, alack,
        I fear my Thisby's promise is forgot.   170
      And thou O wall, O sweet, O lovely wall,
        That stand'st between her father's ground and mine,
      Thou wall, O wall, O sweet and lovely wall,
        Show me thy chink, to blink through with mine eyne.°

*[*WALL *holds up his fingers.]*

    Thanks, courteous wall. Jove shield thee well for this.   175
      But what see I? No Thisby do I see.
    O wicked wall, through whom I see no bliss,
      Cursed by thy stones for thus deceiving me.
THESEUS.   The wall methinks being sensible,° should curse again.°
PYRAMUS.   No in truth sir, he should not. "Deceiving me" is   180
    Thisby's cue: she is to enter now, and I am to spy her
    through the wall. You shall see it will fall pat° as I told
    you: yonder she comes.

Enter THISBY.

THISBY.   O wall, full often hast thou heard my moans,
      For parting my fair Pyramus and me.   185
    My cherry lips have often kissed thy stones;
      Thy stones with lime and hair knit up in thee.

---

153 *interlude:* short play.   161 *right and sinister:* from right to left (he probably uses the
fingers of his right and left hands to form the cranny).   164 *wittiest:* most intelligent.
partition: (1) wall (2) section of a learned book or speech.   174 *eyne:* eyes.   179 *sensible:*
capable of feelings and perception.   *again:* back.   182 *pat:* exactly.

PYRAMUS.   I see a voice: now will I to the chink,
        To spy and I can hear my Thisby's face.
        Thisby?   190
THISBY.   My love thou art, my love I think.
PYRAMUS.   Think what thou wilt, I am thy lover's grace:
        And, like Limander,° am I trusty still.
THISBY.   And I like Helen,° till the Fates me kill.
PYRAMUS.   Not Shafalus to Procrus,° was so true.   195
THISBY.   As Shafalus to Procrus, I to you.
PYRAMUS.   O kiss me through the hole of this vile wall.
THISBY.   I kiss the wall's hole, not your lips at all.
PYRAMUS.   Wilt thou at Ninny's° tomb meet me straightway?
THISBY.   Tide° life, tide death, I come without delay.   200

                                       [*Exeunt* PYRAMUS *and* THISBY.]

WALL.   Thus have I, Wall, my part dischargèd so;
      And being done, thus Wall away doth go.   *Exit.*
THESEUS.   Now is the mural° down between the two neighbours.
DEMETRIUS.   No remedy my lord, when walls are so wilful to hear
    without warning.°   205
HIPPOLYTA.   This is the silliest stuff that ever I heard.
THESEUS.   The best in this kind are but shadows:° and the worst are
    no worse, if imagination amend them.
HIPPOLYTA.   It must be your imagination then, and not theirs.
THESEUS.   If we imagine no worse of them than they of themselves,   210
    they may pass for excellent men. Here come two noble
    beasts in, a man and a lion.

Enter LION *and* MOONSHINE.

LION.   You ladies, you, whose gentle hearts do fear
        The smallest monstrous mouse that creeps on floor,
    May now perchance both quake and tremble here.   215
        When lion rough in wildest rage doth roar.
    Then know that I, as Snug the joiner am
    A lion fell,° nor else no lion's dam:°
    For if I should as lion come in strife
    Into this place, 'twere pity on my life.   220
THESEUS.   A very gentle beast, and of a good conscience.
DEMETRIUS.   The very best at a beast,° my lord, that e'er I saw.
LYSANDER.   This lion is a very fox for his valour.
THESEUS.   True: and a goose for his discretion.
DEMETRIUS.   Not so my lord: for his valour cannot carry his discretion,   225
    and the fox carries the goose.

193 *Limander:* (he means "Leander").   194 *Helen:* (he means "Hero").   195 *Shafalus to Procrus:* (he means "Cephalus" and "Procis" [see Act III, scene 2, 389 n.]).   199 *Ninny:* fool (he means "Ninus").   200 *Tide:* come, betide.   203 *mural:* wall.   205 *without warning:* either (a) without warning the parents or (b) unexpectedly.   207 *in . . . shadows:* of this sort are only plays (or only actors).   218 *fell:* fierce.   *nor . . . dam:* and not a lioness.   222 *best, beast:* (pronounced similarly).

THESEUS.   His discretion, I am sure, cannot carry his valour: for the
goose carries not the fox. It is well: leave it to his discretion,
and let us listen to the moon.

MOONSHINE.   This lanthorn° doth the hornèd moon present—   230

DEMETRIUS.   He should have worn the horns on his head.°

THESEUS.   He is no crescent, and his horns are invisible within the
circumference.

MOONSHINE.   This lanthorn doth the hornèd moon present,
Myself, the man i' th' moon do seem to be.   235

THESEUS.   This is the greatest error of all the rest; the man should
be put into the lanthorn. How is it else the man i' th'
moon?

DEMETRIUS.   He dares not come there for the candle; for you see, it
is already in snuff.°   240

HIPPOLYTA.   I am aweary of this moon. Would he would change.

THESEUS.   It appears, by his small light of discretion, that he is in
the wane: but yet in courtesy, in all reason, we must stay°
the time.

LYSANDER.   Proceed, Moon.   245

MOONSHINE.   All that I have to say, is to tell you that the lanthorn is
the moon, I the man i' th' moon, this thornbush my
thornbush, and this dog my dog.

DEMETRIUS.   Why, all these should be in the lanthorn: for all these are
in the moon. But silence: here comes Thisby.   250

Enter THISBY.

THISBY.   This is old Ninny's tomb. Where is my love?

LION.   Oh!   *The LION roars. THISBY runs off.*

DEMETRIUS.   Well roared, Lion.

THESEUS.   Well run, Thisby.

HIPPOLYTA.   Well shone, Moon. Truly, the moon shines with a good   255
grace.

[The LION shakes THISBY's mantle.]

THESEUS.   Well moused,° Lion.

DEMETRIUS.   And then came Pyramus.

Enter PYRAMUS. [Exit LION.]

LYSANDER.   And so the lion vanished.

PYRAMUS.   Sweet moon, I thank thee for thy sunny beams,   260
I thank thee, moon, for shining now so bright.
For by thy gracious, golden, glittering gleams,
I trust to take of truest Thisby sight.
But stay: O spite!

---

230 *lanthorn:* lantern (once made of horn).   230–231 *hornèd . . . head:* (referring to the
cuckold or deceived husband, who supposedly grew horns).   240 *in snuff:* (1) in need of
snuffing (having a long, burnt-out wick or snuff) (2) in a temper.   243 *stay:* await.
257 *moused:* shaken, as a cat shakes a mouse.

But mark, poor knight,   265
What dreadful dole° is here?
Eyes, do you see!
How can it be!
O dainty duck, O dear!
Thy mantle good,   270
What, stained with blood?
Approach, ye Furies° fell:
O Fates!° come, come:
Cut thread and thrum.°
Quail,° crush, conclude, and quell.°   275

THESEUS.   This passion, and the death of a dear friend, would go
near to make a man look sad.

HIPPOLYTA.   Beshrew° my heart, but I pity the man.

PYRAMUS.   O wherefore Nature, didst thou lions frame?
Since lion vile hath here deflowered my dear.   280
Which is—no, no—which was the fairest dame
That lived, that loved, that liked, that looked with cheer.
Come tears, confound:
Out sword, and wound
The pap° of Pyramus: 285
Ay, that left pap,
Where heart doth hop.   [*Stabs himself.*]
Thus die, I, thus, thus, thus.
Now am I dead,
Now am I fled,   290
My soul is in the sky.
Tongue lose thy light,
Moon° take thy flight,   [*Exit MOONSHINE.*]
Now die, die, die, die, die.   [*Dies.*]

DEMETRIUS.   No die,° but an ace° for him. For he is but one.   295

LYSANDER.   Less than an ace, man. For he is dead, he is nothing.

THESEUS.   With the help of a surgeon, he might yet recover, and
prove an ass.

HIPPOLYTA.   How chance Moonshine is gone before Thisby comes
back and finds her lover?   300

Enter THISBY.

THESEUS.   She will find him by starlight. Here she comes, and her
passion ends the play.

HIPPOLYTA.   Methinks she should not use a long one for such a
Pyramus: I hope she will be brief.

---

266 *dole:* grief.   272 *Furies:* classical spirits of the underworld who avenged murder.
273 *Fates:* three sisters who spun the thread of human destiny, which at will was cut with a
shears.   274 *thrum:* fringelike end of the warp in weaving.   275 *Quail:* subdue.
quell: kill.   278 *Beshrew:* curse (meant lightly).   285 *pap:* breast.   292–293 *Tongue
. . . Moon:* (he reverses the two subjects).   295 *die:* (singular of "dice").   *ace:* a throw of
one at dice.

DEMETRIUS.   A mote will turn the balance, which Pyramus, which   305
    Thisby, is the better: he for a man. God warr'nt° us;
    she for a woman, God bless us.
LYSANDER.   She hath spied him already with those sweet eyes.
DEMETRIUS.   And thus she means,° videlicet°—
THISBY.   Asleep my love?   310
        What, dead, my dove?
          O Pyramus, arise,
            Speak, speak. Quite dumb?
            Dead, dead? A tomb
      Must cover thy sweet eyes.   315
          These lily lips,
          This cherry nose,
    These yellow cowslip° cheeks,
        Are gone, are gone:
        Lovers, make moan: 320
    His eyes were green as leeks.
        O 'Sisters Three,°
        Come, come to me,
    With hands as pale as milk,
      Lay them in gore,   325
      Since you have shore
    With shears his thread of silk.
      Tongue, not a word:
      Come trusty sword,
    Come blade, my breast imbrue:°   *[Stabs herself.]*   330
      And farewell friends:
      Thus Thisby ends:
    Adieu, adieu, adieu.   *[Dies.]*
THESEUS.   Moonshine and Lion are left to bury the dead.
DEMETRIUS.   Ay, and Wall too.   335
BOTTOM.   [*Starts up*] No, I assure you, the wall is down that parted
    their fathers. Will it please you to see the Epilogue, or
    to hear a Bergomask° dance between two of our company?
THESEUS.   No epilogue, I pray you; for your play needs no excuse.
    Never excuse: for when the players are all dead, there   340
    need none to be blamed. Marry, if he that writ it had
    played Pyramus and hanged himself in Thisby's garter,
    it would have been a fine tragedy: and so it is truly, and
    very notably discharged. But come, your Bergomask:
    let your Epilogue alone.   *[A dance.]* 345
    The iron tongue° of midnight hath told° twelve.
    Lovers, to bed, 'tis almost fairy time.°
    I fear we shall outsleep the coming morn,

---

306 *warr'nt:* warrant, protect.   309 *means:* laments.   *videlicet:* namely.   318 *cowslip:*
yellow primrose.   322 *Sisters Three:* the Fates.   330 *imbrue:* stain with gore.
338 *Bergomask:* exaggerated country dance.   346 *iron tongue:* i.e., of the bell.
told: counted, tolled.   347 *fairy time:* (from midnight to daybreak).

As much as we this night have overwatched.
This palpable gross° play hath well beguiled   350
The heavy gait of night. Sweet friends, to bed.
A fortnight hold we this solemnity,
In nightly revels, and new jollity.   *Exeunt.*

Enter PUCK [with a broom].

PUCK.   Now the hungry lion roars,
        And the wolf behowls the moon;   355
    Whilst the heavy° ploughman snores,
        All with weary task fordone.°
    Now the wasted brands° do glow,
        Whilst the screech-owl, screeching loud,
    Puts the wretch that lies in woe°   360
        In remembrance of a shroud.
    Now it is the time of night,
        That the graves, all gaping wide,
    Every one lets forth his sprite,°
        In the church-way paths to glide.   365
    And we fairies, that do run
        By the triple Hecate's° team,°
    From the presence of the sun,
        Following darkness like a dream,
    Now are frolic:° not a mouse   370
    Shall disturb this hallowed house.
    I am sent with broom before,
        To sweep the dust° behind° the door.

Enter KING and QUEEN OF FAIRIES, with all their train.

OBERON.   Through the house give glimmering light,
        By the dead and drowsy fire,   375
    Every elf and fairy sprite,
        Hop as light as bird from brier,
    And this ditty after me,
        Sing, and dance it trippingly.
TITANIA.   First rehearse your song by rote,   380
    To each word a warbling note.
    Hand in hand, with fairy grace,
    Will we sing and bless this place.   [*Song and dance.*]
OBERON.   Now, until the break of day,
    Through this house each fairy stray.   385
    To the best bride-bed will we,
    Which by us shall blessèd be:

350 *palpable gross*: obvious and crude.   356 *heavy*: sleepy.   357 *fordone*: worn out,
"done in."   358 *wasted brands*: burnt logs.   360 *wretch . . . woe*: sick person.
364 *sprite*: spirit, ghost.   367 *triple Hecate*: the moon goddess, identified as Cynthia in
heaven, Diana on earth, and Hecate in hell.   *team*: dragons that pull the chariot of the
night moon.   370 *frolic*: frolicsome.   373 *To sweep the dust*: (Puck often helped with
household chores).   *behind*: from behind.

And the issue° there create,°
Ever shall be fortunate:
So shall all the couples three   390
Ever true in loving be:
And the blots of Nature's hand°
Shall not in their issue° stand.
Never mole, harelip, nor scar,
Nor mark prodigious,° such as are   395
Despisèd in nativity,
Shall upon their children be.
With this field-dew consecrate.
Every fairy take his gait,°
And each several° chamber bless,   400
Through this palace, with sweet peace;
And the owner of its blest,
Ever shall in safety rest.
Trip away: make no stay: *Exeunt [all but PUCK].*   405
Meet me all by break of day.

PUCK.   If we shadows have offended,
Think but this, and all is mended,
That you have but slumbered here,
While these visions did appear.
And this weak and idle° theme,   410
No more yielding but° a dream,
Gentles, do not reprehend.
If you pardon, we will mend.°
And as I am an honest Puck,
If we have unearnèd luck,   415
Now to scape the serpent's tongue,°
We will make amends, ere long:
Else the Puck a liar call.
So, good night unto you all.
Give me your hands,° if we be friends;   420
And Robin shall restore amends.°   *[Exit.]*

388, 393 *issue*: children.   388 *create*: created.   392 *blots . . . hand*: birth defects.
395 *mark prodigious*: unnatural birthmark.   399 *take his gait*: proceed.   400 *several*:
separate.   410 *idle*: foolish.   411 *No . . . but*: yielding nothing more than.
413 *mend*: improve.   416 *serpent's tongue*: hissing of the audience.   420 *hands*:
applause.   421 *restore amends*: do better in the future.

QUESTIONS

Act I

1.   Describe the relationship between Theseus and Hippolyta. What does each
     of them represent? How does Shakespeare show us that they have different
     attitudes toward their marriage?

2.   Characterize Hermia and Lysander. What blocks their relationship? How do they plan to circumvent these obstructions?

3.   What are Helena's feelings about herself? About Hermia? About Demetrius? How might you account for her self-image?

4.   Why have the mechanicals gathered at Quince's house? How does Shakespeare show us that Bottom is eager, ill-educated, energetic, and funny?

Act II

5.   What is Puck's job? What do you find out about his personality, habits, and pastimes in his first conversation?

6.   Why are Titania and Oberon fighting with each other, and what are the specific consequences of their conflict?

7.   What does Oberon plan to do to Titania? Why? What is "love-in-idleness"? What power does it have? What does it symbolize?

8.   Why are Demetrius and Helena in the woods? What does Oberon decide to do to them? What error occurs? What happens to Lysander when Helena awakens him?

Act III

9.   How and why does Puck change Bottom? How is this transformation appropriate? What happens when Bottom awakens Titania? Why?

10.   What does Oberon decide to do when he realizes that Puck has made a mistake? What is Puck's attitude toward the confusion he has created?

11.   What happens when Helena awakens Demetrius? How does this situation reverse the one that began the play? Explain Helena's reaction to the behavior of Demetrius and Lysander.

12.   What real dangers (tragic potential) do the lovers face in Act III? How do Oberon and Puck deal with these dangers? What is their plan? How successful is it?

Act IV

13.   Why does Oberon cure Titania of her infatuation with Bottom? How does the relationship between Oberon and Titania change? How is this change symbolized? Why is it significant?

14.   How are the relationships among the four lovers straightened out? How does each explain his or her feelings? What does Theseus decide about the couples? Why is this significant?

15.   What momentous event occurs offstage and is briefly reported in Act IV, scene 2?

Act V

16.   Describe Pyramus and Thisby. What blocks their relationship? How do they plan to circumvent these obstructions? What happens to them?

17. What is the significance of the fairy masque (a combination of poetry, music, dance, and drama) that ends the play?

18. What does Puck's epilogue suggest about you as a reader or spectator? How does it reinforce the connections among dreaming, imagination, illusion, and drama?

GENERAL QUESTIONS

1. To what extent are the characters in this play conventional and representative types? What is the effect of Shakespeare's style of characterization?

2. Are any of the characters symbolic? If so, what do they symbolize? How does such symbolism reinforce the themes of the play?

3. How does Shakespeare employ language, imagery, and poetic form to define the characters in this play and differentiate among the various groups of characters?

4. To what extent do the two settings—city and woods—structure the play? Where does exposition occur? Complication and catastrophe? The comic resolution? How complete is the resolution? Why is the round-trip journey from one setting to the other necessary for the lovers? The rulers? The "hempen homespuns"?

5. What are the similarities or parallels in plot and theme between *A Midsummer Night's Dream* and "Pyramus and Thisby"? To what degree are they versions of the same play with different endings? Why do you think Shakespeare included the play-within-the-play in *A Midsummer Night's Dream*?

6. In the first soliloquy of the play, Helena discusses love. What kind of love is she talking about? What are its qualities and characteristics? How far do the relationships in the play bear out her ideas about love?

7. How well do the mechanicals understand the nature of dramatic illusion? What sorts of production problems concern them? How do they solve these?

8. What ideas about drama and the ways in which audiences respond to it does *A Midsummer Night's Dream* explore?

9. Compare the play-within-a-play in *A Midsummer Night's Dream* to the one in Act III of *Hamlet*. How are the internal plays and situations similar? Different? What parallels do you see in the connections between each play-within-a-play and the larger play in which each occurs?

THE THEATER OF MOLIÈRE

The seventeenth century was the golden age of French neoclassical theater (called *neo* or *new* classical because it was based on Greek and Latin models). The period was dominated by three playwrights, the tragedians Pierre Corneille (1606–1684) and Jean Racine (1639–1699) and the comic writer Molière. The politically dominant figure of the age was Louis XIV, the "Sun King," the absolute monarch of France. He and his court—a glittering social set of elegant nobles, sparkling wits, would-be wits, and aristocratic ladies- and gentlemen-in-waiting—made Paris the cultural center of France and dictated fashion to the world at large. The ruling class had a profound impact on the drama of the age; since they were the patrons of the theater, their tastes and customs were often mirrored or gently mocked in the plays. More to the point, the values of this class—wit, grace, and privilege—rest at the center of all the drama.

Molière, whose real name was Jean Baptiste Poquelin, was the acknowledged master of comedy in this elegant and courtly age. Born in 1622, he was educated in a Jesuit college and studied law at Orléans. In 1643 he shocked his family by abandoning both the law and his father's prosperous upholstering business and going into the theater, a life that was generally considered sinful and contemptible. He joined a company of actors called The Illustrious Theater, who established themselves in a playhouse, produced a tragedy, and promptly went bankrupt.

The acting company spent the next fourteen years touring the provinces, performing *commedia dell'arte* farces and short comic plays, many by Molière. These years were Molière's real education in the theater; he gradually became a superb actor, writer, and director. More important, he learned about human nature; he saw the world's virtues and vices, follies and excesses, and he learned to write what people would laugh at.

When Molière and his company returned to Paris in 1658, they were invited to perform at the court of Louis XIV. The king was so pleased with Molière's comedy that he gave the company a theater in Paris and became Molière's supporter and protector. For the remainder of his life Molière was the total man of the theater—actor, director, company manager, and playwright.

Molière's personal life was a great deal more troubled than his life in the theater. He was plagued by ill health, and at the age of forty he began an unhappy marriage with Armande Béjart, the twenty-year-old daughter of his former mistress. Nevertheless, his creative efforts were prodigious; he wrote twenty-nine plays, ranging from broad farce to satirical comedies of manners.

His plays both reflect and rebel against the social and theatrical conventions of his age. The reflection is found in his sources, subjects, and awareness of the neoclassical rules of drama. The sources were Roman new comedy, French farce, and Italian *commedia dell'arte*; these taught him about comic characters, tempos, and situations. His inspirations were the manners, morals, and customs of the French aristocracy and the growing middle class.

Molière's rebellion—perhaps innovation would be a better term—is found in his elevation of comedy to the level and seriousness of tragedy. His satiric comedies of manners, such as *The Misanthrope* (1666) and *Tartuffe* (1669) represent the creation of a new form of dry and thoughtful comedy in which the customs and conventions of his world are examined and ridiculed. The laughter in these plays ranges from mocking to gentle, but we are always left with a great deal to think about.

There is very little action in his comedies. The characters tend to be universal types that exemplify the virtues and vices of human nature. What is new here is the thoughtful and detached perspective on the follies and excesses of humanity. Molière found that elusive point of delicate balance from which he could mock the ridiculous conventions, pretenses, habits, and morals of the same social classes that made up his audiences. The mainspring of Molière's satiric comedy is character; the problems and conflicts in his plays grow directly out of the eccentricities and excesses of his characters. And he drew these figures from life, from the posturing of the aristocracy and the pretensions of middle-class social climbers.

The theaters in which Molière's plays were produced were not much different from the older theaters we might find in New York or Chicago today. The auditorium, which held about six hundred spectators, was a long rectangle with galleries or private boxes along each side and a stage across one end. The stage was separated from the audience by a *proscenium arch* that stood in front of the scenery and created a kind of picture frame through which the spectators watched the action.

The stage was illuminated by footlights and large chandeliers containing either candles or oil lamps. Although the scenery could be lavish, Molière favored sparse sets and few props. The actors and actresses (women were never excluded from the French stage) wore contemporary costumes. This convention made Molière's satires all the more effective. Since his actors and actresses were costumed like the social types being mocked, the plays became mirrors reflecting the world outside the theater.

MOLIÈRE, *LOVE IS THE DOCTOR*

Love Is the Doctor (*L'Amour Médecin*) was first performed in 1665 at the palace of Louis XIV at Versailles, where the king himself sometimes joined Molière's casts to indulge his own acting fantasies and to win applause from his courtiers. The play is typical of Molière's comedies, relying heavily on pantomime, dance, and music in the *commedia dell'arte* tradition. (The incidental music by Jean Baptiste Lully has survived and is available on records).

The central character in *Love Is the Doctor*, Sganarelle, also appears in other Molière comedies. Usually Sganarelle tries to beat others, but as often as not he is beaten himself, and therefore he is both the cause and the butt of laughter. His function in *Love Is the Doctor* is characteristic: He is a wealthy businessman and a traditional *pater familias*, with the final word in family matters (not unlike Egeus in *A Midsummer Night's Dream* and Polonius in *Hamlet*). He closely guards his daughter, Lucinda, from suitors to avoid having to pay a massive dowry to a son-in-law who, as he says, might be a perfect stranger.

The plot by Lucinda and her suitor Clitander to marry despite Sganarelle's opposition is an example of the traditional **plot of intrigue.** The main characteristic of the intrigue plot is that the father (or guardian), acting as a blocking agent, chooses another man for the young woman, or, as in *Love Is the Doctor*, tries to prevent marriage entirely. The intrigue is often organized and abetted by a maidservant or *soubrette* (like Lisette in *Love Is the Doctor*), and the goal of the lovers is to outwit the blocker by gaining both marriage and inheritance or dowry—thereby making romantic love socially acceptable. Sometimes the blocker is reconciled by the fact that the young man is independently rich, although that does not happen in this play, for at the end Sganarelle is frustrated and outraged despite the surrounding merriment. With variations, such intrigue plots have furnished the stuff of innumerable French and English romantic plays and novels from Molière's time to our own.

Molière's notable addition to the intrigue plot in *Love Is the Doctor* is his satiric treatment of doctors. Medical practice in the seventeenth century was grounded in the tradition that a healthy body contained a harmonious balance of the four bodily fluids or "humors"—blood, yellow bile, black bile, and phlegm. When one of the humors became excessive or "putrid," the imbalance made the patient sick. Illness, including mental illness, could also be caused by the "adust," or burning, of a particular humor during a high fever. (The understanding of bacterial and viral causes of disease was still two centuries in the future.) When doctors made a diagnosis based on this system, their treatment was to eliminate the noxious pressures created by the offending humor (as the doctors recommend for Lucinda many times in *Love Is the Doctor*). Depending on the humor, they employed one of four methods of purgation: (1) venipuncture, to draw off blood, or "sanguine" (the most common purgation, but the patient, weakened by blood loss, would often die more speedily from the original disease), (2) an emetic, to eliminate yellow bile, or "choler," through vomiting, (3) a laxative, to purge black bile, or "melancholy," and (4) various irritating (and sometimes poisonous) powders, to eliminate "phlegm" through violent sneezing.

With such principles and treatments, medical practitioners were open targets for satire, and *Love Is the Doctor* holds nothing back. Once Lisette reports Lucinda's illness, the play is invaded by Molière's cadre of funny physicians, who, like their real-life counterparts, were bearded men who dressed in black robes and hats. Molière satirizes his doctors on the grounds of cronyism, indifference to the condition of patients, pompousness, exploitation of gullibility, ignorance and indecision, lack of openness to innovation, and simple greed.

Despite the severity of his satire, however, Molière also presents the doctors in a comic-farcical light. Both when they are summoned and then

Molière in the character of Sganarelle.

paid, for example, they perform dances and pantomimes. Even the blatant self-exposure of Dr. Fillpocket ("Dr. Filerin") may be construed as the excess one expects of farce, and therefore honest medical practitioners in Molière's day could have claimed that the doctors in *Love Is the Doctor* represented the exception, not the rule.

Although my translation follows Molière's text faithfully, I have taken latitude in a few instances to emphasize his sharp comic intentions. For example, his introduction of the quack elixir "Orviétan" in Act II, scene 6 has lost its timeliness, and hence it requires explanation, which I have included as part of the dramatic text in preference to creating an extensive footnote. Molière's songs also need slight modification so that they might work in English. Because the names of the doctors are not particularly meaningful, I have given them "tag names." Thus, Drs. *Tomès, De Fonandrès, Macroton, Bahays,* and *Filerin* are, respectively, *Slicer, De Pits, Gouger, Golfer,* and *Fillpocket.* Generally, the medical recommendations of these doctors cannot be translated into modern terms. Readers will therefore need to rely on the brief description given here about medical practice in Molière's day. Alert readers may notice some anachronisms and inconsistencies in the medical terms, such as "pathological" and "psychosomatic"; these are not inadvertent, but are made in the hope that they are consistent with the Molièresque comic spirit.

MOLIÈRE [JEAN BAPTISTE POQUELIN] (1622–1673)

Love Is the Doctor   *(1665) 1666*

Translated by Edgar V. Roberts

CHARACTERS

Sganarelle, *a wealthy Parisian merchant, father of* Lucinda
Aminta, *his neighbor*
Lucretia, *his niece*
Mr. Williams, *his friend, a seller of tapestries*
Mr. Josse, *another friend, a jeweller*
Lucinda, *daughter of* Sganarelle, *in love with* Clitander
Lisette, *maid to* Lucinda, *a soubrette*
Champagne, *an assistant to* Sganarelle, *a dancer*
Dr. Slicer [Tomès]
Dr. De Pits [De Fonandrès]
Dr. Gouger [Macroton]   } *doctors*
Dr. Golfer [Bahays]
Dr. Fillpocket [Filerin]
Clitander, *in love with Lucinda*
A Justice
A Mountebank, *a quack, seller of the cure-all "Orviétan"*
Buffoons and Scaramouches, *assistants to the Mountebank*
The Spirit of Comedy
Musicians
Singers
Dancers
Servants, etc.

The action takes place in Paris, in the house and drawing room of SGANARELLE *[and also on a street in Paris].*

ACT I

Scene 1

Enter SGANARELLE, AMINTA, LUCRETIA, MR. WILLIAMS, *and* MR. JOSSE.

   SGANARELLE.   Life is strange. I agree with that great classical philosopher who said that those who have wealth also have woe,° and that misery breeds more misery. I've been married only once, and my wife is now dead.

1 *woe*: Ecclesiastes 2:9–11.

MR. WILLIAMS. How many wives would you have liked?

SGANARELLE. Don't mock, Mr. Williams; my loss is great, and I'm still sad when I think about her. I never liked her lifestyle, and we argued a great deal, but Death, as they say, settles everything. She's dead and I'm sorry, but if she were alive we would still be fighting. Of all the children that Heaven blessed us with, only my daughter has survived, but she is my greatest sorrow because she is sad beyond belief—in a deep depression I can't get her out of. Beyond that, she won't tell me what's wrong. I'm almost beside myself, and I need your good advice. You [*to* LUCRETIA] are my niece. You [*to* AMINTA] are my neighbor. You [*to* MR. WILLIAMS *and* MR. JOSSE] are my friends and equals. What should I do?

MR. JOSSE. I believe that jewelry is what young women like best, and if I were you I would buy her some nice necklaces, brooches, or rings set with expensive diamonds, rubies, and emeralds.

MR. WILLIAMS. If I were in your position, I'd get her an elegant tapestry showing a landscape or historical scene. The sight of something like that in her room would pick up both her vision and her spirits.

AMINTA. If you ask me, I wouldn't do anything of the sort. Rather, I'd get her married off as soon as possible—maybe to the man who, they say, asked you for her hand some time ago.

LUCRETIA. I don't agree. She's not ready for marriage, and she's not strong enough to bear children. For her, having babies would be a quick way to go six feet under. She's too good for this world, and I think you should send her off to a convent, where she'll be able to do things to suit her special personality.

SGANARELLE. I appreciate your thoughts, but they seem more to your interests than mine. You are a jeweler, Mr. Josse, and your advice would probably make you a handsome profit. You, Mr. Williams, have a tapestry shop, and I think you're trying to get rid of a little excess inventory. I've heard that your boyfriend, neighbor Aminta, is carrying a torch for my daughter, and you'd therefore like to have her married off and out of circulation. And as for you, my dear niece, you know that I have no plans to consent to a marriage for my daughter—I've got my reasons—but your advice to send her to religious orders suggests that you wouldn't mind becoming the only heir to all my money. So, ladies and gentlemen, your advice is perhaps the best in the world, but, if you please, I want none of it. Please go.

[*They leave, grumbling to themselves.* SGANARELLE *then speaks sarcastically to the audience.*]

There you have modern, up-to-date friends, who give their impersonal advice with no hope of gain whatever.

Act I, Scene 2

He remains. Enter LUCINDA.

SGANARELLE. [*Aside.*] That's my daughter taking a walk for exercise. She doesn't see me; she's sighing. Now she's raising her eyes to Heaven. [*To* LUCINDA.] Bless you, Lucinda. What's the matter? Why so sad and sorrowful? Why don't you tell me what's wrong? You can trust your dear old dad, so tell me what's on your mind. Don't worry. Give me a kiss, like a good little girl. [*Aside.*] I can't stand seeing her like this. [*To* LUCINDA.] Do you want me to die with unhappiness because of you? Won't you tell me what's troubling you? Tell me what's wrong and I'll do anything for you, I promise. Just tell me what's making you sad, because I swear on a stack of Bibles that there's nothing I won't do to make you happy. Tell me what you want. Are you jealous of any friends because they seem better dressed? I'll get you clothes that will make theirs seem like rags.—No? Does your room seem bare? I'll let you pick out the best furniture to be found anywhere.—No again? Well, maybe you want to learn music; I'll get you the best piano teacher there is.—Not that either? Maybe you're in love, and would like to be married. [*Lucinda nods her head in agreement.*]

Act I, Scene 3

They remain. Enter Lisette.

LISETTE.   Sir, you've just been chatting with your daughter. Did she tell you what's wrong?

SGANARELLE.   No, she's being bitchy and it's making me mad.

LISETTE.   Let me try; I'll sound her out a little.

SGANARELLE.   It won't work. Since she's so stubborn, let her alone.

LISETTE.   Just let me try. She may be more open with me than you. [*To   5
Lucinda. During Lisette's speech, which Sganarelle also overhears, he gets increasingly irritated with his daughter.*] Now, Madam, let us know what's wrong; don't keep on like this and upset everybody. It seems to me that something really mysterious is bothering you, and if you won't tell your father, maybe you'll tell me. Do you want anything from him? You know that he'll spare no expense for you. Do you want him to give you more freedom? More promenades in the park? More presents to tempt your fancy?—No? Maybe you're angry with someone, then.—No? Well then, maybe you have a secret wish to get married, and you'd like your father's consent. [*Lucinda nods enthusiastically.*]—Ah, that's it; why all the secrecy? Sir, the mystery is solved, and—

SGANARELLE.   [*Interrupting her.*] Get away, you ingrate; I won't talk to you any more. Be as stubborn as you like.

LUCINDA.   Father, since you want me to tell you—

SGANARELLE.   No, I'm finished with you.

LISETTE.   Sir, her sadness—

SGANARELLE.   She's a hussy, and enjoys hurting me.   10

LUCINDA.   Father, I want—

SGANARELLE.   Is this the gratitude I get for bringing you up so well?

LISETTE.   But, sir—

SGANARELLE.   No, I'm so mad I may have a stroke.

LUCINDA.   But, Father—   15

SGANARELLE.   I no longer have a speck of kindness for you.

LISETTE.   But—

SGANARELLE.   She's a cheap wench.

LISETTE.   But—

SGANARELLE.   An ungrateful slut.   20

LISETTE.   But—

SGANARELLE.   A trollop, who won't tell me what's wrong with her.

LISETTE.   It's a husband that she wants!

SGANARELLE. [*Hearing but deliberately ignoring this piece of information.*] I'll turn her out of my house.

LISETTE. A husband!   25

SGANARELLE. I detest her.

LISETTE. [*shouting increasingly more loudly.*] A husband!

SGANARELLE. And I disown her as my daughter.

LISETTE. A husband!

SGANARELLE. No, don't talk to me about it.   30

LISETTE. A husband!

SGANARELLE. Don't talk to me about it.

LISETTE. A husband!

SGANARELLE. Don't talk to me about it.

LISETTE. A husband, a husband, a husband!   35

[*SGANARELLE stalks off.*]

Act I, Scene 4

LISETTE and LUCINDA remain.

LISETTE. It's really true that none are so deaf as those who refuse to hear.

LUCINDA. [*ironically.*] Well, Lisette, you see how wrong I was to hide my feelings, and how all I had to do was to tell my father about everything I wanted.

LISETTE. My God, he's a hard man. I swear, I'd enjoy playing some kind of trick on him to show him up. But why, Madam, did you hide your wishes from me?

LUCINDA. Alas, what would I have gained? I might just as well have kept the secret for the rest of my life. Do you think I didn't foresee what he would do? I know his temper, and I'm in despair about the refusal he gave to the envoy sent to him to propose marriage to me. I've lost hope.

LISETTE. [*As though recalling a forgotten incident.*] What's this? It's that stranger   5
who arranged for the proposal, the one for whom you—

LUCINDA. Perhaps it's not right for me to speak so freely, but I confess, if I had the liberty to choose, he's the one I'd want. We've never spoken together; he's never been able to tell me he loves me. But, in all the places where he's seen me, his looks and gestures have indicated such tenderness, and his formal request for my hand has given me such a sense of his honor, that I can't help believing he loves me. No matter; you see how my father's reaction has hardened all this tenderness.

LISETTE. Well, I have to say, I think you shouldn't have kept things secret from me, but I'll still help you. You need to be certain of your determination—

LUCINDA. But what should I do against my father's authority?—And if he won't listen to my hopes—

LISETTE. Come on now, you can't let yourself be led around like a sheep. As long as you don't offend his honor, you can free yourself at least a little from him. What does he want with you? You're of age, and you're not made of stone. I say again I'll help you in this affair. Your interests are mine, and, you'll see, I know a thing or two—But I see your father; let's go in. Leave everything to me.

[*They hurry off.*]

Act I, Scene 5

Enter SGANARELLE.

SGANARELLE. [*Laughing to himself.*] It's sometimes good to seem not to hear things you hear only too well. I was smart to sidestep that declaration of her hopes that I do not mean to satisfy. Is there anything more tyrannical than that custom by which marriage arrangements make paupers out of fathers?—Anything more futile and ridiculous than to spend your life grubbing and grabbing to get rich, and raising a daughter with care and love, only to be robbed of both of them at the hands of a total stranger, a nobody? No, no, I don't give a damn for that custom, and I'll keep my wealth and my daughter to myself.

Act I, Scene 6

He remains. Enter LISETTE.

LISETTE. [*Pretending not to see SGANARELLE.*]—Oh unhappiness! Oh disgrace! Oh, poor Mr. Sganarelle! Where can I find him?
SGANARELLE. [*Aside.*] What's all this?
LISETTE. Oh unhappy father, what will you do when you learn about this?
SGANARELLE. [*Aside.*] What's going on?
LISETTE. My poor mistress!　　　　　　　　　　　　　　　　　　　　　　5
SGANARELLE. [*Aside.*] I'm lost!
LISETTE. —Oh!
SGANARELLE. [*Running after LISETTE.*] Lisette!
LISETTE. [*Pretending not to hear him, but making sure he hears her.*] What a misfortune!
SGANARELLE. —Lisette!　　　　　　　　　　　　　　　　　　　　　　10
LISETTE. [*Still pretending.*] What bad luck!
SGANARELLE. —Lisette!
LISETTE. [*Pretending yet.*] How ghastly awful!
SGANARELLE. —Lisette!
LISETTE. [*Pretending just now to have noticed him.*] Ah, Sir.　　　15
SGANARELLE. What's going on? What's wrong?
LISETTE. Sir, your daughter—
SGANARELLE. Oh, no!
LISETTE. Sir, sir, don't cry like that. [*Aside.*] You'll make me laugh if you keep on.
SGANARELLE. Tell me quickly.　　　　　　　　　　　　　　　　　20
LISETTE. You daughter was hurt by your words and scared by your anger. [*Dramatizing and exaggerating her following descriptions to the utmost.*] She went to her room and, in despair, she opened the window facing the river—
SGANARELLE. Oh, my God, no!
LISETTE. Then, raising her head heavenward, she said, "No, it's impossible for me to live with the anger of my father, and since he is disowning me, I want to die!"
SGANARELLE. She threw herself out?
LISETTE. No sir. She sorrowfully closed the window, and threw herself on　25
her bed, where she wept bitterly. Suddenly, her face got pale, her eyes rolled in her head, her heart seemed to stop, and she fell into my arms!

SGANARELLE.   Oh, my poor daughter!

LISETTE.   By slapping her face and using smelling salts, I revived her. But she's getting worse, and I don't believe she can last the day.

SGANARELLE.   [*Calling to the offstage servant* CHAMPAGNE.] Champagne! Champagne! Champagne! [*Enter* CHAMPAGNE.] Quickly, go get the doctors, and as many as you can find! There can't be too many for this! Oh, my daughter, my poor daughter!

[*They leave quickly.*]

FIRST ENTR'ACTE

[CHAMPAGNE, *while dancing, knocks on the doors of four doctors, who begin dancing and then ceremoniously enter the house of the patient's father.*]

ACT II

Scene 1

Enter SGANARELLE *and* LISETTE.

LISETTE.   Why do you need four doctors, Sir? Just one alone is enough to kill you.

SGANARELLE.   Be quiet. Four opinions are better than one.

LISETTE.   Can't your daughter die by herself, without the help of these gentlemen?

SGANARELLE.   Do you mean to say that it's the doctor who causes death, and not the disease?

LISETTE.   Absolutely. I know a man who proved beyond doubt that we   5
should never say, "This person died of a raging fever or a galloping consumption," but rather "That person was killed by the incompetence of two druggists and four doctors."

SGANARELLE.   Stop. You'll offend these gentlemen.

LISETTE.   Lord, Sir, our cat needed no drugs or treatment to recover from that jump she made from the rooftop to the street, and she didn't eat or move a muscle for three days. It's lucky for her there are no cat doctors, or they'd have wiped her out with their mindless purging and bleeding.

SGANARELLE.   Will you please keep your impertinent remarks to yourself? Here they are.

LISETTE.   Watch out. They'll tell you what you already know—that your daughter's sick. Only they'll bamboozle you by saying it in Latin!

Act II, Scene 2

Enter DR. SLICER, DR. GOUGER, DR. DE PITS, *and* DR. GOLFER.

SGANARELLE.   Welcome, gentlemen!

DR. SLICER.   [*Pompously.*] We have made our diagnosis of your daughter, and she unquestionably has many impurities in her.

SGANARELLE.   My daughter is impure?

DR. SLICER.   You must understand that it is her body that is full of impurities—many corrupt and putrid humors.°

SGANARELLE.   Oh, thank you, I understand.   5

DR. SLICER.   But, we plan to consult about her.

SGANARELLE.   [To attending servants.] Come, bring chairs for the doctors.

LISETTE.   [To DR. SLICER.] Doctor, is that you?

SGANARELLE.   How do you know Dr. Slicer?

LISETTE.   From having seen him the other day at the home of a good friend   10
of your niece.

DR. SLICER.   How is her coachman?

LISETTE.   Fabulous; he's dead.

DR. SLICER.   Dead?

LISETTE.   Yes, dead.

DR. SLICER.   That cannot be!   15

LISETTE.   I don't know if it couldn't happen, but I do know that it did.

DR. SLICER.   And I tell you he can't be dead.

LISETTE.   And I tell you he's dead and buried.

DR. SLICER.   You've made a mistake.

LISETTE.   I saw it with my own eyes.   20

DR. SLICER.   It's impossible. Hippocrates° says that patients don't die of this disease until the end of the second or third week, and he was sick for only six days.

LISETTE.   Let Hippocrates talk all he wants; the coachman is dead.

SGANARELLE.   [To LISETTE.] Be quiet, chatterbox; we should leave. [To the doctors.] Gentlemen, we will leave you in peace for your consultation. I know it's not customary to pay in advance, but I'll pay you now, before I forget.

[He pays them, and each one, upon receiving the fee, makes a different show of thanks. SGANARELLE and LISETTE then leave.]

Act II, Scene 3

DR. SLICER, DR. GOUGER, DR. DE PITS, and DR. GOLFER remain.

DR. DE PITS.   Paris is an incredibly large city, and a good medical practice requires long trips.

DR. SLICER.   I have an excellent mule for that; you won't believe the distances I make him go each day.

DR. DE PITS.   I have a marvelous horse; he never gets tired.

DR. SLICER.   Do you know the ground my mule has covered today? I was near the Arsenal first. Then I went to the suburb of St. Germain, from there to Le Marais, and then to St. Honoré Gate; after that to St. Jacques, to the Richelieu Gate, and finally here. When I leave, I'll go to the Place Royale.

DR. DE PITS.   My horse has gone to all those places today, and in addition   5
I rode him all the way to Ruel so I could see a patient.

DR. SLICER.   By the way, what position do you gentlemen take in the controversy between Doctors Theophrastus and Artemius? This is a matter that's dividing the whole profession.

4 corrupt and putrid humors: internal illness of body fluids.   21 Hippocrates: Ancient Greek physician, known as the father of medicine.

DR. DE PITS.   I think Artemius is right.

DR. SLICER.   I do too. It's true that his treatment killed the patient, and that the recommendation of Theophrastus was infinitely better, but in the circumstances, Theophrastus was wrong. He should not have ignored the recommendation of Artemius, who was, we must recognize, the senior physician in the case. What do you say about it?

DR. DE PITS.   Proper procedure should always be respected. I think we would be lost without our strict order of authority.

DR. SLICER.   I agree; I'm as severe about this as the devil—unless it's among   10
friends. The other day three of us were consulting with an outside physician about a patient. I stopped the whole business until we proceeded in absolute order. Meanwhile, the people of the house did their best as the illness reached a crisis, but I continued to insist on proper consultative procedure. Before we could end our conference, the patient died—may he rest in peace.

DR. DE PITS.   Insisting on our rights like that is the best way to keep lay people in their place, and show them that we're in control.

DR. SLICER.   A dead person is a dead person, and of no importance; but any neglect of standard operating procedures puts our whole profession in a bad light.

Act II, Scene 4

They remain. Enter SGANARELLE.

SGANARELLE.   Gentlemen, my daughter's condition is becoming serious. Please tell me at once what you have decided.

DR. SLICER.   [*To DR. DE PITS.*] Sir, you speak.

DR. DE PITS.   No, Sir, you speak first.

DR. SLICER.   Please, Sir, don't be modest.

DR. DE PITS.   No, Sir, please, after you.   5

DR. SLICER.   Sir!

DR. DE PITS.   Sir!

SGANARELLE.   With all respect, gentlemen, forget your ceremony and remember our present urgency.

[*All four doctors now speak together.*]

DR. SLICER.   The illness of your daughter—

DR. DE PITS.   The judgment of all these gentlemen together—   10

DR. GOUGER.   After our most exhaustive consultation—

DR. GOLFER.   To consider the case step by step, we—

SGANARELLE.   Gentlemen, please, speak one at a time.

DR. SLICER.   Sir, we have reached a diagnosis of your daughter's illness. My opinion is that it stems from a sanguinary superabundance—too much blood, to you. So my recommendation is blood letting; as soon as possible you should let as much blood from her as you can.

DR. DE PITS.   My best judgment is that her illness results from a putrefaction   15
of humors, caused by too much repletion. So my advice—listen carefully—is that she be given an emetic.

DR. SLICER.   I submit that an emetic will kill her.

Dr. De Pits.   And I believe that a bleeding is contra-indicated; it will bring about instant expiration—in other words, death.

Dr. Slicer.   [*Huffily, to Dr. De Pits.*] You of course are a great authority.

Dr. De Pits.   [*Defensively, to Dr. Slicer.*] Yes, I am; I'll outshine you in any branch of medical knowledge.

Dr. Slicer.   Do you recall that your wrongheaded treatment killed a man   20
the other day?

Dr. De Pits.   Do you recall that your bungling put a woman in her grave just three days ago?

Dr. Slicer.   [*To Sganarelle.*] I've given you my opinion.

Dr. De Pits.   [*To Sganarelle.*] And I've informed you of my professional judgment.

Dr. Slicer.   If you don't bleed your daughter immediately, she'll be a goner.
[*He leaves.*]

Dr. De Pits.   And if you do bleed her, she'll die in a quarter of an hour.   25

[*He leaves.*]

Act II, Scene 5

Sganarelle, Dr. Gouger, and Dr. Golfer remain.

Sganarelle.   Which of the two should I believe, and what should I do with such contrary advice? Gentlemen, I ask you to understand my predicament and tell me objectively what you believe would cure my daughter.

Dr. Gouger.   [*He speaks agonizingly slowly, drawing out his syllables and even stressing ordinarily silent letters.*] Sir, in these matters, we must proceed with circumspection, and, as they say, do nothing rashly, because the mistakes that we may make, according to our master, Hippocrates, may have dangerous consequences.

Dr. Golfer.   [*This one speaks at breakneck speed.*] He's right; we must be careful in what we do. This is not a child's game, and when we fail, it's not easy to repair the damage and restore the dead to life: *Experimentum periculosum: in other words, medicine is a perilous experiment that we learn from as we go along.* That's why we must reason carefully, weigh the alternatives, consider individual cases, examine all the possible causes of the illness, and see what remedies we may bring to the patient.

Sganarelle.   [*Aside.*] One is as slow as a turtle, the other as fast as a jackrabbit.

Dr. Gouger.   [*He is the turtle.*] Therefore, Sir, to get down to the matter, I   5
find that your daughter is sick. She has a chronic sickness which will get worse unless it gets better, for her symptoms indicate a pathological and mordant—that is to say, bad—vapor which penetrates the membranes of the brain. Now this vapor, which is called *atmos* in Greek, is caused by putrid, tenacious, and glutinous humors which are contained in the lower bowel.

Dr. Golfer.   [*He is the jackrabbit.*] And, inasmuch as these humors were engendered there during an extended period, they have turned adust—that is, they have been overcooked, so to speak—and have produced the present pathology of the brain.

Dr. Gouger.   [*Still speaking slowly.*] Therefore, in order that we may draw out, detach, withdraw, expel, and evacuate these said humors, we must recommend an aggressive treatment of purgation. But first, I find, it would not be improper to prescribe anodynes of emollients° and cleansing solutions, together with refreshing medicinal juleps and syrups to be mixed with her herbal tea and her tonic.

DR. GOLFER.   After this, should come purging and bleeding, to be repeated as necessary.

DR. GOUGER.   This does not mean that your daughter won't die after all this, but at least you will have done your best, and may be consoled by the realization that she died in accordance with proper procedures.

DR. GOLFER.   It's much better to die by the rules than to recover in spite   10
of them.

DR. GOUGER.   We are giving you our best professional advice.

DR. GOLFER.   And we have spoken to you as though you were our brother.

SGANARELLE.   [*To Dr. Gouger, drawing out his words.*] I thank you most humbly, Sir. [*To Dr. Golfer, as rapidly as possible.*] To you, Sir, I am infinitely obliged for the care that you have taken.

[*The doctors exit.*]

Act II, Scene 6

Sganarelle, alone.

SGANARELLE.   Now I'm more uncertain than ever. What can I do? [*He ponders this question for a few moments.*] I've got an idea: I've heard about a medicine that can cure everything, which they make down in Orvieto, Italy. It's a marvelous new elixir called "Orviétan." The advertising says it's cured millions of people. I'll buy some for her. It's got to work.

[*He leaves.*]

Act II, Scene 7

A Street. Enter Sganarelle and Mountebank, accompanied by his Buffoons and Scaramouches.

SGANARELLE.   Hello, Sir. Please give me a bottle of your amazing new drug, Orviétan. How much does it cost?

MOUNTEBANK.   [*Singing.*]

> *Would the gold in the richest of mines*
> *Be enough for this all-curing pill?*
> *By its magic it separates the ill*
> *From more ailments than forests have pines.*
>> *Agues and itches,*
>> *Fevers and twitches,*
>> *Plagues and neuroses,*
>> *Funks and psychoses,*
>> *Measles, congestions,*
>> *Strokes and depressions,*
>> *Organs that fail you,*
>> *All things that ail you—*

7 *anodynes of emollients*: soothing lotions.

> *All can be cured by my Orviétan, my Orviétan,*
> *All can be cured by my Orviétan.*

SGANARELLE. Sir, I believe that all the gold in the world is not enough to pay you for your medicine. However, here's five hundred dollars for you.

MOUNTEBANK. [*Singing.*]

> *Sing my praise, for these pills, I surmise—*
> *Such a bargain for such a small cost—*
> *Give new strength to those lives that are tossed*
> *By diseases the heavens devise.*
>> *Agues and itches,*
>> *Fevers and twitches,*
>> *Plagues and neuroses,*
>> *Funks and psychoses,*
>> *Measles, congestions,*
>> *Strokes and depressions,*
>> *Organs that fail you,*
>> *All things that ail you—*
> *All can be cured by my Orviétan, my Orviétan,*
> *All can be cured by my Orviétan.*

[*Exit SGANARELLE.*]

SECOND ENTR'ACTE

A dance by the MOUNTEBANK'S BUFFOONS and SCARAMOUCHES.

ACT III

Scene 1

Enter DR. FILLPOCKET, DR. SLICER, and DR. DE PITS.

DR. FILLPOCKET. Gentlemen, as men of your experience you should be ashamed to have been so imprudent as to quarrel like young blockheads. Don't you see that such open arguments hurt us in the public eye? Isn't it enough that expert critics know all about the controversy and dissension among our authorities and ancient masters, without disclosing our humbug to the world by wrangling in front of spectators? I'm concerned that some members of our profession mismanage their public relations so badly, because lately we've been hurt, and if we're not careful we may ruin ourselves. I have nothing to lose in this, because I've already made my pile. Let it blow, rain, and hail, the dead are dead, and I'm rich enough not to fear the living. But in the long run, our squabbles and disputes don't advance the medical profession. Since Heaven has smiled on us and enabled us to hoodwink the public for centuries, let's not disabuse people by our excesses, but let us go on taking advantage of the gullible—and thereby go on making our bundles. You know we're not the only profession to prey on human vulnerability; it's the major study of half the world's population. Everyone wants to catch people in moments of weakness in order to cash in. Flatterers, for example, benefit from the human need for praise, and so they lay it on with a trowel; some people have made huge fortunes in this way. Alchemists benefit from people's greed by promising mountains of gold to fools stupid enough to invest in their phony technology about making gold out of lead. And people even pour money into those consummate fakers, the psychics, who manipulate the vanity and ambition of their victims by making rosy predictions about the future. But the greatest weakness of humanity is the love of life—yes, our instinct for self-preservation—and we, as doctors, all profit from it, even with our pompous nonsense. We reap gigantic rewards because of the worship and adoration that our profession gains from our patients' fear of death. Let us then preserve the high esteem that human fallibility has given us, and let us, in the eyes of that world of believers out there, agree to take the credit for our cures while we deceive people by convincing them to blame Nature for our blunders. Let's not go about, I say, stupidly destroying the happy continuation of this public misperception which puts bread on our tables; and from the dead, whom we put into the ground, let us raise up our boundless wealth.

DR. SLICER.   [*spellbound.*] You are so right—so very right. But our dispute arose simply from hot blood, which we cannot always control.

DR. FILLPOCKET.   All right, then, gentlemen, put rancor aside, and make your apologies now.

DR. DE PITS.   I agree, if my emetic can be given to our present patient then Dr. Slicer can do as he pleases with the next patient.

DR. FILLPOCKET.   I couldn't say it better myself, and I'm glad to see good   5
sense prevail.

DR. DE PITS.   It's done.

DR. FILLPOCKET.   Shake hands, then. [*DR. DE PITS and DR. SLICER shake hands.*]
Goodbye. And next time, be more careful.

[*Exit DR. FILLPOCKET.*]

Act III, Scene 2

DR. DE PITS and DR. SLICER remain. Enter LISETTE.

LISETTE.   Gentlemen, how can you stand there without seeking a way of getting even for the attack that has just been made against the practice of medicine?

DR. SLICER.   What do you mean?

LISETTE.   A brazen fellow has just had the nerve to practice your profession without a licence; he has just wiped out another fellow with a sword clean through the body.

DR. SLICER.   Listen, you can make fun of us now, but some day you'll be sick, and then we'll get you in our clutches.

LISETTE.   When I'm ready, then I'll give you permission to do me in.   5

[*Exit the doctors.*]

Act III, Scene 3

LISETTE remains. Enter CLITANDER, dressed as a doctor.

CLITANDER.   Well, Lisette, what do you think of my outfit? Do you think I can fool our gentleman with it? Do I look the part of a doctor?

LISETTE. You look fine, but you're late. It's good that Heaven has made me so good-natured. I can't see two lovers sighing for each other without feeling soft myself, and wishing to satisfy their longing. Hang the consequences, I've sworn to free Lucinda from her tyranny and give her to you. I liked you from the first. I'm an authority when it comes to men, and she couldn't have made a better choice than you. True love requires great risks, and we have devised a scheme that we hope will succeed. Our plans are already moving ahead. The man we're dealing with is not one of your brightest in the world, and if we fail now, we can find a thousand other ways to reach our goal. Wait for me alone over there; I'll be right back to get you.

[CLITANDER *leaves.*]

Act III, Scene 4

LISETTE *remains. Enter* SGANARELLE.

LISETTE.   Sir, joy, joy!
SGANARELLE.   What's this?
LISETTE.   Rejoice.
SGANARELLE.   What for?
LISETTE.   And again, I say, rejoice!   5
SGANARELLE.   Tell me what's going on, and then I'll rejoice—maybe.
LISETTE.   No, I want you to rejoice in advance; I want you to sing and dance!
SGANARELLE.   Upon what?
LISETTE.   Upon my word.
SGANARELLE.   Okay, then. [*He sings and dances.*] La lera la la, la lera la. What   10
the devil!
LISETTE.   Sir, your daughter is cured!
SGANARELLE.   My daughter is cured?
LISETTE.   Yes. I am bringing you a doctor, but not just any doctor. He is the most important doctor on earth, who makes miraculous cures and puts all other doctors to shame.
SGANARELLE.   Where is he?
LISETTE.   I'll have him come in. [*She leaves.*]   15
SGANARELLE.   [*Alone.*] Let's see if this one will do better than the others.

Act III, Scene 5

SGANARELLE *remains. Enter* LISETTE *and* CLITANDER *in his doctor's robes.*

LISETTE.   [*Leading* CLITANDER.] Here he is.
SGANARELLE.   This doctor has only a small growth of beard.
LISETTE.   Science is not measured by a beard, and he did not get his degrees because of his chin.
SGANARELLE.   Sir, I'm told that you have effective medications for regular bowel movements.
CLITANDER.   Sir, my remedies are entirely unique. Other doctors use emetics,   5
bleeding, medicines, and enemas, but I cure by words, sounds, letters, signs, and mystical rings.

LISETTE.   What did I tell you?

SGANARELLE.   Here is a great man!

LISETTE.   Sir, since your daughter is up and around, I'll get her over here.

SGANARELLE.   Please do. [*LISETTE leaves.*]

CLITANDER.   [*Taking SGANARELLE's pulse.*] Your daughter is indeed sick.   10

SGANARELLE.   You know that from taking *my* pulse?

CLITANDER.   Yes, because of the sympathetic vibrations passing between father and daughter.

Act III, Scene 6

SGANARELLE and CLITANDER remain. Enter LUCINDA and LISETTE.

LISETTE.   [*To CLITANDER.*] Here, Sir, take this chair. [*To SGANARELLE.*] Let's go and leave them together.

SGANARELLE.   Why? I want to stay here.

LISETTE.   Are you kidding? We should go; a doctor has a hundred questions that it's not right for us to hear.

[*SGANARELLE and LISETTE move to a side of the stage.*]

CLITANDER.   [*Speaking to LUCINDA alone.*] Ah, Madam, I'm so overwhelmed with joy I hardly know how to begin speaking to you! When I could speak only with my eyes, I thought I had hundreds of things to say; but now that I have freedom to say what I want, I feel tongue-tied, and my happiness stifles my words.

LUCINDA.   I feel the same thing, and like you I sense movements of joy   5
that catch in my throat and prevent my speaking.

CLITANDER.   Ah, Madam, I would be so happy if you felt everything I feel, and if I could judge your heart by mine! But, Madam, may I believe that you were the one who thought of this happy stratagem that gives me such joy in your presence?

LUCINDA.   If you don't owe me the idea, at least you should know that I approved it eagerly.

SGANARELLE.   [*To LISETTE.*] He seems very close to her.

LISETTE.   [*To SGANARELLE.*] He's a doctor, and he's studying her facial features.

CLITANDER.   [*To LUCINDA.*] Will you be faithful, Madam, in the promises   10
you make to me?

LUCINDA.   And you, will you be firm in your present resolutions?

CLITANDER.   Ah, Madam, until death, and I'll demonstrate my love by what I'm now about to do.

SGANARELLE.   [*To CLITANDER.*] Well, our patient seems to be perking up.

CLITANDER.   That's because I've already tried one of the remedies of my great art on her. The mind has power over the body, and sickness often begins in the mind. My method is therefore to cure the spirit first before treating the body. Accordingly, I have studied her looks, her facial features, and the lines of her two hands; and by the science bestowed on me by Heaven, I have determined that her sickness is psychosomatic—she is sick in spirit. This disease comes entirely from her disordered imagination, which prompts her depraved wish to be married. My view is that there is nothing more extravagant or ridiculous than this wish for marriage.

SGANARELLE. [*Aside.*] This is indeed a man of skill!   15

CLITANDER. And all my life I have had, and will continue to have, an aversion for it.

SGANARELLE. [*Aside.*] A great physician!

CLITANDER. But, since it's necessary to flatter the imagination of patients, and because I see schizophrenic tendencies in her, and also because it would be perilous not to treat her quickly, I have taken advantage of her weakness and told her that I came here to ask you for her hand in marriage. When she heard that, her appearance changed for the better, her complexion brightened, and her eyes sparkled. I believe that if you keep her in this error for several days, you will see her recover completely.

SGANARELLE. There's nothing I want more.

CLITANDER. Afterwards we'll apply other remedies to cure her of this   20
fantasy entirely.

SGANARELLE. That will be marvellous! [*To LUCINDA.*] Well, daughter, here is a gentleman who wishes to marry you, and I have told him he has my blessing!

LUCINDA. Dear me, is this possible?

SGANARELLE. Yes.

LUCINDA. I'm not dreaming?

SGANARELLE. No, you're not dreaming.   25

LUCINDA. [*To CLITANDER.*] You really want to be my husband?

CLITANDER. Yes, Madam.

LUCINDA. And my father consents?

SGANARELLE. Yes, daughter.

LUCINDA. If this is true, I couldn't be happier!   30

CLITANDER. Don't doubt it, Madam. It is not just today that I began loving you and longing to marry you. I came here only to ask for your hand, and, if you want to know the whole truth exactly as it is, this doctor's costume is nothing more than a false front. I pretended to be a doctor only to come close to you, the more easily to realize my goal of marrying you.

LUCINDA. This all shows me the proofs of your tender love. I am deeply moved by them.

SGANARELLE. [*Aside.*] Oh, the fool! the fool! the fool!

LUCINDA. You approve of this gentleman as my husband, father, and do so willingly?

SGANARELLE. Yes. Give me your hand, and you, Sir, give me yours, too, by   35
way of witness.

CLITANDER. But, Sir—

SGANARELLE. [*Stifling laughter.*] No, no, it's to—it's to ease her mind. Now, join hands. There, it's done.

CLITANDER. Accept as a token of my faith this ring that I give you. [*Speaking low, to SGANARELLE.*] It's a special ring to cure her distracted mind.

LUCINDA. Let us draw up the contract, so that everything will be complete.

CLITANDER. Certainly; I would like that, Madam. [*To SGANARELLE.*] I'll show   40
her the man who writes my prescriptions, and make her believe he's a genuine Justice.

SGANARELLE. Excellent!

CLITANDER. [*Calling offstage.*] You there, send in the Justice I brought with me!

LUCINDA.   What, you brought along a Justice?

CLITANDER.   Yes, Madam.

LUCINDA.   I'm delighted!   45

SGANARELLE.   [*Chuckling.*] Oh, the fool! the fool!

Act III, Scene 7

They all remain. Enter the JUSTICE, *appropriately robed.* CLITANDER *whispers to the* JUSTICE.

SGANARELLE.   [*To the* JUSTICE.] Welcome, Sir. I commission you to draft a contract for these two young people. Please begin writing. [*While the* JUSTICE *is writing,* SGANARELLE *speaks to* LUCINDA.] This will be a contract to end all contracts. [*To the* JUSTICE.] I give her twenty million upon her marriage. Write that down!

LUCINDA.   I'm so overwhelmingly grateful to you, father.

JUSTICE.   [*Giving the contract to* SGANARELLE.] There, it's done; you need only to come and sign.

SGANARELLE.   How's that for a contract speedily finished?

CLITANDER.   [*To* SGANARELLE.] At least, Sir—   5

SGANARELLE.   No, no words of gratitude; say nothing, I beg you. [*Aside to* CLITANDER.] Don't we both know what we're doing? [*To the* JUSTICE.] Come, give him the pen. [*After* CLITANDER *signs,* SGANARELLE *gives the pen to* LUCINDA.] Come, come, sign it. Go ahead; I'll sign too. [*He signs.*]

LUCINDA.   No, no. I want to hold the contract myself.

SGANARELLE.   All right, take it. [*After she has signed.*] Now, are you happy?

LUCINDA.   More than you can imagine!

SGANARELLE.   I'm please. I'm very pleased.   10

CLITANDER.   As for the rest, I not only took the trouble to bring a Justice along, but to celebrate the occasion I brought singers and musicians too. Send them in! These are the people I take with me every day on my rounds; I direct them, with their harmony, to pacify the troubled minds of my patients.

Final Scene

All remain. Enter the SPIRIT OF COMEDY, DANCERS, *and* MUSICIANS.

ALL THREE [COMEDY, DANCERS, *and* MUSICIANS].

If you didn't have music and singing and dancing,
   You'd spend your life with your mind in chains;
For it's we, with our wonderful songs and our prancing,
   Who win the fight against aches and pains.

COMEDY

Do you want to break free,
   In the happiest way,
From the mis'ry and grief
   Of each long day?
      Then sing your song
      The whole day long;
      Throw away your medicine,
      Along with the jar it's in,

>   *And join our throng*
>   *As we sing along.*

ALL THREE

>   *If you didn't have music and singing and dancing,*
>   *You'd spend your life with your mind in chains;*
>   *For it's we, with our wonderful songs and our prancing,*
>   *Who win the fight against aches and pains.*

[*While they are singing and dancing, and amidst all the Games, Smiles, and Pleasures,* CLITANDER *leads* LUCINDA *away.*]

SGANARELLE.   This is a marvelous way to cure someone! But where is my daughter, and where is the doctor?

LISETTE.   They left—to complete the rest of the marriage ritual.

SGANARELLE.   What are you saying? What—what marriage?

LISETTE.   In truth, Sir, the game has been bagged, and what you thought was a joke turns out to be the absolute truth!

SGANARELLE.   [*The* DANCERS *catch hold of him and bring him into the dance by force.*]   5
What's this? The devil! Let me go! Let me go, I tell you! Still more? A plague on everything!

>   [*Finis.*]

QUESTIONS

Act I

1.   What does the opening scene indicate about the ways in which Sganarelle responds to other people? Describe his traits. What do you learn about his economic status? Why is this status important in the development of the plot?

2.   Describe the father-daughter relationship that is brought out in scenes 2 and 3. Why is the relationship made to seem comic and not serious?

3.   Why is it important that we learn about a suitor whom Lucinda likes, and that there has been an "envoy" from him seeking to negotiate a marriage?

4.   Describe the character of Lisette. Is she flat or round, representative or individualized? Why is she important? What is her relationship with Lucinda?

5.   Why does Sganarelle not want his daughter married? What do his reasons disclose about his character? What effect does Sganarelle's behavior toward his daughter have on your attitude toward him at the play's conclusion?

Act II

6.   Why is Sganarelle dramatized as a person with faith in the powers of the medical profession? What is the effect of Lisette's skepticism?

7.   Study the dialogue between Lisette and Dr. Slicer (Act II, scene 2, paragraphs 8–22). Describe how character and speech here produce laughter.

8. At the end of scene 2 a stage direction describes Sganarelle's payment to the doctors. Explain how the pantomime and dance may be used here to augment Molière's satiric presentation of doctors. Be specific.

9. Though Act II, scene 3 is supposedly a medical "consultation" about the condition of Lucinda, the conversation has nothing to do with her. What does Molière achieve by introducing the topics the doctors actually discuss?

10. What treatments do the various doctors prescribe for Lucinda? Though the doctors are contradictory, in what respects are some of them truthful? Why is their telling the truth comic?

11. Explain Sganarelle's role in the scenes with the doctors. What is the effect of these scenes on his seeking out the Mountebank, and also on his reception of Clitander in the next act when Clitander appears disguised as a doctor?

Act III

12. Why does Dr. Fillpocket make such a long speech? How honest is he? Would he give this speech to anyone but fellow doctors? To what degree is Molière's treatment of the speech comic? Serious? True? Partly true? Untrue?

13. What is the stratagem devised by Lisette and Clitander? How is it related to Sganarelle's already proven faith in doctors and medication?

14. Explain the irony of Clitander's confession to Lucinda and also of Sganarelle's responses beginning in Act III, scene 6, and extending to the revelation in the final scene. How is the final scene kept on a light, comic level?

15. How does Sganarelle react to the news that the marriage is real? How is this reaction kept from seeming serious? If you were a director, what might you tell the actor playing Sganarelle to do during the concluding dance? Why?

GENERAL QUESTIONS

1. Who is the protagonist of *Love Is the Doctor*? What conflicts develop? Who and what are the antagonists? Which "side" is triumphant at the end?

2. A traditional topic for laughter is the "biter gets bitten" and the "tables are turned." To what degree does Molière use this topic in the play? How successful is it as a means of developing humor?

3. The critic Harold C. Knutson has observed that in *Love Is the Doctor* we have "a particularly biting commentary on doctors and doctoring," and that one of the modes of satire is that the doctors "drop the mask and betray their callousness" and "contentiousness," and that their "concern" is not with their patients but rather with medical rules and formalities (*Molière: An Archetypal Approach* [Toronto: U. of Toronto Press, 1976, pp. 52–53]. Do you agree or disagree with Professor Knutson's observations? Explain in detail with specific examples from the play.

4. Aside from the medical satire, describe the various doctors as characters. To what degree are they brought to life? Which of the doctors is the most fully developed? Which are most amusing? Why?

BETH HENLEY, *AM I BLUE*

Brought up in Mississippi, Beth Henley attended Southern Methodist University in Texas, where she wrote *Am I Blue* in her sophomore year. She attended an acting school in Illinois and went to Hollywood to attempt an acting career in the movies. She continued working on plays, however, and it is her writing career that has blossomed. Her most notable achievement to date is her "Southern Gothic" play *Crimes of the Heart*, for which she won the Great American Play contest in 1978 and the Pulitzer Prize in 1981. In addition to completing two other full-length plays, she has also seen some of her shorter scripts into production. *Crimes of the Heart* was produced as a film in 1986, starring Diane Keaton, Jessica Lange, Sam Shepard, and Sissy Spacek.

Henley's comedic manner develops out of the eccentricity or "kook-iness" of her main female characters. The comic pattern of behavior is to do something unusual, but to regard the action as more ordinary than ridiculous. One of the characters in *Crimes of the Heart*, for example, after a failed suicide attempt, explains her action by saying that she has been having a "bad day." A character in another play inadvertently sets a house afire, but the outcome, although disastrous, is fortunate. Ashbe of *Am I Blue* is an early original in this pattern, with her liking for hot Kool-Aid and colored marshmallows, her habit of stealing ashtrays and then donating them to a fellow tenant, and her dabbling in voodoo.

Though *Am I Blue* is an amusing play, it deals with serious problems such as the difficulties of adjustment to adulthood, misconceptions about social roles, unfulfilled dreams, general indecision and purposelessness, and the attempt to develop individuality. The larger political and historical context of the year of the supposed events of the play, 1968, is not mentioned by either of the main characters, but one might locate their difficulties in some of the disturbances of that year: the assassinations of Martin Luther King and Robert Kennedy, the several-year-old and seem-ingly endless war in Vietnam, and the many antiwar demonstrations and riots, especially during the Democratic presidential convention in Chicago. Henley is particular in dating the action of *Am I Blue* on November 11–12, 1968; in other words, after all these nationally disturbing events had taken place, and also less than a week after the presidential election. One might note the irony that November 11 had traditionally been called "Armistice Day" (now Veterans Day)—a holiday dedicated to the estab-lishment of peace and stability.

Although Ashbe and John Polk reflect the frustration and disruption of the late 1960s, their lives are their own, seemingly untouched by politics. Ashbe has been left to her own resources at the age of sixteen, with a father who is alcoholic and absent, and a mother who has deserted the home entirely. John Polk is facing a difficult decision about his future. He is also attempting to stay afloat in the swim of fraternity life, and is seeking strength in rum instead of his own character. Nothing earthshaking is claimed for either Ashbe or John Polk at the play's end, but they both develop a degree of recognition, rejecting behaviors imposed by convention, and discovering their own capacities for dignity and friendship.

BETH HENLEY (b. 1952)

Am I Blue°

(1973) 1982

CHARACTERS

> John Polk Richards, *seventeen*
> Ashbe Williams, *sixteen*
> Hilda, *a waitress, thirty-five*
> *Street People:* Barker, Whore, Bum, Clareece

[*Scene: A bar, the street, the living room of a run-down apartment.*]

[*Time: Fall 1968.*]

The scene opens on a street in the New Orleans French Quarter on a rainy, blue bourbon night. Various people—a Whore, Bum, Street Barker, Clareece—appear and disappear along the street. The scene then focuses on a bar where a piano is heard from the back room playing softly and indistinctly "Am I Blue?" The lights go up on John Polk, who sits alone at a table. He is seventeen, a bit overweight and awkward. He wears nice clothes, perhaps a navy sweater with large white monograms. His navy raincoat is slung over an empty chair. While drinking John Polk concentrates on the red and black card that he holds in his hand. As soon as the scene is established, Ashbe enters from the street. She is sixteen, wears a flowered plastic raincoat, a white plastic rain cap, red galoshes, a butterfly barrette, and jeweled cat-eye glasses. She is carrying a bag full of stolen goods. Her hair is very curly. Ashbe makes her way cautiously to John Polk's table. As he sees her coming, he puts the card into his pocket. She sits in the empty chair and pulls his raincoat over her head.

ASHBE. Excuse me . . . do you mind if I sit here please?

JOHN POLK. [*Looks up at her—then down into his glass.*] What are you doing hiding under my raincoat? You're getting it all wet.

ASHBE. Well, I'm very sorry, but after all it is a raincoat. [*He tries to pull off coat.*] It was rude of me I know, but look I just don't want them to recognize me.

JOHN POLK. [*Looking about.*] Who to recognize you?

ASHBE. Well, I stole these two ashtrays from the Screw Inn, ya know right   5
down the street. [*She pulls out two glass commercial ashtrays from her white plastic bag.*] Anyway, I'm scared the manager saw me. They'll be after me I'm afraid.

JOHN POLK. Well, they should be. Look, do you mind giving me back my raincoat? I don't want to be found protecting any thief.

ASHBE. [*Coming out from under coat.*] Thief—would you call Robin Hood a thief?

JOHN POLK. Christ.

First produced in New York City by the Circle Repertory Company.

ASHBE.   [*Back under coat.*] No, you wouldn't. He was valiant—all the time stealing from the rich and giving to the poor.

JOHN POLK.   But your case isn't exactly the same, is it? You're stealing from   10
some crummy little bar and keeping the ashtrays for yourself. Now give me back my coat.

ASHBE.   [*Throws coat at him.*] Sure, take your old coat. I suppose I should have explained—about Miss Marcey. [*Silence.*] Miss Marcey, this cute old lady with a little hump in her back. I always see her in her sun hat and blue print dress. Miss Marcey lives in the apartment building next to ours. I leave all the stolen goods, as gifts on her front steps.

JOHN POLK.   Are you one of those kleptomaniacs? [*He starts checking his wallet.*]

ASHBE.   You mean when people all the time steal and they can't help it?

JOHN POLK.   Yeah.

ASHBE.   Oh, no. I'm not a bit careless. Take my job tonight, my very first   15
night job, if you want to know. Anyway, I've been planning it for two months, trying to decipher which bar most deserved to be stolen from. I finally decided on the Screw Inn. Mainly because of the way they're so mean to Mr. Groves. He works at the magazine rack at Diver's Drugstore and is really very sweet, but he has a drinking problem. I don't think that's fair to be mean to people simply because they have a drinking problem—and, well, anyway, you see I'm not just stealing for personal gain. I mean, I don't even smoke.

JOHN POLK.   Yeah, well, most infants don't, but then again, most infants don't hang around bars.

ASHBE.   I don't see why not, Toulouse Lautrec did.

JOHN POLK.   They'd throw me out.

ASHBE.   Oh, they throw me out too, but I don't accept defeat. [*Slowly moves into him.*] Why it's the very same with my pickpocketing.

[*JOHN POLK sneers, turns away.*]

ASHBE.   It's a very hard act to master. Why every time I've done it, I've   20
been caught.

JOHN POLK.   That's all I need, is to have some slum kid tell me how good it is to steal. Everyone knows it's not.

ASHBE.   [*About his drink.*] That looks good. What is it?

JOHN POLK.   Hey, would you mind leaving me alone—I just wanted to be alone.

ASHBE.   Okay. I'm sorry. How about if I'm quiet?

[*JOHN POLK shrugs. He sips drink, looks around, catches her eye, she smiles and sighs.*]

ASHBE.   I was just looking at your pin. What fraternity are you in?   25

JOHN POLK.   S.A.E.

ASHBE.   Is it a good fraternity?

JOHN POLK.   Sure, it's the greatest.

ASHBE.   I bet you have lots of friends.

JOHN POLK.   Tons.   30

ASHBE.   Are you being serious?

JOHN POLK.   Yes.

ASHBE.   Hmm. Do they have parties and all that?

JOHN POLK. Yeah, lots of parties, booze, honking horns, it's exactly what you would expect.

ASHBE. I wouldn't expect anything. Why did you join? 35

JOHN POLK. I don't know. Well, my brother . . . I guess it was my brother . . . he told me how great it was, how the fraternity was supposed to get you dates, make you study, solve all your problems.

ASHBE. Gee, does it?

JOHN POLK. Doesn't help you study.

ASHBE. How about dates? Do they get you a lot of dates?

JOHN POLK. Some. 40

ASHBE. What were the girls like?

JOHN POLK. I don't know—they were like girls.

ASHBE. Did you have a good time?

JOHN POLK. I had a pretty good time.

ASHBE. Did you make love to any of them? 45

JOHN POLK. [*To self.*] Oh, Christ . . .

ASHBE. I'm sorry . . . I just figured that's why you had the appointment with the whore . . . cause you didn't have anyone else . . . to make love to.

JOHN POLK. How did you know I had the, ah, the appointment?

ASHBE. I saw you put the red card in your pocket when I came up. Those red cards are pretty familiar around here. The house is only about a block or so away. It's one of the best though, really very plush. Only two murders and a knifing in its whole history. Do you go there often?

JOHN POLK. Yeah, I like to give myself a treat. 50

ASHBE. Who do you have?

JOHN POLK. What do you mean?

ASHBE. I mean which girl. [*JOHN POLK gazes into his drink.*] Look, I just thought I might know her is all.

JOHN POLK. Know her, ah, how would you know her?

ASHBE. Well, some of the girls from my high school go there to work when 55
they get out.

JOHN POLK. G.G., her name is G.G.

ASHBE. G.G. . . . Hmm, well, how does she look?

JOHN POLK. I don't know.

ASHBE. Oh, you've never been with her before?

JOHN POLK. No. 60

ASHBE. [*Confidentially.*] Are you one of those kinds that likes a lot of variety?

JOHN POLK. Variety? Sure, I guess I like variety.

ASHBE. Oh, yes, now I remember.

JOHN POLK. What?

ASHBE. G.G., that's just her working name. Her real name is Myrtle Reims, 65
she's Kay Reims' older sister. Kay is in my grade at school.

JOHN POLK. Myrtle? Her name is Myrtle?

ASHBE. I never liked the name either.

JOHN POLK. Myrtle, oh, Christ. Is she pretty?

ASHBE. [*Matter of fact.*] Pretty, no she's not real pretty.

JOHN POLK. What does she look like? 70

ASHBE. Let's see . . . she's, ah, well, Myrtle had acne and there are a few scars left. It's not bad. I think they sort of give her character. Her hair's red, only

I don't think it's really red. It sort of fizzles out all over her head. She's got a pretty good figure . . . big top . . . but the rest of her is kind of skinny.

JOHN POLK.   I wonder if she has a good personality.

ASHBE.   Well, she was a senior when I was a freshman; so I never really knew her. I remember she used to paint her fingernails lots of different colors . . . pink, orange, purple. I don't know, but she kind of scares me. About the only time I ever saw her true personality was around a year ago. I was over at Kay's making a health poster for school. Anyway, Myrtle comes busting in, screaming about how she can't find her spangled bra anywhere. Kay and I just sat on the floor cutting pictures of food out of magazines while she was storming about slamming drawers and swearing. Finally, she found it. It was pretty garish—red with black and gold sequined G's on each cup. That's how I remember the name— G.G.

[*As ASHBE illustrates the placement of the G's she spots HILDA, the waitress, approaching. Ashbe pulls the raincoat over her head and hides on the floor. Hilda enters through the beaded curtains spilling her tray. Hilda is a woman of few words.*]

HILDA.   Shit, damn curtain. Nuther drink?

JOHN POLK.   Mam?   75

HILDA.   [*Points to drink.*] Vodka coke?

JOHN POLK.   No, thank you. I'm not quite finished yet.

HILDA.   Napkins clean.

[*ASHBE pulls her bag off the table. HILDA looks at ASHBE then to JOHN POLK. She walks around the table, as ASHBE is crawling along the floor to escape. ASHBE runs into HILDA's toes.*]

ASHBE.   Are those real gold?

HILDA.   You again. Out.   80

ASHBE.   She wants me to leave. Why should a paying customer leave? [*Back to HILDA.*] Now I'll have a mint julip and easy on the mint.

HILDA.   This pre-teen with you?

JOHN POLK.   Well, I . . . No . . . I . . .

HILDA.   I.D.'s.

ASHBE.   Certainly, I always try to cooperate with the management.   85

HILDA.   [*Looking at JOHN POLK's I.D.*] I.D., 11-12-50. Date: 11-11-68.

JOHN POLK.   Yes, but . . . well, 11-12 is less than two hours away.

HILDA.   Back in two hours.

ASHBE.   I seem to have left my identification in my gold lamé bag.

HILDA.   Well, boo-hoo. [*Motions for ASHBE to leave with a minimum of effort.*   90
She goes back to table.*] No tip.

ASHBE.   You didn't tip her?

JOHN POLK.   I figured the drinks were so expensive . . . I just didn't . . .

HILDA.   No tip!

JOHN POLK.   Look, Miss, I'm sorry. [*Going through his pockets.*] Here would you like a . . . a nickel . . . wait, wait, here's a quarter.

HILDA.   Just move ass, sonny. You too, Barbie.   95

ASHBE.   Ugh, I hate public rudeness. I'm sure I'll refrain from ever coming here again.

HILDA. Think I'll go in the back room and cry.

[*ASHBE and JOHN POLK exit. HILDA picks up tray and exits through the curtain, tripping again.*]

HILDA. Shit. Damn curtain.

[*ASHBE and JOHN POLK are now standing outside under the awning of the bar.*]

ASHBE. Gee, I didn't know it was your birthday tomorrow. Happy birthday! Don't be mad. I thought you were at least twenty or twenty-one, really.

JOHN POLK. It's o.k. Forget it.   100

[*As they begin walking, various blues are heard coming from the nearby bars.*]

ASHBE. It's raining.

JOHN POLK. I know.

ASHBE. Are you going over to the house now?

JOHN POLK. No, not till twelve.

ASHBE. Yeah, the red and black cards—they mean all night. Midnight till   105
morning.

[*At this point a street BARKER beckons the couple into his establishment. Perhaps he is accompanied by a WHORE.*]

BARKER. Hey mister, bring your baby on in, buy her a few drinks, maybe tonight ya get lucky.

ASHBE. Keep walking.

JOHN POLK. What's wrong with the place?

ASHBE. The drinks are watery rot gut, and the show girls are boys . . .

BARKER. Up yours, punk!   110

JOHN POLK. [*Who has now sat down on a street bench.*] Look, just tell me where a cheap bar is. I've got to stay drunk, but I don't have much money left.

ASHBE. Yikes, there aren't too many cheap bars around here, and a lot of them check I.D.'s.

JOHN POLK. Well, do you know of any that don't?

ASHBE. No, not for sure.

JOHN POLK. Oh, God, I need to get drunk.   115

ASHBE. Aren't you?

JOHN POLK. Some, but I'm losing ground fast.

[*By this time a BUM who has been traveling drunkenly down the street falls near the couple and begins throwing up.*]

ASHBE. Oh, I know! You can come to my apartment. It's just down the block. We keep one bottle of rum around. I'll serve you a grand drink, three or four if you like.

JOHN POLK. [*Fretfully.*] No, thanks.

ASHBE. But look, we're getting all wet.   120

JOHN POLK. Sober too, wet and sober.

ASHBE. Oh, come on! Rain's blurring my glasses.

JOHN POLK. Well, how about your parents? What would they say?

ASHBE.   Daddy's out of town and Mama lives in Atlanta; so I'm sure they won't mind. I think we have some cute little marshmallows. [*Pulling on him.*] Won't you really come?

JOHN POLK.   You've probably got some gang of muggers waiting to kill me.   125
Oh, all right . . . what the hell, let's go.

ASHBE.   Hurrah! Come on. It's this way. [*She starts across the stage, stops, and picks up an old hat.*] Hey, look at this hat. Isn't it something! Here, wear it to keep off the rain.

JOHN POLK.   [*Throwing hat back onto street.*] No, thanks, you don't know who's worn it before.

ASHBE.   [*Picking hat back up.*] That makes it all the more exciting. Maybe it was a butcher's who slaughtered his wife or a silver pirate with a black bird on his throat. Who do you guess?

JOHN POLK.   I don't know. Anyway what's the good of guessing? I mean you'll never really know.

ASHBE.   [*Trying the hat on.*] Yeah, probably not.   130

[*At this point ASHBE and JOHN POLK reach the front door.*]

ASHBE.   Here we are.

[*ASHBE begins fumbling for her key. CLAREECE, a teeny-bopper, walks up to JOHN POLK.*]

CLAREECE.   Hey, man, got any spare change?

JOHN POLK.   [*Looking through his pockets.*] Let me see . . . I . . .

ASHBE.   [*Coming up between them, giving CLAREECE a shove.*] Beat it, Clareece.
He's my company.

CLAREECE.   [*Walks away and sneers.*] Oh, shove it, Frizzels.   135

ASHBE.   A lot of jerks live around here. Come on in. [*She opens the door. Lights go up on the living room of a run-down apartment in a run-down apartment house. Besides being merely run-down the room is a malicious pig sty with colors, paper hats, paper dolls, masks, torn up stuffed animals, dead flowers and leaves, dress-up clothes, etc., thrown all about.*] My bones are cold. Do you want a towel to dry off?

JOHN POLK.   Yes, thank you.

ASHBE.   [*She picks up a towel off the floor and tosses it to him.*] Here. [*He begins drying off, as she takes off her rain things; then she begins raking things off the sofa.*] Please do sit down. [*He sits.*] I'm sorry the place is disheveled, but my father's been out of town. I always try to pick up and all before he gets in. Of course, he's pretty used to messes. My mother never was too good at keeping things clean.

JOHN POLK.   When's he coming back?

ASHBE.   Sunday, I believe. Oh, I've been meaning to say . . .   140

JOHN POLK.   What?

ASHBE.   My name's Ashbe Williams.

JOHN POLK.   Ashbe?

ASHBE.   Yeah, Ashbe.

JOHN POLK.   My name's John Polk Richards.   145

ASHBE.   John Polk? They call you John Polk?

JOHN POLK.   It's family.

ASHBE.   [*Putting on socks.*] These are my favorite socks, the red furry ones.
Well, here's some books and magazines to look at while I fix you something to drink. What do you want in your rum?

JOHN POLK. Coke's fine.

ASHBE. I'll see if we have any. I think I'll take some hot Kool-Aid myself. 150

[*She exits to the kitchen.*]

JOHN POLK. Hot Kool-Aid?

ASHBE. It's just Kool-Aid that's been heated, like hot chocolate or hot tea.

JOHN POLK. Sounds great.

ASHBE. Well, I'm used to it. You get so much for your dime, it makes it worth your while. I don't buy presweetened, of course, it's better to sugar your own.

JOHN POLK. I remember once I threw up a lot of grape Kool-Aid when I 155
was a kid. I've hated it ever since. Hey, would you check on the time?

ASHBE. [*She enters carrying a tray with several bottles of food coloring, a bottle of rum, and a huge glass.*] I'm sorry we don't have Coke. I wonder if rum and Kool-Aid is good? Oh, we don't have a clock either.

[*She pours a large amount of rum into the large glass.*]

JOHN POLK. I'll just have it with water then.

ASHBE. [*She finds an almost empty glass of water somewhere in the room and dumps it in with the rum.*] Would you like food coloring in the water? It makes a drink all the more aesthetic. Of course, some people don't care for aesthetics.

JOHN POLK. No, thank you, just plain water.

ASHBE. Are you sure? The taste is entirely the same. I put it in all my 160
water.

JOHN POLK. Well . . .

ASHBE. What color do you want?

JOHN POLK. I don't know.

ASHBE. What's your favorite color?

JOHN POLK. Blue, I guess. 165

[*She puts a few blue drops into the glass. As she has nothing to stir with, she blows into the glass turning the water blue.*]

JOHN POLK. Thanks.

ASHBE. [*Exits. She screams from kitchen.*] Come on, say come on, cat, eat your fresh, good milk.

JOHN POLK. You have a cat?

ASHBE. [*off.*] No.

JOHN POLK. Oh. 170

ASHBE. [*She enters carrying a tray with a cup of hot Kool-Aid and Cheerios and colored marshmallows.*] Here are some Cheerios and some cute, little, colored marshmallows to eat with your drink.

JOHN POLK. Thanks.

ASHBE. I one time smashed all the big white marshmallows in the plastic bag at the grocery store.

JOHN POLK. Why did you do that?

ASHBE. I was angry. Do you like ceramics? 175

JOHN POLK. Yes.

ASHBE. My mother makes them. It's sort of her hobby. She is very talented.

John Polk.   My mother never does anything. Well, I guess she can shuffle the bridge deck okay.

Ashbe.   Actually, my mother is a dancer. She teaches at a school in Atlanta. She's really very talented.

John Polk.   [*Indicates ceramics.*] She must be to do all these.   180

Ashbe.   Well, Madeline, my older sister, did the blue one. Madeline gets to live with Mama.

John Polk.   And you live with your father.

Ashbe.   Yeah, but I get to go visit them sometimes.

John Polk.   You do ceramics too?

Ashbe.   No, I never learned . . . but I have this great potholder set. [*Gets   185 up to show him.*] See, I make lots of multicolored potholders and send them to Mama and Madeline. I also make paper hats. [*Gets material to show him.*] I guess they're more creative, but making potholders is more relaxing. Here would you like to make a hat?

John Polk.   I don't know, I'm a little drunk.

Ashbe.   It's not hard a bit. [*Hands him material.*] Just draw a real pretty design on the paper. It really doesn't have to be pretty, just whatever you want.

John Polk.   It's kind of you to give my creative drives such freedom.

Ashbe.   Ha, ha, ha, I'll work on my potholder set a bit.

John Polk.   What time is it? I've really got to check on the time.   190

Ashbe.   I know. I'll call the time operator.

[*She goes to the phone.*]

John Polk.   How do you get along without a clock?

Ashbe.   Well, I've been late for school a lot. Daddy has a watch. It's 11:03.

John Polk.   I've got a while yet. [*Ashbe twirls back to her chair, drops, and sighs.*] Are you a dancer, too?

Ashbe.   [*Delighted.*] I can't dance a bit, really. I practice a lot is all, at home   195 in the afternoon. I imagine you go to a lot of dances.

John Polk.   Not really, I'm a terrible dancer. I usually get bored or drunk.

Ashbe.   You probably drink too much.

John Polk.   No, it's just since I've come to college. All you do there is drink more beer and write more papers.

Ashbe.   What are you studying for to be?

John Polk.   I don't know.   200

Ashbe.   Why don't you become a rancher?

John Polk.   Dad wants me to help run his soybean farm.

Ashbe.   Soybean farm. Yikes, that's really something. Where is it?

John Polk.   Well, I live in the Delta, Hollybluff, Mississippi. Anyway, Dad feels I should go to business school first; you know, so I'll become, well, management-minded. Pass the blue.

Ashbe.   Is that what you really want to do?   205

John Polk.   I don't know. It would probably be as good as anything else I could do. Dad makes good money. He can take vacations whenever he wants. Sure it'll be a ball.

Ashbe.   I'd hate to have to be management-minded. [*John Polk shrugs.*] I don't mean to hurt your feelings, but I would really hate to be a management mind. [*She starts walking on her knees, twisting her fists in front of her eyes, and making clicking sounds as a management mind would make.*]

JOHN POLK. Cut it out. Just forget it. The farm could burn down, and I wouldn't even have to think about it.

ASHBE. [*After a pause.*] Well, what do you want to talk about?

JOHN POLK. I don't know. 210

ASHBE. When was the last dance you went to?

JOHN POLK. Dances. That's a great subject. Let's see, oh, I don't really remember—it was probably some blind date. God, I hate dates.

ASHBE. Why?

JOHN POLK. Well, they always say that they don't want popcorn, and they wind up eating all of yours.

ASHBE. You mean, you hate dates just because they eat your popcorn? 215
Don't you think that's kind of stingy?

JOHN POLK. It's the principle of the thing. Why can't they just say, yes, I'd like some popcorn when you ask them. But, no, they're always so damn coy.

ASHBE. I'd tell my date if I wanted popcorn. I'm not that immature.

JOHN POLK. Anyway, it's not only the popcorn. It's a lot of little things. I've finished coloring. What do I do now?

ASHBE. Now you have to fold it. Here . . . like this. [*She explains the process with relish.*] Say, that's really something.

JOHN POLK. It's kind of funny looking. [*Putting the hat on.*] Yeah, I like it, 220
but you could never wear it anywhere.

ASHBE. Well, like what anyway?

JOHN POLK. Huh?

ASHBE. The things dates do to you that you don't like, the little things.

JOHN POLK. Oh, well, just the way they wear those false eyelashes and put their hand on your knee when you're trying to parallel park, and keep on giggling and going off to the bathroom with their girl friends. It's obvious they don't want to go out with me. They just want to go out so that they can wear their new clothes and won't have to sit on their ass in the dormitory. They never want to go out with me. I can never even talk to them.

ASHBE. Well, you can talk to me, and I'm a girl. 225

JOHN POLK. Well, I'm really kind of drunk, and you're a stranger . . . well, I probably wouldn't be able to talk to you tomorrow. That makes a difference.

ASHBE. Maybe it does. [*A bit of a pause and then extremely pleased by the idea she says.*] You know we're alike because I don't like dances either.

JOHN POLK. I thought you said you practiced . . . in the afternoons.

ASHBE. Well, I like dancing. I just don't like dances. At least not like . . . well, not like the one our school was having tonight . . . they're so corny.

JOHN POLK. Yeah, most dances are. 230

ASHBE. All they serve is potato chips and fruit punch, and then this stupid baby band plays and everybody dances around thinking they're so hot. I frankly wouldn't dance there. I would prefer to wait till I am invited to an exclusive ball. It doesn't really matter which ball, just one where they have huge, golden chandeliers and silver fountains, and serve delicacies of all sorts and bubble blue champagne. I'll arrive in a pink silk cape. [*Laughing.*] I want to dance in pink!

JOHN POLK. You're mixed up. You're probably one of those people that live in a fantasy world.

ASHBE.   I do not. I accept reality as well as anyone. Anyway, you can talk to me, remember. I know what you mean by the kind of girls it's hard to talk to. There are girls a lot that way in the small clique at my school. Really tacky and mean. They expect everyone to be as stylish as they are, and they won't even speak to you in the hall. I don't mind if they don't speak to me, but I really love the orphans, and it hurts my feelings when they are so mean to them.

JOHN POLK.   What do you mean—they're mean to the "orpheens"? [*Giggles to himself at the wordplay.*]

ASHBE.   Oh, well, they sometimes snicker at the orphans' dresses. The   235
orphans usually have hand-me-down, drab, ugly dresses. Once Shelly Maxwell wouldn't let Glinda borrow her pencil, even though she had two. It hurt her feelings.

JOHN POLK.   Are you best friends with these orphans?

ASHBE.   I hardly know them at all. They're really shy. I just like them a lot. They're the reason I put spells on the girls in the clique.

JOHN POLK.   Spells, what do you mean, witch spells?

ASHBE.   Witch spells? Not really, mostly just voodoo.

JOHN POLK.   Are you kidding? Do you really do voodoo?   240

ASHBE.   Sure, here I'll show you my doll. [*Goes to get doll, comes back with straw voodoo doll. Her air as she returns is one of frightening mystery.*] I know a lot about the subject. Cora, she used to wash dishes in the Moonlight Cafe, told me all about voodoo. She's a real expert on the subject, went to all the meetings and everything. Once she caused a man's throat to rot away and turn almost totally black. She's moved to Chicago now.

JOHN POLK.   It doesn't really work. Does it?

ASHBE.   Well, not always. The thing about voodoo is that both parties have to believe in it for it to work.

JOHN POLK.   Do the girls in school believe in it?

ASHBE.   Not really, I don't think. That's where my main problem comes   245
in. I have to make the clique believe in it, yet I have to be very subtle. Mainly, I give reports in English class or Speech.

JOHN POLK.   Reports?

ASHBE.   On voodoo.

JOHN POLK.   That's really kind of sick, you know.

ASHBE.   Not really. I don't cast spells that'll do any real harm. Mainly, just the kind of thing to make them think . . . to keep them on their toes. [*Blue-drink intoxication begins to take over and JOHN POLK begins laughing.*] What's so funny?

JOHN POLK.   Nothing. I was just thinking what a mean little person you are.   250

ASHBE.   Mean! I'm not mean a bit.

JOHN POLK.   Yes, you are mean . . . [*Picking up color.*] . . . and green too.

ASHBE.   Green?

JOHN POLK.   Yes, green with envy of those other girls; so you play all those mean little tricks.

ASHBE.   Envious of those other girls, that stupid, close-minded little clique!   255

JOHN POLK.   Green as this marshmallow. [*Eats marshmallow.*]

ASHBE.   You think I want to be in some group . . . a sheep like you? A little sheep like you that does everything when he's supposed to do it!

JOHN POLK.   Me a sheep . . . I do what I want!

ASHBE. Ha! I've known you for an hour and already I see you for the sheep you are!

JOHN POLK. Don't take your green meanness out on me. 260

ASHBE. Not only are you a sheep, you are a NORMAL sheep. Give me back my colors! [*Begins snatching colors away.*]

JOHN POLK. [*Pushing colors at her.*] Green and mean! Green and mean! Green and mean!

ASHBE. [*Throwing marshmallows at him.*] That's the reason you're in a fraternity and the reason you're going to manage your mind. And dates . . . you go out on dates merely because it's expected of you even though you have a terrible time. That's the reason you go to the whorehouse to prove you're a normal man. Well, you're much too normal for me.

JOHN POLK. Infant bitch. You think you're really cute.

ASHBE. That really wasn't food coloring in your drink, it was poison! [*She* 265 laughs, he picks up his coat to go, and she stops throwing marshmallows at him.*] Are you going? I was only kidding. For Christ sake, it wasn't really poison. Come on, don't go. Can't you take a little friendly criticism?

JOHN POLK. Look, did you have to bother me tonight? I had enough problems without . . .

[*Phone rings. Both look at phone, it rings for the third time. He stands undecided.*]

ASHBE. Look, wait, we'll make it up. [*She goes to answer phone.*] Hello . . . Daddy. How are you? . . . I'm fine . . . Dad, you sound funny . . . What? . . . Come on, Daddy, you know she's not here. [*Pause.*] Look, I told you I wouldn't call anymore. You've got her number in Atlanta. (*Pause, as she sinks to the floor.*) Why have you started again? . . . Don't say that. I can tell it. I can. Hey, I have to go to bed now, I don't want to talk anymore, okay? [*Hangs up phone, then softly to self.*] Goddamnit.

JOHN POLK. [*He has heard the conversation and is taking off his coat.*] Hey, Ashbe . . . [*She looks at him blankly, her mind far away.*] You want to talk?

ASHBE. No. [*Slight pause.*] Why don't you look at my shell collection? I have this special shell collection. [*She shows him collection.*]

JOHN POLK. They're beautiful, I've never seen colors like this. [*ASHBE is* 270 *silent, he continues to himself.*] I used to go to Biloxi° a lot when I was a kid . . . One time my brother and I, we camped out on the beach. The sky was purple. I remember it was really purple. We ate pork and beans out of a can. I'd always kinda wanted to do that. Every night for about a week after I got home, I dreamt about these waves foaming over my head and face. It was funny. Did you find these shells or buy them?

ASHBE. Some I found, some I bought. I've been trying to decipher their meaning. Here, listen, do you hear that?

JOHN POLK. Yes.

ASHBE. That's the soul of the sea. [*She listens.*] I'm pretty sure it's the soul of the sea. Just imagine when I decipher the language. I'll know all the secrets of the world.

Biloxi: city in southern Mississippi, on the Gulf of Mexico.

JOHN POLK. Yeah, probably you will. [*Looking into the shell.*] You know, you were right.

ASHBE. What do you mean? 275

JOHN POLK. About me, you were right. I am a sheep, a normal one. I've been trying to get out of it, but now I'm as big a sheep as ever.

ASHBE. Oh, it doesn't matter. You're company. It was rude of me to say.

JOHN POLK. No, because it was true. I really didn't want to go into a fraternity, I didn't even want to go to college, and I sure as hell don't want to go back to Hollybluff and work the soybean farm till I'm eighty.

ASHBE. I still say you could work on a ranch.

JOHN POLK. I don't know. I wanted to be a minister or something good, 280 but I don't even know if I believe in God.

ASHBE. Yeah.

JOHN POLK. I never used to worry about being a failure. Now I think about it all the time. It's just I need to do something that's . . . fulfilling.

ASHBE. Fulfilling, yes, I see what you mean. Well, how about college? Isn't it fulfilling? I mean, you take all those wonderful classes, and you have all your very good friends.

JOHN POLK. Friends, yeah, I have some friends.

ASHBE. What do you mean? 285

JOHN POLK. Nothing . . . well, I do mean something. What the hell, let me try to explain. You see it was my "friends," the fraternity guys that set me up with G.G., excuse me, Myrtle, as a gift for my eighteenth birthday.

ASHBE. You mean, you didn't want the appointment?

JOHN POLK. No, I didn't want it. Hey, ah, where did my blue drink go?

ASHBE. [*As she hands him the drink.*] They probably thought you really wanted to go.

JOHN POLK. Yeah, I'm sure they gave a damn what I wanted. They never 290 even asked me. Hell, I would have told them a handkerchief, a pair of argyle socks, but, no, they have to get me a whore just because it's a cool-ass thing to do. They make me sick. I couldn't even stay at the party they gave. All the sweaty T-shirts, and moron sex stories . . . I just couldn't take it.

ASHBE. Is that why you were at the Blue Angel so early?

JOHN POLK. Yeah, I needed to get drunk, but not with them. They're such creeps.

ASHBE. Gosh, so you really don't want to go to Myrtle's?

JOHN POLK. No, I guess not.

ASHBE. Then are you going? 295

JOHN POLK. [*Pause.*] Yes.

ASHBE. That's wrong. You shouldn't go just to please them.

JOHN POLK. Oh, that's not the point anymore, maybe at first it was, but it's not anymore. Now I have go for myself . . . to prove to myself that I'm not afraid.

ASHBE. Afraid? [*Slowly, as she begins to grasp his meaning.*] You mean, you've never slept with a girl before?

JOHN POLK. Well, I've never been in love. 300

ASHBE. [*In amazement.*] You're a virgin?

JOHN POLK. Oh, God.

ASHBE. No, don't feel bad, I am too.

JOHN POLK. I thought I should be in love . . .

ASHBE. Well, you're certainly not in love with Myrtle. I mean, you haven't   305
even met her.

JOHN POLK. I know, but, God, I thought maybe I'd never fall in love. What
then? You should experience everything . . . shouldn't you? Oh, what's it matter,
everything's so screwed.

ASHBE. Screwed? Yeah, I guess it is. I mean, I always thought it would be
fun to have a lot of friends who gave parties and go to dances all dressed up. Like
the dance tonight . . . it might have been fun.

JOHN POLK. Well, why didn't you go?

ASHBE. I don't know. I'm not sure it would have been fun. Anyway, you
can't go . . . alone.

JOHN POLK. Oh, you need a date?   310

ASHBE. Yeah, or something.

JOHN POLK. Say, Ashbe, ya wanna dance here?

ASHBE. No, I think we'd better discuss your dilemma.

JOHN POLK. What dilemma?

ASHBE. Myrtle. It doesn't seem right you should . . .   315

JOHN POLK. Let's forget Myrtle for now. I've got a while yet. Here have
some more of this blue-moon drink.

ASHBE. You're only trying to escape through artificial means.

JOHN POLK. Yeah, you got it. Now come on. Would you like to dance? Hey,
you said you liked to dance.

ASHBE. You're being ridiculous.

JOHN POLK. [*Winking at her.*] Dance?   320

ASHBE. John Polk, I just thought . . .

JOHN POLK. Hmm?

ASHBE. How to solve your problem . . .

JOHN POLK. Well . . .

ASHBE. Make love to me!   325

JOHN POLK. What?!

ASHBE. It all seems logical to me. It would prove you weren't scared, and
you wouldn't be doing it just to impress others.

JOHN POLK. Look, I . . . I mean, I hardly know you . . .

ASHBE. But we've talked. It's better this way, really. I won't be so apt to
point out your mistakes.

JOHN POLK. I'd feel great, stripping a twelve-year-old of her virginity.   330

ASHBE. I'm sixteen! Anyway, I'd be stripping you of yours just as well. I'll
go put on some Tiger Claw perfume. [*She runs out.*]

JOHN POLK. Hey, come back! Tiger Claw perfume, Christ.

ASHBE. [*Entering.*] I think one should have different scents for different
moods.

JOHN POLK. Hey, stop spraying that! You know I'm not going to . . . well,
you'd get neurotic, or pregnant, or some damn thing. Stop spraying, will you!

ASHBE. Pregnant? You really think I could get pregnant?   335

JOHN POLK. Sure, it'd be a delightful possibility.

ASHBE. It really wouldn't be bad. Maybe I would get to go to Tokyo for an
abortion. I've never been to the Orient.

JOHN POLK. Sure getting cut on is always a real treat.

ASHBE. Anyway, I might just want to have my dear baby. I could move to

Atlanta with Mama and Madeline. It'd be wonderful fun. Why I could take him to the supermarket, put him in one of those little baby seats to stroll him about. I'd buy peach baby food and feed it to him with a tiny golden spoon. Why I could take colored pictures of him and send them to you through the mail. Come on . . . [*Starts putting pillows onto the couch.*] Well, I guess you should kiss me for a start. It's only etiquette, everyone begins with it.

JOHN POLK.   I don't think I could even kiss you with a clear conscience. I   340
mean, you're so small with those little cat-eye glasses and curly hair . . . I couldn't even kiss you.

ASHBE.   You couldn't even kiss me? I can't help it if I have to wear glasses. I got the prettiest ones I could find.

JOHN POLK.   Your glasses are fine. Let's forget it, okay?

ASHBE.   I know, my lips are too purple, but if I eat carrots, the dye'll come off and they'll be orange.

JOHN POLK.   I didn't say anything about your lips being too purple.

ASHBE.   Well, what is it? You're just plain chicken, I suppose . . .   345

JOHN POLK.   Sure, right, I'm chicken, totally chicken. Let's forget it. I don't know how, but, somehow, this is probably all my fault.

ASHBE.   You're darn right it's all your fault! I want to have my dear baby or at least get to Japan. I'm so sick of school I could smash every marshmallow in sight! [*She starts smashing.*] Go on to your skinny pimple whore. I hope the skinny whore laughs in your face, which she probably will because you have an easy face to laugh in.

JOHN POLK.   You're absolutely right, she'll probably hoot and howl her damn fizzle red head off. Maybe you can wait outside the door and hear her, give you lots of pleasure, you sadistic, little thief.

ASHBE.   Thief! Was Robin Hood . . . Oh, what's wrong with this world? I just wasn't made for it, is all. I've probably been put in the wrong world, I can see that now.

JOHN POLK.   You're fine in this world.   350

ASHBE.   Sure, everyone just views me as an undesirable lump.

JOHN POLK.   Who?

ASHBE.   You, for one.

JOHN POLK.   [*Pause.*] You mean because I wouldn't make love to you?

ASHBE.   It seems clear to me.   355

JOHN POLK.   But you're wrong, you know.

ASHBE.   [*To self, softly.*] Don't pity me.

JOHN POLK.   The reason I wouldn't wasn't that . . . it's just that . . . well, I like you too much to.

ASHBE.   You like me?

JOHN POLK.   Undesirable lump, Jesus. Your cheeks they're . . . they're . . .   360

ASHBE.   My cheeks? They're what?

JOHN POLK.   They're rosy.

ASHBE.   My cheeks are rosy?

JOHN POLK.   Yeah, your cheeks, they're really rosy.

ASHBE.   Well, they're natural, you know. Say, would you like to dance?   365

JOHN POLK.   Yes.

ASHBE.   I'll turn on the radio. [*She turns on radio. Ethel Waters is heard singing "Honey in the Honeycomb." ASHBE begins snapping her fingers.*] Yikes, let's jazz it out.

[They dance.]

> JOHN POLK.   Hey, I'm not good or anything . . .
> ASHBE.   John Polk.
> JOHN POLK.   Yeah?   370
> ASHBE.   Baby, I think you dance fine!

[They dance on, laughing, saying what they want till end of song. Then a radio announcer comes on and says the 12:00 news will be in five minutes. Billie Holiday, or Terry Pierce, begins singing, "Am I Blue?"]

> JOHN POLK.   Dance?
> ASHBE.   News in five minutes.
> JOHN POLK.   Yeah.
> ASHBE.   That means five minutes till midnight.   375
> JOHN POLK.   Yeah, I know.
> ASHBE.   Then you're not . . .
> JOHN POLK.   Ashbe, I've never danced all night. Wouldn't it be something to . . . to dance all night and watch the rats come out of the gutter?
> ASHBE.   Rats?
> JOHN POLK.   Don't they come out at night? I hear New Orleans has lots of   380
> rats.
> ASHBE.   Yeah, yeah, it's got lots of rats.
> JOHN POLK.   Then let's dance all night and wait for them to come out.
> ASHBE.   All right . . . but, but how about our feet?
> JOHN POLK.   Feet?
> ASHBE.   They'll hurt.   385
> JOHN POLK.   Yeah.
> ASHBE.   *[Smiling.]* Okay, then let's dance.

[He takes her hand, and they dance as lights black out and the music soars and continues to play.]

End.

QUESTIONS

1.   What do Ashbe's actions at the start tell you about her (such as hiding under the coat, stealing and giving the stolen things away, crawling away from the waitress)? What is disclosed by her speeches?

2.   Describe the circumstances of Ashbe and her family. To what degree can her character and behavior be explained by these circumstances?

3.   What is Ashbe's intention in her description of G.G., or Myrtle? What does her description tell you about her? What do you learn about her from her description of the only sort of dance she would like to go to (speech 231)?

4.   What personal, occupational, and social difficulties is John Polk experiencing?

Why is he trying to stay drunk before going to G.G.? What are his reactions to fraternity life and to the family business?

5. Explain the effects of the arguments between Ashbe and John Polk. How does their occasionally taunting each other influence their developing relationship?

6. Why does John Polk not take up Ashbe's invitation to make love? How does this refusal suggest the development of his character? Of Ashbe's character? What may be inferred by their concluding decision to dance the night away?

GENERAL QUESTIONS

1. What is the plot of *Am I Blue*? Who is the protagonist (or protagonists)? Who or what is the antagonist? How is the plot resolved?

2. Describe and analyze the verbal comedy of the play, such as the "two murders and a knifing" (speech 49), Ashbe's description of Myrtle (speeches 71–73), and the inquiry about what to mix with rum (speech 148).

3. What is appealing (or not appealing) about Ashbe and John Polk? To what extent are you to consider them as realistic persons? How might they be seen as symbols, and what might they symbolize?

4. What are the major themes or ideas of the play? To what extent does the comic mode obscure these ideas? To what extent does it bring them out?

5. What is the effect of the setting in the New Orleans French Quarter and the characters to be found there? What is shown about Ashbe and John Polk by their brief interactions with the characters in the bar, especially Hilda, and on the street?

WRITING ABOUT COMEDY

When you plan to write about an aspect of comedy, most of the conventional elements of literature are available as potential topics. You may consider features such as *plot, conflict, character, point of view, setting, style, tone, symbolism,* or *theme* as possible areas of investigation. You might focus on any one of these. You might also consider two or more related elements, such as how language and action define character, how character and symbol convey meaning, or how setting may influence comic structure.

Planning and prewriting strategies for each of these conventional elements are discussed at some length in Chapter 25 (pp. 993–1001) and in other chapters on prose fiction and poetry. As you develop your essay, you will find it helpful to look at the suggestions in these earlier sections.

For the most part, planning and writing about specific features of comedy are much like addressing the same topics in tragedy, realistic drama, short stories, or poetry. However, a few areas of consideration—such as plot, character, and language—are especially significant in comic drama, and may be handled in a distinctive fashion.

Questions for Discovering Ideas

PLOT, CONFLICT, STRUCTURE. What problems, adversities, or abnormal situations are in place at the beginning of the play? How is this initial situation complicated? Do the complications spring mainly from character or from situation? If from character, what aspects of behavior or personality create the problems? If from situation, what sorts of dilemmas or troubles plague the characters? What kind of complications dominate— misunderstandings, disagreements, mistakes in identity, situational problems, or emotional entanglements? To what extent does coincidence contribute to the chaos in the play?

What problems and complications occur early in the play? Who is the comic protagonist (or protagonists) and what is the goal (money, success, marriage, land, freedom)? How is the protagonist blocked (fathers, rivals, laws, customs, his or her own personality)? How threatening is the obstruction? What plans are developed to circumvent the blocking agents? Are the plans sensible or silly? Who initiates and executes the plans? To what extent do plans succeed (or fail)—because of chance and good luck or because of skillful planning and manipulation?

In the later stages of the play, which conflict is central, and whom do the conflicts involve? Do they result from personality clashes or from situations? To what degree are they related to blocking activities? How does the action reach the crisis, and which characters are involved? What choices, decisions, plans, or conclusions become necessary? What events or revelations (of character, emotion, background) produce the catastrophe, and how do these affect characters, circumstances, and relationships?

In the comic resolution, to what extent are loose ends tied up, lives straightened out, order restored, regeneration assured or implied? Does the resolution involve marriage or the prospect of marriage? If so, what does this suggest about the regeneration or continuity and the happiness of the state, the society, the family, and the individuals? Do you find the resolution satisfying or disturbing? Does it leave you happy or thoughtful, or both? Most important, how can you account for your responses to the resolution and the play as a whole? To what extent do they reflect the general aims of the various types of comedy? Are you amused by farce, satisfied by romantic comedy, or disturbed by satire?

CHARACTER. Does the character fill a conventional, representational, or stereotyped role? Does the character represent a social class or dominant eccentricity, or have a structural function? Is he or she a protagonist-lover, an antagonist-blocking agent, a choric figure, a confidant, or a parallel to one of the central figures? Can the character be considered a stock figure? If so, how does the playwright invigorate this character?

Do you find characters who are excessive, eccentric, or irrationally fixated on something? If so, what is the nature of this excess? To what extent does it define the character? What is its effect on the action of the play and on your reactions? To what extent do the play's complications and conflicts develop because of one or more excessive characters? Is this character cured of his or her excesses, or does the excess endure? In other words, do the characters learn and change? If so, why? If not, why not?

LANGUAGE.   Does the language consist of witty turns of phrase, confusions, puns, misunderstandings, or a mixture? Which characters are masters of language and which are mastered by it? Do characters use the same type of language and level of diction consistently? To what extent is language used to expose a character's self-interest or hypocrisy? If the language is witty and sparkling, what specific devices make it work effectively? If it is garbled and filled with misunderstandings, what types of errors does the playwright put into the characters' mouths? To what extent does this language shape your response to characters, to ideas, and to the play as a whole?

Strategies for Organizing Ideas

To develop a central idea, isolate the feature you wish to explore, and consider how it affects the shape and impact of the play. In planning an essay on Shakespeare's *A Midsummer Night's Dream*, for example, you might decide to focus on Puck's character and function. You might also begin to develop a link between Puck's conventional role as a tricky servant with his love of mischief and the chaos he creates in the play. Remember that it is not enough to state, "Puck is a comic character" or "*Love Is the Doctor* is a satiric play." A more focused assertion that also reveals your plan of development is necessary: "Puck is a comic character, modeled on the tricky servant of new comedy, who causes most of the confusion in *A Midsummer Night's Dream*" or "*Love Is the Doctor* satirizes the medical profession on the grounds of ignorance and greed."

You may organize your essay either by grouping related types of details together (such as observations about characters, actions, direct statements, and specific words) or by using the order of the play if you are focusing on only one type of evidence. It is not necessary to use the order of the play, however, even if you are using only one type of evidence. In writing about Puck as a tricky servant and creator of chaos, for example, you might present only one kind of evidence—direct statements by the character—and deal with Puck's remarks as they contribute to your analysis of Puck's character. In this way you can establish your own order, and you will also find it easy to avoid retelling the story of the play.

More often than not, however, you will find that your supporting details represent a variety of types of evidence. In this situation, you might organize the essay so that each topic is treated as having equal importance. For example, you might support an assertion about Puck by referring to his reputation, actions, and attitudes as equally important. Other possible strategies of organization are to demonstrate how the topics are related according to cause and effect, to build the topics from the least to most significant, or to trace how a common image or idea unifies the topic. Whatever the method of development, be consistent in your approach and make sure that the supporting details you use are valid.

A summary of key points is a useful, effective conclusion. In addition, you may show how your conclusions in the body of the essay bear upon larger aspects of the play's meaning.

SAMPLE ESSAY

Setting as Symbol and Comic Structure in *A Midsummer Night's Dream*°

[1]
Shakespeare's *A Midsummer Night's Dream* might superficially be considered light and inconsequential. The changes of mind undergone by the two sets of lovers, the placing of an ass's head on one of the characters, the movement in the forest of unrealistic fairies, the acting of a silly sketch at which many of the characters laugh--all seem both farfetched and far from reality. But the play is real. On a symbolic level it reveals the accidental and somewhat arbitrary origins of love--that most significant of human emotions-- even though it considers this serious subject in the good-natured medium of comedy. To bring out the merriment, and also the message, Shakespeare uses two rather obvious but distinct settings--the city of Athens and the nearby forest.* The journey from the city--the world of order and exposition--to the woods--the world of chaos, complication, and catastrophe--and then back to the city and resolution determines the play's comic structure.†

[2]
At the beginning of the comedy, Athens is presented as a world of daylight, rigid order, and strict law. In this setting, Duke Theseus has absolute authority, fathers are always right, and the law permits Egeus to "dispose" of Hermia "either to this gentleman Demetrius, / Or to her death" (l.1.43–44). This is also the setting for the exposition and the beginning of complication. Here, we meet the various groups of characters (except the fairies), and learn about the initial problem--namely that the relationship between Hermia and Lysander is blocked by a raging father, a rival suitor, and an old law. To flee and then to overcome these obstructions, the characters begin their movement out of the city. Lysander asks Hermia to meet him in the woods:

> Steal forth thy father's house tomorrow night:
> And in the wood, a league without the town,
> Where did I meet thee once with Helena
> To do observance to a morn of May
> There will I stay for thee. (l.1.164–168)

° See p. 1298 for this play.
* Central idea.
† Thesis sentence.

Her agreement begins a journey from Athens to the forest that ultimately includes all four lovers, Egeus, the city rulers, and the "mechanicals."

[3]

The second setting in the play, the woods outside Athens, is the kingdom of Oberon and Titania. It is a world of darkness, moonlight, chaos, madness, and dreams, a world that symbolizes the power of imagination and passion. The disorder in this world has many sources, including Oberon's jealousy, Titania's infatuation with the changeling child, and Puck's delight in mischief and confusion. When the lovers and the mechanicals enter this setting, they leave themselves open to all this disorder and chaos.

[4]

The woods are also the setting for complication, crisis, and catastrophe for the main plot. Confusion dominates the action here. Puck disrupts the mechanicals' rehearsal and transforms Bottom into an ass-headed monster. More important, the passions of the lovers are rearranged several times in this setting by Oberon and Puck through the magic of love-in-idleness, a flower that symbolizes the irrational but overwhelming power of love. Although the first two adjustments of the lovers' feelings are done to help, each has the effect of raising the levels of complication and disorder. Puck gleefully observes that his actions are the cause of the play's confusions:

> OBERON. Stand aside. The noise they make
> Will cause Demetrius to awake.
>
> PUCK. Then will two at once woo one:
> That must needs to be sport alone.
> And those things do best please me
> That befall prepost'rously. (III.2.116–21)

And, of course, Puck is right; the first application of love-in-idleness causes Lysander to fall wildly in love with Helena, and the second does the same to Demetrius.

[5]

The crisis and catastrophe of the main plot also occur in the woods. A crisis is reached when the two lovers challenge each other and the women attack each other. At this point, complication is at a peak, and the fairies must develop a plan to resolve the threats. Thus, Puck misleads the lovers to end their potential duel, and the emotions are readjusted one more time, putting Lysander back in love with Hermia and leaving Demetrius in love with Helena. The catastrophe--the revelation of these newly fixed emotions--occurs the next morning at the edge of the woods, in the presence of Egeus, Theseus, and Hippolyta. Thus, it ends the confusing relationships occurring in the forest, and begins the regularity of relationships that apply in the orderly world of city and society.

[6]

Resolution--the marriages and the mechanicals' production of "Pyramus and Thisby"--occurs back in the first setting, the city representing law and order. But the journey to the second setting has had a significant effect on the urban world both for Theseus and for the lovers. The law has been softened, Egeus overruled, the young lovers allowed to marry as they like, and lives set to right. In the end, this setting also becomes a world of night and the supernatural, but the fairy dance and blessings that close the play only emphasize the harmony and the regenerative implications of the comic resolutions.

Setting, symbolism, and comic pattern thus combine in *A Midsummer Night's Dream* to produce an intricately plotted structure. Each element reinforces the others, bringing the play toward completion though time after time there seems to be no way out of the apparent complication and confusion. [7] The marvel of the play is that the two settings represent, realistically, two opposed states of being, and, dramatically, two distinct stages of comic structure. The journey out of Athens, into the woods, and then back to the city is also a journey from exposition and adversity, through complication, crisis, and catastrophe, and then back to comic resolution.

Commentary on the Essay

This essay deals with three elements of *A Midsummer Night's Dream*: setting, symbol, and comic structure. It demonstrates the way that a number of different topics may be combined in a single essay. The central idea asserts that setting is employed both to symbolize states of mind and to organize the play's comic structure. Consequently, the essay is organized to reflect the journey from the city to the woods and then back to the city. The overall structure of the essay mirrors the stages of traditional dramatic structure (see pp. 993–95).

The body of the essay takes up the settings, their symbolic meaning, and the relationship between setting and structure in the order in which they are mentioned in the thesis sentence. Thus, paragraph 2 deals with Athens both as a world of law and order and as the setting for exposition and the beginnings of complication. The supporting details include circumstance, actions, and dialogue.

Paragraphs 3 through 5 deal with the middle of the journey and of the play. Paragraph 3 discusses the symbolic implications of the forest setting, and paragraphs 4 and 5 take up the connection between the setting and comic structure, specifically complication, crisis, and catastrophe. Again, the supporting details in these paragraphs are a mixture of actions, circumstances, and direct quotations.

Paragraph 6 deals briefly with the return to the city and links this setting with the comic resolution of the play. The concluding paragraph summarizes the connection between setting, symbol, and comic pattern that the essay illustrates.

WRITING TOPICS

1. Write an essay which describes Shakespeare's comic technique in *A Midsummer Night's Dream*. Consider these questions in your essay. Is the basic situation a serious one? How does Shakespeare keep it on a comic level? How does the boisterousness of the low characters influence your perceptions of the high, or courtly, characters? Would the play be as interesting without Bottom

and his crowd, and without the fairies and their involvement? How does the comic outcome depend on the boisterousness and colorfulness provided by the players and the fairies?

2. Though *Love Is the Doctor* is a comedy, it is based on potentially serious subjects, such as the attempts of an overbearing father to control the life of his daughter, the exploitation of gullibility, and the securing of an enormous dowry through deception. Write an essay showing how Molière prevents these topics from bursting through the play's comic tone.

3. Write an essay about the nature of comedy, using *A Midsummer Night's Dream*, *Am I Blue*, and *Love Is the Doctor* as material for your arguments. Deal with some of the following issues: How may comic material be defined? Does the happy outcome of a serious action qualify a play as a comedy, or should no action be serious? When does a play stop being comic and start being tragic? Are jokes necessary? Is farcical action necessary? Where are the edges between comedy and farce, on the one hand, and comedy and tragedy on the other?

4. Write a comic scene of your own between two people, perhaps between a boy and a girl, as in *Am I Blue*, or between a father and daughter, as in *Love Is the Doctor*, or between a person under a spell and a person in normal touch with reality, as in *A Midsummer Night's Dream*. When you've finished, write a short essay to explain the principles on which you've written your scene, such as the reasons for your choice of material, the use you have made of jokes (if any), straightforward dialogue, anger, outrage, amused responses, and so on.

Realistic and Nonrealistic Plays: Varying the Idea of Drama as Imitation

In **realistic drama,** the playwright seeks to put a perfect and detailed illusion of real life in the play and on the stage. The goal is *verisimilitude*— to be true to life. In **nonrealistic drama,** the aim is to present essential features of character and society through techniques that *do not* try to mirror life. From ancient Greek tragedy through Victorian melodrama, plays were explicitly artificial and highly conventionalized. Though the conventions of drama changed from age to age—choruses and masks in Greek tragedy, soliloquies and blank verse in Elizabethan plays, rhymed couplets in French and some English neoclassical drama—these conventions were nonrealistic, and were accepted by audiences and readers as such.

Realistic drama developed in the late nineteenth century in Europe as a reaction against the artificial and romantic plays that then dominated the stage. These escapist love stories and melodramas featured lavish sets, gorgeous costumes, flamboyant acting, conventional plots, and happy endings. The characters were exaggerated and idealized types—noble heroes who saved the day, sweet heroines who swooned at every opportunity, and dastardly villains who twirled their moustaches and leered at the audience in asides as they plotted to foil the hero and steal his money.

In reaction to the escapism and irrelevance of this sort of drama, some nineteenth-century dramatists began to write plays about realistic characters in realistic situations and about the actual problems of contemporary society. The rebellion began slowly, and most of these writers were Europeans, among them Emile Zola, Henrik Ibsen, Maxim Gorki, and George Bernard Shaw. American realists, who came to this tradition somewhat later than the Europeans, include Eugene O'Neill (see p. 1030) and Susan Glaspell (p. 1018).

In keeping with the goal of verisimilitude, realistic plays have many characteristics. A major one is to eliminate traditional but artificial dramatic conventions—such as disguises, overheard conversations, asides, soliloquies, and verse—that do not occur in daily life. The plots are straightforward and have a realistic chronology; the characters look, speak, and act as much like real people as possible. These plays are not set in imaginary or idealized worlds. Rather, their settings are middle-class living rooms, the country houses of the wealthy, the squalid slums of the poor. The plays usually explore ideas about the nature of humanity in conflict with the customs and prejudices of society; realistic drama at its best is a close examination of character in conflict.

The new realism in drama called for equally new and realistic methods of production and action. Most theaters of the nineteenth century already featured a darkened auditorium, a proscenium arch separating the audience from the players, and a picture-frame stage. The spectators watched the play as though the fourth wall of a room had been removed.

The settings and stage directions for the realistic drama became as detailed and lifelike as possible. When the curtain went up, the audience saw a completely furnished room or office, much like the ones in which they themselves lived or worked. Ibsen's lengthy description of the setting for Acts I and II of *An Enemy of the People,* for example, calls for the elaborate duplication of Norwegian middle-class living and dining rooms of the late nineteenth century (1882), complete with a sofa, a coffee table, a burning lamp with an elaborate lampshade, a Scandinavian porcelainized tile heating stove, a dining table with all the china and utensils still on it, and an actual platter of roast beef. Lighting and costumes became equally realistic. Lighting was designed to duplicate the natural light at a particular time of day or the lamps burning in a room at night. Similarly, the lavish and beautiful costumes of nineteenth-century melodrama gave way to detailed realism in dress and makeup.

The most radical and permanent change caused by the new realism was in acting styles. In the Victorian theater, actors stood in one place, assumed a conventional stance, and declaimed or ranted their lines. In realistic drama the acting became more natural. The actors began to combine movement with dialogue and to play "within the scene" to each other rather than to the spectators.

These changes were due, in large measure, to Konstantin Stanislavsky (1863–1938), one of the founders of the Moscow Arts Theater (1898) and the inventor of what we now term *method* acting. Stanislavsky argued that actors had to build characterizations on a lifelong study of inner truths and motivation. He taught actors to search their own lives for the feelings, motivations, and behavior of the characters they portrayed.

THE REBELLION AGAINST REALISM

No sooner had realism taken over the stage than a new nonrealistic drama began to emerge as a reaction against realism. Many playwrights in Europe and America decided that realism had gone too far and that the quest for minutely realistic details had sacrificed the essence of drama—character and universal truth. Playwrights began to explore every avenue of anti-realistic drama. At the same time, new types of stages and theaters began to appear. The **thrust stage,** which projected into the audience, was reintroduced, thus helping to destroy the fourth-wall principle of realistic drama. The **arena stage,** or **theater-in-the-round,** was developed, which also called for new concepts in drama and production.

Playwrights like Luigi Pirandello (1867–1936) and Bertolt Brecht (1898–1956) began to write plays that required only minimal sets or no sets at all. In the same tradition, Thornton Wilder wrote plays (such as *Our Town*) in which the action occurs on a bare stage, with the brick walls, heating pipes, and ropes of the backstage area in full view. Edward Albee's *The Sandbox* is in this tradition, in which the staging reminds us constantly that we are reading or watching a play—an illusion and an imitation—rather than real life.

Nonrealistic drama has moved progressively further away from realism throughout the latter half of the twentieth century. With the development of flexible theaters, in which the seats could be removed from the auditorium while acting areas could be set up throughout the house, the action of plays began to move offstage and into the space once reserved for the audience. In the 1960s and 1970s, acting companies like The Living Theater in New York experimented with plays that began onstage, moved into the audience, and ended on the streets outside the theater. In the mid-1980s, the Old Vic Company in England produced *The Creation*—a series of medieval mystery plays—in which the actors actually mingled among the standing spectators, acting only when their parts were called for. Whenever new scenes were introduced, the spectators were moved aside, so that the acting areas were being newly created and defined by the shifting audience. A production popular early in the 1990s is *Tony and Tina's Wedding*, which is the staging of a wedding and reception. Because performers and audience interact, particularly at the reception, many members of the audience take on impromptu speaking and acting roles. Every performance is therefore spontaneous and unique. Such productions represent the edge of drama; they blur the distinction between the play and the real world to the point where art almost ceases to be art and starts to become life.

ELEMENTS OF REALISTIC AND NONREALISTIC DRAMA

Whereas realistic drama strives as much as possible to be true to life, modern nonrealistic drama is free to deal with human values and problems in a great variety of ways. Realistic drama aims at complete verisimilitude and a minimum of artificial dramatic conventions; nonrealistic drama employs whatever stylized conventions the playwright finds useful.

Realistic plays, like life, unfold chronologically. For this reason, the *story* (as opposed to the *play*) is usually nearing conclusion when the stage action begins. In Susan Glaspell's *Trifles*, for instance, the story includes incidents from Mrs. Wright's childhood, problems with her marriage, and the murder of Mr. Wright. All this, however, is related in conversation; it all occurred *before* the action of the play. Such past events have a profound impact on the present action in a realistic drama, but the play itself presents only the last part of the story.

In nonrealistic drama, the structure of the plot is more fluid. Action can shift from the present to the past with little or no transition; flashbacks can be mixed with present action, or the entire play can dramatize the past through a present perspective. In Tennessee Williams's *The Glass Menagerie*, recollected past action is revealed through the present memories of the narrator. Similarly, the action in Arthur Miller's *Death of a Salesman* constantly shifts between present and past action and fantasy.

The characters in realistic drama are as much like people as possible. They can be representative, symbolic, or even stock characters, but they must sound and act like actual human beings, with names, backgrounds, emotions, and motivations, and they must be consistent. Their responses, considerations, decisions, and character development must be motivated exactly as they would be in real life. Such fidelity to life is apparent in realistic plays like Glaspell's *Trifles* and Ibsen's *An Enemy of the People*.

In modern nonrealistic drama, the characters may be nameless figures who have no background or motivation and who drop in and out of character as the playwright desires. Such is the case in Albee's *The Sandbox*, a play that is nonrealistic to an extreme. Similarly, characters in nonrealistic drama can assume a number of different roles at different times in the play. In *The Glass Menagerie*, for example, Tom is variously a character in the action, a narrator of the action, and a stage manager. As a character, he interacts with Laura and Amanda, but he also provides ongoing narration directly to the audience, and occasionally he gives music and lighting cues to the offstage technicians.

These distinctions do not mean that realistic characters are necessarily round, and nonrealistic ones always flat. The *way* in which a playwright develops characters, realistically or nonrealistically, does not always control the *degree* to which they are developed. Thus, true-to-life characters like Mr. Hale in *Trifles* or the Stockmann children in *An Enemy of the People* can be flat. By the same token, characters that are developed nonrealistically, such as Tom in *The Glass Menagerie* or Willy Loman in *Death of a Salesman*, may have enough depth and scope to be considered fully round.

The language in a realistic play is usually an accurate reproduction of the colloquial diction appropriate to the class or group of people portrayed. There is no poetry, no radical shift in style, and no direct address to the reader or speaker. In *An Enemy of the People*, for instance, Dr. Thomas Stockmann and his wife Katrina consistently speak like middle-class Norwegians (in translation) in the 1880s. Similarly, the characters in Glaspell's *Trifles* sound like Iowa farmers and businesspeople.

Such verisimilitude is not required in nonrealistic drama. Playwrights may employ any linguistic devices that suit their needs. Characters may speak in verse, clichés, or even nonsense sounds. One character may have two or three entirely different styles of speech, as Tom does in *The Glass Menagerie*. Dramatists are free to introduce snippets of poetry or song into the play, and characters can (and frequently do) speak directly to the audience.

Such differences in plot, characterization, and language are matched by differences in production techniques. Whereas the staging of a realistic drama must be as true to life as possible, nonrealistic drama can be staged with few or no realistic effects. Thus, lighting can indicate instantaneous shifts of location, flashbacks, and changes in mood. Spotlights may illuminate and emphasize specific objects and characters in ways that never happen in reality. Nonrealistic plays may call for a virtually bare stage, as in *The Sandbox*. Alternatively, the sets may be symbolic and expressive of mood, employing lighting and semitransparent painted cloth (called a *scrim*) to create the effect of multiple places or times on stage simultaneously. Such expressionistic settings are described in the stage directions for both *Death of a Salesman* and *The Glass Menagerie*.

Perhaps the most important difference between the realistic and modern nonrealistic drama concerns the play's relationships to the theater, the audience, and the world at large. In realistic drama, the play presents a self-contained action in a self-contained world that imitates reality. The illusion of reality is never compromised. The actors never drop out of character, the audience is never addressed, and the play never acknowledges that it is a play. But modern nonrealistic drama tends toward the other extreme; it can be full of devices that break through the illusion on the stage (or the page) and scream out that the play is a play, a work of art, a stylized imitation of something like life. These devices include symbolic characters, poetry, music, minimalist or expressionistic settings, lighting effects, words or images projected onto a wall or screen, action that flows off the stage into the auditorium, and speeches made directly to the spectators or the reader. All these and other devices produce the same general effects: They break the illusion of reality, and remind us that we are reading or watching a play.

THE SPECTRUM OF REALISM

To this point we have been speaking as though realistic and nonrealistic drama were always at opposite extremes. Most plays are not purely realistic or nonrealistic. Rather, the terms represent the opposite ends of a spectrum, and most plays fall somewhere between the two extremes. Both

Trifles and *An Enemy of the People*, for example, are highly realistic plays, yet each modifies its realism through symbolism and selective emphasis. Conversely, *The Sandbox* is nonrealistic, yet the play includes enough realistic elements so that we can understand the correspondence between Albee's art and the real world. Both *Death of a Salesman* and *The Glass Menagerie* fall near the middle of the spectrum; they combine realistic language and characterization with nonrealistic settings, lighting, and structure.

HENRIK IBSEN, *AN ENEMY OF THE PEOPLE*

Henrik Ibsen is one of the masters of the realistic *problem play* in which true-to-life characters come into conflict with the values and prejudices of their societies. His plays embody a vision of human nature and destiny that rises above the limitations of realism, and encompass universal patterns and problems. He was born in the small town of Skien [*shee-en*], Norway, just 70 miles southwest of the capital, Oslo. Although his parents had been wealthy, the family went bankrupt while he was young, and Ibsen struggled against poverty in his early years. He was apprenticed to a pharmacist in 1843, but his real interest was the theater. He wrote his first play in 1850 and spent the next thirteen years writing and working in theaters in Norway, Denmark, and Germany. The success of *The Pretenders* (1863) allowed him to move to Italy, where he lived until his return to Norway in 1891.

Ibsen's early plays were romantic or historical dramas, mostly in verse. His first realistic play, *The League of Youth* (1869), was a prose satire of Norwegian social classes and prejudices. In this play, Ibsen began to employ realistic characters, situations, and problems, and over the next thirteen years he wrote a string of realistic dramas that deal with the troubled relationships between the individual, the family, and the community. These include *A Doll House* (1879), *Ghosts* (1881), and *An Enemy of the People* (1882). In his later plays (for example, *When We Dead Awaken*, 1899) Ibsen moved away from realism toward a combination of symbolic and realistic techniques.

An Enemy of the People, first produced in 1882, is realistic in that it presents an image of believable people confronting the problems of real life and contemporary society. Realism also implies a realistic setting and a story that begins before the opening of the play. *An Enemy of the People* conforms on both counts. The set is realistic not only in the careful and detailed creation of the Stockmann household, the print shop, and the large home of Captain Horster, but in the arrangements within all the interiors. So exacting is Ibsen that a comparison of the living room (Acts I and II) and the study (Act V) shows that the room arrangements and the placements of the doors in the Stockmann house correspond exactly, as though Ibsen had drawn a floor plan before he created his directions for the sets.

The realism is modified to some extent by Ibsen's use of symbols and by his development of polar opposites between the two major characters. The master symbols of the play are the toxic wastes at the nearby town of Mølledal, the town's Therapeutic Spa, Aslaksen's printing business, political manipulation, Stockmann's movement from being first the friend and then the enemy of the people, and the concepts of public opinion and the popular majority. Lesser symbols are the hot toddy, the Mayor's hat and stick, the newspaper *The People's Messenger*, Evensen's horn, the stocks in the Town Spa, and the spring weather at the play's end. Ibsen concentrates the major oppositions of the play in the sibling rivalry and also the ideological divergences of Dr. Thomas Stockmann and his brother, Mayor Peter Stockmann. The inability of these men to reach a compromise with each other, together with their subsequent alienation, is just as much a product of their personal mistrust and hostility as of their conflicting values.

The plot and structure of *An Enemy of the People* reflect Ibsen's awareness of the conventions of the **well-made play,** a form developed and popularized in France in the nineteenth century by Eugène Scribe (1791–1861) and Victorien Sardou (1831–1908). The well-made play follows a rigid structure in which the drama always begins at the climax of the story, thus making necessary a great deal of exposition. The plot is usually built on a secret known to the audience and one or two of the characters but withheld from most of the others. The well-made play thus begins in suspense, and it offers a pattern of increasing tension produced through exposition and the well-timed arrival of new characters (like Vik) and threatening news or props like the Mayor's information about the last will and testament of Morten Kiil. In the course of this action the protagonist of the well-made play moves through a series of high and low points, going eventually from the lowest point, through a **peripeteia** or reversal (Aristotle's concept), to a high point, at which he or she confronts and defeats the villain. Ibsen maintains these structural characteristics throughout *An Enemy of the People*, with the variation that Dr. Stockmann confronts *three* sets of villains in the fifth act (The Mayor, Morten Kiil, and Hovstad and Billing). In addition, because *An Enemy of the People* is a play about ideas, Ibsen concludes the play on new notes of Dr. Stockmann's dedication to growth and the future.

An Enemy of the People demonstrates the force of Ibsen's awareness of modern issues, one of the most significant being the effects of pollution and the conflicts that preservers of the environment have with proponents of business as usual. This issue is joined early in the play, as soon as Dr. Stockmann learns about the toxic wastes percolating through the ground and contaminating the precincts of the Town Spa—on which, we learn, the economic livelihood of the entire town depends.

At first any potential conflict resulting from Dr. Stockmann's discovery seems minor, because his facts are so unassailable. But the issue is raised to a political level with the entry of the local newspaper editor and his publisher. Once The Mayor convinces these men that Dr. Stockmann is distorting the facts to suit his own political goals, the play enlarges into the opposition of the individual and society at large. As these conflicts develop, Ibsen creates two of the great scenes in the history of drama—those scenes in Acts II and III in which Dr. Stockmann and his brother The Mayor divide and argue over the issue of truth and individuality versus interest and collective public opinion. Their conflict comes to a head in the fourth act, in which Ibsen, through Dr. Stockmann, makes a case for recognizing an individual's rights to pursue the truth, regardless of the effects on established interests. The dramatic force of the empty stage at the end of this act, with the cries and jeers of the angry mob reverberating loudly backstage, has not been equaled.

HENRIK IBSEN   (1828–1906)

An Enemy of the People   *1882*

Translated by Edgar V. Roberts

CHARACTERS

Dr. Thomas Stockmann. *A Physician, and Chief Medical Officer of the Town's Therapeutic Spa.*

Mrs. Katrina Stockmann. *His wife.*

Petra Stockmann. *Their daughter, a young woman; a teacher.*

Eilif Stockmann. *Their thirteen-year-old son.*

Morten Stockmann. *Their ten-year-old son.*

Peter Stockmann (THE MAYOR). DR. STOCKMANN'S *older brother, Principal Executive and Chief Constable of the local government, Chief Executive Officer of the Governing Board of the Spa, etc., etc.*

Morten Kiil. *Owner of the tannery at the nearby town of* MØLLEDAL, *and* MRS. STOCKMANN'S *stepfather.*

Captain Horster. *A Ship's Captain, friendly to* DR. STOCKMANN *and his family.*

Hovstad. *Editor-in-Chief of* THE PEOPLE'S MESSENGER.

Billing. *Assistant Editor of the* MESSENGER.

Aslaksen. *Owner of a printing business. Publisher of the* MESSENGER, *Chair of the local Homeowners Association, and Secretary of the Temperance Union.*

Vik. *A stout citizen; a shipowner, and* CAPTAIN HORSTER'S *employer.*

Workers. *Seen in* ASLAKSEN'S *print shop in Act III.*

Local Townspeople. *Men, Women, and Children—of all classes—who attend the meeting in Act IV. Three of these are named:* LAMSTAD (2 CITIZEN); PETTERSEN, *a drunken man; and* SKIPPER EVENSEN, *whose main task is to blow a horn. A number of the other citizens and workers have speaking lines. All react, demonstrate, and shout as a group.*

The location of the play is an unnamed town on the southern coast of Norway. The time and circumstances are those of 1882, the date of the play.

ACT I

SCENE. *It is evening in the living room of DR. and MRS. STOCKMANN. The room is plainly but neatly furnished. At stage right are two doors, the upstage one leading to a hallway, the downstage one to DR. STOCKMANN's study. At upstage left, a door leads to the other family rooms. In the middle of the stage-left wall is a porcelainized tile heating stove, and, farther downstage, a sofa with a mirror above and an oval coffee-table in front. A lamp with a prominent lampshade is burning on the table. An open door in the back wall shows the dining room. BILLING is alone at the dining table, which also holds a lighted lamp. A napkin is tucked into his collar, and MRS. STOCKMANN is serving him from a platter of roast beef. The other chairs are empty, but the table has not yet been cleared of the plates, etc., of the diners who have left the table.*

MRS. STOCKMANN. You see, Mr. Billing, if you come late, you have to settle for cold food.

BILLING. [*speaks while eating.*] This is good, thank you, really fine.

MRS. STOCKMANN.   My husband is very punctual about his meals, you know—

BILLING.   That's all right with me. In fact, I think I enjoy eating more when I'm alone.

MRS. STOCKMANN.   Well, since you feel that way—[*Turns toward sounds at the hallway door.*] That's probably Mr. Hovstad. 5

BILLING.   You're right.

MAYOR PETER STOCKMANN enters, wearing an overcoat and his official hat, and carrying a walking-stick.

THE MAYOR.   Good evening, Katrina.

MRS. STOCKMANN.   [*enters the living room.*] Good evening. How are you? How nice of you to come over!

THE MAYOR.   I was just passing by, and so—[*looks into the dining room*]. But I see you have another guest.

MRS. STOCKMANN.   [*somewhat embarrassed.*] Oh, no, he came by quite by 10 chance. [*Speaks rapidly.*] Won't you have something to eat, too?

THE MAYOR.   Me? No, thank you. With my digestion, I can't eat hot meals at night.

MRS. STOCKMANN.   Not even just this once?

THE MAYOR.   No, my dear, no. I stick to my tea, bread, and butter, which is healthier for me—and cheaper, too.

MRS. STOCKMANN.   [*smiles.*] Now you can't say that Thomas and I are spendthrifts.

THE MAYOR.   No, not you, I'd never say that about *you.* [*Points to the Doctor's* 15 *study.*] Is he in there?

MRS. STOCKMANN.   No, he went walking with the boys after dinner.

THE MAYOR.   I don't think that's a good idea. [*Listens.*] He may be coming now.

MRS. STOCKMANN.   No, not yet. [*A knock at the door.*] Come in! [*EDITOR HOVSTAD enters from the hallway.*] Oh, it's Mr. Hovstad!

HOVSTAD.   Yes. Please excuse me. I was delayed at the printer's. Mr. Mayor, good evening.

THE MAYOR.   [*bows formally.*] Good evening. I suppose you're here on business?   20

HOVSTAD.   Yes, partly. It's about an article for the paper.

THE MAYOR.   As I thought. I understand my brother is a regular contributor to *The People's Messenger*.

HOVSTAD.   Yes, he writes for the *Messenger* on local matters.

MRS. STOCKMANN.   [*to HOVSTAD.*] Would you like—[*Points to the dining room.*]

THE MAYOR.   Yes indeed. I'm sure *I* don't blame him for writing for a   25
sympathetic audience. Besides that, Mr. Hovstad, I have nothing against your paper.

HOVSTAD.   No, I shouldn't think you did.

THE MAYOR.   On the whole, there's a beautiful sense of toleration in the town—genuine public spirit. And it all comes from our mutual interest—an interest that concerns to the highest degree all upright citizens—

HOVSTAD.   The Town Spa, yes.

THE MAYOR.   Precisely—our superb new Therapeutic Baths. Remember this, Mr. Hovstad, the Spa will bring us together. No question about it.

MRS. STOCKMANN.   Thomas says the same thing.   30

THE MAYOR.   Think of how the town has been reviving in the last year! People have now got more money! There's life, and activity! Land and property values are soaring!

HOVSTAD.   Unemployment is going down.

THE MAYOR.   Yes, you're right. Tax rates for maintaining the poor are being lifted, and the middle class is relieved. Moreover, their relief will be greater if we have a good summer—great masses of visitors—and especially flocks of sick people, who will bring fame to our institution.

HOVSTAD.   I hear that the long-range weather forecasts are good.

THE MAYOR.   Things look favorable. We're getting inquiries and reservations   35
for apartments every day.

HOVSTAD.   Well, the Doctor's article will be timely and relevant.

THE MAYOR.   Oh, he's written something new?

HOVSTAD.   This is something he wrote last winter—a commendation of the Spa and a description of its healthful benefits. But I held it for publication until now.

THE MAYOR.   Oh, was there some sort of problem?

HOVSTAD.   No, not that. I thought it better to hold it till now, in the spring,   40
because it's now that people make their summer plans.

THE MAYOR.   Indeed, you're quite right, Mr. Hovstad.

MRS. STOCKMANN.   Yes, Thomas is a tireless booster of the Spa.

THE MAYOR.   Well, he's also one of the staff.

HOVSTAD.   Yes, and more, he was the first to create the idea of the Spa.

THE MAYOR.   Oh he did, did he? I hear that certain people think this, but   45
nevertheless it seems to me that *I* also had a modest role in the undertaking.

MRS. STOCKMANN.   Yes, Thomas always says that.

HOVSTAD.   No one denies your share, Mr. Mayor. You got things going and made the Spa a reality. We all know that. I meant only that the Doctor got the idea first.

THE MAYOR. Oh, yes, the *idea*. My brother has had lots of ideas—unfortunately. But when things get practical, you need different sorts of people, Mr. Hovstad. And I might have expected that here, in this house—

MRS. STOCKMANN. But dear Brother—

HOVSTAD. How could the Mayor—   50

MRS. STOCKMANN. Please go in and have something to eat, Mr. Hovstad. My husband will be back soon.

HOVSTAD. Perhaps just a little something, thank you. [*Goes to the dining room.*]

THE MAYOR. [*lowers his voice.*] Have you ever noticed that these country louts never have any manners?

MRS. STOCKMANN. Now why should you bother yourself about that? Can't you and Thomas, as brothers, share the recognition?

THE MAYOR. I would have thought so, but apparently not everyone seems   55
satisfied with only a share.

MRS. STOCKMANN. Come now—you and Thomas get along so well together. [*Listens to noises in the hallway.*] Here he comes now, I think. [*Goes to the hallway door and opens it.*]

DR. STOCKMANN. [*speaks to various persons while entering amid general noise and laughter.*] Katrina, I've brought another guest. Isn't it great? Now then, Captain Horster, hang your coat on this rack. Oh, you're not wearing an overcoat? Katrina, just think, I met him on our walk and he almost didn't want to come along. [*CAPTAIN HORSTER, followed by DR. STOCKMANN, enters the room and greets MRS. STOCKMANN.*] In with you, boys. [*EILIF and MORTEN enter.*] The walk gave them a new appetite. Join us, Captain Horster, and have some roast beef.

He escorts HORSTER into the dining room. The boys follow them.

MRS. STOCKMANN. But Thomas, do you see—

DR. STOCKMANN. [*turns in the doorway.*] Oh, Peter, it's you. [*Shakes hands with THE MAYOR.*] This is really great!

THE MAYOR. I was just leaving—   60

DR. STOCKMANN. Nonsense. Stay for some hot toddy. You didn't forget the toddy, did you Katrina?

MRS. STOCKMANN. Of course not. The water is boiling just now.

She goes into the dining room.

THE MAYOR. Hot toddy, too—!

DR. STOCKMANN. Yes, have a seat so we can have it in comfort.

THE MAYOR. No, thanks, I never stay at a drinking party.   65

DR. STOCKMANN. But this isn't a party.

THE MAYOR. It seems to me—[*Looks toward the dining room.*] It's amazing how they eat that much food.

DR. STOCKMANN. [*rubs his hands.*] Yes, it's great to see young people eat. They never get filled up, and that's as it should be. They need the food to get strong, Peter, because they're the ones who'll be stirring things up in the future.

THE MAYOR. And just what, as you put it, is going to need "stirring up"?

DR. STOCKMANN. You'll have to ask the young people that—when the time   70
comes. But then, of course, old fogies like you and me won't be around to see it.

THE MAYOR. Really! I'm not sure I like that expression.

DR. STOCKMANN. Don't be so literal, Peter. You know that I'm quite happy. I'm glad to be alive here and now, and to be at the cutting edge. Everything is growing and coming to fruition, and it seems that an entirely new world is emerging around me.

THE MAYOR. You really think so?

DR. STOCKMANN. Yes, but you can't see it the way I do. You've lived here all your life, and you're too used to things. But I was buried all those years up north; I never saw anyone with any new ideas. Well, to me, being here is the same as having flown into the middle of a bustling metropolitan center.

THE MAYOR. A metropolitan center?   75

DR. STOCKMANN. I know what you mean. Ours is a small town. But there's also life here—promise, and countless things to work and struggle for. That's the main thing. [*Calls.*] Katrina, did the mailman come today?

MRS. STOCKMANN. [*in the dining room.*] No, he didn't.

DR. STOCKMANN. And then, Peter, to be well off! When you've lived at just a subsistence level, as we did, you value that.

THE MAYOR. God forbid—

DR. STOCKMANN. It's true. Up there we were often close to the line. But   80 now, we live like kings! We had roast beef today not only for dinner, but also for supper. Come and have some, or at least let me show it to you. Come here—

THE MAYOR. No, no, it's unnecessary.

DR. STOCKMANN. Well, come here, then. Do you see our new tablecloth?

THE MAYOR. Yes, I noticed.

DR. STOCKMANN. And we bought a lampshade. Do you see? Katrina had saved the money for it. It makes the room so cosy. Stand here—no, no, right here—yes, here. Do you see the way it focuses the light downward. I really think that's elegant. Right?

THE MAYOR. Yes, if people can permit such luxury.   85

DR. STOCKMANN. Oh yes, I can afford it. Katrina says I now make almost as much as we spend!

THE MAYOR. Of course, almost!

DR. STOCKMANN. Scientists like me are entitled to a better life, but even then I'm sure that most civil servants live better than I do.

THE MAYOR. Well, yes, a chief officer, a superior court judge—

DR. STOCKMANN. Well then, most businessmen, who spend two or three   90 times more—

THE MAYOR. Their circumstances are not the same as yours.

DR. STOCKMANN. At any rate, I don't waste money. But I can't deny my need to entertain my friends. I was away from everything for so long, and I'm hungry for young, vital, ambitious associates with inquiring and active minds. That description fits everyone enjoying supper in there. You should really get to know Hovstad.

THE MAYOR. By the way, Hovstad told me he was publishing one of your articles.

DR. STOCKMANN. One of my articles?

THE MAYOR. Yes, the one you wrote last winter about the Spa.   95

DR. STOCKMANN. Oh yes, but I don't want that one printed just yet.

THE MAYOR. Not yet? This seems to be a good time.

DR. STOCKMANN. Well, yes, under normal circumstances. [*Paces.*]

THE MAYOR. [*looks at him closely.*] Is something wrong with the present circumstances?

DR. STOCKMANN. [*stops.*] To be frank, Peter, I can't say right now. There really could be some problems—but it's possible that there's no problem at all. It may be no more than my imagination.

THE MAYOR. You're being very mysterious. Is something going on that I don't know about? You should know that I, as Chief Executive Officer of the Governing Board of the Baths—

DR. STOCKMANN. And you should know that I—. But let's not lash out at each other, Peter.

THE MAYOR. Of course not. I don't "lash out" at people, as you put it. But I must insist on orderly procedure, and that only the properly designated officials treat problems that may arise. I cannot tolerate anyone going behind our backs.

DR. STOCKMANN. Did I ever try to go behind anyone's back?

THE MAYOR. Let's just say that you tend to do things in your own way, and that's not very different. Individuals must subordinate their own interests to those of the community—or, to be more accurate, to the authorities who hold the community interest in trust.

DR. STOCKMANN. I'm sure. But what in hell does this have to do with me?

THE MAYOR. My good Thomas, this is what you never seem willing to learn. But look out, because some day, sooner or later, you'll have to pay for it. Now I've told you. Good-bye.

DR. STOCKMANN. Are you crazy? You're on the wrong track!

THE MAYOR. I'm usually not. Please excuse me now. [*Bows toward the dining room.*] Good night, Katrina. Good night, gentlemen. [*Leaves.*]

MRS. STOCKMANN. [*enters from the dining room.*] He's gone?

DR. STOCKMANN. Yes, and in a foul mood.

MRS. STOCKMANN. But dear Thomas, did you provoke him again?

DR. STOCKMANN. No, not at all. And he can't make me give him any report before I'm ready.

MRS. STOCKMANN. What are you making a report about?

DR. STOCKMANN. Don't ask, Katrina.—But why hasn't the mailman come yet?

HOVSTAD, BILLING, and HORSTER enter from the dining room, followed by EILIF and MORTEN.

BILLING. [*stretches.*] Ah! A meal like that makes me feel like a new man, God damn it.

HOVSTAD. The mayor was not his usual sweet self, then?

DR. STOCKMANN. It's just his bad digestion.

HOVSTAD. I think that he couldn't stomach the two of us from the *Messenger.*

MRS. STOCKMANN. I thought that you both carried it off well.

HOVSTAD. Well, I think we have more of a truce than a peace.

BILLING. Yes, that's the right word for it.

DR. STOCKMANN. Let's not forget that Peter is all alone. He has no life, nothing but his job. And then think of the awful tea that he's always pouring into himself—! But now then, boys, sit down at the table. Can we have that hot toddy now, Katrina?

MRS. STOCKMANN. [*goes to the dining room.*] I'll have it right away!

100

105

110

115

120

DR. STOCKMANN.   Sit next to me, Captain Horster. We haven't seen you for   125
a long time—. Please sit down, friends.

They sit at the table. MRS. STOCKMANN carries in a tray with the appropriate glasses, bottles, etc.

MRS. STOCKMANN.   Here you are, gentlemen. This is arrack. This is rum. This is cognac. Just serve yourselves.

DR. STOCKMANN.   [*takes a glass.*] Thank you, we will. [*They all pour drinks for themselves.*] And let's have cigars. Eilif, you know where they are. And Morten, bring me my pipe. [*The boys leave for the room on the right.*] I think Eilif takes a cigar once in a while, but I ignore it. [*Calls out.*] Morten, get my smoking-cap, too. Tell him where it is, Katrina. Ah, he has it. [*The boys bring the things.*] Now, friends. I'll stick with my pipe, you know. This one has seen many a day with me up north. [*They all touch glasses; cries of "skoal," etc.*] Good health! Skoal! Ah, it's good to be warm and comfortable.

MRS. STOCKMANN.   [*sits down and begins knitting.*] Do you sail soon, Captain Horster?

HORSTER.   Yes, I expect as early as next week.

MRS. STOCKMANN.   To America, I suppose?   130

HORSTER.   Yes, that's the schedule.

MRS. STOCKMANN.   Then you can't vote in the next election?

HORSTER.   Is there an election?

MRS. STOCKMANN.   You didn't know?

HORSTER.   No, I usually don't get involved.   135

MRS. STOCKMANN.   You aren't concerned about public affairs?

HORSTER.   No, I don't follow politics.

BILLING.   Even so, people should vote.

HORSTER.   Even if they don't know the issues?

BILLING.   Don't know? What do you mean? Every community is like a large   140
ship; everyone should be ready to be a pilot.

HORSTER.   That may be true on shore, but it won't work on a ship.

HOVSTAD.   It's amazing that sailors have such small concern about what happens on land.

BILLING.   Yes, amazing.

DR. STOCKMANN.   Sailors are like migratory birds, Hovstad; they find their homes anywhere, north or south. And that's one more reason for our own vigilance. Mr. Hovstad, is there anything of local interest in tomorrow's *Messenger?*

HOVSTAD.   No, but I was planning to publish your article the day after   145
tomorrow.

DR. STOCKMANN.   My article, damn it all! —Listen, you'll have to hold that a bit longer.

HOVSTAD.   Really? We have the space, and it's just the right time—

DR. STOCKMANN.   Yes, I understand, but wait just the same.

PETRA enters from the hallway, wearing a hat and coat, and carrying a stack of notebooks.

PETRA.   Good evening.

DR. STOCKMANN.   Good evening, Petra.   150

She greets everyone, and removes her things and puts them on a chair near the door.

PETRA.   I see that you've been having a good time while I've been working like a slave.

DR. STOCKMANN.   Well then, now it's your turn to enjoy.

BILLING.   Can I get you a drink?

PETRA.   [*goes to the table.*] Thanks, I'll do it myself; you always make it too strong. Oh, by the way, Father, I have a letter for you.

Goes to her things on the chair and removes a letter from her coat pocket.

DR. STOCKMANN.   A letter? Who sent it?   155

PETRA.   The mailman delivered it just as I was leaving—

DR. STOCKMANN.   [*gets up and goes to her.*] And you give it to me only now?

PETRA.   I had no time to run upstairs again. Here you are.

DR. STOCKMANN.   [*grabs the letter and looks eagerly at it.*] Let's see, let's see. Yes, this it it—!

MRS. STOCKMANN.   Is this the one you've been expecting, Thomas?   160

DR. STOCKMANN.   Yes. I have to go in—. Where's the lamp, Katrina? Is there no light in my room again?

MRS. STOCKMANN.   Yes, it's lit and it's on your writing desk.

DR. STOCKMANN.   Good, good. Excuse me—just a few minutes—. [*Goes into his study at the right.*]

PETRA.   What's this all about, Mother?

MRS. STOCKMANN.   I don't know. He's been asking about the mailman for   165
the last few days.

BILLING.   Probably a report about an out-of-town patient.

PETRA.   Poor Dad, he may be working too hard. [*Mixes herself a drink.*] This looks so good!

HOVSTAD.   Were you teaching in the evening school too?

PETRA.   [*speaks while holding the glass and drinking.*] Two hours.

BILLING.   And also four hours this morning?   170

PETRA.   Five hours.

MRS. STOCKMANN.   And you still have papers to grade?

PETRA.   A pile, yes.

HORSTER.   You seem overwhelmed with work.

PETRA.   Yes, but that's all right. I feel healthfully tired because of it.   175

BILLING.   You like that?

PETRA.   Yes, because I sleep so well.

MORTEN.   You must be really a bad person, Petra.

PETRA.   Bad?

MORTEN.   Yes, because you work so hard. Mr. Rørlund says work is punish-   180
ment for our sins.

EILIF.   Pooh! What a dumbbell, to swallow garbage like that.

MRS. STOCKMANN.   Now then, Eilif!

BILLING.   [*laughing.*] Kids, anyway!

HOVSTAD.   Don't you like working, Morten?

MORTEN.   Not on your life!   185

HOVSTAD.   Then what would you like to be?

MORTEN.   I'd like to be a Viking.

EILIF.   You'd have to be a heathen, then.

MORTEN.   Well, I could join the heathen church, couldn't I?

BILLING. That's it, Morten. I agree completely.   190

MRS. STOCKMANN. [*signals negatively to* BILLING.] Now, Mr. Billing, you don't believe that.

BILLING. Yes, God damn it! I'm proud to be a heathen. We'll all be heathens before long.

MORTEN. And then we'll be able to do anything we want?

BILLING. Well, you see, Morten—

MRS. STOCKMANN. Boys, you'll have to go to your rooms. You have studying   195
to do for tomorrow.

EILIF. But I want to stay here—

MRS. STOCKMANN. No, no, off you go now.

The boys say good-night and leave through the doorway on the left.

HOVSTAD. Do you think there is any harm in what I was saying?

MRS. STOCKMANN. I'm not sure, but I don't like it.

PETRA. But Mother, you're being foolish about this.   200

MRS. STOCKMANN. You might be right, but I don't like it—not in our own house.

PETRA. There's such great hypocrisy, both at home and at school. At home we can't speak, and at school we have to tell lies to the children.

HORSTER. You tell lies?

PETRA. Yes, don't you realize we have to teach all sorts of things we don't believe?

BILLING. You're quite right.   205

PETRA. If I had enough money I'd start my own school, where things would go differently.

BILLING. Oh, just money—.

HORSTER. If you have ideas about a new school, Miss Stockmann, I'd be happy to offer you rooms. The house my father left me is empty, and there's a huge dining room downstairs.

PETRA. [*laughs.*] Why thank you, but nothing is likely to happen.

HOVSTAD. No, I think Miss Petra is more likely to go into journalism. By   210
the way, have you been able to finish translating that English story you promised for us?

PETRA. No, not yet, but soon, I hope.

DR. STOCKMANN enters from his study, with the open letter in hand.

DR. STOCKMANN. [*waves the letter.*] Well, the town is about to get some real news!

BILLING. Real news?

MRS. STOCKMANN. What do you mean?

DR. STOCKMANN. A major discovery, Katrina.   215

HOVSTAD. Truly?

MRS. STOCKMANN. Your own discovery?

DR. STOCKMANN. Yes, my own. [*Paces.*] Just let them accuse me of imagining things. [*Laughs.*] They'll have to be careful now about what they say.

PETRA. Father, what is it?

DR. STOCKMANN. All in due time. If only Peter were here now! It all shows   220 how human beings can go around and make judgments no better than the blindest of moles—

HOVSTAD.   Doctor, what are you saying?

DR. STOCKMANN.   [*stands at the table.*] I ask, is it or is it not accepted opinion that our town is a healthy place?

HOVSTAD.   It is, yes.

DR. STOCKMANN.   A model for good health, in fact—a center to be accepted enthusiastically for those who are either ill or well?

MRS. STOCKMANN.   Yes, but Thomas, dear—   225

DR. STOCKMANN.   And we've touted it highly. I myself have written pamphlets and articles for the *Messenger*?

HOVSTAD.   Yes, and so?

DR. STOCKMANN.   And we've called our Spa "the artery of our town's blood" and "the center of the town's nervous system," and who the devil knows what other silly phrases—

BILLING.   In an extreme moment, I once said "the town's throbbing heart."

DR. STOCKMANN.   Right. Well, do you know the truth about these curative   230
baths, so marvelous, so magnificent, so highly eulogized—and so expensive? Do you know?

HOVSTAD.   No, but tell us.

MRS. STOCKMANN.   What are they?

DR. STOCKMANN.   The whole thing's a sewer!

PETRA.   The Spa, Father?

MRS. STOCKMANN.   [*at the same time.*] Our baths?   235

HOVSTAD.   But—

BILLING.   Unbelievable!

DR. STOCKMANN.   All the Spa buildings constitute a whited, polluted se-
pulchre°—a threat to public health! All that poisoned runoff up at Mølledal, all that filth, is contaminating the water going to our reservoir! And the same damned, deadly effluent is also filtering out on our shore!

HORSTER.   Do you mean at our Spa buildings, where our visitors take their treatments?

DR. STOCKMANN.   Yes, right there.   240

HOVSTAD.   But Doctor, how do you know all this?

DR. STOCKMANN.   I've suspected something for quite a while, because last year some of the patients had unusual symptoms—typhoid, and gastro-intestinal flu. Now I've studied things thoroughly.

MRS. STOCKMANN.   You're right about those illnesses.

DR. STOCKMANN.   At first we concluded that people were infected before they came here. But this winter I started thinking differently, and began analyzing our water.

MRS. STOCKMANN.   So this is why you've been so busy.   245

DR. STOCKMANN.   Yes, Katrina, I've been busy. But here we don't have much laboratory equipment, so I sent samples of the sea water and drinking water to the University for an exact chemical analysis.

HOVSTAD.   Did they send you a report?

238 *whited, polluted sepulchre:* Matthew 23:27.

DR. STOCKMANN. [*shows the letter.*] This is it. It shows conclusively that our water contains dangerously high levels of bacteria, both for drinking and bathing.

MRS. STOCKMANN. Thank heaven you found out now, before the summer season.

DR. STOCKMANN. Let's all be thankful.   250

HOVSTAD. What are you planning to do now, Doctor?

DR. STOCKMANN. Obviously, to make things right.

HOVSTAD. Is that possible?

DR. STOCKMANN. It must be possible, or else our Spa will be useless. But I have a plan.

MRS. STOCKMANN. But, dear Thomas, why did you keep this so quiet?   255

DR. STOCKMANN. Should I have chattered about it around town without conclusive evidence? I'm not that kind of idiot.

PETRA. But you could have told us.

DR. STOCKMANN. Not to you, not to anyone. But tomorrow you may go and tell the old Badger—

MRS. STOCKMANN. Now Thomas!

DR. STOCKMANN. All right, your stepfather. This will surprise him. He,   260
along with others, thinks I'm balmy, but now they'll see! [*Paces, rubbing his hands.*] This will really get the town stirred up, Katrina. Completely new water lines will have to be installed.

HOVSTAD. [*rises.*] *All* the water lines—?

DR. STOCKMANN. Certainly. The intakes are too low; they'll need to be put on higher ground.

PETRA. So you were right all the time.

DR. STOCKMANN. You remember that, Petra? I wrote against the final plans before work was started. They paid no attention to me then, but they'll pay attention now! I've had a report ready for the Governing Board for the last week, and was only waiting for this. [*Waves the letter.*] I'll send it right away. [*Goes to his office, returning with papers.*] See here, all four sheets, along with an explanatory letter. A newspaper, Katrina, something for wrapping. That's fine. Now give it to—to—[*stamps his foot*]—what's her name? The maid, and tell her to take it to the Mayor.

MRS. STOCKMANN *takes the package and leaves through the dining room.*

PETRA. Father, what will Uncle Peter say about this?   265

DR. STOCKMANN. What can he say? He should be glad that such important facts have been discovered.

HOVSTAD. Would you consent to my publishing an article about this in the *Messenger*?

DR. STOCKMANN. That would be excellent.

HOVSTAD. The public should know, and the sooner the better.

DR. STOCKMANN. Certainly.   270

MRS. STOCKMANN. [*returns.*] She's just gone off with it.

BILLING. Doctor, you're the most important man in town.

DR. STOCKMANN. [*paces happily.*] Oh, come now! I've just been doing my civic duty. I was lucky enough to find the treasure. But just the same—

BILLING. Hovstad, shouldn't the town give Dr. Stockmann some token of gratitude?

HOVSTAD. Well, I'll certainly suggest one.   275

BILLING. And I'll take up the matter with Aslaksen.

DR. STOCKMANN. Dear friends, no nonsense. I won't hear of any ceremonies. And if the Governing Board should recommend a raise, I won't accept it. Katrina, I tell you, I'll turn it down.

MRS. STOCKMANN. Thomas, you're right.

PETRA. [*raises her glass.*] Father, your health!

HOVSTAD and BILLING. Skoal, Doctor! Cheers!   280

HORSTER. [*clinks glasses with DR. STOCKMANN.*]   I hope this affair brings you endless good luck!

DR. STOCKMANN. Thank you, dear friends, thank you. I'm so overwhelmingly glad! Oh what a blessing it is to realize that you've been able to serve your home town and fellow citizens. Hurrah, Katrina!

He embraces her and they do a whirling dance, with MRS. STOCKMANN laughingly protesting. Laughter, applause, and cheers for the DOCTOR. The boys poke their heads in at the door.

ACT II

SCENE. *The same, the next morning. MRS. STOCKMANN, holding a letter, enters from the closed dining-room door. She calls toward the door of the Doctor's study to announce herself.*

MRS. STOCKMANN. Are you in there, Thomas?

DR. STOCKMANN. [*answers from within.*] Yes, I just came in. [*Enters.*] What have you got there?

MRS. STOCKMANN. A letter from your brother. [*Gives it to him.*]

DR. STOCKMANN. Ah, let's see. [*Opens the letter and reads.*] "Find enclosed the materials you sent me"—[*Reads on and mutters.*] Hmm!

MRS. STOCKMANN. Well, what does he say?   5

DR. STOCKMANN. [*puts the papers in a pocket.*] Nothing more than that he'll stop by to see us at about noon.

MRS. STOCKMANN. Well then, be sure to be at home.

DR. STOCKMANN. I will. I've already done my morning rounds.

MRS. STOCKMANN. I wonder what he's going to say.

DR. STOCKMANN. Most probably he'll be unhappy because he didn't discover   10 the problem before I did.

MRS. STOCKMANN. Doesn't that make you nervous?

DR. STOCKMANN. No, he'll probably be broadminded about things, but you know he gets damned anxious about anyone else invading his turf to do something good for the town.

MRS. STOCKMANN. Well, I think you ought to share this with him. Why not let it be known that he was the one who got you going?

DR. STOCKMANN. Fine. It's okay with me. I just want to set things right.

MORTEN KIIL peeks in from the hallway, looks around inquiringly, and chuckles.

MORTEN KIIL. Is it—is it true?   15

MRS. STOCKMANN. Father, how nice.

DR. STOCKMANN. Father Kiil, good morning.

MRS. STOCKMANN.   Please come in.

MORTEN KIIL.   I'll come in if it's true, but I'm going if it's not.

DR. STOCKMANN.   If what is true?   20

MORTEN KIIL.   The crazy story about the water supply. Is it true?

DR. STOCKMANN.   It's true, but how did you hear about it?

MORTEN KILL.   [*enters.*] Petra flew by on her way to school.

DR. STOCKMANN.   Oh she did?

MORTEN KIIL.   Yes, and she says—. I thought she was kidding, but she   25
wouldn't joke about a thing like that.

DR. STOCKMANN.   Certainly not; it's unthinkable.

MORTEN KIIL.   Well, if you believe everything people tell you, they'll make
you a laughing stock before you know it. But it's true, then?

DR. STOCKMANN.   Absolutely true. But please sit down, Father. [*KIIL sits on
the sofa.*] I think the town has been lucky—

MORTEN KIIL.   [*stifles laughter.*] Luck for the town?

DR. STOCKMANN.   Yes, because my discovery was just in time.   30

MORTEN KIIL.   [*still amused.*] Sure, sure sure.—But I never would have
believed that you'd play such hocus-pocus on your own brother.

DR. STOCKMANN.   Hocus-pocus?

MRS. STOCKMANN.   Now really, Father.

MORTEN KIIL.   [*puts his hands and chin on the handle of his walking-cane, and
winks at DR. STOCKMANN.*] Now, what's the story again? Some pernicious monsters
have invaded the water intakes, right?

DR. STOCKMANN.   Right, infectious bacteria.   35

MORTEN KIIL.   And, as Petra says, there are hordes of these—huge hordes—
right?

DR. STOCKMANN.   Right, millions and billions, in fact.

MORTEN KIIL.   But they're invisible, right?

DR. STOCKMANN.   Right.

MORTEN KIIL.   [*laughs.*] Damn it all, I never heard anything better than this!   40

DR. STOCKMANN.   What are you saying?

MORTEN KIIL.   But Mayor Stockmann will never believe it.

DR. STOCKMANN.   We'll see about that.

MORTEN KIIL.   Do you think he's that big a fool—

DR. STOCKMANN.   My hope is that everyone in town will be such "fools," as   45
you say.

MORTEN KIIL.   Everyone in town. It'd serve them right, too. They pressured
me out of town government, they did. They think they know so much, but now
they'll pay. Keep your magic spells going, Stockmann.

DR. STOCKMANN.   Now Mr. Kiil, really—

MORTEN KIIL.   Keep fooling them. [*Gets up.*] If you make the Mayor and
his henchmen believe this, I'll give ten thousand to the poor—just like that.

DR. STOCKMANN.   Now this is very generous.

MORTEN KIIL.   Yes, I'm not wealthy, mind you, but if you pull this off, I'll   50
remember the poor with five thousand—this next Christmas.

EDITOR HOVSTAD enters through the hallway door.

HOVSTAD.   Good morning. [*Sees Morten Kiil.*] Oh, I'm sorry.

DR. STOCKMANN.   Don't be. Come in.

MORTEN KIIL. [*chuckles.*] Aha! He's in on it too?

HOVSTAD. What do you mean?

DR. STOCKMANN. Yes, he knows everything. 55

MORTEN KIIL. I'm not surprised. Get plenty of coverage about this in the papers. Make it big. I'll leave you to your work.

DR. STOCKMANN. Can't you stay?

MORTEN KIIL. No, I've got to go. Keep pushing this hocus-pocus, and, damn it all, you'll never be sorry, I promise you.

MORTEN KIIL leaves. MRS. STOCKMANN follows him out.

DR. STOCKMANN. [*laughs.*] Can you believe it? The old fellow doesn't believe the news about the water lines.

HOVSTAD. Oh, so that's what all this was about. 60

DR. STOCKMANN. Yes. Are you here about the same thing?

HOVSTAD. I am. Can you spare me a few moments, Doctor?

DR. STOCKMANN. Certainly, friend.

HOVSTAD. Has the Mayor contacted you yet?

DR. STOCKMANN. No, but he'll be coming by later. 65

HOVSTAD. I've been thinking a lot about this.

DR. STOCKMANN. And?

HOVSTAD. Well you, as a doctor, see only one side of this, but there are lots of other considerations.

DR. STOCKMANN. What do you mean? Let's sit. No, take the sofa. [*They sit, HOVSTAD on the sofa, DR. STOCKMANN on a chair next to the oval table.*] Now, you were telling me—

HOVSTAD. Yesterday you said that the polluted water came from foul 70 seepage through the ground.

DR. STOCKMANN. Absolutely—toxic seepage from the putrid swamp up at Mølledal.

HOVSTAD. With your leave, Doctor, I believe it's another kind of swamp.

DR. STOCKMANN. What do you mean? What kind of swamp?

HOVSTAD. The swamp on which our whole communal life stands and decays.

DR. STOCKMANN. In the devil's name, Mr. Hovstad, what sort of talk is this? 75

HOVSTAD. Piece by piece, the town has been taken over by a small clique of bureaucrats.

DR. STOCKMANN. Come now, the government is not large.

HOVSTAD. No, the government is just the tip of the iceberg. It's the town bigwigs, the ones with money, that have us in their clutches.

DR. STOCKMANN. Yes, but these are people with brains and dedication.

HOVSTAD. Where were their brains and dedication when the water lines 80 were put where they now lie?

DR. STOCKMANN. Well, I grant the stupidity of that, but things will soon be corrected.

HOVSTAD. Do you think this will be easy?

DR. STOCKMANN. At any rate, easy or not, it'll happen.

HOVSTAD. Yes, but only with the support of the press.

DR. STOCKMANN. But, friend, it won't be needed. I'm sure my brother— 85

HOVSTAD.   Pardon me, Doctor. I have to tell you that I'm planning a series of editorials.

DR. STOCKMANN.   In the paper?

HOVSTAD.   Yes. When I first took over the *Messenger* my idea was to break up the ring of old bootlickers with all the power.

DR. STOCKMANN.   Yes, but you told me you came close to bankruptcy because of this policy.

HOVSTAD.   You're right; I admit it. It was inopportune to undermine public confidence in those men then, because the whole Spa project depended on them. But now things are going well, and we can kiss these pompous crown princes goodbye. 90

DR. STOCKMANN.   Even if they're replaced, they've done the town excellent service.

HOVSTAD.   We'll give them their due. But a writer like me, with the advancement of the people as an objective, can't let this chance slide away to destroy the public's fairy-tale illusions of aristocratic infallibility.

DR. STOCKMANN.   I agree with you there. Fairy tales must go.

HOVSTAD.   I hesitate because the Mayor is your brother, but I'm sure that your priority is to the truth.

DR. STOCKMANN.   That's self-evident. [*Bursts out.*] Yes, but— 95

HOVSTAD.   You must realize that I see nothing to gain for myself in all this.

DR. STOCKMANN.   My friend, who would ever think otherwise?

HOVSTAD.   I was born poor, and that has enabled me to see what the lower classes need. And this is that the people themselves should have a role to play in government, because this, and only this, will bring out their abilities and intelligence and self-esteem—

DR. STOCKMANN.   I understand your point.

HOVSTAD.   You realize that dedicated journalists must take every opportu- 100 nity in the effort to liberate the masses, even though they might be called agitators, or rabble rousers. For me, I'm willing to risk these accusations as long as my conscience is clear.—

DR. STOCKMANN.   Just that, yes! Just that, my dear Mr. Hovstad, but all the same—. [*A knocking at the door.*] The devil! Come in!

ASLAKSEN the printer enters, in a well-worn black suit and a wrinkled white scarf. He holds his hat and his gloves in his hands.

ASLAKSEN.   [*bows.*] Doctor, please excuse my intrusion—

DR. STOCKMANN.   [*rises.*] Well, hello! It's Mr. Aslaksen, the printer.

ASLAKSEN.   Yes, Doctor, you're right.

HOVSTAD.   [*stands.*] Do you want me, Aslaksen? 105

ASLAKSEN.   No, I didn't know you'd be here. I came to see the Doctor.

DR. STOCKMANN.   Well, then, what can I do for you?

ASLAKSEN.   Did I hear things right from Mr. Billing, that you plan to clean up our water systems?

DR. STOCKMANN.   That's right, the ones for the Spa.

ASLAKSEN.   Yes, I understand. Well, I want to give you my support on this. 110

HOVSTAD.   [*to DR. STOCKMANN.*] You see my point.

DR. STOCKMANN.   This is very kind of you, but—

ASLAKSEN.   It would be good to have us local tradesmen behind you.

Together we make a solid majority in town, and it's always good to have the majority with you, Doctor.

DR. STOCKMANN. You're certainly right, but this matter is so non-controversial that it could never become a political issue—

ASLAKSEN. Even so, support would be helpful. Our local politicians never   115
like to do anything that someone else originates. That's why I think we might demonstrate a bit.

HOVSTAD. He has a good point.

DR. STOCKMANN. Demonstrate, you say? But how would you demonstrate?

ASLAKSEN. Naturally, with great moderation, Doctor. I always do things moderately, for to me, moderation is a citizen's first obligation.

DR. STOCKMANN. You are indeed well known for your moderation, Mr. Aslaksen.

ASLAKSEN. I take pride in this. And this water-contamination business is   120
important. The Spa can put the town on the map, and those of us in the trades, and those with rental property, can become rich. This is why we support you. You understand that I speak as Chair of the Homeowners Association—

DR. STOCKMANN. Yes—?

ASLAKSEN. And also as Secretary of the Temperance Union. You knew that this is one of my causes?

DR. STOCKMANN. Oh yes, yes.

ASLAKSEN. Well, you can see that I have many contacts, and with my reputation for moderation I have no small influence in town. You might say, in fact, that I have a certain degree of power.

DR. STOCKMANN. Yes, Mr. Aslaksen, I know.   125

ASLAKSEN. So it would be relatively easy for me to initiate a testimonial.

DR. STOCKMANN. A testimonial?

ASLAKSEN. Yes, public recognition of your importance in an affair of such vital concern to the town. We would need, of course, a statement that would be judicious and moderate—something that would not be disagreeable to our local authorities. With care, I believe that we would not offend anyone.

HOVSTAD. But even if someone were offended—

ASLAKSEN. No, no, Mr. Hovstad, you don't get anywhere by insulting those   130
who have power over you. I once learned that the hard way. But no one can be put off by citizens expressing their views openly and moderately.

DR. STOCKMANN. [*shakes ASLAKSEN's hand.*] Your support is most gratifying, Mr. Aslaksen. May I pour you some sherry?

ASLAKSEN. No thanks, I never touch hard liquor.

DR. STOCKMANN. Well, then, a glass of beer?

ASLAKSEN. Nothing even like that so early in the day. I'm off now to see a few landlords, to get things in motion.

DR. STOCKMANN. This is quite kind of you, Mr. Aslaksen. But are all these   135
cautious steps necessary? Things seem so self-evident.

ASLAKSEN. It's hard to get the authorities moving, Doctor, though sometimes I understand their slowness—

HOVSTAD. We're planning to stir things up in tomorrow's *Messenger,* Aslaksen.

ASLAKSEN. But not too much, Mr. Hovstad. Without moderation, you'll get nowhere; believe me, I've learned that. Well, thank you, Doctor. Be assured that we small-business people stand behind you like a wall. The solid majority is with you, Doctor.

DR. STOCKMANN.   [*shakes* ASLAKSEN's *hand.*] Good Mr. Aslaksen, I'm deeply grateful to you for this. Thank you. Goodbye.

ASLAKSEN.   [*to* HOVSTAD.] I'm going to the print shop. Can you join me, Mr.   140
Hovstad?

HOVSTAD.   Later, I need to stay here a little while longer.

ASLAKSEN.   Good, I'll see you soon, then.

ASLAKSEN *bows and leaves.* DR. STOCKMANN *accompanies him into the hallway, and then returns.*

HOVSTAD.   Well, Doctor, what do you think? Isn't it time to put a little courage into such spineless fence-sitters?

DR. STOCKMANN.   You mean Aslaksen?

HOVSTAD.   Yes, I do. He's a fine enough fellow, but he can't take a decisive   145
step, and there are many just like him. They bend in the wind, this way and that way, and finally they never accomplish anything.

DR. STOCKMANN.   Well, Aslaksen's heart seems in the right place.

HOVSTAD.   Yes, but if he were more decisive he'd be better.

DR. STOCKMANN.   I have to agree with you there.

HOVSTAD.   That's why the time is now so ripe. Public worship of authority must end, and this official blunder with the water contamination must be brought home to the voters.

DR. STOCKMANN.   Well, all right. The common good should be foremost.   150
But before more is done, I'll have to talk to my brother.

HOVSTAD.   In any event, I'll put together a feature article, and if the Mayor won't listen to you—

DR. STOCKMANN.   You don't believe he won't listen?

HOVSTAD.   Anything is possible, and if it happens—

DR. STOCKMANN.   If it happens—if—you can publish my entire report—
every last word.

HOVSTAD.   Do I have your promise on that?   155

DR. STOCKMANN.   [*gives* HOVSTAD *the report.*] Here, take it; there's no harm in your reading it. You can return it later.

HOVSTAD.   Good; I will. Thank you, Doctor, and goodbye.

DR. STOCKMANN.   Goodbye. Everything is going to come out right, Mr. Hovstad, perfectly right.

HOVSTAD.   [*bows and leaves.*] We'll see, we'll see.

DR. STOCKMANN.   [*opens the dining-room door and calls.*] Katrina! Oh it's you,   160
Petra.

PETRA.   [*enters.*] Yes, I just got home from school.

MRS. STOCKMANN.   [*enters.*] Didn't Peter come yet?

DR. STOCKMANN.   No, but I've been talking to Hovstad about the broader significance of the water situation. He's quite excited, and has given me the freedom to publish about it in the *Messenger* whenever it's necessary.

MRS. STOCKMANN.   Will it be necessary?

DR. STOCKMANN.   No, not at all, but it's still gratifying to have support from   165
the open-minded and independent press. Not only this, Katrina, but the Chair of the Homeowners Association has come to see me.

MRS. STOCKMANN.   Well, what was on his mind?

DR. STOCKMANN.   He promised his support, too, and everyone will support me if necessary. Katrina, do you know the support I have in back of me?

MRS. STOCKMANN.   No. What is it?

DR. STOCKMANN.   The solid majority.

MRS. STOCKMANN.   Is that really a good thing for you, Thomas?   170

DR. STOCKMANN.   Yes, I believe so. [*Paces while rubbing his hands.*] Good Lord, how lucky it is to stand this way, as part of a family with one's fellow citizens!

PETRA.   And to be so right about things, father.

DR. STOCKMANN.   Beyond that, to do it for one's own home town!

A doorbell rings.

MRS. STOCKMANN.   That was the doorbell.

DR. STOCKMANN.   It's him, then. [*A knock is heard at the door.*] Come in!   175

THE MAYOR.   [*enters from the hallway.*] Good morning.

DR. STOCKMANN.   Peter, I'm delighted to see you.

MRS. STOCKMANN.   How are you today, Peter?

THE MAYOR.   All right, thank you, [*To DR. STOCKMANN.*] Yesterday evening I received your report about the water condition at the Spa.

DR. STOCKMANN.   Did you finish it?   180

THE MAYOR.   Yes, I did.

DR. STOCKMANN.   Well, what's your response to it?

THE MAYOR.   [*looks at the women.*] Well—

MRS. STOCKMANN.   Come, Petra.

The women leave through the door at the left.

THE MAYOR.   [*pauses briefly before he speaks.*] Did you really need to do your   185 studies behind my back?

DR. STOCKMANN.   Yes, because I had to be sure—

THE MAYOR.   Then you're sure now?

DR. STOCKMANN.   You must realize that I am.

THE MAYOR.   Do you plan to submit your study as an official report to the Governing Board of the Spa?

DR. STOCKMANN.   Yes. Something should be done right away.   190

THE MAYOR.   In your usual manner, you make exaggerations in your report. I cite your claim that patients at our Baths are constantly being poisoned.

DR. STOCKMANN.   Can you say it any other way, Peter? Our water, which we provide to the trusting souls who pay us huge fees to restore them to health, is poison either for drinking or for bathing.

THE MAYOR.   And then you conclude that we must build diversionary drains for these so-called poisons from Mølledal, and also lay new intake mains?

DR. STOCKMANN.   Yes. Can you think of anything else? I can't.

THE MAYOR.   This morning I consulted with our Chief Engineer, and, in   195 jest, as a trial balloon, I asked him about possible costs for such proposals, just in the remote case they might be needed at some future time.

DR. STOCKMANN.   At some future time?

THE MAYOR.   Believe me, he was amused even at the suggestion. Do you have any idea what the new work would cost? His estimate is that the range could be anywhere from twenty-five to thirty million.

DR. STOCKMANN.   That much?

THE MAYOR.   Yes, and worse, the planning and construction would drag out for two years or more.

DR. STOCKMANN.   That long? Two whole years?   200

THE MAYOR.   Or more. And what could we do with the Spa facilities during this time? We'd need to close them. And even after the repairs, do you think anyone would come near them again, with the reputation that they had been hazardous to health?

DR. STOCKMANN.   But Peter, they *are* hazardous.

THE MAYOR.   And all this is happening just as we're getting started. Nearby coastal towns have the same potential for therapeutic baths as ours. Don't you think their public relations people would work overtime to take our clientèle? Where would that put us? We'd probably have to declare the whole extravagant thing a total loss, and then, Thomas, you would have brought your home town to ruin.

DR. STOCKMANN.   Me? Ruin?

THE MAYOR.   The only viable future for this town is the Spa. You know   205
that as well as I do.

DR. STOCKMANN.   Well, what's your solution, then?

THE MAYOR.   I'm not persuaded by your report that the water is as bad as you make it seem.

DR. STOCKMANN.   Peter, it's worse, or at any rate it will be worse once the summer heat sets in.

THE MAYOR.   I told you that you exaggerate the danger. Surely a competent doctor can control noxious elements in the water, or neutralize them if they grow too plentiful.

DR. STOCKMANN.   And so? What else?   210

THE MAYOR.   We must acknowledge that current procedures for securing water cannot be substantially changed. But I believe that the Governing Board, if funding is available, might not be unwilling to institute certain improvements.

DR. STOCKMANN.   Do you believe that I can consent to this kind of underhanded scheme?

THE MAYOR.   An underhanded scheme?

DR. STOCKMANN.   Yes, an underhanded scheme, a lie, an outright crime against the town!

THE MAYOR.   As I've remarked, I've seen no persuasive evidence that the   215
community is in any sort of danger.

DR. STOCKMANN.   Yes you have! There's no choice. You know my report is absolutely truthful, though you won't admit it. You're the one who insisted on the present locations of the intake mains and the Spa buildings, and it's this—your own damned blunder—that you won't admit. Bah! Do you imagine I don't see through you?

THE MAYOR.   Well, let's suppose, then, that you're right. I have the town's interests at heart, and without my present credibility I'm powerless to work for community betterment. For these reasons you must not submit your report. You must hold it back in the public interest. Then later, privately and quietly, we'll exert our best efforts. But for now, nothing—not a word—can be made public about this fatal affair.

DR. STOCKMANN.   My dear Peter, you may not be able to keep it quiet.

THE MAYOR. It must be, and shall be.

DR. STOCKMANN. You can't do it. Too many people already know.   220

THE MAYOR. Know? Who? You can't mean that crew from the *Messenger*?

DR. STOCKMANN. Yes, the open-minded and independent press will let you know your duty.

THE MAYOR. [*pauses before speaking.*] Thomas, you're a thoughtless and impetuous man. Have you considered what might happen to you because of all this?

DR. STOCKMANN. To me?

THE MAYOR. Yes, to you—and to your family.   225

DR. STOCKMANN. What in the devil's name do you mean?

THE MAYOR. As your older brother, have I not always been helpful to you?

DR. STOCKMANN. Yes, and I'm thankful to you.

THE MAYOR. Well, to a degree my own interests have coincided with yours. My hope has been that helping you better yourself financially would give me the power to hold you back on occasions.

DR. STOCKMANN. You mean you did this for yourself?   230

THE MAYOR. Yes, but only to a degree. Any public official is distressed when close relatives do compromising things again and again.

DR. STOCKMANN. You think I do compromising things?

THE MAYOR. Yes, unfortunately, even when you don't mean to. You are naturally combative, Thomas, and you keep none of your thoughts private, whether they're plausible or implausible, but you publish them as soon as you get them either in short articles or whole pamphlets.

DR. STOCKMANN. But isn't a citizen obligated to share new ideas with the public?

THE MAYOR. The public has no need for new ideas. The public is best   235 served by the good, old, recognized ideas they already have.

DR. STOCKMANN. You really believe this?

THE MAYOR. Yes, I do. And now I must speak frankly to you, which I have always avoided because you can be so irritable. The truth is, Thomas, you have no idea of how you hurt yourself by your thoughtless manner. You tear down politicians, and you denounce the government, by claiming that you are ignored or that you are victimized. But with such obstinacy, what else can you expect?

DR. STOCKMANN. So, I'm obstinate, am I?

THE MAYOR. Yes, you're an impossibly obstinate man to work with; I know. You place yourself above all consideration for others, and you have forgotten totally that I am the one you can thank for your position as Chief Medical Officer of the Spa—.

DR. STOCKMANN. But I was the natural one for this position—I and no one   240 else! I originated the idea that the town could become a thriving center for therapeutic baths, and for many years, despite obstructions, I was the one who wrote vigorously to make the Baths a reality.

THE MAYOR. No doubt, but you were too early. Things were not yet right, but you didn't think of that because you were locked away up north. It's a fact, however, that as soon as things came together, I, along with others, took over, and—

DR. STOCKMANN. And created the mess we have now. You fellows certainly did things right!

THE MAYOR. As far as I can see, this whole matter is just another of your habitual ways of attacking people in authority. To you, rebelliousness is a personal way of life. But I've told you, Thomas, that the very existence of the town is now the issue—not to mention my own reputation. And therefore I tell you, Thomas, that I'll be absolute about the demand I'm going to make on you.

DR. STOCKMANN. What's this?

THE MAYOR. Now that you've spoken out when you should have kept quiet, 245
the matter can no longer be hushed up. Rumors will fly, and they'll be used against us. The only thing to do is for you to issue a public denial.

DR. STOCKMANN. Me? But how can I do that?

THE MAYOR. We'll expect that further studies have shown you that things are not as serious or dangerous as your first thoughts had led you to conclude.

DR. STOCKMANN. You expect me to say this?

THE MAYOR. Moreover, you must publicly express your confidence in the integrity of the Governing Board of the Spa, and in their willingness to remedy any possible problems whatever.

DR. STOCKMANN. But you can't set things right now just by cutting and 250
pasting. Peter, I'm giving you my professional judgment.

THE MAYOR. Because you serve the Governing Board, you have no right to an independent professional judgment.

DR. STOCKMANN. [*exclaims incredulously.*] No right?

THE MAYOR. Privately, of course, you may think what you wish. But as an official who must report to the Governing Board, you cannot make a public announcement contrary to Board policy.

DR. STOCKMANN. I've never—. As a doctor, as a scientist, I have no right—?

THE MAYOR. This is not just a matter of science. It's complex, and there 255
are fiscal implications.

DR. STOCKMANN. Complexity and fiscal implications can go to hell! I'm free to speak out on any subject on earth!

THE MAYOR. Be my guest! But not about the Spa. We forbid you that.

DR. STOCKMANN. You forbid me? You? You pack of—

THE MAYOR. I forbid you—I—the Chief Executive Officer of the Governing Board. And when I forbid you, you *must* obey!

DR. STOCKMANN. [*suppresses rage.*] Peter, if we weren't brothers— 260

PETRA. [*enters.*] Father, he can't speak to you like this!

MRS. STOCKMANN. [*enters, trying to restrain* PETRA.] Petra, Petra—

THE MAYOR. So you've been listening!

MRS. STOCKMANN. You were so loud, we couldn't help hearing.

PETRA. Yes, I listened! 265

THE MAYOR. Well, actually, I'm glad—

DR. STOCKMANN. You were talking about forbidding and obeying?

THE MAYOR. Your insolence forced me to speak like that to you.

DR. STOCKMANN. So I am to issue a lie publicly?

THE MAYOR. You must make a statement—something like the one we spoke 270
of.

DR. STOCKMANN. And if I don't—obey?

THE MAYOR. Then we ourselves will issue a statement of reassurance for the public.

DR. STOCKMANN. If you do, I'll have to write against your position. I'll stand behind my conclusions. I'll prove you're wrong and I'm right. What will you do then?

THE MAYOR.   Then I won't be able to prevent your dismissal.

DR. STOCKMANN.   What—?   275

PETRA.   Father—dismissed!

MRS. STOCKMANN.   Fired!

THE MAYOR.   Dismissed as Chief Medical Officer of the Spa. I'll find myself in the position of giving you instant notice, and suspending you from your duties at the Spa.

DR. STOCKMANN.   You'd risk that!

THE MAYOR.   You're the one running the risks!   280

PETRA.   Uncle, this is shocking conduct toward a man like father!

MRS. STOCKMANN.   Petra, will you hold your tongue!

THE MAYOR.   [*to* PETRA.] Oh, so we already speak out with no restraint. I might have expected it. [*To* MRS. STOCKMANN.] My dear Sister-in-Law, you're the least impulsive person here. Use your influence over your husband to persuade him of the dangers he's running for the family and—

DR. STOCKMANN.   Family concerns are mine, and mine only!

THE MAYOR.   —for the family, I was saying, and for the town he lives in.   285

DR. STOCKMANN.   I'm the one who holds the good of the town foremost by trying to disclose the real dangers that face us. I'll show you who loves the town.

THE MAYOR.   You, who in blind defiance go ahead to cut off the town's most important nourishment?

DR. STOCKMANN.   But what gives us our living gives poison to others! Are you insane? We live here by dealing in filth and corruption! Our thriving business life is nourished on lies!

THE MAYOR.   A fairy tale, or worse! Any person who can say such damaging things about his own home town must be an enemy of society!

DR. STOCKMANN.   [*confronts him.*] You dare—   290

MRS. STOCKMANN.   [*stands between them to restrain them.*] Thomas!

PETRA.   [*takes her father's arm.*] Father, control yourself!

THE MAYOR.   I will not be a party to violence! You've been warned; consider yourself—and your family! Goodbye! [*Leaves alone through the hallway.*]

DR. STOCKMANN.   [*paces.*] Must I put up with this, Katrina, and in my own home?

MRS. STOCKMANN.   It's been both shameful and humiliating!   295

PETRA.   I'd like to tell him a thing or two—

DR. STOCKMANN.   I'm at fault for not baring my teeth at him sooner—and biting him. He suggested that I'm an enemy of the town! Me! I'm not going to take this!

MRS. STOCKMANN.   But dear Thomas, your brother has the power—

DR. STOCKMANN.   Yes, but I have the right.

MRS. STOCKMANN.   Yes, right, right. But what good is right without might?   300

PETRA.   Mother, how can you say that?

DR. STOCKMANN.   Don't be absurd, Katrina. When people are free, rightness always implies power. Besides, I have the open-minded and independent press in front of me, and the solid majority behind me. There's a good deal of power here, believe me.

MRS. STOCKMANN.   But God in heaven, Thomas, you don't plan to—

DR. STOCKMANN.   Don't plan to what?

MRS. STOCKMANN.   To set yourself against your brother?   305

DR. STOCKMANN.   ‍What the God damn hell else should I do? Shouldn't I follow what's true and right?

PETRA.   Just what I wanted to say.

MRS. STOCKMANN.   You won't get anywhere. If they oppose you, they'll stop you from doing anything.

DR. STOCKMANN.   Katrina, just wait, and you'll see that I'll take the war to them.

MRS. STOCKMANN.   Yes, you'll drive yourself into your dismissal—that you'll   310 do.

DR. STOCKMANN.   Whatever happens, I'll have fulfilled my obligations to the public—and *I* have been called the enemy of society!

MRS. STOCKMANN.   But think of your family, Thomas—your home—those who depend on you.

PETRA.   Oh Mother, you always think of us first.

MRS. STOCKMANN.   Well, you may talk, but you could take care of yourself, if you had to. But think of the boys, Thomas, and of your own needs, and of me—

DR. STOCKMANN.   Katrina, you're talking nonsense. Do you think I could   315 ever live with myself again if I had to go crawling—like a beaten coward—to Peter and his damned bootlickers?

MRS. STOCKMANN.   I don't know about that, but God help us from the sort of luck we'll all have if you keep up your defiance. You'll be back at zero, with no job and no secure income. We've had our fill of that, Thomas. Think about it, and think of what can happen.

DR. STOCKMANN.   [*squirms and clenches his fists.*] So much for being free but without power. Katrina, it's horrible.

MRS. STOCKMANN.   Yes, they're being horrible to you, it's true. But, God in heaven, there's so much unfairness that people have to endure in the world. [*EILIF and MORTEN, school books in their hands, enter while she is speaking.*] Think of our boys, Thomas, and what may happen to them. Surely you'd never—

DR. STOCKMANN.   [*appears deeply moved.*] The boys—. [*With an effort, he becomes resolute.*] No, I'll never knuckle under, even if the world falls apart! [*Strides toward his office.*]

MRS. STOCKMANN.   [*follows him.*] Thomas, what are you doing?   320

DR. STOCKMANN.   [*turns at the door.*] I want the right to look my own boys in the eyes when they're grown up and free! [*Leaves.*]

MRS. STOCKMANN.   [*begins crying.*] God help and preserve us!

PETRA.   Father is marvelous! He'll never give in!

The boys are dumbfounded, while PETRA cautions them to say nothing.

ACT III

SCENE. *Afternoon. The editorial office of THE PEOPLE'S MESSENGER. On the rear wall, stage left, is the main outside door. At stage right, the rear wall contains the print-shop door, with glass windows through which the print shop may be seen. Several compositors are setting type, and one worker is operating a hand-press. In the stage-right wall is another door. A long table in the middle of the room is spread out with papers, books, etc. There is a downstage window in the stage-left wall, in front of which there is a desk and a high stool where* HOVSTAD *is sitting and writing. Other chairs are at the table and along the walls. The office is generally drab and threadbare; all the furniture is old, nicked, stained, torn, and worn out.* BILLING *enters from the right, holding* DR. STOCKMANN's *manuscript.*

BILLING.   Now this is something!

HOVSTAD.   Did you finish reading it?

BILLING.   [*puts the manuscript on the desk.*] I certainly did.

HOVSTAD.   The Doctor doesn't pull any punches.

BILLING.   None at all. His words are sledgehammer blows!   5

HOVSTAD.   You're right, but these people won't throw in the towel at the first hard punch.

BILLING.   I agree, and for this reason we have to keep slugging away, blow after blow, until we knock out the whole establishment. As I was reading this I could see a dawning revolution.

HOVSTAD.   [*turns toward the print shop.*] Shhh! Don't let Aslaksen hear you.

BILLING.   [*lowers his voice.*] Aslaksen is scared of his own shadow. But you're the one in charge, right? You're printing the Doctor's article?

HOVSTAD.   Yes. Let's hope the Mayor doesn't agree to go along with things   10
first.

BILLING.   That would be Goddamned awkward.

HOVSTAD.   Well, either way we come out ahead. If the Mayor doesn't get on board with the Doctor's suggestions, all the tradespeople and the Homeowners Association will be on his neck. And if he does get on board, he'll alienate most of the shareholders of the Baths, who up to now have been his prime supporters.

BILLING.   Yes, because they'll have to pay through the nose—

HOVSTAD.   You can bet on it. And then the ring will be broken. From then on, in paper after paper, we'll expose the incompetence of the Mayor on one thing or another, and make clear that the town's elective positions—all of them—should be taken over by people with fresh ideas.

BILLING.   You've pictured it! I see it! God damn it, we're at the beginning   15
of a revolution!

A knock at the outside door.

HOVSTAD.   Shh! [*Calls.*] Come in! [*DR. STOCKMANN enters; HOVSTAD rises to greet him.*] Ah, Doctor, welcome!

DR. STOCKMANN.   Go ahead and print, Mr. Hovstad.

HOVSTAD.   You're sure.

BILLING.   Hurrah!

DR. STOCKMANN.   Print away. Yes, I'm sure. They'll have to take it. This   20
town is going to see a knock-down, drag-out fight!

BILLING.   I hope we'll slit their throats, Doctor.

DR. STOCKMANN.   This article is only the start. I have ideas for four or five more already. Where is Aslaksen?

BILLING.   [*goes to the print-shop door and calls.*] Aslaksen, please come in for a moment.

HOVSTAD.   Did you say four or five articles, all about this?

DR. STOCKMANN.   No, not all on the same topic, but all of them stem out of   25
the water-pollution issue. Things follow each other, just like fixing up an old
house. It's just like that.

BILLING.   That's true, God damn it. Once you start, you can't stop until you
tear down the whole rickety structure.

ASLAKSEN.   [*enters.*] Tear down! The Doctor doesn't think the Bath Houses
should be torn down?

HOVSTAD.   Not at all; don't worry.

DR. STOCKMANN.   We have something else in mind. Well, Mr. Hovstad,
what's your response to my article?

HOVSTAD.   It's a masterpiece.   30

DR. STOCKMANN.   Honestly now? I'm very pleased.

HOVSTAD.   It's clear and to the point. It requires no special vocabulary or
expertise. You'll rally all intelligent people.

ASLAKSEN.   And all prudent people, too?

BILLING.   Prudent, imprudent—the whole town.

ASLAKSEN.   Why then, we could certainly risk printing it.   35

DR. STOCKMANN.   Absolutely!

HOVSTAD.   Tomorrow's morning issue will have it.

DR. STOCKMANN.   Yes, in God's name, we shouldn't lose a single day. Mr.
Aslaksen, would you please see to it personally that the printing goes right?

ASLAKSEN.   I'll do it gladly.

DR. STOCKMANN.   Treasure it carefully, as if it were gold—no typographic   40
errors. I'll come in later to read proof. I can't tell you how anxious I am to see
the thing printed, and striking—

BILLING.   Striking—yes, like a flash of lightning—

DR. STOCKMANN.   —and meeting the approval of intelligent citizens. You
won't believe what I've been through since morning. I've been insulted and
menaced, and they've even threatened my basic human rights—

BILLING.   Your basic rights?

DR. STOCKMANN.   —they've tried to humiliate me, make me a coward, and
set personal gain above my deepest, holiest convictions.

BILLING.   This is unspeakable, damn it!   45

HOVSTAD.   Well, you can't expect anything else from this bunch.

DR. STOCKMANN.   But they haven't seen the end of me. With the *Messenger*
as my power base, I'll put things in black and white, and every day I'll fire off one
explosive article after another—

ASLAKSEN.   But, listen—

BILLING.   Hurrah! It's war! It's war!

DR. STOCKMANN.   I'll bring them to the ground! I'll crush them! I'll destroy   50
their bastions in the eyes of all right-thinking people!

ASLAKSEN.   But be moderate, good Doctor. Shoot, but with caution—

BILLING.   No, no, don't spare the dynamite!

DR. STOCKMANN.   [*goes on calmly.*] The issue is no longer just water pipes and
sewers—. No, our entire social structure needs cleansing and disinfecting—

BILLING.   Words of prophecy!

DR. STOCKMANN.   Everywhere, the bumbling incompetents should be put to   55
pasture, and that means *all*. Today I've gotten a sense of a more perfect future—

it's not clear yet, but it's taking shape in my mind. We need new standard bearers, my friends, and new commanding officers at all our outposts.

BILLING. Hear, hear!

DR. STOCKMANN. To make it possible, we must all pull together. With unity, the revolution can be like a ship gliding smoothly from harbor. Am I right?

HOVSTAD. My view is that we're close to getting municipal government into the right hands.

ASLAKSEN. And there'll be no risk as long as we're moderate.

DR. STOCKMANN. To hell with the risk! Everything I do, I do in the name of truth and because of my conscience.

HOVSTAD. Doctor, you've earned our support.

ASLAKSEN. Yes, our support. The Doctor is a true friend—a true benefactor of society.

BILLING. God damn it, Aslaksen, Dr. Stockmann is a friend of the people!

ASLAKSEN. I think the Homeowners Association will soon make use of that expression.

DR. STOCKMANN. [*is moved, and shakes their hands.*] Thank you, thank you, dear friends. This phrase is so stirring; my own brother used a different one, but he'll regret it. I have to go and see a poor devil of a patient now, but I'll come back soon, as I said. Mr. Aslaksen, take care of the manuscript, and set the type carefully. Don't take out any exclamation points. You can add some, if you want. Good, good. For the moment, goodbye, goodbye!

They escort him to the main door, shaking hands, etc. He leaves.

HOVSTAD. This man will be immensely useful.

ASLAKSEN. Yes, but only with regard to the Spa. To follow him in other things might not be politic.

HOVSTAD. Well, that depends—

BILLING. You're always so damned afraid, Aslaksen.

ASLAKSEN. Afraid? On local matters, Mr. Billing, I've learned to be cautious. I've learned this in the game of life. But put me in the area of national politics, even against the Government itself, and see how afraid I am.

BILLING. You're right, I grant. But isn't this contradictory?

ASLAKSEN. No, because I'm a man of conscience. Criticizing the national government is harmless, because the fellows up there don't notice, and they just stay put. But local politicians can be thrown out, and if you *do* get them out you might wind up with a bunch of incompetents—and really hurt not only the Homeowners but everyone.

HOVSTAD. But don't you believe that the improved education of the populace is a necessary consequence of self-government?

ASLAKSEN. Mr. Hovstad, when one's self-interests are at stake, other considerations are not as significant.

HOVSTAD. I hope I'll never hold self-interest first!

BILLING. Hear, hear!

ASLAKSEN. [*smiles, and points to* HOVSTAD's *desk.*] Mr. Sheriff Stensgaard preceded you at that desk.

BILLING. [*spits.*] He was a renegade!

HOVSTAD. I'm not a turncoat, and I hope I never will be.

ASLAKSEN.   A politician should not say "never," Mr. Hovstad. And you, Mr.   80
Billing, you may need to pull in your sails a bit, since you've submitted your
application for the Secretaryship of the Judicial Bench.

BILLING.   I—

HOVSTAD.   Is this true, Billing?

BILLING.   Well, yes, damn it, but you can understand my aim is to be a
gadfly to the establishment.

ASLAKSEN.   This isn't my business. But if you imply that I'm afraid or
contradictory, I remind you that the record of Aslaksen the printer is open. I've
always been consistent, except for becoming more moderate. My heart is always
with the people, but I won't deny that my mind goes with the authorities—the
local ones, that is. [*Leaves through the print-shop door.*]

BILLING.   Hovstad, we've got to get him out.   85

HOVSTAD.   Have you got anyone else in mind to finance our paper and
printing costs?

BILLING.   Damn it all that we don't have financial security!

HOVSTAD.   [*sits at his desk.*] Yes, that would help—

BILLING.   Do you think that Dr. Stockmann—

HOVSTAD.   What's the use? He doesn't have anything.   90

BILLING.   No, but he may be close to a hot prospect. You know—old Morten
Kiil, the one they call the "Badger."

HOVSTAD.   [*speaks while writing.*] Do you know for sure that he's well fixed?

BILLING.   Yes, God damn it! And the Stockmanns stand to inherit. At least
the Stockmann children will get something.

HOVSTAD.   [*faces BILLING directly.*] Are you counting on this?

BILLING.   Counting on it? Naturally, I never count on anything.   95

HOVSTAD.   You're right, and don't plan on the Secretaryship either. You're
not on the final list.

BILLING.   You think I don't know that? Nothing could please me more.
Losing the job will put me in fighting trim, and you need that here in the
boondocks, where nothing ever happens to egg you on.

HOVSTAD.   [*continues to write.*] Of course, of course.

BILLING.   But I'll make a mark yet!— Excuse me; I'm going to write the
appeal to the Homeowners Association now. [*Leaves through the door on the right.*]

HOVSTAD.   [*stays at his desk, chews the end of his pen, and talks slowly to himself.*]   100
So this is how it is. [*A knock at the entrance door.*] Come in! [*PETRA enters. HOVSTAD
rises.*] It's you, here? Why did you come?

PETRA.   Yes. Please excuse me—

HOVSTAD.   [*offers her a chair.*] Please sit down.

PETRA.   No, thank you, I have to go right away.

HOVSTAD.   You have a word from your father, perhaps?

PETRA.   No, I'm here on my own. [*Takes a book out of her coat.*] This is the   105
English story.

HOVSTAD.   Why are you bringing it back?

PETRA.   I won't translate it.

HOVSTAD.   But you gave me your word—

PETRA.   I did, but then I hadn't read it. You haven't read it either?

HOVSTAD.   You know I don't read English, but—   110

PETRA. Well, this is why you need something else. [*Puts the book on the table.*] You can't run this in the *Messenger*.

HOVSTAD. Why not?

PETRA. It contradicts everything you stand for.

HOVSTAD. Well, but then—

PETRA. You don't understand. The story's main theme is that a supernatural   115 power protects the so-called good people in the world and makes everything best for them in the end—and that all the so-called evil people get their punishment.

HOVSTAD. But that's all right. It's what our readers demand.

PETRA. Are you the one to give it to them? You know every single word is a fairy tale; things are not like that in the real world.

HOVSTAD. You're right. But realize that an editor is not totally free. If I want to lead my readers on the important political objectives of liberation and progress, I can't scare them off. A moral story like this one, on the back page, promotes their willingness to accept my editorial opinions on the front page; it makes them more confident.

PETRA. Come now! You set such a web for your readers. You're not a spider!

HOVSTAD. [*smiles.*] No. I thank you for including me in your elevated simile,   120 but the strategy was really Billing's, not mine.

PETRA. Billing's?

HOVSTAD. Yes. In any event, he explained the idea the other day. It's Billing who wants the story. I don't know it myself.

PETRA. But how can Billing, with his emancipated outlook—

HOVSTAD. Well, Billing is many things to many people. I'm told he's also looking for a job in the magistrate's office.

PETRA. I don't believe it. How could he make himself such a conformist?   125

HOVSTAD. Ask him.

PETRA. I would never have thought this of Billing.

HOVSTAD. [*looks at her intently.*] No? Is this so unexpected?

PETRA. Yes. But maybe not. I'm really not sure—

HOVSTAD. We journalists are not heroes, Miss.   130

PETRA. You mean that?

HOVSTAD. Sometimes I think so.

PETRA. I can understand this, under ordinary, everyday circumstances they do. But now, when you've taken a hand in this great cause—

HOVSTAD. You mean this business with your father?

PETRA. Yes. It seems to me that you must think of yourself as a person   135 above most others.

HOVSTAD. Yes, I rather do feel that way today.

PETRA. Of course you do. Why shouldn't you? You've really chosen a noble calling—to prepare the way for unrecognized truths and bold new ways of seeing— or even just to stand up without fear to support an injured man—

HOVSTAD. Yes, especially when the injured man is—how should I say it—

PETRA. You mean when he's so upright and honest?

HOVSTAD. [*softens his tone.*] Rather I mean when that man is your father.   140

PETRA. [*is suddenly struck.*] That?

HOVSTAD. Yes, Miss Petra—Petra.

PETRA.   Is this what's first and foremost to you? Not principle, not truth, not the warmth of my father's great heart?

HOVSTAD.   Yes, of course, all that, too.

PETRA.   No thanks, Hovstad. You're being dishonest, and I can't believe you 145
any more in anything.

HOVSTAD.   Can you be so angry at me when it's because of you—

PETRA.   I'm angry because you haven't been honest with Father. You talked to him as though truth and the common good were uppermost in your mind. You've made fools of both Father and me. You're not what you seem, and I'll never forgive you for that—never!

HOVSTAD.   You shouldn't be so spiteful, Miss Petra, not now, especially.

PETRA.   Why not now?

HOVSTAD.   Your father can't get anywhere without my help. 150

PETRA.   [*stares at him in disgust.*] So you're also like that! Shame!

HOVSTAD.   No, I'm sorry. I just blurted that out. Don't believe what I said!

PETRA.   I know what to believe. Goodbye!

ASLAKSEN.   [*hurries in from the print shop, trying to be secret.*] Hellfire and damnation, Mr. Hovstad!— [*Sees Petra.*] This is bad—

PETRA.   [*points to the book on the desk, and walks toward the main door.*] That's the 155
book. Get someone else to translate it.

HOVSTAD.   [*follows her.*] But Miss—

PETRA.   Goodbye! [*She leaves.*]

ASLAKSEN.   Listen, Mr. Hovstad—

HOVSTAD.   Yes, yes, what is it?

ASLAKSEN.   The Mayor is in the print shop. 160

HOVSTAD.   You say the Mayor?

ASLAKSEN.   Yes. He wants to talk with you. He came in the back way—I guess he didn't want to be seen.

HOVSTAD.   What's this about? No, wait, I'll go myself. [*Goes to the print-shop door and invites the MAYOR in. The Mayor enters.*] Aslaksen, please see that no one—

ASLAKSEN.   I understand. [*Goes into the print room.*]

THE MAYOR.   You were not expecting me, Mr. Hovstad? 165

HOVSTAD.   I certainly wasn't.

THE MAYOR.   [*looks around the room.*] You've made things cosy here. Quite nice.

HOVSTAD.   Well—

THE MAYOR.   And now I come here without an appointment to make a greater demand on your time.

HOVSTAD.   My pleasure, Mr. Mayor. I'm at your service. But let me take 170
your things. [*Puts the MAYOR's hat and walking-stick on a stool.*] Won't you sit down?

THE MAYOR.   [*sits beside the table.*] Thank you. [*HOVSTAD also sits at the table.*] Today, Mr. Hovstad, I've had a—an extremely distressing experience.

HOVSTAD.   Yes, with all the many duties of the Mayor's office—

THE MAYOR.   The one today concerns the Chief Medical Officer of the Spa.

HOVSTAD.   The Doctor?

THE MAYOR.   He has written a sort of report to the Governing Board, 175
claiming that there are supposed shortcomings at the Spa.

HOVSTAD.   No, he said this?

THE MAYOR.   Didn't he tell you? I understood him to say—

HOVSTAD. Well, yes, it's true he let something drop about—

ASLAKSEN. [*enters from the print shop.*] I'll need that manuscript—

HOVSTAD. [*speaks brusquely.*] There—it's on the desk.   180

ASLAKSEN. [*finds it.*] Good.

THE MAYOR. But see, that's it!

ASLAKSEN. Yes, Mr. Mayor, this is the Doctor's article.

HOVSTAD. Oh, is this the one you mean?

THE MAYOR. The same. What do you think of it?   185

HOVSTAD. Well, I'm not an expert, and I've only looked it over briefly.

THE MAYOR. But you're still going to print it?

HOVSTAD. I can't say no to a man with such impressive credentials—

ASLAKSEN. Mr. Mayor, I have no say in the paper's policies.

THE MAYOR. Certainly.   190

ASLAKSEN. I only print the copy put in my hands.

THE MAYOR. As well you should.

ASLAKSEN. [*walks toward the print shop.*] And therefore I must—

THE MAYOR. But stay a moment, Mr. Aslaksen. [ASLAKSEN *remains.*] With your permission, Mr. Hovstad?

HOVSTAD. By all means, Mr. Mayor.   195

THE MAYOR. Mr. Aslaksen, you're a sober and deliberate man.

ASLAKSEN. Your good opinion pleases me, sir.

THE MAYOR. And a man with influence in many circles.

ASLAKSEN. Well, it's mostly among the little people.

THE MAYOR. The small taxpayers are the great majority—here and else-   200
where.

ASLAKSEN. Right.

THE MAYOR. And I don't question that you know the common feelings of most of them. You follow me?

ASLAKSEN. Yes, Mr. Mayor, I think I may safely say I do know them.

THE MAYOR. Yes, and if there's such an admirable spirit of self-sacrifice among citizens of smaller means in our town, then—

ASLAKSEN. What's this?   205

HOVSTAD. Self-sacrifice?

THE MAYOR. This is a beautiful token of public spirit—an overwhelmingly beautiful token. I almost said I didn't expect it. But you know these feelings more thoroughly than I do.

ASLAKSEN. Yes, but Mr. Mayor—

THE MAYOR. And the sacrifice the town will need to make will not be small.

HOVSTAD. The town?   210

ASLAKSEN. But I don't understand—. It's the Spa—.

THE MAYOR. The first estimate for the changes recommended by the Chief Medical Officer is close to thirty million.

ASLAKSEN. That's a huge sum, but—

THE MAYOR. Naturally we'll need to float municipal bonds.

HOVSTAD. [*rises.*] This could never mean that the townspeople—   215

ASLAKSEN. This can't come out of the town's property taxes—out of the empty pockets of the small taxpayers.

THE MAYOR. Yes, my good Mr. Aslaksen, where else can we raise the money?

ASLAKSEN. The people who own the Spa can do it.

THE MAYOR. The shareholders can't extend themselves beyond where they've already gone.

ASLAKSEN. Mr. Mayor, is this completely certain?   220

THE MAYOR. I've assured myself of it. If we want these extensive changes, the town itself must pay for them.

ASLAKSEN. But God damn it to hell—! I'm sorry, your Honor—this is something else!

HOVSTAD. It certainly is!

THE MAYOR. The worst part is that, for at least a couple of years, we'll have to close the Spa entirely.

HOVSTAD. Closed? Entirely closed?   225

ASLAKSEN. For two years?

THE MAYOR. Yes, the work will take two years—at least.

ASLAKSEN. But damn it all, Mr. Mayor, we can never put up with that! How can the Homeowners live?

THE MAYOR. There's no easy answer, Mr. Aslaksen. But what can we do? Do you believe we'll get a single guest if someone goes around and paints the picture that our water is poisoned, that we live in a sewer, that the whole town—

ASLAKSEN. And this is all just imagination?   230

THE MAYOR. With all my best will, I've been able to reach no other conclusion about it.

ASLAKSEN. Well, then, it's totally inexcusable of Dr. Stockmann—I beg your pardon, Mr. Mayor, but—

THE MAYOR. What you're implying is regrettably true, Mr. Aslaksen. My brother has always been an impetuous man.

ASLAKSEN. Mr. Hovstad, can you still support him after this?

HOVSTAD. But who would have believed that—?   235

THE MAYOR. I've prepared an impartial brief reviewing the conditions, and in it I've shown that any possible shortcomings may be addressed without shattering the current budget for the Spa.

HOVSTAD. Do you have a copy, Mr. Mayor?

THE MAYOR. [*reaches into a pocket.*] I do. I brought it along in case—

ASLAKSEN. Oh my God, here he is!

THE MAYOR. Who? My brother?   240

HOVSTAD. Where? Where?

ASLAKSEN. He's coming through the print shop!

THE MAYOR. Unfortunate. I don't want a confrontation here, but I still have a few more things to tell you.

HOVSTAD. [*directs him to the door on the right.*] Go in here for a time.

THE MAYOR. But—?   245

HOVSTAD. No one but Billing is there.

ASLAKSEN. Quickly, Your Honor, he's here now!

THE MAYOR. All right, then, but be quick with him. [*Leaves through the door on the right.* ASLAKSEN *opens it and closes it for him.*]

HOVSTAD. Make as though you're busy, Aslaksen.

HOVSTAD sits at his table and writes. ASLAKSEN *works with papers on a chair at the right.*

DR. STOCKMANN. [*enters from the print shop.*] Here I am again. [*Puts down his*   250
hat and walking-stick.]

HOVSTAD. [*concentrates on his writing.*] Already, Doctor? Aslaksen, hurry up
with the copy we spoke of. Time's getting tight for us.

DR. STOCKMANN. [*to ASLAKSEN.*] I conclude the proofs aren't ready yet.

ASLAKSEN. [*does not look up.*] No, the Doctor shouldn't expect them so soon.

DR. STOCKMANN. No, but I'm naturally impatient. I won't rest for a minute
until I see everything in print.

HOVSTAD. Well, it'll take at least another hour. That's right, isn't it, Aslaksen?   255

ASLAKSEN. I'm afraid so.

DR. STOCKMANN. All right, dear friends. I'll come back again and again if
I need to. When something so important as the welfare of the whole town is at
stake, it's no time to be lazy. [*Begins to leave, but stops and comes back.*] Just one more
thing—

HOVSTAD. Excuse me, but could we do it another time?

DR. STOCKMANN. I'll be done in a moment. It's just this: When people read
my article tomorrow they'll also realize I've spent the whole winter working in the
town's best interest—

HOVSTAD. Yes, but Doctor—   260

DR. STOCKMANN. I know what you'll say, that it was only my duty. Damn it
all, any citizen would do the same. And I agree with you, but my fellow citizens
out there—. God in heaven, think of their high opinion of me—!

ASLAKSEN. Yes, Doctor, the people have thought highly of you, up till now.

DR. STOCKMANN. And that's why I'm afraid that—. This is what I want to
say: If my article creates an incentive, especially for the poor, to take a future
share of town government into their own hands—

HOVSTAD. [*rises, clears throat.*] Doctor, I won't hide this from you—

DR. STOCKMANN. Just as I thought; I knew it. But I won't have it. If anyone   265
is setting something up—

HOVSTAD. Like what?

DR. STOCKMANN. Well, whatever—a demonstration, a testimonial dinner, a
solicitation for a gift—then by all that's sacred, promise me to nip it in the bud.
And you too, Mr. Aslaksen. Am I clear?

HOVSTAD. Doctor, pardon me, but we've got to tell you the plain truth.

MRS. STOCKMANN, in hat and coat, enters from the main outside door.

MRS. STOCKMANN. [*sees the Doctor.*] I was right!

HOVSTAD. [*walks toward her.*] You also, Mrs. Stockmann?   270

DR. STOCKMANN. Katrina, what the hell are you doing here?

MRS. STOCKMANN. You know what I'm doing.

HOVSTAD. Please sit down. Or perhaps—

MRS. STOCKMANN. Please, no thank you. And please don't mind my coming
here for Stockmann, because, I want you to know, I'm the mother of three
children.

DR. STOCKMANN. Claptrap! They know all that!   275

MRS. STOCKMANN. Well, it seems that you haven't been thinking of your
wife and children lately, or else you wouldn't go on like this, leading us into
disaster.

DR. STOCKMANN.   But Katrina, this is insane! Does having a wife and children stop a man from proclaiming the truth—from being a good citizen—from serving his home town?

MRS. STOCKMANN.   All these things, Thomas, but moderately.

ASLAKSEN.   I say that, too. Moderation in everything.

MRS. STOCKMANN.   And because of this, Mr. Hovstad, you are hurting us   280
when you coax my husband away from house and home and make him a dupe in all this.

HOVSTAD.   I'm not making anyone a dupe—

DR. STOCKMANN.   Dupe? Do you think I'm letting myself be used?

MRS. STOCKMANN.   You are. You're the most intelligent man in town, but, Thomas, you're so easy to deceive. [*To HOVSTAD.*] And just think that he loses his position at the Spa as soon as you publish his article—

ASLAKSEN.   What?

HOVSTAD.   Doctor, now see—   285

DR. STOCKMANN.   [*laughs.*] Just let them try! They'll regret it, because the solid majority is backing me!

MRS. STOCKMANN.   Yes, that's the problem, to have something as terrible as that backing you!

DR. STOCKMANN.   Nonsense, Katrina! Go home and look after the house, and leave the community to me. Why are you so afraid when I'm so confident and cheerful? [*Paces, rubbing his hands.*] The people and the truth will be victorious, you can bet on it. I can see it—all the open-minded middle classes forming a triumphant army—! [*Stops at the chair where the MAYOR put his hat and stick.*] Now what the hell is this?

ASLAKSEN.   [*sees the things.*] Oh, my God!

HOVSTAD.   [*likewise.*] Ahem!   290

DR. STOCKMANN.   Here you see the highest authority!

Mockingly holds the MAYOR's hat high in the air.

MRS. STOCKMANN.   The Mayor's hat!

DR. STOCKMANN.   And here's the crook of power, too [*displays the MAYOR's walking-stick*]. How by all the fiends of hell did—

HOVSTAD.   Now, well—

DR. STOCKMANN.   Ah, I understand. He came here to harangue you. [*Laughs.*]   295
He sure came to the right place! And then he saw me in the print shop—. [*Bursts out laughing.*] Did he run, Mr. Aslaksen?

ASLAKSEN.   [*speaks rapidly.*] Oh yes, he ran, Doctor.

DR. STOCKMANN.   Ran away from both his stick and—. Ran away, my foot! Peter doesn't run away from anything. But where the devil did you put him? Aha! In here, naturally. Now you'll see, Katrina!

MRS. STOCKMANN.   Thomas, please—

ASLAKSEN.   Be careful, Doctor.

Still holding the stick, DR. STOCKMANN puts on the MAYOR's hat. He goes to the door at the right, opens it, and salutes as THE MAYOR enters in a rage. BILLING follows.

THE MAYOR.   What do you mean by this clowning?   300

DR. STOCKMANN.   [*paces.*] Have respect, dear Peter. I'm the town's chief authority now!

MRS. STOCKMANN. [*on the verge of tears.*] Thomas, don't—

THE MAYOR. [*follows him.*] Give me my hat and stick!

DR. STOCKMANN. [*as before.*] *You* are only the constable, while *I* am the Mayor—*I* am master of the whole town!

THE MAYOR. Take off that hat! Remember, it's part of an official uniform! 305

DR. STOCKMANN. Piffle! Do you think the people, waking up like a lion, are scared of uniforms? There'll be a revolution in town tomorrow; you'd better know that. You thought you could dismiss me, but I'll dismiss you—from all your posts. You think I can't? Well, listen: I've got the power of the people with me. Hovstad and Billing will thunder in the *People's Messenger,* and Aslaksen the Printer will lead the charge of the entire Homeowners Association—

ASLAKSEN. I won't do it, Doctor.

DR. STOCKMANN. But of course you will—

THE MAYOR. Aha! Mr. Hovstad has perhaps decided to be part of this insurrection, then?

HOVSTAD. No, Mr. Mayor. 310

ASLAKSEN. No, Mr. Hovstad isn't such a fool as to wreck himself and his paper for no more than an insane idea!

DR. STOCKMANN. [*looks around the room.*] What does all this mean?

HOVSTAD. You've put things in a false light, Doctor, and I can't support you any longer.

BILLING. And in light of what the Mayor has just been telling me—

DR. STOCKMANN. False? Let me worry about that. Just print the article, and 315
I'll justify it.

HOVSTAD. I won't print it. I cannot, I will not, and I dare not print it!

DR. STOCKMANN. Dare not? What talk is this? You're the editor, and it's the editors who make editorial decisions, I hope.

HOVSTAD. No, it's the subscribers, Doctor.

THE MAYOR. A good thing, too.

ASLAKSEN. Public opinion—enlightened people—Homeowners and such 320
people—they rule the papers.

DR. STOCKMANN. [*speaks calmly.*] And all this is now against me?

ASLAKSEN. Yes, it is. Printing your article would ruin the community completely.

THE MAYOR. My hat and stick, please. [DR. STOCKMANN *lays the things on the table.* THE MAYOR *takes them.*] Your tenure as the town's chief authority has ended abruptly.

DR. STOCKMANN. No, it's not over yet. [*To* HOVSTAD.] Then it's quite impossible to publish my article in the *Messenger?*

HOVSTAD. Quite impossible, and also because of your family. 325

MRS. STOCKMANN. You needn't bother about the family, Mr. Hovstad.

THE MAYOR. [*takes a sheet of paper from his pocket, and offers it to* HOVSTAD.] If you put this in, it will be sufficient for the guidance of the public. It's an official explanation. Mr. Hovstad, would you please?

HOVSTAD. [*accepts the paper.*] Good. We'll print it right away.

DR. STOCKMANN. But not mine! But you'll find that you can't suppress the truth so easily. Mr. Aslaksen, please publish my manuscript as a pamphlet—at my expense, and under my name. I'll have four hundred copies—no, five hundred! Make it six!

ASLAKSEN.   If you paid me its weight in gold, Doctor, I couldn't use my   330
press for a thing like this. I wouldn't dare, in the light of public opinion. No one
in the whole town will print it!

DR. STOCKMANN.   Then give it back to me.

HOVSTAD.   [*gives him the manuscript.*] Here you are.

DR. STOCKMANN.   [*picks up his hat and stick.*] I'll make it public anyway. I'll
call an open meeting, and all my fellow townspeople will come to hear me read
the truth!

THE MAYOR.   No organization in town would let you rent their hall for this
purpose.

ASLAKSEN.   Not a single one. I'm sure of it.   335

BILLING.   No, God damn it, not one!

MRS. STOCKMANN.   This is a disgrace. Why is everyone turning against you?

DR. STOCKMANN.   [*speaks in anger.*] I'll tell you why. All the men in this town
are no better than old women—like you. They all think only of their families, and
not of the community.

MRS. STOCKMANN.   [*takes his arm.*] Then I'll show them an—old woman—
acting for once as men of power should act. I'll stand with you, Thomas.

DR. STOCKMANN.   Bravely said, Katrina! On my soul, I'll make things public.   340
If I can't rent a hall, I'll hire a drummer to follow me all over town, and I'll shout
out the truth at every corner!

THE MAYOR.   Certainly you're not such a prize idiot as all that!

DR. STOCKMANN.   Oh yes I am!

ASLAKSEN.   You won't find a single voter to back you up.

BILLING.   No, God damn it, you won't!

MRS. STOCKMANN.   Don't give in, Thomas. I'll send the boys with you.   345

DR. STOCKMANN.   That's an inspired idea!

MRS. STOCKMANN.   Morten will love it, and Eilif will go along.

DR. STOCKMANN.   Yes, and Petra, and you too, Katrina.

MRS. STOCKMANN.   No, no, that's not for me. But I'll watch at the window
and support you. That I can do.

DR. STOCKMANN.   [*embraces her and kisses her.*] Thanks for this. Now, my good   350
gentlemen, we'll have a trial by combat! We'll see whether a pack of cowards can
squelch a patriot trying to make the world a cleaner place!

He and MRS. STOCKMANN *leave by the main door.*

THE MAYOR.   [*shakes his head reflectively.*] Now he's made her go crazy too!

ACT IV

SCENE: *The following night. A large room in the home of* CAPTAIN HORSTER. *An anteroom
at the back can be seen through opened folding doors. The entrance door is at the extreme
rear. Three windows are in the wall at stage left, and lighted lamps at these windows illuminate
the room. Downstage from these windows is a table, with candles and a chair. A small podium,
on which there is a table with chair, candles, bell, water, and glass, is set at the middle of the
stage-right wall. There is a door in this wall downstage from the podium, and some chairs
are near it. The room is almost filled with an assortment of townspeople, including a few
women and children, and at the curtain the townsfolk continue entering from the anteroom.*

1 CITIZEN.   [*speaks to another citizen.*] Hello, Lamstad! You here too?

2 CITIZEN.   I always come to public meetings.

3 CITIZEN.   D'you have your whistle?

2 CITIZEN.   You bet. Got yours?

3 CITIZEN.   Right here! And old Skipper Evensen is bringin' a cow-horn!   5

2 CITIZEN.   He's a real joker, that Evensen!

General laughter and noise from the crowd.

4 CITIZEN.   [*meets the three citizens.*] What's going on here tonight?

2 CITIZEN.   Dr. Stockmann is speaking against the Mayor.

4 CITIZEN.   But my God, they're brothers!

1 CITIZEN.   So what? Dr. Stockmann ain't scared.   10

3 CITIZEN.   But he goofed up; I read that in the *Messenger.*

2 CITIZEN.   He's on the wrong side this time, because he couldn't rent the halls of the Homeowners Association or the Downtown Civic Club.

1 CITIZEN.   He couldn't even get the one at the Spa.

2 CITIZEN.   Not on your life, man.

5 CITIZEN.   Whose side are we on here?   15

6 CITIZEN.   Just watch Aslaksen, and follow his lead.

BILLING.   [*comes through the crowd, carrying a writing case.*] Excuse me please. Please let me through. I'm a reporter for the *Messenger.* [*Sits at the table on the left.*]

1 LABORER.   Who's that?

2 LABORER.   Oh, that's Billing. He works at Aslaksen's paper.

MRS. STOCKMANN and PETRA enter from the door at the right, escorted by CAPTAIN HORSTER. EILIF and MORTEN follow them.

HORSTER.   [*points to the chairs.*] Please sit here. Then, if things get out of   20 hand, you can leave easily.

MRS. STOCKMANN.   You're not expecting any trouble?

HORSTER.   With a crowd like this you can't tell. But just sit tight here. You'll be fine!

MRS. STOCKMANN.   [*sits, along with PETRA.*] Letting my husband use the room was so kind.

HORSTER.   Well, since he couldn't get one elsewhere—

PETRA.   It was brave of you, Captain Horster.   25

HORSTER.   Oh, it was nothing.

HOVSTAD and ASLAKSEN enter amid the crowd: "Excuse me!" "Please!" etc.

ASLAKSEN.   [*goes to HORSTER.*] Is the Doctor here yet?

HORSTER.   He's in the next room.

Noise from the crowd at the anteroom door.

HOVSTAD.   Here's the Mayor!

BILLING.   Well I'll be God damned, he's here after all!   30

THE MAYOR enters through the crowd, which parts for him. He bows and greets people as he goes. He takes a stand near the left wall. DR. STOCKMANN then enters from the door at the right, wearing a black frock-coat and a white tie. A few townspeople applaud, but they are quickly restrained. Then perfect silence.

DR. STOCKMANN   [*speaks quietly to* MRS. STOCKMANN.] Are you all right?

MRS. STOCKMANN.   Just fine, thanks. [*Lowers voice.*] Thomas, please don't lose your temper.

DR. STOCKMANN.   No, I'll control myself. [*Takes out his watch and looks at it. Steps to the podium and bows.*] It's quarter past—time to start. [*Takes his manuscript from his pocket.*]

ASLAKSEN.   [*speaks loudly.*] First we should elect someone as Chair!

DR. STOCKMANN.   That won't be necessary.   35

VARIOUS VOICES IN THE CROWD.   Yes! Hear, hear! Elect a Chair! etc.

THE MAYOR.   I too think we should have a Chair!

DR. STOCKMANN.   But I called this meeting to give a lecture, Peter.

THE MAYOR.   [*speaks to the crowd.*] This lecture may lead to controversy, however, and for that we need someone to chair.

VARIOUS VOICES.   A Chair! Elect someone! etc.   40

HOVSTAD.   It seems there is a consensus to elect a Chair!

DR. STOCKMANN.   [*speaks resignedly.*] All right—let the consensus rule.

ASLAKSEN.   Will the Mayor consent to serve? [*Various townspeople applaud. Shouts of "Yes,* MR. MAYOR*!" "He should chair!" etc.*]

THE MAYOR.   You will all understand why I must ask to be excused from serving you. But we do have an acceptable candidate. I recommend to you the President of the Homeowners Association, Mr. Aslaksen!

VARIOUS VOICES.   Yay, Aslaksen! Yes! Hurrah for Aslaksen! etc.   45

DR. STOCKMANN *picks up his manuscript and leaves the podium.*

ASLAKSEN.   As my fellow citizens have such confidence in me, I am not unwilling to accept—

Applause. Cheers. Whistles. etc. ASLAKSEN *mounts the podium.*

BILLING.   [*writes.*] "Mr. Aslaksen was elected by acclamation."

ASLAKSEN.   As your newly elected Chair, permit me a few short words. You all know me as a peaceful and quiet person. I believe in sober moderation, and in—and in moderate sobriety!

VARIOUS TOWNSPEOPLE.   Yes, we know! *Bravo!* etc. [*Light applause.*]

ASLAKSEN.   I am a graduate of the school of hard knocks, and I've learned   50
that the most important virtue of a citizen is moderation—

THE MAYOR.   Hear, hear!

ASLAKSEN.   And furthermore, that discretion and moderation are essential to public service. Therefore I suggest to the distinguished man who has called this meeting that he exert all efforts to keep within the limits of moderation.

7 CITIZEN.   [*stands near the door stage right.*] Let's hear it for the Moderation Party!

VARIOUS VOICES.   Be quiet! Shut your Goddamn mouth! Shh! etc.

ASLAKSEN.   No demonstrations! Please keep order! Is there anyone who   55
wishes to speak?

THE MAYOR.   Mr. Chairman.

ASLAKSEN.   The Honorable Mayor Stockmann has the floor.

THE MAYOR.   Because I am the closest relative of the Chief Medical Officer of the Spa, you will understand my reticence in speaking. But out of my duty as the Chief Executive Officer, and out of my concern for the town, I must present a motion. I believe that no one here considers it in the town's interest to publicize unsubstantiated and dubious reports concerning the sanitary condition of our water supplies.

VARIOUS VOICES. Absolutely not! No, no! No such reports! etc.

THE MAYOR. Therefore I move that this assembly refuse to permit the Chief Medical Officer to give his lecture or discuss it. [*Voice of "Second the motion."*] 60

DR. STOCKMANN. [*angrily.*] Refuse permission?— What's all this?—

MRS. STOCKMANN. [*coughs.*] Ahem!

DR. STOCKMANN. [*collects himself.*] Well, all right for now. Go ahead.

THE MAYOR. In my report printed in the *Messenger*, I laid out the facts so that all impartial citizens might draw their own conclusions. In it you have seen that the Chief Medical Officer's recommendations—in addition to being a direct vote of no confidence in the town's principal citizens—would require unacceptable tax increases for the town, to the extent of many millions.

Cries of indignation and many whistles and catcalls.

ASLAKSEN. [*rings bell.*] Order, gentlemen. [*Stands.*] I rise to support the motion of the Mayor. He's right that there's more to the Doctor's actions than meets the eye. He begins with the Spa, but his real motive is revolution—to get control of the town government. The Doctor of course is honest—no question of that. I too believe in self-government, with the proviso that it does not raise taxes. But higher taxes would result here, and therefore I'll see Dr. Stockmann in hell before I support him on this! Excuse my language, but some things have too high a cost. [*Vigorous approval from all sides.*] 65

HOVSTAD. My position also needs clarification. Dr. Stockmann's analysis at first seemed reasonable, and I judged him worthy of support. But we soon found cause to believe that we had been led astray by false conclusions—

DR. STOCKMANN. False—?

HOVSTAD. Well, not totally reliable conclusions, if you will. The Mayor's statement has established that. I think no one here doubts my devotion to freedom. The record of the *Messenger* on such important political issues is widely recognized. But from wiser and more experienced men I have learned that the paper should take cautious and prudent stands on local issues.

ASLAKSEN. I agree completely with the speaker.

HOVSTAD. And on this current issue, it's certain that there's now a consensus against Dr. Stockmann. Is it not then, gentlemen, an editor's duty to work in tandem with popular sentiment? Is not an editor obligated to work diligently on behalf of the readers whose causes he accepts and reflects? Am I wrong in this? 70

VARIOUS VOICES. No! You're right! Well said! etc.

HOVSTAD. Personally, this public disagreement with Dr. Stockmann, in whose home I have been a guest, has caused me great agony. Till now he has deserved the unconditional respect of his fellow citizens. With so much virtue, his only flaw is his tendency to be ruled by his feelings rather than his judgment.

A SMALL NUMBER OF VOICES. True! Stockmann is okay! Etc.

HOVSTAD. Nevertheless, my overriding concern for the public has directed me to make this break. In addition, there's another reason for which he should be deterred from his present course, and that is concern for his family—

DR. STOCKMANN.   Just stick to water intakes and sewers!   75

HOVSTAD.   —Concern for his wife and children, for whom he has made no security.

MORTEN.   Does he mean us, Mother?

MRS. STOCKMANN.   Shh!

ASLAKSEN.   Gentlemen, are you ready to vote on the Mayor's motion?

DR. STOCKMANN.   There's no need. This evening I don't wish to speak about   80
the filthiness of the Spa. No, you'll hear something different.

THE MAYOR.   [*aside.*] What's next?

PETTERSEN.   [*he is drunk, and stands near the back door.*] I pay taxes, and I want
to talk! My insolent—absolute—unacceptable comment is—

VARIOUS VOICES.   He's plastered! Shut him up! Put that lush out! What an
idiot! Pipe down! Etc. [*Pettersen is ejected.*]

DR. STOCKMANN.   May I speak?

ASLAKSEN.   [*rings the bell.*] Dr. Stockmann has the floor.   85

DR. STOCKMANN.   Thank you. A few days ago, I would have allowed no one
to silence me as has been done tonight. Like a lion, I would have defended my
sacred right to speak. But now this doesn't matter to me, because I have more
important things to say. [*The crowd, one of whom is MORTEN KIIL, moves closer to him.*]
In the last few days I've been thinking things over a good deal, so much that my
head was almost spinning—

THE MAYOR.   [*coughs.*] Ahem!

DR. STOCKMANN.   —but I have put things in order, and that's why I'm in
front of you this evening. I have a unique discovery to tell you about, my fellow
citizens, a revelation far more significant than the pollution of our water and the
contaminated ground at our Therapeutic Spa.

VARIOUS VOICES.   [*shout.*] Not that! Out of order! Not about the Spa! We
won't listen! Etc.

DR. STOCKMANN.   No, my topic tonight is my great discovery of the last few   90
days—that it is our moral life that is polluted and that it is our communal
assumptions that are built on contaminated ground.

VARIOUS VOICES.   [*hushed.*] What's this about? What's he mean? Etc.

THE MAYOR.   What kind of insinuation—!

ASLAKSEN.   [*rings his bell.*] The speaker is cautioned to be moderate.

DR. STOCKMANN.   I was brought up in this town, and I have always loved it.
When I had to leave it I was still not old, and in my exile I thought of it fondly
almost as a place inhabited by angels. [*Brief applause in the crowd.*] In the depressing
hell-hole up north where I practiced for so many years, the people lived far apart,
here and there, among the rocky hills, and I sometimes thought that they didn't
need a physician like myself but rather a veterinarian.

BILLING.   [*puts down his pen.*] Well, God damn it, I never heard—   95

HOVSTAD.   You're insulting the ordinary people!

DR. STOCKMANN.   Now wait! From what I've said, you'll agree that up north
I didn't forget you. I was more like a brooding hen, and what I hatched was—
the plan for our Therapeutic Spa! [*Applause and objections.*] When I was fortunate
enough to return home I thought my life had reached fulfillment. But I had an
ardent, relentless, burning wish, and that was to serve you and to be an asset to
you.

THE MAYOR.   [*looks at the ceiling.*] This is a strange way of doing it!

DR. STOCKMANN. And so, blinded to reality, I was in bliss. However, yesterday morning—no, really the evening before—my blind eyes were opened, and the first thing I saw was the incredible stupidity of our authorities—

Consternation, objections, laughter. MRS. STOCKMANN coughs strongly.

THE MAYOR. Mr. Chairman!　　　　　　　　　　　　　　　　　　　100
ASLAKSEN. [*rings his bell.*] The chair has authority to rule—
DR. STOCKMANN. Let's not quibble about a word, Mr. Aslaksen. I only mean that I began to realize how bull-headed the town leaders had been about the Spa. Generally, I find official types unbearable. They inhibit freedom at every turn. They're no better than goats among newly sprouted trees; they destroy everything. They frustrate a free person at every turn, and I don't see why they shouldn't be exterminated like any pest—.

Uproar in the room.

THE MAYOR. Mr Chairman, can this be allowed?
ASLAKSEN. [*rings his bell.*] Doctor—!
DR. STOCKMANN. I don't know why I didn't see the nature of the official　　105
types before—when each day I could see such a shining example right here in town—my brother Peter—dull in wit, inflexible in prejudice—

Laughter, uproar, whistles. MRS. STOCKMANN coughs continuously. ASLAKSEN rings his bell loudly, etc.

PETTERSEN. [*who has returned.*] Hey, is he talking about me? My name's Pettersen, but damn it to hell if I—
VARIOUS VOICES. [*shout in anger.*] Throw the drunk out! Through the door with 'im! Etc. [*Pettersen is thrown out again.*]
THE MAYOR. Who was that—individual?
1 CITIZEN. I don't know, Mr. Mayor.
2 CITIZEN. He has no business here.　　　　　　　　　　　　　　　　　110
3 CITIZEN. He's probably a lumberman over at—[*The rest cannot be heard.*]
ASLAKSEN. Obviously that man's brain is drowned in beer! [*Laughter.*] Continue, Doctor, but be moderate.
DR. STOCKMANN. So then, neighbors, I will say nothing more about our leading citizens. No one should claim that my main objective is to criticize them, for I take comfort that such parasites—living fossils of a passing age—are racing toward their own extinction. They don't need a doctor's help to hurry them along! No, *they're* not the danger; *they're* not the ones most active in poisoning our moral life and polluting the ground under us. No, *they're* not the worst enemies of truth and freedom.
VARIOUS VOICES. [*speaking from all sides.*] Who then? Who is it? Name them! Etc.
DR. STOCKMANN. Don't worry! I'll name them! This is the great discovery　　115
I made yesterday. [*Raises his voice.*] The most dangerous enemy of truth and freedom among us is the solid majority. Yes, the damned, solid, popular majority! That's it! Now you know!

Tremendous uproar in the room. Most people are shouting, stamping their feet, whistling, booing, hissing, etc. A few older people look slyly at each other and appear to be enjoying themselves. MRS. STOCKMANN *stands anxiously.* EILIF *and* MORTEN *begin quarrelling with some other boys who are demonstrating.* ASLAKSEN *rings his bell and pleads for order.* HOVSTAD *and* BILLING *try to speak, but are drowned out. Finally, things quiet down.*

ASLAKSEN.   As Chair, I ask the speaker to withdraw his immoderate language and apologize to the body.

DR. STOCKMANN.   Not for the world, Mr. Aslaksen! It's the majority in our town who are denying me my free right to speak the truth.

HOVSTAD.   The majority always has right on its side.

BILLING.   And, damn it, it always has truth, too!

DR. STOCKMANN.   The majority is never right—never, I say! Majority rule   120
is nothing more than a fairy tale that all thinking people must oppose. Who forms the majority—the intelligent or the stupid? Is there any doubt that the stupid make up the landslide majority everywhere on earth? But you can throw me in hell if it's ever been part of an eternal plan for the stupid to control the intelligent! [*Outcries, catcalls, disturbance.*] All right, you can shout me down, but you can't answer me. The majority does have *might*—more's the pity—but not *right. I* am right, along with a small number of others. It's the *minority* that's always right! [*More outcries, demonstrations, etc.*]

HOVSTAD.   [*laughs.*] So in the last few days Dr. Stockmann has become an aristocrat!

DR. STOCKMANN.   I've said that I won't waste words on people like that shipwrecked crew of officials behind us. They're no longer even relevant. My thoughts are rather on the few who are creating new and exciting ideas. Such people are in the front ranks, beyond the shortsighted vision of the solid majority. *They* are leading the fight for ideas that are so new and rare that as yet they haven't recruited great numbers to their cause.

HOVSTAD.   Oh, so now the Doctor's a revolutionary!

DR. STOCKMANN.   Yes, in God's name, I am, Mr. Hovstad! I want to revolt against the fairy tale that truth belongs to the majority alone. What are the truths the majority usually flocks around? Old, worn-out, and disintegrating truths. And when a truth gets too old, gentlemen, it's close to being a lie. [*Laughter and scorn at him.*] Yes, believe as you wish, but truths don't live for 969 years, like Methuselah. An average truth can live no more than seventeen or eighteen, or at best twenty years. In fact, truths this old are fading and dying, but it's only then that the majority harvests them for the food of their moral life. As a doctor, I assure you that there's only moral starvation there. All these dead popular beliefs, which are no better than salted meat that's gone rotten, are the cause of our present epidemic of moral scurvy.

ASLAKSEN.   It seems to me that the speaker has wandered away from his   125
text.

THE MAYOR.   I'm in agreement with the Chair.

DR. STOCKMANN.   Peter, you're crazy! I *am* staying on my subject, which is exactly this: It's the mass, the majority—the fiendish, solid majority—that's poisoning the sources of our moral life and passing its waste on the very ground we stand on.

HOVSTAD.   And the great open-minded majority does all this because they're reasonable enough to recognize only secure and sanctioned truths?

DR. STOCKMANN.   Ah, my good Mr. Hovstad, don't pretend to speak about truths! The truths that the mass accepts today are the truths secured by the advance guard at the time of our grandparents. Today's forward thinkers have gone far beyond them. I believe there's only one essential truth, and that is that no society can be healthy if it lives on outmoded, marrowless truths.

HOVSTAD.   Well, instead of standing there with your mind in the blue, why not make it interesting and tell us what you mean by these "marrowless truths" we live on.   130

Support from various parts of the crowd.

DR. STOCKMANN.   Well, I could go on forever, but I might begin with one which is really an outrageous lie but which all the same feeds the *Messenger* and the *Messenger's* readers.

HOVSTAD.   And that is—?

DR. STOCKMANN.   It's the idea given to you from the past and which you transmit mindlessly at every opportunity. It's the falsehood that the crowd, the mass, the majority, form the kernel of the people—in fact, that they *are* the people—and that the common people, the most apathetic and worst prepared in society, have the same right to condemn and approve, to manage and advise, as those few people who are truly enlightened.

BILLING.   I hear this, God damn it, but—

HOVSTAD.   [*shouts at the same time.*] Citizens, remember this!   135

VARIOUS VOICES.   Aren't we the people! So only the aristocrats run things? Etc.

1 LABORER.   Down with him for talking like this!

2 LABORER.   Yeah, throw 'im out!

3 CITIZEN.   [*shouts.*] Toot your horn, Evensen!

Sounds of a loud horn. Whistles and tremendous uproar in the room.

DR. STOCKMANN.   [*speaks when the noise subsides.*] Gentlemen, please listen.   140 Can't you hear the truth for a change? I never expected that you'd all agree with me, but I thought that Mr. Hovstad might, at least after a while. He claims to be a freethinker—

VARIOUS VOICES.   [*in startled but hushed tones.*] He's a freethinker? What? Is Editor Hovstad a freethinker?

HOVSTAD.   [*shouts.*] Prove this, Dr. Stockmann! When did I say this in print?

DR. STOCKMANN.   [*pauses briefly.*] No, damn it, you're right—you've never been that honest. Well, I won't leave you dangling in the wind, Mr. Hovstad. [*To the crowd.*] Let *me* be the freethinker then. I'm going to persuade you logically that the *People's Messenger* misleads you shamelessly by telling you that you—the common folk, the masses—form what is called "The People." This is a lie, for common folk are only the raw material of the people. [*Grumbling, laughter, and commotion in the room.*] Well, consider the differences between thoroughbred and street animals. For instance, a farmyard hen is too scrawny for good eating. And its eggs? A common crow or raven does just as well. But with thoroughbred Spanish or Japanese hens, or well-nourished pheasants or turkeys, the story is different. As further evidence, consider the lives of dogs, which we human beings so closely resemble. Compare an ordinary street mongrel with a registered Collie or Setter which has been bred for many generations. Don't you think these thoroughbred dogs have better brains than the curs? You know the answer. The pups of the well-bred dogs take to training naturally, and do things that common mongrels could never learn. [*Uproar and disapproval all around.*]

9 CITIZEN. [*shouts.*] So you think we're dogs?

10 CITIZEN. We're not animals, *Sir* Doctor!   145

DR. STOCKMANN. Yes, my friend, we really *are*, believe me—the highest animals on earth—but even among us there are just a few really good ones. Among people, there are wide differences between thoroughbreds and mongrels. And the funny thing is that Editor Hovstad totally agrees with me as long as the subject is four-footed creatures—

HOVSTAD. Yes, but they're in a different category.

DR. STOCKMANN. You see! When I apply the principle to us two-legged animals, he refuses the logic. He won't follow his ideas to their necessary conclusion, but rather turns everything upside down, and pontificates in the *Messenger* about the farmyard hens and mongrel curs being the best of the human menagerie! But it's always that way as long as popular bromides control the soul, and people don't free themselves to reach their own highest mental and spiritual distinction.

HOVSTAD. I don't claim distinction of any sort. I come from simple peasants, and I'm proud of my deep roots in the common people he's now insulting.

VARIOUS VOICES. Hurrah for Hovstad! Well said! Etc.   150

DR. STOCKMANN. You recognize that common people are not confined to the lower economic levels. They yelp at our heels wherever we go, even in the highest circles and professions. I cite as an example His Honor, the Mayor. My brother Peter is just as common as anyone in two shoes—.

Laughter and hisses.

THE MAYOR. I protest these personal slurs!

DR. STOCKMANN. [*undisturbed.*] And he's common not because he is—as I am—a descendant of an old Pomeranian pirate. This is, I confess, our common origin—

THE MAYOR. That family legend is not true!

DR. STOCKMANN. But he is low because he uncritically accepts the opinions   155
of his superiors as his own. People like that are intellectual rabble, and this is why my statesmanlike brother Peter is so undistinguished and narrow minded.

THE MAYOR. Mr. Chairman—!

HOVSTAD. So in this country people can be open-minded only if they're distinguished! This is certainly news!

DR. STOCKMANN. Yes, that's *one* of my discoveries. Another is that open-mindedness is virtually the same as morality. This is why it's so indefensible for the *Messenger* to preach day in and day out that the people, the masses, the solid majority, are the guardians of understanding and morality, and that social and political evils are a residue of culture, just as the pollution of our Spa is a residue of the tannery wastes up at Mølledal. [*Uproar and interruptions. Unaffected, he laughs in his exhilaration.*] And yet the *Messenger* preaches on about elevating the masses to their higher destiny! But damn it all, if the *Messenger*'s doctrines were right, then elevating the masses would do no more than drive them straight into the devil's hands! But fortunately this theory is only folklore. No, it's stupidity, poverty, and ugliness that make Old Nick prosper. A house that is not well cleaned and ventilated will soon make its inhabitants lose their moral judgment. Without the oxygen gained from constant cleansing, we lose our conscience. And I conclude that oxygen is lacking in many households here in town, because the popular majority have desensitized their consciences and are willing to build the town's wealth on a cesspool of lies and deceit.

ASLAKSEN. Accusations like this, against the entire town, are outrageous!

10 CITIZEN. I move that the Chair rule the speaker out of order.   160

VARIOUS VOICES. Second! Hear, hear! Out of order! Etc.

DR. STOCKMANN. [*becomes angry.*] If I can't speak here, I'll declare the truth in the streets! I'll write for papers in other towns! The entire country will see what's going on here!

HOVSTAD. It seems that Dr. Stockmann is bent on ruining the town.

DR. STOCKMANN. Yes, I love my home town so much that I prefer its ruin to its living on lies.

ASLAKSEN. Now you've *really* said it!   165

Uproar, shouts, catcalls, etc. MRS. STOCKMANN *coughs, but* DR. STOCKMANN *no longer listens to her.*

HOVSTAD. [*shouts over the noise.*] Any person aiming to destroy the community is a public enemy!

DR. STOCKMANN. [*with rising anger.*] If the community lives on lies, what does its destruction matter? It ought to be pounded to rubble, or its pollution will infect other towns, and, finally, the entire country! And I say, with every fiber of my being, that if things go that far, may the country itself die, and may all its people be eliminated!

11 CITIZEN. This is the talk of a real enemy of the people!

BILLING. That voice—God damn it—that voice is the People's voice!

THE ENTIRE CROWD. [*shouts.*] He's an enemy of the people! He hates his   170
country! He hates all the people! Etc.

ASLAKSEN. I'm deeply disturbed, both publicly and personally, at what we've heard. Dr. Stockmann has revealed an unfortunate part of himself I would never have dreamed possible. But the expression just voiced by one of you conveys the sense of this meeting, and hence I would entertain the following resolution of censure: "This assembly declares that Dr. Thomas Stockmann, Chief Medical Officer of the Spa, is an enemy of the people."

Cries of "So move" and "Second the motion." Tremendous applause and cheers, stamping of feet, etc. A few men surround DR. STOCKMANN *and hiss and menace him.* MRS. STOCKMANN *and* PETRA *stand up.* MORTEN *and* EILIF *begin fighting other boys who have joined the hissing, but they are separated by nearby adults.*

DR. STOCKMANN. [*to those menacing him.*] You fools! I tell you—

ASLAKSEN. [*rings his bell.*] You no longer have the floor, Doctor. We'll take a vote, but as a personal privilege for the Doctor, we'll do it by ballot and not by voice or hand. Mr. Billing, do you have any paper?

BILLING. Yes I do, both blue and white.

ASLAKSEN. [*walks to him.*] That's good, it will make the process easier. Cut   175
it up; yes, like that. [*To the crowd.*] Take blue for no; white for yes. I myself will collect your votes.

The MAYOR *leaves while* ASLAKSEN *and a few others put the ballots in their hats and distribute them.*

1 CITIZEN. [*to* HOVSTAD.] What should we think about the Doctor? Has he gone off his rocker?

HOVSTAD. You know he's always been headstrong.

2 CITIZEN. [*to* BILLING.] Billing, you've been at the house. Did you ever see him drinking?

BILLING. Well, I can't be sure, but there's always liquor on his table.

3 CITIZEN. I think he goes around the bend at times.   180

1 CITIZEN. Has there been any madness in the family?

BILLING. I wouldn't be surprised.

4 CITIZEN. No, it looks like pure spite to me; I think he's out to get someone.

BILLING. Well, he did get turned down on his request for a raise.

THE FOUR CITIZENS. [*agree among themselves.*] Ah, we see it all now!   185

PETTERSEN. [*who has returned again.*] Gimme a blue one! And a white one too!

ANGRY VOICES. There's that lush again! Out with him! Etc.

MORTEN KIIL. [*speaks to* DR. STOCKMANN.] Well, Stockmann, do you see what your hocus-pocus has done for you?

DR. STOCKMANN. I've done my duty as I saw it.

MORTEN KIIL. What did you say about the tanneries at Mølledal?   190

DR. STOCKMANN. You understood me—that they're the source of the toxic waste.

MORTEN KIIL. Including my tannery?

DR. STOCKMANN. Yes, I'm sorry, but yours is the worst.

MORTEN KIIL. Are you going to put this in the paper?

DR. STOCKMANN. I won't hold anything back.   195

MORTEN KIIL. That may cost you plenty, Stockmann. [*Leaves.*]

VIK. [*goes to* HORSTER, *ignoring the women.*] So, Captain, you permit your house to be used by an enemy of the people.

HORSTER. Mr. Vik, I have a right to do as I wish with my own property.

VIK. Well, then, you can't object if I exercise the same right with mine.

HORSTER. Sir, what are you saying?   200

VIK. You'll understand in the morning. [*Turns and walks away.*]

PETRA. Captain Horster, wasn't he your shipowner?

HORSTER. Yes, that was Mr. Vik.

ASLAKSEN. [*ballots in hand, he steps on the podium and rings his bell.*] Order, please! Gentlemen, here are the results. All of you have voted but one—

12 CITIZEN. [*a young man.*] Yeah, that was the drunk!   205

ASLAKSEN. And by a unanimous vote—except for a drunken man—this body of citizens declares that Dr. Thomas Stockmann, Chief Medical Officer of the Spa, is an enemy of the people! [*Applause, outcries.*] Let's have three cheers for our ancient and noble community! [*Cheers.*] Let's also have three cheers for our honorable Mayor, who has put our town above duty to family! [*More cheers.*] Our business is ended. Do I hear a motion to adjourn? [*Cries of* "So move," "Second."] The meeting is now adjourned! [*Steps down.*]

BILLING. Long live our Chair!

THE ENTIRE CROWD. Hurray for Aslaksen the Printer! Etc.

DR. STOCKMANN. Petra, my coat and hat. Captain, do you have space for passengers to the New World?

HORSTER. Yes, Doctor, for you and yours I'll make room.   210

DR. STOCKMANN. [*as* PETRA *helps him with his coat.*] Katrina, boys, let's go. [*He takes his wife's arm.*]

MRS. STOCKMANN. [*lowers her voice.*] Thomas, the back way.

DR. STOCKMANN. There's no back way for me, Katrina. [*Raises his voice.*] You'll be hearing from this enemy of the people again before he shakes the dust of this town from his feet.° I cannot be as charitable as the person who said, "Forgive them, for they know not what they do!"°

ASLAKSEN. Dr. Stockmann, that's blasphemy!

BILLING. Well, God d—. This is too much for a believing person!   215

13 CITIZEN. [*coarsely.*] So he's threatening us, is he?

ANGRY VOICES. Smash his windows! Toss him in the fjord! Etc.

3 CITIZEN. [*shouts.*] Blow your horn, Evensen! Toot, toot!

Loud horn calls, whistles, shouts, general turmoil. HORSTER *leads* DR. STOCKMANN *and his family toward the door at the rear.*

THE WHOLE CROWD. [*howls, etc. at them.*] Enemy of the people! Enemy of the people! Enemy of the people!

BILLING. [*gathers his notes.*] Well, God damn it if I'd go over and have a   220 toddy with the Stockmanns tonight!

The crowd pushes out the rear door. Their noise continues outside. From the street the receding shouts continue: "Enemy of the people," "Enemy of the people!"

ACT V

SCENE: DR. STOCKMANN's *study, the next morning. The room is in general disorder. At the walls are bookcases, along with cabinets containing various specimens. At the rear, a center door leads to the hallway. Downstage in the stage-left wall there is a door to the living room. The two windows in the stage-right wall are completely broken. In the middle of the room is the Doctor's desk, strewn with books, papers, etc.* DR. STOCKMANN, *in dressing gown, slippers, and smoking cap, is using an umbrella to scrape out broken glass and other debris from under a cabinet. Shortly after the curtain he produces a large stone.*

DR. STOCKMANN. [*calls through the living-room door.*] Here's another one, Katrina.

MRS. STOCKMANN. [*offstage.*] I'm sure you'll find more.

DR. STOCKMANN. [*adds the stone to a pile on the desk.*] These stones will be keepsakes. Eilif and Morten will see them every day, and will inherit them when they grow up. [*Rakes under another bookcase.*] Did what's-her-name get the glazier yet?

MRS. STOCKMANN. [*enters.*] Yes, but he wasn't sure he could make it today.

DR. STOCKMANN. You'll soon see that he won't dare to come.   5

MRS. STOCKMANN. Randina—the maid—thought the same. He's afraid because of the neighbors. [*Looks toward the door on the left, and calls.*] What is it, Randina. Yes, I'll take it. [*Leaves and returns immediately.*] It's a letter for you, Thomas.

---

213 *dust . . . feet:* Mark 6:11.   *Forgive . . . do:* Luke 23:34.

DR. STOCKMANN. Thank you. [*Takes the letter, opens it, and reads it quickly.*] Ah, as I expected.

MRS. STOCKMANN. Who's it from?

DR. STOCKMANN. Our landlord. It's a notice to leave.

MRS. STOCKMANN. Can it be? He's such a nice man—   10

DR. STOCKMANN. [*looks at the letter.*] Says he doesn't dare do anything else. His fellow-citizens—public sentiment—dependent on others—can't offend superiors—no choice. You get the picture.

MRS. STOCKMANN. But you see his reasons, Thomas.

DR. STOCKMANN. Yes, I see. I see that the whole town is made up of cowards; they're all afraid of each other. [*Tosses the letter on the desk.*] But, Katrina, it's no matter. We'll sail to America, and then—

MRS. STOCKMANN. Is this the best thing to do, Thomas?

DR. STOCKMANN. Do you think we should stay here, where they've branded   15
me as an enemy of the people, threatened me, and smashed my windows? And look, they've ripped my black trousers!

MRS. STOCKMANN. Oh, dear! That's your best pair.

DR. STOCKMANN. You should never battle for truth and freedom in your Sunday best! It isn't the trousers; you can sew them up again. It's rather the injustice that these scum dared to attack me as though they were my equals. I can never accept that.

MRS. STOCKMANN. Certainly they treated you shabbily, Thomas, but does that justify leaving our own country permanently?

DR. STOCKMANN. Don't you suppose the common mongrels are just as spiteful in other Norwegian towns we could live in? There's not much to choose from. But crap, their snapping at heels isn't the worst! The worst is that everyone in this country is a slave to party—though for that matter it's probably no different anywhere else. In the West, I'm sure, they have the same popular majority, the same pseudo-liberal public opinion, and all that devil's garbage. But, you see, things there are on a huge scale. They may *kill* you, but they don't *torture* you with a thousand cuts, as they do here; they don't put your soul in a vise and squeeze the life out of you. If you need to, though, you can get away there. [*Paces.*] If only I knew of a bargain on an unexplored forest, or a tiny island in the South Seas—

MRS. STOCKMANN. But what of the boys, Thomas?   20

DR. STOCKMANN. [*stops.*] You're so strange, Katrina! Do you want the boys to grow up in a society like ours? Last night you saw that half the people are crazy enough to be in straightjackets, and if the other half haven't lost their minds, it's because they're such blockheads they have nothing to lose.

MRS. STOCKMANN. No, but Thomas, you speak so imprudently.

DR. STOCKMANN. Well, isn't what I'm saying right? Don't they turn everything upside down? Don't they mix up right and wrong? Don't they call everything a lie that I know is the truth? But the most insane thing is that these grown people, who profess to support freedom, go around as a party and try to fool themselves and others into thinking that they're broad-minded and independent. Katrina, have you ever heard the like?

MRS. STOCKMANN. Yes, it's wrong, but— [*PETRA enters from the living room.*] What, already back from school?

PETRA. Yes, I've been dismissed.   25

MRS. STOCKMANN. Dismissed?

DR. STOCKMANN. You too, Petra?

PETRA. Mrs. Busk gave me my walking papers, and I thought it best to go right away.

DR. STOCKMANN. You did right.

MRS. STOCKMANN. Who would have expected that Mrs. Busk was that sort of person? 30

PETRA. She isn't that sort, Mother. I could see how it hurt her. But she didn't dare do anything else, she said, and so I got fired.

DR. STOCKMANN. [*laughs and rubs his hands.*] She didn't dare either. How marvellous!

MRS. STOCKMANN. Well, after the horrible scene last night—

PETRA. That wasn't all. Father, just listen!

DR. STOCKMANN. Well? 35

PETRA. She showed me three letters she had got only this morning.

DR. STOCKMANN. With no signatures, I assume?

PETRA. Yes.

DR. STOCKMANN. Because they didn't *dare* sign their names, Katrina.

PETRA. And two of them reported that a man who had been a guest in our 40
home declared at the Club that I held dangerously liberated views on a number of things—

DR. STOCKMANN. You didn't disavow them, I hope?

PETRA. You know I didn't. Mrs. Busk herself, in private anyway, has liberated views, but because this is coming out about me, she didn't dare keep me.

MRS. STOCKMANN. And one of our guests! That's what you get for your hospitality, Thomas!

DR. STOCKMANN. We can't stay in this pigsty any longer. Pack our things right away, Katrina. The sooner we leave, the better.

MRS. STOCKMANN. Shh! There's someone in the hall. Go see who it is, Petra. 45

PETRA. [*opens the living-room door.*] Oh, it's you, Captain Horster! Please come in.

HORSTER. [*enters.*] Good morning. I wanted to see how you're doing.

DR. STOCKMANN. [*shakes his hand.*] Thank you. You're so kind.

MRS. STOCKMANN. And thank you again for protecting us from the mob, Captain Horster.

PETRA. But how were you able to get back home again? 50

HORSTER. Oh, I managed. I can take care of myself, and that crowd has more bark than bite.

DR. STOCKMANN. Isn't their hangdog cowardice amazing? [*Shows the stones on the desk.*] Look, here are the stones they used to break our windows. Just look! No more than two in this pile have any class as rocks at all; the rest are gravel— just pebbles! And the crowd stood out there milling around, threatening to beat me to a pulp! But for action—action—you just don't see that in this town!

HORSTER. This time, though, it was best for you, Doctor.

DR. STOCKMANN. You're right. But it still makes you mad, because if the country ever gets into a serious all-out fight, you'll see that public opinion will be to run away, Captain Horster, and the solid majority will be scared off like sheep. It's enough to make you sick. But what the hell, it's stupid to go on like this. They've called me the people's enemy, and so I'll *be* the people's enemy.

MRS. STOCKMANN. You can never be that, Thomas. 55

DR. STOCKMANN.   Don't be too sure, Katrina. Being called such an ugly name is the same as being stabbed in the lung. That ghastly name is sitting in my stomach and gnawing at me like a cancer. No medicine can help this.

PETRA.   No, Father, you should just laugh at them.

HORSTER.   Doctor, one day they'll see things your way.

MRS. STOCKMANN.   Yes, as sure as you're standing here.

DR. STOCKMANN.   Sure, when it's too late. Well, they deserve it. Let them   60
roll in their own filth and regret that they once drove a patriot into exile. When do you sail, Captain Horster?

HORSTER.   Well, I came here to tell you—

DR. STOCKMANN.   Is something wrong with the ship?

HORSTER.   No, but what happened is that *I'm* not going along.

PETRA.   You haven't gotten your notice?

HORSTER.   [*smiles.*] Yes, that's it.   65

PETRA.   You too!

MRS. STOCKMANN.   Thomas, do you see?

DR. STOCKMANN.   And all for the sake of truth! If I'd thought for one minute—

HORSTER.   Don't worry. I'll get a post from some shipping line or other out of town.

DR. STOCKMANN.   And here we have the estimable Mr. Vik—a man of wealth   70
and independence. What a God-damned farce!

HORSTER.   Oh, he's right-minded otherwise. He said he would've kept me, if he dared—

DR. STOCKMANN.   But he didn't dare? No, that goes without saying.

HORSTER.   He says it's not easy, being a party man and all—

DR. STOCKMANN.   Now here's a truth from on high! A party is like a meat grinder. It grinds everyone's brains together into a dead-level mash—fatheads and meatheads, all together.

MRS. STOCKMANN.   Thomas, really now!   75

PETRA.   [*to HORSTER.*] If you hadn't taken us home, things might have been different for you.

HORSTER.   I have no regrets.

PETRA.   [*extends her hand.*] Thank you for that!

HORSTER.   [*to DR. STOCKMANN.*] What I came to tell you is that I've another idea, if you're really resolved to leave—

DR. STOCKMANN.   Excellent! The sooner the better—   80

A knock is heard offstage.

MRS. STOCKMANN.   Shh! Someone's knocking.

PETRA.   It must be Uncle.

DR. STOCKMANN.   Ah! [*Calls.*] Come in!

MRS. STOCKMANN.   Dear Thomas, please promise me—

The Mayor enters from the hallway door.

THE MAYOR.   You're busy. I can come back later—   85

DR. STOCKMANN.   Not at all. Come in.

THE MAYOR.   But I'd like to talk to you—just the two of us.

MRS. STOCKMANN.   We'll go to the living room.

HORSTER. And I'll come back later.

DR. STOCKMANN. No, please, Captain, stay with them. I'd like to hear   90
more—

HORSTER. I'll be glad to wait.

He follows Mrs. Stockmann and Petra into the living-room. The Mayor says nothing but looks at the windows.

DR. STOCKMANN. You may find quite a draft here today. Why don't you
put on your hat?

THE MAYOR. Thank you. [*Does so.*] I think I caught a cold last night. I stood
and froze—

DR. STOCKMANN. You did? I thought it was rather warm.

THE MAYOR. I'm sorry I had no power to stop last night's excesses.   95

DR. STOCKMANN. Do you have anything else in particular to tell me?

THE MAYOR. [*takes out a large envelope.*] This letter, from the Governing
Board of the Spa.

DR. STOCKMANN. My notice?

THE MAYOR. Yes, bearing today's date. [*Puts the envelope on the desk.*] This
is painful, but considering public opinion, we didn't dare do anything else.

DR. STOCKMANN. [*smiles.*] Didn't dare? I keep hearing echoes today!   100

THE MAYOR. It's important for you to understand your present position.
You can plan on no future medical practice here in town.

DR. STOCKMANN. The practice be damned to hell! But why are you so sure?

THE MAYOR. The Homeowners Association is circulating a petition from
house to house recommending that responsible citizens stop using your services.
I assure you that not a single family head will refuse to sign. Quite simply, no one
will dare to refuse.

DR. STOCKMANN. I don't doubt you. But what then?

THE MAYOR. My advice is that you'd best leave town for a period.   105

DR. STOCKMANN. Yes, I've been thinking about that.

THE MAYOR. Good. And then after you've thought things out for a time—
say half a year—after mature consideration you might find it fitting to write a
brief apology admitting your mistake—

DR. STOCKMANN. You mean that I might get my post back?

THE MAYOR. Perhaps. It's not impossible.

DR. STOCKMANN. But what about public opinion? You wouldn't dare go   110
against public opinion.

THE MAYOR. Public opinion is variable. And, frankly, it's especially important to us to have some sort of written apology from you.

DR. STOCKMANN. Oh, you're licking your chops for that! But for Christ's
sake, don't you recall what I told you about such dirty tricks?

THE MAYOR. Things were different then. You believed the whole town was
behind you—

DR. STOCKMANN. Yes, and now I believe the whole town's on my neck.
[*Flares up.*] But even if the devil and his great-grandmother were on my neck—!
Never! I say never!

THE MAYOR. Thomas, a family man can't behave as you do. You have no   115
right, Thomas!

DR. STOCKMANN.   No right? There's only one thing in the world that free persons have no right to do, and do you know what that is?

THE MAYOR.   No.

DR. STOCKMANN.   Naturally, but I'll tell you. Free persons have no right to get down and roll in filth—no right to lower themselves to the point where they're spitting in their own faces.

THE MAYOR.   This has a jingle of plausibility, and it would explain your stubbornness if there were nothing else—. But there is—something else.

DR. STOCKMANN.   What are you talking about?   120

THE MAYOR.   You understand me very well. But as your brother, and as a man of perception, I advise you not to be too confident about prospects and hopes that may so easily fall through.

DR. STOCKMANN.   Just what are you getting at?

THE MAYOR.   Do you expect me to believe you know nothing about Mr. Kiil's will?

DR. STOCKMANN.   Well, I know that his small estate will go to a foundation for old working people. But what does that have to do with me?

THE MAYOR.   Well, first, the estate is not small. Mr. Tannerymaster Kiil is   125
a rather wealthy man.

DR. STOCKMANN.   I never had any idea!

THE MAYOR.   Oh—truly? None? You also had no idea that a not insignificant amount of his wealth will go to your children, and that you and your wife will enjoy the interest for life? Didn't he ever tell you?

DR. STOCKMANN.   No, never a blessed word! Rather the reverse. He always blasts away interminably about ridiculously high taxes. But you're sure of all this, Peter?

THE MAYOR.   I have it on the best authority.

DR. STOCKMANN.   Then, praise God, Katrina's secure—and the children too!   130
I'll tell her right away. [*Calls.*] Katrina! Katrina!

THE MAYOR.   [*holds him back.*] Shh! Not a word yet!

MRS. STOCKMANN.   [*opens the door.*] What is it, Thomas?

DR. STOCKMANN.   Not a thing. Wait inside a bit more. [*She closes the door. He begins pacing.*] Secure! And think—they're all secure, and for life. What a blessed feeling—to know you're secure!

THE MAYOR.   Yes, but you're really not. Mr. Kiil the tanner can change his will whenever he wants.

DR. STOCKMANN.   But, my good Peter, he won't. The old Badger is dancing   135
for joy at the way I went after you and your precious cohorts.

THE MAYOR.   [*starts, and looks intently at him.*] This puts things in a new light.

DR. STOCKMANN.   What things?

THE MAYOR.   This whole business was a coordinated maneuver. These wild and reckless slurs that you—in the name of truth—have aimed at our municipal leaders—

DR. STOCKMANN.   Were what?

THE MAYOR.   They were no more than an exchange for being named in   140
that revengeful old man's will.

DR. STOCKMANN.   [*almost speechless.*] Peter, you're the most nauseating scum I've ever known!

THE MAYOR.   This is the end between us. Your dismissal is final, because we now have a weapon against you. [*Leaves.*]

DR. STOCKMANN.   Oh, my God! [*Calls toward the living room.*] Katrina, scrub the floor after him! Have her bring a pail—God damn it—what's-her-name, with the sooty nose—

MRS. STOCKMANN.   [*at the living-room door.*] Thomas, hush, hush!

PETRA.   [*also at the door.*] Father, Grandpa is here, and wants to speak with you alone.   145

DR. STOCKMANN.   Why not? [*Goes to the door. PETRA and MRS. STOCKMANN leave. MORTEN KIIL enters and DR. STOCKMANN closes the door.*] Come in, Father. What is it? Please sit down.

MORTEN KIIL.   No, thank you. [*Looks around.*] You've made it look cosy here today, Stockmann.

DR. STOCKMANN.   Yes, doesn't it look that way?

MORTEN KIIL.   Really fine, and lots of fresh air. Today you have plenty of that ox-ee-gin you talked about yesterday. You have a clear conscience today, I suppose.

DR. STOCKMANN.   Yes, I have.   150

MORTEN KIIL.   I believe it. [*Pats his coat pocket.*] Do you know what I've got here?

DR. STOCKMANN.   A clear conscience too, I hope.

MORTEN KIIL.   Bah! Better than that. [*Takes out a leather folder, opens it, and shows a sheaf of papers.*]

DR. STOCKMANN.   [*looks at him in surprise.*] Shares in the Spa?

MORTEN KIIL.   It wasn't hard to buy 'em today.   155

DR. STOCKMANN.   And you've been out snapping them up—

MORTEN KIIL.   All I could afford.

DR. STOCKMANN.   But, my good Father, the Spa is in such desperate condition!

MORTEN KIIL.   If only you return to sanity, you can put it back in tune soon enough.

DR. STOCKMANN.   Well, you yourself can see I'm doing all I can. But—   160 everyone in town is crazy.

MORTEN KIIL.   You said yesterday that the worst pollution came from my tannery. If that's true, then my grandfather and my father before me and I myself have all been poisoning the town for many years, like three angels of death. Do you believe I can live with that kind of shame?

DR. STOCKMANN.   Well, you'll have to get used to it.

MORTEN KIIL.   No, thanks. I prize my good name and reputation. I hear that people call me "the Badger," which is a sort of pig. But there's no way on earth they'll be right about this. I'm going to live and die with a clean reputation.

DR. STOCKMANN.   How do you plan to do that?

MORTEN KIIL.   You're going to make me clean, Stockmann.   165

DR. STOCKMANN.   Me?

MORTEN KIIL.   Do you know what money I used for the shares? No, you don't, but I'll tell you. It's the money that Katrina, Petra, and the boys will have when I'm gone. Yes, you see, I've been able to salt a little away, despite everything.

DR. STOCKMANN. [*with rising anger.*] You've used Katrina's inheritance for that!

MORTEN KIIL. Yes. Everything is now sunk in the Spa. And now I'll find out, Stockmann, if you're a total lunatic! If you still say that tiny monsters and other such things come from my tannery, it's as though you're cutting wide strips of skin from the bodies of Katrina, and Petra, and the boys. A decent family man couldn't do that—unless he's totally crazy.

DR. STOCKMANN. [*paces.*] But I am totally crazy—totally!   170

MORTEN KIIL. You can't be so raving, foaming crazy that you'd destroy your wife and children.

DR. STOCKMANN. [*stands in front of him.*] Why didn't you ask me before you bought all this trash?

MORTEN KIIL. Once something's done, it's best to finish it.

DR. STOCKMANN. [*paces uneasily.*] If only I weren't so sure—. But I *am* sure! I'm absolutely positive!

MORTEN KIIL. [*weighs the folder in his hand.*] If you hang on to your insane   175
ideas, these will be worthless, you know. [*Returns the folder to his pocket.*]

DR. STOCKMANN. God damn it all! Researchers should be able to unearth a counter-agent, some sort of antidote—

MORTEN KIIL. To kill the tiny monsters?

DR. STOCKMANN. Yes, or to make them harmless.

MORTEN KIIL. Couldn't you try rat poison?

DR. STOCKMANN. Don't be foolish.—But everyone says it's only my imagi-   180
nation. Well, let's have it their way—it's imagination. Didn't the short-sighted curs censure me as an enemy of the people—and weren't they howling to claw my clothes off, too?

MORTEN KIIL. And all the windows they smashed for you!

DR. STOCKMANN. And then there's my family responsibility. I'll take it up with Katrina. She's superb on these things.

MORTEN KIIL. Right, she's a sensible woman; listen to her.

DR. STOCKMANN. [*turns toward him.*] But you, how could you mess things up so totally? To gamble with Katrina's inheritance, and leave me in such a painful bind? When I look at you, I think I'm seeing the devil himself.

MORTEN KIIL. I can see it's time to go. But I want an answer before two   185
o'clock. *Yes* or *no.* With a "no," I'll will everything to my foundation before the day is over.

DR. STOCKMANN. And what does Katrina get then?

MORTEN KIIL. Not even a grain of snuff.

The Hall door opens, showing HOVSTAD *and* ASLAKSEN *waiting to enter.*

MORTEN KIIL. Well, look at this pair!

DR. STOCKMANN. [*glares at them.*] What—? You dare come to see me?

HOVSTAD. Yes, of course.   190

ASLAKSEN. We've come to talk to you.

MORTEN KIIL. [*whispers to* DR. STOCKMANN.] "Yes" or "no," before two o'clock.

Leaves through the hallway door as Hovstad and Aslaksen enter.

ASLAKSEN. [*glances at* HOVSTAD.] Oho!

DR. STOCKMANN. Well, what is it? And be quick!

HOVSTAD. I understand how you feel about our stand toward you last   195
night—

DR. STOCKMANN. Oh, by all the devils in hell, you took a fine stand. You
were as upright as a bent-over crone. "Spineless" is the right word to describe you.

HOVSTAD. Whatever you call it, we couldn't do anything else.

DR. STOCKMANN. You mean you didn't *dare* do anything else. Is that more
like it?

HOVSTAD. Okay, say it your way.

ASLAKSEN. But why didn't you tell us in advance, just a small hint to Mr.   200
Hovstad or me?

DR. STOCKMANN. A hint? About what?

ASLAKSEN. About the idea behind it.

DR. STOCKMANN. I don't follow you.

ASLAKSEN. [*nods confidentially.*] Oh I'm sure you do, Dr. Stockmann.

HOVSTAD. There's no reason to conceal things any longer.   205

DR. STOCKMANN. [*stares from one to the other.*] What in the God-damn hell—?

ASLAKSEN. May I ask, isn't your father-in-law buying up shares in the Spa
all over town?

DR. STOCKMANN. Yes, he's been buying shares today, but—?

ASLAKSEN. It would have been wise to have someone else do it—someone
not so closely related.

HOVSTAD. And you shouldn't have used your own name. No one needed   210
to know where the criticism about the Spa came from. You should have taken me
in with you, Dr. Stockmann.

DR. STOCKMANN. [*stares ahead blankly; a light seems to dawn for him, and he speaks
as though struck from on high.*] Can this be possible? Can such things happen?

ASLAKSEN. [*smiles.*] They can indeed. But only if you have a little—strategy—
if you get my meaning.

HOVSTAD. And you should bring in others, because there's less risk for the
individual when others are with you.

DR. STOCKMANN. [*now composed.*] All right, gentlemen. What is it you want?

ASLAKSEN. Mr. Hovstad should—   215

HOVSTAD. No, *you* should explain, Aslaksen.

ASLAKSEN. Well, now that we understand how things are fitting together,
we thought we could make the *Messenger* available to you.

DR. STOCKMANN. Would you dare that now? What of public opinion? Aren't
you afraid of a storm of criticism?

HOVSTAD. We'll ride that out.

ASLAKSEN. And the Doctor must be ready to reverse positions quickly. As   220
soon as your attack has had its effect—

DR. STOCKMANN. As soon as Mr. Kiil and I have bought all the shares at
panic prices, you mean—?

HOVSTAD. I presume that you have a—scientific purpose?—in wishing to
control the Spa?

DR. STOCKMANN. Oh yes. It was for a *scientific purpose* that I brought the
Old Badger in with me. And so we'll fiddle a bit with the intake pipes, and look
professional while digging samples at the beach, and the town won't be out half a
dollar. Doesn't this sound good?

HOVSTAD. I agree—particularly if you have the *Messenger* with you.

ASLAKSEN.   In a free society the Press is powerful, Doctor.   225

DR. STOCKMANN.   Definitely, and so is public opinion. And you, Mr. Aslaksen, you will act as the conscience of the Homeowners Association?

ASLAKSEN.   Of both the Homeowners Association *and* the Temperance Society. Bank on it.

DR. STOCKMANN.   But gentlemen—. I'm ashamed to ask about it, but what consideration for you—?

HOVSTAD.   You understand that we'd prefer to help you for nothing. But *The People's Messenger* is on wobbly legs. Things are not right, and I really don't want to close the paper now, when there's so much to work for in the larger political scene.

DR. STOCKMANN.   I agree. That would be hard for a *friend* of the people   230
like you. [*Flares up.*] But I'm an *enemy* of the people! [*Searches around.*] Where did I put my stick? Where the hell's the stick?

HOVSTAD.   What's all this?

ASLAKSEN.   You'd never—?

DR. STOCKMANN.   [*stands.*] Well, suppose I don't give you a dime's worth of my shares. Don't forget that the rich stay rich by hanging onto their money!

HOVSTAD.   Well, don't forget that your manipulation of shares can be reported in more than one way!

DR. STOCKMANN.   And you have just the talent for it! If I don't help the   235
Messenger, you'll put a sinister turn on everything. You'll come howling after me and try to choke me the way a hound chokes a rabbit.

HOVSTAD.   That's nature's way; the strongest animals survive.

ASLAKSEN.   And take the nearest food, too.

DR. STOCKMANN.   [*while searching around.*] Then go find yours in a gutter, damn it, because we're about to see which of the three of us is the strongest animal! [*Finds his umbrella and waves it.*] Here you go!

HOVSTAD.   You can't be violent!

ASLAKSEN.   Be careful with that umbrella!   240

DR. STOCKMANN.   Out the window with you, Mr. Hovstad!

HOVSTAD.   [*at the hallway door.*] You're mad!

DR. STOCKMANN.   Out the window, Mr. Aslaksen! I tell you, jump! Distinguish yourself by being first for once!

ASLAKSEN.   [*dodges him at the desk.*] Moderation, Doctor! I'm not strong! I can't do this! [*Shouts.*] Help! Help!

MRS. STOCKMANN, PETRA, and HORSTER from the living-room.

MRS. STOCKMANN.   For the love of God! Thomas, what's going on here?   245

DR. STOCKMANN.   [*swings the umbrella.*] Jump, I tell you! Into the gutter!

HOVSTAD.   This is an unprovoked attack! I call you as a witness, Captain Horster! [*Rushes out down the hall.*]

ASLAKSEN.   [*in confusion.*] If only I knew the way out— [*Slips out through the living-room door.*]

MRS. STOCKMANN.   [*restrains DR. STOCKMANN.*] Thomas, control yourself!

DR. STOCKMANN.   [*throws down the umbrella.*] Damn, they got away after all!   250

MRS. STOCKMANN.   But what was it they wanted with you?

DR. STOCKMANN.   I'll tell you later; I've got to do something else right now. [*Goes to the desk and writes on a card.*] Katrina, what's written here?

MRS. STOCKMANN. [*Reads.*] "No! No! No!" What does it mean?

DR. STOCKMANN. I'll explain that later, too. [*Holds out the card.*] Petra, tell Soot-face to run this over to the Badger as fast as she can. Hurry! [*PETRA takes the card and leaves through the hallway door.*] Today I've been hounded by all the devils of hell! But now I'll use my pen to stab them! My ink will be venom and gall to poison them! My inkpot will crack their skulls!

MRS. STOCKMANN. Yes, but we're leaving the country, Thomas. 255

PETRA returns.

DR. STOCKMANN. Well?

PETRA. She took it.

DR. STOCKMANN. Great! —Leaving, you say? No, I'll be damned if we leave! We're staying where we are, Katrina.

PETRA. We're staying?

MRS. STOCKMANN. Here, in town? 260

DR. STOCKMANN. Yes, here, absolutely. The battlefield is here; the fight will be here; and I'll win here! But we've got to have a roof over our heads. Once you stitch up my trousers, I'll go out to find another house.

HORSTER. But you can share my house.

DR. STOCKMANN. I can?

HORSTER. Absolutely. I've got plenty of room, and I'm almost never home.

MRS. STOCKMANN. Captain Horster, you're so sweet! 265

PETRA. Thank you!

DR. STOCKMANN. [*shakes his hand.*] Thank you, thank you. Well, with that trouble past I can begin things in earnest. There are hundreds of things to look into, Katrina, and I'll be able to do it almost full-time—I meant to tell you earlier—because I've been sacked at the Spa.

MRS. STOCKMANN. [*sighs.*] I expected that.

DR. STOCKMANN. And they're taking away my practice, too. Well, so what? I still have all the poor people, the ones who can't pay, and, God in Heaven, they're the ones who need me most. Well, damn it, those little tyrants will have to listen to me! I'll preach to them both in season and out of season, as it's written somewhere.°

MRS. STOCKMANN. But dearest Thomas, I think you've seen what comes 270 from preaching.

DR. STOCKMANN. Katrina, don't be absurd! Should I let myself be destroyed by public opinion and the solid majority and all that devilish drivel? No thanks! What I want is plain and clear and simple. I only want to pound it into the skulls of these mongrels that the so-called progressive thinkers are the most treacherous enemies of freedom, that party policies wring the neck of every young and promising truth, that political expediency turns morality and justice upside down, and that the result of all this is what they're making life here a total nightmare. Don't you think, Captain Horster, I can make people understand this?

HORSTER. I'm sure you can. I don't know much about such things.

DR. STOCKMANN. Well, you see; listen. The ones to be exterminated are the party bigwigs. A party leader is like the dominant wolf in a pack. To stay on top, he has to keep cutting down his rivals, or otherwise he's finished. Take Hovstad

in season . . . somewhere: 2 Timothy, 4:2.

and Aslaksen, for example. How many rivals have they sent howling—or in any event clawed and bitten until they can do nothing more than join the Homeowners Association or subscribe to *The People's Messenger*? [*Sits at the edge of the desk.*] Come here, Katrina—. See the lovely sunlight streaming in. And breathe in that wonderfully fresh springtime air!

MRS. STOCKMANN.   If only we could live on sunshine and fresh air, Thomas!

DR. STOCKMANN.   I know, you'll have to pinch pennies for a while, but that's   275
minor; things will be all right. What worries me is that there's no one around with the dedication to *real* freedom of thought to take up my work after me.

PETRA.   Father, don't talk like that. You've lots of time. [*EILIF and MORTEN enter from the living room.*] Well hello, here come the boys already.

MRS. STOCKMANN.   Did you get a holiday?

MORTEN.   No. We had a fight with some other boys at recess.

EILIF.   They were the ones who started it!

MORTEN.   Right, and so Mr. Rørlund sent us home for a couple of days.   280

DR. STOCKMANN.   [*snaps his fingers and jumps off the desk.*] That's it! By God, I've got it! You'll never set foot in school again!

BOTH BOYS.   Yay! No more school!

MRS. STOCKMANN.   But Thomas!

DR. STOCKMANN.   I said never! I'll be your teacher. I mean you'll never learn anything in God's creation—

MORTEN.   Hooray!   285

DR. STOCKMANN.   —if I don't turn you into men of distinction and independent minds. Petra, you'll have to help me with this.

PETRA.   Father, count on me.

DR. STOCKMANN.   And I'll hold classes in the very room where they vilified me as an enemy of the people. But we need more; I'll need at least a dozen children to begin with.

MRS. STOCKMANN.   You won't get that kind in this town.

DR. STOCKMANN.   We can. [*To the boys.*] You must know some street kids—   290
society's real castaways?

MORTEN.   Sure thing, Father, I know loads of 'em!

DR. STOCKMANN.   Fine! Bring a few of them to me. This time I'm going to experiment with the mongrels themselves. There may be some remarkable minds there.

MORTEN.   And what will we do once we grow to be men of distinction and independent minds?

DR. STOCKMANN.   Boys, you'll drive all the wolves back into the wilderness!

EILIF looks skeptical; MORTEN jumps and cheers.

MRS. STOCKMANN.   Let's hope it's not the wolves who drive *you* away, Thomas.   295

DR. STOCKMANN.   Don't be foolish, Katrina! Drive me out? —Now, when I'm the strongest man in town?

MRS. STOCKMANN.   The strongest—now?

DR. STOCKMANN.   Yes, and I'll go so far to say that now I'm one of the strongest men in the whole world!

MORTEN.   Right on!

DR. STOCKMANN.   [*lowers his voice.*] Shh! Don't say anything yet, but I've   300
made another great discovery.

MRS. STOCKMANN.   Another one?

DR. STOCKMANN.   Yes, certainly, certainly. [*Gathers them around him, and speaks fervently.*] My discovery, you, see, is that the strongest person in the world is the one who stands most alone.

MRS. STOCKMANN.   [*smiles and shakes her head.*] Oh, Thomas!

PETRA.   [*confidently takes his hands.*] Father!

QUESTIONS

Act I

1. Why does Ibsen bring in The Mayor before Dr. Stockmann?

2. What character traits does The Mayor show in his conversation with Hovstad, and in his conversation with Dr. Stockmann? In what ways are these traits important for the development of the play?

3. Why does Ibsen include the casual conversation scenes before Petra's first entrance and after Dr. Stockmann leaves for his study? What do we learn about the various characters speaking in these scenes?

4. What is Dr. Stockmann's discovery about the Town Spa? To what degree does he seem to be naive about the possible effects of his discovery?

Act II

5. Describe Morten Kiil. What is his relationship with Dr. Stockmann? What level of scientific knowledge does he possess? What is funny about his promises to give money to the poor?

6. During his discussion with Dr. Stockmann, how does Hovstad escalate the issue of the water pollution? Why are these conversations important later on?

7. Who is Aslaksen? What does he represent? Why is he interesting? What is the effect of his constant references to *moderation* here and throughout the play?

8. Describe the development of the scene between Dr. Stockmann and The Mayor. What are The Mayor's responses to Dr. Stockmann's discovery? How valid is The Mayor's position?

9. Assume that speeches 200 through 225 represent a point when genuinely creative discussion and compromise might occur. In light of the characters of the brothers, why does the situation between them deteriorate, bringing about anger rather than understanding?

Act III

10. How do the opening references to boxing and to military ordnance provide a theme for this act?

11. What attitudes toward Dr. Stockmann are brought out in the conversations of Billing, Hovstad, and Aslaksen? What character traits of these men does Ibsen illustrate here?

12. Why does Petra return the story to Hovstad? What is the meaning of the scene between them?

13. Describe the process by which The Mayor undermines Dr. Stockmann's report about the polluted Spa waters. Why does The Mayor, in addition, attack Dr. Stockmann's character?

14. What is the effect on Dr. Stockmann of the entry of his wife? Characterize the relationship between them which emerges at the end of the act.

15. Explain the increasing tension between Dr. Stockmann and The Mayor in the third act. How does the changing allegiance of Hovstad and Aslaksen contribute to this tension, to the point of becoming a rift?

Act IV

16. Why do you think Horster offers Dr. Stockmann his home for the meeting and, later, offers him the home for living and teaching (and earlier had offered the home to Petra for teaching)?

17. How does The Mayor, with Aslaksen, take over the meeting? How does this action contribute to the play's theme against the popular majority?

18. Outline the development of Dr. Stockmann's speeches against the popular majority. What is the basis of his criticism? How many of the ideas he expresses here seem to be connected with Hovstad's ideas in Act II? How many seem to be new here? Why does Dr. Stockmann include The Mayor personally in his attack?

19. Why are the appearances of Pettersen, the drunk, important in the development of the act? Why are the various crowd responses important?

20. At the act's end, why does Dr. Stockmann quote the New Testament passage in which Jesus instructs his disciples how to behave when they meet opposition within a community?

Act V

21. Describe the effect of the verbal pattern "didn't dare not to" in the course of the act. How is this pattern connected to the play's theme about public opinion and the popular majority?

22. What news does The Mayor bring concerning the last will and testament of Morten Kiil? How does this news precipitate the final break between the two brothers?

23. Describe the attitudes of Hovstad and Aslaksen in this act. To what degree have they changed in the play? To what degree do their speeches in this act represent their hypocrisy?

24. What choice does Morton Kiil offer Dr. Stockmann? How might this choice be taken as the crisis and climax of the play? How does his choice here parallel the development of his attitudes in Act III?

25. Why does the play end on the news of Dr. Stockmann's latest discovery? How does the discovery reflect what has happened to him earlier?

GENERAL QUESTIONS

1. Consider *An Enemy of the People* as a realistic drama. What particularly realistic devices does Ibsen utilize (e.g., time, place, the positions and relationships of scenery and properties, motivation)? How heavily does Ibsen rely upon sudden changes and unforeseen developments in the play? What is the effect of such theatrical changes on the play's essential realism?

2. Trace the development of the theme of the *friend/enemy of the people* in the course of the play. How does the term fit Dr. Stockmann, first as a friend, then as an enemy? How might the term be explained as an ironic description of him? What role is he playing at the play's end?

3. Characterize Dr. Stockmann. Consider things such as his idealism, pride, bravery, individuality, temper, political awareness, degree of cooperativeness, attitude toward his wife, general attitude toward his family, and the attitude of others toward him. How correct are The Mayor's opinions about him?

4. Defend the proposition that Dr. Stockmann's attack against the popular majority is more accurately to be explained as an attack against the *political and hypocritical manipulation* of the popular majority.

5. Explain the opposition in the play of minority versus majority rights. What is the connection between individual rights and Dr. Stockmann's insistence on, first, proclaiming and publishing his own professional discoveries and opinions, and, later, educating young children to have "independent minds"? You might also consider the recurring references to public opinion and Dr. Stockmann's attack against political parties in Act V.

6. Explain the symbolic value of Morton Kiil's tannery at Mølledal. What is the realistic meaning of the tannery? What is the extent of its importance in the play's development? Explain the use and meaning of other symbols in the play.

7. Describe the shortcomings and limitations of Dr. Stockmann's arguments in Act IV. Why do some of his ideas seem incorrect and even naive?

8. What do you find in the play that is comic? If the play is a serious one (and it is), why do you think that Ibsen included such opportunities for humor?

9. Write a character study of any one of the major or minor characters in the play.

EDWARD ALBEE, *THE SANDBOX*

Edward Albee was the leading American playwright of the 1960s. His first play, *The Zoo Story*, was written in 1958, first performed in 1959 in Berlin, and published in 1960. This was followed by *The Sandbox* and *The Death of Bessie Smith* (1960), *The American Dream* (1961), and *Who's Afraid of Virginia Woolf?* (1962), Albee's best-known play. This play still stands as the pinnacle of Albee's career; it had a highly successful run in New York City and was awarded the "Tony" as best play in 1963. It was made into a successful film in 1966, featuring Richard Burton and Elizabeth Taylor (who won the Academy Award for her performance). Albee's work after *Who's Afraid of Virginia Woolf?* has met with mixed reactions. *Tiny Alice* (1964) was viewed as confusing and derivative, but *A Delicate Balance* (1966) and *Seascape* (1975) both won Pulitzer Prizes for drama. Other plays and adaptations have had short lives in the theater; one of Albee's more recent works, *The Lady from Dubuque* (1980), survived only twelve performances on Broadway.

Several of Albee's early plays, including *The Sandbox*, represent the playwright's experimentation with nonrealistic staging and with the Theater of the Absurd, a school of drama that evolved in Europe in the 1940s and 1950s. Absurdist dramatists use their plays to examine the foundations of character and existence, stripping away conventions of behavior and accidents of personality. Like the existentialist philosophy on which the absurdist school is based, most plays of the absurd dramatize the assumption that life is irrational. A quality of many absurdist plays is that language, action, and relationships become theatrical games in which the characters demonstrate consciousness of their own fictional existence.

The Sandbox was written in 1959 and first performed in New York City in 1960. Albee's characters are closer to types or symbols than to individualized women and men. Grandma, the protagonist, is in conflict with her family, society, and death; only the last of these conflicts is resolved at the conclusion. Mommy and Daddy represent Albee's vision of the American family reduced to a skeletal form. He employs all the elements of drama to build meaning and impact into *The Sandbox*; plot, character, setting, and symbol all convey the judgment that modern lives and values have become drab and meaningless. In addition, Albee has provided his characters with speeches filled with repetition, parallel speech patterns, idioms, connotative words, and clichés, so that they illustrate in their very own words and expressions the bleak lives they are living.

EDWARD ALBEE   (b. 1928)

The Sandbox   *1960 (1959)*

THE PLAYERS

> The Young Man, 25, *a good-looking, well-built boy in a bathing suit*
> Mommy, 55, *a well-dressed, imposing woman*
> Daddy, 60, *a small man; gray, thin*
> Grandma, 86, *a tiny, wizened woman with bright eyes*
> The Musician, *no particular age, but young would be nice*

Note: When, in the course of the play, MOMMY and DADDY call each other by these names, there should be no suggestion of regionalism. These names are of empty affection and point up the pre-senility and vacuity of their characters.

> *The Scene: A bare stage, with only the following: Near the footlights, far stage-right,*

two simple chairs set side by side, facing the audience; near the footlights, far stage-left, a chair facing stage-right with a music stand before it; farther back, and stage-center, slightly elevated and raked, a large child's sandbox with a toy pail and shovel; the background is the sky, which alters from brightest day to deepest night.

At the beginning, it is brightest day; the YOUNG MAN *is alone on stage, to the rear of the sandbox, and to one side. He is doing calisthenics; he does calisthenics until quite at the very end of the play. These calisthenics, employing the arms only, should suggest the beating and fluttering of wings. The* YOUNG MAN *is, after all, the Angel of Death.*

MOMMY *and* DADDY *enter from stage-left,* MOMMY *first.*

MOMMY.   [*Motioning to Daddy*] Well, here we are; this is the beach.

DADDY.   [*Whining*] I'm cold.

MOMMY.   [*Dismissing him with a little laugh*] Don't be silly; it's as warm as toast. Look at that nice young man over there: *he* doesn't think it's cold. [*Waves to the* YOUNG MAN] Hello.

YOUNG MAN.   [*With an endearing smile*] Hi!

MOMMY.   [*Looking about*] This will do perfectly ... don't you think so,   5
Daddy? There's sand there . . . and the water beyond. What do you think, Daddy?

DADDY.   [*Vaguely*] Whatever you say, Mommy.

MOMMY.   [*With the same little laugh*] Well, of course . . . whatever I say. Then, it's settled, is it?

DADDY.   [*Shrugs*] She's *your* mother, not mine.

MOMMY.   *I* know she's my mother. What do you take me for? [*A pause*] All right, now; let's get on with it. [*She shouts into the wings, stage-left.*] You! Out there! You can come in now.

[*The* MUSICIAN *enters, seats himself in the chair, stage-left, places music on the music stand, is ready to play.* MOMMY *nods approvingly.*]

MOMMY.   Very nice; very nice. Are you ready, Daddy? Let's go get Grandma.   10

DADDY.   Whatever you say, Mommy.

MOMMY.   [*Leading the way out, stage-left*] Of course, whatever I say. [*To the* MUSICIAN] You can begin now. [*The* MUSICIAN *begins playing;* MOMMY *and* DADDY *exit; the* MUSICIAN, *all the while playing, nods to the* YOUNG MAN.]

YOUNG MAN.   [*With the same endearing smile*] Hi!

[*After a moment,* MOMMY *and* DADDY *re-enter, carrying* GRANDMA. *She is borne in by their hands under her armpits; she is quite rigid; her legs are drawn up; her feet do not touch the ground; the expression on her ancient face is that of puzzlement and fear.*]

DADDY.   Where do we put her?

MOMMY.   [*The same little laugh*] Wherever I say, of course. Let me see . . .   15
well . . . all right, over there . . . in the sandbox. [*Pause*] Well, what are you waiting for, Daddy? . . . The sandbox!

[*Together they carry* GRANDMA *over to the sandbox and more or less dump her in.*]

GRANDMA.   [*Righting herself to a sitting position; her voice a cross between a baby's laugh and cry*] Ahhhhhh! Graaaaa!

DADDY.   [*Dusting himself*] What do we do now?

MOMMY.   [*To the* MUSICIAN] You can stop now.

[*The* MUSICIAN *stops.*]

[*Back to* DADDY] What do you mean, what do we do now? We go over there and sit down, of course. [*To the* YOUNG MAN] Hello there.

YOUNG MAN.   [*Again smiling*] Hi!

[MOMMY *and* DADDY *move to the chairs, stage-right, and sit down. A pause*]

GRANDMA.   [*Same as before*] Ahhhhhh! Ah-haaaaaa! Graaaaaa!   20

DADDY.   Do you think . . . do you think she's . . . comfortable?

MOMMY.   [*Impatiently*] How would I know?

DADDY.   [*Pause*] What do we do now?

MOMMY.   [*As if remembering*] We . . . wait. We . . . sit here . . . and we wait . . . that's what we do.

DADDY.   [*After a pause*] Shall we talk to each other?   25

MOMMY.   [*With that little laugh; picking something off her dress*] Well, *you* can talk, if you want to . . . if you can think of anything to *say* . . . if you can think of anything *new*.

DADDY.   [*Thinks*] No . . . I suppose not.

MOMMY.   [*With a triumphant laugh*] Of course not!

GRANDMA.   [*Banging the toy shovel against the pail*] Haaaaaa! Ah-haaaaaa!

MOMMY.   [*Out over the audience*] Be quiet, Grandma . . . just be quiet, and   30
wait.

[GRANDMA *throws a shovelful of sand at* MOMMY.]

MOMMY.   [*Still out over the audience*] She's throwing sand at me! You stop that, Grandma; you stop throwing sand at Mommy! [*To* DADDY] She's throwing sand at me.

[DADDY *looks around at* GRANDMA, *who screams at him.*]

GRANDMA.   GRAAAAA!

MOMMY.   Don't look at her. Just . . . sit here . . . be very still . . . and wait. [*To the* MUSICIAN] You . . . uh . . . you go ahead and do whatever it is you do.

[*The* MUSICIAN *plays.*]
[MOMMY *and* DADDY *are fixed, staring out beyond the audience.* GRANDMA *looks at them, looks at the* MUSICIAN, *looks at the sandbox, throws down the shovel.*]

GRANDMA.   Ah-haaaaaa! Graaaaaa! [*Looks for reaction; gets none. Now . . . directly to the audience*] Honestly! What a way to treat an old woman! Drag her out of the house . . . stick her in a car . . . bring her out here from the city . . . dump her in a pile of sand . . . and leave her here to set. I'm eighty-six years old! I was married when I was seventeen. To a farmer. He died when I was thirty. [*To the* MUSICIAN] Will you stop that, please?

[*The* MUSICIAN *stops playing.*]

I'm a feeble old woman . . . how do you expect anybody to hear me over that peep! peep! peep! [*To herself*] There's no respect around here. [*To the* YOUNG MAN] There's no respect around here!

YOUNG MAN.   [*Same smile*] Hi!   35

GRANDMA.   [*After a pause, a mild double-take, continues, to the audience*] My husband died when I was thirty [*indicates* MOMMY], and I had to raise that big cow over there all by my lonesome. You can imagine what *that* was like. Lordy! [*To the* YOUNG MAN] Where'd they get *you*?

YOUNG MAN.   Oh . . . I've been around for a while.

GRANDMA.   I'll bet you have! Heh, heh, heh. Will you look at you!

YOUNG MAN.   [*Flexing his muscles*] Isn't that something? [*Continues his calisthenics*]

GRANDMA.   Boy, oh boy; I'll say. Pretty good.   40

YOUNG MAN.   [*Sweetly*] I'll say.

GRANDMA.   Where ya from?

YOUNG MAN.   Southern California.

GRANDMA.   [*Nodding*] Figgers; figgers. What's your name, honey?

YOUNG MAN.   I don't know. . . .   45

GRANDMA.   [*To the audience*] Bright, too!

YOUNG MAN.   I mean . . . I mean, they haven't given me one yet . . . the studio . . .

GRANDMA.   [*Giving him the once-over*] You don't say . . . you don't say. Well . . . uh, I've got to talk some more . . . don't you go 'way.

YOUNG MAN.   Oh, no.

GRANDMA.   [*Turning her attention back to the audience*] Fine; fine. [*Then, once*   50 *more, back to the* YOUNG MAN] You're . . . you're an actor, hunh?

YOUNG MAN.   [*Beaming*] Yes. I am.

GRANDMA.   [*To the audience again; shrugs*] I'm smart that way. Anyhow, I had to raise . . . *that* over there all by my lonesome; and what's next to her there . . . that's what she married. Rich? I tell you . . . money, money, money. They took me off the *farm* . . . which was real decent of them . . . and they moved me into the big town house with *them* . . . fixed a nice place for me under the stove . . . gave me an army blanket . . . and my own dish . . . my very own dish! So, what have I got to complain about? Nothing, of course. I'm not complaining. [*She looks up at the sky, shouts to someone off-stage.*] Shouldn't it be getting dark now, dear?

[*The lights dim; night comes on. The* MUSICIAN *begins to play, it becomes deepest night. There are spots on all the players, including the* YOUNG MAN, *who is, of course, continuing his calisthenics.*]

DADDY.   [*Stirring*] It's nighttime.

MOMMY.   Shhhh. Be still . . . wait.

DADDY.   [*Whining*] It's so hot.   55

MOMMY.   Shhhhhh. Be still . . . wait.

GRANDMA.   [*To herself*] That's better. Night. [*To the* MUSICIAN] Honey, do you play all through this part?

[*The* MUSICIAN *nods.*]

Well, keep it nice and soft; that's a good boy.

[*The* MUSICIAN *nods again; plays softly.*]

That's nice.

[*There is an off-stage rumble.*]

DADDY.   [*Starting*] What was that?

MOMMY.   [*Beginning to weep*] It was nothing.

DADDY.   It was ... it was ... thunder ... or a wave breaking ... or   60
something.

MOMMY.   [*Whispering, through her tears*] It was an off-stage rumble ... and
you know what *that* means. ...

DADDY.   I forget. ...

MOMMY.   [*Barely able to talk*] It means the time has come for poor Grandma
... and I can't bear it!

DADDY.   [*Vacantly*] I ... I suppose you've got to be brave.

GRANDMA.   [*Mocking*] That's right, kid; be brave. You'll bear up; you'll get   65
over it.

[*Another off-stage rumble ... louder*]

MOMMY.   Ohhhhhhhhhh ... poor Grandma ... poor Grandma. ...

GRANDMA.   [*To MOMMY*] I'm fine! I'm all right! It hasn't happened yet!

[*A violent off-stage rumble. All the lights go out, save the spot on the YOUNG MAN; the
MUSICIAN stops playing.*]

MOMMY.   Ohhhhhhhhhh ... Ohhhhhhhhhh. ...

[*Silence*]

GRANDMA.   Don't put the lights up yet ... I'm not ready; I'm not quite
ready. [*Silence*] All right, dear ... I'm about done.

[*The lights come up again, to brightest day; the MUSICIAN begins to play. GRANDMA is discovered, still in the sandbox, lying on her side, propped up on an elbow, half covered, busily
shoveling sand over herself.*]

GRANDMA.   [*Muttering*] I don't know how I'm supposed to do anything with   70
this goddam toy shovel. ...

DADDY.   Mommy! It's daylight!

MOMMY.   [*Brightly*] So it is! Well! Our long night is over. We must put away
our tears, take off our mourning ... and face the future. It's our duty.

GRANDMA.   [*Still shoveling; mimicking*] ... take off our mourning ... face the
future. ... Lordy!

[*MOMMY and DADDY rise, stretch. MOMMY waves to the YOUNG MAN.*]

YOUNG MAN.   [*With that smile*] Hi!

[*GRANDMA plays dead. (!) MOMMY and DADDY go over to look at her; she is a little more than
half buried in the sand; the toy shovel is in her hands, which are crossed on her breast.*]

MOMMY.   [*Before the sandbox; shaking her head*] Lovely! It's ... it's hard to be   75
sad ... she looks ... so happy. [*With pride and conviction*] It pays to do things well.
[*To the MUSICIAN*] All right, you can stop now, if you want to. I mean, stay around
for a swim, or something; it's all right with us. [*She sighs heavily.*] Well Daddy ...
off we go.

DADDY.   Brave Mommy!

MOMMY.   Brave Daddy!

[*They exit, stage-left.*]

GRANDMA.   [*After they leave; lying quite still*] It pays to do things well. . . . Boy, oh boy! [*She tries to sit up*] . . . well, kids . . . [*but she finds she can't.*] . . . I . . . I can't get up. I . . . I can't move. . . .

[*The* YOUNG MAN *stops his calisthenics, nods to the* MUSICIAN, *walks over to* GRANDMA, *kneels down by the sandbox.*]

GRANDMA.   I . . . can't move. . . .
YOUNG MAN.   Shhhhh . . . be very still. . . .   80
GRANDMA.   I . . . I can't move. . . .
YOUNG MAN.   Uh . . . ma'am; I . . . I have a line here.
GRANDMA.   Oh, I'm sorry, sweetie; you go right ahead.
YOUNG MAN.   I am . . . uh . . .
GRANDMA.   Take your time, dear.   85
YOUNG MAN.   [*Prepares; delivers the line like a real amateur.*] I am the Angel of Death. I am . . . uh . . . I am come for you.
GRANDMA.   What . . . wha . . . [*Then, with resignation*] . . . ohhh . . . ohhhh, I see.

[*The* YOUNG MAN *bends over, kisses* GRANDMA *gently on the forehead.*]

GRANDMA.   [*Her eyes closed, her hands folded on her breast again, the shovel between her hands, a sweet smile on her face*] Well . . . that was very nice, dear. . . .
YOUNG MAN.   [*Still kneeling*] Shhhhhh . . . be still. . . .
GRANDMA.   What I meant was . . . you did that very well, dear. . . .   90
YOUNG MAN.   [*Blushing*] . . . oh . . .
GRANDMA.   No; I mean it. You've got that . . . you've got a quality.
YOUNG MAN.   [*With his endearing smile*] Oh . . . thank you; thank you very much . . . ma'am.
GRANDMA.   [*Slowly; softly—as the* YOUNG MAN *puts his hands on top of* GRANDMA'S] You're . . . you're welcome . . . dear.

[*Tableau. The* MUSICIAN *continues to play as the curtain slowly comes down.*]

[*Curtain*]

QUESTIONS

1. Why does Mommy say, "This is the beach"? What are the characters waiting for there?

2. Why does Albee indicate that Daddy is *whining*? What is the effect of Daddy's repetition of "Whatever you say, Mommy"?

3. How does Grandma "speak" to Mommy and Daddy? How does she speak to the audience and the Young Man? How do you account for this difference?

4. Albee identifies the Young Man as the Angel of Death; what else does he symbolize or represent? What is Grandma's attitude toward him? How does he treat her?

5. What does the "off-stage rumble" signify?

6. How do Mommy and Daddy react to Grandma's "death"? How would you characterize their language?

7. How does Grandma react to the comments of Mommy and Daddy about her death? What does Grandma reveal about the way Mommy and Daddy deal with death?

GENERAL QUESTIONS

1. How does the setting, described at the beginning of the play, illustrate the level of realism/nonrealism? What props are realistic? Symbolic? What is the realistic/nonrealistic effect of speeches such as Mommy's telling the Musician "You can come in now," Grandma's cueing of the lighting technician, and Mommy's reference to an "off-stage rumble"?

2. Are the characters in this play round or flat? Why don't they have names? What does each symbolize?

3. *The Sandbox* is full of repetition; characters repeat words and even whole lines two or three times. What is the effect of this repetition on your understanding of character, meaning, and level of reality?

4. How does Albee employ diction, speech patterns, connotative words, clichés, and tone to shape character and meaning?

5. How many different generations are presented in *The Sandbox*? Which characters represent each generation? To what extent do the different generations illustrate different phases of American history?

TENNESSEE WILLIAMS, *THE GLASS MENAGERIE*

Many of Tennessee Williams's plays reflect the attitudes and customs that he encountered as he was growing up in Mississippi and Missouri. Until he was eight, his family lived in genteel poverty, mostly in Columbus, Mississippi. In 1919 the family moved to a lower-class neighborhood in St. Louis. Williams, who was sickly and bookish, tried to escape from poverty and family conflicts by writing and going to the movies. One of his few companions during those years was his shy and withdrawn sister, Rose.

Williams began college at the University of Missouri in 1931, but the Depression and family poverty forced him to drop out and go to work in a shoe warehouse. After two years of this, he suffered a nervous collapse, but finally finished college at the University of Iowa. He then began wandering the country, doing odd jobs, but also writing. His first full-length play, *Battle of Angels*, was produced in 1940 but was unsuccessful. He continued to write, however, and was able to get *The Glass Menagerie* staged in 1945. The critical and popular success of this play was the beginning of many good years in the theater. Along with Arthur Miller, during the 1940s and 1950s he dominated the American stage, going on to write many one-act plays and over fifteen full-length dramas (many of which became successful films), including *A Streetcar Named Desire* (1947),

The Rose Tattoo (1951), *Cat on a Hot Tin Roof* (1955), *Suddenly Last Summer* (1958), and *The Night of the Iguana* (1961).

The Glass Menagerie, written in 1944 and produced to rave reviews in Chicago and New York in 1945, is a highly autobiographical play which explores the family dynamics, delusions, and personalities of the Wingfields. Williams originally developed his ideas for the play in a short story called "Portrait of a Girl in Glass" and then in a screenplay for Metro-Goldwyn-Mayer entitled "The Gentleman Caller." In these, and in *The Glass Menagerie*, Laura Wingfield is modeled after his sister, Rose Williams. The least competent member of the family, she is crippled by her own insecurity and her mother's expectations. At every opportunity, Laura withdraws into a world of glass figurines and old phonograph records left by her father when he abandoned the family. Amanda Wingfield is patterned after Williams's mother; she valiantly tries to hold the family together and provide for Laura's future, but her perspectives are skewed by her romanticized memories of a gracious southern past of plantations, formal dances, and "gentleman callers." Tom, a figure based on the playwright himself, is desperate to escape the trap of his impoverished family. He seeks to emulate the long-missing father and move out of the drab Wingfield apartment into adventure and experience.

The play offers a fascinating mixture of realistic and nonrealistic dramatic techniques. The characters (excluding Tom when he narrates) and the language are realistic. This is especially true of Amanda's language, in which Williams skillfully recreates the diction and cadences characteristic of speakers from Mississippi. As he points out in his production notes and stage directions, the play's structure and staging are nonrealistic. Williams employs various devices nonrealistically, including the narrator, music, lighting, and screen projections, to underscore the emotions of his characters and to explore ideas about family and personality.

One of Williams's most effective nonrealistic techniques in *The Glass Menagerie* is its structure as "a memory play," and therefore its illustration of how a first-person narrator may be used in a drama. The characters and the action are neither real nor in the present. Rather, they represent Tom's memories and feelings about events that occurred approximately five years earlier, when America was in the grips of the Great Depression, when the Spanish Civil War had established fascism in Spain, and when World War II was beginning in Europe. As the narrator, Tom exists at the time of the action (1944), but the events he introduces are occurring in about 1939. When Tom becomes a character in the Wingfield household, he is the Tom of this earlier period, quite distinct from his identity as the present narrator. Thus, the action in the apartment is not strictly a realistic recreation of life. Instead, even though the actions and characters seem realistic, they are exaggerated and reshaped as Tom remembers them and regrets them.

TENNESSEE WILLIAMS   (1911–1983)

The Glass Menagerie   *1945*

THE CHARACTERS

Amanda Wingfield (*the mother*)
A little woman of great but confused vitality clinging frantically to another time and place. Her characterization must be carefully created, not copied from type. She is not paranoiac, but her life is paranoia. There is much to admire in Amanda, and as much to love and pity as there is to laugh at. Certainly she has endurance and a kind of heroism, and though her foolishness makes her unwittingly cruel at times, there is tenderness in her slight person.

Laura Wingfield (*her daughter*)
Amanda, having failed to establish contact with reality, continues to live vitally in her illusions, but Laura's situation is even graver. A childhood illness has left her crippled, one leg slightly shorter than the other, and held in a brace. This defect need not be more than suggested on the stage. Stemming from this, Laura's separation increases till she is like a piece of her own glass collection, too exquisitely fragile to move from the shelf.

Tom Wingfield (*her son*)
And the narrator of the play. A poet with a job in a warehouse. His nature is not remorseless, but to escape from a trap he has to act without pity.

Jim O'Connor (*the gentleman caller*)
A nice, ordinary, young man.

PRODUCTION NOTES

Being a "memory play," *The Glass Menagerie* can be presented with unusual freedom of convention. Because of its considerably delicate or tenuous material, atmospheric touches and subtleties of direction play a particularly important part. Expressionism and all other unconventional techniques in drama have only one valid aim, and that is a closer approach to truth. When a play employs unconventional techniques, it is not, or certainly shouldn't be, trying to escape its responsibility of dealing with reality, or interpreting experience, but is actually or should be attempting to find a closer approach, a more penetrating and vivid expression of things as they are. The straight realistic play with its genuine Frigidaire and authentic ice-cubes, its characters who speak exactly as its audience speaks, corresponds to the academic landscape and has the same virtue of a photographic likeness. Everyone should know nowadays the unimportance of the photographic in art: that truth, life, or reality is an organic thing which the poetic imagination can represent or suggest, in essence, only through transformation, through changing into other forms than those which were merely present in appearance.

These remarks are not meant as a preface only to this particular play. They have to do with a conception of a new, plastic theatre which must take the place of the exhausted theatre of realistic conventions if the theatre is to resume vitality as a part of our culture.

THE SCREEN DEVICE: There is *only one important difference between the original and the acting version of the play* and that is the *omission* in the latter of the device that I tentatively included in my *original* script. This device was the use of a screen on which were projected magic-lantern slides bearing images or titles. I do not regret the omission of this device from the original Broadway production. The extraordinary power of Miss Taylor's° performance made it suitable to have the utmost simplicity in the physical production. But I think it may be interesting to some readers to see how this device was conceived. So I am putting it into the published manuscript. These images and legends, projected from behind, were cast on a section of wall between the front-room and dining-room areas, which should be indistinguishable from the rest when not in use.

The purpose of this will probably be apparent. It is to give accent to certain values in each scene. Each scene contains a particular point (or several) which is structurally the most important. In an episodic play, such as this, the basic structure or narrative line may be obscured from the audience; the effect may seem fragmentary rather than architectural. This may not be the fault of the play so much as a lack of attention in the audience. The legend or image upon the screen will strengthen the effect of what is merely allusion in the writing and allow the primary point to be made more simply and lightly than if the entire responsibility were on the spoken lines. Aside from this structural value, I think the screen will have a definite emotional appeal, less definable but just as important. An imaginative producer or director may invent many other uses for this device than those indicated in the present script. In fact the possibilities of the device seem much larger to me than the instance of this play can possibly utilize.

THE MUSIC: Another extra-literary accent in this play is provided by the use of music. A single recurring tune, "The Glass Menagerie,"° is used to give emotional emphasis to suitable passages. This tune is like circus music, not when you are on the grounds or in the immediate vicinity of the parade, but when you are at some distance and very likely thinking of something else. It seems under those circumstances to continue almost interminably and it weaves in and out of your preoccupied consciousness; then it is the lightest, most delicate music in the world and perhaps the saddest. It expresses the surface vivacity of life with the underlying strain of immutable and inexpressible sorrow. When you look at a piece of delicately spun glass you think of two things: how beautiful it is and how easily it can be broken. Both of those ideas should be woven into the recurring tune, which dips in and out of the play as if it were carried on a wind that changes. It serves as a thread of connection and allusion between the narrator with his separate point in time and space and the subject of his story. Between each episode it returns as reference to the emotion, nostalgia, which is the first condition of the play. It is primarily Laura's music and therefore comes out most clearly when the play focuses upon her and the lovely fragility of glass which is her image.

THE LIGHTING: The lighting in the play is not realistic. In keeping with the atmosphere of memory, the stage is dim. Shafts of light are focused on selected areas or actors, sometimes in contradistinction to what is the apparent center. For instance, in the quarrel scene between Tom and Amanda, in which Laura has no active part, the clearest pool of light is on her figure. This is also true of the supper scene, when her silent figure on the sofa should remain the visual center.

Miss Taylor's: The role of Amanda was first played by the American actress Laurette Taylor (1884–1946).   *"The Glass Menagerie":* Original music, including this recurrent theme, was composed for the play by Paul Bowles.

The light upon Laura should be distinct from the others, having a peculiar pristine clarity such as light used in early religious portraits of female saints or madonnas. A certain correspondence to light in religious paintings, such as El Greco's,° where the figures are radiant in atmosphere that is relatively dusky, could be effectively used throughout the play. (It will also permit a more effective use of the screen.) A free, imaginative use of light can be of enormous value in giving a mobile, plastic quality to plays of a more or less static nature.

Tennessee Williams

Scene 1

The Wingfield apartment is in the rear of the building, one of those vast hive-like conglomerations of cellular living-units that flower as warty growths in overcrowded urban centers of lower middle-class population and are symptomatic of the impulse of this largest and fundamentally enslaved section of American society to avoid fluidity and differentiation and to exist and function as one interfused mass of automatism.

The apartment faces an alley and is entered by a fire escape, a structure whose name is a touch of accidental poetic truth, for all of these huge buildings are always burning with the slow and implacable fires of human desperation. The fire escape is part of what we see— that is, the landing of it and steps descending from it.

The scene is memory and is therefore nonrealistic. Memory takes a lot of poetic license. It omits some details; others are exaggerated, according to the emotional value of the articles it touches, for memory is seated predominantly in the heart. The interior is therefore rather dim and poetic.

At the rise of the curtain, the audience is faced with the dark, grim rear wall of the Wingfield tenement. This building is flanked on both sides by dark, narrow alleys which run into murky canyons of tangled clotheslines, garbage cans, and the sinister latticework of neighboring fire escapes. It is up and down these side alleys that exterior entrances and exits are made during the play. At the end of Tom's *opening commentary, the dark tenement wall slowly becomes transparent° and reveals the interior of the ground-floor Wingfield apartment.*

Nearest the audience is the living room, which also serves as a sleeping room for Laura, *the sofa unfolding to make her bed. Just beyond, separated from the living room by a wide arch or second proscenium with transparent faded portieres° (or second curtain), is the dining room. In an old-fashioned whatnot° in the living room are seen scores of transparent glass animals. A blown-up photograph of the father hangs on the wall of the living room, to the left of the archway. It is the face of a very handsome young man in a doughboy's° First World War cap. He is gallantly smiling, ineluctably smiling, as if to say "I will be smiling forever."*

Also hanging on the wall, near the photograph, are a typewriter keyboard chart and a Gregg shorthand diagram. An upright typewriter on a small table stands beneath the charts.

The audience hears and sees the opening scene in the dining room through both the transparent fourth wall of the building and the transparent gauze portieres of the dining-room arch. It is during this revealing scene that the fourth wall slowly ascends, out of sight.

El Greco: Greek painter (ca. 1548–1614) who lived in Spain; typical paintings have elongated and distorted figures and extremely vivid foreground lighting set against a murky background.   *transparent:* The wall is painted on a scrim, a transparent curtain that is opaque when lit from the front and transparent when lit from behind.   *portieres:* curtains hung in a doorway; in production, these may also be painted on a scrim. *whatnot:* a small set of shelves for ornaments.   *doughboy:* popular name for an American infantryman during World War I.

This transparent exterior wall is not brought down again until the very end of the play, during Tom's *final speech.*

The narrator is an undisguised convention of the play. He takes whatever license with dramatic convention is convenient to his purposes.

Tom *enters, dressed as a merchant sailor, and strolls across to the fire escape. There he stops and lights a cigarette. He addresses the audience.*

Tom.   Yes, I have tricks in my pocket, I have things up my sleeve. But I am the opposite of a stage magician. He gives you illusion that has the appearance of truth. I give you truth in the pleasant disguise of illusion.

To begin with, I turn back time. I reverse it to that quaint period, the thirties, when the huge middle class of America was matriculating in a school for the blind. Their eyes had failed them, or they had failed their eyes, and so they were having their fingers pressed forcibly down on the fiery Braille alphabet of a dissolving economy.

In Spain there was revolution. Here there was only shouting and confusion. In Spain there was Guernica.° Here there were disturbances of labor, sometimes pretty violent, in otherwise peaceful cities such as Chicago, Cleveland, Saint Louis . . . This is the social background of the play.

[*Music begins to play.*]

The play is memory. Being a memory play, it is dimly lighted, it is sentimental, it is not realistic. In memory everything seems to happen to music. That explains the fiddle in the wings.

I am the narrator of the play, and also a character in it. The other characters are my mother, Amanda, my sister, Laura, and a gentleman caller who appears in the final scenes. He is the most realistic character in the play, being an emissary from a world of reality that we were somehow set apart from. But since I have a poet's weakness for symbols, I am using this character also as a symbol; he is the long-delayed but always expected something that we live for.

There is a fifth character in the play who doesn't appear except in this larger-than-life-size photograph over the mantel. This is our father who left us a long time ago. He was a telephone man who fell in love with long distances; he gave up his job with the telephone company and skipped the light fantastic out of town . . .

The last we heard of him was a picture postcard from Mazatlan, on the Pacific coast of Mexico, containing a message of two words: "Hello—Goodbye!" and no address.

I think the rest of the play will explain itself. . . .

[Amanda's *voice becomes audible through the portieres.*]

[*Legend on screen:* "Où sont les neiges."°]

Tom *divides the portieres and enters the dining room.* Amanda *and* Laura *are seated at a drop-leaf table. Eating is indicated by gestures without food or utensils.* Amanda *faces the*

Guernica: a Basque town that was destroyed in 1937 by German planes fighting on General Franco's side during the Spanish Civil War. The huge mural *Guernica,* painted by Pablo Picasso, depicts the horror of that bombardment (see p. 367).   *"Où sont les neiges":* "Where are the snows (of yesteryear)," refrain from "The Ballade of Dead Ladies" by the French poet François Villon (ca. 1431–1463).

audience. TOM *and* LAURA *are seated profile. The interior has lit up softly and through the scrim we see* AMANDA *and* LAURA *seated at the table.*]

AMANDA.   [*calling*] Tom?
TOM.   Yes, Mother.
AMANDA.   We can't say grace until you come to the table!
TOM.   Coming, Mother. [*He bows slightly and withdraws, reappearing a few mo-*   5
ments later in his place at the table.]
AMANDA.   [*to her son*] Honey, don't *push* with your *fingers.* If you have to push with something, the thing to push with is a crust of bread. And chew—chew! Animals have secretions in their stomachs which enable them to digest food without mastication, but human beings are supposed to chew their food before they swallow it down. Eat food leisurely, son, and really enjoy it. A well-cooked meal has lots of delicate flavors that have to be held in the mouth for appreciation. So chew your food and give your salivary glands a chance to function!

[TOM *deliberately lays his imaginary fork down and pushes his chair back from the table.*]

TOM.   I haven't enjoyed one bite of this dinner because of your constant directions on how to eat it. It's you that make me rush through meals with your hawklike attention to every bite I take. Sickening—spoils my appetite—all this discussion of—animals' secretion—salivary glands—mastication!
AMANDA.   [*lightly*] Temperament like a Metropolitan star.°

[TOM *rises and walks toward the living room.*]

You're not excused from the table.
TOM.   I'm getting a cigarette.
AMANDA.   You smoke too much.   10

[LAURA *rises.*]

LAURA.   I'll bring in the blanc mange.°

[TOM *remains standing with his cigarette by the portieres.*]

AMANDA.   [*rising*] No, sister, no, sister°—you be the lady this time and I'll be the darky.
LAURA.   I'm already up.
AMANDA.   Resume your seat, little sister—I want you to stay fresh and pretty—for gentlemen callers!
LAURA.   [*sitting down*] I'm not expecting any gentlemen callers.   15
AMANDA.   [*crossing out to the kitchenette, airily*] Sometimes they come when they are least expected! Why, I remember one Sunday afternoon in Blue Mountain°—

---

8 *Metropolitan star:* the Metropolitan Opera in New York City; opera stars are traditionally considered to be highly temperamental.   11 *blanc mange:* a bland molded pudding or custard.   12 *sister:* In the South of Amanda's youth, the oldest daughter in a family was frequently called "sister" by her parents and siblings.   16 *Blue Mountain:* an imaginary town in northwest Mississippi modeled after Clarksville, where Williams spent much of his youth. Blue Mountain (Clarksville) is at the northern edge of the Mississippi Delta, a large fertile plain that supports numerous plantations. This is the recollected world of Amanda's youth—plantations, wealth, black servants, and gentlemen callers who were the sons of cotton planters.

[*She enters the kitchenette.*]

TOM. I know what's coming!
LAURA. Yes. But let her tell it.
TOM. Again?
LAURA. She loves to tell it.   20

[*AMANDA returns with a bowl of dessert.*]

AMANDA. One Sunday afternoon in Blue Mountain—your mother re-
ceived—*seventeen!*—gentlemen callers! Why, sometimes there weren't chairs
enough to accommodate them all. We had to send the nigger over to bring in
folding chairs from the parish house.
TOM. [*remaining at the portieres*] How did you entertain those gentlemen
callers?
AMANDA. I understood the art of conversation!
TOM. I bet you could talk.
AMANDA. Girls in those days *knew* how to talk, I can tell you.   25
TOM. Yes?

[*Image on screen: AMANDA as a girl on a porch, greeting callers.*]

AMANDA. They knew how to entertain their gentlemen callers. It wasn't
enough for a girl to be possessed of a pretty face and a graceful figure—although
I wasn't slighted in either respect. She also needed to have a nimble wit and a
tongue to meet all occasions.
TOM. What did you talk about?
AMANDA. Things of importance going on in the world! Never anything
coarse or common or vulgar.

[*She addresses TOM as though he were seated in the vacant chair at the table though he remains
by the portieres. He plays this scene as though reading from a script.°*]

My callers were gentleman—all! Among my callers were some of the most
prominent young planters of the Mississippi Delta—planters and sons of planters!

[*TOM motions for music and a spot of light on AMANDA. Her eyes lift, her face glows, her
voice becomes rich and elegiac.*

[*Screen legend:* "Où sont les neiges d'antan?"°]

There was young Champ Laughlin who later became vice-president of the
Delta Planters Bank. Hadley Stevenson who was drowned in Moon Lake and left
his widow one hundred and fifty thousand in Government bonds. There were the
Cutrere brothers, Wesley and Bates. Bates was one of my bright particular beaux!
He got in a quarrel with that wild Wainwright boy. They shot it out on the floor
of Moon Lake Casino. Bates was shot through the stomach. Died in the ambulance
on his way to Memphis. His widow was also well provided-for, came into eight or
ten thousand acres, that's all. She married him on the rebound—never loved
her—carried my picture on him the night he died! And there was that boy that

---

29.1 *script:* Here Tom becomes both a character in the play and the stage manager.
29.2 *"Où sont les neiges d'antan?":* Where are the snows of yesteryear? See p. 1477.

every girl in the Delta had set her cap for! That beautiful, brilliant young Fitzhugh boy from Greene County!

TOM.   What did he leave his widow?   30

AMANDA.   He never married! Gracious, you talk as though all of my old admirers had turned up their toes to the daisies!

TOM.   Isn't this the first you've mentioned that still survives?

AMANDA.   That Fitzhugh boy went North and made a fortune—came to be known as the Wolf of Wall Street! He had the Midas touch,° whatever he touched turned to gold! And I could have been Mrs. Duncan J. Fitzhugh, mind you! But— I picked your *father*!

LAURA.   [*rising*] Mother, let me clear the table.

AMANDA.   No, dear, you go in front and study your typewriter chart. Or   35
practice your shorthand a little. Stay fresh and pretty!—It's almost time for our gentlemen callers to start arriving. [*She flounces girlishly toward the kitchenette.*] How many do you suppose we're going to entertain this afternoon?

[TOM *throws down the paper and jumps up with a groan.*]

LAURA.   [*alone in the dining room*] I don't believe we're going to receive any, Mother.

AMANDA.   [*reappearing airily*] What? No one?—not one? You must be joking!

[LAURA *nervously echoes her laugh. She slips in a fugitive manner through the half-open portieres and draws them gently behind her. A shaft of very clear light is thrown on her face against the faded tapestry of the curtains. Faintly the music of "The Glass Menagerie" is heard as she continues lightly:*]

Not one gentleman caller? It can't be true! There must be a flood, there must have been a tornado!

LAURA.   It isn't a flood, it's not a tornado, Mother. I'm just not popular like you were in Blue Mountain. . . .

[TOM *utters another groan.* LAURA *glances at him with a faint, apologetic smile. Her voice catches a little:*]

Mother's afraid I'm going to be an old maid.

[*The scene dims out with the "Glass Menagerie" music.*]

Scene 2

On the dark stage the screen is lighted with the image of blue roses. Gradually LAURA'S figure becomes apparent and the screen goes out. The music subsides.

LAURA *is seated in the delicate ivory chair at the small clawfoot table. She wears a dress of soft violet material for a kimono—her hair is tied back from her forehead with a ribbon. She is washing and polishing her collection of glass.* AMANDA *appears on the fire escape steps. At the sound of her ascent,* LAURA *catches her breath, thrusts the bowl of ornaments away, and seats herself stiffly before the diagram of the typewriter keyboard as though it held her spellbound. Something has happened to* AMANDA. *It is written in her face as she climbs to the landing: a look that is grim and hopeless and a little absurd. She has on one of those cheap*

33 *Midas touch:* In Greek mythology, King Midas was given the power to turn everything he touched into gold.

or imitation velvety-looking cloth coats with imitation fur collar. Her hat is five or six years old, one of those dreadful cloche hats that were worn in the late Twenties, and she is clutching an enormous black patent-leather pocketbook with nickel clasps and initials. This is her full-dress outfit, the one she usually wears to the D.A.R.° Before entering she looks through the door. She purses her lips, opens her eyes very wide, rolls them upward and shakes her head. Then she slowly lets herself in the door. Seeing her mother's expression, LAURA touches her lips with a nervous gesture.

LAURA. Hello, Mother, I was—[*She makes a nervous gesture toward the chart on the wall. AMANDA leans against the shut door and stares at LAURA with a martyred look.*]

AMANDA. Deception? Deception? [*She slowly removes her hat and gloves, continuing the sweet suffering stare. She lets the hat and gloves fall on the floor—a bit of acting.*]

LAURA. [*shakily*] How was the D.A.R. meeting?

[*AMANDA slowly opens her purse and removes a dainty white handkerchief which she shakes out delicately and delicately touches to her lips and nostrils.*]

Didn't you go to the D.A.R. meeting, Mother?

AMANDA. [*faintly, almost inaudibly*] —No.—No. [*then more forcibly:*] I did not have the strength—to go to the D.A.R. In fact, I did not have the courage! I wanted to find a hole in the ground and hide myself in it forever! [*She crosses slowly to the wall and removes the diagram of the typewriter keyboard. She holds it in front of her for a second, staring at it sweetly and sorrowfully—then bites her lips and tears it in two pieces.*]

LAURA. [*faintly*] Why did you do that, Mother?   5

[*AMANDA repeats the same procedure with the chart of the Gregg Alphabet.*]

Why are you—

AMANDA. Why? Why? How old are you, Laura?

LAURA. Mother, you know my age.

AMANDA. I thought you were an adult; it seems that I was mistaken. [*She crosses slowly to the sofa and sinks down and stares at LAURA.*]

LAURA. Please don't stare at me, Mother.

[*AMANDA closes her eyes and lowers her head. There is a ten-second pause.*]

AMANDA. What are we going to do, what is going to become of us, what is   10 the future?

[*There is another pause.*]

LAURA. Has something happened, Mother?

[*AMANDA draws a long breath, takes out the handkerchief again, goes through the dabbing process.*]

Mother, has—something happened?

AMANDA. I'll be all right in a minute, I'm just bewildered—[*She hesitates.*]— by life. . . .

LAURA. Mother, I wish that you would tell me what's happened!

0.2 *D.A.R.:* Daughters of the American Revolution, a patriotic women's organization (founded in 1890) open only to women whose ancestors aided the American Revolution.

AMANDA. As you know, I was supposed to be inducted into my office at the D.A.R. this afternoon.

[*Screen image: A swarm of typewriters.*]

But I stopped off at Rubicam's Business College to speak to your teachers about your having a cold and ask them what progress they thought you were making down there.

LAURA. Oh. . . .   15

AMANDA. I went to the typing instructor and introduced myself as your mother. She didn't know who you were.

"Wingfield," she said, "We don't have any such student enrolled at the school!"

I assured her she did, that you had been going to classes since early in January.

"I wonder," she said, "if you could be talking about that terribly shy little girl who dropped out of school after only a few days' attendance?"

"No," I said, "Laura, my daughter, has been going to school every day for the past six weeks!"

"Excuse me," she said. She took the attendance book out and there was your name, unmistakably printed, and all the dates you were absent until they decided that you had dropped out of school.

I still said, "No, there must have been some mistake! There must have been some mix-up in the records!"

And she said, "No—I remember her perfectly now. Her hands shook so that she couldn't hit the right keys! The first time we gave a speed test, she broke down completely—was sick at the stomach and almost had to be carried into the wash room! After that morning she never showed up any more. We phoned the house but never got any answer"—While I was working at Famous-Barr,° I suppose, demonstrating those—

[*She indicates a brassiere with her hands.*]

Oh! I felt so weak I could barely keep on my feet! I had to sit down while they got me a glass of water! Fifty dollars' tuition, all of our plans—my hopes and ambitions for you—just gone up the spout, just gone up the spout like that.

[*LAURA draws a long breath and gets awkwardly to her feet. She crosses to the Victrola and winds it up.°*]

What are you doing?

LAURA. Oh! [*She releases the handle and returns to her seat.*]

AMANDA. Laura, where have you been going when you've gone out pretending that you were going to business college?

LAURA. I've just been going out walking.

AMANDA. That's not true.   20

LAURA. It is. I just went walking.

AMANDA. Walking? Walking? In winter? Deliberately courting pneumonia in that light coat? Where did you walk to, Laura?

16.8 *Famous-Barr:* a department store in St. Louis.   16.11 *winds it up:* Laura is using a spring-powered (rather than electric) phonograph that has to be rewound frequently.

LAURA.   All sorts of places—mostly in the park.

AMANDA.   Even after you'd started catching that cold?

LAURA.   It was the lesser of two evils, Mother.   25

[*Screen image: Winter scene in a park.*]

I couldn't go back there. I—threw up—on the floor!

AMANDA.   From half past seven till after five every day you mean to tell me you walked around the park, because you wanted to make me think that you were still going to Rubicam's Business College?

LAURA.   It wasn't as bad as it sounds. I went inside places to get warmed up.

AMANDA.   Inside where?

LAURA.   I went in the art museum and the bird houses at the Zoo. I visited the penguins every day! Sometimes I did without lunch and went to the movies. Lately I've been spending most of my afternoons in the Jewel Box, that big glass house where they raise the tropical flowers.

AMANDA.   You did all this to deceive me, just for deception? [*LAURA looks*   30 *down.*] Why?

LAURA.   Mother, when you're disappointed, you get that awful suffering look on your face, like the picture of Jesus' mother in the museum!

AMANDA.   Hush!

LAURA.   I couldn't face it.

[*There is a pause. A whisper of strings is heard. Legend on screen: "The Crust of Humility."*]

AMANDA.   [*hopelessly fingering the huge pocketbook*] So what are we going to do the rest of our lives? Stay home and watch the parades go by? Amuse ourselves with the glass menagerie, darling? Eternally play those worn-out phonograph records your father left as a painful reminder of him? We won't have a business career—we've given that up because it gave us nervous indigestion! [*She laughs wearily.*] What is there left but dependency all our lives? I know so well what becomes of unmarried women who aren't prepared to occupy a position. I've seen such pitiful cases in the South—barely tolerated spinsters living upon the grudging patronage of sister's husband or brother's wife!—stuck away in some little mouse-trap of a room—encouraged by one in-law to visit another—little birdlike women without any nest—eating the crust of humility all their life!

Is that the future that we've mapped out for ourselves? I swear it's the only alternative I can think of! [*She pauses.*] It isn't a very pleasant alternative, is it? [*She pauses again.*] Of course—some girls *do marry.*

[*LAURA twists her hands nervously.*]

Haven't you ever liked some boy?

LAURA.   Yes. I liked one once. [*She rises.*] I came across his picture a while   35 ago.

AMANDA.   [*with some interest*] He gave you his picture?

LAURA.   No, it's in the yearbook.

AMANDA.   [*disappointed*] Oh—a high school boy.

[*Screen image: JIM as the high school hero bearing a silver cup.*]

LAURA.   Yes. His name was Jim. [*She lifts the heavy annual from the claw-foot table.*] Here he is in *The Pirates of Penzance.°*

AMANDA.   [*absently*] The what?   40

LAURA.   The operetta the senior class put on. He had a wonderful voice and we sat across the aisle from each other Mondays, Wednesdays and Fridays in the Aud. Here he is with the silver cup for debating! See his grin?

AMANDA.   [*absently*] He must have had a jolly disposition.

LAURA.   He used to call me—Blue Roses.

[*Screen image: Blue roses.*]

AMANDA.   Why did he call you such a name as that?

LAURA.   When I had that attack of pleurosis—he asked me what was the   45
matter when I came back. I said pleurosis—he thought that I said Blue Roses! So that's what he always called me after that. Whenever he saw me, he'd holler, "Hello, Blue Roses!" I didn't care for the girl that he went out with. Emily Meisenbach. Emily was the best-dressed girl at Soldan. She never struck me, though, as being sincere . . . It says in the Personal Section—they're engaged. That's—six years ago! They must be married by now.

AMANDA.   Girls that aren't cut out for business careers usually wind up married to some nice man. [*She gets up with a spark of revival.*] Sister, that's what you'll do!

[*LAURA utters a startled, doubtful laugh. She reaches quickly for a piece of glass.*]

LAURA.   But, Mother—

AMANDA.   Yes? [*She goes over to the photograph.*]

LAURA.   [*in a tone of frightened apology*] I'm—crippled!

AMANDA.   Nonsense! Laura, I've told you never, never to use that word.   50
Why, you're not crippled, you just have a little defect—hardly noticeable, even! When people have some slight disadvantage like that, they cultivate other things to make up for it—develop charm—and vivacity—and—*charm*! That's all you have to do! [*She turns again to the photograph.*] One thing your father had *plenty of*— was *charm*!

[*The scene fades out with music.*]

Scene 3

[*Legend on screen: "After the fiasco—"*]

TOM speaks from the fire escape landing.]

TOM.   After the fiasco at Rubicam's Business College, the idea of getting a gentleman caller for Laura began to play a more and more important part in Mother's calculations. It became an obsession. Like some archetype of the universal unconscious, the image of the gentleman caller haunted our small apartment. . . .

[*Screen image: A young man at the door of a house with flowers.*]

An evening at home rarely passed without some allusion to this image, this specter,

---

39 *The Pirates of Penzance:* a comic light opera (1879) by W. S. Gilbert and Arthur Sullivan.

this hope. . . . Even when he wasn't mentioned, his presence hung in Mother's preoccupied look and in my sister's frightened, apologetic manner—hung like a sentence passed upon the Wingfields!

Mother was a woman of action as well as words. She began to take logical steps in the planned direction. Late that winter and in the early spring—realizing that extra money would be needed to properly feather the nest and plume the bird—she conducted a vigorous campaign on the telephone, roping in subscribers to one of those magazines for matrons called *The Homemaker's Companion,* the type of journal that features the serialized sublimations of ladies of letters who think in terms of delicate cuplike breasts, slim, tapering waists, rich, creamy thighs, eyes like wood smoke in autumn, fingers that soothe and caress like strains of music, bodies as powerful as Etruscan sculpture.

[*Screen image: The cover of a glamor magazine.*]

AMANDA *enters with the telephone on a long extension cord. She is spotlighted in the dim stage.*]

AMANDA.   Ida Scott? This is Amanda Wingfield! We *missed* you at the D.A.R. last Monday! I said to myself: She's probably suffering with that sinus condition! How is that sinus condition?

Horrors! Heaven have mercy!—You're a Christian martyr, yes, that's what you are, a Christian martyr!

Well, I just now happened to notice that your subscription to the *Companion's* about to expire! Yes, it expires with the next issue, honey!—just when that wonderful new serial by Bessie Mae Hopper is getting off to such an exciting start. Oh, honey, it's something that you can't miss! You remember how *Gone with the Wind*° took everybody by storm? You simply couldn't go out if you hadn't read it. All everybody *talked* was Scarlett O'Hara. Well, this is a book that critics already compare to *Gone with the Wind.* It's the *Gone with the Wind* of the post-World-War generation!—What?—Burning?—Oh, honey, don't let them burn, go take a look in the oven and I'll hold the wire! Heavens—I think she's hung up!

[*The scene dims out.*]

[*Legend on screen: "You think I'm in love with Continental Shoemakers?"*]

[*Before the lights come up again, the violent voices of* TOM *and* AMANDA *are heard. They are quarreling behind the portieres. In front of them stands* LAURA *with clenched hands and panicky expression. A clear pool of light is on her figure throughout this scene.*]

TOM.   What in Christ's name am I—
AMANDA.   [*shrilly*] Don't you use that—
TOM.   —supposed to do!   5
AMANDA.   —expression! Not in my—
TOM.   Ohhh!
AMANDA.   —presence! Have you gone out of your senses?
TOM.   I have, that's true, *driven* out!
AMANDA.   What is the matter with you, you—big—big—IDIOT!   10

2.3 *Gone with the Wind:* popular novel (1936) by Margaret Mitchell (1900–1949), set in the South before, during, and after the Civil War. Scarlett O'Hara was the heroine.

Tom.   Look!—I've got *no thing*, no single thing—

Amanda.   Lower your voice!

Tom.   —in my life here that I can call my own! Everything is—

Amanda.   Stop that shouting!

Tom.   Yesterday you confiscated my books! You had the nerve to—   15

Amanda.   I took that horrible novel back to the library—yes! That hideous book by that insane Mr. Lawrence.°

[*Tom laughs wildly.*]

I cannot control the output of diseased minds or people who cater to them—

[*Tom laughs still more wildly.*]

But I won't allow such filth brought into my house! No, no, no, no, no!

Tom.   House, house! Who pays rent on it, who makes a slave of himself to—

Amanda.   [*fairly screeching*] Don't you DARE to—

Tom.   No, no, *I* mustn't say things! *I've* got to just—

Amanda.   Let me tell you—   20

Tom.   I don't want to hear any more!

[*He tears the portieres open. The dining-room area is lit with turgid smoky red glow. Now we see Amanda; her hair is in metal curlers and she is wearing a very old bathrobe, much too large for her slight figure, a relic of the faithless Mr. Wingfield. The upright typewriter now stands on the drop-leaf table, along with a wild disarray of manuscripts. The quarrel was probably precipitated by Amanda's interruption of Tom's creative labor. A chair lies overthrown on the floor. Their gesticulating shadows are cast on the ceiling by the fiery glow.*]

Amanda.   You *will* hear more, you—

Tom.   No, I won't hear more, I'm going out!

Amanda.   You come right back in—

Tom.   Out, out, out! Because I'm—   25

Amanda.   Come back here, Tom Wingfield! I'm not through talking to you!

Tom.   Oh, go—

Laura.   [*desperately*] —Tom!

Amanda.   You're going to listen, and no more insolence from you! I'm at the end of my patience!

[*He comes back toward her.*]

Tom.   What do you think I'm at? Aren't I supposed to have any patience   30 to reach the end of, Mother? I know, I know. It seems unimportant to you, what I'm *doing*—what I *want* to do—having a little *difference* between them! You don't think that—

Amanda.   I think you've been doing things that you're ashamed of. That's why you act like this. I don't believe that you go every night to the movies. Nobody goes to the movies night after night. Nobody in their right minds goes to the movies as often as you pretend to. People don't go to the movies at nearly midnight, and movies don't let out at two A.M. Come in stumbling. Muttering to yourself like

16 *Lawrence:* D. H. Lawrence (1885–1930), English poet and fiction writer, popularly known as an advocate of passion and sexuality. See "The Horse Dealer's Daughter," p. 372.

a maniac! You get three hours' sleep and then go to work. Oh, I can picture the way you're doing down there. Moping, doping, because you're in no condition.

TOM. [*wildly*] No, I'm in no condition!

AMANDA. What right have you got to jeopardize your job? Jeopardize the security of us all? How do you think we'd manage if you were—

TOM. Listen! You think I'm crazy about the *warehouse*? [*He bends fiercely toward her slight figure.*] You think I'm in love with the Continental Shoemakers? You think I want to spend fifty-five *years* down there in that—*celotex interior*! with—*fluorescent—tubes*! Look! I'd rather somebody picked up a crowbar and battered out my brains—than go back mornings! I *go*! Every time you come in yelling that God damn *"Rise and Shine!"* *"Rise and Shine!"* I say to myself, "How *lucky dead* people are!" But I get up. I *go*! For sixty-five dollars a month I give up all that I dream of doing and being *ever*! And you say self—*self's* all I ever think of. Why, listen, if self is what I thought of, Mother, I'd be where he is—GONE! [*He points to his father's picture.*] As far as the system of transportation reaches! [*He starts past her. She grabs his arm.*] Don't grab at me, Mother!

AMANDA. Where are you going? 35

TOM. I'm going to the *movies*!

AMANDA. I don't believe that lie!

[*TOM crouches toward her, overtowering her tiny figure. She backs away, gasping.*]

TOM. I'm going to opium dens! Yes, opium dens, dens of vice and criminals' hangouts, Mother. I've joined the Hogan Gang,° I'm a hired assassin, I carry a tommy gun in a violin case! I run a string of cat houses in the Valley! They call me Killer, Killer Wingfield, I'm leading a double-life, a simple, honest warehouse worker by day, by night a dynamic *czar* of the *underworld, Mother*. I go to gambling casinos, I spin away fortunes on the roulette table! I wear a patch over one eye and a false mustache, sometimes I put on green whiskers. On those occasions they call me—*El Diablo!*° Oh, I could tell you many things to make you sleepless! My enemies plan to dynamite this place. They're going to blow us all sky-high some night! I'll be glad, very happy, and so will you! You'll go up, up on a broomstick, over Blue Mountain with seventeen gentlemen callers! You ugly—babbling old—witch. . . .

[*He goes through a series of violent, clumsy movements, seizing his overcoat, lunging to the door, pulling it fiercely open. The women watch him, aghast. His arm catches in the sleeve of the coat as he struggles to pull it on. For a moment he is pinioned by the bulky garment. With an outraged groan he tears the coat off again, splitting the shoulder of it, and hurls it across the room. It strikes against the shelf of LAURA's glass collection, and there is a tinkle of shattering glass. LAURA cries out as if wounded.*]

Music.

Screen legend: "The Glass Menagerie."]

LAURA. [*shrilly*] My glass!—menagerie. . . . [*She covers her face and turns away.*]

[*But AMANDA is still stunned and stupefied by the "ugly witch" so that she barely notices this occurrence. Now she recovers her speech.*]

38 *Hogan Gang:* one of the major criminal organizations in St. Louis in the 1930s. *El Diablo:* the devil.

AMANDA.   [*in an awful voice*] I won't speak to you—until you apologize!   40

[*She crosses through the portieres and draws them together behind her. TOM is left with LAURA. LAURA clings weakly to the mantel with her face averted. TOM stares at her stupidly for a moment. Then he crosses to the shelf. He drops awkwardly on his knees to collect the fallen glass, glancing at LAURA as if he would speak but couldn't.*

"The Glass Menagerie" music steals in as the scene dims out.]

Scene 4

The interior of the apartment is dark. There is a faint light in the alley. A deep-voiced bell in a church is tolling the hour of five.

TOM appears at the top of the alley. After each solemn boom of the bell in the tower, he shakes a little noisemaker or rattle as if to express the tiny spasm of man in contrast to the sustained power and dignity of the Almighty. This and the unsteadiness of his advance make it evident that he has been drinking. As he climbs the few steps to the fire escape landing light steals up inside. LAURA appears in the front room in a nightdress. She notices that TOM's bed is empty. TOM fishes in his pockets for his door key, removing a motley assortment of articles in the search, including a shower of movie ticket stubs and an empty bottle. At last he finds the key, but just as he is about to insert it, it slips from his fingers. He strikes a match and crouches below the door.

TOM.   [*bitterly*] One crack—and it falls through!

[*LAURA opens the door.*]

LAURA.   Tom! Tom, what are you doing?
TOM.   Looking for a door key.
LAURA.   Where have you been all this time?
TOM.   I have been to the movies.   5
LAURA.   All this time at the movies?
TOM.   There was a very long program. There was a Garbo° picture and a Mickey Mouse and a travelogue and a newsreel and a preview of coming attractions. And there was an organ solo and a collection for the Milk Fund—simultaneously—which ended up in a terrible fight between a fat lady and an usher!
LAURA.   [*innocently*] Did you have to stay through everything?
TOM.   Of course! And, oh I forgot! There was a big stage show! The headliner on this stage show was Malvolio° the Magician. He performed wonderful tricks, many of them, such as pouring water back and forth between pitchers. First it turned to wine and then it turned to beer and then it turned to whisky. I know it was whisky it finally turned into because he needed somebody to come up out of the audience to help him, and I came up—both shows! It was Kentucky Straight Bourbon. A very generous fellow, he gave souvenirs. [*He pulls from his back pocket a shimmering rainbow-colored scarf.*] He gave me this. This is his magic scarf. You can have it, Laura. You wave it over a canary cage and you get a bowl of goldfish. You wave it over the goldfish bowl and they fly away canaries. . . . But the wonderfullest trick of all was the coffin trick. We nailed him into a coffin and he

7 *Garbo:* Greta Garbo (1905–1990), Swedish star of American silent and early sound films.
9 *Malvolio:* the name, borrowed from a puritanical character in Shakespeare's *Twelfth Night*, means "malevolence" or "ill-will."

got out of the coffin without removing one nail. [*He has come inside.*] There is a trick that would come in handy for me—get me out of this two-by-four situation! [*He flops onto the bed and starts removing his shoes.*]

    LAURA. Tom—shhh!   10

    TOM. What're you shushing me for?

    LAURA. You'll wake up Mother.

    TOM. Goody, goody! Pay 'er back for all those "Rise an' Shines." [*He lies down, groaning.*] You know it don't take much intelligence to get yourself into a nailed-up coffin, Laura. But who in hell ever got himself out of one without removing one nail?

[*As if in answer, the father's grinning photograph lights up. The scene dims out.*]

[*Immediately following, the church bell is heard striking six. At the sixth stroke the alarm clock goes off in* AMANDA's *room, and after a few moments we hear her calling: "Rise and Shine! Rise and Shine! Laura, go tell your brother to rise and shine!"*]

    TOM. [*sitting up slowly*] I'll rise—but I won't shine.

[*The light increases.*]

    AMANDA. Laura, tell your brother his coffee is ready.   15

[LAURA *slips into the front room.*]

    LAURA. Tom!—It's nearly seven. Don't make Mother nervous.

[*He stares at her stupidly.*]

[*Beseechingly.*] Tom, speak to Mother this morning. Make up with her, apologize, speak to her!

    TOM. She won't to me. It's her that started not speaking.

    LAURA. If you just say you're sorry she'll start speaking.

    TOM. Her not speaking—is that such a tragedy?

    LAURA. Please—please!   20

    AMANDA. [*calling from the kitchenette*] Laura, are you going to do what I asked you to do, or do I have to get dressed and go out myself?

    LAURA. Going, going—soon as I get on my coat!

[*She pulls on a shapeless felt hat with a nervous, jerky movement, pleadingly glancing at* TOM. *She rushes awkwardly for her coat. The coat is one of* AMANDA's, *inaccurately made-over, the sleeves too short for* LAURA.]

Butter and what else?

    AMANDA. [*entering from the kitchenette*] Just butter. Tell them to charge it.

    LAURA. Mother, they make such faces when I do that.

    AMANDA. Sticks and stones can break our bones, but the expression on   25 Mr. Garfinkel's face won't harm us! Tell your brother his coffee is getting cold.

    LAURA. [*at the door*] Do what I asked you, will you, will you, Tom?

[*He looks sullenly away.*]

    AMANDA. Laura, go now or just don't go at all!

    LAURA. [*rushing out*] Going—going!

[*A second later she cries out.* TOM *springs up and crosses to the door.* TOM *opens the door.*]

TOM.   Laura?

LAURA.   I'm all right. I slipped, but I'm all right.   30

AMANDA.   [*peering anxiously after her*] If anyone breaks a leg on those fire-escape steps, the landlord ought to be sued for every cent he possesses! [*She shuts the door. Now she remembers she isn't speaking to TOM and returns to the other room.*]

[*As TOM comes listlessly for his coffee, she turns her back to him and stands rigidly facing the window on the gloomy gray vault of the areaway. Its light on her face with its aged but childish features is cruelly sharp, satirical as a Daumier print.*°

The music of "Ave Maria"° *is heard softly.*

TOM glances sheepishly but sullenly at her averted figure and slumps at the table. The coffee is scalding hot; he sips it and gasps and spits it back in the cup. At his gasp, AMANDA catches her breath and half turns. Then she catches herself and turns back to the window. TOM blows on his coffee, glancing sidewise at his mother. She clears her throat. TOM clears his. He starts to rise, sinks back down again, scratches his head, clears his throat again. AMANDA coughs. TOM raises his cup in both hands to blow on it, his eyes staring over the rim of it at his mother for several moments. Then he slowly sets the cup down and awkwardly and hesitantly rises from the chair.]

TOM.   [*hoarsely*] Mother. I—I apologize, Mother.

[*AMANDA draws a quick, shuddering breath. Her face works grotesquely. She breaks into childlike tears.*]

I'm sorry for what I said, for everything that I said, I didn't mean it.

AMANDA.   [*sobbingly*] My devotion has made me a witch and so I make myself hateful to my children!

TOM.   *No, you don't.*

AMANDA.   I worry so much, don't sleep, it makes me nervous!   35

TOM.   [*gently*] I understand that.

AMANDA.   I've had to put up a solitary battle all these years. But you're my right-hand bower!° Don't fall down, don't fail!

TOM.   [*gently*] I try, Mother.

AMANDA.   [*with great enthusiasm*] Try and you will *succeed!* [*The notion makes her breathless.*] Why, you—you're just *full* of natural endowments! Both of my children—they're *unusual* children! Don't you think I know it? I'm so—*proud!* Happy and—feel I've—so much to be thankful for but—promise me one thing, son!

TOM.   What, Mother?   40

AMANDA.   Promise, son, you'll—never be a drunkard!

TOM.   [*turns to her grinning*] I will never be a drunkard, Mother.

AMANDA.   That's what frightened me so, that you'd be drinking! Eat a bowl of Purina!

TOM.   Just coffee, Mother.

AMANDA.   Shredded wheat biscuit?   45

31.1 *Daumier print:* Honoré Daumier (1808–1879), French painter and engraver whose prints frequently satirized his society.   31.2 *"Ave Maria":* a Roman Catholic prayer to the Virgin Mary; the musical setting called for here is by Franz Schubert (1797–1828). 37 *right-hand bower:* or *rightbower;* the Jack of trump in the card game *500,* the second-highest card (below the joker).

Tom. No. No, Mother, just coffee.

Amanda. You can't put in a day's work on an empty stomach. You've got ten minutes—don't gulp! Drinking too-hot liquids makes cancer of the stomach. . . . Put cream in.

Tom. No, thank you.

Amanda. To cool it.

Tom. No! No, thank you, I want it black. 50

Amanda. I know, but it's not good for you. We have to do all that we can to build ourselves up. In these trying times we live in, all that we have to cling to is—each other. . . . That's why it's so important to—Tom, I—I sent out your sister so I could discuss something with you. If you hadn't spoken I would have spoken to you. [*She sits down.*]

Tom. [*gently*] What is it, Mother, that you want to discuss?

Amanda. *Laura!*

[*Tom puts his cup down slowly.*]

Legend on screen "Laura." Music: "The Glass Menagerie."]

Tom. —Oh.—Laura . . .

Amanda. [*touching his sleeve*] You know how Laura is. So quiet but—still 55
water runs deep! She notices things and I think she—broods about them.

[*Tom looks up.*]

A few days ago I came in and she was crying.

Tom. What about?

Amanda. You.

Tom. Me?

Amanda. She has an idea that you're not happy here.

Tom. What gave her that idea? 60

Amanda. What gives her any idea? However, you do act strangely. I—I'm not criticizing, understand *that*! I know your ambitions do not lie in the warehouse, that like everybody in the whole wide world—you've had to—make sacrifices, but—Tom—Tom—life's not easy, it calls for—Spartan endurance! There's so many things in my heart that I cannot describe to you! I've never told you but I—*loved* your father. . . .

Tom. [*gently*] I know that, Mother.

Amanda. And you—when I see you taking after his ways! Staying out late—and—well, you *had* been drinking the night you were in that—terrifying condition! Laura says that you hate the apartment and that you go out nights to get away from it! Is that true, Tom?

Tom. No. You say there's so much in your heart that you can't describe to me. That's true of me, too. There's so much in my heart that I can't describe to *you*! So let's respect each other's—

Amanda. But, why—*why,* Tom—are you always so *restless*? Where do you 65
go to, nights?

Tom. I—go to the movies.

Amanda. Why do you go to the movies so much, Tom?

Tom. I go to the movies because—I like adventure. Adventure is something I don't have much of at work, so I go to the movies.

AMANDA.   But, Tom, you go to the movies *entirely* too *much!*

TOM.   I like a lot of adventure.   70

[AMANDA *looks baffled, then hurt. As the familiar inquisition resumes,* TOM *becomes hard and impatient again.* AMANDA *slips back into her querulous attitude toward him.*

Image on screen: A sailing vessel with Jolly Roger.°]

AMANDA.   Most young men find adventure in their careers.

TOM.   Then most young men are not employed in a warehouse.

AMANDA.   The world is full of young men employed in warehouses and offices and factories.

TOM.   Do all of them find adventure in their careers?

AMANDA.   They do or they do without it! Not everybody has a craze for   75
adventure.

TOM.   Man is by instinct a lover, a hunter, a fighter, and none of those instincts are given much play at the warehouse!

AMANDA.   Man is by instinct! Don't quote instinct to me! Instinct is something that people have got away from! It belongs to animals! Christian adults don't want it!

TOM.   What do Christian adults want, then, Mother?

AMANDA.   Superior things! Things of the mind and the spirit! Only animals have to satisfy instincts! Surely your aims are somewhat higher than theirs! Than monkeys—pigs—

TOM.   I reckon they're not.   80

AMANDA.   You're joking. However, that isn't what I wanted to discuss.

TOM.   [*rising*] I haven't much time.

AMANDA.   [*pushing his shoulders*] Sit down.

TOM.   You want me to punch in red° at the warehouse, Mother?

AMANDA.   You have five minutes. I want to talk about Laura.   85

[*Screen legend: "Plans and Provisions."*]

TOM.   All right! What about Laura?

AMANDA.   We have to be making some plans and provisions for her. She's older than you, two years, and nothing has happened. She just drifts along doing nothing. It frightens me terribly how she just drifts along.

TOM.   I guess she's the type that people call home girls.

AMANDA.   There's no such type, and if there is, it's a pity! That is unless the home is hers, with a husband!

TOM.   What?   90

AMANDA.   Oh, I can see the handwriting on the wall as plain as I see the nose in front of my face! It's terrifying! More and more you remind me of your father! He was out all hours without explanation! —Then *left! Goodbye!* And me with the bag to hold. I saw that letter you got from the Merchant Marine. I know what you're dreaming of. I'm not standing here blindfolded. [*She pauses.*] Very well, then. Then *do* it! But not till there's somebody to take your place.

TOM.   What do you mean?

70.2 *Jolly Roger:* the traditional flag of a pirate ship—a skull and crossed bones on a field of black.   84 *punch in red:* arrive late for work; the time clock stamps late arrival times in red on the time card.

AMANDA.   I mean that as soon as Laura has got somebody to take care of her, married, a home of her own, independent—why, then you'll be free to go wherever you please, on land, on sea, whichever way the wind blows you! But until that time you've got to look out for your sister. I don't say me because I'm old and don't matter! I say for your sister because she's young and dependent.

I put her in business college—a dismal failure! Frightened her so it made her sick at the stomach. I took her over to the Young People's League at the church. Another fiasco. She spoke to nobody, nobody spoke to her. Now all she does is fool with those pieces of glass and play those worn-out records. What kind of a life is that for a girl to lead?

TOM.   What can I do about it?

AMANDA.   Overcome selfishness! Self, self, self is all that you ever think of!   95

[*TOM springs up and crosses to get his coat. It is ugly and bulky. He pulls on a cap with earmuffs.*]

Where is your muffler? Put your wool muffler on!

[*He snatches it angrily from the closet, tosses it around his neck and pulls both ends tight.*]

Tom! I haven't said what I had in mind to ask you.

TOM.   I'm too late to—

AMANDA.   [*catching his arm—very importunately; then shyly*] Down at the warehouse, aren't there some—nice young men?

TOM.   No!

AMANDA.   There *must* be—*some* . . .

TOM.   Mother— [*He gestures.*]   100

AMANDA.   Find out one that's clean-living—doesn't drink and ask him out for sister!

TOM.   What?

AMANDA.   For *sister*! To *meet*! Get *acquainted*!

TOM.   [*stamping to the door*] Oh, my go-osh!

AMANDA.   Will you? [*He opens the door. She says, imploringly:*] Will you?   105

[*He starts down the fire escape.*]

Will you? *Will* you, dear?

TOM.   [*calling back*] Yes!

[*AMANDA closes the door hesitantly and with a troubled but faintly hopeful expression.*

Screen image: The cover of a glamor magazine.

The spotlight picks up AMANDA on the phone.]

AMANDA.   Ella Cartwright? This is Amanda Wingfield! How are you honey? How is that kidney condition?

[*There is a five-second pause.*]

Horrors!

[*There is another pause.*]

You're a Christian martyr, yes, honey, that's what you are, a Christian martyr!

Well, I just now happened to notice in my little red book that your subscription to the *Companion* has just run out! I knew that you wouldn't want to miss out on the wonderful serial starting in this new issue. It's by Bessie Mae Hopper, the first thing she's written since *Honeymoon for Three*. Wasn't that a strange and interesting story? Well, this one is even lovelier, I believe. It has a sophisticated, society background. It's all about the horsey set on Long Island!

[*The light fades out.*]

Scene 5

[*Legend on the screen: "Annunciation."*

Music is heard as the light slowly comes on.

It is early dusk of a spring evening. Supper has just been finished in the Wingfield apartment. AMANDA *and* LAURA, *in light-colored dresses, are removing dishes from the table in the dining room, which is shadowy, their movements formalized almost as a dance or ritual, their moving forms as pale and silent as moths.* TOM, *in white shirt and trousers, rises from the table and crosses toward the fire escape.*]

AMANDA.   [*as he passes her*] Son, will you do me a favor?
TOM.   What?
AMANDA.   Comb your hair! You look so pretty when your hair is combed!

[TOM *slouches on the sofa with the evening paper. Its enormous headline reads: "Franco Triumphs."*°]

There is only one respect in which I would like you to emulate your father.
TOM.   What respect is that?
AMANDA.   The care he always took of his appearance. He never allowed   5
himself to look untidy.

[*He throws down the paper and crosses to the fire escape.*]

Where are you going?
TOM.   I'm going out to smoke.
AMANDA.   You smoke too much. A pack a day at fifteen cents a pack. How much would that amount to in a month? Thirty times fifteen is how much, Tom? Figure it out and you will be astounded at what you could save. Enough to give you a night-school course in accounting at Washington U.!° Just think what a wonderful thing that would be for you, son!

[TOM *is unmoved by the thought.*]

TOM.   I'd rather smoke. [*He steps out on the landing, letting the screen door slam.*]
AMANDA.   [*sharply*] I know! That's the tragedy of it. . . . [*Alone, she turns to look at her husband's picture.*]

[*Dance music: "The World Is Waiting for the Sunrise!"°*]

3.1 *"Franco Triumphs":* Francisco Franco (1892–1975), dictator of Spain from 1939 until his death, was the general of the victorious Falangist armies in the Spanish Civil War (1936–1939).   7 *Washington U:* Washington University, a highly competitive liberal arts school in St. Louis.   9.1 *"The World . . . Sunrise":* popular song written in 1919 by Eugene Lockhart and Ernest Seitz.

TOM. [*to the audience*] Across the alley from us was the Paradise Dance Hall.   10
On evenings in spring the windows and doors were open and the music came
outdoors. Sometimes the lights were turned out except for a large glass sphere
that hung from the ceiling. It would turn slowly about and filter the dusk with
delicate rainbow colors. Then the orchestra played a waltz or a tango, something
that had a slow and sensuous rhythm. Couples would come outside, to the relative
privacy of the alley. You could see them kissing behind ash pits and telephone
poles. This was the compensation for lives that passed like mine, without any
change or adventure. Adventure and change were imminent in this year. They
were waiting around the corner for all these kids. Suspended in the mist over
Berchtesgaden, caught in the folds of Chamberlain's umbrella. In Spain there was
Guernica!° But here there was only hot swing music and liquor, dance halls, bars,
and movies, and sex that hung in the gloom like a chandelier and flooded the
world with brief, deceptive rainbows. . . . All the world was waiting for bombard-
ments!

[AMANDA *turns from the picture and comes outside.*]

AMANDA. [*sighing*] A fire escape landing's a poor excuse for a porch. [*She
spreads a newspaper on a step and sits down, gracefully and demurely as if she were settling
into a swing on a Mississippi veranda.*] What are you looking at?
TOM. The moon.
AMANDA. Is there a moon this evening?
TOM. It's rising over Garfinkel's Delicatessen.
AMANDA. So it is! A little silver slipper of a moon. Have you made a wish   15
on it yet?
TOM. Um-hum.
AMANDA. What did you wish for?
TOM. That's a secret.
AMANDA. A secret, huh? Well, I won't tell mine either. I will be just as
mysterious as you.
TOM. I bet I can guess what yours is.   20
AMANDA. Is my head so transparent?
TOM. You're not a sphinx.°
AMANDA. No, I don't have secrets. I'll tell you what I wished for on the
moon. Success and happiness for my precious children! I wish for that whenever
there's a moon, and when there isn't a moon, I wish for it, too.
TOM. I thought perhaps you wished for a gentleman caller.
AMANDA. Why do you say that?   25
TOM. Don't you remember asking me to fetch one?
AMANDA. I remember suggesting that it would be nice for your sister if you

---

10 *Berchtesgaden . . . Guernica:* The three names mentioned are all foreshadowings of World
War II. Berchtesgaden, a resort in the Bavarian Alps, was Adolf Hitler's favorite residence.
Neville Chamberlain was the British prime minister who signed the Munich Pact with
Hitler in 1938, allowing Nazi Germany to occupy parts of Czechoslovakia. Chamberlain,
who always carried an umbrella, declared that he had ensured "peace in our time." The
bombardment of Guernica during the Spanish Civil War made the name of the town
synonymous with the horrors of war, and especially the killing of civilian women and
children. (See pp. 367, 1477.)   22 *sphinx:* a mythological monster with the head of a
woman and body of a lion, famous for her riddles. See p. 808.

brought home some nice young man from the warehouse. I think that I've made that suggestion more than once.

TOM.   Yes, you have made it repeatedly.

AMANDA.   Well?

TOM.   We are going to have one.   30

AMANDA.   *What?*

TOM.   A gentleman caller!

[*The annunciation is celebrated with music.*

AMANDA *rises.*

Image on screen: A caller with a bouquet.]

AMANDA.   You mean you have asked some nice young man to come over?

TOM.   Yep. I've asked him to dinner.

AMANDA.   You really did?   35

TOM.   I did!

AMANDA.   You did, and did he—*accept?*

TOM.   He did!

AMANDA.   Well, well—well, well! That's—lovely!

TOM.   I thought that you would be pleased.   40

AMANDA.   It's definite then?

TOM.   Very definite.

AMANDA.   Soon?

TOM.   Very soon.

AMANDA.   For heaven's sake, stop putting on and tell me some things, will   45
you?

TOM.   What things do you want me to tell you?

AMANDA.   *Naturally* I would like to know when he's *coming!*

TOM.   He's coming tomorrow.

AMANDA.   *Tomorrow?*

TOM.   Yep. Tomorrow.   50

AMANDA.   But, Tom!

TOM.   Yes, Mother?

AMANDA.   Tomorrow gives me no time!

TOM.   Time for what?

AMANDA.   Preparations! Why didn't you phone me at once, as soon as you   55
asked him, the minute that he accepted? Then, don't you see, I could have been getting ready!

TOM.   You don't have to make any fuss.

AMANDA.   Oh, Tom, Tom, Tom, of course I have to make a fuss! I want things nice, not sloppy! Not thrown together. I'll certainly have to do some fast thinking, won't I?

TOM.   I don't see why you have to think at all.

AMANDA.   You just don't know. We can't have a gentleman caller in a pigsty! All my wedding silver has to be polished, the monogrammed table linen ought to be laundered! The windows have to be washed and fresh curtains put up. And how about clothes? We have to *wear* something, don't we?

TOM.   Mother, this boy is no one to make a fuss over!   60

AMANDA.   Do you realize he's the first young man we've introduced to your sister? It's terrible, disgraceful that poor little sister has never received a single gentleman caller! Tom, come inside! [*She opens the screen door.*]

Tom. What for?

Amanda. I want to ask you some things.

Tom. If you're going to make such a fuss, I'll call it off, I'll tell him not to come!

Amanda. You certainly won't do anything of the kind. Nothing offends people worse than broken engagements. It simply means I'll have to work like a Turk! We won't be brilliant, but we will pass inspection. Come on inside. 65

[*Tom follows her inside, groaning.*]

Sit down.

Tom. Any particular place you would like me to sit?

Amanda. Thank heavens I've got that new sofa! I'm also making payments on a floor lamp I'll have sent out! And put the chintz covers on, they'll brighten things up! Of course I'd hoped to have these walls re-papered. . . . What is the young man's name?

Tom. His name is O'Connor.

Amanda. That, of course, means fish°—tomorrow is Friday! I'll have that salmon loaf—with Durkee's dressing! What does he do? He works at the warehouse?

Tom. Of course! How else would I— 70

Amanda. Tom, he—doesn't drink?

Tom. Why do you ask me that?

Amanda. Your father *did!*

Tom. Don't get started on that!

Amanda. He *does* drink, then? 75

Tom. Not that I know of!

Amanda. Make sure, be certain! The last thing I want for my daughter's a boy who drinks!

Tom. Aren't you being a little bit premature? Mr. O'Connor has not yet appeared on the scene!

Amanda. But will tomorrow. To meet your sister, and what do I know about his character? Nothing! Old maids are better off than wives of drunkards!

Tom. Oh, my God! 80

Amanda. Be still!

Tom. [*leaning forward to whisper*] Lots of fellows meet girls whom they don't marry!

Amanda. Oh, talk sensibly, Tom—and don't be sarcastic! [*She has gotten a hairbrush.*]

Tom. What are you doing?

Amanda. I'm brushing that cowlick down! [*She attacks his hair with the brush.*] 85 What is this young man's position at the warehouse?

Tom. [*submitting grimly to the brush and the interrogation*] This young man's position is that of a shipping clerk, Mother.

Amanda. Sounds to me like a fairly responsible job, the sort of job *you* would be in if you just had more *get-up*. What is his salary? Have you any idea?

---

69 *fish:* Amanda assumes that O'Connor is Catholic. Until the 1960s, Roman Catholics were required by the church to abstain from meat on Fridays.

TOM.   I would judge it to be approximately eighty-five dollars a month.

AMANDA.   Well—not princely, but—

TOM.   Twenty more than I make.   90

AMANDA.   Yes, how well I know! But for a family man, eighty-five dollars a month is not much more than you can just get by on. . . .

TOM.   Yes, but Mr. O'Connor is not a family man.

AMANDA.   He might be, mightn't he? Some time in the future?

TOM.   I see. Plans and provisions.

AMANDA.   You are the only young man that I know of who ignores the fact   95
that the future becomes the present, the present the past, and the past turns into everlasting regret if you don't plan for it!

TOM.   I will think that over and see what I can make of it.

AMANDA.   Don't be supercilious with your mother! Tell me some more about this—what do you call him?

TOM.   James D. O'Connor. The D. is for Delaney.

AMANDA.   Irish on *both* sides! *Gracious*! And he doesn't drink?

TOM.   Shall I call him up and ask him right this minute?   100

AMANDA.   The only way to find out about those things is to make discreet inquiries at the proper moment. When I was a girl in Blue Mountain and it was suspected that a young man drank, the girl whose attentions he had been receiving, if any girl *was*, would sometimes speak to the minister of his church, or rather her father would if her father was living, and sort of feel him out on the young man's character. That is the way such things are discreetly handled to keep a young woman from making a tragic mistake!

TOM.   Then how did you happen to make a tragic mistake?

AMANDA.   That innocent look of your father's had everyone fooled! He *smiled*—the world was *enchanted*! No girl can do worse than put herself at the mercy of a handsome appearance! I hope that Mr. O'Connor is not too good-looking.

TOM.   No, he's not too good-looking. He's covered with freckles and hasn't too much of a nose.

AMANDA.   He's not right-down homely, though?   105

TOM.   Not right-down homely. Just medium homely, I'd say.

AMANDA.   Character's what to look for in a man.

TOM.   That's what I've always said, Mother.

AMANDA.   You've never said anything of the kind and I suspect you would never give it a thought.

TOM.   Don't be so suspicious of me.   110

AMANDA.   At least I hope he's the type that's up and coming.

TOM.   I think he really goes in for self-improvement.

AMANDA.   What reason have you to think so?

TOM.   He goes to night school.

AMANDA.   [*beaming*] Splendid! What does he do, I mean study?   115

TOM.   Radio engineering and public speaking!

AMANDA.   Then he has visions of being advanced in the world! Any young man who studies public speaking is aiming to have an executive job some day! And radio engineering? A thing for the future! Both of these facts are very illuminating. Those are the sort of things that a mother should know concerning any young man who comes to call on her daughter. Seriously or—not.

TOM.   One little warning. He doesn't know about Laura. I didn't let on that we had dark ulterior motives. I just said, why don't you come and have dinner with us? He said okay and that was the whole conversation.

AMANDA.   I bet it was! You're eloquent as an oyster. However, he'll know about Laura when he gets here. When he sees how lovely and sweet and pretty she is, he'll thank his lucky stars he was asked to dinner.

TOM.   Mother, you mustn't expect too much of Laura.   120

AMANDA.   What do you mean?

TOM.   Laura seems all those things to you and me because she's ours and we love her. We don't even notice she's crippled any more.

AMANDA.   Don't say crippled! You know that I never allow that word to be used!

TOM.   But face facts, Mother. She is and—that's not all—

AMANDA.   What do you mean "not all"?   125

TOM.   Laura is very different from other girls.

AMANDA.   I think the difference is all to her advantage.

TOM.   Not quite all—in the eyes of others—strangers—she's terribly shy and lives in a world of her own and those things make her seem a little peculiar to people outside the house.

AMANDA.   Don't say peculiar.

TOM.   Face the facts. She is.   130

[*The dance hall music changes to a tango that has a minor and somewhat ominous tone.*]

AMANDA.   In what way is she peculiar—may I ask?

TOM.   [*gently*] She lives in a world of her own—a world of little glass ornaments, Mother. . . .

[*He gets up. AMANDA remains holding the brush, looking at him, troubled.*]

She plays old phonograph records and—that's about all—[*He glances at himself in the mirror and crosses to the door.*]

AMANDA.   [*sharply*] Where are you going?

TOM.   I'm going to the movies. [*He goes out the screen door.*]

AMANDA.   Not to the movies, every night to the movies! [*She follows quickly   135 to the screen door.*] I don't believe you always go to the movies!

[*He is gone. AMANDA looks worriedly after him for a moment. Then vitality and optimism return and she turns from the door, crossing to the portieres.*]

Laura! Laura!

[*LAURA answers from the kitchenette.*]

LAURA.   Yes, Mother.

AMANDA.   Let those dishes go and come in front!

[*LAURA appears with a dish towel. AMANDA speaks to her gaily.*]

Laura, come here and make a wish on the moon!

[*Screen image: The Moon.*]

LAURA.   [*entering*] Moon—moon?

AMANDA. A little silver slipper of a moon. Look over your left shoulder, Laura, and make a wish!

[*LAURA looks faintly puzzled as if called out of sleep. AMANDA seizes her shoulders and turns her at an angle by the door.*]

Now! Now, darling, *wish!*

LAURA. What shall I wish for, Mother? 140

AMANDA. [*her voice trembling and her eyes suddenly filling with tears*] Happiness! Good fortune!

[*The sound of the violin rises and the stage dims out.*]

Scene 6

[*The light comes up on the fire escape landing. Tom is leaning against the grill, smoking.*
Screen image: The high school hero.]

TOM. And so the following evening I brought Jim home to dinner. I had known Jim slightly in high school. In high school Jim was a hero. He had tremendous Irish good nature and vitality with the scrubbed and polished look of white chinaware. He seemed to move in a continual spotlight. He was a star in basketball, captain of the debating club, president of the senior class and the glee club and he sang the male lead in the annual light operas. He was always running or bounding, never just walking. He seemed always at the point of defeating the law of gravity. He was shooting with such velocity through his adolescence that you would logically expect him to arrive at nothing short of the White House by the time he was thirty. But Jim apparently ran into more interference after his graduation from Soldan. His speed had definitely slowed. Six years after he left high school he was holding a job that wasn't much better than mine.

[*Screen image: The Clerk.*]

He was the only one at the warehouse with whom I was on friendly terms. I was valuable to him as someone who could remember his former glory, who had seen him win basketball games and the silver cup in debating. He knew of my secret practice of retiring to a cabinet of the washroom to work on poems when business was slack in the warehouse. He called me Shakespeare. And while the other boys in the warehouse regarded me with suspicious hostility, Jim took a humorous attitude toward me. Gradually his attitude affected the others, their hostility wore off and they also began to smile at me as people smile at an oddly fashioned dog who trots across their path at some distance.

I knew that Jim and Laura had known each other at Soldan, and I had heard Laura speak admiringly of his voice. I didn't know if Jim remembered her or not. In high school Laura had been as unobtrusive as Jim had been astonishing. If he did remember Laura, it was not as my sister, for when I asked him to dinner, he grinned and said, "You know, Shakespeare, I never thought of you as having folks!"

He was about to discover that I did. . . .

[*Legend on screen: "The accent of a coming foot."*]

[*The light dims out on Tom and comes up in the Wingfield living room—a delicate lemony light. It is about five on a Friday evening of late spring which comes "scattering poems in the sky."*

AMANDA *has worked like a Turk in preparation for the gentleman caller. The results are astonishing. The new floor lamp with its rose silk shade is in place, a colored paper lantern conceals the broken light fixture in the ceiling, new billowing white curtains are at the windows, chintz covers are on the chairs and sofa, a pair of new sofa pillows make their initial appearance. Open boxes and tissue paper are scattered on the floor.*

LAURA *stands in the middle of the room with lifted arms while* AMANDA *crouches before her, adjusting the hem of a new dress, devout and ritualistic. The dress is colored and designed by memory. The arrangement of* LAURA'S *hair is changed; it is softer and more becoming. A fragile, unearthly prettiness has come out in* LAURA: *she is like a piece of translucent glass touched by light, given a momentary radiance, not actual, not lasting.*]

AMANDA. [*impatiently*] Why are you trembling?
LAURA. Mother, you've made me so nervous!
AMANDA. How have I made you nervous?
LAURA. By all this fuss! You make it seem so important!   5
AMANDA. I don't understand you, Laura. You couldn't be satisfied with just sitting home, and yet whenever I try to arrange something for you, you seem to resist it. [*She gets up.*] Now take a look at yourself. No, wait! Wait just a moment— I have an idea!
LAURA. What is it now?

[AMANDA *produces two powder puffs which she wraps in handkerchiefs and stuffs in* LAURA'S *bosom.*]

LAURA. Mother, what are you doing?
AMANDA. They call them "Gay Deceivers"!
LAURA. I won't wear them!   10
AMANDA. You will!
LAURA. Why should I?
AMANDA. Because, to be painfully honest, your chest is flat.
LAURA. You make it seem like we were setting a trap.
AMANDA. All pretty girls are a trap, a pretty trap, and men expect them to   15
be.

[*Legend on screen: "A pretty trap."*]

Now look at yourself, young lady. This is the prettiest you will ever be! [*She stands back to admire* LAURA.] I've got to fix myself now! You're going to be surprised by your mother's appearance!

[AMANDA *crosses through the portieres, humming gaily.* LAURA *moves slowly to the long mirror and stares solemnly at herself. A wind blows the white curtains inward in a slow, graceful motion and with a faint, sorrowful sighing.*]

AMANDA. [*from somewhere behind the portieres*] It isn't dark enough yet.

[LAURA *turns slowly before the mirror with a troubled look.*

Legend on screen: "This is my sister: Celebrate her with strings!" Music plays.]

AMANDA. [*laughing, still not visible*] I'm going to show you something. I'm going to make a spectacular appearance!

LAURA. What is it, Mother?

AMANDA. Possess your soul in patience—you will see! Something I've resurrected from that old trunk! Styles haven't changed so terribly much after all.... [*She parts the portieres.*] Now just look at your mother! [*She wears a girlish frock of yellowed voile with a blue silk sash. She carries a bunch of jonquils—the legend of her youth is nearly revived. Now she speaks feverishly:*] This is the dress in which I led the cotillion. Won the cakewalk twice at Sunset Hill, wore one Spring to the Governor's Ball in Jackson!° See how I sashayed around the ballroom, Laura? [*She raises her skirt and does a mincing step around the room.*] I wore it on Sundays for my gentlemen callers! I had it on the day I met your father.... I had malaria fever all that Spring. The change of climate from East Tennessee to the Delta—weakened resistance. I had a little temperature all the time—not enough to be serious—just enough to make me restless and giddy! Invitations poured in—parties all over the Delta! "Stay in bed," said Mother, "you have a fever!"—but I just wouldn't. I took quinine° but kept on going, going! Evenings, dances! Afternoons, long, long rides! Picnics—lovely! So lovely, that country in May—all lacy with dogwood, literally flooded with jonquils! That was the spring I had the craze for jonquils. Jonquils became an absolute obsession. Mother said, "Honey, there's no more room for jonquils." And still I kept on bringing in more jonquils. Whenever, wherever I saw them, I'd say, "Stop! Stop! I see jonquils!" I made the young men help me gather the jonquils! It was a joke, Amanda and her jonquils. Finally there were no more vases to hold them, every available space was filled with jonquils. No vases to hold them? All right, I'll hold them myself! And then I—[*She stops in front of the picture. Music plays.*] met your father! Malaria fever and jonquils and then—this—boy.... [*She switches on the rose-colored lamp.*] I hope they get here before it starts to rain. [*She crosses the room and places the jonquils in a bowl on the table.*] I gave your brother a little extra change so he and Mr. O'Connor could take the service car home.

LAURA. [*with an altered look*] What did you say his name was?　　20

AMANDA. O'Connor.

LAURA. What is his first name?

AMANDA. I don't remember. Oh, yes, I do. It was—Jim.

[*LAURA sways slightly and catches hold of a chair.*]

Legend on screen: "Not Jim!"]

LAURA. [*faintly*] Not—Jim!

AMANDA. Yes, that was it, it was Jim! I've never known a Jim that wasn't　　25 nice!

[*The music becomes ominous.*]

LAURA. Are you sure his name is Jim O'Connor?

AMANDA. Yes. Why?

LAURA. Is he the one that Tom used to know in high school?

19 *Jackson:* capital of Mississippi. Amanda refers to the social events of her youth. A cotillion is a formal ball, often given for debutantes. The cakewalk is a strutting dance step. 26 *quinine:* long used as a standard drug to control malaria.

AMANDA.   He didn't say so. I think he just got to know him at the warehouse.

LAURA.   There was a Jim O'Connor we both knew in high school—[*Then,* 30
with effort.] If that is the one that Tom is bringing to dinner—you'll have to excuse
me, I won't come to the table.

AMANDA.   What sort of nonsense is this?

LAURA.   You asked me once if I'd ever liked a boy. Don't you remember I
showed you this boy's picture?

AMANDA.   You mean the boy you showed me in the yearbook?

LAURA.   Yes, that boy.

AMANDA.   Laura, Laura, were you in love with that boy? 35

LAURA.   I don't know, Mother. All I know is I couldn't sit at the table if it
was him!

AMANDA.   It won't be him! It isn't the least bit likely. But whether it is or
not, you will come to the table. You will not be excused.

LAURA.   I'll have to be, Mother.

AMANDA.   I don't intend to humor your silliness, Laura. I've had too much
from you and your brother, both! So just sit down and compose yourself till they
come. Tom has forgotten his key so you'll have to let them in, when they arrive.

LAURA.   [*panicky*] Oh, Mother—*you* answer the door! 40

AMANDA.   [*lightly*] I'll be in the kitchen—busy!

LAURA.   Oh, Mother, please answer the door, don't make me do it!

AMANDA.   [*crossing into the kitchenette*] I've got to fix the dressing for the
salmon. Fuss, fuss—silliness!—over a gentleman caller!

[*The door swings shut,* LAURA *is left alone.*

Legend on screen: "Terror!"

*She utters a low moan and turns off the lamp—sits stiffly on the edge of the sofa, knotting
her fingers together.*

Legend on screen: "The Opening of a Door!"

TOM *and* JIM *appear on the fire escape steps and climb to the landing. Hearing their approach,*
LAURA *rises with a panicky gesture. She retreats to the portieres. The doorbell rings.* LAURA
catches her breath and touches her throat. Low drums sound.]

AMANDA.   [*calling*] Laura, sweetheart! The door!

[LAURA *stares at it without moving.*]

JIM.   I think we just beat the rain. 45

TOM.   Uh-huh. [*He rings again, nervously.* JIM *whistles and fishes for a cigarette.*]

AMANDA.   [*very, very gaily*] Laura, that is your brother and Mr. O'Connor!
Will you let them in, darling?

[LAURA *crosses toward the kitchenette door.*]

LAURA.   [*breathlessly*] Mother—you go to the door!

[AMANDA *steps out of the kitchenette and stares furiously at* LAURA. *She points imperiously
at the door.*]

LAURA.   Please, please!

AMANDA. [*in a fierce whisper*] What is the matter with you, you silly thing?   50

LAURA. [*desperately*] Please, you answer it, *please!*

AMANDA. I told you I wasn't going to humor you, Laura. Why have you chosen this moment to lose your mind?

LAURA. Please, please, please, you go!

AMANDA. You'll have to go to the door because I can't.

LAURA. [*despairingly*] I can't either!   55

AMANDA. *Why?*

LAURA. I'm *sick!*

AMANDA. I'm sick, too—of your nonsense! Why can't you and your brother be normal people? Fantastic whims and behavior!

[*Tom gives a long ring.*]

Preposterous goings on! Can you give me one reason—[*She calls out lyrically.*] Coming! Just one second!—why you should be afraid to open a door? Now you answer it, Laura!

LAURA. Oh, oh, oh . . . [*She returns through the portieres, darts to the Victrola, winds it frantically and turns it on.*]

AMANDA. Laura Wingfield, you march right to that door!   60

LAURA. Yes—yes, Mother!

[*A faraway, scratchy rendition of "Dardanella"° softens the air and gives her strength to move through it. She slips to the door and draws it cautiously open. Tom enters with the caller, Jim O'connor.*]

TOM. Laura, this is Jim. Jim, this is my sister, Laura.

JIM. [*stepping inside*] I didn't know that Shakespeare had a sister!

LAURA. [*retreating, stiff and trembling, from the door*] How—how do you do?

JIM. [*heartily, extending his hand*] Okay!   65

[*Laura touches it hesitantly with hers.*]

JIM. Your hand's *cold*, Laura!

LAURA. Yes, well—I've been playing the Victrola. . . .

JIM. Must have been playing classical music on it! You ought to play a little hot swing music to warm you up!

LAURA. Excuse me—I haven't finished playing the Victrola. . . . [*She turns awkwardly and hurries into the front room. She pauses a second by the Victrola. Then she catches her breath and darts through the portieres like a frightened deer.*]

JIM. [*grinning*] What was the matter?   70

TOM. Oh—with Laura? Laura is—terribly shy.

JIM. Shy, huh? It's unusual to meet a shy girl nowadays. I don't believe you ever mentioned you had a sister.

TOM. Well, now you know. I have one. Here is the *Post Dispatch.*° You want a piece of it?

JIM. Uh-huh.

TOM. What piece? The comics?   75

61.1 *"Dardanella":* a popular song and dance tune written in 1919 by Fred Fisher, Felix Bernard, and Johnny S. Black.   73 *Post Dispatch: The St. Louis Post Dispatch,* a newspaper.

JIM.   Sports! [*He glances at it.*] Ole Dizzy Dean° is on his bad behavior.

TOM.   [*uninterested*] Yeah? [*He lights a cigarette and goes over to the fire-escape door.*]

JIM.   Where are *you* going?

TOM.   I'm going out on the terrace.

JIM.   [*going after him*] You know, Shakespeare—I'm going to sell you a bill   80
of goods!

TOM.   What goods?

JIM.   A course I'm taking.

TOM.   Huh?

JIM.   In public speaking! You and me, we're not the warehouse type.

TOM.   Thanks—that's good news. But what has public speaking got to do   85
with it?

JIM.   It fits you for—executive positions!

TOM.   Awww.

JIM.   I tell you it's done a helluva lot for me.

[*Image on screen: Executive at his desk.*]

TOM.   In what respect?

JIM.   In every! Ask yourself what is the difference between you an' me and   90
men in the office down front? Brains?—No!—Ability?—No! Then what? Just one
little thing—

TOM.   What is that one little thing?

JIM.   Primarily it amounts to—social poise! Being able to square up to
people and hold your own on any social level!

AMANDA.   [*from the kitchenette*] Tom?

TOM.   Yes, Mother?

AMANDA.   Is that you and Mr. O'Connor?   95

TOM.   Yes, Mother.

AMANDA.   Well, you just make yourselves comfortable in there.

TOM.   Yes, Mother.

AMANDA.   Ask Mr. O'Connor if he would like to wash his hands.

JIM.   Aw, no—no—thank you—I took care of that at the warehouse. Tom—   100

TOM.   Yes?

JIM.   Mr. Mendoza was speaking to me about you.

TOM.   Favorably?

JIM.   What do you think?

TOM.   Well—   105

JIM.   You're going to be out of a job if you don't wake up.

TOM.   I am waking up—

JIM.   You show no signs.

TOM.   The signs are interior.

[*Image on screen: The sailing vessel with the Jolly Roger again.*]

TOM.   I'm planning to change. [*He leans over the fire escape rail, speaking with*   110
quiet exhilaration. The incandescent marquees and signs of the first-run movie houses light

76 *Dizzy Dean:* Jerome Herman (or Jay Hanna) Dean (1911–1974), outstanding pitcher
with the St. Louis Cardinals (1932–1938).

his face from across the alley. He looks like a voyager.] I'm right at the point of committing myself to a future that doesn't include the warehouse and Mr. Mendoza or even a night-school course in public speaking.

JIM.   What are you gassing about?

TOM.   I'm tired of the movies.

JIM.   Movies!

TOM.   Yes, movies! Look at them—[*a wave toward the marvels of Grand Avenue*] All of those glamorous people—having adventures—hogging it all, gobbling the whole thing up! You know what happens? People go to the *movies* instead of *moving*! Hollywood characters are supposed to have all the adventures for everybody in America, while everybody in America sits in a dark room and watches them have them! Yes, until there's a war. That's when adventure becomes available to the masses! *Everyone's* dish, not only Gable's!° Then the people in the dark room come out of the dark room to have some adventures themselves—goody, goody! It's our turn now, to go to the South Sea Island—to make a safari—to be exotic, far-off! But I'm not patient. I don't want to wait till then. I'm tired of the *movies* and I am *about* to *move*!

JIM.   [*incredulously*] Move?   115

TOM.   Yes.

JIM.   When?

TOM.   Soon!

JIM.   Where? Where?

[*The music seems to answer the question, while* TOM *thinks it over. He searches in his pockets.*]

TOM.   I'm starting to boil inside. I know I seem dreamy, but inside—well,   120
I'm boiling! Whenever I pick up a shoe, I shudder a little thinking how short life is and what I am doing! Whatever that means, I know it doesn't mean shoes—except as something to wear on a traveler's feet! [*He finds what he has been searching for in his pockets and holds out a paper to* JIM.] Look—

JIM.   What?

TOM.   I'm a member.

JIM.   [*reading*] The Union of Merchant Seamen.

TOM.   I paid my dues this month, instead of the light bill.

JIM.   You will regret it when they turn off the lights.   125

TOM.   I won't be here.

JIM.   How about your mother?

TOM.   I'm like my father. The bastard son of a bastard! Did you notice how he's grinning in his picture in there? And he's been absent going on sixteen years!

JIM.   You're just talking, you drip. How does your mother feel about it?

TOM.   Shhh! Here comes Mother! Mother is not acquainted with my plans!   130

AMANDA.   [*coming through the portieres*] Where are you all?

TOM.   On the terrace, Mother.

[*They start inside. She advances to them.* TOM *is distinctly shocked at her appearance. Even* JIM *blinks a little. He is making his first contact with the girlish Southern vivacity and in spite of the night-school course in public speaking is somewhat thrown off the beam by the*

114 *Gable:* Clark Gable (1901–1960), popular American screen actor and matinee idol from the 1930s to his death.

unexpected outlay of social charm. Certain responses are attempted by JIM but are swept aside by AMANDA's gay laughter and chatter. TOM is embarrassed but after the first shock JIM reacts very warmly. He grins and chuckles, is altogether won over.

Image on screen: AMANDA as a girl.]

AMANDA. [*coyly smiling, shaking her girlish ringlets*] Well, well, well, so this is Mr. O'Connor. Introductions entirely unnecessary. I've heard so much about you from my boy. I finally said to him, Tom—good gracious!—why don't you bring this paragon to supper? I'd like to meet this nice young man at the warehouse!— instead of just hearing him sing your praises so much! I don't know why my son is so stand-offish—that's not Southern behavior!

Let's sit down and—I think we could stand a little more air in here! Tom, leave the door open. I felt a nice fresh breeze a moment ago. Where has it gone to? Mmm, so warm already! And not quite summer, even. We're going to burn up when summer really gets started. However, we're having—we're having a very light supper. I think light things are better fo' this time of year. The same as light clothes are. Light clothes an' light food are what warm weather calls fo'. You know our blood gets so thick during th' winter—it takes a while fo' us to *adjust* ourselves!— when the season changes . . . It's come so quick this year. I wasn't prepared. All of sudden—heavens! Already summer! I ran to the trunk an' pulled out this light dress—terribly old! Historical almost! But feels so good—so good an' co-ol, y'know. . . .

TOM. Mother—

AMANDA. Yes, honey?   135

TOM. How about—supper?

AMANDA. Honey, you go ask Sister if supper is ready! You know that Sister is in full charge of supper! Tell her you hungry boys are waiting for it. [*To JIM.*] Have you met Laura?

JIM. She—

AMANDA. Let you in? Oh, good, you've met already! It's rare for a girl as sweet an' pretty as Laura to be domestic! But Laura is, thank heavens, not only pretty but also very domestic. I'm not at all. I never was a bit. I never could make a thing but angel-food cake. Well, in the South we had so many servants. Gone, gone, gone. All vestige of gracious living! Gone completely! I wasn't prepared for what the future brought me. All of my gentlemen callers were sons of planters and so of course I assumed that I would be married to one and raise my family on a large piece of land with plenty of servants. But man proposes—and woman accepts the proposal! to vary that old, old saying a little but—I married no planter! I married a man who worked for the telephone company! That gallantly smiling gentleman over there! [*She points to the picture.*] A telephone man who—fell in love with long-distance! Now he travels and I don't even know where! But what am I going on for about my—tribulations? Tell me yours—I hope you don't have any! Tom?

TOM. [*returning*] Yes, Mother?   140

AMANDA. Is supper nearly ready?

TOM. It looks to me like supper is on the table.

AMANDA. Let me look— [*She rises prettily and looks through the portieres.*] Oh lovely! But where is Sister?

Tom.   Laura is not feeling well and she says that she thinks she'd better not come to the table.

Amanda.   What? Nonsense! Laura? Oh, Laura!   145

Laura.   [*from the kitchenette, faintly*] Yes, Mother.

Amanda.   You really must come to the table. We won't be seated until you come to the table! Come in, Mr. O'Connor. You sit over there and I'll. . . . Laura? Laura Wingfield! You're keeping us waiting, honey! We can't say grace until you come to the table!

[*The kitchenette door is pushed weakly open and* Laura *comes in. She is obviously quite faint, her lips trembling, her eyes wide and staring. She moves unsteadily toward the table.*

Screen legend: "Terror!"

Outside a summer storm is coming on abruptly. The white curtains billow inward at the windows and there is a sorrowful murmur from the deep blue dusk.

Laura *suddenly stumbles; she catches at a chair with a faint moan.*]

Tom.   Laura!

Amanda.   Laura!

[*There is a clap of thunder.*

Screen legend: "Ah!"]

[*despairingly*] Why, Laura, you *are* ill, darling! Tom, help your sister into the living room, dear! Sit in the living room, Laura—rest on the sofa. Well! [*To* Jim *as* Tom *helps his sister to the sofa in the living room.*] Standing over the hot stove made her ill! I told her that it was just too warm this evening, but—

[Tom *comes back to the table.*]

Is Laura all right now?

Tom.   Yes.   150

Amanda.   What is that? Rain? A nice cool rain has come up! [*She gives* Jim *a frightened look.*] I think we may—have grace—now . . . [Tom *looks at her stupidly.*] Tom, honey—you say grace!

Tom.   Oh . . . "For these and all thy mercies—"

[*They bow their heads,* Amanda *stealing a nervous glance at* Jim. *In the living room* Laura, *stretched on the sofa, clenches her hand to her lips, to hold back a shuddering sob.*]

God's Holy Name be praised—

[*The scene dims out.*]

Scene 7

[*It is half an hour later. Dinner is just being finished in the dining room,* Laura *is still huddled upon the sofa, her feet drawn under her, her head resting on a pale blue pillow, her eyes wide and mysteriously watchful. The new floor lamp with its shade of rose-colored silk gives a soft, becoming light to her face, bringing out the fragile, unearthly prettiness which usually escapes attention. From outside there is a steady murmur of rain, but it is slackening and soon stops; the air outside becomes pale and luminous as the moon breaks through the clouds. A moment after the curtain rises, the lights in both rooms flicker and go out.*]

JIM. Hey, there, Mr. Light Bulb!

[*AMANDA laughs nervously.*

Legend on screen: "Suspension of a public service."]

AMANDA. Where was Moses when the lights went out? Ha-ha. Do you know the answer to that one, Mr. O'Connor?

JIM. No, Ma'am, what's the answer?

AMANDA. In the dark!

[*JIM laughs appreciatively.*]

Everybody sit still. I'll light the candles. Isn't it lucky we have them on the table? Where's a match? Which of you gentlemen can provide a match?

JIM. Here.

AMANDA. Thank you, Sir.

JIM. Not at all, Ma'am!

AMANDA. [*as she lights the candles*] I guess the fuse has burnt out. Mr. O'Connor, can you tell a burnt-out fuse? I know I can't and Tom is a total loss when it comes to mechanics. [*They rise from the table and go into the kitchenette, from where their voices are heard.*] Oh, be careful you don't bump into something. We don't want our gentleman caller to break his neck. Now wouldn't that be a fine howdy-do?

JIM. Ha-ha! Where is the fuse-box?

AMANDA. Right here next to the stove. Can you see anything?

JIM. Just a minute.

AMANDA. Isn't electricity a mysterious thing? Wasn't it Benjamin Franklin who tied a key to a kite? We live in such a mysterious universe, don't we? Some people say that science clears up all the mysteries for us. In my opinion it only creates more! Have you found it yet?

JIM. No, Ma'am. All these fuses look okay to me.

AMANDA. Tom!

TOM. Yes, Mother?

AMANDA. That light bill I gave you several days ago. That one I told you we got the notices about?

[*Legend on screen: "Ha!"*]

TOM. Oh—yeah.

AMANDA. You didn't neglect to pay it by any chance?

TOM. Why, I—

AMANDA. Didn't! I might have known it!

JIM. Shakespeare probably wrote a poem on that light bill, Mrs. Wingfield.

AMANDA. I might have known better than to trust him with it! There's such a high price for negligence in this world!

JIM. Maybe the poem will win a ten-dollar prize.

AMANDA.   We'll just have to spend the remainder of the evening in the nineteenth century, before Mr. Edison made the Mazda lamp!°

JIM.   Candlelight is my favorite kind of light.   25

AMANDA.   That shows you're romantic! But that's no excuse for Tom. Well, we got through dinner. Very considerate of them to let us get through dinner before they plunged us into everlasting darkness, wasn't it, Mr. O'Connor?

JIM.   Ha-ha!

AMANDA.   Tom, as a penalty for your carelessness you can help me with the dishes.

JIM.   Let me give you a hand.

AMANDA.   Indeed you will not!   30

JIM.   I ought to be good for something.

AMANDA.   Good for something? [Her tone is rhapsodic.] You? Why, Mr. O'Connor, nobody, nobody's given me this much entertainment in years—as you have!

JIM.   Aw, now, Mrs. Wingfield!

AMANDA.   I'm not exaggerating, not one bit! But Sister is all by her lonesome. You go keep her company in the parlor! I'll give you this lovely old candelabrum that used to be on the altar at the Church of the Heavenly Rest. It was melted a little out of shape when the church burnt down. Lightning struck it one spring. Gypsy Jones was holding a revival at the time and he intimated that the church was destroyed because the Episcopalians gave card parties.

JIM.   Ha-ha.   35

AMANDA.   And how about you coaxing Sister to drink a little wine? I think it would be good for her! Can you carry both at once?

JIM.   Sure. I'm Superman!

AMANDA.   Now, Thomas, get into this apron!

[JIM comes into the dining room, carrying the candelabrum, its candles lighted, in one hand and a glass of wine in the other. The door of the kitchenette swings closed on AMANDA's gay laughter; the flickering light approaches the portieres. LAURA sits up nervously as JIM enters. She can hardly speak from the almost intolerable strain of being alone with a stranger.

Screen legend: "I don't suppose you remember me at all!"

At first, before JIM's warmth overcomes her paralyzing shyness, LAURA's voice is thin and breathless, as though she had just run up a steep flight of stairs. JIM's attitude is gently humorous. While the incident is apparently unimportant, it is to LAURA the climax of her secret life.]

JIM.   Hello there, Laura.

LAURA.   [faintly] Hello.   40

[She clears her throat.]

JIM.   How are you feeling now? Better?

LAURA.   Yes. Yes, thank you.

JIM.   This is for you. A little dandelion wine. [He extends the glass toward her with extravagant gallantry.]

LAURA.   Thank you.

24 Mazda lamp: Thomas A. Edison (1847–1931) developed the first practical incandescent lamp in 1879.

JIM. Drink it—but don't get drunk!   45

[*He laughs heartily.* LAURA *takes the glass uncertainly; she laughs shyly.*]

Where shall I set the candles?
> LAURA. Oh—oh, anywhere . . .
> JIM. How about here on the floor? Any objections?
> LAURA. No.
> JIM. I'll spread a newspaper under to catch the drippings. I like to sit on
the floor. Mind if I do?
> LAURA. Oh, no.   50
> JIM. Give me a pillow?
> LAURA. What?
> JIM. A pillow!
> LAURA. Oh . . . [*She hands him one quickly.*]
> JIM. How about you? Don't you like to sit on the floor?   55
> LAURA. Oh—yes.
> JIM. Why don't you, then?
> LAURA. I—will.
> JIM. Take a pillow!

[*Laura does. She sits on the floor on the other side of the candelabrum.* JIM *crosses his legs
and smiles engagingly at her.*] I can't hardly see you sitting way over there.
> LAURA. I can—see you.   60
> JIM. I know, but that's not fair, I'm in the limelight.

[LAURA *moves her pillow closer.*]

Good! Now I can see you! Comfortable?
> LAURA. Yes.
> JIM. So am I. Comfortable as a cow! Will you have some gum?
> LAURA. No, thank you.
> JIM. I think that I will indulge, with your permission. [*He musingly unwraps*   65
a stick of gum and holds it up.] Think of the fortune made by the guy that invented
the first piece of chewing gum. Amazing, huh? The Wrigley Building° is one of
the sights of Chicago—I saw it when I went up to the Century of Progress.° Did
you take in the Century of Progress?
> LAURA. No, I didn't.
> JIM. Well, it was quite a wonderful exposition. What impressed me most
was the Hall of Science. Gives you an idea of what the future will be in America,
even more wonderful than the present time is! [*There is a pause.* JIM *smiles at her.*]
Your brother tells me you're shy. Is that right—Laura?
> LAURA. I—don't know.
> JIM. I judge you to be an old-fashioned type of girl. Well, I think that's a
pretty good type to be. Hope you don't think I'm being too personal—do you?
> LAURA. [*Hastily, out of embarrassment*] I believe I *will* take a piece of gum, if 70
you—don't mind. [*clearing her throat*] Mr. O'Connor, have you—kept up with your
singing?
> JIM. Singing? Me?

65 *Wrigley Building:* Finished in 1924, this was one of the first skyscrapers in the United
States.   66 *Century of Progress:* a world's fair held in Chicago (1933–1934) to celebrate
the city's centennial.

LAURA.   Yes. I remember what a beautiful voice you had.

JIM.   When did you hear me sing?

[LAURA *does not answer, and in the long pause which follows a man's voice is heard singing offstage.*]

VOICE:

> O blow, ye winds, heigh-ho,
> A-roving I will go!
>> I'm off to my love
>> With a boxing glove—
> Ten thousand miles away!

JIM.   You say you've heard me sing?   75

LAURA.   Oh, Yes! Yes, very often . . . I—don't suppose—you remember me—at all?

JIM.   [*smiling doubtfully*] You know I have an idea I've seen you before. I had that idea soon as you opened the door. It seemed almost like I was about to remember your name. But the name that I started to call you—wasn't a name! And so I stopped myself before I said it.

LAURA.   Wasn't it—Blue Roses?

JIM.   [*springing up, grinning*] Blue Roses! My gosh, yes—Blue Roses! That's what I had on my tongue when you opened the door! Isn't it funny what tricks your memory plays? I didn't connect you with high school somehow or other. But that's where it was; it was high school. I didn't even know you were Shakespeare's sister! Gosh, I'm sorry.

LAURA.   I didn't expect you to. You—barely knew me!   80

JIM.   But we did have a speaking acquaintance, huh?

LAURA.   Yes, we—spoke to each other.

JIM.   When did you recognize me?

LAURA.   Oh, right away!

JIM.   Soon as I came in the door?   85

LAURA.   When I heard your name I thought it was probably you. I knew that Tom used to know you a little in high school. So when you came in the door—well, then I was—sure.

JIM.   Why didn't you *say* something, then?

LAURA.   [*breathlessly*] I didn't know what to say, I was—too surprised!

JIM.   For goodness' sakes! You know, this sure is funny!

LAURA.   Yes! Yes, isn't it, though . . .   90

JIM.   Didn't we have a class in something together?

LAURA.   Yes, we did.

JIM.   What class was that?

LAURA.   It was—singing—chorus!

JIM.   Aw!   95

LAURA.   I sat across the aisle from you in the Aud.

JIM.   Aw!

LAURA.   Mondays, Wednesdays, and Fridays.

JIM.   Now I remember—you always came in late.

LAURA.   Yes, it was so hard for me, getting upstairs. I had that brace on my   100
leg—it clumped so loud!

JIM.   I never heard any clumping.

LAURA. [*wincing at the recollection*] To me it sounded like—thunder!

JIM. Well, well, well, I never even noticed.

LAURA. And everybody was seated before I came in. I had to walk in front of all those people. My seat was in the back row. I had to go clumping all the way up the aisle with everyone watching!

JIM. You shouldn't have been self-conscious. 105

LAURA. I know, but I was. It was always such a relief when the singing started.

JIM. Aw, yes, I've placed you now! I used to call you Blue Roses. How was it that I got started calling you that?

LAURA. I was out of school a little while with pleurosis. When I came back you asked me what was the matter. I said I had pleurosis—you thought that I said *Blue Roses*. That's what you always called me after that!

JIM. I hope you didn't mind.

LAURA. Oh, no—I liked it. You see, I wasn't acquainted with many— 110
people. . . .

JIM. As I remember you sort of stuck by yourself.

LAURA. I—I—never have had much luck at—making friends.

JIM. I don't see why you wouldn't.

LAURA. Well, I—started out badly.

JIM. You mean being— 115

LAURA. Yes, it sort of—stood between me—

JIM. You shouldn't have let it!

LAURA. I know, but it did, and—

JIM. You were shy with people!

LAURA. I tried not to be but never could— 120

JIM. Overcome it?

LAURA. No, I—I never could!

JIM. I guess being shy is something you have to work out of kind of gradually.

LAURA. [*sorrowfully*] Yes—I guess it—

JIM. Takes time! 125

LAURA. Yes—

JIM. People are not so dreadful when you know them. That's what you have to remember! And everybody has problems, not just you, but practically everybody has got some problems. You think of yourself as having the only problems, as being the only one who is disappointed. But just look around you and you will see lots of people as disappointed as you are. For instance, I hoped when I was going to high school that I would be further along at this time, six years later, than I am now. You remember that wonderful write-up I had in *The Torch*?

LAURA. Yes! [*She rises and crosses to the table.*]

JIM. It said I was bound to succeed in anything I went into!

[*LAURA returns with the high school yearbook.*]

Holy Jeez! *The Torch!*

[*He accepts it reverently. They smile across the book with mutual wonder. LAURA crouches beside him and they begin to turn the pages. LAURA's shyness is dissolving in his warmth.*]

LAURA.   Here you are in *The Pirates of Penzance*!   130
JIM.   [*wistfully*] I sang the baritone lead in that operetta.
LAURA.   [*raptly*] So—*beautifully*!
JIM.   [*protesting*] Aw—
LAURA.   Yes, yes—beautifully—beautifully!
JIM.   You heard me?   135
LAURA.   All three times!
JIM.   No!
LAURA.   Yes!
JIM.   All three performances?
LAURA.   [*looking down*] Yes.   140
JIM.   Why?
LAURA.   I—wanted to ask you to—autograph my program. [*She takes the*
program from the back of the yearbook and shows it to him.]
JIM.   Why didn't you ask me to?
LAURA.   You were always surrounded by your own friends so much that I
never had a chance to.
JIM.   You should have just—   145
LAURA.   Well, I—thought you might think I was—
JIM.   Thought I might think you was—what?
LAURA.   Oh—
JIM.   [*with reflective relish*] I was beleaguered by females in those days.
LAURA.   You were terribly popular!   150
JIM.   Yeah—
LAURA.   You had such a—friendly way—
JIM.   I was spoiled in high school.
LAURA.   Everybody—liked you!
JIM.   Including you?   155
LAURA.   I—yes, I—did, too— [*She gently closes the book in her lap.*]
JIM.   Well, well, well! Give me that program, Laura.

[*She hands it to him. He signs it with a flourish.*]

There you are—better late than never!
LAURA.   Oh, I—what a—surprise!
JIM.   My signature isn't worth very much right now. But some day—maybe—
it will increase in value! Being disappointed is one thing and being discouraged is
something else. I am disappointed but I am not discouraged. I'm twenty-three
years old. How old are you?
LAURA.   I'll be twenty-four in June.   160
JIM.   That's not old age!
LAURA.   No, but—
JIM.   You finished high school?
LAURA.   [*with difficulty*] I didn't go back.
JIM.   You mean you dropped out?   165
LAURA.   I made bad grades in my final examinations. [*She rises and replaces*
the book and the program on the table. Her voice is strained.] How is—Emily Meisenbach
getting along?
JIM.   Oh, that kraut-head!
LAURA.   Why do you call her that?

JIM. That's what she was.

LAURA. You're not still—going with her?   170

JIM. I never see her.

LAURA. It was in the "Personal" section that you were—engaged!

JIM. I know, but I wasn't impressed by that—propaganda!

LAURA. It wasn't—the truth?

JIM. Only in Emily's optimistic opinion!   175

LAURA. Oh—

[*Legend:* "What have you done since high school?"]

Jim lights a cigarette and leans indolently back on his elbows smiling at LAURA *with a warmth and charm which lights her inwardly with altar candles. She remains by the table, picks up a piece from the glass menagerie collection, and turns it in her hands to cover her tumult.*]

JIM. [*after several reflective puffs on his cigarette*] What have you done since high school?

[*She seems not to hear him.*]

Huh?

[LAURA *looks up.*]

I said what have you done since high school, Laura?

LAURA. Nothing much.

JIM. You must have been doing something these six long years.

LAURA. Yes.   180

JIM. Well, then, such as what?

LAURA. I took a business course at business college—

JIM. How did that work out?

LAURA. Well, not very—well—I had to drop out, it gave me—indigestion—

[JIM *laughs gently.*]

JIM. What are you doing now?   185

LAURA. I don't do anything—much. Oh, please don't think I sit around doing nothing! My glass collection takes up a good deal of time. Glass is something you have to take good care of.

JIM. What did you say—about glass?

LAURA. Collection I said—I have one—[*She clears her throat and turns away again, acutely shy.*]

JIM. [*abruptly*] You know what I judge to be the trouble with you? Inferiority complex! Know what that is? That's what they call it when someone low-rates himself! I understand it because I had it too. Although my case was not so aggravated as yours seems to be. I had it until I took up public speaking, developed my voice, and learned that I had an aptitude for science. Before that time I never thought of myself as being outstanding in any way whatsoever! Now I've never made a regular study of it, but I have a friend who says I can analyze people better than doctors that make a profession of it. I don't claim that to be necessarily true, but I can sure guess a person's psychology. Laura! [*He takes out his gum.*] Excuse me, Laura. I always take it out when the flavor is gone. I'll use this scrap of paper to wrap it in. I know how it is to get it stuck on a shoe. [*He wraps the gum in paper and puts it in his pocket.*] Yep—that's what I judge to be your principal trouble. A lack of confidence in yourself as a person. You don't have the proper amount of faith in yourself. I'm basing that fact on a number of your remarks and also on certain observations I've made. For instance that clumping you thought was so awful in high school. You say that you even dreaded to walk into class. You see what you did? You dropped out of school, you gave up an education because of a clump, which as far as I know was practically nonexistent! A little physical defect is what you have. Hardly noticeable even! Magnified thousands of times by imagination! You know what my strong advice to you is? Think of yourself as *superior* in some way!

LAURA.   In what way would I think?   190

JIM.   Why, man alive, Laura! Just look about you a little. What do you see? A world full of common people! All of 'em born and all of 'em going to die! Which of them has one-tenth of your good points! Or mine! Or anyone else's, as far as that goes—gosh! Everybody excels in some one thing. Some in many! [*He unconsciously glances at himself in the mirror.*] All you've got to do is discover in *what*! Take me, for instance. [*He adjusts his tie at the mirror.*] My interest happens to lie in electro-dynamics. I'm taking a course in radio engineering at night school, Laura, on top of a fairly responsible job at the warehouse. I'm taking that course and studying public speaking.

LAURA.   Ohhhh.

JIM.   Because I believe in the future of television! [*turning his back to her*] I wish to be ready to go up right along with it. Therefore I'm planning to get in on the ground floor. In fact I've already made the right connections and all that remains is for the industry itself to get under way! Full steam—[*His eyes are starry.*] Knowledge—Zzzzzp! Money—Zzzzzp!—Power! That's the cycle democracy is built on!

[*His attitude is convincingly dynamic.* LAURA *stares at him, even her shyness eclipsed in her absolute wonder. He suddenly grins.*]

I guess you think I think a lot of myself!

LAURA.   No—o-o-o, I—

JIM.   Now how about you? Isn't there something you take more interest in   195
than anything else?

LAURA.   Well, I do—as I said—have my—glass collection—

[*A peal of girlish laughter rings from the kitchenette.*]

JIM.   I'm not right sure I know what you're talking about. What kind of glass is it?

LAURA.   Little articles of it, they're ornaments mostly! Most of them are little animals made out of glass, the tiniest little animals in the world. Mother calls them a glass menagerie! Here's an example of one, if you'd like to see it! This one is one of the oldest. It's nearly thirteen.

[*Music: "The Glass Menagerie."*

He stretches out his hand.]

Oh, be careful—if you breathe, it breaks!

JIM.   I'd better not take it. I'm pretty clumsy with things.

LAURA. Go, on, I trust you with him! [*She places the piece in his palm.*] There 200
now—you're holding him gently! Hold him over the light, he loves the light! You
see how the light shines through him?

JIM. It sure does shine!

LAURA. I shouldn't be partial, but he is my favorite one.

JIM. What kind of a thing is this one supposed to be?

LAURA. Haven't you noticed the single horn on his forehead?

JIM. A unicorn, huh?

LAURA. Mmmm-hmmm! 205

JIM. Unicorns—aren't they extinct in the modern world?

LAURA. I know!

JIM. Poor little fellow, he must feel sort of lonesome.

LAURA. [*smiling*] Well, if he does, he doesn't complain about it. He stays on 210
a shelf with some horses that don't have horns and all of them seem to get along
nicely together.

JIM. How do you know?

LAURA. [*lightly*] I haven't heard any arguments among them!

JIM. [*grinning*] No arguments, huh? Well, that's a pretty good sign! Where
shall I set him?

LAURA. Put him on the table. They all like a change of scenery once in a
while!

JIM. Well, well, well, well—[*He places the glass piece on the table, then raises his* 215
arms and stretches.] Look how big my shadow is when I stretch!

LAURA. Oh, oh, yes—it stretches across the ceiling!

JIM. [*crossing to the door*] I think it's stopped raining. [*He opens the fire-escape*
door and the background music changes to a dance tune.] Where does the music come
from?

LAURA. From the Paradise Dance Hall across the alley.

JIM. How about cutting the rug a little, Miss Wingfield?

LAURA. Oh, I—

JIM. Or is your program filled up? Let me have a look at it. [*He grasps an* 220
imaginary card.] Why, every dance is taken! I'll just have to scratch some out.

[*Waltz music: "La Golondrina"°*]

Ahh, a waltz! [*He executes some sweeping turns by himself, then holds his arms toward*
LAURA.]

LAURA. [*breathlessly*] I—can't dance.

JIM. There you go, that inferiority stuff!

LAURA. I've never danced in my life!

JIM. Come on, try! 225

LAURA. Oh, but I'd step on you!

JIM. I'm not made out of glass.

LAURA. How—how—how do we start?

JIM. Just leave it to me. You hold your arms out a little.

LAURA. Like this? 230

JIM. [*taking her in his arms*] A little bit higher. Right. Now don't tighten up,
that's the main thing about it—relax.

220.1 *"La Golondrina":* a popular Mexican song (1883) written by Narciso Seradell (1843–
1910).

LAURA.   [*laughing breathlessly*] It's hard not to.

JIM.   Okay.

LAURA.   I'm afraid you can't budge me.

JIM.   What do you bet I can't? [*He swings her into motion.*]   235

LAURA.   Goodness, yes, you can!

JIM.   Let yourself go, now, Laura, just let yourself go.

LAURA.   I'm—

JIM.   Come on!

LAURA.   —trying!   240

JIM.   Not so stiff—easy does it!

LAURA.   I know but I'm—

JIM.   Loosen th' backbone! There now, that's a lot better.

LAURA.   Am I?

JIM.   Lots, lots better! [*He moves her about the room in a clumsy waltz.*]   245

LAURA.   Oh, my!

JIM.   Ha-ha!

LAURA.   Oh, my goodness!

JIM.   Ha-ha-ha!

[*They suddenly bump into the table, and the glass piece on it falls to the floor. JIM stops the dance.*]

What did we hit?

LAURA.   Table.   250

JIM.   Did something fall off it? I think—

LAURA.   Yes.

JIM.   I hope that it wasn't the little glass horse with the horn!

LAURA.   Yes. [*She stoops to pick it up.*]

JIM.   Aw, aw, aw. Is it broken?   255

LAURA.   Now it is just like all the other horses.

JIM.   It's lost its—

LAURA.   Horn! It doesn't matter. Maybe it's a blessing in disguise.

JIM.   You'll never forgive me. I bet that that was your favorite piece of glass.

LAURA.   I don't have favorites much. It's no tragedy, Freckles. Glass breaks   260
so easily. No matter how careful you are. The traffic jars the shelves and things
fall off them.

JIM.   Still I'm awfully sorry that I was the cause.

LAURA.   [*smiling*] I'll just imagine he had an operation. The horn was
removed to make him feel less—freakish!

[*They both laugh.*]

Now he will feel more at home with the other horses, the ones that don't
have horns. . . .

JIM.   Ha-ha, that's very funny! [*Suddenly he is serious.*] I'm glad to see that
you have a sense of humor. You know—you're—well—very different! Surprisingly
different from anyone else I know! [*His voice becomes soft and hesitant with a genuine
feeling.*] Do you mind me telling you that?

[*LAURA is abashed beyond speech.*]

I mean it in a nice way—

[LAURA *nods shyly, looking away.*]

You make me feel sort of—I don't know how to put it! I'm usually pretty good at expressing things, but—this is something that I don't know how to say!

[LAURA *touches her throat and clears it—turns the broken unicorn in her hands. His voice becomes softer.*]

Has anyone ever told you that you were pretty?

[*There is a pause, and the music rises slightly.* LAURA *looks up slowly, with wonder, and shakes her head.*]

Well, you are! In a very different way from anyone else. And all the nicer because of the difference, too.

[*His voice becomes low and husky.* LAURA *turns away, nearly faint with the novelty of her emotions.*]

I wish that you were my sister. I'd teach you to have some confidence in yourself. The different people are not like other people, but being different is nothing to be ashamed of. Because other people are not such wonderful people. They're one hundred times one thousand. You're one times one! They walk all over the earth. You just stay here. They're common as—weeds, but—you—well, you're—*Blue Roses*!

[*Image on screen: Blue Roses.*

The music changes.]

> LAURA. But blue is wrong for—roses. . . .
> JIM. It's right for you! You're—pretty!
> LAURA. In what respect am I pretty?
> JIM. In all respects—believe me! Your eyes—your hair—are pretty! Your hands are pretty! [*He catches hold of her hand.*] You think I'm making this up because I'm invited to dinner and have to be nice. Oh, I could do that! I could put on an act for you, Laura, and say lots of things without being very sincere. But this time I am. I'm talking to you sincerely. I happened to notice you had this inferiority complex that keeps you from feeling comfortable with people. Somebody needs to build your confidence up and make you proud instead of shy and turning away and—blushing. Somebody—ought to—*kiss* you, Laura!

265

[*His hand slips slowly up her arm to her shoulder as the music swells tumultuously. He suddenly turns about and kisses her on the lips. When he releases her,* LAURA *sinks on the sofa with a bright, dazed look.* JIM *backs away and fishes in his pocket for a cigarette.*

Legend on screen: "A souvenir."]

Stumblejohn!

[*He lights the cigarette, avoiding her look. There is a peal of girlish laughter from* AMANDA *in the kitchenette.* LAURA *slowly raises and opens her hand. It still contains the little broken glass animal. She looks at it with a tender, bewildered expression.*]

Stumblejohn! I shouldn't have done that—that was way off the beam. You don't smoke, do you?

[*She looks up, smiling, not hearing the question. He sits beside her rather gingerly. She looks at him speechlessly—waiting. He coughs decorously and moves a little further aside as he considers the situation and senses her feelings, dimly, with perturbation. He speaks gently.*]

Would you—care for a mint?

[*She doesn't seem to hear him but her look grows brighter even.*]

Peppermint? Life Saver? My pocket's a regular drugstore—wherever I go. . . . [*He pops a mint in his mouth. Then he gulps and decides to make a clean breast of it. He speaks slowly and gingerly.*] Laura, you know, if I had a sister like you, I'd do the same thing as Tom. I'd bring out fellows and—introduce her to them. The right type of boys—of a type to—appreciate her. Only—well—he made a mistake about me. Maybe I've got no call to be saying this. That may not have been the idea in having me over. But what if it was? There's nothing wrong about that. The only trouble is that in my case—I'm not in a situation to—do the right thing. I can't take down your number and say I'll phone. I can't call up next week and—ask for a date. I thought I had better explain the situation in case you—misunderstood it and—I hurt your feelings. . . .

[*There is a pause. Slowly, very slowly, LAURA's look changes, her eyes returning slowly from his to the glass figure in her palm. AMANDA utters another gay laugh in the kitchenette.*]

LAURA. [*faintly*] You—won't—call again?

JIM. No, Laura, I can't. [*He rises from the sofa.*] As I was just explaining, I've—got strings on me, Laura, I've—been going steady! I go out all the time with a girl named Betty. She's a home-girl like you, and Catholic, and Irish, and in a great many ways we—get along fine. I met her last summer on a moonlight boat trip up the river to Alton,° on the *Majestic*. Well—right away from the start it was—love!

[*Legend: Love!*
LAURA *sways slightly forward and grips the arm of the sofa. He fails to notice, now enrapt in his own comfortable being.*]

Being in love has made a new man of me!

[*Leaning stiffly forward, clutching the arm of the sofa, LAURA struggles visibly with her storm. But JIM is oblivious; she is a long way off.*]

The power of love is really pretty tremendous! Love is something that—changes the whole world, Laura!

[*The storm abates a little and LAURA leans back. He notices her again.*]

It happened that Betty's aunt took sick, she got a wire and had to go to Centralia.° So Tom—when he asked me to dinner—I naturally just accepted the invitation, not knowing that you—that he—that I—[*He stops awkwardly.*] Huh—I'm a stumblejohn!

[*He flops back on the sofa. The holy candles on the altar of LAURA's face have been snuffed out. There is a look of almost infinite desolation. JIM glances at her uneasily.*]

69.1 *Alton:* a city in Illinois about twenty miles north of St. Louis on the Mississippi River.
69.8 *Centralia:* a city in Illinois about sixty miles east of St. Louis.

I wish that you would—say something.

[*She bites her lip which was trembling and then bravely smiles. She opens her hand again on the broken glass figure. Then she gently takes his hand and raises it level with her own. She carefully places the unicorn in the palm of his hand, then pushes his fingers closed upon it.*]

What are you—doing that for? You want me to have him? Laura?

[*She nods.*]

What for?

LAURA. A—souvenir. . . .   270

[*She rises unsteadily and crouches beside the Victrola to wind it up.*

Legend on screen: "Things have a way of turning out so badly!" Or image: "Gentleman caller waving goodbye—gaily."

At this moment AMANDA *rushes brightly back into the living room. She bears a pitcher of fruit punch in an old-fashioned cut-glass pitcher, and a plate of macaroons. The plate has a gold border and poppies painted on it.*]

AMANDA. Well, well, well! Isn't the air delightful after the shower? I've made you children a little liquid refreshment. [*She turns gaily to* JIM.] Jim, do you know that song about lemonade?
"Lemonade, lemonade
Made in the shade and stirred with a spade—
Good enough for any old maid!"

JIM. [*uneasily*] Ha-ha! No—I never heard it.

AMANDA. Why, Laura! You look so serious!

JIM. We were having a serious conversation.

AMANDA. Good! Now you're better acquainted!   275

JIM. [*uncertainly*] Ha-ha! Yes.

AMANDA. You modern young people are much more serious-minded than my generation. I was so gay as a girl!

JIM. You haven't changed, Mrs. Wingfield.

AMANDA. Tonight I'm rejuvenated! The gaiety of the occasion, Mr. O'Connor! [*She tosses her head with a peal of laughter, spilling some lemonade.*] Oooo! I'm baptizing myself!

JIM. Here—let me—   280

AMANDA. [*setting the pitcher down*] There now. I discovered we had some maraschino cherries. I dumped them in, juice and all!

JIM. You shouldn't have gone to that trouble, Mrs. Wingfield.

AMANDA. Trouble, trouble? Why, it was loads of fun! Didn't you hear me cutting up in the kitchen? I bet your ears were burning! I told Tom how outdone with him I was for keeping you to himself so long a time! He should have brought you over much, much sooner! Well, now that you've found your way, I want you to be a very frequent caller! Not just occasional but all the time. Oh, we're going to have a lot of gay times together! I see them coming! Mmm, just breathe that air! So fresh, and the moon's so pretty! I'll skip back out—I know where my place is when young folks are having a—serious conversation!

JIM. Oh, don't go out, Mrs. Wingfield. The fact of the matter is I've got to be going.

AMANDA. Going, now? You're joking! Why, it's only the shank of the   285
evening,° Mr. O'Connor!

JIM. Well, you know how it is.

AMANDA. You mean you're a young workingman and have to keep workingmen's hours. We'll let you off early tonight. But only on the condition that
next time you stay later. What's the best night for you? Isn't Saturday night the
best night for you workingmen?

JIM. I have a couple of time-clocks to punch, Mrs. Wingfield. One at
morning, another one at night!

AMANDA. My, but you *are* ambitious! You work at night, too?

JIM. No, Ma'am, not work but—Betty!   290

[*He crosses deliberately to pick up his hat. The band at the Paradise Dance Hall goes into a
tender waltz.*]

AMANDA. Betty? Betty? Who's—Betty!

[*There is an ominous cracking sound in the sky.*]

JIM. Oh, just a girl. The girl I go steady with!

[*He smiles charmingly. The sky falls.*

Legend: "The Sky Falls."*]

AMANDA. [*a long-drawn exhalation*] Ohhh . . . Is it a serious romance, Mr.
O'Connor?

JIM. We're going to be married the second Sunday in June.

AMANDA. Ohhh—how nice! Tom didn't mention that you were engaged to   295
be married.

JIM. The cat's not out of the bag at the warehouse yet. You know how they
are. They call you Romeo and stuff like that. [*He stops at the oval mirror to put on
his hat. He carefully shapes the brim and the crown to give a discreetly dashing effect.*] It's
been a wonderful evening, Mrs. Wingfield. I guess this is what they mean by
Southern hospitality.

AMANDA. It really wasn't anything at all.

JIM. I hope it don't seem like I'm rushing off. But I promised Betty I'd
pick her up at the Wabash depot, an' by the time I get my jalopy down there her
train'll be in. Some women are pretty upset if you keep 'em waiting.

AMANDA. Yes, I know—the tyranny of women! [*She extends her hand.*] Goodbye, Mr. O'Connor. I wish you luck—and happiness—and success! All three of
them, and so does Laura! Don't you, Laura?

LAURA. Yes!   300

JIM. [*taking LAURA's hand*] Goodbye, Laura. I'm certainly going to treasure
that souvenir. And don't you forget the good advice I gave you. [*He raises his voice
to a cheery shout.*] So long, Shakespeare! Thanks again, ladies. Good night!

[*He grins and ducks jauntily out. Still bravely grimacing, AMANDA closes the door on the
gentleman caller. Then she turns back to the room with a puzzled expression. She and LAURA
don't dare to face each other. LAURA crouches beside the Victrola to wind it.*]

---

285 *shank of the evening*: still early, the best part of the evening.

AMANDA. [*faintly*] Things have a way of turning out so badly. I don't believe that I would play the Victrola. Well, well—well! Our gentleman caller was engaged to be married? [*She raises her voice.*] Tom!

TOM. [*from the kitchenette*] Yes, Mother?

AMANDA. Come in here a minute. I want to tell you something awfully funny.

TOM. [*entering with a macaroon and a glass of the lemonade*] Has the gentleman   305
caller gotten away already?

AMANDA. The gentleman caller has made an early departure. What a wonderful joke you played on us!

TOM. How do you mean?

AMANDA. You didn't mention that he was engaged to be married.

TOM. Jim? Engaged?

AMANDA. That's what he just informed us.   310

TOM. I'll be jiggered! I didn't know about that.

AMANDA. That seems very peculiar.

TOM. What's peculiar about it?

AMANDA. Didn't you call him your best friend down at the warehouse?

TOM. He is, but how did I know?   315

AMANDA. It seems extremely peculiar that you wouldn't know your best friend was going to be married!

TOM. The warehouse is where I work, not where I know things about people!

AMANDA. You don't know things anywhere! You live in a dream; you manufacture illusions!

[*He crosses to the door.*]

Where are you going?

TOM. I'm going to the movies.

AMANDA. That's right, now that you've had us make such fools of ourselves.   320
The effort, the preparations, all the expense! The new floor lamp, the rug, the clothes for Laura! All for what? To entertain some other girl's fiancé! Go to the movies, go! Don't think about us, a mother deserted, an unmarried sister who's crippled and has no job! Don't let anything interfere with your selfish pleasure! Just go, go, go—to the movies!

TOM. All right, I will! The more you shout about my selfishness to me the quicker I'll go, and I won't go to the movies!

AMANDA. Go, then! Go to the moon—you selfish dreamer!

[*TOM smashes his glass on the floor. He plunges out on the fire escape, slamming the door. LAURA screams in fright. The dance-hall music becomes louder. TOM stands on the fire escape, gripping the rail. The moon breaks through the storm clouds, illuminating his face.*]

Legend on screen: "And so goodbye. . ."

TOM's closing speech is timed with what is happening inside the house. We see, as though through soundproof glass, that AMANDA appears to be making a comforting speech to LAURA, who is huddled upon the sofa. Now that we cannot hear the mother's speech, her silliness is gone and she has dignity and tragic beauty. LAURA's hair hides her face until, at the end of the speech, she lifts her head to smile at her mother. AMANDA's gestures are slow and graceful, almost dancelike, as she comforts her daughter. At the end of her speech she glances a moment at the father's picture—then withdraws through the portieres. At the close of TOM's *speech,* LAURA *blows out the candles, ending the play.*]

TOM.   I didn't go to the moon, I went much further—for time is the longest distance between two places. Not long after that I was fired for writing a poem on the lid of a shoe-box. I left Saint Louis. I descended the steps of this fire escape for a last time and followed, from then on, in my father's footsteps, attempting to find in motion what was lost in space. I traveled around a great deal. The cities swept about me like dead leaves, leaves that were brightly colored but torn away from the branches. I would have stopped, but I was pursued by something. It always came upon me unawares, taking me altogether by surprise. Perhaps it was a familiar bit of music. Perhaps it was only a piece of transparent glass. Perhaps I am walking along a street at night, in some strange city, before I have found companions. I pass the lighted window of a shop where perfume is sold. The window is filled with pieces of colored glass, tiny transparent bottles in delicate colors, like bits of a shattered rainbow. Then all at once my sister touches my shoulder. I turn around and look into her eyes. Oh, Laura, Laura, I tried to leave you behind me, but I am more faithful than I intended to be! I reach for a cigarette, I cross the street, I run into the movies or a bar, I buy a drink, I speak to the nearest stranger—anything that can blow your candles out!

[LAURA *bends over the candles.*]

For nowadays the world is lit by lightning! Blow out your candles, Laura— and so goodbye. . . .

[*She blows the candles out.*]

QUESTIONS

1.   What does the setting described in the opening stage direction tell you about the Wingfields? Consider especially the adjectives Williams employs and the symbolism of the alley and the fire escape.

2.   Who is the "fifth character" in the play and how is his presence established? In what ways is Tom a parallel to this character?

3.   What does Amanda reveal about her past in scene 1? How does Williams reveal that Amanda often dwells in the past?

4.   What happened to Laura at Rubicam's Business College? How can you account for her behavior? What plan of Amanda's did she upset?

5.   What new plan for Laura's future does Amanda begin to develop in scene 2? Why is the plan impracticable? Why is the image of Jim introduced here?

6.   Summarize the argument between Tom and Amanda in scene 3. What does Amanda assert about Tom? What does he claim about his life? Why is Laura spotlighted throughout the argument?

7.   What sort of agreement does Amanda try to reach with Tom about Laura in scene 4?

8.   How does Amanda react to the news of a gentleman caller? How does Laura react? Describe Laura's feelings toward Jim during the conversation and the

dancing in scene 7. Describe his feelings toward her. How and why do his feelings change after the kiss?

9. Explain the symbolism of the unicorn (both whole and broken). Why does Laura give it to Jim as a souvenir?

10. What is Tom's situation at the close of the play? To what degree has he achieved his dreams of escape and adventure?

11. Describe Amanda's and Laura's situations at the close of the play. What is the significance of Laura's blowing out of the candles? What future can you predict for these women? Why?

GENERAL QUESTIONS

1. What are the most striking nonrealistic aspects of the play? Explain why each is nonrealistic and how each contributes to the impact and meaning of the play. Which is the most effective? Why?

2. Which characters in the play, if any, learn or change in significant ways? To what extent do the characters succeed or fail in their goals? What means do they use to escape the harsh realities they face?

3. Consider the distinction between Tom as a character and as narrator. How and why is the language of the narrator different from that of the character? What does the character dream about and strive for? What has the narrator learned about these dreams and strivings?

4. As the title suggests, Laura and her fantasy world are central to the play. Explain the reasons for Laura's inability to deal with reality. What is the symbolic significance of her glass menagerie?

5. Williams says that there is much to admire, pity, and laugh at in Amanda. What aspects of her character are admirable? Pitiable? Laughable? Which reaction is dominant for you at the close of the play? Why?

6. In his opening speech, Tom calls Jim "the most realistic character in the play." In what ways is Jim realistic? How are his dreams and goals more (or less) realistic than Tom's?

7. At the opening of the play, Tom (as narrator) mentions the "social background," and he remarks on it throughout. Discuss this background, especially the events occurring in Europe, and the ways it relates to the play's action.

8. Discuss the line of religious allusion and imagery that runs through the play. Consider especially Malvolio the Magician, the "Ave Maria," the "Annunciation," the Paradise Dance Hall, and Laura's candles. What is the effect of these references on the play's level of reality?

WRITING ABOUT REALISTIC AND NONREALISTIC DRAMA

In planning and writing an essay about a realistic or nonrealistic play, your attention will be focused on the traditional elements of drama—plot, character, perspective, setting, language, tone, symbol, and theme. Conventional approaches to these were discussed earlier (pp. 993–1001); you may want to review this material. You will also be concerned, however, with the relative degrees of realism or nonrealism with which the elements are presented and developed, and the ways in which this variable affects the impact and meaning of the play.

You will be dealing with four related areas of exploration for this type of essay: (1) the elements or aspects of the play that you find most interesting, significant, and effective; (2) the feelings, ideas, and effects created or emphasized through these features; (3) the degree to which these elements or aspects may be considered realistic (or nonrealistic); and (4) the extent to which the impact or meaning of the play depends on the realism or nonrealism of the elements under consideration. The introduction of a new variable into your planning—the spectrum of realism and its impact on the play—thus creates new ways to study and consider drama. Think about the following questions as you plan your essay.

Questions for Discovering Ideas

PLOT. Does the play unfold in a chronological order that imitates reality, or does it mix past and present action? Is the action true to life or stylized? Are the conflicts resolved realistically, or does the playwright employ a conventional and perhaps improbable happy (or sad) ending? How does the realistic or nonrealistic development of these aspects affect the impact and meaning of the play?

CHARACTER. Are the characters presented and developed in a predominantly realistic manner? Are they symbolic, representative, or stereotyped? Round or flat? Are they motivated by lifelike considerations, or simply by the requirements of the play? In *The Glass Menagerie*, for example, Amanda is presented as a realistic character who lives only within the world of the past action, but the narrator is cast in the artificial role of speaking directly to the audience. Are the characters consistent, or do they drop in and out of character? Is their clothing and makeup (as described in the stage directions) an imitation of real life, or is it theatrical and nonrealistic? Are all the characters developed in the same manner, or are there differences in the degree of realism you find in each? Is there one character who is more or less realistic than any of the others? If so, what impact does this have on the play?

PERSPECTIVE. In realistic drama, in which the point of view tends to be objective, one of the few ways to impose a somewhat subjective point of view is to give all or most of the lines to a single character; Eugene O'Neill uses such a device in *Before Breakfast* (pp. 1030–35), in which Mrs. Rowland has the only speaking part. When you encounter such a play, consider why the character is given most of the dialogue and how the device shapes or distorts your perception of the play. In nonrealistic drama, the playwright has the freedom to unfold the play through whatever perspective he or she chooses. In such a case, consider which characters speak directly to the audience or the reader. How extensive is such direct address? Is there a single character who does most of this talking? If so, what is he or she like? What does the character tell you about himself or herself? About the other characters in the play? The background? Plot? Action? Setting? Staging? How accurate and objective is this character? Above all else, how does this direct address shape and control your responses?

SETTING. To what degree do the stage directions present the setting as realistic or nonrealistic? Do the playwright's directions call in minute detail for the reproduction of an actual room or place? If less than a fully realistic setting is described, how far does the playwright go in reducing the setting to the bare stage? How much of the physical theater (brick walls, pipes, wires, lights, backstage ropes) does the playwright indicate that he or she wants you to see or imagine? To what extent do you find symbolic, impressionistic and nonrealistic devices such as transparent walls? Most important, how does the setting and its degree of realism (or nonrealism) contribute to the impact and meaning of the play? How do the stage directions describe the lighting? Is lighting used realistically, to recreate the natural illumination in a room, or nonrealistically, to isolate and emphasize specific places, objects, characters, or actions?

LANGUAGE. Is the language colloquial and appropriate for the characters, or do you find nonrealistic devices such as verse, song, or unnatural and patterned repetition? In *An Enemy of the People*, for example, the dialogue is consistently imitative of real life, but in *The Sandbox* we find inarticulate noises, strings of clichés, and much repetition. Does each character maintain a consistent style and level of diction, or do you find a single character speaking in different voices? How do these aspects of language determine the extent to which the play effectively communicates ideas and emotions to you? As you deal with language, also consider the significance of other aspects of sound indicated in the stage directions, such as sound effects or music.

SYMBOLISM. Since symbols operate in life as they do in art, there is room for symbolism in the realistic plays of Glaspell and Ibsen as well as in the relatively nonrealistic dramas of Miller and Williams. Are symbols in the play introduced through realistic or nonrealistic techniques? You can focus your exploration directly on the symbol and its meaning (the water pollution in *An Enemy of the People*) or the nonrealistic methods through which it is established (the blue roses in *The Glass Menagerie*).

THEME.   What are the important concepts in the play and how are they conveyed? Here you should give special consideration to significantly realistic or nonrealistic techniques. In dealing with a realistic play like *Trifles* or *An Enemy of the People*, you might explore the ways in which realism in character, action, and setting contribute to the emergence of the play's ideas. Conversely, you might consider how Williams employs a strikingly nonrealistic device, such as the music of the screen projections, to convey and emphasize the themes of *The Glass Menagerie*.

Strategies for Organizing Ideas

The central idea will normally assert a connection between a specific aspect of the play, its relative realism or nonrealism, and the impact or effect it produces. It is inadequate to assert as a central idea that "Mrs. Katrina Stockmann is a realistic character" or that "Tom is a nonrealistic character." A better central idea would link Mrs. Stockmann's realistic character or Tom's nonrealistic one to the effect the character has on the play. In working on an essay about Tom, for example, you might assert, "The development of Tom as a nonrealistic narrator and realistic character unifies *The Glass Menagerie* and gives the play a coherent and subjective point of view."

The supporting details may be organized in any fashion that produces a logical and convincing essay. If you deal with several topics, you can treat them in sequence. If you are writing about the ways in which nonrealistic devices emphasize meaning in *The Glass Menagerie*, for example, you might treat the setting, the lighting, and the screen device in a series of paragraphs. When the essay focuses on just one element, you may organize your supporting details to reflect the order in which they occur in the play.

The concluding paragraph should bring the essay to an assertive and convincing close. A summary of your major points is always appropriate here. You might also raise larger issues or make broader connections not only about the topics you considered, but also about the play as a whole. Finally, this is a good place to reconsider the play's general level of realistic or nonrealistic techniques, and the impact it creates.

SAMPLE ESSAY

Realism and Nonrealism in Tom's Triple Role in *The Glass Menagerie*°

In *The Glass Menagerie*, Tennessee Williams combines realistic and nonrealistic elements to explore the personalities and conflicts of the Wingfield family. One of the most effective nonrealistic elements in the play is

° See page 1474 for this play.

[1] Williams's use of Tom in three different roles to unify the play's theme and to provide a subjective and overall perspective.* As realistic character within the action, nonrealistic stage manager of the action, and nonrealistic narrator of the entire play, Tom combines three functions that significantly shape our perception of the drama.†

[2] As a realistic character involved in the recollected action of the play, Tom is ensnared by the economic and emotional demands of his family and his job. In the opening description of the characters, Williams defines Tom as trapped when he notes that "To escape from a trap he [Tom] has to act without pity." In addition, the character repeatedly expresses his feelings of entrapment and the need to escape from his dull, stifling life. He discusses these things with his mother in scene 3, with Laura in scene 4, and, above all, with Jim in scene 6. Here, we see that Tom craves escape and adventure. He tells Jim, "I'm planning a change." And he clearly expresses his desire to move out of the prison house of the family:

> It's our turn now, to go the South Sea Island--to make a safari--to be exotic, far off! But I'm not patient. I don't want to wait till then, I'm tired of the *movies* and I am *about to move*! (speech 114)

> I'm starting to boil inside. I know I seem dreamy, but inside--well, I'm boiling. (speech 120)

As these passages indicate, Tom as a character repeatedly directs us to one of the central ideas in the play--the need to escape. His strivings define a major line of the realistic thought and action in *The Glass Menagerie*.

[3] Tom's realism as a character is deeply undercut by his momentary role as a stage manager in scene 1. Here, he speaks with Amanda "as though reading from a script." In this same scene, "Tom motions for music and a spot of light on Amanda." Although this device is abandoned, the image of Tom holding an imaginary script and giving cues to the musicians and the lighting technicians breaks any possible illusions that the play is imitating real life. The role as manager emphasizes the fact that what we are reading or watching is a play designed for the stage and for live actors carrying out conventional stage roles.

[4] Tom's part in shaping and unifying the play becomes most explicit in his nonrealistic function as narrator. In this role, he stands completely outside the action occurring in the Wingfield apartment, and speaks directly to us. He introduces the characters, provides background, and supplies an ongoing retrospective commentary on the dramatized events. Most important, Tom as the narrator provides two central functions in the play, thematic unity and a subjective and overriding perspective on the action. First, the narrator speaks truths that his character in its past role has not yet learned. As the past character, Tom strives toward freedom and adventure. As the present narrator, however, he recognizes that escape from the past is impossible. At the close

---

* Central idea.
† Thesis sentence.

of the play, he tells us that he remains trapped, even as he wanders through the streets of strange cities: "Then all at once my sister touches my shoulder. I turn around and look into her eyes. Oh, Laura, Laura, I tried to leave you behind me, but I am more faithful than I intended to be!" (speech 323). The narrator, unlike the character, understands that the past always controls the present; he thus provides a final perspective on the central theme of escape.

[5]   The second striking aspect of Tom's function as narrator concerns his complete control of the play. Because he is the narrator, the action in *The Glass Menagerie* represents Tom's memories of events, rather than the events themselves. In his first speech, Tom tells us that "The play is memory. Being a memory play, it is dimly lighted, it is sentimental, it is not realistic." Since the events which occur on stage from the past emerge from Tom's memory, it is he who provides an overriding unity and perspective. We see everything through his mind and from his point of view. Tom as a nonrealistic narrator holds the central stage action together and shapes our response to everything we experience.

[6]   Williams thus uses Tom in three distinct ways to create unity and perspective. As a realistic character aching to leave the confines of home, Tom embodies the theme of escape. As a nonrealistic stage manager, he illustrates the artificiality of the dramatic literary form and stresses the legendary nature of the action. As the play's narrator, he imposes a subjective but coherent control over the action and offers thematic resolution. The nonrealistic aspects of his roles mesh perfectly with other devices that Williams employs non-realistically, especially the slides, music, and lighting.

[7]   Whether realistic or unrealistic, however, *The Glass Menagerie* is about life--its desires, its dreams, its need for independent action, its disappointments, and its poignancy. If Williams did not dramatize these issues, all the technique on earth would not make a great play. But he does dramatize them, and as a result the freedom of action and character he achieves through the combination of roles for Tom enables him to achieve a remarkable unity of topic, merging past with present and reality with unreality. It is as though the play, within moments, is able to present and review all of a significant and crucial portion in the life of a family. Williams's use of Tom, then, is a major reason for which *The Glass Menagerie* is a powerful and great modern drama.

Commentary on the Essay

This essay discusses theme and perspective, or point of view, as they are shaped by Tom's various roles in *The Glass Menagerie*. The primary focus is on character, but a number of distinct topics are taken up in connection with this element because the essay concerns Tom as a character, stage director, and narrator.

The introductory paragraph supplies an overview for the essay, providing title, author, and general observation, isolating the central idea about the merging of realism and nonrealism, and claiming unity and perspective for the use Williams makes of the character of Tom. The thesis sentence lists the three aspects of Tom's role that the essay will investigate.

The body of the essay (paragraphs 2 through 5) takes up these three roles in the order listed in the introduction. Notice that this order does not reflect the sequence in which these occur in the play. Rather, they are organized to reflect a progression from the most realistic to the most nonrealistic aspects of Tom's three different functions. Thus, paragraph 2 discusses Tom as a realistic character and connects him to one of the play's central themes—entrapment and the desire to escape. Paragraphs 3, 4, and 5 shift to a consideration of Tom first as stage manager and second as narrator. These paragraphs explain the nonrealistic nature of these roles, and explore the effects of Tom as the nonrealistic figure.

Throughout the body, direct quotation of dialogue or action as indicated in the stage directions is employed as supporting evidence. Quotation is used to validate specific points and is documented either within parentheses or in the body of discourse itself.

The conclusion of the essay (paragraphs 6 and 7) provides a review-summary of the three roles that Tom plays and the effects that each produces in connection with theme, unity, and perspective. In addition, it suggests a connection between the nonrealistic aspects of Tom's roles and the play's great power.

WRITING TOPICS

1. The detail initiating the action in *An Enemy of the People* is Dr. Stockmann's discovery that the foul-smelling, mucky effluent of the tanneries at nearby Mølledal is contaminating the town water. With this contamination as a starting point for a definition of realism, consider the other almost relentlessly realistic elements of the play, along with other realistic elements in other plays in the chapter. Why does it often seem necessary for realism to be unpleasant or grim? What realistic elements are not unpleasant, but may actually point toward satisfaction and happiness?

2. Compare the families of Mommy and Daddy in *The Sandbox*, the Stockmanns in *An Enemy of the People*, and the Wingfields in *The Glass Menagerie*. To what degree do the families seem to have normal (realistic) family internal squabbles? To what degree do they seem idealized or representative (non-realistic)? Why?

3. In an essay, compare the sets described in *The Sandbox* and *The Glass Menagerie*. What elements of realism are common to them? What is unrealistic about them, and why? To what extent do you think the sets would have similar effects on the audience? Why?

4. The screen device described in Tennessee Williams's production notes (see pp. 1474–75) is omitted from most productions of *The Glass Menagerie*. Write an essay considering the advantages or disadvantages of including reference to this device in the printed text. How are you affected by the screen images as you read the play? How effective would they be in a stage production?

5. Write an essay investigating Williams's symbolism in *The Glass Menagerie*. To what end does Williams use symbolism? Which characters, places, objects,

and actions are symbolic, and what do they symbolize? If these elements are symbolic, to what degree are they also realistic? If there were no basis in realism, how successful would they be as symbols?

6. Write two separate versions of a scene of your own. (Some possible topics: a woman confronts her boyfriend upon learning that he has been seeing someone else; a man has an interview with his boss and learns that he must be let go; an army lieutenant tells his platoon that they are about to be attacked; a woman realizes that she is the best salesperson in the firm.) First, aim for total reality, and second, for total unreality. What differences do you think your differing intentions require of you as a practicing dramatist? What different requirements are made on your dialogue, on your action, on your setting, and on your costuming and suggested makeup for your actors? What elements do you think are the most unrealistic in your unrealistic version, and why do you believe you make them so unrealistic? Does the lack of realism, in your judgment, make your scene either more or less dramatic? Write an introductory essay to your two versions explaining these and other principles of your dramatic composition.

29

Film: Drama on the Silver and Color Screens

Film is the word most often used for motion pictures, although other common words are *picture* and (more likely) *movie*. It is a specialized type of drama, using the dramatic techniques of dialogue, monologue, and action and employing movement and spectacle. Unlike drama, it embodies techniques from photography and lighting, film chemistry, sound, and editing. Because movies are dramatic, you may study them from a purely literary approach, such as character, structure, tone, ideas, or symbolism. In addition, the techniques of film are so specialized that you will also need to take at least some of these techniques into account.

FILM: A BRIEF HISTORY

Film arose out of technologies developed in the late nineteenth century. The first of these was the creation of a flexible substance—celluloid, or film—that could accept the silver iodide emulsions that in the early years of photography had been applied to glass. The other significant inventions were the movie camera and the movie projector. Once these were in place early in the twentieth century, and once producers and directors decided to use the medium for full-length dramas, film as we know it came into existence.

Although the earliest filmmakers thought of moving pictures as something to be seen privately, it soon became apparent that the development of large filmmaking studios, national distribution, and a system of local movie theaters could become extremely lucrative. The history of film is hence just as much a history of the film *business* as of the art and development of film dramas and film acting. With the production of D. W. Griffith's *Birth of a Nation* in 1915, which realized an enormous profit on a relatively small investment, film as an industry had come of age.

The first motion pictures were on black and white film and were silent. Producers realized that large profits required easily recognized actors with "big names," and hence the "star system" made national figures out of actors like Mary Pickford, Charlie Chaplin, and Rudolph Valentino. In 1928 the first talking picture, *Lights of New York*, was made. In 1932, with the first technicolor film, *La Cucaracha*, all the present basic tools of the filmmaker were available.

For a time after the end of World War II, the growth of television inhibited the power of the large studios. Soon, however, many films were developed specifically for television viewing, and popular pictures were released for television use. In the last decade, with the technology of videotape and laser technology, home viewing has become a normal feature of American homes. Today, film rental outlets may be found in shopping districts everywhere. The result is that virtually the entire corpus of movies, from the origins to the present, are within the reach of everyone with a VCR and a television set. The hopes of early dramatists, such as Shakespeare, were to fill their theater for a number of consecutive performances, thus reaching perhaps several thousand persons. Film writers today, however, can reach millions in the first-run movie houses, and many millions more on television reruns and videocassettes.

FILM AND STAGE PLAYS

While the film we speak about is a form of drama, there are a number of important differences between a film and the stage production of a play. A play may be produced many times, in many different places, with many different people. In bringing a play to life, the producer and director not only employ actors, but also use artists, scene designers, carpenters, painters, lighting technicians, costume makers, choreographers, and music directors and musicians. Each production is therefore different from every other, because not only the actors, but also the appurtenances of the staging, are unique.

A film, however, because of high production costs, and also because it reaches a mass audience, usually exists in only one version ("remakes" excepted). Thus, Shakespeare's play *Hamlet* has been staged innumerable times since Shakespeare's actors first produced it at the beginning of the seventeenth century; Orson Welles's *Citizen Kane* (1941) is in only one form, however, and, though it was restored and reedited for distribution in 1991, it will not undergo any substantial changes.

As might be expected, then, stage and movie productions are radically different. In a play, actors enter, speak to each other, and remain in front of the audience until they exit. The stage itself limits what can be done. However, the makers of a film have few such limitations, and the absence of restrictions permits the inclusion of any detail whatever, from a car chase to a scene in the Napoleonic wars. If there is to be a scene on a desert island, the filmmaker goes to such an island and presents it in all its reality, complete with beach, palm trees, huts, and authentic natives-turned-actors. Nothing is left to your imagination. If the scene is a distant planet, obviously the filmmaker cannot go on location there, but instead creates a working location in the studio, with lighting, props, costumes, and special effects. Film, in short, enables a dramatic production to approach almost complete imaginative freedom.

THE PAINTER, THE PHOTOGRAPHER, AND THE FILMMAKER

To the degree that film is confined to a screen, it may visually be compared to the art of the painter and the still photographer. There is a whole language of visual art. One object in a painting may take on special relationships to others as the artist directs the eyes of the observer. A color used in one part may be balanced with the same color, or its complement, in another part. Painters and photographers may introduce certain colors and details as symbols, and may suggest allegorical inter-pretations through the inclusion of mythical figures or universally recog-nized objects. Particular effects may be achieved with the use of textures of the paint and control over shutter speed, focus, and various techniques of development. The techniques and effects are extensive.

The filmmaker is able to utilize most of the resources of the still photographer and many of those of the painter, and may augment these with special effects. Artistically, the most confining aspect of film is the rectangular screen, but aside from that, film is unrestricted. With a basis in a dramatic text called a "filmscript" or "shooting script," it uses words and their effects, but it also employs the language of visual art, and especially the particular vividness and power of moving pictures. When considering film, then, you should realize that film communicates not just by words, but also by various techniques. The visual presentation is inseparable from the medium of film itself.

TECHNIQUES

There are many techniques of film, and a full description and documen-tation of them can, and has, become extensive.* In evaluating film, however, you need to familiarize yourself only with those aspects of

---

* See, for example, Ephraim Katz, *The Film Encyclopedia* (New York: Crowell, 1979); Daniel Talbot, ed., *Film: An Anthology* (Berkeley: University of California Press, 1969); Louis D. Giannetti, *Understanding Movies*, 5th ed. (Englewood Cliffs, NJ: Prentice Hall, 1990); John Wyver, *The Moving Image* (Oxford: Basil Blackwell, 1989); and James Monaco, *How to Read a Film*, rev. ed. (New York: Oxford University Press, 1981).

technique that have an immediate bearing on your responses and interpretations.

EDITING OR *MONTAGE*: THE HEART OF THE FILMMAKER'S CRAFT

A finished film is not a continuous work, filmed from start to end, but is instead a composite. The putting together of the film is the process of *editing*, or **montage** (assemblage, mounting, construction), which is a cutting and gluing. Depending on the flexibility of the filmscript, the various scenes of the film are planned before shooting begins, but the major task of montage is done in a studio, by special film editors.

If we again compare film with a stage play, we may note that a theatrical production moves continuously, with pauses only for intermissions and scene changes. Your perception of the action is caused by your distance from the stage (perhaps aided by opera glasses or binoculars). Also, even as you move your eyes from one character to another, you still perceive the entire stage. In a film, however, the directors and editors *create* these continuous perceptions for you by piecing together different parts. The editors begin with many "takes" (separately filmed scenes, including many versions of the same scenes). What they select, or mount, will be the film, and we never see the discarded scenes. Thus, it is editing that puts everything together.

THE USES OF MONTAGE

NARRATIVE CONTINUITY. The first use of montage, already suggested, is narrative continuity. For example, a climb up a steep cliff may be shown at the bottom, middle, and top (with backward slips and falls to show the danger of the climb and to make viewers catch their breaths). All such narrative sequences result from the assembling of individual pieces, each one representing phases of the activity. A classic example of a large number of separate parts forming a narrative unit is the well-known shower murder in Alfred Hitchcock's *Psycho* (1959), where a forty-five-second sequence is made up of more than seventy different shots (e.g., the woman in the shower, the murderer behind the curtain, the attack, the slumping figure, the running water, the dead woman's eye, the bathtub drain, etc.).

EXPLANATION OF CHARACTER AND MOTIVATION. Montage is used in "flashbacks" to explain present, ongoing actions or characteristics, or to illustrate a character's thoughts and memories, or in brief examples from the unremembered past of a character suffering from amnesia. It also supplies direct visual explanation of character. A famous example occurs in Welles's *Citizen Kane* (1941) (the subject of the sample essay, p. 1551). The concluding scene shows overhead views of Kane's vast collection of statues and mementos. At the very end, the camera focuses on a raging incinerator, into which workmen have thrown his boyhood sled, which bears the brand name "Rosebud" (and which we have fleetingly seen him playing with as a boy). Because "Rosebud" is Kane's dying word, which everyone in the film is trying to learn about, this final scene shows that Kane's last thoughts are about his vanished boyhood, before he was taken away from his parents, and that his unhappy life has resulted from feelings of rejection and personal pain.

DIRECTORIAL COMMENTARY.   In addition, montage is used symbolically as commentary, as in an early sequence in Charlie Chaplin's *Modern Times* (1936), which shows a large group of workers rushing to their factory jobs. Immediately following this scene is a view of a large, milling herd of sheep. By this symbolic montage, Chaplin suggests that the men are being herded and dehumanized by modern industry.

OTHER USES.   Montage may also produce other characteristics through camera work, development, and special effects. For example, filmmakers may reverse an action to emphasize its illogicality or ridiculousness. Editing may also speed up action (which makes even the most serious things funny), or slow things down. It may also blend one scene with another, or juxtapose two or more actions in quick succession, or in split screen, to show what people may be doing while they are separated. The possibilities for creativity and uniqueness are extensive.

VISUAL TECHNIQUES

The Camera

While editing or montage is a finishing technique, the work of film begins with the camera, which permits great freedom in the presentation of characters and actions. In a film, the visual viewpoint may shift. Thus, a film may begin with a distant shot of the actors—a "longshot"—much like the view of actors on stage. Then the camera may zoom in to give a closeup, or zoom out to present a wide and complete panorama. Usually a speaking actor will be the subject of a closeup, but the camera may also show closeups of other actors who are reacting. You must decide on the effects of closeups and longshots yourself, but it should be plain that the frequent use of either—or of middle-distance photographs—is a means by which film directors control perceptions of their characters and situations.

The camera may also move from character to character, or from character to object. In this way a film may show a series of reactions to an event. It may also concentrate your attention on a character's attitude, or it may be a visual commentary on his or her actions. If a man and woman are in love, as an example, the camera may shift, either directly or through montage, from the couple to flowers and trees, thus associating their love visually with objects of beauty and growth. Should the flowers be wilted and the trees leafless, however, the visual commentary might be that the love is doomed and hopeless.

The camera may also create unique effects. Slow motion, for example, can focus on a certain aspect of a person's character. The concentrated focus on a child running happily in a meadow (as in *The Color Purple* [1985] by Steven Spielberg) suggests the joy inherent in such movement. Surprisingly, speed is sometimes indicated by slow motion, which emphasizes strong muscular effort (as in the running scenes in Hugh Hudson's *Chariots of Fire* [1981]).

Many other camera techniques bear on action and character. The focus may be sharp at one point, indistinct at another. Moving a speaking character out of focus may suggest that listeners are bored. Sharp or blurred focus may also show that a character has seen things exactly or inexactly. In action sequences, the camera may be mounted in a moving vehicle to "track" or follow running human beings or horses, speeding bicycles and cars (as in Woody Allen's *Annie Hall*), or moving sailboats, canoes, speedboats, or rowboats. A camera operator on foot may also be the tracker, or the camera may track ground movement from an aircraft. Movement may also be captured by a rotating camera that follows a moving object or character. Then, too, the camera may be fixed while the moving object goes from one side to the other.

Light, Shadow, and Color

As in the theater, the filmmaker uses light, shadow, and color to reinforce ideas and to create realistic and symbolic effects. A scene in sunshine, which brings out colors, and the same scene in rain and clouds or in twilight, all of which mute colors, create different moods. Characters in bright light are presumably open and frank, whereas characters in shadow may be hiding something, particularly in black and white films. Flashing or strobe lights might show a changeable or sinister character or situation.

Colors, of course, have much the same meaning that they have in any other artistic medium. Blue sky and clear light suggest happiness; greenish light may indicate something ghoulish. A memorable control of color occurs midway through David O. Selznick's *Gone With the Wind* (1939), when Scarlet O'Hara reflects upon the devastation of her plantation home, Tara. She resolves never to be hungry again, and as she speaks she is silhouetted against a flaming orange sky—an angry background which suggests how totally the way of life she knew as a young woman has been destroyed. As in this example, you may expect colors to underscore the story of the film. Thus, lovers may wear clothing with the same or complementary colors; people who are not "right" for each other may wear clashing colors.

ACTION AND THE HUMAN BODY

Action

The strength of film is direct action. Actions of all sorts—running, swimming, driving a car, fighting, embracing and kissing, or even just sitting; chases, trick effects, ambushes—all these and more create a sense of immediate reality, and all are tied (or should be) to narrative development. Scenes of action may run on for several minutes, with little or no accompanying dialogue, to carry on the story or to convey ideas about the interests and abilities of the characters.

The Body

Closely related to the portrayal of action is the way in which film shows the human body (and animal bodies), together with bodily motion and gesture (or body language). The view or perspective that the filmmaker presents is particularly important. A torso shot of a character may stress no more than the content alone of that character's speech. A closeup shot, however, with the character's head filling the screen, may put emphasis on motives as well as content. The camera may also distort ordinary expectations of reality. With wide-angle lenses and closeups, for example, human subjects may be made to seem bizarre or grotesque, as with the faces in the crowd in Woody Allen's *Stardust Memories* (1980). Sometimes the camera creates other bodily distortions, enlarging certain limbs, for example, as with the forest dweller in Ingmar Bergman's *Virgin Spring* (1959), or throwing into unnatural prominence a scolding mouth or a suspicious eye. If distortion is used, it invites interpretation: The filmmaker may be asserting that certain human beings, even supposedly normal ones, are odd, sinister, intimidating, or psychotic.

SOUND

Dialogue and Music

The first business of the sound track is the spoken dialogue, which is "mixed" in editing to be synchronized with the action. There are also many other elements in the sound track. Music, the most important, creates and augments moods. A melody in a major or minor key, or in a slow or fast tempo, may affect our perception of actions. If a character is thinking deeply, muted strings may create a complementary sound. But if the character is going insane, the music may become discordant and percussive.

Sometimes, music gives a film a special identity. In Hudson's *Chariots of Fire*, for example, Vangelis Papathanassiou wrote music that has become separately popular, but which is always identified with the film. In addition, musical accompaniments may directly render dramatic statement, without dialogue. An example occurs in Welles's *Citizen Kane*. Beginning that portion of the narrative derived from the autobiography of a character who is now dead (the scene first focuses on his statue), the musical sound track by Bernard Herrmann quotes the "Dies Irae" theme from the traditional mass for the dead. The instrumentation, however, makes the music funny, and we do not grieve but rather smile. Herrmann, incidentally, varies this theme elsewhere in the film, usually for comic effect.

Special Sound Effects

Special sound effects may also augment a film's action. The sound of a blow, for example, may be enhanced electronically to cause an impact similar to the force of the blow itself (as in the boxing scenes from the many *Rocky* films). At times some sounds, such as the noises of wailing people, squeaking or slamming doors, marching feet, or moving vehicles, may be filtered through an electronic apparatus to create weird or ghostly effects. Often a character's words may echo rapidly and sickeningly to show dismay or anguish. In a word, sound is a vital part of film.

ORSON WELLES AND HERMAN J. MANKIEWICZ, SHOT 71 FROM THE SHOOTING SCRIPT OF *CITIZEN KANE*

Orson Welles (1915–1985) developed an early interest in the theater. As a youth he traveled extensively, even spending some time in Spain as a bullfighter. In 1937 he co-founded the Mercury Theatre, specializing in hour-long Sunday evening radio dramatizations. In 1938 he achieved early immortality by acting in and directing a version of H. G. Wells's *The War of the Worlds*. This production created a near panic in the nation among listeners who did not understand they were hearing a dramatic production, not a series of real news broadcasts about invaders from the planet Mars.

Within a few years Welles assembled many of the actors of the Mercury Theatre in the writing and production, with Herman J. Mankiewicz (1897–1953), of *Citizen Kane* (1941), which was based on the life of the newspaper magnate William Randolph Hearst. Hearst tried unsuccessfully to suppress the picture, which went forward to massive critical acclaim. Because of financial and technical problems, Welles was never again to reach the heights of *Citizen Kane*.

In 1958 a poll of international critics listed *Citizen Kane* as one of the twelve best films ever made. Its use of the format similar to *The March of Time* (a popular news feature series that ran regularly in movie theaters), deep-focus camera work, unusual camera angles, contrasts of light and shadow, and its employment of four separate points of view, together with its relentless insights into the major figure—all combined to make it a pioneering work in the history of film. Today, it is one of the touchstones in any discussion of movies.

The scene included here occurs about two-thirds of the way through the film. It is vital because it is a major indicator of Kane's personal decline. At first imbued with ideals for informing and reforming society, Kane (Orson Welles) becomes publisher of a newspaper and assumes public-minded editorial policies. A high point in his career is his running for governor of the state, but because news of his secret love affair becomes public, he loses the election. The scene occurs right after the loss. His most loyal supporter and co-worker, Jedediah Leland (Joseph Cotten), confronts him and asks for a transfer to Chicago. The unspoken issue in the scene is that both men know that their friendship has been lost not because of the election, but because of Kane's misperceptions of people and his desertion of his earlier ideals.

The scene is taken from the so-called shooting script, which in film most closely corresponds to a dramatic text, and it is the full version, with copious directions for the actors. A comparison of this "shot," or scene, with the filmed version will show that some of the dialogue has been trimmed for purposes of pacing and speed. The shortening indicates a major characteristic of film (and the production of plays), namely, to keep speeches to no more than the essentials in order to keep the action moving and hold the audience's attention.

The scene is reprinted from *The Citizen Kane Book* (Boston: Little, Brown & Co., 1971), pp. 228–231.

ORSON WELLES (1915–1985)
AND HERMAN J. MANKIEWICZ (1897–1953)

Shot 71 of the Shooting Script of *Citizen Kane*   *(1941)*

RKO Radio Pictures. A Mercury Production. Producer and Director, Orson Welles. Photographer, Gregg Toland. Editor, Robert Wise. Art Director, Van Nest Polglase. Music, Bernard Herrmann. Special Effects, Vernon L. Walker.

Dissolve In

71 Int. Kane's Office—"Inquirer"—Night—1916

KANE looks up from his desk as there is a knock on the door.

KANE. Come in.

LELAND enters.

KANE. (*Surprised*) I thought I heard somebody knock.

LELAND. (*A bit drunk*) I knocked. (*He looks at him defiantly*)

KANE. (*Trying to laugh it off*) Oh! An official visit of state, eh? (*Waves his hand*) Sit down, Jedediah.

LELAND. (*Sitting down angrily*) I'm drunk.   5

KANE. Good! It's high time—

LELAND. You don't have to be amusing.

KANE. All right. Tell you what I'll do. I'll get drunk, too.

LELAND. (*Thinks this over*) No. That wouldn't help. Besides, you never get drunk. (*Pauses*) I want to talk to you—about—about—(*He can't get it out*)

KANE. (*Looks at him sharply a moment*) If you've got yourself drunk to talk to 10
me about Susan Alexander—I'm not interested.

LELAND. She's not important. What's much more important—(*He keeps glaring at Kane*)

KANE. (*As if genuinely surprised*) Oh! (*He gets up*) I frankly didn't think I'd have to listen to that lecture from you. (*Pauses*) I've betrayed the sacred cause of reform, is that it? I've set back the sacred cause of reform in this state twenty years. Don't tell me, Jed, *you*—

Despite his load,° LELAND manages to achieve a dignity about the silent contempt with which he looks at KANE.

KANE. (*An outburst*) What makes the sacred cause of reform so sacred? Why does the sacred cause of reform have to be exempt from all the other facts of life? Why do the laws of this state have to be executed by a man on a white charger?

LELAND lets the storm ride over his head.

KANE. (*Cont'd*) (*Calming down*) But, if that's the way they want it—they've made their choice. The people of this state obviously prefer Mr. Rogers to me. (*His lips tighten*) So be it.

LELAND. You talk about the people as though they belong to you. As long 15
as I can remember you've talked about giving the people their rights as though you could make them a present of liberty—in reward for services rendered. You remember the workingman? You used to write an awful lot about the workingman. Well, he's turning into something called organized labor, and you're not going to like that a bit when you find out it means that he thinks he's entitled to something as his right and not your gift. (*He pauses*) And listen, Charles. When your precious underprivileged really do get together—that's going to add up to something bigger—than your privilege—and then I don't know what you'll do. Sail away to a desert island, probably, and lord it over the monkeys.

KANE. Don't worry about it too much, Jed. There's sure to be a few of them there to tell me where I'm wrong.

Load: i.e., a heavy amount of liquor.

LELAND.   You may not always be that lucky. (*Pauses*) Charlie, why can't you get to look at things less personally? Everything doesn't have to be between you and—the personal note doesn't always—

KANE.   (*Violently*) The personal note is all there is to it. It's all there ever is to it. It's all there ever is to anything! Stupidity in our government—crookedness— even just complacency and self-satisfaction and an unwillingness to believe that anything done by a certain class of people can be wrong—you can't fight those things impersonally. They're not impersonal crimes against the people. They're being done by actual persons—with actual names and positions and—the right of the American people to their own country is not an academic issue, Jed, that you debate—and then the judges retire to return a verdict—and the winners give a dinner for the losers.

LELAND.   You almost convince me, almost. The truth is, Charlie, you just don't care about anything except you. You just want to convince people that you love them so much that they should love you back. Only you want love on your own terms. It's something to be played your way—according to your rules. And if anything goes wrong and you're hurt—then the game stops, and you've got to be soothed and nursed, no matter what else is happening—and no matter who else is hurt!

They look at each other.

KANE.   (*Trying to kid him into a better humor*) Hey, Jedediah!   20

LELAND is not to be seduced.

LELAND.   Charlie, I wish you'd let me work on the Chicago paper—you said yourself you were looking for someone to do dramatic criticism there—

KANE.   You're more valuable here.

There is silence.

LELAND.   Well, Charlie, then I'm afraid there's nothing I can do but to ask you to accept—

KANE.   (*Harshly*) All right. You can go to Chicago.

LELAND.   Thank you.   25

There is an awkward pause. KANE opens a drawer of his desk and takes out a bottle and two glasses.

KANE.   I guess I'd better *try* to get drunk, anyway.

KANE hands JED a glass, which he makes no move to take.

KANE.   (*Cont'd*) But I warn you, Jedediah, you're not going to like it in Chicago. The wind comes howling in off the lake, and the Lord only knows if they've ever heard of lobster Newburg.

LELAND.   Will a week from Saturday be all right?

KANE.   (*Wearily*) Anytime you say.

LELAND.   Thank you.   30

KANE looks at him intently and lifts the glass.

KANE.   A toast, Jedediah—to love on *my* terms. Those are the only terms anybody knows—his own.

Dissolve

QUESTIONS

1. What do you learn about the past and present relationship of Kane and Leland in this scene? What do Leland's speeches indicate about Kane's attitudes toward people? About Kane's shortcomings?

2. Basing your conclusions on this scene, why do you think the film is named *Citizen Kane*, and not something like *The Life of an American Tycoon* or *The Perils of Wealth*?

3. This scene is one of the revolutionary ones in the film because Welles and Toland (the principal photographer) shot it from floor height, emphasizing the distance from the camera to the heads of the characters. What effect do you think this vantage point has on viewers of the film? If you have seen the picture, what do you think the camera angles and the lighting contribute to the thoughts and characterizations of the characters?

ARTHUR LAURENTS, A SCENE FROM *THE TURNING POINT*

Arthur Laurents is one of the most successful dramatists and screenplay writers of the postwar period. Among his achievements in film are *The Snake Pit* (1948), *Anastasia* (1956), and *The Way We Were* (1973). His plays *West Side Story* (1957) and *Gypsy* (1959) had long Broadway runs as musicals, and also became successful films. *The Turning Point* (1977) received the Golden Globe Award, the National Board of Review Best Picture, and the Writers Guild of America Award as the best film of that year. In addition, Laurents created a novelization of the story.

   The Turning Point takes place against the background of ballet and the life of ballerinas. Deedee Rodgers (Shirley Maclaine) and Emma Jacklin (Anne Bancroft) had been close friends when they were beginning their careers as dancers with the American Ballet Theater. Deedee married, but before she had a chance to become a star, she became pregnant and had a daughter, Emilia. She left the company and moved to Oklahoma, having two more children and establishing a successful ballet school with her husband, Wayne (Tom Skerrit), also a dancer.

   During the following seventeen years, Deedee has believed she could have become a star if she had not become a mother. She has also nursed a grudge against Emma for having urged her to have the baby. In this way, Deedee believes, Emma pushed her aside when the two women had competed for the once-in-a-lifetime opportunity to dance in a new ballet, *Anna Karenina*, by the company's principal choreographer, Michael (James Mitchell). Emma, who won the role, went on to become famous as the company's prima ballerina. However, she has lived her life alone, her principal companions being the three dogs she keeps in her elegant apartment.

   As the film opens, the ballet company comes to perform in Oklahoma

City. Deedee's first daughter, Emilia (Leslie Browne), is now a promising dancer, and with Emma's help and support she becomes a star with the company during the following summer in New York. The scene included here occurs after a gala performance by the company, in which Emilia has brilliantly performed her first major solo dance, and in which Emma has done a solo from *Anna Karenina*, perhaps for the last time.

At the reception after the gala, Emma makes a show of acknowledging Emilia, a gesture which angers Deedee and leads her to conclude that for a number of months Emma has been trying to gain undue influence over Emilia. Shortly after this, the company's director, Adelaide (Martha Scott) asks Emma to create a new production of Tchaikowsky's *Sleeping Beauty* ballet, but *not* to dance in it. This request hits Emma with full force, for she now recognizes that she is getting old and is about to be pushed aside by dancers who, like Emilia, are young and strong. She rushes out and stops at the nearby bar, where she encounters Deedee. The scene, which is virtually a short play all by itself, then develops, as the long pent-up frustration, apprehension, and guilt of both women emerge.

ARTHUR LAURENTS   (b. 1918)

A Scene from *The Turning Point*   *(1977)*

Twentieth Century Fox. Producers, Herbert Ross and Arthur Laurents. Executive Producer, Nora Kaye. Photography, Robert Surtees. Film editor, William Reynolds. Music adapter, John Lanchbery. Director, Herbert Ross.

[SCENE] Interior Bar—Rainbow Room

DEEDEE is alone at the bar, drinking champagne. As EMMA, on her way to the Ladies' room, comes toward her, DEEDEE smiles and does a half-curtsy. EMMA stops and smiles back. Then she tosses her evening bag onto the bar.

EMMA.   (*to the bartender*).   Champagne, please.

Declaration of war accepted. During the following, they both get refills, but they do not guzzle; there is no need for them to get drunk. Emotionally, each is ready to burst anyway. They (and we) are unaware of the bartender and he is unaware of them. For despite the lines, despite what each feels underneath, they are totally charming: two smiling, lovely, delightful friends having a chat.

DEEDEE.   Remember the fairy tales we used to take turns reading to Emilia? Like the one about the two princesses? Every time one opened her mouth, out came diamonds and rubies. Every time the other opened her mouth, out came newts and hoptoads. Newts and hoptoads—(*taps her chest*)—coming out.

EMMA.   One of those little toads has already made an appearance.

DEEDEE.   Really! When?

EMMA.   In my dressing room. When you said I shouldn't have bought Emilia   5 that dress. Twice, you said it. Just before a performance. . . . I danced better tonight than I have in years.

DEEDEE.   So I heard.

EMMA.   Oh, another little toad! You've kept quite a few bottled up all these years, haven't you?

DEEDEE.   Ohhh—embalmed, really.

EMMA.   I think not. Why don't you let them out? I don't have a performance tomorrow.

DEEDEE looks at her, then accepts the challenge. She puts her glass down on the bar and holds out her hands with her fists clenched.

DEEDEE.   Okay. Pick.   10

EMMA puts her glass down and points to a fist. DEEDEE opens it.

DEEDEE.   Ah, a tiny one. I'd practically forgotten him. (*Looks up now.*) Why'd you make your best pal doubt herself and her hubby, Emma? Why'd you take the chance of lousing up her marriage? Why'd you say: "You better have that baby. It's the only way you can hold on to Wayne." I'm just curious now.

EMMA.   You have a curious memory. but don't we all? As I remember, I said if you had an abortion, you might lose Wayne.

DEEDEE.   Sweet, but inaccurate. I've remembered your exact words for lo, these too many moons. I eventually figured out why you said 'em. Because you also said: "Forget Michael's ballet, there'll be others." You clever little twinkletoes! You knew a ballet like that comes once in a career. You wanted it real bad, so you lied to make sure you got what you wanted.

EMMA.   I've never had to lie to get what I wanted, Deedee. I'm too good.

DEEDEE.   Really?   15

EMMA.   Oh, yes.

DEEDEE.   Well, I suppose if you said "bullshit," you'd say it in French.

Close shot.

EMMA.   If that word came as naturally to me as it does to you, I'd have used it several times by now. In English. I think it's more appropriate that you say it— to yourself. For trying to blame *me* for what you did, for example. The choice was yours. It's much too late to regret it now, Deedee.

DEEDEE.   And the same to you, Emma me darlin'.

EMMA.   I certainly don't regret mine.   20

DEEDEE.   Then why are you trying to become a mother at your age?

EMMA.   Ooh, that's not a little toad. That's a rather large bullfrog. I don't want to be anybody's mother. I think of Emilia as a friend. And one reason I tried to help—stupid me!—I thought it would make you happy if your daughter became what you wanted to be and couldn't be.

DEEDEE.   Meaning you. It's so lovely to be you.

EMMA.   Obviously, you think so.

DEEDEE.   Oh, no no no no no no!   25

EMMA.   No no no no?

DEEDEE.   No; alas. And I doubt if Emilia could become you. Oh, she's as talented. She works as hard. But there's one thing, dearest friend, that you are that she, poor darling, is not.

EMMA. And what, pray tell, is that?

DEEDEE. A killer. You'll walk over anybody and still get a good night's sleep. That's what got you where you are, Emma.

She is smiling adorably. EMMA smiles back, finishes her drink, pushes the glass to the bartender, keeps smiling until it is refilled, then picks it up. They are both smiling, almost laughing as EMMA looks at her drink, looks at DEEDEE, then throws the champagne in DEEDEE's face. A moment. Then DEEDEE sets down her glass.

DEEDEE. Good girl.   30

She picks up her evening bag and starts out of the bar toward the exit and the elevators. The cool reaction infuriates EMMA. She puts down her glass and starts after DEEDEE.

Interior corridor outside Rainbow Room

EMMA comes through the entrance to the Rainbow Room just as DEEDEE steps into an elevator.

EMMA. Deedee!

She runs for the elevator and just gets in as the doors are closing.

Interior elevator—Rockefeller Center

EMMA. I'm sick to death of your jealousy and resentment!

DEEDEE. So am I.

EMMA. Then stop blaming your goddamn life on me! You picked it!

DEEDEE. You did. You took away the choice, you didn't give me the chance   35
to find out if I was good enough.

EMMA. I can tell you now: you weren't.

The elevator doors open and DEEDEE strides out, EMMA after her.

Exterior Rockefeller Plaza—Night

EMMA is fast after DEEDEE, their heels clicking on the stone.

EMMA. You knew it yourself. That's why you married Wayne!

DEEDEE (*whirls around*). I loved him!

EMMA. So much that you said to hell with your career!

DEEDEE. Yes!   40

EMMA. And got pregnant to prove you meant it!

DEEDEE. Yes!

EMMA. Lie to yourself, not to me. You got married because you knew you were second-rate; you got pregnant because Wayne was a ballet dancer, and that meant queer!

DEEDEE. *He wasn't!*

EMMA. Still afraid someone will think he is? You were terrified then! You   45
had to *prove* he was a man! *That's* why you had a baby!

DEEDEE. That's a goddamn lie!

EMMA. It's the goddamn truth! You saddled him with a baby and blew his career! And now she's grown up and better than you ever were and you're jealous!

DEEDEE. You're certifiable! You'll use anything for an excuse.

EMMA.   What's that an excuse for?

DEEDEE.   Trying to take away my child!   50

EMMA.   I return the compliment: you're a liar!

DEEDEE.   And you're a user. You have been your whole life! Me, Michael—pretending to love him!—Adelaide and now Emilia!

EMMA.   How Emilia?!

DEEDEE.   "How Emilia." That display five minutes ago: curtsy! Applause! Embrace! For *you*, not her! You were using her so everyone'd say: "Emma's so gracious, Emma's so wonderful!"

EMMA.   Untrue!   55

DEEDEE.   You *are* wonderful! You're amazing! It's incredible how you keep going on. You're over the hill; you know it and *you're* terrified. All you've got are your scrapbooks and your old toe shoes and those stupid, ridiculous dogs! What are you going to fill in with, Emma? Not my daughter. You keep your goddam hands off!

EMMA.   I'm better for her than you are.

DEEDEE.   Like hell!

EMMA.   She came to me because her mother wasn't there. Her mother was too busy screwing her head off!

DEEDEE.   You bitch!   60

She whacks EMMA with her evening bag. For a moment, EMMA is too startled to move. But as DEEDEE lifts her bag again, EMMA blocks it with one hand and with the other whacks DEEDEE with her evening bag. They both go at it: rarely hitting, ducking blows, slamming out blindly with their evening bags.

Exterior Rockefeller Center—Night

There they are, these two ladies in their evening gowns, each making a last pass, a last weak attempt to hit the other, and missing. They are panting, exhausted, and at last, they stop and just stand there, breathing hard.

Close shot—Their breath is coming back. DEEDEE smiles.

DEEDEE.   If there'd been a photographer handy, you'd have a whole new career.

EMMA.   I must look awful.

DEEDEE.   No: beautiful. I don't know how you do it.

EMMA has taken out a mirror and is looking in it.

EMMA.   If I can borrow your comb, I'll show you. Oh, I lost an earring.

DEEDEE (*handing her a comb*).   I'm sorry.   65

EMMA.   I'm not.

DEEDEE.   Really?

EMMA.   Yes.

She returns the comb, and they start walking, looking for the lost earring. The following is very quiet:

DEEDEE.   Jealousy is poison. Makes you a monster.

EMMA.   Well, it does make one unfair. (*Smiles.*) Two.   70

DEEDEE.   Two?

EMMA.   Me, too.

DEEDEE (*a second, then laughs*).   Emma, you made a good joke!

EMMA.   Yes, I did. . . . I'm really not so humorless.

DEEDEE.   Listen, you got off some really good ones before. Oh, look!   75

She picks up the earring and gives it to EMMA.

EMMA.   How did it get over here? Thank you.

DEEDEE.   You also hit a couple of bull's-eyes before.

EMMA.   So did you.

DEEDEE.   Sit?

EMMA.   Oh, please.   80

They sit on the rim of the fountain.

EMMA.   I don't really remember what I said about having the baby. But I do know I would have said anything to make sure I got that ballet. . . . I had to have it, Deedee. I just had to.

DEEDEE.   My God. Oh Emma. Emma, I didn't know how much all I wanted was for you to say just that. . . . Let's have a drink!

EMMA.   Absolutely!

They get up. EMMA links her arm through DEEDEE's as they start walking.

EMMA.   It's good.

DEEDEE.   You bet.

EMMA.   I'm glad Wayne's coming.   85

DEEDEE.   Me, too. . . . How's with Carter?

EMMA.   Ça va. . . . *That's* bullshit in French.

DEEDEE laughs and walks toward the street, to a taxi. But EMMA has stopped, turned toward the entrance to the party.

DEEDEE.   Not back to the party?

EMMA.   I have to.   90

DEEDEE (*nods, understands*).   Call me when you wake up.

EMMA.   If not before.

They smile—and walk in opposite directions.

QUESTIONS

1.   Despite the fact that the two women carry their anger so far as to strike each other, what does the scene show about the nature of friendship? What key admissions do the women make to effect their reconciliation?

2.   The film omits the last ten speeches of the script (concluding with "to say just that" in speech 82). Justify eliminating these last speeches.

3.   What is the effect of the fact that the locations of this scene move from the interior bar to the exterior plaza? Granted the actions of the two women, why can the scene not be in a single location (as it would necessarily be if written for the theater)? On the basis of your answers, what conclusions can

you draw about the comparative freedoms and limitations of film and theater?

4. View the film *The Turning Point,* and compare the details of the script with the final filmed version of the scene. Explain the purpose and nature of the changes in the film. If you had the freedom of a film director, what other liberties might you take in the performance? Why?

WRITING ABOUT FILM

Obviously the first requirement is to see the film, either in a theater or with videocassette. No matter how you see it, you should do so at least twice, making notes as you go, because your discussion takes on value the more thoroughly you know the material. Write down the names of the scriptwriter, director, composer, special effects editor, chief photographer, and major actresses and actors. If particular speeches are worth quoting, remember the general circumstances of the quotation, and also, if possible, key words. Take notes on costume and color, or (if the film is in black and white) light and shade. You will need to rely on memory, but if you have videotape, you may easily check important details.

If you have no other instructions, you might decide on usual literary subjects like plot, structure, character, ideas, or setting. Remember, however, to consider not only dialogue and action, but also film techniques.

Questions for Discovering Ideas

ACTION

To what degree is action important? Is there much repetition of actions, say in slow motion? Are the moving actors (and animals) viewed closely or distantly? Why?

What sorts of actions are stressed (chases, concealment, gun battles, love-making, etc.)? What does the type of action contribute to the film?

What do closeups show about character and motivation (smiles and laughter of happiness, frowns of disapproval, leers of desire, pinched features showing anxiety, etc.)?

What actions indicate seasonal conditions (cold by a character's stamping of feet, warmth by the character's removing a coat or shirt)? What connection do these actions have to the film's general ideas?

Does the action show any changing of mood, from sadness to happiness, or from indecision to decision?

CINEMATOGRAPHIC TECHNIQUES

What notable techniques are used (colors, lighting, etc.)? What is their relationship to the film's characterizations and themes?

What characterizes the use of the camera (tracking, closeups, distant shots, camera angles, etc.)? How do the camera perspectives reinforce or detract from the film's theme and plot?

How does the editing (the sequencing of scenes) reinforce or detract from story and theme?

What scene or scenes best exemplify how the cinematographic techniques interact with the theme, plot, characters, setting, and so on? Why?

ACTING

How well do the actors adapt to the medium of film? How convincing are their performances?

How well do the actors control their facial expressions and body movement? Are they graceful? Awkward?

What does their appearance lend to your understanding of their characters?

Does it seem that the actors are genuinely creating their roles, or just reading through the parts?

Strategies for Organizing Ideas

Any of the organizing strategies discussed in the chapters on drama are equally valid for an essay on a film. You will need to choose which elements you find important, and develop them in a visual context. For example, if you want to write about the effects of a character on the plot, you need to develop your argument using the evidence of camera techniques, montage, sound effects, and the like.

When discussing film techniques, be sure to have good notes, so that your supporting details are accurate. A good method is to concentrate on technique in only a few scenes. If you analyze the effects of montage, for example, you may use your stop-action control (for a videocassette recorder) to go over the scene a number of times.

In the conclusion of your essay, you might evaluate the effectiveness of the cinematic form to story and idea. Are all the devices of film used in the best possible way? Is anything overdone? Is anything underplayed? Is the film good, bad, or indifferent up to a point, and then does it change? How? Why?

SAMPLE ESSAY

Orson Welles's *Citizen Kane*: Whittling a Giant Down to Size

Citizen Kane (1941) is a well-crafted film in black and white. The script is by Herman Mankiewicz and Orson Welles, with photography by Gregg Toland, music by Bernard Herrmann, direction and production by Welles, and the leading role by Welles. It is the story of a wealthy and powerful man,

[1]   Charles Foster Kane, who exemplifies the American dream of economic self-sufficiency, self-determination, and self, period. The film does not explore the "greatness" of the hero, however, but rather exposes him as a misguided, unhappy person who tries to buy love and remake reality.* All aspects of the picture--characterization, structure, and technique--are directed to this goal.†

[2]   At the film's heart is the deterioration of Kane, the newly deceased newspaper magnate and millionaire. He is not all bad, for he begins well and then goes downward, in a tragic sequence. For example, the view we see of him as a child, being taken away from home, invites sympathy. When we next see him as a young man, he idealistically takes over a daily newspaper, the *Inquirer*. This idealism makes him admirable but also makes his deterioration tragic. As he says to Thatcher in a moment of insight, he could have been a great person if he had not been wealthy. His corruption begins when he tries to alter the world to suit himself, such as his demented attempt to make an opera star out of his second wife, Susan, and his related attempt to shape critical praise for her despite her terrible singing. Even though he builds an opera house for her, and also sponsors many performances, he cannot change reality. This tampering with truth indicates how completely he loses his youthful integrity.

[3]   The structure is progressively arranged to bring out such weaknesses. The film flows out of the opening obituary newsreel, from which we learn that Kane's dying word was the name "Rosebud" (the brand name of his boyhood sled, which is spoken at the beginning by a person [Kane] whose mouth is shown in closeup). The newsreel director, wanting to get the inside story, assigns a reporter named Thompson to learn about "Rosebud." Thompson's search unifies the rest of the film; he goes from place to place and person to person to collect materials and conduct interviews which disclose Kane's increasing strangeness and alienation. At the end, although the camera leaves Thompson to focus on the burning sled, he has been successful in uncovering the story of Kane's deterioration (even though he himself never learns what "Rosebud" means). Both the sled and the reporter therefore tie together the many aspects of the film.

[4]   It is through Thompson's searches that the film presents the flashback accounts of Kane's deterioration. The separate persons being interviewed (including Thatcher's handwritten account) each contribute something different to the narrative because their experiences with Kane have all been unique. As a result of these individual points of view, the story is quite intricate. We learn in the Bernstein section, for example, that Jedediah proudly saves a copy of Kane's declaration about truth in reporting. We do not learn in Jedediah's interview, however, that he, Jedediah, sends the copy back to Kane as an indictment of Kane's betrayal of principle. Rather, it is in *Susan's* account that we learn about the return, even though she herself understands nothing about it. This subtlety, so typical of the film, marks the ways in which the biography of Kane is perceptively revealed.

* Central idea.
† Thesis sentence.

[5] Thus, the major importance of these narrating characters is to reveal and reflect Kane's disintegration. Jedediah (Joseph Cotten) is a person of principle who works closely with Kane, but after the lost election he rebels when he understands the falseness of Kane's personal life. He is totally alienated after Kane completes the unfinished attack on Susan's performance. Jedediah's change, or perhaps his assertion of principle, thus reveals Kane's increasing corruption. Susan, Kane's second wife (Dorothy Comingore), is naive, sincere, and warm, but her drinking, her attempted suicide, and her final separation show the harm of Kane's warped visions. Bernstein (Everett Sloane), the first person Thompson interviews, is a solitary figure who is uncritical of Kane, but it is he who first touches the theme about the mystery of Kane's motivations. Bernstein also takes on life when he speaks poignantly of his forty-five-year memory of the girl in white. Even though this revelation is brief, it suggests layers of feeling and longing.

[6] In addition to these perceptive structural characterizations, *Citizen Kane* is a masterpiece of film technique. The camera images are sharp, with clear depths of field. In keeping with Kane's disintegration and mysteriousness, the screen is rarely bright. Instead, the film makes strong use of darkness and contrasts, almost to the point at times of blurring distinctions between people. Unique in Gregg Toland's camera work are the many shots taken from waist high or below, which distort the bodies of the characters by distancing their heads--suggesting that the characters are preoccupied with their own concerns and oblivious to normal perspectives. Nowhere is this distortion better exemplified than in the scene between Kane and Jedediah in the empty rooms after the lost election, when Jedediah asks permission to leave for Chicago.

[7] As might be expected in a film so dominated by its central figure, the many symbols create strong statements about character. The most obvious is the sled, "Rosebud," the dominating symbol of the need for love and acceptance in childhood. Another notable symbol is glass and, in one scene, ice. In the party scene, two ice statues are in the foreground of the employees of the *Inquirer.* In another scene, a bottle looms large in front of Jedediah, who is drunk. In another, a pill bottle and drinking glass are in front of Susan, who has just used them in her suicide attempt. The suggestion of these carefully photographed symbols is that life is brittle and temporary. Particularly symbolic is the bizarre entertainment in the party scene. Because Kane joins the dancing and singing, the action suggests that he is doing no more than taking a role in life, never being himself or knowing himself. Symbols that frame the film are the wire fence and the "No Trespassing" sign at both beginning and end. These symbols suggest that even if we understand a little about Kane, or anyone, there are boundaries we cannot pass, depths we can never reach.

There are also amusing symbols which suggest not only the diminution of Kane, but also of the other characters. An example is Bernstein's high-backed chair, which makes him look like a small child. Similarly, the gigantic fireplace at Xanadu makes both Kane and Susan seem like pygmies--a symbol that great wealth dwarfs and dehumanizes people. Especially comic is Kane's picnic at Xanadu. In going into the country, Kane and his friends do

[8]
not walk, but ride in a long line of cars--more like a funeral procession than a picnic--and they stay overnight in a massive tent. Quite funny is the increasing distance between Kane and Emily, his first wife, in the rapid-fire shots that portray their developing separation. Even more comic is the vast distance at Xanadu between Kane and Susan when they discuss their life together. They are so far apart that they must shout to be heard. Amusing as these symbols of diminution and alienation are, however, they are also pathetic, because at first Kane finds closeness with both his wives.

[9]
In all respects, *Citizen Kane* is a masterly film. This is not to say that the characters are likable, or that the amusing parts make it a comedy. Instead, the film pursues truth, suggesting that greatness and wealth cannot give happiness. It is relentless in whittling away at its major figure. Kane is likable at times, and he is enormously generous (as shown when he sends Jedediah $25,000 in severance pay). But these high moments show the contrasting depths to which Kane falls, with the general point being that people who are powerful and great may deteriorate even at their height. The goal of the newsreel director at the beginning is to get at the "real story" behind the public man. There is more to any person than a two-hour film can reveal, but within its limits, *Citizen Kane* gets at the real story, and the real story is both sad and disturbing.

Commentary on the Essay

The writer's major point is that the film diminishes the major figure, Kane. In this respect the essay illustrates the analysis of *character* (Chapter 4, pp. 137–95), and it therefore emphasizes how film may be considered as a form of literature. Also shown in the essay are other methods of literary analysis: *structure* (pp. 96–135) and *symbolism* (pp. 326–61). Of these topics, only the use of symbols, because they are visually presented in the film, is unique to the medium of film as opposed to the medium of words.

Any one of the topics might be developed as a separate essay. There is more than enough about the character of Susan, for example, to sustain a complete essay, and the film's structure could be extensively explored. *Citizen Kane* itself as a repository of film techniques is rich enough for an exhaustive, book-length account.

Because the essay is about a film, the unique aspect of the introductory paragraph is the opening brief description (stressing the medium of black and white), and the credits to the script writers, principal photographer, composer, and director. Unlike works written by a single author, film is a collaborative medium, and therefore it is appropriate to recognize the separate efforts of the principal contributors.

Paragraph 2 begins the body, and carries out a brief analysis of the major character. Paragraphs 3 through 5 discuss various aspects of the film's structure (the second topic announced in the thesis sentence) as they bear on Kane. In paragraph 3 the unifying importance of the sled and the reporter, Thompson, is explained. Paragraph 4 focuses on the film's use of flashback as a structural technique; paragraph 5 discusses three of the flashback characters as they either intentionally or unintentionally reveal Kane's flaws.

In paragraphs 6 through 8, the topic is film technique, the third and last topic of the thesis sentence. Paragraph 6 focuses on light, camera angles, and distortion; paragraph 7 treats visual symbols; paragraph 8 continues the topic of symbols, but extends it to amusing ones.

The final paragraph, 9, restates the central idea, and also relates the theme of deterioration to the larger issue of how great wealth and power affect character. Thus, as a conclusion, this paragraph not only presents a summary, but also notes the film's general ideas.

WRITING TOPICS

1. Select a single film technique that particularly interests you, such as the use of color, the control of light, or the photographing of action, and write an essay describing how it is used in a film. For best results, use a videocassette for your study. As much as possible, try to explain how the technique is used throughout the film. Determine constant and contrasting features, the relationship of the technique to the development of story and character, and so on.

2. Write an essay explaining the ways in which all the film techniques of a particular scene are employed (i.e., camera angles, closeups or longshots, tracking, on-camera and off-camera speeches, lighting, depth of field, etc.). For your study, you will have to rerun your scene a number of times, trying to notice elements for the first time, and also reinforcing your first observations.

3. Pick out a recent news story that interests you, and write a dramatic scene about it. Once you have written your scene, consider how you would do it for a film, and provide directions for the actors and for the camera (e.g., "As Character A speaks, his facial actions show that he is lying; the camera zooms slowly in on his face, with a corresponding loss of focus," or, "As Character A speaks, the camera focuses on Character B's exchanging disapproving glances with Character C," and so on. When you have finished your scene to your satisfaction, write an explanation of what your directions are designed to bring out about story and character.

Appendix A: Taking Examinations on Literature

Taking an examination on literature is not difficult if you prepare correctly. Preparing means (1) studying the material assigned in conjunction with the comments made in class by your instructor and by fellow students in discussion, (2) developing and reinforcing your own thoughts, (3) anticipating the questions by writing your own practice answers to these questions, and (4) understanding the precise function of the test in your education.

You should realize that the test is not designed to plague you or to hold down your grade. The grade you receive is a reflection of your achievement in the course. If your grades are low, you can improve them by studying coherently and systematically. Those students who can easily do satisfactory work might do superior work if they improved their method of preparation. From whatever level you begin, you can increase your achievement by improving your method of study.

Your instructor has three major concerns in evaluating your tests (assuming literate English): (1) to see the extent of your command over the subject material of the course ("How good is your retention?"), (2) to see how well you are able to think about the material ("How well are you educating yourself?"), and (3) to see how well you respond to a question or deal with an issue.

Many elements go into writing good answers on tests, but this last point, about responsiveness, is the most important. A major cause of low exam grades is that students really do not *answer* the questions asked. Does that seem surprising? The problem is that some students do no more than retell a story or restate an argument, never confronting the issues in the question. This is the common problem that has been treated throughout this book. Therefore, if you are asked, "Why does . . . ," be sure to emphasize the *why*, and use the *does* only to exemplify the *why*. If the question is about organization, focus on that. If a problem has been raised, deal with the problem. In short, always *respond* directly to the question or instruction. Let us compare two answers to the same question.

   Question: *How does the setting of Jackson's "The Lottery" figure in the development of the story?*

A	B
The setting of Jackson's "The Lottery" is a major element in the development of the story. The scene is laid in the village square, between the bank and the post office. There are many flowers blooming, and the grass is green. A pile of stones is set up in the square. Into this place, just before ten o'clock in the morning, come the villagers to hold their annual lottery. There are 300 of them—children, men, and housewives. In the center of the square the black lottery box is set up on a three-legged stool. This box has been around for years, and looks broken and shabby. The setting requires that the villagers gather around the box, and that the male head representing each village family draw a slip of paper for that family. Once they have all drawn, it is discovered that Bill Hutchinson is the "winner." He is not a lucky winner, however, because his family of five has to draw again individually. Bill's wife Tessie draws the black spot that Bill had drawn for the family. Then all the villagers in the square fall upon her to stone her to death, because that is the fate of the "winner." The setting here is therefore all-important in the development of the story.	The setting of Jackson's "The Lottery" is a major element in the development of the story. As a setting for all the action, the town square of the unnamed village is large enough to contain all 300 villagers, piles of stones which they can pick up and hurl, and the black box on a three-legged stool. As a setting in time, the entire action takes place within a two-hour period between ten in the morning and noon. As a seasonal setting, the date of June 27, specifically mentioned as the day of the action, suggests an anachronistic and mindless but nevertheless cruel early summer ritual. As a setting in character and society, the homey, simple lifestyle of the people indicates inertia and fallibility, not sophistication and innovativeness. It is *likely* that such people would preserve cruel and meaningless customs without thinking about their horrible effects. In all respects, then, the setting in place, time, season, and culture is all-important in the development of the story.

   While column A begins well and introduces important details of the story's setting, it does not stress how these details are used in the story's development. It is also cluttered with details having no bearing on the question. On the other hand, column B, focusing directly on the connection, stresses how four aspects of setting relate to the story. Because of this emphasis, B is shorter than A. That is, with the focus directly on the issue, there is no need for irrelevant narrative details. Thus, A is unresponsive and unnecessarily long; B is responsive and includes details only if they exemplify the major points.

PREPARATION

Your problem is how best to prepare yourself to have a knowledgeable and ready mind at examination time. If you simply cram facts into your head for the examination in hopes that you will be able to adjust to whatever questions are asked, you will likely flounder.

Read and Reread

Above all, keep in mind that your preparation should begin not on the night before the exam, but as soon as the course begins. When each assignment is given, you should complete it by the date due, for you will understand the classroom discussion only if you know the material (see also the guides for study in Chapter 1, pp. 13–15). Then, about a week before the exam, you should review each assignment, preferably rereading everything completely. With this preparation, your study on the night before the exam will be fruitful, for it might be viewed as a climax of preparation, not the entire preparation itself.

Make Your Own Questions: Go on the Attack

Just to read or reread is too passive to give you the masterly preparation you want for an exam. You should instead go on the attack by trying to anticipate the specific conditions of the test. The best way to reach this goal is to compose and answer your own practice questions. Do not waste your time trying to guess the question you think your instructor might ask. That might happen—and wouldn't you be happy if it did?—but do not turn your study into a game of chance. One of the most important things you can do is to arrange the subject matter by asking yourself questions that help you get things straight.

How can you make your own questions? It is not as hard as you might think. Your instructor may have announced certain topics or ideas to be tested on the exam. You might develop questions from these. Or you might apply general questions to the specifics of your assignments, as in the following examples:

1. *About a character and the interactions of characters (see also Chapter 4, pp. 137–95).* What sort of character is A? How does A grow or change in the work? What does A learn, or not learn, that brings about the conclusion? To what degree is A representative of any particular type, or of any idea? How does B influence A? Does a change in C bring about any corresponding change in A?

2. *About technical and structural questions.* These may be quite broad, covering everything from *point of view* (Chapter 5) to *prosody* (Chapter 18). The best guide here is to study those technical aspects that have been discussed in class, for it is unlikely that you will be asked to go beyond the levels expected in classroom discussion.

3. *About events or situations (see also Chapter 3 on plot and structure, pp. 94–135).* What relationship does episode *A* have to situation *B*? Does *C*'s thinking about situation *D* have any influence on the outcome of event *E*?

4. *About a problem (see also Chapter 26, pp. 1277–85).* Why is character *A* or situation *X* this way and not that way? Is the conclusion justified by the ideas and events leading up to it?

Adapt Your Notes to Make Questions

One of the best ways to construct questions is to adapt your classroom notes, for notes are the fullest record you have about your instructor's views of the subject material. As you work with your notes, you should refer to passages from the text that were studied by the class or stressed by your instructor. If there is time, memorize as many important phrases or lines as you can; plan to incorporate these into your answers as evidence to support the points you make. Remember that it is good to work not only with main ideas from your notes, but also with matters such as style, imagery, and organization.

Obviously, you cannot make questions from all your notes, and you will therefore need to select from those that seem most important. As an example, here is a short note from a classroom discussion of *Hamlet:* "In a major respect, a study in how private problems get public, how a court conspiracy may produce disastrous consequences." It is not difficult to devise practice questions from this note:

1. In what ways is *Hamlet* not only about private problems, but also public ones?

2. Why should the consequences of Claudius's murder of Hamlet's father be considered disastrous?

The principle shown here is that exam questions should never be asked just about *what*, but should rather get into the issues of *why*. Observe that the first question therefore adapts the words *in what ways* to the phrasing of the note. For the second, the word *why* has been adapted. Either question would force pointed study, and neither would ask you merely to describe events. Question 1 would require you to consider the wider political effects of Hamlet's hostility toward Claudius, including his murder of Polonius and the subsequent madness of Ophelia. Question 2, with its emphasis on disaster, would lead you to consider not only the ruination of the hopes and lives of those in the play, but also the importance of Young Fortinbras and the eventual establishment of Norwegian control over Denmark after Claudius and Hamlet are gone. If you spent fifteen or twenty minutes writing practice answers to these questions, you could be confident in taking an examination on the material, for it is likely that you could adapt your answers to any exam question about the personal and political implications of Claudius's murder of his brother.

Work with Questions Even When Time Is Short

Whatever your subject, you should spend as much study time as possible making and answering your own questions. You should not forget, of course, to work with your own remarks and ideas that you will have developed in the journal entries you have made when doing your regular assignments (see Chapter 1, pp. 13–21). Many of these will give you additional ideas for your own questions, which you may practice along with the questions you develop from your notes.

Obviously, with the limited time you have before your examination, you will not be able to create your own questions and answers indefinitely. Even so, do not give up on the question method. If time is too short for full practice answers, write out the main heads, or topics, of an answer. When the press of time (or the need for sleep) no longer permits you to make even such a brief outline answer, keep thinking of questions, and think about the answers on the way to the exam. *Try never to read passively or unresponsively, but always with a creative question-and-answer goal.* Think of studying as prewriting experience.

The time you spend in this way will be valuable, for as you practice, you will develop control and therefore confidence. If you have ever known anyone who has had difficulty with tests, or who has claimed a phobia about them, you may find that a major cause has been *passive* rather than *active* preparation. It is a fact that test questions compel thought, arrangement, and responsiveness; but a passively prepared student is not ready for this challenge and therefore writes answers that are unresponsive and filled with summary. The grade, needless to say, is low, and the student's fear of tests is reinforced.

It seems clear that active, creative study is the best way to break such long-standing patterns of fear or uncertainty, because it is the best form of preparation. There is no moral case to make against practice question-and-answer study, either, for everyone has the right and obligation to prepare—and all of this is preparation—in the best way possible.

Study with a Classmate

Often the thoughts of another person can help you understand the material to be tested. Find a fellow student with whom you can work, for both of you together can help each other individually. In view of the need for steady preparation throughout a course, regular discussions about the material are a good idea. Also you might make your joint study systematic by setting aside a specific evening or afternoon for work sessions. Make the effort; working with someone else can be stimulating and rewarding.

TWO BASIC TYPES OF QUESTIONS ABOUT LITERATURE

Generally, you will find two types of questions on literature exams. Keep them in mind as you prepare. The first type is *factual,* or *mainly objective,* and the second is *general, comprehensive, broad,* or *mainly subjective.* In a literature course very few questions are purely objective, except for multiple-choice questions.

Factual Questions

MULTIPLE-CHOICE QUESTIONS. These questions are mainly factual. In a literature course, your instructor will most likely reserve them for short quizzes, usually on days when an assignment is due, to make sure that you are keeping up with the reading. Multiple choice tests your knowledge of facts, and it also tests your ingenuity in perceiving subtleties of phrasing, but on a literature exam this type of question is rare.

IDENTIFICATION QUESTIONS. These questions are more interesting and challenging because they require you both to know details and also to develop thoughts about them. This type of question will frequently be used as a check on the depth and scope of your reading. In fact, an entire exam could be composed of only identification questions, each demanding perhaps five minutes to write. Typical examples of what you might be asked to identify are as follows:

1. *A character.* It is necessary to describe briefly the character's position, main activity, and significance. Let us assume that "Prince Prospero" is the character to be identified. Our answer should mention that he is the prince (position) who invites a thousand followers to his castle to enjoy themselves while keeping out the plague of the red death in Poe's "The Masque of the Red Death" (main activity). He is the major cause of the action, and he embodies the story's theme that pride is vain and that death is inescapable (significance). Under the category of "significance," of course, you might develop as many ideas as you have time for, but the short illustration here is a general model for most examinations.

2. *Incidents or situations,* which may be illustrated as follows: "A woman mourns the death of her husband." After giving the location of the situation or incident (Mrs. Popov in Chekhov's play *The Bear* or the Widow in "The Widow of Ephesus"), try to demonstrate its significance in the work. (That is, in *The Bear* Mrs. Popov is mourning the death of her husband, and in the course of the play Chekhov uses her feelings to show amusingly that life with real emotion is stronger than duty to the dead. Very much the same point is made in "The Widow of Ephesus.")

3. *Things, places, and dates.* Your instructor may ask you to identify a cavalry

charge (Twain's "Luck"), a village square (Jackson's "The Lottery"), or the dates of Mansfield's "Miss Brill" (1920) or Amy Lowell's "Patterns" (1916). For dates, you may be given a leeway of five or ten years if you must guess. What is important about a date is not so much exactness as historical and intellectual perspective. The date of "Patterns," for example, was the third year of World War I, and the poem consequently reflects a reaction against the protracted and senseless loss of life that war was producing. Thus, to claim "World War I" as the date of the poem would likely be acceptable as an answer, if it happens that you cannot remember the exact date.

4. *Quotations.* You should remember enough of the text to identify a passage taken from it, or at least to make an informed guess. Generally, you should (1) locate the quotation, if you remember it, or else describe the probable location, (2) show the ways in which the quotation is typical of the content and style of the work you have read, and (3) describe the importance of the passage. You can often salvage much from a momentary lapse of memory by writing a reasoned and careful explanation of your guess. Even if your guess is wrong, the knowledge and cogency of your explanation should earn points.

TECHNICAL AND ANALYTICAL QUESTIONS AND PROBLEMS.   In a scale of ascending importance, the third and most difficult type of factual question is on those matters with which this book has been concerned: technique, analysis, and problems. You might be asked to discuss the *setting, images, point of view,* or *principal idea* of a work; you might be asked about a *specific problem;* or you might be asked to analyze a poem that may or may not be duplicated for your benefit (if it is not duplicated, woe to students who have not studied their assignments). Questions like these assume that you have technical knowledge; they also ask you to examine the text within the limitations imposed by the terms.

Obviously, technical questions occur more frequently in advanced courses than in elementary ones, and the questions become more subtle as the courses become more advanced. Instructors of elementary courses may use main-idea or special-problem questions, but will probably not use many of the others unless they state their intentions to do so in advance, or unless technical terms have been studied in class.

Questions of this type are fairly long, perhaps with from fifteen to twenty-five minutes allowed for each. If you have two or more of these questions, try to space your time sensibly; do not devote 80 percent of your time to one question and leave only 20 percent for the rest.

Basis of Judging Factual Questions

IDENTIFICATION QUESTIONS.   In all factual questions, your instructor is testing (1) your factual command, and (2) your quickness in relating a part of the whole. Thus, suppose you are identifying the incident "A man kills a canary." It is correct to say that Susan Glaspell's play *Trifles* (pp. 1018–28; see also "A Jury of Her Peers," pp. 158–72) is the location of incident, that the dead farmer John Wright was the killer, and that the canary belonged to his wife. Knowledge of these details clearly establishes that you know the facts. But a strong answer must go further. Even in the brief time you have for short answers, you should always aim to connect the facts to (1) major causation in the work, (2) an important idea or ideas, (3) the development of the work, and (4) for a quotation, the style. Time is short and you must be selective, but if you can make your answer move from facts to significance, you will always fashion superior responses. Along these lines, let us look at an answer identifying the action from *Trifles:*

> The action is from Glaspell's *Trifles*. The man who kills the bird is Mr. Wright, and the owner is Mrs. Wright. The killing is important because it is shown as the final indignity in Mrs. Wright's long-developing rage, which prompts her to strangle Wright in his sleep. It is thus the cause not only of the murder but also of the investigation bringing the officers and their wives on stage. In fact, the wringing of the bird's neck makes the play possible because it is the wives who discover the dead bird, and it is the means by which Glaspell highlights them as the major characters in the play. Because the husband's brutal act shows how bleak the life of Mrs. Wright actually was, it dramatizes the lonely plight of women in a male-dominated way of life like that on the Wright farm. The discovery also raises the issue of legality and morality, because the two wives decide to conceal the evidence, therefore protecting Mrs. Wright from conviction and punishment.

Any of the points in this answer could be developed as a separate essay, but the paragraph is successful as a short answer because it goes beyond fact to deal with significance. Clearly, such answers are possible at the time of an exam only if you have devoted considerable thought to the various works beforehand. The more thinking and practicing you do before an exam, the better your answers will be. You may remember this advice as a virtual axiom: *You cannot write really superior answers if you do not think extensively before the exam.* By studying well beforehand, you will be able to reduce surprise on an exam to an absolute minimum.

LONGER FACTUAL QUESTIONS. More extended factual questions also require more thoroughly developed organization. Remember that here your knowledge of essay writing is important, for the quality of your composition will determine a major share of your instructor's evaluation of your answers. It is therefore best to take several minutes to gather your thoughts together before you begin to write, because *a ten-minute planned answer is preferable to a twenty-five-minute unplanned answer.* You do not need to write every possible fact on each particular question. Of greater importance is the use to which you put the facts you know and the organization of your answer. Use a sheet of scratch paper to jot down the facts you remember and your ideas about them in relation to the question.

Then put them together, phrase a thesis sentence, and use your facts to exemplify and support your thesis.

It is always necessary to begin your answer pointedly, using key words or phrases from the question or direction if possible, so that your answer will have thematic shape. You should never begin an answer with "Because" and then go on from there without referring again to the question. To be most responsive during the short time available for an exam, you should use the question as your guide for your answer. Let us suppose that you have the following question on your test: "How does Glaspell use details in *Trifles* to reveal the character of Mrs. Wright?" The most common way to go astray on such a question, and the easiest thing to do also, is to concentrate on Mrs. Wright's character rather than on how Glaspell uses detail to bring out her character. The word *how* makes a vast difference in the nature of the final answer, and hence a good method on the exam is to duplicate key phrases in the question to ensure that you make your major points clear. Here is an opening sentence that uses the key words and phrases (underlined here) from the question to direct thought and provide focus:

> Glaspell uses details of setting, marital relationships, and personal habits to reveal the character of Mrs. Wright as a person of great but unfulfilled potential whom anger has finally overcome.

Because this sentence repeats the key phrases from the question, and also because it promises to show *how* the details are to be focused on the character, it suggests that the answer to follow will be responsive.

General or Comprehensive Questions

General or comprehensive questions are particularly important on final examinations, when your instructor is interested in testing your total comprehension of the course material. Considerable time is usually allowed for answering this type of question, which may be phrased in a number of ways:

1. A direct question asking about philosophy, underlying attitudes, main ideas, characteristics of style, backgrounds, and so on. Here are some possible questions in this category:
   "What use do_____, _____, and _____ make of the topic of _____?"
   "Define and characterize the short story as a genre of literature."
   "Explain the use of dialogue by Hawthorne, Welty, and Maupassant."
   "Contrast the technique of point of view as used by _____, _____, and _____."

2. A "comment" question, often based on an extensive quotation, borrowed from a critic or written by your instructor for the occasion, about a broad class of writers, or about a literary movement, or the like. Your instructor

may ask you to treat this question broadly (taking in many writers) or else to apply the quotation to a specific writer.

3. A "suppose" question, such as "What advice might Mrs. Wright of *Trifles* give the speakers of Lowell's 'Patterns' and Keats's 'Bright Star'?", or "What might the speaker of Rossetti's poem 'Echo' say if she learned that her dead lover was Goodman Brown of Hawthorne's 'Young Goodman Brown'?" Although suppose questions might seem whimsical at first sight, they have a serious design and should prompt original and radical thinking. The first question, for example, should cause a test writer to bring out, from Mrs. Wright's perspective, that the love of both speakers was/is potential, not actual. She would likely sympathize with the speaker's loss in "Patterns," but might also say the lost married life might not have been as totally happy as the speaker assumes. For the speaker of "Bright Star," a male, Mrs. Wright might say that the steadfast love sought by him should also be linked to kindness and tolerance as well as passion.

Although "suppose" questions, and answers, are speculative, the need to respond to them causes a detailed consideration of the works involved, and in this respect the suppose question is a salutary means of learning. Needless to say, it is difficult to prepare for a suppose question, which you may therefore regard as a test not only of your knowledge, but also of your inventiveness and ingenuity.

Basis of Judging General Questions

When answering broad, general questions, you are in fact dealing with an unstructured situation, and you must not only supply an *answer* but—equally important—you must also create a *structure* within which your answer can have meaning. You might say that you make up your own specific question out of the original general question. If you were asked to "Consider the role of women as seen in Lowell, Mansfield, and Glaspell," for example, you would do well to structure the question by focusing on a number of clearly defined topics. A possible way to begin answering such a question might be this:

Lowell, Mansfield, and Glaspell present a view of female resilience by demonstrating inner control, power of adaptation, and endurance.

With this sort of focus you would be able to proceed point by point, introducing supporting data as you form your answer.

As a general rule, the best method for answering a comprehensive question is comparison-contrast (see also Appendix B, pp. 1567–82). The reason is that in dealing with, say, a general question on Rossetti, Chekhov, and Keats, it is too easy to write *three* separate essays rather than *one*. Thus, you should try to create a topic like "The treatment of real or idealized love," or "The difficulties in male-female relationships," and then develop your answer point by point rather than writer by writer. By creating your answer in this way, you can bring in references to each or all of the writers as they become relevant to your main idea. But if you were to treat each writer separately, your comprehensive answer would lose focus and effectiveness, and it would be needlessly repetitive.

Remember these things, then: In judging your response to a general question, your instructor is interested in seeing (1) how effectively you perceive and explain the significant issues in the question, (2) how intelligently and clearly you organize your answer, (3) how relevantly and persuasively you use materials from the work as supporting evidence.

Bear in mind that in answering comprehensive questions, though you are ostensibly free, the freedom you have been extended is that of creating your own structure. The underlying idea of the comprehensive, general question is that you possess special knowledge and insights that cannot be discovered by more factual questions. You must therefore formulate your own responses to the material and introduce evidence that reflects your own insights and command of information.

A final word, always: Good luck.

Appendix B: Comparison-Contrast and Extended Comparison-Contrast: Learning by Seeing Things Together

A comparison-contrast essay is used to compare and contrast different authors, two or more works by the same author, different drafts of the same work, or characters, incidents, techniques, and ideas in the same work or in different works. The virtue of comparison-contrast is that it enables the study of works in perspective. No matter what works you consider together, the method helps you isolate and highlight individual characteristics, for the quickest way to get at the essence of one thing is to compare it with another. Similarities are brought out by comparison, and differences are shown by contrast. In other words, you can enhance your understanding of what a thing *is* by using comparison-contrast to determine what it *is not*.

For example, our understanding of Shakespeare's Sonnet 30, "When to the Sessions of Sweet Silent Thought" (p. 627) may be enhanced if we compare it with Christina Rossetti's poem "Echo" (p. 698). Both poems treat personal recollections of past experiences, told by a speaker to a listener who is not intended to be the reader. They also both refer to persons, now dead, with whom the speakers were closely involved.

There are important differences, however. Shakespeare's speaker numbers the dead persons as friends whom he laments generally, whereas Rossetti refers specifically to one person with whom the speaker was in love. Rossetti's topic is the sorrow of dead love, the irrevocability of the past, and the present loneliness of the speaker. Shakespeare includes the references to dead friends as a way of accounting for present sorrows, but then his speaker turns to the present, and asserts that thinking about the "dear friend" being addressed enables him to restore past "losses" and end all "sorrows." In Rossetti's poem, there is no reconciliation of past and present, and instead the speaker focuses entirely upon the sadness of the present moment. Though both poems are retrospective, then, Shakespeare's poem looks toward the present while Rossetti's looks to the past.

While more could be said, this example shows how the comparison-contrast method enables us to identify leading similarities and distinguishing differences in both works. It is undeniable that you may overcome difficulty with one work by comparing and contrasting it with another work on a comparable subject.

CLARIFY YOUR INTENTION

When planning a comparison-contrast essay, you should first decide on your goal, for you may use the method in a number of ways. One objective may be *the equal and mutual illumination of two (or more) works.* For example, an essay comparing Welty's "A Worn Path" (p. 119) with Hawthorne's "Young Goodman Brown" (p. 332) might be designed (1) to compare ideas, characters, or methods in these stories equally, without stressing or favoring either. But you might also wish (2) to emphasize "Young Goodman Brown," and therefore you would use "A Worn Path" as material for highlighting Hawthorne's story. In addition, you might also use the comparison-contrast method (3) to show your liking of one story at the expense of another, or (4) to emphasize a method or idea that you think is especially noteworthy or appropriate.

A first task is therefore to decide what to emphasize. The first sample essay (p. 1574) gives "equal time" to both works being considered, without any claims for the superiority of either. Unless you want to pursue a different rhetorical goal, this essay is a suitable model for most comparisons.

FIND COMMON GROUNDS FOR COMPARISON

The second stage in prewriting for this essay is to select a common ground for discussion. It is pointless to compare dissimilar things, for the resulting conclusions will not have much value. Instead, find a common ground. Compare like with like: idea with idea, characterization with characterization, imagery with imagery, point of view with point of view, tone with tone, problem with problem. Nothing much can be learned from a comparison of "Welty's view of courage and Chekhov's view of love," but a comparison of "The relationship of love to stability and courage in Chekhov and Welty" suggests common ground, with the promise of important things to be learned through the examination of similarities and differences.

In seeking common ground, you will need to be inventive and creative. For instance, if you compare de Maupassant's "The Necklace" and Chekhov's *The Bear*, these two works at first seem dissimilar. Yet a common ground can be found, such as "The Treatment of Self-Deceit,"

"The Effects of Chance on Human Affairs," "The View of Women," and so on. Although other works may seem even more dissimilar than these, it is usually possible to find a common ground for comparison and contrast. Much of your success with this type of essay depends on your finding a workable basis—a common denominator—for comparison.

METHODS OF COMPARISON

Let us assume that you have decided on your rhetorical purpose and on the basis or bases of your comparison. You have done your reading, taken notes, and have a rough idea of what to say. The remaining problem is the treatment of your material.

A common way is to make your points first about one work and then about the other. Unfortunately, this method makes your paper seem like two big lumps. ("Work 1" takes up one half of your paper, and "work 2" takes up the other half.) Also, the method involves repetition because you must repeat many points when you treat the second subject.

A better method therefore is to treat the major aspects of your main idea, and to refer to the two (or more) works as they support your arguments. Thus, you refer constantly to *both* works, sometimes within the same sentence, and remind your reader of the point of your discussion. There are reasons for the superiority of this method: (1) You do not repeat your points needlessly, for you document them as you raise them. (2) By constantly referring to the two works, you make your points without requiring a reader with a poor memory to reread previous sections.

As a model, here is a paragraph on "Natural References as a Basis of Comparison in Frost's 'Desert Places' and Shakespeare's Sonnet 73 ['That Time of Year Thou Mayst in Me Behold']" (pp. 743 and 690). The virtue of the paragraph is that it uses material from both poems simultaneously (as nearly as the time sequence of sentences allows) as the substance for the development of the ideas.

> [1] Both writers link their ideas to events occurring in the natural world. [2] Night as a parallel with death is common to both poems, with Frost speaking about it in his first line, and Shakespeare introducing it in his seventh. [3] Along with night, Frost emphasizes the onset of winter and snow as a time of death and desolation. [4] With this natural description, Frost also symbolically refers to empty, secret, dead places in the inner spirit— crannies of the soul where bleak winter snowfalls correspond to selfishness and indifference to others. [5] By contrast, Shakespeare uses the fall season, with the yellowing and dropping of leaves and also the flying away of birds, to stress the closeness of real death and therefore also the need to love fully during the time remaining. [6] Both poems therefore share a sense of gloom, because both present death as inevitable and final, just like the oncoming season of barrenness and waste. [7] Because Shakespeare's sonnet is addressed

to a listener who is also a loved one, however, it is more outgoing than the more introspective poem of Frost. [8] Frost turns the snow, the night, and the emptiness of the universe inwardly in order to show the speaker's inner bleakness, and by extension, the bleakness of many human spirits. [9] Shakespeare instead uses the bleakness of seasons, night, and dying fires to state the need for loving "well." [10] The poems thus use common and similar references for different purposes and effects.

The paragraph links Shakespeare's references to nature with those of Frost. Five sentences speak of both authors together; three speak of Frost alone, and two of Shakespeare alone, but all the sentences are unified topically. This interweaving of references indicates that the writer has learned both poems well enough to think of them at the same time, and it also enables the writing to be more pointed and succinct than if the works were separately treated.

You can learn from this example: If you develop your essay by putting your two subjects constantly together, you will write economically and pointedly (not only for essays, but also for tests). Beyond that, if you digest the material as successfully as this method indicates, you demonstrate that you are fulfilling a major educational goal—the assimilation and *use* of material. Too often, because you learn things separately (in separate works and courses, at separate times), you tend also to compartmentalize them. But instead, you should always try to relate them, to *synthesize* them. Comparison and contrast help in this process of putting together, of seeing things not as fragments but as parts of wholes.

AVOID THE "TENNIS-BALL" METHOD

As you make your comparison, do not confuse an interlocking method with a "tennis-ball" method, in which you bounce your subject back and forth constantly and repetitively, almost as though you were hitting observations back and forth over a net. The tennis-ball method is shown in the following example from a comparison of the characters Mathilde (Maupassant's "The Necklace") and Miss Brill (Mansfield's "Miss Brill"):

> Mathilde is a young married woman, while Miss Brill is single and getting older. Mathilde has at least some kind of social life, even though she doesn't have more than one friend, while Miss Brill leads a life of solitude. Mathilde's daydreams are responsible for her misfortune, but the shattering of Miss Brill's is done by someone from the outside. Therefore, Mathilde is made unhappy because of her own shortcomings, but Miss Brill is a helpless victim. In Mathilde's case the focus is on adversity not only causing trouble but also strengthening character. In Miss Brill's case the focus is on the weak getting hurt and becoming weaker.

Imagine the effect of an entire essay written in this boring "1,2—1,2—1,2" order. Aside from the repetition and unvaried patterning of subjects, the tennis-ball method does not permit much illustrative development. You should not feel so cramped that you cannot take two or more sentences to develop a point about one writer or subject before you include comparative references to another. If you remember to interlock the two subjects of comparison, however, as in the paragraph about Frost and Shakespeare, your method will give you the freedom to develop your topics fully.

THE EXTENDED COMPARISON-CONTRAST ESSAY

For a longer essay about a number of works—such as a limited research paper, comprehensive exam questions, and the sort of extended essay required at the end of a semester—comparison-contrast is an essential method. You may wish to compare the works on the basis of elements such as ideas, plot, structure, character, metaphor, point of view, or setting. Because of the larger number of works, however, you will need to modify the way in which you employ the comparison-contrast method. Let us assume that you are dealing with not just two works but six, seven, or more. You need first to find a common ground which you may use as your central, unifying idea, just as you do for a comparison of only two works. Once you establish the common ground, you should classify or group your works on the basis of the similarities and differences which they exemplify with regard to the topic. The idea is to get two *groups* for comparison, not just two works.

Let us assume that three or four works treat a topic in one way, while two or three do it in another (e.g., either criticism or praise of wealth and trade, or the joys or sorrows of love, or the enthusiasm or disillusion-ment of youth). In writing about these works, you might treat the topic itself in a straightforward comparison-contrast method, but use details from the works within the groupings as the material which you use for illustration and argument.

To make your essay as specific as possible, it is probably best to stress only two major works with each of your subpoints. Once you have established these points in detail, there is no need to go into similar detail with all the other works you are studying. Instead, you may refer to the other works briefly, with your purpose being to strengthen your points but not to create more and more examples. Once you go to another subpoint, you may use different works for illustration, so that by the end of your essay you will have given due attention to each work in your assignment. In this way—by treating many works in comparative groups of twos—you can keep your essay reasonably brief, for there is no need for unproductive detail.

For illustration, the second sample essay shows how this grouping may be done (p. 1577). There, six works are included in a general category of how love and service offer guidance and stability. This group is contrasted with another group of four works (including two characters from one of the works in the first group), in which love is shown as an escape or retreat.

DOCUMENTATION AND THE EXTENDED COMPARISON-CONTRAST ESSAY

For the longer comparison-contrast essay you may find a problem in documentation. Generally you do not need to locate page numbers for references to major traits, ideas, and actions. For example, if you refer to the end of Poe's "The Masque of the Red Death," where Prince Prospero rushes through his suite of seven rooms and dies in the last, you may assume that your reader also knows about this action. You do not need to do any more than make the reference.

But if you quote lines or passages, or if you cite actions or characters in special ways, you may need to use parenthetical page references, as described in Joseph Gibaldi and Walter S. Achtert, *MLA Handbook for Writers of Research Papers*, 3rd ed. (discussed in Appendix C, pp. 1597–99). If you are using lines or parts of lines of poetry, use line numbers parenthetically, as in the second sample essay. Be guided by the following principle: If you make a specific reference that you think your reader might want to examine in more detail, supply the line or page number. If you refer to minor details that might easily be unnoticed or forgotten, also supply the line or page number. Otherwise, if you refer to major ideas, actions, or characterizations, be sure to make your internal reference clear enough so that your reader can easily recall it from his or her memory of the work.

WRITING COMPARISON-CONTRAST ESSAYS

Organizing Your Essay

First, narrow and simplify your subject so that you can handle it conveniently. Should your subject be a comparison of Amy Lowell and Wilfred Owen (as in the first sample essay), pick out one or two of each poet's poems on the same or a similar topic, and write your essay about these. For the longer comparison-contrast essay, you will need no more than one work by each author. Be wary, however, of the limitations of your selection, because generalizations made from one or two works may not apply to all works of the same writer.

Once you have found an organizing principle along with the relevant works, begin to refine and focus the direction of your essay. As you study each work, note common or contrasting elements, and use these to form your central idea. At the same time, you can select the most illustrative works and classify them according to your topic, such as war (first sample essay) or love (second).

INTRODUCTION. State the works, authors, characters, or ideas which you are considering. Then show how you have narrowed the topic. Your central idea should briefly highlight the principal grounds of comparison and contrast, such as that both works treat a common topic, exhibit a similar idea, use a similar form, develop an identical attitude, and so on, and also that major or minor differences help to make the works unique. You may also assert that one work is superior to the other, if you wish to make this judgment and defend it.

BODY. The body depends on the works and your basis of comparison (ideas and essays, depictions of character, uses of setting, qualities of style, or uses of point of view, and so on). For a comparison-contrast treatment on such a basis, your goal should be to shed light on both (or more) of the works you are treating. For example, you might examine a number of stories that are written in the first-person point of view (see Chapter 5, pp. 198–200). An essay on this topic might compare the ways each author uses this point of view to achieve similar or distinct effects. Or you might compare a group of poems that employ similar images, symbols, or ironic methods. Sometimes, the process can be as simple as identifying female or male protagonists, and comparing the ways in which their characters are developed. Another approach is to compare the *subjects*, as opposed to the *theme*. You might identify works dealing with general subjects like love, death, youth, race, or war. Such groupings provide a basis of excellent comparisons and contrasts.

As you develop the body, remember to keep comparison-contrast foremost. That is, your discussions of point of view, metaphorical language, and so on should not so much explain these topics as topics, but rather explore similarities and differences about the works you are comparing. Let us say that your topic is an idea. You of course need to explain the idea, but only enough to establish points of similarity or difference. As you develop such an essay, you might illustrate your arguments by referring to related uses of elements like setting, characterization, rhythm or rhyme, symbolism, point of view, or metaphor. When you introduce these new subjects, you will be right on target as long as you use them comparatively.

CONCLUSION. Here you may reflect on other ideas or techniques in the works you have compared, make observations about similar qualities, or summarize briefly the grounds of your comparison. The conclusion of an extended comparison-contrast essay should represent a final bringing together of your materials. In the body of your essay, you may not have referred to all the works in each paragraph. However, in your conclusion you should try to include them all. If your writers belong to any "period" or "school" (information about such topics would require research and the use of correct documentation), you also might show how they relate to these larger movements. References of this sort provide an obvious common ground for comparison and contrast.

SAMPLE ESSAY (TWO WORKS)

The Treatment of Responses to War in Amy Lowell's "Patterns" and Wilfred Owen's "Anthem for Doomed Youth"[°]

[1] "Patterns" and "Anthem for Doomed Youth" are both powerful and unique condemnations of war.[*] Owen's short poem speaks broadly and generally about the ugliness of war and also about large groups of bereaved people; Lowell's longer poem focuses upon the personal grief of just one person. In a real sense, Lowell's poem begins where Owen's ends, a fact which accounts for both the similarities and differences between the two works. The antiwar themes may be compared on the basis of their subjects, their lengths, their concreteness, and their use of a common major metaphor.[†]

[2] "Anthem for Doomed Youth" attacks war more directly than "Patterns." Owen's opening line, "What passing bells for those who die as cattle," suggests that in war human beings are depersonalized before they are slaughtered, like so much meat, while his observations about the "monstrous" guns and the "shrill, demented" shells unambiguously condemn the horrors of war. By contrast, in "Patterns" warfare is far away, on another continent, intruding only when the messenger delivers the letter stating that the speaker's fiancé has been killed (lines 63–64). Similar news governs the last six lines of Owen's poem, quietly describing how those at home respond to the news that their loved ones have died in war. Thus, the antiwar focus in "Patterns" is the contrast between the calm, peaceful life of the speaker's garden and the anguish of her responses, while in Owen's poem the stress is more the external horrors of war which bring about the need for ceremonies honoring the dead.

Another difference, which is surprising, is that Owen's poem is less than one-seventh as long as Lowell's. "Patterns" is an interior monologue or meditation of 107 lines, but it could not be shorter and still be convincing. In the poem the speaker thinks about the present and past, and contemplates the future loneliness to which her intended husband's death has doomed her.

[°] For these poems, see pp. 932 and 604.
[*] Central idea.
[†] Thesis sentence.

[3] Her final outburst, "Christ, what are patterns for?", can make no sense if she does not explain her situation as extensively as she does. On the other hand, "Anthem for Doomed Youth" is brief--a 14-line sonnet--because it is more general and less personal than "Patterns." Although Owen's speaker shows great sympathy, he or she views the sorrows of others distantly, unlike Lowell, who goes right into the mind and spirit of the grieving woman. Owen's use, in his last six lines, of phrases like "tenderness of patient minds" and "drawing down of blinds" is a short but powerful representation of deep grief. He gives no further detail even though thousands of individual stories might be told. In contrast, Lowell tells one of these stories as she focuses on her solitary speaker's lost hopes and dreams. Thus, the contrasting lengths of the poems are governed by each poet's treatment of the topic.

[4] Despite these differences of approach and length, both poems are similarly concrete and real. Owen moves from the real scenes and sounds of far-off battlefields to the homes of the many soldiers who have been killed in battle, whereas Lowell's scene is a single place--the garden of the estate where the speaker has just received news of her lover's death. Her speaker walks on real gravel along garden paths which contain daffodils, squills, a fountain, and a lime tree. She thinks of her clothing and her ribboned shoes, and also of her fiancé's boots, sword hilts, and buttons. The images in Owen's poem are equally real, but are not associated with individuals as in "Patterns." Thus, his images refer to cattle, bells, rifle shots, shells, bugles, candles, and window blinds. While both poems thus reflect reality, Owen's details are more general and public, whereas Lowell's are more personal and intimate.

[5] Along with this concreteness, the poems share a major metaphor: that cultural patterns both control and frustrate human wishes and hopes. In "Patterns" this metaphor is shown in warfare itself (line 106), which is the supremely destructive political structure, or pattern. Further examples of the metaphor are found in details about clothing (particularly the speaker's stiff, confining gown in lines 5, 18, 21, 73, and 100, but also the lover's military boots in lines 46 and 49); the orderly, formal garden paths in which the speaker is walking (lines 1, 93); her restraint at hearing about her lover's death; and her courtesy, despite her grief, in ordering refreshment for the messenger (line 69). Within such rigid patterns, her hopes for happiness have vanished, along with the sensuous spontaneity symbolized by her lover's plans to make love with her on a "shady seat' in the garden (lines 85–89). The metaphor of the constricting pattern may also be seen in "Anthem for Doomed Youth," except that in this poem the pattern is the funeral, not love or marriage. Owen's speaker contrasts the calm, peaceful tolling of "passing bells" (line 1) with the frightening sounds of war represented by the "monstrous anger of the guns," "the rifles' rapid rattle," and "the demented choirs of wailing shells" (lines 2–8). Thus, while Lowell uses the metaphor to reveal the irony of hope and desire being destroyed by war, Owen uses it to reveal the irony of war's nullification and perversion of peaceful ceremonies.

Though the poems in these ways share topics and some aspects of treatment, they are distinct and individual. "Patterns" is visual and kinesthetic, whereas "Anthem for Doomed Youth" is strongly auditory. Both poems con-

[6] clude on powerfully emotional although different notes. Owen's poem dwells on the pathos and sadness that war brings to many unnamed people, while Lowell's expresses the most intimate thoughts of a particular woman in the first agony of sorrow. Although neither poem directly attacks the usual platitudes and justifications for war (the needs to mobilize, to sacrifice, to achieve peace through fighting, and so on), the attack is there by implication, for both poems make their appeal by stressing how war destroys the relationships that make life worth living. For this reason, despite their differences, both "Patterns" and "Anthem for Doomed Youth," are parallel antiwar poems, and both are strong portrayals of human feeling.

Commentary on the Essay

This example illustrates how approximately "equal time" may be given to the similarities and differences of each work being compared. Because the essay shifts constantly from one work to the next, particular phrases may be noticed. When the works are similar or even identical, terms are "common," "share," "and," "similar," "also," and "both." For comparative situations, words like "longer," and "more" are useful. Differences are marked by "by contrast," "while," "whereas," "different," "dissimilar," and "on the other hand." Transitions from paragraph to paragraph are no different in this type of essay from those in other essays. Thus, "despite," "along with this concreteness," and "in these ways" are used here, but they could be used anywhere for the same transitional purpose.

The central idea—that the poems mutually condemn war—is brought out in the introductory paragraph, together with the supporting idea that the poems blend into each other because both show responses to news of battle casualties.

Paragraph 2, the first in the body, discusses how each poem brings out its attack on warfare. Paragraph 3 explains the differing lengths of the poems as a function of differences in perspective. Because Owen's sonnet views war and its effects at a distance, it is brief, while Lowell's interior monologue views death intimately, needing more detail and greater length. Paragraph 4, on the topic of concreteness and reality, shows how "equal time" may be given to two works without the bouncing back and forth of the "tennis-ball" method. Three of the sentences in this paragraph (3, 4, and 6) are devoted exclusively to details in one or the other poem, while sentences 1, 2, 5, and 7 refer to both works, stressing points of broad or specific comparison. The scheme demonstrates that the two works are, in effect, interlocked within the paragraph.

Paragraph 5, the last in the body, considers the similar and dissimilar ways in which the poems treat the common metaphor of cultural patterns.

The final paragraph summarizes the central idea, and it also stresses the ways in which both poems, while being similar, are distinct and unique.

SAMPLE ESSAY (EXTENDED COMPARISON-CONTRAST)

The Complexity of Love and Devoted Service

[1] On the surface, sexual attraction, love, and devoted duty are simple, and their results should be good. When love works and is in balance, a person loves and devotes attention to someone, or serves a cause with respect and willingness. Such devotion leads to stability and a healthy sense of identity. It is a way of saying "yes." When love and devotion do not work, the effect is extreme unhappiness, a way of saying "no." Love, in short, is not simple. It is complex, and its results are not uniformly good.° This idea can be traced in a comparison of ten works: Shakespeare's Sonnet 116, Keats's "Bright Star," Rossetti's "Echo," Arnold's "Dover Beach," Hardy's "Channel Firing," Owen's "Anthem for Doomed Youth," Chekhov's The Bear, Glaspell's Trifles, Updike's "A & P," and Welty's "A Worn Path."* The complexity in these works is that love and devotion do not operate in a vacuum but rather in the context of personal, philosophical, economic, and national difficulties. The works show that love and devotion may be forces for stability and refuge, but also for harm.†

[2] Love as an ideal and stabilizing force is a major principle asserted by Shakespeare in Sonnet 116, Keats in the sonnet "Bright Star," and Rossetti in "Echo." All three writers think of love as a constant, and associate it with guidance and illumination. Shakespeare states that love gives lovers strength and stability in a complex world of opposition and difficulty. Such love is like a "star" (obviously the North Star) that guides wandering ships (line 7), and like a "fixed mark" that stands against the shaking of life's tempests (lines 5 and 6). Fixity is also the condition stressed by Keats in "Bright Star," where the speaker contrasts his own apparent instability with his desire to be as steadfast in his loving as the star is in the sky (line 1). Rossetti refers to love as a light in darkness (stanza 1), even though the light, to her speaker, has been snuffed out by the death of her beloved.

[3] For these three writers, then, love grows out of the need for stability and guidance, just as it also supplies this need. To this degree, love is a simplifying force, but it simplifies primarily because the darkness and the "tempests" complicating life are so strong. Such love is one of the best things that happens to human beings, because it fulfills them and prepares them to face life. It is fair to say that all the writers being considered here, either directly or indirectly, are working with this same positive assumption about love.

The desire to seek identity in love is so strong that it can also cause people to do strange and funny things. The two major characters in Chekhov's short comedy-farce The Bear are examples, as is Sammy of Updike's story

---

° Central idea.

* For the texts of these works, see pp. 732, 629, 698, 559, 562, 604, 1007, 1018, 65, and 119.

† Thesis sentence.

[4] " A & P." Sammy watches the three girls in the store with great sexual curiosity, and within minutes after they leave, he quits his job in a gesture that combines sexual adoration, chivalric respect, and his own individuality. A similar quick change is shown by Chekhov's Mrs. Popov and Smirnov, who as *The Bear* opens are enmeshed in their own confusions. She is devoted to the memory of her dead husband, while he is disillusioned and cynical about women because of mismanaged love affairs. But Chekhov makes them go through hoops for love. As the two argue, insult each other, and reach the point of dueling with real pistols, their need for love overcomes their anger. In their case, as in Sammy's, it is as though the impulse for love and admiration overcomes all the contrary influences, because the common need for a stabilizing base is so strong.

[5] Either seriously or comically, then, love and love interest are like a rudder, guiding people in powerful and conflicting currents. The results may be sudden and passionate kisses, as with Chekhov's characters, or they may be the establishment of a new condition or ideal, as in Shakespeare, Keats, and Rossetti, and in the decision that Updike's Sammy makes. All these works, however, demonstrate that love shapes lives in ways that go beyond a person's immediate intentions.

[6] This thought is somewhat like the view presented by Eudora Welty in "A Worn Path." Welty's story describes how love is manifested in loving service, in this respect being not only a guide, but a controlling force. A poor grandmother, Phoenix Jackson, has a hard life in caring for her incurably ill grandson. The walk she takes along the "worn path" to Natchez symbolizes the hardships she endures because of her single-minded love. Her care is the closest thing to pure simplicity that may be found in all the works examined, with the possible exception of the sudden falling in love in Chekhov's play.

[7] Even Phoenix's devoted service, however, does not solve problems, but rather brings them out. She is not surrounded by the joyless, loveless, violent world described by Hardy in "Channel Firing," Owen in "Anthem for Doomed Youth," and Arnold in "Dover Beach," but her life is nevertheless quite grim. She is poor and ignorant, and her grandson has nowhere to go but down. If she would only think deeply about her condition, she might be as despairing as Arnold and Hardy. But her strength is her ability either to accept her difficult life or to ignore the grimness of it. With her service as her "star" and "ever-fixèd mark," to recall Shakespeare's words in Sonnet 116, she stays cheerful and lives in friendship with the animals and the woods. Her life has meaning and dignity.

[8] Arnold's view of love and devotion under such bad conditions marks a departure from the views of love's power as a guiding and governing force. For Arnold, the public world seems to be so far gone that there is nothing left but personal relationships. Thus love is not so much a guide as a refuge, a condition accepted for sanity and safety. After describing what he considers the worldwide shrinking of the "Sea of Faith" (i.e., the loss of absolute belief in the existence of a personal and caring God), his speaker states:

Ah, love, let us be true
To one another! for the world, which seems
To lie before us like a land of dreams,
So various, so beautiful, so new,
Hath really neither joy, nor love, nor light,
Nor certitude, nor peace, nor help for pain;
And we are here as on a darkling plain
Swept with confused alarms of struggle and flight
Where ignorant armies clash by night.

(lines 29–37)

Here the word *true* should be underlined, as Shakespeare emphasizes "*true* minds" and as Welty gives us in Phoenix a portrait of *true* service. "True" in Arnold's poem involves the creation of a small area of fidelity and certainty in the world of horrible naval gunnery and rattling rifles of "Channel Firing" and "Anthem for Doomed Youth," where there is only madness and death. Love is not so much a guide as a condition of hope, a retreat where truth can still have meaning.

[9]   In practice, perhaps, Arnold's idea of love as a refuge is not different from the view that love is a guide. Once the truthful pledge is made, it is a force for goodness, at least for the lovers making the pledge, just as love creates stability and purpose for Shakespeare, Chekhov, Welty, and Keats. Yet Arnold's view is weaker. It does not come from within, as with the longing of Rossetti's speaker, the gesture of support that Updike's Sammy makes for the rights of the young ladies to wear nothing but bathing suits in a public place, or the abrupt love of Chekhov's major characters. Rather, Arnold's appeal for truth and fidelity results from a philosophical decision to ignore political and philosophical forces, which are beyond control, and to seek meaning and fidelity only in small and private relationships.

[10]   Thus far love and devotion have been considered more or less as ideals, but the ideal is always subject to the reality of human personality. A major idea is hence that the character of a person may turn love sour and damage life. In the set of works being considered here, such destructiveness is brought out best by Susan Glaspell in *Trifles* (and in the other version of the story, "A Jury of Her Peers"). Ideally, the love of John and Minnie Wright should give them the strength and stability to live satisfactory if not happy lives on their isolated small farm. Instead, John has used his power to suppress Minnie's femininity and love of song. The result is her simmering anger for the thirty years of their life together, resulting in the outburst of her strangling John in his sleep.

[11]   Minnie's anger is not dissimilar to that of Mrs. Popov, whose dead husband Nicolai had been neglectful and unfaithful. John, however, is not unfaithful, but masterful and cruel, thus justifying Minnie's rage. Mrs. Popov has some of the same rage, but submerges it at the start of *The Bear* by devoting her life to the role of a grieving (but angry) widow. She of course is more fortunate than Minnie, for fate takes her husband Nicolai while Minnie, in

desperation and presumed rage, takes the burden of eliminating her husband herself. Even though neither husband appears in *The Bear* and *Trifles*, they both demonstrate the worst possible result of love--its use for personal power rather than for mutual understanding, tenderness, and devoted caring.

[12] John Wright and Nicolai Popov are minor compared with those unseen, unnamed, and distant persons firing the big guns during the "gunnery practice out at sea" of Hardy's "Channel Firing" (line 10) and also those who create "the monstrous anger of the guns" of Owen's "Anthem for Doomed Youth" (line 2). Neither poet treats the gunners as individuals but as an evil collective force made up of persons who, under the sheltering claim of devoted service to country, are "striving strong to make / Red war yet redder" (Hardy, lines 13, 14) and to create great hordes of "these who die as cattle" (Owen, line 1). For them, love of country is a last refuge and not a guide, and it is therefore a misuse of devoted service. In their blind obedience, as Hardy's God says, they are not much better than the dead because they do nothing "for Christés sake" (line 15). They operate the ships and fill the columns of Arnold's "ignorant armies," and, like Wright and Nicolai, they have forsaken the guidance that love should give while they pursue mindless and destructive ends.

[13] In summary, love and devotion as seen in these various works may be compared with a continuous line formed out of the human need for love and for the stability and guidance that love offers. At one end love is totally good and ideal; at the other it becomes totally bad. Shakespeare, Keats, Rossetti, Welty, Chekhov's Smirnov and Mrs. Popov, and Updike's Sammy are at the end that is good. Still at the good end, but moving toward the center, is Arnold's use of love as a refuge. On the other side of the line are Chekhov's Nicolai Popov and Glaspell's John Wright, while all the way at the bad end are the insensible and invisible gunners in Hardy's "Channel Firing" and Owen's "Anthem for Doomed Youth."

[14] The difficulty noted in all the works, and a major problem in life, is to keep oneself on the stabilizing, constructive part of the line. Although in his farce Chekhov causes love to win against gigantic odds, he shows the problem most vividly of all the authors studied. Under normal conditions, people like Mrs. Popov and Smirnov would not find love. Instead, they would continue following their destructive and false guides. They would be unhappy and disillusioned, and would continue to spread talk about their own confused ideas (as Smirnov actually does almost right up to his sudden conversion to loving Mrs. Popov). Like the military and naval forces of Arnold and Hardy, they would then wind up at the destructive end of the line.

[15] Change, death, opposition, confusion, anger, resignation, economic difficulty, illness--these are only some of the forces that attack people as they try to find meaning and stability in love and service as in Sonnet 116, "Bright Star," "Echo," the major characters in *The Bear*, "A Worn Path," and, to smaller degrees, "A & P" and "Dover Beach." If confusion wins, they are locked into harmful positions, like the gunners in "Channel Firing" and "Anthem for Doomed Youth" and like Nicolai Popov of *The Bear* and John Wright of *Trifles*. Thus, love is complicated by circumstances, and is not by itself alone the

simple force for good that it should ideally be. The works compared and contrasted here have shown these difficulties and complexities.

Commentary on the Essay

This essay, combining for discussion all three of the genres, is visualized as an assignment at the end of a unit of study. The expectation prompting the assignment is that a fairly large number of literary works can be profitably compared on the basis of a unifying subject, idea, or technique. For this sample, the works—six poems, two stories, and two plays—are compared and contrasted on the common ground or central idea of the complexity of love and service. The essay develops this central idea in three major sections: (1) love as an ideal and guide, in paragraphs 2 to 7, (2) love as a refuge or escape, in paragraphs 8 and 9, and (3) love as an excuse for doing harm, as in paragraphs 10 to 12.

The various works are grouped generally according to these sections. Thus, Sonnet 116, "Bright Star," "Echo," *The Bear*, "A & P," and "A Worn Path" are together in the first group—love as an ideal and guide. "Dover Beach" and "Channel Firing" are considered in the second section, but are also introduced for comparison in paragraph 7 as part of a point about the nature of Phoenix's condition in "A Worn Path." Similarly, some of the works in the first group are included as subjects of comparison and contrast in all the sections.

It is obviously impossible that all works being considered can be discussed in detail in every paragraph of a comparison-contrast essay. Thus, in paragraph 2 of this essay, only three works are introduced on the common topic, not all ten, and paragraph 3 consists of a reflection on these three works. Paragraph 4 introduces two works on a slightly different point ("strange and funny things") than that of paragraphs 2 and 3. Paragraph 5 is like the third paragraph because it, too, serves as a point of reflection—this time about all the works considered to that point. The form of comparison and contrast throughout the essay might hence be thought of as one of expansion (when a number of works are introduced) and contraction (when there are just a few).

Paragraph 6 introduces references to just one work, Welty's "A Worn Path," with a brief comparison of only one other work at the end. The seventh paragraph continues the subject of the sixth and introduces two additional works for comparison.

Paragraph 8 illustrates how virtually the entire number of works being studied may be focused on a single topic—here, the use of love as refuge or retreat, with the central work of the paragraph being "Dover Beach." The first sentence contrasts Arnold's view with the common idea in the six works in the first group—that love is a guide. The fifth sentence shows how Arnold is similar in one respect to Shakespeare and Welty, and the sixth sentence shows a similarity of Arnold with Owen and Hardy. The paragraph thus brings together most of the works being studied, either through specific mention or general allusion. Like paragraph 8, paragraph 9 uses Arnold's "Dover Beach" as the key work, with reference to a number of other works for comparison.

The third major section of the essay, consisting of paragraphs 10 to 12, is devoted primarily to four works, although the general ideal of love, as established early in the essay, provides the overall thematic linkage.

The technique of comparison-contrast used in this way shows how the various works may be defined and distinguished in relation to the common idea. Paragraph 13, the first in the conclusion, summarizes these distinctions by suggesting a continuous line along which each of the works may be placed. Paragraphs 14 and 15 continue the summary by showing the prominence of complicating difficulties, and, by implication, the importance of love and devoted duty.

One may readily grant that an extended comparison-contrast essay does not present a "full treatment" of each of the works. Indeed, the works are unique, and there are many elements that would not yield to the comparison-contrast method. In "Channel Firing," for example, there are ideas that human beings need eternal rest and not eternal life, that God is amused by—or indifferent to—human affairs, that religious service may be futile, and that war itself is the supreme form of cruelty. To introduce the poem into the comparison-contrast structure, however, requires questioning the motives for patriotic duty of the distant gunners. While this consideration forms a link with the other works, it is not necessarily the major idea in Hardy's poem. So it is with the other works, each of which could be the subject of analysis from a number of separate standpoints. The effect of the comparison of all the works collectively, however, is the enhanced understanding of each of the works separately. To achieve such an understanding and explain it is the major goal of the extended comparison-contrast method.

Appendix C: Writing and Documenting the Research Essay

Research, as distinguished from criticism, refers to using primary and secondary sources for assistance in solving a literary problem. That is, in discussing a work you consult only the work itself (the *primary source*), whereas in doing research, you consult not only the work but many other works that were written about it or that may shed light on it (*secondary sources*). Typical research tasks are to find out more about the historical period in which a story was written or about prevailing opinions of the times or about what modern (or earlier) critics have said.

It is obvious that a certain amount of research is always necessary in any critical job, or in any essay. Looking up words in a dictionary, for example, is only minimal research. More vigorous research—the type we are considering here—involves introductions, critical articles, encyclopedias, biographies, critical studies, histories, and the like.

In general, students and scholars do research to uncover some of the accumulated "lore" of our civilization. This lore—the knowledge that currently exists—may be compared to a large cone that is constantly being filled. At the beginnings of human existence there was little knowledge, and the cone was at its narrowest point. As civilization progressed, people learned more and more, and the cone began to fill. Each time a new piece of information or a new conclusion was recorded, a little more knowledge or lore was in effect poured into the cone, which accordingly became slightly fuller and wider. Though at present our cone of knowledge is quite full, it seems capable of infinite growth. Knowledge keeps piling up and new disciplines keep developing. It becomes more and more difficult for one person to accumulate more than a small portion of the entirety. Indeed, historians generally agree that the last person to know virtually everything about every existing discipline was Aristotle—2,400 years ago.

If you grant that you cannot learn everything, you can make a positive start by recognizing that research can provide two things: (1) a systematic understanding of a portion of the knowledge filling the cone, and (2) an understanding of, and ability to handle, the methods by which you might someday be able to make your own contributions.

Thus far we have been speaking broadly about the relevance of research to any discipline. The chemist, the anthropologist, the ecologist, the marine biologist—all employ research. Our topic here, however, is **literary research,** the systematic study of library sources in order to illuminate a topic connected with a work of literature.

SELECTING A TOPIC

Frequently your instructor will ask for a research essay on a specific topic. However, if you have only a general research assignment, your first problem is to make your own selection. It may be helpful to have a general notion of the kind of research essay you would find most congenial. Here are some possibilities.

1. *A particular work.* You might treat character (for example, "The Character of Bottom in *A Midsummer Night's Dream,*" or "The Question of Whether Willie Loman Is a Hero or Antihero in *Death of a Salesman*"), or tone, ideas, form, problems, and the like. A research paper on a single work is similar to an essay on the same work, except that the research paper takes into account more views and facts than those you are likely to have without the research.

2. *A particular author.* This essay is about an idea or some facet of style, imagery, setting, or tone of the author, tracing the origins and development of the topic through a number of different stories, poems, or plays. An example might be "The Idea of the True Self as Developed by Frost in His Poetry Before 1920." This type of paper is suitable if you are writing on a poet whose works are short, though a topic like "Shakespeare's Idea of the Relationships Between Men and Women as Dramatized in *A Midsummer Night's Dream* and *Hamlet*" might also be possible.

3. *A paper based on comparison and contrast.* There are two types:
    a. *An idea or artistic quality common to two or more authors.* Your intention might be to show points of similarity or contrast, or else to show that one author's work may be read as a criticism of another's. A possible subject of such a paper might be "The Theme of Ineffectuality in Behn, Eliot, Steinbeck, and Williams," or "Behn's Anti-Male Poems in the Context of Male-Dominated Lyric Poetry of the Seventeenth Century." Consult the second sample essay in Appendix B for an example of this type.
    b. *Different critical views of a particular work or body of works.* Sometimes much is to be gained from an examination of differing critical opinions on topics like "The Meaning of Shirley Jackson's 'The Lottery,'" "The Interpretations of Gray's *Elegy,*" or "The Question of Hamlet's Hesitation." Such a study would attempt to determine the critical opinion and taste to which a work did or did not appeal, and it might also aim at conclusions about whether the work was in the advance or rear guard of its time.

4. *The influence of an idea, author, philosophy, political situation, or artistic movement on specific works of an author or authors.* A paper on influences can be specific and to the point, as in "Details of Early Twentieth-Century Mexican-American Culture as Reflected in Parédes's 'The Hammon and the Beans,'" or else it can be more abstract and critical, as in "The Influence of Early Twentieth-Century Oppression of Mexican Americans on the Narrator of 'The Hammon and the Beans.'"

5. *The origin of a particular work or type of work.* One avenue of research for such an essay might be to examine an author's biography to discover the germination and development of a work—for example, "'The Old Chief Mshlanga' as an Outgrowth of Lessing's Life in Rhodesia-Zimbabwe." Another way of discovering origins might be to relate a work to a particular type or tradition: "*Hamlet* as Revenge Tragedy," or "*Love Is the Doctor* and Its Origins in the Tradition of Italian Comedy."

If you consider these types, an idea of what to write may come to you. Perhaps you have particularly liked one author, or several authors. If so, you might start to think along the lines of types 1, 2 and 3. If you are interested in influences or in origins, then types 4 or 5 may suit you better.

If you still cannot decide on a topic after rereading the works you have liked, then you should carry your search for a topic into your school library. Look up your author or authors in the card or computer catalog. Your first goal should be to find a relatively recent book-length critical study published by a university press. Use your judgment here: Look for a title indicating that the book is a general one dealing with the author's major works rather than just one work. Study those chapters relevant to the work or works you have chosen. Most writers of critical studies describe their purpose and plan in their introductions or first chapters, so begin with the first part of the book. If there is no separate chapter on the primary text, use the index and go to the relevant pages. Reading in this way will give you enough knowledge about the issues and ideas raised by the work to enable you to select a promising topic. Once you make your decision, you are ready to go ahead and develop a working bibliography.

SETTING UP A BIBLIOGRAPHY

The best way to develop a working bibliography of books and articles is to begin with major critical studies of the writer or writers. Again, go to the catalogue and pick out books that have been published by university presses. These books usually contain selective bibliographies. Be particularly careful to read the chapters on your primary work or works and to look for the footnotes or endnotes. Quite often you can save time if you record the names of books and articles listed in these notes. Then refer to the bibliographies included at the ends of the books, and select likely looking titles. Now, look at the dates of publication of the critical books. Let us suppose that you have been looking at three, published in 1951, 1963, and 1987. The chances are that the bibliography in a book published in 1987 will be complete up through about 1985, for the writer will usually have completed the manuscript about two years before the book actually was published. What you should do then is to gather a bibliography of works published since 1985; you may assume that writers of critical works will have done the selecting for you of the most relevant works published before that time.

Bibliographical Guides

Fortunately for students doing literary research, the Modern Language Association (MLA) of America has been providing a virtually complete bibliography of literary studies for years, not just in English and American literatures, but in the literatures of many foreign languages. The MLA started achieving completeness in the late 1950s, and by 1969 had reached such an advanced state that it divided the bibliography into four parts, which are bound together in library editions. Most university and college libraries have a set of these bibliographies on open shelves or tables.

There are, of course, many other bibliographies useful for students doing literary research, such as the *Essay and General Literature Index*, the *International Index*, and various specific indexes. There are many more than can be mentioned here meaningfully. For most purposes, however, the *MLA International Bibliography* is more than adequate. Remember that as you progress in your reading, the notes and bibliographies in the works you consult also will constitute an unfolding bibliography. For the sample research essay in this chapter, for example, a number of entries were discovered not from the bibliographies, but from the reference lists in critical works.

The *MLA International Bibliography* is conveniently organized by period and author. If your author is Gwendolyn Brooks, for example, look her up under "American Literature V. Twentieth Century," the relevant listing of all twentieth-century American writers. If your author is Shakespeare, refer to "English Literature VI. Renaissance and Elizabethan." You will find most books and articles listed under the author's last name. For special help for students and researchers, the MLA provides an exhaustive topics list that is keyed to the bibliographical entries. Using these topics, you may locate important works that you might miss with only the authors' list. In the MLA bibliographies, journal references are abbreviated, but a lengthy list explaining abbreviations appears at the beginning of the volume. Using the MLA bibliographies, begin with the most recent one and then go backward to your stopping point. Be sure to get the complete information, especially volume numbers and years of publication, for each article and book. You are now ready to find your sources and to take notes.

Online Computerized Library Services

In recent years, localized and nationwide online reference services are becoming increasingly more available through most libraries and library systems. You therefore have the possibility of access to the collections of large research libraries, such as the Library of Congress, which can be of immense value to you for extended research essays. If you learn of the existence of books in such collections that your own library does not have, you may be able to use the Interlibrary Loan Service to acquire the copy you need. Also, many associated libraries, such as state colleges and urban public libraries, have pooled their resources in online systems. If you can use the services of a network of county libraries, for example, you may be able to locate works that are not available in your college or local library. Usually, with time, the libraries will accommodate as many of your needs as they can. Librarians are immensely helpful and cooperative people.

You may use a personal computer yourself to gain access to the online service of a large library, provided that you have a modem, a telecommunications program, the correct telephone number and other entry information, the ability to follow the program codes, and patience and persistence. Once you gain access, you may ask for books by specific authors, or for books about specific topics. If your topic is *Shakespeare*, for example, you may ask for books by and about him. The request for general critical works about Shakespeare from a large urban university library produced a list of 396 items, including all the pertinent bibliographical information. The same library disclosed the presence of 113 works containing specific material about *Hamlet*. Once you have such materials on your screen, you may select and list only the most likely looking titles—the ones you think will be most important to you. Such a list comprises a fairly comprehensive search bibliography, which you may use once you physically enter the library to begin collecting and using materials.

If you gain access to online services, you should be careful to determine the year when the computerization began. Many libraries have a recent commencement date—like 1973, for example, or 1978. For completeness, therefore, you would need to use the complete catalog for items published before these years.

TAKING NOTES AND PARAPHRASING MATERIAL

There are many ways to taking notes, but the consensus is that the best method is to use note cards. If you have never used cards before, you might profit from consulting any one of a number of handbooks and special workbooks on research. A lucid and methodical explanation of using cards and taking notes can be found in Glenn Leggett et al., *Prentice-Hall Handbook for Writers*, 10th ed. (Englewood Cliffs, NJ: Prentice Hall, 1988). The principal virtue of using cards is that they may be classified, numbered, renumbered, shuffled, tried out in one place, rejected, and then used in another place (or thrown away), and arranged in order when you start to write.

Taking Notes

WRITE THE SOURCE ON EACH CARD. As you take notes, write down the source of your information on each card. This may sound like a lot of bother, but it is easier than going back to the library to locate the correct source after you have begun your essay. You can save time if you take the complete data on one card—a "master card" for that source—and then make up an abbreviation for your notes. Here is an example, which also, you will observe, includes the location where the reference was originally found (e.g., card catalog, computer search, bibliography in a book, the *MLA International Bibliography*, etc.). Notice that the author's name goes first.

Donovan, Josephine, ed. Feminist   PN
    Literary Criticism: <u>Explorations</u>   98
    <u>in Theory</u>. Lexington: The University   W64
    Press of Kentucky, 1975.   F4

    DONOVAN
    Card Catalogue, "Women"

If you plan to write many notes from this book, then the name "Donovan" will serve as identification. Be sure not to lose your complete master cards because you will need them when you prepare your list of works cited. If possible, you may wish to put the complete bibliographical data in a computer file.

RECORD THE PAGE NUMBER FOR EACH NOTE. It would be hard to guess how much exasperation has been caused by the failure to record page numbers in notes. Be sure to get the page number down first, *before* you begin to take your note, and, to be doubly sure, write the page number again at the end of your note. If the detail you are noting goes from one page to the next in your source, record the exact spot where the page changes, as in this example:

Heilbrun and Stimson, in DONOVAN, pp. 63–64

[63] After the raising of the feminist consciousness
it is necessary to develop/ [64] "the growth of moral perception"
through anger and the correction of social inequity.

The reason for such care is that you may wish to use only a part of a note you have taken, and when there are two pages you will need to be accurate in locating what goes where.

RECORD ONLY ONE FACT OR OPINION PER CARD. Record only one thing on each card—one quotation, one paraphrase, one observation—*never two or more*. You might be tempted to fill up the entire card, but such a try at economy often gets you in trouble because you might want to use different details recorded on the same card in other spots, which may mean copying the material again or else using scissors to chop up your original card. If you have only one entry per card, you will avoid such hassles and also retain the freedom you need.

USE QUOTATION MARKS FOR ALL QUOTED MATERIAL. A major problem in taking notes is to distinguish copied material from your own words. Here you must be extremely cautious. *Always put quotation marks around every direct quotation you copy verbatim from a source.* Make the quotation marks immediately, before you forget, so that you will always know that the words of your notes within quotation marks are the words of another writer.

Often, as you take a note, you may use some of your own words and some of the words from your source. In cases like this it is even more important to be cautious. Put quotation marks around *every word* that you take directly from the source, even if you find yourself literally with a note that resembles a picket fence. Later, when you begin writing your paper, your memory of what is yours and not yours will become dim, and if you use another's words in your own paper but do not grant recognition, you lay yourself open to the charge of plagiarism. Statistics are not available, but it is clear that a great deal of plagiarism is caused not by deliberate deception but rather by sloppy note-taking habits.

Paraphrasing

When you take notes, it is best to paraphrase the sources. A paraphrase is a restatement in your own words, and because of this it is actually a first step in the writing of the essay. Chapter 2 in this book has a full treatment on making a précis or abridgement (pp. 87–93). If you work on this technique, you will be well prepared to paraphrase for your research paper.

A big problem in paraphrasing is to capture the idea in the source without duplicating the words. The best way to do this is to read and reread the passage you are noting. Turn over the book or journal and write out the idea *in your own words* as accurately as you can. Once you have this note, compare it with the original and make corrections to improve your thought and emphasis. Add a short quotation if you believe it is needed, but be sure to use quotation marks. If your paraphrase is too close to the original, *throw out the note and try again*. It is worth making this effort, because often you can transform much of your note directly to the appropriate place in your research paper.

To see the problems of paraphrase, let us look at a paragraph of criticism and then see how a student doing research might take notes on it. The paragraph is by Maynard Mack, from an essay entitled "The World of Hamlet," originally published in *The Yale Review* 41 (1952) and reprinted in *Twentieth Century Interpretations of Hamlet*, ed. David Bevington (Englewood Cliffs, NJ: Prentice-Hall, 1968), p. 57.

> The powerful sense of mortality in *Hamlet* is conveyed to us, I think, in three ways. First, there is the play's emphasis on human weakness, the instability of human purpose, the subjection of humanity to fortune—all that we might call the aspect of failure in man. Hamlet opens this theme in Act I, when he describes how from that single blemish, perhaps not even the victim's fault, a man's whole character may take corruption. Claudius dwells on it again, to an extent that goes far beyond the needs of the occasion, while engaged in seducing Laertes to step behind the arras of a seemer's world and dispose of Hamlet by a trick. Time qualifies everything, Claudius says, including love, including purpose. As for love—it has a "plurisy" in it and dies of its own too much. As for purpose—"That we would do, We should do when we would, for the 'would' changes, And hath abatements and delays as many As there are tongues, are hands, are accidents; And then this 'should' is like a spendthrift's sigh, That hurts by easing." The player-king, in his long speeches to his queen in the play within the play, sets the matter in a still darker light. She means these protestations of undying love, he knows, but our purposes depend on our memory, and our memory fades fast. Or else, he suggests, we propose something to ourselves in a condition of strong feeling, but then the feeling goes, and with it the resolve. Or else our fortunes change, he adds, and with these our loves: "The great man

down, you mark his favorite flies." The subjection of human aims to fortune is a reiterated theme in *Hamlet*, as subsequently in *Lear*. Fortune is the harlot goddess in whose secret parts men like Rosencrantz and Guildenstern live and thrive; the strumpet who threw down Troy and Hecuba and Priam; the outrageous foe whose slings and arrows a man of principle must suffer or seek release in suicide. Horatio suffers them with composure: he is one of the blessed few "Whose blood and judgment are so well co-mingled That there are not a pipe for fortune's finger To sound what stop she please." For Hamlet the task is of a greater difficulty.

Because taking notes necessarily forces a shortening of this or any criticism, it also requires you to discriminate, judge, interpret, and select; good note-taking is no easy task. There are some things that can guide you, however, when you go through the many sources you uncover.

THINK OF THE PURPOSE OF YOUR RESEARCH PAPER. You may not know exactly what you are "fishing for" when you start to take notes, for you cannot prejudge what your essay will contain. Research is a form of discovery. But soon you will notice patterns or large topics that your sources constantly explore. If you can accept one of these as your major topic, or focus of interest, you may use that as your guide in all further note-taking.

For example, suppose you are taking notes on *Hamlet* criticism, and after a certain amount of reading you have decided to focus on "Shakespeare's Tragic Views in *Hamlet*." This decision would prompt you to take a note when you come to Mack's thought about mortality and death in the passage just quoted. In this instance, the following note would suffice:

Mack, in Bevington, 57   Death and
                                                Mortality

Mack cites three ways in which *Hamlet* stresses death and mortality.
The first (57) is an emphasis on human shortcomings and
"weakness." Corruption, loss of memory and enthusiasm, bad luck,
misery--all suit the sense of the closeness of death to life. 57

Let us now suppose that you want a fuller note, in the expectation that you need not just the topic but also some of Mack's detail. Such a note might look like this:

Mack, in Bevington,   57   Death and
                                                                      Mortality

The first of Mack's "three ways" in which a "powerful sense of
mortality" is shown in *Hamlet* is the illustration of human "weakness,"
"instability," and helplessness before fate. In support, Mack refers to
Hamlet's early speech on a single fault leading to corruption, also to
Claudius's speech (in the scene persuading Laertes to trick Hamlet).
The player-king also talks about his queen's forgetfulness and
therefore inconstancy by default. As slaves to fortune, Rosencrantz
and Guildenstern are examples. Horatio is not a slave, however.
Hamlet's case is by far the worst of all.   57

When the actual essay is being written, any part of this note would be
useful. The words are almost all the note-taker's own, and the few
quotations are within quotation marks. Note that Mack, the critic, is
properly recognized as the source of the criticism, so that you could adapt
the note easily when you are doing your writing. The key here is that
your taking of notes should be guided by your developing plan for your
essay.

Note-taking is part of your thinking and composing process. You
may not know whether you will be able to use each note that you take,
and you will always exclude many notes when you write your essay. You
will certainly find, however, that taking notes is easier once you have
determined your purpose.

TITLE YOUR NOTES.   To help plan and develop the various parts of
your essay, write a title for each of your notes, in the upper right corner
of the card, as in the examples in this chapter. This practice is a form of
outlining. Let us assume that you have chosen to study the importance of
the Ghost in the play. As you do research, you discover that there are
conflicting views about how the Ghost should be understood. Here is a
note about one of the questionable qualities of this character:

Prosser, 133, 134   Negative, Devilish

   [133] When describing his pain and suffering as a dead spirit, the
Ghost is not specific but emphasizes the horror. He should, if a good
spirit, try to use his suffering to urge repentance and salvation for
Hamlet. [134] This emphasis is a sign that he is closer in nature to a
devil than to a soul earning its way to redemption.

Notice that the title classifies the topic of the note. If you use such classifications while taking notes, a number of like-titled cards could form the substance of a section in your essay about the negative qualities of the Ghost in *Hamlet*. In addition, once you decide that "Negative, Devilish" is one of the topics you plan to explore, the topic itself will guide you in further study and note-taking.

WRITE YOUR OWN THOUGHTS AS THEY OCCUR TO YOU.   As you take your notes, you will have many of your own thoughts. Do not let these go, on the chance of remembering them later (maybe), but write them down immediately. Often you may notice a detail that your source does not mention, or you may get a hint for an idea that the critic does not develop. Often, too, you may get thoughts which can serve as "bridges" between details in your notes or as introductions or concluding observations. Be sure to title your comment and also to mark it as your own thought. Here is such a note, which is related to the importance of the Ghost in the structure of *Hamlet*:

My Own   Structure

  Shakespeare does a superb job with the Ghost. His
characterization shows many qualities of a living human being, and
the Ghost is fully integrated in the play's structure.

Please observe that some of the ideas and language from this note are used in paragraphs 9 and 10 of the sample research essay (p. 1606–7).

SORT YOUR CARDS INTO GROUPS.   If you have taken your notes well, your essay will have been forming in your mind already. The titles of your cards will suggest areas to be developed as you do your planning and initial drafting. Once you have assembled a stack of note cards derived from a reasonable number of sources (your instructor may have assigned a minimum number), you can sort them into groups according to the topics and titles. For the sample essay, after some shuffling and retitling, the following groups of cards were assembled:

1.   Importance in the action
2.   Importance in themes
3.   Condition as a spirit
    a.   Good signs
    b.   Negative, devilish signs

4.   Human traits

5.   Importance in the structure

6.   Effect on other characters

If you look at the major sections of the sample essay, you will see that the topics are closely adapted from these groups of cards. In other words, the arrangement of the cards is an effective means of outlining and organizing a research essay.

ARRANGE THE CARDS IN EACH GROUP.   There is still much to be done with these individual groups. You cannot use the details as they happen to fall randomly in your "deal." You need to decide which notes are relevant. You might also need to retitle some cards and use them elsewhere. Of those that remain in the group, you will need to lay them out in a logical order to be used in the essay.

Once you have your cards in order, you can write whatever comments or transitions are needed to move from detail to detail. Write this material directly on the cards, and be sure to use a different color ink so that you can distinguish later between the original note and what you add now. Here is an example of such a "developed" note card:

Campbell, 127   Negative, Devilish

Shakespeare's Ghost reflects the general uncertainty at the time about how ghosts were to be interpreted.   127

This may be the best way to answer the questions about the Ghost's ambiguous nature. Moreover, Shakespeare may have been trying to be more lifelike than consistent with his Ghost.

By adding such commentary to your note cards, you will facilitate the actual writing of your first draft. In many instances, the note and the comment may be moved directly into the paper with minor adjustments (material from this note and comment appears in paragraph 5 of the sample essay).

BE CREATIVE AND ORIGINAL IN RESEARCH PAPERS. This is not to say you can always transfer your notes directly into your essay. The major trap to avoid in a research paper is that your use of sources can become an end in itself and therefore a shortcut for your own thinking and writing. Quite often students introduce details in a research paper the way a master of ceremonies introduces performers in a variety show. This is unfortunate because it is the *student* whose essay will be judged, even though the sources, like the performers, do all the work. Thus, it is important to be creative and original in a research essay, and do your own thinking and writing, even though you are relying heavily on your sources. Here are four ways in which research papers may offer chances for originality.

1. Selection. In each major section of your essay you will include many details from your sources. To be creative you should select different but related details and avoid overlapping or repetition. The essay will be judged on the basis of the thoroughness with which you make your point with different details (which in turn will represent the completeness of your research). Even though you are relying on published materials and cannot be original on that score, your selection can be original because you bring *these* materials together for the first time, and because you emphasize some details and minimize others. Inevitably, your assemblage of details from your sources will be unique and therefore original.

2. Development. Your arrangement of your various points is an obvious area of originality: One detail seems naturally to precede another, and certain conclusions stem out of certain details. As you present the details, conclusions, and arguments from your sources, you may also add your own original stamp by using supporting details that are different from those in your sources. You may also wish to add your own emphasis to particular points—an emphasis that you do not find in your sources.

Naturally, the words that you use will be original. Your topic sentences, for example, will all be your own. As you introduce details and conclusions, you will need to write "bridges" to get yourself from point to point. These may be introductory remarks or transitions. In other words, as you write, you are not just stringing things out but are actively tying thoughts together in a variety of creative ways. Your success in these efforts will constitute your greatest originality.

3. Explanation of controversial views. Closely related to your selection is that in your research you may have found conflicting or differing views on a topic. If you make it a point to describe and distinguish these views, and explain the reasons for the differences, you are presenting material originally. To see how differing views may be handled, see paragraphs 4 and 5 of the sample essay.

4. Creation of your own insights and positions. There are three possibilities here, all related to how well you have learned the primary texts on which your research in secondary sources is based.

a. *Your own interpretations and ideas.* An important part of taking notes is to make your own points precisely when they occur to you. Often you can expand these as truly original parts of your essay. Your originality does not need to be extensive; it may consist of no more than a single insight. Here is such a card, which was written during the research on the Ghost in *Hamlet*:

My Own   introductory

The Ghost is minor in the action but major in the play. He is seen twice in scene 1, but this scene is really all about him. (Also about his appearances before the play opens.) In scene 4 of Act 1 he comes again and leads Hamlet off to scene 5--the biggest for him as an acting and speaking character. He speaks after this only from under the stage, and then a small appearance (but important) in 3.4, and that's all. But he is dominant because he set everything in motion and therefore his presence is felt everywhere in the play.

The originality here is built around the idea of the small role but dominant significance of the Ghost. The discovery is not unusual or startling, but it nevertheless represents original thought about *Hamlet*. When modified and adapted (and put into full sentences with proper punctuation), the material of the card supplies much of the opening paragraph of the sample essay. You can see that here the development of a *my own* note card is an important part of the prewriting stage for a research essay.

b.   *Gaps in the sources.* As you read your secondary sources it may dawn on you that a certain obvious conclusion is not being made, or that a certain detail is not being stressed. Here is an area which you can develop on your own. Your conclusion may involve a particular interpretation or major point of comparison, or it may rest on a particularly important but understressed word or fact. In the sample essay, for example, the writer discusses the idea that the Ghost's commands to Hamlet make it impossible for him to solve problems through negotiation or research—the ways he might have chosen as prince and student. The commands force him instead into a pattern requiring murder. Most critics observe that Hamlet's life is changed because of the Ghost but have not quite stressed this aspect of the change. Given such a critical "vacuum" (assuming that you cannot read all the articles about some of your topics, where your discovery may already have been published a number of times), it is right to begin filling it with your own insights. A great deal of scholarship is created in this way.

c.   *Disputes with the sources.* Your sources may present arguments that you wish to dispute. As you develop your disagreement, you will be arguing originally, for you will be using details in a different way from that of the critic or critics whom you are disputing, and your conclusions will be your own. This area of originality is similar to the laying out of controversial critical views, except that you furnish one of the opposing views yourself. The approach is limited because it is difficult to find many substantive points of interpretation on which there are not already clearly delineated opposing views. Paragraph 5 of the sample research essay shows a small point of disagreement (about whether Shakespeare was concerned with consistency in presenting the Ghost's spirit nature), but one that is nevertheless original.

DOCUMENTATION SYSTEMS

It is essential to acknowledge—to *document*—all sources from which you have *quoted or paraphrased* factual and interpretive information. If you do not grant recognition, you run the risk of being challenged for presenting other people's work as your own. This is plagiarism. As the means of documentation, there are many reference systems, some using parenthetical references, and others using footnotes or endnotes. Whatever system is used, documentation almost always includes a carefully prepared list of *works cited*, or a *bibliography*.

We will first discuss the list of works cited, and then review the two major reference systems for use in a research paper: (1) Parenthetical references, preferred by the Modern Language Association (MLA) since 1984, are described in Joseph Gibaldi and Walter S. Achtert, *MLA Handbook for Writers of Research Papers*, 3rd ed., 1988, and (2) Footnotes or endnotes, recommended by the MLA before 1984, and still widely required today.

List of Works Cited (Bibliography)

The key to any reference system is a carefully prepared list of *Works Cited* that is included at the end of the essay. *Works Cited* means exactly that; the list should contain just those books and articles which you have actually *used* within your essay. If, on the other hand, your instructor has required that you use footnotes or endnotes, you may extend your concluding list to be a complete bibliography of works both cited and also consulted but not actually used. *Always* check your instructor's preferences.

For the *Works Cited* list, you should include the following information in each entry:

FOR A BOOK

1. The author's name, last name first, period.

2. Title, underlined, period.

3. City of publication (not state), colon; publisher (easily recognized abbreviations or key words may be used unless they seem awkward or strange; see the *MLA Handbook*, 213–216), comma; date, period.

FOR AN ARTICLE

1. The author's name, last name first, period.

2. Title of article in quotation marks, period.

3. Name of journal or periodical, underlined, followed by volume number in Arabic (*not* Roman) numbers with no punctuation, followed by the year of publication within parentheses, colon. For a daily paper or weekly magazine, omit the parentheses and cite the date in the British style (day, month, year; i.e., 29 Feb. 1988) followed by a colon. Inclusive page numbers, period (without any preceding "p." or "pp.").

The list of works cited should be arranged alphabetically by author, with unsigned articles being listed by title. Bibliographical lists are begun at the left margin, with subsequent lines being indented, so that the key locating word—usually the author's last name—may be easily seen. The many unpredictable and complex combinations, including ways to describe works of art, musical or other performances, and films, are detailed extensively in the *MLA Handbook* (86–154). Here are two model entries:

BOOK: Alpers, Antony. Katherine Mansfield, A Biography. New York: Knopf, 1953.

ARTICLE: Hankin, Cheryl. "Fantasy and the Sense of an Ending in the Work of Katherine Mansfield." Modern Fiction Studies 24 (1978): 465–74.

Parenthetical References to the List of Works Cited

Within the text of the essay, you may refer parenthetically to the list of works cited. The parenthetical reference system recommended in the *MLA Handbook* (155–77) involves the insertion of the author's last name and the relevant page number or numbers into the body of the essay. If the author's name is mentioned in the discussion, only the page number or numbers are given in parentheses. Here are two examples:

Pope believed in the idea that the universe is a whole, a totally unified body, which provides a "viable benevolent system for the salvation of everyone who does good" (Kallich 24).

Martin Kallich draws attention to Pope's belief in the idea that the universe is a whole, a totally unified body, which provides a "viable benevolent system for the salvation of everyone who does good" (24).

For a fuller discussion of the types of in-text references and the format to use, see the *MLA Handbook*, 155–161.

Footnotes and Endnotes

The most formal system of documentation still widely used is that of *footnotes* (references at the bottom of each page) or *endnotes* (references listed numerically at the end of the essay). If your instructor wants you to use one of these formats, do the following: The first time you quote or refer to the source, make a note with the details in this order.

FOR A BOOK

1. The author's name, first name or initial first, comma.
2. The title: underlined for a book, no punctuation. If you are referring to a work (article, story, poem) in a collection, use quotation marks for that, but underline the title of the book. (Use a comma after the title if an editor, translator, or edition follows.)
3. The name of the editor or translator, if relevant. Abbreviate "editor" or "edited by" as *ed.*, "editors" as *eds.* Use *trans.* for "translator" or "translated by."
4. The edition (if indicated), abbreviated thus: *2nd ed., 3rd ed.,* and so on.
5. The publication facts should be given in parentheses, without any preceding or following punctuation, in the following order:
    a. City (but *not* the state) of publication, colon.
    b. Publisher (clear abbreviations are acceptable), comma.
    c. Year of publication, comma.
6. The page number(s), for example, 65, 6–10, 15–19, 295–307, 311–16. If you are referring to longer works, such as novels or longer stories that may have division or chapter numbers, include these numbers for readers who may be using an edition different from yours.

FOR AN ARTICLE

1. The author, first name or initials first, comma.
2. The title of the article, in quotation marks, comma.
3. The name of the journal, underlined, no punctuation.
4. The volume number, in Arabic letters, no punctuation.
5. The year of publication in parentheses, colon. For newspaper and journal articles, omit the parentheses, and include day, month, and year (in the British style), colon.
6. The page number(s); for example, 65, 6–10, 34–36, 98–102, 345–47.

For later notes to the same work, use the last name of the author as the reference unless you are referring to two or more works by the same author. Thus, if you refer to only one work by, say, Joseph Conrad, the name "Conrad" will be enough for all later references. Should you be referring to other works by Conrad, however, you will also need to make a short reference to the specific works to distinguish them, such as "Conrad, 'Youth,'" and "Conrad, 'The Secret Sharer.'"

Footnotes are placed at the bottom of each page, and endnotes are included in separate page(s) at the end of the essay. The first lines of both footnotes and endnotes should be paragraph indented, and continuing lines should be flush with the left margin. Both endnote and footnote numbers are positioned slightly above the line (as superior numbers) like this(^{12}). Generally, you may single-space footnotes and endnotes, and leave a space between them, but be sure to ask your instructor about what is acceptable. For more detailed coverage of footnoting practices, see the *MLA Handbook*, 185–200.

SMALL CAPS Sample Footnotes. In the following examples, book titles and periodicals, which are usually *italicized* in print, are shown underlined, as they would be in your typewritten or carefully handwritten essay.

[1] James Anderson Winn, John Dryden and His World (New Haven: Yale UP, 1987), 299.

[2] Susan Gubar, "The Birth of the Artist as Heroine: (Re)production, the Kunstlerroman Tradition, and the Fiction of Katherine Mansfield," in The Representation of Women in Fiction, eds. Carolyn G. Heilbrun and Margaret R. Higonnet, Selected Papers from the English Institute, 1981 (Baltimore: Johns Hopkins UP, 1982), 25.

[3] John O'Meara, "Hamlet and the Fortunes of Sorrowful Imagination: A Reexamination of the Genesis and Fate of the Ghost," Cahiers Élisabéthain 35 (1989), 21.

[4] Gubar 29.

[5] Winn 55.

[6] O'Meara 17.

As a principle, you do not need to repeat in a note any material you have already mentioned in your own discourse. For example, if you recognize the author and title of your source, then the note should merely give no more than the data about publication. Here is an example:

In The Fiction of Katherine Mansfield, Marvin Magalaner points out that Mansfield was as skillful in the development of epiphanies (that is, the use of highly significant though perhaps unobtrusive actions or statements to reveal the depths of a particular character) as Joyce himself, the "inventor" of the technique.[9]

---

[9] (Carbondale: Southern Illinois UP, 1971), 130.

Other Reference Systems

There are many other reference systems and style manuals, which have been adopted by various disciplines (e.g., mathematics, medicine, psychology) to serve their own particular needs. If you receive no instructions from your instructors in other courses, you may adapt the systems described here. If you need to use the documentation methods of other fields, however, use the *MLA Handbook*, 201–202 for guidance about what style manual to select.

Some Final Advice

As long as all you want from a reference is the page number of a quotation or a parahrase, the parenthetical system described briefly here—and detailed fully in the *MLA Handbook*—is the most suitable and convenient one you can use. It saves your reader the trouble of searching the bottom of the page or of thumbing through pages at the end to find a reference in a long list of notes. However, you may wish to use footnotes or endnotes if you need to add more details or refer your readers to other materials that you are not using.

Whatever method you follow, *there is an unchanging need to grant recognition to sources*. Remember that whenever you begin to write and make references, you might forget a number of specific details about documentation, and you will certainly discover that you have many questions. Be sure then to ask your instructor, who is your final authority.

ORGANIZING YOUR ESSAY

Introduction

For a research essay, the introduction may be expanded beyond the length of that for an ordinary essay because of the need to relate the problem of research to your topic. You may wish to bring in relevant historical or biographical information (see, for example, the introduction of the sample essay). You might also wish to summarize critical opinion or describe any relevant critical problems about your topic. The idea is to lead your reader into your topic by providing interesting and significant materials that you have found during your research. Because of the greater length of most research essays, some instructors require a topic outline, which is in effect a brief table of contents. This pattern is observed in the sample essay. *Because the inclusion of any outline is a matter of choice with various instructors, be sure that you understand whether your instructor requires it.*

Body, Conclusion

Your development, both for the body and the conclusion, will be governed by your choice of topic. Consult the relevant chapters in this book about what to include for whatever approach or approaches you select (setting, idea, point of view, character, tone, or any other).

In length, the research essay may be anywhere from five to fifteen or more pages. It seems reasonable to assume an essay on only one work may be shorter than one based on several. If you narrow the scope of your topic, as suggested in the approaches we describe, you can readily keep your essay within the assigned length. The sample research paper, for example, illustrates the first approach by being limited to only one character in one play. Were you to write on characters in a number of other plays by Shakespeare (the second approach), you could limit your total number of pages by stressing comparative treatments and by avoiding excessive detail about problems pertaining to only one work. In short, you will decide to include or exclude materials by compromising between the importance of the materials and the limits of your assignment.

Although you limit your topic yourself in consultation with your instructor, you may encounter problems because you will be dealing not with one text alone but with many. Naturally the sources will provide you with details and also with many of your ideas. The problem is to handle the many strands without piling on too many details, and also without being led into digressions. It is important therefore to keep your central idea foremost, for the constant stressing of your central idea will help you in both selecting relevant materials and rejecting irrelevant ones.

Because of the sources, there is a problem about authority, and that problem is to quote, paraphrase, and otherwise adapt the materials of others without plagiarism. Your reader will automatically assume that everything you write is your own unless you indicate otherwise. You leave yourself open to a charge of plagiarism, however, if you give no recognition to details, interpretations, or specific language that you clearly derive from a source. To handle this problem, you must be especially careful in the use of quotation marks and in the granting of recognition. Most commonly, if you are simply presenting details and facts, you can write straightforwardly and let parenthetical references suffice as your authority, as the following sentence from the sample essay shows.

> Thus he is most emphatic that Hamlet should not kill her along with Claudius (Fisch 80), and he also voices concern about the reputation and future of Denmark (Gottschalk, "Scanning" 165).

Here the parenthetical references to secondary texts are sufficient recognition of authority beyond your own.

If you are using an interpretation that is unique to a particular writer, however, or you are relying on a significant quotation from your source, you should grant recognition as an essential part of your discussion, as in this sentence:

> A. C. Bradley (126) suggests that these speeches indicate Shakespeare's master touch in the development of the Ghost's character.

Here the idea of the critic is singled out specially for acknowledgment. If you grant recognition in this way, no confusion can possibly arise about the authority underlying your essay.

SAMPLE RESEARCH ESSAY

The Ghost in Shakespeare's *Hamlet*

OUTLINE

  I. INTRODUCTION
    A. THE IMPORTANCE OF THE GHOST IN *HAMLET*
    B. THE GHOST'S INFLUENCE UPON THE PLAY'S THEMES
 II. THE GHOST'S STATUS AS A SPIRIT
III. THE GHOST'S CHARACTER
 IV. THE GHOST'S IMPORTANCE IN THE STRUCTURE OF THE PLAY
  V. THE GHOST'S EFFECT
 VI. CONCLUSION

I. Introduction

A. The Importance of the Ghost in *Hamlet*

[1]   Even though the Ghost of old Hamlet is present in only a few scenes of *Hamlet*, he is nevertheless a dominant presence throughout the play.* He is seen twice in the first scene, and this entire scene itself is about the meaning of these and earlier appearances. He enters again in the fourth scene of the first act, when he beckons and leads Hamlet off stage, in this way providing an early illustration of Hamlet's courage (Edgar 257). In the fifth scene of Act I he finally speaks, to describe how his brother Claudius murdered him and to urge his son, Hamlet, to kill Claudius in retribution. His appeal for revenge causes the rest of the play's action. After some words which he speaks from underground (i.e., under the stage), he does not enter again until the fourth scene of Act III, in the Queen's closet or bedroom, when he reveals

* Central idea.

himself to Hamlet--but not to Gertrude--to reproach the Prince for not having yet killed Claudius. The Ghost is not present at the play's end, but the actions he sets in motion are concluded there, and hence his effect remains dominant throughout.

B.   The Ghost's influence upon the Play's Themes

[2]

Not only is the Ghost dominant, he is also directly linked to many of the play's themes. Jean Paris observes that *Hamlet* is one of Shakespeare's plays that reveals "an intensification of interior suffering" (85). Hamlet's anguished soliloquies, together with the pain of Ophelia and Laertes (and even that of Claudius himself) may thus be traced to the Ghost. The commands the Ghost makes to Hamlet are direct and urgent, and therefore the Ghost introduces another of the play's major themes--that of responsibility, whether personal, political, or conjugal (McFarland 15). Hamlet of course does not rush right out to kill Claudius, despite the Ghost's urgings, and therefore his hesitation--this great "Sphinx of Modern Literature" (Jones 22)--has become one of the weaknesses cited most frequently about Hamlet's character. The Ghost's scary presence also poses questions about the power of superstition, terror, and fear (Campbell 211). Beyond these, deeply within the psychological realm, the Ghost has been cited as a "confirmation" of the influence of "psychic residues in governing and shaping human life" (McFarland 34), not to mention the significance of the Oedipus complex in the development of Hamlet's character.

[3]

Because the Ghost is so important, one hardly needs to justify a study of him. His importance may be traced in his spirit nature, his influence upon the play's structure, and his effect upon Hamlet and therefore indirectly upon all the major characters in the play.†

II.   The Ghost's Status as a Spirit

[4]

The Ghost is an apparition of questionable status. When Hamlet first sees the Ghost he raises a question about whether the vision is "a spirit of health, or goblin damned" (I.4.40). Horatio adds the idea that Hamlet is "desperate with imagination" (I.4.87), thus casting doubt upon the Ghost's reality, even though everyone on stage shares Hamlet's vision. When speaking with Hamlet, the Ghost is vague about his out-of-earth location, complaining that he is suffering hellish fires, but intimating that he will do so only until his earthly sins are purged away. In the meanwhile, he says, he is able to walk the earth for a certain time, presumably only at night (but is his visit in III.4 made in the daytime?). Surprising as it might seem, this detail about where ghosts spend their time reflects Renaissance controversies about Protestantism and Catholicism. Showing a ghost of someone long dead who was returning from Purgatory might have been interpreted as a ratification of Catholic doctrine. It was apparently safest for Protestant writers to show a ghost only of a person who was "freshly dead or on the point of death" (O'Meara 15), and leave the precise details a little vague.

† Thesis sentence.

The status and existence of ghosts therefore reflects uncertainties during the Elizabethan period. Lily Campbell offers a number of ways in which Elizabethans dealt with these uncertainties. First, James I of England (when still James VI of Scotland), in writing about departed spirits, emphasized that the Devil himself could choose the shape of loved ones in order to deceive living persons and lead them to damnation. It is this danger that Hamlet specifically describes. Second, as already mentioned, Elizabethan Catholic [5] teaching held it possible for souls in Purgatory to return to earth for a time to communicate with the living. Third, scientifically oriented thinkers interpreted ghostly appearances as a sign of madness or deep melancholia (121), or what O'Meara calls "sorrowful imagination" (19). There were apparently a number of "tests" that might have enabled people to determine whether ghosts were authentic, and not creations of the Devil or products of a sick imagination. Most of these required that the spirit in question be good, comforting, and sweet (Campbell 123).

The Ghost of King Hamlet passes parts of these tests, but fails others. Even though he has redeeming qualities (Campbell 126), he also imposes a duty of revenge on Hamlet, something that no ghost trying to reach Heaven would ever do (Prosser 136; McFarland 36). Although the Ghost describes the pain of a soul in Purgatory, he does so with a desire to horrify, not to urge Hamlet to commit himself to Christian repentance and salvation. Again, this description is an indication that he is closer in nature to the Devil than to a soul earning its way to redemption (Prosser 133–34). Another sign suggesting that the Ghost is a devilish spirit is that he withholds his appearance from Gertrude when he shows himself to Hamlet in III.4 (Campbell 124; Prosser [6] 200). Hamlet of course creates his own test of the Ghost by getting the traveling actors to perform "The Murder of Gonzago." Once he sees the king's disturbance at the play, he concludes that the Ghost is real, and not just a "figment of his melancholy imagination" (Harrison 883). However, perhaps the best answer to the conflicting signs about the Ghost is provided by Lily Campbell, who suggests that the ambiguity is a reflection of the general uncertainty about ghosts among Shakespeare's contemporaries (127). In other words, there was no unanimity about the nature and purposes of ghosts at the time Shakespeare wrote, and Shakespeare, if he was even concerned about theological issues of ghostly consistency, was reflecting common understanding and attitudes.

III. The Ghost's Character

Uncertainty aside, the likely fact is that Shakespeare as a dramatist is probably presenting a lifelike rendering of what he thought a ghost would be like. He inherited a tradition of noisy, bloodthirsty ghosts from his sources-- what Harold Fisch calls a "Senecan ghost" (91). There was also a tradition of the "hungry ghost," spirits who prowled about the earth "searching for the life they were deprived of" (Austin 93). In keeping with this tradition, Shakespeare's Ghost is bloodthirsty, although ironically not as bloodthirsty as Ham- [7] let himself (Gottschalk 166). The Ghost is also surrounded by awe and horror (DeLuca 147), and is genuinely frightening, both to the soldiers at the beginning of the play, and also to Hamlet in III.4 (Charney, *Style* 167–168). In addition, his speeches are designed to evoke grief, fear, and despair (Prosser 135). This effect also refers to readers and viewers; a famous example is James Boswell's testimony that Dr. Johnson, when young, was "terrified" when he read "the speech of the ghost when alone" (52). It would seem that horror is the main effect that Shakespeare was trying to create with the Ghost.

But the Ghost is not only an imitation of the Senecan ghost. He is real, and well drawn as an individual person by Shakespeare (Alexander 30). Indeed, Shakespeare has toned down the Ghost from one in an earlier play, perhaps one of the sources used for *Hamlet*, which was described by Shakespeare's contemporary Thomas Lodge (1558?–1625). Lodge talked about "ye ghost which cried so miserally [pitifully, sorrowfully] at ye theator . . . *Hamlet, reuenge.*" The Ghost in Shakespeare's *Hamlet* is preoccupied with vengeance (Allman 243), but as a former king he is concerned about his country, [8] and as a former loving husband he is also considerate of Hamlet's mother, Gertrude. Thus he is most emphatic that Hamlet should not kill her along with Claudius (Fisch 80), and he also voices concern about the reputation and future of Denmark (Gottschalk 165). Paul Gottschalk draws attention to this redeeming dimension as an indication that the Ghost is concerned with "restoration" as well as "retaliation" (166), a view not shared by Norman Austin, who calls the Ghost "the spirit of ruin" (105).

Indeed, the Ghost has many qualities of a living human being as opposed to those of either a bad or a good spirit. For example, he is witty, as Maurice Charney observes about the following interchange between the Ghost and Hamlet just at the beginning of the revelation speeches in I.5.6–7:

HAMLET.   Speak, I am bound to hear.
GHOST.   So art thou to revenge, when thou shalt hear.

[9]

In other words, even though the Ghost may have come "with airs from heaven, or blasts from hell" (I.4.41), he is still mentally alert enough to make a pun out of Hamlet's word "bound" (Charney, *Style,* 118). To this quickness may be added his shrewd ability to judge his son's character. He knows that Hamlet may neglect duty, and hence his last words in I.5 are "remember me," and his first words in III.4 are "Do not forget." A. C. Bradley suggests that these speeches indicate Shakespeare's master touch in the development of the Ghost's character (126).

The Ghost also shows other human traits. He feels strong remorse about his lifelong crimes and "imperfections" for which his sudden death did not give him time to atone. It is this awareness that has made him, naturally enough, bitter and vengeful. Also, he has a sense of appropriateness that extends to what he wears. Thus, at the beginning he appears on the parapets dressed in full armor. This battle uniform is in keeping with the location, and [10] also with his vengeful mission urging Hamlet to kill Claudius (Aldus 54). The armor is in fact intimidating, a means of enforcing the idea that the Ghost in death has become a "spirit of hatred" (Austin 99). By contrast, in the closet scene he wears a dressing gown ("in his habit as he lived," III.4.135), as though he is prepared for ordinary palace activities of both business and leisure (Charney, *Style* 26).

IV. The Ghost's Importance in the Structure of the Play

Shakespeare's great strength as a dramatist is shown not only in his giving the Ghost such a round, full character, but also in integrating him fully within the play's structure. Peter Alexander observes that the Ghost is "indispensable" as the mechanism of the plot and the source of communication to set things in motion (29). He is also a director and organizer as well as an informer--a figure who keeps the action moving until there is no stopping [11] it (Aldus 100). A careful study of his speeches shows that he is a manipulator, playing upon his son's emotions to make him see that his role, as a living person, is to carry out the necessary revenge. And the Ghost is persistent, because his return to Hamlet in III.4 to "whet thy almost blunted purpose" (line 111) is the mark of a managerial type who gets nervous and then intervenes when he sees his directions being neglected by the one entrusted to carry them out.

The Ghost is also significant as a part of some of the other major structures of the play. During the imagined period when the events at Elsinore are taking place, there is a national mobilization going on in preparation for possible war against Norway (Alexander 34). This note of future warfare and impending political change reminds the audience that the events being witnessed have important political consequences. Indeed, King Hamlet, when [12] alive, had conquered the Norwegian king Fortinbras in single combat. Now, with the Danish state being torn by the internal anguish following Claudius's fratricide, the state lies weak and exposed--an easy prey to the Norwegians. Structurally the beginning and ending of *Hamlet* are marked by the fear of war and the political takeover by Young Fortinbras of Norway. It is therefore ironic that the Ghost in death is responsible for the fall of the state he so courageously defended in life.

There is an additional major structure involving the Ghost. Maurice Charney observes that the Ghost is significant in the "symmetrical" poison plots in the play (39). The first of these plots, the poisoning of King Hamlet, is described by the Ghost himself in I.5. The poisoning of the Player King in [13] III.2 is a reenactment of the first murder, and it occurs in approximately the middle of the action. The final poisonings--of Gertrude, Laertes, Claudius, and finally Hamlet himself--occurs in V.2, the play's last scene. These actions have value as a set of symbolic frames which measure the progressive deterioration of the play's major characters.

V. The Ghost's Effect

Beyond the Ghost's practical and structural importance in the action, he has profound psychological influence, mainly negative, on the characters. Roy Walker describes him as a "prologue" to the "omen" of Hamlet himself, who is the agent of the "dread purpose" of vengeance (220). Because Hamlet is already suffering depression and melancholia, this murderous mission

opens the wounds of his vulnerability (Campbell 127–28). Literally, Hamlet
must give up everything he has ever learned, even "the movement of existence
itself," so that he may carry out the Ghost's commandment (McFarland 32–
33). In an invasive, overpowering manner, Hamlet's melancholy influences
his love for Ophelia, his possible friendship with Laertes, and his relationship
with his mother (Kott 49; Kirsch 31). No one escapes. The effect is like waves
radiating outward, with the Ghost at the center as a relentless destructive
force.

[14]

These effects occur because, almost literally, Hamlet himself cannot
escape (Allman 218). In Act I, scene 5 the Ghost, who has gone underground,
follows him and hears his conversations with Horatio and the guards--an obvious symbolic representation of the Ghost's pervasive power. He therefore
represents "dimensions of reality" beyond what we see on the stage, a mysterious world "elsewhere" that dominates the very souls of living persons
(Charney, "Asides" 127). As a result of this ever-present force, which as far
as Hamlet is concerned might become visible at any moment, Hamlet is denied the healing that might normally occur after the death of a parent (Kirsch
26). The steady pressure toward vengeance disrupts any movement to mental
health, and creates what Kirsch calls a "pathology of depression" (26) that
inhibits Hamlet's actions (Bradley 123), causes his Oedipal preoccupation
with the sexuality of his parents (Kirsch 22), and brings about his desire for
the oblivion that suicide might bring (Kirsch 27).

[15]

It is, finally, this power over his son that gives the Ghost the greatest
influence in the play. Once the Ghost has appeared, Hamlet can never be
the same. He loses the dignity and composure that he has assumed as his
right as a Prince of Denmark and as a student in quest of knowlege (McFarland
38). Rather than attack problems that he might have solved normally and
easily with negotiations and research, he must sink into acts of murder. Is it
any wonder that he hesitates? What could be more normal than hesitation
under such circumstances? Despite all his reflection and hesitation, finally
the web of vengeance woven by the Ghost closes in on all those caught in
it, and the consequence is that Hamlet becomes not only a murderer, but a
victim (Allman 254). There is no solution but the final one--real death, which
is the literal conclusion of the symbolic death represented by the Ghost when
he first appears on the Elsinore battlements.

[16]

VI. Conclusion

The Ghost is real in terms of the play's action and structure. He is seen
by the characters on the stage, and when he speaks we hear him. He is made
round and full by Shakespeare, and his motivation is direct and clear, even
though the signs of his status as a spirit are presented ambiguously. But the
Ghost is more. He has been made a Ghost by the greed and envy of Claudius,
and in this respect he becomes in the play either a conscious or unwitting
agent of the "unseen Fates or forces" of his own doom (Walker 220). What
he brings is the unavoidable horror that seems somehow to be just beneath
the surface of good, moral people, waiting for the license to reach out and
destroy. Once the forces are released, there is no holding them, and the
tragedy of *Hamlet* is that there is no way to win against such odds.

[17]

WORKS CITED

Alexander, Peter. Hamlet: Father and Son. Oxford: Clarendon, 1955.

Aldus, P. J. Mousetrap: Structure and Meaning in Hamlet. Toronto: U of Toronto P, 1977.

Allman, Eileen Jorge. Player-King and Adversary. Baton Rouge: Louisiana State UP, 1980.

Austin, Norman. "Hamlet's Hungry Ghost." Shenandoah 37.1 (1987): 78–105.

Boswell, James. Boswell's Life of Johnson. 1952. London: Oxford UP, 1957.

Bradley, A. C. Shakespearean Tragedy. 1904. London: Macmillan, 1950.

Campbell, Lily B. Shakespeare's Tragic Heroes: Slaves of Passion. New York: Barnes & Noble, 1959.

Charney, Maurice. "Asides, Soliloquies, and Offstage Speech in Hamlet," Shakespeare and the Sense of Performance: Essays in the Tradition of Performance Criticism in Honor of Bernard Beckerman. Ed. Marvin and Ruth Thompson. Newark: U of Delaware P, 1989: 116–31.

--- Style in Hamlet. Princeton: Princeton UP, 1969.

DeLuca, Diana Macintyre. "The Movements of the Ghost in Hamlet," Shakespeare Quarterly 24 (1973): 147–54.

Edgar, Irving I. Shakespeare, Medicine and Psychiatry. New York: Philosophical Library, 1970.

Fisch, Harold. Hamlet and the Word. New York: Ungar, 1971.

Gottschalk, Paul. "Hamlet and the Scanning of Revenge." Shakespeare Quarterly 24 (1973): 155–70.

Harrison, G. B., ed. Shakespeare: The Complete Works. 1948. New York: Harcourt, 1968.

Jones, Ernest. Hamlet and Oedipus. 1949. New York: Doubleday, 1954.

Kirsch, Arthur. "Hamlet's Grief." ELH 48 (1981): 17–36.

Kott, Jan. Shakespeare Our Contemporary. Trans. Boleslaw Taborski. 1967. London: Methuen, 1970.

McFarland, Thomas. Tragic Meanings in Shakespeare. New York: Random House, 1966.

O'Meara, John. "Hamlet and the Fortunes of Sorrowful Imagination: A Reexamination of the Genesis and Fate of the Ghost." Cahiers Élisabéthain 35 (1989): 15–25.

Paris, Jean. Shakespeare. Trans. Richard Seaver. New York: Grove, 1960.

Prosser, Eleanor. Hamlet and Revenge. 2nd ed. Stanford: Stanford UP, 1971.

Walker, Roy. "Hamlet: The Opening Scene." Shakespeare: Modern Essays in Criticism. Ed. Leonard F. Dean. New York: Oxford UP, 1961.

Commentary on the Essay

This sample essay illustrates an assignment requiring about twenty sources (there are twenty-two) and about 2,500 words. The sources were located through an examination of a library catalog, the *MLA International*

Bibliography, library bookshelves, and the bibliographies in some of the listed books. They represent the range of materials available in a college library with a selective, not exhaustive, set of holdings. Two of the sources (Austin, O'Meara) were obtained through the Interlibrary Loan Service because they were recent publications and also because their titles suggested that they should not be overlooked.

The writing itself is all derived and developed out of the sources listed, with originality being provided by the structure and development of the essay, additional observations not existing in the sources, and transitions. The outline is placed appropriately at the beginning, and it indicates the major divisions to follow. If you are asked for an outline, be sure to find out from your instructor if the topics alone are sufficient, or if more is required.

Because the essay is about only one work—and one topic about that work—it demonstrates the first approach to a problem in research, as outlined on page 1584. The essay is eclectic in dealing with the subject, introducing discussions of ideas, character, style, and structure. The goal is to cover the ground fairly completely, within the confines of the assignment, and hence the various topics may be justified. A shorter research assignment might deal with no more than, say, the Ghost's character, ignoring the other topics introduced into this essay. On the other hand, a longer essay might deal further with the philosophical and theological meanings of ghosts during the Elizabethan period, or a more detailed study of all the traits of the Ghost's character, and so on.

The central idea of the sample essay is stressed in paragraph 1, along with an assertion that the Ghost is a major influence in the play, together with a concession that the Ghost is only a minor character in the action. The research for this paragraph is derived primarily from a close reading of the play itself. Paragraph 2, continuing the exploration of the central idea, demonstrates that the Ghost figures in the major themes of *Hamlet*. Paragraph 3 is mainly functional, being used as the location of the thesis sentence.

Part II of the essay, containing paragraphs 4 through 6, is on the topic of the Ghost's status as a spirit. Part III, with four paragraphs (7–10), actually continues Part II but is concerned with the Ghost's human rather than spiritual characteristics. Part IV, with paragraphs 11–13, deals with the significance of the Ghost in four of the major structures which dominate the play. Part V, with three paragraphs, considers the negative and inexorable influence the Ghost has upon the major figures of *Hamlet*, with the emphasis being the character of Hamlet as the transferring agent of the Ghost's destructive revenge. The concluding paragraph (17) summarizes much of the essay, with its final idea being concerned with the Ghost's influence upon the nature of *Hamlet* as a tragedy.

The list of works cited is the basis of all references in the text of the essay, in accord with the *MLA Handbook for Writers of Research Papers*, 3rd. ed. By tracing these parenthetical references, an interested reader could verify and examine any of the ideas contained in the essay, or else could branch out into a completely new research project.

Glossary/Index

Abstract diction   Language describing qualities that pertain broadly to many things rather than to one or a few (e.g., "good," "interesting," "neat," and so on); distinguished from *concrete diction*. 268–69, 580

Accentual (or sprung) rhythm (prosody)   Lines relying not on traditional meters but rather on strong stresses. 683

Actions (incidents)   The events or occurrences in a work. 58, 65, 94

Allegory   A complete *narrative* that may also be applied to a parallel set of external situations that may be political, moral, religious, or philosophical. 64, 65, 328–61

Alliteration (prosody)   The repetition of identical consonant sounds (most often the sounds beginning words) in close proximity (e.g., "pensive poets," "grown grey"), 685–86

Allusion   Unacknowledged references and quotations. Authors assume that readers will recognize the original sources, and relate their meaning to the new context. 330, 771–73

Amphibrach (prosody)   A three-syllable *foot* consisting of a light, heavy, and light stress. 682

Amphimacer, or cretic (prosody)   A three-syllable *foot* consisting of a heavy, light, and heavy stress. 682

Anagnorisis, or recognition   That point at which a dramatic character experiences increased self-knowledge and understanding. 1049–50

Analytical sentence outline   A scheme or plan for an essay, arranged according to topics (A, B, C, etc.) and with the topics expressed in sentences. 27–28

Anapaest (prosody)   A three-syllable *foot* consisting of two light stresses climaxed by a heavy stress. 681

Antagonist   The person, idea, force, or general set of circumstances opposing the *protagonist*, an essential element of *plot*. 59, 94, 139, 995

Anticipation   See *procatalepsis*.

Antithesis   A rhetorical device of opposition, in which one idea or word is established, and then the opposite idea or word is expressed, as in "I burn and freeze." 585

Apostrophe   The addressing of a discourse to a real or imagined person who is not present; also, a speech to an abstraction. 628–29

Apron (thrust) stage   A stage that projects outward into the spectator area, thus increasing the area for action; a characteristic feature of Elizabethan stages and many recent ones. 991, 1205, 1401

Archetype   A character, action, or situation that is a prototype or pattern of human

1613

life generally; a situation that occurs over and over again in literature, such as a quest, an initiation, or an attempt to overcome evil. Many *myths* are archetypes. 798

Arena stage   An acting area, either high or low, surrounded by the audience. 1205, 1401

Aside   A short speech delivered by a character to another character or to the audience, the convention being that the other characters on stage cannot hear it; the speaker usually reveals his or her thoughts or plans. 996

Assertion   A sentence putting an *idea* (the subject) into operation (the predicate); necessary for both developing and understanding the idea. 362

Assonance (prosody)   The repetition of identical vowel sounds in different words in close proximity, as in the *deep green sea*. 685

Atmosphere, or **mood**   The emotional aura invoked by a work. 62, 246

Audience, or **intended reader**   The intended group of readers for whom a writer writes. 991

Auditory images   References to sound. 603

Authorial voice   (*See also* Speaker, Point of view, *and* Third-Person Point of View). The *voice* or *speaker* used by authors when seemingly speaking for themselves. The use of the term makes it possible to discuss a narration or presentation without identifying the ideas absolutely with those of the author. 61, 196

Bacchius, or **Bacchic (prosody)**   A three-syllable *foot* consisting of a light stress followed by two heavy stresses, as in "he won't go." 682

Ballad, Ballad Measure (prosody)   A ballad is a narrative poem composed of *quatrains* in which lines of iambic tetrameter alternate with iambic trimeter, rhyming *X-A-X-A*. 690, 727–28

Beat, or **Accent (prosody)**   The heavy stresses or accents in lines of poetry. The number of beats in a line usually dictates the meter of the line (five beats in a pentameter line, etc.). 679

Blank verse (prosody)   Unrhymed iambic pentameter. 724

Blocking agent   A person, circumstance, or attitude that obstructs the union of lovers. 1292

Blocking   In the performance of a play, the grouping and movement of characters on stage. 990

Box set   In the modern theater, a realistic setting of a single room from which the "fourth wall" is missing, so that the stage resembles a three-dimensional picture. 1204

Brainstorming   The exploration, discovery, and development of details to be used in a composition. 17–21

Business (stage business)   The gestures, expressions, and general activity (beyond blocking) of actors on stage. Usually, business is designed to create laughter. It may sometimes be spontaneous and unrehearsed. 1052

Cacophony (prosody)   Meaning "bad sound," *cacophony* refers to words combining sharp or harsh sounds. 686–87

Cadence group (prosody, style)   A coherent word group spoken as a single rhythmical unit, such as a noun phrase ("our sacred honor") or prepositional phrase ("of parting day"). 683

Caesura, caesurae (prosody)   The pause(s) separating phrases within lines of poetry, an important aspect of poetic *rhythm*. 683–84

Carpe diem poetry   Poetry concerned with the shortness of life and the need to act in or enjoy the present. *Carpe diem* means "seize the day." 823

Catastrophe   The "turning downward" of the dramatic plot, the fourth stage in the structure after the climax. The dénouement of a play, in which things are explained and put into place. 994–95

Catharsis (purgation)   The stimulation and subsequent elimination of pity, sympathy, fear, and other strong emotions that, according to Aristotle, occur as one watches or reads an effective tragedy. 1047

Central idea (1) The thesis or main idea of an essay. (2) The theme of a literary work. 59–60, 65

Character An extended verbal representation of a human being, the inner self that determines thought, speech, and behavior. 58, 137–95, 540

Chiasmus, or **antimetabole** A rhetorical pattern in which words and ideas are repeated in the sequence A-B-B-A, as in "I love life and devote my life to love." 273–74, 585

Choragos The leader of the chorus in classical Greek drama. 1052

Choric figure A character who remains detached from the action and who provides commentary. See also *raisonneur.* 995

Chorus In classical Greek drama, a group of actors chanting or speaking in unison, probably while moving in a stately dance. The chorus introduces, responds, and comments on the action, and provides transitions from episode to episode. 1052

Chronology ("logic of time"). The sequence of events in a work, with emphasis upon the complex intertwining of cause and effect. 59

Clerihew A humorous closed-form poem in four lines, rhyming A-A-B-B, usually about a real or literary famous person. 731

Cliché rhymes (prosody) Rhymes, such as *moon* and *June* or *trees* and *breeze*, that have been so widely used as to become trite. 687

Climax (Greek for *ladder*) The high point of *conflict* and tension preceding the resolution of a drama or story; the point of decision, of inevitability and no return. The climax is sometimes merged with the *crisis* in the consideration of dramatic and narrative structure. 97–98, 994

Closed-form poetry (prosody) Poetry written in specific and traditional patterns produced through rhyme, meter, line length, and line groupings. 723–24

Colonnade A line of columns installed at the Great Theater of Dionysius in ancient Athens to form a permanent scenic backdrop. 1052

Comedy A literary work in which confusions and doubts are resolved satisfactorily if not happily. Usually, comedy is characterized by smiles and laughter. 991, 1291–1398

Comedy of manners A form of comedy, usually regular (five acts or three acts), in which social customs and conventions are measured against human needs. 1295

Comedy of the Absurd A modern form of comedy dramatizing the apparent pointlessness, ambiguity, uncertainty, and absurdity of existence. 1295

Commedia dell'arte Broadly humorous farce, developed in sixteenth-century Italy, featuring stock characters, stock situations, and much improvised dialogue. 1294

Commentary, analysis, or **interpretation** Passages of explanation and reflection about the meaning of actions, thoughts, dialogue, historical movements, and so on. 63

Common ground of assent Those interests, concerns, and assumptions that the writer assumes in common with readers so that an effective and persuasive tone may be maintained. 659

Common measure (prosody) A closed poetic quatrain, rhyming A-B-A-B, in which lines of iambic tetrameter alternate with iambic trimeter. See also *ballad measure.* 728

Comparison-contrast A technique of analyzing two or more works in order to determine similarities and differences in topic, treatment, and quality. *Appendix A,* 1567–81

Complex sentence A main clause together with a subordinate or dependent clause. 271

Complication A stage of narrative and dramatic structure in which the major *conflicts* are brought out; the *rising action* of a *drama.* 994, 997

Compound sentence Two simple sentences joined by a conjunction. 271

Compound-complex sentence A compound sentence also integrating one or more dependent or subordinate clauses. 271

Concrete diction Words that describe specific qualities or properties, such as an ice-cream sundae being "cold," "sweet," and "creamy." These words are *concrete, while the words* "good" or "neat" as applied to the sundae would be *abstract.* 60, 268–69, 580 See also *abstract diction.*

Concrete poetry   Poetry created not only to express ideas and emotions but also to create visual shapes. 737

Conflict   The opposition between two characters, between large groups of people, or between *protagonists*and larger forces such as natural objects, ideas, modes of behavior, public opinion, and the like. Conflict may also be internal and psychological, involving choices facing a *protagonist.* It is the essence of *plot.* 58–59, 94–96, 993–94

Connotation   The meanings that words suggest beyond their bare dictionary definitions. 269–70

Consonant segments   Sounds produced as a result of the touching or close proximity of the tongue or the lips in relation to the teeth or palate (e.g., *p, f, sh, ch*); contrasted with *vowel segments.*   685–86

Contextual symbol   See *Private Symbol.*

Convention   An accepted feature of a genre, such as the point of view in a story, the form of a poem (e.g., sonnet, ode), the competence or brilliance of the detective in detective fiction, the impenetrability of disguise and concealment in a Shakespearean play, or the chorus in Greek drama. 1002

Cosmic irony (irony of fate)   *Situational irony* that is connected to a pessimistic or fatalistic view of life. 304

Costumes   The clothes worn by actors, designed to indicate things such as historical period, social status, economic level, etc. 990

Cothurni **(buskins)**   Thick-soled boots worn by actors in ancient Greek tragedy, designed, according to tradition, to distinguish the actors by making them tall. 1052

Couplet (prosody)   Two successive rhyming lines. 724–25

Crisis   The point of uncertainty and tension—the *turning point*—that results from the *conflicts*and difficulties brought about through the complications of the *plot.* The crisis leads to the *climax*—that is, to the decision made by the protagonist to resolve the conflict. Sometimes the *crisis* and the *climax* are considered as two elements of the same stage of plot development. 97, 994

Cultural (universal) symbols   *Symbols* recognized and shared as a result of a common social and cultural heritage. 327, 766, 999

Cumulatio, **or accumulation**   The parallel building up of much detail; a short way of introducing a considerable amount of material. 273

Dactyl (prosody)   A three-syllable *foot* consisting of a heavy stress followed by two lights, such as "This is the." 682

Dactyllic, or **triple rhyme (prosody)**   Rhyming *dactyls.* 689

Decorum   A quality of language and behavior that is thought to be appropriate, suitable, and fitting both to the literary medium (such as epic poetry or a detective story) and also to subject and character. 581, 997–98

Denotation   The standard dictionary meaning of a word. 269–70, 577–79

Description   The exposition of scenes, actions, attitudes, and feelings. 62–63

Device   A rhetorical figure or strategy. 622

Dénouement (untying), or **resolution**   The final stage of *plot* development, in which mysteries are explained, characters find their destinies, and the work is completed. Usually the dénouement is done as speedily as possible, for it occurs after all conflicts are ended. 98, 995

Dialect   The speech of a particular region or social group, usually characterized by unique words, expressions, and pronunciation. When a dialect becomes widespread in government, business, education, and literature, it is claimed as the standard of the particular language. 582–83

Dialogue   The speech of two or more characters in a story, play, or poem. 62–63, 65, 544, 990

Diction   Word choice, types of words, and the level of language. 266–70, 580–83

Diction, Formal (high)   Proper, elevated, elaborate, and often polysyllabic language. 267, 581

Diction, Informal (low)   Relaxed, conversational, and familiar language, utilizing contractions and elisions, and sometimes employing slang and grammatical mistakes. 267, 581–82

Diction, neutral (middle)   Correct language characterized by directness and simplicity, 267, 581

Digraph (prosody)   Two alphabetical letters spelling one sound, as in *digraph*, where ph spells the f sound. 678

Dilemma   Two choices facing a *protagonist*, usually in a tragic situation, with either choice being unacceptable or damaging; a cause of both internal and external *conflict*. 95

Dimeter (prosody)   A line consisting of two metrical feet. 679

Dionysia   The religious festivals in ancient Greece which celebrated the god Dionysus. Greek drama developed as a major features of these festivals. 1050

Dipody, dipodic foot, or syzygy (prosody)   The submergence of two normal *feet*, usually iambs or trochees, under a stronger beat, so that a "galloping" or "rollicking" rhythm results. 682

Director (stage)   In a dramatic production, the person in charge of guiding and instructing the actors in matters of speech delivery and stage movements. 991

Domestic tragedy   A tragedy of domestic life usually involving middle-class characters. 1049

Donnée   (French for "given") The given action of set of assumptions on which a work of literature is based. 56–57

Double dactyl   A comic closed-form poem in two quatrains, written in dactylic dimeter. The second line must be a proper name, and the sixth or seventh a single word. 731

Double entendre ("double meaning")   Deliberate ambiguity, often sexual. 303–304

Double or **trochaic rhyme (prosody)**   Two-syllable trochaic rhymes. 191

Double plot   Two different but related lines of action going on at the same time, usually in a play. 993

Drama   An individual play; also, plays considered as a group; one of the three major *genres* of literature. 4, 989 ff.

Dramatic convention   See *Convention.*

Dramatic irony   A special kind of *situational irony* in which a character perceives his or her plight in a limited way while the audience and one or more of the other characters understand it entirely. 64, 304–305, 661, 999

Dramatic monologue   A type of poem derived from the theater, in which a speaker addresses an internal listener or the reader at length. The form is related to the soliloquy. 545

Dramatic (objective) point of view   A third-person *narration* reporting speech and action, but rigorously excluding commentary on the actions and thoughts of the characters. 61, 201, 203, 996

Dying rhyme (prosody)   See *falling rhyme.*

Dynamic character   A character who undergoes adaptation, change, or growth, unlike the *static character,* who remains constant. In a *short story,* there is usually only one dynamic character, whereas in a *novel* there may be many. 139, 995

Echoic words (prosody)   Words echoing the actions they describe, such as *buzz, bump,* and *slap*; important in the device of *onomatopoeia.* 686

Editing   See *Montage.*

Enclosing method   See *Framing method.*

End-stopped line (prosody)   A line ending in a full pause, usually indicated with a period or semi-colon. 683

Framing (enclosing) method   The same features of topic or setting used at both the beginning and ending of a work so as to "frame" or "enclose" the work. 246

Free verse (prosody)   Poetry that, for rhythm, uses not metrical feet but rather the natural rhythms of phrases and normal pauses. 734

French scene   A numbering system for a play in which a new scene is numbered whenever characters enter or leave the stage. (As in Molière's *Love Is the Doctor*, 1358.) 993

Freytag Pyramid   A scheme developed by Gustav Freytag to show how the five stages of dramatic plot structure go up and down like the sides of a pyramid. 994

Full-length play   A drama, either a tragedy or comedy (usually not a farce) designed for a full evening's performance, containing either five or three acts. 992

Gallery   The upper seats at the back and sides of a theater. 1097

General language   Words referring to broad classes of persons or things; distinguished from *specific language*. 268–69, 580

Genre   A type of literature, such as *fiction*, *poetry*, or *drama*; also a type of work, such as detective fiction, epic poetry, tragedy, etc. 4

Graph, Graphics (spelling)   Writing or spelling; the appearance of words on a page, as opposed to their actual sounds. 678

Gustatory images   References to impressions of taste. 604

Haiku   A poetic form derived from Japanese, traditionally containing three lines of 5, 7, and 5 syllables. Very short poems of two or three lines are often considered *haiku*. 729

Half rhyme   See *Slant rhyme*.

Hamartia   A Greek word describing the error or frailty that causes the downfall of a tragic protagonist. (In the New Testament, *hamartia is* usually translated as *sin*.) 1048

Heavy-stress rhyme   A *rhyme*, such as rhyming iambs or anapests, ending with a strong stress. 191

Heptameter, or the septenary (prosody)   A line consisting of seven metrical *feet*. 679

Hero, heroine   The major male and female *protagonists* in a narrative or drama; the terms are often used to describe leading characters in adventures and romances. 139

Heroic couplet (prosody)   Two successive rhyming lines of iambic pentameter; the second line is commonly end-stopped. Couplets written from 1660–1800 are usually termed "heroic," regardless of their topic matter. 725

Hexameter (prosody)   A line consisting of six metrical *feet*. 679

High comedy   Elegant comedies characterized by wit and sophistication, in which the complications grow out of character; also, a *comedy of manners*.   1294

Hovering accent   See *Spondee*.

Hymn (prosody),   A religious song, consisting of one and usually many more replicating rhythmical stanzas, 728

Hyperbole   A rhetorical figure in which emphasis is achieved through exaggeration. 303, 632

Iamb   (prosody)   A two-syllable *foot* consisting of a light stress followed by a heavy stress (e.g., *the winds*). 680

Iambic pentameter (prosody)   A line consisting of five iambic *feet*. 192

Idea   A concept, thought, opinion, or belief; in literature, a unifying, centralizing conception or *theme*. 362–409, 819–43

Idiom   A phrase or style of speaking, characteristic of a particular group, class, region, or nation, whose meaning cannot be derived from an analysis of constituent parts; e.g., to stand *on* line or to stand *in* line. 582

Image, Imagery   Language, making for vividness, that triggers the mind to fuse together memories of sights (*visual*), sounds (*auditory*), tastes (*gustatory*), smells (*olfac-*

tory), and sensations of touch (*tactile*). The word "image" refers to a single mental picture, such as Coleridge's image of a damsel playing a dulcimer (in "Kubla Khan"). "Imagery" refers to images throughout a work or throughout the works of a writer or group of writers. 4, 600–602

Imaginative literature   Literature based in the imagination of the writer, usually comprising *fiction, poetry,* and *drama.* 4

Imitation   The theory that literature is derived from life and is an imaginative duplication of life experiences; closely connected to *realism* and *verisimilitude.* 56

Imperfect foot (prosody)   A metrical *foot* consisting of a single syllable, either heavily or lightly stressed. 682

Incidents   See *Actions.*

Internal rhyme   The occurrence of rhyming words within a single line of verse. 689

Intrigue plot   The dramatic rendering of how a young woman and her lover foil the blocking mechanisms of a parent or guardian, often aided by a maidservant or *soubrette.* 1356

Invention   The process of discovering and determining materials to be included in a composition, whether a theme or an imaginative work; a vital phase of *prewriting.* 17–21

Ironic comedy   A form of comedy in which characters seem to be in the grips of uncontrollable forces. The dominant tone is therefore one of irony. 1295

Irony   Broadly, a means of indirection. Language that states the opposite of what is intended is *verbal irony.* The placement of characters in a state of ignorance is *dramatic irony,* while an emphasis on powerlessness is *situational irony.* 63–65, 303–305, 659–62, 999

Italian or **Petrarchan sonnet**   An iambic pentameter poem of fourteen lines, divided between the first eight lines (the *octet*) and the last six (the *sestet*). 727

Jargon   Words and phrases that are characteristic of a particular profession, trade, or pursuit such as medicine, football, or the military. 583

Kinesthetic images   Words describing human or animal motion and activity. 605

Kinetic images   Words describing general motion. 605

Lighting (stage)   The general word describing the many types, positions, directions, and intensities of artificial lights used in the theater. 991, 1205

Limerick   A five-line poetic closed form in which two lines of anapaestic trimeter are followed by two in anapaestic dimeter and a final line in trimeter, rhyming *3a-3a-2b-2b-3a,* often used in comic and bawdy verse. 730–31

Limited, or **limited-omniscient point of view**   A third-person narration in which the actions, and often the thoughts, of the protagonist are the focus of attention. 61, 201–203

Listener (internal audience)   A character or characters who serve as the audience to whom a story or poem is spoken, and whose presence influences the content of the work, as in Browning's "My Last Duchess" or Paley's "Goodbye and Good Luck." 543

Literature   Written compositions (but also, in preliterate societies, oral compositions) designed to engage readers emotionally as well as intellectually, with the major genres being *fiction, poetry, drama,* and *nonfiction prose,* and with many separate sub-forms. 3–4 (3–1712)

Longshot (film)   A distant camera view, including not only characters but also their surroundings; distinguished from a *closeup.* 1537

Loose sentence (style)   A straightforward sentence, usually in subject-verb-object order, with no climax and no surprises. 271

Low comedy   Crude, violent, and physical comedies, characterized by sight gags, bawdy jokes, and outrageous situations. 1294

Lyric A short poem written in a repeating stanzaic form, often designed to be set to music; a *song*. 728

Main plot The central and major line of causation and action in a literary work. 993

Major mover A major participant in a work's action, who either causes things to happen or who is the subject of major events. If the first-person narrator is also a major mover, such as the *protagonist*, that fact gives first-hand authenticity to the narration. 205

Makeup (stage) The materials, such as cosmetics, wigs, and padding, applied to an actor to change appearance for a specific role, such as a youth, an aged person, or a hunchback. 990

Malapropism The comic use of an improperly pronounced word, so that what comes out is another but incorrect word. Examples are *odorous* for *odious*, or *pineapple* for *pinnacle*. The new word must be close enough to the correct word so that the resemblance and error may be immediately recognized. The name is derived from *Mrs. Malaprop*, a character created by Richard Brinsley Sheridan. 302

Masculine rhyme (prosody) See *Rising rhyme*.

Meaning That which is to be understood in a work; the total combination of ideas, actions, descriptions, and effects. 819–43

Mechanics of verse See *Prosody*.

Melodrama A sentimental form of tragedy with an artificially happy ending. 992

Metaphor *Figurative language* which makes the direct verbal equation of two or more things that may at first seem unlike each other. 62, 622–28

Metaphorical language See *Figurative language*.

Metaphysical conceit An elaborate and extended metaphor or simile that links two apparently unrelated fields or subjects. The term is commonly used to describe the metaphorical language of a number of early seventeenth-century poets, particularly John Donne. 845–46

Meter (prosody) The number of *feet* within a line of traditional verse, such as *iambic pentameter* referring to a line containing five *iambs*. 679

Metonymy A rhetorical figure in which one thing is used as a substitute for another with which it is closely identified. 630

Metrical foot See *Foot*.

Mimesis, mimetic The theory which holds that literature is imitative of life, and derived directly from it. 989

Miracle play A medieval play dramatizing a miracle or miracles performed by a saint. An outgrowth of the earlier medieval *mystery play* (q.v.). 1095

Monologue A long speech spoken by a single character to himself or herself, to the audience, or to an off-stage character. 990

Montage (film) The editing or assembling of the various camera "takes," or separate filmed scenes, to make a continuous film. 1536–37

Mood (*See* Atmosphere)

Morality play A type of medieval and early Renaissance play that dramatizes the way to live a pious life. 990, 1095

Motif Meaning "something that moves," a *motif* is sometimes used in reference to a main idea or theme in a single work or in many works, such as a *carpe diem* theme, or a comparison of lovers to little worlds. 819. See also *Archetype*.

Music of poetry (prosody) Broadly, the rhythms, sounds, and rhymes of poetry; *prosody*. 677

Mystery play Medieval drama that enacted events from the Bible, such as the killing of Abel by Cain, the problems of Noah, the anger of Herod, and so on. The word is derived from the *masters,*or leading citizens, who sponsored the plays in the towns where they were performed. 990, 1095

Myth, Mythology A story that embodies truths about human experience and that codifies social and cultural values; also, myths considered collectively. 4, 329–30, 795–818

Mythical reader   See *Audience.*

Narration, narrative fiction   The relating or recounting of a sequence of events or actions. While a *narration* may be reportorial and historical, *narrative fiction* is primarily creative and imaginative. 4, 53, 60, 65, 94

Narrative ballad   A poem in ballad measure telling a story. 526

Narrative fiction   See *Prose Fiction.*

Narrator   See *Speaker.*

New comedy   Witty and sometimes robust comedy, romantic rather than satirical in purpose, and dependent on plot rather than language and character. Originated by the Greek dramatist Menander and later modified in Rome by Plautus and Terence. 1292

Nonfiction prose   A *genre* consisting of essays, articles, and books that are concerned with real as opposed to fictional things; one of the major *genres* of literature. 4–5

Nonrealistic character   An undeveloped and often symbolic character without full motivation or individual identity. 995–96

Nonrealistic drama   Dreamlike, fantastic, symbolic, and otherwise artificial plays that make no attempt to present an imitation of everyday reality. 999, 1399

Novel   A long work of fictional prose. 4, 55

Objective point of view   See *Dramatic point of view.*

Octameter   A line consisting of eight metrical feet. 679

Octave (prosody)   The first eight lines of an Italian sonnet, unified by rhythm, rhyme, and topic. 727

Ode (prosody)   A stanzaic poetic form (usually long, to contrast it with the *song*) with varying line lengths and sometimes intricate *rhyme* schemes. 728–29

Old comedy   Satirical comedy full of personal invective and improvisation, exemplified by the plays of the Greek comic writer Aritosphanes. 1291–92

Olfactory imagery   Language describing smells. 604

Omniscient point of view   A *third-person narrative* in which the *speaker* or *narrator*, with no apparent limitations, may describe intentions, actions, reactions, locations, and speeches of any or all of the characters, and may also describe their innermost thoughts (when necessary). 61, 201, 203

One-act play   A short play of one act, usually with one major scene and continuous action. 992

Onomatopoeia (prosody)   A blending of consonant and vowel sounds designed to imitate or suggest the activity being described. 686

Open-form poetry   Poems that avoid traditional structural patterns, such as rhyme or meter, in favor of other methods of organization. 723, 734–35

Orchestra (Greek theater)   (1) The central circle where the chorus performed in ancient Greek theaters. (2) The ground or first-floor area in a modern theater where the audience sits. 1050

Organic unity   The interdependence of all elements of a work, including character, actions, speeches, descriptions, thoughts, and observations. The concept of organized unity presupposes that everything in a literary work is absolutely essential; to eliminate anything is to destroy the work. 58–59

Outline   A formal pattern for a written composition.

Overstatement   See *Hyperbole.*

Parable   A short *allegory* designed to illustrate a religious truth, most often associated with Jesus as recorded in the Gospels. 4, 54, 329

Parados   (1) Two aisles on each side of the orchestra in ancient Greek theaters along which actors could enter or exit. (2) The first lyrical ode chanted by the chorus in Greek tragedy. 1052–53

Paradox A rhetorical figure embodying a seeming contradiction that is nevertheless true. 628

Parallelism (style) A rhetorical structure in which the same grammatical forms are repeated. 272–73, 584

Paranomasia See *Pun.*

Paraphrase A brief restatement, in one's own words, of all or part of a literary work; a précis. 87–92, 525, 533–35

Pentameter (prosody) A line consisting of five metrical *feet.* 679

Perfect rhyme See *Exact rhyme.*

Performance (stage) An individual production of a play, either for an evening or for an extended period, comprising acting, movement, lighting, sound effects, staging and scenery, ticket sales, and the accommodation of the audience. 990

Periodic sentence A sentence arranged to build toward a climactic and sometimes surprising idea. 271–72

Peripeteia, or **reversal** A sudden reversal, when the action of a work, particularly a play, veers around quickly to its opposite. 1049, 1405

Persona (The Greek word for **mask.** See also *Speaker.*) The narrator or speaker of a *story* or *poem.* 61, 196, 541, 1052

Personification A rhetorical figure in which human characteristics are attributed to nonhuman things or abstractions. 629

Phonetic, phonetics (prosody) The *actual pronunciation* of sounds, as distinguished from spelling or *graphics.* 678

Plausibility See *Verisimilitude.*

Play See *Drama.*

Playwright A writer of plays. 990

Plot The plan or groundwork for a story, with the actions resulting from believable and authentic human responses to a *conflict.* It is causation, conflict, response, opposition, and interaction that make a *plot* out of a series of *actions.* 58–59, 65, 94–135, 993, 1296

Poem, poet, poetry *Poetry* is a variable literary genre which is, foremost, characterized by the rhythmical qualities of language. While poems may be short (including *epigrams* and *haiku* of just a few lines) or long (*epics* of thousands of lines), the essence of poetry is compression, economy, and force, in contrast with the expansiveness of prose. There is no bar to the topics that poets may consider, and poems may range from the personal and lyric to the public and discursive. A *poem* is one poetic work. A *poet* is a person who writes poems. *Poetry* may refer to the poems of one writer, to poems of a number of writers, to all poems generally, or to the aesthetics of poetry considered as an art. 4, 519

Point of view The *speaker, voice, narrator,* or *persona* of a work; the position from which details are perceived and related; a centralizing mind or intelligence; not to be confused with *opinion* or *belief.* 60–61, 196–240, 541, 996

Point-of-view character The central figure or *protagonist* in a *limited-point-of-view narration,* the character about whom events turn, the focus of attention in the narration. 202

Postulate (premise) The assumption on which a work of literature is based, such as a level of absolute, literal reality, or as a dreamlike, fanciful set of events. 56–57

Précis A shortening, or cutting down, of a narrative into its essential parts, a synopsis, abridgment, paraphrase, condensation, or epitome. 87–92

Private (contextual) symbol A symbol which is derived not from common historical, cultural, or religious materials, but which is rather developed within the context of an individual work. 327–28, 767–69, 999

Probability (plausibility) The standard of judgment requiring that literature should be about what is probable, common, normal, and usual. 142–43

Repetition   Repeating the same word, phrase, sentence, or the like for rhetorical impact and effect. 584

Representative character,   A *flat character* with the qualities of all other members of a group (i.e., clerks, cowboys, detectives, etc.); a *stereotype*. 139–40

Research, literary   The use of both primary and secondary sources for assistance in treating a literary subject. 1583–1611

Resolution   *See Dénouement.*

Response   A reader's intellectual and emotional reactions to a literary work. 41–49

Revenge tragedy   A popular type of English Renaissance drama, developed by Thomas Kyd, in which a person is called upon (often by a ghost) to avenge the murder of a loved one. Shakespeare's *Hamlet* is in the tradition of revenge tragedy. 1098

Reversal   See *Peripeteia.*

Rhetoric   The art of persuasive writing; broadly, the art of all effective writing. 270–74

Rhetorical Figure   See *Figurative Language.*

Rhetorical substitution   See *Substitution.*

Rhyme (prosody)   The repetition of identical concluding syllables in different words, most often at the ends of lines. 687–90

Rhyme scheme (prosody)   The pattern of *rhyme*, usually indicated by assigning a letter of the alphabet to each rhyming sound. 690

Rhythm (prosody, style)   The varying speed, intensity, elevation, pitch, loudness, and expressiveness of speech, especially poetry. 678

Rising action   The action in a play before the climax. 994

Rising rhyme (prosody)   Rhymes produced with one syllable words, like *sky* and *fly,* or with multisyllabic words in which the accent falls on the last syllable, such as *decline* and *confine.* 688

Romance   (1) Lengthy Spanish and French stories of the sixteenth and seventeenth centuries. (2) Modern formulaic stories describing the growth of an enthusiastic love relationship. 4, 55

Romantic comedy   Sympathetic comedy that presents the adventures of young lovers trying to overcome opposition and achieve a successful union. 1295

Round character   A character who profits from experience and undergoes a change or development; usually but not necessarily the *protagonist*. 138–39, 995

Run-on line   See *Enjambement.*

Satire   An attack on human follies or vices, as measured positively against a normative religious, moral, or social standard. 662–63

Satiric comedy   A form of comedy designed to correct social and individual behavior by ridiculing human vices and follies. 1294–95

Satyr play   A short comic interlude performed during the Dionysian Festival in ancient Greece. 1050. See also *Trilogy.*

Scansion (prosody)   The act of determining the prevailing *rhythm* of a poem. 679

Scene   (1) In a play, a part or division (of an act, as in *Hamlet*, or entire play, as in *Death of a Salesman*) in which there is a unity of subject, setting, and (often) actors. (2) In a film, a unit of continuous action in one location. 992

Scenery   The artificial environment created on stage to produce the illusion of a specific or generalized place and time. 991

Second-person point of view   A *narration* in which a second-person listener ("you") is the *protagonist* and the speaker is someone with knowledge the protagonist does not possess or understand about his or her own actions (e.g., doctor, parent, rejected lover, etc.). 200, 203

Segment (prosody)   The smallest meaningful unit of sound, such as the *l, u,* and *v* sounds in "love." Segments are to be distinguished from spellings. 677

Semivowel segments   Midway between the consonants and vowels, the semivowel sgements are *y, w,* and *h*. 677

Septenary See *Heptameter*.

Sequence (literally, "a following") The events in a work as they take place in time, from beginning to end. 59, 65, 94

Sestet (1) A six-line stanza or unit of poetry. (2) The last six lines of an *Italian* sonnet. 729

Setting The natural, manufactured, and cultural environment in which characters live and move, including all the artifacts they use in their lives. 28–29, 39–40, 241–65, 997

Shakespearean sonnet See *English sonnet*.

Shaped verse Poetry written so that the lines or words of the poem form a recognizable shape, such as a pair of wings or a geometrical figure. 737

Short story A compact, concentrated work of *narrative fiction* that may also contain description, dialogue, and commentary. Poe used the term "brief prose tale" for the short story, and emphasized that it should create a major, unified impact. 4, 55–56

Sight rhyme See *Eye rhyme*.

Simile A figure of comparison, using "like" with nouns and "as" with clauses, as in "the trees were bent by the wind *like actors bowing after a performance*." 622–28

Simple sentence (style) A complete sentence containing one subject and one verb, together with modifiers and complements. 271

Situational irony A type of *irony* emphasizing that human beings are enmeshed in forces beyond their comprehension and control. 64, 65, 304, 660–61, 999

Skene The building behind the orchestra in ancient Greek theaters, used as dressing rooms and off-stage areas. 1051

Slang Informal and nonstandard vocabulary. Some slang is a permanent part of the language (e.g., phrases like "I'll be damned," "Go jump in the lake," and our many four-letter words). Other slang is spontaneous, rising within a group (jargon), and often then being replaced when new slang emerges. 583

Slant rhyme (prosody) A *near rhyme*, in which the consonant sounds are identical, but not the vowels, such as "should" and "food," "slum" and "slam." 689

Slapstick comedy A type of low farce in which the humor depends almost entirely on physical actions and sight gags. 1294

Social drama A type of problem play that deals with current social issues and the place of individuals in society. 992

Soliloquy A speech made by a character, alone on stage, directly to the audience, the convention being that the character is revealing thoughts and feelings. A soliloquy is to be distinguished from an *aside*, which is made to the audience (or confidentially to another character) when other character are present. 996, 1002, 1098

Song (prosody) A lyric poem with a number of repeating stanzas, written to be set to music. 728

Sonnet A poem of fourteen lines in *iambic pentameter*. 727

Speaker The *narrator* of a story or poem, the *point of view*, often an independent character who is completely imagined and consistently maintained by the author. In addition to narrating the essential events of the work (justifying status as the *narrator*), the speaker may also introduce other aspects of his or her knowledge, and may interject judgments and opinions. Often the character of the speaker is of as much interest as the *actions* or *incidents*. 60–61, 196, 540–43

Specific language (style) Words referring to a real thing or things that may be readily perceived or imagined; distinguished from *general language*. 60, 268–69, 580

Speeches See *Dialogue*.

Spondee (prosody) A two-syllable *foot* consisting of successive, equally heavy accents (e.g., "men's eyes"). 681

Sprung, or **accentual rhythm (prosody),** A method of accenting, developed by Gerard Manley Hopkins, in which major stresses are "sprung" from the poetic line. 683

Stage business See *Business*.

Stage convention See *Convention.*

Stage directions A playwright's instructions concerning lighting, scenery, blocking, tone of voice, action, entrances and exits, and the like. 990

Stanza (prosody), A group of poetic lines corresponding to paragraphs in prose; the meters and rhymes are usually repeating or systematic. 193

Stanza A poetic unit made up of lines grouped together by rhyme and/or meter. In a *song* or *hymn,* the patterns established in the first stanza are usually repeated throughout the poem, but in an *ode* the subsequent stanzas may be varied. 723

Stasimon A choral ode chanted by the chorus in Greek tragedy. 1053

Static character A character who undergoes no change; contrasted with a *dynamic character.* 139–40, 995

Stereotype A character who is so ordinary and unoriginal that he or she seems to have been cast in a mold; a *representative* character. 139–40, 995–96

Stock character A *flat character* in a standard role with standard *traits,* such as the irate police captain, the bored hotel clerk, etc.; a stereotype. 139–40, 996

Stop sound The consonant sound produced by the momentary stoppage and release of breath either when the lips touch each other or when the tongue touches the teeth or palate, as in *p, t, d, g,*and *k.*

Story A narrative, usually fictional, centering on a major character, and rendering a complete action. 55

Stress (prosody) The emphasis given to a syllable, either strong or light. 679, 712–14. See also *beat.*

Strong-stress rhythm See *Heavy-stress rhythm.*

Structure The arrangement and placement of materials in a work. 59, 96–135

Style The manipulation of language, the placement of words in the service of content. 60, 65, 266–98

Subject The topic that a literary work addresses, such as love, marriage, war, death, and the like. 819, 1000

Subplot A secondary line of action in a literary work that often comments directly or obliquely on the main plot. 993

Substitution *Formal substitution* is the use of an actual variant foot within a line, such as an anapaest being used in place of an iamb. *Rhetorical substitution* is the manipulation of the *caesura* to create the effect of a series of differing feet. 684–85

Syllable (prosody) A separately pronounced part of a word (e.g., the *eat* and *ing* parts of "eating") or, in some cases, a complete word (e.g., *the, when, flounced*). 679

Symbol, symbolism A specific word, idea, or object that may stand for ideas, values, persons, or ways of life. 62, 64, 65, 326–61, 765–94, 999

Symbolic character A character whose primary function is symbolic, even though the character also retains normal or realistic qualities. 995–96

Synecdoche A rhetorical figure in which a part stands for a whole, or a whole for a part. 630

Synesthesia A rhetorical figure uniting or fusing separate sensations or feelings; the description of one type of perception or thought with words that are appropriate to another. 630–31

Syntax Word order and sentence structure. A mark of style is a writer's syntactical patterning (regular patterns and variations), depending on the rhetorical needs of the literary work. 583–85

Syzygy See *Dipodic.*

Tactile image Language describing touching and feeling. 604

Tenor (figurative language) The sense, or meaning, of a *metaphor, symbol*or other *rhetorical figure.* 625. See *Vehicle.*

Tercet A three-line unit or stanza of poetry, often rhyming *A-A-A* or *A-B-A.* 725

Terza rima (prosody) A three-line stanza form with the pattern *A-B-A, B-C-B,* etc. 726

Tetrameter (prosody)   A line consisting of four metrical *feet.* 679

Theater in the round   A modern theater arrangement, often outdoors, in which the audience totally surrounds the stage, with all actors entering and exiting along the aisles; an *arena stage.* 991, 1205, 1401

Theme   (1) The major or central idea of a work. (2) An essay, a short composition developing an interpretation or advancing an argument. (3) The main point or idea that a writer of an essay asserts and illustrates. 59–60, 65, 362–409, 819–43, 1000

Thesis statement, or **thesis sentence**   An introductory sentence which names the topics to be developed in the body of an essay. 24–25

Third-person point of view   A third-person method of *narration* (i.e., *she, he, it, they, them,* etc.), in which the *speaker* or *narrator* is not a part of the story, as with the *first-person point of view.* Because the third-person speaker may exhibit great knowledge and understanding, together with other qualities of character, he or she is often virtually identified with the author, but this identification is not easily decided. 61, 200–203. See also *Authorial Voice, Omniscient Point of View.*

Third-person objective point of view   See *Dramatic point of view.*

Thrust stage   See *Apron stage.*

Tiring house   An enclosed area in an Elizabethan theater in which actors changed costumes and awaited their cues, and in which stage properties were kept. 1097

Tone   The methods used by writers to control attitudes. 63–64, 299–325, 654–56, 998, 1049–50

Topic sentence   The sentence determining the subject matter of a paragraph. 25–26

Traditional poetry   Verse which follows regular patterns such as iambs, trochees, stanzas, etc. Closed-form poetry. 724–34

Tragedy   A drama (or other literary work) that recounts the fall of an individual who, while undergoing suffering, deals responsibly with the situations and dilemmas that he or she faces, and thus demonstrates the value of human effort. 991, 1046–1290

Tragic flaw   See *Hamartia.*

Tragicomedy   A literary work—drama or story—containing a mixture of tragic and comic elements. 992

Trait, traits   A typical mode of behavior; the study of major traits provides a guide to the description of *character.* 137–38

Trilogy   A group of three literary works, usually related or unified. Ancient Athenian dramatists wrote a *trilogy* (three tragedies), together with a *satyr play,* for submission at the Dionysiac festival. 1050

Trimeter (prosody)   A line consisting of three metrical *feet.* 679

Triple rhyme   See *Dactylic rhyme.*

Triplet   See *Tercet.*

Trochaic (double) rhyme   Rhyming trochees such as *flower* and *shower.* 688–89

Trochee, trochaic (prosody)   A two-syllable *foot* consisting of a heavy followed by a light stress. 680–81

Trope   A short dramatic dialogue inserted into the Church mass during the early middle ages. 1095

Tudor interlude   A short tragedy, comedy, or history play written during the reigns of the English Kings Henry VII and Henry VIII (i.e., the first half of the sixteenth century). 1095

Understatement   The deliberate underplaying or undervaluing of a thing to create emphasis. 303, 632

Unit set   A series of platforms, rooms, stairs, and exits that form the locations for all of a play's actions. A unit set enables scenes to change rapidly, without the drawing of a curtain and the placement of new sets. 997

Unities   The unities of place, time, and action that, according to Aristotle, were observed by the dramatists of his time. Later critics held that the unities were to be observed scrupulously, but Shakespeare and subsequent critics either did not know them or ignored them. 1054

Universal symbol   See *Cultural symbols.*

Value, values   The expression of an idea or ideas that concurrently asserts their importance and desirability as goals, standards, and ideals. 363

Vehicle   The image or reference of a *rhetorical figure*, such as a *metaphor* or *simile*; it is the vehicle that carries or embodies the *tenor* (q.v.). 625

Verbal irony   Language stating the opposite of what is meant. 64, 303, 662, 999

Verisimilitude (i.e., **"like truth"**) or **realism**   A characteristic whereby the setting, circumstances, characters, dialogue, actions, and outcomes in a work are designed to seem true, lifelike, real, plausible, and probable. 56–57, 142–43, 245

Versification   See *Prosody.*

Villanelle   A closed poetic form of nineteen lines, composed of five triplets and a quatrain. The form requires that whole lines be repeated in a specific order and that only two rhyming sounds occur throughout. 726

Visual image   Language describing things that can be seen. 602–603

Visual poetry   Poetry that draws much of its power from the appearance of the verse on the page. 737. See also *Concrete verse* and *Shaped verse.*

Voice   See *Speaker.*

Vowel sounds, or **segments**   Continuant sounds produced by the resonation of the voice in the space between the tongue and the top of the mouth, such as the *ee* in *feel,* the *eh* in *bet,* and the *oo* in *cool.* 677, 685–87

Well-made play   A type of play developed in nineteenth-century France. The action of a well-made play begins at the climax, and the conflict depends on a secret. 1405

Word counts (style)   An elementary method of describing a writer's style by counting the lengths of words, sentences, and paragraphs. 270–71

Credits

Frank O'Connor. "First Confession" from *Collected Stories* by Frank O'Connor. Copyright 1951 by Frank O'Connor. Reprinted by permission of Alfred A. Knopf, Inc. and Joan Daves.

Frank O'Hara. "Poem" from *Meditations in an Emergency* by Frank O'Hara. Copyright © 1957 by Frank O'Hara. Reprinted by permission of Grove Press, Inc.

Sharon Olds. "35/10" from *The Dead and the Living* by Sharon Olds. Copyright © 1983 by Sharon Olds. Reprinted by permission of Alfred A. Knopf, Inc.

Tillie Olsen. "I Stand Here Ironing" excerpted from the book *Tell Me a Riddle* by Tillie Olsen. Copyright © 1956 by Tillie Olsen. Reprinted by permission of Delacorte Press/Seymour Lawrence.

Eugene O'Neill. "Before Breakfast" from *The Plays of Eugene O'Neill*. Copyright 1924 by Boni & Liveright, Inc. Reprinted by permission of Random House, Inc.

Simon Ortiz. "A Story of How a Wall Stands" by Simon Ortiz is reprinted by permission of the author.

Wilfred Owen. "Dulce et Decorum Est" from *The Collected Poems of Wilfred Owen*, edited by C. D. Lewis. Copyright © 1963 by Chatto & Windus, Ltd. Reprinted by permission of New Directions Publishing Corporation, the Estate of C. D. Lewis, and Chatto & Windus, Ltd.

Wilfred Owen. "Anthem for Doomed Youth" from *The Collected Poems of Wilfred Owen*, edited by C. D. Lewis. Copyright © 1960 by The Hogarth Press. Reprinted by permission of New Directions Publishing Corporation, the Estate of C. D. Lewis and The Hogarth Press.

Cynthia Ozick. "The Shawl" from *The Shawl* by Cynthia Ozick. Copyright © 1980, 1983 by Cynthia Ozick. Reprinted by permission of Alfred A. Knopf, Inc. Originally appeared in *The New Yorker*.

Grace Paley. "Goodbye and Good Luck" from *The Little Disturbances of Man* by Grace Paley. Copyright © 1956, renewed 1984 by Grace Paley. Reprinted by permission of Viking Penguin, Inc.

Américo Parédes. "Guitarreros" by Américo Parédes in *The Southwest Review*, Vol. 49 (Autumn 1964). Reprinted by permission of the author.

Américo Parédes. "The Hammon and the Beans" by Américo Parédes in *The Texas Observer*, April 18, 1963. Reprinted by permission of the author.

Dorothy Parker. "Panelope" and "Résumé" from *The Portable Dorothy Parker*. Copyright 1926, 1928, renewed 1954, © 1956 by Dorothy Parker. Reprinted by permission of Viking Penguin, Inc., a division of Penguin Books USA Inc.

Linda Pastan. "Ethics" from *Waiting for My Life*, Poems by Linda Pastan. Copyright © 1981 by Linda Pastan. Reprinted by permission of W. W. Norton & Company, Inc.

Linda Pastan. "Marks" from *The Five Stages of Grief*, Poems by Linda Pastan. Copyright © 1978 by Linda Pastan. Reprinted by permission of W. W. Norton & Company, Inc.

Marge Piercy. "The Secretary Chant" and "A Work of Artifice" from *Circles on the Water* by Marge Piercy. Copyright © 1969, 1971, 1973 by Marge Piercy. Reprinted by permission of Alfred A. Knopf, Inc.

Marge Piercy. "Wellfleet Sabbath" from *Available Light* by Marge Piercy. Copyright © 1988 by Middlemarsh, Inc. Reprinted by permission of Alfred A. Knopf, Inc.

Marge Piercy. "Will We Work Together?" from *The Moon Is Always Female* by Marge Piercy. Copyright © 1980 by Marge Piercy. Reprinted by permission of Alfred A. Knopf, Inc.

Sylvia Plath. "Metaphors" from *Collected Poems of Sylvia Plath*. Copyright © 1960 by Ted Hughes. Reprinted by permission of Harper & Row, Publishers, Inc. Published by Faber and Faber, London. Copyright by Ted Hughes 1971, 1981 and reprinted by permission of Olwyn Hughes Literary Agency.

Sylvia Plath. "Last Words" and "Mirror" from *Crossing the Water* by Sylvia Plath. Copyright © 1963, 1971 by Ted Hughes. Reprinted by permission of Harper & Row, Publishers, Inc. From *Collected Poems* by Sylvia Plath. Copyright © 1971, 1981 by Ted Hughes. Published by Faber and Faber, London, and reprinted by permission of Olwyn Hughes Literary Agency.

Katherine Anne Porter. "The Jilting of Granny Weatherall" from *Flowering Judas and Other Stories* by Katherine Anne Porter. Copyright 1930 and renewed © 1958 by Katherine Anne Porter. Reprinted by permission of Harcourt Brace Jovanovich, Inc.

Ezra Pound. "The River-Merchant's Wife: A Letter" and "In a Station of the Metro" from *Personae* by Ezra Pound. Copyright 1926 by Ezra Pound. Reprinted by permission of New Directions Publishing Corporation.

E. J. Pratt. "The Shark" by E. J. Pratt. Reprinted by permission of the University of Toronto Press.

Thomas Rabbitt. "Gargoyle" from *The Booth Interstate* by Thomas Rabbitt. Copyright © 1981 by Thomas Rabbitt. Reprinted by permission of Alfred A. Knopf, Inc.

Dudley Randall. "Ballad of Birmingham" from *Poem Counter Poem* by Dudley Randall. Copyright © 1966. Reprinted by permission of Broadside Press.

John Crowe Ransom. "Bells for John Whiteside's Daughter" from *Selected Poems, Third Edition, Revised and Enlarged* by John Crowe Ransom. Copyright 1924 by Alfred A. Knopf, Inc. and renewed by John Crowe Ransom. Reprinted by permission of Alfred A. Knopf, Inc.

Henry Reed. "Naming of Parts" from *A Map of Verona* by Henry Reed. Reprinted by permission of the Peters Fraser & Dunlop Group Ltd.

Adrienne Rich. "Diving Into the Wreck" from *The Fact of a Doorframe, Poems Selected and New, 1950–1984*, by Adrienne Rich. Copyright © 1984 by Adrienne Rich. Copyright © 1975, 1978 by W. W. Norton & Company, Inc. Copyright © 1981 by Adrienne Rich. Reprinted by permission of W. W. Norton & Company, Inc.

Theodore Roethke. "I Knew a Woman" and "The Waking" from *The Collected Poems of Theodore Roethke*. Copyright 1948, 1953, 1954 by Theodore Roethke. Reprinted by permission of Doubleday & Company, Inc.

Theodore Roethke. "My Papa's Waltz" from *The Collected Poems of Theodore Roethke*. Copyright 1942 by Hearst Magazine, Inc. Reprinted by permission of Doubleday & Company, Inc.

Theodore Roethke. "Dolor" from *The Collected Poems of Theodore Roethke*. Copyright 1943 by Modern Poetry Association, Inc. Reprinted by permission of Doubleday & Company, Inc.

Muriel Rukeyser. "Myth" from *Breaking Open* by Muriel Rukeyser. Copyright © 1973 by Muriel Rukeyser. Reprinted by permission of International Creative Management, Inc.

Luis Omar Salinas. "In a Farmhouse" in *From the Barrio: A Chicano Anthology* by Luis Omar Salinas and Lillian Faderman. Copyright © 1973 by Luis Omar Salinas. Reprinted by permission of Harper & Row, Publishers, Inc.

Carl Sandburg. "Chicago" from *Chicago Poems* by Carl Sandburg. Copyright 1916 by Holt, Rinehart and Winston, Inc. and renewed 1944 by Carl Sandburg. Reprinted by permission of Harcourt Brace Jovanovich, Inc.

Sonia Sanchez. "right on: white america" from *The Poetry of Black America* by Sonia Sanchez. Reprinted by permission of A. Adoff.

Siegfried Sassoon. "Dreamers" from *Collected Poems* by Siegfried Sassoon. Copyright 1918, 1920 by E. P. Dutton & Co. Copyright 1936, 1946, 1947, 1948 by Siegfried Sassoon. Reprinted by permission of Viking Penguin Inc. and George Sassoon.

Virginia Scott. "Snow" from *The Witness Box* by Virginia Scott. Copyright © 1984 by Virginia Scott. Reprinted by permission of Virginia Scott and Motherroot Publications.

Index of Authors, Titles, and First Lines

INDEX OF KEY TERMS